TheStreet Ratings'
Guide to Bond and
Money Market
Mutual Funds

TheStreet Ratings' Guide to Bond and Money Market Mutual Funds

A Quarterly Compilation of Investment Ratings
and Analyses Covering Fixed Income Funds

Spring 2017

GREY HOUSE PUBLISHING

TheStreet, Inc.
14 Wall Street, 15th Floor
New York, NY 10005
800-706-2501

TheStreet Ratings

Published by Grey House Publishing, Inc. located at 4919 Route 22, Amenia, NY, 12501; telephone 518-789-8700. Grey House Publishing neither guarantees the accuracy of the data contained herein nor assumes any responsibility for errors, omissions or discrepancies. Grey House Publishing accepts no payment for listing; inclusion in the publication of any organization agency, institution, publication, service or individual does not imply endorsement of the publisher.

Grey House Publishing
4919 Route 22
PO Box 56
Amenia, NY 12501-0056

Edition No. 70, Spring 2017

ISBN: 978-1-68217-427-2
ISSN: 2158-5997

Contents

Terms and Conditions

This Document is prepared strictly for the confidential use of our customer(s). It has been provided to you at your specific request. It is not directed to, or intended for distribution to or use by, any person or entity who is a citizen or resident of or located in any locality, state, country or other jurisdiction where such distribution, publication, availability or use would be contrary to law or regulation or which would subject TheStreet Ratings or its affiliates to any registration or licensing requirement within such jurisdiction.

No part of the analysts' compensation was, is, or will be, directly or indirectly, related to the specific recommendations or views expressed in this research report.

This Document is not intended for the direct or indirect solicitation of business. TheStreet, Inc. and its affiliates disclaims any and all liability to any person or entity for any loss or damage caused, in whole or in part, by any error (negligent or otherwise) or other circumstances involved in, resulting from or relating to the procurement, compilation, analysis, interpretation, editing, transcribing, publishing and/or dissemination or transmittal of any information contained herein.

TheStreet has not taken any steps to ensure that the securities or investment vehicle referred to in this report are suitable for any particular investor. The investment or services contained or referred to in this report may not be suitable for you and it is recommended that you consult an independent investment advisor if you are in doubt about such investments or investment services. Nothing in this report constitutes investment, legal, accounting or tax advice or a representation that any investment or strategy is suitable or appropriate to your individual circumstances or otherwise constitutes a personal recommendation to you.

The ratings and other opinions contained in this Document must be construed solely as statements of opinion from TheStreet, Inc., and not statements of fact. Each rating or opinion must be weighed solely as a factor in your choice of an institution and should not be construed as a recommendation to buy, sell or otherwise act with respect to the particular product or company involved.

Past performance should not be taken as an indication or guarantee of future performance, and no representation or warranty, expressed or implied, is made regarding future performance. Information, opinions and estimates contained in this report reflect a judgment at its original date of publication and are subject to change without notice. TheStreet Ratings offers a notification service for rating changes on companies you specify. For more information call 1-800-706-2501 or visit www.thestreet.com/ratings. The price, value and income from any of the securities or financial instruments mentioned in this report can fall as well as rise.

This Document and the information contained herein is copyrighted by TheStreet, Inc. Any copying, displaying, selling, distributing or otherwise delivering of this information or any part of this Document to any other person, without the express written consent of TheStreet, Inc. except by a reviewer or editor who may quote brief passages in connection with a review or a news story, is prohibited.

Welcome to TheStreet Ratings
Guide to Bond and Money Market Mutual Funds

With the growing popularity of mutual fund investing, consumers need a reliable source to help them track and evaluate the performance of their mutual fund holdings. Plus, they need a way of identifying and monitoring other funds as potential new investments. Unfortunately, the hundreds of performance and risk measures available – multiplied by the vast number of mutual fund investments on the market today – can make this a daunting task for even the most sophisticated investor.

TheStreet Investment Ratings simplify the evaluation process. We condense all of the available mutual fund data into a single composite opinion of each fund's risk-adjusted performance. This allows you to instantly identify those funds that have historically done well and those that have underperformed the market. While there is no guarantee of future performance, TheStreet Investment Ratings provide a solid framework for making informed investment decisions.

TheStreet Ratings' Mission Statement

TheStreet Ratings' mission is to empower consumers, professionals, and institutions with high quality advisory information for selecting or monitoring a financial investments.

In doing so, TheStreet Ratings will adhere to the highest ethical standards by maintaining our independent, unbiased outlook and approach to advising our customers.

Why rely on TheStreet Ratings?

Our mission is to provide fair, objective information to help professionals and consumers alike make educated purchasing decisions.

At TheStreet Ratings, objectivity and total independence are never compromised. We never take a penny from rated companies for issuing our ratings, and we publish them without regard for the companies' preferences. TheStreet's ratings are more frequently reviewed and updated than any other ratings, so you can be sure that the information you receive is accurate and current.

Our rating scale, from A to E, is easy to understand as follows:

	Rating	Description
Top 10% of mutual funds	A	Excellent
Next 20% of mutual funds	B	Good
Middle 40% of mutual funds	C	Fair
Next 20% of mutual funds	D	Weak
Bottom 10% of mutual funds	E	Very Weak

In addition, a plus or minus sign designates that a fund is in the top third or bottom third of funds with the same letter grade.

Thank you for your trust and purchase of this Guide. If you have any comments, or wish to review other products from TheStreet Ratings, please call 1-800-706-2501 or visit www.thestreetratings.com. We look forward to hearing from you.

How to Use This Guide

The purpose of the *Guide to Bond and Money Market Mutual Funds* is to provide investors with a reliable source of investment ratings and analyses on a timely basis. We realize that past performance is an important factor to consider when making the decision to purchase shares in a mutual fund. The ratings and analyses in this Guide can make that evaluation easier when you are considering:

- corporate bond funds

- municipal bond funds

- government bond funds

- money market funds

However, this Guide does not include funds with significant investments in equity securities since they are not comparable investments to funds invested primarily in fixed income securities. The rating for a particular fund indicates our opinion regarding that fund's past risk-adjusted performance.

When evaluating a specific mutual fund, we recommend you follow these steps:

Step 1   **Confirm the fund name and ticker symbol.** To ensure you evaluate the correct mutual fund, verify the fund's exact name and ticker symbol as it was given to you in its prospectus or appears on your account statement. Many funds have similar names, so you want to make sure the fund you look up is really the one you are interested in evaluating. For a definition of the most commonly used share classes see page 537.

Step 2   **Check the fund's Investment Rating.** Turn to Section I, the Index of Bond and Money Market Mutual Funds, and locate the fund you are evaluating. This section contains all bond and money market mutual funds analyzed by TheStreet Ratings including those that did not receive an Investment Rating. All funds are listed in alphabetical order by the name of the fund with the ticker symbol following the name for additional verification. Once you have located your specific fund, the first column after the ticker symbol shows its Investment Rating. Turn to *About TheStreet Investment Ratings* on page 7 for information about what this rating means.

Step 3   **Analyze the supporting data.** Following TheStreet Investment Rating are some of the various measures we have used in rating the fund. Refer to the Section I introduction (beginning on page 17) to see what each of these factors measures. In most cases, lower rated funds will have a low performance rating and/or a low risk rating (i.e., high volatility). Bear in mind, however, that TheStreet Investment Rating is the result of a complex computer-generated analysis which cannot be reproduced using only the data provided here.

When looking to identify a mutual fund that achieves your specific investing goals, we recommend the following:

Step 4   **Take our Investor Profile Quiz.** Turn to page 529 of the Appendix and take our Investor Profile Quiz to help determine your level of risk tolerance. After you have scored yourself, the last page of the quiz will refer you to the risk category in Section VII (Top-Rated Bond Mutual Funds by Risk Category) that is best for you. There you can choose a fund that has historically provided top notch returns while keeping the risk at a level that is suited to your investment style.

Step 5   **View the 100 top performing funds.** If your priority is to achieve the highest return, regardless of the amount of risk, turn to Section V which lists the top 100 bond mutual funds with the best financial performance. Keep in mind that past performance alone is not always a true indicator of the future since these funds have already experienced a run up in price and could be due for a correction.

Step 6   **View the 100 funds with the lowest risk.** On the other hand, if capital preservation is your top priority, turn to Section VI which lists the top 100 bond mutual funds with the lowest risk. These funds will have lower performance ratings than most other funds, but can provide a safe harbor for your savings.

Step 7   **View the top-rated funds by fund type.** If you are looking to invest in a particular type of mutual fund (e.g., corporate high yield or a U.S. Government agency fund), turn to Section VIII, Top-Rated Bond Mutual Funds by Fund Type. There you will find the top 100 bond mutual funds with the highest performance rating in each category. Please be careful to also consider the risk component when selecting a fund from one of these lists.

Step 8   **Refer back to Section I.** Once you have identified a particular fund that interests you, refer back to Section I, the Index of Bond and Money Market Mutual Funds, for a more thorough analysis.

Always remember:

Step 9   **Read our warnings and cautions.** In order to use TheStreet Investment Ratings most effectively, we strongly recommend you consult the Important Warnings and Cautions listed on page 13. These are more than just "standard disclaimers." They are very important factors you should be aware of before using this Guide.

Step 10   **Stay up to date.** Periodically review the latest TheStreet Investment Ratings for the funds that you own to make sure they are still in line with your investment goals and level of risk tolerance. For information on how to acquire follow-up reports on a particular mutual fund, call 1-800-706-2501 or visit www.thestreetratings.com.

Data Source: Thomson Wealth Management
1455 Research Boulevard
Rockville, MD 20850

Date of data analyzed: Feb. 28, 2017

About TheStreet Investment Ratings

TheStreet Investment Ratings represent a completely independent, unbiased opinion of a mutual fund's historical risk-adjusted performance. Each fund's rating is based on two primary components:

Primary Component #1

A fund's **Performance Rating** is based on its total return to shareholders over the last trailing three years, including share price appreciation and distributions to shareholders. This total return figure is stated net of the expenses and fees charged by the fund, and we also make additional adjustments for any front-end or deferred sales loads. In the case of funds investing in municipal or other tax-free securities, the tax-free return is adjusted to its taxable equivalent based on the maximum marginal U.S. tax rate (35%).

This adjusted return is then weighted to give more recent performance a slightly greater emphasis. Thus, two mutual funds may have provided identical returns to their shareholders over the last three years, but the one with the better performance in the last 12 months will receive a slightly higher performance rating.

Primary Component #2

The **Risk Rating** is based on the level of volatility in the fund's monthly returns, also over the last trailing three years. We use a statistical measure – standard deviation from the mean – as our barometer of volatility. Funds with more volatility relative to other mutual funds are considered riskier, and thus receive a lower risk rating. By contrast, funds with a very stable returns are considered less risky and receive a higher risk rating.

In addition to past volatility, the risk rating component also takes into consideration the credit risk of the fund's underlying investments and its relative exposure to interest rate risk.

Rarely will you ever find a mutual fund that has both a very high Performance Rating and, at the same time, a very high Risk Rating. Therefore, the funds that receive the highest overall Investment Ratings are those that combine the ideal combination of both primary components. There is always a tradeoff between risk and reward. That is why we suggest you assess your own personal risk tolerance using the quiz on page 529 as a part of your decision-making process.

Keep in mind that while TheStreet Investment Ratings use the same rating scale as TheStreet Financial Strength Ratings of financial institutions, the two ratings have totally independent meanings. The Financial Strength Ratings assess the *future* financial stability of an insurer or bank as a way of helping investors place their money with a financially sound company and minimize the risk of loss. These ratings are derived without regard to the performance of the individual investments offered by the insurance companies, banks, or thrifts.

On the other hand, the Investment Ratings employ a ranking system to evaluate both safety and performance. Based on these measures, funds are divided into points, and an individual performance rating and a risk rating are assigned to each fund. Then these measures are combined to derive a fund's composite point ranking. Finally, TheStreet Investment Ratings are assigned to their corresponding point rankings as shown on page 3.

How Our Ratings Differ From Those of Other Services

Balanced approach: TheStreet Investment Ratings are designed to meet the needs of aggressive *as well as* conservative investors. We realize that your investment goals can be different from those of other investors based upon your age, income, and tolerance for risk. Therefore, our ratings balance a fund's performance against the amount of risk it poses to identify those funds that have achieved the optimum mix of both factors. Some of these top funds have achieved excellent returns with only average risk. Others have achieved average returns with only moderate risk. Whatever your personal preferences, we can help you identify a top-notch fund that meets your investing style.

Other investment rating firms give a far greater weight to performance and insufficient consideration to risk. In effect, they are betting too heavily on a continuation of the prevailing economic climate and not giving enough consideration to the risk of a decline. While performance is obviously a very important factor to consider, we believe that the riskiness of a fund is also very important. Therefore, we weigh these two components more equally when assigning TheStreet Investment Ratings.

But we don't stop there. We also assign a separate performance rating and risk rating to each fund so you can focus on the component that is most important to you. In fact, Sections V, VI, and VII are designed specifically to help you select the best mutual funds based on these two factors. No other source gives you the cream of the crop in this manner.

Easy to use: Unlike those of other services, TheStreet Investment Ratings are extremely intuitive and easy to use. Our rating scale (A to E) is easily understood by members of the general public based on their familiarity with school grades. So, there are no stars to count and no numbering systems to interpret.

More funds: *TheStreet Ratings Guide to Bond and Money Market Mutual Funds* tracks more mutual funds than any other publication – with updates that come out more frequently than those of other rating agencies. We've included almost 7,100 funds in this edition, all of which are updated every three months. Compare that to other investment rating agencies, such as Morningstar, where coverage stops after the top 1,500 funds and it takes five months for a fund to cycle through their publication's update process.

Recency: Recognizing that every fund's performance is going to have its peaks and valleys, superior long-term performance is a major consideration in TheStreet Investment Ratings. Even so, we do not give a fund a top rating solely because it did well 10 or 15 years ago. Times change and the top performing funds in the current economic environment are often very different from those of a decade ago. Thus, our ratings are designed to keep you abreast of the best funds available *today* and in the *near future,* not the distant past.

No bias toward load funds: In keeping with our conservative, consumer-oriented nature, we adjust the performance for so-called "load" funds differently from other rating agencies. We spread the impact to you of front-end loads and back-end loads (a.k.a. deferred sales charges) over a much shorter period in our evaluation of a fund. Thus our performance rating, as well as the overall TheStreet Investment Rating, more fully reflects the actual returns the typical investor experiences when placing money in a load fund.

Peer Comparison of Mutual Fund Investment Ratings

TheStreet Ratings	Morningstar	Lipper / Barra
A+, A, A-	Five stars	√
B+, B, B-	Four stars	2
C+, C, C-	Three stars	3
D+, D, D-	Two stars	4
E+, E, E-	One star	5

What Our Ratings Mean

A   **Excellent**. The mutual fund has an excellent track record for maximizing performance while minimizing risk, thus delivering the best possible combination of total return on investment and reduced volatility. It has made the most of the recent economic environment to maximize risk-adjusted returns compared to other mutual funds. While past performance is just an indication – not a guarantee – we believe this fund is among the most likely to deliver superior performance relative to risk in the future.

B   **Good.** The mutual fund has a good track record for balancing performance with risk. Compared to other mutual funds, it has achieved above-average returns given the level of risk in its underlying investments. While the risk-adjusted performance of any mutual fund is subject to change, we believe that this fund has proven to be a good investment in the recent past.

C   **Fair.** In the trade-off between performance and risk, the mutual fund has a track record which is about average. It is neither significantly better nor significantly worse than most other mutual funds. With some funds in this category, the total return may be better than average, but this can be misleading since the higher return was achieved with higher than average risk. With other funds, the risk may be lower than average, but the returns are also lower. In short, based on recent history, there is no particular advantage to investing in this fund.

D   **Weak.** The mutual fund has underperformed the universe of other funds given the level of risk in its underlying investments, resulting in a weak risk-adjusted performance. Thus, its investment strategy and/or management has not been attuned to capitalize on the recent economic environment. While the risk-adjusted performance of any mutual fund is subject to change, we believe that this fund has proven to be a bad investment over the recent past.

E   **Very Weak.** The mutual fund has significantly underperformed most other funds given the level of risk in its underlying investments, resulting in a very weak risk-adjusted performance. Thus, its investment strategy and/or management has done just the opposite of what was needed to maximize returns in the recent economic environment. While the risk-adjusted performance of any mutual fund is subject to change, we believe this fund has proven to be a very bad investment in the recent past.

+   **The plus sign** is an indication that the fund is in the top third of its letter grade.

-   **The minus sign** is an indication that the fund is in the bottom third of its letter grade.

U   **Unrated.** The mutual fund is unrated because it is too new to make a reliable assessment of its risk-adjusted performance. Typically, a fund must be established for at least three years before it is eligible to receive a TheStreet Investment Rating.

Important Warnings And Cautions

1. **A rating alone cannot tell the whole story.** Please read the explanatory information contained here, in the section introductions and in the appendix. It is provided in order to give you an understanding of our rating methodology as well as to paint a more complete picture of a mutual fund's strengths and weaknesses.

2. **Investment ratings shown in this directory were current as of the publication date.** In the meantime, the rating may have been updated based on more recent data. TheStreet Ratings offers a notification service for ratings changes on companies that you specify. For more information call 1-800-706-2501 or visit www.thestreet.com/ratings.

3. **When deciding to buy or sell shares in a specific mutual fund, your decision must be based on a wide variety of factors in addition to TheStreet Investment Rating.** These include any charges you may incur from switching funds, to what degree it meets your long-term planning needs, and what other choices are available to you.

4. **TheStreet Investment Ratings represent our opinion of a mutual fund's past risk-adjusted performance.** As such, a high rating means we feel that the mutual fund has performed very well for its shareholders compared to other mutual funds. A high rating is not a guarantee that a fund will continue to perform well, nor is a low rating a prediction of continued weak performance. TheStreet Investment Ratings are not deemed to be a recommendation concerning the purchase or sale of any mutual fund.

5. **A mutual fund's individual performance is not the only factor in determining its rating.** Since TheStreet Investment Ratings are based on performance relative to other funds, it is possible for a fund's rating to be upgraded or downgraded based strictly on the improved or deteriorated performance of other funds.

6. **All funds that have the same TheStreet Investment Rating should be considered to be essentially equal from a risk/reward perspective.** This is true regardless of any differences in the underlying numbers which might appear to indicate greater strengths.

7. **Our rating standards are more consumer-oriented than those used by other rating agencies.** We make more conservative assumptions about the amortization of loads and other fees as we attempt to identify those funds that have historically provided superior returns with only little or moderate risk.

8. **We are an independent rating agency and do not depend on the cooperation of the managers operating the mutual funds we rate.** Our data are derived, for the most part, from price quotes obtained and documented on the open market. This is supplemented by information collected from the mutual fund prospectuses and regulatory filings. Although we seek to maintain an open line of communication with the mutual fund managers, we do not grant them the right to stop or influence publication of the ratings. This policy stems from the fact that this Guide is designed for the information of the consumer.

9. **This Guide does not cover stock funds.** Because stock funds represent a whole separate class of investments with unique risk profiles and performance expectations, they are excluded from this publication.

Section I

Index of Bond and Money Market Mutual Funds

An analysis of all rated and unrated

Fixed Income Mutual Funds

Funds are listed in alphabetical order.

Section I Contents

Left Pages

1. Fund Type

The mutual fund's peer category based on its investment objective as stated in its prospectus.

COH	Corporate - High Yield	MMT	Money Market - Treas.
COI	Corporate - Inv. Grade	MTG	Mortgage
EM	Emerging Market	MUH	Municipal - High Yield
GEN	General	MUI	Municipal - Insured
GEI	General - Inv. Grade	MUN	Municipal - National
GEL	General - Long Term	MUS	Municipal - Single State
GES	General - Short & Interm.	USL	U.S. Gov.- Long Term
GL	Global	USS	U.S. Gov. - Short & Interm
LP	Loan Participation	USA	U.S. Gov. - Agency
MMF	Money Mkt - Tax Exempt	US	U.S. Gov. - Treasury

A blank fund type means that the mutual fund has not yet been categorized.

2. Fund Name

The name of the mutual fund as stated in its prospectus, which can sometimes differ slightly from the name that the company uses for advertising. If you cannot find the particular mutual fund you are interested in, or if you have any doubts regarding the precise name, verify the information with your broker or on your account statement. Also, use the fund's ticker symbol for confirmation. (See column 3.)

3. Ticker Symbol

The unique alphabetic symbol used for identifying and trading a specific mutual fund. No two funds can have the same ticker symbol, and the ticker symbol for mutual funds always ends with an "X".

A handful of funds currently show no associated ticker symbol. This means that the fund is either small or new since the NASD assigns a ticker symbol only to funds with at least $25 million in assets or 1,000 shareholders.

4. Overall Investment Rating

Our overall rating is measured on a scale from A to E based on each fund's risk-adjusted performance. Please see page 11 for specific descriptions of each letter grade. Also, refer to page 7 for information on how our ratings are derived. Most important, when using this rating, please be sure to consider the warnings beginning on page 13 regarding the ratings' limitations and the underlying assumptions.

5. Phone

The telephone number of the company managing the fund. Call this number to receive a prospectus or other information about the fund.

6.	**Performance Rating/Points**	A letter grade rating based solely on the mutual fund's financial performance over the trailing three years, without any consideration for the amount of risk the fund poses. Like the overall Investment Rating, the Performance Rating is measured on a scale from A to E for ease of interpretation. The points score indicates where the Performance Rating falls on a scale of 0 to 10.
		In the case of funds investing in municipal or other tax-free securities, this rating is based on the taxable equivalent return of the fund assuming the maximum marginal U.S. tax rate (35%).
7.	**3-Month Total Return**	The total return the fund has provided to investors over the preceding three months. This total return figure is computed based on the fund's dividend distributions and share price appreciation/depreciation during the period, net of the expenses and fees it imposes on its shareholders. Although the total return figure does not reflect an adjustment for any loads the fund may carry, such adjustments have been made in deriving TheStreet Investment Ratings. The 3-Month Total Return shown here is not annualized.
8.	**6-Month Total Return**	The total return the fund has provided investors over the preceding six months, not annualized.
9.	**1-Year Total Return**	The total return the fund has provided investors over the preceding twelve months.
10.	**1-Year Total Return Percentile**	The fund's percentile rank based on its one-year performance compared to that of all other fixed income funds in existence for at least one year. A score of 99 is the best possible, indicating that the fund outperformed 99% of the other mutual funds. Zero is the worst possible percentile score.
		In the case of funds investing in municipal or other tax-free securities, this percentile rank is based on the taxable equivalent return of the fund assuming the maximum marginal U.S. tax rate (35%).
11.	**3-Year Total Return**	The total annual return the fund has provided investors over the preceding three years.
12.	**3-Year Total Return Percentile**	The fund's percentile rank based on its three-year performance compared to that of all other fixed income funds in existence for at least three years. A score of 99 is the best possible, indicating that the fund outperformed 99% of the other mutual funds. Zero is the worst possible percentile score.
		In the case of funds investing in municipal or other tax-free securities, this percentile rank is based on the taxable equivalent return of the fund assuming the maximum marginal U.S. tax rate (35%).
13.	**5-Year Total Return**	The total annual return the fund has provided investors over the preceding five years.

14. 5-Year Total Return Percentile

The fund's percentile rank based on its five-year performance compared to that of all other fixed income funds in existence for at least five years. A score of 99 is the best possible, indicating that the fund outperformed 99% of the other mutual funds. Zero is the worst possible percentile score.

In the case of funds investing in municipal or other tax-free securities, this percentile rank is based on the taxable equivalent return of the fund assuming the maximum marginal U.S. tax rate (35%).

15. Dividend Yield

Distributions provided to fund investors over the preceding 12 months, expressed as a percent of the fund's current share price. The dividend yield of a fund may have little correlation to the amount of dividends the fund has received from its underlying investments. Rather, dividend distributions are based on a fund's need to pass earnings from both dividends and gains on the sale of investments along to shareholders. Thus, these dividend distributions are included as a part of the fund's total return.

Keep in mind that a higher dividend yield means more current income, as opposed to capital appreciation, which in turn means a higher tax liability in the year of the distribution.

16. Expense Ratio

The expense ratio is taken directly from each fund's annual report with no further calculation. It indicates the percentage of the fund's assets that are deducted each fiscal year to cover its expenses, although for practical purposes, it is actually accrued daily. Typical fund expenses include 12b-1 fees, management fees, administrative fees, operating costs, and all other asset-based costs incurred by the fund. Brokerage costs incurred by the fund to buy or sell the underlying securities, as well as any sales loads levied on investors, are not included in the expense ratio.

If a mutual fund's net assets are small, its expense ratio can be quite high because the fund must cover its expenses from a smaller asset base. Conversely, as the net assets of the fund grow, the expense percentage ideally should diminish since the expenses are being spread across a larger asset base.

Funds with higher expense ratios are generally less attractive since the expense ratio represents a hurdle that must be met before the investment becomes profitable to its shareholders. Since a fund's expenses affect its total return though, they are already factored into its Investment Rating.

Right Pages

1. Risk Rating/Points

A letter grade rating based solely on the mutual fund's risk as determined by its monthly performance volatility over the trailing three years and the underlying credit risk and interest rate risk of its investment portfolio. The risk rating does not take into consideration the overall financial performance the fund has achieved or the total return it has provided to its shareholders. Like the overall Investment Rating, the Risk Rating is measured on a scale from A to E for ease of interpretation. The points score indicates where the Risk Rating falls on a scale of 0 to 10.

2. Standard Deviation

A statistical measure of the amount of volatility in a fund's monthly performance over the last trailing 36 months. In absolute terms, standard deviation provides a historical measure of a fund's deviation from its mean, or average, monthly total return over the period.

A high standard deviation indicates a high degree of volatility in the past, which usually means you should expect to see a high degree of volatility in the future as well. This translates into higher risk since a large negative swing could easily become a sizable loss in the event you need to liquidate your shares.

3. Average Duration

Expressed in years, duration is a measure of a fund's sensitivity to interest rate fluctuations, or its level of interest rate risk.

The longer a fund's duration, the more sensitive the fund is to shifts in interest rates. For example, a fund with a duration of eight years is twice as sensitive to a change in rates as a fund with a four year duration.

4. Net Asset Value (NAV)

The fund's share price as of the date indicated. A fund's NAV is computed by dividing the value of the fund's asset holdings, less accrued fees and expenses, by the number of its shares outstanding.

5. Net Assets

The total value (stated in millions of dollars) of all of the fund's asset holdings including stocks, bonds, cash, and other financial instruments, less accrued expenses and fees.

Larger funds have the advantage of being able to spread their expenses over a greater asset base so that the effect per share is lessened. On the other hand, if a fund becomes too large, it can be more difficult for the fund manager to buy and sell investments for the benefit of shareholders.

6. Cash %

The percentage of the fund's assets held in cash and cash equivalent assets as of the last reporting period. Investments in this area will tend to hamper the fund's returns while adding to its stability during market swings.

7. Government Bonds %

The percentage of the fund's assets invested in U.S. government and U.S. government agency bonds as of the last reporting period. These investments carry little or no credit risk, but also tend to offer lower than average yields.

8.	**Municipal Bonds %**	The percentage of the fund's assets invested as of the last reporting period in bonds issued by state and local governments. The quality of municipal bonds can vary greatly, so it is important to check TheStreet Risk Rating for funds with a high concentration of assets in this category.
9.	**Corporate Bonds %**	The percentage of the fund's assets invested as of the last reporting period in bonds issued by corporations. This includes both high yield corporate bonds (i.e. junk bonds) and investment grade corporate bonds, so it is important to check TheStreet Risk Rating for funds with a high concentration of assets in this category.
10.	**Other %**	The percentage of the fund's assets invested as of the last reporting period in other types of financial instruments such as convertible or equity securities.
11.	**Portfolio Turnover Ratio**	The average annual portion of the fund's holdings that have been moved from one specific investment to another over the past three years. This indicates the amount of buying and selling the fund manager engages in. A portfolio turnover ratio of 100% signifies that on average, the entire value of the fund's assets is turned over once during the course of a year.
		A high portfolio turnover ratio has implications for shareholders since the fund is required to pass all realized earnings along to shareholders each year. Thus a high portfolio turnover ratio will result in higher annual distributions for shareholders, effectively increasing their annual taxable income. In contrast, a low turnover ratio means a higher level of unrealized gains that will not be taxable until you sell your shares in the fund.
12.	**Average Coupon Rate**	The average overall interest rate being received on the fund's fixed income investments based on a weighted average of each individual bond's stated interest rate, or coupon rate.
		Interest payments are only one factor contributing to a fund's overall performance. However, the higher the average coupon rate, the higher the level of realized gains that the fund will have to distribute to its shareholders in the form of a taxable dividend distribution.
13.	**Manager Quality Percentile**	The manager quality percentile is based on a ranking of the fund's alpha, a statistical measure representing the difference between a fund's actual returns and its expected performance given its level of risk. Fund managers who have been able to exceed the fund's statistically expected performance receive a high percentile rank with 99 representing the best possible score. At the other end of the spectrum, fund managers who actually have detracted from the fund's expected performance receive a low percentile rank with 0 representing the worst possible score.
14.	**Manager Tenure**	The number of years the current manager has been managing the fund. Since fund managers who deliver substandard returns are usually replaced, a long tenure is usually a good sign that shareholders are satisfied that the fund is achieving its stated objectives.

15. Initial Purchase Minimum

The minimum investment amount, stated in dollars, that the fund management company requires in order for you to initially purchase shares in the fund. In theory, funds with high purchase minimums are able to keep expenses down because they have fewer accounts to administer. Don't be misled, however, by the misconception that a fund with a high purchase minimum will deliver superior results simply because it is designed for "high rollers."

Additional Purchase Minimum

The minimum subsequent fund purchase, stated in dollars, that you could make once you have opened an existing account. This minimum may be lowered or waived if you participate in an electronic transfer plan where shares of the fund are automatically purchased at regularly scheduled intervals.

17. Front-End Load

A fee charged on all new investments in the fund, stated as a percentage of the initial investment. Thus a fund with a 4% front-end load means that only 96% of your initial investment is working for you while the other 4% is immediately sacrificed to the fund company. It is generally best to avoid funds that charge a front-end load since there is usually a comparable no-load fund available to serve as an alternative.

While a fund's total return does not reflect the expense to shareholders of a front-end load, we have factored this fee into our evaluation when deriving its Investment Rating.

18. Back-End Load

Also known as a deferred sales charge, this fee is levied when you sell the fund, and is stated as a percentage of your total sales price. For instance, investing in a fund with a 5% back-end load means that you will only receive 95% of your total investment when you sell the fund. The remaining 5% goes to the fund company. As with front-end loads, it is generally best to avoid funds that charge a back-end load since there is usually a comparable no-load fund available to serve as an alternative.

While a fund's total return does not reflect the expense to shareholders of a back-end load, we have factored this fee into our evaluation when deriving its Investment Rating.

Fund Type	Fund Name	Ticker Symbol	Overall Investment Rating	Phone	Perfor-mance Rating/Pts	3 Mo	6 Mo	1Yr / Pct	Annualized 3Yr / Pct	Annualized 5Yr / Pct	Dividend Yield	Expense Ratio
COH	1290 High Yield Bond A	TNHAX	U	(888) 310-0416	U /	5.13	6.51	19.80 /96	--	--	5.55	1.99
COH	1290 High Yield Bond C	TNHCX	U	(888) 310-0416	U /	5.19	6.63	20.08 /96	--	--	6.04	2.74
COH	1290 High Yield Bond I	TNHIX	U	(888) 310-0416	U /	5.19	6.63	20.10 /96	--	--	6.04	1.74
COH	1290 High Yield Bond R	TNHRX	U	(888) 310-0416	U /	5.06	6.36	19.49 /95	--	--	5.59	2.24
MUS	1919 Maryland Tax-Free Income A	LMMDX	B+	(844) 828-1919	C / 4.6	1.29	-0.86	1.39 /50	2.72 /77	2.10 /61	3.21	0.93
MUS	1919 Maryland Tax-Free Income C	LMMCX	A	(844) 828-1919	C+ / 5.8	1.09	-1.13	0.83 /43	2.15 /66	1.52 /47	2.79	1.52
MUS	1919 Maryland Tax-Free Income I	LMMIX	A+	(844) 828-1919	B- / 7.3	1.33	-0.72	1.54 /52	2.89 /80	2.27 /65	3.50	0.89
COI	AAM Select Income A	CPUAX	D+	(888) 966-9661	C+ / 6.0	2.48	-1.27	7.58 /73	3.95 /75	--	2.83	1.71
COI	AAM Select Income C	CPUCX	D+	(888) 966-9661	C+ / 6.0	2.19	-1.63	6.80 /72	3.21 /64	--	2.19	2.46
COI	AAM Select Income I	CPUIX	C	(888) 966-9661	B- / 7.3	2.54	-1.14	7.81 /74	4.22 /78	--	3.14	1.46
COI	AAM/HIMCO Short Duration A	ASDAX	U	(888) 966-9661	U /	1.01	1.24	3.40 /59	--	--	1.97	1.28
COI	AAM/HIMCO Short Duration C	ASDCX	U	(888) 966-9661	U /	0.84	0.89	2.68 /54	--	--	1.32	2.03
COI	AAM/HIMCO Short Duration I	ASDIX	U	(888) 966-9661	U /	1.06	1.36	3.76 /61	--	--	2.27	1.03
GES	AB All Mkt Real Return 1	AMTOX	E-	(800) 221-5672	E- / 0.1	3.84	6.29	23.44 /98	-6.59 / 0	-4.00 / 0	2.47	1.16
GES	AB All Mkt Real Return 2	AMTTX	E-	(800) 221-5672	E- / 0.1	3.88	6.40	23.83 /99	-6.35 / 0	-3.75 / 0	2.65	0.92
GES	AB All Mkt Real Return A	AMTAX	E-	(800) 221-5672	E- / 0.0	3.85	6.26	23.44 /98	-6.72 / 0	-4.09 / 0	2.16	1.42
GES	AB All Mkt Real Return Adv	AMTYX	E-	(800) 221-5672	E- / 0.1	3.86	6.40	23.66 /99	-6.46 / 0	-3.82 / 0	2.50	1.17
GES	AB All Mkt Real Return C	ACMTX	E-	(800) 221-5672	E- / 0.1	3.73	5.89	22.46 /98	-7.39 / 0	-4.76 / 0	1.40	2.16
GES	AB All Mkt Real Return I	AMTIX	E-	(800) 221-5672	E- / 0.1	3.92	6.48	23.87 /99	-6.37 / 0	-3.76 / 0	2.68	0.96
GES	AB All Mkt Real Return K	AMTKX	E-	(800) 221-5672	E- / 0.1	3.80	6.24	23.29 /98	-6.70 / 0	-4.06 / 0	2.32	1.34
GES	AB All Mkt Real Return R	AMTRX	E-	(800) 221-5672	E- / 0.1	3.73	6.04	23.05 /98	-6.95 / 0	-4.31 / 0	2.13	1.64
COI	AB Bond Inflation Strat 1	ABNOX	D	(800) 221-5672	C / 5.1	1.69	0.93	5.98 /70	1.84 /40	1.12 /29	2.11	0.87
COI	AB Bond Inflation Strat 2	ABNTX	D	(800) 221-5672	C / 5.3	1.71	0.97	6.10 /70	1.94 /42	1.24 /30	2.22	0.77
COI	AB Bond Inflation Strat A	ABNAX	E+	(800) 221-5672	C- / 3.0	1.63	0.79	5.76 /69	1.64 /37	0.92 /26	1.58	1.31
COI	AB Bond Inflation Strat Adv	ABNYX	D	(800) 221-5672	C / 5.2	1.67	0.98	6.09 /70	1.93 /42	1.21 /30	1.97	1.06
COI	AB Bond Inflation Strat C	ABNCX	D-	(800) 221-5672	C- / 3.6	1.47	0.44	4.99 /67	0.94 /27	0.21 /18	1.24	2.07
COI	AB Bond Inflation Strat I	ANBIX	D	(800) 221-5672	C / 5.3	1.78	1.02	6.06 /70	1.97 /42	1.24 /31	2.11	0.76
COI	AB Bond Inflation Strat K	ABNKX	D	(800) 221-5672	C / 4.8	1.62	0.88	5.76 /69	1.70 /38	0.98 /27	1.74	1.17
COI	AB Bond Inflation Strat R	ABNRX	D-	(800) 221-5672	C / 4.4	1.57	0.76	5.57 /69	1.45 /34	0.73 /24	1.66	1.50
GL	AB Bond Inflation Strat Z	ABNZX	U	(800) 221-5672	U /	1.70	0.97	6.08 /70	--	--	2.21	0.84
COI	AB Corporate Income	ACISX	C	(800) 221-5672	B- / 7.2	2.08	-1.78	5.92 /70	3.90 /74	4.31 /76	3.51	N/A
* GL	AB Global Bond A	ANAGX	B	(800) 221-5672	C / 5.2	1.42	-0.99	4.46 /64	3.68 /71	3.21 /61	2.05	0.85
GL	AB Global Bond Adv	ANAYX	A+	(800) 221-5672	B- / 7.1	1.36	-0.99	4.72 /65	3.97 /75	3.51 /66	2.39	0.60
GL ●	AB Global Bond B	ANABX	B+	(800) 221-5672	C+ / 5.7	1.22	-1.48	3.65 /60	2.91 /59	2.46 /49	1.37	1.63
GL	AB Global Bond C	ANACX	B+	(800) 221-5672	C+ / 5.9	1.23	-1.36	3.79 /61	2.96 /60	2.50 /49	1.38	1.60
GL	AB Global Bond I	ANAIX	A+	(800) 221-5672	B- / 7.2	1.48	-0.87	4.72 /66	3.98 /75	3.54 /66	2.39	0.59
GL	AB Global Bond K	ANAKX	A	(800) 221-5672	C+ / 6.8	1.39	-1.03	4.49 /65	3.66 /71	3.21 /61	2.05	0.95
GL	AB Global Bond R	ANARX	A-	(800) 221-5672	C+ / 6.4	1.31	-1.20	4.15 /63	3.33 /66	2.86 /55	1.72	1.27
GL	AB Global Bond Z	ANAZX	A+	(800) 221-5672	B- / 7.3	1.50	-0.84	4.90 /66	4.08 /76	3.49 /65	2.44	0.53
MMT	AB Government Exchange Reserves	AEAXX	C-	(800) 221-5672	D- / 1.2	0.08	0.09	0.22 /26	0.14 /15	0.13 /16	0.22	N/A
MMT ●	AB Government Exchange Reserves	AEBXX	C-	(800) 221-5672	D- / 1.1	0.07	0.07	0.19 /25	0.12 /14	0.11 /15	0.19	N/A
MMT	AB Government Exchange Reserves	AECXX	C-	(800) 221-5672	D- / 1.2	0.08	0.09	0.21 /26	0.13 /14	0.12 /16	0.21	N/A
MMT	AB Government Exchange Reserves	AIEXX	C-	(800) 221-5672	D- / 1.3	0.10	0.14	0.29 /29	0.17 /16	0.15 /17	0.29	N/A
MMT	AB Government Exchange Reserves	AEKXX	C-	(800) 221-5672	D- / 1.2	0.09	0.11	0.26 /28	0.14 /15	0.13 /16	0.26	N/A
MMT	AB Government Exchange Reserves	AREXX	C-	(800) 221-5672	D- / 1.2	0.09	0.12	0.26 /28	0.14 /15	0.12 /16	0.26	N/A
MMT	AB Govt Reserves 1	AGRXX	C-	(800) 221-5672	E+ / 0.9	0.07	0.11	0.17 /25	0.07 /11	--	0.17	N/A
* GL	AB High Income A	AGDAX	B-	(800) 221-5672	A / 9.3	5.46	5.71	20.70 /97	4.76 /83	6.95 /96	5.61	0.85
GL	AB High Income Adv	AGDYX	B	(800) 221-5672	A+ / 9.8	5.64	5.96	20.95 /97	5.08 /85	7.28 /97	6.09	0.60
GL ●	AB High Income B	AGDBX	B	(800) 221-5672	A / 9.4	5.21	5.25	19.54 /95	3.93 /74	6.13 /93	5.05	1.63
GL	AB High Income C	AGDCX	B	(800) 221-5672	A / 9.4	5.32	5.37	19.67 /95	3.95 /75	6.13 /93	5.07	1.60
GL	AB High Income I	AGDIX	B+	(800) 221-5672	A+ / 9.8	5.64	5.98	21.00 /97	5.12 /86	7.33 /97	6.13	0.54
GL	AB High Income K	AGDKX	B	(800) 221-5672	A+ / 9.7	5.56	5.82	20.64 /97	4.77 /83	6.96 /96	5.82	0.94

● Denotes fund is closed to new investors
* Denotes fund is included in Section II

www.thestreetratings.com

RISK			NET ASSETS		ASSET							FUND MANAGER		MINIMUM		LOADS	
Risk Rating/Pts	3 Yr Avg Standard Deviation	Avg Duration	NAV As of 2/28/17	Total $(Mil)	Cash %	Gov. Bond %	Muni. Bond %	Corp. Bond %	Other %	Portfolio Turnover Ratio	Avg Coupon Rate	Manager Quality Pct	Manager Tenure (Years)	Initial Purch. $	Additional Purch. $	Front End Load	Back End Load
U /	N/A	3.4	9.32	1	2	0	0	96	2	79	0.0	N/A	3	2,000	100	4.5	0.0
U /	N/A	3.4	9.32	N/A	2	0	0	96	2	79	0.0	N/A	3	2,000	100	0.0	0.0
U /	N/A	3.4	9.32	29	2	0	0	96	2	79	0.0	N/A	3	1,000,000	0	0.0	0.0
U /	N/A	3.4	9.32	N/A	2	0	0	96	2	79	0.0	N/A	3	0	0	0.0	0.0
B+ / 8.3	2.0	5.4	15.92	86	1	0	98	0	1	5	4.9	73	10	1,000	50	4.3	0.0
B+ / 8.3	1.9	5.4	15.92	21	1	0	98	0	1	5	4.9	60	10	1,000	50	0.0	0.0
B+ / 8.4	1.9	5.4	15.93	17	1	0	98	0	1	5	4.9	77	10	1,000,000	0	0.0	0.0
C- / 3.2	3.8	7.4	10.00	12	4	13	2	66	15	45	0.0	68	4	2,500	500	3.0	2.0
C- / 3.3	3.8	7.4	10.00	2	4	13	2	66	15	45	0.0	36	4	2,500	500	0.0	2.0
C- / 3.2	3.8	7.4	10.01	39	4	13	2	66	15	45	0.0	73	4	25,000	5,000	0.0	2.0
U /	N/A	1.0	9.96	10	3	0	0	62	35	37	0.0	N/A	3	2,500	500	2.5	1.0
U /	N/A	1.0	9.95	2	3	0	0	62	35	37	0.0	N/A	3	2,500	500	0.0	1.0
U /	N/A	1.0	9.97	68	3	0	0	62	35	37	0.0	N/A	3	25,000	5,000	0.0	1.0
E- / 0.0	13.6	N/A	8.36	583	4	31	0	0	65	119	0.0	0	2	5,000	0	0.0	0.0
E- / 0.0	13.5	N/A	8.54	N/A	4	31	0	0	65	119	0.0	0	2	0	0	0.0	0.0
E- / 0.0	13.6	N/A	8.51	14	4	31	0	0	65	119	0.0	0	2	2,500	50	4.3	0.0
E- / 0.0	13.6	N/A	8.48	28	4	31	0	0	65	119	0.0	0	2	0	0	0.0	0.0
E- / 0.0	13.5	N/A	8.49	3	4	31	0	0	65	119	0.0	0	2	2,500	50	0.0	0.0
E- / 0.0	13.5	N/A	8.42	17	4	31	0	0	65	119	0.0	0	2	0	0	0.0	0.0
E- / 0.0	13.5	N/A	8.41	2	4	31	0	0	65	119	0.0	0	2	0	0	0.0	0.0
E- / 0.0	13.6	N/A	8.41	N/A	4	31	0	0	65	119	0.0	0	2	0	0	0.0	0.0
C- / 3.8	3.6	4.0	10.74	240	0	66	0	17	17	41	1.9	15	7	5,000	0	0.0	0.0
C- / 3.9	3.5	4.0	10.74	60	0	66	0	17	17	41	1.9	18	7	0	0	0.0	0.0
C- / 3.8	3.6	4.0	10.86	26	0	66	0	17	17	41	1.9	11	7	2,500	50	4.3	0.0
C- / 3.9	3.5	4.0	10.88	85	0	66	0	17	17	41	1.9	19	7	0	0	0.0	0.0
C- / 3.9	3.6	4.0	10.64	5	0	66	0	17	17	41	1.9	4	7	2,500	50	0.0	0.0
C- / 3.8	3.6	4.0	10.79	N/A	0	66	0	17	17	41	1.9	19	7	0	0	0.0	0.0
C- / 3.9	3.5	4.0	10.84	3	0	66	0	17	17	41	1.9	14	7	0	0	0.0	0.0
C- / 3.9	3.5	4.0	10.84	1	0	66	0	17	17	41	1.9	10	7	0	0	0.0	0.0
U /	N/A	4.0	10.77	14	0	66	0	17	17	41	1.9	N/A	7	0	0	0.0	0.0
D+ / 2.9	4.1	N/A	11.10	61	2	5	0	90	3	59	0.0	54	7	0	0	0.0	0.0
B- / 7.1	2.7	5.7	8.38	1,291	3	57	1	26	13	113	3.8	94	25	2,500	50	4.3	0.0
B- / 7.1	2.7	5.7	8.37	3,642	3	57	1	26	13	113	3.8	95	25	0	0	0.0	0.0
B- / 7.1	2.7	5.7	8.38	1	3	57	1	26	13	113	3.8	93	25	2,500	50	0.0	0.0
C+ / 6.9	2.8	5.7	8.41	318	3	57	1	26	13	113	3.8	93	25	2,500	50	0.0	0.0
B- / 7.1	2.7	5.7	8.37	713	3	57	1	26	13	113	3.8	95	25	0	0	0.0	0.0
C+ / 6.9	2.8	5.7	8.38	33	3	57	1	26	13	113	3.8	94	25	0	0	0.0	0.0
C+ / 6.9	2.8	5.7	8.38	85	3	57	1	26	13	113	3.8	94	25	0	0	0.0	0.0
B- / 7.0	2.7	5.7	8.38	274	3	57	1	26	13	113	3.8	95	25	0	0	0.0	0.0
A+ / 9.9	N/A	N/A	1.00	156	100	0	0	0	0	0	0.2	48	N/A	2,500	50	0.0	0.0
A+ / 9.9	N/A	N/A	1.00	3	100	0	0	0	0	0	0.2	46	N/A	2,500	50	0.0	0.0
A+ / 9.9	N/A	N/A	1.00	17	100	0	0	0	0	0	0.2	47	N/A	2,500	50	0.0	0.0
A+ / 9.9	N/A	N/A	1.00	11	100	0	0	0	0	0	0.3	50	N/A	0	0	0.0	0.0
A+ / 9.9	N/A	N/A	1.00	46	100	0	0	0	0	0	0.3	48	N/A	0	0	0.0	0.0
A+ / 9.9	N/A	N/A	1.00	6	100	0	0	0	0	0	0.3	48	N/A	0	0	0.0	0.0
A+ / 9.9	N/A	N/A	1.00	609	100	0	0	0	0	0	0.2	43	N/A	100,000	0	0.0	0.0
D / 1.8	5.4	3.9	8.86	2,039	1	27	0	52	20	45	5.9	97	15	2,500	50	4.3	0.0
D / 1.8	5.4	3.9	8.88	3,935	1	27	0	52	20	45	5.9	97	15	0	0	0.0	0.0
D / 1.9	5.3	3.9	8.94	2	1	27	0	52	20	45	5.9	95	15	2,500	50	0.0	0.0
D / 1.8	5.4	3.9	8.97	1,293	1	27	0	52	20	45	5.9	95	15	2,500	50	0.0	0.0
D / 1.8	5.3	3.9	8.88	295	1	27	0	52	20	45	5.9	98	15	0	0	0.0	0.0
D / 1.8	5.4	3.9	8.87	115	1	27	0	52	20	45	5.9	97	15	0	0	0.0	0.0

	99 Pct = Best 0 Pct = Worst		Overall		PERFORMANCE			Total Return % through 2/28/17			Incl. in Returns	
Fund Type	Fund Name	Ticker Symbol	Investment Rating	Phone	Perfor- mance Rating/Pts	3 Mo	6 Mo	1Yr / Pct	3Yr / Pct Annualized	5Yr / Pct	Dividend Yield	Expense Ratio
*MUH	AB High Income Municipal A	ABTHX	B	(800) 221-5672	A / 9.4	2.73	-4.92	0.97 /44	6.01 /98	5.19 /98	4.01	0.88
MUH	AB High Income Municipal Adv	ABTYX	B+	(800) 221-5672	A+ / 9.8	2.70	-4.80	1.22 /48	6.26 /99	5.47 /99	4.40	0.63
MUH	AB High Income Municipal C	ABTFX	B	(800) 221-5672	A / 9.4	2.54	-5.19	0.30 /32	5.24 /97	4.44 /96	3.36	1.63
GL	AB High Income R	AGDRX	B	(800) 221-5672	A+ / 9.6	5.37	5.51	20.23 /96	4.38 /79	6.57 /95	5.48	1.27
GL	AB High Income Z	AGDZX	B+	(800) 221-5672	A+ / 9.8	5.65	5.98	21.02 /97	5.15 /86	7.20 /97	6.15	0.53
GL	AB High Yield A	HIYAX	U	(800) 221-5672	U /	4.76	5.39	--	--	--	0.00	2.87
GL	AB High Yield Adv	HIYYX	U	(800) 221-5672	U /	4.90	5.70	--	--	--	0.00	2.80
GL	AB High Yield C	HIYCX	U	(800) 221-5672	U /	4.65	5.08	--	--	--	0.00	4.45
GL	AB High Yield I	HIYIX	U	(800) 221-5672	U /	4.90	5.70	--	--	--	0.00	2.02
GL	AB High Yield K	HIYKX	U	(800) 221-5672	U /	4.83	5.58	--	--	--	0.00	2.29
GL	AB High Yield R	HIYRX	U	(800) 221-5672	U /	4.66	5.34	--	--	--	0.00	2.76
COH	AB High Yield Z	HIYZX	C+	(800) 221-5672	A / 9.5	4.90	5.71	19.63 /95	4.23 /78	7.23 /97	9.03	2.01
COI	AB Income A	AKGAX	U	(800) 221-5672	U /	3.28	1.09	--	--	--	0.00	N/A
GL	AB Income Advisor	ACGYX	A	(800) 221-5672	B / 8.2	3.35	1.35	6.84 /72	4.41 /80	4.05 /73	4.61	0.96
COI	AB Income C	AKGCX	U	(800) 221-5672	U /	3.21	0.83	--	--	--	0.00	N/A
MUS	AB Interm CA Muni A	AICAX	D	(800) 221-5672	D / 2.0	1.69	-2.04	-0.59 / 8	1.46 /47	1.22 /40	1.82	0.81
MUN	AB Interm CA Muni Advisor	AICYX	U		U /	1.75	-1.98	--	--	--	0.00	N/A
MUS	AB Interm CA Muni C	ACMCX	D	(800) 221-5672	D / 2.0	1.50	-2.41	-1.33 / 2	0.71 /29	0.49 /24	1.11	1.57
MUN	AB Interm Diversif Muni A	AIDAX	D	(800) 221-5672	D / 1.9	1.65	-2.02	-0.56 / 9	1.44 /47	1.26 /41	1.77	0.81
MUN	AB Interm Diversif Muni Adv	AIDYX	U	(800) 221-5672	U /	1.71	-1.90	-0.48 /10	--	--	1.97	0.57
MUN●	AB Interm Diversif Muni B	AIDBX	D	(800) 221-5672	D / 1.9	1.45	-2.40	-1.31 / 2	0.65 /28	0.50 /24	1.05	1.59
MUN	AB Interm Diversif Muni C	AIMCX	D	(800) 221-5672	D / 2.0	1.46	-2.31	-1.30 / 2	0.70 /29	0.53 /25	1.06	1.57
MUS	AB Interm NY Muni A	ANIAX	D+	(800) 221-5672	D+ / 2.5	1.70	-2.01	-0.41 /11	1.73 /55	1.30 /42	1.90	0.80
MUN	AB Interm NY Muni Advisor	ANIYX	U		U /	1.85	-1.88	--	--	--	0.00	N/A
MUS ●	AB Interm NY Muni B	ANYBX	D	(800) 221-5672	D+ / 2.4	1.49	-2.44	-1.22 / 3	0.93 /34	0.54 /25	1.06	1.57
MUS	AB Interm NY Muni C	ANMCX	D+	(800) 221-5672	D+ / 2.6	1.59	-2.30	-1.08 / 4	1.01 /36	0.57 /26	1.20	1.55
GEI	AB Intermediate Bond A	ABQUX	C-	(800) 221-5672	C- / 4.0	1.41	-1.40	3.66 /60	2.93 /60	2.82 /55	2.25	1.03
GEI	AB Intermediate Bond Adv	ABQYX	B+	(800) 221-5672	C+ / 6.2	1.36	-1.30	3.90 /62	3.19 /64	3.10 /59	2.58	0.77
GEI ●	AB Intermediate Bond B	ABQBX	C	(800) 221-5672	C / 4.5	1.13	-1.77	2.89 /56	2.18 /46	2.09 /43	1.59	1.80
GEI	AB Intermediate Bond C	ABQCX	C	(800) 221-5672	C / 4.5	1.23	-1.77	2.90 /56	2.19 /46	2.11 /44	1.60	1.78
GEI	AB Intermediate Bond I	ABQIX	B+	(800) 221-5672	C+ / 6.2	1.47	-1.18	4.02 /62	3.23 /65	3.12 /60	2.60	0.75
GEI	AB Intermediate Bond K	ABQKX	B	(800) 221-5672	C+ / 5.9	1.41	-1.40	3.66 /61	2.98 /61	2.87 /56	2.34	1.08
GEI	AB Intermediate Bond R	ABQRX	C+	(800) 221-5672	C / 5.4	1.35	-1.52	3.50 /60	2.69 /56	2.59 /51	2.10	1.38
COI	AB Intermediate Bond Z	ABQZX	B+	(800) 221-5672	C+ / 6.2	1.38	-1.28	3.91 /62	3.19 /64	2.97 /57	2.59	0.71
COH	AB Limited Dur High Inc A	ALHAX	C-	(800) 221-5672	C+ / 6.1	2.30	2.57	10.42 /80	3.01 /61	4.63 /80	3.35	1.08
COH	AB Limited Dur High Inc Adv	ALHYX	B-	(800) 221-5672	B / 7.7	2.36	2.70	10.71 /80	3.34 /66	4.94 /83	3.75	0.84
COH	AB Limited Dur High Inc C	ALHCX	C	(800) 221-5672	C+ / 6.6	2.21	2.29	9.72 /78	2.31 /48	3.88 /71	2.77	1.84
COH	AB Limited Dur High Inc I	ALIHX	B-	(800) 221-5672	B / 7.7	2.36	2.71	10.72 /81	3.34 /66	4.97 /84	3.77	1.38
COH	AB Limited Dur High Inc K	ALHKX	C+	(800) 221-5672	B- / 7.4	2.29	2.56	10.40 /80	3.02 /61	4.66 /80	3.49	1.71
COH	AB Limited Dur High Inc R	ALHRX	C+	(800) 221-5672	B- / 7.2	2.23	2.44	10.13 /79	2.76 /57	4.40 /77	3.24	2.02
MUN	AB Muni Bond Inf Str 1	AUNOX	B+	(800) 221-5672	C+ / 5.6	2.99	1.37	3.27 /67	1.27 /42	0.92 /33	1.93	0.67
MUN	AB Muni Bond Inf Str 2	AUNTX	A-	(800) 221-5672	C+ / 5.8	2.91	1.42	3.27 /67	1.34 /44	1.00 /35	2.04	0.57
MUN	AB Muni Bond Inf Str A	AUNAX	C-	(800) 221-5672	C- / 3.1	2.84	1.29	3.10 /66	1.06 /37	0.72 /29	1.72	0.87
MUN	AB Muni Bond Inf Str Adv	AUNYX	A-	(800) 221-5672	C+ / 5.9	3.00	1.50	3.35 /67	1.36 /45	1.02 /36	2.01	0.61
MUN	AB Muni Bond Inf Str C	AUNCX	C-	(800) 221-5672	C- / 3.2	2.66	0.91	2.23 /59	0.35 /21	--	1.02	1.61
*MUH	AB Municipal Income	MISHX	B+	(800) 221-5672	A+ / 9.9	2.73	-4.32	1.95 /56	6.93 /99	6.25 /99	4.01	0.01
MUS	AB Municipal Income CA A	ALCAX	C	(800) 221-5672	C+ / 6.4	1.92	-3.25	-0.40 /11	3.68 /90	3.15 /82	3.22	0.80
MUS	AB Municipal Income CA Adv	ALCVX	B+	(800) 221-5672	B / 8.2	1.99	-3.13	-0.15 /15	3.95 /92	3.44 /87	3.58	0.55
MUS ●	AB Municipal Income CA B	ALCBX	C	(800) 221-5672	C+ / 6.4	1.74	-3.62	-1.14 / 3	2.92 /81	2.42 /69	2.55	1.56
MUS	AB Municipal Income CA C	ACACX	C+	(800) 221-5672	C+ / 6.4	1.74	-3.53	-1.14 / 3	2.92 /81	2.42 /69	2.55	1.56
MUS	AB Municipal Income II AZ A	AAZAX	B-	(800) 221-5672	C+ / 6.9	1.78	-2.88	0.33 /33	3.83 /91	2.99 /80	3.01	0.96
MUS ●	AB Municipal Income II AZ B	AAZBX	B-	(800) 221-5672	C+ / 6.9	1.69	-3.16	-0.42 /11	3.11 /83	2.26 /65	2.34	1.71

RISK			NET ASSETS		ASSET							FUND MANAGER		MINIMUM		LOADS	
Risk Rating/Pts	3 Yr Avg Standard Deviation	Avg Dura-tion	NAV As of 2/28/17	Total $(Mil)	Cash %	Gov. Bond %	Muni. Bond %	Corp. Bond %	Other %	Portfolio Turnover Ratio	Avg Coupon Rate	Manager Quality Pct	Manager Tenure (Years)	Initial Purch. $	Additional Purch. $	Front End Load	Back End Load
D /1.9	4.8	6.3	11.07	781	0	0	100	0	0	14	0.0	77	7	2,500	50	3.0	0.0
D /1.9	4.7	6.3	11.06	1,325	0	0	100	0	0	14	0.0	80	7	0	0	0.0	0.0
D /1.9	4.8	6.3	11.07	314	0	0	100	0	0	14	0.0	59	7	2,500	50	0.0	0.0
D /1.8	5.3	3.9	8.86	88	1	27	0	52	20	45	5.9	96	15	0	0	0.0	0.0
D /1.8	5.3	3.9	8.88	128	1	27	0	52	20	45	5.9	98	15	0	0	0.0	0.0
U /	N/A	4.7	9.73	4	18	3	0	71	8	56	6.0	N/A	3	2,500	50	4.3	0.0
U /	N/A	4.7	9.74	3	18	3	0	71	8	56	6.0	N/A	3	0	0	0.0	0.0
U /	N/A	4.7	9.73	1	18	3	0	71	8	56	6.0	N/A	3	2,500	50	0.0	0.0
U /	N/A	4.7	9.74	18	18	3	0	71	8	56	6.0	N/A	3	0	0	0.0	0.0
U /	N/A	4.7	9.74	N/A	18	3	0	71	8	56	6.0	N/A	3	0	0	0.0	0.0
U /	N/A	4.7	9.73	N/A	18	3	0	71	8	56	6.0	N/A	3	0	0	0.0	0.0
D- /1.1	5.6	4.7	9.73	64	18	3	0	71	8	56	6.0	35	3	0	0	0.0	0.0
U /	N/A	4.9	8.03	9	0	77	0	10	13	34	7.3	N/A	30	2,500	50	4.3	0.0
C /4.9	3.2	4.9	8.04	911	0	77	0	10	13	34	7.3	96	30	0	0	0.0	0.0
U /	N/A	4.9	8.05	3	0	77	0	10	13	34	7.3	N/A	30	2,500	50	0.0	0.0
B /7.7	2.4	4.2	14.22	85	0	5	94	0	1	12	5.0	10	15	2,500	50	3.0	0.0
U /	N/A	4.2	14.22	6	0	5	94	0	1	12	5.0	N/A	15	0	0	0.0	0.0
B /7.6	2.5	4.2	14.22	23	0	5	94	0	1	12	5.0	3	15	2,500	50	0.0	0.0
B /7.7	2.4	4.0	14.32	382	0	4	94	0	2	11	5.0	10	28	2,500	50	3.0	0.0
U /	N/A	4.0	14.30	1,063	0	4	94	0	2	11	5.0	N/A	28	0	0	0.0	0.0
B /7.7	2.4	4.0	14.32	N/A	0	4	94	0	2	11	5.0	3	28	2,500	50	0.0	0.0
B /7.7	2.4	4.0	14.32	94	0	4	94	0	2	11	5.0	4	28	2,500	50	0.0	0.0
B /7.6	2.5	4.2	13.96	151	2	4	92	0	2	17	5.0	15	18	2,500	50	0.0	0.0
U /	N/A	4.2	13.96	14	2	4	92	0	2	17	5.0	N/A	18	0	0	0.0	0.0
B /7.6	2.5	4.2	13.96	N/A	2	4	92	0	2	17	5.0	4	18	2,500	50	0.0	0.0
B /7.6	2.5	4.2	13.97	52	2	4	92	0	2	17	5.0	5	18	2,500	50	0.0	0.0
C+ /6.2	2.9	4.9	11.01	231	0	25	0	29	46	128	3.7	62	12	2,500	50	4.3	0.0
C+ /6.3	2.9	4.9	11.01	60	0	25	0	29	46	128	3.7	70	12	0	0	0.0	0.0
C+ /6.4	2.8	4.9	11.01	1	0	25	0	29	46	128	3.7	29	12	2,500	50	0.0	0.0
C+ /6.1	2.9	4.9	10.99	39	0	25	0	29	46	128	3.7	28	12	2,500	50	0.0	0.0
C+ /6.5	2.8	4.9	11.03	3	0	25	0	29	46	128	3.7	71	12	0	0	0.0	0.0
C+ /6.2	2.9	4.9	11.02	5	0	25	0	29	46	128	3.7	63	12	0	0	0.0	0.0
C+ /6.1	2.9	4.9	11.01	3	0	25	0	29	46	128	3.7	54	12	0	0	0.0	0.0
C+ /6.5	2.8	4.9	11.03	18	0	25	0	29	46	128	3.7	68	12	0	0	0.0	0.0
C- /3.7	3.2	2.5	10.39	28	1	21	0	69	9	57	4.6	66	6	2,500	50	4.3	0.0
C- /3.8	3.1	2.5	10.38	286	1	21	0	69	9	57	4.6	73	6	0	0	0.0	0.0
C- /3.7	3.2	2.5	10.39	31	1	21	0	69	9	57	4.6	34	6	2,500	50	0.0	0.0
C- /3.7	3.2	2.5	10.39	N/A	1	21	0	69	9	57	4.6	73	6	0	0	0.0	0.0
C- /3.8	3.1	2.5	10.39	N/A	1	21	0	69	9	57	4.6	66	6	0	0	0.0	0.0
C- /3.7	3.2	2.5	10.39	N/A	1	21	0	69	9	57	4.6	58	6	0	0	0.0	0.0
B- /7.3	2.6	2.2	10.26	359	0	1	95	3	1	9	0.0	22	7	5,000	0	0.0	0.0
B- /7.5	2.5	2.2	10.26	179	0	1	95	3	1	9	0.0	27	7	0	0	0.0	0.0
B- /7.4	2.6	2.2	10.29	59	0	1	95	3	1	9	0.0	19	7	2,500	50	3.0	0.0
B- /7.3	2.6	2.2	10.30	193	0	1	95	3	1	9	0.0	25	7	0	0	0.0	0.0
B- /7.5	2.5	2.2	10.27	13	0	1	95	3	1	9	0.0	6	7	2,500	50	0.0	0.0
D /1.9	4.7	N/A	11.16	1,571	4	0	95	0	1	8	0.0	85	7	0	0	0.0	0.0
C /4.3	3.4	4.8	11.09	456	0	0	99	0	1	13	4.5	50	22	2,500	50	3.0	0.0
C /4.3	3.4	4.8	11.09	126	0	0	99	0	1	13	4.5	60	22	0	0	0.0	0.0
C /4.3	3.4	4.8	11.09	N/A	0	0	99	0	1	13	4.5	19	22	2,500	50	0.0	0.0
C /4.4	3.4	4.8	11.09	89	0	0	99	0	1	13	4.5	20	22	2,500	50	0.0	0.0
C /4.8	3.2	4.8	10.98	100	1	0	98	0	1	11	5.4	63	22	2,500	50	3.0	0.0
C /4.8	3.2	4.8	10.97	N/A	1	0	98	0	1	11	5.4	29	22	2,500	50	0.0	0.0

Fund Type	Fund Name	Ticker Symbol	Overall Investment Rating	Phone	Performance Rating/Pts	Total Return % through 2/28/17					Incl. in Returns	
	99 Pct = Best / 0 Pct = Worst					3 Mo	6 Mo	1Yr / Pct	Annualized 3Yr / Pct	5Yr / Pct	Dividend Yield	Expense Ratio
MUS	AB Municipal Income II AZ C	AAZCX	B-	(800) 221-5672	C+ / 6.9	1.69	-3.16	-0.42 /11	3.11 /83	2.26 /65	2.33	1.71
MUS	AB Municipal Income II MA A	AMAAX	C	(800) 221-5672	C / 5.6	1.67	-2.81	-0.29 /13	3.26 /85	2.47 /70	3.02	0.87
MUN	AB Municipal Income II MA Adv	AMAYX	U	(800) 221-5672	U /	1.74	-2.77	--	--	--	0.00	0.62
MUS ●	AB Municipal Income II MA B	AMABX	C	(800) 221-5672	C+ / 5.7	1.49	-3.17	-1.03 / 4	2.52 /74	1.76 /53	2.36	1.64
MUS	AB Municipal Income II MA C	AMACX	C	(800) 221-5672	C+ / 5.7	1.49	-3.18	-1.04 / 4	2.51 /73	1.74 /52	2.36	1.63
MUS	AB Municipal Income II MN A	AMNAX	C+	(800) 221-5672	C / 5.4	1.62	-2.60	-0.14 /15	3.10 /83	2.49 /70	2.82	1.08
MUS ●	AB Municipal Income II MN B	AMNBX	C+	(800) 221-5672	C / 5.5	1.44	-2.95	-0.88 / 5	2.38 /71	1.79 /54	2.13	1.84
MUS	AB Municipal Income II MN C	AMNCX	C+	(800) 221-5672	C / 5.4	1.44	-2.96	-0.88 / 5	2.34 /70	1.77 /53	2.13	1.84
MUS	AB Municipal Income II NJ A	ANJAX	C	(800) 221-5672	C+ / 6.2	2.12	-2.78	0.77 /41	3.34 /86	2.67 /74	3.32	0.99
MUS ●	AB Municipal Income II NJ B	ANJBX	C	(800) 221-5672	C+ / 6.2	1.94	-3.13	0.03 /20	2.59 /75	1.92 /57	2.66	1.78
MUS	AB Municipal Income II NJ C	ANJCX	C	(800) 221-5672	C+ / 6.2	1.82	-3.14	0.01 /18	2.59 /75	1.92 /57	2.65	1.74
MUS	AB Municipal Income II OH A	AOHAX	C+	(800) 221-5672	C+ / 6.5	2.14	-2.56	0.40 /35	3.53 /88	2.28 /66	2.78	0.99
MUS ●	AB Municipal Income II OH B	AOHBX	C+	(800) 221-5672	C+ / 6.5	1.96	-2.92	-0.34 /12	2.78 /78	1.56 /48	2.11	1.75
MUS	AB Municipal Income II OH C	AOHCX	C+	(800) 221-5672	C+ / 6.4	1.85	-3.02	-0.45 /10	2.74 /78	1.55 /47	2.10	1.74
MUS	AB Municipal Income II PA A	APAAX	C+	(800) 221-5672	C+ / 6.5	1.91	-2.49	0.23 /30	3.58 /89	2.71 /74	2.87	1.03
MUS ●	AB Municipal Income II PA B	APABX	C+	(800) 221-5672	C+ / 6.5	1.72	-2.86	-0.52 / 9	2.79 /78	1.97 /58	2.19	1.88
MUS	AB Municipal Income II PA C	APACX	C+	(800) 221-5672	C+ / 6.4	1.71	-2.87	-0.55 / 9	2.78 /78	1.96 /58	2.16	1.78
MUS	AB Municipal Income II VA A	AVAAX	A-	(800) 221-5672	C+ / 6.9	1.97	-2.38	0.48 /37	3.77 /90	2.73 /75	2.96	0.87
MUN	AB Municipal Income II VA Adv	AVAYX	U	(800) 221-5672	U /	2.04	-2.25	--	--	--	0.00	0.62
MUS ●	AB Municipal Income II VA B	AVABX	B+	(800) 221-5672	C+ / 6.8	1.78	-2.83	-0.35 /12	2.98 /81	2.00 /59	2.29	1.65
MUS	AB Municipal Income II VA C	AVACX	B+	(800) 221-5672	C+ / 6.8	1.79	-2.75	-0.35 /12	2.99 /82	2.00 /59	2.30	1.62
* MUN	AB Municipal Income Natl A	ALTHX	C	(800) 221-5672	C+ / 6.5	1.99	-3.36	0.26 /31	3.61 /89	3.01 /80	2.98	0.80
MUN	AB Municipal Income Natl Adv	ALTVX	B+	(800) 221-5672	B / 8.2	2.05	-3.24	0.51 /37	3.89 /92	3.30 /85	3.33	0.55
MUN ●	AB Municipal Income Natl B	ALTBX	C	(800) 221-5672	C+ / 6.5	1.81	-3.77	-0.53 / 9	2.88 /80	2.29 /66	2.26	1.58
MUN	AB Municipal Income Natl C	ALNCX	C	(800) 221-5672	C+ / 6.5	1.81	-3.72	-0.49 /10	2.86 /80	2.28 /66	2.30	1.56
MUS	AB Municipal Income NY A	ALNYX	C	(800) 221-5672	C+ / 5.8	1.99	-3.19	-0.06 /17	3.31 /86	2.32 /67	2.84	0.83
MUS	AB Municipal Income NY Adv	ALNVX	B+	(800) 221-5672	B / 7.7	2.05	-3.06	0.19 /28	3.58 /89	2.58 /72	3.18	0.58
MUS ●	AB Municipal Income NY B	ALNBX	C	(800) 221-5672	C+ / 5.9	1.81	-3.45	-0.80 / 6	2.56 /74	1.59 /49	2.16	1.61
MUS	AB Municipal Income NY C	ANYCX	C-	(800) 221-5672	C+ / 5.8	1.81	-3.55	-0.80 / 6	2.53 /74	1.57 /48	2.16	1.58
GEI	AB Short Duration A	ADPAX	D	(800) 221-5672	E- / 0.2	0.26	-0.18	0.42 /31	0.24 /17	0.16 /17	0.48	0.96
GEI ●	AB Short Duration B	ADPBX	D	(800) 221-5672	E / 0.5	0.10	-0.31	0.12 /23	-0.03 / 5	-0.09 / 4	0.29	1.72
GEI	AB Short Duration C	ADPCX	D	(800) 221-5672	E / 0.5	0.12	-0.28	0.13 /23	-0.01 / 5	-0.06 / 5	0.30	1.72
MUN	AB Tax Aware Fxd Inc A	ATTAX	D+	(800) 221-5672	C / 5.1	2.02	-3.23	0.11 /25	2.94 /81	--	1.96	2.18
MUN	AB Tax Aware Fxd Inc Adv	ATTYX	B	(800) 221-5672	B- / 7.3	2.08	-3.11	0.35 /34	3.21 /84	--	2.28	1.92
MUN	AB Tax Aware Fxd Inc C	ATCCX	D+	(800) 221-5672	C / 5.1	1.83	-3.59	-0.64 / 8	2.18 /66	--	1.25	2.85
GEN	AB Taxable MS Income	CSHTX	B-	(800) 221-5672	C- / 3.2	0.61	0.35	1.96 /48	1.22 /31	1.58 /36	2.05	N/A
GL	AB Unconstrained Bond A	AGSAX	C	(800) 221-5672	C / 4.7	3.97	3.39	7.97 /74	2.06 /44	2.44 /48	3.21	1.01
GL	AB Unconstrained Bond Adv	AGSIX	A-	(800) 221-5672	C+ / 6.8	4.04	3.52	8.26 /75	2.35 /49	2.74 /53	3.61	0.76
GL ●	AB Unconstrained Bond B	AGSBX	C+	(800) 221-5672	C / 5.1	3.76	2.99	7.13 /73	1.30 /32	1.74 /38	2.59	1.76
GL	AB Unconstrained Bond C	AGCCX	C+	(800) 221-5672	C / 5.2	3.77	2.99	7.15 /73	1.32 /32	1.75 /38	2.60	1.77
GL	AB Unconstrained Bond I	AGLIX	A-	(800) 221-5672	C+ / 6.8	4.06	3.54	8.31 /75	2.37 /49	2.76 /54	3.66	0.78
GL	AB Unconstrained Bond K	AGSKX	B+	(800) 221-5672	C+ / 6.4	3.92	3.33	7.97 /74	2.06 /44	2.47 /49	3.25	1.12
GL	AB Unconstrained Bond R	AGSRX	B	(800) 221-5672	C+ / 6.0	3.87	3.29	7.65 /74	1.84 /40	2.24 /45	2.95	1.46
GL	Aberdeen Asia Bond A	AEEAX	E	(866) 667-9231	D / 2.0	2.56	-3.19	5.04 /67	1.35 /33	0.49 /21	0.00	1.04
GL	Aberdeen Asia Bond C	AEECX	E	(866) 667-9231	D+ / 2.5	2.41	-3.55	4.37 /64	0.57 /21	-0.26 / 4	0.00	1.81
GL	Aberdeen Asia Bond Inst Service	ABISX	E+	(866) 667-9231	C- / 3.9	2.67	-3.10	5.26 /68	1.40 /33	0.51 /21	0.00	0.90
GL	Aberdeen Asia Bond Instituitonal	CSABX	E+	(866) 667-9231	C / 4.3	2.76	-2.99	5.45 /68	1.62 /37	0.76 /24	0.00	0.85
GL	Aberdeen Asia Bond R	AEERX	E	(866) 667-9231	C- / 3.4	2.58	-3.31	4.85 /66	1.09 /29	0.22 /19	0.00	1.25
EM	Aberdeen Emerging Markets Debt A	AKFAX	D+	(866) 667-9231	B+ / 8.5	6.15	0.82	17.99 /94	4.27 /78	--	0.00	1.62
EM	Aberdeen Emerging Markets Debt C	AKFCX	C-	(866) 667-9231	B+ / 8.8	6.07	0.62	17.27 /92	3.58 /70	--	0.00	2.42
EM	Aberdeen Emerging Markets Debt	AKFIX	C	(866) 667-9231	A / 9.4	6.36	1.13	18.35 /94	4.50 /81	--	0.00	1.35
EM	Aberdeen Emerging Markets Debt IS	AKFSX	C	(866) 667-9231	A / 9.5	6.35	1.02	18.47 /94	4.60 /82	--	0.00	1.35

● Denotes fund is closed to new investors
* Denotes fund is included in Section II

www.thestreetratings.com

RISK			NET ASSETS		ASSET					Portfolio Turnover Ratio	Avg Coupon Rate	FUND MANAGER		MINIMUM		LOADS	
Risk Rating/Pts	3 Yr Avg Standard Deviation	Avg Dura-tion	NAV As of 2/28/17	Total $(Mil)	Cash %	Gov. Bond %	Muni. Bond %	Corp. Bond %	Other %			Manager Quality Pct	Manager Tenure (Years)	Initial Purch. $	Additional Purch. $	Front End Load	Back End Load
C /4.8	3.2	4.8	10.97	23	1	0	98	0	1	11	5.4	30	22	2,500	50	0.0	0.0
C /5.1	3.1	4.8	11.21	176	1	0	98	0	1	15	5.2	45	22	2,500	50	3.0	0.0
U /	N/A	4.8	11.20	22	1	0	98	0	1	15	5.2	N/A	22	0	0	0.0	0.0
C /5.2	3.1	4.8	11.19	N/A	1	0	98	0	1	15	5.2	17	22	2,500	50	0.0	0.0
C /5.2	3.1	4.8	11.19	53	1	0	98	0	1	15	5.2	17	22	2,500	50	0.0	0.0
C+ /5.9	2.9	4.6	10.18	64	1	0	98	0	1	10	5.2	43	22	2,500	50	3.0	0.0
C+ /6.0	2.9	4.6	10.19	N/A	1	0	98	0	1	10	5.2	17	22	2,500	50	0.0	0.0
C+ /5.9	2.9	4.6	10.19	15	1	0	98	0	1	10	5.2	16	22	2,500	50	0.0	0.0
C /4.4	3.3	4.9	9.60	82	1	0	98	0	1	14	4.9	33	22	2,500	50	3.0	0.0
C /4.4	3.3	4.9	9.60	N/A	1	0	98	0	1	14	4.9	14	22	2,500	50	0.0	0.0
C /4.4	3.3	4.9	9.60	27	1	0	98	0	1	14	4.9	14	22	2,500	50	0.0	0.0
C /4.8	3.2	5.0	9.88	73	0	0	98	0	2	13	5.2	53	22	2,500	50	3.0	0.0
C /4.9	3.2	5.0	9.87	N/A	0	0	98	0	2	13	5.2	20	22	2,500	50	0.0	0.0
C /4.9	3.2	5.0	9.87	24	0	0	98	0	2	13	5.2	20	22	2,500	50	0.0	0.0
C /4.8	3.2	4.7	10.37	76	0	1	98	0	1	11	5.1	56	22	2,500	50	3.0	0.0
C /4.7	3.2	4.7	10.37	N/A	0	1	98	0	1	11	5.1	20	22	2,500	50	0.0	0.0
C /4.8	3.2	4.7	10.37	20	0	1	98	0	1	11	5.1	21	22	2,500	50	0.0	0.0
C+ /6.0	2.9	4.7	11.04	167	1	0	98	0	1	7	5.1	68	22	2,500	50	3.0	0.0
U /	N/A	4.7	11.04	10	1	0	98	0	1	7	5.1	N/A	22	0	0	0.0	0.0
C+ /5.9	2.9	4.7	11.02	N/A	1	0	98	0	1	7	5.1	34	22	2,500	50	0.0	0.0
C+ /5.8	2.9	4.7	11.01	53	1	0	98	0	1	7	5.1	34	22	2,500	50	0.0	0.0
C- /4.2	3.4	4.7	10.12	614	0	0	99	0	1	13	5.4	41	22	2,500	50	3.0	0.0
C- /4.1	3.5	4.7	10.12	458	0	0	99	0	1	13	5.4	54	22	0	0	0.0	0.0
C- /4.1	3.5	4.7	10.11	N/A	0	0	99	0	1	13	5.4	16	22	2,500	50	0.0	0.0
C- /4.2	3.4	4.7	10.11	143	0	0	99	0	1	13	5.4	16	22	2,500	50	0.0	0.0
C /4.5	3.3	4.8	9.83	443	0	0	99	0	1	16	5.0	32	22	2,500	50	3.0	0.0
C /4.4	3.3	4.8	9.83	72	0	0	99	0	1	16	5.0	47	22	0	0	0.0	0.0
C /4.5	3.3	4.8	9.82	1	0	0	99	0	1	16	5.0	13	22	2,500	50	0.0	0.0
C /4.5	3.3	4.8	9.82	83	0	0	99	0	1	16	5.0	12	22	2,500	50	0.0	0.0
A+ /9.6	0.7	2.1	11.70	23	4	34	0	23	39	76	1.6	27	12	2,500	50	4.3	0.0
A+ /9.7	0.7	2.1	11.67	N/A	4	34	0	23	39	76	1.6	20	12	2,500	50	0.0	0.0
A+ /9.7	0.7	2.1	11.67	10	4	34	0	23	39	76	1.6	20	12	2,500	50	0.0	0.0
C /4.5	3.3	5.3	10.58	9	4	0	92	2	2	36	0.0	21	4	2,500	50	3.0	0.0
C /4.5	3.3	5.3	10.58	47	4	0	92	2	2	36	0.0	29	4	0	0	0.0	0.0
C /4.4	3.3	5.3	10.58	2	4	0	92	2	2	36	0.0	7	4	2,500	50	0.0	0.0
A /9.3	0.9	N/A	9.84	98	1	41	0	35	23	109	0.0	64	7	0	0	0.0	0.0
C+ /6.2	2.9	4.6	8.62	42	8	38	0	33	21	137	2.3	86	21	2,500	50	4.3	0.0
C+ /6.2	2.9	4.6	8.61	164	8	38	0	33	21	137	2.3	88	21	0	0	0.0	0.0
C+ /6.2	2.9	4.6	8.63	N/A	8	38	0	33	21	137	2.3	80	21	2,500	50	0.0	0.0
C+ /6.3	2.9	4.6	8.62	19	8	38	0	33	21	137	2.3	80	21	2,500	50	0.0	0.0
C+ /6.2	2.9	4.6	8.60	47	8	38	0	33	21	137	2.3	88	21	0	0	0.0	0.0
C+ /6.4	2.8	4.6	8.65	N/A	8	38	0	33	21	137	2.3	86	21	0	0	0.0	0.0
C+ /6.3	2.9	4.6	8.63	1	8	38	0	33	21	137	2.3	85	21	0	0	0.0	0.0
D- /1.4	5.8	5.7	10.01	1	6	44	0	40	10	96	5.0	90	10	1,000	50	4.3	0.0
D- /1.3	5.9	5.7	9.79	N/A	6	44	0	40	10	96	5.0	84	10	1,000	50	0.0	0.0
D- /1.3	5.9	5.7	10.01	8	6	44	0	40	10	96	5.0	90	10	1,000,000	0	0.0	0.0
D- /1.4	5.8	5.7	10.06	13	6	44	0	40	10	96	5.0	91	10	1,000,000	0	0.0	0.0
D- /1.3	5.9	5.7	9.94	N/A	6	44	0	40	10	96	5.0	88	10	0	0	0.0	0.0
E /0.5	7.6	6.9	9.84	N/A	3	75	1	15	6	103	0.0	97	5	1,000	50	4.3	0.0
E /0.5	7.6	6.9	9.78	N/A	3	75	1	15	6	103	0.0	96	5	1,000	50	0.0	0.0
E /0.5	7.6	6.9	9.87	18	3	75	1	15	6	103	0.0	98	5	1,000,000	0	0.0	0.0
E /0.5	7.6	6.9	9.88	N/A	3	75	1	15	6	103	0.0	98	5	1,000,000	0	0.0	0.0

I. Index of Bond and Money Market Mutual Funds

Fund Type	Fund Name	Ticker Symbol	Overall Investment Rating	Phone	Performance Rating/Pts	3 Mo	6 Mo	1Yr / Pct	3Yr / Pct	5Yr / Pct	Dividend Yield	Expense Ratio
							Total Return % through 2/28/17		Annualized		Incl. in Returns	
EM	Aberdeen Emerging Markets Debt R	AKFRX	C	(866) 667-9231	A- / 9.2	6.16	0.82	17.87 /93	4.10 /76	--	0.00	1.85
GL	Aberdeen Global High Income A	BJBHX	D-	(866) 667-9231	C+ / 5.6	4.69	4.42	16.14 /90	0.06 /10	4.18 /75	5.10	1.04
GL	Aberdeen Global High Income I	JHYIX	D-	(866) 667-9231	C+ / 6.0	4.69	4.47	16.26 /91	0.31 /19	4.44 /78	5.71	0.76
GL	Aberdeen Global Unconstrained FI A	CUGAX	E	(866) 667-9231	D / 2.1	1.33	1.03	9.55 /78	0.43 /20	0.69 /23	0.00	2.06
GL	Aberdeen Global Unconstrained FI C	CGBCX	E	(866) 667-9231	D+ / 2.6	1.15	0.74	8.80 /76	-0.26 / 4	-0.03 / 5	0.00	2.92
GL	Aberdeen Global Unconstrained FI I	AGCIX	E+	(866) 667-9231	C / 4.3	1.42	1.22	9.91 /79	0.73 /23	1.00 /27	0.00	1.87
GL	Aberdeen Global Unconstrained FI IS	CGFIX	E+	(866) 667-9231	C- / 4.1	1.42	1.12	9.74 /78	0.55 /21	0.82 /25	0.00	1.92
MUN	Aberdeen Tax-Free Income A	NTFAX	D	(866) 667-9231	D+ / 2.3	1.46	-2.18	-0.56 / 9	2.04 /63	1.96 /58	2.86	1.02
MUN	Aberdeen Tax-Free Income C	GTICX	C-	(866) 667-9231	C- / 3.1	1.28	-2.44	-1.19 / 3	1.29 /43	1.23 /40	2.24	1.82
MUN	Aberdeen Tax-Free Income Inst	ABEIX	A-	(866) 667-9231	C+ / 5.7	1.53	-2.05	-0.29 /13	2.30 /69	2.22 /64	3.26	0.75
MUN	Aberdeen Tax-Free Income IS	ABESX	A-	(866) 667-9231	C+ / 5.7	1.52	-2.06	-0.30 /13	2.31 /69	--	3.25	0.75
MUN	Aberdeen Tax-Free Income R	ABERX	B-	(866) 667-9231	C / 4.4	1.40	-2.30	-0.80 / 6	1.80 /57	--	2.74	1.25
GL	Aberdeen Total Return Bond A	BJBGX	C+	(866) 667-9231	C / 5.0	1.14	-1.85	3.30 /58	2.53 /52	2.08 /43	0.98	0.71
GL	Aberdeen Total Return Bond I	JBGIX	B-	(866) 667-9231	C / 5.5	1.14	-1.75	3.54 /60	2.78 /57	2.34 /47	1.26	0.45
USS	Access Cap Community Invs A	ACASX	C-	(800) 422-2766	D / 2.0	0.25	-0.97	-0.06 /17	1.95 /42	1.62 /36	2.51	1.06
USS	Access Cap Community Invs I	ACCSX	B	(800) 422-2766	C- / 4.2	0.34	-0.90	0.31 /29	2.33 /49	1.95 /41	2.98	0.63
COH	Access Flex Bear High Yield Inv	AFBIX	E-	(888) 776-3637	E- / 0.0	-3.91	-4.96	-14.53 / 0	-8.63 / 0	-11.20 / 0	0.00	2.60
COH	Access Flex Bear High Yield Svc	AFBSX	E-	(888) 776-3637	E- / 0.0	-4.15	-5.32	-15.21 / 0	-9.49 / 0	-12.06 / 0	0.00	3.60
COH	Access Flex High Yield Inv	FYAIX	C	(888) 776-3637	B / 7.9	2.76	2.43	9.88 /79	3.60 /70	5.64 /90	2.15	1.77
COH	Access Flex High Yield Svc	FYASX	D	(888) 776-3637	C+ / 6.8	2.50	1.97	8.86 /76	2.57 /53	4.60 /80	1.14	2.77
MMT●	Active Assets Government Trust	AISXX	C-	(800) 869-6397	D- / 1.2	0.11	0.18	0.32 /29	0.13 /14	0.08 /14	0.32	N/A
MMT●	Active Assets Prime Trust S	AVIXX	C-	(800) 869-6397	D- / 1.2	0.06	0.09	0.26 /28	0.14 /15	0.11 /15	0.26	N/A
COI	Advantus Strategic Credit Inc A	ABSNX	U	(800) 665-6005	U /	2.20	2.21	4.67 /65	--	--	2.02	1.51
COI	Advantus Strategic Credit Inc Inst	VBSIX	U	(800) 665-6005	U /	2.27	2.35	4.71 /65	--	--	2.16	1.26
GES	AdvisorOne CLS Flexible Income N	CLFLX	A-	(866) 811-0225	C+ / 5.8	2.12	0.23	5.52 /69	2.42 /50	2.34 /47	2.50	1.24
MTG	Advisors Series Trust PIA MBS Bond	PMTGX	B	(800) 251-1970	C- / 4.2	0.37	-1.45	0.44 /32	2.38 /50	2.00 /42	2.88	0.31
GEN	Advisory Research Strategic Income	ADVNX	B-	(888) 665-1414	C+ / 6.9	2.99	-0.09	6.08 /70	3.83 /73	--	4.19	1.14
COH	AIG Flexible Credit A	SHNAX	D	(800) 858-8850	C+ / 6.5	3.27	3.44	11.72 /83	3.11 /63	5.17 /86	3.93	1.48
COH	AIG Flexible Credit C	SHNCX	C-	(800) 858-8850	B- / 7.1	2.80	3.11	10.96 /81	2.45 /51	4.49 /79	3.50	2.12
COH	AIG Flexible Credit W	SHNWX	U	(800) 858-8850	U /	3.02	3.55	11.95 /83	--	--	4.34	1.29
MMT	AIG Govt Money Market I	NAIXX	U	(800) 858-8850	U /	--	--	--	--	--	0.01	N/A
LP	AIG Sr Floating Rate A	SASFX	B	(800) 858-8850	C+ / 6.9	2.59	4.47	13.03 /85	3.01 /61	4.16 /74	3.54	1.79
LP	AIG Sr Floating Rate C	NFRCX	B+	(800) 858-8850	B / 7.7	2.64	4.32	12.85 /85	2.74 /57	3.88 /71	3.39	2.19
GES	AIG Strategic Bond A	SDIAX	D-	(800) 858-8850	C / 5.4	3.08	0.59	10.50 /80	2.73 /56	3.63 /68	3.12	1.34
GES	AIG Strategic Bond B	SDIBX	D	(800) 858-8850	C+ / 6.2	2.91	0.25	9.77 /78	2.05 /44	2.95 /57	2.62	2.01
GES	AIG Strategic Bond C	NAICX	D	(800) 858-8850	C+ / 6.0	2.60	-0.02	9.77 /78	1.98 /43	2.91 /56	2.65	1.98
GEL	AIG Strategic Bond W	SDIWX	U	(800) 858-8850	U /	3.12	0.68	10.70 /80	--	--	3.46	1.15
USS	AIG US Gov Sec A	SGTAX	E+	(800) 858-8850	E- / 0.1	-0.12	-4.05	-2.83 / 0	0.69 /23	0.02 / 7	1.68	1.36
USS	AIG US Gov Sec C	NASBX	E+	(800) 858-8850	E- / 0.2	-0.28	-4.46	-3.56 / 0	0.04 / 9	-0.63 / 3	1.10	2.03
MUS	Alabama Tax Free Bond	ALABX	C-	(866) 738-1125	D / 2.0	1.19	-0.91	-0.40 /11	0.48 /24	0.68 /28	1.24	0.82
EM	AllianzGI Emerging Markets Dbt Inst	AGMIX	U	(800) 988-8380	U /	4.69	2.83	15.21 /89	--	--	5.27	1.60
EM	AllianzGI Emerging Markets Debt A	AGMAX	U	(800) 988-8380	U /	4.66	2.75	14.97 /88	--	--	4.68	1.85
EM	AllianzGI Emerging Markets Debt C	AGMCX	U	(800) 988-8380	U /	4.46	2.32	14.08 /87	--	--	4.29	2.59
EM	AllianzGI Emerging Markets Debt P	AGMPX	U	(800) 988-8380	U /	4.70	2.76	15.09 /89	--	--	5.11	1.59
COH	AllianzGI High Yield Bond A	AYBAX	D	(800) 988-8380	B- / 7.5	4.20	4.98	19.30 /95	2.60 /54	5.15 /85	5.39	1.03
COH	AllianzGI High Yield Bond Admn	AYBVX	C-	(800) 988-8380	B+ / 8.4	4.21	5.06	19.34 /95	2.36 /49	5.05 /84	5.88	0.98
COH	AllianzGI High Yield Bond C	AYBCX	D	(800) 988-8380	B / 7.8	4.02	4.71	18.47 /94	1.89 /41	4.40 /77	4.90	1.68
COH	AllianzGI High Yield Bond Inst	AYBIX	C	(800) 988-8380	B+ / 8.9	4.31	5.20	19.86 /96	2.99 /61	5.53 /89	6.11	0.63
COH	AllianzGI High Yield Bond P	AYBPX	C	(800) 988-8380	B+ / 8.8	4.32	5.20	19.76 /96	2.96 /60	5.48 /88	6.12	0.64
COH	AllianzGI High Yield Bond R	AYBRX	D+	(800) 988-8380	B / 8.0	4.02	4.75	18.99 /95	2.07 /44	4.74 /81	5.59	1.46
COH	AllianzGI Short Dur High Inc A	ASHAX	C+	(800) 988-8380	B / 7.6	2.00	2.60	11.91 /83	3.77 /72	4.44 /78	4.95	0.86
COH	AllianzGI Short Dur High Inc C	ASHCX	B-	(800) 988-8380	B / 8.0	2.01	2.48	11.65 /82	3.50 /69	4.14 /74	4.82	1.15

● Denotes fund is closed to new investors
* Denotes fund is included in Section II

RISK			NET ASSETS		ASSET					Portfolio Turnover Ratio	Avg Coupon Rate	FUND MANAGER		MINIMUM		LOADS	
Risk Rating/Pts	3 Yr Avg Standard Deviation	Avg Dura-tion	NAV As of 2/28/17	Total $(Mil)	Cash %	Gov. Bond %	Muni. Bond %	Corp. Bond %	Other %			Manager Quality Pct	Manager Tenure (Years)	Initial Purch. $	Additional Purch. $	Front End Load	Back End Load
E / 0.5	7.6	6.9	9.83	2	3	75	1	15	6	103	0.0	97	5	0	0	0.0	0.0
D / 1.6	5.6	N/A	8.92	206	4	2	0	87	7	72	0.0	61	15	1,000	50	0.0	0.0
D / 1.6	5.6	N/A	8.37	256	4	2	0	87	7	72	0.0	69	15	1,000,000	0	0.0	0.0
D+ / 2.4	4.6	-0.3	10.15	1	1	9	0	85	5	174	5.7	82	8	1,000	50	4.3	0.0
D+ / 2.4	4.6	-0.3	9.96	N/A	1	9	0	85	5	174	5.7	72	8	1,000	50	0.0	0.0
D+ / 2.4	4.6	-0.3	10.25	4	1	9	0	85	5	174	5.7	84	8	1,000,000	0	0.0	0.0
D+ / 2.4	4.5	-0.3	10.19	11	1	9	0	85	5	174	5.7	82	8	1,000,000	0	0.0	0.0
B / 7.6	2.4	4.8	9.88	9	0	0	99	0	1	11	4.8	21	4	1,000	50	4.3	0.0
B / 7.7	2.4	4.8	9.87	1	0	0	99	0	1	11	4.8	8	4	1,000	50	0.0	0.0
B / 7.6	2.4	4.8	9.89	77	0	0	99	0	1	11	4.8	28	4	1,000,000	0	0.0	0.0
B / 7.6	2.5	4.8	9.89	N/A	0	0	99	0	1	11	4.8	28	4	1,000,000	0	0.0	0.0
B / 7.7	2.4	4.8	9.89	N/A	0	0	99	0	1	11	4.8	16	4	0	0	0.0	0.0
C+ / 6.0	2.9	4.7	13.13	66	2	17	4	32	45	151	0.0	92	15	1,000	50	0.0	0.0
C+ / 6.3	2.9	4.7	12.94	404	2	17	4	32	45	151	0.0	93	15	1,000,000	0	0.0	0.0
B+ / 8.6	1.8	2.9	9.03	23	0	0	2	0	98	13	0.0	75	11	2,500	100	3.8	0.0
B+ / 8.6	1.7	2.9	9.02	576	0	0	2	0	98	13	0.0	80	11	1,000,000	10,000	0.0	0.0
D / 1.6	5.1	N/A	39.06	1	100	0	0	0	0	0	0.0	0	12	15,000	0	0.0	0.0
D / 1.6	5.1	N/A	34.89	N/A	100	0	0	0	0	0	0.0	0	12	15,000	0	0.0	0.0
D / 2.1	4.4	N/A	33.27	30	48	51	0	0	1	2,247	0.0	76	13	15,000	0	0.0	0.0
D / 2.1	4.4	N/A	32.50	6	48	51	0	0	1	2,247	0.0	47	13	15,000	0	0.0	0.0
A+ / 9.9	N/A	N/A	1.00	5,757	100	0	0	0	0	0	0.3	47	N/A	2,000,000	0	0.0	0.0
A+ / 9.9	N/A	N/A	1.00	9	100	0	0	0	0	0	0.3	48	N/A	5,000	0	0.0	0.0
U /	N/A	N/A	10.04	N/A	0	0	0	0	100	96	0.0	N/A	3	1,000	100	0.0	0.0
U /	N/A	N/A	10.04	26	0	0	0	0	100	96	0.0	N/A	3	100,000	1,000	0.0	0.0
B- / 7.5	2.5	N/A	10.25	188	0	29	4	45	22	19	0.0	71	3	2,500	250	0.0	0.0
B+ / 8.3	2.0	2.3	9.53	83	0	11	0	0	89	161	0.0	38	11	1,000	50	0.0	0.0
C / 4.9	3.2	4.5	9.40	9	6	0	0	46	48	26	0.0	86	14	2,500	500	0.0	2.0
D+ / 2.5	3.9	2.1	3.46	150	0	0	0	66	34	52	5.3	54	16	500	100	4.8	0.0
D+ / 2.6	3.9	2.1	3.48	75	0	0	0	66	34	52	5.3	25	16	500	100	0.0	0.0
U /	N/A	2.1	3.46	151	0	0	0	66	34	52	5.3	N/A	3	50,000	0	0.0	0.0
U /	N/A	N/A	1.00	13	100	0	0	0	0	0	0.0	N/A	N/A	0	0	0.0	0.0
C / 5.0	3.1	N/A	8.12	131	2	0	0	75	23	48	0.0	88	8	500	100	3.8	0.0
C / 4.9	3.2	N/A	8.12	155	2	0	0	75	23	48	0.0	86	8	500	100	0.0	0.0
D+ / 2.8	4.1	6.0	3.41	166	3	9	0	60	28	108	5.1	69	15	500	100	4.8	0.0
D+ / 2.8	4.2	6.0	3.41	30	3	9	0	60	28	108	5.1	47	15	500	100	0.0	0.0
D+ / 2.8	4.2	6.0	3.42	133	3	9	0	60	28	108	5.1	46	15	500	100	0.0	0.0
U /	N/A	6.0	3.41	36	3	9	0	60	28	108	5.1	N/A	15	50,000	0	0.0	0.0
C+ / 6.6	2.6	7.6	9.17	150	0	53	0	0	47	36	3.2	16	3	500	100	4.8	0.0
C+ / 6.5	2.6	7.6	9.16	20	0	53	0	0	47	36	3.2	6	3	500	100	0.0	0.0
B+ / 8.8	1.5	2.9	10.35	27	1	0	98	0	1	13	0.0	12	24	5,000	0	0.0	0.0
U /	N/A	N/A	14.78	41	3	37	0	54	6	123	0.0	N/A	3	1,000,000	0	0.0	0.0
U /	N/A	N/A	14.83	N/A	3	37	0	54	6	123	0.0	N/A	3	1,000	50	3.8	0.0
U /	N/A	N/A	14.88	N/A	3	37	0	54	6	123	0.0	N/A	3	1,000	50	0.0	0.0
U /	N/A	N/A	14.80	N/A	3	37	0	54	6	123	0.0	N/A	3	1,000,000	0	0.0	0.0
E+ / 0.8	6.0	N/A	9.31	60	3	0	0	95	2	59	0.0	3	21	1,000	50	3.8	0.0
E+ / 0.8	6.2	N/A	8.86	2	3	0	0	95	2	59	0.0	1	21	1,000,000	0	0.0	0.0
E+ / 0.9	6.0	N/A	9.30	13	3	0	0	95	2	59	0.0	1	21	1,000	50	0.0	0.0
E+ / 0.8	6.0	N/A	9.00	207	3	0	0	95	2	59	0.0	5	21	1,000,000	0	0.0	0.0
E+ / 0.9	6.0	N/A	8.97	54	3	0	0	95	2	59	0.0	5	21	1,000,000	0	0.0	0.0
E+ / 0.8	6.0	N/A	8.95	1	3	0	0	95	2	59	0.0	1	21	0	0	0.0	0.0
C- / 3.4	3.4	N/A	15.24	234	4	0	0	95	1	63	0.0	79	4	1,000	50	2.3	0.0
C- / 3.4	3.4	N/A	15.22	147	4	0	0	95	1	63	0.0	75	4	1,000	50	0.0	0.0

Fund Type	Fund Name	Ticker Symbol	Overall Investment Rating	Phone	Performance Rating/Pts	3 Mo	6 Mo	1Yr / Pct	3Yr / Pct	5Yr / Pct	Dividend Yield	Expense Ratio
COH	AllianzGI Short Dur High Inc Inst	ASHIX	B+	(800) 988-8380	B+ / 8.5	2.14	2.75	12.32 / 84	4.04 / 76	4.72 / 81	5.34	0.59
COH	AllianzGI Short Dur High Inc P	ASHPX	B	(800) 988-8380	B+ / 8.5	2.13	2.72	12.20 / 84	3.97 / 75	4.64 / 80	5.30	0.64
GEI	AlphaCentric Bond Rotation A	BDRAX	U	(844) 223-8637	U /	4.40	1.85	2.64 / 54	--	--	1.96	2.94
GEI	AlphaCentric Bond Rotation C	BDRCX	U	(844) 223-8637	U /	5.07	2.40	2.87 / 56	--	--	1.34	3.69
GEI	AlphaCentric Bond Rotation I	BDRIX	U	(844) 223-8637	U /	4.46	1.95	2.86 / 56	--	--	2.26	4.69
GEN	AlphaCentric Income Opportunities A	IOFAX	U	(844) 223-8637	U /	2.35	5.45	12.01 / 83	--	--	4.14	2.26
GEN	AlphaCentric Income Opportunities C	IOFCX	U	(844) 223-8637	U /	2.18	5.12	11.19 / 82	--	--	3.80	3.01
GEN	AlphaCentric Income Opportunities I	IOFIX	U	(844) 223-8637	U /	2.40	5.56	12.23 / 84	--	--	4.56	2.01
MUH	Alpine HY Managed Duration Muni A	AAHMX	A+	(888) 785-5578	B- / 7.2	1.22	-1.11	2.02 / 57	3.81 / 91	--	2.95	1.37
MUH	Alpine HY Managed Duration Muni	AHYMX	A+	(888) 785-5578	B+ / 8.6	1.28	-1.08	2.28 / 60	4.05 / 93	--	3.28	1.12
MUN	Alpine Ultra Short Muni Inc A	ATOAX	C	(888) 785-5578	D- / 1.4	0.13	0.16	0.38 / 35	0.33 / 21	0.32 / 21	0.48	1.18
MUN	Alpine Ultra Short Muni Inc Inst	ATOIX	C+	(888) 785-5578	D+ / 2.5	0.29	0.38	0.73 / 41	0.61 / 27	0.57 / 26	0.73	0.93
GL	Altegris Futures Evolution Strat A	EVOAX	D	(877) 772-5838	B / 7.9	2.69	-3.34	-6.84 / 0	8.67 / 98	4.74 / 81	6.68	1.97
GL	Altegris Futures Evolution Strat I	EVOIX	C-	(877) 772-5838	A / 9.3	2.76	-3.14	-6.53 / 0	8.94 / 98	5.03 / 84	7.37	1.72
GL	Altegris Futures Evolution Strat N	EVONX	C-	(877) 772-5838	A- / 9.1	2.69	-3.34	-6.84 / 0	8.63 / 98	4.75 / 81	7.10	1.97
GEN	Amana Participation Institutional	AMIPX	U	(800) 732-6262	U /	1.29	-0.58	3.69 / 61	--	--	2.22	0.72
GEN	Amana Participation Investor	AMAPX	U	(800) 732-6262	U /	1.24	-0.68	3.43 / 59	--	--	2.27	1.12
COH	American Beacon Crescent SD HI A	ACHAX	U	(800) 658-5811	U /	3.25	4.01	13.04 / 85	--	--	4.33	1.56
COH	American Beacon Crescent SD HI C	ACHCX	U	(800) 658-5811	U /	2.95	3.63	12.05 / 83	--	--	3.69	2.09
COH	American Beacon Crescent SD HI	ACHIX	U	(800) 658-5811	U /	3.24	4.10	13.34 / 86	--	--	4.82	1.28
COH	American Beacon Crescent SD HI Inv	ACHPX	U	(800) 658-5811	U /	3.25	4.01	13.05 / 85	--	--	4.46	1.47
COH	American Beacon Crescent SD HI Y	ACHYX	U	(800) 658-5811	U /	3.22	4.16	13.23 / 86	--	--	4.72	1.30
GL	American Beacon Flexible Bond A	AFXAX	D-	(800) 658-5811	D / 1.9	2.06	2.03	6.29 / 71	0.77 / 24	1.39 / 33	1.91	1.53
GL	American Beacon Flexible Bond C	AFXCX	D	(800) 658-5811	D+ / 2.6	1.86	1.62	5.48 / 68	0.02 / 7	0.61 / 23	1.25	2.27
GL	American Beacon Flexible Bond Inst	AFXIX	C+	(800) 658-5811	C / 4.6	2.21	2.25	6.82 / 72	1.19 / 31	1.85 / 40	2.30	1.14
GL	American Beacon Flexible Bond Inv	AFPX	C	(800) 658-5811	C- / 4.0	2.16	2.05	6.41 / 71	0.84 / 25	1.47 / 34	2.04	1.43
GL	American Beacon Flexible Bond Y	AFXYX	C	(800) 658-5811	C / 4.4	2.10	2.15	6.67 / 72	1.08 / 29	1.73 / 38	2.27	1.20
COI	American Beacon GH Quality Bd Inst	GHQIX	U	(800) 658-5811	U /	0.79	-2.69	--	--	--	0.00	N/A
COI	American Beacon GH Quality Bd Inv	GHQPX	U	(800) 658-5811	U /	0.79	-2.69	--	--	--	0.00	N/A
COI	American Beacon GH Quality Bd Y	GHQYX	U	(800) 658-5811	U /	0.79	-2.60	--	--	--	0.00	N/A
COH	American Beacon SiM Hi Yld Opps A	SHOAX	C	(800) 658-5811	B+ / 8.6	4.28	5.50	19.41 / 95	4.62 / 82	7.09 / 96	5.41	1.25
COH	American Beacon SiM Hi Yld Opps C	SHOCX	C+	(800) 658-5811	B+ / 8.9	4.08	5.11	18.64 / 94	3.87 / 74	6.37 / 94	4.99	2.00
COH	American Beacon SiM Hi Yld Opps	SHOIX	B-	(800) 658-5811	A+ / 9.6	4.26	5.58	19.88 / 96	5.05 / 85	7.70 / 98	6.05	0.92
COH	American Beacon SiM Hi Yld Opps	SHYPX	B-	(800) 658-5811	A / 9.5	4.40	5.76	19.83 / 96	4.75 / 83	7.26 / 97	5.76	1.19
COH	American Beacon SiM Hi Yld Opps Y	SHOYX	B-	(800) 658-5811	A / 9.5	4.36	5.67	19.96 / 96	4.97 / 85	7.46 / 97	6.00	0.92
LP	American Beacon Sound Pt FR Inc A	SOUAX	U	(800) 658-5811	U /	1.06	1.66	4.11 / 63	--	--	0.00	1.69
LP	American Beacon Sound Pt FR Inc C	SOUCX	U	(800) 658-5811	U /	1.06	1.76	4.21 / 63	--	--	0.00	2.57
LP	American Beacon Sound Pt FR Inc I	SPFLX	U	(800) 658-5811	U /	2.39	2.99	5.37 / 68	--	--	0.00	1.28
LP	American Beacon Sound Pt FR Inc	SPFPX	U	(800) 658-5811	U /	2.40	3.00	5.27 / 68	--	--	0.00	1.33
LP	American Beacon Sound Pt FR Inc	SPFRX	U	(800) 658-5811	U /	2.39	3.00	5.37 / 68	--	--	0.00	1.51
LP	American Beacon Sound Pt FR Inc Y	SPFYX	U	(800) 658-5811	U /	11.32	11.97	14.67 / 88	--	--	0.00	1.44
MUH	American Century CA Hi-Yld Muni A	CAYAX	C-	(800) 345-6488	B / 7.6	2.63	-4.47	0.31 / 33	4.94 / 97	4.53 / 96	3.14	0.75
MUH	American Century CA Hi-Yld Muni C	CAYCX	C+	(800) 345-6488	B / 8.2	2.45	-4.82	-0.43 / 10	4.12 / 94	3.76 / 91	2.51	1.50
MUH	American Century CA Hi-Yld Muni Ins	BCHIX	B+	(800) 345-6488	A / 9.5	2.75	-4.35	0.67 / 40	5.38 / 98	4.98 / 97	3.75	0.30
MUH	American Century CA Hi-Yld Muni Inv	BCHYX	B	(800) 345-6488	A / 9.4	2.70	-4.35	0.56 / 38	5.20 / 97	4.79 / 97	3.54	0.50
MUS	American Century CA IT TxFr Bd A	BCIAX	D-	(800) 345-6488	D / 2.1	2.04	-3.04	-0.74 / 6	2.08 / 64	2.07 / 60	2.06	0.72
MUS	American Century CA IT TxFr Bd C	BCIYX	D-	(800) 345-6488	C- / 3.1	1.94	-3.32	-1.39 / 2	1.32 / 44	1.32 / 42	1.40	1.47
MUS	American Century CA IT TxFr Bd Inst	BCTIX	B	(800) 345-6488	C+ / 6.1	2.15	-2.82	-0.29 / 13	2.54 / 74	2.53 / 71	2.62	0.27
MUS	American Century CA IT TxFr Bd Inv	BCITX	C+	(800) 345-6488	C+ / 5.6	2.19	-2.92	-0.49 / 10	2.33 / 70	2.34 / 67	2.42	0.47
MUS	American Century CA Lg Term T/F A	ALTAX	D-	(800) 345-6488	C / 4.6	2.20	-4.10	-0.43 / 10	3.29 / 85	3.11 / 82	3.07	0.72
MUS	American Century CA Lg Term T/F C	ALTCX	D	(800) 345-6488	C / 5.5	2.11	-4.37	-1.08 / 4	2.52 / 74	2.36 / 68	2.44	1.47
MUS	American Century CA Lg Term T/F	BCLIX	B	(800) 345-6488	B / 7.8	2.32	-3.88	0.02 / 19	3.73 / 90	3.57 / 88	3.67	0.27

● Denotes fund is closed to new investors
* Denotes fund is included in Section II

RISK			NET ASSETS		ASSET					Portfolio Turnover Ratio	Avg Coupon Rate	FUND MANAGER		MINIMUM		LOADS	
Risk Rating/Pts	3 Yr Avg Standard Deviation	Avg Duration	NAV As of 2/28/17	Total $(Mil)	Cash %	Gov. Bond %	Muni. Bond %	Corp. Bond %	Other %			Manager Quality Pct	Manager Tenure (Years)	Initial Purch. $	Additional Purch. $	Front End Load	Back End Load
C- /3.4	3.4	N/A	15.21	410	4	0	0	95	1	63	0.0	81	4	1,000,000	0	0.0	0.0
C- /3.4	3.4	N/A	15.20	821	4	0	0	95	1	63	0.0	81	4	1,000,000	0	0.0	0.0
U /	N/A	N/A	9.58	8	2	49	48	0	1	476	0.0	N/A	2	2,500	50	4.8	0.0
U /	N/A	N/A	9.65	N/A	2	49	48	0	1	476	0.0	N/A	2	2,500	50	0.0	0.0
U /	N/A	N/A	9.59	N/A	2	49	48	0	1	476	0.0	N/A	2	2,500	50	0.0	0.0
U /	N/A	N/A	11.41	78	6	3	0	7	84	6	0.0	N/A	2	2,500	50	4.8	0.0
U /	N/A	N/A	11.39	16	6	3	0	7	84	6	0.0	N/A	2	2,500	50	0.0	0.0
U /	N/A	N/A	11.42	315	6	3	0	7	84	6	0.0	N/A	2	2,500	50	0.0	0.0
B /7.7	1.9	N/A	10.17	39	1	0	98	0	1	132	0.0	85	N/A	2,500	0	2.5	0.8
B /7.7	1.9	N/A	10.17	138	1	0	98	0	1	132	0.0	87	N/A	250,000	0	0.0	0.8
A+ /9.9	0.2	N/A	10.09	211	0	0	100	0	0	143	0.0	54	N/A	2,500	0	0.5	0.3
A+ /9.9	0.2	N/A	10.04	910	0	0	100	0	0	143	0.0	63	N/A	250,000	0	0.0	0.3
E- /0.1	12.2	N/A	9.75	74	32	6	1	16	45	59	0.0	99	6	2,500	250	5.8	1.0
E- /0.1	12.1	N/A	9.73	385	32	6	1	16	45	59	0.0	99	6	1,000,000	500	0.0	1.0
E- /0.1	12.2	N/A	9.74	105	32	6	1	16	45	59	0.0	99	6	2,500	250	0.0	1.0
U /	N/A	N/A	10.07	24	73	0	0	26	1	0	0.0	N/A	2	100,000	25	0.0	2.0
U /	N/A	N/A	10.03	9	73	0	0	26	1	0	0.0	N/A	2	5,000	25	0.0	2.0
U /	N/A	2.9	9.69	1	5	0	0	65	30	72	0.0	N/A	N/A	2,500	50	2.5	0.0
U /	N/A	2.9	9.69	1	5	0	0	65	30	72	0.0	N/A	N/A	1,000	50	0.0	0.0
U /	N/A	2.9	9.69	52	5	0	0	65	30	72	0.0	N/A	N/A	250,000	50	0.0	0.0
U /	N/A	2.9	9.70	3	5	0	0	65	30	72	0.0	N/A	N/A	2,500	50	0.0	0.0
U /	N/A	2.9	9.69	6	5	0	0	65	30	72	0.0	N/A	N/A	100,000	50	0.0	0.0
C+ /6.9	2.7	1.3	9.55	8	0	36	0	30	34	162	0.0	74	6	2,500	50	4.8	0.0
C+ /6.7	2.8	1.3	9.54	3	0	36	0	30	34	162	0.0	52	6	1,000	50	0.0	0.0
C+ /6.9	2.7	1.3	9.61	84	0	36	0	30	34	162	0.0	80	6	250,000	50	0.0	0.0
C+ /6.8	2.8	1.3	9.60	3	0	36	0	30	34	162	0.0	75	6	2,500	50	0.0	0.0
C+ /6.8	2.8	1.3	9.60	27	0	36	0	30	34	162	0.0	78	6	100,000	50	0.0	0.0
U /	N/A	4.8	9.85	126	0	0	0	0	100	0	0.0	N/A	1	250,000	50	0.0	0.0
U /	N/A	4.8	9.85	9	0	0	0	0	100	0	0.0	N/A	1	2,500	50	0.0	0.0
U /	N/A	4.8	9.85	3	0	0	0	0	100	0	0.0	N/A	1	100,000	50	0.0	0.0
D- /1.4	5.3	4.1	9.73	89	4	2	0	87	7	57	0.0	67	6	2,500	50	4.8	2.0
D- /1.4	5.3	4.1	9.77	75	4	2	0	87	7	57	0.0	33	6	1,000	50	0.0	2.0
D- /1.4	5.3	4.1	9.72	353	4	2	0	87	7	57	0.0	76	6	250,000	50	0.0	2.0
D- /1.4	5.3	4.1	9.69	136	4	2	0	87	7	57	0.0	69	6	2,500	50	0.0	2.0
D- /1.4	5.3	4.1	9.72	587	4	2	0	87	7	57	0.0	74	6	100,000	50	0.0	2.0
U /	N/A	0.4	10.35	25	0	0	0	0	100	168	0.0	N/A	3	2,500	50	2.5	0.0
U /	N/A	0.4	10.36	21	0	0	0	0	100	168	0.0	N/A	3	1,000	50	0.0	0.0
U /	N/A	0.4	10.35	163	0	0	0	0	100	168	0.0	N/A	3	250,000	0	0.0	0.0
U /	N/A	0.4	10.33	83	0	0	0	0	100	168	0.0	N/A	3	2,500	50	0.0	0.0
U /	N/A	0.4	10.34	9	0	0	0	0	100	168	0.0	N/A	3	2,500	0	0.0	0.0
U /	N/A	0.4	10.36	243	0	0	0	0	100	168	0.0	N/A	3	100,000	50	0.0	0.0
D /2.2	4.3	5.8	10.31	117	0	0	99	0	1	19	4.8	61	30	5,000	50	4.5	0.0
D /2.2	4.3	5.8	10.31	32	0	0	99	0	1	19	4.8	26	30	5,000	50	0.0	0.0
D /2.2	4.3	5.8	10.30	122	0	0	99	0	1	19	4.8	72	30	5,000,000	0	0.0	0.0
D /2.2	4.3	5.8	10.31	749	0	0	99	0	1	19	4.8	69	30	5,000	50	0.0	0.0
C+ /5.8	2.9	4.7	11.74	37	0	0	99	0	1	23	4.5	10	15	5,000	50	4.5	0.0
C /5.4	3.0	4.7	11.75	18	0	0	99	0	1	23	4.5	3	15	5,000	50	0.0	0.0
C+ /5.8	2.9	4.7	11.74	300	0	0	99	0	1	23	4.5	20	15	5,000,000	0	0.0	0.0
C /5.5	3.0	4.7	11.74	1,226	0	0	99	0	1	23	4.5	14	15	5,000	50	0.0	0.0
C- /3.7	3.6	5.7	11.45	7	0	0	100	0	0	24	4.7	21	20	5,000	50	4.5	0.0
C- /3.7	3.7	5.7	11.46	6	0	0	100	0	0	24	4.7	7	20	5,000	50	0.0	0.0
C- /3.7	3.7	5.7	11.45	N/A	0	0	100	0	0	24	4.7	34	20	5,000,000	0	0.0	0.0

99 Pct = Best
0 Pct = Worst

Fund Type	Fund Name	Ticker Symbol	Overall Investment Rating	Phone	Performance Rating/Pts	3 Mo	6 Mo	1Yr / Pct	Annualized 3Yr / Pct	Annualized 5Yr / Pct	Dividend Yield	Expense Ratio
MUS	American Century CA Lg Term T/F	BCLTX	B-	(800) 345-6488	B / 7.6	2.36	-3.89	-0.09 /16	3.55 /88	3.38 /86	3.47	0.47
GEI	American Century Core Plus Fd A	ACCQX	D	(800) 345-6488	C- / 3.2	1.43	-1.83	3.13 /57	2.53 /52	2.11 /44	2.44	0.92
GEI	American Century Core Plus Fd C	ACCKX	D+	(800) 345-6488	C- / 3.7	1.15	-2.20	2.36 /52	1.73 /38	1.33 /32	1.80	1.67
GEI	American Century Core Plus Fd Inst	ACCUX	B	(800) 345-6488	C+ / 5.8	1.44	-1.62	3.59 /60	2.96 /60	2.55 /50	3.01	0.47
GEI	American Century Core Plus Fd Inv	ACCNX	B-	(800) 345-6488	C / 5.5	1.49	-1.62	3.39 /59	2.78 /57	2.37 /47	2.81	0.67
GEI	American Century Core Plus Fd R	ACCPX	C	(800) 345-6488	C / 4.6	1.27	-1.96	2.88 /56	2.24 /47	1.84 /39	2.30	1.17
GEI	American Century Diversified Bd A	ADFAX	D-	(800) 345-6488	D+ / 2.3	1.05	-2.41	1.49 /44	2.22 /47	1.87 /40	1.94	0.85
GEI	American Century Diversified Bd C	CDBCX	D-	(800) 345-6488	D+ / 2.9	0.86	-2.68	0.73 /36	1.46 /34	1.11 /29	1.27	1.60
GEI	American Century Diversified Bd I	ACBPX	C+	(800) 345-6488	C / 5.0	1.16	-2.10	1.94 /48	2.72 /56	2.35 /47	2.49	0.40
GEI	American Century Diversified Bd Inv	ADFIX	C	(800) 345-6488	C / 4.7	1.11	-2.20	1.83 /47	2.51 /52	2.15 /44	2.29	0.60
GEI	American Century Diversified Bd R	ADVRX	D+	(800) 345-6488	C- / 3.8	0.99	-2.53	1.23 /42	1.97 /42	1.62 /36	1.78	1.10
COI	American Century Diversified Bd R6	ADDVX	C+	(800) 345-6488	C / 5.0	1.17	-2.08	1.99 /49	2.73 /56	--	2.54	0.35
EM	American Century Em Mkts Debt A	AEDQX	U	(800) 345-6488	U /	3.40	1.04	10.92 /81	--	--	3.13	1.22
EM	American Century Em Mkts Debt C	AEDHX	U	(800) 345-6488	U /	3.21	0.57	10.11 /79	--	--	2.54	1.97
EM	American Century Em Mkts Debt Inst	AEDJX	U	(800) 345-6488	U /	3.51	1.26	11.40 /82	--	--	3.72	0.77
EM	American Century Em Mkts Debt Inv	AEDVX	U	(800) 345-6488	U /	3.46	1.16	11.30 /82	--	--	3.52	0.97
EM	American Century Em Mkts Debt R	AEDWX	U	(800) 345-6488	U /	3.44	0.91	10.76 /81	--	--	3.03	1.47
EM	American Century Em Mkts Debt R6	AEXDX	U	(800) 345-6488	U /	3.52	1.29	11.46 /82	--	--	3.77	0.72
USA	American Century Ginnie Mae A	BGNAX	D-	(800) 345-6488	E / 0.5	0.25	-1.36	-0.22 /14	1.43 /34	1.11 /29	2.06	0.80
USA	American Century Ginnie Mae C	BGNCX	D+	(800) 345-6488	D / 1.6	-0.03	-1.72	-0.96 / 4	0.68 /23	0.35 /20	1.40	1.55
USA	American Century Ginnie Mae I	AGMNX	B-	(800) 345-6488	C- / 3.6	0.36	-1.05	0.23 /27	1.89 /41	1.58 /36	2.61	0.35
USA	American Century Ginnie Mae Inv	BGNMX	C+	(800) 345-6488	C- / 3.2	0.31	-1.24	0.03 /19	1.69 /38	1.36 /32	2.41	0.55
USA	American Century Ginnie Mae R	AGMWX	C-	(800) 345-6488	D+ / 2.3	0.09	-1.48	-0.47 /10	1.15 /30	0.85 /25	1.91	1.05
GL	American Century Global Bond A	AGBAX	C	(800) 345-6488	C- / 3.6	1.09	-1.74	2.72 /55	2.92 /60	2.63 /51	0.85	1.21
GL	American Century Global Bond C	AGBTX	C+	(800) 345-6488	C- / 4.2	0.94	-2.12	1.97 /49	2.16 /46	1.89 /40	0.14	1.96
GL	American Century Global Bond Inst	AGBNX	A	(800) 345-6488	C+ / 6.2	1.24	-1.48	3.17 /58	3.39 /67	3.11 /59	1.33	0.76
GL	American Century Global Bond Inv	AGBVX	A-	(800) 345-6488	C+ / 6.0	1.14	-1.59	2.97 /56	3.18 /64	2.89 /56	1.14	0.96
GL	American Century Global Bond R	AGBRX	B	(800) 345-6488	C / 5.0	1.04	-1.90	2.47 /53	2.65 /55	2.39 /48	0.64	1.46
GL	American Century Global Bond R6	AGBDX	A-	(800) 345-6488	C+ / 6.3	1.29	-1.43	3.22 /58	3.44 /68	--	1.38	0.71
USS	American Century Govt Bond A	ABTAX	E+	(800) 345-6488	E / 0.4	0.42	-2.63	-1.02 / 4	1.40 /33	0.86 /25	1.55	0.72
USS	American Century Govt Bond C	ABTCX	E+	(800) 345-6488	E+ / 0.8	0.24	-2.99	-1.85 / 1	0.61 /22	0.09 /14	0.86	1.47
USS	American Century Govt Bond Inst	ABTIX	C-	(800) 345-6488	C- / 3.2	0.54	-2.41	-0.57 / 9	1.85 /40	1.32 /32	2.08	0.27
USS	American Century Govt Bond Inv	CPTNX	D+	(800) 345-6488	D+ / 2.8	0.49	-2.51	-0.86 / 5	1.65 /37	1.12 /29	1.88	0.47
USS	American Century Govt Bond R	ABTRX	D-	(800) 345-6488	D / 2.0	0.36	-2.66	-1.26 / 3	1.14 /30	0.61 /23	1.37	0.97
MUH	American Century High Yld Muni A	AYMAX	C-	(800) 345-6488	B- / 7.4	2.50	-4.31	0.67 /40	4.67 /96	4.18 /95	3.16	0.85
MUH	American Century High Yld Muni C	AYMCX	C	(800) 345-6488	B / 7.9	2.31	-4.57	-0.08 /16	3.89 /92	3.41 /86	2.53	1.60
MUH	American Century High Yld Muni Inst	AYMIX	B+	(800) 345-6488	A / 9.4	2.61	-4.10	1.12 /46	5.14 /97	4.65 /97	3.77	0.40
MUH	American Century High Yld Muni Inv	ABHYX	B	(800) 345-6488	A / 9.3	2.56	-4.19	0.92 /44	4.93 /97	4.44 /96	3.56	0.60
COH	American Century High-Yield A	AHYVX	D	(800) 345-6488	B- / 7.2	4.08	3.92	17.53 /93	2.75 /57	5.03 /84	4.65	1.10
COH	American Century High-Yield C	AHDCX	D	(800) 345-6488	B- / 7.5	3.89	3.53	16.66 /91	1.99 /43	4.25 /75	4.14	1.85
COH	American Century High-Yield Inst	ACYIX	C	(800) 345-6488	B+ / 8.8	4.20	4.15	18.05 /94	3.21 /64	5.51 /88	5.30	0.65
COH	American Century High-Yield Inv	ABHIX	C-	(800) 345-6488	B+ / 8.5	3.97	3.87	17.62 /93	2.95 /60	5.26 /86	5.11	0.85
COH	American Century High-Yield R	AHYRX	D+	(800) 345-6488	B / 8.1	4.02	3.79	17.24 /92	2.49 /51	4.77 /81	4.62	1.35
COH	American Century High-Yield R6	AHYDX	C	(800) 345-6488	B+ / 8.8	4.22	4.18	18.14 /94	3.21 /64	--	5.35	0.60
GEI	American Century Infl Adj Bd A	AIAVX	E+	(800) 345-6488	C- / 3.3	1.22	-0.65	3.44 /59	1.12 /29	0.02 / 7	1.60	0.72
GEI	American Century Infl Adj Bd C	AINOX	E	(800) 345-6488	D / 2.0	1.08	-1.05	2.65 /54	0.34 /19	-0.74 / 2	0.92	1.47
GEI	American Century Infl Adj Bd Inst	AIANX	E+	(800) 345-6488	C- / 4.1	1.37	-0.50	3.90 /62	1.58 /36	0.47 /21	2.13	0.27
GEI	American Century Infl Adj Bd Inv	ACITX	E+	(800) 345-6488	C- / 3.7	1.35	-0.52	3.69 /61	1.36 /33	0.26 /19	1.92	0.47
GEI	American Century Infl Adj Bd R	AIARX	E+	(800) 345-6488	D+ / 2.8	1.17	-0.87	3.16 /58	0.84 /25	-0.24 / 4	1.42	0.97
MUN	American Century Int Tax-Fr Bd A	TWWOX	E+	(800) 345-6488	D / 1.7	1.87	-3.00	-0.76 / 6	1.86 /59	1.67 /51	2.18	0.72
MUN	American Century Int Tax-Fr Bd C	TWTCX	D-	(800) 345-6488	D+ / 2.5	1.68	-3.37	-1.50 / 2	1.10 /38	0.91 /33	1.52	1.47
MUN	American Century Int Tax-Fr Bd Inst	AXBIX	B-	(800) 345-6488	C+ / 5.7	1.98	-2.79	-0.31 /12	2.32 /69	2.13 /62	2.75	0.27

● Denotes fund is closed to new investors
* Denotes fund is included in Section II

www.thestreetratings.com

RISK			NET ASSETS		ASSET					Portfolio Turnover Ratio	Avg Coupon Rate	FUND MANAGER		MINIMUM		LOADS	
Risk Rating/Pts	3 Yr Avg Standard Deviation	Avg Duration	NAV As of 2/28/17	Total $(Mil)	Cash %	Gov. Bond %	Muni. Bond %	Corp. Bond %	Other %			Manager Quality Pct	Manager Tenure (Years)	Initial Purch. $	Additional Purch. $	Front End Load	Back End Load
C- / 3.7	3.7	5.7	11.46	311	0	0	100	0	0	24	4.7	28	20	5,000	50	0.0	0.0
C+ / 6.4	2.8	5.5	10.74	28	0	22	1	37	40	145	3.9	51	11	2,500	50	4.5	0.0
C+ / 6.1	2.9	5.5	10.73	7	0	22	1	37	40	145	3.9	17	11	2,500	50	0.0	0.0
C+ / 6.4	2.8	5.5	10.73	3	0	22	1	37	40	145	3.9	65	11	5,000,000	50	0.0	0.0
C+ / 6.5	2.8	5.5	10.74	87	0	22	1	37	40	145	3.9	61	11	2,500	50	0.0	0.0
C+ / 6.3	2.9	5.5	10.73	2	0	22	1	37	40	145	3.9	32	11	2,500	50	0.0	0.0
C+ / 6.0	2.9	5.5	10.71	424	0	33	1	29	37	174	3.4	27	16	2,500	50	4.5	0.0
C+ / 6.0	2.9	5.5	10.71	69	0	33	1	29	37	174	3.4	10	16	2,500	50	0.0	0.0
C+ / 6.2	2.9	5.5	10.71	2,901	0	33	1	29	37	174	3.4	53	16	5,000,000	50	0.0	0.0
C+ / 6.1	2.9	5.5	10.71	2,260	0	33	1	29	37	174	3.4	39	16	2,500	50	0.0	0.0
C+ / 6.0	2.9	5.5	10.71	14	0	33	1	29	37	174	3.4	19	16	2,500	50	0.0	0.0
C+ / 6.2	2.9	5.5	10.71	164	0	33	1	29	37	174	3.4	55	16	0	0	0.0	0.0
U /	N/A	4.6	10.26	6	11	5	0	79	5	97	4.9	N/A	3	2,500	50	4.5	0.0
U /	N/A	4.6	10.24	1	11	5	0	79	5	97	4.9	N/A	3	2,500	50	0.0	0.0
U /	N/A	4.6	10.27	6	11	5	0	79	5	97	4.9	N/A	3	5,000,000	50	0.0	0.0
U /	N/A	4.6	10.27	3	11	5	0	79	5	97	4.9	N/A	3	2,500	50	0.0	0.0
U /	N/A	4.6	10.26	1	11	5	0	79	5	97	4.9	N/A	3	2,500	50	0.0	0.0
U /	N/A	4.6	10.27	18	11	5	0	79	5	97	4.9	N/A	3	0	0	0.0	0.0
B+ / 8.6	1.7	2.8	10.55	64	0	2	0	0	98	308	3.9	65	11	2,500	50	4.5	0.0
B+ / 8.7	1.6	2.8	10.55	8	0	2	0	0	98	308	3.9	31	13	2,500	50	0.0	0.0
B+ / 8.7	1.7	2.8	10.55	73	0	2	0	0	98	308	3.9	75	11	5,000,000	50	0.0	0.0
B+ / 8.6	1.7	2.8	10.55	940	0	2	0	0	98	308	3.9	71	11	2,500	50	0.0	0.0
B+ / 8.6	1.7	2.8	10.54	7	0	2	0	0	98	308	3.9	55	11	2,500	50	0.0	0.0
B- / 7.3	2.6	6.7	10.05	9	0	48	1	24	27	106	3.5	93	5	2,500	50	4.5	0.0
B- / 7.3	2.6	6.7	9.97	4	0	48	1	24	27	106	3.5	89	5	2,500	50	0.0	0.0
B- / 7.2	2.6	6.7	10.10	870	0	48	1	24	27	106	3.5	94	5	5,000,000	50	0.0	0.0
B- / 7.3	2.6	6.7	10.08	268	0	48	1	24	27	106	3.5	93	5	2,500	50	0.0	0.0
B- / 7.3	2.6	6.7	10.02	N/A	0	48	1	24	27	106	3.5	92	5	2,500	50	0.0	0.0
B- / 7.0	2.7	6.7	10.10	113	0	48	1	24	27	106	3.5	94	5	0	0	0.0	0.0
B- / 7.2	2.7	4.6	10.97	95	0	42	0	0	58	280	3.2	32	15	2,500	50	4.5	0.0
B- / 7.1	2.7	4.6	10.96	4	0	42	0	0	58	280	3.2	11	15	2,500	50	0.0	0.0
B- / 7.2	2.7	4.6	10.97	191	0	42	0	0	58	280	3.2	57	15	5,000,000	50	0.0	0.0
B- / 7.3	2.6	4.6	10.97	594	0	42	0	0	58	280	3.2	50	15	2,500	50	0.0	0.0
B- / 7.0	2.7	4.6	10.97	3	0	42	0	0	58	280	3.2	23	15	2,500	50	0.0	0.0
D+ / 2.3	4.1	5.7	9.32	53	0	0	99	0	1	41	5.0	60	19	5,000	50	4.5	0.0
D+ / 2.4	4.1	5.7	9.32	21	0	0	99	0	1	41	5.0	27	19	5,000	50	0.0	0.0
D+ / 2.3	4.1	5.7	9.32	83	0	0	99	0	1	41	5.0	72	19	5,000,000	0	0.0	0.0
D+ / 2.3	4.1	5.7	9.32	349	0	0	99	0	1	41	5.0	68	19	5,000	50	0.0	0.0
D- / 1.0	5.9	3.8	5.78	23	0	0	0	97	3	24	6.1	4	9	2,500	50	4.5	0.0
E+ / 0.9	5.9	3.8	5.78	10	0	0	0	97	3	24	6.1	1	9	2,500	50	0.0	0.0
E+ / 0.9	5.9	3.8	5.78	522	0	0	0	97	3	24	6.1	7	9	5,000,000	50	0.0	0.0
D- / 1.0	5.9	3.8	5.77	314	0	0	0	97	3	24	6.1	5	9	2,500	50	0.0	0.0
E+ / 0.9	5.9	3.8	5.78	1	0	0	0	97	3	24	6.1	2	9	2,500	50	0.0	0.0
E+ / 0.9	5.9	3.8	5.77	86	0	0	0	97	3	24	6.1	7	9	0	0	0.0	0.0
D+ / 2.9	4.1	6.4	11.67	284	0	85	0	4	11	14	1.5	4	11	2,500	50	0.0	0.0
C- / 3.0	4.1	6.4	11.68	16	0	85	0	4	11	14	1.5	1	11	2,500	50	0.0	0.0
D+ / 2.9	4.1	6.4	11.69	1,190	0	85	0	4	11	14	1.5	6	11	5,000,000	50	0.0	0.0
D+ / 2.9	4.1	6.4	11.70	1,678	0	85	0	4	11	14	1.5	5	11	2,500	50	0.0	0.0
C- / 3.1	4.1	6.4	11.72	27	0	85	0	4	11	14	1.5	2	11	2,500	50	0.0	0.0
C+ / 6.1	2.9	4.7	11.19	72	0	0	100	0	0	32	4.8	8	11	5,000	50	4.5	0.0
C+ / 6.0	2.9	4.7	11.18	15	0	0	100	0	0	32	4.8	3	11	5,000	50	0.0	0.0
C+ / 6.1	2.9	4.7	11.19	1,575	0	0	100	0	0	32	4.8	16	11	5,000,000	0	0.0	0.0

99 Pct = Best
0 Pct = Worst

Fund Type	Fund Name	Ticker Symbol	Overall Investment Rating	Phone	PERFORMANCE Perfor-mance Rating/Pts	Total Return % through 2/28/17 3 Mo	6 Mo	1Yr / Pct	Annualized 3Yr / Pct	5Yr / Pct	Incl. in Returns Dividend Yield	Expense Ratio
MUN	American Century Int Tax-Fr Bd Inv	TWTIX	C+	(800) 345-6488	C / 5.2	1.93	-2.88	-0.42 / 11	2.12 / 65	1.93 / 57	2.54	0.47
GL	American Century Intl Bond A	AIBDX	E-	(800) 345-6488	E- / 0.0	1.00	-8.11	-1.38 / 2	-3.66 / 1	-2.36 / 1	0.00	1.06
GL	American Century Intl Bond C	AIQCX	E-	(800) 345-6488	E- / 0.0	0.76	-8.47	-2.22 / 1	-4.39 / 0	-3.09 / 1	0.00	1.81
GL	American Century Intl Bond Inst	AIDIX	E-	(800) 345-6488	E- / 0.0	1.16	-7.90	-0.97 / 4	-3.23 / 1	-1.91 / 1	0.00	0.61
GL	American Century Intl Bond Inv	BEGBX	E-	(800) 345-6488	E- / 0.0	0.99	-8.06	-1.21 / 3	-3.44 / 1	-2.12 / 1	0.00	0.81
GL	American Century Intl Bond R	AIBRX	E-	(800) 345-6488	E- / 0.0	0.92	-8.21	-1.63 / 1	-3.89 / 0	-2.59 / 1	0.00	1.31
GL	American Century Intl Bond R6	AIDDX	E-	(800) 345-6488	E- / 0.0	1.16	-7.83	-0.89 / 5	-3.18 / 1	--	0.00	0.56
US	American Century MA Real Rtn A	ASIDX	E-	(800) 345-6488	E- / 0.2	4.42	2.98	9.50 / 78	-1.49 / 2	-1.47 / 2	0.00	1.43
US	American Century MA Real Rtn C	ASIZX	E	(800) 345-6488	E / 0.4	4.25	2.64	8.61 / 75	-2.22 / 2	-2.20 / 1	0.00	2.18
US	American Century MA Real Rtn Inst	ASINX	E	(800) 345-6488	D+ / 2.6	4.59	3.16	10.00 / 79	-1.04 / 3	-1.01 / 2	0.00	0.98
US	American Century MA Real Rtn Inv	ASIOX	E	(800) 345-6488	D+ / 2.3	4.50	3.17	9.80 / 78	-1.24 / 2	-1.22 / 2	0.00	1.18
US	American Century MA Real Rtn R	ASIUX	E	(800) 345-6488	D- / 1.5	4.36	2.79	9.25 / 77	-1.75 / 2	-1.71 / 1	0.00	1.68
GEN	American Century NT Diver Bd Inst	ACLDX	C	(800) 345-6488	C / 5.0	1.16	-2.13	1.90 / 48	2.69 / 56	2.28 / 46	2.26	0.40
COI	American Century NT Diver Bd R6	ACDDX	C+	(800) 345-6488	C / 5.0	1.18	-2.11	1.86 / 48	2.74 / 57	--	2.31	0.35
MMT	American Century Prime MM A	ACAXX	C-	(800) 345-6488	E+ / 0.9	0.08	0.13	0.16 / 24	0.06 / 10	0.04 / 10	0.16	N/A
MMT	American Century Prime MM C	ARCXX	C-	(800) 345-6488	E+ / 0.9	0.08	0.13	0.16 / 24	0.06 / 10	0.04 / 10	0.16	N/A
MMT	American Century Prime MM Inv	BPRXX	C-	(800) 345-6488	E+ / 0.9	0.08	0.13	0.16 / 24	0.06 / 10	0.04 / 10	0.16	N/A
GEI	American Century SD Inf Prot Bd A	APOAX	D-	(800) 345-6488	E+ / 0.7	0.97	1.17	2.90 / 56	0.11 / 13	-0.12 / 4	0.17	0.82
GEI	American Century SD Inf Prot Bd C	APOCX	D-	(800) 345-6488	E / 0.4	0.82	0.82	2.17 / 50	-0.63 / 3	-0.85 / 2	0.00	1.57
GEI	American Century SD Inf Prot Bd Ins	APISX	C	(800) 345-6488	D+ / 2.7	1.11	1.31	3.31 / 58	0.53 / 21	0.32 / 20	0.62	0.37
GEI	American Century SD Inf Prot Bd Inv	APOIX	C-	(800) 345-6488	D+ / 2.5	1.11	1.31	3.23 / 58	0.35 / 19	0.14 / 16	0.42	0.57
GEI	American Century SD Inf Prot Bd R	APORX	D	(800) 345-6488	D / 1.7	0.97	0.97	2.67 / 54	-0.16 / 5	-0.37 / 3	0.00	1.07
GEI	American Century SD Inf Prot Bd R6	APODX	C	(800) 345-6488	D+ / 2.8	1.06	1.36	3.47 / 59	0.59 / 22	0.32 / 20	0.67	0.32
GL	American Century Sh Dur St Inc A	ASADX	U	(800) 345-6488	U /	1.67	2.19	7.22 / 73	--	--	2.42	1.06
GL	American Century Sh Dur St Inc C	ASCDX	U	(800) 345-6488	U /	1.49	1.81	6.42 / 71	--	--	1.74	1.81
GL	American Century Sh Dur St Inc Inst	ASDJX	U	(800) 345-6488	U /	1.79	2.41	7.70 / 74	--	--	2.92	0.61
GL	American Century Sh Dur St Inc Inv	ASDVX	U	(800) 345-6488	U /	1.74	2.31	7.48 / 73	--	--	2.72	0.81
GL	American Century Sh Dur St Inc R	ASDRX	U	(800) 345-6488	U /	1.61	2.06	6.95 / 72	--	--	2.23	1.31
GL	American Century Sh Dur St Inc R6	ASXDX	U	(800) 345-6488	U /	1.80	2.44	7.75 / 74	--	--	2.96	0.56
GEI	American Century Sh Duration A	ACSQX	C	(800) 345-6488	D / 1.9	0.55	0.30	1.88 / 48	0.89 / 26	0.82 / 25	1.34	0.85
GEI	American Century Sh Duration C	ACSKX	C-	(800) 345-6488	D- / 1.5	0.37	-0.07	1.02 / 40	0.13 / 14	0.05 / 10	0.62	1.60
GEI	American Century Sh Duration Inst	ACSUX	B+	(800) 345-6488	C- / 3.5	0.66	0.53	2.33 / 52	1.34 / 32	1.28 / 31	1.82	0.40
GEI	American Century Sh Duration Inv	ACSNX	B	(800) 345-6488	C- / 3.2	0.61	0.43	2.13 / 50	1.14 / 30	1.08 / 28	1.62	0.60
GEI	American Century Sh Duration R	ACSPX	C+	(800) 345-6488	D+ / 2.4	0.49	0.28	1.62 / 45	0.67 / 23	0.58 / 22	1.13	1.10
USS	American Century Sh-Term Govt A	TWAVX	D	(800) 345-6488	E / 0.3	0.11	-0.31	-0.24 / 14	0.04 / 9	-0.07 / 4	0.38	0.80
USS	American Century Sh-Term Govt C	TWACX	D	(800) 345-6488	E- / 0.2	0.00	-0.64	-0.85 / 5	-0.67 / 3	-0.80 / 2	0.00	1.55
USS	American Century Sh-Term Govt Inst	TWUOX	C	(800) 345-6488	D / 1.9	0.22	-0.08	0.22 / 26	0.51 / 21	0.38 / 20	0.84	0.35
USS	American Century Sh-Term Govt Inv	TWUSX	C-	(800) 345-6488	D- / 1.5	0.17	-0.19	0.01 / 17	0.31 / 19	0.18 / 18	0.64	0.55
USS	American Century Sh-Term Govt R	TWARX	D	(800) 345-6488	E / 0.4	0.15	-0.36	-0.47 / 10	-0.19 / 4	-0.31 / 4	0.05	1.05
GEL	American Century Strategic Inc A	ASIQX	U	(800) 345-6488	U /	2.95	1.76	9.27 / 77	--	--	3.02	1.11
GEL	American Century Strategic Inc C	ASIHX	U	(800) 345-6488	U /	2.77	1.39	8.58 / 75	--	--	2.42	1.86
GEL	American Century Strategic Inc Inst	ASIJX	U	(800) 345-6488	U /	3.07	1.99	9.88 / 79	--	--	3.60	0.66
GEL	American Century Strategic Inc Inv	ASIEX	U	(800) 345-6488	U /	3.02	1.89	9.55 / 78	--	--	3.41	0.86
GEL	American Century Strategic Inc R	ASIWX	U	(800) 345-6488	U /	2.89	1.64	9.00 / 76	--	--	2.91	1.36
GEL	American Century Strategic Inc R6	ASIPX	U	(800) 345-6488	U /	3.08	2.01	9.82 / 79	--	--	3.65	0.61
MMT	American Century US Govt MM A	AGQXX	U	(800) 345-6488	U /	0.03	0.05	0.05 / 20	--	--	0.05	N/A
USL	American Century VP Infl Prot I	APTIX	D-	(800) 345-6488	C- / 4.2	1.31	-0.38	4.48 / 64	1.62 / 37	0.72 / 24	2.13	0.47
*USL	American Century VP Infl Prot II	AIPTX	D-	(800) 345-6488	C- / 3.9	1.35	-0.48	4.26 / 63	1.39 / 33	0.48 / 21	1.82	0.72
US	American Century Zero Cpn 2020	ACTEX	D-	(800) 345-6488	C- / 3.5	0.30	-1.74	-0.69 / 7	2.03 / 44	1.49 / 34	3.03	0.80
US	American Century Zero Cpn 2020 Inv	BTTTX	D-	(800) 345-6488	C- / 3.9	0.36	-1.61	-0.44 / 10	2.29 / 48	1.75 / 38	3.16	0.55
GEI	American Century Zero Cpn 2025	ACTVX	E+	(800) 345-6488	C / 5.2	0.64	-5.93	-3.22 / 0	4.01 / 75	2.53 / 50	3.39	0.80
GEI	American Century Zero Cpn 2025 Inv	BTTRX	E+	(800) 345-6488	C+ / 5.6	0.70	-5.80	-2.97 / 0	4.27 / 78	2.78 / 54	3.50	0.55

● Denotes fund is closed to new investors
* Denotes fund is included in Section II

RISK			NET ASSETS		ASSET					Portfolio Turnover Ratio	Avg Coupon Rate	FUND MANAGER		MINIMUM		LOADS	
Risk Rating/Pts	3 Yr Avg Standard Deviation	Avg Dura-tion	NAV As of 2/28/17	Total $(Mil)	Cash %	Gov. Bond %	Muni. Bond %	Corp. Bond %	Other %			Manager Quality Pct	Manager Tenure (Years)	Initial Purch. $	Additional Purch. $	Front End Load	Back End Load
C+ / 6.0	2.9	4.7	11.19	1,554	0	0	100	0	0	32	4.8	12	11	5,000	50	0.0	0.0
E / 0.5	7.4	7.8	12.12	18	5	75	3	12	5	40	2.9	8	8	2,500	50	4.5	0.0
E / 0.5	7.4	7.8	11.88	1	5	75	3	12	5	40	2.9	2	8	2,500	50	0.0	0.0
E / 0.5	7.4	7.8	12.24	392	5	75	3	12	5	40	2.9	16	8	5,000,000	50	0.0	0.0
E / 0.5	7.4	7.8	12.21	424	5	75	3	12	5	40	2.9	11	8	2,500	50	0.0	0.0
E / 0.5	7.4	7.8	12.07	N/A	5	75	3	12	5	40	2.9	6	8	2,500	50	0.0	0.0
E / 0.5	7.4	7.8	12.24	57	5	75	3	12	5	40	2.9	17	8	0	0	0.0	0.0
D / 2.0	5.1	1.5	9.68	4	3	51	0	6	40	152	1.8	2	7	2,500	50	5.8	0.0
D / 2.0	5.1	1.5	9.33	2	3	51	0	6	40	152	1.8	1	7	2,500	50	0.0	0.0
D / 2.0	5.1	1.5	9.79	1	3	51	0	6	40	152	1.8	5	7	5,000,000	0	0.0	0.0
D / 2.0	5.1	1.5	9.75	12	3	51	0	6	40	152	1.8	4	7	2,500	50	0.0	0.0
D / 2.0	5.1	1.5	9.57	N/A	3	51	0	6	40	152	1.8	2	7	2,500	50	0.0	0.0
C+ / 6.0	2.9	5.0	10.69	2,714	0	35	1	27	37	207	4.2	50	11	0	0	0.0	0.0
C+ / 6.1	2.9	5.0	10.69	307	0	35	1	27	37	207	4.2	54	11	0	0	0.0	0.0
A+ / 9.9	N/A	N/A	1.00	25	100	0	0	0	0	0	0.2	42	N/A	2,500	50	0.0	0.0
A+ / 9.9	N/A	N/A	1.00	10	100	0	0	0	0	0	0.2	42	N/A	2,500	50	0.0	0.0
A+ / 9.9	N/A	N/A	1.00	1,263	100	0	0	0	0	0	0.2	42	N/A	2,500	50	0.0	0.0
B+ / 8.3	2.0	2.4	10.19	47	0	88	0	3	9	36	1.0	13	11	2,500	50	2.3	0.0
B+ / 8.3	1.9	2.4	9.88	28	0	88	0	3	9	36	1.0	5	11	2,500	50	0.0	0.0
B / 8.2	2.0	2.4	10.36	650	0	88	0	3	9	36	1.0	21	11	5,000,000	50	0.0	0.0
B / 8.2	2.0	2.4	10.29	523	0	88	0	3	9	36	1.0	17	11	2,500	50	0.0	0.0
B+ / 8.3	2.0	2.4	10.39	12	0	88	0	3	9	36	1.0	8	11	2,500	50	0.0	0.0
B+ / 8.3	2.0	2.4	10.36	197	0	88	0	3	9	36	1.0	24	11	0	0	0.0	0.0
U /	N/A	0.9	9.62	10	4	0	0	64	32	19	4.0	N/A	N/A	2,500	50	2.3	0.0
U /	N/A	0.9	9.62	1	4	0	0	64	32	19	4.0	N/A	N/A	2,500	50	0.0	0.0
U /	N/A	0.9	9.62	7	4	0	0	64	32	19	4.0	N/A	N/A	5,000,000	50	0.0	0.0
U /	N/A	0.9	9.62	11	4	0	0	64	32	19	4.0	N/A	N/A	2,500	50	0.0	0.0
U /	N/A	0.9	9.62	1	4	0	0	64	32	19	4.0	N/A	N/A	2,500	50	0.0	0.0
U /	N/A	0.9	9.62	1	4	0	0	64	32	19	4.0	N/A	N/A	0	0	0.0	0.0
A+ / 9.6	0.8	1.9	10.26	51	0	22	0	49	29	73	2.7	59	N/A	2,500	50	2.3	0.0
A / 9.5	0.8	1.9	10.26	16	0	22	0	49	29	73	2.7	23	N/A	2,500	50	0.0	0.0
A+ / 9.6	0.8	1.9	10.26	61	0	22	0	49	29	73	2.7	72	N/A	5,000,000	50	0.0	0.0
A+ / 9.6	0.8	1.9	10.26	244	0	22	0	49	29	73	2.7	67	N/A	2,500	50	0.0	0.0
A / 9.5	0.8	1.9	10.27	1	0	22	0	49	29	73	2.7	50	N/A	2,500	50	0.0	0.0
A / 9.5	0.8	1.9	9.59	11	1	64	0	0	35	99	1.4	22	15	2,500	50	2.3	0.0
A / 9.5	0.8	1.9	9.30	1	1	64	0	0	35	99	1.4	8	15	2,500	50	0.0	0.0
A / 9.5	0.8	1.9	9.59	24	1	64	0	0	35	99	1.4	42	15	5,000,000	50	0.0	0.0
A+ / 9.6	0.8	1.9	9.59	202	1	64	0	0	35	99	1.4	32	15	2,500	50	0.0	0.0
A / 9.5	0.8	1.9	9.56	1	1	64	0	0	35	99	1.4	17	15	2,500	50	0.0	0.0
U /	N/A	3.4	9.80	1	6	1	0	61	32	25	4.7	N/A	N/A	2,500	50	4.5	0.0
U /	N/A	3.4	9.80	1	6	1	0	61	32	25	4.7	N/A	N/A	2,500	50	0.0	0.0
U /	N/A	3.4	9.80	1	6	1	0	61	32	25	4.7	N/A	N/A	5,000,000	50	0.0	0.0
U /	N/A	3.4	9.80	8	6	1	0	61	32	25	4.7	N/A	N/A	2,500	50	0.0	0.0
U /	N/A	3.4	9.80	1	6	1	0	61	32	25	4.7	N/A	N/A	2,500	50	0.0	0.0
U /	N/A	3.4	9.80	1	6	1	0	61	32	25	4.7	N/A	N/A	0	0	0.0	0.0
U /	N/A	N/A	1.00	99	100	0	0	0	0	0	0.1	N/A	N/A	2,500	50	0.0	0.0
C- / 3.4	3.9	6.9	10.26	86	0	64	0	16	20	23	2.6	51	10	0	0	0.0	0.0
C- / 3.4	3.9	6.9	10.24	590	0	64	0	16	20	23	2.6	36	10	0	0	0.0	0.0
C- / 4.2	3.4	4.0	98.60	6	0	100	0	0	0	43	0.0	57	11	2,500	50	0.0	0.0
C- / 4.2	3.4	4.0	103.15	164	0	100	0	0	0	43	0.0	65	11	2,500	50	0.0	0.0
E+ / 0.7	6.8	9.1	91.74	2	0	100	0	0	0	55	0.0	5	11	2,500	50	0.0	0.0
E+ / 0.7	6.8	9.1	96.09	141	0	100	0	0	0	55	0.0	6	11	2,500	50	0.0	0.0

Fund Type	Fund Name	Ticker Symbol	Overall Investment Rating	Phone	Performance Rating/Pts	3 Mo	6 Mo	1Yr / Pct	3Yr / Pct	5Yr / Pct	Dividend Yield	Expense Ratio
	99 Pct = Best 0 Pct = Worst				PERFORMANCE Total Return % through 2/28/17 Annualized						Incl. in Returns	
COI	American Fds College Enroll 529A	CENAX	C-	(800) 421-0180	D / 1.9	0.49	-0.11	0.69 / 36	1.22 / 31	--	1.36	0.78
COI	American Fds College Enroll 529B	CENBX	D+	(800) 421-0180	D / 1.6	0.20	-0.50	-0.10 / 16	0.44 / 20	--	0.00	1.53
COI	American Fds College Enroll 529C	CENCX	D+	(800) 421-0180	D / 1.7	0.30	-0.50	--	0.45 / 20	--	0.60	1.53
COI	American Fds College Enroll 529E	CENEX	C	(800) 421-0180	D+ / 2.5	0.48	-0.13	0.58 / 35	1.00 / 28	--	1.18	1.00
COI	American Fds College Enroll 529F1	CENFX	C+	(800) 421-0180	C- / 3.3	0.55	0.05	0.95 / 39	1.48 / 35	--	1.65	0.53
USL	American Fds Ins Ser USGAAA Sec		C	(800) 421-0180	C / 4.4	0.82	-0.73	0.33 / 30	2.43 / 50	1.69 / 37	1.63	N/A
USL	American Fds Ins Ser USGAAA Sec		C-	(800) 421-0180	C- / 3.6	0.68	-1.04	-0.21 / 14	1.91 / 41	1.11 / 29	1.11	0.85
MUS	American Fds Tax-Exempt Fd of NY	NYAAX	C	(800) 421-0180	C+ / 6.0	2.27	-3.29	0.32 / 33	3.53 / 88	2.84 / 77	2.42	0.72
MUS ●	American Fds Tax-Exempt Fd of NY	NYABX	B-	(800) 421-0180	B- / 7.1	2.29	-3.23	0.30 / 32	3.07 / 83	2.23 / 64	2.49	1.39
MUS	American Fds Tax-Exempt Fd of NY	NYACX	C	(800) 421-0180	C+ / 6.2	2.07	-3.67	-0.47 / 10	2.69 / 77	1.98 / 58	1.71	1.51
MUS	American Fds Tax-Exempt Fd of NY	NYAEX	B	(800) 421-0180	B / 7.7	2.27	-3.28	0.36 / 34	3.52 / 88	2.79 / 76	2.56	0.72
MUS	American Fds Tax-Exempt Fd of NY	NYAFX	B+	(800) 421-0180	B / 7.9	2.30	-3.23	0.45 / 36	3.65 / 89	2.94 / 79	2.66	0.58
MUN	American Fds Tax-Exempt Fd of NY	TFNYX	B	(800) 421-0180	B / 7.7	2.28	-3.28	0.33 / 33	3.53 / 88	2.84 / 77	2.52	0.48
MUN	American Fds TxEx Preservation C	TEPCX	C-	(800) 421-0180	D+ / 2.8	1.42	-2.19	-0.88 / 5	1.05 / 37	--	1.47	1.46
GEI	American Funds Bd Fd of Amer 529A	CFAAX	D-	(800) 421-0180	C- / 3.1	1.26	-1.48	2.15 / 50	2.35 / 49	2.20 / 45	1.53	0.69
GEI ●	American Funds Bd Fd of Amer 529B	CFABX	D	(800) 421-0180	C- / 3.3	1.06	-1.87	1.33 / 43	1.55 / 36	1.41 / 33	0.78	1.50
GEI	American Funds Bd Fd of Amer 529C	CFACX	D	(800) 421-0180	C- / 3.3	1.07	-1.85	1.37 / 43	1.57 / 36	1.43 / 33	0.82	1.45
GEI	American Funds Bd Fd of Amer 529E	CFAEX	D+	(800) 421-0180	C / 4.3	1.21	-1.58	1.94 / 48	2.13 / 45	1.98 / 42	1.38	0.90
GEI	American Funds Bd Fd of Amer	CFAFX	C	(800) 421-0180	C / 5.0	1.32	-1.36	2.38 / 52	2.58 / 53	2.44 / 48	1.82	0.46
* GEI	American Funds Bd Fd of Amer A	ABNDX	D	(800) 421-0180	C- / 3.2	1.28	-1.44	2.22 / 51	2.44 / 51	2.30 / 46	1.61	0.61
GEI ●	American Funds Bd Fd of Amer B	BFABX	D	(800) 421-0180	C- / 3.5	1.09	-1.81	1.45 / 44	1.67 / 37	1.53 / 35	0.90	1.37
GEI	American Funds Bd Fd of Amer C	BFACX	D	(800) 421-0180	C- / 3.4	1.09	-1.83	1.42 / 44	1.63 / 37	1.49 / 34	0.87	1.40
GEI	American Funds Bd Fd of Amer F1	BFAFX	C-	(800) 421-0180	C / 4.7	1.27	-1.46	2.19 / 51	2.41 / 50	2.27 / 46	1.64	0.64
GEI	American Funds Bd Fd of Amer F2	ABNFX	C	(800) 421-0180	C / 5.2	1.34	-1.32	2.48 / 53	2.69 / 56	2.55 / 50	1.92	0.36
COI	American Funds Bd Fd of Amer F3	BFFAX	C-	(800) 421-0180	C / 4.8	1.30	-1.43	2.24 / 51	2.44 / 51	2.30 / 46	1.68	0.26
GEI	American Funds Bd Fd of Amer R1	RBFAX	D	(800) 421-0180	C- / 3.5	1.09	-1.82	1.46 / 44	1.67 / 37	1.53 / 35	0.91	1.37
GEI	American Funds Bd Fd of Amer R2	RBFBX	D	(800) 421-0180	C- / 3.5	1.09	-1.84	1.47 / 44	1.68 / 38	1.54 / 35	0.92	1.35
COI	American Funds Bd Fd of Amer R2E	RBEBX	D+	(800) 421-0180	C- / 4.2	1.17	-1.66	1.77 / 47	2.08 / 45	1.83 / 39	1.22	1.05
GEI	American Funds Bd Fd of Amer R3	RBFCX	D+	(800) 421-0180	C / 4.3	1.21	-1.59	1.92 / 48	2.13 / 45	1.98 / 42	1.37	0.91
GEI	American Funds Bd Fd of Amer R4	RBFEX	C-	(800) 421-0180	C / 4.8	1.28	-1.44	2.23 / 51	2.45 / 51	2.30 / 46	1.68	0.60
GEI	American Funds Bd Fd of Amer R5	RBFFX	C+	(800) 421-0180	C / 5.3	1.36	-1.29	2.53 / 53	2.75 / 57	2.60 / 51	1.97	0.31
COI	American Funds Bd Fd of Amer R5E	RBFHX	C	(800) 421-0180	C / 4.9	1.34	-1.35	2.39 / 52	2.51 / 52	2.34 / 47	1.84	0.48
GEI	American Funds Bd Fd of Amer R6	RBFGX	C+	(800) 421-0180	C / 5.4	1.37	-1.27	2.59 / 54	2.80 / 58	2.66 / 52	2.03	0.25
GL	American Funds Cap World Bond	CCWAX	E-	(800) 421-0180	E- / 0.2	2.03	-4.29	1.91 / 48	-0.40 / 4	0.38 / 20	1.51	1.03
GL ●	American Funds Cap World Bond	CCWBX	E	(800) 421-0180	E- / 0.2	1.84	-4.66	1.12 / 41	-1.18 / 2	-0.41 / 3	0.39	1.85
GL	American Funds Cap World Bond	CCWCX	E	(800) 421-0180	E- / 0.2	1.80	-4.68	1.15 / 41	-1.16 / 2	-0.40 / 3	0.80	1.80
GL	American Funds Cap World Bond	CCWEX	E	(800) 421-0180	E / 0.3	1.95	-4.40	1.70 / 46	-0.58 / 3	0.18 / 18	1.40	1.21
GL	American Funds Cap World Bond	CCWFX	E	(800) 421-0180	E / 0.5	2.05	-4.20	2.16 / 50	-0.17 / 4	0.60 / 22	1.81	0.81
* GL	American Funds Cap World Bond A	CWBFX	E-	(800) 421-0180	E- / 0.2	2.06	-4.27	2.00 / 49	-0.31 / 4	0.46 / 21	1.59	0.94
GL ●	American Funds Cap World Bond B	WBFBX	E	(800) 421-0180	E- / 0.2	1.87	-4.60	1.19 / 42	-1.07 / 3	-0.30 / 4	0.52	1.72
GL	American Funds Cap World Bond C	CWBCX	E	(800) 421-0180	E- / 0.2	1.82	-4.64	1.16 / 41	-1.11 / 3	-0.34 / 3	0.85	1.74
GL	American Funds Cap World Bond F1	WBFFX	E	(800) 421-0180	E / 0.4	2.08	-4.22	1.96 / 49	-0.31 / 4	0.47 / 21	1.18	0.94
GL	American Funds Cap World Bond F2	BFWFX	E	(800) 421-0180	E+ / 0.9	2.10	-4.12	2.27 / 51	-0.02 / 5	0.75 / 24	1.97	0.65
GL	American Funds Cap World Bond F3	WFBFX	E	(800) 421-0180	E / 0.4	2.06	-4.27	2.00 / 49	-0.31 / 4	0.46 / 21	1.65	0.55
GL	American Funds Cap World Bond R1	RCWAX	E	(800) 421-0180	E- / 0.2	1.84	-4.63	1.22 / 42	-1.05 / 3	-0.27 / 4	0.92	1.68
GL	American Funds Cap World Bond R2	RCWBX	E	(800) 421-0180	E- / 0.2	1.84	-4.60	1.23 / 42	-1.08 / 3	-0.31 / 4	0.93	1.64
GL	American Funds Cap World Bond	RCEBX	E	(800) 421-0180	E / 0.3	1.93	-4.47	1.58 / 45	-0.51 / 3	0.10 / 15	1.34	1.33
GL	American Funds Cap World Bond R3	RCWCX	E	(800) 421-0180	E / 0.3	1.96	-4.39	1.69 / 46	-0.60 / 3	0.17 / 17	1.39	1.20
GL	American Funds Cap World Bond R4	RCWEX	E	(800) 421-0180	E / 0.4	2.09	-4.23	2.06 / 49	-0.26 / 4	0.51 / 21	1.71	0.90
GL	American Funds Cap World Bond R5	RCWFX	E	(800) 421-0180	D- / 1.2	2.11	-4.08	2.32 / 52	0.03 / 8	0.81 / 25	2.02	0.59
GL	American Funds Cap World Bond	RCWHX	E	(800) 421-0180	E / 0.5	2.07	-4.20	2.18 / 50	-0.24 / 4	0.51 / 21	1.88	0.73
GL	American Funds Cap World Bond R6	RCWGX	E	(800) 421-0180	D- / 1.3	2.12	-4.05	2.38 / 52	0.08 / 11	0.86 / 26	2.08	0.53

● Denotes fund is closed to new investors
* Denotes fund is included in Section II

www.thestreetratings.com

RISK			NET ASSETS		ASSET					Portfolio Turnover Ratio	Avg Coupon Rate	FUND MANAGER		MINIMUM		LOADS	
Risk Rating/Pts	3 Yr Avg Standard Deviation	Avg Duration	NAV As of 2/28/17	Total $(Mil)	Cash %	Gov. Bond %	Muni. Bond %	Corp. Bond %	Other %			Manager Quality Pct	Manager Tenure (Years)	Initial Purch. $	Additional Purch. $	Front End Load	Back End Load
B+ / 8.8	1.5	N/A	9.87	225	0	41	0	19	40	12	0.0	50	5	250	50	2.5	0.0
B+ / 8.8	1.5	N/A	9.89	N/A	0	41	0	19	40	12	0.0	18	5	250	50	0.0	0.0
B+ / 8.8	1.5	N/A	9.81	107	0	41	0	19	40	12	0.0	17	5	250	50	0.0	0.0
B+ / 8.8	1.5	N/A	9.85	17	0	41	0	19	40	12	0.0	35	5	250	50	0.0	0.0
B+ / 8.8	1.5	N/A	9.89	44	0	41	0	19	40	12	0.0	59	5	250	50	0.0	0.0
C+ / 6.6	2.8	3.8	12.15	N/A	0	0	0	0	100	901	2.0	75	7	0	0	0.0	0.0
C+ / 6.8	2.8	3.8	12.05	55	0	0	0	0	100	901	2.0	64	7	0	0	0.0	0.0
C / 4.3	3.4	6.4	10.63	158	2	0	97	0	1	14	4.6	37	7	1,000	50	3.8	0.0
C / 4.3	3.4	6.4	10.63	N/A	2	0	97	0	1	14	4.6	23	7	1,000	50	0.0	0.0
C / 4.3	3.4	6.4	10.63	13	2	0	97	0	1	14	4.6	14	7	1,000	50	0.0	0.0
C / 4.3	3.4	6.4	10.63	2	2	0	97	0	1	14	4.6	37	7	1,000	50	0.0	0.0
C / 4.3	3.4	6.4	10.63	28	2	0	97	0	1	14	4.6	48	7	1,000	50	0.0	0.0
C / 4.3	3.4	6.4	10.63	N/A	2	0	97	0	1	14	4.6	37	7	250	50	0.0	0.0
B / 7.9	2.2	4.3	9.72	56	0	0	99	0	1	6	4.7	8	5	250	50	0.0	0.0
C+ / 5.7	3.0	5.1	12.82	916	0	46	0	30	24	401	2.7	30	28	250	50	3.8	0.0
C+ / 5.6	3.0	5.1	12.82	1	0	46	0	30	24	401	2.7	10	28	250	50	0.0	0.0
C+ / 5.6	3.0	5.1	12.82	317	0	46	0	30	24	401	2.7	11	28	250	50	0.0	0.0
C+ / 5.6	3.0	5.1	12.82	47	0	46	0	30	24	401	2.7	23	28	250	50	0.0	0.0
C+ / 5.7	3.0	5.1	12.82	80	0	46	0	30	24	401	2.7	39	28	250	50	0.0	0.0
C+ / 5.7	3.0	5.1	12.82	19,312	0	46	0	30	24	401	2.7	33	28	250	50	3.8	0.0
C+ / 5.6	3.0	5.1	12.82	9	0	46	0	30	24	401	2.7	12	28	250	50	0.0	0.0
C+ / 5.6	3.0	5.1	12.82	1,230	0	46	0	30	24	401	2.7	12	28	250	50	0.0	0.0
C+ / 5.7	3.0	5.1	12.82	766	0	46	0	30	24	401	2.7	32	28	250	50	0.0	0.0
C+ / 5.7	3.0	5.1	12.82	3,720	0	46	0	30	24	401	2.7	49	28	250	50	0.0	0.0
C+ / 5.7	3.0	5.1	12.82	N/A	0	46	0	30	24	401	2.7	34	28	250	50	0.0	0.0
C+ / 5.6	3.0	5.1	12.82	40	0	46	0	30	24	401	2.7	12	28	250	50	0.0	0.0
C+ / 5.6	3.0	5.1	12.82	498	0	46	0	30	24	401	2.7	12	28	250	50	0.0	0.0
C+ / 5.6	3.0	5.1	12.82	11	0	46	0	30	24	401	2.7	22	28	250	50	0.0	0.0
C+ / 5.6	3.0	5.1	12.82	651	0	46	0	30	24	401	2.7	23	28	250	50	0.0	0.0
C+ / 5.7	3.0	5.1	12.82	559	0	46	0	30	24	401	2.7	33	28	250	50	0.0	0.0
C+ / 5.7	3.0	5.1	12.82	157	0	46	0	30	24	401	2.7	52	28	250	50	0.0	0.0
C+ / 5.7	3.0	5.1	12.82	1	0	46	0	30	24	401	2.7	36	28	250	50	0.0	0.0
C+ / 5.7	3.0	5.1	12.82	4,052	0	46	0	30	24	401	2.7	54	28	250	50	0.0	0.0
D / 2.0	5.1	6.5	19.37	289	0	66	0	28	6	138	3.6	78	18	250	50	3.8	0.0
D / 2.0	5.1	6.5	19.27	N/A	0	66	0	28	6	138	3.6	60	18	250	50	0.0	0.0
D / 2.0	5.1	6.5	19.10	108	0	66	0	28	6	138	3.6	61	18	250	50	0.0	0.0
D / 2.0	5.1	6.5	19.24	15	0	66	0	28	6	138	3.6	75	18	250	50	0.0	0.0
D / 2.0	5.1	6.5	19.26	35	0	66	0	28	6	138	3.6	81	18	250	50	0.0	0.0
D / 2.0	5.1	6.5	19.32	5,791	0	66	0	28	6	138	3.6	79	18	250	50	3.8	0.0
D / 2.0	5.1	6.5	19.21	2	0	66	0	28	6	138	3.6	64	18	250	50	0.0	0.0
D / 2.0	5.1	6.5	18.97	326	0	66	0	28	6	138	3.6	62	18	250	50	0.0	0.0
D / 2.0	5.1	6.5	19.28	318	0	66	0	28	6	138	3.6	79	18	250	50	0.0	0.0
D / 2.0	5.1	6.5	19.29	2,075	0	66	0	28	6	138	3.6	82	18	250	50	0.0	0.0
D / 2.0	5.1	6.5	19.32	1	0	66	0	28	6	138	3.6	79	18	250	50	0.0	0.0
D / 2.0	5.1	6.5	19.10	10	0	66	0	28	6	138	3.6	64	18	250	50	0.0	0.0
D / 2.0	5.1	6.5	19.09	131	0	66	0	28	6	138	3.6	64	18	250	50	0.0	0.0
D / 2.0	5.1	6.5	19.27	2	0	66	0	28	6	138	3.6	76	18	250	50	0.0	0.0
D / 2.0	5.1	6.5	19.28	140	0	66	0	28	6	138	3.6	75	18	250	50	0.0	0.0
D / 2.0	5.1	6.5	19.31	108	0	66	0	28	6	138	3.6	80	18	250	50	0.0	0.0
D / 2.0	5.1	6.5	19.34	78	0	66	0	28	6	138	3.6	82	18	250	50	0.0	0.0
D / 2.0	5.1	6.5	19.30	N/A	0	66	0	28	6	138	3.6	80	18	250	50	0.0	0.0
D / 2.0	5.1	6.5	19.33	2,817	0	66	0	28	6	138	3.6	83	18	250	50	0.0	0.0

I. Index of Bond and Money Market Mutual Funds

					PERFORMANCE						Incl. in Returns	
	99 Pct = Best 0 Pct = Worst		Overall		Perfor-	Total Return % through 2/28/17							
		Ticker	Investment		mance				Annualized		Dividend	Expense
Fund		Symbol	Rating	Phone	Rating/Pts	3 Mo	6 Mo	1Yr / Pct	3Yr / Pct	5Yr / Pct	Yield	Ratio
Type	Fund Name											
COI	American Funds Corporate Bond	COBAX	D+	(800) 421-0180	C+ / 6.3	1.92	-1.91	6.16 /71	4.13 /77	--	1.99	1.26
COI	American Funds Corporate Bond	COBBX	C	(800) 421-0180	B- / 7.1	1.95	-1.81	6.08 /70	3.76 /72	--	1.98	1.97
COI	American Funds Corporate Bond	COBCX	C-	(800) 421-0180	C+ / 6.8	1.75	-2.24	5.56 /69	3.59 /70	--	1.50	1.97
COI	American Funds Corporate Bond	COBEX	C	(800) 421-0180	B- / 7.2	1.88	-1.96	6.01 /70	3.91 /74	--	1.92	1.43
COI	American Funds Corporate Bond	COBFX	C+	(800) 421-0180	B- / 7.5	1.99	-1.76	6.35 /71	4.19 /77	--	2.24	0.96
COI	American Funds Corporate Bond A	BFCAX	C-	(800) 421-0180	C+ / 6.9	1.94	-1.85	6.46 /71	4.58 /82	--	2.26	1.17
COI	American Funds Corporate Bond B	BFCBX	C	(800) 421-0180	B- / 7.1	1.92	-1.81	6.08 /70	3.76 /72	--	1.98	1.89
COI	American Funds Corporate Bond C	BFCCX	C-	(800) 421-0180	C+ / 6.8	1.76	-2.22	5.56 /69	3.59 /70	--	1.50	1.92
COI	American Funds Corporate Bond F1	BFCFX	C	(800) 421-0180	B- / 7.4	1.91	-1.90	6.20 /71	4.14 /77	--	2.10	1.17
COI	American Funds Corporate Bond F2	BFCGX	C+	(800) 421-0180	B / 7.9	2.00	-1.74	6.59 /72	4.62 /82	--	2.47	0.89
COI	American Funds Corporate Bond F3	CFBFX	C+	(800) 421-0180	B / 7.9	1.96	-1.84	6.48 /71	4.58 /82	--	2.36	0.81
COI	American Funds Corporate Bond R1	RCBAX	C	(800) 421-0180	B- / 7.1	1.96	-1.80	6.10 /70	3.76 /72	--	2.01	1.82
COI	American Funds Corporate Bond R2	RCBBX	C	(800) 421-0180	B- / 7.0	1.84	-1.96	5.90 /70	3.70 /71	--	1.81	2.04
COI	American Funds Corporate Bond R2E	RCBGX	C	(800) 421-0180	B- / 7.3	2.00	-1.75	6.22 /71	3.91 /74	--	2.12	1.64
COI	American Funds Corporate Bond R3	RCBCX	C	(800) 421-0180	B- / 7.3	1.90	-1.87	6.13 /71	3.95 /75	--	2.04	1.64
COI	American Funds Corporate Bond R4	RCBDX	C	(800) 421-0180	B- / 7.2	1.99	-1.77	6.17 /71	3.79 /73	--	2.07	1.11
COI	American Funds Corporate Bond R5	RCBEX	C+	(800) 421-0180	B / 7.9	2.00	-1.75	6.59 /72	4.62 /82	--	2.46	0.82
COI	American Funds Corporate Bond R5E	RCBHX	C+	(800) 421-0180	B / 7.9	2.01	-1.74	6.60 /72	4.62 /82	--	2.47	0.95
COI	American Funds Corporate Bond R6	RCBFX	C+	(800) 421-0180	B / 7.9	1.97	-1.80	6.54 /72	4.60 /82	--	2.42	0.79
EM	American Funds Emerg Mkt Bd 529A	CBNAX	U	(800) 421-0180	U /	6.78	1.05	--	--	--	0.00	1.37
EM	American Funds Emerg Mkt Bd 529B	CBNBX	U	(800) 421-0180	U /	6.90	1.22	--	--	--	0.00	2.13
EM	American Funds Emerg Mkt Bd 529C	CBNCX	U	(800) 421-0180	U /	6.62	0.83	--	--	--	0.00	2.07
EM	American Funds Emerg Mkt Bd 529E	CBNEX	U	(800) 421-0180	U /	6.77	1.04	--	--	--	0.00	1.55
EM	American Funds Emerg Mkt Bd	CBNFX	U	(800) 421-0180	U /	6.86	1.20	--	--	--	0.00	1.08
EM	American Funds Emerg Mkt Bd A	EBNAX	U	(800) 421-0180	U /	6.79	1.07	--	--	--	0.00	1.24
EM	American Funds Emerg Mkt Bd B	EBNBX	U	(800) 421-0180	U /	6.90	1.28	--	--	--	0.00	2.04
EM	American Funds Emerg Mkt Bd C	EBNCX	U	(800) 421-0180	U /	6.61	0.75	--	--	--	0.00	2.02
EM	American Funds Emerg Mkt Bd F1	EBNEX	U	(800) 421-0180	U /	6.79	1.07	--	--	--	0.00	1.25
EM	American Funds Emerg Mkt Bd F2	EBNFX	U	(800) 421-0180	U /	6.83	1.13	--	--	--	0.00	0.95
EM	American Funds Emerg Mkt Bd F3	EBNGX	U	(800) 421-0180	U /	6.79	1.06	--	--	--	0.00	1.06
EM	American Funds Emerg Mkt Bd R1	REGAX	U	(800) 421-0180	U /	6.74	1.08	--	--	--	0.00	1.97
EM	American Funds Emerg Mkt Bd R2	REGBX	U	(800) 421-0180	U /	6.69	0.90	--	--	--	0.00	2.18
EM	American Funds Emerg Mkt Bd R2E	REGHX	U	(800) 421-0180	U /	6.87	1.21	--	--	--	0.00	1.60
EM	American Funds Emerg Mkt Bd R3	REGCX	U	(800) 421-0180	U /	6.79	1.10	--	--	--	0.00	1.55
EM	American Funds Emerg Mkt Bd R4	REGEX	U	(800) 421-0180	U /	6.86	1.20	--	--	--	0.00	1.20
EM	American Funds Emerg Mkt Bd R5	REGFX	U	(800) 421-0180	U /	6.87	1.21	--	--	--	0.00	0.91
EM	American Funds Emerg Mkt Bd R5E	REGJX	U	(800) 421-0180	U /	6.87	1.22	--	--	--	0.00	1.00
EM	American Funds Emerg Mkt Bd R6	REGGX	U	(800) 421-0180	U /	6.84	1.18	--	--	--	0.00	0.84
* MUH	American Funds High Inc Muni Bnd A	AMHIX	B	(800) 421-0180	B+ / 8.9	2.36	-3.32	1.75 /54	5.43 /98	5.38 /98	3.68	0.67
MUH ●	American Funds High Inc Muni Bnd B	ABHMX	B+	(800) 421-0180	A- / 9.1	2.18	-3.66	1.04 /45	4.69 /96	4.63 /97	3.11	1.38
MUH	American Funds High Inc Muni Bnd C	AHICX	B+	(800) 421-0180	A- / 9.1	2.17	-3.68	0.99 /45	4.64 /96	4.58 /96	3.06	1.43
MUH	American Funds High Inc Muni Bnd	ABHFX	A-	(800) 421-0180	A+ / 9.6	2.34	-3.36	1.68 /54	5.35 /98	5.29 /98	3.75	0.74
MUH	American Funds High Inc Muni Bnd	AHMFX	A-	(800) 421-0180	A+ / 9.7	2.40	-3.23	1.94 /56	5.63 /98	5.56 /99	4.02	0.48
MUH	American Funds High Inc Muni Bnd	HIMFX	A-	(800) 421-0180	A+ / 9.6	2.36	-3.33	1.74 /54	5.43 /98	5.38 /98	3.81	0.39
COH	American Funds High Income Tr	CITAX	D+	(800) 421-0180	B / 8.0	4.75	5.80	21.31 /97	2.73 /56	5.05 /84	5.09	0.81
COH ●	American Funds High Income Tr	CITBX	D+	(800) 421-0180	B / 8.1	4.53	5.37	20.33 /96	1.91 /41	4.22 /75	4.51	1.62
COH	American Funds High Income Tr	CITCX	D+	(800) 421-0180	B / 8.2	4.55	5.40	20.39 /96	1.94 /42	4.24 /75	4.55	1.57
COH	American Funds High Income Tr	CITEX	C-	(800) 421-0180	B+ / 8.7	4.70	5.70	21.07 /97	2.52 /52	4.82 /82	5.10	1.00
COH	American Funds High Income Tr	CITFX	C	(800) 421-0180	A- / 9.1	4.81	5.92	21.58 /98	2.96 /60	5.28 /87	5.50	0.58
* COH	American Funds High Income Tr A	AHITX	D+	(800) 421-0180	B / 8.1	4.77	5.84	21.40 /97	2.82 /58	5.14 /85	5.16	0.71
COH ●	American Funds High Income Tr B	AHTBX	D+	(800) 421-0180	B+ / 8.3	4.56	5.43	20.48 /97	2.05 /44	4.35 /77	4.62	1.48
COH	American Funds High Income Tr C	AHTCX	D+	(800) 421-0180	B+ / 8.3	4.56	5.42	20.45 /96	2.01 /43	4.31 /76	4.60	1.51

● Denotes fund is closed to new investors
* Denotes fund is included in Section II

www.thestreetratings.com

RISK			NET ASSETS		ASSET							FUND MANAGER		MINIMUM		LOADS	
Risk Rating/Pts	3 Yr Avg Standard Deviation	Avg Dura-tion	NAV As of 2/28/17	Total $(Mil)	Cash %	Gov. Bond %	Muni. Bond %	Corp. Bond %	Other %	Portfolio Turnover Ratio	Avg Coupon Rate	Manager Quality Pct	Manager Tenure (Years)	Initial Purch. $	Additional Purch. $	Front End Load	Back End Load
C- / 3.0	4.1	6.7	10.18	4	0	0	0	0	100	295	3.1	63	5	250	50	3.8	0.0
C- / 3.0	4.1	6.7	10.18	N/A	0	0	0	0	100	295	3.1	51	5	250	50	0.0	0.0
C- / 3.0	4.1	6.7	10.18	2	0	0	0	0	100	295	3.1	36	5	250	50	0.0	0.0
C- / 3.0	4.1	6.7	10.18	N/A	0	0	0	0	100	295	3.1	56	5	250	50	0.0	0.0
C- / 3.0	4.1	6.7	10.18	1	0	0	0	0	100	295	3.1	64	5	250	50	0.0	0.0
D+ / 2.9	4.1	6.7	10.18	138	0	0	0	0	100	295	3.1	73	5	250	50	3.8	0.0
C- / 3.1	4.1	6.7	10.18	N/A	0	0	0	0	100	295	3.1	51	5	250	50	0.0	0.0
C- / 3.0	4.1	6.7	10.18	7	0	0	0	0	100	295	3.1	36	5	250	50	0.0	0.0
C- / 3.0	4.1	6.7	10.18	2	0	0	0	0	100	295	3.1	63	5	250	50	0.0	0.0
C- / 3.0	4.1	6.7	10.18	5	0	0	0	0	100	295	3.1	74	5	250	50	0.0	0.0
D+ / 2.9	4.1	6.7	10.18	N/A	0	0	0	0	100	295	3.1	73	5	250	50	0.0	0.0
C- / 3.0	4.1	6.7	10.18	N/A	0	0	0	0	100	295	3.1	51	5	250	50	0.0	0.0
C- / 3.0	4.1	6.7	10.18	N/A	0	0	0	0	100	295	3.1	47	5	250	50	0.0	0.0
C- / 3.1	4.1	6.7	10.18	N/A	0	0	0	0	100	295	3.1	56	5	250	50	0.0	0.0
C- / 3.0	4.1	6.7	10.18	N/A	0	0	0	0	100	295	3.1	58	5	250	50	0.0	0.0
C- / 3.0	4.1	6.7	10.18	N/A	0	0	0	0	100	295	3.1	51	5	250	50	0.0	0.0
C- / 3.0	4.1	6.7	10.18	N/A	0	0	0	0	100	295	3.1	74	5	250	50	0.0	0.0
C- / 3.0	4.1	6.7	10.18	N/A	0	0	0	0	100	295	3.1	74	5	250	50	0.0	0.0
D+ / 2.9	4.1	6.7	10.18	N/A	0	0	0	0	100	295	3.1	74	5	250	50	0.0	0.0
U /	N/A	6.4	10.08	1	0	0	0	0	100	0	13.4	N/A	N/A	250	50	3.8	0.0
U /	N/A	6.4	10.08	N/A	0	0	0	0	100	0	13.4	N/A	N/A	250	50	0.0	0.0
U /	N/A	6.4	10.08	N/A	0	0	0	0	100	0	13.4	N/A	N/A	250	50	0.0	0.0
U /	N/A	6.4	10.08	N/A	0	0	0	0	100	0	13.4	N/A	N/A	250	50	0.0	0.0
U /	N/A	6.4	10.08	69	0	0	0	0	100	0	13.4	N/A	N/A	250	50	3.8	0.0
U /	N/A	6.4	10.08	N/A	0	0	0	0	100	0	13.4	N/A	N/A	250	50	0.0	0.0
U /	N/A	6.4	10.08	1	0	0	0	0	100	0	13.4	N/A	N/A	250	50	0.0	0.0
U /	N/A	6.4	10.08	2	0	0	0	0	100	0	13.4	N/A	N/A	250	50	0.0	0.0
U /	N/A	6.4	10.08	13	0	0	0	0	100	0	13.4	N/A	N/A	250	50	0.0	0.0
U /	N/A	6.4	10.08	N/A	0	0	0	0	100	0	13.4	N/A	N/A	250	50	0.0	0.0
U /	N/A	6.4	10.08	N/A	0	0	0	0	100	0	13.4	N/A	N/A	250	50	0.0	0.0
U /	N/A	6.4	10.08	N/A	0	0	0	0	100	0	13.4	N/A	N/A	250	50	0.0	0.0
U /	N/A	6.4	10.08	N/A	0	0	0	0	100	0	13.4	N/A	N/A	250	50	0.0	0.0
U /	N/A	6.4	10.08	N/A	0	0	0	0	100	0	13.4	N/A	N/A	250	50	0.0	0.0
U /	N/A	6.4	10.08	N/A	0	0	0	0	100	0	13.4	N/A	N/A	250	50	0.0	0.0
U /	N/A	6.4	10.08	N/A	0	0	0	0	100	0	13.4	N/A	N/A	250	50	0.0	0.0
U /	N/A	6.4	10.08	N/A	0	0	0	0	100	0	13.4	N/A	N/A	250	50	0.0	0.0
D+ / 2.8	3.7	6.9	15.41	3,407	1	0	98	0	1	21	4.9	82	23	250	50	3.8	0.0
D+ / 2.8	3.7	6.9	15.41	N/A	1	0	98	0	1	21	4.9	72	23	250	50	0.0	0.0
D+ / 2.8	3.7	6.9	15.41	229	1	0	98	0	1	21	4.9	71	23	250	50	0.0	0.0
D+ / 2.8	3.7	6.9	15.41	219	1	0	98	0	1	21	4.9	81	23	250	50	0.0	0.0
D+ / 2.8	3.7	6.9	15.41	845	1	0	98	0	1	21	4.9	83	23	250	50	0.0	0.0
D+ / 2.8	3.7	6.9	15.41	N/A	1	0	98	0	1	21	4.9	82	23	250	50	0.0	0.0
E+ / 0.8	6.2	3.4	10.46	321	0	4	0	88	8	76	6.8	2	28	250	50	3.8	0.0
E+ / 0.8	6.2	3.4	10.46	N/A	0	4	0	88	8	76	6.8	1	28	250	50	0.0	0.0
E+ / 0.8	6.2	3.4	10.46	104	0	4	0	88	8	76	6.8	1	28	250	50	0.0	0.0
E+ / 0.8	6.2	3.4	10.46	18	0	4	0	88	8	76	6.8	2	28	250	50	0.0	0.0
E+ / 0.8	6.2	3.4	10.46	26	0	4	0	88	8	76	6.8	4	28	250	50	0.0	0.0
E+ / 0.8	6.2	3.4	10.46	11,925	0	4	0	88	8	76	6.8	3	28	250	50	3.8	0.0
E+ / 0.8	6.2	3.4	10.46	5	0	4	0	88	8	76	6.8	1	28	250	50	0.0	0.0
E+ / 0.8	6.2	3.4	10.46	834	0	4	0	88	8	76	6.8	1	28	250	50	0.0	0.0

						PERFORMANCE					Incl. in Returns	
							Total Return % through 2/28/17					
									Annualized		Dividend	Expense
Fund Type	Fund Name	Ticker Symbol	Overall Investment Rating	Phone	Perfor- mance Rating/Pts	3 Mo	6 Mo	1Yr / Pct	3Yr / Pct	5Yr / Pct	Yield	Ratio
COH	American Funds High Income Tr F1	AHTFX	C	(800) 421-0180	B+ / 8.9	4.76	5.82	21.36 /97	2.78 /57	5.10 /85	5.33	0.74
COH	American Funds High Income Tr F2	AHIFX	C	(800) 421-0180	A- / 9.2	4.83	5.96	21.69 /98	3.05 /62	5.37 /87	5.59	0.48
COH	American Funds High Income Tr F3	HIGFX	C	(800) 421-0180	A- / 9.0	4.77	5.83	21.39 /97	2.82 /58	5.14 /85	5.34	0.36
COH	American Funds High Income Tr R1	RITAX	D+	(800) 421-0180	B+ / 8.3	4.57	5.43	20.46 /96	2.01 /43	4.32 /76	4.61	1.50
COH	American Funds High Income Tr R2	RITBX	D+	(800) 421-0180	B / 8.2	4.57	5.41	20.48 /97	1.99 /43	4.29 /76	4.62	1.47
COH	American Funds High Income Tr R2E	RTEHX	C-	(800) 421-0180	B+ / 8.7	4.65	5.59	20.84 /97	2.48 /51	4.76 /81	4.91	1.16
COH	American Funds High Income Tr R3	RITCX	C-	(800) 421-0180	B+ / 8.7	4.69	5.67	21.02 /97	2.48 /51	4.79 /82	5.05	1.02
COH	American Funds High Income Tr R4	RITEX	C	(800) 421-0180	A- / 9.0	4.77	5.83	21.39 /97	2.80 /58	5.12 /85	5.35	0.73
COH	American Funds High Income Tr R5	RITFX	C	(800) 421-0180	A- / 9.2	4.84	5.99	21.75 /98	3.11 /63	5.43 /88	5.64	0.42
COH	American Funds High Income Tr R5E	RITHX	C	(800) 421-0180	A- / 9.0	4.82	5.93	21.57 /98	2.88 /59	5.18 /86	5.49	0.59
COH	American Funds High Income Tr R6	RITGX	C	(800) 421-0180	A- / 9.2	4.86	6.02	21.82 /98	3.17 /64	5.49 /88	5.69	0.36
GEI	American Funds Infl Lnk Bond 529A	CNLAX	D-	(800) 421-0180	C- / 4.0	1.16	0.33	4.50 /65	2.14 /45	—	0.91	0.67
GEI	American Funds Infl Lnk Bond 529B	CNLBX	D-	(800) 421-0180	C- / 4.2	1.03	0.10	3.93 /62	1.67 /38	—	0.00	1.63
GEI	American Funds Infl Lnk Bond 529C	CNLCX	E+	(800) 421-0180	C- / 3.7	0.89	-0.15	3.48 /59	1.34 /32	—	0.57	1.57
GEI	American Funds Infl Lnk Bond 529E	CNLEX	D-	(800) 421-0180	C / 4.5	1.04	0.11	4.05 /62	1.83 /40	—	0.82	1.00
GEI	American Funds Infl Lnk Bond 529F1	CNLFX	D-	(800) 421-0180	C / 5.1	1.10	0.27	4.54 /65	2.18 /46	—	0.97	0.58
GEI	American Funds Infl Lnk Bond A	BFIAX	D-	(800) 421-0180	C- / 4.1	1.12	0.29	4.34 /64	2.21 /46	—	0.87	0.77
GEI	American Funds Infl Lnk Bond B	BFIBX	D-	(800) 421-0180	C- / 4.1	0.93	0.00	3.83 /61	1.57 /36	—	0.00	1.52
GEI	American Funds Infl Lnk Bond C	BFICX	E+	(800) 421-0180	C- / 3.8	1.00	-0.04	3.59 /60	1.40 /33	—	0.47	1.51
GEI	American Funds Infl Lnk Bond F1	BFIFX	D-	(800) 421-0180	C / 4.9	1.15	0.32	4.38 /64	2.07 /44	—	0.92	0.74
GEI	American Funds Infl Lnk Bond F2	BFIGX	D	(800) 421-0180	C / 5.5	1.26	0.43	4.70 /65	2.40 /50	—	1.03	0.51
GEI	American Funds Infl Lnk Bond F3	FILBX	D-	(800) 421-0180	C / 5.1	1.12	0.29	4.34 /64	2.21 /47	—	0.89	0.43
GEI	American Funds Infl Lnk Bond R1	RILAX	E+	(800) 421-0180	C- / 3.8	0.93	-0.11	3.51 /60	1.46 /34	—	0.10	1.62
GEI	American Funds Infl Lnk Bond R2	RILBX	E+	(800) 421-0180	C- / 3.8	0.90	-0.14	3.49 /60	1.43 /34	—	0.58	1.53
GEI	American Funds Infl Lnk Bond R2E	RILGX	D-	(800) 421-0180	C / 4.7	1.05	0.13	4.28 /63	1.95 /42	—	0.93	1.17
GEI	American Funds Infl Lnk Bond R3	RILCX	D-	(800) 421-0180	C / 4.4	1.09	0.15	4.00 /62	1.79 /39	—	0.86	1.06
GEI	American Funds Infl Lnk Bond R4	RILDX	D-	(800) 421-0180	C / 4.9	1.12	0.30	4.35 /64	2.08 /45	—	0.90	0.74
GEI	American Funds Infl Lnk Bond R5	RILEX	D	(800) 421-0180	C / 5.5	1.22	0.40	4.67 /65	2.40 /50	—	1.00	0.48
GEI	American Funds Infl Lnk Bond R5E	RILHX	D	(800) 421-0180	C / 5.3	1.16	0.33	4.50 /65	2.29 /48	—	0.83	0.63
GEI	American Funds Infl Lnk Bond R6	RILFX	D	(800) 421-0180	C / 5.5	1.16	0.44	4.71 /65	2.41 /50	—	1.03	0.42
COI	American Funds Ins Ser Bond 4		D+	(800) 421-0180	C- / 4.2	1.06	-2.03	1.84 /48	2.13 /45	1.52 /35	1.57	0.88
GL	American Funds Ins Ser Glb Bond 1A		E	(800) 421-0180	D- / 1.0	1.98	-3.90	2.43 /53	-0.02 / 5	0.69 /23	0.80	0.82
GL	American Funds Ins Ser Glb Bond 4		E	(800) 421-0180	E / 0.3	1.93	-4.11	2.02 /49	-0.51 / 3	0.32 /20	0.47	1.07
COH	American Funds Ins Ser Hg Inc Bd		C+	(800) 421-0180	A / 9.5	5.21	6.85	23.02 /98	3.66 /71	5.58 /89	6.05	N/A
MTG	American Funds Ins Ser Mtge 1A		A-	(800) 421-0180	C / 5.4	0.55	0.64	1.55 /45	2.83 /58	2.23 /45	1.90	N/A
MTG	American Funds Ins Ser Mtge 4		B	(800) 421-0180	C / 4.5	0.42	0.42	1.06 /40	2.30 /48	1.61 /36	1.33	0.97
GEI	American Funds Intm Bd Fd Amr	CBOAX	D	(800) 421-0180	D / 1.6	0.52	-0.43	0.52 /33	1.05 /28	0.95 /27	1.09	0.70
GEI ●	American Funds Intm Bd Fd Amr	CBOBX	D	(800) 421-0180	D- / 1.1	0.26	-0.87	-0.31 /13	0.26 /18	0.16 /17	0.36	1.48
GEI	American Funds Intm Bd Fd Amr	CBOCX	D	(800) 421-0180	D- / 1.1	0.27	-0.86	-0.28 /13	0.27 /18	0.18 /18	0.39	1.46
GEI	American Funds Intm Bd Fd Amr	CBOEX	C-	(800) 421-0180	D / 2.2	0.47	-0.53	0.31 /29	0.84 /25	0.73 /24	0.91	0.90
GEI	American Funds Intm Bd Fd Amr	CBOFX	C	(800) 421-0180	C- / 3.0	0.58	-0.32	0.75 /37	1.28 /32	1.18 /30	1.34	0.47
* GEI	American Funds Intm Bd Fd Amr A	AIBAX	D+	(800) 421-0180	D / 1.8	0.54	-0.40	0.59 /35	1.14 /30	1.04 /28	1.16	0.61
GEI ●	American Funds Intm Bd Fd Amr B	IBFBX	D	(800) 421-0180	D- / 1.4	0.28	-0.83	-0.22 /14	0.38 /20	0.28 /19	0.45	1.35
GEI	American Funds Intm Bd Fd Amr C	IBFCX	D	(800) 421-0180	D- / 1.3	0.27	-0.84	-0.24 /14	0.33 /19	0.24 /19	0.43	1.39
GEI	American Funds Intm Bd Fd Amr F1	IBFFX	C	(800) 421-0180	D+ / 2.6	0.52	-0.43	0.54 /34	1.09 /29	0.99 /27	1.14	0.66
GEI	American Funds Intm Bd Fd Amr F2	IBAFX	C+	(800) 421-0180	C- / 3.1	0.59	-0.29	0.83 /38	1.37 /33	1.27 /31	1.42	0.37
COI	American Funds Intm Bd Fd Amr F3	IFBFX	C	(800) 421-0180	D+ / 2.6	0.48	-0.45	0.54 /34	1.12 /29	1.03 /28	1.21	0.26
GEI	American Funds Intm Bd Fd Amr R1	RBOAX	D	(800) 421-0180	D- / 1.4	0.28	-0.84	-0.22 /14	0.35 /19	0.25 /19	0.45	1.37
GEI	American Funds Intm Bd Fd Amr R2	RBOBX	D	(800) 421-0180	D- / 1.3	0.28	-0.84	-0.21 /14	0.33 /19	0.25 /19	0.46	1.37
COI	American Funds Intm Bd Fd Amr R2E	REBBX	C-	(800) 421-0180	D / 2.2	0.34	-0.70	0.08 /21	0.86 /25	0.63 /23	0.75	1.05
GEI	American Funds Intm Bd Fd Amr R3	RBOCX	C-	(800) 421-0180	D / 2.2	0.46	-0.56	0.28 /28	0.81 /24	0.71 /24	0.88	0.92
GEI	American Funds Intm Bd Fd Amr R4	RBOEX	C	(800) 421-0180	D+ / 2.7	0.53	-0.40	0.58 /35	1.13 /29	1.03 /28	1.18	0.62

● Denotes fund is closed to new investors
* Denotes fund is included in Section II

www.thestreetratings.com

RISK			NET ASSETS		ASSET							FUND MANAGER		MINIMUM		LOADS	
Risk Rating/Pts	3 Yr Avg Standard Deviation	Avg Dura-tion	NAV As of 2/28/17	Total $(Mil)	Cash %	Gov. Bond %	Muni. Bond %	Corp. Bond %	Other %	Portfolio Turnover Ratio	Avg Coupon Rate	Manager Quality Pct	Manager Tenure (Years)	Initial Purch. $	Additional Purch. $	Front End Load	Back End Load
E+ / 0.8	6.2	3.4	10.46	673	0	4	0	88	8	76	6.8	3	28	250	50	0.0	0.0
E+ / 0.8	6.2	3.4	10.46	1,389	0	4	0	88	8	76	6.8	4	28	250	50	0.0	0.0
E+ / 0.8	6.2	3.4	10.46	3	0	4	0	88	8	76	6.8	3	28	250	50	0.0	0.0
E+ / 0.8	6.2	3.4	10.46	16	0	4	0	88	8	76	6.8	1	28	250	50	0.0	0.0
E+ / 0.8	6.2	3.4	10.46	180	0	4	0	88	8	76	6.8	1	28	250	50	0.0	0.0
E+ / 0.8	6.2	3.4	10.46	4	0	4	0	88	8	76	6.8	2	28	250	50	0.0	0.0
E+ / 0.8	6.2	3.4	10.46	196	0	4	0	88	8	76	6.8	2	28	250	50	0.0	0.0
E+ / 0.8	6.2	3.4	10.46	161	0	4	0	88	8	76	6.8	3	28	250	50	0.0	0.0
E+ / 0.8	6.2	3.4	10.46	80	0	4	0	88	8	76	6.8	4	28	250	50	0.0	0.0
E+ / 0.8	6.2	3.4	10.46	N/A	0	4	0	88	8	76	6.8	3	28	250	50	0.0	0.0
E+ / 0.8	6.2	3.4	10.46	1,472	0	4	0	88	8	76	6.8	5	28	250	50	0.0	0.0
C- / 3.3	3.9	4.8	9.73	12	0	96	0	1	3	295	0.9	22	5	250	50	2.5	0.0
C- / 3.3	3.9	4.8	9.78	N/A	0	96	0	1	3	295	0.9	12	5	250	50	0.0	0.0
C- / 3.3	3.9	4.8	9.63	3	0	96	0	1	3	295	0.9	7	5	250	50	0.0	0.0
C- / 3.3	3.9	4.8	9.70	N/A	0	96	0	1	3	295	0.9	15	5	250	50	0.0	0.0
C- / 3.3	3.9	4.8	9.74	1	0	96	0	1	3	295	0.9	24	5	250	50	0.0	0.0
C- / 3.3	4.0	4.8	9.72	399	0	96	0	1	3	295	0.9	24	5	250	50	2.5	0.0
C- / 3.2	4.0	4.8	9.75	N/A	0	96	0	1	3	295	0.9	10	5	250	50	0.0	0.0
C- / 3.2	4.0	4.8	9.65	14	0	96	0	1	3	295	0.9	8	5	250	50	0.0	0.0
C- / 3.2	4.0	4.8	9.72	32	0	96	0	1	3	295	0.9	20	5	250	50	0.0	0.0
C- / 3.3	4.0	4.8	9.75	275	0	96	0	1	3	295	0.9	29	5	250	50	0.0	0.0
C- / 3.3	4.0	4.8	9.72	N/A	0	96	0	1	3	295	0.9	24	5	250	50	0.0	0.0
C- / 3.2	4.0	4.8	9.71	N/A	0	96	0	1	3	295	0.9	8	5	250	50	0.0	0.0
C- / 3.2	4.0	4.8	9.62	2	0	96	0	1	3	295	0.9	8	5	250	50	0.0	0.0
C- / 3.3	3.9	4.8	9.72	1	0	96	0	1	3	295	0.9	17	5	250	50	0.0	0.0
C- / 3.3	4.0	4.8	9.67	3	0	96	0	1	3	295	0.9	14	5	250	50	0.0	0.0
C- / 3.3	4.0	4.8	9.72	3	0	96	0	1	3	295	0.9	20	5	250	50	0.0	0.0
C- / 3.3	3.9	4.8	9.75	1	0	96	0	1	3	295	0.9	29	5	250	50	0.0	0.0
C- / 3.3	4.0	4.8	9.73	N/A	0	96	0	1	3	295	0.9	27	5	250	50	0.0	0.0
C- / 3.3	3.9	4.8	9.75	1,809	0	96	0	1	3	295	0.9	30	5	250	50	0.0	0.0
C / 5.5	3.0	5.3	10.79	104	0	0	0	0	100	434	3.0	23	N/A	0	0	0.0	0.0
D / 2.0	5.0	6.4	11.42	N/A	0	0	0	0	100	159	3.7	82	4	0	0	0.0	0.0
D / 2.0	5.1	6.4	11.28	12	0	0	0	0	100	159	3.7	76	4	0	0	0.0	0.0
E+ / 0.8	6.2	3.3	10.49	N/A	0	0	0	0	100	54	7.7	10	24	0	0	0.0	0.0
B / 8.1	2.1	1.8	10.62	N/A	0	0	0	0	100	1,103	3.0	68	7	0	0	0.0	0.0
B / 8.0	2.1	1.8	10.53	9	0	0	0	0	100	1,103	3.0	50	7	0	0	0.0	0.0
B+ / 8.5	1.8	2.9	13.39	374	0	65	0	18	17	173	2.0	24	8	250	50	2.5	0.0
B+ / 8.5	1.8	2.9	13.38	N/A	0	65	0	18	17	173	2.0	8	8	250	50	0.0	0.0
B+ / 8.5	1.8	2.9	13.38	63	0	65	0	18	17	173	2.0	8	8	250	50	0.0	0.0
B+ / 8.5	1.8	2.9	13.39	18	0	65	0	18	17	173	2.0	18	8	250	50	0.0	0.0
B+ / 8.5	1.8	2.9	13.39	83	0	65	0	18	17	173	2.0	31	8	250	50	0.0	0.0
B+ / 8.5	1.8	2.9	13.39	7,075	0	65	0	18	17	173	2.0	26	8	250	50	2.5	0.0
B+ / 8.5	1.8	2.9	13.38	1	0	65	0	18	17	173	2.0	9	8	250	50	0.0	0.0
B+ / 8.5	1.8	2.9	13.38	85	0	65	0	18	17	173	2.0	9	8	250	50	0.0	0.0
B+ / 8.5	1.8	2.9	13.39	230	0	65	0	18	17	173	2.0	25	8	250	50	0.0	0.0
B+ / 8.5	1.8	2.9	13.39	802	0	65	0	18	17	173	2.0	34	8	250	50	0.0	0.0
B+ / 8.5	1.8	2.9	13.38	1	0	65	0	18	17	173	2.0	29	8	250	50	0.0	0.0
B+ / 8.5	1.8	2.9	13.38	8	0	65	0	18	17	173	2.0	9	8	250	50	0.0	0.0
B+ / 8.5	1.8	2.9	13.38	112	0	65	0	18	17	173	2.0	9	8	250	50	0.0	0.0
B+ / 8.4	1.8	2.9	13.37	3	0	65	0	18	17	173	2.0	21	8	250	50	0.0	0.0
B+ / 8.5	1.8	2.9	13.39	150	0	65	0	18	17	173	2.0	17	8	250	50	0.0	0.0
B+ / 8.5	1.8	2.9	13.39	119	0	65	0	18	17	173	2.0	26	8	250	50	0.0	0.0

Fund Type	Fund Name	Ticker Symbol	Overall Investment Rating	Phone	Perfor-mance Rating/Pts	Total Return % through 2/28/17					Incl. in Returns	
	99 Pct = Best 0 Pct = Worst					3 Mo	6 Mo	1Yr / Pct	Annualized 3Yr / Pct	5Yr / Pct	Dividend Yield	Expense Ratio
GEI	American Funds Intm Bd Fd Amr R5	RBOFX	C+	(800) 421-0180	C- / 3.2	0.61	-0.26	0.88 / 38	1.43 / 34	1.33 / 32	1.48	0.32
COI	American Funds Intm Bd Fd Amr R5E	RBOHX	C	(800) 421-0180	D+ / 2.8	0.59	-0.32	0.73 / 36	1.20 / 31	1.08 / 28	1.33	0.49
GEI	American Funds Intm Bd Fd Amr R6	RBOGX	C+	(800) 421-0180	C- / 3.3	0.62	-0.23	0.94 / 39	1.48 / 35	1.38 / 33	1.54	0.27
* MUN	American Funds Ltd Term T/E Bond	LTEBX	D+	(800) 421-0180	D / 2.0	1.42	-1.32	-0.25 / 14	1.24 / 41	1.54 / 47	2.00	0.59
MUN ●	American Funds Ltd Term T/E Bond	LTXBX	D+	(800) 421-0180	D / 1.9	1.25	-1.66	-0.93 / 5	0.54 / 25	0.84 / 31	1.36	1.29
MUN	American Funds Ltd Term T/E Bond	LTXCX	D+	(800) 421-0180	D / 1.8	1.23	-1.68	-0.97 / 4	0.49 / 24	0.79 / 30	1.31	1.33
MUN	American Funds Ltd Term T/E Bond	LTXFX	C+	(800) 421-0180	C- / 3.4	1.40	-1.36	-0.32 / 12	1.16 / 39	1.46 / 45	1.98	0.67
MUN	American Funds Ltd Term T/E Bond	LTEFX	B	(800) 421-0180	C- / 4.0	1.46	-1.23	-0.06 / 17	1.41 / 46	1.72 / 52	2.25	0.41
MUN	American Funds Ltd Term T/E Bond	FLTEX	C+	(800) 421-0180	C- / 3.6	1.43	-1.31	-0.23 / 14	1.24 / 41	1.54 / 47	2.06	0.31
MTG	American Funds Mortgage Fund	CMFAX	C	(800) 421-0180	C- / 3.0	0.51	0.22	0.99 / 39	2.38 / 50	1.79 / 39	1.42	0.76
MTG ●	American Funds Mortgage Fund	CMFBX	C+	(800) 421-0180	C- / 3.4	0.42	-0.15	0.25 / 27	1.64 / 37	1.02 / 28	0.75	1.60
MTG	American Funds Mortgage Fund	CMFCX	C	(800) 421-0180	C- / 3.3	0.41	-0.17	0.22 / 26	1.59 / 36	0.99 / 27	0.71	1.55
MTG	American Funds Mortgage Fund	CMFEX	B	(800) 421-0180	C- / 4.1	0.44	0.00	0.76 / 37	2.13 / 45	1.52 / 35	1.25	1.01
MTG	American Funds Mortgage Fund	CMFFX	A-	(800) 421-0180	C / 5.0	0.65	0.33	1.32 / 43	2.64 / 55	2.01 / 42	1.71	0.55
MTG	American Funds Mortgage Fund A	MFAAX	C+	(800) 421-0180	C- / 3.2	0.61	0.25	1.16 / 41	2.50 / 52	1.89 / 40	1.50	0.68
MTG ●	American Funds Mortgage Fund B	MFABX	C+	(800) 421-0180	C- / 3.4	0.32	-0.23	0.29 / 28	1.67 / 38	1.08 / 28	0.79	1.44
MTG	American Funds Mortgage Fund C	MFACX	C+	(800) 421-0180	C- / 3.4	0.32	-0.14	0.28 / 28	1.64 / 37	1.05 / 28	0.77	1.48
MTG	American Funds Mortgage Fund F1	MFAEX	B+	(800) 421-0180	C / 4.8	0.60	0.24	1.06 / 40	2.49 / 51	1.87 / 40	1.55	0.67
MTG	American Funds Mortgage Fund F2	MFAFX	A-	(800) 421-0180	C / 5.2	0.68	0.38	1.34 / 43	2.77 / 57	2.14 / 44	1.82	0.41
USA	American Funds Mortgage Fund F3	AFFMX	B+	(800) 421-0180	C / 4.8	0.64	0.28	1.19 / 42	2.51 / 52	1.89 / 40	1.58	0.31
MTG	American Funds Mortgage Fund R1	RMAAX	B-	(800) 421-0180	C- / 4.0	0.42	-0.15	0.29 / 28	2.08 / 45	1.57 / 36	0.78	1.48
MTG	American Funds Mortgage Fund R2	RMABX	C+	(800) 421-0180	C- / 3.3	0.43	-0.14	0.33 / 30	1.61 / 36	1.12 / 29	0.82	1.44
MTG	American Funds Mortgage Fund R2E	RMBEX	B	(800) 421-0180	C / 4.6	0.41	0.12	1.01 / 40	2.39 / 50	1.57 / 36	1.60	1.27
MTG	American Funds Mortgage Fund R3	RMACX	B-	(800) 421-0180	C- / 4.2	0.54	0.07	0.73 / 37	2.15 / 46	1.62 / 36	1.22	1.00
MTG	American Funds Mortgage Fund R4	RMAEX	B+	(800) 421-0180	C / 4.9	0.61	0.25	1.17 / 41	2.55 / 53	1.94 / 41	1.56	0.65
MTG	American Funds Mortgage Fund R5	RMAFX	A-	(800) 421-0180	C / 5.3	0.69	0.40	1.37 / 43	2.81 / 58	2.18 / 44	1.85	0.39
USS	American Funds Mortgage Fund R5E	RMAHX	B+	(800) 421-0180	C / 4.9	0.67	0.34	1.24 / 42	2.57 / 53	1.93 / 41	1.73	0.54
MTG	American Funds Mortgage Fund R6	RMAGX	A	(800) 421-0180	C / 5.4	0.71	0.43	1.44 / 44	2.88 / 59	2.25 / 45	1.93	0.31
GEI	American Funds Preservation 529A	CPPAX	D+	(800) 421-0180	D / 1.7	0.58	-0.41	0.96 / 39	1.05 / 28	--	1.18	0.73
GEI	American Funds Preservation 529B	CPPBX	D	(800) 421-0180	D- / 1.3	0.33	-0.86	0.12 / 23	0.25 / 17	--	0.27	1.55
GEI	American Funds Preservation 529C	CPPCX	D	(800) 421-0180	D- / 1.4	0.39	-0.77	0.19 / 25	0.29 / 18	--	0.44	1.52
GEI	American Funds Preservation 529E	CPPEX	C-	(800) 421-0180	D+ / 2.3	0.53	-0.61	0.71 / 36	0.82 / 25	--	0.96	0.98
GEI	American Funds Preservation 529F1	CPPFX	C+	(800) 421-0180	C- / 3.1	0.64	-0.28	1.17 / 41	1.28 / 32	--	1.42	0.52
* GEI	American Funds Preservation A	PPVAX	D+	(800) 421-0180	D / 1.8	0.59	-0.49	0.97 / 39	1.09 / 29	--	1.19	0.71
GEI	American Funds Preservation B	PPVBX	D	(800) 421-0180	D- / 1.4	0.33	-0.84	0.17 / 25	0.32 / 19	--	0.31	1.46
GEI	American Funds Preservation C	PPVCX	D	(800) 421-0180	D- / 1.5	0.31	-0.85	0.15 / 24	0.34 / 19	--	0.50	1.44
GEI	American Funds Preservation F1	PPVFX	C	(800) 421-0180	D+ / 2.7	0.59	-0.49	0.97 / 39	1.10 / 29	--	1.21	0.71
GEI	American Funds Preservation F2	PPEFX	C+	(800) 421-0180	C- / 3.2	0.66	-0.35	1.24 / 42	1.35 / 33	--	1.49	0.44
COI	American Funds Preservation F3	PPFFX	C	(800) 421-0180	D+ / 2.7	0.62	-0.46	1.00 / 39	1.10 / 29	--	1.25	0.34
GEI	American Funds Preservation R1	RPPVX	D	(800) 421-0180	D- / 1.5	0.40	-0.87	0.23 / 27	0.33 / 19	--	0.47	1.45
GEI	American Funds Preservation R2	RPPBX	D+	(800) 421-0180	D- / 1.5	0.34	-0.84	0.19 / 25	0.33 / 19	--	0.54	1.45
COI	American Funds Preservation R2E	RPBEX	C-	(800) 421-0180	D+ / 2.3	0.37	-0.71	0.50 / 33	0.87 / 25	--	0.85	1.11
GEI	American Funds Preservation R3	RPPCX	C-	(800) 421-0180	D / 2.2	0.54	-0.63	0.69 / 36	0.81 / 24	--	0.94	1.01
GEI	American Funds Preservation R4	RPPEX	C	(800) 421-0180	D+ / 2.8	0.61	-0.48	1.00 / 39	1.12 / 29	--	1.25	0.70
GEI	American Funds Preservation R5	RPPFX	C+	(800) 421-0180	C- / 3.2	0.57	-0.33	1.29 / 43	1.38 / 33	--	1.53	0.40
COI	American Funds Preservation R5E	RGMFX	C	(800) 421-0180	D+ / 2.9	0.64	-0.40	1.12 / 41	1.16 / 30	--	1.37	0.57
GEI	American Funds Preservation R6	RPPGX	C+	(800) 421-0180	C- / 3.3	0.59	-0.30	1.24 / 42	1.45 / 34	--	1.59	0.34
GES	American Funds Sh-T Bd of Amr	CAAFX	D	(800) 421-0180	E / 0.5	0.35	0.13	0.91 / 39	0.54 / 21	0.42 / 21	0.86	0.66
GES ●	American Funds Sh-T Bd of Amr	CBAMX	D	(800) 421-0180	E / 0.4	0.18	-0.20	0.13 / 23	-0.21 / 4	-0.35 / 3	0.20	1.44
GES ●	American Funds Sh-T Bd of Amr	CCAMX	D	(800) 421-0180	E / 0.4	0.16	-0.23	0.08 / 21	-0.27 / 4	-0.43 / 3	0.15	1.51
GES	American Funds Sh-T Bd of Amr	CEAMX	C-	(800) 421-0180	D / 1.6	0.27	-0.02	0.58 / 35	0.24 / 17	0.08 / 13	0.55	0.99
GES	American Funds Sh-T Bd of Amr	CFAMX	C+	(800) 421-0180	D / 2.2	0.38	0.20	1.05 / 40	0.68 / 23	0.56 / 22	1.01	0.52

● Denotes fund is closed to new investors
* Denotes fund is included in Section II

www.thestreetratings.com

Risk Rating/Pts	3 Yr Avg Standard Deviation	Avg Duration	NAV As of 2/28/17	Total $(Mil)	Cash %	Gov. Bond %	Muni. Bond %	Corp. Bond %	Other %	Portfolio Turnover Ratio	Avg Coupon Rate	Manager Quality Pct	Manager Tenure (Years)	Initial Purch. $	Additional Purch. $	Front End Load	Back End Load
B+ / 8.5	1.8	2.9	13.39	34	0	65	0	18	17	173	2.0	36	8	250	50	0.0	0.0
B+ / 8.5	1.8	2.9	13.39	N/A	0	65	0	18	17	173	2.0	32	8	250	50	0.0	0.0
B+ / 8.5	1.8	2.9	13.39	3,998	0	65	0	18	17	173	2.0	41	8	250	50	0.0	0.0
B+ / 8.5	1.8	3.1	15.65	2,989	0	0	99	0	1	16	4.3	18	24	250	50	2.5	0.0
B+ / 8.5	1.8	3.1	15.65	N/A	0	0	99	0	1	16	4.3	7	24	250	50	0.0	0.0
B+ / 8.5	1.8	3.1	15.65	28	0	0	99	0	1	16	4.3	6	24	250	50	0.0	0.0
B+ / 8.5	1.8	3.1	15.65	86	0	0	99	0	1	16	4.3	17	24	250	50	0.0	0.0
B+ / 8.5	1.8	3.1	15.65	351	0	0	99	0	1	16	4.3	23	24	250	50	0.0	0.0
B+ / 8.5	1.8	3.1	15.65	N/A	0	0	99	0	1	16	4.3	19	24	250	50	0.0	0.0
B / 8.2	2.0	2.2	10.09	19	0	27	0	12	61	1,041	2.9	54	7	250	50	3.8	0.0
B+ / 8.3	2.0	2.2	10.05	N/A	0	27	0	12	61	1,041	2.9	21	7	250	50	0.0	0.0
B / 8.1	2.1	2.2	10.05	6	0	27	0	12	61	1,041	2.9	19	7	250	50	0.0	0.0
B / 8.2	2.0	2.2	10.09	1	0	27	0	12	61	1,041	2.9	37	7	250	50	0.0	0.0
B / 8.2	2.0	2.2	10.10	7	0	27	0	12	61	1,041	2.9	62	7	250	50	0.0	0.0
B / 8.2	2.0	2.2	10.10	216	0	27	0	12	61	1,041	2.9	58	7	250	50	3.8	0.0
B / 8.1	2.1	2.2	10.06	N/A	0	27	0	12	61	1,041	2.9	21	7	250	50	0.0	0.0
B / 8.2	2.0	2.2	10.06	25	0	27	0	12	61	1,041	2.9	21	7	250	50	0.0	0.0
B+ / 8.3	2.0	2.2	10.10	16	0	27	0	12	61	1,041	2.9	59	7	250	50	0.0	0.0
B / 8.1	2.1	2.2	10.10	42	0	27	0	12	61	1,041	2.9	64	7	250	50	0.0	0.0
B / 8.2	2.0	2.2	10.10	N/A	0	27	0	12	61	1,041	2.9	80	7	250	50	0.0	0.0
B / 8.2	2.0	2.2	10.07	3	0	27	0	12	61	1,041	2.9	36	7	250	50	0.0	0.0
B / 8.2	2.0	2.2	10.05	3	0	27	0	12	61	1,041	2.9	20	7	250	50	0.0	0.0
B / 8.2	2.1	2.2	10.08	N/A	0	27	0	12	61	1,041	2.9	54	7	250	50	0.0	0.0
B / 8.1	2.1	2.2	10.09	23	0	27	0	12	61	1,041	2.9	35	7	250	50	0.0	0.0
B / 8.2	2.0	2.2	10.10	2	0	27	0	12	61	1,041	2.9	60	7	250	50	0.0	0.0
B / 8.0	2.1	2.2	10.10	1	0	27	0	12	61	1,041	2.9	64	7	250	50	0.0	0.0
B+ / 8.3	2.0	2.2	10.10	N/A	0	27	0	12	61	1,041	2.9	81	7	250	50	0.0	0.0
B / 8.2	2.0	2.2	10.10	2,641	0	27	0	12	61	1,041	2.9	69	7	250	50	0.0	0.0
B+ / 8.7	1.7	3.3	9.91	74	0	46	1	25	28	2	2.7	26	5	250	50	2.5	0.0
B+ / 8.7	1.6	3.3	9.92	N/A	0	46	1	25	28	2	2.7	10	5	250	50	0.0	0.0
B+ / 8.7	1.6	3.3	9.90	34	0	46	1	25	28	2	2.7	10	5	250	50	0.0	0.0
B+ / 8.7	1.6	3.3	9.90	3	0	46	1	25	28	2	2.7	21	5	250	50	0.0	0.0
B+ / 8.7	1.7	3.3	9.91	15	0	46	1	25	28	2	2.7	34	5	250	50	0.0	0.0
B+ / 8.7	1.6	3.3	9.91	785	0	46	1	25	28	2	2.7	28	5	250	50	2.5	0.0
B+ / 8.6	1.7	3.3	9.92	N/A	0	46	1	25	28	2	2.7	10	5	250	50	0.0	0.0
B+ / 8.7	1.6	3.3	9.89	168	0	46	1	25	28	2	2.7	10	5	250	50	0.0	0.0
B+ / 8.7	1.6	3.3	9.91	27	0	46	1	25	28	2	2.7	29	5	250	50	0.0	0.0
B+ / 8.7	1.6	3.3	9.91	49	0	46	1	25	28	2	2.7	40	5	250	50	0.0	0.0
B+ / 8.7	1.6	3.3	9.91	N/A	0	46	1	25	28	2	2.7	30	5	250	50	0.0	0.0
B+ / 8.7	1.6	3.3	9.90	1	0	46	1	25	28	2	2.7	10	5	250	50	0.0	0.0
B+ / 8.8	1.5	3.3	9.88	16	0	46	1	25	28	2	2.7	11	5	250	50	0.0	0.0
B+ / 8.7	1.6	3.3	9.90	2	0	46	1	25	28	2	2.7	25	5	250	50	0.0	0.0
B+ / 8.7	1.6	3.3	9.90	16	0	46	1	25	28	2	2.7	21	5	250	50	0.0	0.0
B+ / 8.7	1.6	3.3	9.91	9	0	46	1	25	28	2	2.7	31	5	250	50	0.0	0.0
B+ / 8.7	1.6	3.3	9.91	1	0	46	1	25	28	2	2.7	45	5	250	50	0.0	0.0
B+ / 8.7	1.7	3.3	9.92	N/A	0	46	1	25	28	2	2.7	32	5	250	50	0.0	0.0
B+ / 8.8	1.5	3.3	9.91	10	0	46	1	25	28	2	2.7	51	5	250	50	0.0	0.0
A / 9.5	0.8	1.6	9.95	305	0	44	1	25	30	301	1.6	36	6	250	50	2.5	0.0
A / 9.4	0.8	1.6	9.84	N/A	0	44	1	25	30	301	1.6	15	6	250	50	0.0	0.0
A / 9.4	0.8	1.6	9.81	65	0	44	1	25	30	301	1.6	13	6	250	50	0.0	0.0
A / 9.5	0.8	1.6	9.94	17	0	44	1	25	30	301	1.6	26	6	250	50	0.0	0.0
A / 9.4	0.8	1.6	9.95	61	0	44	1	25	30	301	1.6	46	6	250	50	0.0	0.0

					PERFORMANCE							Incl. in Returns	
	99 Pct = Best 0 Pct = Worst				Perfor-	Total Return % through 2/28/17							
					mance					Annualized		Dividend	Expense
Fund Type	Fund Name	Ticker Symbol	Overall Investment Rating	Phone	Rating/Pts	3 Mo	6 Mo	1Yr / Pct	3Yr / Pct	5Yr / Pct		Yield	Ratio
*GES	American Funds Sh-T Bd of Amr A	ASBAX	D	(800) 421-0180	E+ / 0.8	0.45	0.25	1.04 /40	0.63 /22	0.50 /21		0.88	0.62
GES ●	American Funds Sh-T Bd of Amr B	AMSBX	D	(800) 421-0180	E / 0.5	0.28	-0.09	0.27 /28	-0.07 / 5	-0.21 / 4		0.24	1.31
GES ●	American Funds Sh-T Bd of Amr C	ASBCX	D	(800) 421-0180	E / 0.4	0.16	-0.22	0.10 /22	-0.22 / 4	-0.36 / 3		0.17	1.45
GES	American Funds Sh-T Bd of Amr F1	ASBFX	C	(800) 421-0180	D / 1.9	0.32	0.09	0.82 /37	0.47 /20	0.35 /20		0.79	0.72
GES	American Funds Sh-T Bd of Amr F2	SBFFX	C+	(800) 421-0180	D+ / 2.4	0.49	0.32	1.20 /42	0.78 /24	0.65 /23		1.06	0.46
USA	American Funds Sh-T Bd of Amr F3	FSBTX	C	(800) 421-0180	D / 2.2	0.47	0.27	1.06 /40	0.63 /22	0.50 /21		0.92	0.35
GES	American Funds Sh-T Bd of Amr R1	RAMAX	D	(800) 421-0180	E / 0.4	0.16	-0.23	0.09 /22	-0.23 / 4	-0.38 / 3		0.16	1.45
GES	American Funds Sh-T Bd of Amr R2	RAMBX	D	(800) 421-0180	E / 0.4	0.16	-0.23	0.13 /23	-0.21 / 4	-0.37 / 3		0.20	1.46
COI	American Funds Sh-T Bd of Amr R2E	RAAEX	C-	(800) 421-0180	D / 1.6	0.21	-0.03	0.47 /33	0.29 /18	0.03 / 8		0.44	1.22
GES	American Funds Sh-T Bd of Amr R3	RAMCX	C-	(800) 421-0180	D- / 1.5	0.26	-0.05	0.55 /34	0.23 /17	0.07 /13		0.52	1.00
GES	American Funds Sh-T Bd of Amr R4	RAMEX	C	(800) 421-0180	D / 2.0	0.33	0.11	0.86 /38	0.50 /21	0.38 /20		0.82	0.70
GES	American Funds Sh-T Bd of Amr R5	RAMFX	C+	(800) 421-0180	D+ / 2.5	0.51	0.35	1.25 /42	0.83 /25	0.69 /23		1.11	0.41
USS	American Funds Sh-T Bd of Amr R5E	RAAGX	C	(800) 421-0180	D / 2.2	0.47	0.26	0.98 /39	0.65 /22	0.51 /22		0.94	0.58
GES	American Funds Sh-T Bd of Amr R6	RMMGX	C+	(800) 421-0180	D+ / 2.5	0.42	0.28	1.21 /42	0.88 /26	0.73 /24		1.17	0.35
*MUN	American Funds ST T/E Bnd Fd A	ASTEX	D	(800) 421-0180	E / 0.5	1.08	-0.42	0.20 /29	0.52 /24	0.70 /28		1.06	0.59
MUN	American Funds ST T/E Bnd Fd F1	FSTTX	C-	(800) 421-0180	D / 1.8	1.03	-0.54	-0.03 /17	0.30 /20	0.47 /24		0.86	0.81
MUN	American Funds ST T/E Bnd Fd F2	ASTFX	C	(800) 421-0180	D+ / 2.4	1.09	-0.41	0.23 /30	0.56 /25	0.73 /29		1.12	0.56
MUN	American Funds ST T/E Bnd Fd F3	SFTEX	C	(800) 421-0180	D+ / 2.3	1.09	-0.42	0.21 /29	0.53 /25	0.70 /28		1.09	0.45
GEN	American Funds Strategic Bond 529A	CANAX	U	(800) 421-0180	U /	1.80	0.11	--	--	--		0.00	1.31
GEN	American Funds Strategic Bond 529B	CANBX	U	(800) 421-0180	U /	1.75	0.02	--	--	--		0.00	2.07
GEN	American Funds Strategic Bond 529C	CANCX	U	(800) 421-0180	U /	1.57	-0.27	--	--	--		0.00	2.01
GEN	American Funds Strategic Bond 529E	CANEX	U	(800) 421-0180	U /	1.76	0.06	--	--	--		0.00	1.49
GEN	American Funds Strategic Bond	CANFX	U	(800) 421-0180	U /	1.88	0.26	--	--	--		0.00	1.02
GEN	American Funds Strategic Bond A	ANBAX	U	(800) 421-0180	U /	1.82	0.14	--	--	--		0.00	1.16
GEN	American Funds Strategic Bond B	ANBBX	U	(800) 421-0180	U /	1.77	-0.09	--	--	--		0.00	1.96
GEN	American Funds Strategic Bond C	ANBCX	U	(800) 421-0180	U /	1.57	-0.26	--	--	--		0.00	1.94
GEN	American Funds Strategic Bond F1	ANBEX	U	(800) 421-0180	U /	1.72	0.15	--	--	--		0.00	1.17
GEN	American Funds Strategic Bond F2	ANBFX	U	(800) 421-0180	U /	1.88	0.28	--	--	--		0.00	0.87
GEL	American Funds Strategic Bond F3	ANBGX	U	(800) 421-0180	U /	1.82	0.14	--	--	--		0.00	0.76
GEN	American Funds Strategic Bond R1	RANAX	U	(800) 421-0180	U /	1.67	0.07	--	--	--		0.00	1.89
GEN	American Funds Strategic Bond R2	RANBX	U	(800) 421-0180	U /	1.71	-0.05	--	--	--		0.00	2.10
GEN	American Funds Strategic Bond R2E	RANHX	U	(800) 421-0180	U /	1.88	0.27	--	--	--		0.00	1.52
GEN	American Funds Strategic Bond R3	RANCX	U	(800) 421-0180	U /	1.70	0.03	--	--	--		0.00	1.47
GEN	American Funds Strategic Bond R4	RANEX	U	(800) 421-0180	U /	1.72	0.10	--	--	--		0.00	1.12
GEN	American Funds Strategic Bond R5	RANFX	U	(800) 421-0180	U /	1.87	0.35	--	--	--		0.00	0.83
GEN	American Funds Strategic Bond R5E	RANJX	U	(800) 421-0180	U /	1.88	0.28	--	--	--		0.00	0.92
GEN	American Funds Strategic Bond R-6	RANGX	U	(800) 421-0180	U /	1.90	0.32	--	--	--		0.00	0.76
*MUN	American Funds T/E Bd of America A	AFTEX	C+	(800) 421-0180	C+ / 5.9	1.97	-2.93	0.28 /32	3.50 /88	3.32 /85		3.02	0.54
MUN●	American Funds T/E Bd of America B	TEBFX	B-	(800) 421-0180	C+ / 6.3	1.81	-3.27	-0.44 /10	2.74 /78	2.56 /72		2.39	1.28
MUN	American Funds T/E Bd of America C	TEBCX	C+	(800) 421-0180	C+ / 6.2	1.78	-3.31	-0.51 / 9	2.69 /77	2.51 /71		2.32	1.33
MUN	American Funds T/E Bd of America	AFTFX	B+	(800) 421-0180	B- / 7.4	1.94	-2.99	0.13 /26	3.36 /86	3.19 /83		2.98	0.67
MUN	American Funds T/E Bd of America	TEAFX	A	(800) 421-0180	B / 7.9	2.01	-2.87	0.41 /35	3.64 /89	3.46 /87		3.27	0.40
MUN	American Funds T/E Bd of America	TFEBX	A-	(800) 421-0180	B / 7.7	1.97	-2.94	0.28 /32	3.50 /88	3.32 /85		3.12	0.31
*MUS	American Funds Tax-Exempt of CA A	TAFTX	C	(800) 421-0180	C+ / 6.0	2.29	-3.39	-0.24 /14	3.62 /89	3.70 /90		2.96	0.60
MUS ●	American Funds Tax-Exempt of CA B	TECBX	C	(800) 421-0180	C+ / 6.4	2.11	-3.73	-0.95 / 5	2.87 /80	2.95 /79		2.34	1.34
MUS	American Funds Tax-Exempt of CA C	TECCX	C	(800) 421-0180	C+ / 6.2	2.10	-3.77	-1.02 / 4	2.81 /79	2.89 /78		2.26	1.39
MUS	American Funds Tax-Exempt of CA	TECFX	B	(800) 421-0180	B- / 7.5	2.26	-3.45	-0.37 /11	3.49 /88	3.57 /88		2.94	0.73
MUS	American Funds Tax-Exempt of CA	TEFEX	B+	(800) 421-0180	B / 7.9	2.32	-3.33	-0.12 /16	3.75 /90	3.83 /91		3.20	0.48
MUN	American Funds Tax-Exempt of CA	EXCAX	B	(800) 421-0180	B / 7.7	2.30	-3.38	-0.24 /14	3.62 /89	3.70 /90		3.07	0.37
MUN	American Funds TxEx Preservation A	TEPAX	C	(800) 421-0180	D+ / 2.9	1.50	-1.93	-0.28 /13	1.75 /56	--		2.13	0.75
MUN	American Funds TxEx Preservation B	TEPBX	C-	(800) 421-0180	D+ / 2.8	1.38	-2.16	-0.86 / 5	1.06 /37	--		1.18	1.47
MUN	American Funds TxEx Preservation	TEPFX	B	(800) 421-0180	C / 4.6	1.50	-1.92	-0.25 /14	1.75 /56	--		2.22	0.72

● Denotes fund is closed to new investors
* Denotes fund is included in Section II

www.thestreetratings.com

Risk Rating/Pts	3 Yr Avg Standard Deviation	Avg Duration	NAV As of 2/28/17	Total $(Mil)	Cash %	Gov. Bond %	Muni. Bond %	Corp. Bond %	Other %	Portfolio Turnover Ratio	Avg Coupon Rate	Manager Quality Pct	Manager Tenure (Years)	Initial Purch. $	Additional Purch. $	Front End Load	Back End Load
A /9.5	0.8	1.6	9.96	3,157	0	44	1	25	30	301	1.6	42	6	250	50	2.5	0.0
A /9.4	0.9	1.6	9.89	1	0	44	1	25	30	301	1.6	16	6	250	50	0.0	0.0
A /9.4	0.9	1.6	9.84	82	0	44	1	25	30	301	1.6	14	6	250	50	0.0	0.0
A /9.4	0.8	1.6	9.95	133	0	44	1	25	30	301	1.6	32	6	250	50	0.0	0.0
A /9.4	0.8	1.6	9.96	443	0	44	1	25	30	301	1.6	51	6	250	50	0.0	0.0
A /9.4	0.8	1.6	9.96	1	0	44	1	25	30	301	1.6	52	6	250	50	0.0	0.0
A /9.5	0.8	1.6	9.83	5	0	44	1	25	30	301	1.6	14	6	250	50	0.0	0.0
A /9.4	0.8	1.6	9.83	44	0	44	1	25	30	301	1.6	14	6	250	50	0.0	0.0
A /9.5	0.8	1.6	9.95	N/A	0	44	1	25	30	301	1.6	30	6	250	50	0.0	0.0
A /9.5	0.8	1.6	9.94	56	0	44	1	25	30	301	1.6	25	6	250	50	0.0	0.0
A /9.4	0.8	1.6	9.95	34	0	44	1	25	30	301	1.6	33	6	250	50	0.0	0.0
A /9.4	0.8	1.6	9.96	11	0	44	1	25	30	301	1.6	54	6	250	50	0.0	0.0
A /9.4	0.8	1.6	9.96	N/A	0	44	1	25	30	301	1.6	53	6	250	50	0.0	0.0
A /9.4	0.9	1.6	9.95	1,163	0	44	1	25	30	301	1.6	55	6	250	50	0.0	0.0
A- /9.1	1.1	2.1	10.11	737	0	0	98	0	2	21	3.6	21	8	250	50	2.5	0.0
A- /9.1	1.1	2.1	10.11	12	0	0	98	0	2	21	3.6	16	8	250	50	0.0	0.0
A- /9.1	1.1	2.1	10.11	84	0	0	98	0	2	21	3.6	22	8	250	50	0.0	0.0
A- /9.1	1.1	2.1	10.11	N/A	0	0	98	0	2	21	3.6	21	8	250	50	0.0	0.0
U /	N/A	4.8	10.20	5	0	0	0	0	100	0	1.8	N/A	1	250	50	3.8	0.0
U /	N/A	4.8	10.21	N/A	0	0	0	0	100	0	1.8	N/A	1	250	50	0.0	0.0
U /	N/A	4.8	10.17	2	0	0	0	0	100	0	1.8	N/A	1	250	50	0.0	0.0
U /	N/A	4.8	10.20	N/A	0	0	0	0	100	0	1.8	N/A	1	250	50	0.0	0.0
U /	N/A	4.8	10.21	3	0	0	0	0	100	0	1.8	N/A	1	250	50	0.0	0.0
U /	N/A	4.8	10.21	228	0	0	0	0	100	0	1.8	N/A	1	250	50	3.8	0.0
U /	N/A	4.8	10.20	N/A	0	0	0	0	100	0	1.8	N/A	1	250	50	0.0	0.0
U /	N/A	4.8	10.17	13	0	0	0	0	100	0	1.8	N/A	1	250	50	0.0	0.0
U /	N/A	4.8	10.20	5	0	0	0	0	100	0	1.8	N/A	1	250	50	0.0	0.0
U /	N/A	4.8	10.21	51	0	0	0	0	100	0	1.8	N/A	1	250	50	0.0	0.0
U /	N/A	4.8	10.21	N/A	0	0	0	0	100	0	1.8	N/A	1	250	50	0.0	0.0
U /	N/A	4.8	10.20	N/A	0	0	0	0	100	0	1.8	N/A	1	250	50	0.0	0.0
U /	N/A	4.8	10.19	1	0	0	0	0	100	0	1.8	N/A	1	250	50	0.0	0.0
U /	N/A	4.8	10.22	N/A	0	0	0	0	100	0	1.8	N/A	1	250	50	0.0	0.0
U /	N/A	4.8	10.20	N/A	0	0	0	0	100	0	1.8	N/A	1	250	50	0.0	0.0
U /	N/A	4.8	10.20	1	0	0	0	0	100	0	1.8	N/A	1	250	50	0.0	0.0
U /	N/A	4.8	10.22	N/A	0	0	0	0	100	0	1.8	N/A	1	250	50	0.0	0.0
U /	N/A	4.8	10.22	N/A	0	0	0	0	100	0	1.8	N/A	1	250	50	0.0	0.0
U /	N/A	4.8	10.22	24	0	0	0	0	100	0	1.8	N/A	1	250	50	0.0	0.0
C /5.2	3.1	5.7	12.80	9,326	0	0	98	0	2	13	4.8	55	38	250	50	3.8	0.0
C /5.2	3.1	5.7	12.80	1	0	0	98	0	2	13	4.8	21	38	250	50	0.0	0.0
C /5.2	3.1	5.7	12.80	487	0	0	98	0	2	13	4.8	20	38	250	50	0.0	0.0
C /5.2	3.1	5.7	12.80	478	0	0	98	0	2	13	4.8	49	38	250	50	0.0	0.0
C /5.2	3.1	5.7	12.80	3,092	0	0	98	0	2	13	4.8	60	38	250	50	0.0	0.0
C /5.2	3.1	5.7	12.80	3	0	0	98	0	2	13	4.8	55	38	250	50	0.0	0.0
C /4.3	3.4	6.3	17.35	1,593	1	0	98	0	1	11	4.7	47	31	1,000	50	3.8	0.0
C /4.3	3.4	6.3	17.35	N/A	1	0	98	0	1	11	4.7	18	31	1,000	50	0.0	0.0
C /4.3	3.4	6.3	17.35	88	1	0	98	0	1	11	4.7	16	31	1,000	50	0.0	0.0
C /4.3	3.4	6.3	17.35	75	1	0	98	0	1	11	4.7	36	31	1,000	50	0.0	0.0
C /4.3	3.4	6.3	17.35	260	1	0	98	0	1	11	4.7	54	31	1,000	50	0.0	0.0
C /4.3	3.4	6.3	17.35	N/A	1	0	98	0	1	11	4.7	47	31	1,000	50	0.0	0.0
B /8.0	2.1	4.3	9.73	318	0	0	99	0	1	6	4.7	21	5	250	50	2.5	0.0
B /8.0	2.1	4.3	9.78	N/A	0	0	99	0	1	6	4.7	8	5	250	50	0.0	0.0
B /8.0	2.1	4.3	9.73	9	0	0	99	0	1	6	4.7	22	5	250	50	0.0	0.0

I. Index of Bond and Money Market Mutual Funds

| | | | | | PERFORMANCE | | | | | | Incl. in Returns | |
| | | | | | | Total Return % through 2/28/17 | | | Annualized | | | |
Fund Type	Fund Name	Ticker Symbol	Overall Investment Rating	Phone	Perfor-mance Rating/Pts	3 Mo	6 Mo	1Yr / Pct	3Yr / Pct	5Yr / Pct	Dividend Yield	Expense Ratio
MUN	American Funds TxEx Preservation	TXEFX	A-	(800) 421-0180	C / 5.3	1.57	-1.80	-0.01 /17	2.04 /63	--	2.47	0.47
MUN	American Funds TxEx Preservation	TYEFX	B	(800) 421-0180	C / 4.6	1.53	-1.90	-0.26 /13	1.76 /56	--	2.21	0.36
USS	American Funds U.S. Govt Sec 529A	CGTAX	D-	(800) 421-0180	D / 1.9	0.55	-1.19	-0.40 /11	1.83 /40	1.21 /30	1.05	0.71
USS ●	American Funds U.S. Govt Sec 529B	CGTBX	D-	(800) 421-0180	D / 2.1	0.37	-1.60	-1.18 / 3	1.04 /28	0.43 /21	0.37	1.50
USS	American Funds U.S. Govt Sec 529C	CGTCX	D-	(800) 421-0180	D / 2.1	0.44	-1.52	-1.09 / 4	1.07 /29	0.44 /21	0.39	1.47
USS	American Funds U.S. Govt Sec 529E	CGTEX	D	(800) 421-0180	C- / 3.0	0.57	-1.30	-0.63 / 8	1.59 /36	0.97 /27	0.86	0.94
USS	American Funds U.S. Govt Sec	CGTFX	C-	(800) 421-0180	C- / 3.7	0.61	-1.08	-0.18 /15	2.05 /44	1.43 /33	1.32	0.49
MMT	American Funds US Gov Mny Mkt A	AFAXX	U	(800) 421-0180	U /	--	--	--	--	--	0.02	N/A
MMT	American Funds US Gov Mny Mkt F3	USGXX	D+	(800) 421-0180	E+ / 0.6	0.02	0.02	0.02 /19	0.01 / 6	--	0.02	N/A
MMT	American Funds US Gov Mny Mkt R6	RAFXX	U	(800) 421-0180	U /	--	--	--	--	--	0.02	N/A
*USS	American Funds US Govt Sec A	AMUSX	D-	(800) 421-0180	D / 1.9	0.57	-1.16	-0.34 /12	1.90 /41	1.29 /31	1.11	0.63
USS ●	American Funds US Govt Sec B	UGSBX	D-	(800) 421-0180	D+ / 2.3	0.45	-1.50	-1.05 / 4	1.16 /30	0.55 /22	0.43	1.38
USS	American Funds US Govt Sec C	UGSCX	D-	(800) 421-0180	D / 2.2	0.45	-1.51	-1.14 / 3	1.10 /30	0.50 /21	0.41	1.42
USS	American Funds US Govt Sec F1	UGSFX	C-	(800) 421-0180	C- / 3.5	0.56	-1.17	-0.36 /12	1.90 /41	1.29 /31	1.13	0.65
USS	American Funds US Govt Sec F2	GVTFX	C	(800) 421-0180	C- / 3.9	0.63	-1.04	-0.09 /16	2.16 /46	1.54 /35	1.41	0.38
USA	American Funds US Govt Sec F3	USGFX	C-	(800) 421-0180	C- / 3.5	0.59	-1.14	-0.32 /12	1.90 /41	1.29 /31	1.17	0.38
USS	American Funds US Govt Sec R1	RGVAX	D-	(800) 421-0180	D / 2.2	0.46	-1.51	-1.05 / 4	1.15 /30	0.53 /22	0.43	1.39
USS	American Funds US Govt Sec R2	RGVBX	D-	(800) 421-0180	D / 2.2	0.46	-1.50	-1.09 / 4	1.13 /29	0.52 /22	0.47	1.37
USL	American Funds US Govt Sec R2E	RGEVX	D	(800) 421-0180	C- / 3.1	0.53	-1.37	-0.75 / 6	1.68 /38	0.91 /26	0.74	1.07
USS	American Funds US Govt Sec R3	RGVCX	D	(800) 421-0180	C- / 3.0	0.56	-1.31	-0.64 / 8	1.59 /36	0.97 /27	0.85	0.95
USS	American Funds US Govt Sec R4	RGVEX	C-	(800) 421-0180	C- / 3.5	0.57	-1.15	-0.32 /12	1.92 /42	1.30 /31	1.17	0.62
USS	American Funds US Govt Sec R5	RGVFX	C	(800) 421-0180	C- / 4.1	0.72	-0.94	0.04 /20	2.24 /47	1.61 /36	1.46	0.32
USL	American Funds US Govt Sec R5E	RGVJX	C-	(800) 421-0180	C- / 3.6	0.69	-1.08	-0.18 /15	1.97 /42	1.33 /32	1.31	0.50
USS	American Funds US Govt Sec R6	RGVGX	C	(800) 421-0180	C- / 4.1	0.66	-0.98	0.02 /18	2.27 /48	1.65 /37	1.52	0.27
GEI	American Ind Carret Core+ A	IBFSX	D	(866) 410-2006	D+ / 2.6	0.87	-1.59	1.82 /47	2.24 /47	2.13 /44	2.09	1.07
GEI	American Ind Carret Core+ I	IIISX	B-	(866) 410-2006	C / 4.9	0.96	-1.43	2.08 /50	2.59 /54	2.48 /49	2.54	0.72
MUS	American Ind KS Tax Exempt Bond A	IKSTX	C+	(866) 410-2006	C- / 3.8	1.30	-1.71	-0.19 /15	2.68 /76	2.20 /63	2.46	0.99
MUS	American Ind KS Tax Exempt Bond C	IKTEX	B+	(866) 410-2006	C / 5.0	1.24	-2.02	-0.79 / 6	2.07 /64	1.58 /48	1.96	1.60
MUS	American Ind KS Tax Exempt Bond I	SEKSX	A+	(866) 410-2006	B- / 7.2	1.40	-1.52	0.20 /29	3.07 /83	2.59 /72	2.97	0.60
USS	American Ind US Infl Protected A	FNIHX	E	(866) 410-2006	D- / 1.1	0.99	-0.96	2.63 /54	1.07 /29	0.02 / 7	0.76	1.14
GEI	American Ind US Infl Protected C	FCIHX	E	(866) 410-2006	D / 2.2	0.92	-1.18	2.09 /50	0.58 /21	-0.52 / 3	0.23	1.69
USS	American Ind US Infl Protected Inst	FFIHX	E+	(866) 410-2006	C- / 3.8	1.15	-0.71	3.00 /56	1.52 /35	0.45 /21	1.36	0.69
GEI	American Ind US Infl Protected Prm	AIIPX	E+	(866) 410-2006	C- / 3.6	1.06	-0.71	2.90 /56	1.39 /33	0.35 /20	1.17	0.84
MTG	AMF Ultra Short Mortgage Fund	ASARX	C	(800) 527-3713	D / 1.6	0.28	0.14	-0.04 /17	0.34 /19	0.80 /25	1.65	1.15
GEI	AMG GW&K Core Bond I	MBDFX	D-	(800) 548-4539	C- / 3.9	1.22	-2.66	1.56 /45	1.98 /43	2.45 /49	2.08	0.62
COI	AMG GW&K Core Bond N	MBGVX	U	(800) 548-4539	U /	1.14	-2.83	1.13 /41	--	--	1.74	0.94
COI	AMG GW&K Core Bond Z	MBDLX	U	(800) 548-4539	U /	1.24	-2.63	1.63 /46	--	--	2.15	0.54
GEI	AMG GW&K Enhanced Core Bond C	MFDCX	E+	(800) 548-4539	D / 1.8	0.87	-2.76	1.70 /46	0.40 /20	1.38 /33	1.39	1.62
COI	AMG GW&K Enhanced Core Bond I	MFDSX	D-	(800) 548-4539	C- / 3.3	1.09	-2.22	2.71 /55	1.37 /33	2.35 /47	2.40	0.72
GEI	AMG GW&K Enhanced Core Bond N	MFDAX	D-	(800) 548-4539	C- / 3.0	1.05	-2.41	2.56 /53	1.16 /30	2.14 /44	2.24	0.87
GEI	AMG GW&K Enhanced Core Bond Z	MFDYX	D-	(800) 548-4539	C- / 3.4	1.12	-2.28	2.81 /55	1.41 /33	2.41 /48	2.50	0.62
MUH	AMG GW&K Muni Enhanced Yield I	GWMEX	C+	(800) 548-4539	A+ / 9.7	2.90	-5.76	0.66 /40	5.82 /98	4.64 /97	2.99	0.73
MUH	AMG GW&K Muni Enhanced Yield N	GWMNX	C+	(800) 548-4539	A / 9.4	2.78	-5.98	0.17 /28	5.35 /98	4.18 /95	2.48	1.08
MUH	AMG GW&K Muni Enhanced Yield S	GWMRX	C+	(800) 548-4539	A+ / 9.6	2.89	-5.77	0.61 /39	5.76 /98	4.54 /96	2.92	0.83
MUN	AMG GW&K Municipal Bond I	GWMIX	C	(800) 548-4539	C+ / 6.7	2.53	-3.20	-0.96 / 4	2.98 /82	2.82 /77	1.50	0.45
MUN	AMG GW&K Municipal Bond N	GWMTX	D+	(800) 548-4539	C+ / 5.8	2.44	-3.32	-1.29 / 2	2.51 /73	2.36 /68	1.10	0.78
MUN	AMG GW&K Municipal Bond S	GWMSX	C-	(800) 548-4539	C+ / 6.4	2.49	-3.28	-1.12 / 3	2.81 /79	2.65 /73	1.35	0.56
USS	AMG Mgrs Amundi Intmd Gov N	MGIDX	B	(800) 548-4539	C- / 4.2	0.22	-1.20	0.47 /33	2.37 /49	2.13 /44	1.21	0.96
USS	AMG Mgrs Amundi Short DurGov N	MGSDX	C+	(800) 548-4539	D / 2.0	0.16	0.42	1.25 /42	0.46 /20	0.62 /23	1.14	0.80
GEN	AMG Mgrs DoubleLine Core+ Bd I	ADLIX	A	(800) 548-4539	C+ / 6.8	1.72	-0.51	4.84 /66	3.48 /68	3.64 /68	3.41	0.83
GEN	AMG Mgrs DoubleLine Core+ Bd N	ADBLX	A	(800) 548-4539	C+ / 6.4	1.56	-0.73	4.58 /65	3.22 /64	3.38 /63	3.16	1.08
GL	AMG Mgrs Global Income Opp N	MGGBX	E	(800) 548-4539	D / 2.2	3.11	-3.59	6.82 /72	0.20 /16	1.52 /35	0.00	1.09

● Denotes fund is closed to new investors
* Denotes fund is included in Section II

www.thestreetratings.com

RISK			NET ASSETS		ASSET					Portfolio Turnover Ratio	Avg Coupon Rate	FUND MANAGER		MINIMUM		LOADS	
Risk Rating/Pts	3 Yr Avg Standard Deviation	Avg Dura-tion	NAV As of 2/28/17	Total $(Mil)	Cash %	Gov. Bond %	Muni. Bond %	Corp. Bond %	Other %			Manager Quality Pct	Manager Tenure (Years)	Initial Purch. $	Additional Purch. $	Front End Load	Back End Load
B /8.0	2.2	4.3	9.73	32	0	0	99	0	1	6	4.7	30	5	250	50	0.0	0.0
B /8.0	2.1	4.3	9.73	N/A	0	0	99	0	1	6	4.7	22	5	250	50	0.0	0.0
C+ /6.9	2.7	3.8	13.70	135	0	80	0	0	20	693	1.8	55	7	250	50	3.8	0.0
C+ /6.7	2.8	3.8	13.65	N/A	0	80	0	0	20	693	1.8	20	7	250	50	0.0	0.0
C+ /6.8	2.8	3.8	13.66	51	0	80	0	0	20	693	1.8	21	7	250	50	0.0	0.0
C+ /6.6	2.8	3.8	13.70	9	0	80	0	0	20	693	1.8	37	7	250	50	0.0	0.0
C+ /6.8	2.8	3.8	13.70	14	0	80	0	0	20	693	1.8	62	7	250	50	0.0	0.0
U /	N/A	N/A	1.00	12,374	100	0	0	0	0	0	0.0	38	N/A	1,000	50	0.0	0.0
A+ /9.9	N/A	N/A	1.00	N/A	100	0	0	0	0	0	0.0	38	N/A	1,000	50	0.0	0.0
U /	N/A	N/A	1.00	592	100	0	0	0	0	0	0.0	38	N/A	1,000	50	0.0	0.0
C+ /6.8	2.8	3.8	13.70	2,789	0	80	0	0	20	693	1.8	57	7	250	50	3.8	0.0
C+ /6.7	2.8	3.8	13.68	2	0	80	0	0	20	693	1.8	23	7	250	50	0.0	0.0
C+ /6.7	2.8	3.8	13.67	276	0	80	0	0	20	693	1.8	21	7	250	50	0.0	0.0
C+ /6.8	2.8	3.8	13.70	226	0	80	0	0	20	693	1.8	57	7	250	50	0.0	0.0
C+ /6.9	2.8	3.8	13.70	297	0	80	0	0	20	693	1.8	65	7	250	50	0.0	0.0
C+ /6.8	2.8	3.8	13.70	N/A	0	80	0	0	20	693	1.8	57	7	250	50	0.0	0.0
C+ /6.7	2.8	3.8	13.68	10	0	80	0	0	20	693	1.8	23	7	250	50	0.0	0.0
C+ /6.6	2.8	3.8	13.67	124	0	80	0	0	20	693	1.8	22	7	250	50	0.0	0.0
C+ /6.5	2.8	3.8	13.70	3	0	80	0	0	20	693	1.8	56	7	250	50	0.0	0.0
C+ /6.7	2.8	3.8	13.70	146	0	80	0	0	20	693	1.8	37	7	250	50	0.0	0.0
C+ /6.8	2.8	3.8	13.70	250	0	80	0	0	20	693	1.8	58	7	250	50	0.0	0.0
C+ /6.8	2.8	3.8	13.71	59	0	80	0	0	20	693	1.8	67	7	250	50	0.0	0.0
C+ /6.7	2.8	3.8	13.70	N/A	0	80	0	0	20	693	1.8	65	7	250	50	0.0	0.0
C+ /6.8	2.8	3.8	13.70	4,676	0	80	0	0	20	693	1.8	68	7	250	50	0.0	0.0
B- /7.2	2.7	5.2	10.85	1	9	19	0	41	31	61	0.0	35	11	5,000	250	4.3	0.0
B- /7.1	2.7	5.2	10.77	49	9	19	0	41	31	61	0.0	55	11	3,000,000	5,000	0.0	0.0
B /8.0	2.1	4.9	10.89	12	1	1	96	0	2	10	0.0	62	17	5,000	250	4.3	0.0
B /8.0	2.2	4.9	10.89	1	1	1	96	0	2	10	0.0	31	17	5,000	250	0.0	0.0
B /8.0	2.1	4.9	10.89	170	1	1	96	0	2	10	0.0	72	17	3,000,000	5,000	0.0	0.0
D+ /2.6	4.0	8.3	10.67	16	0	98	0	0	2	173	0.0	17	11	5,000	250	4.3	0.0
D+ /2.6	4.0	8.3	10.44	12	0	98	0	0	2	173	0.0	2	11	5,000	250	0.0	0.0
D+ /2.6	4.0	8.3	10.71	268	0	98	0	0	2	173	0.0	29	11	20,000,000	5,000	0.0	0.0
D+ /2.6	4.0	8.3	10.68	2	0	98	0	0	2	173	0.0	6	11	250,000	5,000	0.0	0.0
A+ /9.7	0.7	1.2	7.11	115	0	0	0	0	100	22	3.2	33	8	10,000	0	0.0	0.0
C- /4.2	3.4	5.9	10.03	376	1	15	6	45	33	48	4.6	12	2	100,000	100	0.0	0.0
U /	N/A	5.9	10.02	N/A	1	15	6	45	33	48	4.6	N/A	2	2,000	100	0.0	0.0
U /	N/A	5.9	10.03	6	1	15	6	45	33	48	4.6	N/A	2	5,000,000	1,000	0.0	0.0
C /4.6	3.3	6.3	9.72	7	0	7	6	54	33	57	4.9	2	5	2,000	100	0.0	0.0
C /4.7	3.2	6.3	9.77	36	0	7	6	54	33	57	4.9	8	5	100,000	100	0.0	0.0
C /4.9	3.2	6.3	9.73	16	0	7	6	54	33	57	4.9	8	5	2,000	100	0.0	0.0
C /4.8	3.2	6.3	9.76	24	0	7	6	54	33	57	4.9	11	5	5,000,000	100,000	0.0	0.0
D- /1.0	5.3	13.7	9.49	202	0	1	97	0	2	120	5.2	57	12	100,000	100	0.0	0.0
D- /1.0	5.3	13.7	9.50	8	0	1	97	0	2	120	5.2	33	12	2,000	100	0.0	0.0
D- /1.0	5.3	13.7	9.51	16	0	1	97	0	2	120	5.2	57	12	100,000	100	0.0	0.0
C- /3.4	3.8	6.6	11.44	782	0	2	95	0	3	78	5.0	11	8	100,000	100	0.0	0.0
C- /3.5	3.8	6.6	11.38	36	0	2	95	0	3	78	5.0	6	8	2,000	100	0.0	0.0
C- /3.4	3.8	6.6	11.40	166	0	2	95	0	3	78	5.0	9	8	100,000	100	0.0	0.0
B+ /8.4	1.9	N/A	10.67	158	0	0	0	0	100	21	0.0	80	25	2,000	100	0.0	0.0
A+ /9.8	0.5	N/A	9.63	226	0	0	0	0	100	51	0.0	61	25	2,000	100	0.0	0.0
B- /7.1	2.7	5.2	10.59	426	4	14	0	41	41	78	3.3	80	6	100,000	50	0.0	0.0
B- /7.1	2.7	5.2	10.59	250	4	14	0	41	41	78	3.3	78	6	2,500	50	0.0	0.0
D- /1.0	6.3	5.9	19.59	15	2	45	0	50	3	53	5.1	86	15	2,000	100	0.0	1.0

Fund Type	Fund Name	Ticker Symbol	Overall Investment Rating	Phone	Performance Rating/Pts	3 Mo	6 Mo	1Yr / Pct	Annualized 3Yr / Pct	Annualized 5Yr / Pct	Dividend Yield	Expense Ratio
COH	AMG Mgrs High Yield I	MHHYX	C+	(800) 548-4539	A- / 9.2	4.80	4.70	20.07 / 96	4.09 / 76	6.22 / 94	5.45	1.24
COH	AMG Mgrs High Yield N	MHHAX	C	(800) 548-4539	A- / 9.0	4.77	4.58	19.76 / 96	3.85 / 73	5.96 / 92	5.21	1.49
COI	AMG Mgrs Loomis Sayles Bond I	MGBIX	C+	(800) 548-4539	C+ / 6.6	2.70	-0.50	7.58 / 73	2.76 / 57	3.94 / 71	3.76	0.89
* GEL	AMG Mgrs Loomis Sayles Bond N	MGFIX	C	(800) 548-4539	C+ / 6.4	2.64	-0.54	7.44 / 73	2.66 / 55	3.86 / 70	3.68	0.89
COI	Anfield Universal Fixed Income A	AFLEX	C+	(866) 851-2525	C- / 3.2	1.09	1.83	4.97 / 66	2.30 / 48	--	2.19	1.81
COI	Anfield Universal Fixed Income C	AFLKX	B+	(866) 851-2525	C- / 4.2	0.97	1.54	4.37 / 64	1.44 / 34	--	1.65	2.56
COI	Anfield Universal Fixed Income I	AFLIX	A+	(866) 851-2525	C+ / 6.0	1.15	1.97	5.32 / 68	2.56 / 53	--	2.55	1.56
GEN	Angel Oak Flexible Income A	ANFLX	U	(877) 625-3042	U /	1.44	2.88	11.07 / 81	--	--	3.79	1.49
GEL	Angel Oak Flexible Income C	AFLCX	U	(877) 625-3042	U /	1.22	2.55	10.35 / 80	--	--	3.66	2.34
GEN	Angel Oak Flexible Income Inst	ANFIX	U	(877) 625-3042	U /	1.38	3.02	11.38 / 82	--	--	4.14	1.28
COH	Angel Oak High Yield Opps A	ANHAX	C+	(877) 625-3042	A / 9.5	4.46	4.83	20.86 / 97	4.70 / 83	--	4.57	1.22
COI	Angel Oak High Yield Opps Inst	ANHIX	B	(877) 625-3042	A+ / 9.7	4.41	4.84	20.93 / 97	4.75 / 83	6.31 / 94	4.87	0.97
GL	Angel Oak Multi Strategy Income C	ANGCX	U	(877) 625-3042	U /	0.96	2.67	8.11 / 75	--	--	4.97	2.21
GL	Angel Oak Multi Strategy Income I	ANGIX	A+	(877) 625-3042	B / 7.6	1.19	3.16	9.21 / 77	3.46 / 68	--	5.51	1.19
GEI	API Multi Asset Income A	APIUX	D	(800) 544-6060	B / 7.7	5.70	6.56	23.71 / 99	2.42 / 50	5.54 / 89	6.56	2.54
GEI	API Multi Asset Income L	AFFIX	D+	(800) 544-6060	B+ / 8.6	5.49	6.28	23.06 / 98	1.93 / 42	5.02 / 84	6.92	3.04
COI ●	AQR Multi-Strategy Alternative I	ASAIX	B	(866) 290-2688	A- / 9.1	2.64	4.26	1.28 / 43	6.33 / 94	4.67 / 80	0.86	2.46
COI ●	AQR Multi-Strategy Alternative N	ASANX	B-	(866) 290-2688	B+ / 8.9	2.55	4.17	1.08 / 40	6.09 / 92	4.40 / 77	0.86	2.73
MUS	Aquila Churchill Tax-Free of KY A	CHTFX	C	(800) 437-1020	C- / 3.7	1.60	-2.33	-0.45 / 10	2.61 / 75	2.27 / 65	2.67	0.73
MUS	Aquila Churchill Tax-Free of KY C	CHKCX	C+	(800) 437-1020	C- / 4.0	1.49	-2.74	-1.29 / 2	1.74 / 55	1.43 / 45	1.91	1.58
MUS	Aquila Churchill Tax-Free of KY I	CHKIX	A-	(800) 437-1020	C+ / 5.9	1.67	-2.40	-0.59 / 8	2.47 / 73	2.14 / 62	2.64	0.92
MUS	Aquila Churchill Tax-Free of KY Y	CHKYX	A	(800) 437-1020	C+ / 6.6	1.74	-2.25	-0.30 / 13	2.77 / 78	2.45 / 69	2.93	0.58
* MUN	Aquila Hawaiian Tax Free Trust A	HULAX	D+	(800) 437-1020	D+ / 2.7	1.94	-2.20	-0.62 / 8	2.15 / 66	1.71 / 51	1.95	0.83
MUN	Aquila Hawaiian Tax Free Trust C	HULCX	C-	(800) 437-1020	C- / 3.2	1.74	-2.59	-1.41 / 2	1.34 / 44	0.91 / 33	1.21	1.63
MUN	Aquila Hawaiian Tax Free Trust Y	HULYX	B+	(800) 437-1020	C+ / 5.9	1.98	-2.10	-0.41 / 11	2.38 / 71	1.92 / 57	2.23	0.63
MUI	Aquila Narragansett TxFr Income A	NITFX	C-	(800) 437-1020	C / 5.1	1.90	-2.84	-0.31 / 13	3.31 / 86	2.60 / 72	2.53	0.85
MUI	Aquila Narragansett TxFr Income C	NITCX	C	(800) 437-1020	C / 5.5	1.69	-3.24	-1.15 / 3	2.44 / 72	1.73 / 52	1.76	1.70
MUI	Aquila Narragansett TxFr Income I	NITIX	B+	(800) 437-1020	B- / 7.2	1.86	-2.82	-0.36 / 12	3.20 / 84	2.46 / 70	2.49	1.05
MUI	Aquila Narragansett TxFr Income Y	NITYX	A-	(800) 437-1020	B- / 7.5	1.94	-2.76	-0.16 / 15	3.47 / 87	2.75 / 75	2.78	0.70
MUS	Aquila Tax-Free Fd for Utah A	UTAHX	C	(800) 437-1020	C / 5.4	1.83	-2.91	-0.37 / 11	3.47 / 87	3.23 / 84	2.48	0.87
MUS	Aquila Tax-Free Fd for Utah C	UTACX	C+	(800) 437-1020	C+ / 5.9	1.63	-3.29	-1.17 / 3	2.63 / 76	2.40 / 68	1.77	1.67
MUS	Aquila Tax-Free Fd for Utah Y	UTAYX	A	(800) 437-1020	B / 7.9	1.97	-2.70	-0.06 / 17	3.71 / 90	3.46 / 87	2.79	0.67
MUS	Aquila Tax-Free Fd of Colorado A	COTFX	C+	(800) 437-1020	C / 4.6	1.70	-2.17	-0.43 / 10	3.01 / 82	2.46 / 70	2.51	0.69
MUS	Aquila Tax-Free Fd of Colorado C	COTCX	C+	(800) 437-1020	C / 4.7	1.56	-2.64	-1.38 / 2	2.05 / 63	1.50 / 46	1.65	1.64
MUS	Aquila Tax-Free Fd of Colorado Y	COTYX	A+	(800) 437-1020	B- / 7.1	1.70	-2.14	-0.37 / 11	3.08 / 83	2.51 / 71	2.67	0.64
MUS	Aquila Tax-Free Tr of Arizona A	AZTFX	C+	(800) 437-1020	C / 4.8	1.53	-2.83	-0.33 / 12	3.21 / 85	2.82 / 77	2.83	0.71
MUS	Aquila Tax-Free Tr of Arizona C	AZTCX	C+	(800) 437-1020	C / 5.3	1.41	-3.15	-1.17 / 3	2.38 / 71	1.96 / 58	2.08	1.56
MUS	Aquila Tax-Free Tr of Arizona Y	AZTYX	A	(800) 437-1020	B- / 7.4	1.66	-2.66	-0.17 / 15	3.37 / 86	2.98 / 79	3.10	0.56
MUS	Aquila Tax-Free Trust of Oregon A	ORTFX	C	(800) 437-1020	C- / 3.7	1.71	-2.45	-0.65 / 7	2.64 / 76	2.26 / 65	2.35	0.74
MUS	Aquila Tax-Free Trust of Oregon C	ORTCX	C	(800) 437-1020	C- / 4.0	1.49	-2.86	-1.49 / 2	1.78 / 57	1.39 / 44	1.58	1.59
MUS	Aquila Tax-Free Trust of Oregon Y	ORTYX	A	(800) 437-1020	C+ / 6.6	1.74	-2.38	-0.50 / 9	2.80 / 79	2.39 / 68	2.60	0.59
COH	Aquila Three Peaks High Inc A	ATPAX	C+	(800) 437-1020	C+ / 5.6	2.57	2.42	5.86 / 70	3.49 / 68	4.47 / 78	3.52	1.20
COH	Aquila Three Peaks High Inc C	ATPCX	B-	(800) 437-1020	C+ / 6.2	2.37	2.02	5.03 / 67	2.67 / 55	3.64 / 68	2.88	2.01
COH	Aquila Three Peaks High Inc I	ATIPX	B	(800) 437-1020	C+ / 6.9	2.54	2.36	5.75 / 69	3.37 / 67	4.41 / 77	3.56	1.28
COH	Aquila Three Peaks High Inc Y	ATPYX	B+	(800) 437-1020	B- / 7.2	2.62	2.53	6.21 / 71	3.70 / 71	4.70 / 81	3.87	1.01
COI	AR 529 Gift College Inv Inc		C-	(800) 662-7447	D+ / 2.7	0.58	-1.29	0.95 / 39	1.16 / 30	0.65 / 23	0.00	0.75
GEL	Arbitrage Credit Opportunities A	AGCAX	D+	(800) 295-4485	D / 1.6	0.49	1.38	3.89 / 62	1.24 / 31	--	1.99	1.95
GEN	Arbitrage Credit Opportunities C	ARCCX	C	(800) 295-4485	D+ / 2.5	0.29	0.95	3.12 / 57	0.49 / 21	--	1.30	2.70
GEN	Arbitrage Credit Opportunities I	ACFIX	C+	(800) 295-4485	C- / 3.3	0.57	1.41	4.12 / 63	1.47 / 34	--	2.38	1.70
GEN	Arbitrage Credit Opportunities R	ARCFX	C+	(800) 295-4485	D+ / 2.9	0.49	1.38	3.96 / 62	1.22 / 31	--	2.12	1.95
GEN	Archer Income Fund	ARINX	B	(800) 494-2755	C / 5.2	1.22	-0.41	4.97 / 66	2.37 / 49	1.84 / 39	2.78	1.77
COH	Artisan High Income Advisor	APDFX	U	(800) 344-1770	U /	4.34	5.54	20.74 / 97	--	--	6.23	0.93

● Denotes fund is closed to new investors
* Denotes fund is included in Section II

www.thestreetratings.com

Risk Rating/Pts	3 Yr Avg Standard Deviation	Avg Duration	NAV As of 2/28/17	Total $(Mil)	Cash %	Gov. Bond %	Muni. Bond %	Corp. Bond %	Other %	Portfolio Turnover Ratio	Avg Coupon Rate	Manager Quality Pct	Manager Tenure (Years)	Initial Purch. $	Additional Purch. $	Front End Load	Back End Load
D- / 1.0	5.9	4.9	7.92	3	3	1	0	90	6	42	6.5	25	16	100,000	100	0.0	2.0
D- / 1.0	5.8	4.9	7.84	20	3	1	0	90	6	42	6.5	19	16	2,000	100	0.0	2.0
C / 4.3	3.4	5.6	26.63	788	1	34	1	53	11	10	5.2	50	23	100,000	100	0.0	0.0
C / 4.4	3.4	5.6	26.63	1,223	1	34	1	53	11	10	5.2	66	23	2,000	100	0.0	0.0
B+ / 8.9	1.4	2.0	10.07	10	1	0	0	61	38	26	0.0	84	4	2,500	500	5.8	0.0
B+ / 8.9	1.4	2.0	10.09	N/A	1	0	0	61	38	26	0.0	73	4	2,500	500	0.0	0.0
B+ / 8.8	1.5	2.0	10.08	100	1	0	0	61	38	26	0.0	85	4	100,000	1,000	0.0	0.0
U /	N/A	N/A	9.46	7	0	0	0	22	78	101	0.0	N/A	3	1,000	100	2.3	0.0
U /	N/A	N/A	9.40	1	0	0	0	22	78	101	0.0	N/A	3	1,000	100	0.0	0.0
U /	N/A	N/A	9.45	166	0	0	0	22	78	101	0.0	N/A	3	1,000,000	100	0.0	0.0
D- / 1.1	5.7	4.0	11.98	1	1	0	0	98	1	35	6.9	61	8	1,000	100	2.3	0.0
D / 1.6	5.6	4.0	11.94	49	1	0	0	98	1	35	6.9	88	8	1,000,000	100	0.0	0.0
U /	N/A	N/A	11.21	52	7	0	0	1	92	44	0.0	N/A	6	1,000	100	0.0	0.0
C+ / 6.9	2.7	N/A	11.27	4,224	7	0	0	1	92	44	0.0	93	6	1,000,000	100	0.0	0.0
E / 0.3	8.5	8.4	10.41	159	0	4	4	34	58	101	5.3	85	20	1,000	100	5.8	0.0
E / 0.3	8.4	8.4	9.88	378	0	4	4	34	58	101	5.3	81	20	1,000	100	0.0	0.0
D+ / 2.3	4.7	4.7	9.67	2,360	61	0	0	0	39	208	0.0	97	6	5,000,000	0	0.0	0.0
D+ / 2.3	4.7	4.7	9.62	472	61	0	0	0	39	208	0.0	96	6	1,000,000	0	0.0	0.0
B / 7.6	2.5	4.4	10.55	186	1	0	98	0	1	7	0.0	36	8	1,000	0	4.0	0.0
B- / 7.5	2.6	4.4	10.55	9	1	0	98	0	1	7	0.0	12	8	1,000	0	0.0	0.0
B- / 7.5	2.6	4.4	10.55	8	1	0	98	0	1	7	0.0	30	8	0	0	0.0	0.0
B- / 7.5	2.6	4.4	10.56	53	1	0	98	0	1	7	0.0	47	8	0	0	0.0	0.0
B- / 7.2	2.7	4.5	11.34	664	1	0	96	0	3	16	5.3	18	32	1,000	0	4.0	0.0
B- / 7.2	2.7	4.5	11.33	49	1	0	96	0	3	16	5.3	6	32	1,000	0	0.0	0.0
B- / 7.1	2.7	4.5	11.36	50	1	0	96	0	3	16	5.3	24	32	0	0	0.0	0.0
C / 5.3	3.1	5.3	10.60	127	0	0	98	0	2	19	0.0	47	17	1,000	0	4.0	0.0
C / 5.3	3.1	5.3	10.60	13	0	0	98	0	2	19	0.0	15	17	1,000	0	0.0	0.0
C / 5.2	3.1	5.3	10.60	N/A	0	0	98	0	2	19	0.0	37	17	0	0	0.0	0.0
C / 5.2	3.1	5.3	10.60	105	0	0	98	0	2	19	0.0	55	17	0	0	0.0	0.0
C / 5.5	3.0	5.9	10.25	215	0	1	98	0	1	20	0.0	56	8	1,000	0	4.0	0.0
C / 5.5	3.0	5.9	10.24	74	0	1	98	0	1	20	0.0	20	8	1,000	0	0.0	0.0
C / 5.5	3.0	5.9	10.29	124	0	1	98	0	1	20	0.0	64	8	0	0	0.0	0.0
C+ / 6.9	2.7	4.9	10.52	210	3	0	96	0	1	10	0.0	51	30	1,000	0	4.0	0.0
C+ / 6.8	2.8	4.9	10.50	21	3	0	96	0	1	10	0.0	14	30	1,000	0	0.0	0.0
B- / 7.1	2.7	4.9	10.55	83	3	0	96	0	1	10	0.0	55	30	0	0	0.0	0.0
C+ / 6.4	2.8	5.8	10.59	231	0	0	97	0	3	10	0.0	55	31	1,000	0	4.0	0.0
C+ / 6.2	2.9	5.8	10.59	17	0	0	97	0	3	10	0.0	18	31	1,000	0	0.0	0.0
C+ / 6.2	2.9	5.8	10.61	43	0	0	97	0	3	10	0.0	59	31	0	0	0.0	0.0
B- / 7.1	2.7	5.0	11.00	415	0	0	99	0	1	7	0.0	32	31	1,000	0	4.0	0.0
B- / 7.1	2.7	5.0	10.99	39	0	0	99	0	1	7	0.0	10	31	1,000	0	0.0	0.0
B- / 7.1	2.7	5.0	10.99	185	0	0	99	0	1	7	0.0	37	31	0	0	0.0	0.0
C / 5.5	2.5	4.2	8.57	53	4	0	0	95	1	120	0.0	85	11	1,000	0	4.0	1.0
C / 5.4	2.5	4.2	8.57	16	4	0	0	95	1	120	0.0	78	11	1,000	0	0.0	0.0
C / 5.2	2.6	4.2	8.57	2	4	0	0	95	1	120	0.0	84	11	0	0	0.0	1.0
C / 5.1	2.6	4.2	8.58	174	4	0	0	95	1	120	0.0	86	11	0	0	0.0	1.0
B / 7.9	2.2	N/A	13.79	46	25	48	0	12	15	0	0.0	17	12	25	10	0.0	0.0
B+ / 8.7	1.6	1.3	9.76	N/A	26	0	0	54	20	181	0.0	77	7	2,000	0	3.3	2.0
B+ / 8.8	1.5	1.3	9.71	1	26	0	0	54	20	181	0.0	60	7	2,000	0	0.0	0.0
B+ / 8.7	1.6	1.3	9.76	45	26	0	0	54	20	181	0.0	80	7	100,000	0	0.0	2.0
B+ / 8.7	1.6	1.3	9.78	12	26	0	0	54	20	181	0.0	77	7	2,000	0	0.0	2.0
B- / 7.3	2.6	N/A	19.36	12	9	0	21	62	8	14	0.0	65	6	2,500	100	0.0	0.5
U /	N/A	N/A	10.04	1,452	0	0	0	83	17	69	0.0	N/A	3	250,000	0	0.0	2.0

99 Pct = Best
0 Pct = Worst

Fund Type	Fund Name	Ticker Symbol	Overall Investment Rating	Phone	Performance Rating/Pts	3 Mo	6 Mo	1Yr / Pct	3Yr / Pct	5Yr / Pct	Dividend Yield	Expense Ratio
COH	Artisan High Income Investor	ARTFX	U	(800) 344-1770	U /	4.39	5.54	20.63 /97	--	--	6.03	1.09
GL	Ashmore Em Mkts Hard Curr Debt A	ESDAX	C+	(866) 876-8294	A+ / 9.7	5.64	2.41	16.84 /92	6.88 /95	5.05 /84	6.88	3.81
GL	Ashmore Em Mkts Hard Curr Debt C	ESDCX	C+	(866) 876-8294	A+ / 9.8	5.59	2.13	15.38 /89	6.25 /93	4.33 /76	5.77	4.49
GL	Ashmore Em Mkts Hard Curr Debt	ESDIX	C+	(866) 876-8294	A+ / 9.9	5.73	2.65	16.50 /91	6.86 /95	5.06 /85	6.72	3.49
GL	Ashmore Emerg Mkts Corp Dbt A	ECDAX	C+	(866) 876-8294	A+ / 9.8	7.13	9.90	28.76 /99	4.94 /85	5.42 /88	7.03	1.55
GL	Ashmore Emerg Mkts Corp Dbt C	ECDCX	C+	(866) 876-8294	A+ / 9.8	6.94	9.38	27.91 /99	4.16 /77	4.63 /80	6.68	2.30
GL	Ashmore Emerg Mkts Corp Dbt Inst	EMCIX	C+	(866) 876-8294	A+ / 9.9	7.10	9.91	29.15 /99	5.23 /87	5.69 /90	7.54	1.30
GL	Ashmore Emerg Mkts Loc Cur Bd A	ELBAX	E-	(866) 876-8294	E / 0.5	7.29	1.59	16.10 /90	-2.14 / 2	-2.74 / 1	2.91	1.51
GL	Ashmore Emerg Mkts Loc Cur Bd C	ELBCX	E-	(866) 876-8294	D- / 1.0	7.00	1.17	15.25 /89	-2.88 / 1	-3.47 / 0	2.57	2.26
GL	Ashmore Emerg Mkts Loc Cur Bd Inst	ELBIX	E	(866) 876-8294	D+ / 2.8	7.18	1.60	16.33 /91	-1.92 / 2	-2.49 / 1	3.19	1.26
EM	Ashmore Emerg Mkts Sht Dur A	ESFAX	U	(866) 876-8294	U /	5.81	8.70	27.79 /99	--	--	8.84	1.65
EM	Ashmore Emerg Mkts Sht Dur Inst	ESFIX	U	(866) 876-8294	U /	5.85	8.81	28.07 /99	--	--	9.46	1.41
GL	Ashmore Emerg Mkts Total Rtn A	EMKAX	C-	(866) 876-8294	B+ / 8.8	7.35	4.11	23.07 /98	3.36 /67	2.59 /51	6.46	1.37
GL	Ashmore Emerg Mkts Total Rtn C	EMKCX	C-	(866) 876-8294	B+ / 8.9	7.16	3.73	22.18 /98	2.59 /54	1.83 /39	6.00	2.12
GL	Ashmore Emerg Mkts Total Rtn Inst	EMKIX	C	(866) 876-8294	A / 9.5	7.46	4.23	23.46 /98	3.67 /71	2.85 /55	6.97	1.12
MUN	Aspiriant Risk Managed Municipal Bd	RMMBX	U	(877) 997-9971	U /	1.46	-2.75	0.60 /39	--	--	2.81	0.49
GEI	Ave Maria Bond	AVEFX	A+	(866) 283-6274	C+ / 6.2	1.22	0.82	4.92 /66	2.85 /59	3.47 /65	1.34	0.51
GEN	Avenue Credit Strategies Inst	ACSBX	E-	(877) 525-7445	E / 0.3	4.18	5.14	17.68 /93	-3.45 / 1	--	4.93	1.45
GEN	Avenue Credit Strategies Inv	ACSAX	E-	(877) 525-7445	E- / 0.2	4.13	5.03	17.35 /93	-3.69 / 1	--	4.66	1.76
COI	Baird Aggregate Bond Inst	BAGIX	B-	(866) 442-2473	C+ / 5.9	1.23	-1.84	2.75 /55	3.19 /64	3.32 /62	2.44	0.30
* COI	Baird Aggregate Bond Inv	BAGSX	C+	(866) 442-2473	C / 5.4	1.13	-1.99	2.50 /53	2.90 /59	3.06 /59	2.12	0.55
MUN	Baird Core Interm Muni Bd Inst	BMNIX	U	(866) 442-2473	U /	1.68	-2.08	0.98 /45	--	--	1.82	0.30
MUN	Baird Core Interm Muni Bd Inv	BMNSX	U	(866) 442-2473	U /	1.72	-2.20	0.84 /43	--	--	1.58	0.55
GEI	Baird Core Plus Bond Inst	BCOIX	B+	(866) 442-2473	C+ / 6.5	1.52	-1.30	4.43 /64	3.38 /67	3.40 /64	2.80	0.30
* GEI	Baird Core Plus Bond Inv	BCOSX	B	(866) 442-2473	C+ / 6.1	1.48	-1.38	4.18 /63	3.12 /63	3.15 /60	2.44	0.55
GEI	Baird Interm Bond Inst	BIMIX	B	(866) 442-2473	C / 4.5	0.99	-0.99	2.09 /50	2.21 /47	2.54 /50	2.25	0.30
GEI	Baird Interm Bond Inv	BIMSX	C+	(866) 442-2473	C- / 4.0	0.97	-1.08	1.84 /48	1.95 /42	2.29 /46	1.90	0.55
GEI	Baird Quality Interm Muni Bd Inst	BMBIX	C-	(866) 442-2473	C- / 3.2	1.82	-1.97	-0.56 / 9	1.71 /38	1.65 /37	2.22	0.30
GEI	Baird Quality Interm Muni Bd Inv	BMBSX	C-	(866) 442-2473	D+ / 2.8	1.80	-2.05	-0.80 / 6	1.45 /34	1.39 /33	1.91	0.55
GES	Baird Short-Term Bond Inst	BSBIX	B	(866) 442-2473	C- / 3.6	0.55	0.21	2.25 /51	1.47 /34	1.84 /39	1.60	0.30
COI	Baird Short-Term Bond Inv	BSBSX	B-	(866) 442-2473	C- / 3.2	0.49	0.08	2.00 /49	1.22 /31	--	1.36	0.55
MUN	Baird Short-Term Municipal Bd Inst	BTMIX	U	(866) 442-2473	U /	1.33	-0.24	0.76 /41	--	--	1.42	0.30
MUN	Baird Short-Term Municipal Bd Inv	BTMSX	U	(866) 442-2473	U /	1.26	-0.36	0.54 /38	--	--	1.20	0.55
GEI	Baird Ultra Short Bond Inst	BUBIX	B-	(866) 442-2473	D+ / 2.7	0.38	0.62	1.75 /47	0.90 /26	--	1.03	0.30
GEI	Baird Ultra Short Bond Investor	BUBSX	C+	(866) 442-2473	D+ / 2.3	0.32	0.51	1.52 /45	0.66 /22	--	0.81	0.55
COI	Barings Active Short Duration Bd A	BXDAX	U		U /	0.77	0.65	2.56 /53	--	--	1.58	1.18
COI	Barings Active Short Duration Bd C	BXDCX	U		U /	0.61	0.53	2.58 /54	--	--	1.70	4.94
COI	Barings Active Short Duration Bd I	BXDIX	U		U /	0.83	0.78	2.82 /55	--	--	1.83	0.96
COI	Barings Active Short Duration Bd Y	BXDYX	U		U /	0.83	0.88	2.82 /55	--	--	1.83	0.87
EM	Barings Em Mkts Local Curr Debt A	BXLAX	U		U /	3.25	-4.04	10.04 /79	--	--	4.73	8.55
EM	Barings Em Mkts Local Curr Debt C	BXLCX	U		U /	3.06	-4.40	9.23 /77	--	--	4.16	9.30
EM	Barings Em Mkts Local Curr Debt I	BXLIX	U		U /	3.31	-3.92	10.31 /80	--	--	5.18	4.03
EM	Barings Em Mkts Local Curr Debt Y	BXLYX	U		U /	3.31	-3.92	10.31 /80	--	--	5.18	4.03
EM	Barings EmMkt Dbt Blended Tot Rtn	BXEAX	U		U /	8.45	2.52	12.56 /84	--	--	4.59	6.82
EM	Barings EmMkt Dbt Blended Tot Rtn	BXECX	U		U /	8.26	2.14	11.73 /83	--	--	4.06	7.57
EM	Barings EmMkt Dbt Blended Tot Rtn I	BXEIX	U		U /	8.52	2.64	12.84 /85	--	--	5.02	2.58
EM	Barings EmMkt Dbt Blended Tot Rtn	BXEYX	U		U /	8.52	2.64	12.84 /85	--	--	5.02	2.58
GL	Barings Global Cr Inc Opty A	BXIAX	B-		A / 9.3	5.20	7.51	22.75 /98	4.49 /81	--	5.71	1.90
GL	Barings Global Cr Inc Opty C	BXICX	B-		A / 9.4	4.90	7.01	21.74 /98	3.69 /71	--	5.23	2.91
GL	Barings Global Cr Inc Opty I	BXITX	B		A+ / 9.7	5.16	7.54	22.93 /98	4.71 /83	--	6.18	1.54
GL	Barings Global Cr Inc Opty Y	BXIYX	B		A+ / 9.7	5.16	7.54	22.93 /98	4.71 /83	--	6.18	1.55
GL	Barings Global Floating Rate A	BXFAX	B+		B / 7.6	2.94	5.89	14.42 /87	3.51 /69	--	4.63	1.72

● Denotes fund is closed to new investors
* Denotes fund is included in Section II

RISK			NET ASSETS		ASSET					Portfolio Turnover Ratio	Avg Coupon Rate	FUND MANAGER		MINIMUM		LOADS	
Risk Rating/Pts	3 Yr Avg Standard Deviation	Avg Dura-tion	NAV As of 2/28/17	Total $(Mil)	Cash %	Gov. Bond %	Muni. Bond %	Corp. Bond %	Other %			Manager Quality Pct	Manager Tenure (Years)	Initial Purch. $	Additional Purch. $	Front End Load	Back End Load
U /	N/A	N/A	10.05	557	0	0	0	83	17	69	0.0	N/A	3	1,000	0	0.0	2.0
E+ / 0.8	6.8	5.7	8.57	N/A	3	73	0	18	6	68	0.0	99	7	1,000	50	4.0	0.0
E+ / 0.8	6.7	5.7	8.53	N/A	3	73	0	18	6	68	0.0	99	7	1,000	50	0.0	0.0
E+ / 0.8	6.7	5.7	8.52	7	3	73	0	18	6	68	0.0	99	7	1,000,000	5,000	0.0	0.0
E- / 0.2	9.6	3.4	8.23	10	3	5	0	72	20	81	0.0	97	N/A	1,000	50	4.0	0.0
E- / 0.2	9.6	3.4	8.22	6	3	5	0	72	20	81	0.0	96	N/A	1,000	50	0.0	0.0
E- / 0.2	9.6	3.4	8.57	257	3	5	0	72	20	81	0.0	98	N/A	1,000,000	5,000	0.0	0.0
E- / 0.0	12.5	N/A	7.06	1	30	66	0	0	4	83	0.0	69	7	1,000	50	4.0	0.0
E- / 0.0	12.5	N/A	7.03	N/A	30	66	0	0	4	83	0.0	36	7	1,000	50	0.0	0.0
E- / 0.0	12.5	N/A	7.31	80	30	66	0	0	4	83	0.0	74	7	1,000,000	5,000	0.0	0.0
U /	N/A	1.9	10.49	20	0	0	0	0	100	73	0.0	N/A	3	1,000	50	4.0	0.0
U /	N/A	1.9	10.30	128	0	0	0	0	100	73	0.0	N/A	3	1,000,000	5,000	0.0	0.0
E- / 0.2	9.7	5.4	8.04	4	9	61	0	20	10	91	0.0	97	N/A	1,000	50	4.0	0.0
E- / 0.2	9.7	5.4	8.03	3	9	61	0	20	10	91	0.0	95	N/A	1,000	50	0.0	0.0
E- / 0.2	9.7	5.4	8.16	834	9	61	0	20	10	91	0.0	97	N/A	1,000,000	5,000	0.0	0.0
U /	N/A	N/A	10.00	979	7	0	84	6	3	0	0.0	N/A	2	0	0	0.0	0.0
B+ / 8.3	2.0	3.2	11.29	261	8	32	0	43	17	25	3.5	85	14	2,500	0	0.0	0.0
E / 0.4	7.8	3.2	8.93	131	23	0	0	51	26	206	0.0	0	5	1,000,000	0	0.0	2.0
E / 0.4	7.8	3.2	8.93	266	23	0	0	51	26	206	0.0	0	5	5,000	0	0.0	2.0
C+ / 6.0	2.9	5.5	10.77	10,420	1	17	1	42	39	40	0.0	67	17	25,000	0	0.0	0.0
C+ / 5.9	2.9	5.5	11.12	841	1	17	1	42	39	40	0.0	59	17	2,500	100	0.0	0.0
U /	N/A	4.7	10.07	114	7	0	90	0	3	0	0.0	N/A	2	25,000	0	0.0	0.0
U /	N/A	4.7	10.07	1	7	0	90	0	3	0	0.0	N/A	2	2,500	100	0.0	0.0
C+ / 6.0	2.9	5.4	11.11	10,347	1	12	1	51	35	34	0.0	72	17	25,000	0	0.0	0.0
C+ / 5.8	3.0	5.4	11.55	2,935	1	12	1	51	35	34	0.0	66	17	2,500	100	0.0	0.0
B / 7.9	2.2	4.1	11.03	2,238	1	35	2	46	16	39	0.0	57	17	25,000	0	0.0	0.0
B / 7.9	2.2	4.1	11.50	98	1	35	2	46	16	39	0.0	44	17	2,500	100	0.0	0.0
B- / 7.5	2.5	4.5	11.52	934	0	0	98	0	2	9	0.0	30	16	25,000	0	0.0	0.0
B- / 7.5	2.5	4.5	11.79	136	0	0	98	0	2	9	0.0	21	16	2,500	100	0.0	0.0
A / 9.4	0.9	1.9	9.68	4,157	1	16	2	59	22	38	0.0	71	13	25,000	0	0.0	0.0
A / 9.4	0.9	1.9	9.68	110	1	16	2	59	22	38	0.0	63	13	2,500	100	0.0	0.0
U /	N/A	2.4	10.05	59	4	0	94	0	2	0	0.0	N/A	2	25,000	0	0.0	0.0
U /	N/A	2.4	10.04	5	4	0	94	0	2	0	0.0	N/A	2	2,500	100	0.0	0.0
A+ / 9.9	0.4	0.5	10.04	523	2	14	2	67	15	66	0.0	71	4	25,000	0	0.0	0.0
A+ / 9.9	0.4	0.5	10.04	15	2	14	2	67	15	66	0.0	63	4	2,500	100	0.0	0.0
U /	N/A	1.6	9.97	103	0	0	0	0	100	219	0.0	N/A	2	1,000	250	0.0	0.0
U /	N/A	1.6	9.96	N/A	0	0	0	0	100	219	0.0	N/A	2	1,000	250	0.0	0.0
U /	N/A	1.6	9.97	N/A	0	0	0	0	100	219	0.0	N/A	2	500,000	250	0.0	0.0
U /	N/A	1.6	9.97	166	0	0	0	0	100	219	0.0	N/A	2	100,000	250	0.0	0.0
U /	N/A	N/A	10.07	N/A	0	0	0	0	100	38	0.0	N/A	2	1,000	250	4.0	0.0
U /	N/A	N/A	10.07	N/A	0	0	0	0	100	38	0.0	N/A	2	1,000	250	0.0	0.0
U /	N/A	N/A	10.07	2	0	0	0	0	100	38	0.0	N/A	2	500,000	250	0.0	0.0
U /	N/A	N/A	10.07	2	0	0	0	0	100	38	0.0	N/A	2	100,000	250	0.0	0.0
U /	N/A	5.4	10.17	N/A	0	0	0	0	100	83	0.0	N/A	2	1,000	250	4.0	0.0
U /	N/A	5.4	10.17	N/A	0	0	0	0	100	83	0.0	N/A	2	1,000	250	0.0	0.0
U /	N/A	5.4	10.17	5	0	0	0	0	100	83	0.0	N/A	2	500,000	250	0.0	0.0
U /	N/A	5.4	10.17	5	0	0	0	0	100	83	0.0	N/A	2	100,000	250	0.0	0.0
D / 1.8	5.4	2.1	9.54	23	6	0	0	62	32	58	0.0	95	4	1,000	250	3.8	1.0
D / 1.8	5.4	2.1	9.52	5	6	0	0	62	32	58	0.0	94	4	1,000	250	0.0	1.0
D / 1.8	5.4	2.1	9.53	27	6	0	0	62	32	58	0.0	96	4	500,000	250	0.0	1.0
D / 1.8	5.4	2.1	9.53	87	6	0	0	62	32	58	0.0	96	4	100,000	250	0.0	1.0
C / 4.7	3.2	0.5	9.62	39	8	0	0	54	38	63	0.0	93	4	1,000	250	3.0	1.0

					PERFORMANCE						Incl. in Returns	
							Total Return % through 2/28/17					
									Annualized		Dividend	Expense
Fund Type	Fund Name	Ticker Symbol	Overall Investment Rating	Phone	Perfor-mance Rating/Pts	3 Mo	6 Mo	1Yr / Pct	3Yr / Pct	5Yr / Pct	Yield	Ratio
GL	Barings Global Floating Rate C	BXFCX	B+		B / 7.7	2.87	5.55	13.66 /86	2.80 /58	—	4.09	2.50
GL	Barings Global Floating Rate I	BXFIX	A		B+ / 8.7	3.11	6.00	14.84 /88	3.83 /73	—	5.03	1.29
GL	Barings Global Floating Rate Y	BXFYX	A		B+ / 8.7	3.11	6.11	14.84 /88	3.82 /73	—	5.03	1.27
GL	Barings Global High Yield A	BXGAX	U		U /	5.79	7.48	21.02 /97	--	—	5.72	7.14
GL	Barings Global High Yield C	BXGCX	U		U /	5.59	6.97	20.11 /96	--	—	5.23	7.89
GL	Barings Global High Yield I	BXGIX	U		U /	5.85	7.61	21.32 /97	--	—	6.18	1.51
GL	Barings Global High Yield Y	BXGYX	U		U /	5.85	7.61	21.32 /97	--	—	6.18	1.51
COI	Barings Total Return Bond A	BXTAX	U		U /	1.69	-1.20	4.06 /62	--	—	2.49	5.65
COI	Barings Total Return Bond C	BXTCX	U		U /	1.50	-1.56	3.29 /58	--	—	1.84	6.43
COI	Barings Total Return Bond I	BXTIX	U		U /	1.75	-1.07	4.32 /64	--	—	2.84	1.42
COI	Barings Total Return Bond Y	BXTYX	U		U /	1.75	-1.07	4.32 /64	--	—	2.84	1.41
COH	Barings US High Yield A	BXHAX	U		U /	5.48	6.64	19.95 /96	--	—	5.79	5.47
COH	Barings US High Yield C	BXHCX	U		U /	5.29	6.25	19.06 /95	--	—	5.31	7.30
COH	Barings US High Yield I	BXHIX	U		U /	5.55	6.77	20.24 /96	--	—	6.26	1.38
COH	Barings US High Yield Y	BXHYX	U		U /	5.55	6.77	20.24 /96	--	—	6.26	1.42
MUN	BBH Intermediate Municipal Bond I	BBIIX	U	(800) 625-5759	U /	1.42	-1.85	1.05 /46	--	—	1.86	0.78
MUN	BBH Intermediate Municipal Bond N	BBINX	U	(800) 625-5759	U /	1.39	-1.92	0.89 /43	--	—	1.70	1.15
GL	BBH Limited Duration Class I	BBBIX	A-	(800) 625-5759	C- / 4.0	0.74	1.60	3.64 /60	1.38 /33	1.66 /37	2.18	0.28
GL	BBH Limited Duration Class N	BBBMX	B+	(800) 625-5759	C- / 3.7	0.78	1.50	3.44 /59	1.20 /31	1.47 /34	1.99	0.48
MMT	BBH US Government Money Market	BBSXX	D+	(800) 625-5759	E+ / 0.7	0.05	0.06	0.09 /22	0.04 / 9	0.03 / 9	0.09	N/A
MMT	BBH US Government Money Market	BBMXX	U	(800) 625-5759	U /	--	--	--	--	—	0.01	N/A
*GES	Berwyn Income Fund	BERIX	C-	(800) 992-6757	C+ / 6.6	1.49	1.91	9.76 /78	2.69 /56	5.65 /90	1.61	0.67
MUS	Bishop Street HI Muni Bond A	BHIAX	D	(800) 262-9565	C- / 3.5	1.94	-2.72	-0.57 / 9	2.26 /68	1.83 /55	2.13	1.23
MUS	Bishop Street HI Muni Bond Inst	BSHIX	B	(800) 262-9565	C+ / 6.1	2.01	-2.60	-0.32 /12	2.52 /74	2.09 /61	2.46	0.98
GEI	Bishop Street High Grade Inc Inst	BSHGX	D-	(800) 262-9565	C- / 3.6	0.88	-3.22	-0.03 /17	2.07 /44	1.88 /40	2.22	1.21
GEI	BlackRock Alloc Target Srs C	BRACX	C	(800) 441-7762	B- / 7.1	2.05	-1.97	5.75 /69	3.76 /72	4.27 /76	3.48	0.14
MUN	BlackRock Alloc Target Srs E	BATEX	U	(800) 441-7762	U /	3.22	-3.56	3.46 /68	--	—	4.33	0.31
*GEI	BlackRock Alloc Target Srs M	BRAMX	B+	(800) 441-7762	C / 5.0	0.56	-1.13	0.83 /38	2.83 /58	2.92 /56	3.02	0.12
GL	BlackRock Alloc Target Srs P	BATPX	E-	(800) 441-7762	E- / 0.2	0.21	6.00	5.05 /67	-2.76 / 1	—	0.00	0.16
GEI	BlackRock Alloc Target Srs S	BRASX	A	(800) 441-7762	C / 4.7	0.99	1.30	3.66 /61	1.95 /42	2.47 /49	3.29	0.31
MTG	BlackRock Bd Alloc Target Srs A	BATAX	U	(800) 441-7762	U /	1.87	2.39	10.80 /81	--	—	5.99	0.91
MUS	BlackRock CA Muni Opptys A	MECMX	B	(800) 441-7762	B- / 7.3	2.74	-2.29	1.12 /46	4.27 /95	3.54 /88	2.49	0.77
MUS ●	BlackRock CA Muni Opptys A1	MDCMX	A+	(800) 441-7762	A- / 9.1	2.86	-2.13	1.34 /49	4.43 /95	3.69 /90	2.74	0.63
MUS	BlackRock CA Muni Opptys C	MFCMX	B+	(800) 441-7762	B / 7.8	2.63	-2.57	0.44 /36	3.51 /88	2.77 /76	1.83	1.54
MUS	BlackRock CA Muni Opptys Inst	MACMX	A+	(800) 441-7762	A- / 9.2	2.88	-2.08	1.44 /51	4.53 /96	3.78 /91	2.84	0.52
MUS ●	BlackRock CA Muni Opptys Inv C1	MCCMX	A	(800) 441-7762	B+ / 8.5	2.73	-2.37	0.84 /43	3.91 /92	3.17 /83	2.23	1.14
MMT	BlackRock Cash:Prime Cap	BCPXX	C	(800) 441-7762	D / 1.6	0.16	0.29	0.51 /33	0.26 /18	0.21 /18	0.50	N/A
MMT	BlackRock Cash:Prime Premium	BPSXX	C	(800) 441-7762	D- / 1.5	0.16	0.28	0.49 /33	0.23 /17	0.18 /18	0.47	N/A
GEI	BlackRock Core Bond Inst	BFMCX	B-	(800) 441-7762	C / 5.0	1.07	-1.74	1.57 /45	2.76 /57	2.95 /57	2.42	0.58
GEI	BlackRock Core Bond Inv A	BCBAX	D	(800) 441-7762	D+ / 2.9	1.11	-1.87	1.26 /42	2.47 /51	2.63 /51	2.03	0.87
GEI	BlackRock Core Bond Inv C	BCBCX	D+	(800) 441-7762	C- / 3.2	0.82	-2.25	0.51 /33	1.68 /38	1.86 /40	1.36	1.60
GEI	BlackRock Core Bond K	CCBBX	B-	(800) 441-7762	C / 5.1	1.08	-1.71	1.62 /46	2.83 /58	3.03 /58	2.47	0.45
GEI	BlackRock Core Bond R	BCBRX	C	(800) 441-7762	C- / 4.1	0.94	-1.99	1.01 /40	2.17 /46	2.35 /47	1.86	1.15
GEI	BlackRock Core Bond Svc	CMCBX	C	(800) 441-7762	C / 4.5	1.01	-1.97	1.26 /42	2.42 /50	2.61 /51	2.11	0.88
GEI	BlackRock CoreAlpha Bond Inst	BCRIX	C-	(800) 441-7762	C / 4.7	0.77	-2.66	1.30 /43	2.65 /55	2.28 /46	2.71	0.36
COI	BlackRock CoreAlpha Bond Inv A	BCRAX	D-	(800) 441-7762	D+ / 2.4	0.69	-2.91	0.95 /39	2.29 /48	—	2.26	0.71
COI	BlackRock CoreAlpha Bond Inv C	BCRCX	D-	(800) 441-7762	D+ / 2.9	0.50	-3.19	0.20 /26	1.56 /36	—	1.59	1.46
COI	BlackRock CoreAlpha Bond K	BCRKX	U	(800) 441-7762	U /	0.79	-2.73	--	--	—	0.00	0.31
COI	BlackRock CoRI 2015 Inst	BCVIX	D	(800) 441-7762	B / 7.7	1.76	-6.98	0.46 /32	5.83 /91	—	3.08	1.69
COI	BlackRock CoRI 2015 Inv A	BCVAX	E+	(800) 441-7762	C+ / 6.3	1.68	-7.08	0.20 /26	5.57 /89	—	2.71	2.06
COI	BlackRock CoRI 2017 Inst	BCWIX	D	(800) 441-7762	B / 8.0	1.54	-7.47	0.25 /27	6.20 /93	—	3.11	1.65
COI	BlackRock CoRI 2017 Inv A	BCWAX	D-	(800) 441-7762	C+ / 6.6	1.56	-7.56	0.09 /22	5.96 /92	—	2.39	2.03

● Denotes fund is closed to new investors
* Denotes fund is included in Section II

RISK			NET ASSETS		ASSET							FUND MANAGER		MINIMUM		LOADS	
Risk Rating/Pts	3 Yr Avg Standard Deviation	Avg Dura-tion	NAV As of 2/28/17	Total $(Mil)	Cash %	Gov. Bond %	Muni. Bond %	Corp. Bond %	Other %	Portfolio Turnover Ratio	Avg Coupon Rate	Manager Quality Pct	Manager Tenure (Years)	Initial Purch. $	Additional Purch. $	Front End Load	Back End Load
C / 4.7	3.2	0.5	9.59	9	8	0	0	54	38	63	0.0	91	4	1,000	250	0.0	1.0
C / 4.7	3.2	0.5	9.64	21	8	0	0	54	38	63	0.0	94	4	500,000	250	0.0	1.0
C / 4.7	3.2	0.5	9.64	112	8	0	0	54	38	63	0.0	94	4	100,000	250	0.0	1.0
U /	N/A	N/A	10.43	N/A	0	0	0	0	100	83	0.0	N/A	2	1,000	250	4.0	0.0
U /	N/A	N/A	10.43	N/A	0	0	0	0	100	83	0.0	N/A	2	1,000	250	0.0	0.0
U /	N/A	N/A	10.43	13	0	0	0	0	100	83	0.0	N/A	2	500,000	250	0.0	0.0
U /	N/A	N/A	10.43	14	0	0	0	0	100	83	0.0	N/A	2	100,000	250	0.0	0.0
U /	N/A	5.4	10.00	N/A	0	0	0	0	100	434	0.0	N/A	2	1,000	250	4.0	0.0
U /	N/A	5.4	10.00	N/A	0	0	0	0	100	434	0.0	N/A	2	1,000	250	0.0	0.0
U /	N/A	5.4	10.00	12	0	0	0	0	100	434	0.0	N/A	2	500,000	250	0.0	0.0
U /	N/A	5.4	10.00	16	0	0	0	0	100	434	0.0	N/A	2	100,000	250	0.0	0.0
U /	N/A	4.2	10.60	2	0	0	0	0	100	78	0.0	N/A	2	1,000	250	4.0	0.0
U /	N/A	4.2	10.60	N/A	0	0	0	0	100	78	0.0	N/A	2	1,000	250	0.0	0.0
U /	N/A	4.2	10.60	16	0	0	0	0	100	78	0.0	N/A	2	500,000	250	0.0	0.0
U /	N/A	4.2	10.60	15	0	0	0	0	100	78	0.0	N/A	2	100,000	250	0.0	0.0
U /	N/A	4.3	10.19	58	1	0	98	0	1	40	0.0	N/A	3	5,000,000	25,000	0.0	1.0
U /	N/A	4.3	10.20	20	1	0	98	0	1	40	0.0	N/A	3	5,000	500	0.0	1.0
A+ / 9.7	0.7	0.6	10.16	5,826	0	12	9	35	44	53	0.0	79	6	5,000,000	25,000	0.0	0.0
A+ / 9.7	0.7	0.6	10.17	46	0	12	9	35	44	53	0.0	77	6	25,000	25,000	0.0	0.0
A+ / 9.9	N/A	N/A	1.00	1,799	100	0	0	0	0	0	0.1	40	N/A	5,000,000	0	0.0	0.0
U /	N/A	N/A	1.00	65	100	0	0	0	0	0	0.0	N/A	N/A	100,000	0	0.0	0.0
C- / 3.4	3.8	2.8	13.74	1,741	7	13	0	50	30	45	0.0	82	15	1,000	250	0.0	1.0
C+ / 6.1	2.9	5.3	10.53	22	0	0	99	0	1	28	0.0	15	10	1,000	0	3.0	0.0
C+ / 6.2	2.9	5.3	10.53	122	0	0	99	0	1	28	0.0	21	10	1,000	0	0.0	0.0
C / 4.6	3.2	5.7	9.70	62	0	22	9	58	11	24	0.0	15	11	1,000	0	0.0	0.0
C- / 3.4	3.9	N/A	10.35	415	0	11	2	83	4	53	0.0	66	8	0	0	0.0	0.0
U /	N/A	N/A	10.46	128	0	0	99	0	1	44	0.0	N/A	3	0	0	0.0	0.0
B / 8.2	2.0	N/A	9.72	596	5	12	0	0	83	1,789	0.0	77	6	0	0	0.0	0.0
D / 1.9	5.3	N/A	9.36	123	50	1	0	15	34	0	0.0	0	8	0	0	0.0	0.0
A / 9.4	0.9	N/A	9.54	193	0	1	0	36	63	270	0.0	80	8	0	0	0.0	0.0
U /	N/A	N/A	10.15	248	0	0	0	0	100	45	0.0	N/A	2	0	0	0.0	0.0
C / 4.6	3.3	N/A	12.34	410	0	0	97	0	3	119	0.0	75	24	1,000	50	4.3	0.0
C / 4.5	3.3	N/A	12.36	125	0	0	97	0	3	119	0.0	77	24	0	0	0.0	0.0
C / 4.5	3.3	N/A	12.36	114	0	0	97	0	3	119	0.0	55	24	1,000	50	0.0	0.0
C / 4.6	3.3	N/A	12.36	515	0	0	97	0	3	119	0.0	78	24	2,000,000	0	0.0	0.0
C / 4.5	3.3	N/A	12.36	13	0	0	97	0	3	119	0.0	66	24	0	0	0.0	0.0
A+ / 9.9	0.1	N/A	1.00	16	100	0	0	0	0	0	0.5	53	N/A	25,000,000	0	0.0	0.0
A+ / 9.9	0.1	N/A	1.00	4	100	0	0	0	0	0	0.5	52	N/A	10,000,000	0	0.0	0.0
C+ / 6.8	2.8	5.0	9.59	1,755	0	37	0	26	37	594	2.5	58	7	2,000,000	0	0.0	0.0
C+ / 6.8	2.8	5.0	9.61	495	0	37	0	26	37	594	2.5	44	7	1,000	50	4.0	0.0
C+ / 6.8	2.8	5.0	9.56	97	0	37	0	26	37	594	2.5	16	7	1,000	50	0.0	0.0
C+ / 6.8	2.8	5.0	9.62	697	0	37	0	26	37	594	2.5	60	7	5,000,000	0	0.0	0.0
C+ / 6.8	2.8	5.0	9.61	4	0	37	0	26	37	594	2.5	29	7	100	0	0.0	0.0
C+ / 6.7	2.8	5.0	9.59	63	0	37	0	26	37	594	2.5	37	7	5,000	0	0.0	0.0
C+ / 5.7	3.0	N/A	10.26	352	0	10	0	33	57	540	0.0	N/A	10	2,000,000	0	0.0	0.0
C+ / 5.6	3.0	N/A	10.26	2	0	10	0	33	57	540	0.0	29	10	1,000	50	4.0	0.0
C+ / 5.7	3.0	N/A	10.26	N/A	0	10	0	33	57	540	0.0	11	10	1,000	50	0.0	0.0
U /	N/A	N/A	10.26	N/A	0	10	0	33	57	540	0.0	N/A	10	5,000,000	0	0.0	0.0
E / 0.4	7.6	12.5	10.58	11	1	60	0	38	1	52	1.6	26	3	2,000,000	0	0.0	0.0
E / 0.4	7.6	12.5	10.56	N/A	1	60	0	38	1	52	1.6	19	3	1,000	50	4.0	0.0
E / 0.3	8.6	13.2	10.25	10	1	61	0	36	2	47	2.6	17	3	2,000,000	0	0.0	0.0
E- / 0.2	8.6	13.2	10.27	N/A	1	61	0	36	2	47	2.6	12	3	1,000	50	4.0	0.0

Fund Type	Fund Name	Ticker Symbol	Overall Investment Rating	Phone	PERFORMANCE Perfor-mance Rating/Pts	Total Return % through 2/28/17 3 Mo	6 Mo	1Yr / Pct	Annualized 3Yr / Pct	5Yr / Pct	Incl. in Returns Dividend Yield	Expense Ratio
COI	BlackRock CoRI 2019 Inst	BCXIX	D+	(800) 441-7762	B+ / 8.4	1.75	-8.73	0.11 / 22	6.85 / 95	--	3.20	1.58
COI	BlackRock CoRI 2019 Inv A	BCXAX	D-	(800) 441-7762	B- / 7.1	1.68	-8.89	-0.24 / 14	6.58 / 95	--	2.76	1.92
COI	BlackRock CoRI 2021 Inst	BCYIX	D+	(800) 441-7762	B+ / 8.7	1.96	-10.03	0.24 / 27	7.29 / 96	--	3.37	1.58
COI	BlackRock CoRI 2021 Inv A	BCYAX	D-	(800) 441-7762	B- / 7.4	2.00	-10.12	0.08 / 21	7.06 / 96	--	2.93	1.88
COI	BlackRock CoRI 2023 Inst	BCZIX	C-	(800) 441-7762	B+ / 8.9	2.14	-11.25	0.63 / 35	7.75 / 97	--	3.33	1.45
COI	BlackRock CoRI 2023 Inv A	BCZAX	D	(800) 441-7762	B / 7.8	2.08	-11.28	0.48 / 33	7.54 / 97	--	2.97	1.55
GES	BlackRock Crdt Strategies Inc Inst	BMSIX	A+	(800) 441-7762	B / 8.1	3.16	2.83	10.03 / 79	3.76 / 72	5.08 / 85	4.31	0.81
GES	BlackRock Crdt Strategies Inc Inv A	BMSAX	A	(800) 441-7762	B- / 7.2	3.10	2.81	9.75 / 78	3.53 / 69	4.82 / 82	3.96	1.11
GES	BlackRock Crdt Strategies Inc Inv C	BMSCX	B+	(800) 441-7762	B- / 7.0	2.91	2.32	8.93 / 76	2.73 / 56	4.02 / 73	3.32	1.84
LP	BlackRock Crdt Strategies Inc K	BMSKX	U	(800) 441-7762	U /	3.17	2.86	--	--	--	0.00	N/A
EM	BlackRock Emg Mkts Flex Dyn Bd	BEDIX	B	(800) 441-7762	A+ / 9.9	4.21	6.23	17.82 / 93	7.12 / 96	4.57 / 79	4.27	1.52
EM	BlackRock Emg Mkts Flex Dyn Bd	BAEDX	B	(800) 441-7762	A+ / 9.8	4.15	6.09	17.51 / 93	6.80 / 95	4.26 / 76	3.84	1.83
EM	BlackRock Emg Mkts Flex Dyn Bd	BCEDX	B	(800) 441-7762	A+ / 9.8	3.96	5.70	16.64 / 91	6.00 / 92	3.48 / 65	3.29	2.66
EM	BlackRock Emg Mkts Flex Dyn Bd K	BREDX	B	(800) 441-7762	A+ / 9.9	4.22	6.26	18.05 / 94	7.22 / 96	4.67 / 80	4.35	1.39
LP	BlackRock Floating Rate Inc Inst	BFRIX	A+	(800) 441-7762	B / 7.8	1.99	3.51	9.91 / 79	3.53 / 69	4.45 / 78	4.19	0.69
* LP	BlackRock Floating Rate Inc Inv A	BFRAX	A+	(800) 441-7762	C+ / 6.9	1.92	3.35	9.56 / 78	3.24 / 65	4.15 / 74	3.78	1.02
LP	BlackRock Floating Rate Inc Inv C	BFRCX	A+	(800) 441-7762	C+ / 6.7	1.74	3.09	8.79 / 76	2.50 / 52	3.39 / 64	3.18	1.72
LP ●	BlackRock Floating Rate Inc Inv C1	BFRPX	A+	(800) 441-7762	B- / 7.0	1.80	3.12	9.08 / 77	2.77 / 57	3.66 / 68	3.44	1.46
LP	BlackRock Floating Rate Inc K	BFRKX	U	(800) 441-7762	U /	2.01	3.64	--	--	--	0.00	0.64
GL	BlackRock Glbl Long/Short Crd Iv A	BGCAX	D+	(800) 441-7762	D+ / 2.3	1.80	2.52	5.93 / 70	0.87 / 25	2.50 / 49	0.00	2.30
GL	BlackRock Glbl Long/Short Crd Iv C	BGCCX	C-	(800) 441-7762	D+ / 2.7	1.62	2.14	5.14 / 67	0.13 / 14	1.73 / 38	0.00	3.07
GL	BlackRock Glbl Long/Short Cred Inst	BGCIX	B	(800) 441-7762	C / 4.5	1.89	2.71	6.22 / 71	1.15 / 30	2.77 / 54	0.00	2.09
MTG	BlackRock GNMA Port Inst	BGNIX	B	(800) 441-7762	C- / 4.1	0.32	-1.02	0.59 / 35	2.23 / 47	2.00 / 42	2.89	0.70
MTG	BlackRock GNMA Port Inv A	BGPAX	C-	(800) 441-7762	D / 1.9	0.26	-1.15	0.29 / 28	1.90 / 41	1.65 / 37	2.48	0.95
MTG	BlackRock GNMA Port Inv C	BGPCX	C-	(800) 441-7762	D / 2.2	-0.03	-1.52	-0.47 / 10	1.10 / 29	0.88 / 26	1.82	1.70
MTG	BlackRock GNMA Port K	BBGPX	B	(800) 441-7762	C- / 4.1	0.23	-1.01	0.62 / 35	2.23 / 47	2.01 / 42	2.93	0.58
MTG	BlackRock GNMA Port Svc	BGPSX	C+	(800) 441-7762	C- / 3.5	0.16	-1.16	0.27 / 28	1.86 / 41	1.65 / 37	2.57	1.04
COH	BlackRock High Yield Bond Inst	BHYIX	C+	(800) 441-7762	A / 9.4	4.79	5.78	18.21 / 94	4.11 / 76	6.91 / 96	5.58	0.60
* COH	BlackRock High Yield Bond Inv A	BHYAX	C-	(800) 441-7762	B+ / 8.4	4.57	5.47	17.67 / 93	3.75 / 72	6.55 / 95	5.06	0.94
COH ●	BlackRock High Yield Bond Inv B	BHYBX	C-	(800) 441-7762	B+ / 8.4	4.28	4.93	16.65 / 91	2.83 / 58	5.63 / 89	4.30	1.81
COH ●	BlackRock High Yield Bond Inv B1	BHYDX	C	(800) 441-7762	B+ / 8.8	4.56	5.32	17.20 / 92	3.23 / 65	6.02 / 92	4.75	1.76
COH	BlackRock High Yield Bond Inv C	BHYCX	C	(800) 441-7762	B+ / 8.7	4.50	5.21	16.93 / 92	3.04 / 62	5.79 / 91	4.54	1.68
COH ●	BlackRock High Yield Bond Inv C1	BHYEX	C	(800) 441-7762	B+ / 8.8	4.41	5.31	17.14 / 92	3.19 / 64	5.96 / 92	4.72	1.50
COH	BlackRock High Yield Bond K	BRHYX	C+	(800) 441-7762	A / 9.4	4.67	5.67	18.29 / 94	4.19 / 77	6.99 / 96	5.65	0.54
COH	BlackRock High Yield Bond R	BHYRX	C+	(800) 441-7762	A- / 9.0	4.62	5.43	17.44 / 93	3.49 / 68	6.26 / 94	4.95	1.24
COH	BlackRock High Yield Bond Svc	BHYSX	C+	(800) 441-7762	A- / 9.2	4.57	5.60	17.85 / 93	3.80 / 73	6.58 / 95	5.29	0.91
MUH	BlackRock High Yld Muni Inst	MAYHX	B+	(800) 441-7762	A+ / 9.9	3.44	-4.14	1.94 / 56	6.73 / 99	5.33 / 98	4.26	0.66
MUH	BlackRock High Yld Muni Inv A	MDYHX	B	(800) 441-7762	A / 9.5	3.38	-4.27	1.68 / 54	6.46 / 99	5.06 / 98	3.83	0.91
MUH	BlackRock High Yld Muni Inv C	MCYHX	B	(800) 441-7762	A+ / 9.7	3.18	-4.61	0.93 / 44	5.66 / 98	4.29 / 95	3.23	1.67
GEI	BlackRock Impact Bond Inst	BIIIX	U	(800) 441-7762	U /	1.24	-1.59	--	--	--	0.00	N/A
GEI	BlackRock Impact Bond Investor A	BIAAX	U	(800) 441-7762	U /	1.18	-1.71	--	--	--	0.00	N/A
GEI	BlackRock Impact Bond Investor C	BIACX	U	(800) 441-7762	U /	0.99	-2.09	--	--	--	0.00	N/A
GEI	BlackRock Impact Bond K	BIAKX	U	(800) 441-7762	U /	1.25	-1.57	--	--	--	0.00	N/A
GES	BlackRock Inflation Prot Bond Inst	BPRIX	E+	(800) 441-7762	C- / 3.4	1.13	-0.41	3.58 / 60	1.15 / 30	0.43 / 21	1.18	0.53
GES	BlackRock Inflation Prot Bond Inv A	BPRAX	E	(800) 441-7762	D- / 1.0	0.96	-0.62	3.25 / 58	0.84 / 25	0.10 / 15	1.05	0.88
GES	BlackRock Inflation Prot Bond Inv C	BPRCX	E	(800) 441-7762	D / 1.8	0.79	-0.97	2.51 / 53	0.13 / 14	-0.60 / 3	0.91	1.56
GES	BlackRock Inflation Prot Bond K	BPLBX	E+	(800) 441-7762	C- / 3.6	1.05	-0.42	3.64 / 60	1.27 / 32	0.53 / 22	1.20	0.43
GES	BlackRock Inflation Prot Bond Svc	BPRSX	E+	(800) 441-7762	C- / 3.0	1.04	-0.52	3.33 / 59	0.87 / 25	0.14 / 16	1.10	0.84
MMF	BlackRock Liqdty CA Mny Admin	BLCXX	U	(800) 441-7762	U /	--	--	--	--	--	0.21	N/A
MMF	BlackRock Liqdty CA Mny Inst	MUCXX	C	(800) 441-7762	D / 1.7	0.22	0.33	0.43 / 36	0.15 / 17	0.10 / 17	0.43	N/A
MMF	BlackRock Liqdty CA Money PC	BCAXX	U	(800) 441-7762	U /	--	--	--	--	--	0.12	N/A
MMF	BlackRock Liqdty CA Money Prem	BLBXX	U	(800) 441-7762	U /	--	--	--	--	--	0.01	N/A

● Denotes fund is closed to new investors
* Denotes fund is included in Section II

www.thestreetratings.com

RISK			NET ASSETS		ASSET					Portfolio Turnover Ratio	Avg Coupon Rate	FUND MANAGER		MINIMUM		LOADS	
Risk Rating/Pts	3 Yr Avg Standard Deviation	Avg Dura-tion	NAV As of 2/28/17	Total $(Mil)	Cash %	Gov. Bond %	Muni. Bond %	Corp. Bond %	Other %			Manager Quality Pct	Manager Tenure (Years)	Initial Purch. $	Additional Purch. $	Front End Load	Back End Load
E- / 0.2	9.9	15.2	10.27	10	1	63	0	35	1	58	2.6	12	3	2,000,000	0	0.0	0.0
E- / 0.2	9.9	15.2	10.27	1	1	63	0	35	1	58	2.6	8	3	1,000	50	4.0	0.0
E- / 0.2	11.0	17.1	10.18	10	1	60	0	37	2	93	2.6	6	3	2,000,000	0	0.0	0.0
E- / 0.2	11.0	17.1	10.17	1	1	60	0	37	2	93	2.6	4	3	1,000	50	4.0	0.0
E- / 0.0	12.4	19.0	11.14	11	1	56	0	41	2	110	2.1	2	3	2,000,000	0	0.0	0.0
E- / 0.0	12.3	19.0	11.12	3	1	56	0	41	2	110	2.1	2	3	1,000	50	4.0	0.0
C+ / 5.7	3.0	0.3	10.19	234	3	0	0	25	72	101	4.7	92	5	2,000,000	0	0.0	0.0
C+ / 6.1	2.9	0.3	10.19	118	3	0	0	25	72	101	4.7	91	5	1,000	50	2.5	0.0
C+ / 5.7	3.0	0.3	10.19	32	3	0	0	25	72	101	4.7	85	5	1,000	50	0.0	0.0
U /	N/A	0.3	10.19	N/A	3	0	0	25	72	101	4.7	N/A	5	5,000,000	0	0.0	0.0
D- / 1.4	5.8	-4.0	9.69	34	12	61	0	24	3	421	174.7	99	6	2,000,000	0	0.0	0.0
D- / 1.4	5.8	-4.0	9.68	16	12	61	0	24	3	421	174.7	99	6	1,000	50	4.0	0.0
D- / 1.3	5.9	-4.0	9.68	5	12	61	0	24	3	421	174.7	98	6	1,000	50	0.0	0.0
D- / 1.3	5.9	-4.0	9.69	56	12	61	0	24	3	421	174.7	99	6	5,000,000	0	0.0	0.0
B / 7.8	2.3	0.1	10.26	2,510	3	0	0	12	85	72	5.0	91	8	2,000,000	0	0.0	0.0
B / 7.8	2.3	0.1	10.26	643	3	0	0	12	85	72	5.0	90	8	1,000	50	2.5	0.0
B / 7.8	2.4	0.1	10.26	142	3	0	0	12	85	72	5.0	85	8	1,000	50	0.0	0.0
B / 7.8	2.4	0.1	10.26	41	3	0	0	12	85	72	5.0	88	8	0	0	0.0	0.0
U /	N/A	0.1	10.26	194	3	0	0	12	85	72	5.0	N/A	8	5,000,000	0	0.0	0.0
B / 8.1	2.1	N/A	10.19	325	6	0	0	48	46	253	0.0	71	6	1,000	50	4.0	0.0
B / 8.1	2.1	N/A	10.02	160	6	0	0	48	46	253	0.0	45	6	1,000	50	0.0	0.0
B / 8.0	2.1	N/A	10.24	3,500	6	0	0	48	46	253	0.0	76	6	2,000,000	0	0.0	0.0
B+ / 8.6	1.7	2.2	9.65	419	0	1	0	0	99	1,139	3.8	53	8	2,000,000	0	0.0	0.0
B+ / 8.6	1.7	2.2	9.69	198	0	1	0	0	99	1,139	3.8	34	8	1,000	50	4.0	0.0
B+ / 8.6	1.7	2.2	9.64	85	0	1	0	0	99	1,139	3.8	12	8	1,000	50	0.0	0.0
B+ / 8.6	1.8	2.2	9.61	18	0	1	0	0	99	1,139	3.8	52	8	5,000,000	0	0.0	0.0
B+ / 8.6	1.7	2.2	9.63	11	0	1	0	0	99	1,139	3.8	33	8	5,000	0	0.0	0.0
D- / 1.2	5.5	1.2	7.78	9,167	0	0	0	84	16	90	10.5	37	10	2,000,000	0	0.0	0.0
D- / 1.2	5.5	1.2	7.77	3,589	0	0	0	84	16	90	10.5	25	10	1,000	50	4.0	0.0
D- / 1.3	5.5	1.2	7.78	N/A	0	0	0	84	16	90	10.5	7	10	0	0	0.0	0.0
D- / 1.3	5.5	1.2	7.78	N/A	0	0	0	84	16	90	10.5	13	10	0	0	0.0	0.0
D- / 1.3	5.5	1.2	7.79	499	0	0	0	84	16	90	10.5	10	10	1,000	50	0.0	0.0
D- / 1.3	5.5	1.2	7.79	48	0	0	0	84	16	90	10.5	12	10	0	0	0.0	0.0
D- / 1.2	5.6	1.2	7.78	5,333	0	0	0	84	16	90	10.5	41	10	5,000,000	0	0.0	0.0
D- / 1.3	5.5	1.2	7.78	124	0	0	0	84	16	90	10.5	18	10	100	0	0.0	0.0
D- / 1.3	5.5	1.2	7.78	464	0	0	0	84	16	90	10.5	27	10	5,000	0	0.0	0.0
D / 1.7	4.7	8.8	9.36	474	0	0	99	0	1	19	4.8	84	11	2,000,000	0	0.0	0.0
D / 1.7	4.7	8.8	9.34	204	0	0	99	0	1	19	4.8	82	11	1,000	50	4.3	0.0
D / 1.7	4.7	8.8	9.37	65	0	0	99	0	1	19	4.8	72	11	1,000	50	0.0	0.0
U /	N/A	N/A	9.71	19	0	0	0	0	100	0	0.0	N/A	1	2,000,000	0	0.0	0.0
U /	N/A	N/A	9.71	N/A	0	0	0	0	100	0	0.0	N/A	1	1,000	50	4.0	0.0
U /	N/A	N/A	9.71	N/A	0	0	0	0	100	0	0.0	N/A	1	1,000	50	0.0	0.0
U /	N/A	N/A	9.71	N/A	0	0	0	0	100	0	0.0	N/A	1	5,000,000	0	0.0	0.0
D+ / 2.9	3.9	7.7	10.77	1,521	0	99	0	0	1	45	3.6	5	7	2,000,000	0	0.0	0.0
C- / 3.0	3.9	7.7	10.52	357	0	99	0	0	1	45	3.6	4	7	1,000	50	4.0	0.0
D+ / 2.9	3.9	7.7	10.21	182	0	99	0	0	1	45	3.6	1	7	1,000	50	0.0	0.0
D+ / 2.9	3.9	7.7	10.59	422	0	99	0	0	1	45	3.6	6	7	5,000,000	0	0.0	0.0
D+ / 2.9	3.9	7.7	10.64	36	0	99	0	0	1	45	3.6	4	7	5,000	0	0.0	0.0
U /	N/A	N/A	1.00	N/A	100	0	0	0	0	0	0.2	N/A	N/A	5,000	0	0.0	0.0
A+ / 9.9	0.1	N/A	1.00	38	100	0	0	0	0	0	0.4	50	N/A	3,000,000	0	0.0	0.0
U /	N/A	N/A	1.00	4	100	0	0	0	0	0	0.1	43	N/A	0	0	0.0	0.0
U /	N/A	N/A	1.00	N/A	100	0	0	0	0	0	0.0	N/A	N/A	0	0	0.0	0.0

Fund Type	Fund Name	Ticker Symbol	Overall Investment Rating	Phone	Performance Rating/Pts	3 Mo	6 Mo	1Yr / Pct	3Yr / Pct	5Yr / Pct	Dividend Yield	Expense Ratio
			99 Pct = Best			Total Return % through 2/28/17			Annualized		Incl. in Returns	
MMF	BlackRock Liqdty CA Money Select	BCBXX	U	(800) 441-7762	U /	--	--	--	--	--	0.11	N/A
MMT	BlackRock Liqdty FedFd Admin	BLFXX	C-	(800) 441-7762	D- / 1.0	0.08	0.14	0.22 /27	0.09 /12	0.06 /12	0.22	N/A
MMT	BlackRock Liqdty FedFd Cash Mgmt		U	(800) 441-7762	U /	--	--	--	--	--	0.05	N/A
MMT	BlackRock Liqdty FedFd Cash Rsv	BFRXX	D+	(800) 441-7762	E+ / 0.7	0.02	0.04	0.06 /21	0.03 / 8	0.02 / 7	0.06	N/A
MMT	BlackRock Liqdty FedFd Dlr	TDDXX	D+	(800) 441-7762	E+ / 0.7	0.05	0.07	0.09 /22	0.04 / 9	0.03 / 9	0.09	N/A
MMT	BlackRock Liqdty FedFd Inst	TFDXX	C-	(800) 441-7762	D- / 1.3	0.11	0.19	0.32 /29	0.13 /14	0.08 /14	0.32	N/A
MMT	BlackRock Liqdty FedFd Prem	BUPXX	U	(800) 441-7762	U /	--	--	--	--	--	0.05	N/A
MMT	BlackRock Liqdty FedFd Prvte Client	BRPXX	U	(800) 441-7762	U /	--	--	--	--	--	0.05	N/A
MMT	BlackRock Liqdty FedFd Select	BFBXX	U	(800) 441-7762	U /	--	--	--	--	--	0.05	N/A
MMF	BlackRock Liqdty MuniCash Port D	MCDXX	C-		D- / 1.4	0.08	0.26	0.27 /31	0.10 /15	0.06 /14	0.25	N/A
MMF	BlackRock Liqdty MuniCash Port Inst	MCSXX	C	(800) 441-7762	D / 1.8	0.14	0.38	0.48 /37	0.17 /18	0.13 /18	0.46	N/A
MMF	BlackRock Liqdty MuniFd Cash Mgmt	BCMXX	U	(800) 441-7762	U /	--	--	--	--	--	0.02	N/A
MMF	BlackRock Liqdty MuniFd Premier	BLSXX	U	(800) 441-7762	U /	--	--	--	--	--	0.01	N/A
MMF	BlackRock Liqdty MuniFund Select	BMBXX	U	(800) 441-7762	U /	--	--	--	--	--	0.02	N/A
MMF	BlackRock Liqdty NY Money Admin	BLNXX	U	(800) 441-7762	U /	--	--	--	--	--	0.25	N/A
MMF	BlackRock Liqdty NY Money Inst	MUNXX	C	(800) 441-7762	D / 1.7	0.11	0.23	0.47 /36	0.17 /18	0.11 /17	0.47	N/A
MMF	BlackRock Liqdty NY Money Prem	BNBXX	U	(800) 441-7762	U /	--	--	--	--	--	0.16	N/A
MMF	BlackRock Liqdty NY Money Prv Cl	BYPXX	U	(800) 441-7762	U /	--	--	--	--	--	0.16	N/A
MMT	BlackRock Liqdty TempFd Admin	BTMXX	C	(800) 441-7762	D- / 1.5	0.17	0.33	0.49 /33	0.19 /16	0.13 /16	0.44	N/A
MMT	BlackRock Liqdty TempFd Cash	BRRXX	C-	(800) 441-7762	D- / 1.0	0.12	0.20	0.21 /26	0.08 /11	0.06 /12	0.16	N/A
MMT	BlackRock Liqdty TempFd Csh Mgmt	BRTXX	C-	(800) 441-7762	E+ / 0.9	0.10	0.16	0.16 /24	0.07 /11	0.05 /11	0.11	N/A
MMT	BlackRock Liqdty TempFd Dollar	TDOXX	C-	(800) 441-7762	D- / 1.3	0.16	0.27	0.35 /30	0.14 /15	0.09 /14	0.30	N/A
MMT	BlackRock Liqdty TempFd Inst	TMPXX	C	(800) 441-7762	D / 1.7	0.22	0.39	0.60 /35	0.26 /18	0.20 /18	0.55	N/A
MMT	BlackRock Liqdty TempFd Premier	BFPXX	D+	(800) 441-7762	E+ / 0.7	0.02	0.07	0.07 /21	0.03 / 8	0.02 / 7	0.02	N/A
MMT	BlackRock Liqdty TempFd Priv Client	BTVXX	C-	(800) 441-7762	E+ / 0.9	0.10	0.16	0.16 /24	0.06 /10	0.04 /10	0.11	N/A
MMT	BlackRock Liqdty TempFd Select	BTBXX	D+	(800) 441-7762	E+ / 0.7	0.03	0.08	0.08 /21	0.04 / 9	0.02 / 7	0.03	N/A
MMT	BlackRock Liqdty T-Fund Ptf Admin	BTAXX	D+	(800) 441-7762	E+ / 0.9	0.07	0.10	0.15 /24	0.06 /10	0.04 /10	0.15	N/A
MMT	BlackRock Liqdty Treas Tr Fd Admin	BITXX	D+	(800) 441-7762	E+ / 0.8	0.06	0.08	0.12 /23	0.04 / 9	0.03 / 9	0.12	N/A
MMT	BlackRock Liqdty Treas Tr Fd Inst	TTTXX	C-	(800) 221-8120	D- / 1.0	0.09	0.13	0.22 /27	0.08 /11	0.05 /11	0.22	N/A
GEI	BlackRock Low Duration Bond Inst	BFMSX	B+	(800) 441-7762	C- / 3.7	0.92	0.84	2.24 /51	1.40 /33	1.99 /42	1.80	0.50
* GEI	BlackRock Low Duration Bond Inv A	BLDAX	C	(800) 441-7762	D / 2.1	0.75	0.70	1.93 /48	1.07 /29	1.65 /37	1.46	0.84
GEI ●	BlackRock Low Duration Bond Inv A1	CMGAX	B-	(800) 441-7762	D+ / 2.9	0.79	0.78	2.11 /50	1.21 /31	1.82 /39	1.65	0.67
GEI	BlackRock Low Duration Bond Inv C	BLDCX	C	(800) 441-7762	D / 1.9	0.67	0.33	1.18 /42	0.32 /19	0.91 /26	0.75	1.57
GEI ●	BlackRock Low Duration Bond Inv C2	CLDCX	C+	(800) 441-7762	D+ / 2.8	0.72	0.63	1.78 /47	0.88 /26	1.48 /34	1.35	0.97
COI ●	BlackRock Low Duration Bond Inv C3	BLDFX	C	(800) 441-7762	D / 1.9	0.70	0.37	1.23 /42	0.36 /19	0.92 /26	0.81	1.55
GEI	BlackRock Low Duration Bond K	CLDBX	B+	(800) 441-7762	C- / 3.7	0.93	0.86	2.29 /51	1.45 /34	2.04 /43	1.85	0.42
COI	BlackRock Low Duration Bond R	BLDPX	C+	(800) 441-7762	D+ / 2.6	0.69	0.58	1.67 /46	0.80 /24	1.32 /32	1.25	1.14
GEI	BlackRock Low Duration Bond Svc	CMGBX	B-	(800) 441-7762	C- / 3.0	0.75	0.70	1.93 /48	1.04 /28	1.63 /37	1.49	0.86
GEI	BlackRock Managed Income Inst	BLDIX	A	(800) 441-7762	B+ / 8.5	2.31	1.54	9.31 /77	4.52 /81	3.88 /71	2.81	0.97
GEI	BlackRock Managed Income Inv A	BLADX	A-	(800) 441-7762	B / 8.1	2.24	1.41	8.89 /76	4.17 /77	3.53 /66	2.54	1.29
GEI	BlackRock Managed Income K	BLDRX	A	(800) 441-7762	B+ / 8.6	2.42	1.57	9.35 /77	4.62 /82	3.99 /72	2.87	0.87
MUN ●	BlackRock National Municpal K	BNMLX	A+	(800) 441-7762	B+ / 8.3	2.09	-1.99	0.84 /43	3.81 /91	3.58 /88	3.20	0.51
MUN	BlackRock Natl Muni Inst	MANLX	A+	(800) 441-7762	B / 8.2	2.18	-2.02	0.75 /41	3.71 /90	3.48 /87	3.10	0.60
* MUN	BlackRock Natl Muni Inv A	MDNLX	B+	(800) 441-7762	C+ / 6.0	2.11	-2.13	0.66 /40	3.53 /88	3.31 /85	2.79	0.85
MUN ●	BlackRock Natl Muni Inv B	MBNLX	A	(800) 441-7762	B- / 7.0	1.89	-2.46	0.06 /22	2.98 /82	2.78 /76	2.40	1.39
MUN	BlackRock Natl Muni Inv C	MFNLX	A	(800) 441-7762	C+ / 6.6	1.92	-2.49	-0.09 /16	2.76 /78	2.54 /71	2.15	1.54
MUN ●	BlackRock Natl Muni Inv C1	MCNLX	A+	(800) 441-7762	B- / 7.0	1.88	-2.39	0.02 /19	2.96 /81	2.72 /75	2.35	1.34
MUN	BlackRock Natl Muni Svc	BNMSX	A+	(800) 441-7762	B / 7.8	2.02	-2.14	0.54 /38	3.51 /88	3.17 /83	2.89	0.80
MUS	BlackRock NJ Muni Bond Inst	MANJX	C+	(800) 441-7762	B / 8.1	2.05	-4.11	0.31 /33	3.95 /92	3.34 /85	3.59	0.81
MUS	BlackRock NJ Muni Bond Inv A	MENJX	D	(800) 441-7762	C+ / 5.9	1.98	-4.21	0.13 /26	3.81 /91	3.21 /83	3.26	0.99
MUS ●	BlackRock NJ Muni Bond Inv A1	MDNJX	C+	(800) 441-7762	B / 8.1	2.02	-4.22	0.27 /31	3.94 /92	3.35 /85	3.55	0.83
MUS	BlackRock NJ Muni Bond Inv C	MFNJX	C-	(800) 441-7762	C+ / 6.6	1.80	-4.57	-0.54 / 9	3.02 /82	2.42 /69	2.62	1.73

● Denotes fund is closed to new investors
* Denotes fund is included in Section II

www.thestreetratings.com

RISK			NET ASSETS		ASSET							FUND MANAGER		MINIMUM		LOADS	
Risk Rating/Pts	3 Yr Avg Standard Deviation	Avg Dura- tion	NAV As of 2/28/17	Total $(Mil)	Cash %	Gov. Bond %	Muni. Bond %	Corp. Bond %	Other %	Portfolio Turnover Ratio	Avg Coupon Rate	Manager Quality Pct	Manager Tenure (Years)	Initial Purch. $	Additional Purch. $	Front End Load	Back End Load
U /	N/A	N/A	1.00	6	100	0	0	0	0	0	0.1	42	N/A	0	0	0.0	0.0
A+ / 9.9	N/A	N/A	1.00	2,004	100	0	0	0	0	0	0.2	45	N/A	5,000	0	0.0	0.0
U /	N/A	N/A	1.00	164	100	0	0	0	0	0	0.1	40	N/A	5,000	0	0.0	0.0
A+ / 9.9	N/A	N/A	1.00	864	100	0	0	0	0	0	0.1	40	N/A	5,000	0	0.0	0.0
A+ / 9.9	N/A	N/A	1.00	2,355	100	0	0	0	0	0	0.1	40	N/A	5,000	0	0.0	0.0
A+ / 9.9	N/A	N/A	1.00	79,377	100	0	0	0	0	0	0.3	47	N/A	3,000,000	0	0.0	0.0
U /	N/A	N/A	1.00	N/A	100	0	0	0	0	0	0.1	40	N/A	0	0	0.0	0.0
U /	N/A	N/A	1.00	2	100	0	0	0	0	0	0.1	40	N/A	0	0	0.0	0.0
U /	N/A	N/A	1.00	245	100	0	0	0	0	0	0.1	40	N/A	0	0	0.0	0.0
A+ / 9.9	0.1	N/A	1.00	1	100	0	0	0	0	0	0.3	N/A	N/A	5,000	0	0.0	0.0
A+ / 9.9	0.1	N/A	1.00	2,569	100	0	0	0	0	0	0.5	50	N/A	3,000,000	0	0.0	0.0
U /	N/A	N/A	1.00	N/A	100	0	0	0	0	0	0.0	40	N/A	5,000	0	0.0	0.0
U /	N/A	N/A	1.00	N/A	100	0	0	0	0	0	0.0	39	N/A	0	0	0.0	0.0
U /	N/A	N/A	1.00	6	100	0	0	0	0	0	0.0	40	N/A	0	0	0.0	0.0
U /	N/A	N/A	1.00	N/A	100	0	0	0	0	0	0.3	N/A	N/A	5,000	0	0.0	0.0
A+ / 9.9	0.1	N/A	1.00	19	100	0	0	0	0	0	0.5	50	N/A	3,000,000	0	0.0	0.0
U /	N/A	N/A	1.00	N/A	100	0	0	0	0	0	0.2	42	N/A	0	0	0.0	0.0
U /	N/A	N/A	1.00	N/A	100	0	0	0	0	0	0.2	42	N/A	0	0	0.0	0.0
A+ / 9.9	0.1	N/A	1.00	15	100	0	0	0	0	0	0.4	50	N/A	5,000	0	0.0	0.0
A+ / 9.9	0.1	N/A	1.00	4	100	0	0	0	0	0	0.2	43	N/A	5,000	0	0.0	0.0
A+ / 9.9	N/A	N/A	1.00	805	100	0	0	0	0	0	0.1	42	N/A	5,000	0	0.0	0.0
A+ / 9.9	0.1	N/A	1.00	98	100	0	0	0	0	0	0.3	46	N/A	5,000	0	0.0	0.0
A+ / 9.9	0.1	N/A	1.00	12,271	100	0	0	0	0	0	0.6	53	N/A	3,000,000	0	0.0	0.0
A+ / 9.9	N/A	N/A	1.00	N/A	100	0	0	0	0	0	0.0	40	N/A	0	0	0.0	0.0
A+ / 9.9	N/A	N/A	1.00	2	100	0	0	0	0	0	0.1	41	N/A	0	0	0.0	0.0
A+ / 9.9	N/A	N/A	1.00	N/A	100	0	0	0	0	0	0.0	40	N/A	0	0	0.0	0.0
A+ / 9.9	N/A	N/A	1.00	431	100	0	0	0	0	0	0.2	42	N/A	5,000	0	0.0	0.0
A+ / 9.9	N/A	N/A	1.00	463	100	0	0	0	0	0	0.1	40	N/A	5,000	0	0.0	0.0
A+ / 9.9	N/A	N/A	1.00	20,904	100	0	0	0	0	0	0.2	44	N/A	3,000,000	0	0.0	0.0
A / 9.5	0.8	2.0	9.63	2,978	0	23	0	28	49	316	2.6	71	9	2,000,000	0	0.0	0.0
A / 9.5	0.8	2.0	9.62	887	0	23	0	28	49	316	2.6	64	9	1,000	50	2.3	0.0
A / 9.5	0.8	2.0	9.63	11	0	23	0	28	49	316	2.6	68	9	0	0	1.0	0.0
A / 9.5	0.8	2.0	9.62	335	0	23	0	28	49	316	2.6	28	9	1,000	50	0.0	0.0
A / 9.5	0.8	2.0	9.62	6	0	23	0	28	49	316	2.6	58	9	0	0	0.0	0.0
A / 9.5	0.8	2.0	9.62	16	0	23	0	28	49	316	2.6	29	9	0	0	0.0	0.0
A+ / 9.6	0.8	2.0	9.62	749	0	23	0	28	49	316	2.6	72	9	5,000,000	0	0.0	0.0
A / 9.5	0.8	2.0	9.62	5	0	23	0	28	49	316	2.6	55	9	100	0	0.0	0.0
A / 9.5	0.8	2.0	9.62	57	0	23	0	28	49	316	2.6	63	9	5,000	0	0.0	0.0
C / 4.6	3.3	6.7	10.02	32	3	16	1	74	6	67	4.1	87	8	2,000,000	0	0.0	0.0
C / 4.6	3.3	6.7	10.02	48	3	16	1	74	6	67	4.1	84	8	1,000	50	0.0	0.0
C / 4.7	3.2	6.7	10.05	55	3	16	1	74	6	67	4.1	87	8	5,000,000	0	0.0	0.0
B- / 7.1	2.7	N/A	10.77	538	0	0	99	0	1	83	0.0	75	21	5,000,000	0	0.0	0.0
B- / 7.0	2.7	N/A	10.77	2,955	0	0	99	0	1	83	0.0	72	21	2,000,000	0	0.0	0.0
B- / 7.0	2.7	N/A	10.78	2,327	0	0	99	0	1	83	0.0	68	21	1,000	50	4.3	0.0
C+ / 6.9	2.7	N/A	10.76	1	0	0	99	0	1	83	0.0	51	21	0	0	0.0	0.0
B- / 7.0	2.7	N/A	10.78	426	0	0	99	0	1	83	0.0	36	21	1,000	50	0.0	0.0
B- / 7.2	2.7	N/A	10.77	55	0	0	99	0	1	83	0.0	53	21	0	0	0.0	0.0
B- / 7.1	2.7	N/A	10.76	3	0	0	99	0	1	83	0.0	69	21	5,000	0	0.0	0.0
D+ / 2.9	4.1	N/A	10.87	132	0	0	99	0	1	7	3.7	28	11	2,000,000	0	0.0	0.0
C- / 3.0	4.1	N/A	10.88	79	0	0	99	0	1	7	3.7	25	11	1,000	50	4.3	0.0
C- / 3.0	4.1	N/A	10.88	23	0	0	99	0	1	7	3.7	29	11	0	0	0.0	0.0
C- / 3.1	4.1	N/A	10.87	31	0	0	99	0	1	7	3.7	9	11	1,000	50	0.0	0.0

Fund Type	Fund Name	Ticker Symbol	Overall Investment Rating	Phone	Performance Rating/Pts	3 Mo	6 Mo	1Yr / Pct	3Yr / Pct	5Yr / Pct	Dividend Yield	Expense Ratio
MUS	BlackRock NJ Muni Bond Inv C1	MCNJX	C	(800) 441-7762	B- / 7.3	1.90	-4.38	-0.15 / 15	3.42 / 87	2.83 / 77	3.02	1.32
MUS	BlackRock NJ Muni Bond Svc	MSNJX	C+	(800) 441-7762	B / 7.9	1.98	-4.21	0.13 / 26	3.81 / 91	3.21 / 83	3.41	1.05
MUS	BlackRock NY Muni Oppty Inst	MANKX	A	(800) 441-7762	A+ / 9.6	2.61	-3.04	2.24 / 59	5.29 / 98	4.00 / 93	3.18	0.76
MUS	BlackRock NY Muni Oppty Inv A	MENKX	B	(800) 441-7762	B+ / 8.4	2.64	-3.16	2.08 / 58	5.04 / 97	3.75 / 91	2.80	1.01
MUS ●	BlackRock NY Muni Oppty Inv A1	MDNKX	B	(800) 441-7762	B+ / 8.7	2.68	-3.09	2.22 / 59	5.16 / 97	3.89 / 92	2.94	0.86
MUS	BlackRock NY Muni Oppty Inv C	MFNKX	B+	(800) 441-7762	B+ / 8.8	2.45	-3.44	1.32 / 49	4.29 / 95	3.00 / 80	2.16	1.76
MUS ●	BlackRock NY Muni Oppty Inv C1	MCNKX	A-	(800) 441-7762	A- / 9.2	2.55	-3.33	1.72 / 54	4.65 / 96	3.40 / 86	2.57	1.35
MUS	BlackRock PA Muni Bond Inst	MAPYX	A	(800) 441-7762	B+ / 8.9	2.18	-3.24	0.70 / 40	4.50 / 96	3.37 / 86	4.11	0.87
MUS	BlackRock PA Muni Bond Inv A	MEPYX	C+	(800) 441-7762	B- / 7.0	2.12	-3.34	0.50 / 37	4.30 / 95	3.18 / 83	3.73	1.04
MUS ●	BlackRock PA Muni Bond Inv A1	MDPYX	A	(800) 441-7762	B+ / 8.9	2.07	-3.27	0.57 / 38	4.47 / 96	3.35 / 85	4.06	0.87
MUS	BlackRock PA Muni Bond Inv C	MFPYX	B-	(800) 441-7762	B- / 7.4	1.93	-3.71	-0.27 / 13	3.50 / 88	2.38 / 68	3.11	1.76
MUS ●	BlackRock PA Muni Bond Inv C1	MCPYX	B+	(800) 441-7762	B / 8.1	2.03	-3.52	0.13 / 26	3.92 / 92	2.80 / 76	3.52	1.36
MUS	BlackRock PA Muni Bond Svc	MSPYX	A-	(800) 441-7762	B+ / 8.7	2.03	-3.34	0.50 / 37	4.33 / 95	3.20 / 83	3.90	1.12
MMT	BlackRock Select Treasury Str Inst	MLSXX	C-	(800) 441-7762	D- / 1.2	0.11	0.15	0.23 / 27	0.12 / 14	0.12 / 16	0.23	N/A
GEI	BlackRock Short Obligations Inst	BISOX	B-	(800) 441-7762	D+ / 2.5	0.41	0.68	1.45 / 44	0.79 / 24	---	1.00	0.58
COI	BlackRock Short Obligations K	BBSOX	B-	(800) 441-7762	D+ / 2.6	0.32	0.70	1.49 / 44	0.86 / 25	---	1.04	0.99
MUN	BlackRock Short Term Muni Inst	MALMX	C	(800) 441-7762	D / 2.0	0.91	-0.14	0.09 / 23	0.34 / 21	0.42 / 23	0.54	0.52
MUN	BlackRock Short Term Muni Inv A	MELMX	D	(800) 441-7762	E- / 0.2	0.95	-0.17	-0.18 / 15	0.06 / 12	0.17 / 19	0.26	0.71
MUN●	BlackRock Short Term Muni Inv A1	MDLMX	C	(800) 441-7762	D / 1.7	0.89	-0.19	-0.02 / 17	0.22 / 19	0.32 / 21	0.43	0.55
MUN	BlackRock Short Term Muni Inv C	MFLMX	D	(800) 441-7762	E- / 0.2	0.65	-0.56	-0.96 / 4	-0.72 / 3	-0.63 / 3	0.00	1.48
MUN	BlackRock Short-Term Muni K	MPLMX	C	(800) 441-7762	D / 2.0	0.92	-0.12	0.10 / 24	0.34 / 21	0.42 / 23	0.55	0.42
GEI	BlackRock ST Inf Prot Sec Idx Inst	BIIPX	U	(800) 441-7762	U /	0.83	0.97	2.39 / 52	---	---	1.86	N/A
GEI	BlackRock ST Inf Prot Sec Idx Inv A	BAIPX	U	(800) 441-7762	U /	0.70	0.81	2.08 / 50	---	---	1.66	N/A
GEI	BlackRock ST Inf Prot Sec Idx K	BKIPX	U	(800) 441-7762	U /	0.73	0.88	2.33 / 52	---	---	1.90	N/A
MUN	BlackRock Strat Muni Opps Instl	MAMTX	A-	(800) 441-7762	B+ / 8.6	2.95	-2.84	1.83 / 55	3.88 / 92	3.52 / 88	2.57	0.73
*MUN	BlackRock Strat Muni Opps Inv A	MEMTX	C	(800) 441-7762	C+ / 6.3	2.81	-2.94	1.53 / 52	3.62 / 89	3.28 / 84	2.26	0.95
MUN●	BlackRock Strat Muni Opps Inv A1	MDMTX	B+	(800) 441-7762	B+ / 8.4	2.84	-2.88	1.67 / 54	3.76 / 90	3.41 / 86	2.50	0.80
MUN	BlackRock Strat Muni Opps Inv C	MFMTX	C+	(800) 441-7762	B- / 7.0	2.71	-3.31	0.84 / 43	2.86 / 80	2.50 / 70	1.58	1.71
GL	BlackRock Strategic Global Bd Inst	MAWIX	E+	(800) 441-7762	C- / 3.6	2.52	-2.10	5.58 / 69	1.01 / 28	2.32 / 46	2.71	1.17
GL	BlackRock Strategic Global Bd Inv A	MDWIX	E	(800) 441-7762	D- / 1.5	2.28	-2.39	5.32 / 68	0.77 / 24	2.09 / 43	2.36	1.41
GL	BlackRock Strategic Global Bd Inv C	MHWIX	E	(800) 441-7762	D / 1.9	2.10	-2.75	4.53 / 65	0.01 / 5	1.31 / 32	1.70	2.23
GL	BlackRock Strategic Global Bd K	MKWIX	U	(800) 441-7762	U /	2.36	-2.24	5.45 / 68	---	---	2.76	1.03
GL ●	BlackRock Strategic Global Bond C1	MCWIX	E	(800) 441-7762	D / 2.2	2.32	-2.49	4.74 / 66	0.21 / 17	1.46 / 34	1.90	1.95
GEI	BlackRock Total Return Inst	MAHQX	B	(800) 441-7762	C+ / 6.3	1.50	-1.20	2.91 / 56	3.40 / 67	4.03 / 73	2.81	0.55
*GEI	BlackRock Total Return Inv A	MDHQX	D+	(800) 441-7762	C- / 4.1	1.42	-1.45	2.56 / 53	3.08 / 62	3.69 / 68	2.37	0.86
GEI ●	BlackRock Total Return Inv A1	MEHQX	B-	(800) 441-7762	C+ / 6.1	1.38	-1.36	2.75 / 55	3.27 / 65	3.89 / 71	2.66	0.66
GEI ●	BlackRock Total Return Inv B	MBHQX	C	(800) 441-7762	C / 4.9	1.21	-1.68	2.12 / 50	2.58 / 53	3.07 / 59	2.04	1.54
GEI	BlackRock Total Return Inv C	MFHQX	C-	(800) 441-7762	C / 4.6	1.25	-1.77	1.89 / 48	2.40 / 50	3.02 / 58	1.80	1.59
GEI ●	BlackRock Total Return Inv C1	MCHQX	C	(800) 441-7762	C / 4.8	1.27	-1.64	1.99 / 49	2.49 / 51	3.12 / 60	1.90	1.43
GEI ●	BlackRock Total Return Inv C2	MHHQX	C+	(800) 441-7762	C / 5.3	1.35	-1.57	2.31 / 52	2.81 / 58	3.39 / 64	2.22	1.15
GEI	BlackRock Total Return K	MPHQX	B+	(800) 441-7762	C+ / 6.3	1.43	-1.25	2.97 / 56	3.45 / 68	4.11 / 74	2.87	0.45
GEI	BlackRock Total Return R	MRCBX	C+	(800) 441-7762	C / 5.3	1.35	-1.57	2.30 / 51	2.81 / 58	3.43 / 64	2.22	1.13
GEI	BlackRock Total Return Service	MSHQX	B-	(800) 441-7762	C+ / 5.9	1.43	-1.43	2.59 / 54	3.14 / 63	3.76 / 69	2.50	0.79
USS	BlackRock US Govt Bond Inst	PNIGX	C+	(800) 441-7762	C- / 3.8	0.59	-1.87	0.05 / 20	2.13 / 45	1.69 / 37	2.08	0.92
USS	BlackRock US Govt Bond Inv A	CIGAX	D	(800) 441-7762	D / 1.7	0.52	-2.08	-0.24 / 14	1.83 / 40	1.37 / 33	1.70	1.10
USS	BlackRock US Govt Bond Inv B1	BIGEX	D+	(800) 441-7762	D+ / 2.4	0.30	-2.33	-0.74 / 6	1.28 / 32	0.85 / 25	1.27	2.00
USS	BlackRock US Govt Bond Inv C	BIGCX	D	(800) 441-7762	D / 2.0	0.34	-2.36	-1.00 / 4	1.03 / 28	0.58 / 22	1.00	1.91
USS ●	BlackRock US Govt Bond Inv C1	BIGHX	D	(800) 441-7762	D / 2.2	0.29	-2.36	-0.81 / 6	1.19 / 31	0.76 / 24	1.20	1.74
USS	BlackRock US Govt Bond R	BGBRX	C-	(800) 441-7762	D+ / 2.8	0.46	-2.21	-0.50 / 9	1.54 / 35	1.08 / 28	1.51	1.41
USS	BlackRock US Govt Bond Svc	PIGSX	C	(800) 441-7762	C- / 3.4	0.52	-2.08	-0.16 / 15	1.93 / 42	1.49 / 34	1.86	1.14
GEI	BlackRock US Total Bond Index Fund	WFBIX	C-	(800) 441-7762	C / 4.6	0.95	-2.33	1.24 / 42	2.53 / 52	2.05 / 43	2.17	0.09
GEI	BlackRock US Total Bond Index Inst	BMOIX	C-	(800) 441-7762	C / 4.5	0.93	-2.26	1.20 / 42	2.48 / 51	2.00 / 42	2.12	0.15

● Denotes fund is closed to new investors
* Denotes fund is included in Section II

RISK			NET ASSETS		ASSET							FUND MANAGER		MINIMUM		LOADS	
Risk Rating/Pts	3 Yr Avg Standard Deviation	Avg Dura-tion	NAV As of 2/28/17	Total $(Mil)	Cash %	Gov. Bond %	Muni. Bond %	Corp. Bond %	Other %	Portfolio Turnover Ratio	Avg Coupon Rate	Manager Quality Pct	Manager Tenure (Years)	Initial Purch. $	Additional Purch. $	Front End Load	Back End Load
D+ / 2.9	4.1	N/A	10.87	7	0	0	99	0	1	7	3.7	15	11	0	0	0.0	0.0
D+ / 2.9	4.1	N/A	10.87	9	0	0	99	0	1	7	3.7	24	11	5,000	0	0.0	0.0
C- / 3.2	4.0	6.4	11.02	211	0	0	98	0	2	20	4.8	79	11	2,000,000	0	0.0	0.0
C- / 3.1	4.0	6.4	11.03	250	0	0	98	0	2	20	4.8	74	11	1,000	50	4.3	0.0
C- / 3.2	4.0	6.4	11.03	114	0	0	98	0	2	20	4.8	76	11	0	0	4.0	0.0
C- / 3.2	4.0	6.4	11.03	85	0	0	98	0	2	20	4.8	55	11	1,000	50	0.0	0.0
C- / 3.1	4.0	6.4	11.03	6	0	0	98	0	2	20	4.8	65	11	0	0	0.0	0.0
C- / 4.0	3.5	N/A	11.07	295	0	0	99	0	1	19	5.1	72	11	2,000,000	0	0.0	0.0
C- / 4.0	3.5	N/A	11.08	94	0	0	99	0	1	19	5.1	68	11	1,000	50	4.3	0.0
C- / 4.1	3.5	N/A	11.08	15	0	0	99	0	1	19	5.1	72	11	0	0	0.0	0.0
C- / 4.0	3.5	N/A	11.08	34	0	0	99	0	1	19	5.1	33	11	1,000	50	0.0	0.0
C- / 4.0	3.5	N/A	11.07	4	0	0	99	0	1	19	5.1	57	11	0	0	0.0	0.0
C- / 4.1	3.5	N/A	11.08	1	0	0	99	0	1	19	5.1	69	11	5,000	0	0.0	0.0
A+ / 9.9	N/A	N/A	1.00	590	100	0	0	0	0	0	0.2	48	N/A	10,000,000	1,000	0.0	0.0
A+ / 9.9	0.2	N/A	10.03	48	26	0	0	49	25	184	0.0	68	5	2,000,000	0	0.0	0.0
A+ / 9.9	0.2	N/A	10.04	30	26	0	0	49	25	184	0.0	69	5	5,000,000	0	0.0	0.0
A+ / 9.6	0.8	1.7	10.13	401	0	0	99	0	1	67	4.4	27	10	2,000,000	0	0.0	0.0
A / 9.5	0.8	1.7	10.14	91	0	0	99	0	1	67	4.4	18	10	1,000	50	3.0	0.0
A / 9.5	0.8	1.7	10.14	21	0	0	99	0	1	67	4.4	23	10	0	0	0.0	0.0
A+ / 9.6	0.8	1.7	9.88	28	0	0	99	0	1	67	4.4	7	10	1,000	50	0.0	0.0
A / 9.5	0.8	1.7	10.13	3	0	0	99	0	1	67	4.4	28	10	5,000,000	0	0.0	0.0
U /	N/A	N/A	10.10	1	0	0	0	0	100	0	0.0	N/A	N/A	5,000,000	0	0.0	0.0
U /	N/A	N/A	10.09	N/A	0	0	0	0	100	0	0.0	N/A	N/A	1,000	50	0.0	0.0
U /	N/A	N/A	10.09	11	0	0	0	0	100	0	0.0	N/A	N/A	5,000,000	0	0.0	0.0
C- / 4.0	3.5	N/A	11.31	3,179	0	0	97	1	2	174	4.4	61	11	2,000,000	0	0.0	0.0
C- / 4.0	3.5	N/A	11.30	1,091	0	0	97	1	2	174	4.4	52	11	1,000	50	4.3	0.0
C- / 4.0	3.5	N/A	11.30	31	0	0	97	1	2	174	4.4	57	11	0	0	0.0	0.0
C- / 3.9	3.5	N/A	11.31	260	0	0	97	1	2	174	4.4	19	11	1,000	50	0.0	0.0
D+ / 2.6	4.4	6.0	5.89	84	0	56	1	33	10	477	4.4	87	6	2,000,000	0	0.0	0.0
D+ / 2.6	4.4	6.0	5.88	63	0	56	1	33	10	477	4.4	86	6	1,000	50	4.0	0.0
D+ / 2.6	4.4	6.0	5.88	13	0	56	1	33	10	477	4.4	79	6	1,000	50	0.0	0.0
U /	N/A	6.0	5.88	16	0	56	1	33	10	477	4.4	N/A	6	5,000,000	0	0.0	0.0
D+ / 2.6	4.4	6.0	5.88	3	0	56	1	33	10	477	4.4	81	6	0	0	0.0	0.0
C+ / 6.0	2.9	4.9	11.66	3,370	0	28	4	24	44	841	2.8	72	7	2,000,000	0	0.0	0.0
C+ / 5.7	3.0	4.9	11.66	2,029	0	28	4	24	44	841	2.8	63	7	1,000	50	4.0	0.0
C+ / 5.8	3.0	4.9	11.65	32	0	28	4	24	44	841	2.8	69	7	0	0	0.0	0.0
C+ / 5.8	3.0	4.9	11.65	2	0	28	4	24	44	841	2.8	43	7	0	0	0.0	0.0
C+ / 5.7	3.0	4.9	11.65	444	0	28	4	24	44	841	2.8	32	7	1,000	50	0.0	0.0
C+ / 6.1	2.9	4.9	11.66	59	0	28	4	24	44	841	2.8	37	7	0	0	0.0	0.0
C+ / 5.9	2.9	4.9	11.65	4	0	28	4	24	44	841	2.8	56	7	0	0	0.0	0.0
C+ / 6.1	2.9	4.9	11.65	2,995	0	28	4	24	44	841	2.8	74	7	5,000,000	0	0.0	0.0
C+ / 5.8	3.0	4.9	11.66	124	0	28	4	24	44	841	2.8	55	7	100	0	0.0	0.0
C+ / 5.9	2.9	4.9	11.66	114	0	28	4	24	44	841	2.8	66	7	5,000	0	0.0	0.0
B / 7.7	2.4	4.3	10.43	152	0	47	0	8	45	929	1.6	69	N/A	2,000,000	0	0.0	0.0
B / 7.6	2.5	4.3	10.45	421	0	47	0	8	45	929	1.6	60	N/A	1,000	50	4.0	0.0
B / 7.7	2.4	4.3	10.41	N/A	0	47	0	8	45	929	1.6	33	N/A	0	0	0.0	0.0
B / 7.7	2.4	4.3	10.44	46	0	47	0	8	45	929	1.6	25	N/A	1,000	50	0.0	0.0
B / 7.7	2.4	4.3	10.43	50	0	47	0	8	45	929	1.6	30	N/A	0	0	0.0	0.0
B / 7.7	2.4	4.3	10.45	23	0	47	0	8	45	929	1.6	51	N/A	100	0	0.0	0.0
B / 7.7	2.4	4.3	10.42	5	0	47	0	8	45	929	1.6	64	N/A	5,000	0	0.0	0.0
C+ / 5.8	3.0	N/A	10.07	478	0	43	1	24	32	356	0.0	35	8	1	1	0.0	0.0
C+ / 5.8	3.0	N/A	10.07	115	0	43	1	24	32	356	0.0	33	8	2,000,000	0	0.0	0.0

I. Index of Bond and Money Market Mutual Funds

						PERFORMANCE					Incl. in Returns	
						Perfor-mance Rating/Pts	Total Return % through 2/28/17			Annualized	Dividend	Expense
Fund Type	Fund Name	Ticker Symbol	Overall Investment Rating	Phone			3 Mo	6 Mo	1Yr / Pct	3Yr / Pct	5Yr / Pct	Yield	Ratio
GEI	BlackRock US Total Bond Index Inv A	BMOAX	D+	(800) 441-7762		C- / 4.0	0.88	-2.47	0.86 /38	2.21 /47	1.73 /38	1.88	0.40
MMT	BlackRock-Lq Federal Tr Admin	BFTXX	D+	(800) 441-7762		E+ / 0.9	0.07	0.10	0.14 /24	0.06 /10	0.04 /10	0.14	N/A
MMT	BlackRock-Lq Federal Tr Dollar	TSDXX	D+	(800) 441-7762		E+ / 0.6	0.03	0.03	0.03 /19	0.02 / 7	0.02 / 7	0.03	N/A
MMT	BlackRock-Lq Federal Tr Instl	TFFXX	C-	(800) 441-7762		D- / 1.1	0.09	0.15	0.25 /27	0.10 /13	0.06 /12	0.25	N/A
MMT	BlackRock-Lq TempCash Dollar	TCDXX	D+	(800) 441-7762		E+ / 0.9	0.06	0.09	0.14 /24	0.06 /10	0.05 /11	0.14	N/A
MMT	BlackRock-Lq TempCash Instl	TMCXX	C	(800) 441-7762		D- / 1.4	0.12	0.21	0.39 /31	0.19 /16	0.16 /17	0.39	N/A
MMT	BlackRock-Lq T-Fund Instl	TSTXX	C-	(800) 441-7762		D- / 1.1	0.09	0.15	0.25 /27	0.10 /13	0.07 /13	0.25	N/A
MMT	BlackRock-Money Market Prtfl Instl	PNIXX	C	(800) 441-7762		D / 1.6	0.22	0.37	0.58 /35	0.23 /17	0.14 /16	0.58	N/A
MMT	BlackRock-Money Market Prtf Inv A	PINXX	C-	(800) 441-7762		D- / 1.1	0.13	0.19	0.25 /27	0.10 /13	0.06 /12	0.25	N/A
MMT ●	BlackRock-Money Market Prtf Inv B	CIBXX	C-	(800) 441-7762		E+ / 0.9	0.05	0.10	0.16 /24	0.07 /11	0.04 /10	0.16	N/A
MMT ●	BlackRock-Money Market Prtf Inv C	BMCXX	D+	(800) 441-7762		E+ / 0.9	0.03	0.05	0.12 /23	0.07 /11	0.04 /10	0.12	N/A
MMT	BlackRock-Money Market Prtf Svc	PNPXX	C-	(800) 441-7762		D- / 1.2	0.14	0.22	0.30 /29	0.12 /14	0.07 /13	0.30	N/A
MMT	BMO Govt Money Market Y	MGYXX	D+	(800) 236-3863		E+ / 0.6	0.02	0.02	0.03 /19	0.02 / 7	0.01 / 5	0.03	N/A
MUN	BMO Intermediate Tax Free A	BITAX	B-	(800) 236-3863		C / 4.8	1.70	-2.46	0.10 /24	2.91 /80	2.60 /72	2.32	0.58
MUN	BMO Intermediate Tax Free I	MIITX	A+	(800) 236-3863		B- / 7.3	1.76	-2.26	0.34 /33	3.16 /84	2.93 /79	2.64	0.33
MUN	BMO Intermediate Tax Free Y	MITFX	A+	(800) 236-3863		C+ / 6.9	1.70	-2.46	0.10 /24	2.93 /81	2.72 /75	2.40	0.58
COH	BMO Monegy High Yield Bond A	BMHAX	D+	(800) 236-3863		B- / 7.1	4.08	3.76	13.75 /86	2.96 /60	4.69 /81	4.91	1.22
GL	BMO Monegy High Yield Bond I	MHBNX	C+	(800) 236-3863		B+ / 8.4	4.14	3.89	14.02 /87	3.26 /65	5.06 /85	5.31	0.97
MTG	BMO Mortgage Income A	BMTAX	C-	(800) 236-3863		D+ / 2.8	0.37	-1.52	0.71 /36	2.36 /49	1.76 /38	2.71	0.86
USS	BMO Mortgage Income I	MGIIX	B+	(800) 236-3863		C / 4.7	0.43	-1.40	0.95 /39	2.60 /54	2.13 /44	3.06	0.61
USS	BMO Mortgage Income Y	MRGIX	B	(800) 236-3863		C- / 4.2	0.37	-1.52	0.70 /36	2.38 /50	1.88 /40	2.81	0.86
MMT	BMO Prime Money Market Premier	MAIXX	C-	(800) 236-3863		D- / 1.3	0.13	0.23	0.37 /30	0.15 /15	0.13 /16	0.37	N/A
MMT	BMO Prime Money Market Y	MARXX	D+	(800) 236-3863		E+ / 0.8	0.07	0.10	0.13 /23	0.05 / 9	0.03 / 9	0.13	N/A
MUN	BMO Short Tax Free Y	MTFYX	B+	(800) 236-3863		C- / 4.0	0.93	-0.34	0.25 /31	1.30 /43	--	1.11	0.78
MUN	BMO Short Term Tax Free A	BASFX	C+	(800) 236-3863		D+ / 2.6	0.93	-0.34	0.25 /31	1.28 /42	--	1.09	0.78
MUN	BMO Short Term Tax Free I	MTFIX	A-	(800) 236-3863		C / 4.5	1.07	-0.27	0.50 /37	1.48 /48	--	1.26	0.53
COI	BMO Short-Term Income A	BTMAX	C	(800) 236-3863		D / 2.0	0.49	0.32	1.67 /46	0.97 /27	1.14 /29	1.32	0.72
GEI	BMO Short-Term Income I	MSIFX	B	(800) 236-3863		C- / 3.3	0.55	0.44	1.93 /48	1.25 /31	1.55 /35	1.59	0.47
GEI	BMO Short-Term Income Y	MSINX	B-	(800) 236-3863		D+ / 2.8	0.49	0.32	1.67 /46	0.99 /27	1.25 /31	1.34	0.72
MMF	BMO T/F Money Market Premier	MFIXX	C	(800) 236-3863		D / 1.7	0.13	0.29	0.43 /36	0.17 /18	0.15 /19	0.43	N/A
COI	BMO TCH Core Plus Bond A	BATCX	D	(800) 236-3863		C / 5.3	1.70	-0.85	7.32 /73	3.03 /61	3.46 /65	2.61	0.60
GEI	BMO TCH Core Plus Bond I	MCBIX	C+	(800) 236-3863		B- / 7.0	1.76	-0.72	7.59 /73	3.31 /66	3.82 /70	2.95	0.35
GEI	BMO TCH Core Plus Bond Y	MCYBX	C	(800) 236-3863		C+ / 6.7	1.70	-0.85	7.32 /73	3.06 /62	3.58 /67	2.70	0.60
COI	BMO TCH Corporate Income A	BATIX	C+	(800) 236-3863		B / 8.2	2.90	0.64	15.31 /89	4.45 /80	4.78 /82	2.99	0.73
COI	BMO TCH Corporate Income I	MCIIX	B-	(800) 236-3863		A- / 9.1	2.93	0.70	15.46 /89	4.60 /80	5.02 /84	3.21	0.48
COI	BMO TCH Corporate Income Y	MCIYX	B-	(800) 236-3863		A- / 9.0	2.90	0.64	15.31 /89	4.47 /80	4.90 /83	3.10	0.73
EM	BMO TCH Emerging Markets Bond A	BAMEX	D	(800) 236-3863		B / 7.6	4.08	0.39	14.35 /87	4.38 /79	--	0.00	2.84
EM	BMO TCH Emerging Markets Bond I	MEBIX	C-	(800) 236-3863		B+ / 8.6	4.08	0.40	14.34 /87	4.51 /81	--	3.14	2.59
COI	BMO TCH Intermediate Income A	BAIIX	C-	(800) 236-3863		C / 4.6	1.21	0.06	7.63 /74	2.43 /50	2.25 /45	2.05	0.87
GEI	BMO TCH Intermediate Income I	MIBIX	B	(800) 236-3863		C+ / 6.5	1.28	0.27	8.01 /74	2.71 /56	2.62 /51	2.38	0.62
MUN	BMO Ultra Sht Tax-Free A	BAUSX	D+	(800) 236-3863		E / 0.5	0.37	0.32	0.57 /38	0.46 /23	0.51 /25	0.55	0.64
MUN	BMO Ultra Sht Tax-Free I	MUISX	B	(800) 236-3863		C- / 3.1	0.43	0.55	0.92 /44	0.77 /30	0.87 /32	0.81	0.39
MUN	BMO Ultra Sht Tax-Free Y	MUYSX	C+	(800) 236-3863		D+ / 2.3	0.37	0.32	0.57 /38	0.48 /24	0.62 /27	0.56	0.64
GEI	BNY Mellon Bond Inv	MIBDX	C	(800) 645-6561		C- / 4.0	1.13	-1.97	1.71 /46	2.02 /43	1.84 /39	2.61	0.81
* GEI	BNY Mellon Bond M	MPBFX	C+	(800) 645-6561		C / 4.4	1.11	-1.92	1.90 /48	2.25 /47	2.09 /43	2.88	0.56
GEI	BNY Mellon Corporate Bond Inv	BYMIX	B+	(800) 645-6561		C+ / 6.9	2.09	-0.13	6.48 /72	3.31 /66	--	3.37	0.81
GEI	BNY Mellon Corporate Bond M	BYMMX	A-	(800) 645-6561		B- / 7.2	2.14	0.07	6.74 /72	3.60 /70	--	3.61	0.56
MMT	BNY Mellon Government Mny Mkt Inv	MLOXX	U	(800) 645-6561		U /	--	--	--	--	--	0.01	N/A
MMT	BNY Mellon Government Mny Mkt M	MLMXX	D+	(800) 645-6561		E+ / 0.8	0.06	0.08	0.10 /22	0.04 / 9	0.02 / 7	0.10	N/A
GEI	BNY Mellon Inter Bond Inv	MIIDX	C+	(800) 645-6561		D+ / 2.9	0.83	-0.79	1.49 /44	1.13 /29	1.07 /28	1.81	0.81
* GEI	BNY Mellon Inter Bond M	MPIBX	C+	(800) 645-6561		C- / 3.3	0.82	-0.73	1.76 /47	1.37 /33	1.32 /32	2.08	0.56
MUS	BNY Mellon MA Inter Mun Bd Inv	MMBIX	C-	(800) 645-6561		C / 4.4	2.08	-2.86	-0.64 / 8	1.77 /56	1.48 /46	2.12	0.79

● Denotes fund is closed to new investors
* Denotes fund is included in Section II

www.thestreetratings.com

Risk Rating/Pts	3 Yr Avg Standard Deviation	Avg Duration	NAV As of 2/28/17	Total $(Mil)	Cash %	Gov. Bond %	Muni. Bond %	Corp. Bond %	Other %	Portfolio Turnover Ratio	Avg Coupon Rate	Manager Quality Pct	Manager Tenure (Years)	Initial Purch. $	Additional Purch. $	Front End Load	Back End Load
C+ / 5.6	3.0	N/A	10.06	95	0	43	1	24	32	356	0.0	24	8	1,000	50	0.0	0.0
A+ / 9.9	N/A	N/A	1.00	41	100	0	0	0	0	0	0.1	42	N/A	5,000	0	0.0	0.0
A+ / 9.9	N/A	N/A	1.00	152	100	0	0	0	0	0	0.0	38	N/A	5,000	0	0.0	0.0
A+ / 9.9	N/A	N/A	1.00	3,163	100	0	0	0	0	0	0.3	45	N/A	3,000,000	0	0.0	0.0
A+ / 9.9	N/A	N/A	1.00	25	100	0	0	0	0	0	0.1	42	N/A	5,000	0	0.0	0.0
A+ / 9.9	N/A	N/A	1.00	154	100	0	0	0	0	0	0.4	51	N/A	3,000,000	0	0.0	0.0
A+ / 9.9	N/A	N/A	1.00	45,436	100	0	0	0	0	0	0.3	N/A	N/A	3,000,000	0	0.0	0.0
A+ / 9.9	0.1	N/A	1.00	582	100	0	0	0	0	0	0.6	52	9	2,000,000	0	0.0	0.0
A+ / 9.9	0.1	N/A	1.00	126	100	0	0	0	0	0	0.3	45	9	1,000	50	0.0	0.0
A+ / 9.9	N/A	N/A	1.00	N/A	100	0	0	0	0	0	0.2	43	9	1,000	50	0.0	0.0
A+ / 9.9	N/A	N/A	1.00	27	100	0	0	0	0	0	0.1	43	9	1,000	50	0.0	0.0
A+ / 9.9	0.1	N/A	1.00	6	100	0	0	0	0	0	0.3	46	9	5,000	0	0.0	0.0
A+ / 9.9	N/A	N/A	1.00	843	100	0	0	0	0	0	0.0	38	5	1,000	50	0.0	0.0
B- / 7.3	2.6	4.3	11.15	2	0	0	99	0	1	42	4.2	50	2	1,000	50	3.5	0.0
B- / 7.2	2.7	4.3	11.15	541	0	0	99	0	1	42	4.2	58	2	1,000,000	0	0.0	0.0
B- / 7.2	2.6	4.3	11.15	1,057	0	0	99	0	1	42	4.2	51	2	1,000	50	0.0	0.0
D / 2.0	4.5	4.2	9.59	31	2	0	0	97	1	51	6.3	22	6	1,000	50	3.5	0.0
D+ / 2.4	4.5	4.2	9.59	20	2	0	0	97	1	51	6.3	94	6	1,000,000	0	0.0	0.0
B / 8.1	2.1	2.8	9.16	N/A	1	2	0	0	97	13	3.9	35	N/A	1,000	50	3.5	0.0
B / 8.1	2.1	2.8	9.15	18	1	2	0	0	97	13	3.9	81	N/A	1,000,000	0	0.0	0.0
B / 8.1	2.1	2.8	9.16	75	1	2	0	0	97	13	3.9	78	N/A	1,000	50	0.0	0.0
A+ / 9.9	0.1	N/A	1.00	235	100	0	0	0	0	0	0.4	49	5	10,000,000	0	0.0	0.0
A+ / 9.9	N/A	N/A	1.00	221	100	0	0	0	0	0	0.1	41	5	1,000	50	0.0	0.0
A / 9.3	1.0	2.0	10.14	18	0	0	99	0	1	39	3.4	58	5	1,000	50	0.0	0.0
A / 9.3	1.0	2.0	10.14	2	0	0	99	0	1	39	3.4	57	5	1,000	50	2.0	0.0
A- / 9.2	1.1	2.0	10.15	162	0	0	99	0	1	39	3.4	61	5	1,000,000	0	0.0	0.0
A+ / 9.6	0.7	1.9	9.36	N/A	0	19	0	51	30	64	2.1	61	5	1,000	50	2.0	0.0
A+ / 9.7	0.7	1.9	9.38	191	0	19	0	51	30	64	2.1	68	5	1,000,000	0	0.0	0.0
A+ / 9.6	0.7	1.9	9.36	52	0	19	0	51	30	64	2.1	60	5	1,000	50	0.0	0.0
A+ / 9.9	0.1	N/A	1.00	299	100	0	0	0	0	0	0.4	50	2	10,000,000	0	0.0	0.0
C- / 4.0	3.5	4.3	11.61	2	2	18	0	43	37	39	3.6	51	9	1,000	50	3.5	0.0
C- / 4.0	3.5	4.3	11.61	480	2	18	0	43	37	39	3.6	73	9	1,000,000	0	0.0	0.0
C- / 4.0	3.5	4.3	11.61	501	2	18	0	43	37	39	3.6	67	9	1,000	50	0.0	0.0
D / 2.1	4.9	5.2	12.96	1	2	8	0	88	2	62	4.0	74	9	1,000	50	3.5	0.0
D / 2.1	4.9	5.2	12.94	122	2	8	0	88	2	62	4.0	76	9	1,000,000	0	0.0	0.0
D / 2.1	4.9	5.2	12.96	110	2	8	0	88	2	62	4.0	74	9	1,000	50	0.0	0.0
E+ / 0.7	7.0	6.0	10.20	N/A	3	39	0	56	2	44	5.3	97	4	1,000	50	3.5	2.0
E+ / 0.7	7.0	6.0	9.89	13	3	39	0	56	2	44	5.3	97	4	1,000,000	0	0.0	2.0
C+ / 5.9	2.9	2.5	10.62	19	0	18	0	54	28	50	3.3	56	4	1,000	50	3.5	0.0
C+ / 5.7	3.0	2.5	10.61	58	0	18	0	54	28	50	3.3	75	4	1,000,000	0	0.0	0.0
A+ / 9.9	0.2	0.4	10.07	1	0	0	99	0	1	56	2.0	56	2	1,000	50	2.0	0.0
A+ / 9.9	0.2	0.4	10.07	558	0	0	99	0	1	56	2.0	66	2	1,000,000	0	0.0	0.0
A+ / 9.9	0.2	0.4	10.07	46	0	0	99	0	1	56	2.0	56	2	1,000	50	0.0	0.0
B- / 7.1	2.7	5.1	12.63	9	0	17	7	44	32	72	0.0	28	12	10,000	100	0.0	0.0
B- / 7.1	2.7	5.1	12.65	992	0	17	7	44	32	72	0.0	36	12	10,000	100	0.0	0.0
C+ / 5.9	2.9	5.1	12.83	2	0	3	6	89	2	35	0.0	75	5	10,000	100	0.0	0.0
C+ / 5.9	2.9	5.1	12.84	778	0	3	6	89	2	35	0.0	79	5	10,000	100	0.0	0.0
U /	N/A	N/A	1.00	14	100	0	0	0	0	0	0.0	N/A	N/A	10,000	100	0.0	0.0
A+ / 9.9	N/A	N/A	1.00	735	100	0	0	0	0	0	0.1	40	N/A	10,000	100	0.0	0.0
B+ / 8.7	1.7	3.2	12.53	6	0	40	5	53	2	33	0.0	28	11	10,000	100	0.0	0.0
B+ / 8.7	1.6	3.2	12.52	851	0	40	5	53	2	33	0.0	37	11	10,000	100	0.0	0.0
C+ / 5.6	3.0	4.6	12.51	11	0	0	99	0	1	29	0.0	6	11	10,000	100	0.0	0.0

Fund Type	Fund Name	Ticker Symbol	Overall Investment Rating	Phone	Performance Rating/Pts	3 Mo	6 Mo	1Yr / Pct	3Yr / Pct	5Yr / Pct	Dividend Yield	Expense Ratio
MUS	BNY Mellon MA Inter Mun Bd M	MMBMX	C	(800) 645-6561	C / 5.1	2.22	-2.74	-0.39 /11	2.05 /63	1.75 /52	2.38	0.54
GL	BNY Mellon Muni Opptys Fd Inv	MOTIX	C+	(800) 645-6561	C+ / 6.2	1.78	-2.94	1.08 /40	3.79 /73	3.50 /66	3.37	0.96
GL	BNY Mellon Muni Opptys Fd M	MOTMX	C+	(800) 645-6561	C+ / 6.7	1.84	-2.82	1.41 /44	4.08 /76	3.75 /69	3.62	0.71
MMF	BNY Mellon National Muni MM Inv	MNTXX	D+	(800) 645-6561	E+ / 0.7	0.03	0.06	0.07 /23	0.02 / 8	0.01 / 7	0.07	N/A
MMF	BNY Mellon National Muni MM M	MOMXX	C-	(800) 645-6561	D- / 1.2	0.09	0.18	0.22 /30	0.08 /14	0.05 /14	0.22	N/A
MUI	BNY Mellon National ST Muni Bd Inv	MINSX	C-	(800) 645-6561	D / 1.7	0.94	-0.33	0.21 /29	0.19 /18	0.32 /21	0.62	0.76
*MUI	BNY Mellon National ST Muni Bd M	MPSTX	C	(800) 645-6561	D / 2.2	0.92	-0.28	0.38 /35	0.44 /23	0.54 /25	0.87	0.51
MUN	BNY Mellon Natl Int Muni Inv	MINMX	C	(800) 645-6561	C / 5.2	2.11	-2.75	-0.44 /10	2.10 /65	1.98 /58	2.29	0.75
*MUN	BNY Mellon Natl Int Muni M	MPNIX	C+	(800) 645-6561	C+ / 5.8	2.10	-2.63	-0.19 /15	2.33 /70	2.22 /64	2.54	0.50
MUN	BNY Mellon NY Int TxEx Inv	MNYIX	C+	(800) 645-6561	C / 5.5	1.90	-2.85	-0.35 /12	2.28 /69	1.83 /55	2.17	0.97
MUS	BNY Mellon NY Int TxEx M	MNYMX	B	(800) 645-6561	C+ / 6.2	1.96	-2.82	-0.10 /16	2.54 /74	2.08 /61	2.42	0.72
MUI	BNY Mellon PA Inter Muni Bond Inv	MIPAX	C	(800) 645-6561	C / 4.6	1.87	-2.83	-0.35 /12	1.84 /58	1.46 /45	2.22	0.94
MUI	BNY Mellon PA Inter Muni Bond M	MPPIX	C+	(800) 645-6561	C / 5.4	2.02	-2.63	-0.10 /16	2.13 /65	1.70 /51	2.47	0.69
USS	BNY Mellon ST US Gov Sec Inv	MISTX	D	(800) 645-6561	E / 0.5	0.13	-0.45	-0.32 /12	0.02 / 7	-0.06 / 5	0.79	0.80
USS	BNY Mellon ST US Gov Sec M	MPSUX	C-	(800) 645-6561	D- / 1.3	0.26	-0.34	-0.09 /16	0.27 /18	0.18 /18	1.02	0.55
EM	Bradesco LA Hard Curr Bd Inst	BHCIX	D-	(888) 739-1390	B- / 7.3	4.65	2.57	17.42 /93	2.19 /46	--	3.51	2.42
EM	Bradesco LA Hard Curr Bd Retail	BHCRX	U	(888) 739-1390	U /	4.67	2.49	17.18 /92	--	--	3.24	2.67
GL	Brandes Core Plus Fixed Inc A	BCPAX	C-	(800) 237-7119	C- / 3.4	1.14	-1.09	4.32 /64	2.25 /47	--	2.24	1.06
GL	Brandes Core Plus Fixed Inc I	BCPIX	B	(800) 237-7119	C / 5.4	1.21	-0.98	4.51 /65	2.53 /52	3.18 /60	2.52	0.86
GL	Brandes Credit Focus Yield A	BCFAX	C	(800) 237-7119	C / 4.7	1.49	0.48	8.61 /76	2.37 /49	2.86 /55	2.75	1.53
GL	Brandes Credit Focus Yield I	BCFIX	A-	(800) 237-7119	C+ / 6.6	1.45	0.51	8.79 /76	2.64 /55	3.11 /59	3.13	1.33
COH	Brandes Separately Mgd Acct Res	SMARX	B	(800) 237-7119	B+ / 8.6	2.20	1.07	13.04 /85	4.22 /78	5.71 /90	4.76	0.74
*GEN	Bridge Builder Core Bond	BBTBX	C+	(855) 823-3611	C / 5.5	1.18	-1.86	2.32 /52	2.99 /61	--	2.61	0.37
COI	Bridge Builder Core Plus Bond	BBCPX	U	(855) 823-3611	U /	0.48	-2.57	1.79 /47	--	--	1.22	0.44
MUN	Bridge Builder Municipal Bond	BBMUX	U	(855) 823-3611	U /	1.22	-3.24	-0.73 / 7	--	--	0.97	0.44
GEI	Brown Advisory Interm Income Adv	BAIAX	C+	(800) 540-6807	C- / 3.4	0.75	-1.23	1.26 /42	1.63 /37	1.27 /31	1.85	0.86
GEI	Brown Advisory Interm Income Inv	BIAIX	B-	(800) 540-6807	C- / 3.8	0.70	-1.17	1.49 /44	1.88 /41	1.51 /35	2.07	0.61
MUS	Brown Advisory Maryland Bond Inv	BIAMX	B-	(800) 540-6807	C / 4.4	1.65	-2.21	-0.19 /15	1.70 /54	1.37 /44	2.23	0.49
MTG	Brown Advisory Mortgage Sec Ins	BAFZX	U	(800) 540-6807	U /	0.47	-1.83	0.11 /22	--	--	2.24	0.51
MTG	Brown Advisory Mortgage Sec Inv	BIAZX	C+	(800) 540-6807	C- / 3.9	0.56	-1.76	0.15 /24	2.23 /47	--	2.18	0.46
GEL	Brown Advisory Strategic Bond Adv	BATBX	C+	(800) 540-6807	C- / 4.1	1.21	1.04	6.38 /71	1.10 /29	1.07 /28	2.24	1.01
MUN	Brown Advisory Tax Exempt Bd Inv	BIAEX	B	(800) 540-6807	C / 5.2	1.36	-2.55	0.26 /31	2.06 /64	--	2.83	0.49
GL	Brown Advisory Total Return Instl	BAFTX	U	(800) 540-6807	U /	1.45	-1.78	3.67 /61	--	--	2.50	0.51
GL	Brown Advisory Total Return Inv	BIATX	U	(800) 540-6807	U /	1.44	-1.81	3.61 /60	--	--	2.45	0.56
GEN	BTS Tactical Fixed Income A	BTFAX	C	(877) 287-9820	B- / 7.1	3.47	3.26	9.99 /79	4.38 /79	--	2.68	2.18
GEN	BTS Tactical Fixed Income C	BTFCX	C+	(877) 287-9820	B / 7.6	3.24	2.95	9.25 /77	3.61 /70	--	1.82	2.93
COH	Buffalo High Yield Fund	BUFHX	C+	(800) 492-8332	B / 7.7	3.16	3.21	10.54 /80	3.75 /72	5.51 /89	4.29	1.03
MUS	CA Tax-Free Income Direct	CFNTX	B	(800) 955-9988	C / 5.5	1.70	-2.47	-0.48 /10	2.27 /68	2.36 /68	2.43	0.69
COH	Calamos High Income A	CHYDX	D-	(800) 582-6959	C+ / 6.8	4.25	4.99	16.48 /91	2.44 /51	4.47 /78	4.61	1.29
COH ●	Calamos High Income B	CAHBX	D	(800) 582-6959	B- / 7.2	4.02	4.53	15.50 /89	1.66 /37	3.68 /68	3.82	2.03
COH	Calamos High Income C	CCHYX	D	(800) 582-6959	B- / 7.2	4.08	4.60	15.60 /89	1.67 /38	3.70 /69	3.90	2.04
COH	Calamos High Income I	CIHYX	C-	(800) 582-6959	B+ / 8.3	4.31	5.12	16.77 /91	2.70 /56	4.73 /81	5.09	1.04
COH	Calamos High Income R	CHYRX	D+	(800) 582-6959	B / 7.7	4.16	4.85	16.06 /90	2.15 /46	4.19 /75	4.60	1.54
GEI	Calamos Total Return Bond A	CTRAX	D+	(800) 582-6959	C- / 3.2	1.03	-1.56	2.81 /55	2.41 /50	2.24 /45	2.14	1.12
GEI ●	Calamos Total Return Bond B	CTXBX	C-	(800) 582-6959	C- / 3.6	0.85	-1.92	2.05 /49	1.65 /37	1.48 /34	1.47	1.87
GEI	Calamos Total Return Bond C	CTRCX	C-	(800) 582-6959	C- / 3.5	0.85	-2.01	1.95 /48	1.62 /37	1.46 /34	1.47	1.87
GEI	Calamos Total Return Bond I	CTRIX	B	(800) 582-6959	C / 5.2	1.00	-1.53	2.96 /56	2.64 /55	2.47 /49	2.48	0.87
GEI	Calamos Total Return Bond R	CTRRX	C	(800) 582-6959	C- / 4.2	0.87	-1.78	2.26 /51	2.06 /44	1.91 /41	1.97	1.37
GEI	Calvert Bond Portfolio A	CSIBX	D-	(800) 368-2745	C- / 3.2	1.15	-1.30	3.91 /62	2.78 /57	2.80 /54	2.34	0.89
GEI	Calvert Bond Portfolio C	CSBCX	D-	(800) 368-2745	C- / 3.3	0.94	-1.69	3.00 /56	1.92 /42	1.94 /41	1.53	1.73
GEI	Calvert Bond Portfolio I	CBDIX	B-	(800) 368-2745	C+ / 6.4	1.31	-1.06	4.27 /63	3.29 /66	3.34 /63	2.78	0.53
GEI	Calvert Bond Portfolio Y	CSIYX	C+	(800) 368-2745	C+ / 6.1	1.27	-1.11	4.21 /63	3.07 /62	3.09 /59	2.67	0.62

● Denotes fund is closed to new investors
* Denotes fund is included in Section II

www.thestreetratings.com

RISK			NET ASSETS		ASSET							FUND MANAGER		MINIMUM		LOADS	
Risk Rating/Pts	3 Yr Avg Standard Deviation	Avg Dura-tion	NAV As of 2/28/17	Total $(Mil)	Cash %	Gov. Bond %	Muni. Bond %	Corp. Bond %	Other %	Portfolio Turnover Ratio	Avg Coupon Rate	Manager Quality Pct	Manager Tenure (Years)	Initial Purch. $	Additional Purch. $	Front End Load	Back End Load
C / 5.5	3.0	4.6	12.52	284	0	0	99	0	1	29	0.0	10	11	10,000	100	0.0	0.0
C / 4.7	3.2	3.5	12.85	17	0	0	100	0	0	32	0.0	95	9	10,000	100	0.0	0.0
C / 4.7	3.2	3.5	12.85	1,194	0	0	100	0	0	32	0.0	95	9	10,000	100	0.0	0.0
A+ / 9.9	N/A	N/A	1.00	N/A	100	0	0	0	0	0	0.1	39	N/A	10,000	100	0.0	0.0
A+ / 9.9	N/A	N/A	1.00	540	100	0	0	0	0	0	0.2	44	N/A	10,000	100	0.0	0.0
A / 9.4	0.8	1.8	12.76	8	0	0	99	0	1	51	0.0	19	2	10,000	100	0.0	0.0
A / 9.4	0.9	1.8	12.76	911	0	0	99	0	1	51	0.0	26	2	10,000	100	0.0	0.0
C+ / 5.6	3.0	4.5	13.36	51	0	0	100	0	0	19	0.0	10	17	10,000	100	0.0	0.0
C+ / 5.6	3.0	4.5	13.37	2,034	0	0	100	0	0	19	0.0	15	17	10,000	100	0.0	0.0
C+ / 5.8	2.9	4.5	10.99	13	1	0	98	0	1	37	0.0	15	10	10,000	100	0.0	0.0
C+ / 5.9	2.9	4.5	10.98	154	1	0	98	0	1	37	0.0	20	10	10,000	100	0.0	0.0
C+ / 6.0	2.9	4.6	11.98	6	1	0	98	0	1	26	0.0	8	17	10,000	100	0.0	0.0
C+ / 6.0	2.9	4.6	12.00	222	1	0	98	0	1	26	0.0	12	17	10,000	100	0.0	0.0
A+ / 9.6	0.8	1.8	11.69	2	0	60	4	1	35	100	0.0	23	17	10,000	100	0.0	0.0
A / 9.5	0.8	1.8	11.71	208	0	60	4	1	35	100	0.0	30	17	10,000	100	0.0	0.0
E+ / 0.7	7.1	N/A	9.76	16	0	0	0	0	100	50	0.0	92	4	1,000,000	0	0.0	2.0
U /	N/A	N/A	9.79	N/A	0	0	0	0	100	50	0.0	N/A	4	1,000	250	0.0	2.0
C+ / 6.8	2.8	4.7	9.15	2	5	56	0	27	12	36	3.6	90	10	2,500	500	3.8	0.0
B- / 7.0	2.7	4.7	9.20	98	5	56	0	27	12	36	3.6	92	10	100,000	500	0.0	0.0
C+ / 6.4	2.8	3.5	10.21	2	4	36	0	53	7	34	4.5	91	17	2,500	500	3.8	0.0
C+ / 6.5	2.8	3.5	10.20	29	4	36	0	53	7	34	4.5	92	17	100,000	500	0.0	0.0
D+ / 2.8	3.7	4.3	8.89	165	1	16	0	61	22	54	4.9	85	12	0	0	0.0	0.0
C+ / 5.9	2.9	5.4	10.09	10,790	1	23	0	30	46	238	0.0	60	4	0	0	0.0	0.0
U /	N/A	5.3	10.02	5,595	0	22	0	35	43	197	0.0	N/A	2	0	0	0.0	0.0
U /	N/A	4.8	10.02	2,270	0	0	0	0	100	21	0.0	N/A	2	0	0	0.0	0.0
B+ / 8.3	2.0	3.7	10.35	8	0	17	10	27	46	68	5.0	34	25	2,000	100	0.0	0.0
B+ / 8.3	2.0	3.7	10.56	133	0	17	10	27	46	68	5.0	50	25	5,000	100	0.0	0.0
B / 7.6	2.5	4.2	10.52	177	1	0	98	0	1	80	4.7	12	3	5,000	100	0.0	0.0
U /	N/A	N/A	9.85	360	0	0	1	0	99	244	0.0	N/A	4	1,000,000	100	0.0	0.0
B / 7.7	2.4	N/A	9.86	1	0	0	1	0	99	244	0.0	27	4	5,000	100	0.0	0.0
B / 7.8	2.3	1.6	9.58	1	0	6	2	9	83	288	0.0	61	6	2,000	100	0.0	0.0
B- / 7.3	2.6	4.3	9.85	246	1	0	98	0	1	119	0.0	18	5	5,000	100	0.0	0.0
U /	N/A	5.6	9.94	99	0	5	2	28	65	218	0.0	N/A	2	1,000,000	100	0.0	0.0
U /	N/A	5.6	9.94	3	0	5	2	28	65	218	0.0	N/A	2	5,000	100	0.0	0.0
C- / 3.1	4.0	N/A	10.51	282	33	0	0	65	2	660	0.0	93	4	1,000	100	5.0	1.0
C- / 3.1	4.0	N/A	10.44	91	33	0	0	65	2	660	0.0	90	4	1,000	100	0.0	1.0
C- / 3.3	3.4	3.1	11.24	238	2	1	0	73	24	44	0.0	79	14	2,500	100	0.0	2.0
B- / 7.0	2.7	4.4	11.44	78	0	0	99	0	1	19	4.4	20	14	1,000	100	0.0	0.0
D- / 1.2	5.6	4.8	8.83	42	1	0	0	97	2	44	6.2	4	18	2,500	50	4.8	0.0
D- / 1.2	5.6	4.8	9.37	N/A	1	0	0	97	2	44	6.2	1	18	2,500	50	0.0	0.0
D- / 1.1	5.6	4.8	9.26	17	1	0	0	97	2	44	6.2	1	18	2,500	50	0.0	0.0
D- / 1.2	5.6	4.8	8.83	9	1	0	0	97	2	44	6.2	5	18	1,000,000	0	0.0	0.0
D- / 1.2	5.5	4.8	8.81	N/A	1	0	0	97	2	44	6.2	2	18	0	0	0.0	0.0
C+ / 6.8	2.8	5.0	10.34	52	2	6	0	91	1	54	3.4	52	10	2,500	50	3.8	0.0
B- / 7.1	2.7	5.0	10.34	N/A	2	6	0	91	1	54	3.4	21	10	2,500	50	0.0	0.0
B- / 7.0	2.7	5.0	10.33	14	2	6	0	91	1	54	3.4	20	10	2,500	50	0.0	0.0
B- / 7.0	2.7	5.0	10.33	21	2	6	0	91	1	54	3.4	61	10	1,000,000	0	0.0	0.0
B- / 7.0	2.7	5.0	10.31	N/A	2	6	0	91	1	54	3.4	33	10	0	0	0.0	0.0
C / 5.3	3.1	5.1	15.94	352	4	12	3	49	32	154	3.7	55	4	2,000	250	3.8	2.0
C / 5.4	3.0	5.1	15.84	30	4	12	3	49	32	154	3.7	20	4	2,000	250	0.0	2.0
C / 5.4	3.0	5.1	15.96	431	4	12	3	49	32	154	3.7	70	4	1,000,000	0	0.0	0.0
C / 5.3	3.1	5.1	16.06	111	4	12	3	49	32	154	3.7	64	4	2,000	250	0.0	0.0

99 Pct = Best
0 Pct = Worst

Fund Type	Fund Name	Ticker Symbol	Overall Investment Rating	Phone	Performance Rating/Pts	3 Mo	6 Mo	1Yr / Pct	3Yr / Pct	5Yr / Pct	Dividend Yield	Expense Ratio
COI	Calvert Green Bond A	CGAFX	C-	(800) 368-2745	D+ / 2.7	1.01	-1.00	3.05 /57	2.54 /52	--	1.67	1.16
COI	Calvert Green Bond I	CGBIX	A	(800) 368-2745	C+ / 5.9	1.10	-0.81	3.44 /59	2.97 /60	--	2.11	0.78
COI	Calvert Green Bond Y	CGYFX	A-	(800) 368-2745	C+ / 5.6	1.07	-0.87	3.30 /58	2.83 /58	--	1.98	1.02
COH	Calvert High Yield Bond A	CYBAX	D-	(800) 368-2745	C+ / 5.7	2.70	3.22	14.54 /88	2.45 /51	5.42 /88	4.90	1.39
COH	Calvert High Yield Bond C	CHBCX	D-	(800) 368-2745	C+ / 5.8	2.52	2.83	13.68 /86	1.53 /35	4.42 /77	4.28	2.35
COH	Calvert High Yield Bond I	CYBIX	C	(800) 368-2745	B / 7.9	2.79	3.41	14.91 /88	2.80 /58	5.81 /91	5.49	0.95
COH	Calvert High Yield Bond Y	CYBYX	C-	(800) 368-2745	B / 7.8	2.79	3.35	14.83 /88	2.72 /56	5.68 /90	5.10	1.07
GEI	Calvert Income A	CFICX	D	(800) 368-2745	C / 5.3	2.07	-1.46	6.33 /71	2.75 /57	3.26 /62	3.22	1.06
GEI	Calvert Income C	CIFCX	D-	(800) 368-2745	C- / 4.1	1.88	-1.85	5.51 /69	2.02 /43	2.51 /50	2.44	1.75
GEI	Calvert Income I	CINCX	C	(800) 368-2745	C+ / 6.9	2.17	-1.27	6.79 /72	3.31 /66	3.85 /70	3.59	0.66
GEI	Calvert Income R	CICRX	D	(800) 368-2745	C / 5.5	1.94	-1.68	5.86 /70	2.34 /49	2.94 /56	2.73	1.76
GEI	Calvert Income Y	CIFYX	C-	(800) 368-2745	C+ / 6.5	2.18	-1.31	6.69 /72	2.99 /61	3.54 /66	3.47	0.73
GEI	Calvert Long Term Income A	CLDAX	E+	(800) 368-2745	C+ / 5.9	2.67	-4.89	5.47 /68	4.70 /83	4.56 /79	2.92	1.13
COI	Calvert Long Term Income I	CLDIX	D+	(800) 368-2745	B / 8.1	2.86	-4.64	6.01 /70	5.13 /86	4.82 /82	3.56	N/A
COI	Calvert Short Duration Income A	CSDAX	C-	(800) 368-2745	D / 1.8	0.73	0.16	3.66 /61	1.29 /32	1.98 /42	1.97	0.95
COI	Calvert Short Duration Income C	CDICX	C-	(800) 368-2745	D / 1.7	0.56	-0.22	2.90 /56	0.55 /21	1.24 /31	1.28	1.63
COI	Calvert Short Duration Income I	CDSIX	A-	(800) 368-2745	C / 4.5	0.84	0.35	4.04 /62	1.81 /40	2.50 /49	2.40	0.51
COI	Calvert Short Duration Income Y	CSDYX	B+	(800) 368-2745	C- / 4.2	0.87	0.37	4.01 /62	1.60 /36	2.30 /46	2.32	0.62
MUN	Calvert TF Responsible Impact Bd A	CTTLX	C	(800) 368-2745	C+ / 5.9	2.27	-3.41	-0.27 /13	2.45 /72	2.08 /61	2.71	0.96
MUN	Calvert TF Responsible Impact Bd C	CTTCX	D-	(800) 368-2745	C- / 3.8	2.07	-3.76	-1.02 / 4	1.63 /52	1.22 /40	1.94	26.82
MUN	Calvert TF Responsible Impact Bd I	CTTIX	C+	(800) 368-2745	C+ / 6.5	2.36	-3.18	0.14 /26	2.66 /76	2.20 /63	3.06	4.53
MUN	Calvert TF Responsible Impact Bd Y	CTTYX	C	(800) 368-2745	C+ / 6.2	2.27	-3.28	-0.01 /17	2.59 /75	2.16 /62	2.97	5.34
GEI	Calvert Ultra-Short Inc A	CULAX	C+	(800) 368-2745	D+ / 2.4	0.45	0.80	2.43 /53	0.92 /26	1.11 /29	1.09	0.87
GEI	Calvert Ultra-Short Inc I	CULIX	B+	(800) 368-2745	C- / 3.6	0.53	0.97	2.80 /55	1.28 /32	1.32 /32	1.47	1.13
GEI	Calvert Ultra-Short Inc Y	CULYX	B+	(800) 368-2745	C- / 3.3	0.46	0.89	2.67 /54	1.15 /30	1.34 /32	1.41	0.56
MUS	Capital Group California Core Muni	CCCMX	B	(800) 421-0180	C / 4.8	1.85	-2.11	-0.27 /13	1.88 /59	1.91 /56	1.93	0.41
MUN	Capital Group California Sh-Tm Muni	CCSTX	C	(800) 421-0180	D+ / 2.4	1.31	-0.50	-0.11 /16	0.61 /27	0.80 /30	1.02	0.45
GES	Capital Group Core Bond	CCBPX	C	(800) 421-0180	C- / 3.3	0.69	-1.14	0.91 /39	1.54 /35	1.38 /33	1.54	0.41
MUN	Capital Group Core Municipal	CCMPX	B-	(800) 421-0180	C- / 3.8	1.43	-1.63	-0.28 /13	1.35 /45	1.54 /47	2.01	0.40
MUN	Capital Group Short-Term Municipal	CSTMX	C+	(800) 421-0180	D+ / 2.7	1.35	-0.44	0.35 /34	0.67 /28	0.86 /32	1.22	0.44
MMT	Cash Reserve Government Inst	ABPXX	D+	(800) 728-3337	E+ / 0.8	0.03	0.05	0.13 /23	0.06 /10	0.04 /10	0.13	N/A
MMT	Cash Reserve Government Shares	ABRXX	U	(800) 728-3337	U /	--	--	--	--	--	0.01	N/A
COI	Catalyst Insider Income A	IIXAX	U	(866) 447-4228	U /	0.85	1.21	5.29 /68	--	--	1.66	14.21
COI	Catalyst Insider Income C	IIXCX	U	(866) 447-4228	U /	0.68	0.69	4.54 /65	--	--	1.13	14.96
COI	Catalyst Insider Income I	IIXIX	U	(866) 447-4228	U /	1.03	1.44	5.63 /69	--	--	1.95	13.96
GEN	Catalyst Princeton Uncon Hdg Inc A	HIFAX	U	(866) 447-4228	U /	0.09	2.86	20.00 /96	--	--	4.14	19.04
GEN	Catalyst Princeton Uncon Hdg Inc C	HIFCX	U	(866) 447-4228	U /	-0.15	2.37	19.12 /95	--	--	3.83	19.79
GEN	Catalyst Princeton Uncon Hdg Inc I	HIFIX	U	(866) 447-4228	U /	0.06	2.90	20.21 /96	--	--	4.62	18.79
LP	Catalyst/Princeton Float Rate Inc A	CFRAX	D-	(866) 447-4228	C / 5.4	3.42	4.48	16.50 /91	1.46 /34	--	4.50	1.77
LP	Catalyst/Princeton Float Rate Inc C	CFRCX	D-	(866) 447-4228	C+ / 6.2	3.36	4.23	15.70 /90	0.74 /24	--	4.03	2.54
LP	Catalyst/Princeton Float Rate Inc I	CFRIX	C-	(866) 447-4228	B- / 7.4	3.60	4.72	16.94 /92	1.72 /38	--	4.97	1.47
COH	Catalyst/SMH High Income A	HIIFX	E	(866) 447-4228	C- / 3.3	5.53	11.38	46.00 /99	-5.28 / 0	-1.69 / 1	5.70	1.76
COH	Catalyst/SMH High Income C	HIICX	E	(866) 447-4228	C- / 4.0	5.34	10.99	44.94 /99	-5.99 / 0	-2.42 / 1	5.31	2.51
COH	Catalyst/SMH High Income I	HIIIX	E+	(866) 447-4228	C+ / 5.7	5.87	11.50	46.35 /99	-5.09 / 0	--	6.20	1.51
MTG	Catalyst/Stone Beach Income Oppty	IOXAX	U	(866) 447-4228	U /	0.19	0.33	1.96 /49	--	--	2.84	6.59
MTG	Catalyst/Stone Beach Income Oppty	IOXCX	U	(866) 447-4228	U /	0.00	0.05	1.20 /42	--	--	2.26	7.34
MTG	Catalyst/Stone Beach Income Oppty I	IOXIX	U	(866) 447-4228	U /	0.24	0.55	2.22 /51	--	--	3.26	6.34
GEI	Cavalier Adaptive Income Adv	CADAX	B-	(877) 773-3863	C+ / 6.6	5.50	3.25	8.66 /76	2.02 /43	1.97 /41	2.02	3.45
GEI	Cavalier Adaptive Income Inst	CADTX	A-	(877) 773-3863	B / 7.7	5.77	3.84	9.82 /79	3.02 /61	2.99 /58	2.86	2.45
GL	Cavalier Hedged High Income Adv	CAHIX	C	(877) 773-3863	B / 8.2	7.87	6.86	11.31 /82	2.83 /58	--	0.69	3.49
GL	Cavalier Hedged High Income Inst	CHIIX	B-	(877) 773-3863	A- / 9.1	8.00	7.32	12.38 /84	3.85 /73	--	0.85	2.49
COI	Cavanal Hill Bond A	AABOX	D	(800) 762-7085	D / 2.0	0.56	-2.59	-0.65 / 7	1.60 /36	2.29 /46	1.67	0.76

● Denotes fund is closed to new investors
* Denotes fund is included in Section II

www.thestreetratings.com

Risk Rating/Pts	3 Yr Avg Standard Deviation	Avg Duration	NAV As of 2/28/17	Total $(Mil)	Cash %	Gov. Bond %	Muni. Bond %	Corp. Bond %	Other %	Portfolio Turnover Ratio	Avg Coupon Rate	Manager Quality Pct	Manager Tenure (Years)	Initial Purch. $	Additional Purch. $	Front End Load	Back End Load
B /7.7	2.4	4.2	15.19	30	4	22	12	40	22	243	3.1	62	4	2,000	250	3.8	2.0
B /7.7	2.4	4.2	15.19	18	4	22	12	40	22	243	3.1	73	4	1,000,000	0	0.0	0.0
B /7.6	2.5	4.2	15.22	20	4	22	12	40	22	243	3.1	69	4	2,000	250	0.0	0.0
D /1.9	4.7	2.5	27.47	61	5	0	0	79	16	129	6.6	12	4	2,000	250	3.8	2.0
D /1.9	4.7	2.5	27.86	6	5	0	0	79	16	129	6.6	3	4	2,000	250	0.0	2.0
D /1.9	4.7	2.5	27.09	69	5	0	0	79	16	129	6.6	19	4	1,000,000	0	0.0	0.0
D /1.9	4.7	2.5	28.78	30	5	0	0	79	16	129	6.6	17	4	2,000	250	0.0	0.0
C- /3.4	3.6	7.2	16.23	326	0	0	0	66	34	155	4.4	33	4	2,000	250	0.0	2.0
C- /3.4	3.6	7.2	16.23	73	0	0	0	66	34	155	4.4	13	4	2,000	250	0.0	2.0
C- /3.4	3.6	7.2	16.25	46	0	0	0	66	34	155	4.4	61	4	1,000,000	0	0.0	0.0
C- /3.4	3.6	7.2	16.36	3	0	0	0	66	34	155	4.4	21	4	0	0	0.0	0.0
C- /3.4	3.6	7.2	16.42	98	0	0	0	66	34	155	4.4	49	4	2,000	250	0.0	0.0
E /0.5	7.0	12.8	16.56	73	4	16	3	58	19	244	4.3	10	4	2,000	250	3.8	2.0
E+ /0.6	7.0	12.8	16.57	10	4	16	3	58	19	244	4.3	13	4	1,000,000	0	0.0	0.0
A- /9.0	1.3	2.2	16.04	362	3	8	0	50	39	147	3.2	56	4	2,000	250	2.8	2.0
A- /9.0	1.3	2.2	15.98	116	3	8	0	50	39	147	3.2	22	4	2,000	250	0.0	2.0
A- /9.0	1.3	2.2	16.13	307	3	8	0	50	39	147	3.2	71	4	1,000,000	0	0.0	0.0
A- /9.0	1.3	2.2	16.18	319	3	8	0	50	39	147	3.2	65	4	2,000	250	0.0	0.0
C /4.4	3.4	4.6	15.58	127	0	0	100	0	0	41	4.6	11	1	2,000	250	0.0	0.0
C /4.4	3.3	4.6	15.59	1	0	0	100	0	0	41	4.6	4	1	2,000	250	0.0	0.0
C /4.4	3.3	4.6	15.61	8	0	0	100	0	0	41	4.6	16	1	1,000,000	0	0.0	0.0
C /4.4	3.3	4.6	15.60	8	0	0	100	0	0	41	4.6	14	1	2,000	250	0.0	0.0
A+ /9.8	0.5	0.3	15.62	389	6	0	1	51	42	64	2.4	72	5	2,000	250	1.3	0.0
A+ /9.8	0.5	0.3	15.63	84	6	0	1	51	42	64	2.4	78	5	1,000,000	0	0.0	0.0
A+ /9.8	0.5	0.3	15.66	299	6	0	1	51	42	64	2.4	76	5	2,000	250	0.0	0.0
B- /7.5	2.5	N/A	10.48	331	1	0	95	0	4	11	0.0	16	7	25,000	0	0.0	0.0
A- /9.0	1.3	N/A	10.18	113	6	0	93	0	1	19	0.0	19	7	25,000	0	0.0	0.0
B /8.1	2.1	N/A	10.11	368	0	49	2	26	23	86	0.0	28	7	25,000	0	0.0	0.0
B+ /8.3	2.0	N/A	10.31	401	0	0	99	0	1	18	0.0	18	1	25,000	0	0.0	0.0
A- /9.0	1.2	N/A	10.06	169	1	0	90	0	9	24	0.0	22	7	25,000	0	0.0	0.0
A+ /9.9	N/A	N/A	1.00	43	100	0	0	0	0	0	0.1	42	N/A	1,000,000	0	0.0	0.0
U /	N/A	N/A	1.00	71	100	0	0	0	0	0	0.0	N/A	N/A	1,500	0	0.0	0.0
U /	N/A	N/A	9.25	1	8	0	0	67	25	52	0.0	N/A	3	2,500	50	4.8	0.0
U /	N/A	N/A	9.24	N/A	8	0	0	67	25	52	0.0	N/A	3	2,500	50	0.0	0.0
U /	N/A	N/A	9.26	N/A	8	0	0	67	25	52	0.0	N/A	3	2,500	50	0.0	0.0
U /	N/A	N/A	9.34	N/A	8	3	0	83	6	484	0.0	N/A	3	2,500	50	4.8	0.0
U /	N/A	N/A	9.31	1	8	3	0	83	6	484	0.0	N/A	3	2,500	50	0.0	0.0
U /	N/A	N/A	9.32	1	8	3	0	83	6	484	0.0	N/A	3	2,500	50	0.0	0.0
D /2.0	5.0	N/A	9.45	7	0	0	0	22	78	44	0.0	76	5	2,500	50	4.8	0.0
D /2.0	5.1	N/A	9.43	7	0	0	0	22	78	44	0.0	56	5	2,500	50	0.0	0.0
D /2.0	5.1	N/A	9.45	22	0	0	0	22	78	44	0.0	79	5	2,500	50	0.0	0.0
E- /0.0	15.4	N/A	3.91	28	12	0	0	77	11	26	0.0	0	9	2,500	50	4.8	0.0
E- /0.0	15.3	N/A	3.91	15	12	0	0	77	11	26	0.0	0	9	2,500	50	0.0	0.0
E- /0.0	15.3	N/A	3.91	21	12	0	0	77	11	26	0.0	0	9	2,500	50	0.0	0.0
U /	N/A	N/A	9.63	1	11	0	0	0	89	78	0.0	N/A	N/A	2,500	50	5.8	0.0
U /	N/A	N/A	9.62	N/A	11	0	0	0	89	78	0.0	N/A	N/A	2,500	50	0.0	0.0
U /	N/A	N/A	9.63	4	11	0	0	0	89	78	0.0	N/A	N/A	2,500	50	0.0	0.0
C /5.1	3.1	N/A	10.08	2	0	33	0	29	38	247	0.0	66	1	250	50	0.0	0.0
C /5.0	3.1	N/A	10.41	5	0	33	0	29	38	247	0.0	82	1	250	50	0.0	0.0
D /1.9	5.2	N/A	10.08	1	4	61	0	33	2	327	0.0	93	1	250	50	0.0	0.0
D /1.9	5.2	N/A	10.16	5	4	61	0	33	2	327	0.0	95	1	250	50	0.0	0.0
B- /7.2	2.7	5.3	9.41	N/A	4	48	0	2	46	107	2.2	24	24	0	0	2.0	0.0

Fund Type	Fund Name	Ticker Symbol	Overall Investment Rating	Phone	Performance Rating/Pts	3 Mo	6 Mo	1Yr / Pct	3Yr / Pct	5Yr / Pct	Dividend Yield	Expense Ratio
	99 Pct = Best, 0 Pct = Worst							Total Return % through 2/28/17	Annualized		Incl. in Returns	
GEI	Cavanal Hill Bond Inst	AIBNX	C-	(800) 762-7085	C- / 3.2	0.62	-2.57	-0.40 /11	1.86 /41	2.52 /50	1.97	0.66
GEI	Cavanal Hill Bond NL Inv	APBDX	D+	(800) 762-7085	D+ / 2.8	0.55	-2.69	-0.77 / 6	1.62 /37	2.28 /46	1.69	0.91
MMT	Cavanal Hill Gvt Secs Mny Mkt Admn	APCXX	U	(800) 762-7085	U /	--	--	--	--	--	0.01	N/A
MMT	Cavanal Hill Gvt Secs Mny Mkt Inst	APHXX	D+	(800) 762-7085	E+ / 0.8	0.06	0.09	0.12 /23	0.05 / 9	0.03 / 9	0.12	N/A
MMT	Cavanal Hill Gvt Secs Mny Mkt Prem	APPXX	D+	(800) 762-7085	E+ / 0.9	0.07	0.11	0.15 /24	0.06 /10	--	0.15	N/A
MUN	Cavanal Hill Intmdt TxFr Bd A	AATFX	C	(800) 762-7085	D+ / 2.8	1.47	-1.41	-0.33 /12	1.51 /48	1.44 /45	2.30	0.83
MUN	Cavanal Hill Intmdt TxFr Bd Instl	AITEX	B+	(800) 762-7085	C / 4.8	1.55	-1.26	-0.02 /17	1.76 /56	1.59 /49	2.66	0.73
MUN	Cavanal Hill Intmdt TxFr Bd NL Inv	APTFX	B	(800) 762-7085	C- / 4.2	1.48	-1.39	-0.29 /13	1.52 /49	1.32 /47	2.39	0.98
GEI	Cavanal Hill Limited Dur NL A	AASTX	C-	(800) 762-7085	D- / 1.4	0.22	-0.20	0.51 /33	0.82 /25	1.53 /35	1.23	0.74
GEI	Cavanal Hill Limited Dur NL Inst	AISTX	B-	(800) 762-7085	D+ / 2.7	0.38	0.03	0.88 /38	1.08 /29	1.77 /38	1.51	0.64
GEI	Cavanal Hill Limited Dur NL Inv	APSTX	C+	(800) 762-7085	D / 2.2	0.20	-0.23	0.56 /34	0.80 /24	1.50 /34	1.19	0.89
GEI	Cavanal Hill Moderate Dur Inst	AIFBX	C	(800) 762-7085	C- / 3.0	0.87	-1.14	0.40 /31	1.42 /33	3.36 /63	2.25	0.74
GEI	Cavanal Hill Moderate Dur NoLd Inv	APFBX	C-	(800) 762-7085	D+ / 2.5	0.80	-1.28	0.02 /18	1.17 /30	3.10 /59	1.95	0.99
COI	Cavanal Hill Moderate Duration A	AAIBX	D+	(800) 762-7085	D / 1.9	0.80	-1.08	0.15 /24	1.17 /30	3.14 /60	1.95	0.84
MMT	Cavanal Hill US Treasury Instl	APKXX	D+	(800) 762-7085	E+ / 0.7	0.05	0.07	0.09 /22	0.03 / 8	0.02 / 7	0.09	N/A
MMT	Cavanal Hill US Treasury Ser	APJXX	D+	(800) 762-7085	E+ / 0.6	0.02	0.03	0.03 /19	0.01 / 6	0.01 / 5	0.03	N/A
MUN	Centre Active US Tax Exempt Inst	DHBIX	C	(800) 955-7175	C- / 3.8	1.41	-2.85	-1.83 / 1	1.73 /55	1.17 /39	2.33	0.84
MUN	Centre Active US Tax Exempt Inv	DHBRX	D-	(800) 955-7175	D- / 1.0	1.34	-2.96	-2.06 / 1	1.47 /47	1.04 /36	2.00	1.09
US	Centre Active US Treasury Inst	DHTUX	E	(855) 298-4236	E / 0.4	0.31	-3.30	-3.58 / 0	0.48 /21	--	2.59	1.02
US	Centre Active US Treasury Inv	DHTRX	E	(855) 298-4236	E / 0.3	0.14	-3.53	-3.90 / 0	0.19 /16	--	2.49	0.95
* GEI	CGCM Core Fixed Inc	TIIUX	C+	(800) 444-4273	C / 5.1	1.32	-1.80	2.50 /53	2.68 /55	2.86 /55	2.72	0.54
COH	CGCM High Yield	THYUX	D+	(800) 444-4273	B / 8.1	4.50	5.65	19.81 /96	1.91 /41	5.01 /84	6.09	0.90
GEI	CGCM Inflation-Linked Fixed Income	TILUX	U	(800) 444-4273	U /	1.46	0.06	--	--	--	0.00	0.63
GL	CGCM Intl Fixed Inc	TIFUX	B	(800) 444-4273	B- / 7.5	0.98	-1.23	5.26 /68	4.40 /80	3.81 /70	1.10	0.87
MUN	CGCM Municipal Bd	TMUUX	C-	(800) 444-4273	C+ / 6.4	1.93	-3.57	-0.41 /11	2.79 /78	2.31 /66	2.87	0.66
GEI	CGCM Ultra-Short Term Fixed	TSDUX	U	(800) 444-4273	U /	0.60	1.39	--	--	--	0.00	0.60
GES	Changing Parameters	CPMPX	A-	(866) 618-3456	B+ / 8.7	3.67	3.26	12.45 /84	4.05 /76	4.61 /80	2.19	2.37
COH	Chartwell Short Duration Hi Yld I	CWFIX	U	(866) 585-6552	U /	2.10	2.70	9.92 /79	--	--	3.46	2.16
GL	Chou Income	CHOIX	C	(877) 682-6352	A / 9.4	8.62	13.77	41.85 /99	0.26 /18	9.67 /99	12.25	2.36
MMT	CitizensSelect Treas Secs MM Ham	CEAXX	C-	(800) 645-6561	E+ / 0.9	0.08	0.13	0.19 /25	0.07 /11	0.04 /10	0.19	N/A
MMT	CitizensSelect Treas Secs MM Prem	CEBXX	D+	(800) 645-6561	E+ / 0.6	0.03	0.04	0.04 /20	0.01 / 6	0.01 / 5	0.04	N/A
MUN	Clearwater Tax-Exempt Bond	QWVQX	A	(888) 228-0935	A+ / 9.8	3.02	-2.45	2.26 /59	6.08 /99	5.17 /98	4.58	0.66
GEI	CM Advisors Fixed Income	CMFIX	A+	(800) 664-4888	C+ / 6.3	1.50	2.11	7.95 /74	2.36 /49	1.92 /41	3.16	0.81
COH	CMG Tactical Bond A	CHYAX	U	(866) 264-9456	U /	3.68	2.32	8.33 /75	--	--	1.68	2.14
MUI	CNR CA Tax-Exempt Bond N	CCTEX	C	(888) 889-0799	C- / 3.1	1.59	-1.80	-0.63 / 8	1.08 /37	1.28 /41	1.10	1.00
MUI	CNR CA Tax-Exempt Bond Servicing	CNTIX	C+	(888) 889-0799	C- / 3.6	1.56	-1.68	-0.45 /10	1.31 /43	1.52 /47	1.38	0.75
COI	CNR Corporate Bond N	CCBAX	C+	(888) 889-0799	D+ / 2.7	0.81	-0.30	2.56 /54	0.83 /25	1.34 /32	1.47	1.09
COI	CNR Corporate Bond Servicing	CNCIX	C+	(888) 889-0799	C- / 3.1	0.78	-0.18	2.77 /55	1.07 /29	1.61 /36	1.77	0.84
* GEI	CNR Fixed Income Opportunities N	RIMOX	B+	(888) 889-0799	A- / 9.1	3.52	4.90	15.63 /90	4.16 /77	5.58 /89	5.94	1.12
USS	CNR Government Bond Institutional	CNIGX	C-	(888) 889-0799	D / 2.0	0.38	-0.53	0.06 /21	0.69 /23	0.50 /21	0.95	0.57
USS	CNR Government Bond N	CGBAX	D	(888) 889-0799	E+ / 0.6	0.26	-0.77	-0.53 / 9	0.16 /15	-0.02 / 5	0.45	1.07
USS	CNR Government Bond Servicing	CNBIX	D+	(888) 889-0799	D- / 1.5	0.23	-0.74	-0.29 /13	0.41 /20	0.25 /19	0.70	0.82
MMT	CNR Government MM N	CNGXX	U	(888) 889-0799	U /	--	--	--	--	--	0.03	N/A
MMT	CNR Government MM S	CNFXX	U	(888) 889-0799	U /	--	--	--	--	--	0.03	N/A
MMT	CNR Government MM Servicing	CNIXX	U	(888) 889-0799	U /	0.02	0.02	0.04 /20	0.02 / 7	0.02 / 7	0.04	N/A
COH	CNR High Yield Bond Institutional	CNIHX	C+	(888) 889-0799	A+ / 9.6	4.11	5.77	21.72 /98	4.36 /79	6.52 /95	5.67	0.83
COH	CNR High Yield Bond N	CHBAX	C+	(888) 889-0799	A / 9.4	3.98	5.61	21.23 /97	3.88 /74	6.00 /92	5.28	1.33
COH	CNR High Yield Bond Servicing	CHYIX	C+	(888) 889-0799	A / 9.5	4.05	5.64	21.42 /97	4.10 /76	6.25 /94	5.43	1.08
COI	CNR Intermediate Fixed Income Inst	CNRIX	A-	(888) 889-0799	C / 5.0	1.18	-0.50	3.09 /57	2.36 /49	--	2.44	0.53
GEI	CNR Intermediate Fixed Income N	RIMCX	B	(888) 889-0799	C- / 4.1	1.04	-0.76	2.54 /53	1.84 /40	2.31 /46	1.94	1.03
MUH	CNR Municipal High Income N	CNRNX	C+	(888) 889-0799	B+ / 8.8	3.62	-4.69	0.27 /31	4.44 /95	--	3.77	1.09
MUH	CNR Municipal High Income	CNRMX	B-	(888) 889-0799	A- / 9.2	3.68	-4.48	0.52 /37	4.73 /96	--	4.02	0.85

● Denotes fund is closed to new investors
* Denotes fund is included in Section II

www.thestreetratings.com

RISK			NET ASSETS		ASSET								FUND MANAGER		MINIMUM		LOADS	
Risk Rating/Pts	3 Yr Avg Standard Deviation	Avg Duration	NAV As of 2/28/17	Total $(Mil)	Cash %	Gov. Bond %	Muni. Bond %	Corp. Bond %	Other %	Portfolio Turnover Ratio	Avg Coupon Rate	Manager Quality Pct	Manager Tenure (Years)	Initial Purch. $	Additional Purch. $	Front End Load	Back End Load
B- / 7.2	2.6	5.3	9.40	130	4	48	0	2	46	107	2.2	24	24	100,000	100	0.0	0.0
B- / 7.2	2.7	5.3	9.42	8	4	48	0	2	46	107	2.2	18	24	1,000	0	0.0	0.0
U /	N/A	N/A	1.00	781	100	0	0	0	0	0	0.0	N/A	N/A	1,000	0	0.0	0.0
A+ / 9.9	N/A	N/A	1.00	261	100	0	0	0	0	0	0.1	41	N/A	100,000	0	0.0	0.0
A+ / 9.9	N/A	N/A	1.00	90	100	0	0	0	0	0	0.2	42	N/A	1,000	0	0.0	0.0
B+ / 8.3	2.0	3.1	10.97	3	11	0	88	0	1	8	4.1	20	24	0	0	2.0	0.0
B+ / 8.3	2.0	3.1	10.97	32	11	0	88	0	1	8	4.1	27	24	100,000	100	0.0	0.0
B+ / 8.3	2.0	3.1	10.96	5	11	0	88	0	1	8	4.1	21	24	1,000	0	0.0	0.0
A+ / 9.6	0.7	2.0	9.52	1	4	41	0	10	45	80	1.9	54	23	0	0	2.0	0.0
A+ / 9.6	0.8	2.0	9.52	82	4	41	0	10	45	80	1.9	62	23	100,000	100	0.0	0.0
A+ / 9.6	0.7	2.0	9.52	20	4	41	0	10	45	80	1.9	52	23	1,000	0	0.0	0.0
B+ / 8.5	1.8	4.1	10.34	42	5	45	0	5	45	129	2.1	34	24	100,000	100	0.0	0.0
B+ / 8.5	1.8	4.1	10.34	12	5	45	0	5	45	129	2.1	25	24	1,000	0	0.0	0.0
B+ / 8.4	1.9	4.1	10.34	2	5	45	0	5	45	129	2.1	29	24	0	0	2.0	0.0
A+ / 9.9	N/A	N/A	1.00	240	100	0	0	0	0	0	0.1	40	N/A	100,000	0	0.0	0.0
A+ / 9.9	N/A	N/A	1.00	28	100	0	0	0	0	0	0.0	38	N/A	10,000	0	0.0	0.0
B- / 7.2	2.7	4.2	9.99	7	2	4	92	0	2	6	4.6	13	2	100,000	100	0.0	0.0
B- / 7.2	2.6	4.2	10.05	26	2	4	92	0	2	6	4.6	9	2	5,000	100	3.0	0.0
C / 4.5	3.3	N/A	9.89	4	4	95	0	0	1	2	0.0	11	3	1,000,000	10,000	0.0	0.0
C / 4.6	3.3	N/A	9.82	54	4	95	0	0	1	2	0.0	7	3	5,000	1,000	0.0	0.0
C+ / 6.2	2.9	4.0	8.07	712	1	32	0	28	39	245	0.0	53	12	100	0	0.0	0.0
E+ / 0.9	6.0	N/A	3.87	325	5	0	0	93	2	64	0.0	1	12	100	0	0.0	0.0
U /	N/A	N/A	10.16	165	0	0	0	0	100	0	0.0	N/A	1	100	0	0.0	0.0
C / 4.3	3.4	N/A	7.61	173	3	47	4	23	23	199	0.0	96	3	100	0	0.0	0.0
C- / 3.4	3.4	11.2	9.19	60	4	0	95	0	1	16	0.0	15	12	100	0	0.0	0.0
U /	N/A	N/A	10.02	170	0	0	0	0	100	0	0.0	N/A	1	100	0	0.0	0.0
C- / 3.9	3.6	N/A	10.26	65	12	11	14	31	32	694	0.0	91	10	2,500	100	0.0	0.0
U /	N/A	N/A	9.69	22	3	0	0	96	1	52	0.0	N/A	3	1,000,000	0	0.0	2.0
E- / 0.0	13.1	N/A	8.18	18	21	0	0	50	29	7	0.0	64	7	5,000	500	0.0	2.0
A+ / 9.9	N/A	N/A	1.00	190	100	0	0	0	0	0	0.2	42	N/A	1,000,000,00	0	0.0	0.0
A+ / 9.9	N/A	N/A	1.00	87	100	0	0	0	0	0	0.0	38	N/A	1,000,000,00	0	0.0	0.0
C- / 3.4	3.9	N/A	9.95	491	1	0	96	0	3	19	0.0	85	17	1,000	1,000	0.0	0.0
B / 8.2	2.1	2.9	11.57	67	4	46	0	48	2	18	0.0	79	6	2,500	0	0.0	0.0
U /	N/A	N/A	9.84	1	3	0	0	90	7	1,413	0.0	N/A	3	5,000	1,000	5.8	0.0
B / 8.1	2.1	4.1	10.55	10	2	0	97	0	1	25	4.9	10	8	0	0	0.0	0.0
B / 8.2	2.0	4.1	10.51	86	2	0	97	0	1	25	4.9	15	8	0	0	0.0	0.0
B+ / 8.9	1.4	2.6	10.41	5	2	1	7	86	4	30	0.0	27	16	0	0	0.0	0.0
B+ / 8.9	1.4	2.6	10.39	127	2	1	7	86	4	30	0.0	35	16	0	0	0.0	0.0
D+ / 2.8	4.2	N/A	25.98	2,371	6	5	0	52	37	124	0.0	95	6	0	0	0.0	0.0
A- / 9.0	1.2	2.4	10.49	47	2	83	0	0	15	37	0.0	36	14	1,000,000	0	0.0	0.0
A- / 9.0	1.2	2.4	10.50	2	2	83	0	0	15	37	0.0	19	14	0	0	0.0	0.0
A- / 9.1	1.2	2.4	10.48	82	2	83	0	0	15	37	0.0	27	14	0	0	0.0	0.0
U /	N/A	N/A	1.00	3,633	100	0	0	0	0	0	0.0	N/A	N/A	0	0	0.0	0.0
U /	N/A	N/A	1.00	846	100	0	0	0	0	0	0.0	N/A	N/A	0	0	0.0	0.0
U /	N/A	N/A	1.00	1,002	100	0	0	0	0	0	0.0	N/A	N/A	0	0	0.0	0.0
D- / 1.1	5.7	4.8	8.01	40	2	0	0	89	9	69	0.0	45	6	1,000,000	0	0.0	0.0
D- / 1.1	5.7	4.8	8.01	19	2	0	0	89	9	69	0.0	25	6	0	0	0.0	0.0
D- / 1.1	5.7	4.8	8.01	18	2	0	0	89	9	69	0.0	32	6	0	0	0.0	0.0
B+ / 8.4	1.9	N/A	26.23	4	0	14	1	74	11	25	0.0	68	4	1,000,000	0	0.0	0.0
B+ / 8.4	1.9	N/A	26.20	253	0	14	1	74	11	25	0.0	55	4	0	0	0.0	0.0
D / 1.8	4.9	N/A	10.47	621	1	2	96	0	1	28	0.0	22	1	0	0	0.0	0.0
D / 1.8	4.9	N/A	10.48	442	1	2	96	0	1	28	0.0	31	1	0	0	0.0	0.0

Fund Type	Fund Name	Ticker Symbol	Overall Investment Rating	Phone	Perfor-mance Rating/Pts	3 Mo	6 Mo	1Yr / Pct	3Yr / Pct	5Yr / Pct	Dividend Yield	Expense Ratio
	99 Pct = Best 0 Pct = Worst							Total Return % through 2/28/17	Annualized		Incl. in Returns	
GEI	CO 529 CollegeInvest Bond Index		D	(800) 662-7447	C- / 4.1	1.18	-2.46	1.11 /41	2.23 /47	1.81 /39	0.00	0.52
GEI	CO 529 CollegeInvest Income Port		C+	(800) 662-7447	C- / 3.5	0.70	-1.17	1.20 /42	1.66 /37	1.07 /28	0.00	0.52
GEN	Cohen & Steers LD Pref and Inc A	LPXAX	U	(800) 330-7348	U /	2.76	1.87	7.98 /74	--	--	3.62	1.90
GEN	Cohen & Steers LD Pref and Inc C	LPXCX	U	(800) 330-7348	U /	2.67	1.61	7.44 /73	--	--	3.19	2.55
GEN	Cohen & Steers LD Pref and Inc I	LPXIX	U	(800) 330-7348	U /	2.71	1.92	8.27 /75	--	--	3.96	1.65
GEN	Cohen & Steers LD Pref and Inc R	LPXRX	U	(800) 330-7348	U /	2.64	1.69	7.77 /74	--	--	3.51	2.05
GEN	Cohen & Steers LD Pref and Inc Z	LPXZX	U	(800) 330-7348	U /	2.71	1.92	8.27 /75	--	--	3.96	1.55
GL	Cohen and Steers Pref Sec and Inc Z	CPXZX	U	(800) 330-7348	U /	4.24	0.65	11.01 /81	--	--	5.51	0.84
* GEI	Cohen and Steers Pref Sec&Inc A	CPXAX	A-	(800) 330-7348	A / 9.3	4.19	0.51	10.71 /80	6.99 /96	8.28 /99	5.00	1.19
GEI	Cohen and Steers Pref Sec&Inc C	CPXCX	A-	(800) 330-7348	A / 9.5	4.03	0.17	9.93 /79	6.28 /93	7.59 /97	4.58	1.84
GEI	Cohen and Steers Pref Sec&Inc I	CPXIX	A	(800) 330-7348	A+ / 9.8	4.24	0.64	10.99 /81	7.35 /97	8.65 /99	5.50	0.94
GL	Cohen and Steers Pref Sec&Inc R	CPRRX	U	(800) 330-7348	U /	4.16	0.45	10.60 /80	--	--	5.14	1.34
*MUS	Colorado Bond Shares Tax-Exempt	HICOX	A+	(800) 572-0069	C+ / 6.6	0.72	-0.80	2.01 /57	3.88 /92	3.71 /90	4.11	0.58
GEI	Columbia Abs Rtn Currency & Inc A	RARAX	C+	(800) 345-6611	A+ / 9.9	4.77	4.67	9.25 /77	12.23 /99	5.21 /86	0.00	1.75
GEI ●	Columbia Abs Rtn Currency & Inc B	CARBX	C+	(800) 345-6611	A+ / 9.9	4.53	4.22	8.41 /75	11.36 /99	4.41 /77	0.00	2.50
GEI	Columbia Abs Rtn Currency & Inc C	RARCX	C+	(800) 345-6611	A+ / 9.9	4.54	4.23	8.42 /75	11.37 /99	4.42 /77	0.00	2.50
GEI	Columbia Abs Rtn Currency & Inc I	RVAIX	C+	(800) 345-6611	A+ / 9.9	4.82	4.91	9.75 /78	12.68 /99	5.64 /90	0.00	1.34
GEI	Columbia Abs Rtn Currency & Inc W	RACWX	C+	(800) 345-6611	A+ / 9.9	4.70	4.70	9.30 /77	12.21 /99	5.18 /86	0.00	1.75
GEI	Columbia Abs Rtn Currency & Inc Z	CACZX	C+	(800) 345-6611	A+ / 9.9	4.80	4.80	9.55 /78	12.51 /99	5.47 /88	0.00	1.50
MUS	Columbia AMT Fr NY Intm Muni Bd A	LNYAX	D+	(800) 345-6611	C- / 3.2	1.73	-2.88	-0.89 / 5	2.16 /66	1.86 /55	2.73	0.97
MUS ●	Columbia AMT Fr NY Intm Muni Bd B	LNYBX	D+	(800) 345-6611	C- / 3.1	1.54	-3.25	-1.64 / 1	1.40 /46	1.10 /37	2.04	1.72
MUS	Columbia AMT Fr NY Intm Muni Bd C	LNYCX	C	(800) 345-6611	C- / 3.9	1.61	-3.03	-1.34 / 2	1.70 /54	1.42 /44	2.35	1.72
MUN	Columbia AMT Fr NY Intm Muni Bd	CNYIX	B+	(800) 345-6611	C+ / 5.7	1.79	-2.69	-0.65 / 8	2.41 /72	2.11 /61	3.06	0.72
MUN	Columbia AMT Fr NY Intm Muni Bd	CNYUX	B+	(800) 345-6611	C+ / 5.8	1.81	-2.71	-0.62 / 8	2.42 /72	2.12 /62	3.16	N/A
MUS ●	Columbia AMT Fr NY Intm Muni Bd V	GANYX	D	(800) 345-6611	D+ / 2.3	1.75	-2.76	-0.80 / 6	2.26 /68	1.96 /58	2.77	0.87
MUS	Columbia AMT Fr NY Intm Muni Bd Z	GNYTX	B+	(800) 345-6611	C+ / 5.7	1.79	-2.69	-0.65 / 8	2.41 /72	2.12 /62	3.06	0.72
MUS	Columbia AMT-Fr CA Intm Muni Bd A	NACMX	D-	(800) 345-6611	C- / 3.9	2.02	-3.25	-0.69 / 7	2.50 /73	2.49 /70	2.44	0.93
MUS ●	Columbia AMT-Fr CA Intm Muni Bd B	CCIBX	D-	(800) 345-6611	C- / 3.8	1.74	-3.62	-1.53 / 2	1.70 /54	1.70 /51	1.75	1.68
MUS	Columbia AMT-Fr CA Intm Muni Bd C	CCICX	D-	(800) 345-6611	C- / 3.9	1.74	-3.62	-1.43 / 2	1.73 /55	1.72 /52	1.75	1.68
MUN	Columbia AMT-Fr CA Intm Muni Bd	CCMRX	C+	(800) 345-6611	C+ / 6.5	1.99	-3.15	-0.45 /10	2.79 /78	2.74 /75	2.77	0.68
MUN	Columbia AMT-Fr CA Intm Muni Bd	CNBRX	C+	(800) 345-6611	C+ / 6.6	2.02	-3.12	-0.46 /10	2.85 /79	2.80 /76	2.87	0.55
MUS	Columbia AMT-Fr CA Intm Muni Bd Z	NCMAX	C+	(800) 345-6611	C+ / 6.4	1.99	-3.15	-0.54 / 9	2.76 /78	2.72 /75	2.77	0.68
MUS	Columbia AMT-Fr CT Intm Muni Bd A	LCTAX	D-	(800) 345-6611	D+ / 2.3	1.66	-2.79	-0.95 / 5	1.76 /56	1.59 /49	2.64	0.99
MUS ●	Columbia AMT-Fr CT Intm Muni Bd B	LCTBX	D-	(800) 345-6611	D+ / 2.3	1.57	-3.16	-1.70 / 1	1.00 /35	0.83 /31	1.95	1.74
MUS	Columbia AMT-Fr CT Intm Muni Bd C	LCTCX	D	(800) 345-6611	C- / 3.0	1.55	-3.00	-1.39 / 2	1.30 /43	1.16 /39	2.26	1.74
MUN	Columbia AMT-Fr CT Intm Muni Bd	CCTMX	C+	(800) 345-6611	C / 4.9	1.83	-2.66	-0.60 / 8	2.03 /63	1.86 /55	2.99	0.74
MUS	Columbia AMT-Fr CT Intm Muni Bd V	GCBAX	D-	(800) 345-6611	D- / 1.5	1.79	-2.74	-0.85 / 5	1.86 /59	1.70 /51	2.69	0.89
MUS	Columbia AMT-Fr CT Intm Muni Bd Z	SCTEX	C+	(800) 345-6611	C / 4.9	1.73	-2.66	-0.70 / 7	2.02 /63	1.85 /55	2.98	0.74
MUS	Columbia AMT-Fr GA Intm Muni Bd A	NGIMX	D	(800) 345-6611	D+ / 2.4	1.72	-2.92	-0.94 / 5	1.84 /58	1.66 /50	2.52	1.03
MUS ●	Columbia AMT-Fr GA Intm Muni Bd B	NGITX	D	(800) 345-6611	D+ / 2.3	1.43	-3.38	-1.78 / 1	1.05 /37	0.88 /32	1.83	1.78
MUS	Columbia AMT-Fr GA Intm Muni Bd C	NGINX	D-	(800) 345-6611	D+ / 2.3	1.53	-3.29	-1.78 / 1	1.05 /37	0.88 /32	1.83	1.78
MUN	Columbia AMT-Fr GA Intm Muni Bd	CGIMX	C+	(800) 345-6611	C / 5.1	1.89	-2.72	-0.70 / 7	2.10 /65	1.92 /57	2.86	0.78
MUS	Columbia AMT-Fr GA Intm Muni Bd Z	NGAMX	B-	(800) 345-6611	C / 5.0	1.79	-2.80	-0.70 / 7	2.10 /65	1.92 /57	2.86	0.78
MUH	Columbia AMT-Fr Intm Muni Bond A	LITAX	D-	(800) 345-6611	C- / 3.9	1.85	-2.95	-0.53 / 9	2.45 /72	2.26 /65	2.94	0.87
MUH ●	Columbia AMT-Fr Intm Muni Bond B	LITBX	D-	(800) 345-6611	C- / 4.2	1.68	-3.17	-1.07 / 4	1.79 /57	1.62 /49	2.37	1.52
MUH	Columbia AMT-Fr Intm Muni Bond C	LITCX	D-	(800) 345-6611	C- / 4.0	1.59	-3.26	-1.17 / 3	1.76 /56	1.78 /53	2.37	1.52
MUN	Columbia AMT-Fr Intm Muni Bond R4	CIMRX	B	(800) 345-6611	C+ / 6.2	1.80	-2.85	-0.33 /12	2.62 /76	2.45 /69	3.24	0.67
MUN	Columbia AMT-Fr Intm Muni Bond R5	CTMRX	B+	(800) 345-6611	C+ / 6.5	1.92	-2.72	-0.15 /15	2.75 /78	2.56 /72	3.33	0.53
MUH ●	Columbia AMT-Fr Intm Muni Bond V	GIMAX	E+	(800) 345-6611	D+ / 2.9	1.86	-2.92	-0.48 /10	2.51 /73	2.31 /66	2.94	0.82
MUH	Columbia AMT-Fr Intm Muni Bond Z	SETMX	C	(800) 345-6611	C+ / 6.2	1.80	-2.85	-0.33 /12	2.63 /76	2.46 /70	3.24	0.67
MUS	Columbia AMT-Fr MA Intm Muni Bd A	LMIAX	D-	(800) 345-6611	D+ / 2.5	1.87	-2.94	-1.23 / 3	1.93 /60	1.64 /50	2.74	0.96
MUS ●	Columbia AMT-Fr MA Intm Muni Bd B	LMIBX	D-	(800) 345-6611	D+ / 2.6	1.78	-3.30	-1.88 / 1	1.20 /40	0.88 /32	2.06	1.71

● Denotes fund is closed to new investors
* Denotes fund is included in Section II

www.thestreetratings.com

Risk Rating/Pts	3 Yr Avg Standard Deviation	Avg Dura-tion	NAV As of 2/28/17	Total $(Mil)	Cash %	Gov. Bond %	Muni. Bond %	Corp. Bond %	Other %	Portfolio Turnover Ratio	Avg Coupon Rate	Manager Quality Pct	Manager Tenure (Years)	Initial Purch. $	Additional Purch. $	Front End Load	Back End Load
C /5.1	3.1	N/A	15.49	37	0	46	1	25	28	0	0.0	21	13	25	15	0.0	0.0
B /8.0	2.1	N/A	14.34	247	25	51	0	12	12	0	0.0	30	13	25	15	0.0	0.0
U /	N/A	N/A	10.09	32	0	0	0	0	100	0	0.0	N/A	2	0	0	2.0	0.0
U /	N/A	N/A	10.08	4	0	0	0	0	100	0	0.0	N/A	2	0	0	0.0	0.0
U /	N/A	N/A	10.09	127	0	0	0	0	100	0	0.0	N/A	2	100,000	0	0.0	0.0
U /	N/A	N/A	10.09	N/A	0	0	0	0	100	0	0.0	N/A	2	0	0	0.0	0.0
U /	N/A	N/A	10.09	N/A	0	0	0	0	100	0	0.0	N/A	2	0	0	0.0	0.0
U /	N/A	N/A	13.79	N/A	3	0	0	55	42	46	0.0	N/A	7	0	0	0.0	0.0
C- /3.0	4.1	N/A	13.77	932	3	0	0	55	42	46	0.0	96	7	1,000	250	4.5	0.0
C- /3.0	4.1	N/A	13.70	860	3	0	0	55	42	46	0.0	95	7	1,000	250	0.0	0.0
C- /3.0	4.1	N/A	13.80	4,632	3	0	0	55	42	46	0.0	97	7	100,000	0	0.0	0.0
U /	N/A	N/A	13.79	4	3	0	0	55	42	46	0.0	N/A	7	0	0	0.0	0.0
B+ /8.8	1.5	5.7	8.93	1,072	17	0	64	1	18	17	4.5	89	27	500	0	4.8	0.0
E- /0.1	11.6	0.1	10.95	21	98	0	0	0	2	0	0.6	99	11	10,000	0	3.0	0.0
E- /0.2	11.6	0.1	10.27	N/A	98	0	0	0	2	0	0.6	99	11	10,000	0	0.0	0.0
E- /0.1	11.6	0.1	10.26	3	98	0	0	0	2	0	0.6	99	11	10,000	0	0.0	0.0
E- /0.1	11.6	0.1	11.35	26	98	0	0	0	2	0	0.6	99	11	0	0	0.0	0.0
E- /0.1	11.6	0.1	10.90	N/A	98	0	0	0	2	0	0.6	99	11	500	0	0.0	0.0
E- /0.2	11.6	0.1	11.28	11	98	0	0	0	2	0	0.6	99	11	2,000	0	0.0	0.0
C+ /6.8	2.8	5.2	11.79	20	1	0	98	0	1	13	4.7	16	19	2,000	0	3.0	0.0
C+ /6.8	2.8	5.2	11.79	N/A	1	0	98	0	1	13	4.7	5	19	2,000	0	0.0	0.0
C+ /6.9	2.7	5.2	11.79	21	1	0	98	0	1	13	4.7	8	19	2,000	0	0.0	0.0
C+ /6.8	2.8	5.2	11.78	1	1	0	98	0	1	13	4.7	22	19	0	0	0.0	0.0
B- /7.0	2.7	5.2	11.81	N/A	1	0	98	0	1	13	4.7	23	19	0	0	0.0	0.0
B- /7.0	2.7	5.2	11.79	7	1	0	98	0	1	13	4.7	19	19	2,000	0	4.8	0.0
B- /7.0	2.7	5.2	11.79	201	1	0	98	0	1	13	4.7	23	19	2,000	0	0.0	0.0
C /4.7	3.2	5.4	10.33	42	1	0	98	0	1	8	4.3	13	6	2,000	0	3.0	0.0
C /4.7	3.2	5.4	10.32	N/A	1	0	98	0	1	8	4.3	4	6	2,000	0	0.0	0.0
C /4.8	3.2	5.4	10.32	15	1	0	98	0	1	8	4.3	5	6	2,000	0	0.0	0.0
C /4.9	3.2	5.4	10.30	1	1	0	98	0	1	8	4.3	20	6	0	0	0.0	0.0
C /4.6	3.3	5.4	10.27	5	1	0	98	0	1	8	4.3	19	6	0	0	0.0	0.0
C /4.7	3.2	5.4	10.30	357	1	0	98	0	1	8	4.3	18	6	2,000	0	0.0	0.0
C+ /6.7	2.8	5.0	10.55	8	4	0	95	0	1	12	4.7	9	15	2,000	0	3.0	0.0
C+ /6.4	2.8	5.0	10.55	N/A	4	0	95	0	1	12	4.7	3	15	2,000	0	0.0	0.0
C+ /6.6	2.8	5.0	10.55	5	4	0	95	0	1	12	4.7	4	15	2,000	0	0.0	0.0
C+ /6.7	2.8	5.0	10.54	1	4	0	95	0	1	12	4.7	13	15	0	0	0.0	0.0
C+ /6.4	2.8	5.0	10.54	11	4	0	95	0	1	12	4.7	9	15	2,000	0	4.8	0.0
C+ /6.6	2.8	5.0	10.55	111	4	0	95	0	1	12	4.7	12	15	2,000	0	0.0	0.0
C+ /6.8	2.8	5.3	10.41	20	2	0	97	0	1	13	4.7	10	6	2,000	0	3.0	0.0
C+ /6.9	2.7	5.3	10.41	N/A	2	0	97	0	1	13	4.7	3	6	2,000	0	0.0	0.0
C+ /6.7	2.8	5.3	10.41	4	2	0	97	0	1	13	4.7	3	6	2,000	0	0.0	0.0
C+ /6.6	2.8	5.3	10.40	N/A	2	0	97	0	1	13	4.7	14	6	0	0	0.0	0.0
C+ /6.9	2.7	5.3	10.41	47	2	0	97	0	1	13	4.7	15	6	2,000	0	0.0	0.0
C /4.3	2.9	5.5	10.44	230	0	0	99	0	1	6	4.7	19	8	2,000	0	3.0	0.0
C /4.3	2.9	5.5	10.44	N/A	0	0	99	0	1	6	4.7	8	8	2,000	0	0.0	0.0
C /4.3	2.9	5.5	10.44	52	0	0	99	0	1	6	4.7	7	8	2,000	0	0.0	0.0
C+ /6.1	2.9	5.5	10.43	11	0	0	99	0	1	6	4.7	24	8	0	0	0.0	0.0
C+ /6.1	2.9	5.5	10.43	11	0	0	99	0	1	6	4.7	27	8	0	0	0.0	0.0
C- /4.2	2.9	5.5	10.44	14	0	0	99	0	1	6	4.7	20	8	2,000	0	4.8	0.0
C /4.3	2.9	5.5	10.44	1,756	0	0	99	0	1	6	4.7	24	8	2,000	0	0.0	0.0
C+ /6.0	2.9	5.4	10.53	23	2	0	97	0	1	16	4.9	9	8	2,000	0	3.0	0.0
C+ /6.0	2.9	5.4	10.54	N/A	2	0	97	0	1	16	4.9	3	8	2,000	0	0.0	0.0

Fund Type	Fund Name	Ticker Symbol	Overall Investment Rating	Phone	Performance Rating/Pts	3 Mo	6 Mo	1Yr / Pct	3Yr / Pct	5Yr / Pct	Dividend Yield	Expense Ratio
									Annualized	Annualized	Incl. in Returns	
MUS	Columbia AMT-Fr MA Intm Muni Bd C	LMICX	D	(800) 345-6611	C- / 3.3	1.75	-3.16	-1.67 / 1	1.47 /47	1.20 /40	2.37	1.71
MUN	Columbia AMT-Fr MA Intm Muni Bd	CMANX	C+	(800) 345-6611	C / 5.2	2.03	-2.82	-0.89 / 5	2.21 /67	1.91 /57	3.08	0.71
MUN	Columbia AMT-Fr MA Intm Muni Bd	CMAUX	C+	(800) 345-6611	C / 5.4	2.05	-2.77	-0.80 / 6	2.25 /68	1.93 /57	3.16	N/A
MUS ●	Columbia AMT-Fr MA Intm Muni Bd V	GMBAX	D-	(800) 345-6611	D / 1.9	1.99	-2.89	-1.04 / 4	2.06 /64	1.76 /53	2.79	0.86
MUS	Columbia AMT-Fr MA Intm Muni Bd Z	SEMAX	C+	(800) 345-6611	C / 5.2	2.03	-2.82	-0.89 / 5	2.21 /67	1.91 /57	3.08	0.71
MUS	Columbia AMT-Fr MD Intm Muni Bd A	NMDMX	D	(800) 345-6611	C- / 3.0	1.89	-2.72	-0.49 /10	2.01 /62	1.77 /53	2.48	1.02
MUS ●	Columbia AMT-Fr MD Intm Muni Bd B	NMITX	D	(800) 345-6611	C- / 3.0	1.69	-3.08	-1.23 / 3	1.25 /42	1.01 /35	1.78	1.77
MUS	Columbia AMT-Fr MD Intm Muni Bd	NMINX	D	(800) 345-6611	C- / 3.0	1.70	-3.08	-1.23 / 3	1.25 /42	1.01 /35	1.79	1.77
MUN	Columbia AMT-Fr MD Intm Muni Bd	CMDMX	B	(800) 345-6611	C+ / 5.7	1.94	-2.60	-0.25 /14	2.30 /69	1.97 /58	2.80	0.77
MUS	Columbia AMT-Fr MD Intm Muni Bd Z	NMDBX	B-	(800) 345-6611	C+ / 5.6	1.95	-2.60	-0.24 /14	2.27 /68	2.02 /59	2.81	0.77
MUS	Columbia AMT-Fr NC Intm Muni Bd A	NNCIX	D-	(800) 345-6611	D / 2.1	1.81	-3.11	-1.05 / 4	1.69 /54	1.55 /47	2.37	0.96
MUS ●	Columbia AMT-Fr NC Intm Muni Bd B	NNITX	D-	(800) 345-6611	D / 2.0	1.52	-3.47	-1.79 / 1	0.93 /34	0.80 /30	1.67	1.71
MUS	Columbia AMT-Fr NC Intm Muni Bd C	NNINX	D-	(800) 345-6611	D / 2.0	1.52	-3.57	-1.89 / 1	0.93 /34	0.78 /30	1.67	1.71
MUN	Columbia AMT-Fr NC Intm Muni Bd	CNCEX	C	(800) 345-6611	C / 4.6	1.77	-3.09	-0.90 / 5	1.94 /61	1.79 /54	2.71	0.71
MUS	Columbia AMT-Fr NC Intm Muni Bd Z	NNIBX	C	(800) 345-6611	C / 4.6	1.87	-2.99	-0.81 / 6	1.94 /61	1.81 /54	2.70	0.71
MUS	Columbia AMT-Fr OR Inter Muni Bd A	COEAX	D+	(800) 345-6611	C- / 3.2	1.81	-2.67	-0.57 / 9	2.11 /65	1.81 /54	2.53	0.84
MUS ●	Columbia AMT-Fr OR Inter Muni Bd B	COEBX	D+	(800) 345-6611	C- / 3.1	1.54	-3.03	-1.32 / 2	1.34 /44	1.05 /36	1.83	1.59
MUS	Columbia AMT-Fr OR Inter Muni Bd	CORCX	C	(800) 345-6611	C- / 3.9	1.61	-2.89	-1.02 / 4	1.66 /53	1.38 /44	2.14	1.59
MUN	Columbia AMT-Fr OR Inter Muni Bd	CORMX	B+	(800) 345-6611	C+ / 5.8	1.79	-2.55	-0.32 /12	2.36 /70	2.07 /60	2.86	1.59
MUN	Columbia AMT-Fr OR Inter Muni Bd	CODRX	B+	(800) 345-6611	C+ / 6.0	1.88	-2.46	-0.20 /14	2.40 /71	2.10 /61	2.91	0.55
MUS	Columbia AMT-Fr OR Inter Muni Bd Z	CMBFX	B+	(800) 345-6611	C+ / 5.8	1.79	-2.55	-0.32 /12	2.36 /70	2.06 /60	2.86	0.59
MUS	Columbia AMT-Fr SC Intm Muni Bd A	NSCIX	D-	(800) 345-6611	D+ / 2.9	1.96	-3.06	-0.94 / 5	2.06 /64	1.87 /56	2.73	0.97
MUS ●	Columbia AMT-Fr SC Intm Muni Bd B	NISCX	D-	(800) 345-6611	D+ / 2.9	1.78	-3.41	-1.67 / 1	1.29 /43	1.13 /38	2.04	1.72
MUS	Columbia AMT-Fr SC Intm Muni Bd C	NSICX	D-	(800) 345-6611	D+ / 2.9	1.77	-3.41	-1.58 / 1	1.29 /43	1.13 /38	2.04	1.72
MUN	Columbia AMT-Fr SC Intm Muni Bd	CSICX	C+	(800) 345-6611	C / 5.5	2.03	-2.94	-0.60 / 8	2.31 /69	2.14 /62	3.06	0.72
MUS	Columbia AMT-Fr SC Intm Muni Bd Z	NSCMX	C+	(800) 345-6611	C / 5.5	2.03	-2.93	-0.59 / 8	2.31 /69	2.14 /62	3.06	0.72
MUS	Columbia AMT-Fr VA Intm Muni Bd A	NVAFX	C-	(800) 345-6611	C- / 3.0	1.68	-2.45	-0.70 / 7	2.04 /63	1.69 /51	2.70	0.95
MUS ●	Columbia AMT-Fr VA Intm Muni Bd B	NVANX	C-	(800) 345-6611	C- / 3.1	1.59	-2.72	-1.35 / 2	1.31 /43	0.95 /34	2.01	1.70
MUS	Columbia AMT-Fr VA Intm Muni Bd C	NVRCX	C-	(800) 345-6611	C- / 3.1	1.59	-2.72	-1.35 / 2	1.31 /43	0.95 /34	2.02	1.70
MUN	Columbia AMT-Fr VA Intm Muni Bd	CAIVX	B+	(800) 345-6611	C+ / 5.9	1.85	-2.23	-0.35 /12	2.36 /70	1.96 /58	3.05	0.70
MUS	Columbia AMT-Fr VA Intm Muni Bd Z	NVABX	B+	(800) 345-6611	C+ / 5.7	1.84	-2.24	-0.36 /12	2.32 /69	1.94 /57	3.04	0.70
COI	Columbia Bond A	CNDAX	D	(800) 345-6611	C- / 3.0	1.23	-1.92	2.70 /55	2.57 /53	2.08 /43	1.81	1.01
COI ●	Columbia Bond B	CNDBX	D	(800) 345-6611	C- / 3.7	1.04	-2.29	1.93 /48	1.81 /40	1.32 /32	1.14	1.76
COI	Columbia Bond C	CNDCX	D	(800) 345-6611	C- / 3.8	1.05	-2.29	1.93 /48	1.83 /40	1.39 /33	1.15	1.76
COI	Columbia Bond I	CBNIX	C+	(800) 345-6611	C+ / 5.7	1.33	-1.72	3.11 /57	2.99 /61	2.51 /50	2.31	0.56
COI	Columbia Bond R	CBFRX	C-	(800) 345-6611	C / 4.6	1.17	-2.05	2.44 /53	2.32 /48	1.82 /39	1.65	1.26
COI	Columbia Bond R4	CNDRX	C+	(800) 345-6611	C / 5.4	1.30	-1.81	2.84 /56	2.83 /58	2.33 /47	2.15	0.76
COI	Columbia Bond R5	CNFRX	C+	(800) 345-6611	C / 5.5	1.32	-1.76	2.94 /56	2.91 /59	2.40 /48	2.26	0.61
COI ●	Columbia Bond V	CNDTX	D	(800) 345-6611	C- / 3.1	1.14	-2.00	2.68 /54	2.63 /54	2.18 /44	1.91	0.91
COI	Columbia Bond W	CBDWX	C	(800) 345-6611	C / 5.0	1.23	-1.92	2.70 /55	2.57 /53	2.10 /44	1.90	1.01
COI	Columbia Bond Y	CBFYX	C+	(800) 345-6611	C+ / 5.7	1.33	-1.73	3.11 /57	2.99 /61	2.49 /49	2.31	0.56
COI	Columbia Bond Z	UMMGX	C+	(800) 345-6611	C / 5.4	1.29	-1.80	2.95 /56	2.83 /58	2.33 /47	2.15	0.76
MUS	Columbia CA Tax Exempt A	CLMPX	C	(800) 345-6611	B- / 7.1	1.87	-3.89	-0.22 /14	4.15 /94	4.01 /93	3.60	0.88
MUS ●	Columbia CA Tax Exempt B	CCABX	C	(800) 345-6611	B- / 7.1	1.68	-4.25	-0.97 / 4	3.37 /86	3.24 /84	2.94	1.63
MUS	Columbia CA Tax Exempt C	CCAOX	C+	(800) 345-6611	B- / 7.5	1.76	-4.22	-0.67 / 7	3.68 /90	3.55 /88	3.25	1.63
MUN	Columbia CA Tax Exempt R4	CCARX	B+	(800) 345-6611	B+ / 8.7	1.94	-3.89	0.03 /20	4.41 /95	4.22 /95	3.98	0.63
MUN	Columbia CA Tax Exempt R5	CCAUX	B+	(800) 345-6611	B+ / 8.5	2.07	-3.74	0.07 /23	4.25 /94	4.07 /94	3.99	N/A
MUS	Columbia CA Tax Exempt Z	CCAZX	B+	(800) 345-6611	B+ / 8.7	1.93	-3.89	0.03 /20	4.41 /95	4.27 /95	3.97	0.63
*GEI	Columbia CMG Ultra Short Term	CMGUX	C+	(800) 345-6611	D / 2.2	0.26	0.49	1.15 /41	0.63 /22	0.63 /23	0.92	0.26
USS	Columbia Corporate Income A	LIIAX	D-	(800) 345-6611	C / 5.2	2.26	-0.81	10.81 /81	2.78 /57	3.58 /67	2.52	0.98
USS ●	Columbia Corporate Income B	CIOBX	D-	(800) 345-6611	C+ / 6.0	2.08	-1.18	9.99 /79	2.04 /44	2.81 /54	1.90	1.73
USS	Columbia Corporate Income C	CIOCX	D	(800) 345-6611	C+ / 6.2	2.11	-1.10	10.15 /79	2.20 /46	2.96 /57	2.05	1.73

● Denotes fund is closed to new investors
* Denotes fund is included in Section II

www.thestreetratings.com

RISK			NET ASSETS		ASSET							FUND MANAGER		MINIMUM		LOADS	
Risk Rating/Pts	3 Yr Avg Standard Deviation	Avg Dura-tion	NAV As of 2/28/17	Total $(Mil)	Cash %	Gov. Bond %	Muni. Bond %	Corp. Bond %	Other %	Portfolio Turnover Ratio	Avg Coupon Rate	Manager Quality Pct	Manager Tenure (Years)	Initial Purch. $	Additional Purch. $	Front End Load	Back End Load
C+ / 6.0	2.9	5.4	10.53	10	2	0	97	0	1	16	4.9	5	8	2,000	0	0.0	0.0
C+ / 6.0	2.9	5.4	10.53	4	2	0	97	0	1	16	4.9	14	8	0	0	0.0	0.0
C+ / 6.1	2.9	5.4	10.56	N/A	2	0	97	0	1	16	4.9	15	8	0	0	0.0	0.0
C+ / 6.0	2.9	5.4	10.54	18	2	0	97	0	1	16	4.9	11	8	2,000	0	4.8	0.0
C+ / 6.0	2.9	5.4	10.54	203	2	0	97	0	1	16	4.9	14	8	2,000	0	0.0	0.0
C+ / 6.3	2.8	5.2	10.55	16	2	0	97	0	1	13	4.8	12	6	2,000	0	3.0	0.0
C+ / 6.5	2.8	5.2	10.56	N/A	2	0	97	0	1	13	4.8	4	6	2,000	0	0.0	0.0
C+ / 6.2	2.9	5.2	10.55	3	2	0	97	0	1	13	4.8	4	6	2,000	0	0.0	0.0
C+ / 6.4	2.8	5.2	10.55	N/A	2	0	97	0	1	13	4.8	17	6	0	0	0.0	0.0
C+ / 6.2	2.9	5.2	10.55	58	2	0	97	0	1	13	4.8	16	6	2,000	0	0.0	0.0
C+ / 6.4	2.8	5.6	10.29	20	1	0	98	0	1	11	4.9	7	6	2,000	0	3.0	0.0
C+ / 6.6	2.8	5.6	10.29	N/A	1	0	98	0	1	11	4.9	2	6	2,000	0	0.0	0.0
C+ / 6.3	2.9	5.6	10.28	7	1	0	98	0	1	11	4.9	2	6	2,000	0	0.0	0.0
C+ / 6.2	2.9	5.6	10.27	3	1	0	98	0	1	11	4.9	10	6	0	0	0.0	0.0
C+ / 6.3	2.8	5.6	10.28	165	1	0	98	0	1	11	4.9	10	6	2,000	0	0.0	0.0
C+ / 6.9	2.7	5.0	12.31	52	2	0	97	0	1	9	4.3	15	14	2,000	0	3.0	0.0
B- / 7.0	2.7	5.0	12.30	N/A	2	0	97	0	1	9	4.3	5	14	2,000	0	0.0	0.0
B- / 7.0	2.7	5.0	12.31	26	2	0	97	0	1	9	4.3	8	14	2,000	0	0.0	0.0
B- / 7.0	2.7	5.0	12.31	1	2	0	97	0	1	9	4.3	21	14	0	0	0.0	0.0
B- / 7.0	2.7	5.0	12.30	37	2	0	97	0	1	9	4.3	23	14	0	0	0.0	0.0
B- / 7.1	2.7	5.0	12.31	332	2	0	97	0	1	9	4.3	22	14	2,000	0	0.0	0.0
C / 5.4	3.0	5.7	10.12	24	2	0	97	0	1	16	4.9	9	6	2,000	0	3.0	0.0
C / 5.5	3.0	5.7	10.13	N/A	2	0	97	0	1	16	4.9	3	6	2,000	0	0.0	0.0
C / 5.5	3.0	5.7	10.13	14	2	0	97	0	1	16	4.9	3	6	2,000	0	0.0	0.0
C / 5.5	3.0	5.7	10.12	1	2	0	97	0	1	16	4.9	14	6	0	0	0.0	0.0
C / 5.4	3.0	5.7	10.13	87	2	0	97	0	1	16	4.9	14	6	2,000	0	0.0	0.0
B- / 7.2	2.6	5.0	10.75	39	2	0	97	0	1	12	4.5	16	6	2,000	0	3.0	0.0
B- / 7.3	2.6	5.0	10.76	N/A	2	0	97	0	1	12	4.5	6	6	2,000	0	0.0	0.0
B- / 7.2	2.6	5.0	10.76	5	2	0	97	0	1	12	4.5	6	6	2,000	0	0.0	0.0
B- / 7.2	2.7	5.0	10.75	1	2	0	97	0	1	12	4.5	24	6	0	0	0.0	0.0
B- / 7.2	2.7	5.0	10.75	153	2	0	97	0	1	12	4.5	22	6	2,000	0	0.0	0.0
C+ / 6.0	2.9	5.4	8.44	56	0	22	1	30	47	428	2.9	45	7	2,000	0	4.8	0.0
C+ / 5.9	2.9	5.4	8.44	N/A	0	22	1	30	47	428	2.9	16	7	2,000	0	0.0	0.0
C+ / 5.6	3.0	5.4	8.43	10	0	22	1	30	47	428	2.9	16	7	2,000	0	0.0	0.0
C+ / 5.7	3.0	5.4	8.46	N/A	0	22	1	30	47	428	2.9	61	7	0	0	0.0	0.0
C+ / 5.7	3.0	5.4	8.44	1	0	22	1	30	47	428	2.9	29	7	0	0	0.0	0.0
C+ / 6.0	2.9	5.4	8.43	1	0	22	1	30	47	428	2.9	57	7	0	0	0.0	0.0
C+ / 5.8	3.0	5.4	8.41	1	0	22	1	30	47	428	2.9	59	7	0	0	0.0	0.0
C+ / 6.2	2.9	5.4	8.42	10	0	22	1	30	47	428	2.9	51	7	2,000	0	4.8	0.0
C+ / 5.9	2.9	5.4	8.45	N/A	0	22	1	30	47	428	2.9	44	7	500	0	0.0	0.0
C+ / 5.7	3.0	5.4	8.45	30	0	22	1	30	47	428	2.9	61	7	0	0	0.0	0.0
C+ / 5.8	3.0	5.4	8.44	378	0	22	1	30	47	428	2.9	56	7	2,000	0	0.0	0.0
C- / 3.5	3.6	7.6	7.61	353	3	0	96	0	1	13	4.6	60	7	2,000	0	3.0	0.0
C- / 3.4	3.6	7.6	7.61	N/A	3	0	96	0	1	13	4.6	25	7	2,000	0	0.0	0.0
C- / 3.5	3.6	7.6	7.61	51	3	0	96	0	1	13	4.6	36	7	2,000	0	0.0	0.0
C- / 3.5	3.6	7.6	7.61	1	3	0	96	0	1	13	4.6	67	7	0	0	0.0	0.0
C- / 3.4	3.6	7.6	7.63	1	3	0	96	0	1	13	4.6	63	7	0	0	0.0	0.0
C- / 3.4	3.6	7.6	7.61	108	3	0	96	0	1	13	4.6	67	7	2,000	0	0.0	0.0
A+ / 9.9	0.3	0.5	9.01	1,795	2	12	2	48	36	82	1.8	62	5	3,000,000	2,500	0.0	0.0
D+ / 2.3	4.6	7.4	10.09	96	15	0	0	84	1	50	4.2	84	7	2,000	0	4.8	0.0
D / 2.2	4.6	7.4	10.09	N/A	15	0	0	84	1	50	4.2	76	7	2,000	0	0.0	0.0
D / 2.2	4.6	7.4	10.09	11	15	0	0	84	1	50	4.2	78	7	2,000	0	0.0	0.0

Fund Type	Fund Name	Ticker Symbol	Overall Investment Rating	Phone	Performance Rating/Pts	PERFORMANCE Total Return % through 2/28/17					Incl. in Returns	
	99 Pct = Best 0 Pct = Worst					3 Mo	6 Mo	1Yr / Pct	Annualized 3Yr / Pct	5Yr / Pct	Dividend Yield	Expense Ratio
COI	Columbia Corporate Income I	CPTIX	C-	(800) 345-6611	B- / 7.4	2.37	-0.61	11.26 /82	3.22 /64	4.02 /73	3.05	0.52
COI	Columbia Corporate Income R4	CIFRX	C-	(800) 345-6611	B- / 7.3	2.33	-0.59	11.10 /81	3.07 /62	3.86 /71	2.89	0.73
COI	Columbia Corporate Income R5	CPIRX	C-	(800) 345-6611	B- / 7.4	2.36	-0.54	11.34 /82	3.20 /64	3.97 /72	3.00	0.57
COI	Columbia Corporate Income W	CPIWX	D+	(800) 345-6611	B- / 7.0	2.27	-0.81	10.82 /81	2.78 /57	3.58 /67	2.65	0.98
COI	Columbia Corporate Income Y	CRIYX	C-	(800) 345-6611	B- / 7.5	2.37	-0.61	11.26 /82	3.25 /65	4.01 /73	3.05	0.52
USS	Columbia Corporate Income Z	SRINX	C-	(800) 345-6611	B- / 7.3	2.33	-0.69	11.09 /81	3.07 /62	3.84 /70	2.89	0.73
GEI	Columbia Diversified Real Return A	CDRAX	U	(800) 345-6611	U /	2.09	2.62	13.00 /85	--	--	1.97	2.69
GEI	Columbia Diversified Real Return C	CDRCX	U	(800) 345-6611	U /	1.80	2.24	12.04 /83	--	--	1.34	3.44
GEI	Columbia Diversified Real Return R4	CDRRX	U	(800) 345-6611	U /	2.05	2.75	13.17 /85	--	--	2.32	2.44
GEI	Columbia Diversified Real Return R5	CDRFX	U	(800) 345-6611	U /	2.04	2.62	13.13 /85	--	--	2.28	2.48
GEI	Columbia Diversified Real Return W	CDTWX	U	(800) 345-6611	U /	1.99	2.52	12.91 /85	--	--	2.08	2.69
GEI	Columbia Diversified Real Return Z	CDRZX	U	(800) 345-6611	U /	2.06	2.65	13.18 /85	--	--	2.33	2.44
EM	Columbia Emerging Markets Bond A	REBAX	C-	(800) 345-6611	B+ / 8.5	5.82	0.57	16.23 /91	4.77 /83	3.97 /72	2.59	1.14
EM	● Columbia Emerging Markets Bond B	CMBBX	C-	(800) 345-6611	B+ / 8.8	5.54	0.19	15.28 /89	3.97 /75	3.19 /60	2.00	1.89
EM	Columbia Emerging Markets Bond C	REBCX	C-	(800) 345-6611	B+ / 8.9	5.57	0.19	15.36 /89	3.99 /75	3.21 /61	2.00	1.89
EM	Columbia Emerging Markets Bond I	RSMIX	C+	(800) 345-6611	A+ / 9.6	5.85	0.82	16.81 /92	5.27 /87	4.49 /79	3.22	0.66
EM	● Columbia Emerging Markets Bond K	CMKRX	C	(800) 345-6611	A / 9.5	5.89	0.68	16.48 /91	5.01 /85	4.20 /75	2.93	0.96
EM	Columbia Emerging Markets Bond R	CMBRX	C	(800) 345-6611	A- / 9.2	5.67	0.35	15.84 /90	4.49 /81	3.72 /69	2.48	1.39
EM	Columbia Emerging Markets Bond R4	CEBSX	C	(800) 345-6611	A / 9.5	5.88	0.69	16.48 /91	5.05 /85	4.19 /75	2.96	0.89
EM	Columbia Emerging Markets Bond R5	CEBRX	C+	(800) 345-6611	A+ / 9.6	5.94	0.79	16.75 /91	5.26 /87	4.38 /77	3.17	0.71
EM	Columbia Emerging Markets Bond W	REMWX	C	(800) 345-6611	A / 9.4	5.83	0.65	16.24 /91	4.78 /83	4.00 /72	2.72	1.14
EM	Columbia Emerging Markets Bond Y	CEBYX	C+	(800) 345-6611	A+ / 9.6	5.85	0.73	16.69 /91	5.27 /87	4.42 /77	3.22	0.66
EM	Columbia Emerging Markets Bond Z	CMBZX	C	(800) 345-6611	A / 9.5	5.88	0.69	16.50 /91	5.05 /85	4.24 /75	2.96	0.89
LP	Columbia Floating Rate A	RFRAX	A	(800) 345-6611	B- / 7.1	1.95	3.61	11.84 /83	3.29 /66	4.52 /79	3.70	1.06
LP	● Columbia Floating Rate B	RSFBX	A	(800) 345-6611	B- / 7.1	1.76	3.34	11.12 /81	2.55 /53	3.74 /69	3.07	1.81
LP	Columbia Floating Rate C	RFRCX	A	(800) 345-6611	B- / 7.1	1.64	3.23	11.00 /81	2.52 /52	3.74 /69	3.08	1.81
LP	Columbia Floating Rate I	RFRIX	A+	(800) 345-6611	B+ / 8.3	2.03	3.90	12.35 /84	3.69 /71	4.90 /83	4.15	0.71
LP	● Columbia Floating Rate K	CFERX	A+	(800) 345-6611	B / 8.0	1.95	3.75	12.01 /83	3.38 /67	4.61 /80	3.86	1.01
LP	Columbia Floating Rate R	CFRRX	A	(800) 345-6611	B / 7.7	1.88	3.48	11.68 /83	3.07 /62	4.26 /76	3.57	1.31
LP	Columbia Floating Rate R4	CFLRX	A+	(800) 345-6611	B / 8.2	1.90	3.74	12.13 /83	3.54 /69	4.71 /81	4.06	0.81
LP	Columbia Floating Rate R5	RFRFX	A+	(800) 345-6611	B / 8.2	1.90	3.75	12.14 /84	3.60 /70	4.85 /82	4.10	0.76
LP	Columbia Floating Rate W	RFRWX	A+	(800) 345-6611	B / 7.9	1.93	3.69	11.89 /83	3.35 /66	4.55 /79	3.76	1.06
LP	Columbia Floating Rate Y	CFRYX	A+	(800) 345-6611	B / 8.1	1.92	3.79	12.23 /84	3.49 /69	4.65 /80	4.16	0.71
LP	Columbia Floating Rate Z	CFRZX	A+	(800) 345-6611	B / 8.2	2.01	3.74	12.12 /83	3.58 /70	4.78 /82	4.05	0.81
GL	Columbia Global Bond A	IGBFX	E-	(800) 345-6611	E- / 0.0	1.63	-5.39	0.72 /36	-2.45 / 2	-2.00 / 1	0.00	1.35
GL	● Columbia Global Bond B	IGLOX	E-	(800) 345-6611	E- / 0.0	1.46	-5.75	--	-3.17 / 1	-2.74 / 1	0.00	2.10
GL	Columbia Global Bond C	AGBCX	E-	(800) 345-6611	E- / 0.0	1.48	-5.66	--	-3.15 / 1	-2.74 / 1	0.00	2.10
GL	Columbia Global Bond I	AGBIX	E-	(800) 345-6611	E- / 0.1	1.81	-5.05	1.26 /42	-1.96 / 2	-1.57 / 1	0.00	0.88
GL	● Columbia Global Bond K	RGBRX	E-	(800) 345-6611	E- / 0.1	1.62	-5.37	0.89 /38	-2.28 / 2	-1.87 / 1	0.00	1.18
GL	Columbia Global Bond R	RBGRX	E-	(800) 345-6611	E- / 0.1	1.64	-5.42	0.54 /34	-2.66 / 1	-2.22 / 1	0.00	1.60
GL	Columbia Global Bond W	RGBWX	E-	(800) 345-6611	E- / 0.1	1.63	-5.39	0.72 /36	-2.45 / 2	-2.03 / 1	0.00	1.35
GL	Columbia Global Bond Y	CGBYX	E-	(800) 345-6611	E- / 0.1	1.81	-5.22	1.08 /40	-2.02 / 2	-1.64 / 1	0.00	0.88
GL	Columbia Global Bond Z	CGBZX	E-	(800) 345-6611	E- / 0.1	1.62	-5.36	0.89 /38	-2.19 / 2	-1.77 / 1	0.00	1.10
MMT	Columbia Government Money Market	IDSXX	D+	(800) 345-6611	E+ / 0.6	0.00	0.03	0.04 /20	0.02 / 7	0.02 / 7	0.04	N/A
MMT	● Columbia Government Money Market	ACBXX	D+	(800) 345-6611	E+ / 0.6	0.00	0.03	0.04 /20	0.02 / 7	0.02 / 7	0.04	N/A
MMT	Columbia Government Money Market	RCCXX	D+	(800) 345-6611	E+ / 0.6	0.00	0.04	0.04 /20	0.02 / 7	0.02 / 7	0.04	N/A
MMT	Columbia Government Money Market	RCIXX	D+	(800) 345-6611	E+ / 0.7	0.04	0.08	0.09 /22	0.04 / 9	0.03 / 9	0.09	N/A
MMT	Columbia Government Money Market	RVRXX	D+	(800) 345-6611	E+ / 0.6	0.00	0.03	0.04 /20	0.02 / 7	0.02 / 7	0.04	N/A
MMT	Columbia Government Money Market	CMRXX	D+	(800) 345-6611	E+ / 0.7	0.04	0.07	0.09 /22	0.04 / 9	0.03 / 9	0.09	N/A
MMT	Columbia Government Money Market	RCWXX	D+	(800) 345-6611	E+ / 0.6	0.00	0.04	0.04 /20	0.02 / 7	0.02 / 7	0.04	N/A
MMT	Columbia Government Money Market	IDYXX	D+	(800) 345-6611	E+ / 0.6	0.00	0.03	0.04 /20	0.02 / 7	0.02 / 7	0.04	N/A
*COH	Columbia High Yield Bond A	INEAX	C-	(800) 345-6611	B / 7.9	4.01	3.60	13.75 /86	4.28 /78	6.18 /93	4.49	1.06

● Denotes fund is closed to new investors
* Denotes fund is included in Section II

www.thestreetratings.com

I. Index of Bond and Money Market Mutual Funds

RISK			NET ASSETS		ASSET							FUND MANAGER		MINIMUM		LOADS	
Risk Rating/Pts	3 Yr Avg Standard Deviation	Avg Duration	NAV As of 2/28/17	Total $(Mil)	Cash %	Gov. Bond %	Muni. Bond %	Corp. Bond %	Other %	Portfolio Turnover Ratio	Avg Coupon Rate	Manager Quality Pct	Manager Tenure (Years)	Initial Purch. $	Additional Purch. $	Front End Load	Back End Load
D+ / 2.3	4.5	7.4	10.09	530	15	0	0	84	1	50	4.2	31	7	0	0	0.0	0.0
D+ / 2.3	4.5	7.4	10.08	13	15	0	0	84	1	50	4.2	26	7	0	0	0.0	0.0
D+ / 2.3	4.5	7.4	10.08	2	15	0	0	84	1	50	4.2	31	7	0	0	0.0	0.0
D+ / 2.3	4.6	7.4	10.09	7	15	0	0	84	1	50	4.2	18	7	500	0	0.0	0.0
D+ / 2.3	4.6	7.4	10.09	5	15	0	0	84	1	50	4.2	31	7	0	0	0.0	0.0
D / 2.2	4.6	7.4	10.09	594	15	0	0	84	1	50	4.2	86	7	2,000	0	0.0	0.0
U /	N/A	N/A	9.56	N/A	17	27	0	21	35	32	0.0	N/A	3	2,000	0	4.8	0.0
U /	N/A	N/A	9.56	N/A	17	27	0	21	35	32	0.0	N/A	3	2,000	0	0.0	0.0
U /	N/A	N/A	9.56	N/A	17	27	0	21	35	32	0.0	N/A	3	0	0	0.0	0.0
U /	N/A	N/A	9.55	N/A	17	27	0	21	35	32	0.0	N/A	3	100,000	0	0.0	0.0
U /	N/A	N/A	9.54	N/A	17	27	0	21	35	32	0.0	N/A	3	500	0	0.0	0.0
U /	N/A	N/A	9.56	1	17	27	0	21	35	32	0.0	N/A	3	2,000	0	0.0	0.0
E+ / 0.6	7.5	7.0	11.55	112	4	55	3	35	3	44	6.9	98	6	2,000	0	4.8	0.0
E+ / 0.6	7.5	7.0	11.53	N/A	4	55	3	35	3	44	6.9	97	6	2,000	0	0.0	0.0
E+ / 0.6	7.5	7.0	11.48	21	4	55	3	35	3	44	6.9	97	6	2,000	0	0.0	0.0
E+ / 0.6	7.5	7.0	11.56	170	4	55	3	35	3	44	6.9	99	6	0	0	0.0	0.0
E+ / 0.6	7.5	7.0	11.55	N/A	4	55	3	35	3	44	6.9	98	6	0	0	0.0	0.0
E+ / 0.6	7.5	7.0	11.54	25	4	55	3	35	3	44	6.9	98	6	0	0	0.0	0.0
E+ / 0.6	7.5	7.0	11.57	2	4	55	3	35	3	44	6.9	98	6	0	0	0.0	0.0
E+ / 0.6	7.5	7.0	11.56	37	4	55	3	35	3	44	6.9	99	6	0	0	0.0	0.0
E+ / 0.6	7.5	7.0	11.54	2	4	55	3	35	3	44	6.9	98	6	500	0	0.0	0.0
E+ / 0.6	7.5	7.0	11.56	3	4	55	3	35	3	44	6.9	99	6	0	0	0.0	0.0
E / 0.5	7.5	7.0	11.56	72	4	55	3	35	3	44	6.9	98	6	2,000	0	0.0	0.0
C+ / 6.6	2.8	0.3	9.08	517	4	0	0	28	68	25	4.7	89	11	5,000	0	3.0	0.0
C+ / 6.1	2.9	0.3	9.09	1	4	0	0	28	68	25	4.7	85	11	5,000	0	0.0	0.0
C+ / 6.4	2.8	0.3	9.08	103	4	0	0	28	68	25	4.7	84	11	5,000	0	0.0	0.0
C+ / 6.1	2.9	0.3	9.08	110	4	0	0	28	68	25	4.7	92	11	0	0	0.0	0.0
C+ / 6.2	2.9	0.3	9.10	N/A	4	0	0	28	68	25	4.7	90	11	0	0	0.0	0.0
C+ / 6.1	2.9	0.3	9.09	7	4	0	0	28	68	25	4.7	88	11	0	0	0.0	0.0
C+ / 6.2	2.9	0.3	9.06	17	4	0	0	28	68	25	4.7	91	11	0	0	0.0	0.0
C+ / 6.5	2.8	0.3	9.11	19	4	0	0	28	68	25	4.7	91	11	0	0	0.0	0.0
C+ / 6.4	2.8	0.3	9.10	N/A	4	0	0	28	68	25	4.7	90	11	500	0	0.0	0.0
C+ / 6.6	2.8	0.3	9.08	12	4	0	0	28	68	25	4.7	91	11	0	0	0.0	0.0
C+ / 6.3	2.9	0.3	9.07	318	4	0	0	28	68	25	4.7	91	11	2,000	0	0.0	0.0
D / 1.8	5.5	6.5	5.62	63	7	46	0	34	13	129	5.3	9	4	2,000	0	4.8	0.0
D / 1.7	5.5	6.5	5.57	N/A	7	46	0	34	13	129	5.3	3	4	2,000	0	0.0	0.0
D / 1.8	5.5	6.5	5.50	2	7	46	0	34	13	129	5.3	3	4	2,000	0	0.0	0.0
D / 1.7	5.5	6.5	5.64	N/A	7	46	0	34	13	129	5.3	19	4	0	0	0.0	0.0
D / 1.7	5.5	6.5	5.64	N/A	7	46	0	34	13	129	5.3	12	4	0	0	0.0	0.0
D / 1.7	5.5	6.5	5.58	N/A	7	46	0	34	13	129	5.3	6	4	0	0	0.0	0.0
D / 1.8	5.5	6.5	5.62	N/A	7	46	0	34	13	129	5.3	9	4	500	0	0.0	0.0
D / 1.8	5.5	6.5	5.63	N/A	7	46	0	34	13	129	5.3	17	4	0	0	0.0	0.0
D / 1.7	5.5	6.5	5.65	1	7	46	0	34	13	129	5.3	13	4	2,000	0	0.0	0.0
A+ / 9.9	N/A	N/A	1.00	848	100	0	0	0	0	0	0.0	39	N/A	2,000	0	0.0	0.0
A+ / 9.9	N/A	N/A	1.00	1	100	0	0	0	0	0	0.0	39	N/A	2,000	0	0.0	0.0
A+ / 9.9	N/A	N/A	1.00	23	100	0	0	0	0	0	0.0	39	N/A	2,000	0	0.0	0.0
A+ / 9.9	N/A	N/A	1.00	1	100	0	0	0	0	0	0.1	40	N/A	0	0	0.0	0.0
A+ / 9.9	N/A	N/A	1.00	5	100	0	0	0	0	0	0.0	39	N/A	0	0	0.0	0.0
A+ / 9.9	N/A	N/A	1.00	1	100	0	0	0	0	0	0.1	40	N/A	0	0	0.0	0.0
A+ / 9.9	N/A	N/A	1.00	N/A	100	0	0	0	0	0	0.0	39	N/A	500	0	0.0	0.0
A+ / 9.9	N/A	N/A	1.00	191	100	0	0	0	0	0	0.0	39	N/A	2,000	0	0.0	0.0
D / 1.8	5.0	4.2	2.97	1,134	5	0	0	92	3	51	6.2	66	7	2,000	0	4.8	0.0

Data as of February 28, 2017

99 Pct = Best
0 Pct = Worst

Fund Type	Fund Name	Ticker Symbol	Overall Investment Rating	Phone	Performance Rating/Pts	3 Mo	6 Mo	1Yr / Pct	3Yr / Pct	5Yr / Pct	Dividend Yield	Expense Ratio
COH ●	Columbia High Yield Bond B	IEIBX	C	(800) 345-6611	B+ / 8.3	3.82	3.22	12.91 / 85	3.50 / 69	5.39 / 87	3.98	1.81
COH	Columbia High Yield Bond C	APECX	C	(800) 345-6611	B+ / 8.3	3.84	3.22	12.56 / 84	3.52 / 69	5.44 / 88	3.98	1.81
COH	Columbia High Yield Bond I	RSHIX	B-	(800) 345-6611	A- / 9.2	4.12	3.80	13.81 / 86	4.58 / 82	6.61 / 95	5.10	0.66
COH ●	Columbia High Yield Bond K	RSHYX	C+	(800) 345-6611	A- / 9.0	4.03	3.64	13.44 / 86	4.27 / 78	6.29 / 94	4.80	0.96
COH	Columbia High Yield Bond R	CHBRX	C+	(800) 345-6611	B+ / 8.7	3.59	3.12	13.06 / 85	3.91 / 74	5.84 / 91	4.48	1.31
COH	Columbia High Yield Bond R4	CYLRX	C+	(800) 345-6611	A- / 9.1	3.71	3.37	13.59 / 86	4.43 / 80	6.38 / 94	4.97	0.81
COH	Columbia High Yield Bond R5	RSHRX	B-	(800) 345-6611	A- / 9.2	4.10	3.77	13.75 / 86	4.53 / 81	6.49 / 95	5.04	0.71
COH	Columbia High Yield Bond W	RHYWX	C+	(800) 345-6611	B+ / 8.9	4.04	3.61	13.60 / 86	4.21 / 78	6.14 / 93	4.85	1.06
COH	Columbia High Yield Bond Y	CHYYX	B-	(800) 345-6611	A- / 9.2	4.12	3.80	13.81 / 86	4.58 / 82	6.54 / 95	5.09	0.66
COH	Columbia High Yield Bond Z	CHYZX	C+	(800) 345-6611	A- / 9.1	4.08	3.73	13.65 / 86	4.42 / 80	6.37 / 94	4.96	0.81
MUH	Columbia High Yield Municipal A	LHIAX	B	(800) 345-6611	B+ / 8.9	2.48	-3.08	1.48 / 51	5.23 / 97	4.84 / 97	4.18	0.94
MUH ●	Columbia High Yield Municipal B	CHMBX	B	(800) 345-6611	B+ / 8.9	2.29	-3.36	0.81 / 42	4.45 / 95	4.07 / 94	3.54	1.69
MUH	Columbia High Yield Municipal C	CHMCX	B	(800) 345-6611	A- / 9.0	2.32	-3.31	0.91 / 44	4.56 / 96	4.19 / 95	3.64	1.69
MUH	Columbia High Yield Municipal R4	CHIYX	B+	(800) 345-6611	A+ / 9.7	2.53	-2.98	1.68 / 54	5.44 / 98	5.06 / 98	4.52	0.74
MUH	Columbia High Yield Municipal R5	CHMYX	A-	(800) 345-6611	A+ / 9.7	2.55	-2.95	1.76 / 55	5.53 / 98	5.14 / 98	4.60	0.62
MUH	Columbia High Yield Municipal Z	SRHMX	B+	(800) 345-6611	A+ / 9.7	2.53	-2.99	1.68 / 54	5.44 / 98	5.05 / 98	4.52	0.74
*COH	Columbia Income Opportunities A	AIOAX	D+	(800) 345-6611	B- / 7.5	3.92	3.12	12.63 / 84	4.00 / 75	5.66 / 90	4.17	1.13
COH ●	Columbia Income Opportunities B	AIOBX	C-	(800) 345-6611	B / 7.9	3.63	2.64	11.80 / 83	3.22 / 64	4.87 / 83	3.65	1.88
COH	Columbia Income Opportunities C	RIOCX	C-	(800) 345-6611	B / 7.9	3.74	2.74	11.80 / 83	3.22 / 64	4.93 / 83	3.65	1.88
COH	Columbia Income Opportunities I	AOPIX	C+	(800) 345-6611	A- / 9.0	4.03	3.23	13.09 / 85	4.45 / 80	6.11 / 93	4.80	0.65
COH ●	Columbia Income Opportunities K	COPRX	C+	(800) 345-6611	B+ / 8.8	3.95	3.18	12.74 / 85	4.14 / 77	5.79 / 91	4.50	0.95
COH	Columbia Income Opportunities R	CIORX	C	(800) 345-6611	B+ / 8.5	3.86	3.00	12.46 / 84	3.78 / 72	5.42 / 88	4.14	1.38
COH	Columbia Income Opportunities R4	CPPRX	C+	(800) 345-6611	B+ / 8.9	3.97	3.25	12.99 / 85	4.29 / 78	5.90 / 91	4.62	0.88
COH	Columbia Income Opportunities R5	CEPRX	C+	(800) 345-6611	A- / 9.0	4.01	3.31	13.14 / 85	4.40 / 80	6.00 / 92	4.74	0.70
COH	Columbia Income Opportunities W	CIOWX	C+	(800) 345-6611	B+ / 8.7	3.93	3.03	12.64 / 84	4.00 / 75	5.69 / 90	4.39	1.13
COH	Columbia Income Opportunities Y	CIOYX	C+	(800) 345-6611	A- / 9.1	4.02	3.34	13.20 / 85	4.48 / 80	6.13 / 93	4.79	0.65
COH	Columbia Income Opportunities Z	CIOZX	C+	(800) 345-6611	B+ / 8.9	3.98	3.25	13.00 / 85	4.29 / 78	5.94 / 92	4.62	0.88
GEI	Columbia Inflation Protected Sec A	APSAX	E+	(800) 345-6611	C- / 3.7	1.85	1.41	10.09 / 79	1.02 / 28	0.33 / 20	0.00	1.03
GEI ●	Columbia Inflation Protected Sec B	APSBX	E+	(800) 345-6611	C- / 3.7	1.66	0.99	9.29 / 77	0.31 / 19	-0.40 / 3	0.00	1.78
GEI ●	Columbia Inflation Protected Sec C	RIPCX	E+	(800) 345-6611	C- / 3.8	1.78	1.10	9.30 / 77	0.35 / 19	-0.37 / 3	0.00	1.78
GEI	Columbia Inflation Protected Sec I	AIPIX	D-	(800) 345-6611	C+ / 5.6	1.94	1.61	10.49 / 80	1.43 / 34	0.74 / 24	0.00	0.63
GEI ●	Columbia Inflation Protected Sec K	CISRX	E+	(800) 345-6611	C / 5.1	1.95	1.51	10.20 / 79	1.16 / 30	0.45 / 21	0.00	0.93
GEI	Columbia Inflation Protected Sec R	RIPRX	E+	(800) 345-6611	C / 4.5	1.86	1.31	9.80 / 78	0.80 / 24	0.08 / 13	0.00	1.28
GEI	Columbia Inflation Protected Sec R5	CFSRX	D-	(800) 345-6611	C / 5.5	1.95	1.62	10.43 / 80	1.39 / 33	0.64 / 23	0.00	0.68
GEI	Columbia Inflation Protected Sec W	RIPWX	E+	(800) 345-6611	C / 4.9	1.95	1.51	10.07 / 79	1.06 / 28	0.34 / 20	0.00	1.03
GEI	Columbia Inflation Protected Sec Z	CIPZX	E+	(800) 345-6611	C / 5.3	1.95	1.51	10.29 / 79	1.25 / 31	0.56 / 22	0.00	0.78
GEI	Columbia Limited Duration Credit A	ALDAX	D	(800) 345-6611	C- / 3.7	0.96	0.59	8.39 / 75	1.47 / 34	2.05 / 43	1.69	0.88
GEI ●	Columbia Limited Duration Credit B	ALDBX	D	(800) 345-6611	C- / 3.7	0.78	0.22	7.58 / 73	0.75 / 24	1.29 / 31	1.00	1.63
GEI	Columbia Limited Duration Credit C	RDCLX	D	(800) 345-6611	C- / 3.8	0.78	0.32	7.70 / 74	0.75 / 24	1.29 / 31	1.00	1.63
GEI	Columbia Limited Duration Credit I	ALDIX	C	(800) 345-6611	C / 5.5	0.94	0.77	8.78 / 76	1.84 / 40	2.42 / 48	2.10	0.47
GEI ●	Columbia Limited Duration Credit K	CLDRX	C-	(800) 345-6611	C / 5.0	0.87	0.62	8.44 / 75	1.54 / 35	2.11 / 44	1.81	0.77
COI	Columbia Limited Duration Credit R4	CDLRX	C	(800) 345-6611	C / 5.4	0.92	0.72	8.66 / 76	1.76 / 39	2.26 / 45	1.99	0.63
COI	Columbia Limited Duration Credit R5	CTLRX	C	(800) 345-6611	C / 5.5	1.03	0.74	8.72 / 76	1.83 / 40	2.35 / 47	2.05	0.52
GEI	Columbia Limited Duration Credit W	RLDWX	C-	(800) 345-6611	C / 5.0	0.96	0.59	8.50 / 75	1.51 / 35	2.05 / 43	1.75	0.88
COI	Columbia Limited Duration Credit Y	CLDYX	C	(800) 345-6611	C+ / 5.6	0.94	0.77	8.78 / 76	1.85 / 40	2.35 / 47	2.10	0.47
COI	Columbia Limited Duration Credit Z	CLDZX	C	(800) 345-6611	C / 5.4	0.92	0.72	8.66 / 76	1.73 / 38	2.29 / 46	1.99	0.63
MUS	Columbia Minnesota Tax-Exempt A	IMNTX	C+	(800) 345-6611	C+ / 6.4	1.89	-3.10	0.05 / 21	3.59 / 89	3.12 / 82	3.09	0.80
MUS ●	Columbia Minnesota Tax-Exempt B	IDSMX	C+	(800) 345-6611	C+ / 6.4	1.89	-3.28	-0.69 / 7	2.81 / 79	2.39 / 68	2.42	1.55
MUS	Columbia Minnesota Tax-Exempt C	RMTCX	C+	(800) 345-6611	C+ / 6.3	1.70	-3.46	-0.70 / 7	2.81 / 79	2.35 / 67	2.42	1.55
MUN	Columbia Minnesota Tax-Exempt R4	CLONX	A	(800) 345-6611	B / 8.2	1.95	-2.80	0.30 / 32	3.91 / 92	3.37 / 86	3.44	0.55
MUN	Columbia Minnesota Tax-Exempt R5	CADOX	A	(800) 345-6611	B / 8.1	1.95	-2.98	0.12 / 25	3.86 / 91	3.30 / 85	3.46	0.55
MUS	Columbia Minnesota Tax-Exempt Z	CMNZX	A	(800) 345-6611	B+ / 8.3	2.14	-2.80	0.30 / 32	3.91 / 92	3.42 / 86	3.44	0.55

● Denotes fund is closed to new investors
* Denotes fund is included in Section II

I. Index of Bond and Money Market Mutual Funds

RISK			NET ASSETS		ASSET					Portfolio Turnover Ratio	Avg Coupon Rate	FUND MANAGER		MINIMUM		LOADS	
Risk Rating/Pts	3 Yr Avg Standard Deviation	Avg Dura- tion	NAV As of 2/28/17	Total $(Mil)	Cash %	Gov. Bond %	Muni. Bond %	Corp. Bond %	Other %			Manager Quality Pct	Manager Tenure (Years)	Initial Purch. $	Additional Purch. $	Front End Load	Back End Load
D /1.7	5.0	4.2	2.97	3	5	0	0	92	3	51	6.2	31	7	2,000	0	0.0	0.0
D /1.8	4.9	4.2	2.95	89	5	0	0	92	3	51	6.2	36	7	2,000	0	0.0	0.0
D /1.7	5.0	4.2	2.96	307	5	0	0	92	3	51	6.2	73	7	0	0	0.0	0.0
D /1.8	5.0	4.2	2.97	36	5	0	0	92	3	51	6.2	68	7	0	0	0.0	0.0
D /1.7	5.0	4.2	2.97	25	5	0	0	92	3	51	6.2	55	7	0	0	0.0	0.0
D /1.7	5.0	4.2	2.98	57	5	0	0	92	3	51	6.2	71	7	0	0	0.0	0.0
D /1.7	5.0	4.2	2.96	79	5	0	0	92	3	51	6.2	73	7	0	0	0.0	0.0
D /1.7	5.0	4.2	2.94	N/A	5	0	0	92	3	51	6.2	63	7	500	0	0.0	0.0
D /1.7	5.0	4.2	2.96	54	5	0	0	92	3	51	6.2	73	7	0	0	0.0	0.0
D /1.7	5.0	4.2	2.96	285	5	0	0	92	3	51	6.2	70	7	2,000	0	0.0	0.0
D+ /2.5	3.8	7.2	10.49	160	1	0	98	0	1	10	5.0	80	8	2,000	0	3.0	0.0
D+ /2.5	3.7	7.2	10.49	N/A	1	0	98	0	1	10	5.0	67	8	2,000	0	0.0	0.0
D+ /2.5	3.7	7.2	10.49	54	1	0	98	0	1	10	5.0	70	8	2,000	0	0.0	0.0
D+ /2.5	3.7	7.2	10.50	3	1	0	98	0	1	10	5.0	82	8	0	0	0.0	0.0
D+ /2.5	3.7	7.2	10.48	5	1	0	98	0	1	10	5.0	83	8	0	0	0.0	0.0
D+ /2.5	3.8	7.2	10.49	577	1	0	98	0	1	10	5.0	82	8	2,000	0	0.0	0.0
D /1.7	5.1	4.3	9.94	1,529	6	0	0	92	2	53	6.0	58	14	2,000	0	4.8	0.0
D /1.7	5.0	4.3	9.93	3	6	0	0	92	2	53	6.0	24	14	2,000	0	0.0	0.0
D /1.7	5.0	4.3	9.93	97	6	0	0	92	2	53	6.0	25	14	2,000	0	0.0	0.0
D /1.7	5.0	4.3	9.95	340	6	0	0	92	2	53	6.0	71	14	0	0	0.0	0.0
D /1.7	5.0	4.3	9.97	1	6	0	0	92	2	53	6.0	62	14	0	0	0.0	0.0
D /1.7	5.0	4.3	9.95	2	6	0	0	92	2	53	6.0	49	14	0	0	0.0	0.0
D /1.7	5.0	4.3	9.98	10	6	0	0	92	2	53	6.0	67	14	0	0	0.0	0.0
D /1.7	5.0	4.3	9.97	95	6	0	0	92	2	53	6.0	69	14	0	0	0.0	0.0
D /1.7	5.0	4.3	9.94	1	6	0	0	92	2	53	6.0	59	14	500	0	0.0	0.0
D /1.7	5.0	4.3	9.96	4	6	0	0	92	2	53	6.0	71	14	1,000,000	0	0.0	0.0
D /1.7	5.0	4.3	9.97	634	6	0	0	92	2	53	6.0	67	14	2,000	0	0.0	0.0
D /1.7	5.5	5.8	9.38	67	0	82	0	12	6	60	1.6	5	5	5,000	0	3.0	0.0
D /1.7	5.5	5.8	9.18	N/A	0	82	0	12	6	60	1.6	2	5	5,000	0	0.0	0.0
D /1.8	5.4	5.8	9.17	8	0	82	0	12	6	60	1.6	2	5	5,000	0	0.0	0.0
D /1.7	5.5	5.8	9.48	81	0	82	0	12	6	60	1.6	11	5	0	0	0.0	0.0
D /1.7	5.5	5.8	9.40	N/A	0	82	0	12	6	60	1.6	7	5	0	0	0.0	0.0
D /1.7	5.5	5.8	9.30	6	0	82	0	12	6	60	1.6	4	5	0	0	0.0	0.0
D /1.7	5.5	5.8	9.42	N/A	0	82	0	12	6	60	1.6	10	5	0	0	0.0	0.0
D /1.8	5.5	5.8	9.40	N/A	0	82	0	12	6	60	1.6	6	5	500	0	0.0	0.0
D /1.6	5.6	5.8	9.43	14	0	82	0	12	6	60	1.6	7	5	2,000	0	0.0	0.0
C /5.1	3.1	3.0	9.83	353	5	2	0	90	3	49	3.3	69	14	2,000	0	3.0	0.0
C /5.3	3.1	3.0	9.83	N/A	5	2	0	90	3	49	3.3	44	14	2,000	0	0.0	0.0
C /5.1	3.1	3.0	9.83	49	5	2	0	90	3	49	3.3	N/A	14	2,000	0	0.0	0.0
C /5.3	3.1	3.0	9.83	122	5	2	0	90	3	49	3.3	77	14	0	0	0.0	0.0
C /5.3	3.1	3.0	9.85	N/A	5	2	0	90	3	49	3.3	72	14	0	0	0.0	0.0
C /5.2	3.1	3.0	9.83	52	5	2	0	90	3	49	3.3	56	14	0	0	0.0	0.0
C /5.3	3.0	3.0	9.84	61	5	2	0	90	3	49	3.3	59	14	0	0	0.0	0.0
C /5.2	3.1	3.0	9.85	1	5	2	0	90	3	49	3.3	71	14	500	0	0.0	0.0
C /5.2	3.1	3.0	9.83	3	5	2	0	90	3	49	3.3	59	14	0	0	0.0	0.0
C /5.2	3.1	3.0	9.83	104	5	2	0	90	3	49	3.3	55	14	2,000	0	0.0	0.0
C /5.0	3.1	6.5	5.42	471	0	0	99	0	1	8	4.9	57	10	2,000	0	3.0	0.0
C /4.7	3.2	6.5	5.43	N/A	0	0	99	0	1	8	4.9	21	10	2,000	0	0.0	0.0
C /5.0	3.1	6.5	5.42	73	0	0	99	0	1	8	4.9	22	10	2,000	0	0.0	0.0
C /5.4	3.0	6.5	5.42	3	0	0	99	0	1	8	4.9	69	10	0	0	0.0	0.0
C /5.3	3.1	6.5	5.41	1	0	0	99	0	1	8	4.9	67	10	100,000	0	0.0	0.0
C /4.9	3.2	6.5	5.42	41	0	0	99	0	1	8	4.9	66	10	2,000	0	0.0	0.0

Fund Type	Fund Name	Ticker Symbol	Overall Investment Rating	Phone	Perfor-mance Rating/Pts	3 Mo	6 Mo	1Yr / Pct	3Yr / Pct	5Yr / Pct	Dividend Yield	Expense Ratio
* COI	Columbia MMrg Tot Rtn Bd Strat A	CMCPX	B-	(800) 345-6611	C / 4.9	1.44	-1.64	3.10 /57	2.43 /51	--	2.02	0.81
COI	Columbia MMrg Tot Rtn Bd Strat Z	CTRZX	B-	(800) 345-6611	C / 5.0	1.48	-1.61	3.13 /57	2.44 /51	--	2.04	N/A
MUS	Columbia NY Tax-Exempt A	COLNX	C+	(800) 345-6611	B- / 7.0	2.04	-3.43	0.25 /31	3.95 /92	3.28 /84	3.04	0.91
MUS ●	Columbia NY Tax-Exempt B	CNYBX	C+	(800) 345-6611	C+ / 6.9	1.72	-3.92	-0.64 / 8	3.18 /84	2.51 /71	2.37	1.66
MUS	Columbia NY Tax-Exempt C	CNYCX	C+	(800) 345-6611	B- / 7.4	1.79	-3.77	-0.34 /12	3.49 /88	2.82 /77	2.67	1.66
MUN	Columbia NY Tax-Exempt R4	CNYEX	B+	(800) 345-6611	B+ / 8.5	1.97	-3.45	0.36 /34	4.21 /94	3.46 /87	3.40	0.66
MUN	Columbia NY Tax-Exempt R5	CNYRX	B+	(800) 345-6611	B+ / 8.6	2.11	-3.44	0.39 /35	4.20 /94	3.50 /87	3.43	0.59
MUN	Columbia NY Tax-Exempt Z	CNYZX	B+	(800) 345-6611	B+ / 8.6	2.11	-3.44	0.36 /34	4.21 /94	3.52 /88	3.39	0.66
GEI	Columbia Short Term Bond A	NSTRX	C	(800) 345-6611	D / 1.9	0.44	0.15	1.46 /44	0.65 /22	0.86 /26	0.74	0.88
GEI ●	Columbia Short Term Bond B	NSTFX	C	(800) 345-6611	D / 1.8	0.27	-0.10	1.15 /41	0.35 /19	0.47 /21	0.44	1.63
GEI	Columbia Short Term Bond C	NSTIX	C-	(800) 345-6611	D- / 1.3	0.30	-0.14	0.90 /39	0.10 /13	0.40 /20	0.19	1.63
GEI	Columbia Short Term Bond I	CTMIX	B-	(800) 345-6611	C- / 3.0	0.54	0.34	1.86 /48	1.05 /28	1.25 /31	1.14	0.44
GEI ●	Columbia Short Term Bond K	CBRFX	C+	(800) 345-6611	D+ / 2.4	0.36	0.09	1.45 /44	0.72 /23	0.93 /26	0.84	0.74
GEI	Columbia Short Term Bond R	CSBRX	C	(800) 345-6611	D / 1.9	0.38	0.03	1.20 /42	0.40 /20	0.60 /22	0.49	1.13
COI	Columbia Short Term Bond R4	CMDRX	C+	(800) 345-6611	D+ / 2.7	0.40	0.18	1.71 /46	0.90 /26	1.11 /29	0.99	0.63
COI	Columbia Short Term Bond R5	CCBRX	B-	(800) 345-6611	D+ / 2.8	0.43	0.22	1.71 /46	0.97 /27	1.17 /30	1.09	0.49
GEI	Columbia Short Term Bond W	CSBWX	C+	(800) 345-6611	D+ / 2.3	0.45	0.15	1.46 /44	0.65 /22	0.86 /26	0.75	0.88
GEI	Columbia Short Term Bond Y	CSBYX	B-	(800) 345-6611	C- / 3.0	0.54	0.24	1.86 /48	1.05 /28	1.25 /31	1.14	0.44
GEI	Columbia Short Term Bond Z	NSTMX	B-	(800) 345-6611	D+ / 2.7	0.40	0.18	1.71 /46	0.90 /26	1.11 /29	0.99	0.63
MUN	Columbia Sh-Term Muni Bd A	NSMMX	D	(800) 345-6611	E+ / 0.6	0.86	-0.35	--	0.27 /20	0.47 /24	0.86	0.88
MUN●	Columbia Sh-Term Muni Bd B	NSMNX	D	(800) 345-6611	E / 0.3	0.67	-0.73	-0.73 / 7	-0.47 / 4	-0.29 / 4	0.14	1.63
MUN	Columbia Sh-Term Muni Bd C	NSMUX	D	(800) 345-6611	E / 0.3	0.77	-0.63	-0.72 / 7	-0.44 / 4	-0.27 / 4	0.14	1.63
MUN	Columbia Sh-Term Muni Bd R4	CSMTX	C+	(800) 345-6611	D+ / 2.5	1.02	-0.13	0.35 /34	0.55 /25	0.72 /29	1.12	0.63
MUN	Columbia Sh-Term Muni Bd R5	CNNRX	C+	(800) 345-6611	D+ / 2.6	1.04	-0.18	0.35 /34	0.62 /27	0.80 /30	1.22	0.49
MUN	Columbia Sh-Term Muni Bd Z	NSMIX	C+	(800) 345-6611	D+ / 2.4	1.02	-0.13	0.25 /31	0.55 /25	0.73 /29	1.12	0.63
* GES	Columbia Strategic Income A	COSIX	C	(800) 345-6611	C+ / 6.6	2.44	1.49	10.61 /80	3.68 /71	4.08 /73	2.80	1.05
GES ●	Columbia Strategic Income B	CLSBX	C+	(800) 345-6611	B- / 7.2	2.25	1.12	9.80 /78	2.97 /60	3.31 /62	2.21	1.80
GES	Columbia Strategic Income C	CLSCX	C	(800) 345-6611	B- / 7.2	2.08	1.12	9.79 /78	2.95 /60	3.36 /63	2.21	1.80
GES ●	Columbia Strategic Income K	CSIVX	B	(800) 345-6611	B / 8.2	2.49	1.74	10.91 /81	3.86 /73	4.19 /75	3.09	0.92
GES	Columbia Strategic Income R	CSNRX	B-	(800) 345-6611	B / 7.7	2.36	1.36	10.27 /79	3.46 /68	3.84 /70	2.68	1.30
GL	Columbia Strategic Income R4	CMNRX	B	(800) 345-6611	B / 8.2	2.37	1.64	10.88 /81	3.95 /75	4.29 /76	3.24	0.80
GES	Columbia Strategic Income R5	CTIVX	B	(800) 345-6611	B+ / 8.3	2.38	1.68	10.97 /81	4.06 /76	4.45 /78	3.33	0.67
GES	Columbia Strategic Income W	CTTWX	B-	(800) 345-6611	B / 8.0	2.44	1.49	10.62 /80	3.75 /72	4.11 /74	2.94	1.05
GL	Columbia Strategic Income Y	CPHUX	B	(800) 345-6611	B+ / 8.4	2.58	1.72	11.06 /81	4.12 /76	4.42 /77	3.39	0.62
GES	Columbia Strategic Income Z	LSIZX	B	(800) 345-6611	B+ / 8.3	2.54	1.64	10.87 /81	4.00 /75	4.34 /77	3.23	0.80
* MUN	Columbia Strategic Municipal Inc A	INTAX	B-	(800) 345-6611	B / 7.9	2.17	-3.56	0.89 /43	4.56 /96	4.11 /94	3.61	0.82
MUN●	Columbia Strategic Municipal Inc B	ITEBX	B-	(800) 345-6611	B / 7.9	1.98	-3.92	0.13 /26	3.78 /91	3.34 /85	2.95	1.57
MUN	Columbia Strategic Municipal Inc C	RTCEX	B-	(800) 345-6611	B / 7.9	1.98	-3.92	0.13 /26	3.78 /91	3.34 /85	2.95	1.57
MUN	Columbia Strategic Municipal Inc R4	CATRX	A-	(800) 345-6611	A / 9.3	2.24	-3.45	1.13 /46	4.83 /97	4.32 /95	3.98	0.57
MUN	Columbia Strategic Municipal Inc R5	CADNX	A-	(800) 345-6611	A / 9.3	2.25	-3.44	1.13 /47	4.83 /97	4.28 /95	3.98	0.57
MUN	Columbia Strategic Municipal Inc Z	CATZX	A	(800) 345-6611	A / 9.3	2.23	-3.45	1.13 /47	4.83 /97	4.37 /96	3.98	0.57
* MUN	Columbia Tax-Exempt A	COLTX	C	(800) 345-6611	C+ / 6.7	1.93	-3.70	0.17 /28	3.81 /91	3.38 /86	3.98	0.72
MUN●	Columbia Tax-Exempt B	CTEBX	C	(800) 345-6611	C+ / 6.7	1.82	-4.00	-0.58 / 8	3.04 /82	2.62 /73	3.32	1.47
MUN	Columbia Tax-Exempt C	COLCX	C	(800) 345-6611	C+ / 6.9	1.77	-4.02	-0.55 / 9	3.20 /84	2.79 /76	3.43	1.47
MUN	Columbia Tax-Exempt R4	CTERX	B+	(800) 345-6611	B+ / 8.3	1.98	-3.61	0.30 /32	4.02 /93	3.54 /88	4.31	0.52
MUN	Columbia Tax-Exempt R5	CADMX	B	(800) 345-6611	B+ / 8.4	2.07	-3.59	0.42 /36	4.08 /93	3.55 /88	4.36	0.50
MUN	Columbia Tax-Exempt Z	CTEZX	B	(800) 345-6611	B+ / 8.3	1.98	-3.61	0.38 /35	4.02 /93	3.59 /89	4.31	0.52
* COI	Columbia Total Return Bond A	LIBAX	C	(800) 345-6611	C / 4.7	1.44	-1.38	4.45 /64	2.91 /59	2.60 /51	2.49	0.90
COI ●	Columbia Total Return Bond B	LIBBX	C+	(800) 345-6611	C / 4.6	1.26	-1.74	3.67 /61	2.14 /45	1.86 /40	1.81	1.65
COI	Columbia Total Return Bond C	LIBCX	C	(800) 345-6611	C / 4.7	1.26	-1.74	3.67 /61	2.18 /46	1.95 /41	1.81	1.65
COI	Columbia Total Return Bond I	CIMIX	B+	(800) 345-6611	C+ / 6.5	1.53	-1.20	4.82 /66	3.28 /65	2.99 /58	2.93	0.50
COI ●	Columbia Total Return Bond K	CIBKX	B	(800) 345-6611	C+ / 6.0	1.57	-1.24	4.51 /65	2.97 /60	2.73 /53	2.62	0.80

● Denotes fund is closed to new investors
* Denotes fund is included in Section II

Risk Rating/Pts	3 Yr Avg Standard Deviation	Avg Duration	NAV As of 2/28/17	Total $(Mil)	Cash %	Gov. Bond %	Muni. Bond %	Corp. Bond %	Other %	Portfolio Turnover Ratio	Avg Coupon Rate	Manager Quality Pct	Manager Tenure (Years)	Initial Purch. $	Additional Purch. $	Front End Load	Back End Load
C+ / 6.9	2.7	5.2	9.99	7,059	4	21	0	30	45	289	3.0	43	5	100	0	0.0	0.0
C+ / 6.9	2.7	5.2	10.00	N/A	4	21	0	30	45	289	3.0	44	5	100	0	0.0	0.0
C- / 3.7	3.5	7.2	7.36	163	4	0	95	0	1	9	4.7	57	7	2,000	0	3.0	0.0
C- / 3.8	3.4	7.2	7.35	N/A	4	0	95	0	1	9	4.7	25	7	2,000	0	0.0	0.0
C- / 3.7	3.4	7.2	7.35	30	4	0	95	0	1	9	4.7	34	7	2,000	0	0.0	0.0
C- / 3.8	3.4	7.2	7.34	N/A	4	0	95	0	1	9	4.7	66	7	0	0	0.0	0.0
C- / 3.8	3.4	7.2	7.33	1	4	0	95	0	1	9	4.7	66	7	0	0	0.0	0.0
C- / 3.7	3.5	7.2	7.35	25	4	0	95	0	1	9	4.7	64	7	2,000	0	0.0	0.0
A+ / 9.6	0.8	1.6	9.99	337	4	16	1	36	43	73	2.2	N/A	13	2,000	0	1.0	0.0
A+ / 9.6	0.7	1.6	9.98	1	4	16	1	36	43	73	2.2	32	13	2,000	0	0.0	0.0
A+ / 9.6	0.8	1.6	9.97	62	4	16	1	36	43	73	2.2	22	13	2,000	0	0.0	0.0
A+ / 9.6	0.7	1.6	9.97	387	4	16	1	36	43	73	2.2	64	13	0	0	0.0	0.0
A+ / 9.6	0.8	1.6	9.96	N/A	4	16	1	36	43	73	2.2	50	13	0	0	0.0	0.0
A+ / 9.6	0.7	1.6	9.99	4	4	16	1	36	43	73	2.2	33	13	0	0	0.0	0.0
A+ / 9.6	0.8	1.6	9.97	10	4	16	1	36	43	73	2.2	56	13	0	0	0.0	0.0
A+ / 9.6	0.7	1.6	9.96	17	4	16	1	36	43	73	2.2	60	13	0	0	0.0	0.0
A+ / 9.6	0.8	1.6	9.99	2	4	16	1	36	43	73	2.2	46	13	500	0	0.0	0.0
A+ / 9.6	0.7	1.6	9.97	24	4	16	1	36	43	73	2.2	63	13	0	0	0.0	0.0
A+ / 9.7	0.7	1.6	9.97	983	4	16	1	36	43	73	2.2	60	13	2,000	0	0.0	0.0
A / 9.4	0.9	1.8	10.35	119	1	0	98	0	1	37	3.9	20	5	2,000	0	1.0	0.0
A / 9.4	0.9	1.8	10.34	N/A	1	0	98	0	1	37	3.9	7	5	2,000	0	0.0	0.0
A / 9.4	0.9	1.8	10.35	15	1	0	98	0	1	37	3.9	8	5	2,000	0	0.0	0.0
A / 9.4	0.9	1.8	10.36	1	1	0	98	0	1	37	3.9	29	5	0	0	0.0	0.0
A / 9.4	0.9	1.8	10.35	16	1	0	98	0	1	37	3.9	31	5	0	0	0.0	0.0
A / 9.4	0.9	1.8	10.36	1,409	1	0	98	0	1	37	3.9	29	5	2,000	0	0.0	0.0
C- / 3.5	3.8	4.1	5.98	1,713	0	11	0	45	44	168	4.8	91	7	2,000	0	4.8	0.0
C- / 3.5	3.7	4.1	5.98	3	0	11	0	45	44	168	4.8	87	7	2,000	0	0.0	0.0
C- / 3.4	3.8	4.1	5.98	326	0	11	0	45	44	168	4.8	87	7	2,000	0	0.0	0.0
C- / 3.4	3.8	4.1	5.89	N/A	0	11	0	45	44	168	4.8	92	7	0	0	0.0	0.0
C- / 3.5	3.8	4.1	6.02	6	0	11	0	45	44	168	4.8	90	7	0	0	0.0	0.0
C- / 3.5	3.8	4.1	5.88	65	0	11	0	45	44	168	4.8	95	7	0	0	0.0	0.0
C- / 3.5	3.7	4.1	5.89	129	0	11	0	45	44	168	4.8	93	7	0	0	0.0	0.0
C- / 3.5	3.8	4.1	5.98	N/A	0	11	0	45	44	168	4.8	91	7	500	0	0.0	0.0
C- / 3.5	3.8	4.1	5.88	13	0	11	0	45	44	168	4.8	95	7	0	0	0.0	0.0
C- / 3.5	3.8	4.1	5.89	917	0	11	0	45	44	168	4.8	93	7	2,000	0	0.0	0.0
C- / 3.5	3.6	7.5	3.96	677	1	0	98	0	1	11	4.9	72	10	2,000	0	3.0	0.0
C- / 3.5	3.6	7.5	3.96	N/A	1	0	98	0	1	11	4.9	46	10	2,000	0	0.0	0.0
C- / 3.3	3.7	7.5	3.96	42	1	0	98	0	1	11	4.9	35	10	2,000	0	0.0	0.0
C- / 3.4	3.6	7.5	3.95	10	1	0	98	0	1	11	4.9	75	10	0	0	0.0	0.0
C- / 3.3	3.8	7.5	3.95	8	1	0	98	0	1	11	4.9	74	10	100,000	0	0.0	0.0
C- / 3.5	3.6	7.5	3.95	167	1	0	98	0	1	11	4.9	76	10	2,000	0	0.0	0.0
C- / 3.6	3.5	7.3	13.45	3,009	1	0	98	0	1	14	5.1	52	15	2,000	0	3.0	0.0
C- / 3.6	3.5	7.3	13.44	1	1	0	98	0	1	14	5.1	18	15	2,000	0	0.0	0.0
C- / 3.6	3.5	7.3	13.44	113	1	0	98	0	1	14	5.1	24	15	2,000	0	0.0	0.0
C- / 3.7	3.5	7.3	13.44	9	1	0	98	0	1	14	5.1	60	15	0	0	0.0	0.0
C- / 3.5	3.6	7.3	13.45	1	1	0	98	0	1	14	5.1	60	15	100,000	0	0.0	0.0
C- / 3.6	3.5	7.3	13.45	729	1	0	98	0	1	14	5.1	59	15	2,000	0	0.0	0.0
C+ / 6.3	2.9	5.6	9.01	893	0	12	1	44	43	458	3.6	60	5	2,000	0	3.0	0.0
C+ / 6.6	2.8	5.6	9.01	3	0	12	1	44	43	458	3.6	27	5	2,000	0	0.0	0.0
C+ / 6.3	2.9	5.6	9.01	51	0	12	1	44	43	458	3.6	27	5	2,000	0	0.0	0.0
C+ / 6.4	2.8	5.6	9.02	443	0	12	1	44	43	458	3.6	71	5	0	0	0.0	0.0
C+ / 6.4	2.8	5.6	9.01	3	0	12	1	44	43	458	3.6	62	5	0	0	0.0	0.0

| | | | | | | | | Total Return % through 2/28/17 | | Incl. in Returns | |
Fund Type	Fund Name	Ticker Symbol	Overall Investment Rating	Phone	Perfor-mance Rating/Pts	3 Mo	6 Mo	1Yr / Pct	3Yr / Pct (Annualized)	5Yr / Pct	Dividend Yield	Expense Ratio
COI	Columbia Total Return Bond R	CIBRX	B	(800) 345-6611	C / 5.5	1.38	-1.50	4.07 /62	2.65 /55	2.35 /47	2.32	1.15
COI	Columbia Total Return Bond R4	CBNRX	B+	(800) 345-6611	C+/ 6.3	1.51	-1.15	4.71 /65	3.16 /63	2.85 /55	2.82	0.65
COI	Columbia Total Return Bond R5	CTBRX	B+	(800) 345-6611	C+/ 6.4	1.52	-1.23	4.77 /66	3.23 /65	2.92 /56	2.87	0.55
COI	Columbia Total Return Bond W	CIBWX	B	(800) 345-6611	C+/ 5.9	1.34	-1.48	4.33 /64	2.87 /59	2.59 /51	2.57	0.90
COI	Columbia Total Return Bond Y	CTBYX	A-	(800) 345-6611	C+/ 6.5	1.54	-1.09	4.82 /66	3.28 /65	2.98 /57	2.93	0.50
COI	Columbia Total Return Bond Z	SRBFX	A-	(800) 345-6611	C+/ 6.4	1.62	-1.14	4.70 /65	3.20 /64	2.88 /56	2.81	0.65
* USS	Columbia US Government Mortgage	AUGAX	B-	(800) 345-6611	C- / 3.9	0.88	-0.17	2.34 /52	2.60 /54	2.65 /52	1.97	0.97
USS ●	Columbia US Government Mortgage	AUGBX	B-	(800) 345-6611	C- / 3.8	0.69	-0.72	1.57 /45	1.77 /39	1.84 /39	1.27	1.72
USS	Columbia US Government Mortgage	AUGCX	B-	(800) 345-6611	C- / 3.9	0.69	-0.54	1.57 /45	1.83 /40	1.88 /40	1.27	1.72
USS	Columbia US Government Mortgage I	RVGIX	A	(800) 345-6611	C+/ 5.7	0.79	-0.16	2.56 /54	2.94 /60	3.00 /58	2.43	0.52
USS ●	Columbia US Government Mortgage	RSGYX	A	(800) 345-6611	C / 5.3	0.90	-0.13	2.44 /53	2.69 /56	2.70 /53	2.13	0.82
MTG	Columbia US Government Mortgage	CUGUX	A-	(800) 345-6611	C / 4.9	0.63	-0.48	2.08 /50	2.49 /51	2.48 /49	1.77	1.22
MTG	Columbia US Government Mortgage	CUVRX	A	(800) 345-6611	C / 5.4	0.75	-0.23	2.40 /52	2.79 /58	2.82 /55	2.28	0.72
MTG	Columbia US Government Mortgage	CGVRX	A+	(800) 345-6611	C+/ 5.8	0.96	0.00	2.70 /55	2.95 /60	2.94 /57	2.38	0.57
MTG	Columbia US Government Mortgage	CGMWX	A-	(800) 345-6611	C / 5.1	0.89	-0.16	2.35 /52	2.60 /54	2.69 /53	2.04	0.97
MTG	Columbia US Government Mortgage	CUGYX	A	(800) 345-6611	C+/ 5.8	0.98	0.02	2.75 /55	2.94 /60	2.85 /55	2.43	0.52
MTG	Columbia US Government Mortgage	CUGZX	A	(800) 345-6611	C / 5.4	0.75	-0.23	2.40 /52	2.79 /58	--	2.28	0.72
MUN	Columbia US Social Bond A	CONAX	U	(800) 345-6611	U /	2.31	-3.68	-0.18 /15	--	--	1.90	1.39
MUN	Columbia US Social Bond C	CONCX	U	(800) 345-6611	U /	2.11	-4.05	-0.94 / 5	--	--	1.17	2.14
MUN	Columbia US Social Bond R4	CONFX	U	(800) 345-6611	U /	2.37	-3.56	0.08 /23	--	--	2.22	1.14
MUN	Columbia US Social Bond R5	COVNX	U	(800) 345-6611	U /	2.37	-3.56	-0.04 /17	--	--	2.20	1.13
MUN	Columbia US Social Bond Z	CONZX	U	(800) 345-6611	U /	2.37	-3.56	0.07 /23	--	--	2.21	1.14
US	Columbia US Treasury Index A	LUTAX	E+	(800) 345-6611	D+/ 2.5	0.60	-3.37	-1.49 / 2	1.56 /36	0.99 /27	1.27	0.66
US ●	Columbia US Treasury Index B	LUTBX	E	(800) 345-6611	D- / 1.1	0.41	-3.73	-2.22 / 1	0.81 /24	0.24 /19	0.51	1.41
US	Columbia US Treasury Index C	LUTCX	E+	(800) 345-6611	D- / 1.3	0.42	-3.71	-2.17 / 1	0.87 /26	0.34 /20	0.56	1.41
US	Columbia US Treasury Index I	CUTIX	E+	(800) 345-6611	D+/ 2.8	0.63	-3.30	-1.34 / 2	1.73 /38	1.19 /30	1.43	0.41
US	Columbia US Treasury Index R5	CUTRX	E+	(800) 345-6611	D+/ 2.8	0.63	-3.31	-1.35 / 2	1.73 /39	1.19 /30	1.43	0.41
US	Columbia US Treasury Index W	CTIWX	E+	(800) 345-6611	D+/ 2.4	0.57	-3.33	-1.59 / 1	1.51 /35	0.94 /27	1.18	0.66
US	Columbia US Treasury Index Z	IUTIX	E+	(800) 345-6611	D+/ 2.8	0.63	-3.30	-1.34 / 2	1.73 /39	1.19 /30	1.43	0.41
* GEI	Commerce Bond	CFBNX	A-	(800) 995-6365	C+/ 5.9	1.48	-0.94	3.98 /62	2.89 /59	3.14 /60	3.40	0.68
MUI	Commerce Kansas T/F Intm Bond	KTXIX	B+	(800) 995-6365	C+/ 5.7	1.56	-2.62	-0.43 /10	2.37 /71	1.97 /58	2.19	0.85
MUS	Commerce Missouri T/F Intm Bd	CFMOX	B	(800) 995-6365	C+/ 5.9	1.92	-2.25	-0.10 /16	2.31 /69	2.00 /59	2.46	0.67
MUN	Commerce National T/F Intm Bd	CFNLX	C+	(800) 995-6365	C+/ 5.8	2.04	-2.63	-0.16 /15	2.34 /70	2.21 /64	2.23	0.65
USS	Commerce Short Term Govt	CFSTX	C-	(800) 995-6365	D / 2.0	0.39	-0.35	0.40 /31	0.62 /22	0.80 /25	1.69	0.83
COI	Cornerstone Advisors Core Plus Bd I	CACTX	U		U /	2.24	0.38	--	--	--	0.00	0.49
GEI	Cornerstone Advisors Inc Oppty Inst	CAIOX	D+		B+/ 8.5	5.80	5.42	28.38 /99	0.98 /27	--	4.52	0.92
COH	Counterpoint Tactical Income A	CPATX	U	(844) 273-8637	U /	4.26	3.98	16.33 /91	--	--	3.08	2.38
COH	Counterpoint Tactical Income C	CPCTX	U	(844) 273-8637	U /	4.10	3.56	15.36 /89	--	--	2.45	3.13
COH	Counterpoint Tactical Income I	CPITX	U	(844) 273-8637	U /	4.31	4.09	16.52 /91	--	--	3.48	2.13
GEI	CRA Qualified Investment CRA	CRAIX	C	(877) 272-1977	C- / 3.2	0.44	-2.10	-0.78 / 6	1.86 /41	1.32 /32	2.25	0.91
GEI	CRA Qualified Investment Inst	CRANX	C+	(877) 272-1977	C- / 4.0	0.55	-1.79	-0.33 /12	2.32 /48	1.77 /38	2.72	0.46
GEI	CRA Qualified Investment Retail	CRATX	C	(877) 272-1977	C- / 3.4	0.36	-2.06	-0.68 / 7	1.97 /42	1.42 /33	2.36	0.81
GEI	Credit Suisse Cmdty Rtn Strat A	CRSAX	E-	(877) 927-2874	E- / 0.0	2.87	6.82	16.51 /91	-12.70 / 0	-10.08 / 0	0.00	1.11
GEI	Credit Suisse Cmdty Rtn Strat C	CRSCX	E-	(877) 927-2874	E- / 0.0	2.61	6.32	15.72 /90	-13.35 / 0	-10.76 / 0	0.00	1.86
GEI	Credit Suisse Cmdty Rtn Strat Inst	CRSOX	E-	(877) 927-2874	E- / 0.0	2.82	6.90	16.67 /91	-12.51 / 0	-9.89 / 0	0.00	0.86
GEI	Credit Suisse Commdty Ret Str	CCRSX	E-	(877) 927-2874	E- / 0.0	2.55	6.76	16.32 /91	-12.69 / 0	-10.11 / 0	0.00	1.09
COH	Credit Suisse Floating Rate HI A	CHIAX	B-	(877) 927-2874	B- / 7.3	2.31	4.34	12.68 /84	3.84 /73	4.63 /80	4.12	1.02
COH ●	Credit Suisse Floating Rate HI B	CHOBX	B	(877) 927-2874	B / 7.8	2.26	3.95	11.98 /83	3.17 /64	3.96 /72	3.60	1.77
COH	Credit Suisse Floating Rate HI C	CHICX	B	(877) 927-2874	B / 7.7	2.12	3.96	11.83 /83	3.07 /62	3.86 /71	3.60	1.77
COH	Credit Suisse Floating Rate HI Inst	CSHIX	A	(877) 927-2874	B+/ 8.8	2.53	4.48	13.00 /85	4.08 /76	4.92 /83	4.57	0.77
GEN	Credit Suisse Strategic Income A	CSOAX	B	(877) 927-2874	A+/ 9.7	5.29	8.56	24.42 /99	5.36 /88	--	6.10	1.40
GEN	Credit Suisse Strategic Income C	CSOCX	B	(877) 927-2874	A+/ 9.8	5.21	8.17	23.52 /99	4.58 /82	--	5.71	2.15

99 Pct = Best
0 Pct = Worst

RISK			NET ASSETS		ASSET							FUND MANAGER		MINIMUM		LOADS	
Risk Rating/Pts	3 Yr Avg Standard Deviation	Avg Dura-tion	NAV As of 2/28/17	Total $(Mil)	Cash %	Gov. Bond %	Muni. Bond %	Corp. Bond %	Other %	Portfolio Turnover Ratio	Avg Coupon Rate	Manager Quality Pct	Manager Tenure (Years)	Initial Purch. $	Additional Purch. $	Front End Load	Back End Load
C+ / 6.7	2.8	5.6	9.01	2	0	12	1	44	43	458	3.6	54	5	0	0	0.0	0.0
C+ / 6.6	2.8	5.6	9.00	18	0	12	1	44	43	458	3.6	69	5	0	0	0.0	0.0
C+ / 6.6	2.8	5.6	9.00	26	0	12	1	44	43	458	3.6	70	5	0	0	0.0	0.0
C+ / 6.5	2.8	5.6	9.01	127	0	12	1	44	43	458	3.6	60	5	500	0	0.0	0.0
C+ / 6.7	2.8	5.6	9.02	19	0	12	1	44	43	458	3.6	72	5	0	0	0.0	0.0
C+ / 6.6	2.8	5.6	9.02	937	0	12	1	44	43	458	3.6	70	5	2,000	0	0.0	0.0
B+ / 8.5	1.8	3.3	5.42	653	0	0	0	2	98	328	4.0	83	8	2,000	0	3.0	0.0
B+ / 8.4	1.9	3.3	5.42	N/A	0	0	0	2	98	328	4.0	73	8	2,000	0	0.0	0.0
B+ / 8.5	1.8	3.3	5.43	46	0	0	0	2	98	328	4.0	75	8	2,000	0	0.0	0.0
B+ / 8.5	1.8	3.3	5.41	759	0	0	0	2	98	328	4.0	86	8	0	0	0.0	0.0
B+ / 8.6	1.8	3.3	5.41	1	0	0	0	2	98	328	4.0	84	8	0	0	0.0	0.0
B+ / 8.5	1.8	3.3	5.41	N/A	0	0	0	2	98	328	4.0	67	8	0	0	0.0	0.0
B+ / 8.5	1.8	3.3	5.41	79	0	0	0	2	98	328	4.0	72	8	0	0	0.0	0.0
B+ / 8.6	1.8	3.3	5.42	27	0	0	0	2	98	328	4.0	76	8	0	0	0.0	0.0
B+ / 8.4	1.8	3.3	5.43	14	0	0	0	2	98	328	4.0	69	8	500	0	0.0	0.0
B+ / 8.4	1.9	3.3	5.39	63	0	0	0	2	98	328	4.0	75	8	0	0	0.0	0.0
B+ / 8.5	1.8	3.3	5.41	441	0	0	0	2	98	328	4.0	72	8	2,000	0	0.0	0.0
U /	N/A	7.0	9.94	5	3	0	86	9	2	26	4.4	N/A	2	2,000	0	3.0	0.0
U /	N/A	7.0	9.94	1	3	0	86	9	2	26	4.4	N/A	2	2,000	0	0.0	0.0
U /	N/A	7.0	9.94	N/A	3	0	86	9	2	26	4.4	N/A	2	0	0	0.0	0.0
U /	N/A	7.0	9.94	1	3	0	86	9	2	26	4.4	N/A	2	0	0	0.0	0.0
U /	N/A	7.0	9.94	27	3	0	86	9	2	26	4.4	N/A	2	2,000	0	0.0	0.0
C- / 4.2	3.4	6.2	11.02	52	0	99	0	0	1	91	1.9	28	7	2,000	0	0.0	0.0
C- / 4.2	3.4	6.2	11.02	N/A	0	99	0	0	1	91	1.9	10	7	2,000	0	0.0	0.0
C- / 4.2	3.4	6.2	11.02	8	0	99	0	0	1	91	1.9	12	7	2,000	0	0.0	0.0
C- / 4.2	3.4	6.2	11.02	265	0	99	0	0	1	91	1.9	35	7	0	0	0.0	0.0
C- / 4.2	3.4	6.2	11.00	25	0	99	0	0	1	91	1.9	34	7	0	0	0.0	0.0
C- / 4.2	3.4	6.2	11.02	28	0	99	0	0	1	91	1.9	27	7	500	0	0.0	0.0
C- / 4.2	3.4	6.2	11.02	298	0	99	0	0	1	91	1.9	35	7	2,000	0	0.0	0.0
B- / 7.4	2.6	5.2	19.88	1,078	2	6	8	45	39	17	5.5	69	23	1,000	250	0.0	0.0
B- / 7.2	2.7	5.2	19.14	131	1	0	98	0	1	11	0.0	24	17	1,000	250	0.0	0.0
C+ / 6.5	2.8	5.0	19.26	332	0	0	99	0	1	21	5.2	19	18	1,000	250	0.0	0.0
C / 5.0	3.1	5.6	19.29	317	4	0	95	0	1	27	0.0	14	18	1,000	250	0.0	0.0
A- / 9.1	1.1	2.2	17.17	103	1	69	0	0	30	35	0.0	36	23	1,000	250	0.0	0.0
U /	N/A	5.5	9.93	414	0	0	0	0	100	0	0.0	N/A	1	2,000	0	0.0	0.0
E- / 0.2	10.7	N/A	9.53	210	30	16	0	26	28	35	0.0	22	5	2,000	0	0.0	0.0
U /	N/A	N/A	11.21	78	99	0	0	0	1	123	0.0	N/A	3	5,000	250	4.5	1.0
U /	N/A	N/A	11.15	26	99	0	0	0	1	123	0.0	N/A	3	5,000	250	0.0	1.0
U /	N/A	N/A	11.22	167	99	0	0	0	1	123	0.0	N/A	3	100,000	10,000	0.0	1.0
B / 7.8	2.3	6.3	10.55	1,542	0	4	19	0	77	22	0.0	36	8	500,000	0	0.0	0.0
B / 7.9	2.3	6.3	10.54	335	0	4	19	0	77	22	0.0	60	8	500,000	0	0.0	0.0
B / 7.8	2.3	6.3	10.53	73	0	4	19	0	77	22	0.0	44	8	2,500	1,000	0.0	0.0
E- / 0.0	13.6	N/A	5.01	90	20	77	0	2	1	151	0.0	0	11	2,500	100	4.8	0.0
E- / 0.0	13.7	N/A	4.71	7	20	77	0	2	1	151	0.0	0	11	2,500	100	0.0	0.0
E- / 0.0	13.7	N/A	5.11	3,690	20	77	0	2	1	151	0.0	0	11	250,000	100,000	0.0	0.0
E- / 0.0	13.7	N/A	4.42	357	0	77	0	2	21	113	0.0	0	11	0	0	0.0	0.0
C / 4.3	2.9	0.5	6.90	260	5	0	0	53	42	48	5.0	85	12	2,500	100	4.8	0.0
C- / 4.2	2.9	0.5	6.94	2	5	0	0	53	42	48	5.0	79	12	2,500	100	0.0	0.0
C / 4.3	2.9	0.5	6.92	121	5	0	0	53	42	48	5.0	78	12	2,500	100	0.0	0.0
C / 4.4	2.9	0.5	6.87	2,724	5	0	0	53	42	48	5.0	86	12	250,000	100,000	0.0	0.0
D / 1.7	5.5	1.6	10.15	26	5	0	0	37	58	73	6.7	98	5	2,500	100	4.8	0.0
D / 1.7	5.5	1.6	10.15	11	5	0	0	37	58	73	6.7	96	5	2,500	100	0.0	0.0

					PERFORMANCE							
	99 Pct = Best 0 Pct = Worst						Total Return % through 2/28/17				Incl. in Returns	
		Ticker	Overall Investment		Perfor- mance				Annualized		Dividend	Expense
Fund Type	Fund Name	Symbol	Rating	Phone	Rating/Pts	3 Mo	6 Mo	1Yr / Pct	3Yr / Pct	5Yr / Pct	Yield	Ratio
GEN	Credit Suisse Strategic Income I	CSOIX	B+	(877) 927-2874	A+ / 9.9	5.46	8.70	24.89 /99	5.66 /90	--	6.65	1.15
GEI	Croft Income	CLINX	C-	(800) 551-0990	D / 1.9	0.48	-0.12	3.32 /58	0.66 /22	0.98 /27	1.39	1.64
GL	Crow Point Alternative Income	AAIFX	E	(855) 282-1100	E / 0.4	0.56	-1.34	2.92 /56	-0.63 / 3	-0.62 / 3	1.29	4.16
USS	CT 529 Advisor Mny Mkt 529 Ptf A		C-	(888) 843-7824	D- / 1.3	0.10	0.20	0.40 /31	0.16 /15	0.10 /15	0.00	1.11
USS	CT 529 Advisor Mny Mkt 529 Ptf C		U	(888) 843-7824	U /	--	--	--	--	--	0.00	1.86
USS	CT 529 Advisor Mny Mkt 529 Ptf E		C-	(888) 843-7824	D- / 1.3	0.10	0.20	0.40 /31	0.16 /15	0.10 /15	0.00	0.86
COI	CT 529 Hartford Inf Plus 529 Ptf A		E+	(888) 843-7824	D / 1.6	1.28	0.45	3.35 /59	0.65 /22	-0.36 / 3	0.00	1.16
COI	CT 529 Hartford Inf Plus 529 Ptf C		E+	(888) 843-7824	D / 1.7	1.05	0.09	2.61 /54	-0.09 / 5	-1.10 / 2	0.00	1.91
COI	CT 529 Hartford Inf Plus 529 Ptf E		D-	(888) 843-7824	C- / 3.3	1.35	0.62	3.67 /61	0.92 /26	-0.11 / 4	0.00	0.91
GEL	CT 529 Hartford TR Bond 529 Ptf A		D	(888) 843-7824	C- / 3.7	1.43	-1.31	4.16 /63	2.24 /47	2.39 /48	0.00	1.15
GEL	CT 529 Hartford TR Bond 529 Ptf C		D	(888) 843-7824	C- / 3.7	1.33	-1.72	3.43 /59	1.48 /35	1.62 /36	0.00	1.90
GEL	CT 529 Hartford TR Bond 529 Ptf E		C	(888) 843-7824	C / 5.4	1.58	-1.21	4.44 /64	2.50 /52	2.64 /52	0.00	0.90
GEI	Cutler Fixed Income Fund	CALFX	E	(888) 288-5374	D / 1.9	-0.79	-3.10	-0.31 /13	1.03 /28	0.71 /24	11.92	1.36
USS	Davis Government Bond A	RFBAX	D	(800) 279-0279	E- / 0.2	-0.03	-0.63	-0.45 /10	0.32 /19	0.13 /16	0.64	1.05
USS ●	Davis Government Bond B	VRPFX	D	(800) 279-0279	E- / 0.2	-0.38	-1.30	-1.67 / 1	-0.68 / 3	-0.82 / 2	0.00	1.92
USS	Davis Government Bond C	DGVCX	D-	(800) 279-0279	E- / 0.2	-0.19	-1.11	-1.29 / 3	-0.45 / 4	-0.66 / 3	0.00	1.75
USS	Davis Government Bond Y	DGVYX	C-	(800) 279-0279	D / 1.8	0.01	-0.73	-0.40 /11	0.63 /22	0.49 /21	0.90	0.57
MMT ●	Davis Government MM B		D+	(800) 279-0279	E+ / 0.8	0.01	0.02	0.05 /21	0.06 /10	0.05 /11	0.05	N/A
MMT	Davis Government MM C		D+	(800) 279-0279	E+ / 0.8	0.01	0.02	0.05 /21	0.06 /10	0.05 /11	0.05	N/A
MMT	Davis Government MM Y		D+	(800) 279-0279	E+ / 0.8	0.01	0.02	0.05 /21	0.06 /10	0.05 /11	0.05	N/A
COH	DDJ Opportunistic Hi Yld I	DDJCX	U	(866) 759-5679	U /	5.49	7.65	18.84 /95	--	--	7.78	1.88
COH	DDJ Opportunistic Hi Yld II	DDJRX	U	(866) 759-5679	U /	5.32	7.52	18.45 /94	--	--	7.56	2.13
COH	DDJ Opportunistic Hi Yld Inst	DDJIX	U	(866) 759-5679	U /	5.42	7.66	18.92 /95	--	--	7.96	1.78
GEN	Deer Park Total Return Credit A	DPFAX	U	(888) 868-9501	U /	2.45	5.96	12.21 /84	--	--	4.56	N/A
GEN	Deer Park Total Return Credit I	DPFNX	U	(888) 868-9501	U /	2.51	6.08	12.48 /84	--	--	5.08	N/A
COI	Delaware Corporate Bond A	DGCAX	D-	(800) 523-1918	C / 4.7	3.03	-1.00	6.75 /72	2.90 /59	4.23 /75	3.23	0.96
COI	Delaware Corporate Bond C	DGCCX	D-	(800) 523-1918	C / 5.4	2.84	-1.37	5.96 /70	2.14 /45	3.45 /64	2.63	1.71
COI	Delaware Corporate Bond I	DGCIX	C-	(800) 523-1918	C+ / 6.9	3.09	-0.88	7.01 /72	3.16 /63	4.48 /78	3.63	0.71
COI	Delaware Corporate Bond R	DGCRX	D	(800) 523-1918	C+ / 6.3	2.96	-1.12	6.67 /72	2.71 /56	3.97 /72	3.13	1.21
* GES	Delaware Diversified Income A	DPDFX	D-	(800) 523-1918	D+ / 2.9	1.79	-1.25	3.65 /60	2.15 /46	2.43 /48	3.13	0.90
GES	Delaware Diversified Income C	DPCFX	D	(800) 523-1918	C- / 3.5	1.61	-1.51	2.88 /56	1.39 /33	1.67 /37	2.52	1.65
GES	Delaware Diversified Income I	DPFFX	C	(800) 523-1918	C / 5.2	1.85	-1.02	4.03 /62	2.40 /50	2.69 /53	3.53	0.65
GES	Delaware Diversified Income R	DPRFX	D+	(800) 523-1918	C / 4.4	1.73	-1.27	3.51 /60	1.89 /41	2.17 /44	3.02	1.15
GEL	Delaware Diversified Income R6	DPZRX	U	(800) 523-1918	U /	1.81	-1.10	--	--	--	0.00	N/A
EM	Delaware Emerging Markets Debt A	DEDAX	C-	(800) 523-1918	B / 8.1	5.24	1.66	15.18 /89	4.24 /78	--	3.77	2.05
EM	Delaware Emerging Markets Debt C	DEDCX	C+	(800) 523-1918	A- / 9.0	5.24	1.66	15.18 /89	4.14 /77	--	3.95	2.80
EM	Delaware Emerging Markets Debt	DEDIX	C+	(800) 523-1918	A- / 9.1	5.12	1.66	15.17 /89	4.28 /78	--	3.95	1.80
EM	Delaware Emerging Markets Debt R	DEDRX	C+	(800) 523-1918	A- / 9.1	5.24	1.66	15.18 /89	4.21 /78	--	3.95	2.30
COI	Delaware Extended Duration Bd A	DEEAX	D-	(800) 523-1918	C+ / 6.9	3.98	-4.09	7.49 /73	4.72 /83	5.49 /88	3.28	1.00
COI	Delaware Extended Duration Bd C	DEECX	D-	(800) 523-1918	B- / 7.3	3.79	-4.45	6.87 /72	3.94 /74	4.70 /81	2.68	1.75
COI	Delaware Extended Duration Bd I	DEEIX	D+	(800) 523-1918	B+ / 8.4	4.05	-3.98	7.76 /74	4.98 /85	5.75 /90	3.69	0.75
COI	Delaware Extended Duration Bd R	DEERX	D	(800) 523-1918	B / 7.8	3.91	-4.21	7.21 /73	4.46 /80	5.22 /86	3.18	1.25
COI	Delaware Extended Duration Bd R6	DEZRX	U	(800) 523-1918	U /	4.23	-3.94	--	--	--	0.00	0.67
LP	Delaware Floating Rate Fd A	DDFAX	C+	(800) 523-1918	D+ / 2.8	1.29	1.93	5.42 /68	1.03 /28	1.79 /39	1.93	0.97
LP	Delaware Floating Rate Fd C	DDFCX	C	(800) 523-1918	D+ / 2.7	1.23	1.55	4.63 /65	0.28 /18	1.04 /28	1.25	1.72
LP	Delaware Floating Rate Fd Inst	DDFLX	B+	(800) 523-1918	C / 4.4	1.48	2.05	5.68 /69	1.28 /32	2.05 /43	2.23	0.72
LP	Delaware Floating Rate Fd R	DDFFX	B-	(800) 523-1918	C- / 3.6	1.35	1.80	5.15 /67	0.78 /24	1.54 /35	1.74	1.22
COH	Delaware High-Yield Bond	DPHYX	C-	(800) 523-1918	B / 8.2	4.29	4.42	16.79 /92	2.64 /55	6.01 /92	5.87	0.56
COH	Delaware High-Yield Opps A	DHOAX	D-	(800) 523-1918	C+ / 6.0	4.39	4.70	16.96 /92	1.63 /37	5.14 /85	5.16	1.14
COH	Delaware High-Yield Opps C	DHOCX	D-	(800) 523-1918	C+ / 6.4	4.19	4.03	16.08 /90	0.80 /24	4.38 /77	4.68	1.89
COH	Delaware High-Yield Opps I	DHOIX	D	(800) 523-1918	B / 7.7	4.44	4.82	17.24 /92	1.88 /41	5.42 /88	5.63	0.89
COH	Delaware High-Yield Opps R	DHIRX	D-	(800) 523-1918	B- / 7.1	4.31	4.29	16.63 /91	1.31 /32	4.90 /83	5.16	1.39

● Denotes fund is closed to new investors
* Denotes fund is included in Section II

RISK Risk Rating/Pts	3 Yr Avg Standard Deviation	Avg Dura-tion	NET ASSETS NAV As of 2/28/17	Total $(Mil)	ASSET Cash %	Gov. Bond %	Muni. Bond %	Corp. Bond %	Other %	Portfolio Turnover Ratio	Avg Coupon Rate	FUND MANAGER Manager Quality Pct	Manager Tenure (Years)	MINIMUM Initial Purch. $	Additional Purch. $	LOADS Front End Load	Back End Load
D /1.7	5.5	1.6	10.15	78	5	0	0	37	58	73	6.7	98	5	250,000	100,000	0.0	0.0
A- /9.0	1.3	1.6	9.66	13	18	32	0	46	4	20	3.3	40	22	2,000	100	0.0	2.0
C /4.4	3.3	N/A	8.24	7	80	0	0	12	8	162	0.0	29	1	2,500	100	0.0	0.0
A+ /9.9	0.1	N/A	10.05	5	0	0	0	0	100	0	0.0	49	7	50	25	0.0	0.0
U /	N/A	N/A	10.05	5	0	0	0	0	100	0	0.0	47	7	50	25	0.0	0.0
A+ /9.9	0.1	N/A	10.05	3	0	0	0	0	100	0	0.0	49	7	50	25	0.0	0.0
C /4.9	3.2	N/A	11.12	2	0	92	0	0	8	0	0.0	5	7	50	25	3.0	0.0
C /5.0	3.1	N/A	10.60	2	0	92	0	0	8	0	0.0	1	7	50	25	0.0	0.0
C /4.9	3.2	N/A	11.30	N/A	0	92	0	0	8	0	0.0	7	7	50	25	0.0	0.0
C /5.5	3.0	N/A	12.03	3	0	20	1	29	50	0	0.0	31	7	50	25	3.0	0.0
C /5.3	3.0	N/A	11.46	3	0	20	1	29	50	0	0.0	11	7	50	25	0.0	0.0
C /5.3	3.0	N/A	12.22	1	0	20	1	29	50	0	0.0	43	7	50	25	0.0	0.0
D+ /2.5	4.5	N/A	8.68	17	7	22	0	3	68	71	0.0	8	30	2,500	0	0.0	0.0
A /9.4	0.8	1.5	5.36	28	7	0	0	0	93	25	3.0	31	18	1,000	25	4.8	0.0
A /9.3	0.9	1.5	5.30	1	7	0	0	0	93	25	3.0	8	18	1,000	25	0.0	0.0
A /9.3	1.0	1.5	5.35	9	7	0	0	0	93	25	3.0	10	18	1,000	25	0.0	0.0
A /9.3	0.9	1.5	5.40	3	7	0	0	0	93	25	3.0	51	18	5,000,000	25	0.0	0.0
A+ /9.9	N/A	N/A	1.00	5	100	0	0	0	0	0	0.1	42	18	1,000	25	0.0	0.0
A+ /9.9	N/A	N/A	1.00	5	100	0	0	0	0	0	0.1	42	18	1,000	25	0.0	0.0
A+ /9.9	N/A	N/A	1.00	10	100	0	0	0	0	0	0.1	42	18	5,000,000	25	0.0	0.0
U /	N/A	N/A	10.00	1	0	0	0	0	100	72	0.0	N/A	2	1,000,000	50,000	0.0	1.0
U /	N/A	N/A	9.99	N/A	0	0	0	0	100	72	0.0	N/A	2	5,000	2,500	0.0	1.0
U /	N/A	N/A	10.00	7	0	0	0	0	100	72	0.0	N/A	2	5,000,000	0	0.0	1.0
U /	N/A	N/A	10.98	20	0	0	0	0	100	28	0.0	N/A	2	2,500	100	5.8	0.0
U /	N/A	N/A	10.99	122	0	0	0	0	100	28	0.0	N/A	2	100,000	100	0.0	0.0
D+ /2.7	4.1	7.5	5.78	255	4	0	0	89	7	217	4.6	19	10	1,000	100	4.5	0.0
D+ /2.7	4.1	7.5	5.78	152	4	0	0	89	7	217	4.6	7	10	1,000	100	0.0	0.0
D+ /2.7	4.1	7.5	5.78	554	4	0	0	89	7	217	4.6	26	10	0	0	0.0	0.0
D+ /2.7	4.1	7.5	5.79	26	4	0	0	89	7	217	4.6	16	10	0	0	0.0	0.0
C /5.4	3.0	5.8	8.67	994	1	5	1	49	44	240	4.4	28	16	1,000	100	4.5	0.0
C /5.5	3.0	5.8	8.67	776	1	5	1	49	44	240	4.4	11	16	1,000	100	0.0	0.0
C+ /5.6	3.0	5.8	8.68	2,710	1	5	1	49	44	240	4.4	41	16	0	0	0.0	0.0
C /5.5	3.0	5.8	8.67	67	1	5	1	49	44	240	4.4	21	16	0	0	0.0	0.0
U /	N/A	5.8	8.68	N/A	1	5	1	49	44	240	4.4	N/A	16	0	0	0.0	0.0
D /1.6	5.7	5.5	8.54	N/A	5	29	1	61	4	232	5.8	97	4	1,000	100	4.5	0.0
D- /1.5	5.7	5.5	8.54	N/A	5	29	1	61	4	232	5.8	97	4	1,000	100	0.0	0.0
D- /1.5	5.7	5.5	8.54	21	5	29	1	61	4	232	5.8	97	4	0	0	0.0	0.0
D- /1.5	5.7	5.5	8.54	N/A	5	29	1	61	4	232	5.8	97	4	0	0	0.0	0.0
E /0.4	7.3	14.0	6.39	215	1	0	4	93	2	219	4.8	5	10	1,000	100	4.5	0.0
E /0.4	7.3	14.0	6.39	30	1	0	4	93	2	219	4.8	1	10	1,000	100	0.0	0.0
E /0.4	7.3	14.0	6.38	384	1	0	4	93	2	219	4.8	7	10	0	0	0.0	0.0
E /0.4	7.3	14.0	6.40	21	1	0	4	93	2	219	4.8	3	10	0	0	0.0	0.0
U /	N/A	14.0	6.39	8	1	0	4	93	2	219	4.8	N/A	10	0	0	0.0	0.0
B+ /8.9	1.4	0.2	8.38	51	1	5	2	47	45	90	3.1	68	7	1,000	100	2.8	0.0
B+ /8.8	1.5	0.2	8.38	45	1	5	2	47	45	90	3.1	33	7	1,000	100	0.0	0.0
B+ /8.8	1.5	0.2	8.38	194	1	5	2	47	45	90	3.1	73	7	0	0	0.0	0.0
B+ /8.8	1.5	0.2	8.38	1	1	5	2	47	45	90	3.1	59	7	0	0	0.0	0.0
D- /1.2	5.6	4.3	7.72	244	4	0	0	89	7	119	6.6	5	5	1,000,000	0	0.0	0.0
E+ /0.9	5.9	4.3	3.85	163	0	0	0	93	7	109	6.8	1	5	1,000	100	4.5	0.0
E+ /0.9	6.0	4.3	3.85	43	0	0	0	93	7	109	6.8	0	5	1,000	100	0.0	0.0
E+ /0.9	6.0	4.3	3.85	90	0	0	0	93	7	109	6.8	1	5	0	0	0.0	0.0
E+ /0.9	5.9	4.3	3.86	8	0	0	0	93	7	109	6.8	1	5	0	0	0.0	0.0

Data as of February 28, 2017

Fund Type	Fund Name	Ticker Symbol	Overall Investment Rating	Phone	Perfor-mance Rating/Pts	3 Mo	6 Mo	1Yr / Pct	3Yr / Pct	5Yr / Pct	Dividend Yield	Expense Ratio
GEI	Delaware Investments Ultrasht A	DLTAX	U	(800) 523-1918	U /	0.31	0.21	0.92 /39	--	--	0.68	0.89
GEI	Delaware Investments Ultrasht C	DLTCX	U	(800) 523-1918	U /	0.31	0.21	0.92 /39	--	--	0.70	1.64
COI	Delaware Investments Ultrasht Inst	DULTX	U	(800) 523-1918	U /	0.31	0.21	0.82 /37	--	--	0.69	0.64
GEI ●	Delaware Investments Ultrasht L	DLTLX	U	(800) 523-1918	U /	0.31	0.21	0.92 /39	--	--	0.70	0.64
USS	Delaware Limited-Term Diver Inc A	DTRIX	C-	(800) 523-1918	D / 2.1	0.43	-0.26	1.81 /47	1.30 /32	0.76 /24	1.87	0.92
USS	Delaware Limited-Term Diver Inc C	DTICX	C-	(800) 523-1918	D / 1.9	0.34	-0.56	1.07 /40	0.45 /20	-0.07 / 4	1.07	1.67
USS	Delaware Limited-Term Diver Inc I	DTINX	B-	(800) 523-1918	C- / 3.5	0.46	-0.19	2.08 /50	1.45 /34	0.93 /26	2.08	0.67
USS	Delaware Limited-Term Diver Inc R	DLTRX	C+	(800) 523-1918	D+ / 2.7	0.46	-0.32	1.58 /45	0.99 /27	0.43 /21	1.57	1.17
MUH	Delaware MN HY Muni Bond A	DVMHX	D+	(800) 523-1918	C+ / 5.6	1.84	-2.92	0.45 /36	3.59 /89	3.09 /81	3.08	0.98
MUH	Delaware MN HY Muni Bond C	DVMMX	C	(800) 523-1918	C+ / 6.6	1.75	-3.18	-0.29 /13	2.85 /79	2.34 /67	2.45	1.73
MUN	Delaware MN HY Muni Bond Inst	DMHIX	A+	(800) 523-1918	B+ / 8.3	1.90	-2.71	0.70 /40	3.90 /92	--	3.48	0.73
MUH	Delaware Natl HY Muni Bd A	CXHYX	B	(800) 523-1918	A / 9.3	3.02	-3.85	1.84 /55	6.07 /99	5.22 /81	3.69	0.94
MUH	Delaware Natl HY Muni Bd C	DVHCX	B	(800) 523-1918	A / 9.5	2.73	-4.27	1.09 /46	5.27 /98	4.43 /96	3.09	1.69
MUH	Delaware Natl HY Muni Bd Inst	DVHIX	B+	(800) 523-1918	A+ / 9.9	3.06	-3.76	2.11 /58	6.35 /99	5.47 /99	4.12	0.69
GEI	Delaware Pooled Trust Core Plus FI	DCPFX	C	(800) 523-1918	C / 4.9	1.49	-1.41	2.29 /51	2.47 /51	2.66 /52	2.65	0.60
USS	Delaware Strategic Income Fund A	DEGGX	D-	(800) 523-1918	D+ / 2.4	1.41	-1.58	1.98 /49	2.07 /44	2.32 /46	2.60	1.21
USS	Delaware Strategic Income Fund C	DUGCX	D	(800) 523-1918	C- / 3.0	1.23	-1.94	1.22 /42	1.31 /32	1.56 /35	1.96	1.96
USS	Delaware Strategic Income Fund I	DUGIX	C	(800) 523-1918	C / 4.7	1.48	-1.45	2.23 /51	2.32 /48	2.58 /51	2.97	0.96
USS	Delaware Strategic Income Fund R	DUGRX	D+	(800) 523-1918	C- / 3.8	1.47	-1.69	1.73 /46	1.81 /40	2.07 /43	2.46	1.46
MUS	Delaware Tax Free Arizona Fund A	VAZIX	B-	(800) 523-1918	C+ / 6.8	1.89	-2.75	0.51 /37	4.18 /94	2.98 /79	3.15	0.96
MUS	Delaware Tax Free Arizona Fund C	DVACX	B+	(800) 523-1918	B- / 7.4	1.70	-3.18	-0.23 /14	3.40 /87	2.21 /64	2.53	1.71
MUN	Delaware Tax Free Arizona Inst	DAZIX	A+	(800) 523-1918	B+ / 8.9	1.86	-2.71	0.76 /41	4.44 /95	--	3.55	0.71
MUS	Delaware Tax Free California A	DVTAX	C+	(800) 523-1918	B- / 7.3	2.49	-3.21	0.41 /35	4.53 /96	3.85 /92	3.30	1.01
MUS	Delaware Tax Free California C	DVFTX	B	(800) 523-1918	B / 7.9	2.30	-3.56	-0.34 /12	3.78 /91	3.09 /81	2.69	1.76
MUN	Delaware Tax Free California Inst	DCTIX	A	(800) 523-1918	A / 9.3	2.64	-3.09	0.66 /40	4.80 /97	--	3.71	0.76
MUS	Delaware Tax Free Colorado A	VCTFX	C+	(800) 523-1918	C+ / 6.6	1.82	-3.11	0.37 /34	4.13 /94	2.94 /79	3.42	0.96
MUS	Delaware Tax Free Colorado C	DVCTX	B	(800) 523-1918	B- / 7.2	1.63	-3.46	-0.37 /11	3.35 /86	2.16 /63	2.80	1.71
MUN	Delaware Tax Free Colorado Inst	DCOIX	A	(800) 523-1918	B+ / 8.8	1.89	-2.99	0.71 /40	4.39 /95	--	3.83	0.71
MUS	Delaware Tax Free Idaho A	VIDAX	C+	(800) 523-1918	C / 4.7	1.58	-2.59	-0.09 /16	3.22 /85	1.90 /56	2.98	0.99
MUS	Delaware Tax Free Idaho C	DVICX	B	(800) 523-1918	C+ / 5.6	1.39	-2.96	-0.84 / 5	2.43 /72	1.14 /38	2.35	1.74
MUN	Delaware Tax Free Idaho Inst	DTIDX	A+	(800) 523-1918	B / 7.7	1.73	-2.39	0.25 /31	3.51 /88	--	3.37	0.74
MUS	Delaware Tax Free Minnesota A	DEFFX	B-	(800) 523-1918	C / 5.1	1.78	-2.61	0.17 /28	3.37 /86	2.79 /76	3.06	0.95
MUS	Delaware Tax Free Minnesota C	DMOCX	B+	(800) 523-1918	C+ / 6.1	1.59	-2.96	-0.57 / 9	2.60 /75	2.03 /60	2.43	1.70
MUN	Delaware Tax Free Minnesota Inst	DMNIX	A+	(800) 523-1918	B / 7.9	1.84	-2.49	0.42 /36	3.66 /90	--	3.46	0.70
MUS	Delaware Tax Free MN Intmdt A	DXCCX	C+	(800) 523-1918	C / 4.4	1.63	-2.51	-0.16 /15	2.54 /74	2.16 /63	2.82	0.97
MUS	Delaware Tax Free MN Intmdt C	DVSCX	C+	(800) 523-1918	C- / 4.0	1.42	-2.92	-0.90 / 5	1.70 /54	1.32 /42	2.03	1.72
MUN	Delaware Tax Free MN Intmdt Inst	DMIIX	A	(800) 523-1918	C+ / 6.5	1.67	-2.44	0.08 /23	2.71 /77	--	3.05	0.72
MUS	Delaware Tax Free New York A	FTNYX	C+	(800) 523-1918	C+ / 6.9	1.97	-3.36	0.19 /28	4.33 /95	3.35 /85	2.98	1.02
MUS	Delaware Tax Free New York C	DVFNX	B-	(800) 523-1918	B- / 7.4	1.70	-3.73	-0.57 / 9	3.55 /88	2.56 /72	2.36	1.77
MUN	Delaware Tax Free New York Inst	DTNIX	A	(800) 523-1918	B+ / 8.9	1.95	-3.24	0.44 /36	4.54 /96	--	3.38	0.77
MUS	Delaware Tax-Free Pennsylvania A	DELIX	B	(800) 523-1918	C+ / 6.6	1.91	-2.85	0.75 /41	4.06 /93	3.07 /81	3.39	0.94
MUS	Delaware Tax-Free Pennsylvania C	DPTCX	B+	(800) 523-1918	B- / 7.2	1.72	-3.21	-0.13 /15	3.27 /85	2.29 /66	2.77	1.70
MUN	Delaware Tax-Free Pennsylvania Inst	DTPIX	A+	(800) 523-1918	B+ / 8.8	1.97	-2.74	0.87 /43	4.31 /95	--	3.80	0.70
MUN	Delaware Tax-Free USA A	DMTFX	C	(800) 523-1918	C+ / 6.2	2.44	-3.10	0.30 /32	3.89 /92	3.41 /86	3.42	0.95
MUN	Delaware Tax-Free USA C	DUSCX	C+	(800) 523-1918	B- / 7.0	2.34	-3.38	-0.37 /11	3.11 /83	2.64 /73	2.81	1.70
MUN	Delaware Tax-Free USA I	DTFIX	A	(800) 523-1918	B+ / 8.6	2.58	-2.95	0.57 /38	4.14 /94	3.66 /89	3.83	0.70
MUN	Delaware Tax-Free USA Intmdt A	DMUSX	D	(800) 523-1918	C- / 3.9	2.20	-3.05	-0.51 / 9	2.38 /71	2.11 /61	2.77	0.92
MUN	Delaware Tax-Free USA Intmdt C	DUICX	D-	(800) 523-1918	C- / 3.4	1.99	-3.46	-1.43 / 2	1.48 /48	1.23 /40	1.98	1.67
MUN	Delaware Tax-Free USA Intmdt Inst	DUSIX	C+	(800) 523-1918	C+ / 6.0	2.23	-3.01	-0.41 /11	2.50 /73	2.25 /65	3.01	0.67
COI	Delaware VIP Capital Reserves Svc		C+	(800) 523-1918	C- / 3.0	0.60	-0.37	1.57 /45	1.19 /31	0.92 /26	1.46	0.85
MMF ●	DEU CAT Tax Exempt Cash Prmr	SCIXX	C	(800) 728-3337	D / 1.7	0.13	0.34	0.46 /36	0.17 /18	0.12 /18	0.46	N/A
MMF ●	DEU T/E Cash Mngd	TXMXX	C-	(800) 728-3337	D- / 1.3	0.05	0.19	0.21 /29	0.09 /15	0.06 /14	0.21	N/A

● Denotes fund is closed to new investors
* Denotes fund is included in Section II

www.thestreetratings.com

RISK			NET ASSETS		ASSET							FUND MANAGER		MINIMUM		LOADS	
Risk Rating/Pts	3 Yr Avg Standard Deviation	Avg Dura-tion	NAV As of 2/28/17	Total $(Mil)	Cash %	Gov. Bond %	Muni. Bond %	Corp. Bond %	Other %	Portfolio Turnover Ratio	Avg Coupon Rate	Manager Quality Pct	Manager Tenure (Years)	Initial Purch. $	Additional Purch. $	Front End Load	Back End Load
U /	N/A	0.7	10.00	10	34	1	0	33	32	123	1.5	N/A	19	1,000	100	2.0	0.0
U /	N/A	0.7	10.00	8	34	1	0	33	32	123	1.5	N/A	19	1,000	100	0.0	0.0
U /	N/A	0.7	10.00	N/A	34	1	0	33	32	123	1.5	N/A	19	0	0	0.0	0.0
U /	N/A	0.7	10.00	69	34	1	0	33	32	123	1.5	N/A	19	0	0	0.0	0.0
A- / 9.0	1.3	1.9	8.48	420	0	0	1	42	57	94	2.8	66	18	1,000	100	2.8	0.0
A- / 9.0	1.3	1.9	8.48	113	0	0	1	42	57	94	2.8	28	18	1,000	100	0.0	0.0
A- / 9.0	1.2	1.9	8.48	369	0	0	1	42	57	94	2.8	71	18	0	0	0.0	0.0
A- / 9.0	1.3	1.9	8.49	5	0	0	1	42	57	94	2.8	57	18	0	0	0.0	0.0
C- / 4.0	3.0	4.9	10.64	105	0	0	99	0	1	15	5.1	62	14	1,000	100	4.5	0.0
C- / 4.1	3.0	4.9	10.67	33	0	0	99	0	1	15	5.1	29	14	1,000	100	0.0	0.0
C+ / 5.9	2.9	4.9	10.64	35	0	0	99	0	1	15	5.1	72	14	0	0	0.0	0.0
D / 2.2	4.4	6.2	10.77	207	1	0	98	0	1	13	5.7	82	14	1,000	100	4.5	0.0
D / 2.2	4.3	6.2	10.81	101	1	0	98	0	1	13	5.7	71	14	1,000	100	0.0	0.0
D / 2.1	4.4	6.2	10.87	861	1	0	98	0	1	13	5.7	84	14	0	0	0.0	0.0
C+ / 6.1	2.9	5.9	10.08	139	0	2	1	44	53	310	3.9	38	15	1,000,000	0	0.0	0.0
C+ / 6.2	2.9	5.9	8.29	56	3	3	1	50	43	316	4.0	65	20	1,000	100	4.5	0.0
C+ / 6.1	2.9	5.9	8.30	7	3	3	1	50	43	316	4.0	31	20	1,000	100	0.0	0.0
C+ / 6.2	2.9	5.9	8.30	43	3	3	1	50	43	316	4.0	71	20	0	0	0.0	0.0
C+ / 5.9	2.9	5.9	8.32	6	3	3	1	50	43	316	4.0	56	20	0	0	0.0	0.0
C / 4.8	3.2	4.7	11.32	66	1	0	98	0	1	14	5.2	72	14	1,000	100	4.5	0.0
C / 4.9	3.2	4.7	11.35	6	1	0	98	0	1	14	5.2	50	14	1,000	100	0.0	0.0
C / 5.0	3.1	4.7	11.32	7	1	0	98	0	1	14	5.2	77	14	0	0	0.0	0.0
C- / 3.9	3.6	5.3	11.99	55	5	0	94	0	1	18	5.3	70	14	1,000	100	4.5	0.0
C- / 3.9	3.6	5.3	12.01	17	5	0	94	0	1	18	5.3	41	14	1,000	100	0.0	0.0
C- / 3.8	3.6	5.3	11.99	22	5	0	94	0	1	18	5.3	74	14	0	0	0.0	0.0
C / 4.5	3.3	4.8	11.09	166	0	0	99	0	1	6	5.2	68	14	1,000	100	4.5	0.0
C / 4.5	3.3	4.8	11.12	16	0	0	99	0	1	6	5.2	35	14	1,000	100	0.0	0.0
C / 4.5	3.3	4.8	11.09	16	0	0	99	0	1	6	5.2	73	14	0	0	0.0	0.0
C+ / 6.7	2.8	4.5	11.31	67	3	0	96	0	1	11	5.0	57	14	1,000	100	4.5	0.0
C+ / 6.8	2.8	4.5	11.30	29	3	0	96	0	1	11	5.0	22	14	1,000	100	0.0	0.0
C+ / 6.7	2.8	4.5	11.32	9	3	0	96	0	1	11	5.0	65	14	0	0	0.0	0.0
C+ / 6.9	2.8	4.7	12.34	433	0	0	99	0	1	15	5.3	62	14	1,000	100	4.5	0.0
C+ / 6.8	2.8	4.7	12.38	51	0	0	99	0	1	15	5.3	27	14	1,000	100	0.0	0.0
C+ / 6.9	2.7	4.7	12.34	69	0	0	99	0	1	15	5.3	70	14	0	0	0.0	0.0
B- / 7.4	2.6	4.4	10.98	69	0	0	100	0	0	14	5.1	31	14	1,000	100	2.8	0.0
B- / 7.3	2.6	4.4	11.01	12	0	0	100	0	0	14	5.1	10	14	1,000	100	0.0	0.0
B- / 7.4	2.6	4.4	10.99	18	0	0	100	0	0	14	5.1	37	14	0	0	0.0	0.0
C- / 4.1	3.5	5.0	11.40	45	0	0	99	0	1	8	5.1	68	14	1,000	100	4.5	0.0
C- / 4.2	3.4	5.0	11.37	19	0	0	99	0	1	8	5.1	38	14	1,000	100	0.0	0.0
C- / 4.1	3.4	5.0	11.39	27	0	0	99	0	1	8	5.1	73	14	0	0	0.0	0.0
C / 5.3	3.1	4.8	8.01	403	0	0	99	0	1	14	5.3	72	14	1,000	100	4.5	0.0
C / 5.1	3.1	4.8	8.01	34	0	0	99	0	1	14	5.3	43	14	1,000	100	0.0	0.0
C / 5.0	3.1	4.8	8.00	29	0	0	99	0	1	14	5.3	75	14	0	0	0.0	0.0
C / 4.4	3.4	5.2	11.51	427	0	0	99	0	1	33	5.5	58	14	1,000	100	4.5	0.0
C- / 4.2	3.4	5.2	11.52	29	0	0	99	0	1	33	5.5	22	14	1,000	100	0.0	0.0
C- / 4.2	3.4	5.2	11.60	49	0	0	99	0	1	33	5.5	65	14	0	0	0.0	0.0
C / 5.0	3.1	4.9	11.83	164	1	0	98	0	1	35	5.2	12	14	1,000	100	2.8	0.0
C / 4.9	3.1	4.9	11.82	45	1	0	98	0	1	35	5.2	3	14	1,000	100	0.0	0.0
C / 5.0	3.1	4.9	11.94	366	1	0	98	0	1	35	5.2	15	14	0	0	0.0	0.0
A- / 9.0	1.4	2.3	9.78	1,329	0	7	1	39	53	128	2.4	N/A	17	0	0	0.0	0.0
A+ / 9.9	0.1	N/A	1.00	31	100	0	0	0	0	0	0.5	50	N/A	1,000,000	0	0.0	0.0
A+ / 9.9	0.1	N/A	1.00	65	100	0	0	0	0	0	0.2	N/A	N/A	100,000	1,000	0.0	0.0

Fund Type	Fund Name	Ticker Symbol	Overall Investment Rating	Phone	Performance Rating/Pts	3 Mo	6 Mo	1Yr / Pct	3Yr / Pct (Annualized)	5Yr / Pct (Annualized)	Dividend Yield	Expense Ratio
MMF●	DEU Tax Free Money Fund	DTBXX	C	(800) 728-3337	D / 1.6	0.10	0.29	0.39 / 35	0.15 / 17	0.10 / 17	0.39	N/A
MMF●	DEU Tax Free Money Fund S	DTCXX	C	(800) 728-3337	D / 1.6	0.09	0.27	0.36 / 34	0.14 / 17	0.09 / 16	0.36	N/A
MUS	Deutsche CA Tax Free Inc A	KCTAX	C-	(800) 728-3337	C+ / 6.1	2.32	-3.66	-0.61 / 8	3.45 / 87	3.30 / 85	3.34	0.92
MUS	Deutsche CA Tax Free Inc C	KCTCX	D+	(800) 728-3337	C+ / 5.9	2.15	-3.92	-1.38 / 2	2.68 / 76	2.52 / 71	2.66	1.69
MUS	Deutsche CA Tax Free Inc S	SDCSX	B-	(800) 728-3337	B / 7.7	2.25	-3.55	-0.50 / 9	3.71 / 90	3.52 / 88	3.69	0.78
MMT●	Deutsche Cash Investment Trust A	DOAXX	D+	(800) 728-3337	E+ / 0.6	0.02	0.03	0.03 / 19	0.02 / 7	0.01 / 5	0.03	N/A
MMT●	Deutsche Cash Investment Trust C	DOCXX	U	(800) 728-3337	U /	--	--	--	--	--	0.02	N/A
MMT●	Deutsche Cash Investment Trust S	DOSXX	D+	(800) 728-3337	E+ / 0.8	0.08	0.12	0.14 / 24	0.05 / 9	0.04 / 10	0.14	N/A
MMT	Deutsche CAT GASP - Govt Cash	DBBXX	C-	(800) 728-3337	D- / 1.3	0.11	0.19	0.33 / 30	0.15 / 15	0.10 / 15	0.33	N/A
MMT	Deutsche CAT GASP - Govt Cash	DCMXX	D+	(800) 728-3337	E+ / 0.7	0.06	0.08	0.09 / 22	0.04 / 9	0.03 / 9	0.09	N/A
MMT	Deutsche CAT GASP - Money	DTGXX	C-	(800) 728-3337	D- / 1.0	0.09	0.15	0.24 / 27	0.09 / 12	0.06 / 12	0.24	N/A
MMT	Deutsche CAT GASP - Svc	CAGXX	U	(800) 728-3337	U /	--	--	--	--	--	0.01	N/A
MMT●	Deutsche CAT Tax-Exempt Port Svc	CHSXX	U	(800) 728-3337	U /	--	--	--	--	--	0.10	N/A
MMF●	Deutsche CAT-TEP TF Inv Shs	DTDXX	U	(800) 728-3337	U /	--	--	--	--	--	0.11	N/A
GES	Deutsche Core Fixed Income A	SFXAX	C-	(800) 728-3337	C- / 3.1	1.46	-1.44	2.83 / 55	2.44 / 51	2.56 / 50	1.52	1.07
GES	Deutsche Core Fixed Income C	SFXCX	C	(800) 728-3337	C- / 3.7	1.27	-1.81	2.08 / 50	1.67 / 38	1.80 / 39	0.85	1.80
GES	Deutsche Core Fixed Income Inst	MFINX	B+	(800) 728-3337	C / 5.4	1.52	-1.31	3.10 / 57	2.70 / 56	2.83 / 55	1.85	0.75
GES	Deutsche Core Fixed Income R	SFXRX	C+	(800) 728-3337	C / 4.5	1.40	-1.53	2.50 / 53	2.19 / 46	2.31 / 46	1.37	1.48
GES	Deutsche Core Fixed Income S	SFXSX	B	(800) 728-3337	C / 5.3	1.60	-1.27	3.00 / 57	2.63 / 55	2.75 / 54	1.75	0.81
GEI	Deutsche Core Plus Income A	SZIAX	D-	(800) 728-3337	C- / 3.3	2.65	-0.53	3.90 / 62	2.26 / 47	2.35 / 47	2.22	1.10
GEI	Deutsche Core Plus Income C	SZICX	D	(800) 728-3337	C- / 3.8	2.37	-0.99	3.13 / 57	1.46 / 34	1.57 / 36	1.57	1.90
GEI	Deutsche Core Plus Income Inst	SZIIX	C	(800) 728-3337	C+ / 5.6	2.63	-0.51	4.17 / 63	2.49 / 52	2.59 / 51	2.57	0.74
GEI	Deutsche Core Plus Income S	SCSBX	C	(800) 728-3337	C+ / 5.6	2.72	-0.41	4.16 / 63	2.52 / 52	2.60 / 51	2.57	0.85
EM	Deutsche Enh Emg Mrkts Fxd Inc A	SZEAX	E	(800) 728-3337	D+ / 2.7	4.13	0.54	10.98 / 81	0.52 / 21	1.63 / 37	4.33	1.29
EM	Deutsche Enh Emg Mrkts Fxd Inc C	SZECX	E	(800) 728-3337	C- / 3.4	3.93	0.16	10.13 / 79	-0.19 / 4	0.87 / 26	3.79	2.02
EM	Deutsche Enh Emg Mrkts Fxd Inc Inst	SZEIX	E+	(800) 728-3337	C / 5.1	4.21	0.69	11.35 / 82	0.86 / 25	1.99 / 42	4.86	0.85
EM	Deutsche Enh Emg Mrkts Fxd Inc S	SCEMX	E+	(800) 728-3337	C / 5.0	4.20	0.67	11.26 / 82	0.81 / 24	1.89 / 40	4.78	1.00
GL	Deutsche Enhanced Global Bond A	SZGAX	E+	(800) 728-3337	D / 1.8	3.49	-0.76	3.89 / 62	1.04 / 28	1.41 / 33	1.84	1.31
GL	Deutsche Enhanced Global Bond C	SZGCX	E+	(800) 728-3337	D+ / 2.3	3.30	-1.24	3.12 / 57	0.28 / 18	0.66 / 23	1.18	2.07
GL	Deutsche Enhanced Global Bond S	SSTGX	D-	(800) 728-3337	C- / 4.0	3.55	-0.64	4.27 / 63	1.29 / 32	1.68 / 37	2.17	1.01
GES	Deutsche Fixed Income Opps A	SDUAX	D+	(800) 728-3337	D+ / 2.6	2.05	2.05	6.49 / 72	0.63 / 22	1.62 / 36	1.71	0.94
GES	Deutsche Fixed Income Opps C	SDUCX	D+	(800) 728-3337	D+ / 2.4	1.86	1.65	5.67 / 69	-0.12 / 5	0.86 / 26	1.00	1.70
GES	Deutsche Fixed Income Opps Instl	MGSFX	C+	(800) 728-3337	C- / 4.2	2.12	2.18	6.77 / 72	0.90 / 26	1.87 / 40	2.02	0.69
GEL	Deutsche Fixed Income Opps R6	SDURX	U	(800) 728-3337	U /	2.12	2.16	6.58 / 72	--	--	1.96	0.75
GES	Deutsche Fixed Income Opps S	SDUSX	C+	(800) 728-3337	C- / 4.0	2.12	2.15	6.70 / 72	0.81 / 24	1.81 / 39	1.95	0.77
LP	Deutsche Floating Rate A	DFRAX	D-	(800) 728-3337	D+ / 2.5	1.41	2.84	7.83 / 74	0.35 / 19	2.43 / 48	4.51	1.16
LP	Deutsche Floating Rate C	DFRCX	E+	(800) 728-3337	D+ / 2.3	1.10	2.34	7.01 / 73	-0.42 / 4	1.66 / 37	3.89	1.91
LP	Deutsche Floating Rate Inst	DFRTX	D	(800) 728-3337	C- / 4.0	1.47	2.97	8.10 / 75	0.58 / 21	2.70 / 53	4.89	0.88
LP	Deutsche Floating Rate R6	DFRRX	U	(800) 728-3337	U /	1.48	2.98	8.12 / 75	--	--	4.90	0.82
LP	Deutsche Floating Rate S	DFRPX	D	(800) 728-3337	C- / 3.9	1.45	2.92	8.00 / 74	0.50 / 21	2.59 / 51	4.79	1.01
COH	Deutsche Global High Income A	SGHAX	C-	(800) 728-3337	B / 8.1	4.40	4.24	16.61 / 91	4.45 / 80	6.12 / 93	4.55	1.08
COH	Deutsche Global High Income C	SGHCX	C	(800) 728-3337	B+ / 8.4	4.19	3.84	15.68 / 90	3.67 / 71	5.36 / 87	4.03	1.83
COH	Deutsche Global High Income Inst	MGHYX	B-	(800) 728-3337	A / 9.3	4.48	4.40	16.99 / 92	4.76 / 83	6.48 / 95	5.04	0.78
COH	Deutsche Global High Income S	SGHSX	C+	(800) 728-3337	A- / 9.2	4.43	4.19	16.78 / 92	4.63 / 82	6.35 / 94	4.95	0.88
USL	Deutsche Global Inflation A	TIPAX	E	(800) 728-3337	D+ / 2.3	0.80	-1.75	2.88 / 56	1.44 / 34	-0.07 / 4	0.41	1.07
USL	Deutsche Global Inflation C	TIPCX	E	(800) 728-3337	D / 2.1	0.60	-2.04	2.03 / 49	0.66 / 22	-0.81 / 2	0.31	1.79
USL	Deutsche Global Inflation Inst	TIPIX	E+	(800) 728-3337	C- / 3.9	0.90	-1.56	3.13 / 57	1.69 / 38	0.21 / 18	0.47	0.69
USL	Deutsche Global Inflation S	TIPSX	E+	(800) 728-3337	C- / 3.9	0.90	-1.56	3.13 / 57	1.69 / 38	0.18 / 18	0.47	0.84
USA	Deutsche GNMA A	GGGGX	C-	(800) 728-3337	D / 2.0	-0.09	-0.62	0.44 / 32	1.58 / 36	1.01 / 27	2.63	0.82
USA	Deutsche GNMA C	GCGGX	C-	(800) 728-3337	D / 2.0	-0.28	-0.98	-0.30 / 13	0.82 / 25	0.25 / 19	1.95	1.57
USA	Deutsche GNMA Institutional	GIGGX	B	(800) 728-3337	C- / 3.7	0.06	-0.45	0.77 / 37	1.89 / 41	1.30 / 31	3.02	0.57
USA	Deutsche GNMA R	GRGGX	C	(800) 728-3337	D+ / 2.7	-0.10	-0.71	0.20 / 26	1.27 / 32	--	2.37	1.24

● Denotes fund is closed to new investors
* Denotes fund is included in Section II

www.thestreetratings.com

RISK			NET ASSETS		ASSET							FUND MANAGER		MINIMUM		LOADS	
Risk Rating/Pts	3 Yr Avg Standard Deviation	Avg Dura-tion	NAV As of 2/28/17	Total $(Mil)	Cash %	Gov. Bond %	Muni. Bond %	Corp. Bond %	Other %	Portfolio Turnover Ratio	Avg Coupon Rate	Manager Quality Pct	Manager Tenure (Years)	Initial Purch. $	Additional Purch. $	Front End Load	Back End Load
A+ / 9.9	0.1	N/A	1.00	149	100	0	0	0	0	0	0.4	49	N/A	1,000	50	0.0	0.0
A+ / 9.9	0.1	N/A	1.00	56	100	0	0	0	0	0	0.4	49	N/A	2,500	50	0.0	0.0
C- / 3.7	3.7	5.0	7.46	497	0	0	99	0	1	21	0.0	25	18	1,000	50	2.8	0.0
C- / 3.7	3.7	5.0	7.41	45	0	0	99	0	1	21	0.0	8	18	1,000	50	0.0	0.0
C- / 3.6	3.7	5.0	7.44	441	0	0	99	0	1	21	0.0	31	18	2,500	50	0.0	0.0
A+ / 9.9	N/A	N/A	1.00	82	100	0	0	0	0	0	0.0	38	N/A	1,000	50	0.0	0.0
U /	N/A	N/A	1.00	29	100	0	0	0	0	0	0.0	N/A	N/A	1,000	50	0.0	0.0
A+ / 9.9	N/A	N/A	1.00	200	100	0	0	0	0	0	0.1	41	N/A	2,500	50	0.0	0.0
A+ / 9.9	N/A	N/A	1.00	4,122	100	0	0	0	0	0	0.3	49	N/A	1,000,000	0	0.0	0.0
A+ / 9.9	N/A	N/A	1.00	212	100	0	0	0	0	0	0.1	40	N/A	100,000	1,000	0.0	0.0
A+ / 9.9	N/A	N/A	1.00	145	100	0	0	0	0	0	0.2	45	N/A	1,000	50	0.0	0.0
U /	N/A	N/A	1.00	33	100	0	0	0	0	0	0.0	N/A	N/A	1,000	100	0.0	0.0
U /	N/A	N/A	1.00	40	100	0	0	0	0	0	0.1	42	N/A	1,000	100	0.0	0.0
U /	N/A	N/A	1.00	9	100	0	0	0	0	0	0.1	43	N/A	2,000	0	0.0	0.0
B- / 7.3	2.6	5.2	9.95	59	7	5	0	39	49	178	0.0	54	3	1,000	50	4.5	0.0
B- / 7.3	2.6	5.2	9.95	9	7	5	0	39	49	178	0.0	20	3	1,000	50	0.0	0.0
B- / 7.3	2.6	5.2	9.95	73	7	5	0	39	49	178	0.0	62	3	1,000,000	0	0.0	0.0
B- / 7.3	2.6	5.2	10.00	N/A	7	5	0	39	49	178	0.0	37	3	0	0	0.0	0.0
B- / 7.2	2.6	5.2	9.95	40	7	5	0	39	49	178	0.0	60	3	2,500	50	0.0	0.0
C / 5.0	3.1	5.5	10.70	50	0	16	1	34	49	270	0.0	35	5	1,000	50	4.5	0.0
C / 5.1	3.1	5.5	10.70	2	0	16	1	34	49	270	0.0	14	5	1,000	50	0.0	0.0
C / 5.1	3.1	5.5	10.65	29	0	16	1	34	49	270	0.0	52	5	1,000,000	0	0.0	0.0
C / 5.0	3.1	5.5	10.70	122	0	16	1	34	49	270	0.0	52	5	2,500	50	0.0	0.0
E+ / 0.9	6.4	5.5	9.41	4	1	43	2	52	2	67	0.0	82	6	1,000	50	4.5	0.0
E+ / 0.9	6.4	5.5	9.43	2	1	43	2	52	2	67	0.0	73	6	1,000	50	0.0	0.0
E+ / 0.9	6.4	5.5	9.40	48	1	43	2	52	2	67	0.0	85	6	1,000,000	0	0.0	0.0
E+ / 0.9	6.4	5.5	9.41	61	1	43	2	52	2	67	0.0	85	6	2,500	50	0.0	0.0
C- / 3.5	3.8	6.3	9.15	14	7	43	2	40	8	320	0.0	84	6	1,000	50	4.5	0.0
C- / 3.5	3.8	6.3	9.15	2	7	43	2	40	8	320	0.0	77	6	1,000	50	0.0	0.0
C- / 3.5	3.7	6.3	9.14	56	7	43	2	40	8	320	0.0	86	6	2,500	50	0.0	0.0
B / 7.7	2.4	1.7	8.59	72	6	6	0	59	29	61	0.0	74	7	1,000	50	2.8	0.0
B / 7.7	2.4	1.7	8.59	27	6	6	0	59	29	61	0.0	51	7	1,000	50	0.0	0.0
B / 7.7	2.4	1.7	8.60	36	6	6	0	59	29	61	0.0	77	7	1,000,000	0	0.0	0.0
U /	N/A	1.7	8.59	N/A	6	6	0	59	29	61	0.0	N/A	7	0	0	0.0	0.0
B / 7.8	2.4	1.7	8.60	53	6	6	0	59	29	61	0.0	77	7	2,500	50	0.0	0.0
C / 5.5	3.0	N/A	8.42	177	0	0	0	20	80	36	0.0	27	10	1,000	50	2.8	0.0
C / 5.3	3.1	N/A	8.46	157	0	0	0	20	80	36	0.0	10	10	1,000	50	0.0	0.0
C+ / 5.6	3.0	N/A	8.42	99	0	0	0	20	80	36	0.0	34	10	1,000,000	0	0.0	0.0
U /	N/A	N/A	8.42	N/A	0	0	0	20	80	36	0.0	N/A	10	0	0	0.0	0.0
C / 5.5	3.0	N/A	8.41	174	0	0	0	20	80	36	0.0	30	10	2,500	50	0.0	0.0
D / 1.6	5.1	4.5	6.85	69	0	1	0	96	3	67	0.0	65	11	1,000	50	4.5	2.0
D / 1.7	5.0	4.5	6.88	23	0	1	0	96	3	67	0.0	34	11	1,000	50	0.0	2.0
D / 1.6	5.1	4.5	6.83	50	0	1	0	96	3	67	0.0	73	11	1,000,000	0	0.0	2.0
D / 1.6	5.1	4.5	6.88	297	0	1	0	96	3	67	0.0	70	11	2,500	50	0.0	2.0
D+ / 2.3	4.4	8.9	10.10	9	0	99	0	0	1	185	0.0	22	7	1,000	50	2.8	0.0
D+ / 2.3	4.4	8.9	10.08	5	0	99	0	0	1	185	0.0	7	7	1,000	50	0.0	0.0
D+ / 2.3	4.4	8.9	10.09	69	0	99	0	0	1	185	0.0	30	7	1,000,000	0	0.0	0.0
D+ / 2.3	4.4	8.9	10.09	11	0	99	0	0	1	185	0.0	30	7	2,500	50	0.0	0.0
B+ / 8.8	1.5	3.4	13.82	47	0	8	0	0	92	339	0.0	74	2	1,000	50	2.8	0.0
B+ / 8.8	1.5	3.4	13.83	30	0	8	0	0	92	339	0.0	54	2	1,000	50	0.0	0.0
B+ / 8.8	1.5	3.4	13.84	9	0	8	0	0	92	339	0.0	79	2	1,000,000	0	0.0	0.0
B+ / 8.8	1.5	3.4	13.85	1	0	8	0	0	92	339	0.0	68	2	0	0	0.0	0.0

99 Pct = Best
0 Pct = Worst

Fund Type	Fund Name	Ticker Symbol	Overall Investment Rating	Phone	Performance Rating/Pts	Total Return % through 2/28/17			Annualized		Incl. in Returns	
						3 Mo	6 Mo	1Yr / Pct	3Yr / Pct	5Yr / Pct	Dividend Yield	Expense Ratio
USA	Deutsche GNMA R6	GRRGX	U	(800) 728-3337	U /	0.04	-0.43	0.74 /37	--	--	2.93	0.78
USA	Deutsche GNMA S	SGINX	B	(800) 728-3337	C- / 3.7	0.05	-0.41	0.73 /37	1.88 /41	1.26 /31	2.98	0.55
MMT	Deutsche Government Cash Mgmt	BICXX	C-	(800) 728-3337	E+ / 0.9	0.07	0.11	0.19 /25	0.08 /11	0.05 /11	0.19	N/A
MMT	Deutsche Government Cash Rsrvs	BIRXX	C-	(800) 728-3337	D- / 1.1	0.08	0.13	0.23 /27	0.11 /13	0.08 /14	0.23	N/A
MMT	Deutsche Govt Mny Mkt Ser Inst	ICAXX	C-	(800) 728-3337	D- / 1.4	0.11	0.19	0.35 /30	0.18 /16	0.15 /17	0.35	N/A
*COH	Deutsche High Income A	KHYAX	D	(800) 728-3337	B- / 7.3	4.29	4.52	17.10 /92	3.52 /69	5.82 /91	4.80	0.94
COH	Deutsche High Income C	KHYCX	C-	(800) 728-3337	B / 7.7	4.31	4.34	16.16 /90	2.79 /58	5.05 /84	4.26	1.72
COH	Deutsche High Income Institutional	KHYIX	C+	(800) 728-3337	B+ / 8.8	4.35	4.86	17.34 /93	3.84 /73	6.13 /93	5.24	0.70
COH	Deutsche High Income R	KHYRX	C	(800) 728-3337	B+ / 8.7	4.20	4.56	16.68 /91	3.21 /64	--	4.68	1.38
COH	Deutsche High Income R6	KHYQX	U	(800) 728-3337	U /	4.32	4.82	17.24 /92	--	--	5.16	0.85
COH	Deutsche High Income S	KHYSX	C+	(800) 728-3337	A- / 9.0	4.33	4.61	17.01 /92	3.69 /71	--	5.18	0.77
MUN	Deutsche Interm Tax/AMT Free A	SZMAX	C-	(800) 728-3337	C- / 3.8	1.90	-2.39	-0.58 / 8	2.30 /69	1.96 /58	2.25	0.79
MUN	Deutsche Interm Tax/AMT Free C	SZMCX	D+	(800) 728-3337	C- / 3.6	1.71	-2.84	-1.34 / 2	1.53 /49	1.18 /39	1.53	1.55
MUN	Deutsche Interm Tax/AMT Free Inst	SZMIX	B+	(800) 728-3337	C+ / 6.2	1.96	-2.35	-0.33 /12	2.56 /74	2.23 /64	2.57	0.53
MUN	Deutsche Interm Tax/AMT Free S	SCMTX	B+	(800) 728-3337	C+ / 6.2	1.96	-2.35	-0.35 /12	2.55 /74	2.19 /63	2.55	0.62
GEI	Deutsche Ltd Maturity Qual Inc Inst	DLTIX	U	(800) 728-3337	U /	0.28	0.62	0.97 /39	--	--	0.87	1.20
GEI	Deutsche Ltd Maturity Qual Inc Inv	DLTVX	U	(800) 728-3337	U /	0.26	0.57	0.87 /38	--	--	0.77	1.38
MUS	Deutsche MA Tax Free A	SQMAX	C-	(800) 728-3337	C / 5.3	1.95	-3.20	-0.32 /12	3.02 /82	2.38 /68	3.20	0.99
MUS	Deutsche MA Tax Free C	SQMCX	D+	(800) 728-3337	C / 5.1	1.84	-3.56	-1.00 / 4	2.25 /68	1.63 /50	2.52	1.76
MUS	Deutsche MA Tax Free S	SCMAX	B	(800) 728-3337	B- / 7.3	2.02	-3.08	-0.07 /16	3.28 /85	2.64 /73	3.55	0.80
*MUN	Deutsche Managed Municipal Bd A	SMLAX	C+	(800) 728-3337	C+ / 6.7	2.25	-3.18	0.11 /25	3.67 /90	3.22 /84	3.44	0.80
MUN	Deutsche Managed Municipal Bd C	SMLCX	C	(800) 728-3337	C+ / 6.3	1.94	-3.66	-0.78 / 6	2.83 /79	2.40 /68	2.73	1.59
MUN	Deutsche Managed Municipal Bd Inst	SMLIX	B+	(800) 728-3337	B+ / 8.3	2.30	-3.08	0.34 /33	3.91 /92	3.46 /87	3.78	0.56
MUN	Deutsche Managed Municipal Bd S	SCMBX	B+	(800) 728-3337	B / 8.2	2.30	-3.18	0.20 /29	3.88 /92	3.42 /86	3.74	0.64
MMT●	Deutsche Money Market	KMMXX	C-	(800) 728-3337	D- / 1.0	0.08	0.12	0.18 /25	0.07 /11	0.04 /10	0.18	N/A
MUS	Deutsche NY Tax Free Inc A	KNTAX	C	(800) 728-3337	C+ / 6.1	1.97	-3.30	0.31 /33	3.32 /86	2.60 /72	3.29	0.96
MUS	Deutsche NY Tax Free Inc C	KNTCX	C	(800) 728-3337	C+ / 5.9	1.69	-3.75	-0.44 /10	2.55 /74	1.81 /54	2.62	1.76
MUS	Deutsche NY Tax Free Inc S	SNWYX	B+	(800) 728-3337	B / 7.8	1.94	-3.27	0.56 /38	3.58 /89	2.83 /77	3.64	0.79
GEI	Deutsche Short Duration A	PPIAX	C-	(800) 728-3337	D / 1.8	0.90	0.74	3.22 /58	0.72 /23	1.30 /31	2.53	0.87
GEI	Deutsche Short Duration C	PPLCX	C-	(800) 728-3337	D / 1.7	0.71	0.36	2.44 /53	-0.03 / 5	0.52 /22	1.84	1.63
GEI	Deutsche Short Duration Institution	PPILX	B-	(800) 728-3337	C- / 3.3	0.96	0.98	3.47 /59	0.98 /27	1.55 /35	2.84	0.61
COI	Deutsche Short Duration R6	PPLZX	U	(800) 728-3337	U /	0.96	0.86	3.35 /59	--	--	2.85	0.76
GEI	Deutsche Short Duration S	DBPIX	B-	(800) 728-3337	C- / 3.3	0.85	0.86	3.35 /59	0.98 /27	1.53 /35	2.85	0.69
MUN	Deutsche Short Term Muni Bond A	SRMAX	D	(800) 728-3337	E / 0.5	0.90	-0.47	-0.01 /17	0.55 /25	0.60 /26	1.15	0.89
MUN	Deutsche Short Term Muni Bond C	SRMCX	D	(800) 728-3337	E / 0.3	0.61	-0.84	-0.86 / 5	-0.23 / 4	-0.17 / 4	0.42	1.67
MUN	Deutsche Short Term Muni Bond Inst	MGSMX	C+	(800) 728-3337	D+ / 2.9	0.96	-0.35	0.24 /30	0.81 /31	0.86 /32	1.43	0.64
MUN	Deutsche Short Term Muni Bond S	SRMSX	C+	(800) 728-3337	D+ / 2.7	0.94	-0.30	0.14 /26	0.70 /29	0.75 /29	1.33	0.76
MUH	Deutsche Strat High Yield T/F A	NOTAX	C+	(800) 728-3337	B / 7.7	2.09	-3.24	1.31 /49	4.25 /94	3.55 /88	3.94	0.97
MUH	Deutsche Strat High Yield T/F C	NOTCX	C+	(800) 728-3337	B / 7.6	1.90	-3.52	0.56 /38	3.48 /87	2.80 /76	3.28	1.73
MUH	Deutsche Strat High Yield T/F Inst	NOTIX	B+	(800) 728-3337	A- / 9.1	2.15	-3.10	1.50 /52	4.51 /96	3.81 /91	4.32	0.75
MUH	Deutsche Strat High Yield T/F S	SHYTX	B+	(800) 728-3337	A- / 9.1	2.15	-3.12	1.57 /52	4.52 /96	3.81 /91	4.31	0.78
*USS	Deutsche Strategic Govt Sec A	KUSAX	C-	(800) 728-3337	D / 2.1	-0.12	-0.63	0.35 /30	1.66 /37	1.05 /28	2.70	0.81
USS	Deutsche Strategic Govt Sec C	KUSCX	C-	(800) 728-3337	D / 2.1	-0.19	-1.01	-0.31 /13	0.91 /26	0.27 /19	1.96	1.60
USS	Deutsche Strategic Govt Sec Inst	KUSIX	B	(800) 728-3337	C- / 3.7	-0.06	-0.50	0.73 /37	1.90 /41	1.27 /31	3.03	0.56
USS	Deutsche Strategic Govt Sec S	KUSMX	B-	(800) 728-3337	C- / 3.6	-0.09	-0.56	0.62 /35	1.82 /40	1.19 /30	2.91	0.67
GEI	Deutsche Ultra-Short Invest Gr Inst	DUSNX	U	(800) 728-3337	U /	0.31	0.67	1.49 /44	--	--	1.06	1.21
GEI	Deutsche Ultra-Short Invest Gr Inv	DUSVX	U	(800) 728-3337	U /	0.28	0.62	1.39 /44	--	--	0.96	1.38
GES	Deutsche Unconstrained Income A	KSTAX	D-	(800) 728-3337	C / 4.4	3.78	1.48	7.90 /74	1.67 /38	2.88 /56	3.24	1.06
GES	Deutsche Unconstrained Income C	KSTCX	D-	(800) 728-3337	C- / 4.2	3.57	1.10	7.06 /73	0.84 /25	2.07 /43	2.59	1.81
GEL	Deutsche Unconstrained Income Inst	KSTIX	U	(800) 728-3337	U /	3.62	1.63	8.14 /75	--	--	3.56	1.03
GES	Deutsche Unconstrained Income S	KSTSX	C-	(800) 728-3337	C+ / 5.8	3.59	1.55	8.06 /74	1.78 /39	3.04 /58	3.49	0.88
GEI	Deutsche US Bond Index A	BONDX	D-	(800) 728-3337	D+ / 2.9	0.94	-2.34	0.89 /38	2.20 /46	1.79 /39	2.42	0.85

● Denotes fund is closed to new investors
* Denotes fund is included in Section II

www.thestreetratings.com

Risk Rating/Pts	3 Yr Avg Standard Deviation	Avg Duration	NAV As of 2/28/17	Total $(Mil)	Cash %	Gov. Bond %	Muni. Bond %	Corp. Bond %	Other %	Portfolio Turnover Ratio	Avg Coupon Rate	Manager Quality Pct	Manager Tenure (Years)	Initial Purch. $	Additional Purch. $	Front End Load	Back End Load
U /	N/A	3.4	13.84	N/A	0	8	0	0	92	339	0.0	N/A	2	0	0	0.0	0.0
B+ / 8.8	1.5	3.4	13.85	1,131	0	8	0	0	92	339	0.0	79	2	2,500	50	0.0	0.0
A+ / 9.9	N/A	N/A	1.00	2,094	100	0	0	0	0	0	0.2	44	N/A	1,000,000	0	0.0	0.0
A+ / 9.9	N/A	N/A	1.00	632	100	0	0	0	0	0	0.2	N/A	N/A	10,000,000	0	0.0	0.0
A+ / 9.9	N/A	N/A	1.00	11,206	100	0	0	0	0	0	0.4	51	N/A	1,000,000	0	0.0	0.0
D- / 1.5	5.2	4.4	4.77	797	1	1	0	96	2	71	0.0	23	11	1,000	50	4.5	2.0
D- / 1.5	5.2	4.4	4.78	78	1	1	0	96	2	71	0.0	9	11	1,000	50	0.0	2.0
D / 1.6	5.1	4.4	4.78	74	1	1	0	96	2	71	0.0	36	11	1,000,000	0	0.0	2.0
D- / 1.5	5.2	4.4	4.77	1	1	1	0	96	2	71	0.0	16	11	0	0	0.0	0.0
U /	N/A	4.4	4.78	N/A	1	1	0	96	2	71	0.0	N/A	11	0	0	0.0	2.0
D- / 1.5	5.2	4.4	4.77	25	1	1	0	96	2	71	0.0	29	11	2,500	50	0.0	0.0
C+ / 6.8	2.8	4.3	11.76	237	0	0	99	0	1	41	0.0	19	27	1,000	50	2.8	0.0
C+ / 6.5	2.8	4.3	11.75	54	0	0	99	0	1	41	0.0	6	27	1,000	50	0.0	0.0
C+ / 6.5	2.8	4.3	11.76	869	0	0	99	0	1	41	0.0	25	27	1,000,000	0	0.0	0.0
C+ / 6.6	2.8	4.3	11.76	639	0	0	99	0	1	41	0.0	24	27	2,500	50	0.0	0.0
U /	N/A	0.2	10.01	10	0	0	0	0	100	161	0.0	N/A	2	1,000,000	0	0.0	0.0
U /	N/A	0.2	10.01	N/A	0	0	0	0	100	161	0.0	N/A	2	100,000	0	0.0	0.0
C / 4.6	3.2	5.0	14.23	79	0	0	98	0	2	28	0.0	25	28	1,000	50	2.8	0.0
C / 4.7	3.2	5.0	14.23	17	0	0	98	0	2	28	0.0	9	28	1,000	50	0.0	0.0
C / 4.6	3.2	5.0	14.23	330	0	0	98	0	2	28	0.0	34	28	2,500	50	0.0	0.0
C- / 4.1	3.5	4.9	9.04	1,848	0	0	99	0	1	29	0.0	43	29	1,000	50	2.8	0.0
C- / 4.1	3.5	4.9	9.03	268	0	0	99	0	1	29	0.0	15	29	1,000	50	0.0	0.0
C- / 4.1	3.5	4.9	9.04	166	0	0	99	0	1	29	0.0	55	29	1,000,000	0	0.0	0.0
C- / 4.0	3.5	4.9	9.05	2,777	0	0	99	0	1	29	0.0	53	29	2,500	50	0.0	0.0
A+ / 9.9	N/A	N/A	1.00	561	100	0	0	0	0	0	0.2	42	N/A	1,000	50	0.0	0.0
C / 4.6	3.3	4.8	10.57	128	0	0	99	0	1	32	0.0	34	18	1,000	50	2.8	0.0
C / 4.6	3.3	4.8	10.56	20	0	0	99	0	1	32	0.0	14	18	1,000	50	0.0	0.0
C / 4.6	3.3	4.8	10.56	222	0	0	99	0	1	32	0.0	52	18	2,500	50	0.0	0.0
A- / 9.1	1.1	2.0	8.69	205	0	21	0	43	36	58	0.0	62	11	1,000	50	2.8	0.0
A- / 9.1	1.1	2.0	8.68	118	0	21	0	43	36	58	0.0	28	11	1,000	50	0.0	0.0
A- / 9.1	1.1	2.0	8.70	38	0	21	0	43	36	58	0.0	70	11	1,000,000	0	0.0	0.0
U /	N/A	2.0	8.70	N/A	0	21	0	43	36	58	0.0	N/A	11	0	0	0.0	0.0
A- / 9.2	1.1	2.0	8.71	487	0	21	0	43	36	58	0.0	71	11	2,500	50	0.0	0.0
A- / 9.2	1.0	1.9	10.11	143	0	0	99	0	1	81	0.0	24	14	1,000	50	2.0	0.0
A / 9.3	1.0	1.9	10.10	18	0	0	99	0	1	81	0.0	8	14	1,000	50	0.0	0.0
A / 9.3	1.0	1.9	10.11	37	0	0	99	0	1	81	0.0	32	14	1,000,000	0	0.0	0.0
A / 9.3	1.0	1.9	10.10	125	0	0	99	0	1	81	0.0	28	14	2,500	50	0.0	0.0
C- / 3.1	3.5	5.0	12.09	309	0	0	99	0	1	36	0.0	67	19	1,000	50	2.8	0.0
C- / 3.2	3.5	5.0	12.10	116	0	0	99	0	1	36	0.0	35	19	1,000	50	0.0	0.0
C- / 3.2	3.5	5.0	12.10	247	0	0	99	0	1	36	0.0	73	19	1,000,000	0	0.0	0.0
C- / 3.2	3.5	5.0	12.10	1,289	0	0	99	0	1	36	0.0	73	19	2,500	50	0.0	0.0
B+ / 8.8	1.5	3.4	7.91	838	0	6	0	0	94	368	0.0	75	3	1,000	50	2.8	0.0
B+ / 8.9	1.4	3.4	7.93	25	0	6	0	0	94	368	0.0	58	3	1,000	50	0.0	0.0
B+ / 8.8	1.5	3.4	7.89	5	0	6	0	0	94	368	0.0	78	3	1,000,000	0	0.0	0.0
B+ / 8.8	1.5	3.4	7.91	44	0	6	0	0	94	368	0.0	78	3	2,500	50	0.0	0.0
U /	N/A	0.3	10.02	10	0	0	0	0	100	132	0.0	N/A	2	1,000,000	0	0.0	0.0
U /	N/A	0.3	10.02	N/A	0	0	0	0	100	132	0.0	N/A	2	100,000	0	0.0	0.0
C- / 4.1	3.4	4.3	4.60	243	2	29	0	40	29	177	0.0	56	11	1,000	50	2.8	0.0
C- / 4.2	3.4	4.3	4.63	47	2	29	0	40	29	177	0.0	21	11	1,000	50	0.0	0.0
U /	N/A	4.3	4.60	5	2	29	0	40	29	177	0.0	N/A	11	1,000,000	0	0.0	0.0
C / 4.4	3.3	4.3	4.60	54	2	29	0	40	29	177	0.0	61	11	2,500	50	0.0	0.0
C+ / 5.8	2.9	5.4	9.47	10	1	44	1	26	28	27	0.0	25	20	1,000	50	2.8	0.0

99 Pct = Best
0 Pct = Worst

Fund Type	Fund Name	Ticker Symbol	Overall Investment Rating	Phone	Perfor-mance Rating/Pts	3 Mo	6 Mo	1Yr / Pct	3Yr / Pct	5Yr / Pct	Dividend Yield	Expense Ratio
GEI	Deutsche US Bond Index Inst	BTUSX	C-	(800) 728-3337	C / 4.5	1.00	-2.21	1.14 /41	2.46 /51	2.07 /43	2.75	0.62
GEI	Deutsche US Bond Index S	BONSX	C-	(800) 728-3337	C / 4.3	0.98	-2.26	1.04 /40	2.41 /50	1.97 /41	2.64	0.70
LP	Deutsche Variable NAV Money Cap	VNVXX	C+	(800) 728-3337	D / 1.9	0.22	0.45	0.78 /37	0.43 /20	0.36 /20	0.76	0.51
MUN	DFA CA Int Trm Muni Bd Inst	DCIBX	B+	(800) 984-9472	C+ / 5.8	1.88	-1.43	-0.36 /12	2.26 /68	2.12 /62	1.35	0.23
*MUS	DFA CA Sht Trm Muni Bd Inst	DFCMX	C+	(800) 984-9472	D+ / 2.7	0.99	-0.37	-0.04 /17	0.73 /29	0.76 /30	0.83	0.22
GL	DFA Diversified Fixed Income Instl	DFXIX	U		U /	0.72	-1.55	--	--	--	0.00	N/A
* GL	DFA Five Year Glbl Fixed Inc Inst	DFGBX	C+	(800) 984-9472	C- / 3.7	0.75	-0.87	0.97 /39	1.82 /40	1.98 /42	1.67	0.27
* US	DFA Infltn Protected Sec Port Inst	DIPSX	E+	(800) 984-9472	C / 4.3	1.44	-0.51	3.02 /57	1.85 /40	0.74 /24	1.71	0.12
*USS	DFA Intmdt Govt Fx Inc Inst	DFIGX	E+	(800) 984-9472	C- / 3.6	0.78	-3.34	-1.27 / 3	2.32 /48	1.75 /38	1.98	0.12
*MUN	DFA Intmdt Term Municipal Bd Inst	DFTIX	B+	(800) 984-9472	C / 5.5	1.82	-1.42	-0.38 /11	2.14 /66	--	1.30	0.23
* GL	DFA Int-Term Extended Quality Inst	DFTEX	D+	(800) 984-9472	C+ / 6.7	1.75	-2.77	3.70 /61	3.78 /72	3.32 /62	2.95	0.22
* GL	DFA Investment Grade Portfolio	DFAPX	D	(800) 984-9472	C / 5.2	1.13	-2.19	1.53 /45	2.92 /60	2.48 /49	2.10	0.22
GEI	DFA LTIP Institutional	DRXIX	D-	(800) 984-9472	B- / 7.5	1.72	-6.12	6.62 /72	4.53 /81	--	2.45	16.11
MUN	DFA Municipal Bond Institutional	DFMPX	U	(800) 984-9472	U /	1.77	-1.06	-0.21 /14	--	--	1.07	0.37
GEI	DFA Municipal Real Return Port Inst	DMREX	U	(800) 984-9472	U /	2.68	0.68	2.40 /52	--	--	1.15	0.35
MUN	DFA NY Municipal Bond Institutional	DNYMX	U	(800) 984-9472	U /	1.23	-0.71	0.20 /29	--	--	0.99	0.25
*GES	DFA One-Yr Fixed Inc Inst	DFIHX	C+	(800) 984-9472	D / 2.0	0.31	0.32	0.79 /37	0.48 /21	0.52 /22	0.78	0.17
* GL	DFA S/T Extended Quality Port Inst	DFEQX	B-	(800) 984-9472	C- / 3.6	0.71	-0.33	1.92 /48	1.54 /35	1.65 /37	1.73	0.22
* GL	DFA Selectively Hedged Glb FI Ptf	DFSHX	E+	(800) 984-9472	D / 1.7	1.42	-0.04	4.47 /64	-0.37 / 4	0.07 /13	1.60	0.17
* GEI	DFA Short Dur Real Ret Port Instl	DFAIX	C+	(800) 984-9472	C- / 3.7	1.42	1.73	4.47 /64	0.96 /27	--	1.40	0.24
*MUN	DFA Short Term Municipal Bd Inst	DFSMX	C+	(800) 984-9472	D+ / 2.7	1.12	-0.34	0.03 /20	0.73 /29	0.68 /28	0.92	0.22
*USS	DFA Short-Term Government Inst	DFFGX	C	(800) 984-9472	D+ / 2.3	0.27	-0.63	-0.14 /15	0.98 /27	0.87 /26	1.01	0.19
COI	DFA Social Fixed Income Instl	DSFIX	U		U /	1.10	-2.22	--	--	--	0.00	N/A
COI	DFA Targeted Credit Institutional	DTCPX	U	(800) 984-9472	U /	0.95	-0.46	3.00 /57	--	--	2.06	0.23
* GL	DFA Two Year Glbl Fixed Inc Inst	DFGFX	C+	(800) 984-9472	D / 2.1	0.35	0.25	0.85 /38	0.62 /22	0.63 /23	0.85	0.18
* GL	DFA World ex US Govt Fxd Inc Inst	DWFIX	C	(800) 984-9472	B / 7.9	1.18	-2.64	1.88 /48	5.40 /88	4.46 /78	2.51	0.22
COI	Diamond Hill Core Bond A	DHRAX	U		U /	0.96	-1.80	--	--	--	0.00	N/A
COI	Diamond Hill Core Bond I	DHRIX	U		U /	1.02	-1.59	--	--	--	0.00	N/A
COI	Diamond Hill Core Bond Y	DHRYX	U		U /	1.04	-1.64	--	--	--	0.00	N/A
COI	Diamond Hill Corporate Credit A	DSIAX	B+	(614) 255-3333	A- / 9.0	3.52	3.18	15.58 /89	5.22 /86	5.60 /89	5.22	0.94
COI	Diamond Hill Corporate Credit C	DSICX	B+	(614) 255-3333	A- / 9.1	3.43	2.95	14.88 /88	4.43 /80	4.81 /82	4.78	1.69
COI	Diamond Hill Corporate Credit I	DHSTX	A	(614) 255-3333	A+ / 9.6	3.70	3.43	16.10 /90	5.51 /89	5.88 /91	5.73	0.64
GEL	Diamond Hill Corporate Credit Y	DSIYX	A		A+ / 9.7	3.64	3.49	16.13 /90	5.61 /89	6.02 /92	5.84	0.54
COH	Diamond Hill High Yield A	DHHAX	U		U /	4.52	4.28	20.54 /97	--	--	5.90	0.99
COH	Diamond Hill High Yield I	DHHIX	U		U /	4.59	4.41	20.84 /97	--	--	6.35	0.69
COH	Diamond Hill High Yield Y	DHHYX	U		U /	4.61	4.46	20.96 /97	--	--	6.44	0.59
COI	Diamond Hill Short Duration TR A	DHEAX	U		U /	0.99	1.32	--	--	--	0.00	N/A
COI	Diamond Hill Short Duration TR I	DHEIX	U		U /	1.04	1.46	--	--	--	0.00	N/A
COI	Diamond Hill Short Duration TR Y	DHEYX	U		U /	1.07	1.50	--	--	--	0.00	N/A
US	Direxion Mo 7-10 Year Tr Bl 2X Inv	DXKLX	E	(800) 851-0511	D+ / 2.4	0.89	-10.63	-8.47 / 0	3.22 /65	1.44 /33	0.00	1.38
US	Direxion Mo 7-10 Year Tr Br 2X Inv	DXKSX	E-	(800) 851-0511	E- / 0.0	-1.94	8.54	3.05 /57	-8.69 / 0	-7.30 / 0	0.00	1.41
GL	Dodge & Cox Global Bond	DODLX	D-	(800) 621-3979	C+ / 6.2	3.26	2.09	13.15 /85	1.31 /32	--	1.66	1.41
* GEI	Dodge & Cox Income Fund	DODIX	A	(800) 621-3979	C+ / 6.7	1.68	-0.05	6.70 /72	3.06 /62	3.38 /63	3.07	0.43
COI	Domini Impact Bond Inst	DSBIX	D	(800) 498-1351	C- / 3.6	0.99	-2.23	2.69 /54	2.22 /47	1.70 /37	2.48	1.22
COI	Domini Impact Bond Inv	DSBFX	D	(800) 498-1351	C- / 3.2	1.00	-2.37	2.48 /53	1.98 /43	1.45 /34	2.18	1.19
GL	DoubleLine Core Fixed Income I	DBLFX	A	(877) 354-6311	C+ / 6.5	1.41	-1.06	3.97 /62	3.40 /67	3.49 /65	2.91	0.73
* GL	DoubleLine Core Fixed Income N	DLFNX	A-	(877) 354-6311	C+ / 6.1	1.45	-1.10	3.81 /61	3.15 /63	3.23 /61	2.65	0.48
EM	DoubleLine Em Mkts Fxd Inc I	DBLEX	C+	(877) 354-6311	A+ / 9.7	3.70	2.56	18.63 /94	5.35 /87	4.95 /84	4.28	0.90
EM	DoubleLine Em Mkts Fxd Inc N	DLENX	C+	(877) 354-6311	A+ / 9.6	3.63	2.43	18.33 /94	5.08 /85	4.67 /80	4.04	1.15
GEN	DoubleLine Flexible Income I	DFLEX	U	(877) 354-6311	U /	1.76	1.94	7.91 /74	--	--	3.53	0.89
GEN	DoubleLine Flexible Income N	DLINX	U	(877) 354-6311	U /	1.60	1.72	7.54 /73	--	--	3.29	1.14
LP	DoubleLine Floating Rate I	DBFRX	A+	(877) 354-6311	C+ / 6.3	1.46	2.50	6.85 /72	2.82 /58	--	3.54	0.66

● Denotes fund is closed to new investors
* Denotes fund is included in Section II

www.thestreetratings.com

RISK Rating/Pts	3 Yr Avg Standard Deviation	Avg Dura-tion	NAV As of 2/28/17	Total $(Mil)	Cash %	Gov. Bond %	Muni. Bond %	Corp. Bond %	Other %	Portfolio Turnover Ratio	Avg Coupon Rate	Manager Quality Pct	Manager Tenure (Years)	Initial Purch. $	Additional Purch. $	Front End Load	Back End Load
C+ / 5.7	3.0	5.4	9.47	55	1	44	1	26	28	27	0.0	32	20	1,000,000	0	0.0	0.0
C+ / 6.2	2.9	5.4	9.48	25	1	44	1	26	28	27	0.0	33	20	2,500	50	0.0	0.0
A+ / 9.9	0.1	N/A	1.00	44	0	0	0	0	100	0	0.0	59	N/A	1,000,000	0	0.0	0.0
B- / 7.0	2.7	4.6	10.50	289	0	0	99	0	1	4	4.6	26	6	0	0	0.0	0.0
A- / 9.1	1.2	2.6	10.30	943	0	0	98	0	2	20	4.8	27	10	0	0	0.0	0.0
U /	N/A	N/A	9.76	294	0	0	0	0	100	0	0.0	N/A	1	0	0	0.0	0.0
B / 8.1	2.1	3.7	10.94	12,772	0	26	8	62	4	41	2.1	86	18	0	0	0.0	0.0
D+ / 2.3	4.5	7.9	11.86	3,802	0	99	0	0	1	19	1.5	38	11	0	0	0.0	0.0
C- / 3.5	3.8	5.7	12.44	4,040	1	95	0	0	4	17	4.6	48	7	0	0	0.0	0.0
B- / 7.1	2.7	4.8	10.14	1,459	0	0	99	0	1	3	4.8	23	5	0	0	0.0	0.0
D+ / 2.5	4.4	6.9	10.66	1,483	1	6	0	89	4	28	3.8	95	7	0	0	0.0	0.0
C- / 4.1	3.5	N/A	10.80	6,766	1	44	0	53	2	7	0.0	93	6	0	0	0.0	0.0
E- / 0.2	10.6	N/A	9.38	88	2	97	0	0	1	4	0.0	1	4	0	0	0.0	0.0
U /	N/A	5.0	10.14	280	3	0	96	0	1	2	4.6	N/A	2	0	0	0.0	0.0
U /	N/A	4.8	9.91	616	1	0	98	0	1	0	3.9	N/A	3	0	0	0.0	0.0
U /	N/A	N/A	10.19	72	0	0	0	0	100	1	0.0	N/A	2	0	0	0.0	0.0
A+ / 9.9	0.4	1.0	10.30	7,089	0	44	4	38	14	64	1.2	54	34	0	0	0.0	0.0
B+ / 8.8	1.5	2.8	10.80	4,978	1	11	1	84	3	25	2.6	83	9	0	0	0.0	0.0
C- / 4.0	3.5	2.8	9.57	1,053	2	14	1	81	2	54	2.8	63	N/A	0	0	0.0	0.0
B / 7.9	2.2	N/A	9.95	993	1	13	1	82	3	62	0.0	44	4	0	0	0.0	0.0
A- / 9.0	1.2	2.6	10.19	2,237	0	0	97	0	3	11	4.7	27	15	0	0	0.0	0.0
B+ / 8.9	1.4	2.8	10.62	2,130	0	99	0	0	1	51	1.9	50	29	0	0	0.0	0.0
U /	N/A	N/A	9.79	89	0	0	0	0	100	47	0.0	N/A	1	0	0	0.0	0.0
U /	N/A	N/A	9.97	416	0	0	0	0	100	21	0.0	N/A	2	0	0	0.0	0.0
A+ / 9.8	0.5	1.5	9.97	4,911	8	56	4	28	4	87	1.4	66	18	0	0	0.0	0.0
D / 2.2	4.5	8.2	10.02	816	3	87	8	0	2	48	2.7	98	6	0	0	0.0	0.0
U /	N/A	5.1	9.76	2	0	0	0	0	100	0	0.0	N/A	1	2,500	100	3.5	0.0
U /	N/A	5.1	9.76	8	0	0	0	0	100	0	0.0	N/A	1	2,500	100	0.0	0.0
U /	N/A	5.1	9.76	30	0	0	0	0	100	0	0.0	N/A	1	500,000	100	0.0	0.0
C- / 3.3	4.0	4.4	11.27	82	2	0	0	93	5	48	0.0	93	11	2,500	100	3.5	0.0
C- / 3.2	4.0	4.4	11.24	29	2	0	0	93	5	48	0.0	90	11	2,500	100	0.0	0.0
C- / 3.2	4.0	4.4	11.24	443	2	0	0	93	5	48	0.0	94	11	2,500	100	0.0	0.0
C- / 3.3	4.0	4.4	11.23	24	2	0	0	93	5	48	0.0	96	11	500,000	100	0.0	0.0
U /	N/A	N/A	10.84	N/A	2	0	0	97	1	0	0.0	N/A	2	2,500	100	3.5	0.0
U /	N/A	N/A	10.84	27	2	0	0	97	1	0	0.0	N/A	2	2,500	100	0.0	0.0
U /	N/A	N/A	10.84	8	2	0	0	97	1	0	0.0	N/A	2	500,000	100	0.0	0.0
U /	N/A	1.6	10.07	N/A	0	0	0	0	100	0	0.0	N/A	1	2,500	100	2.3	0.0
U /	N/A	1.6	10.07	18	0	0	0	0	100	0	0.0	N/A	1	2,500	100	0.0	0.0
U /	N/A	1.6	10.07	218	0	0	0	0	100	0	0.0	N/A	1	500,000	0	0.0	0.0
E- / 0.2	11.0	N/A	34.14	14	23	43	1	10	23	0	0.0	1	11	25,000	500	0.0	0.0
E- / 0.2	11.1	N/A	30.38	5	67	24	0	0	9	0	0.0	0	13	25,000	500	0.0	0.0
D / 1.9	5.2	3.0	10.57	113	0	20	3	58	19	55	4.8	87	3	2,500	100	0.0	0.0
B- / 7.1	2.7	4.0	13.74	47,060	2	16	4	42	36	24	4.5	78	28	2,500	100	0.0	0.0
C+ / 5.8	3.0	4.4	11.12	5	0	16	3	26	55	297	2.5	28	2	500,000	0	0.0	2.0
C+ / 5.8	2.9	4.4	11.15	143	0	16	3	26	55	297	2.5	21	2	2,500	100	0.0	2.0
B- / 7.1	2.7	4.4	10.87	6,839	4	19	3	31	43	70	3.7	94	7	100,000	100	0.0	0.0
B- / 7.0	2.7	4.4	10.87	1,065	4	19	3	31	43	70	3.7	94	7	2,000	100	0.0	0.0
D- / 1.0	6.3	3.6	10.50	760	1	11	0	87	1	75	5.2	98	7	100,000	100	0.0	0.0
D- / 1.0	6.3	3.6	10.50	204	1	11	0	87	1	75	5.2	98	7	2,000	100	0.0	0.0
U /	N/A	1.4	9.82	556	4	9	0	26	61	42	4.3	N/A	3	100,000	100	0.0	0.0
U /	N/A	1.4	9.81	148	4	9	0	26	61	42	4.3	N/A	3	2,000	100	0.0	0.0
B+ / 8.4	1.9	0.3	9.93	277	7	0	0	16	77	70	4.5	88	4	100,000	100	0.0	1.0

Fund Type	Fund Name	Ticker Symbol	Overall Investment Rating	Phone	Performance Rating/Pts	3 Mo	6 Mo	1Yr / Pct	Annualized 3Yr / Pct	5Yr / Pct	Dividend Yield	Expense Ratio
			99 Pct = Best / 0 Pct = Worst					Total Return % through 2/28/17			Incl. in Returns	
LP	DoubleLine Floating Rate N	DLFRX	A+	(877) 354-6311	C+ / 6.0	1.40	2.37	6.57 / 72	2.60 / 54	--	3.29	0.91
GL	DoubleLine Global Bond I	DBLGX	U	(877) 354-6311	U /	0.91	-5.72	-1.89 / 1	--	--	0.39	0.93
GL	DoubleLine Global Bond N	DLGBX	U	(877) 354-6311	U /	0.81	-5.84	-2.12 / 1	--	--	0.24	1.18
COI	DoubleLine Long Dur Tot Rtn Bd I	DBLDX	U	(877) 354-6311	U /	1.17	-8.15	-2.49 / 0	--	--	3.26	0.84
COI	DoubleLine Long Dur Tot Rtn Bd N	DLLDX	U	(877) 354-6311	U /	1.00	-8.28	-2.84 / 0	--	--	2.98	1.09
EM	DoubleLine Low Dur Em Mkts FI I	DBLLX	U	(877) 354-6311	U /	2.06	0.89	8.54 / 75	--	--	3.06	0.84
EM	DoubleLine Low Dur Em Mkts FI N	DELNX	U	(877) 354-6311	U /	1.99	0.76	8.27 / 75	--	--	2.82	1.09
COI	DoubleLine Low Duration Bond I	DBLSX	A	(877) 354-6311	C / 4.5	0.86	0.90	3.45 / 59	1.86 / 41	2.03 / 42	2.49	0.44
* COI	DoubleLine Low Duration Bond N	DLSNX	A-	(877) 354-6311	C- / 4.1	0.80	0.88	3.30 / 58	1.61 / 36	1.81 / 39	2.25	0.69
GES	DoubleLine Total Return Bond I	DBLTX	A	(877) 354-6311	C+ / 5.6	0.85	-0.65	1.37 / 43	3.13 / 63	3.68 / 68	3.74	0.47
* GES	DoubleLine Total Return Bond N	DLTNX	A-	(877) 354-6311	C / 5.1	0.70	-0.78	1.11 / 41	2.85 / 59	3.43 / 64	3.49	0.72
GEI	DoubleLine Ultra Short Bond I	DBULX	U	(877) 354-6311	U /	0.24	0.28	--	--	--	0.00	0.82
GEI	DoubleLine Ultra Short Bond N	DLUSX	U	(877) 354-6311	U /	0.20	0.20	--	--	--	0.00	1.07
MUN	Dreyfus AMT Free Muni Bond A	DMUAX	D	(800) 645-6561	C / 5.4	2.36	-3.57	-0.40 / 11	3.61 / 89	3.05 / 81	2.82	0.94
MUN	Dreyfus AMT Free Muni Bond C	DMUCX	C-	(800) 645-6561	C+ / 6.3	2.17	-3.93	-1.14 / 3	2.84 / 79	2.28 / 66	2.18	1.70
MUN	Dreyfus AMT Free Muni Bond I	DMBIX	B	(800) 645-6561	B / 8.1	2.42	-3.45	-0.08 / 16	3.87 / 92	3.32 / 85	3.20	0.71
MUN	Dreyfus AMT Free Muni Bond Y	DMUYX	B+	(800) 645-6561	B+ / 8.3	2.43	-3.38	0.09 / 23	3.98 / 93	--	3.46	3.31
MUN	Dreyfus AMT Free Muni Bond Z	DRMBX	B	(800) 645-6561	B / 8.0	2.41	-3.46	-0.17 / 15	3.84 / 91	3.26 / 84	3.18	0.71
MMF	Dreyfus AMT-F NY Muni Csh Mgmt	DAYXX	C-	(800) 645-6561	D- / 1.0	0.07	0.13	0.15 / 27	0.05 / 11	0.03 / 11	0.15	N/A
MMF	Dreyfus AMT-F NY Muni Csh Mgmt	DIYXX	C-	(800) 645-6561	D- / 1.3	0.09	0.18	0.24 / 30	0.08 / 14	0.05 / 14	0.24	N/A
MMF	Dreyfus AMT-F NY Muni Csh Mgmt	DVYXX	D+	(800) 645-6561	E+ / 0.7	0.03	0.06	0.06 / 22	0.02 / 8	0.01 / 7	0.06	N/A
MMF	Dreyfus AMT-F NY Muni Csh Mgmt	DPYXX	U	(800) 645-6561	U /	--	--	--	--	--	0.02	N/A
MMF	Dreyfus AMT-Free T/E Cash Mgmt	DEAXX	C-	(800) 645-6561	D- / 1.2	0.07	0.15	0.19 / 29	0.07 / 13	0.04 / 12	0.19	N/A
MMF	Dreyfus AMT-Free T/E Cash Mgmt	DEIXX	C-	(800) 645-6561	D- / 1.4	0.10	0.21	0.29 / 32	0.10 / 15	0.06 / 14	0.29	N/A
MMF	Dreyfus AMT-Free T/E Cash Mgmt	DEVXX	D+	(800) 645-6561	E+ / 0.9	0.04	0.09	0.10 / 24	0.04 / 10	0.02 / 9	0.10	N/A
MMF	Dreyfus AMT-Free T/E Cash Mgmt	DEPXX	U	(800) 645-6561	U /	--	--	--	--	--	0.03	N/A
MMT	Dreyfus Basic Money Market	DBAXX	C-	(800) 645-6561	D- / 1.1	0.12	0.19	0.25 / 27	0.09 / 12	0.05 / 11	0.25	N/A
COI	Dreyfus Bond Market Index I	DBIRX	C-	(800) 645-6561	C / 4.4	1.10	-2.29	1.16 / 41	2.42 / 50	1.99 / 42	2.44	0.16
* COI	Dreyfus Bond Market Index Inv	DBMIX	D+	(800) 645-6561	C- / 3.9	0.94	-2.42	0.91 / 39	2.13 / 45	1.73 / 38	2.19	0.41
MMF	Dreyfus CA AMT Fr Mun Csh Mgmt	DAIXX	U	(800) 645-6561	U /	--	--	--	--	--	0.22	N/A
MMF	Dreyfus CA AMT Fr Mun Csh Mgmt	DFPXX	U	(800) 645-6561	U /	--	--	--	--	--	0.22	N/A
MMF	Dreyfus CA AMT Free Mun Csh	DIIXX	U	(800) 645-6561	U /	--	--	--	--	--	0.27	N/A
MUS	Dreyfus CA AMT Free Muni A	DCAAX	D+	(800) 645-6561	C+ / 5.9	2.95	-3.48	-0.38 / 11	3.76 / 90	3.07 / 81	3.07	0.93
MUS	Dreyfus CA AMT Free Muni C	DCACX	C-	(800) 645-6561	C+ / 6.6	2.76	-3.91	-1.21 / 3	2.95 / 81	2.30 / 66	2.44	1.70
MUS	Dreyfus CA AMT Free Muni I	DCMIX	B	(800) 645-6561	B+ / 8.4	3.01	-3.43	-0.14 / 15	4.02 / 93	3.33 / 85	3.48	0.69
MUN	Dreyfus CA AMT Free Muni Y	DCAYX	B	(800) 645-6561	B+ / 8.4	3.02	-3.42	-0.11 / 16	4.03 / 93	--	3.50	0.65
MUS	Dreyfus CA AMT Free Muni Z	DRCAX	B	(800) 645-6561	B+ / 8.3	3.00	-3.44	-0.16 / 15	3.98 / 93	3.29 / 85	3.45	0.72
MMT	Dreyfus Cash Mgmt Fund Admin	DACXX	C-	(800) 645-6561	D- / 1.3	0.14	0.23	0.32 / 29	0.12 / 14	0.07 / 13	0.29	N/A
MMT	Dreyfus Cash Mgmt Fund Agency	DMCXX	C-	(800) 645-6561	D- / 1.3	0.15	0.24	0.36 / 30	0.14 / 15	0.09 / 14	0.33	N/A
MMT	Dreyfus Cash Mgmt Fund Inst	DICXX	C	(800) 645-6561	D- / 1.4	0.16	0.27	0.42 / 31	0.18 / 16	0.13 / 16	0.39	N/A
MMT	Dreyfus Cash Mgmt Fund Inv	DVCXX	C-	(800) 645-6561	E+ / 0.9	0.11	0.16	0.18 / 25	0.06 / 10	0.04 / 10	0.15	N/A
MMT	Dreyfus Cash Mgmt Fund Part	DPCXX	D+	(800) 645-6561	E+ / 0.7	0.06	0.08	0.09 / 22	0.03 / 8	0.02 / 7	0.07	N/A
MUS	Dreyfus CT Muni A	PSCTX	D-	(800) 645-6561	C- / 3.6	1.91	-3.48	-0.88 / 5	2.88 / 80	1.91 / 57	2.62	0.91
MUS	Dreyfus CT Muni C	PMCCX	D-	(800) 645-6561	C / 4.5	1.72	-3.85	-1.64 / 1	2.10 / 65	1.13 / 38	1.96	1.68
MUS	Dreyfus CT Muni I	DTCIX	C+	(800) 645-6561	C+ / 6.9	1.97	-3.37	-0.64 / 8	3.13 / 84	2.16 / 63	2.99	0.67
MUN	Dreyfus CT Muni Y	DPMYX	C+	(800) 645-6561	B- / 7.0	1.97	-3.35	-0.61 / 8	3.15 / 84	--	3.02	0.64
MUS ●	Dreyfus CT Muni Z	DPMZX	C+	(800) 645-6561	C+ / 6.9	1.97	-3.37	-0.67 / 7	3.10 / 83	2.12 / 62	2.97	0.71
EM	Dreyfus Eme Mkts Dbt LC A	DDBAX	E-	(800) 782-6620	E- / 0.0	7.18	-0.26	11.43 / 82	-4.81 / 0	-3.53 / 0	0.00	1.27
EM	Dreyfus Eme Mkts Dbt LC C	DDBCX	E-	(800) 782-6620	E- / 0.0	6.95	-0.72	10.47 / 80	-5.57 / 0	-4.29 / 0	0.00	2.04
EM	Dreyfus Eme Mkts Dbt LC I	DDBIX	E-	(800) 782-6620	E- / 0.1	7.11	-0.26	11.65 / 82	-4.56 / 0	-3.29 / 1	0.00	1.00
EM	Dreyfus Eme Mkts Dbt LC Y	DDBYX	E-	(800) 782-6620	E- / 0.1	7.29	-0.09	11.93 / 83	-4.47 / 0	--	0.00	0.90
LP	Dreyfus Floating Rate Income A	DFLAX	B+	(800) 782-6620	C+ / 6.2	1.60	2.88	10.22 / 79	2.58 / 53	--	3.57	1.04

● Denotes fund is closed to new investors
* Denotes fund is included in Section II

www.thestreetratings.com

Risk Rating/Pts	3 Yr Avg Standard Deviation	Avg Duration	NAV As of 2/28/17	Total $(Mil)	Cash %	Gov. Bond %	Muni. Bond %	Corp. Bond %	Other %	Portfolio Turnover Ratio	Avg Coupon Rate	Manager Quality Pct	Manager Tenure (Years)	Initial Purch. $	Additional Purch. $	Front End Load	Back End Load
B+ / 8.4	1.9	0.3	9.95	111	7	0	0	16	77	70	4.5	86	4	2,000	100	0.0	1.0
U /	N/A	N/A	10.00	440	0	0	0	0	100	0	0.0	N/A	2	100,000	100	0.0	0.0
U /	N/A	N/A	9.99	24	0	0	0	0	100	0	0.0	N/A	2	2,000	100	0.0	0.0
U /	N/A	13.6	9.86	53	2	21	0	0	77	52	2.8	N/A	3	100,000	100	0.0	0.0
U /	N/A	13.6	9.85	11	2	21	0	0	77	52	2.8	N/A	3	2,000	100	0.0	0.0
U /	N/A	2.6	9.86	130	0	20	0	79	1	39	4.7	N/A	3	100,000	100	0.0	0.0
U /	N/A	2.6	9.87	217	0	20	0	79	1	39	4.7	N/A	3	2,000	100	0.0	0.0
A / 9.5	0.8	1.1	10.04	2,549	6	11	0	31	52	66	3.3	80	6	100,000	100	0.0	0.0
A+ / 9.6	0.8	1.1	10.04	1,521	6	11	0	31	52	66	3.3	77	6	2,000	100	0.0	0.0
B+ / 8.3	2.0	2.6	10.64	44,457	1	11	0	4	84	15	3.7	80	7	100,000	100	0.0	0.0
B / 8.2	2.0	2.6	10.63	10,091	1	11	0	4	84	15	3.7	77	7	2,000	100	0.0	0.0
U /	N/A	0.3	10.01	8	0	0	0	0	100	0	0.0	N/A	1	100,000	100	0.0	0.0
U /	N/A	0.3	10.02	N/A	0	0	0	0	100	0	0.0	N/A	1	2,000	100	0.0	0.0
C- / 3.7	3.7	5.3	13.85	459	1	0	98	0	1	8	0.0	28	5	1,000	100	4.5	0.0
C- / 3.7	3.7	5.3	13.85	33	1	0	98	0	1	8	0.0	10	5	1,000	100	0.0	0.0
C- / 3.8	3.6	5.3	13.86	303	1	0	98	0	1	8	0.0	42	5	1,000	100	0.0	0.0
C- / 3.7	3.7	5.3	13.86	N/A	1	0	98	0	1	8	0.0	48	5	1,000,000	0	0.0	0.0
C- / 3.7	3.7	5.3	13.86	181	1	0	98	0	1	8	0.0	36	5	1,000	100	0.0	0.0
A+ / 9.9	N/A	N/A	1.00	14	100	0	0	0	0	0	0.2	42	N/A	10,000,000	0	0.0	0.0
A+ / 9.9	N/A	N/A	1.00	72	100	0	0	0	0	0	0.2	44	N/A	10,000,000	0	0.0	0.0
A+ / 9.9	N/A	N/A	1.00	126	100	0	0	0	0	0	0.1	39	N/A	10,000,000	0	0.0	0.0
U /	N/A	N/A	1.00	N/A	100	0	0	0	0	0	0.0	N/A	N/A	10,000,000	0	0.0	0.0
A+ / 9.9	N/A	N/A	1.00	N/A	100	0	0	0	0	0	0.2	44	N/A	10,000,000	0	0.0	0.0
A+ / 9.9	0.1	N/A	1.00	676	100	0	0	0	0	0	0.3	46	N/A	10,000,000	0	0.0	0.0
A+ / 9.9	N/A	N/A	1.00	40	100	0	0	0	0	0	0.1	41	N/A	10,000,000	0	0.0	0.0
U /	N/A	N/A	1.00	1	100	0	0	0	0	0	0.0	39	N/A	10,000,000	0	0.0	0.0
A+ / 9.9	N/A	N/A	1.00	142	100	0	0	0	0	0	0.3	44	N/A	25,000	1,000	0.0	0.0
C+ / 5.7	3.0	5.5	10.29	1,399	0	46	0	24	30	145	0.0	35	7	10,000	1,000	0.0	0.0
C+ / 5.9	2.9	5.5	10.28	1,042	0	46	0	24	30	145	0.0	27	7	2,500	100	0.0	0.0
U /	N/A	N/A	1.00	12	100	0	0	0	0	0	0.2	43	N/A	10,000,000	0	0.0	0.0
U /	N/A	N/A	1.00	4	100	0	0	0	0	0	0.2	43	N/A	10,000,000	0	0.0	0.0
U /	N/A	N/A	1.00	6	100	0	0	0	0	0	0.3	45	N/A	10,000,000	0	0.0	0.0
C- / 3.4	3.9	5.3	15.00	82	0	0	99	0	1	11	0.0	28	8	1,000	100	4.5	0.0
C- / 3.4	3.9	5.3	14.99	17	0	0	99	0	1	11	0.0	9	8	1,000	100	0.0	0.0
C- / 3.4	3.9	5.3	14.99	49	0	0	99	0	1	11	0.0	36	8	1,000	100	0.0	0.0
C- / 3.4	3.9	5.3	14.99	3	0	0	99	0	1	11	0.0	36	8	1,000,000	0	0.0	0.0
C- / 3.4	3.9	5.3	15.00	817	0	0	99	0	1	11	0.0	35	8	1,000	100	0.0	0.0
A+ / 9.9	0.1	N/A	1.00	134	100	0	0	0	0	0	0.3	N/A	26	10,000,000	0	0.0	0.0
A+ / 9.9	0.1	N/A	1.00	8	100	0	0	0	0	0	0.3	46	26	10,000,000	0	0.0	0.0
A+ / 9.9	0.1	N/A	1.00	3,042	100	0	0	0	0	0	0.4	49	26	10,000,000	0	0.0	0.0
A+ / 9.9	N/A	N/A	1.00	146	100	0	0	0	0	0	0.2	41	26	10,000,000	0	0.0	0.0
A+ / 9.9	N/A	N/A	1.00	20	100	0	0	0	0	0	0.1	39	26	10,000,000	0	0.0	0.0
C- / 4.1	3.5	5.1	11.61	148	1	0	98	0	1	10	0.0	16	7	1,000	100	4.5	0.0
C- / 4.1	3.5	5.1	11.59	11	1	0	98	0	1	10	0.0	5	7	1,000	100	0.0	0.0
C- / 4.0	3.5	5.1	11.61	13	1	0	98	0	1	10	0.0	21	7	1,000	100	0.0	0.0
C- / 4.1	3.4	5.1	11.61	1	1	0	98	0	1	10	0.0	23	7	1,000,000	0	0.0	0.0
C- / 4.2	3.4	5.1	11.61	88	1	0	98	0	1	10	0.0	21	7	1,000	100	0.0	0.0
E- / 0.1	12.1	5.4	11.50	3	3	84	0	12	1	30	0.0	2	9	1,000	100	4.5	2.0
E- / 0.1	12.1	5.4	11.08	3	3	84	0	12	1	30	0.0	1	9	1,000	100	0.0	2.0
E- / 0.1	12.1	5.4	11.60	39	3	84	0	12	1	30	0.0	3	9	1,000	100	0.0	2.0
E- / 0.1	12.1	5.4	11.63	7	3	84	0	12	1	30	0.0	3	9	1,000,000	0	0.0	2.0
C+ / 6.6	2.8	0.3	12.19	15	5	0	0	20	75	66	0.0	85	4	1,000	100	2.5	0.0

99 Pct = Best
0 Pct = Worst

Fund Type	Fund Name	Ticker Symbol	Overall Investment Rating	Phone	Perfor-mance Rating/Pts	3 Mo	6 Mo	1Yr / Pct	3Yr / Pct	5Yr / Pct	Dividend Yield	Expense Ratio
LP	Dreyfus Floating Rate Income C	DFLCX	B	(800) 782-6620	C+ / 6.0	1.42	2.53	9.48 /78	1.79 /39	--	2.98	1.84
LP	Dreyfus Floating Rate Income I	DFLIX	A+	(800) 782-6620	B- / 7.3	1.68	3.05	10.50 /80	2.84 /58	--	3.99	0.77
LP	Dreyfus Floating Rate Income Y	DFLYX	A+	(800) 782-6620	B- / 7.3	1.69	3.08	10.56 /80	2.86 /59	--	4.03	0.75
MMF	Dreyfus General CA Muni MM A	GCAXX	U	(800) 645-6561	U /	--	--	--	--	--	0.01	N/A
MMF	Dreyfus General CA Muni MM B	GENXX	U	(800) 645-6561	U /	--	--	--	--	--	0.01	N/A
MMT	Dreyfus General Govt Secs MM A	GGSXX	U	(800) 645-6561	U /	--	--	--	--	--	0.01	N/A
MMT	Dreyfus General Govt Secs MM B	GSBXX	U	(800) 645-6561	U /	--	--	--	--	--	0.01	N/A
MMT	Dreyfus General Money Market A	GMMXX	D+	(800) 645-6561	E+ / 0.6	0.04	0.04	0.05 /21	0.02 / 7	0.02 / 7	0.05	N/A
MMT	Dreyfus General Money Market B	GMBXX	U	(800) 645-6561	U /	--	--	--	--	--	0.01	N/A
MMT	Dreyfus General Money Mkt Dreyfus	GMGXX	U	(800) 645-6561	U /	0.04	0.06	0.06 /21	--	--	0.06	N/A
MMF	Dreyfus General Municipal MM A	GTMXX	U	(800) 645-6561	U /	--	--	--	--	--	0.06	N/A
MMF	Dreyfus General Municipal MM B	GBMXX	U	(800) 645-6561	U /	--	--	--	--	--	0.02	N/A
MMF	Dreyfus General NY AMT-Fr Muni	GNMXX	U	(800) 645-6561	U /	--	--	--	--	--	0.02	N/A
MMF	Dreyfus General NY AMT-Fr Muni	GNYXX	U	(800) 645-6561	U /	--	--	--	--	--	0.01	N/A
MMT	Dreyfus General Treas Secs MM A	GTAXX	U	(800) 645-6561	U /	--	--	--	--	--	0.01	N/A
MMT	Dreyfus General Treas Secs MM B	GTBXX	U	(800) 645-6561	U /	--	--	--	--	--	0.01	N/A
MMT	Dreyfus General Treas Secs MM Dr	GTFXX	U	(800) 645-6561	U /	--	--	--	--	--	0.01	N/A
GL	Dreyfus Global Dynamic Bond A	DGDAX	C	(800) 782-6620	D+ / 2.4	1.23	0.11	3.68 /61	1.68 /38	2.63 /51	3.21	1.99
GL	Dreyfus Global Dynamic Bond C	DGDCX	C+	(800) 782-6620	D+ / 2.9	0.98	-0.25	2.95 /56	0.88 /26	1.86 /40	2.81	2.74
GL	Dreyfus Global Dynamic Bond I	DGDIX	A-	(800) 782-6620	C / 4.7	1.29	0.24	4.06 /62	1.91 /42	2.86 /55	3.56	1.70
GL	Dreyfus Global Dynamic Bond Y	DGDYX	A-	(800) 782-6620	C / 4.7	1.31	0.26	3.99 /62	1.97 /42	--	3.58	1.31
USA	Dreyfus GNMA Fund A	GPGAX	D-	(800) 782-6620	E / 0.5	0.08	-1.53	-0.03 /17	1.43 /34	1.16 /29	1.96	1.03
USA	Dreyfus GNMA Fund C	GPNCX	D	(800) 782-6620	D- / 1.4	-0.19	-1.99	-0.92 / 5	0.60 /22	0.34 /20	1.21	1.83
USA	Dreyfus GNMA Fund I	GPNIX	U	(800) 782-6620	U /	0.08	-1.63	--	--	--	0.00	N/A
USA	Dreyfus GNMA Fund Y	GPNYX	U	(800) 782-6620	U /	0.09	-1.43	0.30 /29	--	--	2.39	0.75
USA ●	Dreyfus GNMA Fund Z	DRGMX	C+	(800) 782-6620	C- / 3.0	0.05	-1.48	0.07 /21	1.53 /35	1.28 /31	2.15	0.91
MMT	Dreyfus Govt Cash Mgmt Admin	DAGXX	C-	(800) 645-6561	D- / 1.0	0.08	0.13	0.19 /25	0.07 /11	0.05 /11	0.19	N/A
MMT	Dreyfus Govt Cash Mgmt Agency	DGMXX	C-	(800) 645-6561	D- / 1.0	0.09	0.15	0.23 /27	0.09 /12	0.06 /12	0.23	N/A
MMT	Dreyfus Govt Cash Mgmt Inst	DGCXX	C-	(800) 645-6561	D- / 1.2	0.11	0.18	0.30 /29	0.11 /13	0.07 /13	0.30	N/A
MMT	Dreyfus Govt Cash Mgmt Inv	DGVXX	D+	(800) 645-6561	E+ / 0.7	0.04	0.05	0.06 /21	0.03 / 8	0.02 / 7	0.06	N/A
MMT	Dreyfus Govt Cash Mgmt Part	DPGXX	U	(800) 645-6561	U /	--	--	--	--	--	0.02	N/A
MMT	Dreyfus Govt Secs Cash Mgmt Admn	DAPXX	D+	(800) 645-6561	E+ / 0.8	0.06	0.08	0.12 /23	0.04 / 9	0.03 / 9	0.12	N/A
MMT	Dreyfus Govt Secs Cash Mgmt Agcy	DRPXX	D+	(800) 645-6561	E+ / 0.9	0.07	0.10	0.16 /24	0.06 /10	0.03 / 9	0.16	N/A
MMT	Dreyfus Govt Secs Cash Mgmt Inst	DIPXX	C-	(800) 645-6561	D- / 1.0	0.09	0.14	0.24 /27	0.09 /12	0.05 /11	0.24	N/A
MMT	Dreyfus Govt Secs Cash Mgmt Inv	DVPXX	D+	(800) 645-6561	E+ / 0.6	0.02	0.03	0.03 /19	0.01 / 6	0.01 / 5	0.03	N/A
MMT	Dreyfus Govt Secs Cash Mgmt Part	DGPXX	U	(800) 645-6561	U /	--	--	--	--	--	0.01	N/A
COH	Dreyfus High Yield A	DPLTX	D	(800) 782-6620	B / 7.6	4.28	4.94	17.95 /93	3.14 /63	5.67 /90	4.91	0.96
COH	Dreyfus High Yield C	PTHIX	D+	(800) 782-6620	B / 8.0	4.09	4.39	17.07 /92	2.38 /50	4.89 /83	4.42	1.71
COH	Dreyfus High Yield I	DLHRX	C	(800) 782-6620	B+ / 8.9	4.35	4.90	18.24 /94	3.38 /67	5.95 /92	5.39	0.71
MUH	Dreyfus High Yld Muni Bd A	DHYAX	C	(800) 645-6561	B+ / 8.9	5.15	-3.81	2.69 /63	5.88 /98	4.77 /97	4.00	1.03
MUH	Dreyfus High Yld Muni Bd C	DHYCX	C+	(800) 645-6561	A- / 9.2	4.86	-4.26	1.86 /56	5.05 /97	3.97 /93	3.54	1.80
MUH	Dreyfus High Yld Muni Bd I	DYBIX	B-	(800) 645-6561	A+ / 9.8	5.22	-3.71	2.96 /65	6.15 /99	5.04 /98	4.46	0.80
MUH	Dreyfus High Yld Muni Bd Y	DHYYX	B-	(800) 645-6561	A+ / 9.8	5.23	-3.68	2.94 /65	6.16 /99	--	4.34	0.76
MUH	Dreyfus High Yld Muni Bd Z	DHMBX	B-	(800) 645-6561	A+ / 9.8	5.19	-3.76	2.75 /63	6.01 /98	4.89 /97	4.52	0.93
GEI	Dreyfus Infl Adjusted Sec I	DIASX	E+	(800) 645-6561	C- / 3.0	1.06	0.05	2.24 /51	0.99 /27	0.10 /15	1.03	0.54
GEI	Dreyfus Infl Adjusted Sec Inv	DIAVX	E+	(800) 645-6561	D+ / 2.6	1.00	-0.05	2.04 /49	0.75 /24	-0.18 / 4	0.91	0.76
GEI	Dreyfus Infl Adjusted Sec Y	DAIYX	E+	(800) 645-6561	C- / 3.1	1.08	0.07	2.36 /52	1.05 /28	--	1.06	0.44
MMT	Dreyfus Inst Pref Govt Mny Mkt Agcy	DRGXX	C-	(800) 426-9363	D- / 1.0	0.08	0.11	0.19 /26	0.07 /11	0.04 /10	0.19	N/A
MMT	Dreyfus Inst Pref Govt Mny Mkt Clsc	DLSXX	U	(800) 426-9363	U /	--	--	--	--	--	0.01	N/A
MMT	Dreyfus Inst Pref Govt Mny Mkt Ham	DSHXX	C-	(800) 426-9363	D- / 1.2	0.10	0.16	0.29 /29	0.11 /13	0.08 /14	0.29	N/A
MMT	Dreyfus Inst Pref Govt Mny Mkt Inst	DSVXX	C-	(800) 426-9363	D- / 1.3	0.11	0.19	0.34 /30	0.16 /15	0.12 /16	0.34	N/A
MMT	Dreyfus Inst Pref Govt Mny Mkt Prem	DERXX	D+	(800) 426-9363	E+ / 0.6	0.04	0.04	0.05 /21	0.02 / 7	0.01 / 5	0.05	N/A

● Denotes fund is closed to new investors
* Denotes fund is included in Section II

www.thestreetratings.com

I. Index of Bond and Money Market Mutual Funds

Risk Rating/Pts	3 Yr Avg Standard Deviation	Avg Duration	NAV As of 2/28/17	Total $(Mil)	Cash %	Gov. Bond %	Muni. Bond %	Corp. Bond %	Other %	Portfolio Turnover Ratio	Avg Coupon Rate	Manager Quality Pct	Manager Tenure (Years)	Initial Purch. $	Additional Purch. $	Front End Load	Back End Load
C+ / 6.4	2.8	0.3	12.17	3	5	0	0	20	75	66	0.0	77	4	1,000	100	0.0	0.0
C+ / 6.7	2.8	0.3	12.17	25	5	0	0	20	75	66	0.0	86	4	1,000	100	0.0	0.0
C+ / 6.8	2.8	0.3	12.16	713	5	0	0	20	75	66	0.0	87	4	1,000,000	0	0.0	0.0
U /	N/A	N/A	1.00	74	100	0	0	0	0	0	0.0	N/A	N/A	2,500	100	0.0	0.0
U /	N/A	N/A	1.00	20	100	0	0	0	0	0	0.0	N/A	N/A	2,500	100	0.0	0.0
U /	N/A	N/A	1.00	87	100	0	0	0	0	0	0.0	N/A	N/A	2,500	100	0.0	0.0
U /	N/A	N/A	1.00	2,544	100	0	0	0	0	0	0.0	N/A	N/A	2,500	100	0.0	0.0
A+ / 9.9	N/A	N/A	1.00	1,208	100	0	0	0	0	0	0.1	39	N/A	2,500	100	0.0	0.0
U /	N/A	N/A	1.00	8,230	100	0	0	0	0	0	0.0	N/A	N/A	2,500	100	0.0	0.0
U /	N/A	N/A	1.00	N/A	100	0	0	0	0	0	0.1	N/A	N/A	2,500	100	0.0	0.0
U /	N/A	N/A	1.00	359	100	0	0	0	0	0	0.1	40	N/A	2,500	100	0.0	0.0
U /	N/A	N/A	1.00	456	100	0	0	0	0	0	0.0	38	N/A	2,500	100	0.0	0.0
U /	N/A	N/A	1.00	113	100	0	0	0	0	0	0.0	N/A	N/A	2,500	100	0.0	0.0
U /	N/A	N/A	1.00	76	100	0	0	0	0	0	0.0	N/A	N/A	2,500	100	0.0	0.0
U /	N/A	N/A	1.00	9	100	0	0	0	0	0	0.0	N/A	N/A	2,500	100	0.0	0.0
U /	N/A	N/A	1.00	3,840	100	0	0	0	0	0	0.0	N/A	N/A	2,500	100	0.0	0.0
U /	N/A	N/A	1.00	523	100	0	0	0	0	0	0.0	N/A	N/A	2,500	100	0.0	0.0
B+ / 8.8	1.5	3.3	12.00	1	0	48	1	43	8	141	0.0	84	6	1,000	100	4.5	0.0
B+ / 8.7	1.6	3.3	11.89	1	0	48	1	43	8	141	0.0	75	6	1,000	100	0.0	0.0
B+ / 8.7	1.6	3.3	12.02	3	0	48	1	43	8	141	0.0	86	6	1,000	100	0.0	0.0
B+ / 8.7	1.6	3.3	12.02	35	0	48	1	43	8	141	0.0	86	6	1,000,000	0	0.0	0.0
B+ / 8.6	1.7	2.2	15.00	40	0	6	0	3	91	279	0.0	65	2	1,000	100	4.5	0.0
B+ / 8.6	1.8	2.2	14.99	4	0	6	0	3	91	279	0.0	28	2	1,000	100	0.0	0.0
U /	N/A	2.2	15.00	4	0	6	0	3	91	279	0.0	N/A	2	1,000	100	0.0	0.0
U /	N/A	2.2	15.00	N/A	0	6	0	3	91	279	0.0	N/A	2	1,000,000	0	0.0	0.0
B+ / 8.6	1.8	2.2	15.00	366	0	6	0	3	91	279	0.0	67	2	1,000	100	0.0	0.0
A+ / 9.9	N/A	N/A	1.00	3,386	100	0	0	0	0	0	0.2	43	N/A	10,000,000	0	0.0	0.0
A+ / 9.9	N/A	N/A	1.00	85	100	0	0	0	0	0	0.2	44	N/A	10,000,000	0	0.0	0.0
A+ / 9.9	N/A	N/A	1.00	48,181	100	0	0	0	0	0	0.3	46	N/A	10,000,000	0	0.0	0.0
A+ / 9.9	N/A	N/A	1.00	1,553	100	0	0	0	0	0	0.1	39	N/A	10,000,000	0	0.0	0.0
U /	N/A	N/A	1.00	105	100	0	0	0	0	0	0.0	N/A	N/A	10,000,000	0	0.0	0.0
A+ / 9.9	N/A	N/A	1.00	384	100	0	0	0	0	0	0.1	40	N/A	10,000,000	0	0.0	0.0
A+ / 9.9	N/A	N/A	1.00	13	100	0	0	0	0	0	0.2	42	N/A	10,000,000	0	0.0	0.0
A+ / 9.9	N/A	N/A	1.00	3,989	100	0	0	0	0	0	0.2	44	N/A	10,000,000	0	0.0	0.0
A+ / 9.9	N/A	N/A	1.00	388	100	0	0	0	0	0	0.0	38	N/A	10,000,000	0	0.0	0.0
U /	N/A	N/A	1.00	326	100	0	0	0	0	0	0.0	N/A	N/A	10,000,000	0	0.0	0.0
D- / 1.1	5.7	3.8	6.32	162	0	5	0	90	5	54	0.0	8	7	1,000	100	4.5	0.0
D- / 1.0	5.7	3.8	6.32	59	0	5	0	90	5	54	0.0	2	7	1,000	100	0.0	0.0
D- / 1.1	5.7	3.8	6.32	982	0	5	0	90	5	54	0.0	11	7	1,000	100	0.0	0.0
D- / 1.2	5.3	7.1	11.80	48	1	0	98	0	1	12	0.0	62	6	1,000	100	4.5	2.0
D- / 1.2	5.3	7.1	11.79	19	1	0	98	0	1	12	0.0	26	6	1,000	100	0.0	2.0
D- / 1.2	5.3	7.1	11.78	35	1	0	98	0	1	12	0.0	69	6	1,000	100	0.0	2.0
D- / 1.2	5.3	7.1	11.79	3	1	0	98	0	1	12	0.0	70	6	1,000,000	0	0.0	2.0
D- / 1.2	5.4	7.1	11.78	60	1	0	98	0	1	12	0.0	65	6	1,000	100	0.0	2.0
C- / 3.5	3.2	20.0	12.68	20	0	99	0	0	1	60	0.0	9	12	1,000	100	0.0	0.0
C- / 3.5	3.3	20.0	12.64	17	0	99	0	0	1	60	0.0	6	12	10,000	100	0.0	0.0
C- / 3.5	3.2	20.0	12.69	100	0	99	0	0	1	60	0.0	9	12	1,000,000	0	0.0	0.0
A+ / 9.9	N/A	N/A	1.00	11	100	0	0	0	0	0	0.2	42	N/A	500,000,000	0	0.0	0.0
U /	N/A	N/A	1.00	2	100	0	0	0	0	0	0.0	N/A	N/A	500,000,000	0	0.0	0.0
A+ / 9.9	N/A	N/A	1.00	1,489	100	0	0	0	0	0	0.3	N/A	N/A	500,000,000	0	0.0	0.0
A+ / 9.9	N/A	N/A	1.00	3,371	100	0	0	0	0	0	0.3	49	N/A	500,000,000	0	0.0	0.0
A+ / 9.9	N/A	N/A	1.00	127	100	0	0	0	0	0	0.1	38	N/A	500,000,000	0	0.0	0.0

Fund Type	Fund Name	Ticker Symbol	Overall Investment Rating	Phone	Performance Rating/Pts	3 Mo	6 Mo	1Yr / Pct	3Yr / Pct	5Yr / Pct	Dividend Yield	Expense Ratio
MMT	Dreyfus Inst Preferred Govt Plus MM		C	(800) 645-6561	D- / 1.4	0.11	0.18	0.35 /30	0.20 /16	0.16 /17	0.35	N/A
MMT	Dreyfus Inst Resrv Prf MM Hmltn Shs	DRSXX	C-	(800) 645-6561	D- / 1.4	0.16	0.27	0.41 /31	0.16 /15	0.12 /16	0.40	N/A
MMT	Dreyfus Inst Tr Agcy Cash Adv Agcy	DGYXX	D+	(800) 426-9363	E+ / 0.8	0.06	0.08	0.13 /23	0.05 / 9	0.03 / 9	0.13	N/A
MMT	Dreyfus Inst Tr Agcy Cash Adv Clsc	DSSXX	U	(800) 426-9363	U /	--	--	--	--	--	0.01	N/A
MMT	Dreyfus Inst Tr Agcy Cash Adv Ham	DHLXX	C-	(800) 426-9363	D- / 1.0	0.09	0.13	0.23 /27	0.08 /11	0.05 /11	0.23	N/A
MMT	Dreyfus Inst Tr Agcy Cash Adv Inst	DNSXX	C-	(800) 426-9363	D- / 1.1	0.10	0.16	0.28 /28	0.10 /13	0.07 /13	0.28	N/A
MMT	Dreyfus Inst Tr Agcy Cash Adv Prem	DRRXX	D+	(800) 426-9363	E+ / 0.6	0.03	0.03	0.04 /20	0.01 / 6	0.01 / 5	0.04	N/A
MMT	Dreyfus Inst Trs Secs Csh Adv Ham	DHMXX	D+	(800) 426-9363	E+ / 0.8	0.07	0.11	0.16 /24	0.05 / 9	0.03 / 9	0.16	N/A
MMT	Dreyfus Inst Trs Secs Csh Adv Inst	DUPXX	C-	(800) 426-9363	D- / 1.0	0.08	0.13	0.20 /26	0.07 /11	0.04 /10	0.20	N/A
MMT	Dreyfus Inst Trs Secs Csh Adv Prem	DMEXX	U	(800) 426-9363	U /	0.01	0.01	0.02 /19	0.01 / 6	--	0.02	N/A
GEI	Dreyfus Interm Term Inc A	DRITX	E+	(800) 645-6561	D / 1.6	1.37	-1.90	2.19 /51	1.48 /35	2.02 /42	1.96	0.92
GEI	Dreyfus Interm Term Inc C	DTECX	D-	(800) 645-6561	D / 2.2	1.19	-2.25	1.46 /44	0.74 /24	1.28 /31	1.32	1.65
GEI	Dreyfus Interm Term Inc I	DITIX	D+	(800) 645-6561	C- / 4.0	1.53	-1.74	2.54 /53	1.84 /40	2.33 /47	2.39	0.63
COI	Dreyfus Interm Term Inc Y	DITYX	D+	(800) 645-6561	C- / 4.1	1.54	-1.71	2.59 /54	1.90 /41	--	2.44	0.54
*MUN	Dreyfus Intermediate Muni Bd	DITEX	C+	(800) 645-6561	C+ / 6.3	2.20	-2.87	-0.48 /10	2.66 /76	2.39 /68	2.52	0.74
GL	Dreyfus Intl Bond A	DIBAX	E-	(800) 645-6561	E- / 0.1	3.10	-5.23	2.43 /53	-0.56 / 3	0.53 /22	0.31	1.12
GL	Dreyfus Intl Bond C	DIBCX	E-	(800) 645-6561	E- / 0.2	2.96	-5.42	1.93 /48	-1.15 / 2	-0.10 / 4	0.06	1.77
GL	Dreyfus Intl Bond I	DIBRX	E-	(800) 645-6561	E+ / 0.9	3.22	-4.93	2.98 /56	-0.15 / 5	0.91 /26	0.60	0.74
GL	Dreyfus Intl Bond Y	DIBYX	E	(800) 645-6561	D- / 1.3	3.25	-4.94	3.03 /57	-0.06 / 5	--	0.64	0.67
MMT	Dreyfus Liquid Assets 1	DLAXX	D+	(800) 645-6561	E+ / 0.6	0.02	0.02	0.03 /19	0.01 / 6	0.01 / 5	0.03	N/A
MMT	Dreyfus Liquid Assets Z	DLZXX	U	(800) 645-6561	U /	--	--	--	--	--	0.01	N/A
MUS	Dreyfus MA Muni A	PSMAX	E+	(800) 782-6620	C- / 3.0	1.84	-3.85	-1.43 / 2	2.69 /77	1.90 /56	2.43	0.95
MUS	Dreyfus MA Muni C	PCMAX	D-	(800) 782-6620	C- / 3.8	1.64	-4.15	-2.22 / 1	1.88 /59	1.12 /38	1.72	1.75
MUS ●	Dreyfus MA Muni Z	PMAZX	C	(800) 782-6620	C+ / 6.4	1.90	-3.74	-1.21 / 3	2.92 /81	2.13 /62	2.79	0.73
MUN	Dreyfus Muni Bond Opp A	PTEBX	D	(800) 782-6620	C+ / 5.6	2.46	-3.73	-0.41 /11	3.74 /90	3.13 /82	2.94	0.92
MUN	Dreyfus Muni Bond Opp C	DMBCX	C-	(800) 782-6620	C+ / 6.5	2.26	-4.08	-1.16 / 3	2.95 /81	2.34 /67	2.29	1.69
MUN	Dreyfus Muni Bond Opp I	DMBVX	U	(800) 782-6620	U /	2.43	-3.61	--	--	--	0.00	N/A
MUN	Dreyfus Muni Bond Opp Y	DMBYX	U	(800) 782-6620	U /	2.37	-3.83	--	--	--	0.00	N/A
MUN●	Dreyfus Muni Bond Opp Z	DMBZX	B-	(800) 782-6620	B / 7.9	2.47	-3.70	-0.36 /12	3.80 /91	3.17 /83	3.14	0.87
MMF	Dreyfus Muni Cash Mgmt Plus Admin	DAMXX	C	(800) 645-6561	D / 1.8	0.07	0.11	0.58 /39	0.20 /19	0.12 /18	0.58	N/A
MMF	Dreyfus Muni Cash Mgmt Plus Inst	DIMXX	C	(800) 645-6561	D / 1.8	0.08	0.13	0.61 /39	0.21 /19	0.13 /18	0.60	N/A
MMF	Dreyfus Muni Cash Mgmt Plus Inv	DVMXX	C	(800) 645-6561	D / 1.7	0.04	0.06	0.53 /38	0.18 /18	0.11 /17	0.53	N/A
MMF	Dreyfus Muni Cash Mgmt Plus Part	DMPXX	U	(800) 645-6561	U /	--	--	--	--	--	0.48	N/A
*MUN	Dreyfus Municipal Bond	DRTAX	B-	(800) 645-6561	B / 7.8	2.45	-3.46	-0.09 /16	3.68 /90	3.08 /81	3.14	0.73
MUS	Dreyfus NJ Muni Bond A	DRNJX	C-	(800) 645-6561	C+ / 5.7	2.25	-3.18	0.33 /33	3.60 /89	2.61 /73	3.14	0.95
MUS	Dreyfus NJ Muni Bond C	DCNJX	C	(800) 645-6561	C+ / 6.5	2.07	-3.55	-0.42 /11	2.83 /79	1.86 /55	2.51	1.71
MUS	Dreyfus NJ Muni Bond I	DNMIX	B+	(800) 645-6561	B / 8.2	2.23	-3.13	0.51 /37	3.86 /91	2.85 /77	3.54	0.71
MUN	Dreyfus NJ Muni Bond Y	DNJYX	B+	(800) 645-6561	B / 8.2	2.32	-3.06	0.58 /38	3.83 /91	--	3.54	0.71
MUS ●	Dreyfus NJ Muni Bond Z	DZNJX	B+	(800) 782-6620	B / 8.1	2.23	-3.15	0.46 /36	3.80 /91	2.79 /76	3.49	0.77
MUS	Dreyfus NY AMT Free Muni Bd A	PSNYX	D	(800) 645-6561	C / 4.9	2.36	-3.63	-0.37 /11	3.37 /86	2.42 /69	2.66	0.91
MUS	Dreyfus NY AMT Free Muni Bd C	PNYCX	C-	(800) 645-6561	C+ / 5.8	2.17	-4.00	-1.12 / 4	2.59 /75	1.63 /50	2.01	1.67
MUS	Dreyfus NY AMT Free Muni Bd I	DNYIX	B	(800) 645-6561	B / 7.7	2.42	-3.52	-0.13 /15	3.62 /89	2.68 /74	3.04	0.66
MUN	Dreyfus NY AMT Free Muni Bd Y	DNYYX	B-	(800) 645-6561	B / 7.6	2.40	-3.55	-0.12 /16	3.54 /88	--	3.05	0.64
*MUS	Dreyfus NY Tax Exempt Bond	DRNYX	B	(800) 645-6561	B / 7.7	2.30	-3.10	0.16 /27	3.51 /88	2.41 /69	3.13	0.73
GEI	Dreyfus Opportunistic Fixed Inc A	DSTAX	E	(800) 782-6620	E- / 0.2	2.59	2.04	5.60 /69	-1.06 / 3	1.23 /30	2.70	0.89
GEI	Dreyfus Opportunistic Fixed Inc C	DSTCX	E	(800) 782-6620	E / 0.3	2.49	1.71	4.92 /66	-1.79 / 2	0.49 /21	2.26	1.65
GEI	Dreyfus Opportunistic Fixed Inc I	DSTRX	E	(800) 782-6620	D / 1.9	2.75	2.32	6.00 /70	-0.78 / 3	1.52 /35	3.01	0.63
GEL	Dreyfus Opportunistic Fixed Inc Y	DSTYX	E	(800) 782-6620	D / 2.0	2.77	2.34	6.00 /70	-0.71 / 3	--	3.10	0.58
MUS	Dreyfus PA Muni A	PTPAX	C-	(800) 782-6620	C / 5.5	2.03	-3.32	0.35 /34	3.57 /88	2.80 /76	2.79	0.95
MUS	Dreyfus PA Muni C	PPACX	C	(800) 782-6620	C+ / 6.4	1.84	-3.68	-0.41 /11	2.81 /79	2.02 /59	2.13	1.72
MUS ●	Dreyfus PA Muni Z	DPENX	B+	(800) 782-6620	B / 8.1	2.08	-3.21	0.58 /38	3.82 /91	3.03 /80	3.15	0.74
MMT	Dreyfus Prime Money Market B	CZBXX	C-	(800) 645-6561	D- / 1.2	0.14	0.23	0.30 /29	0.10 /13	0.06 /12	0.30	N/A

99 Pct = Best
0 Pct = Worst

● Denotes fund is closed to new investors
* Denotes fund is included in Section II

www.thestreetratings.com

RISK			NET ASSETS		ASSET							FUND MANAGER		MINIMUM		LOADS	
Risk Rating/Pts	3 Yr Avg Standard Deviation	Avg Dura-tion	NAV As of 2/28/17	Total $(Mil)	Cash %	Gov. Bond %	Muni. Bond %	Corp. Bond %	Other %	Portfolio Turnover Ratio	Avg Coupon Rate	Manager Quality Pct	Manager Tenure (Years)	Initial Purch. $	Additional Purch. $	Front End Load	Back End Load
A+ / 9.9	N/A	N/A	1.00	1,601	100	0	0	0	0	0	0.4	51	N/A	1,000,000,00	0	0.0	0.0
A+ / 9.9	0.1	N/A	1.00	306	100	0	0	0	0	0	0.4	49	N/A	1,000,000,00	0	0.0	0.0
A+ / 9.9	N/A	N/A	1.00	3	100	0	0	0	0	0	0.1	41	N/A	275,000,000	0	0.0	0.0
U /	N/A	N/A	1.00	3	100	0	0	0	0	0	0.0	N/A	N/A	275,000,000	0	0.0	0.0
A+ / 9.9	N/A	N/A	1.00	211	100	0	0	0	0	0	0.2	44	N/A	275,000,000	0	0.0	0.0
A+ / 9.9	N/A	N/A	1.00	277	100	0	0	0	0	0	0.3	N/A	N/A	275,000,000	0	0.0	0.0
A+ / 9.9	N/A	N/A	1.00	290	100	0	0	0	0	0	0.2	38	N/A	275,000,000	0	0.0	0.0
A+ / 9.9	N/A	N/A	1.00	143	100	0	0	0	0	0	0.2	41	N/A	275,000,000	0	0.0	0.0
A+ / 9.9	N/A	N/A	1.00	589	100	0	0	0	0	0	0.2	43	N/A	275,000,000	0	0.0	0.0
U /	N/A	N/A	1.00	327	100	0	0	0	0	0	0.0	N/A	N/A	275,000,000	0	0.0	0.0
C+ / 5.9	2.9	5.5	13.35	460	0	35	1	33	31	270	0.0	12	9	1,000	100	4.5	0.0
C+ / 6.0	2.9	5.5	13.35	19	0	35	1	33	31	270	0.0	4	9	1,000	100	0.0	0.0
C+ / 5.9	2.9	5.5	13.35	237	0	35	1	33	31	270	0.0	19	9	1,000	100	0.0	0.0
C+ / 5.8	3.0	5.5	13.36	46	0	35	1	33	31	270	0.0	17	9	1,000,000	0	0.0	0.0
C / 4.7	3.2	4.9	13.53	726	0	0	99	0	1	14	0.0	16	6	2,500	100	0.0	0.0
D- / 1.0	6.1	7.4	15.03	93	0	68	0	20	12	127	0.0	79	11	1,000	100	4.5	0.0
D- / 1.0	6.1	7.4	14.68	45	0	68	0	20	12	127	0.0	68	11	1,000	100	0.0	0.0
D- / 1.0	6.1	7.4	15.15	642	0	68	0	20	12	127	0.0	83	11	1,000	100	0.0	0.0
D- / 1.0	6.1	7.4	15.15	31	0	68	0	20	12	127	0.0	83	11	1,000,000	0	0.0	0.0
A+ / 9.9	N/A	N/A	1.00	475	100	0	0	0	0	0	0.0	38	N/A	2,500	100	0.0	0.0
U /	N/A	N/A	1.00	142	100	0	0	0	0	0	0.0	N/A	N/A	0	0	0.0	0.0
C- / 4.0	3.5	5.4	11.41	28	0	0	99	0	1	13	0.0	11	6	1,000	100	4.5	0.0
C- / 4.0	3.5	5.4	11.42	2	0	0	99	0	1	13	0.0	3	6	1,000	100	0.0	0.0
C- / 4.0	3.5	5.4	11.41	128	0	0	99	0	1	13	0.0	15	6	1,000	100	0.0	0.0
C- / 3.5	3.8	5.4	12.70	167	0	0	99	0	1	19	0.0	29	5	1,000	100	4.5	0.0
C- / 3.5	3.8	5.4	12.73	10	0	0	99	0	1	19	0.0	10	5	1,000	100	0.0	0.0
U /	N/A	5.4	12.70	5	0	0	99	0	1	19	0.0	N/A	5	1,000	100	0.0	0.0
U /	N/A	5.4	12.70	N/A	0	0	99	0	1	19	0.0	N/A	5	1,000,000	0	0.0	0.0
C- / 3.5	3.8	5.4	12.70	199	0	0	99	0	1	19	0.0	31	5	1,000	100	0.0	0.0
A+ / 9.9	0.3	N/A	1.00	N/A	100	0	0	0	0	0	0.6	50	21	10,000,000	0	0.0	0.0
A+ / 9.9	0.3	N/A	1.00	4	100	0	0	0	0	0	0.6	50	21	10,000,000	0	0.0	0.0
A+ / 9.9	0.3	N/A	1.00	178	100	0	0	0	0	0	0.5	49	21	10,000,000	0	0.0	0.0
U /	N/A	N/A	1.00	1	100	0	0	0	0	0	0.5	49	21	10,000,000	0	0.0	0.0
C- / 3.6	3.7	5.2	11.58	1,357	0	0	99	0	1	16	0.0	29	8	2,500	100	0.0	0.0
C- / 4.0	3.5	5.1	12.73	342	1	0	98	0	1	8	0.0	36	8	1,000	100	4.5	0.0
C- / 4.0	3.5	5.1	12.72	10	1	0	98	0	1	8	0.0	14	8	1,000	100	0.0	0.0
C- / 4.1	3.4	5.1	12.73	15	1	0	98	0	1	8	0.0	55	8	1,000	100	0.0	0.0
C- / 4.0	3.5	5.1	12.73	N/A	1	0	98	0	1	8	0.0	52	8	1,000,000	0	0.0	0.0
C- / 4.1	3.5	5.1	12.73	103	1	0	98	0	1	8	0.0	52	8	1,000	100	0.0	0.0
C- / 3.8	3.6	5.4	14.68	297	1	0	98	0	1	25	0.0	24	8	1,000	100	4.5	0.0
C- / 3.8	3.6	5.4	14.68	30	1	0	98	0	1	25	0.0	8	8	1,000	100	0.0	0.0
C- / 3.9	3.6	5.4	14.68	74	1	0	98	0	1	25	0.0	32	8	1,000	100	0.0	0.0
C- / 3.8	3.6	5.4	14.68	N/A	1	0	98	0	1	25	0.0	29	8	1,000,000	0	0.0	0.0
C- / 4.2	3.4	5.3	14.67	1,133	1	0	98	0	1	12	0.0	36	8	2,500	100	0.0	0.0
C- / 3.1	4.1	1.4	11.28	42	0	38	2	32	28	159	1.9	8	7	1,000	100	4.5	0.0
C- / 3.1	4.1	1.4	11.25	24	0	38	2	32	28	159	1.9	3	7	1,000	100	0.0	0.0
C- / 3.0	4.1	1.4	11.28	73	0	38	2	32	28	159	1.9	12	7	1,000	100	0.0	0.0
C- / 3.0	4.1	1.4	11.27	13	0	38	2	32	28	159	1.9	14	7	1,000,000	0	0.0	0.0
C / 4.3	3.4	5.3	16.06	100	1	0	98	0	1	12	0.0	45	5	1,000	100	4.5	0.0
C / 4.3	3.4	5.3	16.07	5	1	0	98	0	1	12	0.0	16	5	1,000	100	0.0	0.0
C / 4.3	3.4	5.3	16.06	49	1	0	98	0	1	12	0.0	56	5	1,000	100	0.0	0.0
A+ / 9.9	0.1	N/A	1.00	8	100	0	0	0	0	0	0.3	45	N/A	1,000,000	0	0.0	0.0

Fund Type	Fund Name	Ticker Symbol	Overall Investment Rating	Phone	Performance Rating/Pts	3 Mo	6 Mo	1Yr / Pct	3Yr / Pct	5Yr / Pct	Dividend Yield	Expense Ratio
MMT	Dreyfus Prime Money Market Citizens	CZAXX	C	(800) 645-6561	D- / 1.4	0.18	0.30	0.45 / 32	0.16 / 15	0.10 / 15	0.45	N/A
MUI	Dreyfus Sh-Intmd Muni Bd A	DMBAX	D-	(800) 645-6561	E / 0.4	1.46	-0.62	-0.30 / 13	0.43 / 22	0.63 / 27	0.67	0.86
MUI	Dreyfus Sh-Intmd Muni Bd D	DSIBX	C	(800) 645-6561	D+ / 2.4	1.50	-0.55	-0.07 / 16	0.58 / 26	0.78 / 30	0.84	0.72
MUI	Dreyfus Sh-Intmd Muni Bd I	DIMIX	C	(800) 645-6561	D+ / 2.6	1.52	-0.58	-0.05 / 17	0.68 / 28	0.88 / 32	0.94	0.64
MUN	Dreyfus Sh-Intmd Muni Bd Y	DMYBX	C	(800) 645-6561	D+ / 2.6	1.52	-0.58	-0.04 / 17	0.69 / 28	--	0.94	0.65
GEI	Dreyfus Short Term Inc D	DSTIX	C-	(800) 782-6620	D / 2.0	0.59	-0.13	1.36 / 43	0.43 / 20	1.02 / 28	1.06	0.95
GEI ●	Dreyfus Short Term Inc P	DSHPX	C-	(800) 782-6620	D / 1.9	0.57	-0.27	1.26 / 42	0.35 / 19	0.95 / 27	0.97	1.06
MUN	Dreyfus Tax Sensitive Tot Ret Bd A	DSDAX	D-	(800) 645-6561	D+ / 2.3	1.91	-2.84	-0.43 / 11	2.11 / 65	1.92 / 57	1.93	0.89
MUN	Dreyfus Tax Sensitive Tot Ret Bd C	DSDCX	D-	(800) 645-6561	C- / 3.3	1.78	-3.15	-1.12 / 4	1.36 / 45	1.16 / 39	1.27	1.69
MUN	Dreyfus Tax Sensitive Tot Ret Bd I	SDITX	C+	(800) 645-6561	C+ / 5.9	2.02	-2.71	-0.18 / 15	2.37 / 71	2.19 / 63	2.28	0.58
MUN	Dreyfus Tax Sensitive Tot Ret Bd Y	SDYTX	C+	(800) 645-6561	C+ / 5.9	2.02	-2.67	-0.14 / 15	2.37 / 71	--	2.28	0.59
MMT	Dreyfus Treas & Agn Cash Mgt Adm	DTAXX	D+	(800) 645-6561	E+ / 0.8	0.06	0.09	0.14 / 24	0.05 / 9	0.04 / 10	0.14	N/A
MMT	Dreyfus Treas & Agn Cash Mgt Agn	DYAXX	C-	(800) 645-6561	E+ / 0.9	0.07	0.11	0.17 / 25	0.07 / 11	0.04 / 10	0.17	N/A
MMT	Dreyfus Treas & Agn Cash Mgt Inst	DTRXX	C-	(800) 645-6561	D- / 1.1	0.09	0.14	0.24 / 27	0.10 / 13	0.06 / 12	0.24	N/A
MMT	Dreyfus Treas & Agn Cash Mgt Inv	DTVXX	D+	(800) 645-6561	E+ / 0.6	0.03	0.03	0.04 / 20	0.02 / 7	0.02 / 7	0.04	N/A
MMT	Dreyfus Treas & Agn Cash Mgt Prm	DYPXX	U	(800) 645-6561	U /	0.02	0.02	0.02 / 19	0.01 / 6	0.01 / 5	0.02	N/A
MMT	Dreyfus Treas Sec Csh Mgt Admin	DARXX	D+	(800) 645-6561	E+ / 0.8	0.06	0.08	0.10 / 22	0.04 / 9	0.02 / 7	0.10	N/A
MMT	Dreyfus Treas Sec Csh Mgt Agency	DSAXX	D+	(800) 645-6561	E+ / 0.8	0.07	0.10	0.14 / 24	0.05 / 9	0.03 / 9	0.14	N/A
MMT	Dreyfus Treas Sec Csh Mgt Inst	DIRXX	C-	(800) 645-6561	D- / 1.0	0.08	0.13	0.21 / 26	0.08 / 11	0.05 / 11	0.21	N/A
MMT	Dreyfus Treas Sec Csh Mgt Inv	DVRXX	D+	(800) 645-6561	E+ / 0.6	0.02	0.02	0.03 / 19	0.01 / 6	0.01 / 5	0.03	N/A
USS	Dreyfus Ultra Short Income D	DSDDX	D	(800) 645-6561	E / 0.5	0.12	0.19	0.43 / 32	-0.21 / 4	--	0.33	0.72
USS	Dreyfus Ultra Short Income Instl	DSYDX	C-	(800) 645-6561	D- / 1.4	0.22	0.49	0.90 / 39	0.09 / 12	--	0.70	0.45
USS	Dreyfus Ultra Short Income Z	DSIGX	D+	(800) 645-6561	E+ / 0.9	0.16	0.36	0.66 / 36	-0.03 / 5	0.04 / 10	0.46	0.65
US	Dreyfus US Treasury Intermediate	DRGIX	D	(800) 645-6561	D / 1.6	0.30	-1.78	-1.04 / 4	0.67 / 23	0.41 / 20	0.77	0.66
US	Dreyfus US Treasury Long Term	DRGBX	E+	(800) 645-6561	C+ / 6.1	1.59	-11.09	-4.72 / 0	5.29 / 87	2.53 / 50	2.49	0.66
GL	Dreyfus/Standish Global Fixed Inc A	DHGAX	D+	(800) 645-6561	C- / 3.1	1.40	-1.47	1.68 / 46	2.61 / 54	3.28 / 62	1.44	0.82
GL	Dreyfus/Standish Global Fixed Inc C	DHGCX	C-	(800) 645-6561	C- / 3.8	1.27	-1.80	0.99 / 39	1.88 / 41	2.52 / 50	0.82	1.55
GL	Dreyfus/Standish Global Fixed Inc I	SDGIX	B	(800) 645-6561	C / 5.5	1.50	-1.31	2.02 / 49	2.92 / 60	3.58 / 67	1.80	0.52
GL	Dreyfus/Standish Global Fixed Inc Y	DSDYX	B	(800) 645-6561	C+ / 5.6	1.50	-1.26	2.07 / 49	2.98 / 61	--	1.85	0.48
LP	Driehaus Select Credit Fund	DRSLX	E-	(800) 560-6111	E- / 0.1	1.59	1.84	9.42 / 78	-3.53 / 1	-0.36 / 3	4.73	1.40
COI	Dunham Corporate/Government	DACGX	D-	(888) 338-6426	D / 1.8	1.49	-1.78	3.44 / 59	1.45 / 34	1.91 / 41	2.20	1.31
COI	Dunham Corporate/Government	DCCGX	D	(888) 338-6426	C- / 3.9	1.37	-2.03	4.72 / 66	1.49 / 35	1.77 / 38	3.59	1.81
COI	Dunham Corporate/Government	DNCGX	C-	(888) 338-6426	C- / 4.0	1.62	-1.59	3.78 / 61	1.63 / 37	2.23 / 45	2.56	1.06
LP	Dunham Floating Rate Bond A	DAFRX	B	(888) 338-6426	C / 4.7	1.85	3.00	8.59 / 75	2.36 / 49	--	3.33	1.52
LP	Dunham Floating Rate Bond C	DCFRX	A	(888) 338-6426	C+ / 5.9	1.78	2.81	8.24 / 75	1.90 / 41	--	2.96	2.02
LP	Dunham Floating Rate Bond N	DNFRX	A+	(888) 338-6426	C+ / 6.9	1.93	3.14	8.98 / 76	2.62 / 54	--	3.75	1.27
COH	Dunham High-Yield Bond A	DAHYX	D-	(888) 338-6426	C / 5.4	3.51	3.67	13.36 / 86	1.86 / 41	3.69 / 68	4.06	1.27
COH	Dunham High-Yield Bond C	DCHYX	C-	(888) 338-6426	B / 7.7	5.30	5.34	14.96 / 88	2.07 / 44	3.63 / 68	3.73	1.77
COH	Dunham High-Yield Bond N	DNHYX	C-	(888) 338-6426	B / 7.8	4.55	4.78	14.64 / 88	2.44 / 51	4.32 / 76	4.51	1.02
GEI	Dunham International Oppty Bd A	DAIOX	E-	(888) 338-6426	E- / 0.0	1.34	-7.78	-0.91 / 5	-3.89 / 0	--	0.00	1.63
GEI	Dunham International Oppty Bd C	DCIOX	E-	(888) 338-6426	E- / 0.0	1.12	-8.07	-1.37 / 2	-4.38 / 0	--	0.00	2.13
GEI	Dunham International Oppty Bd N	DNIOX	E-	(888) 338-6426	E- / 0.0	1.33	-7.75	-0.69 / 7	-3.68 / 1	--	0.00	1.38
EM	DuPont Capital Emerging Mkts Dbt I	DCDEX	C+	(888) 739-1390	A+ / 9.8	4.22	-0.56	14.15 / 87	7.64 / 97	--	5.44	3.34
MUS	Dupree AL Tax Free Income	DUALX	A+	(800) 866-0614	B- / 7.5	1.59	-2.56	0.50 / 37	3.36 / 86	3.01 / 80	3.08	0.78
USL	Dupree Interm Government Bond	DPIGX	D-	(800) 866-0614	C / 4.8	0.43	-2.19	-0.90 / 5	3.10 / 63	2.08 / 43	2.51	0.53
*MUS	Dupree KY Tax Free Income	KYTFX	A	(800) 866-0614	C+ / 6.6	1.69	-2.64	0.11 / 25	2.73 / 77	2.56 / 72	3.13	0.55
MUS	Dupree KY Tax Free Short-to-Med	KYSMX	C-	(800) 866-0614	D+ / 2.5	1.84	-2.03	-0.76 / 6	0.85 / 32	1.01 / 35	1.89	0.72
MUS	Dupree MS Tax Free Income	DUMSX	A-	(800) 866-0614	B / 8.0	1.80	-2.57	0.36 / 34	3.73 / 90	3.13 / 82	2.90	0.88
MUS	Dupree NC Tax Free Income	NTFIX	B	(800) 866-0614	C+ / 6.9	1.85	-3.30	-0.14 / 15	3.02 / 82	2.74 / 75	2.79	0.70
MUS	Dupree NC Tax Free Sh-to-Med	NTSMX	D+	(800) 866-0614	D / 2.0	1.51	-1.72	-0.91 / 5	0.63 / 27	0.88 / 32	1.49	0.83
MUN	Dupree Taxable Muni Bd Srs	DUTMX	A	(800) 866-0614	A+ / 9.6	0.84	-2.13	2.08 / 58	5.31 / 98	4.96 / 97	4.80	0.86
MUS	Dupree TN Tax-Free Income	TNTIX	A	(800) 866-0614	C+ / 6.7	1.52	-2.78	-0.12 / 16	2.91 / 80	2.64 / 73	2.91	0.71

● Denotes fund is closed to new investors
* Denotes fund is included in Section II

www.thestreetratings.com

RISK			NET ASSETS		ASSET							FUND MANAGER		MINIMUM		LOADS	
Risk Rating/Pts	3 Yr Avg Standard Deviation	Avg Dura-tion	NAV As of 2/28/17	Total $(Mil)	Cash %	Gov. Bond %	Muni. Bond %	Corp. Bond %	Other %	Portfolio Turnover Ratio	Avg Coupon Rate	Manager Quality Pct	Manager Tenure (Years)	Initial Purch. $	Additional Purch. $	Front End Load	Back End Load
A+ / 9.9	0.1	N/A	1.00	6	100	0	0	0	0	0	0.5	49	N/A	1,000,000	0	0.0	0.0
B+ / 8.9	1.4	2.5	12.94	61	1	0	98	0	1	21	0.0	12	8	1,000	100	2.5	0.0
B+ / 8.9	1.4	2.5	12.94	276	1	0	98	0	1	21	0.0	17	8	2,500	100	0.0	0.0
B+ / 8.8	1.4	2.5	12.94	161	1	0	98	0	1	21	0.0	18	8	1,000	100	0.0	0.0
B+ / 8.8	1.4	2.5	12.94	N/A	1	0	98	0	1	21	0.0	18	8	1,000,000	0	0.0	0.0
A- / 9.1	1.2	2.4	10.35	172	0	64	0	30	6	200	0.0	23	9	2,500	100	0.0	0.0
A- / 9.1	1.1	2.4	10.36	N/A	0	64	0	30	6	200	0.0	22	9	100,000	100	0.0	0.0
C / 5.4	3.0	4.7	22.61	15	1	0	93	2	4	29	0.0	10	16	1,000	100	4.5	0.0
C / 5.3	3.0	4.7	22.62	1	1	0	93	2	4	29	0.0	3	16	1,000	100	0.0	0.0
C / 5.3	3.0	4.7	22.62	227	1	0	93	2	4	29	0.0	14	16	1,000	100	0.0	0.0
C / 5.4	3.0	4.7	22.62	7	1	0	93	2	4	29	0.0	15	16	1,000,000	0	0.0	0.0
A+ / 9.9	N/A	N/A	1.00	285	100	0	0	0	0	0	0.1	41	21	10,000,000	0	0.0	0.0
A+ / 9.9	N/A	N/A	1.00	5	100	0	0	0	0	0	0.2	43	21	10,000,000	0	0.0	0.0
A+ / 9.9	N/A	N/A	1.00	16,822	100	0	0	0	0	0	0.2	45	21	10,000,000	0	0.0	0.0
A+ / 9.9	N/A	N/A	1.00	1,746	100	0	0	0	0	0	0.0	38	21	10,000,000	0	0.0	0.0
U /	N/A	N/A	1.00	15	100	0	0	0	0	0	0.0	N/A	21	10,000,000	0	0.0	0.0
A+ / 9.9	N/A	N/A	1.00	3,106	100	0	0	0	0	0	0.1	40	N/A	10,000,000	0	0.0	0.0
A+ / 9.9	N/A	N/A	1.00	30	100	0	0	0	0	0	0.1	41	N/A	10,000,000	0	0.0	0.0
A+ / 9.9	N/A	N/A	1.00	29,197	100	0	0	0	0	0	0.2	43	N/A	10,000,000	0	0.0	0.0
A+ / 9.9	N/A	N/A	1.00	1,986	100	0	0	0	0	0	0.0	38	N/A	10,000,000	0	0.0	0.0
A+ / 9.7	0.6	1.0	10.07	14	8	1	0	89	2	59	0.0	29	1	2,500	100	0.0	0.0
A+ / 9.8	0.6	1.0	10.07	18	8	1	0	89	2	59	0.0	45	1	1,000,000	0	0.0	0.0
A+ / 9.8	0.6	1.0	10.08	78	8	1	0	89	2	59	0.0	35	1	2,500	100	0.0	0.0
B / 8.0	2.1	3.9	13.21	61	0	99	0	0	1	231	0.0	23	9	2,500	100	0.0	0.0
E- / 0.2	10.5	17.4	18.40	67	0	99	0	0	1	129	0.0	37	9	2,500	100	0.0	0.0
C+ / 6.9	2.7	6.7	21.18	323	2	72	0	15	11	178	0.0	91	11	1,000	100	4.5	0.0
C+ / 6.8	2.8	6.7	21.07	94	2	72	0	15	11	178	0.0	86	11	1,000	100	0.0	0.0
C+ / 6.9	2.7	6.7	21.22	2,164	2	72	0	15	11	178	0.0	92	11	1,000	100	0.0	0.0
C+ / 6.9	2.7	6.7	21.23	146	2	72	0	15	11	178	0.0	93	11	1,000,000	0	0.0	0.0
D / 1.8	5.4	0.8	8.03	62	25	0	0	41	34	77	0.0	0	7	25,000	5,000	0.0	0.0
C+ / 6.5	2.8	5.2	13.67	5	1	21	3	40	35	58	5.0	16	4	5,000	100	4.5	0.0
C / 4.9	3.2	5.2	13.58	3	1	21	3	40	35	58	5.0	14	4	5,000	100	0.0	0.0
C+ / 6.4	2.8	5.2	13.69	46	1	21	3	40	35	58	5.0	20	4	100,000	0	0.0	0.0
B / 7.7	2.4	N/A	9.77	13	0	0	0	25	75	62	0.0	84	4	5,000	100	4.5	0.0
B / 7.7	2.4	N/A	9.78	5	0	0	0	25	75	62	0.0	80	4	5,000	100	0.0	0.0
B / 7.7	2.4	N/A	9.78	106	0	0	0	25	75	62	0.0	86	4	100,000	0	0.0	0.0
D / 1.8	4.9	N/A	9.15	11	2	2	0	94	2	62	0.0	3	12	5,000	100	4.5	0.0
D / 1.7	5.0	N/A	9.18	8	2	2	0	94	2	62	0.0	4	12	5,000	100	0.0	0.0
D / 1.8	4.9	N/A	9.15	81	2	2	0	94	2	62	0.0	7	12	100,000	0	0.0	0.0
E+ / 0.6	7.3	N/A	8.82	2	3	55	2	34	6	64	0.0	0	4	5,000	100	4.5	0.0
E+ / 0.6	7.3	N/A	8.70	1	3	55	2	34	6	64	0.0	0	4	5,000	100	0.0	0.0
E+ / 0.6	7.3	N/A	8.86	25	3	55	2	34	6	64	0.0	0	4	100,000	0	0.0	0.0
E / 0.5	7.6	N/A	9.55	6	0	0	0	0	100	25	0.0	99	4	1,000,000	100,000	0.0	2.0
C+ / 6.9	2.7	4.1	12.20	27	0	0	100	0	0	5	5.0	64	16	100	0	0.0	0.0
C- / 3.6	3.7	5.7	10.25	16	0	100	0	0	0	2	5.6	76	18	100	0	0.0	0.0
C+ / 6.8	2.8	5.1	7.70	982	0	0	100	0	0	12	5.0	33	18	100	0	0.0	0.0
B / 7.8	2.3	3.9	5.28	74	0	0	100	0	0	26	4.6	6	18	100	0	0.0	0.0
C / 4.9	3.2	4.7	12.00	12	0	0	100	0	0	3	5.1	63	17	100	0	0.0	0.0
C / 5.0	3.1	5.4	11.40	139	0	0	100	0	0	6	5.0	30	13	100	0	0.0	0.0
B+ / 8.4	1.9	3.5	10.76	22	0	0	100	0	0	24	4.7	7	13	100	0	0.0	0.0
C- / 3.2	3.5	10.8	10.50	12	0	0	100	0	0	11	6.7	88	7	100	0	0.0	0.0
C+ / 6.7	2.8	5.4	11.34	107	0	0	100	0	0	10	5.0	44	13	100	0	0.0	0.0

Fund Type	Fund Name	Ticker Symbol	Overall Investment Rating	Phone	Performance Rating/Pts	3 Mo	6 Mo	1Yr / Pct	3Yr / Pct	5Yr / Pct	Dividend Yield	Expense Ratio
MUS	Dupree TN Tax-Free Sh-to-Med	TTSMX	C	(800) 866-0614	C- / 3.0	1.36	-1.41	-0.67 / 7	1.04 /36	1.02 /36	1.57	0.86
COI	Eagle Investment Grade Bond A	EGBAX	D+	(800) 421-4184	D / 2.0	0.86	-0.61	1.47 /44	1.59 /36	1.32 /32	1.35	1.36
COI	Eagle Investment Grade Bond C	EGBCX	C-	(800) 421-4184	D / 2.2	0.67	-1.00	0.67 /36	0.81 /24	0.51 /22	0.61	2.12
COI	Eagle Investment Grade Bond I	EGBLX	B-	(800) 421-4184	C- / 4.0	0.93	-0.47	1.74 /47	1.87 /41	1.57 /36	1.66	1.09
COI	Eagle Investment Grade Bond R3	EGBRX	C	(800) 421-4184	C- / 3.1	0.86	-0.68	1.19 /42	1.30 /32	1.02 /28	1.13	1.69
COI	Eagle Investment Grade Bond R5	EGBTX	B-	(800) 421-4184	C- / 4.0	1.00	-0.47	1.74 /47	1.87 /41	1.59 /36	1.67	1.01
COI	Eagle Investment Grade Bond R6	EGBUX	U	(800) 421-4184	U /	0.96	-0.42	1.84 /48	--	--	1.77	0.99
MUN	Eaton Vance AMT-Free Muni Income	ETMBX	C+	(800) 262-1122	C+ / 6.9	1.92	-3.29	0.41 /35	4.38 /95	3.65 /89	3.72	0.90
MUN ●	Eaton Vance AMT-Free Muni Income	EBMBX	B-	(800) 262-1122	B / 7.6	1.74	-3.58	-0.36 /12	3.61 /89	2.88 /78	3.13	1.65
MUN	Eaton Vance AMT-Free Muni Income	ECMBX	B-	(800) 262-1122	B / 7.6	1.74	-3.57	-0.35 /12	3.61 /89	2.88 /78	3.13	1.65
MUN	Eaton Vance AMT-Free Muni Income	EVMBX	A	(800) 262-1122	A- / 9.0	1.91	-3.12	0.65 /39	4.61 /96	3.89 /92	4.16	0.65
MUS	Eaton Vance AZ Municipal Income A	ETAZX	D+	(800) 262-1122	C / 4.9	1.85	-2.88	0.66 /40	3.31 /86	2.73 /75	2.99	0.69
MUS ●	Eaton Vance AZ Municipal Income B	EVAZX	C	(800) 262-1122	C+ / 6.0	1.56	-3.35	-0.13 /15	2.56 /74	1.96 /58	2.37	1.44
MUS	Eaton Vance AZ Municipal Income C	ECAZX	C	(800) 262-1122	C+ / 6.1	1.66	-3.25	-0.13 /15	2.56 /74	1.98 /58	2.37	1.44
MUS	Eaton Vance AZ Municipal Income I	EIAZX	B+	(800) 262-1122	B / 7.9	1.90	-2.78	0.86 /43	3.55 /88	2.95 /79	3.34	0.49
MUN	Eaton Vance CA Municipal Opptys A	EACAX	C	(800) 262-1122	B- / 7.0	1.84	-4.01	0.25 /31	4.59 /96	3.77 /91	2.51	0.88
MUN	Eaton Vance CA Municipal Opptys C	ECCAX	B-	(800) 262-1122	B / 7.7	1.65	-4.29	-0.49 /10	3.84 /91	3.00 /80	1.86	1.63
MUN	Eaton Vance CA Municipal Opptys I	EICAX	A	(800) 262-1122	A- / 9.2	1.91	-3.89	0.50 /37	4.89 /97	4.03 /93	2.89	0.63
COI	Eaton Vance Core Bond A	EAGIX	D-	(800) 262-1122	D / 2.1	1.25	-2.00	1.79 /47	2.06 /44	2.15 /44	2.41	0.96
COI	Eaton Vance Core Bond I	EIGIX	C	(800) 262-1122	C / 4.6	1.42	-1.88	2.14 /50	2.31 /48	2.40 /48	2.78	0.71
USS	Eaton Vance Core Plus Bond A	EBABX	C	(800) 262-1122	B+ / 8.6	3.57	2.20	16.06 /90	4.91 /84	3.78 /70	3.34	1.14
USS	Eaton Vance Core Plus Bond C	ECBAX	C+	(800) 262-1122	B+ / 8.9	3.38	1.82	15.20 /89	4.14 /77	3.02 /58	2.77	1.89
USS	Eaton Vance Core Plus Bond I	EIBAX	B-	(800) 262-1122	A / 9.5	3.64	2.23	16.36 /91	5.15 /86	4.02 /73	3.74	0.89
MUN	Eaton Vance CT Municipal Income A	ETCTX	C+	(800) 262-1122	C / 5.4	1.30	-2.63	0.48 /37	3.55 /88	2.52 /71	3.13	0.72
MUN ●	Eaton Vance CT Municipal Income B	EVCTX	B	(800) 262-1122	C+ / 6.3	1.11	-3.02	-0.28 /13	2.78 /78	1.75 /53	2.52	1.47
MUN	Eaton Vance CT Municipal Income C	ECCTX	B	(800) 262-1122	C+ / 6.3	1.11	-3.01	-0.28 /13	2.78 /78	1.73 /52	2.52	1.47
MUN	Eaton Vance CT Municipal Income I	EICTX	A+	(800) 262-1122	B / 8.1	1.35	-2.54	0.68 /40	3.76 /90	2.71 /74	3.49	0.52
GL	Eaton Vance Dvsfd Currency Income	EAIIX	E+	(800) 262-1122	E+ / 0.6	3.16	2.24	5.38 /68	0.16 /15	-0.46 / 3	5.00	1.30
GL	Eaton Vance Dvsfd Currency Income	ECIMX	E+	(800) 262-1122	D / 1.9	2.98	1.88	4.54 /65	-0.56 / 3	-1.07 / 2	4.45	2.00
GL	Eaton Vance Dvsfd Currency Income	EIIMX	D	(800) 262-1122	C- / 3.5	3.25	2.27	5.64 /69	0.44 /20	-0.20 / 4	5.61	1.00
EM	Eaton Vance Em Mkts Debt Oppts A	EADOX	D-	(800) 262-1122	C+ / 6.4	3.51	1.57	14.46 /87	2.82 /58	--	4.97	1.64
EM	Eaton Vance Em Mkts Debt Oppts I	EIDOX	C-	(800) 262-1122	B / 8.2	3.68	1.79	15.08 /89	3.18 /64	--	5.31	1.39
EM	Eaton Vance Em Mkts Debt Oppts R6	EELDX	C-	(800) 262-1122	B / 8.1	3.59	1.81	15.02 /88	3.09 /62	--	5.34	1.34
EM	Eaton Vance Emer Market Local Inc	EEIAX	E	(800) 262-1122	C- / 3.4	6.81	0.70	17.57 /93	-0.11 / 5	-2.49 / 1	9.67	1.43
EM	Eaton Vance Emer Market Local Inc	EEICX	E	(800) 262-1122	C- / 4.2	6.57	0.39	16.96 /92	-0.81 / 3	-3.05 / 1	9.17	2.13
EM	Eaton Vance Emer Market Local Inc I	EEIIX	E+	(800) 262-1122	C+ / 6.0	6.89	0.85	18.05 /94	0.20 /16	-2.25 / 1	10.57	1.13
* LP	Eaton Vance Float Rate Advtage A	EAFAX	B+	(800) 262-1122	B+ / 8.5	2.67	5.23	15.82 /90	3.87 /74	4.93 /83	4.53	1.36
LP	Eaton Vance Float Rate Advtage	EVFAX	A-	(800) 262-1122	B+ / 8.9	2.67	5.23	15.82 /90	3.87 /74	4.93 /83	4.63	1.37
LP ●	Eaton Vance Float Rate Advtage B	EBFAX	B+	(800) 262-1122	B+ / 8.7	2.58	5.06	15.41 /89	3.51 /69	4.55 /79	4.31	1.71
LP	Eaton Vance Float Rate Advtage C	ECFAX	B+	(800) 262-1122	B+ / 8.5	2.55	4.98	15.27 /89	3.35 /66	4.41 /77	4.15	1.86
LP	Eaton Vance Float Rate Advtage I	EIFAX	A	(800) 262-1122	A- / 9.2	2.73	5.35	16.10 /90	4.12 /76	5.19 /86	4.87	1.12
* LP	Eaton Vance Floating Rate A	EVBLX	B+	(800) 262-1122	B / 7.6	2.56	4.67	13.62 /86	3.21 /64	3.98 /72	3.72	1.03
LP	Eaton Vance Floating Rate Adv	EABLX	A	(800) 262-1122	B / 8.2	2.50	4.65	13.57 /86	3.22 /65	3.98 /72	3.81	1.03
LP ●	Eaton Vance Floating Rate B	EBBLX	B	(800) 262-1122	B- / 7.3	2.32	4.15	12.75 /85	2.42 /50	3.21 /61	3.08	1.78
LP	Eaton Vance Floating Rate C	ECBLX	B+	(800) 262-1122	B- / 7.4	2.31	4.26	12.74 /85	2.45 /51	3.21 /61	3.08	1.78
LP	Eaton Vance Floating Rate Inst	EIBLX	A	(800) 262-1122	B+ / 8.4	2.56	4.78	13.85 /87	3.44 /68	4.24 /75	4.05	0.78
LP	Eaton Vance Floating Rate R6	ESBLX	A	(800) 262-1122	B+ / 8.5	2.69	4.91	13.99 /87	3.49 /69	4.27 /76	4.05	N/A
MUN	Eaton Vance Floating-Rte Muni Inc A	EXFLX	D	(800) 262-1122	E / 0.4	0.26	0.22	0.72 /41	0.26 /20	0.14 /19	0.70	0.61
MUN	Eaton Vance Floating-Rte Muni Inc I	EILMX	C+	(800) 262-1122	D / 2.2	0.29	0.19	0.87 /43	0.38 /21	0.28 /21	0.87	0.46
LP	Eaton Vance Flt-Rate and Hi Inc A	EVFHX	B+	(800) 262-1122	B / 7.9	2.71	4.64	13.86 /87	3.46 /68	4.43 /78	3.94	1.07
LP	Eaton Vance Flt-Rate and Hi Inc Adv	EAFHX	A-	(800) 262-1122	B+ / 8.4	2.70	4.57	13.83 /86	3.41 /67	4.41 /77	4.03	1.07
LP ●	Eaton Vance Flt-Rate and Hi Inc B	EBFHX	B	(800) 262-1122	B / 7.6	2.52	4.19	13.01 /85	2.64 /55	3.63 /68	3.30	1.82

● Denotes fund is closed to new investors
* Denotes fund is included in Section II

www.thestreetratings.com

I. Index of Bond and Money Market Mutual Funds

RISK			NET ASSETS		ASSET							FUND MANAGER		MINIMUM		LOADS	
Risk Rating/Pts	3 Yr Avg Standard Deviation	Avg Dura- tion	NAV As of 2/28/17	Total $(Mil)	Cash %	Gov. Bond %	Muni. Bond %	Corp. Bond %	Other %	Portfolio Turnover Ratio	Avg Coupon Rate	Manager Quality Pct	Manager Tenure (Years)	Initial Purch. $	Additional Purch. $	Front End Load	Back End Load
B+ / 8.4	1.9	3.5	10.67	11	0	0	100	0	0	7	4.6	14	18	100	0	0.0	0.0
B+ / 8.3	2.0	5.1	14.78	16	0	26	0	43	31	90	2.7	44	7	1,000	0	3.8	0.0
B+ / 8.3	2.0	5.1	14.75	19	0	26	0	43	31	90	2.7	16	7	1,000	0	0.0	0.0
B+ / 8.3	2.0	5.1	14.81	11	0	26	0	43	31	90	2.7	57	7	2,500,000	0	0.0	0.0
B+ / 8.3	2.0	5.1	14.78	N/A	0	26	0	43	31	90	2.7	28	7	0	0	0.0	0.0
B+ / 8.3	2.0	5.1	14.80	N/A	0	26	0	43	31	90	2.7	58	7	0	0	0.0	0.0
U /	N/A	5.1	14.85	1	0	26	0	43	31	90	2.7	N/A	7	0	0	0.0	0.0
C- / 4.1	3.5	4.6	9.03	181	4	0	95	0	1	21	5.0	72	12	1,000	0	4.8	0.0
C- / 4.0	3.5	4.6	8.97	N/A	4	0	95	0	1	21	5.0	N/A	12	1,000	0	0.0	0.0
C- / 4.0	3.5	4.6	8.98	41	4	0	95	0	1	21	5.0	N/A	12	1,000	0	0.0	0.0
C- / 4.1	3.5	4.6	9.86	124	4	0	95	0	1	21	5.0	76	12	250,000	0	0.0	0.0
C / 4.7	3.2	5.0	9.45	45	1	0	98	0	1	14	4.9	42	13	1,000	0	4.8	0.0
C / 4.7	3.2	5.0	10.50	N/A	1	0	98	0	1	14	4.9	17	13	1,000	0	0.0	0.0
C / 4.7	3.2	5.0	10.51	6	1	0	98	0	1	14	4.9	17	13	1,000	0	0.0	0.0
C / 4.7	3.2	5.0	9.45	13	1	0	98	0	1	14	4.9	55	13	250,000	0	0.0	0.0
C- / 3.5	3.8	6.1	10.25	133	0	0	100	0	0	219	4.2	68	3	1,000	0	4.8	0.0
C- / 3.5	3.7	6.1	9.48	31	0	0	100	0	0	219	4.2	36	3	1,000	0	0.0	0.0
C- / 3.5	3.7	6.1	10.26	110	0	0	100	0	0	219	4.2	74	3	250,000	0	0.0	0.0
C+ / 6.4	2.8	5.6	9.75	37	0	34	0	29	37	159	3.4	25	7	1,000	0	4.8	0.0
C+ / 6.2	2.9	5.6	9.74	109	0	34	0	29	37	159	3.4	33	7	250,000	0	0.0	0.0
D / 1.6	5.6	4.4	11.69	22	21	17	0	29	33	71	4.9	94	8	1,000	0	4.8	0.0
D / 1.6	5.6	4.4	11.69	14	21	17	0	29	33	71	4.9	93	8	1,000	0	0.0	0.0
D / 1.6	5.6	4.4	11.68	19	21	17	0	29	33	71	4.9	95	8	250,000	0	0.0	0.0
C+ / 6.0	2.9	4.7	10.13	64	0	0	99	0	1	7	5.1	65	3	1,000	0	4.8	0.0
C+ / 5.9	2.9	4.7	10.08	1	0	0	99	0	1	7	5.1	30	3	1,000	0	0.0	0.0
C+ / 5.9	2.9	4.7	10.09	6	0	0	99	0	1	7	5.1	30	3	1,000	0	0.0	0.0
C+ / 5.9	2.9	4.7	10.13	14	0	0	99	0	1	7	5.1	70	3	250,000	0	0.0	0.0
C+ / 5.7	3.0	1.0	8.81	33	5	50	0	0	45	38	0.0	65	9	1,000	0	4.8	0.0
C+ / 5.8	2.9	1.0	8.81	18	5	50	0	0	45	38	0.0	32	9	1,000	0	0.0	0.0
C+ / 5.7	3.0	1.0	8.78	57	5	50	0	0	45	38	0.0	72	9	250,000	0	0.0	0.0
D- / 1.1	6.2	3.4	9.25	N/A	8	76	0	4	12	85	0.0	94	N/A	1,000	0	4.8	0.0
D- / 1.1	6.2	3.4	9.28	1	8	76	0	4	12	85	0.0	95	N/A	250,000	0	0.0	0.0
D- / 1.1	6.2	3.4	9.25	68	8	76	0	4	12	85	0.0	94	N/A	1,000,000	0	0.0	0.0
E- / 0.1	11.7	5.3	6.17	89	3	79	0	11	7	73	0.0	89	9	1,000	0	4.8	0.0
E- / 0.1	11.7	5.3	6.24	33	3	79	0	11	7	73	0.0	83	9	1,000	0	0.0	0.0
E- / 0.1	11.7	5.3	6.17	182	3	79	0	11	7	73	0.0	90	9	250,000	0	0.0	0.0
C- / 3.6	3.7	0.3	10.89	1,826	0	0	0	77	23	38	4.8	91	21	1,000	0	2.3	0.0
C- / 3.6	3.7	0.3	10.89	151	0	0	0	77	23	38	4.8	91	21	1,000	0	0.0	0.0
C- / 3.6	3.7	0.3	10.91	7	0	0	0	77	23	38	4.8	89	21	1,000	0	0.0	0.0
C- / 3.6	3.7	0.3	10.87	1,178	0	0	0	77	23	38	4.8	88	21	1,000	0	0.0	0.0
C- / 3.6	3.7	0.3	10.89	3,589	0	0	0	77	23	38	4.8	92	21	250,000	0	0.0	0.0
C / 4.8	3.2	0.3	9.31	1,177	4	0	0	67	29	27	4.8	88	16	1,000	0	2.3	0.0
C / 4.9	3.2	0.3	9.00	374	4	0	0	67	29	27	4.8	88	16	1,000	0	0.0	0.0
C / 4.8	3.2	0.3	8.98	7	4	0	0	67	29	27	4.8	82	16	1,000	0	0.0	0.0
C / 4.8	3.2	0.3	8.99	703	4	0	0	67	29	27	4.8	82	16	1,000	0	0.0	0.0
C / 4.8	3.2	0.3	9.00	5,361	4	0	0	67	29	27	4.8	89	16	250,000	0	0.0	0.0
C / 4.8	3.2	0.3	9.01	265	4	0	0	67	29	27	4.8	89	16	1,000,000	0	0.0	0.0
A+ / 9.8	0.4	0.3	9.80	159	3	0	95	0	2	7	1.6	37	13	1,000	0	2.3	0.0
A+ / 9.8	0.4	0.3	9.80	118	3	0	95	0	2	7	1.6	46	13	250,000	0	0.0	0.0
C / 4.5	3.3	0.9	9.44	315	9	0	0	69	22	13	5.1	90	17	1,000	0	2.3	0.0
C / 4.5	3.3	0.9	8.87	197	9	0	0	69	22	13	5.1	89	17	1,000	0	0.0	0.0
C / 4.5	3.3	0.9	8.86	2	9	0	0	69	22	13	5.1	84	17	1,000	0	0.0	0.0

Data as of February 28, 2017

99 Pct = Best
0 Pct = Worst

Fund Type	Fund Name	Ticker Symbol	Overall Investment Rating	Phone	Performance Rating/Pts	3 Mo	6 Mo	1Yr / Pct	3Yr / Pct	5Yr / Pct	Dividend Yield	Expense Ratio
LP	Eaton Vance Flt-Rate and Hi Inc C	ECFHX	B	(800) 262-1122	B / 7.6	2.52	4.19	12.88 /85	2.64 /55	3.61 /67	3.30	1.82
LP	Eaton Vance Flt-Rate and Hi Inc I	EIFHX	A	(800) 262-1122	B+ / 8.6	2.65	4.58	13.98 /87	3.67 /71	4.65 /80	4.27	0.82
LP	Eaton Vance Flt-Rate and Hi Inc R6	ESFHX	A	(800) 262-1122	B+ / 8.5	2.75	4.74	14.10 /87	3.49 /69	4.46 /78	4.25	0.76
MUN	Eaton Vance GA Municipal Income A	ETGAX	C	(800) 262-1122	C / 5.3	1.81	-3.00	0.27 /31	3.54 /88	2.74 /75	2.88	0.70
MUN●	Eaton Vance GA Municipal Income B	EVGAX	C+	(800) 262-1122	C+ / 6.3	1.67	-3.39	-0.53 / 9	2.80 /79	1.96 /58	2.25	1.46
MUN	Eaton Vance GA Municipal Income C	ECGAX	B-	(800) 262-1122	C+ / 6.3	1.67	-3.39	-0.53 / 9	2.80 /79	1.98 /58	2.25	1.45
MUN	Eaton Vance GA Municipal Income I	EIGAX	A	(800) 262-1122	B / 8.0	1.86	-3.00	0.36 /34	3.75 /90	2.92 /79	3.23	0.50
GL	Eaton Vance Glb Mac Abslut Ret A	EAGMX	B	(800) 262-1122	C / 4.7	1.13	0.80	5.03 /67	3.24 /65	1.93 /41	3.40	1.07
GL	Eaton Vance Glb Mac Abslut Ret C	ECGMX	A	(800) 262-1122	C+ / 5.6	0.95	0.56	4.35 /64	2.56 /53	1.23 /30	2.81	1.77
GL	Eaton Vance Glb Mac Abslut Ret I	EIGMX	A+	(800) 262-1122	B- / 7.0	1.09	0.95	5.25 /68	3.58 /70	2.24 /45	3.90	0.77
GL	Eaton Vance Glb Mac Abslut Ret R	ERGMX	A+	(800) 262-1122	C+ / 6.4	1.07	0.70	4.80 /66	3.06 /62	1.74 /38	3.36	1.27
USS	Eaton Vance Govt Obligation A	EVGOX	D	(800) 262-1122	E / 0.3	0.67	0.20	0.49 /33	0.90 /26	0.78 /25	3.16	1.18
USS ●	Eaton Vance Govt Obligation B	EMGOX	D+	(800) 262-1122	D- / 1.0	0.48	-0.17	-0.26 /13	0.15 /15	0.02 / 7	2.56	1.94
USS	Eaton Vance Govt Obligation C	ECGOX	D+	(800) 262-1122	D- / 1.2	0.48	-0.17	-0.26 /13	0.19 /16	0.02 / 7	2.56	1.93
USS	Eaton Vance Govt Obligation I	EIGOX	B-	(800) 262-1122	C- / 3.0	0.73	0.48	0.89 /38	1.20 /31	1.03 /28	3.56	0.93
USS	Eaton Vance Govt Obligation R	ERGOX	C	(800) 262-1122	D / 2.2	0.76	0.23	0.38 /31	0.69 /23	0.54 /22	3.06	1.43
COH	Eaton Vance High Inc Opp Fund A	ETHIX	C+	(800) 262-1122	B+ / 8.5	4.05	4.26	14.99 /88	4.72 /83	7.02 /96	5.10	0.90
COH ●	Eaton Vance High Inc Opp Fund B	EVHIX	C+	(800) 262-1122	B+ / 8.8	3.85	3.87	14.12 /87	3.94 /74	6.23 /94	4.63	1.65
COH	Eaton Vance High Inc Opp Fund C	ECHIX	C+	(800) 262-1122	B+ / 8.8	3.86	3.87	13.86 /87	3.93 /74	6.22 /94	4.63	1.65
COH	Eaton Vance High Inc Opp Fund I	EIHIX	B	(800) 262-1122	A / 9.5	4.10	4.37	15.25 /89	4.98 /85	7.29 /97	5.59	0.65
MUN	Eaton Vance High Yield Muni Inc A	ETHYX	B+	(800) 262-1122	A- / 9.1	1.82	-4.43	1.03 /45	6.27 /99	5.42 /99	3.82	0.86
MUN●	Eaton Vance High Yield Muni Inc B	EVHYX	B+	(800) 262-1122	A / 9.5	1.64	-4.70	0.27 /31	5.49 /98	4.64 /97	3.23	1.61
MUN	Eaton Vance High Yield Muni Inc C	ECHYX	B+	(800) 262-1122	A / 9.5	1.57	-4.82	0.18 /28	5.47 /98	4.65 /97	3.23	1.61
MUN	Eaton Vance High Yield Muni Inc I	EIHYX	A-	(800) 262-1122	A+ / 9.8	1.88	-4.20	1.29 /49	6.54 /99	5.68 /99	4.26	0.61
*COH	Eaton Vance Income Fd of Boston A	EVIBX	C	(800) 262-1122	B / 8.0	3.90	4.28	14.93 /88	4.15 /77	6.10 /93	5.44	1.00
COH ●	Eaton Vance Income Fd of Boston B	EBIBX	C+	(800) 262-1122	B+ / 8.4	3.71	3.72	14.07 /87	3.37 /67	5.31 /87	4.98	1.75
COH	Eaton Vance Income Fd of Boston C	ECIBX	C+	(800) 262-1122	B+ / 8.5	3.70	3.89	14.05 /87	3.42 /67	5.30 /87	4.98	1.75
COH	Eaton Vance Income Fd of Boston I	EIBIX	B-	(800) 262-1122	A- / 9.2	3.96	4.22	15.21 /89	4.41 /80	6.36 /94	5.95	0.75
COH	Eaton Vance Income Fd of Boston R	ERIBX	C+	(800) 262-1122	B+ / 8.9	3.83	3.97	14.64 /88	3.89 /74	5.83 /91	5.47	1.25
COH	Eaton Vance Income Fd of Boston R6	EIBRX	B-	(800) 262-1122	A- / 9.2	3.98	4.27	15.31 /89	4.39 /79	6.24 /94	6.04	0.66
MUN	Eaton Vance MA Municipal Income A	ETMAX	D-	(800) 262-1122	C / 4.7	2.12	-3.50	-0.42 /11	3.38 /86	2.84 /77	3.21	0.77
MUN	Eaton Vance MA Municipal Income C	ECMMX	D+	(800) 262-1122	C+ / 5.6	1.81	-3.97	-1.27 / 3	2.57 /75	2.05 /60	2.59	1.52
MUN	Eaton Vance MA Municipal Income I	EIMAX	B-	(800) 262-1122	B / 7.7	2.17	-3.41	-0.22 /14	3.59 /89	3.04 /80	3.57	0.57
MUN	Eaton Vance MD Municipal Income A	ETMDX	C+	(800) 262-1122	C- / 4.2	1.81	-1.92	0.52 /37	2.90 /80	2.48 /70	3.33	0.76
MUN●	Eaton Vance MD Municipal Income B	EVMYX	B+	(800) 262-1122	C / 5.3	1.54	-2.30	-0.28 /13	2.12 /65	1.69 /52	2.76	1.51
MUN	Eaton Vance MD Municipal Income C	ECMDX	B+	(800) 262-1122	C / 5.3	1.54	-2.30	-0.19 /15	2.11 /65	1.71 /52	2.74	1.51
MUN	Eaton Vance MD Municipal Income I	EIMDX	A+	(800) 262-1122	B- / 7.4	1.86	-1.81	0.72 /41	3.11 /83	2.67 /74	3.70	0.56
MUS	Eaton Vance MN Municipal Income A	ETMNX	C-	(800) 262-1122	C- / 3.4	1.80	-2.90	-0.30 /13	2.73 /77	2.52 /71	2.79	0.69
MUS ●	Eaton Vance MN Municipal Income B	EVMNX	C+	(800) 262-1122	C / 4.6	1.64	-3.25	-1.02 / 4	1.99 /62	1.75 /53	2.16	1.45
MUS	Eaton Vance MN Municipal Income C	ECMNX	C+	(800) 262-1122	C / 4.6	1.64	-3.15	-1.02 / 4	1.99 /62	1.77 /53	2.16	1.44
MUS	Eaton Vance MN Municipal Income I	EIMNX	A	(800) 262-1122	C+ / 6.8	1.85	-2.80	-0.10 /16	2.93 /81	2.73 /75	3.13	0.49
MUS	Eaton Vance MO Municipal Income A	ETMOX	B-	(800) 262-1122	C+ / 6.1	1.43	-2.70	0.85 /43	3.88 /92	2.95 /79	3.39	0.71
MUS ●	Eaton Vance MO Municipal Income B	EVMOX	A-	(800) 262-1122	B- / 7.0	1.19	-3.10	0.15 /27	3.11 /83	2.19 /63	2.79	1.46
MUS	Eaton Vance MO Municipal Income C	ECMOX	A-	(800) 262-1122	B- / 7.0	1.19	-3.10	0.15 /27	3.11 /83	2.19 /63	2.79	1.46
MUS	Eaton Vance MO Municipal Income I	EIMOX	A+	(800) 262-1122	B+ / 8.6	1.48	-2.59	1.16 /47	4.12 /94	3.18 /83	3.76	0.51
COI	Eaton Vance Multisector Income A	EVBAX	C-	(800) 262-1122	A- / 9.1	7.50	8.94	32.89 /99	2.29 /48	—	2.21	0.95
GEL	Eaton Vance Multisector Income C	EVBCX	C	(800) 262-1122	A / 9.4	7.32	8.55	31.98 /99	1.55 /36	—	1.63	1.70
COI	Eaton Vance Multisector Income I	EVBIX	C	(800) 262-1122	A+ / 9.7	7.67	9.18	33.36 /99	2.57 /53	—	2.55	0.70
GEL	Eaton Vance Multisector Income R	EVBRX	C	(800) 262-1122	A+ / 9.6	7.52	8.81	32.60 /99	2.02 /43	—	2.12	1.20
GEL	Eaton Vance Multisector Income R6	EVBSX	C	(800) 262-1122	A+ / 9.7	7.58	9.10	33.28 /99	2.63 /55	—	2.61	0.64
GES	Eaton Vance Mult-Str Absolute Rtn A	EADDX	C-	(800) 262-1122	D / 2.0	0.73	0.44	2.89 /56	1.62 /37	0.92 /26	1.05	1.24
GES ●	Eaton Vance Mult-Str Absolute Rtn B	EBDDX	C	(800) 262-1122	D+ / 2.7	0.60	0.02	2.05 /49	0.86 /25	0.20 /18	0.40	1.99

● Denotes fund is closed to new investors
* Denotes fund is included in Section II

www.thestreetratings.com

RISK			NET ASSETS		ASSET							FUND MANAGER		MINIMUM		LOADS	
Risk Rating/Pts	3 Yr Avg Standard Deviation	Avg Dura-tion	NAV As of 2/28/17	Total $(Mil)	Cash %	Gov. Bond %	Muni. Bond %	Corp. Bond %	Other %	Portfolio Turnover Ratio	Avg Coupon Rate	Manager Quality Pct	Manager Tenure (Years)	Initial Purch. $	Additional Purch. $	Front End Load	Back End Load
C /4.5	3.3	0.9	8.85	157	9	0	0	69	22	13	5.1	84	17	1,000	0	0.0	0.0
C /4.6	3.3	0.9	8.87	927	9	0	0	69	22	13	5.1	91	17	250,000	0	0.0	0.0
C /4.4	3.3	0.9	8.87	14	9	0	0	69	22	13	5.1	90	17	1,000,000	0	0.0	0.0
C /5.3	3.1	5.0	8.47	40	4	0	95	0	1	7	5.1	60	10	1,000	0	4.8	0.0
C /5.1	3.1	5.0	9.05	N/A	4	0	95	0	1	7	5.1	24	10	1,000	0	0.0	0.0
C /5.2	3.1	5.0	9.06	7	4	0	95	0	1	7	5.1	25	10	1,000	0	0.0	0.0
C /5.2	3.1	5.0	8.49	28	4	0	95	0	1	7	5.1	65	10	250,000	0	0.0	0.0
B /7.9	2.3	1.2	9.04	427	17	62	0	1	20	97	0.0	92	20	1,000	0	4.8	0.0
B /7.9	2.2	1.2	9.08	237	17	62	0	1	20	97	0.0	88	20	1,000	0	0.0	0.0
B /7.9	2.2	1.2	9.02	5,069	17	62	0	1	20	97	0.0	93	20	250,000	0	0.0	0.0
B /7.9	2.2	1.2	9.06	1	17	62	0	1	20	97	0.0	91	20	1,000	0	0.0	0.0
A /9.5	0.8	2.0	6.38	280	3	6	0	0	91	33	5.5	63	3	1,000	0	4.8	0.0
A /9.4	0.8	2.0	6.38	4	3	6	0	0	91	33	5.5	28	3	1,000	0	0.0	0.0
A /9.4	0.8	2.0	6.37	83	3	6	0	0	91	33	5.5	30	3	1,000	0	0.0	0.0
A /9.5	0.8	2.0	6.38	85	3	6	0	0	91	33	5.5	71	3	250,000	0	0.0	0.0
A /9.4	0.9	2.0	6.36	30	3	6	0	0	91	33	5.5	56	3	1,000	0	0.0	0.0
D /1.9	4.7	3.3	4.55	436	10	0	0	84	6	39	6.4	77	21	1,000	0	4.8	0.0
D /1.9	4.8	3.3	4.56	6	10	0	0	84	6	39	6.4	58	21	1,000	0	0.0	0.0
D /1.9	4.7	3.3	4.55	138	10	0	0	84	6	39	6.4	61	21	1,000	0	0.0	0.0
D /1.9	4.8	3.3	4.56	848	10	0	0	84	6	39	6.4	80	21	250,000	0	0.0	0.0
D+ /2.7	4.3	6.0	8.68	373	4	0	95	0	1	27	5.2	84	13	1,000	0	4.8	0.0
D+ /2.7	4.3	6.0	8.65	2	4	0	95	0	1	27	5.2	77	13	1,000	0	0.0	0.0
D+ /2.7	4.2	6.0	8.03	190	4	0	95	0	1	27	5.2	76	13	1,000	0	0.0	0.0
D+ /2.7	4.3	6.0	8.69	559	4	0	95	0	1	27	5.2	86	13	250,000	0	0.0	0.0
D /1.9	4.7	3.3	5.80	1,600	7	0	0	87	6	34	6.4	65	16	1,000	0	4.8	0.0
D /1.9	4.7	3.3	5.80	12	7	0	0	87	6	34	6.4	30	16	1,000	0	0.0	0.0
D /1.9	4.7	3.3	5.81	253	7	0	0	87	6	34	6.4	33	16	1,000	0	0.0	0.0
D /1.9	4.7	3.3	5.80	4,554	7	0	0	87	6	34	6.4	72	16	250,000	0	0.0	0.0
D /2.0	4.6	3.3	5.80	45	7	0	0	87	6	34	6.4	59	16	1,000	0	0.0	0.0
D /1.9	4.7	3.3	5.80	92	7	0	0	87	6	34	6.4	71	16	1,000,000	0	0.0	0.0
C- /3.8	3.6	5.2	8.79	106	1	0	98	0	1	17	4.9	26	7	1,000	0	4.8	0.0
C- /3.7	3.7	5.2	8.79	21	1	0	98	0	1	17	4.9	9	7	1,000	0	0.0	0.0
C- /3.8	3.6	5.2	8.79	40	1	0	98	0	1	17	4.9	33	7	250,000	0	0.0	0.0
B /7.7	2.4	3.8	8.82	40	4	0	95	0	1	11	5.0	58	13	1,000	0	4.8	0.0
B /7.7	2.4	3.8	9.61	N/A	4	0	95	0	1	11	5.0	24	13	1,000	0	0.0	0.0
B /7.7	2.4	3.8	9.62	15	4	0	95	0	1	11	5.0	24	13	1,000	0	0.0	0.0
B /7.7	2.4	3.8	8.84	9	4	0	95	0	1	11	5.0	65	13	250,000	0	0.0	0.0
C+ /6.9	2.7	4.3	9.35	68	0	0	99	0	1	12	4.4	33	13	1,000	0	4.8	0.0
C+ /6.7	2.8	4.3	10.06	N/A	0	0	99	0	1	12	4.4	12	13	1,000	0	0.0	0.0
C+ /6.8	2.8	4.3	10.06	12	0	0	99	0	1	12	4.4	13	13	1,000	0	0.0	0.0
C+ /6.9	2.7	4.3	9.35	66	0	0	99	0	1	12	4.4	46	13	250,000	0	0.0	0.0
C+ /5.7	3.0	5.1	9.39	57	1	0	98	0	1	10	4.0	71	25	1,000	0	4.8	0.0
C+ /5.9	2.9	5.1	10.38	N/A	1	0	98	0	1	10	4.0	47	25	1,000	0	0.0	0.0
C+ /5.9	2.9	5.1	10.37	9	1	0	98	0	1	10	4.0	48	25	1,000	0	0.0	0.0
C+ /5.6	3.0	5.1	9.41	5	1	0	98	0	1	10	4.0	76	25	250,000	0	0.0	0.0
E- /0.2	10.7	N/A	10.60	132	5	15	0	35	45	74	5.4	4	4	1,000	0	4.8	0.0
E- /0.2	10.7	N/A	10.58	114	5	15	0	35	45	74	5.4	53	4	1,000	0	0.0	0.0
E- /0.2	10.7	N/A	10.61	305	5	15	0	35	45	74	5.4	6	4	250,000	0	0.0	0.0
E- /0.2	10.7	N/A	10.60	1	5	15	0	35	45	74	5.4	67	4	1,000	0	0.0	0.0
E- /0.2	10.7	N/A	10.61	5	5	15	0	35	45	74	5.4	78	4	1,000,000	0	0.0	0.0
B+ /8.9	1.4	2.5	8.70	72	67	4	0	16	13	44	7.2	71	13	1,000	0	4.8	0.0
B+ /8.8	1.5	2.5	8.69	1	67	4	0	16	13	44	7.2	40	13	1,000	0	0.0	0.0

					PERFORMANCE						Incl. in Returns	
					Perfor-mance Rating/Pts	Total Return % through 2/28/17			Annualized		Dividend Yield	Expense Ratio
Fund Type	Fund Name	Ticker Symbol	Overall Investment Rating	Phone		3 Mo	6 Mo	1Yr / Pct	3Yr / Pct	5Yr / Pct		
GES	Eaton Vance Mult-Str Absolute Rtn C	ECDDX	C+	(800) 262-1122	D+ / 2.7	0.60	0.03	2.19 /51	0.88 /26	0.21 /18	0.42	1.99
GES	Eaton Vance Mult-Str Absolute Rtn I	EIDDX	B+	(800) 262-1122	C / 4.4	0.79	0.46	3.03 /57	1.88 /41	1.13 /29	1.36	0.99
MUN	Eaton Vance Municipal Opp A	EMOAX	C+	(800) 262-1122	B- / 7.5	1.95	-3.69	0.05 /21	4.95 /97	3.90 /92	1.76	0.97
MUN	Eaton Vance Municipal Opp C	EMOCX	B-	(800) 262-1122	B / 8.1	1.76	-4.13	-0.70 / 7	4.11 /94	3.09 /81	1.08	1.72
MUN	Eaton Vance Municipal Opp I	EMOIX	A	(800) 262-1122	A / 9.4	2.01	-3.56	0.38 /35	5.24 /97	4.17 /95	2.10	0.72
MUN	Eaton Vance Nat Ltd Mat Muni Inc A	EXNAX	C+	(800) 262-1122	C- / 4.2	1.86	-2.24	-0.48 /10	2.32 /69	2.08 /61	2.81	0.66
MUN●	Eaton Vance Nat Ltd Mat Muni Inc B	ELNAX	C	(800) 262-1122	C- / 3.8	1.67	-2.60	-1.22 / 3	1.55 /50	1.34 /43	2.10	1.41
MUN	Eaton Vance Nat Ltd Mat Muni Inc C	EZNAX	C	(800) 262-1122	C- / 3.7	1.63	-2.63	-1.23 / 3	1.54 /49	1.32 /43	2.11	1.41
MUN	Eaton Vance Nat Ltd Mat Muni Inc I	EINAX	A	(800) 262-1122	C+ / 6.1	1.89	-2.16	-0.33 /12	2.50 /73	2.26 /65	3.02	0.51
*MUN	Eaton Vance National Muni Inc A	EANAX	B+	(800) 262-1122	B+ / 8.3	1.89	-2.71	2.02 /57	5.15 /97	3.98 /93	3.64	0.76
MUN●	Eaton Vance National Muni Inc B	EVHMX	A-	(800) 262-1122	B+ / 8.8	1.60	-3.17	1.15 /47	4.34 /95	3.19 /83	3.05	1.51
MUN	Eaton Vance National Muni Inc C	ECHMX	A-	(800) 262-1122	B+ / 8.9	1.70	-3.07	1.26 /48	4.37 /95	3.21 /83	3.05	1.51
MUN	Eaton Vance National Muni Inc I	EIHMX	A	(800) 262-1122	A+ / 9.7	1.95	-2.59	2.27 /60	5.42 /98	4.24 /95	4.08	0.51
MUN	Eaton Vance NC Muni Inc A	ETNCX	C	(800) 262-1122	C+ / 5.8	1.61	-2.93	0.12 /25	3.82 /91	2.86 /77	3.11	0.77
MUN●	Eaton Vance NC Muni Inc B	EVNCX	B-	(800) 262-1122	C+ / 6.7	1.37	-3.27	-0.61 / 8	3.06 /83	2.10 /61	2.51	1.52
MUN	Eaton Vance NC Muni Inc C	ECNCX	B-	(800) 262-1122	C+ / 6.7	1.37	-3.27	-0.62 / 8	3.06 /83	2.10 /61	2.50	1.52
MUN	Eaton Vance NC Muni Inc I	EINCX	A	(800) 262-1122	B+ / 8.4	1.54	-2.82	0.32 /33	4.03 /93	3.04 /80	3.47	0.57
MUN	Eaton Vance NJ Muni Inc A	ETNJX	C-	(800) 262-1122	C- / 4.2	1.33	-3.15	0.13 /26	3.14 /84	3.04 /80	3.42	0.75
MUN	Eaton Vance NJ Muni Inc C	ECNJX	C+	(800) 262-1122	C / 5.3	1.12	-3.61	-0.69 / 7	2.36 /70	2.26 /65	2.82	1.50
MUN	Eaton Vance NJ Muni Inc I	EINJX	A	(800) 262-1122	B- / 7.3	1.38	-3.15	0.22 /30	3.35 /86	3.24 /84	3.79	0.55
MUN	Eaton Vance NY Muni Inc A	ETNYX	C-	(800) 262-1122	C+ / 6.2	2.16	-3.56	0.21 /29	4.03 /93	3.54 /88	3.02	0.76
MUN	Eaton Vance NY Muni Inc C	ECNYX	C+	(800) 262-1122	B- / 7.0	1.86	-4.01	-0.54 / 9	3.22 /85	2.74 /75	2.40	1.51
MUN	Eaton Vance NY Muni Inc I	EINYX	A-	(800) 262-1122	B+ / 8.6	2.20	-3.46	0.40 /35	4.24 /94	3.74 /90	3.37	0.56
MUS	Eaton Vance NY Muni Oppty A	EXNYX	D	(800) 262-1122	D+ / 2.8	1.95	-3.08	-0.74 / 6	1.74 /55	1.51 /46	2.68	0.75
MUS	Eaton Vance NY Muni Oppty C	EZNYX	D-	(800) 262-1122	D+ / 2.4	1.83	-3.36	-1.44 / 2	1.00 /35	0.75 /29	1.97	1.50
MUS	Eaton Vance NY Muni Oppty I	ENYIX	C+	(800) 262-1122	C / 4.6	1.99	-3.01	-0.59 / 8	1.89 /59	1.67 /51	2.89	0.60
MUN	Eaton Vance OH Muni Inc A	ETOHX	C-	(800) 262-1122	C+ / 5.7	1.89	-3.38	0.12 /25	3.79 /91	2.93 /79	3.37	0.74
MUN	Eaton Vance OH Muni Inc C	ECOHX	C	(800) 262-1122	C+ / 6.6	1.59	-3.75	-0.63 / 8	2.98 /82	2.14 /62	2.77	1.49
MUN	Eaton Vance OH Muni Inc I	EIOHX	B+	(800) 262-1122	B / 8.2	1.82	-3.39	0.21 /29	3.96 /92	3.12 /82	3.75	0.54
MUS	Eaton Vance OR Municipal Income A	ETORX	B-	(800) 262-1122	B- / 7.2	1.61	-2.52	1.42 /51	4.39 /95	1.96 /58	3.39	0.75
MUS ●	Eaton Vance OR Municipal Income B	EVORX	B+	(800) 262-1122	B / 7.8	1.48	-2.82	0.64 /39	3.60 /89	1.21 /40	2.80	1.50
MUS	Eaton Vance OR Municipal Income C	ECORX	B+	(800) 262-1122	B / 7.8	1.47	-2.82	0.64 /39	3.60 /89	1.21 /40	2.80	1.50
MUS	Eaton Vance OR Municipal Income I	EIORX	A+	(800) 262-1122	A- / 9.1	1.67	-2.43	1.51 /52	4.56 /96	2.16 /63	3.77	0.55
MUN	Eaton Vance PA Muni Inc A	ETPAX	C	(800) 262-1122	C- / 4.2	1.76	-2.74	0.03 /20	3.05 /83	2.93 /79	3.57	0.77
MUN●	Eaton Vance PA Muni Inc B	EVPAX	B	(800) 262-1122	C / 5.2	1.55	-3.16	-0.81 / 6	2.27 /68	2.15 /62	2.98	1.52
MUN	Eaton Vance PA Muni Inc C	ECPAX	B	(800) 262-1122	C / 5.4	1.55	-3.05	-0.70 / 7	2.31 /69	2.16 /63	2.98	1.52
MUN	Eaton Vance PA Muni Inc I	EIPAX	A+	(800) 262-1122	B- / 7.3	1.81	-2.73	0.25 /31	3.26 /85	3.12 /82	3.96	0.57
MUN	Eaton Vance SC Municipal Income A	EASCX	C	(800) 262-1122	C+ / 6.5	1.66	-2.88	0.65 /39	4.12 /94	2.88 /78	3.04	0.73
MUN●	Eaton Vance SC Municipal Income B	EVSCX	B-	(800) 262-1122	B- / 7.4	1.53	-3.19	-0.07 /16	3.38 /86	2.10 /61	2.42	1.48
MUN	Eaton Vance SC Municipal Income C	ECSCX	B-	(800) 262-1122	B- / 7.3	1.42	-3.19	-0.06 /17	3.35 /86	2.10 /61	2.42	1.48
MUN	Eaton Vance SC Municipal Income I	EISCX	A	(800) 262-1122	B+ / 8.8	1.71	-2.78	0.85 /43	4.33 /95	3.08 /81	3.40	0.53
USS	Eaton Vance Sh Duration Gov Inc A	EALDX	C+	(800) 262-1122	D+ / 2.8	0.51	1.23	2.26 /51	1.47 /34	1.32 /32	2.07	0.99
USS ●	Eaton Vance Sh Duration Gov Inc B	EBLDX	C+	(800) 262-1122	D+ / 2.5	0.33	0.85	1.51 /45	0.72 /23	0.56 /22	1.38	1.75
USS	Eaton Vance Sh Duration Gov Inc C	ECLDX	C+	(800) 262-1122	D+ / 2.7	0.36	0.93	1.66 /46	0.87 /26	0.71 /24	1.52	1.59
USS	Eaton Vance Sh Duration Gov Inc I	EILDX	A-	(800) 262-1122	C- / 4.1	0.57	1.35	2.52 /53	1.72 /38	1.57 /36	2.37	0.74
MUS	Eaton Vance Short Dur Muni Opptys	EXMAX	C+	(800) 262-1122	C- / 4.2	1.72	-1.85	-0.10 /16	2.23 /68	1.63 /50	2.49	0.77
MUS	Eaton Vance Short Dur Muni Opptys	EZMAX	C	(800) 262-1122	C- / 3.7	1.48	-2.35	-0.86 / 5	1.45 /47	0.86 /32	1.79	1.52
MUS	Eaton Vance Short Dur Muni Opptys I	EMAIX	A	(800) 262-1122	C+ / 6.1	1.76	-1.78	0.14 /26	2.38 /71	1.78 /53	2.70	0.62
COI	Eaton Vance Short Dur Real Return A	EARRX	C	(800) 262-1122	C- / 3.2	1.45	2.85	6.43 /71	0.92 /26	1.04 /28	2.03	1.24
COI	Eaton Vance Short Dur Real Return	ECRRX	C-	(800) 262-1122	D+ / 2.8	1.21	2.32	5.60 /69	0.11 /13	0.27 /19	1.29	1.99
COI	Eaton Vance Short Dur Real Return I	EIRRX	B-	(800) 262-1122	C / 4.5	1.52	2.88	6.62 /72	1.13 /30	1.27 /31	2.35	0.99
*GL	Eaton Vance Short Dur Strat Inc A	ETSIX	C+	(800) 262-1122	C+ / 6.7	1.90	3.58	9.53 /78	2.98 /61	2.75 /54	3.81	1.06

● Denotes fund is closed to new investors
* Denotes fund is included in Section II

www.thestreetratings.com

Risk Rating/Pts	3 Yr Avg Standard Deviation	Avg Duration	NAV As of 2/28/17	Total $(Mil)	Cash %	Gov. Bond %	Muni. Bond %	Corp. Bond %	Other %	Portfolio Turnover Ratio	Avg Coupon Rate	Manager Quality Pct	Manager Tenure (Years)	Initial Purch. $	Additional Purch. $	Front End Load	Back End Load
B+ /8.8	1.4	2.5	8.69	21	67	4	0	16	13	44	7.2	N/A	13	1,000	0	0.0	0.0
B+ /8.8	1.5	2.5	8.69	21	67	4	0	16	13	44	7.2	75	13	250,000	0	0.0	0.0
C- /3.2	4.0	5.6	11.65	180	1	0	98	0	1	58	4.2	71	6	1,000	0	4.8	0.0
C- /3.3	4.0	5.6	11.64	53	1	0	98	0	1	58	4.2	43	6	1,000	0	0.0	0.0
C- /3.2	4.0	5.6	11.67	497	1	0	98	0	1	58	4.2	77	6	250,000	0	0.0	0.0
B- /7.2	2.7	4.2	9.85	225	0	0	99	0	1	10	4.5	23	3	1,000	0	2.3	0.0
B- /7.3	2.6	4.2	9.86	N/A	0	0	99	0	1	10	4.5	9	3	1,000	0	0.0	0.0
B- /7.2	2.7	4.2	9.24	101	0	0	99	0	1	10	4.5	8	3	1,000	0	0.0	0.0
B- /7.3	2.6	4.2	9.86	285	0	0	99	0	1	10	4.5	31	3	250,000	0	0.0	0.0
C- /3.7	3.7	5.2	9.77	1,670	1	0	98	0	1	71	5.6	81	4	1,000	0	4.8	0.0
C- /3.7	3.7	5.2	9.76	12	1	0	98	0	1	71	5.6	68	4	1,000	0	0.0	0.0
C- /3.7	3.7	5.2	9.77	519	1	0	98	0	1	71	5.6	68	4	1,000	0	0.0	0.0
C- /3.7	3.7	5.2	9.77	698	1	0	98	0	1	71	5.6	83	4	250,000	0	0.0	0.0
C /4.6	3.2	4.8	8.99	76	1	0	98	0	1	8	5.2	63	3	1,000	0	4.8	0.0
C /4.8	3.2	4.8	9.67	N/A	1	0	98	0	1	8	5.2	31	3	1,000	0	0.0	0.0
C /4.7	3.2	4.8	9.67	19	1	0	98	0	1	8	5.2	30	3	1,000	0	0.0	0.0
C /4.8	3.2	4.8	9.01	31	1	0	98	0	1	8	5.2	70	3	250,000	0	0.0	0.0
C+ /6.2	2.9	4.6	9.08	109	0	0	99	0	1	17	4.2	55	7	1,000	0	4.8	0.0
C+ /5.9	2.9	4.6	9.47	23	0	0	99	0	1	17	4.2	20	7	1,000	0	0.0	0.0
C+ /6.0	2.9	4.6	9.08	27	0	0	99	0	1	17	4.2	60	7	250,000	0	0.0	0.0
C- /3.9	3.6	5.2	9.95	262	0	0	98	0	2	38	4.7	57	22	1,000	0	4.8	0.0
C- /3.9	3.5	5.2	9.95	75	0	0	98	0	2	38	4.7	23	22	1,000	0	0.0	0.0
C- /3.9	3.6	5.2	9.95	98	0	0	98	0	2	38	4.7	63	22	250,000	0	0.0	0.0
C+ /6.8	2.8	5.6	9.78	53	0	0	97	2	1	9	4.8	9	3	1,000	0	2.3	0.0
C+ /6.6	2.8	5.6	9.30	23	0	0	97	2	1	9	4.8	3	3	1,000	0	0.0	0.0
C+ /6.8	2.8	5.6	9.78	17	0	0	97	2	1	9	4.8	11	3	250,000	0	0.0	0.0
C- /4.1	3.5	5.7	8.90	124	3	0	96	0	1	9	5.2	54	N/A	1,000	0	4.8	0.0
C- /3.9	3.5	5.7	8.89	24	3	0	96	0	1	9	5.2	19	N/A	1,000	0	0.0	0.0
C- /3.9	3.5	5.7	8.90	23	3	0	96	0	1	9	5.2	58	N/A	250,000	0	0.0	0.0
C /4.4	3.3	5.7	8.61	84	0	0	99	0	1	8	4.6	75	3	1,000	0	4.8	0.0
C /4.4	3.3	5.7	9.42	1	0	0	99	0	1	8	4.6	56	3	1,000	0	0.0	0.0
C /4.4	3.3	5.7	9.43	13	0	0	99	0	1	8	4.6	55	3	1,000	0	0.0	0.0
C /4.4	3.4	5.7	8.60	19	0	0	99	0	1	8	4.6	77	3	250,000	0	0.0	0.0
C+ /6.9	2.7	4.7	8.69	137	0	0	100	0	0	8	4.4	54	10	1,000	0	4.8	0.0
B- /7.0	2.7	4.7	8.99	1	0	0	100	0	0	8	4.4	20	10	1,000	0	0.0	0.0
B- /7.1	2.7	4.7	9.00	32	0	0	100	0	0	8	4.4	23	10	1,000	0	0.0	0.0
B- /7.1	2.7	4.7	8.72	50	0	0	100	0	0	8	4.4	62	10	250,000	0	0.0	0.0
C- /4.1	3.4	5.3	9.19	67	1	0	98	0	1	6	5.1	67	3	1,000	0	4.8	0.0
C- /4.1	3.5	5.3	9.75	N/A	1	0	98	0	1	6	5.1	35	3	1,000	0	0.0	0.0
C- /4.1	3.4	5.3	9.75	28	1	0	98	0	1	6	5.1	33	3	1,000	0	0.0	0.0
C- /4.2	3.4	5.3	9.20	34	1	0	98	0	1	6	5.1	72	3	250,000	0	0.0	0.0
A /9.3	0.9	0.5	8.28	175	5	0	0	1	94	45	3.2	83	3	1,000	0	2.3	0.0
A /9.3	0.9	0.5	8.29	N/A	5	0	0	1	94	45	3.2	74	3	1,000	0	0.0	0.0
A /9.5	0.8	0.5	8.29	70	5	0	0	1	94	45	3.2	76	3	1,000	0	0.0	0.0
A /9.5	0.8	0.5	8.27	209	5	0	0	1	94	45	3.2	85	3	250,000	0	0.0	0.0
B- /7.4	2.6	4.4	9.83	25	0	0	100	0	0	9	4.5	25	3	1,000	0	2.3	0.0
B /7.6	2.5	4.4	9.41	9	0	0	100	0	0	9	4.5	9	3	1,000	0	0.0	0.0
B- /7.5	2.5	4.4	9.83	7	0	0	100	0	0	9	4.5	30	3	250,000	0	0.0	0.0
B /7.8	2.3	1.9	9.91	21	14	56	0	23	7	83	2.2	41	N/A	1,000	0	2.3	0.0
B /7.8	2.3	1.9	9.85	8	14	56	0	23	7	83	2.2	14	N/A	1,000	0	0.0	0.0
B /7.8	2.3	1.9	9.89	72	14	56	0	23	7	83	2.2	54	N/A	250,000	0	0.0	0.0
C /4.6	3.3	1.2	7.38	867	11	28	0	31	30	10	0.0	90	27	1,000	0	2.3	0.0

Fund Type	Fund Name	Ticker Symbol	Overall Investment Rating	Phone	Perfor-mance Rating/Pts	3 Mo	6 Mo	1Yr / Pct	3Yr / Pct	5Yr / Pct	Dividend Yield	Expense Ratio
GL	● Eaton Vance Short Dur Strat Inc B	EVSGX	C+	(800) 262-1122	C+ / 6.4	1.77	3.14	8.72 /76	2.22 /47	2.02 /42	3.15	1.81
GL	Eaton Vance Short Dur Strat Inc C	ECSIX	C+	(800) 262-1122	C+ / 6.4	1.77	3.14	8.72 /76	2.22 /47	2.00 /42	3.15	1.81
GL	Eaton Vance Short Dur Strat Inc I	ESIIX	B+	(800) 262-1122	B / 7.6	1.97	3.71	9.81 /78	3.24 /65	3.00 /58	4.14	0.81
GL	Eaton Vance Short Dur Strat Inc R	ERSIX	B-	(800) 262-1122	B- / 7.1	1.84	3.45	9.24 /77	2.72 /56	2.50 /49	3.65	1.31
GL	Eaton Vance Sht Duration High Inc A	ESHAX	A+	(800) 262-1122	B- / 7.2	2.34	3.45	10.23 /79	3.40 /67	--	4.05	1.79
GL	Eaton Vance Sht Duration High Inc I	ESHIX	A+	(800) 262-1122	B / 8.1	2.51	3.58	10.50 /80	3.71 /72	--	4.39	1.54
MUN	Eaton Vance TABS 1 to10 Y Ldr MB	EALBX	U	(800) 262-1122	U /	1.79	-2.12	-0.50 / 9	--	--	1.12	2.10
MUN	Eaton Vance TABS 1 to10 Y Ldr MB	ECLBX	U	(800) 262-1122	U /	1.59	-2.49	-1.25 / 3	--	--	0.40	2.85
MUN	Eaton Vance TABS 1 to10 Y Ldr MB I	EILBX	U	(800) 262-1122	U /	1.85	-2.00	-0.25 /14	--	--	1.42	1.85
MUN	Eaton Vance TABS 10to20 Y Ldr MB	EATTX	U	(800) 262-1122	U /	2.90	-5.14	-0.24 /14	--	--	2.35	4.00
MUN	Eaton Vance TABS 10to20 Y Ldr MB	ECTTX	U	(800) 262-1122	U /	2.71	-5.49	-0.89 / 5	--	--	1.69	4.75
MUN	Eaton Vance TABS 10to20 Y Ldr MB	EITTX	U	(800) 262-1122	U /	3.06	-4.93	0.11 /25	--	--	2.73	3.75
MUN	Eaton Vance TABS 5to15 Yr Ldr MB	EALTX	C	(800) 262-1122	B / 7.7	2.93	-4.09	-0.45 /10	5.13 /97	4.39 /96	1.41	0.84
MUN	Eaton Vance TABS 5to15 Yr Ldr MB	ECLTX	C+	(800) 262-1122	B+ / 8.4	2.66	-4.45	-1.22 / 3	4.34 /95	3.60 /89	0.69	1.59
MUN	Eaton Vance TABS 5to15 Yr Ldr MB I	EILTX	B	(800) 262-1122	A / 9.5	2.91	-4.06	-0.29 /13	5.35 /98	4.62 /97	1.74	0.59
MUN	Eaton Vance TABS Int-Term Muni Bd	EITAX	D	(800) 262-1122	C / 5.0	2.27	-3.63	-0.63 / 8	2.81 /79	2.50 /70	1.59	0.99
MUN	Eaton Vance TABS Int-Term Muni Bd	EITCX	D-	(800) 262-1122	C / 4.4	2.00	-3.99	-1.45 / 2	2.02 /63	1.72 /52	0.86	1.74
MUN	Eaton Vance TABS Int-Term Muni Bd	ETIIX	C+	(800) 262-1122	C+ / 6.9	2.24	-3.51	-0.38 /11	3.07 /83	2.75 /75	1.88	0.74
MUN	Eaton Vance TABS ST Muni Bond A	EABSX	D	(800) 262-1122	D- / 1.3	1.68	-1.55	-0.77 / 6	0.94 /34	0.95 /34	1.21	0.89
MUN	Eaton Vance TABS ST Muni Bond C	ECBSX	D-	(800) 262-1122	E / 0.5	1.39	-1.92	-1.60 / 1	0.18 /18	0.19 /19	0.49	1.65
MUN	Eaton Vance TABS ST Muni Bond I	EIBSX	C+	(800) 262-1122	C- / 3.4	1.74	-1.42	-0.61 / 8	1.19 /40	1.20 /40	1.49	0.64
MUN	Eaton Vance VA Municipal Income A	ETVAX	B+	(800) 262-1122	C / 5.3	1.72	-1.75	1.35 /50	3.27 /85	2.61 /73	3.48	0.76
MUN●	Eaton Vance VA Municipal Income B	EVVAX	A	(800) 262-1122	C+ / 6.3	1.57	-2.10	0.59 /39	2.52 /74	1.85 /55	2.89	1.51
MUN	Eaton Vance VA Municipal Income C	ECVAX	A	(800) 262-1122	C+ / 6.2	1.45	-2.21	0.58 /38	2.48 /73	1.83 /55	2.89	1.51
MUN	Eaton Vance VA Municipal Income I	EVAIX	A+	(800) 262-1122	B / 8.0	1.76	-1.65	1.56 /52	3.48 /87	2.81 /76	3.85	0.56
GEI	Elfun Income	EINFX	B-	(800) 843-2639	C+ / 5.6	1.41	-1.78	3.69 /61	2.80 /58	2.72 /53	2.37	0.32
* MUN	Elfun Tax Exempt Income	ELFTX	A-	(800) 843-2639	B / 8.1	2.04	-2.76	0.44 /36	3.75 /90	2.93 /79	3.95	0.20
COI	Estabrook Investment Grade Fxd In I	EEFIX	B	(888) 739-1390	C / 4.6	1.51	-0.33	4.72 /66	2.12 /45	3.18 /60	2.14	1.41
EM	EuroPac International Bond A	EPIBX	E-	(888) 558-5851	E- / 0.0	3.70	-2.17	5.72 /69	-4.84 / 0	-3.25 / 1	0.00	1.48
GL	EuroPac International Bond I	EPBIX	E-	(888) 558-5851	E- / 0.0	3.81	-2.04	5.96 /70	-4.61 / 0	--	0.00	1.23
GEI	Fairholme Focused Income	FOCIX	C+	(866) 202-2263	A+ / 9.9	3.04	19.02	42.47 /99	6.55 /94	10.45 /99	4.63	1.01
GEI	FCI Bond Fund	FCIZX	C	(800) 408-4682	C- / 3.0	0.78	-1.32	1.53 /45	1.58 /36	1.92 /41	1.92	0.84
COI	FDP BlacRock Franklin Temp TR Inst	MAFFX	C+	(800) 441-7762	C / 4.8	1.48	-1.30	4.42 /64	2.08 /45	2.51 /50	2.45	0.69
COI	FDP BlacRock Franklin Temp TR Inv	MDFFX	D	(800) 441-7762	D+ / 2.7	1.42	-1.33	4.16 /63	1.86 /41	2.28 /46	2.12	0.94
COI	FDP BlacRock Franklin Temp TR Inv	MCFFX	C-	(800) 441-7762	C- / 3.5	1.28	-1.60	3.58 /60	1.29 /32	1.71 /38	1.64	1.50
MTG	Federated Adj Rate Sec Inst	FEUGX	C	(800) 341-7400	D / 1.7	0.30	0.38	0.70 /36	0.28 /18	0.33 /20	0.70	1.03
MTG	Federated Adj Rate Secs Svc	FASSX	C-	(800) 341-7400	D- / 1.2	0.24	0.28	0.49 /33	0.07 /11	0.10 /15	0.49	1.04
* COI	Federated Bond Fund A	FDBAX	C-	(800) 341-7400	C+ / 6.6	3.09	0.28	10.31 /80	3.71 /72	4.27 /76	3.85	1.01
COI	Federated Bond Fund B	FDBBX	C	(800) 341-7400	B- / 7.0	2.96	-0.04	9.46 /78	2.87 /59	3.44 /64	3.18	1.75
COI	Federated Bond Fund C	FDBCX	C	(800) 341-7400	B- / 7.0	2.97	-0.13	9.47 /78	2.84 /59	3.42 /64	3.20	1.75
COI	Federated Bond Fund Class IS	FDBIX	B-	(800) 341-7400	B / 8.1	3.15	0.39	10.54 /80	3.91 /74	4.47 /78	4.25	0.75
COI	Federated Bond Fund F	ISHIX	C+	(800) 341-7400	B- / 7.5	3.06	0.27	10.32 /80	3.64 /70	4.22 /75	3.94	1.00
MMT	Federated CA Muni Cash Cap	CCCXX	C	(800) 341-7400	D- / 1.5	0.08	0.42	0.46 /32	0.19 /16	0.12 /16	0.46	N/A
MMF	Federated CA Muni Cash Svc	CACXX	C	(800) 341-7400	D / 1.6	0.06	0.36	0.37 /34	0.16 /18	0.11 /17	0.36	N/A
MMT	Federated CA Muni Cash Tr Cash II	CALXX	U	(800) 341-7400	U /	--	--	--	--	--	0.29	N/A
MMT	Federated CA Muni Cash Tr Cash	CCSXX	U	(800) 341-7400	U /	--	--	--	--	--	0.25	N/A
MMF	Federated CA Muni Cash Tr Wealth	CAIXX	C	(800) 341-7400	D / 1.9	0.12	0.48	0.57 /38	0.22 /19	0.15 /19	0.57	N/A
COI	Federated Corporate Bond Strat	FCSPX	C	(800) 341-7400	B / 8.1	3.05	-0.82	10.08 /79	4.09 /76	4.49 /79	4.22	0.35
MMF	Federated CT Muni Cash Svc	FCTXX	U	(800) 341-7400	U /	--	--	--	--	--	0.03	N/A
MMT	Federated Edward Jones MM Inv	JNSXX	U	(800) 341-7400	U /	--	--	--	--	--	0.01	N/A
MMT	Federated Edward Jones MM Retr	JRSXX	U	(800) 341-7400	U /	--	--	--	--	--	0.01	N/A
COI	Federated Emerging Mkt Debt A	IHIAX	E+	(800) 341-7400	C / 5.2	6.56	2.00	11.94 /83	1.84 /40	2.21 /45	2.84	1.81

● Denotes fund is closed to new investors
* Denotes fund is included in Section II

www.thestreetratings.com

RISK			NET ASSETS		ASSET					Portfolio Turnover Ratio	Avg Coupon Rate	FUND MANAGER		MINIMUM		LOADS	
Risk Rating/Pts	3 Yr Avg Standard Deviation	Avg Dura-tion	NAV As of 2/28/17	Total $(Mil)	Cash %	Gov. Bond %	Muni. Bond %	Corp. Bond %	Other %			Manager Quality Pct	Manager Tenure (Years)	Initial Purch. $	Additional Purch. $	Front End Load	Back End Load
C /4.5	3.3	1.2	6.96	22	11	28	0	31	30	10	0.0	85	27	1,000	0	0.0	0.0
C /4.6	3.3	1.2	6.96	565	11	28	0	31	30	10	0.0	85	27	1,000	0	0.0	0.0
C /4.6	3.3	1.2	7.37	770	11	28	0	31	30	10	0.0	92	27	250,000	0	0.0	0.0
C /4.5	3.3	1.2	7.39	3	11	28	0	31	30	10	0.0	89	27	1,000	0	0.0	0.0
B- /7.1	2.7	1.5	9.82	6	0	0	0	0	100	67	5.9	94	4	1,000	0	2.3	0.0
B- /7.0	2.7	1.5	9.84	36	0	0	0	0	100	67	5.9	94	4	250,000	0	0.0	0.0
U /	N/A	3.9	10.17	5	3	0	96	0	1	0	4.3	N/A	2	1,000	0	4.8	0.0
U /	N/A	3.9	10.17	3	3	0	96	0	1	0	4.3	N/A	2	1,000	0	0.0	0.0
U /	N/A	3.9	10.18	39	3	0	96	0	1	0	4.3	N/A	2	250,000	0	0.0	0.0
U /	N/A	6.5	10.30	1	12	0	87	0	1	0	4.4	N/A	2	1,000	0	4.8	0.0
U /	N/A	6.5	10.31	N/A	12	0	87	0	1	0	4.4	N/A	2	1,000	0	0.0	0.0
U /	N/A	6.5	10.31	7	12	0	87	0	1	0	4.4	N/A	2	250,000	0	0.0	0.0
D /2.2	4.8	6.2	11.97	144	7	0	92	0	1	41	4.6	48	7	1,000	0	4.8	0.0
D /2.2	4.8	6.2	11.96	52	7	0	92	0	1	41	4.6	18	7	1,000	0	0.0	0.0
D /2.2	4.8	6.2	11.95	299	7	0	92	0	1	41	4.6	57	7	250,000	0	0.0	0.0
C- /3.6	3.7	5.3	12.13	57	2	0	97	0	1	62	4.1	10	7	1,000	0	2.3	0.0
C- /3.7	3.7	5.3	12.12	34	2	0	97	0	1	62	4.1	3	7	1,000	0	0.0	0.0
C- /3.7	3.6	5.3	12.14	430	2	0	97	0	1	62	4.1	16	7	250,000	0	0.0	0.0
B /8.0	2.1	3.5	10.42	193	0	0	98	0	2	47	4.3	9	7	1,000	0	2.3	0.0
B /8.2	2.1	3.5	10.39	69	0	0	98	0	2	47	4.3	3	7	1,000	0	0.0	0.0
B /8.0	2.1	3.5	10.42	205	0	0	98	0	2	47	4.3	12	7	250,000	0	0.0	0.0
B /7.7	2.4	5.0	7.95	57	2	0	97	0	1	13	5.3	72	10	1,000	0	4.8	0.0
B /7.7	2.4	5.0	8.80	N/A	2	0	97	0	1	13	5.3	49	10	1,000	0	0.0	0.0
B /7.7	2.4	5.0	8.80	5	2	0	97	0	1	13	5.3	49	10	1,000	0	0.0	0.0
B /7.7	2.4	5.0	7.97	17	2	0	97	0	1	13	5.3	75	10	250,000	0	0.0	0.0
C+ /6.2	2.9	5.4	11.36	275	0	25	0	39	36	278	6.2	61	N/A	500	100	0.0	0.0
C /4.6	3.3	6.7	11.54	1,494	0	1	98	0	1	22	5.1	58	N/A	500	100	0.0	0.0
B /7.8	2.3	N/A	10.12	33	0	0	0	0	100	113	0.0	53	7	100,000	100	0.0	1.0
E /0.4	7.9	N/A	8.13	44	3	61	3	29	4	26	0.0	1	7	2,500	250	4.5	2.0
E /0.4	7.9	N/A	8.18	1	3	61	3	29	4	26	0.0	1	7	15,000	2,500	0.0	2.0
E- /0.0	13.0	N/A	12.55	279	17	4	0	62	17	67	0.0	99	8	25,000	2,500	0.0	0.0
B /7.9	2.2	N/A	10.38	39	1	29	0	63	7	29	0.0	26	12	250,000	100	0.0	1.0
C+ /6.7	2.8	N/A	10.16	7	2	16	1	37	44	315	0.0	30	12	2,000,000	0	0.0	0.0
C+ /6.9	2.7	N/A	10.17	79	2	16	1	37	44	315	0.0	25	12	1,000	50	4.0	0.0
C+ /6.9	2.7	N/A	10.17	98	2	16	1	37	44	315	0.0	11	12	1,000	50	0.0	0.0
A+ /9.9	0.4	0.5	9.69	288	0	1	0	0	99	19	1.7	48	22	1,000,000	0	0.0	0.0
A+ /9.9	0.4	0.5	9.69	22	0	1	0	0	99	19	1.7	34	22	1,000,000	0	0.0	0.0
C- /3.2	4.0	6.3	9.20	642	0	0	0	96	4	14	5.3	61	4	1,500	100	4.5	0.0
C- /3.1	4.1	6.3	9.26	32	0	0	0	96	4	14	5.3	23	4	1,500	100	0.0	0.0
C- /3.2	4.0	6.3	9.26	102	0	0	0	96	4	14	5.3	24	4	1,500	100	0.0	0.0
C- /3.1	4.0	6.3	9.20	236	0	0	0	96	4	14	5.3	66	4	1,000,000	0	0.0	0.0
C- /3.1	4.0	6.3	9.27	170	0	0	0	96	4	14	5.3	58	4	1,500	100	1.0	0.0
A+ /9.9	0.2	N/A	1.00	35	100	0	0	0	0	0	0.5	56	21	25,000	0	0.0	0.0
A+ /9.9	0.2	N/A	1.00	145	100	0	0	0	0	0	0.4	55	21	10,000	0	0.0	0.0
U /	N/A	N/A	1.00	7	100	0	0	0	0	0	0.3	54	21	10,000	0	0.0	0.0
U /	N/A	N/A	1.00	57	100	0	0	0	0	0	0.3	53	21	1,000	0	0.0	0.0
A+ /9.9	0.2	N/A	1.00	91	100	0	0	0	0	0	0.6	57	21	25,000	0	0.0	0.0
D /2.1	4.7	7.6	10.85	81	1	6	0	91	2	26	4.6	45	7	0	0	0.0	0.0
U /	N/A	N/A	1.00	23	100	0	0	0	0	0	0.0	40	21	10,000	0	0.0	0.0
U /	N/A	N/A	1.00	15,833	100	0	0	0	0	0	0.0	N/A	N/A	0	0	0.0	0.0
U /	N/A	N/A	1.00	5,139	100	0	0	0	0	0	0.0	N/A	N/A	0	0	0.0	0.0
E /0.3	8.5	4.7	8.47	38	1	53	5	38	3	134	0.0	7	4	1,500	100	4.5	0.0

						PERFORMANCE					Incl. in Returns	
							Total Return % through 2/28/17					
			Overall		Perfor-				Annualized		Dividend	Expense
Fund		Ticker	Investment		mance						Yield	Ratio
Type	Fund Name	Symbol	Rating	Phone	Rating/Pts	3 Mo	6 Mo	1Yr / Pct	3Yr / Pct	5Yr / Pct		
COI ●	Federated Emerging Mkt Debt B	IHIBX	E+	(800) 341-7400	C+ / 5.8	6.39	1.62	11.00 /81	1.09 /29	1.45 /34	2.24	2.55
COI	Federated Emerging Mkt Debt C	IHICX	E+	(800) 341-7400	C+ / 5.9	6.40	1.75	11.17 /82	1.09 /29	1.46 /34	2.25	2.55
EM	Federated Emerging Mkt Debt Inst	EMDIX	D-	(800) 341-7400	B- / 7.2	6.74	2.13	12.20 /84	2.12 /45	2.50 /49	3.21	1.56
MMF	Federated FL Muni Cash Tr Wealth	FLMXX	C-	(800) 341-7400	D- / 1.0	0.04	0.08	0.09 /24	0.06 /12	0.05 /14	0.09	N/A
MMF	Federated FL Muni Cash Tr-Cash II	FLCXX	U	(800) 341-7400	U /	--	--	--	--	--	0.01	N/A
LP	Federated Floating Rt Str Inc A	FRSAX	A+	(800) 341-7400	C+ / 6.9	1.90	3.09	9.25 /77	3.16 /63	3.65 /68	3.29	1.22
LP	Federated Floating Rt Str Inc C	FRICX	A+	(800) 341-7400	C+ / 6.7	1.73	2.76	8.55 /75	2.51 /52	--	2.74	1.86
GL	Federated Floating Rt Str Inc Inst	FFRSX	A+	(800) 341-7400	B / 7.8	1.98	3.37	9.63 /78	3.52 /69	4.01 /73	3.71	0.87
USS	Federated Fund for US Govt Sec A	FUSGX	D+	(800) 341-7400	D / 1.7	0.31	-1.43	0.27 /28	1.88 /41	1.50 /34	2.21	0.92
USS ●	Federated Fund for US Govt Sec B	FUSBX	C-	(800) 341-7400	D+ / 2.3	0.26	-1.67	-0.36 /12	1.15 /30	0.76 /24	1.53	1.67
USS	Federated Fund for US Govt Sec C	FUSCX	C-	(800) 341-7400	D+ / 2.3	0.13	-1.80	-0.49 /10	1.15 /30	0.76 /24	1.54	1.67
MMF	Federated GA Muni Cash Tr	GAMXX	C-	(800) 341-7400	D- / 1.1	0.07	0.13	0.14 /27	0.07 /13	0.05 /14	0.14	N/A
GL	Federated Global Total Return Bd A	FTIIX	E-	(800) 341-7400	E- / 0.0	-0.37	-9.53	-3.72 / 0	-2.95 / 1	-2.25 / 1	2.41	2.21
GL ●	Federated Global Total Return Bd B	FTBBX	E-	(800) 341-7400	E- / 0.0	-0.50	-9.80	-4.46 / 0	-3.66 / 1	-2.96 / 1	1.86	2.70
GL	Federated Global Total Return Bd C	FTIBX	E-	(800) 341-7400	E- / 0.0	-0.46	-9.86	-4.47 / 0	-3.68 / 1	-2.97 / 1	1.92	2.71
USS	Federated Gov Ultrash Dur Inst	FGUSX	C	(800) 341-7400	D / 1.7	0.16	0.28	0.62 /35	0.29 /18	0.30 /20	0.51	0.51
USS	Federated Gov Ultrashort Dur A	FGUAX	D	(800) 341-7400	E / 0.3	0.15	0.06	0.18 /25	-0.14 / 5	-0.14 / 4	0.07	1.01
GEI	Federated Gov Ultrashort Dur R6	FGULX	C	(800) 341-7400	D / 1.7	0.16	0.19	0.64 /35	0.30 /19	0.30 /20	0.52	0.53
USS	Federated Gov Ultrashort Dur Svc	FEUSX	C	(800) 341-7400	D- / 1.5	0.23	0.23	0.52 /33	0.19 /16	0.20 /18	0.41	0.77
USS	Federated Govt Inc Securities A	FGOAX	D-	(800) 341-7400	E+ / 0.8	0.31	-1.95	-0.26 /13	1.66 /37	1.33 /32	2.04	1.18
USS ●	Federated Govt Inc Securities B	FGOBX	D	(800) 341-7400	D / 1.9	0.24	-2.33	-0.91 / 5	0.93 /26	0.58 /22	1.36	1.93
USS	Federated Govt Inc Securities C	FGOCX	D	(800) 341-7400	D / 1.9	0.12	-2.32	-0.91 / 5	0.93 /26	0.58 /22	1.36	1.93
USS	Federated Govt Inc Securities F	FGOIX	C-	(800) 341-7400	D+ / 2.6	0.32	-1.95	-0.26 /13	1.67 /38	1.34 /32	2.12	1.18
USS	Federated Govt Income Trust Inst	FICMX	C+	(800) 341-7400	C- / 3.7	0.47	-1.27	0.13 /23	1.96 /42	1.55 /35	2.11	0.86
USS	Federated Govt Income Trust Svc	FITSX	C+	(800) 341-7400	C- / 3.3	0.42	-1.37	-0.07 /16	1.76 /39	1.35 /32	1.90	0.85
MMT	Federated Govt Obl Cap	GOCXX	C-	(800) 341-7400	E+ / 0.9	0.07	0.11	0.17 /25	0.07 /11	0.04 /10	0.17	N/A
MMT	Federated Govt Obl Instl	GOIXX	C-	(800) 341-7400	D- / 1.2	0.10	0.17	0.28 /28	0.11 /13	0.07 /13	0.27	N/A
MMT	Federated Govt Obl Premier	GOFXX	U	(800) 341-7400	U /	0.11	0.19	0.32 /29	--	--	0.32	N/A
MMT	Federated Govt Obl Svc	GOSXX	D+	(800) 341-7400	E+ / 0.6	0.04	0.05	0.05 /21	0.02 / 7	0.02 / 7	0.05	N/A
MMT	Federated Govt Obl Tr	GORXX	U	(800) 341-7400	U /	--	--	--	--	--	0.01	N/A
MMT	Federated Govt Obl Tx-Mgd Auto	GOAXX	U	(800) 341-7400	U /	0.02	0.02	0.03 /19	--	--	0.03	N/A
MMT	Federated Govt Obl Tx-Mgd Instl	GOTXX	C-	(800) 341-7400	D- / 1.1	0.09	0.16	0.27 /28	0.11 /13	0.07 /13	0.27	N/A
MMT	Federated Govt Obl Tx-Mgd Svc	GTSXX	D+	(800) 341-7400	E+ / 0.6	0.03	0.04	0.04 /20	0.02 / 7	0.02 / 7	0.04	N/A
*COH	Federated High Income Bond A	FHIIX	C	(800) 341-7400	B+ / 8.6	4.61	4.52	17.79 /93	4.27 /78	6.14 /93	4.76	1.01
COH	Federated High Income Bond B	FHBBX	C	(800) 341-7400	B+ / 8.8	4.27	3.99	16.94 /92	3.45 /68	5.33 /87	4.26	1.79
COH	Federated High Income Bond C	FHICX	C	(800) 341-7400	B+ / 8.9	4.42	4.13	16.95 /92	3.46 /68	5.33 /87	4.27	1.76
GL	Federated High Yield Strat Port	FHYSX	B+	(800) 341-7400	A+ / 9.8	4.72	5.06	19.17 /95	5.68 /90	7.46 /97	6.16	0.52
COH	Federated High Yield Trust A	FHYAX	C	(800) 341-7400	A- / 9.0	5.14	5.16	19.96 /96	5.11 /86	8.12 /98	4.34	1.13
COH	Federated High Yield Trust C	FHYCX	C	(800) 341-7400	A- / 9.2	4.96	4.62	19.11 /95	4.29 /78	7.32 /97	3.84	1.87
COH	Federated High Yield Trust Ins	FHTIX	C+	(800) 341-7400	A+ / 9.7	5.22	5.30	20.33 /96	5.28 /87	8.26 /98	4.78	0.87
COH	Federated High Yield Trust Svc	FHYTX	C+	(800) 341-7400	A+ / 9.6	5.16	5.17	20.02 /96	5.02 /85	8.09 /98	4.55	1.11
MMT	Federated Inst Money Mkt Mgt Cap	MMLXX	C-	(800) 341-7400	D- / 1.3	0.10	0.16	0.33 /30	0.15 /15	0.11 /15	0.33	N/A
MMT	Federated Inst Money Mkt Mgt Inst	MMPXX	C	(800) 341-7400	D- / 1.5	0.13	0.21	0.43 /32	0.24 /17	0.19 /18	0.43	N/A
MMT	Federated Inst Money Mkt Mgt Svc	MMSXX	C-	(800) 341-7400	D- / 1.0	0.06	0.09	0.19 /26	0.08 /11	0.05 /11	0.19	N/A
MMT	Federated Inst Prime 60 Day Prem	FMTXX	C-	(800) 341-7400	D- / 1.1	0.15	0.23	0.28 /28	0.09 /12	0.06 /12	0.28	N/A
USA	Federated Inst Prime Obl Automated	PBAXX	U	(800) 341-7400	U /	0.04	0.05	0.09 /22	--	--	0.10	0.64
MMT	Federated Inst Prime Obl Capital	POPXX	C-	(800) 341-7400	D- / 1.4	0.11	0.19	0.38 /31	0.16 /15	--	0.38	N/A
MMT	Federated Inst Prime Obl Inst	POIXX	C	(800) 341-7400	D- / 1.4	0.12	0.22	0.44 /32	0.20 /16	0.16 /17	0.43	N/A
MMT	Federated Inst Prime Obl Service	PRSXX	C-	(800) 341-7400	D- / 1.0	0.08	0.11	0.20 /26	0.08 /11	0.05 /11	0.19	N/A
MMT	Federated Inst Prime Obl Trust	POLXX	D+	(800) 341-7400	E+ / 0.7	0.02	0.04	0.07 /21	0.04 / 9	0.03 / 9	0.06	N/A
MMT	Federated Inst Prime Value Obl Cap	PVCXX	C	(800) 341-7400	D- / 1.4	0.19	0.28	0.44 /32	0.18 /16	0.13 /16	0.41	N/A
MMT	Federated Inst Prime Value Obl Inst	PVOXX	C	(800) 341-7400	D / 1.6	0.21	0.33	0.54 /34	0.26 /18	0.21 /18	0.51	N/A

● Denotes fund is closed to new investors
* Denotes fund is included in Section II

www.thestreetratings.com

Risk Rating/Pts	3 Yr Avg Standard Deviation	Avg Duration	NAV As of 2/28/17	Total $(Mil)	Cash %	Gov. Bond %	Muni. Bond %	Corp. Bond %	Other %	Portfolio Turnover Ratio	Avg Coupon Rate	Manager Quality Pct	Manager Tenure (Years)	Initial Purch. $	Additional Purch. $	Front End Load	Back End Load
E / 0.3	8.4	4.7	8.44	3	1	53	5	38	3	134	0.0	2	4	1,500	100	0.0	0.0
E / 0.3	8.4	4.7	8.43	10	1	53	5	38	3	134	0.0	2	4	1,500	100	0.0	0.0
E / 0.3	8.4	4.7	8.49	12	1	53	5	38	3	134	0.0	92	4	1,000,000	0	0.0	0.0
A+ / 9.9	N/A	N/A	1.00	30	100	0	0	0	0	0	0.1	43	N/A	10,000	0	0.0	0.0
U /	N/A	N/A	1.00	3	100	0	0	0	0	0	0.0	41	N/A	10,000	0	0.0	0.0
B / 8.2	2.1	0.1	10.02	346	73	0	0	15	12	25	7.6	90	2	1,500	100	2.0	0.0
B / 8.2	2.1	0.1	10.03	41	73	0	0	15	12	25	7.6	86	2	1,500	100	0.0	0.0
B / 8.2	2.0	0.1	10.02	430	73	0	0	15	12	25	7.6	93	2	1,000,000	0	0.0	0.0
B+ / 8.4	1.9	2.2	7.39	298	0	2	0	0	98	28	3.7	72	14	1,500	100	4.5	0.0
B+ / 8.3	1.9	2.2	7.40	6	0	2	0	0	98	28	3.7	47	14	1,500	100	0.0	0.0
B / 8.2	2.0	2.2	7.39	27	0	2	0	0	98	28	3.7	42	14	1,500	100	0.0	0.0
A+ / 9.9	N/A	N/A	1.00	92	100	0	0	0	0	0	0.1	44	N/A	10,000	0	0.0	0.0
E / 0.5	7.2	8.3	9.50	18	3	75	0	12	10	87	0.0	21	15	1,500	100	4.5	0.0
E / 0.5	7.3	8.3	9.18	1	3	75	0	12	10	87	0.0	8	15	1,500	100	0.0	0.0
E / 0.5	7.3	8.3	9.09	2	3	75	0	12	10	87	0.0	7	15	1,500	100	0.0	0.0
A+ / 9.9	0.3	0.2	9.87	570	0	16	0	0	84	8	0.9	54	20	1,000,000	0	0.0	0.0
A+ / 9.9	0.3	0.2	9.82	9	0	16	0	0	84	8	0.9	31	20	1,500	100	2.0	0.0
A+ / 9.9	0.3	0.2	9.87	2	0	16	0	0	84	8	0.9	54	20	0	0	0.0	0.0
A+ / 9.9	0.3	0.2	9.87	278	0	16	0	0	84	8	0.9	47	20	1,000,000	0	0.0	0.0
B / 7.8	2.3	3.9	8.79	40	0	25	0	0	75	36	3.2	58	14	1,500	100	4.5	0.0
B / 7.8	2.4	3.9	8.77	2	0	25	0	0	75	36	3.2	23	14	1,500	100	0.0	0.0
B / 7.7	2.4	3.9	8.80	11	0	25	0	0	75	36	3.2	23	14	1,500	100	0.0	0.0
B / 7.8	2.3	3.9	8.77	148	0	25	0	0	75	36	3.2	57	14	1,500	100	1.0	0.0
B+ / 8.4	1.9	2.3	10.16	412	0	0	0	0	100	307	3.8	74	17	1,000,000	0	0.0	0.0
B+ / 8.4	1.9	2.3	10.16	35	0	0	0	0	100	307	3.8	70	17	0	0	0.0	0.0
A+ / 9.9	N/A	N/A	1.00	2,679	100	0	0	0	0	0	0.2	43	23	500,000	0	0.0	0.0
A+ / 9.9	N/A	N/A	1.00	26,369	100	0	0	0	0	0	0.3	N/A	23	500,000	0	0.0	0.0
U /	N/A	N/A	1.00	32,485	100	0	0	0	0	0	0.3	N/A	23	5,000,000	0	0.0	0.0
A+ / 9.9	N/A	N/A	1.00	8,771	100	0	0	0	0	0	0.1	39	23	500,000	0	0.0	0.0
U /	N/A	N/A	1.00	1,202	100	0	0	0	0	0	0.0	N/A	23	500,000	0	0.0	0.0
U /	N/A	N/A	1.00	2	100	0	0	0	0	0	0.0	N/A	N/A	25,000	0	0.0	0.0
A+ / 9.9	N/A	N/A	1.00	3,390	100	0	0	0	0	0	0.3	N/A	N/A	500,000	0	0.0	0.0
A+ / 9.9	N/A	N/A	1.00	3,208	100	0	0	0	0	0	0.0	39	N/A	500,000	0	0.0	0.0
D- / 1.3	5.4	3.6	7.65	650	0	0	0	98	2	23	6.3	51	30	1,500	100	4.5	0.0
D- / 1.3	5.4	3.6	7.63	35	0	0	0	98	2	23	6.3	17	30	1,500	100	0.0	0.0
D- / 1.3	5.4	3.6	7.63	151	0	0	0	98	2	23	6.3	17	30	1,500	100	0.0	0.0
D / 1.9	5.3	N/A	13.39	41	100	0	0	0	0	25	0.0	98	9	0	0	0.0	0.0
E+ / 0.7	6.3	4.0	6.91	133	3	0	0	88	9	37	6.5	58	33	1,500	100	4.5	2.0
E+ / 0.7	6.4	4.0	6.90	45	3	0	0	88	9	37	6.5	21	33	1,500	100	0.0	2.0
E+ / 0.7	6.4	4.0	6.88	258	3	0	0	88	9	37	6.5	62	33	1,000,000	0	0.0	2.0
E+ / 0.7	6.4	4.0	6.89	628	3	0	0	88	9	37	6.5	54	33	1,000,000	0	0.0	2.0
A+ / 9.9	N/A	N/A	1.00	N/A	100	0	0	0	0	0	0.3	49	N/A	500,000	0	0.0	0.0
A+ / 9.9	0.1	N/A	1.00	247	100	0	0	0	0	0	0.4	53	N/A	500,000	0	0.0	0.0
A+ / 9.9	N/A	N/A	1.00	1	100	0	0	0	0	0	0.2	43	N/A	500,000	0	0.0	0.0
A+ / 9.9	0.1	N/A	1.00	9	100	0	0	0	0	0	0.3	44	26	5,000,000	0	0.0	0.0
U /	N/A	N/A	1.00	N/A	0	0	0	0	100	0	0.0	N/A	26	25,000	0	0.0	0.0
A+ / 9.9	0.1	N/A	1.00	15	100	0	0	0	0	0	0.4	49	26	500,000	0	0.0	0.0
A+ / 9.9	0.1	N/A	1.00	738	100	0	0	0	0	0	0.4	51	26	500,000	0	0.0	0.0
A+ / 9.9	N/A	N/A	1.00	42	100	0	0	0	0	0	0.2	44	26	500,000	0	0.0	0.0
A+ / 9.9	N/A	N/A	1.00	1	100	0	0	0	0	0	0.1	41	26	500,000	0	0.0	0.0
A+ / 9.9	0.1	N/A	1.00	25	100	0	0	0	0	0	0.4	49	N/A	500,000	0	0.0	0.0
A+ / 9.9	0.1	N/A	1.00	2,875	100	0	0	0	0	0	0.5	53	N/A	500,000	0	0.0	0.0

Fund Type	Fund Name	Ticker Symbol	Overall Investment Rating	Phone	Performance Rating/Pts	3 Mo	6 Mo	1Yr / Pct	3Yr / Pct	5Yr / Pct	Dividend Yield	Expense Ratio
MMT	Federated Inst Prime Value Obl Svc	PVSXX	C-	(800) 341-7400	D- / 1.2	0.15	0.20	0.29 / 29	0.11 / 13	0.07 / 13	0.26	N/A
MMF	Federated Inst Tx Fr Cash Tr Prmr	FTFXX	C	(800) 341-7400	D / 1.6	0.13	0.27	0.39 / 35	0.14 / 17	0.08 / 16	0.39	N/A
COH	Federated Instl High Yld Bond	FIHBX	B-	(800) 341-7400	A / 9.5	4.74	4.74	18.69 / 94	5.14 / 86	6.97 / 96	5.60	0.58
COH	Federated Instl High Yld Bond R6	FIHLX	U	(800) 341-7400	U /	4.74	4.75	--	--	--	0.00	0.53
COI	Federated Interm Corp Bd Instl	FIIFX	A-	(800) 341-7400	C / 5.5	1.61	-0.31	4.75 / 66	2.47 / 51	3.34 / 63	3.21	0.98
MUN	Federated Interm Muni Trust Inst	FIMTX	B	(800) 341-7400	C+ / 6.5	1.87	-2.95	0.25 / 31	2.72 / 77	2.38 / 68	2.28	0.97
MUN	Federated Interm Muni Trust Y	FIMYX	B	(800) 341-7400	C+ / 6.8	1.91	-2.96	0.33 / 33	2.87 / 80	2.54 / 71	2.46	0.71
COI	Federated Intermediate Corp Bd Svc	INISX	B	(800) 341-7400	C / 5.1	1.55	-0.43	4.49 / 65	2.21 / 47	3.09 / 59	2.95	1.22
GL	Federated International Bond Str	FIBPX	E+	(800) 341-7400	C- / 4.1	2.23	-3.44	5.06 / 67	1.58 / 36	1.78 / 39	4.52	2.04
MMF	Federated MA Muni Cash Svc	MMCXX	U	(800) 341-7400	U /	--	--	--	--	--	0.10	N/A
MMF	Federated MA Muni Csh Tr Cash Ser	FMCXX	U	(800) 341-7400	U /	--	--	--	--	--	0.05	N/A
MUS	Federated MI Interm Muni Tr	MMIFX	D+	(800) 341-7400	C- / 3.8	1.85	-2.54	-0.88 / 5	2.43 / 72	2.20 / 63	2.28	0.91
MMF	Federated MI Muni Cash Svc	MIMXX	C-	(800) 341-7400	D- / 1.1	0.04	0.13	0.13 / 26	0.06 / 12	0.04 / 12	0.13	N/A
MMF	Federated MI Muni Cash Tr Wealth	MINXX	C-	(800) 341-7400	D- / 1.4	0.08	0.21	0.23 / 30	0.10 / 15	0.06 / 14	0.23	N/A
MMF	Federated MN Muni Cash Tr Cash	MNMXX	U	(800) 341-7400	U /	--	--	--	--	--	0.01	N/A
MMF	Federated MN Muni Cash Tr Wealth	FEMXX	C-	(800) 341-7400	D- / 1.3	0.09	0.18	0.24 / 30	0.09 / 15	0.06 / 14	0.24	N/A
MTG	Federated Mortgage Fund Inst	FGFIX	A-	(800) 341-7400	C / 4.9	0.51	-1.05	2.00 / 49	2.62 / 54	2.10 / 44	2.75	0.65
MTG	Federated Mortgage Strat	FMBPX	B+	(800) 341-7400	C / 5.0	0.54	-1.09	1.16 / 41	2.77 / 57	2.14 / 44	2.70	0.30
MTG	Federated Mortgage Svc	FGFSX	B+	(800) 341-7400	C / 4.5	0.54	-1.10	1.80 / 47	2.31 / 48	1.79 / 39	2.44	1.15
*MUH	Federated Muni & Stock Advantage A	FMUAX	B-	(800) 341-7400	A- / 9.1	4.33	2.76	9.80 / 89	4.20 / 94	5.98 / 99	2.09	1.07
MUH	Federated Muni & Stock Advantage B	FMNBX	B+	(800) 341-7400	A+ / 9.6	4.22	2.38	9.08 / 87	3.46 / 87	5.19 / 98	1.48	1.82
MUH	Federated Muni & Stock Advantage C	FMUCX	B	(800) 341-7400	A+ / 9.6	4.14	2.39	8.99 / 86	3.43 / 87	5.18 / 98	1.48	1.82
MUH	Federated Muni & Stock Advantage F	FMUFX	B+	(800) 341-7400	A+ / 9.8	4.33	2.76	9.80 / 89	4.20 / 94	5.98 / 99	2.19	1.07
MUH	Federated Muni High Yield Advn A	FMOAX	B-	(800) 341-7400	B+ / 8.7	2.42	-3.53	1.34 / 49	5.50 / 98	4.91 / 97	3.85	1.03
MUH	Federated Muni High Yield Advn B	FMOBX	B	(800) 341-7400	A- / 9.1	2.23	-3.89	0.59 / 39	4.72 / 96	4.13 / 94	3.27	1.78
MUH	Federated Muni High Yield Advn C	FMNCX	B	(800) 341-7400	A- / 9.1	2.23	-3.99	0.59 / 39	4.71 / 96	4.13 / 94	3.27	1.78
MUH	Federated Muni High Yield Advn F	FHTFX	B+	(800) 341-7400	A / 9.5	2.42	-3.64	1.34 / 49	5.46 / 98	4.91 / 97	4.00	1.03
MUH	Federated Muni High Yield Advn Ins	FMYIX	B+	(800) 341-7400	A+ / 9.7	2.37	-3.52	1.49 / 51	5.69 / 98	5.06 / 98	4.30	0.78
MUN	Federated Muni Securities Fd A	LMSFX	C-	(800) 341-7400	C / 5.4	2.14	-3.16	0.49 / 37	3.47 / 87	2.93 / 79	2.90	0.94
MUN●	Federated Muni Securities Fd B	LMSBX	C	(800) 341-7400	C+ / 6.2	1.93	-3.47	-0.25 / 14	2.64 / 76	2.10 / 61	2.18	1.69
MUN	Federated Muni Securities Fd C	LMSCX	C	(800) 341-7400	C+ / 6.2	1.93	-3.47	-0.34 / 12	2.64 / 76	2.10 / 61	2.18	1.69
MUN	Federated Muni Securities Fd F	LMFFX	B	(800) 341-7400	B / 7.7	2.14	-3.07	0.49 / 37	3.50 / 88	2.93 / 79	3.01	0.94
*MUI	Federated Muni Ultrashrt A	FMUUX	D	(800) 341-7400	E / 0.3	0.21	0.22	0.52 / 37	0.06 / 12	0.16 / 19	0.41	0.98
MUI	Federated Muni Ultrashrt Inst	FMUSX	B-	(800) 341-7400	D+ / 2.5	0.32	0.45	0.97 / 44	0.51 / 24	0.61 / 27	0.86	0.47
MMF	Federated Municipal Obl Cap	MFCXX	C	(800) 341-7400	D / 1.7	0.19	0.31	0.41 / 35	0.16 / 18	0.11 / 17	0.41	N/A
MMF	Federated Municipal Obl Cash II	MODXX	U	(800) 341-7400	U /	--	--	--	--	--	0.08	N/A
MMF	Federated Municipal Obl Cash Series	MFSXX	U	(800) 341-7400	U /	--	--	--	--	--	0.07	N/A
MMF	Federated Municipal Obl Investment	MOIXX	U	(800) 341-7400	U /	0.08	0.09	0.09 / 24	--	--	0.09	N/A
MMF	Federated Municipal Obl Svc	MOSXX	C	(800) 341-7400	D- / 1.5	0.15	0.24	0.27 / 31	0.12 / 16	0.08 / 16	0.27	N/A
MMF	Federated Municipal Obl Trust	MOTXX	U	(800) 341-7400	U /	0.11	0.13	0.14 / 27	--	--	0.14	N/A
MMF	Federated Municipal Obl Wealth	MOFXX	C	(800) 341-7400	D / 1.8	0.21	0.36	0.51 / 37	0.19 / 19	0.14 / 19	0.51	N/A
MMF	Federated NC Muni Cash Tr	NCMXX	U	(800) 341-7400	U /	--	--	--	--	--	0.04	N/A
MMF	Federated NJ Muni Cash Svc	NJSXX	D+	(800) 341-7400	E+ / 0.8	0.03	0.05	0.05 / 21	0.03 / 9	0.02 / 9	0.05	N/A
MMF	Federated NJ Muni Cash Tr Wealth	NJMXX	C-	(800) 341-7400	D- / 1.0	0.07	0.12	0.12 / 25	0.05 / 11	0.04 / 12	0.12	N/A
MMF	Federated NY Muni Cash Svc	FNTXX	C-	(800) 341-7400	D- / 1.0	0.06	0.11	0.12 / 25	0.05 / 11	0.04 / 12	0.12	N/A
MMF	Federated NY Muni Cash Tr Wealth	NISXX	C	(800) 341-7400	D- / 1.4	0.11	0.22	0.29 / 32	0.11 / 16	0.08 / 16	0.29	N/A
MMF	Federated NY Muni Cash Tr-Cash II	NYCXX	U	(800) 341-7400	U /	--	--	--	--	--	0.02	N/A
MUS	Federated NY Muni Income Fd A	NYIFX	C-	(800) 341-7400	C / 4.8	1.98	-2.76	0.60 / 39	3.13 / 84	2.74 / 75	2.74	1.35
MUS ●	Federated NY Muni Income Fd B	NYIBX	C+	(800) 341-7400	C+ / 5.7	1.79	-3.12	-0.15 / 15	2.36 / 70	1.98 / 58	2.11	2.10
MMF	Federated OH Muni Cash Svc	OHTXX	U	(800) 341-7400	U /	--	--	--	--	--	0.28	N/A
MMF	Federated OH Muni Cash Tr Cash II	FOHXX	U	(800) 341-7400	U /	--	--	--	--	--	0.26	N/A
MMF	Federated OH Muni Cash Tr Wealth	OHIXX	C	(800) 341-7400	D / 1.6	0.10	0.36	0.37 / 34	0.13 / 16	0.08 / 16	0.37	N/A

● Denotes fund is closed to new investors
* Denotes fund is included in Section II

www.thestreetratings.com

RISK			NET ASSETS		ASSET					Portfolio	Avg	FUND MANAGER		MINIMUM		LOADS	
Risk Rating/Pts	3 Yr Avg Standard Deviation	Avg Dura-tion	NAV As of 2/28/17	Total $(Mil)	Cash %	Gov. Bond %	Muni. Bond %	Corp. Bond %	Other %	Portfolio Turnover Ratio	Avg Coupon Rate	Manager Quality Pct	Manager Tenure (Years)	Initial Purch. $	Additional Purch. $	Front End Load	Back End Load
A+ / 9.9	0.1	N/A	1.00	234	100	0	0	0	0	0	0.3	45	N/A	500,000	0	0.0	0.0
A+ / 9.9	0.1	N/A	1.00	255	100	0	0	0	0	0	0.4	49	N/A	25,000	0	0.0	0.0
D- / 1.3	5.5	3.8	10.06	5,673	2	0	0	97	1	23	6.3	74	15	1,000,000	0	0.0	2.0
U /	N/A	3.8	10.06	418	2	0	0	97	1	23	6.3	N/A	15	0	0	0.0	2.0
B / 7.6	2.5	4.4	9.25	190	0	2	0	97	1	28	4.3	58	4	1,000,000	0	0.0	0.0
C / 5.3	3.0	4.9	9.96	85	0	0	100	0	0	36	0.0	23	22	1,000,000	0	0.0	0.0
C / 5.1	3.1	4.9	9.95	6	0	0	100	0	0	36	0.0	25	22	100,000	0	0.0	0.0
B / 7.6	2.5	4.4	9.25	23	0	2	0	97	1	28	4.3	45	4	1,000,000	0	0.0	0.0
D / 1.8	5.4	5.1	14.14	13	57	40	0	2	1	33	0.0	92	9	0	0	0.0	0.0
U /	N/A	N/A	1.00	58	100	0	0	0	0	0	0.1	44	N/A	10,000	0	0.0	0.0
U /	N/A	N/A	1.00	60	100	0	0	0	0	0	0.1	42	N/A	1,000	0	0.0	0.0
C+ / 6.1	2.9	4.6	11.08	109	0	0	99	0	1	12	0.0	19	19	1,500	100	3.0	0.0
A+ / 9.9	0.1	N/A	1.00	25	100	0	0	0	0	0	0.1	43	22	10,000	0	0.0	0.0
A+ / 9.9	0.1	N/A	1.00	4	100	0	0	0	0	0	0.2	N/A	21	10,000	0	0.0	0.0
U /	N/A	N/A	1.00	18	100	0	0	0	0	0	0.0	N/A	21	10,000	0	0.0	0.0
A+ / 9.9	N/A	N/A	1.00	42	100	0	0	0	0	0	0.2	45	21	25,000	0	0.0	0.0
B+ / 8.5	1.8	2.0	9.57	153	2	4	0	0	94	57	3.6	65	14	1,000,000	0	0.0	0.0
B / 8.1	2.1	N/A	9.92	86	3	0	0	1	96	20	0.0	56	10	0	0	0.0	0.0
B+ / 8.4	1.9	2.0	9.57	13	2	4	0	0	94	57	3.6	53	14	1,000,000	0	0.0	0.0
D / 2.1	4.5	6.2	12.87	654	0	0	58	0	42	55	0.0	92	14	1,500	100	5.5	0.0
D / 2.1	4.5	6.2	12.87	26	0	0	58	0	42	55	0.0	88	14	1,500	100	0.0	0.0
D / 2.1	4.5	6.2	12.86	347	0	0	58	0	42	55	0.0	88	14	1,500	100	0.0	0.0
D / 2.1	4.5	6.2	12.87	215	0	0	58	0	42	55	0.0	92	14	1,500	100	1.0	0.0
D+ / 2.4	3.8	7.5	8.78	217	0	0	99	0	1	10	0.0	81	8	1,500	100	4.5	0.0
D+ / 2.4	3.8	7.5	8.77	10	0	0	99	0	1	10	0.0	69	8	1,500	100	0.0	0.0
D+ / 2.4	3.9	7.5	8.77	69	0	0	99	0	1	10	0.0	68	8	1,500	100	0.0	0.0
D+ / 2.4	3.9	7.5	8.77	199	0	0	99	0	1	10	0.0	80	8	1,500	100	1.0	0.0
D+ / 2.4	3.8	7.5	8.76	117	0	0	99	0	1	10	0.0	83	8	1,000,000	0	0.0	0.0
C / 4.4	3.4	6.1	10.38	307	1	0	98	0	1	25	0.0	36	21	1,500	100	4.5	0.0
C / 4.4	3.3	6.1	10.39	4	1	0	98	0	1	25	0.0	14	21	1,500	100	0.0	0.0
C / 4.4	3.3	6.1	10.39	18	1	0	98	0	1	25	0.0	13	21	1,500	100	0.0	0.0
C / 4.4	3.4	6.1	10.38	28	1	0	98	0	1	25	0.0	37	21	1,500	100	0.0	0.0
A+ / 9.9	0.3	0.3	9.99	803	0	0	98	0	2	29	0.0	33	17	1,500	100	2.0	0.0
A+ / 9.9	0.3	0.3	9.99	1,753	0	0	98	0	2	29	0.0	57	17	1,000,000	0	0.0	0.0
A+ / 9.9	0.1	N/A	1.00	254	100	0	0	0	0	0	0.4	50	N/A	500,000	0	0.0	0.0
U /	N/A	N/A	1.00	94	100	0	0	0	0	0	0.1	N/A	N/A	25,000	0	0.0	0.0
U /	N/A	N/A	1.00	110	100	0	0	0	0	0	0.1	N/A	N/A	10,000	250	0.0	0.0
U /	N/A	N/A	1.00	67	100	0	0	0	0	0	0.1	N/A	N/A	1,500	100	0.0	0.0
A+ / 9.9	0.1	N/A	1.00	405	100	0	0	0	0	0	0.3	47	N/A	500,000	0	0.0	0.0
U /	N/A	N/A	1.00	N/A	100	0	0	0	0	0	0.1	N/A	N/A	500,000	0	0.0	0.0
A+ / 9.9	0.1	N/A	1.00	616	100	0	0	0	0	0	0.5	51	N/A	500,000	0	0.0	0.0
U /	N/A	N/A	1.00	96	100	0	0	0	0	0	0.0	40	N/A	10,000	0	0.0	0.0
A+ / 9.9	N/A	N/A	1.00	10	100	0	0	0	0	0	0.1	39	N/A	25,000	0	0.0	0.0
A+ / 9.9	N/A	N/A	1.00	5	100	0	0	0	0	0	0.1	41	N/A	25,000	0	0.0	0.0
A+ / 9.9	N/A	N/A	1.00	43	100	0	0	0	0	0	0.1	42	N/A	10,000	0	0.0	0.0
A+ / 9.9	0.1	N/A	1.00	77	100	0	0	0	0	0	0.3	46	N/A	10,000	0	0.0	0.0
U /	N/A	N/A	1.00	8	100	0	0	0	0	0	0.0	N/A	N/A	10,000	0	0.0	0.0
C / 5.4	3.0	5.8	10.27	27	1	0	98	0	1	10	0.0	36	22	1,500	100	4.5	0.0
C / 5.4	3.0	5.8	10.27	2	1	0	98	0	1	10	0.0	15	22	1,500	100	0.0	0.0
U /	N/A	N/A	1.00	11	100	0	0	0	0	0	0.3	52	26	10,000	0	0.0	0.0
U /	N/A	N/A	1.00	17	100	0	0	0	0	0	0.3	52	26	10,000	0	0.0	0.0
A+ / 9.9	0.1	N/A	1.00	28	100	0	0	0	0	0	0.4	53	26	10,000	0	0.0	0.0

Fund Type	Fund Name	Ticker Symbol	Overall Investment Rating	Phone	Performance Rating/Pts	3 Mo	6 Mo	1Yr / Pct	3Yr / Pct	5Yr / Pct	Dividend Yield	Expense Ratio
					PERFORMANCE — Total Return % through 2/28/17 (Annualized 3Yr/5Yr); Incl. in Returns							
MUH	Federated Ohio Municipal Inc Fund	OMIFX	C-	(800) 341-7400	C+ / 6.1	1.85	-3.14	0.16 /27	2.82 /79	2.53 /71	2.74	1.30
MUH	Federated Ohio Municipal Inc Fund A	OMIAX	D-	(800) 341-7400	C / 4.3	1.98	-2.98	0.40 /35	2.98 /82	2.68 /74	2.79	0.90
MMF	Federated PA Muni Cash Svc	FPAXX	D+	(800) 341-7400	E+ / 0.9	0.02	0.05	0.06 /22	0.05 /11	0.04 /12	0.06	N/A
MMF	Federated PA Muni Cash Tr Wealth	PAMXX	C-	(800) 341-7400	D- / 1.2	0.07	0.15	0.17 /28	0.08 /14	0.06 /14	0.17	N/A
MUS	Federated PA Muni Income Fund A	PAMFX	C-	(800) 341-7400	C / 5.2	1.90	-2.99	0.87 /43	3.32 /86	2.90 /78	2.91	0.88
MUS ●	Federated PA Muni Income Fund B	FPABX	C+	(800) 341-7400	C+ / 6.1	1.71	-3.27	0.09 /24	2.56 /74	2.12 /62	2.25	1.63
MMT	Federated Prime Cash Obl	PTAXX	U	(800) 341-7400	U /	0.11	0.14	0.19 /26	--	--	0.19	N/A
MMT	Federated Prime Cash Obl Cap	PCCXX	C-	(800) 341-7400	D- / 1.4	0.16	0.24	0.39 /31	0.15 /15	0.10 /15	0.39	N/A
MMT	Federated Prime Cash Obl Cash II	PCDXX	U	(800) 341-7400	U /	0.02	0.02	0.03 /20	--	--	0.03	N/A
MMT	Federated Prime Cash Obl Cash Srs	PTSXX	U	(800) 341-7400	U /	--	--	--	--	--	0.01	N/A
MMT	Federated Prime Cash Obl R	PTRXX	U	(800) 341-7400	U /	--	--	--	--	--	0.01	N/A
MMT	Federated Prime Cash Obl Svc	PRCXX	C-	(800) 341-7400	D- / 1.1	0.13	0.17	0.24 /27	0.09 /12	0.06 /12	0.24	N/A
MMT	Federated Prime Cash Obl Trust	PTTXX	U	(800) 341-7400	U /	0.07	0.07	0.08 /21	--	--	0.08	N/A
MMT	Federated Prime Cash Obl Wealth	PCOXX	C	(800) 341-7400	D- / 1.5	0.19	0.29	0.49 /33	0.22 /17	0.17 /17	0.49	N/A
GL	Federated Prudent DollarBear A	PSAFX	E-	(800) 341-7400	E / 0.0	-0.11	-5.80	-3.29 / 0	-5.52 / 0	-4.82 / 0	0.00	1.73
GL	Federated Prudent DollarBear C	FPGCX	E-	(800) 341-7400	E / 0.0	-0.33	-6.17	-3.96 / 0	-6.23 / 0	-5.52 / 0	0.00	2.48
GL	Federated Prudent DollarBear IS	FPGIX	E-	(800) 341-7400	E / 0.0	0.00	-5.62	-2.94 / 0	-5.27 / 0	-4.55 / 0	0.00	1.48
GEI	Federated Real Return Bond A	RRFAX	E+	(800) 341-7400	D / 1.7	0.82	1.99	5.81 /70	0.68 /23	0.24 /19	1.37	2.09
GEI	Federated Real Return Bond C	RRFCX	E+	(800) 341-7400	D / 2.2	0.65	1.64	4.98 /67	-0.06 / 5	-0.51 / 3	0.89	2.84
GEI	Federated Real Return Bond Inst	RRFIX	D-	(800) 341-7400	C- / 3.9	0.89	2.13	6.00 /70	0.93 /26	0.49 /21	1.62	1.86
MUN	Federated Sh Int Dur Muni A	FMTAX	D	(800) 341-7400	E+ / 0.7	0.91	-0.64	-0.24 /14	0.35 /21	0.58 /26	0.83	1.04
MUN	Federated Sh Int Dur Muni Inst	FSHIX	B-	(800) 341-7400	C- / 3.1	1.03	-0.40	0.36 /34	0.85 /32	1.08 /37	1.34	0.79
MUN	Federated Short Int Dur Muni Svc	FSHSX	C	(800) 341-7400	D+ / 2.4	0.97	-0.52	0.12 /25	0.60 /26	0.84 /31	1.10	1.04
GES	Federated Short Term Inc A	FTIAX	C-	(800) 341-7400	D- / 1.4	0.34	0.07	1.14 /41	0.37 /19	0.60 /22	0.77	1.33
GES	Federated Short Term Inc Inst	FSTIX	B-	(800) 341-7400	D+ / 2.8	0.49	0.38	1.77 /47	0.97 /27	1.19 /30	1.40	0.84
GES	Federated Short Term Inc Svc	FSISX	C+	(800) 341-7400	D+ / 2.5	0.43	0.26	1.53 /45	0.80 /24	0.99 /27	1.17	0.98
GES	Federated Short Term Inc Y	FSTYX	B	(800) 341-7400	C- / 3.1	0.52	0.44	1.90 /48	1.13 /30	1.35 /32	1.53	0.58
COI	Federated Sht-Interm Tot Ret B A	FGCAX	C+	(800) 341-7400	C- / 3.4	0.71	-0.11	3.52 /60	1.44 /34	--	1.89	0.80
COI	Federated Sht-Interm Tot Ret B Inst	FGCIX	B	(800) 341-7400	C- / 4.2	0.77	0.01	3.88 /62	1.69 /38	1.80 /39	2.16	0.58
COI	Federated Sht-Interm Tot Ret B R6	SRBRX	C+	(800) 341-7400	C- / 3.2	0.77	-0.08	3.30 /58	1.03 /28	--	1.79	0.53
COI	Federated Sht-Interm Tot Ret B Svc	FGCSX	B-	(800) 341-7400	C- / 3.8	0.71	-0.12	3.52 /60	1.41 /33	1.53 /35	1.91	0.83
GES	Federated Strategic Income Fund A	STIAX	D+	(800) 341-7400	B- / 7.2	3.81	2.68	14.08 /87	3.45 /68	3.77 /69	3.90	1.09
GES	Federated Strategic Income Fund B	SINBX	C-	(800) 341-7400	B / 7.6	3.62	2.42	13.25 /86	2.68 /55	2.98 /57	3.35	1.86
GES	Federated Strategic Income Fund C	SINCX	C-	(800) 341-7400	B / 7.6	3.62	2.30	13.25 /86	2.68 /56	2.98 /57	3.35	1.84
GES	Federated Strategic Income Fund F	STFSX	C	(800) 341-7400	B / 8.1	3.72	2.70	14.05 /87	3.44 /68	3.75 /69	4.07	1.09
GES	Federated Strategic Income Fund IS	STISX	C+	(800) 341-7400	B+ / 8.7	3.90	2.83	14.32 /87	3.73 /72	4.01 /73	4.35	0.83
MMF	Federated T/F Oblig Fund Wealth	TBIXX	C	(800) 341-7400	D / 1.8	0.14	0.46	0.57 /38	0.21 /19	0.13 /18	0.57	N/A
MMF	Federated Tax-Free Oblig Svc	TBSXX	C	(800) 341-7400	D- / 1.5	0.07	0.33	0.35 /34	0.13 /16	0.08 /16	0.35	N/A
COI	Federated Tot Ret Bd A	TLRAX	D+	(800) 341-7400	C- / 3.7	1.63	-1.12	4.82 /66	2.56 /53	2.41 /48	2.72	0.99
COI	Federated Tot Ret Bd B	TLRBX	C	(800) 341-7400	C / 4.6	1.50	-1.39	4.25 /63	2.00 /43	1.85 /40	2.29	1.55
COI	Federated Tot Ret Bd C	TLRCX	C	(800) 341-7400	C / 4.7	1.50	-1.37	4.28 /63	2.03 /44	1.88 /40	2.33	1.51
COI	Federated Tot Ret Bd Inst	FTRBX	A-	(800) 341-7400	C+ / 6.5	1.77	-0.85	5.39 /68	3.12 /63	2.96 /57	3.40	0.48
COI	Federated Tot Ret Bd R	FTRKX	C+	(800) 341-7400	C / 5.3	1.59	-1.20	4.64 /65	2.41 /50	2.26 /46	2.67	1.14
COI	Federated Tot Ret Bd R6	FTRLX	A-	(800) 341-7400	C+ / 6.4	1.68	-0.85	5.31 /68	3.09 /62	2.94 /57	3.41	0.44
COI	Federated Tot Ret Bond Svc	FTRFX	B+	(800) 341-7400	C+ / 6.0	1.70	-1.00	5.08 /67	2.81 /58	2.67 /52	3.10	0.97
USS	Federated Tot Ret Gov Bd Inst	FTRGX	D-	(800) 341-7400	D+ / 2.9	0.42	-2.70	-0.64 / 8	1.67 /38	1.27 /31	1.97	0.49
USS	Federated Tot Ret Gov Bd R6	FTGLX	U	(800) 341-7400	U /	0.42	-2.69	--	--	--	0.00	0.45
USS	Federated Tot Ret Gov Bond Svc	FTGSX	D-	(800) 341-7400	D+ / 2.3	0.33	-2.86	-0.98 / 4	1.32 /32	0.92 /26	1.62	0.99
USA	Federated Treas Oblig Automated	TOAXX	U	(800) 341-7400	U /	--	--	--	--	--	0.02	0.64
MMT	Federated Treas Oblig Cap	TOCXX	D+	(800) 341-7400	E+ / 0.8	0.06	0.09	0.13 /23	0.05 / 9	0.04 /10	0.13	N/A
MMT	Federated Treas Oblig Instl	TOIXX	C-	(800) 341-7400	D- / 1.1	0.09	0.14	0.23 /27	0.09 /12	0.06 /12	0.23	N/A
MMT	Federated Treas Oblig Svc	TOSXX	D+	(800) 341-7400	E+ / 0.6	0.03	0.03	0.04 /20	0.02 / 7	0.02 / 7	0.04	N/A

99 Pct = Best
0 Pct = Worst

● Denotes fund is closed to new investors
* Denotes fund is included in Section II

www.thestreetratings.com

RISK			NET ASSETS		ASSET							FUND MANAGER		MINIMUM		LOADS	
Risk Rating/Pts	3 Yr Avg Standard Deviation	Avg Dura-tion	NAV As of 2/28/17	Total $(Mil)	Cash %	Gov. Bond %	Muni. Bond %	Corp. Bond %	Other %	Portfolio Turnover Ratio	Avg Coupon Rate	Manager Quality Pct	Manager Tenure (Years)	Initial Purch. $	Additional Purch. $	Front End Load	Back End Load
C- / 3.8	3.1	5.7	11.05	102	0	0	99	0	1	13	0.0	24	22	1,500	100	1.0	0.0
C- / 3.8	3.1	5.7	11.05	61	0	0	99	0	1	13	0.0	28	22	1,500	100	4.5	0.0
A+ / 9.9	N/A	N/A	1.00	34	100	0	0	0	0	0	0.1	42	N/A	10,000	0	0.0	0.0
A+ / 9.9	N/A	N/A	1.00	12	100	0	0	0	0	0	0.2	45	N/A	10,000	0	0.0	0.0
C / 5.2	3.1	6.2	10.78	184	0	0	98	0	2	14	0.0	49	22	1,500	100	4.5	0.0
C / 5.1	3.1	6.2	10.79	2	0	0	98	0	2	14	0.0	17	22	1,500	100	0.0	0.0
U /	N/A	N/A	1.00	492	100	0	0	0	0	0	0.2	N/A	21	25,000	0	0.0	0.0
A+ / 9.9	0.1	N/A	1.00	175	100	0	0	0	0	0	0.4	48	21	500,000	0	0.0	0.0
U /	N/A	N/A	1.00	1,281	100	0	0	0	0	0	0.0	N/A	21	25,000	0	0.0	0.0
U /	N/A	N/A	1.00	30	100	0	0	0	0	0	0.0	N/A	21	10,000	250	0.0	0.0
U /	N/A	N/A	1.00	160	100	0	0	0	0	0	0.0	N/A	21	0	0	0.0	0.0
A+ / 9.9	N/A	N/A	1.00	1,280	100	0	0	0	0	0	0.2	44	21	500,000	0	0.0	0.0
U /	N/A	N/A	1.00	35	100	0	0	0	0	0	0.1	N/A	21	500,000	0	0.0	0.0
A+ / 9.9	0.1	N/A	1.00	2,474	100	0	0	0	0	0	0.5	51	21	500,000	0	0.0	0.0
D- / 1.2	6.1	0.1	9.42	46	5	79	0	8	8	10	0.0	0	3	1,500	100	4.5	0.0
D- / 1.2	6.1	0.1	8.98	2	5	79	0	8	8	10	0.0	0	3	1,500	100	0.0	0.0
D- / 1.2	6.1	0.1	9.58	4	5	79	0	8	8	10	0.0	0	3	1,000,000	0	0.0	0.0
C / 4.7	3.2	4.1	10.44	11	1	92	0	5	2	35	1.1	28	11	1,500	100	4.5	0.0
C / 4.8	3.2	4.1	10.29	5	1	92	0	5	2	35	1.1	11	11	1,500	100	0.0	0.0
C / 4.7	3.2	4.1	10.49	14	1	92	0	5	2	35	1.1	38	11	1,000,000	0	0.0	0.0
A- / 9.1	1.1	1.8	10.24	246	0	0	97	0	3	15	0.0	16	21	1,500	100	1.0	0.0
A- / 9.2	1.1	1.8	10.24	828	0	0	97	0	3	15	0.0	31	21	1,000,000	0	0.0	0.0
A- / 9.1	1.1	1.8	10.24	33	0	0	97	0	3	15	0.0	23	21	1,000,000	0	0.0	0.0
A+ / 9.7	0.6	1.5	8.50	61	8	3	0	35	54	15	2.0	34	22	1,500	100	1.0	0.0
A+ / 9.7	0.6	1.5	8.50	452	8	3	0	35	54	15	2.0	63	22	1,000,000	0	0.0	0.0
A+ / 9.8	0.6	1.5	8.50	75	8	3	0	35	54	15	2.0	59	22	1,000,000	0	0.0	0.0
A+ / 9.7	0.6	1.5	8.50	402	8	3	0	35	54	15	2.0	67	22	100,000	0	0.0	0.0
B+ / 8.6	1.7	2.6	10.33	30	7	30	0	52	11	30	2.6	52	4	1,500	100	1.0	0.0
B+ / 8.6	1.7	2.6	10.33	242	7	30	0	52	11	30	2.6	61	4	1,000,000	0	0.0	0.0
B+ / 8.6	1.7	2.6	10.32	22	7	30	0	52	11	30	2.6	30	4	250	100	0.0	0.0
B+ / 8.6	1.7	2.6	10.32	35	7	30	0	52	11	30	2.6	51	4	1,000,000	0	0.0	0.0
D / 2.1	4.9	3.6	9.06	372	0	0	0	67	33	17	5.3	87	4	1,500	100	4.5	0.0
D / 2.1	4.9	3.6	9.05	55	0	0	0	67	33	17	5.3	81	4	1,500	100	0.0	0.0
D / 2.2	4.8	3.6	9.05	153	0	0	0	67	33	17	5.3	81	4	1,500	100	0.0	0.0
D / 2.1	4.9	3.6	9.00	68	0	0	0	67	33	17	5.3	87	4	1,500	100	1.0	0.0
D / 2.2	4.8	3.6	9.01	126	0	0	0	67	33	17	5.3	89	4	1,000,000	0	0.0	0.0
A+ / 9.9	0.1	N/A	1.00	1,970	100	0	0	0	0	0	0.6	52	N/A	500,000	0	0.0	0.0
A+ / 9.9	0.1	N/A	1.00	239	100	0	0	0	0	0	0.4	48	N/A	500,000	0	0.0	0.0
C+ / 6.4	2.8	5.1	10.86	333	13	16	0	45	26	30	3.9	44	4	1,500	100	4.5	0.0
C+ / 6.4	2.8	5.1	10.86	18	13	16	0	45	26	30	3.9	21	4	1,500	100	0.0	0.0
C+ / 6.4	2.8	5.1	10.86	85	13	16	0	45	26	30	3.9	22	4	1,500	100	0.0	0.0
C+ / 6.6	2.8	5.1	10.86	5,803	13	16	0	45	26	30	3.9	66	4	1,000,000	0	0.0	0.0
C+ / 6.4	2.8	5.1	10.86	61	13	16	0	45	26	30	3.9	34	4	0	0	0.0	0.0
C+ / 6.6	2.8	5.1	10.85	139	13	16	0	45	26	30	3.9	66	4	0	0	0.0	0.0
C+ / 6.5	2.8	5.1	10.86	543	13	16	0	45	26	30	3.9	57	4	1,000,000	0	0.0	0.0
C+ / 5.7	3.0	5.8	10.77	435	0	44	0	0	56	82	2.4	36	14	1,000,000	0	0.0	0.0
U /	N/A	5.8	10.77	25	0	44	0	0	56	82	2.4	N/A	14	0	0	0.0	0.0
C+ / 5.7	3.0	5.8	10.77	84	0	44	0	0	56	82	2.4	24	14	1,000,000	0	0.0	0.0
U /	N/A	N/A	1.00	1,427	0	0	0	0	100	0	0.0	N/A	24	25,000	0	0.0	0.0
A+ / 9.9	N/A	N/A	1.00	1,894	100	0	0	0	0	0	0.1	41	24	500,000	0	0.0	0.0
A+ / 9.9	N/A	N/A	1.00	23,161	100	0	0	0	0	0	0.2	45	24	500,000	0	0.0	0.0
A+ / 9.9	N/A	N/A	1.00	4,386	100	0	0	0	0	0	0.0	39	24	500,000	0	0.0	0.0

Fund Type	Fund Name	Ticker Symbol	Overall Investment Rating	Phone	Performance Rating/Pts	3 Mo	6 Mo	1Yr / Pct	3Yr / Pct	5Yr / Pct	Dividend Yield	Expense Ratio
MMT	Federated Treas Oblig Tr	TOTXX	U	(800) 341-7400	U /	--	--	--	--	--	0.01	N/A
MMT	Federated Trust For US Trs Obl Inst	TTOXX	C-	(800) 341-7400	D- / 1.1	0.09	0.14	0.24 / 27	0.09 / 12	0.05 / 11	0.24	N/A
GES	Federated Ultra Short Bd A	FULAX	D+	(800) 341-7400	E+ / 0.8	0.33	0.43	1.44 / 44	0.41 / 20	0.64 / 23	0.76	1.06
GES	Federated Ultra Short Bd Inst	FULIX	B	(800) 341-7400	C- / 3.0	0.46	0.70	2.00 / 49	1.00 / 28	1.19 / 30	1.32	0.51
GES	Federated Ultra Short Bond Svc	FULBX	C+	(800) 341-7400	D / 2.2	0.35	0.48	1.54 / 45	0.55 / 21	0.74 / 24	0.87	1.01
USS	Federated US Gvt Sec:1-3yrs Svc	FSGIX	D	(800) 341-7400	E / 0.4	0.03	-0.23	--	-0.27 / 4	-0.43 / 3	0.68	1.01
USS	Federated US Gvt Sec:2-5yrs Svc	FIGIX	D-	(800) 341-7400	E+ / 0.6	0.10	-1.25	-0.68 / 7	0.24 / 17	-0.08 / 4	1.06	0.89
MMT	Federated US Trs Csh Res Instl	UTIXX	C-	(800) 341-7400	D- / 1.0	0.08	0.13	0.21 / 26	0.08 / 11	0.05 / 11	0.21	N/A
MMT	Federated US Trs Csh Res Svc	TISXX	D+	(800) 341-7400	E+ / 0.6	0.02	0.02	0.03 / 20	0.01 / 6	0.01 / 5	0.03	N/A
USS	Federated USG Sec:1-3yrs Inst	FSGVX	D+	(800) 341-7400	E+ / 0.9	0.12	-0.05	0.35 / 30	0.06 / 10	-0.08 / 4	1.03	0.75
USS	Federated USG Sec:1-3yrs Y	FSGTX	C-	(800) 341-7400	D- / 1.4	0.15	0.01	0.49 / 33	0.21 / 17	0.07 / 13	1.17	0.50
USS	Federated USG Sec:2-5yrs Inst	FIGTX	D	(800) 341-7400	D- / 1.5	0.16	-1.14	-0.46 / 10	0.47 / 21	0.15 / 17	1.29	0.85
USS	Federated USG Sec:2-5yrs R	FIGKX	D-	(800) 341-7400	E / 0.3	-0.01	-1.39	-1.06 / 4	-0.14 / 5	-0.48 / 3	0.58	1.27
MMF	Federated VA Muni Cash Svc	VACXX	U	(800) 341-7400	U /	--	--	--	--	--	0.12	N/A
MMF	Federated VA Muni Cash Tr Cash	VCSXX	U	(800) 341-7400	U /	--	--	--	--	--	0.09	N/A
MMF	Federated VA Muni Cash Tr Wealth	VAIXX	C-	(800) 341-7400	D- / 1.3	0.13	0.19	0.20 / 29	0.08 / 14	0.05 / 14	0.20	N/A
GES	Fidelity Adv 529 High Income A	FHCAX	C-	(800) 522-7297	B / 7.9	4.22	4.47	18.28 / 94	3.47 / 68	5.25 / 86	0.00	1.27
GES	Fidelity Adv 529 High Income C	FHPCX	C-	(800) 522-7297	B / 8.2	4.02	4.07	17.28 / 92	2.59 / 54	4.38 / 77	0.00	2.12
GES	Fidelity Adv 529 High Income D	FHIDX	C	(800) 522-7297	B+ / 8.7	4.15	4.32	17.87 / 93	3.10 / 63	4.89 / 83	0.00	1.62
GES	Fidelity Adv 529 High Income P	FHIPX	C	(800) 522-7297	B+ / 8.5	4.09	4.22	17.60 / 93	2.85 / 59	4.63 / 80	0.00	1.87
GEI	Fidelity Adv 529 Inflatn-Prot Bd A	FIPEX	E	(800) 522-7297	E / 0.5	1.09	-0.95	2.40 / 52	1.02 / 28	-0.07 / 4	0.00	0.85
GEI	Fidelity Adv 529 Inflatn-Prot Bd C	FICPX	E	(800) 522-7297	D / 1.6	0.89	-1.34	1.52 / 45	0.18 / 16	-0.91 / 2	0.00	1.70
GEI	Fidelity Adv 529 Inflatn-Prot Bd D	FIDDX	E+	(800) 522-7297	D+ / 2.4	1.09	-1.06	2.07 / 50	0.68 / 23	-0.41 / 3	0.00	1.20
GEI	Fidelity Adv 529 Inflatn-Prot Bd P	FIPPX	E	(800) 522-7297	D / 1.9	0.92	-1.29	1.80 / 47	0.42 / 20	-0.67 / 2	0.00	1.45
GEI	Fidelity Adv 529 Ltd Term Bond A	FLTAX	D+	(800) 522-7297	D / 1.6	0.66	-0.36	2.08 / 50	1.19 / 31	1.49 / 34	0.00	0.88
GEI	Fidelity Adv 529 Ltd Term Bond C	FLBCX	C-	(800) 522-7297	D / 1.7	0.41	-0.81	1.17 / 41	0.32 / 19	0.62 / 23	0.00	1.73
GEI	Fidelity Adv 529 Ltd Term Bond D	FLDDX	C	(800) 522-7297	D+ / 2.5	0.57	-0.56	1.67 / 46	0.81 / 25	1.12 / 29	0.00	1.23
GEI	Fidelity Adv 529 Ltd Term Bond P	FLTPX	C-	(800) 522-7297	D / 2.1	0.53	-0.65	1.46 / 44	0.57 / 21	0.89 / 26	0.00	1.48
USS	Fidelity Adv 529 Money Market P	FMMPX	U	(800) 522-7297	U /	--	--	--	--	--	0.00	1.34
GES	Fidelity Adv 529 Strat Inc A	FBBGX	D+	(800) 522-7297	C+ / 6.4	3.55	1.58	11.26 / 82	3.25 / 65	3.70 / 69	0.00	1.13
GES	Fidelity Adv 529 Strat Inc C	FSXMX	C-	(800) 522-7297	C+ / 6.8	3.29	1.13	10.27 / 79	2.37 / 49	2.83 / 55	0.00	1.98
GES	Fidelity Adv 529 Strat Inc P	FSXPX	C	(800) 522-7297	B- / 7.1	3.32	1.28	10.51 / 80	2.61 / 54	3.07 / 59	0.00	1.73
MUS	Fidelity Adv CA Muni Inc A	FCMAX	D	(800) 522-7297	C / 5.1	1.97	-3.82	-0.70 / 7	3.45 / 87	3.35 / 85	2.72	0.80
MUS	Fidelity Adv CA Muni Inc C	FCMKX	D+	(800) 522-7297	C+ / 5.7	1.78	-4.19	-1.46 / 2	2.67 / 76	2.57 / 72	2.06	1.55
MUS	Fidelity Adv CA Muni Inc I	FCMQX	B-	(800) 522-7297	B / 7.7	2.04	-3.70	-0.46 / 10	3.70 / 90	3.59 / 89	3.08	0.55
MUS	Fidelity Adv CA Muni Inc T	FCMTX	D	(800) 522-7297	C / 5.1	1.98	-3.86	-0.74 / 6	3.47 / 87	3.39 / 86	2.75	0.74
EM	Fidelity Adv Emerging Mkts Inc A	FMKAX	C+	(800) 522-7297	A+ / 9.7	6.38	2.81	18.36 / 94	6.62 / 95	5.33 / 87	4.86	1.18
EM	Fidelity Adv Emerging Mkts Inc C	FMKCX	C+	(800) 522-7297	A+ / 9.7	6.14	2.42	17.46 / 93	5.83 / 91	4.55 / 79	4.33	1.93
EM	Fidelity Adv Emerging Mkts Inc I	FMKIX	C+	(800) 522-7297	A+ / 9.9	6.49	2.97	18.72 / 95	6.92 / 96	5.64 / 90	5.35	0.89
EM	Fidelity Adv Emerging Mkts Inc T	FAEMX	C+	(800) 522-7297	A+ / 9.6	6.32	2.79	18.28 / 94	6.56 / 95	5.29 / 87	4.82	1.22
*LP	Fidelity Adv Float-Rate Hi-Inc A	FFRAX	C+	(800) 522-7297	C+ / 6.3	1.97	3.54	12.18 / 84	2.71 / 56	3.37 / 63	3.49	0.99
LP	Fidelity Adv Float-Rate Hi-Inc C	FFRCX	C+	(800) 522-7297	C+ / 6.2	1.78	3.15	11.34 / 82	1.94 / 42	2.59 / 51	2.85	1.74
LP	Fidelity Adv Float-Rate Hi-Inc I	FFRIX	B+	(800) 522-7297	B- / 7.4	2.03	3.66	12.45 / 84	2.95 / 60	3.61 / 67	3.82	0.75
LP	Fidelity Adv Float-Rate Hi-Inc T	FFRTX	C+	(800) 522-7297	C+ / 6.2	1.85	3.50	11.97 / 83	2.62 / 54	3.25 / 61	3.41	1.08
GL	Fidelity Adv Global Bond A	FGBZX	E-	(800) 544-8544	E- / 0.1	2.24	-4.35	3.34 / 59	-1.02 / 3	--	1.85	1.46
GL	Fidelity Adv Global Bond C	FGBYX	E-	(800) 544-8544	E- / 0.1	2.03	-4.74	2.47 / 53	-1.78 / 2	--	1.17	2.25
GL	Fidelity Adv Global Bond I	FGBIX	E	(800) 544-8544	E / 0.3	2.30	-4.24	3.60 / 60	-0.77 / 3	--	2.19	1.14
GL	Fidelity Adv Global Bond T	FGBWX	E-	(800) 544-8544	E- / 0.1	2.27	-4.33	3.36 / 59	-1.01 / 3	--	1.87	1.48
USS	Fidelity Adv Govt Inc A	FVIAX	E+	(800) 522-7297	E / 0.5	0.44	-2.78	-1.14 / 3	1.58 / 36	1.18 / 30	1.27	0.76
USS	Fidelity Adv Govt Inc C	FVICX	E+	(800) 522-7297	D- / 1.3	0.25	-3.15	-1.90 / 1	0.80 / 24	0.41 / 20	0.54	1.54
USS	Fidelity Adv Govt Inc I	FVIIX	D	(800) 522-7297	C- / 3.1	0.51	-2.65	-0.88 / 5	1.85 / 40	1.45 / 34	1.60	0.50
USS	Fidelity Adv Govt Inc T	FVITX	E+	(800) 522-7297	E / 0.5	0.44	-2.78	-1.14 / 3	1.59 / 36	1.20 / 30	1.27	0.76

99 Pct = Best
0 Pct = Worst

● Denotes fund is closed to new investors
* Denotes fund is included in Section II

www.thestreetratings.com

RISK			NET ASSETS		ASSET							FUND MANAGER		MINIMUM		LOADS	
Risk Rating/Pts	3 Yr Avg Standard Deviation	Avg Dura-tion	NAV As of 2/28/17	Total $(Mil)	Cash %	Gov. Bond %	Muni. Bond %	Corp. Bond %	Other %	Portfolio Turnover Ratio	Avg Coupon Rate	Manager Quality Pct	Manager Tenure (Years)	Initial Purch. $	Additional Purch. $	Front End Load	Back End Load
U /	N/A	N/A	1.00	950	100	0	0	0	0	0	0.0	N/A	24	500,000	0	0.0	0.0
A+ / 9.9	N/A	N/A	1.00	293	100	0	0	0	0	0	0.2	44	N/A	25,000	0	0.0	0.0
A+ / 9.8	0.4	0.7	9.11	295	8	0	1	32	59	30	1.8	52	19	1,500	100	2.0	0.0
A+ / 9.9	0.4	0.7	9.11	2,556	8	0	1	32	59	30	1.8	71	19	1,000,000	0	0.0	0.0
A+ / 9.8	0.4	0.7	9.11	44	8	0	1	32	59	30	1.8	58	19	1,000,000	0	0.0	0.0
A+ / 9.6	0.7	1.7	10.33	6	0	89	0	0	11	150	1.2	17	4	1,000,000	0	0.0	0.0
B+ / 8.4	1.9	3.7	10.88	49	0	91	0	0	9	233	1.3	13	4	1,000,000	0	0.0	0.0
A+ / 9.9	N/A	N/A	1.00	13,616	100	0	0	0	0	0	0.2	44	23	25,000	0	0.0	0.0
A+ / 9.9	N/A	N/A	1.00	2,183	100	0	0	0	0	0	0.0	38	23	25,000	0	0.0	0.0
A+ / 9.6	0.7	1.7	10.34	66	0	89	0	0	11	150	1.2	26	4	1,000,000	0	0.0	0.0
A+ / 9.6	0.7	1.7	10.34	69	0	89	0	0	11	150	1.2	31	4	100,000	0	0.0	0.0
B+ / 8.4	1.9	3.7	10.88	392	0	91	0	0	9	233	1.3	17	4	1,000,000	0	0.0	0.0
B+ / 8.4	1.9	3.7	10.88	12	0	91	0	0	9	233	1.3	7	4	250	100	0.0	0.0
U /	N/A	N/A	1.00	112	100	0	0	0	0	0	0.1	44	N/A	10,000	0	0.0	0.0
U /	N/A	N/A	1.00	97	100	0	0	0	0	0	0.1	42	N/A	1,000	0	0.0	0.0
A+ / 9.9	0.1	N/A	1.00	3	100	0	0	0	0	0	0.2	45	N/A	25,000	0	0.0	0.0
D- / 1.4	5.8	N/A	26.66	15	2	0	0	94	4	10	0.0	89	12	1,000	50	4.8	0.0
D- / 1.4	5.8	N/A	23.55	6	2	0	0	94	4	10	0.0	83	12	1,000	50	0.0	0.0
D- / 1.4	5.8	N/A	25.33	N/A	2	0	0	94	4	10	0.0	87	12	1,000	50	0.0	0.0
D- / 1.4	5.8	N/A	24.45	N/A	2	0	0	94	4	10	0.0	85	12	1,000	50	0.0	0.0
D+ / 2.8	4.2	N/A	16.63	13	0	99	0	0	1	12	0.0	2	12	1,000	50	4.8	0.0
D+ / 2.8	4.1	N/A	14.72	6	0	99	0	0	1	12	0.0	1	12	1,000	50	0.0	0.0
D+ / 2.9	4.1	N/A	15.80	N/A	0	99	0	0	1	12	0.0	1	12	1,000	50	0.0	0.0
D+ / 2.8	4.1	N/A	15.28	N/A	0	99	0	0	1	12	0.0	1	12	1,000	50	0.0	0.0
B+ / 8.9	1.4	N/A	16.69	22	1	14	0	68	17	15	0.0	45	12	1,000	50	3.8	0.0
B+ / 8.9	1.4	N/A	14.75	11	1	14	0	68	17	15	0.0	14	12	1,000	50	0.0	0.0
B+ / 8.9	1.4	N/A	15.86	2	1	14	0	68	17	15	0.0	27	12	1,000	50	0.0	0.0
B+ / 8.9	1.4	N/A	15.30	N/A	1	14	0	68	17	15	0.0	20	12	1,000	50	0.0	0.0
U /	N/A	N/A	11.28	1	0	0	0	0	100	34	0.0	36	12	1,000	50	0.0	0.0
C- / 3.0	4.1	N/A	18.67	46	8	29	0	11	52	9	0.0	82	12	1,000	50	4.8	0.0
D+ / 2.9	4.1	N/A	16.96	27	8	29	0	11	52	9	0.0	69	12	1,000	50	0.0	0.0
C- / 3.0	4.1	N/A	17.45	1	8	29	0	11	52	9	0.0	74	12	1,000	50	0.0	0.0
C- / 3.8	3.6	6.2	12.79	47	1	0	98	0	1	11	0.0	27	1	2,500	0	4.0	0.0
C- / 3.9	3.6	6.2	12.77	31	1	0	98	0	1	11	0.0	10	1	2,500	0	0.0	0.0
C- / 3.9	3.6	6.2	12.80	59	1	0	98	0	1	11	0.0	35	1	2,500	0	0.0	0.0
C- / 3.9	3.6	6.2	12.82	9	1	0	98	0	1	11	0.0	28	1	2,500	0	4.0	0.0
E / 0.4	7.5	5.9	14.20	244	3	74	0	20	3	105	0.0	99	22	2,500	0	4.0	1.0
E+ / 0.6	7.5	5.9	14.31	105	3	74	0	20	3	105	0.0	99	22	2,500	0	0.0	1.0
E+ / 0.6	7.5	5.9	13.93	4,077	3	74	0	20	3	105	0.0	99	22	2,500	0	0.0	1.0
E+ / 0.6	7.5	5.9	14.14	87	3	74	0	20	3	105	0.0	99	22	2,500	0	4.0	1.0
C / 5.1	3.1	0.3	9.69	796	2	1	0	54	43	46	0.0	85	4	2,500	0	2.8	1.0
C / 5.1	3.1	0.3	9.69	584	2	1	0	54	43	46	0.0	78	4	2,500	0	0.0	1.0
C / 5.1	3.1	0.3	9.67	1,961	2	1	0	54	43	46	0.0	87	4	2,500	0	0.0	1.0
C / 5.2	3.1	0.3	9.67	172	2	1	0	54	43	46	0.0	84	4	2,500	0	2.8	1.0
D / 1.8	5.3	6.8	8.78	5	0	32	0	24	44	110	0.0	66	5	2,500	0	4.0	0.0
D / 1.8	5.4	6.8	8.76	3	0	32	0	24	44	110	0.0	33	5	2,500	0	0.0	0.0
D / 1.8	5.4	6.8	8.78	2	0	32	0	24	44	110	0.0	72	5	2,500	0	0.0	0.0
D / 1.9	5.3	6.8	8.78	3	0	32	0	24	44	110	0.0	67	5	2,500	0	4.0	0.0
C+ / 6.1	2.9	5.3	10.22	220	3	48	0	0	49	93	0.0	34	10	2,500	0	4.0	0.0
C+ / 6.0	2.9	5.3	10.22	78	3	48	0	0	49	93	0.0	12	10	2,500	0	0.0	0.0
C+ / 6.0	2.9	5.3	10.22	475	3	48	0	0	49	93	0.0	51	10	2,500	0	0.0	0.0
C+ / 5.8	2.9	5.3	10.22	167	3	48	0	0	49	93	0.0	33	10	2,500	0	4.0	0.0

Fund Type	Fund Name	Ticker Symbol	Overall Investment Rating	Phone	Performance Rating/Pts	Total Return % through 2/28/17					Incl. in Returns	
									Annualized		Dividend Yield	Expense Ratio
						3 Mo	6 Mo	1Yr / Pct	3Yr / Pct	5Yr / Pct		
*COH	Fidelity Adv Hi Income Advantage A	FAHDX	C+	(800) 522-7297	A / 9.5	6.30	6.57	22.41 /98	5.20 /86	7.61 /97	4.14	1.04
COH	Fidelity Adv Hi Income Advantage C	FAHEX	C+	(800) 522-7297	A+ / 9.6	6.11	6.17	21.53 /98	4.42 /80	6.80 /96	3.60	1.79
COH	Fidelity Adv Hi Income Advantage I	FAHCX	C+	(800) 522-7297	A+ / 9.8	6.39	6.66	22.71 /98	5.45 /88	7.85 /98	4.55	0.80
COH	Fidelity Adv Hi Income Advantage T	FAHYX	C+	(800) 522-7297	A / 9.5	6.28	6.55	22.44 /98	5.20 /86	7.61 /97	4.15	1.03
COH	Fidelity Adv High Income A	FHIAX	D+	(800) 522-7297	B / 7.9	4.14	4.44	18.48 /94	3.59 /70	5.41 /88	4.64	1.04
COH	Fidelity Adv High Income C	FHNCX	C-	(800) 522-7297	B / 8.2	4.09	4.18	17.62 /93	2.84 /59	4.62 /80	4.09	1.80
COH	Fidelity Adv High Income I	FHNIX	C	(800) 522-7297	A- / 9.1	4.33	4.68	18.70 /95	3.83 /73	5.63 /89	5.04	0.82
COH	Fidelity Adv High Income T	FHITX	D+	(800) 522-7297	B / 8.0	4.27	4.56	18.47 /94	3.61 /70	5.39 /87	4.61	1.06
GES	Fidelity Adv Inflation-Protect Bd A	FIPAX	E	(800) 522-7297	D- / 1.4	1.10	-0.89	2.54 /53	1.10 /29	0.02 / 7	0.00	0.78
GES	Fidelity Adv Inflation-Protect Bd C	FIPCX	E	(800) 522-7297	D / 1.8	0.88	-1.27	1.76 /47	0.33 /19	-0.74 / 2	0.00	1.55
GES	Fidelity Adv Inflation-Protect Bd I	FIPIX	E+	(800) 522-7297	C- / 3.5	1.19	-0.77	2.77 /55	1.38 /33	0.28 /19	0.07	0.52
GES	Fidelity Adv Inflation-Protect Bd T	FIPTX	E	(800) 522-7297	D- / 1.2	1.10	-0.89	2.45 /53	1.05 /28	-0.01 / 5	0.00	0.83
MUN	Fidelity Adv Interm Municipal Inc A	FZIAX	D	(800) 522-7297	D+ / 2.5	1.56	-2.77	-0.40 /11	2.09 /65	1.99 /59	2.16	0.69
MUN	Fidelity Adv Interm Municipal Inc C	FZICX	D+	(800) 522-7297	C- / 3.1	1.37	-3.13	-1.14 / 3	1.32 /44	1.22 /40	1.48	1.44
MUN	Fidelity Adv Interm Municipal Inc I	FZIIX	B+	(800) 522-7297	C+ / 5.7	1.62	-2.64	-0.15 /15	2.34 /70	2.24 /64	2.50	0.44
MUN	Fidelity Adv Interm Municipal Inc T	FZITX	D	(800) 522-7297	D+ / 2.6	1.57	-2.75	-0.37 /11	2.13 /65	2.02 /59	2.19	0.65
GL	Fidelity Adv International Bond A	FINWX	E-	(800) 544-8544	E- / 0.0	2.68	-5.96	2.76 /55	-3.28 / 1	--	1.71	1.42
GL	Fidelity Adv International Bond C	FINRX	E-	(800) 544-8544	E- / 0.0	2.37	-6.32	2.04 /49	-4.02 / 0	--	1.05	2.25
GL	Fidelity Adv International Bond I	FINOX	E-	(800) 544-8544	E- / 0.1	2.62	-5.94	3.03 /57	-3.04 / 1	--	2.05	1.15
GL	Fidelity Adv International Bond T	FINTX	E-	(800) 544-8544	E- / 0.0	2.69	-5.95	2.77 /55	-3.28 / 1	--	1.72	1.49
GEI	Fidelity Adv Invt Grade Bond A	FGBAX	D	(800) 522-7297	C- / 3.7	1.42	-1.40	4.93 /66	2.44 /51	2.36 /47	2.02	0.77
GEI	Fidelity Adv Invt Grade Bond C	FGBCX	D	(800) 522-7297	C- / 4.0	1.23	-1.89	4.12 /63	1.63 /37	1.60 /36	1.34	1.54
GEI	Fidelity Adv Invt Grade Bond I	FGBPX	C	(800) 522-7297	C+ / 5.7	1.49	-1.38	5.07 /67	2.67 /55	2.64 /52	2.38	0.50
GEI	Fidelity Adv Invt Grade Bond T	FGBTX	D-	(800) 522-7297	C- / 3.6	1.42	-1.54	4.76 /66	2.37 /49	2.34 /47	1.99	0.81
COI	Fidelity Adv Limited Term Bond	FJRLX	B	(800) 522-7297	C- / 3.8	0.75	-0.11	2.46 /53	1.58 /36	1.88 /40	1.57	0.45
GEI	Fidelity Adv Limited Term Bond A	FDIAX	C-	(800) 522-7297	D / 2.1	0.67	-0.26	2.16 /50	1.26 /31	1.58 /36	1.23	0.76
GEI	Fidelity Adv Limited Term Bond C	FNBCX	C-	(800) 522-7297	D / 1.9	0.48	-0.73	1.37 /43	0.46 /20	0.79 /25	0.48	1.53
GEI	Fidelity Adv Limited Term Bond I	EFIPX	B	(800) 522-7297	C- / 3.7	0.73	-0.22	2.41 /52	1.53 /35	1.84 /39	1.52	0.50
GEI	Fidelity Adv Limited Term Bond T	FTBRX	C-	(800) 522-7297	D / 2.0	0.67	-0.35	2.15 /50	1.23 /31	1.57 /36	1.22	0.76
MUN	Fidelity Adv Ltd Term Muni Inc A	FASHX	D-	(800) 522-7297	E / 0.3	1.15	-1.30	-0.57 / 9	0.57 /26	0.76 /30	1.08	0.81
MUN	Fidelity Adv Ltd Term Muni Inc C	FCSHX	D-	(800) 522-7297	E / 0.3	0.96	-1.67	-1.31 / 2	-0.15 / 5	0.01 / 7	0.36	1.55
MUN	Fidelity Adv Ltd Term Muni Inc I	FISHX	C	(800) 522-7297	D+ / 2.7	1.22	-1.17	-0.32 /12	0.86 /32	1.02 /36	1.37	0.55
MUN	Fidelity Adv Ltd Term Muni Inc T	FTSHX	D-	(800) 522-7297	E / 0.4	1.16	-1.29	-0.54 / 9	0.61 /27	0.80 /30	1.12	0.77
MTG	Fidelity Adv Mortgage Secs A	FMGAX	C-	(800) 522-7297	D+ / 2.4	0.41	-1.31	0.31 /29	2.28 /48	1.94 /41	1.85	0.79
MTG	Fidelity Adv Mortgage Secs C	FOMCX	C	(800) 522-7297	D+ / 2.9	0.31	-1.60	-0.36 /12	1.56 /36	1.22 /30	1.17	1.54
MTG	Fidelity Adv Mortgage Secs I	FMSCX	B+	(800) 522-7297	C / 4.7	0.49	-1.17	0.69 /36	2.61 /54	2.24 /45	2.22	0.50
MTG	Fidelity Adv Mortgage Secs T	FMSAX	C-	(800) 522-7297	D+ / 2.5	0.50	-1.23	0.39 /31	2.31 /48	1.97 /42	1.84	0.80
MUH	Fidelity Adv Muni Income A	FAMUX	D-	(800) 522-7297	C / 5.0	1.95	-4.09	-0.64 / 8	3.40 /87	3.07 /81	2.73	0.81
MUH	Fidelity Adv Muni Income C	FAMCX	D-	(800) 522-7297	C+ / 5.6	1.76	-4.44	-1.37 / 2	2.62 /76	2.31 /66	2.08	1.56
MUH	Fidelity Adv Muni Income I	FMPIX	C	(800) 522-7297	B / 7.6	2.02	-3.93	-0.34 /12	3.66 /90	3.34 /85	3.10	0.56
MUH	Fidelity Adv Muni Income T	FAHIX	D-	(800) 522-7297	C / 5.0	1.94	-4.08	-0.62 / 8	3.41 /87	3.10 /82	2.75	0.79
MUS	Fidelity Adv NY Muni Income A	FNMAX	D+	(800) 522-7297	C / 5.3	2.05	-3.60	-0.49 /10	3.46 /87	2.73 /75	2.50	0.79
MUS	Fidelity Adv NY Muni Income C	FNYCX	C-	(800) 522-7297	C+ / 6.0	1.86	-3.96	-1.23 / 3	2.70 /77	1.96 /58	1.83	1.53
MUS	Fidelity Adv NY Muni Income I	FEMIX	B	(800) 522-7297	B / 7.8	2.11	-3.48	-0.24 /14	3.73 /90	2.98 /79	2.86	0.54
MUS	Fidelity Adv NY Muni Income T	FNYPX	D+	(800) 522-7297	C / 5.5	2.14	-3.50	-0.43 /11	3.55 /88	2.79 /76	2.55	0.73
COI	Fidelity Adv Short-Term Bond A	FBNAX	U	(800) 544-8544	U /	0.41	0.01	--	--	--	0.00	0.66
COI	Fidelity Adv Short-Term Bond C	FANCX	U	(800) 544-8544	U /	0.09	-0.49	--	--	--	0.00	1.52
COI	Fidelity Adv Short-Term Bond I	FBNIX	U	(800) 544-8544	U /	0.45	0.08	--	--	--	0.00	0.51
COI	Fidelity Adv Short-Term Bond T	FBNTX	U	(800) 544-8544	U /	0.41	0.00	--	--	--	0.00	0.67
*GES	Fidelity Adv Strategic Income A	FSTAX	C-	(800) 522-7297	C+ / 6.8	3.58	1.71	11.45 /82	3.38 /67	3.84 /70	3.04	1.00
GES	Fidelity Adv Strategic Income C	FSRCX	C	(800) 522-7297	B- / 7.1	3.40	1.33	10.55 /80	2.62 /54	3.07 /59	2.44	1.75
GES	Fidelity Adv Strategic Income I	FSRIX	C+	(800) 522-7297	B / 8.1	3.61	1.75	11.62 /82	3.61 /70	4.07 /73	3.42	0.78

● Denotes fund is closed to new investors
* Denotes fund is included in Section II

www.thestreetratings.com

RISK			NET ASSETS		ASSET							FUND MANAGER		MINIMUM		LOADS	
Risk Rating/Pts	3 Yr Avg Standard Deviation	Avg Dura-tion	NAV As of 2/28/17	Total $(Mil)	Cash %	Gov. Bond %	Muni. Bond %	Corp. Bond %	Other %	Portfolio Turnover Ratio	Avg Coupon Rate	Manager Quality Pct	Manager Tenure (Years)	Initial Purch. $	Additional Purch. $	Front End Load	Back End Load
E+ / 0.6	6.7	3.8	11.09	612	2	0	0	74	24	46	0.0	55	8	2,500	0	4.0	1.0
E+ / 0.6	6.8	3.8	11.07	166	2	0	0	74	24	46	0.0	21	8	2,500	0	0.0	1.0
E+ / 0.6	6.7	3.8	10.40	704	2	0	0	74	24	46	0.0	62	8	2,500	0	0.0	1.0
E+ / 0.6	6.8	3.8	11.15	419	2	0	0	74	24	46	0.0	54	8	2,500	0	4.0	1.0
D- / 1.0	5.9	3.6	7.89	226	1	0	0	94	5	61	0.0	13	16	2,500	0	4.0	1.0
E+ / 0.9	5.9	3.6	7.87	99	1	0	0	94	5	61	0.0	4	16	2,500	0	0.0	1.0
D- / 1.0	5.8	3.6	7.91	382	1	0	0	94	5	61	0.0	18	16	2,500	0	0.0	1.0
D- / 1.0	5.9	3.6	7.88	64	1	0	0	94	5	61	0.0	14	16	2,500	0	4.0	1.0
C- / 3.0	4.1	5.8	11.93	93	0	99	0	0	1	29	0.0	3	13	2,500	0	4.0	0.0
D+ / 2.9	4.1	5.8	11.38	53	0	99	0	0	1	29	0.0	1	13	2,500	0	0.0	0.0
D+ / 2.8	4.1	5.8	12.04	192	0	99	0	0	1	29	0.0	4	13	2,500	0	0.0	0.0
D+ / 2.9	4.1	5.8	11.93	27	0	99	0	0	1	29	0.0	3	13	2,500	0	4.0	0.0
B- / 7.2	2.7	4.7	10.27	131	7	0	92	0	1	14	0.0	17	11	2,500	0	4.0	0.0
B- / 7.0	2.7	4.7	10.27	60	7	0	92	0	1	14	0.0	5	11	2,500	0	0.0	0.0
B- / 7.2	2.7	4.7	10.28	777	7	0	92	0	1	14	0.0	22	11	2,500	0	0.0	0.0
B- / 7.0	2.7	4.7	10.26	19	7	0	92	0	1	14	0.0	16	11	2,500	0	4.0	0.0
E / 0.4	7.5	7.4	8.36	4	10	50	0	15	25	94	0.0	12	5	2,500	0	4.0	0.0
E / 0.4	7.5	7.4	8.34	3	10	50	0	15	25	94	0.0	4	5	2,500	0	0.0	0.0
E / 0.4	7.5	7.4	8.36	2	10	50	0	15	25	94	0.0	17	5	2,500	0	0.0	0.0
E / 0.4	7.5	7.4	8.36	3	10	50	0	15	25	94	0.0	12	5	2,500	0	4.0	0.0
C / 5.1	3.1	5.6	7.84	72	0	33	1	36	30	48	0.0	36	13	2,500	0	4.0	0.0
C / 5.0	3.1	5.6	7.85	27	0	33	1	36	30	48	0.0	13	13	2,500	0	0.0	0.0
C / 4.9	3.2	5.6	7.85	596	0	33	1	36	30	48	0.0	50	13	2,500	0	0.0	0.0
C / 4.9	3.2	5.6	7.84	22	0	33	1	36	30	48	0.0	32	13	2,500	0	4.0	0.0
B+ / 8.9	1.4	2.6	11.49	1,439	1	12	0	70	17	50	0.0	60	8	2,500	0	0.0	0.0
B+ / 8.9	1.4	2.6	11.46	350	1	12	0	70	17	50	0.0	51	8	2,500	0	2.8	0.0
B+ / 8.9	1.4	2.6	11.43	87	1	12	0	70	17	50	0.0	17	8	2,500	0	0.0	0.0
B+ / 8.9	1.4	2.6	11.49	553	1	12	0	70	17	50	0.0	60	8	2,500	0	0.0	0.0
B+ / 8.9	1.4	2.6	11.46	181	1	12	0	70	17	50	0.0	47	8	2,500	0	2.8	0.0
B+ / 8.7	1.6	2.6	10.53	301	4	0	95	0	1	30	0.0	10	14	2,500	0	2.8	0.0
B+ / 8.7	1.6	2.6	10.51	50	4	0	95	0	1	30	0.0	4	14	2,500	0	0.0	0.0
B+ / 8.7	1.5	2.6	10.52	298	4	0	95	0	1	30	0.0	17	14	2,500	0	0.0	0.0
B+ / 8.7	1.6	2.6	10.51	19	4	0	95	0	1	30	0.0	11	14	2,500	0	2.8	0.0
B / 8.2	2.0	2.9	11.18	39	0	0	0	0	100	404	0.0	33	9	2,500	0	4.0	0.0
B / 8.1	2.1	2.9	11.17	16	0	0	0	0	100	404	0.0	13	9	2,500	0	0.0	0.0
B / 8.2	2.0	2.9	11.17	76	0	0	0	0	100	404	0.0	53	9	2,500	0	0.0	0.0
B / 8.1	2.1	2.9	11.21	21	0	0	0	0	100	404	0.0	32	9	2,500	0	4.0	0.0
D+ / 2.8	3.7	6.6	12.93	347	1	0	98	0	1	22	0.0	22	11	2,500	0	4.0	0.0
D+ / 2.7	3.7	6.6	12.96	119	1	0	98	0	1	22	0.0	7	11	2,500	0	0.0	0.0
D+ / 2.8	3.7	6.6	12.86	689	1	0	98	0	1	22	0.0	29	11	2,500	0	0.0	0.0
D+ / 2.8	3.7	6.6	12.97	170	1	0	98	0	1	22	0.0	21	11	2,500	0	4.0	0.0
C- / 4.2	3.4	6.3	13.10	48	2	0	97	0	1	17	0.0	33	15	2,500	0	4.0	0.0
C- / 4.2	3.4	6.3	13.10	33	2	0	97	0	1	17	0.0	13	15	2,500	0	0.0	0.0
C- / 4.2	3.4	6.3	13.09	49	2	0	97	0	1	17	0.0	49	15	2,500	0	0.0	0.0
C- / 4.2	3.4	6.3	13.12	8	2	0	97	0	1	17	0.0	35	15	2,500	0	4.0	0.0
U /	N/A	1.7	8.61	198	0	0	0	0	100	138	0.0	N/A	10	2,500	0	1.5	0.0
U /	N/A	1.7	8.60	76	0	0	0	0	100	138	0.0	N/A	10	2,500	0	0.0	0.0
U /	N/A	1.7	8.61	401	0	0	0	0	100	138	0.0	N/A	10	2,500	0	0.0	0.0
U /	N/A	1.7	8.61	89	0	0	0	0	100	138	0.0	N/A	10	2,500	0	1.5	0.0
C- / 3.0	4.1	4.9	12.13	3,120	8	29	0	10	53	88	0.0	83	18	2,500	0	4.0	0.0
D+ / 2.9	4.1	4.9	12.10	1,379	8	29	0	10	53	88	0.0	74	18	2,500	0	0.0	0.0
C- / 3.0	4.1	4.9	12.29	2,955	8	29	0	10	53	88	0.0	85	18	2,500	0	0.0	0.0

99 Pct = Best
0 Pct = Worst

Fund Type	Fund Name	Ticker Symbol	Overall Investment Rating	Phone	Perfor- mance Rating/Pts	3 Mo	6 Mo	1Yr / Pct	3Yr / Pct	5Yr / Pct	Dividend Yield	Expense Ratio
GES	Fidelity Adv Strategic Income T	FSIAX	C-	(800) 522-7297	C+ / 6.8	3.59	1.63	11.36 /82	3.35 /66	3.83 /70	3.05	1.00
COI	Fidelity Advisor Corporate Bond A	FCBAX	D-	(800) 522-7297	C+ / 5.7	2.35	-1.43	7.72 /74	3.37 /67	3.61 /67	2.76	0.79
COI	Fidelity Advisor Corporate Bond C	FCCCX	D	(800) 522-7297	C+ / 6.1	2.16	-1.72	6.91 /72	2.62 /54	2.82 /55	2.11	1.54
COI	Fidelity Advisor Corporate Bond I	FCBIX	C	(800) 522-7297	B- / 7.4	2.42	-1.29	8.03 /74	3.67 /71	3.89 /71	3.16	0.50
COI	Fidelity Advisor Corporate Bond T	FCBTX	D-	(800) 522-7297	C / 5.5	2.33	-1.47	7.63 /74	3.30 /66	3.54 /66	2.68	0.87
GL	Fidelity Advisor Glbl Hi Income A	FGHAX	D+	(800) 522-7297	B / 7.7	4.85	2.97	17.28 /92	3.59 /70	5.70 /90	4.28	1.38
GL	Fidelity Advisor Glbl Hi Income C	FGHCX	C-	(800) 522-7297	B / 8.0	4.66	2.59	16.41 /91	2.85 /59	4.90 /83	3.73	2.20
GL	Fidelity Advisor Glbl Hi Income I	FGHIX	C+	(800) 522-7297	B+ / 8.9	4.91	3.09	17.57 /93	3.85 /73	5.97 /92	4.70	1.10
GL	Fidelity Advisor Glbl Hi Income T	FGHTX	D+	(800) 522-7297	B / 7.7	4.85	2.97	17.28 /92	3.62 /70	5.68 /90	4.28	1.48
MUN	Fidelity Advisor Muni Inc 2017 A	FAMMX	D	(800) 544-8544	E / 0.3	0.15	0.00	0.03 /20	0.34 /21	0.77 /30	0.56	0.65
MUN	Fidelity Advisor Muni Inc 2017 I	FAVIX	C+	(800) 544-8544	D+ / 2.4	0.21	0.12	0.28 /32	0.59 /26	1.02 /36	0.83	0.40
MUN	Fidelity Advisor Muni Inc 2019 A	FAPAX	D+	(800) 544-8544	D / 1.8	0.97	-0.71	-0.14 /15	1.15 /39	1.57 /48	1.21	0.65
MUN	Fidelity Advisor Muni Inc 2019 I	FACIX	B	(800) 544-8544	C- / 4.1	1.03	-0.59	0.11 /25	1.40 /46	1.82 /54	1.50	0.40
MUN	Fidelity Advisor Muni Inc 2021 A	FOMAX	D+	(800) 544-8544	C / 4.6	2.22	-1.67	-0.51 / 9	2.53 /74	2.40 /68	1.70	0.65
MUN	Fidelity Advisor Muni Inc 2021 I	FOMIX	B	(800) 544-8544	C+ / 6.8	2.28	-1.55	-0.27 /13	2.79 /78	2.65 /73	2.00	0.40
MUN	Fidelity Advisor Muni Inc 2023 A	FSODX	D	(800) 544-8544	C+ / 5.9	2.08	-3.18	-0.74 / 6	3.35 /86	--	1.72	0.65
MUN	Fidelity Advisor Muni Inc 2023 I	FSWTX	C+	(800) 544-8544	B / 7.7	2.14	-3.06	-0.49 /10	3.61 /89	--	2.03	0.40
COI	Fidelity Advisor Series ShTm Fd	FYATX	U	(800) 522-7297	U /	0.45	0.08	1.52 /45	--	--	1.14	0.45
* GEI	Fidelity Advisor Total Bond A	FEPAX	C-	(800) 522-7297	C / 4.8	1.87	-0.77	5.83 /70	2.99 /61	2.89 /56	2.44	0.75
GEI	Fidelity Advisor Total Bond C	FCEPX	C	(800) 522-7297	C / 5.2	1.67	-1.15	5.03 /67	2.24 /47	2.11 /44	1.78	1.52
GEI	Fidelity Advisor Total Bond I	FEPIX	B	(800) 522-7297	C+ / 6.7	1.84	-0.75	6.01 /70	3.22 /65	3.14 /60	2.80	0.50
GEI	Fidelity Advisor Total Bond T	FEPTX	C-	(800) 522-7297	C / 4.8	1.87	-0.78	5.83 /70	2.98 /61	2.86 /55	2.43	0.77
COI	Fidelity Advisor Total Bond Z	FBKWX	U	(800) 544-8544	U /	1.87	-0.68	6.15 /71	--	--	2.94	0.36
US	Fidelity AZ Inter Treas Index		E+	(800) 544-8544	C- / 3.4	0.81	-3.59	-2.07 / 1	2.27 /48	1.47 /34	0.00	0.35
MUS	Fidelity AZ Muni Income Fd	FSAZX	B+	(800) 544-8544	B / 8.1	2.19	-3.29	-0.17 /15	3.91 /92	3.29 /85	2.67	0.55
MMF	Fidelity AZ Muni Money Market	FSAXX	C-	(800) 544-8544	D- / 1.3	0.06	0.20	0.21 /29	0.08 /14	0.05 /14	0.21	N/A
MMF	Fidelity CA AMT T/F MM Fd	FSPXX	C	(800) 544-8544	D- / 1.4	0.10	0.21	0.28 /32	0.10 /15	0.07 /15	0.28	N/A
MMF	Fidelity CA AMT T/F MM I	FSBXX	C	(800) 544-8544	D- / 1.5	0.12	0.25	0.36 /34	0.13 /16	0.08 /16	0.36	N/A
MMF	Fidelity CA AMT T/F MM Svc	FSSXX	C-	(800) 544-8544	D- / 1.1	0.06	0.12	0.14 /27	0.06 /12	0.04 /12	0.14	N/A
*MUS	Fidelity CA Ltd Term Tax-Free Bd	FCSTX	B	(800) 544-8544	C- / 4.0	1.55	-1.17	-0.27 /13	1.40 /46	1.46 /45	1.60	0.48
MMF	Fidelity CA Muni Money Market	FCFXX	C-	(800) 544-8544	D- / 1.1	0.06	0.12	0.15 /27	0.06 /12	0.04 /12	0.15	N/A
MUS	Fidelity CA Municipal Inc	FCTFX	B	(800) 544-8544	B / 7.8	2.06	-3.66	-0.37 /11	3.77 /90	3.68 /90	3.18	0.46
MMT	Fidelity Cash-MM III	FCOXX	C-	(800) 544-8544	D- / 1.3	0.15	0.25	0.33 /30	0.12 /14	0.08 /14	0.32	N/A
MMF	Fidelity Cash-Tax Exempt I	FTCXX	C	(800) 522-7297	D / 1.8	0.13	0.26	0.45 /36	0.19 /19	0.12 /18	0.45	N/A
*GEN	Fidelity Conservative Inc Bond	FCONX	C+	(800) 544-8544	D / 2.2	0.34	0.58	1.19 /42	0.57 /21	0.67 /23	0.86	0.40
GEN	Fidelity Conservative Inc Bond Inst	FCNVX	C+	(800) 544-8544	D+ / 2.3	0.37	0.63	1.29 /43	0.67 /23	0.77 /25	0.96	0.35
MUN	Fidelity Consrv Inc Muni Bd	FCRDX	C+	(800) 522-7297	D / 2.1	0.48	0.08	0.36 /34	0.40 /22	--	0.64	0.40
MUN	Fidelity Consrv Inc Muni Bd Inst	FMNDX	C+	(800) 522-7297	D+ / 2.3	0.51	0.13	0.46 /36	0.50 /24	--	0.74	0.35
COI	Fidelity Corporate Bond Fund	FCBFX	C	(800) 522-7297	B- / 7.4	2.44	-1.27	8.08 /74	3.72 /72	3.95 /72	3.21	0.45
MUS	Fidelity CT Muni Income Fd	FICNX	C	(800) 544-8544	C+ / 6.8	2.03	-3.81	-1.00 / 4	3.16 /84	2.45 /69	2.61	0.48
MMF	Fidelity CT Muni Money Market	FCMXX	C-	(800) 544-8544	D- / 1.0	0.06	0.12	0.12 /25	0.05 /11	0.03 /11	0.12	N/A
US	Fidelity DE Inter Treasury Index		E+	(800) 544-8544	C- / 3.3	0.76	-3.66	-2.11 / 1	2.25 /47	1.47 /34	0.00	0.35
LP	Fidelity Floating Rate High Income	FFRHX	B+	(800) 544-8544	B- / 7.4	1.94	3.58	12.39 /84	3.00 /61	3.64 /68	3.87	0.71
*COH	Fidelity Focused High Income	FHIFX	C	(800) 544-8544	B+ / 8.5	3.71	3.50	14.52 /88	3.70 /71	4.94 /83	4.35	0.85
GL	Fidelity Global Bond Fund	FGBFX	E-	(800) 544-8544	E / 0.3	2.30	-4.24	3.48 /60	-0.81 / 3	--	2.19	1.09
GL	Fidelity Global High Income	FGHNX	C+	(800) 522-7297	B+ / 8.9	4.91	3.09	17.57 /93	3.85 /73	5.98 /92	4.70	1.20
*USA	Fidelity GNMA Fund	FGMNX	B	(800) 544-8544	C / 4.3	0.35	-0.85	0.69 /36	2.33 /49	1.95 /41	2.00	0.45
MMT	Fidelity Government Cash Reserves	FDRXX	D+	(800) 544-8544	E+ / 0.8	0.06	0.09	0.13 /23	0.05 /10	0.04 /10	0.13	N/A
USS	Fidelity Government Income Fund	FGOVX	D	(800) 544-8544	C- / 3.2	0.52	-2.63	-0.74 / 7	1.90 /41	1.51 /35	1.64	0.45
MMT	Fidelity Government Port I	FIGXX	C-	(800) 544-8544	D- / 1.2	0.10	0.17	0.29 /29	0.11 /13	0.07 /13	0.29	N/A
MMT	Fidelity Government Port II	FCVXX	D+	(800) 544-8544	E+ / 0.8	0.06	0.09	0.14 /24	0.05 /10	0.04 /10	0.14	N/A
MMT	Fidelity Government Port III	FCGXX	D+	(800) 544-8544	E+ / 0.6	0.04	0.04	0.05 /21	0.02 / 7	0.02 / 7	0.05	N/A

● Denotes fund is closed to new investors
* Denotes fund is included in Section II

www.thestreetratings.com

RISK			NET ASSETS		ASSET					Portfolio Turnover Ratio	Avg Coupon Rate	FUND MANAGER		MINIMUM		LOADS	
Risk Rating/Pts	3 Yr Avg Standard Deviation	Avg Dura-tion	NAV As of 2/28/17	Total $(Mil)	Cash %	Gov. Bond %	Muni. Bond %	Corp. Bond %	Other %			Manager Quality Pct	Manager Tenure (Years)	Initial Purch. $	Additional Purch. $	Front End Load	Back End Load
D+ / 2.9	4.1	4.9	12.12	973	8	29	0	10	53	88	0.0	82	18	2,500	0	4.0	0.0
D+ / 2.6	4.2	7.1	11.40	42	7	1	2	88	2	40	0.0	28	7	2,500	0	4.0	0.0
D+ / 2.6	4.2	7.1	11.40	19	7	1	2	88	2	40	0.0	10	7	2,500	0	0.0	0.0
D+ / 2.6	4.2	7.1	11.40	156	7	1	2	88	2	40	0.0	38	7	2,500	0	0.0	0.0
D+ / 2.6	4.2	7.1	11.40	9	7	1	2	88	2	40	0.0	25	7	2,500	0	4.0	0.0
D- / 1.3	6.0	3.8	9.50	8	6	1	0	89	4	41	0.0	95	6	2,500	0	4.0	1.0
D- / 1.3	6.0	3.8	9.50	4	6	1	0	89	4	41	0.0	94	6	2,500	0	0.0	1.0
D- / 1.3	6.0	3.8	9.50	2	6	1	0	89	4	41	0.0	95	6	2,500	0	0.0	1.0
D- / 1.3	6.0	3.8	9.50	2	6	1	0	89	4	41	0.0	95	6	2,500	0	4.0	1.0
A+ / 9.7	0.6	0.6	10.44	9	0	0	100	0	0	9	0.0	43	6	10,000	100	2.8	0.0
A+ / 9.7	0.6	0.6	10.44	20	0	0	100	0	0	9	0.0	56	6	10,000	100	2.8	0.0
B+ / 8.5	1.8	2.5	10.64	9	0	0	100	0	0	5	0.0	27	6	10,000	100	2.8	0.0
B+ / 8.5	1.8	2.5	10.64	22	0	0	100	0	0	5	0.0	36	6	10,000	100	0.0	0.0
C / 5.1	3.1	4.1	10.90	12	0	0	100	0	0	4	0.0	23	6	10,000	100	2.8	0.0
C / 5.1	3.1	4.1	10.90	19	0	0	100	0	0	4	0.0	31	6	10,000	100	0.0	0.0
C- / 3.2	4.0	5.8	10.09	5	0	0	100	0	0	19	0.0	16	4	10,000	100	2.8	0.0
C- / 3.2	4.0	5.8	10.09	11	0	0	100	0	0	19	0.0	22	4	10,000	100	0.0	0.0
U /	N/A	1.8	9.98	207	0	2	0	70	28	115	0.0	N/A	2	0	0	0.0	0.0
C / 5.2	3.1	5.3	10.62	1,210	0	28	1	32	39	134	0.0	66	13	2,500	0	4.0	0.0
C / 5.3	3.1	5.3	10.62	180	0	28	1	32	39	134	0.0	32	13	2,500	0	0.0	0.0
C / 5.2	3.1	5.3	10.59	3,152	0	28	1	32	39	134	0.0	71	13	2,500	0	0.0	0.0
C / 5.2	3.1	5.3	10.60	164	0	28	1	32	39	134	0.0	65	13	2,500	0	4.0	0.0
U /	N/A	5.3	10.59	710	0	28	1	32	39	134	0.0	N/A	13	0	0	0.0	0.0
D+ / 2.4	4.5	N/A	16.10	3	0	99	0	0	1	3	0.0	34	11	50	25	0.0	0.0
C- / 4.0	3.5	6.2	11.91	170	2	0	97	0	1	7	0.0	53	7	10,000	0	0.0	0.0
A+ / 9.9	0.1	N/A	1.00	175	100	0	0	0	0	0	0.2	47	11	5,000	0	0.0	0.0
A+ / 9.9	0.1	N/A	1.00	319	100	0	0	0	0	0	0.3	46	2	25,000	0	0.0	0.0
A+ / 9.9	0.1	N/A	1.00	874	100	0	0	0	0	0	0.4	48	2	1,000,000	0	0.0	0.0
A+ / 9.9	N/A	N/A	1.00	N/A	100	0	0	0	0	0	0.1	44	2	1,000,000	0	0.0	0.0
B+ / 8.5	1.8	3.1	10.59	765	1	0	98	0	1	20	0.0	25	1	10,000	0	0.0	0.0
A+ / 9.9	N/A	N/A	1.00	3,556	100	0	0	0	0	0	0.2	42	2	5,000	0	0.0	0.0
C- / 3.8	3.6	6.2	12.77	1,725	1	0	98	0	1	11	0.0	37	1	10,000	0	0.0	0.0
A+ / 9.9	0.1	N/A	1.00	89	100	0	0	0	0	0	0.3	46	6	1,000,000	0	0.0	0.0
A+ / 9.9	0.1	N/A	1.00	2,196	100	0	0	0	0	0	0.5	51	N/A	1,000,000	0	0.0	0.0
A+ / 9.9	0.2	0.3	10.04	1,739	10	0	10	79	1	54	0.0	63	2	2,500	0	0.0	0.0
A+ / 9.9	0.2	0.3	10.04	4,559	10	0	10	79	1	54	0.0	66	2	1,000,000	0	0.0	0.0
A+ / 9.9	0.3	0.7	10.03	188	0	0	100	0	0	32	0.0	47	4	10,000	0	0.0	0.0
A+ / 9.9	0.3	0.7	10.03	1,021	0	0	100	0	0	32	0.0	52	4	1,000,000	0	0.0	0.0
D+ / 2.6	4.2	7.1	11.40	911	7	1	2	88	2	40	0.0	45	7	2,500	0	0.0	0.0
C- / 3.7	3.7	6.3	11.32	397	3	0	96	0	1	13	0.0	17	15	10,000	0	0.0	0.0
A+ / 9.9	N/A	N/A	1.00	913	100	0	0	0	0	0	0.1	43	2	5,000	0	0.0	0.0
D+ / 2.4	4.6	N/A	15.81	3	0	99	0	0	1	57	0.0	32	11	50	25	0.0	0.0
C / 5.1	3.1	0.3	9.67	6,999	2	1	0	54	43	46	0.0	87	4	2,500	0	0.0	1.0
D- / 1.4	5.3	3.9	8.62	594	6	0	0	92	2	47	0.0	31	13	2,500	0	0.0	1.0
D / 1.8	5.4	6.8	8.78	42	0	32	0	24	44	110	0.0	72	5	2,500	0	0.0	0.0
D- / 1.3	6.0	3.8	9.50	84	6	1	0	89	4	41	0.0	95	6	2,500	0	0.0	1.0
B+ / 8.5	1.8	2.7	11.44	5,586	0	0	0	0	100	304	0.0	80	13	2,500	0	0.0	0.0
A+ / 9.9	N/A	N/A	1.00	136,008	100	0	0	0	0	0	0.1	41	5	2,500	0	0.0	0.0
C+ / 5.8	3.0	5.3	10.21	3,472	3	48	0	0	49	93	0.0	52	10	2,500	0	0.0	0.0
A+ / 9.9	N/A	N/A	1.00	33,106	100	0	0	0	0	0	0.3	46	2	1,000,000	0	0.0	0.0
A+ / 9.9	N/A	N/A	1.00	906	100	0	0	0	0	0	0.1	43	2	1,000,000	0	0.0	0.0
A+ / 9.9	N/A	N/A	1.00	2,908	100	0	0	0	0	0	0.1	39	2	1,000,000	0	0.0	0.0

Fund Type	Fund Name	Ticker Symbol	Overall Investment Rating	Phone	Perfor-mance Rating/Pts	3 Mo	6 Mo	1Yr / Pct	3Yr / Pct	5Yr / Pct	Dividend Yield	Expense Ratio
MMT	Fidelity Government Port Select	FGEXX	C-	(800) 544-8544	D- / 1.1	0.09	0.14	0.24 /27	0.09 /12	0.06 /12	0.24	N/A
*COI	Fidelity High Income	SPHIX	C+	(800) 544-8544	A / 9.4	5.57	5.74	21.79 /98	3.96 /75	5.91 /91	5.28	0.73
GEI	Fidelity Infl PB Idx Inst	FIPBX	E+	(800) 544-8544	C / 4.3	1.33	-0.57	3.30 /58	1.83 /40	--	0.10	0.06
GEI	Fidelity Infl PB Idx Inv	FSIQX	E+	(800) 544-8544	C- / 4.1	1.30	-0.62	3.23 /58	1.71 /38	--	0.03	0.19
GEI	Fidelity Infl PB Idx IP	FIPDX	E+	(800) 544-8544	C / 4.3	1.33	-0.57	3.32 /58	1.84 /40	--	0.12	0.05
GEI	Fidelity Infl PB Idx Pr	FSIYX	E+	(800) 544-8544	C- / 4.2	1.32	-0.59	3.28 /58	1.80 /40	--	0.08	0.09
GEI	Fidelity Inflation-Protected Bd	FINPX	E+	(800) 544-8544	C- / 3.7	1.21	-0.65	2.91 /56	1.44 /34	0.35 /20	0.14	0.45
MMT	Fidelity Inst MM-Treasury Only II	FOXXX	D+	(800) 544-8544	E+ / 0.7	0.04	0.05	0.06 /21	0.03 / 8	0.02 / 7	0.06	N/A
MMT	Fidelity Inst MM-Treasury Only III	FOIXX	D+	(800) 544-8544	E+ / 0.6	0.02	0.02	0.03 /20	0.02 / 7	0.01 / 5	0.03	N/A
USA	Fidelity Inst MM-Treasury Only Inst	FRSXX	U	(800) 544-8544	U /	0.09	0.15	0.25 /27	--	--	0.25	0.18
MUN	Fidelity Intermd Muni Inc	FLTMX	B+	(800) 544-8544	C+ / 6.0	1.64	-2.61	-0.08 /16	2.42 /72	2.30 /66	2.58	0.36
*GEI	Fidelity Intermediate Bond	FTHRX	B-	(800) 544-8544	C- / 4.2	1.01	-1.00	2.23 /51	2.01 /43	2.13 /44	2.14	0.45
*USS	Fidelity Intermediate Government	FSTGX	D+	(800) 544-8544	D+ / 2.3	0.36	-1.56	-0.69 / 7	1.18 /30	1.05 /28	1.23	0.45
GL	Fidelity International Bond Rtl	FINUX	E-	(800) 544-8544	E- / 0.1	2.62	-5.94	3.03 /57	-3.08 / 1	--	2.05	1.11
US	Fidelity Intrm Treasury Inv	FIBIX	E+	(800) 544-8544	C- / 3.4	0.82	-3.61	-2.09 / 1	2.33 /49	1.56 /35	1.78	0.19
US	Fidelity Intrm Treasury Pr	FIBAX	E+	(800) 544-8544	C- / 3.6	0.84	-3.57	-1.99 / 1	2.43 /51	1.66 /37	1.88	0.09
GEI	Fidelity Investment Grade Bond Fd	FBNDX	C+	(800) 544-8544	C+ / 6.0	1.63	-1.24	5.26 /68	2.77 /57	2.72 /53	2.43	0.45
US	Fidelity Lg-T Tre Bd In Inv	FLBIX	D-	(800) 544-8544	C+ / 6.8	1.79	-11.42	-4.66 / 0	6.00 /92	3.19 /60	2.70	0.19
US	Fidelity Lg-T Tre Bd In Pr	FLBAX	D-	(800) 544-8544	B- / 7.0	1.82	-11.37	-4.57 / 0	6.10 /93	3.29 /62	2.80	0.09
USS	Fidelity Limited Term Government	FFXSX	C-	(800) 544-8544	D / 1.9	0.20	-0.79	-0.38 /11	0.70 /23	0.66 /23	0.88	0.45
MUN	Fidelity Limited Term Municipal Inc	FSTFX	C+	(800) 544-8544	D+ / 2.9	1.24	-1.14	-0.25 /14	0.89 /33	1.08 /37	1.45	0.48
MMF	Fidelity MA AMT T/F MM Fd	FMSXX	C	(800) 544-8544	D- / 1.5	0.10	0.19	0.25 /31	0.13 /16	0.09 /17	0.25	N/A
MMF	Fidelity MA AMT T/F MM Inst	FMAXX	C	(800) 544-8544	D / 1.6	0.12	0.24	0.34 /34	0.16 /18	0.11 /18	0.34	N/A
MMF	Fidelity MA AMT T/F MM Svc	FMHXX	C-	(800) 544-8544	D- / 1.2	0.06	0.12	0.13 /26	0.09 /15	0.06 /14	0.13	N/A
US	Fidelity MA Intr Treas Index		E+	(800) 544-8544	C- / 3.3	0.82	-3.63	-2.15 / 1	2.25 /47	1.47 /34	0.00	0.35
*MUS	Fidelity MA Muni Inc Fd	FDMMX	C+	(800) 544-8544	B- / 7.4	1.89	-3.98	-0.61 / 8	3.56 /88	2.87 /77	2.91	0.46
MUS	Fidelity MD Muni Income Fd	SMDMX	B	(800) 544-8544	B / 7.6	2.07	-3.37	-0.12 /16	3.51 /88	2.60 /72	2.50	0.55
*MUS	Fidelity MI Muni Inc	FMHTX	B	(800) 544-8544	B- / 7.5	1.99	-3.21	-0.48 /10	3.54 /88	2.89 /78	2.89	0.49
MMF	Fidelity MI Tax-Free Money Market	FMIXX	U	(800) 544-8544	U /	--	--	--	--	--	0.18	N/A
MMT	Fidelity MM Port I	FMPXX	C	(800) 522-7297	D / 1.7	0.22	0.38	0.58 /35	0.26 /18	0.20 /18	0.58	N/A
MMT	Fidelity MM Port II	FCIXX	C	(800) 522-7297	D- / 1.4	0.18	0.30	0.43 /32	0.16 /15	0.10 /15	0.43	N/A
MMT	Fidelity MM Port Inst	FNSXX	C	(800) 544-8544	D / 1.8	0.23	0.40	0.62 /35	0.30 /19	0.24 /19	0.62	N/A
MMT	Fidelity MM Port Select	FMYXX	C	(800) 544-8544	D- / 1.5	0.20	0.35	0.53 /34	0.21 /17	0.16 /17	0.53	N/A
MMT	Fidelity MM Prime MM Select	FDIXX	C	(800) 544-8544	D- / 1.5	0.19	0.35	0.53 /34	0.21 /17	0.14 /17	0.47	N/A
MMF	Fidelity MM Tax Exempt Select	FSXXX	C	(800) 544-8544	D / 1.7	0.12	0.24	0.40 /35	0.17 /18	0.11 /18	0.40	N/A
MMT	Fidelity MM Treas Only Select	FTYXX	D+	(800) 544-8544	E+ / 0.9	0.07	0.10	0.16 /24	0.06 /10	0.04 /10	0.16	N/A
MMT	Fidelity MM Treasury I	FISXX	C-	(800) 544-8544	D- / 1.1	0.09	0.15	0.24 /27	0.10 /13	0.06 /12	0.24	N/A
MMT	Fidelity MM Treasury II	FCEXX	D+	(800) 544-8544	E+ / 0.7	0.05	0.07	0.09 /22	0.04 / 9	0.03 / 9	0.09	N/A
MMT	Fidelity MM Treasury III	FCSXX	D+	(800) 544-8544	E+ / 0.6	0.03	0.03	0.04 /20	0.02 / 7	0.02 / 7	0.04	N/A
MMT	Fidelity MM Treasury Instl	FRBXX	U	(800) 544-8544	U /	0.10	0.17	0.28 /28	--	--	0.28	N/A
MMT	Fidelity MM Treasury Select	FTUXX	C-	(800) 544-8544	D- / 1.0	0.08	0.12	0.19 /26	0.08 /11	0.05 /11	0.19	N/A
*MUS	Fidelity MN Muni Inc	FIMIX	B+	(800) 544-8544	C+ / 6.7	2.02	-2.72	-0.06 /17	2.83 /79	2.34 /67	2.56	0.50
MTG	Fidelity Mortgage Securities	FMSFX	B+	(800) 544-8544	C / 4.7	0.50	-1.14	0.74 /37	2.66 /55	2.29 /46	2.27	0.45
MUN●	Fidelity Muni Inc 2017	FMIFX	C+	(800) 544-8544	D+ / 2.4	0.21	0.12	0.28 /32	0.59 /26	1.02 /36	0.83	0.40
MUN	Fidelity Muni Inc 2019	FMCFX	B	(800) 544-8544	C- / 4.1	1.03	-0.59	0.11 /25	1.40 /46	1.82 /54	1.50	0.40
MUN	Fidelity Muni Inc 2021	FOCFX	B	(800) 544-8544	C+ / 6.8	2.28	-1.55	-0.27 /13	2.79 /78	2.65 /73	2.00	0.40
MUN	Fidelity Muni Inc 2023	FCHPX	C+	(800) 544-8544	B / 7.7	2.14	-3.06	-0.49 /10	3.61 /89	--	2.03	0.40
*MUH	Fidelity Municipal Inc	FHIGX	C+	(800) 544-8544	B / 7.8	2.02	-3.86	-0.13 /15	3.77 /91	3.37 /86	3.28	0.48
MMF	Fidelity Municipal MM Fund	FTEXX	C-	(800) 544-8544	D- / 1.3	0.08	0.17	0.20 /29	0.08 /14	0.05 /14	0.20	N/A
MMT	Fidelity NC Cap Mgmt Tr Govt Port		C-	(800) 544-8544	D- / 1.3	0.10	0.17	0.34 /30	0.15 /15	0.11 /15	0.34	N/A
USS	Fidelity NC Cap Mgmt Tr Term Port		C	(800) 544-8544	D / 1.7	0.20	0.36	0.62 /35	0.29 /18	0.24 /19	0.61	0.26
*EM	Fidelity New Markets Income	FNMIX	C+	(800) 544-8544	A+ / 9.9	6.48	3.00	18.72 /95	7.02 /96	5.74 /90	5.42	0.86

RISK			NET ASSETS		ASSET							FUND MANAGER		MINIMUM		LOADS	
Risk Rating/Pts	3 Yr Avg Standard Deviation	Avg Dura-tion	NAV As of 2/28/17	Total $(Mil)	Cash %	Gov. Bond %	Muni. Bond %	Corp. Bond %	Other %	Portfolio Turnover Ratio	Avg Coupon Rate	Manager Quality Pct	Manager Tenure (Years)	Initial Purch. $	Additional Purch. $	Front End Load	Back End Load
A+ / 9.9	N/A	N/A	1.00	1,025	100	0	0	0	0	0	0.2	45	2	1,000,000	0	0.0	0.0
D- / 1.1	6.2	3.5	8.91	4,659	4	0	0	88	8	33	0.0	81	17	2,500	0	0.0	1.0
D+ / 2.8	4.2	5.8	9.80	134	0	100	0	0	0	25	0.0	8	3	5,000,000	0	0.0	0.0
D+ / 2.7	4.2	5.8	9.80	10	0	100	0	0	0	25	0.0	6	3	2,500	0	0.0	0.0
D+ / 2.8	4.2	5.8	9.80	573	0	100	0	0	0	25	0.0	8	3	100,000,000	0	0.0	0.0
D+ / 2.7	4.2	5.8	9.80	587	0	100	0	0	0	25	0.0	7	3	10,000	0	0.0	0.0
D+ / 2.9	4.1	5.8	12.08	1,524	0	99	0	0	1	29	0.0	5	13	2,500	0	0.0	0.0
A+ / 9.9	N/A	N/A	1.00	162	100	0	0	0	0	0	0.1	39	N/A	1,000,000	0	0.0	0.0
A+ / 9.9	N/A	N/A	1.00	1,026	100	0	0	0	0	0	0.0	38	N/A	1,000,000	0	0.0	0.0
U /	N/A	N/A	1.00	4,951	0	0	0	0	100	0	0.0	N/A	N/A	10,000,000	0	0.0	0.0
B- / 7.0	2.7	4.7	10.26	4,912	7	0	92	0	1	14	0.0	23	11	10,000	0	0.0	0.0
B / 7.9	2.2	4.0	10.84	3,141	3	37	0	49	11	58	0.0	50	4	2,500	0	0.0	0.0
B / 7.9	2.2	3.8	10.47	611	0	67	0	0	33	117	0.0	33	9	2,500	0	0.0	0.0
E / 0.4	7.5	7.4	8.36	42	10	50	0	15	25	94	0.0	16	5	2,500	0	0.0	0.0
D+ / 2.4	4.6	6.6	10.70	53	0	99	0	0	1	48	0.0	35	3	2,500	0	0.0	0.0
D+ / 2.4	4.6	6.6	10.70	1,449	0	99	0	0	1	48	0.0	43	3	10,000	0	0.0	0.0
C / 4.9	3.2	5.6	7.85	8,476	0	33	1	36	30	48	0.0	54	13	2,500	0	0.0	0.0
E- / 0.1	11.5	18.2	12.80	42	0	99	0	0	1	71	0.0	53	3	2,500	0	0.0	0.0
E- / 0.1	11.5	18.2	12.80	1,026	0	99	0	0	1	71	0.0	57	3	10,000	0	0.0	0.0
B+ / 8.9	1.4	2.6	9.94	378	0	74	0	0	26	102	0.0	32	9	2,500	0	0.0	0.0
B+ / 8.7	1.6	2.6	10.51	2,798	4	0	95	0	1	30	0.0	16	14	10,000	0	0.0	0.0
A+ / 9.9	0.1	N/A	1.00	202	100	0	0	0	0	0	0.3	48	2	25,000	0	0.0	0.0
A+ / 9.9	0.1	N/A	1.00	616	100	0	0	0	0	0	0.3	50	2	1,000,000	0	0.0	0.0
A+ / 9.9	0.1	N/A	1.00	N/A	100	0	0	0	0	0	0.1	N/A	2	1,000,000	0	0.0	0.0
D+ / 2.4	4.6	N/A	15.95	28	0	99	0	0	1	0	0.0	32	11	50	25	0.0	0.0
C- / 3.8	3.6	6.8	12.02	2,119	3	0	96	0	1	11	0.0	29	7	10,000	0	0.0	0.0
C- / 4.1	3.5	6.4	11.18	220	1	0	98	0	1	9	0.0	33	15	10,000	0	0.0	0.0
C / 4.5	3.3	5.9	11.99	654	1	0	98	0	1	11	0.0	47	1	10,000	0	0.0	0.0
U /	N/A	N/A	1.00	546	100	0	0	0	0	0	0.2	44	11	5,000	0	0.0	0.0
A+ / 9.9	0.1	N/A	1.00	7,124	100	0	0	0	0	0	0.6	54	6	1,000,000	0	0.0	0.0
A+ / 9.9	0.1	N/A	1.00	15	100	0	0	0	0	0	0.4	49	6	1,000,000	0	0.0	0.0
A+ / 9.9	0.1	N/A	1.00	9,352	100	0	0	0	0	0	0.6	55	6	10,000,000	0	0.0	0.0
A+ / 9.9	0.1	N/A	1.00	10	100	0	0	0	0	0	0.5	51	6	1,000,000	0	0.0	0.0
A+ / 9.9	0.1	N/A	1.00	28	100	0	0	0	0	0	0.5	51	2	1,000,000	0	0.0	0.0
A+ / 9.9	0.1	N/A	1.00	N/A	100	0	0	0	0	0	0.4	50	N/A	1,000,000	0	0.0	0.0
A+ / 9.9	N/A	N/A	1.00	99	100	0	0	0	0	0	0.2	43	N/A	1,000,000	0	0.0	0.0
A+ / 9.9	N/A	N/A	1.00	9,103	100	0	0	0	0	0	0.2	46	15	1,000,000	0	0.0	0.0
A+ / 9.9	N/A	N/A	1.00	281	100	0	0	0	0	0	0.1	40	15	1,000,000	0	0.0	0.0
A+ / 9.9	N/A	N/A	1.00	2,635	100	0	0	0	0	0	0.0	38	15	1,000,000	0	0.0	0.0
U /	N/A	N/A	1.00	6,703	100	0	0	0	0	0	0.3	N/A	N/A	10,000,000	0	0.0	0.0
A+ / 9.9	N/A	N/A	1.00	260	100	0	0	0	0	0	0.2	44	15	1,000,000	0	0.0	0.0
C+ / 5.8	3.0	5.6	11.48	527	1	0	98	0	1	13	0.0	28	7	10,000	0	0.0	0.0
B+ / 8.3	2.0	2.9	11.21	943	0	0	0	0	100	404	0.0	56	9	2,500	0	0.0	0.0
A+ / 9.7	0.6	0.6	10.44	66	0	0	100	0	0	9	0.0	57	6	10,000	0	0.0	0.0
B+ / 8.5	1.8	2.5	10.64	50	0	0	100	0	0	5	0.0	36	6	10,000	0	0.0	0.0
C / 5.1	3.1	4.1	10.90	33	0	0	100	0	0	4	0.0	31	6	10,000	0	0.0	0.0
C- / 3.2	4.0	5.8	10.09	14	0	0	100	0	0	19	0.0	22	4	10,000	0	0.0	0.0
D+ / 2.8	3.7	6.6	12.91	5,417	1	0	98	0	1	14	0.0	33	7	10,000	0	0.0	0.0
A+ / 9.9	N/A	N/A	1.00	13,068	100	0	0	0	0	0	0.2	44	14	5,000	0	0.0	0.0
A+ / 9.9	N/A	N/A	1.00	5,398	100	0	0	0	0	0	0.3	49	4	0	0	0.0	0.0
A+ / 9.9	0.1	0.1	9.68	2,442	20	3	0	74	3	902	0.0	54	2	0	0	0.0	0.0
E / 0.4	7.5	5.9	16.09	5,231	3	73	0	20	4	110	0.0	99	22	2,500	0	0.0	1.0

Fund Type	Fund Name	Ticker Symbol	Overall Investment Rating	Phone	Perfor-mance Rating/Pts	3 Mo	6 Mo	1Yr / Pct	3Yr / Pct	5Yr / Pct	Dividend Yield	Expense Ratio
						Total Return % through 2/28/17			Annualized		Incl. in Returns	
US	Fidelity NH Inter Treas Index		E+	(800) 544-8544	C- / 3.4	0.82	-3.57	-2.09 / 1	2.27 / 48	1.47 / 34	0.00	0.35
MMF	Fidelity NJ AMT T/F MM Inst	FSKXX	C	(800) 544-8544	D / 1.6	0.13	0.25	0.36 / 34	0.15 / 17	0.10 / 17	0.36	N/A
MMF	Fidelity NJ AMT T/F MM Svc	FNNXX	C-	(800) 544-8544	D- / 1.1	0.07	0.12	0.14 / 27	0.07 / 13	0.05 / 14	0.13	N/A
*MUS	Fidelity NJ Muni Income Fd	FNJHX	C-	(800) 544-8544	C+ / 6.6	1.37	-4.04	0.10 / 24	2.91 / 80	2.51 / 71	3.07	0.48
MMF	Fidelity NJ Municipal Money Market	FNJXX	C-	(800) 544-8544	D- / 1.0	0.06	0.11	0.12 / 25	0.05 / 12	0.03 / 11	0.12	N/A
MMF	Fidelity NY AMT T/F MM Inst	FNKXX	C	(800) 544-8544	D / 1.6	0.13	0.26	0.36 / 34	0.16 / 18	0.10 / 17	0.36	N/A
MMF	Fidelity NY AMT T/F MM Svc	FNOXX	C-	(800) 544-8544	D- / 1.2	0.07	0.13	0.14 / 27	0.08 / 14	0.06 / 15	0.14	N/A
MUS	Fidelity NY Muni Inc Fd	FTFMX	B+	(800) 544-8544	B / 7.9	2.13	-3.37	-0.16 / 15	3.80 / 91	3.07 / 81	2.93	0.46
*MUS	Fidelity OH Muni Inc	FOHFX	B	(800) 544-8544	B / 8.2	2.02	-3.75	-0.22 / 14	4.08 / 93	3.40 / 86	2.80	0.48
MUS	Fidelity PA Muni Inc	FPXTX	A-	(800) 544-8544	B / 7.8	1.83	-2.98	0.27 / 31	3.64 / 89	3.15 / 82	3.02	0.49
MMF	Fidelity PA Muni MM Fd	FPTXX	C-	(800) 544-8544	D- / 1.0	0.05	0.12	0.12 / 25	0.05 / 12	0.03 / 11	0.12	N/A
MMT	Fidelity Prime MM I	FIDXX	C	(800) 522-7297	D / 1.6	0.20	0.38	0.58 / 35	0.24 / 17	0.17 / 18	0.52	N/A
MMT	Fidelity Prime MM II	FDOXX	C	(800) 522-7297	D- / 1.4	0.17	0.29	0.42 / 32	0.16 / 15	0.10 / 15	0.37	N/A
MMT	Fidelity Prime MM III	FCDXX	C-	(800) 522-7297	D- / 1.3	0.14	0.24	0.32 / 29	0.12 / 14	0.07 / 13	0.27	N/A
MMT	Fidelity Prime MM Inst	FIPXX	C	(800) 544-8544	D / 1.7	0.20	0.38	0.60 / 35	0.28 / 18	0.21 / 19	0.56	N/A
MMT	Fidelity Retirement Government MM	FRTXX	D+	(800) 544-8544	E+ / 0.7	0.05	0.07	0.08 / 21	0.04 / 9	0.03 / 9	0.08	N/A
US	Fidelity S/T TyBd In Inv	FSBIX	C-	(800) 544-8544	D / 1.9	0.30	-0.80	-0.25 / 14	0.72 / 23	0.62 / 23	0.95	0.19
US	Fidelity S/T TyBd In Pr	FSBAX	C-	(800) 544-8544	D / 2.1	0.32	-0.75	-0.15 / 15	0.83 / 25	0.72 / 24	1.05	0.09
US	Fidelity SAI Lg-T Tre Bd In	FBLTX	U	(800) 544-8544	U /	1.88	-11.88	-4.77 / 0	--	--	2.71	0.17
*EM	Fidelity Series Emerg Mrkts Dbt	FEDCX	C+	(800) 522-7297	A+ / 9.9	5.58	2.91	18.86 / 95	6.93 / 96	5.95 / 92	6.00	0.82
EM	Fidelity Series Emerg Mrkts Dbt F	FEDFX	C+	(800) 522-7297	A+ / 9.9	5.61	2.96	18.98 / 95	7.05 / 96	6.07 / 93	6.11	0.72
COI	Fidelity Series Float Rate Hi Inc	FFHCX	B	(800) 544-8544	B / 7.8	2.22	4.23	13.97 / 87	2.83 / 58	4.72 / 81	4.35	0.75
COI	Fidelity Series Float Rate Hi Inc F	FFHFX	B	(800) 544-8544	B / 7.9	2.24	4.28	14.10 / 87	2.94 / 60	4.83 / 82	4.46	0.64
GEI	Fidelity Series Inf-Pro Bd Idx	FSIPX	D-	(800) 544-8544	C- / 3.1	1.16	0.26	2.56 / 54	0.99 / 27	0.32 / 20	0.05	0.20
*GEI	Fidelity Series Inf-Pro Bd Idx F	FFIPX	D-	(800) 544-8544	C- / 3.6	1.35	0.58	2.97 / 56	1.22 / 31	0.52 / 22	0.44	0.05
US	Fidelity Series Long Tm Treas Bd	FTLTX	U	(800) 544-8544	U /	1.86	-11.42	--	--	--	0.00	N/A
US	Fidelity Series Long Tm Treas Bd F	FFTTX	U	(800) 544-8544	U /	1.89	-11.36	--	--	--	0.00	N/A
COI	Fidelity Series Short-Term Credit	FYBTX	U	(800) 544-8544	U /	0.46	0.05	1.56 / 45	--	--	1.08	0.45
COI	Fidelity Series Short-Term Credit F	FYCTX	U	(800) 544-8544	U /	0.49	0.10	1.66 / 46	--	--	1.18	0.35
GL	Fidelity Short Dur High Inc	FSAHX	C-	(800) 544-8544	B- / 7.4	3.18	3.80	15.05 / 89	2.36 / 49	--	4.14	0.96
GL	Fidelity Short Dur High Inc A	FSBHX	D-	(800) 544-8544	C+ / 5.7	3.11	3.67	14.77 / 88	2.11 / 45	--	3.74	1.24
GL	Fidelity Short Dur High Inc C	FSDHX	D-	(800) 544-8544	C+ / 6.1	2.92	3.29	13.92 / 87	1.35 / 33	--	3.17	2.00
GL	Fidelity Short Dur High Inc I	FSFHX	C-	(800) 544-8544	B- / 7.4	3.17	3.79	15.05 / 89	2.36 / 49	--	4.14	0.99
GL	Fidelity Short Dur High Inc T	FSEHX	D-	(800) 544-8544	C+ / 5.7	3.11	3.67	14.77 / 88	2.11 / 45	--	3.74	1.25
GEI ●	Fidelity Short-Term Bond	FSHBX	C+	(800) 544-8544	D+ / 2.6	0.34	-0.01	1.25 / 42	0.95 / 27	1.12 / 29	1.01	0.45
MMT	Fidelity Spartan Money Market	SPRXX	C	(800) 544-8544	D- / 1.4	0.16	0.28	0.43 / 32	0.16 / 15	0.10 / 15	0.43	N/A
MMT	Fidelity Spartan Money Market Prem	FZDXX	C	(800) 544-8544	D / 1.6	0.19	0.34	0.56 / 34	0.22 / 17	0.13 / 16	0.55	N/A
MMT	Fidelity Spartan US Govt MM	SPAXX	D+	(800) 544-8544	E+ / 0.7	0.04	0.06	0.07 / 21	0.03 / 8	0.02 / 7	0.07	N/A
MMT	Fidelity Spartan US Govt MM	FZCXX	C-	(800) 544-8544	E+ / 0.9	0.07	0.11	0.17 / 25	0.07 / 11	0.04 / 10	0.17	N/A
*GEI	Fidelity Srs Inv Grade Bond	FSIGX	C+	(800) 544-8544	C+ / 6.0	1.55	-1.44	4.20 / 63	2.94 / 60	2.65 / 52	2.66	0.45
GEI	Fidelity Srs Inv Grade Bond F	FIBFX	C+	(800) 544-8544	C+ / 6.1	1.66	-1.31	4.38 / 64	3.07 / 62	2.77 / 54	2.75	0.35
GEI	Fidelity Strat Adv Core Inc MM	FWHBX	C+	(800) 544-8544	C+ / 5.6	1.51	-1.42	3.58 / 60	2.77 / 57	--	2.24	1.00
GEI	Fidelity Strat Adv Core Inc MM L	FQANX	B-	(800) 544-8544	C+ / 5.7	1.61	-1.32	3.68 / 61	2.80 / 58	--	2.23	1.00
GEI	Fidelity Strat Adv Core Inc MM N	FQAOX	C+	(800) 544-8544	C / 5.1	1.45	-1.54	3.32 / 58	2.51 / 52	--	1.99	1.25
*COI	Fidelity Strat Adv Short Duration	FAUDX	B	(800) 544-8544	C- / 3.1	0.52	0.63	2.27 / 51	1.03 / 28	1.04 / 28	1.35	0.76
GEN	Fidelity Strat Advs Inc Opp FOF	FSADX	B-	(800) 544-8544	A / 9.3	5.01	5.63	19.73 / 95	4.01 / 75	--	5.52	2.22
GEL	Fidelity Strat Advs Inc Opp FOF F	FLTSX	B-	(800) 544-8544	A / 9.3	5.02	5.64	19.73 / 96	4.01 / 75	--	5.52	2.21
GEN	Fidelity Strat Advs Inc Opp FOF L	FQAFX	B-	(800) 544-8544	A / 9.3	5.01	5.63	19.73 / 96	4.01 / 75	--	5.51	2.22
GEN	Fidelity Strat Advs Inc Opp FOF N		C+	(800) 544-8544	B+ / 8.9	4.81	5.36	19.27 / 95	3.39 / 67	--	5.28	2.47
*GEI	Fidelity Strategic Advisers Cor Inc	FPCIX	B+	(800) 544-8544	C+ / 6.1	1.80	-0.84	4.60 / 65	2.93 / 60	2.96 / 57	2.81	0.73
*COH	Fidelity Strategic Advisers Inc Opp	FPIOX	C+	(800) 544-8544	A- / 9.2	4.86	5.45	18.95 / 95	3.65 / 71	6.09 / 93	5.17	1.14
*GL	Fidelity Strategic Income Fund	FSICX	C+	(800) 544-8544	B / 8.1	3.64	1.72	11.62 / 82	3.60 / 70	4.10 / 74	3.39	0.71

● Denotes fund is closed to new investors
* Denotes fund is included in Section II

www.thestreetratings.com

I. Index of Bond and Money Market Mutual Funds

RISK			NET ASSETS		ASSET							FUND MANAGER		MINIMUM		LOADS	
Risk Rating/Pts	3 Yr Avg Standard Deviation	Avg Dura-tion	NAV As of 2/28/17	Total $(Mil)	Cash %	Gov. Bond %	Muni. Bond %	Corp. Bond %	Other %	Portfolio Turnover Ratio	Avg Coupon Rate	Manager Quality Pct	Manager Tenure (Years)	Initial Purch. $	Additional Purch. $	Front End Load	Back End Load
D+ / 2.4	4.6	N/A	15.94	57	0	99	0	0	1	0	0.0	33	11	50	25	0.0	0.0
A+ / 9.9	0.1	N/A	1.00	151	100	0	0	0	0	0	0.4	49	7	1,000,000	0	0.0	0.0
A+ / 9.9	N/A	N/A	1.00	N/A	100	0	0	0	0	0	0.1	44	7	1,000,000	0	0.0	0.0
C- / 3.4	3.8	6.2	11.53	523	0	0	99	0	1	7	0.0	11	1	10,000	0	0.0	0.0
A+ / 9.9	N/A	N/A	1.00	1,328	100	0	0	0	0	0	0.1	41	7	5,000	0	0.0	0.0
A+ / 9.9	0.1	N/A	1.00	648	100	0	0	0	0	0	0.4	50	6	1,000,000	0	0.0	0.0
A+ / 9.9	N/A	N/A	1.00	N/A	100	0	0	0	0	0	0.1	46	6	1,000,000	0	0.0	0.0
C- / 4.2	3.4	6.3	13.11	1,559	2	0	97	0	1	17	0.0	52	15	10,000	0	0.0	0.0
C- / 3.5	3.8	6.9	11.95	652	0	0	99	0	1	17	0.0	48	1	10,000	0	0.0	0.0
C / 5.1	3.1	6.2	11.01	456	2	0	97	0	1	17	0.0	59	15	10,000	0	0.0	0.0
A+ / 9.9	N/A	N/A	1.00	382	100	0	0	0	0	0	0.1	43	6	5,000	0	0.0	0.0
A+ / 9.9	0.1	N/A	1.00	777	100	0	0	0	0	0	0.5	52	2	1,000,000	0	0.0	0.0
A+ / 9.9	0.1	N/A	1.00	36	100	0	0	0	0	0	0.4	49	2	1,000,000	0	0.0	0.0
A+ / 9.9	0.1	N/A	1.00	8	100	0	0	0	0	0	0.3	N/A	2	1,000,000	0	0.0	0.0
A+ / 9.9	0.1	N/A	1.00	9,726	100	0	0	0	0	0	0.6	54	2	10,000,000	0	0.0	0.0
A+ / 9.9	N/A	N/A	1.00	9,770	100	0	0	0	0	0	0.1	40	N/A	100,000	0	0.0	0.0
B+ / 8.8	1.5	2.7	10.39	148	0	99	0	0	1	41	0.0	36	3	2,500	0	0.0	0.0
B+ / 8.8	1.5	2.7	10.39	1,257	0	99	0	0	1	41	0.0	44	3	10,000	0	0.0	0.0
U /	N/A	19.1	9.86	763	0	0	0	0	100	0	0.0	N/A	2	0	0	0.0	0.0
E+ / 0.7	7.1	5.6	10.24	603	6	70	2	20	2	41	0.0	99	6	0	0	0.0	0.0
E+ / 0.7	7.1	5.6	10.24	698	6	70	2	20	2	41	0.0	99	6	0	0	0.0	0.0
C- / 3.8	3.6	0.2	9.54	206	7	0	0	57	36	46	0.0	85	6	0	0	0.0	0.0
C- / 3.8	3.6	0.2	9.54	239	7	0	0	57	36	46	0.0	86	6	0	0	0.0	0.0
C / 4.4	3.3	3.7	9.87	1,014	0	100	0	0	0	33	0.0	7	3	0	0	0.0	0.0
C / 4.5	3.3	3.7	9.88	1,249	0	100	0	0	0	33	0.0	11	3	0	0	0.0	0.0
U /	N/A	18.2	8.59	11	0	0	0	0	100	0	0.0	N/A	1	0	0	0.0	0.0
U /	N/A	18.2	8.59	11	0	0	0	0	100	0	0.0	N/A	1	0	0	0.0	0.0
U /	N/A	1.8	9.97	1,033	0	2	0	70	28	112	0.0	N/A	2	0	0	0.0	0.0
U /	N/A	1.8	9.97	1,098	0	2	0	70	28	112	0.0	N/A	2	0	0	0.0	0.0
D / 2.2	4.9	2.1	9.55	89	4	0	0	92	4	56	0.0	90	1	2,500	0	0.0	1.0
D / 2.2	4.8	2.1	9.55	9	4	0	0	92	4	56	0.0	89	1	2,500	0	4.0	1.0
D / 2.2	4.9	2.1	9.55	5	4	0	0	92	4	56	0.0	83	1	2,500	0	0.0	1.0
D / 2.2	4.9	2.1	9.55	10	4	0	0	92	4	56	0.0	90	1	2,500	0	0.0	1.0
D / 2.2	4.8	2.1	9.55	3	4	0	0	92	4	56	0.0	89	1	2,500	0	4.0	1.0
A+ / 9.6	0.8	1.7	8.60	5,546	0	0	0	0	100	138	0.0	58	10	2,500	0	0.0	0.0
A+ / 9.9	0.1	N/A	1.00	2,132	100	0	0	0	0	0	0.4	49	N/A	2,500	0	0.0	0.0
A+ / 9.9	0.1	N/A	1.00	6,193	100	0	0	0	0	0	0.6	52	N/A	100,000	0	0.0	0.0
A+ / 9.9	N/A	N/A	1.00	62,162	100	0	0	0	0	0	0.1	39	5	2,500	0	0.0	0.0
A+ / 9.9	N/A	N/A	1.00	2,409	100	0	0	0	0	0	0.2	44	5	100,000	0	0.0	0.0
C / 5.1	3.1	5.6	11.18	11,859	0	20	2	44	34	121	0.0	58	9	0	0	0.0	0.0
C / 5.1	3.1	5.6	11.19	11,672	0	20	2	44	34	121	0.0	62	9	0	0	0.0	0.0
C+ / 6.0	2.9	N/A	9.85	39	0	0	0	0	100	74	0.0	56	5	0	0	0.0	0.0
C+ / 6.1	2.9	N/A	9.86	N/A	0	0	0	0	100	74	0.0	58	5	0	0	0.0	0.0
C+ / 6.1	2.9	N/A	9.85	N/A	0	0	0	0	100	74	0.0	N/A	5	0	0	0.0	0.0
A+ / 9.8	0.5	N/A	10.04	9,093	11	8	2	51	28	33	0.0	69	6	0	0	0.0	0.0
D / 1.6	5.6	N/A	10.14	8	5	0	0	83	12	65	0.0	92	5	0	0	0.0	1.0
D / 1.6	5.6	N/A	10.14	N/A	5	0	0	83	12	65	0.0	92	5	0	0	0.0	1.0
D / 1.7	5.6	N/A	10.14	N/A	5	0	0	83	12	65	0.0	92	5	0	0	0.0	1.0
D / 1.6	5.6	N/A	10.14	N/A	5	0	0	83	12	65	0.0	89	5	0	0	0.0	1.0
C+ / 6.5	2.8	N/A	10.50	30,089	0	28	2	29	41	69	0.0	66	10	0	0	0.0	0.0
D- / 1.2	5.6	N/A	9.56	3,302	6	0	0	82	12	10	0.0	19	10	0	0	0.0	0.0
D+ / 2.8	4.2	4.8	10.87	7,669	7	29	0	10	54	88	0.0	95	18	2,500	0	0.0	0.0

Data as of February 28, 2017

Fund Type	Fund Name	Ticker Symbol	Overall Investment Rating	Phone	Performance Rating/Pts	3 Mo	6 Mo	1Yr / Pct	3Yr / Pct	5Yr / Pct	Dividend Yield	Expense Ratio
MMF	Fidelity Tax Exempt MM Dly Mny	FDEXX	U	(800) 522-7297	U /	--	--	--	--	--	0.11	N/A
MMF	Fidelity Tax Exempt MM Premium	FZEXX	C	(800) 522-7297	D- / 1.4	0.10	0.20	0.30 /33	0.11 /16	0.07 /15	0.30	N/A
MMF	Fidelity Tax Exempt MM TxFr MM	FMOXX	C-	(800) 544-8544	D- / 1.2	0.07	0.14	0.19 /29	0.07 /13	0.05 /14	0.19	N/A
*MUN	Fidelity Tax Free Bond Fd	FTABX	B	(800) 544-8544	B / 8.1	1.98	-3.70	0.10 /24	3.89 /92	3.51 /88	3.28	0.46
GEI	Fidelity Total Bond Fund	FTBFX	B	(800) 544-8544	C+ / 6.8	1.85	-0.63	6.05 /70	3.31 /66	3.19 /60	2.85	0.45
MMT	Fidelity Treasury Mny Mkt Dly Mny	FDUXX	U	(800) 522-7297	U /	--	--	--	--	--	0.01	N/A
MMT	Fidelity Treasury Money Market Fund	FZFXX	D+	(800) 522-7297	E+ / 0.6	0.03	0.03	0.04 /20	0.02 / 7	0.02 / 7	0.04	N/A
MMT	Fidelity Treasury Only Money Market	FDLXX	D+	(800) 544-8544	E+ / 0.6	0.02	0.02	0.03 /20	0.02 / 7	0.01 / 5	0.03	N/A
GEI	Fidelity US Bond Idx F	FUBFX	C-	(800) 544-8544	C / 4.7	1.11	-2.21	1.28 /43	2.63 /55	2.22 /45	2.50	0.03
COI	Fidelity US Bond Idx Inst	FXSTX	C-	(800) 544-8544	C / 4.7	1.11	-2.21	1.27 /42	2.61 /54	2.21 /45	2.49	0.04
GEI	Fidelity US Bond Idx Inv	FBIDX	D+	(800) 544-8544	C / 4.4	0.99	-2.35	1.15 /41	2.47 /51	2.04 /43	2.37	0.15
COI	Fidelity US Bond Idx IP	FXNAX	C-	(800) 544-8544	C / 4.7	1.11	-2.21	1.28 /43	2.63 /55	2.22 /45	2.50	0.03
COI	Fidelity US Bond Idx Pr	FSITX	C-	(800) 544-8544	C / 4.7	1.10	-2.22	1.26 /42	2.59 /54	2.18 /44	2.48	0.05
MMT	Fidelity US Treasury Income Port I	FSIXX	C-	(800) 544-8544	D- / 1.0	0.08	0.13	0.21 /26	0.08 /12	0.05 /11	0.21	N/A
GL	Fiera Cap STRONG Nations Curr Inst	SCAFX	E-	(855) 722-3637	E- / 0.0	1.08	-1.58	1.26 /42	-3.49 / 1	--	0.00	1.08
MMT	Financial Sq Treas Instr Cap	GCIXX	D+	(800) 526-7384	E+ / 0.7	0.05	0.06	0.09 /22	0.03 / 8	0.02 / 7	0.09	N/A
MMT	First American Gov Oblig D	FGDXX	U	(800) 677-3863	U /	0.01	0.01	0.01 /18	0.01 / 6	0.01 / 5	0.01	N/A
MMT	First American Gov Oblig Inst Inv	FVIXX	D+	(800) 677-3863	E+ / 0.9	0.07	0.10	0.16 /24	0.06 /10	0.04 /10	0.16	N/A
MMT	First American Gov Oblig Y	FGVXX	D+	(800) 677-3863	E+ / 0.6	0.04	0.04	0.04 /20	0.02 / 7	0.02 / 7	0.04	N/A
MMT	First American Gov Oblig Z	FGZXX	C-	(800) 677-3863	D- / 1.1	0.10	0.16	0.28 /28	0.10 /13	0.07 /13	0.28	N/A
MMT	First American Inst Prime Oblig T	FIUXX	C-	(800) 677-3863	E+ / 0.9	0.10	0.12	0.16 /24	0.07 /11	0.04 /10	0.16	N/A
MMT	First American Inst Prime Oblig V	FPIXX	C-	(800) 677-3863	D- / 1.1	0.12	0.17	0.26 /28	0.11 /13	0.06 /12	0.26	N/A
MMT	First American Inst Prime Oblig Y	FAIXX	D+	(800) 677-3863	E+ / 0.8	0.08	0.10	0.12 /23	0.05 /10	0.03 / 9	0.12	N/A
MMT	First American Inst Prime Oblig Z	FPZXX	C-	(800) 677-3863	D- / 1.4	0.14	0.22	0.36 /30	0.15 /15	0.10 /15	0.36	N/A
MMF	First American Retail T/F Oblig A	FTAXX	U	(800) 677-3863	U /	--	--	--	--	--	0.01	N/A
MMF	First American Retail T/F Oblig V	FHIXX	C-	(800) 677-3863	D- / 1.3	0.10	0.20	0.25 /31	0.08 /14	0.05 /14	0.25	N/A
MMF	First American Retail T/F Oblig Y	FFCXX	C-	(800) 677-3863	D- / 1.0	0.06	0.12	0.13 /26	0.04 /11	0.03 /11	0.13	N/A
MMF	First American Retail T/F Oblig Z	FTZXX	C	(800) 677-3863	D- / 1.5	0.12	0.25	0.34 /34	0.11 /16	0.07 /15	0.34	N/A
MMT	First American Treas Oblig Inst Inv	FLIXX	D+	(800) 677-3863	E+ / 0.8	0.07	0.09	0.13 /23	0.05 /10	0.03 / 9	0.13	N/A
MMT	First American Treas Oblig Res	STSXX	U	(800) 677-3863	U /	--	--	--	--	--	0.01	N/A
MMT	First American Treas Oblig Y	FOCXX	D+	(800) 677-3863	E+ / 0.6	0.03	0.03	0.03 /20	0.01 / 6	0.01 / 5	0.03	N/A
MMT	First American Treas Oblig Z	FUZXX	C-	(800) 677-3863	D- / 1.1	0.10	0.15	0.25 /28	0.09 /12	0.06 /12	0.25	N/A
MMT	First American US Treas MM Inst Inv	FUIXX	D+	(800) 677-3863	E+ / 0.6	0.05	0.06	0.07 /21	0.02 / 7	0.01 / 5	0.07	N/A
MMT	First American US Treas Money Mkt	FOYXX	U	(800) 677-3863	U /	0.01	0.01	0.01 /18	--	--	0.01	N/A
MMT	First American US Treas Money Mkt	FOZXX	C-	(800) 677-3863	E+ / 0.9	0.07	0.12	0.17 /25	0.06 /11	0.04 /10	0.17	N/A
GL	First Eagle High Yield A	FEHAX	D	(800) 334-2143	B / 7.6	3.19	5.18	23.99 /99	2.27 /48	4.84 /82	5.22	1.16
GL	First Eagle High Yield C	FEHCX	D	(800) 334-2143	B / 8.0	3.01	4.80	22.95 /98	1.52 /35	4.06 /73	4.76	1.91
COH	First Eagle High Yield I	FEHIX	C-	(800) 334-2143	B+ / 8.9	3.27	5.33	24.20 /99	2.56 /53	5.17 /86	5.76	0.87
MUI	First Inv CA Tax Exempt A	FICAX	D+	(800) 423-4026	C / 4.8	1.93	-3.01	-0.18 /15	3.65 /89	3.23 /84	3.30	1.05
MUN	First Inv CA Tax Exempt Adv	FICJX	A	(800) 423-4026	B+ / 8.3	1.94	-2.85	0.16 /27	3.98 /93	--	3.86	0.75
MUI	First Inv CA Tax Exempt B	FICFX	C	(800) 423-4026	C+ / 5.6	1.37	-3.82	-1.52 / 2	2.63 /76	2.30 /66	2.88	1.85
MUN	First Inv CA Tax Exempt Inst	FICLX	A	(800) 423-4026	B / 8.1	1.94	-2.85	0.16 /27	3.84 /91	--	3.86	0.73
MUI	First Inv CT Tax Exempt A	FICTX	C	(800) 423-4026	C- / 3.1	1.36	-2.14	-0.08 /16	2.84 /79	2.22 /64	3.08	1.06
MUN	First Inv CT Tax Exempt Adv	FICYX	A+	(800) 423-4026	C+ / 6.6	1.38	-2.06	0.11 /25	2.76 /78	--	3.34	0.92
MUI	First Inv CT Tax Exempt B	FICUX	B+	(800) 423-4026	C / 4.9	1.15	-2.54	-0.80 / 6	2.10 /65	1.48 /46	2.45	1.79
MUN	First Inv CT Tax Exempt Inst	FICZX	A+	(800) 423-4026	B- / 7.1	1.43	-1.96	0.19 /28	3.04 /82	--	3.29	0.75
*COH	First Inv Fund for Income A	FIFIX	D-	(800) 423-4026	C+ / 5.9	3.28	3.27	12.67 /84	2.78 /57	4.98 /84	4.52	1.23
COH ●	First Inv Fund for Income Adv	FIFKX	C	(800) 423-4026	B / 8.0	3.76	3.40	13.44 /86	3.05 /62	--	5.04	0.95
COH	First Inv Fund for Income B	FIFJX	D	(800) 423-4026	C+ / 6.7	3.03	2.78	12.06 /83	1.89 /41	4.15 /74	3.84	2.03
COH	First Inv Fund for Income Inst	FIFLX	C	(800) 423-4026	B / 8.2	3.81	3.51	13.66 /86	3.25 /65	--	5.26	0.80
USS	First Inv Government A	FIGVX	E+	(800) 423-4026	E- / 0.1	0.16	-2.74	-1.52 / 2	0.59 /22	0.41 /21	1.79	1.19
USL ●	First Inv Government Adv	FIHUX	D	(800) 423-4026	D / 1.8	0.24	-2.57	-1.23 / 3	0.91 /26	--	2.20	0.89

Risk Rating/Pts	3 Yr Avg Standard Deviation	Avg Dura-tion	NAV As of 2/28/17	Total $(Mil)	Cash %	Gov. Bond %	Muni. Bond %	Corp. Bond %	Other %	Portfolio Turnover Ratio	Avg Coupon Rate	Manager Quality Pct	Manager Tenure (Years)	Initial Purch. $	Additional Purch. $	Front End Load	Back End Load
U /	N/A	N/A	1.00	142	100	0	0	0	0	0	0.1	41	6	1,000	0	0.0	0.0
A+ / 9.9	0.1	N/A	1.00	770	100	0	0	0	0	0	0.3	46	6	100,000	0	0.0	0.0
A+ / 9.9	N/A	N/A	1.00	3,920	100	0	0	0	0	0	0.2	44	6	5,000	0	0.0	0.0
C- / 3.8	3.6	6.6	11.33	3,153	2	0	97	0	1	9	0.0	46	7	25,000	0	0.0	0.0
C / 5.3	3.1	5.3	10.61	21,516	0	28	1	32	39	134	0.0	73	13	2,500	0	0.0	0.0
U /	N/A	N/A	1.00	3,572	100	0	0	0	0	0	0.0	N/A	6	1,000	0	0.0	0.0
A+ / 9.9	N/A	N/A	1.00	8,684	100	0	0	0	0	0	0.0	39	6	2,500	0	0.0	0.0
A+ / 9.9	N/A	N/A	1.00	3,859	100	0	0	0	0	0	0.0	38	2	25,000	0	0.0	0.0
C / 5.2	3.1	5.6	11.55	3,633	0	42	1	24	33	63	0.0	35	3	0	0	0.0	0.0
C / 5.3	3.1	5.6	11.55	3,832	0	42	1	24	33	63	0.0	45	3	5,000,000	0	0.0	0.0
C / 5.3	3.0	5.6	11.55	369	0	42	1	24	33	63	0.0	30	3	2,500	0	0.0	0.0
C / 5.2	3.1	5.6	11.55	12,157	0	42	1	24	33	63	0.0	44	3	100,000,000	0	0.0	0.0
C / 5.2	3.1	5.6	11.55	8,335	0	42	1	24	33	63	0.0	41	3	10,000	0	0.0	0.0
A+ / 9.9	N/A	N/A	1.00	7,734	100	0	0	0	0	0	0.2	44	N/A	1,000,000	0	0.0	0.0
D / 2.0	5.0	N/A	16.82	74	14	69	16	0	1	238	0.0	2	5	100,000	10,000	0.0	0.0
A+ / 9.9	N/A	N/A	1.00	582	100	0	0	0	0	0	0.1	39	N/A	10,000,000	0	0.0	0.0
U /	N/A	N/A	1.00	3,761	100	0	0	0	0	0	0.0	N/A	N/A	0	0	0.0	0.0
A+ / 9.9	N/A	N/A	1.00	1,438	100	0	0	0	0	0	0.2	43	N/A	0	0	0.0	0.0
A+ / 9.9	N/A	N/A	1.00	7,647	100	0	0	0	0	0	0.0	38	N/A	0	0	0.0	0.0
A+ / 9.9	N/A	N/A	1.00	14,765	100	0	0	0	0	0	0.3	N/A	N/A	10,000,000	0	0.0	0.0
A+ / 9.9	N/A	N/A	1.00	109	100	0	0	0	0	0	0.2	43	N/A	0	0	0.0	0.0
A+ / 9.9	N/A	N/A	1.00	58	100	0	0	0	0	0	0.3	N/A	N/A	0	0	0.0	0.0
A+ / 9.9	N/A	N/A	1.00	332	100	0	0	0	0	0	0.1	41	N/A	0	0	0.0	0.0
A+ / 9.9	0.1	N/A	1.00	253	100	0	0	0	0	0	0.4	49	N/A	10,000,000	0	0.0	0.0
U /	N/A	N/A	1.00	37	100	0	0	0	0	0	0.0	N/A	N/A	2,500	100	0.0	0.0
A+ / 9.9	N/A	N/A	1.00	1	100	0	0	0	0	0	0.3	46	N/A	0	0	0.0	0.0
A+ / 9.9	N/A	N/A	1.00	298	100	0	0	0	0	0	0.1	41	N/A	0	0	0.0	0.0
A+ / 9.9	0.1	N/A	1.00	49	100	0	0	0	0	0	0.3	46	N/A	10,000,000	0	0.0	0.0
A+ / 9.9	N/A	N/A	1.00	677	100	0	0	0	0	0	0.1	41	N/A	0	0	0.0	0.0
U /	N/A	N/A	1.00	101	100	0	0	0	0	0	0.0	N/A	N/A	0	0	0.0	0.0
A+ / 9.9	N/A	N/A	1.00	2,654	100	0	0	0	0	0	0.0	38	N/A	0	0	0.0	0.0
A+ / 9.9	N/A	N/A	1.00	4,861	100	0	0	0	0	0	0.3	46	N/A	10,000,000	0	0.0	0.0
A+ / 9.9	N/A	N/A	1.00	33	100	0	0	0	0	0	0.1	39	N/A	0	0	0.0	0.0
U /	N/A	N/A	1.00	624	100	0	0	0	0	0	0.0	N/A	N/A	0	0	0.0	0.0
A+ / 9.9	N/A	N/A	1.00	300	100	0	0	0	0	0	0.2	43	N/A	10,000,000	0	0.0	0.0
E+ / 0.7	7.2	4.5	9.08	141	8	0	0	77	15	37	0.0	90	N/A	2,500	100	4.5	0.0
E+ / 0.7	7.1	4.5	9.07	108	8	0	0	77	15	37	0.0	85	N/A	2,500	100	0.0	0.0
E / 0.5	7.1	4.5	9.08	301	8	0	0	77	15	37	0.0	1	N/A	1,000,000	100	0.0	0.0
C / 5.1	3.1	4.6	12.63	50	0	0	99	0	1	76	5.2	60	26	1,000	0	5.8	0.0
C / 5.2	3.1	4.6	12.60	6	0	0	99	0	1	76	5.2	70	26	1,000	0	0.0	0.0
C / 5.0	3.1	4.6	12.46	N/A	0	0	99	0	1	76	5.2	18	26	1,000	0	0.0	0.0
C / 5.1	3.1	4.6	12.60	N/A	0	0	99	0	1	76	5.2	65	26	2,000,000	0	0.0	0.0
B / 7.8	2.3	3.4	13.22	35	1	0	98	0	1	25	5.0	60	26	1,000	0	5.8	0.0
B / 7.8	2.3	3.4	13.13	N/A	1	0	98	0	1	25	5.0	58	26	1,000	0	0.0	0.0
B / 7.8	2.3	3.4	13.22	N/A	1	0	98	0	1	25	5.0	26	26	1,000	0	0.0	0.0
B / 7.8	2.3	3.4	13.32	N/A	1	0	98	0	1	25	5.0	66	26	2,000,000	0	0.0	0.0
D / 1.9	4.8	4.0	2.50	569	0	1	0	90	9	55	9.4	15	8	1,000	0	5.8	0.0
D / 1.8	4.8	4.0	2.50	61	0	1	0	90	9	55	9.4	20	8	1,000	0	0.0	0.0
D / 1.9	4.6	4.0	2.50	3	0	1	0	90	9	55	9.4	5	8	1,000	0	0.0	0.0
D / 1.8	5.0	4.0	2.51	76	0	1	0	90	9	55	9.4	23	8	2,000,000	0	0.0	0.0
B / 7.8	2.3	4.8	10.46	243	1	29	0	0	70	97	3.2	16	5	1,000	0	5.8	0.0
B / 7.8	2.3	4.8	10.48	68	1	29	0	0	70	97	3.2	28	5	1,000	0	0.0	0.0

					PERFORMANCE						Incl. in Returns	
	99 Pct = Best 0 Pct = Worst		Overall			Total Return % through 2/28/17					Dividend	Expense
		Ticker	Investment		Perfor- mance				Annualized			
Fund Type	Fund Name	Symbol	Rating	Phone	Rating/Pts	3 Mo	6 Mo	1Yr / Pct	3Yr / Pct	5Yr / Pct	Yield	Ratio
USS	First Inv Government B	FIGYX	E+	(800) 423-4026	E- / 0.2	-0.14	-3.23	-2.43 / 0	-0.24 / 4	-0.38 / 3	1.06	2.02
USL	First Inv Government Inst	FIHVX	D	(800) 423-4026	D / 2.2	0.29	-2.21	-0.75 / 6	1.13 /30	--	2.38	0.76
COI	First Inv Investment Grade A	FIIGX	D-	(800) 423-4026	C- / 3.1	1.50	-1.56	4.31 /64	2.67 /55	3.20 /61	3.34	1.15
COI ●	First Inv Investment Grade Advisor	FIIJX	C	(800) 423-4026	C+ / 6.2	1.66	-1.43	4.72 /66	3.04 /62	--	3.73	0.84
COI	First Inv Investment Grade B	FIIHX	D-	(800) 423-4026	C- / 4.1	1.34	-1.99	3.50 /60	1.77 /39	2.36 /47	2.53	2.03
COI	First Inv Investment Grade Inst	FIIKX	C	(800) 423-4026	C+ / 6.2	1.61	-1.44	4.75 /66	3.06 /62	--	3.97	0.74
COH	First Inv Life Srs Fd For Income		C	(800) 423-4026	B / 8.2	3.65	3.65	13.42 /86	3.21 /64	5.35 /87	5.33	0.86
COI	First Inv Ltd Dur Hi Qual Bd A	FLDKX	U	(800) 423-4026	U /	0.46	-0.75	0.33 /30	--	--	2.11	1.32
COI	First Inv Ltd Dur Hi Qual Bd Adv	FLDLX	U	(800) 423-4026	U /	0.54	-0.59	0.64 /35	--	--	2.55	1.09
COI	First Inv Ltd Dur Hi Qual Bd Inst	FLDMX	U	(800) 423-4026	U /	0.57	-0.53	0.76 /37	--	--	2.67	0.92
MUI	First Inv MA Tax Exempt A	FIMAX	C-	(800) 423-4026	C- / 3.4	1.45	-2.48	-0.10 /16	3.02 /82	2.27 /65	3.14	1.13
MUN	First Inv MA Tax Exempt Adv	FIMHX	A+	(800) 423-4026	B- / 7.5	1.51	-2.34	0.24 /30	3.37 /86	--	3.59	0.85
MUI	First Inv MA Tax Exempt B	FIMGX	B	(800) 423-4026	C / 5.4	1.27	-2.82	-0.77 / 6	2.31 /69	1.57 /48	2.65	1.83
MUN	First Inv MA Tax Exempt Inst	FIMJX	A+	(800) 423-4026	B- / 7.3	1.51	-2.34	0.24 /30	3.25 /85	--	3.59	0.80
MUI	First Inv MI Tax Exempt A	FTMIX	B+	(800) 423-4026	C / 5.2	1.28	-1.73	0.06 /22	3.77 /91	2.45 /69	3.54	1.13
MUN	First Inv MI Tax Exempt Adv	FTMLX	A+	(800) 423-4026	B+ / 8.6	1.25	-1.61	0.22 /30	4.19 /94	--	3.99	0.92
MUI	First Inv MI Tax Exempt B	FTMJX	A+	(800) 423-4026	C+ / 6.8	1.11	-2.08	-0.70 / 7	3.02 /82	1.71 /52	3.07	1.84
MUN	First Inv MI Tax Exempt Inst	FTMMX	A+	(800) 423-4026	B+ / 8.4	1.35	-1.53	0.39 /35	3.97 /93	--	4.01	0.81
MUI	First Inv MN Tax Exempt A	FIMNX	D+	(800) 423-4026	D / 2.1	1.28	-1.67	-0.20 /14	2.30 /69	2.11 /61	3.22	1.11
MUN	First Inv MN Tax Exempt Adv	FIMQX	A+	(800) 423-4026	C+ / 6.4	1.36	-1.52	0.10 /24	2.59 /75	--	3.72	0.85
MUI	First Inv MN Tax Exempt B	FIMOX	C+	(800) 423-4026	C- / 3.8	1.08	-1.99	-0.90 / 5	1.54 /49	1.34 /43	2.62	1.86
MUN	First Inv MN Tax Exempt Inst	FIMRX	A+	(800) 423-4026	C+ / 6.4	1.44	-1.44	0.10 /24	2.56 /74	--	3.71	0.80
MUI	First Inv NC Tax Exempt A	FMTNX	C-	(800) 423-4026	D+ / 2.6	1.31	-1.79	-0.53 / 9	2.63 /76	1.98 /59	3.36	1.10
MUN	First Inv NC Tax Exempt Adv	FMTTX	A+	(800) 423-4026	C+ / 6.9	1.38	-1.65	-0.21 /14	2.96 /81	--	3.80	0.80
MUI	First Inv NC Tax Exempt B	FMTQX	B	(800) 423-4026	C- / 4.2	1.06	-2.22	-1.30 / 2	1.82 /58	1.22 /40	2.84	1.88
MUN	First Inv NC Tax Exempt Inst	FMTUX	A+	(800) 423-4026	C+ / 6.7	1.38	-1.66	-0.21 /14	2.81 /79	--	3.81	0.79
MUI	First Inv NJ Tax Exempt A	FINJX	D+	(800) 423-4026	C- / 3.7	1.87	-2.62	0.45 /36	3.03 /82	2.24 /64	3.20	1.05
MUN	First Inv NJ Tax Exempt Adv	FINLX	A	(800) 423-4026	B / 7.6	1.96	-2.53	0.78 /42	3.36 /86	--	3.74	0.74
MUI	First Inv NJ Tax Exempt B	FINKX	C+	(800) 423-4026	C / 5.4	1.68	-3.01	-0.36 /12	2.23 /68	1.46 /45	2.66	1.84
MUN	First Inv NJ Tax Exempt Inst	FINNX	A-	(800) 423-4026	B- / 7.4	1.97	-2.46	0.73 /41	3.17 /84	--	3.77	0.74
MUI	First Inv NY Tax Exempt A	FNYFX	C+	(800) 423-4026	C- / 3.9	1.51	-2.25	-0.01 /17	3.20 /84	2.41 /69	3.51	1.01
MUN	First Inv NY Tax Exempt Adv	FNYHX	A+	(800) 423-4026	B / 7.8	1.64	-2.07	0.28 /32	3.51 /88	--	3.96	0.71
MUI	First Inv NY Tax Exempt B	FNYGX	A-	(800) 423-4026	C+ / 5.9	1.40	-2.54	-0.72 / 7	2.48 /73	1.68 /51	3.01	1.73
MUN	First Inv NY Tax Exempt Inst	FNYJX	A+	(800) 423-4026	B / 7.6	1.63	-2.07	0.28 /32	3.40 /87	--	3.95	0.69
MUI	First Inv OH Tax Exempt A	FIOHX	C+	(800) 423-4026	C- / 4.0	1.25	-2.12	-0.16 /15	3.28 /85	2.49 /70	3.14	1.10
MUN	First Inv OH Tax Exempt Adv	FIOKX	A	(800) 423-4026	C+ / 6.5	1.23	-2.30	-0.31 /13	2.78 /78	--	3.24	0.96
MUI	First Inv OH Tax Exempt B	FIOJX	B+	(800) 423-4026	C / 5.4	1.06	-2.57	-1.04 / 4	2.36 /70	1.63 /50	2.27	2.03
MUN	First Inv OH Tax Exempt Inst	FIOLX	A+	(800) 423-4026	B / 7.7	1.31	-2.05	0.03 /20	3.54 /88	--	3.26	0.79
MUI	First Inv OR Tax Exempt A	FTORX	D-	(800) 423-4026	C- / 3.1	1.82	-3.07	-0.24 /14	2.91 /80	1.98 /59	2.84	1.06
MUN	First Inv OR Tax Exempt Adv	FTOTX	A-	(800) 423-4026	B- / 7.2	1.93	-2.95	0.08 /23	3.20 /84	--	3.42	0.75
MUI	First Inv OR Tax Exempt B	FTOBX	C	(800) 423-4026	C / 4.9	1.71	-3.17	-0.83 / 6	2.13 /66	1.24 /41	2.25	1.86
MUN	First Inv OR Tax Exempt Inst	FTOUX	A-	(800) 423-4026	B- / 7.1	1.88	-2.98	0.09 /24	3.10 /83	--	3.51	0.74
MUI	First Inv PA Tax Exempt A	FTPAX	B+	(800) 423-4026	C / 4.9	1.42	-1.20	0.78 /42	3.45 /87	2.83 /77	3.59	1.06
MUN	First Inv PA Tax Exempt Adv	FTPEX	A+	(800) 423-4026	B+ / 8.3	1.48	-1.08	1.02 /45	3.73 /90	--	4.05	0.78
MUI	First Inv PA Tax Exempt B	FTPDX	A+	(800) 423-4026	C+ / 6.3	1.25	-1.64	-0.08 /16	2.59 /75	2.02 /59	3.11	1.88
MUN	First Inv PA Tax Exempt Inst	FTPFX	A+	(800) 423-4026	B / 8.1	1.48	-1.08	0.95 /44	3.58 /89	--	4.06	0.75
*MUI	First Inv Tax Exempt Income A	FITAX	C	(800) 423-4026	C- / 3.4	1.35	-1.88	-0.03 /17	2.94 /81	2.59 /72	3.85	1.00
MUN	First Inv Tax Exempt Income Adv	FITDX	A+	(800) 423-4026	B- / 7.5	1.52	-1.65	0.33 /33	3.29 /85	--	4.35	0.69
MUI	First Inv Tax Exempt Income B	FITCX	B+	(800) 423-4026	C / 5.1	1.17	-2.24	-0.85 / 5	2.19 /67	1.84 /55	3.37	1.76
MUN	First Inv Tax Exempt Income Inst	FITEX	A+	(800) 423-4026	C+ / 6.8	1.42	-2.35	-0.40 /11	2.99 /82	--	4.37	0.67
MUI	First Inv Tax Exempt Opps A	EIITX	C	(800) 423-4026	C / 4.9	1.57	-2.62	-0.02 /17	3.72 /90	3.00 /80	3.14	1.04
MUN	First Inv Tax Exempt Opps Adv	EIIAX	A+	(800) 423-4026	B / 8.2	1.60	-2.51	0.15 /27	3.91 /92	--	3.44	0.86

● Denotes fund is closed to new investors
* Denotes fund is included in Section II

RISK			NET ASSETS		ASSET					Portfolio Turnover Ratio	Avg Coupon Rate	FUND MANAGER		MINIMUM		LOADS	
Risk Rating/Pts	3 Yr Avg Standard Deviation	Avg Dura-tion	NAV As of 2/28/17	Total $(Mil)	Cash %	Gov. Bond %	Muni. Bond %	Corp. Bond %	Other %			Manager Quality Pct	Manager Tenure (Years)	Initial Purch. $	Additional Purch. $	Front End Load	Back End Load
B /7.8	2.3	4.8	10.43	2	1	29	0	0	70	97	3.2	5	5	1,000	0	0.0	0.0
B /7.8	2.3	4.8	10.54	1	1	29	0	0	70	97	3.2	36	5	2,000,000	0	0.0	0.0
C /4.7	3.2	5.4	9.61	464	1	1	0	97	1	37	7.7	30	8	1,000	0	5.8	0.0
C /4.6	3.3	5.4	9.66	91	1	1	0	97	1	37	7.7	50	8	1,000	0	0.0	0.0
C /4.5	3.3	5.4	9.55	3	1	1	0	97	1	37	7.7	9	8	1,000	0	0.0	0.0
C /4.5	3.3	5.4	9.63	32	1	1	0	97	1	37	7.7	50	8	2,000,000	0	0.0	0.0
D /1.9	4.7	N/A	6.17	103	0	1	0	90	9	45	0.0	26	8	0	0	0.0	0.0
U /	N/A	2.7	9.50	58	3	8	0	58	31	54	3.5	N/A	3	1,000	0	5.8	0.0
U /	N/A	2.7	9.53	54	3	8	0	58	31	54	3.5	N/A	3	1,000	0	0.0	0.0
U /	N/A	2.7	9.54	23	3	8	0	58	31	54	3.5	N/A	3	2,000,000	0	0.0	0.0
C+ /6.7	2.8	3.9	11.74	23	1	0	98	0	1	14	5.1	51	26	1,000	0	5.8	0.0
C+ /6.8	2.8	3.9	11.77	1	1	0	98	0	1	14	5.1	63	26	1,000	0	0.0	0.0
C+ /6.9	2.7	3.9	11.71	N/A	1	0	98	0	1	14	5.1	21	26	1,000	0	0.0	0.0
C+ /6.8	2.8	3.9	11.77	N/A	1	0	98	0	1	14	5.1	60	26	2,000,000	0	0.0	0.0
B- /7.5	2.5	3.4	11.98	19	2	0	97	0	1	32	5.3	79	26	1,000	0	5.8	0.0
B- /7.4	2.6	3.4	12.02	N/A	2	0	97	0	1	32	5.3	83	26	1,000	0	0.0	0.0
B- /7.5	2.6	3.4	11.93	N/A	2	0	97	0	1	32	5.3	64	26	1,000	0	0.0	0.0
B- /7.4	2.6	3.4	11.97	N/A	2	0	97	0	1	32	5.3	81	26	2,000,000	0	0.0	0.0
B /8.1	2.1	2.9	11.95	20	0	0	100	0	0	20	5.1	51	26	1,000	0	5.8	0.0
B /8.1	2.1	2.9	11.95	1	0	0	100	0	0	20	5.1	61	26	1,000	0	0.0	0.0
B /8.2	2.1	2.9	11.89	N/A	0	0	100	0	0	20	5.1	19	26	1,000	0	0.0	0.0
B /8.1	2.1	2.9	11.97	N/A	0	0	100	0	0	20	5.1	60	26	2,000,000	0	0.0	0.0
B /8.2	2.1	3.1	13.22	24	0	0	100	0	0	10	5.1	64	25	1,000	0	5.8	0.0
B /8.1	2.1	3.1	13.25	3	0	0	100	0	0	10	5.1	72	25	1,000	0	0.0	0.0
B /8.2	2.1	3.1	13.18	N/A	0	0	100	0	0	10	5.1	28	25	1,000	0	0.0	0.0
B /8.1	2.1	3.1	13.22	N/A	0	0	100	0	0	10	5.1	68	25	2,000,000	0	0.0	0.0
C+ /6.0	2.9	4.4	12.75	48	0	0	99	0	1	48	5.3	37	26	1,000	0	5.8	0.0
C+ /5.6	3.0	4.4	12.73	2	0	0	99	0	1	48	5.3	54	26	1,000	0	0.0	0.0
C+ /5.8	2.9	4.4	12.68	N/A	0	0	99	0	1	48	5.3	14	26	1,000	0	0.0	0.0
C+ /5.7	3.0	4.4	12.71	N/A	0	0	99	0	1	48	5.3	N/A	26	2,000,000	0	0.0	0.0
B- /7.5	2.5	4.0	14.26	154	1	0	98	0	1	36	5.1	64	26	1,000	0	5.8	0.0
B- /7.5	2.5	4.0	14.26	7	1	0	98	0	1	36	5.1	72	26	1,000	0	0.0	0.0
B- /7.5	2.6	4.0	14.24	1	1	0	98	0	1	36	5.1	31	26	1,000	0	0.0	0.0
B- /7.5	2.6	4.0	14.28	N/A	1	0	98	0	1	36	5.1	69	26	2,000,000	0	0.0	0.0
B /7.7	2.4	3.3	12.38	21	1	0	98	0	1	29	5.1	70	26	1,000	0	5.8	0.0
B- /7.5	2.5	3.3	12.19	N/A	1	0	98	0	1	29	5.1	53	26	1,000	0	0.0	0.0
B /7.6	2.5	3.3	12.36	N/A	1	0	98	0	1	29	5.1	32	26	1,000	0	0.0	0.0
B /7.6	2.5	3.3	12.49	N/A	1	0	98	0	1	29	5.1	75	26	2,000,000	0	0.0	0.0
C+ /5.6	3.0	4.6	13.36	51	0	0	100	0	0	27	4.8	30	25	1,000	0	5.8	0.0
C+ /5.6	3.0	4.6	13.32	3	0	0	100	0	0	27	4.8	45	25	1,000	0	0.0	0.0
C+ /5.8	3.0	4.6	13.31	N/A	0	0	100	0	0	27	4.8	12	25	1,000	0	0.0	0.0
C+ /5.7	3.0	4.6	13.32	N/A	0	0	100	0	0	27	4.8	40	25	2,000,000	0	0.0	0.0
B /7.9	2.2	3.0	13.02	34	0	0	99	0	1	58	5.2	78	26	1,000	0	5.8	0.0
B /8.0	2.2	3.0	13.03	1	0	0	99	0	1	58	5.2	82	26	1,000	0	0.0	0.0
B /7.9	2.2	3.0	12.92	N/A	0	0	99	0	1	58	5.2	60	26	1,000	0	0.0	0.0
B /8.0	2.2	3.0	13.00	N/A	0	0	99	0	1	58	5.2	80	26	2,000,000	0	0.0	0.0
B /7.9	2.3	3.5	9.51	612	0	0	100	0	0	11	5.2	66	26	1,000	0	5.8	0.0
B /7.8	2.3	3.5	9.51	39	0	0	100	0	0	11	5.2	73	26	1,000	0	0.0	0.0
B /7.9	2.3	3.5	9.47	1	0	0	100	0	0	11	5.2	33	26	1,000	0	0.0	0.0
B /7.7	2.4	3.5	9.47	4	0	0	100	0	0	11	5.2	62	26	2,000,000	0	0.0	0.0
C+ /5.8	3.0	4.0	16.58	271	0	0	100	0	0	59	5.2	67	26	1,000	0	5.8	0.0
C+ /6.0	2.9	4.0	16.59	6	0	0	100	0	0	59	5.2	72	26	1,000	0	0.0	0.0

Data as of February 28, 2017

					PERFORMANCE							
99 Pct = Best					Perfor-	Total Return % through 2/28/17					Incl. in Returns	
0 Pct = Worst			Overall		mance				Annualized		Dividend	Expense
Fund Type	Fund Name	Ticker Symbol	Investment Rating	Phone	Rating/Pts	3 Mo	6 Mo	1Yr / Pct	3Yr / Pct	5Yr / Pct	Yield	Ratio
MUI	First Inv Tax Exempt Opps B	EIIUX	B+	(800) 423-4026	C+ / 6.6	1.34	-2.98	-0.77 / 6	2.97 /81	2.25 /65	2.63	1.78
MUN	First Inv Tax Exempt Opps Inst	EIINX	A+	(800) 423-4026	B+ / 8.3	1.65	-2.45	0.27 /31	3.93 /92	--	3.42	0.71
MUI	First Inv VA Tax Exempt A	FIVAX	D	(800) 423-4026	D+ / 2.9	1.64	-3.05	-0.36 /12	2.83 /79	2.07 /60	2.90	1.05
MUN	First Inv VA Tax Exempt Adv	FIVCX	A-	(800) 423-4026	C+ / 6.8	1.74	-2.95	-0.15 /15	2.97 /81	--	3.14	0.96
MUI	First Inv VA Tax Exempt B	FIVBX	D+	(800) 423-4026	C- / 3.9	1.39	-3.58	-1.51 / 2	1.77 /56	1.13 /38	2.07	2.01
MUN	First Inv VA Tax Exempt Inst	FIVDX	A-	(800) 423-4026	C+ / 6.9	1.72	-2.93	-0.07 /16	3.00 /82	--	3.12	0.73
LP	First Investors Floating Rate A	FRFDX	C	(800) 423-4026	C- / 3.0	1.22	2.18	7.12 /73	1.84 /40	--	2.90	1.33
LP	First Investors Floating Rate Adv	FRFEX	A	(800) 423-4026	C+ / 5.7	1.16	2.28	7.33 /73	2.02 /43	--	3.27	1.03
LP	First Investors Floating Rate Inst	FRFNX	A	(800) 423-4026	C+ / 6.1	1.21	2.37	7.54 /73	2.29 /48	--	3.46	0.90
GL	First Investors Intl Opptys Bd A	FIOBX	E-	(800) 423-4026	E- / 0.1	3.40	-3.81	3.46 /59	-1.42 / 2	--	0.18	1.38
GL ●	First Investors Intl Opptys Bd Adv	FIODX	E-	(800) 423-4026	E / 0.3	3.50	-3.58	3.69 /61	-1.13 / 3	--	0.19	1.04
GL	First Investors Intl Opptys Bd Inst	FIOEX	E-	(800) 423-4026	E / 0.4	3.60	-3.46	4.04 /62	-0.97 / 3	--	0.20	0.90
GEN ●	First Investors Strategic Inc Adv	FSIHX	C	(800) 423-4026	C+ / 5.9	2.34	1.31	7.21 /73	2.09 /45	--	3.39	0.86
MUN	First Security Municipal Bond A	FSARX	U		U /	2.55	-4.01	-1.07 / 4	--	--	2.28	9.13
MUN	First Security Municipal Bond Inst	FIFSX	U		U /	2.55	-4.01	-0.97 / 4	--	--	2.32	9.13
LP	First Trust Short Duration HI A	FDHAX	C+	(800) 621-1675	C+ / 6.5	2.75	2.61	10.61 /80	3.04 /62	--	3.91	1.26
LP	First Trust Short Duration HI C	FDHCX	C+	(800) 621-1675	C+ / 6.7	2.57	2.36	9.93 /79	2.30 /48	--	3.43	2.01
LP	First Trust Short Duration HI I	FDHIX	B+	(800) 621-1675	B / 7.8	2.82	2.87	11.03 /81	3.34 /66	--	4.42	1.01
GEI	First Western Fixed Income Inst	FWFIX	A+	(800) 292-6775	C+ / 6.0	1.35	-0.36	3.33 /59	3.03 /61	--	2.83	0.95
COH	First Western Sh Dur Hi Yld Cr Inst	FWSHX	U	(800) 292-6775	U /	4.18	5.60	17.10 /92	--	--	5.80	2.39
COI	First Western Sht Duration Bd Inst	FWSBX	A	(800) 292-6775	C / 4.3	0.87	0.76	2.73 /55	1.85 /40	--	2.30	0.89
* GEI	FPA New Income Inc	FPNIX	B-	(800) 982-4372	D+ / 2.8	0.96	1.05	2.94 /56	1.30 /32	1.41 /33	2.30	0.58
* USS	Franklin Adjustable US Govt Sec A	FISAX	D	(800) 342-5236	E / 0.3	0.19	0.36	0.50 /33	-0.04 / 5	0.20 /18	1.54	0.91
GEI	Franklin Adjustable US Govt Sec A1	FAUGX	U	(800) 342-5236	U /	0.24	0.57	0.67 /36	--	--	1.71	0.75
USS	Franklin Adjustable US Govt Sec Adv	FAUZX	C	(800) 342-5236	D / 1.7	0.26	0.62	0.76 /37	0.22 /17	0.45 /21	1.84	0.66
USS	Franklin Adjustable US Govt Sec C	FCSCX	D	(800) 342-5236	E / 0.4	0.23	0.30	0.24 /27	-0.39 / 4	-0.20 / 4	1.20	1.31
GEI	Franklin Adjustable US Govt Sec R6		C	(800) 342-5236	D / 1.6	0.29	0.55	0.87 /38	0.18 /16	--	1.94	0.53
MUS	Franklin Alabama Tax-Free Inc A	FRALX	A-	(800) 342-5236	C+ / 6.3	1.56	-1.84	1.67 /54	3.63 /89	2.76 /75	3.26	0.71
MUS	Franklin Alabama Tax-Free Inc C	FALEX	A+	(800) 342-5236	B- / 7.3	1.42	-2.08	1.11 /46	3.06 /83	2.19 /63	2.82	1.26
*MUS	Franklin Arizona Tax-Free Inc A	FTAZX	C+	(800) 342-5236	C+ / 6.0	1.45	-2.59	0.75 /41	3.66 /90	2.91 /78	3.34	0.62
MUS	Franklin Arizona Tax-Free Inc Adv	FAZZX	A	(800) 321-8563	B / 8.1	1.48	-2.53	0.85 /43	3.76 /90	3.03 /80	3.59	0.52
MUS	Franklin Arizona Tax-Free Inc C	FAZIX	B	(800) 342-5236	B- / 7.0	1.29	-2.91	0.19 /28	3.07 /83	2.34 /67	2.87	1.17
*MUS	Franklin CA Interm Tax-Free A	FKCIX	C-	(800) 342-5236	C+ / 5.7	2.03	-3.06	-0.43 /11	3.07 /83	2.88 /78	2.63	0.63
MUS	Franklin CA Interm Tax-Free Adv	FRCZX	B-	(800) 321-8563	B- / 7.1	2.05	-3.01	-0.33 /12	3.16 /84	2.97 /79	2.78	0.53
MUS	Franklin CA Interm Tax-Free C	FCCIX	C-	(800) 342-5236	C+ / 5.9	1.97	-3.24	-0.90 / 5	2.52 /74	2.32 /67	2.11	1.18
* MUH	Franklin California H/Y Muni A	FCAMX	C+	(800) 342-5236	B+ / 8.9	2.57	-4.65	1.16 /47	5.83 /98	5.23 /98	3.53	0.65
MUH	Franklin California H/Y Muni Adv	FVCAX	B	(800) 321-8563	A+ / 9.7	2.50	-4.58	1.26 /48	5.93 /98	5.35 /98	3.78	0.55
MUH	Franklin California H/Y Muni C	FCAHX	B	(800) 342-5236	A / 9.4	2.41	-4.79	0.69 /40	5.28 /98	4.68 /97	3.09	1.20
*MUS	Franklin California Tx-Fr Inc A	FKTFX	C+	(800) 342-5236	B / 7.9	2.71	-3.84	1.22 /48	4.88 /97	4.25 /95	3.42	0.57
MUS	Franklin California Tx-Fr Inc Adv	FCAVX	B+	(800) 321-8563	A / 9.4	2.89	-3.80	1.32 /49	4.99 /97	4.36 /96	3.69	0.48
MUS	Franklin California Tx-Fr Inc C	FRCTX	B	(800) 342-5236	B+ / 8.7	2.71	-4.13	0.65 /39	4.35 /95	3.68 /90	3.00	1.13
*MUS	Franklin Colorado Tax-Free Inc A	FRCOX	B+	(800) 342-5236	C+ / 6.7	1.79	-1.95	1.30 /49	3.88 /92	2.87 /77	3.58	0.65
MUS	Franklin Colorado Tax-Free Inc Adv	FCOZX	A+	(800) 321-8563	B+ / 8.6	1.82	-1.89	1.40 /50	3.99 /93	2.98 /79	3.84	0.55
MUS	Franklin Colorado Tax-Free Inc C	FCOIX	A	(800) 342-5236	B- / 7.5	1.63	-2.19	0.73 /41	3.30 /86	2.30 /66	3.14	1.20
MUS	Franklin CT Tax-Free Inc A	FXCTX	C	(800) 342-5236	C / 4.4	1.24	-2.53	0.82 /42	2.91 /80	1.87 /56	3.31	0.69
MUS	Franklin CT Tax-Free Inc Adv	FCNZX	A	(800) 321-8563	B- / 7.2	1.36	-2.39	1.00 /45	3.04 /83	1.99 /59	3.55	0.59
MUS	Franklin CT Tax-Free Inc C	FCTIX	B	(800) 342-5236	C+ / 5.7	1.09	-2.78	0.25 /31	2.33 /70	1.32 /43	2.86	1.24
EM	Franklin Emg Mkt Debt Opportunities	FEMDX	C+	(800) 342-5236	A / 9.5	5.64	3.91	18.26 /94	4.50 /81	4.72 /81	0.00	1.09
* MUN	Franklin Fdrl Lmtd Trm T/F Inc A	FFTFX	D	(800) 342-5236	E / 0.4	0.59	-0.09	0.05 /21	0.45 /23	0.69 /28	0.80	0.69
MUN	Franklin Fdrl Lmtd Trm T/F Inc Adv	FTFZX	C+	(800) 342-5236	D+ / 2.6	0.71	-0.03	0.28 /32	0.63 /27	0.85 /32	0.95	0.54
* MUN	Franklin Fed Interm-Trm T/F Inc A	FKITX	C-	(800) 342-5236	C- / 4.0	1.81	-2.45	-0.71 / 7	2.28 /69	2.17 /63	2.45	0.66
MUN	Franklin Fed Interm-Trm T/F Inc Adv	FITZX	B-	(800) 321-8563	C+ / 5.6	1.75	-2.48	-0.62 / 8	2.34 /70	2.26 /65	2.60	0.56

● Denotes fund is closed to new investors
* Denotes fund is included in Section II

I. Index of Bond and Money Market Mutual Funds

RISK			NET ASSETS		ASSET					Portfolio Turnover Ratio	Avg Coupon Rate	FUND MANAGER		MINIMUM		LOADS	
Risk Rating/Pts	3 Yr Avg Standard Deviation	Avg Dura-tion	NAV As of 2/28/17	Total $(Mil)	Cash %	Gov. Bond %	Muni. Bond %	Corp. Bond %	Other %			Manager Quality Pct	Manager Tenure (Years)	Initial Purch. $	Additional Purch. $	Front End Load	Back End Load
C+ / 5.8	2.9	4.0	16.49	2	0	0	100	0	0	59	5.2	35	26	1,000	0	0.0	0.0
C+ / 5.9	2.9	4.0	16.67	N/A	0	0	100	0	0	59	5.2	72	26	2,000,000	0	0.0	0.0
C+ / 6.4	2.8	4.7	12.89	46	1	0	98	0	1	26	5.1	32	26	1,000	0	5.8	0.0
C+ / 6.1	2.9	4.7	12.87	N/A	1	0	98	0	1	26	5.1	36	26	1,000	0	0.0	0.0
C+ / 6.1	2.9	4.7	12.77	N/A	1	0	98	0	1	26	5.1	8	26	1,000	0	0.0	0.0
C+ / 6.3	2.9	4.7	12.97	N/A	1	0	98	0	1	26	5.1	40	26	2,000,000	0	0.0	0.0
B / 7.9	2.2	N/A	9.69	65	7	0	0	46	47	38	0.0	80	4	1,000	0	5.8	0.0
B / 8.0	2.2	N/A	9.68	66	7	0	0	46	47	38	0.0	82	4	1,000	0	0.0	0.0
B / 8.0	2.2	N/A	9.67	20	7	0	0	46	47	38	0.0	84	4	2,000,000	0	0.0	0.0
E+ / 0.6	7.4	N/A	8.83	59	5	81	0	13	1	72	0.0	66	5	1,000	0	5.8	0.0
E+ / 0.6	7.4	N/A	8.88	57	5	81	0	13	1	72	0.0	73	5	1,000	0	0.0	0.0
E+ / 0.6	7.4	N/A	8.93	5	5	81	0	13	1	72	0.0	76	5	2,000,000	0	0.0	0.0
C / 4.6	3.3	N/A	9.45	1	9	14	5	54	18	49	0.0	69	4	1,000	0	0.0	0.0
U /	N/A	N/A	9.96	13	23	0	76	0	1	26	0.0	N/A	2	5,000	1,000	2.0	0.0
U /	N/A	N/A	9.97	2	23	0	76	0	1	26	0.0	N/A	2	25,000	1,000	0.0	0.0
C / 4.7	3.2	1.6	20.14	73	3	0	0	31	66	62	0.0	88	5	2,500	50	3.5	0.0
C / 4.6	3.3	1.6	20.12	23	3	0	0	31	66	62	0.0	82	5	2,500	50	0.0	0.0
C / 4.6	3.3	1.6	20.14	136	3	0	0	31	66	62	0.0	90	5	0	0	0.0	0.0
B+ / 8.4	1.9	N/A	9.77	66	4	9	2	40	45	38	0.0	80	5	1,000	100	0.0	0.0
U /	N/A	N/A	10.27	42	3	0	0	96	1	103	0.0	N/A	2	100,000	0	0.0	0.0
A+ / 9.6	0.8	N/A	9.95	132	3	0	2	48	47	45	0.0	78	4	1,000	100	0.0	0.0
A+ / 9.6	0.7	1.3	10.02	4,927	1	8	0	6	85	44	2.6	73	13	1,500	100	0.0	2.0
A+ / 9.8	0.4	0.8	8.37	632	3	0	0	0	97	11	2.7	33	26	1,000	0	2.3	0.0
U /	N/A	0.8	8.37	149	3	0	0	0	97	11	2.7	N/A	26	0	0	2.3	0.0
A+ / 9.9	0.4	0.8	8.38	212	3	0	0	0	97	11	2.7	51	26	1,000,000	0	0.0	0.0
A+ / 9.8	0.4	0.8	8.37	245	3	0	0	0	97	11	2.7	22	26	1,000	0	0.0	0.0
A+ / 9.8	0.4	0.8	8.38	2	3	0	0	0	97	11	2.7	47	26	0	0	0.0	0.0
C+ / 6.8	2.8	4.4	11.16	228	4	0	95	0	1	11	5.1	74	28	1,000	0	4.3	0.0
C+ / 6.8	2.8	4.4	11.30	56	4	0	95	0	1	11	5.1	59	28	1,000	0	0.0	0.0
C / 5.2	3.1	4.6	10.78	776	1	0	98	0	1	13	5.1	65	25	1,000	0	4.3	0.0
C / 5.1	3.1	4.6	10.81	80	1	0	98	0	1	13	5.1	68	25	1,000	0	0.0	0.0
C / 5.1	3.1	4.6	10.95	119	1	0	98	0	1	13	5.1	36	25	1,000	0	0.0	0.0
C / 4.3	3.4	5.2	11.93	940	0	0	99	0	1	4	5.1	23	25	1,000	0	2.3	0.0
C / 4.3	3.4	5.2	11.96	571	0	0	99	0	1	4	5.1	26	25	1,000	0	0.0	0.0
C- / 4.2	3.4	5.2	11.98	268	0	0	99	0	1	4	5.1	10	25	1,000	0	0.0	0.0
D / 1.8	4.7	7.0	10.64	1,367	0	0	99	0	1	12	5.5	75	23	1,000	0	4.3	0.0
D / 1.9	4.6	7.0	10.66	610	0	0	99	0	1	12	5.5	77	23	1,000	0	0.0	0.0
D / 1.9	4.6	7.0	10.72	368	0	0	99	0	1	12	5.5	63	23	1,000	0	0.0	0.0
D+ / 2.7	4.3	6.8	7.39	12,536	0	0	98	0	2	9	5.2	60	26	1,000	0	4.3	0.0
D+ / 2.6	4.3	6.8	7.38	1,328	0	0	98	0	2	9	5.2	62	26	1,000	0	0.0	0.0
D+ / 2.7	4.3	6.8	7.38	1,666	0	0	98	0	2	9	5.2	33	26	1,000	0	0.0	0.0
C+ / 6.1	2.9	4.1	11.66	560	0	0	99	0	1	5	5.2	74	25	1,000	0	4.3	0.0
C+ / 5.9	2.9	4.1	11.66	67	0	0	99	0	1	5	5.2	75	25	1,000	0	0.0	0.0
C+ / 5.9	2.9	4.1	11.79	115	0	0	99	0	1	5	5.2	59	25	1,000	0	0.0	0.0
C+ / 6.5	2.8	4.2	10.42	227	0	0	98	0	2	8	5.1	51	29	1,000	0	4.3	0.0
C+ / 6.3	2.9	4.2	10.42	22	0	0	98	0	2	8	5.1	54	29	1,000	0	0.0	0.0
C+ / 6.5	2.8	4.2	10.50	62	0	0	98	0	2	8	5.1	24	29	1,000	0	0.0	0.0
E+ / 0.7	7.0	4.3	11.31	505	7	46	4	31	12	22	6.8	97	11	1,000,000	0	0.0	0.0
A+ / 9.7	0.7	1.3	10.37	835	0	0	100	0	0	23	3.9	32	14	1,000	0	2.3	0.0
A+ / 9.7	0.7	1.3	10.37	284	0	0	100	0	0	23	3.9	43	14	1,000	0	0.0	0.0
C+ / 6.0	2.9	4.5	12.11	1,966	0	0	99	0	1	7	5.0	16	25	1,000	0	2.3	0.0
C+ / 6.1	2.9	4.5	12.13	1,914	0	0	99	0	1	7	5.0	17	25	1,000	0	0.0	0.0

| | | | | | | Total Return % through 2/28/17 | | | | | Incl. in Returns | |
| | 99 Pct = Best 0 Pct = Worst | | Overall | | Perfor- | | | | Annualized | | Dividend | Expense |
Fund Type	Fund Name	Ticker Symbol	Investment Rating	Phone	mance Rating/Pts	3 Mo	6 Mo	1Yr / Pct	3Yr / Pct	5Yr / Pct	Yield	Ratio
MUN	Franklin Fed Interm-Trm T/F Inc C	FCITX	D+	(800) 342-5236	C- / 4.0	1.67	-2.79	-1.25 / 3	1.71 /55	1.60 /49	1.94	1.21
*MUN	Franklin Federal Tax-Free Inc A	FKTIX	B	(800) 342-5236	C+ / 6.2	1.49	-2.54	0.56 /38	3.76 /90	3.21 /83	3.68	0.61
MUN	Franklin Federal Tax-Free Inc Adv	FAFTX	A+	(800) 321-8563	B+ / 8.4	1.51	-2.49	0.97 /44	3.97 /93	3.38 /86	4.26	0.51
MUN	Franklin Federal Tax-Free Inc C	FRFTX	A	(800) 342-5236	B- / 7.4	1.43	-2.74	0.34 /33	3.31 /86	2.72 /75	3.53	1.16
COI	Franklin Flexible Alpha Bond A	FABFX	U	(800) 342-5236	U /	-0.51	-0.71	1.52 /45	--	--	0.77	4.13
COI	Franklin Flexible Alpha Bond Adv	FZBAX	U	(800) 342-5236	U /	-0.62	-0.73	1.41 /44	--	--	0.79	3.88
COI	Franklin Flexible Alpha Bond C	FABDX	U	(800) 342-5236	U /	-0.73	-1.02	0.80 /37	--	--	0.47	4.53
COI	Franklin Flexible Alpha Bond R	FABMX	U	(800) 342-5236	U /	-0.62	-0.60	1.45 /44	--	--	0.73	4.38
COI	Franklin Flexible Alpha Bond R6	FABNX	U	(800) 342-5236	U /	-0.63	-0.73	1.42 /44	--	--	0.80	4.14
*LP	Franklin Floating Rate Dly-Acc A	FAFRX	B	(800) 342-5236	B- / 7.5	1.55	3.74	14.02 /87	3.19 /64	3.93 /71	4.01	0.86
LP	Franklin Floating Rate Dly-Acc Adv	FDAAX	A-	(800) 321-8563	B+ / 8.3	1.62	3.88	14.32 /87	3.41 /67	4.19 /75	4.35	0.61
LP	Franklin Floating Rate Dly-Acc C	FCFRX	B+	(800) 342-5236	B / 7.6	1.47	3.56	13.60 /86	2.79 /58	3.52 /66	3.73	1.26
LP	Franklin Floating Rate Dly-Acc R6	FFRDX	A	(800) 342-5236	B+ / 8.4	1.64	3.93	14.41 /87	3.49 /69	4.25 /75	4.43	0.73
*MUS	Franklin Florida Tax-Free Inc A	FRFLX	B	(800) 342-5236	C+ / 6.2	1.61	-1.77	1.02 /45	3.60 /89	2.41 /69	3.74	0.64
MUS	Franklin Florida Tax-Free Inc C	FRFIX	A	(800) 342-5236	B- / 7.1	1.46	-2.08	0.46 /36	3.03 /82	1.84 /55	3.28	1.19
MUS	Franklin Georgia Tax-Free Inc A	FTGAX	B	(800) 342-5236	C+ / 5.8	1.29	-2.36	0.68 /40	3.56 /88	2.83 /77	3.33	0.67
MUS	Franklin Georgia Tax-Free Inc C	FGAIX	A-	(800) 342-5236	C+ / 6.9	1.14	-2.60	0.12 /25	3.01 /82	2.26 /65	2.86	1.22
GL	Franklin Global Government Bond A	FGGAX	E	(800) 321-8563	E- / 0.0	0.47	-6.71	-3.77 / 0	-1.56 / 2	--	0.48	2.17
GL	Franklin Global Government Bond		E	(800) 321-8563	E- / 0.1	0.38	-6.62	-3.62 / 0	-1.44 / 2	--	0.65	1.92
GL	Franklin Global Government Bond C		E	(800) 321-8563	E- / 0.0	0.23	-7.00	-4.27 / 0	-2.14 / 2	--	0.20	2.57
GL	Franklin Global Government Bond R		E	(800) 321-8563	E- / 0.1	0.46	-6.47	-3.58 / 0	-1.81 / 2	--	0.26	2.42
GL	Franklin Global Government Bond R6		E	(800) 321-8563	E- / 0.1	0.39	-6.62	-3.60 / 0	-1.48 / 2	--	0.68	2.83
*COH	Franklin High Income A	FHAIX	D+	(800) 342-5236	B+ / 8.4	5.78	6.70	27.58 /99	2.20 /46	5.26 /86	5.34	0.79
COH	Franklin High Income Adv	FVHIX	C	(800) 321-8563	A / 9.3	5.81	6.76	26.95 /99	2.35 /49	5.41 /88	5.71	0.64
COH	Franklin High Income C	FCHIX	C-	(800) 342-5236	B+ / 8.8	5.58	6.35	26.60 /99	1.65 /37	4.79 /82	5.06	1.29
COH	Franklin High Income R	FHIRX	C-	(800) 342-5236	B+ / 8.9	5.58	6.38	26.60 /99	1.79 /39	4.91 /83	5.16	1.14
COH	Franklin High Income R6	FHRRX	C	(800) 342-5236	A / 9.4	6.43	7.42	27.98 /99	2.50 /52	5.52 /89	5.86	0.48
*MUH	Franklin High Yld Tax-Free Inc A	FRHIX	C	(800) 342-5236	B / 7.7	1.92	-3.54	1.19 /47	4.76 /96	3.74 /90	4.20	0.67
MUH	Franklin High Yld Tax-Free Inc Adv	FHYVX	B+	(800) 321-8563	A / 9.3	2.04	-3.47	1.38 /50	4.91 /97	3.85 /92	4.47	0.57
MUH	Franklin High Yld Tax-Free Inc C	FHYIX	B-	(800) 342-5236	B+ / 8.5	1.75	-3.74	0.62 /39	4.21 /94	3.17 /83	3.75	1.22
MUS	Franklin Kentucky Tax-Free Inc A	FRKYX	B+	(800) 342-5236	C+ / 5.6	1.26	-1.87	0.85 /43	3.38 /86	2.62 /73	3.46	0.76
MUS	Franklin Louisiana Tax-Free Inc A	FKLAX	C+	(800) 342-5236	C+ / 5.7	1.88	-2.37	0.43 /36	3.49 /88	2.49 /70	3.45	0.69
MUS	Franklin Louisiana Tax-Free Inc C	FLAIX	B	(800) 342-5236	C+ / 6.8	1.71	-2.69	-0.14 /15	2.93 /81	1.92 /57	2.98	1.24
*GEI	Franklin Low Dur Totl Return A	FLDAX	C+	(800) 342-5236	D+ / 2.7	0.97	1.17	3.85 /61	1.13 /30	1.40 /33	1.79	0.97
GEI	Franklin Low Dur Totl Return Adv	FLDZX	B+	(800) 321-8563	C- / 3.9	0.99	1.15	3.99 /62	1.34 /32	1.63 /37	1.97	0.72
COI	Franklin Low Dur Totl Return C	FLDCX	C+	(800) 342-5236	D+ / 2.9	0.80	0.92	3.39 /59	0.71 /23	--	1.48	1.37
COI	Franklin Low Dur Totl Return R6	FLRRX	B+	(800) 342-5236	C- / 4.2	1.01	1.27	4.15 /63	1.47 /35	1.68 /37	2.03	0.55
MUS	Franklin MA Tax-Free Inc A	FMISX	B	(800) 342-5236	C+ / 6.7	1.43	-2.54	0.61 /39	4.08 /93	2.81 /76	3.17	0.66
MUS	Franklin MA Tax-Free Inc Adv	FMAHX	A+	(800) 321-8563	B+ / 8.7	1.46	-2.49	0.71 /40	4.21 /94	2.91 /78	3.42	0.56
MUS	Franklin MA Tax-Free Inc C	FMAIX	A	(800) 342-5236	B / 7.7	1.37	-2.78	0.13 /26	3.56 /88	2.25 /65	2.71	1.21
MUS	Franklin Maryland Tax-Free Inc A	FMDTX	C	(800) 342-5236	C+ / 5.7	1.77	-2.23	1.30 /49	3.34 /86	2.20 /63	3.44	0.67
MUS	Franklin Maryland Tax-Free Inc Adv	FMDZX	A	(800) 321-8563	B / 7.9	1.80	-2.09	1.49 /51	3.47 /87	2.32 /67	3.69	0.57
MUS	Franklin Maryland Tax-Free Inc C	FMDIX	B	(800) 342-5236	C+ / 6.8	1.60	-2.46	0.72 /41	2.78 /78	1.64 /50	2.97	1.22
*MUI	Franklin MI Tax-Free Inc A	FTTMX	C	(800) 342-5236	C / 5.2	1.46	-2.33	1.23 /48	3.19 /84	2.43 /69	3.38	0.64
MUI	Franklin MI Tax-Free Inc C	FRMTX	B	(800) 342-5236	C+ / 6.4	1.31	-2.64	0.66 /40	2.61 /75	1.85 /55	2.92	1.19
MUI	Franklin Michigan Tax-Free Inc Adv	FMTFX	A	(800) 321-8563	B / 7.6	1.49	-2.35	1.32 /49	3.28 /85	2.53 /71	3.62	0.54
*MUS	Franklin Missouri Tax-Free Inc A	FRMOX	B-	(800) 342-5236	C / 5.5	1.33	-1.80	0.93 /44	3.30 /86	2.24 /64	3.45	0.64
MUS	Franklin Missouri Tax-Free Inc Adv	FRMZX	A+	(800) 321-8563	B / 7.8	1.36	-1.74	1.04 /45	3.44 /87	2.34 /67	3.71	0.54
MUS	Franklin Missouri Tax-Free Inc C	FMOIX	A-	(800) 342-5236	C+ / 6.7	1.19	-2.05	0.37 /34	2.77 /78	1.69 /51	3.01	1.19
*MUI	Franklin MN Tax-Free Inc A	FMINX	C+	(800) 342-5236	C / 4.3	1.83	-2.00	0.10 /24	2.84 /79	2.35 /67	2.92	0.64
MUI	Franklin MN Tax-Free Inc Adv	FMNZX	A+	(800) 321-8563	B- / 7.0	1.86	-1.94	0.20 /29	2.94 /81	2.45 /69	3.15	0.54
MUI	Franklin MN Tax-Free Inc C	FMNIX	B+	(800) 342-5236	C+ / 5.6	1.68	-2.25	-0.45 /10	2.27 /69	1.78 /53	2.46	1.19

● Denotes fund is closed to new investors
* Denotes fund is included in Section II

www.thestreetratings.com

RISK			NET ASSETS		ASSET							FUND MANAGER		MINIMUM		LOADS	
Risk Rating/Pts	3 Yr Avg Standard Deviation	Avg Dura-tion	NAV As of 2/28/17	Total $(Mil)	Cash %	Gov. Bond %	Muni. Bond %	Corp. Bond %	Other %	Portfolio Turnover Ratio	Avg Coupon Rate	Manager Quality Pct	Manager Tenure (Years)	Initial Purch. $	Additional Purch. $	Front End Load	Back End Load
C+ / 6.0	2.9	4.5	12.14	431	0	0	99	0	1	7	5.0	7	25	1,000	0	0.0	0.0
C+ / 5.9	2.9	4.3	12.05	9,552	0	0	99	0	1	6	5.3	69	30	1,000	0	4.3	0.0
C+ / 5.9	2.9	4.3	12.06	1,488	0	0	99	0	1	6	5.3	74	30	1,000	0	0.0	0.0
C+ / 5.9	2.9	4.3	12.05	1,443	0	0	99	0	1	6	5.3	57	30	1,000	0	0.0	0.0
U /	N/A	1.0	9.85	10	0	0	0	0	100	40	0.0	N/A	2	1,000	0	4.3	0.0
U /	N/A	1.0	9.84	N/A	0	0	0	0	100	40	0.0	N/A	2	0	0	0.0	0.0
U /	N/A	1.0	9.80	N/A	0	0	0	0	100	40	0.0	N/A	2	1,000	0	4.3	0.0
U /	N/A	1.0	9.84	N/A	0	0	0	0	100	40	0.0	N/A	2	1,000	0	0.0	0.0
U /	N/A	1.0	9.84	N/A	0	0	0	0	100	40	0.0	N/A	2	1,000,000	0	0.0	0.0
C / 4.5	3.3	0.2	8.89	1,465	7	0	0	60	33	34	4.8	87	4	1,000	0	2.3	0.0
C / 4.5	3.3	0.2	8.89	1,428	7	0	0	60	33	34	4.8	88	4	1,000,000	0	0.0	0.0
C / 4.5	3.3	0.2	8.89	590	7	0	0	60	33	34	4.8	84	4	1,000	0	0.0	0.0
C / 4.5	3.3	0.2	8.89	16	7	0	0	60	33	34	4.8	89	4	1,000,000	0	0.0	0.0
C+ / 6.2	2.9	4.0	10.88	643	0	0	99	0	1	5	5.3	71	30	1,000	0	4.3	0.0
C+ / 6.5	2.8	4.0	11.10	91	0	0	99	0	1	5	5.3	56	30	1,000	0	0.0	0.0
C+ / 6.2	2.9	4.4	11.99	433	1	0	98	0	1	5	5.1	67	21	1,000	0	4.3	0.0
C+ / 6.3	2.9	4.4	12.16	129	1	0	98	0	1	5	5.1	50	21	1,000	0	0.0	0.0
D+ / 2.7	4.2	N/A	9.06	12	6	93	0	0	1	38	0.0	24	4	1,000	0	4.3	0.0
D+ / 2.7	4.2	N/A	9.08	N/A	6	93	0	0	1	38	0.0	28	4	0	0	0.0	0.0
D+ / 2.7	4.2	N/A	9.02	N/A	6	93	0	0	1	38	0.0	10	4	1,000	0	0.0	0.0
D+ / 2.8	4.2	N/A	9.08	N/A	6	93	0	0	1	38	0.0	17	4	1,000	0	0.0	0.0
D+ / 2.8	4.2	N/A	9.06	N/A	6	93	0	0	1	38	0.0	26	4	1,000,000	0	0.0	0.0
E / 0.3	8.0	4.0	1.91	2,848	3	0	0	92	5	19	6.8	0	26	1,000	0	4.3	0.0
E / 0.3	7.9	4.0	1.91	474	3	0	0	92	5	19	6.8	0	26	1,000	0	0.0	0.0
E / 0.3	7.9	4.0	1.93	579	3	0	0	92	5	19	6.8	0	26	1,000	0	0.0	0.0
E / 0.4	7.7	4.0	1.94	204	3	0	0	92	5	19	6.8	0	26	1,000	0	0.0	0.0
E / 0.3	8.0	4.0	1.91	32	3	0	0	92	5	19	6.8	0	26	1,000	0	0.0	0.0
D+ / 2.6	3.9	5.7	10.25	5,039	0	0	99	0	1	12	5.6	71	24	1,000	0	4.3	0.0
D+ / 2.5	3.9	5.7	10.30	1,853	0	0	99	0	1	12	5.6	72	24	1,000	0	0.0	0.0
D+ / 2.6	3.9	5.7	10.44	1,024	0	0	99	0	1	12	5.6	55	24	1,000	0	0.0	0.0
B- / 7.5	2.6	4.0	11.01	168	1	0	98	0	1	6	5.2	72	21	1,000	0	4.3	0.0
C / 5.3	3.1	4.7	11.15	345	1	0	98	0	1	4	5.2	59	21	1,000	0	4.3	0.0
C / 5.3	3.1	4.7	11.32	68	1	0	98	0	1	4	5.2	31	21	1,000	0	0.0	0.0
A- / 9.2	1.0	1.4	9.86	1,471	0	21	0	43	36	45	2.4	71	13	1,000	0	2.3	0.0
A- / 9.2	1.0	1.4	9.90	298	0	21	0	43	36	45	2.4	75	13	1,000,000	0	0.0	0.0
A- / 9.2	1.0	1.4	9.83	208	0	21	0	43	36	45	2.4	51	13	1,000	0	0.0	0.0
A- / 9.2	1.0	1.4	9.91	512	0	21	0	43	36	45	2.4	74	13	1,000,000	0	0.0	0.0
C / 5.5	3.0	4.4	11.63	391	0	0	99	0	1	5	4.9	75	28	1,000	0	4.3	0.0
C / 5.4	3.0	4.4	11.63	19	0	0	99	0	1	5	4.9	77	28	1,000	0	0.0	0.0
C / 5.5	3.0	4.4	11.77	60	0	0	99	0	1	5	4.9	63	28	1,000	0	0.0	0.0
C / 5.2	3.1	4.6	11.10	361	1	0	98	0	1	10	5.1	57	28	1,000	0	4.3	0.0
C / 5.2	3.1	4.6	11.11	32	1	0	98	0	1	10	5.1	62	28	1,000	0	0.0	0.0
C / 5.2	3.1	4.6	11.31	115	1	0	98	0	1	10	5.1	31	28	1,000	0	0.0	0.0
C+ / 5.6	3.0	4.5	11.52	867	2	0	97	0	1	12	5.2	59	28	1,000	0	4.3	0.0
C+ / 5.7	3.0	4.5	11.69	142	2	0	97	0	1	12	5.2	31	28	1,000	0	0.0	0.0
C+ / 5.7	3.0	4.5	11.55	58	2	0	97	0	1	12	5.2	62	28	1,000	0	0.0	0.0
C+ / 6.5	2.8	4.2	11.74	871	0	0	99	0	1	8	5.1	66	25	1,000	0	4.3	0.0
C+ / 6.5	2.8	4.2	11.75	71	0	0	99	0	1	8	5.1	70	25	1,000	0	0.0	0.0
C+ / 6.5	2.8	4.2	11.86	170	0	0	99	0	1	8	5.1	49	25	1,000	0	0.0	0.0
B- / 7.2	2.6	3.9	12.27	709	0	0	100	0	0	9	4.7	46	28	1,000	0	4.3	0.0
B- / 7.2	2.6	3.9	12.28	149	0	0	100	0	0	9	4.7	52	28	1,000	0	0.0	0.0
B- / 7.3	2.6	3.9	12.40	223	0	0	100	0	0	9	4.7	22	28	1,000	0	0.0	0.0

Fund Type	Fund Name	Ticker Symbol	Overall Investment Rating	Phone	Performance Rating/Pts	Total Return % through 2/28/17 3 Mo	6 Mo	1Yr / Pct	Annualized 3Yr / Pct	5Yr / Pct	Incl. in Returns Dividend Yield	Expense Ratio
	99 Pct = Best / 0 Pct = Worst											
MMT	Franklin Money R6	FRRXX	U	(800) 342-5236	U /	0.01	0.01	0.01 /18	--	--	0.01	N/A
*MUS	Franklin NC Tax-Free Inc A	FXNCX	B-	(800) 342-5236	C /4.8	1.58	-1.68	1.18 /47	2.95 /81	1.83 /55	3.37	0.64
MUS	Franklin NC Tax-Free Inc Adv	FNCZX	A+	(800) 321-8563	B- /7.4	1.70	-1.62	1.28 /49	3.05 /83	1.95 /58	3.62	0.54
MUS	Franklin NC Tax-Free Inc C	FNCIX	A-	(800) 342-5236	C+ /6.1	1.51	-2.00	0.61 /39	2.37 /71	1.28 /42	2.91	1.19
*MUN	Franklin New Jersey TaxFree Inc A	FRNJX	C+	(800) 342-5236	C /5.0	1.22	-1.99	1.43 /51	3.04 /83	2.01 /59	3.76	0.64
MUN	Franklin New Jersey TaxFree Inc Adv	FNJZX	A+	(800) 321-8563	B- /7.5	1.25	-1.94	1.53 /52	3.14 /84	2.12 /62	4.02	0.54
MUN	Franklin New Jersey TaxFree Inc C	FNIIX	A-	(800) 342-5236	C+ /6.3	1.08	-2.23	0.94 /44	2.50 /73	1.46 /45	3.31	1.19
*MUS	Franklin New York Tax-Free Inc A	FNYTX	B	(800) 342-5236	C /4.7	1.34	-2.00	0.61 /39	3.02 /82	2.25 /65	3.44	0.61
MUS	Franklin New York Tax-Free Inc Adv	FNYAX	A+	(800) 321-8563	B- /7.4	1.46	-1.95	0.80 /42	3.15 /84	2.36 /68	3.68	0.51
MUS	Franklin New York Tax-Free Inc C	FNYIX	A	(800) 342-5236	C+ /6.1	1.29	-2.20	0.14 /26	2.46 /73	1.68 /51	3.02	1.16
*MUS	Franklin NY Interm Tax-Free Inc A	FKNIX	D+	(800) 342-5236	C /4.7	1.97	-2.79	-0.74 / 7	2.62 /76	2.23 /64	2.50	0.65
MUS	Franklin NY Interm Tax-Free Inc Adv	FNYZX	C+	(800) 321-8563	C+ /6.3	1.98	-2.74	-0.66 / 7	2.71 /77	2.34 /67	2.64	0.55
MUS	Franklin NY Interm Tax-Free Inc C	FKNCX	D+	(800) 342-5236	C /4.7	1.82	-3.06	-1.30 / 2	2.07 /64	1.67 /51	1.97	1.20
MUI	Franklin Ohio Ins Tax-Free Inc Adv	FROZX	A+	(800) 321-8563	B+ /8.4	1.70	-2.32	0.61 /39	3.98 /93	3.06 /81	3.35	0.53
*MUI	Franklin Ohio Tax-Free Inc A	FTOIX	B	(800) 342-5236	C+ /6.4	1.67	-2.37	0.51 /37	3.86 /91	2.94 /79	3.12	0.63
MUI	Franklin Ohio Tax-Free Inc C	FOITX	A-	(800) 342-5236	B- /7.3	1.43	-2.69	-0.05 /17	3.30 /86	2.37 /68	2.65	1.18
*MUS	Franklin Oregon Tax-Free Inc A	FRORX	C	(800) 342-5236	C+ /5.6	1.71	-2.53	0.89 /43	3.41 /87	2.23 /64	3.29	0.63
MUS	Franklin Oregon Tax-Free Inc Adv	FOFZX	A-	(800) 321-8563	B /7.8	1.74	-2.47	0.99 /45	3.51 /88	2.33 /67	3.53	0.53
MUS	Franklin Oregon Tax-Free Inc C	FORIX	B	(800) 342-5236	C+ /6.7	1.55	-2.76	0.32 /33	2.85 /79	1.67 /51	2.82	1.18
*MUS	Franklin PA Tax-Free Inc A	FRPAX	A-	(800) 342-5236	C+ /6.6	1.45	-1.72	1.61 /53	3.79 /91	2.61 /73	3.57	0.64
MUS	Franklin PA Tax-Free Inc Adv	FPFZX	A+	(800) 321-8563	B+ /8.5	1.48	-1.67	1.71 /54	3.89 /92	2.71 /74	3.82	0.54
MUS	Franklin PA Tax-Free Inc C	FRPTX	A	(800) 342-5236	B- /7.4	1.30	-2.07	1.04 /45	3.21 /85	2.04 /60	3.12	1.19
COI	Franklin Payout 2017 Advisor	FPOBX	U	(800) 342-5236	U /	0.33	0.43	1.74 /47	--	--	1.13	4.25
COI	Franklin Payout 2017 R6	FPOKX	U	(800) 342-5236	U /	0.33	0.43	1.74 /47	--	--	1.13	4.11
COI	Franklin Payout 2018 Advisor	FPODX	U	(800) 342-5236	U /	0.40	0.10	2.11 /50	--	--	1.39	4.17
COI	Franklin Payout 2018 R6	FPOLX	U	(800) 342-5236	U /	0.40	0.10	2.11 /50	--	--	1.39	4.03
COI	Franklin Payout 2019 Advisor	FPOFX	U	(800) 342-5236	U /	0.63	-0.16	2.74 /55	--	--	1.81	3.71
COI	Franklin Payout 2019 R6	FPOEX	U	(800) 342-5236	U /	0.62	-0.16	2.74 /55	--	--	1.81	3.57
COI	Franklin Payout 2020 Advisor	FPOHX	U	(800) 342-5236	U /	0.99	-0.76	3.23 /58	--	--	1.97	3.73
COI	Franklin Payout 2020 R6	FPOGX	U	(800) 342-5236	U /	0.99	-0.77	3.22 /58	--	--	1.97	3.59
COI	Franklin Payout 2021 Advisor	FPOJX	U	(800) 342-5236	U /	0.89	-1.52	2.59 /54	--	--	2.16	3.70
COI	Franklin Payout 2021 R6	FPOMX	U	(800) 342-5236	U /	0.88	-1.52	2.59 /54	--	--	2.16	3.56
GEI	Franklin Real Return A	FRRAX	E	(800) 342-5236	E /0.3	1.89	1.59	7.34 /73	-0.65 / 3	-0.07 / 4	0.00	1.12
GEI	Franklin Real Return Adv	FARRX	E+	(800) 342-5236	D+ /2.5	1.98	1.68	7.64 /74	-0.41 / 4	0.17 /17	0.00	0.87
GEI	Franklin Real Return C	FRRCX	E	(800) 342-5236	D- /1.3	1.81	1.30	6.86 /72	-1.08 / 3	-0.48 / 3	0.00	1.52
GEI	Franklin Real Return R6	FRRRX	E+	(800) 342-5236	D+ /2.7	1.98	1.78	7.85 /74	-0.26 / 4	0.29 /19	0.00	0.73
*GEN	Franklin Strategic Income A	FRSTX	D-	(800) 342-5236	C /4.7	3.10	2.45	11.31 /82	1.77 /39	3.34 /63	1.92	0.92
GEN	Franklin Strategic Income Adv	FKSAX	C-	(800) 321-8563	C+ /6.8	3.17	2.58	11.70 /83	2.03 /44	3.62 /67	2.25	0.67
GEN	Franklin Strategic Income C	FSGCX	D	(800) 342-5236	C+ /5.7	3.01	2.15	10.88 /81	1.33 /32	2.93 /56	1.62	1.32
GEN	Franklin Strategic Income R	FKSRX	D+	(800) 342-5236	C+ /6.0	3.06	2.23	11.09 /81	1.49 /35	3.08 /59	1.77	1.17
GL	Franklin Strategic Income R6	FGKNX	C	(800) 342-5236	C+ /6.9	3.20	2.65	11.75 /83	2.17 /46	3.64 /68	2.39	0.53
MTG	Franklin Strategic Mortgage Port A	FSMFX	C	(800) 342-5236	D+ /2.6	0.64	-0.99	0.88 /38	2.35 /49	2.80 /54	2.19	1.01
MTG ●	Franklin Strategic Mortgage Port A1	FSMIX	C+	(800) 342-5236	C- /3.1	0.72	-0.85	1.15 /41	2.64 /55	3.07 /59	2.44	0.76
MTG	Franklin Strategic Mortgage Port Ad	FSMZX	B+	(800) 342-5236	C /4.8	0.72	-0.75	1.15 /41	2.61 /54	3.06 /59	2.55	0.76
MTG	Franklin Strategic Mortgage Port C		B-		C- /3.7	0.46	-1.16	0.41 /31	1.95 /42	2.40 /48	1.92	1.41
MUS	Franklin Tennessee Muni Bond A	FRTIX	C+	(800) 342-5236	C /5.0	1.67	-2.27	0.86 /43	3.14 /84	2.29 /66	3.27	0.72
*GEI	Franklin Total Return A	FKBAX	D	(800) 342-5236	D+ /2.8	1.58	-1.38	3.78 /61	2.02 /43	2.45 /49	1.86	0.94
GEI	Franklin Total Return Adv	FBDAX	C+	(800) 321-8563	C /5.0	1.63	-1.28	4.12 /63	2.30 /48	2.72 /53	2.08	0.69
GEI	Franklin Total Return C	FCTLX	C-	(800) 342-5236	C- /3.9	1.40	-1.63	3.36 /59	1.60 /36	2.04 /43	1.74	1.34
GEI	Franklin Total Return R	FTRRX	C	(800) 342-5236	C- /4.2	1.53	-1.47	3.54 /60	1.77 /39	2.20 /45	1.81	1.19
COI	Franklin Total Return R6	FRERX	C+	(800) 342-5236	C /5.2	1.56	-1.23	4.19 /63	2.41 /50	2.81 /54	2.14	0.53
*USS	Franklin US Government Sec A	FKUSX	D	(800) 342-5236	E+ /0.8	0.14	-1.02	0.04 /20	1.46 /34	1.20 /30	2.99	0.76

● Denotes fund is closed to new investors
* Denotes fund is included in Section II

www.thestreetratings.com

RISK			NET ASSETS		ASSET							FUND MANAGER		MINIMUM		LOADS	
Risk Rating/Pts	3 Yr Avg Standard Deviation	Avg Dura-tion	NAV As of 2/28/17	Total $(Mil)	Cash %	Gov. Bond %	Muni. Bond %	Corp. Bond %	Other %	Portfolio Turnover Ratio	Avg Coupon Rate	Manager Quality Pct	Manager Tenure (Years)	Initial Purch. $	Additional Purch. $	Front End Load	Back End Load
U /	N/A	N/A	1.00	56	100	0	0	0	0	0	0.0	N/A	13	1,000	0	0.0	0.0
B- / 7.3	2.6	3.9	11.70	759	1	0	98	0	1	7	5.1	60	30	1,000	0	4.3	0.0
B- / 7.2	2.7	3.9	11.70	99	1	0	98	0	1	7	5.1	62	30	1,000	0	0.0	0.0
B- / 7.1	2.7	3.9	11.88	198	1	0	98	0	1	7	5.1	29	30	1,000	0	0.0	0.0
C+ / 6.7	2.8	3.7	11.45	752	0	0	99	0	1	5	5.2	59	29	1,000	0	4.3	0.0
C+ / 6.6	2.8	3.7	11.46	94	0	0	99	0	1	5	5.2	62	29	1,000	0	0.0	0.0
C+ / 6.7	2.8	3.7	11.60	217	0	0	99	0	1	5	5.2	32	29	1,000	0	0.0	0.0
B- / 7.5	2.5	3.7	11.21	3,970	1	0	98	0	1	4	5.2	64	28	1,000	0	4.3	0.0
B- / 7.5	2.6	3.7	11.22	281	1	0	98	0	1	4	5.2	66	28	1,000	0	0.0	0.0
B- / 7.4	2.6	3.7	11.20	641	1	0	98	0	1	4	5.2	35	28	1,000	0	0.0	0.0
C / 4.9	3.2	5.0	11.53	533	0	0	99	0	1	3	4.9	17	25	1,000	50	2.3	0.0
C / 4.9	3.2	5.0	11.56	393	0	0	99	0	1	3	4.9	19	25	1,000	0	0.0	0.0
C / 4.9	3.2	5.0	11.57	176	0	0	99	0	1	3	4.9	8	25	1,000	50	0.0	0.0
C+ / 5.6	3.0	4.2	12.57	125	0	0	99	0	1	7	5.0	72	18	1,000	0	0.0	0.0
C+ / 5.6	3.0	4.2	12.56	1,142	0	0	99	0	1	7	5.0	70	18	1,000	0	4.3	0.0
C+ / 5.7	3.0	4.2	12.72	330	0	0	99	0	1	7	5.0	55	18	1,000	0	0.0	0.0
C / 5.2	3.1	4.7	11.60	967	4	0	95	0	1	12	5.2	55	17	1,000	0	4.3	0.0
C / 5.2	3.1	4.7	11.61	78	4	0	95	0	1	12	5.2	58	17	1,000	0	0.0	0.0
C / 5.1	3.1	4.7	11.77	197	4	0	95	0	1	12	5.2	27	17	1,000	0	0.0	0.0
C+ / 6.4	2.8	4.0	10.12	951	0	0	100	0	0	5	5.2	76	31	1,000	0	4.3	0.0
C+ / 6.4	2.8	4.0	10.13	67	0	0	100	0	0	5	5.2	77	31	1,000	0	0.0	0.0
C+ / 6.4	2.8	4.0	10.24	283	0	0	100	0	0	5	5.2	63	31	1,000	0	0.0	0.0
U /	N/A	1.1	10.01	2	2	13	1	79	5	4	3.2	N/A	2	1,000,000	0	0.0	0.0
U /	N/A	1.1	10.01	2	2	13	1	79	5	4	3.2	N/A	2	1,000,000	0	0.0	0.0
U /	N/A	2.0	10.03	2	0	0	0	0	100	3	3.4	N/A	2	1,000,000	0	0.0	0.0
U /	N/A	2.0	10.03	2	0	0	0	0	100	3	3.4	N/A	2	1,000,000	0	0.0	0.0
U /	N/A	2.9	10.08	2	0	0	0	0	100	0	3.2	N/A	2	1,000,000	0	0.0	0.0
U /	N/A	2.9	10.08	2	0	0	0	0	100	0	3.2	N/A	2	1,000,000	0	0.0	0.0
U /	N/A	3.7	10.07	2	1	22	0	75	2	4	3.6	N/A	1	1,000,000	0	0.0	0.0
U /	N/A	3.7	10.07	2	1	22	0	75	2	4	3.6	N/A	1	1,000,000	0	0.0	0.0
U /	N/A	4.6	10.12	2	0	0	0	0	100	0	3.4	N/A	2	1,000	0	0.0	0.0
U /	N/A	4.6	10.12	2	0	0	0	0	100	0	3.4	N/A	2	1,000,000	0	0.0	0.0
C- / 3.0	4.1	1.5	10.24	164	5	68	0	7	20	32	2.7	3	13	1,000	0	4.3	0.0
C- / 3.0	4.1	1.5	10.29	37	5	68	0	7	20	32	2.7	4	13	1,000,000	0	0.0	0.0
C- / 3.1	4.0	1.5	10.13	39	5	68	0	7	20	32	2.7	1	13	1,000	0	0.0	0.0
C- / 3.0	4.1	1.5	10.31	6	5	68	0	7	20	32	2.7	5	13	1,000,000	0	0.0	0.0
C- / 3.3	4.0	3.6	9.78	4,007	0	15	1	48	36	88	4.8	69	23	1,000	0	4.3	0.0
C- / 3.2	4.0	3.6	9.79	962	0	15	1	48	36	88	4.8	74	23	1,000	0	0.0	0.0
C- / 3.2	4.0	3.6	9.77	1,443	0	15	1	48	36	88	4.8	55	23	1,000	0	0.0	0.0
C- / 3.1	4.0	3.6	9.74	158	0	15	1	48	36	88	4.8	61	23	1,000	0	0.0	0.0
C- / 3.2	4.0	3.6	9.79	474	0	15	1	48	36	88	4.8	89	23	1,000,000	0	0.0	0.0
B+ / 8.4	1.9	2.5	9.35	29	0	6	0	0	94	552	3.6	53	24	1,000	0	4.3	0.0
B+ / 8.4	1.9	2.5	9.36	48	0	6	0	0	94	552	3.6	62	24	1,000	0	4.3	0.0
B+ / 8.4	1.9	2.5	9.35	6	0	6	0	0	94	552	3.6	62	24	1,000	0	0.0	0.0
B+ / 8.4	1.9	2.5	9.35	8	0	6	0	0	94	552	3.6	31	24	1,000	0	0.0	0.0
C+ / 6.3	2.9	4.4	11.13	284	1	0	98	0	1	5	5.1	56	21	1,000	0	4.3	0.0
C+ / 6.7	2.8	5.6	9.72	3,304	0	16	1	37	46	287	3.6	36	19	1,000	0	4.3	0.0
C+ / 6.3	2.9	5.6	9.77	784	0	16	1	37	46	287	3.6	52	19	1,000,000	0	0.0	0.0
C+ / 6.3	2.9	5.6	9.66	414	0	16	1	37	46	287	3.6	21	19	1,000	0	0.0	0.0
C+ / 6.6	2.8	5.6	9.69	54	0	16	1	37	46	287	3.6	27	19	1,000	0	0.0	0.0
C+ / 6.5	2.8	5.6	9.77	103	0	16	1	37	46	287	3.6	46	19	1,000,000	0	0.0	0.0
B+ / 8.9	1.4	2.6	6.19	3,913	1	0	0	0	99	92	4.2	71	24	1,000	0	4.3	0.0

Fund Type	Fund Name	Ticker Symbol	Overall Investment Rating	Phone	Performance Rating/Pts	Total Return % through 2/28/17		1Yr / Pct	Annualized 3Yr / Pct	5Yr / Pct	Incl. in Returns Dividend Yield	Expense Ratio
						3 Mo	6 Mo					
USS	Franklin US Government Sec Adv	FUSAX	C+	(800) 321-8563	C- / 3.2	0.17	-0.94	0.19 /25	1.61 /37	1.34 /32	3.27	0.61
USS	Franklin US Government Sec C	FRUGX	C-	(800) 342-5236	D / 2.1	0.01	-1.27	-0.45 /10	0.96 /27	0.69 /23	2.64	1.26
USS	Franklin US Government Sec R	FUSRX	C-	(800) 342-5236	D / 2.2	0.05	-1.19	-0.47 /10	1.05 /28	0.80 /25	2.77	1.11
USA	Franklin US Government Sec R6	FGORX	B-	(800) 342-5236	C- / 3.4	0.21	-0.87	0.32 /29	1.74 /39	1.41 /33	3.40	0.47
*MUS	Franklin Virginia Tax-Free Inc A	FRVAX	B+	(800) 342-5236	C+ / 5.9	1.48	-1.74	1.49 /51	3.37 /86	2.30 /66	3.41	0.65
MUS	Franklin Virginia Tax-Free Inc Adv	FRVZX	A+	(800) 321-8563	B / 8.0	1.51	-1.77	1.59 /53	3.47 /87	2.40 /68	3.66	0.55
MUS	Franklin Virginia Tax-Free Inc C	FVAIX	A	(800) 342-5236	C+ / 6.9	1.42	-1.98	0.92 /44	2.82 /79	1.74 /52	2.95	1.20
GL	Frost Conservative Allocation Inv	FDSFX	E+	(866) 777-7818	C / 4.3	2.71	0.84	7.27 /73	1.62 /37	3.28 /62	0.55	2.71
GEI	Frost Credit Inst	FCFIX	B	(866) 777-7818	A / 9.4	4.08	5.78	19.00 /95	4.13 /77	--	5.10	0.83
GEI	Frost Credit Inv	FCFAX	B	(866) 777-7818	A / 9.3	3.92	5.55	18.61 /94	3.84 /73	--	4.87	1.08
COI	Frost Low Duration Bond Inst	FILDX	B	(866) 777-7818	C- / 3.4	0.73	0.57	1.91 /48	1.29 /32	1.47 /34	1.80	0.47
COI	Frost Low Duration Bond Inv	FADLX	B-	(866) 777-7818	C- / 3.0	0.67	0.55	1.76 /47	1.07 /29	1.24 /31	1.55	0.72
MUN	Frost Municipal Bond Inst	FIMUX	B+	(866) 777-7818	C / 5.1	1.84	-2.17	-0.55 / 9	2.06 /64	1.88 /56	2.35	0.52
MUN	Frost Municipal Bond Inv	FAUMX	B-	(866) 777-7818	C / 4.6	1.88	-2.20	-0.70 / 7	1.81 /57	1.63 /50	2.10	0.77
GEI	Frost Total Return Bond Inst	FIJEX	A+	(866) 777-7818	C+ / 6.9	1.74	1.33	7.28 /73	3.05 /62	4.48 /78	3.88	0.52
GEI	Frost Total Return Bond Inv	FATRX	A+	(866) 777-7818	C+ / 6.6	1.68	1.20	7.02 /73	2.80 /58	4.22 /75	3.63	0.77
GEI	FX Strategy A	FXFAX	C-	(855) 397-8728	A- / 9.2	-3.24	15.36	4.86 /66	7.25 /96	0.61 /23	0.00	1.79
MMT	Gabelli US Treasury Money Mkt A	GBAXX	C-	(800) 422-3554	D- / 1.2	0.10	0.16	0.27 /28	0.10 /13	0.07 /13	0.27	N/A
MMT	Gabelli US Treasury Money Mkt AAA	GABXX	C-	(800) 422-3554	D- / 1.2	0.10	0.16	0.28 /28	0.10 /13	0.07 /13	0.28	N/A
MMT	Gabelli US Treasury Money Mkt C	GBCXX	C-	(800) 422-3554	D- / 1.2	0.10	0.16	0.27 /28	0.10 /13	0.07 /13	0.27	N/A
*GES	GE RSP Income	GESLX	B-	(800) 242-0134	C+ / 5.6	1.37	-1.77	3.49 /60	2.86 /59	2.76 /54	2.41	0.17
MMF	General AMT-Free Municipal MM A	DLTXX	U	(800) 645-6561	U /	--	--	--	--	--	0.04	N/A
MMF	General AMT-Free Municipal MM B	DMBXX	U	(800) 645-6561	U /	--	--	--	--	--	0.01	N/A
MMF	General AMT-Free Municipal MM Dr	DLRXX	C-	(800) 645-6561	D- / 1.0	0.06	0.12	0.13 /26	0.05 /12	0.03 /11	0.13	N/A
MMF	General New Jersey Municipal MM A	DNJXX	U	(800) 645-6561	U /	--	--	--	--	--	0.06	N/A
MMT	General Treasury and Agency MM A	DUIXX	U	(800) 645-6561	U /	--	--	--	--	--	0.01	N/A
MMT	General Treasury and Agency MM	DUTXX	U	(800) 645-6561	U /	--	--	--	--	--	0.02	N/A
USS	Glenmede Core Fixed Income Port	GTCGX	C	(800) 442-8299	C- / 3.7	0.83	-2.06	0.51 /33	1.99 /43	1.62 /36	2.01	0.53
MUH	Glenmede High Yield Municipal Ptf	GHYMX	U	(800) 442-8299	U /	2.26	-4.40	1.14 /47	--	--	2.47	1.18
MUN	Glenmede Intermediate Muni Port	GTCMX	B-	(800) 442-8299	C / 4.3	1.87	-1.67	-0.13 /15	1.58 /51	1.47 /46	1.56	0.23
MUN	Glenmede Shrt Trm Tax Aware Fx Inc	GTAWX	U	(800) 442-8299	U /	0.96	-0.13	--	--	--	0.00	N/A
GEI	GMO Core Plus Bond III	GUGAX	D		C / 4.8	1.22	-1.80	2.44 /53	2.49 /52	3.60 /67	3.78	0.64
GEI	GMO Core Plus Bond IV	GPBFX	D		C / 5.0	1.25	-1.76	2.55 /53	2.56 /53	3.68 /68	3.94	0.59
GL	GMO Currency Hedged Intl Bond III	GMHBX	C+		B+ / 8.4	1.27	-2.79	2.79 /55	5.93 /91	6.04 /92	3.42	1.02
*EM ●	GMO Emerging Country Debt III	GMCDX	C+		A+ / 9.9	6.80	1.55	19.47 /95	7.56 /97	7.87 /98	6.77	0.54
EM ●	GMO Emerging Country Debt IV	GMDFX	C+		A+ / 9.9	6.80	1.58	19.50 /95	7.60 /97	7.92 /98	6.83	0.49
*GEI	GMO Opportunistic Income VI	GMODX	A+		B / 7.8	1.92	3.81	7.62 /74	4.08 /76	3.64 /68	2.49	0.50
*US	GMO US Treasury	GUSTX	C		D / 1.6	0.14	0.25	0.49 /33	0.25 /18	0.20 /18	0.44	0.10
GEI	Goldman Sachs Bond A	GSFAX	C-	(800) 526-7384	C- / 3.3	1.53	-1.68	2.51 /53	2.45 /51	3.20 /61	2.36	1.02
GEI	Goldman Sachs Bond C	GSFCX	C	(800) 526-7384	C- / 3.6	1.34	-2.05	1.74 /47	1.65 /37	2.43 /48	1.69	1.77
GEI	Goldman Sachs Bond Institutional	GSNIX	B+	(800) 526-7384	C / 5.4	1.51	-1.52	2.76 /55	2.77 /57	3.55 /66	2.80	0.68
GEI	Goldman Sachs Bond IR	GSNTX	B	(800) 526-7384	C / 5.2	1.49	-1.57	2.77 /55	2.68 /56	3.47 /65	2.71	0.77
GEI	Goldman Sachs Bond R	GSNRX	C+	(800) 526-7384	C / 4.3	1.37	-1.81	2.16 /50	2.13 /45	2.93 /56	2.21	1.28
COI	Goldman Sachs Bond R6	GSFUX	U	(800) 526-7384	U /	1.52	-1.60	2.77 /55	--	--	2.81	0.71
GEI	Goldman Sachs Bond Service	GSNSX	C+	(800) 526-7384	C / 4.5	1.39	-1.76	2.25 /51	2.26 /47	3.05 /59	2.30	1.19
GEI	Goldman Sachs Core Fixed Inc A	GCFIX	C-	(800) 526-7384	C- / 3.3	1.47	-1.66	2.20 /51	2.48 /51	2.43 /48	2.12	0.85
GEI	Goldman Sachs Core Fixed Inc C	GCFCX	C-	(800) 526-7384	C- / 3.5	1.28	-2.10	1.44 /44	1.68 /38	1.65 /37	1.45	1.60
GEI	Goldman Sachs Core Fixed Inc Inst	GSFIX	B+	(800) 526-7384	C / 5.4	1.55	-1.48	2.55 /53	2.82 /58	2.78 /54	2.55	0.51
GEI	Goldman Sachs Core Fixed Inc IR	GDFTX	B	(800) 526-7384	C / 5.3	1.53	-1.53	2.46 /53	2.73 /56	2.68 /52	2.45	0.60
GEI	Goldman Sachs Core Fixed Inc R	GDFRX	C+	(800) 526-7384	C / 4.3	1.31	-1.87	1.85 /48	2.19 /46	2.16 /44	1.95	1.11
COI	Goldman Sachs Core Fixed Inc R6	GCFUX	U	(800) 526-7384	U /	1.55	-1.47	2.57 /54	--	--	2.57	0.49
GEI	Goldman Sachs Core Fixed Inc Svc	GSCSX	C+	(800) 526-7384	C / 4.5	1.33	-1.82	1.94 /48	2.28 /48	2.24 /45	2.04	1.01

● Denotes fund is closed to new investors
* Denotes fund is included in Section II

RISK			NET ASSETS		ASSET					Portfolio Turnover Ratio	Avg Coupon Rate	FUND MANAGER		MINIMUM		LOADS	
Risk Rating/Pts	3 Yr Avg Standard Deviation	Avg Dura-tion	NAV As of 2/28/17	Total $(Mil)	Cash %	Gov. Bond %	Muni. Bond %	Corp. Bond %	Other %			Manager Quality Pct	Manager Tenure (Years)	Initial Purch. $	Additional Purch. $	Front End Load	Back End Load
B+ / 8.9	1.4	2.6	6.21	752	1	0	0	0	99	92	4.2	74	24	1,000	0	0.0	0.0
B+ / 8.9	1.4	2.6	6.15	941	1	0	0	0	99	92	4.2	56	24	1,000	0	0.0	0.0
B+ / 8.8	1.4	2.6	6.18	54	1	0	0	0	99	92	4.2	59	24	1,000	0	0.0	0.0
B+ / 8.9	1.4	2.6	6.21	572	1	0	0	0	99	92	4.2	76	24	1,000,000	0	0.0	0.0
B- / 7.0	2.7	3.8	11.31	523	0	0	99	0	1	5	5.1	69	30	1,000	0	4.3	0.0
C+ / 6.9	2.7	3.8	11.31	71	0	0	99	0	1	5	5.1	70	30	1,000	0	0.0	0.0
C+ / 6.9	2.7	3.8	11.49	108	0	0	99	0	1	5	5.1	50	30	1,000	0	0.0	0.0
D+ / 2.8	4.2	N/A	10.72	1	4	25	1	16	54	67	0.0	85	6	2,500	500	0.0	2.0
D / 2.1	4.9	2.3	9.91	145	5	0	0	42	53	36	0.0	93	5	1,000,000	0	0.0	0.0
D / 2.1	4.9	2.3	9.89	12	5	0	0	42	53	36	0.0	92	5	2,500	500	0.0	0.0
A / 9.5	0.8	2.5	10.23	244	2	28	2	20	48	36	0.0	68	15	1,000,000	0	0.0	0.0
A / 9.5	0.8	2.5	10.24	22	2	28	2	20	48	36	0.0	62	15	2,500	500	0.0	0.0
B / 7.6	2.4	4.5	10.34	271	0	2	92	1	5	5	0.0	21	15	1,000,000	0	0.0	0.0
B / 7.6	2.5	4.5	10.34	6	0	2	92	1	5	5	0.0	15	15	2,500	500	0.0	0.0
B / 8.0	2.1	4.4	10.44	1,730	2	26	3	19	50	32	0.0	83	15	1,000,000	0	0.0	0.0
B / 8.0	2.1	4.4	10.44	277	2	26	3	19	50	32	0.0	81	15	2,500	500	0.0	0.0
E- / 0.0	26.3	N/A	10.14	N/A	33	14	2	25	26	40	0.0	99	6	5,000	2,000	5.8	0.0
A+ / 9.9	N/A	N/A	1.00	6	100	0	0	0	0	0	0.3	N/A	25	3,000	0	0.0	0.0
A+ / 9.9	N/A	N/A	1.00	1,707	100	0	0	0	0	0	0.3	N/A	25	10,000	0	0.0	0.0
A+ / 9.9	N/A	N/A	1.00	4	100	0	0	0	0	0	0.3	N/A	25	3,000	0	0.0	0.0
C+ / 6.2	2.9	6.0	11.46	2,417	0	28	0	37	35	271	5.9	61	N/A	0	0	0.0	0.0
U /	N/A	N/A	1.00	1	100	0	0	0	0	0	0.0	39	N/A	100,000	0	0.0	0.0
U /	N/A	N/A	1.00	59	100	0	0	0	0	0	0.0	38	N/A	2,500	100	0.0	0.0
A+ / 9.9	N/A	N/A	1.00	13	100	0	0	0	0	0	0.1	43	N/A	10,000	100	0.0	0.0
U /	N/A	N/A	1.00	102	100	0	0	0	0	0	0.1	43	N/A	2,500	100	0.0	0.0
U /	N/A	N/A	1.00	215	100	0	0	0	0	0	0.0	N/A	N/A	100,000	0	0.0	0.0
U /	N/A	N/A	1.00	74	100	0	0	0	0	0	0.0	N/A	N/A	100,000	0	0.0	0.0
B / 7.6	2.5	5.0	10.98	475	2	31	1	39	27	24	0.0	65	18	1,000	0	0.0	0.0
U /	N/A	8.3	9.96	148	0	0	0	0	100	73	0.0	N/A	2	0	0	0.0	0.0
B / 7.8	2.3	N/A	10.89	305	0	0	99	0	1	34	5.1	15	6	0	0	0.0	0.0
U /	N/A	N/A	9.98	30	0	0	0	0	100	0	0.0	N/A	1	0	0	0.0	0.0
C- / 3.7	3.7	4.7	21.10	22	0	56	0	13	31	21	5.4	36	3	0	0	0.0	0.0
C- / 3.6	3.7	4.7	21.15	61	0	56	0	13	31	21	5.4	40	3	125,000,000	0	0.0	0.0
D / 2.0	5.0	5.3	26.50	59	0	93	0	0	7	69	6.3	98	3	0	0	0.0	0.0
E / 0.4	7.9	4.7	28.99	1,067	0	76	0	6	18	20	8.3	99	23	0	0	0.5	0.5
E / 0.4	7.9	4.7	28.95	3,018	0	76	0	6	18	20	8.3	99	23	125,000,000	0	0.5	0.5
A- / 9.1	1.2	N/A	25.78	1,511	0	0	0	0	100	66	0.0	95	3	300,000,000	0	0.4	0.4
A+ / 9.9	0.1	N/A	25.00	2,666	0	99	0	0	1	0	0.0	52	3	0	0	0.0	0.0
B- / 7.3	2.6	6.2	10.17	118	0	25	1	25	49	588	0.0	57	11	1,000	50	3.8	0.0
B- / 7.3	2.6	6.2	10.16	20	0	25	1	25	49	588	0.0	21	11	1,000	50	0.0	0.0
B- / 7.4	2.6	6.2	10.16	314	0	25	1	25	49	588	0.0	67	11	1,000,000	0	0.0	0.0
B- / 7.3	2.6	6.2	10.13	45	0	25	1	25	49	588	0.0	63	11	0	0	0.0	0.0
B- / 7.3	2.6	6.2	10.15	25	0	25	1	25	49	588	0.0	37	11	0	0	0.0	0.0
U /	N/A	6.2	10.16	51	0	25	1	25	49	588	0.0	N/A	11	0	0	0.0	0.0
B- / 7.3	2.6	6.2	10.16	1	0	25	1	25	49	588	0.0	49	11	0	0	0.0	0.0
B- / 7.2	2.7	4.9	10.44	146	0	27	0	29	44	450	0.0	52	17	1,000	50	3.8	0.0
B- / 7.1	2.7	4.9	10.49	17	0	27	0	29	44	450	0.0	18	17	1,000	50	0.0	0.0
B- / 7.3	2.6	4.9	10.48	791	0	27	0	29	44	450	0.0	64	17	1,000,000	0	0.0	0.0
B- / 7.3	2.6	4.9	10.45	39	0	27	0	29	44	450	0.0	61	17	0	0	0.0	0.0
B- / 7.3	2.6	4.9	10.44	9	0	27	0	29	44	450	0.0	35	17	0	0	0.0	0.0
U /	N/A	4.9	10.48	57	0	27	0	29	44	450	0.0	N/A	17	0	0	0.0	0.0
B- / 7.2	2.6	4.9	10.48	2	0	27	0	29	44	450	0.0	37	17	0	0	0.0	0.0

99 Pct = Best
0 Pct = Worst

Fund Type	Fund Name	Ticker Symbol	Overall Investment Rating	Phone	Performance Rating/Pts	3 Mo	6 Mo	1Yr / Pct	3Yr / Pct	5Yr / Pct	Dividend Yield	Expense Ratio
EM	Goldman Sachs Dyn Em Mkts Debt A	GDDAX	E	(800) 526-7384	D+ / 2.8	6.06	0.26	12.86 /85	0.77 /24	--	4.43	2.98
EM	Goldman Sachs Dyn Em Mkts Debt C	GDDCX	E	(800) 526-7384	C- / 3.6	5.85	0.01	11.99 /83	0.14 /14	--	3.89	3.79
EM	Goldman Sachs Dyn Em Mkts Debt	GDDIX	E+	(800) 526-7384	C / 5.3	6.01	0.31	13.08 /85	1.20 /31	--	4.99	2.45
EM	Goldman Sachs Dyn Em Mkts Debt	GIRDX	E+	(800) 526-7384	C / 5.3	6.12	0.38	13.14 /85	1.14 /30	--	4.90	2.63
EM	Goldman Sachs Dyn Em Mkts Debt R	GDDRX	E+	(800) 526-7384	C / 4.4	5.98	0.26	12.55 /84	0.65 /22	--	4.40	3.18
MUN	Goldman Sachs Dynamic Muni Inc A	GSMIX	C	(800) 526-7384	C+ / 6.6	2.46	-2.21	2.00 /57	3.54 /88	3.13 /82	3.14	0.99
MUN	Goldman Sachs Dynamic Muni Inc C	GSMUX	C+	(800) 526-7384	B- / 7.0	2.27	-2.57	1.24 /48	2.77 /78	2.38 /68	2.50	1.75
MUN	Goldman Sachs Dynamic Muni Inc	GSMTX	A-	(800) 526-7384	B+ / 8.7	2.54	-2.05	2.35 /60	3.89 /92	3.50 /87	3.61	0.65
MUN	Goldman Sachs Dynamic Muni Inc IR	GUIRX	A-	(800) 526-7384	B+ / 8.6	2.58	-2.04	2.31 /60	3.79 /91	3.40 /86	3.50	0.74
MUN	Goldman Sachs Dynamic Muni Inc Sv	GSMEX	B	(800) 526-7384	B / 7.9	2.41	-2.27	1.85 /56	3.38 /86	2.98 /79	3.10	1.16
EM	Goldman Sachs Emg Mkts Debt A	GSDAX	C-	(800) 526-7384	B+ / 8.5	5.10	-0.39	12.35 /84	6.06 /92	5.17 /86	4.41	1.27
EM	Goldman Sachs Emg Mkts Debt C	GSCDX	C	(800) 526-7384	B+ / 8.8	4.82	-0.84	11.52 /82	5.27 /87	4.39 /77	3.87	2.02
EM	Goldman Sachs Emg Mkts Debt Inst	GSDIX	C+	(800) 526-7384	A / 9.5	5.09	-0.29	12.72 /85	6.42 /94	5.51 /89	4.95	0.93
EM	Goldman Sachs Emg Mkts Debt IR	GSIRX	C+	(800) 526-7384	A / 9.5	5.07	-0.34	12.62 /84	6.32 /94	5.43 /88	4.86	1.02
EM	Goldman Sachs Emg Mkts Debt R6	GSIUX	U	(800) 526-7384	U /	5.10	-0.29	12.74 /85	--	--	4.97	0.92
GEI	Goldman Sachs Enhanced Inc A	GEIAX	C-	(800) 526-7384	D- / 1.3	0.51	0.68	1.67 /46	0.33 /19	0.40 /20	0.79	0.72
GEI	Goldman Sachs Enhanced Inc Admin	GEADX	C+	(800) 526-7384	D / 2.1	0.53	0.62	1.76 /47	0.42 /20	0.48 /21	0.89	0.62
GEI	Goldman Sachs Enhanced Inc Inst	GEIIX	B-	(800) 526-7384	D+ / 2.5	0.59	0.85	2.02 /49	0.67 /23	0.73 /24	1.14	0.37
GEI	Goldman Sachs Enhanced Inc IR	GHIRX	C+	(800) 526-7384	D+ / 2.4	0.57	0.70	1.82 /47	0.58 /21	0.62 /23	1.05	0.47
GEI	Goldman Sachs Enhanced Inc R6	GEIUX	U	(800) 526-7384	U /	0.59	0.76	1.92 /48	--	--	1.16	0.38
MMT	Goldman Sachs Fin Sq Fed Adm	FIOXX	U	(800) 526-7384	U /	0.04	0.05	0.06 /21	--	--	0.06	N/A
MMT	Goldman Sachs Fin Sq Fed Cap	FIKXX	U	(800) 526-7384	U /	0.06	0.10	0.14 /24	--	--	0.14	N/A
MMT	Goldman Sachs Fin Sq Fed Inst	FIRXX	U	(800) 526-7384	U /	0.10	0.17	0.29 /29	--	--	0.29	N/A
MMT	Goldman Sachs Fin Sq Fed Prf	FIHXX	U	(800) 526-7384	U /	0.08	0.12	0.19 /26	--	--	0.19	N/A
MMT	Goldman Sachs Fin Sq Fed Prm	FIQXX	U	(800) 526-7384	U /	0.02	0.02	0.02 /19	--	--	0.02	N/A
MMT	Goldman Sachs Fin Sq Fed Sel	FIJXX	U	(800) 526-7384	U /	0.09	0.16	0.26 /28	--	--	0.26	N/A
MMT	Goldman Sachs Fin Sq Govt Adm	FOAXX	D+	(800) 526-7384	E+ / 0.7	0.05	0.06	0.08 /21	0.03 / 8	0.02 / 7	0.08	N/A
MMT	Goldman Sachs Fin Sq Govt Cap	GCGXX	C-	(800) 526-7384	E+ / 0.9	0.07	0.11	0.17 /25	0.07 /11	0.04 /10	0.17	N/A
MMT	Goldman Sachs Fin Sq Govt Inst	FGTXX	C-	(800) 526-7384	D- / 1.3	0.11	0.19	0.33 /30	0.13 /14	0.09 /15	0.32	N/A
MMT	Goldman Sachs Fin Sq Govt Prf	GPGXX	C-	(800) 526-7384	D- / 1.1	0.09	0.14	0.22 /27	0.09 /12	0.05 /11	0.22	N/A
MMT	Goldman Sachs Fin Sq Govt Prm	GGPXX	D+	(800) 526-7384	E+ / 0.6	0.02	0.03	0.04 /20	0.02 / 7	0.01 / 5	0.04	N/A
MMT	Goldman Sachs Fin Sq Govt R6		U	(800) 526-7384	U /	0.11	0.19	0.32 /30	--	--	0.32	N/A
MMT	Goldman Sachs Fin Sq Govt Sel	GSGXX	C-	(800) 526-7384	D- / 1.2	0.10	0.17	0.30 /29	0.12 /14	0.07 /13	0.29	N/A
MMT	Goldman Sachs Fin Sq MM Adm	FADXX	C-	(800) 526-7384	D- / 1.2	0.14	0.20	0.28 /28	0.11 /13	0.07 /13	0.25	N/A
MMT	Goldman Sachs Fin Sq MM Capital	GCKXX	C-	(800) 526-7384	D- / 1.3	0.16	0.24	0.37 /30	0.14 /15	0.09 /15	0.35	N/A
MMT	Goldman Sachs Fin Sq MM CM	GSCXX	D+	(800) 526-7384	E+ / 0.6	0.01	0.03	0.04 /20	0.02 / 7	0.01 / 5	0.02	N/A
MMT	Goldman Sachs Fin Sq MM Inst	FSMXX	C	(800) 526-7384	D / 1.6	0.20	0.32	0.53 /34	0.26 /18	0.20 /18	0.50	N/A
MMT	Goldman Sachs Fin Sq MM Prf	GPMXX	C	(800) 526-7384	D- / 1.4	0.17	0.27	0.42 /32	0.17 /16	0.11 /15	0.40	N/A
MMT	Goldman Sachs Fin Sq MM Prm	GPRXX	C-	(800) 526-7384	D- / 1.1	0.11	0.15	0.23 /27	0.09 /12	0.06 /12	0.21	N/A
MMT	Goldman Sachs Fin Sq MM Res	GREXX	D+	(800) 526-7384	E+ / 0.8	0.04	0.06	0.14 /24	0.06 /11	0.04 /10	0.12	N/A
MMT	Goldman Sachs Fin Sq MM Sel	GSMXX	C	(800) 526-7384	D / 1.6	0.19	0.30	0.50 /33	0.23 /17	0.17 /18	0.47	N/A
MMT	Goldman Sachs Fin Sq MM Svc	FSVXX	D+	(800) 526-7384	E+ / 0.8	0.08	0.10	0.10 /22	0.04 / 9	0.02 / 7	0.07	N/A
MMT	Goldman Sachs Fin Sq Pr Oblg Adm	FBAXX	C-	(800) 526-7384	D- / 1.2	0.14	0.21	0.28 /28	0.11 /13	0.07 /13	0.25	N/A
MMT	Goldman Sachs Fin Sq Pr Oblg CM	GFOXX	D+	(800) 526-7384	E+ / 0.8	0.04	0.06	0.13 /23	0.06 /11	0.04 /10	0.09	N/A
MMT	Goldman Sachs Fin Sq Pr Oblg Cptl	GCPXX	C-	(800) 526-7384	D- / 1.4	0.17	0.26	0.38 /31	0.15 /15	0.09 /15	0.35	N/A
MMT	Goldman Sachs Fin Sq Pr Oblg Inst	FPOXX	C	(800) 526-7384	D / 1.6	0.21	0.33	0.53 /34	0.23 /17	0.16 /17	0.50	N/A
MMT	Goldman Sachs Fin Sq Pr Oblg Prf	GPPXX	C	(800) 526-7384	D- / 1.4	0.18	0.29	0.44 /32	0.17 /16	0.11 /15	0.40	N/A
MMT	Goldman Sachs Fin Sq Pr Oblg Prm	GOPXX	C-	(800) 526-7384	D- / 1.2	0.13	0.18	0.25 /28	0.10 /13	0.06 /12	0.21	N/A
MMT	Goldman Sachs Fin Sq Pr Oblg Res	GBRXX	D+	(800) 526-7384	E+ / 0.7	0.06	0.07	0.08 /22	0.03 / 8	0.02 / 7	0.04	N/A
MMT	Goldman Sachs Fin Sq Pr Oblg Sel	GSPXX	C	(800) 526-7384	D- / 1.5	0.19	0.32	0.50 /33	0.20 /16	0.14 /17	0.47	N/A
MMT	Goldman Sachs Fin Sq Pr Oblg Svc	FBSXX	D+	(800) 526-7384	E+ / 0.8	0.07	0.10	0.10 /22	0.04 / 9	0.03 / 9	0.07	N/A
MMT	Goldman Sachs Fin Sq Tre Instr Adm	FRAXX	D+	(800) 526-7384	E+ / 0.6	0.03	0.03	0.03 /20	0.01 / 6	0.01 / 5	0.03	N/A

● Denotes fund is closed to new investors
* Denotes fund is included in Section II

RISK			NET ASSETS		ASSET							FUND MANAGER		MINIMUM		LOADS	
Risk Rating/Pts	3 Yr Avg Standard Deviation	Avg Dura-tion	NAV As of 2/28/17	Total $(Mil)	Cash %	Gov. Bond %	Muni. Bond %	Corp. Bond %	Other %	Portfolio Turnover Ratio	Avg Coupon Rate	Manager Quality Pct	Manager Tenure (Years)	Initial Purch. $	Additional Purch. $	Front End Load	Back End Load
E /0.3	8.5	N/A	8.36	N/A	18	55	1	23	3	98	0.0	90	4	1,000	50	4.5	2.0
E /0.3	8.4	N/A	8.39	N/A	18	55	1	23	3	98	0.0	86	4	1,000	50	0.0	2.0
E /0.3	8.4	N/A	8.38	21	18	55	1	23	3	98	0.0	92	4	1,000,000	0	0.0	2.0
E /0.3	8.4	N/A	8.37	N/A	18	55	1	23	3	98	0.0	92	4	0	0	0.0	2.0
E /0.3	8.5	N/A	8.39	N/A	18	55	1	23	3	98	0.0	90	4	0	0	0.0	2.0
C- /4.0	3.2	8.1	15.46	216	0	0	99	0	1	15	0.0	59	18	1,000	50	3.8	0.0
C- /4.0	3.2	8.1	15.47	43	0	0	99	0	1	15	0.0	25	18	1,000	50	0.0	0.0
C- /4.0	3.2	8.1	15.46	735	0	0	99	0	1	15	0.0	69	18	1,000,000	0	0.0	0.0
C- /4.0	3.2	8.1	15.45	59	0	0	99	0	1	15	0.0	67	18	0	0	0.0	0.0
C- /4.1	3.2	8.1	15.54	N/A	0	0	99	0	1	15	0.0	54	18	0	0	0.0	0.0
D- /1.0	6.1	7.2	12.73	120	0	69	1	20	10	99	0.0	99	14	1,000	50	4.5	2.0
D- /1.0	6.1	7.2	12.72	32	0	69	1	20	10	99	0.0	98	14	1,000	50	0.0	2.0
D- /1.0	6.1	7.2	12.74	1,584	0	69	1	20	10	99	0.0	99	14	1,000,000	0	0.0	2.0
D- /1.0	6.1	7.2	12.74	48	0	69	1	20	10	99	0.0	99	14	0	0	0.0	2.0
U /	N/A	7.2	12.74	25	0	69	1	20	10	99	0.0	N/A	14	0	0	0.0	0.0
A+ /9.8	0.4	0.6	9.45	35	3	13	0	68	16	60	0.0	55	9	1,000	50	1.5	0.0
A+ /9.8	0.4	0.6	9.47	N/A	3	13	0	68	16	60	0.0	58	9	0	0	0.0	0.0
A+ /9.8	0.4	0.6	9.44	440	3	13	0	68	16	60	0.0	66	9	1,000,000	0	0.0	0.0
A+ /9.9	0.4	0.6	9.43	1	3	13	0	68	16	60	0.0	63	9	0	0	0.0	0.0
U /	N/A	0.6	9.44	N/A	3	13	0	68	16	60	0.0	N/A	9	0	0	0.0	0.0
U /	N/A	N/A	1.00	41	100	0	0	0	0	0	0.1	N/A	N/A	10,000,000	0	0.0	0.0
U /	N/A	N/A	1.00	9	100	0	0	0	0	0	0.1	N/A	N/A	10,000,000	0	0.0	0.0
U /	N/A	N/A	1.00	703	100	0	0	0	0	0	0.3	N/A	N/A	10,000,000	0	0.0	0.0
U /	N/A	N/A	1.00	N/A	100	0	0	0	0	0	0.2	N/A	N/A	10,000,000	0	0.0	0.0
U /	N/A	N/A	1.00	N/A	100	0	0	0	0	0	0.0	N/A	N/A	10,000,000	0	0.0	0.0
U /	N/A	N/A	1.00	N/A	100	0	0	0	0	0	0.3	N/A	N/A	10,000,000	0	0.0	0.0
A+ /9.9	N/A	N/A	1.00	3,958	100	0	0	0	0	0	0.1	39	N/A	10,000,000	0	0.0	0.0
A+ /9.9	N/A	N/A	1.00	1,390	100	0	0	0	0	0	0.2	43	N/A	10,000,000	0	0.0	0.0
A+ /9.9	N/A	N/A	1.00	92,233	100	0	0	0	0	0	0.3	47	N/A	10,000,000	0	0.0	0.0
A+ /9.9	N/A	N/A	1.00	724	100	0	0	0	0	0	0.2	44	N/A	10,000,000	0	0.0	0.0
A+ /9.9	N/A	N/A	1.00	66	100	0	0	0	0	0	0.0	39	N/A	10,000,000	0	0.0	0.0
U /	N/A	N/A	1.00	12	100	0	0	0	0	0	0.3	N/A	N/A	0	0	0.0	0.0
A+ /9.9	N/A	N/A	1.00	2,526	100	0	0	0	0	0	0.3	46	N/A	10,000,000	0	0.0	0.0
A+ /9.9	0.1	N/A	1.00	9	100	0	0	0	0	0	0.3	46	N/A	10,000,000	0	0.0	0.0
A+ /9.9	0.1	N/A	1.00	N/A	100	0	0	0	0	0	0.4	47	N/A	10,000,000	0	0.0	0.0
A+ /9.9	N/A	N/A	1.00	N/A	100	0	0	0	0	0	0.0	39	N/A	10,000,000	0	0.0	0.0
A+ /9.9	0.1	N/A	1.00	1,615	100	0	0	0	0	0	0.5	53	N/A	10,000,000	0	0.0	0.0
A+ /9.9	0.1	N/A	1.00	N/A	100	0	0	0	0	0	0.4	49	N/A	10,000,000	0	0.0	0.0
A+ /9.9	N/A	N/A	1.00	N/A	100	0	0	0	0	0	0.2	44	N/A	10,000,000	0	0.0	0.0
A+ /9.9	N/A	N/A	1.00	N/A	100	0	0	0	0	0	0.1	41	N/A	10,000,000	0	0.0	0.0
A+ /9.9	0.1	N/A	1.00	8	100	0	0	0	0	0	0.5	52	N/A	10,000,000	0	0.0	0.0
A+ /9.9	N/A	N/A	1.00	1	100	0	0	0	0	0	0.1	39	N/A	10,000,000	0	0.0	0.0
A+ /9.9	0.1	N/A	1.00	4	100	0	0	0	0	0	0.3	46	N/A	10,000,000	0	0.0	0.0
A+ /9.9	N/A	N/A	1.00	N/A	100	0	0	0	0	0	0.1	43	N/A	10,000,000	0	0.0	0.0
A+ /9.9	0.1	N/A	1.00	N/A	100	0	0	0	0	0	0.4	48	N/A	10,000,000	0	0.0	0.0
A+ /9.9	0.1	N/A	1.00	780	100	0	0	0	0	0	0.5	52	N/A	10,000,000	0	0.0	0.0
A+ /9.9	0.1	N/A	1.00	1	100	0	0	0	0	0	0.4	50	N/A	10,000,000	0	0.0	0.0
A+ /9.9	N/A	N/A	1.00	N/A	100	0	0	0	0	0	0.2	46	N/A	10,000,000	0	0.0	0.0
A+ /9.9	N/A	N/A	1.00	N/A	100	0	0	0	0	0	0.0	40	N/A	10,000,000	0	0.0	0.0
A+ /9.9	0.1	N/A	1.00	N/A	100	0	0	0	0	0	0.5	51	N/A	10,000,000	0	0.0	0.0
A+ /9.9	N/A	N/A	1.00	1	100	0	0	0	0	0	0.1	40	N/A	10,000,000	0	0.0	0.0
A+ /9.9	N/A	N/A	1.00	2,013	100	0	0	0	0	0	0.0	38	N/A	10,000,000	0	0.0	0.0

Fund Type	Fund Name	Ticker Symbol	Overall Investment Rating	Phone	Perfor-mance Rating/Pts	Total Return % through 2/28/17 3 Mo	6 Mo	1Yr / Pct	Annualized 3Yr / Pct	5Yr / Pct	Incl. in Returns Dividend Yield	Expense Ratio
	99 Pct = Best *0 Pct = Worst*											
MMT	Goldman Sachs Fin Sq Tre Instr Inst	FTIXX	C-	(800) 526-7384	D- / 1.1	0.09	0.14	0.24 /27	0.09 /12	0.05 /11	0.24	N/A
MMT	Goldman Sachs Fin Sq Tre Instr Prf	GPIXX	D+	(800) 526-7384	E+ / 0.8	0.06	0.09	0.14 /24	0.05 /10	0.03 / 9	0.14	N/A
MMT	Goldman Sachs Fin Sq Tre Instr Sel	GSIXX	C-	(800) 526-7384	D- / 1.0	0.08	0.12	0.21 /26	0.08 /12	0.05 /11	0.21	N/A
MMT	Goldman Sachs Fin Sq Treas Sol	FVAXX	D+	(800) 526-7384	E+ / 0.6	0.03	0.03	0.03 /20	0.02 / 7	0.01 / 5	0.03	N/A
MMT	Goldman Sachs Fin Sq Treas Sol	GCFXX	D+	(800) 526-7384	E+ / 0.7	0.05	0.07	0.09 /22	0.04 / 9	0.02 / 7	0.09	N/A
MMT	Goldman Sachs Fin Sq Treas Sol Inst	FEDXX	C-	(800) 526-7384	D- / 1.1	0.09	0.14	0.24 /27	0.10 /13	0.06 /12	0.24	N/A
MMT	Goldman Sachs Fin Sq Treas Sol Prf	GPFXX	C-	(800) 526-7384	E+ / 0.9	0.07	0.09	0.14 /24	0.06 /11	0.04 /10	0.14	N/A
MMT	Goldman Sachs Fin Sq Treas Sol	GFPXX	U	(800) 526-7384	U /	--	--	--	--	--	0.01	N/A
MMT	Goldman Sachs Fin Sq Treas Sol Sel	GSFXX	C-	(800) 526-7384	D- / 1.0	0.08	0.13	0.21 /26	0.08 /12	0.05 /11	0.21	N/A
MMT	Goldman Sachs Finan Sq Trs Oblg	GCTXX	D+	(800) 526-7384	E+ / 0.8	0.05	0.07	0.11 /23	0.04 / 9	0.03 / 9	0.11	N/A
MMT	Goldman Sachs Finan Sq Trs Oblg	GPOXX	C-	(800) 526-7384	E+ / 0.9	0.07	0.09	0.16 /24	0.06 /11	0.04 /10	0.16	N/A
MMT	Goldman Sachs Finan Sq Trs Oblg	GTPXX	U	(800) 526-7384	U /	--	--	--	--	--	0.01	N/A
GL	Goldman Sachs Glbl Income A	GSGIX	C+	(800) 526-7384	C- / 3.7	0.98	-1.65	2.13 /50	2.80 /58	3.31 /62	0.91	1.15
GL	Goldman Sachs Glbl Income C	GSLCX	C+	(800) 526-7384	C- / 3.9	0.82	-2.00	1.33 /43	2.03 /44	2.52 /50	0.22	1.90
GL	Goldman Sachs Glbl Income Inst	GSGLX	A	(800) 526-7384	C+ / 5.8	1.06	-1.57	2.48 /53	3.15 /63	3.66 /68	1.28	0.81
GL	Goldman Sachs Glbl Income IR	GBIRX	A-	(800) 526-7384	C+ / 5.6	1.04	-1.61	2.31 /52	3.04 /62	3.54 /66	1.19	0.90
GL	Goldman Sachs Glbl Income R6	GBIUX	U	(800) 526-7384	U /	1.07	-1.48	2.50 /53	--	--	1.30	0.79
GL	Goldman Sachs Glbl Income Svc	GGISX	B	(800) 526-7384	C / 4.7	0.94	-1.82	1.90 /48	2.49 /52	3.06 /59	0.78	1.29
USS	Goldman Sachs Govt Income A	GSGOX	D-	(800) 526-7384	E+ / 0.8	0.48	-2.29	-0.70 / 7	1.49 /35	1.15 /29	1.69	1.05
USS	Goldman Sachs Govt Income C	GSOCX	D-	(800) 526-7384	D- / 1.5	0.30	-2.65	-1.44 / 2	0.74 /24	0.40 /20	0.99	1.80
USS	Goldman Sachs Govt Income Inst	GSOIX	C-	(800) 526-7384	C- / 3.3	0.57	-2.07	-0.37 /11	1.84 /40	1.49 /34	2.10	0.71
USS	Goldman Sachs Govt Income IR	GSOTX	C-	(800) 526-7384	C- / 3.1	0.55	-2.17	-0.46 /10	1.75 /39	1.40 /33	2.01	0.80
USS	Goldman Sachs Govt Income R	GSORX	D	(800) 526-7384	D+ / 2.3	0.49	-2.35	-0.89 / 5	1.26 /31	0.91 /26	1.50	1.30
USS	Goldman Sachs Govt Income R6	GSOUX	U	(800) 526-7384	U /	0.64	-2.06	-0.28 /13	--	--	2.12	0.70
USS	Goldman Sachs Govt Income Svc	GSOSX	D	(800) 526-7384	D+ / 2.4	0.45	-2.38	-0.87 / 5	1.33 /32	0.98 /27	1.59	1.21
MTG	Goldman Sachs Hi Qual Fltg R A	GSAMX	C-	(800) 526-7384	D- / 1.1	0.62	0.98	1.87 /48	0.18 /16	0.24 /19	0.68	0.88
MTG	Goldman Sachs Hi Qual Fltg R Inst	GSARX	C+	(800) 526-7384	D+ / 2.3	0.59	1.04	2.05 /49	0.44 /20	0.54 /22	0.98	0.54
MTG	Goldman Sachs Hi Qual Fltg R IR	GTATX	C+	(800) 526-7384	D / 2.1	0.56	0.98	1.95 /48	0.31 /19	0.42 /21	0.88	0.63
GEI	Goldman Sachs Hi Qual Fltg R R6	GTAUX	U	(800) 526-7384	U /	0.71	1.16	2.18 /51	--	--	1.00	0.53
MTG	Goldman Sachs Hi Qual Fltg R Svc	GSASX	U	(800) 526-7384	U /	0.58	0.90	1.65 /46	--	0.11 /15	0.49	1.04
COH	Goldman Sachs High Yield A	GSHAX	D	(800) 526-7384	B- / 7.3	4.75	5.65	19.09 /95	3.10 /63	5.77 /91	4.84	1.06
COH	Goldman Sachs High Yield C	GSHCX	D+	(800) 526-7384	B / 7.7	4.55	5.25	18.38 /94	2.34 /49	4.98 /84	4.35	1.81
COH	Goldman Sachs High Yield Inst	GSHIX	C	(800) 526-7384	B+ / 8.8	4.83	5.82	19.64 /95	3.46 /68	6.10 /93	5.40	0.72
COH	Goldman Sachs High Yield IR	GSHTX	C	(800) 526-7384	B+ / 8.8	4.97	5.93	19.54 /95	3.37 /67	6.03 /92	5.31	0.81
MUH	Goldman Sachs High Yield Muni A	GHYAX	B	(800) 526-7384	A / 9.4	3.35	-2.08	4.89 /73	6.19 /99	5.65 /99	4.22	0.93
MUH	Goldman Sachs High Yield Muni C	GHYCX	B+	(800) 526-7384	A+ / 9.6	3.16	-2.44	4.11 /71	5.40 /98	4.87 /97	3.66	1.68
MUH	Goldman Sachs High Yield Muni Inst	GHYIX	B+	(800) 526-7384	A+ / 9.9	3.42	-1.95	5.19 /74	6.49 /99	5.96 /99	4.71	0.59
MUH	Goldman Sachs High Yield Muni IR	GYIRX	B+	(800) 526-7384	A+ / 9.9	3.50	-1.98	5.24 /74	6.44 /99	5.93 /99	4.65	0.68
COH	Goldman Sachs High Yield R	GSHRX	C-	(800) 526-7384	B+ / 8.3	4.69	5.52	18.99 /95	2.84 /59	5.51 /89	4.83	1.31
COH	Goldman Sachs High Yield R6	GSHUX	U	(800) 526-7384	U /	4.83	5.82	19.64 /95	--	--	5.42	0.70
COH	Goldman Sachs High Yield Svc	GSHSX	C-	(800) 526-7384	B+ / 8.4	4.87	5.56	19.10 /95	2.94 /60	5.60 /89	4.92	1.22
LP	Goldman Sachs HY Floating Rate A	GFRAX	A-	(800) 526-7384	C+ / 6.2	1.69	2.35	9.66 /78	2.64 /55	3.44 /64	3.74	0.98
LP	Goldman Sachs HY Floating Rate C	GFRCX	A-	(800) 526-7384	C+ / 5.9	1.51	1.87	8.85 /76	1.88 /41	2.69 /53	3.09	1.74
LP	Goldman Sachs HY Floating Rate	GSFRX	A+	(800) 526-7384	B- / 7.3	1.78	2.52	10.03 /79	2.99 /61	3.82 /70	4.16	0.65
LP	Goldman Sachs HY Floating Rate IR	GFRIX	A+	(800) 526-7384	B- / 7.2	1.76	2.37	9.93 /79	2.87 /59	3.72 /69	4.08	0.74
LP	Goldman Sachs HY Floating Rate R	GFRRX	A	(800) 526-7384	C+ / 6.6	1.63	2.12	9.40 /77	2.36 /49	3.19 /60	3.59	1.22
GEI	Goldman Sachs Infl Prot Secs A	GSAPX	E	(800) 526-7384	D / 2.1	1.22	-0.60	3.30 /58	1.37 /33	0.39 /20	1.00	0.89
GEI	Goldman Sachs Infl Prot Secs C	GSCFX	E+	(800) 526-7384	D+ / 2.3	0.98	-1.06	2.49 /53	0.59 /22	-0.36 / 3	0.62	1.64
GEI	Goldman Sachs Infl Prot Secs Inst	GSIPX	D-	(800) 526-7384	C- / 4.2	1.30	-0.53	3.69 /61	1.72 /38	0.73 /24	1.25	0.56
GEI	Goldman Sachs Infl Prot Secs IR	GSTPX	E+	(800) 526-7384	C- / 4.1	1.29	-0.56	3.56 /60	1.62 /37	0.62 /23	1.21	0.64
GEI	Goldman Sachs Infl Prot Secs R	GSRPX	E+	(800) 526-7384	C- / 3.2	1.08	-0.81	3.03 /57	1.09 /29	0.12 /16	0.87	1.15
GEI	Goldman Sachs Infl Prot Secs R6	GSRUX	U	(800) 526-7384	U /	1.20	-0.52	3.61 /60	--	--	1.27	0.60

● Denotes fund is closed to new investors
* Denotes fund is included in Section II

Risk Rating/Pts	3 Yr Avg Standard Deviation	Avg Duration	NAV As of 2/28/17	Total $(Mil)	Cash %	Gov. Bond %	Muni. Bond %	Corp. Bond %	Other %	Portfolio Turnover Ratio	Avg Coupon Rate	Manager Quality Pct	Manager Tenure (Years)	Initial Purch. $	Additional Purch. $	Front End Load	Back End Load
A+ / 9.9	N/A	N/A	1.00	44,794	100	0	0	0	0	0	0.2	44	N/A	10,000,000	0	0.0	0.0
A+ / 9.9	N/A	N/A	1.00	59	100	0	0	0	0	0	0.1	41	N/A	10,000,000	0	0.0	0.0
A+ / 9.9	N/A	N/A	1.00	20	100	0	0	0	0	0	0.2	44	N/A	10,000,000	0	0.0	0.0
A+ / 9.9	N/A	N/A	1.00	161	100	0	0	0	0	0	0.0	38	N/A	10,000,000	0	0.0	0.0
A+ / 9.9	N/A	N/A	1.00	283	100	0	0	0	0	0	0.1	40	N/A	10,000,000	0	0.0	0.0
A+ / 9.9	N/A	N/A	1.00	8,731	100	0	0	0	0	0	0.2	46	N/A	10,000,000	0	0.0	0.0
A+ / 9.9	N/A	N/A	1.00	75	100	0	0	0	0	0	0.1	41	N/A	10,000,000	0	0.0	0.0
U /	N/A	N/A	1.00	N/A	100	0	0	0	0	0	0.0	N/A	N/A	10,000,000	0	0.0	0.0
A+ / 9.9	N/A	N/A	1.00	11	100	0	0	0	0	0	0.2	45	N/A	10,000,000	0	0.0	0.0
A+ / 9.9	N/A	N/A	1.00	283	100	0	0	0	0	0	0.1	40	N/A	10,000,000	0	0.0	0.0
A+ / 9.9	N/A	N/A	1.00	82	100	0	0	0	0	0	0.2	43	N/A	10,000,000	0	0.0	0.0
U /	N/A	N/A	1.00	N/A	100	0	0	0	0	0	0.0	N/A	N/A	10,000,000	0	0.0	0.0
B / 7.8	2.3	6.5	12.22	170	0	49	1	18	32	261	0.0	92	22	1,000	50	3.8	0.0
B / 7.7	2.4	6.5	12.12	22	0	49	1	18	32	261	0.0	88	22	1,000	50	0.0	0.0
B / 7.8	2.4	6.5	12.20	611	0	49	1	18	32	261	0.0	93	22	1,000,000	0	0.0	0.0
B / 7.7	2.4	6.5	12.18	65	0	49	1	18	32	261	0.0	93	22	0	0	0.0	0.0
U /	N/A	6.5	12.20	6	0	49	1	18	32	261	0.0	N/A	22	0	0	0.0	0.0
B / 7.7	2.4	6.5	12.13	3	0	49	1	18	32	261	0.0	90	22	0	0	0.0	0.0
B / 7.6	2.5	4.6	14.67	135	0	49	1	1	49	590	0.0	43	4	1,000	50	3.8	0.0
B / 7.6	2.5	4.6	14.67	9	0	49	1	1	49	590	0.0	16	4	1,000	50	0.0	0.0
B / 7.6	2.5	4.6	14.65	124	0	49	1	1	49	590	0.0	59	4	1,000,000	0	0.0	0.0
B / 7.6	2.5	4.6	14.66	5	0	49	1	1	49	590	0.0	56	4	0	0	0.0	0.0
B / 7.6	2.5	4.6	14.66	21	0	49	1	1	49	590	0.0	31	4	0	0	0.0	0.0
U /	N/A	4.6	14.65	18	0	49	1	1	49	590	0.0	N/A	4	0	0	0.0	0.0
B / 7.6	2.5	4.6	14.63	54	0	49	1	1	49	590	0.0	33	4	0	0	0.0	0.0
A+ / 9.8	0.5	0.1	8.72	11	1	12	6	1	80	71	0.0	56	9	1,000	50	1.5	0.0
A+ / 9.8	0.4	0.1	8.71	390	1	12	6	1	80	71	0.0	66	9	1,000,000	0	0.0	0.0
A+ / 9.8	0.4	0.1	8.69	N/A	1	12	6	1	80	71	0.0	62	9	0	0	0.0	0.0
U /	N/A	0.1	8.72	N/A	1	12	6	1	80	71	0.0	N/A	9	0	0	0.0	0.0
U /	0.5	0.1	8.76	1	1	12	6	1	80	71	0.0	N/A	9	0	0	0.0	0.0
D- / 1.1	5.7	3.8	6.62	325	0	1	0	91	8	46	0.0	8	8	1,000	50	4.5	2.0
D- / 1.1	5.6	3.8	6.63	49	0	1	0	91	8	46	0.0	3	8	1,000	50	0.0	2.0
D- / 1.1	5.7	3.8	6.64	3,519	0	1	0	91	8	46	0.0	13	8	1,000,000	0	0.0	2.0
D- / 1.1	5.7	3.8	6.64	34	0	1	0	91	8	46	0.0	12	8	0	0	0.0	2.0
D / 2.1	4.2	8.8	9.31	236	0	0	99	0	1	11	0.0	88	17	1,000	50	4.5	2.0
D / 2.1	4.2	8.8	9.31	68	0	0	99	0	1	11	0.0	82	17	1,000	50	0.0	2.0
D / 2.1	4.2	8.8	9.31	4,160	0	0	99	0	1	11	0.0	90	17	1,000,000	0	0.0	2.0
D / 2.0	4.2	8.8	9.32	39	0	0	99	0	1	11	0.0	89	17	0	0	0.0	2.0
D- / 1.1	5.6	3.8	6.62	15	0	1	0	91	8	46	0.0	6	8	0	0	0.0	2.0
U /	N/A	3.8	6.65	185	0	1	0	91	8	46	0.0	N/A	8	0	0	0.0	2.0
D- / 1.1	5.7	3.8	6.62	12	0	1	0	91	8	46	0.0	6	8	0	0	0.0	2.0
B- / 7.2	2.7	0.7	9.76	7	0	3	0	88	9	42	0.0	86	6	1,000	50	2.3	0.0
B- / 7.2	2.7	0.7	9.76	2	0	3	0	88	9	42	0.0	80	6	1,000	50	0.0	0.0
B- / 7.2	2.7	0.7	9.77	3,797	0	3	0	88	9	42	0.0	88	6	1,000,000	0	0.0	0.0
B- / 7.2	2.7	0.7	9.77	4	0	3	0	88	9	42	0.0	87	6	0	0	0.0	0.0
B- / 7.1	2.7	0.7	9.76	N/A	0	3	0	88	9	42	0.0	84	6	0	0	0.0	0.0
C- / 3.1	3.8	7.9	10.48	76	1	98	0	0	1	171	0.0	7	10	1,000	50	3.8	0.0
C- / 3.2	3.8	7.9	10.33	7	1	98	0	0	1	171	0.0	2	10	1,000	50	0.0	0.0
C- / 3.2	3.8	7.9	10.60	195	1	98	0	0	1	171	0.0	11	10	1,000,000	0	0.0	0.0
C- / 3.1	3.8	7.9	10.54	12	1	98	0	0	1	171	0.0	9	10	0	0	0.0	0.0
C- / 3.1	3.8	7.9	10.44	18	1	98	0	0	1	171	0.0	4	10	0	0	0.0	0.0
U /	N/A	7.9	10.59	1	1	98	0	0	1	171	0.0	N/A	10	0	0	0.0	0.0

					PERFORMANCE						Incl. in Returns	
			99 Pct = Best 0 Pct = Worst			Total Return % through 2/28/17						
			Overall		Perfor-				Annualized		Dividend	Expense
Fund		Ticker	Investment		mance						Yield	Ratio
Type	Fund Name	Symbol	Rating	Phone	Rating/Pts	3 Mo	6 Mo	1Yr / Pct	3Yr / Pct	5Yr / Pct		
GL	Goldman Sachs Inv Gr Cdt A	GSGAX	D-	(800) 526-7384	C / 4.5	2.08	-1.98	5.67 /69	2.81 /58	3.52 /66	2.87	0.86
GL	Goldman Sachs Inv Gr Cdt Inst	GSGDX	D+	(800) 526-7384	C+ / 6.5	2.17	-1.82	6.02 /70	3.16 /63	3.85 /70	3.33	0.52
GL	Goldman Sachs Inv Gr Cdt IR	GTIRX	D+	(800) 526-7384	C+ / 6.5	2.25	-1.86	5.92 /70	3.10 /63	3.78 /70	3.23	0.61
COI	Goldman Sachs Inv Gr Cdt R6	GTIUX	U	(800) 526-7384	U /	2.28	-1.81	6.15 /71	--	--	3.33	0.50
GL	Goldman Sachs Inv Gr Cdt SA-Inst	GSCPX	D+	(800) 526-7384	C+ / 6.5	2.17	-1.92	5.90 /70	3.16 /63	3.85 /70	3.33	0.52
MMF	Goldman Sachs Inv Tx Ex MM Adm	FEAXX	C-	(800) 526-7384	D- / 1.2	0.11	0.17	0.18 /28	0.06 /12	0.04 /12	0.18	N/A
MMF	Goldman Sachs Inv Tx Ex MM CM	GXCXX	U	(800) 526-7384	U /	--	--	--	--	--	0.11	N/A
MMT	Goldman Sachs Inv Tx Ex MM Cptl	GCXXX	C-	(800) 526-7384	D- / 1.1	0.13	0.21	0.24 /27	0.09 /12	0.05 /11	0.24	N/A
MMF	Goldman Sachs Inv Tx Ex MM Inst	FTXXX	C	(800) 526-7384	D / 1.6	0.17	0.28	0.38 /35	0.13 /16	0.09 /17	0.38	N/A
MMF	Goldman Sachs Inv Tx Ex MM Pfd	GPTXX	C	(800) 526-7384	D- / 1.5	0.15	0.25	0.30 /33	0.11 /16	0.07 /15	0.30	N/A
MMF	Goldman Sachs Inv Tx Ex MM Prm	GXPXX	D+	(800) 526-7384	E+ / 0.8	0.04	0.08	0.08 /23	0.03 /10	0.02 / 9	0.08	N/A
MMF	Goldman Sachs Inv Tx Ex MM Res	GXRXX	U	(800) 526-7384	U /	--	--	--	--	--	0.07	N/A
MMF	Goldman Sachs Inv Tx Ex MM Sel	GSTXX	C	(800) 526-7384	D / 1.6	0.17	0.28	0.36 /34	0.13 /16	0.08 /16	0.36	N/A
MMF	Goldman Sachs Inv Tx Ex MM Svc	FESXX	U	(800) 526-7384	U /	--	--	--	--	--	0.07	N/A
EM	Goldman Sachs Local Emg Mkt Debt	GAMDX	E-	(800) 526-7384	E- / 0.1	7.01	-0.54	12.70 /84	-3.74 / 1	-3.37 / 0	5.32	1.40
EM	Goldman Sachs Local Emg Mkt Debt	GCMDX	E-	(800) 526-7384	E- / 0.1	6.62	-1.07	11.66 /82	-4.49 / 0	-4.13 / 0	4.81	2.15
EM	Goldman Sachs Local Emg Mkt Debt	GIMDX	E-	(800) 526-7384	E- / 0.1	6.91	-0.56	12.86 /85	-3.47 / 1	-3.07 / 1	5.89	1.06
EM	Goldman Sachs Local Emg Mkt Debt	GLIRX	E-	(800) 526-7384	E- / 0.1	6.90	-0.59	12.80 /85	-3.60 / 1	-3.19 / 1	5.83	1.14
USS	Goldman Sachs Short Dur Gov A	GSSDX	D	(800) 526-7384	E / 0.5	0.11	-0.08	0.53 /34	0.32 /19	0.30 /20	1.52	0.91
USS	Goldman Sachs Short Dur Gov C	GSDCX	D	(800) 526-7384	E / 0.5	0.01	-0.18	0.23 /27	-0.07 / 5	-0.06 / 5	1.14	1.66
USS	Goldman Sachs Short Dur Gov Inst	GSTGX	C+	(800) 526-7384	D / 2.1	0.19	0.09	0.87 /38	0.66 /22	0.64 /23	1.88	0.57
USS	Goldman Sachs Short Dur Gov IR	GTDTX	C+	(800) 526-7384	D / 2.0	0.17	0.15	0.79 /37	0.57 /21	0.57 /22	1.79	0.66
USS	Goldman Sachs Short Dur Gov R6	GSTUX	U	(800) 526-7384	U /	0.20	0.10	0.89 /38	--	--	1.90	0.55
USS	Goldman Sachs Short Dur Gov Svc	GSDSX	C-	(800) 526-7384	D- / 1.3	0.07	-0.06	0.47 /33	0.16 /15	0.16 /17	1.38	1.07
GEI	Goldman Sachs Short Dur Income A	GDIAX	C	(800) 526-7384	D+ / 2.5	0.90	0.11	2.67 /54	1.05 /28	1.56 /35	1.81	0.94
GEI	Goldman Sachs Short Dur Income C	GDICX	C	(800) 526-7384	D+ / 2.5	0.91	0.01	2.37 /52	0.68 /23	1.18 /30	1.44	1.69
GEI	Goldman Sachs Short Dur Income	GDFIX	B	(800) 526-7384	C- / 3.8	0.99	0.28	3.02 /57	1.42 /33	1.95 /41	2.18	0.60
GEI	Goldman Sachs Short Dur Income IR	GSSRX	B	(800) 526-7384	C- / 3.6	1.07	0.33	2.93 /56	1.33 /32	1.86 /40	2.08	0.69
GEI	Goldman Sachs Short Dur Income R	GIFRX	C+	(800) 526-7384	D+ / 2.8	0.84	-0.01	2.42 /52	0.83 /25	1.35 /32	1.59	1.19
COI	Goldman Sachs Short Dur Income R6	GDIUX	U	(800) 526-7384	U /	1.08	0.27	3.10 /57	--	--	2.15	0.63
MUN	Goldman Sachs Short Dur T/F A	GSDTX	C-	(800) 526-7384	D / 1.8	1.04	-0.62	0.43 /36	0.68 /28	0.68 /28	0.98	0.76
MUN	Goldman Sachs Short Dur T/F C	GSTCX	C-	(800) 526-7384	D / 1.7	0.94	-0.82	0.03 /20	0.28 /20	0.27 /21	0.59	1.51
MUN	Goldman Sachs Short Dur T/F Inst	GSDUX	B	(800) 526-7384	C- / 3.7	1.21	-0.38	0.74 /41	1.05 /37	1.02 /36	1.31	0.42
MUN	Goldman Sachs Short Dur T/F IR	GDIRX	B-	(800) 526-7384	C- / 3.4	1.10	-0.50	0.68 /40	0.96 /35	0.94 /34	1.24	0.51
MUN	Goldman Sachs Short Dur T/F Svc	GSFSX	C	(800) 526-7384	D+ / 2.3	1.09	-0.63	0.24 /30	0.55 /25	0.52 /25	0.81	0.92
USA	Goldman Sachs Short-Term Consv	GPPAX	C+	(800) 526-7384	D / 2.0	0.21	0.51	1.03 /40	0.45 /20	--	0.73	2.44
USA	Goldman Sachs Short-Term Consv	GPPIX	C+	(800) 526-7384	D+ / 2.4	0.37	0.63	1.29 /43	0.70 /23	--	0.98	2.10
* GL	Goldman Sachs Strategic Income A	GSZAX	E+	(800) 526-7384	E+ / 0.9	1.54	2.19	6.40 /71	-0.05 / 5	3.03 /58	1.68	0.91
GL	Goldman Sachs Strategic Income C	GSZCX	E+	(800) 526-7384	D / 1.6	1.38	1.84	5.64 /69	-0.78 / 3	2.29 /46	1.04	1.66
GL	Goldman Sachs Strategic Income Inst	GSZIX	D-	(800) 526-7384	C- / 3.3	1.62	2.36	6.76 /72	0.29 /18	3.38 /63	2.07	0.57
GL	Goldman Sachs Strategic Income IR	GZIRX	D-	(800) 526-7384	C- / 3.2	1.60	2.31	6.66 /72	0.20 /16	3.29 /62	1.99	0.66
GL	Goldman Sachs Strategic Income R	GSZRX	E+	(800) 526-7384	D+ / 2.3	1.59	2.06	6.14 /71	-0.29 / 4	2.78 /54	1.50	1.16
MTG	Goldman Sachs US Mtge A	GSUAX	C-	(800) 526-7384	D+ / 2.5	0.42	-1.20	0.50 /33	2.27 /48	2.39 /48	2.25	0.98
MTG	Goldman Sachs US Mtge Inst	GSUIX	B+	(800) 526-7384	C / 4.7	0.41	-1.12	0.75 /37	2.62 /54	2.73 /53	2.68	0.64
MTG	Goldman Sachs US Mtge IR	GGIRX	B+	(800) 526-7384	C / 4.5	0.38	-1.17	0.66 /36	2.49 /52	2.66 /52	2.59	0.73
MTG	Goldman Sachs US Mtge R6	GGIUX	U	(800) 526-7384	U /	0.51	-1.02	0.86 /38	--	--	2.69	0.66
MTG	Goldman Sachs US Mtge SA-Inst	GSUPX	B+	(800) 526-7384	C / 4.7	0.50	-1.03	0.75 /37	2.62 /54	2.74 /53	2.68	0.64
GEI	Great Lakes Bond Institutional	GLBNX	C	(855) 278-2020	C / 4.8	1.34	-2.24	3.18 /58	2.39 /50	--	2.24	0.75
COI	Great-West Bond Index Init	MXBIX	D+	(866) 831-7129	C- / 4.0	0.79	-2.48	0.67 /36	2.23 /47	1.86 /40	0.98	0.50
COI	Great-West Bond Index Inst	MXCOX	U	(866) 831-7129	U /	0.90	-2.29	1.02 /40	--	--	2.48	0.15
COI	Great-West Bond Index L	MXBJX	D	(866) 831-7129	C- / 3.5	0.71	-2.65	0.32 /29	1.97 /42	1.59 /36	3.07	0.75
COI	Great-West Federated Bond Init	MXFDX	B	(866) 831-7129	C+ / 5.7	1.59	-1.13	5.58 /69	2.57 /53	2.32 /46	2.28	0.70

● Denotes fund is closed to new investors
* Denotes fund is included in Section II

Risk Rating/Pts	3 Yr Avg Standard Deviation	Avg Duration	NAV As of 2/28/17	Total $(Mil)	Cash %	Gov. Bond %	Muni. Bond %	Corp. Bond %	Other %	Portfolio Turnover Ratio	Avg Coupon Rate	Manager Quality Pct	Manager Tenure (Years)	Initial Purch. $	Additional Purch. $	Front End Load	Back End Load
D+ / 2.8	4.0	7.1	9.10	32	0	13	3	82	2	79	0.0	93	14	1,000	50	3.8	0.0
D+ / 2.8	4.0	7.1	9.10	139	0	13	3	82	2	79	0.0	94	14	1,000,000	0	0.0	0.0
D+ / 2.8	4.0	7.1	9.11	4	0	13	3	82	2	79	0.0	94	14	0	0	0.0	0.0
U /	N/A	7.1	9.11	N/A	0	13	3	82	2	79	0.0	N/A	14	0	0	0.0	0.0
D+ / 2.8	4.0	7.1	9.10	250	0	13	3	82	2	79	0.0	94	14	100,000,000	0	0.0	0.0
A+ / 9.9	0.1	N/A	1.00	5	100	0	0	0	0	0	0.2	45	N/A	10,000,000	0	0.0	0.0
U /	N/A	N/A	1.00	N/A	100	0	0	0	0	0	0.1	43	N/A	10,000,000	0	0.0	0.0
A+ / 9.9	0.1	N/A	1.00	N/A	100	0	0	0	0	0	0.2	N/A	N/A	10,000,000	0	0.0	0.0
A+ / 9.9	0.1	N/A	1.00	921	100	0	0	0	0	0	0.4	49	N/A	10,000,000	0	0.0	0.0
A+ / 9.9	0.1	N/A	1.00	N/A	100	0	0	0	0	0	0.3	46	N/A	10,000,000	0	0.0	0.0
A+ / 9.9	N/A	N/A	1.00	N/A	100	0	0	0	0	0	0.1	41	N/A	10,000,000	0	0.0	0.0
U /	N/A	N/A	1.00	5	100	0	0	0	0	0	0.1	40	N/A	10,000,000	0	0.0	0.0
A+ / 9.9	0.1	N/A	1.00	N/A	100	0	0	0	0	0	0.4	48	N/A	10,000,000	0	0.0	0.0
U /	N/A	N/A	1.00	1	100	0	0	0	0	0	0.1	41	N/A	10,000,000	0	0.0	0.0
E- / 0.0	12.4	N/A	6.22	101	6	76	0	3	15	100	0.0	12	9	1,000	50	4.5	2.0
E- / 0.1	12.3	N/A	6.22	6	6	76	0	3	15	100	0.0	4	9	1,000	50	0.0	2.0
E- / 0.1	12.4	N/A	6.21	346	6	76	0	3	15	100	0.0	18	9	1,000,000	0	0.0	2.0
E- / 0.1	12.4	N/A	6.20	17	6	76	0	3	15	100	0.0	15	9	0	0	0.0	2.0
A+ / 9.7	0.7	2.0	9.98	140	0	54	0	0	46	227	0.0	36	9	1,000	50	1.5	0.0
A+ / 9.7	0.7	2.0	9.92	29	0	54	0	0	46	227	0.0	24	9	1,000	50	0.0	0.0
A+ / 9.7	0.7	2.0	9.95	1,045	0	54	0	0	46	227	0.0	57	9	1,000,000	0	0.0	0.0
A+ / 9.7	0.7	2.0	9.99	25	0	54	0	0	46	227	0.0	54	9	0	0	0.0	0.0
U /	N/A	2.0	9.95	76	0	54	0	0	46	227	0.0	N/A	9	0	0	0.0	0.0
A+ / 9.7	0.7	2.0	9.94	26	0	54	0	0	46	227	0.0	31	9	0	0	0.0	0.0
A- / 9.1	1.1	2.5	9.96	9	0	8	2	56	34	161	0.0	57	5	1,000	50	1.5	0.0
A- / 9.0	1.2	2.5	9.97	1	0	8	2	56	34	161	0.0	34	5	1,000	50	0.0	0.0
A- / 9.1	1.1	2.5	9.98	553	0	8	2	56	34	161	0.0	68	5	1,000,000	0	0.0	0.0
A- / 9.1	1.2	2.5	9.98	2	0	8	2	56	34	161	0.0	65	5	0	0	0.0	0.0
A- / 9.1	1.2	2.5	9.98	N/A	0	8	2	56	34	161	0.0	45	5	0	0	0.0	0.0
U /	N/A	2.5	9.98	N/A	0	8	2	56	34	161	0.0	N/A	5	0	0	0.0	0.0
A- / 9.1	1.2	2.1	10.52	125	0	0	100	0	0	24	0.0	23	18	1,000	50	1.5	0.0
A- / 9.1	1.2	2.1	10.51	24	0	0	100	0	0	24	0.0	14	18	1,000	50	0.0	0.0
A- / 9.0	1.2	2.1	10.51	4,439	0	0	100	0	0	24	0.0	34	18	1,000,000	0	0.0	0.0
A- / 9.1	1.2	2.1	10.51	10	0	0	100	0	0	24	0.0	32	18	0	0	0.0	0.0
A- / 9.0	1.2	2.1	10.51	N/A	0	0	100	0	0	24	0.0	19	18	0	0	0.0	0.0
A+ / 9.9	0.2	0.3	10.02	N/A	0	0	0	0	100	39	0.0	60	3	0	0	0.0	0.0
A+ / 9.9	0.2	0.3	10.02	155	0	0	0	0	100	39	0.0	67	3	1,000,000	0	0.0	0.0
C / 5.0	3.1	-0.5	9.69	864	3	33	2	27	35	212	0.0	26	7	1,000	50	3.8	0.0
C / 4.8	3.2	-0.5	9.70	466	3	33	2	27	35	212	0.0	9	7	1,000	50	0.0	0.0
C / 5.0	3.1	-0.5	9.69	6,527	3	33	2	27	35	212	0.0	42	7	1,000,000	0	0.0	0.0
C / 4.8	3.2	-0.5	9.69	177	3	33	2	27	35	212	0.0	35	7	0	0	0.0	0.0
C / 4.8	3.2	-0.5	9.69	10	3	33	2	27	35	212	0.0	19	7	0	0	0.0	0.0
B+ / 8.4	1.9	2.8	10.47	51	0	16	0	0	84	956	0.0	43	14	1,000	50	3.8	0.0
B+ / 8.4	1.8	2.8	10.49	63	0	16	0	0	84	956	0.0	61	14	1,000,000	0	0.0	0.0
B+ / 8.4	1.9	2.8	10.49	23	0	16	0	0	84	956	0.0	55	14	0	0	0.0	0.0
U /	N/A	2.8	10.50	1	0	16	0	0	84	956	0.0	N/A	14	0	0	0.0	0.0
B+ / 8.4	1.9	2.8	10.47	223	0	16	0	0	84	956	0.0	59	14	100,000,000	0	0.0	0.0
C+ / 5.7	3.0	6.4	9.77	116	4	8	15	53	20	68	3.6	35	5	100,000	100	0.0	0.0
C+ / 5.7	3.0	5.5	13.65	336	0	41	1	24	34	40	3.0	30	13	0	0	0.0	0.0
U /	N/A	5.5	9.75	868	0	41	1	24	34	40	3.0	N/A	13	0	0	0.0	0.0
C+ / 5.9	2.9	5.5	8.83	180	0	41	1	24	34	40	3.0	24	13	0	0	0.0	0.0
C+ / 6.3	2.9	5.1	10.66	32	0	18	0	51	31	49	3.8	47	14	0	0	0.0	0.0

Fund Type	Fund Name	Ticker Symbol	Overall Investment Rating	Phone	Performance Rating/Pts	3 Mo	6 Mo	1Yr / Pct	3Yr / Pct	5Yr / Pct	Dividend Yield	Expense Ratio
	99 Pct = Best							Total Return % through 2/28/17	Annualized		Incl. in Returns	
COI	Great-West Federated Bond Inst	MXIUX	U	(866) 831-7129	U /	1.74	-0.88	5.95 /70	--	--	3.11	0.35
COI	Great-West Loomis Sayles Bond Init	MXLMX	C-	(866) 831-7129	B / 7.7	3.42	1.96	15.20 /89	2.55 /53	5.32 /87	2.25	0.90
GEL	Great-West Loomis Sayles Bond Inst	MXUGX	U	(866) 831-7129	U /	3.61	2.27	15.67 /90	--	--	4.08	0.55
COH	Great-West Putnam High Yld Bd Init	MXHYX	C+	(866) 831-7129	A / 9.3	4.10	4.17	19.39 /95	3.94 /74	6.17 /93	6.04	1.10
COH	Great-West Putnam High Yld Bd Inst	MXFRX	U	(866) 831-7129	U /	4.08	4.35	19.78 /96	--	--	5.46	0.75
COI	Great-West Short Duration Bd Init	MXSDX	B-	(866) 831-7129	C- / 3.1	0.81	0.12	2.20 /51	1.11 /29	1.77 /38	1.48	0.60
COI	Great-West Short Duration Bd Inst	MXXJX	U	(866) 831-7129	U /	0.92	0.37	2.64 /54	--	--	2.19	0.25
COI	Great-West Short Duration Bd L	MXTDX	B-	(866) 831-7129	C- / 3.1	0.80	0.17	2.28 /51	1.11 /29	--	1.60	0.85
GL	Great-West TempletonGlobal Bd Init	MXGBX	E+	(866) 831-7129	C / 4.8	4.68	5.99	8.38 /75	0.51 /21	1.54 /35	1.26	1.30
GL	Great-West TempletonGlobal Bd Inst	MXZMX	U	(866) 831-7129	U /	4.71	6.14	8.83 /76	--	--	1.26	0.95
MTG	Great-West US Govt Mtg Secs Init	MXGMX	C+	(866) 831-7129	C- / 3.5	0.33	-1.76	-0.10 /16	1.98 /43	1.69 /37	1.76	0.60
MTG	Great-West US Govt Mtg Secs Inst	MXDQX	U	(866) 831-7129	U /	0.47	-1.48	0.30 /29	--	--	2.70	0.25
* LP	Guggenheim Floating Rate Strat A	GIFAX	A+	(800) 820-0888	C+ / 6.8	1.49	2.89	9.26 /77	3.50 /69	5.17 /86	3.60	1.19
LP	Guggenheim Floating Rate Strat C	GIFCX	A+	(800) 820-0888	C+ / 6.8	1.30	2.51	8.45 /75	2.72 /56	4.38 /77	2.97	1.91
LP	Guggenheim Floating Rate Strat Inst	GIFIX	A+	(800) 820-0888	B / 7.9	1.55	3.01	9.51 /78	3.74 /72	5.41 /88	3.94	0.85
LP	Guggenheim Floating Rate Strat P	GIFPX	U	(800) 820-0888	U /	1.48	2.89	9.25 /77	--	--	3.70	1.04
COH	Guggenheim High Yield A	SIHAX	C+	(800) 820-0888	A- / 9.2	4.34	6.22	21.15 /97	4.98 /85	7.64 /97	5.68	1.27
COH	Guggenheim High Yield C	SIHSX	B-	(800) 820-0888	A / 9.3	4.21	5.90	20.30 /96	4.20 /78	6.84 /96	5.16	2.01
COH	Guggenheim High Yield Inst	SHYIX	B	(800) 820-0888	A+ / 9.7	4.54	6.51	21.68 /98	5.28 /87	7.93 /98	6.25	0.94
COH	Guggenheim High Yield P	SIHPX	U	(800) 820-0888	U /	4.49	6.43	21.42 /97	--	--	5.96	3.36
USS	Guggenheim Investment Grade Bd A	SIUSX	A+	(800) 820-0888	C+ / 6.5	1.83	0.03	6.20 /71	4.14 /77	4.59 /80	3.27	1.17
USS	Guggenheim Investment Grade Bd C	SDICX	A+	(800) 820-0888	C+ / 6.8	1.60	-0.33	5.37 /68	3.38 /67	3.82 /70	2.67	1.99
COI	Guggenheim Investment Grade Bd	GIUSX	A+	(800) 820-0888	B / 7.9	1.88	0.20	6.46 /71	4.40 /80	--	3.71	0.94
COI	Guggenheim Investment Grade Bd P	SIUPX	U	(800) 820-0888	U /	1.78	0.05	6.14 /71	--	--	3.41	3.29
COI	Guggenheim Limited Duration P	GILPX	U	(800) 820-0888	U /	1.03	1.71	5.36 /68	--	--	2.78	0.94
* GEL	Guggenheim Macro Opportunities A	GIOAX	A+	(800) 820-0888	B / 8.0	2.52	4.68	14.16 /87	4.09 /76	5.75 /90	4.48	1.57
GEL	Guggenheim Macro Opportunities C	GIOCX	A+	(800) 820-0888	B / 8.2	2.33	4.25	13.30 /86	3.32 /66	4.97 /84	3.93	2.29
GEL	Guggenheim Macro Opportunities	GIOIX	A+	(800) 820-0888	A- / 9.2	2.60	4.86	14.57 /88	4.45 /80	6.10 /93	5.03	1.25
MUN	Guggenheim Municipal Income A	GIJAX	C-	(800) 820-0888	C+ / 5.9	1.62	-3.25	-0.36 /12	3.71 /90	3.31 /85	2.00	1.17
MUN	Guggenheim Municipal Income P	GIJPX	U	(800) 820-0888	U /	1.53	-3.33	-0.35 /12	--	--	2.09	3.17
* GEI	Guggenheim Total Return Bond A	GIBAX	A+	(800) 820-0888	C+ / 6.8	1.81	0.17	6.95 /72	4.32 /79	5.46 /88	3.52	1.10
GEI	Guggenheim Total Return Bond C	GIBCX	A+	(800) 820-0888	B- / 7.1	1.59	-0.19	6.16 /71	3.55 /69	4.69 /81	2.92	1.80
GEI	Guggenheim Total Return Bond Inst	GIBIX	A+	(800) 820-0888	B / 8.2	1.85	0.35	7.33 /73	4.68 /83	5.82 /91	4.03	0.76
COI	Guggenheim Total Return Bond P	GIBLX	U	(800) 820-0888	U /	1.78	0.19	7.03 /73	--	--	3.74	1.02
MMT	Guggenheim US Govt MM MM	RYFXX	U	(800) 820-0888	U /	--	--	--	--	--	0.01	N/A
GEI	GuideMark Core Fixed Inc Inst	GICFX	C-	(888) 278-5809	C / 4.4	1.11	-2.03	2.05 /49	2.24 /47	1.98 /42	2.29	0.74
GEI	GuideMark Core Fixed Inc Svc	GMCOX	D	(888) 278-5809	C- / 3.6	0.93	-2.33	1.52 /45	1.81 /40	1.49 /34	1.66	1.32
GL	GuideMark Opptnstc Fxd Inc Inst	GIOFX	D+	(888) 278-5809	C+ / 6.0	3.72	5.94	9.01 /76	1.31 /32	2.53 /50	3.11	1.15
GL	GuideMark Opptnstc Fxd Inc Svc	GMIFX	D-	(888) 278-5809	C / 5.1	3.54	5.63	8.26 /75	0.85 /25	2.03 /43	1.72	1.70
MUI	GuideMark Tax-Exempt Fixed Inc Svc	GMTEX	B	(888) 278-5809	C+ / 6.8	1.92	-2.81	-0.44 /10	2.99 /82	2.27 /65	2.76	1.42
GL	GuidePath Flexible Income Alloc Ins	GIXFX	B+	(888) 278-5809	C+ / 5.8	1.97	-0.11	4.74 /66	2.58 /53	--	2.55	0.83
GL	GuidePath Flexible Income Alloc Svc	GPIFX	C+	(888) 278-5809	C / 4.4	1.81	-0.33	4.13 /63	1.71 /38	--	1.95	1.43
COI	GuideStone Ex-Duration Bond Inst	GEDYX	D+	(888) 984-8433	B+ / 8.5	3.20	-5.34	8.36 /75	5.33 /87	5.19 /86	5.01	0.60
COI	GuideStone Ex-Duration Bond Inv	GEDZX	D	(888) 984-8433	B / 8.1	3.07	-5.79	7.74 /74	4.96 /85	4.87 /83	2.05	0.85
COH	GuideStone Flexible Income Inv	GFLZX	C	(888) 984-8433	C / 5.5	1.46	2.58	8.01 /74	1.68 /38	--	3.09	1.19
GL	GuideStone Global Bond Inst	GGBEX	U	(888) 984-8433	U /	3.83	1.84	14.67 /88	--	--	4.11	0.63
GL	GuideStone Global Bond Inv	GGBFX	D+	(888) 984-8433	B- / 7.5	3.76	1.70	14.34 /87	2.54 /52	3.46 /65	3.83	0.87
GEI	GuideStone Infl Protected Bd Inst	GIPYX	U	(888) 984-8433	U /	0.95	-0.58	2.93 /56	--	--	1.24	0.42
GL	GuideStone Infl Protected Bd Inv	GIPZX	E+	(888) 984-8433	C- / 3.0	0.91	-0.68	2.61 /54	1.00 /28	0.06 /12	0.63	0.68
COI	GuideStone Low-Duration Bond Inst	GLDYX	B	(888) 984-8433	C- / 3.3	0.57	0.51	2.24 /51	1.23 /31	1.47 /34	1.55	0.38
COI	GuideStone Low-Duration Bond Inv	GLDZX	B-	(888) 984-8433	D+ / 2.8	0.51	0.36	1.87 /48	0.94 /27	1.23 /30	0.95	0.65
COI	GuideStone Med-Duration Bond Inst	GMDYX	B-	(888) 984-8433	C / 5.5	1.57	-1.48	3.42 /59	2.78 /57	2.86 /55	2.66	0.45

● Denotes fund is closed to new investors
* Denotes fund is included in Section II

www.thestreetratings.com

RISK			NET ASSETS		ASSET					Portfolio Turnover Ratio	Avg Coupon Rate	FUND MANAGER		MINIMUM		LOADS	
Risk Rating/Pts	3 Yr Avg Standard Deviation	Avg Duration	NAV As of 2/28/17	Total $(Mil)	Cash %	Gov. Bond %	Muni. Bond %	Corp. Bond %	Other %	Portfolio Turnover Ratio	Avg Coupon Rate	Manager Quality Pct	Manager Tenure (Years)	Initial Purch. $	Additional Purch. $	Front End Load	Back End Load
U /	N/A	5.1	9.83	403	0	18	0	51	31	49	3.8	N/A	14	0	0	0.0	0.0
D /1.9	5.2	4.5	13.19	315	1	34	2	46	17	35	4.7	35	23	0	0	0.0	0.0
U /	N/A	4.5	9.66	428	1	34	2	46	17	35	4.7	N/A	23	0	0	0.0	0.0
D- /1.0	5.8	3.4	8.28	9	1	1	0	86	12	56	5.9	20	8	0	0	0.0	0.0
U /	N/A	3.4	9.77	308	1	1	0	86	12	56	5.9	N/A	8	0	0	0.0	0.0
A /9.3	1.0	2.3	10.31	51	0	0	0	80	20	74	2.4	58	14	0	0	0.0	0.0
U /	N/A	2.3	9.92	143	0	0	0	80	20	74	2.4	N/A	14	0	0	0.0	0.0
A- /9.2	1.0	2.3	9.51	N/A	0	0	0	80	20	74	2.4	57	14	0	0	0.0	0.0
D /1.8	5.4	0.7	8.50	53	17	75	0	0	8	49	4.3	55	12	0	0	0.0	0.0
U /	N/A	0.7	9.34	302	17	75	0	0	8	49	4.3	N/A	12	0	0	0.0	0.0
B /7.9	2.2	3.3	11.90	203	0	3	0	2	95	42	3.4	19	24	0	0	0.0	0.0
U /	N/A	3.3	9.65	195	0	3	0	2	95	42	3.4	N/A	24	0	0	0.0	0.0
B /8.0	2.2	0.3	26.11	536	1	0	0	22	77	35	4.3	91	6	2,500	100	3.0	0.0
B /8.0	2.1	0.3	26.10	219	1	0	0	22	77	35	4.3	87	6	2,500	100	0.0	0.0
B /8.0	2.2	0.3	26.13	2,385	1	0	0	22	77	35	4.3	92	6	2,000,000	0	0.0	0.0
U /	N/A	0.3	26.12	228	1	0	0	22	77	35	4.3	N/A	6	0	0	0.0	0.0
D /1.7	5.1	2.4	11.46	115	0	2	0	73	25	55	7.4	78	5	2,500	100	4.0	2.0
D /1.7	5.0	2.4	11.56	28	0	2	0	73	25	55	7.4	61	5	2,500	100	0.0	2.0
D /1.6	5.1	2.4	9.35	215	0	2	0	73	25	55	7.4	81	5	2,000,000	0	0.0	2.0
U /	N/A	2.4	11.47	12	0	2	0	73	25	55	7.4	N/A	5	0	0	0.0	2.0
B /8.0	2.1	4.4	18.27	162	0	16	1	17	66	100	2.6	93	5	2,500	100	4.0	0.0
B /8.0	2.1	4.4	18.19	31	0	16	1	17	66	100	2.6	89	5	2,500	100	0.0	0.0
B /8.0	2.1	4.4	18.24	105	0	16	1	17	66	100	2.6	90	5	2,000,000	0	0.0	0.0
U /	N/A	4.4	18.28	2	0	16	1	17	66	100	2.6	N/A	5	0	0	0.0	0.0
U /	N/A	0.8	24.74	24	6	0	0	29	65	39	2.4	N/A	4	0	0	0.0	0.0
C+ /6.4	2.8	-0.1	26.58	828	2	1	0	32	65	61	3.9	94	6	2,500	100	4.0	0.0
C+ /6.3	2.9	-0.1	26.56	375	2	1	0	32	65	61	3.9	91	6	2,500	100	0.0	0.0
C+ /6.4	2.8	-0.1	26.61	3,250	2	1	0	32	65	61	3.9	94	6	2,000,000	0	0.0	0.0
C /4.3	3.4	5.7	12.40	32	6	0	93	0	1	61	3.7	58	5	2,500	100	4.0	0.0
U /	N/A	5.7	12.39	N/A	6	0	93	0	1	61	3.7	N/A	5	0	0	0.0	0.0
B /7.9	2.3	4.4	26.64	639	0	10	4	31	55	86	2.2	89	6	2,500	100	4.0	0.0
B /7.9	2.2	4.4	26.64	222	0	10	4	31	55	86	2.2	84	6	2,500	100	0.0	0.0
B /7.9	2.2	4.4	26.67	4,049	0	10	4	31	55	86	2.2	91	6	2,000,000	0	0.0	0.0
U /	N/A	4.4	26.64	301	0	10	4	31	55	86	2.2	N/A	6	0	0	0.0	0.0
U /	N/A	N/A	1.00	516	100	0	0	0	0	0	0.0	N/A	24	0	0	0.0	0.0
C+ /6.1	2.9	N/A	9.30	9	0	10	0	37	53	157	0.0	28	7	0	0	0.0	0.0
C+ /6.0	2.9	N/A	9.37	150	0	10	0	37	53	157	0.0	16	7	0	0	0.0	0.0
C- /3.3	4.0	N/A	9.36	9	1	55	0	6	38	41	0.0	73	6	0	0	0.0	0.0
C- /3.3	4.0	N/A	9.44	60	1	55	0	6	38	41	0.0	61	6	0	0	0.0	0.0
C /5.4	3.0	N/A	11.29	33	0	0	0	0	100	12	0.0	30	11	0	0	0.0	0.0
B- /7.1	2.7	N/A	9.77	N/A	5	34	0	27	34	148	0.0	92	5	0	0	0.0	0.0
B- /7.3	2.6	N/A	9.70	101	5	34	0	27	34	148	0.0	87	5	0	0	0.0	0.0
E /0.5	7.6	N/A	17.26	118	2	40	2	52	4	42	0.0	6	16	1,000,000	0	0.0	0.0
E /0.5	7.6	N/A	17.26	119	2	40	2	52	4	42	0.0	4	16	1,000	100	0.0	0.0
C /5.2	2.6	N/A	9.60	156	4	0	0	25	71	50	0.0	36	4	1,000	100	0.0	0.0
U /	N/A	8.7	9.92	355	7	24	1	57	11	30	0.0	N/A	11	1,000,000	0	0.0	0.0
D /1.6	5.3	8.7	9.92	94	7	24	1	57	11	30	0.0	93	11	1,000	100	0.0	0.0
U /	N/A	N/A	10.37	202	1	98	0	0	1	45	0.0	N/A	3	1,000,000	0	0.0	0.0
C- /3.4	3.8	N/A	10.38	83	1	98	0	0	1	45	0.0	83	3	1,000	100	0.0	0.0
A+ /9.7	0.6	N/A	13.39	602	0	23	1	42	34	746	0.0	71	9	1,000,000	0	0.0	0.0
A+ /9.7	0.6	N/A	13.39	281	0	23	1	42	34	746	0.0	63	9	1,000	100	0.0	0.0
C+ /6.2	2.9	N/A	14.61	855	0	28	1	28	43	346	0.0	56	16	1,000,000	0	0.0	0.0

Fund Type	Fund Name	Ticker Symbol	Overall Investment Rating	Phone	Performance Rating/Pts	3 Mo	6 Mo	1Yr / Pct	3Yr / Pct	5Yr / Pct	Dividend Yield	Expense Ratio
								Total Return % through 2/28/17	Annualized		Incl. in Returns	
COI	GuideStone Med-Duration Bond Inv	GMDZX	C	(888) 984-8433	C / 4.9	1.43	-1.72	2.99 /56	2.46 /51	2.63 /52	1.54	0.73
MMT	GuideStone Money Market Inst	GMYXX	C-	(888) 984-8433	D- / 1.3	0.10	0.17	0.29 /29	0.15 /15	0.11 /15	0.29	N/A
MMT	GuideStone Money Market Inv	GMZXX	D+	(888) 984-8433	E+ / 0.7	0.04	0.05	0.06 /21	0.03 / 8	0.03 / 9	0.06	N/A
MUN	Gurtin CA Muni Opport Val Inst	GCMFX	A+	(844) 342-5763	B / 7.8	0.94	-1.58	0.30 /32	3.54 /88	3.89 /92	1.84	0.79
MUN	Gurtin California Muni Int Val Inst	GCMVX	U	(844) 342-5763	U /	2.22	-2.94	-0.56 / 9	--	--	1.35	1.02
MUN	Gurtin National Mun Opport Val Inst	GNMFX	A+	(844) 342-5763	B / 7.9	1.14	-0.92	0.93 /44	3.45 /87	3.61 /89	1.76	0.93
MUN	Gurtin National Muni Int Value Inst	GNMVX	U	(844) 342-5763	U /	1.93	-2.78	-0.22 /14	--	--	1.38	1.04
MUN	Hancock Horizon LA Tax Fr Inc C	HHLCX	A-	(888) 346-6300	A / 9.5	2.49	-2.51	1.26 /48	5.00 /97	--	2.89	2.32
MUS	Hancock Horizon LA Tax Fr Inc Inst	HHLTX	A-	(888) 346-6300	A / 9.4	2.33	-2.83	0.75 /41	5.03 /97	3.01 /80	2.56	1.57
MUS	Hancock Horizon LA Tax Fr Inc Inv	HHLAX	C+	(888) 346-6300	B / 7.8	2.33	-2.90	0.50 /37	4.76 /96	2.76 /75	2.56	1.57
MUN	Hancock Horizon MS Tax-Fr Inc C	HAMCX	C-	(888) 346-6300	B- / 7.2	2.18	-4.22	-1.31 / 2	3.52 /88	--	1.88	2.07
MUS	Hancock Horizon MS Tax-Fr Inc Inst	HHMTX	B-	(888) 346-6300	B+ / 8.5	2.44	-3.74	-0.31 /13	4.22 /94	2.51 /71	2.93	1.10
MUS	Hancock Horizon MS Tax-Fr Inc Inv	HIMAX	D	(888) 346-6300	C+ / 6.3	2.31	-3.87	-0.57 / 9	3.96 /92	2.27 /65	2.55	1.35
GEI	Harbor Bond Admin	HRBDX	C-	(800) 422-1050	C / 5.3	2.07	-0.72	4.24 /63	2.35 /49	2.69 /53	2.58	0.85
* GEI	Harbor Bond Inst	HABDX	C	(800) 422-1050	C+ / 5.8	2.23	-0.50	4.52 /65	2.62 /54	2.96 /57	2.84	0.60
COH	Harbor High Yield Bond Admin	HYFRX	C-	(800) 422-1050	B / 8.2	4.20	4.41	15.48 /89	3.11 /63	4.80 /82	4.91	0.96
COH	Harbor High Yield Bond Inst	HYFAX	C	(800) 422-1050	B+ / 8.5	4.38	4.55	15.91 /90	3.41 /67	5.06 /85	5.15	0.71
COH	Harbor High Yield Bond Inv	HYFIX	C-	(800) 422-1050	B / 8.1	4.17	4.26	15.44 /89	3.01 /61	4.67 /80	4.77	1.08
COH	Harbor High Yield Bond Ret	HNHYX	U	(800) 422-1050	U /	4.39	4.59		--	--	0.00	0.66
MMT	Harbor Money Market Admin	HRMXX	C	(800) 422-1050	D- / 1.4	0.12	0.21	0.38 /31	0.19 /16	0.15 /17	0.38	N/A
MMT	Harbor Money Market Inst	HARXX	C	(800) 422-1050	D- / 1.4	0.12	0.21	0.38 /31	0.19 /16	0.15 /17	0.38	N/A
US	Harbor Real Return Admin	HRRRX	E+	(800) 422-1050	C- / 3.6	1.56	0.15	4.83 /66	1.02 /28	0.27 /19	0.04	1.04
US	Harbor Real Return Inst	HARRX	E+	(800) 422-1050	C- / 4.1	1.55	0.25	5.04 /67	1.30 /32	0.53 /22	0.35	0.79
GL	Hartford Emg Markets Local Debt A	HLDAX	E-	(888) 843-7824	E- / 0.2	6.64	-0.13	13.53 /86	-2.62 / 1	-1.12 / 2	4.20	1.54
GL	Hartford Emg Markets Local Debt C	HLDCX	E-	(888) 843-7824	E- / 0.2	6.45	-0.37	12.69 /84	-3.32 / 1	-1.85 / 1	3.65	2.30
GL	Hartford Emg Markets Local Debt I	HLDIX	E-	(888) 843-7824	D / 1.6	6.72	0.14	13.86 /87	-2.31 / 2	-0.86 / 2	4.68	1.19
GL	Hartford Emg Markets Local Debt R3	HLDRX	E-	(888) 843-7824	E / 0.3	6.73	-0.02	13.25 /86	-2.99 / 1	-1.48 / 2	4.44	1.82
GL	Hartford Emg Markets Local Debt R4	HLDSX	E-	(888) 843-7824	E+ / 0.6	6.67	-0.02	13.61 /86	-2.62 / 1	-1.13 / 2	4.75	1.52
GL	Hartford Emg Markets Local Debt R5	HLDTX	E-	(888) 843-7824	D- / 1.4	6.80	0.24	13.83 /87	-2.46 / 2	-0.91 / 2	6.28	1.22
GL	Hartford Emg Markets Local Debt Y	HLDYX	E-	(888) 843-7824	D / 1.6	6.63	0.06	13.90 /87	-2.31 / 2	-0.80 / 2	4.82	1.12
* LP	Hartford Floating Rate A	HFLAX	C+	(888) 843-7824	B- / 7.4	2.85	5.30	14.73 /88	2.99 /61	4.07 /73	3.77	0.99
LP ●	Hartford Floating Rate B	HFLBX	C+	(888) 843-7824	B- / 7.4	2.66	4.92	13.89 /87	2.21 /47	3.27 /62	3.16	1.85
LP	Hartford Floating Rate C	HFLCX	C+	(888) 843-7824	B- / 7.4	2.67	4.93	13.92 /87	2.24 /47	3.31 /62	3.19	1.74
GL	Hartford Floating Rate High Inc A	HFHAX	C	(888) 843-7824	B / 7.9	3.28	5.65	17.79 /93	3.00 /61	4.78 /82	4.34	1.13
GL	Hartford Floating Rate High Inc C	HFHCX	C	(888) 843-7824	B / 7.9	3.09	5.26	16.92 /92	2.23 /47	4.00 /72	3.75	1.90
GL	Hartford Floating Rate High Inc I	HFHIX	B-	(888) 843-7824	B+ / 8.9	3.34	5.78	18.20 /94	3.25 /65	5.06 /85	4.71	0.88
GL	Hartford Floating Rate High Inc R3	HFHRX	C+	(888) 843-7824	B+ / 8.4	3.21	5.50	17.45 /93	2.73 /56	4.47 /78	4.19	1.50
GL	Hartford Floating Rate High Inc R4	HFHSX	B-	(888) 843-7824	B+ / 8.7	3.29	5.66	17.80 /93	3.02 /61	4.78 /82	4.46	1.20
GL	Hartford Floating Rate High Inc R5	HFHTX	B	(888) 843-7824	A- / 9.1	3.36	5.81	18.15 /94	3.67 /71	5.30 /87	4.74	0.90
GL	Hartford Floating Rate High Inc Y	HFHYX	B-	(888) 843-7824	B+ / 8.9	3.36	5.81	18.17 /94	3.31 /66	5.08 /85	4.76	0.79
LP	Hartford Floating Rate I	HFLIX	B+	(888) 843-7824	B+ / 8.5	2.92	5.45	15.03 /88	3.23 /65	4.34 /77	4.16	0.72
LP	Hartford Floating Rate R3	HFLRX	B-	(888) 843-7824	B / 7.9	2.66	5.16	14.41 /87	2.72 /56	3.80 /70	3.65	1.38
LP	Hartford Floating Rate R4	HFLSX	B	(888) 843-7824	B / 8.1	2.73	5.18	14.59 /88	2.94 /60	4.05 /73	3.89	1.07
LP	Hartford Floating Rate R5	HFLTX	B+	(888) 843-7824	B+ / 8.5	2.92	5.46	15.07 /89	3.28 /66	4.36 /77	4.18	0.79
LP	Hartford Floating Rate Y	HFLYX	B+	(888) 843-7824	B+ / 8.6	2.94	5.49	15.14 /89	3.34 /66	4.42 /78	4.22	0.66
COH	Hartford High Yield A	HAHAX	D+	(888) 843-7824	B / 7.6	4.62	4.45	16.42 /91	3.33 /66	5.37 /87	4.53	1.17
COH ●	Hartford High Yield B	HAHBX	C-	(888) 843-7824	B / 7.9	4.31	3.94	15.47 /89	2.56 /53	4.58 /79	4.02	2.07
COH	Hartford High Yield C	HAHCX	C-	(888) 843-7824	B / 8.0	4.45	3.93	15.61 /89	2.56 /53	4.57 /79	4.02	1.85
COH	Hartford High Yield HLS IA		C+	(888) 843-7824	A / 9.3	4.78	4.91	17.97 /93	3.90 /74	5.87 /91	6.06	0.76
COH	Hartford High Yield HLS IB		C+	(888) 843-7824	A- / 9.1	4.73	4.73	17.63 /93	3.64 /70	5.60 /89	5.85	1.01
COH	Hartford High Yield I	HAHIX	C+	(888) 843-7824	B+ / 8.9	4.67	4.43	16.65 /91	3.58 /70	5.61 /89	4.99	0.85
COH	Hartford High Yield R3	HAHRX	C	(888) 843-7824	B+ / 8.4	4.41	4.16	16.09 /90	3.02 /61	5.06 /85	4.46	1.49

Risk Rating/Pts	3 Yr Avg Standard Deviation	Avg Duration	NAV As of 2/28/17	Total $(Mil)	Cash %	Gov. Bond %	Muni. Bond %	Corp. Bond %	Other %	Portfolio Turnover Ratio	Avg Coupon Rate	Manager Quality Pct	Manager Tenure (Years)	Initial Purch. $	Additional Purch. $	Front End Load	Back End Load
C+ / 6.1	2.9	N/A	14.61	219	0	28	1	28	43	346	0.0	35	16	1,000	100	0.0	0.0
A+ / 9.9	N/A	N/A	1.00	253	100	0	0	0	0	0	0.3	49	N/A	1,000,000	0	0.0	0.0
A+ / 9.9	N/A	N/A	1.00	967	100	0	0	0	0	0	0.1	40	N/A	1,000	100	0.0	0.0
B+ / 8.4	1.9	N/A	9.99	197	0	0	0	0	100	5	0.0	82	N/A	250,000	0	0.0	0.0
U /	N/A	N/A	9.92	69	0	0	0	0	100	5	0.0	N/A	N/A	250,000	0	0.0	0.0
B+ / 8.6	1.8	N/A	9.99	118	0	0	0	0	100	59	0.0	82	N/A	250,000	0	0.0	0.0
U /	N/A	N/A	9.94	169	0	0	0	0	100	59	0.0	N/A	2	250,000	0	0.0	0.0
D+ / 2.9	3.9	7.8	16.93	N/A	0	0	0	0	100	16	0.0	75	6	1,000	100	0.0	0.0
D+ / 2.9	3.9	7.8	16.83	4	0	0	0	0	100	16	0.0	76	6	1,000	100	0.0	0.0
D+ / 2.9	3.9	7.8	16.83	3	0	0	0	0	100	16	0.0	70	6	1,000	100	4.0	0.0
D+ / 2.6	4.3	5.4	16.29	N/A	0	0	0	0	100	6	0.0	13	6	1,000	100	0.0	0.0
D+ / 2.7	4.3	5.4	16.26	8	0	0	0	0	100	6	0.0	31	6	1,000	100	0.0	0.0
D+ / 2.7	4.3	5.4	16.26	7	0	0	0	0	100	6	0.0	24	6	1,000	100	4.0	0.0
C / 4.6	3.3	5.6	11.52	33	0	34	2	19	45	592	3.3	31	3	50,000	0	0.0	0.0
C / 4.6	3.3	5.6	11.52	2,260	0	34	2	19	45	592	3.3	48	3	1,000	0	0.0	0.0
D- / 1.3	5.4	3.5	10.25	5	1	0	0	95	4	58	6.1	11	15	50,000	0	0.0	1.0
D- / 1.4	5.3	3.5	10.24	1,675	1	0	0	95	4	58	6.1	18	15	1,000	0	0.0	1.0
D- / 1.3	5.4	3.5	10.25	80	1	0	0	95	4	58	6.1	10	15	2,500	0	0.0	1.0
U /	N/A	3.5	10.25	19	1	0	0	95	4	58	6.1	N/A	15	0	0	0.0	0.0
A+ / 9.9	N/A	N/A	1.00	1	100	0	0	0	0	0	0.4	51	14	50,000	0	0.0	0.0
A+ / 9.9	N/A	N/A	1.00	115	100	0	0	0	0	0	0.4	51	14	1,000	0	0.0	0.0
D+ / 2.3	4.6	7.7	9.42	2	0	86	0	6	8	611	1.4	22	12	50,000	0	0.0	0.0
D / 2.2	4.6	7.7	9.42	105	0	86	0	6	8	611	1.4	31	12	1,000	0	0.0	0.0
E- / 0.2	11.3	5.0	7.30	5	9	65	0	23	3	18	7.7	35	6	5,000	50	4.5	0.0
E- / 0.2	11.3	5.0	7.30	2	9	65	0	23	3	18	7.7	15	6	5,000	50	0.0	0.0
E- / 0.2	11.2	5.0	7.29	22	9	65	0	23	3	18	7.7	55	6	5,000	50	0.0	0.0
E- / 0.2	11.3	5.0	7.28	N/A	9	65	0	23	3	18	7.7	21	6	0	0	0.0	0.0
E- / 0.2	11.3	5.0	7.28	N/A	9	65	0	23	3	18	7.7	35	6	0	0	0.0	0.0
E- / 0.2	11.3	5.0	7.08	N/A	9	65	0	23	3	18	7.7	44	6	0	0	0.0	0.0
E- / 0.2	11.2	5.0	7.25	70	9	65	0	23	3	18	7.7	55	6	250,000	0	0.0	0.0
C- / 3.5	3.8	0.3	8.73	853	0	3	0	49	48	40	5.8	85	N/A	2,000	50	3.0	0.0
C- / 3.6	3.7	0.3	8.72	3	0	3	0	49	48	40	5.8	79	N/A	0	0	0.0	0.0
C- / 3.6	3.7	0.3	8.72	1,191	0	3	0	49	48	40	5.8	79	N/A	2,000	50	0.0	0.0
D+ / 2.3	4.7	0.5	10.02	128	0	0	0	73	27	75	6.6	93	N/A	2,000	50	3.0	0.0
D+ / 2.3	4.7	0.5	10.02	91	0	0	0	73	27	75	6.6	89	N/A	2,000	50	0.0	0.0
D+ / 2.3	4.7	0.5	10.03	236	0	0	0	73	27	75	6.6	93	N/A	2,000	50	0.0	0.0
D+ / 2.4	4.6	0.5	10.01	N/A	0	0	0	73	27	75	6.6	92	N/A	0	0	0.0	0.0
D+ / 2.4	4.6	0.5	10.00	1	0	0	0	73	27	75	6.6	93	N/A	0	0	0.0	0.0
D+ / 2.4	4.5	0.5	10.00	2	0	0	0	73	27	75	6.6	94	N/A	0	0	0.0	0.0
D+ / 2.4	4.6	0.5	10.00	4	0	0	0	73	27	75	6.6	94	N/A	250,000	0	0.0	0.0
C- / 3.5	3.8	0.3	8.74	1,779	0	3	0	49	48	40	5.8	87	N/A	2,000	50	0.0	0.0
C- / 3.5	3.8	0.3	8.75	11	0	3	0	49	48	40	5.8	83	N/A	0	0	0.0	0.0
C- / 3.6	3.7	0.3	8.72	8	0	3	0	49	48	40	5.8	85	N/A	0	0	0.0	0.0
C- / 3.6	3.7	0.3	8.73	2	0	3	0	49	48	40	5.8	88	N/A	0	0	0.0	0.0
C- / 3.5	3.7	0.3	8.72	370	0	3	0	49	48	40	5.8	88	N/A	250,000	0	0.0	0.0
D- / 1.4	5.3	4.2	7.45	249	2	2	0	90	6	47	6.0	17	5	2,000	50	4.5	0.0
D- / 1.4	5.3	4.2	7.40	1	2	2	0	90	6	47	6.0	6	5	0	0	0.0	0.0
D- / 1.4	5.3	4.2	7.42	60	2	2	0	90	6	47	6.0	6	5	2,000	50	0.0	0.0
D- / 1.3	5.4	4.2	8.33	248	4	0	0	92	4	34	7.3	29	5	0	0	0.0	0.0
D- / 1.3	5.4	4.2	8.19	78	4	0	0	92	4	34	7.3	21	5	0	0	0.0	0.0
D- / 1.4	5.3	4.2	7.48	55	2	2	0	90	6	47	6.0	23	5	2,000	50	0.0	0.0
D- / 1.4	5.3	4.2	7.44	3	2	2	0	90	6	47	6.0	11	5	0	0	0.0	0.0

					PERFORMANCE						Incl. in Returns	
	99 Pct = Best 0 Pct = Worst					Total Return % through 2/28/17						
			Overall		Perfor-				Annualized		Dividend	Expense
Fund Type	Fund Name	Ticker Symbol	Investment Rating	Phone	mance Rating/Pts	3 Mo	6 Mo	1Yr / Pct	3Yr / Pct	5Yr / Pct	Yield	Ratio
COH	Hartford High Yield R4	HAHSX	C+	(888) 843-7824	B+ / 8.8	4.62	4.43	16.54 /91	3.36 /67	5.39 /87	4.72	1.18
COH	Hartford High Yield R5	HAHTX	C+	(888) 843-7824	A- / 9.0	4.70	4.47	16.78 /92	3.64 /71	5.68 /90	5.04	0.87
COH	Hartford High Yield Y	HAHYX	C+	(888) 843-7824	A- / 9.0	4.58	4.50	16.86 /92	3.69 /71	5.71 /90	5.08	0.75
US	Hartford Inflation Plus A	HIPAX	E+	(888) 843-7824	D- / 1.2	1.27	0.54	3.56 /60	0.86 /25	-0.19 / 4	1.12	0.94
US ●	Hartford Inflation Plus B	HIPBX	E+	(888) 843-7824	D / 1.9	1.06	0.19	2.73 /55	0.09 /12	-0.93 / 2	0.00	1.78
US	Hartford Inflation Plus C	HIPCX	E+	(888) 843-7824	D / 1.9	1.07	0.20	2.75 /55	0.09 /12	-0.93 / 2	0.39	1.66
US	Hartford Inflation Plus I	HIPIX	E+	(888) 843-7824	D / 2.2	-0.18	-0.72	2.31 /52	0.61 /22	-0.22 / 4	0.00	0.73
US	Hartford Inflation Plus R3	HIPRX	D-	(888) 843-7824	D+ / 2.5	1.14	0.39	3.17 /58	0.51 /21	-0.55 / 3	0.85	1.25
US	Hartford Inflation Plus R4	HIPSX	E+	(888) 843-7824	D / 2.0	0.09	-0.64	2.25 /51	0.43 /20	-0.47 / 3	0.00	0.95
US	Hartford Inflation Plus R5	HIPTX	E+	(888) 843-7824	D / 2.2	-0.18	-0.72	2.31 /52	0.61 /22	-0.22 / 4	0.00	0.66
US	Hartford Inflation Plus Y	HIPYX	E+	(888) 843-7824	D+ / 2.3	-0.09	-0.71	2.40 /52	0.68 /23	-0.14 / 4	0.00	0.54
MUN	Hartford Municipal Income A	HMKAX	U	(888) 843-7824	U /	2.08	-3.72	-0.07 /16	--	--	2.05	1.12
MUN	Hartford Municipal Income C	HMKCX	U	(888) 843-7824	U /	1.89	-4.07	-0.81 / 6	--	--	1.39	1.84
MUN	Hartford Municipal Income I	HMKIX	U	(888) 843-7824	U /	2.14	-3.59	0.19 /28	--	--	2.41	0.84
MUH	Hartford Municipal Opportunities A	HHMAX	D-	(888) 843-7824	C / 4.7	2.22	-3.22	-0.03 /17	3.22 /85	3.20 /83	2.37	0.70
MUH ●	Hartford Municipal Opportunities B	HHMBX	D	(888) 843-7824	C+ / 5.6	1.91	-3.59	-0.78 / 6	2.45 /72	2.43 /69	1.71	1.52
MUH	Hartford Municipal Opportunities C	HHMCX	D	(888) 843-7824	C+ / 5.6	1.91	-3.69	-0.78 / 6	2.45 /72	2.43 /69	1.71	1.46
MUH	Hartford Municipal Opportunities I	HHMIX	C+	(888) 843-7824	B / 7.6	2.16	-3.21	0.22 /30	3.47 /87	3.45 /87	2.74	0.45
MUN	Hartford Municipal Real Return A	HTNAX	C+	(888) 843-7824	C- / 4.1	2.24	-0.27	2.56 /62	2.25 /68	1.92 /57	2.65	0.79
MUN ●	Hartford Municipal Real Return B	HTNBX	B-	(888) 843-7824	C / 4.9	1.95	-0.64	1.81 /55	1.46 /47	1.15 /38	2.03	1.61
MUN	Hartford Municipal Real Return C	HTNCX	B-	(888) 843-7824	C / 4.9	1.95	-0.75	1.81 /55	1.45 /47	1.15 /38	2.03	1.54
MUN	Hartford Municipal Real Return I	HTNIX	A+	(888) 843-7824	B- / 7.2	2.18	-0.25	2.82 /64	2.50 /73	2.17 /63	3.02	0.56
MUN	Hartford Municipal Real Return Y	HTNYX	A+	(888) 843-7824	B- / 7.2	2.19	-0.25	2.82 /64	2.47 /73	2.17 /63	3.03	0.49
MUN	Hartford Municipal Short Duration A	HMJAX	U	(888) 843-7824	U /	0.90	-1.21	-0.35 /12	--	--	1.00	1.12
MUN	Hartford Municipal Short Duration C	HMJCX	U	(888) 843-7824	U /	0.82	-1.47	-1.09 / 4	--	--	0.30	1.82
MUN	Hartford Municipal Short Duration I	HMJIX	U	(888) 843-7824	U /	0.96	-1.08	-0.10 /16	--	--	1.31	0.78
MTG	Hartford Quality Bond A	HQBAX	D	(888) 843-7824	D / 2.2	0.45	-2.30	0.07 /21	2.38 /50	--	1.50	1.24
MTG	Hartford Quality Bond C	HQBCX	D+	(888) 843-7824	D+ / 2.7	0.16	-2.69	-0.68 / 7	1.58 /36	--	0.82	1.99
MTG	Hartford Quality Bond I	HQBIX	C+	(888) 843-7824	C / 4.4	0.41	-2.18	0.32 /29	2.62 /54	--	1.82	0.95
MTG	Hartford Quality Bond R3	HQBRX	C	(888) 843-7824	C- / 3.7	0.38	-2.45	-0.26 /13	2.17 /46	--	1.24	1.64
MTG	Hartford Quality Bond R4	HQBSX	C+	(888) 843-7824	C / 4.3	0.45	-2.05	-0.02 /17	2.53 /52	--	1.37	1.34
MTG	Hartford Quality Bond R5	HQBTX	B-	(888) 843-7824	C / 4.8	0.42	-2.09	0.19 /25	2.85 /59	--	1.68	1.04
MTG	Hartford Quality Bond Y	HQBYX	C+	(888) 843-7824	C / 4.6	0.53	-2.12	0.43 /32	2.69 /56	--	1.93	0.95
EM	Hartford Schroders Em Mkt MS Bd A	SMSVX	D	(888) 843-7824	B / 7.7	6.61	1.68	16.86 /92	3.45 /68	--	3.17	1.46
EM	Hartford Schroders Em Mkt MS Bd I	SMSNX	C-	(888) 843-7824	B+ / 8.9	6.58	1.66	17.00 /92	3.62 /70	--	3.53	1.15
EM	Hartford Schroders Em Mkt MS Bd	SMSRX	U	(888) 843-7824	U /	6.59	1.80	17.22 /92	--	--	3.62	1.01
GL	Hartford Schroders EMD & Cur A	SARVX	E	(888) 843-7824	D+ / 2.9	3.23	0.39	9.29 /77	0.99 /27	1.32 /32	0.00	1.60
GL	Hartford Schroders EMD & Cur I	SARNX	E+	(888) 843-7824	C / 5.1	3.23	0.49	9.53 /78	1.19 /31	1.56 /35	0.00	1.30
GL	Hartford Schroders Gl Strat Bd A	SGBVX	U	(888) 843-7824	U /	1.25	2.84	5.18 /67	--	--	3.59	1.31
GL	Hartford Schroders Gl Strat Bd I	SGBNX	U	(888) 843-7824	U /	1.19	2.83	5.49 /68	--	--	3.95	1.00
MUN	Hartford Schroders Tax Aware Bd A	STWVX	U	(888) 843-7824	U /	1.63	-2.34	2.37 /60	--	--	2.08	0.96
COI	Hartford Schroders Tax Aware Bd I	STWTX	B	(888) 843-7824	B / 7.8	1.68	-2.14	2.78 /55	5.09 /86	4.49 /79	2.40	0.69
* COI	Hartford Short Duration A	HSDAX	C+	(888) 843-7824	C- / 3.0	0.90	0.65	3.50 /60	1.40 /33	1.81 /39	1.77	0.90
COI ●	Hartford Short Duration B	HSDBX	B+	(888) 843-7824	C- / 4.0	0.89	0.66	3.60 /60	1.47 /35	1.95 /41	1.81	1.78
COI	Hartford Short Duration C	HSDCX	C+	(888) 843-7824	D+ / 2.6	0.72	0.29	2.74 /55	0.65 /22	1.05 /28	1.07	1.60
COI	Hartford Short Duration I	HSDIX	A-	(888) 843-7824	C / 4.3	0.97	0.79	3.80 /61	1.70 /38	2.12 /44	2.09	0.54
COI	Hartford Short Duration R3	HSDRX	B-	(888) 843-7824	C- / 3.4	0.82	0.50	3.20 /58	1.13 /30	1.51 /35	1.51	1.23
COI	Hartford Short Duration R4	HSDSX	B+	(888) 843-7824	C- / 3.9	0.90	0.65	3.51 /60	1.43 /34	1.83 /39	1.81	0.92
COI	Hartford Short Duration R5	HSDTX	A-	(888) 843-7824	C / 4.3	0.97	0.80	3.82 /61	1.70 /38	2.11 /44	2.11	0.62
COI	Hartford Short Duration Y	HSDYX	A-	(888) 843-7824	C / 4.5	0.99	0.82	3.87 /62	1.79 /39	2.18 /44	2.16	0.51
COH	Hartford SMART529 High Yld 529 A		D+	(888) 843-7824	B- / 7.4	4.47	4.26	16.25 /91	3.16 /64	5.19 /86	0.00	1.85
COH	Hartford SMART529 High Yld 529 B		C-	(888) 843-7824	B / 8.0	4.30	3.97	15.66 /90	2.59 /54	4.61 /80	0.00	2.40

● Denotes fund is closed to new investors
* Denotes fund is included in Section II

RISK			NET ASSETS		ASSET							FUND MANAGER		MINIMUM		LOADS	
Risk Rating/Pts	3 Yr Avg Standard Deviation	Avg Dura-tion	NAV As of 2/28/17	Total $(Mil)	Cash %	Gov. Bond %	Muni. Bond %	Corp. Bond %	Other %	Portfolio Turnover Ratio	Avg Coupon Rate	Manager Quality Pct	Manager Tenure (Years)	Initial Purch. $	Additional Purch. $	Front End Load	Back End Load
D- / 1.5	5.2	4.2	7.46	2	2	2	0	90	6	47	6.0	18	5	0	0	0.0	0.0
D- / 1.4	5.3	4.2	7.44	1	2	2	0	90	6	47	6.0	25	5	0	0	0.0	0.0
D- / 1.4	5.3	4.2	7.43	14	2	2	0	90	6	47	6.0	26	5	250,000	0	0.0	0.0
C / 5.0	3.1	5.6	10.90	221	0	92	0	1	7	70	1.8	30	2	2,000	50	4.5	0.0
C / 5.1	3.1	5.6	10.52	3	0	92	0	1	7	70	1.8	11	2	0	0	0.0	0.0
C / 4.9	3.1	5.6	10.47	135	0	92	0	1	7	70	1.8	10	2	2,000	50	0.0	0.0
C / 4.8	3.2	5.6	11.08	64	0	92	0	1	7	70	1.8	22	2	2,000	50	0.0	0.0
C / 5.1	3.1	5.6	10.71	54	0	92	0	1	7	70	1.8	19	2	0	0	0.0	0.0
C / 5.0	3.1	5.6	10.89	16	0	92	0	1	7	70	1.8	18	2	0	0	0.0	0.0
C / 4.7	3.2	5.6	11.05	3	0	92	0	1	7	70	1.8	21	2	0	0	0.0	0.0
C / 4.6	3.2	5.6	11.11	117	0	92	0	1	7	70	1.8	23	2	250,000	0	0.0	0.0
U /	N/A	5.7	10.04	12	7	0	92	0	1	0	2.3	N/A	2	2,000	50	4.5	0.0
U /	N/A	5.7	10.04	3	7	0	92	0	1	0	2.3	N/A	2	2,000	50	0.0	0.0
U /	N/A	5.7	10.04	6	7	0	92	0	1	0	2.3	N/A	2	2,000	50	0.0	0.0
C- / 3.4	3.4	5.1	8.45	243	1	0	97	0	2	22	2.1	27	5	2,000	50	4.5	0.0
C- / 3.5	3.3	5.1	8.44	1	1	0	97	0	2	22	2.1	11	5	0	0	0.0	0.0
C- / 3.4	3.3	5.1	8.45	113	1	0	97	0	2	22	2.1	10	5	2,000	50	0.0	0.0
C- / 3.4	3.3	5.1	8.46	293	1	0	97	0	2	22	2.1	37	5	2,000	50	0.0	0.0
B- / 7.2	2.6	4.5	9.19	103	3	1	94	0	2	21	2.0	49	N/A	2,000	50	4.5	0.0
B- / 7.2	2.6	4.5	9.10	N/A	3	1	94	0	2	21	2.0	17	N/A	0	0	0.0	0.0
B- / 7.2	2.6	4.5	9.13	21	3	1	94	0	2	21	2.0	18	N/A	2,000	50	0.0	0.0
B- / 7.2	2.6	4.5	9.21	43	3	1	94	0	2	21	2.0	60	N/A	0	0	0.0	0.0
B- / 7.3	2.6	4.5	9.16	17	3	1	94	0	2	21	2.0	58	N/A	250,000	0	0.0	0.0
U /	N/A	2.4	9.96	8	12	0	87	0	1	0	1.5	N/A	2	2,000	50	4.5	0.0
U /	N/A	2.4	9.96	4	12	0	87	0	1	0	1.5	N/A	2	2,000	50	0.0	0.0
U /	N/A	2.4	9.96	7	12	0	87	0	1	0	1.5	N/A	2	2,000	50	0.0	0.0
B- / 7.2	2.6	3.8	9.93	14	8	1	0	0	91	84	2.4	20	5	2,000	50	4.5	0.0
B- / 7.3	2.6	3.8	9.85	4	8	1	0	0	91	84	2.4	6	5	2,000	50	0.0	0.0
B- / 7.3	2.6	3.8	9.94	6	8	1	0	0	91	84	2.4	27	5	2,000	50	0.0	0.0
B- / 7.3	2.6	3.8	9.91	N/A	8	1	0	0	91	84	2.4	15	5	0	0	0.0	0.0
B- / 7.3	2.6	3.8	9.94	N/A	8	1	0	0	91	84	2.4	24	5	0	0	0.0	0.0
B- / 7.3	2.6	3.8	9.94	N/A	8	1	0	0	91	84	2.4	36	5	0	0	0.0	0.0
B- / 7.2	2.7	3.8	9.95	106	8	1	0	0	91	84	2.4	27	5	250,000	0	0.0	0.0
E / 0.3	8.7	6.3	9.72	2	2	58	3	34	3	147	0.0	97	4	5,000	50	4.5	0.0
E / 0.3	8.7	6.3	9.70	9	2	58	3	34	3	147	0.0	97	4	5,000	50	0.0	0.0
U /	N/A	6.3	9.72	54	2	58	3	34	3	147	0.0	N/A	4	5,000,000	0	0.0	0.0
D- / 1.4	5.8	N/A	10.24	3	3	93	0	0	4	163	0.0	89	6	5,000	50	4.5	0.0
D- / 1.4	5.8	N/A	10.23	70	3	93	0	0	4	163	0.0	90	6	5,000	50	0.0	0.0
U /	N/A	0.6	8.98	N/A	0	31	2	54	13	140	0.0	N/A	1	2,500	1,000	4.5	0.0
U /	N/A	0.6	9.02	N/A	0	31	2	54	13	140	0.0	N/A	1	250,000	1,000	0.0	0.0
U /	N/A	5.2	10.91	11	0	11	54	34	1	42	0.0	N/A	6	2,000	50	4.5	0.0
C- / 3.8	3.6	5.2	10.93	106	0	11	54	34	1	42	0.0	88	6	2,000	50	0.0	0.0
A- / 9.1	1.1	1.8	9.86	517	0	1	0	65	34	41	2.1	66	5	2,000	50	2.0	0.0
A- / 9.1	1.1	1.8	9.92	2	0	1	0	65	34	41	2.1	68	5	0	0	0.0	0.0
A- / 9.1	1.1	1.8	9.86	117	0	1	0	65	34	41	2.1	33	5	2,000	50	0.0	0.0
A- / 9.1	1.1	1.8	9.88	207	0	1	0	65	34	41	2.1	74	5	2,000	50	0.0	0.0
A- / 9.1	1.1	1.8	9.84	1	0	1	0	65	34	41	2.1	59	5	0	0	0.0	0.0
A- / 9.1	1.1	1.8	9.85	1	0	1	0	65	34	41	2.1	68	5	0	0	0.0	0.0
A- / 9.1	1.1	1.8	9.84	N/A	0	1	0	65	34	41	2.1	74	5	0	0	0.0	0.0
A- / 9.1	1.1	1.8	9.84	45	0	1	0	65	34	41	2.1	76	5	250,000	0	0.0	0.0
D- / 1.4	5.3	N/A	21.03	6	4	0	0	87	9	15	0.0	14	13	250	25	4.5	0.0
D- / 1.4	5.3	N/A	19.65	N/A	4	0	0	87	9	15	0.0	6	13	250	25	0.0	0.0

Fund Type	Fund Name	Ticker Symbol	Overall Investment Rating	Phone	Performance Rating/Pts	3 Mo	6 Mo	1Yr / Pct	3Yr / Pct	5Yr / Pct	Dividend Yield	Expense Ratio
COH	Hartford SMART529 High Yld 529 C		C-	(888) 843-7824	B / 7.8	4.24	3.85	15.42 /89	2.40 /50	4.41 /77	0.00	2.59
COH	Hartford SMART529 High Yld 529 E		C+	(888) 843-7824	B+ / 8.8	4.52	4.37	16.56 /91	3.42 /67	5.45 /88	0.00	1.19
US	Hartford SMART529 Infl Plus 529 A		E	(888) 843-7824	E / 0.5	1.23	0.48	3.36 /59	0.66 /22	-0.35 / 3	0.00	1.85
US	Hartford SMART529 Infl Plus 529 B		E+	(888) 843-7824	D / 2.0	1.10	0.22	2.83 /55	0.11 /13	-0.90 / 2	0.00	2.40
US	Hartford SMART529 Infl Plus 529 C		E+	(888) 843-7824	D / 1.7	1.05	0.15	2.59 /54	-0.08 / 5	-1.08 / 2	0.00	2.59
US	Hartford SMART529 Infl Plus 529 E		D-	(888) 843-7824	C- / 3.3	1.32	0.66	3.65 /60	0.93 /26	-0.09 / 4	0.00	1.19
GEI	Hartford SMART529 Tot Ret Bd 529		D-	(888) 843-7824	C- / 3.1	1.46	-1.37	4.16 /63	2.24 /47	2.40 /48	0.00	1.85
GEI	Hartford SMART529 Tot Ret Bd 529		D	(888) 843-7824	C- / 4.1	1.34	-1.59	3.61 /60	1.70 /38	1.85 /40	0.00	2.40
GEI	Hartford SMART529 Tot Ret Bd 529		D	(888) 843-7824	C- / 3.7	1.25	-1.70	3.38 /59	1.49 /35	1.64 /37	0.00	2.59
GEI	Hartford SMART529 Tot Ret Bd 529		C	(888) 843-7824	C / 5.4	1.51	-1.21	4.39 /64	2.50 /52	2.65 /52	0.00	1.19
GL	Hartford Strategic Income A	HSNAX	D+	(888) 843-7824	C+ / 6.9	4.33	2.04	12.69 /84	3.28 /66	3.71 /69	4.46	1.03
GL ●	Hartford Strategic Income B	HSNBX	C-	(888) 843-7824	B / 7.6	4.31	2.02	12.63 /84	2.82 /58	3.14 /60	4.64	1.85
GL	Hartford Strategic Income C	HSNCX	C-	(888) 843-7824	B- / 7.2	4.12	1.63	11.88 /83	2.52 /52	2.96 /57	3.86	1.74
GL	Hartford Strategic Income I	HSNIX	C+	(888) 843-7824	B+ / 8.3	4.38	2.16	12.95 /85	3.54 /69	3.97 /72	4.92	0.73
GL	Hartford Strategic Income R3	HSNRX	C	(888) 843-7824	B / 7.7	4.27	1.90	12.35 /84	2.98 /61	3.39 /64	4.36	1.41
GL	Hartford Strategic Income R4	HSNSX	C	(888) 843-7824	B / 8.1	4.42	2.13	12.79 /85	3.32 /66	3.74 /69	4.64	1.08
GL	Hartford Strategic Income R5	HSNTX	C+	(888) 843-7824	B+ / 8.4	4.42	2.32	13.06 /85	3.61 /70	4.03 /73	4.99	0.75
GEL	Hartford Strategic Income R6	HSNVX	U	(888) 843-7824	U /	4.43	2.24	13.00 /85	--	--	5.06	0.69
GL	Hartford Strategic Income Y	HSNYX	C+	(888) 843-7824	B+ / 8.4	4.43	2.23	12.99 /85	3.66 /71	4.07 /73	5.05	0.64
* GEI	Hartford Total Return Bond A	ITBAX	D-	(888) 843-7824	C- / 3.3	1.61	-1.23	4.26 /63	2.35 /49	2.51 /50	2.52	0.88
GEI ●	Hartford Total Return Bond B	ITBBX	D	(888) 843-7824	C- / 3.8	1.33	-1.72	3.39 /59	1.56 /36	1.73 /38	1.87	1.87
GEI	Hartford Total Return Bond C	HABCX	D	(888) 843-7824	C- / 3.9	1.33	-1.68	3.40 /59	1.61 /37	1.75 /38	1.90	1.60
COI	Hartford Total Return Bond HLS IA		B-	(888) 843-7824	C+ / 6.2	1.72	-0.97	5.04 /67	2.97 /60	3.03 /58	2.61	0.52
COI	Hartford Total Return Bond HLS IB		C+	(888) 843-7824	C+ / 5.9	1.73	-1.06	4.86 /66	2.73 /56	2.79 /54	2.32	0.77
GEI	Hartford Total Return Bond I	ITBIX	C+	(888) 843-7824	C+ / 5.7	1.67	-1.13	4.54 /65	2.66 /55	2.80 /54	2.90	0.57
GEI	Hartford Total Return Bond R3	ITBRX	C-	(888) 843-7824	C / 4.6	1.52	-1.43	3.91 /62	2.03 /44	2.19 /45	2.33	1.17
GEI	Hartford Total Return Bond R4	ITBUX	C	(888) 843-7824	C / 5.1	1.50	-1.28	4.25 /63	2.35 /49	2.50 /49	2.65	0.85
GEI	Hartford Total Return Bond R5	ITBTX	C+	(888) 843-7824	C+ / 5.7	1.67	-1.14	4.55 /65	2.66 /55	2.81 /54	2.94	0.56
COI	Hartford Total Return Bond R6	ITBVX	U	(888) 843-7824	U /	1.70	-1.06	4.69 /65	--	--	3.07	0.51
GEI	Hartford Total Return Bond Y	HABYX	C+	(888) 843-7824	C+ / 5.9	1.60	-1.09	4.66 /65	2.77 /57	2.91 /56	3.05	0.45
COI	Hartford Ultrashort Bd HLS IA		C+	(888) 843-7824	D / 2.0	0.30	0.40	1.07 /40	0.43 /20	--	0.46	0.43
GES	Hartford Unconstrained Bond A	HTIAX	D+	(888) 843-7824	C- / 3.3	2.16	2.23	7.61 /74	1.51 /35	1.69 /37	3.22	1.17
GES ●	Hartford Unconstrained Bond B	HTIBX	C	(888) 843-7824	C- / 3.9	2.08	1.86	6.82 /72	0.75 /24	0.95 /27	2.64	2.11
GES	Hartford Unconstrained Bond C	HTICX	C-	(888) 843-7824	C- / 3.9	1.97	1.85	6.80 /72	0.72 /23	0.93 /26	2.64	1.86
COI	Hartford Unconstrained Bond I	HTIIX	B+	(888) 843-7824	C+ / 5.6	2.23	2.24	7.76 /74	1.74 /39	1.93 /41	3.62	0.81
COI	Hartford Unconstrained Bond R3	HTIRX	C+	(888) 843-7824	C / 4.7	2.09	2.07	7.30 /73	1.21 /31	1.41 /33	3.08	1.45
COI	Hartford Unconstrained Bond R4	HTISX	B	(888) 843-7824	C / 5.2	2.16	2.23	7.61 /74	1.51 /35	1.71 /38	3.37	1.14
COI	Hartford Unconstrained Bond R5	HTITX	B+	(888) 843-7824	C+ / 5.8	2.35	2.38	7.94 /74	1.81 /40	2.02 /42	3.67	0.83
GES	Hartford Unconstrained Bond Y	HTIYX	B+	(888) 843-7824	C+ / 5.7	2.24	2.38	7.94 /74	1.78 /39	1.98 /42	3.67	0.73
USS	Hartford US Govt Sec HLS Fd IA	HAUSX	C	(888) 843-7824	C- / 3.4	0.39	-1.43	0.19 /25	1.78 /39	1.53 /35	1.96	0.51
USS	Hartford US Govt Sec HLS Fd IB	HBUSX	C-	(888) 843-7824	C- / 3.0	0.29	-1.53	0.02 /18	1.54 /36	1.29 /31	1.69	0.76
GL	Hartford US Govt Securities HLS IA		C	(888) 843-7824	C- / 3.4	0.39	-1.43	0.19 /25	1.78 /39	1.53 /35	1.96	0.51
GL	Hartford World Bond A	HWDAX	D-	(888) 843-7824	E+ / 0.6	0.59	-0.87	1.74 /47	1.18 /30	2.07 /43	0.05	1.08
GL	Hartford World Bond C	HWDCX	D+	(888) 843-7824	D / 1.8	0.39	-1.16	0.99 /39	0.43 /20	1.33 /32	0.00	1.77
GL	Hartford World Bond I	HWDIX	C+	(888) 843-7824	C- / 3.4	0.58	-0.77	1.96 /49	1.43 /34	2.32 /46	0.08	0.77
GL	Hartford World Bond R3	HWDRX	C	(888) 843-7824	D+ / 2.4	0.59	-0.96	1.52 /45	0.86 /25	1.74 /38	0.04	1.39
GL	Hartford World Bond R4	HWDSX	C+	(888) 843-7824	D+ / 2.9	0.59	-0.87	1.74 /47	1.14 /30	2.06 /43	0.06	1.08
GL	Hartford World Bond R5	HWDTX	C+	(888) 843-7824	C- / 3.4	0.68	-0.67	2.07 /50	1.45 /34	2.35 /47	0.09	0.83
GL	Hartford World Bond R6	HWDVX	U	(888) 843-7824	U /	0.68	-0.67	2.17 /50	--	--	0.09	0.74
GL	Hartford World Bond Y	HWDYX	B-	(888) 843-7824	C- / 3.6	0.68	-0.67	2.17 /50	1.56 /36	2.45 /49	0.09	0.67
EM	Harvest Fds Intermediate Bond A	HXIAX	C	(866) 777-7818	B / 8.0	2.66	0.84	9.14 /77	5.72 /90	--	3.14	1.73
EM	Harvest Fds Intermediate Bond Inst	HXIIX	B-	(866) 777-7818	A- / 9.0	2.73	0.87	9.18 /77	5.81 /91	--	3.51	1.47

● Denotes fund is closed to new investors
* Denotes fund is included in Section II

www.thestreetratings.com

RISK			NET ASSETS		ASSET							FUND MANAGER		MINIMUM		LOADS	
Risk Rating/Pts	3 Yr Avg Standard Deviation	Avg Dura-tion	NAV As of 2/28/17	Total $(Mil)	Cash %	Gov. Bond %	Muni. Bond %	Corp. Bond %	Other %	Portfolio Turnover Ratio	Avg Coupon Rate	Manager Quality Pct	Manager Tenure (Years)	Initial Purch. $	Additional Purch. $	Front End Load	Back End Load
D- / 1.4	5.3	N/A	19.16	1	4	0	0	87	9	15	0.0	5	13	250	25	0.0	0.0
D- / 1.4	5.3	N/A	21.75	1	4	0	0	87	9	15	0.0	19	13	250	25	0.0	0.0
C / 4.9	3.2	N/A	14.77	4	0	92	0	0	8	15	0.0	23	13	250	25	4.5	0.0
C / 4.9	3.2	N/A	13.79	N/A	0	92	0	0	8	15	0.0	10	13	250	25	0.0	0.0
C / 5.0	3.1	N/A	13.46	1	0	92	0	0	8	15	0.0	8	13	250	25	0.0	0.0
C / 4.9	3.2	N/A	15.32	1	0	92	0	0	8	15	0.0	31	13	250	25	0.0	0.0
C / 5.5	3.0	N/A	18.03	17	0	20	1	29	50	9	0.0	31	15	250	25	4.5	0.0
C / 5.4	3.0	N/A	16.66	1	0	20	1	29	50	9	0.0	16	15	250	25	0.0	0.0
C / 5.4	3.0	N/A	16.20	4	0	20	1	29	50	9	0.0	11	15	250	25	0.0	0.0
C / 5.5	3.0	N/A	18.77	1	0	20	1	29	50	9	0.0	45	15	250	25	0.0	0.0
D / 2.2	4.9	5.3	8.76	115	0	29	1	34	36	55	4.8	95	5	2,000	50	4.5	0.0
D / 2.2	4.9	5.3	8.78	2	0	29	1	34	36	55	4.8	94	5	0	0	0.0	0.0
D / 2.1	4.9	5.3	8.79	69	0	29	1	34	36	55	4.8	93	5	2,000	50	0.0	0.0
D / 2.2	4.9	5.3	8.79	33	0	29	1	34	36	55	4.8	95	5	2,000	50	0.0	0.0
D / 2.2	4.9	5.3	8.75	N/A	0	29	1	34	36	55	4.8	94	5	0	0	0.0	0.0
D / 2.2	4.8	5.3	8.77	N/A	0	29	1	34	36	55	4.8	95	5	0	0	0.0	0.0
D / 2.2	4.8	5.3	8.76	N/A	0	29	1	34	36	55	4.8	95	5	0	0	0.0	0.0
U /	N/A	5.3	8.75	N/A	0	29	1	34	36	55	4.8	N/A	5	0	0	0.0	0.0
D / 2.2	4.9	5.3	8.75	156	0	29	1	34	36	55	4.8	95	5	250,000	0	0.0	0.0
C / 5.5	3.0	5.4	10.31	736	0	14	0	27	59	41	3.2	35	5	2,000	50	4.5	0.0
C / 5.5	3.0	5.4	10.22	3	0	14	0	27	59	41	3.2	13	5	0	0	0.0	0.0
C+ / 5.6	3.0	5.4	10.32	65	0	14	0	27	59	41	3.2	14	5	2,000	50	0.0	0.0
C+ / 5.7	3.0	5.4	11.23	2,218	0	0	0	0	100	66	3.5	59	5	0	0	0.0	0.0
C+ / 5.6	3.0	5.4	11.17	262	0	0	0	0	100	66	3.5	48	5	0	0	0.0	0.0
C+ / 5.6	3.0	5.4	10.32	176	0	14	0	27	59	41	3.2	55	5	2,000	50	0.0	0.0
C+ / 5.6	3.0	5.4	10.50	6	0	14	0	27	59	41	3.2	25	5	0	0	0.0	0.0
C+ / 5.7	3.0	5.4	10.48	14	0	14	0	27	59	41	3.2	36	5	0	0	0.0	0.0
C / 5.5	3.0	5.4	10.48	1	0	14	0	27	59	41	3.2	53	5	0	0	0.0	0.0
U /	N/A	5.4	10.47	N/A	0	14	0	27	59	41	3.2	N/A	5	0	0	0.0	0.0
C / 5.5	3.0	5.4	10.47	1,078	0	14	0	27	59	41	3.2	57	5	250,000	0	0.0	0.0
A+ / 9.9	0.3	0.6	10.06	521	0	0	0	0	100	35	1.1	55	4	0	0	0.0	0.0
C+ / 6.7	2.8	2.5	9.60	44	0	7	0	16	77	38	3.1	72	5	2,000	50	4.5	0.0
C+ / 6.9	2.7	2.5	9.60	N/A	0	7	0	16	77	38	3.1	47	5	0	0	0.0	0.0
C+ / 6.8	2.8	2.5	9.62	10	0	7	0	16	77	38	3.1	44	5	2,000	50	0.0	0.0
B- / 7.0	2.7	2.5	9.60	5	0	7	0	16	77	38	3.1	61	5	2,000	50	0.0	0.0
C+ / 6.9	2.7	2.5	9.59	N/A	0	7	0	16	77	38	3.1	36	5	0	0	0.0	0.0
B- / 7.0	2.7	2.5	9.59	1	0	7	0	16	77	38	3.1	55	5	0	0	0.0	0.0
C+ / 6.9	2.8	2.5	9.59	3	0	7	0	16	77	38	3.1	63	5	0	0	0.0	0.0
C+ / 6.9	2.8	2.5	9.57	7	0	7	0	16	77	38	3.1	77	5	250,000	0	0.0	0.0
B / 7.8	2.3	3.9	10.35	359	0	32	0	0	68	42	1.8	61	5	0	0	0.0	0.0
B / 7.9	2.2	3.9	10.33	78	0	32	0	0	68	42	1.8	54	5	0	0	0.0	0.0
B / 7.8	2.3	3.9	10.35	367	0	32	0	0	68	42	1.8	86	5	0	0	0.0	0.0
B+ / 8.7	1.6	1.1	10.29	392	4	66	1	12	17	122	1.7	81	6	2,000	50	4.5	0.0
B+ / 8.7	1.7	1.1	10.20	134	4	66	1	12	17	122	1.7	69	6	2,000	50	0.0	0.0
B+ / 8.6	1.7	1.1	10.32	2,187	4	66	1	12	17	122	1.7	83	6	2,000	50	0.0	0.0
B+ / 8.6	1.7	1.1	10.27	2	4	66	1	12	17	122	1.7	77	6	0	0	0.0	0.0
B+ / 8.7	1.7	1.1	10.30	1	4	66	1	12	17	122	1.7	80	6	0	0	0.0	0.0
B+ / 8.6	1.7	1.1	10.32	2	4	66	1	12	17	122	1.7	83	6	0	0	0.0	0.0
U /	N/A	1.1	10.34	1	4	66	1	12	17	122	1.7	N/A	6	0	0	0.0	0.0
B+ / 8.7	1.7	1.1	10.34	519	4	66	1	12	17	122	1.7	84	6	250,000	0	0.0	0.0
D / 2.1	4.9	3.9	10.11	26	5	0	0	91	4	210	0.0	98	4	2,500	100	4.3	1.5
D / 2.2	4.8	3.9	10.09	27	5	0	0	91	4	210	0.0	98	4	1,000,000	0	0.0	1.5

Fund Type	Fund Name	Ticker Symbol	Overall Investment Rating	Phone	Performance Rating/Pts	3 Mo	6 Mo	1Yr / Pct	3Yr / Pct	5Yr / Pct	Dividend Yield	Expense Ratio
COI	HC Capital US Corp FI Sec HC Strat	HCXSX	C	(800) 242-9596	C+ / 6.7	1.76	-1.70	6.19 /71	3.36 /67	2.69 /53	2.68	0.19
USL	HC Capital US Govt FI Sec HC Strat	HCUSX	D-	(800) 242-9596	D+ / 2.8	0.62	-2.80	-1.18 / 3	1.67 /38	0.63 /23	1.41	0.19
MTG	HC Capital US Mtg/Asst Bckd FI Str	HCASX	B-	(800) 242-9596	C- / 3.8	0.44	-1.37	0.08 /21	2.06 /44	1.74 /38	2.70	0.21
GL	HC Inflation Protected Secs HC Adv	HCPAX	U	(800) 242-9596	U /	1.23	-0.58	3.05 /57	--	--	2.13	0.40
GL	HC Inflation Protected Secs HC Str	HCPBX	U	(800) 242-9596	U /	1.23	-0.58	3.04 /57	--	--	2.12	0.15
GL	Henderson High Yield Opp A	HYOAX	B	(866) 443-6337	A / 9.5	5.13	6.79	19.58 /95	5.56 /89	--	5.20	1.25
GL	Henderson High Yield Opp C	HYOCX	B	(866) 443-6337	A+ / 9.6	4.96	6.44	18.59 /94	4.75 /83	--	4.74	2.06
GL	Henderson High Yield Opp I	HYOIX	B+	(866) 443-6337	A+ / 9.8	5.22	6.96	19.75 /96	5.81 /91	--	5.66	1.05
GL	Henderson High Yield Opp R6	HYORX	U	(866) 443-6337	U /	5.24	6.88	19.73 /96	--	--	5.74	0.99
GEI	Henderson Strategic Income A	HFAAX	B	(866) 443-6337	C+ / 6.9	2.94	0.72	8.37 /75	4.33 /79	5.59 /89	2.40	1.06
GEI	Henderson Strategic Income C	HFACX	B+	(866) 443-6337	B- / 7.3	2.76	0.34	7.48 /73	3.53 /69	4.80 /82	1.79	1.82
GEI	Henderson Strategic Income I	HFAIX	A	(866) 443-6337	B+ / 8.4	3.01	0.85	8.54 /75	4.55 /81	5.85 /91	2.78	0.81
GEL	Henderson Strategic Income R6	HFARX	U	(866) 443-6337	U /	2.92	0.77	8.61 /76	--	--	2.84	0.75
GEI	Highland Fixed Income A	HFBAX	B	(877) 665-1287	C / 4.7	2.00	0.10	6.17 /71	2.83 /58	2.36 /47	2.65	0.94
GEI	Highland Fixed Income C	HFBCX	B	(877) 665-1287	C / 5.1	1.82	-0.34	5.40 /68	2.04 /44	1.59 /36	2.03	1.69
GEI	Highland Fixed Income Y	HFBYX	A+	(877) 665-1287	C+ / 6.7	2.06	0.23	6.45 /71	3.09 /62	2.64 /52	3.02	0.69
LP	Highland Floating Rate Opps A	HFRAX	D	(877) 665-1287	B- / 7.5	4.93	7.40	21.26 /97	1.84 /40	6.92 /96	5.09	1.73
LP	Highland Floating Rate Opps C	HFRCX	D+	(877) 665-1287	B / 7.8	4.66	6.99	20.50 /97	1.29 /32	6.37 /94	4.81	2.23
LP	Highland Floating Rate Opps Z	HFRZX	C	(877) 665-1287	B+ / 8.7	5.03	7.44	21.51 /98	2.19 /46	7.30 /97	5.61	1.38
MUN	Highland Tax-Exempt A	HTXAX	D-	(877) 665-1287	C- / 3.1	1.63	-2.38	-0.62 / 8	2.44 /72	1.92 /57	1.82	1.06
MUN	Highland Tax-Exempt C	HTXCX	D	(877) 665-1287	C- / 3.9	1.44	-2.75	-1.37 / 2	1.66 /53	1.17 /39	1.14	1.81
MUN	Highland Tax-Exempt Y	HTXYX	B-	(877) 665-1287	C+ / 6.4	1.69	-2.23	-0.34 /12	2.68 /77	2.18 /63	2.15	0.81
GL	Holbrook Income I	HOBIX	U	(877) 345-8646	U /	2.28	2.60	--	--	--	0.00	N/A
GL	Holbrook Income Investor	HOBEX	U	(877) 345-8646	U /	2.16	2.43	--	--	--	0.00	N/A
*GES	Homestead Short Term Bond	HOSBX	A+	(800) 258-3030	C+ / 6.3	3.90	3.68	5.27 /68	2.34 /49	2.47 /49	4.76	0.74
USS	Homestead Short Term Govt Sec	HOSGX	C-	(800) 258-3030	D / 1.9	0.13	-0.43	-0.07 /16	0.64 /22	0.60 /23	0.88	0.77
GL	Horizon Active Income A	AIHAX	U	(800) 773-3863	U /	2.35	-2.62	0.46 /32	--	--	1.89	1.50
GL	Horizon Active Income N	AIMNX	E	(800) 773-3863	E+ / 0.6	2.40	-2.98	-0.20 /14	0.11 /13	--	1.76	1.50
*COH	Hotchkis and Wiley High Yield A	HWHAX	C	(866) 493-8637	A- / 9.0	5.69	6.44	23.14 /98	4.13 /77	6.85 /96	5.66	0.99
COH	Hotchkis and Wiley High Yield C	HWHCX	C	(866) 493-8637	A- / 9.1	5.46	6.11	22.51 /98	3.41 /67	--	5.22	1.74
COH	Hotchkis and Wiley High Yield I	HWHIX	C+	(866) 493-8637	A+ / 9.6	5.73	6.64	23.43 /98	4.40 /80	7.17 /97	6.12	0.74
GL	HSBC Emerging Markets Local Debt	HBMAX	E-	(800) 728-8183	E- / 0.1	5.81	-0.97	10.41 /80	-3.10 / 1	-3.75 / 0	0.67	2.06
GL	HSBC Emerging Markets Local Debt I	HBMIX	E-	(800) 728-8183	E- / 0.2	5.88	-0.89	10.65 /80	-2.80 / 1	-3.43 / 0	0.77	1.71
GL	HSBC Euro High Yield Bond A	HEYAX	U	(800) 782-8183	U /	3.07	1.81	12.05 /83	--	--	2.81	1.48
GL	HSBC Euro High Yield Bond I	HEYIX	U	(800) 782-8183	U /	3.18	1.95	12.31 /84	--	--	3.00	1.13
GL	HSBC Global High Income Bond A	HBIAX	U	(800) 782-8183	U /	2.90	0.50	10.04 /79	--	--	3.39	1.56
GL	HSBC Global High Income Bond I	HBIIX	U	(800) 782-8183	U /	3.02	0.64	10.51 /80	--	--	3.69	1.21
GL	HSBC Global High Yield Bond A	HBYAX	U	(800) 782-8183	U /	4.05	3.62	15.75 /90	--	--	4.51	1.65
GL	HSBC Global High Yield Bond I	HBYIX	U	(800) 782-8183	U /	4.07	3.78	16.15 /90	--	--	4.88	1.30
MMT	HSBC US Government Money Market	FTRXX	U	(800) 728-8183	U /	--	--	--	--	--	0.01	N/A
MMT●	HSBC US Government Money Market	HUBXX	U	(800) 728-8183	U /	--	--	--	--	--	0.01	N/A
MMT	HSBC US Government Money Market	HGDXX	D+	(800) 728-8183	E+ / 0.6	0.02	0.02	0.03 /20	0.03 / 8	0.02 / 8	0.03	N/A
MMT	HSBC US Government Money Market	HGIXX	C-	(800) 728-8183	D- / 1.3	0.11	0.18	0.30 /29	0.13 /14	0.08 /14	0.30	N/A
MMT	HSBC US Government Money Market	RGYXX	C-	(800) 728-8183	D- / 1.0	0.08	0.13	0.19 /26	0.09 /12	0.06 /12	0.19	N/A
MMT	HSBC US Treasury Money Market D	HTDXX	U	(800) 728-8183	U /	--	--	--	--	--	0.01	N/A
MMT	HSBC US Treasury Money Market I	HBIXX	C-	(800) 728-8183	D- / 1.0	0.10	0.15	0.22 /27	0.08 /12	0.05 /11	0.22	N/A
MMT	HSBC US Treasury Money Market Y	HTYXX	D+	(800) 728-8183	E+ / 0.8	0.07	0.09	0.11 /23	0.04 / 9	0.02 / 8	0.11	N/A
COH	Hundredfold Select Alternative Svc	SFHYX	B+	(855) 582-8006	A- / 9.2	5.61	5.93	14.09 /87	4.14 /77	5.07 /85	2.74	3.10
USS	Hussman Strategic Total Return	HSTRX	E+	(800) 487-7626	C / 4.8	1.52	-2.16	3.60 /60	2.77 /57	0.57 /22	0.25	0.81
GEI	IA 529 CSI Bond Index Port		D	(800) 662-7447	C / 4.3	1.21	-2.39	1.27 /43	2.37 /49	1.96 /41	0.00	0.34
GEL	IA 529 CSI Conservative Income Port		C+	(800) 662-7447	C- / 3.8	0.66	-1.09	1.32 /43	1.85 /40	1.24 /31	0.00	0.34
COI	ICON Bond A	IOBAX	B-	(800) 764-0442	C / 4.8	2.01	0.48	6.91 /72	2.98 /61	3.12 /60	2.95	1.51

● Denotes fund is closed to new investors
* Denotes fund is included in Section II

Risk Rating/Pts	3 Yr Avg Standard Deviation	Avg Duration	NAV As of 2/28/17	Total $(Mil)	Cash %	Gov. Bond %	Muni. Bond %	Corp. Bond %	Other %	Portfolio Turnover Ratio	Avg Coupon Rate	Manager Quality Pct	Manager Tenure (Years)	Initial Purch. $	Additional Purch. $	Front End Load	Back End Load
C- /3.3	3.9	N/A	9.91	268	0	0	0	0	100	64	0.0	34	N/A	0	0	0.0	0.0
C /5.4	3.0	N/A	9.79	229	0	0	0	0	100	50	0.0	37	N/A	0	0	0.0	0.0
B+ /8.3	1.9	N/A	9.60	202	0	0	0	0	100	15	0.0	29	4	0	0	0.0	0.0
U /	N/A	N/A	10.14	N/A	5	94	0	0	1	21	0.0	N/A	3	0	0	0.0	0.0
U /	N/A	N/A	10.15	485	5	94	0	0	1	21	0.0	N/A	3	0	0	0.0	0.0
D /1.9	5.2	N/A	10.12	12	6	0	0	92	2	174	0.0	98	4	500	0	4.8	0.0
D /1.9	5.2	N/A	10.09	3	6	0	0	92	2	174	0.0	97	4	500	0	0.0	0.0
D /1.9	5.1	N/A	10.08	23	6	0	0	92	2	174	0.0	98	4	0	0	0.0	0.0
U /	N/A	N/A	10.07	23	6	0	0	92	2	174	0.0	N/A	4	0	0	0.0	0.0
C /5.0	3.1	N/A	9.39	61	9	4	0	74	13	110	0.0	90	9	500	0	4.8	0.0
C /4.9	3.2	N/A	9.34	44	9	4	0	74	13	110	0.0	84	9	500	0	0.0	0.0
C /5.0	3.1	N/A	9.36	325	9	4	0	74	13	110	0.0	90	9	0	0	0.0	0.0
U /	N/A	N/A	9.36	1	9	4	0	74	13	110	0.0	N/A	9	0	0	0.0	0.0
B /7.6	2.5	5.1	12.92	111	0	15	7	45	33	46	5.2	75	3	500	100	4.3	0.0
B- /7.5	2.5	5.1	12.93	4	0	15	7	45	33	46	5.2	53	3	500	100	0.0	0.0
B /7.6	2.5	5.1	12.91	24	0	15	7	45	33	46	5.2	79	3	1,000,000	0	0.0	0.0
D- /1.3	5.9	N/A	7.40	269	0	0	0	53	47	53	8.4	68	5	2,500	50	3.5	0.0
D- /1.3	5.9	N/A	7.39	236	0	0	0	53	47	53	8.4	53	5	2,500	50	0.0	0.0
D- /1.3	5.9	N/A	7.39	307	0	0	0	53	47	53	8.4	77	5	2,500	50	0.0	0.0
C /5.3	2.8	7.0	11.47	13	5	6	87	0	2	26	5.5	22	3	500	100	4.3	0.0
C /5.3	2.8	7.0	11.46	1	5	6	87	0	2	26	5.5	7	3	500	100	0.0	0.0
C /5.4	2.8	7.0	12.44	N/A	5	6	87	0	2	26	5.5	29	3	1,000,000	0	0.0	0.0
U /	N/A	0.8	10.17	N/A	0	0	0	0	100	0	0.0	N/A	1	100,000	2,500	0.0	0.0
U /	N/A	0.8	10.17	N/A	0	0	0	0	100	0	0.0	N/A	1	2,500	2,500	0.0	0.0
B+ /8.3	1.9	2.6	5.21	536	0	5	19	47	29	20	0.0	83	26	500	0	0.0	0.0
A- /9.1	1.1	2.2	5.17	74	0	57	0	32	11	32	0.0	37	22	500	0	0.0	0.0
U /	N/A	N/A	9.70	N/A	0	0	0	0	100	324	0.0	N/A	4	2,500	250	5.8	0.0
C- /3.9	3.5	N/A	9.67	186	0	0	0	0	100	324	0.0	70	4	2,500	250	0.0	0.0
E+ /0.9	6.0	3.7	12.25	523	2	0	0	91	7	45	6.8	24	8	2,500	100	3.8	2.0
E+ /0.8	6.0	3.7	12.33	3	2	0	0	91	7	45	6.8	9	8	2,500	100	0.0	2.0
E+ /0.9	6.0	3.7	12.33	2,078	2	0	0	91	7	45	6.8	34	8	1,000,000	100	0.0	2.0
E- /0.1	11.8	4.3	7.06	N/A	22	76	0	1	1	186	0.0	22	2	1,000	100	4.8	0.0
E- /0.1	11.8	4.3	7.07	30	22	76	0	1	1	186	0.0	33	2	1,000,000	0	0.0	0.0
U /	N/A	N/A	10.85	N/A	0	0	0	0	100	20	0.0	N/A	1	1,000	100	4.8	0.0
U /	N/A	N/A	10.88	28	0	0	0	0	100	20	0.0	N/A	1	1,000	0	0.0	0.0
U /	N/A	N/A	10.13	N/A	0	0	0	0	100	47	0.0	N/A	2	1,000	100	4.8	0.0
U /	N/A	N/A	10.16	27	0	0	0	0	100	47	0.0	N/A	2	1,000,000	0	0.0	0.0
U /	N/A	N/A	10.05	2	0	0	0	0	100	50	0.0	N/A	2	1,000	100	4.8	0.0
U /	N/A	N/A	10.08	27	0	0	0	0	100	50	0.0	N/A	2	1,000,000	0	0.0	0.0
U /	N/A	N/A	1.00	2	100	0	0	0	0	0	0.0	N/A	N/A	1,000	100	0.0	0.0
U /	N/A	N/A	1.00	N/A	100	0	0	0	0	0	0.0	N/A	N/A	0	0	0.0	0.0
A+ /9.9	N/A	N/A	1.00	1,790	100	0	0	0	0	0	0.0	40	N/A	1,000	100	0.0	0.0
A+ /9.9	N/A	N/A	1.00	6,642	100	0	0	0	0	0	0.3	47	N/A	25,000,000	5,000,000	0.0	0.0
A+ /9.9	N/A	N/A	1.00	2,575	100	0	0	0	0	0	0.2	45	N/A	5,000,000	0	0.0	0.0
U /	N/A	N/A	1.00	224	100	0	0	0	0	0	0.0	N/A	N/A	1,000	100	0.0	0.0
A+ /9.9	N/A	N/A	1.00	730	100	0	0	0	0	0	0.2	45	N/A	25,000,000	5,000,000	0.0	0.0
A+ /9.9	N/A	N/A	1.00	672	100	0	0	0	0	0	0.1	40	N/A	5,000,000	0	0.0	0.0
D+ /2.6	3.9	N/A	22.72	38	26	0	0	50	24	358	0.0	82	13	5,000	1,000	0.0	0.0
D- /1.0	6.3	N/A	12.04	401	12	70	0	1	17	129	0.0	71	15	1,000	100	0.0	1.5
C /5.1	3.1	N/A	16.78	37	0	46	1	25	28	0	0.0	26	14	25	25	0.0	0.0
B /8.1	2.1	N/A	15.36	140	25	49	1	13	12	0	0.0	43	14	25	25	0.0	0.0
B- /7.3	2.6	4.6	9.40	7	7	2	0	65	26	141	5.4	76	6	1,000	100	4.8	0.0

Fund Type	Fund Name	Ticker Symbol	Overall Investment Rating	Phone	Perfor-mance Rating/Pts	3 Mo	6 Mo	1Yr / Pct	3Yr / Pct	5Yr / Pct	Dividend Yield	Expense Ratio
	99 Pct = Best							Total Return % through 2/28/17	Annualized		Incl. in Returns	
GES	ICON Bond C	IOBCX	A-	(800) 764-0442	C+ / 6.0	1.95	0.33	6.34 /71	2.42 /50	2.53 /50	2.60	2.34
GES	ICON Bond S	IOBZX	A+	(800) 764-0442	B- / 7.0	2.05	0.59	7.17 /73	3.26 /65	3.38 /63	3.36	1.06
GEL	ID 529 IDeal CSP Income Port		C	(800) 662-7447	C- / 3.0	0.64	-1.18	1.13 /41	1.31 /32	0.73 /24	0.00	0.84
MMT	IFT-Money Market Portf	INFXX	D+	(800) 321-8563	E+ / 0.7	0.05	0.05	0.05 /21	0.02 / 7	0.01 / 6	0.05	N/A
COI	Insight Invest Grade Bond Inst	CWBIX	A-	(866) 678-6242	C+ / 6.5	1.64	-0.89	5.34 /68	3.46 /68	3.48 /65	2.88	1.29
COH	Integrity High Income A	IHFAX	C-	(800) 601-5593	B+ / 8.5	4.52	4.30	19.13 /95	3.86 /73	5.91 /91	4.85	1.67
COH	Integrity High Income C	IHFCX	C	(800) 601-5593	B+ / 8.7	4.45	4.04	18.18 /94	3.08 /62	5.15 /85	4.32	2.41
COH	Integrity High Income I	IHFIX	U	(800) 601-5593	U /	4.72	4.55	--	--	--	0.00	N/A
COH	Intrepid Income Institutional	ICMUX	D	(866) 996-3863	C / 5.1	1.03	1.33	9.68 /78	1.98 /43	2.86 /56	2.98	0.96
MUS	Invesco California Tax-Free Inc A	CLFAX	C-	(800) 959-4246	C+ / 6.9	2.10	-4.12	-0.14 /15	4.37 /95	3.69 /90	3.46	0.94
MUS ●	Invesco California Tax-Free Inc B	CLFBX	B	(800) 959-4246	B+ / 8.7	2.18	-4.06	-0.11 /16	4.41 /95	3.76 /91	3.60	0.94
MUS	Invesco California Tax-Free Inc C	CLFCX	C+	(800) 959-4246	B / 7.8	2.06	-4.32	-0.70 / 7	3.85 /91	3.17 /83	3.09	1.44
MUS	Invesco California Tax-Free Inc Y	CLFDX	B+	(800) 959-4246	B+ / 8.9	2.25	-3.97	0.12 /25	4.63 /96	3.96 /93	3.86	0.69
COI	Invesco Conservative Income Instl	ICIFX	U	(800) 959-4246	U /	0.27	0.45	1.11 /41	--	--	1.01	0.59
* GEI	Invesco Core Plus Bond A	ACPSX	C	(800) 959-4246	C+ / 5.6	1.94	-0.79	5.52 /69	3.68 /71	3.66 /68	2.87	0.95
GEI ●	Invesco Core Plus Bond B	CPBBX	C+	(800) 959-4246	C+ / 6.1	1.83	-1.17	4.73 /66	2.91 /59	2.89 /56	2.24	1.70
GEI	Invesco Core Plus Bond C	CPCFX	C+	(800) 959-4246	C+ / 6.1	1.84	-1.16	4.74 /66	2.91 /59	2.89 /56	2.25	1.70
GEI	Invesco Core Plus Bond R	CPBRX	B	(800) 959-4246	C+ / 6.8	1.97	-0.92	5.26 /68	3.42 /68	3.41 /64	2.74	1.20
GEI	Invesco Core Plus Bond R5	CPIIX	B+	(800) 959-4246	B- / 7.4	2.12	-0.63	5.92 /70	3.98 /75	3.93 /71	3.28	0.63
COI	Invesco Core Plus Bond R6	CPBFX	B+	(800) 959-4246	B- / 7.5	2.12	-0.61	6.00 /70	4.06 /76	3.97 /72	3.36	0.53
GEI	Invesco Core Plus Bond Y	CPBYX	B+	(800) 959-4246	B- / 7.3	2.09	-0.66	5.78 /69	3.94 /74	3.94 /72	3.25	0.70
* GEI	Invesco Corporate Bond A	ACCBX	C-	(800) 959-4246	B- / 7.2	3.30	-0.11	9.98 /79	4.28 /78	4.73 /81	3.43	0.90
GEI ●	Invesco Corporate Bond B	ACCDX	C+	(800) 959-4246	B+ / 8.3	3.30	-0.10	9.97 /79	4.28 /78	4.73 /81	3.58	0.90
GEI	Invesco Corporate Bond C	ACCEX	C-	(800) 959-4246	B- / 7.5	3.03	-0.60	9.17 /77	3.49 /69	3.96 /72	2.60	1.64
COI	Invesco Corporate Bond R	ACCZX	C	(800) 959-4246	B / 8.0	3.10	-0.37	9.70 /78	3.97 /75	4.47 /78	3.33	1.15
COI	Invesco Corporate Bond R5	ACCWX	B-	(800) 959-4246	B+ / 8.7	3.25	-0.07	10.33 /80	4.65 /82	5.15 /85	3.91	0.54
COI	Invesco Corporate Bond R6	ICBFX	B-	(800) 959-4246	B+ / 8.7	3.41	0.11	10.43 /80	4.74 /83	5.16 /86	4.00	0.46
GEI	Invesco Corporate Bond Y	ACCHX	C+	(800) 959-4246	B+ / 8.5	3.22	-0.11	10.24 /79	4.49 /81	4.99 /84	3.83	0.65
EM	Invesco Emerg Mkts Flexible Bond A	IAEMX	E-	(800) 959-4246	E- / 0.0	2.49	1.09	7.67 /74	-4.59 / 0	-4.03 / 0	2.86	1.89
EM ●	Invesco Emerg Mkts Flexible Bond B	IBEMX	E-	(800) 959-4246	E- / 0.0	2.30	0.55	6.87 /72	-5.31 / 0	-4.76 / 0	2.25	2.64
EM	Invesco Emerg Mkts Flexible Bond C	ICEMX	E-	(800) 959-4246	E- / 0.0	2.30	0.71	6.87 /72	-5.30 / 0	-4.75 / 0	2.25	2.64
EM	Invesco Emerg Mkts Flexible Bond R	IREMX	E-	(800) 959-4246	E- / 0.0	2.43	0.96	7.41 /73	-4.84 / 0	-4.30 / 0	2.74	2.14
EM	Invesco Emerg Mkts Flexible Bond	IIEMX	E-	(800) 959-4246	E- / 0.1	2.56	1.22	7.94 /74	-4.31 / 0	-3.77 / 0	3.23	1.34
EM	Invesco Emerg Mkts Flexible Bond	IFEMX	E-	(800) 959-4246	E- / 0.1	2.40	1.06	7.95 /74	-4.36 / 0	-3.85 / 0	3.24	1.33
EM	Invesco Emerg Mkts Flexible Bond Y	IYEMX	E-	(800) 959-4246	E- / 0.1	2.56	1.21	7.94 /74	-4.35 / 0	-3.81 / 0	3.23	1.64
* LP	Invesco Floating Rate A	AFRAX	B-	(800) 959-4246	B / 7.6	2.72	4.97	14.94 /88	3.10 /63	4.53 /79	4.22	1.12
LP	Invesco Floating Rate C	AFRCX	B-	(800) 959-4246	B / 7.8	2.60	4.72	14.42 /87	2.59 /54	4.02 /73	3.84	1.62
LP	Invesco Floating Rate R	AFRRX	B	(800) 959-4246	B / 8.0	2.66	4.70	14.64 /88	2.81 /58	4.25 /75	4.09	1.37
LP	Invesco Floating Rate R5	AFRIX	B+	(800) 959-4246	B+ / 8.6	2.78	5.10	15.39 /89	3.37 /67	4.83 /82	4.58	0.86
LP	Invesco Floating Rate R6	AFRFX	B+	(800) 959-4246	B+ / 8.6	2.81	5.16	15.20 /89	3.38 /67	4.82 /82	4.67	0.77
LP	Invesco Floating Rate Y	AFRYX	B+	(800) 959-4246	B+ / 8.6	2.79	5.10	15.24 /89	3.36 /67	4.79 /82	4.57	0.87
MMT	Invesco Gov and Agency Corp	AGCXX	C-	(800) 959-4246	D- / 1.2	0.10	0.17	0.29 /29	0.12 /14	0.08 /14	0.29	N/A
MMT	Invesco Gov and Agency CshMgt		C-	(800) 959-4246	D- / 1.1	0.09	0.14	0.24 /27	0.10 /13	0.07 /13	0.24	N/A
MMT	Invesco Gov and Agency Inst	AGPXX	C-	(800) 959-4246	D- / 1.3	0.11	0.18	0.32 /30	0.14 /15	0.09 /15	0.32	N/A
MMT	Invesco Gov and Agency Psnl		C-	(800) 959-4246	E+ / 0.9	0.03	0.07	0.13 /23	0.07 /11	0.05 /11	0.13	N/A
MMT	Invesco Gov and Agency Pvt	GPVXX	C-	(800) 959-4246	E+ / 0.9	0.04	0.07	0.14 /24	0.07 /11	0.05 /11	0.14	N/A
MMT	Invesco Gov and Agency Res		C-	(800) 959-4246	D- / 1.0	0.07	0.10	0.17 /25	0.08 /12	0.06 /12	0.17	N/A
MMT	Invesco Gov and Agency Rsv		C-	(800) 959-4246	E+ / 0.9	0.03	0.07	0.13 /23	0.07 /11	0.05 /11	0.13	N/A
MMT ●	Invesco Govt Money Market AX	ACZXX	D+	(800) 959-4246	E+ / 0.7	0.01	0.01	0.01 /18	0.04 / 9	0.05 /11	0.01	N/A
MMT	Invesco Govt Money Market CRS	AIMXX	D+	(800) 959-4246	E+ / 0.7	0.01	0.01	0.01 /18	0.04 / 9	0.05 /11	0.01	N/A
MMT ●	Invesco Govt Money Market Investor	INAXX	D+	(800) 959-4246	E+ / 0.7	0.04	0.04	0.04 /20	0.05 /10	0.05 /11	0.04	N/A
MMT	Invesco Govt Money Market Y		D+	(800) 959-4246	E+ / 0.7	0.04	0.04	0.04 /20	0.05 /10	0.05 /11	0.04	N/A

● Denotes fund is closed to new investors
* Denotes fund is included in Section II

www.thestreetratings.com

RISK			NET ASSETS		ASSET							FUND MANAGER		MINIMUM		LOADS	
Risk Rating/Pts	3 Yr Avg Standard Deviation	Avg Dura-tion	NAV As of 2/28/17	Total $(Mil)	Cash %	Gov. Bond %	Muni. Bond %	Corp. Bond %	Other %	Portfolio Turnover Ratio	Avg Coupon Rate	Manager Quality Pct	Manager Tenure (Years)	Initial Purch. $	Additional Purch. $	Front End Load	Back End Load
B- / 7.4	2.6	4.6	9.48	4	7	2	0	65	26	141	5.4	71	6	1,000	100	0.0	0.0
B- / 7.4	2.6	4.6	9.44	71	7	2	0	65	26	141	5.4	82	6	1,000	100	0.0	0.0
B / 7.9	2.2	N/A	12.54	56	25	48	0	12	15	0	0.0	20	10	25	25	0.0	0.0
A+ / 9.9	N/A	N/A	1.00	19,858	100	0	0	0	0	0	0.1	38	N/A	100,000	0	0.0	0.0
C+ / 6.6	2.8	N/A	10.03	40	3	14	2	48	33	46	0.0	75	7	100,000	0	0.0	1.0
D- / 1.1	5.7	N/A	7.80	26	5	0	0	93	2	41	0.0	21	9	1,000	50	4.3	0.0
D- / 1.1	5.7	N/A	7.82	5	5	0	0	93	2	41	0.0	7	9	1,000	50	0.0	0.0
U /	N/A	N/A	7.80	1	5	0	0	93	2	41	0.0	N/A	9	1,000	50	0.0	0.0
C- / 3.9	3.0	1.8	9.31	81	34	0	0	58	8	52	0.0	36	7	250,000	100	0.0	2.0
C- / 3.2	3.8	7.6	11.90	330	2	0	97	0	1	7	5.2	59	8	1,000	50	4.3	0.0
C- / 3.1	3.8	7.6	12.02	10	2	0	97	0	1	7	5.2	59	8	1,000	50	0.0	0.0
C- / 3.1	3.9	7.6	11.98	51	2	0	97	0	1	7	5.2	31	8	1,000	50	0.0	0.0
C- / 3.1	3.8	7.6	11.95	38	2	0	97	0	1	7	5.2	65	8	1,000	50	0.0	0.0
U /	N/A	N/A	10.01	104	26	0	0	43	31	84	0.0	N/A	3	1,000,000	0	0.0	0.0
C / 5.3	3.1	5.6	10.79	716	0	23	0	47	30	518	1.3	78	8	1,000	50	4.3	0.0
C / 5.3	3.1	5.6	10.79	5	0	23	0	47	30	518	1.3	61	8	1,000	50	0.0	0.0
C / 5.3	3.1	5.6	10.79	113	0	23	0	47	30	518	1.3	62	8	1,000	50	0.0	0.0
C / 5.3	3.1	5.6	10.79	9	0	23	0	47	30	518	1.3	74	8	0	0	0.0	0.0
C / 5.3	3.1	5.6	10.79	4	0	23	0	47	30	518	1.3	81	8	10,000,000	0	0.0	0.0
C / 5.2	3.1	5.6	10.79	1,101	0	23	0	47	30	518	1.3	79	8	10,000,000	0	0.0	0.0
C / 5.2	3.1	5.6	10.80	652	0	23	0	47	30	518	1.3	80	8	1,000	50	0.0	0.0
D+ / 2.4	4.4	7.0	7.31	947	3	9	0	83	5	202	10.4	77	7	1,000	50	4.3	0.0
D+ / 2.4	4.4	7.0	7.32	10	3	9	0	83	5	202	10.4	77	7	1,000	50	0.0	0.0
D+ / 2.4	4.4	7.0	7.36	85	3	9	0	83	5	202	10.4	57	7	1,000	50	0.0	0.0
D+ / 2.4	4.4	7.0	7.31	7	3	9	0	83	5	202	10.4	51	7	0	0	0.0	0.0
D+ / 2.4	4.4	7.0	7.31	5	3	9	0	83	5	202	10.4	72	7	10,000,000	0	0.0	0.0
D+ / 2.4	4.4	7.0	7.32	29	3	9	0	83	5	202	10.4	73	7	10,000,000	0	0.0	0.0
D+ / 2.4	4.4	7.0	7.32	234	3	9	0	83	5	202	10.4	79	7	1,000	50	0.0	0.0
E / 0.5	7.6	4.9	6.56	5	7	41	1	41	10	266	7.1	0	2	1,000	50	4.3	0.0
E / 0.4	7.7	4.9	6.55	N/A	7	41	1	41	10	266	7.1	0	2	1,000	50	0.0	0.0
E / 0.5	7.6	4.9	6.56	1	7	41	1	41	10	266	7.1	0	2	1,000	50	0.0	0.0
E / 0.5	7.6	4.9	6.55	N/A	7	41	1	41	10	266	7.1	0	2	0	0	0.0	0.0
E / 0.5	7.6	4.9	6.56	N/A	7	41	1	41	10	266	7.1	0	2	10,000,000	0	0.0	0.0
E / 0.5	7.6	4.9	6.55	60	7	41	1	41	10	266	7.1	0	2	10,000,000	0	0.0	0.0
E / 0.5	7.6	4.9	6.56	N/A	7	41	1	41	10	266	7.1	0	2	1,000	50	0.0	0.0
C- / 3.6	3.7	N/A	7.62	729	0	0	0	21	79	70	0.0	87	11	1,000	50	2.5	0.0
C- / 3.6	3.7	N/A	7.59	473	0	0	0	21	79	70	0.0	83	11	1,000	50	0.0	0.0
C- / 3.6	3.7	N/A	7.63	7	0	0	0	21	79	70	0.0	84	11	0	0	0.0	0.0
C- / 3.5	3.8	N/A	7.63	2	0	0	0	21	79	70	0.0	88	11	10,000,000	0	0.0	0.0
C- / 3.6	3.7	N/A	7.61	566	0	0	0	21	79	70	0.0	88	11	10,000,000	0	0.0	0.0
C- / 3.6	3.7	N/A	7.61	913	0	0	0	21	79	70	0.0	88	11	1,000	50	0.0	0.0
A+ / 9.9	N/A	N/A	1.00	320	100	0	0	0	0	0	0.3	47	N/A	1,000,000	0	0.0	0.0
A+ / 9.9	N/A	N/A	1.00	141	100	0	0	0	0	0	0.2	N/A	N/A	1,000,000	0	0.0	0.0
A+ / 9.9	N/A	N/A	1.00	22,167	100	0	0	0	0	0	0.3	48	N/A	1,000,000	0	0.0	0.0
A+ / 9.9	N/A	N/A	1.00	17	100	0	0	0	0	0	0.1	44	N/A	1,000	0	0.0	0.0
A+ / 9.9	N/A	N/A	1.00	436	100	0	0	0	0	0	0.1	44	N/A	100,000	0	0.0	0.0
A+ / 9.9	N/A	N/A	1.00	368	100	0	0	0	0	0	0.2	45	N/A	1,000,000	0	0.0	0.0
A+ / 9.9	N/A	N/A	1.00	394	100	0	0	0	0	0	0.1	44	N/A	1,000	0	0.0	0.0
A+ / 9.9	N/A	N/A	1.00	103	100	0	0	0	0	0	0.0	43	N/A	1,000	50	0.0	0.0
A+ / 9.9	N/A	N/A	1.00	843	100	0	0	0	0	0	0.0	43	N/A	1,000	50	0.0	0.0
A+ / 9.9	N/A	N/A	1.00	123	100	0	0	0	0	0	0.0	43	N/A	1,000	50	0.0	0.0
A+ / 9.9	N/A	N/A	1.00	27	100	0	0	0	0	0	0.0	43	N/A	1,000	50	0.0	0.0

						Total Return % through 2/28/17			Annualized		Incl. in Returns	
Fund Type	Fund Name	Ticker Symbol	Overall Investment Rating	Phone	Perfor-mance Rating/Pts	3 Mo	6 Mo	1Yr / Pct	3Yr / Pct	5Yr / Pct	Dividend Yield	Expense Ratio
*COH	Invesco High Yield A	AMHYX	D	(800) 959-4246	B- / 7.2	3.96	3.79	15.91 /90	3.00 /61	5.70 /90	4.96	1.03
COH ●	Invesco High Yield B	AHYBX	D	(800) 959-4246	B- / 7.5	4.02	3.40	15.03 /88	2.24 /47	4.91 /83	4.46	1.78
COH ●	Invesco High Yield C	AHYCX	D	(800) 959-4246	B- / 7.5	3.78	3.41	15.09 /89	2.21 /47	4.90 /83	4.46	1.78
COH ●	Invesco High Yield Investor	HYINX	C-	(800) 959-4246	B+ / 8.3	3.98	3.57	15.95 /90	2.95 /60	5.72 /90	5.22	1.01
*MUH	Invesco High Yield Municipal A	ACTHX	B+	(800) 959-4246	A+ / 9.7	2.74	-3.53	2.53 /62	6.92 /99	5.74 /99	4.84	0.93
MUH●	Invesco High Yield Municipal B	ACTGX	B+	(800) 959-4246	A+ / 9.9	2.73	-3.59	2.54 /62	6.91 /99	5.74 /99	5.06	0.93
MUH	Invesco High Yield Municipal C	ACTFX	B+	(800) 959-4246	A+ / 9.8	2.55	-3.91	1.86 /56	6.15 /99	4.96 /97	4.29	1.66
MUH	Invesco High Yield Municipal R5	ACTNX	B+	(800) 959-4246	A+ / 9.9	2.79	-3.43	2.64 /62	7.10 /99	5.92 /99	5.27	0.72
MUH	Invesco High Yield Municipal Y	ACTDX	B+	(800) 959-4246	A+ / 9.9	2.91	-3.39	2.89 /64	7.18 /99	6.00 /99	5.32	0.68
COH	Invesco High Yield R5	AHIYX	C	(800) 959-4246	B+ / 8.6	4.06	3.97	16.32 /91	3.26 /65	6.02 /92	5.51	0.69
COH	Invesco High Yield R6	HYIFX	C	(800) 959-4246	B+ / 8.7	4.08	3.77	16.42 /91	3.35 /66	6.06 /92	5.60	0.60
COH	Invesco High Yield Y	AHHYX	C	(800) 959-4246	B+ / 8.7	4.27	3.92	16.44 /91	3.34 /66	6.01 /92	5.41	0.78
GEI	Invesco Income Allocation A	ALAAX	C+	(800) 959-4246	B+ / 8.5	4.19	2.53	12.91 /85	5.42 /88	6.66 /95	3.00	1.06
GEI ●	Invesco Income Allocation B	BLIAX	B	(800) 959-4246	A- / 9.0	4.08	2.24	12.15 /84	4.69 /83	5.91 /91	2.45	1.81
GEI	Invesco Income Allocation C	CLIAX	B	(800) 959-4246	A- / 9.0	4.09	2.24	12.16 /84	4.66 /82	5.90 /91	2.45	1.81
GEI	Invesco Income Allocation R	RLIAX	B	(800) 959-4246	A / 9.3	4.12	2.49	12.73 /85	5.16 /86	6.40 /95	2.93	1.31
GEI	Invesco Income Allocation R5	ILAAX	B+	(800) 959-4246	A+ / 9.6	4.35	2.75	13.29 /86	5.72 /90	6.96 /96	3.42	0.78
GEI	Invesco Income Allocation Y	ALAYX	B+	(800) 959-4246	A+ / 9.6	4.26	2.66	13.19 /85	5.69 /90	6.94 /96	3.42	0.81
*MUN	Invesco Intm Term Municipal Inc A	VKLMX	C	(800) 959-4246	C / 5.2	1.62	-3.32	-0.30 /13	2.94 /81	2.66 /74	2.57	0.90
MUN●	Invesco Intm Term Municipal Inc B	VKLBX	B	(800) 959-4246	C+ / 6.7	1.61	-3.32	-0.33 /12	2.94 /81	2.65 /73	2.64	0.90
MUN	Invesco Intm Term Municipal Inc C	VKLCX	C-	(800) 959-4246	C / 4.8	1.44	-3.70	-1.06 / 4	2.19 /67	1.90 /56	1.86	1.65
MUN	Invesco Intm Term Municipal Inc Y	VKLIX	B+	(800) 959-4246	B- / 7.1	1.69	-3.20	-0.05 /17	3.20 /84	2.92 /79	2.90	0.65
*MUN	Invesco Limited Term Muni Inc A	ATFAX	C-	(800) 959-4246	D / 2.2	1.40	-1.59	-0.51 / 9	1.43 /46	1.70 /51	1.74	0.61
MUN●	Invesco Limited Term Muni Inc A2	AITFX	B-	(800) 959-4246	C- / 3.8	1.46	-1.55	-0.35 /12	1.65 /52	1.94 /57	2.02	0.36
MUN	Invesco Limited Term Muni Inc C	ATFCX	D+	(800) 959-4246	D / 1.9	1.21	-1.96	-1.26 / 3	0.64 /27	--	1.02	1.36
MUN	Invesco Limited Term Muni Inc R5	ATFIX	B	(800) 959-4246	C / 4.4	1.45	-1.55	-0.33 /12	1.68 /53	1.96 /58	2.06	0.31
MUN	Invesco Limited Term Muni Inc Y	ATFYX	B+	(800) 959-4246	C / 4.5	1.46	-1.47	-0.27 /13	1.68 /53	1.94 /57	2.04	0.36
MMT	Invesco Liquid Assets Corp	LPCXX	C	(800) 959-4246	D / 1.6	0.17	0.35	0.55 /34	0.24 /17	0.18 /18	0.52	N/A
MMT	Invesco Liquid Assets CshMgt	LPMXX	C	(800) 959-4246	D- / 1.5	0.18	0.33	0.50 /33	0.20 /16	0.14 /17	0.47	N/A
MMT	Invesco Liquid Assets Inst	LAPXX	C	(800) 959-4246	D / 1.7	0.18	0.36	0.58 /35	0.27 /18	0.21 /19	0.54	N/A
MMT	Invesco Liquid Assets Psnl	LPPXX	C-	(800) 959-4246	D- / 1.0	0.05	0.15	0.21 /26	0.08 /12	0.06 /12	0.17	N/A
MMT	Invesco Liquid Assets Pvt	LPVXX	C-	(800) 959-4246	D- / 1.2	0.10	0.22	0.29 /29	0.11 /13	0.07 /13	0.25	N/A
MMT	Invesco Liquid Assets Rs	LRCXX	C-	(800) 959-4246	D- / 1.4	0.16	0.27	0.38 /31	0.15 /15	0.09 /15	0.35	N/A
MMT	Invesco Liquid Assets Rsv	LPRXX	C-	(800) 959-4246	D- / 1.0	0.04	0.15	0.20 /26	0.08 /12	0.05 /11	0.17	N/A
GL	Invesco Multi-Asset Income A	PIAFX	B-	(800) 959-4246	A+ / 9.7	5.87	1.85	17.23 /92	7.15 /96	6.36 /94	4.30	1.13
GL	Invesco Multi-Asset Income C	PICFX	B	(800) 959-4246	A+ / 9.8	5.68	1.46	16.36 /91	6.35 /94	5.57 /89	3.83	1.88
GL	Invesco Multi-Asset Income R	PIRFX	B	(800) 959-4246	A+ / 9.8	5.71	1.72	16.83 /92	6.85 /95	6.08 /93	4.31	1.38
GL	Invesco Multi-Asset Income R5	IPNFX	B	(800) 959-4246	A+ / 9.9	5.83	1.97	17.39 /93	7.38 /97	6.63 /95	4.79	0.75
GL	Invesco Multi-Asset Income R6	PIFFX	B	(800) 959-4246	A+ / 9.9	5.94	1.97	17.51 /93	7.42 /97	6.60 /95	4.79	0.75
GL	Invesco Multi-Asset Income Y	PIYFX	B	(800) 959-4246	A+ / 9.9	5.94	1.97	17.51 /93	7.38 /97	6.61 /95	4.79	0.88
*MUN	Invesco Municipal Income A	VKMMX	C	(800) 959-4246	C+ / 6.6	2.14	-3.61	0.29 /32	4.09 /93	3.50 /87	3.81	0.93
MUN●	Invesco Municipal Income B	VMIBX	C+	(800) 959-4246	B- / 7.2	1.95	-3.99	-0.47 /10	3.32 /86	2.73 /75	3.20	1.68
MUN	Invesco Municipal Income C	VMICX	C+	(800) 959-4246	B- / 7.2	1.95	-4.01	-0.48 /10	3.32 /86	2.71 /75	3.20	1.68
MUN	Invesco Municipal Income Inv	VMINX	B+	(800) 959-4246	B+ / 8.6	2.16	-3.56	0.39 /35	4.21 /94	--	4.09	0.82
MUN	Invesco Municipal Income Y	VMIIX	B+	(800) 959-4246	B+ / 8.8	2.20	-3.49	0.54 /38	4.35 /95	3.77 /91	4.24	0.68
MUS	Invesco NY Tax Free Income A	VNYAX	C-	(800) 959-4246	C+ / 6.0	1.87	-3.98	-0.44 /10	3.94 /92	2.91 /78	3.21	1.00
MUS ●	Invesco NY Tax Free Income B	VBNYX	B	(800) 959-4246	B / 8.0	1.87	-3.97	-0.49 /10	3.94 /92	2.91 /78	3.36	1.00
MUS	Invesco NY Tax Free Income C	VNYCX	C	(800) 959-4246	C+ / 6.6	1.68	-4.35	-1.26 / 3	3.16 /84	2.14 /62	2.57	1.75
MUS	Invesco NY Tax Free Income Y	VNYYX	B+	(800) 959-4246	B+ / 8.4	1.87	-3.86	-0.26 /14	4.20 /94	3.16 /82	3.61	0.75
MUS	Invesco PA Tax Free Income A	VKMPX	C+	(800) 959-4246	C+ / 6.7	1.72	-3.28	0.64 /39	4.12 /94	3.14 /82	3.39	1.08
MUS ●	Invesco PA Tax Free Income B	VKPAX	A-	(800) 959-4246	B+ / 8.5	1.72	-3.26	0.65 /39	4.10 /93	3.13 /82	3.55	1.08
MUS	Invesco PA Tax Free Income C	VKPCX	B-	(800) 959-4246	B- / 7.2	1.52	-3.64	-0.11 /16	3.35 /86	2.38 /68	2.77	1.83

● Denotes fund is closed to new investors
* Denotes fund is included in Section II

www.thestreetratings.com

Risk Rating/Pts	3 Yr Avg Standard Deviation	Avg Dura-tion	NAV As of 2/28/17	Total $(Mil)	Cash %	Gov. Bond %	Muni. Bond %	Corp. Bond %	Other %	Portfolio Turnover Ratio	Avg Coupon Rate	Manager Quality Pct	Manager Tenure (Years)	Initial Purch. $	Additional Purch. $	Front End Load	Back End Load
D- /1.1	5.6	4.1	4.21	826	3	1	0	93	3	84	9.0	8	7	1,000	50	4.3	0.0
D- /1.1	5.6	4.1	4.22	6	3	1	0	93	3	84	9.0	2	7	1,000	50	0.0	0.0
D- /1.1	5.7	4.1	4.20	101	3	1	0	93	3	84	9.0	2	7	1,000	50	0.0	0.0
D- /1.1	5.6	4.1	4.21	105	3	1	0	93	3	84	9.0	7	7	1,000	50	0.0	0.0
D /2.0	4.3	8.3	9.87	4,907	1	0	98	0	1	14	5.9	88	15	1,000	50	4.3	0.0
D /1.9	4.4	8.3	9.91	37	1	0	98	0	1	14	5.9	88	15	1,000	50	0.0	0.0
D /1.9	4.4	8.3	9.84	1,172	1	0	98	0	1	14	5.9	83	15	1,000	50	0.0	0.0
D /1.9	4.3	8.3	9.86	1	1	0	98	0	1	14	5.9	89	15	10,000,000	0	0.0	0.0
D /1.9	4.4	8.3	9.89	1,861	1	0	98	0	1	14	5.9	89	15	1,000	50	0.0	0.0
D- /1.2	5.6	4.1	4.20	88	3	1	0	93	3	84	9.0	11	7	10,000,000	0	0.0	0.0
D- /1.2	5.6	4.1	4.20	157	3	1	0	93	3	84	9.0	13	7	10,000,000	0	0.0	0.0
D- /1.3	5.4	4.1	4.23	198	3	1	0	93	3	84	9.0	15	7	1,000	50	0.0	0.0
D+ /2.3	4.7	4.5	11.44	385	0	15	0	24	61	1	7.8	93	3	1,000	50	5.5	0.0
D+ /2.3	4.7	4.5	11.47	2	0	15	0	24	61	1	7.8	89	3	1,000	50	0.0	0.0
D+ /2.3	4.7	4.5	11.46	130	0	15	0	24	61	1	7.8	89	3	1,000	50	0.0	0.0
D+ /2.3	4.7	4.5	11.45	5	0	15	0	24	61	1	7.8	92	3	0	0	0.0	0.0
D+ /2.3	4.7	4.5	11.45	1	0	15	0	24	61	1	7.8	93	3	10,000,000	0	0.0	0.0
D+ /2.3	4.7	4.5	11.44	40	0	15	0	24	61	1	7.8	93	3	1,000	50	0.0	0.0
C /5.4	3.0	5.6	10.97	701	0	0	98	0	2	7	4.7	29	12	1,000	50	2.5	0.0
C /5.5	3.0	5.6	11.19	3	0	0	98	0	2	7	4.7	30	12	1,000	50	0.0	0.0
C /5.5	3.0	5.6	10.94	235	0	0	98	0	2	7	4.7	12	12	1,000	50	0.0	0.0
C /5.4	3.0	5.6	10.96	271	0	0	98	0	2	7	4.7	41	12	1,000	50	0.0	0.0
B+ /8.4	1.9	3.5	11.31	1,275	0	0	97	0	3	13	4.2	21	6	1,000	50	2.5	0.0
B+ /8.4	1.9	3.5	11.31	72	0	0	97	0	3	13	4.2	27	6	1,000	50	1.0	0.0
B+ /8.4	1.9	3.5	11.30	391	0	0	97	0	3	13	4.2	7	6	1,000	50	0.0	0.0
B+ /8.3	1.9	3.5	11.30	11	0	0	97	0	3	13	4.2	28	6	10,000,000	0	0.0	0.0
B+ /8.4	1.9	3.5	11.30	801	0	0	97	0	3	13	4.2	28	6	1,000	50	0.0	0.0
A+ /9.9	0.1	N/A	1.00	9	100	0	0	0	0	0	0.5	53	N/A	1,000,000	0	0.0	0.0
A+ /9.9	0.1	N/A	1.00	7	100	0	0	0	0	0	0.5	52	N/A	1,000,000	0	0.0	0.0
A+ /9.9	0.1	N/A	1.00	292	100	0	0	0	0	0	0.5	54	N/A	10,000,000	0	0.0	0.0
A+ /9.9	N/A	N/A	1.00	N/A	100	0	0	0	0	0	0.2	N/A	N/A	1,000	0	0.0	0.0
A+ /9.9	0.1	N/A	1.00	11	100	0	0	0	0	0	0.3	46	N/A	100,000	0	0.0	0.0
A+ /9.9	0.1	N/A	1.00	1	100	0	0	0	0	0	0.4	50	N/A	1,000,000	0	0.0	0.0
A+ /9.9	N/A	N/A	1.00	1	100	0	0	0	0	0	0.2	N/A	N/A	1,000	0	0.0	0.0
D- /1.4	5.8	4.7	10.78	111	3	15	0	36	46	101	5.7	99	4	1,000	50	5.5	0.0
D- /1.5	5.7	4.7	10.77	34	3	15	0	36	46	101	5.7	99	4	1,000	50	0.0	0.0
D- /1.5	5.7	4.7	10.77	1	3	15	0	36	46	101	5.7	99	4	0	0	0.0	0.0
D- /1.5	5.7	4.7	10.78	N/A	3	15	0	36	46	101	5.7	99	4	10,000,000	0	0.0	0.0
D- /1.5	5.7	4.7	10.78	53	3	15	0	36	46	101	5.7	99	4	10,000,000	0	0.0	0.0
D- /1.5	5.7	4.7	10.78	69	3	15	0	36	46	101	5.7	99	4	1,000	50	0.0	0.0
C- /3.7	3.5	7.5	13.22	1,924	0	0	98	0	2	12	5.3	61	12	1,000	50	4.3	0.0
C- /3.6	3.5	7.5	13.19	6	0	0	98	0	2	12	5.3	26	12	1,000	50	0.0	0.0
C- /3.7	3.5	7.5	13.16	251	0	0	98	0	2	12	5.3	26	12	1,000	50	0.0	0.0
C- /3.7	3.5	7.5	13.23	108	0	0	98	0	2	12	5.3	64	12	1,000	50	0.0	0.0
C- /3.6	3.5	7.5	13.22	524	0	0	98	0	2	12	5.3	68	12	1,000	50	0.0	0.0
C- /3.6	3.5	7.8	15.42	124	1	0	98	0	1	7	5.1	56	10	1,000	50	4.3	0.0
C- /3.6	3.5	7.8	15.45	1	1	0	98	0	1	7	5.1	55	10	1,000	50	0.0	0.0
C- /3.6	3.5	7.8	15.40	28	1	0	98	0	1	7	5.1	21	10	1,000	50	0.0	0.0
C- /3.6	3.5	7.8	15.40	18	1	0	98	0	1	7	5.1	64	10	1,000	50	0.0	0.0
C- /4.1	3.3	7.1	16.18	112	2	0	97	0	1	12	5.2	70	8	1,000	50	4.3	0.0
C- /4.1	3.2	7.1	16.21	1	2	0	97	0	1	12	5.2	70	8	1,000	50	0.0	0.0
C- /4.2	3.2	7.1	16.20	11	2	0	97	0	1	12	5.2	41	8	1,000	50	0.0	0.0

					PERFORMANCE						Incl. in Returns	
99 Pct = Best 0 Pct = Worst			Overall		Perfor-mance	Total Return % through 2/28/17			Annualized		Dividend	Expense
Fund Type	Fund Name	Ticker Symbol	Investment Rating	Phone	Rating/Pts	3 Mo	6 Mo	1Yr / Pct	3Yr / Pct	5Yr / Pct	Yield	Ratio
MUS	Invesco PA Tax Free Income Y	VKPYX	A	(800) 959-4246	B+ / 8.8	1.72	-3.15	0.83 /43	4.36 /95	3.40 /86	3.80	0.83
MMT	Invesco Premier Portfolio Inst	IPPXX	C	(800) 959-4246	D- / 1.5	0.17	0.32	0.51 /33	0.22 /17	0.16 /17	0.45	N/A
MMF	Invesco Premier Tax-Ex Port Inst	PEIXX	C	(800) 959-4246	D- / 1.5	0.12	0.24	0.34 /34	0.12 /16	0.08 /16	0.34	N/A
MMT	Invesco Premier US Gv Mny Port Inst	IUGXX	C-	(800) 959-4246	D- / 1.2	0.10	0.17	0.29 /29	0.12 /14	0.08 /14	0.29	N/A
USS	Invesco Quality Income A	VKMGX	C+	(800) 959-4246	C- / 3.3	0.43	-0.79	1.19 /42	2.83 /58	2.48 /49	3.23	0.96
USS ●	Invesco Quality Income B	VUSBX	B-	(800) 959-4246	C- / 3.9	0.24	-1.18	0.41 /31	2.08 /45	1.72 /38	2.60	1.72
USS	Invesco Quality Income C	VUSCX	C+	(800) 959-4246	C- / 3.9	0.24	-1.18	0.49 /33	2.07 /44	1.71 /38	2.60	1.72
MTG	Invesco Quality Income R5	VUSJX	A	(800) 959-4246	C+ / 5.8	0.61	-0.59	1.65 /46	3.19 /64	2.81 /54	3.74	0.68
USS	Invesco Quality Income Y	VUSIX	A	(800) 959-4246	C+ / 5.6	0.49	-0.66	1.45 /44	3.11 /63	2.75 /54	3.62	0.72
LP	Invesco Senior Loan A	VSLAX	B-	(800) 959-4246	A- / 9.0	3.91	6.82	20.95 /97	3.89 /74	6.11 /93	4.69	1.92
LP	Invesco Senior Loan B	VSLBX	B	(800) 959-4246	A / 9.4	3.91	6.82	20.95 /97	3.74 /72	6.01 /92	4.85	2.67
LP	Invesco Senior Loan C	VSLCX	B	(800) 959-4246	A- / 9.1	3.72	6.58	20.22 /96	3.17 /64	5.37 /87	4.14	2.67
LP	Invesco Senior Loan IB	XPRTX	B+	(800) 959-4246	A+ / 9.6	3.97	7.12	21.43 /97	4.16 /77	6.36 /94	5.08	1.67
LP	Invesco Senior Loan IC	XSLCX	B+	(800) 959-4246	A / 9.5	3.78	6.88	21.08 /97	3.95 /75	6.20 /93	4.95	1.82
MUH	Invesco Sh Dur High Yield Muni A	ISHAX	U	(800) 959-4246	U /	1.83	-2.37	2.90 /64	--	--	3.23	1.47
MUH	Invesco Sh Dur High Yield Muni C	ISHCX	U	(800) 959-4246	U /	1.74	-2.65	2.23 /59	--	--	2.54	2.22
MUH	Invesco Sh Dur High Yield Muni R5	ISHFX	U	(800) 959-4246	U /	2.00	-2.15	3.36 /67	--	--	3.56	1.20
MUH	Invesco Sh Dur High Yield Muni Y	ISHYX	U	(800) 959-4246	U /	1.90	-2.24	3.26 /67	--	--	3.56	1.22
US	Invesco Sh Dur Infl Pro A	LMTAX	C-	(800) 959-4246	D / 1.9	0.88	0.88	2.04 /49	0.89 /26	0.53 /22	1.23	0.90
US ●	Invesco Sh Dur Infl Pro A2	SHTIX	C	(800) 959-4246	D+ / 2.6	0.90	0.93	2.14 /50	0.95 /27	0.57 /22	1.34	0.80
US	Invesco Sh Dur Infl Pro R5	ALMIX	C+	(800) 959-4246	C- / 3.2	0.96	1.02	2.31 /52	1.04 /28	0.64 /23	1.52	0.59
US	Invesco Sh Dur Infl Pro Y	LMTYX	C+	(800) 959-4246	C- / 3.1	0.84	1.01	2.29 /51	0.99 /27	0.61 /23	1.51	0.65
GEI	Invesco Short Term Bond A	STBAX	C+	(800) 959-4246	D+ / 2.9	0.73	0.36	3.39 /59	1.49 /35	1.74 /38	1.65	0.68
GEI	Invesco Short Term Bond C	STBCX	B-	(800) 959-4246	C- / 3.3	0.76	0.18	3.03 /57	1.14 /30	1.41 /33	1.35	1.18
GEI	Invesco Short Term Bond R	STBRX	B-	(800) 959-4246	C- / 3.3	0.64	0.18	2.90 /56	1.14 /30	1.38 /33	1.34	1.03
GEI	Invesco Short Term Bond R5	ISTBX	A-	(800) 959-4246	C- / 4.2	0.80	0.49	3.54 /60	1.71 /38	1.94 /41	1.96	0.43
COI	Invesco Short Term Bond R6	ISTFX	A-	(800) 959-4246	C / 4.3	0.80	0.49	3.66 /61	1.76 /39	1.94 /41	1.96	0.42
GEI	Invesco Short Term Bond Y	STBYX	B+	(800) 959-4246	C- / 4.1	0.77	0.43	3.42 /59	1.64 /37	1.89 /40	1.84	0.53
US	Invesco Sht Dur Inflation Prot R6	SDPSX	U	(800) 959-4246	U /	0.87	1.03	2.32 /52	--	--	1.53	0.49
MMT	Invesco STIC Prime Corp	SSCXX	C	(800) 959-4246	D- / 1.5	0.14	0.22	0.38 /31	0.20 /16	0.15 /17	0.37	N/A
MMT	Invesco STIC Prime CshMgt	SCNXX	C-	(800) 959-4246	D- / 1.4	0.13	0.20	0.33 /30	0.18 /16	0.13 /16	0.33	N/A
MMT	Invesco STIC Prime Inst	SRIXX	C	(800) 959-4246	D- / 1.5	0.15	0.24	0.41 /31	0.21 /17	0.16 /17	0.41	N/A
MMT	Invesco STIC Prime Psnl	SPEXX	C-	(800) 959-4246	D- / 1.2	0.06	0.11	0.20 /26	0.13 /14	0.10 /15	0.20	N/A
MMT	Invesco STIC Prime Pvt	SPVXX	C-	(800) 959-4246	D- / 1.2	0.08	0.13	0.22 /27	0.14 /15	0.11 /16	0.22	N/A
MMT	Invesco STIC Prime Rs	SRSXX	C-	(800) 959-4246	D- / 1.3	0.11	0.16	0.26 /28	0.14 /15	0.11 /16	0.26	N/A
MMT	Invesco STIC Prime Rsv	SPSXX	C-	(800) 959-4246	D- / 1.2	0.06	0.11	0.20 /26	0.13 /14	0.10 /15	0.20	N/A
GEI	Invesco Strategic Real Return A	SRRAX	U	(800) 959-4246	U /	2.40	1.98	9.21 /77	--	--	3.31	2.57
GEI	Invesco Strategic Real Return C	SRRCX	U	(800) 959-4246	U /	2.21	1.50	8.40 /75	--	--	2.65	3.32
GEI	Invesco Strategic Real Return R	SRRQX	U	(800) 959-4246	U /	2.34	1.86	8.94 /76	--	--	3.15	2.82
GEI	Invesco Strategic Real Return R5	SRRFX	U	(800) 959-4246	U /	2.46	2.01	9.48 /78	--	--	3.64	2.37
GEI	Invesco Strategic Real Return R6	SRRSX	U	(800) 959-4246	U /	2.57	2.11	9.59 /78	--	--	3.64	2.37
GEI	Invesco Strategic Real Return Y	SRRYX	U	(800) 959-4246	U /	2.46	2.01	9.48 /78	--	--	3.64	2.32
MMF	Invesco Tax-Exempt Cash A	ACSXX	C	(800) 959-4246	D- / 1.4	0.01	0.18	0.18 /28	0.13 /16	0.11 /18	0.18	N/A
MMF ●	Invesco Tax-Exempt Cash Inv	TEIXX	C	(800) 959-4246	D- / 1.5	0.01	0.19	0.19 /29	0.14 /17	0.12 /18	0.19	N/A
MMF	Invesco Tax-Exempt Cash Y		C	(800) 959-4246	D- / 1.5	0.01	0.19	0.19 /29	0.14 /17	0.12 /18	0.19	N/A
MMF	Invesco Tax-Free Cash Rsv Corp	TFOXX	C	(800) 959-4246	D- / 1.5	0.11	0.23	0.31 /33	0.11 /16	0.09 /17	0.31	N/A
MMF	Invesco Tax-Free Cash Rsv CshMgt		C-	(800) 959-4246	D- / 1.4	0.10	0.21	0.27 /32	0.10 /15	0.08 /16	0.27	N/A
MMF	Invesco Tax-Free Cash Rsv Inst	TFPXX	C	(800) 959-4246	D- / 1.5	0.12	0.25	0.34 /34	0.12 /16	0.10 /17	0.34	N/A
MMF	Invesco Tax-Free Cash Rsv Psnl		C-	(800) 959-4246	D- / 1.2	0.08	0.16	0.20 /29	0.07 /13	0.07 /16	0.20	N/A
MMF	Invesco Tax-Free Cash Rsv Pvt	TRCXX	C-	(800) 959-4246	D- / 1.3	0.08	0.17	0.21 /30	0.08 /14	0.07 /16	0.21	N/A
MMF	Invesco Tax-Free Cash Rsv Rs		C-	(800) 959-4246	D- / 1.3	0.09	0.18	0.23 /30	0.08 /14	0.07 /16	0.23	N/A
MMF	Invesco Tax-Free Cash Rsv Rsv		C-	(800) 959-4246	D- / 1.3	0.08	0.16	0.20 /29	0.08 /14	0.07 /16	0.20	N/A

● Denotes fund is closed to new investors
* Denotes fund is included in Section II

www.thestreetratings.com

RISK			NET ASSETS		ASSET							FUND MANAGER		MINIMUM		LOADS	
Risk Rating/Pts	3 Yr Avg Standard Deviation	Avg Dura-tion	NAV As of 2/28/17	Total $(Mil)	Cash %	Gov. Bond %	Muni. Bond %	Corp. Bond %	Other %	Portfolio Turnover Ratio	Avg Coupon Rate	Manager Quality Pct	Manager Tenure (Years)	Initial Purch. $	Additional Purch. $	Front End Load	Back End Load
C- /4.2	3.2	7.1	16.19	6	2	0	97	0	1	12	5.2	75	8	1,000	50	0.0	0.0
A+ /9.9	0.1	N/A	1.00	657	100	0	0	0	0	0	0.5	52	N/A	1,000,000	0	0.0	0.0
A+ /9.9	0.1	N/A	1.00	55	100	0	0	0	0	0	0.3	48	N/A	1,000,000	0	0.0	0.0
A+ /9.9	N/A	N/A	1.00	6,574	100	0	0	0	0	0	0.3	46	N/A	1,000,000	0	0.0	0.0
B /8.1	2.1	3.6	12.08	384	0	0	0	3	97	500	3.7	83	7	1,000	50	4.3	0.0
B+ /8.3	2.0	3.6	12.02	1	0	0	0	3	97	500	3.7	75	7	1,000	50	0.0	0.0
B /8.2	2.1	3.6	12.00	15	0	0	0	3	97	500	3.7	75	7	1,000	50	0.0	0.0
B /8.1	2.1	3.6	12.13	144	0	0	0	3	97	500	3.7	70	7	10,000,000	0	0.0	0.0
B+ /8.3	2.0	3.6	12.13	72	0	0	0	3	97	500	3.7	86	7	1,000	50	0.0	0.0
D /2.2	4.8	N/A	6.68	121	0	0	0	52	48	51	0.0	89	10	1,000	100	3.3	0.0
D /2.2	4.8	N/A	6.68	2	0	0	0	52	48	51	0.0	88	10	1,000	100	0.0	0.0
D+ /2.3	4.7	N/A	6.70	118	0	0	0	52	48	51	0.0	85	10	1,000	100	0.0	0.0
D /2.2	4.8	N/A	6.69	552	0	0	0	52	48	51	0.0	91	10	1,000	100	0.0	0.0
D /2.2	4.8	N/A	6.68	47	0	0	0	52	48	51	0.0	90	10	1,000	100	0.0	0.0
U /	N/A	N/A	10.18	50	0	0	0	0	100	69	0.0	N/A	2	1,000	50	2.5	0.0
U /	N/A	N/A	10.17	25	0	0	0	0	100	69	0.0	N/A	2	1,000	50	0.0	0.0
U /	N/A	N/A	10.20	N/A	0	0	0	0	100	69	0.0	N/A	2	10,000,000	0	0.0	0.0
U /	N/A	N/A	10.19	14	0	0	0	0	100	69	0.0	N/A	2	1,000	50	0.0	0.0
B+ /8.9	1.4	3.1	10.58	41	0	99	0	0	1	199	0.7	61	8	1,000	50	2.5	0.0
A- /9.0	1.3	3.1	10.59	22	0	99	0	0	1	199	0.7	65	8	1,000	50	1.0	0.0
B+ /8.9	1.4	3.1	10.60	1	0	99	0	0	1	199	0.7	65	8	10,000,000	0	0.0	0.0
A- /9.0	1.4	3.1	10.59	10	0	99	0	0	1	199	0.7	64	8	1,000	50	0.0	0.0
A- /9.2	1.1	1.9	8.61	434	0	23	0	57	20	200	2.4	72	8	1,000	50	2.5	0.0
A- /9.2	1.1	1.9	8.61	450	0	23	0	57	20	200	2.4	64	8	1,000	50	0.0	0.0
A- /9.2	1.0	1.9	8.62	7	0	23	0	57	20	200	2.4	62	8	0	0	0.0	0.0
A- /9.2	1.0	1.9	8.60	1	0	23	0	57	20	200	2.4	76	8	10,000,000	0	0.0	0.0
A- /9.2	1.1	1.9	8.62	499	0	23	0	57	20	200	2.4	75	8	10,000,000	0	0.0	0.0
A- /9.2	1.0	1.9	8.61	130	0	23	0	57	20	200	2.4	75	8	1,000	50	0.0	0.0
U /	N/A	3.1	10.59	719	0	99	0	0	1	199	0.7	N/A	8	10,000,000	0	0.0	0.0
A+ /9.9	0.2	N/A	1.00	N/A	100	0	0	0	0	0	0.4	57	N/A	1,000,000	0	0.0	0.0
A+ /9.9	0.1	N/A	1.00	1	100	0	0	0	0	0	0.3	51	N/A	1,000,000	0	0.0	0.0
A+ /9.9	0.1	N/A	1.00	321	100	0	0	0	0	0	0.4	52	N/A	1,000,000	0	0.0	0.0
A+ /9.9	N/A	N/A	1.00	1	100	0	0	0	0	0	0.2	49	N/A	1,000	0	0.0	0.0
A+ /9.9	N/A	N/A	1.00	2	100	0	0	0	0	0	0.2	49	N/A	100,000	0	0.0	0.0
A+ /9.9	N/A	N/A	1.00	N/A	100	0	0	0	0	0	0.3	49	N/A	1,000,000	0	0.0	0.0
A+ /9.9	N/A	N/A	1.00	1	100	0	0	0	0	0	0.2	49	N/A	1,000	0	0.0	0.0
U /	N/A	N/A	9.73	12	2	44	0	27	27	35	0.0	N/A	3	1,000	50	2.5	0.0
U /	N/A	N/A	9.72	1	2	44	0	27	27	35	0.0	N/A	3	1,000	50	0.0	0.0
U /	N/A	N/A	9.73	N/A	2	44	0	27	27	35	0.0	N/A	3	0	0	0.0	0.0
U /	N/A	N/A	9.73	N/A	2	44	0	27	27	35	0.0	N/A	3	10,000,000	0	0.0	0.0
U /	N/A	N/A	9.74	N/A	2	44	0	27	27	35	0.0	N/A	3	10,000,000	0	0.0	0.0
U /	N/A	N/A	9.73	9	2	44	0	27	27	35	0.0	N/A	3	1,000	50	0.0	0.0
A+ /9.9	0.1	N/A	1.00	31	100	0	0	0	0	0	0.2	49	N/A	1,000	50	0.0	0.0
A+ /9.9	0.1	N/A	1.00	6	100	0	0	0	0	0	0.2	49	N/A	1,000	50	0.0	0.0
A+ /9.9	0.1	N/A	1.00	5	100	0	0	0	0	0	0.2	49	N/A	1,000	50	0.0	0.0
A+ /9.9	0.1	N/A	1.00	N/A	100	0	0	0	0	0	0.3	47	N/A	1,000,000	0	0.0	0.0
A+ /9.9	N/A	N/A	1.00	36	100	0	0	0	0	0	0.3	N/A	N/A	1,000,000	0	0.0	0.0
A+ /9.9	0.1	N/A	1.00	96	100	0	0	0	0	0	0.3	47	N/A	1,000,000	0	0.0	0.0
A+ /9.9	N/A	N/A	1.00	2	100	0	0	0	0	0	0.2	45	N/A	10,000	0	0.0	0.0
A+ /9.9	N/A	N/A	1.00	20	100	0	0	0	0	0	0.2	45	N/A	100,000	0	0.0	0.0
A+ /9.9	N/A	N/A	1.00	2	100	0	0	0	0	0	0.2	46	N/A	1,000,000	0	0.0	0.0
A+ /9.9	N/A	N/A	1.00	22	100	0	0	0	0	0	0.2	45	N/A	10,000	0	0.0	0.0

I. Index of Bond and Money Market Mutual Funds

			99 Pct = Best 0 Pct = Worst		PERFORMANCE						Incl. in Returns	
			Overall		Perfor-	Total Return % through 2/28/17					Dividend	Expense
Fund		Ticker	Investment		mance				Annualized			
Type	Fund Name	Symbol	Rating	Phone	Rating/Pts	3 Mo	6 Mo	1Yr / Pct	3Yr / Pct	5Yr / Pct	Yield	Ratio
MMT	Invesco Treasury Corp	TYCXX	C-	(800) 959-4246	D- / 1.1	0.08	0.13	0.24 /27	0.10 /13	0.07 /13	0.24	N/A
MMT	Invesco Treasury CshMgt		C-	(800) 959-4246	D- / 1.0	0.07	0.11	0.19 /26	0.08 /12	0.06 /12	0.19	N/A
MMT	Invesco Treasury Inst	TRPXX	C-	(800) 959-4246	D- / 1.2	0.09	0.15	0.27 /28	0.11 /13	0.08 /14	0.27	N/A
MMT	Invesco Treasury Psnl		D+	(800) 959-4246	E+ / 0.8	0.02	0.05	0.10 /22	0.05 /10	0.04 /10	0.10	N/A
MMT	Invesco Treasury Pvt	TPFXX	U	(800) 959-4246	U /	--	--	--	--	--	0.10	N/A
MMT	Invesco Treasury Rs		C-	(800) 959-4246	E+ / 0.9	0.05	0.08	0.13 /23	0.06 /11	0.04 /10	0.13	N/A
MMT	Invesco Treasury Rsv		D+	(800) 959-4246	E+ / 0.8	0.02	0.05	0.10 /22	0.05 /10	0.04 /10	0.10	N/A
MMT	Invesco Trs Obligations Corp	TACXX	C-	(800) 959-4246	D- / 1.0	0.07	0.10	0.16 /24	0.10 /13	0.07 /13	0.16	N/A
MMT	Invesco Trs Obligations CshMgt		C-	(800) 959-4246	D- / 1.0	0.06	0.08	0.14 /24	0.09 /12	0.07 /13	0.14	N/A
MMT	Invesco Trs Obligations Inst	TSPXX	C-	(800) 959-4246	D- / 1.1	0.08	0.11	0.19 /26	0.11 /14	0.08 /14	0.19	N/A
MMT	Invesco Trs Obligations Prvt	TXPXX	U	(800) 959-4246	U /	--	--	--	--	--	0.12	N/A
MMT	Invesco Trs Obligations Psnl		U	(800) 959-4246	U /	--	--	--	--	--	0.12	N/A
MMT	Invesco Trs Obligations Res		C-	(800) 959-4246	D- / 1.0	0.04	0.07	0.13 /23	0.09 /12	0.06 /12	0.13	N/A
MMT	Invesco Trs Obligations Rsv		U	(800) 959-4246	U /	--	--	--	--	--	0.12	N/A
* USS	Invesco US Government A	AGOVX	E+	(800) 959-4246	E / 0.5	0.28	-2.20	-0.14 /15	1.51 /35	0.98 /27	1.83	0.95
USS ●	Invesco US Government B	AGVBX	D-	(800) 959-4246	D / 1.6	0.09	-2.67	-0.89 / 5	0.75 /24	0.23 /19	1.14	1.70
USS	Invesco US Government C	AGVCX	D-	(800) 959-4246	D / 1.7	0.20	-2.57	-0.89 / 5	0.76 /24	0.25 /19	1.14	1.70
USS ●	Invesco US Government Investor	AGIVX	D	(800) 959-4246	D+ / 2.9	0.29	-2.18	-0.12 /16	1.53 /35	1.01 /27	1.93	1.20
USS	Invesco US Government R	AGVRX	D	(800) 959-4246	D+ / 2.4	0.22	-2.32	-0.39 /11	1.26 /31	0.73 /24	1.65	0.93
USS	Invesco US Government R5	AGOIX	C-	(800) 959-4246	C- / 3.5	0.37	-2.03	0.20 /26	1.92 /42	1.36 /32	2.26	0.59
USS	Invesco US Government Y	AGVYX	D+	(800) 959-4246	C- / 3.3	0.46	-2.07	0.11 /23	1.81 /40	1.26 /31	2.17	0.70
GL	Invesco World Bond A	AUBAX	E-	(800) 959-4246	E- / 0.1	1.86	-6.35	4.88 /66	-1.37 / 2	0.11 /15	2.10	1.72
GL ●	Invesco World Bond B	AUBBX	E-	(800) 959-4246	E- / 0.1	1.65	-6.66	4.09 /63	-2.12 / 2	-0.63 / 3	1.30	2.47
GL	Invesco World Bond C	AUBCX	E-	(800) 959-4246	E- / 0.1	1.65	-6.67	4.09 /63	-2.13 / 2	-0.66 / 3	1.30	2.47
GL	Invesco World Bond R5	AUBIX	E-	(800) 959-4246	E- / 0.2	1.87	-6.29	5.08 /67	-1.15 / 2	0.33 /20	2.49	1.16
GL	Invesco World Bond R6	AUBFX	E-	(800) 959-4246	E- / 0.2	1.97	-6.20	5.18 /67	-1.11 / 3	0.33 /20	2.49	1.16
GL	Invesco World Bond Y	AUBYX	E-	(800) 959-4246	E- / 0.2	1.97	-6.20	5.19 /67	-1.15 / 2	0.35 /20	2.49	1.47
MMT	Investors Deutsche Treasury Inst	ICTXX	C-	(800) 728-3337	D- / 1.2	0.11	0.18	0.29 /29	0.11 /14	0.07 /13	0.29	N/A
MMT	Investors Deutsche Treasury Inv	ITVXX	U	(800) 728-3337	U /	--	--	--	--	--	0.03	N/A
MMT	Investors Deutsche Trs Deut US TM	IUSXX	C-	(800) 728-3337	D- / 1.0	0.09	0.13	0.18 /25	0.07 /11	0.04 /10	0.18	N/A
GEN	Iron Strategic Income Fd Inst	IFUNX	D-	(800) 408-4682	C- / 4.1	3.24	2.43	8.47 /75	0.77 /24	2.85 /55	2.12	1.77
GEN	Iron Strategic Income Fd Inv	IRNIX	E+	(800) 408-4682	C- / 3.5	3.13	2.23	8.01 /74	0.41 /20	2.48 /49	1.85	2.12
GL	Ivy Apollo Strategic Income A	IAPOX	U	(800) 777-6472	U /	2.46	2.26	9.40 /77	--	--	3.29	1.55
GL	Ivy Apollo Strategic Income C	ICPOX	U	(800) 777-6472	U /	2.29	2.01	8.76 /76	--	--	2.82	2.16
GL	Ivy Apollo Strategic Income I	IIPOX	U	(800) 777-6472	U /	2.64	2.52	9.83 /79	--	--	3.78	1.29
GL	Ivy Apollo Strategic Income N	IRPOX	U	(800) 777-6472	U /	2.64	2.53	9.83 /79	--	--	3.79	1.15
GL	Ivy Apollo Strategic Income Y	IYPOX	U	(800) 777-6472	U /	2.57	2.39	9.56 /78	--	--	3.54	1.54
GEI	Ivy Bond A	IBOAX	D	(800) 777-6472	C- / 3.8	2.00	-0.78	4.55 /65	3.00 /61	3.10 /59	2.32	1.02
GEI ●	Ivy Bond B	IBOBX	C-	(800) 777-6472	C / 4.6	1.77	-1.22	3.55 /60	2.03 /44	2.12 /44	1.50	1.96
GEI	Ivy Bond C	IBOCX	C	(800) 777-6472	C / 4.9	1.83	-1.11	3.83 /61	2.24 /47	2.33 /47	1.77	1.78
GEI	Ivy Bond Fund Y	IBOYX	B	(800) 777-6472	C+ / 6.3	2.02	-0.73	4.64 /65	3.06 /62	3.15 /60	2.55	0.98
GEI	Ivy Bond I	IVBIX	B+	(800) 777-6472	C+ / 6.6	2.11	-0.59	4.91 /66	3.32 /66	3.42 /64	2.81	0.74
COI	Ivy Bond N	IBNDX	B+	(800) 777-6472	C+ / 6.8	2.12	-0.53	5.04 /67	3.45 /68	3.49 /65	2.94	0.59
COI	Ivy Bond R	IYBDX	C+	(800) 777-6472	C+ / 5.7	1.94	-0.89	4.28 /63	2.70 /56	--	2.20	1.34
EM	Ivy Emerging Mkts Loc Curr Debt A	IECAX	U	(800) 777-6472	U /	4.19	-1.86	10.34 /80	--	--	0.00	2.00
EM	Ivy Emerging Mkts Loc Curr Debt C	IECCX	U	(800) 777-6472	U /	3.89	-2.22	9.44 /78	--	--	0.00	2.50
EM	Ivy Emerging Mkts Loc Curr Debt E	IECEX	U	(800) 777-6472	U /	4.19	-1.86	10.34 /80	--	--	0.00	1.72
EM	Ivy Emerging Mkts Loc Curr Debt I	IECIX	U	(800) 777-6472	U /	4.28	-1.74	10.69 /80	--	--	0.00	1.62
EM	Ivy Emerging Mkts Loc Curr Debt N	IMMCX	U	(800) 777-6472	U /	4.16	-1.74	10.69 /80	--	--	0.00	1.47
EM	Ivy Emerging Mkts Loc Curr Debt R	IECRX	U	(800) 777-6472	U /	4.09	-1.98	10.00 /79	--	--	0.00	2.33
EM	Ivy Emerging Mkts Loc Curr Debt Y	IECYX	U	(800) 777-6472	U /	4.19	-1.86	10.34 /80	--	--	0.00	1.86
GEI	Ivy Fond E	IVBEX	D	(800) 777-6472	C- / 3.8	2.00	-0.77	4.55 /65	2.94 /60	3.03 /58	2.33	1.32

● Denotes fund is closed to new investors
* Denotes fund is included in Section II

www.thestreetratings.com

RISK			NET ASSETS		ASSET							FUND MANAGER		MINIMUM		LOADS	
Risk Rating/Pts	3 Yr Avg Standard Deviation	Avg Dura-tion	NAV As of 2/28/17	Total $(Mil)	Cash %	Gov. Bond %	Muni. Bond %	Corp. Bond %	Other %	Portfolio Turnover Ratio	Avg Coupon Rate	Manager Quality Pct	Manager Tenure (Years)	Initial Purch. $	Additional Purch. $	Front End Load	Back End Load
A+ / 9.9	N/A	N/A	1.00	918	100	0	0	0	0	0	0.2	46	N/A	1,000,000	0	0.0	0.0
A+ / 9.9	N/A	N/A	1.00	377	100	0	0	0	0	0	0.2	45	N/A	1,000,000	0	0.0	0.0
A+ / 9.9	N/A	N/A	1.00	17,309	100	0	0	0	0	0	0.3	N/A	N/A	1,000,000	0	0.0	0.0
A+ / 9.9	N/A	N/A	1.00	151	100	0	0	0	0	0	0.1	41	N/A	1,000	0	0.0	0.0
U /	N/A	N/A	1.00	542	100	0	0	0	0	0	0.1	41	N/A	100,000	0	0.0	0.0
A+ / 9.9	N/A	N/A	1.00	458	100	0	0	0	0	0	0.1	43	N/A	1,000,000	0	0.0	0.0
A+ / 9.9	N/A	N/A	1.00	157	100	0	0	0	0	0	0.1	41	N/A	1,000	0	0.0	0.0
A+ / 9.9	0.1	N/A	1.00	N/A	100	0	0	0	0	0	0.2	N/A	N/A	1,000,000	0	0.0	0.0
A+ / 9.9	N/A	N/A	1.00	2	100	0	0	0	0	0	0.1	46	N/A	1,000,000	0	0.0	0.0
A+ / 9.9	0.1	N/A	1.00	1,287	100	0	0	0	0	0	0.2	47	N/A	1,000,000	0	0.0	0.0
U /	N/A	N/A	1.00	1	100	0	0	0	0	0	0.1	46	N/A	100,000	0	0.0	0.0
U /	N/A	N/A	1.00	N/A	100	0	0	0	0	0	0.1	46	N/A	1,000	0	0.0	0.0
A+ / 9.9	N/A	N/A	1.00	N/A	100	0	0	0	0	0	0.1	46	N/A	1,000,000	0	0.0	0.0
U /	N/A	N/A	1.00	77	100	0	0	0	0	0	0.1	46	N/A	1,000	0	0.0	0.0
C+ / 6.9	2.7	5.0	8.84	559	1	42	0	7	50	61	2.6	35	8	1,000	50	4.3	0.0
C+ / 6.8	2.8	5.0	8.87	5	1	42	0	7	50	61	2.6	14	8	1,000	50	0.0	0.0
C+ / 6.8	2.8	5.0	8.84	41	1	42	0	7	50	61	2.6	13	8	1,000	50	0.0	0.0
C+ / 6.9	2.7	5.0	8.85	35	1	42	0	7	50	61	2.6	36	8	1,000	50	0.0	0.0
C+ / 6.7	2.8	5.0	8.85	6	1	42	0	7	50	61	2.6	26	8	0	0	0.0	0.0
B- / 7.0	2.7	5.0	8.85	1	1	42	0	7	50	61	2.6	58	8	10,000,000	0	0.0	0.0
C+ / 6.8	2.8	5.0	8.86	12	1	42	0	7	50	61	2.6	53	8	1,000	50	0.0	0.0
E+ / 0.6	7.3	7.9	10.02	24	4	51	4	28	13	246	7.2	75	7	1,000	50	4.3	0.0
E+ / 0.6	7.2	7.9	10.01	N/A	4	51	4	28	13	246	7.2	54	7	1,000	50	0.0	0.0
E+ / 0.6	7.3	7.9	10.00	4	4	51	4	28	13	246	7.2	54	7	1,000	50	0.0	0.0
E+ / 0.6	7.3	7.9	10.01	N/A	4	51	4	28	13	246	7.2	78	7	10,000,000	0	0.0	0.0
E+ / 0.6	7.3	7.9	10.02	N/A	4	51	4	28	13	246	7.2	79	7	10,000,000	0	0.0	0.0
E+ / 0.6	7.3	7.9	10.01	7	4	51	4	28	13	246	7.2	78	7	1,000	50	0.0	0.0
A+ / 9.9	N/A	N/A	1.00	2,133	100	0	0	0	0	0	0.3	47	N/A	1,000,000	0	0.0	0.0
U /	N/A	N/A	1.00	131	100	0	0	0	0	0	0.0	39	N/A	2,000	0	0.0	0.0
A+ / 9.9	N/A	N/A	1.00	109	100	0	0	0	0	0	0.2	44	N/A	2,500	50	0.0	0.0
C- / 3.7	3.7	N/A	10.72	126	53	0	0	34	13	673	0.0	66	11	10,000	1,000	0.0	1.0
C- / 3.8	3.6	N/A	10.79	9	53	0	0	34	13	673	0.0	54	11	10,000	1,000	0.0	1.0
U /	N/A	3.0	10.24	116	0	0	0	0	100	42	5.1	N/A	2	750	0	5.8	0.0
U /	N/A	3.0	10.24	10	0	0	0	0	100	42	5.1	N/A	2	750	0	0.0	0.0
U /	N/A	3.0	10.25	252	0	0	0	0	100	42	5.1	N/A	2	0	0	0.0	0.0
U /	N/A	3.0	10.25	6	0	0	0	0	100	42	5.1	N/A	2	0	0	0.0	0.0
U /	N/A	3.0	10.25	7	0	0	0	0	100	42	5.1	N/A	2	0	0	0.0	0.0
C+ / 5.8	3.0	5.5	10.65	215	0	11	1	47	41	213	4.1	63	14	750	0	5.8	0.0
C+ / 5.8	3.0	5.5	10.65	6	0	11	1	47	41	213	4.1	23	14	750	0	0.0	0.0
C+ / 5.8	3.0	5.5	10.65	29	0	11	1	47	41	213	4.1	29	14	750	0	0.0	0.0
C+ / 5.8	3.0	5.5	10.65	5	0	11	1	47	41	213	4.1	65	14	0	0	0.0	0.0
C+ / 5.8	3.0	5.5	10.65	462	0	11	1	47	41	213	4.1	71	10	0	0	0.0	0.0
C+ / 5.8	3.0	5.5	10.65	2	0	11	1	47	41	213	4.1	72	14	0	0	0.0	0.0
C+ / 5.8	3.0	5.5	10.65	6	0	11	1	47	41	213	4.1	51	14	0	0	0.0	0.0
U /	N/A	5.1	8.96	12	4	79	0	11	6	74	4.9	N/A	2	750	0	5.8	0.0
U /	N/A	5.1	8.81	2	4	79	0	11	6	74	4.9	N/A	2	750	0	0.0	0.0
U /	N/A	5.1	8.96	2	4	79	0	11	6	74	4.9	N/A	2	750	0	5.8	0.0
U /	N/A	5.1	9.01	30	4	79	0	11	6	74	4.9	N/A	2	0	0	0.0	0.0
U /	N/A	5.1	9.01	1	4	79	0	11	6	74	4.9	N/A	2	0	0	0.0	0.0
U /	N/A	5.1	8.91	2	4	79	0	11	6	74	4.9	N/A	2	0	0	0.0	0.0
U /	N/A	5.1	8.96	3	4	79	0	11	6	74	4.9	N/A	2	0	0	0.0	0.0
C+ / 5.8	3.0	5.5	10.65	4	0	11	1	47	41	213	4.1	61	10	750	0	5.8	0.0

I. Index of Bond and Money Market Mutual Funds

Spring 2017

99 Pct = Best
0 Pct = Worst

Fund Type	Fund Name	Ticker Symbol	Overall Investment Rating	Phone	Performance Rating/Pts	3 Mo	6 Mo	1Yr / Pct	3Yr / Pct	5Yr / Pct	Dividend Yield	Expense Ratio
GL	Ivy Global Bond A	IVSAX	E+	(800) 777-6472	C- / 3.7	2.92	2.76	10.48 / 80	1.57 / 36	2.18 / 44	1.95	1.29
GL ●	Ivy Global Bond B	IVSBX	D-	(800) 777-6472	C / 4.7	2.74	2.37	9.55 / 78	0.80 / 24	1.42 / 33	1.35	2.16
GL	Ivy Global Bond C	IVSCX	D-	(800) 777-6472	C / 4.8	2.73	2.47	9.66 / 78	0.80 / 24	1.44 / 33	1.33	1.91
GL	Ivy Global Bond I	IVSIX	D	(800) 777-6472	C+ / 6.4	2.98	2.89	10.76 / 81	1.82 / 40	2.46 / 49	2.31	0.90
GL	Ivy Global Bond N	IVBDX	D	(800) 777-6472	C+ / 6.4	2.97	2.87	10.74 / 81	1.81 / 40	2.46 / 49	2.30	0.76
GL	Ivy Global Bond R	IYGOX	D-	(800) 777-6472	C / 5.2	2.80	2.49	9.95 / 79	1.07 / 29	--	1.58	1.49
GL	Ivy Global Bond Y	IVSYX	D	(800) 777-6472	C+ / 6.0	2.92	2.76	10.48 / 80	1.56 / 36	2.18 / 44	2.07	1.16
MMT	Ivy Government Money Market A	WRAXX	U	(800) 777-6472	U /	--	--	--	--	--	0.03	N/A
MMT ●	Ivy Government Money Market B	WRBXX	U	(800) 777-6472	U /	--	--	--	--	--	0.02	N/A
MMT	Ivy Government Money Market C	WRCXX	U	(800) 777-6472	U /	--	--	--	--	--	0.02	N/A
MMT	Ivy Government Money Market E	IVEXX	U	(800) 777-6472	U /	--	--	--	--	--	0.02	N/A
*COH	Ivy High Income A	WHIAX	C-	(800) 777-6472	B+ / 8.6	5.00	7.64	23.90 / 99	3.39 / 67	6.68 / 96	6.83	0.96
COH ●	Ivy High Income B	WHIBX	C	(800) 777-6472	A- / 9.1	4.75	7.24	22.99 / 98	2.63 / 55	5.89 / 91	6.53	1.70
COH	Ivy High Income C	WRHIX	C	(800) 777-6472	A- / 9.1	4.82	7.25	23.03 / 98	2.68 / 56	5.94 / 92	6.57	1.66
COH	Ivy High Income E	IVHEX	D+	(800) 777-6472	B+ / 8.3	4.93	7.51	23.63 / 99	3.13 / 63	6.33 / 94	6.63	1.30
COH	Ivy High Income I	IVHIX	C+	(800) 777-6472	A+ / 9.6	5.06	7.76	24.21 / 99	3.66 / 71	6.95 / 96	7.49	0.70
COH	Ivy High Income N	IHIFX	C+	(800) 777-6472	A+ / 9.7	5.10	7.87	24.43 / 99	3.81 / 73	7.04 / 96	7.66	0.56
COH	Ivy High Income R	IYHIX	C	(800) 777-6472	A / 9.3	4.90	7.45	23.48 / 99	3.06 / 62	--	6.92	1.30
COH	Ivy High Income Y	WHIYX	C+	(800) 777-6472	A / 9.5	5.00	7.62	23.91 / 99	3.40 / 67	6.69 / 96	7.26	0.95
*GES	Ivy Limited-Term Bond A	WLTAX	C-	(800) 777-6472	D / 1.8	0.68	-0.58	1.75 / 47	1.05 / 28	0.96 / 27	1.61	0.88
GES ●	Ivy Limited-Term Bond B	WLTBX	D	(800) 777-6472	D- / 1.4	0.44	-1.03	0.88 / 38	0.21 / 17	0.11 / 15	0.79	1.71
GES	Ivy Limited-Term Bond C	WLBCX	D+	(800) 777-6472	D / 1.7	0.48	-0.96	0.99 / 39	0.30 / 19	0.21 / 18	0.90	1.61
GES	Ivy Limited-Term Bond E	IVLEX	D+	(800) 777-6472	D / 1.7	0.65	-0.63	1.63 / 46	0.93 / 26	0.84 / 25	1.50	1.03
GES	Ivy Limited-Term Bond I	ILTIX	C+	(800) 777-6472	C- / 3.2	0.73	-0.47	1.99 / 49	1.30 / 32	1.21 / 30	1.89	0.64
COI	Ivy Limited-Term Bond N	ILMDX	B-	(800) 777-6472	C- / 3.5	0.77	-0.39	2.14 / 50	1.43 / 34	1.29 / 31	2.04	0.49
COI	Ivy Limited-Term Bond R	IYLTX	C-	(800) 777-6472	D / 2.2	0.58	-0.76	1.37 / 43	0.69 / 23	--	1.28	1.24
GES	Ivy Limited-Term Bond Y	WLTYX	C+	(800) 777-6472	D+ / 2.8	0.68	-0.58	1.75 / 47	1.05 / 28	0.96 / 27	1.66	0.89
MUN	Ivy Municipal Bond A	WMBAX	C	(800) 777-6472	C- / 3.8	1.50	-2.48	0.11 / 25	2.66 / 76	2.40 / 68	2.23	0.99
MUN ●	Ivy Municipal Bond B	WMBBX	B-	(800) 777-6472	C / 4.5	1.31	-2.86	-0.65 / 8	1.88 / 59	1.63 / 50	1.55	1.73
MUN	Ivy Municipal Bond C	WMBCX	B-	(800) 777-6472	C / 4.5	1.31	-2.85	-0.64 / 8	1.89 / 60	1.64 / 50	1.56	1.73
MUN	Ivy Municipal Bond I	IMBIX	A+	(800) 777-6472	C+ / 6.8	1.55	-2.39	0.30 / 32	2.87 / 80	2.61 / 73	2.52	0.78
MUN	Ivy Municipal Bond Y	WMBYX	A	(800) 777-6472	C+ / 6.4	1.50	-2.48	0.11 / 25	2.66 / 76	2.40 / 69	2.33	1.03
MUH	Ivy Municipal High Income A	IYIAX	B	(800) 777-6472	B+ / 8.6	2.10	-2.37	1.94 / 56	5.18 / 97	4.01 / 93	4.15	0.88
MUH ●	Ivy Municipal High Income B	IYIBX	B+	(800) 777-6472	B+ / 8.9	1.93	-2.72	1.20 / 48	4.38 / 95	3.22 / 84	3.58	1.64
MUH	Ivy Municipal High Income C	IYICX	B+	(800) 777-6472	A- / 9.0	1.94	-2.69	1.24 / 48	4.43 / 95	3.26 / 84	3.63	1.60
MUH	Ivy Municipal High Income I	WYMHX	A	(800) 777-6472	A+ / 9.7	2.17	-2.26	2.16 / 58	5.38 / 98	4.20 / 95	4.56	0.69
MUH	Ivy Municipal High Income Y	IYIYX	A	(800) 777-6472	A+ / 9.6	2.10	-2.37	1.94 / 56	5.19 / 97	4.02 / 93	4.34	0.95
GEI	J Hancock Absolute Ret Curr A	JCUAX	E	(800) 257-3336	D / 2.1	-1.16	2.73	3.18 / 58	1.09 / 29	2.47 / 49	0.00	1.38
GEI	J Hancock Absolute Ret Curr I	JCUIX	E	(800) 257-3336	C- / 3.9	-1.12	2.87	3.53 / 60	1.42 / 33	2.86 / 56	0.00	1.06
GEI	J Hancock Absolute Ret Curr NAV		E	(800) 257-3336	C- / 4.1	-1.11	2.95	3.60 / 60	1.51 / 35	3.01 / 58	0.00	0.95
GEI	J Hancock Active Bond 1	JIADX	B+	(800) 257-3336	C+ / 6.2	1.78	-0.93	4.31 / 64	3.08 / 62	3.61 / 67	3.11	0.70
GEI	J Hancock Active Bond NAV		B+	(800) 257-3336	C+ / 6.3	1.79	-0.91	4.36 / 64	3.14 / 63	3.64 / 68	3.17	0.65
*GEI	J Hancock Bond A	JHNBX	C+	(800) 257-3336	C / 4.9	1.89	-0.76	5.24 / 68	3.16 / 64	4.11 / 74	3.02	0.93
GEI ●	J Hancock Bond B	JHBBX	C+	(800) 257-3336	C / 5.4	1.72	-1.10	4.51 / 65	2.45 / 51	3.38 / 63	2.45	1.63
GEI	J Hancock Bond C	JHCBX	C+	(800) 257-3336	C / 5.3	1.72	-1.17	4.51 / 65	2.42 / 50	3.38 / 63	2.45	1.63
GEI	J Hancock Bond I	JHBIX	A	(800) 257-3336	C+ / 6.9	1.97	-0.67	5.50 / 69	3.46 / 68	4.45 / 78	3.46	0.61
COI	J Hancock Bond NAV		U	(800) 257-3336	U /	1.99	-0.61	5.69 / 69	--	--	3.58	0.50
COI	J Hancock Bond R2	JHRBX	A-	(800) 257-3336	C+ / 6.4	1.87	-0.80	5.15 / 67	3.08 / 62	4.12 / 74	3.06	1.02
COI	J Hancock Bond R4	JBFRX	U	(800) 257-3336	U /	2.00	-0.61	5.50 / 69	--	--	3.33	0.87
COI	J Hancock Bond R6	JHBSX	A	(800) 257-3336	B- / 7.1	2.06	-0.49	5.75 / 69	3.62 / 70	4.60 / 80	3.57	0.52
MUS	J Hancock CA Tax Free Income A	TACAX	D	(800) 257-3336	C+ / 6.3	2.45	-4.11	0.10 / 24	3.91 / 92	3.58 / 89	3.47	0.84
MUS ●	J Hancock CA Tax Free Income B	TSCAX	D+	(800) 257-3336	C+ / 6.8	2.16	-4.55	-0.73 / 7	3.13 / 84	2.81 / 76	2.84	1.69

● Denotes fund is closed to new investors
* Denotes fund is included in Section II

www.thestreetratings.com

I. Index of Bond and Money Market Mutual Funds

RISK			NET ASSETS		ASSET					Portfolio Turnover Ratio	Avg Coupon Rate	FUND MANAGER		MINIMUM		LOADS	
Risk Rating/Pts	3 Yr Avg Standard Deviation	Avg Dura-tion	NAV As of 2/28/17	Total $(Mil)	Cash %	Gov. Bond %	Muni. Bond %	Corp. Bond %	Other %			Manager Quality Pct	Manager Tenure (Years)	Initial Purch. $	Additional Purch. $	Front End Load	Back End Load
D+ / 2.6	4.4	2.5	9.67	51	2	20	1	68	9	14	5.0	86	9	750	0	5.8	0.0
D+ / 2.6	4.4	2.5	9.66	3	2	20	1	68	9	14	5.0	79	9	750	0	0.0	0.0
D+ / 2.6	4.4	2.5	9.67	16	2	20	1	68	9	14	5.0	79	9	750	0	0.0	0.0
D+ / 2.6	4.4	2.5	9.67	81	2	20	1	68	9	14	5.0	88	9	0	0	0.0	0.0
D+ / 2.6	4.4	2.5	9.67	3	2	20	1	68	9	14	5.0	88	9	0	0	0.0	0.0
D+ / 2.5	4.4	2.5	9.65	1	2	20	1	68	9	14	5.0	82	9	0	0	0.0	0.0
D+ / 2.5	4.4	2.5	9.67	3	2	20	1	68	9	14	5.0	86	9	0	0	0.0	0.0
U /	N/A	N/A	1.00	158	100	0	0	0	0	0	0.0	N/A	17	750	0	0.0	0.0
U /	N/A	N/A	1.00	6	100	0	0	0	0	0	0.0	N/A	17	750	0	0.0	0.0
U /	N/A	N/A	1.00	29	100	0	0	0	0	0	0.0	N/A	17	750	0	0.0	0.0
U /	N/A	N/A	1.00	6	100	0	0	0	0	0	0.0	N/A	17	750	0	0.0	0.0
E+ / 0.7	6.3	3.1	7.64	1,397	1	0	0	77	22	29	7.5	8	3	750	0	5.8	0.0
E+ / 0.7	6.3	3.1	7.64	81	1	0	0	77	22	29	7.5	2	3	750	0	0.0	0.0
E+ / 0.7	6.4	3.1	7.64	989	1	0	0	77	22	29	7.5	3	3	750	0	0.0	0.0
E+ / 0.7	6.4	3.1	7.64	10	1	0	0	77	22	29	7.5	5	3	750	0	5.8	0.0
E+ / 0.7	6.3	3.1	7.64	1,652	1	0	0	77	22	29	7.5	11	3	0	0	0.0	0.0
E+ / 0.7	6.3	3.1	7.64	32	1	0	0	77	22	29	7.5	14	3	0	0	0.0	0.0
E+ / 0.7	6.3	3.1	7.64	70	1	0	0	77	22	29	7.5	5	3	0	0	0.0	0.0
E+ / 0.7	6.4	3.1	7.64	430	1	0	0	77	22	29	7.5	8	3	0	0	0.0	0.0
B+ / 8.7	1.5	2.9	10.81	575	0	10	2	66	22	46	3.2	30	3	750	0	2.5	0.0
B+ / 8.7	1.5	2.9	10.81	11	0	10	2	66	22	46	3.2	10	3	750	0	0.0	0.0
B+ / 8.7	1.5	2.9	10.81	94	0	10	2	66	22	46	3.2	11	3	750	0	0.0	0.0
B+ / 8.7	1.5	2.9	10.81	5	0	10	2	66	22	46	3.2	26	3	750	0	2.5	0.0
B+ / 8.7	1.5	2.9	10.81	899	0	10	2	66	22	46	3.2	41	3	0	0	0.0	0.0
B+ / 8.7	1.5	2.9	10.81	86	0	10	2	66	22	46	3.2	50	3	0	0	0.0	0.0
B+ / 8.7	1.5	2.9	10.81	1	0	10	2	66	22	46	3.2	19	3	0	0	0.0	0.0
B+ / 8.7	1.5	2.9	10.81	18	0	10	2	66	22	46	3.2	30	3	0	0	0.0	0.0
B- / 7.5	2.6	5.7	11.84	74	0	0	94	3	3	4	3.8	38	17	750	0	4.3	0.0
B- / 7.5	2.6	5.7	11.84	2	0	0	94	3	3	4	3.8	15	17	750	0	0.0	0.0
B- / 7.5	2.6	5.7	11.84	26	0	0	94	3	3	4	3.8	15	17	750	0	0.0	0.0
B- / 7.5	2.6	5.7	11.84	102	0	0	94	3	3	4	3.8	53	17	0	0	0.0	0.0
B- / 7.5	2.6	5.7	11.84	1	0	0	94	3	3	4	3.8	38	17	0	0	0.0	0.0
C- / 3.3	3.5	6.8	5.14	273	1	0	95	2	2	4	5.5	84	8	750	0	4.3	0.0
C- / 3.3	3.5	6.8	5.14	12	1	0	95	2	2	4	5.5	75	8	750	0	0.0	0.0
C- / 3.3	3.5	6.8	5.14	192	1	0	95	2	2	4	5.5	76	8	750	0	0.0	0.0
C- / 3.3	3.5	6.8	5.14	617	1	0	95	2	2	4	5.5	85	8	0	0	0.0	0.0
C- / 3.3	3.5	6.8	5.14	15	1	0	95	2	2	4	5.5	84	8	0	0	0.0	0.0
E+ / 0.7	7.1	N/A	9.41	18	0	99	0	0	1	0	0.0	87	6	1,000	0	3.0	0.0
E+ / 0.7	7.2	N/A	9.67	361	0	99	0	0	1	0	0.0	89	6	250,000	0	0.0	0.0
E+ / 0.7	7.2	N/A	9.78	740	0	99	0	0	1	0	0.0	90	6	0	0	0.0	0.0
C+ / 6.6	2.8	5.2	10.06	343	0	16	0	42	42	80	3.1	70	12	0	0	0.0	0.0
C+ / 6.5	2.8	5.2	10.05	1,752	0	16	0	42	42	80	3.1	70	12	0	0	0.0	0.0
C+ / 6.3	2.9	5.0	15.80	1,690	2	14	0	47	37	56	0.0	73	15	1,000	0	4.0	0.0
C+ / 6.3	2.9	5.0	15.80	17	2	14	0	47	37	56	0.0	53	15	1,000	0	0.0	0.0
C+ / 6.3	2.9	5.0	15.80	303	2	14	0	47	37	56	0.0	52	15	1,000	0	0.0	0.0
C+ / 6.6	2.8	5.0	15.80	3,800	2	14	0	47	37	56	0.0	78	15	250,000	0	0.0	0.0
U /	N/A	5.0	15.82	2	2	14	0	47	37	56	0.0	N/A	15	0	0	0.0	0.0
C+ / 6.7	2.8	5.0	15.82	51	2	14	0	47	37	56	0.0	67	15	0	0	0.0	0.0
U /	N/A	5.0	15.83	28	2	14	0	47	37	56	0.0	N/A	15	0	0	0.0	0.0
C+ / 6.3	2.9	5.0	15.83	156	2	14	0	47	37	56	0.0	77	15	1,000,000	0	0.0	0.0
D+ / 2.5	4.0	10.9	10.71	218	1	0	98	0	1	20	0.0	30	2	1,000	0	4.0	0.0
D+ / 2.5	3.9	10.9	10.71	1	1	0	98	0	1	20	0.0	11	2	1,000	0	0.0	0.0

Fund Type	Fund Name	Ticker Symbol	Overall Investment Rating	Phone	PERFORMANCE Perfor-mance Rating/Pts	Total Return % through 2/28/17 3 Mo	6 Mo	1Yr / Pct	Annualized 3Yr / Pct	5Yr / Pct	Incl. in Returns Dividend Yield	Expense Ratio
	99 Pct = Best 0 Pct = Worst											
MUS	J Hancock CA Tax Free Income C	TCCAX	D+	(800) 257-3336	C+ / 6.8	2.26	-4.47	-0.64 / 8	3.13 /84	2.81 /76	2.84	1.69
GEI	J Hancock Core Bond 1	JICDX	C-	(800) 257-3336	C / 4.5	1.09	-2.05	1.50 /45	2.44 /51	2.42 /48	1.82	0.67
GEI	J Hancock Core Bond NAV		C-	(800) 257-3336	C / 4.6	1.11	-2.02	1.55 /45	2.47 /51	2.48 /49	1.87	0.62
EM	J Hancock Emerg Markets Debt A	JMKAX	C-	(800) 257-3336	B+ / 8.8	6.03	0.45	17.97 /93	4.66 /82	3.99 /72	5.37	1.24
EM	J Hancock Emerg Markets Debt C	JMKCX	U	(800) 257-3336	U /	5.83	0.09	17.27 /92	--	--	4.89	1.94
EM	J Hancock Emerg Markets Debt I	JMKIX	C	(800) 257-3336	A+ / 9.6	6.10	0.61	18.31 /94	5.01 /85	4.37 /77	5.90	0.93
EM	J Hancock Emerg Markets Debt NAV		C	(800) 257-3336	A+ / 9.6	6.13	0.66	18.47 /94	5.16 /86	--	6.02	0.81
EM	J Hancock Emerg Markets Debt R2	JHEMX	U	(800) 257-3336	U /	6.07	0.53	18.30 /94	--	--	5.76	1.33
EM	J Hancock Emerg Markets Debt R4	JHMDX	U	(800) 257-3336	U /	6.09	0.58	18.41 /94	--	--	5.85	1.18
EM	J Hancock Emerg Markets Debt R6	JEMIX	U	(800) 257-3336	U /	6.13	0.66	18.61 /94	--	--	6.02	0.83
GEI	J Hancock Fltng Rate Inc 1	JFIHX	C+	(800) 257-3336	B / 7.8	2.92	4.90	16.00 /90	2.41 /50	3.91 /71	5.40	0.78
GEI	J Hancock Fltng Rate Inc A	JFIAX	C-	(800) 257-3336	C+ / 6.7	2.82	4.71	15.56 /89	2.03 /44	3.47 /65	4.91	1.16
GEI ●	J Hancock Fltng Rate Inc B	JFIBX	C-	(800) 257-3336	C+ / 6.6	2.52	4.22	14.61 /88	1.31 /32	2.72 /53	4.36	1.86
GEI	J Hancock Fltng Rate Inc C	JFIGX	C-	(800) 257-3336	C+ / 6.6	2.64	4.34	14.71 /88	1.34 /33	2.78 /54	4.35	1.86
GEI	J Hancock Fltng Rate Inc I	JFIIX	C+	(800) 257-3336	B / 7.8	2.90	4.87	15.91 /90	2.38 /50	3.84 /70	5.34	0.84
GEI	J Hancock Fltng Rate Inc NAV		C+	(800) 257-3336	B / 7.9	2.93	4.93	16.04 /90	2.47 /51	3.94 /72	5.45	0.73
LP	J Hancock Fltng Rate Inc R6	JFIRX	C+	(800) 257-3336	B / 7.9	2.92	4.92	16.04 /90	2.47 /51	3.90 /71	5.45	0.75
GL	J Hancock Global Bond 1	JIGDX	E	(800) 257-3336	E+ / 0.8	1.50	-5.40	1.75 /47	0.21 /17	0.90 /26	2.57	0.82
GL	J Hancock Global Bond NAV		E	(800) 257-3336	D- / 1.1	1.56	-5.35	1.89 /48	0.26 /18	0.95 /27	2.62	0.77
GEI	J Hancock Global Income A	JYGAX	D	(800) 257-3336	B / 7.8	5.37	2.41	16.13 /90	3.61 /70	4.06 /73	4.89	1.31
GEI	J Hancock Global Income I	JYGIX	C	(800) 257-3336	A- / 9.1	5.56	2.57	16.51 /91	3.96 /75	4.38 /77	5.41	1.01
GEI	J Hancock Global Income NAV		C	(800) 257-3336	A- / 9.2	5.48	2.62	16.64 /91	4.07 /76	4.52 /79	5.52	0.89
USS	J Hancock Government Inc A	JHGIX	D-	(800) 257-3336	E / 0.5	0.40	-2.41	-0.47 /10	1.44 /34	1.56 /35	2.12	1.10
USS ●	J Hancock Government Inc B	TSGIX	D-	(800) 257-3336	D- / 1.3	0.31	-2.79	-1.24 / 3	0.67 /23	0.77 /25	1.41	1.85
USS	J Hancock Government Inc C	TCGIX	D-	(800) 257-3336	D- / 1.3	0.21	-2.89	-1.24 / 3	0.67 /23	0.77 /25	1.42	1.85
COH	J Hancock High Yield 1	JIHDX	C	(800) 257-3336	A- / 9.1	4.74	6.17	24.91 /99	2.55 /53	5.87 /91	6.13	0.79
COH	J Hancock High Yield A	JHHBX	D+	(800) 257-3336	B / 8.1	5.01	5.67	20.68 /97	2.96 /60	7.03 /96	5.70	0.98
COH ●	J Hancock High Yield B	TSHYX	C-	(800) 257-3336	B+ / 8.3	4.82	5.28	19.75 /96	2.16 /46	6.21 /94	5.19	1.73
COH	J Hancock High Yield C	JHYCX	C-	(800) 257-3336	B+ / 8.4	4.83	5.59	19.79 /96	2.19 /46	6.24 /94	5.22	1.73
COH	J Hancock High Yield I	JYHIX	C	(800) 257-3336	A- / 9.2	5.10	5.82	21.05 /97	3.22 /65	7.28 /97	6.20	0.71
MUH	J Hancock High Yield Muni Bond A	JHTFX	C	(800) 257-3336	B / 7.6	2.01	-3.53	1.46 /51	4.55 /96	3.55 /88	4.65	0.98
MUH●	J Hancock High Yield Muni Bond B	TSHTX	C	(800) 257-3336	B / 8.0	1.82	-3.89	0.71 /40	3.78 /91	2.78 /76	4.06	1.73
MUH	J Hancock High Yield Muni Bond C	JCTFX	C	(800) 257-3336	B / 8.0	1.82	-3.89	0.71 /40	3.78 /91	2.78 /76	4.06	1.73
COH	J Hancock High Yield NAV		C	(800) 257-3336	A- / 9.2	4.81	6.14	24.95 /99	2.63 /55	5.93 /92	6.24	0.74
* GL	J Hancock Income A	JHFIX	C	(800) 257-3336	C- / 3.0	1.52	-0.70	3.23 /58	2.12 /45	3.45 /64	2.78	0.82
GL ●	J Hancock Income B	STIBX	C+	(800) 257-3336	C- / 3.5	1.35	-1.05	2.51 /53	1.41 /33	2.73 /53	2.19	1.52
GL	J Hancock Income C	JSTCX	C+	(800) 257-3336	C- / 3.5	1.35	-1.05	2.51 /53	1.40 /33	2.73 /53	2.19	1.52
GL	J Hancock Income I	JSTIX	B+	(800) 257-3336	C / 5.3	1.60	-0.40	3.71 /61	2.43 /51	3.79 /70	3.20	0.50
GL	J Hancock Income R1	JSTRX	B-	(800) 257-3336	C- / 4.1	1.43	-0.87	2.88 /56	1.77 /39	3.10 /59	2.55	1.16
GEL	J Hancock Income R2	JSNSX	B	(800) 257-3336	C / 4.5	1.50	-0.75	3.14 /57	2.03 /44	3.44 /64	2.80	0.91
GL	J Hancock Income R3	JSNHX	B	(800) 257-3336	C / 4.3	1.46	-0.66	3.15 /58	1.88 /41	3.21 /61	2.66	1.06
GL	J Hancock Income R4	JSNFX	B+	(800) 257-3336	C / 4.9	1.56	-0.63	3.39 /59	2.28 /48	3.63 /68	3.05	0.76
GL	J Hancock Income R5	JSNVX	A-	(800) 257-3336	C / 5.3	1.61	-0.53	3.60 /60	2.48 /51	3.83 /70	3.26	0.46
GEL	J Hancock Income R6	JSNWX	A-	(800) 257-3336	C / 5.4	1.63	-0.50	3.67 /61	2.55 /53	3.89 /71	3.32	0.41
GEI	J Hancock Inv Quality Bond 1	JIQBX	C	(800) 257-3336	C / 5.5	1.66	-1.27	4.23 /63	2.60 /54	2.61 /51	2.13	0.68
GEI	J Hancock Inv Quality Bond NAV		C	(800) 257-3336	C+ / 5.6	1.68	-1.24	4.29 /64	2.63 /55	2.65 /52	2.18	0.63
GEI	J Hancock Invest Gr Bond A	TAUSX	C-	(800) 257-3336	C- / 3.5	1.34	-1.54	2.78 /55	2.64 /55	3.07 /59	2.57	0.88
GEI ●	J Hancock Invest Gr Bond B	TSUSX	C-	(800) 257-3336	C- / 3.8	1.15	-2.00	1.91 /48	1.84 /40	2.30 /46	1.92	1.63
GEI	J Hancock Invest Gr Bond C	TCUSX	C-	(800) 257-3336	C- / 3.8	1.15	-2.00	1.91 /48	1.84 /40	2.30 /46	1.92	1.63
GEI	J Hancock Invest Gr Bond I	TIUSX	B	(800) 257-3336	C+ / 5.6	1.40	-1.51	2.94 /56	2.91 /60	3.34 /63	2.94	0.62
COI	J Hancock Invest Gr Bond R2	JIGBX	U	(800) 257-3336	U /	1.31	-1.59	2.73 /55	--	--	2.63	1.02
COI	J Hancock Invest Gr Bond R4	JIGMX	U	(800) 257-3336	U /	1.37	-1.59	2.93 /56	--	--	2.83	0.87

● Denotes fund is closed to new investors
* Denotes fund is included in Section II

www.thestreetratings.com

RISK			NET ASSETS		ASSET					Portfolio	Avg	FUND MANAGER		MINIMUM		LOADS	
Risk Rating/Pts	3 Yr Avg Standard Deviation	Avg Dura-tion	NAV As of 2/28/17	Total $(Mil)	Cash %	Gov. Bond %	Muni. Bond %	Corp. Bond %	Other %	Portfolio Turnover Ratio	Avg Coupon Rate	Manager Quality Pct	Manager Tenure (Years)	Initial Purch. $	Additional Purch. $	Front End Load	Back End Load
D+ / 2.5	4.0	10.9	10.71	33	1	0	98	0	1	20	0.0	11	2	1,000	0	0.0	0.0
C+ / 5.7	3.0	5.5	12.92	194	0	33	0	21	46	471	2.8	31	10	0	0	0.0	0.0
C+ / 5.7	3.0	5.5	12.90	1,351	0	33	0	21	46	471	2.8	32	10	0	0	0.0	0.0
E / 0.4	8.1	N/A	9.44	2	9	43	0	46	2	26	0.0	98	4	1,000	0	4.0	0.0
U /	N/A	N/A	9.44	N/A	9	43	0	46	2	26	0.0	N/A	4	1,000	0	0.0	0.0
E / 0.4	8.1	N/A	9.45	8	9	43	0	46	2	26	0.0	98	4	250,000	0	0.0	0.0
E / 0.4	8.1	N/A	9.44	662	9	43	0	46	2	26	0.0	99	4	0	0	0.0	0.0
U /	N/A	N/A	9.44	N/A	9	43	0	46	2	26	0.0	N/A	4	0	0	0.0	0.0
U /	N/A	N/A	9.44	N/A	9	43	0	46	2	26	0.0	N/A	4	0	0	0.0	0.0
U /	N/A	N/A	9.44	N/A	9	43	0	46	2	26	0.0	N/A	4	1,000,000	0	0.0	0.0
C- / 3.2	4.0	0.5	8.64	27	2	0	0	52	46	35	4.1	88	10	0	0	0.0	0.0
C- / 3.2	4.0	0.5	8.65	146	2	0	0	52	46	35	4.1	85	10	1,000	0	2.5	0.0
C- / 3.2	4.0	0.5	8.65	17	2	0	0	52	46	35	4.1	78	10	1,000	0	0.0	0.0
C- / 3.3	3.9	0.5	8.69	142	2	0	0	52	46	35	4.1	79	10	1,000	0	0.0	0.0
C- / 3.2	4.0	0.5	8.65	184	2	0	0	52	46	35	4.1	87	10	250,000	0	0.0	0.0
C- / 3.2	4.0	0.5	8.65	1,401	2	0	0	52	46	35	4.1	88	10	0	0	0.0	0.0
C- / 3.1	4.0	0.5	8.65	N/A	2	0	0	52	46	35	4.1	82	10	1,000,000	0	0.0	0.0
D / 1.6	5.6	6.3	12.02	59	0	42	3	29	26	71	3.9	86	2	0	0	0.0	0.0
D / 1.6	5.6	6.3	12.01	434	0	42	3	29	26	71	3.9	86	2	0	0	0.0	0.0
E+ / 0.9	6.5	5.3	9.48	7	2	47	0	47	4	74	7.6	82	8	1,000	0	4.0	0.0
E+ / 0.9	6.5	5.3	9.48	1	2	47	0	47	4	74	7.6	84	8	250,000	0	0.0	0.0
E+ / 0.9	6.4	5.3	9.48	310	2	47	0	47	4	74	7.6	85	8	0	0	0.0	0.0
B / 7.7	2.4	4.2	9.38	254	0	39	0	0	61	60	0.0	48	19	1,000	0	4.0	0.0
B / 7.6	2.4	4.2	9.38	3	0	39	0	0	61	60	0.0	16	19	1,000	0	0.0	0.0
B / 7.7	2.4	4.2	9.38	14	0	39	0	0	61	60	0.0	17	19	1,000	0	0.0	0.0
E / 0.5	7.1	3.9	8.36	355	1	0	0	90	9	58	8.2	1	11	0	0	0.0	0.0
E+ / 0.9	5.9	3.5	3.54	384	2	0	0	92	6	89	0.0	6	8	1,000	0	4.0	0.0
E+ / 0.9	6.0	3.5	3.54	15	2	0	0	92	6	89	0.0	2	8	1,000	0	0.0	0.0
D- / 1.0	5.8	3.5	3.54	127	2	0	0	92	6	89	0.0	2	8	1,000	0	0.0	0.0
E+ / 0.8	6.1	3.5	3.53	219	2	0	0	92	6	89	0.0	7	8	250,000	0	0.0	0.0
D+ / 2.4	3.7	9.5	7.93	141	2	2	94	0	2	22	0.0	70	2	1,000	0	4.0	0.0
D+ / 2.4	3.7	9.5	7.93	5	2	2	94	0	2	22	0.0	37	2	1,000	0	0.0	0.0
D+ / 2.4	3.7	9.5	7.93	43	2	2	94	0	2	22	0.0	37	2	1,000	0	0.0	0.0
E / 0.5	7.1	3.9	8.27	151	1	0	0	90	9	58	8.2	1	11	0	0	0.0	0.0
B / 8.1	2.1	3.6	6.43	691	2	26	4	45	23	37	0.0	89	18	1,000	0	4.0	0.0
B / 8.0	2.2	3.6	6.43	78	2	26	4	45	23	37	0.0	84	18	1,000	0	0.0	0.0
B / 8.1	2.1	3.6	6.43	352	2	26	4	45	23	37	0.0	84	18	1,000	0	0.0	0.0
B / 7.9	2.2	3.6	6.42	3,276	2	26	4	45	23	37	0.0	91	18	250,000	0	0.0	0.0
B / 7.9	2.2	3.6	6.45	14	2	26	4	45	23	37	0.0	87	18	0	0	0.0	0.0
B / 7.9	2.2	3.6	6.42	13	2	26	4	45	23	37	0.0	62	18	0	0	0.0	0.0
B / 8.1	2.1	3.6	6.43	6	2	26	4	45	23	37	0.0	87	18	0	0	0.0	0.0
B / 7.9	2.2	3.6	6.43	141	2	26	4	45	23	37	0.0	90	18	0	0	0.0	0.0
B / 8.0	2.2	3.6	6.42	16	2	26	4	45	23	37	0.0	91	18	0	0	0.0	0.0
B / 7.9	2.3	3.6	6.42	265	2	26	4	45	23	37	0.0	73	18	1,000,000	0	0.0	0.0
C / 5.3	3.0	5.4	12.23	77	0	14	0	23	63	66	6.6	N/A	7	0	0	0.0	0.0
C / 5.3	3.1	5.4	12.21	329	0	14	0	23	63	66	6.6	46	7	0	0	0.0	0.0
C+ / 6.7	2.8	4.5	10.41	340	1	15	0	39	45	63	0.0	54	19	1,000	0	4.0	0.0
C+ / 6.6	2.8	4.5	10.41	5	1	15	0	39	45	63	0.0	19	19	1,000	0	0.0	0.0
C+ / 6.5	2.8	4.5	10.41	34	1	15	0	39	45	63	0.0	19	19	1,000	0	0.0	0.0
C+ / 6.7	2.8	4.5	10.41	301	1	15	0	39	45	63	0.0	63	19	250,000	0	0.0	0.0
U /	N/A	4.5	10.41	1	1	15	0	39	45	63	0.0	N/A	19	0	0	0.0	0.0
U /	N/A	4.5	10.41	N/A	1	15	0	39	45	63	0.0	N/A	19	0	0	0.0	0.0

Fund Type	Fund Name	Ticker Symbol	Overall Investment Rating	Phone	Perfor-mance Rating/Pts	3 Mo	6 Mo	1Yr / Pct	3Yr / Pct	5Yr / Pct	Dividend Yield	Expense Ratio
COI	J Hancock Invest Gr Bond R6	JIGEX	U	(800) 257-3336	U /	1.43	-1.45	3.06 /57	--	--	3.06	0.52
MMT	J Hancock Money Market A	JHMXX	U	(800) 257-3336	U /	--	--	--	--	--	0.01	N/A
MMT●	J Hancock Money Market B	TSMXX	U	(800) 257-3336	U /	--	--	--	--	--	0.01	N/A
MMT●	J Hancock Money Market C	JMCXX	U	(800) 257-3336	U /	--	--	--	--	--	0.01	N/A
GEI	J Hancock Real Return Bond 1	JIRRX	E+	(800) 257-3336	C- / 3.8	1.61	-0.11	4.52 /65	1.19 /31	0.43 /21	1.90	0.80
GEI	J Hancock Real Return Bond NAV		E+	(800) 257-3336	C- / 3.9	1.56	-0.09	4.61 /65	1.24 /31	0.47 /21	1.97	0.75
USS	J Hancock Sh Tm Govt Inc NAV		C-	(800) 257-3336	D / 1.7	0.27	-0.68	-0.33 /12	0.50 /21	0.42 /21	1.67	0.62
GEL	J Hancock Short Duration Opp A	JMBAX	D	(800) 257-3336	C / 4.4	2.12	1.80	8.77 /76	1.58 /36	2.42 /48	2.89	1.19
GEL	J Hancock Short Duration Opp I	JMBIX	C	(800) 257-3336	C+ / 6.1	2.20	2.07	9.14 /77	1.92 /42	2.73 /53	3.29	0.87
GEL	J Hancock Short Duration Opp NAV		C+	(800) 257-3336	C+ / 6.3	2.33	2.13	9.37 /77	2.05 /44	2.92 /56	3.40	0.76
* GL	J Hancock Strat Income Opp A	JIPAX	B+	(800) 257-3336	C / 4.9	2.00	0.95	5.87 /70	2.86 /59	4.00 /73	2.08	1.11
GL	J Hancock Strat Income Opp C	JIPCX	A-	(800) 257-3336	C / 5.3	1.83	0.60	5.13 /67	2.14 /45	3.28 /62	1.48	1.81
GL	J Hancock Strat Income Opp I	JIPIX	A+	(800) 257-3336	C+ / 6.9	2.08	1.01	6.20 /71	3.19 /64	4.35 /77	2.48	0.79
GL	J Hancock Strat Income Opp NAV		A+	(800) 257-3336	C+ / 6.9	2.11	1.07	6.22 /71	3.19 /64	4.40 /77	2.59	0.68
GL	J Hancock Strat Income Opp R2	JIPPX	A+	(800) 257-3336	C+ / 6.3	1.99	0.92	5.80 /70	2.80 /58	3.97 /72	2.10	1.20
GEI	J Hancock Strat Income Opp R6	JIPRX	A+	(800) 257-3336	B- / 7.0	2.01	1.07	6.21 /71	3.28 /66	4.42 /78	2.59	0.70
MUN	J Hancock Tax Free Bond A	TAMBX	D-	(800) 257-3336	C / 5.5	2.20	-3.71	-0.12 /16	3.48 /87	2.79 /76	3.58	0.92
MUN●	J Hancock Tax Free Bond B	TSMBX	D	(800) 257-3336	C+ / 6.1	2.01	-4.06	-0.87 / 5	2.71 /77	2.02 /59	2.95	1.67
MUN	J Hancock Tax Free Bond C	TBMBX	D	(800) 257-3336	C+ / 6.0	1.90	-4.16	-0.97 / 4	2.68 /77	2.02 /59	2.96	1.67
COH	J Hancock US High Yield Bd 1	JIHLX	B-	(800) 257-3336	A+ / 9.7	4.99	5.54	20.86 /97	4.65 /82	5.94 /92	5.92	0.85
COH	J Hancock US High Yield Bd NAV		B-	(800) 257-3336	A+ / 9.7	5.01	5.57	20.94 /97	4.71 /83	6.00 /92	5.98	0.80
GL	J Hancock VIT Active Bond NAV		A	(800) 257-3336	C+ / 6.7	1.80	-0.82	4.82 /66	3.41 /67	3.97 /72	3.80	0.64
GL	J Hancock VIT Core Bond NAV		C	(800) 257-3336	C / 4.9	1.15	-1.93	1.79 /47	2.63 /55	2.57 /51	2.11	0.63
GL	J Hancock VIT Global Bond I		E	(800) 257-3336	E+ / 0.7	1.48	-5.50	1.64 /46	0.21 /17	0.74 /24	0.00	0.83
GL	J Hancock VIT Global Bond NAV		E	(800) 257-3336	E+ / 0.9	1.48	-5.51	1.73 /46	0.25 /18	0.78 /25	0.00	0.78
COH	J Hancock VIT High Yield I		C	(800) 257-3336	A- / 9.0	4.86	5.87	24.20 /99	2.44 /51	5.91 /91	6.78	0.80
COH	J Hancock VIT High Yield NAV		C	(800) 257-3336	A- / 9.0	4.73	5.79	24.13 /99	2.47 /51	5.92 /92	6.93	0.75
GEL	J Hancock VIT Inv Qual Bd I		C	(800) 257-3336	C / 5.5	1.65	-1.13	4.47 /64	2.55 /53	2.68 /52	2.24	0.69
GEL	J Hancock VIT Inv Qual Bd II		C	(800) 257-3336	C / 5.1	1.55	-1.29	4.16 /63	2.34 /49	2.47 /49	2.04	0.89
GEL	J Hancock VIT Inv Qual Bd NAV		C+	(800) 257-3336	C+ / 5.6	1.65	-1.18	4.44 /64	2.61 /54	2.74 /53	2.30	0.64
GES	J Hancock VIT Strat Inc Opps I	JESNX	A+	(800) 257-3336	B- / 7.2	2.18	1.13	6.29 /71	3.47 /68	4.76 /81	2.41	0.75
GES	J Hancock VIT Strat Inc Opps II		A+	(800) 257-3336	C+ / 6.9	2.10	1.03	6.07 /70	3.25 /65	4.55 /79	2.21	0.95
GES	J Hancock VIT Strat Inc Opps NAV		A+	(800) 257-3336	B- / 7.2	2.19	1.17	6.36 /71	3.53 /69	4.81 /82	2.47	0.70
GEI	J Hancock VIT Total Bd Mkt B NAV		D+	(800) 257-3336	C / 4.5	0.99	-2.34	1.16 /41	2.48 /51	2.05 /43	2.75	0.51
GEN	J Hancock VIT Value I	JEVLX	C	(800) 257-3336	A+ / 9.9	7.36	11.79	32.97 /99	6.07 /92	11.88 /99	0.62	0.89
GEN	J Hancock VIT Value II		C	(800) 257-3336	A+ / 9.9	7.30	11.67	32.70 /99	5.85 /91	11.65 /99	0.46	1.09
GEN	J Hancock VIT Value NAV		C	(800) 257-3336	A+ / 9.9	7.37	11.85	33.01 /99	6.12 /93	11.94 /99	0.66	0.84
MUS	Jamestown VA Tax Exempt	JTEVX	C	(866) 738-1126	C- / 3.3	1.66	-2.08	-0.74 / 7	1.23 /41	1.01 /35	1.87	0.90
GEI	Janus Aspen Flexible Bond Inst	JAFLX	C+	(800) 295-2687	C / 4.3	1.11	-1.65	2.12 /50	2.16 /46	2.83 /55	2.89	0.62
GEI	Janus Aspen Flexible Bond Svc		C	(800) 295-2687	C- / 3.9	0.99	-1.85	1.83 /47	1.90 /41	2.56 /50	2.46	0.88
EM	Janus Emerging Markets A	JMFAX	D+	(800) 295-2687	B+ / 8.8	7.82	5.47	29.19 /99	2.84 /59	-0.15 / 4	0.53	1.98
EM	Janus Emerging Markets C	JMFCX	C-	(800) 295-2687	A / 9.3	7.76	5.25	28.38 /99	2.11 /45	-0.88 / 2	0.20	2.77
EM ●	Janus Emerging Markets D	JMFDX	C	(800) 295-2687	A+ / 9.7	7.94	5.71	29.59 /99	3.15 /63	0.10 /15	0.97	1.68
EM	Janus Emerging Markets I	JMFIX	C	(800) 295-2687	A+ / 9.7	8.00	5.66	29.76 /99	3.27 /65	0.28 /19	1.04	1.56
EM	Janus Emerging Markets S	JMFSX	C	(800) 295-2687	A+ / 9.6	7.80	5.58	29.42 /99	3.01 /61	-0.05 / 5	0.00	2.01
EM	Janus Emerging Markets T	JMFTX	C	(800) 295-2687	A+ / 9.7	7.89	5.67	29.50 /99	3.04 /62	0.03 / 8	0.94	1.79
MMT●	Janus Fd Inc-Govt MM D	JGVXX	U	(800) 295-2687	U /	0.01	0.01	0.01 /18	--	--	0.01	N/A
* GEI	Janus Flexible Bond A	JDFAX	D-	(800) 295-2687	D / 2.0	1.03	-1.79	1.90 /48	1.93 /42	2.56 /50	2.38	0.81
GEI	Janus Flexible Bond C	JFICX	D+	(800) 295-2687	D+ / 2.9	0.96	-2.03	1.30 /43	1.24 /31	1.83 /39	1.80	1.53
COI ●	Janus Flexible Bond D	JANFX	C+	(800) 295-2687	C / 4.3	1.09	-1.68	2.13 /50	2.13 /45	2.76 /54	2.72	0.60
GEI	Janus Flexible Bond I	JFLEX	C+	(800) 295-2687	C / 4.4	1.19	-1.56	2.27 /51	2.20 /46	2.81 /54	2.76	0.56
COI	Janus Flexible Bond N	JDFNX	C+	(800) 295-2687	C / 4.6	1.13	-1.60	2.38 /52	2.29 /48	2.91 /56	2.88	0.44

● Denotes fund is closed to new investors
* Denotes fund is included in Section II

www.thestreetratings.com

I. Index of Bond and Money Market Mutual Funds

RISK	3 Yr Avg Standard Deviation	Avg Dura-tion	NET ASSETS NAV As of 2/28/17	Total $(Mil)	ASSET Cash %	Gov. Bond %	Muni. Bond %	Corp. Bond %	Other %	Portfolio Turnover Ratio	Avg Coupon Rate	FUND MANAGER Manager Quality Pct	Manager Tenure (Years)	MINIMUM Initial Purch. $	Additional Purch. $	LOADS Front End Load	Back End Load
U /	N/A	4.5	10.41	2	1	15	0	39	45	63	0.0	N/A	19	1,000,000	0	0.0	0.0
U /	N/A	N/A	1.00	490	100	0	0	0	0	0	0.0	N/A	N/A	1,000	0	0.0	0.0
U /	N/A	N/A	1.00	5	100	0	0	0	0	0	0.0	N/A	N/A	1,000	0	0.0	0.0
U /	N/A	N/A	1.00	21	100	0	0	0	0	0	0.0	N/A	N/A	1,000	0	0.0	0.0
D+ /2.5	4.5	6.9	11.28	80	0	83	0	6	11	58	2.6	4	9	0	0	0.0	0.0
D+ /2.5	4.4	6.9	11.14	978	0	83	0	6	11	58	2.6	4	9	0	0	0.0	0.0
A- /9.1	1.1	N/A	9.47	231	2	82	0	0	16	72	0.0	32	N/A	0	0	0.0	0.0
C /4.6	3.3	2.2	9.67	31	1	8	0	63	28	52	5.2	74	8	1,000	0	2.5	0.0
C /4.7	3.2	2.2	9.66	31	1	8	0	63	28	52	5.2	79	8	250,000	0	0.0	0.0
C /4.6	3.3	2.2	9.68	1,160	1	8	0	63	28	52	5.2	80	8	0	0	0.0	0.0
B /7.9	2.2	2.8	10.70	585	5	25	3	45	22	44	0.0	92	11	1,000	0	4.0	0.0
B /7.9	2.2	2.8	10.70	402	5	25	3	45	22	44	0.0	88	11	1,000	0	0.0	0.0
B /7.8	2.3	2.8	10.70	3,413	5	25	3	45	22	44	0.0	93	11	250,000	0	0.0	0.0
B /7.9	2.3	2.8	10.69	1,868	5	25	3	45	22	44	0.0	93	11	0	0	0.0	0.0
B /7.9	2.3	2.8	10.71	19	5	25	3	45	22	44	0.0	91	11	0	0	0.0	0.0
B /7.9	2.2	2.8	10.70	34	5	25	3	45	22	44	0.0	87	11	1,000,000	0	0.0	0.0
D+ /2.7	3.7	10.9	9.72	511	0	0	99	0	1	13	0.0	24	2	1,000	0	4.0	0.0
D+ /2.8	3.7	10.9	9.72	5	0	0	99	0	1	13	0.0	9	2	1,000	0	0.0	0.0
D+ /2.7	3.7	10.9	9.71	54	0	0	99	0	1	13	0.0	8	2	1,000	0	0.0	0.0
D- /1.2	5.6	4.7	11.39	86	0	1	0	94	5	59	6.2	60	12	0	0	0.0	0.0
D- /1.2	5.6	4.7	11.38	217	0	1	0	94	5	59	6.2	62	12	0	0	0.0	0.0
C+ /6.6	2.8	5.2	9.59	539	0	15	0	43	42	60	0.0	94	12	0	0	0.0	0.0
C+ /5.7	3.0	5.5	13.16	1,009	0	31	1	22	46	425	2.9	92	10	0	0	0.0	0.0
D /1.6	5.6	6.4	12.38	39	0	52	5	21	22	81	4.1	86	2	0	0	0.0	0.0
D /1.6	5.6	6.4	12.34	461	0	52	5	21	22	81	4.1	86	2	0	0	0.0	0.0
E+ /0.6	7.0	3.9	5.39	88	3	1	0	87	9	74	8.5	1	20	0	0	0.0	0.0
E+ /0.6	6.9	3.9	5.31	100	3	1	0	87	9	74	8.5	1	20	0	0	0.0	0.0
C /5.4	3.0	5.4	11.12	158	0	12	0	26	62	97	6.7	N/A	7	0	0	0.0	0.0
C+ /5.7	3.0	5.4	11.12	82	0	12	0	26	62	97	6.7	34	7	0	0	0.0	0.0
C /5.5	3.0	5.4	11.08	53	0	12	0	26	62	97	6.7	50	7	0	0	0.0	0.0
B /7.8	2.3	2.8	13.59	480	3	23	3	46	25	49	0.0	88	13	0	0	0.0	0.0
B /7.8	2.3	2.8	13.62	46	3	23	3	46	25	49	0.0	86	13	0	0	0.0	0.0
B /7.8	2.3	2.8	13.55	67	3	23	3	46	25	49	0.0	88	13	0	0	0.0	0.0
C /5.2	3.1	5.4	10.16	172	0	45	1	23	31	67	5.6	30	12	0	0	0.0	0.0
E- /0.0	13.8	N/A	22.17	482	0	3	0	0	97	26	0.0	99	20	0	0	0.0	0.0
E- /0.0	13.8	N/A	22.06	27	0	3	0	0	97	26	0.0	99	20	0	0	0.0	0.0
E- /0.0	13.8	N/A	22.14	33	0	3	0	0	97	26	0.0	99	20	0	0	0.0	0.0
B /7.8	2.3	3.6	9.96	25	6	0	93	0	1	11	0.0	8	12	5,000	0	0.0	0.0
B- /7.0	2.7	5.5	11.74	333	0	24	0	41	35	111	3.7	31	10	0	0	0.0	0.0
B- /7.1	2.7	5.5	12.75	400	0	24	0	41	35	111	3.7	24	10	0	0	0.0	0.0
E- /0.0	15.5	N/A	8.68	N/A	3	0	0	0	97	95	0.0	96	5	2,500	0	5.8	0.0
E- /0.0	15.5	N/A	8.57	N/A	3	0	0	0	97	95	0.0	95	5	2,500	0	0.0	0.0
E- /0.0	15.5	N/A	8.63	11	3	0	0	0	97	95	0.0	97	5	2,500	0	0.0	0.0
E- /0.0	15.5	N/A	8.66	41	3	0	0	0	97	95	0.0	97	5	1,000,000	0	0.0	0.0
E- /0.0	15.5	N/A	8.71	N/A	3	0	0	0	97	95	0.0	96	5	2,500	0	0.0	0.0
E- /0.0	15.5	N/A	8.64	8	3	0	0	0	97	95	0.0	97	5	2,500	0	0.0	0.0
U /	N/A	N/A	1.00	157	100	0	0	0	0	0	0.0	N/A	8	2,500	100	0.0	0.0
B- /7.1	2.7	5.5	10.34	616	1	28	0	38	33	99	3.7	25	10	2,500	0	4.8	0.0
B- /7.1	2.7	5.5	10.35	331	1	28	0	38	33	99	3.7	10	10	2,500	0	0.0	0.0
B- /7.1	2.7	5.5	10.34	633	1	28	0	38	33	99	3.7	32	10	2,500	100	0.0	0.0
B- /7.1	2.7	5.5	10.35	5,366	1	28	0	38	33	99	3.7	34	10	1,000,000	0	0.0	0.0
B- /7.0	2.7	5.5	10.34	551	1	28	0	38	33	99	3.7	37	10	0	0	0.0	0.0

Data as of February 28, 2017

Fund Type	Fund Name	Ticker Symbol	Overall Investment Rating	Phone	Performance Rating/Pts	3 Mo	6 Mo	1Yr / Pct	3Yr / Pct	5Yr / Pct	Dividend Yield	Expense Ratio
	99 Pct = Best						Total Return % through 2/28/17		Annualized		Incl. in Returns	
GEI	Janus Flexible Bond R	JDFRX	C-	(800) 295-2687	C- / 3.4	0.94	-1.97	1.62 /46	1.56 /36	2.18 /44	2.12	1.20
GEI	Janus Flexible Bond S	JADFX	C	(800) 295-2687	C- / 3.8	1.00	-1.84	1.88 /48	1.82 /40	2.43 /48	2.38	0.94
GEI	Janus Flexible Bond T	JAFIX	C	(800) 295-2687	C- / 4.2	1.07	-1.72	2.03 /49	2.05 /44	2.67 /52	2.63	0.69
GL	Janus Global Bond A	JGBAX	E	(800) 295-2687	E- / 0.1	1.23	-5.12	--	-0.25 / 4	1.01 /27	1.56	1.07
GL	Janus Global Bond C	JGBCX	E	(800) 295-2687	E- / 0.2	0.95	-5.55	-0.78 / 6	-1.01 / 3	0.24 /19	0.94	1.81
GL •	Janus Global Bond D	JGBDX	E	(800) 295-2687	E / 0.3	1.18	-5.02	0.09 /22	-0.08 / 5	1.13 /29	1.85	0.93
GL	Janus Global Bond I	JGBIX	E	(800) 295-2687	E / 0.4	1.29	-5.01	0.14 /24	-0.01 / 5	1.26 /31	1.90	0.80
GL	Janus Global Bond N	JGLNX	E	(800) 295-2687	E / 0.4	1.22	-4.95	0.25 /27	0.08 /11	1.28 /31	2.01	0.71
GL	Janus Global Bond S	JGBSX	E	(800) 295-2687	E / 0.3	1.11	-5.14	-0.14 /15	-0.21 / 4	0.96 /27	1.60	1.22
GL	Janus Global Bond T	JHBTX	E	(800) 295-2687	E / 0.3	1.27	-5.05	0.11 /23	-0.15 / 5	1.08 /28	1.76	0.96
GL	Janus Global Unconstrained Bond A	JUCAX	U	(800) 295-2687	U /	0.70	1.33	4.54 /65	--	--	4.38	1.02
GL	Janus Global Unconstrained Bond C	JUCCX	U	(800) 295-2687	U /	0.51	0.97	3.80 /61	--	--	3.87	1.80
GL	Janus Global Unconstrained Bond D	JUCDX	U	(800) 295-2687	U /	0.70	1.36	4.58 /65	--	--	4.63	1.02
GL	Janus Global Unconstrained Bond I	JUCIX	U	(800) 295-2687	U /	0.76	1.46	4.81 /66	--	--	4.86	0.76
GL	Janus Global Unconstrained Bond N	JUCNX	U	(800) 295-2687	U /	0.77	1.49	4.85 /66	--	--	4.89	0.74
GL	Janus Global Unconstrained Bond S	JUCSX	U	(800) 295-2687	U /	0.77	1.26	4.49 /65	--	--	4.44	1.24
GL	Janus Global Unconstrained Bond T	JUCTX	U	(800) 295-2687	U /	0.72	1.37	4.61 /65	--	--	4.66	0.99
COH	Janus High Yield N	JHYNX	B-	(800) 295-2687	A- / 9.2	4.45	5.28	16.34 /91	3.99 /75	6.20 /93	5.95	0.63
GL	Janus High-Yield A	JHYAX	C	(800) 295-2687	B / 7.8	4.36	5.11	15.91 /90	3.61 /70	5.84 /91	5.32	1.00
GL	Janus High-Yield C	JDHCX	C+	(800) 295-2687	B+ / 8.3	4.19	4.73	15.12 /89	2.91 /60	5.08 /85	4.93	1.71
GL •	Janus High-Yield D	JNHYX	B	(800) 295-2687	A- / 9.1	4.41	5.19	16.16 /90	3.83 /73	6.07 /93	5.80	0.78
GL	Janus High-Yield I	JHYFX	B	(800) 295-2687	A- / 9.1	4.44	5.24	16.26 /91	3.88 /74	6.13 /93	5.89	0.70
GL	Janus High-Yield R	JHYRX	C+	(800) 295-2687	B+ / 8.5	4.26	4.89	15.48 /89	3.17 /64	5.43 /88	5.22	1.38
GL	Janus High-Yield S	JDHYX	B-	(800) 295-2687	B+ / 8.8	4.33	4.90	15.76 /90	3.45 /68	5.69 /90	5.48	1.13
GL	Janus High-Yield T	JAHYX	B	(800) 295-2687	A- / 9.0	4.39	5.15	16.05 /90	3.74 /72	5.95 /92	5.71	0.87
MMT •	Janus Money Market D	JNMXX	U	(800) 295-2687	U /	--	--	--	--	--	0.03	N/A
GL	Janus Multi Sector Income A	JMUAX	A+	(800) 295-2687	B- / 7.3	2.48	2.73	9.86 /79	4.32 /79	--	4.67	1.52
GL	Janus Multi Sector Income C	JMUCX	A+	(800) 295-2687	B / 7.8	2.41	2.46	9.18 /77	3.62 /70	--	4.19	2.27
GL	Janus Multi Sector Income D	JMUDX	A+	(800) 295-2687	B+ / 8.7	2.63	2.92	10.16 /79	4.51 /81	--	5.07	1.41
GL	Janus Multi Sector Income I	JMUIX	A+	(800) 295-2687	B+ / 8.8	2.66	2.87	10.29 /79	4.63 /82	--	5.18	1.03
GL	Janus Multi Sector Income N	JMTNX	A+	(800) 295-2687	B+ / 8.8	2.65	2.97	10.29 /80	4.67 /82	--	5.19	1.28
GL	Janus Multi Sector Income S	JMUSX	A+	(800) 295-2687	B+ / 8.7	2.95	3.18	10.31 /80	4.40 /80	--	5.21	1.80
GL	Janus Multi Sector Income T	JMUTX	A+	(800) 295-2687	B+ / 8.6	2.61	2.77	9.95 /79	4.41 /80	--	4.98	1.55
COI	Janus Short Term Bond N	JSHNX	C+	(800) 295-2687	D+ / 2.9	0.72	0.42	1.75 /47	0.98 /27	1.47 /34	1.41	0.59
GL	Janus Short-Term Bond A	JSHAX	D	(800) 295-2687	E+ / 0.7	0.31	-0.06	1.45 /44	0.57 /21	1.13 /29	1.08	0.90
GL	Janus Short-Term Bond C	JSHCX	D	(800) 295-2687	E / 0.5	0.13	-0.43	0.71 /36	-0.07 / 5	0.38 /20	0.37	1.67
GL •	Janus Short-Term Bond D	JNSTX	C+	(800) 295-2687	D+ / 2.6	0.69	0.35	1.61 /45	0.83 /25	1.27 /31	1.27	0.76
GL	Janus Short-Term Bond I	JSHIX	C+	(800) 295-2687	D+ / 2.5	0.37	0.06	1.70 /46	0.80 /24	1.37 /33	1.35	0.65
GL	Janus Short-Term Bond S	JSHSX	C	(800) 295-2687	D / 2.1	0.61	-0.14	1.29 /43	0.55 /21	0.98 /27	0.95	1.09
GL	Janus Short-Term Bond T	JASBX	C+	(800) 295-2687	D+ / 2.4	0.66	0.30	1.50 /45	0.73 /24	1.16 /29	1.16	0.84
GEI	JNL/PPM America Strategic Income		C	(800) 392-2909	B / 7.6	3.21	2.93	14.41 /87	2.54 /53	--	0.00	0.76
GEI	JNL/PPM America Total Return A		C-	(800) 392-2909	C+ / 5.6	1.54	-0.87	6.57 /72	2.32 /48	2.46 /49	3.09	0.85
GL	John Hancock Glbl Sht Dur Crdt NAV		C+	(800) 257-3336	B+ / 8.6	3.65	4.35	16.84 /92	3.20 /64	--	5.37	0.81
GL	John Hancock II Asia Pac TR Bd NA		C-	(800) 257-3336	C+ / 6.6	2.38	-0.60	6.71 /72	3.03 /61	--	1.57	0.81
GES	Johnson Fixed Income	JFINX	C+	(800) 541-0170	C / 5.0	0.84	-2.08	2.10 /50	2.73 /56	2.26 /46	1.97	0.85
GES	Johnson Institutional Core Bond	JIBFX	B-	(800) 541-0170	C+ / 5.6	1.05	-1.90	2.61 /54	3.06 /62	2.50 /49	2.55	0.30
GES	Johnson Institutional Intrmdt Bond	JIBEX	B	(800) 541-0170	C / 4.5	0.92	-1.00	2.81 /55	2.15 /46	1.92 /41	2.32	0.30
GES	Johnson Institutional Short Dur Bd	JIBDX	B-	(800) 541-0170	D+ / 2.8	0.53	0.05	1.69 /46	1.01 /28	1.05 /28	1.61	0.30
MUN	Johnson Municipal Income	JMUNX	B+	(800) 541-0170	C / 5.3	1.51	-1.85	-0.39 /11	2.13 /66	2.09 /61	1.82	0.65
MMT	JPMorgan 100% US Tr Sc MM	VPIXX	D+	(800) 480-4111	E+ / 0.8	0.07	0.10	0.15 /24	0.05 /10	0.03 / 9	0.15	N/A
MMT	JPMorgan 100% US Tr Sc MM Cptl	CJTXX	C-	(800) 480-4111	D- / 1.0	0.09	0.14	0.23 /27	0.08 /12	0.05 /11	0.23	N/A
MMT	JPMorgan 100% US Tr Sc MM Prem	VHPXX	D+	(800) 480-4111	E+ / 0.6	0.02	0.02	0.02 /19	0.01 / 6	0.01 / 6	0.02	N/A

• Denotes fund is closed to new investors
* Denotes fund is included in Section II

www.thestreetratings.com

RISK			NET ASSETS		ASSET					Portfolio Turnover Ratio	Avg Coupon Rate	FUND MANAGER		MINIMUM		LOADS	
Risk Rating/Pts	3 Yr Avg Standard Deviation	Avg Dura-tion	NAV As of 2/28/17	Total $(Mil)	Cash %	Gov. Bond %	Muni. Bond %	Corp. Bond %	Other %			Manager Quality Pct	Manager Tenure (Years)	Initial Purch. $	Additional Purch. $	Front End Load	Back End Load
B- / 7.2	2.7	5.5	10.35	41	1	28	0	38	33	99	3.7	16	10	2,500	0	0.0	0.0
B- / 7.2	2.7	5.5	10.35	56	1	28	0	38	33	99	3.7	22	10	2,500	0	0.0	0.0
C+ / 6.9	2.7	5.5	10.34	1,429	1	28	0	38	33	99	3.7	27	10	2,500	0	0.0	0.0
D+ / 2.5	4.5	5.8	9.34	11	5	53	0	29	13	125	3.2	76	6	2,500	0	4.8	0.0
D+ / 2.5	4.5	5.8	9.34	4	5	53	0	29	13	125	3.2	56	6	2,500	0	0.0	0.0
D+ / 2.5	4.5	5.8	9.33	10	5	53	0	29	13	125	3.2	78	6	2,500	100	0.0	0.0
D+ / 2.5	4.4	5.8	9.33	26	5	53	0	29	13	125	3.2	79	6	1,000,000	0	0.0	0.0
D+ / 2.5	4.5	5.8	9.32	179	5	53	0	29	13	125	3.2	80	6	0	0	0.0	0.0
D+ / 2.5	4.5	5.8	9.34	1	5	53	0	29	13	125	3.2	77	6	2,500	0	0.0	0.0
D+ / 2.5	4.5	5.8	9.34	6	5	53	0	29	13	125	3.2	77	6	2,500	0	0.0	0.0
U /	N/A	1.2	9.60	108	0	0	0	0	100	149	5.2	N/A	3	2,500	0	4.8	0.0
U /	N/A	1.2	9.59	56	0	0	0	0	100	149	5.2	N/A	3	2,500	0	0.0	0.0
U /	N/A	1.2	9.60	16	0	0	0	0	100	149	5.2	N/A	3	2,500	100	0.0	0.0
U /	N/A	1.2	9.60	1,473	0	0	0	0	100	149	5.2	N/A	3	1,000,000	0	0.0	0.0
U /	N/A	1.2	9.60	5	0	0	0	0	100	149	5.2	N/A	3	0	0	0.0	0.0
U /	N/A	1.2	9.60	1	0	0	0	0	100	149	5.2	N/A	3	2,500	0	0.0	0.0
U /	N/A	1.2	9.59	190	0	0	0	0	100	149	5.2	N/A	3	2,500	0	0.0	0.0
D / 1.9	4.7	3.5	8.58	27	7	0	0	86	7	66	7.1	63	9	0	0	0.0	0.0
D / 2.2	4.8	3.5	8.58	64	7	0	0	86	7	66	7.1	94	9	2,500	0	4.8	0.0
D+ / 2.3	4.7	3.5	8.58	46	7	0	0	86	7	66	7.1	93	9	2,500	0	0.0	0.0
D+ / 2.3	4.7	3.5	8.58	367	7	0	0	86	7	66	7.1	95	9	2,500	100	0.0	0.0
D+ / 2.3	4.7	3.5	8.58	579	7	0	0	86	7	66	7.1	95	9	1,000,000	0	0.0	0.0
D+ / 2.3	4.7	3.5	8.57	1	7	0	0	86	7	66	7.1	94	9	2,500	0	0.0	0.0
D+ / 2.3	4.7	3.5	8.59	2	7	0	0	86	7	66	7.1	94	9	2,500	0	0.0	0.0
D+ / 2.3	4.7	3.5	8.58	992	7	0	0	86	7	66	7.1	95	9	2,500	0	0.0	0.0
U /	N/A	N/A	1.00	967	100	0	0	0	0	0	0.0	38	8	2,500	100	0.0	0.0
B- / 7.5	2.6	N/A	9.82	10	3	11	0	54	32	76	0.0	95	3	2,500	0	4.8	0.0
B- / 7.4	2.6	N/A	9.83	4	3	11	0	54	32	76	0.0	94	3	2,500	0	0.0	0.0
B- / 7.4	2.6	N/A	9.83	16	3	11	0	54	32	76	0.0	96	3	2,500	100	0.0	0.0
B- / 7.4	2.6	N/A	9.82	35	3	11	0	54	32	76	0.0	96	3	1,000,000	0	0.0	0.0
B- / 7.4	2.6	N/A	9.83	2	3	11	0	54	32	76	0.0	96	3	0	0	0.0	0.0
B- / 7.4	2.6	N/A	9.83	2	3	11	0	54	32	76	0.0	96	3	2,500	0	0.0	0.0
B- / 7.4	2.6	N/A	9.82	10	3	11	0	54	32	76	0.0	96	3	2,500	0	0.0	0.0
A / 9.4	0.9	1.8	3.03	33	0	34	0	56	10	78	2.4	58	10	0	0	0.0	0.0
A / 9.3	1.0	1.8	3.02	128	0	34	0	56	10	78	2.4	67	10	2,500	0	2.5	0.0
A / 9.5	0.8	1.8	3.02	48	0	34	0	56	10	78	2.4	44	10	2,500	0	0.0	0.0
A- / 9.2	1.0	1.8	3.03	186	0	34	0	56	10	78	2.4	74	10	2,500	100	0.0	0.0
A / 9.3	1.0	1.8	3.02	489	0	34	0	56	10	78	2.4	73	10	1,000,000	0	0.0	0.0
A / 9.3	0.9	1.8	3.02	3	0	34	0	56	10	78	2.4	68	10	2,500	0	0.0	0.0
A- / 9.2	1.0	1.8	3.03	1,269	0	34	0	56	10	78	2.4	72	10	2,500	0	0.0	0.0
D+ / 2.3	4.7	5.0	11.59	116	4	0	0	84	12	76	5.7	81	5	0	0	0.0	0.0
C / 4.3	3.4	5.4	11.85	1,171	3	12	0	58	27	88	4.5	53	8	0	0	0.0	0.0
D / 1.9	5.2	N/A	9.20	327	0	0	0	0	100	56	0.0	94	4	0	0	0.0	0.0
C- / 3.2	4.0	N/A	9.43	386	3	44	0	51	2	54	0.0	94	4	0	0	0.0	0.0
C+ / 6.3	2.9	5.5	16.82	312	2	23	6	53	16	37	4.2	55	24	2,000	100	0.0	0.0
C+ / 6.2	2.9	5.6	15.83	133	2	23	4	53	18	30	4.2	65	17	1,000,000	100	0.0	0.0
B / 8.2	2.0	3.8	15.63	113	1	25	5	58	11	33	4.1	61	17	1,000,000	100	0.0	0.0
A+ / 9.6	0.8	1.8	15.02	137	0	0	0	0	100	42	3.6	60	17	1,000,000	100	0.0	0.0
B / 7.8	2.3	4.4	17.20	93	3	0	96	0	1	13	4.5	27	22	2,000	100	0.0	0.0
A+ / 9.9	N/A	N/A	1.00	1,849	100	0	0	0	0	0	0.2	41	N/A	5,000,000	0	0.0	0.0
A+ / 9.9	N/A	N/A	1.00	11,628	100	0	0	0	0	0	0.2	45	N/A	50,000,000	0	0.0	0.0
A+ / 9.9	N/A	N/A	1.00	858	100	0	0	0	0	0	0.0	38	N/A	1,000,000	0	0.0	0.0

Fund Type	Fund Name	Ticker Symbol	Overall Investment Rating	Phone	Performance Rating/Pts	3 Mo	6 Mo	1Yr / Pct	3Yr / Pct	5Yr / Pct	Dividend Yield	Expense Ratio
	99 Pct = Best *0 Pct = Worst*							Total Return % through 2/28/17	Annualized		Incl. in Returns	
MMF	JPMorgan CA Mun MM Morgan	VCAXX	C-	(800) 480-4111	E+ / 0.9	0.05	0.08	0.08 / 23	0.04 / 11	0.03 / 11	0.08	N/A
MMF	JPMorgan CA Mun MM Svc	JCVXX	U	(800) 480-4111	U /	--	--	--	--	--	0.04	N/A
MUH	JPMorgan CA Tax Free Bond A	JCBAX	E+	(800) 480-4111	D+ / 2.5	2.07	-2.91	-0.95 / 5	2.09 / 65	2.11 / 61	2.39	0.94
MUH	JPMorgan CA Tax Free Bond C	JCBCX	D-	(800) 480-4111	C- / 3.7	1.95	-3.10	-1.46 / 2	1.57 / 50	1.60 / 49	1.98	1.46
MUH	JPMorgan CA Tax Free Bond I	JPICX	D+	(800) 480-4111	C / 5.2	2.04	-2.83	-0.86 / 5	2.19 / 67	2.21 / 64	2.64	0.72
MUH	JPMorgan CA Tax Free Bond Sel	JPCBX	D	(800) 480-4111	C / 5.1	2.09	-2.79	-0.90 / 5	2.16 / 66	2.17 / 63	2.53	0.54
* GEI	JPMorgan Core Bond A	PGBOX	D	(800) 480-4111	D+ / 2.5	0.85	-2.21	0.91 / 39	2.20 / 46	2.01 / 42	2.19	0.99
GEI	JPMorgan Core Bond C	OBOCX	D	(800) 480-4111	C- / 3.0	0.76	-2.44	0.40 / 31	1.57 / 36	1.38 / 33	1.58	1.46
GEI	JPMorgan Core Bond R2	JCBZX	C-	(800) 480-4111	C- / 3.7	0.87	-2.33	0.75 / 37	1.98 / 43	1.78 / 39	2.03	1.35
GEI	JPMorgan Core Bond R5	JCBRX	C+	(800) 480-4111	C / 4.6	1.02	-2.07	1.30 / 43	2.53 / 52	2.33 / 47	2.59	0.53
GEI	JPMorgan Core Bond R6	JCBUX	C+	(800) 480-4111	C / 4.8	1.04	-2.01	1.40 / 44	2.61 / 54	2.42 / 48	2.69	0.42
GEI	JPMorgan Core Bond Sel	WOBDX	C	(800) 480-4111	C / 4.4	1.00	-2.02	1.18 / 42	2.42 / 50	2.20 / 45	2.47	0.72
* GL	JPMorgan Core Plus Bond A	ONIAX	C	(800) 480-4111	C- / 4.0	1.34	-1.35	3.34 / 59	2.82 / 58	3.13 / 60	2.36	1.03
GL	JPMorgan Core Plus Bond C	OBDCX	C+	(800) 480-4111	C / 4.4	1.06	-1.65	2.64 / 54	2.12 / 45	2.43 / 48	1.77	1.50
GL	JPMorgan Core Plus Bond L	JCBIX	B+	(800) 480-4111	C+ / 5.9	1.28	-1.21	3.46 / 59	3.04 / 62	3.37 / 63	2.70	0.70
GL	JPMorgan Core Plus Bond R2	JCPZX	B-	(800) 480-4111	C / 4.8	1.12	-1.53	2.91 / 56	2.36 / 49	2.69 / 53	2.03	1.42
GL	JPMorgan Core Plus Bond R6	JCPUX	A-	(800) 480-4111	C+ / 6.1	1.31	-1.16	3.68 / 61	3.16 / 64	3.47 / 65	2.78	0.43
GL	JPMorgan Core Plus Bond Sel	HLIPX	B+	(800) 480-4111	C+ / 6.0	1.41	-1.09	3.74 / 61	2.98 / 61	3.27 / 62	2.71	0.56
GEI	JPMorgan Corporate Bond A	CBRAX	D	(800) 480-4111	C+ / 5.8	2.25	-1.82	6.08 / 70	3.66 / 71	--	2.44	1.11
GEI	JPMorgan Corporate Bond C	CBRCX	D+	(800) 480-4111	C+ / 6.4	2.23	-1.97	5.59 / 69	3.14 / 63	--	2.07	1.87
GEI	JPMorgan Corporate Bond R6	CBFVX	C	(800) 480-4111	B- / 7.4	2.44	-1.65	6.54 / 72	4.01 / 75	--	2.87	0.42
GEI	JPMorgan Corporate Bond Sel	CBFSX	C	(800) 480-4111	B- / 7.4	2.42	-1.60	6.44 / 71	3.95 / 75	--	2.78	0.74
EM	JPMorgan Emerg Mkt Corp Debt A	JEMAX	C+	(800) 480-4111	B / 8.1	3.59	1.41	12.79 / 85	4.61 / 82	--	3.80	2.35
EM	JPMorgan Emerg Mkt Corp Debt C	JEFMX	C+	(800) 480-4111	B+ / 8.5	3.43	1.13	12.21 / 84	4.07 / 76	--	3.45	3.56
EM	JPMorgan Emerg Mkt Corp Debt R6	JCDRX	B	(800) 480-4111	A / 9.3	3.71	1.56	13.32 / 86	5.06 / 85	--	4.41	0.93
EM	JPMorgan Emerg Mkt Corp Debt Sel	JEDSX	B	(800) 480-4111	A- / 9.1	3.64	1.43	13.02 / 85	4.85 / 84	--	4.16	1.51
EM	JPMorgan Emerg Mkt Debt A	JEDAX	D	(800) 480-4111	B- / 7.5	5.17	-0.42	11.14 / 81	4.16 / 77	3.95 / 72	4.52	1.60
EM	JPMorgan Emerg Mkt Debt C	JEDCX	C-	(800) 480-4111	B / 7.9	4.96	-0.66	10.50 / 80	3.62 / 70	3.42 / 64	4.23	1.99
EM	JPMorgan Emerg Mkt Debt R5	JEMRX	C	(800) 480-4111	B+ / 8.9	5.39	-0.08	11.63 / 82	4.65 / 82	4.43 / 78	5.07	0.95
EM	JPMorgan Emerg Mkt Debt R6	JEMVX	C+	(800) 480-4111	B+ / 8.9	5.32	-0.14	11.66 / 82	4.70 / 83	4.46 / 78	5.19	0.85
EM	JPMorgan Emerg Mkt Debt Sel	JEMDX	C	(800) 480-4111	B+ / 8.7	5.26	-0.29	11.39 / 82	4.41 / 80	4.20 / 75	4.93	1.15
EM	JPMorgan Emg Mkts Strat Debt A	JECAX	E-	(800) 480-4111	E- / 0.1	4.77	1.67	12.48 / 84	-3.47 / 1	--	0.87	1.97
EM	JPMorgan Emg Mkts Strat Debt C	JECCX	E-	(800) 480-4111	E- / 0.1	4.60	1.45	11.97 / 83	-3.96 / 0	--	0.93	2.49
EM	JPMorgan Emg Mkts Strat Debt R2	JECZX	E-	(800) 480-4111	E- / 0.2	4.72	1.60	12.35 / 84	-3.71 / 1	--	0.96	2.26
EM	JPMorgan Emg Mkts Strat Debt R5	JECRX	E-	(800) 480-4111	E / 0.3	4.98	1.91	13.04 / 85	-3.04 / 1	--	1.16	1.55
EM	JPMorgan Emg Mkts Strat Debt R6	JECUX	E-	(800) 480-4111	E / 0.3	4.99	1.93	13.04 / 85	-3.02 / 1	--	1.17	1.03
EM	JPMorgan Emg Mkts Strat Debt Sel	JECSX	E-	(800) 480-4111	E / 0.3	4.94	1.86	12.76 / 85	-3.23 / 1	--	1.10	1.27
MMT	JPMorgan Federal MM Agency	VFIXX	C-	(800) 480-4111	D- / 1.0	0.08	0.13	0.20 / 26	0.08 / 12	0.05 / 11	0.20	N/A
MMT	JPMorgan Federal MM Inst	JFMXX	C-	(800) 480-4111	D- / 1.1	0.09	0.15	0.25 / 28	0.10 / 13	0.06 / 12	0.25	N/A
MMT	JPMorgan Federal MM Morgan	VFVXX	U	(800) 480-4111	U /	0.01	0.01	0.02 / 19	0.01 / 6	0.01 / 6	0.02	N/A
MMT	JPMorgan Federal MM Prem	VFPXX	D+	(800) 480-4111	E+ / 0.7	0.04	0.04	0.04 / 20	0.02 / 7	0.02 / 8	0.04	N/A
MMT	JPMorgan Federal MM Res	JFRXX	U	(800) 480-4111	U /	--	--	--	--	--	0.01	N/A
LP	JPMorgan Floating Rate Income A	JPHAX	C	(800) 480-4111	C+ / 5.8	2.02	3.25	11.56 / 82	1.94 / 42	3.61 / 67	4.03	1.23
LP	JPMorgan Floating Rate Income C	JPHCX	C	(800) 480-4111	C+ / 5.9	1.91	3.00	11.03 / 81	1.42 / 33	3.06 / 59	3.63	1.74
LP	JPMorgan Floating Rate Income R6	JPHRX	B-	(800) 480-4111	B- / 7.0	2.10	3.42	11.94 / 83	2.25 / 47	--	4.45	0.67
LP	JPMorgan Floating Rate Income Sel	JPHSX	B-	(800) 480-4111	C+ / 6.9	2.09	3.37	11.82 / 83	2.18 / 46	3.85 / 70	4.35	0.92
GL	JPMorgan Global Bond Opptys A	GBOAX	C+	(800) 480-4111	C+ / 6.9	3.51	1.64	10.57 / 80	3.52 / 69	--	4.36	1.28
GL	JPMorgan Global Bond Opptys C	GBOCX	B-	(800) 480-4111	B- / 7.4	3.32	1.35	10.05 / 79	3.09 / 62	--	4.14	1.77
GL	JPMorgan Global Bond Opptys R6	GBONX	B+	(800) 480-4111	B+ / 8.3	3.61	1.74	10.97 / 81	3.95 / 75	--	4.90	0.70
GL	JPMorgan Global Bond Opptys Select	GBOSX	B+	(800) 480-4111	B / 8.1	3.47	1.67	10.72 / 81	3.77 / 72	--	4.77	0.96
* USS	JPMorgan Government Bond A	OGGAX	E+	(800) 480-4111	D / 1.8	0.54	-2.32	-0.57 / 9	1.92 / 42	1.35 / 32	2.03	1.14
USS	JPMorgan Government Bond C	OGVCX	D-	(800) 480-4111	D / 2.1	0.29	-2.74	-1.36 / 2	1.18 / 30	0.61 / 23	1.40	1.53

● Denotes fund is closed to new investors
* Denotes fund is included in Section II

www.thestreetratings.com

RISK			NET ASSETS		ASSET							FUND MANAGER		MINIMUM		LOADS	
Risk Rating/Pts	3 Yr Avg Standard Deviation	Avg Dura-tion	NAV As of 2/28/17	Total $(Mil)	Cash %	Gov. Bond %	Muni. Bond %	Corp. Bond %	Other %	Portfolio Turnover Ratio	Avg Coupon Rate	Manager Quality Pct	Manager Tenure (Years)	Initial Purch. $	Additional Purch. $	Front End Load	Back End Load
A+ / 9.9	N/A	N/A	1.00	7	100	0	0	0	0	0	0.1	41	N/A	1,000	25	0.0	0.0
U /	N/A	N/A	1.00	167	100	0	0	0	0	0	0.0	40	N/A	10,000,000	0	0.0	0.0
C- / 4.2	2.9	5.1	10.78	79	2	3	92	0	3	8	4.1	11	13	1,000	50	3.8	0.0
C- / 4.1	3.0	5.1	10.69	69	2	3	92	0	3	8	4.1	5	13	1,000	50	0.0	0.0
C- / 4.1	2.9	5.1	10.55	141	2	3	92	0	3	8	4.1	12	13	3,000,000	0	0.0	0.0
C- / 4.1	3.0	5.1	10.78	27	2	3	92	0	3	8	4.1	12	13	1,000,000	0	0.0	0.0
C+ / 6.7	2.8	5.5	11.55	2,571	0	27	0	25	48	22	2.8	29	2	1,000	50	3.8	0.0
C+ / 6.6	2.8	5.5	11.63	915	0	27	0	25	48	22	2.8	13	2	1,000	50	0.0	0.0
C+ / 6.7	2.8	5.5	11.54	113	0	27	0	25	48	22	2.8	23	2	0	0	0.0	0.0
C+ / 6.7	2.8	5.5	11.53	437	0	27	0	25	48	22	2.8	47	2	0	0	0.0	0.0
C+ / 6.8	2.8	5.5	11.56	11,482	0	27	0	25	48	22	2.8	52	2	15,000,000	0	0.0	0.0
C+ / 6.6	2.8	5.5	11.55	12,046	0	27	0	25	48	22	2.8	37	2	1,000,000	0	0.0	0.0
B- / 7.0	2.7	5.7	8.22	1,074	1	25	1	29	44	45	3.6	93	11	1,000	50	3.8	0.0
B- / 7.1	2.7	5.7	8.26	277	1	25	1	29	44	45	3.6	90	11	1,000	50	0.0	0.0
B- / 7.0	2.7	5.7	8.22	1,307	1	25	1	29	44	45	3.6	93	11	3,000,000	0	0.0	0.0
B- / 7.1	2.7	5.7	8.21	35	1	25	1	29	44	45	3.6	91	11	0	0	0.0	0.0
B- / 7.0	2.7	5.7	8.22	4,548	1	25	1	29	44	45	3.6	94	11	15,000,000	0	0.0	0.0
B- / 7.0	2.7	5.7	8.22	1,188	1	25	1	29	44	45	3.6	93	11	1,000,000	0	0.0	0.0
D+ / 2.7	4.2	N/A	9.99	165	0	0	0	0	100	74	0.0	57	4	1,000	50	3.8	0.0
D+ / 2.8	4.2	N/A	9.99	1	0	0	0	0	100	74	0.0	31	4	1,000	50	0.0	0.0
D+ / 2.7	4.2	N/A	10.01	1,740	0	0	0	0	100	74	0.0	68	4	15,000,000	0	0.0	0.0
D+ / 2.7	4.3	N/A	10.01	43	0	0	0	0	100	74	0.0	65	4	1,000,000	0	0.0	0.0
D+ / 2.3	4.7	4.9	10.37	1	0	5	0	93	2	83	5.6	97	4	1,000	50	3.8	0.0
D+ / 2.3	4.7	4.9	10.37	N/A	0	5	0	93	2	83	5.6	96	4	1,000	50	0.0	0.0
D+ / 2.3	4.7	4.9	10.37	236	0	5	0	93	2	83	5.6	98	4	15,000,000	0	0.0	0.0
D+ / 2.3	4.7	4.9	10.39	2	0	5	0	93	2	83	5.6	97	4	1,000,000	0	0.0	0.0
D- / 1.3	6.0	7.0	8.15	48	0	80	0	17	3	147	6.4	97	1	1,000	50	3.8	0.0
D- / 1.3	6.0	7.0	8.12	8	0	80	0	17	3	147	6.4	96	1	1,000	50	0.0	0.0
D- / 1.3	6.0	7.0	8.24	1	0	80	0	17	3	147	6.4	98	1	0	0	0.0	0.0
D- / 1.3	6.0	7.0	8.18	850	0	80	0	17	3	147	6.4	98	1	15,000,000	0	0.0	0.0
D- / 1.2	6.0	7.0	8.16	63	0	80	0	17	3	147	6.4	97	1	1,000,000	0	0.0	0.0
E- / 0.2	10.7	N/A	8.17	N/A	17	66	0	14	3	189	0.0	8	5	1,000	50	3.8	0.0
E- / 0.2	10.7	N/A	8.02	N/A	17	66	0	14	3	189	0.0	4	5	1,000	50	0.0	0.0
E- / 0.2	10.7	N/A	8.10	N/A	17	66	0	14	3	189	0.0	6	5	0	0	0.0	0.0
E- / 0.2	10.6	N/A	8.29	N/A	17	66	0	14	3	189	0.0	15	5	0	0	0.0	0.0
E- / 0.2	10.6	N/A	8.30	51	17	66	0	14	3	189	0.0	16	5	15,000,000	0	0.0	0.0
E- / 0.2	10.7	N/A	8.23	4	17	66	0	14	3	189	0.0	11	5	1,000,000	0	0.0	0.0
A+ / 9.9	N/A	N/A	1.00	133	100	0	0	0	0	0	0.2	44	N/A	5,000,000	0	0.0	0.0
A+ / 9.9	N/A	N/A	1.00	2,767	100	0	0	0	0	0	0.3	46	N/A	10,000,000	0	0.0	0.0
U /	N/A	N/A	1.00	53	100	0	0	0	0	0	0.0	N/A	N/A	1,000	25	0.0	0.0
A+ / 9.9	N/A	N/A	1.00	109	100	0	0	0	0	0	0.0	39	N/A	1,000,000	0	0.0	0.0
U /	N/A	N/A	1.00	N/A	100	0	0	0	0	0	0.0	N/A	N/A	10,000,000	25	0.0	0.0
C / 4.5	3.3	N/A	9.48	107	8	0	0	27	65	41	0.0	78	6	1,000	50	2.3	0.0
C / 4.4	3.3	N/A	9.45	29	8	0	0	27	65	41	0.0	68	6	1,000	50	0.0	0.0
C / 4.6	3.3	N/A	9.48	915	8	0	0	27	65	41	0.0	81	6	15,000,000	0	0.0	0.0
C / 4.5	3.3	N/A	9.48	1,075	8	0	0	27	65	41	0.0	80	6	1,000,000	0	0.0	0.0
C- / 4.1	3.5	N/A	10.13	146	2	13	0	57	28	71	0.0	94	5	1,000	50	3.8	0.0
C- / 4.2	3.4	N/A	10.09	58	2	13	0	57	28	71	0.0	93	5	1,000	50	0.0	0.0
C- / 4.1	3.5	N/A	10.15	147	2	13	0	57	28	71	0.0	95	5	15,000,000	0	0.0	0.0
C- / 4.1	3.4	N/A	10.14	1,201	2	13	0	57	28	71	0.0	95	5	1,000,000	0	0.0	0.0
C+ / 5.6	3.0	5.2	10.54	529	1	49	0	0	50	15	2.5	52	21	1,000	50	3.8	0.0
C+ / 5.6	3.0	5.2	10.50	68	1	49	0	0	50	15	2.5	20	21	1,000	50	0.0	0.0

Fund Type	Fund Name	Ticker Symbol	Overall Investment Rating	Phone	Performance Rating/Pts	3 Mo	6 Mo	1Yr / Pct	3Yr / Pct	5Yr / Pct	Dividend Yield	Expense Ratio
	99 Pct = Best							Total Return % through 2/28/17	Annualized		Incl. in Returns	
USS	JPMorgan Government Bond R2	JGBZX	D-	(800) 480-4111	D+ / 2.9	0.48	-2.44	-0.82 / 6	1.66 /37	1.11 /29	1.85	1.42
USL	JPMorgan Government Bond R6	OGGYX	U	(800) 480-4111	U /	0.65	-2.12	--	--	--	0.00	0.43
USS	JPMorgan Government Bond Sel	HLGAX	D	(800) 480-4111	C- / 3.7	0.52	-2.27	-0.38 /11	2.18 /46	1.63 /37	2.40	0.82
*COH	JPMorgan High Yield A	OHYAX	C-	(800) 480-4111	B / 8.1	4.40	4.45	18.04 /94	3.48 /68	5.76 /90	5.00	0.72
COH	JPMorgan High Yield C	OGHCX	C	(800) 480-4111	B+ / 8.6	4.41	4.33	17.53 /93	2.94 /60	5.19 /86	4.65	1.86
COH	JPMorgan High Yield R2	JHYZX	C	(800) 480-4111	B+ / 8.7	4.33	4.34	17.74 /93	3.15 /63	5.44 /88	4.94	1.83
COH	JPMorgan High Yield R5	JYHRX	C+	(800) 480-4111	A- / 9.2	4.45	4.59	18.40 /94	3.76 /72	6.03 /92	5.42	0.89
COH	JPMorgan High Yield R6	JHYUX	C+	(800) 480-4111	A- / 9.2	4.48	4.64	18.49 /94	3.81 /73	6.10 /93	5.48	0.77
COH	JPMorgan High Yield Sel	OHYFX	C+	(800) 480-4111	A- / 9.1	4.44	4.58	18.40 /94	3.68 /71	5.98 /92	5.40	1.13
COI	JPMorgan Inflation Managed Bond A	JIMAX	D	(800) 480-4111	D / 1.7	1.14	0.84	3.63 /60	0.85 /25	0.69 /23	1.55	1.15
COI	JPMorgan Inflation Managed Bond C	JIMCX	D	(800) 480-4111	D / 2.1	0.92	0.56	3.05 /57	0.21 /17	0.04 /10	1.04	1.53
COI	JPMorgan Inflation Managed Bond	JIMRX	C+	(800) 480-4111	C- / 3.6	1.19	1.04	3.95 /62	1.09 /29	0.92 /26	1.82	0.58
GEI	JPMorgan Inflation Managed Bond	JIMMX	C+	(800) 480-4111	C- / 3.8	1.21	0.98	4.05 /62	1.17 /30	0.98 /27	1.91	0.46
COI	JPMorgan Inflation Managed Bond	JRBSX	C	(800) 480-4111	C- / 3.5	1.18	0.93	3.83 /61	1.01 /28	0.84 /25	1.80	0.72
GEI	JPMorgan Intermediate T/F Bd A	JITAX	D-	(800) 480-4111	D / 1.8	1.90	-2.77	-0.78 / 6	1.81 /40	1.61 /36	2.12	0.93
GEI	JPMorgan Intermediate T/F Bd C	JITCX	D-	(800) 480-4111	D / 2.1	1.74	-3.01	-1.39 / 2	1.15 /30	0.94 /27	1.64	1.43
GEI	JPMorgan Intermediate T/F Bd Inst	JITIX	C-	(800) 480-4111	C- / 3.7	1.94	-2.64	-0.59 / 8	2.06 /44	1.86 /40	2.54	0.66
GEI	JPMorgan Intermediate T/F Bd Sel	VSITX	D+	(800) 480-4111	C- / 3.6	2.03	-2.56	-0.55 / 9	2.00 /43	1.79 /39	2.48	0.51
GEI	JPMorgan Limited Duration Bd A	ONUAX	C	(800) 480-4111	D / 1.6	0.36	0.17	1.13 /41	0.86 /25	1.98 /42	0.90	0.97
GEI	JPMorgan Limited Duration Bd C	OGUCX	C	(800) 480-4111	D / 1.7	0.24	-0.08	0.63 /35	0.34 /19	1.45 /34	0.43	1.46
GEI	JPMorgan Limited Duration Bd R6	JUSUX	B	(800) 480-4111	C- / 3.2	0.37	0.39	1.58 /45	1.29 /32	2.42 /48	1.37	0.39
GEI	JPMorgan Limited Duration Bd Sel	HLGFX	B	(800) 480-4111	D+ / 2.9	0.42	0.39	1.47 /44	1.09 /29	2.23 /45	1.16	0.65
MMT	JPMorgan Liquid Assets MM Agency	AJLXX	C	(800) 480-4111	D- / 1.5	0.20	0.30	0.45 /32	0.18 /16	0.13 /16	0.45	N/A
MMT	JPMorgan Liquid Assets MM C	OPCXX	D+	(800) 480-4111	E+ / 0.7	0.03	0.04	0.04 /20	0.02 / 8	0.02 / 8	0.04	N/A
MMT	JPMorgan Liquid Assets MM Cptl	CJLXX	C	(800) 480-4111	D / 1.6	0.22	0.34	0.53 /34	0.25 /18	0.20 /18	0.53	N/A
MMT	JPMorgan Liquid Assets MM Inst	IJLXX	C	(800) 480-4111	D- / 1.5	0.21	0.33	0.50 /33	0.22 /17	0.17 /18	0.50	N/A
MMT	JPMorgan Liquid Assets MM Inv	HLPXX	C-	(800) 480-4111	D- / 1.1	0.14	0.19	0.21 /26	0.08 /12	0.05 /11	0.21	N/A
MMT	JPMorgan Liquid Assets MM Morg	MJLXX	C-	(800) 480-4111	E+ / 0.9	0.12	0.16	0.16 /24	0.06 /11	0.04 /10	0.16	N/A
MMT	JPMorgan Liquid Assets MM Prem	PJLXX	C-	(800) 480-4111	D- / 1.2	0.15	0.21	0.26 /28	0.10 /13	0.06 /12	0.26	N/A
MMT	JPMorgan Liquid Assets MM Rsv	HPIXX	D+	(800) 480-4111	E+ / 0.8	0.09	0.12	0.12 /23	0.05 /10	0.03 / 9	0.12	N/A
GEI	JPMorgan Managed Income Instl	JMGIX	C+	(800) 480-4111	D / 2.2	0.29	0.54	1.18 /42	0.63 /22	0.60 /23	0.96	0.36
GEI	JPMorgan Managed Income Select	JMGSX	C+	(800) 480-4111	D / 2.1	0.29	0.52	1.01 /40	0.54 /21	0.51 /22	0.89	0.59
MTG	JPMorgan Mortgage Backed Sec A	OMBAX	C	(800) 480-4111	D+ / 2.9	0.50	-0.81	0.78 /37	2.39 /50	2.24 /45	2.38	1.00
MTG	JPMorgan Mortgage Backed Sec C	OBBCX	C+	(800) 480-4111	C- / 3.6	0.39	-1.07	0.22 /26	1.91 /42	1.73 /38	2.05	1.52
MTG	JPMorgan Mortgage Backed Sec R6	JMBUX	A-	(800) 480-4111	C / 5.1	0.62	-0.62	1.13 /41	2.78 /57	2.64 /52	2.96	0.47
MTG	JPMorgan Mortgage Backed Sec Sel	OMBIX	A-	(800) 480-4111	C / 4.9	0.58	-0.70	1.06 /40	2.65 /55	2.50 /49	2.80	0.73
MUN	JPMorgan Muni Income A	OTBAX	D+	(800) 480-4111	C- / 3.5	2.06	-2.48	-0.40 /11	2.42 /72	2.14 /62	2.39	1.00
MUN	JPMorgan Muni Income C	OMICX	C-	(800) 480-4111	C / 4.4	1.94	-2.77	-0.87 / 5	1.83 /58	1.56 /48	1.92	1.51
MUN	JPMorgan Muni Income Sel	HLTAX	B+	(800) 480-4111	C+ / 6.5	2.03	-2.47	-0.16 /15	2.67 /76	2.39 /68	2.74	0.73
MMF	JPMorgan Muni MM Agency	JMAXX	C	(800) 480-4111	D- / 1.5	0.12	0.24	0.33 /33	0.12 /16	0.08 /16	0.33	N/A
MMF	JPMorgan Muni MM Inst	IJMXX	C	(800) 480-4111	D- / 1.5	0.14	0.27	0.37 /34	0.13 /16	0.10 /17	0.37	N/A
MMF	JPMorgan Muni MM Morgan	MJMXX	U	(800) 480-4111	U /	--	--	--	--	--	0.08	N/A
MMF	JPMorgan Muni MM Prem	HTOXX	C-	(800) 480-4111	D- / 1.1	0.08	0.15	0.16 /28	0.06 /13	0.04 /12	0.16	N/A
MMF	JPMorgan Muni MM Rsv	OGIXX	U	(800) 480-4111	U /	--	--	--	--	--	0.04	N/A
MMF	JPMorgan Muni MM Svc	SJMXX	U	(800) 480-4111	U /	--	--	--	--	--	0.03	N/A
MMF	JPMorgan NY Mun MM Morgan	VNYXX	D+	(800) 480-4111	E+ / 0.8	0.03	0.05	0.06 /22	0.03 /10	0.02 / 9	0.06	N/A
MMF	JPMorgan NY Muni MM Svc	JNVXX	U	(800) 480-4111	U /	--	--	--	--	--	0.02	N/A
MUS	JPMorgan NY T/F Bond A	VANTX	D	(800) 480-4111	D / 1.8	1.68	-2.37	-0.72 / 7	1.61 /51	1.57 /48	2.79	0.94
MUS	JPMorgan NY T/F Bond C	JCNTX	D	(800) 480-4111	D+ / 2.4	1.55	-2.65	-1.21 / 3	0.92 /34	0.89 /33	2.25	1.45
MUS	JPMorgan NY T/F Bond Inst	JNYIX	B	(800) 480-4111	C / 4.7	1.73	-2.26	-0.50 / 9	1.85 /59	1.82 /54	3.12	0.70
MUS	JPMorgan NY T/F Bond Sel	VINTX	C+	(800) 480-4111	C / 4.3	1.59	-2.40	-0.58 / 9	1.73 /55	1.68 /51	3.03	0.54
MUI	JPMorgan OH Municipal A	ONOHX	D	(800) 480-4111	D / 2.2	1.78	-2.26	-0.59 / 8	1.85 /59	1.66 /50	2.67	0.98

● Denotes fund is closed to new investors
* Denotes fund is included in Section II

www.thestreetratings.com

RISK			NET ASSETS		ASSET								FUND MANAGER		MINIMUM		LOADS	
Risk Rating/Pts	3 Yr Avg Standard Deviation	Avg Dura-tion	NAV As of 2/28/17	Total $(Mil)	Cash %	Gov. Bond %	Muni. Bond %	Corp. Bond %	Other %	Portfolio Turnover Ratio	Avg Coupon Rate	Manager Quality Pct	Manager Tenure (Years)	Initial Purch. $	Additional Purch. $	Front End Load	Back End Load
C+ / 5.6	3.0	5.2	10.53	58	1	49	0	0	50	15	2.5	35	21	0	0	0.0	0.0
U /	N/A	5.2	10.53	70	1	49	0	0	50	15	2.5	N/A	21	15,000,000	0	0.0	0.0
C / 5.5	3.0	5.2	10.53	640	1	49	0	0	50	15	2.5	61	21	1,000,000	0	0.0	0.0
D- / 1.2	5.6	4.2	7.44	981	0	1	0	90	9	52	0.0	15	19	1,000	50	3.8	0.0
D- / 1.1	5.6	4.2	7.46	212	0	1	0	90	9	52	0.0	6	19	1,000	50	0.0	0.0
D- / 1.2	5.6	4.2	7.43	9	0	1	0	90	9	52	0.0	9	19	0	0	0.0	0.0
D- / 1.1	5.6	4.2	7.49	70	0	1	0	90	9	52	0.0	20	19	0	0	0.0	0.0
D- / 1.2	5.5	4.2	7.48	5,509	0	1	0	90	9	52	0.0	23	19	15,000,000	0	0.0	0.0
D- / 1.2	5.6	4.2	7.48	6,439	0	1	0	90	9	52	0.0	18	19	1,000,000	0	0.0	0.0
B / 7.8	2.3	3.0	10.34	27	0	29	0	33	38	27	3.1	18	7	1,000	50	3.8	0.0
B / 7.8	2.3	3.0	10.29	6	0	29	0	33	38	27	3.1	8	7	1,000	50	0.0	0.0
B / 7.8	2.3	3.0	10.39	1	0	29	0	33	38	27	3.1	25	7	0	0	0.0	0.0
B / 7.9	2.3	3.0	10.36	855	0	29	0	33	38	27	3.1	36	7	15,000,000	0	0.0	0.0
B / 7.8	2.3	3.0	10.34	563	0	29	0	33	38	27	3.1	22	7	1,000,000	0	0.0	0.0
C+ / 6.4	2.8	5.0	10.94	177	1	1	96	0	2	15	4.5	28	12	1,000	50	3.8	0.0
C+ / 6.3	2.8	5.0	10.68	63	1	1	96	0	2	15	4.5	11	12	1,000	50	0.0	0.0
C+ / 6.5	2.8	5.0	10.75	3,556	1	1	96	0	2	15	4.5	36	12	3,000,000	0	0.0	0.0
C+ / 6.3	2.9	5.0	10.78	283	1	1	96	0	2	15	4.5	33	12	1,000,000	0	0.0	0.0
A+ / 9.8	0.5	1.1	9.99	150	1	0	1	15	83	23	1.8	63	22	1,000	50	2.3	0.0
A+ / 9.8	0.5	1.1	9.88	41	1	0	1	15	83	23	1.8	37	22	1,000	50	0.0	0.0
A+ / 9.8	0.5	1.1	10.00	757	1	0	1	15	83	23	1.8	73	22	15,000,000	0	0.0	0.0
A+ / 9.8	0.5	1.1	9.99	239	1	0	1	15	83	23	1.8	70	22	1,000,000	0	0.0	0.0
A+ / 9.9	0.1	N/A	1.00	36	100	0	0	0	0	0	0.5	50	N/A	5,000,000	0	0.0	0.0
A+ / 9.9	N/A	N/A	1.00	33	100	0	0	0	0	0	0.0	39	N/A	1,000	25	0.0	0.0
A+ / 9.9	0.1	N/A	1.00	105	100	0	0	0	0	0	0.5	53	N/A	50,000,000	0	0.0	0.0
A+ / 9.9	0.1	N/A	1.00	286	100	0	0	0	0	0	0.5	51	N/A	10,000,000	0	0.0	0.0
A+ / 9.9	0.1	N/A	1.00	4	100	0	0	0	0	0	0.2	44	N/A	1,000,000	0	0.0	0.0
A+ / 9.9	N/A	N/A	1.00	144	100	0	0	0	0	0	0.2	42	N/A	1,000	25	0.0	0.0
A+ / 9.9	0.1	N/A	1.00	156	100	0	0	0	0	0	0.3	45	N/A	1,000,000	0	0.0	0.0
A+ / 9.9	N/A	N/A	1.00	8	100	0	0	0	0	0	0.1	40	N/A	10,000,000	0	0.0	0.0
A+ / 9.9	0.2	0.5	10.02	8,117	2	4	0	75	19	106	1.4	65	7	3,000,000	0	0.0	0.0
A+ / 9.9	0.2	0.5	10.02	2	2	4	0	75	19	106	1.4	62	7	1,000,000	0	0.0	0.0
B+ / 8.4	1.9	3.4	11.45	143	0	0	0	0	100	16	3.6	59	12	1,000	50	3.8	0.0
B+ / 8.4	1.8	3.4	11.15	18	0	0	0	0	100	16	3.6	35	12	1,000	50	0.0	0.0
B+ / 8.4	1.9	3.4	11.17	1,176	0	0	0	0	100	16	3.6	70	12	15,000,000	0	0.0	0.0
B+ / 8.5	1.8	3.4	11.18	1,022	0	0	0	0	100	16	3.6	68	12	1,000,000	0	0.0	0.0
C+ / 6.2	2.9	4.9	9.70	77	0	2	95	0	3	22	4.7	19	11	1,000	50	3.8	0.0
C+ / 6.0	2.9	4.9	9.61	17	0	2	95	0	3	22	4.7	8	11	1,000	50	0.0	0.0
C+ / 6.4	2.8	4.9	9.63	177	0	2	95	0	3	22	4.7	27	11	1,000,000	0	0.0	0.0
A+ / 9.9	0.1	N/A	1.00	36	100	0	0	0	0	0	0.3	47	N/A	5,000,000	0	0.0	0.0
A+ / 9.9	0.1	N/A	1.00	303	100	0	0	0	0	0	0.4	49	N/A	10,000,000	0	0.0	0.0
U /	N/A	N/A	1.00	313	100	0	0	0	0	0	0.1	42	N/A	1,000	25	0.0	0.0
A+ / 9.9	N/A	N/A	1.00	32	100	0	0	0	0	0	0.2	44	N/A	1,000,000	0	0.0	0.0
U /	N/A	N/A	1.00	N/A	100	0	0	0	0	0	0.0	40	N/A	10,000,000	0	0.0	0.0
U /	N/A	N/A	1.00	364	100	0	0	0	0	0	0.0	39	N/A	10,000,000	0	0.0	0.0
A+ / 9.9	N/A	N/A	1.00	304	100	0	0	0	0	0	0.1	40	N/A	1,000	25	0.0	0.0
U /	N/A	N/A	1.00	57	100	0	0	0	0	0	0.0	N/A	N/A	10,000,000	0	0.0	0.0
B / 7.6	2.5	4.5	6.84	148	0	0	98	0	2	11	4.7	11	12	1,000	50	3.8	0.0
B / 7.6	2.5	4.5	6.84	107	0	0	98	0	2	11	4.7	4	12	1,000	50	0.0	0.0
B / 7.6	2.5	4.5	6.87	119	0	0	98	0	2	11	4.7	16	12	3,000,000	0	0.0	0.0
B / 7.6	2.5	4.5	6.87	43	0	0	98	0	2	11	4.7	13	12	1,000,000	0	0.0	0.0
B- / 7.5	2.5	4.6	10.59	47	0	0	98	0	2	8	4.7	15	23	1,000	50	3.8	0.0

Fund Type	Fund Name	Ticker Symbol	Overall Investment Rating	Phone	Performance Rating/Pts	3 Mo	6 Mo	1Yr / Pct	3Yr / Pct	5Yr / Pct	Dividend Yield	Expense Ratio
MUI	JPMorgan OH Municipal C	JOMCX	C-	(800) 480-4111	C- / 3.1	1.74	-2.53	-1.19 / 3	1.24 /42	1.05 /36	2.13	1.49
MUI	JPMorgan OH Municipal Sel	HLOMX	B+	(800) 480-4111	C / 5.3	1.86	-2.16	-0.36 /12	2.11 /65	1.92 /57	3.03	0.74
MMT	JPMorgan Prime MM Agency	VMIXX	C	(800) 480-4111	D- / 1.5	0.19	0.32	0.48 /33	0.19 /16	0.13 /16	0.48	N/A
MMT	JPMorgan Prime MM C	JXCXX	D+	(800) 480-4111	E+ / 0.6	0.02	0.02	0.03 /20	0.02 / 8	0.01 / 6	0.03	N/A
MMT	JPMorgan Prime MM Capital	CJPXX	C	(800) 480-4111	D / 1.7	0.21	0.36	0.57 /34	0.25 /18	0.19 /18	0.57	N/A
MMT	JPMorgan Prime MM IM	JIMXX	C	(800) 480-4111	D / 1.7	0.21	0.36	0.58 /35	0.27 /18	--	0.58	N/A
MMT	JPMorgan Prime MM Inst	JINXX	C	(800) 480-4111	D / 1.6	0.20	0.35	0.54 /34	0.22 /17	0.17 /18	0.54	N/A
MMT	JPMorgan Prime MM Morgan	VMVXX	C-	(800) 480-4111	D- / 1.1	0.13	0.19	0.22 /27	0.08 /12	0.05 /11	0.22	N/A
MMT	JPMorgan Prime MM Prem	VPMXX	C-	(800) 480-4111	D- / 1.2	0.14	0.22	0.29 /29	0.11 /14	0.07 /13	0.29	N/A
MMT	JPMorgan Prime MM Rsv	JRVXX	D+	(800) 480-4111	E+ / 0.8	0.08	0.11	0.12 /23	0.05 /10	0.03 / 9	0.12	N/A
* GEI	JPMorgan Short Duration Bond A	OGLVX	D	(800) 480-4111	E / 0.4	0.29	-0.21	0.55 /34	0.43 /20	0.47 /21	0.61	0.92
GEI	JPMorgan Short Duration Bond C	OSTCX	D	(800) 480-4111	E / 0.5	0.16	-0.44	0.05 /20	-0.07 / 5	-0.02 / 5	0.13	1.41
GEI	JPMorgan Short Duration Bond R6	JSDUX	C+	(800) 480-4111	D+ / 2.6	0.50	0.13	1.15 /41	0.97 /27	0.98 /27	1.13	0.35
GEI	JPMorgan Short Duration Bond Sel	HLLVX	C+	(800) 480-4111	D / 2.2	0.35	-0.09	0.90 /39	0.71 /23	0.72 /24	0.88	0.66
COH	JPMorgan Short Duration Hi Yld A	JSDHX	C	(800) 480-4111	B- / 7.2	3.01	4.12	13.06 /85	2.84 /59	--	4.27	1.26
COH	JPMorgan Short Duration Hi Yld C	JSDCX	C	(800) 480-4111	B- / 7.2	2.89	3.78	12.54 /84	2.31 /48	--	3.91	1.89
COH	JPMorgan Short Duration Hi Yld R6	JSDRX	C+	(800) 480-4111	B / 8.2	3.00	4.21	13.51 /86	3.20 /64	--	4.75	0.70
COH	JPMorgan Short Duration Hi Yld Sel	JSDSX	C+	(800) 480-4111	B / 8.0	2.96	4.11	13.34 /86	3.07 /62	--	4.60	0.95
MUN	JPMorgan Short Term Muni Bond A	OSTAX	D-	(800) 480-4111	E / 0.4	1.48	-1.70	-0.69 / 7	0.51 /24	0.49 /24	0.93	0.87
MUN	JPMorgan Short Term Muni Bond C	STMCX	D-	(800) 480-4111	E / 0.4	1.34	-1.94	-1.27 / 3	-0.04 / 5	-0.03 / 5	0.44	1.40
MUN	JPMorgan Short Term Muni Bond Inst	JIMIX	C	(800) 480-4111	C- / 3.0	1.58	-1.45	-0.20 /14	0.97 /35	0.97 /34	1.44	0.62
MUN	JPMorgan Short Term Muni Bond Sel	PGUIX	C-	(800) 480-4111	D+ / 2.5	1.59	-1.51	-0.37 /12	0.75 /30	0.75 /29	1.27	0.47
GL	JPMorgan SmartAllocation Income A	SAIAX	D-	(800) 480-4111	D+ / 2.9	1.58	-1.75	3.46 /59	2.00 /43	--	2.24	1.98
GL	JPMorgan SmartAllocation Income C	SAICX	D-	(800) 480-4111	C- / 3.5	1.45	-2.02	2.85 /56	1.47 /35	--	1.87	3.90
GL	JPMorgan SmartAllocation Income	SAIRX	D	(800) 480-4111	C / 4.0	1.51	-1.89	3.14 /57	1.75 /39	--	2.09	4.09
GL	JPMorgan SmartAllocation Income	SIARX	C-	(800) 480-4111	C / 5.1	1.69	-1.54	3.86 /61	2.43 /51	--	2.79	3.29
GL	JPMorgan SmartAllocation Income	SINRX	C	(800) 480-4111	C / 5.3	1.70	-1.52	3.91 /62	2.50 /52	--	2.83	0.79
GL	JPMorgan SmartAllocation Income	SIASX	C-	(800) 480-4111	C / 4.8	1.61	-1.65	3.64 /60	2.24 /47	--	2.58	3.85
* GL	JPMorgan Strategic Income Opp A	JSOAX	B+	(800) 480-4111	C+ / 5.8	2.73	3.29	11.60 /82	2.34 /49	3.15 /60	3.84	1.28
GL	JPMorgan Strategic Income Opp C	JSOCX	A	(800) 480-4111	C+ / 6.4	2.61	2.96	10.97 /81	1.81 /40	2.63 /52	3.51	1.71
GL	JPMorgan Strategic Income Opp R5	JSORX	A+	(800) 480-4111	B / 7.6	2.92	3.52	12.16 /84	2.81 /58	3.63 /68	4.42	0.71
GL	JPMorgan Strategic Income Opp Sel	JSOSX	A+	(800) 480-4111	B- / 7.3	2.79	3.34	11.86 /83	2.58 /53	3.39 /64	4.23	0.92
GEN	JPMorgan Tax Aware High Inc A	JTIAX	C-	(800) 480-4111	C- / 3.4	1.87	-2.04	1.07 /40	2.75 /57	2.55 /50	2.57	1.18
GEN	JPMorgan Tax Aware High Inc C	JTICX	C+	(800) 480-4111	C- / 4.1	1.76	-2.28	0.58 /35	2.24 /47	2.04 /43	2.18	1.70
GEN	JPMorgan Tax Aware High Inc Sel	JTISX	B	(800) 480-4111	C / 5.1	1.90	-2.00	1.17 /41	2.85 /59	2.67 /52	2.77	0.93
MUN	JPMorgan Tax Aware Inc Opps A	JTAAX	D	(800) 480-4111	E+ / 0.6	1.42	0.01	1.74 /54	0.77 /30	1.00 /35	1.47	1.13
MUN	JPMorgan Tax Aware Inc Opps C	JTACX	C	(800) 480-4111	D / 1.9	1.31	-0.27	1.23 /48	0.14 /17	0.34 /22	0.93	1.65
MUN	JPMorgan Tax Aware Inc Opps Sel	JTASX	B+	(800) 480-4111	C- / 3.8	1.49	0.10	1.89 /56	0.88 /33	1.10 /37	1.68	0.89
MUI	JPMorgan Tax Aware Real Return A	TXRAX	D-	(800) 480-4111	D- / 1.3	2.17	0.24	2.78 /63	0.66 /28	0.46 /24	2.45	0.97
MUI	JPMorgan Tax Aware Real Return C	TXRCX	D	(800) 480-4111	D+ / 2.3	2.15	0.07	2.28 /60	0.04 /10	-0.18 / 4	1.95	1.49
MUI	JPMorgan Tax Aware Real Return	TXRIX	C+	(800) 480-4111	C / 4.5	2.33	0.46	3.14 /66	0.91 /33	0.71 /29	2.78	0.56
MUN	JPMorgan Tax Aware Real Return R6	TXRRX	B-	(800) 480-4111	C / 4.7	2.25	0.41	3.13 /66	1.01 /36	--	2.88	0.45
MUI	JPMorgan Tax Aware Real Return	TXRSX	C+	(800) 480-4111	C- / 4.1	2.23	0.34	2.93 /65	0.77 /30	0.55 /25	2.69	0.73
MUN	JPMorgan Tax Aware Real Return	JTARX	C-	(800) 480-4111	C / 4.9	2.75	0.83	3.02 /65	1.03 /36	0.67 /28	2.68	1.01
MUN	JPMorgan Tax Free Bond A	PMBAX	D+	(800) 480-4111	C / 5.3	1.81	-3.82	-0.03 /17	3.38 /86	2.99 /80	3.11	0.97
MUN	JPMorgan Tax Free Bond C	JTFCX	C-	(800) 480-4111	C+ / 6.1	1.77	-4.07	-0.66 / 7	2.71 /77	2.30 /66	2.60	1.47
MUN	JPMorgan Tax Free Bond Sel	PRBIX	B-	(800) 480-4111	B / 7.6	1.87	-3.74	0.09 /24	3.55 /88	3.16 /83	3.44	0.71
MMF	JPMorgan Tax Free MM Agency	VTIXX	C	(800) 480-4111	D- / 1.4	0.11	0.21	0.27 /32	0.10 /15	0.07 /16	0.27	N/A
MMF	JPMorgan Tax Free MM Direct	JTDXX	C-	(800) 480-4111	D- / 1.3	0.10	0.19	0.24 /31	0.09 /15	0.06 /15	0.24	N/A
MMF	JPMorgan Tax Free MM Inst	JTFXX	C	(800) 480-4111	D- / 1.5	0.12	0.23	0.32 /33	0.12 /16	0.08 /16	0.32	N/A
MMF	JPMorgan Tax Free MM Morgan	VTMXX	D+	(800) 480-4111	E+ / 0.8	0.03	0.05	0.05 /22	0.03 /10	0.02 / 9	0.05	N/A
MMF	JPMorgan Tax Free MM Prem	VXPXX	C-	(800) 480-4111	D- / 1.0	0.06	0.12	0.12 /25	0.05 /12	0.04 /12	0.12	N/A

| RISK | | | NET ASSETS | | ASSET | | | | | | | FUND MANAGER | | MINIMUM | | LOADS | |
Risk Rating/Pts	3 Yr Avg Standard Deviation	Avg Duration	NAV As of 2/28/17	Total $(Mil)	Cash %	Gov. Bond %	Muni. Bond %	Corp. Bond %	Other %	Portfolio Turnover Ratio	Avg Coupon Rate	Manager Quality Pct	Manager Tenure (Years)	Initial Purch. $	Additional Purch. $	Front End Load	Back End Load
B- /7.5	2.6	4.6	10.65	27	0	0	98	0	2	8	4.7	6	23	1,000	50	0.0	0.0
B- /7.4	2.6	4.6	10.52	47	0	0	98	0	2	8	4.7	19	23	1,000,000	0	0.0	0.0
A+ /9.9	0.1	N/A	1.00	1,003	100	0	0	0	0	0	0.5	50	N/A	5,000,000	0	0.0	0.0
A+ /9.9	N/A	N/A	1.00	4	100	0	0	0	0	0	0.0	38	N/A	1,000	25	0.0	0.0
A+ /9.9	0.1	N/A	1.00	20,087	100	0	0	0	0	0	0.6	53	N/A	50,000,000	0	0.0	0.0
A+ /9.9	0.1	N/A	1.00	2,011	100	0	0	0	0	0	0.6	54	N/A	50,000,000	0	0.0	0.0
A+ /9.9	0.1	N/A	1.00	6,081	100	0	0	0	0	0	0.5	52	N/A	10,000,000	0	0.0	0.0
A+ /9.9	N/A	N/A	1.00	534	100	0	0	0	0	0	0.2	44	N/A	1,000	25	0.0	0.0
A+ /9.9	0.1	N/A	1.00	687	100	0	0	0	0	0	0.3	46	N/A	1,000,000	0	0.0	0.0
A+ /9.9	N/A	N/A	1.00	99	100	0	0	0	0	0	0.1	40	N/A	10,000,000	0	0.0	0.0
A /9.5	0.8	1.8	10.81	536	0	55	0	23	22	45	2.1	30	11	1,000	50	2.3	0.0
A /9.5	0.8	1.8	10.88	90	0	55	0	23	22	45	2.1	16	11	1,000	50	0.0	0.0
A /9.5	0.8	1.8	10.83	2,564	0	55	0	23	22	45	2.1	58	11	15,000,000	0	0.0	0.0
A+ /9.6	0.8	1.8	10.83	2,863	0	55	0	23	22	45	2.1	47	11	1,000,000	0	0.0	0.0
D+ /2.9	3.6	N/A	9.59	4	0	0	0	82	18	42	0.0	47	4	1,000	50	2.3	0.0
D+ /2.9	3.6	N/A	9.57	1	0	0	0	82	18	42	0.0	23	4	1,000	50	0.0	0.0
D+ /2.9	3.6	N/A	9.58	35	0	0	0	82	18	42	0.0	61	4	15,000,000	0	0.0	0.0
C- /3.0	3.6	N/A	9.58	125	0	0	0	82	18	42	0.0	58	4	1,000,000	0	0.0	0.0
B+ /8.4	1.9	3.5	10.48	31	0	0	99	0	1	39	4.1	6	11	1,000	50	2.3	0.0
B+ /8.4	1.9	3.5	10.56	14	0	0	99	0	1	39	4.1	3	11	1,000	50	0.0	0.0
B+ /8.4	1.9	3.5	10.53	1,889	0	0	99	0	1	39	4.1	11	11	3,000,000	0	0.0	0.0
B+ /8.4	1.9	3.5	10.51	144	0	0	99	0	1	39	4.1	8	11	1,000,000	0	0.0	0.0
C /5.1	3.1	N/A	14.69	1	41	11	0	31	17	16	0.0	90	5	500	50	3.8	0.0
C /5.2	3.1	N/A	14.65	N/A	41	11	0	31	17	16	0.0	86	5	500	50	0.0	0.0
C /5.3	3.1	N/A	14.68	N/A	41	11	0	31	17	16	0.0	88	5	0	0	0.0	0.0
C /5.1	3.1	N/A	14.71	N/A	41	11	0	31	17	16	0.0	92	5	0	0	0.0	0.0
C /5.3	3.1	N/A	14.72	188	41	11	0	31	17	16	0.0	92	5	15,000,000	0	0.0	0.0
C /5.3	3.1	N/A	14.75	N/A	41	11	0	31	17	16	0.0	91	5	1,000,000	0	0.0	0.0
B- /7.1	2.7	1.7	11.69	1,531	2	1	0	70	27	51	4.6	89	9	1,000	50	3.8	0.0
B- /7.0	2.7	1.7	11.65	1,126	2	1	0	70	27	51	4.6	85	9	1,000	50	0.0	0.0
B- /7.0	2.7	1.7	11.73	570	2	1	0	70	27	51	4.6	91	9	0	0	0.0	0.0
B- /7.1	2.7	1.7	11.71	9,191	2	1	0	70	27	51	4.6	90	9	1,000,000	0	0.0	0.0
B- /7.4	2.6	4.7	10.82	44	0	0	82	2	16	19	4.6	69	10	1,000	50	3.8	0.0
B- /7.4	2.6	4.7	10.80	21	0	0	82	2	16	19	4.6	54	10	1,000	50	0.0	0.0
B- /7.4	2.6	4.7	10.82	36	0	0	82	2	16	19	4.6	71	10	1,000,000	0	0.0	0.0
A- /9.2	1.0	2.1	10.14	66	0	0	85	6	9	133	3.0	37	6	1,000	50	3.8	0.0
A- /9.2	1.0	2.1	10.03	10	0	0	85	6	9	133	3.0	18	6	1,000	50	0.0	0.0
A- /9.2	1.0	2.1	10.14	166	0	0	85	6	9	133	3.0	48	6	1,000,000	0	0.0	0.0
B- /7.3	2.6	3.3	9.52	52	0	0	98	0	2	7	4.4	11	12	1,000	50	3.8	0.0
B- /7.1	2.7	3.3	9.50	30	0	0	98	0	2	7	4.4	5	12	1,000	50	0.0	0.0
B- /7.1	2.7	3.3	9.54	1,098	0	0	98	0	2	7	4.4	15	12	3,000,000	0	0.0	0.0
B- /7.3	2.6	3.3	9.54	115	0	0	98	0	2	7	4.4	18	12	15,000,000	0	0.0	0.0
B- /7.3	2.6	3.3	9.53	121	0	0	98	0	2	7	4.4	13	12	1,000,000	0	0.0	0.0
C /5.5	3.0	N/A	10.00	10	1	2	94	0	3	32	0.0	13	10	0	0	0.0	0.0
C- /4.1	3.5	6.6	11.93	149	1	3	92	1	3	94	4.3	29	12	1,000	50	3.8	0.0
C- /4.0	3.5	6.6	11.84	32	1	3	92	1	3	94	4.3	12	12	1,000	50	0.0	0.0
C- /4.0	3.5	6.6	11.88	142	1	3	92	1	3	94	4.3	33	12	1,000,000	0	0.0	0.0
A+ /9.9	N/A	N/A	1.00	438	100	0	0	0	0	0	0.3	47	N/A	5,000,000	0	0.0	0.0
A+ /9.9	N/A	N/A	1.00	N/A	100	0	0	0	0	0	0.2	N/A	N/A	0	0	0.0	0.0
A+ /9.9	0.1	N/A	1.00	10,567	100	0	0	0	0	0	0.3	47	N/A	10,000,000	0	0.0	0.0
A+ /9.9	N/A	N/A	1.00	12	100	0	0	0	0	0	0.1	40	N/A	1,000	25	0.0	0.0
A+ /9.9	N/A	N/A	1.00	1,713	100	0	0	0	0	0	0.1	43	N/A	1,000,000	0	0.0	0.0

Fund Type	Fund Name	Ticker Symbol	Overall Investment Rating	Phone	Performance Rating/Pts	3 Mo	6 Mo	1Yr / Pct	3Yr / Pct	5Yr / Pct	Dividend Yield	Expense Ratio
MMF	JPMorgan Tax Free MM Rsv	RTJXX	U	(800) 480-4111	U /	--	--	--	--	--	0.02	N/A
GEI	JPMorgan Total Return A	JMTAX	C	(800) 480-4111	C / 4.4	1.98	-1.02	5.03 /67	2.77 /57	3.36 /63	2.46	1.11
GEI	JPMorgan Total Return C	JMTCX	C+	(800) 480-4111	C / 4.8	1.82	-1.36	4.35 /64	2.10 /45	2.66 /52	1.90	1.61
COI	JPMorgan Total Return R2	JMTTX	U	(800) 480-4111	U /	1.85	-1.28	4.50 /65	--	--	2.05	1.46
GEI	JPMorgan Total Return R5	JMTRX	B+	(800) 480-4111	C+ / 6.3	2.02	-0.94	5.21 /68	2.99 /61	3.56 /67	2.74	0.68
COI	JPMorgan Total Return R6	JMTIX	U	(800) 480-4111	U /	1.94	-1.00	5.17 /67	--	--	2.80	0.52
GEI	JPMorgan Total Return Sel	JMTSX	B+	(800) 480-4111	C+ / 6.1	2.00	-0.98	5.12 /67	2.86 /59	3.44 /64	2.65	0.81
US	JPMorgan Treasury and Agency A	OTABX	D-	(800) 480-4111	E / 0.3	0.13	-0.66	-0.27 /13	0.20 /16	0.12 /16	0.52	1.03
US	JPMorgan Treasury and Agency Sel	OGTFX	C-	(800) 480-4111	D / 1.7	0.31	-0.52	-0.03 /17	0.46 /20	0.38 /20	0.76	0.77
MUN	JPMorgan Ultra-Short Municipal A	USMSX	U	(800) 480-4111	U /	0.47	0.36	--	--	--	0.00	0.92
MUN	JPMorgan Ultra-Short Municipal Sel	USMTX	U	(800) 480-4111	U /	0.50	0.43	--	--	--	0.00	0.65
GL	JPMorgan Unconstrained Debt A	JSIAX	B-	(800) 480-4111	C- / 4.1	2.17	1.10	6.76 /72	2.06 /44	2.71 /53	2.83	1.15
GL	JPMorgan Unconstrained Debt C	JINCX	B+	(800) 480-4111	C / 4.9	2.06	0.97	6.32 /71	1.57 /36	2.21 /45	2.51	1.67
GL	JPMorgan Unconstrained Debt R2	JISZX	A-	(800) 480-4111	C / 5.2	2.09	1.05	6.51 /72	1.79 /39	2.45 /49	2.70	2.47
GL	JPMorgan Unconstrained Debt R5	JSIRX	A+	(800) 480-4111	C+ / 6.4	2.25	1.40	7.32 /73	2.51 /52	3.16 /60	3.37	0.66
GL	JPMorgan Unconstrained Debt R6	JSIMX	A+	(800) 480-4111	C+ / 6.5	2.27	1.43	7.36 /73	2.57 /53	3.23 /61	3.41	0.60
GL	JPMorgan Unconstrained Debt Select	JSISX	A+	(800) 480-4111	C+ / 6.1	2.24	1.35	7.16 /73	2.35 /49	2.98 /57	3.21	0.85
MMT	JPMorgan US Govt MM Agency	OGAXX	C-	(800) 480-4111	D- / 1.0	0.09	0.13	0.22 /27	0.08 /12	0.05 /11	0.22	N/A
MMT	JPMorgan US Govt MM Cptl	OGVXX	C-	(800) 480-4111	D- / 1.3	0.11	0.19	0.33 /30	0.13 /14	0.08 /14	0.33	N/A
MMT	JPMorgan US Govt MM Direct	JGDXX	C-	(800) 480-4111	D- / 1.0	0.08	0.12	0.19 /26	0.07 /11	0.05 /11	0.19	N/A
MMT	JPMorgan US Govt MM Eagle	JJGXX	U	(800) 480-4111	U /	--	--	--	--	--	0.01	N/A
MMT	JPMorgan US Govt MM IM	MGMXX	C-	(800) 480-4111	D- / 1.3	0.11	0.19	0.33 /30	0.13 /14	--	0.33	N/A
MMT	JPMorgan US Govt MM Inst	IJGXX	C-	(800) 480-4111	D- / 1.2	0.10	0.17	0.30 /29	0.11 /14	0.07 /13	0.30	N/A
MMT	JPMorgan US Govt MM Investor	JGMXX	D+	(800) 480-4111	E+ / 0.6	0.03	0.03	0.03 /20	0.02 / 8	0.01 / 6	0.03	N/A
MMT	JPMorgan US Govt MM Morgan	MJGXX	U	(800) 480-4111	U /	0.01	0.01	0.02 /19	0.01 / 6	0.01 / 6	0.02	N/A
MMT	JPMorgan US Govt MM Prem	OGSXX	D+	(800) 480-4111	E+ / 0.7	0.04	0.05	0.06 /21	0.03 / 8	0.02 / 8	0.06	N/A
MMT	JPMorgan US Govt MM Rsv	RJGXX	U	(800) 480-4111	U /	--	--	--	--	--	0.01	N/A
MMT	JPMorgan US Govt MM Svc	SJGXX	U	(800) 480-4111	U /	--	--	--	--	--	0.01	N/A
MMT	JPMorgan US Treas Plus MM Agency	AJTXX	C-	(800) 480-4111	D- / 1.0	0.08	0.12	0.18 /25	0.07 /11	0.04 /10	0.18	N/A
MMT	JPMorgan US Treas Plus MM Direct	JUDXX	D+	(800) 480-4111	E+ / 0.8	0.07	0.10	0.14 /24	0.05 /10	0.03 / 9	0.14	N/A
MMT	JPMorgan US Treas Plus MM IM	MJPXX	C-	(800) 480-4111	D- / 1.2	0.10	0.16	0.28 /28	0.11 /14	--	0.28	N/A
MMT	JPMorgan US Treas Plus MM Inst	IJTXX	C-	(800) 480-4111	D- / 1.1	0.09	0.14	0.23 /27	0.09 /12	0.05 /11	0.23	N/A
MMT	JPMorgan US Treas Plus MM Inv	HGOXX	D+	(800) 480-4111	E+ / 0.6	0.02	0.02	0.02 /19	0.01 / 6	--	0.02	N/A
MMT	JPMorgan US Treas Plus MM Prem	PJTXX	D+	(800) 480-4111	E+ / 0.6	0.03	0.03	0.03 /20	0.01 / 6	0.01 / 6	0.03	N/A
MUS	Kansas Municipal	KSMUX	B-	(800) 601-5593	C / 4.7	1.76	-2.42	0.10 /24	2.57 /75	2.25 /65	2.77	1.18
COI	Knights of Columbus Core Bond Inst	KCCIX	U	(844) 523-8637	U /	1.28	-1.43	2.29 /51	--	--	2.38	1.19
COI	Knights of Columbus Core Bond Inv	KCCVX	U	(844) 523-8637	U /	1.18	-1.51	--	--	--	0.00	N/A
COI	Knights of Columbus Core Bond S	KCCSX	U	(844) 523-8637	U /	1.27	-1.44	2.25 /51	--	--	2.35	1.31
COI	Knights of Columbus Ltd Dur Bd Inst	KCLIX	U	(844) 523-8637	U /	0.53	0.25	1.42 /44	--	--	1.21	1.22
COI	Knights of Columbus Ltd Dur Bd Inv	KCLVX	U	(844) 523-8637	U /	0.34	-0.03	--	--	--	0.00	N/A
COI	Knights of Columbus Ltd Dur Bd S	KCLSX	U	(844) 523-8637	U /	0.42	0.13	1.28 /43	--	--	1.17	1.48
*GEI	KP Fixed Income Instl	KPFIX	A-	(855) 457-3637	C+ / 5.7	1.41	-1.13	3.55 /60	2.84 /59	--	2.24	0.35
COI	KS 529 LearningQuest ESP Dvsd Bd		D-	(800) 345-6488	D / 2.0	0.95	-2.50	1.37 /43	2.01 /43	1.70 /38	0.00	1.03
COI	KS 529 LearningQuest ESP Dvsd Bd		D-	(800) 345-6488	D+ / 2.7	0.88	-2.68	0.73 /37	1.29 /32	0.95 /27	0.00	1.78
GL	KS 529 LearningQuest ESP If Pr Bd		D-	(800) 345-6488	E- / 0.2	1.05	1.20	2.74 /55	-0.10 / 5	-0.32 / 3	0.00	0.96
GL	KS 529 LearningQuest ESP If Pr Bd		D-	(800) 345-6488	E / 0.3	0.80	0.64	1.95 /48	-0.89 / 3	-1.08 / 2	0.00	1.71
MMT	KS 529 LearningQuest ESP MM Port		D+	(800) 345-6488	E+ / 0.7	0.03	0.05	0.05 /21	0.02 / 8	0.02 / 8	0.05	N/A
GL	KS 529 LearningQuest ESP ShTm A		D-	(800) 345-6488	E- / 0.2	0.44	-1.15	0.29 /28	0.24 /17	0.15 /17	0.00	0.97
GL	KS 529 LearningQuest ESP ShTm C		D-	(800) 345-6488	E / 0.3	0.16	-1.43	-0.48 /10	-0.53 / 3	-0.60 / 3	0.00	1.72
GL	KS 529 LearningQuest ESP ShTm		C-	(800) 345-6488	D / 1.9	0.41	-0.93	0.81 /37	0.54 /21	0.46 /21	0.00	0.55
COI	KS 529 LearningQuest ESP Tot Bd		D	(800) 345-6488	C / 4.4	1.13	-2.43	1.26 /42	2.40 /50	1.98 /42	0.00	0.25
GL	KS 529 Schwab CSP Short-Term		C-	(800) 345-6488	D / 2.0	0.51	-0.86	1.02 /40	0.56 /21	0.65 /23	0.00	0.68

RISK			NET ASSETS		ASSET							FUND MANAGER		MINIMUM		LOADS	
Risk Rating/Pts	3 Yr Avg Standard Deviation	Avg Dura-tion	NAV As of 2/28/17	Total $(Mil)	Cash %	Gov. Bond %	Muni. Bond %	Corp. Bond %	Other %	Portfolio Turnover Ratio	Avg Coupon Rate	Manager Quality Pct	Manager Tenure (Years)	Initial Purch. $	Additional Purch. $	Front End Load	Back End Load
U /	N/A	N/A	1.00	2,650	100	0	0	0	0	0	0.0	39	N/A	10,000,000	0	0.0	0.0
C+ / 6.6	2.8	5.3	9.90	185	2	8	0	61	29	418	3.8	64	9	1,000	50	3.8	0.0
C+ / 6.3	2.9	5.3	9.87	40	2	8	0	61	29	418	3.8	33	9	1,000	50	0.0	0.0
U /	N/A	5.3	9.91	1	2	8	0	61	29	418	3.8	N/A	9	0	0	0.0	0.0
C+ / 6.6	2.8	5.3	9.92	11	2	8	0	61	29	418	3.8	70	9	0	0	0.0	0.0
U /	N/A	5.3	9.91	24	2	8	0	61	29	418	3.8	N/A	9	15,000,000	0	0.0	0.0
C+ / 6.5	2.8	5.3	9.92	300	2	8	0	61	29	418	3.8	66	9	1,000,000	0	0.0	0.0
A- / 9.2	1.1	2.2	9.34	20	0	90	0	9	1	24	1.8	26	N/A	1,000	50	2.3	0.0
A- / 9.1	1.1	2.2	9.34	71	0	90	0	9	1	24	1.8	34	N/A	1,000,000	0	0.0	0.0
U /	N/A	0.7	10.02	1	0	0	0	0	100	0	3.0	N/A	1	1,000	50	2.3	0.0
U /	N/A	0.7	10.02	31	0	0	0	0	100	0	3.0	N/A	1	1,000,000	0	0.0	0.0
B / 8.1	2.1	3.8	9.89	62	5	4	0	42	49	181	4.6	88	7	1,000	50	3.8	0.0
B / 8.0	2.2	3.8	9.84	9	5	4	0	42	49	181	4.6	84	7	1,000	50	0.0	0.0
B / 8.1	2.1	3.8	9.88	N/A	5	4	0	42	49	181	4.6	86	7	0	0	0.0	0.0
B / 8.0	2.1	3.8	9.92	3	5	4	0	42	49	181	4.6	90	7	0	0	0.0	0.0
B / 8.0	2.1	3.8	9.92	389	5	4	0	42	49	181	4.6	90	7	15,000,000	0	0.0	0.0
B / 8.1	2.1	3.8	9.91	2,272	5	4	0	42	49	181	4.6	89	7	1,000,000	0	0.0	0.0
A+ / 9.9	N/A	N/A	1.00	12,888	100	0	0	0	0	0	0.2	45	N/A	5,000,000	0	0.0	0.0
A+ / 9.9	N/A	N/A	1.00	86,186	100	0	0	0	0	0	0.3	47	N/A	50,000,000	0	0.0	0.0
A+ / 9.9	N/A	N/A	1.00	194	100	0	0	0	0	0	0.2	44	N/A	0	0	0.0	0.0
U /	N/A	N/A	1.00	1,215	100	0	0	0	0	0	0.0	N/A	N/A	1,000	0	0.0	0.0
A+ / 9.9	N/A	N/A	1.00	590	100	0	0	0	0	0	0.3	47	N/A	50,000,000	0	0.0	0.0
A+ / 9.9	N/A	N/A	1.00	36,865	100	0	0	0	0	0	0.3	47	N/A	10,000,000	0	0.0	0.0
A+ / 9.9	N/A	N/A	1.00	920	100	0	0	0	0	0	0.0	38	N/A	1,000,000	0	0.0	0.0
U /	N/A	N/A	1.00	2,460	100	0	0	0	0	0	0.0	N/A	N/A	1,000	25	0.0	0.0
A+ / 9.9	N/A	N/A	1.00	7,765	100	0	0	0	0	0	0.1	39	N/A	1,000,000	0	0.0	0.0
U /	N/A	N/A	1.00	120	100	0	0	0	0	0	0.0	N/A	N/A	10,000,000	0	0.0	0.0
U /	N/A	N/A	1.00	2,439	100	0	0	0	0	0	0.0	N/A	N/A	10,000,000	0	0.0	0.0
A+ / 9.9	N/A	N/A	1.00	838	100	0	0	0	0	0	0.2	43	N/A	5,000,000	0	0.0	0.0
A+ / 9.9	N/A	N/A	1.00	6	100	0	0	0	0	0	0.1	42	N/A	0	0	0.0	0.0
A+ / 9.9	N/A	N/A	1.00	7,448	100	0	0	0	0	0	0.3	N/A	N/A	50,000,000	0	0.0	0.0
A+ / 9.9	N/A	N/A	1.00	14,811	100	0	0	0	0	0	0.2	45	N/A	10,000,000	0	0.0	0.0
A+ / 9.9	N/A	N/A	1.00	71	100	0	0	0	0	0	0.0	37	N/A	1,000,000	0	0.0	0.0
A+ / 9.9	N/A	N/A	1.00	249	100	0	0	0	0	0	0.0	38	N/A	1,000,000	0	0.0	0.0
B- / 7.4	2.6	4.3	10.69	60	3	0	96	0	1	12	4.8	34	21	1,000	50	2.5	0.0
U /	N/A	6.4	9.93	53	0	0	0	0	100	55	0.0	N/A	2	25,000	250	0.0	2.0
U /	N/A	6.4	9.93	N/A	0	0	0	0	100	55	0.0	N/A	2	1,000	0	0.0	2.0
U /	N/A	6.4	9.93	N/A	0	0	0	0	100	55	0.0	N/A	2	100,000	0	0.0	2.0
U /	N/A	2.5	9.98	65	0	0	0	0	100	76	0.0	N/A	2	25,000	250	0.0	2.0
U /	N/A	2.5	9.97	N/A	0	0	0	0	100	76	0.0	N/A	2	1,000	0	0.0	2.0
U /	N/A	2.5	9.98	N/A	0	0	0	0	100	76	0.0	N/A	2	100,000	0	0.0	2.0
B- / 7.5	2.5	N/A	9.96	1,296	10	42	0	22	26	533	0.0	68	3	0	0	0.0	0.0
C+ / 6.1	2.9	N/A	7.42	1	0	33	1	29	37	0	0.0	22	N/A	100	50	4.5	0.0
C+ / 6.2	2.9	N/A	6.90	2	0	33	1	29	37	0	0.0	8	N/A	100	50	0.0	0.0
B+ / 8.3	2.0	N/A	6.76	N/A	0	82	0	11	7	0	0.0	54	N/A	100	50	4.5	0.0
B / 8.2	2.1	N/A	6.28	N/A	0	82	0	11	7	0	0.0	19	N/A	100	50	0.0	0.0
A+ / 9.9	N/A	N/A	1.00	58	100	0	0	0	0	0	0.1	39	14	500	50	0.0	0.0
A- / 9.1	1.2	N/A	6.85	22	0	72	2	13	13	0	0.0	63	N/A	500	50	4.5	0.0
A- / 9.0	1.2	N/A	6.22	11	0	72	2	13	13	0	0.0	28	N/A	500	50	0.0	0.0
A- / 9.1	1.2	N/A	7.43	287	0	72	2	15	11	0	0.0	71	N/A	500	50	0.0	0.0
C / 4.9	3.1	N/A	8.02	15	3	45	1	27	24	0	0.0	29	N/A	500	50	0.0	0.0
A- / 9.1	1.1	N/A	13.83	177	0	0	0	0	100	0	0.0	72	N/A	1,000	50	0.0	0.0

						PERFORMANCE					Incl. in Returns	
							Total Return % through 2/28/17					
				Overall		Perfor-				Annualized		Dividend	Expense
Fund Type	Fund Name	Ticker Symbol	Investment Rating	Phone		mance Rating/Pts	3 Mo	6 Mo	1Yr / Pct	3Yr / Pct	5Yr / Pct	Yield	Ratio
GL	Laudus Mondrian Global Govt Fxd Inc	LMGDX	E-	(800) 407-0256	E- / 0.2	2.42	-5.94	2.54 /53	-1.57 / 2	--	0.00	2.23
GL	Laudus Mondrian Intl Govt Fxd Inc	LIFNX	E-	(800) 407-0256	E- / 0.0	0.82	-9.05	-2.67 / 0	-3.16 / 1	-2.78 / 1	0.01	0.81
GL	Lazard Emerg Mkts Multi Asset Inst	EMMIX	E+	(800) 821-6474	C / 5.4	6.48	2.42	20.69 /97	-0.39 / 4	-1.39 / 2	0.92	1.32
GL	Lazard Emerg Mkts Multi Asset Open	EMMOX	E+	(800) 821-6474	C / 4.9	6.30	2.24	20.31 /96	-0.71 / 3	-1.71 / 1	0.64	2.96
EM	Lazard Emerging Markets Income	LEIIX	U	(800) 821-6474	U /	4.79	0.25	7.12 /73	--	--	2.03	2.55
EM	Lazard Emerging Markets Income	LEIOX	U	(800) 821-6474	U /	4.76	0.17	6.90 /72	--	--	0.00	12.19
EM	Lazard Explorer Total Ret Ptf Instl	LETIX	E+	(800) 821-6474	C / 4.5	4.27	0.56	9.77 /78	0.94 /27	--	4.57	1.11
EM	Lazard Explorer Total Ret Ptf Open	LETOX	E+	(800) 821-6474	C- / 4.0	4.17	0.39	9.36 /77	0.62 /22	--	4.22	1.61
GL	Lazard Global Fixed Inc Pfolio Inst	LZGIX	E	(800) 821-6474	E- / 0.1	1.01	-5.00	-0.20 /14	-1.28 / 2	--	2.27	4.26
GL	Lazard Global Fixed Inc Pfolio Open	LZGOX	E	(800) 821-6474	E- / 0.1	0.93	-5.14	-0.50 / 9	-1.57 / 2	--	1.96	27.72
COH	Lazard US Corporate Income Inst	LZHYX	C	(800) 821-6474	B / 8.1	2.86	2.60	11.18 /82	3.95 /75	5.51 /89	4.67	0.69
COH	Lazard US Corporate Income Open	LZHOX	C	(800) 821-6474	B / 7.7	2.78	2.45	10.59 /80	3.58 /70	5.16 /86	4.38	1.69
COI	Lazard US Short Dur Fixed Inc Inst	UMNIX	C+	(800) 821-6474	D / 2.1	0.35	0.28	1.22 /42	0.50 /21	0.38 /20	1.32	0.48
COI	Lazard US Short Dur Fixed Inc Open	UMNOX	C+	(800) 821-6474	D / 2.1	0.37	0.13	1.02 /40	0.61 /22	0.34 /20	1.02	42.51
COI	Leader Short-Term Bond A	LCAMX	D-	(800) 711-9164	E / 0.3	1.76	0.95	3.14 /57	-0.95 / 3	--	2.16	1.43
COI	Leader Short-Term Bond C	LCMCX	E+	(800) 711-9164	E- / 0.2	1.63	0.80	2.63 /54	-1.43 / 2	--	1.70	1.93
GEI	Leader Short-Term Bond Inst	LCCIX	D	(800) 711-9164	D / 1.7	1.87	1.33	3.66 /61	-0.42 / 4	2.04 /43	2.71	0.93
GEI	Leader Short-Term Bond Inv	LCCMX	D-	(800) 711-9164	E / 0.4	1.75	1.06	3.17 /58	-0.94 / 3	1.52 /35	2.22	1.43
GEI	Leader Total Return A	LCATX	E	(800) 711-9164	D+ / 2.9	2.63	2.50	12.59 /84	-0.50 / 4	--	3.27	1.56
GEI	Leader Total Return C	LCCTX	E	(800) 711-9164	D+ / 2.8	2.50	2.35	12.22 /84	-0.98 / 3	--	2.84	2.06
GL	Leader Total Return Inst	LCTIX	E+	(800) 711-9164	C / 4.5	2.77	2.86	13.31 /86	0.03 / 8	3.97 /72	3.81	1.06
GL	Leader Total Return Inv	LCTRX	E+	(800) 711-9164	C- / 3.6	2.63	2.60	12.69 /84	-0.49 / 4	3.49 /65	3.31	1.56
MUS	Lee Fnl Hawaii-Muni Bond Inv	SURFX	A+		B- / 7.1	1.50	-2.27	-0.09 /16	3.13 /84	2.81 /76	2.46	1.05
GL	Legg Mason BW Global Flex Income	LFLAX	U	(877) 534-4627	U /	4.71	1.98	--	--	--	0.00	N/A
GL	Legg Mason BW Global Flex Income I	LFLIX	U	(877) 534-4627	U /	4.77	2.02	--	--	--	0.00	N/A
GL	Legg Mason BW Global Flex Income	LFLSX	B	(877) 534-4627	B+ / 8.8	4.78	2.14	12.51 /84	4.17 /77	--	1.81	N/A
GL	Legg Mason BW Global High Yield A	LBHAX	D	(877) 534-4627	B- / 7.3	5.90	4.15	16.71 /91	2.76 /57	--	4.03	1.80
GL	Legg Mason BW Global High Yield C	LBHCX	D	(877) 534-4627	B / 7.6	5.74	3.71	15.81 /90	2.00 /43	--	3.56	2.69
GL	Legg Mason BW Global High Yield FI	LBHFX	C-	(877) 534-4627	B+ / 8.5	5.93	4.12	16.80 /92	2.78 /57	--	4.28	1.87
GL	Legg Mason BW Global High Yield I	LMYIX	C	(877) 534-4627	B+ / 8.7	5.99	4.21	17.01 /92	3.07 /62	--	4.56	1.38
GL	Legg Mason BW Global High Yield IS	LMZIX	C	(877) 534-4627	B+ / 8.8	6.01	4.24	17.06 /92	3.14 /63	5.81 /91	4.60	1.28
GL	Legg Mason BW Global Opportunities	LOBAX	E	(877) 534-4627	D / 1.8	4.17	-2.60	5.94 /70	0.72 /23	--	0.00	1.10
GEI	Legg Mason CO Sc Ch All Fixed Inc		C-	(877) 534-4627	C+ / 5.6	2.53	-0.45	6.44 /71	3.27 /65	3.32 /63	0.00	0.82
GEI	Legg Mason CO Sc Ch All Fixed Inc		C	(877) 534-4627	C+ / 5.9	2.35	-0.74	5.70 /69	2.54 /53	2.60 /51	0.00	1.52
GEI	Legg Mason CO Sc Ch All Fixed Inc		C	(877) 534-4627	C+ / 6.2	2.38	-0.67	5.89 /70	2.76 /57	2.81 /54	0.00	1.32
GEI	Legg Mason CO Sc Ch All Fixed Inc		C+	(877) 534-4627	C+ / 6.5	2.45	-0.55	6.11 /70	2.96 /60	3.02 /58	0.00	1.09
GEI	Legg Mason WY Sch Ch Fix Inc 80%		B-	(877) 534-4627	C / 4.8	2.41	2.00	6.26 /71	2.50 /52	3.49 /65	0.00	0.86
GEI	Legg Mason WY Sch Ch Fix Inc 80%		B	(877) 534-4627	C / 5.1	2.24	1.65	5.48 /68	1.79 /39	2.77 /54	0.00	1.56
GEI	Legg Mason WY Sch Ch Fix Inc 80%		B+	(877) 534-4627	C / 5.4	2.23	1.72	5.69 /69	1.99 /43	2.97 /57	0.00	1.36
GEI	Legg Mason WY Sch Ch Fix Inc 80%		A-	(877) 534-4627	C+ / 5.8	2.31	1.89	5.88 /70	2.17 /46	3.16 /60	0.00	1.09
GEI	LeggMason CO SC Yr to Enr Le Th 1		D	(877) 534-4627	E / 0.3	0.58	0.00	1.23 /42	0.36 /19	0.32 /20	0.00	0.71
GEI	LeggMason CO SC Yr to Enr Le Th 1		D	(877) 534-4627	E / 0.4	0.40	-0.32	0.48 /33	-0.34 / 4	-0.38 / 3	0.00	1.41
GEI	LeggMason CO SC Yr to Enr Le Th 1		D	(877) 534-4627	E / 0.5	0.46	-0.23	0.70 /36	-0.13 / 5	-0.18 / 4	0.00	1.21
GEI	LeggMason CO SC Yr to Enr Le Th 1		D	(877) 534-4627	E+ / 0.8	0.53	-0.15	0.83 /38	-0.07 / 5	-0.12 / 4	0.00	1.09
GEI	LeggMason CO Sch Ch Fix Inc 80%		B-	(877) 534-4627	C / 4.8	2.41	2.00	6.26 /71	2.50 /52	3.49 /65	0.00	0.81
GEI	LeggMason CO Sch Ch Fix Inc 80%		B	(877) 534-4627	C / 5.1	2.24	1.65	5.48 /68	1.79 /39	2.77 /54	0.00	1.51
GEI	LeggMason CO Sch Ch Fix Inc 80%		B+	(877) 534-4627	C / 5.4	2.23	1.72	5.69 /69	1.99 /43	2.97 /57	0.00	1.31
GEI	LeggMason CO Sch Ch Fix Inc 80%		A-	(877) 534-4627	C+ / 5.8	2.31	1.89	5.88 /70	2.17 /46	3.16 /60	0.00	1.09
MMT	LeggMason CO Schr Ch Cash Rsv A		U	(877) 534-4627	U /	--	--	--	--	--	0.01	N/A
MMT	LeggMason CO Schr Ch Cash Rsv B		U	(877) 534-4627	U /	--	--	--	--	--	0.01	N/A
MMT	LeggMason CO Schr Ch Cash Rsv C		U	(877) 534-4627	U /	--	--	--	--	--	0.01	N/A
MMT	LeggMason CO Schr Ch Cash Rsv O		U	(877) 534-4627	U /	--	--	--	--	--	0.01	N/A

● Denotes fund is closed to new investors
* Denotes fund is included in Section II

www.thestreetratings.com

Risk Rating/Pts	3 Yr Avg Standard Deviation	Avg Duration	NAV As of 2/28/17	Total $(Mil)	Cash %	Gov. Bond %	Muni. Bond %	Corp. Bond %	Other %	Portfolio Turnover Ratio	Avg Coupon Rate	Manager Quality Pct	Manager Tenure (Years)	Initial Purch. $	Additional Purch. $	Front End Load	Back End Load
E /0.5	7.6	N/A	8.87	8	2	97	0	0	1	42	0.0	71	N/A	100	0	0.0	0.0
E /0.4	7.7	6.4	9.22	104	1	93	0	0	6	31	0.0	20	N/A	100	0	0.0	0.0
E- /0.1	11.9	N/A	8.51	196	4	24	0	0	72	109	0.0	81	6	100,000	50	0.0	1.0
E- /0.1	11.9	N/A	8.52	1	4	24	0	0	72	109	0.0	78	6	2,500	50	0.0	1.0
U /	N/A	1.1	8.68	12	0	0	0	0	100	175	2.3	N/A	3	100,000	50	0.0	1.0
U /	N/A	1.1	8.81	N/A	0	0	0	0	100	175	2.3	N/A	3	2,500	50	0.0	1.0
D /1.9	5.2	5.1	8.90	256	34	37	0	27	2	262	6.2	83	4	100,000	50	0.0	1.0
D /1.9	5.2	5.1	8.95	1	34	37	0	27	2	262	6.2	81	4	2,500	50	0.0	1.0
D /2.1	4.9	4.6	8.69	4	4	51	11	32	2	60	4.2	58	5	100,000	50	0.0	1.0
D /2.2	4.9	4.6	8.69	N/A	4	51	11	32	2	60	4.2	40	5	2,500	50	0.0	1.0
D /2.2	4.3	3.5	4.91	306	0	2	0	96	2	17	5.7	71	14	100,000	50	0.0	1.0
D+ /2.3	4.2	3.5	4.93	8	0	2	0	96	2	17	5.7	63	14	2,500	50	0.0	1.0
A+ /9.8	0.4	1.6	9.86	104	1	7	5	37	50	57	2.7	51	6	100,000	50	0.0	0.0
A+ /9.8	0.6	1.6	9.88	N/A	1	7	5	37	50	57	2.7	57	6	2,500	50	0.0	0.0
B /7.9	2.3	1.9	9.00	11	27	1	0	49	23	107	3.2	4	12	2,500	100	1.5	0.0
B /7.8	2.3	1.9	9.04	7	27	1	0	49	23	107	3.2	2	12	2,500	100	0.0	0.0
B /7.9	2.2	1.9	9.09	126	27	1	0	49	23	107	3.2	16	12	2,000,000	0	0.0	0.0
B /7.9	2.3	1.9	9.02	111	27	1	0	49	23	107	3.2	7	12	2,500	100	0.0	0.0
D /2.0	5.0	2.4	9.60	6	6	15	0	26	53	209	3.6	7	7	2,500	100	1.5	0.0
D /2.0	5.1	2.4	9.68	3	6	15	0	26	53	209	3.6	4	7	2,500	100	0.0	0.0
D /2.0	5.1	2.4	9.58	26	6	15	0	26	53	209	3.6	59	7	2,000,000	0	0.0	0.0
D /2.0	5.1	2.4	9.62	15	6	15	0	26	53	209	3.6	31	7	2,500	100	0.0	0.0
B /7.6	2.5	5.6	11.03	168	2	0	97	0	1	18	5.2	65	2	10,000	100	0.0	0.0
U /	N/A	5.5	10.27	N/A	0	0	0	0	100	0	5.1	N/A	1	1,000	50	4.3	0.0
U /	N/A	5.5	10.27	N/A	0	0	0	0	100	0	5.1	N/A	1	1,000,000	0	0.0	0.0
D+ /2.7	4.3	5.5	10.28	7	0	0	0	0	100	0	5.1	96	1	0	0	0.0	0.0
D- /1.2	6.1	4.4	9.03	N/A	10	0	0	79	11	96	6.3	94	8	1,000	50	4.3	0.0
D- /1.2	6.1	4.4	9.02	1	10	0	0	79	11	96	6.3	91	8	1,000	50	0.0	0.0
D- /1.2	6.1	4.4	9.03	N/A	10	0	0	79	11	96	6.3	94	8	0	0	0.0	0.0
D- /1.2	6.1	4.4	9.02	3	10	0	0	79	11	96	6.3	94	8	1,000,000	0	0.0	0.0
D- /1.2	6.1	4.4	9.02	39	10	0	0	79	11	96	6.3	94	8	0	0	0.0	0.0
E /0.4	7.7	5.7	10.43	13	2	78	0	15	5	59	4.6	90	11	1,000	50	4.3	0.0
C /4.4	3.4	N/A	22.31	19	0	37	0	35	28	0	0.0	70	16	250	50	3.5	0.0
C /4.4	3.3	N/A	20.02	1	0	37	0	35	28	0	0.0	45	16	250	50	0.0	0.0
C /4.5	3.3	N/A	20.68	14	0	37	0	35	28	0	0.0	56	16	250	50	0.0	0.0
C /4.5	3.3	N/A	21.71	2	0	37	0	35	28	0	0.0	62	16	250	50	0.0	0.0
B- /7.3	2.6	N/A	17.82	315	0	0	0	0	100	0	0.0	83	18	250	50	3.5	0.0
B- /7.5	2.6	N/A	15.98	15	0	0	0	0	100	0	0.0	76	18	250	50	0.0	0.0
B- /7.5	2.5	N/A	16.53	257	0	0	0	0	100	0	0.0	79	18	250	50	0.0	0.0
B- /7.4	2.6	N/A	17.28	40	0	0	0	0	100	0	0.0	81	18	250	50	0.0	0.0
A /9.3	1.0	N/A	13.99	142	0	0	0	0	100	0	0.0	24	18	250	50	3.5	0.0
A /9.3	1.0	N/A	12.57	7	0	0	0	0	100	0	0.0	9	18	250	50	0.0	0.0
A /9.3	0.9	N/A	12.97	140	0	0	0	0	100	0	0.0	13	18	250	50	0.0	0.0
A- /9.2	1.0	N/A	13.32	19	0	0	0	0	100	0	0.0	13	18	250	50	0.0	0.0
B- /7.3	2.6	N/A	17.82	315	0	0	0	0	100	0	0.0	83	18	250	50	3.5	0.0
B- /7.5	2.6	N/A	15.98	15	0	0	0	0	100	0	0.0	76	18	250	50	0.0	0.0
B- /7.5	2.5	N/A	16.53	257	0	0	0	0	100	0	0.0	79	18	250	50	0.0	0.0
B- /7.4	2.6	N/A	17.28	40	0	0	0	0	100	0	0.0	81	18	250	50	0.0	0.0
U /	N/A	N/A	1.00	37	100	0	0	0	0	0	0.0	N/A	12	250	50	0.0	0.0
U /	N/A	N/A	1.00	1	100	0	0	0	0	0	0.0	N/A	12	250	50	0.0	0.0
U /	N/A	N/A	1.00	33	100	0	0	0	0	0	0.0	N/A	12	250	50	0.0	0.0
U /	N/A	N/A	1.00	4	100	0	0	0	0	0	0.0	N/A	12	250	50	0.0	0.0

I. Index of Bond and Money Market Mutual Funds

99 Pct = Best
0 Pct = Worst

Fund Type	Fund Name	Ticker Symbol	Overall Investment Rating	Phone	Performance Rating/Pts	3 Mo	6 Mo	1Yr / Pct	3Yr / Pct	5Yr / Pct	Dividend Yield	Expense Ratio
GEI	LeggMason WY SC Yr To Enr Le Th		D	(877) 534-4627	E / 0.3	0.58	0.00	1.23 /42	0.36 /19	0.32 /20	0.00	0.86
GEI	LeggMason WY SC Yr To Enr Le Th		D	(877) 534-4627	E / 0.4	0.40	-0.32	0.48 /33	-0.34 / 4	-0.38 / 3	0.00	1.56
GEI	LeggMason WY SC Yr To Enr Le Th		D	(877) 534-4627	E / 0.5	0.46	-0.23	0.70 /36	-0.13 / 5	-0.18 / 4	0.00	1.36
GEI	LeggMason WY SC Yr To Enr Le Th		D	(877) 534-4627	E+ / 0.8	0.53	-0.15	0.83 /38	-0.07 / 5	-0.12 / 4	0.00	1.09
GEI	LeggMason WY Sch Ch All Fixed Inc		C-	(877) 534-4627	C+ / 5.6	2.53	-0.45	6.44 /71	3.27 /65	3.32 /63	0.00	0.82
GEI	LeggMason WY Sch Ch All Fixed Inc		C	(877) 534-4627	C+ / 5.9	2.35	-0.74	5.70 /69	2.54 /53	2.60 /51	0.00	1.52
GEI	LeggMason WY Sch Ch All Fixed Inc		C	(877) 534-4627	C+ / 6.2	2.38	-0.67	5.89 /70	2.76 /57	2.81 /54	0.00	1.32
GEI	LeggMason WY Sch Ch All Fixed Inc		C+	(877) 534-4627	C+ / 6.5	2.45	-0.55	6.11 /70	2.96 /60	3.02 /58	0.00	1.09
GEI	Leland Currency Strategy A	GHCAX	U	(877) 270-2848	U /	3.47	1.75	-3.49 / 0	--	--	0.00	16.35
GEI	Leland Currency Strategy C	GHCCX	U	(877) 270-2848	U /	3.34	1.42	-4.18 / 0	--	--	0.00	17.10
GEI	Leland Currency Strategy I	GHCIX	U	(877) 270-2848	U /	3.46	1.83	-3.32 / 0	--	--	0.00	16.10
GEI	LKCM Fixed Income Institutional	LKFIX	C+	(800) 688-5526	C- / 3.3	0.82	-0.88	2.85 /56	1.56 /36	1.81 /39	2.12	0.73
GL	LM BW Absolute Return Opptys FI	LBAFX	D	(877) 534-4627	C+ / 6.1	3.20	2.85	6.43 /71	2.15 /46	2.85 /55	0.00	1.12
GL	LM BW Global Opportunities Bond A	GOBAX	E	(877) 534-4627	D / 2.0	4.27	-2.51	6.14 /71	0.92 /26	1.65 /37	0.00	0.92
GL	LM BW Global Opportunities Bond C	LGOCX	E	(877) 534-4627	D+ / 2.3	3.92	-3.00	5.18 /67	0.11 /13	0.86 /26	0.00	1.68
GL	LM BW Global Opportunities Bond C1	GOBCX	E	(877) 534-4627	C- / 3.0	4.11	-2.71	5.67 /69	0.46 /20	1.19 /30	0.00	1.35
GL	LM BW Global Opportunities Bond FI	GOBFX	E	(877) 534-4627	C- / 3.7	4.22	-2.54	6.11 /70	0.86 /25	1.60 /36	0.00	0.95
GL	LM BW Global Opportunities Bond I	GOBIX	E	(877) 534-4627	C- / 4.2	4.29	-2.43	6.38 /71	1.17 /30	1.90 /41	0.00	0.69
GL	LM BW Global Opportunities Bond IS	GOBSX	E+	(877) 534-4627	C / 4.3	4.28	-2.43	6.48 /72	1.28 /32	2.01 /42	0.00	0.56
GL	LM BW Global Opportunities Bond R	LBORX	E	(877) 534-4627	C- / 3.2	4.09	-2.71	5.75 /69	0.56 /21	1.33 /32	0.00	1.26
GL	LM BW International Opptys Bd A	LWOAX	E-	(877) 534-4627	E- / 0.2	4.24	-3.15	5.23 /68	-0.44 / 4	1.27 /31	0.00	0.99
GL	LM BW International Opptys Bd C	LIOCX	E-	(877) 534-4627	E / 0.3	4.02	-3.55	4.41 /64	-1.19 / 2	0.49 /21	0.00	1.81
GL	LM BW International Opptys Bd FI	LWOFX	E	(877) 534-4627	D / 1.8	4.23	-3.15	5.22 /68	-0.39 / 4	1.32 /32	0.00	1.05
GL	LM BW International Opptys Bd I	LWOIX	E	(877) 534-4627	D / 2.1	4.31	-2.96	5.50 /69	-0.17 / 4	1.53 /35	0.00	0.81
GL	LM BW International Opptys Bd IS	LMOTX	E	(877) 534-4627	D / 2.2	4.31	-2.96	5.59 /69	-0.08 / 5	1.60 /36	0.00	0.66
GL	LM BW International Opptys Bd R	LWORX	E-	(877) 534-4627	E+ / 0.9	4.17	-3.25	4.96 /66	-0.69 / 3	1.00 /27	0.00	1.42
GEI	LM Capital Opportunistic Bond Inst	LMCOX	C-	(866) 777-7818	C / 5.1	1.46	-1.77	2.94 /56	2.58 /53	--	2.94	3.04
GEN	Logan Circle Part Core Plus I		U	(866) 777-7818	U /	1.73	-1.14	4.23 /63	--	--	2.61	4.72
GEN	Logan Circle Part Core Plus R		U	(866) 777-7818	U /	1.73	-1.23	4.01 /62	--	--	2.61	4.97
GES	Loomis Sayles Bond Admin	LBFAX	D	(800) 633-3330	B- / 7.0	4.18	2.17	14.29 /87	1.80 /40	4.07 /73	1.85	1.14
GES	Loomis Sayles Bond Inst	LSBDX	D+	(800) 633-3330	B- / 7.5	4.27	2.47	14.90 /88	2.32 /48	4.62 /80	2.31	0.64
COI	Loomis Sayles Bond N	LSBNX	D+	(800) 633-3330	B / 7.6	4.37	2.51	14.99 /88	2.40 /50	--	2.38	0.57
* GES	Loomis Sayles Bond Ret	LSBRX	D	(800) 633-3330	B- / 7.3	4.30	2.35	14.68 /88	2.02 /44	4.33 /76	2.07	0.89
* GEI	Loomis Sayles Fixed Inc Fd	LSFIX	C	(800) 633-3330	B / 8.0	4.37	2.82	15.01 /88	2.80 /58	5.26 /86	3.40	0.57
GL	Loomis Sayles Glbl Bd Inst	LSGBX	E	(800) 633-3330	E / 0.5	1.93	-4.23	4.30 /64	-0.51 / 4	0.48 /21	0.35	0.78
GL	Loomis Sayles Glbl Bd Ret	LSGLX	E	(800) 633-3330	E / 0.3	1.85	-4.37	4.07 /62	-0.76 / 3	0.24 /19	0.27	1.03
COH	Loomis Sayles High Income A	NEFHX	C-	(800) 225-5478	B+ / 8.8	4.61	4.79	21.71 /98	3.82 /73	6.26 /94	3.30	1.14
COH	Loomis Sayles High Income C	NEHCX	C-	(800) 225-5478	B+ / 8.9	4.40	4.37	20.74 /97	3.03 /61	5.44 /88	2.71	1.89
COH	Loomis Sayles High Income Y	NEHYX	C+	(800) 225-5478	A / 9.5	4.69	4.95	22.09 /98	4.02 /76	6.50 /95	3.70	0.89
USL	Loomis Sayles Infl Prot Sec Inst	LSGSX	E+	(800) 633-3330	C- / 3.4	1.18	-0.51	3.03 /57	1.26 /31	0.40 /20	1.46	0.80
GEI	Loomis Sayles Infl Prot Sec Rtl	LIPRX	E+	(800) 633-3330	D+ / 2.9	1.12	-0.63	2.70 /55	0.95 /27	0.12 /16	0.84	1.03
*COH	Loomis Sayles Inst High Income Inst	LSHIX	C+	(800) 633-3330	A+ / 9.7	5.61	7.02	27.63 /99	3.85 /73	8.00 /98	5.54	0.68
COI	Loomis Sayles Intm Dur Bd A	LSDRX	D+	(800) 225-5478	D / 2.2	0.82	-1.15	2.12 /50	1.90 /41	2.11 /44	1.77	0.71
COI	Loomis Sayles Intm Dur Bd C	LSCDX	U	(800) 225-5478	U /	0.54	-1.49	--	--	--	0.00	1.47
GEI	Loomis Sayles Intm Dur Bd Y	LSDIX	B	(800) 225-5478	C / 4.5	0.88	-0.93	2.38 /52	2.19 /46	2.37 /47	2.10	0.47
GEI	Loomis Sayles Invst Gr Fix Inc I	LSIGX	C-	(800) 633-3330	C+ / 6.6	3.39	0.94	9.28 /77	2.38 /50	3.65 /68	2.37	0.48
MUN	Lord Abbett AMT Free Municipal Bd A	LATAX	C+	(888) 522-2388	B / 7.6	2.10	-3.99	0.40 /35	4.21 /94	3.37 /86	3.12	0.89
MUN	Lord Abbett AMT Free Municipal Bd	LATCX	C+	(888) 522-2388	B- / 7.5	2.01	-4.29	-0.22 /14	3.56 /88	2.69 /74	2.55	1.53
MUN	Lord Abbett AMT Free Municipal Bd F	LATFX	B+	(888) 522-2388	B+ / 8.7	2.19	-3.94	0.50 /37	4.31 /95	3.47 /87	3.29	0.79
MUN	Lord Abbett AMT Free Municipal Bd I	LMCIX	B+	(888) 522-2388	B+ / 8.8	2.22	-3.89	0.61 /39	4.42 /95	3.58 /89	3.40	0.69
*COH	Lord Abbett Bond Debenture A	LBNDX	B-	(888) 522-2388	A / 9.3	4.11	4.50	18.04 /94	4.84 /84	6.50 /95	4.40	0.82
COH ●	Lord Abbett Bond Debenture B	LBNBX	C+	(888) 522-2388	A- / 9.2	3.89	4.09	17.22 /92	4.02 /76	5.72 /90	3.74	1.62

● Denotes fund is closed to new investors
* Denotes fund is included in Section II

www.thestreetratings.com

RISK			NET ASSETS		ASSET							FUND MANAGER		MINIMUM		LOADS	
Risk Rating/Pts	3 Yr Avg Standard Deviation	Avg Dura- tion	NAV As of 2/28/17	Total $(Mil)	Cash %	Gov. Bond %	Muni. Bond %	Corp. Bond %	Other %	Portfolio Turnover Ratio	Avg Coupon Rate	Manager Quality Pct	Manager Tenure (Years)	Initial Purch. $	Additional Purch. $	Front End Load	Back End Load
A /9.3	1.0	N/A	13.99	142	0	0	0	0	100	0	0.0	24	N/A	250	50	3.5	0.0
A /9.3	1.0	N/A	12.57	7	0	0	0	0	100	0	0.0	9	N/A	250	50	0.0	0.0
A /9.3	0.9	N/A	12.97	140	0	0	0	0	100	0	0.0	13	N/A	250	50	0.0	0.0
A- /9.2	1.0	N/A	13.32	19	0	0	0	0	100	0	0.0	13	N/A	250	50	0.0	0.0
C /4.4	3.4	N/A	22.31	19	0	0	0	0	100	0	0.0	70	17	250	50	3.5	0.0
C /4.4	3.3	N/A	20.02	1	0	0	0	0	100	0	0.0	45	17	250	50	0.0	0.0
C /4.5	3.3	N/A	20.68	14	0	0	0	0	100	0	0.0	56	17	250	50	0.0	0.0
C /4.5	3.3	N/A	21.71	2	0	0	0	0	100	0	0.0	62	17	250	50	0.0	0.0
U /	N/A	N/A	11.63	7	100	0	0	0	0	0	0.0	N/A	3	2,500	250	5.8	1.0
U /	N/A	N/A	11.45	1	100	0	0	0	0	0	0.0	N/A	3	2,500	250	0.0	1.0
U /	N/A	N/A	11.66	13	100	0	0	0	0	0	0.0	N/A	3	5,000,000	10,000	0.0	1.0
B+ /8.4	1.9	3.3	10.72	231	0	25	0	73	2	29	2.9	53	20	2,000	1,000	0.0	1.0
D+ /2.3	4.7	N/A	11.92	3	3	67	0	21	9	30	0.0	89	6	0	0	0.0	0.0
E /0.4	7.7	5.7	10.46	258	2	78	0	15	5	59	4.6	91	11	1,000	50	4.3	0.0
E /0.5	7.7	5.7	10.28	22	2	78	0	15	5	59	4.6	86	11	1,000	50	0.0	0.0
E /0.4	7.7	5.7	10.35	11	2	78	0	15	5	59	4.6	89	11	1,000	50	0.0	0.0
E /0.4	7.7	5.7	10.33	72	2	78	0	15	5	59	4.6	91	11	0	0	0.0	0.0
E /0.4	7.7	5.7	10.41	1,047	2	78	0	15	5	59	4.6	92	11	1,000,000	0	0.0	0.0
E /0.4	7.7	5.7	10.42	1,556	2	78	0	15	5	59	4.6	93	11	0	0	0.0	0.0
E /0.4	7.7	5.7	10.39	16	2	78	0	15	5	59	4.6	89	11	0	0	0.0	0.0
E /0.4	8.0	5.4	11.06	11	4	81	0	12	3	73	4.5	83	8	1,000	50	4.3	0.0
E /0.4	8.0	5.4	10.88	N/A	4	81	0	12	3	73	4.5	75	8	1,000	50	0.0	0.0
E /0.4	8.0	5.4	11.08	14	4	81	0	12	3	73	4.5	84	8	0	0	0.0	0.0
E /0.4	8.0	5.4	11.13	58	4	81	0	12	3	73	4.5	86	8	1,000,000	0	0.0	0.0
E /0.4	8.1	5.4	11.14	13	4	81	0	12	3	73	4.5	87	8	0	0	0.0	0.0
E /0.4	8.0	5.4	11.00	N/A	4	81	0	12	3	73	4.5	81	8	0	0	0.0	0.0
C /5.1	3.1	5.7	9.98	10	0	22	0	53	25	16	0.0	37	4	1,000,000	0	0.0	0.0
U /	N/A	6.5	9.90	11	0	23	0	32	45	798	0.0	N/A	3	5,000,000	0	0.0	0.0
U /	N/A	6.5	9.90	N/A	0	23	0	32	45	798	0.0	N/A	3	500,000	0	0.0	0.0
D- /1.5	5.7	3.6	13.83	177	5	26	1	45	23	13	4.4	62	26	0	0	0.0	0.0
D- /1.4	5.8	3.6	13.95	9,659	5	26	1	45	23	13	4.4	75	26	100,000	50	0.0	0.0
D- /1.5	5.7	3.6	13.94	191	5	26	1	45	23	13	4.4	27	26	1,000,000	0	0.0	0.0
D- /1.4	5.8	3.6	13.89	3,891	5	26	1	45	23	13	4.4	69	26	2,500	50	0.0	0.0
D /1.9	5.3	4.0	13.39	1,088	3	23	2	58	14	14	4.7	81	22	3,000,000	50,000	0.0	0.0
D /1.9	5.3	6.5	15.62	531	0	52	1	30	17	120	3.4	78	17	100,000	0	0.0	0.0
D /1.9	5.3	6.5	15.39	293	0	52	1	30	17	120	3.4	74	17	2,500	50	0.0	0.0
E+ /0.6	6.8	4.3	4.31	35	4	6	0	75	15	38	5.7	7	15	2,500	100	4.3	0.0
E+ /0.6	6.7	4.3	4.32	12	4	6	0	75	15	38	5.7	2	15	2,500	100	0.0	0.0
E+ /0.6	6.8	4.3	4.30	127	4	6	0	75	15	38	5.7	9	15	100,000	100	0.0	0.0
D+ /2.7	4.0	8.6	10.49	37	0	96	0	2	2	61	0.7	26	5	100,000	0	0.0	0.0
D+ /2.7	4.0	8.6	10.47	2	0	96	0	2	2	61	0.7	3	5	2,500	50	0.0	0.0
E /0.4	7.7	4.0	6.81	761	9	10	0	59	22	17	5.2	4	21	3,000,000	50,000	0.0	0.0
B /8.1	2.1	4.1	10.24	20	0	0	0	0	100	151	2.5	48	12	2,500	100	4.3	0.0
U /	N/A	4.1	10.24	3	0	0	0	0	100	151	2.5	N/A	12	2,500	100	0.0	0.0
B /8.1	2.1	4.1	10.24	152	0	0	0	0	100	151	2.5	60	12	100,000	0	0.0	0.0
C- /3.1	4.1	4.2	12.11	409	2	35	0	48	15	23	4.2	69	23	3,000,000	50,000	0.0	0.0
C- /3.3	4.0	6.5	15.72	129	0	0	99	0	1	9	5.2	48	7	1,000	0	2.3	0.0
C- /3.2	4.0	6.5	15.72	26	0	0	99	0	1	9	5.2	20	7	1,000	0	0.0	0.0
C- /3.2	4.0	6.5	15.72	57	0	0	99	0	1	9	5.2	52	7	0	0	0.0	0.0
C- /3.2	4.0	6.5	15.73	1	0	0	99	0	1	9	5.2	56	7	1,000,000	0	0.0	0.0
D /1.6	5.1	4.5	8.09	4,173	1	3	1	74	21	119	0.0	76	4	1,000	0	2.3	0.0
D /1.6	5.1	4.5	8.12	42	1	3	1	74	21	119	0.0	56	4	1,000	0	0.0	0.0

					PERFORMANCE						Incl. in Returns	
99 Pct = Best / 0 Pct = Worst					Perfor-mance Rating/Pts	Total Return % through 2/28/17			Annualized		Dividend Yield	Expense Ratio
Fund Type	Fund Name	Ticker Symbol	Overall Investment Rating	Phone		3 Mo	6 Mo	1Yr / Pct	3Yr / Pct	5Yr / Pct		
COH	Lord Abbett Bond Debenture C	BDLAX	C+	(888) 522-2388	A / 9.3	3.94	4.18	17.27 /92	4.18 /77	5.82 /91	3.90	1.45
COH	Lord Abbett Bond Debenture F	LBDFX	B	(888) 522-2388	A+ / 9.6	4.13	4.56	18.17 /94	4.94 /85	6.67 /96	4.59	0.72
COH	Lord Abbett Bond Debenture I	LBNYX	B	(888) 522-2388	A+ / 9.6	4.17	4.62	18.35 /94	5.05 /85	6.75 /96	4.69	0.62
COH	Lord Abbett Bond Debenture P	LBNPX	B	(888) 522-2388	A / 9.5	4.03	4.43	17.98 /93	4.79 /84	6.48 /95	4.46	1.07
COH	Lord Abbett Bond Debenture R2	LBNQX	B-	(888) 522-2388	A / 9.4	4.00	4.30	17.58 /93	4.43 /80	6.14 /93	4.12	1.22
COH	Lord Abbett Bond Debenture R3	LBNRX	B-	(888) 522-2388	A / 9.4	4.03	4.36	17.72 /93	4.54 /81	6.26 /94	4.22	1.12
GEL	Lord Abbett Bond Debenture R4	LBNSX	U	(888) 522-2388	U /	4.09	4.34	17.98 /93	--	--	4.45	0.87
GEL	Lord Abbett Bond Debenture R5	LBNTX	U	(888) 522-2388	U /	4.17	4.62	18.50 /94	--	--	4.69	0.62
GEL	Lord Abbett Bond Debenture R6	LBNVX	U	(888) 522-2388	U /	4.06	4.53	18.45 /94	--	--	4.78	0.53
GEI	Lord Abbett Core Fixed Income A	LCRAX	D+	(888) 522-2388	C- / 3.6	1.03	-2.06	2.20 /51	2.31 /48	2.24 /45	2.25	0.86
GEI	● Lord Abbett Core Fixed Income B	LCRBX	D	(888) 522-2388	C- / 3.2	0.83	-2.45	1.50 /45	1.50 /35	1.43 /33	1.51	1.66
GEI	Lord Abbett Core Fixed Income C	LCRCX	D+	(888) 522-2388	C- / 3.4	0.88	-2.38	1.58 /45	1.68 /38	1.60 /36	1.68	1.48
GEI	Lord Abbett Core Fixed Income F	LCRFX	C+	(888) 522-2388	C / 4.7	1.06	-2.01	2.31 /52	2.41 /50	2.34 /47	2.41	0.76
GEI	Lord Abbett Core Fixed Income I	LCRYX	C+	(888) 522-2388	C / 4.9	1.08	-1.96	2.42 /52	2.52 /52	2.44 /48	2.52	0.66
GEI	● Lord Abbett Core Fixed Income P	LCRPX	C-	(888) 522-2388	C- / 4.2	0.97	-2.16	2.09 /50	2.09 /45	2.01 /42	2.10	1.11
GEI	Lord Abbett Core Fixed Income R2	LCRQX	C-	(888) 522-2388	C- / 3.9	1.03	-2.25	1.90 /48	1.94 /42	1.85 /40	1.92	1.26
GEI	Lord Abbett Core Fixed Income R3	LCRRX	C-	(888) 522-2388	C- / 4.0	0.96	-2.29	1.91 /48	2.01 /43	1.94 /41	2.02	1.16
COI	Lord Abbett Core Fixed Income R4	LCRSX	U	(888) 522-2388	U /	1.02	-2.08	2.17 /50	--	--	2.27	0.91
COI	Lord Abbett Core Fixed Income R5	LCRTX	U	(888) 522-2388	U /	1.08	-1.96	2.44 /53	--	--	2.54	0.66
COI	Lord Abbett Core Fixed Income R6	LCRVX	U	(888) 522-2388	U /	1.11	-1.90	2.63 /54	--	--	2.63	0.56
COI	Lord Abbett Core Plus Bond F	LPLFX	U	(888) 522-2388	U /	1.98	-0.16	7.55 /73	--	--	3.61	0.84
EM	Lord Abbett Em Mkts Corp Debt A	LCDAX	B+	(888) 522-2388	A / 9.3	3.91	0.96	11.45 /82	6.11 /93	--	4.21	1.70
EM	Lord Abbett Em Mkts Corp Debt C	LEDCX	B	(888) 522-2388	A- / 9.2	3.73	0.62	10.71 /80	5.35 /87	--	3.65	2.42
EM	Lord Abbett Em Mkts Corp Debt F	LCDFX	B+	(888) 522-2388	A+ / 9.6	4.00	1.01	11.53 /82	6.22 /93	--	4.38	1.60
EM	Lord Abbett Em Mkts Corp Debt I	LCDIX	B+	(888) 522-2388	A+ / 9.6	3.96	1.07	11.68 /83	6.33 /94	--	4.51	1.50
EM	Lord Abbett Em Mkts Corp Debt R2	LCDQX	B+	(888) 522-2388	A+ / 9.6	3.96	1.07	11.68 /83	6.33 /94	--	4.51	2.10
EM	Lord Abbett Em Mkts Corp Debt R3	LCDRX	B+	(888) 522-2388	A+ / 9.6	3.96	1.07	11.68 /83	6.33 /94	--	4.51	2.00
EM	Lord Abbett Em Mkts Corp Debt R4	LCDSX	U	(888) 522-2388	U /	3.90	0.95	11.41 /82	--	--	4.27	1.75
EM	Lord Abbett Em Mkts Corp Debt R5	LCDTX	U	(888) 522-2388	U /	3.96	1.07	11.68 /83	--	--	4.51	1.50
EM	Lord Abbett Em Mkts Corp Debt R6	LCDVX	U	(888) 522-2388	U /	3.98	1.11	11.77 /83	--	--	4.59	1.42
EM	Lord Abbett Em Mkts Local Bond A	LEMAX	E-	(888) 522-2388	E- / 0.1	5.94	-0.81	11.40 /82	-4.16 / 0	--	6.32	3.22
EM	Lord Abbett Em Mkts Local Bond C	LEMCX	E-	(888) 522-2388	E- / 0.1	5.78	-1.12	10.69 /80	-4.84 / 0	--	5.81	3.94
EM	Lord Abbett Em Mkts Local Bond F	LEMFX	E-	(888) 522-2388	E- / 0.1	5.97	-0.77	11.51 /82	-4.07 / 0	--	6.57	3.12
EM	Lord Abbett Em Mkts Local Bond I	LEMLX	E-	(888) 522-2388	E- / 0.1	6.00	-0.71	11.62 /82	-3.96 / 0	--	6.67	3.02
EM	Lord Abbett Em Mkts Local Bond R2	LEMQX	E-	(888) 522-2388	E- / 0.1	6.00	-0.62	11.62 /82	-3.96 / 0	--	6.67	3.62
EM	Lord Abbett Em Mkts Local Bond R3	LEMRX	E-	(888) 522-2388	E- / 0.1	6.00	-0.62	11.62 /82	-3.96 / 0	--	6.67	3.52
EM	Lord Abbett Em Mkts Local Bond R4	LEMKX	U	(888) 522-2388	U /	5.95	-0.80	11.41 /82	--	--	6.48	3.27
EM	Lord Abbett Em Mkts Local Bond R5	LEMTX	U	(888) 522-2388	U /	6.02	-0.68	11.69 /83	--	--	6.73	3.02
EM	Lord Abbett Em Mkts Local Bond R6	LEMVX	U	(888) 522-2388	U /	6.03	-0.65	11.76 /83	--	--	6.80	2.96
GL	Lord Abbett Emerg Mkts Currency A	LDMAX	E-	(888) 522-2388	E- / 0.2	2.67	0.22	10.04 /79	-2.23 / 2	-1.70 / 1	3.22	0.98
GL	● Lord Abbett Emerg Mkts Currency B	LDMBX	E-	(888) 522-2388	E- / 0.2	2.46	-0.17	9.14 /77	-3.04 / 1	-2.49 / 1	2.50	1.78
GL	Lord Abbett Emerg Mkts Currency C	LDMCX	E-	(888) 522-2388	E- / 0.2	2.51	-0.07	9.56 /78	-2.85 / 1	-2.31 / 1	2.69	1.59
GL	Lord Abbett Emerg Mkts Currency F	LDMFX	E-	(888) 522-2388	E / 0.4	2.88	0.26	10.35 /80	-2.14 / 2	-1.57 / 1	3.39	0.88
GL	Lord Abbett Emerg Mkts Currency I	LDMYX	E-	(888) 522-2388	E / 0.4	2.72	0.31	10.49 /80	-2.05 / 2	-1.51 / 2	3.50	0.78
GL	Lord Abbett Emerg Mkts Currency R2	LDMQX	E-	(888) 522-2388	E- / 0.2	2.56	0.02	9.81 /78	-2.61 / 1	-2.08 / 1	2.90	1.38
GL	Lord Abbett Emerg Mkts Currency R3	LDMRX	E-	(888) 522-2388	E- / 0.2	2.60	0.07	9.95 /79	-2.52 / 1	-1.95 / 1	3.01	1.28
GL	Lord Abbett Emerg Mkts Currency R4	LDMSX	U	(888) 522-2388	U /	2.66	0.21	10.24 /79	--	--	3.28	1.03
GL	Lord Abbett Emerg Mkts Currency R5	LDMTX	U	(888) 522-2388	U /	2.72	0.34	10.31 /80	--	--	3.53	0.78
GL	Lord Abbett Emerg Mkts Currency R6	LDMVX	U	(888) 522-2388	U /	2.74	0.37	10.40 /80	--	--	3.62	0.76
*LP	Lord Abbett Floating Rate A	LFRAX	A+	(888) 522-2388	B / 7.7	2.12	3.80	11.78 /83	3.73 /72	4.86 /83	4.39	0.80
LP	Lord Abbett Floating Rate C	LARCX	A+	(888) 522-2388	B / 7.6	2.07	3.60	11.08 /81	3.07 /62	4.19 /75	3.87	1.44
LP	Lord Abbett Floating Rate F	LFRFX	A+	(888) 522-2388	B+ / 8.4	2.25	3.97	11.89 /83	3.83 /73	4.99 /84	4.58	0.70

● Denotes fund is closed to new investors
* Denotes fund is included in Section II

RISK			NET ASSETS		ASSET					Portfolio Turnover Ratio	Avg Coupon Rate	FUND MANAGER		MINIMUM		LOADS	
Risk Rating/Pts	3 Yr Avg Standard Deviation	Avg Dura-tion	NAV As of 2/28/17	Total $(Mil)	Cash %	Gov. Bond %	Muni. Bond %	Corp. Bond %	Other %	Portfolio Turnover Ratio	Avg Coupon Rate	Manager Quality Pct	Manager Tenure (Years)	Initial Purch. $	Additional Purch. $	Front End Load	Back End Load
D / 1.6	5.1	4.5	8.11	1,905	1	3	1	74	21	119	0.0	60	4	1,000	0	0.0	0.0
D / 1.6	5.1	4.5	8.08	3,185	1	3	1	74	21	119	0.0	77	4	0	0	0.0	0.0
D / 1.6	5.1	4.5	8.05	475	1	3	1	74	21	119	0.0	79	4	1,000,000	0	0.0	0.0
D / 1.6	5.1	4.5	8.27	37	1	3	1	74	21	119	0.0	75	4	0	0	0.0	0.0
D / 1.6	5.1	4.5	8.09	6	1	3	1	74	21	119	0.0	67	4	0	0	0.0	0.0
D / 1.7	5.1	4.5	8.08	132	1	3	1	74	21	119	0.0	71	4	0	0	0.0	0.0
U /	N/A	4.5	8.09	3	1	3	1	74	21	119	0.0	N/A	4	0	0	0.0	0.0
U /	N/A	4.5	8.06	22	1	3	1	74	21	119	0.0	N/A	4	0	0	0.0	0.0
U /	N/A	4.5	8.05	18	1	3	1	74	21	119	0.0	N/A	4	0	0	0.0	0.0
C+ / 6.4	2.8	5.6	10.85	459	0	41	0	15	44	494	0.0	32	19	1,500	0	2.3	0.0
C+ / 6.5	2.8	5.6	10.82	3	0	41	0	15	44	494	0.0	12	19	1,000	0	0.0	0.0
C+ / 6.4	2.8	5.6	10.80	78	0	41	0	15	44	494	0.0	15	19	1,500	0	0.0	0.0
C+ / 6.6	2.8	5.6	10.85	420	0	41	0	15	44	494	0.0	37	19	0	0	0.0	0.0
C+ / 6.5	2.8	5.6	10.85	160	0	41	0	15	44	494	0.0	N/A	19	1,000,000	0	0.0	0.0
C+ / 6.4	2.8	5.6	10.89	N/A	0	41	0	15	44	494	0.0	26	19	0	0	0.0	0.0
C+ / 6.4	2.8	5.6	10.86	1	0	41	0	15	44	494	0.0	21	19	0	0	0.0	0.0
C+ / 6.4	2.8	5.6	10.85	19	0	41	0	15	44	494	0.0	23	19	0	0	0.0	0.0
U /	N/A	5.6	10.85	1	0	41	0	15	44	494	0.0	N/A	19	0	0	0.0	0.0
U /	N/A	5.6	10.85	N/A	0	41	0	15	44	494	0.0	N/A	19	0	0	0.0	0.0
U /	N/A	5.6	10.85	36	0	41	0	15	44	494	0.0	N/A	19	0	0	0.0	0.0
U /	N/A	5.0	15.10	5	0	0	0	0	100	0	0.0	N/A	2	0	0	0.0	0.0
D+ / 2.5	4.4	N/A	15.43	8	4	4	0	90	2	148	0.0	99	4	1,000	0	2.3	0.0
D+ / 2.5	4.4	N/A	15.43	1	4	4	0	90	2	148	0.0	98	4	1,000	0	0.0	0.0
D+ / 2.5	4.5	N/A	15.44	16	4	4	0	90	2	148	0.0	99	4	0	0	0.0	0.0
D+ / 2.5	4.5	N/A	15.43	9	4	4	0	90	2	148	0.0	99	4	1,000,000	0	0.0	0.0
D+ / 2.5	4.4	N/A	15.43	N/A	4	4	0	90	2	148	0.0	99	4	0	0	0.0	0.0
D+ / 2.5	4.4	N/A	15.43	N/A	4	4	0	90	2	148	0.0	99	4	0	0	0.0	0.0
U /	N/A	N/A	15.43	N/A	4	4	0	90	2	148	0.0	N/A	4	0	0	0.0	0.0
U /	N/A	N/A	15.43	N/A	4	4	0	90	2	148	0.0	N/A	4	0	0	0.0	0.0
U /	N/A	N/A	15.43	N/A	4	4	0	90	2	148	0.0	N/A	4	0	0	0.0	0.0
E- / 0.1	11.7	N/A	10.33	7	4	90	0	5	1	62	0.0	5	4	1,000	0	2.3	0.0
E- / 0.1	11.6	N/A	10.33	N/A	4	90	0	5	1	62	0.0	2	4	1,000	0	0.0	0.0
E- / 0.1	11.6	N/A	10.32	N/A	4	90	0	5	1	62	0.0	5	4	0	0	0.0	0.0
E- / 0.1	11.6	N/A	10.33	2	4	90	0	5	1	62	0.0	6	4	1,000,000	0	0.0	0.0
E- / 0.1	11.6	N/A	10.33	N/A	4	90	0	5	1	62	0.0	6	4	0	0	0.0	0.0
E- / 0.1	11.6	N/A	10.33	N/A	4	90	0	5	1	62	0.0	6	4	0	0	0.0	0.0
U /	N/A	N/A	10.32	N/A	4	90	0	5	1	62	0.0	N/A	4	0	0	0.0	0.0
U /	N/A	N/A	10.32	N/A	4	90	0	5	1	62	0.0	N/A	4	0	0	0.0	0.0
U /	N/A	N/A	10.32	N/A	4	90	0	5	1	62	0.0	N/A	4	0	0	0.0	0.0
E / 0.5	7.5	0.1	5.26	19	4	3	1	40	52	52	2.4	18	10	1,000	0	2.3	0.0
E / 0.5	7.6	0.1	5.28	N/A	4	3	1	40	52	52	2.4	5	10	1,000	0	0.0	0.0
E / 0.5	7.6	0.1	5.29	4	4	3	1	40	52	52	2.4	7	10	1,000	0	0.0	0.0
E / 0.5	7.7	0.1	5.26	7	4	3	1	40	52	52	2.4	20	10	0	0	0.0	0.0
E / 0.4	7.7	0.1	5.25	254	4	3	1	40	52	52	2.4	23	10	1,000,000	0	0.0	0.0
E / 0.5	7.6	0.1	5.27	N/A	4	3	1	40	52	52	2.4	10	10	0	0	0.0	0.0
E / 0.5	7.6	0.1	5.25	N/A	4	3	1	40	52	52	2.4	11	10	0	0	0.0	0.0
U /	N/A	0.1	5.26	N/A	4	3	1	40	52	52	2.4	N/A	10	0	0	0.0	0.0
U /	N/A	0.1	5.25	N/A	4	3	1	40	52	52	2.4	N/A	10	0	0	0.0	0.0
U /	N/A	0.1	5.25	N/A	4	3	1	40	52	52	2.4	N/A	10	0	0	0.0	0.0
B- / 7.3	2.6	0.5	9.26	3,523	2	0	0	13	85	77	0.0	92	5	1,500	0	2.3	0.0
B- / 7.4	2.6	0.5	9.27	1,676	2	0	0	13	85	77	0.0	88	5	1,500	0	0.0	0.0
B- / 7.4	2.6	0.5	9.26	5,014	2	0	0	13	85	77	0.0	92	5	0	0	0.0	0.0

99 Pct = Best
0 Pct = Worst

Fund Type	Fund Name	Ticker Symbol	Overall Investment Rating	Phone	Performance Rating/Pts	3 Mo	6 Mo	1Yr / Pct	Annualized 3Yr / Pct	Annualized 5Yr / Pct	Dividend Yield	Expense Ratio
LP	Lord Abbett Floating Rate I	LFRIX	A+	(888) 522-2388	B+ / 8.5	2.27	4.02	11.99 / 83	3.94 / 74	5.07 / 85	4.68	0.60
LP	Lord Abbett Floating Rate R2	LFRRX	A+	(888) 522-2388	B / 7.8	2.02	3.61	11.34 / 82	3.29 / 66	4.43 / 78	4.11	1.20
LP	Lord Abbett Floating Rate R3	LRRRX	A+	(888) 522-2388	B / 8.0	2.15	3.77	11.46 / 82	3.43 / 68	4.56 / 79	4.21	1.10
LP	Lord Abbett Floating Rate R4	LRRKX	U	(888) 522-2388	U /	2.21	3.89	11.85 / 83	--	--	4.44	0.85
LP	Lord Abbett Floating Rate R5	LRRTX	U	(888) 522-2388	U /	2.28	4.03	12.00 / 83	--	--	4.69	0.60
LP	Lord Abbett Floating Rate R6	LRRVX	U	(888) 522-2388	U /	2.18	3.94	12.07 / 83	--	--	4.75	0.54
*COH	Lord Abbett High Yield A	LHYAX	B-	(888) 522-2388	A+ / 9.7	5.03	5.91	21.58 / 98	5.57 / 89	7.79 / 98	5.65	0.94
COH ●	Lord Abbett High Yield B	LHYBX	B-	(888) 522-2388	A+ / 9.7	4.84	5.51	20.71 / 97	4.79 / 84	6.96 / 96	5.04	1.74
COH	Lord Abbett High Yield C	LHYCX	B-	(888) 522-2388	A+ / 9.7	4.74	5.58	20.70 / 97	4.89 / 84	7.07 / 96	5.16	1.59
COH	Lord Abbett High Yield F	LHYFX	B-	(888) 522-2388	A+ / 9.8	4.92	5.96	21.71 / 98	5.67 / 90	7.89 / 98	5.87	0.84
COH	Lord Abbett High Yield I	LAHYX	B-	(888) 522-2388	A+ / 9.9	4.93	6.00	21.76 / 98	5.79 / 90	7.98 / 98	5.98	0.74
MUH	Lord Abbett High Yield Muni Bd F	HYMFX	A-	(888) 522-2388	A+ / 9.9	2.89	-2.48	3.69 / 69	6.03 / 99	5.42 / 99	4.49	0.77
COH ●	Lord Abbett High Yield P	LHYPX	B-	(888) 522-2388	A+ / 9.8	4.92	5.89	21.23 / 97	5.33 / 87	7.52 / 97	5.56	1.19
COH	Lord Abbett High Yield R2	LHYQX	B-	(888) 522-2388	A+ / 9.8	4.91	5.83	21.19 / 97	5.22 / 87	7.37 / 97	5.42	1.34
COH	Lord Abbett High Yield R3	LHYRX	B-	(888) 522-2388	A+ / 9.8	4.93	5.88	21.31 / 97	5.32 / 87	7.48 / 97	5.52	1.24
COH	Lord Abbett High Yield R4	LHYSX	B-	(888) 522-2388	A+ / 9.8	5.02	5.89	21.54 / 98	5.53 / 89	7.75 / 98	5.76	0.99
COH	Lord Abbett High Yield R5	LHYTX	U	(888) 522-2388	U /	5.07	6.01	21.77 / 98	--	--	5.99	0.74
COH	Lord Abbett High Yield R6	LHYVX	U	(888) 522-2388	U /	5.09	6.19	22.04 / 98	--	--	6.07	0.68
*COI	Lord Abbett Income A	LAGVX	C	(888) 522-2388	B / 7.7	3.08	0.70	12.18 / 84	3.84 / 73	4.64 / 80	3.64	0.90
COI ●	Lord Abbett Income B	LAVBX	C	(888) 522-2388	B- / 7.5	2.87	0.30	11.69 / 83	3.14 / 63	3.81 / 70	2.93	1.70
COI	Lord Abbett Income C	LAUSX	C	(888) 522-2388	B / 7.7	2.91	0.40	11.85 / 83	3.32 / 66	3.96 / 72	3.10	1.54
COI	Lord Abbett Income F	LAUFX	C+	(888) 522-2388	B+ / 8.4	3.10	0.74	12.28 / 84	3.94 / 75	4.73 / 81	3.81	0.80
COI	Lord Abbett Income I	LAUYX	B-	(888) 522-2388	B+ / 8.5	3.13	0.80	12.40 / 84	4.05 / 76	4.77 / 82	3.92	0.70
COI	Lord Abbett Income R2	LAUQX	C+	(888) 522-2388	B / 7.9	2.95	0.51	12.06 / 83	3.44 / 68	4.22 / 75	3.32	1.30
COI	Lord Abbett Income R3	LAURX	C+	(888) 522-2388	B / 7.9	3.00	0.55	11.81 / 83	3.54 / 69	4.33 / 76	3.43	1.20
COI	Lord Abbett Income R4	LAUKX	U	(888) 522-2388	U /	2.70	0.32	12.13 / 83	--	--	3.68	0.95
COI	Lord Abbett Income R5	LAUTX	U	(888) 522-2388	U /	3.13	0.80	12.41 / 84	--	--	3.93	0.70
COI	Lord Abbett Income R6	LAUVX	U	(888) 522-2388	U /	3.16	0.85	12.52 / 84	--	--	4.03	0.59
GEN	Lord Abbett Inflation Focused A	LIFAX	E	(888) 522-2388	D / 1.8	1.09	6.12	9.21 / 77	-0.84 / 3	0.12 / 16	4.03	0.96
GEN	Lord Abbett Inflation Focused C	LIFCX	E	(888) 522-2388	D / 1.8	0.94	5.79	8.54 / 75	-1.45 / 2	-0.55 / 3	3.52	1.59
GEN	Lord Abbett Inflation Focused F	LIFFX	E+	(888) 522-2388	D+ / 2.9	1.11	6.24	9.30 / 77	-0.74 / 3	0.22 / 19	4.20	0.86
GEN	Lord Abbett Inflation Focused I	LIFIX	E+	(888) 522-2388	C- / 3.1	1.14	6.31	9.51 / 78	-0.61 / 3	0.34 / 20	4.31	0.76
GEN	Lord Abbett Inflation Focused R2	LIFQX	E	(888) 522-2388	D / 2.0	0.99	5.91	8.69 / 76	-1.23 / 2	-0.19 / 4	3.74	1.36
GEN	Lord Abbett Inflation Focused R3	LIFRX	E	(888) 522-2388	D / 2.2	1.02	5.97	8.90 / 76	-1.10 / 3	-0.13 / 4	3.84	1.26
GEI	Lord Abbett Inflation Focused R4	LIFKX	U	(888) 522-2388	U /	1.16	6.17	9.14 / 77	--	--	4.05	1.01
GEI	Lord Abbett Inflation Focused R5	LIFTX	U	(888) 522-2388	U /	1.14	6.22	9.33 / 77	--	--	4.31	0.76
GEI	Lord Abbett Inflation Focused R6	LIFVX	U	(888) 522-2388	U /	1.20	6.34	9.57 / 78	--	--	4.53	0.53
*MUN	Lord Abbett Interm Tax Free A	LISAX	D+	(888) 522-2388	C / 5.2	1.93	-3.26	-0.55 / 9	2.87 / 80	2.61 / 73	2.47	0.71
MUN●	Lord Abbett Interm Tax Free B	LISBX	D	(888) 522-2388	C / 4.7	1.82	-3.56	-1.25 / 3	2.08 / 64	1.82 / 54	1.71	1.51
MUN	Lord Abbett Interm Tax Free C	LISCX	D+	(888) 522-2388	C / 5.0	1.77	-3.48	-1.18 / 3	2.23 / 68	1.96 / 58	1.88	1.34
MUN	Lord Abbett Interm Tax Free F	LISFX	C+	(888) 522-2388	C+ / 6.8	1.95	-3.13	-0.46 / 10	2.97 / 81	2.71 / 75	2.62	0.61
MUN	Lord Abbett Interm Tax Free I	LAIIX	B-	(888) 522-2388	B- / 7.0	2.07	-3.08	-0.27 / 13	3.10 / 83	2.81 / 76	2.72	0.51
MUN●	Lord Abbett Interm Tax Free P	LISPX	C	(888) 522-2388	C+ / 6.1	1.96	-3.28	-0.69 / 7	2.62 / 76	2.39 / 68	2.28	0.96
MUH	Lord Abbett Sh Dur Hi Yld Muni Bd A	SDHAX	U	(888) 522-2388	U /	1.78	-2.50	0.44 / 36	--	--	2.61	1.71
MUH	Lord Abbett Sh Dur Hi Yld Muni Bd C	SDHCX	U	(888) 522-2388	U /	1.59	-2.86	-0.39 / 11	--	--	1.89	2.51
MUH	Lord Abbett Sh Dur Hi Yld Muni Bd F	SDHFX	U	(888) 522-2388	U /	1.80	-2.45	0.53 / 38	--	--	2.76	1.61
MUH	Lord Abbett Sh Dur Hi Yld Muni Bd I	SDHIX	U	(888) 522-2388	U /	1.82	-2.41	0.56 / 38	--	--	2.86	1.51
*GEI	Lord Abbett Shrt Duration Inc A	LALDX	B+	(888) 522-2388	C- / 4.0	0.96	1.01	4.69 / 65	1.98 / 43	2.57 / 51	3.83	0.60
GEI ●	Lord Abbett Shrt Duration Inc B	LLTBX	B	(888) 522-2388	C- / 3.7	0.76	0.62	4.11 / 63	1.18 / 30	1.77 / 38	3.11	1.40
GEI	Lord Abbett Shrt Duration Inc C	LDLAX	B	(888) 522-2388	C- / 3.9	0.80	0.70	4.27 / 63	1.34 / 33	1.91 / 41	3.28	1.25
GEI	Lord Abbett Shrt Duration Inc F	LDLFX	A	(888) 522-2388	C / 5.1	0.98	1.06	5.03 / 67	2.08 / 45	2.67 / 52	4.00	0.50
GEI	Lord Abbett Shrt Duration Inc I	LLDYX	A	(888) 522-2388	C / 5.3	1.00	1.11	5.14 / 67	2.18 / 46	2.77 / 54	4.11	0.40

● Denotes fund is closed to new investors
* Denotes fund is included in Section II

RISK			NET ASSETS		ASSET							FUND MANAGER		MINIMUM		LOADS	
Risk Rating/Pts	3 Yr Avg Standard Deviation	Avg Dura-tion	NAV As of 2/28/17	Total $(Mil)	Cash %	Gov. Bond %	Muni. Bond %	Corp. Bond %	Other %	Portfolio Turnover Ratio	Avg Coupon Rate	Manager Quality Pct	Manager Tenure (Years)	Initial Purch. $	Additional Purch. $	Front End Load	Back End Load
B- / 7.4	2.6	0.5	9.27	851	2	0	0	13	85	77	0.0	93	5	1,000,000	0	0.0	0.0
B- / 7.4	2.6	0.5	9.27	1	2	0	0	13	85	77	0.0	90	5	0	0	0.0	0.0
B- / 7.4	2.6	0.5	9.27	39	2	0	0	13	85	77	0.0	90	5	0	0	0.0	0.0
U /	N/A	0.5	9.27	4	2	0	0	13	85	77	0.0	N/A	5	0	0	0.0	0.0
U /	N/A	0.5	9.28	2	2	0	0	13	85	77	0.0	N/A	5	0	0	0.0	0.0
U /	N/A	0.5	9.27	17	2	0	0	13	85	77	0.0	N/A	5	0	0	0.0	0.0
D- / 1.1	5.6	4.4	7.67	1,673	1	1	0	83	15	93	0.0	78	7	1,500	0	2.3	0.0
D- / 1.1	5.7	4.4	7.64	4	1	1	0	83	15	93	0.0	60	7	1,000	0	0.0	0.0
D- / 1.1	5.6	4.4	7.63	499	1	1	0	83	15	93	0.0	66	7	1,500	0	0.0	0.0
D- / 1.1	5.6	4.4	7.66	2,104	1	1	0	83	15	93	0.0	79	7	0	0	0.0	0.0
D- / 1.1	5.6	4.4	7.70	1,992	1	1	0	83	15	93	0.0	81	7	1,000,000	0	0.0	0.0
D+ / 2.4	3.9	7.4	11.64	471	1	0	98	0	1	27	5.5	86	13	0	0	0.0	0.0
D- / 1.1	5.7	4.4	7.78	N/A	1	1	0	83	15	93	0.0	74	7	0	0	0.0	0.0
D- / 1.1	5.7	4.4	7.72	14	1	1	0	83	15	93	0.0	72	7	0	0	0.0	0.0
D- / 1.1	5.7	4.4	7.72	79	1	1	0	83	15	93	0.0	74	7	0	0	0.0	0.0
D- / 1.1	5.7	4.4	7.67	34	1	1	0	83	15	93	0.0	77	7	0	0	0.0	0.0
U /	N/A	4.4	7.70	28	1	1	0	83	15	93	0.0	N/A	7	0	0	0.0	0.0
U /	N/A	4.4	7.71	124	1	1	0	83	15	93	0.0	N/A	7	0	0	0.0	0.0
D+ / 2.6	4.4	5.7	2.82	890	2	17	1	59	21	191	0.0	63	19	1,500	0	2.3	0.0
D+ / 2.6	4.3	5.7	2.83	3	2	17	1	59	21	191	0.0	34	19	500	0	0.0	0.0
D+ / 2.6	4.3	5.7	2.84	248	2	17	1	59	21	191	0.0	47	19	1,500	0	0.0	0.0
D+ / 2.5	4.5	5.7	2.82	515	2	17	1	59	21	191	0.0	64	19	0	0	0.0	0.0
D+ / 2.6	4.4	5.7	2.82	87	2	17	1	59	21	191	0.0	69	19	1,000,000	0	0.0	0.0
D+ / 2.6	4.4	5.7	2.85	2	2	17	1	59	21	191	0.0	54	19	0	0	0.0	0.0
D+ / 2.5	4.5	5.7	2.83	54	2	17	1	59	21	191	0.0	51	19	0	0	0.0	0.0
U /	N/A	5.7	2.82	2	2	17	1	59	21	191	0.0	N/A	19	0	0	0.0	0.0
U /	N/A	5.7	2.82	N/A	2	17	1	59	21	191	0.0	N/A	19	0	0	0.0	0.0
U /	N/A	5.7	2.82	4	2	17	1	59	21	191	0.0	N/A	19	0	0	0.0	0.0
D+ / 2.5	4.5	2.0	12.20	211	5	3	0	46	46	79	0.0	66	6	1,500	0	2.3	0.0
D+ / 2.5	4.5	2.0	12.22	53	5	3	0	46	46	79	0.0	37	6	1,500	0	0.0	0.0
D+ / 2.5	4.5	2.0	12.21	354	5	3	0	46	46	79	0.0	69	6	0	0	0.0	0.0
D+ / 2.5	4.5	2.0	12.21	431	5	3	0	46	46	79	0.0	72	6	1,000,000	0	0.0	0.0
D+ / 2.5	4.5	2.0	12.19	N/A	5	3	0	46	46	79	0.0	53	6	0	0	0.0	0.0
D+ / 2.4	4.5	2.0	12.20	N/A	5	3	0	46	46	79	0.0	58	6	0	0	0.0	0.0
U /	N/A	2.0	12.21	N/A	5	3	0	46	46	79	0.0	N/A	6	0	0	0.0	0.0
U /	N/A	2.0	12.20	N/A	5	3	0	46	46	79	0.0	N/A	6	0	0	0.0	0.0
U /	N/A	2.0	12.20	N/A	5	3	0	46	46	79	0.0	N/A	6	0	0	0.0	0.0
C / 4.6	3.3	5.1	10.65	1,682	0	0	99	0	1	8	4.9	21	11	1,000	0	2.3	0.0
C / 4.5	3.3	5.1	10.65	1	0	0	99	0	1	8	4.9	7	11	1,000	0	0.0	0.0
C / 4.6	3.3	5.1	10.64	585	0	0	99	0	1	8	4.9	9	11	1,000	0	0.0	0.0
C / 4.5	3.3	5.1	10.65	1,623	0	0	99	0	1	8	4.9	23	11	0	0	0.0	0.0
C / 4.6	3.3	5.1	10.66	334	0	0	99	0	1	8	4.9	28	11	1,000,000	0	0.0	0.0
C / 4.5	3.3	5.1	10.66	N/A	0	0	99	0	1	8	4.9	15	11	0	0	0.0	0.0
U /	N/A	3.3	14.97	65	0	0	88	0	12	12	4.8	N/A	2	1,000	0	2.3	0.0
U /	N/A	3.3	14.97	8	0	0	88	0	12	12	4.8	N/A	2	1,000	0	0.0	0.0
U /	N/A	3.3	14.97	69	0	0	88	0	12	12	4.8	N/A	2	0	0	0.0	0.0
U /	N/A	3.3	14.97	17	0	0	88	0	12	12	4.8	N/A	2	1,000,000	0	0.0	0.0
A- / 9.0	1.3	2.0	4.31	10,725	0	2	0	47	51	50	0.0	80	19	1,500	0	2.3	0.0
A- / 9.0	1.4	2.0	4.32	12	0	2	0	47	51	50	0.0	66	19	1,000	0	0.0	0.0
A- / 9.0	1.4	2.0	4.34	6,565	0	2	0	47	51	50	0.0	70	19	1,500	0	0.0	0.0
B+ / 8.9	1.4	2.0	4.31	14,405	0	2	0	47	51	50	0.0	81	19	0	0	0.0	0.0
B+ / 8.9	1.4	2.0	4.31	6,182	0	2	0	47	51	50	0.0	82	19	1,000,000	0	0.0	0.0

Fund Type	Fund Name	Ticker Symbol	Overall Investment Rating	Phone	Performance Rating/Pts	3 Mo	6 Mo	1Yr / Pct	3Yr / Pct	5Yr / Pct	Dividend Yield	Expense Ratio
GEI	Lord Abbett Shrt Duration Inc R2	LDLQX	B+	(888) 522-2388	C- / 4.2	0.86	0.81	4.28 /63	1.51 /35	2.17 /44	3.52	1.00
GEI	Lord Abbett Shrt Duration Inc R3	LDLRX	A-	(888) 522-2388	C / 4.6	1.12	1.09	4.63 /65	1.69 /38	2.28 /46	3.61	0.90
COI	Lord Abbett Shrt Duration Inc R4	LDLKX	U	(888) 522-2388	U /	0.94	0.98	4.64 /65	--	--	3.86	0.65
COI	Lord Abbett Shrt Duration Inc R5	LDLTX	U	(888) 522-2388	U /	1.01	1.11	4.91 /66	--	--	4.12	0.40
COI	Lord Abbett Shrt Duration Inc R6	LDLVX	U	(888) 522-2388	U /	1.02	1.14	4.97 /66	--	--	4.18	0.33
*MUN	Lord Abbett Shrt Duration Tax-Fr A	LSDAX	D-	(888) 522-2388	E / 0.4	1.05	-1.11	-0.51 / 9	0.54 /25	0.75 /29	1.06	0.70
MUN	Lord Abbett Shrt Duration Tax-Fr C	LSDCX	D-	(888) 522-2388	E / 0.4	0.96	-1.35	-1.06 / 4	-0.07 / 5	0.13 /18	0.47	1.32
MUN	Lord Abbett Shrt Duration Tax-Fr F	LSDFX	C	(888) 522-2388	D+ / 2.3	1.14	-1.00	-0.35 /12	0.65 /28	0.86 /32	1.19	0.60
MUN	Lord Abbett Shrt Duration Tax-Fr I	LISDX	C	(888) 522-2388	D+ / 2.6	1.17	-0.95	-0.25 /14	0.75 /30	0.96 /34	1.29	0.50
MUS	Lord Abbett Tax Free CA A	LCFIX	B-	(888) 522-2388	B / 8.2	2.43	-3.93	0.34 /34	4.65 /96	4.13 /94	3.19	0.82
MUS	Lord Abbett Tax Free CA C	CALAX	B-	(888) 522-2388	B / 8.2	2.37	-4.15	-0.21 /14	4.02 /93	3.48 /87	2.61	1.45
MUS	Lord Abbett Tax Free CA F	LCFFX	B+	(888) 522-2388	A- / 9.1	2.46	-3.89	0.43 /36	4.75 /96	4.22 /95	3.36	0.72
MUN	Lord Abbett Tax Free CA I	CAILX	B+	(888) 522-2388	A- / 9.2	2.49	-3.85	0.53 /38	4.82 /97	4.32 /95	3.47	0.62
*MUN	Lord Abbett Tax Free Natl A	LANSX	B-	(888) 522-2388	B / 7.9	2.24	-3.85	0.36 /34	4.41 /95	3.85 /92	3.40	0.77
MUN ●	Lord Abbett Tax Free Natl B	LANBX	C+	(888) 522-2388	B- / 7.5	2.12	-4.20	-0.42 /11	3.61 /89	3.05 /81	2.65	1.57
MUN	Lord Abbett Tax Free Natl C	LTNSX	C+	(888) 522-2388	B / 7.8	2.17	-4.13	-0.25 /14	3.80 /91	3.22 /84	2.83	1.40
MUN	Lord Abbett Tax Free Natl F	LANFX	B+	(888) 522-2388	B+ / 8.9	2.26	-3.89	0.46 /36	4.51 /96	3.95 /93	3.57	0.67
MUN	Lord Abbett Tax Free Natl I	LTNIX	B+	(888) 522-2388	A- / 9.0	2.38	-3.75	0.54 /38	4.60 /96	4.04 /93	3.66	0.57
MUS	Lord Abbett Tax Free NJ A	LANJX	C	(888) 522-2388	B- / 7.2	1.83	-3.80	0.82 /42	3.84 /91	3.17 /83	3.07	0.86
MUS	Lord Abbett Tax Free NJ F	LNJFX	B	(888) 522-2388	B+ / 8.4	2.07	-3.56	1.13 /47	4.01 /93	3.26 /84	3.24	0.76
MUN	Lord Abbett Tax Free NJ I	LINJX	B	(888) 522-2388	B+ / 8.6	2.08	-3.53	1.01 /45	4.15 /94	3.40 /86	3.33	0.66
MUS	Lord Abbett Tax Free NY A	LANYX	B-	(888) 522-2388	B / 7.6	2.33	-3.50	0.54 /38	4.10 /93	3.40 /86	2.66	0.80
MUS	Lord Abbett Tax Free NY C	NYLAX	B-	(888) 522-2388	B- / 7.5	2.17	-3.73	-0.11 /16	3.47 /87	2.76 /75	2.07	1.44
MUS	Lord Abbett Tax Free NY F	LNYFX	B+	(888) 522-2388	B+ / 8.6	2.35	-3.45	0.64 /39	4.20 /94	3.50 /87	2.82	0.70
MUN	Lord Abbett Tax Free NY I	NYLIX	A-	(888) 522-2388	B+ / 8.8	2.38	-3.40	0.73 /41	4.34 /95	3.63 /89	2.92	0.60
*GEI	Lord Abbett Total Return A	LTRAX	C+	(888) 522-2388	C / 4.7	1.45	-1.46	4.17 /63	2.78 /57	2.95 /57	2.66	0.83
GEI ●	Lord Abbett Total Return B	LTRBX	C-	(888) 522-2388	C / 4.3	1.25	-1.85	3.25 /58	1.97 /43	2.12 /44	1.93	1.63
GEI	Lord Abbett Total Return C	LTRCX	C	(888) 522-2388	C / 4.6	1.29	-1.77	3.51 /60	2.13 /45	2.29 /46	2.08	1.48
GEI	Lord Abbett Total Return F	LTRFX	B+	(888) 522-2388	C+ / 5.9	1.38	-1.42	4.16 /63	2.88 /59	3.03 /58	2.82	0.73
GEI	Lord Abbett Total Return I	LTRYX	B+	(888) 522-2388	C+ / 6.0	1.50	-1.35	4.38 /64	2.99 /61	3.16 /60	2.93	0.63
GEI ●	Lord Abbett Total Return P	LTRPX	C+	(888) 522-2388	C / 5.2	1.29	-1.67	3.80 /61	2.52 /52	2.68 /52	2.47	1.08
GEI	Lord Abbett Total Return R2	LTRQX	C+	(888) 522-2388	C / 4.9	1.26	-1.65	3.66 /61	2.37 /49	2.53 /50	2.33	1.23
GEI	Lord Abbett Total Return R3	LTRRX	C+	(888) 522-2388	C / 5.1	1.28	-1.61	3.76 /61	2.48 /51	2.63 /52	2.43	1.13
COI	Lord Abbett Total Return R4	LTRKX	U	(888) 522-2388	U /	1.44	-1.48	4.13 /63	--	--	2.68	0.88
COI	Lord Abbett Total Return R5	LTRTX	U	(888) 522-2388	U /	1.51	-1.34	4.34 /64	--	--	2.99	0.63
COI	Lord Abbett Total Return R6	LTRHX	U	(888) 522-2388	U /	1.43	-1.39	4.47 /64	--	--	3.02	0.51
*MUH	Lord Abbett Tx Fr High Yld Muni A	HYMAX	B+	(888) 522-2388	A+ / 9.7	2.87	-2.53	3.59 /69	5.90 /98	5.30 /98	4.29	0.87
MUH	Lord Abbett Tx Fr High Yld Muni C	HYMCX	B+	(888) 522-2388	A+ / 9.7	2.72	-2.91	2.96 /65	5.24 /97	4.64 /97	3.76	1.50
MUH	Lord Abbett Tx Fr High Yld Muni I	HYMIX	A-	(888) 522-2388	A+ / 9.9	2.92	-2.46	3.78 /70	6.06 /99	5.45 /99	4.57	0.67
MUH ●	Lord Abbett Tx Fr High Yld Muni P	HYMPX	B+	(888) 522-2388	A+ / 9.8	2.81	-2.63	3.37 /67	5.70 /98	5.10 /98	4.17	1.12
MMT	Lord Abbett US G and G Spns MM A	LACXX	U	(888) 522-2388	U /	0.00	0.01	0.02 /19	0.02 / 8	0.02 / 8	0.02	N/A
MMT	Lord Abbett US G and G Spns MM C	LCCXX	U	(888) 522-2388	U /	0.00	0.01	0.02 /19	0.02 / 8	0.02 / 8	0.02	N/A
GEI	LWAS DFA Two Year Fixed Income	DFCFX	C+	(800) 984-9472	D / 2.0	0.28	0.23	0.79 /37	0.57 /21	0.52 /22	0.79	0.29
USS	LWAS DFA Two Year Government	DFYGX	C	(800) 984-9472	D / 1.8	0.20	0.00	0.38 /31	0.41 /20	0.34 /20	0.58	0.28
COI	Madison Core Bond A	MBOAX	D+	(800) 877-6089	D+ / 2.7	0.98	-1.62	2.65 /54	2.28 /48	1.51 /35	2.12	0.90
COI ●	Madison Core Bond B	MBOBX	C-	(800) 877-6089	C- / 3.3	0.79	-1.98	1.89 /48	1.52 /35	0.78 /25	1.46	1.65
COI	Madison Core Bond R6	MCBRX	B	(800) 877-6089	C / 5.2	1.06	-1.48	3.02 /57	2.62 /54	--	2.48	0.52
COI	Madison Core Bond Y	MBOYX	B	(800) 877-6089	C / 5.0	1.06	-1.49	2.93 /56	2.53 /52	1.77 /38	2.49	0.65
GEI	Madison Corporate Bond Y	COINX	C	(800) 877-6089	C+ / 6.6	1.92	-1.60	6.14 /71	3.18 /64	2.70 /53	2.86	0.65
COH	Madison High Income A	MHNAX	D	(800) 877-6089	B- / 7.3	4.08	4.45	14.86 /88	3.29 /66	4.82 /82	4.49	1.01
COH ●	Madison High Income B	MHNBX	D+	(800) 877-6089	B / 7.6	3.76	4.09	13.96 /87	2.47 /51	4.00 /73	3.83	1.76
COH	Madison High Income Y	MHNYX	C	(800) 877-6089	B+ / 8.8	4.09	4.53	15.06 /89	3.58 /70	5.09 /85	5.24	0.76

● Denotes fund is closed to new investors
* Denotes fund is included in Section II

RISK			NET ASSETS		ASSET							FUND MANAGER		MINIMUM		LOADS	
Risk Rating/Pts	3 Yr Avg Standard Deviation	Avg Dura-tion	NAV As of 2/28/17	Total $(Mil)	Cash %	Gov. Bond %	Muni. Bond %	Corp. Bond %	Other %	Portfolio Turnover Ratio	Avg Coupon Rate	Manager Quality Pct	Manager Tenure (Years)	Initial Purch. $	Additional Purch. $	Front End Load	Back End Load
A- / 9.0	1.3	2.0	4.31	28	0	2	0	47	51	50	0.0	74	19	0	0	0.0	0.0
A- / 9.0	1.3	2.0	4.32	283	0	2	0	47	51	50	0.0	76	19	0	0	0.0	0.0
U /	N/A	2.0	4.32	48	0	2	0	47	51	50	0.0	N/A	19	0	0	0.0	0.0
U /	N/A	2.0	4.30	18	0	2	0	47	51	50	0.0	N/A	19	0	0	0.0	0.0
U /	N/A	2.0	4.31	205	0	2	0	47	51	50	0.0	N/A	19	0	0	0.0	0.0
A- / 9.0	1.3	2.2	15.56	875	0	0	99	0	1	23	3.8	15	9	1,000	0	2.3	0.0
A- / 9.0	1.3	2.2	15.57	161	0	0	99	0	1	23	3.8	6	9	1,000	0	0.0	0.0
A- / 9.0	1.3	2.2	15.57	653	0	0	99	0	1	23	3.8	18	9	0	0	0.0	0.0
A- / 9.0	1.3	2.2	15.57	73	0	0	99	0	1	23	3.8	20	9	1,000,000	0	0.0	0.0
C- / 3.1	4.1	6.7	10.77	202	1	0	98	0	1	8	5.2	59	11	1,000	0	2.3	0.0
D+ / 2.9	4.1	6.7	10.78	49	1	0	98	0	1	8	5.2	29	11	1,000	0	0.0	0.0
C- / 3.1	4.1	6.7	10.77	47	1	0	98	0	1	8	5.2	62	11	0	0	0.0	0.0
C- / 3.0	4.1	6.7	10.76	5	1	0	98	0	1	8	5.2	64	11	1,000,000	0	0.0	0.0
C- / 3.3	3.9	6.4	11.12	1,461	1	0	98	0	1	16	5.2	58	11	1,000	0	2.3	0.0
C- / 3.3	3.9	6.4	11.18	2	1	0	98	0	1	16	5.2	23	11	1,000	0	0.0	0.0
C- / 3.3	3.9	6.4	11.14	179	1	0	98	0	1	16	5.2	28	11	1,000	0	0.0	0.0
C- / 3.3	3.9	6.4	11.11	312	1	0	98	0	1	16	5.2	60	11	0	0	0.0	0.0
C- / 3.3	3.9	6.4	11.12	9	1	0	98	0	1	16	5.2	63	11	1,000,000	0	0.0	0.0
C- / 3.3	4.0	6.2	4.86	87	1	0	98	0	1	13	5.1	30	11	1,000	0	2.3	0.0
C- / 3.2	4.0	6.2	4.87	9	1	0	98	0	1	13	5.1	35	11	0	0	0.0	0.0
C- / 3.3	4.0	6.2	4.87	N/A	1	0	98	0	1	13	5.1	N/A	11	1,000,000	0	0.0	0.0
C- / 3.7	3.6	6.0	11.17	270	1	0	98	0	1	20	5.1	56	11	1,000	0	2.3	0.0
C- / 3.8	3.6	6.0	11.16	60	1	0	98	0	1	20	5.1	27	11	1,000	0	0.0	0.0
C- / 3.7	3.7	6.0	11.18	44	1	0	98	0	1	20	5.1	59	11	0	0	0.0	0.0
C- / 3.8	3.6	6.0	11.18	1	1	0	98	0	1	20	5.1	64	11	1,000,000	0	0.0	0.0
C+ / 6.5	2.8	5.4	10.34	1,292	0	35	0	23	42	443	0.0	62	19	1,500	0	2.3	0.0
C+ / 6.2	2.9	5.4	10.32	6	0	35	0	23	42	443	0.0	25	19	1,000	0	0.0	0.0
C+ / 6.4	2.8	5.4	10.33	199	0	35	0	23	42	443	0.0	31	19	1,500	0	0.0	0.0
C+ / 6.7	2.8	5.4	10.33	1,006	0	35	0	23	42	443	0.0	66	19	0	0	0.0	0.0
C+ / 6.5	2.8	5.4	10.36	308	0	35	0	23	42	443	0.0	68	19	1,000,000	0	0.0	0.0
C+ / 6.5	2.8	5.4	10.38	1	0	35	0	23	42	443	0.0	54	19	0	0	0.0	0.0
C+ / 6.7	2.8	5.4	10.33	9	0	35	0	23	42	443	0.0	48	19	0	0	0.0	0.0
C+ / 6.5	2.8	5.4	10.33	138	0	35	0	23	42	443	0.0	52	19	0	0	0.0	0.0
U /	N/A	5.4	10.34	43	0	35	0	23	42	443	0.0	N/A	19	0	0	0.0	0.0
U /	N/A	5.4	10.34	29	0	35	0	23	42	443	0.0	N/A	19	0	0	0.0	0.0
U /	N/A	5.4	10.34	71	0	35	0	23	42	443	0.0	N/A	19	0	0	0.0	0.0
D+ / 2.3	4.0	7.4	11.63	1,128	1	0	98	0	1	27	5.5	85	13	1,000	0	2.3	0.0
D+ / 2.3	4.0	7.4	11.63	395	1	0	98	0	1	27	5.5	80	13	1,000	0	0.0	0.0
D+ / 2.3	4.0	7.4	11.61	50	1	0	98	0	1	27	5.5	87	13	1,000,000	0	0.0	0.0
D+ / 2.4	3.9	7.4	11.64	N/A	1	0	98	0	1	27	5.5	84	13	0	0	0.0	0.0
U /	N/A	N/A	1.00	492	100	0	0	0	0	0	0.0	N/A	N/A	1,000	0	0.0	0.0
U /	N/A	N/A	1.00	51	100	0	0	0	0	0	0.0	N/A	N/A	1,000	0	0.0	0.0
A+ / 9.8	0.5	1.6	9.99	80	0	35	4	58	3	93	1.5	53	N/A	0	0	0.0	0.0
A+ / 9.7	0.6	1.8	9.85	111	0	99	0	0	1	118	0.9	42	16	0	0	0.0	0.0
B- / 7.4	2.6	5.0	9.98	34	1	25	8	32	34	39	25.5	42	8	1,000	50	4.5	0.0
B- / 7.5	2.6	5.0	9.99	2	1	25	8	32	34	39	25.5	16	8	1,000	50	0.0	0.0
B- / 7.4	2.6	5.0	9.99	2	1	25	8	32	34	39	25.5	59	8	500,000	50,000	0.0	0.0
B- / 7.4	2.6	5.0	9.95	177	1	25	8	32	34	39	25.5	55	8	25,000	50	0.0	0.0
C- / 3.8	3.6	6.7	11.47	24	2	0	2	94	2	36	26.7	59	10	25,000	50	0.0	0.0
D- / 1.3	5.4	3.6	6.14	21	6	6	0	85	3	73	17.3	16	1	1,000	50	4.5	0.0
D- / 1.3	5.4	3.6	6.31	2	6	6	0	85	3	73	17.3	5	1	1,000	50	0.0	0.0
D- / 1.3	5.4	3.6	6.03	1	6	6	0	85	3	73	17.3	23	1	25,000	50	0.0	0.0

						PERFORMANCE							
							Total Return % through 2/28/17					Incl. in Returns	
										Annualized		Dividend	Expense
Fund Type	Fund Name	Ticker Symbol	Overall Investment Rating	Phone		Performance Rating/Pts	3 Mo	6 Mo	1Yr / Pct	3Yr / Pct	5Yr / Pct	Yield	Ratio
GEI	Madison High Quality Bond Y	MIIBX	C	(800) 877-6089		D+ / 2.3	0.48	-0.96	0.12 / 23	0.93 / 26	0.84 / 25	1.10	0.49
MUN	Madison Tax Free National Y	GTFHX	B-	(800) 877-6089		C+ / 6.9	1.96	-2.65	-0.47 / 10	3.04 / 83	2.31 / 66	2.35	0.75
MUS	Madison Tax Free Virginia Y	GTVAX	A-	(800) 877-6089		C+ / 6.2	1.61	-2.28	-0.49 / 10	2.61 / 76	1.97 / 58	2.15	0.85
MUS	Maine Municipal	MEMUX	D-	(800) 601-5593		D+ / 2.4	1.08	-3.72	-1.38 / 2	1.88 / 59	1.69 / 51	2.37	1.30
MUN	MainStay California Tx Fr Opp A	MSCAX	B-	(800) 624-6782		B+ / 8.6	2.02	-4.83	0.49 / 37	5.75 / 98	--	3.00	0.86
MUN	MainStay California Tx Fr Opp C	MSCCX	B+	(800) 624-6782		A / 9.4	1.95	-4.97	0.20 / 29	5.35 / 98	--	2.85	1.19
MUN	MainStay California Tx Fr Opp I	MCOIX	A-	(800) 624-6782		A+ / 9.7	2.09	-4.71	0.74 / 41	6.02 / 98	--	3.41	0.61
MUN	MainStay California Tx Fr Opp Inv	MSCVX	B-	(800) 624-6782		B+ / 8.5	2.01	-4.85	0.45 / 36	5.68 / 98	--	2.97	0.94
LP	MainStay Floating Rate A	MXFAX	A	(800) 624-6782		C+ / 6.3	1.94	3.33	10.07 / 79	2.83 / 58	3.59 / 67	3.39	1.06
LP ●	MainStay Floating Rate B	MXFBX	A	(800) 624-6782		C+ / 6.3	1.74	2.93	9.36 / 77	2.07 / 44	2.81 / 55	2.75	1.81
LP	MainStay Floating Rate C	MXFCX	A-	(800) 624-6782		C+ / 6.2	1.74	2.82	9.25 / 77	2.04 / 44	2.81 / 55	2.76	1.81
LP	MainStay Floating Rate I	MXFIX	A+	(800) 624-6782		B- / 7.5	2.01	3.34	10.35 / 80	3.08 / 62	3.85 / 70	3.75	0.81
LP	MainStay Floating Rate Inv	MXFNX	A	(800) 624-6782		C+ / 6.3	1.93	3.20	10.06 / 79	2.84 / 59	3.58 / 67	3.39	1.06
LP	MainStay Floating Rate R3	MXFHX	U	(800) 624-6782		U /	1.86	3.04	9.54 / 78	--	--	3.02	1.41
GL	MainStay Global High Income A	MGHAX	D+	(800) 624-6782		B+ / 8.4	5.69	0.87	18.00 / 94	4.29 / 78	4.16 / 74	4.79	1.23
GL ●	MainStay Global High Income B	MGHBX	D+	(800) 624-6782		B+ / 8.6	5.55	0.42	17.00 / 92	3.36 / 67	3.21 / 61	4.18	2.16
GL	MainStay Global High Income C	MHYCX	D+	(800) 624-6782		B+ / 8.6	5.44	0.42	16.86 / 92	3.35 / 67	3.21 / 61	4.18	2.16
GL	MainStay Global High Income I	MGHIX	C	(800) 624-6782		A / 9.4	5.75	0.99	18.28 / 94	4.55 / 81	4.41 / 77	5.25	0.98
GL	MainStay Global High Income Inv	MGHHX	D	(800) 624-6782		B / 8.2	5.59	0.68	17.74 / 93	4.10 / 76	3.97 / 72	4.58	1.41
USS	MainStay Government Fund A	MGVAX	D-	(800) 624-6782		E / 0.4	0.17	-2.20	-0.66 / 7	1.40 / 33	1.09 / 29	1.89	1.00
USS ●	MainStay Government Fund B	MCSGX	D-	(800) 624-6782		E / 0.5	-0.09	-2.69	-1.66 / 1	0.35 / 19	0.11 / 15	0.95	2.03
USS	MainStay Government Fund C	MGVCX	D-	(800) 624-6782		E / 0.5	0.03	-2.58	-1.55 / 1	0.39 / 20	0.11 / 15	0.95	2.03
USS	MainStay Government Fund I	MGOIX	C	(800) 624-6782		D+ / 2.9	0.23	-2.06	-0.41 / 11	1.60 / 36	1.33 / 32	2.21	0.75
USS	MainStay Government Fund Inv	MGVNX	D-	(800) 624-6782		E / 0.3	0.10	-2.32	-0.91 / 5	1.10 / 29	0.84 / 25	1.64	1.28
COH	MainStay High Yield Corp Bond A	MHCAX	C+	(800) 624-6782		A- / 9.0	3.69	4.58	19.69 / 95	4.72 / 83	6.28 / 94	5.86	0.96
COH ●	MainStay High Yield Corp Bond B	MKHCX	C+	(800) 624-6782		A- / 9.2	3.50	4.17	18.56 / 94	3.87 / 74	5.42 / 88	5.34	1.77
*COH	MainStay High Yield Corp Bond C	MYHCX	C+	(800) 624-6782		A- / 9.2	3.68	4.35	18.76 / 95	3.92 / 74	5.45 / 88	5.33	1.77
COH	MainStay High Yield Corp Bond I	MHYIX	B	(800) 624-6782		A+ / 9.7	3.93	4.89	19.96 / 96	5.04 / 85	6.54 / 95	6.37	0.71
COH	MainStay High Yield Corp Bond Inv	MHHIX	C+	(800) 624-6782		A- / 9.0	3.85	4.56	19.55 / 95	4.66 / 82	6.25 / 94	5.85	1.02
COH	MainStay High Yield Corp Bond R1	MHHRX	B	(800) 624-6782		A+ / 9.6	3.91	4.65	19.86 / 96	4.88 / 84	--	6.27	0.81
COH	MainStay High Yield Corp Bond R2	MHYRX	B	(800) 624-6782		A+ / 9.6	3.67	4.53	19.56 / 95	4.61 / 82	6.14 / 93	6.03	1.06
COH	MainStay High Yield Corp Bond R3	MHYTX	U	(800) 624-6782		U /	3.80	4.42	19.31 / 95	--	--	5.82	1.31
COH	MainStay High Yield Corp Bond R6	MHYSX	B	(800) 624-6782		A+ / 9.7	3.98	4.80	20.20 / 96	5.12 / 86	--	6.55	0.58
MUH	MainStay High Yield Muni Bond A	MMHAX	B+	(800) 624-6782		A+ / 9.8	3.75	-3.05	3.28 / 67	7.25 / 99	6.31 / 99	3.89	0.92
MUH	MainStay High Yield Muni Bond C	MMHDX	B+	(800) 624-6782		A+ / 9.9	3.56	-3.43	2.48 / 61	6.40 / 99	5.49 / 99	3.28	1.69
MUH	MainStay High Yield Muni Bond I	MMHIX	B+	(800) 624-6782		A+ / 9.9	3.73	-2.93	3.53 / 68	7.48 / 99	6.58 / 99	4.32	0.67
MUH	MainStay High Yield Muni Bond Inv	MMHVX	B+	(800) 624-6782		A+ / 9.8	3.66	-3.06	3.25 / 67	7.20 / 99	6.29 / 99	3.86	0.94
GEI	MainStay Indexed Bond A	MIXAX	D-	(800) 624-6782		D+ / 2.3	0.80	-2.66	0.88 / 38	1.88 / 41	1.50 / 34	2.18	0.74
GEI	MainStay Indexed Bond I	MIXIX	C-	(800) 624-6782		C- / 4.1	0.90	-2.47	1.25 / 42	2.23 / 47	1.86 / 40	2.61	0.49
GEI	MainStay Indexed Bond Inv	MIXNX	D-	(800) 624-6782		D / 2.1	0.87	-2.62	0.72 / 36	1.73 / 39	1.36 / 32	2.01	0.98
MMT ●	MainStay Money Market Fund A	MMAXX	D+	(800) 624-6782		E+ / 0.6	0.02	0.03	0.03 / 20	0.02 / 8	0.01 / 6	0.03	N/A
MMT ●	MainStay Money Market Fund B	MKMXX	U	(800) 624-6782		U /	--	--	--	--	--	0.02	N/A
MMT ●	MainStay Money Market Fund C	MSCXX	U	(800) 624-6782		U /	--	--	--	--	--	0.02	N/A
MMT ●	MainStay Money Market Fund Inv	MKTXX	U	(800) 624-6782		U /	--	--	--	--	--	0.02	N/A
MUN	MainStay NY Tax Free Opp A	MNOAX	B-	(800) 624-6782		B / 7.9	1.70	-4.44	0.50 / 37	5.20 / 97	--	3.35	0.87
MUN	MainStay NY Tax Free Opp C	MNOCX	A-	(800) 624-6782		A- / 9.0	1.62	-4.58	0.10 / 24	4.87 / 97	--	3.19	1.18
MUN	MainStay NY Tax Free Opp I	MNOIX	A	(800) 624-6782		A+ / 9.6	1.86	-4.23	0.74 / 41	5.50 / 98	--	3.75	0.62
MUN	MainStay NY Tax Free Opp Inv	MNOVX	B-	(800) 624-6782		B / 7.9	1.79	-4.36	0.56 / 38	5.18 / 97	--	3.32	0.93
COH	MainStay Sht Duration Hi Yield A	MDHAX	B	(800) 624-6782		B / 8.2	2.27	3.29	13.35 / 86	4.27 / 78	--	4.70	1.00
COH	MainStay Sht Duration Hi Yield C	MDHCX	B-	(800) 624-6782		B / 8.0	2.06	2.87	12.53 / 84	3.38 / 67	--	4.02	1.87
COH	MainStay Sht Duration Hi Yield I	MDHIX	A-	(800) 624-6782		A- / 9.0	2.33	3.31	13.63 / 86	4.53 / 81	--	5.08	0.75
COH	MainStay Sht Duration Hi Yield Inv	MDHVX	B-	(800) 624-6782		B / 8.0	2.25	3.25	13.37 / 86	4.15 / 77	--	4.60	1.12

● Denotes fund is closed to new investors
* Denotes fund is included in Section II

www.thestreetratings.com

99 Pct = Best
0 Pct = Worst

RISK Rating/Pts	3 Yr Avg Standard Deviation	Avg Dura-tion	NAV As of 2/28/17	Total $(Mil)	Cash %	Gov. Bond %	Muni. Bond %	Corp. Bond %	Other %	Portfolio Turnover Ratio	Avg Coupon Rate	Manager Quality Pct	Manager Tenure (Years)	Initial Purch. $	Additional Purch. $	Front End Load	Back End Load
B+ /8.8	1.5	2.8	10.94	100	1	60	0	37	2	25	43.8	26	17	25,000	50	0.0	0.0
C /4.6	3.2	5.2	10.77	26	2	0	97	0	1	9	23.8	26	20	25,000	50	0.0	0.0
B- /7.0	2.7	5.3	11.41	22	3	0	96	0	1	12	24.7	29	20	25,000	50	0.0	0.0
C+ /5.9	2.9	5.1	10.74	20	2	0	97	0	1	2	4.4	8	14	1,000	50	2.5	0.0
D+ /2.7	4.3	N/A	10.06	103	0	0	99	0	1	27	0.0	80	4	25,000	0	4.5	0.0
D+ /2.7	4.3	N/A	10.06	26	0	0	99	0	1	27	0.0	74	4	2,500	50	0.0	0.0
D+ /2.6	4.3	N/A	10.06	151	0	0	99	0	1	27	0.0	82	4	5,000,000	0	0.0	0.0
D+ /2.6	4.3	N/A	10.06	N/A	0	0	99	0	1	27	0.0	79	4	2,500	50	4.5	0.0
B- /7.1	2.7	N/A	9.37	365	0	3	0	60	37	36	0.0	87	13	25,000	0	3.0	0.0
B- /7.1	2.7	N/A	9.38	9	0	3	0	60	37	36	0.0	81	13	1,000	50	0.0	0.0
B- /7.0	2.7	N/A	9.37	168	0	3	0	60	37	36	0.0	80	13	1,000	50	0.0	0.0
B- /7.0	2.7	N/A	9.37	915	0	3	0	60	37	36	0.0	89	13	5,000,000	0	0.0	0.0
B- /7.1	2.7	N/A	9.37	30	0	3	0	60	37	36	0.0	87	13	1,000	50	3.0	0.0
U /	N/A	N/A	9.37	N/A	0	3	0	60	37	36	0.0	N/A	13	0	0	0.0	0.0
E /0.3	8.3	3.6	10.46	101	4	54	1	38	3	38	0.0	98	6	25,000	0	4.5	0.0
E /0.3	8.3	3.6	10.28	7	4	54	1	38	3	38	0.0	96	6	1,000	50	0.0	0.0
E /0.4	8.3	3.6	10.29	32	4	54	1	38	3	38	0.0	96	6	1,000	50	0.0	0.0
E /0.3	8.3	3.6	10.47	11	4	54	1	38	3	38	0.0	98	6	5,000,000	0	0.0	0.0
E /0.4	8.3	3.6	10.55	25	4	54	1	38	3	38	0.0	98	6	1,000	50	4.5	0.0
B+ /8.3	2.0	4.6	8.33	81	1	17	0	0	82	41	0.0	58	6	25,000	0	4.5	0.0
B /8.2	2.0	4.6	8.33	6	1	17	0	0	82	41	0.0	16	6	1,000	50	0.0	0.0
B /8.2	2.0	4.6	8.33	13	1	17	0	0	82	41	0.0	17	6	1,000	50	0.0	0.0
B+ /8.3	2.0	4.6	8.41	10	1	17	0	0	82	41	0.0	64	6	5,000,000	0	0.0	0.0
B+ /8.3	2.0	4.6	8.36	37	1	17	0	0	82	41	0.0	44	6	1,000	50	4.5	0.0
D /1.6	5.1	3.5	5.81	3,662	5	0	0	90	5	41	0.0	71	4	25,000	0	4.5	0.0
D /1.6	5.1	3.5	5.78	130	5	0	0	90	5	41	0.0	37	4	1,000	50	0.0	0.0
D /1.6	5.1	3.5	5.79	744	5	0	0	90	5	41	0.0	38	4	1,000	50	0.0	0.0
D /1.6	5.1	3.5	5.82	5,914	5	0	0	90	5	41	0.0	76	4	5,000,000	0	0.0	0.0
D /1.6	5.1	3.5	5.86	293	5	0	0	90	5	41	0.0	70	4	1,000	50	4.5	0.0
D /1.6	5.1	3.5	5.81	N/A	5	0	0	90	5	41	0.0	74	4	0	0	0.0	0.0
D /1.6	5.1	3.5	5.81	11	5	0	0	90	5	41	0.0	69	4	0	0	0.0	0.0
U /	N/A	3.5	5.81	N/A	5	0	0	90	5	41	0.0	N/A	4	0	0	0.0	0.0
D /1.6	5.1	3.5	5.81	64	5	0	0	90	5	41	0.0	77	4	250,000	0	0.0	0.0
D /2.0	4.6	N/A	12.17	776	0	0	99	0	1	41	0.0	90	7	25,000	0	4.5	0.0
D /2.0	4.6	N/A	12.14	381	0	0	99	0	1	41	0.0	84	7	2,500	50	0.0	0.0
D /2.0	4.5	N/A	12.17	1,640	0	0	99	0	1	41	0.0	91	7	5,000,000	0	0.0	0.0
D /2.0	4.5	N/A	12.15	4	0	0	99	0	1	41	0.0	90	7	2,500	50	4.5	0.0
C+ /6.0	2.9	4.5	10.61	31	0	38	1	26	35	89	0.0	17	13	25,000	0	3.0	0.0
C+ /6.1	2.9	4.5	10.62	158	0	38	1	26	35	89	0.0	27	13	5,000,000	0	0.0	0.0
C+ /5.8	3.0	4.5	10.67	5	0	38	1	26	35	89	0.0	13	13	1,000	50	3.0	0.0
A+ /9.9	N/A	N/A	1.00	224	100	0	0	0	0	0	0.0	38	8	25,000	0	0.0	0.0
U /	N/A	N/A	1.00	49	100	0	0	0	0	0	0.0	N/A	8	1,000	50	0.0	0.0
U /	N/A	N/A	1.00	41	100	0	0	0	0	0	0.0	N/A	8	1,000	50	0.0	0.0
U /	N/A	N/A	1.00	57	100	0	0	0	0	0	0.0	N/A	8	1,000	50	0.0	0.0
C- /3.4	3.9	N/A	10.20	115	0	0	99	0	1	28	0.0	79	5	25,000	0	4.5	0.0
C- /3.3	3.9	N/A	10.20	41	0	0	99	0	1	28	0.0	73	5	2,500	50	0.0	0.0
C- /3.3	3.9	N/A	10.21	55	0	0	99	0	1	28	0.0	81	5	5,000,000	0	0.0	0.0
C- /3.4	3.9	N/A	10.21	N/A	0	0	99	0	1	28	0.0	78	5	2,500	50	4.5	0.0
C- /3.4	3.3	N/A	9.96	180	4	0	0	88	8	50	0.0	83	5	25,000	0	3.0	0.0
C- /3.4	3.3	N/A	9.96	55	4	0	0	88	8	50	0.0	72	5	2,500	50	0.0	0.0
C- /3.4	3.4	N/A	9.96	525	4	0	0	88	8	50	0.0	85	5	5,000,000	0	0.0	0.0
C- /3.4	3.4	N/A	9.96	7	4	0	0	88	8	50	0.0	82	5	2,500	50	3.0	0.0

99 Pct = Best
0 Pct = Worst

Fund Type	Fund Name	Ticker Symbol	Overall Investment Rating	Phone	Performance Rating/Pts	3 Mo	6 Mo	1Yr / Pct	Annualized 3Yr / Pct	Annualized 5Yr / Pct	Dividend Yield	Expense Ratio
COH	MainStay Sht Duration Hi Yield R2	MDHRX	B+	(800) 624-6782	B+ / 8.8	2.24	3.24	13.37 / 86	4.16 / 77	--	4.75	1.10
COH	MainStay Sht Duration Hi Yield R3	MDHTX	U	(800) 624-6782	U /	2.18	3.11	13.07 / 85	--	--	4.50	1.35
GES	MainStay Tax Adv Sht-Tm Bd A	MSTAX	C	(800) 624-6782	D / 1.6	0.53	-0.22	0.30 / 29	0.61 / 22	0.51 / 22	0.71	0.85
GES	MainStay Tax Adv Sht-Tm Bd I	MSTIX	C+	(800) 624-6782	D+ / 2.3	0.49	-0.20	0.45 / 32	0.83 / 25	0.75 / 24	0.96	0.60
GES	MainStay Tax Adv Sht-Tm Bd	MYTBX	D	(800) 624-6782	E / 0.5	0.43	-0.51	-0.09 / 16	0.20 / 16	0.13 / 16	0.32	1.20
MUN	MainStay Tax Free Bond Fund A	MTBAX	C	(800) 624-6782	C+ / 6.8	1.64	-4.22	0.33 / 33	4.42 / 95	3.85 / 92	3.00	0.81
MUN ●	MainStay Tax Free Bond Fund B	MKTBX	B	(800) 624-6782	B+ / 8.3	1.58	-4.32	0.10 / 24	4.15 / 94	3.56 / 88	2.90	1.07
MUN	MainStay Tax Free Bond Fund C	MTFCX	B	(800) 624-6782	B+ / 8.3	1.58	-4.23	0.20 / 29	4.18 / 94	3.56 / 88	2.90	1.07
MUN	MainStay Tax Free Bond Fund I	MTBIX	A-	(800) 624-6782	A- / 9.0	1.70	-4.00	0.68 / 40	4.71 / 96	4.11 / 94	3.40	0.56
MUN	MainStay Tax Free Bond Fund Inv	MKINX	C	(800) 624-6782	C+ / 6.9	1.64	-4.18	0.36 / 34	4.44 / 95	3.82 / 91	3.02	0.82
GEI	MainStay Total Return Bond A	MTMAX	D	(800) 624-6782	D+ / 2.8	1.64	-1.24	4.61 / 65	1.98 / 43	2.47 / 49	2.49	1.08
GEI ●	MainStay Total Return Bond B	MTMBX	D	(800) 624-6782	C- / 3.5	1.41	-1.70	3.92 / 62	1.22 / 31	1.67 / 37	1.94	1.76
GEI	MainStay Total Return Bond C	MTMCX	D+	(800) 624-6782	C- / 3.5	1.41	-1.70	3.92 / 62	1.22 / 31	1.67 / 37	1.94	1.76
GEI	MainStay Total Return Bond I	MTMIX	C+	(800) 624-6782	C / 5.3	1.72	-1.17	4.95 / 66	2.33 / 49	2.82 / 55	2.93	0.83
GEI	MainStay Total Return Bond Inv	MTMNX	D	(800) 624-6782	D+ / 2.9	1.69	-1.23	4.78 / 66	2.01 / 43	2.45 / 49	2.56	1.01
COI	MainStay Total Return Bond R1	MTMRX	C+	(800) 624-6782	C / 5.1	1.69	-1.22	4.84 / 66	2.23 / 47	--	2.83	0.93
COI	MainStay Total Return Bond R2	MTRTX	C	(800) 624-6782	C / 4.6	1.63	-1.35	4.42 / 64	1.94 / 42	--	2.52	1.18
COI	MainStay Total Return Bond R3	MTRVX	U	(800) 624-6782	U /	1.57	-1.46	4.31 / 64	--	--	2.32	1.43
COI	MainStay Total Return Bond R6	MTRDX	U	(800) 624-6782	U /	1.72	-1.15	5.01 / 67	--	--	2.98	0.53
GL	MainStay Unconstrained Bond A	MASAX	E+	(800) 624-6782	C / 4.4	2.38	2.23	11.93 / 83	1.63 / 37	3.63 / 68	3.87	1.01
GL ●	MainStay Unconstrained Bond B	MASBX	D-	(800) 624-6782	C / 5.0	2.19	1.97	11.13 / 81	0.87 / 26	2.81 / 55	3.31	1.78
GL	MainStay Unconstrained Bond C	MSICX	D-	(800) 624-6782	C / 4.9	2.19	1.85	11.14 / 81	0.84 / 25	2.79 / 54	3.31	1.78
GL	MainStay Unconstrained Bond I	MSDIX	D+	(800) 624-6782	C+ / 6.6	2.44	2.48	12.34 / 84	1.89 / 41	3.91 / 71	4.30	0.76
GL	MainStay Unconstrained Bond Inv	MSYDX	E+	(800) 624-6782	C / 4.3	2.35	2.32	11.95 / 83	1.61 / 37	3.56 / 67	3.82	1.03
COI	Manning & Napier Core Bond I	EXCIX	U	(800) 466-3863	U /	1.11	-1.02	3.22 / 58	--	--	1.98	0.48
COI	Manning & Napier Core Bond S	EXCRX	C+	(800) 466-3863	C- / 4.2	1.03	-1.18	3.02 / 57	1.85 / 40	2.47 / 49	1.59	0.73
MUN	Manning & Napier Diversified TE Srs	EXDVX	D+	(800) 466-3863	D / 2.2	1.85	-1.69	-0.81 / 6	0.67 / 28	0.73 / 29	1.09	0.57
GL	Manning & Napier Glb Fxd Inc Srs I	MNGIX	E	(800) 466-3863	E- / 0.1	1.42	-3.03	1.98 / 49	-1.84 / 2	--	0.00	0.73
GL	Manning & Napier Glb Fxd Inc Srs S	MNGSX	E	(800) 466-3863	E- / 0.1	1.42	-3.04	1.87 / 48	-1.94 / 2	--	0.00	0.88
GL	Manning & Napier High Yield Bond I	MNHAX	B	(800) 466-3863	A / 9.5	5.05	4.73	18.56 / 94	4.41 / 80	--	7.42	0.68
COI	Manning & Napier Unconstrained Bd I	MNCPX	A-	(800) 466-3863	C / 5.2	1.39	0.86	5.51 / 69	1.99 / 43	--	2.42	0.52
* COI	Manning & Napier Unconstrained Bd	EXCPX	B+	(800) 466-3863	C / 4.8	1.36	0.82	5.30 / 68	1.77 / 39	2.74 / 53	1.93	0.77
USS	Manor Bond Fund	MNRBX	D-	(800) 787-3334	E- / 0.2	0.19	-2.09	-1.81 / 1	-0.38 / 4	-0.40 / 3	0.17	1.00
GEI	MassMutual Premier Core Bond A	MMCBX	D-	(800) 542-6767	D / 2.1	1.29	-1.74	2.83 / 55	1.84 / 40	2.00 / 42	2.64	0.87
GEI	MassMutual Premier Core Bond Adm	MCBLX	C-	(800) 542-6767	C / 4.4	1.24	-1.67	2.95 / 56	2.09 / 45	2.26 / 46	3.09	0.72
COI	MassMutual Premier Core Bond I	MCZZX	C	(800) 542-6767	C / 5.0	1.35	-1.44	3.34 / 59	2.41 / 50	2.57 / 51	3.37	0.42
GEI	MassMutual Premier Core Bond R3	MCBNX	D+	(800) 542-6767	C- / 3.8	1.24	-1.82	2.65 / 54	1.69 / 38	1.80 / 39	2.69	1.12
COI	MassMutual Premier Core Bond R4	MCZRX	U	(800) 542-6767	U /	1.25	-1.69	2.89 / 56	--	--	3.03	0.87
GEI	MassMutual Premier Core Bond R5	MCBDX	C	(800) 542-6767	C / 4.8	1.24	-1.54	3.22 / 58	2.28 / 48	2.42 / 48	3.25	0.52
GEI	MassMutual Premier Core Bond Svc	MCBYX	C	(800) 542-6767	C / 4.7	1.37	-1.52	3.17 / 58	2.20 / 46	2.36 / 47	3.11	0.62
GEI	MassMutual Premier Diversified Bd A	MDVAX	D	(800) 542-6767	D+ / 2.8	1.62	-1.25	3.69 / 61	2.15 / 46	2.69 / 53	1.99	1.11
COI	MassMutual Premier Diversified Bd I	MDBZX	B	(800) 542-6767	C+ / 5.7	1.67	-1.10	4.19 / 63	2.72 / 56	3.50 / 66	2.48	0.56
GEI	MassMutual Premier Dvsfd Bd Adm	MDBLX	C+	(800) 542-6767	C / 5.2	1.66	-1.20	3.83 / 61	2.41 / 50	2.95 / 57	2.33	0.86
GEI	MassMutual Premier Dvsfd Bd Svc	MDBYX	C+	(800) 542-6767	C / 5.3	1.67	-1.18	3.94 / 62	2.48 / 51	3.03 / 58	2.43	0.76
COI	MassMutual Premier Dvsfd Bond R4	MDBFX	U	(800) 542-6767	U /	1.55	-1.33	3.74 / 61	--	--	2.32	1.01
GEI	MassMutual Premier Dvsfd Bond R5	MDBSX	B-	(800) 542-6767	C / 5.5	1.70	-1.18	4.00 / 62	2.58 / 53	3.10 / 59	2.57	0.66
COH	MassMutual Premier High Yield A	MPHAX	C+	(800) 542-6767	A- / 9.1	5.36	6.40	19.70 / 95	4.82 / 84	7.72 / 98	5.39	1.13
COH	MassMutual Premier High Yield Adm	MPHLX	B	(800) 542-6767	A+ / 9.8	5.52	6.67	20.12 / 96	5.12 / 86	8.01 / 98	5.98	0.88
COH	MassMutual Premier High Yield I	MPHZX	B	(800) 542-6767	A+ / 9.8	5.53	6.79	20.40 / 96	5.41 / 88	8.36 / 99	6.20	0.58
COH	MassMutual Premier High Yield R3	MPHNX	B	(800) 542-6767	A+ / 9.7	5.33	6.36	19.60 / 95	4.66 / 82	7.51 / 97	5.68	1.28
COH	MassMutual Premier High Yield R4	MPHRX	U	(800) 542-6767	U /	5.46	6.63	19.92 / 96	--	--	6.04	1.03
COH	MassMutual Premier High Yield R5	MPHSX	B	(800) 542-6767	A+ / 9.8	5.52	6.78	20.32 / 96	5.31 / 87	8.22 / 98	6.08	0.68

● Denotes fund is closed to new investors
* Denotes fund is included in Section II

www.thestreetratings.com

Risk Rating/Pts	3 Yr Avg Standard Deviation	Avg Duration	NAV As of 2/28/17	Total $(Mil)	Cash %	Gov. Bond %	Muni. Bond %	Corp. Bond %	Other %	Portfolio Turnover Ratio	Avg Coupon Rate	Manager Quality Pct	Manager Tenure (Years)	Initial Purch. $	Additional Purch. $	Front End Load	Back End Load
C- / 3.4	3.4	N/A	9.96	N/A	4	0	0	88	8	50	0.0	82	5	0	0	0.0	0.0
U /	N/A	N/A	9.97	N/A	4	0	0	88	8	50	0.0	N/A	5	0	0	0.0	0.0
A+ / 9.6	0.7	2.0	9.56	173	1	44	0	53	2	66	0.0	42	2	25,000	0	1.0	0.0
A+ / 9.7	0.7	2.0	9.55	194	1	44	0	53	2	66	0.0	55	2	5,000,000	0	0.0	0.0
A+ / 9.6	0.7	2.0	9.58	4	1	44	0	53	2	66	0.0	24	2	1,000	50	1.0	0.0
C- / 3.4	3.7	7.2	9.82	1,269	0	0	99	0	1	47	0.0	69	8	25,000	0	4.5	0.0
C- / 3.4	3.7	7.2	9.82	19	0	0	99	0	1	47	0.0	62	8	1,000	50	0.0	0.0
C- / 3.4	3.6	7.2	9.83	255	0	0	99	0	1	47	0.0	64	8	1,000	50	0.0	0.0
C- / 3.4	3.7	7.2	9.83	856	0	0	99	0	1	47	0.0	75	8	5,000,000	0	0.0	0.0
C- / 3.4	3.7	7.2	9.87	16	0	0	99	0	1	47	0.0	70	8	1,000	50	4.5	0.0
C+ / 6.4	2.8	3.7	10.51	295	5	14	0	56	25	21	0.0	33	6	25,000	0	4.5	0.0
C+ / 6.2	2.9	3.7	10.52	6	5	14	0	56	25	21	0.0	12	6	1,000	50	0.0	0.0
C+ / 6.4	2.8	3.7	10.53	24	5	14	0	56	25	21	0.0	13	6	1,000	50	0.0	0.0
C+ / 6.3	2.9	3.7	10.51	862	5	14	0	56	25	21	0.0	53	6	5,000,000	0	0.0	0.0
C+ / 6.1	2.9	3.7	10.57	9	5	14	0	56	25	21	0.0	32	6	1,000	50	4.5	0.0
C+ / 6.3	2.9	3.7	10.51	4	5	14	0	56	25	21	0.0	30	6	0	0	0.0	0.0
C+ / 6.3	2.9	3.7	10.50	N/A	5	14	0	56	25	21	0.0	21	6	0	0	0.0	0.0
U /	N/A	3.7	10.51	N/A	5	14	0	56	25	21	0.0	N/A	6	0	0	0.0	0.0
U /	N/A	3.7	10.51	N/A	5	14	0	56	25	21	0.0	N/A	6	250,000	0	0.0	0.0
D+ / 2.3	4.2	4.3	8.81	325	7	0	0	84	9	15	0.0	85	8	25,000	0	4.5	0.0
D+ / 2.7	4.2	4.3	8.77	18	7	0	0	84	9	15	0.0	78	8	1,000	50	0.0	0.0
D+ / 2.7	4.3	4.3	8.76	200	7	0	0	84	9	15	0.0	77	8	1,000	50	0.0	0.0
D+ / 2.8	4.2	4.3	8.82	822	7	0	0	84	9	15	0.0	87	8	5,000,000	0	0.0	0.0
D+ / 2.7	4.3	4.3	8.88	31	7	0	0	84	9	15	0.0	85	8	1,000	50	4.5	0.0
U /	N/A	N/A	9.86	71	0	0	0	0	100	88	0.0	N/A	12	10,000,000	0	0.0	0.0
B / 7.8	2.3	N/A	10.62	119	0	0	0	0	100	88	0.0	35	12	2,000	0	0.0	0.0
B / 8.0	2.1	N/A	10.98	307	3	0	96	0	1	33	0.0	6	2	2,000	0	0.0	0.0
D+ / 2.6	4.4	N/A	9.29	7	3	50	0	39	8	54	0.0	16	5	1,000,000	0	0.0	0.0
D+ / 2.6	4.4	N/A	9.26	177	3	50	0	39	8	54	0.0	13	5	2,000	0	0.0	0.0
D / 1.9	5.3	N/A	8.92	24	4	0	0	95	1	109	0.0	96	14	1,000,000	0	0.0	0.0
B / 8.1	2.1	N/A	9.38	51	5	4	0	76	15	81	0.0	62	12	10,000,000	0	0.0	0.0
B / 8.2	2.0	N/A	10.43	835	5	4	0	76	15	81	0.0	57	12	2,000	0	0.0	0.0
B+ / 8.8	1.5	2.1	10.30	1	5	94	0	0	1	0	2.1	7	19	1,000	25	0.0	0.0
C+ / 5.7	3.0	5.4	10.55	131	0	4	1	43	52	330	3.3	18	22	0	0	4.8	0.0
C+ / 6.1	2.9	5.4	10.63	80	0	4	1	43	52	330	3.3	27	22	0	0	0.0	0.0
C+ / 6.0	2.9	5.4	10.73	488	0	4	1	43	52	330	3.3	32	22	0	0	0.0	0.0
C+ / 5.9	2.9	5.4	10.76	1	0	4	1	43	52	330	3.3	16	22	0	0	0.0	0.0
U /	N/A	5.4	10.50	16	0	4	1	43	52	330	3.3	N/A	22	0	0	0.0	0.0
C+ / 6.1	2.9	5.4	10.76	394	0	4	1	43	52	330	3.3	34	22	0	0	0.0	0.0
C+ / 6.1	2.9	5.4	10.71	78	0	4	1	43	52	330	3.3	30	22	0	0	0.0	0.0
C+ / 6.2	2.9	5.4	9.95	36	0	4	0	48	48	314	3.3	30	18	0	0	4.8	0.0
C+ / 6.5	2.8	5.4	10.63	23	0	4	0	48	48	314	3.3	55	18	0	0	0.0	0.0
C+ / 6.2	2.9	5.4	9.96	31	0	4	0	48	48	314	3.3	43	18	0	0	0.0	0.0
C+ / 6.3	2.9	5.4	9.98	16	0	4	0	48	48	314	3.3	50	18	0	0	0.0	0.0
U /	N/A	5.4	9.87	4	0	4	0	48	48	314	3.3	N/A	18	0	0	0.0	0.0
C+ / 6.5	2.8	5.4	9.85	78	0	4	0	48	48	314	3.3	55	18	0	0	0.0	0.0
D / 1.6	5.2	3.6	9.13	30	2	0	0	93	5	50	7.7	75	7	0	0	5.8	0.0
D / 1.6	5.2	3.6	9.15	31	2	0	0	93	5	50	7.7	79	7	0	0	0.0	0.0
D / 1.6	5.1	3.6	9.23	238	2	0	0	93	5	50	7.7	82	7	0	0	0.0	0.0
D / 1.6	5.1	3.6	9.25	18	2	0	0	93	5	50	7.7	72	7	0	0	0.0	0.0
U /	N/A	3.6	9.05	26	2	0	0	93	5	50	7.7	N/A	7	0	0	0.0	0.0
D / 1.6	5.1	3.6	9.28	58	2	0	0	93	5	50	7.7	81	7	0	0	0.0	0.0

Fund Type	Fund Name	Ticker Symbol	Overall Investment Rating	Phone	Performance Rating/Pts	3 Mo	6 Mo	1Yr / Pct	3Yr / Pct	5Yr / Pct	Dividend Yield	Expense Ratio
COH	MassMutual Premier High Yield Svc	DLHYX	B	(800) 542-6767	A+ / 9.8	5.38	6.64	20.16 /96	5.19 /86	8.12 /98	5.95	0.78
GEI	MassMutual Premier Infl-PI A	MPSAX	E	(800) 542-6767	D / 1.9	1.18	-0.64	3.48 /60	1.51 /35	0.35 /20	2.10	1.22
GEI	MassMutual Premier Infl-PI Adm	MIPLX	D-	(800) 542-6767	C / 4.3	1.28	-0.50	3.73 /61	1.77 /39	0.57 /22	2.47	0.97
GEI	MassMutual Premier Infl-PI I	MIPZX	D-	(800) 542-6767	C / 4.8	1.37	-0.33	4.03 /62	2.07 /44	0.89 /26	2.74	0.67
GEI	MassMutual Premier Infl-PI R3	MIPNX	E+	(800) 542-6767	C- / 3.6	1.10	-0.72	3.30 /58	1.33 /32	0.12 /16	2.32	1.37
GEI	MassMutual Premier Infl-PI R4	MIPRX	U	(800) 542-6767	U /	1.17	-0.57	3.47 /59	--	--	2.49	1.12
GEI	MassMutual Premier Infl-PI R5	MIPSX	D-	(800) 542-6767	C / 4.6	1.27	-0.43	3.83 /61	1.96 /42	0.76 /24	2.65	0.77
GEI	MassMutual Premier Infl-PI Svc	MIPYX	D-	(800) 542-6767	C / 4.4	1.25	-0.46	3.72 /61	1.86 /41	0.68 /23	2.54	0.87
GEI	MassMutual Premier Short Dur Bd A	MSHAX	C	(800) 542-6767	D / 2.0	0.71	0.61	2.41 /52	1.28 /32	1.35 /32	1.82	0.95
GEI	MassMutual Premier Short Dur Bd	MSTLX	B+	(800) 542-6767	C- / 3.9	0.75	0.75	2.65 /54	1.51 /35	1.60 /36	2.13	0.70
COI	MassMutual Premier Short Dur Bd I	MSTZX	A-	(800) 542-6767	C / 4.4	0.89	0.89	2.97 /56	1.85 /40	1.93 /41	2.45	0.40
GEI	MassMutual Premier Short Dur Bd R3	MSDNX	B-	(800) 542-6767	C- / 3.2	0.70	0.61	2.30 /51	1.11 /29	1.13 /29	1.88	1.10
COI	MassMutual Premier Short Dur Bd R4	MPSDX	U	(800) 542-6767	U /	0.77	0.67	2.55 /53	--	--	2.04	0.85
GEI	MassMutual Premier Short Dur Bd R5	MSTDX	B+	(800) 542-6767	C- / 4.2	0.79	0.88	2.86 /56	1.73 /39	1.78 /39	2.34	0.50
GEI	MassMutual Premier Short Dur Bd	MSBYX	B+	(800) 542-6767	C- / 4.1	0.76	0.85	2.84 /56	1.63 /37	1.70 /38	2.22	0.60
MMT	MassMutual Premier US Gv Mny Mkt	MKSXX	D+	(800) 542-6767	E+ / 0.6	0.02	0.02	0.02 /19	0.01 / 6	0.01 / 6	0.02	N/A
COI	MassMutual Select Total Ret Bd A	MPTRX	U	(800) 542-6767	U /	0.80	-1.73	1.60 /45	--	--	2.10	0.89
GL	MassMutual Select Total Ret Bd Adm	MSPLX	C+	(800) 542-6767	C- / 4.0	0.90	-1.64	1.80 /47	1.96 /42	2.44 /48	2.30	0.64
GL	MassMutual Select Total Ret Bd I	MSPZX	B-	(800) 542-6767	C / 4.5	1.07	-1.45	2.18 /51	2.27 /48	2.79 /54	2.66	0.34
GL	MassMutual Select Total Ret Bd R3	MSPNX	C	(800) 542-6767	C- / 3.3	0.84	-1.79	1.45 /44	1.55 /36	2.08 /43	1.95	1.04
GL	MassMutual Select Total Ret Bd R4	MSPGX	C	(800) 542-6767	C- / 3.7	0.93	-1.69	1.73 /46	1.79 /39	2.33 /47	2.12	0.79
GL	MassMutual Select Total Ret Bd R5	MSPSX	C+	(800) 542-6767	C / 4.3	0.96	-1.47	2.07 /50	2.16 /46	2.65 /52	2.56	0.44
GL	MassMutual Select Total Ret Bd Svc	MSPHX	C+	(800) 542-6767	C- / 4.2	0.95	-1.57	1.95 /48	2.06 /44	2.54 /50	2.44	0.54
GEI	MassMutual Strategic Bond A	MSBAX	D	(800) 542-6767	C / 4.4	1.78	-1.48	4.54 /65	3.20 /64	3.08 /59	2.12	1.14
GEI	MassMutual Strategic Bond Adm	MSBLX	C+	(800) 542-6767	C+ / 6.7	1.90	-1.36	4.74 /66	3.45 /68	3.34 /63	2.53	0.89
COI	MassMutual Strategic Bond I	MSBZX	B	(800) 542-6767	B- / 7.0	1.94	-1.21	5.09 /67	3.76 /72	3.61 /67	2.77	0.59
GEI	MassMutual Strategic Bond R3	MSBNX	C+	(800) 542-6767	C+ / 6.1	1.82	-1.48	4.39 /64	3.07 /62	2.86 /56	2.27	1.29
COI	MassMutual Strategic Bond R4	MSBRX	U	(800) 542-6767	U /	1.84	-1.43	4.71 /65	--	--	2.39	1.04
GEI	MassMutual Strategic Bond R5	MBSSX	B-	(800) 542-6767	B- / 7.0	1.94	-1.21	5.09 /67	3.67 /71	3.56 /67	2.67	0.69
GEI	MassMutual Strategic Bond Service	MBSYX	B-	(800) 542-6767	C+ / 6.8	1.89	-1.26	4.94 /66	3.58 /70	3.46 /65	2.52	0.79
EM	Matthews Asia Strategic Income Inst	MINCX	C+	(800) 789-2742	B+ / 8.4	2.82	0.78	11.44 /82	4.12 /77	4.30 /76	4.06	1.09
EM	Matthews Asia Strategic Income Inv	MAINX	C+	(800) 789-2742	B / 8.2	2.85	0.75	11.27 /82	3.89 /74	4.09 /74	3.81	1.28
MUN	McDonnell Intermediate Muni Bond A	MIMAX	D-	(800) 225-5478	D+ / 2.9	1.96	-3.13	-0.97 / 4	2.07 /64	--	1.29	1.12
MUN	McDonnell Intermediate Muni Bond C	MIMCX	D-	(800) 225-5478	C- / 3.0	1.77	-3.49	-1.71 / 1	1.35 /45	--	0.57	1.88
MUN	McDonnell Intermediate Muni Bond Y	MIMYX	C	(800) 225-5478	C+ / 5.6	2.02	-3.00	-0.62 / 8	2.37 /71	--	1.59	0.85
USA	MD Sass Sht Trm US Gv Agcy Inc	MDSIX	C	(855) 637-3863	D / 1.9	0.27	-0.37	0.16 /24	0.55 /21	0.60 /23	2.90	0.59
GL	Meeder Total Return Bond Retail	FLBDX	C	(800) 325-3539	C / 4.4	2.54	0.19	5.60 /69	1.41 /33	2.18 /45	3.08	1.76
GES	Metropolitan West Alpha Trak 500 M	MWATX	C+	(800) 496-8298	A+ / 9.9	12.66	17.56	35.34 /99	13.01 /99	16.54 /99	1.95	2.65
LP	Metropolitan West Floating Rt Inc I	MWFLX	A+	(800) 496-8298	B- / 7.2	1.47	2.84	7.74 /74	3.21 /64	--	3.48	0.74
LP	Metropolitan West Floating Rt Inc M	MWFRX	A+	(800) 496-8298	B- / 7.0	1.42	2.64	7.53 /73	3.01 /61	--	3.28	1.08
COH	Metropolitan West High Yield Bond I	MWHIX	C-	(800) 496-8298	C+ / 6.9	3.25	3.72	11.16 /82	2.12 /45	5.01 /84	3.70	0.62
COH	Metropolitan West High Yield Bond M	MWHYX	D	(800) 496-8298	C+ / 6.6	3.08	3.59	10.88 /81	1.86 /41	4.75 /81	3.46	0.88
GEI	Metropolitan West Interm Bond I	MWIIX	C+	(800) 496-8298	C- / 3.5	0.71	-1.00	1.21 /42	1.62 /37	2.76 /54	1.60	0.46
GEI	Metropolitan West Interm Bond M	MWIMX	C+	(800) 496-8298	C- / 3.1	0.66	-1.02	1.05 /40	1.41 /33	2.53 /50	1.35	0.70
GEI	Metropolitan West Low Dur Bd Adm	MWLNX	C+	(800) 496-8298	D+ / 2.4	0.48	0.38	1.39 /44	0.76 /24	1.94 /41	1.07	0.72
GEI	Metropolitan West Low Dur Bd I	MWLIX	B	(800) 496-8298	C- / 3.0	0.50	0.50	1.67 /46	1.08 /29	2.28 /46	1.37	0.39
* GEI	Metropolitan West Low Dur Bd M	MWLDX	B-	(800) 496-8298	D+ / 2.6	0.46	0.39	1.45 /44	0.86 /25	2.09 /43	1.16	0.62
GEI	Metropolitan West Strategic Inc I	MWSIX	A	(800) 496-8298	C / 5.1	1.14	1.29	4.34 /64	2.10 /45	4.35 /77	3.50	1.54
GEI	Metropolitan West Strategic Inc M	MWSTX	A	(800) 496-8298	C / 4.6	1.07	1.15	4.08 /62	1.82 /40	4.07 /73	3.25	1.87
GEI	Metropolitan West Tot Ret Bond Adm	MWTNX	C+	(800) 496-8298	C- / 4.2	0.89	-1.89	1.45 /44	2.18 /46	3.36 /63	1.62	0.79
GEI	Metropolitan West Tot Ret Bond I	MWTIX	B	(800) 496-8298	C / 4.8	0.97	-1.73	1.75 /47	2.55 /53	3.75 /69	1.92	0.44
* GEI	Metropolitan West Tot Ret Bond M	MWTRX	B-	(800) 496-8298	C / 4.4	1.01	-1.75	1.52 /45	2.34 /49	3.54 /66	1.69	0.67

● Denotes fund is closed to new investors
* Denotes fund is included in Section II

www.thestreetratings.com

RISK			NET ASSETS		ASSET							FUND MANAGER		MINIMUM		LOADS	
Risk Rating/Pts	3 Yr Avg Standard Deviation	Avg Dura-tion	NAV As of 2/28/17	Total $(Mil)	Cash %	Gov. Bond %	Muni. Bond %	Corp. Bond %	Other %	Portfolio Turnover Ratio	Avg Coupon Rate	Manager Quality Pct	Manager Tenure (Years)	Initial Purch. $	Additional Purch. $	Front End Load	Back End Load
D /1.6	5.1	3.6	9.28	47	2	0	0	93	5	50	7.7	80	7	0	0	0.0	0.0
C- /3.0	4.1	5.8	10.24	22	0	52	0	20	28	46	2.4	6	14	0	0	4.8	0.0
C- /3.0	4.1	5.8	10.48	16	0	52	0	20	28	46	2.4	9	14	0	0	0.0	0.0
C- /3.1	4.1	5.8	10.40	124	0	52	0	20	28	46	2.4	15	14	0	0	0.0	0.0
C- /3.1	4.1	5.8	10.20	4	0	52	0	20	28	46	2.4	5	14	0	0	0.0	0.0
U /	N/A	5.8	10.18	6	0	52	0	20	28	46	2.4	N/A	14	0	0	0.0	0.0
C- /3.1	4.0	5.8	10.40	67	0	52	0	20	28	46	2.4	13	14	0	0	0.0	0.0
C- /3.1	4.0	5.8	10.37	59	0	52	0	20	28	46	2.4	11	14	0	0	0.0	0.0
A- /9.1	1.1	1.6	10.09	56	0	3	0	47	50	87	2.7	63	19	0	0	3.5	0.0
A- /9.1	1.1	1.6	10.15	30	0	3	0	47	50	87	2.7	69	19	0	0	0.0	0.0
A- /9.1	1.1	1.6	10.22	260	0	3	0	47	50	87	2.7	75	19	0	0	0.0	0.0
A- /9.2	1.1	1.6	10.17	6	0	3	0	47	50	87	2.7	58	19	0	0	0.0	0.0
U /	N/A	1.6	10.21	11	0	3	0	47	50	87	2.7	N/A	19	0	0	0.0	0.0
A- /9.1	1.1	1.6	10.25	194	0	3	0	47	50	87	2.7	74	19	0	0	0.0	0.0
A- /9.1	1.1	1.6	10.19	51	0	3	0	47	50	87	2.7	72	19	0	0	0.0	0.0
A+ /9.9	N/A	N/A	1.00	311	100	0	0	0	0	0	0.0	38	8	0	0	0.0	0.0
U /	N/A	N/A	9.75	4	0	31	1	23	45	264	0.0	N/A	N/A	0	0	4.8	0.0
B /7.6	2.5	N/A	9.74	66	0	31	1	23	45	264	0.0	88	N/A	0	0	0.0	0.0
B /7.6	2.5	N/A	9.78	319	0	31	1	23	45	264	0.0	90	N/A	0	0	0.0	0.0
B /7.6	2.5	N/A	9.74	43	0	31	1	23	45	264	0.0	85	N/A	0	0	0.0	0.0
B /7.6	2.5	N/A	9.81	251	0	31	1	23	45	264	0.0	87	N/A	0	0	0.0	0.0
B /7.6	2.5	N/A	9.76	110	0	31	1	23	45	264	0.0	90	N/A	0	0	0.0	0.0
B /7.6	2.5	N/A	9.80	144	0	31	1	23	45	264	0.0	89	N/A	0	0	0.0	0.0
C /4.8	3.2	5.8	10.21	47	1	35	0	28	36	207	4.1	66	13	0	0	4.8	0.0
C /4.7	3.2	5.8	10.23	52	1	35	0	28	36	207	4.1	71	13	0	0	0.0	0.0
C /4.7	3.2	5.8	10.25	99	1	35	0	28	36	207	4.1	74	13	0	0	0.0	0.0
C /4.8	3.2	5.8	10.11	10	1	35	0	28	36	207	4.1	63	13	0	0	0.0	0.0
U /	N/A	5.8	10.18	38	1	35	0	28	36	207	4.1	N/A	13	0	0	0.0	0.0
C /4.7	3.2	5.8	10.26	69	1	35	0	28	36	207	4.1	76	13	0	0	0.0	0.0
C /4.8	3.2	5.8	10.26	45	1	35	0	28	36	207	4.1	74	13	0	0	0.0	0.0
D /2.2	4.8	4.5	10.63	14	3	28	0	59	10	50	0.0	96	6	100,000	100	0.0	0.0
D /2.2	4.8	4.5	10.64	56	3	28	0	59	10	50	0.0	96	6	2,500	100	0.0	0.0
C /4.9	3.2	N/A	9.97	5	7	0	92	0	1	20	0.0	8	5	2,500	100	3.0	0.0
C /4.8	3.2	N/A	9.97	4	7	0	92	0	1	20	0.0	2	5	2,500	100	0.0	0.0
C /4.9	3.2	N/A	9.98	43	7	0	92	0	1	20	0.0	11	5	100,000	100	0.0	0.0
A /9.4	0.9	N/A	9.53	44	2	16	0	0	82	182	0.0	45	6	10,000	1,000	0.0	0.0
C+ /6.2	2.9	N/A	9.40	185	0	0	0	0	100	295	0.0	85	6	2,500	100	0.0	0.0
E- /0.2	10.9	0.6	8.96	18	2	23	0	23	52	59	5.3	99	19	5,000	0	0.0	0.0
B+ /8.6	1.7	0.2	10.08	199	7	4	0	68	21	66	3.8	90	4	3,000,000	50,000	0.0	0.0
B+ /8.6	1.7	0.2	10.08	23	7	4	0	68	21	66	3.8	89	4	5,000	0	0.0	0.0
D+ /2.5	4.0	2.2	9.60	544	2	8	0	84	6	139	5.2	16	15	3,000,000	50,000	0.0	0.0
D+ /2.5	4.0	2.2	9.60	358	2	8	0	84	6	139	5.2	11	15	5,000	0	0.0	0.0
B+ /8.7	1.7	3.5	10.38	1,061	0	44	0	29	27	309	2.0	51	15	3,000,000	50,000	0.0	0.0
B+ /8.6	1.8	3.5	10.39	99	0	44	0	29	27	309	2.0	34	15	5,000	0	0.0	0.0
A+ /9.8	0.5	1.4	11.27	7	0	38	0	19	43	119	1.9	61	20	2,500	0	0.0	0.0
A+ /9.8	0.5	1.4	8.72	1,764	0	38	0	19	43	119	1.9	70	20	3,000,000	50,000	0.0	0.0
A+ /9.8	0.5	1.4	8.72	1,302	0	38	0	19	43	119	1.9	63	20	5,000	0	0.0	0.0
A- /9.1	1.1	1.5	8.05	70	0	4	0	19	77	20	3.7	84	14	3,000,000	50,000	0.0	0.0
A- /9.2	1.1	1.5	8.06	45	0	4	0	19	77	20	3.7	81	14	5,000	0	0.0	0.0
B- /7.5	2.5	4.9	10.60	736	0	37	0	21	42	303	2.6	37	20	2,500	0	0.0	0.0
B- /7.5	2.5	4.9	10.59	49,084	0	37	0	21	42	303	2.6	57	20	3,000,000	50,000	0.0	0.0
B- /7.5	2.5	4.9	10.60	15,316	0	37	0	21	42	303	2.6	49	20	5,000	0	0.0	0.0

Fund Type	Fund Name	Ticker Symbol	Overall Investment Rating	Phone	Performance Rating/Pts	3 Mo	6 Mo	1Yr / Pct	3Yr / Pct	5Yr / Pct	Dividend Yield	Expense Ratio
COI	Metropolitan West Tot Ret Bond Plan	MWTSX	B	(800) 496-8298	C / 4.9	1.03	-1.67	1.81 /47	2.61 /54	3.80 /70	1.99	0.38
GEI	Metropolitan West Ultra Short Bnd I	MWUIX	C+	(800) 496-8298	D / 2.2	0.25	0.54	1.04 /40	0.66 /23	1.61 /36	1.11	0.51
GEI	Metropolitan West Ultra Short Bnd M	MWUSX	C+	(800) 496-8298	D / 2.1	0.44	0.46	1.11 /41	0.57 /21	1.45 /34	0.95	0.69
GEL	Metropolitan West Uncons Bond I	MWCIX	A+	(800) 496-8298	C+ / 5.8	1.24	1.54	4.73 /66	2.50 /52	4.46 /78	2.44	0.74
* GEL	Metropolitan West Uncons Bond M	MWCRX	A+	(800) 496-8298	C / 5.3	1.16	1.38	4.49 /65	2.20 /46	4.20 /75	2.14	1.05
GL	MFS Absolute Return Fund A	MRNAX	E	(800) 225-2606	E / 0.3	1.30	0.24	4.04 /62	0.01 / 5	0.11 /15	0.60	1.42
GL	MFS Absolute Return Fund B	MRNBX	E	(800) 225-2606	E / 0.4	1.14	-0.04	3.25 /58	-0.75 / 3	-0.64 / 3	0.06	2.17
GL	MFS Absolute Return Fund C	MRNCX	E	(800) 225-2606	E / 0.5	1.25	-0.05	3.36 /59	-0.75 / 3	-0.63 / 3	0.06	2.17
GL	MFS Absolute Return Fund I	MRNIX	E+	(800) 225-2606	D+ / 2.5	1.47	0.47	4.28 /64	0.29 /18	0.37 /20	0.87	1.17
GL	MFS Absolute Return Fund R1	MRNRX	E	(800) 225-2606	E / 0.5	1.25	-0.04	3.36 /59	-0.71 / 3	-0.62 / 3	0.06	2.17
GL	MFS Absolute Return Fund R2	MRNSX	E+	(800) 225-2606	D / 1.7	1.24	0.12	3.77 /61	-0.25 / 4	-0.14 / 4	0.37	1.67
GL	MFS Absolute Return Fund R3	MRNTX	E+	(800) 225-2606	D / 2.1	1.41	0.35	4.14 /63	0.04 / 9	0.13 /16	0.62	1.42
GL	MFS Absolute Return Fund R4	MRNUX	E+	(800) 225-2606	D+ / 2.5	1.47	0.47	4.40 /64	0.29 /18	0.38 /20	0.87	1.17
MUS	MFS AL Municipal Bond Fund A	MFALX	B	(800) 225-2606	C+ / 6.1	1.74	-2.69	0.21 /29	3.75 /90	2.78 /76	3.46	1.06
MUS	MFS AL Municipal Bond Fund B	MBABX	A-	(800) 225-2606	C+ / 6.7	1.55	-3.06	-0.63 / 8	2.97 /81	2.00 /59	2.84	1.81
MUN	MFS AL Municipal Bond Fund I	MLALX	U	(800) 225-2606	U /	1.84	-2.50	--	--	--	0.00	0.81
MUS	MFS AR Municipal Bond Fund A	MFARX	C	(800) 225-2606	C / 5.3	1.66	-2.72	-0.24 /14	3.44 /87	2.20 /63	3.14	0.90
MUS	MFS AR Municipal Bond Fund B	MBARX	C+	(800) 225-2606	C+ / 6.0	1.46	-3.09	-0.99 / 4	2.66 /76	1.42 /44	2.50	1.65
MUN	MFS AR Municipal Bond Fund I	MARLX	U	(800) 225-2606	U /	1.69	-2.61	--	--	--	0.00	0.65
MUS	MFS CA Municipal Bond Fund A	MCFTX	B-	(800) 225-2606	B / 7.8	2.11	-3.42	0.66 /40	4.87 /97	3.98 /93	3.43	0.88
MUS	MFS CA Municipal Bond Fund B	MBCAX	B	(800) 225-2606	B / 8.2	1.91	-3.80	-0.11 /16	4.08 /93	3.19 /83	2.79	1.63
MUS	MFS CA Municipal Bond Fund C	MCCAX	B	(800) 225-2606	B / 8.0	1.88	-3.84	-0.24 /14	3.92 /92	3.04 /80	2.64	1.63
MUN	MFS CA Municipal Bond Fund I	MCAVX	U	(800) 225-2606	U /	2.20	-3.47	--	--	--	0.00	0.63
* GEI	MFS Corporate Bond A	MFBFX	D	(800) 225-2606	C / 5.0	2.02	-1.53	5.95 /70	3.31 /66	3.72 /69	3.11	0.82
GEI	MFS Corporate Bond B	MFBBX	D	(800) 225-2606	C / 5.5	1.83	-1.91	5.16 /67	2.54 /53	2.95 /57	2.50	1.57
GEI	MFS Corporate Bond C	MFBCX	D	(800) 225-2606	C+ / 5.6	1.83	-1.91	5.24 /68	2.57 /53	2.96 /57	2.50	1.57
GEI	MFS Corporate Bond I	MBDIX	C+	(800) 225-2606	B- / 7.0	2.09	-1.41	6.21 /71	3.57 /69	3.96 /72	3.51	0.57
GEI	MFS Corporate Bond R1	MFBGX	D	(800) 225-2606	C+ / 5.6	1.83	-1.91	5.24 /68	2.56 /53	2.96 /57	2.50	1.57
GEI	MFS Corporate Bond R2	MBRRX	C-	(800) 225-2606	C+ / 6.3	1.96	-1.66	5.68 /69	3.05 /62	3.46 /65	3.00	1.07
GEI	MFS Corporate Bond R3	MFBHX	C	(800) 225-2606	C+ / 6.7	2.02	-1.53	5.95 /70	3.31 /66	3.72 /69	3.25	0.82
GEI	MFS Corporate Bond R4	MFBJX	C+	(800) 225-2606	B- / 7.1	2.16	-1.40	6.29 /71	3.59 /70	3.98 /72	3.50	0.57
COI	MFS Corporate Bond R6	MFBKX	C+	(800) 225-2606	B- / 7.1	2.10	-1.37	6.30 /71	3.67 /71	--	3.59	0.46
EM	MFS Emerging Markets Debt A	MEDAX	C-	(800) 225-2606	B / 7.7	4.08	-0.39	11.63 /82	4.62 /82	4.13 /74	4.29	1.10
EM	MFS Emerging Markets Debt B	MEDBX	C-	(800) 225-2606	B / 8.1	3.94	-0.69	10.85 /81	3.86 /73	3.37 /63	3.74	1.85
EM	MFS Emerging Markets Debt C	MEDCX	C-	(800) 225-2606	B / 8.0	3.95	-0.76	10.78 /81	3.84 /73	3.37 /63	3.74	1.85
EM	MFS Emerging Markets Debt I	MEDIX	C+	(800) 225-2606	A- / 9.0	4.22	-0.21	11.92 /83	4.88 /84	4.39 /77	4.73	0.85
EM	MFS Emerging Markets Debt R1	MEDDX	C-	(800) 225-2606	B / 8.0	3.94	-0.69	10.85 /81	3.83 /73	3.36 /63	3.74	1.85
EM	MFS Emerging Markets Debt R2	MEDEX	C	(800) 225-2606	B+ / 8.5	4.07	-0.51	11.33 /82	4.34 /79	3.88 /71	4.24	1.35
EM	MFS Emerging Markets Debt R3	MEDFX	C+	(800) 225-2606	B+ / 8.8	4.15	-0.39	11.63 /82	4.60 /82	4.12 /74	4.48	1.10
EM	MFS Emerging Markets Debt R4	MEDGX	C+	(800) 225-2606	A- / 9.0	4.21	-0.27	11.90 /83	4.86 /84	4.39 /77	4.73	0.85
EM	MFS Emerging Markets Debt R6	MEDHX	C+	(800) 225-2606	A- / 9.1	4.24	-0.16	12.00 /83	4.99 /85	4.50 /79	4.81	0.74
EM	MFS Emerging Mkts Debt Loc Curr A	EMLAX	E-	(800) 225-2606	E- / 0.1	6.08	0.09	12.97 /85	-3.02 / 1	-3.22 / 1	4.06	1.48
EM	MFS Emerging Mkts Debt Loc Curr B	EMLBX	E-	(800) 225-2606	E- / 0.2	6.04	-0.32	12.08 /83	-3.71 / 1	-3.93 / 0	3.46	2.23
EM	MFS Emerging Mkts Debt Loc Curr C	EMLCX	E-	(800) 225-2606	E- / 0.2	5.89	-0.43	11.95 /83	-3.74 / 1	-3.95 / 0	3.50	2.23
EM	MFS Emerging Mkts Debt Loc Curr I	EMLIX	E-	(800) 225-2606	E / 0.4	6.15	0.07	13.08 /85	-2.82 / 1	-3.01 / 1	4.49	1.23
EM	MFS Emerging Mkts Debt Loc Curr	EMLJX	E-	(800) 225-2606	E- / 0.2	5.88	-0.28	12.12 /83	-3.73 / 1	-3.93 / 0	3.50	2.23
EM	MFS Emerging Mkts Debt Loc Curr	EMLKX	E-	(800) 225-2606	E- / 0.2	6.17	-0.03	12.67 /84	-3.21 / 1	-3.44 / 0	3.99	1.73
EM	MFS Emerging Mkts Debt Loc Curr	EMLLX	E-	(800) 225-2606	E / 0.3	6.24	0.09	12.95 /85	-2.97 / 1	-3.20 / 1	4.24	1.48
EM	MFS Emerging Mkts Debt Loc Curr	EMLMX	E-	(800) 225-2606	E / 0.4	6.14	0.07	13.07 /85	-2.77 / 1	-2.98 / 1	4.49	1.23
EM	MFS Emerging Mkts Debt Loc Curr	EMLNX	E-	(800) 225-2606	E / 0.5	6.18	0.12	13.16 /85	-2.70 / 1	--	4.58	1.18
MUS	MFS GA Municipal Bond Fund A	MMGAX	C+	(800) 225-2606	C+ / 5.8	1.66	-2.70	0.13 /26	3.62 /89	2.58 /72	3.02	1.03
MUS	MFS GA Municipal Bond Fund B	MBGAX	B	(800) 225-2606	C+ / 6.5	1.47	-3.04	-0.61 / 8	2.84 /79	1.80 /54	2.39	1.78

● Denotes fund is closed to new investors
* Denotes fund is included in Section II

www.thestreetratings.com

RISK			NET ASSETS		ASSET								FUND MANAGER		MINIMUM		LOADS	
Risk Rating/Pts	3 Yr Avg Standard Deviation	Avg Dura-tion	NAV As of 2/28/17	Total $(Mil)	Cash %	Gov. Bond %	Muni. Bond %	Corp. Bond %	Other %	Portfolio Turnover Ratio	Avg Coupon Rate	Manager Quality Pct	Manager Tenure (Years)	Initial Purch. $	Additional Purch. $	Front End Load	Back End Load
B /7.6	2.5	4.9	9.97	13,559	0	37	0	21	42	303	2.6	63	20	25,000,000	50,000	0.0	0.0
A+ /9.9	0.3	0.6	4.27	72	4	26	0	19	51	37	1.9	65	14	3,000,000	50,000	0.0	0.0
A+ /9.9	0.4	0.6	4.27	68	4	26	0	19	51	37	1.9	61	14	5,000	0	0.0	0.0
A /9.3	0.9	1.4	11.88	1,932	1	11	2	20	66	23	3.5	86	6	3,000,000	50,000	0.0	0.0
A /9.3	1.0	1.4	11.89	1,432	1	11	2	20	66	23	3.5	84	6	5,000	0	0.0	0.0
C /4.3	3.4	0.6	9.47	3	4	7	0	72	17	36	1.9	66	6	1,000	50	4.3	0.0
C /4.3	3.4	0.6	9.39	1	4	7	0	72	17	36	1.9	32	6	1,000	50	0.0	0.0
C /4.3	3.4	0.6	9.39	1	4	7	0	72	17	36	1.9	32	6	1,000	50	0.0	0.0
C /4.4	3.4	0.6	9.49	1	4	7	0	72	17	36	1.9	73	6	0	0	0.0	0.0
C /4.3	3.4	0.6	9.41	N/A	4	7	0	72	17	36	1.9	33	6	0	0	0.0	0.0
C- /4.2	3.4	0.6	9.47	N/A	4	7	0	72	17	36	1.9	58	6	0	0	0.0	0.0
C- /4.2	3.4	0.6	9.48	N/A	4	7	0	72	17	36	1.9	67	6	0	0	0.0	0.0
C- /4.2	3.4	0.6	9.48	N/A	4	7	0	72	17	36	1.9	73	6	0	0	0.0	0.0
C+ /6.3	2.9	5.2	10.12	54	0	0	98	0	2	16	5.1	70	18	1,000	50	4.3	0.0
C+ /6.4	2.8	5.2	10.12	1	0	0	98	0	2	16	5.1	40	18	1,000	50	0.0	0.0
U /	N/A	5.2	9.65	6	0	0	98	0	2	16	5.1	N/A	18	0	0	0.0	0.0
C /5.4	3.0	5.2	9.73	144	0	0	99	0	1	11	4.8	56	18	1,000	50	4.3	0.0
C /5.3	3.0	5.2	9.74	6	0	0	99	0	1	11	4.8	21	18	1,000	50	0.0	0.0
U /	N/A	5.2	9.66	11	0	0	99	0	1	11	4.8	N/A	18	0	0	0.0	0.0
C- /3.7	3.7	6.0	5.94	251	0	0	98	0	2	18	4.9	75	18	1,000	50	4.3	0.0
C- /3.5	3.8	6.0	5.94	3	0	0	98	0	2	18	4.9	51	18	1,000	50	0.0	0.0
C- /3.6	3.7	6.0	5.96	35	0	0	98	0	2	18	4.9	41	18	1,000	50	0.0	0.0
U /	N/A	6.0	9.67	42	0	0	98	0	2	18	4.9	N/A	18	0	0	0.0	0.0
C- /3.6	3.7	6.8	13.88	1,551	1	3	0	93	3	30	4.4	61	12	1,000	50	4.3	0.0
C- /3.6	3.7	6.8	13.85	64	1	3	0	93	3	30	4.4	27	12	1,000	50	0.0	0.0
C- /3.6	3.7	6.8	13.84	250	1	3	0	93	3	30	4.4	28	12	1,000	50	0.0	0.0
C- /3.6	3.7	6.8	13.87	1,846	1	3	0	93	3	30	4.4	69	12	0	0	0.0	0.0
C- /3.6	3.7	6.8	13.85	7	1	3	0	93	3	30	4.4	28	12	0	0	0.0	0.0
C- /3.6	3.7	6.8	13.88	53	1	3	0	93	3	30	4.4	52	12	0	0	0.0	0.0
C- /3.6	3.7	6.8	13.88	61	1	3	0	93	3	30	4.4	61	12	0	0	0.0	0.0
C- /3.6	3.7	6.8	13.89	160	1	3	0	93	3	30	4.4	70	12	0	0	0.0	0.0
C- /3.6	3.7	6.8	13.87	56	1	3	0	93	3	30	4.4	61	12	0	0	0.0	0.0
D- /1.5	5.7	6.6	14.76	411	5	61	1	29	4	67	5.9	98	19	1,000	50	4.3	0.0
D- /1.5	5.7	6.6	14.83	29	5	61	1	29	4	67	5.9	96	19	1,000	50	0.0	0.0
D- /1.5	5.8	6.6	14.81	198	5	61	1	29	4	67	5.9	96	19	1,000	50	0.0	0.0
D- /1.5	5.7	6.6	14.73	4,162	5	61	1	29	4	67	5.9	98	19	0	0	0.0	0.0
D- /1.5	5.7	6.6	14.83	1	5	61	1	29	4	67	5.9	96	19	0	0	0.0	0.0
D- /1.5	5.7	6.6	14.82	25	5	61	1	29	4	67	5.9	97	19	0	0	0.0	0.0
D- /1.5	5.7	6.6	14.77	48	5	61	1	29	4	67	5.9	98	19	0	0	0.0	0.0
D- /1.5	5.7	6.6	14.77	66	5	61	1	29	4	67	5.9	98	19	0	0	0.0	0.0
D- /1.5	5.7	6.6	14.76	806	5	61	1	29	4	67	5.9	98	19	0	0	0.0	0.0
E- /0.1	12.0	5.8	6.79	2	0	82	0	13	5	80	7.2	24	6	1,000	0	4.3	0.0
E- /0.1	12.1	5.8	6.80	N/A	0	82	0	13	5	80	7.2	9	6	1,000	0	0.0	0.0
E- /0.1	12.0	5.8	6.79	1	0	82	0	13	5	80	7.2	9	6	1,000	0	0.0	0.0
E- /0.1	12.0	5.8	6.78	2	0	82	0	13	5	80	7.2	32	6	0	0	0.0	0.0
E- /0.1	12.0	5.8	6.80	N/A	0	82	0	13	5	80	7.2	9	6	0	0	0.0	0.0
E- /0.1	12.0	5.8	6.80	N/A	0	82	0	13	5	80	7.2	19	6	0	0	0.0	0.0
E- /0.1	12.1	5.8	6.80	N/A	0	82	0	13	5	80	7.2	27	6	0	0	0.0	0.0
E- /0.1	12.0	5.8	6.79	N/A	0	82	0	13	5	80	7.2	33	6	0	0	0.0	0.0
E- /0.1	12.0	5.8	6.79	309	0	82	0	13	5	80	7.2	35	6	0	0	0.0	0.0
C+ /5.7	3.0	5.3	10.69	60	0	0	99	0	1	11	5.1	63	18	1,000	50	4.3	0.0
C+ /5.8	3.0	5.3	10.73	1	0	0	99	0	1	11	5.1	29	18	1,000	50	0.0	0.0

Fund Type	Fund Name	Ticker Symbol	Overall Investment Rating	Phone	Performance Rating/Pts	3 Mo	6 Mo	1Yr / Pct	3Yr / Pct	5Yr / Pct	Dividend Yield	Expense Ratio
MUN	MFS GA Municipal Bond Fund I	MGATX	U	(800) 225-2606	U /	1.81	-2.52	--	--	--	0.00	0.78
GL	MFS Global Bond Fund A	MGBAX	E-	(800) 225-2606	E- / 0.2	1.18	-5.56	1.37 / 43	-1.09 / 3	-1.32 / 2	1.34	1.24
GL	MFS Global Bond Fund B	MGBBX	E-	(800) 225-2606	E- / 0.1	0.99	-5.96	0.49 / 33	-1.81 / 2	-2.04 / 1	0.63	1.99
GL	MFS Global Bond Fund C	MGBDX	E-	(800) 225-2606	E- / 0.1	1.11	-5.85	0.61 / 35	-1.77 / 2	-2.04 / 1	0.63	1.99
GL	MFS Global Bond Fund I	MGBJX	E-	(800) 225-2606	E- / 0.2	1.25	-5.47	1.51 / 45	-0.82 / 3	-1.08 / 2	1.66	0.99
GL	MFS Global Bond Fund R1	MGBKX	E-	(800) 225-2606	E- / 0.1	1.11	-5.85	0.61 / 35	-1.77 / 2	-2.02 / 1	0.63	1.99
GL	MFS Global Bond Fund R2	MGBLX	E-	(800) 225-2606	E- / 0.1	1.12	-5.72	1.00 / 40	-1.32 / 2	-1.57 / 1	1.15	1.49
GL	MFS Global Bond Fund R3	MGBMX	E-	(800) 225-2606	E- / 0.2	1.31	-5.48	1.37 / 43	-1.03 / 3	-1.30 / 2	1.40	1.24
GL	MFS Global Bond Fund R4	MGBNX	E-	(800) 225-2606	E- / 0.2	1.25	-5.47	1.62 / 46	-0.82 / 3	-1.05 / 2	1.66	0.99
GL	MFS Global Bond Fund R6	MGBOX	E-	(800) 225-2606	E- / 0.2	1.28	-5.42	1.75 / 47	-0.68 / 3	--	1.79	0.83
COH	MFS Global High Yield A	MHOAX	C+	(800) 225-2606	A- / 9.1	4.73	4.37	17.65 / 93	3.73 / 72	5.63 / 89	5.23	1.15
COH	MFS Global High Yield B	MHOBX	C-	(800) 225-2606	B+ / 8.4	4.53	3.98	16.76 / 91	2.91 / 60	4.81 / 82	4.74	1.90
COH	MFS Global High Yield C	MHOCX	C-	(800) 225-2606	B+ / 8.5	4.37	3.99	16.80 / 92	2.95 / 60	4.81 / 82	4.74	1.90
COH	MFS Global High Yield I	MHOIX	C+	(800) 225-2606	A / 9.3	4.79	4.50	17.94 / 93	3.94 / 75	5.86 / 91	5.70	0.90
COH	MFS Global High Yield R1	MHORX	C	(800) 225-2606	B+ / 8.5	4.53	4.15	16.76 / 91	2.96 / 60	4.81 / 82	4.74	1.90
COH	MFS Global High Yield R2	MHOSX	C	(800) 225-2606	B+ / 8.9	4.66	4.24	17.34 / 93	3.42 / 68	5.33 / 87	5.22	1.40
COH	MFS Global High Yield R3	MHOTX	C+	(800) 225-2606	A- / 9.1	4.73	4.37	17.65 / 93	3.73 / 72	5.59 / 89	5.46	1.15
COH	MFS Global High Yield R4	MHOUX	C+	(800) 225-2606	A- / 9.2	4.78	4.50	17.88 / 93	3.90 / 74	5.99 / 92	5.70	0.90
COH	MFS Global High Yield R6	MHOVX	C+	(800) 225-2606	A / 9.3	4.83	4.56	18.08 / 94	4.04 / 76	5.98 / 92	5.79	0.80
GL	MFS Global Multi-Asset A	GLMAX	E	(800) 225-2606	D+ / 2.9	3.56	1.74	11.64 / 82	0.91 / 26	1.70 / 38	0.00	2.51
GL	MFS Global Multi-Asset B	GLMBX	E+	(800) 225-2606	C- / 4.0	3.32	1.34	10.81 / 81	0.14 / 14	0.92 / 26	0.00	3.26
GL	MFS Global Multi-Asset C	GLMCX	E+	(800) 225-2606	C- / 4.1	3.32	1.34	10.81 / 81	0.17 / 15	0.94 / 27	0.00	3.26
GL	MFS Global Multi-Asset I	GLMIX	E+	(800) 225-2606	C+ / 5.8	3.64	1.84	12.05 / 83	1.16 / 30	1.96 / 41	0.00	2.26
GL	MFS Global Multi-Asset R1	GLMRX	E+	(800) 225-2606	C- / 4.1	3.30	1.34	10.91 / 81	0.17 / 15	0.93 / 26	0.00	3.26
GL	MFS Global Multi-Asset R2	GLMSX	E+	(800) 225-2606	C / 4.9	3.47	1.65	11.47 / 82	0.65 / 22	1.43 / 33	0.00	2.76
GL	MFS Global Multi-Asset R3	GLMTX	E+	(800) 225-2606	C / 5.3	3.56	1.75	11.65 / 82	0.91 / 26	1.69 / 37	0.00	2.51
GL	MFS Global Multi-Asset R4	GLMUX	E+	(800) 225-2606	C+ / 5.7	3.52	1.84	11.92 / 83	1.13 / 30	1.94 / 41	0.00	2.26
*USS	MFS Government Securities Fund A	MFGSX	E+	(800) 225-2606	E / 0.4	0.33	-2.62	-0.96 / 4	1.42 / 34	1.00 / 27	2.29	0.88
USS	MFS Government Securities Fund B	MFGBX	D-	(800) 225-2606	E+ / 0.8	0.14	-3.10	-1.81 / 1	0.63 / 22	0.22 / 19	1.62	1.63
USS	MFS Government Securities Fund C	MFGDX	D-	(800) 225-2606	E+ / 0.8	0.14	-3.08	-1.80 / 1	0.63 / 22	0.20 / 18	1.62	1.63
USS	MFS Government Securities Fund I	MGSIX	C-	(800) 225-2606	D+ / 2.9	0.39	-2.50	-0.71 / 7	1.64 / 37	1.23 / 30	2.65	0.63
USS	MFS Government Securities Fund R1	MFGGX	D-	(800) 225-2606	D- / 1.0	0.24	-3.00	-1.71 / 1	0.66 / 22	0.24 / 19	1.62	1.63
USS	MFS Government Securities Fund R2	MGVSX	D	(800) 225-2606	D / 2.1	0.37	-2.75	-1.21 / 3	1.17 / 30	0.74 / 24	2.13	1.13
USS	MFS Government Securities Fund R3	MFGHX	D	(800) 225-2606	D+ / 2.4	0.33	-2.72	-1.06 / 4	1.39 / 33	0.98 / 27	2.39	0.88
USS	MFS Government Securities Fund R4	MFGJX	C-	(800) 225-2606	D+ / 2.9	0.39	-2.50	-0.71 / 7	1.64 / 37	1.23 / 30	2.65	0.63
USL	MFS Government Securities Fund R6	MFGKX	C-	(800) 225-2606	C- / 3.1	0.41	-2.46	-0.61 / 8	1.75 / 39	--	2.76	0.52
COH	MFS High Income Fund 529A	EAHIX	C+	(800) 225-2606	A- / 9.0	3.99	4.10	17.44 / 93	3.72 / 72	5.63 / 89	5.01	0.70
COH	MFS High Income Fund 529B	EMHBX	C-	(800) 225-2606	B+ / 8.4	4.09	4.00	16.89 / 92	2.93 / 60	4.89 / 83	4.48	1.05
COH	MFS High Income Fund 529C	EMHCX	C-	(800) 225-2606	B+ / 8.4	4.09	3.70	16.52 / 91	2.94 / 60	4.83 / 82	4.49	1.80
COH	MFS High Income Fund A	MHITX	C-	(800) 225-2606	B / 8.2	4.30	4.42	17.82 / 93	3.76 / 72	5.73 / 90	5.03	0.95
COH	MFS High Income Fund B	MHIBX	C-	(800) 225-2606	B+ / 8.4	4.11	3.72	16.57 / 91	2.99 / 61	4.89 / 83	4.54	1.70
COH	MFS High Income Fund C	MHICX	C	(800) 225-2606	B+ / 8.5	4.10	4.02	16.91 / 92	2.99 / 61	4.88 / 83	4.53	1.70
COH	MFS High Income Fund I	MHIIX	C+	(800) 225-2606	A- / 9.2	4.37	4.25	17.76 / 93	4.01 / 75	5.93 / 92	5.50	0.70
COH	MFS High Income Fund R1	MHIGX	C	(800) 225-2606	B+ / 8.5	4.11	4.03	16.58 / 91	2.99 / 61	4.88 / 83	4.54	1.70
COH	MFS High Income Fund R2	MIHRX	C	(800) 225-2606	B+ / 8.8	3.93	3.99	17.19 / 92	3.40 / 67	5.35 / 87	5.03	1.20
COH	MFS High Income Fund R3	MHIHX	C+	(800) 225-2606	A- / 9.1	4.30	4.42	17.82 / 93	3.76 / 72	5.73 / 90	5.25	0.95
COH	MFS High Income Fund R4	MHIJX	C+	(800) 225-2606	A / 9.3	4.36	4.55	18.11 / 94	4.02 / 76	5.93 / 92	5.49	0.70
COH	MFS High Income Fund R6	MHIKX	C+	(800) 225-2606	A / 9.3	4.39	4.60	18.23 / 94	4.11 / 76	--	5.59	0.61
USS	MFS Inflation Adjusted Bond A	MIAAX	E	(800) 225-2606	E+ / 0.9	1.02	-1.00	2.44 / 53	1.06 / 28	-0.06 / 5	1.58	1.02
USS	MFS Inflation Adjusted Bond B	MIABX	E	(800) 225-2606	D / 1.8	0.83	-1.47	1.69 / 46	0.30 / 19	-0.82 / 2	0.90	1.77
USS	MFS Inflation Adjusted Bond C	MIACX	E	(800) 225-2606	D / 1.6	0.80	-1.43	1.59 / 45	0.22 / 17	-0.91 / 2	0.79	1.77
USS	MFS Inflation Adjusted Bond I	MIAIX	E+	(800) 225-2606	C- / 3.2	1.05	-1.02	2.60 / 54	1.21 / 31	0.08 / 13	1.80	0.77

● Denotes fund is closed to new investors
* Denotes fund is included in Section II

www.thestreetratings.com

RISK			NET ASSETS		ASSET							FUND MANAGER		MINIMUM		LOADS	
Risk Rating/Pts	3 Yr Avg Standard Deviation	Avg Duration	NAV As of 2/28/17	Total $(Mil)	Cash %	Gov. Bond %	Muni. Bond %	Corp. Bond %	Other %	Portfolio Turnover Ratio	Avg Coupon Rate	Manager Quality Pct	Manager Tenure (Years)	Initial Purch. $	Additional Purch. $	Front End Load	Back End Load
U /	N/A	5.3	9.70	7	0	0	99	0	1	11	5.1	N/A	18	0	0	0.0	0.0
D- /1.5	5.8	6.9	8.60	11	9	43	0	39	9	56	4.0	70	7	1,000	50	0.0	0.0
D- /1.5	5.7	6.9	8.55	1	9	43	0	39	9	56	4.0	41	7	1,000	50	0.0	0.0
D- /1.4	5.8	6.9	8.56	2	9	43	0	39	9	56	4.0	N/A	7	1,000	50	0.0	0.0
D- /1.4	5.8	6.9	8.55	4	9	43	0	39	9	56	4.0	76	7	0	0	0.0	0.0
D- /1.4	5.8	6.9	8.56	N/A	9	43	0	39	9	56	4.0	47	7	0	0	0.0	0.0
D- /1.4	5.8	6.9	8.55	N/A	9	43	0	39	9	56	4.0	64	7	0	0	0.0	0.0
D- /1.4	5.8	6.9	8.56	N/A	9	43	0	39	9	56	4.0	72	7	0	0	0.0	0.0
D- /1.4	5.8	6.9	8.56	N/A	9	43	0	39	9	56	4.0	76	7	0	0	0.0	0.0
D- /1.4	5.8	6.9	8.55	622	9	43	0	39	9	56	4.0	78	7	0	0	0.0	0.0
D- /1.2	5.5	3.7	6.24	218	67	3	0	29	1	16	6.3	21	12	1,000	50	0.0	0.0
D- /1.2	5.5	3.7	6.25	15	67	3	0	29	1	16	6.3	7	12	1,000	50	0.0	0.0
D- /1.2	5.5	3.7	6.23	66	67	3	0	29	1	16	6.3	7	12	1,000	50	0.0	0.0
D- /1.2	5.5	3.7	6.24	114	67	3	0	29	1	16	6.3	28	12	0	0	0.0	0.0
D- /1.3	5.5	3.7	6.25	N/A	67	3	0	29	1	16	6.3	8	12	0	0	0.0	0.0
D- /1.2	5.5	3.7	6.25	N/A	67	3	0	29	1	16	6.3	15	12	0	0	0.0	0.0
D- /1.2	5.5	3.7	6.24	9	67	3	0	29	1	16	6.3	22	12	0	0	0.0	0.0
D- /1.2	5.6	3.7	6.27	7	67	3	0	29	1	16	6.3	25	12	0	0	0.0	0.0
D- /1.2	5.6	3.7	6.23	4	67	3	0	29	1	16	6.3	30	12	0	0	0.0	0.0
E+ /0.9	6.4	N/A	9.13	5	9	30	0	20	41	54	0.0	85	6	1,000	50	5.8	0.0
D- /1.0	6.4	N/A	8.84	1	9	30	0	20	41	54	0.0	78	6	1,000	50	0.0	0.0
E+ /0.9	6.4	N/A	8.84	1	9	30	0	20	41	54	0.0	78	6	1,000	50	0.0	0.0
E+ /0.9	6.4	N/A	9.22	14	9	30	0	20	41	54	0.0	87	6	0	0	0.0	0.0
E+ /0.9	6.4	N/A	8.87	N/A	9	30	0	20	41	54	0.0	78	6	0	0	0.0	0.0
E+ /0.9	6.4	N/A	9.06	N/A	9	30	0	20	41	54	0.0	83	6	0	0	0.0	0.0
E+ /0.9	6.4	N/A	9.12	1	9	30	0	20	41	54	0.0	85	6	0	0	0.0	0.0
E+ /0.9	6.4	N/A	9.21	N/A	9	30	0	20	41	54	0.0	87	6	0	0	0.0	0.0
B- /7.4	2.6	4.5	9.84	684	0	41	0	2	57	88	3.4	35	11	1,000	0	4.3	0.0
B- /7.3	2.6	4.5	9.82	18	0	41	0	2	57	88	3.4	12	11	1,000	0	0.0	0.0
B- /7.3	2.6	4.5	9.85	42	0	41	0	2	57	88	3.4	13	11	1,000	0	0.0	0.0
B- /7.4	2.6	4.5	9.83	43	0	41	0	2	57	88	3.4	51	11	0	0	0.0	0.0
B- /7.3	2.6	4.5	9.83	3	0	41	0	2	57	88	3.4	13	11	0	0	0.0	0.0
B- /7.3	2.6	4.5	9.83	111	0	41	0	2	57	88	3.4	26	11	0	0	0.0	0.0
B- /7.3	2.6	4.5	9.83	88	0	41	0	2	57	88	3.4	33	11	0	0	0.0	0.0
B- /7.4	2.6	4.5	9.84	64	0	41	0	2	57	88	3.4	51	11	0	0	0.0	0.0
B- /7.5	2.6	4.5	9.83	1,036	0	41	0	2	57	88	3.4	58	11	0	0	0.0	0.0
D- /1.3	5.4	3.7	3.45	4	0	1	0	94	5	36	6.3	24	11	250	0	0.0	0.0
D- /1.2	5.5	3.7	3.46	N/A	0	1	0	94	5	36	6.3	7	11	250	0	0.0	0.0
D- /1.2	5.6	3.7	3.46	1	0	1	0	94	5	36	6.3	7	11	250	0	0.0	0.0
D- /1.3	5.4	3.7	3.46	508	0	1	0	94	5	36	6.3	24	11	1,000	50	4.3	0.0
D- /1.2	5.6	3.7	3.46	22	0	1	0	94	5	36	6.3	7	11	1,000	50	0.0	0.0
D- /1.3	5.4	3.7	3.47	66	0	1	0	94	5	36	6.3	9	11	1,000	50	0.0	0.0
D- /1.2	5.5	3.7	3.45	142	0	1	0	94	5	36	6.3	30	11	0	0	0.0	0.0
D- /1.2	5.5	3.7	3.46	1	0	1	0	94	5	36	6.3	8	11	0	0	0.0	0.0
D- /1.3	5.4	3.7	3.45	15	0	1	0	94	5	36	6.3	16	11	0	0	0.0	0.0
D- /1.3	5.4	3.7	3.46	7	0	1	0	94	5	36	6.3	25	11	0	0	0.0	0.0
D- /1.3	5.4	3.7	3.46	N/A	0	1	0	94	5	36	6.3	34	11	0	0	0.0	0.0
D- /1.3	5.4	3.7	3.46	797	0	1	0	94	5	36	6.3	36	11	0	0	0.0	0.0
C- /3.1	4.1	6.8	10.39	49	0	99	0	0	1	23	1.0	16	14	1,000	0	4.3	0.0
C- /3.1	4.0	6.8	10.34	9	0	99	0	0	1	23	1.0	5	14	1,000	0	0.0	0.0
C- /3.2	4.0	6.8	10.35	12	0	99	0	0	1	23	1.0	5	14	1,000	0	0.0	0.0
C- /3.1	4.1	6.8	10.40	20	0	99	0	0	1	23	1.0	18	14	0	0	0.0	0.0

Fund Type	Fund Name	Ticker Symbol	Overall Investment Rating	Phone	Perfor-mance Rating/Pts	Total Return % through 2/28/17			Annualized		Incl. in Returns	
	99 Pct = Best 0 Pct = Worst					3 Mo	6 Mo	1Yr / Pct	3Yr / Pct	5Yr / Pct	Dividend Yield	Expense Ratio
USS	MFS Inflation Adjusted Bond R1	MIALX	E	(800) 225-2606	D / 1.7	0.90	-1.43	1.69 /46	0.22 /17	-0.90 / 2	0.79	1.77
USS	MFS Inflation Adjusted Bond R2	MIATX	E+	(800) 225-2606	D+ / 2.4	0.93	-1.27	2.09 /50	0.70 /23	-0.42 / 3	1.30	1.27
USS	MFS Inflation Adjusted Bond R3	MIAHX	E+	(800) 225-2606	D+ / 2.8	0.99	-1.05	2.34 /52	0.97 /27	-0.14 / 4	1.55	1.02
USS	MFS Inflation Adjusted Bond R4	MIAJX	E+	(800) 225-2606	C- / 3.2	1.05	-0.92	2.60 /54	1.21 /31	0.10 /15	1.80	0.77
GEI	MFS Inflation Adjusted Bond R6	MIAKX	E+	(800) 225-2606	C- / 3.4	1.07	-0.87	2.68 /54	1.31 /32	--	1.88	0.67
GEI	MFS Limited Maturity 529A	EALMX	C-	(800) 225-2606	D- / 1.2	0.53	0.15	1.57 /45	0.65 /22	1.00 /27	1.20	0.95
GEI	MFS Limited Maturity 529B	EBLMX	D+	(800) 225-2606	E+ / 0.8	0.34	-0.23	0.80 /37	-0.06 / 5	0.27 /19	0.46	1.70
GEI	MFS Limited Maturity 529C	ELDCX	D	(800) 225-2606	E / 0.5	0.32	-0.27	0.72 /36	-0.14 / 5	0.15 /17	0.38	1.70
GEI	MFS Limited Maturity A	MQLFX	C-	(800) 225-2606	D- / 1.3	0.55	0.18	1.63 /46	0.70 /23	1.05 /28	1.25	0.85
GEI	● MFS Limited Maturity B	MQLBX	D	(800) 225-2606	E+ / 0.6	0.18	-0.38	0.68 /36	-0.06 / 5	0.29 /20	0.51	1.60
GEI	MFS Limited Maturity C	MQLCX	D	(800) 225-2606	E / 0.5	0.16	-0.42	0.60 /35	-0.15 / 5	0.20 /18	0.43	1.60
GEI	MFS Limited Maturity I	MQLIX	C+	(800) 225-2606	D+ / 2.6	0.42	0.08	1.61 /45	0.85 /25	1.17 /30	1.43	0.60
GEI	MFS Limited Maturity Initial		B-	(800) 225-2606	D+ / 2.9	0.59	0.29	1.78 /47	0.99 /27	1.13 /29	1.38	0.45
GEI	MFS Limited Maturity R1	MQLGX	D	(800) 225-2606	E / 0.5	0.16	-0.42	0.76 /37	-0.15 / 5	0.20 /18	0.43	1.60
GEI	MFS Limited Maturity R2	MLMRX	C+	(800) 225-2606	D / 2.1	0.48	0.05	1.37 /43	0.51 /21	0.80 /25	1.03	1.10
GEI	MFS Limited Maturity R3	MQLHX	C+	(800) 225-2606	D+ / 2.3	0.35	-0.04	1.52 /45	0.66 /23	0.98 /27	1.18	0.85
GEI	MFS Limited Maturity R4	MQLJX	B-	(800) 225-2606	D+ / 2.7	0.59	0.25	1.78 /47	0.86 /25	1.20 /30	1.43	0.60
COI	MFS Limited Maturity R6	MQLKX	B-	(800) 225-2606	D+ / 2.7	0.43	0.12	1.68 /46	0.93 /26	--	1.51	0.52
MUS	MFS MA Municipal Bond A	MFSSX	B-	(800) 225-2606	C+ / 6.4	1.72	-2.68	0.21 /29	3.94 /92	2.60 /73	3.54	0.88
MUS	MFS MA Municipal Bond B	MBMAX	B	(800) 225-2606	B- / 7.0	1.52	-3.05	-0.55 / 9	3.14 /84	1.82 /54	2.90	1.63
MUN	MFS MA Municipal Bond I	MTALX	U	(800) 225-2606	U /	1.75	-2.65	--	--	--	0.00	0.63
MUS	MFS MD Municipal Bond A	MFSMX	B+	(800) 225-2606	C+ / 5.7	1.65	-2.31	0.61 /39	3.48 /88	2.35 /67	3.38	0.98
MUS	MFS MD Municipal Bond B	MBMDX	A	(800) 225-2606	C+ / 6.4	1.46	-2.67	-0.05 /17	2.71 /77	1.59 /49	2.76	1.73
MUN	MFS MD Municipal Bond I	MMDIX	U	(800) 225-2606	U /	1.68	-2.14	--	--	--	0.00	0.73
MUS	MFS MS Municipal Bond A	MISSX	C-	(800) 225-2606	C / 5.2	1.67	-3.29	-0.16 /15	3.44 /87	2.54 /71	3.36	0.96
MUS	MFS MS Municipal Bond B	MBMSX	C+	(800) 225-2606	C+ / 6.1	1.50	-3.61	-0.92 / 5	2.75 /78	1.84 /55	2.81	1.71
MUN	MFS MS Municipal Bond I	MMSTX	U	(800) 225-2606	U /	1.67	-3.18	--	--	--	0.00	0.71
* MUH	MFS Municipal High Income A	MMHYX	B+	(800) 225-2606	A / 9.4	2.54	-3.16	1.91 /56	6.12 /99	5.03 /98	4.15	0.71
MUH	MFS Municipal High Income B	MMHBX	B+	(800) 225-2606	A+ / 9.6	2.36	-3.51	1.27 /48	5.30 /98	4.21 /95	3.55	1.71
MUH	MFS Municipal High Income C	MMHCX	B+	(800) 225-2606	A / 9.4	2.31	-3.62	0.92 /44	5.07 /97	3.99 /93	3.33	1.71
MUH	MFS Municipal High Income I	MMIIX	A-	(800) 225-2606	A+ / 9.8	2.53	-3.16	2.03 /57	6.11 /99	5.05 /98	4.33	0.71
* MUN	MFS Municipal Income A	MFIAX	B	(800) 225-2606	B- / 7.1	1.91	-2.64	0.87 /43	4.25 /94	3.40 /86	3.43	0.78
MUN	MFS Municipal Income A1	MMIDX	B+	(800) 225-2606	B- / 7.5	2.10	-2.50	1.13 /47	4.51 /96	3.68 /90	3.68	0.53
MUN	MFS Municipal Income B	MMIBX	B+	(800) 225-2606	B- / 7.4	1.72	-3.10	--	3.42 /87	2.63 /73	2.81	1.53
MUN	MFS Municipal Income B1	MMIGX	A-	(800) 225-2606	B / 8.0	1.90	-2.88	0.35 /34	3.71 /90	2.90 /78	3.04	0.53
MUN	MFS Municipal Income C	MMICX	B+	(800) 225-2606	B- / 7.5	1.72	-2.99	0.11 /25	3.45 /87	2.62 /73	2.80	1.53
MUN	MFS Municipal Income I	MIMIX	A+	(800) 225-2606	A- / 9.1	1.98	-2.52	1.12 /46	4.51 /96	3.65 /89	3.83	0.53
* MUN	MFS Municipal Lmtd Maturity A	MTLFX	C-	(800) 225-2606	D+ / 2.4	1.39	-1.46	-0.04 /17	1.45 /47	1.36 /43	1.91	0.80
MUN	● MFS Municipal Lmtd Maturity B	MTLBX	C-	(800) 225-2606	D / 2.1	1.21	-1.83	-0.79 / 6	0.69 /28	0.60 /26	1.19	1.55
MUN	MFS Municipal Lmtd Maturity C	MTLCX	D+	(800) 225-2606	D / 2.0	1.18	-1.88	-0.88 / 5	0.63 /27	0.53 /25	1.09	1.55
MUN	MFS Municipal Lmtd Maturity I	MTLIX	B+	(800) 225-2606	C / 4.6	1.56	-1.27	0.23 /30	1.64 /52	1.53 /47	2.10	0.55
MUS	MFS NC Municipal Bond A	MSNCX	B-	(800) 225-2606	C+ / 5.7	1.62	-2.65	0.12 /25	3.58 /89	2.40 /69	3.36	0.87
MUS	MFS NC Municipal Bond B	MBNCX	B+	(800) 225-2606	C+ / 6.4	1.43	-2.94	-0.64 / 8	2.81 /79	1.66 /50	2.74	1.62
MUS	MFS NC Municipal Bond C	MCNCX	B+	(800) 225-2606	C+ / 6.4	1.43	-2.94	-0.56 / 9	2.80 /79	1.65 /50	2.73	1.62
MUN	MFS NC Municipal Bond I	MNCLX	U	(800) 225-2606	U /	1.61	-2.52	--	--	--	0.00	0.62
MUS	MFS NY Municipal Bond A	MSNYX	C+	(800) 225-2606	C+ / 6.8	2.09	-3.12	0.37 /34	4.16 /94	2.90 /78	3.47	0.88
MUS	MFS NY Municipal Bond B	MBNYX	B-	(800) 225-2606	B- / 7.3	1.92	-3.47	-0.36 /12	3.40 /87	2.14 /62	2.87	1.63
MUS	MFS NY Municipal Bond C	MCNYX	B	(800) 225-2606	B- / 7.4	1.92	-3.38	-0.27 /13	3.43 /87	2.15 /62	2.87	1.63
MUN	MFS NY Municipal Bond I	MNYLX	U	(800) 225-2606	U /	2.19	-2.95	--	--	--	0.00	0.63
MUS	MFS PA Municipal Bond A	MFPAX	B	(800) 225-2606	B- / 7.1	1.76	-2.71	0.87 /43	4.24 /94	3.11 /82	3.52	0.94
MUS	MFS PA Municipal Bond B	MBPAX	B+	(800) 225-2606	B / 7.6	1.66	-2.97	0.11 /25	3.48 /88	2.32 /67	2.88	1.69
MUN	MFS PA Municipal Bond I	MPALX	U	(800) 225-2606	U /	1.82	-2.59	--	--	--	0.00	0.69

● Denotes fund is closed to new investors
* Denotes fund is included in Section II

www.thestreetratings.com

RISK			NET ASSETS		ASSET					Portfolio Turnover Ratio	Avg Coupon Rate	FUND MANAGER		MINIMUM		LOADS	
Risk Rating/Pts	3 Yr Avg Standard Deviation	Avg Duration	NAV As of 2/28/17	Total $(Mil)	Cash %	Gov. Bond %	Muni. Bond %	Corp. Bond %	Other %			Manager Quality Pct	Manager Tenure (Years)	Initial Purch. $	Additional Purch. $	Front End Load	Back End Load
C- /3.1	4.0	6.8	10.34	N/A	0	99	0	0	1	23	1.0	5	14	0	0	0.0	0.0
C- /3.1	4.1	6.8	10.37	1	0	99	0	0	1	23	1.0	9	14	0	0	0.0	0.0
C- /3.2	4.0	6.8	10.39	2	0	99	0	0	1	23	1.0	14	14	0	0	0.0	0.0
C- /3.1	4.0	6.8	10.40	1	0	99	0	0	1	23	1.0	19	14	0	0	0.0	0.0
C- /3.1	4.0	6.8	10.42	1,135	0	99	0	0	1	23	1.0	5	14	0	0	0.0	0.0
A+ /9.6	0.7	1.6	5.98	84	0	10	0	71	19	30	2.0	50	N/A	250	0	2.5	0.0
A+ /9.6	0.8	1.6	5.96	4	0	10	0	71	19	30	2.0	18	N/A	250	0	0.0	0.0
A+ /9.6	0.7	1.6	5.98	42	0	10	0	71	19	30	2.0	17	N/A	250	0	0.0	0.0
A+ /9.7	0.7	1.6	5.98	496	0	10	0	71	19	30	2.0	52	N/A	1,000	50	2.5	0.0
A+ /9.7	0.7	1.6	5.96	6	0	10	0	71	19	30	2.0	19	N/A	1,000	50	0.0	0.0
A+ /9.7	0.6	1.6	5.97	100	0	10	0	71	19	30	2.0	17	N/A	1,000	50	0.0	0.0
A+ /9.7	0.6	1.6	5.95	258	0	10	0	71	19	30	2.0	58	N/A	0	0	0.0	0.0
A+ /9.7	0.7	1.6	10.22	465	0	5	0	73	22	26	2.2	62	N/A	0	0	0.0	0.0
A+ /9.7	0.7	1.6	5.96	N/A	0	10	0	71	19	30	2.0	17	N/A	0	0	0.0	0.0
A+ /9.6	0.7	1.6	5.98	4	0	10	0	71	19	30	2.0	39	N/A	0	0	0.0	0.0
A+ /9.7	0.7	1.6	5.98	3	0	10	0	71	19	30	2.0	50	N/A	0	0	0.0	0.0
A+ /9.7	0.7	1.6	5.98	7	0	10	0	71	19	30	2.0	58	N/A	0	0	0.0	0.0
A+ /9.7	0.7	1.6	5.96	519	0	10	0	71	19	30	2.0	59	N/A	0	0	0.0	0.0
C /5.3	3.1	5.3	11.03	208	0	0	98	0	2	15	5.0	69	18	1,000	50	4.3	0.0
C /5.1	3.1	5.3	11.05	3	0	0	98	0	2	15	5.0	35	18	1,000	50	0.0	0.0
U /	N/A	5.3	9.65	21	0	0	98	0	2	15	5.0	N/A	18	0	0	0.0	0.0
B- /7.0	2.7	5.2	10.77	81	0	0	98	0	2	10	5.4	66	18	1,000	50	4.3	0.0
C+ /6.9	2.7	5.2	10.77	2	0	0	98	0	2	10	5.4	32	18	1,000	50	0.0	0.0
U /	N/A	5.2	9.72	6	0	0	98	0	2	10	5.4	N/A	18	0	0	0.0	0.0
C /4.8	3.2	5.9	9.64	85	0	0	98	0	2	17	5.1	49	18	1,000	50	4.3	0.0
C /4.9	3.2	5.9	9.65	1	0	0	98	0	2	17	5.1	20	18	1,000	50	0.0	0.0
U /	N/A	5.9	9.63	5	0	0	98	0	2	17	5.1	N/A	18	0	0	0.0	0.0
D+ /2.6	3.9	6.9	8.07	1,646	0	0	99	0	1	17	5.4	86	15	1,000	50	4.3	0.0
D+ /2.6	3.8	6.9	8.08	26	0	0	99	0	1	17	5.4	79	15	1,000	50	0.0	0.0
D+ /2.6	3.8	6.9	8.08	286	0	0	99	0	1	17	5.4	76	15	1,000	50	0.0	0.0
D+ /2.6	3.8	6.9	8.07	1,714	0	0	99	0	1	17	5.4	86	15	0	0	0.0	0.0
C /5.0	3.1	5.9	8.64	1,225	1	1	94	2	2	22	5.1	74	19	1,000	50	4.3	0.0
C /4.9	3.2	5.9	8.65	509	1	1	94	2	2	22	5.1	77	19	1,000	50	4.3	0.0
C /4.8	3.2	5.9	8.65	24	1	1	94	2	2	22	5.1	46	19	1,000	50	0.0	0.0
C /4.7	3.2	5.9	8.66	N/A	1	1	94	2	2	22	5.1	58	19	1,000	50	0.0	0.0
C /5.1	3.1	5.9	8.67	184	1	1	94	2	2	22	5.1	52	19	1,000	50	0.0	0.0
C /5.0	3.1	5.9	8.63	956	1	1	94	2	2	22	5.1	78	19	0	0	0.0	0.0
B+ /8.4	1.9	3.3	8.07	632	0	0	97	0	3	24	4.5	21	17	1,000	50	2.5	0.0
B+ /8.3	1.9	3.3	8.06	2	0	0	97	0	3	24	4.5	7	17	1,000	50	0.0	0.0
B+ /8.4	1.9	3.3	8.08	131	0	0	97	0	3	24	4.5	7	17	1,000	50	0.0	0.0
B+ /8.3	1.9	3.3	8.07	880	0	0	97	0	3	24	4.5	27	17	0	0	0.0	0.0
C+ /6.2	2.9	5.1	11.60	264	0	0	99	0	1	9	5.2	65	18	1,000	50	4.3	0.0
C+ /6.1	2.9	5.1	11.59	3	0	0	99	0	1	9	5.2	31	18	1,000	50	0.0	0.0
C+ /6.4	2.8	5.1	11.60	58	0	0	99	0	1	9	5.2	32	18	1,000	50	0.0	0.0
U /	N/A	5.1	9.67	36	0	0	99	0	1	9	5.2	N/A	18	0	0	0.0	0.0
C /4.3	3.4	5.8	10.93	123	0	0	99	0	1	13	5.3	66	18	1,000	50	4.3	0.0
C /4.3	3.4	5.8	10.90	5	0	0	99	0	1	13	5.3	33	18	1,000	50	0.0	0.0
C /4.3	3.4	5.8	10.92	26	0	0	99	0	1	13	5.3	34	18	1,000	50	0.0	0.0
U /	N/A	5.8	9.67	50	0	0	99	0	1	13	5.3	N/A	18	0	0	0.0	0.0
C /4.9	3.2	5.6	10.19	99	0	0	99	0	1	16	5.2	73	18	1,000	50	4.3	0.0
C /4.7	3.2	5.6	10.22	5	0	0	99	0	1	16	5.2	50	18	1,000	50	0.0	0.0
U /	N/A	5.6	9.71	19	0	0	99	0	1	16	5.2	N/A	18	0	0	0.0	0.0

					PERFORMANCE						
99 Pct = Best 0 Pct = Worst					Perfor-mance Rating/Pts	Total Return % through 2/28/17			Annualized		Incl. in Returns	
Fund Type	Fund Name	Ticker Symbol	Overall Investment Rating	Phone		3 Mo	6 Mo	1Yr / Pct	3Yr / Pct	5Yr / Pct	Dividend Yield	Expense Ratio
MUS	MFS SC Municipal Bond A	MFSCX	C-	(800) 225-2606	C / 5.4	1.83	-2.82	-0.22 /14	3.50 /88	2.28 /66	3.02	0.89
MUS	MFS SC Municipal Bond B	MBSCX	C+	(800) 225-2606	C+ / 6.1	1.55	-3.19	-1.05 / 4	2.73 /78	1.52 /47	2.38	1.64
MUN	MFS SC Municipal Bond I	MTSCX	U	(800) 225-2606	U /	1.81	-2.73	--	--	--	0.00	0.64
GES	MFS Strategic Income A	MFIOX	C+	(800) 225-2606	C+ / 6.8	2.66	0.47	9.18 /77	2.71 /56	3.64 /68	3.46	1.11
GES	MFS Strategic Income B	MIOBX	C-	(800) 225-2606	C+ / 5.8	2.47	0.08	8.41 /75	1.98 /43	2.93 /56	2.86	1.86
GES	MFS Strategic Income C	MIOCX	C-	(800) 225-2606	C+ / 5.8	2.48	0.08	8.25 /75	1.98 /43	2.93 /56	2.86	1.86
GES	MFS Strategic Income I	MFIIX	B-	(800) 225-2606	B- / 7.2	2.86	0.72	9.43 /78	2.96 /60	3.93 /71	3.83	0.86
MUS	MFS TN Municipal Bond A	MSTNX	C-	(800) 225-2606	C / 5.1	1.57	-2.81	0.06 /22	3.33 /86	2.27 /65	3.14	0.94
MUS	MFS TN Municipal Bond B	MBTNX	C+	(800) 225-2606	C+ / 5.9	1.38	-3.17	-0.69 / 7	2.56 /75	1.51 /46	2.51	1.69
MUN	MFS TN Municipal Bond I	MTNLX	U	(800) 225-2606	U /	1.68	-2.71	--	--	--	0.00	0.69
GEI	MFS Total Return Bond 529A	EARBX	D+	(800) 225-2606	C- / 3.2	1.26	-1.69	3.00 /57	2.48 /51	2.79 /54	2.69	0.99
GEI	MFS Total Return Bond 529B	EBRBX	D+	(800) 225-2606	C- / 3.4	0.93	-2.21	2.01 /49	1.57 /36	1.87 /40	1.93	1.74
GEI	MFS Total Return Bond 529C	ECRBX	D+	(800) 225-2606	C- / 3.5	1.03	-2.12	2.11 /50	1.57 /36	1.87 /40	1.92	1.74
*GEI	MFS Total Return Bond A	MRBFX	D+	(800) 225-2606	C- / 3.3	1.26	-1.68	3.03 /57	2.52 /52	2.79 /54	2.72	0.89
GEI	MFS Total Return Bond B	MRBBX	C-	(800) 225-2606	C- / 3.7	0.97	-2.14	2.16 /50	1.73 /39	2.03 /43	2.08	1.64
GEI	MFS Total Return Bond C	MRBCX	C-	(800) 225-2606	C- / 3.5	1.04	-2.10	2.06 /49	1.62 /37	1.92 /41	1.98	1.64
GEI	MFS Total Return Bond I	MRBIX	B-	(800) 225-2606	C / 5.3	1.30	-1.60	3.19 /58	2.65 /55	2.95 /57	2.99	0.64
GEI	MFS Total Return Bond R1	MRBGX	C-	(800) 225-2606	C- / 3.6	1.04	-2.09	2.16 /50	1.66 /37	1.93 /41	1.97	1.64
GEI	MFS Total Return Bond R2	MRRRX	C	(800) 225-2606	C / 4.3	1.08	-1.94	2.58 /54	2.13 /45	2.43 /48	2.48	1.14
GEI	MFS Total Return Bond R3	MRBHX	C+	(800) 225-2606	C / 4.9	1.24	-1.73	2.93 /56	2.42 /50	2.71 /53	2.74	0.89
GEI	MFS Total Return Bond R4	MRBJX	B-	(800) 225-2606	C / 5.3	1.30	-1.60	3.19 /58	2.68 /56	2.95 /57	2.99	0.64
GEI	MFS Total Return Bond R6	MRBKX	B-	(800) 225-2606	C / 5.4	1.32	-1.56	3.29 /58	2.75 /57	3.04 /58	3.09	0.53
MMT●	MFS US Government Cash Reserve	MACXX	U	(800) 225-2606	U /	0.00	0.01	0.01 /18	--	--	0.01	N/A
MMT●	MFS US Government Cash Reserve	MRBXX	U	(800) 225-2606	U /	0.00	0.01	0.01 /18	--	--	0.01	N/A
MMT●	MFS US Government Cash Reserve	MRCXX	U	(800) 225-2606	U /	0.00	0.01	0.01 /18	--	--	0.01	N/A
MMT●	MFS US Government Cash Reserve	MSRXX	U	(800) 225-2606	U /	0.00	0.01	0.01 /18	--	--	0.01	N/A
MMT●	MFS US Government Cash Reserve	MCRXX	U	(800) 225-2606	U /	0.00	0.01	0.01 /18	--	--	0.01	N/A
MMT●	MFS US Government Cash Reserve	MCCXX	U	(800) 225-2606	U /	0.00	0.01	0.01 /18	--	--	0.01	N/A
MMT●	MFS US Government Cash Reserve	CRVXX	U	(800) 225-2606	U /	0.00	0.01	0.01 /18	--	--	0.01	N/A
MMT●	MFS US Government Cash Reserve	CRMXX	U	(800) 225-2606	U /	0.00	0.01	0.01 /18	--	--	0.01	N/A
MMT●	MFS US Government Cash Reserve	CRJXX	U	(800) 225-2606	U /	0.00	0.01	0.01 /18	--	--	0.01	N/A
MMT●	MFS US Government Cash Reserve	CRKXX	U	(800) 225-2606	U /	0.00	0.01	0.01 /18	--	--	0.01	N/A
MMT●	MFS US Government Money Market	MCMXX	D+	(800) 225-2606	E+ / 0.7	0.00	0.07	0.07 /21	0.02 / 8	0.01 / 6	0.07	N/A
MUS	MFS VA Municipal Bond A	MSVAX	C+	(800) 225-2606	C+ / 5.8	1.80	-2.50	0.14 /26	3.59 /89	2.56 /72	3.43	0.89
MUS	MFS VA Municipal Bond B	MBVAX	B+	(800) 225-2606	C+ / 6.5	1.72	-2.76	-0.59 / 8	2.83 /79	1.80 /54	2.83	1.64
MUS	MFS VA Municipal Bond C	MVACX	B	(800) 225-2606	C+ / 6.5	1.63	-2.85	-0.60 / 8	2.82 /79	1.80 /54	2.83	1.64
MUN	MFS VA Municipal Bond I	MIVAX	U	(800) 225-2606	U /	1.98	-2.34	--	--	--	0.00	0.64
MUS	MFS WV Municipal Bond A	MFWVX	B-	(800) 225-2606	C+ / 5.8	1.81	-2.28	0.19 /28	3.57 /88	2.23 /64	3.16	0.93
MUS	MFS WV Municipal Bond B	MBWVX	B+	(800) 225-2606	C+ / 6.6	1.62	-2.56	-0.48 /10	2.83 /79	1.47 /46	2.53	1.68
MUN	MFS WV Municipal Bond I	MWVIX	U	(800) 225-2606	U /	1.89	-2.11	--	--	--	0.00	0.68
MTG	Mgd Acct Srs BlackRock US Mtg Inst	MSUMX	A	(800) 441-7762	C+ / 5.8	0.67	-0.77	1.98 /49	3.18 /64	3.49 /65	2.85	0.61
MTG	Mgd Acct Srs BlackRock US Mtg Inv	BMPAX	C+	(800) 441-7762	C- / 3.6	0.61	-0.90	1.69 /46	2.89 /59	3.21 /61	2.47	0.94
MTG	Mgd Acct Srs BlackRock US Mtg Inv	BMPCX	B	(800) 441-7762	C- / 4.1	0.52	-1.17	1.03 /40	2.16 /46	2.46 /49	1.81	1.65
COI	Miller Intermediate Bond A	MIFAX	U	(877) 441-4434	U /	1.22	2.32	11.02 /81	--	--	1.13	2.05
COI	Miller Intermediate Bond C	MIFCX	U	(877) 441-4434	U /	1.08	1.98	10.27 /79	--	--	0.47	2.80
COI	Miller Intermediate Bond I	MIFIX	U	(877) 441-4434	U /	1.25	2.48	11.32 /82	--	--	1.47	1.80
GL	Mirae Global Dynamic Bond A	MAGDX	C-	(888) 335-3417	C / 4.9	2.39	0.23	5.83 /70	3.09 /62	3.01 /58	2.49	5.27
GL	Mirae Global Dynamic Bond C	MCGDX	C	(888) 335-3417	C / 5.5	2.19	-0.14	5.06 /67	2.28 /48	2.23 /45	1.87	5.96
GL	Mirae Global Dynamic Bond I	MDBIX	B+	(888) 335-3417	B- / 7.0	2.44	0.44	6.07 /70	3.34 /66	3.26 /62	2.84	2.11
COI	MN Rainier Interm Fixed Income Inst	RAIFX	U	(800) 248-6314	U /	0.71	-1.38	0.29 /28	--	--	1.98	0.81
GEI	MN Rainier Interm Fixed Income Orig	RIMFX	C-	(800) 248-6314	D+ / 2.6	0.59	-1.62	0.04 /20	1.23 /31	1.59 /36	1.81	0.71
GEL	MO 529 MOST CSP Direct Vngd Csv		B-	(800) 662-7447	C- / 4.0	0.77	-0.96	1.55 /45	1.92 /42	1.30 /31	0.00	0.55

● Denotes fund is closed to new investors
* Denotes fund is included in Section II

www.thestreetratings.com

Risk Rating/Pts	3 Yr Avg Standard Deviation	Avg Dura-tion	NAV As of 2/28/17	Total $(Mil)	Cash %	Gov. Bond %	Muni. Bond %	Corp. Bond %	Other %	Portfolio Turnover Ratio	Avg Coupon Rate	Manager Quality Pct	Manager Tenure (Years)	Initial Purch. $	Additional Purch. $	Front End Load	Back End Load
C /4.9	3.2	5.3	11.93	171	0	0	99	0	1	8	5.1	53	18	1,000	50	4.3	0.0
C /4.9	3.1	5.3	11.92	4	0	0	99	0	1	8	5.1	20	18	1,000	50	0.0	0.0
U /	N/A	5.3	9.66	12	0	0	99	0	1	8	5.1	N/A	18	0	0	0.0	0.0
C- /4.2	3.4	5.1	6.56	201	34	16	0	42	8	21	5.0	73	6	1,000	0	0.0	0.0
C /4.3	3.4	5.1	6.52	22	34	16	0	42	8	21	5.0	52	6	1,000	0	0.0	0.0
C- /4.2	3.4	5.1	6.50	35	34	16	0	42	8	21	5.0	52	6	1,000	0	0.0	0.0
C /4.4	3.3	5.1	6.56	48	34	16	0	42	8	21	5.0	77	6	0	0	0.0	0.0
C /5.4	3.0	5.4	10.36	92	0	0	99	0	1	14	5.1	51	18	1,000	50	4.3	0.0
C /5.3	3.0	5.4	10.35	1	0	0	99	0	1	14	5.1	19	18	1,000	50	0.0	0.0
U /	N/A	5.4	9.68	18	0	0	99	0	1	14	5.1	N/A	18	0	0	0.0	0.0
C+ /6.8	2.8	5.4	10.63	7	0	19	1	44	36	53	3.7	50	11	250	0	4.3	0.0
C+ /6.7	2.8	5.4	10.65	N/A	0	19	1	44	36	53	3.7	15	11	250	0	0.0	0.0
C+ /6.6	2.8	5.4	10.65	4	0	19	1	44	36	53	3.7	14	11	250	0	0.0	0.0
C+ /6.7	2.8	5.4	10.64	1,680	0	19	1	44	36	53	3.7	52	11	1,000	50	4.3	0.0
C+ /6.6	2.8	5.4	10.65	26	0	19	1	44	36	53	3.7	18	11	1,000	50	0.0	0.0
C+ /6.7	2.8	5.4	10.65	141	0	19	1	44	36	53	3.7	16	11	1,000	50	0.0	0.0
C+ /6.5	2.8	5.4	10.64	1,216	0	19	1	44	36	53	3.7	55	11	0	0	0.0	0.0
C+ /6.6	2.8	5.4	10.66	3	0	19	1	44	36	53	3.7	16	11	0	0	0.0	0.0
C+ /6.7	2.8	5.4	10.63	49	0	19	1	44	36	53	3.7	29	11	0	0	0.0	0.0
C+ /6.8	2.8	5.4	10.64	94	0	19	1	44	36	53	3.7	N/A	11	0	0	0.0	0.0
C+ /6.6	2.8	5.4	10.64	128	0	19	1	44	36	53	3.7	56	11	0	0	0.0	0.0
C+ /6.6	2.8	5.4	10.64	1,407	0	19	1	44	36	53	3.7	59	11	0	0	0.0	0.0
U /	N/A	N/A	1.00	13	100	0	0	0	0	0	0.0	N/A	15	250	0	0.0	0.0
U /	N/A	N/A	1.00	N/A	100	0	0	0	0	0	0.0	N/A	15	250	0	0.0	0.0
U /	N/A	N/A	1.00	7	100	0	0	0	0	0	0.0	N/A	15	250	0	0.0	0.0
U /	N/A	N/A	1.00	120	100	0	0	0	0	0	0.0	N/A	15	1,000	0	0.0	0.0
U /	N/A	N/A	1.00	22	100	0	0	0	0	0	0.0	N/A	15	1,000	0	0.0	0.0
U /	N/A	N/A	1.00	45	100	0	0	0	0	0	0.0	N/A	15	1,000	0	0.0	0.0
U /	N/A	N/A	1.00	12	100	0	0	0	0	0	0.0	N/A	15	0	0	0.0	0.0
U /	N/A	N/A	1.00	50	100	0	0	0	0	0	0.0	N/A	15	0	0	0.0	0.0
U /	N/A	N/A	1.00	34	100	0	0	0	0	0	0.0	N/A	15	0	0	0.0	0.0
U /	N/A	N/A	1.00	3	100	0	0	0	0	0	0.0	N/A	15	0	0	0.0	0.0
A+ /9.9	N/A	N/A	1.00	342	100	0	0	0	0	0	0.1	39	15	1,000	0	0.0	0.0
C+ /5.8	3.0	5.2	11.12	228	0	0	99	0	1	9	5.1	63	18	1,000	50	4.3	0.0
C+ /6.0	2.9	5.2	11.12	1	0	0	99	0	1	9	5.1	30	18	1,000	50	0.0	0.0
C+ /5.7	3.0	5.2	11.12	26	0	0	99	0	1	9	5.1	29	18	1,000	50	0.0	0.0
U /	N/A	5.2	9.67	39	0	0	99	0	1	9	5.1	N/A	18	0	0	0.0	0.0
C+ /6.0	2.9	5.1	11.02	111	0	0	98	0	2	9	5.1	64	18	1,000	50	4.3	0.0
C+ /6.0	2.9	5.1	11.02	1	0	0	98	0	2	9	5.1	30	18	1,000	50	0.0	0.0
U /	N/A	5.1	9.70	5	0	0	98	0	2	9	5.1	N/A	18	0	0	0.0	0.0
B+ /8.4	1.9	0.9	10.29	213	0	1	0	0	99	2,669	4.9	74	8	2,000,000	0	0.0	0.0
B+ /8.3	1.9	0.9	10.27	71	0	1	0	0	99	2,669	4.9	67	8	1,000	50	4.0	0.0
B+ /8.3	2.0	0.9	10.28	23	0	1	0	0	99	2,669	4.9	34	8	1,000	50	0.0	0.0
U /	N/A	N/A	16.47	N/A	0	0	0	0	100	40	0.0	N/A	3	2,500	100	5.8	0.0
U /	N/A	N/A	16.56	N/A	0	0	0	0	100	40	0.0	N/A	3	2,500	100	0.0	0.0
U /	N/A	N/A	16.48	165	0	0	0	0	100	40	0.0	N/A	3	1,000,000	100	0.0	0.0
C+ /5.6	3.0	3.4	10.33	1	4	30	0	56	10	94	0.0	94	5	2,000	100	4.5	0.0
C /5.5	3.0	3.4	10.29	1	4	30	0	56	10	94	0.0	91	5	2,000	100	0.0	0.0
C /5.4	3.0	3.4	10.34	14	4	30	0	56	10	94	0.0	94	5	250,000	25,000	0.0	0.0
U /	N/A	N/A	11.98	13	0	37	0	62	1	101	6.9	N/A	N/A	100,000	1,000	0.0	0.0
B /8.1	2.1	N/A	11.97	4	0	37	0	62	1	101	6.9	19	N/A	2,500	250	0.0	0.0
B+ /8.3	1.9	N/A	14.41	185	25	48	1	13	13	0	0.0	55	11	25	25	0.0	0.0

			99 Pct = Best 0 Pct = Worst		PERFORMANCE						Incl. in Returns	
						Total Return % through 2/28/17						
									Annualized			
Fund Type	Fund Name	Ticker Symbol	Overall Investment Rating	Phone	Perfor- mance Rating/Pts	3 Mo	6 Mo	1Yr / Pct	3Yr / Pct	5Yr / Pct	Dividend Yield	Expense Ratio
COI	MO 529 MOST CSP Direct Vngd		B	(800) 662-7447	B- / 7.1	2.23	-0.30	5.62 /69	3.57 /69	3.86 /71	0.00	0.55
COI	Monteagle Fixed Income Inst	MFHRX	D+	(888) 263-5593	D+ / 2.5	0.44	-1.67	-0.02 /17	1.20 /31	0.78 /25	1.25	1.08
MMF	Morgan Stanley CA T/F Dly Inc MM R	DSCXX	U	(800) 869-6397	U /	--	--	--	--	--	0.07	N/A
GES	Morgan Stanley Gl Fxd Inc Opps A	DINAX	D	(800) 869-6397	C / 4.5	2.35	1.64	8.45 /75	2.23 /47	4.11 /74	3.28	1.04
GES ●	Morgan Stanley Gl Fxd Inc Opps B	DINBX	D	(800) 869-6397	C / 5.0	2.15	1.04	7.60 /73	1.49 /35	3.32 /63	2.66	1.88
GEI	Morgan Stanley Gl Fxd Inc Opps C	MSIPX	U	(800) 869-6397	U /	2.19	1.09	7.52 /73	--	--	2.75	1.74
GES	Morgan Stanley Gl Fxd Inc Opps I	DINDX	B-	(800) 869-6397	C+ / 6.7	2.42	1.77	8.69 /76	2.60 /54	4.43 /78	3.69	0.70
GEI	Morgan Stanley Gl Fxd Inc Opps IS	MGFOX	C+	(800) 869-6397	C+ / 6.7	2.43	1.62	8.77 /76	2.59 /54	--	3.77	0.64
GES ●	Morgan Stanley Gl Fxd Inc Opps L	DINCX	C	(800) 869-6397	C+ / 6.0	2.30	1.51	8.20 /75	1.99 /43	3.79 /70	3.19	1.26
USS	Morgan Stanley Mortgage Sec Tr A	MTGAX	A+	(800) 869-6397	C+ / 6.8	1.68	1.74	7.28 /73	4.23 /78	4.92 /83	4.44	1.58
USS ●	Morgan Stanley Mortgage Sec Tr B	MTGBX	A+	(800) 869-6397	B- / 7.4	1.55	1.44	6.73 /72	3.66 /71	4.32 /76	4.07	2.61
MTG	Morgan Stanley Mortgage Sec Tr C	MSMTX	U	(800) 869-6397	U /	1.50	1.36	6.49 /72	--	--	3.88	15.92
USS	Morgan Stanley Mortgage Sec Tr I	MTGDX	A+	(800) 869-6397	B+ / 8.4	1.79	1.93	7.63 /74	4.63 /82	5.30 /87	5.04	1.35
USS ●	Morgan Stanley Mortgage Sec Tr L	MTGCX	A+	(800) 869-6397	B / 7.7	1.62	1.61	7.04 /73	4.01 /75	4.61 /80	4.39	1.81
MMF	Morgan Stanley Mun Mny Mkt R	DWNXX	U	(800) 869-6397	U /	--	--	--	--	--	0.03	N/A
MMF	Morgan Stanley T/F Daily Inc MM R	DSTXX	U	(800) 869-6397	U /	--	--	--	--	--	0.06	N/A
MMT	Morgan Stanley US Govt Mny Tr R	DWGXX	D+	(800) 869-6397	E+ / 0.6	0.02	0.02	0.03 /20	0.02 / 8	0.01 / 6	0.03	N/A
USS	Morgan Stanley US Govt Sec Tr A	USGAX	D+	(800) 869-6397	D+ / 2.5	0.56	-1.92	1.11 /41	2.36 /49	1.93 /41	2.63	0.94
USS ●	Morgan Stanley US Govt Sec Tr B	USGBX	B-	(800) 869-6397	C / 4.3	0.57	-1.91	1.13 /41	2.37 /49	1.94 /41	2.77	0.90
USL	Morgan Stanley US Govt Sec Tr C	MSGVX	U	(800) 869-6397	U /	0.36	-2.39	0.32 /29	--	--	1.94	4.26
USS	Morgan Stanley US Govt Sec Tr I	USGDX	B	(800) 869-6397	C / 4.8	0.64	-1.86	1.46 /44	2.68 /56	2.21 /45	3.10	0.71
USS ●	Morgan Stanley US Govt Sec Tr L	USGCX	C+	(800) 869-6397	C- / 3.8	0.49	-2.03	0.85 /38	2.05 /44	1.57 /36	2.47	1.22
GEI	MSIF Corporate Bond A	MIGAX	C	(800) 354-8185	A- / 9.1	2.40	1.38	16.90 /92	5.62 /89	5.33 /87	2.62	1.88
COI	MSIF Corporate Bond C	MSBOX	U	(800) 354-8185	U /	2.30	1.05	16.00 /90	--	--	2.02	38.20
GEI	MSIF Corporate Bond I	MPFDX	B-	(800) 354-8185	A+ / 9.8	2.47	1.60	17.21 /92	6.41 /94	5.88 /91	2.99	1.15
GEI ●	MSIF Corporate Bond L	MGILX	C+	(800) 354-8185	A+ / 9.6	2.40	1.27	16.59 /91	5.78 /90	5.28 /87	2.38	1.73
EM	MSIF EM Fixed Income Oppty A	MEAPX	D+	(800) 354-8185	B+ / 8.3	5.90	2.00	16.06 /90	4.81 /84	--	5.32	2.49
EM	MSIF EM Fixed Income Oppty C	MSEDX	U	(800) 354-8185	U /	5.72	1.62	15.12 /89	--	--	4.73	6.28
EM	MSIF EM Fixed Income Oppty I	MEAIX	C	(800) 354-8185	A / 9.4	6.12	2.18	16.45 /91	5.20 /86	--	5.79	1.82
EM	MSIF EM Fixed Income Oppty IS	MRDPX	C	(800) 354-8185	A / 9.4	6.00	2.19	16.33 /91	5.17 /86	--	5.81	1.86
EM ●	MSIF EM Fixed Income Oppty L	MEALX	C-	(800) 354-8185	A- / 9.0	5.85	1.87	15.68 /90	4.53 /81	--	5.21	2.94
COH	MSIF High Yield A	MSYPX	C	(800) 354-8185	B+ / 8.8	4.29	5.88	20.24 /96	4.09 /76	8.40 /99	6.03	1.53
COH	MSIF High Yield C	MSHDX	U	(800) 354-8185	U /	4.10	5.48	19.39 /95	--	--	5.60	2.15
COH	MSIF High Yield I	MSYIX	C+	(800) 354-8185	A+ / 9.6	4.38	6.05	20.63 /97	4.44 /80	8.72 /99	6.62	1.17
COH	MSIF High Yield IS	MSHYX	U	(800) 354-8185	U /	4.28	6.07	20.67 /97	--	--	6.65	1.57
COH ●	MSIF High Yield L	MSYLX	C+	(800) 354-8185	A / 9.4	4.22	5.73	19.93 /96	3.82 /73	8.12 /98	6.05	1.84
COI	MSIF Short Duration Income A	MLDAX	B+	(800) 354-8185	C / 5.5	1.06	4.30	8.64 /76	2.73 /56	2.38 /47	1.59	1.12
COI ●	MSIF Short Duration Income C	MSLDX	U	(800) 354-8185	U /	0.82	3.87	7.79 /74	--	--	0.86	6.63
GES	MSIF Short Duration Income I	MPLDX	A+	(800) 354-8185	B- / 7.3	1.13	4.44	8.91 /76	3.03 /61	2.61 /51	1.89	0.53
COI	MSIF Short Duration Income IS	MSDSX	U	(800) 354-8185	U /	1.14	4.47	8.96 /76	--	--	1.93	N/A
COI ●	MSIF Short Duration Income L	MSJLX	A	(800) 354-8185	C+ / 6.6	1.00	4.18	8.36 /75	2.37 /49	--	1.39	1.70
USS	MSIF Trust Core Plus Fix Inc A	MFXAX	B-	(800) 354-8185	B+ / 8.6	1.57	1.73	12.57 /84	5.58 /89	5.13 /85	2.79	1.07
COI	MSIF Trust Core Plus Fix Inc C	MSCKX	U	(800) 354-8185	U /	1.39	1.40	11.78 /83	--	--	2.37	14.06
USS	MSIF Trust Core Plus Fix Inc I	MPFIX	B+	(800) 354-8185	A / 9.5	1.66	1.90	12.93 /85	5.95 /92	5.45 /88	3.21	0.73
COI ●	MSIF Trust Core Plus Fix Inc L	MSIOX	B	(800) 354-8185	A- / 9.2	1.50	1.55	12.31 /84	5.31 /87	--	2.68	1.76
GL	MSIF Ultra Short Inc A	MUAIX	U	(800) 354-8185	U /	0.18	0.31	--	--	--	0.00	N/A
GL	MSIF Ultra Short Inc I	MUIIX	U	(800) 354-8185	U /	0.23	0.41	--	--	--	0.00	N/A
GL	MSIF Ultra Short Inc IR	MULSX	U	(800) 354-8185	U /	0.24	0.53	--	--	--	0.00	N/A
MMT	MSILF Govt Portfolio Adm	MGOXX	C-	(800) 354-8185	D- / 1.0	0.07	0.11	0.16 /24	0.08 /12	0.07 /13	0.16	N/A
MMT	MSILF Govt Portfolio Adv	MAYXX	D+	(800) 354-8185	E+ / 0.8	0.05	0.06	0.07 /21	0.05 /10	0.05 /11	0.07	N/A
MMT	MSILF Govt Portfolio Cash Mgmt	MSGXX	C-	(800) 354-8185	D- / 1.0	0.07	0.11	0.16 /24	0.08 /12	0.07 /13	0.16	N/A
MMT	MSILF Govt Portfolio Inst	MVRXX	C-	(800) 354-8185	D- / 1.3	0.11	0.18	0.31 /29	0.14 /15	0.10 /15	0.31	N/A

● Denotes fund is closed to new investors
* Denotes fund is included in Section II

RISK			NET ASSETS		ASSET					Portfolio Turnover Ratio	Avg Coupon Rate	FUND MANAGER		MINIMUM		LOADS	
Risk Rating/Pts	3 Yr Avg Standard Deviation	Avg Duration	NAV As of 2/28/17	Total $(Mil)	Cash %	Gov. Bond %	Muni. Bond %	Corp. Bond %	Other %			Manager Quality Pct	Manager Tenure (Years)	Initial Purch. $	Additional Purch. $	Front End Load	Back End Load
C /4.9	3.2	N/A	16.53	256	0	42	1	19	38	0	0.0	76	11	25	25	0.0	0.0
B /7.8	2.3	4.5	10.37	51	0	0	0	0	100	12	5.6	18	14	50,000	0	0.0	0.0
U /	N/A	N/A	1.00	32	100	0	0	0	0	0	0.1	40	N/A	5,000	100	0.0	0.0
C /4.7	3.2	2.2	5.49	80	0	24	4	36	36	120	4.5	77	4	1,000	100	4.3	0.0
C /4.4	3.4	2.2	5.51	1	0	24	4	36	36	120	4.5	57	4	1,000	100	0.0	0.0
U /	N/A	2.2	5.48	22	0	24	4	36	36	120	4.5	N/A	4	1,000	100	0.0	0.0
C /4.8	3.2	2.2	5.55	185	0	24	4	36	36	120	4.5	81	4	5,000,000	0	0.0	0.0
C /4.6	3.3	2.2	5.55	197	0	24	4	36	36	120	4.5	81	4	10,000,000	0	0.0	0.0
C /4.7	3.2	2.2	5.49	9	0	24	4	36	36	120	4.5	73	4	1,000	100	0.0	0.0
B /8.0	2.1	3.6	8.49	52	0	0	0	4	96	253	3.2	93	3	1,000	100	4.3	0.0
B /8.1	2.1	3.6	8.31	N/A	0	0	0	4	96	253	3.2	91	3	1,000	100	0.0	0.0
U /	N/A	3.6	8.42	1	0	0	0	4	96	253	3.2	N/A	3	1,000	100	0.0	0.0
B /8.0	2.2	3.6	8.34	34	0	0	0	4	96	253	3.2	94	3	5,000,000	0	0.0	0.0
B /8.0	2.1	3.6	8.42	2	0	0	0	4	96	253	3.2	93	3	1,000	100	0.0	0.0
U /	N/A	N/A	1.00	20	100	0	0	0	0	0	0.0	38	N/A	5,000	100	0.0	0.0
U /	N/A	N/A	1.00	62	100	0	0	0	0	0	0.1	40	N/A	5,000	100	0.0	0.0
A+ /9.9	N/A	N/A	1.00	1,330	100	0	0	0	0	0	0.0	38	N/A	1,000	50	0.0	0.0
B /7.8	2.3	4.6	8.70	42	0	16	10	4	70	464	3.4	76	5	1,000	100	4.3	0.0
B /7.8	2.3	4.6	8.70	371	0	16	10	4	70	464	3.4	77	5	1,000	100	0.0	0.0
U /	N/A	4.6	8.77	1	0	16	10	4	70	464	3.4	N/A	5	1,000	100	0.0	0.0
B /7.8	2.3	4.6	8.70	80	0	16	10	4	70	464	3.4	80	5	5,000,000	0	0.0	0.0
B /7.9	2.3	4.6	8.77	12	0	16	10	4	70	464	3.4	71	5	1,000	100	0.0	0.0
E+ /0.9	6.2	7.2	12.04	8	0	1	5	91	3	41	0.0	88	6	1,000	0	4.3	0.0
U /	N/A	7.2	12.00	N/A	0	1	5	91	3	41	0.0	N/A	6	1,000	0	0.0	0.0
D- /1.0	6.2	7.2	12.03	33	0	1	5	91	3	41	0.0	92	6	5,000,000	0	0.0	0.0
E+ /0.9	6.2	7.2	12.03	2	0	1	5	91	3	41	0.0	89	6	1,000	0	0.0	0.0
E /0.5	7.6	5.1	9.41	1	5	56	0	37	2	111	5.5	98	5	1,000	0	4.3	2.0
U /	N/A	5.1	9.39	N/A	5	56	0	37	2	111	5.5	N/A	5	1,000	0	0.0	2.0
E /0.5	7.6	5.1	9.43	21	5	56	0	37	2	111	5.5	99	5	5,000,000	0	0.0	2.0
E /0.5	7.6	5.1	9.43	1	5	56	0	37	2	111	5.5	99	5	10,000,000	0	0.0	2.0
E /0.5	7.6	5.1	9.40	1	5	56	0	37	2	111	5.5	98	5	1,000	0	0.0	2.0
D- /1.1	5.6	3.3	10.12	62	0	0	0	98	2	74	0.0	42	5	1,000	0	4.3	0.0
U /	N/A	3.3	10.11	3	0	0	0	98	2	74	0.0	N/A	5	1,000	0	0.0	0.0
D- /1.1	5.7	3.3	10.13	54	0	0	0	98	2	74	0.0	57	5	5,000,000	0	0.0	0.0
U /	N/A	3.3	10.13	1	0	0	0	98	2	74	0.0	N/A	5	10,000,000	0	0.0	0.0
D- /1.1	5.6	3.3	10.12	1	0	0	0	98	2	74	0.0	29	5	1,000	0	0.0	0.0
B- /7.4	2.6	0.9	8.16	64	1	8	0	75	16	66	0.0	86	6	1,000	0	4.3	0.0
U /	N/A	0.9	8.12	N/A	1	8	0	75	16	66	0.0	N/A	6	1,000	0	0.0	0.0
B- /7.3	2.6	0.9	8.14	97	1	8	0	75	16	66	0.0	90	6	5,000,000	0	0.0	0.0
U /	N/A	0.9	8.14	N/A	1	8	0	75	16	66	0.0	N/A	6	10,000,000	0	0.0	0.0
B- /7.3	2.6	0.9	8.14	N/A	1	8	0	75	16	66	0.0	83	6	1,000	0	0.0	0.0
D+ /2.4	4.5	5.2	10.92	45	0	16	12	29	43	262	7.7	95	6	1,000	0	4.3	0.0
U /	N/A	5.2	10.86	5	0	16	12	29	43	262	7.7	N/A	6	1,000	0	0.0	0.0
D+ /2.4	4.5	5.2	10.90	233	0	16	12	29	43	262	7.7	96	6	5,000,000	0	0.0	0.0
D+ /2.4	4.5	5.2	10.91	1	0	16	12	29	43	262	7.7	87	6	1,000	0	0.0	0.0
U /	N/A	N/A	10.00	1,095	0	0	0	0	100	0	0.0	N/A	1	1,000	0	0.0	0.0
U /	N/A	N/A	10.00	1,076	0	0	0	0	100	0	0.0	N/A	1	5,000,000	0	0.0	0.0
U /	N/A	N/A	10.01	374	0	0	0	0	100	0	0.0	N/A	1	10,000,000	0	0.0	0.0
A+ /9.9	N/A	N/A	1.00	168	100	0	0	0	0	0	0.2	45	N/A	10,000,000	0	0.0	0.0
A+ /9.9	N/A	N/A	1.00	1,113	100	0	0	0	0	0	0.1	42	N/A	10,000,000	0	0.0	0.0
A+ /9.9	N/A	N/A	1.00	96	100	0	0	0	0	0	0.2	45	N/A	1,000,000	0	0.0	0.0
A+ /9.9	N/A	N/A	1.00	52,124	100	0	0	0	0	0	0.3	48	N/A	10,000,000	0	0.0	0.0

99 Pct = Best
0 Pct = Worst

Fund Type	Fund Name	Ticker Symbol	Overall Investment Rating	Phone	Performance Rating/Pts	3 Mo	6 Mo	1Yr / Pct	3Yr / Pct	5Yr / Pct	Dividend Yield	Expense Ratio
MMT	MSILF Govt Portfolio Inv	MVVXX	C-	(800) 354-8185	D- / 1.1	0.08	0.13	0.21 /26	0.10 /13	0.08 /14	0.21	N/A
MMT	MSILF Govt Portfolio IS	MGSXX	C-	(800) 354-8185	D- / 1.2	0.10	0.16	0.26 /28	0.12 /14	0.09 /15	0.26	N/A
MMT	MSILF Govt Sec Portfolio Adm	MGAXX	D+	(800) 354-8185	E+ / 0.7	0.05	0.06	0.08 /22	0.03 / 9	0.02 / 8	0.08	N/A
MMT	MSILF Govt Sec Portfolio Adv	MVAXX	D+	(800) 354-8185	E+ / 0.7	0.03	0.03	0.04 /20	0.02 / 8	0.01 / 6	0.04	N/A
MMT	MSILF Govt Sec Portfolio Cash Mgmt	MCHXX	D+	(800) 354-8185	E+ / 0.7	0.05	0.07	0.08 /22	0.03 / 9	0.02 / 8	0.08	N/A
MMT	MSILF Govt Sec Portfolio Inst	MUIXX	C-	(800) 354-8185	D- / 1.1	0.09	0.14	0.22 /27	0.09 /12	0.06 /12	0.22	N/A
MMT	MSILF Govt Sec Portfolio Inv	MVIXX	D+	(800) 354-8185	E+ / 0.8	0.07	0.09	0.12 /23	0.05 /10	0.03 / 9	0.12	N/A
MMT	MSILF Govt Sec Portfolio IS	MSVXX	C-	(800) 354-8185	E+ / 0.9	0.08	0.12	0.17 /25	0.07 /11	0.04 /10	0.17	N/A
MMT	MSILF Govt Sec Portfolio Part	MGPXX	D+	(800) 354-8185	E+ / 0.7	0.03	0.04	0.04 /20	0.02 / 8	0.02 / 8	0.04	N/A
MMT	MSILF Money Mkt Adm	MANXX	C-	(800) 354-8185	D- / 1.0	0.00	0.04	0.19 /26	0.09 /13	0.06 /12	0.19	N/A
MMT	MSILF Money Mkt Adv	MVSXX	C-	(800) 354-8185	D- / 1.4	0.17	0.29	0.39 /31	0.15 /15	0.09 /15	0.32	N/A
MMT	MSILF Money Mkt Cshmgt	MSHXX	C	(800) 354-8185	D- / 1.4	0.19	0.28	0.43 /32	0.17 /16	0.11 /16	0.41	N/A
MMT	MSILF Money Mkt Inst	MPUXX	C	(800) 354-8185	D / 1.8	0.22	0.37	0.60 /35	0.30 /19	0.23 /19	0.56	N/A
MMT	MSILF Money Mkt Inv	MIOXX	C-	(800) 354-8185	D- / 1.1	0.00	0.05	0.23 /27	0.12 /14	0.09 /15	0.23	N/A
MMT	MSILF Money Mkt IS	MMRXX	C	(800) 354-8185	D / 1.6	0.21	0.33	0.53 /34	0.24 /17	0.18 /18	0.51	N/A
MMT	MSILF Money Mkt Part	MMNXX	C-	(800) 354-8185	E+ / 0.9	0.10	0.13	0.13 /23	0.05 /10	0.03 / 9	0.11	N/A
MMT	MSILF Prime Portfolio Adm	MPMXX	C-	(800) 354-8185	D- / 1.0	0.00	0.04	0.16 /24	0.09 /13	0.06 /13	0.16	N/A
MMT	MSILF Prime Portfolio Adv	MAVXX	C-	(800) 354-8185	E+ / 0.9	0.00	0.09	0.16 /24	0.08 /12	0.05 /11	0.16	N/A
MMT	MSILF Prime Portfolio Inst	MPFXX	C	(800) 354-8185	D / 1.7	0.22	0.37	0.57 /34	0.25 /18	0.20 /18	0.53	N/A
MMT	MSILF Prime Portfolio Inv	MPVXX	C-	(800) 354-8185	D- / 1.0	0.00	0.03	0.17 /25	0.10 /13	0.07 /13	0.17	N/A
MMT	MSILF Prime Portfolio IS	MPEXX	C	(800) 354-8185	D- / 1.5	0.13	0.31	0.48 /33	0.20 /16	0.15 /17	0.48	N/A
MMT	MSILF Prime Portfolio Part	MPNXX	U	(800) 354-8185	U /	--	--	--	--	--	0.02	N/A
MMF	MSILF T/E Portfolio Adm	MXAXX	U	(800) 354-8185	U /	--	--	--	--	--	0.30	N/A
MMF	MSILF T/E Portfolio Adv	MADXX	C-	(800) 354-8185	D- / 1.4	0.00	0.09	0.31 /33	0.11 /16	0.07 /16	0.31	N/A
MMF	MSILF T/E Portfolio Cshmgt	MTMXX	C	(800) 354-8185	D- / 1.5	0.08	0.15	0.40 /35	0.14 /17	0.09 /17	0.40	N/A
MMF	MSILF T/E Portfolio Inst	MTXXX	C	(800) 354-8185	D / 1.8	0.11	0.23	0.54 /38	0.19 /19	0.12 /18	0.54	N/A
MMF	MSILF T/E Portfolio Inst Select	MXSXX	C	(800) 354-8185	D / 1.7	0.10	0.20	0.50 /37	0.17 /18	0.11 /18	0.50	N/A
MMF	MSILF T/E Portfolio Inv	MXIXX	U	(800) 354-8185	U /	--	--	--	--	--	0.33	N/A
MMF	MSILF T/E Portfolio Part	MXPXX	U	(800) 354-8185	U /	--	--	--	--	--	0.23	N/A
MMT	MSILF Treasury Portfolio Adm	MTTXX	D+	(800) 354-8185	E+ / 0.8	0.06	0.08	0.11 /23	0.06 /11	0.05 /11	0.11	N/A
MMT	MSILF Treasury Portfolio Adv	MAOXX	D+	(800) 354-8185	E+ / 0.7	0.03	0.03	0.04 /20	0.03 / 9	0.03 / 9	0.04	N/A
MMT	MSILF Treasury Portfolio Cshmgt	MREXX	D+	(800) 354-8185	E+ / 0.9	0.06	0.08	0.11 /23	0.06 /11	0.05 /11	0.11	N/A
MMT	MSILF Treasury Portfolio Inst	MISXX	C-	(800) 354-8185	D- / 1.2	0.09	0.15	0.26 /28	0.12 /14	0.08 /14	0.26	N/A
MMT	MSILF Treasury Portfolio Inv	MTNXX	C-	(800) 354-8185	D- / 1.0	0.07	0.10	0.16 /24	0.08 /12	0.06 /13	0.16	N/A
MMT	MSILF Treasury Portfolio IS	MTSXX	C-	(800) 354-8185	D- / 1.1	0.08	0.12	0.21 /26	0.10 /13	0.07 /13	0.21	N/A
MMT	MSILF Treasury Securities Admin	MAMXX	D+	(800) 354-8185	E+ / 0.7	0.05	0.06	0.08 /22	0.03 / 9	0.02 / 8	0.08	N/A
MMT	MSILF Treasury Securities Adv	MVYXX	D+	(800) 354-8185	E+ / 0.6	0.03	0.03	0.03 /20	0.02 / 8	0.02 / 8	0.03	N/A
MMT	MSILF Treasury Securities Cshmgt	MHSXX	D+	(800) 354-8185	E+ / 0.7	0.05	0.06	0.08 /22	0.03 / 9	0.02 / 8	0.08	N/A
MMT	MSILF Treasury Securities Inst	MSUXX	C-	(800) 354-8185	D- / 1.1	0.09	0.14	0.23 /27	0.09 /13	0.06 /13	0.23	N/A
MMT	MSILF Treasury Securities Inv	MNVXX	D+	(800) 354-8185	E+ / 0.9	0.06	0.09	0.13 /23	0.05 /10	0.03 / 9	0.13	N/A
MMT	MSILF Treasury Securities IS	MSSXX	C-	(800) 354-8185	E+ / 0.9	0.08	0.11	0.18 /25	0.07 /11	0.05 /11	0.18	N/A
COI	Mutual of America Inst Bond	MABOX	C+	(800) 914-8716	C / 5.4	1.29	-1.26	3.75 /61	2.63 /55	2.50 /49	3.09	1.95
COH	Muzinich Credit Opportunities A	MZCRX	U	(855) 689-4642	U /	2.20	0.91	--	--	--	0.00	1.25
COH	Muzinich Credit Opportunities Inst	MZCIX	U	(855) 689-4642	U /	2.13	0.96	6.33 /71	--	--	2.91	0.97
COH	Muzinich Credit Opportunities SIns	MZCSX	A+	(855) 689-4642	B- / 7.1	2.13	0.96	6.37 /71	3.66 /71	--	2.95	0.90
COI	Muzinich Low Duration SInst	MZLSX	U	(855) 689-4642	U /	2.81	1.74	--	--	--	0.00	0.74
COH	Muzinich US HiYld Corp Bond SInst	MZHSX	U	(855) 689-4642	U /	3.76	3.53	--	--	--	0.00	1.04
GL	Nationwide Amundi Global Hi Yld A	NWXIX	U	(800) 848-0920	U /	5.20	5.87	19.35 /95	--	--	6.56	1.33
GL	Nationwide Amundi Global Hi Yld C	NWXJX	U	(800) 848-0920	U /	5.01	5.58	18.46 /94	--	--	5.98	2.08
GL	Nationwide Amundi Global Hi Yld Ins	NWXKX	U	(800) 848-0920	U /	5.27	6.10	19.76 /96	--	--	6.94	0.83
GL	Nationwide Amundi Global Hi Yld IS	NWXLX	U	(800) 848-0920	U /	5.37	6.10	19.76 /96	--	--	6.94	1.08
GL	Nationwide Amundi Strat Inc A	NWXEX	U	(800) 848-0920	U /	4.29	5.19	17.36 /93	--	--	5.08	2.05

• Denotes fund is closed to new investors
* Denotes fund is included in Section II

www.thestreetratings.com

RISK	3 Yr Avg Standard Deviation	Avg Dura-tion	NET ASSETS NAV As of 2/28/17	Total $(Mil)	ASSET Cash %	Gov. Bond %	Muni. Bond %	Corp. Bond %	Other %	Portfolio Turnover Ratio	Avg Coupon Rate	FUND MANAGER Manager Quality Pct	Manager Tenure (Years)	MINIMUM Initial Purch. $	Additional Purch. $	LOADS Front End Load	Back End Load
A+ / 9.9	N/A	N/A	1.00	79	100	0	0	0	0	0	0.2	N/A	N/A	10,000,000	0	0.0	0.0
A+ / 9.9	N/A	N/A	1.00	1,398	100	0	0	0	0	0	0.3	47	N/A	10,000,000	0	0.0	0.0
A+ / 9.9	N/A	N/A	1.00	N/A	100	0	0	0	0	0	0.1	39	N/A	10,000,000	0	0.0	0.0
A+ / 9.9	N/A	N/A	1.00	N/A	100	0	0	0	0	0	0.0	38	N/A	10,000,000	0	0.0	0.0
A+ / 9.9	N/A	N/A	1.00	2	100	0	0	0	0	0	0.1	39	N/A	1,000,000	0	0.0	0.0
A+ / 9.9	N/A	N/A	1.00	70	100	0	0	0	0	0	0.2	45	N/A	10,000,000	0	0.0	0.0
A+ / 9.9	N/A	N/A	1.00	N/A	100	0	0	0	0	0	0.1	42	N/A	10,000,000	0	0.0	0.0
A+ / 9.9	N/A	N/A	1.00	N/A	100	0	0	0	0	0	0.2	43	N/A	10,000,000	0	0.0	0.0
A+ / 9.9	N/A	N/A	1.00	23,274	100	0	0	0	0	0	0.0	38	N/A	10,000,000	0	0.0	0.0
A+ / 9.9	N/A	N/A	1.00	N/A	100	0	0	0	0	0	0.2	N/A	N/A	10,000,000	0	0.0	0.0
A+ / 9.9	0.1	N/A	1.00	N/A	100	0	0	0	0	0	0.3	47	N/A	10,000,000	0	0.0	0.0
A+ / 9.9	0.1	N/A	1.00	35	100	0	0	0	0	0	0.4	49	N/A	1,000,000	0	0.0	0.0
A+ / 9.9	0.1	N/A	1.00	338	100	0	0	0	0	0	0.6	55	N/A	200,000,000	0	0.0	0.0
A+ / 9.9	N/A	N/A	1.00	N/A	100	0	0	0	0	0	0.2	48	N/A	10,000,000	0	0.0	0.0
A+ / 9.9	0.1	N/A	1.00	N/A	100	0	0	0	0	0	0.5	53	N/A	10,000,000	0	0.0	0.0
A+ / 9.9	N/A	N/A	1.00	N/A	100	0	0	0	0	0	0.1	42	N/A	10,000,000	0	0.0	0.0
A+ / 9.9	N/A	N/A	1.00	N/A	100	0	0	0	0	0	0.2	N/A	N/A	10,000,000	0	0.0	0.0
A+ / 9.9	N/A	N/A	1.00	N/A	100	0	0	0	0	0	0.2	46	N/A	10,000,000	0	0.0	0.0
A+ / 9.9	0.1	N/A	1.00	2,817	100	0	0	0	0	0	0.5	53	N/A	10,000,000	0	0.0	0.0
A+ / 9.9	N/A	N/A	1.00	N/A	100	0	0	0	0	0	0.2	47	N/A	10,000,000	0	0.0	0.0
A+ / 9.9	0.1	N/A	1.00	40	100	0	0	0	0	0	0.5	51	N/A	10,000,000	0	0.0	0.0
U /	N/A	N/A	1.00	N/A	100	0	0	0	0	0	0.0	40	N/A	10,000,000	0	0.0	0.0
U /	N/A	N/A	1.00	N/A	100	0	0	0	0	0	0.3	47	N/A	10,000,000	0	0.0	0.0
A+ / 9.9	0.1	N/A	1.00	N/A	100	0	0	0	0	0	0.3	47	N/A	10,000,000	0	0.0	0.0
A+ / 9.9	0.1	N/A	1.00	30	100	0	0	0	0	0	0.4	49	N/A	1,000,000	0	0.0	0.0
A+ / 9.9	0.1	N/A	1.00	118	100	0	0	0	0	0	0.5	51	N/A	10,000,000	0	0.0	0.0
A+ / 9.9	0.1	N/A	1.00	N/A	100	0	0	0	0	0	0.5	50	N/A	10,000,000	0	0.0	0.0
U /	N/A	N/A	1.00	N/A	100	0	0	0	0	0	0.3	47	N/A	10,000,000	0	0.0	0.0
U /	N/A	N/A	1.00	N/A	100	0	0	0	0	0	0.2	45	N/A	10,000,000	0	0.0	0.0
A+ / 9.9	N/A	N/A	1.00	2	100	0	0	0	0	0	0.1	43	N/A	10,000,000	0	0.0	0.0
A+ / 9.9	N/A	N/A	1.00	507	100	0	0	0	0	0	0.0	40	N/A	10,000,000	0	0.0	0.0
A+ / 9.9	N/A	N/A	1.00	62	100	0	0	0	0	0	0.1	43	N/A	1,000,000	0	0.0	0.0
A+ / 9.9	N/A	N/A	1.00	16,879	100	0	0	0	0	0	0.3	47	N/A	10,000,000	0	0.0	0.0
A+ / 9.9	N/A	N/A	1.00	15	100	0	0	0	0	0	0.2	45	N/A	10,000,000	0	0.0	0.0
A+ / 9.9	N/A	N/A	1.00	242	100	0	0	0	0	0	0.2	46	N/A	10,000,000	0	0.0	0.0
A+ / 9.9	N/A	N/A	1.00	N/A	100	0	0	0	0	0	0.1	39	N/A	10,000,000	0	0.0	0.0
A+ / 9.9	N/A	N/A	1.00	N/A	100	0	0	0	0	0	0.0	38	N/A	10,000,000	0	0.0	0.0
A+ / 9.9	N/A	N/A	1.00	98	100	0	0	0	0	0	0.1	40	N/A	1,000,000	0	0.0	0.0
A+ / 9.9	N/A	N/A	1.00	19,195	100	0	0	0	0	0	0.2	45	N/A	10,000,000	0	0.0	0.0
A+ / 9.9	N/A	N/A	1.00	59	100	0	0	0	0	0	0.1	42	N/A	10,000,000	0	0.0	0.0
A+ / 9.9	N/A	N/A	1.00	275	100	0	0	0	0	0	0.2	44	N/A	10,000,000	0	0.0	0.0
C+ / 5.8	3.0	5.0	9.89	18	1	7	0	57	35	16	3.6	55	21	25,000	5,000	0.0	0.0
U /	N/A	4.0	10.64	N/A	4	7	0	80	9	473	0.0	N/A	4	10,000	100	4.3	1.0
U /	N/A	4.0	10.64	85	4	7	0	80	9	473	0.0	N/A	4	1,000,000	100	0.0	1.0
B- / 7.1	2.2	4.0	10.64	184	4	7	0	80	9	473	0.0	88	4	100,000,000	100	0.0	1.0
U /	N/A	N/A	10.00	269	0	0	0	0	100	0	0.0	N/A	1	5,000,000	100	0.0	1.0
U /	N/A	3.9	10.60	85	0	0	0	0	100	0	0.0	N/A	1	5,000,000	100	0.0	1.0
U /	N/A	4.3	10.48	N/A	0	0	0	0	100	96	0.0	N/A	2	2,000	100	2.3	0.0
U /	N/A	4.3	10.48	N/A	0	0	0	0	100	96	0.0	N/A	2	2,000	100	0.0	0.0
U /	N/A	4.3	10.49	148	0	0	0	0	100	96	0.0	N/A	2	1,000,000	0	0.0	0.0
U /	N/A	4.3	10.49	N/A	0	0	0	0	100	96	0.0	N/A	2	50,000	0	0.0	0.0
U /	N/A	3.7	10.36	N/A	0	0	0	0	100	192	0.0	N/A	2	2,000	100	2.3	0.0

Fund Type	Fund Name	Ticker Symbol	Overall Investment Rating	Phone	Performance Rating/Pts	Total Return % through 2/28/17			Annualized		Incl. in Returns	
						3 Mo	6 Mo	1Yr / Pct	3Yr / Pct	5Yr / Pct	Dividend Yield	Expense Ratio
GL	Nationwide Amundi Strat Inc C	NWXFX	U	(800) 848-0920	U /	4.10	4.91	16.50 /91	--	--	4.48	2.80
GL	Nationwide Amundi Strat Inc Ins Svc	NWXHX	U	(800) 848-0920	U /	4.35	5.33	17.66 /93	--	--	5.44	1.80
GL	Nationwide Amundi Strat Inc R6	NWXGX	U	(800) 848-0920	U /	4.35	5.33	17.66 /93	--	--	5.44	1.55
COI	Nationwide Bond A	NBDAX	D	(800) 848-0920	C- / 3.4	1.19	-2.06	2.79 /55	2.09 /45	2.64 /52	2.14	0.89
COI	Nationwide Bond C	GBDCX	D-	(800) 848-0920	C- / 3.0	1.00	-2.52	2.02 /49	1.28 /32	1.89 /40	1.42	1.65
GEI	Nationwide Bond Index A	GBIAX	D-	(800) 848-0920	D+ / 2.7	0.79	-2.56	0.71 /36	1.98 /43	1.58 /36	1.93	0.68
GEI	Nationwide Bond Index C	GBICX	D-	(800) 848-0920	D+ / 2.5	0.62	-2.88	0.05 /20	1.31 /32	0.93 /26	1.31	1.36
GEI	Nationwide Bond Index R6	GBXIX	C-	(800) 848-0920	C / 4.3	0.89	-2.37	1.12 /41	2.41 /50	1.99 /42	2.40	0.27
COI	Nationwide Bond Inst Svc	MUIBX	C-	(800) 848-0920	C / 4.7	1.25	-2.04	3.04 /57	2.32 /48	2.90 /56	2.43	0.63
COI	Nationwide Bond R	GBDRX	D	(800) 848-0920	C- / 3.6	0.99	-2.36	2.24 /51	1.66 /37	2.32 /46	1.75	1.33
COI	Nationwide Bond R6	NWIBX	C-	(800) 848-0920	C / 4.8	1.26	-1.91	3.09 /57	2.39 /50	--	2.47	0.58
COI	Nationwide Core Plus Bond A	NWCPX	C+	(800) 848-0920	C- / 3.8	1.58	-1.02	3.83 /61	2.72 /56	--	2.82	0.83
COI	Nationwide Core Plus Bond Inst Svc	NWCSX	A	(800) 848-0920	C+ / 6.1	1.65	-0.88	4.09 /63	3.01 /61	--	3.19	0.59
GEI	Nationwide Core Plus Bond R6	NWCIX	A	(800) 848-0920	C+ / 6.2	1.67	-0.73	4.31 /64	3.08 /62	3.47 /65	3.30	0.49
USS	Nationwide Govt Bond A	NUSAX	E	(800) 848-0920	E / 0.3	0.21	-3.82	-2.15 / 1	0.76 /24	0.62 /23	1.35	1.16
USS	Nationwide Govt Bond C	GGBCX	E	(800) 848-0920	E / 0.3	0.15	-4.05	-2.72 / 0	0.08 /11	-0.03 / 5	0.69	1.83
USS	Nationwide Govt Bond Inst Svc	NAUGX	E+	(800) 848-0920	D / 1.8	0.38	-3.59	-1.78 / 1	1.05 /28	0.92 /26	1.67	0.87
USS	Nationwide Govt Bond R	GGBRX	E	(800) 848-0920	E / 0.4	0.22	-3.91	-2.43 / 0	0.37 /19	0.28 /19	0.98	1.53
MMT	Nationwide Govt Money Market R6	GMIXX	U	(800) 848-0920	U /	--	--	--	--	--	0.05	N/A
COH	Nationwide High Yield Bond A	GGHAX	D-	(800) 848-0920	C+ / 6.7	4.40	4.45	15.68 /90	2.35 /49	4.97 /84	4.81	1.78
COH	Nationwide High Yield Bond C	GHHCX	D	(800) 848-0920	B- / 7.2	4.25	4.18	15.05 /89	1.78 /39	4.43 /78	4.54	2.29
COH	Nationwide High Yield Bond Inst Svc	GGYSX	C-	(800) 848-0920	B / 8.0	4.23	4.52	15.81 /90	2.50 /52	--	5.20	1.61
COH	Nationwide High Yield Bond R6	GGYIX	C-	(800) 848-0920	B / 8.2	4.29	4.44	16.03 /90	2.65 /55	5.24 /86	5.37	1.41
GEI	Nationwide HighMark Bond A	NWJGX	D+	(800) 848-0920	C- / 3.8	1.08	-1.84	3.08 /57	2.28 /48	2.38 /47	1.96	0.90
GEI	Nationwide HighMark Bond C	NWJHX	C-	(800) 848-0920	C- / 4.0	0.98	-1.97	2.66 /54	1.84 /40	1.94 /41	1.59	1.35
GEI	Nationwide HighMark Bond IS	NWJJX	C	(800) 848-0920	C / 4.9	1.09	-1.74	3.17 /58	2.40 /50	2.56 /50	2.12	0.74
COI	Nationwide HighMark Bond R6	NWJIX	C+	(800) 848-0920	C / 5.2	1.16	-1.62	3.42 /59	2.61 /54	--	2.36	0.50
MUS	Nationwide HighMark CA Int TF Bd A	NWJKX	D-	(800) 848-0920	D+ / 2.5	2.18	-2.70	-1.44 / 2	1.66 /53	1.80 /54	1.93	0.89
MUS	Nationwide HighMark CA Int TF Bd C	NWJLX	D-	(800) 848-0920	D+ / 2.9	2.18	-2.93	-1.82 / 1	1.24 /42	1.35 /43	1.50	1.38
MUS	Nationwide HighMark CA Int TF Bd IS	NWJNX	C-	(800) 848-0920	C / 4.7	2.33	-2.58	-1.12 / 4	1.92 /60	2.04 /60	2.19	0.66
MUN	Nationwide HighMark CA Int TF Bd	NWJMX	C	(800) 848-0920	C / 4.8	2.35	-2.53	-1.12 / 4	1.99 /62	--	2.28	0.57
MUN	Nationwide HighMark Natl Int TFB A	NWJOX	E+	(800) 848-0920	D- / 1.4	2.28	-2.82	-1.50 / 2	1.15 /39	1.40 /44	1.56	1.08
MUN	Nationwide HighMark Natl Int TFB C	NWJPX	E+	(800) 848-0920	D / 1.8	2.06	-3.14	-1.96 / 1	0.69 /29	0.94 /34	1.11	1.57
MUN	Nationwide HighMark Natl Int TFB IS	NWJRX	D	(800) 848-0920	C- / 3.6	2.35	-2.69	-1.23 / 3	1.41 /46	1.66 /50	1.86	0.85
MUN	Nationwide HighMark Natl Int TFB R6	NWJQX	D	(800) 848-0920	C- / 3.6	2.27	-2.76	-1.19 / 3	1.45 /47	--	1.90	0.77
GEI	Nationwide HighMark Sht Term Bd A	NWJSX	C-	(800) 848-0920	D- / 1.4	0.39	-0.15	1.52 /45	0.71 /23	0.84 /25	1.09	0.78
GEI	Nationwide HighMark Sht Term Bd C	NWJTX	C-	(800) 848-0920	D / 1.6	0.36	-0.30	1.09 /40	0.23 /17	0.39 /20	0.59	1.29
GEI	Nationwide HighMark Sht Term Bd IS	NWJVX	C+	(800) 848-0920	D+ / 2.8	0.55	0.08	1.88 /48	0.98 /27	1.11 /29	1.36	0.53
COI	Nationwide HighMark Sht Term Bd	NWJUX	C+	(800) 848-0920	D+ / 2.9	0.47	0.12	1.96 /49	1.03 /28	--	1.44	0.45
GEI	Nationwide Infl-Prot Secs A	NIFAX	E+	(800) 848-0920	D+ / 2.7	1.24	-0.71	3.05 /57	1.44 /34	--	0.00	0.84
GEI	Nationwide Infl-Prot Secs R6	NIFIX	E+	(800) 848-0920	C- / 4.1	1.23	-0.71	3.25 /58	1.69 /38	--	0.00	0.34
MUN	Nationwide Ziegler Wisconsin TE A	NWJWX	D	(800) 848-0920	C- / 3.3	1.74	-2.19	0.90 /44	1.65 /53	0.96 /34	2.80	1.03
MUN	Nationwide Ziegler Wisconsin TE C	NWKGX	D	(800) 848-0920	C- / 3.7	1.72	-2.33	0.51 /37	1.22 /41	0.50 /25	2.37	1.53
MUN	Nationwide Ziegler Wisconsin TE IS	NWJZX	C+	(800) 848-0920	C / 5.4	1.91	-2.06	1.17 /47	1.91 /60	1.21 /40	3.14	0.78
MUN	Nationwide Ziegler Wisconsin TE R6	NWJYX	C+	(800) 848-0920	C / 5.5	1.82	-2.04	1.20 /48	1.96 /61	--	3.17	0.74
USS	Natixis Loomis Say Ltd Trm Gv&Agy	NEFLX	D	(800) 225-5478	E / 0.5	0.25	-0.53	0.10 /22	0.65 /22	0.84 /25	1.48	0.77
USS	Natixis Loomis Say Ltd Trm Gv&Agy	NECLX	D	(800) 225-5478	E / 0.4	0.06	-0.90	-0.65 / 8	-0.09 / 5	0.09 /14	0.76	1.53
USS	Natixis Loomis Say Ltd Trm Gv&Agy	NELYX	C	(800) 225-5478	D+ / 2.3	0.22	-0.49	0.35 /30	0.91 /26	1.08 /28	1.76	0.52
* GEI	Natixis Loomis Sayles Cor Pl Bd A	NEFRX	D-	(800) 225-5478	C / 4.4	2.00	-0.93	7.98 /74	2.51 /52	3.48 /65	2.92	0.74
GEI	Natixis Loomis Sayles Cor Pl Bd C	NECRX	D-	(800) 225-5478	C / 4.9	1.81	-1.25	7.17 /73	1.73 /39	2.72 /53	2.29	1.49
COI	Natixis Loomis Sayles Cor Pl Bd N	NERNX	C-	(800) 225-5478	C+ / 6.7	2.08	-0.75	8.38 /75	2.84 /59	--	3.37	0.40
GEI	Natixis Loomis Sayles Cor Pl Bd Y	NERYX	D+	(800) 225-5478	C+ / 6.5	2.05	-0.88	8.20 /75	2.72 /56	3.74 /69	3.28	0.49

● Denotes fund is closed to new investors
* Denotes fund is included in Section II

www.thestreetratings.com

Risk Rating/Pts	3 Yr Avg Standard Deviation	Avg Dura-tion	NAV As of 2/28/17	Total $(Mil)	Cash %	Gov. Bond %	Muni. Bond %	Corp. Bond %	Other %	Portfolio Turnover Ratio	Avg Coupon Rate	Manager Quality Pct	Manager Tenure (Years)	Initial Purch. $	Additional Purch. $	Front End Load	Back End Load
U /	N/A	3.7	10.36	N/A	0	0	0	0	100	192	0.0	N/A	2	2,000	100	0.0	0.0
U /	N/A	3.7	10.36	28	0	0	0	0	100	192	0.0	N/A	2	50,000	0	0.0	0.0
U /	N/A	3.7	10.36	N/A	0	0	0	0	100	192	0.0	N/A	2	1,000,000	0	0.0	0.0
C / 5.5	2.8	7.4	9.63	12	0	0	0	51	49	116	0.0	27	13	2,000	100	2.3	0.0
C / 5.4	2.8	7.4	9.64	3	0	0	0	51	49	116	0.0	9	13	2,000	100	0.0	0.0
C+ / 5.7	3.0	5.5	10.98	194	1	41	1	26	31	147	0.0	18	8	2,000	100	2.3	0.0
C+ / 5.8	3.0	5.5	10.98	2	1	41	1	26	31	147	0.0	7	8	2,000	100	0.0	0.0
C+ / 5.7	3.0	5.5	10.96	751	1	41	1	26	31	147	0.0	30	8	1,000,000	0	0.0	0.0
C / 5.4	2.8	7.4	9.64	52	0	0	0	51	49	116	0.0	34	13	50,000	0	0.0	0.0
C / 5.4	2.8	7.4	9.63	N/A	0	0	0	51	49	116	0.0	15	13	0	0	0.0	0.0
C / 5.4	2.8	7.4	9.65	494	0	0	0	51	49	116	0.0	37	13	1,000,000	0	0.0	0.0
B- / 7.5	2.5	1.1	10.20	5	1	7	0	49	43	91	0.0	63	15	2,000	100	4.3	0.0
B- / 7.5	2.5	1.1	10.21	6	1	7	0	49	43	91	0.0	71	15	50,000	0	0.0	0.0
B- / 7.5	2.5	1.1	10.21	1,144	1	7	0	49	43	91	0.0	73	15	1,000,000	0	0.0	0.0
C / 4.4	3.4	6.2	9.92	14	1	62	0	4	33	30	0.0	9	20	2,000	100	2.3	0.0
C / 4.5	3.3	6.2	9.92	1	1	62	0	4	33	30	0.0	3	20	2,000	100	0.0	0.0
C / 4.3	3.4	6.2	9.93	29	1	62	0	4	33	30	0.0	13	20	50,000	0	0.0	0.0
C / 4.4	3.3	6.2	9.93	1	1	62	0	4	33	30	0.0	5	20	0	0	0.0	0.0
U /	N/A	N/A	1.00	365	100	0	0	0	0	0	0.1	38	N/A	1,000,000	0	0.0	0.0
D- / 1.3	5.5	4.1	5.91	18	3	0	0	95	2	64	8.0	4	7	2,000	100	4.3	0.0
D- / 1.3	5.4	4.1	5.94	4	3	0	0	95	2	64	8.0	2	7	2,000	100	0.0	0.0
D- / 1.3	5.5	4.1	5.95	2	3	0	0	95	2	64	8.0	5	7	50,000	0	0.0	0.0
D- / 1.3	5.5	4.1	5.94	4	3	0	0	95	2	64	8.0	6	7	1,000,000	0	0.0	0.0
C+ / 6.1	2.9	5.1	10.63	27	2	19	4	44	31	57	7.0	32	4	2,000	100	2.3	0.0
C+ / 6.2	2.9	5.1	10.57	7	2	19	4	44	31	57	7.0	20	4	2,000	100	0.0	0.0
C+ / 6.1	2.9	5.1	10.83	224	2	19	4	44	31	57	7.0	38	4	50,000	0	0.0	0.0
C+ / 6.4	2.8	5.1	10.83	216	2	19	4	44	31	57	7.0	48	4	1,000,000	0	0.0	0.0
C+ / 5.9	2.9	4.8	9.99	51	1	0	98	0	1	20	0.0	6	4	2,000	100	2.3	0.0
C+ / 5.6	3.0	4.8	9.96	28	1	0	98	0	1	20	0.0	3	4	2,000	100	0.0	0.0
C+ / 5.8	2.9	4.8	10.05	38	1	0	98	0	1	20	0.0	9	4	50,000	0	0.0	0.0
C+ / 5.9	2.9	4.8	10.05	52	1	0	98	0	1	20	0.0	10	4	1,000,000	0	0.0	0.0
C / 5.3	3.0	4.9	10.52	8	0	0	99	0	1	28	0.0	3	21	2,000	100	2.3	0.0
C / 5.5	3.0	4.9	10.53	4	0	0	99	0	1	28	0.0	1	21	2,000	100	0.0	0.0
C / 5.4	3.0	4.9	10.53	9	0	0	99	0	1	28	0.0	4	21	50,000	0	0.0	0.0
C / 5.5	3.0	4.9	10.52	21	0	0	99	0	1	28	0.0	5	21	1,000,000	0	0.0	0.0
A / 9.4	0.9	1.7	9.94	67	1	6	0	63	30	48	0.0	44	13	2,000	100	2.3	0.0
A / 9.4	0.8	1.7	10.07	16	1	6	0	63	30	48	0.0	24	13	2,000	100	0.0	0.0
A / 9.4	0.9	1.7	9.96	52	1	6	0	63	30	48	0.0	57	13	50,000	0	0.0	0.0
A / 9.3	0.9	1.7	9.96	226	1	6	0	63	30	48	0.0	56	13	1,000,000	0	0.0	0.0
D+ / 2.9	3.9	7.6	9.79	1	0	99	0	0	1	30	0.0	6	5	2,000	100	2.3	0.0
C- / 3.0	3.9	7.6	9.85	200	0	99	0	0	1	30	0.0	10	5	1,000,000	0	0.0	0.0
C+ / 5.8	2.9	5.1	9.80	81	5	0	94	0	1	10	4.7	8	8	2,000	100	2.3	0.0
C+ / 5.8	2.9	5.1	9.79	9	5	0	94	0	1	10	4.7	5	8	2,000	100	0.0	0.0
C+ / 5.7	3.0	5.1	9.80	1	5	0	94	0	1	10	4.7	12	8	50,000	0	0.0	0.0
C+ / 6.0	2.9	5.1	9.80	N/A	5	0	94	0	1	10	4.7	14	8	1,000,000	0	0.0	0.0
A- / 9.2	1.0	2.0	11.36	383	1	28	0	0	71	109	2.3	41	16	2,500	100	2.3	0.0
A- / 9.2	1.0	2.0	11.37	59	1	28	0	0	71	109	2.3	16	16	2,500	100	0.0	0.0
A- / 9.2	1.0	2.0	11.39	358	1	28	0	0	71	109	2.3	56	16	100,000	100	0.0	0.0
D+ / 2.9	4.1	6.3	12.82	740	1	31	0	42	26	143	3.7	38	21	2,500	100	4.3	0.0
D+ / 2.9	4.1	6.3	12.82	289	1	31	0	42	26	143	3.7	15	21	2,500	100	0.0	0.0
D+ / 2.9	4.1	6.3	12.92	1,921	1	31	0	42	26	143	3.7	26	21	1,000,000	0	0.0	0.0
D+ / 2.9	4.1	6.3	12.91	2,909	1	31	0	42	26	143	3.7	53	21	100,000	0	0.0	0.0

Fund Type	Fund Name	Ticker Symbol	Overall Investment Rating	Phone	Performance Rating/Pts	3 Mo	6 Mo	1Yr / Pct	3Yr / Pct	5Yr / Pct	Dividend Yield	Expense Ratio
COI	Natixis Loomis Sayles Inv Gr Bd Adm	LIGAX	D-	(800) 225-5478	C / 5.0	2.51	0.09	8.33 /75	1.41 /33	2.78 /54	2.14	1.08
* GEI	Natixis Loomis Sayles Invst Gr Bd A	LIGRX	E+	(800) 225-5478	C- / 3.6	2.52	0.08	8.54 /75	1.63 /37	3.01 /58	2.24	0.83
GEI	Natixis Loomis Sayles Invst Gr Bd C	LGBCX	E+	(800) 225-5478	C- / 4.1	2.45	-0.22	7.70 /74	0.90 /26	2.25 /45	1.62	1.58
COI	Natixis Loomis Sayles Invst Gr Bd N	LGBNX	D	(800) 225-5478	C+ / 6.0	2.71	0.27	8.95 /76	2.02 /44	--	2.71	0.47
GEI	Natixis Loomis Sayles Invst Gr Bd Y	LSIIX	D	(800) 225-5478	C+ / 5.8	2.68	0.30	8.81 /76	1.90 /41	3.29 /62	2.59	0.58
LP	Natixis Loomis Sayles Sen FR & FI A	LSFAX	B-	(800) 225-5478	B / 7.9	2.23	3.97	15.39 /89	3.77 /72	5.31 /87	5.24	1.08
LP	Natixis Loomis Sayles Sen FR & FI C	LSFCX	B-	(800) 225-5478	B / 8.0	2.05	3.61	14.60 /88	2.98 /61	4.53 /79	4.72	1.83
LP	Natixis Loomis Sayles Sen FR & FI Y	LSFYX	A-	(800) 225-5478	A- / 9.0	2.28	4.20	15.78 /90	4.03 /76	5.58 /89	5.66	0.83
GES	Natixis Loomis Sayles Strat Alpha A	LABAX	B	(800) 225-5478	C / 5.1	1.50	2.61	9.64 /78	2.46 /51	3.17 /60	1.97	1.10
GES	Natixis Loomis Sayles Strat Alpha C	LABCX	B+	(800) 225-5478	C+ / 5.6	1.21	2.25	8.76 /76	1.70 /38	2.38 /48	1.34	1.85
GES	Natixis Loomis Sayles Strat Alpha Y	LASYX	A+	(800) 225-5478	B- / 7.0	1.47	2.43	9.83 /79	2.70 /56	3.42 /64	2.32	0.85
* GEL	Natixis Loomis Sayles Strat Inc A	NEFZX	D-	(800) 225-5478	C+ / 6.4	4.61	3.18	15.67 /90	2.19 /46	5.24 /86	2.57	0.94
GEL	Natixis Loomis Sayles Strat Inc Adm	NEZAX	D	(800) 225-5478	B- / 7.4	4.58	3.08	15.38 /89	1.95 /42	4.99 /84	2.47	1.19
GEL	Natixis Loomis Sayles Strat Inc C	NECZX	D-	(800) 225-5478	C+ / 6.8	4.44	2.82	14.83 /88	1.44 /34	4.47 /78	1.92	1.69
GEL	Natixis Loomis Sayles Strat Inc N	NEZNX	D+	(800) 225-5478	B / 8.0	4.70	3.29	16.00 /90	2.53 /52	--	3.01	0.62
GEL	Natixis Loomis Sayles Strat Inc Y	NEZYX	D+	(800) 225-5478	B / 7.9	4.68	3.25	15.90 /90	2.45 /51	5.50 /88	2.93	0.69
MUN	Navigator Duration Neutral Bond A	NDNAX	D-	(877) 766-2264	D / 1.8	1.75	0.26	2.31 /60	0.95 /34	--	1.25	1.71
MUN	Navigator Duration Neutral Bond C	NDNCX	D-	(877) 766-2264	D / 2.0	1.51	-0.19	1.45 /51	0.13 /16	--	0.64	2.46
MUN	Navigator Duration Neutral Bond I	NDNIX	C	(877) 766-2264	C / 4.8	1.82	0.39	2.48 /61	1.19 /40	--	1.56	1.46
MUS	Nebraska Municipal	NEMUX	D+	(800) 601-5593	C / 4.4	1.47	-3.76	-0.82 / 6	2.72 /77	2.17 /63	2.44	1.21
GEN	Neiman Tactical Income A	NTAFX	E+		D- / 1.1	3.00	1.59	7.18 /73	0.43 /20	--	3.14	2.12
EM	Neuberger Berman Emg Mkts Debt A	NERAX	E	(800) 877-9700	C / 4.3	5.80	-0.20	13.11 /85	1.20 /31	--	5.09	1.53
EM	Neuberger Berman Emg Mkts Debt C	NERCX	E+	(800) 877-9700	C / 4.7	5.48	-0.69	12.14 /84	0.40 /20	--	4.58	2.21
EM	Neuberger Berman Emg Mkts Debt	NERIX	D-	(800) 877-9700	C+ / 6.5	5.77	-0.14	13.39 /86	1.53 /35	--	5.69	1.07
LP	Neuberger Berman Floating Rt Inc A	NFIAX	B-	(800) 877-9700	C / 5.1	1.51	2.51	9.54 /78	2.49 /52	3.47 /65	3.25	1.22
LP	Neuberger Berman Floating Rt Inc C	NFICX	B	(800) 877-9700	C+ / 5.6	1.32	2.13	8.73 /76	1.73 /39	2.70 /53	2.66	1.96
LP	Neuberger Berman Floating Rt Inc I	NFIIX	A	(800) 877-9700	B- / 7.2	1.61	2.71	9.96 /79	2.88 /59	3.86 /71	3.77	0.84
COH	Neuberger Berman High Inc Bd A	NHIAX	D	(800) 877-9700	B- / 7.3	4.14	4.03	16.59 /91	2.91 /60	5.36 /87	4.87	1.09
COH	Neuberger Berman High Inc Bd C	NHICX	D	(800) 877-9700	B / 7.6	3.94	3.76	15.70 /90	2.16 /46	4.61 /80	4.36	1.82
COH	Neuberger Berman High Inc Bd Inst	NHILX	C	(800) 877-9700	B+ / 8.8	4.35	4.34	16.98 /92	3.35 /67	5.79 /91	5.43	0.69
COH ●	Neuberger Berman High Inc Bd Inv	NHINX	C	(800) 877-9700	B+ / 8.6	4.24	4.20	16.75 /91	3.17 /64	5.65 /90	5.35	0.84
COH	Neuberger Berman High Inc Bd R3	NHIRX	C-	(800) 877-9700	B / 8.1	4.05	3.82	16.19 /90	2.67 /55	5.11 /85	4.76	1.32
COH	Neuberger Berman High Inc Bd R6	NRHIX	C	(800) 877-9700	B+ / 8.8	4.25	4.38	17.08 /92	3.43 /68	--	5.52	0.62
MUN	Neuberger Berman Muni Int Bd A	NMNAX	D-	(800) 877-9700	D+ / 2.3	1.44	-2.75	-0.79 / 6	2.07 /64	1.88 /56	1.63	1.04
MUN	Neuberger Berman Muni Int Bd C	NMNCX	D	(800) 877-9700	C- / 3.0	1.34	-3.03	-1.53 / 2	1.33 /44	1.14 /38	0.94	1.80
MUN	Neuberger Berman Muni Int Bd Inst	NMNLX	B+	(800) 877-9700	C+ / 6.0	1.63	-2.57	-0.42 /11	2.47 /73	2.27 /66	2.08	0.66
MUN●	Neuberger Berman Muni Int Bd Inv	NMUIX	B	(800) 877-9700	C / 5.5	1.59	-2.64	-0.57 / 9	2.32 /69	2.12 /62	1.93	0.84
MUN	Neuberger Berman NY Muni Inc Inst	NMIIX	A-	(800) 877-9700	C+ / 6.5	1.82	-2.44	-0.15 /15	2.68 /77	--	2.27	0.89
GEI	Neuberger Berman Short Dur Bd A	NSHAX	D	(800) 877-9700	E / 0.3	0.26	-0.30	0.35 /30	0.28 /18	0.78 /25	1.00	1.41
GEI	Neuberger Berman Short Dur Bd C	NSHCX	D	(800) 877-9700	E / 0.3	0.08	-0.67	-0.40 /11	-0.46 / 4	0.03 / 8	0.27	2.17
GEI	Neuberger Berman Short Dur Bd Inst	NSHLX	C+	(800) 877-9700	D / 2.2	0.36	-0.07	0.75 /37	0.69 /23	1.17 /30	1.40	1.05
GEI ●	Neuberger Berman Short Dur Bd Inv	NSBIX	C	(800) 877-9700	D / 1.8	0.18	-0.30	0.42 /31	0.44 /20	0.97 /27	1.19	1.28
GEI ●	Neuberger Berman Short Dur Bd Tr	NSBTX	C	(800) 877-9700	D / 1.8	0.28	-0.26	0.42 /31	0.40 /20	0.88 /26	1.09	1.44
COH	Neuberger Berman Short Dur HI A	NHSAX	D-	(800) 877-9700	C / 4.6	2.25	2.57	9.43 /78	2.08 /45	--	3.65	1.22
COH	Neuberger Berman Short Dur HI C	NHSCX	D-	(800) 877-9700	C / 5.1	2.06	2.19	8.63 /76	1.29 /32	--	3.09	1.99
COH	Neuberger Berman Short Dur HI Inst	NHSIX	C-	(800) 877-9700	C+ / 6.8	2.34	2.76	9.72 /78	2.46 /51	--	4.18	0.81
GES	Neuberger Berman Strat Inc A	NSTAX	D	(800) 877-9700	C / 5.2	2.73	0.63	9.24 /77	2.68 /56	3.62 /67	2.98	1.09
GES	Neuberger Berman Strat Inc C	NSTCX	C-	(800) 877-9700	C+ / 5.9	2.56	0.37	8.49 /75	1.96 /42	2.90 /56	2.42	1.82
GES	Neuberger Berman Strat Inc Inst	NSTLX	C+	(800) 877-9700	B- / 7.3	2.84	0.83	9.69 /78	3.09 /63	4.03 /73	3.51	0.69
GL	Neuberger Berman Strat Inc R6	NRSIX	C+	(800) 877-9700	B- / 7.3	2.86	0.86	9.77 /78	3.13 /63	--	3.58	0.62
GES ●	Neuberger Berman Strat Inc Tr	NSTTX	C+	(800) 877-9700	C+ / 6.9	2.75	0.74	9.41 /77	2.73 /57	3.67 /68	3.16	1.05
GEI	Neuberger Core Bond A	NCRAX	D	(800) 877-9700	D+ / 2.7	1.19	-1.82	2.30 /51	2.24 /47	1.92 /41	2.21	1.01

● Denotes fund is closed to new investors
* Denotes fund is included in Section II

www.thestreetratings.com

RISK			NET ASSETS		ASSET					Portfolio Turnover Ratio	Avg Coupon Rate	FUND MANAGER		MINIMUM		LOADS	
Risk Rating/Pts	3 Yr Avg Standard Deviation	Avg Dura-tion	NAV As of 2/28/17	Total $(Mil)	Cash %	Gov. Bond %	Muni. Bond %	Corp. Bond %	Other %			Manager Quality Pct	Manager Tenure (Years)	Initial Purch. $	Additional Purch. $	Front End Load	Back End Load
D+ / 2.6	4.4	4.0	10.97	30	2	28	0	56	14	11	4.7	7	21	0	0	0.0	0.0
D+ / 2.5	4.4	4.0	10.99	955	2	28	0	56	14	11	4.7	31	21	2,500	100	4.3	0.0
D+ / 2.5	4.4	4.0	10.89	845	2	28	0	56	14	11	4.7	12	21	2,500	100	0.0	0.0
D+ / 2.5	4.4	4.0	10.99	1,108	2	28	0	56	14	11	4.7	18	21	1,000,000	0	0.0	0.0
D+ / 2.6	4.4	4.0	11.00	3,256	2	28	0	56	14	11	4.7	48	21	100,000	100	0.0	0.0
C- / 3.5	3.8	N/A	9.98	432	3	0	0	67	30	67	0.0	91	6	2,500	100	3.5	0.0
C- / 3.5	3.8	N/A	9.95	326	3	0	0	67	30	67	0.0	86	6	2,500	100	0.0	0.0
C- / 3.5	3.8	N/A	9.99	1,858	3	0	0	67	30	67	0.0	92	6	100,000	100	0.0	0.0
B- / 7.3	2.6	N/A	9.94	69	13	6	0	51	30	72	0.0	87	7	2,500	100	4.3	0.0
B- / 7.4	2.6	N/A	9.89	43	13	6	0	51	30	72	0.0	81	7	2,500	100	0.0	0.0
B- / 7.4	2.6	N/A	9.93	1,091	13	6	0	51	30	72	0.0	89	7	100,000	100	0.0	0.0
D- / 1.0	6.4	3.3	14.50	2,229	3	24	1	46	26	17	4.4	73	22	2,500	100	4.3	0.0
D- / 1.0	6.4	3.3	14.45	142	3	24	1	46	26	17	4.4	69	22	0	0	0.0	0.0
D- / 1.0	6.4	3.3	14.62	2,977	3	24	1	46	26	17	4.4	52	22	2,500	100	0.0	0.0
D- / 1.0	6.4	3.3	14.48	137	3	24	1	46	26	17	4.4	78	22	1,000,000	0	0.0	0.0
D- / 1.0	6.4	3.3	14.48	5,235	3	24	1	46	26	17	4.4	77	22	100,000	100	0.0	0.0
C+ / 6.2	2.9	N/A	10.21	1	11	0	88	0	1	97	0.0	63	4	5,000	500	3.8	0.0
C+ / 6.2	2.9	N/A	10.09	N/A	11	0	88	0	1	97	0.0	25	4	5,000	500	0.0	0.0
C+ / 6.3	2.9	N/A	10.18	55	11	0	88	0	1	97	0.0	69	4	25,000	0	0.0	0.0
C / 5.1	3.1	4.9	10.28	51	4	0	95	0	1	7	4.7	23	21	1,000	50	2.5	0.0
C / 5.1	3.1	N/A	9.34	13	13	24	0	46	17	269	0.0	15	4	2,500	100	5.8	0.0
E / 0.3	9.1	6.0	8.70	N/A	5	68	0	24	3	80	7.9	93	N/A	1,000	100	4.3	0.0
E / 0.3	9.1	6.0	8.69	N/A	5	68	0	24	3	80	7.9	89	N/A	1,000	100	0.0	0.0
E / 0.3	9.1	6.0	8.69	125	5	68	0	24	3	80	7.9	94	N/A	1,000,000	0	0.0	0.0
C+ / 6.7	2.8	0.3	9.96	22	4	0	1	71	24	64	4.5	84	8	1,000	100	4.3	0.0
C+ / 6.7	2.8	0.3	9.96	24	4	0	1	71	24	64	4.5	76	8	1,000	100	0.0	0.0
C+ / 6.6	2.8	0.3	9.96	313	4	0	1	71	24	64	4.5	87	8	1,000,000	0	0.0	0.0
D- / 1.1	5.6	4.0	8.83	79	2	1	0	93	4	72	6.1	7	12	1,000	100	4.3	0.0
D- / 1.2	5.6	4.0	8.85	29	2	1	0	93	4	72	6.1	2	12	1,000	100	0.0	0.0
D- / 1.1	5.6	4.0	8.85	3,014	2	1	0	93	4	72	6.1	13	12	1,000,000	0	0.0	0.0
D- / 1.1	5.7	4.0	8.83	128	2	1	0	93	4	72	6.1	10	12	2,000	100	0.0	0.0
D- / 1.1	5.6	4.0	8.84	13	2	1	0	93	4	72	6.1	5	12	0	0	0.0	0.0
D- / 1.2	5.6	4.0	8.85	758	2	1	0	93	4	72	6.1	15	12	0	0	0.0	0.0
C+ / 6.5	2.8	4.9	11.62	5	1	0	98	0	1	44	3.9	13	7	1,000	100	4.0	0.0
C+ / 6.8	2.8	4.9	11.63	4	1	0	98	0	1	44	3.9	5	7	1,000	100	0.0	0.0
C+ / 6.7	2.8	4.9	11.63	182	1	0	98	0	1	44	3.9	23	7	1,000,000	0	0.0	0.0
C+ / 6.6	2.8	4.9	11.64	14	1	0	98	0	1	44	3.9	19	7	2,000	100	0.0	0.0
C+ / 6.5	2.8	5.0	17.18	60	0	0	99	0	1	28	4.7	28	4	1,000,000	0	0.0	0.0
A+ / 9.7	0.7	1.7	7.44	4	5	20	0	32	43	104	1.7	30	11	1,000	100	2.5	0.0
A+ / 9.7	0.7	1.7	7.44	2	5	20	0	32	43	104	1.7	10	11	1,000	100	0.0	0.0
A+ / 9.7	0.6	1.7	7.81	53	5	20	0	32	43	104	1.7	53	11	1,000,000	0	0.0	0.0
A+ / 9.7	0.6	1.7	7.81	26	5	20	0	32	43	104	1.7	35	11	2,000	100	0.0	0.0
A+ / 9.7	0.6	1.7	7.45	2	5	20	0	32	43	104	1.7	33	11	1,000	100	0.0	0.0
C- / 3.0	3.6	1.9	9.77	4	1	0	0	89	10	51	5.7	19	5	1,000	100	4.3	0.0
C- / 3.0	3.6	1.9	9.76	1	1	0	0	89	10	51	5.7	6	5	1,000	100	0.0	0.0
C- / 3.0	3.6	1.9	9.76	85	1	0	0	89	10	51	5.7	31	5	1,000,000	0	0.0	0.0
C- / 3.9	3.6	4.9	11.01	271	0	26	0	37	37	363	3.1	75	9	1,000	100	4.3	0.0
C- / 3.9	3.5	4.9	11.00	167	0	26	0	37	37	363	3.1	58	9	1,000	100	0.0	0.0
C- / 3.9	3.6	4.9	11.00	1,518	0	26	0	37	37	363	3.1	81	9	1,000,000	0	0.0	0.0
C- / 3.9	3.5	4.9	10.99	214	0	26	0	37	37	363	3.1	94	9	0	0	0.0	0.0
C- / 3.8	3.6	4.9	11.00	25	0	26	0	37	37	363	3.1	76	9	1,000	100	0.0	0.0
B- / 7.0	2.7	5.2	10.26	24	0	38	0	26	36	148	2.9	34	9	1,000	100	4.3	0.0

Fund Type	Fund Name	Ticker Symbol	Overall Investment Rating	Phone	Performance Rating/Pts	Total Return % through 2/28/17 3 Mo	6 Mo	1Yr / Pct	Annualized 3Yr / Pct	5Yr / Pct	Incl. in Returns Dividend Yield	Expense Ratio
											99 Pct = Best	0 Pct = Worst
GEI	Neuberger Core Bond C	NCRCX	C-	(800) 877-9700	C- / 3.3	1.00	-2.18	1.63 /46	1.51 /35	1.18 /30	1.55	1.76
GEI	Neuberger Core Bond Inst	NCRLX	B	(800) 877-9700	C / 5.2	1.29	-1.62	2.81 /55	2.65 /55	2.35 /47	2.71	0.62
GEI ●	Neuberger Core Bond Inv	NCRIX	C+	(800) 877-9700	C / 4.5	1.19	-1.82	2.40 /52	2.24 /47	1.94 /41	2.31	1.15
MUH	Neuberger Municipal High Inc A	NMHAX	U	(800) 877-9700	U /	2.67	-4.50	0.34 /34	--	--	3.04	1.38
MUH	Neuberger Municipal High Inc C	NMHCX	U	(800) 877-9700	U /	2.48	-4.85	-0.31 /13	--	--	2.41	2.13
MUH	Neuberger Municipal High Inc Inst	NMHIX	U	(800) 877-9700	U /	2.76	-4.33	0.80 /42	--	--	3.56	1.01
GEI	New Covenant Income	NCICX	B	(877) 835-4531	C- / 4.1	0.76	-1.06	1.75 /47	2.02 /44	1.70 /38	1.89	0.98
MUS	New Hampshire Municipal	NHMUX	E	(800) 601-5593	E / 0.5	1.70	-4.80	-2.52 / 0	1.44 /47	1.30 /42	2.07	1.68
GL	NJ 529 NJBest CSP Income Port		B-	(800) 342-5236	C / 4.4	2.00	1.74	4.94 /66	1.36 /33	1.56 /35	0.00	0.96
COH	Nomura High Yield I	NPHIX	C+	(800) 535-2726	A / 9.5	4.63	6.00	21.94 /98	4.32 /79	--	5.53	2.95
GEI	North Country Intermediate Bond	NCBDX	D	(888) 350-2990	D+ / 2.5	0.51	-2.60	0.36 /30	1.27 /32	1.29 /31	1.77	0.85
GES	Northeast Investors Trust	NTHEX	E+	(800) 225-6704	C / 4.8	4.34	6.98	35.60 /99	-3.55 / 1	2.53 /50	6.22	1.27
MUS	Northern AZ Tax Exempt	NOAZX	B	(800) 595-9111	B- / 7.4	2.39	-2.83	0.01 /18	3.28 /85	2.95 /79	2.71	0.60
*MTG	Northern Bond Index	NOBOX	C-	(800) 595-9111	C / 4.5	1.07	-2.30	1.17 /41	2.50 /52	2.08 /43	2.60	0.18
MUS	Northern CA Intermediate T/E	NCITX	C	(800) 595-9111	C+ / 6.5	2.49	-3.28	-0.80 / 6	2.81 /79	2.65 /74	2.47	0.51
MUS	Northern CA T/E Bond	NCATX	B+	(800) 595-9111	B+ / 8.5	2.31	-3.75	-0.45 /10	4.32 /95	3.97 /93	3.00	0.62
GEI	Northern Core Bond	NOCBX	C-	(800) 637-1380	C / 4.5	1.02	-2.29	1.65 /46	2.42 /50	2.42 /48	2.07	0.47
* GL	Northern Fixed Income	NOFIX	C	(800) 595-9111	C / 5.3	1.49	-1.67	3.31 /58	2.66 /55	2.82 /55	2.60	0.49
MUH	Northern High Yield Muni	NHYMX	B	(800) 595-9111	A- / 9.0	2.25	-4.17	0.17 /28	4.77 /97	4.20 /95	3.69	0.84
*COH	Northern HY Fixed Income	NHFIX	C	(800) 595-9111	B+ / 8.4	4.52	5.63	17.51 /93	3.23 /65	5.79 /91	5.73	0.82
MMT	Northern Inst Fds Prime Oblg Pf Shs	NPAXX	C	(800) 637-1380	D / 1.6	0.18	0.36	0.57 /34	0.24 /17	0.17 /18	0.55	N/A
MMT	Northern Inst Treasury Port Shares	NITXX	C-	(800) 637-1380	D- / 1.2	0.10	0.16	0.28 /28	0.11 /14	0.07 /13	0.28	N/A
MMF	Northern Instl Muni Port Shares	NMUXX	C	(800) 637-1380	D- / 1.5	0.11	0.26	0.35 /34	0.13 /16	0.08 /16	0.35	N/A
USA	Northern Instl US Gvt Select WC	WCGXX	U	(800) 637-1380	U /	0.09	0.16	0.26 /28	--	--	0.26	0.21
* MUN	Northern Intermed Tax Exempt	NOITX	C+	(800) 595-9111	C+ / 6.0	2.08	-2.87	-0.32 /12	2.46 /73	2.20 /63	1.96	0.51
EM	Northern Multi Mgr EM Debt Oppty	NMEDX	E	(800) 595-9111	D+ / 2.7	5.40	-0.83	11.27 /82	-0.25 / 4	--	1.38	1.12
GEI	Northern Multi-Mgr HY Oppty	NMHYX	C+	(800) 595-9111	A / 9.4	4.95	6.40	21.69 /98	4.03 /76	6.19 /93	5.44	0.98
GEI	Northern Short Bond	BSBAX	C+	(800) 637-1380	D+ / 2.8	0.73	0.36	2.06 /49	0.86 /25	1.14 /29	1.46	0.43
USS	Northern Short-Int US Govt	NSIUX	C-	(800) 595-9111	D / 1.8	0.22	-1.11	-0.52 / 9	0.66 /23	0.43 /21	0.80	0.49
* MUH	Northern Short-Interm Tax-Ex	NSITX	C-	(800) 595-9111	D+ / 2.6	1.45	-0.77	-0.29 /13	0.73 /29	0.76 /30	1.18	0.49
* MUN	Northern Tax Exempt	NOTEX	B+	(800) 595-9111	B / 8.1	2.12	-3.03	0.19 /28	3.80 /91	3.25 /84	3.07	0.49
*MTG	Northern Tax-Advtged Ult-Sh Fxd Inc	NTAUX	C+	(800) 595-9111	D / 2.2	0.50	0.31	1.03 /40	0.61 /22	0.74 /24	0.83	0.26
* GEI	Northern Ultra-Short Fixed Income	NUSFX	B-	(800) 595-9111	D+ / 2.8	0.48	0.47	1.83 /47	0.92 /26	1.05 /28	1.13	0.26
USS	Northern US Government	NOUGX	D	(800) 595-9111	D / 2.1	0.27	-2.04	-1.13 / 3	1.15 /30	0.70 /24	1.03	0.83
US	Northern US Treasury Index	BTIAX	E+	(800) 637-1380	D+ / 2.9	0.57	-3.38	-1.43 / 2	1.81 /40	1.22 /30	1.55	0.26
* MUN	Nuveen All Amer Muni A	FLAAX	C	(800) 257-8787	B / 7.6	2.66	-3.91	0.67 /40	4.72 /96	4.09 /94	3.58	0.70
MUN	Nuveen All Amer Muni C	FACCX	C+	(800) 257-8787	B / 8.0	2.35	-4.31	-0.13 /15	3.87 /92	--	2.92	1.50
MUN●	Nuveen All Amer Muni C2	FAACX	B-	(800) 257-8787	B+ / 8.4	2.51	-4.19	0.13 /26	4.14 /94	3.53 /88	3.18	1.25
MUN	Nuveen All Amer Muni I	FAARX	B+	(800) 257-8787	A / 9.3	2.70	-3.79	0.96 /44	4.92 /97	4.29 /95	3.93	0.50
MUN	Nuveen All Amer Muni R6	FAAWX	U	(800) 257-8787	U /	2.70	-3.79	--	--	--	0.00	0.47
MUS	Nuveen AZ Muni Bond A	FAZTX	C-	(800) 257-8787	C+ / 6.1	1.94	-3.42	0.26 /31	3.80 /91	3.00 /80	2.82	0.87
MUN	Nuveen AZ Muni Bond C	FZCCX	C	(800) 257-8787	C+ / 6.6	1.73	-3.73	-0.55 / 9	2.96 /81	--	2.10	1.67
MUS ●	Nuveen AZ Muni Bond C2	FAZCX	C+	(800) 257-8787	B- / 7.1	1.80	-3.69	-0.29 /13	3.23 /85	2.44 /69	2.38	1.42
MUS	Nuveen AZ Muni Bond I	NMARX	B+	(800) 257-8787	B+ / 8.3	1.99	-3.30	0.46 /36	4.01 /93	3.21 /83	3.14	0.67
MUH	Nuveen CA High Yield Muni Bd A	NCHAX	C+	(800) 257-8787	A / 9.5	3.31	-5.67	0.25 /31	6.67 /99	6.69 /99	3.92	0.85
MUN	Nuveen CA High Yield Muni Bd C	NAWSX	B-	(800) 257-8787	A+ / 9.6	3.21	-5.96	-0.44 /10	5.87 /98	--	3.26	1.65
MUH●	Nuveen CA High Yield Muni Bd C2	NCHCX	C+	(800) 257-8787	A+ / 9.7	3.28	-5.85	-0.30 /13	6.10 /99	6.10 /99	3.52	1.41
MUH	Nuveen CA High Yield Muni Bd I	NCHRX	C+	(800) 257-8787	A+ / 9.9	3.36	-5.58	0.44 /36	6.97 /99	6.96 /99	4.29	0.65
MUS	Nuveen CA Muni Bond A	NCAAX	C+	(800) 257-8787	B / 8.2	2.66	-3.91	0.36 /34	5.18 /97	4.84 /97	3.19	0.76
MUN	Nuveen CA Muni Bond C	NAKFX	B-	(800) 257-8787	B+ / 8.5	2.45	-4.26	-0.39 /11	4.31 /95	--	2.48	1.56
MUS ●	Nuveen CA Muni Bond C2	NCACX	B	(800) 257-8787	B+ / 8.8	2.52	-4.21	-0.22 /14	4.58 /96	4.27 /95	2.73	1.31
MUS	Nuveen CA Muni Bond I	NCSPX	B+	(800) 257-8787	A+ / 9.6	2.80	-3.75	0.61 /39	5.38 /98	5.07 /98	3.49	0.56

● Denotes fund is closed to new investors
* Denotes fund is included in Section II

www.thestreetratings.com

RISK			NET ASSETS		ASSET							FUND MANAGER		MINIMUM		LOADS	
Risk Rating/Pts	3 Yr Avg Standard Deviation	Avg Dura-tion	NAV As of 2/28/17	Total $(Mil)	Cash %	Gov. Bond %	Muni. Bond %	Corp. Bond %	Other %	Portfolio Turnover Ratio	Avg Coupon Rate	Manager Quality Pct	Manager Tenure (Years)	Initial Purch. $	Additional Purch. $	Front End Load	Back End Load
B- /7.0	2.7	5.2	10.28	4	0	38	0	26	36	148	2.9	15	9	1,000	100	0.0	0.0
B- /7.1	2.7	5.2	10.30	311	0	38	0	26	36	148	2.9	59	9	1,000,000	0	0.0	0.0
B- /7.2	2.6	5.2	10.28	11	0	38	0	26	36	148	2.9	38	9	2,000	100	0.0	0.0
U /	N/A	8.0	9.93	1	0	0	99	0	1	75	4.5	N/A	2	1,000	100	4.3	0.0
U /	N/A	8.0	9.94	N/A	0	0	99	0	1	75	4.5	N/A	2	1,000	100	0.0	0.0
U /	N/A	8.0	9.93	94	0	0	99	0	1	75	4.5	N/A	2	1,000,000	0	0.0	0.0
B+ /8.3	2.0	3.6	23.13	302	0	19	2	33	46	202	0.0	57	3	500	100	0.0	0.0
C- /4.1	3.5	6.1	10.42	7	0	0	100	0	0	23	4.1	2	14	1,000	50	2.5	0.0
B /7.6	2.5	N/A	16.35	22	0	0	0	0	100	0	0.0	80	14	25	25	0.0	0.0
E+ /0.9	5.9	4.4	9.68	111	4	0	0	89	7	116	0.0	30	5	250,000	1,000	0.0	2.0
B- /7.4	2.6	N/A	10.14	77	0	38	0	58	4	51	0.0	11	14	1,000	100	0.0	0.0
E- /0.0	12.7	6.5	4.74	324	5	1	0	68	26	4	7.8	2	N/A	1,000	0	0.0	0.0
C /4.3	3.4	5.3	10.53	103	3	0	96	0	1	61	4.9	28	18	2,500	50	0.0	0.0
C+ /5.8	2.9	5.4	10.51	2,569	0	42	1	26	31	89	3.6	17	10	2,500	50	0.0	0.0
C- /3.9	3.5	5.2	10.56	467	1	0	98	0	1	82	4.5	13	18	2,500	50	0.0	0.0
C- /3.4	3.8	5.4	11.49	181	4	0	95	0	1	132	4.4	57	20	2,500	50	0.0	0.0
C+ /5.7	3.0	5.4	10.19	259	4	16	0	36	44	680	3.7	31	6	2,500	50	0.0	0.0
C /5.4	3.0	5.4	10.17	1,191	8	13	0	48	31	555	4.7	92	6	2,500	50	0.0	0.0
D+ /2.6	3.8	5.5	8.68	494	6	0	93	0	1	7	5.9	71	19	2,500	50	0.0	0.0
D- /1.3	5.4	4.0	6.89	4,706	4	0	0	91	5	80	7.6	15	10	2,500	50	0.0	2.0
A+ /9.9	0.1	N/A	1.00	1,710	100	0	0	0	0	0	0.6	52	N/A	20,000,000	0	0.0	0.0
A+ /9.9	N/A	N/A	1.00	9,756	100	0	0	0	0	0	0.3	47	N/A	5,000,000	0	0.0	0.0
A+ /9.9	0.1	N/A	1.00	811	100	0	0	0	0	0	0.4	49	N/A	5,000,000	0	0.0	0.0
U /	N/A	N/A	1.00	274	0	0	0	0	100	0	0.0	N/A	N/A	5,000,000	0	0.0	0.0
C /4.9	3.2	4.6	10.39	2,790	3	0	96	0	1	128	4.2	14	19	2,500	50	0.0	0.0
E /0.3	8.4	6.1	9.26	91	6	82	0	10	2	203	0.0	83	4	100,000	50	0.0	2.0
D- /1.4	5.8	3.4	10.05	353	15	1	0	74	10	73	7.2	92	5	2,500	50	0.0	2.0
A /9.4	0.9	1.9	18.88	487	3	12	0	61	24	268	2.8	56	7	2,500	50	0.0	0.0
B+ /8.7	1.5	2.8	9.82	145	0	60	0	0	40	784	1.2	28	4	2,500	50	0.0	0.0
B /8.2	1.5	2.5	10.35	1,063	1	0	98	0	1	20	4.3	15	10	2,500	50	0.0	0.0
C /4.3	3.4	4.7	10.56	1,114	3	0	96	0	1	112	4.9	56	19	2,500	50	0.0	0.0
A+ /9.9	0.3	0.9	10.14	3,507	0	0	76	21	3	52	2.7	58	8	2,500	50	0.0	0.0
A+ /9.8	0.5	1.0	10.21	2,115	6	9	0	71	14	51	1.4	65	5	2,500	50	0.0	0.0
B /7.7	2.4	3.9	9.65	24	5	78	0	0	17	602	1.5	28	4	2,500	50	0.0	0.0
C- /4.2	3.4	6.3	21.39	111	1	98	0	0	1	69	1.8	37	8	2,500	50	0.0	0.0
D+ /2.8	4.0	7.6	11.33	1,273	0	0	99	0	1	13	4.9	64	7	3,000	100	4.2	0.0
D+ /2.8	4.0	7.6	11.33	165	0	0	99	0	1	13	4.9	28	7	3,000	100	0.0	0.0
D+ /2.9	3.9	7.6	11.33	271	0	0	99	0	1	13	4.9	43	7	3,000	100	0.0	0.0
D+ /2.8	3.9	7.6	11.38	1,501	0	0	99	0	1	13	4.9	70	7	100,000	0	0.0	0.0
U /	N/A	7.6	11.38	7	0	0	99	0	1	13	4.9	N/A	7	5,000,000	0	0.0	0.0
C- /4.0	3.3	7.4	10.62	52	6	0	93	0	1	9	5.1	58	6	3,000	100	4.2	0.0
C- /4.0	3.3	7.4	10.62	5	6	0	93	0	1	9	5.1	23	6	3,000	100	0.0	0.0
C- /3.9	3.3	7.4	10.62	6	6	0	93	0	1	9	5.1	29	6	3,000	100	0.0	0.0
C- /4.0	3.3	7.4	10.65	58	6	0	93	0	1	9	5.1	65	6	100,000	0	0.0	0.0
E+ /0.9	5.6	9.6	9.35	412	0	0	98	0	2	9	4.4	73	11	3,000	100	4.2	0.0
D- /1.2	5.6	9.6	9.35	68	0	0	98	0	2	9	4.4	50	11	3,000	100	0.0	0.0
E+ /0.8	5.7	9.6	9.34	42	0	0	98	0	2	9	4.4	56	11	3,000	100	0.0	0.0
E+ /0.8	5.7	9.6	9.34	294	0	0	98	0	2	9	4.4	77	11	100,000	0	0.0	0.0
D+ /2.7	4.1	7.7	11.00	441	0	0	99	0	1	22	4.8	73	14	3,000	100	4.2	0.0
D+ /2.7	4.1	7.7	10.96	85	0	0	99	0	1	22	4.8	48	14	3,000	100	0.0	0.0
D+ /2.7	4.0	7.7	10.97	51	0	0	99	0	1	22	4.8	59	14	3,000	100	0.0	0.0
D+ /2.7	4.1	7.7	11.01	696	0	0	99	0	1	22	4.8	76	14	100,000	0	0.0	0.0

Fund Type	Fund Name	Ticker Symbol	Overall Investment Rating	Phone	Perfor-mance Rating/Pts	Total Return % through 2/28/17			Annualized		Incl. in Returns	
						3 Mo	6 Mo	1Yr / Pct	3Yr / Pct	5Yr / Pct	Dividend Yield	Expense Ratio
MUS	Nuveen CO Muni Bond A	FCOTX	C	(800) 257-8787	B- / 7.0	2.15	-3.69	0.23 /30	4.33 /95	3.78 /91	3.16	0.84
MUN	Nuveen CO Muni Bond C	FAFKX	C+	(800) 257-8787	B- / 7.3	1.94	-4.02	-0.59 / 8	3.49 /88	--	2.46	1.64
MUS ●	Nuveen CO Muni Bond C2	FCOCX	B-	(800) 257-8787	B / 7.8	2.00	-3.82	-0.25 /14	3.79 /91	3.22 /84	2.71	1.39
MUS	Nuveen CO Muni Bond I	FCORX	A-	(800) 257-8787	B+ / 8.9	2.19	-3.53	0.49 /37	4.55 /96	3.98 /93	3.48	0.64
GES	Nuveen Core Bond A	FAIIX	D-	(800) 257-8787	D / 2.0	0.90	-2.82	1.47 /44	1.58 /36	1.82 /39	2.36	0.85
COI	Nuveen Core Bond C	NTIBX	D-	(800) 257-8787	D / 2.0	0.71	-3.11	0.68 /36	0.81 /25	1.07 /28	1.64	1.61
GES	Nuveen Core Bond I	FINIX	D	(800) 257-8787	C- / 3.6	0.97	-2.71	1.72 /46	1.80 /40	2.06 /43	2.69	0.59
COI	Nuveen Core Bond R6	NTIFX	U	(800) 257-8787	U /	1.07	-2.61	1.83 /48	--	--	2.69	0.58
GEI	Nuveen Core Plus Bond A	FAFIX	D-	(800) 257-8787	C / 4.3	2.24	-0.17	8.62 /76	2.20 /46	3.08 /59	3.74	0.85
GEI	Nuveen Core Plus Bond C	FFAIX	D	(800) 257-8787	C / 4.8	2.05	-0.55	7.86 /74	1.46 /34	2.31 /46	3.18	1.63
GEI	Nuveen Core Plus Bond I	FFIIX	C	(800) 257-8787	C+ / 6.5	2.31	-0.03	8.94 /76	2.48 /51	3.34 /63	4.19	0.63
GEI	Nuveen Core Plus Bond R3	FFISX	C-	(800) 257-8787	C+ / 5.9	2.36	-0.10	8.55 /75	2.01 /43	2.87 /56	3.67	1.13
COI	Nuveen Core Plus Bond R6	FPCFX	U	(800) 257-8787	U /	2.31	-0.03	8.93 /76	--	--	4.18	0.57
MUS	Nuveen CT Muni Bond A	FCTTX	C-	(800) 257-8787	C / 5.2	1.85	-3.27	-0.15 /15	3.42 /87	2.60 /73	3.17	0.79
MUN	Nuveen CT Muni Bond C	FDCDX	C	(800) 257-8787	C+ / 5.8	1.65	-3.66	-0.93 / 5	2.59 /75	--	2.51	1.59
MUS ●	Nuveen CT Muni Bond C2	FCTCX	C+	(800) 257-8787	C+ / 6.4	1.71	-3.55	-0.71 / 7	2.85 /79	2.03 /60	2.74	1.34
MUS	Nuveen CT Muni Bond I	FCTRX	A-	(800) 257-8787	B / 7.8	1.91	-3.24	0.07 /23	3.64 /89	2.80 /76	3.53	0.59
MUS	Nuveen GA Muni Bond A	FGATX	D+	(800) 257-8787	C / 4.3	1.43	-3.43	-0.20 /14	3.06 /83	3.06 /81	3.33	0.83
MUN	Nuveen GA Muni Bond C	FGCCX	C-	(800) 257-8787	C / 4.9	1.32	-3.76	-1.01 / 4	2.24 /68	--	2.65	1.62
MUS ●	Nuveen GA Muni Bond C2	FGACX	C	(800) 257-8787	C+ / 5.6	1.37	-3.74	-0.77 / 6	2.51 /73	2.51 /71	2.90	1.38
MUS	Nuveen GA Muni Bond I	FGARX	B+	(800) 257-8787	B- / 7.2	1.57	-3.28	0.06 /22	3.28 /85	3.28 /84	3.66	0.63
GL	Nuveen High Income Bond A	FJSIX	C	(800) 257-8787	A- / 9.2	6.39	9.72	32.82 /99	2.50 /52	5.75 /90	6.40	1.08
GL	Nuveen High Income Bond C	FCSIX	C	(800) 257-8787	A / 9.4	6.08	9.21	31.74 /99	1.69 /38	4.96 /84	6.05	1.84
GL	Nuveen High Income Bond I	FJSYX	C+	(800) 257-8787	A+ / 9.8	6.44	9.82	33.03 /99	2.73 /57	6.03 /92	6.93	0.83
GL	Nuveen High Income Bond R3	FANSX	C	(800) 257-8787	A+ / 9.6	6.24	9.62	32.29 /99	2.18 /46	5.44 /88	6.50	1.34
* MUH	Nuveen High Yield Muni Bond A	NHMAX	B-	(800) 257-8787	A+ / 9.7	3.31	-4.57	2.45 /61	6.80 /99	6.98 /99	5.35	0.83
MUH	Nuveen High Yield Muni Bond C	NHCCX	B	(800) 257-8787	A+ / 9.8	3.15	-4.92	1.63 /53	5.96 /98	--	4.74	1.62
MUH ●	Nuveen High Yield Muni Bond C2	NHMCX	B	(800) 257-8787	A+ / 9.8	3.16	-4.78	1.89 /56	6.22 /99	6.41 /99	5.01	1.38
MUH	Nuveen High Yield Muni Bond I	NHMRX	B	(800) 257-8787	A+ / 9.9	3.36	-4.47	2.66 /63	7.02 /99	7.21 /99	5.80	0.63
MUH	Nuveen High Yield Muni Bond R6	NHMFX	U	(800) 257-8787	U /	3.36	-4.41	--	--	--	0.00	0.60
MUN	Nuveen Infl Protected Muni Bd A	NITAX	C-	(800) 257-8787	C / 5.4	2.65	0.38	3.37 /67	2.18 /67	1.76 /53	2.39	1.05
MUN	Nuveen Infl Protected Muni Bd C	NAADX	C-	(800) 257-8787	C / 5.1	2.34	-0.05	2.50 /61	1.36 /45	--	1.62	1.85
MUN ●	Nuveen Infl Protected Muni Bd C2	NIPCX	C+	(800) 257-8787	C+ / 5.9	2.50	0.18	2.79 /64	1.64 /52	1.20 /40	1.90	1.60
MUN	Nuveen Infl Protected Muni Bd I	NIPIX	B+	(800) 257-8787	B- / 7.3	2.69	0.46	3.54 /68	2.38 /71	1.96 /58	2.63	0.85
GL	Nuveen Inflation Protected Sec A	FAIPX	E	(800) 257-8787	D- / 1.5	1.64	-0.90	2.69 /55	1.14 /30	0.31 /20	1.23	0.97
GL	Nuveen Inflation Protected Sec C	FCIPX	E	(800) 257-8787	D / 1.6	0.93	-1.79	1.40 /44	0.27 /18	-0.41 / 3	0.46	1.72
GL	Nuveen Inflation Protected Sec I	FYIPX	E+	(800) 257-8787	C- / 3.7	1.69	-0.85	2.90 /56	1.46 /34	0.66 /23	1.42	0.72
GL	Nuveen Inflation Protected Sec R3	FRIPX	E+	(800) 257-8787	D+ / 2.7	1.59	-1.04	2.37 /52	0.81 /25	0.08 /14	1.15	1.23
GL	Nuveen Inflation Protected Sec R6	FISFX	U	(800) 257-8787	U /	1.78	-0.75	3.10 /57	--	--	1.43	0.51
USS	Nuveen Intermediate Government Bd	FIGAX	D-	(800) 257-8787	E- / 0.2	0.06	-2.34	-1.63 / 1	0.54 /21	0.59 /22	1.19	0.98
USS	Nuveen Intermediate Government Bd	FYGYX	D	(800) 257-8787	D / 1.8	0.25	-2.09	-1.25 / 3	0.81 /25	0.86 /26	1.50	0.73
USS	Nuveen Intermediate Govt Bd C	FYGCX	D-	(800) 257-8787	E / 0.3	-0.01	-2.59	-2.25 / 1	-0.17 / 5	-0.13 / 4	0.46	1.73
USS	Nuveen Intermediate Govt Bd R3	FYGRX	D-	(800) 257-8787	E / 0.5	0.11	-2.36	-1.79 / 1	0.34 /19	0.36 /20	0.95	1.23
* MUN	Nuveen Intmdt Duration Muni Bond A	NMBAX	D-	(800) 257-8787	C- / 4.2	2.16	-3.43	-0.64 / 8	2.63 /76	2.52 /71	2.74	0.68
MUN	Nuveen Intmdt Duration Muni Bond C	NNCCX	D-	(800) 257-8787	C- / 4.0	1.96	-3.81	-1.41 / 2	1.80 /57	--	2.02	1.48
MUN ●	Nuveen Intmdt Duration Muni Bond	NNSCX	D	(800) 257-8787	C / 4.8	2.02	-3.68	-1.15 / 3	2.10 /65	1.96 /58	2.29	1.24
MUN	Nuveen Intmdt Duration Muni Bond I	NUVBX	C+	(800) 257-8787	C+ / 6.6	2.21	-3.32	-0.45 /10	2.86 /80	2.72 /75	3.01	0.49
MUS	Nuveen KS Muni Bond A	FKSTX	C-	(800) 257-8787	C / 5.5	1.35	-3.58	-0.77 / 6	3.75 /90	2.83 /77	3.63	0.84
MUN	Nuveen KS Muni Bond C	FAFOX	C	(800) 257-8787	C+ / 6.2	1.14	-3.99	-1.56 / 1	2.95 /81	--	2.97	1.64
MUS ●	Nuveen KS Muni Bond C2	FCKSX	C+	(800) 257-8787	C+ / 6.6	1.21	-3.94	-1.40 / 2	3.19 /84	2.27 /66	3.23	1.39
MUS	Nuveen KS Muni Bond I	FRKSX	B+	(800) 257-8787	B / 7.9	1.41	-3.55	-0.64 / 8	3.96 /92	3.04 /80	4.00	0.64
MUS	Nuveen KY Muni Bond A	FKYTX	B-	(800) 257-8787	C / 5.3	1.69	-2.56	-0.19 /15	3.42 /87	2.71 /75	3.56	0.80

● Denotes fund is closed to new investors
* Denotes fund is included in Section II

www.thestreetratings.com

RISK			NET ASSETS		ASSET					Portfolio Turnover Ratio	Avg Coupon Rate	FUND MANAGER		MINIMUM		LOADS	
Risk Rating/Pts	3 Yr Avg Standard Deviation	Avg Dura-tion	NAV As of 2/28/17	Total $(Mil)	Cash %	Gov. Bond %	Muni. Bond %	Corp. Bond %	Other %			Manager Quality Pct	Manager Tenure (Years)	Initial Purch. $	Additional Purch. $	Front End Load	Back End Load
C- / 3.5	3.6	7.6	10.59	92	1	0	98	0	1	6	4.7	65	6	3,000	100	4.2	0.0
C- / 3.6	3.5	7.6	10.56	13	1	0	98	0	1	6	4.7	32	6	3,000	100	0.0	0.0
C- / 3.6	3.5	7.6	10.57	10	1	0	98	0	1	6	4.7	48	6	3,000	100	0.0	0.0
C- / 3.5	3.5	7.6	10.58	99	1	0	98	0	1	6	4.7	71	6	100,000	0	0.0	0.0
C+ / 5.8	2.9	4.8	9.69	14	1	13	1	40	45	75	4.2	12	17	3,000	100	3.0	0.0
C+ / 6.2	2.9	4.8	9.66	2	1	13	1	40	45	75	4.2	4	17	3,000	100	0.0	0.0
C+ / 6.0	2.9	4.8	9.65	78	1	13	1	40	45	75	4.2	18	17	100,000	0	0.0	0.0
U /	N/A	4.8	9.67	58	1	13	1	40	45	75	4.2	N/A	17	5,000,000	0	0.0	0.0
C- / 3.7	3.6	4.5	10.97	59	2	0	1	57	40	79	4.2	57	15	3,000	100	4.3	0.0
C- / 3.7	3.6	4.5	10.92	8	2	0	1	57	40	79	4.2	24	15	3,000	100	0.0	0.0
C- / 3.8	3.6	4.5	10.95	275	2	0	1	57	40	79	4.2	65	15	100,000	0	0.0	0.0
C- / 3.8	3.6	4.5	11.03	3	2	0	1	57	40	79	4.2	49	15	0	0	0.0	0.0
U /	N/A	4.5	10.96	24	2	0	1	57	40	79	4.2	N/A	15	5,000,000	0	0.0	0.0
C / 4.9	3.2	7.0	10.51	154	0	0	99	0	1	12	5.1	48	6	3,000	100	4.2	0.0
C / 5.0	3.1	7.0	10.49	6	0	0	99	0	1	12	5.1	17	6	3,000	100	0.0	0.0
C / 5.0	3.1	7.0	10.50	35	0	0	99	0	1	12	5.1	24	6	3,000	100	0.0	0.0
C / 5.0	3.1	7.0	10.54	68	0	0	99	0	1	12	5.1	58	6	100,000	0	0.0	0.0
C+ / 5.6	3.0	6.5	10.73	90	1	0	98	0	1	16	5.3	38	10	3,000	100	4.2	0.0
C / 5.4	3.0	6.5	10.69	10	1	0	98	0	1	16	5.3	13	10	3,000	100	0.0	0.0
C / 5.3	3.1	6.5	10.69	23	1	0	98	0	1	16	5.3	18	10	3,000	100	0.0	0.0
C / 5.5	3.0	6.5	10.70	47	1	0	98	0	1	16	5.3	52	10	100,000	0	0.0	0.0
E / 0.3	8.3	4.4	7.95	198	7	0	0	83	10	91	7.9	91	12	3,000	100	4.8	0.0
E / 0.3	8.3	4.4	7.93	49	7	0	0	83	10	91	7.9	87	12	3,000	100	0.0	0.0
E / 0.3	8.3	4.4	7.97	236	7	0	0	83	10	91	7.9	92	12	100,000	0	0.0	0.0
E / 0.4	8.3	4.4	8.11	1	7	0	0	83	10	91	7.9	90	12	0	0	0.0	0.0
D- / 1.4	4.9	9.4	16.68	4,389	1	0	96	1	2	14	5.8	83	17	3,000	100	4.2	0.0
D- / 1.4	4.9	9.4	16.67	843	1	0	96	1	2	14	5.8	74	17	3,000	100	0.0	0.0
D- / 1.4	4.9	9.4	16.67	1,065	1	0	96	1	2	14	5.8	78	17	3,000	100	0.0	0.0
D- / 1.4	4.9	9.4	16.68	6,509	1	0	96	1	2	14	5.8	85	17	100,000	0	0.0	0.0
U /	N/A	9.4	16.68	37	1	0	96	1	2	14	5.8	N/A	17	5,000,000	0	0.0	0.0
C / 4.8	3.2	4.5	10.59	30	0	0	100	0	0	1	4.3	34	6	3,000	100	3.0	0.0
C / 4.9	3.1	4.5	10.58	1	0	0	100	0	0	1	4.3	13	6	3,000	100	0.0	0.0
C / 4.9	3.2	4.5	10.59	5	0	0	100	0	0	1	4.3	19	6	3,000	100	0.0	0.0
C / 4.9	3.2	4.5	10.61	43	0	0	100	0	0	1	4.3	48	6	100,000	0	0.0	0.0
C- / 3.2	4.0	4.3	11.07	117	0	90	0	3	7	26	0.0	85	13	3,000	100	4.3	0.0
C- / 3.2	4.0	4.3	10.89	14	0	90	0	3	7	26	0.0	76	13	3,000	100	0.0	0.0
C- / 3.2	4.0	4.3	11.20	476	0	90	0	3	7	26	0.0	88	13	100,000	0	0.0	0.0
C- / 3.1	4.1	4.3	10.97	10	0	90	0	3	7	26	0.0	82	13	0	0	0.0	0.0
U /	N/A	4.3	11.24	23	0	90	0	3	7	26	0.0	N/A	13	5,000,000	0	0.0	0.0
B / 8.1	2.1	3.7	8.65	11	6	75	2	0	17	58	4.6	17	15	3,000	100	3.0	0.0
B / 8.0	2.1	3.7	8.66	50	6	75	2	0	17	58	4.6	22	15	100,000	0	0.0	0.0
B / 8.0	2.2	3.7	8.67	1	6	75	2	0	17	58	4.6	5	15	3,000	100	0.0	0.0
B / 8.0	2.1	3.7	8.66	N/A	6	75	2	0	17	58	4.6	12	15	0	0	0.0	0.0
C- / 4.2	3.4	5.6	9.02	1,049	1	0	98	0	1	18	4.5	12	10	3,000	100	3.0	0.0
C / 4.3	3.4	5.6	9.03	46	1	0	98	0	1	18	4.5	4	10	3,000	100	0.0	0.0
C / 4.3	3.4	5.6	9.04	88	1	0	98	0	1	18	4.5	6	10	3,000	100	0.0	0.0
C / 4.4	3.4	5.6	9.05	3,953	1	0	98	0	1	18	4.5	18	10	100,000	0	0.0	0.0
C / 4.5	3.3	6.2	10.59	146	1	0	98	0	1	11	5.4	57	6	3,000	100	4.2	0.0
C / 4.5	3.3	6.2	10.57	13	1	0	98	0	1	11	5.4	23	6	3,000	100	0.0	0.0
C / 4.4	3.3	6.2	10.57	36	1	0	98	0	1	11	5.4	29	6	3,000	100	0.0	0.0
C / 4.4	3.3	6.2	10.63	36	1	0	98	0	1	11	5.4	64	6	100,000	0	0.0	0.0
C+ / 6.6	2.8	5.6	10.81	285	1	0	98	0	1	10	5.3	62	10	3,000	100	4.2	0.0

Fund Type	Fund Name	Ticker Symbol	Overall Investment Rating	Phone	Performance Rating/Pts	3 Mo	6 Mo	1Yr / Pct	3Yr / Pct	5Yr / Pct	Dividend Yield	Expense Ratio
MUN	Nuveen KY Muni Bond C	FKCCX	B	(800) 257-8787	C+ / 5.9	1.48	-2.96	-1.09 / 4	2.57 / 75	--	2.89	1.59
MUS ●	Nuveen KY Muni Bond C2	FKYCX	B+	(800) 257-8787	C+ / 6.4	1.55	-2.83	-0.82 / 6	2.83 / 79	2.12 / 62	3.17	1.35
MUS	Nuveen KY Muni Bond I	FKYRX	A+	(800) 257-8787	B / 7.8	1.65	-2.45	-0.07 / 16	3.61 / 89	2.90 / 78	3.94	0.60
MUS	Nuveen LA Muni Bond A	FTLAX	D	(800) 257-8787	C / 5.3	1.34	-4.95	-1.51 / 2	3.86 / 91	3.16 / 83	3.46	0.84
MUN	Nuveen LA Muni Bond C	FAFLX	D+	(800) 257-8787	C+ / 6.0	1.23	-5.27	-2.30 / 1	3.06 / 83	--	2.80	1.64
MUS ●	Nuveen LA Muni Bond C2	FTLCX	C-	(800) 257-8787	C+ / 6.5	1.29	-5.17	-2.07 / 1	3.32 / 86	2.60 / 73	3.05	1.39
MUS	Nuveen LA Muni Bond I	FTLRX	C+	(800) 257-8787	B / 7.8	1.40	-4.84	-1.30 / 2	4.07 / 93	3.37 / 86	3.82	0.64
*MUN	Nuveen Ltd Term Muni A	FLTDX	D-	(800) 257-8787	D- / 1.1	1.39	-1.99	-0.92 / 5	1.07 / 37	1.29 / 42	1.78	0.63
MUN	Nuveen Ltd Term Muni C	FAFJX	D-	(800) 257-8787	E+ / 0.9	1.28	-2.31	-1.64 / 1	0.40 / 22	--	1.00	1.43
MUN ●	Nuveen Ltd Term Muni C2	FLTCX	D+	(800) 257-8787	D / 2.0	1.29	-2.09	-1.21 / 3	0.72 / 29	0.95 / 34	1.44	0.98
MUN	Nuveen Ltd Term Muni I	FLTRX	C+	(800) 257-8787	C- / 3.5	1.53	-1.82	-0.67 / 7	1.30 / 43	1.52 / 47	2.00	0.43
MUS	Nuveen MA Muni Bond A	NMAAX	C+	(800) 257-8787	C+ / 6.3	1.84	-2.88	0.55 / 38	3.84 / 91	3.15 / 82	2.97	0.81
MUN	Nuveen MA Muni Bond C	NAAGX	B-	(800) 257-8787	C+ / 6.7	1.64	-3.31	-0.27 / 13	2.98 / 82	--	2.28	1.61
MUS ●	Nuveen MA Muni Bond C2	NMACX	B	(800) 257-8787	B- / 7.2	1.70	-3.19	-0.03 / 17	3.26 / 85	2.56 / 72	2.52	1.36
MUS	Nuveen MA Muni Bond I	NBMAX	A	(800) 257-8787	B+ / 8.5	1.89	-2.79	0.73 / 41	4.03 / 93	3.35 / 86	3.28	0.61
MUS	Nuveen MD Muni Bond A	NMDAX	B	(800) 257-8787	C+ / 6.3	2.08	-2.43	0.62 / 39	3.75 / 90	2.69 / 74	3.26	0.83
MUN	Nuveen MD Muni Bond C	NACCX	B+	(800) 257-8787	C+ / 6.7	1.79	-2.92	-0.26 / 14	2.89 / 80	--	2.62	1.63
MUS ●	Nuveen MD Muni Bond C2	NMDCX	A	(800) 257-8787	B- / 7.2	1.85	-2.80	0.06 / 22	3.16 / 84	2.11 / 62	2.84	1.38
MUS	Nuveen MD Muni Bond I	NMMDX	A+	(800) 257-8787	B+ / 8.4	2.04	-2.41	0.74 / 41	3.95 / 92	2.89 / 78	3.63	0.63
MUS	Nuveen MI Muni Bond A	FMITX	C	(800) 257-8787	C+ / 6.5	2.13	-3.18	0.07 / 23	4.02 / 93	3.44 / 87	3.13	0.84
MUN	Nuveen MI Muni Bond C	FAFNX	C+	(800) 257-8787	B- / 7.0	1.93	-3.59	-0.72 / 7	3.19 / 84	--	2.45	1.64
MUS ●	Nuveen MI Muni Bond C2	FLMCX	C+	(800) 257-8787	B- / 7.4	1.99	-3.55	-0.55 / 9	3.46 / 87	2.87 / 78	2.71	1.39
MUS	Nuveen MI Muni Bond I	NMMIX	A-	(800) 257-8787	B+ / 8.6	2.19	-3.08	0.28 / 32	4.24 / 94	3.64 / 89	3.48	0.64
MUS	Nuveen Minnesota Intmdt Muni Bd A	FAMAX	C-	(800) 257-8787	C / 4.6	1.89	-2.76	-0.28 / 13	2.75 / 78	2.45 / 69	2.76	0.82
MUN	Nuveen Minnesota Intmdt Muni Bd C	NIBCX	C-	(800) 257-8787	C / 4.4	1.69	-3.07	-1.08 / 4	1.90 / 60	--	2.04	1.61
MUS	Nuveen Minnesota Intmdt Muni Bd	FACMX	C+	(800) 257-8787	C / 5.3	1.77	-2.97	-0.73 / 7	2.26 / 68	1.99 / 59	2.37	1.27
MUN ●	Nuveen Minnesota Intmdt Muni Bd	NIBMX	C	(800) 257-8787	C / 5.1	1.75	-3.05	-0.85 / 5	2.17 / 66	1.89 / 56	2.27	1.37
MUS	Nuveen Minnesota Intmdt Muni Bd I	FAMTX	A-	(800) 257-8787	C+ / 6.9	1.94	-2.68	-0.02 / 17	2.97 / 81	2.67 / 74	3.04	0.62
MUS	Nuveen Minnesota Municipal Bond A	FJMNX	C-	(800) 257-8787	C+ / 6.5	2.47	-3.63	-0.13 / 15	4.06 / 93	3.35 / 86	3.17	0.82
MUN	Nuveen Minnesota Municipal Bond C	NTCCX	C	(800) 257-8787	B- / 7.1	2.35	-3.95	-0.83 / 6	3.26 / 85	--	2.50	1.62
MUS	Nuveen Minnesota Municipal Bond	FCMNX	C+	(800) 257-8787	B / 7.6	2.45	-3.79	-0.50 / 9	3.63 / 89	2.91 / 78	2.85	1.28
MUN ●	Nuveen Minnesota Municipal Bond	NMBCX	C	(800) 257-8787	B- / 7.4	2.41	-3.82	-0.58 / 9	3.51 / 88	2.80 / 76	2.75	1.38
MUS	Nuveen Minnesota Municipal Bond I	FYMNX	B	(800) 257-8787	B+ / 8.6	2.52	-3.54	0.07 / 23	4.28 / 95	3.56 / 88	3.51	0.62
MUS	Nuveen MO Muni Bond A	FMOTX	C+	(800) 257-8787	C+ / 6.7	2.09	-2.96	0.85 / 43	3.98 / 93	3.39 / 86	3.34	0.79
MUN	Nuveen MO Muni Bond C	FAFPX	C+	(800) 257-8787	B- / 7.0	1.89	-3.35	0.06 / 22	3.11 / 83	--	2.70	1.58
MUS ●	Nuveen MO Muni Bond C2	FMOCX	B	(800) 257-8787	B- / 7.5	1.96	-3.22	0.32 / 33	3.41 / 87	2.83 / 77	2.96	1.34
MUS	Nuveen MO Muni Bond I	FMMRX	A-	(800) 257-8787	B+ / 8.7	2.14	-2.86	1.06 / 46	4.17 / 94	3.59 / 89	3.71	0.59
MUS	Nuveen NC Muni Bond A	FLNCX	D	(800) 257-8787	C / 4.9	1.96	-3.74	-0.30 / 13	3.34 / 86	2.87 / 78	2.86	0.79
MUN	Nuveen NC Muni Bond C	FDCCX	D+	(800) 257-8787	C+ / 5.6	1.75	-4.14	-1.11 / 4	2.54 / 74	--	2.15	1.59
MUS ●	Nuveen NC Muni Bond C2	FCNCX	C-	(800) 257-8787	C+ / 6.1	1.81	-4.03	-0.89 / 5	2.78 / 78	2.31 / 66	2.38	1.34
MUS	Nuveen NC Muni Bond I	FCNRX	B-	(800) 257-8787	B / 7.6	2.01	-3.62	-0.10 / 16	3.54 / 88	3.08 / 81	3.17	0.59
MUS	Nuveen Nebraska Municipal Bond A	FNTAX	D	(800) 257-8787	C+ / 5.7	2.00	-3.55	-0.30 / 13	3.69 / 90	2.66 / 74	3.17	0.91
MUN	Nuveen Nebraska Municipal Bond C	NAAFX	D+	(800) 257-8787	C+ / 6.0	1.79	-3.88	-1.12 / 4	2.73 / 78	--	2.47	1.71
MUS	Nuveen Nebraska Municipal Bond C1	FNTCX	C	(800) 257-8787	B- / 7.0	1.88	-3.73	-0.71 / 7	3.23 / 85	2.21 / 64	2.82	1.37
MUN ●	Nuveen Nebraska Municipal Bond C2	NCNBX	C	(800) 257-8787	C+ / 6.8	1.84	-3.75	-0.78 / 6	3.14 / 84	2.11 / 62	2.71	1.47
MUS	Nuveen Nebraska Municipal Bond I	FNTYX	B-	(800) 257-8787	B / 8.2	2.14	-3.38	-0.04 / 17	3.93 / 92	2.88 / 78	3.48	0.71
MUS	Nuveen NJ Muni Bond A	NNJAX	D	(800) 257-8787	C+ / 6.1	2.38	-4.10	0.46 / 36	3.81 / 91	3.42 / 87	3.35	0.81
MUN	Nuveen NJ Muni Bond C	NJCCX	D+	(800) 257-8787	C+ / 6.6	2.17	-4.44	-0.35 / 12	2.97 / 81	--	2.68	1.60
MUS ●	Nuveen NJ Muni Bond C2	NNJCX	C-	(800) 257-8787	B- / 7.1	2.14	-4.39	-0.09 / 16	3.21 / 85	2.84 / 77	2.94	1.36
MUS	Nuveen NJ Muni Bond I	NMNJX	C+	(800) 257-8787	B+ / 8.3	2.33	-4.07	0.58 / 38	4.02 / 93	3.64 / 89	3.70	0.61
MUS	Nuveen NM Muni Bond A	FNMTX	C-	(800) 257-8787	C / 5.0	1.74	-2.85	-0.04 / 17	3.29 / 85	2.22 / 64	2.98	0.87
MUN	Nuveen NM Muni Bond C	FNCCX	C+	(800) 257-8787	C+ / 5.8	1.63	-3.14	-0.74 / 7	2.50 / 73	--	2.28	1.66

● Denotes fund is closed to new investors
* Denotes fund is included in Section II

www.thestreetratings.com

RISK			NET ASSETS		ASSET							FUND MANAGER		MINIMUM		LOADS	
Risk Rating/Pts	3 Yr Avg Standard Deviation	Avg Dura-tion	NAV As of 2/28/17	Total $(Mil)	Cash %	Gov. Bond %	Muni. Bond %	Corp. Bond %	Other %	Portfolio Turnover Ratio	Avg Coupon Rate	Manager Quality Pct	Manager Tenure (Years)	Initial Purch. $	Additional Purch. $	Front End Load	Back End Load
C+ / 6.4	2.8	5.6	10.80	8	1	0	98	0	1	10	5.3	24	10	3,000	100	0.0	0.0
C+ / 6.4	2.8	5.6	10.80	40	1	0	98	0	1	10	5.3	32	10	3,000	100	0.0	0.0
C+ / 6.7	2.8	5.6	10.80	37	1	0	98	0	1	10	5.3	68	10	100,000	0	0.0	0.0
C- / 3.3	3.9	6.8	10.94	90	1	0	97	0	2	5	5.2	32	6	3,000	100	4.2	0.0
C- / 3.3	3.9	6.8	10.89	9	1	0	97	0	2	5	5.2	11	6	3,000	100	0.0	0.0
C- / 3.2	4.0	6.8	10.89	19	1	0	97	0	2	5	5.2	15	6	3,000	100	0.0	0.0
C- / 3.3	4.0	6.8	10.97	20	1	0	97	0	2	5	5.2	39	6	100,000	0	0.0	0.0
B / 8.1	2.1	3.2	10.88	1,212	0	0	98	0	2	20	3.9	10	11	3,000	100	2.5	0.0
B / 8.1	2.1	3.2	10.84	114	0	0	98	0	2	20	3.9	4	11	3,000	100	0.0	0.0
B / 8.2	2.0	3.2	10.85	393	0	0	98	0	2	20	3.9	6	11	3,000	100	0.0	0.0
B / 8.1	2.1	3.2	10.84	2,918	0	0	98	0	2	20	3.9	14	11	100,000	0	0.0	0.0
C / 4.9	3.2	6.8	10.01	118	0	0	99	0	1	12	5.0	64	6	3,000	100	4.2	0.0
C / 4.9	3.2	6.8	9.92	8	0	0	99	0	1	12	5.0	27	6	3,000	100	0.0	0.0
C / 5.0	3.1	6.8	9.93	20	0	0	99	0	1	12	5.0	37	6	3,000	100	0.0	0.0
C / 5.0	3.1	6.8	10.00	171	0	0	99	0	1	12	5.0	70	6	100,000	0	0.0	0.0
C+ / 6.0	2.9	6.9	10.57	66	0	0	99	0	1	18	4.1	69	1	3,000	100	4.2	0.0
C+ / 5.9	2.9	6.9	10.52	13	0	0	99	0	1	18	4.1	32	1	3,000	100	0.0	0.0
C+ / 6.0	2.9	6.9	10.53	26	0	0	99	0	1	18	4.1	48	1	3,000	100	0.0	0.0
C+ / 6.1	2.9	6.9	10.57	80	0	0	99	0	1	18	4.1	73	1	100,000	0	0.0	0.0
C- / 3.9	3.4	7.1	11.37	115	0	0	99	0	1	5	4.7	62	10	3,000	100	4.2	0.0
C- / 3.8	3.4	7.1	11.34	11	0	0	99	0	1	5	4.7	26	10	3,000	100	0.0	0.0
C- / 3.8	3.4	7.1	11.34	18	0	0	99	0	1	5	4.7	34	10	3,000	100	0.0	0.0
C- / 3.9	3.4	7.1	11.36	57	0	0	99	0	1	5	4.7	69	10	100,000	0	0.0	0.0
C+ / 5.8	2.9	6.2	10.30	96	1	0	98	0	1	11	4.6	26	23	3,000	100	3.0	0.0
C+ / 6.0	2.9	6.2	10.24	13	1	0	98	0	1	11	4.6	9	23	3,000	100	0.0	0.0
C+ / 5.8	3.0	6.2	10.33	2	1	0	98	0	1	11	4.6	14	23	3,000	100	0.0	0.0
C+ / 5.8	3.0	6.2	10.26	6	1	0	98	0	1	11	4.6	12	23	3,000	100	0.0	0.0
C+ / 6.0	2.9	6.2	10.25	212	1	0	98	0	1	11	4.6	34	23	100,000	0	0.0	0.0
C- / 3.1	3.8	8.4	11.50	165	1	0	98	0	1	6	4.2	49	1	3,000	100	4.2	0.0
D+ / 2.9	3.8	8.4	11.49	27	1	0	98	0	1	6	4.2	17	1	3,000	100	0.0	0.0
C- / 3.0	3.8	8.4	11.46	12	1	0	98	0	1	6	4.2	27	1	3,000	100	0.0	0.0
D+ / 2.9	3.8	8.4	11.51	8	1	0	98	0	1	6	4.2	23	1	3,000	100	0.0	0.0
C- / 3.1	3.8	8.4	11.49	134	1	0	98	0	1	6	4.2	59	1	100,000	0	0.0	0.0
C- / 4.0	3.3	7.3	11.19	211	0	0	99	0	1	9	4.3	64	6	3,000	100	4.2	0.0
C- / 4.1	3.3	7.3	11.15	19	0	0	99	0	1	9	4.3	27	6	3,000	100	0.0	0.0
C- / 4.1	3.2	7.3	11.16	25	0	0	99	0	1	9	4.3	41	6	3,000	100	0.0	0.0
C- / 4.1	3.3	7.3	11.18	218	0	0	99	0	1	9	4.3	69	6	100,000	0	0.0	0.0
C- / 3.8	3.4	7.2	10.76	166	1	0	98	0	1	6	4.4	30	10	3,000	100	4.2	0.0
C- / 3.8	3.4	7.2	10.76	20	1	0	98	0	1	6	4.4	10	10	3,000	100	0.0	0.0
C- / 3.8	3.4	7.2	10.77	33	1	0	98	0	1	6	4.4	16	10	3,000	100	0.0	0.0
C- / 3.8	3.4	7.2	10.81	270	1	0	98	0	1	6	4.4	38	10	100,000	0	0.0	0.0
C- / 3.2	3.5	10.4	10.60	26	1	0	98	0	1	8	4.9	44	1	3,000	100	4.2	0.0
C- / 3.3	3.4	10.4	10.57	3	1	0	98	0	1	8	4.9	13	1	3,000	100	0.0	0.0
C- / 3.3	3.4	10.4	10.53	2	1	0	98	0	1	8	4.9	26	1	3,000	100	0.0	0.0
C- / 3.3	3.4	10.4	10.61	4	1	0	98	0	1	8	4.9	23	1	3,000	100	0.0	0.0
C- / 3.2	3.5	10.4	10.62	27	1	0	98	0	1	8	4.9	56	1	100,000	0	0.0	0.0
D+ / 2.7	4.0	7.9	11.19	154	1	0	98	0	1	16	4.2	25	6	3,000	100	4.2	0.0
D+ / 2.7	4.0	7.9	11.14	16	1	0	98	0	1	16	4.2	8	6	3,000	100	0.0	0.0
D+ / 2.8	4.0	7.9	11.14	36	1	0	98	0	1	16	4.2	11	6	3,000	100	0.0	0.0
D+ / 2.7	4.0	7.9	11.22	115	1	0	98	0	1	16	4.2	31	6	100,000	0	0.0	0.0
C / 5.4	3.0	6.5	10.27	50	1	0	98	0	1	9	5.0	50	6	3,000	100	4.2	0.0
C / 5.4	3.0	6.5	10.29	3	1	0	98	0	1	9	5.0	18	6	3,000	100	0.0	0.0

Fund Type	Fund Name	Ticker Symbol	Overall Investment Rating	Phone	Perfor-mance Rating/Pts	3 Mo	6 Mo	1Yr / Pct	3Yr / Pct	5Yr / Pct	Dividend Yield	Expense Ratio
MUS ●	Nuveen NM Muni Bond C2	FNMCX	B-	(800) 257-8787	C+ / 6.2	1.60	-3.10	-0.55 / 9	2.69 /77	1.65 /50	2.58	1.42
MUS	Nuveen NM Muni Bond I	FNMRX	A-	(800) 257-8787	B / 7.6	1.79	-2.72	0.18 /28	3.47 /87	2.43 /69	3.32	0.66
GEN	Nuveen NWQ Flexible Income A	NWQAX	C+	(800) 257-8787	A- / 9.2	5.16	2.08	14.85 /88	5.93 /91	6.37 /94	4.90	1.19
GEN	Nuveen NWQ Flexible Income C	NWQCX	B-	(800) 257-8787	A / 9.4	4.92	1.70	13.98 /87	5.14 /86	5.58 /89	4.42	1.93
GEN	Nuveen NWQ Flexible Income I	NWQIX	B	(800) 257-8787	A+ / 9.8	5.23	2.21	15.13 /89	6.19 /93	6.66 /96	5.39	0.94
GEL	Nuveen NWQ Flexible Income R6	NQWFX	U	(800) 257-8787	U /	5.21	2.23	--	--	--	0.00	1.05
MUS	Nuveen NY Muni Bond A	NNYAX	C	(800) 257-8787	C+ / 6.8	2.19	-3.42	0.56 /38	4.13 /94	3.09 /81	3.41	0.78
MUN	Nuveen NY Muni Bond C	NAJPX	C+	(800) 257-8787	B- / 7.1	1.89	-3.82	-0.34 /12	3.28 /85	--	2.74	1.58
MUS ●	Nuveen NY Muni Bond C2	NNYCX	B-	(800) 257-8787	B- / 7.5	1.96	-3.69	-0.07 /16	3.54 /88	2.51 /71	3.01	1.33
MUS	Nuveen NY Muni Bond I	NTNYX	B+	(800) 257-8787	B+ / 8.7	2.15	-3.31	0.68 /40	4.31 /95	3.28 /84	3.78	0.58
MUS	Nuveen OH Muni Bond A	FOHTX	D+	(800) 257-8787	C+ / 6.0	2.13	-3.79	-0.07 /16	3.79 /91	3.27 /84	3.10	0.79
MUN	Nuveen OH Muni Bond C	FAFMX	C-	(800) 257-8787	C+ / 6.5	1.93	-4.20	-0.87 / 5	2.97 /81	--	2.43	1.58
MUS ●	Nuveen OH Muni Bond C2	FOHCX	C	(800) 257-8787	B- / 7.1	2.08	-3.99	-0.55 / 9	3.25 /85	2.72 /75	2.66	1.34
MUS	Nuveen OH Muni Bond I	NXOHX	B	(800) 257-8787	B+ / 8.3	2.29	-3.61	0.14 /26	4.02 /93	3.49 /87	3.46	0.59
MUS	Nuveen Oregon Intmdt Muni Bd A	FOTAX	D-	(800) 257-8787	C- / 3.4	2.04	-3.12	-0.74 / 7	2.25 /68	1.85 /55	2.35	0.83
MUN	Nuveen Oregon Intmdt Muni Bd C	NAFOX	D-	(800) 257-8787	C- / 3.0	1.67	-3.60	-1.61 / 1	1.36 /45	--	1.54	1.62
MUN ●	Nuveen Oregon Intmdt Muni Bd C2	NIMOX	D	(800) 257-8787	C- / 3.9	1.83	-3.38	-1.37 / 2	1.68 /53	1.28 /42	1.78	1.38
MUS	Nuveen Oregon Intmdt Muni Bd I	FORCX	C	(800) 257-8787	C+ / 5.8	2.02	-3.09	-0.64 / 8	2.44 /72	2.03 /60	2.53	0.62
MUS	Nuveen PA Muni Bond A	FPNTX	D	(800) 257-8787	C+ / 5.9	1.99	-4.44	-0.49 /10	3.89 /92	3.38 /86	3.31	0.81
MUN	Nuveen PA Muni Bond C	FPCCX	D+	(800) 257-8787	C+ / 6.3	1.78	-4.88	-1.32 / 2	3.02 /82	--	2.60	1.60
MUS ●	Nuveen PA Muni Bond C2	FPMBX	C	(800) 257-8787	C+ / 6.9	1.84	-4.75	-1.08 / 4	3.33 /86	2.82 /77	2.85	1.36
MUS	Nuveen PA Muni Bond I	NBPAX	B-	(800) 257-8787	B / 8.2	2.04	-4.29	-0.24 /14	4.10 /94	3.60 /89	3.63	0.61
USS	Nuveen Preferred Securities A	NPSAX	A	(800) 257-8787	A- / 9.0	4.29	2.43	11.35 /82	6.19 /93	8.02 /98	5.18	1.06
USS	Nuveen Preferred Securities C	NPSCX	A	(800) 257-8787	A / 9.3	4.15	2.05	10.59 /80	5.41 /88	7.22 /97	4.70	1.81
USS	Nuveen Preferred Securities I	NPSRX	A+	(800) 257-8787	A+ / 9.7	4.35	2.55	11.69 /83	6.46 /94	8.29 /99	5.68	0.81
COI	Nuveen Preferred Securities R3	NPSTX	A+	(800) 257-8787	A / 9.5	4.26	2.30	11.17 /82	5.94 /91	7.76 /98	5.19	1.31
GEL	Nuveen Preferred Securities R6	NPSFX	U	(800) 257-8787	U /	4.41	2.61	--	--	--	0.00	0.75
* MUH	Nuveen Short Dur Hi Yld Muni A	NVHAX	C	(800) 257-8787	C+ / 6.6	1.50	-3.76	0.43 /36	3.64 /89	--	3.35	0.83
MUH	Nuveen Short Dur Hi Yld Muni C	NVCCX	C-	(800) 257-8787	C+ / 6.3	1.28	-4.07	-0.30 /13	2.84 /79	--	2.58	1.63
MUH ●	Nuveen Short Dur Hi Yld Muni C2	NVHCX	C	(800) 257-8787	C+ / 6.8	1.35	-4.04	-0.14 /15	3.08 /83	--	2.86	1.38
MUH	Nuveen Short Dur Hi Yld Muni I	NVHIX	B	(800) 257-8787	B / 8.1	1.54	-3.67	0.70 /40	3.86 /91	--	3.61	0.63
GEI	Nuveen Short Term Bond A	FALTX	C	(800) 257-8787	D / 2.0	0.60	0.39	2.42 /52	0.92 /26	1.55 /35	1.54	0.76
GEI	Nuveen Short Term Bond C	FBSCX	C	(800) 257-8787	D / 1.7	0.40	-0.01	1.61 /45	0.16 /15	0.80 /25	0.79	1.51
GEI	Nuveen Short Term Bond I	FLTIX	B	(800) 257-8787	C- / 3.3	0.66	0.51	2.67 /54	1.16 /30	1.81 /39	1.83	0.51
COI	Nuveen Short Term Bond R3	NSSRX	C+	(800) 257-8787	D+ / 2.4	0.52	0.23	2.11 /50	0.61 /22	1.27 /31	1.28	1.01
COI	Nuveen Short Term Bond R6	NSSFX	U	(800) 257-8787	U /	0.66	0.61	2.77 /55	--	--	1.82	0.47
MUN	Nuveen Short Term Municipal Bond A	FSHAX	D	(800) 257-8787	E / 0.5	0.94	-0.31	0.06 /22	0.56 /25	0.91 /33	0.93	0.70
MUN	Nuveen Short Term Municipal Bond C	NAAEX	D	(800) 257-8787	E / 0.5	0.75	-0.70	-0.71 / 7	-0.03 / 5	--	0.18	1.50
MUN ●	Nuveen Short Term Municipal Bond	NSVCX	C-	(800) 257-8787	D- / 1.4	0.85	-0.49	-0.30 /13	0.20 /19	0.53 /25	0.60	1.05
MUN	Nuveen Short Term Municipal Bond I	FSHYX	C+	(800) 257-8787	D+ / 2.8	1.09	-0.22	0.24 /30	0.74 /30	1.11 /38	1.13	0.50
COI	Nuveen Strategic Income A	FCDDX	D	(800) 257-8787	C+ / 6.3	3.00	1.21	13.35 /86	2.81 /58	4.39 /77	4.80	0.92
COI	Nuveen Strategic Income C	FCBCX	D	(800) 257-8787	C+ / 6.7	2.72	0.82	12.54 /84	2.04 /44	3.61 /67	4.25	1.67
COI	Nuveen Strategic Income I	FCBYX	C	(800) 257-8787	B / 7.8	2.96	1.32	13.75 /86	3.08 /62	4.67 /80	5.35	0.67
COI	Nuveen Strategic Income R3	FABSX	C-	(800) 257-8787	B- / 7.3	2.93	1.09	13.04 /85	2.54 /53	4.13 /74	4.77	1.17
GEL	Nuveen Strategic Income R6	FSFRX	U	(800) 257-8787	U /	3.06	1.42	13.71 /86	--	--	5.23	0.60
MUN	Nuveen Strategic Municipal Opptys A	NSAOX	U	(800) 257-8787	U /	2.58	-5.82	-0.01 /17	--	--	2.78	1.33
MUN	Nuveen Strategic Municipal Opptys C	NSCOX	U	(800) 257-8787	U /	2.47	-6.12	-0.81 / 6	--	--	2.02	2.13
MUN	Nuveen Strategic Municipal Opptys I	NSIOX	U	(800) 257-8787	U /	2.62	-5.64	0.16 /27	--	--	3.04	1.13
GEI	Nuveen Symphony Credit Oppty A	NCOAX	C	(800) 257-8787	A- / 9.1	5.01	8.00	25.98 /99	3.49 /69	6.33 /94	6.69	1.02
GEI	Nuveen Symphony Credit Oppty C	NCFCX	C+	(800) 257-8787	A / 9.3	4.82	7.62	25.05 /99	2.72 /56	5.53 /89	6.33	1.77
GEI	Nuveen Symphony Credit Oppty I	NCOIX	C+	(800) 257-8787	A+ / 9.7	5.12	8.18	26.35 /99	3.75 /72	6.59 /95	7.25	0.77
COH	Nuveen Symphony Credit Oppty R6	NCSRX	U	(800) 257-8787	U /	5.11	8.18	26.44 /99	--	--	7.24	0.69

● Denotes fund is closed to new investors
* Denotes fund is included in Section II

www.thestreetratings.com

RISK			NET ASSETS		ASSET							FUND MANAGER		MINIMUM		LOADS	
Risk Rating/Pts	3 Yr Avg Standard Deviation	Avg Duration	NAV As of 2/28/17	Total $(Mil)	Cash %	Gov. Bond %	Muni. Bond %	Corp. Bond %	Other %	Portfolio Turnover Ratio	Avg Coupon Rate	Manager Quality Pct	Manager Tenure (Years)	Initial Purch. $	Additional Purch. $	Front End Load	Back End Load
C /5.4	3.0	6.5	10.27	9	1	0	98	0	1	9	5.0	23	6	3,000	100	0.0	0.0
C /5.3	3.0	6.5	10.33	19	1	0	98	0	1	9	5.0	56	6	100,000	0	0.0	0.0
D- /1.5	5.7	N/A	21.83	118	5	0	0	54	41	37	0.0	95	2	3,000	100	4.8	0.0
D- /1.5	5.7	N/A	21.79	88	5	0	0	54	41	37	0.0	93	2	3,000	100	0.0	0.0
D- /1.5	5.7	N/A	21.86	206	5	0	0	54	41	37	0.0	95	2	100,000	0	0.0	0.0
U /	N/A	N/A	21.92	N/A	5	0	0	54	41	37	0.0	N/A	2	5,000,000	0	0.0	0.0
C- /3.6	3.5	7.3	10.85	320	0	0	99	0	1	25	4.4	62	6	3,000	100	4.2	0.0
C- /3.7	3.5	7.3	10.83	32	0	0	99	0	1	25	4.4	26	6	3,000	100	0.0	0.0
C- /3.7	3.5	7.3	10.84	62	0	0	99	0	1	25	4.4	36	6	3,000	100	0.0	0.0
C- /3.7	3.5	7.3	10.86	376	0	0	99	0	1	25	4.4	68	6	100,000	0	0.0	0.0
C- /3.3	3.7	7.4	11.35	298	0	0	99	0	1	9	5.1	34	10	3,000	100	4.2	0.0
C- /3.4	3.7	7.4	11.29	23	0	0	99	0	1	9	5.1	13	10	3,000	100	0.0	0.0
C- /3.3	3.7	7.4	11.32	51	0	0	99	0	1	9	5.1	18	10	3,000	100	0.0	0.0
C- /3.4	3.7	7.4	11.32	207	0	0	99	0	1	9	5.1	51	10	100,000	0	0.0	0.0
C /5.0	3.1	6.0	10.13	52	3	0	96	0	1	11	4.7	10	20	3,000	100	3.0	0.0
C /5.1	3.1	6.0	10.07	4	3	0	96	0	1	11	4.7	3	20	3,000	100	0.0	0.0
C /5.0	3.1	6.0	10.11	7	3	0	96	0	1	11	4.7	5	20	3,000	100	0.0	0.0
C /5.0	3.1	6.0	10.14	144	3	0	96	0	1	11	4.7	13	20	100,000	0	0.0	0.0
C- /3.2	3.8	7.7	10.77	133	1	0	98	0	1	16	4.7	36	6	3,000	100	4.2	0.0
C- /3.2	3.8	7.7	10.72	21	1	0	98	0	1	16	4.7	12	6	3,000	100	0.0	0.0
C- /3.2	3.8	7.7	10.73	35	1	0	98	0	1	16	4.7	19	6	3,000	100	0.0	0.0
C- /3.2	3.8	7.7	10.75	157	1	0	98	0	1	16	4.7	52	6	100,000	0	0.0	0.0
C- /4.0	3.5	4.6	17.22	484	2	0	0	69	29	15	0.0	98	11	3,000	100	4.8	0.0
C- /4.0	3.5	4.6	17.24	263	2	0	0	69	29	15	0.0	96	11	3,000	100	0.0	0.0
C- /4.0	3.5	4.6	17.23	2,069	2	0	0	69	29	15	0.0	98	11	100,000	0	0.0	0.0
C- /4.0	3.5	4.6	17.35	2	2	0	0	69	29	15	0.0	95	11	0	0	0.0	0.0
U /	N/A	4.6	17.24	6	2	0	0	69	29	15	0.0	N/A	11	5,000,000	0	0.0	0.0
C- /3.6	3.2	N/A	9.84	762	2	0	96	0	2	28	0.0	59	4	3,000	100	2.5	0.0
C- /3.6	3.2	N/A	9.84	121	2	0	96	0	2	28	0.0	25	4	3,000	100	0.0	0.0
C- /3.5	3.2	N/A	9.84	35	2	0	96	0	2	28	0.0	31	4	3,000	100	0.0	0.0
C- /3.5	3.3	N/A	9.85	2,343	2	0	96	0	2	28	0.0	65	4	100,000	0	0.0	0.0
A /9.5	0.8	1.2	9.85	101	4	8	1	44	43	43	4.9	64	13	3,000	100	2.3	0.0
A+ /9.6	0.8	1.2	9.89	31	4	8	1	44	43	43	4.9	30	13	3,000	100	0.0	0.0
A /9.5	0.8	1.2	9.86	364	4	8	1	44	43	43	4.9	70	13	100,000	0	0.0	0.0
A /9.5	0.8	1.2	9.87	N/A	4	8	1	44	43	43	4.9	46	13	0	0	0.0	0.0
U /	N/A	1.2	9.88	95	4	8	1	44	43	43	4.9	N/A	13	5,000,000	0	0.0	0.0
A /9.3	0.9	1.9	10.05	190	0	0	99	0	1	24	3.8	29	15	3,000	100	2.5	0.0
A /9.3	0.9	1.9	10.03	11	0	0	99	0	1	24	3.8	13	15	3,000	100	0.0	0.0
A /9.3	0.9	1.9	10.04	13	0	0	99	0	1	24	3.8	18	15	3,000	100	0.0	0.0
A /9.3	1.0	1.9	10.06	433	0	0	99	0	1	24	3.8	32	15	100,000	0	0.0	0.0
D /2.2	4.8	4.3	10.66	177	2	4	0	78	16	56	5.5	33	17	3,000	100	4.3	0.0
D /2.2	4.8	4.3	10.60	81	2	4	0	78	16	56	5.5	13	17	3,000	100	0.0	0.0
D /2.2	4.8	4.3	10.65	481	2	4	0	78	16	56	5.5	50	17	100,000	0	0.0	0.0
D /2.2	4.8	4.3	10.70	7	2	4	0	78	16	56	5.5	26	17	0	0	0.0	0.0
U /	N/A	4.3	10.67	29	2	4	0	78	16	56	5.5	N/A	17	5,000,000	0	0.0	0.0
U /	N/A	N/A	9.93	12	0	0	100	0	0	59	0.0	N/A	3	3,000	100	3.0	0.0
U /	N/A	N/A	9.93	2	0	0	100	0	0	59	0.0	N/A	3	3,000	100	0.0	0.0
U /	N/A	N/A	9.94	71	0	0	100	0	0	59	0.0	N/A	3	100,000	0	0.0	0.0
E+ /0.8	6.7	3.1	20.76	101	8	0	0	86	6	42	0.0	91	7	3,000	100	4.8	0.0
E+ /0.8	6.7	3.1	20.73	86	8	0	0	86	6	42	0.0	86	7	3,000	100	0.0	0.0
E+ /0.8	6.7	3.1	20.77	434	8	0	0	86	6	42	0.0	92	7	100,000	0	0.0	0.0
U /	N/A	3.1	20.81	8	8	0	0	86	6	42	0.0	N/A	7	5,000,000	0	0.0	0.0

Fund Type	Fund Name	Ticker Symbol	Overall Investment Rating	Phone	Performance Rating/Pts	Total Return % through 2/28/17					Incl. in Returns	
									Annualized		Dividend Yield	Expense Ratio
						3 Mo	6 Mo	1Yr / Pct	3Yr / Pct	5Yr / Pct		
LP	Nuveen Symphony Floating Rt Inc A	NFRAX	B	(800) 257-8787	B- / 7.3	2.83	4.71	13.27 /86	3.09 /63	5.08 /85	5.02	0.96
LP	Nuveen Symphony Floating Rt Inc C	NFFCX	B	(800) 257-8787	B- / 7.3	2.65	4.33	12.43 /84	2.32 /48	4.28 /76	4.44	1.71
LP	Nuveen Symphony Floating Rt Inc I	NFRIX	A	(800) 257-8787	B+ / 8.3	2.89	4.83	13.54 /86	3.34 /66	5.34 /87	5.41	0.70
LP	Nuveen Symphony Floating Rt Inc R6	NFRFX	U	(800) 257-8787	U /	2.90	4.89	13.66 /86	--	—	5.41	0.68
COH	Nuveen Symphony High Yield Bond A	NSYAX	D	(800) 257-8787	B- / 7.4	5.48	7.36	19.81 /96	2.33 /49	—	5.12	1.61
COH	Nuveen Symphony High Yield Bond	NSYCX	D	(800) 257-8787	B / 7.9	5.31	7.00	19.00 /95	1.56 /36	—	4.69	2.34
COH	Nuveen Symphony High Yield Bond I	NSYIX	C-	(800) 257-8787	B+ / 8.9	5.54	7.49	20.11 /96	2.58 /53	—	5.62	1.36
COH	Nuveen Symphony High Yield Bond	NSYFX	U	(800) 257-8787	U /	5.66	7.57	--	--	—	0.00	1.32
MUS	Nuveen TN Muni Bond A	FTNTX	C-	(800) 257-8787	C+ / 5.8	2.32	-2.93	0.08 /23	3.57 /88	3.08 /81	3.15	0.82
MUN	Nuveen TN Muni Bond C	FTNDX	C	(800) 257-8787	C+ / 6.2	2.11	-3.41	-0.72 / 7	2.70 /77	—	2.47	1.61
MUS ●	Nuveen TN Muni Bond C2	FTNCX	C+	(800) 257-8787	C+ / 6.8	2.18	-3.28	-0.47 /10	2.98 /82	2.52 /71	2.73	1.37
MUS	Nuveen TN Muni Bond I	FTNRX	B+	(800) 257-8787	B / 8.1	2.37	-2.91	0.28 /32	3.75 /90	3.29 /85	3.50	0.62
MUS	Nuveen VA Muni Bond A	FVATX	C+	(800) 257-8787	C+ / 6.4	2.23	-2.97	0.46 /36	3.86 /91	2.90 /78	2.83	0.79
MUN	Nuveen VA Muni Bond C	FVCCX	B-	(800) 257-8787	C+ / 6.9	2.02	-3.28	-0.34 /12	3.03 /82	—	2.14	1.59
MUS ●	Nuveen VA Muni Bond C2	FVACX	B	(800) 257-8787	B- / 7.2	1.99	-3.26	-0.11 /16	3.26 /85	2.33 /67	2.38	1.34
MUS	Nuveen VA Muni Bond I	NMVAX	A	(800) 257-8787	B+ / 8.6	2.28	-2.81	0.71 /40	4.07 /93	3.10 /82	3.13	0.59
MUS	Nuveen WI Muni Bond A	FWIAX	D-	(800) 257-8787	C / 5.0	1.05	-4.82	-1.57 / 1	3.77 /91	2.42 /69	3.29	0.86
MUN	Nuveen WI Muni Bond C	FWCCX	D	(800) 257-8787	C+ / 5.7	0.85	-5.20	-2.33 / 0	2.97 /81	—	2.62	1.66
MUS ●	Nuveen WI Muni Bond C2	FWICX	D+	(800) 257-8787	C+ / 6.2	0.91	-5.18	-2.12 / 1	3.18 /84	1.84 /55	2.85	1.42
MUS	Nuveen WI Muni Bond I	FWIRX	C+	(800) 257-8787	B / 7.6	1.11	-4.79	-1.44 / 2	3.99 /93	2.60 /73	3.65	0.66
COI	NY 529 CSP Direct Bd Mkt Idx Port		D+	(800) 662-7447	C / 4.5	1.23	-2.37	1.35 /43	2.48 /51	2.06 /43	0.00	0.25
GEI	NY 529 CSP Direct Inf-Prot Secs		E+	(800) 662-7447	C / 4.3	1.40	-0.48	3.35 /59	1.83 /40	0.69 /23	0.00	0.25
COH	Oaktree High Yield Bond Adv	OHYDX	U		U /	4.02	3.76	16.98 /92	--	—	5.09	4.14
COH	Oaktree High Yield Bond Inst	OHYIX	U		U /	3.98	3.89	17.27 /92	--	—	5.33	3.89
USA	OH CollegeAdv 529 BR GNMA Opt A		D+	(800) 441-7762	D / 1.7	0.16	-1.28	0.08 /21	1.76 /39	1.49 /34	0.00	1.08
USA	OH CollegeAdv 529 BR GNMA Opt C		C-	(800) 441-7762	D / 2.1	0.00	-1.60	-0.60 / 8	0.99 /27	0.74 /24	0.00	1.83
MUH	OH CollegeAdv 529 BR Hi Yd Bd Opt		B-	(800) 441-7762	A+ / 9.8	4.70	5.53	17.67 /99	3.63 /89	6.39 /99	0.00	1.21
MUH	OH CollegeAdv 529 BR Hi Yd Bd Opt		B-	(800) 441-7762	A+ / 9.8	4.43	5.11	16.78 /99	2.83 /79	5.57 /99	0.00	1.96
USS	OH CollegeAdv 529 BR Inf Pr Bd Op		E	(800) 441-7762	E / 0.5	1.00	-0.65	2.97 /56	0.67 /23	-0.07 / 4	0.00	0.93
USS	OH CollegeAdv 529 BR Inf Pr Bd Op		E	(800) 441-7762	D- / 1.4	0.88	-0.95	2.32 /52	-0.06 / 5	-0.80 / 2	0.00	1.68
MMT	OH CollegeAdv 529 BR Mny Mkt Opt		D+	(800) 441-7762	E+ / 0.7	0.02	0.04	0.09 /22	0.04 / 9	0.02 / 8	0.09	N/A
MMT	OH CollegeAdv 529 BR Mny Mkt Opt		D+	(800) 441-7762	E+ / 0.7	0.02	0.04	0.09 /22	0.04 / 9	0.02 / 8	0.09	N/A
GEI	OH CollegeAdv 529 BR WF TR Bd		D-	(800) 441-7762	D / 2.0	0.88	-2.31	0.96 /39	1.94 /42	1.90 /41	0.00	1.24
GEI	OH CollegeAdv 529 BR WF TR Bd		D-	(800) 441-7762	D+ / 2.4	0.76	-2.68	0.25 /27	1.19 /31	1.16 /29	0.00	1.99
MUS	Oklahoma Municipal	OKMUX	D	(800) 601-5593	C / 4.6	1.74	-3.35	-0.40 /11	2.65 /76	2.21 /64	2.33	1.19
* GEI	Old Westbury Fixed Income	OWFIX	D	(800) 607-2200	D / 2.0	0.62	-1.60	-0.12 /16	0.83 /25	0.97 /27	1.33	0.74
* MUN	Old Westbury Muni Bond	OWMBX	C-	(800) 607-2200	C- / 3.0	1.52	-2.15	-0.83 / 6	1.11 /38	1.02 /36	1.13	0.70
* MUS	Oppenheimer Rochester CA Muni A	OPCAX	A-	(888) 470-0862	A / 9.3	2.23	-1.29	4.11 /71	5.61 /98	5.51 /99	4.97	1.22
MUS ●	Oppenheimer Rochester CA Muni B	OCABX	A	(888) 470-0862	A / 9.5	2.03	-1.67	3.31 /67	4.82 /97	4.66 /97	4.43	1.98
MUS	Oppenheimer Rochester CA Muni C	OCACX	A	(888) 470-0862	A / 9.5	2.05	-1.79	3.22 /66	4.80 /97	4.71 /97	4.47	1.97
MUS	Oppenheimer Rochester CA Muni Y	OCAYX	A	(888) 470-0862	A+ / 9.9	2.29	-1.18	4.36 /72	5.87 /98	5.76 /99	5.47	0.96
* MUH	Oppeneheimer Rochester Hi Yld Mun	ORNAX	B+	(888) 470-0862	A+ / 9.9	4.15	-1.02	7.13 /81	7.47 /99	6.59 /99	5.97	0.99
MUH ●	Oppeneheimer Rochester Hi Yld Mun	ORNBX	B+	(888) 470-0862	A+ / 9.9	3.93	-1.38	6.44 /79	6.68 /99	5.80 /99	5.48	1.74
MUH	Oppeneheimer Rochester Hi Yld Mun	ORNCX	B+	(888) 470-0862	A+ / 9.9	3.83	-1.39	6.36 /78	6.65 /99	5.79 /99	5.54	1.74
MUH	Oppeneheimer Rochester Hi Yld Mun	ORNYX	B+	(888) 470-0862	A+ / 9.9	4.04	-0.95	7.30 /82	7.64 /99	6.76 /99	6.43	0.84
MUS	Oppenheimer Rochester LT CA	OLCAX	B+	(888) 470-0862	C+ / 5.8	1.53	-1.01	2.29 /60	2.56 /75	2.55 /71	3.48	0.91
MUS ●	Oppenheimer Rochester LT CA	OLCBX	B	(888) 470-0862	C / 5.0	1.29	-1.64	1.45 /51	1.70 /54	1.68 /51	2.68	1.69
MUS	Oppenheimer Rochester LT CA	OLCCX	B-	(888) 470-0862	C / 5.3	1.35	-1.38	1.53 /52	1.80 /57	1.78 /53	2.81	1.67
MUS	Oppenheimer Rochester LT CA	OLCYX	A+	(888) 470-0862	B- / 7.4	1.58	-0.89	2.53 /62	2.80 /79	2.79 /76	3.80	0.67
MUS	Oppenheimer Rochester NJ Muni A	ONJAX	C+	(888) 470-0862	B+ / 8.5	1.75	-1.17	3.98 /71	4.86 /97	3.11 /82	4.39	0.97
MUS ●	Oppenheimer Rochester NJ Muni B	ONJBX	B	(888) 470-0862	A- / 9.0	1.55	-1.54	3.17 /66	4.11 /94	2.31 /66	3.82	1.74
MUS	Oppenheimer Rochester NJ Muni C	ONJCX	B	(888) 470-0862	A- / 9.0	1.56	-1.54	3.09 /66	4.08 /93	2.33 /67	3.84	1.72

● Denotes fund is closed to new investors
* Denotes fund is included in Section II

www.thestreetratings.com

RISK			NET ASSETS		ASSET					Portfolio Turnover Ratio	Avg Coupon Rate	FUND MANAGER		MINIMUM		LOADS	
Risk Rating/Pts	3 Yr Avg Standard Deviation	Avg Dura-tion	NAV As of 2/28/17	Total $(Mil)	Cash %	Gov. Bond %	Muni. Bond %	Corp. Bond %	Other %			Manager Quality Pct	Manager Tenure (Years)	Initial Purch. $	Additional Purch. $	Front End Load	Back End Load
C /4.7	3.2	0.9	19.99	249	4	0	0	78	18	40	0.0	88	6	3,000	100	3.0	0.0
C /4.7	3.2	0.9	19.99	86	4	0	0	78	18	40	0.0	82	6	3,000	100	0.0	0.0
C /4.7	3.2	0.9	20.00	1,103	4	0	0	78	18	40	0.0	89	6	100,000	0	0.0	0.0
U /	N/A	0.9	20.02	2	4	0	0	78	18	40	0.0	N/A	6	5,000,000	0	0.0	0.0
E+ /0.7	6.6	N/A	17.12	2	0	0	0	92	8	74	0.0	2	5	3,000	100	4.8	0.0
E+ /0.7	6.6	N/A	17.07	1	0	0	0	92	8	74	0.0	1	5	3,000	100	0.0	0.0
E+ /0.7	6.6	N/A	17.12	9	0	0	0	92	8	74	0.0	2	5	100,000	0	0.0	0.0
U /	N/A	N/A	17.17	1	0	0	0	92	8	74	0.0	N/A	5	5,000,000	0	0.0	0.0
C /4.3	3.4	6.9	11.68	270	1	0	98	0	1	10	4.6	42	10	3,000	100	4.2	0.0
C /4.3	3.4	6.9	11.64	22	1	0	98	0	1	10	4.6	14	10	3,000	100	0.0	0.0
C /4.3	3.4	6.9	11.66	72	1	0	98	0	1	10	4.6	20	10	3,000	100	0.0	0.0
C /4.3	3.4	6.9	11.66	98	1	0	98	0	1	10	4.6	53	10	100,000	0	0.0	0.0
C /4.6	3.3	6.8	10.98	193	0	0	99	0	1	15	4.2	62	1	3,000	100	4.2	0.0
C /4.7	3.2	6.8	10.97	21	0	0	99	0	1	15	4.2	26	1	3,000	100	0.0	0.0
C /4.6	3.3	6.8	10.96	38	0	0	99	0	1	15	4.2	33	1	3,000	100	0.0	0.0
C /4.6	3.2	6.8	10.95	163	0	0	99	0	1	15	4.2	68	1	100,000	0	0.0	0.0
C- /3.4	3.8	6.8	10.40	60	1	0	98	0	1	10	4.7	33	6	3,000	100	4.2	0.0
C- /3.4	3.8	6.8	10.40	7	1	0	98	0	1	10	4.7	11	6	3,000	100	0.0	0.0
C- /3.4	3.9	6.8	10.40	10	1	0	98	0	1	10	4.7	15	6	3,000	100	0.0	0.0
C- /3.4	3.9	6.8	10.42	47	1	0	98	0	1	10	4.7	43	6	100,000	0	0.0	0.0
C /5.1	3.1	N/A	16.50	260	0	46	1	25	28	0	0.0	33	8	25	25	0.0	0.0
D+ /2.9	4.1	N/A	16.64	234	1	98	0	0	1	0	0.0	8	N/A	25	25	0.0	0.0
U /	N/A	N/A	10.21	1	0	0	0	0	100	46	0.0	N/A	3	25,000	2,500	0.0	0.0
U /	N/A	N/A	10.21	26	0	0	0	0	100	46	0.0	N/A	3	1,000,000	100,000	0.0	0.0
B+ /8.6	1.7	N/A	12.35	5	0	4	0	0	96	0	0.0	74	N/A	25	25	4.0	0.0
B+ /8.6	1.7	N/A	11.68	3	0	4	0	0	96	0	0.0	53	N/A	25	25	0.0	0.0
D- /1.2	5.5	N/A	18.71	21	4	0	0	79	17	0	0.0	94	N/A	25	25	4.0	0.0
D- /1.2	5.5	N/A	17.68	8	4	0	0	79	17	0	0.0	91	N/A	25	25	0.0	0.0
C- /3.3	3.9	N/A	12.15	8	0	99	0	0	1	0	0.0	12	N/A	25	25	4.0	0.0
C- /3.4	3.9	N/A	11.49	4	0	99	0	0	1	0	0.0	4	N/A	25	25	0.0	0.0
A+ /9.9	N/A	N/A	1.00	91	100	0	0	0	0	0	0.1	40	8	25	25	0.0	0.0
A+ /9.9	N/A	N/A	1.00	31	100	0	0	0	0	0	0.1	40	8	25	25	0.0	0.0
C+ /5.8	2.9	N/A	12.68	34	0	33	0	20	47	0	0.0	18	N/A	25	25	4.0	0.0
C /5.5	3.0	N/A	12.00	14	0	33	0	20	47	0	0.0	6	N/A	25	25	0.0	0.0
C /4.9	3.2	5.0	11.55	47	3	0	96	0	1	11	4.7	18	21	1,000	50	2.5	0.0
B /7.9	1.9	8.5	11.11	780	0	59	1	30	10	67	0.0	14	5	1,000	100	0.0	0.0
B /7.7	2.4	6.3	11.85	2,055	0	5	94	0	1	44	0.0	7	19	1,000	100	0.0	0.0
C- /3.3	4.0	5.6	8.27	869	0	0	100	0	0	15	0.0	86	15	1,000	50	4.8	0.0
C- /3.3	4.0	5.6	8.28	1	0	0	100	0	0	15	0.0	79	15	1,000	50	0.0	0.0
C- /3.3	3.9	5.6	8.23	243	0	0	100	0	0	15	0.0	79	15	1,000	50	0.0	0.0
C- /3.3	3.9	5.6	8.27	191	0	0	100	0	0	15	0.0	88	15	1,000	50	0.0	0.0
D /1.7	5.0	6.8	7.09	3,110	0	0	99	0	1	20	0.0	91	15	1,000	50	4.8	0.0
D /1.7	5.0	6.8	7.13	20	0	0	99	0	1	20	0.0	87	15	1,000	50	0.0	0.0
D /1.7	5.0	6.8	7.06	1,294	0	0	99	0	1	20	0.0	87	15	1,000	50	0.0	0.0
D /1.7	5.0	6.8	7.08	1,045	0	0	99	0	1	20	0.0	92	15	1,000	50	0.0	0.0
B- /7.2	2.7	3.5	3.20	255	0	0	99	0	1	13	0.0	59	13	1,000	50	2.3	0.0
B- /7.3	2.6	3.5	3.30	N/A	0	0	99	0	1	13	0.0	22	13	1,000	50	0.0	0.0
C+ /6.8	2.8	3.5	3.19	130	0	0	99	0	1	13	0.0	25	13	1,000	50	0.0	0.0
B- /7.1	2.7	3.5	3.21	166	0	0	99	0	1	13	0.0	67	13	1,000	50	0.0	0.0
D+ /2.5	4.5	5.4	9.38	229	0	0	100	0	0	11	0.0	84	15	1,000	50	4.8	0.0
D+ /2.5	4.4	5.4	9.41	2	0	0	100	0	0	11	0.0	77	15	1,000	50	0.0	0.0
D+ /2.5	4.5	5.4	9.39	113	0	0	100	0	0	11	0.0	75	15	1,000	50	0.0	0.0

Fund Type	Fund Name	Ticker Symbol	Overall Investment Rating	Phone	Performance Rating/Pts	3 Mo	6 Mo	1Yr / Pct	3Yr / Pct	5Yr / Pct	Dividend Yield	Expense Ratio
					PERFORMANCE — Total Return % through 2/28/17				Annualized		Incl. in Returns	
MUS	Oppenheimer Rochester NJ Muni Y	ONJYX	A-	(888) 470-0862	A+ / 9.7	1.78	-1.10	4.13 /71	5.01 /97	3.27 /84	4.75	0.81
MUS	Oppenheimer Rochester PA Muni A	OPATX	A	(888) 470-0862	A+ / 9.7	2.83	0.07	5.37 /75	6.05 /99	3.84 /91	5.21	0.97
MUS ●	Oppenheimer Rochester PA Muni B	OPABX	A	(888) 470-0862	A+ / 9.8	2.64	-0.21	4.68 /73	5.29 /98	3.05 /81	4.71	1.73
MUS	Oppenheimer Rochester PA Muni C	OPACX	A	(888) 470-0862	A+ / 9.8	2.64	-0.21	4.70 /73	5.27 /98	3.07 /81	4.73	1.72
MUS	Oppenheimer Rochester PA Muni Y	OPAYX	A	(888) 470-0862	A+ / 9.9	2.86	0.24	5.62 /76	6.23 /99	4.01 /93	5.62	0.82
GEI	Oppenheimer Rochester UI Sht Dur	OSDIX	U	(888) 470-0862	U /	0.29	1.74	2.49 /53	--	--	1.06	0.37
GL	Oppenheimer Rochester UI Sht Dur	OSDYX	C+	(888) 470-0862	D+ / 2.4	0.29	0.55	1.29 /43	0.71 /23	0.64 /23	1.09	0.39
USL	Oppenheimer 529 BS FI Port 4		B-	(888) 470-0862	C- / 3.5	0.78	-0.48	2.16 /50	1.45 /34	1.26 /31	0.00	0.68
USL	Oppenheimer 529 BS FI Port A		C-	(888) 470-0862	D / 1.9	1.02	-0.29	2.98 /56	1.13 /30	0.83 /25	0.00	0.78
USL	Oppenheimer 529 BS FI Port C		C	(888) 470-0862	D+ / 2.6	0.75	-0.59	2.59 /54	0.80 /24	0.54 /22	0.00	1.03
USL	Oppenheimer 529 BS FI Port G		C+	(888) 470-0862	C- / 3.2	0.96	-0.31	2.81 /55	1.11 /29	0.82 /25	0.00	0.78
USL	Oppenheimer 529 BS FI Port H		B-	(888) 470-0862	C- / 3.6	0.93	-0.20	3.07 /57	1.34 /33	1.06 /28	0.00	0.53
USL	Oppenheimer 529 BS Idx FI Port 4		C+	(888) 470-0862	C- / 3.2	0.74	-1.15	0.96 /39	1.48 /35	1.32 /32	0.00	0.22
GEI	Oppenheimer 529 SE AC Div Bond A		D-	(888) 470-0862	D / 1.8	0.94	-2.47	1.11 /41	1.90 /41	1.56 /35	0.00	1.00
GEI	Oppenheimer 529 SE AC Div Bond B		D-	(888) 470-0862	D+ / 2.4	0.80	-2.80	0.37 /30	1.15 /30	0.80 /25	0.00	2.06
GEI	Oppenheimer 529 SE AC Div Bond C		D-	(888) 470-0862	D+ / 2.4	0.80	-2.79	0.43 /32	1.17 /30	0.80 /25	0.00	2.06
GES	Oppenheimer 529 SE Global Str Inc		D	(888) 470-0862	C / 4.8	3.30	1.65	9.35 /77	2.33 /49	3.15 /60	0.00	1.02
GES	Oppenheimer 529 SE Global Str Inc		D+	(888) 470-0862	C / 5.5	3.10	1.27	8.53 /75	1.57 /36	2.38 /48	0.00	1.94
GES	Oppenheimer 529 SE Global Str Inc		D+	(888) 470-0862	C / 5.5	3.12	1.27	8.55 /75	1.57 /36	2.38 /48	0.00	1.94
GES	Oppenheimer 529 SE Inst Mny Mkt A		U	(888) 470-0862	U /	--	--	--	--	--	0.00	0.35
GES	Oppenheimer 529 SE Inst Mny Mkt C		U	(888) 470-0862	U /	--	--	--	--	--	0.00	1.65
GEI	Oppenheimer 529 SE School Yrs 3		C+	(888) 470-0862	C- / 3.8	1.53	0.57	4.77 /66	1.09 /29	1.54 /35	0.00	1.95
GEI	Oppenheimer 529 SE School Yrs A		C	(888) 470-0862	C- / 3.1	1.73	0.95	5.58 /69	1.87 /41	2.31 /46	0.00	0.94
GEI	Oppenheimer 529 SE Ultra Cons 3		C+	(888) 470-0862	C / 5.5	2.27	1.45	7.15 /73	1.84 /40	2.61 /51	0.00	1.91
GEI	Oppenheimer 529 SE Ultra Cons A		C	(888) 470-0862	C / 4.8	2.53	1.85	7.99 /74	2.59 /54	3.38 /64	0.00	1.01
GES	Oppenheimer 529 TEP School Yrs		B+	(888) 470-0862	C / 4.4	1.38	0.61	3.86 /62	1.70 /38	2.03 /43	0.00	0.54
* GEI	Oppenheimer Core Bond A	OPIGX	D	(888) 470-0862	C- / 3.3	1.37	-1.82	2.56 /54	2.79 /58	3.56 /67	2.30	0.96
GEI ●	Oppenheimer Core Bond B	OIGBX	C-	(888) 470-0862	C- / 3.9	1.02	-2.36	1.73 /46	1.93 /42	2.73 /53	1.59	1.74
GEI	Oppenheimer Core Bond C	OPBCX	C-	(888) 470-0862	C- / 3.9	1.02	-2.35	1.74 /47	1.93 /42	2.73 /53	1.60	1.72
COI	Oppenheimer Core Bond I	OPBIX	B	(888) 470-0862	C+ / 5.9	1.31	-1.79	2.93 /56	3.10 /63	--	2.77	0.52
GEI	Oppenheimer Core Bond R	OPBNX	C	(888) 470-0862	C / 4.7	1.15	-2.11	2.25 /51	2.44 /51	3.24 /61	2.10	1.21
GEI	Oppenheimer Core Bond Y	OPBYX	B-	(888) 470-0862	C+ / 5.6	1.29	-1.86	2.82 /55	3.00 /61	3.72 /69	2.67	0.71
COI	Oppenheimer Corporate Bond A	OFIAX	E+	(888) 470-0862	C / 4.4	2.24	-1.49	6.36 /71	2.93 /60	4.20 /75	2.54	1.04
COI	Oppenheimer Corporate Bond C	OFICX	D-	(888) 470-0862	C / 5.2	2.15	-1.85	5.57 /69	2.20 /46	3.45 /65	1.92	1.79
COI	Oppenheimer Corporate Bond I	OFIIX	C-	(888) 470-0862	B- / 7.0	2.35	-1.27	6.83 /72	3.42 /68	--	3.12	0.58
COI	Oppenheimer Corporate Bond R	OFINX	D	(888) 470-0862	C+ / 6.1	2.18	-1.61	6.09 /70	2.71 /56	3.96 /72	2.42	1.29
COI	Oppenheimer Corporate Bond Y	OFIYX	C-	(888) 470-0862	C+ / 6.8	2.40	-1.28	6.73 /72	3.25 /65	4.47 /78	2.92	0.78
EM	Oppenheimer Em Mkts Local Debt A	OEMAX	E	(888) 470-0862	C- / 3.5	7.20	1.72	15.90 /90	0.05 / 9	-0.79 / 2	9.60	1.69
EM	Oppenheimer Em Mkts Local Debt C	OEMCX	E	(888) 470-0862	C- / 4.1	6.85	1.20	14.88 /88	-0.73 / 3	-1.56 / 2	9.33	2.38
EM	Oppenheimer Em Mkts Local Debt I	OEMIX	E+	(888) 470-0862	C+ / 6.1	7.15	1.78	16.21 /91	0.41 /20	-0.48 / 3	10.50	1.11
EM	Oppenheimer Em Mkts Local Debt R	OEMNX	E+	(888) 470-0862	C / 5.0	7.13	1.59	15.62 /89	-0.20 / 4	-1.04 / 2	9.83	1.88
EM	Oppenheimer Em Mkts Local Debt Y	OEMYX	E+	(888) 470-0862	C+ / 6.0	7.12	1.87	16.25 /91	0.35 /19	-0.49 / 3	10.39	1.35
GL	Oppenheimer Global High Yield A	OGYAX	D	(888) 470-0862	C+ / 6.9	4.65	4.19	16.04 /90	2.65 /55	--	4.39	1.75
GL	Oppenheimer Global High Yield C	OGYCX	D+	(888) 470-0862	B- / 7.3	4.36	3.84	15.12 /89	1.91 /42	--	3.93	2.60
GL	Oppenheimer Global High Yield I	OGYIX	C+	(888) 470-0862	B+ / 8.5	4.73	4.37	16.44 /91	3.01 /61	--	4.94	1.28
GL	Oppenheimer Global High Yield R	OGYNX	C-	(888) 470-0862	B / 7.9	4.58	4.07	15.76 /90	2.40 /50	--	4.37	2.39
GL	Oppenheimer Global High Yield Y	OGYYX	C	(888) 470-0862	B+ / 8.5	4.72	4.35	16.39 /91	2.96 /60	--	4.90	1.51
* GES	Oppenheimer Global Strategic Inc A	OPSIX	D	(888) 470-0862	C / 4.9	3.34	1.68	9.42 /78	2.39 /50	3.22 /61	3.57	1.04
GES ●	Oppenheimer Global Strategic Inc B	OPSGX	D+	(888) 470-0862	C+ / 5.6	3.14	1.29	8.57 /75	1.62 /37	2.38 /48	3.00	1.79
GES	Oppenheimer Global Strategic Inc C	OSICX	D+	(888) 470-0862	C+ / 5.6	3.16	1.30	8.61 /76	1.62 /37	2.44 /49	3.01	1.79
GEI	Oppenheimer Global Strategic Inc I	OSIIX	C+	(888) 470-0862	B- / 7.2	3.46	1.90	9.92 /79	2.83 /58	3.58 /67	4.18	0.60
GES	Oppenheimer Global Strategic Inc R	OSINX	C	(888) 470-0862	C+ / 6.4	3.28	1.55	9.14 /77	2.14 /45	2.90 /56	3.50	1.29

● Denotes fund is closed to new investors
* Denotes fund is included in Section II

www.thestreetratings.com

RISK			NET ASSETS		ASSET					FUND MANAGER			MINIMUM		LOADS	
Risk Rating/Pts	3 Yr Avg Standard Deviation	Avg Dura-tion	NAV As of 2/28/17	Total $(Mil)	Cash %	Gov. Bond %	Muni. Bond %	Corp. Bond %	Other %	Portfolio Turnover Ratio	Avg Coupon Rate	Manager Quality Pct	Manager Tenure (Years)	Initial Purch. $	Additional Purch. $	Front End Load	Back End Load
D+ / 2.6	4.4	5.4	9.39	33	0	0	100	0	0	11	0.0	85	15	1,000	50	0.0	0.0
C- / 3.2	4.0	6.6	10.40	506	0	0	100	0	0	6	0.0	91	15	1,000	50	4.8	0.0
C- / 3.2	4.0	6.6	10.40	4	0	0	100	0	0	6	0.0	87	15	1,000	50	0.0	0.0
C- / 3.2	4.0	6.6	10.38	208	0	0	100	0	0	6	0.0	87	15	1,000	50	0.0	0.0
C- / 3.3	4.0	6.6	10.41	42	0	0	100	0	0	6	0.0	92	15	1,000	50	0.0	0.0
U /	N/A	0.4	5.07	10	0	0	0	0	100	90	0.0	N/A	6	5,000,000	0	0.0	0.0
A+ / 9.9	0.3	0.4	5.01	418	0	0	0	0	100	90	0.0	68	6	250,000	0	0.0	0.0
B+ / 8.8	1.5	N/A	10.39	28	0	0	0	0	100	0	0.0	68	10	25	15	0.0	0.0
B+ / 8.7	1.6	N/A	6.92	4	0	0	0	0	100	0	0.0	62	10	25	15	3.5	0.0
B+ / 8.8	1.5	N/A	6.74	8	0	0	0	0	100	0	0.0	52	10	25	15	0.0	0.0
B+ / 8.8	1.5	N/A	9.50	8	0	0	0	0	100	0	0.0	63	10	25	15	0.0	0.0
B+ / 8.8	1.5	N/A	9.73	4	0	0	0	0	100	0	0.0	69	10	25	15	0.0	0.0
B+ / 8.4	1.8	N/A	13.70	93	0	0	0	0	100	0	0.0	62	10	25	15	0.0	0.0
C+ / 6.1	2.9	N/A	18.17	3	0	0	0	0	100	0	0.0	19	12	250	25	4.8	0.0
C+ / 6.1	2.9	N/A	16.30	N/A	0	0	0	0	100	0	0.0	6	12	250	25	0.0	0.0
C+ / 6.2	2.9	N/A	16.36	1	0	0	0	0	100	0	0.0	7	12	250	25	0.0	0.0
C- / 3.8	3.6	N/A	43.84	12	0	0	0	0	100	0	0.0	69	12	250	25	4.8	0.0
C- / 3.8	3.6	N/A	39.94	N/A	0	0	0	0	100	0	0.0	36	12	250	25	0.0	0.0
C- / 3.8	3.6	N/A	39.99	3	0	0	0	0	100	0	0.0	36	12	250	25	0.0	0.0
U /	N/A	N/A	23.38	20	0	0	0	0	100	0	0.0	39	12	250	25	4.8	0.0
U /	N/A	N/A	22.16	6	0	0	0	0	100	0	0.0	37	12	250	25	0.0	0.0
B / 8.2	2.0	N/A	24.61	3	0	0	0	0	100	0	0.0	53	12	250	25	0.0	0.0
B / 8.2	2.0	N/A	27.61	8	0	0	0	0	100	0	0.0	74	12	250	25	4.8	0.0
C+ / 5.6	3.0	N/A	12.59	3	0	0	0	0	100	0	0.0	75	12	250	25	0.0	0.0
C+ / 5.7	3.0	N/A	13.79	9	0	0	0	0	100	0	0.0	83	12	250	25	4.8	0.0
B+ / 8.8	1.5	N/A	13.19	7	0	0	0	0	100	0	0.0	72	12	250	25	0.0	0.0
C+ / 6.1	2.9	2.1	6.81	601	1	3	0	50	46	85	0.0	58	8	1,000	0	4.8	0.0
C+ / 6.4	2.8	2.1	6.80	4	1	3	0	50	46	85	0.0	22	8	1,000	0	0.0	0.0
C+ / 6.5	2.8	2.1	6.81	123	1	3	0	50	46	85	0.0	22	8	1,000	0	0.0	0.0
C+ / 6.6	2.8	2.1	6.80	681	1	3	0	50	46	85	0.0	68	8	5,000,000	0	0.0	0.0
C+ / 6.3	2.9	2.1	6.80	66	1	3	0	50	46	85	0.0	41	8	1,000	0	0.0	0.0
C+ / 6.3	2.9	2.1	6.76	178	1	3	0	50	46	85	0.0	65	8	1,000	0	0.0	0.0
D+ / 2.7	4.1	7.0	10.73	131	6	0	0	91	3	73	0.0	19	7	1,000	50	4.8	0.0
D+ / 2.7	4.1	7.0	10.73	34	6	0	0	91	3	73	0.0	7	7	1,000	50	0.0	0.0
D+ / 2.7	4.0	7.0	10.73	N/A	6	0	0	91	3	73	0.0	35	7	5,000,000	0	0.0	0.0
D+ / 2.7	4.0	7.0	10.74	14	6	0	0	91	3	73	0.0	15	7	1,000	50	0.0	0.0
D+ / 2.7	4.1	7.0	10.73	12	6	0	0	91	3	73	0.0	29	7	1,000	50	0.0	0.0
E- / 0.2	10.9	4.7	7.17	47	0	72	0	27	1	108	0.0	89	2	1,000	0	4.8	0.0
E- / 0.2	10.8	4.7	7.17	11	0	72	0	27	1	108	0.0	84	2	1,000	0	0.0	0.0
E- / 0.2	10.8	4.7	7.16	6	0	72	0	27	1	108	0.0	91	2	5,000,000	0	0.0	0.0
E- / 0.2	10.9	4.7	7.17	2	0	72	0	27	1	108	0.0	88	2	1,000	0	0.0	0.0
E- / 0.2	10.8	4.7	7.17	26	0	72	0	27	1	108	0.0	91	2	0	0	0.0	0.0
D / 1.8	5.4	4.3	9.54	30	3	0	0	95	2	54	0.0	93	2	1,000	0	4.8	0.0
D / 1.8	5.4	4.3	9.53	7	3	0	0	95	2	54	0.0	89	2	1,000	0	0.0	0.0
D / 1.8	5.4	4.3	9.54	10	3	0	0	95	2	54	0.0	94	2	5,000,000	0	0.0	0.0
D / 1.8	5.4	4.3	9.54	1	3	0	0	95	2	54	0.0	92	2	1,000	0	0.0	0.0
D / 1.8	5.4	4.3	9.54	1	3	0	0	95	2	54	0.0	94	2	0	0	0.0	0.0
C- / 3.7	3.7	4.3	3.94	3,388	1	14	0	52	33	78	0.0	70	8	1,000	0	4.8	0.0
C- / 3.9	3.6	4.3	3.95	31	1	14	0	52	33	78	0.0	48	8	1,000	0	0.0	0.0
C- / 3.7	3.7	4.3	3.93	792	1	14	0	52	33	78	0.0	36	8	1,000	0	0.0	0.0
C- / 3.8	3.6	4.3	3.92	47	1	14	0	52	33	78	0.0	78	8	5,000,000	0	0.0	0.0
C- / 3.7	3.6	4.3	3.94	138	1	14	0	52	33	78	0.0	64	8	1,000	0	0.0	0.0

99 Pct = Best
0 Pct = Worst

Fund Type	Fund Name	Ticker Symbol	Overall Investment Rating	Phone	Performance Rating/Pts	3 Mo	6 Mo	1Yr / Pct	3Yr / Pct	5Yr / Pct	Dividend Yield	Expense Ratio
GES	Oppenheimer Global Strategic Inc Y	OSIYX	C+	(888) 470-0862	B- / 7.0	3.41	1.54	9.70 /78	2.56 /53	3.46 /65	4.00	0.79
MMT	Oppenheimer Govt Cash Reserves A	CRSXX	U	(888) 470-0862	U /	--	--	--	--	--	0.01	N/A
MMT ●	Oppenheimer Govt Cash Reserves B	CRBXX	U	(888) 470-0862	U /	--	--	--	--	--	0.01	N/A
MMT	Oppenheimer Govt Cash Reserves C	CSCXX	U	(888) 470-0862	U /	--	--	--	--	--	0.01	N/A
MMT	Oppenheimer Govt Cash Reserves R	CSNXX	U	(888) 470-0862	U /	--	--	--	--	--	0.01	N/A
MMT	Oppenheimer Govt Money Market A	OMBXX	U	(888) 470-0862	U /	--	--	--	--	--	0.01	N/A
MMT	Oppenheimer Govt Money Market Y	OMYXX	U	(888) 470-0862	U /	--	--	--	--	--	0.01	N/A
MMT	Oppenheimer Insti Govt MM E	IOEXX	C	(888) 470-0862	D- / 1.5	0.11	0.18	0.41 /31	0.23 /17	0.20 /18	0.41	N/A
MMT	Oppenheimer Insti Govt MM L	IOLXX	C-	(888) 470-0862	D- / 1.4	0.10	0.16	0.36 /30	0.18 /16	0.14 /17	0.36	N/A
* GL	Oppenheimer Intl Bond A	OIBAX	E+	(888) 470-0862	C- / 3.4	3.48	-1.44	9.42 /78	1.57 /36	1.55 /35	4.36	1.02
GL ●	Oppenheimer Intl Bond B	OIBBX	E+	(888) 470-0862	C- / 4.1	3.30	-1.65	8.62 /76	0.79 /24	0.74 /24	3.82	1.77
GL	Oppenheimer Intl Bond C	OIBCX	E+	(888) 470-0862	C- / 4.1	3.30	-1.65	8.63 /76	0.80 /24	0.81 /25	3.82	1.77
GL	Oppenheimer Intl Bond I	OIBIX	D-	(888) 470-0862	C+ / 6.1	3.60	-1.23	9.91 /79	2.01 /43	1.98 /42	5.02	0.57
GL	Oppenheimer Intl Bond R	OIBNX	E+	(888) 470-0862	C / 4.9	3.43	-1.57	9.17 /77	1.31 /32	1.24 /31	4.33	1.27
GL	Oppenheimer Intl Bond Y	OIBYX	D-	(888) 470-0862	C+ / 5.6	3.37	-1.32	9.50 /78	1.76 /39	1.77 /39	4.84	0.77
USS	Oppenheimer Limited Term Govt A	OPGVX	D	(888) 470-0862	E / 0.5	0.24	-0.36	0.24 /27	0.62 /22	0.78 /25	1.57	0.93
USS ●	Oppenheimer Limited Term Govt B	OGSBX	D	(888) 470-0862	E / 0.4	0.04	-0.75	-0.34 /12	-0.15 / 5	-0.04 / 5	0.79	1.69
USS	Oppenheimer Limited Term Govt C	OLTCX	D	(888) 470-0862	E / 0.4	0.04	-0.75	-0.56 / 9	-0.18 / 4	-0.04 / 5	0.80	1.67
USA	Oppenheimer Limited Term Govt I	OLTIX	C+	(888) 470-0862	D+ / 2.6	0.32	-0.20	0.79 /37	0.99 /27	--	1.93	0.48
USS	Oppenheimer Limited Term Govt R	OLTNX	C-	(888) 470-0862	D / 1.6	0.17	-0.51	0.17 /25	0.36 /19	0.49 /21	1.30	1.18
USS	Oppenheimer Limited Term Govt Y	OLTYX	C+	(888) 470-0862	D+ / 2.4	0.32	-0.21	0.55 /34	0.93 /26	1.12 /29	1.91	0.68
* USS	Oppenheimer Limited-Term Bond A	OUSGX	C+	(888) 470-0862	D+ / 2.6	0.63	0.26	2.79 /55	1.33 /32	1.62 /36	2.05	0.90
USS ●	Oppenheimer Limited-Term Bond B	UGTBX	C	(888) 470-0862	D / 2.2	0.65	0.07	1.95 /48	0.53 /21	0.84 /25	1.27	1.66
USS	Oppenheimer Limited-Term Bond C	OUSCX	C	(888) 470-0862	D+ / 2.3	0.65	0.07	1.96 /49	0.54 /21	0.84 /25	1.28	1.65
USL	Oppenheimer Limited-Term Bond I	OUSIX	B+	(888) 470-0862	C / 4.3	0.95	0.67	3.17 /58	1.74 /39	--	2.47	0.46
USS	Oppenheimer Limited-Term Bond R	OUSNX	C+	(888) 470-0862	C- / 3.0	0.56	0.11	2.48 /53	1.02 /28	1.34 /32	1.79	1.15
USS	Oppenheimer Limited-Term Bond Y	OUSYX	B+	(888) 470-0862	C- / 3.9	0.68	0.36	2.98 /56	1.51 /35	1.86 /40	2.28	0.65
* MUS	Oppenheimer Ltd Term NY Muni A	LTNYX	D-	(888) 470-0862	C / 4.7	2.18	0.00	2.22 /59	1.88 /59	1.21 /40	3.48	0.85
MUS ●	Oppenheimer Ltd Term NY Muni B	LTBBX	D-	(888) 470-0862	C- / 4.1	1.65	-0.38	1.46 /51	1.12 /38	0.35 /22	2.81	1.61
MUS	Oppenheimer Ltd Term NY Muni C	LTNCX	D-	(888) 470-0862	C- / 4.1	1.66	-0.38	1.47 /51	1.13 /39	0.39 /23	2.83	1.60
MUN	Oppenheimer Ltd Term NY Muni Y	LTBYX	C	(888) 470-0862	C+ / 6.7	2.24	0.12	2.47 /61	2.13 /66	1.45 /45	3.81	0.60
MUN ●	Oppenheimer Rochester AMT-Fr	OTFBX	A	(888) 470-0862	A+ / 9.8	2.78	-1.79	2.82 /64	5.53 /98	5.15 /98	4.78	1.73
MUN	Oppenheimer Rochester AMT-Fr	OMFCX	A	(888) 470-0862	A+ / 9.8	2.78	-1.93	2.83 /64	5.48 /98	5.18 /98	4.79	1.73
MUN	Oppenheimer Rochester AMT-Fr	OMFYX	A	(888) 470-0862	A+ / 9.9	3.17	-1.29	3.99 /71	6.61 /99	6.27 /99	5.77	0.73
* MUS	Oppenheimer Rochester AMT-Fr NY	OPNYX	B+	(888) 470-0862	A / 9.3	2.39	-1.80	4.42 /72	5.65 /98	3.89 /92	4.37	0.96
MUS ●	Oppenheimer Rochester AMT-Fr NY	ONYBX	B+	(888) 470-0862	A+ / 9.6	2.19	-2.17	3.61 /69	4.85 /97	3.05 /81	3.79	1.73
MUS	Oppenheimer Rochester AMT-Fr NY	ONYCX	B+	(888) 470-0862	A / 9.5	2.20	-2.26	3.54 /68	4.82 /97	3.09 /81	3.81	1.71
MUN	Oppenheimer Rochester AMT-Fr NY	ONYYX	A-	(888) 470-0862	A+ / 9.9	2.44	-1.77	4.57 /73	5.89 /98	4.13 /94	4.82	0.71
* MUN	Oppenheimer Rochester AMT-Free	OPTAX	A-	(888) 470-0862	A+ / 9.7	3.10	-1.40	3.73 /69	6.34 /99	6.00 /99	5.25	0.98
MUS ●	Oppenheimer Rochester AZ Muni A	ORAZX	B	(888) 470-0862	B+ / 8.7	2.14	1.55	6.14 /78	4.48 /96	2.83 /77	4.11	1.60
MUS ●	Oppenheimer Rochester AZ Muni B	ORBZX	B+	(888) 470-0862	A- / 9.2	1.95	1.17	5.35 /75	3.70 /90	2.07 /60	3.57	2.38
MUS ●	Oppenheimer Rochester AZ Muni C	ORCZX	B+	(888) 470-0862	A- / 9.2	1.95	1.17	5.35 /75	3.70 /90	2.06 /60	3.57	2.36
MUN ●	Oppenheimer Rochester AZ Muni Y	ORYZX	A	(888) 470-0862	A+ / 9.7	2.23	1.55	6.24 /78	4.53 /96	2.89 /78	4.31	1.34
MUN	Oppenheimer Rochester Int Term Mu	ORRWX	C	(888) 470-0862	C+ / 6.8	2.39	-3.72	-0.08 /16	3.65 /89	2.78 /76	1.99	1.18
MUN	Oppenheimer Rochester Int Term Mu	ORRCX	C-	(888) 470-0862	C+ / 6.2	2.20	-4.10	-0.85 / 5	2.80 /79	1.96 /58	1.24	1.94
MUN	Oppenheimer Rochester Int Term Mu	ORRYX	B	(888) 470-0862	B / 8.1	2.44	-3.62	0.14 /26	3.88 /92	3.01 /80	2.26	0.95
* MUN	Oppenheimer Rochester Ltd Term M	OPITX	C	(888) 470-0862	C / 5.4	1.16	0.53	3.43 /68	2.10 /65	1.98 /59	3.75	0.92
MUN ●	Oppenheimer Rochester Ltd Term M	OIMBX	C-	(888) 470-0862	C / 4.8	0.75	0.15	2.66 /63	1.31 /44	1.15 /39	3.08	1.68
MUN	Oppenheimer Rochester Ltd Term M	OITCX	C-	(888) 470-0862	C / 4.7	0.76	-0.06	2.67 /63	1.30 /43	1.17 /39	3.11	1.67
MUN	Oppenheimer Rochester Ltd Term M	OPIYX	B+	(888) 470-0862	B- / 7.0	1.00	0.43	3.45 /68	2.31 /69	2.19 /63	4.09	0.67
MUS ●	Oppenheimer Rochester MA Muni A	ORMAX	B	(888) 470-0862	B+ / 8.3	2.49	-0.35	3.50 /68	4.66 /96	3.05 /81	4.24	1.64
MUS ●	Oppenheimer Rochester MA Muni B	ORBAX	B+	(888) 470-0862	B+ / 8.8	2.20	-0.73	2.62 /62	3.85 /91	2.26 /65	3.70	2.47

● Denotes fund is closed to new investors
* Denotes fund is included in Section II

www.thestreetratings.com

RISK			NET ASSETS		ASSET							FUND MANAGER		MINIMUM		LOADS	
Risk Rating/Pts	3 Yr Avg Standard Deviation	Avg Dura- tion	NAV As of 2/28/17	Total $(Mil)	Cash %	Gov. Bond %	Muni. Bond %	Corp. Bond %	Other %	Portfolio Turnover Ratio	Avg Coupon Rate	Manager Quality Pct	Manager Tenure (Years)	Initial Purch. $	Additional Purch. $	Front End Load	Back End Load
C- / 3.7	3.7	4.3	3.93	380	1	14	0	52	33	78	0.0	73	8	1,000	0	0.0	0.0
U /	N/A	N/A	1.00	406	100	0	0	0	0	0	0.0	N/A	7	1,000	0	0.0	0.0
U /	N/A	N/A	1.00	7	100	0	0	0	0	0	0.0	N/A	7	1,000	0	0.0	0.0
U /	N/A	N/A	1.00	218	100	0	0	0	0	0	0.0	N/A	7	1,000	0	0.0	0.0
U /	N/A	N/A	1.00	154	100	0	0	0	0	0	0.0	N/A	7	1,000	0	0.0	0.0
U /	N/A	N/A	1.00	1,946	100	0	0	0	0	0	0.0	N/A	7	1,000	0	0.0	0.0
U /	N/A	N/A	1.00	96	100	0	0	0	0	0	0.0	N/A	7	0	0	0.0	0.0
A+ / 9.9	N/A	N/A	1.00	6,678	100	0	0	0	0	0	0.4	53	11	0	0	0.0	0.0
A+ / 9.9	N/A	N/A	1.00	841	100	0	0	0	0	0	0.4	50	11	1,000,000	0	0.0	0.0
D / 2.0	5.0	4.6	5.72	1,413	0	62	0	32	6	128	0.0	90	4	1,000	0	4.8	0.0
D / 2.0	5.0	4.6	5.70	12	0	62	0	32	6	128	0.0	85	4	1,000	0	0.0	0.0
D / 2.0	5.0	4.6	5.70	422	0	62	0	32	6	128	0.0	85	4	1,000	0	0.0	0.0
D / 2.1	5.0	4.6	5.71	1,284	0	62	0	32	6	128	0.0	92	4	5,000,000	0	0.0	0.0
D / 2.0	5.0	4.6	5.70	131	0	62	0	32	6	128	0.0	89	4	1,000	0	0.0	0.0
D / 2.0	5.0	4.6	5.71	1,992	0	62	0	32	6	128	0.0	91	4	1,000	0	0.0	0.0
A / 9.3	1.0	2.1	4.42	498	0	44	0	0	56	211	0.0	45	8	1,000	0	2.3	0.0
A- / 9.2	1.0	2.1	4.42	4	0	44	0	0	56	211	0.0	16	8	1,000	0	0.0	0.0
A- / 9.2	1.0	2.1	4.41	149	0	44	0	0	56	211	0.0	15	8	1,000	0	0.0	0.0
A- / 9.2	1.0	2.1	4.42	361	0	44	0	0	56	211	0.0	60	8	1,000,000	0	0.0	0.0
A / 9.3	0.9	2.1	4.42	28	0	44	0	0	56	211	0.0	31	8	1,000	0	0.0	0.0
A / 9.3	1.0	2.1	4.43	56	0	44	0	0	56	211	0.0	59	8	1,000	0	0.0	0.0
A- / 9.2	1.0	2.1	4.54	696	0	1	0	71	28	55	0.0	74	8	1,000	0	2.3	0.0
A- / 9.1	1.1	2.1	4.54	6	0	1	0	71	28	55	0.0	48	8	1,000	0	0.0	0.0
A- / 9.1	1.1	2.1	4.54	161	0	1	0	71	28	55	0.0	50	8	1,000	0	0.0	0.0
A- / 9.1	1.1	2.1	4.56	200	0	1	0	71	28	55	0.0	80	8	1,000,000	0	0.0	0.0
A- / 9.1	1.1	2.1	4.54	35	0	1	0	71	28	55	0.0	67	8	1,000	0	0.0	0.0
A- / 9.2	1.0	2.1	4.56	285	0	1	0	71	28	55	0.0	77	8	1,000	0	0.0	0.0
C- / 3.8	3.6	3.7	2.98	1,602	0	0	99	0	1	9	0.0	29	15	1,000	50	2.3	0.0
C- / 3.8	3.6	3.7	2.97	4	0	0	99	0	1	9	0.0	12	15	1,000	50	0.0	0.0
C- / 3.8	3.6	3.7	2.96	667	0	0	99	0	1	9	0.0	12	15	1,000	50	0.0	0.0
C- / 3.9	3.6	3.7	2.98	181	0	0	99	0	1	9	0.0	37	15	0	0	0.0	0.0
C- / 3.0	4.1	6.1	6.78	4	0	0	99	0	1	16	0.0	84	15	1,000	0	0.0	0.0
C- / 3.0	4.1	6.1	6.77	387	0	0	99	0	1	16	0.0	83	15	1,000	0	0.0	0.0
D+ / 2.9	4.1	6.1	6.81	360	0	0	99	0	1	16	0.0	90	15	1,000	0	0.0	0.0
D+ / 2.5	4.4	6.3	11.08	914	0	0	98	0	2	34	0.0	84	15	1,000	0	4.8	0.0
D+ / 2.5	4.5	6.3	11.09	1	0	0	98	0	2	34	0.0	75	15	1,000	0	0.0	0.0
D+ / 2.4	4.5	6.3	11.08	119	0	0	98	0	2	34	0.0	73	15	1,000	0	0.0	0.0
D+ / 2.5	4.5	6.3	11.09	64	0	0	98	0	2	34	0.0	85	15	1,000	0	0.0	0.0
D+ / 2.8	4.2	6.1	6.83	1,218	0	0	99	0	1	16	0.0	89	15	1,000	0	4.8	0.0
D+ / 2.8	4.1	3.6	10.50	21	0	0	100	0	0	3	0.0	87	11	1,000	0	4.8	0.0
C- / 3.0	4.1	3.6	10.49	1	0	0	100	0	0	3	0.0	81	11	1,000	0	0.0	0.0
D+ / 2.9	4.1	3.6	10.50	11	0	0	100	0	0	3	0.0	81	11	1,000	0	0.0	0.0
C- / 3.0	4.1	3.6	10.51	3	0	0	100	0	0	3	0.0	87	11	1,000	0	0.0	0.0
C- / 3.7	3.7	5.4	4.31	133	0	0	100	0	0	24	0.0	33	7	1,000	0	2.3	0.0
C- / 3.6	3.7	5.4	4.30	38	0	0	100	0	0	24	0.0	11	7	1,000	0	0.0	0.0
C- / 3.7	3.7	5.4	4.31	49	0	0	100	0	0	24	0.0	48	7	1,000	0	0.0	0.0
C / 5.3	3.0	2.2	4.50	963	0	0	100	0	0	10	0.0	68	15	1,000	0	2.3	0.0
C+ / 5.7	3.0	2.2	4.49	6	0	0	100	0	0	10	0.0	42	15	1,000	0	0.0	0.0
C+ / 5.6	3.0	2.2	4.47	542	0	0	100	0	0	10	0.0	35	15	1,000	0	0.0	0.0
C / 5.5	3.0	2.2	4.49	252	0	0	100	0	0	10	0.0	73	15	1,000	0	0.0	0.0
C- / 3.6	3.7	5.5	10.28	24	0	0	100	0	0	5	0.0	83	11	1,000	0	4.8	0.0
C- / 3.5	3.8	5.5	10.27	N/A	0	0	100	0	0	5	0.0	74	11	1,000	0	0.0	0.0

Fund Type	Fund Name	Ticker Symbol	Overall Investment Rating	Phone	Performance Rating/Pts	3 Mo	6 Mo	1Yr / Pct	3Yr / Pct	5Yr / Pct	Dividend Yield	Expense Ratio
MUS ●	Oppenheimer Rochester MA Muni C	ORCAX	B+	(888) 470-0862	B+ / 8.8	2.31	-0.72	2.64 /62	3.86 /92	2.27 /66	3.71	2.40
MUS ●	Oppenheimer Rochester MA Muni Y	ORYAX	A	(888) 470-0862	A / 9.5	2.49	-0.35	3.40 /68	4.64 /96	3.06 /81	4.46	1.39
MUS ●	Oppenheimer Rochester MD Muni A	ORMDX	C	(888) 470-0862	B+ / 8.3	1.62	0.66	5.85 /76	4.29 /95	2.27 /66	4.84	1.28
MUS ●	Oppenheimer Rochester MD Muni B	ORYBX	C+	(888) 470-0862	B+ / 8.9	1.44	0.28	5.07 /74	3.54 /88	1.52 /47	4.34	2.11
MUS ●	Oppenheimer Rochester MD Muni C	ORYCX	C+	(888) 470-0862	B+ / 8.9	1.44	0.39	5.19 /74	3.53 /88	1.49 /46	4.35	2.04
MUN ●	Oppenheimer Rochester MD Muni Y	ORYYX	B	(888) 470-0862	A+ / 9.6	1.62	0.66	5.96 /77	4.34 /95	2.29 /66	5.08	1.02
MUS ●	Oppenheimer Rochester MI Muni A	ORMIX	C+	(888) 470-0862	B- / 7.1	1.75	-0.40	3.66 /69	3.81 /91	2.25 /65	4.53	1.28
MUS ●	Oppenheimer Rochester MI Muni B	ORMBX	B-	(888) 470-0862	B / 7.7	1.44	-0.90	2.77 /63	3.03 /82	1.46 /45	4.00	2.03
MUS ●	Oppenheimer Rochester MI Muni C	ORMCX	B-	(888) 470-0862	B / 7.8	1.57	-0.89	2.90 /64	3.05 /83	1.47 /46	4.01	2.03
MUS ●	Oppenheimer Rochester MI Muni Y	ORMYX	A-	(888) 470-0862	B+ / 8.9	1.75	-0.53	3.67 /69	3.82 /91	2.24 /65	4.77	1.03
MUS ●	Oppenheimer Rochester MN Muni A	OPAMX	B	(888) 470-0862	B- / 7.0	1.80	-2.76	0.71 /40	4.39 /95	3.92 /92	3.50	1.07
MUS ●	Oppenheimer Rochester MN Muni B	OPBMX	A-	(888) 470-0862	B / 7.7	1.70	-3.12	0.04 /21	3.62 /89	3.16 /83	2.90	1.83
MUS ●	Oppenheimer Rochester MN Muni C	OPCMX	A-	(888) 470-0862	B / 7.7	1.70	-3.12	0.04 /21	3.62 /89	3.16 /83	2.91	1.82
MUN ●	Oppenheimer Rochester MN Muni Y	OPYMX	A+	(888) 470-0862	B+ / 8.9	1.81	-2.72	0.79 /42	4.47 /96	3.99 /93	3.75	0.82
*MUS	Oppenheimer Rochester Muni A	RMUNX	B+	(888) 470-0862	A+ / 9.7	3.07	-0.54	6.99 /81	5.99 /98	3.99 /93	5.46	0.86
MUS ●	Oppenheimer Rochester Muni B	RMUBX	B+	(888) 470-0862	A+ / 9.8	2.86	-0.96	6.10 /77	5.10 /97	3.08 /81	4.88	1.72
MUS	Oppenheimer Rochester Muni C	RMUCX	B+	(888) 470-0862	A+ / 9.8	2.86	-0.96	6.18 /78	5.11 /97	3.11 /82	4.89	1.71
MUS	Oppenheimer Rochester Muni Y	RMUYX	B+	(888) 470-0862	A+ / 9.9	3.11	-0.41	7.22 /81	6.17 /99	4.15 /94	5.88	0.71
MUS ●	Oppenheimer Rochester NC Muni A	OPNCX	B+	(888) 470-0862	B+ / 8.8	2.36	-0.30	4.13 /71	4.95 /97	2.87 /78	4.42	1.46
MUS ●	Oppenheimer Rochester NC Muni B	OPCBX	A-	(888) 470-0862	A- / 9.2	2.17	-0.58	3.35 /67	4.19 /94	2.07 /60	3.88	2.24
MUS ●	Oppenheimer Rochester NC Muni C	OPCCX	A-	(888) 470-0862	A- / 9.2	2.17	-0.67	3.35 /67	4.17 /94	2.11 /62	3.89	2.21
MUN ●	Oppenheimer Rochester NC Muni Y	OPCYX	A	(888) 470-0862	A+ / 9.7	2.35	-0.21	4.23 /72	5.01 /97	2.92 /79	4.65	1.21
MUS ●	Oppenheimer Rochester Ohio Muni A	OROHX	B+	(888) 470-0862	A- / 9.0	3.05	-1.33	4.02 /71	5.23 /97	4.29 /95	4.68	1.14
MUS ●	Oppenheimer Rochester Ohio Muni B	OROBX	A-	(888) 470-0862	A / 9.4	2.86	-1.61	3.24 /67	4.45 /95	3.51 /88	4.16	1.92
MUS ●	Oppenheimer Rochester Ohio Muni C	OROCX	A-	(888) 470-0862	A / 9.4	2.86	-1.70	3.25 /67	4.46 /95	3.52 /88	4.16	1.90
MUS ●	Oppenheimer Rochester Ohio Muni Y	OROYX	A	(888) 470-0862	A+ / 9.8	3.04	-1.24	4.02 /71	5.26 /98	4.34 /96	4.93	0.90
MUN	Oppenheimer Rochester Sht Term	ORSTX	B+	(888) 470-0862	C- / 4.1	0.90	-0.04	0.82 /42	1.93 /60	1.91 /57	1.59	0.85
MUN	Oppenheimer Rochester Sht Term	ORSCX	B	(888) 470-0862	C- / 3.7	0.99	-0.42	0.06 /22	1.17 /40	1.13 /38	0.87	1.61
MUN	Oppenheimer Rochester Sht Term	ORSYX	A+	(888) 470-0862	C+ / 6.0	0.96	0.08	1.07 /46	2.09 /65	2.16 /63	1.87	0.60
MUS ●	Oppenheimer Rochester VA Muni A	ORVAX	C+	(888) 470-0862	A+ / 9.7	4.18	0.12	9.27 /87	5.37 /98	2.85 /77	5.86	1.55
MUS ●	Oppenheimer Rochester VA Muni B	ORVBX	C+	(888) 470-0862	A+ / 9.8	4.00	-0.26	8.48 /85	4.59 /96	2.09 /61	5.42	2.32
MUS ●	Oppenheimer Rochester VA Muni C	ORVCX	C+	(888) 470-0862	A+ / 9.8	4.01	-0.26	8.49 /85	4.60 /96	2.07 /60	5.43	2.31
MUS ●	Oppenheimer Rochester VA Muni Y	ORVYX	C+	(888) 470-0862	A+ / 9.9	4.19	0.13	9.29 /87	5.41 /98	2.89 /78	6.18	1.32
LP	Oppenheimer Sen Floating Rate Pl A	OSFAX	C+	(888) 470-0862	B+ / 8.3	3.13	6.36	18.23 /94	3.47 /68	—	4.63	2.06
LP	Oppenheimer Sen Floating Rate Pl C	OSFCX	B-	(888) 470-0862	B+ / 8.3	2.93	5.94	17.30 /92	2.68 /56	—	4.04	2.82
LP	Oppenheimer Sen Floating Rate Pl I	OSFIX	B+	(888) 470-0862	A / 9.3	3.11	6.54	18.63 /94	3.88 /74	—	5.14	1.56
LP	Oppenheimer Sen Floating Rate Pl Y	OSFYX	B+	(888) 470-0862	A- / 9.2	3.08	6.49	18.39 /94	3.73 /72	—	5.05	1.77
*LP	Oppenheimer Sen-Floating Rate A	OOSAX	B+	(888) 470-0862	B+ / 8.3	2.70	6.24	16.53 /91	3.76 /72	4.75 /81	4.45	1.11
LP ●	Oppenheimer Sen-Floating Rate B	OOSBX	A-	(888) 470-0862	B+ / 8.6	2.70	6.11	16.09 /90	3.24 /65	4.21 /75	4.12	1.62
LP	Oppenheimer Sen-Floating Rate C	OOSCX	B+	(888) 470-0862	B+ / 8.4	2.51	5.84	15.81 /90	2.98 /61	4.06 /73	3.88	1.87
LP	Oppenheimer Sen-Floating Rate I	OOSIX	A	(888) 470-0862	A- / 9.2	2.78	6.42	16.93 /92	4.08 /76	5.03 /84	4.91	0.80
LP	Oppenheimer Sen-Floating Rate R	OOSNX	A	(888) 470-0862	B+ / 8.8	2.76	6.11	16.40 /91	3.50 /69	4.48 /78	4.36	1.37
LP	Oppenheimer Sen-Floating Rate Y	OOSYX	A	(888) 470-0862	A- / 9.2	2.89	6.51	16.99 /92	4.05 /76	5.04 /84	4.84	0.87
*GL	Opportunistic Income A	ENIAX	A+	(800) 342-5734	C+ / 5.9	1.20	2.23	5.36 /68	2.38 /50	3.11 /59	2.73	0.53
GEI	Optimum Fixed Income A	OAFIX	D	(800) 523-1918	D / 2.2	1.59	-0.93	3.13 /57	1.74 /39	1.81 /39	1.80	1.17
GEI	Optimum Fixed Income C	OCFIX	D+	(800) 523-1918	D+ / 2.9	1.48	-1.26	2.36 /52	1.01 /28	1.09 /29	1.14	1.92
GEI	Optimum Fixed Income I	OIFIX	C+	(800) 523-1918	C / 4.5	1.64	-0.78	3.28 /58	2.00 /43	2.09 /43	2.15	0.92
*GES	Osterweis Strategic Income	OSTIX	B+	(800) 700-3316	B+ / 8.6	2.57	4.23	15.03 /88	3.51 /69	4.90 /83	5.16	0.83
GL	PACE Global Fx Inc Inve A	PWFAX	E-	(888) 793-8637	E- / 0.1	1.15	-7.98	-0.77 / 6	-0.28 / 4	-0.61 / 3	2.65	1.28
GL	PACE Global Fx Inc Inve C	PWFCX	E-	(888) 793-8637	E- / 0.1	1.02	-8.11	-1.14 / 3	-0.74 / 3	-1.09 / 2	2.27	1.76
GL	PACE Global Fx Inc Inve P	PCGLX	E-	(888) 793-8637	E- / 0.2	1.19	-7.81	-0.57 / 9	-0.09 / 5	-0.41 / 3	2.98	1.08
GL	PACE Global Fx Inc Inve Y	PWFYX	E-	(888) 793-8637	E- / 0.2	1.19	-7.84	-0.57 / 9	-0.09 / 5	-0.41 / 3	3.00	1.07

● Denotes fund is closed to new investors
* Denotes fund is included in Section II

www.thestreetratings.com

RISK			NET ASSETS		ASSET					Portfolio	Avg	FUND MANAGER		MINIMUM		LOADS	
Risk Rating/Pts	3 Yr Avg Standard Deviation	Avg Dura-tion	NAV As of 2/28/17	Total $(Mil)	Cash %	Gov. Bond %	Muni. Bond %	Corp. Bond %	Other %	Portfolio Turnover Ratio	Avg Coupon Rate	Manager Quality Pct	Manager Tenure (Years)	Initial Purch. $	Additional Purch. $	Front End Load	Back End Load
C- / 3.5	3.8	5.5	10.25	14	0	0	100	0	0	5	0.0	73	11	1,000	0	0.0	0.0
C- / 3.5	3.8	5.5	10.27	7	0	0	100	0	0	5	0.0	83	11	1,000	0	0.0	0.0
D / 1.7	5.6	4.4	9.59	18	0	0	100	0	0	17	0.0	82	11	1,000	0	4.8	0.0
D / 1.7	5.6	4.4	9.57	N/A	0	0	100	0	0	17	0.0	71	11	1,000	0	0.0	0.0
D / 1.7	5.5	4.4	9.56	18	0	0	100	0	0	17	0.0	72	11	1,000	0	0.0	0.0
D / 1.7	5.5	4.4	9.60	2	0	0	100	0	0	17	0.0	82	11	1,000	0	0.0	0.0
C- / 3.8	3.6	4.2	8.23	24	0	0	100	0	0	24	0.0	80	11	1,000	0	4.8	0.0
C- / 3.7	3.7	4.2	8.22	N/A	0	0	100	0	0	24	0.0	65	11	1,000	0	0.0	0.0
C- / 3.7	3.7	4.2	8.21	13	0	0	100	0	0	24	0.0	66	11	1,000	0	0.0	0.0
C- / 3.7	3.7	4.2	8.21	1	0	0	100	0	0	24	0.0	79	11	1,000	0	0.0	0.0
C / 5.1	3.1	4.7	12.73	75	0	0	100	0	0	14	0.0	78	11	1,000	0	4.8	0.0
C / 5.0	3.1	4.7	12.72	1	0	0	100	0	0	14	0.0	60	11	1,000	0	0.0	0.0
C / 5.0	3.1	4.7	12.72	34	0	0	100	0	0	14	0.0	60	11	1,000	0	0.0	0.0
C / 5.2	3.1	4.7	12.73	21	0	0	100	0	0	14	0.0	79	11	1,000	0	0.0	0.0
D / 2.1	5.0	7.0	14.88	4,510	0	0	99	0	1	13	0.0	87	15	1,000	50	4.8	0.0
D / 2.1	5.0	7.0	14.86	8	0	0	99	0	1	13	0.0	79	15	1,000	50	0.0	0.0
D / 2.1	5.0	7.0	14.85	886	0	0	99	0	1	13	0.0	79	15	1,000	50	0.0	0.0
D / 2.1	5.0	7.0	14.89	285	0	0	99	0	1	13	0.0	88	15	1,000	50	0.0	0.0
C- / 3.1	4.0	5.2	10.89	33	0	0	100	0	0	7	0.0	86	11	1,000	0	4.8	0.0
C- / 3.1	4.0	5.2	10.89	N/A	0	0	100	0	0	7	0.0	79	11	1,000	0	0.0	0.0
C- / 3.1	4.0	5.2	10.89	23	0	0	100	0	0	7	0.0	79	11	1,000	0	0.0	0.0
C- / 3.1	4.1	5.2	10.89	6	0	0	100	0	0	7	0.0	86	11	1,000	0	0.0	0.0
C- / 3.1	4.1	5.5	10.06	39	0	0	100	0	0	3	0.0	81	11	1,000	0	4.8	0.0
C- / 3.1	4.0	5.5	10.05	N/A	0	0	100	0	0	3	0.0	71	11	1,000	0	0.0	0.0
C- / 3.1	4.1	5.5	10.04	18	0	0	100	0	0	3	0.0	71	11	1,000	0	0.0	0.0
C- / 3.1	4.0	5.5	10.05	7	0	0	100	0	0	3	0.0	82	11	1,000	0	0.0	0.0
A- / 9.2	1.0	1.4	3.73	432	0	0	99	0	1	51	0.0	74	7	1,000	0	2.3	0.0
A- / 9.1	1.2	1.4	3.73	109	0	0	99	0	1	51	0.0	N/A	7	1,000	0	0.0	0.0
A- / 9.2	1.1	1.4	3.73	463	0	0	99	0	1	51	0.0	77	7	1,000	0	0.0	0.0
E+ / 0.6	7.0	7.5	8.23	50	0	0	100	0	0	15	0.0	77	11	1,000	0	4.8	0.0
E+ / 0.6	7.0	7.5	8.21	1	0	0	100	0	0	15	0.0	60	11	1,000	0	0.0	0.0
E+ / 0.7	7.0	7.5	8.20	21	0	0	100	0	0	15	0.0	62	11	1,000	0	0.0	0.0
E+ / 0.7	7.0	7.5	8.22	7	0	0	100	0	0	15	0.0	78	11	1,000	0	0.0	0.0
D+ / 2.7	4.3	0.3	9.55	33	0	0	0	25	75	69	0.0	89	4	1,000	50	3.5	0.0
D+ / 2.8	4.2	0.3	9.55	15	0	0	0	25	75	69	0.0	83	4	1,000	50	0.0	0.0
D+ / 2.7	4.2	0.3	9.56	1	0	0	0	25	75	69	0.0	91	4	5,000,000	0	0.0	0.0
D+ / 2.8	4.2	0.3	9.55	23	0	0	0	25	75	69	0.0	90	4	0	0	0.0	0.0
C- / 4.0	3.5	0.1	8.20	4,556	1	3	0	24	72	28	0.0	90	18	1,000	50	3.5	0.0
C- / 4.0	3.5	0.1	8.21	26	1	3	0	24	72	28	0.0	87	18	1,000	50	0.0	0.0
C- / 4.0	3.5	0.1	8.21	2,945	1	3	0	24	72	28	0.0	85	18	1,000	50	0.0	0.0
C- / 4.0	3.5	0.1	8.18	1,198	1	3	0	24	72	28	0.0	92	18	5,000,000	0	0.0	0.0
C- / 4.0	3.5	0.1	8.20	53	1	3	0	24	72	28	0.0	89	18	1,000	50	0.0	0.0
C- / 4.0	3.5	0.1	8.19	5,772	1	3	0	24	72	28	0.0	92	18	0	0	0.0	0.0
A- / 9.2	1.0	2.6	8.22	2,207	1	3	0	11	85	35	0.0	88	10	100,000	1,000	0.0	0.0
B- / 7.3	2.6	5.2	9.38	35	0	17	2	34	47	536	4.1	25	10	1,000	100	4.5	0.0
B- / 7.2	2.6	5.2	9.38	125	0	17	2	34	47	536	4.1	9	10	1,000	100	0.0	0.0
B- / 7.3	2.6	5.2	9.37	1,740	0	17	2	34	47	536	4.1	34	10	0	0	0.0	0.0
C- / 3.7	3.7	1.2	11.35	5,381	2	21	0	72	5	31	0.0	93	15	5,000	100	0.0	0.0
E+ / 0.8	6.5	7.9	9.67	39	2	45	2	42	9	38	3.3	84	22	1,000	100	4.5	1.0
E+ / 0.8	6.5	7.9	9.68	3	2	45	2	42	9	38	3.3	80	22	1,000	100	0.0	1.0
E+ / 0.8	6.5	7.9	9.67	454	2	45	2	42	9	38	3.3	86	22	10,000	500	0.0	1.0
E+ / 0.8	6.5	7.9	9.64	3	2	45	2	42	9	38	3.3	86	22	5,000,000	0	0.0	1.0

I. Index of Bond and Money Market Mutual Funds

Fund Type	Fund Name	Ticker Symbol	Overall Investment Rating	Phone	Perfor-mance Rating/Pts	3 Mo	6 Mo	1Yr / Pct	Annualized 3Yr / Pct	Annualized 5Yr / Pct	Dividend Yield	Expense Ratio
COH	PACE High Yield Invst A	PHIAX	C	(888) 793-8637	B+ / 8.8	4.85	5.70	20.85 /97	3.94 /75	6.22 /94	5.28	1.26
COH	PACE High Yield Invst C	PHYCX	C+	(888) 793-8637	A- / 9.2	4.72	5.43	20.27 /96	3.45 /68	5.73 /90	5.05	1.75
COH	PACE High Yield Invst P	PHYPX	C+	(888) 793-8637	A / 9.5	4.77	5.76	20.97 /97	4.13 /77	6.43 /95	5.65	1.11
COH	PACE High Yield Invst Y	PHDYX	C+	(888) 793-8637	A+ / 9.6	4.87	5.76	21.13 /97	4.20 /78	6.48 /95	5.69	1.03
GEI	PACE Intrm Fixed Inc Inve A	PIFAX	D	(888) 793-8637	D- / 1.1	0.72	-0.77	1.49 /44	1.32 /32	1.37 /33	1.21	1.03
GEI	PACE Intrm Fixed Inc Inve C	PIICX	C-	(888) 793-8637	D+ / 2.3	0.58	-1.02	0.97 /39	0.81 /25	0.86 /26	0.75	1.53
GEI	PACE Intrm Fixed Inc Inve P	PCIFX	C+	(888) 793-8637	C- / 3.5	0.78	-0.64	1.75 /47	1.55 /36	1.63 /37	1.52	0.83
GEI	PACE Intrm Fixed Inc Inve Y	PIFYX	C+	(888) 793-8637	C- / 3.6	0.78	-0.64	1.75 /47	1.58 /36	1.63 /37	1.52	0.94
USS	PACE Mtg Backed Sec Fixed Inc Inv	PFXAX	C-	(888) 793-8637	D+ / 2.4	0.80	-1.06	1.29 /43	2.26 /48	1.74 /38	2.36	1.07
USS	PACE Mtg Backed Sec Fixed Inc Inv	PFXCX	C+	(888) 793-8637	C- / 3.4	0.67	-1.38	0.70 /36	1.72 /38	1.23 /30	1.96	1.60
USS	PACE Mtg Backed Sec Fixed Inc Inv	PCGTX	B+	(888) 793-8637	C / 4.7	0.86	-1.01	1.46 /44	2.49 /52	1.98 /42	2.73	0.91
USS	PACE Mtg Backed Sec Fixed Inc Inv	PFXYX	B+	(888) 793-8637	C / 4.7	0.86	-0.93	1.46 /44	2.49 /52	2.00 /42	2.73	0.89
MUN	PACE Muni Fxd Inc Inve A	PMUAX	E+	(888) 793-8637	D+ / 2.6	2.21	-3.02	-0.82 / 6	2.32 /69	2.02 /59	2.39	0.92
MUN	PACE Muni Fxd Inc Inve C	PMUCX	D	(888) 793-8637	C- / 4.2	2.08	-3.27	-1.33 / 2	1.81 /57	1.50 /46	1.99	1.42
MUN	PACE Muni Fxd Inc Inve P	PCMNX	C	(888) 793-8637	C+ / 6.1	2.27	-2.98	-0.58 / 9	2.58 /75	2.27 /66	2.75	0.67
MUN	PACE Muni Fxd Inc Inve Y	PMUYX	C	(888) 793-8637	C+ / 6.0	2.26	-2.99	-0.62 / 8	2.53 /74	2.24 /65	2.72	0.72
COI	PACE Strat Fxd Inc Inve A	PBNAX	D-	(888) 793-8637	C- / 4.2	2.38	-1.01	5.10 /67	2.84 /59	2.63 /52	2.90	1.10
COI	PACE Strat Fxd Inc Inve C	PBNCX	D	(888) 793-8637	C / 5.4	2.33	-1.25	4.64 /65	2.38 /50	2.16 /44	2.51	1.60
COI	PACE Strat Fxd Inc Inve P	PCSIX	C	(888) 793-8637	C+ / 6.5	2.45	-0.96	5.34 /68	3.10 /63	2.89 /56	3.26	0.88
COI	PACE Strat Fxd Inc Inve Y	PSFYX	C	(888) 793-8637	C+ / 6.5	2.52	-0.88	5.32 /68	3.06 /62	2.87 /56	3.23	0.97
GES	Pacific Advisors Inc & Eq A	PADIX	D-	(800) 282-6693	C+ / 5.8	2.13	1.99	9.50 /78	3.73 /72	5.59 /89	0.24	2.81
GES	Pacific Advisors Inc & Eq C	PIECX	D	(800) 282-6693	C+ / 6.4	1.95	1.61	8.68 /76	2.96 /60	4.80 /82	0.00	3.56
MUN	Pacific Capital T/F Sh-Interm Y	PTFSX	C+	(888) 739-1390	C- / 3.2	1.38	-0.79	-0.07 /16	0.95 /34	0.89 /33	1.24	0.35
MUI	Pacific Capital Tax-Free Secs Y	PTXFX	B+	(888) 739-1390	C+ / 6.7	2.13	-2.55	-0.38 /11	2.86 /80	2.44 /69	2.50	0.30
MTG	Pacific Financial Tactical Inst	PFGTX	C	(888) 451-8734	D+ / 2.4	1.60	1.18	3.10 /57	0.26 /18	1.84 /39	1.79	2.31
MTG	Pacific Financial Tactical Inv	PFTLX	D	(888) 451-8734	E+ / 0.6	1.31	0.77	2.30 /52	-0.50 / 4	1.07 /28	0.97	3.06
GEI	Pacific Funds Core Income Class A	PLIAX	D	(800) 722-2333	C- / 3.7	1.75	-0.85	5.26 /68	2.37 /49	3.38 /64	2.53	1.14
GL	Pacific Funds Core Income Class Adv	PLIDX	C+	(800) 722-2333	C+ / 6.0	1.91	-0.63	5.62 /69	2.66 /55	3.63 /68	2.89	0.89
LP	Pacific Funds Core Income Class C	PLNCX	C-	(800) 722-2333	C- / 4.2	1.56	-1.13	4.56 /65	1.64 /37	2.61 /51	1.88	1.89
GEI	Pacific Funds Core Income Class I	PLIIX	B-	(800) 722-2333	C+ / 6.0	1.82	-0.70	5.57 /69	2.67 /55	3.64 /68	2.94	0.74
COI	Pacific Funds Core Income Class P		U	(800) 722-2333	U /	1.79	-0.74	5.49 /69	--	--	2.87	0.74
LP	Pacific Funds Floating Rate Inc A	PLFLX	A+	(800) 722-2333	B- / 7.0	2.86	4.68	10.53 /80	3.17 /64	4.72 /81	3.85	1.30
LP	Pacific Funds Floating Rate Inc Adv	PLFDX	A+	(800) 722-2333	B / 8.1	2.92	4.80	10.78 /81	3.42 /68	4.96 /84	4.21	1.05
LP	Pacific Funds Floating Rate Inc C	PLBCX	A+	(800) 722-2333	B- / 7.0	2.69	4.32	9.74 /78	2.38 /50	3.94 /72	3.26	2.05
LP	Pacific Funds Floating Rate Inc I	PLFRX	A+	(800) 722-2333	B / 8.1	2.93	4.83	10.85 /81	3.44 /68	5.01 /84	4.26	0.90
LP	Pacific Funds Floating Rate Inc P		A+	(800) 722-2333	B / 8.0	2.81	4.69	10.79 /81	3.36 /67	--	4.20	0.90
COH	Pacific Funds High Income A	PLAHX	D+	(800) 722-2333	B / 8.0	5.38	6.25	20.70 /97	2.83 /58	--	5.12	1.32
COH	Pacific Funds High Income Adv	PLHYX	C	(800) 722-2333	A- / 9.1	5.34	6.27	20.89 /97	3.06 /62	--	5.61	1.07
COH	Pacific Funds High Income C	PLCHX	D+	(800) 722-2333	B+ / 8.3	5.10	5.77	19.75 /96	2.04 /44	--	4.67	2.07
COH	Pacific Funds High Income I	PLHIX	C	(800) 722-2333	A- / 9.2	5.39	6.34	21.00 /97	3.09 /63	6.01 /92	5.69	0.92
COH	Pacific Funds High Income P		U	(800) 722-2333	U /	5.27	6.21	20.84 /97	--	--	5.65	0.92
COH	Pacific Funds Ltd Dur Hi Inc A	PLLDX	E+	(800) 722-2333	C- / 3.7	2.60	3.16	10.20 /79	0.80 /24	--	3.81	1.45
COH	Pacific Funds Ltd Dur Hi Inc Adv	PLLYX	D-	(800) 722-2333	C / 5.3	2.67	3.18	10.36 /80	1.05 /28	--	4.19	1.20
COH	Pacific Funds Ltd Dur Hi Inc C	PLLCX	E+	(800) 722-2333	C- / 3.7	2.43	2.80	9.42 /78	0.06 /10	--	3.21	2.20
COH	Pacific Funds Ltd Dur Hi Inc I	PLLIX	D-	(800) 722-2333	C / 5.4	2.56	3.20	10.41 /80	1.06 /29	--	4.23	1.05
COI	Pacific Funds Shrt Duration Inc A	PLADX	C	(800) 722-2333	D+ / 2.3	0.97	0.52	3.12 /57	1.23 /31	--	1.65	1.06
COI	Pacific Funds Shrt Duration Inc Adv	PLDSX	B	(800) 722-2333	C- / 4.0	1.03	0.65	3.37 /59	1.48 /35	--	1.95	0.81
COI	Pacific Funds Shrt Duration Inc C	PLCSX	C	(800) 722-2333	D+ / 2.3	0.78	0.15	2.36 /52	0.49 /21	--	0.96	1.81
COI	Pacific Funds Shrt Duration Inc I	PLSDX	B+	(800) 722-2333	C- / 4.0	1.04	0.76	3.42 /59	1.52 /35	2.65 /52	2.00	0.66
GEL	Pacific Funds Strategic Income A	PLSTX	D	(800) 722-2333	C+ / 6.6	3.14	2.64	14.02 /87	2.85 /59	--	3.51	1.30
GEL	Pacific Funds Strategic Income Adv	PLSFX	C	(800) 722-2333	B / 8.1	3.20	2.66	14.30 /87	3.08 /62	--	3.91	1.05
GEL	Pacific Funds Strategic Income C	PLCNX	D+	(800) 722-2333	B- / 7.0	2.96	2.27	13.21 /85	2.07 /44	--	2.95	2.05

• Denotes fund is closed to new investors
* Denotes fund is included in Section II

www.thestreetratings.com

Risk Rating/Pts	3 Yr Avg Standard Deviation	Avg Dura-tion	NAV As of 2/28/17	Total $(Mil)	Cash %	Gov. Bond %	Muni. Bond %	Corp. Bond %	Other %	Portfolio Turnover Ratio	Avg Coupon Rate	Manager Quality Pct	Manager Tenure (Years)	Initial Purch. $	Additional Purch. $	Front End Load	Back End Load
D- /1.1	5.7	3.9	10.04	4	2	0	0	93	5	103	6.6	25	2	1,000	100	4.5	0.0
D- /1.1	5.7	3.9	10.03	3	2	0	0	93	5	103	6.6	13	2	1,000	100	0.0	0.0
D- /1.1	5.7	3.9	10.06	430	2	0	0	93	5	103	6.6	31	2	10,000	500	0.0	0.0
D- /1.1	5.7	3.9	10.08	1	2	0	0	93	5	103	6.6	32	2	5,000,000	0	0.0	0.0
B+ /8.5	1.8	3.3	12.20	18	25	37	0	26	12	284	2.5	31	5	1,000	100	4.5	0.0
B+ /8.4	1.8	3.3	12.22	1	25	37	0	26	12	284	2.5	16	5	1,000	100	0.0	0.0
B+ /8.4	1.9	3.3	12.20	390	25	37	0	26	12	284	2.5	38	5	10,000	500	0.0	0.0
B+ /8.5	1.8	3.3	12.20	N/A	25	37	0	26	12	284	2.5	N/A	5	5,000,000	0	0.0	0.0
B /8.2	2.0	2.3	12.82	38	0	1	0	0	99	1,383	2.9	77	4	1,000	100	4.5	0.0
B /8.2	2.1	2.3	12.83	11	0	1	0	0	99	1,383	2.9	67	4	1,000	100	0.0	0.0
B /8.2	2.1	2.3	12.82	384	0	1	0	0	99	1,383	2.9	80	4	10,000	500	0.0	0.0
B /8.2	2.0	2.3	12.82	47	0	1	0	0	99	1,383	2.9	80	4	5,000,000	0	0.0	0.0
C /4.5	3.3	5.0	12.86	48	1	0	98	0	1	15	5.0	9	17	1,000	100	4.5	0.0
C /4.5	3.3	5.0	12.86	9	1	0	98	0	1	15	5.0	4	17	1,000	100	0.0	0.0
C /4.4	3.3	5.0	12.86	325	1	0	98	0	1	15	5.0	13	17	10,000	500	0.0	0.0
C /4.5	3.3	5.0	12.86	N/A	1	0	98	0	1	15	5.0	12	17	5,000,000	0	0.0	0.0
C- /4.0	3.5	6.6	13.60	13	0	36	1	32	31	133	3.4	32	2	1,000	100	4.5	0.0
C- /3.9	3.5	6.6	13.61	9	0	36	1	32	31	133	3.4	17	2	1,000	100	0.0	0.0
C- /4.0	3.5	6.6	13.59	816	0	36	1	32	31	133	3.4	46	2	10,000	500	0.0	0.0
C- /3.9	3.6	6.6	13.58	2	0	36	1	32	31	133	3.4	39	2	5,000,000	0	0.0	0.0
D /2.1	5.0	4.6	12.51	15	2	0	0	46	52	22	5.1	93	16	1,000	25	4.8	2.0
D /2.1	5.0	4.6	11.95	3	2	0	0	46	52	22	5.1	89	16	10,000	500	0.0	2.0
B+ /8.8	1.5	N/A	10.12	70	3	1	91	0	5	19	0.0	21	13	0	0	0.0	0.0
C+ /5.6	3.0	N/A	10.10	305	1	0	95	0	4	18	0.0	28	13	0	0	0.0	0.0
A- /9.0	1.4	N/A	9.60	8	24	11	1	7	57	122	0.0	29	10	5,000	250	0.0	0.0
A- /9.0	1.3	N/A	9.35	82	24	11	1	7	57	122	0.0	11	10	5,000	250	0.0	0.0
C+ /5.7	3.0	5.3	10.54	164	3	13	0	68	16	74	0.0	56	1	1,000	50	4.3	0.0
C /5.5	3.0	5.3	10.57	334	3	13	0	68	16	74	0.0	93	1	0	0	0.0	0.0
C+ /5.7	3.0	5.3	10.55	124	3	13	0	68	16	74	0.0	78	1	1,000	50	0.0	0.0
C+ /5.9	2.9	5.3	10.55	4	3	13	0	68	16	74	0.0	66	1	500,000	0	0.0	0.0
U /	N/A	5.3	10.58	122	3	13	0	68	16	74	0.0	N/A	1	0	0	0.0	0.0
B- /7.4	2.6	0.4	10.19	198	0	1	0	9	90	99	0.0	89	6	1,000	50	3.0	0.0
B- /7.5	2.6	0.4	10.22	416	0	1	0	9	90	99	0.0	91	6	0	0	0.0	0.0
B- /7.4	2.6	0.4	10.17	175	0	1	0	9	90	99	0.0	84	6	1,000	50	0.0	0.0
B- /7.4	2.6	0.4	10.20	244	0	1	0	9	90	99	0.0	91	6	500,000	0	0.0	0.0
B- /7.4	2.6	0.4	10.19	1	0	1	0	9	90	99	0.0	90	6	0	0	0.0	0.0
E+ /0.7	6.5	4.0	10.39	6	7	0	0	87	6	54	0.0	2	6	1,000	50	4.3	0.0
E+ /0.7	6.4	4.0	10.39	3	7	0	0	87	6	54	0.0	4	6	0	0	0.0	0.0
E+ /0.7	6.5	4.0	10.37	5	7	0	0	87	6	54	0.0	1	6	1,000	50	0.0	0.0
E+ /0.7	6.4	4.0	10.31	5	7	0	0	87	6	54	0.0	3	6	500,000	0	0.0	0.0
U /	N/A	4.0	10.29	10	7	0	0	87	6	54	0.0	N/A	6	0	0	0.0	0.0
D+ /2.6	3.9	1.6	9.16	6	6	0	0	59	35	48	0.0	2	4	1,000	50	3.0	0.0
D+ /2.6	3.9	1.6	9.15	2	6	0	0	59	35	48	0.0	4	4	0	0	0.0	0.0
D+ /2.5	3.9	1.6	9.14	3	6	0	0	59	35	48	0.0	1	4	1,000	50	0.0	0.0
D+ /2.6	3.9	1.6	9.15	23	6	0	0	59	35	48	0.0	4	4	500,000	0	0.0	0.0
B+ /8.9	1.4	1.9	10.32	67	5	6	0	77	12	41	0.0	57	6	1,000	50	3.0	0.0
B+ /8.9	1.4	1.9	10.32	160	5	6	0	77	12	41	0.0	65	6	0	0	0.0	0.0
A- /9.0	1.3	1.9	10.30	44	5	6	0	77	12	41	0.0	25	6	1,000	50	0.0	0.0
A- /9.0	1.3	1.9	10.31	3	5	6	0	77	12	41	0.0	67	6	500,000	0	0.0	0.0
D /2.2	4.8	4.1	10.73	67	1	0	0	83	16	94	0.0	83	6	1,000	50	4.3	0.0
D /2.2	4.8	4.1	10.73	203	1	0	0	83	16	94	0.0	85	6	0	0	0.0	0.0
D /2.2	4.8	4.1	10.71	49	1	0	0	83	16	94	0.0	75	6	1,000	50	0.0	0.0

Data as of February 28, 2017

Fund Type	Fund Name	Ticker Symbol	Overall Investment Rating	Phone	Performance Rating/Pts	3 Mo	6 Mo	1Yr / Pct	3Yr / Pct	5Yr / Pct	Dividend Yield	Expense Ratio
	99 Pct = Best				PERFORMANCE		Total Return % through 2/28/17		Annualized		Incl. in Returns	
	0 Pct = Worst											
GEN	Pacific Funds Strategic Income I	PLSRX	C	(800) 722-2333	B / 8.1	3.23	2.70	14.33 /87	3.13 /63	6.29 /94	3.98	0.90
GL	Palmer Square Income Plus	PSYPX	C-	(866) 933-9033	B- / 7.5	1.91	3.70	15.78 /90	2.87 /59	--	4.21	0.86
GEI	Parnassus Income Fd-Fixed Inc	PRFIX	C+	(800) 999-3505	C / 4.4	1.29	-1.51	2.04 /49	2.19 /46	1.56 /35	2.19	0.79
COI	Parnassus Income Fd-Fixed Inc Inst	PFPLX	U	(800) 999-3505	U /	1.34	-1.36	2.23 /51	--	--	2.38	0.50
COH	Pax High Yield A	PXHAX	D	(800) 767-1729	B / 7.6	5.64	6.81	21.17 /97	2.29 /48	4.84 /82	5.16	0.97
COH	Pax High Yield I	PXHIX	C	(800) 767-1729	B+ / 8.9	5.73	6.96	21.55 /98	2.55 /53	5.11 /85	5.64	0.72
COH	Pax High Yield Inv	PAXHX	C-	(800) 767-1729	B+ / 8.7	5.65	6.82	21.20 /97	2.25 /47	4.82 /82	5.40	0.97
COH	Pax High Yield R	PXHRX	C-	(800) 767-1729	B+ / 8.5	5.58	6.84	20.86 /97	2.05 /44	4.62 /80	5.15	1.22
MUS	Payden CA Muni Inc Investor	PYCRX	C+	(888) 409-8007	C / 5.2	1.69	-2.72	-0.65 / 8	2.15 /66	2.26 /65	1.76	0.70
MMT	Payden Cash Rsv MM Investor	PBHXX	C-	(888) 409-8007	E+ / 0.9	0.07	0.10	0.16 /24	0.06 /11	0.04 /10	0.16	N/A
COI	Payden Core Bond Adviser	PYCWX	A-	(888) 409-8007	C+ / 6.0	1.63	-1.07	3.90 /62	2.97 /60	3.08 /59	2.77	0.84
GEI	Payden Core Bond Investor	PYCBX	A	(888) 409-8007	C+ / 6.3	1.69	-0.95	4.14 /63	3.22 /65	3.40 /64	3.01	0.59
COI	Payden Corporate Bond Investor	PYACX	B+	(888) 409-8007	B+ / 8.8	3.03	-0.26	8.28 /75	5.17 /86	5.29 /87	3.06	0.78
EM	Payden Em Mkts Corp Bd Adv	PYCAX	B	(888) 409-8007	B+ / 8.8	3.66	1.30	11.44 /82	4.46 /80	--	3.91	1.58
EM	Payden Em Mkts Corp Bd Inv	PYCEX	B	(888) 409-8007	B+ / 8.9	3.72	1.31	11.59 /82	4.66 /82	--	4.13	1.33
EM	Payden Em Mkts Corp Bd SI	PYCIX	B	(888) 409-8007	A- / 9.0	3.74	1.26	11.68 /83	4.78 /84	--	4.23	1.33
EM	Payden Emerg Mkts Bond Investor	PYEMX	C+	(888) 409-8007	A+ / 9.6	5.14	0.30	13.89 /87	5.83 /91	4.82 /82	5.43	0.76
EM	Payden Emerging Market Bond Adv	PYEWX	C+	(888) 409-8007	A / 9.5	5.08	0.19	13.61 /86	5.58 /89	4.55 /79	5.28	1.01
EM	Payden Emerging Market Bond SI	PYEIX	C+	(888) 409-8007	A+ / 9.6	5.24	0.40	13.98 /87	5.91 /91	--	5.51	0.76
EM	Payden Emerging Markets Lcl Bd Adv	PYEAX	E-	(888) 409-8007	E / 0.4	6.81	0.51	13.01 /85	-2.86 / 1	-3.48 / 0	5.05	1.25
EM	Payden Emerging Markets Lcl Bd Inv	PYELX	E-	(888) 409-8007	E+ / 0.6	6.88	0.49	13.11 /85	-2.61 / 1	-3.23 / 1	5.30	1.00
LP	Payden Floating Rate Adv	PYFAX	A+	(888) 409-8007	B- / 7.1	1.24	2.34	7.97 /74	3.16 /64	--	3.27	1.09
LP	Payden Floating Rate Inv	PYFRX	A+	(888) 409-8007	B- / 7.3	1.29	2.56	8.24 /75	3.35 /67	--	3.51	0.84
LP	Payden Floating Rate SI	PYFIX	A+	(888) 409-8007	B- / 7.5	1.32	2.62	8.46 /75	3.50 /69	--	3.62	0.84
GL	Payden Global Fixed Inc Investor	PYGFX	A+	(888) 409-8007	C+ / 6.7	1.29	-1.14	3.50 /60	3.73 /72	3.75 /69	1.42	0.92
GL	Payden Global Low Duration Investor	PYGSX	B-	(888) 409-8007	C- / 3.0	0.62	0.49	2.11 /50	0.98 /27	1.69 /37	1.19	0.69
USA	Payden GNMA Adv	PYGWX	B-	(888) 409-8007	C- / 3.8	0.07	-1.35	0.33 /30	2.07 /44	1.49 /34	2.76	0.92
USA	Payden GNMA Investor	PYGNX	B	(888) 409-8007	C- / 4.2	0.13	-1.13	0.58 /35	2.33 /49	1.77 /39	3.01	0.67
COH	Payden High Income Adviser	PYHWX	C	(888) 409-8007	B / 8.2	3.42	3.01	12.01 /83	3.50 /69	5.15 /86	4.97	0.94
COH	Payden High Income Investor	PYHRX	C+	(888) 409-8007	B+ / 8.4	3.66	3.31	12.32 /84	3.68 /71	5.37 /87	5.22	0.69
USS	Payden Kravitz Cash Bal Plan Adv	PKCBX	B	(888) 409-8007	C- / 3.9	1.19	0.90	4.74 /66	1.20 /31	1.55 /35	1.67	1.71
USS	Payden Kravitz Cash Bal Plan Ret	PKCRX	B-	(888) 409-8007	C- / 3.5	1.11	0.70	4.47 /64	0.94 /27	1.29 /31	1.71	1.96
USS	Payden Kravitz Cash Bal Plan SI	PKBIX	B+	(888) 409-8007	C / 4.3	1.21	0.92	4.91 /66	1.45 /34	1.79 /39	1.68	1.46
GEI	Payden Limited Maturity Investor	PYLMX	B-	(888) 409-8007	D+ / 2.6	0.46	0.60	1.70 /46	0.79 /24	0.87 /26	0.95	0.57
* GEI	Payden Low Duration Investor	PYSBX	B	(888) 409-8007	C- / 3.1	0.61	0.52	2.17 /50	1.04 /28	1.41 /33	1.25	0.57
USS	Payden US Government Adv	PYUWX	C-	(888) 409-8007	D / 1.9	0.15	-0.76	-0.10 /16	0.65 /22	0.58 /22	1.43	0.84
US	Payden US Government Investor	PYUSX	C	(888) 409-8007	D / 2.2	0.31	-0.64	0.14 /24	0.90 /26	0.85 /25	1.68	0.59
LP	PENN Cap Senior Flt Rte Income Inst	PFRNX	U	(844) 302-7366	U /	1.71	2.97	7.50 /73	--	--	3.67	2.80
GL	PENN Capital Opportunistic HY Inst	PHYNX	U	(844) 302-7366	U /	5.82	7.76	20.39 /96	--	--	6.38	5.15
MUN	Performance Trust Muni Bond Inst	PTIMX	C+	(800) 737-3676	B+ / 8.3	2.80	-4.11	-0.07 /17	4.69 /96	4.85 /97	2.37	0.86
MUN	Performance Trust Muni Bond Rtl	PTRMX	C+	(800) 737-3676	B / 8.0	2.75	-4.19	-0.28 /13	4.49 /96	--	2.29	1.11
* GEI	Performance Trust Strategic Bond	PTIAX	A+	(800) 737-3676	B / 7.8	2.32	0.56	5.50 /69	5.01 /85	5.75 /90	5.59	0.89
US	Permanent Portfolio Short-Tm Trs I	PRTBX	D	(800) 531-5142	E / 0.3	0.06	-0.08	-0.14 /15	-0.45 / 4	-0.51 / 3	0.00	1.21
COI	Permanent Portfolio Versatile Bd A	PRVDX	U	(800) 531-5142	U /	1.98	4.96	--	--	--	0.00	1.47
COI	Permanent Portfolio Versatile Bd C	PRVHX	U	(800) 531-5142	U /	1.80	4.60	--	--	--	0.00	2.22
COH	Permanent Portfolio Versatile Bd I	PRVBX	C	(800) 531-5142	A- / 9.1	2.05	5.10	19.94 /96	3.59 /70	4.11 /74	2.90	1.22
GL	PF Currency Strategies P		D-	(800) 722-2333	C+ / 6.5	1.38	0.31	2.17 /50	3.55 /69	--	11.82	0.90
EM	PF Emerging Mkts Debt P		C	(800) 722-2333	A+ / 9.7	7.78	4.13	22.85 /98	4.44 /80	--	11.19	1.07
GEI	PF Inflation Managed P		E+	(800) 722-2333	C- / 3.5	1.60	0.22	4.33 /64	1.02 /28	0.33 /20	0.00	0.79
COI	PF Managed Bond P		C	(800) 722-2333	C+ / 6.6	2.07	-0.99	5.12 /67	3.28 /66	3.19 /61	1.41	0.64
GEI	PF Short Duration Bond P		C+	(800) 722-2333	D+ / 2.7	0.44	0.24	2.19 /51	0.86 /25	1.03 /28	0.94	0.65
MMT	PFM Government Select Series CO		C	(800) 338-3383	D- / 1.5	0.10	0.17	0.42 /32	0.23 /17	0.22 /19	0.42	N/A

● Denotes fund is closed to new investors
* Denotes fund is included in Section II

www.thestreetratings.com

RISK			NET ASSETS		ASSET					Portfolio Turnover Ratio	Avg Coupon Rate	FUND MANAGER		MINIMUM		LOADS	
Risk Rating/Pts	3 Yr Avg Standard Deviation	Avg Dura-tion	NAV As of 2/28/17	Total $(Mil)	Cash %	Gov. Bond %	Muni. Bond %	Corp. Bond %	Other %			Manager Quality Pct	Manager Tenure (Years)	Initial Purch. $	Additional Purch. $	Front End Load	Back End Load
D /2.2	4.8	4.1	10.67	2	1	0	0	83	16	94	0.0	86	6	500,000	0	0.0	0.0
D /2.0	5.1	N/A	9.84	355	16	0	0	45	39	59	0.0	89	3	1,000,000	0	0.0	2.0
B- /7.5	2.5	4.6	16.54	194	5	23	0	47	25	36	3.0	37	4	2,000	50	0.0	0.0
U /	N/A	4.6	16.54	28	5	23	0	47	25	36	3.0	N/A	4	100,000	50	0.0	0.0
E+ /0.9	6.0	4.0	6.87	6	2	0	0	92	6	78	6.8	2	2	1,000	50	4.5	0.0
E+ /0.9	5.9	4.0	6.84	171	2	0	0	92	6	78	6.8	3	2	250,000	0	0.0	0.0
E+ /0.9	6.0	4.0	6.86	232	2	0	0	92	6	78	6.8	2	2	1,000	50	0.0	0.0
E+ /0.9	6.0	4.0	6.87	1	2	0	0	92	6	78	6.8	1	2	0	0	0.0	0.0
C+ /6.3	2.9	4.4	10.00	54	0	0	99	0	1	57	4.3	14	N/A	5,000	250	0.0	0.0
A+ /9.9	N/A	N/A	1.00	352	100	0	0	0	0	0	0.2	43	N/A	5,000	250	0.0	0.0
B- /7.1	2.7	5.1	10.56	23	0	17	2	43	38	57	3.8	67	20	5,000	250	0.0	0.0
B- /7.0	2.7	5.1	10.58	678	0	17	2	43	38	57	3.8	74	20	100,000	250	0.0	0.0
C- /3.2	3.8	7.5	11.03	138	1	3	0	92	4	145	4.5	84	N/A	5,000	250	0.0	0.0
D+ /2.7	4.3	5.0	10.10	N/A	1	16	1	79	3	74	5.3	96	4	5,000	250	0.0	0.0
D+ /2.6	4.3	5.0	10.07	4	1	16	1	79	3	74	5.3	97	4	100,000	250	0.0	0.0
D+ /2.6	4.4	5.0	10.08	36	1	16	1	79	3	74	5.3	97	4	50,000,000	250	0.0	0.0
D- /1.0	6.2	7.2	13.79	475	2	78	0	18	2	46	6.2	99	17	100,000	250	0.0	0.0
D- /1.0	6.1	7.2	13.80	93	2	78	0	18	2	46	6.2	99	17	5,000	250	0.0	0.0
D- /1.0	6.2	7.2	13.78	588	2	78	0	18	2	46	6.2	99	17	50,000,000	250	0.0	0.0
E- /0.2	11.3	5.6	6.77	N/A	1	78	0	18	3	68	7.0	29	N/A	5,000	250	0.0	0.0
E- /0.2	11.3	5.6	6.77	154	1	78	0	18	3	68	7.0	38	N/A	100,000	250	0.0	0.0
B /8.0	2.1	0.3	10.04	N/A	8	0	0	21	71	41	4.3	89	4	5,000	250	0.0	0.0
B /8.0	2.1	0.3	10.03	43	8	0	0	21	71	41	4.3	91	4	100,000	250	0.0	0.0
B /7.9	2.2	0.3	10.04	131	8	0	0	21	71	41	4.3	91	4	50,000,000	250	0.0	0.0
B /7.6	2.5	6.6	8.98	125	0	46	0	42	12	76	2.7	94	9	5,000	250	0.0	0.0
A+ /9.7	0.7	1.4	10.04	130	0	24	0	55	21	41	1.8	75	N/A	5,000	250	0.0	0.0
B+ /8.4	1.8	2.4	9.57	19	0	0	0	0	100	12	4.5	77	N/A	5,000	250	0.0	0.0
B+ /8.5	1.8	2.4	9.58	246	0	0	0	0	100	12	4.5	80	N/A	100,000	250	0.0	0.0
D /2.0	4.6	3.9	6.56	12	0	0	0	93	7	44	6.1	51	5	5,000	250	0.0	0.0
D /1.9	4.6	3.9	6.54	573	0	0	0	93	7	44	6.1	56	5	100,000	250	0.0	0.0
B+ /8.8	1.5	1.4	10.27	53	4	8	0	40	48	55	3.2	76	N/A	25,000	0	0.0	0.0
B+ /8.8	1.5	1.4	9.87	36	4	8	0	40	48	55	3.2	72	N/A	25,000	0	0.0	0.0
B+ /8.8	1.5	1.4	10.44	115	4	8	0	40	48	55	3.2	79	N/A	25,000	0	0.0	0.0
A+ /9.9	0.4	0.6	9.47	500	0	25	1	50	24	39	1.4	66	N/A	5,000	250	0.0	0.0
A+ /9.7	0.6	1.6	10.09	847	1	31	0	46	22	41	2.0	67	N/A	5,000	250	0.0	0.0
A- /9.0	1.3	2.3	10.48	N/A	0	6	0	1	93	35	2.5	34	N/A	5,000	250	0.0	0.0
A- /9.0	1.2	2.3	10.48	124	0	6	0	1	93	35	2.5	56	N/A	100,000	250	0.0	0.0
U /	N/A	N/A	10.24	22	0	0	0	0	100	0	0.0	N/A	2	1,000,000	100	0.0	2.0
U /	N/A	N/A	10.68	9	1	0	0	97	2	0	0.0	N/A	2	1,000,000	100	0.0	2.0
D+ /2.5	4.4	N/A	23.55	151	1	0	98	0	1	14	0.0	40	6	1,000,000	500	0.0	2.0
D+ /2.5	4.4	N/A	23.57	25	1	0	98	0	1	14	0.0	32	6	2,500	500	0.0	2.0
B /8.2	2.1	N/A	22.48	834	0	0	39	2	59	46	0.0	93	7	5,000	500	0.0	2.0
A+ /9.9	0.2	0.2	64.70	17	0	100	0	0	0	0	0.2	20	14	1,000	100	0.0	0.0
U /	N/A	7.1	59.60	N/A	0	0	0	0	100	4	0.0	N/A	14	1,000	100	4.0	0.0
U /	N/A	7.1	59.54	N/A	0	0	0	0	100	4	0.0	N/A	14	1,000	100	0.0	0.0
E+ /0.8	6.0	7.1	59.65	12	0	0	0	0	100	4	0.0	37	14	1,000	100	0.0	0.0
E+ /0.6	7.4	N/A	9.32	84	0	0	0	0	100	82	0.0	93	5	0	0	0.0	0.0
E- /0.2	9.3	N/A	9.35	49	4	68	0	24	4	80	0.0	98	5	0	0	0.0	0.0
D+ /2.8	4.2	N/A	8.91	12	0	89	0	1	10	89	0.0	3	9	0	0	0.0	0.0
C- /4.1	3.5	N/A	10.62	836	0	26	3	24	47	370	0.0	57	3	0	0	0.0	0.0
A /9.3	0.9	N/A	9.88	126	2	7	0	46	45	98	0.0	57	6	0	0	0.0	0.0
A+ /9.9	0.1	N/A	1.00	177	100	0	0	0	0	0	0.4	53	N/A	50,000	0	0.0	0.0

Fund Type	Fund Name	Ticker Symbol	Overall Investment Rating	Phone	Performance Rating/Pts	3 Mo	6 Mo	1Yr / Pct	3Yr / Pct	5Yr / Pct	Dividend Yield	Expense Ratio
COI	PIA BBB Bond MACS	PBBBX	C-	(800) 251-1970	B- / 7.4	2.61	-1.55	8.50 /75	3.65 /71	3.77 /69	3.86	0.16
COH	PIA High Yield Institutional	PHYSX	B	(800) 251-1970	A+ / 9.6	4.31	4.85	18.33 /94	4.80 /84	6.74 /96	6.01	0.93
MTG	PIA Short-Term Securities Adv	PIASX	C+	(800) 251-1970	D+ / 2.4	0.29	0.34	1.68 /46	0.72 /23	0.57 /22	1.07	0.41
MUS	PIMCO CA Interm Muni Bond A	PCMBX	D	(800) 426-0107	C- / 3.3	1.94	-2.83	-0.84 / 5	1.96 /61	1.93 /57	2.10	0.78
MUS	PIMCO CA Interm Muni Bond C	PCFCX	D-	(800) 426-0107	D+ / 2.8	1.76	-3.19	-1.58 / 1	1.20 /40	1.17 /39	1.39	1.53
MUS	PIMCO CA Interm Muni Bond D	PCIDX	C-	(800) 426-0107	C / 4.7	1.95	-2.83	-0.84 / 5	1.96 /61	1.93 /57	2.15	0.78
MUS	PIMCO CA Interm Muni Bond Inst	PCIMX	C+	(800) 426-0107	C+ / 5.6	2.03	-2.67	-0.52 / 9	2.29 /69	2.26 /65	2.48	0.45
MUS	PIMCO CA Interm Muni Bond P	PCIPX	C	(800) 426-0107	C / 5.3	2.00	-2.72	-0.62 / 8	2.19 /67	2.16 /63	2.38	0.55
MUS	PIMCO CA Sh Duration Muni Inc A	PCDAX	D	(800) 426-0107	E / 0.3	0.90	-0.57	-0.28 /13	0.23 /19	0.24 /20	0.61	0.73
MUS	PIMCO CA Sh Duration Muni Inc C	PCSCX	D	(800) 426-0107	E / 0.5	0.82	-0.72	-0.58 / 9	-0.07 / 5	-0.06 / 5	0.33	1.03
MUS	PIMCO CA Sh Duration Muni Inc D	PCDDX	C-	(800) 426-0107	D- / 1.5	0.90	-0.57	-0.28 /13	0.23 /19	0.24 /20	0.63	0.73
MUS	PIMCO CA Sh Duration Muni Inc Inst	PCDIX	C+	(800) 426-0107	D+ / 2.5	1.00	-0.38	0.11 /25	0.63 /27	0.64 /27	1.03	0.33
MUS	PIMCO CA Sh Duration Muni Inc P	PCDPX	C	(800) 426-0107	D+ / 2.3	0.97	-0.43	0.02 /19	0.53 /25	0.54 /25	0.93	0.43
MUN	PIMCO California Municipal Bd A	PCTTX	C	(800) 426-0107	B- / 7.4	2.66	-4.54	0.55 /38	4.08 /93	—	2.54	0.79
MUN	PIMCO California Municipal Bd C	PCTGX	C-	(800) 426-0107	B- / 7.1	2.47	-4.90	-0.20 /14	3.31 /86	—	1.83	1.54
MUN	PIMCO California Municipal Bd D	PCTDX	C+	(800) 426-0107	B+ / 8.4	2.65	-4.54	0.55 /38	4.08 /93	—	2.60	0.79
MUN	PIMCO California Municipal Bd Inst	PCTIX	B	(800) 426-0107	B+ / 8.9	2.74	-4.38	0.90 /44	4.44 /95	—	2.95	0.44
MUN	PIMCO California Municipal Bd P	PCTPX	B-	(800) 426-0107	B+ / 8.7	2.72	-4.43	0.80 /42	4.34 /95	—	2.85	0.54
GEI	PIMCO Credit Absolute Return A	PZCRX	C-	(800) 426-0107	C+ / 5.8	2.77	3.80	12.21 /84	2.17 /46	2.98 /57	2.68	1.33
GEI	PIMCO Credit Absolute Return C	PCCRX	C	(800) 426-0107	C+ / 6.1	2.66	3.50	11.31 /82	1.43 /34	2.23 /45	2.34	2.08
GEI	PIMCO Credit Absolute Return D	PDCRX	C+	(800) 426-0107	B- / 7.1	2.73	3.78	12.07 /83	2.18 /46	2.98 /57	2.96	1.33
GEI	PIMCO Credit Absolute Return Inst	PCARX	B	(800) 426-0107	B- / 7.5	2.97	4.01	12.65 /84	2.62 /54	3.41 /64	3.15	0.93
GEI	PIMCO Credit Absolute Return P	PPCRX	B-	(800) 426-0107	B- / 7.4	2.89	4.01	12.52 /84	2.49 /52	3.30 /62	3.12	1.03
GES	PIMCO Diversified Income A	PDVAX	C	(800) 426-0107	B / 8.2	3.81	1.77	13.45 /86	4.51 /81	4.86 /83	4.25	1.16
GES	PIMCO Diversified Income Admin	PDAAX	B-	(800) 426-0107	A- / 9.1	3.85	1.84	13.62 /86	4.66 /82	5.01 /84	4.56	1.01
GES	PIMCO Diversified Income C	PDICX	C+	(800) 426-0107	B+ / 8.3	3.62	1.39	12.61 /84	3.73 /72	4.08 /74	3.68	1.91
GES	PIMCO Diversified Income D	PDVDX	B-	(800) 426-0107	A- / 9.0	3.81	1.77	13.45 /86	4.51 /81	4.85 /82	4.41	1.16
GES	PIMCO Diversified Income Inst	PDIIX	B	(800) 426-0107	A / 9.3	3.91	1.96	13.89 /87	4.92 /84	5.27 /87	4.80	0.76
GES	PIMCO Diversified Income P	PDVPX	B	(800) 426-0107	A- / 9.2	3.88	1.92	13.78 /86	4.82 /84	5.17 /86	4.70	0.86
EM	PIMCO EM Corporate Bond A	PECZX	D-	(800) 426-0107	C+ / 6.7	5.02	4.30	16.82 /92	1.99 /43	3.14 /60	3.98	1.35
EM	PIMCO EM Corporate Bond C	PECCX	D-	(800) 426-0107	C+ / 6.9	4.83	3.92	15.95 /90	1.23 /31	2.37 /47	3.42	2.10
EM	PIMCO EM Corporate Bond Inst	PEMIX	D+	(800) 426-0107	B / 8.2	5.13	4.50	17.28 /92	2.39 /50	3.55 /66	4.52	0.95
EM	PIMCO EM Corporate Bond P	PMIPX	D	(800) 426-0107	B / 8.1	5.10	4.45	17.16 /92	2.29 /48	3.45 /65	4.43	1.05
EM	PIMCO Em Mkts Full Spectrum Bd A	PFSSX	E	(800) 426-0107	D+ / 2.9	6.13	1.65	15.63 /90	-0.53 / 3	—	4.59	2.28
EM	PIMCO Em Mkts Full Spectrum Bd C	PFSCX	E	(800) 426-0107	C- / 3.2	5.94	1.26	14.76 /88	-1.28 / 2	—	4.02	3.03
EM	PIMCO Em Mkts Full Spectrum Bd	PFSIX	E+	(800) 426-0107	C / 5.2	6.24	1.85	16.09 /90	-0.13 / 5	—	5.16	1.88
EM	PIMCO Em Mkts Full Spectrum Bd P	PFSPX	E+	(800) 426-0107	C / 5.0	6.21	1.80	15.97 /90	-0.23 / 4	—	5.06	1.98
EM	PIMCO Emerging Local Bond A	PELAX	E-	(800) 426-0107	E- / 0.1	6.96	0.38	14.35 /87	-3.27 / 1	-3.50 / 0	5.00	1.30
EM	PIMCO Emerging Local Bond Admin	PEBLX	E-	(800) 426-0107	E / 0.4	7.00	0.46	14.55 /88	-3.08 / 1	-3.31 / 0	5.38	1.15
EM	PIMCO Emerging Local Bond C	PELCX	E-	(800) 426-0107	E- / 0.2	6.76	0.02	13.51 /86	-3.99 / 0	-4.22 / 0	4.45	2.05
EM	PIMCO Emerging Local Bond D	PLBDX	E-	(800) 426-0107	E / 0.3	6.96	0.38	14.35 /87	-3.28 / 1	-3.50 / 0	5.20	1.30
EM	PIMCO Emerging Local Bond Inst	PELBX	E-	(800) 426-0107	E+ / 0.8	7.06	0.58	14.84 /88	-2.84 / 1	-3.07 / 1	5.62	0.90
EM	PIMCO Emerging Local Bond P	PELPX	E-	(800) 426-0107	E / 0.5	7.04	0.53	14.72 /88	-2.94 / 1	-3.17 / 1	5.53	1.00
EM	PIMCO Emerging Markets Bond A	PAEMX	C-	(800) 426-0107	B+ / 8.8	5.93	1.46	17.97 /93	4.41 /80	3.73 /69	4.95	1.20
EM	PIMCO Emerging Markets Bond	PEBAX	C	(800) 426-0107	A / 9.4	5.96	1.51	18.10 /94	4.54 /81	3.88 /71	5.25	1.08
EM	PIMCO Emerging Markets Bond C	PEBCX	C-	(800) 426-0107	B+ / 8.9	5.73	1.09	17.10 /92	3.64 /71	2.96 /57	4.42	1.95
EM	PIMCO Emerging Markets Bond D	PEMDX	C	(800) 426-0107	A / 9.4	5.93	1.46	17.97 /93	4.41 /80	3.73 /69	5.14	1.20
EM	PIMCO Emerging Markets Bond Inst	PEBIX	C	(800) 426-0107	A / 9.5	6.02	1.64	18.40 /94	4.81 /84	4.14 /74	5.50	0.83
EM	PIMCO Emerging Markets Bond P	PEMPX	C	(800) 426-0107	A / 9.5	6.00	1.59	18.29 /94	4.70 /83	4.03 /73	5.41	0.93
GL	PIMCO Emerging Markets Currency	PLMAX	E-	(800) 426-0107	E- / 0.2	5.09	1.73	11.00 /81	-1.92 / 2	-1.57 / 2	2.37	1.26
GL	PIMCO Emerging Markets Currency	PDEVX	E	(800) 426-0107	D / 1.8	5.06	1.74	11.09 /81	-1.79 / 2	-1.44 / 2	2.55	1.11
GL	PIMCO Emerging Markets Currency	PLMCX	E-	(800) 426-0107	E / 0.3	4.90	1.36	10.18 /79	-2.65 / 1	-2.31 / 1	1.73	2.01

● Denotes fund is closed to new investors
* Denotes fund is included in Section II

www.thestreetratings.com

RISK			NET ASSETS		ASSET							FUND MANAGER		MINIMUM		LOADS	
Risk Rating/Pts	3 Yr Avg Standard Deviation	Avg Dura-tion	NAV As of 2/28/17	Total $(Mil)	Cash %	Gov. Bond %	Muni. Bond %	Corp. Bond %	Other %	Portfolio Turnover Ratio	Avg Coupon Rate	Manager Quality Pct	Manager Tenure (Years)	Initial Purch. $	Additional Purch. $	Front End Load	Back End Load
D / 2.1	4.7	7.6	9.22	221	1	11	0	87	1	18	0.0	24	14	1,000	50	0.0	0.0
D / 1.9	4.8	3.3	10.32	170	4	0	0	95	1	26	0.0	77	7	1,000,000	100	0.0	0.0
A+ / 9.8	0.5	1.0	10.03	165	0	37	0	44	19	60	0.0	62	N/A	1,000	50	0.0	0.0
C+ / 5.6	3.0	4.9	9.69	48	4	0	95	0	1	24	4.6	9	2	1,000	50	2.3	0.0
C+ / 5.6	3.0	4.9	9.69	11	4	0	95	0	1	24	4.6	3	2	1,000	50	0.0	0.0
C+ / 5.6	3.0	4.9	9.69	3	4	0	95	0	1	24	4.6	9	2	1,000	50	0.0	0.0
C+ / 5.6	3.0	4.9	9.69	43	4	0	95	0	1	24	4.6	15	2	1,000,000	0	0.0	0.0
C+ / 5.6	3.0	4.9	9.69	29	4	0	95	0	1	24	4.6	13	2	1,000,000	0	0.0	0.0
A / 9.3	1.0	2.0	9.88	31	4	0	95	0	1	42	3.5	17	6	1,000	50	2.3	0.0
A / 9.3	1.0	2.0	9.88	3	4	0	95	0	1	42	3.5	11	6	1,000	50	0.0	0.0
A / 9.3	1.0	2.0	9.88	2	4	0	95	0	1	42	3.5	17	6	1,000	50	0.0	0.0
A / 9.3	1.0	2.0	9.88	78	4	0	95	0	1	42	3.5	29	6	1,000,000	0	0.0	0.0
A / 9.3	1.0	2.0	9.88	12	4	0	95	0	1	42	3.5	26	6	1,000,000	0	0.0	0.0
D+ / 2.5	4.3	7.9	10.51	6	1	0	98	0	1	89	4.9	26	2	1,000	50	2.3	0.0
D+ / 2.5	4.3	7.9	10.51	2	1	0	98	0	1	89	4.9	10	2	1,000	50	0.0	0.0
D+ / 2.5	4.3	7.9	10.51	1	1	0	98	0	1	89	4.9	26	2	1,000	50	0.0	0.0
D+ / 2.5	4.3	7.9	10.51	3	1	0	98	0	1	89	4.9	41	2	1,000,000	0	0.0	0.0
D+ / 2.5	4.3	7.9	10.51	1	1	0	98	0	1	89	4.9	35	2	1,000,000	0	0.0	0.0
C- / 4.2	3.4	1.1	9.97	9	23	11	0	30	36	110	4.1	85	6	1,000	50	3.8	0.0
C- / 4.2	3.4	1.1	9.86	7	23	11	0	30	36	110	4.1	77	6	1,000	50	0.0	0.0
C- / 4.2	3.4	1.1	9.93	11	23	11	0	30	36	110	4.1	84	6	1,000	50	0.0	0.0
C- / 4.2	3.4	1.1	9.95	346	23	11	0	30	36	110	4.1	88	6	1,000,000	0	0.0	0.0
C- / 4.1	3.5	1.1	9.92	27	23	11	0	30	36	110	4.1	87	6	1,000,000	0	0.0	0.0
D / 2.1	4.9	5.5	10.75	166	3	16	1	52	28	99	5.0	88	1	1,000	50	3.8	0.0
D / 2.1	4.9	5.5	10.75	12	3	16	1	52	28	99	5.0	89	1	1,000,000	0	0.0	0.0
D / 2.1	4.9	5.5	10.75	105	3	16	1	52	28	99	5.0	82	1	1,000	50	0.0	0.0
D / 2.1	4.9	5.5	10.75	55	3	16	1	52	28	99	5.0	88	1	1,000	50	0.0	0.0
D / 2.1	4.9	5.5	10.75	2,345	3	16	1	52	28	99	5.0	90	1	1,000,000	0	0.0	0.0
D / 2.1	4.9	5.5	10.75	80	3	16	1	52	28	99	5.0	90	1	1,000,000	0	0.0	0.0
E+ / 0.6	7.3	4.4	10.61	1	6	3	0	89	2	69	6.3	90	1	1,000	50	3.8	0.0
E+ / 0.6	7.3	4.4	10.61	1	6	3	0	89	2	69	6.3	85	1	1,000	50	0.0	0.0
E+ / 0.6	7.3	4.4	10.61	144	6	3	0	89	2	69	6.3	92	1	1,000,000	0	0.0	0.0
E+ / 0.6	7.3	4.4	10.61	1	6	3	0	89	2	69	6.3	92	1	1,000,000	0	0.0	0.0
E- / 0.2	9.6	N/A	7.57	1	16	42	0	40	2	42	0.0	80	4	1,000	50	3.8	0.0
E- / 0.2	9.6	N/A	7.57	N/A	16	42	0	40	2	42	0.0	67	4	1,000	50	0.0	0.0
E- / 0.2	9.6	N/A	7.57	359	16	42	0	40	2	42	0.0	84	4	1,000,000	0	0.0	0.0
E- / 0.2	9.6	N/A	7.57	1	16	42	0	40	2	42	0.0	83	4	1,000,000	0	0.0	0.0
E- / 0.1	12.4	5.0	7.21	38	8	73	0	14	5	58	5.5	20	11	1,000	50	3.8	0.0
E- / 0.1	12.4	5.0	7.21	9	8	73	0	14	5	58	5.5	26	11	1,000,000	0	0.0	0.0
E- / 0.1	12.4	5.0	7.21	20	8	73	0	14	5	58	5.5	7	11	1,000	50	0.0	0.0
E- / 0.1	12.4	5.0	7.21	31	8	73	0	14	5	58	5.5	20	11	1,000	50	0.0	0.0
E- / 0.1	12.4	5.0	7.21	3,728	8	73	0	14	5	58	5.5	34	11	1,000,000	0	0.0	0.0
E- / 0.1	12.4	5.0	7.21	69	8	73	0	14	5	58	5.5	31	11	1,000,000	0	0.0	0.0
E / 0.3	8.5	6.4	10.40	151	0	50	0	31	19	43	5.8	98	5	1,000	50	3.8	0.0
E / 0.3	8.5	6.4	10.40	5	0	50	0	31	19	43	5.8	98	5	1,000,000	0	0.0	0.0
E / 0.3	8.5	6.4	10.40	66	0	50	0	31	19	43	5.8	96	5	1,000	50	0.0	0.0
E / 0.3	8.5	6.4	10.40	147	0	50	0	31	19	43	5.8	98	5	1,000	50	0.0	0.0
E / 0.3	8.5	6.4	10.40	1,401	0	50	0	31	19	43	5.8	98	5	1,000,000	0	0.0	0.0
E / 0.3	8.5	6.4	10.40	114	0	50	0	31	19	43	5.8	98	5	1,000,000	0	0.0	0.0
E / 0.5	7.6	0.7	8.91	13	23	40	0	31	6	64	4.5	26	12	1,000	50	3.8	0.0
E / 0.5	7.6	0.7	8.91	N/A	23	40	0	31	6	64	4.5	30	12	1,000,000	0	0.0	0.0
E / 0.5	7.6	0.7	8.91	6	23	40	0	31	6	64	4.5	9	12	1,000	50	0.0	0.0

Fund Type	Fund Name	Ticker Symbol	Overall Investment Rating	Phone	PERFORMANCE Performance Rating/Pts	Total Return % through 2/28/17 3 Mo	6 Mo	1Yr / Pct	Annualized 3Yr / Pct	5Yr / Pct	Incl. in Returns Dividend Yield	Expense Ratio
	99 Pct = Best											
	0 Pct = Worst											
GL	PIMCO Emerging Markets Currency	PLMDX	E	(800) 426-0107	D / 1.6	5.09	1.73	11.00 / 81	-1.92 / 2	-1.57 / 2	2.46	1.26
GL	PIMCO Emerging Markets Currency	PLMIX	E	(800) 426-0107	D / 2.2	5.19	1.93	11.44 / 82	-1.52 / 2	-1.18 / 2	2.86	0.86
GL	PIMCO Emerging Markets Currency	PLMPX	E	(800) 426-0107	D / 2.0	5.17	1.88	11.33 / 82	-1.62 / 2	-1.28 / 2	2.76	0.96
GEI	PIMCO Extended Duration Inst	PEDIX	C-	(800) 426-0107	A- / 9.2	2.60	-16.44	-5.85 / 0	9.56 / 99	4.41 / 77	2.78	0.53
GEI	PIMCO Extended Duration P	PEDPX	C-	(800) 426-0107	A- / 9.1	2.58	-16.49	-5.95 / 0	9.45 / 99	4.30 / 76	2.66	0.63
* GEI	PIMCO Fixed Income SHares C	FXICX	D+	(800) 988-8380	C+ / 5.7	2.86	2.24	6.15 / 71	1.98 / 43	3.65 / 68	4.48	0.03
GL	PIMCO Fixed Income SHares LD	FXIDX	A+	(800) 988-8380	C+ / 6.9	0.93	1.77	6.48 / 72	3.19 / 64	--	4.32	0.24
* GEI	PIMCO Fixed Income SHares M	FXIMX	C	(800) 988-8380	B / 8.0	2.83	-2.01	9.26 / 77	4.29 / 79	4.60 / 80	4.42	0.06
US	PIMCO Fixed Income SHares R	FXIRX	D-	(800) 988-8380	C / 5.1	2.30	1.19	8.44 / 75	1.40 / 33	1.49 / 34	3.58	0.16
MUN	PIMCO Fixed Income SHares TE	FXIEX	B+	(800) 988-8380	B / 7.6	2.41	-2.99	1.25 / 48	3.26 / 85	--	3.23	N/A
GES	PIMCO Floating Income C	PFNCX	C-	(800) 426-0107	B / 7.9	3.32	4.57	16.86 / 92	2.36 / 49	3.53 / 66	2.97	1.26
GL	PIMCO Foreign Bd Fd (Unhgd) A	PFUAX	E-	(800) 426-0107	E- / 0.1	2.52	-4.83	4.04 / 62	-1.08 / 3	-0.22 / 4	1.49	0.92
GL	PIMCO Foreign Bd Fd (Unhgd)	PFUUX	E-	(800) 426-0107	E / 0.3	2.56	-4.76	4.20 / 63	-0.93 / 3	-0.07 / 5	1.70	0.77
GL	PIMCO Foreign Bd Fd (Unhgd) C	PFRCX	E-	(800) 426-0107	E- / 0.1	2.33	-5.18	3.26 / 58	-1.81 / 2	-0.96 / 2	0.77	1.67
GL	PIMCO Foreign Bd Fd (Unhgd) D	PFBDX	E-	(800) 426-0107	E / 0.3	2.52	-4.83	4.04 / 62	-1.08 / 3	-0.22 / 4	1.55	0.92
GL	PIMCO Foreign Bd Fd (Unhgd) Inst	PFUIX	E-	(800) 426-0107	E / 0.4	2.62	-4.65	4.46 / 64	-0.68 / 3	0.18 / 18	1.95	0.52
GL	PIMCO Foreign Bd Fd (Unhgd) P	PFUPX	E-	(800) 426-0107	E / 0.4	2.59	-4.69	4.35 / 64	-0.78 / 3	0.08 / 14	1.85	0.62
GL	PIMCO Foreign Bond (US Hedged) A	PFOAX	B-	(800) 426-0107	B- / 7.5	1.32	-0.03	5.65 / 69	5.27 / 87	5.42 / 88	0.97	0.91
GL	PIMCO Foreign Bond (US Hedged)	PFRAX	A-	(800) 426-0107	B+ / 8.6	1.36	0.04	5.81 / 70	5.43 / 88	5.58 / 89	1.16	0.76
GL	PIMCO Foreign Bond (US Hedged) C	PFOCX	B	(800) 426-0107	B / 7.6	1.06	-0.47	4.74 / 66	4.46 / 80	4.62 / 80	0.24	1.66
GL	PIMCO Foreign Bond (US Hedged) D	PFODX	A-	(800) 426-0107	B+ / 8.5	1.32	-0.03	5.65 / 69	5.27 / 87	5.42 / 88	1.01	0.91
GL	PIMCO Foreign Bond (US Hedged)	PFORX	A	(800) 426-0107	B+ / 8.8	1.42	0.16	6.07 / 70	5.69 / 90	5.84 / 91	1.40	0.51
GL	PIMCO Foreign Bond (US Hedged) P	PFBPX	A	(800) 426-0107	B+ / 8.7	1.40	0.11	5.97 / 70	5.59 / 89	5.73 / 90	1.31	0.61
GL	PIMCO Foreign Bond (US Hedged) R	PFRRX	B+	(800) 426-0107	B / 8.2	1.26	-0.16	5.39 / 68	5.01 / 85	5.16 / 86	0.77	1.16
GL	PIMCO Glb Advantage Strategy Bd A	PGSAX	E	(800) 426-0107	E+ / 0.7	3.20	0.81	8.66 / 76	-0.47 / 4	0.27 / 19	1.58	1.14
GL	PIMCO Glb Advantage Strategy Bd C	PAFCX	E	(800) 426-0107	D- / 1.4	3.01	0.45	7.86 / 74	-1.21 / 2	-0.47 / 3	0.91	1.89
GL	PIMCO Glb Advantage Strategy Bd D	PGSDX	E	(800) 426-0107	D+ / 2.6	3.20	0.81	8.66 / 76	-0.47 / 4	0.27 / 19	1.64	1.14
GL	PIMCO Glb Advantage Strategy Bd I	PSAIX	E+	(800) 426-0107	C- / 3.3	3.30	1.01	9.09 / 77	-0.07 / 5	0.68 / 23	2.03	0.74
GL	PIMCO Glb Advantage Strategy Bd P	PGBPX	E+	(800) 426-0107	C- / 3.2	3.28	0.96	8.98 / 76	-0.17 / 5	0.57 / 22	1.94	0.84
GL	PIMCO Glb Advantage Strategy Bd R	PSBRX	E	(800) 426-0107	D / 2.2	3.14	0.69	8.39 / 75	-0.71 / 3	0.03 / 8	1.40	1.39
GL	PIMCO Global Bond (Unhedged)	PADMX	E	(800) 426-0107	D+ / 2.3	2.12	-3.35	4.11 / 63	0.46 / 20	1.00 / 27	1.85	0.82
GL	PIMCO Global Bond (Unhedged) D	PGBDX	E	(800) 426-0107	D / 2.1	2.08	-3.42	3.96 / 62	0.31 / 19	0.85 / 25	1.70	0.97
GL	PIMCO Global Bond (Unhedged) Inst	PIGLX	E	(800) 426-0107	D+ / 2.7	2.18	-3.23	4.37 / 64	0.71 / 23	1.26 / 31	2.10	0.57
GL	PIMCO Global Bond (Unhedged) P	PGOPX	E	(800) 426-0107	D+ / 2.6	2.16	-3.28	4.27 / 63	0.61 / 22	1.16 / 29	2.00	0.67
GL	PIMCO Global Bond (US Hedged) A	PAIIX	B-	(800) 426-0107	C+ / 6.7	1.56	-0.14	5.47 / 68	4.48 / 80	4.34 / 77	2.16	0.92
GL	PIMCO Global Bond (US Hedged)	PGDAX	A-	(800) 426-0107	B / 7.9	1.59	-0.09	5.58 / 69	4.58 / 82	4.45 / 78	2.34	0.82
GL	PIMCO Global Bond (US Hedged) C	PCIIX	B-	(800) 426-0107	B- / 7.0	1.38	-0.50	4.68 / 65	3.70 / 71	3.56 / 67	1.49	1.67
GL	PIMCO Global Bond (US Hedged)	PGBIX	A-	(800) 426-0107	B / 8.2	1.65	0.04	5.84 / 70	4.84 / 84	4.71 / 81	2.59	0.57
GL	PIMCO Global Bond (US Hedged) P	PGNPX	A-	(800) 426-0107	B / 8.1	1.63	-0.01	5.74 / 69	4.74 / 83	4.60 / 80	2.49	0.67
USA	PIMCO GNMA A	PAGNX	C-	(800) 426-0107	D / 2.2	0.62	-0.95	0.65 / 36	1.97 / 43	1.57 / 36	2.46	0.90
USA	PIMCO GNMA C	PCGNX	C	(800) 426-0107	D+ / 2.6	0.44	-1.31	-0.08 / 16	1.22 / 31	0.82 / 25	1.81	1.65
USA	PIMCO GNMA D	PGNDX	B-	(800) 426-0107	C- / 3.8	0.62	-0.95	0.65 / 36	1.97 / 43	1.57 / 36	2.55	0.90
USA	PIMCO GNMA Inst	PDMIX	B+	(800) 426-0107	C / 4.5	0.72	-0.75	1.05 / 40	2.38 / 50	1.97 / 42	2.95	0.50
USA	PIMCO GNMA P	PPGNX	B+	(800) 426-0107	C / 4.3	0.69	-0.80	0.95 / 39	2.28 / 48	1.87 / 40	2.85	0.60
MMT	PIMCO Government Money Market A	AMAXX	C-	(800) 426-0107	D- / 1.0	0.06	0.11	0.18 / 25	0.08 / 12	0.06 / 13	0.17	N/A
MMT	PIMCO Government Money Market C	AMGXX	C-	(800) 426-0107	D- / 1.0	0.06	0.10	0.17 / 25	0.08 / 12	0.06 / 13	0.17	N/A
MMT	PIMCO Government Money Market M	PGFXX	C-	(800) 426-0107	D- / 1.3	0.09	0.18	0.32 / 30	0.14 / 15	0.10 / 15	0.32	N/A
MMT	PIMCO Government Money Market P	PGPXX	C-	(800) 426-0107	D- / 1.1	0.07	0.13	0.22 / 27	0.10 / 13	0.07 / 13	0.22	N/A
*COH	PIMCO High Yield A	PHDAX	C	(800) 426-0107	B+ / 8.4	4.28	4.06	15.65 / 90	4.19 / 77	5.83 / 91	4.75	0.91
COH	PIMCO High Yield Admin	PHYAX	C+	(800) 426-0107	A- / 9.2	4.30	4.11	15.77 / 90	4.29 / 79	5.94 / 92	5.03	0.81
COH	PIMCO High Yield C	PHDCX	C	(800) 426-0107	B+ / 8.6	4.09	3.68	14.80 / 88	3.42 / 68	5.05 / 84	4.21	1.66
COH	PIMCO High Yield D	PHYDX	C+	(800) 426-0107	A- / 9.2	4.28	4.06	15.65 / 90	4.19 / 77	5.83 / 91	4.93	0.91

● Denotes fund is closed to new investors
* Denotes fund is included in Section II

www.thestreetratings.com

RISK			NET ASSETS		ASSET							FUND MANAGER		MINIMUM		LOADS	
Risk Rating/Pts	3 Yr Avg Standard Deviation	Avg Dura-tion	NAV As of 2/28/17	Total $(Mil)	Cash %	Gov. Bond %	Muni. Bond %	Corp. Bond %	Other %	Portfolio Turnover Ratio	Avg Coupon Rate	Manager Quality Pct	Manager Tenure (Years)	Initial Purch. $	Additional Purch. $	Front End Load	Back End Load
E /0.5	7.6	0.7	8.91	14	23	40	0	31	6	64	4.5	26	12	1,000	50	0.0	0.0
E /0.5	7.6	0.7	8.91	3,967	23	40	0	31	6	64	4.5	N/A	12	1,000,000	0	0.0	0.0
E /0.5	7.6	0.7	8.91	7	23	40	0	31	6	64	4.5	37	12	1,000,000	0	0.0	0.0
E- /0.0	17.7	26.6	7.55	1,131	0	0	0	0	100	96	0.4	0	10	1,000,000	0	0.0	0.0
E- /0.0	17.7	26.6	7.55	11	0	0	0	0	100	96	0.4	0	10	1,000,000	0	0.0	0.0
C- /3.7	3.7	N/A	10.15	1,349	0	35	1	38	26	95	0.0	78	1	0	0	0.0	0.0
B /8.0	2.2	N/A	9.78	40	0	7	0	59	34	1,135	0.0	92	4	0	0	0.0	0.0
D /1.8	5.5	N/A	10.13	1,362	0	21	12	16	51	473	0.0	48	1	0	0	0.0	0.0
D /1.9	5.1	N/A	9.29	161	0	80	0	8	12	126	0.0	53	10	0	0	0.0	0.0
C /4.9	3.2	N/A	9.84	89	2	9	87	0	2	72	0.0	61	5	0	0	0.0	0.0
D /1.6	5.6	0.5	8.43	86	3	10	1	50	36	118	5.0	90	1	1,000	50	0.0	0.0
E /0.5	7.3	7.8	9.47	64	0	53	7	20	20	327	2.3	79	3	1,000	50	3.8	0.0
E /0.5	7.3	7.8	9.47	32	0	53	7	20	20	327	2.3	81	3	1,000,000	0	0.0	0.0
E /0.5	7.3	7.8	9.47	19	0	53	7	20	20	327	2.3	65	3	1,000	50	0.0	0.0
E /0.5	7.3	7.8	9.47	365	0	53	7	20	20	327	2.3	79	3	1,000	50	0.0	0.0
E+ /0.6	7.3	7.8	9.47	584	0	53	7	20	20	327	2.3	83	3	1,000,000	0	0.0	0.0
E+ /0.6	7.3	7.8	9.47	65	0	53	7	20	20	327	2.3	82	3	1,000,000	0	0.0	0.0
C- /4.1	3.3	7.9	10.51	456	0	52	4	12	32	313	1.8	97	3	1,000	50	3.8	0.0
C- /4.1	3.3	7.9	10.51	92	0	52	4	12	32	313	1.8	97	3	1,000,000	0	0.0	0.0
C- /4.1	3.3	7.9	10.50	105	0	52	4	12	32	313	1.8	96	3	1,000	50	0.0	0.0
C- /4.1	3.3	7.9	10.51	1,195	0	52	4	12	32	313	1.8	97	3	1,000	50	0.0	0.0
C- /4.1	3.3	7.9	10.51	4,930	0	52	4	12	32	313	1.8	98	3	1,000,000	0	0.0	0.0
C- /4.1	3.3	7.9	10.51	1,444	0	52	4	12	32	313	1.8	98	3	1,000,000	0	0.0	0.0
C- /4.1	3.3	7.9	10.51	45	0	52	4	12	32	313	1.8	97	3	0	0	0.0	0.0
D /2.1	4.9	5.4	10.44	9	0	40	6	22	32	263	3.0	67	6	1,000	50	3.8	0.0
D /2.1	4.9	5.4	10.44	6	0	40	6	22	32	263	3.0	34	6	1,000	50	0.0	0.0
D /2.1	4.9	5.4	10.44	4	0	40	6	22	32	263	3.0	67	6	1,000	50	0.0	0.0
D /2.1	4.9	5.4	10.44	493	0	40	6	22	32	263	3.0	76	6	1,000,000	0	0.0	0.0
D /2.1	4.9	5.4	10.44	4	0	40	6	22	32	263	3.0	74	6	1,000,000	0	0.0	0.0
D /2.1	4.9	5.4	10.44	3	0	40	6	22	32	263	3.0	60	6	0	0	0.0	0.0
D /1.9	5.2	6.9	9.13	108	0	38	4	18	40	380	2.3	87	3	1,000,000	0	0.0	0.0
D /1.9	5.2	6.9	9.13	15	0	38	4	18	40	380	2.3	86	3	1,000	50	0.0	0.0
D /1.9	5.2	6.9	9.13	350	0	38	4	18	40	380	2.3	88	3	1,000,000	0	0.0	0.0
D /1.9	5.2	6.9	9.13	1	0	38	4	18	40	380	2.3	88	3	1,000,000	0	0.0	0.0
C /4.8	3.2	6.8	10.21	78	0	39	3	20	38	354	2.2	96	3	1,000	50	3.8	0.0
C /4.8	3.2	6.8	10.21	8	0	39	3	20	38	354	2.2	96	3	1,000,000	0	0.0	0.0
C /4.8	3.2	6.8	10.21	23	0	39	3	20	38	354	2.2	94	3	1,000	50	0.0	0.0
C /4.8	3.2	6.8	10.21	568	0	39	3	20	38	354	2.2	97	3	1,000,000	0	0.0	0.0
C /4.8	3.2	6.8	10.21	69	0	39	3	20	38	354	2.2	96	3	1,000,000	0	0.0	0.0
B+ /8.6	1.8	3.0	11.14	174	0	0	0	0	100	1,609	2.9	76	5	1,000	50	3.8	0.0
B+ /8.6	1.8	3.0	11.14	77	0	0	0	0	100	1,609	2.9	58	5	1,000	50	0.0	0.0
B+ /8.6	1.8	3.0	11.14	83	0	0	0	0	100	1,609	2.9	76	5	1,000	50	0.0	0.0
B+ /8.6	1.8	3.0	11.14	296	0	0	0	0	100	1,609	2.9	81	5	1,000,000	0	0.0	0.0
B+ /8.6	1.8	3.0	11.14	65	0	0	0	0	100	1,609	2.9	80	5	1,000,000	0	0.0	0.0
A+ /9.9	N/A	N/A	1.00	131	100	0	0	0	0	0	0.2	45	6	1,000	50	0.0	0.0
A+ /9.9	N/A	N/A	1.00	61	100	0	0	0	0	0	0.2	45	6	1,000	50	0.0	0.0
A+ /9.9	0.1	N/A	1.00	547	100	0	0	0	0	0	0.3	48	6	1,000,000	0	0.0	0.0
A+ /9.9	N/A	N/A	1.00	3	100	0	0	0	0	0	0.2	N/A	6	1,000,000	0	0.0	0.0
D- /1.5	5.2	3.5	8.96	583	5	0	0	92	3	32	6.3	56	7	1,000	50	3.8	0.0
D- /1.5	5.2	3.5	8.96	589	5	0	0	92	3	32	6.3	60	7	1,000,000	0	0.0	0.0
D- /1.5	5.2	3.5	8.96	325	5	0	0	92	3	32	6.3	22	7	1,000	50	0.0	0.0
D- /1.5	5.2	3.5	8.96	371	5	0	0	92	3	32	6.3	56	7	1,000	50	0.0	0.0

Fund Type	Fund Name	Ticker Symbol	Overall Investment Rating	Phone	Performance Rating/Pts	3 Mo	6 Mo	1Yr / Pct	3Yr / Pct	5Yr / Pct	Dividend Yield	Expense Ratio
COH	PIMCO High Yield Inst	PHIYX	B-	(800) 426-0107	A / 9.4	4.37	4.24	16.05 / 90	4.55 / 81	6.20 / 93	5.27	0.56
MUH	PIMCO High Yield Muni Bond A	PYMAX	B+	(800) 426-0107	A+ / 9.6	3.24	-3.67	2.36 / 60	5.95 / 98	5.05 / 98	3.70	0.86
MUH	PIMCO High Yield Muni Bond C	PYMCX	B	(800) 426-0107	A / 9.5	3.05	-4.03	1.60 / 53	5.16 / 97	4.27 / 95	3.02	1.61
MUH	PIMCO High Yield Muni Bond D	PYMDX	B+	(800) 426-0107	A+ / 9.8	3.24	-3.67	2.36 / 60	5.95 / 98	5.06 / 98	3.78	0.86
MUH	PIMCO High Yield Muni Bond Inst	PHMIX	B+	(800) 426-0107	A+ / 9.9	3.32	-3.53	2.66 / 63	6.27 / 99	5.37 / 98	4.09	0.56
MUH	PIMCO High Yield Muni Bond P	PYMPX	B+	(800) 426-0107	A+ / 9.8	3.29	-3.58	2.56 / 62	6.16 / 99	5.26 / 98	3.99	0.66
COH	PIMCO High Yield P	PHLPX	C+	(800) 426-0107	A / 9.3	4.34	4.18	15.93 / 90	4.45 / 80	6.10 / 93	5.17	0.66
COH	PIMCO High Yield R	PHYRX	C+	(800) 426-0107	A- / 9.0	4.21	3.93	15.37 / 89	3.93 / 74	5.57 / 89	4.69	1.16
GL	PIMCO High Yield Spectrum A	PHSAX	C+	(800) 426-0107	A- / 9.1	5.33	5.50	19.90 / 96	4.42 / 80	6.86 / 96	5.74	0.96
GL	PIMCO High Yield Spectrum C	PHSCX	C+	(800) 426-0107	A- / 9.2	5.14	5.11	19.02 / 95	3.64 / 71	6.07 / 93	5.25	1.71
GL	PIMCO High Yield Spectrum D	PHSDX	B-	(800) 426-0107	A+ / 9.6	5.33	5.50	19.90 / 96	4.41 / 80	6.86 / 96	5.97	0.96
GL	PIMCO High Yield Spectrum Inst	PHSIX	B	(800) 426-0107	A+ / 9.7	5.42	5.68	20.31 / 96	4.78 / 84	7.23 / 97	6.30	0.61
GL	PIMCO High Yield Spectrum P	PHSPX	B	(800) 426-0107	A+ / 9.7	5.40	5.63	20.20 / 96	4.68 / 83	7.13 / 97	6.21	0.71
* GEI	PIMCO Income Fund A	PONAX	A+	(800) 426-0107	B+ / 8.8	3.06	4.20	10.72 / 81	5.53 / 89	8.03 / 98	4.87	0.85
GEI	PIMCO Income Fund Adm	PIINX	A+	(800) 426-0107	A / 9.5	3.09	4.28	10.88 / 81	5.69 / 90	8.20 / 98	5.21	0.70
GEI	PIMCO Income Fund C	PONCX	A+	(800) 426-0107	B+ / 8.9	2.87	3.82	9.92 / 79	4.77 / 83	7.30 / 97	4.35	1.60
GEI	PIMCO Income Fund D	PONDX	A+	(800) 426-0107	A / 9.4	3.07	4.23	10.79 / 81	5.60 / 89	8.13 / 98	5.12	0.79
GEI	PIMCO Income Fund Inst	PIMIX	A+	(800) 426-0107	A+ / 9.6	3.16	4.40	11.15 / 81	5.94 / 92	8.44 / 99	5.44	0.45
GEI	PIMCO Income Fund P	PONPX	A+	(800) 426-0107	A / 9.5	3.13	4.35	11.04 / 81	5.84 / 91	8.34 / 99	5.35	0.55
GEI	PIMCO Income Fund R	PONRX	A+	(800) 426-0107	A / 9.3	2.99	4.07	10.44 / 80	5.27 / 87	7.78 / 98	4.82	1.10
* COI	PIMCO Investment Grade Corp A	PBDAX	C-	(800) 426-0107	B- / 7.2	2.82	-0.72	7.71 / 74	4.52 / 81	4.91 / 83	3.27	0.93
COI	PIMCO Investment Grade Corp	PGCAX	C+	(800) 426-0107	B+ / 8.3	2.86	-0.65	7.87 / 74	4.67 / 82	5.07 / 85	3.54	0.78
COI	PIMCO Investment Grade Corp C	PBDCX	C	(800) 426-0107	B- / 7.3	2.63	-1.08	6.92 / 72	3.74 / 72	4.13 / 74	2.65	1.68
COI	PIMCO Investment Grade Corp D	PBDDX	C+	(800) 426-0107	B / 8.2	2.82	-0.72	7.71 / 74	4.52 / 81	4.91 / 83	3.40	0.93
COI	PIMCO Investment Grade Corp Inst	PIGIX	B-	(800) 426-0107	B+ / 8.6	2.92	-0.52	8.14 / 75	4.93 / 84	5.33 / 87	3.79	0.53
COI	PIMCO Investment Grade Corp P	PBDPX	B-	(800) 426-0107	B+ / 8.5	2.90	-0.57	8.03 / 74	4.83 / 84	5.23 / 86	3.69	0.63
COI	PIMCO Long Dur Total Return D	PLRDX	U	(800) 426-0107	U /	4.07	-5.86	6.47 / 71	--	--	3.83	0.95
GEI	PIMCO Long Dur Total Return Inst	PLRIX	C-	(800) 426-0107	A- / 9.1	4.17	-5.68	6.91 / 72	6.28 / 93	4.80 / 82	4.25	0.55
GEI	PIMCO Long Dur Total Return P	PLRPX	C-	(800) 426-0107	A- / 9.0	4.15	-5.73	6.80 / 72	6.18 / 93	4.69 / 81	4.15	0.65
GEI	PIMCO Long Term Credit Inst	PTCIX	C+	(800) 426-0107	A+ / 9.8	4.92	-3.23	13.18 / 85	7.28 / 96	7.24 / 97	5.54	0.65
GEI	PIMCO Long Term Credit P	PLCPX	C+	(800) 426-0107	A+ / 9.8	4.89	-3.28	12.98 / 85	7.14 / 96	7.11 / 97	5.36	0.75
USL	PIMCO Long Term US Govt A	PFGAX	E+	(800) 426-0107	C / 4.9	1.86	-11.09	-3.95 / 0	5.46 / 88	2.99 / 58	2.34	0.89
USL	PIMCO Long Term US Govt Admin	PLGBX	D-	(800) 426-0107	C+ / 6.6	1.89	-11.05	-3.85 / 0	5.56 / 89	3.10 / 59	2.54	0.79
USL	PIMCO Long Term US Govt C	PFGCX	E+	(800) 426-0107	C / 5.2	1.68	-11.42	-4.66 / 0	4.67 / 82	2.22 / 45	1.64	1.64
USL	PIMCO Long Term US Govt D	PLGDX	U	(800) 426-0107	U /	1.86	-11.10	-3.98 / 0	--	--	2.40	0.89
USL	PIMCO Long Term US Govt Inst	PGOVX	D-	(800) 426-0107	C+ / 6.9	1.95	-10.92	-3.60 / 0	5.83 / 91	3.35 / 63	2.82	0.54
USL	PIMCO Long Term US Govt P	PLTPX	D-	(800) 426-0107	C+ / 6.8	1.92	-10.99	-3.71 / 0	5.72 / 90	3.25 / 62	2.70	0.64
* GEI	PIMCO Low Duration A	PTLAX	C-	(800) 426-0107	D / 1.7	0.81	0.64	2.41 / 52	0.63 / 22	1.30 / 31	1.73	0.85
GEI	PIMCO Low Duration Admin	PLDAX	C+	(800) 426-0107	D+ / 2.7	0.83	0.69	2.50 / 53	0.72 / 23	1.39 / 33	1.86	0.76
GEI	PIMCO Low Duration C	PTLCX	C-	(800) 426-0107	D / 2.1	0.74	0.49	2.10 / 50	0.33 / 19	0.99 / 27	1.48	1.15
GEI	PIMCO Low Duration D	PLDDX	C+	(800) 426-0107	D+ / 2.6	0.82	0.67	2.46 / 53	0.68 / 23	1.35 / 32	1.82	0.80
GEI	PIMCO Low Duration ESG Admin	PDRAX	C+	(800) 426-0107	D+ / 2.7	0.89	0.77	2.32 / 52	0.72 / 23	1.39 / 33	1.66	0.77
GEI	PIMCO Low Duration ESG Inst	PLDIX	B-	(800) 426-0107	C- / 3.1	0.95	0.90	2.57 / 54	0.97 / 27	1.64 / 37	1.91	0.52
COI	● PIMCO Low Duration ESG P	PLUPX	C+	(800) 426-0107	C- / 3.0	0.93	0.85	2.47 / 53	0.87 / 26	1.54 / 35	1.81	0.62
GEI	PIMCO Low Duration II Admin	PDFAX	C+	(800) 426-0107	D+ / 2.5	0.69	0.31	2.52 / 53	0.61 / 22	1.07 / 28	1.56	0.79
GEI	PIMCO Low Duration II Inst	PLDTX	C+	(800) 426-0107	D+ / 2.9	0.75	0.43	2.77 / 55	0.86 / 25	1.33 / 32	1.81	0.54
GES	PIMCO Low Duration Income A	PFIAX	C-	(800) 426-0107	B / 7.7	3.40	4.72	17.21 / 92	2.67 / 55	3.84 / 70	3.19	0.96
GES	PIMCO Low Duration Income D	PFIDX	C	(800) 426-0107	B+ / 8.3	3.40	4.72	17.21 / 92	2.67 / 55	3.84 / 70	3.26	0.96
GES	PIMCO Low Duration Income Inst	PFIIX	C+	(800) 426-0107	B+ / 8.7	3.50	4.93	17.67 / 93	3.07 / 62	4.25 / 75	3.64	0.56
GES	PIMCO Low Duration Income P	PFTPX	C	(800) 426-0107	B+ / 8.6	3.48	4.88	17.56 / 93	2.97 / 60	4.15 / 74	3.55	0.66
GEI	PIMCO Low Duration Inst	PTLDX	C+	(800) 426-0107	C- / 3.2	0.90	0.81	2.76 / 55	0.97 / 27	1.64 / 37	2.11	0.51
GEI	PIMCO Low Duration P	PLDPX	C+	(800) 426-0107	C- / 3.0	0.87	0.76	2.65 / 54	0.87 / 26	1.54 / 35	2.01	0.61

● Denotes fund is closed to new investors
* Denotes fund is included in Section II

www.thestreetratings.com

Risk Rating/Pts	RISK 3 Yr Avg Standard Deviation	Avg Duration	NET ASSETS NAV As of 2/28/17	Total $(Mil)	ASSET Cash %	Gov. Bond %	Muni. Bond %	Corp. Bond %	Other %	Portfolio Turnover Ratio	Avg Coupon Rate	FUND MANAGER Manager Quality Pct	Manager Tenure (Years)	MINIMUM Initial Purch. $	Additional Purch. $	LOADS Front End Load	Back End Load
D- /1.5	5.2	3.5	8.96	8,861	5	0	0	92	3	32	6.3	67	7	1,000,000	0	0.0	0.0
D /2.1	4.4	6.5	8.77	255	6	0	92	0	2	58	4.3	80	2	1,000	50	2.3	0.0
D /2.1	4.4	6.5	8.77	88	6	0	92	0	2	58	4.3	68	2	1,000	50	0.0	0.0
D /2.1	4.4	6.5	8.77	34	6	0	92	0	2	58	4.3	80	2	1,000	50	0.0	0.0
D /2.2	4.4	6.5	8.77	235	6	0	92	0	2	58	4.3	83	2	1,000,000	0	0.0	0.0
D /2.2	4.4	6.5	8.77	104	6	0	92	0	2	58	4.3	82	2	1,000,000	0	0.0	0.0
D- /1.5	5.2	3.5	8.96	468	5	0	0	92	3	32	6.3	64	7	1,000,000	0	0.0	0.0
D- /1.5	5.2	3.5	8.96	35	5	0	0	92	3	32	6.3	43	7	0	0	0.0	0.0
D- /1.5	5.7	3.2	10.00	38	5	0	0	93	2	30	7.0	96	7	1,000	50	3.8	0.0
D- /1.5	5.7	3.2	10.00	10	5	0	0	93	2	30	7.0	95	7	1,000	50	0.0	0.0
D- /1.5	5.7	3.2	10.00	82	5	0	0	93	2	30	7.0	96	7	1,000	50	0.0	0.0
D- /1.5	5.7	3.2	10.00	1,783	5	0	0	93	2	30	7.0	97	7	1,000,000	0	0.0	0.0
D- /1.5	5.7	3.2	10.00	144	5	0	0	93	2	30	7.0	97	7	1,000,000	0	0.0	0.0
B- /7.5	2.6	2.6	12.20	8,615	4	26	0	20	50	52	2.6	96	10	1,000	50	3.8	0.0
B- /7.5	2.6	2.6	12.20	326	4	26	0	20	50	52	2.6	96	10	1,000,000	0	0.0	0.0
B- /7.4	2.6	2.6	12.20	7,768	4	26	0	20	50	52	2.6	94	10	1,000	50	0.0	0.0
B- /7.5	2.6	2.6	12.20	11,223	4	26	0	20	50	52	2.6	96	10	1,000	50	0.0	0.0
B- /7.5	2.6	2.6	12.20	31,448	4	26	0	20	50	52	2.6	97	10	1,000,000	0	0.0	0.0
B- /7.5	2.6	2.6	12.20	15,678	4	26	0	20	50	52	2.6	96	10	1,000,000	0	0.0	0.0
B- /7.4	2.6	2.6	12.20	312	4	26	0	20	50	52	2.6	95	10	0	0	0.0	0.0
D+ /2.7	4.3	6.7	10.35	1,001	0	24	0	64	12	87	4.1	72	15	1,000	50	3.8	0.0
D+ /2.7	4.3	6.7	10.35	177	0	24	0	64	12	87	4.1	75	15	1,000,000	0	0.0	0.0
D+ /2.7	4.3	6.7	10.35	589	0	24	0	64	12	87	4.1	46	15	1,000	50	0.0	0.0
D+ /2.7	4.3	6.7	10.35	652	0	24	0	64	12	87	4.1	72	15	1,000	50	0.0	0.0
D+ /2.7	4.3	6.7	10.35	6,254	0	24	0	64	12	87	4.1	78	15	1,000,000	0	0.0	0.0
D+ /2.7	4.3	6.7	10.35	1,464	0	24	0	64	12	87	4.1	77	15	1,000,000	0	0.0	0.0
U /	N/A	14.4	10.70	9	0	0	0	0	100	59	4.7	N/A	10	1,000	50	0.0	0.0
E /0.3	8.5	14.4	10.70	2,734	0	0	0	0	100	59	4.7	13	10	1,000,000	0	0.0	0.0
E /0.3	8.5	14.4	10.70	10	0	0	0	0	100	59	4.7	11	10	1,000	50	0.0	0.0
E /0.3	8.3	12.8	11.71	2,778	0	0	0	0	100	124	5.7	69	8	1,000,000	0	0.0	0.0
E /0.3	8.3	12.8	11.71	41	0	0	0	0	100	124	5.7	65	8	1,000,000	0	0.0	0.0
E- /0.1	11.1	17.9	6.02	103	0	86	0	1	13	101	3.5	14	10	1,000	50	3.8	0.0
E- /0.1	11.1	17.9	6.02	21	0	86	0	1	13	101	3.5	16	10	1,000,000	0	0.0	0.0
E- /0.1	11.1	17.9	6.02	26	0	86	0	1	13	101	3.5	5	10	1,000	50	0.0	0.0
U /	N/A	17.9	6.02	8	0	86	0	1	13	101	3.5	N/A	10	1,000	50	0.0	0.0
E- /0.2	11.1	17.9	6.02	1,481	0	86	0	1	13	101	3.5	22	10	1,000,000	0	0.0	0.0
E- /0.2	11.1	17.9	6.02	38	0	86	0	1	13	101	3.5	19	10	1,000,000	0	0.0	0.0
A- /9.0	1.2	1.9	9.86	864	0	25	0	32	43	186	2.1	50	3	1,000	50	2.3	0.0
A- /9.0	1.2	1.9	9.86	125	0	25	0	32	43	186	2.1	54	3	1,000,000	0	0.0	0.0
A- /9.0	1.2	1.9	9.86	468	0	25	0	32	43	186	2.1	32	3	1,000	50	0.0	0.0
A- /9.0	1.2	1.9	9.86	689	0	25	0	32	43	186	2.1	53	3	1,000	50	0.0	0.0
A- /9.1	1.1	1.9	9.49	5	0	25	1	29	45	257	1.9	55	3	1,000,000	0	0.0	0.0
A- /9.1	1.1	1.9	9.49	117	0	25	1	29	45	257	1.9	64	3	1,000,000	0	0.0	0.0
A- /9.1	1.1	1.9	9.49	34	0	25	1	29	45	257	1.9	57	3	1,000,000	0	0.0	0.0
A- /9.1	1.1	1.9	9.75	9	0	19	1	31	49	282	2.0	49	3	1,000,000	0	0.0	0.0
A- /9.1	1.1	1.9	9.75	312	0	19	1	31	49	282	2.0	59	3	1,000,000	0	0.0	0.0
D /1.6	5.6	0.5	8.43	144	3	10	1	50	36	118	5.0	92	1	1,000	50	2.3	0.0
D /1.6	5.6	0.5	8.43	42	3	10	1	50	36	118	5.0	91	1	1,000	50	0.0	0.0
D /1.6	5.6	0.5	8.43	90	3	10	1	50	36	118	5.0	93	1	1,000,000	0	0.0	0.0
D /1.6	5.6	0.5	8.43	42	3	10	1	50	36	118	5.0	93	1	1,000,000	0	0.0	0.0
A- /9.0	1.2	1.9	9.86	6,146	0	25	0	32	43	186	2.1	63	3	1,000,000	0	0.0	0.0
A- /9.0	1.2	1.9	9.86	687	0	25	0	32	43	186	2.1	60	3	1,000,000	0	0.0	0.0

99 Pct = Best
0 Pct = Worst

Fund Type	Fund Name	Ticker Symbol	Overall Investment Rating	Phone	Perfor- mance Rating/Pts	3 Mo	6 Mo	1Yr / Pct	3Yr / Pct	5Yr / Pct	Dividend Yield	Expense Ratio
GEI	PIMCO Low Duration R	PLDRX	C	(800) 426-0107	D / 2.1	0.75	0.52	2.15 / 50	0.38 / 20	1.04 / 28	1.52	1.10
COI	PIMCO Moderate Duration Admin	PMAOX	U	(800) 426-0107	U /	1.80	0.20	3.28 / 58	--	--	1.25	0.73
GEI	PIMCO Moderate Duration Fund P	PMOPX	B-	(800) 426-0107	C / 4.6	1.80	0.20	3.36 / 59	1.89 / 41	2.56 / 50	1.92	0.58
GEI	PIMCO Moderate Duration Inst	PMDRX	B	(800) 426-0107	C / 4.7	1.82	0.25	3.46 / 59	1.99 / 43	2.66 / 52	2.02	0.48
MTG	PIMCO Mortgage Opportunities A	PMZAX	A+	(800) 426-0107	C+ / 6.2	1.74	2.09	5.94 / 70	3.64 / 71	--	4.61	1.09
MTG	PIMCO Mortgage Opportunities C	PMZCX	A+	(800) 426-0107	C+ / 6.4	1.56	1.71	5.16 / 67	2.87 / 59	--	4.04	1.84
MTG	PIMCO Mortgage Opportunities D	PMZDX	A+	(800) 426-0107	B- / 7.3	1.74	2.09	5.95 / 70	3.64 / 71	--	4.79	1.09
MTG	PIMCO Mortgage Opportunities Inst	PMZIX	A+	(800) 426-0107	B / 7.7	1.84	2.29	6.37 / 71	4.05 / 76	--	5.19	0.69
MTG	PIMCO Mortgage Opportunities P	PMZPX	A+	(800) 426-0107	B / 7.6	1.82	2.24	6.24 / 71	3.94 / 75	--	5.07	0.79
MTG	PIMCO Mortgage-Backd Sec A	PMRAX	C+	(800) 426-0107	C- / 3.7	1.11	-0.11	1.80 / 47	2.71 / 56	2.43 / 48	2.65	0.90
MTG	PIMCO Mortgage-Backd Sec Admin	PMTAX	A	(800) 426-0107	C / 5.5	1.15	-0.04	1.95 / 48	2.86 / 59	2.58 / 51	2.90	0.75
MTG	PIMCO Mortgage-Backd Sec C	PMRCX	B-	(800) 426-0107	C- / 4.0	0.92	-0.48	1.04 / 40	1.94 / 42	1.67 / 37	2.00	1.65
MTG	PIMCO Mortgage-Backd Sec D	PTMDX	A	(800) 426-0107	C / 5.2	1.11	-0.11	1.80 / 47	2.71 / 56	2.43 / 48	2.75	0.90
MTG	PIMCO Mortgage-Backd Sec Inst	PTRIX	A+	(800) 426-0107	C+ / 6.0	1.21	0.08	2.20 / 51	3.12 / 63	2.84 / 55	3.15	0.50
MTG	PIMCO Mortgage-Backd Sec P	PMRPX	A	(800) 426-0107	C+ / 5.8	1.18	0.03	2.10 / 50	3.01 / 61	2.74 / 53	3.05	0.60
MUN	PIMCO Municipal Bond A	PMLAX	C+	(800) 426-0107	B- / 7.4	2.35	-3.53	0.71 / 40	3.94 / 92	3.47 / 87	2.98	0.76
MUN	PIMCO Municipal Bond C	PMLCX	C+	(800) 426-0107	B- / 7.5	2.23	-3.77	0.21 / 29	3.42 / 87	2.95 / 79	2.54	1.26
MUN	PIMCO Municipal Bond D	PMBDX	B+	(800) 426-0107	B+ / 8.3	2.35	-3.53	0.71 / 40	3.94 / 92	3.47 / 87	3.04	0.76
MUN	PIMCO Municipal Bond Inst	PFMIX	B+	(800) 426-0107	B+ / 8.8	2.43	-3.38	1.02 / 45	4.26 / 94	3.79 / 91	3.36	0.45
MUN	PIMCO Municipal Bond P	PMUPX	B+	(800) 426-0107	B+ / 8.6	2.41	-3.43	0.92 / 44	4.16 / 94	3.69 / 90	3.26	0.55
MUN	PIMCO Natl Intmdt Mncpl Bd A	PMNTX	D	(800) 426-0107	C- / 4.2	1.82	-3.39	-0.61 / 8	2.45 / 72	--	1.86	0.80
MUN	PIMCO Natl Intmdt Mncpl Bd C	PMNNX	D	(800) 426-0107	C / 4.4	1.69	-3.62	-1.10 / 4	1.94 / 61	--	1.40	1.30
MUN	PIMCO Natl Intmdt Mncpl Bd D	PMNDX	C-	(800) 426-0107	C+ / 5.7	1.82	-3.39	-0.61 / 8	2.45 / 72	--	1.91	0.80
MUN	PIMCO Natl Intmdt Mncpl Bd Inst	PMNIX	C+	(800) 426-0107	C+ / 6.5	1.90	-3.22	-0.26 / 14	2.80 / 79	--	2.26	0.45
MUN	PIMCO Natl Intmdt Mncpl Bd P	PMNPX	C+	(800) 426-0107	C+ / 6.3	1.88	-3.27	-0.36 / 12	2.70 / 77	--	2.16	0.55
MUS	PIMCO NY Muni Bond A	PNYAX	C+	(800) 426-0107	B- / 7.0	2.16	-3.19	0.31 / 33	3.64 / 89	2.91 / 78	2.98	0.78
MUS	PIMCO NY Muni Bond C	PBFCX	C+	(800) 426-0107	C+ / 6.6	1.97	-3.55	-0.43 / 11	2.87 / 80	2.14 / 62	2.29	1.53
MUS	PIMCO NY Muni Bond D	PNYDX	B+	(800) 426-0107	B / 7.8	2.16	-3.19	0.31 / 33	3.64 / 89	2.91 / 78	3.05	0.78
MUS	PIMCO NY Muni Bond Inst	PNYIX	A-	(800) 426-0107	B+ / 8.4	2.24	-3.03	0.64 / 39	3.98 / 93	3.25 / 84	3.38	0.45
MUS	PIMCO NY Muni Bond P	PNYPX	A-	(800) 426-0107	B / 8.2	2.22	-3.08	0.54 / 38	3.88 / 92	3.14 / 82	3.28	0.55
* GEI	PIMCO Real Return A	PRTNX	E	(800) 426-0107	D / 2.1	1.59	-0.10	4.85 / 66	1.07 / 29	0.42 / 21	0.66	0.98
GEI	PIMCO Real Return Administrative	PARRX	E+	(800) 426-0107	C- / 3.9	1.63	-0.03	5.01 / 67	1.22 / 31	0.57 / 22	0.83	0.83
GEI	PIMCO Real Return Asset Inst	PRAIX	D-	(800) 426-0107	C+ / 6.6	2.40	-2.82	7.91 / 74	3.00 / 61	1.21 / 30	1.50	0.73
GEI	PIMCO Real Return Asset P	PRTPX	D-	(800) 426-0107	C+ / 6.5	2.38	-2.87	7.81 / 74	2.90 / 59	1.11 / 29	1.40	0.83
GEI	PIMCO Real Return C	PRTCX	E	(800) 426-0107	D+ / 2.8	1.47	-0.34	4.34 / 64	0.57 / 21	-0.08 / 4	0.19	1.48
GEI	PIMCO Real Return D	PRRDX	E+	(800) 426-0107	C- / 3.7	1.59	-0.10	4.85 / 66	1.07 / 29	0.42 / 21	0.69	0.98
GEI	PIMCO Real Return Institutional	PRRIX	E+	(800) 426-0107	C / 4.3	1.69	0.10	5.27 / 68	1.44 / 34	0.81 / 25	1.08	0.58
COI	PIMCO Real Return Ltd Duration D	PPDRX	U	(800) 426-0107	U /	0.91	1.36	3.44 / 59	--	--	1.55	1.01
COI	PIMCO Real Return Ltd Duration Inst	PPIRX	U	(800) 426-0107	U /	1.00	1.56	4.03 / 62	--	--	2.11	0.61
COI	PIMCO Real Return Ltd Duration P	PPPRX	U	(800) 426-0107	U /	0.98	1.51	3.89 / 62	--	--	1.98	0.71
GEI	PIMCO Real Return P	PRLPX	E+	(800) 426-0107	C- / 4.2	1.67	0.05	5.16 / 67	1.37 / 33	0.72 / 24	0.98	0.68
GEI	PIMCO Real Return R	PRRRX	E+	(800) 426-0107	C- / 3.3	1.53	-0.22	4.59 / 65	0.82 / 25	0.17 / 17	0.44	1.23
COI	PIMCO Senior Floating Rate Fd A	PSRZX	A-	(800) 426-0107	C+ / 5.6	1.49	2.55	8.96 / 76	2.59 / 54	3.51 / 66	3.32	1.02
COI	PIMCO Senior Floating Rate Fd C	PSRWX	B+	(800) 426-0107	C / 5.2	1.31	2.17	8.16 / 75	1.83 / 40	2.75 / 54	2.66	1.77
COI	PIMCO Senior Floating Rate Fd D	PSRDX	A+	(800) 426-0107	C+ / 6.5	1.49	2.55	8.96 / 76	2.59 / 54	3.51 / 66	3.40	1.02
COI	PIMCO Senior Floating Rate Fd Inst	PSRIX	A+	(800) 426-0107	C+ / 6.8	1.57	2.70	9.29 / 77	2.90 / 59	3.82 / 70	3.69	0.72
COI	PIMCO Senior Floating Rate Fd P	PSRPX	A+	(800) 426-0107	C+ / 6.7	1.54	2.65	9.18 / 77	2.79 / 58	3.72 / 69	3.59	0.82
COI	PIMCO Short Asset Investment A	PAIAX	C	(800) 426-0107	D / 1.6	0.40	0.85	1.63 / 46	0.68 / 23	--	0.98	0.70
COI	PIMCO Short Asset Investment	PAIQX	B-	(800) 426-0107	D+ / 2.6	0.43	0.91	1.73 / 46	0.79 / 24	--	1.11	0.60
COI	PIMCO Short Asset Investment D	PAIUX	C+	(800) 426-0107	D+ / 2.4	0.40	0.86	1.63 / 46	0.69 / 23	--	1.01	0.70
COI	PIMCO Short Asset Investment Inst	PAIDX	B	(800) 426-0107	C- / 3.1	0.49	1.03	1.98 / 49	1.04 / 28	--	1.35	0.35
COI	PIMCO Short Asset Investment M	PAMSX	U	(800) 426-0107	U /	0.48	1.03	1.98 / 49	--	--	1.35	0.35

● Denotes fund is closed to new investors
* Denotes fund is included in Section II

RISK			NET ASSETS		ASSET							FUND MANAGER		MINIMUM		LOADS	
Risk Rating/Pts	3 Yr Avg Standard Deviation	Avg Dura-tion	NAV As of 2/28/17	Total $(Mil)	Cash %	Gov. Bond %	Muni. Bond %	Corp. Bond %	Other %	Portfolio Turnover Ratio	Avg Coupon Rate	Manager Quality Pct	Manager Tenure (Years)	Initial Purch. $	Additional Purch. $	Front End Load	Back End Load
A- /9.0	1.2	1.9	9.86	79	0	25	0	32	43	186	2.1	34	3	0	0	0.0	0.0
U /	N/A	4.2	10.21	N/A	0	0	0	0	100	217	2.8	N/A	3	1,000,000	0	0.0	0.0
B /7.7	2.4	4.2	10.15	6	0	0	0	0	100	217	2.8	50	3	1,000,000	0	0.0	0.0
B /7.7	2.4	4.2	10.15	1,358	0	0	0	0	100	217	2.8	54	3	1,000,000	0	0.0	0.0
B+ /8.9	1.4	N/A	10.97	59	0	22	0	2	76	1,146	0.0	90	5	1,000	50	3.8	0.0
B+ /8.9	1.4	N/A	10.97	24	0	22	0	2	76	1,146	0.0	84	5	1,000	50	0.0	0.0
B+ /8.9	1.4	N/A	10.97	81	0	22	0	2	76	1,146	0.0	90	5	1,000	50	0.0	0.0
B+ /8.9	1.4	N/A	10.97	1,990	0	22	0	2	76	1,146	0.0	92	5	1,000,000	0	0.0	0.0
B+ /8.9	1.4	N/A	10.97	299	0	22	0	2	76	1,146	0.0	91	5	1,000,000	0	0.0	0.0
B+ /8.4	1.9	2.5	10.45	23	0	0	0	1	99	1,930	2.5	63	5	1,000	50	3.8	0.0
B+ /8.4	1.9	2.5	10.45	4	0	0	0	1	99	1,930	2.5	67	5	1,000,000	0	0.0	0.0
B+ /8.4	1.9	2.5	10.45	9	0	0	0	1	99	1,930	2.5	29	5	1,000	50	0.0	0.0
B+ /8.4	1.9	2.5	10.45	37	0	0	0	1	99	1,930	2.5	63	5	1,000	50	0.0	0.0
B+ /8.4	1.9	2.5	10.45	116	0	0	0	1	99	1,930	2.5	73	5	1,000,000	0	0.0	0.0
B+ /8.4	1.9	2.5	10.45	8	0	0	0	1	99	1,930	2.5	71	5	1,000,000	0	0.0	0.0
C- /3.6	3.7	6.1	9.63	256	0	0	98	0	2	85	4.6	48	2	1,000	50	2.3	0.0
C- /3.6	3.7	6.1	9.63	111	0	0	98	0	2	85	4.6	25	2	1,000	50	0.0	0.0
C- /3.6	3.7	6.1	9.63	11	0	0	98	0	2	85	4.6	48	2	1,000	50	0.0	0.0
C- /3.6	3.7	6.1	9.63	156	0	0	98	0	2	85	4.6	61	2	1,000,000	0	0.0	0.0
C- /3.6	3.7	6.1	9.63	114	0	0	98	0	2	85	4.6	57	2	1,000,000	0	0.0	0.0
C /4.6	3.3	4.8	10.36	23	6	0	93	0	1	41	4.4	12	2	1,000	50	2.3	0.0
C /4.6	3.3	4.8	10.36	5	6	0	93	0	1	41	4.4	6	2	1,000	50	0.0	0.0
C /4.6	3.3	4.8	10.36	2	6	0	93	0	1	41	4.4	12	2	1,000	50	0.0	0.0
C /4.6	3.3	4.8	10.36	13	6	0	93	0	1	41	4.4	19	2	1,000,000	0	0.0	0.0
C /4.6	3.3	4.8	10.36	16	6	0	93	0	1	41	4.4	17	2	1,000,000	0	0.0	0.0
C /4.4	3.3	6.1	11.11	97	5	0	94	0	1	36	4.5	49	2	1,000	50	2.3	0.0
C /4.4	3.3	6.1	11.11	18	5	0	94	0	1	36	4.5	18	2	1,000	50	0.0	0.0
C /4.4	3.3	6.1	11.11	12	5	0	94	0	1	36	4.5	49	2	1,000	50	0.0	0.0
C /4.4	3.3	6.1	11.11	52	5	0	94	0	1	36	4.5	62	2	1,000,000	0	0.0	0.0
C /4.4	3.3	6.1	11.11	11	5	0	94	0	1	36	4.5	59	2	1,000,000	0	0.0	0.0
D /2.1	4.7	7.6	11.09	1,747	0	82	0	5	13	102	1.7	2	10	1,000	50	3.8	0.0
D /2.1	4.7	7.6	11.09	572	0	82	0	5	13	102	1.7	3	10	1,000,000	0	0.0	0.0
E /0.3	8.1	16.9	8.39	258	0	0	0	0	100	107	2.6	1	10	1,000,000	0	0.0	0.0
E /0.3	8.1	16.9	8.39	12	0	0	0	0	100	107	2.6	1	10	1,000,000	0	0.0	0.0
D /2.1	4.7	7.6	11.09	715	0	82	0	5	13	102	1.7	1	10	1,000	50	0.0	0.0
D /2.1	4.7	7.6	11.09	727	0	82	0	5	13	102	1.7	2	10	1,000	50	0.0	0.0
D /2.1	4.7	7.6	11.09	5,867	0	82	0	5	13	102	1.7	5	10	1,000,000	0	0.0	0.0
U /	N/A	2.7	9.91	N/A	0	0	0	0	100	42	0.7	N/A	2	1,000	50	0.0	0.0
U /	N/A	2.7	9.91	5	0	0	0	0	100	42	0.7	N/A	2	1,000,000	0	0.0	0.0
U /	N/A	2.7	9.91	N/A	0	0	0	0	100	42	0.7	N/A	2	1,000,000	0	0.0	0.0
D /2.1	4.7	7.6	11.09	838	0	82	0	5	13	102	1.7	4	10	1,000,000	0	0.0	0.0
D /2.1	4.7	7.6	11.09	322	0	82	0	5	13	102	1.7	2	10	0	0	0.0	0.0
B /7.8	2.3	0.7	9.95	85	8	0	0	76	16	31	4.3	83	6	1,000	50	2.3	1.0
B /7.8	2.3	0.7	9.95	55	8	0	0	76	16	31	4.3	75	6	1,000	50	0.0	1.0
B /7.8	2.3	0.7	9.95	15	8	0	0	76	16	31	4.3	83	6	1,000	50	0.0	1.0
B /7.8	2.3	0.7	9.95	1,106	8	0	0	76	16	31	4.3	86	6	1,000,000	0	0.0	1.0
B /7.8	2.3	0.7	9.95	14	8	0	0	76	16	31	4.3	85	6	1,000,000	0	0.0	1.0
A+ /9.9	0.3	N/A	10.05	148	12	8	2	60	18	256	2.2	67	5	1,000	50	2.3	0.0
A+ /9.9	0.3	N/A	10.05	14	12	8	2	60	18	256	2.2	70	5	1,000,000	0	0.0	0.0
A+ /9.9	0.3	N/A	10.05	22	12	8	2	60	18	256	2.2	67	5	1,000	50	0.0	0.0
A+ /9.9	0.3	N/A	10.05	983	12	8	2	60	18	256	2.2	75	5	1,000,000	0	0.0	0.0
U /	N/A	N/A	10.05	N/A	12	8	2	60	18	256	2.2	N/A	5	1,000,000	0	0.0	0.0

Fund Type	Fund Name	Ticker Symbol	Overall Investment Rating	Phone	Perfor-mance Rating/Pts	3 Mo	6 Mo	1Yr / Pct	3Yr / Pct	5Yr / Pct	Dividend Yield	Expense Ratio
COI	PIMCO Short Asset Investment P	PAIPX	B	(800) 426-0107	D+ / 2.9	0.46	0.98	1.88 / 48	0.94 / 27	--	1.25	0.45
MUN	PIMCO Short Duration Muni Inc A	PSDAX	D	(800) 426-0107	E / 0.4	1.11	-0.59	-0.10 / 16	0.39 / 22	0.48 / 24	0.83	0.73
MUN	PIMCO Short Duration Muni Inc C	PSDCX	D	(800) 426-0107	E+ / 0.9	1.04	-0.74	-0.39 / 11	0.10 / 15	0.18 / 19	0.56	1.03
MUN	PIMCO Short Duration Muni Inc D	PSDDX	C	(800) 426-0107	D / 2.0	1.11	-0.59	-0.10 / 16	0.39 / 22	0.47 / 24	0.85	0.73
MUN	PIMCO Short Duration Muni Inc Inst	PSDIX	C+	(800) 426-0107	C- / 3.0	1.21	-0.40	0.30 / 32	0.80 / 31	0.88 / 32	1.25	0.33
MUN	PIMCO Short Duration Muni Inc P	PSDPX	C+	(800) 426-0107	D+ / 2.7	1.19	-0.45	0.20 / 29	0.69 / 29	0.78 / 30	1.15	0.43
* GEI	PIMCO Short Term A	PSHAX	C+	(800) 426-0107	C- / 3.0	0.60	1.30	3.42 / 59	1.40 / 33	1.41 / 33	1.47	0.72
GEI	PIMCO Short Term Admin	PSFAX	B+	(800) 426-0107	C- / 3.9	0.60	1.30	3.42 / 59	1.40 / 33	1.41 / 33	1.51	0.72
GEI	PIMCO Short Term C	PFTCX	B	(800) 426-0107	C- / 3.4	0.53	1.15	3.12 / 57	1.09 / 29	1.11 / 29	1.21	0.97
GEI	PIMCO Short Term D	PSHDX	B+	(800) 426-0107	C- / 3.9	0.60	1.30	3.42 / 59	1.40 / 33	1.41 / 33	1.51	0.72
GEI	PIMCO Short Term Inst	PTSHX	A-	(800) 426-0107	C / 4.3	0.66	1.42	3.68 / 61	1.65 / 37	1.67 / 37	1.75	0.47
GEI	PIMCO Short Term P	PTSPX	B+	(800) 426-0107	C- / 4.1	0.63	1.37	3.58 / 60	1.55 / 36	1.56 / 35	1.65	0.57
GEI	PIMCO Short Term R	PTSRX	B	(800) 426-0107	C- / 3.5	0.54	1.18	3.17 / 58	1.14 / 30	1.16 / 30	1.26	0.97
MTG	PIMCO StkPlus Intl (DH) A	PIPAX	C	(800) 426-0107	A+ / 9.9	9.09	13.59	26.71 / 99	6.07 / 92	10.96 / 99	0.72	1.16
MTG	PIMCO StkPlus Intl (DH) C	PIPCX	C	(800) 426-0107	A+ / 9.9	8.78	13.24	25.68 / 99	5.28 / 87	10.13 / 99	0.34	1.91
MTG	PIMCO StkPlus Intl (DH) D	PIPDX	C	(800) 426-0107	A+ / 9.9	9.08	13.58	26.67 / 99	6.11 / 93	10.96 / 99	0.76	1.16
MTG	PIMCO StkPlus Intl (DH) I	PISIX	C	(800) 426-0107	A+ / 9.9	9.08	13.81	27.22 / 99	6.52 / 94	11.42 / 99	0.99	0.76
USS	PIMCO StocksPLUS Short A	PSSAX	E-	(800) 426-0107	E- / 0.0	-5.23	-6.28	-14.51 / 0	-9.78 / 0	-11.51 / 0	0.00	1.08
USS	PIMCO StocksPLUS Short C	PSSCX	E-	(800) 426-0107	E- / 0.0	-5.44	-6.63	-15.20 / 0	-10.38 / 0	-12.18 / 0	0.00	1.83
USS	PIMCO StocksPLUS Short D	PSSDX	E-	(800) 426-0107	E- / 0.0	-5.24	-6.30	-14.55 / 0	-9.74 / 0	-11.48 / 0	0.00	1.08
USS	PIMCO StocksPLUS Short I	PSTIX	E-	(800) 426-0107	E- / 0.0	-5.07	-6.10	-14.21 / 0	-9.32 / 0	-11.13 / 0	0.00	0.68
USS	PIMCO StocksPLUS Short P	PSPLX	E-	(800) 426-0107	E- / 0.0	-5.18	-6.21	-14.31 / 0	-9.43 / 0	-11.28 / 0	0.00	0.78
* GEI	PIMCO Total Return A	PTTAX	D-	(800) 426-0107	C- / 3.4	2.21	-0.70	3.51 / 60	2.18 / 46	2.57 / 51	2.48	0.86
GEI	PIMCO Total Return Admin	PTRAX	D+	(800) 426-0107	C / 5.2	2.24	-0.63	3.65 / 60	2.33 / 49	2.71 / 53	2.72	0.72
GEI	PIMCO Total Return C	PTTCX	D-	(800) 426-0107	C- / 3.7	2.02	-1.06	2.75 / 55	1.42 / 34	1.80 / 39	1.83	1.61
GEI	PIMCO Total Return D	PTTDX	D+	(800) 426-0107	C / 5.1	2.23	-0.65	3.61 / 60	2.29 / 48	2.67 / 52	2.68	0.76
GEI	PIMCO Total Return ESG Admin	PRFAX	D+	(800) 426-0107	C / 5.0	2.12	-0.75	3.75 / 61	2.19 / 46	2.48 / 49	2.63	0.80
GEI	PIMCO Total Return ESG P	PRAPX	C-	(800) 426-0107	C / 5.2	2.16	-0.67	3.91 / 62	2.35 / 49	2.64 / 52	2.78	0.65
GEI	PIMCO Total Return Fund II P	PMTPX	C-	(800) 426-0107	C / 5.0	2.13	-0.82	4.00 / 62	2.19 / 46	2.34 / 47	3.28	0.66
GEI	PIMCO Total Return II Admin	PRADX	D+	(800) 426-0107	C / 4.8	2.09	-0.89	3.85 / 61	2.04 / 44	2.19 / 45	3.13	0.81
GEI	PIMCO Total Return II Inst	PMBIX	C-	(800) 426-0107	C / 5.2	2.16	-0.77	4.11 / 63	2.30 / 48	2.45 / 49	3.38	0.56
GEI	PIMCO Total Return III Inst	PTSAX	C-	(800) 426-0107	C / 5.4	2.18	-0.62	4.01 / 62	2.46 / 51	2.74 / 53	2.88	0.55
GEI	PIMCO Total Return Inst	PTTRX	C-	(800) 426-0107	C+ / 5.6	2.30	-0.51	3.91 / 62	2.58 / 53	2.97 / 57	2.97	0.47
COI	PIMCO Total Return IV A	PTUZX	D-	(800) 426-0107	D+ / 2.7	1.56	-1.02	3.44 / 59	1.80 / 40	2.27 / 46	2.10	0.86
COI	PIMCO Total Return IV C	PTUCX	D-	(800) 426-0107	C- / 3.1	1.38	-1.38	2.68 / 54	1.09 / 29	1.58 / 36	1.43	1.61
COI	PIMCO Total Return IV Inst	PTUIX	C-	(800) 426-0107	C / 4.8	1.65	-0.85	3.80 / 61	2.15 / 46	2.62 / 51	2.53	0.51
COI	PIMCO Total Return IV P	PTUPX	D+	(800) 426-0107	C / 4.7	1.63	-0.91	3.68 / 61	2.04 / 44	2.52 / 50	2.41	0.61
GEI	PIMCO Total Return P	PTTPX	C-	(800) 426-0107	C / 5.4	2.28	-0.55	3.81 / 61	2.48 / 51	2.86 / 56	2.87	0.57
GEI	PIMCO Total Return R	PTRRX	D	(800) 426-0107	C / 4.5	2.14	-0.82	3.25 / 58	1.93 / 42	2.31 / 46	2.33	1.11
GEI	PIMCO Unconstrained Bond A	PUBAX	C-	(800) 426-0107	C / 5.3	3.10	4.38	10.74 / 81	1.95 / 42	2.24 / 45	1.71	1.39
GEI	PIMCO Unconstrained Bond C	PUBCX	C-	(800) 426-0107	C / 5.5	2.91	4.00	9.81 / 79	1.15 / 30	1.50 / 34	1.06	2.14
GEI	PIMCO Unconstrained Bond D	PUBDX	C+	(800) 426-0107	C+ / 6.7	3.10	4.38	10.74 / 81	1.95 / 42	2.24 / 45	1.77	1.39
GEI	PIMCO Unconstrained Bond Inst	PFIUX	B	(800) 426-0107	B- / 7.2	3.20	4.59	11.18 / 82	2.36 / 49	2.65 / 52	2.16	0.99
GEI	PIMCO Unconstrained Bond P	PUCPX	B-	(800) 426-0107	B- / 7.1	3.17	4.53	11.06 / 81	2.25 / 47	2.54 / 50	2.06	1.09
GEI	PIMCO Unconstrained Bond R	PUBRX	C+	(800) 426-0107	C+ / 6.4	3.03	4.25	10.46 / 80	1.70 / 38	1.99 / 42	1.53	1.64
MUN	PIMCO Unconstrained Tax Mnged Bd	ATMAX	B	(800) 426-0107	B / 7.6	4.34	4.93	9.78 / 89	2.19 / 67	2.25 / 65	2.04	1.11
MUN	PIMCO Unconstrained Tax Mnged Bd	ATMCX	B	(800) 426-0107	B / 7.8	4.15	4.54	8.97 / 86	1.40 / 46	1.56 / 48	1.39	1.86
MUN	PIMCO Unconstrained Tax Mnged Bd	ATMDX	A	(800) 426-0107	A- / 9.0	4.34	4.92	9.78 / 89	2.18 / 67	2.24 / 65	2.11	1.86
MUN	PIMCO Unconstrained Tax Mnged Bd	PUTIX	A+	(800) 426-0107	A / 9.4	4.45	5.13	10.22 / 90	2.59 / 75	2.65 / 74	2.50	0.71
MUN	PIMCO Unconstrained Tax Mnged Bd	PUTPX	A+	(800) 426-0107	A / 9.3	4.42	5.08	10.11 / 89	2.49 / 73	2.55 / 71	2.40	0.81
EM	PIMCO VIT Emerging Mkt Bond Adm		C	(800) 426-0107	A / 9.4	5.84	1.02	16.61 / 91	4.62 / 82	3.92 / 71	5.11	1.00
* MUN	Pioneer AMT-Free Muni A	PBMFX	C-	(800) 225-6292	B- / 7.1	3.08	-4.33	-0.08 / 16	4.49 / 96	4.27 / 95	2.71	0.83

● Denotes fund is closed to new investors
* Denotes fund is included in Section II

Risk Rating/Pts	3 Yr Avg Standard Deviation	Avg Duration	NAV As of 2/28/17	Total $(Mil)	Cash %	Gov. Bond %	Muni. Bond %	Corp. Bond %	Other %	Portfolio Turnover Ratio	Avg Coupon Rate	Manager Quality Pct	Manager Tenure (Years)	Initial Purch. $	Additional Purch. $	Front End Load	Back End Load
A+ / 9.9	0.3	N/A	10.05	109	12	8	2	60	18	256	2.2	73	5	1,000,000	0	0.0	0.0
A- / 9.2	1.0	1.9	8.40	89	3	0	96	0	1	31	2.9	19	3	1,000	50	2.3	0.0
A- / 9.2	1.0	1.9	8.40	12	3	0	96	0	1	31	2.9	13	3	1,000	50	0.0	0.0
A- / 9.2	1.0	1.9	8.40	2	3	0	96	0	1	31	2.9	19	3	1,000	50	0.0	0.0
A- / 9.2	1.0	1.9	8.40	53	3	0	96	0	1	31	2.9	32	3	1,000,000	0	0.0	0.0
A- / 9.2	1.0	1.9	8.40	35	3	0	96	0	1	31	2.9	28	3	1,000,000	0	0.0	0.0
A- / 9.2	1.0	N/A	9.82	876	0	13	0	65	22	1,753	2.7	83	6	1,000	50	2.3	0.0
A- / 9.2	1.0	N/A	9.82	1,668	0	13	0	65	22	1,753	2.7	83	6	1,000,000	0	0.0	0.0
A- / 9.2	1.0	N/A	9.82	177	0	13	0	65	22	1,753	2.7	81	6	1,000	50	0.0	0.0
A- / 9.2	1.0	N/A	9.82	493	0	13	0	65	22	1,753	2.7	83	6	1,000	50	0.0	0.0
A- / 9.2	1.0	N/A	9.82	6,745	0	13	0	65	22	1,753	2.7	85	6	1,000,000	0	0.0	0.0
A- / 9.2	1.0	N/A	9.82	1,714	0	13	0	65	22	1,753	2.7	84	6	1,000,000	0	0.0	0.0
A- / 9.2	1.0	N/A	9.82	117	0	13	0	65	22	1,753	2.7	81	6	0	0	0.0	0.0
E- / 0.0	13.7	5.6	7.60	301	2	58	0	20	20	499	4.7	98	2	1,000	50	3.8	0.0
E- / 0.0	13.7	5.6	7.06	153	2	58	0	20	20	499	4.7	98	2	1,000	50	0.0	0.0
E- / 0.0	13.7	5.6	7.61	235	2	58	0	20	20	499	4.7	99	2	1,000	50	0.0	0.0
E- / 0.0	13.7	5.6	7.95	1,493	2	58	0	20	20	499	4.7	99	2	1,000,000	0	0.0	0.0
E / 0.3	8.3	5.9	9.25	29	1	39	1	19	40	524	0.0	0	3	1,000	50	3.8	0.0
E / 0.3	8.3	5.9	8.87	12	1	39	1	19	40	524	0.0	0	3	1,000	50	0.0	0.0
E / 0.4	8.2	5.9	9.22	30	1	39	1	19	40	524	0.0	0	3	1,000	50	0.0	0.0
E / 0.3	8.4	5.9	9.54	1,748	1	39	1	19	40	524	0.0	0	3	1,000,000	0	0.0	0.0
E / 0.3	8.4	5.9	9.52	36	1	39	1	19	40	524	0.0	0	3	1,000,000	0	0.0	0.0
C / 4.4	3.3	5.6	10.15	5,628	0	37	2	16	45	478	3.1	25	3	1,000	50	3.8	0.0
C / 4.4	3.3	5.6	10.15	3,752	0	37	2	16	45	478	3.1	30	3	1,000	50	0.0	0.0
C / 4.4	3.3	5.6	10.15	3,242	0	37	2	16	45	478	3.1	9	3	1,000	50	0.0	0.0
C / 4.4	3.3	5.6	10.15	4,416	0	37	2	16	45	478	3.1	28	3	1,000	50	0.0	0.0
C / 4.6	3.3	5.6	9.02	26	0	36	4	18	42	454	3.5	27	3	1,000,000	0	0.0	0.0
C / 4.6	3.3	5.6	9.02	44	0	36	4	18	42	454	3.5	32	3	1,000,000	0	0.0	0.0
C / 5.0	3.1	5.6	9.60	11	0	25	2	18	55	516	3.7	25	3	1,000,000	0	0.0	0.0
C / 5.0	3.1	5.6	9.60	13	0	25	2	18	55	516	3.7	20	3	1,000,000	0	0.0	0.0
C / 5.0	3.1	5.6	9.60	734	0	25	2	18	55	516	3.7	28	3	1,000,000	0	0.0	0.0
C / 4.6	3.3	5.6	9.02	990	0	36	4	18	42	454	3.5	35	3	1,000,000	0	0.0	0.0
C / 4.5	3.3	5.6	10.15	52,559	0	37	2	16	45	478	3.1	42	3	1,000,000	0	0.0	0.0
C / 5.2	3.1	5.6	10.30	15	11	45	6	16	22	449	2.5	15	3	1,000	50	3.8	0.0
C / 5.2	3.1	5.6	10.30	3	11	45	6	16	22	449	2.5	5	3	1,000	50	0.0	0.0
C / 5.2	3.1	5.6	10.30	1,438	11	45	6	16	22	449	2.5	24	3	1,000,000	0	0.0	0.0
C / 5.2	3.1	5.6	10.30	1	11	45	6	16	22	449	2.5	20	3	1,000,000	0	0.0	0.0
C / 4.4	3.3	5.6	10.15	3,459	0	37	2	16	45	478	3.1	35	3	1,000,000	0	0.0	0.0
C / 4.4	3.3	5.6	10.15	1,176	0	37	2	16	45	478	3.1	18	3	0	0	0.0	0.0
C / 4.6	3.3	2.9	10.84	230	0	36	1	23	40	389	4.5	84	3	1,000	50	3.8	0.0
C / 4.5	3.3	2.9	10.84	262	0	36	1	23	40	389	4.5	76	3	1,000	50	0.0	0.0
C / 4.6	3.3	2.9	10.84	102	0	36	1	23	40	389	4.5	84	3	1,000	50	0.0	0.0
C / 4.6	3.3	2.9	10.84	2,635	0	36	1	23	40	389	4.5	87	3	1,000,000	0	0.0	0.0
C / 4.5	3.3	2.9	10.84	300	0	36	1	23	40	389	4.5	86	3	1,000,000	0	0.0	0.0
C / 4.5	3.3	2.9	10.84	8	0	36	1	23	40	389	4.5	82	3	0	0	0.0	0.0
C- / 4.2	3.4	N/A	10.43	24	0	8	77	1	14	441	3.8	84	2	1,000	50	3.8	0.0
C- / 4.2	3.4	N/A	10.43	5	0	8	77	1	14	441	3.8	75	2	1,000	50	0.0	0.0
C- / 4.2	3.4	N/A	10.43	6	0	8	77	1	14	441	3.8	84	2	1,000	50	0.0	0.0
C / 4.3	3.4	N/A	10.43	68	0	8	77	1	14	441	3.8	87	2	1,000,000	0	0.0	0.0
C / 4.3	3.4	N/A	10.43	9	0	8	77	1	14	441	3.8	86	2	1,000,000	0	0.0	0.0
E / 0.4	7.8	6.4	12.93	230	6	53	0	35	6	28	5.9	98	3	0	0	0.0	0.0
D+ / 2.6	4.4	6.6	14.27	684	0	0	99	0	1	21	4.4	33	11	1,000	100	4.5	0.0

					PERFORMANCE						Incl. in Returns	
99 Pct = Best *0 Pct = Worst*			Overall Investment Rating		Perfor-mance Rating/Pts	Total Return % through 2/28/17			Annualized		Dividend Yield	Expense Ratio
Fund Type	Fund Name	Ticker Symbol		Phone		3 Mo	6 Mo	1Yr / Pct	3Yr / Pct	5Yr / Pct		
MUN	Pioneer AMT-Free Muni C	MNBCX	C	(800) 225-6292	B / 7.6	2.91	-4.60	-0.77 / 6	3.71 /90	3.51 /88	2.07	1.56
MUN	Pioneer AMT-Free Muni Y	PBYMX	B+	(800) 225-6292	A- / 9.2	3.23	-4.09	0.24 /30	4.82 /97	4.56 /96	3.10	0.64
*GEI	Pioneer Bond Fund A	PIOBX	B-	(800) 225-6292	C- / 4.2	1.39	-0.47	4.94 /66	2.90 /59	3.51 /66	2.83	0.98
GEI	Pioneer Bond Fund C	PCYBX	B+	(800) 225-6292	C / 4.8	1.11	-0.86	4.09 /63	2.11 /45	2.66 /52	2.23	1.60
COI	Pioneer Bond Fund K	PBFKX	A+	(800) 225-6292	C+ / 6.7	1.49	-0.18	5.34 /68	3.31 /66	3.81 /70	3.35	0.47
GEI	Pioneer Bond Fund R	PBFRX	A	(800) 225-6292	C+ / 5.7	1.33	-0.58	4.66 /65	2.62 /54	3.17 /60	2.71	1.21
GEI	Pioneer Bond Fund Y	PICYX	A+	(800) 225-6292	C+ / 6.5	1.47	-0.35	5.25 /68	3.18 /64	3.74 /69	3.24	0.59
GL	Pioneer Dynamic Credit A	RCRAX	C	(800) 225-6292	C+ / 6.8	3.92	3.70	14.10 /87	2.92 /60	4.32 /76	5.92	1.19
GL	Pioneer Dynamic Credit C	RCRCX	C+	(800) 225-6292	B- / 7.2	3.73	3.30	13.12 /85	2.14 /45	3.52 /66	5.43	1.95
GL	Pioneer Dynamic Credit Y	RCRYX	B+	(800) 225-6292	B+ / 8.4	4.10	3.97	14.44 /87	3.24 /65	4.66 /80	6.52	0.96
COH	Pioneer Floating Rate Fund Class A	FLARX	B+	(800) 225-6292	C / 5.2	1.59	2.64	8.44 /75	2.80 /58	3.71 /69	3.41	1.10
COH	Pioneer Floating Rate Fund Class C	FLRCX	A-	(800) 225-6292	C+ / 6.0	1.39	2.25	7.79 /74	2.10 /45	2.97 /57	2.83	1.84
LP	Pioneer Floating Rate Fund Class K	FLRKX	A+	(800) 225-6292	B- / 7.3	1.67	2.80	8.78 /76	3.21 /64	3.98 /72	3.89	0.73
COH	Pioneer Floating Rate Fund Class Y	FLYRX	A+	(800) 225-6292	B- / 7.3	1.66	2.80	8.77 /76	3.21 /64	4.10 /74	3.89	0.82
GL	Pioneer Global High Yield A	PGHYX	D-	(800) 225-6292	C+ / 6.3	4.57	4.29	18.35 /94	1.73 /39	4.02 /73	5.46	1.17
GL	Pioneer Global High Yield C	PGYCX	D-	(800) 225-6292	C+ / 6.9	4.41	3.93	17.57 /93	1.05 /28	3.30 /62	5.04	1.87
GL	Pioneer Global High Yield Y	GHYYX	D+	(800) 225-6292	B / 7.9	4.58	4.46	18.62 /94	2.02 /44	4.29 /76	5.98	0.87
GL	Pioneer Global Multisector Income A	PGABX	D-	(800) 225-6292	C- / 3.1	1.74	-1.35	5.43 /68	2.03 /44	2.06 /43	2.75	2.67
GL	Pioneer Global Multisector Income C	PGCBX	D-	(800) 225-6292	C- / 3.4	1.51	-1.87	4.41 /64	1.13 /30	1.17 /30	2.01	2.56
GL	Pioneer Global Multisector Income Y	PGYBX	C-	(800) 225-6292	C / 5.4	1.79	-1.30	5.56 /69	2.30 /48	2.31 /46	3.13	1.39
MUH	Pioneer High Income Municipal A	PIMAX	B	(800) 225-6292	A / 9.5	4.01	-2.57	3.01 /65	6.07 /99	5.50 /99	5.06	0.87
MUH	Pioneer High Income Municipal C	HICMX	B+	(800) 225-6292	A+ / 9.7	3.66	-2.95	2.08 /58	5.26 /98	4.68 /97	4.51	1.63
MUH	Pioneer High Income Municipal Y	HIMYX	B+	(800) 225-6292	A+ / 9.9	4.09	-2.41	3.16 /66	6.26 /99	5.67 /99	5.48	0.71
*COH	Pioneer High Yield A	TAHYX	D	(800) 225-6292	B / 7.8	4.82	5.57	19.80 /96	2.87 /59	6.02 /92	4.60	1.17
COH	Pioneer High Yield C	PYICX	D+	(800) 225-6292	B / 8.2	4.77	5.22	19.01 /95	2.17 /46	5.29 /87	4.13	1.89
COH	Pioneer High Yield R	TYHRX	C-	(800) 225-6292	B+ / 8.6	4.78	5.48	19.46 /95	2.57 /53	5.67 /90	4.42	1.51
COH	Pioneer High Yield Y	TYHYX	C	(800) 225-6292	A- / 9.1	4.89	5.71	20.13 /96	3.21 /64	6.38 /94	5.10	0.88
*GL	Pioneer Multi-Asset Ultrasht Inc A	MAFRX	C+	(800) 225-6292	D / 2.2	0.48	1.03	2.52 /53	1.08 /29	1.29 /31	1.65	0.63
GL	Pioneer Multi-Asset Ultrasht Inc C	MCFRX	B-	(800) 225-6292	D+ / 2.7	0.40	0.87	2.20 /51	0.77 /24	0.93 /26	1.37	0.94
GL	Pioneer Multi-Asset Ultrasht Inc C2	MAUCX	B-	(800) 225-6292	D+ / 2.7	0.40	0.87	2.20 /51	0.77 /24	0.93 /26	1.37	0.94
GL	Pioneer Multi-Asset Ultrasht Inc K	MAUKX	B+	(800) 225-6292	C- / 3.6	0.54	1.14	2.74 /55	1.33 /32	1.50 /34	1.90	0.42
GL	Pioneer Multi-Asset Ultrasht Inc Y	MYFRX	B+	(800) 225-6292	C- / 3.4	0.51	0.98	2.55 /53	1.18 /30	1.43 /33	1.81	0.51
GEI	Pioneer Short Term Income A	STABX	C+	(800) 225-6292	D+ / 2.3	0.62	0.82	2.33 /52	1.20 /31	1.69 /37	1.84	0.79
GEI	Pioneer Short Term Income C	PSHCX	B	(800) 225-6292	D+ / 2.9	0.56	0.69	2.07 /50	0.95 /27	1.30 /31	1.63	1.05
COI	Pioneer Short Term Income C2	STIIX	B	(800) 225-6292	D+ / 2.9	0.46	0.59	2.09 /50	0.93 /26	1.34 /32	1.65	1.04
COI	Pioneer Short Term Income K	STIKX	A-	(800) 225-6292	C- / 3.8	0.70	0.98	2.74 /55	1.47 /35	1.85 /40	2.19	0.50
GEI	Pioneer Short Term Income Y	PSHYX	B+	(800) 225-6292	C- / 3.7	0.68	0.93	2.65 /54	1.42 /34	1.95 /41	2.09	0.59
*GES	Pioneer Strategic Income A	PSRAX	B	(800) 225-6292	C+ / 6.2	2.37	1.32	9.79 /78	3.34 /66	4.12 /74	3.20	1.05
GES	Pioneer Strategic Income C	PSRCX	B+	(800) 225-6292	C+ / 6.8	2.23	0.97	9.09 /77	2.66 /55	3.43 /64	2.69	1.72
GEN	Pioneer Strategic Income K	STRKX	A+	(800) 225-6292	B / 8.0	2.48	1.54	10.24 /79	3.81 /73	4.52 /79	3.78	0.61
GES	Pioneer Strategic Income R	STIRX	A-	(800) 225-6292	B- / 7.1	2.24	1.12	9.39 /77	2.98 /61	3.76 /69	3.00	1.38
GES	Pioneer Strategic Income Y	STRYX	A+	(800) 225-6292	B / 7.9	2.45	1.47	10.12 /79	3.66 /71	4.44 /78	3.66	0.73
MMT	Plan Investment Government	PIFXX	C-	(800) 441-7762	D- / 1.2	0.10	0.16	0.26 /28	0.11 /14	0.09 /15	0.26	N/A
MMT	Plan Investment Money Market Port	PIMXX	C-	(800) 441-7762	D- / 1.4	0.10	0.20	0.34 /30	0.16 /15	0.12 /16	0.35	N/A
GEI	Plan Investment Ultrashort Dur Gvt	PIFUX	C	(800) 621-9215	D / 1.7	0.12	0.16	0.44 /32	0.32 /19	--	0.16	0.61
GEI	PMC Core Fixed Income Fund	PMFIX	C	(866) 762-7338	C- / 4.2	1.28	-1.58	3.12 /57	1.92 /42	1.99 /42	1.77	1.41
MMT	PNC Advtg Inst Treasury MM Inst	PAIXX	D+	(800) 551-2145	E+ / 0.9	0.07	0.09	0.11 /23	0.05 /10	0.03 / 9	0.11	N/A
GES	PNC Bond A	PAAAX	D-	(800) 551-2145	D / 1.9	1.14	-2.29	1.28 /43	1.90 /41	1.68 /37	1.85	0.91
GES	PNC Bond C	PFDCX	D-	(800) 551-2145	D+ / 2.4	0.97	-2.56	0.53 /34	1.05 /28	0.88 /26	1.19	1.63
GES	PNC Bond I	PFDIX	C-	(800) 551-2145	C- / 4.0	1.21	-2.17	1.53 /45	2.01 /43	1.88 /40	2.19	0.63
MMT	PNC Government Money Market A	PGAXX	C-	(800) 551-2145	D- / 1.1	0.09	0.14	0.20 /26	0.09 /13	0.06 /13	0.20	N/A
MMT	PNC Government Money Market Adv	PAGXX	U	(800) 551-2145	U /	0.09	0.14	0.20 /26	--	--	0.20	N/A

● Denotes fund is closed to new investors
* Denotes fund is included in Section II

www.thestreetratings.com

RISK			NET ASSETS		ASSET							FUND MANAGER		MINIMUM		LOADS	
Risk Rating/Pts	3 Yr Avg Standard Deviation	Avg Dura-tion	NAV As of 2/28/17	Total $(Mil)	Cash %	Gov. Bond %	Muni. Bond %	Corp. Bond %	Other %	Portfolio Turnover Ratio	Avg Coupon Rate	Manager Quality Pct	Manager Tenure (Years)	Initial Purch. $	Additional Purch. $	Front End Load	Back End Load
D+ / 2.6	4.4	6.6	14.16	59	0	0	99	0	1	21	4.4	13	11	1,000	500	0.0	0.0
D+ / 2.6	4.4	6.6	14.24	478	0	0	99	0	1	21	4.4	53	11	5,000,000	0	0.0	0.0
B / 8.0	2.1	4.3	9.67	1,181	0	8	1	35	56	43	3.7	79	19	1,000	100	4.5	0.0
B / 8.0	2.1	4.3	9.56	112	0	8	1	35	56	43	3.7	64	19	1,000	500	0.0	0.0
B / 8.1	2.1	4.3	9.67	460	0	8	1	35	56	43	3.7	81	19	5,000,000	0	0.0	0.0
B / 8.1	2.1	4.3	9.76	172	0	8	1	35	56	43	3.7	76	19	0	0	0.0	0.0
B / 8.0	2.1	4.3	9.58	2,376	0	8	1	35	56	43	3.7	82	19	5,000,000	0	0.0	0.0
C- / 3.6	3.7	3.8	9.43	36	4	0	0	64	32	56	5.3	93	6	1,000	100	4.5	0.0
C- / 3.5	3.8	3.8	9.40	39	4	0	0	64	32	56	5.3	89	6	1,000	500	0.0	0.0
C- / 3.6	3.7	3.8	9.47	198	4	0	0	64	32	56	5.3	94	6	5,000,000	0	0.0	0.0
B- / 7.4	2.1	0.4	6.81	202	0	8	0	60	32	51	4.3	80	10	1,000	100	4.5	0.0
B- / 7.4	2.1	0.4	6.82	87	0	8	0	60	32	51	4.3	70	10	1,000	500	0.0	0.0
B / 8.1	2.1	0.4	6.81	N/A	0	8	0	60	32	51	4.3	90	10	5,000,000	0	0.0	0.0
B- / 7.5	2.0	0.4	6.83	545	0	8	0	60	32	51	4.3	84	10	5,000,000	0	0.0	0.0
D- / 1.0	6.3	3.7	8.85	191	0	10	1	73	16	40	6.3	88	16	1,000	100	4.5	0.0
D- / 1.0	6.3	3.7	8.83	171	0	10	1	73	16	40	6.3	83	16	1,000	500	0.0	0.0
D- / 1.0	6.3	3.7	8.69	274	0	10	1	73	16	40	6.3	90	16	5,000,000	0	0.0	0.0
C / 4.7	3.2	4.6	10.42	24	2	45	4	27	22	37	4.1	90	10	1,000	100	4.5	0.0
C / 4.8	3.2	4.6	10.45	10	2	45	4	27	22	37	4.1	84	10	1,000	500	0.0	0.0
C / 4.7	3.2	4.6	10.51	18	2	45	4	27	22	37	4.1	91	10	5,000,000	0	0.0	0.0
D / 2.0	4.6	6.0	7.21	254	0	0	99	0	1	20	6.2	81	11	1,000	100	4.5	0.0
D / 2.0	4.6	6.0	7.21	145	0	0	99	0	1	20	6.2	71	11	1,000	500	0.0	0.0
D / 2.0	4.6	6.0	7.12	163	0	0	99	0	1	20	6.2	83	11	5,000,000	0	0.0	0.0
E+ / 0.8	6.2	3.4	9.72	547	0	4	0	68	28	41	5.4	4	10	1,000	100	4.5	0.0
E+ / 0.8	6.2	3.4	9.93	252	0	4	0	68	28	41	5.4	1	10	1,000	500	0.0	0.0
E+ / 0.8	6.2	3.4	11.01	30	0	4	0	68	28	41	5.4	3	10	0	0	0.0	0.0
E+ / 0.8	6.2	3.4	9.73	223	0	4	0	68	28	41	5.4	7	10	5,000,000	0	0.0	0.0
A+ / 9.9	0.4	0.3	9.98	762	5	3	0	32	60	58	2.1	76	N/A	1,000	100	2.5	0.0
A+ / 9.9	0.4	0.3	9.97	559	5	3	0	32	60	58	2.1	69	N/A	1,000	500	0.0	0.0
A+ / 9.9	0.4	0.3	9.97	10	5	3	0	32	60	58	2.1	69	N/A	1,000	500	0.0	0.0
A+ / 9.9	0.4	0.3	9.99	59	5	3	0	32	60	58	2.1	79	N/A	5,000,000	0	0.0	0.0
A+ / 9.9	0.4	0.3	9.98	1,731	5	3	0	32	60	58	2.1	77	N/A	5,000,000	0	0.0	0.0
A+ / 9.8	0.4	1.2	9.53	172	0	7	1	40	52	44	2.4	74	11	1,000	100	2.5	0.0
A+ / 9.8	0.5	1.2	9.51	85	0	7	1	40	52	44	2.4	68	11	1,000	500	0.0	0.0
A+ / 9.8	0.5	1.2	9.51	3	0	7	1	40	52	44	2.4	67	11	1,000	500	0.0	0.0
A+ / 9.8	0.5	1.2	9.54	16	0	7	1	40	52	44	2.4	78	11	5,000,000	0	0.0	0.0
A+ / 9.8	0.5	1.2	9.51	286	0	7	1	40	52	44	2.4	77	11	5,000,000	0	0.0	0.0
C+ / 6.2	2.9	4.1	10.73	1,201	0	14	1	44	41	43	4.6	86	18	1,000	100	4.5	0.0
C+ / 5.9	2.9	4.1	10.50	821	0	14	1	44	41	43	4.6	80	18	1,000	500	0.0	0.0
C+ / 5.9	2.9	4.1	10.75	316	0	14	1	44	41	43	4.6	89	18	5,000,000	0	0.0	0.0
C+ / 5.9	2.9	4.1	10.90	228	0	14	1	44	41	43	4.6	83	18	0	0	0.0	0.0
C+ / 6.2	2.9	4.1	10.73	3,303	0	14	1	44	41	43	4.6	88	18	5,000,000	0	0.0	0.0
A+ / 9.9	N/A	N/A	1.00	464	100	0	0	0	0	0	0.3	N/A	N/A	0	0	0.0	0.0
A+ / 9.9	N/A	N/A	1.00	19	100	0	0	0	0	0	0.4	50	N/A	0	0	0.0	0.0
A+ / 9.9	0.3	0.9	10.02	41	1	46	0	0	53	88	0.0	48	5	1,000,000	0	0.0	0.0
C+ / 6.5	2.8	N/A	16.64	279	6	34	0	27	33	100	0.0	24	8	1,000	50	0.0	0.0
A+ / 9.9	N/A	N/A	1.00	497	100	0	0	0	0	0	0.1	42	N/A	3,000,000	0	0.0	0.0
C+ / 6.4	2.8	5.4	10.23	3	0	25	0	38	37	111	0.0	20	15	1,000	50	4.5	0.0
C+ / 6.5	2.8	5.4	10.20	N/A	0	25	0	38	37	111	0.0	6	15	1,000	50	0.0	0.0
C+ / 6.4	2.8	5.4	10.20	52	0	25	0	38	37	111	0.0	24	15	0	0	0.0	0.0
A+ / 9.9	N/A	N/A	1.00	483	100	0	0	0	0	0	0.2	46	N/A	1,000	50	0.0	0.0
U /	N/A	N/A	1.00	6	100	0	0	0	0	0	0.2	N/A	N/A	0	0	0.0	0.0

Fund Type	Fund Name	Ticker Symbol	Overall Investment Rating	Phone	Performance Rating/Pts	3 Mo	6 Mo	1Yr / Pct	Annualized 3Yr / Pct	Annualized 5Yr / Pct	Dividend Yield	Expense Ratio
MMT	PNC Government Money Market I	PKIXX	C-	(800) 551-2145	D- / 1.1	0.09	0.14	0.21 / 26	0.09 / 13	0.06 / 13	0.20	N/A
USS	PNC Government Mortgage A	POMAX	D-	(800) 551-2145	E / 0.5	0.34	-1.63	-0.55 / 9	1.53 / 35	1.04 / 28	2.13	1.08
USS	PNC Government Mortgage C	PGTCX	D	(800) 551-2145	D / 1.7	0.17	-1.98	-1.27 / 3	0.76 / 24	0.29 / 20	1.50	1.80
USS	PNC Government Mortgage I	PTGIX	C	(800) 551-2145	C- / 3.3	0.41	-1.49	-0.27 / 13	1.77 / 39	1.28 / 31	2.52	0.80
GES	PNC Intermediate Bond A	PBFAX	D-	(800) 551-2145	E / 0.4	0.87	-1.28	0.99 / 39	1.06 / 29	1.15 / 29	1.25	0.81
GES	PNC Intermediate Bond C	PIBCX	D	(800) 551-2145	D- / 1.4	0.69	-1.62	0.28 / 28	0.30 / 19	0.41 / 21	0.60	1.53
GES	PNC Intermediate Bond I	PIKIX	C	(800) 551-2145	C- / 3.0	0.94	-1.23	1.26 / 42	1.27 / 32	1.39 / 33	1.59	0.53
MUN	PNC Intermediate Tax Exempt Bond	PTBIX	D	(800) 551-2145	C- / 4.1	1.88	-3.00	-0.63 / 8	2.56 / 75	2.20 / 64	2.07	0.92
MUN	PNC Intermediate Tax Exempt Bond	PITCX	D	(800) 551-2145	C- / 3.8	1.61	-3.41	-1.40 / 2	1.70 / 54	1.38 / 44	1.36	1.64
MUN	PNC Intermediate Tax Exempt Bond I	PTIIX	C+	(800) 551-2145	C+ / 6.2	1.84	-2.97	-0.49 / 10	2.65 / 76	2.35 / 67	2.37	0.64
GEI	PNC Ltd Maturity Bond A	PLFAX	D	(800) 551-2145	E / 0.5	0.23	-0.18	0.43 / 32	0.40 / 20	0.42 / 21	0.66	0.77
GEI	PNC Ltd Maturity Bond C	PFLCX	D	(800) 551-2145	E / 0.4	0.06	-0.63	-0.33 / 12	-0.23 / 4	-0.13 / 4	0.02	1.49
GEI	PNC Ltd Maturity Bond I	PMYIX	C	(800) 551-2145	D / 1.9	0.30	-0.16	0.58 / 35	0.46 / 20	0.57 / 22	0.93	0.49
MUS	PNC MD Tax Exempt Bond A	PDATX	D-	(800) 551-2145	D+ / 2.5	1.41	-3.13	-1.21 / 3	1.97 / 62	1.36 / 43	1.94	0.95
MUS	PNC MD Tax Exempt Bond C	PDACX	D-	(800) 551-2145	D+ / 2.5	1.24	-3.46	-1.97 / 1	1.21 / 41	0.62 / 27	1.30	1.67
MUS	PNC MD Tax Exempt Bond I	PDITX	C+	(800) 551-2145	C / 5.1	1.48	-2.99	-0.93 / 5	2.19 / 67	1.61 / 49	2.28	0.67
MUS	PNC Ohio Intermediate Tax-Ex Bond	POXAX	E+	(800) 551-2145	D+ / 2.3	1.66	-2.87	-1.19 / 3	1.80 / 57	1.49 / 46	1.75	0.98
MUS	PNC Ohio Intermediate Tax-Ex Bond	POXCX	D-	(800) 551-2145	D+ / 2.5	1.58	-3.14	-1.80 / 1	1.12 / 38	0.79 / 30	1.08	1.70
MUS	PNC Ohio Intermediate Tax-Ex Bond	POXIX	C-	(800) 551-2145	C / 4.9	1.72	-2.73	-0.90 / 5	2.07 / 64	1.76 / 53	2.09	0.70
MUN	PNC Tax Exempt Limited Mat Bond A	PDLAX	D-	(800) 551-2145	E / 0.4	1.37	-1.25	-0.66 / 7	0.70 / 29	0.69 / 28	1.12	0.84
MUN	PNC Tax Exempt Limited Mat Bond I	PDLIX	C+	(800) 551-2145	C- / 3.0	1.44	-1.11	-0.39 / 11	0.97 / 35	0.96 / 34	1.44	0.56
GEI	PNC Total Return Advantage A	PTVAX	D-	(800) 551-2145	D / 2.1	1.41	-1.67	3.05 / 57	1.73 / 39	1.98 / 42	2.09	0.87
GEI	PNC Total Return Advantage C	PTVCX	D	(800) 551-2145	D+ / 2.7	1.22	-2.02	2.31 / 52	1.00 / 28	1.25 / 31	1.45	1.59
GEI	PNC Total Return Advantage I	PTVIX	C	(800) 551-2145	C / 4.4	1.48	-1.54	3.33 / 59	1.98 / 43	2.24 / 45	2.46	0.59
MMT	PNC Treasury Money Market A	PRAXX	D+	(800) 551-2145	E+ / 0.9	0.07	0.10	0.13 / 23	0.05 / 10	0.04 / 10	0.13	N/A
MMT	PNC Treasury Money Market I	PDIXX	D+	(800) 551-2145	E+ / 0.9	0.07	0.10	0.13 / 23	0.05 / 10	0.04 / 10	0.13	N/A
GEI	PNC Ultra Short Bond A	PSBAX	D+	(800) 551-2145	E / 0.5	0.26	0.18	0.60 / 35	0.14 / 14	0.10 / 15	0.49	0.60
GEI	PNC Ultra Short Bond I	PNCIX	C+	(800) 551-2145	D / 1.8	0.23	0.32	0.78 / 37	0.38 / 20	0.36 / 20	0.78	0.32
GEI	Power Income A	PWRAX	D	(877) 779-7462	C- / 3.0	3.02	2.11	8.23 / 75	1.26 / 31	2.88 / 56	0.57	1.70
GEI	Power Income C	PWRCX	U	(877) 779-7462	U /	2.74	1.74	7.33 / 73	--	--	0.43	2.45
GEI	Power Income I	PWRIX	B	(877) 779-7462	C / 5.5	3.12	2.26	8.50 / 75	1.52 / 35	3.15 / 60	0.65	1.45
GES	Praxis Impact Bond A	MIIAX	D	(800) 977-2947	D / 1.9	0.93	-1.85	1.34 / 43	2.22 / 47	2.08 / 43	2.16	0.98
GES	Praxis Impact Bond I	MIIIX	C+	(800) 977-2947	C- / 4.0	1.04	-1.66	1.66 / 46	2.60 / 54	2.46 / 49	2.67	0.54
GEI	Principal Bond Market Index Inst	PNIIX	C	(800) 222-5852	C / 4.6	0.96	-2.40	0.96 / 39	2.59 / 54	2.07 / 43	1.76	0.28
GEI	Principal Bond Market Index J	PBIJX	D	(800) 222-5852	C- / 3.2	0.78	-2.64	0.41 / 31	1.71 / 38	1.32 / 32	1.22	0.70
GEI	Principal Bond Market Index R1	PBIMX	D-	(800) 222-5852	D+ / 2.6	0.74	-2.78	0.18 / 25	1.33 / 32	0.97 / 27	0.99	1.17
GEI	Principal Bond Market Index R2	PBINX	D-	(800) 222-5852	D+ / 2.8	0.75	-2.76	0.29 / 28	1.44 / 34	1.10 / 29	1.01	1.04
GEI	Principal Bond Market Index R3	PBOIX	D-	(800) 222-5852	C- / 3.1	0.84	-2.69	0.46 / 32	1.63 / 37	1.27 / 31	1.28	0.86
GEI	Principal Bond Market Index R4	PBIPX	D	(800) 222-5852	C- / 3.5	0.89	-2.54	0.61 / 35	1.85 / 40	1.48 / 34	1.42	0.67
GEI	Principal Bond Market Index R5	PBIQX	D+	(800) 222-5852	C- / 3.6	0.92	-2.50	0.73 / 37	1.94 / 42	1.59 / 36	1.54	0.55
MUS	Principal CA Municipal A	SRCMX	C	(800) 222-5852	B- / 7.5	2.90	-4.37	-0.02 / 17	4.63 / 96	4.25 / 95	2.81	0.81
MUS	Principal CA Municipal C	SRCCX	C	(800) 222-5852	B / 7.6	2.69	-4.83	-0.84 / 5	3.72 / 90	3.27 / 84	2.08	1.74
MUN	Principal CA Municipal Inst	PCMFX	B	(800) 222-5852	A- / 9.1	2.94	-4.37	0.15 / 27	4.74 / 96	4.32 / 95	3.10	95.60
MUN	Principal CA Municipal P	PLBTX	U	(800) 222-5852	U /	3.06	-4.25	0.23 / 30	--	--	3.18	0.60
GL	Principal Capital Securities S	PCSFX	U	(800) 222-5852	U /	4.43	3.56	13.06 / 85	--	--	4.95	0.11
GEI	Principal Core Plus Bond A	PRBDX	D	(800) 222-5852	C- / 3.3	1.57	-1.47	3.74 / 61	2.24 / 47	2.41 / 48	2.12	1.01
GEI	Principal Core Plus Bond C	PBMCX	D	(800) 222-5852	C- / 3.4	1.36	-1.89	2.75 / 55	1.35 / 33	1.55 / 35	1.33	2.02
GEI	Principal Core Plus Bond Inst	PMSIX	B	(800) 222-5852	C / 5.5	1.67	-1.28	4.04 / 62	2.62 / 54	2.81 / 55	2.59	0.50
GEI	Principal Core Plus Bond J	PBMJX	C+	(800) 222-5852	C / 4.9	1.57	-1.42	3.80 / 61	2.28 / 48	2.42 / 48	2.27	0.82
GEI	Principal Core Plus Bond R1	PBOMX	C-	(800) 222-5852	C- / 4.0	1.45	-1.71	3.14 / 57	1.73 / 39	1.91 / 41	1.71	1.38
GEI	Principal Core Plus Bond R2	PBMNX	C	(800) 222-5852	C / 4.3	1.50	-1.57	3.31 / 58	1.89 / 41	2.05 / 43	1.87	1.25
GEI	Principal Core Plus Bond R3	PBMMX	C	(800) 222-5852	C / 4.5	1.54	-1.57	3.48 / 60	2.06 / 44	2.23 / 45	2.04	1.07

● Denotes fund is closed to new investors
* Denotes fund is included in Section II

99 Pct = Best
0 Pct = Worst

RISK			NET ASSETS		ASSET							FUND MANAGER		MINIMUM		LOADS	
Risk Rating/Pts	3 Yr Avg Standard Deviation	Avg Dura-tion	NAV As of 2/28/17	Total $(Mil)	Cash %	Gov. Bond %	Muni. Bond %	Corp. Bond %	Other %	Portfolio Turnover Ratio	Avg Coupon Rate	Manager Quality Pct	Manager Tenure (Years)	Initial Purch. $	Additional Purch. $	Front End Load	Back End Load
A+ / 9.9	N/A	N/A	1.00	9,312	100	0	0	0	0	0	0.2	46	N/A	0	0	0.0	0.0
B+ / 8.3	2.0	2.7	8.99	8	0	8	0	0	92	13	0.0	62	15	1,000	50	4.5	0.0
B+ / 8.3	2.0	2.7	8.98	1	0	8	0	0	92	13	0.0	27	15	1,000	50	0.0	0.0
B / 8.1	2.1	2.7	8.99	39	0	8	0	0	92	13	0.0	67	15	0	0	0.0	0.0
B / 8.1	2.1	3.9	10.87	4	1	32	0	43	24	87	0.0	17	15	1,000	50	4.5	0.0
B / 8.1	2.1	3.9	10.91	N/A	1	32	0	43	24	87	0.0	5	15	1,000	50	0.0	0.0
B / 8.1	2.1	3.9	10.86	214	1	32	0	43	24	87	0.0	21	15	0	0	0.0	0.0
C / 4.9	3.2	5.1	9.39	3	3	0	95	0	2	22	0.0	15	10	1,000	50	3.0	0.0
C / 5.3	3.1	5.1	9.29	N/A	3	0	95	0	2	22	0.0	5	10	1,000	50	0.0	0.0
C / 5.2	3.1	5.1	9.42	75	3	0	95	0	2	22	0.0	19	10	0	0	0.0	0.0
A+ / 9.6	0.7	1.9	10.16	2	6	29	0	34	31	75	0.0	31	15	1,000	50	2.0	0.0
A+ / 9.6	0.7	1.9	10.15	1	6	29	0	34	31	75	0.0	14	15	1,000	50	0.0	0.0
A+ / 9.7	0.7	1.9	10.12	306	6	29	0	34	31	75	0.0	34	15	0	0	0.0	0.0
C+ / 6.3	2.9	4.9	10.70	N/A	3	0	96	0	1	18	0.0	11	10	1,000	50	3.0	0.0
C+ / 6.2	2.9	4.9	10.70	N/A	3	0	96	0	1	18	0.0	4	10	1,000	50	0.0	0.0
C+ / 6.4	2.8	4.9	10.71	37	3	0	96	0	1	18	0.0	15	10	0	0	0.0	0.0
C / 5.3	3.0	5.2	10.41	4	2	0	97	0	1	20	0.0	6	8	1,000	50	3.0	0.0
C / 5.1	3.1	5.2	10.39	1	2	0	97	0	1	20	0.0	2	8	1,000	50	0.0	0.0
C / 5.2	3.1	5.2	10.44	33	2	0	97	0	1	20	0.0	9	8	0	0	0.0	0.0
B+ / 8.6	1.7	3.2	10.33	N/A	2	0	97	0	1	29	0.0	11	10	1,000	50	3.0	0.0
B+ / 8.6	1.7	3.2	10.32	126	2	0	97	0	1	29	0.0	17	10	0	0	0.0	0.0
C+ / 6.6	2.8	5.4	10.70	18	0	29	0	31	40	53	0.0	20	15	1,000	50	4.5	0.0
C+ / 6.6	2.8	5.4	10.72	1	0	29	0	31	40	53	0.0	7	15	1,000	50	0.0	0.0
C+ / 6.5	2.8	5.4	10.69	150	0	29	0	31	40	53	0.0	26	15	0	0	0.0	0.0
A+ / 9.9	N/A	N/A	1.00	171	100	0	0	0	0	0	0.1	42	N/A	1,000	50	0.0	0.0
A+ / 9.9	N/A	N/A	1.00	1,021	100	0	0	0	0	0	0.1	42	N/A	0	0	0.0	0.0
A+ / 9.9	0.3	1.0	9.95	1	0	32	0	37	31	91	0.0	37	15	1,000	50	1.0	0.0
A+ / 9.9	0.3	1.0	9.93	435	0	32	0	37	31	91	0.0	53	15	0	0	0.0	0.0
C+ / 6.6	2.8	N/A	10.23	34	3	3	0	79	15	238	0.0	70	7	1,000	100	5.0	0.0
U /	N/A	N/A	10.12	4	3	3	0	79	15	238	0.0	N/A	7	2,500	500	0.0	0.0
C+ / 6.6	2.8	N/A	10.25	177	3	3	0	79	15	238	0.0	75	7	100,000	0	0.0	0.0
B- / 7.4	2.6	4.7	10.36	82	0	30	2	40	28	23	0.0	35	23	2,500	100	3.8	2.0
B- / 7.4	2.6	4.7	10.31	384	0	30	2	40	28	23	0.0	58	23	100,000	0	0.0	2.0
C+ / 6.1	2.9	5.5	10.92	1,819	0	42	1	24	33	152	3.1	47	8	0	0	0.0	0.0
C+ / 6.0	2.9	5.5	10.74	31	0	42	1	24	33	152	3.1	13	8	1,000	100	0.0	0.0
C+ / 5.8	3.0	5.5	10.74	2	0	42	1	24	33	152	3.1	7	8	0	0	0.0	0.0
C+ / 6.0	2.9	5.5	10.76	3	0	42	1	24	33	152	3.1	9	8	0	0	0.0	0.0
C+ / 5.8	3.0	5.5	10.72	19	0	42	1	24	33	152	3.1	11	8	0	0	0.0	0.0
C+ / 6.1	2.9	5.5	10.74	36	0	42	1	24	33	152	3.1	17	8	0	0	0.0	0.0
C+ / 6.1	2.9	5.5	10.78	22	0	42	1	24	33	152	3.1	18	8	0	0	0.0	0.0
D+ / 2.6	4.4	6.5	10.32	290	0	0	99	0	1	28	4.9	45	4	1,000	100	3.8	0.0
D+ / 2.6	4.4	6.5	10.34	43	0	0	99	0	1	28	4.9	14	4	1,000	100	0.0	0.0
D+ / 2.6	4.3	6.5	10.32	12	0	0	99	0	1	28	4.9	52	4	0	0	0.0	0.0
U /	N/A	6.5	10.32	57	0	0	99	0	1	28	4.9	N/A	4	0	0	0.0	0.0
U /	N/A	N/A	10.07	331	6	0	0	81	13	9	0.0	N/A	3	0	0	0.0	0.0
C+ / 6.3	2.9	5.5	10.88	92	0	14	0	43	43	168	3.6	33	17	1,000	100	3.8	0.0
C+ / 6.3	2.8	5.5	10.88	9	0	14	0	43	43	168	3.6	11	17	1,000	100	0.0	0.0
C+ / 6.7	2.8	5.5	10.87	3,401	0	14	0	43	43	168	3.6	57	17	1,000,000	0	0.0	0.0
C+ / 6.6	2.8	5.5	10.95	150	0	14	0	43	43	168	3.6	36	17	1,000	100	0.0	0.0
C+ / 6.6	2.8	5.5	10.87	5	0	14	0	43	43	168	3.6	19	17	0	0	0.0	0.0
C+ / 6.6	2.8	5.5	10.77	9	0	14	0	43	43	168	3.6	23	17	0	0	0.0	0.0
C+ / 6.5	2.8	5.5	10.81	21	0	14	0	43	43	168	3.6	28	17	0	0	0.0	0.0

Fund Type	Fund Name	Ticker Symbol	Overall Investment Rating	Phone	Performance Rating/Pts	3 Mo	6 Mo	1Yr / Pct	3Yr / Pct	5Yr / Pct	Dividend Yield	Expense Ratio
GEI	Principal Core Plus Bond R4	PBMSX	C+	(800) 222-5852	C / 4.9	1.65	-1.45	3.69 /61	2.27 /48	2.43 /48	2.18	0.88
GEI	Principal Core Plus Bond R5	PBMPX	C+	(800) 222-5852	C / 5.1	1.61	-1.41	3.80 /61	2.37 /49	2.54 /50	2.35	0.76
COH	Principal Dynamic HY Exp A	PDYAX	U	(800) 222-5852	U /	2.49	5.08	15.85 /90	--	--	4.65	1.72
COH	Principal Dynamic HY Exp Instl	PDYIX	U	(800) 222-5852	U /	2.62	5.24	16.32 /91	--	--	4.93	1.37
* GL	Principal Glb Divers Income A	PGBAX	C+	(800) 222-5852	B+ / 8.3	4.80	3.63	14.19 /87	4.27 /78	6.21 /94	5.09	1.09
GL	Principal Glb Divers Income C	PGDCX	C+	(800) 222-5852	B+ / 8.5	4.65	3.19	13.34 /86	3.49 /69	5.41 /88	4.58	1.85
GL	Principal Glb Divers Income Inst	PGDIX	B	(800) 222-5852	A / 9.3	4.98	3.81	14.62 /88	4.62 /82	6.57 /95	5.62	0.78
GL	Principal Glb Divers Income P	PGDPX	B	(800) 222-5852	A / 9.3	4.90	3.79	14.49 /88	4.54 /81	6.48 /95	5.58	0.83
MTG	Principal Govt & High Qual Bd A	CMPGX	C-	(800) 222-5852	D+ / 2.5	0.21	-1.27	0.01 /17	1.84 /40	1.72 /38	3.75	0.90
MTG	Principal Govt & High Qual Bd C	CCUGX	D+	(800) 222-5852	D / 2.0	-0.11	-1.72	-0.88 / 5	0.98 /27	0.89 /26	2.92	1.66
MTG	Principal Govt & High Qual Bd Inst	PMRIX	B-	(800) 222-5852	C- / 3.9	0.26	-1.09	0.22 /26	2.13 /45	2.02 /42	4.04	0.52
MTG	Principal Govt & High Qual Bd J	PMRJX	C+	(800) 222-5852	C- / 3.3	0.19	-1.23	-0.08 /16	1.80 /40	1.64 /37	3.73	0.80
MTG	Principal Govt & High Qual Bd P	PGSPX	C+	(800) 222-5852	C- / 3.6	0.20	-1.20	0.10 /22	1.96 /42	1.84 /39	3.82	0.75
MTG	Principal Govt & High Qual Bd R1	PMGRX	C-	(800) 222-5852	D+ / 2.6	0.07	-1.46	-0.45 /10	1.35 /33	1.23 /30	3.25	1.38
MTG	Principal Govt & High Qual Bd R2	PFMRX	C-	(800) 222-5852	D+ / 2.8	0.10	-1.40	-0.32 /12	1.48 /35	1.38 /33	3.39	1.25
MTG	Principal Govt & High Qual Bd R3	PRCMX	C	(800) 222-5852	C- / 3.1	0.15	-1.31	-0.14 /15	1.66 /37	1.56 /35	3.57	1.07
MTG	Principal Govt & High Qual Bd R4	PMRDX	C+	(800) 222-5852	C- / 3.4	0.19	-1.22	-0.04 /17	1.85 /40	1.74 /38	3.77	0.88
MTG	Principal Govt & High Qual Bd R5	PMREX	C+	(800) 222-5852	C- / 3.6	0.13	-1.25	0.07 /21	1.94 /42	1.86 /40	3.89	0.76
* COH	Principal High Yield A	CPHYX	C+	(800) 222-5852	A- / 9.2	5.12	6.16	19.56 /95	4.48 /80	6.51 /95	5.21	0.88
COH	Principal High Yield C	CCHIX	C+	(800) 222-5852	A / 9.3	5.02	5.85	18.79 /95	3.73 /72	5.73 /90	4.63	1.63
COH	Principal High Yield Fund I A	PYHAX	D+	(800) 222-5852	B / 7.7	4.24	4.15	17.17 /92	3.20 /64	5.51 /89	4.85	1.23
COH	Principal High Yield Fund I Inst	PYHIX	C	(800) 222-5852	A- / 9.0	4.33	4.35	17.61 /93	3.58 /70	5.89 /91	5.41	0.65
COH	Principal High Yield Inst	PHYTX	B-	(800) 222-5852	A+ / 9.7	5.09	6.35	20.04 /96	4.78 /84	6.82 /96	5.71	0.60
COH	Principal High Yield P	PYHPX	B-	(800) 222-5852	A+ / 9.7	5.20	6.31	19.91 /96	4.74 /83	6.76 /96	5.70	0.71
COI	Principal Income Fd A	CMPIX	C	(800) 222-5852	C / 4.8	1.92	-0.48	5.58 /69	2.51 /52	3.20 /61	3.04	0.88
COI	Principal Income Fd C	CNMCX	C-	(800) 222-5852	C / 4.3	1.60	-0.98	4.70 /65	1.67 /38	2.36 /47	2.28	1.67
COI	Principal Income Fd Inst	PIOIX	B	(800) 222-5852	C+ / 6.3	1.90	-0.39	5.97 /70	2.88 /59	3.56 /67	3.48	0.50
COI	Principal Income Fd J	PIOJX	C+	(800) 222-5852	C+ / 5.9	1.95	-0.43	5.68 /69	2.55 /53	3.18 /60	3.20	0.79
COI	Principal Income Fd P	PIMPX	B	(800) 222-5852	C+ / 6.1	1.86	-0.49	5.80 /70	2.71 /56	3.40 /64	3.32	0.67
COI	Principal Income Fd R1	PIOMX	C	(800) 222-5852	C / 5.0	1.79	-0.71	5.05 /67	2.03 /44	2.68 /52	2.61	1.37
COI	Principal Income Fd R2	PIONX	C	(800) 222-5852	C / 5.2	1.82	-0.65	5.29 /68	2.16 /46	2.83 /55	2.74	1.24
COI	Principal Income Fd R3	PIOOX	C+	(800) 222-5852	C / 5.4	1.76	-0.66	5.37 /68	2.30 /48	3.00 /58	2.92	1.06
COI	Principal Income Fd R4	PIOPX	C+	(800) 222-5852	C+ / 5.9	1.92	-0.47	5.68 /69	2.53 /52	3.21 /61	3.11	0.87
COI	Principal Income Fd R5	PIOQX	B-	(800) 222-5852	C+ / 6.0	1.95	-0.41	5.71 /69	2.63 /55	3.32 /63	3.24	0.75
COI	Principal Income Fd R6	PICNX	U	(800) 222-5852	U /	2.01	-0.38	5.96 /70	--	--	3.48	1.22
GEI	Principal Infl Prot A	PITAX	E	(800) 222-5852	E / 0.5	0.77	-0.99	2.47 /53	0.71 /23	-0.07 / 5	0.73	0.95
GEI	Principal Infl Prot C	PPOCX	E	(800) 222-5852	D- / 1.0	0.63	-1.32	1.77 /47	-0.05 / 5	-0.81 / 2	0.62	2.08
GEI	Principal Infl Prot Inst	PIPIX	E+	(800) 222-5852	C- / 3.3	0.88	-0.86	2.93 /56	1.19 /31	0.42 /21	0.87	0.39
GEI	Principal Infl Prot J	PIPJX	E	(800) 222-5852	D / 2.1	0.72	-1.19	2.21 /51	0.47 /21	-0.23 / 4	0.71	1.03
GEI	Principal Infl Prot R1	PISPX	E	(800) 222-5852	D / 1.8	0.67	-1.27	2.05 /49	0.30 /19	-0.45 / 3	0.66	1.27
GEI	Principal Infl Prot R2	PBSAX	E	(800) 222-5852	D / 2.0	0.74	-1.20	2.24 /51	0.44 /20	-0.33 / 3	0.73	1.14
GEI	Principal Infl Prot R3	PIFPX	E	(800) 222-5852	D+ / 2.3	0.77	-1.03	2.38 /52	0.60 /22	-0.15 / 4	0.76	0.96
GEI	Principal Infl Prot R4	PIFSX	E+	(800) 222-5852	D+ / 2.7	0.80	-0.97	2.65 /54	0.84 /25	0.04 /10	0.79	0.77
GEI	Principal Infl Prot R5	PBPPX	E+	(800) 222-5852	D+ / 2.9	0.82	-0.94	2.77 /55	0.94 /27	0.15 /17	0.81	0.65
MMT	Principal Mny Mrkt A	PCSXX	D+	(800) 222-5852	E+ / 0.7	0.08	0.10	0.10 /22	0.03 / 9	0.02 / 8	0.10	N/A
MMT	Principal Mny Mrkt C	PPCXX	D+	(800) 222-5852	E+ / 0.7	0.05	0.06	0.06 /21	0.02 / 8	0.01 / 6	0.06	N/A
MMT	Principal Mny Mrkt Inst	PVMXX	U	(800) 222-5852	U /	--	--	--	--	--	0.05	N/A
MMT	Principal Mny Mrkt J	PMJXX	D+	(800) 222-5852	E+ / 0.7	0.07	0.08	0.08 /22	0.03 / 9	0.02 / 8	0.08	N/A
MUN	Principal Opportunistic Muni C	PMODX	B	(800) 222-5852	A / 9.3	2.36	-5.96	0.08 /23	5.22 /97	--	2.79	1.97
MUH	Principal Opportunistic Muni Inst	POMFX	B	(800) 222-5852	A+ / 9.8	2.51	-5.57	1.08 /46	6.18 /99	--	3.83	0.83
MUH	Principal Opportunistic Muni P	PMOQX	B+	(800) 222-5852	A+ / 9.8	2.61	-5.54	1.12 /46	6.32 /99	--	3.86	1.06
MUN	Principal Opportunistic Munil A	PMOAX	B	(800) 222-5852	A- / 9.1	2.54	-5.60	0.83 /43	6.04 /99	--	3.43	1.11

RISK			NET ASSETS		ASSET							FUND MANAGER		MINIMUM		LOADS	
Risk Rating/Pts	3 Yr Avg Standard Deviation	Avg Dura-tion	NAV As of 2/28/17	Total $(Mil)	Cash %	Gov. Bond %	Muni. Bond %	Corp. Bond %	Other %	Portfolio Turnover Ratio	Avg Coupon Rate	Manager Quality Pct	Manager Tenure (Years)	Initial Purch. $	Additional Purch. $	Front End Load	Back End Load
C+ / 6.4	2.8	5.5	11.02	18	0	14	0	43	43	168	3.6	35	17	0	0	0.0	0.0
C+ / 6.5	2.8	5.5	10.82	59	0	14	0	43	43	168	3.6	43	17	0	0	0.0	0.0
U /	N/A	0.9	9.37	8	1	0	0	48	51	113	5.5	N/A	3	1,000	100	3.8	0.0
U /	N/A	0.9	9.42	7	1	0	0	48	51	113	5.5	N/A	3	0	0	0.0	0.0
D / 2.1	5.0	3.8	13.84	1,945	3	15	0	36	46	101	6.2	96	7	1,000	100	3.8	0.0
D / 2.1	5.0	3.8	13.76	2,343	3	15	0	36	46	101	6.2	95	7	1,000	100	0.0	0.0
D / 2.1	5.0	3.8	13.79	3,894	3	15	0	36	46	101	6.2	97	7	1,000,000	0	0.0	0.0
D / 2.1	4.9	3.8	13.77	3,160	3	15	0	36	46	101	6.2	97	7	0	0	0.0	0.0
B / 8.1	2.1	3.0	10.54	292	0	7	0	0	93	31	3.5	20	7	1,000	100	2.3	0.0
B / 8.2	2.1	3.0	10.53	57	0	7	0	0	93	31	3.5	6	7	1,000	100	0.0	0.0
B / 8.2	2.1	3.0	10.55	994	0	7	0	0	93	31	3.5	30	7	1,000,000	0	0.0	0.0
B / 8.2	2.1	3.0	10.56	129	0	7	0	0	93	31	3.5	20	7	1,000	100	0.0	0.0
B / 8.1	2.1	3.0	10.58	17	0	7	0	0	93	31	3.5	25	7	0	0	0.0	0.0
B / 8.2	2.0	3.0	10.56	2	0	7	0	0	93	31	3.5	11	7	0	0	0.0	0.0
B / 8.1	2.1	3.0	10.56	14	0	7	0	0	93	31	3.5	12	7	0	0	0.0	0.0
B / 8.1	2.1	3.0	10.56	13	0	7	0	0	93	31	3.5	16	7	0	0	0.0	0.0
B / 8.2	2.1	3.0	10.56	15	0	7	0	0	93	31	3.5	21	7	0	0	0.0	0.0
B / 8.1	2.1	3.0	10.56	23	0	7	0	0	93	31	3.5	24	7	0	0	0.0	0.0
D- / 1.4	5.4	3.4	7.47	987	1	2	0	89	8	43	6.5	59	5	1,000	100	3.8	0.0
D- / 1.3	5.4	3.4	7.55	376	1	2	0	89	8	43	6.5	25	5	1,000	100	0.0	0.0
D- / 1.1	5.6	4.0	9.99	6	3	0	0	88	9	52	6.2	10	10	1,000	100	3.8	0.0
D- / 1.1	5.6	4.0	10.00	1,084	3	0	0	88	9	52	6.2	17	10	1,000,000	0	0.0	0.0
D- / 1.3	5.4	3.4	7.42	1,704	1	2	0	89	8	43	6.5	67	5	1,000,000	0	0.0	0.0
D- / 1.3	5.4	3.4	7.47	609	1	2	0	89	8	43	6.5	66	5	0	0	0.0	0.0
C+ / 5.8	3.0	4.9	9.52	256	0	16	0	58	26	13	4.0	37	12	1,000	100	2.3	0.0
C+ / 5.8	3.0	4.9	9.57	65	0	16	0	58	26	13	4.0	13	12	1,000	100	0.0	0.0
C+ / 5.7	3.0	4.9	9.54	2,674	0	16	0	58	26	13	4.0	58	12	1,000,000	0	0.0	0.0
C+ / 5.7	3.0	4.9	9.54	98	0	16	0	58	26	13	4.0	39	12	1,000	100	0.0	0.0
C+ / 5.9	2.9	4.9	9.54	29	0	16	0	58	26	13	4.0	53	12	0	0	0.0	0.0
C+ / 5.6	3.0	4.9	9.55	21	0	16	0	58	26	13	4.0	20	12	0	0	0.0	0.0
C+ / 5.6	3.0	4.9	9.56	3	0	16	0	58	26	13	4.0	24	12	0	0	0.0	0.0
C+ / 6.0	2.9	4.9	9.56	31	0	16	0	58	26	13	4.0	31	12	0	0	0.0	0.0
C+ / 5.6	3.0	4.9	9.56	28	0	16	0	58	26	13	4.0	37	12	0	0	0.0	0.0
C+ / 5.7	3.0	4.9	9.54	50	0	16	0	58	26	13	4.0	46	12	0	0	0.0	0.0
U /	N/A	4.9	9.54	7	0	16	0	58	26	13	4.0	N/A	12	0	0	0.0	0.0
D+ / 2.9	3.9	7.8	8.45	15	1	98	0	0	1	62	7.0	2	7	1,000	100	3.8	Back
D+ / 2.9	3.9	7.8	8.09	4	1	98	0	0	1	62	7.0	1	7	1,000	100	0.0	0.0
C- / 3.0	3.9	7.8	8.55	1,524	1	98	0	0	1	62	7.0	5	7	1,000,000	0	0.0	0.0
D+ / 2.9	3.9	7.8	8.26	8	1	98	0	0	1	62	7.0	2	7	1,000	100	0.0	0.0
C- / 3.0	3.9	7.8	8.13	1	1	98	0	0	1	62	7.0	1	7	0	0	0.0	0.0
D+ / 2.9	3.9	7.8	8.18	1	1	98	0	0	1	62	7.0	2	7	0	0	0.0	0.0
D+ / 2.8	3.9	7.8	8.27	6	1	98	0	0	1	62	7.0	2	7	0	0	0.0	0.0
C- / 3.0	3.9	7.8	8.36	2	1	98	0	0	1	62	7.0	3	7	0	0	0.0	0.0
C- / 3.0	3.9	7.8	8.43	4	1	98	0	0	1	62	7.0	4	7	0	0	0.0	0.0
A+ / 9.9	N/A	N/A	1.00	467	100	0	0	0	0	0	0.1	39	17	1,000	100	0.0	0.0
A+ / 9.9	N/A	N/A	1.00	18	100	0	0	0	0	0	0.1	38	17	1,000	100	0.0	0.0
U /	N/A	N/A	1.00	N/A	100	0	0	0	0	0	0.1	39	17	1,000,000	0	0.0	0.0
A+ / 9.9	N/A	N/A	1.00	261	100	0	0	0	0	0	0.1	39	17	1,000	100	0.0	0.0
D / 2.1	4.9	6.8	10.22	16	2	0	97	0	1	54	5.4	56	5	1,000	100	0.0	0.0
D / 1.8	4.9	6.8	10.22	1	2	0	97	0	1	54	5.4	79	5	0	0	0.0	0.0
D / 1.8	4.9	6.8	10.24	58	2	0	97	0	1	54	5.4	80	5	0	0	0.0	0.0
D / 2.2	4.9	6.8	10.23	40	2	0	97	0	1	54	5.4	77	5	1,000	100	3.8	0.0

						PERFORMANCE					Incl. in Returns	
							Total Return % through 2/28/17					
	99 Pct = Best		Overall		Perfor-				Annualized		Dividend	Expense
Fund	0 Pct = Worst	Ticker	Investment		mance						Yield	Ratio
Type	Fund Name	Symbol	Rating	Phone	Rating/Pts	3 Mo	6 Mo	1Yr / Pct	3Yr / Pct	5Yr / Pct		
*USS	Principal Preferred Sec A	PPSAX	A+	(800) 222-5852	A- / 9.0	3.98	1.93	9.14 /77	6.30 /93	7.09 /96	4.23	1.07
USS	Principal Preferred Sec C	PRFCX	A+	(800) 222-5852	A- / 9.2	3.91	1.58	8.35 /75	5.52 /89	6.30 /94	3.68	1.82
USS	Principal Preferred Sec Inst	PPSIX	A+	(800) 222-5852	A+ / 9.6	4.08	2.01	9.42 /78	6.59 /95	7.41 /97	4.73	0.76
USS	Principal Preferred Sec J	PPSJX	A+	(800) 222-5852	A / 9.5	3.99	1.91	9.08 /77	6.25 /93	6.98 /96	4.54	1.06
COI	Principal Preferred Sec P	PPSPX	A+	(800) 222-5852	A+ / 9.6	4.07	1.98	9.38 /77	6.53 /94	7.34 /97	4.69	0.83
USS	Principal Preferred Sec R1	PUSAX	A+	(800) 222-5852	A / 9.3	3.80	1.62	8.48 /75	5.72 /90	6.52 /95	3.95	1.58
USS	Principal Preferred Sec R2	PPRSX	A+	(800) 222-5852	A / 9.4	3.96	1.69	8.67 /76	5.90 /91	6.68 /96	4.11	1.45
USS	Principal Preferred Sec R3	PNARX	A+	(800) 222-5852	A / 9.5	3.98	1.86	8.93 /76	6.09 /92	6.88 /96	4.25	1.27
USS	Principal Preferred Sec R4	PQARX	A+	(800) 222-5852	A / 9.5	4.05	1.97	9.16 /77	6.27 /93	7.08 /96	4.46	1.08
USS	Principal Preferred Sec R5	PPARX	A+	(800) 222-5852	A+ / 9.6	4.05	1.91	9.13 /77	6.40 /94	7.20 /97	4.55	0.96
GEL	Principal Preferred Sec R6	PPREX	A+	(800) 222-5852	A+ / 9.6	4.07	2.00	9.41 /78	6.59 /95	7.41 /97	4.72	N/A
MTG	Principal Real Estate Dbt Inc A	PRDYX	U	(800) 222-5852	U /	1.38	-1.67	5.85 /70	--	--	2.55	1.14
MTG	Principal Real Estate Dbt Inc Inst	PRDIX	U	(800) 222-5852	U /	1.38	-1.59	5.19 /67	--	--	3.19	0.84
MTG	Principal Real Estate Dbt Inc P	PDIFX	U	(800) 222-5852	U /	1.34	-1.67	5.04 /67	--	--	3.04	0.89
MTG	Principal Real Estate Dbt Inc R6	PRDHX	U	(800) 222-5852	U /	1.48	-1.50	5.29 /68	--	--	3.17	N/A
GEI	Principal Short-Term Income Fd A	SRHQX	C+	(800) 222-5852	D+ / 2.6	0.75	0.36	2.36 /52	1.37 /33	1.75 /38	1.64	0.68
GEI	Principal Short-Term Income Fd C	STCCX	C	(800) 222-5852	D / 2.0	0.53	-0.15	1.47 /44	0.43 /20	0.87 /26	0.80	1.57
GEI	Principal Short-Term Income Fd Inst	PSHIX	B+	(800) 222-5852	C- / 3.9	0.82	0.41	2.62 /54	1.61 /37	2.01 /42	1.94	0.43
GEI	Principal Short-Term Income Fd J	PSJIX	B	(800) 222-5852	C- / 3.4	0.76	0.29	2.36 /52	1.31 /32	1.65 /37	1.68	0.70
COI	Principal Short-Term Income Fd P	PSTPX	B+	(800) 222-5852	C- / 3.8	0.80	0.37	2.54 /53	1.49 /35	1.91 /41	1.86	0.52
GEI	Principal Short-Term Income Fd R1	PSIMX	C+	(800) 222-5852	D+ / 2.5	0.60	-0.02	1.75 /47	0.74 /24	1.14 /29	1.07	1.30
GEI	Principal Short-Term Income Fd R2	PSINX	C+	(800) 222-5852	D+ / 2.7	0.63	0.04	1.88 /48	0.87 /26	1.27 /31	1.20	1.17
GEI	Principal Short-Term Income Fd R3	PSIOX	B-	(800) 222-5852	C- / 3.0	0.68	0.21	2.06 /49	1.05 /28	1.47 /34	1.38	0.99
GEI	Principal Short-Term Income Fd R4	PSIPX	B	(800) 222-5852	C- / 3.3	0.73	0.31	2.26 /51	1.25 /31	1.67 /37	1.58	0.80
GEI	Principal Short-Term Income Fd R5	PSIQX	B	(800) 222-5852	C- / 3.5	0.75	0.29	2.37 /52	1.36 /33	1.79 /39	1.69	0.68
MUN	Principal Tax-Exempt Bond Fd A	PTEAX	C-	(800) 222-5852	C+ / 6.4	2.38	-4.59	-0.27 /13	3.97 /93	3.32 /85	3.71	0.81
MUN	Principal Tax-Exempt Bond Fd C	PTBCX	C-	(800) 222-5852	C+ / 6.6	2.02	-4.96	-1.21 / 3	3.16 /84	2.50 /70	2.99	1.78
MUN	Principal Tax-Exempt Bond Fd Inst	PITEX	B	(800) 222-5852	B / 8.2	2.28	-4.50	-0.22 /14	4.08 /93	3.39 /86	4.04	0.60
MUN	Principal Tax-Exempt Bond Fd P	PTETX	U	(800) 222-5852	U /	2.31	-4.46	-0.13 /16	--	--	4.14	0.61
MMT	ProFunds Govt Money Market Inv	MPIXX	U	(888) 776-3637	U /	--	--	--	--	--	0.02	N/A
MMT	ProFunds Govt Money Market Svc	MPSXX	U	(888) 776-3637	U /	--	--	--	--	--	0.02	N/A
MTG	ProFunds-Falling US Dollar Inv	FDPIX	E-	(888) 776-3637	E- / 0.0	-0.42	-6.36	-5.44 / 0	-9.62 / 0	-6.71 / 0	0.00	2.43
MTG	ProFunds-Falling US Dollar Svc	FDPSX	E-	(888) 776-3637	E- / 0.0	-0.70	-6.79	-6.29 / 0	-10.51 / 0	-7.63 / 0	0.00	3.43
USA	ProFunds-US Government Plus Inv	GVPIX	E+	(888) 776-3637	C+ / 6.6	2.64	-17.03	-7.80 / 0	6.63 /95	2.51 /50	0.00	1.27
USA	ProFunds-US Government Plus Svc	GVPSX	E+	(888) 776-3637	C / 5.0	2.40	-17.40	-8.64 / 0	5.62 /89	1.47 /34	0.00	2.27
GEI	Prudential Absolute Return Bond A	PADAX	B-	(800) 225-1852	C- / 4.2	2.75	2.29	8.08 /74	2.05 /44	2.50 /50	2.02	1.24
GEI	Prudential Absolute Return Bond C	PADCX	B	(800) 225-1852	C / 4.9	2.56	1.92	7.27 /73	1.30 /32	1.75 /38	1.39	1.99
GEI	Prudential Absolute Return Bond Q	PADQX	A+	(800) 225-1852	C+ / 6.6	2.83	2.48	8.33 /75	2.35 /49	2.81 /55	2.46	0.84
GEI	Prudential Absolute Return Bond Z	PADZX	A+	(800) 225-1852	C+ / 6.6	2.91	2.51	8.42 /75	2.34 /49	2.78 /54	2.35	0.99
MUS	Prudential CA Muni Income A	PBCAX	D	(800) 225-1852	C / 5.3	2.01	-3.87	-0.36 /12	3.48 /88	3.23 /84	3.34	0.92
MUS ●	Prudential CA Muni Income B	PCAIX	C+	(800) 225-1852	B- / 7.0	1.95	-3.99	-0.60 / 8	3.22 /85	2.97 /79	3.23	1.17
MUS	Prudential CA Muni Income C	PCICX	C-	(800) 225-1852	C+ / 6.0	1.83	-4.31	-1.09 / 4	2.72 /77	2.47 /70	2.72	1.67
MUS	Prudential CA Muni Income Z	PCIZX	B	(800) 225-1852	B / 7.8	2.09	-3.83	-0.09 /16	3.75 /90	3.50 /87	3.76	0.67
COI	Prudential Core Bond A	TPCAX	E+	(800) 225-1852	D- / 1.1	1.15	-2.04	2.31 /52	1.28 /32	1.57 /36	2.12	1.00
COI	Prudential Core Bond C	TPCCX	D-	(800) 225-1852	D / 1.9	0.86	-2.50	1.54 /45	0.54 /21	0.84 /25	1.45	1.75
COI	Prudential Core Bond Q	TPCQX	D+	(800) 225-1852	C- / 3.6	1.22	-1.89	2.60 /54	1.57 /36	1.87 /40	2.50	0.69
COI	Prudential Core Bond R	TPCRX	D-	(800) 225-1852	D+ / 2.6	1.09	-2.17	2.05 /49	0.98 /27	1.21 /30	1.96	1.50
GEI	Prudential Core Bond Z	TAIBX	D+	(800) 225-1852	C- / 3.6	1.22	-2.01	2.57 /54	1.56 /36	1.86 /40	2.47	0.75
GEI	Prudential Core Short-Term Bond Fd		B+	(800) 225-1852	C- / 3.5	0.53	0.90	2.01 /49	1.38 /33	2.32 /46	1.89	0.07
MTG	Prudential Corporate Bond A	PCWAX	C-	(800) 225-1852	C+ / 6.0	2.32	-1.34	7.44 /73	3.76 /72	2.66 /52	2.75	1.52
MTG	Prudential Corporate Bond C	PCWCX	C-	(800) 225-1852	C+ / 6.3	2.05	-1.72	6.56 /72	2.90 /59	1.84 /39	2.14	2.27
MTG	Prudential Corporate Bond Q	PCWQX	B-	(800) 225-1852	B- / 7.5	2.29	-1.23	7.62 /74	3.92 /74	2.85 /55	3.14	1.21

● Denotes fund is closed to new investors
* Denotes fund is included in Section II

www.thestreetratings.com

RISK			NET ASSETS		ASSET					Portfolio Turnover Ratio	Avg Coupon Rate	FUND MANAGER		MINIMUM		LOADS	
Risk Rating/Pts	3 Yr Avg Standard Deviation	Avg Dura-tion	NAV As of 2/28/17	Total $(Mil)	Cash %	Gov. Bond %	Muni. Bond %	Corp. Bond %	Other %			Manager Quality Pct	Manager Tenure (Years)	Initial Purch. $	Additional Purch. $	Front End Load	Back End Load
C /4.5	3.3	4.6	10.23	715	3	1	0	63	33	14	6.4	97	15	1,000	100	3.8	0.0
C /4.4	3.3	4.6	10.22	784	3	1	0	63	33	14	6.4	96	15	1,000	100	0.0	0.0
C /4.5	3.3	4.6	10.16	2,358	3	1	0	63	33	14	6.4	98	15	0	0	0.0	0.0
C /4.5	3.3	4.6	9.97	49	3	1	0	63	33	14	6.4	97	15	1,000	100	0.0	0.0
C /4.5	3.3	4.6	10.15	1,587	3	1	0	63	33	14	6.4	95	15	0	0	0.0	0.0
C /4.5	3.3	4.6	10.11	2	3	1	0	63	33	14	6.4	96	15	0	0	0.0	0.0
C /4.5	3.3	4.6	10.06	1	3	1	0	63	33	14	6.4	97	15	0	0	0.0	0.0
C /4.5	3.3	4.6	10.10	3	3	1	0	63	33	14	6.4	97	15	0	0	0.0	0.0
C /4.4	3.3	4.6	10.08	3	3	1	0	63	33	14	6.4	97	15	0	0	0.0	0.0
C /4.5	3.3	4.6	10.12	4	3	1	0	63	33	14	6.4	97	15	0	0	0.0	0.0
C /4.5	3.3	4.6	10.16	N/A	3	1	0	63	33	14	6.4	96	15	0	0	0.0	0.0
U /	N/A	5.4	9.66	1	1	0	0	5	94	20	4.2	N/A	3	1,000	100	3.8	0.0
U /	N/A	5.4	9.55	171	1	0	0	5	94	20	4.2	N/A	3	0	0	0.0	0.0
U /	N/A	5.4	9.55	N/A	1	0	0	5	94	20	4.2	N/A	3	0	0	0.0	0.0
U /	N/A	5.4	9.56	N/A	1	0	0	5	94	20	4.2	N/A	3	0	0	0.0	0.0
A /9.3	0.9	1.9	12.19	364	1	6	0	61	32	54	2.7	67	7	1,000	100	2.3	0.0
A /9.3	0.9	1.9	12.19	84	1	6	0	61	32	54	2.7	27	7	1,000	100	0.0	0.0
A /9.4	0.9	1.9	12.18	3,048	1	6	0	61	32	54	2.7	73	7	1,000,000	0	0.0	0.0
A /9.4	0.9	1.9	12.18	143	1	6	0	61	32	54	2.7	66	7	1,000	100	0.0	0.0
A /9.3	0.9	1.9	12.18	106	1	6	0	61	32	54	2.7	70	7	0	0	0.0	0.0
A /9.4	0.9	1.9	12.18	1	1	6	0	61	32	54	2.7	41	7	0	0	0.0	0.0
A /9.4	0.9	1.9	12.18	2	1	6	0	61	32	54	2.7	51	7	0	0	0.0	0.0
A /9.3	0.9	1.9	12.19	15	1	6	0	61	32	54	2.7	57	7	0	0	0.0	0.0
A /9.3	0.9	1.9	12.19	12	1	6	0	61	32	54	2.7	64	7	0	0	0.0	0.0
A /9.4	0.9	1.9	12.19	10	1	6	0	61	32	54	2.7	68	7	0	0	0.0	0.0
C- /3.2	4.0	5.5	7.14	288	3	0	95	0	2	34	5.3	31	4	1,000	100	3.8	0.0
C- /3.4	3.9	5.5	7.16	27	3	0	95	0	2	34	5.3	13	4	1,000	100	0.0	0.0
C- /3.3	4.0	5.5	7.14	4	3	0	95	0	2	34	5.3	37	4	0	0	0.0	0.0
U /	N/A	5.5	7.13	38	3	0	95	0	2	34	5.3	N/A	4	0	0	0.0	0.0
U /	N/A	N/A	1.00	356	100	0	0	0	0	0	0.0	N/A	N/A	15,000	100	0.0	0.0
U /	N/A	N/A	1.00	16	100	0	0	0	0	0	0.0	N/A	N/A	5,000	100	0.0	0.0
E+ /0.7	7.1	N/A	16.50	1	100	0	0	0	0	0	0.0	0	8	15,000	100	0.0	0.0
E+ /0.7	7.1	N/A	15.64	N/A	100	0	0	0	0	0	0.0	0	8	5,000	100	0.0	0.0
E- /0.0	17.0	N/A	52.47	27	82	12	0	5	1	409	0.0	3	8	15,000	100	0.0	0.0
E- /0.0	17.1	N/A	49.04	1	82	12	0	5	1	409	0.0	1	8	5,000	100	0.0	0.0
B /7.7	2.4	0.8	9.71	129	2	4	0	53	41	38	3.9	81	6	2,500	100	4.5	0.0
B /7.7	2.4	0.8	9.74	108	2	4	0	53	41	38	3.9	68	6	2,500	100	0.0	0.0
B /7.8	2.3	0.8	9.72	194	2	4	0	53	41	38	3.9	83	6	0	0	0.0	0.0
B /7.8	2.4	0.8	9.76	1,164	2	4	0	53	41	38	3.9	83	6	0	0	0.0	0.0
C- /3.9	3.6	6.9	10.52	117	0	0	99	0	1	20	4.8	29	13	2,500	100	4.0	0.0
C- /3.9	3.6	6.9	10.52	4	0	0	99	0	1	20	4.8	22	13	2,500	100	0.0	0.0
C- /3.9	3.6	6.9	10.52	34	0	0	99	0	1	20	4.8	11	13	2,500	100	0.0	0.0
C- /3.8	3.6	6.9	10.52	47	0	0	99	0	1	20	4.8	36	13	0	0	0.0	0.0
C+ /6.1	2.9	5.4	9.89	51	0	0	0	0	100	224	3.1	9	2	2,500	100	4.5	0.0
C+ /6.2	2.9	5.4	9.89	3	0	0	0	0	100	224	3.1	3	2	2,500	100	0.0	0.0
C+ /6.1	2.9	5.4	9.89	133	0	0	0	0	100	224	3.1	13	2	0	0	0.0	0.0
C+ /6.1	2.9	5.4	9.89	N/A	0	0	0	0	100	224	3.1	6	2	0	0	0.0	0.0
C+ /6.2	2.9	5.4	9.89	84	0	0	0	0	100	224	3.1	13	2	0	0	0.0	0.0
A+ /9.9	0.3	0.2	9.28	3,052	7	0	0	46	47	25	1.6	79	N/A	2,500	100	0.0	0.0
C- /3.7	3.7	7.0	11.14	1	3	0	0	95	2	165	3.8	70	2	2,500	100	4.5	0.0
C- /3.8	3.6	7.0	11.11	1	3	0	0	95	2	165	3.8	36	2	2,500	100	0.0	0.0
C- /3.8	3.6	7.0	11.11	N/A	3	0	0	95	2	165	3.8	74	2	0	0	0.0	0.0

					PERFORMANCE							
99 Pct = Best 0 Pct = Worst					Perfor-	Total Return % through 2/28/17					Incl. in Returns	
			Overall		mance				Annualized		Dividend	Expense
Fund Type	Fund Name	Ticker Symbol	Investment Rating	Phone	Rating/Pts	3 Mo	6 Mo	1Yr / Pct	3Yr / Pct	5Yr / Pct	Yield	Ratio
MTG	Prudential Corporate Bond R	PCWRX	C+	(800) 225-1852	C+ / 6.9	2.17	-1.48	7.07 /73	3.30 /66	2.18 /45	2.62	2.02
MTG	Prudential Corporate Bond Z	TGMBX	B-	(800) 225-1852	B- / 7.5	2.30	-1.23	7.52 /73	3.92 /74	2.85 /55	3.13	1.27
GL	Prudential Emg Mkts Debt Loc Curr A	EMDAX	E-	(800) 225-1852	E- / 0.2	7.02	-0.67	11.55 /82	-2.36 / 2	-2.66 / 1	5.49	2.31
GL	Prudential Emg Mkts Debt Loc Curr C	EMDCX	E-	(800) 225-1852	E- / 0.2	6.93	-0.89	11.15 /81	-3.03 / 1	-3.26 / 1	4.91	3.06
GL	Prudential Emg Mkts Debt Loc Curr Q	EMDQX	E-	(800) 225-1852	D / 1.7	7.01	-0.49	11.98 /83	-1.97 / 2	-2.25 / 1	6.02	2.01
GL	Prudential Emg Mkts Debt Loc Curr Z	EMDZX	E-	(800) 225-1852	D / 1.7	7.16	-0.39	12.04 /83	-2.02 / 2	-2.30 / 1	5.91	2.06
LP	Prudential Floating Rate Inc A	FRFAX	A+	(800) 225-1852	C+ / 6.7	1.80	3.35	10.46 /80	3.21 /64	4.24 /75	3.87	1.29
LP	Prudential Floating Rate Inc C	FRFCX	A+	(800) 225-1852	C+ / 6.7	1.61	2.97	9.64 /78	2.41 /50	3.44 /64	3.27	2.04
LP	Prudential Floating Rate Inc Q	PFRIX	A+	(800) 225-1852	B / 8.0	1.99	3.52	10.79 /81	3.59 /70	4.57 /79	4.31	0.94
LP	Prudential Floating Rate Inc Z	FRFZX	A+	(800) 225-1852	B / 7.9	1.87	3.49	10.76 /81	3.49 /69	4.50 /79	4.28	1.04
GL	Prudential Global Total Return A	GTRAX	E-	(800) 225-1852	E / 0.4	3.23	-5.00	2.83 /55	0.93 /26	2.12 /44	3.36	1.05
GL	● Prudential Global Total Return B	PBTRX	E	(800) 225-1852	D- / 1.4	3.05	-5.35	2.08 /50	0.19 /16	1.33 /32	2.77	1.80
GL	Prudential Global Total Return C	PCTRX	E	(800) 225-1852	D- / 1.5	3.05	-5.36	2.07 /50	0.24 /17	1.36 /33	2.76	1.80
GL	Prudential Global Total Return Q	PGTQX	E	(800) 225-1852	C- / 3.6	3.27	-4.80	3.13 /57	1.55 /36	2.62 /51	3.81	0.67
GL	Prudential Global Total Return Z	PZTRX	E	(800) 225-1852	C- / 3.3	3.28	-4.72	3.39 /59	1.28 /32	2.39 /48	3.75	0.80
USS	Prudential Government Income A	PGVAX	E+	(800) 225-1852	D- / 1.0	0.62	-2.68	-0.24 /14	1.74 /39	1.51 /35	1.10	0.99
USS	● Prudential Government Income B	PBGPX	D-	(800) 225-1852	D / 1.9	0.33	-3.04	-1.01 / 4	0.98 /27	0.74 /24	0.37	1.74
USS	Prudential Government Income C	PRICX	D-	(800) 225-1852	D / 1.9	0.33	-3.03	-1.01 / 4	0.98 /27	0.76 /24	0.37	1.74
USL	Prudential Government Income Q	PGIQX	D+	(800) 225-1852	C- / 3.5	0.62	-2.48	--	1.99 /43	1.77 /39	1.50	N/A
USS	Prudential Government Income R	JDRVX	D-	(800) 225-1852	D+ / 2.6	0.45	-2.80	-0.49 /10	1.48 /35	1.24 /31	0.90	1.49
USS	Prudential Government Income Z	PGVZX	C-	(800) 225-1852	C- / 3.5	0.58	-2.56	--	1.99 /43	1.77 /39	1.40	0.74
MMT	Prudential Government Money Mkt A	PBMXX	U	(800) 225-1852	U /	--	--	--	--	--	0.02	N/A
MMT	● Prudential Government Money Mkt B	MJBXX	U	(800) 225-1852	U /	--	--	--	--	--	0.02	N/A
MMT	Prudential Government Money Mkt C	MJCXX	U	(800) 225-1852	U /	--	--	--	--	--	0.02	N/A
MMT	Prudential Government Money Mkt Z	PMZXX	U	(800) 225-1852	U /	--	--	--	--	--	0.02	N/A
*COH	Prudential High Yield A	PBHAX	C+	(800) 225-1852	A- / 9.2	5.30	5.36	20.00 /96	4.84 /84	6.53 /95	5.76	0.82
COH	● Prudential High Yield B	PBHYX	C+	(800) 225-1852	A / 9.5	4.98	5.11	19.20 /95	4.32 /79	6.01 /92	5.55	1.32
COH	Prudential High Yield C	PRHCX	C+	(800) 225-1852	A / 9.4	4.92	4.98	18.91 /95	4.06 /76	5.74 /90	5.32	1.57
COH	Prudential High Yield Q	PHYQX	B-	(800) 225-1852	A+ / 9.8	5.20	5.37	20.20 /96	5.17 /86	6.88 /96	6.39	0.45
COH	Prudential High Yield R	JDYRX	C+	(800) 225-1852	A+ / 9.6	5.05	5.05	19.49 /95	4.52 /81	6.27 /94	5.80	1.32
COH	Prudential High Yield Z	PHYZX	B-	(800) 225-1852	A+ / 9.8	5.17	5.51	20.32 /96	5.13 /86	6.82 /96	6.31	0.57
MUH	Prudential Muni High Income A	PRHAX	B-	(800) 225-1852	B+ / 8.8	2.89	-3.49	1.40 /50	5.43 /98	4.72 /97	3.89	0.87
MUH	● Prudential Muni High Income B	PMHYX	B+	(800) 225-1852	A / 9.5	2.73	-3.70	1.07 /46	5.17 /97	4.47 /96	3.81	1.12
MUH	Prudential Muni High Income C	PHICX	B	(800) 225-1852	A- / 9.1	2.71	-3.93	0.58 /38	4.66 /96	3.95 /93	3.31	1.62
MUH	Prudential Muni High Income Z	PHIZX	B+	(800) 225-1852	A+ / 9.7	2.87	-3.45	1.60 /53	5.68 /98	4.98 /98	4.36	0.62
*MUN	Prudential National Muni A	PRNMX	C-	(800) 225-1852	C+ / 5.6	2.11	-3.10	0.38 /35	3.41 /87	2.98 /79	3.40	0.84
MUN	● Prudential National Muni B	PBHMX	B-	(800) 225-1852	B- / 7.1	2.04	-3.21	0.14 /26	3.13 /84	2.71 /75	3.28	1.09
MUN	Prudential National Muni C	PNMCX	C	(800) 225-1852	C+ / 6.1	1.93	-3.50	-0.39 /11	2.63 /76	2.21 /64	2.80	1.59
MUN	Prudential National Muni Z	DNMZX	B+	(800) 225-1852	B / 8.0	2.17	-2.98	0.63 /39	3.67 /90	3.23 /84	3.80	0.59
COI	Prudential Short Dur Mtl Sec Bd A	SDMAX	C+	(800) 225-1852	C- / 3.2	1.44	0.49	4.26 /63	1.74 /39	--	2.42	1.27
COI	Prudential Short Dur Mtl Sec Bd C	SDMCX	C+	(800) 225-1852	C- / 3.3	1.25	0.23	3.49 /60	1.03 /28	--	1.76	2.02
COI	Prudential Short Dur Mtl Sec Bd Q	SDMQX	A-	(800) 225-1852	C / 4.9	1.39	0.62	4.41 /64	1.99 /43	--	2.76	0.92
COI	Prudential Short Dur Mtl Sec Bd Z	SDMZX	A	(800) 225-1852	C / 5.2	1.70	0.81	4.72 /66	2.08 /45	--	2.73	1.02
COH	Prudential Short Duration HY Inc A	HYSAX	C+	(800) 225-1852	C+ / 6.5	2.48	2.16	8.91 /76	3.26 /65	--	5.56	1.08
COH	Prudential Short Duration HY Inc C	HYSCX	C+	(800) 225-1852	C+ / 6.6	2.30	1.89	8.10 /75	2.49 /52	--	5.00	1.83
COH	Prudential Short Duration HY Inc Q	HYSQX	B+	(800) 225-1852	B / 7.8	2.68	2.44	9.39 /77	3.63 /70	--	6.07	0.74
COH	Prudential Short Duration HY Inc Z	HYSZX	B+	(800) 225-1852	B / 7.8	2.66	2.40	9.31 /77	3.56 /69	--	6.00	0.83
*COI	Prudential Short-Term Corp Bond A	PBSMX	C	(800) 225-1852	D+ / 2.4	0.86	-0.10	2.76 /55	1.49 /35	1.91 /41	2.30	0.77
COI	● Prudential Short-Term Corp Bond B	PSMBX	C	(800) 225-1852	D+ / 2.5	0.67	-0.47	2.08 /50	0.73 /24	1.15 /29	1.62	1.52
COI	Prudential Short-Term Corp Bond C	PIFCX	C	(800) 225-1852	D+ / 2.5	0.67	-0.47	1.99 /49	0.74 /24	1.15 /29	1.62	1.52
COI	Prudential Short-Term Corp Bond Q	PSTQX	B+	(800) 225-1852	C / 4.4	1.03	0.08	3.20 /58	1.91 /42	2.29 /46	2.72	0.42
COI	Prudential Short-Term Corp Bond R	JDTRX	B-	(800) 225-1852	C- / 3.3	0.80	-0.22	2.50 /53	1.24 /31	1.66 /37	2.12	1.27

● Denotes fund is closed to new investors
* Denotes fund is included in Section II

www.thestreetratings.com

RISK			NET ASSETS		ASSET							FUND MANAGER		MINIMUM		LOADS	
Risk Rating/Pts	3 Yr Avg Standard Deviation	Avg Dura-tion	NAV As of 2/28/17	Total $(Mil)	Cash %	Gov. Bond %	Muni. Bond %	Corp. Bond %	Other %	Portfolio Turnover Ratio	Avg Coupon Rate	Manager Quality Pct	Manager Tenure (Years)	Initial Purch. $	Additional Purch. $	Front End Load	Back End Load
C- / 3.8	3.6	7.0	11.11	N/A	3	0	0	95	2	165	3.8	59	2	0	0	0.0	0.0
C- / 3.8	3.6	7.0	11.11	20	3	0	0	95	2	165	3.8	74	2	0	0	0.0	0.0
E- / 0.1	12.4	5.9	6.23	3	3	86	0	9	2	196	7.0	64	6	2,500	100	4.5	0.0
E- / 0.1	12.3	5.9	6.29	1	3	86	0	9	2	196	7.0	30	6	2,500	100	0.0	0.0
E- / 0.1	12.2	5.9	6.30	N/A	3	86	0	9	2	196	7.0	72	6	0	0	0.0	0.0
E- / 0.1	12.2	5.9	6.31	26	3	86	0	9	2	196	7.0	72	6	0	0	0.0	0.0
B- / 7.4	2.6	1.8	9.95	70	4	0	0	14	82	55	4.9	89	6	2,500	100	3.3	0.0
B- / 7.3	2.6	1.8	9.95	54	4	0	0	14	82	55	4.9	84	6	2,500	100	0.0	0.0
B- / 7.3	2.6	1.8	9.96	32	4	0	0	14	82	55	4.9	91	6	0	0	0.0	0.0
B- / 7.5	2.6	1.8	9.96	366	4	0	0	14	82	55	4.9	91	6	0	0	0.0	0.0
E+ / 0.9	6.2	8.5	6.39	156	1	49	1	22	27	86	3.7	91	15	2,500	100	4.5	0.0
E+ / 0.9	6.2	8.5	6.39	4	1	49	1	22	27	86	3.7	87	15	2,500	100	0.0	0.0
E+ / 0.8	6.2	8.5	6.38	30	1	49	1	22	27	86	3.7	87	15	2,500	100	0.0	0.0
E+ / 0.9	6.2	8.5	6.47	234	1	49	1	22	27	86	3.7	93	15	0	0	0.0	0.0
E+ / 0.9	6.1	8.5	6.43	309	1	49	1	22	27	86	3.7	93	15	0	0	0.0	0.0
C+ / 6.5	2.8	4.7	9.55	329	0	39	1	10	50	778	3.0	49	14	2,500	100	4.5	0.0
C+ / 6.4	2.8	4.7	9.56	2	0	39	1	10	50	778	3.0	18	14	2,500	100	0.0	0.0
C+ / 6.4	2.8	4.7	9.57	11	0	39	1	10	50	778	3.0	18	14	2,500	100	0.0	0.0
C+ / 6.5	2.8	4.7	9.52	34	0	39	1	10	50	778	3.0	61	14	0	0	0.0	0.0
C+ / 6.2	2.9	4.7	9.56	16	0	39	1	10	50	778	3.0	32	14	0	0	0.0	0.0
C+ / 6.7	2.8	4.7	9.53	96	0	39	1	10	50	778	3.0	60	14	0	0	0.0	0.0
U /	N/A	N/A	1.00	459	100	0	0	0	0	0	0.0	N/A	N/A	2,500	100	0.0	0.0
U /	N/A	N/A	1.00	17	100	0	0	0	0	0	0.0	N/A	N/A	2,500	100	0.0	0.0
U /	N/A	N/A	1.00	14	100	0	0	0	0	0	0.0	N/A	N/A	2,500	100	0.0	0.0
U /	N/A	N/A	1.00	96	100	0	0	0	0	0	0.0	N/A	N/A	0	0	0.0	0.0
D- / 1.2	5.6	3.9	5.57	1,334	1	0	0	95	4	28	6.6	64	16	2,500	100	4.5	0.0
D- / 1.1	5.6	3.9	5.56	177	1	0	0	95	4	28	6.6	39	16	2,500	100	0.0	0.0
D- / 1.1	5.6	3.9	5.56	264	1	0	0	95	4	28	6.6	29	16	2,500	100	0.0	0.0
D- / 1.2	5.5	3.9	5.57	1,495	1	0	0	95	4	28	6.6	73	16	0	0	0.0	0.0
D- / 1.2	5.6	3.9	5.56	62	1	0	0	95	4	28	6.6	55	16	0	0	0.0	0.0
D- / 1.1	5.6	3.9	5.58	2,568	1	0	0	95	4	28	6.6	71	16	0	0	0.0	0.0
D / 2.2	4.1	7.4	10.07	346	0	0	100	0	0	7	5.1	78	13	2,500	100	4.0	0.0
D+ / 2.3	4.0	7.4	10.07	45	0	0	100	0	0	7	5.1	75	13	2,500	100	0.0	0.0
D+ / 2.3	4.0	7.4	10.07	121	0	0	100	0	0	7	5.1	63	13	2,500	100	0.0	0.0
D / 2.2	4.1	7.4	10.05	333	0	0	100	0	0	7	5.1	81	13	0	0	0.0	0.0
C / 4.6	3.3	6.5	14.78	570	0	0	99	0	1	17	4.9	38	13	2,500	100	4.0	0.0
C / 4.4	3.3	6.5	14.82	21	0	0	99	0	1	17	4.9	26	13	2,500	100	0.0	0.0
C / 4.5	3.3	6.5	14.81	31	0	0	99	0	1	17	4.9	14	13	2,500	100	0.0	0.0
C / 4.6	3.3	6.5	14.77	41	0	0	99	0	1	17	4.9	55	13	0	0	0.0	0.0
B+ / 8.6	1.7	2.3	9.65	12	7	4	0	52	37	66	3.9	65	4	2,500	100	3.3	0.0
B+ / 8.6	1.7	2.3	9.66	9	7	4	0	52	37	66	3.9	33	4	2,500	100	0.0	0.0
B+ / 8.7	1.7	2.3	9.65	158	7	4	0	52	37	66	3.9	71	4	0	0	0.0	0.0
B+ / 8.6	1.7	2.3	9.68	12	7	4	0	52	37	66	3.9	73	4	0	0	0.0	0.0
C / 4.7	2.7	1.9	9.09	390	2	0	0	91	7	58	6.6	78	5	2,500	100	3.3	0.0
C / 4.6	2.8	1.9	9.09	380	2	0	0	91	7	58	6.6	61	5	2,500	100	0.0	0.0
C / 4.7	2.7	1.9	9.10	48	2	0	0	91	7	58	6.6	82	5	0	0	0.0	0.0
C / 4.7	2.7	1.9	9.10	1,490	2	0	0	91	7	58	6.6	81	5	0	0	0.0	0.0
B+ / 8.9	1.4	2.7	11.05	1,348	0	0	0	88	12	49	3.2	58	18	2,500	100	3.3	0.0
B+ / 8.9	1.4	2.7	11.05	19	0	0	0	88	12	49	3.2	23	18	2,500	100	0.0	0.0
B+ / 8.9	1.4	2.7	11.05	1,401	0	0	0	88	12	49	3.2	24	18	2,500	100	0.0	0.0
B+ / 8.9	1.4	2.7	11.09	554	0	0	0	88	12	49	3.2	69	18	0	0	0.0	0.0
B+ / 8.9	1.4	2.7	11.05	173	0	0	0	88	12	49	3.2	46	18	0	0	0.0	0.0

Fund Type	Fund Name	Ticker Symbol	Overall Investment Rating	Phone	Performance Rating/Pts	3 Mo	6 Mo	1Yr / Pct	3Yr / Pct	5Yr / Pct	Dividend Yield	Expense Ratio
COI	Prudential Short-Term Corp Bond Z	PIFZX	B+	(800) 225-1852	C- / 4.2	1.01	0.03	3.11 /57	1.75 /39	2.17 /44	2.62	0.52
MUH	Prudential Sht Dur Muni High Inc A	PDSAX	U	(800) 225-1852	U /	1.44	-2.76	-0.35 /12	--	--	1.99	1.11
MUH	Prudential Sht Dur Muni High Inc C	PDSCX	U	(800) 225-1852	U /	1.26	-3.02	-1.00 / 4	--	--	1.29	1.86
MUH	Prudential Sht Dur Muni High Inc Z	PDSZX	U	(800) 225-1852	U /	1.51	-2.54	-0.10 /16	--	--	2.31	0.86
* GES	Prudential Total Return Bond A	PDBAX	D	(800) 225-1852	C / 4.9	2.29	-1.48	4.72 /66	3.42 /68	3.55 /66	2.48	0.80
GES ●	Prudential Total Return Bond B	PRDBX	C-	(800) 225-1852	C+ / 5.9	2.09	-1.79	4.14 /63	2.86 /59	3.02 /58	2.10	1.55
GES	Prudential Total Return Bond C	PDBCX	D+	(800) 225-1852	C / 5.4	2.10	-1.92	3.88 /62	2.62 /54	2.76 /54	1.85	1.55
GES	Prudential Total Return Bond Q	PTRQX	C+	(800) 225-1852	B- / 7.1	2.31	-1.39	5.01 /67	3.77 /72	3.91 /71	2.94	0.43
GES	Prudential Total Return Bond R	DTBRX	C-	(800) 225-1852	C+ / 6.2	2.22	-1.67	4.38 /64	3.13 /63	3.27 /62	2.35	1.30
GES	Prudential Total Return Bond Z	PDBZX	C+	(800) 225-1852	B- / 7.0	2.36	-1.36	5.01 /67	3.67 /71	3.82 /70	2.86	0.55
GL	Putnam Absolute Return 100 A	PARTX	B	(800) 225-1581	C- / 3.8	1.66	2.07	5.32 /68	1.15 /30	1.41 /33	2.42	0.67
GL	Putnam Absolute Return 100 B	PARPX	B	(800) 225-1581	C- / 3.8	1.61	1.91	5.06 /67	0.92 /26	1.22 /30	2.29	0.87
GL	Putnam Absolute Return 100 C	PARQX	C+	(800) 225-1581	D+ / 2.9	1.48	1.69	4.52 /65	0.40 /20	0.66 /23	1.57	1.42
GL	Putnam Absolute Return 100 M	PARZX	B	(800) 225-1581	C- / 3.8	1.75	2.05	5.31 /68	1.11 /29	1.37 /33	2.41	0.72
GL	Putnam Absolute Return 100 R	PRARX	B	(800) 225-1581	C- / 3.8	1.64	1.94	5.07 /67	0.88 /26	1.16 /30	2.32	0.92
GL	Putnam Absolute Return 100 Y	PARYX	A-	(800) 225-1581	C / 4.6	1.74	2.14	5.60 /69	1.39 /33	1.66 /37	2.72	0.42
GL	Putnam Absolute Return 300 A	PTRNX	D+	(800) 225-1581	C / 4.6	2.65	4.25	9.10 /77	0.93 /26	2.11 /44	2.98	0.84
GL	Putnam Absolute Return 300 B	PTRBX	D+	(800) 225-1581	C / 4.8	2.67	4.17	8.81 /76	0.76 /24	1.91 /41	2.83	1.04
GL	Putnam Absolute Return 300 C	PTRGX	D-	(800) 225-1581	C- / 3.8	2.47	3.75	8.16 /75	0.19 /16	1.35 /32	2.11	1.59
GL	Putnam Absolute Return 300 M	PZARX	D+	(800) 225-1581	C / 4.7	2.73	4.23	8.98 /76	0.91 /26	2.08 /43	2.97	0.89
GL	Putnam Absolute Return 300 R	PTRKX	D+	(800) 225-1581	C / 4.6	2.49	4.08	8.69 /76	0.68 /23	1.84 /39	2.55	1.09
GL	Putnam Absolute Return 300 Y	PYTRX	C	(800) 225-1581	C / 5.5	2.67	4.36	9.33 /77	1.20 /31	2.36 /47	3.33	0.59
GL	Putnam Absolute Return 500 A	PJMDX	D-	(800) 225-1581	C- / 3.0	2.51	2.70	4.95 /66	1.96 /42	2.85 /55	0.00	1.15
GL	Putnam Absolute Return 500 B	PJMBX	D	(800) 225-1581	C- / 4.1	2.27	2.27	4.13 /63	1.19 /31	2.08 /43	0.00	1.90
GL	Putnam Absolute Return 500 C	PJMCX	D	(800) 225-1581	C- / 4.2	2.37	2.37	4.15 /63	1.22 /31	2.09 /43	0.00	1.90
GL	Putnam Absolute Return 500 M	PJMMX	D-	(800) 225-1581	C- / 3.1	2.35	2.35	4.42 /64	1.43 /34	2.34 /47	0.00	1.65
GL	Putnam Absolute Return 500 R	PJMRX	D+	(800) 225-1581	C / 5.0	2.37	2.55	4.66 /65	1.72 /38	2.59 /51	0.00	1.40
GL	Putnam Absolute Return 500 Y	PJMYX	C	(800) 225-1581	C+ / 5.9	2.59	2.88	5.22 /68	2.23 /47	3.12 /60	0.00	0.90
GL	Putnam Absolute Return 700 A	PDMAX	D-	(800) 225-1581	C / 5.2	3.54	4.18	8.43 /75	2.82 /58	3.83 /70	0.00	1.30
GL	Putnam Absolute Return 700 B	PDMBX	D	(800) 225-1581	C+ / 6.3	3.35	3.83	7.55 /73	2.06 /44	3.05 /59	0.00	2.05
GL	Putnam Absolute Return 700 C	PDMCX	D	(800) 225-1581	C+ / 6.3	3.36	3.83	7.56 /73	2.07 /44	3.05 /59	0.00	2.05
GL	Putnam Absolute Return 700 M	PDMMX	D-	(800) 225-1581	C / 5.3	3.42	3.99	7.79 /74	2.32 /48	3.32 /63	0.00	1.80
GL	Putnam Absolute Return 700 R	PDMRX	D+	(800) 225-1581	B- / 7.0	3.49	4.14	8.13 /75	2.61 /54	3.59 /67	0.00	1.55
GL	Putnam Absolute Return 700 Y	PDMYX	C-	(800) 225-1581	B- / 7.5	3.62	4.35	8.70 /76	3.11 /63	4.10 /74	0.00	1.05
USS	Putnam American Government A	PAGVX	D-	(800) 225-1581	E / 0.3	0.88	-1.58	0.33 /30	0.70 /23	1.16 /30	2.11	0.93
USS	Putnam American Government B	PAMBX	D-	(800) 225-1581	E / 0.4	0.58	-1.98	-0.43 /11	-0.05 / 5	0.41 /21	1.44	1.68
USS	Putnam American Government C	PAMIX	D-	(800) 225-1581	E / 0.4	0.58	-1.95	-0.41 /11	-0.05 / 5	0.41 /21	1.46	1.68
USS	Putnam American Government M	PAMMX	D-	(800) 225-1581	E / 0.3	0.80	-1.69	0.17 /25	0.46 /20	0.92 /26	1.84	1.18
USS	Putnam American Government R	PAMRX	D+	(800) 225-1581	D / 1.7	0.81	-1.71	0.17 /25	0.46 /20	0.90 /26	1.91	1.18
USL	Putnam American Government R5	PAMDX	C-	(800) 225-1581	D+ / 2.5	0.95	-1.44	0.62 /35	1.01 /28	--	2.49	0.61
USL	Putnam American Government R6	PAMEX	C	(800) 225-1581	D+ / 2.5	0.87	-1.38	0.75 /37	1.05 /28	--	2.62	0.54
USS	Putnam American Government Y	PATYX	C-	(800) 225-1581	D+ / 2.3	0.83	-1.56	0.61 /35	0.93 /26	1.41 /33	2.48	0.68
MUI	Putnam AMT Free Ins Mun A	PPNAX	C	(800) 225-1581	C / 5.5	1.78	-3.26	-0.19 /15	3.50 /88	2.94 /79	3.12	0.80
MUI	Putnam AMT Free Ins Mun B	PTFIX	C+	(800) 225-1581	C+ / 6.4	1.69	-3.55	-0.80 / 6	2.88 /80	2.31 /66	2.62	1.41
MUI	Putnam AMT Free Ins Mun C	PAMTX	C+	(800) 225-1581	C+ / 6.0	1.58	-3.68	-1.02 / 4	2.72 /77	2.15 /62	2.46	1.56
MUI	Putnam AMT Free Ins Mun M	PPMTX	C-	(800) 225-1581	C / 5.3	1.77	-3.38	-0.45 /10	3.23 /85	2.67 /74	2.88	1.06
MUI	Putnam AMT Free Ins Mun Y	PAMYX	A-	(800) 225-1581	B / 7.9	1.84	-3.21	0.04 /21	3.76 /90	3.18 /83	3.49	0.56
MUS	Putnam AZ Tax Exempt Inc A	PTAZX	C-	(800) 225-1581	C / 4.8	1.70	-2.85	-0.44 /10	3.19 /84	2.42 /69	2.69	0.96
MUS	Putnam AZ Tax Exempt Inc B	PAZBX	C+	(800) 225-1581	C+ / 5.7	1.54	-3.15	-1.07 / 4	2.54 /74	1.78 /53	2.15	1.59
MUS	Putnam AZ Tax Exempt Inc C	PAZCX	C	(800) 225-1581	C / 5.3	1.50	-3.22	-1.22 / 3	2.38 /71	1.64 /50	1.99	1.74
MUS	Putnam AZ Tax Exempt Inc M	PAZMX	D+	(800) 225-1581	C / 4.5	1.63	-2.98	-0.72 / 7	2.89 /80	2.15 /62	2.42	1.24
MUS	Putnam AZ Tax Exempt Inc Y	PAZYX	B+	(800) 225-1581	B- / 7.4	1.75	-2.74	-0.33 /12	3.41 /87	2.66 /74	3.02	0.74

● Denotes fund is closed to new investors
* Denotes fund is included in Section II

Risk Rating/Pts	3 Yr Avg Standard Deviation	Avg Duration	NAV As of 2/28/17	Total $(Mil)	Cash %	Gov. Bond %	Muni. Bond %	Corp. Bond %	Other %	Portfolio Turnover Ratio	Avg Coupon Rate	Manager Quality Pct	Manager Tenure (Years)	Initial Purch. $	Additional Purch. $	Front End Load	Back End Load
B+ / 8.8	1.5	2.7	11.08	6,503	0	0	0	88	12	49	3.2	64	18	0	0	0.0	0.0
U /	N/A	3.8	10.01	41	14	0	85	0	1	19	4.4	N/A	3	2,500	100	3.3	0.0
U /	N/A	3.8	10.01	22	14	0	85	0	1	19	4.4	N/A	3	2,500	100	0.0	0.0
U /	N/A	3.8	10.01	57	14	0	85	0	1	19	4.4	N/A	3	0	0	0.0	0.0
C- / 3.9	3.5	5.8	14.30	3,061	0	12	1	47	40	102	3.6	61	15	2,500	100	4.5	0.0
C- / 3.9	3.5	5.8	14.29	37	0	12	1	47	40	102	3.6	34	15	2,500	100	0.0	0.0
C- / 3.9	3.5	5.8	14.28	556	0	12	1	47	40	102	3.6	26	15	2,500	100	0.0	0.0
C- / 3.9	3.5	5.8	14.27	6,441	0	12	1	47	40	102	3.6	70	15	0	0	0.0	0.0
C- / 3.9	3.6	5.8	14.32	642	0	12	1	47	40	102	3.6	50	15	0	0	0.0	0.0
C- / 3.9	3.6	5.8	14.25	9,685	0	12	1	47	40	102	3.6	67	15	0	0	0.0	0.0
B+ / 8.9	1.4	0.3	9.99	77	4	3	0	58	35	129	2.6	76	9	500	0	1.0	0.0
A- / 9.0	1.4	0.3	9.96	2	4	3	0	58	35	129	2.6	72	9	500	0	0.0	0.0
A- / 9.0	1.3	0.3	9.96	18	4	3	0	58	35	129	2.6	58	9	500	0	0.0	0.0
B+ / 8.9	1.4	0.3	9.97	2	4	3	0	58	35	129	2.6	76	9	500	0	0.8	0.0
B+ / 8.9	1.4	0.3	10.05	N/A	4	3	0	58	35	129	2.6	71	9	500	0	0.0	0.0
A- / 9.0	1.4	0.3	10.01	58	4	3	0	58	35	129	2.6	79	9	500	0	0.0	0.0
C / 4.9	3.2	0.4	9.77	204	0	4	0	37	59	428	4.8	70	9	500	0	1.0	0.0
C / 4.8	3.2	0.4	9.73	7	0	4	0	37	59	428	4.8	65	9	500	0	0.0	0.0
C / 4.9	3.2	0.4	9.72	78	0	4	0	37	59	428	4.8	39	9	500	0	0.0	0.0
C / 5.1	3.1	0.4	9.74	6	0	4	0	37	59	428	4.8	69	9	500	0	0.8	0.0
C / 5.0	3.1	0.4	9.81	N/A	0	4	0	37	59	428	4.8	63	9	500	0	0.0	0.0
C / 4.9	3.2	0.4	9.78	131	0	4	0	37	59	428	4.8	75	9	500	0	0.0	0.0
C / 4.7	3.2	2.1	11.02	290	22	1	0	17	60	522	2.1	84	9	500	0	5.8	0.0
C / 4.7	3.2	2.1	10.83	27	22	1	0	17	60	522	2.1	76	9	500	0	0.0	0.0
C / 4.8	3.2	2.1	10.80	165	22	1	0	17	60	522	2.1	77	9	500	0	0.0	0.0
C / 4.6	3.3	2.1	10.87	7	22	1	0	17	60	522	2.1	79	9	500	0	3.5	0.0
C / 4.7	3.2	2.1	11.24	1	22	1	0	17	60	522	2.1	82	9	500	0	0.0	0.0
C / 4.8	3.2	2.1	11.08	369	22	1	0	17	60	522	2.1	86	9	500	0	0.0	0.0
D+ / 2.3	4.7	3.0	11.71	294	0	1	0	22	77	578	3.3	90	9	500	0	5.8	0.0
D+ / 2.3	4.7	3.0	11.40	27	0	1	0	22	77	578	3.3	85	9	500	0	0.0	0.0
D+ / 2.3	4.7	3.0	11.38	169	0	1	0	22	77	578	3.3	85	9	500	0	0.0	0.0
D / 2.2	4.8	3.0	11.48	6	0	1	0	22	77	578	3.3	87	9	500	0	3.5	0.0
D+ / 2.3	4.7	3.0	11.57	2	0	1	0	22	77	578	3.3	89	9	500	0	0.0	0.0
D+ / 2.3	4.7	3.0	11.75	544	0	1	0	22	77	578	3.3	91	9	500	0	0.0	0.0
B+ / 8.5	1.8	5.9	8.61	370	0	28	0	0	72	993	4.6	33	10	500	0	4.0	0.0
B+ / 8.6	1.8	5.9	8.53	4	0	28	0	0	72	993	4.6	14	10	500	0	0.0	0.0
B+ / 8.6	1.8	5.9	8.57	14	0	28	0	0	72	993	4.6	14	10	500	0	0.0	0.0
B+ / 8.5	1.8	5.9	8.69	1	0	28	0	0	72	993	4.6	26	10	500	0	3.3	0.0
B+ / 8.5	1.8	5.9	8.63	4	0	28	0	0	72	993	4.6	26	10	500	0	0.0	0.0
B+ / 8.5	1.8	5.9	8.60	1	0	28	0	0	72	993	4.6	54	10	0	0	0.0	0.0
B+ / 8.5	1.8	5.9	8.58	6	0	28	0	0	72	993	4.6	55	10	0	0	0.0	0.0
B+ / 8.5	1.8	5.9	8.58	27	0	28	0	0	72	993	4.6	48	10	500	0	0.0	0.0
C / 5.0	3.1	6.5	14.94	328	0	0	100	0	0	11	4.8	53	15	500	0	4.0	0.0
C / 4.9	3.2	6.5	14.96	2	0	0	100	0	0	11	4.8	23	15	500	0	0.0	0.0
C / 5.0	3.1	6.5	14.98	32	0	0	100	0	0	11	4.8	20	15	500	0	0.0	0.0
C / 5.0	3.1	6.5	14.99	1	0	0	100	0	0	11	4.8	35	15	500	0	3.3	0.0
C / 5.0	3.1	6.5	14.95	46	0	0	100	0	0	11	4.8	62	15	500	0	0.0	0.0
C / 5.4	3.0	6.0	9.00	38	0	0	100	0	0	13	5.0	41	15	500	0	4.0	0.0
C / 5.3	3.0	6.0	8.99	1	0	0	100	0	0	13	5.0	18	15	500	0	0.0	0.0
C / 5.3	3.0	6.0	9.01	3	0	0	100	0	0	13	5.0	15	15	500	0	0.0	0.0
C / 5.3	3.1	6.0	9.02	1	0	0	100	0	0	13	5.0	28	15	500	0	3.3	0.0
C / 5.2	3.1	6.0	9.01	3	0	0	100	0	0	13	5.0	53	15	0	0	0.0	0.0

					PERFORMANCE							
	99 Pct = Best 0 Pct = Worst				Perfor- mance Rating/Pts	Total Return % through 2/28/17					Incl. in Returns	
									Annualized		Dividend	Expense
Fund Type	Fund Name	Ticker Symbol	Overall Investment Rating	Phone		3 Mo	6 Mo	1Yr / Pct	3Yr / Pct	5Yr / Pct	Yield	Ratio
*MUS	Putnam CA Tax Exempt Income A	PCTEX	C-	(800) 225-1581	C+ / 6.4	2.20	-3.32	0.19 /28	3.87 /92	3.47 /87	3.33	0.74
MUS	Putnam CA Tax Exempt Income B	PCTBX	C+	(800) 225-1581	B- / 7.1	2.04	-3.62	-0.44 /10	3.22 /85	2.82 /77	2.83	1.37
MUS	Putnam CA Tax Exempt Income C	PCTCX	C	(800) 225-1581	C+ / 6.8	1.99	-3.67	-0.59 / 8	3.08 /83	2.66 /74	2.64	1.52
MUS	Putnam CA Tax Exempt Income M	PCLMX	C-	(800) 225-1581	C+ / 6.2	2.13	-3.46	-0.09 /16	3.63 /89	3.18 /83	3.09	1.02
MUS	Putnam CA Tax Exempt Income Y	PCIYX	B+	(800) 225-1581	B+ / 8.5	2.25	-3.20	0.29 /32	4.13 /94	3.70 /90	3.69	0.52
*GES	Putnam Diversified Income A	PDINX	E+	(800) 225-1581	C / 5.3	3.32	6.20	15.03 /89	1.18 /30	3.84 /70	5.19	0.98
GES	Putnam Diversified Income B	PSIBX	D-	(800) 225-1581	C / 5.5	3.02	5.72	13.99 /87	0.39 /20	3.06 /59	4.74	1.73
GES	Putnam Diversified Income C	PDVCX	D-	(800) 225-1581	C+ / 5.6	3.04	5.76	14.10 /87	0.39 /20	3.05 /59	4.77	1.73
GES	Putnam Diversified Income M	PDVMX	E+	(800) 225-1581	C / 5.1	3.17	6.05	14.57 /88	0.93 /26	3.58 /67	5.15	1.23
GES	Putnam Diversified Income R	PDVRX	D-	(800) 225-1581	C+ / 6.4	3.15	6.00	14.63 /88	0.90 /26	3.58 /67	5.26	1.23
GEL	Putnam Diversified Income R6	PDVGX	D	(800) 225-1581	B- / 7.2	3.29	6.29	15.24 /89	1.53 /35	--	5.80	0.64
GES	Putnam Diversified Income Y	PDVYX	D	(800) 225-1581	B- / 7.0	3.27	6.24	15.11 /89	1.42 /34	4.08 /74	5.68	0.73
EM	Putnam Emerging Markets Income A	PEMWX	D	(800) 225-1581	B / 7.7	5.28	-0.32	15.25 /89	3.86 /73	--	3.28	2.40
EM	Putnam Emerging Markets Income B	PEMHX	D	(800) 225-1581	B / 8.0	5.20	-0.58	14.52 /88	3.11 /63	--	2.75	3.15
EM	Putnam Emerging Markets Income C	PEMJX	D	(800) 225-1581	B / 8.0	5.20	-0.60	14.52 /88	3.11 /63	--	2.77	3.15
EM	Putnam Emerging Markets Income M	PEMKX	D	(800) 225-1581	B / 7.7	5.33	-0.36	15.08 /89	3.63 /70	--	3.05	2.65
EM	Putnam Emerging Markets Income Y	PEMOX	C-	(800) 225-1581	B+ / 8.9	5.35	-0.08	15.68 /90	4.12 /77	--	3.66	2.15
COH	Putnam Floating Rate Income A	PFLRX	C+	(800) 225-1581	C+ / 6.6	1.34	2.71	10.39 /80	2.50 /52	3.92 /71	3.60	1.02
COH	Putnam Floating Rate Income B	PFRBX	C+	(800) 225-1581	C+ / 6.6	1.29	2.62	10.18 /79	2.29 /48	3.72 /69	3.44	1.22
COH	Putnam Floating Rate Income C	PFICX	C-	(800) 225-1581	C+ / 5.9	1.27	2.33	9.57 /78	1.73 /39	3.15 /60	2.89	1.77
COH	Putnam Floating Rate Income M	PFLMX	C+	(800) 225-1581	C+ / 6.6	1.33	2.69	10.34 /80	2.45 /51	3.87 /71	3.56	1.07
COH	Putnam Floating Rate Income R	PFLLX	C+	(800) 225-1581	C+ / 6.6	1.28	2.59	10.12 /79	2.24 /47	3.66 /68	3.39	1.27
COH	Putnam Floating Rate Income Y	PFRYX	B-	(800) 225-1581	B- / 7.2	1.40	2.85	10.67 /80	2.76 /57	4.18 /75	3.89	0.77
GL	Putnam Global Income A	PGGIX	E	(800) 225-1581	D / 1.7	2.82	-1.53	6.24 /71	0.62 /22	1.77 /39	3.12	1.17
GL	Putnam Global Income B	PGLBX	E	(800) 225-1581	D / 2.1	2.64	-1.91	5.47 /68	-0.13 / 5	1.01 /27	2.50	1.92
GL	Putnam Global Income C	PGGLX	E	(800) 225-1581	D / 2.0	2.64	-1.91	5.38 /68	-0.15 / 5	1.01 /27	2.51	1.92
GL	Putnam Global Income M	PGGMX	E	(800) 225-1581	D / 1.6	2.80	-1.58	6.05 /70	0.38 /20	1.53 /35	2.94	1.42
GL	Putnam Global Income R	PGBRX	E+	(800) 225-1581	D+ / 2.9	2.74	-1.67	6.00 /70	0.37 /19	1.52 /35	2.84	1.42
GL	Putnam Global Income R5	PGGDX	E+	(800) 225-1581	C- / 3.9	3.01	-1.27	6.68 /72	0.93 /26	--	3.58	0.83
GL	Putnam Global Income R6	PGGEX	E+	(800) 225-1581	C- / 3.9	2.93	-1.33	6.66 /72	0.99 /27	--	3.64	0.76
GL	Putnam Global Income Y	PGGYX	E+	(800) 225-1581	C- / 3.7	2.88	-1.40	6.51 /72	0.85 /25	2.01 /42	3.50	0.92
MMT	Putnam Government Money Market I	PGKXX	U	(800) 225-1581	U /	0.01	0.01	--	--	--	0.00	N/A
COH	Putnam High Yield Advantage A	PHYIX	D+	(800) 225-1581	B / 8.0	3.84	4.22	19.31 /95	3.55 /69	5.79 /91	5.25	1.04
COH	Putnam High Yield Advantage B	PHYBX	C-	(800) 225-1581	B / 8.2	3.73	3.93	18.52 /94	2.75 /57	4.98 /84	4.89	1.79
COH	Putnam High Yield Advantage C	PHYLX	C-	(800) 225-1581	B / 8.2	3.76	3.96	18.40 /94	2.77 /57	5.00 /84	4.94	1.79
COH	Putnam High Yield Advantage M	PHYMX	D+	(800) 225-1581	B / 7.8	3.80	4.13	18.90 /95	3.24 /65	5.51 /89	5.12	1.29
COH	Putnam High Yield Advantage R	PFJAX	C	(800) 225-1581	B+ / 8.7	3.80	4.13	18.90 /95	3.29 /66	5.51 /89	5.29	1.29
COH	Putnam High Yield Advantage Y	PHAYX	C+	(800) 225-1581	A- / 9.1	4.06	4.47	19.62 /95	3.82 /73	6.04 /92	5.41	0.79
*COH	Putnam High Yield Trust A	PHIGX	C-	(800) 225-1581	B+ / 8.4	4.03	4.75	19.68 /95	3.62 /70	6.05 /92	4.70	1.02
COH	Putnam High Yield Trust B	PHBBX	C	(800) 225-1581	B+ / 8.7	3.97	4.35	18.82 /95	2.88 /59	5.26 /87	4.18	1.77
COH	Putnam High Yield Trust C	PCHYX	C-	(800) 225-1581	B+ / 8.6	3.86	4.25	18.66 /94	2.82 /58	5.25 /86	4.21	1.77
COH	Putnam High Yield Trust M	PHIMX	C-	(800) 225-1581	B+ / 8.3	3.92	4.56	19.25 /95	3.35 /67	5.78 /91	4.46	1.27
COH	Putnam High Yield Trust R	PHDRX	C	(800) 225-1581	A- / 9.0	4.04	4.59	19.38 /95	3.39 /67	5.77 /91	4.77	1.27
COH	Putnam High Yield Trust Y	PHYYX	C+	(800) 225-1581	A / 9.3	4.07	4.76	19.84 /96	3.87 /74	6.29 /94	5.28	0.77
*GES	Putnam Income Fund A	PINCX	D+	(800) 225-1581	C- / 3.0	2.83	0.31	6.01 /70	1.46 /34	3.50 /66	3.19	0.86
GES	Putnam Income Fund B	PNCBX	C-	(800) 225-1581	C- / 3.4	2.68	-0.06	5.29 /68	0.71 /23	2.74 /53	2.62	1.61
GES	Putnam Income Fund C	PUICX	D+	(800) 225-1581	C- / 3.4	2.66	-0.07	5.27 /68	0.68 /23	2.71 /53	2.60	1.61
GES	Putnam Income Fund M	PNCMX	D	(800) 225-1581	D+ / 2.9	2.86	0.23	5.98 /70	1.20 /31	3.25 /62	3.12	1.11
GES	Putnam Income Fund R	PIFRX	C	(800) 225-1581	C- / 4.2	2.79	0.21	5.84 /70	1.17 /30	3.23 /61	3.14	1.11
COI	Putnam Income Fund R5	PINFX	B-	(800) 225-1581	C / 5.1	2.89	0.48	6.46 /71	1.73 /39	--	3.63	0.57
COI	Putnam Income Fund R6	PINHX	B-	(800) 225-1581	C / 5.4	3.03	0.62	6.59 /72	1.83 /40	--	3.61	0.50
GES	Putnam Income Fund Y	PNCYX	B-	(800) 225-1581	C / 5.0	2.83	0.41	6.30 /71	1.67 /38	3.75 /69	3.49	0.61

● Denotes fund is closed to new investors
* Denotes fund is included in Section II

www.thestreetratings.com

| RISK | | | NET ASSETS | | ASSET | | | | | | | FUND MANAGER | | MINIMUM | | LOADS | |
Risk Rating/Pts	3 Yr Avg Standard Deviation	Avg Dura-tion	NAV As of 2/28/17	Total $(Mil)	Cash %	Gov. Bond %	Muni. Bond %	Corp. Bond %	Other %	Portfolio Turnover Ratio	Avg Coupon Rate	Manager Quality Pct	Manager Tenure (Years)	Initial Purch. $	Additional Purch. $	Front End Load	Back End Load
C- /3.6	3.5	7.3	8.02	1,150	0	0	100	0	0	16	4.7	53	15	500	0	4.0	0.0
C- /3.7	3.5	7.3	8.01	4	0	0	100	0	0	16	4.7	24	15	500	0	0.0	0.0
C- /3.7	3.5	7.3	8.07	54	0	0	100	0	0	16	4.7	20	15	500	0	0.0	0.0
C- /3.7	3.5	7.3	8.00	4	0	0	100	0	0	16	4.7	37	15	500	0	3.3	0.0
C- /3.7	3.5	7.3	8.04	75	0	0	100	0	0	16	4.7	62	15	500	0	0.0	0.0
D- /1.4	5.8	0.3	7.05	1,285	0	6	0	25	69	835	6.3	93	23	500	0	4.0	0.0
D- /1.4	5.8	0.3	6.97	51	0	6	0	25	69	835	6.3	89	23	500	0	0.0	0.0
D- /1.4	5.8	0.3	6.92	616	0	6	0	25	69	835	6.3	89	23	500	0	0.0	0.0
D- /1.4	5.8	0.3	6.92	135	0	6	0	25	69	835	6.3	92	23	500	0	3.3	0.0
D- /1.4	5.8	0.3	6.96	3	0	6	0	25	69	835	6.3	92	23	500	0	0.0	0.0
D- /1.4	5.8	0.3	6.98	11	0	6	0	25	69	835	6.3	94	23	0	0	0.0	0.0
D- /1.4	5.8	0.3	6.97	1,216	0	6	0	25	69	835	6.3	94	23	500	0	0.0	0.0
E /0.4	8.2	5.6	9.00	12	2	53	1	42	2	48	5.6	97	4	500	0	4.0	0.0
E /0.4	8.3	5.6	8.98	N/A	2	53	1	42	2	48	5.6	96	4	500	0	0.0	0.0
E /0.3	8.3	5.6	8.99	1	2	53	1	42	2	48	5.6	96	4	500	0	0.0	0.0
E /0.4	8.3	5.6	9.01	N/A	2	53	1	42	2	48	5.6	97	4	500	0	3.3	0.0
E /0.4	8.2	5.6	9.00	5	2	53	1	42	2	48	5.6	98	4	500	0	0.0	0.0
C- /4.2	2.9	0.4	8.63	339	3	0	0	66	31	46	4.5	64	12	500	0	1.0	0.0
C /4.3	2.9	0.4	8.63	17	3	0	0	66	31	46	4.5	58	12	500	0	0.0	0.0
C- /4.2	2.9	0.4	8.63	100	3	0	0	66	31	46	4.5	29	12	500	0	0.0	0.0
C- /4.2	2.9	0.4	8.63	4	3	0	0	66	31	46	4.5	62	12	500	0	0.8	0.0
C /4.3	2.9	0.4	8.63	1	3	0	0	66	31	46	4.5	56	12	500	0	0.0	0.0
C- /4.2	2.9	0.4	8.64	360	3	0	0	66	31	46	4.5	70	12	500	0	0.0	0.0
D+ /2.9	4.1	5.3	11.83	141	0	33	0	22	45	551	4.4	82	23	500	0	4.0	0.0
C- /3.0	4.1	5.3	11.77	4	0	33	0	22	45	551	4.4	71	23	500	0	0.0	0.0
C- /3.0	4.1	5.3	11.77	19	0	33	0	22	45	551	4.4	71	23	500	0	0.0	0.0
D+ /2.9	4.1	5.3	11.71	8	0	33	0	22	45	551	4.4	79	23	500	0	3.3	0.0
D+ /2.9	4.1	5.3	11.82	3	0	33	0	22	45	551	4.4	79	23	0	0	0.0	0.0
D+ /2.8	4.1	5.3	11.83	N/A	0	33	0	22	45	551	4.4	84	23	0	0	0.0	0.0
D+ /2.9	4.1	5.3	11.83	6	0	33	0	22	45	551	4.4	85	23	0	0	0.0	0.0
D+ /2.9	4.1	5.3	11.82	66	0	33	0	22	45	551	4.4	84	23	0	0	0.0	0.0
U /	N/A	N/A	1.00	N/A	100	0	0	0	0	0	0.0	N/A	N/A	5,000,000	0	0.0	0.0
E+ /0.9	5.9	3.5	5.92	315	4	0	0	92	4	42	6.1	11	15	500	0	4.0	1.0
D- /1.0	5.9	3.5	5.77	15	4	0	0	92	4	42	6.1	4	15	500	0	0.0	1.0
D- /1.0	5.8	3.5	5.75	22	4	0	0	92	4	42	6.1	4	15	500	0	0.0	1.0
D- /1.0	5.8	3.5	5.90	78	4	0	0	92	4	42	6.1	8	15	500	0	3.3	1.0
D- /1.0	5.8	3.5	5.90	24	4	0	0	92	4	42	6.1	9	15	500	0	0.0	1.0
D- /1.0	5.8	3.5	6.21	101	4	0	0	92	4	42	6.1	18	15	0	0	0.0	1.0
D- /1.0	5.9	3.4	7.77	795	4	0	0	88	8	42	6.0	13	15	500	0	4.0	0.0
D- /1.0	5.8	3.4	7.76	12	4	0	0	88	8	42	6.0	5	15	500	0	0.0	0.0
D- /1.0	5.8	3.4	7.69	48	4	0	0	88	8	42	6.0	4	15	500	0	0.0	0.0
D- /1.0	5.8	3.4	7.81	13	4	0	0	88	8	42	6.0	9	15	500	0	3.3	0.0
D- /1.0	5.9	3.4	7.59	8	4	0	0	88	8	42	6.0	9	15	500	0	0.0	0.0
D- /1.0	5.9	3.4	7.58	280	4	0	0	88	8	42	6.0	18	15	500	0	0.0	0.0
B- /7.0	2.7	5.9	6.87	749	0	0	0	21	79	981	5.5	59	10	500	0	4.0	0.0
C+ /6.8	2.8	5.9	6.80	23	0	0	0	21	79	981	5.5	24	10	500	0	0.0	0.0
C+ /6.6	2.8	5.9	6.81	158	0	0	0	21	79	981	5.5	22	10	500	0	0.0	0.0
C+ /6.8	2.8	5.9	6.70	84	0	0	0	21	79	981	5.5	49	10	500	0	3.3	0.0
C+ /6.6	2.8	5.9	6.81	22	0	0	0	21	79	981	5.5	42	10	0	0	0.0	0.0
B- /7.0	2.7	5.9	6.95	5	0	0	0	21	79	981	5.5	55	10	0	0	0.0	0.0
C+ /6.7	2.8	5.9	6.98	72	0	0	0	21	79	981	5.5	56	10	0	0	0.0	0.0
B- /7.0	2.7	5.9	6.97	573	0	0	0	21	79	981	5.5	66	10	0	0	0.0	0.0

Fund Type	Fund Name	Ticker Symbol	Overall Investment Rating	Phone	Perfor-mance Rating/Pts	3 Mo	6 Mo	1Yr / Pct	3Yr / Pct	5Yr / Pct	Dividend Yield	Expense Ratio
	99 Pct = Best				PERFORMANCE			Total Return % through 2/28/17	Annualized		Incl. in Returns	
MUN	Putnam Intermediate-Term Muni Inc	PIMEX	E+	(800) 225-1581	E / 0.5	1.69	-2.95	-1.14 / 3	1.52 / 49	--	1.27	1.73
MUN	Putnam Intermediate-Term Muni Inc	PIMBX	D-	(800) 225-1581	D / 2.2	1.54	-3.14	-1.63 / 1	0.95 / 34	--	0.72	2.33
MUN	Putnam Intermediate-Term Muni Inc	PIMFX	D-	(800) 225-1581	D / 1.9	1.61	-3.21	-1.78 / 1	0.80 / 31	--	0.57	2.48
MUN	Putnam Intermediate-Term Muni Inc	PIMMX	D	(800) 225-1581	C- / 3.1	1.63	-2.97	-1.29 / 3	1.31 / 44	--	1.07	1.98
MUN	Putnam Intermediate-Term Muni Inc	PIMYX	D-	(800) 225-1581	D / 2.2	1.76	-2.83	-0.90 / 5	1.78 / 57	--	1.53	1.48
MUS	Putnam MA Tax Exempt Inc II A	PXMAX	C	(800) 225-1581	C / 5.1	1.54	-2.90	0.07 / 23	3.25 / 85	2.32 / 67	2.82	0.78
MUS	Putnam MA Tax Exempt Inc II B	PMABX	B-	(800) 225-1581	C+ / 6.1	1.38	-3.10	-0.44 / 10	2.61 / 76	1.69 / 51	2.31	1.40
MUS	Putnam MA Tax Exempt Inc II C	PMMCX	C+	(800) 225-1581	C+ / 5.7	1.34	-3.27	-0.59 / 8	2.48 / 73	1.55 / 48	2.14	1.55
MUS	Putnam MA Tax Exempt Inc II M	PMAMX	C-	(800) 225-1581	C / 4.8	1.47	-3.03	-0.20 / 14	2.96 / 81	2.05 / 60	2.58	1.05
MUS	Putnam MA Tax Exempt Inc II Y	PMAYX	A	(800) 225-1581	B / 7.7	1.59	-2.68	0.41 / 35	3.51 / 88	2.57 / 72	3.17	0.55
MUS	Putnam MI Tax Exempt Inc II A	PXMIX	C+	(800) 225-1581	C / 4.8	1.59	-2.53	-0.11 / 16	3.11 / 84	2.35 / 68	2.68	0.90
MUS	Putnam MI Tax Exempt Inc II B	PMEBX	B+	(800) 225-1581	C+ / 5.9	1.54	-2.73	-0.62 / 8	2.51 / 74	1.74 / 52	2.16	1.52
MUS	Putnam MI Tax Exempt Inc II C	PMGCX	B	(800) 225-1581	C / 5.5	1.39	-2.80	-0.78 / 6	2.35 / 70	1.58 / 48	2.00	1.67
MUS	Putnam MI Tax Exempt Inc II M	PMIMX	C+	(800) 225-1581	C / 4.7	1.62	-2.56	-0.28 / 13	2.86 / 80	2.09 / 61	2.42	1.17
MUS	Putnam MI Tax Exempt Inc II Y	PMIYX	A+	(800) 225-1581	B- / 7.5	1.64	-2.42	0.12 / 25	3.37 / 86	2.60 / 73	3.03	0.67
MUS	Putnam MN Tax Exempt Inc II A	PXMNX	B-	(800) 225-1581	C / 4.5	1.51	-2.37	0.04 / 21	2.94 / 81	2.52 / 71	2.77	0.86
MUS	Putnam MN Tax Exempt Inc II B	PMTBX	B+	(800) 225-1581	C / 5.5	1.36	-2.58	-0.59 / 8	2.32 / 69	1.89 / 56	2.25	1.48
MUS	Putnam MN Tax Exempt Inc II C	PMOCX	B	(800) 225-1581	C / 5.2	1.43	-2.65	-0.63 / 8	2.20 / 67	1.73 / 52	2.09	1.63
MUS	Putnam MN Tax Exempt Inc II M	PMNMX	C+	(800) 225-1581	C / 4.3	1.45	-2.51	-0.23 / 14	2.67 / 76	2.24 / 65	2.53	1.13
MUS	Putnam MN Tax Exempt Inc II Y	PMNYX	A+	(800) 225-1581	B- / 7.3	1.57	-2.15	0.27 / 31	3.21 / 85	2.77 / 76	3.11	0.63
MMT	Putnam Money Market A	PDDXX	D+	(800) 225-1581	E+ / 0.8	0.08	0.09	0.10 / 22	0.04 / 9	0.03 / 9	0.10	N/A
MMT	Putnam Money Market M	PTMXX	D+	(800) 225-1581	E+ / 0.7	0.04	0.04	0.05 / 21	0.02 / 8	0.02 / 8	0.05	N/A
MMT	Putnam Money Market T	PMMXX	D+	(800) 225-1581	E+ / 0.6	0.02	0.02	0.03 / 20	0.02 / 8	0.01 / 6	0.03	N/A
MTG	Putnam Mortgage Opportunities I	PMOTX	U	(800) 225-1581	U /	2.41	4.83	12.10 / 83	--	--	2.88	2.12
MUS	Putnam NJ Tax Exempt Income A	PTNJX	D-	(800) 225-1581	C- / 4.0	1.63	-3.15	-0.04 / 17	2.76 / 78	2.05 / 60	3.27	0.81
MUS	Putnam NJ Tax Exempt Income B	PNJBX	D+	(800) 225-1581	C / 4.9	1.47	-3.45	-0.66 / 7	2.13 / 66	1.44 / 45	2.77	1.43
MUS	Putnam NJ Tax Exempt Income C	PNJCX	D	(800) 225-1581	C / 4.5	1.43	-3.52	-0.81 / 6	1.97 / 62	1.26 / 41	2.60	1.58
MUS	Putnam NJ Tax Exempt Income M	PNJMX	D-	(800) 225-1581	C- / 3.7	1.56	-3.38	-0.31 / 13	2.48 / 73	1.77 / 53	3.02	1.08
MUS	Putnam NJ Tax Exempt Income Y	PNJYX	B	(800) 225-1581	B- / 7.0	1.68	-3.04	0.19 / 28	3.03 / 82	2.29 / 66	3.64	0.58
*MUS	Putnam NY Tax Exempt Income A	PTEIX	C+	(800) 225-1581	C+ / 5.8	1.91	-2.88	0.22 / 30	3.53 / 88	2.60 / 73	3.20	0.75
MUS	Putnam NY Tax Exempt Income B	PEIBX	B-	(800) 225-1581	C+ / 6.6	1.75	-3.19	-0.41 / 11	2.89 / 80	1.97 / 58	2.69	1.38
MUS	Putnam NY Tax Exempt Income C	PNNCX	B-	(800) 225-1581	C+ / 6.2	1.71	-3.26	-0.56 / 9	2.73 / 78	1.81 / 54	2.53	1.53
MUS	Putnam NY Tax Exempt Income M	PNYMX	C	(800) 225-1581	C / 5.5	1.84	-3.01	-0.07 / 17	3.24 / 85	2.32 / 67	2.94	1.03
MUS	Putnam NY Tax Exempt Income Y	PNYYX	A	(800) 225-1581	B / 8.0	1.84	-2.78	0.32 / 33	3.76 / 90	2.83 / 77	3.56	0.53
MUS	Putnam OH Tax Exempt Inc II A	PXOHX	C-	(800) 225-1581	C / 4.5	1.72	-2.73	-0.04 / 17	2.96 / 81	2.36 / 68	2.80	0.82
MUS	Putnam OH Tax Exempt Inc II B	POXBX	C+	(800) 225-1581	C / 5.5	1.57	-3.03	-0.66 / 7	2.33 / 70	1.73 / 52	2.28	1.44
MUS	Putnam OH Tax Exempt Inc II C	POOCX	C	(800) 225-1581	C / 5.0	1.53	-3.10	-0.81 / 6	2.17 / 66	1.57 / 48	2.12	1.59
MUS	Putnam OH Tax Exempt Inc II M	POHMX	C-	(800) 225-1581	C- / 4.2	1.65	-2.86	-0.42 / 11	2.68 / 77	2.08 / 61	2.55	1.09
MUS	Putnam OH Tax Exempt Inc II Y	POTYX	A	(800) 225-1581	B- / 7.3	1.78	-2.62	0.19 / 29	3.23 / 85	2.59 / 72	3.14	0.59
MUS	Putnam PA Tax Exempt Income A	PTEPX	B-	(800) 225-1581	C / 5.3	1.47	-2.75	0.03 / 20	3.35 / 86	2.51 / 71	3.05	0.82
MUS	Putnam PA Tax Exempt Income B	PPNBX	B+	(800) 225-1581	C+ / 6.1	1.20	-3.05	-0.59 / 8	2.69 / 77	1.86 / 56	2.55	1.44
MUS	Putnam PA Tax Exempt Income C	PPNCX	B+	(800) 225-1581	C+ / 5.8	1.16	-3.12	-0.74 / 7	2.56 / 75	1.71 / 52	2.38	1.59
MUS	Putnam PA Tax Exempt Income M	PPAMX	C+	(800) 225-1581	C / 4.9	1.28	-2.98	-0.34 / 12	3.04 / 83	2.22 / 64	2.81	1.09
MUS	Putnam PA Tax Exempt Income Y	PPTYX	A+	(800) 225-1581	B / 7.8	1.52	-2.63	0.26 / 31	3.59 / 89	2.75 / 75	3.41	0.59
*COI	Putnam Short Duration Income A	PSDTX	C+	(800) 225-1581	D / 2.2	0.33	0.53	1.21 / 42	0.61 / 22	0.67 / 23	0.80	0.54
COI	Putnam Short Duration Income B	PSDBX	C	(800) 225-1581	D / 1.6	0.23	0.33	0.82 / 38	0.22 / 17	0.28 / 19	0.41	0.94
COI	Putnam Short Duration Income C	PSDLX	C	(800) 225-1581	D / 1.6	0.23	0.33	0.82 / 38	0.22 / 17	0.28 / 19	0.41	0.94
COI	Putnam Short Duration Income M	PSDGX	C+	(800) 225-1581	D / 2.1	0.21	0.50	1.17 / 41	0.56 / 21	0.60 / 23	0.76	0.59
COI	Putnam Short Duration Income R	PSDRX	C	(800) 225-1581	D / 1.6	0.23	0.33	0.82 / 38	0.22 / 17	0.28 / 19	0.41	0.94
GEI	Putnam Short Duration Income R6	PSDQX	C+	(800) 225-1581	D+ / 2.4	0.25	0.58	1.32 / 43	0.71 / 23	--	0.91	0.43
COI	Putnam Short Duration Income Y	PSDYX	C+	(800) 225-1581	D+ / 2.4	0.35	0.58	1.31 / 43	0.71 / 23	0.79 / 25	0.91	0.44
MUN	Putnam Short-Term Municipal Inc A	PSMEX	D	(800) 225-1581	E / 0.5	0.69	-0.46	-0.21 / 14	0.31 / 21	--	0.59	1.54

● Denotes fund is closed to new investors
* Denotes fund is included in Section II

www.thestreetratings.com

RISK			NET ASSETS		ASSET								FUND MANAGER		MINIMUM		LOADS	
Risk Rating/Pts	3 Yr Avg Standard Deviation	Avg Dura-tion	NAV As of 2/28/17	Total $(Mil)	Cash %	Gov. Bond %	Muni. Bond %	Corp. Bond %	Other %	Portfolio Turnover Ratio	Avg Coupon Rate	Manager Quality Pct	Manager Tenure (Years)	Initial Purch. $	Additional Purch. $	Front End Load	Back End Load
C+ / 6.5	2.8	5.0	10.07	14	2	0	97	0	1	16	4.6	6	4	500	0	4.0	0.0
C+ / 6.6	2.8	5.0	10.08	N/A	2	0	97	0	1	16	4.6	3	4	500	0	0.0	0.0
C+ / 6.3	2.9	5.0	10.08	1	2	0	97	0	1	16	4.6	2	4	500	0	0.0	0.0
C+ / 6.6	2.8	5.0	10.08	N/A	2	0	97	0	1	16	4.6	5	4	500	0	0.0	0.0
C+ / 6.5	2.8	5.0	10.07	1	2	0	97	0	1	16	4.6	9	4	500	0	3.3	0.0
C / 5.5	3.0	6.1	9.52	209	0	0	100	0	0	15	4.7	49	15	500	0	4.0	0.0
C / 5.5	3.0	6.1	9.51	3	0	0	100	0	0	15	4.7	21	15	500	0	0.0	0.0
C / 5.4	3.0	6.1	9.54	28	0	0	100	0	0	15	4.7	18	15	500	0	0.0	0.0
C+ / 5.6	3.0	6.1	9.52	2	0	0	100	0	0	15	4.7	32	15	500	0	3.3	0.0
C / 5.4	3.0	6.1	9.55	49	0	0	100	0	0	15	4.7	59	15	0	0	0.0	0.0
C+ / 6.7	2.8	5.8	9.01	60	0	0	99	0	1	9	4.8	53	15	500	0	4.0	0.0
C+ / 6.5	2.8	5.8	9.01	1	0	0	99	0	1	9	4.8	24	15	500	0	0.0	0.0
C+ / 6.8	2.8	5.8	9.02	4	0	0	99	0	1	9	4.8	21	15	500	0	0.0	0.0
C+ / 6.7	2.8	5.8	9.02	N/A	0	0	99	0	1	9	4.8	37	15	500	0	3.3	0.0
C+ / 6.7	2.8	5.8	9.03	12	0	0	99	0	1	9	4.8	63	15	0	0	0.0	0.0
B- / 7.4	2.6	5.8	9.20	78	0	0	100	0	0	15	4.7	55	15	500	0	4.0	0.0
B- / 7.5	2.6	5.8	9.17	1	0	0	100	0	0	15	4.7	25	15	500	0	0.0	0.0
B- / 7.4	2.6	5.8	9.19	18	0	0	100	0	0	15	4.7	21	15	500	0	0.0	0.0
B- / 7.4	2.6	5.8	9.19	N/A	0	0	100	0	0	15	4.7	37	15	500	0	3.3	0.0
B- / 7.5	2.5	5.8	9.22	9	0	0	100	0	0	15	4.7	64	15	0	0	0.0	0.0
A+ / 9.9	N/A	N/A	1.00	815	100	0	0	0	0	0	0.1	40	N/A	500	0	0.0	0.0
A+ / 9.9	N/A	N/A	1.00	27	100	0	0	0	0	0	0.1	39	N/A	500	0	0.0	0.0
A+ / 9.9	N/A	N/A	1.00	3	100	0	0	0	0	0	0.0	38	N/A	500	0	0.0	0.0
U /	N/A	0.5	9.90	10	0	0	0	0	100	1,074	6.1	N/A	2	5,000,000	0	0.0	0.0
C / 4.7	3.2	6.0	9.09	135	0	0	100	0	0	18	4.6	19	15	500	0	4.0	0.0
C / 4.8	3.2	6.0	9.08	3	0	0	100	0	0	18	4.6	8	15	500	0	0.0	0.0
C / 4.7	3.2	6.0	9.10	21	0	0	100	0	0	18	4.6	6	15	500	0	0.0	0.0
C / 4.7	3.2	6.0	9.09	2	0	0	100	0	0	18	4.6	13	15	500	0	3.3	0.0
C / 4.9	3.2	6.0	9.11	22	0	0	100	0	0	18	4.6	28	15	0	0	0.0	0.0
C / 5.2	3.1	6.6	8.43	888	0	0	99	0	1	22	4.9	56	15	500	0	4.0	0.0
C / 5.2	3.1	6.6	8.41	10	0	0	99	0	1	22	4.9	26	15	500	0	0.0	0.0
C / 5.3	3.1	6.6	8.43	64	0	0	99	0	1	22	4.9	22	15	500	0	0.0	0.0
C / 5.3	3.1	6.6	8.44	2	0	0	99	0	1	22	4.9	42	15	500	0	3.3	0.0
C / 5.5	3.0	6.6	8.43	88	0	0	99	0	1	22	4.9	66	15	0	0	0.0	0.0
C+ / 5.9	2.9	6.1	8.91	110	0	0	100	0	0	11	4.7	34	15	500	0	4.0	0.0
C+ / 5.7	3.0	6.1	8.90	2	0	0	100	0	0	11	4.7	15	15	500	0	0.0	0.0
C+ / 5.8	2.9	6.1	8.91	11	0	0	100	0	0	11	4.7	12	15	500	0	0.0	0.0
C+ / 6.1	2.9	6.1	8.91	1	0	0	100	0	0	11	4.7	25	15	500	0	3.3	0.0
C+ / 5.9	2.9	6.1	8.92	12	0	0	100	0	0	11	4.7	50	15	0	0	0.0	0.0
C+ / 6.8	2.8	6.2	9.00	152	0	0	100	0	0	12	4.9	62	15	500	0	4.0	0.0
C+ / 6.7	2.8	6.2	8.98	4	0	0	100	0	0	12	4.9	31	15	500	0	0.0	0.0
C+ / 6.9	2.7	6.2	9.00	24	0	0	100	0	0	12	4.9	28	15	500	0	0.0	0.0
C+ / 6.8	2.8	6.2	9.00	4	0	0	100	0	0	12	4.9	52	15	500	0	3.3	0.0
C+ / 6.7	2.8	6.2	9.01	10	0	0	100	0	0	12	4.9	68	15	0	0	0.0	0.0
A+ / 9.9	0.2	0.1	10.05	3,532	1	0	0	92	7	51	1.1	64	6	500	0	0.0	0.0
A+ / 9.9	0.2	0.1	10.04	2	1	0	0	92	7	51	1.1	50	6	500	0	0.0	0.0
A+ / 9.9	0.2	0.1	10.04	20	1	0	0	92	7	51	1.1	50	6	500	0	0.0	0.0
A+ / 9.9	0.2	0.1	10.04	12	1	0	0	92	7	51	1.1	63	6	500	0	0.0	0.0
A+ / 9.9	0.2	0.1	10.04	3	1	0	0	92	7	51	1.1	50	6	500	0	0.0	0.0
A+ / 9.9	0.2	0.1	10.06	3	1	0	0	92	7	51	1.1	67	6	0	0	0.0	0.0
A+ / 9.9	0.2	0.1	10.06	2,190	1	0	0	92	7	51	1.1	66	6	0	0	0.0	0.0
A+ / 9.7	0.7	1.6	9.97	14	3	0	96	0	1	46	3.7	26	4	500	0	1.0	0.0

99 Pct = Best
0 Pct = Worst

Fund Type	Fund Name	Ticker Symbol	Overall Investment Rating	Phone	Performance Rating/Pts	3 Mo	6 Mo	1Yr / Pct	3Yr / Pct (Annualized)	5Yr / Pct (Annualized)	Dividend Yield	Expense Ratio
MUN	Putnam Short-Term Municipal Inc B	PSMFX	D+	(800) 225-1581	E+ / 0.9	0.74	-0.46	-0.41 /11	0.11 /16	--	0.39	1.74
MUN	Putnam Short-Term Municipal Inc C	PSMTX	D	(800) 225-1581	E / 0.4	0.63	-0.67	-0.67 / 7	-0.21 / 4	--	0.03	2.29
MUN	Putnam Short-Term Municipal Inc M	PSMMX	D	(800) 225-1581	E+ / 0.7	0.78	-0.39	-0.26 /14	0.26 /20	--	0.54	1.59
MUN	Putnam Short-Term Municipal Inc Y	PSMYX	C+	(800) 225-1581	D+ / 2.3	0.86	-0.24	0.04 /21	0.56 /25	--	0.84	1.29
*MUN	Putnam Tax Exempt Income A	PTAEX	B-	(800) 225-1581	C+ / 5.9	1.76	-2.90	0.37 /34	3.55 /88	2.98 /80	3.56	0.75
MUN	Putnam Tax Exempt Income B	PTBEX	B	(800) 225-1581	C+ / 6.6	1.60	-3.20	-0.27 /13	2.86 /80	2.33 /67	3.05	1.38
MUN	Putnam Tax Exempt Income C	PTECX	B	(800) 225-1581	C+ / 6.3	1.56	-3.27	-0.42 /11	2.74 /78	2.19 /63	2.89	1.53
MUN	Putnam Tax Exempt Income M	PTXMX	C+	(800) 225-1581	C+ / 5.6	1.80	-3.03	0.08 /23	3.25 /85	2.70 /74	3.28	1.03
MUN	Putnam Tax Exempt Income Y	PTEYX	A+	(800) 225-1581	B / 8.1	1.81	-2.79	0.58 /38	3.77 /91	3.22 /84	3.92	0.53
*COH	Putnam Tax-Free Hi-Yield A	PTHAX	D	(800) 225-1581	C+ / 6.3	2.45	-3.44	1.42 /44	5.34 /87	4.56 /79	4.01	0.83
COH	Putnam Tax-Free Hi-Yield B	PTHYX	D+	(800) 225-1581	C+ / 6.9	2.29	-3.73	0.80 /37	4.71 /83	3.94 /72	3.53	1.45
COH	Putnam Tax-Free Hi-Yield C	PTCCX	D+	(800) 225-1581	C+ / 6.7	2.25	-3.80	0.65 /36	4.56 /81	3.77 /70	3.37	1.60
COH	Putnam Tax-Free Hi-Yield M	PTYMX	D	(800) 225-1581	C+ / 6.2	2.38	-3.57	1.15 /41	5.06 /85	4.28 /76	3.77	1.10
COH	Putnam Tax-Free Hi-Yield Y	PTFYX	C	(800) 225-1581	B / 7.8	2.49	-3.31	1.65 /46	5.60 /89	4.82 /82	4.39	0.60
*USS	Putnam US Govt Income Tr A	PGSIX	D	(800) 225-1581	D- / 1.4	0.69	0.37	2.05 /49	1.11 /29	1.72 /38	2.85	0.85
USS	Putnam US Govt Income Tr B	PGSBX	C-	(800) 225-1581	D / 1.9	0.43	0.00	1.23 /42	0.37 /19	0.98 /27	2.24	1.58
USS	Putnam US Govt Income Tr C	PGVCX	C-	(800) 225-1581	D / 1.9	0.50	-0.01	1.30 /43	0.36 /19	0.97 /27	2.23	1.60
USS	Putnam US Govt Income Tr M	PGSMX	D	(800) 225-1581	D- / 1.3	0.62	0.24	1.77 /47	0.87 /26	1.48 /34	2.60	1.09
USS	Putnam US Govt Income Tr R	PGVRX	C	(800) 225-1581	D+ / 2.7	0.62	0.23	1.79 /47	0.88 /26	1.48 /34	2.72	1.10
USS	Putnam US Govt Income Tr Y	PUSYX	B-	(800) 225-1581	C- / 3.5	0.68	0.51	2.28 /51	1.35 /33	1.98 /42	3.28	0.60
COI	Quality Income	SQIFX	C+	(800) 332-5580	D / 1.9	0.23	0.11	1.00 /40	0.39 /20	--	0.89	0.90
GL	Quantified Managed Income Investor	QBDSX	D-	(855) 747-9555	C / 4.4	2.30	0.57	6.64 /72	1.22 /31	--	0.99	1.73
GL	Quantified Managed IncomeAdvisor	QBDAX	U	(855) 747-9555	U /	2.13	0.18	--	--	--	0.00	2.33
EM	RBC BlueBay Em Mkt Corporate Bd	RECAX	C-	(800) 422-2766	B- / 7.2	4.46	2.40	13.11 /85	4.12 /77	--	3.55	35.45
EM	RBC BlueBay Em Mkt Corporate Bd I	RBECX	C+	(800) 422-2766	B+ / 8.6	4.52	2.50	13.30 /86	4.39 /79	4.42 /78	3.98	1.74
EM	RBC BlueBay EM Unconstrained FI I	RUFIX	U	(800) 422-2766	U /	1.46	0.75	11.32 /82	--	--	6.57	2.50
EM	RBC BlueBay Emerg Mkt Select Bd A	RESAX	E-	(800) 422-2766	D- / 1.4	5.05	-1.14	10.52 /80	0.24 /17	--	0.00	3.84
EM	RBC BlueBay Emerg Mkt Select Bd I	RBESX	E	(800) 422-2766	C- / 3.5	5.04	-1.13	10.74 /81	0.42 /20	0.23 /19	0.00	1.14
GL	RBC BlueBay Global High Yield Bd A	RHYAX	C	(800) 422-2766	C+ / 6.9	3.39	3.84	11.57 /82	3.94 /75	--	3.92	2.38
GL	RBC BlueBay Global High Yield Bd I	RGHYX	B+	(800) 422-2766	B+ / 8.5	3.67	4.27	12.17 /84	4.30 /79	6.12 /93	4.22	1.33
COI	RBC Short Duration Fixed Income F	RSHFX	U	(800) 422-2766	U /	0.73	0.45	3.04 /57	--	--	1.69	1.70
COI	RBC Short Duration Fixed Income I	RSDIX	B+	(800) 422-2766	C- / 4.1	0.76	0.50	3.15 /58	1.66 /37	--	1.79	1.37
COI	RBC Ultra-Short Fixed Income F	RULFX	U	(800) 422-2766	U /	0.50	0.78	2.23 /51	--	--	1.50	1.25
COI	RBC Ultra-Short Fixed Income I	RUSIX	B+	(800) 422-2766	C- / 3.5	0.53	0.73	2.24 /51	1.33 /32	--	1.61	1.13
MMT	RBC US Govt Money Market Fd Inst	TUGXX	C-	(800) 422-2766	D- / 1.3	0.11	0.20	0.33 /30	0.13 /14	0.08 /14	0.33	N/A
MMT	RBC US Govt Money Market Fd Inst	TIMXX	C-	(800) 422-2766	D- / 1.1	0.09	0.15	0.23 /27	0.09 /13	0.06 /13	0.23	N/A
MMT	RBC US Govt Money Market Fd Inv	TUIXX	U	(800) 422-2766	U /	--	--	--	--	--	0.01	N/A
MMT	RBC US Govt Money Market Fd Rsv	TURXX	U	(800) 422-2766	U /	--	--	--	--	--	0.01	N/A
MMT	RBC US Govt Money Market Fd Sel	TUSXX	U	(800) 422-2766	U /	--	--	--	--	--	0.01	N/A
MMT	Ready Assets USA Govt Money	MGRXX	U	(800) 441-7762	U /	--	--	--	--	--	0.01	N/A
COH	Redwood Managed Volatility I	RWDIX	C		B+ / 8.3	3.10	2.20	16.82 /92	3.10 /63	--	4.79	2.17
COH	Redwood Managed Volatility N	RWDNX	C		B / 8.1	3.01	2.12	16.59 /91	2.87 /59	--	4.58	2.43
COH	Redwood Managed Volatility Y	RWDYX	C		B / 8.2	3.09	2.25	16.89 /92	3.27 /65	--	4.76	2.16
GEI	RidgeWorth Seix Core Bond A	STGIX	D-	(888) 784-3863	D+ / 2.9	1.29	-1.85	2.31 /52	2.54 /53	1.93 /41	1.67	0.65
GEI	RidgeWorth Seix Core Bond I	STIGX	C	(888) 784-3863	C / 5.2	1.32	-1.87	2.36 /52	2.72 /56	2.16 /44	1.90	0.48
COI	RidgeWorth Seix Core Bond IS	STGZX	C	(888) 784-3863	C / 5.2	1.36	-1.80	2.60 /54	2.70 /56	2.15 /44	2.03	0.34
GEI	RidgeWorth Seix Core Bond R	SCIGX	C-	(888) 784-3863	C / 4.5	1.22	-2.06	2.04 /49	2.31 /48	1.73 /38	1.48	0.88
COH	RidgeWorth Seix Corporate Bond A	SAINX	D	(888) 784-3863	B- / 7.0	3.42	-0.28	10.51 /80	4.11 /76	3.56 /67	2.57	1.11
COH	RidgeWorth Seix Corporate Bond C	STIFX	C-	(888) 784-3863	B- / 7.5	3.26	-0.63	9.78 /78	3.43 /68	2.85 /55	2.01	1.80
COH	RidgeWorth Seix Corporate Bond I	STICX	C+	(888) 784-3863	B+ / 8.5	3.50	-0.27	10.82 /81	4.39 /80	3.85 /70	2.95	0.83
LP	RidgeWorth Seix Fltng Rt Hg Inc A	SFRAX	B	(888) 784-3863	B- / 7.5	2.16	4.10	13.62 /86	3.30 /66	4.28 /76	4.28	0.92
LP	RidgeWorth Seix Fltng Rt Hg Inc C	SFRCX	B-	(888) 784-3863	B- / 7.5	1.90	3.80	12.96 /85	2.66 /55	3.65 /68	3.82	1.51

● Denotes fund is closed to new investors
* Denotes fund is included in Section II

www.thestreetratings.com

RISK			NET ASSETS		ASSET							FUND MANAGER		MINIMUM		LOADS	
Risk Rating/Pts	3 Yr Avg Standard Deviation	Avg Duration	NAV As of 2/28/17	Total $(Mil)	Cash %	Gov. Bond %	Muni. Bond %	Corp. Bond %	Other %	Portfolio Turnover Ratio	Avg Coupon Rate	Manager Quality Pct	Manager Tenure (Years)	Initial Purch. $	Additional Purch. $	Front End Load	Back End Load
A+ / 9.6	0.7	1.6	9.97	N/A	3	0	96	0	1	46	3.7	20	4	500	0	0.0	0.0
A+ / 9.6	0.7	1.6	9.97	N/A	3	0	96	0	1	46	3.7	12	4	500	0	0.0	0.0
A+ / 9.6	0.7	1.6	9.97	N/A	3	0	96	0	1	46	3.7	25	4	500	0	0.8	0.0
A+ / 9.6	0.7	1.6	9.97	6	3	0	96	0	1	46	3.7	34	4	500	0	0.0	0.0
C+ / 5.9	2.9	6.4	8.50	826	0	0	99	0	1	21	5.0	62	15	500	0	4.0	0.0
C+ / 5.6	3.0	6.4	8.50	6	0	0	99	0	1	21	5.0	28	15	500	0	0.0	0.0
C+ / 5.9	2.9	6.4	8.52	37	0	0	99	0	1	21	5.0	27	15	500	0	0.0	0.0
C / 5.5	3.0	6.4	8.53	6	0	0	99	0	1	21	5.0	48	15	500	0	3.3	0.0
C+ / 5.9	2.9	6.4	8.52	46	0	0	99	0	1	21	5.0	69	15	500	0	0.0	0.0
D+ / 2.4	3.8	7.2	12.29	739	0	0	98	1	1	25	5.1	96	15	500	0	4.0	1.0
D+ / 2.5	3.8	7.2	12.32	11	0	0	98	1	1	25	5.1	95	15	500	0	0.0	1.0
D+ / 2.4	3.8	7.2	12.32	72	0	0	98	1	1	25	5.1	95	15	500	0	0.0	1.0
D+ / 2.4	3.8	7.2	12.29	8	0	0	98	1	1	25	5.1	96	15	500	0	3.3	1.0
D+ / 2.4	3.8	7.2	12.34	122	0	0	98	1	1	25	5.1	97	15	500	0	0.0	1.0
B+ / 8.6	1.7	3.2	13.03	697	0	0	0	0	100	1,272	6.2	78	10	500	0	4.0	0.0
B+ / 8.7	1.7	3.2	12.96	13	0	0	0	0	100	1,272	6.2	61	10	500	0	0.0	0.0
B+ / 8.7	1.7	3.2	12.91	50	0	0	0	0	100	1,272	6.2	60	10	500	0	0.0	0.0
B+ / 8.6	1.7	3.2	13.09	13	0	0	0	0	100	1,272	6.2	74	10	500	0	3.3	0.0
B+ / 8.6	1.7	3.2	12.90	19	0	0	0	0	100	1,272	6.2	74	10	500	0	0.0	0.0
B+ / 8.7	1.7	3.2	12.90	92	0	0	0	0	100	1,272	6.2	80	10	500	0	0.0	0.0
A+ / 9.9	0.4	1.0	9.83	74	4	15	7	14	60	90	3.4	53	5	5,000	100	0.0	0.0
C- / 3.9	3.5	N/A	9.46	45	13	24	20	8	35	718	0.0	83	4	10,000	1,000	0.0	0.0
U /	N/A	N/A	9.38	N/A	13	24	20	8	35	718	0.0	N/A	4	10,000	1,000	0.0	0.0
D / 2.2	4.8	4.9	9.98	1	19	3	0	77	1	220	0.0	96	6	2,500	100	4.3	2.0
D / 2.2	4.8	4.9	9.98	21	19	3	0	77	1	220	0.0	97	6	1,000,000	10,000	0.0	2.0
U /	N/A	N/A	9.73	16	0	0	0	0	100	1,227	0.0	N/A	3	1,000,000	10,000	0.0	2.0
E / 0.4	8.0	N/A	9.56	N/A	21	74	0	3	2	279	0.0	87	6	2,500	100	4.3	2.0
E / 0.4	8.0	N/A	9.59	17	21	74	0	3	2	279	0.0	88	6	1,000,000	10,000	0.0	2.0
C- / 3.5	3.8	N/A	10.13	N/A	12	0	0	77	11	84	0.0	95	1	2,500	100	4.3	2.0
C- / 3.5	3.8	N/A	10.17	36	12	0	0	77	11	84	0.0	95	1	1,000,000	10,000	0.0	2.0
U /	N/A	1.8	9.97	1	0	0	0	67	33	50	0.0	N/A	4	10,000	1,000	0.0	0.0
A- / 9.2	1.0	1.8	9.97	17	0	0	0	67	33	50	0.0	73	4	10,000	1,000	0.0	0.0
U /	N/A	1.0	9.90	1	4	0	0	61	35	41	0.0	N/A	4	10,000	1,000	0.0	0.0
A+ / 9.8	0.5	1.0	9.89	14	4	0	0	61	35	41	0.0	75	4	10,000	1,000	0.0	0.0
A+ / 9.9	N/A	N/A	1.00	3,773	100	0	0	0	0	0	0.3	47	N/A	10,000,000	0	0.0	0.0
A+ / 9.9	N/A	N/A	1.00	937	100	0	0	0	0	0	0.2	46	N/A	1,000,000	0	0.0	0.0
U /	N/A	N/A	1.00	411	100	0	0	0	0	0	0.0	N/A	N/A	0	0	0.0	0.0
U /	N/A	N/A	1.00	2,133	100	0	0	0	0	0	0.0	N/A	N/A	0	0	0.0	0.0
U /	N/A	N/A	1.00	1,736	100	0	0	0	0	0	0.0	N/A	N/A	0	0	0.0	0.0
U /	N/A	N/A	1.00	56	100	0	0	0	0	0	0.0	38	16	5,000	1,000	0.0	0.0
D / 1.9	4.7	N/A	15.47	55	2	0	3	86	9	111	0.0	40	4	250,000	1,000	0.0	0.0
D / 1.9	4.6	N/A	15.45	28	2	0	3	86	9	111	0.0	31	4	10,000	500	0.0	0.0
D / 1.9	4.6	N/A	15.55	243	2	0	3	86	9	111	0.0	53	4	20,000,000	1,000	0.0	1.0
C+ / 5.9	2.9	5.5	10.61	10	0	35	0	27	38	232	3.0	37	13	2,000	1,000	4.8	0.0
C+ / 5.6	3.0	5.5	10.61	203	0	35	0	27	38	232	3.0	48	13	0	0	0.0	0.0
C / 5.4	3.0	5.5	10.61	1	0	35	0	27	38	232	3.0	46	13	2,500,000	0	0.0	0.0
C+ / 5.6	3.0	5.5	10.62	3	0	35	0	27	38	232	3.0	27	13	0	0	0.0	0.0
D / 1.8	4.7	7.9	8.76	1	2	1	0	96	1	84	3.9	83	13	2,000	1,000	4.8	0.0
D / 1.8	4.7	7.9	8.72	8	2	1	0	96	1	84	3.9	77	13	5,000	1,000	0.0	0.0
D / 1.8	4.7	7.9	8.72	12	2	1	0	96	1	84	3.9	86	13	0	0	0.0	0.0
C- / 4.2	3.4	0.3	8.79	167	0	0	0	58	42	33	4.7	89	11	2,000	1,000	2.5	0.0
C- / 4.1	3.5	0.3	8.79	57	0	0	0	58	42	33	4.7	85	11	5,000	1,000	0.0	0.0

99 Pct = Best
0 Pct = Worst

Fund Type	Fund Name	Ticker Symbol	Overall Investment Rating	Phone	Performance Rating/Pts	3 Mo	6 Mo	1Yr / Pct	3Yr / Pct	5Yr / Pct	Dividend Yield	Expense Ratio
LP	RidgeWorth Seix Fltng Rt Hg Inc I	SAMBX	A-	(888) 784-3863	B+ / 8.5	2.24	4.26	13.97 /87	3.57 /70	4.58 /80	4.69	0.62
LP	RidgeWorth Seix Fltng Rt Hg Inc IS	SFRZX	A-	(888) 784-3863	B+ / 8.5	2.15	4.19	13.95 /87	3.65 /71	4.63 /80	4.80	0.51
MUS	RidgeWorth Seix GA Tax Ex Bond A	SGTEX	D	(888) 784-3863	C / 4.3	1.83	-3.23	-0.12 /16	3.14 /84	2.65 /74	2.48	0.75
MUS	RidgeWorth Seix GA Tax Ex Bond I	SGATX	B	(888) 784-3863	B- / 7.3	1.96	-3.09	-0.01 /17	3.27 /85	2.79 /76	2.71	0.68
MUS	RidgeWorth Seix Hi Grade Muni Bd A	SFLTX	C-	(888) 784-3863	C+ / 6.3	2.55	-2.88	0.66 /40	3.94 /92	3.71 /90	1.90	0.80
MUS	RidgeWorth Seix Hi Grade Muni Bd I	SCFTX	A-	(888) 784-3863	B+ / 8.6	2.51	-2.81	0.81 /42	4.09 /93	3.85 /92	2.15	0.70
COH	RidgeWorth Seix High Income A	SAHIX	D+	(888) 784-3863	B+ / 8.3	4.43	4.93	22.00 /98	3.35 /67	5.87 /91	5.47	1.03
COH	RidgeWorth Seix High Income I	STHTX	C	(888) 784-3863	A / 9.4	4.49	5.05	22.10 /98	3.59 /70	6.12 /93	5.97	0.79
COH	RidgeWorth Seix High Income IS	STHZX	C+	(888) 784-3863	A / 9.4	4.53	5.14	22.30 /98	3.72 /72	6.20 /93	6.13	0.63
COH	RidgeWorth Seix High Income R	STHIX	C	(888) 784-3863	A- / 9.1	4.38	5.00	21.78 /98	3.14 /63	5.68 /90	5.56	1.20
COH	RidgeWorth Seix High Yield A	HYPSX	D	(888) 784-3863	B- / 7.3	3.89	4.21	17.66 /93	2.93 /60	5.31 /87	5.07	0.84
COH	RidgeWorth Seix High Yield I	SAMHX	C	(888) 784-3863	B+ / 8.7	4.00	4.39	17.86 /93	3.13 /63	5.56 /89	5.51	0.61
COH	RidgeWorth Seix High Yield IS	HYIZX	U	(888) 784-3863	U /	3.90	4.32	--	--	--	0.00	0.54
COH	RidgeWorth Seix High Yield R	HYLSX	C-	(888) 784-3863	B+ / 8.3	3.77	4.06	17.25 /92	2.68 /56	5.06 /85	5.12	1.04
MUN	RidgeWorth Seix Inv Grade T/E Bd A	SISIX	D-	(888) 784-3863	D+ / 2.9	1.89	-2.69	-0.17 /15	2.45 /72	2.33 /67	2.07	0.94
MUN	RidgeWorth Seix Inv Grade T/E Bd I	STTBX	B	(888) 784-3863	C+ / 6.4	2.02	-2.62	0.06 /22	2.63 /76	2.50 /70	2.33	0.69
US	RidgeWorth Seix Ltd Dur I	SAMLX	C+	(888) 784-3863	D+ / 2.5	0.32	1.28	1.74 /47	0.68 /23	0.65 /23	0.61	0.47
MUS	RidgeWorth Seix NC Tax Exempt A	SNCIX	D	(888) 784-3863	C- / 3.9	1.75	-3.21	-0.20 /15	3.00 /82	2.44 /69	2.02	0.81
MUS	RidgeWorth Seix NC Tax Exempt I	CNCFX	B	(888) 784-3863	B- / 7.1	1.89	-3.12	0.06 /22	3.15 /84	2.59 /72	2.27	0.73
MUS	RidgeWorth Seix Short-Trm Muni Bd	CMDTX	C+	(888) 784-3863	D+ / 2.5	1.07	-0.12	0.27 /31	0.55 /25	0.85 /32	0.74	0.63
MUS	RidgeWorth Seix Short-Trm Muni Bd	SMMAX	D	(888) 784-3863	E / 0.4	1.06	-0.18	0.12 /25	0.43 /23	0.70 /28	0.57	0.73
GEI	RidgeWorth Seix Sh-Term Bond A	STSBX	D	(888) 784-3863	E / 0.4	0.25	-0.31	0.39 /31	0.37 /19	0.68 /23	0.58	0.81
GEI	RidgeWorth Seix Sh-Term Bond C	SCBSX	D	(888) 784-3863	E / 0.4	0.10	-0.59	-0.30 /13	-0.13 / 5	0.05 /10	0.01	1.58
GEI	RidgeWorth Seix Sh-Term Bond I	SSBTX	C	(888) 784-3863	D / 2.0	0.30	-0.22	0.49 /33	0.57 /21	0.89 /26	0.79	0.68
COI	RidgeWorth Seix Total Return Bd A	CBPSX	D-	(888) 784-3863	D+ / 2.7	1.18	-1.98	2.17 /50	2.45 /51	1.95 /41	1.63	0.71
COI	RidgeWorth Seix Total Return Bd I	SAMFX	C-	(888) 784-3863	C / 5.2	1.27	-1.86	2.44 /53	2.73 /57	2.22 /45	1.96	0.45
COI	RidgeWorth Seix Total Return Bd IS	SAMZX	C	(888) 784-3863	C / 5.4	1.30	-1.79	2.58 /54	2.85 /59	2.30 /46	2.10	0.31
COI	RidgeWorth Seix Total Return Bd R	SCBLX	D	(888) 784-3863	C- / 4.1	1.12	-2.15	1.82 /47	2.08 /45	1.62 /36	1.35	1.06
GEI	RidgeWorth Seix Ultra Short Bond I	SISSX	B-	(888) 784-3863	D+ / 2.6	0.39	0.65	1.70 /46	0.78 /24	0.93 /26	1.08	0.38
* USS	RidgeWorth Seix US Gvt Sec US Bd I	SIGVX	C+	(888) 784-3863	D / 2.0	0.26	0.50	0.87 /38	0.50 /21	0.57 /22	0.97	0.41
GEI	RidgeWorth Seix US Gvt Sec US Bd	SIGZX	U	(888) 784-3863	U /	0.30	0.57	--	--	--	0.00	N/A
MTG	RidgeWorth Seix US Mtg A	SLTMX	C	(888) 784-3863	C- / 3.1	0.37	-1.19	0.10 /22	2.33 /49	1.75 /38	1.53	1.10
MTG	RidgeWorth Seix US Mtg C	SCLFX	C-	(888) 784-3863	D+ / 2.8	0.19	-1.56	-0.64 / 8	1.53 /35	0.97 /27	0.82	1.79
MTG	RidgeWorth Seix US Mtg I	SLMTX	B	(888) 784-3863	C / 4.4	0.43	-1.09	0.31 /29	2.51 /52	1.95 /41	1.78	0.86
MUS	RidgeWorth Seix VA Interm Muni A	CVIAX	D+	(888) 784-3863	D+ / 2.8	1.75	-2.12	0.09 /24	2.33 /70	1.92 /57	2.21	0.76
MUS	RidgeWorth Seix VA Interm Muni I	CRVTX	A-	(888) 784-3863	C+ / 6.1	1.79	-2.15	0.22 /30	2.41 /72	2.06 /60	2.46	0.68
COI	River Canyon Total Return Bond Inst	RCTIX	U	(800) 245-0371	U /	3.29	3.37	7.27 /73	--	--	2.22	1.83
GEI ●	RiverNorth/DoubleLine Strat Inc I	RNSIX	A+	(888) 848-7549	B+ / 8.4	2.88	2.13	10.78 /81	4.68 /83	5.41 /88	4.96	1.40
GEI ●	RiverNorth/DoubleLine Strat Inc R	RNDLX	A	(888) 848-7549	B / 8.1	2.72	1.90	10.38 /80	4.41 /80	5.13 /85	4.71	1.65
GEI	RiverNorth/Oaktree High Income I	RNHIX	B-	(888) 848-7549	B+ / 8.8	4.28	5.12	17.78 /93	3.78 /73	--	4.66	1.82
GEI	RiverNorth/Oaktree High Income R	RNOTX	C+	(888) 848-7549	B+ / 8.6	4.22	4.99	17.52 /93	3.51 /69	--	4.43	2.07
COH ●	RiverPark Sht-Tm Hi Yield Instl	RPHIX	A+	(888) 564-4517	C / 5.5	0.67	1.41	3.44 /59	2.57 /53	3.09 /59	2.76	0.87
COH ●	RiverPark Sht-Tm High Yield Rtl	RPHYX	A	(888) 564-4517	C / 5.0	0.61	1.29	3.20 /58	2.25 /47	2.80 /54	2.53	1.18
COH	Robinson Opportunistic Income A	RBNAX	U	(800) 207-7108	U /	7.14	6.39	27.81 /99	--	--	6.41	N/A
COH	Robinson Opportunistic Income C	RBNCX	U	(800) 207-7108	U /	6.98	6.05	26.80 /99	--	--	6.21	N/A
COH	Robinson Opportunistic Income Inst	RBNNX	U	(800) 207-7108	U /	7.21	6.53	28.09 /99	--	--	7.00	N/A
MUN	Robinson Tax Advantaged Income A	ROBAX	U	(800) 207-7108	U /	3.51	-5.33	1.06 /46	--	--	3.81	3.31
MUN	Robinson Tax Advantaged Income C	ROBCX	U	(800) 207-7108	U /	3.32	-5.68	0.32 /33	--	--	3.28	4.06
MUN	Robinson Tax Advantaged Income	ROBNX	U	(800) 207-7108	U /	3.57	-5.21	1.31 /49	--	--	4.29	3.06
COI	Rockefeller Core Taxable Bond Instl	RCFIX	C+	(855) 369-6209	C- / 4.1	0.78	-1.85	1.67 /46	2.10 /45	--	1.61	0.74
MUN	Rockefeller Int TxEx Natl Bd Instl	RCTEX	C	(855) 369-6209	C- / 3.1	1.22	-1.93	-0.62 / 8	1.11 /38	--	0.79	0.85
MUN	Rockefeller Int TxEx NY Bd Instl	RCNYX	C-	(855) 369-6209	D+ / 2.6	1.40	-1.91	-0.80 / 6	0.91 /33	--	0.57	0.85

● Denotes fund is closed to new investors
* Denotes fund is included in Section II

www.thestreetratings.com

I. Index of Bond and Money Market Mutual Funds

Risk Rating/Pts	3 Yr Avg Standard Deviation	Avg Duration	NAV As of 2/28/17	Total $(Mil)	Cash %	Gov. Bond %	Muni. Bond %	Corp. Bond %	Other %	Portfolio Turnover Ratio	Avg Coupon Rate	Manager Quality Pct	Manager Tenure (Years)	Initial Purch. $	Additional Purch. $	Front End Load	Back End Load
C- / 4.1	3.4	0.3	8.79	4,210	0	0	0	58	42	33	4.7	91	11	0	0	0.0	0.0
C- / 4.2	3.4	0.3	8.79	1,302	0	0	0	58	42	33	4.7	91	11	2,500,000	0	0.0	0.0
C / 4.4	3.3	5.7	10.51	4	0	0	94	0	6	41	5.0	27	14	2,000	1,000	4.8	0.0
C / 4.4	3.3	5.7	10.50	93	0	0	94	0	6	41	5.0	31	14	0	0	0.0	0.0
C- / 3.8	3.6	5.7	11.69	12	0	0	86	0	14	171	4.2	52	23	2,000	1,000	4.8	0.0
C- / 3.8	3.6	5.7	11.68	80	0	0	86	0	14	171	4.2	59	23	0	0	0.0	0.0
E+ / 0.6	6.7	3.3	6.53	67	0	7	0	88	5	77	6.8	4	6	2,000	1,000	4.8	0.0
E+ / 0.7	6.7	3.3	6.52	542	0	7	0	88	5	77	6.8	5	6	0	0	0.0	0.0
E+ / 0.7	6.6	3.3	6.52	16	0	7	0	88	5	77	6.8	6	6	2,500,000	0	0.0	0.0
E+ / 0.7	6.6	3.3	6.53	15	0	7	0	88	5	77	6.8	3	6	0	0	0.0	0.0
D- / 1.0	5.8	3.1	8.21	5	0	5	0	91	4	76	6.3	5	10	2,000	1,000	4.8	0.0
D- / 1.0	5.7	3.1	8.42	486	0	5	0	91	4	76	6.3	8	10	0	0	0.0	0.0
U /	N/A	3.1	8.42	43	0	5	0	91	4	76	6.3	N/A	10	2,500,000	0	0.0	0.0
D- / 1.0	5.7	3.1	8.41	N/A	0	5	0	91	4	76	6.3	4	10	0	0	0.0	0.0
C+ / 5.8	3.0	5.1	11.66	21	0	0	88	0	12	139	4.8	18	25	2,000	1,000	4.8	0.0
C+ / 5.8	3.0	5.1	11.65	534	0	0	88	0	12	139	4.8	23	25	0	0	0.0	0.0
A+ / 9.8	0.5	0.1	9.93	7	0	0	0	0	100	50	0.9	67	15	0	0	0.0	0.0
C / 4.8	3.2	5.7	10.01	2	0	4	86	1	9	42	4.8	27	12	2,000	1,000	4.8	0.0
C / 4.6	3.2	5.7	10.04	24	0	4	86	1	9	42	4.8	31	12	0	0	0.0	0.0
A- / 9.2	1.0	1.7	9.94	26	0	3	91	1	5	82	4.1	25	6	0	0	0.0	0.0
A- / 9.2	1.0	1.7	9.94	2	0	3	91	1	5	82	4.1	22	6	2,000	1,000	2.5	0.0
A / 9.5	0.8	1.9	9.96	2	0	45	0	28	27	87	1.9	28	3	2,000	1,000	2.5	0.0
A / 9.4	0.8	1.9	9.95	1	0	45	0	28	27	87	1.9	14	3	5,000	1,000	0.0	0.0
A / 9.5	0.8	1.9	9.93	52	0	45	0	28	27	87	1.9	35	3	0	0	0.0	0.0
C / 5.2	3.1	5.5	10.81	28	0	37	0	25	38	181	3.4	31	15	2,000	1,000	4.8	0.0
C / 5.2	3.1	5.5	10.46	785	0	37	0	25	38	181	3.4	48	15	0	0	0.0	0.0
C / 5.3	3.1	5.5	10.46	105	0	37	0	25	38	181	3.4	55	15	2,500,000	0	0.0	0.0
C / 5.3	3.1	5.5	10.46	42	0	37	0	25	38	181	3.4	20	15	0	0	0.0	0.0
A+ / 9.9	0.4	0.3	9.96	132	0	4	0	45	51	59	1.9	66	3	0	0	0.0	0.0
A+ / 9.9	0.2	0.3	10.02	1,344	0	2	0	0	98	52	1.6	61	3	0	0	0.0	0.0
U /	N/A	0.3	10.03	12	0	2	0	0	98	52	1.6	N/A	3	2,500,000	0	0.0	0.0
B / 8.1	2.1	2.4	11.10	4	0	3	0	0	97	223	3.9	32	10	2,000	1,000	2.5	0.0
B / 8.0	2.1	2.4	11.12	5	0	3	0	0	97	223	3.9	11	10	5,000	1,000	0.0	0.0
B / 8.1	2.1	2.4	11.12	18	0	3	0	0	97	223	3.9	41	10	0	0	0.0	0.0
B- / 7.2	2.6	4.8	9.54	4	0	0	92	0	8	48	4.8	25	6	2,000	1,000	4.8	0.0
B- / 7.1	2.7	4.8	9.54	47	0	0	92	0	8	48	4.8	26	6	0	0	0.0	0.0
U /	N/A	N/A	10.20	27	15	0	0	0	85	19	0.0	N/A	3	100,000	10,000	0.0	0.0
C / 5.4	3.0	N/A	10.60	1,950	0	21	3	24	52	36	0.0	92	7	100,000	100	0.0	2.0
C+ / 5.6	3.0	N/A	10.61	220	0	21	3	24	52	36	0.0	91	7	5,000	100	0.0	2.0
D / 2.2	4.8	N/A	9.72	81	0	1	0	70	29	40	0.0	92	5	100,000	100	0.0	2.0
D / 2.2	4.8	N/A	9.71	8	0	1	0	70	29	40	0.0	90	5	5,000	100	0.0	2.0
A- / 9.0	0.7	1.3	9.79	683	0	0	0	79	21	114	0.0	87	7	100,000	100	0.0	0.0
A- / 9.0	0.7	1.3	9.76	246	0	0	0	79	21	114	0.0	84	7	1,000	100	0.0	0.0
U /	N/A	N/A	11.27	4	0	0	0	0	100	0	0.0	N/A	2	2,500	100	5.8	0.0
U /	N/A	N/A	11.25	2	0	0	0	0	100	0	0.0	N/A	2	2,500	100	0.0	0.0
U /	N/A	N/A	11.27	58	0	0	0	0	100	0	0.0	N/A	2	1,000,000	100,000	0.0	0.0
U /	N/A	N/A	9.70	31	0	0	97	0	3	92	0.0	N/A	3	2,500	100	5.8	0.0
U /	N/A	N/A	9.69	11	0	0	97	0	3	92	0.0	N/A	3	2,500	100	0.0	0.0
U /	N/A	N/A	9.70	95	0	0	97	0	3	92	0.0	N/A	3	1,000,000	100,000	0.0	0.0
B / 7.7	2.4	N/A	10.01	80	0	0	0	0	100	88	0.0	48	1	1,000,000	10,000	0.0	0.0
B+ / 8.3	2.0	N/A	9.99	79	0	0	0	0	100	43	0.0	12	1	1,000,000	10,000	0.0	0.0
B+ / 8.3	2.0	N/A	9.94	35	0	0	0	0	100	51	0.0	9	1	1,000,000	10,000	0.0	0.0

99 Pct = Best
0 Pct = Worst

Fund Type	Fund Name	Ticker Symbol	Overall Investment Rating	Phone	Performance Rating/Pts	3 Mo	6 Mo	1Yr / Pct	Annualized 3Yr / Pct	Annualized 5Yr / Pct	Dividend Yield	Expense Ratio
GL	Russell Investments Glbl Opp Crd A	RGCAX	D+	(800) 832-6688	B- / 7.4	4.45	2.10	14.68 /88	3.35 /67	4.29 /76	3.98	1.59
GL	Russell Investments Glbl Opp Crd C	RGCCX	D+	(800) 832-6688	B / 7.6	4.27	1.72	13.77 /86	2.58 /53	3.51 /66	3.43	2.34
GL	Russell Investments Glbl Opp Crd E	RCCEX	C	(800) 832-6688	B+ / 8.4	4.48	2.14	14.70 /88	3.33 /66	4.29 /76	3.85	1.59
GL	Russell Investments Glbl Opp Crd S	RGCSX	C	(800) 832-6688	B+ / 8.6	4.50	2.23	14.91 /88	3.60 /70	4.53 /79	4.37	1.34
GL	Russell Investments Glbl Opp Crd Y	RGCYX	C	(800) 832-6688	B+ / 8.7	4.52	2.27	15.00 /88	3.64 /71	4.61 /80	4.44	1.14
COI	Russell Investments Inv Grd Bd A	RFAAX	D-	(800) 832-6688	D+ / 2.6	0.77	-2.72	1.21 /42	2.30 /48	2.11 /44	1.80	0.81
COI	Russell Investments Inv Grd Bd C	RFACX	D-	(800) 832-6688	D+ / 2.9	0.63	-3.08	0.51 /33	1.55 /36	1.35 /32	1.12	1.56
COI	Russell Investments Inv Grd Bd E	RFAEX	D+	(800) 832-6688	C- / 4.2	0.78	-2.71	1.26 /42	2.31 /48	2.13 /44	1.82	0.81
COI ●	Russell Investments Inv Grd Bd I	RFASX	C-	(800) 832-6688	C / 4.7	0.85	-2.60	1.54 /45	2.64 /55	2.45 /49	2.20	0.48
COI	Russell Investments Inv Grd Bd R6	RIGRX	U	(800) 832-6688	U /	0.87	-2.55	--	--	--	0.00	0.41
COI	Russell Investments Inv Grd Bd S	RFATX	C-	(800) 832-6688	C / 4.6	0.83	-2.60	1.46 /44	2.56 /53	2.37 /47	2.12	0.56
COI	Russell Investments Inv Grd Bd Y	RFAYX	C-	(800) 832-6688	C / 4.9	0.88	-2.54	1.66 /46	2.76 /57	2.57 /51	2.32	0.36
GEI	Russell Investments Sht Dur Bd A	RSBTX	D+	(800) 832-6688	D- / 1.2	0.40	0.12	2.42 /52	0.95 /27	1.35 /32	1.39	1.01
GEI	Russell Investments Sht Dur Bd C	RSBCX	C-	(800) 832-6688	D / 1.8	0.26	-0.21	1.68 /46	0.21 /17	0.60 /23	0.71	1.76
GEI	Russell Investments Sht Dur Bd E	RSBEX	B-	(800) 832-6688	D+ / 2.9	0.41	0.13	2.42 /52	0.96 /27	1.36 /33	1.34	1.01
COI	Russell Investments Sht Dur Bd R6	RDBRX	U	(800) 832-6688	U /	0.52	0.32	--	--	--	0.00	0.61
GEI	Russell Investments Sht Dur Bd S	RFBSX	B	(800) 832-6688	C- / 3.4	0.51	0.30	2.73 /55	1.22 /31	1.62 /36	1.70	0.76
GEI	Russell Investments Sht Dur Bd Y	RSBYX	B	(800) 832-6688	C- / 3.4	0.47	0.28	2.75 /55	1.28 /32	1.70 /38	1.77	0.56
GEI	Russell Investments Strat Bd A	RFDAX	D-	(800) 832-6688	C- / 3.0	1.04	-2.34	2.24 /51	2.37 /49	2.58 /51	1.43	1.05
GEI	Russell Investments Strat Bd C	RFCCX	D-	(800) 832-6688	C- / 3.3	0.84	-2.72	1.57 /45	1.62 /37	1.82 /39	0.73	1.80
GEI	Russell Investments Strat Bd E	RFCEX	D	(800) 832-6688	C / 4.5	0.97	-2.33	2.28 /51	2.36 /49	2.57 /51	1.43	1.05
GEI ●	Russell Investments Strat Bd I	RFCSX	C-	(800) 832-6688	C / 5.0	1.03	-2.22	2.47 /53	2.67 /55	2.87 /56	1.80	0.72
COI	Russell Investments Strat Bd R6	RSBRX	U	(800) 832-6688	U /	1.14	-2.16	--	--	--	0.00	0.65
GEI	Russell Investments Strat Bd S	RFCTX	D+	(800) 832-6688	C / 5.0	1.10	-2.20	2.49 /53	2.62 /54	2.83 /55	1.73	0.80
GEI	Russell Investments Strat Bd Y	RFCYX	C-	(800) 832-6688	C / 5.2	1.15	-2.15	2.68 /54	2.78 /57	3.00 /58	1.91	0.60
MUN	Russell Investments Tax Exmp Bd A	RTEAX	C-	(800) 832-6688	C- / 3.4	1.71	-2.61	-0.36 /12	2.42 /72	2.05 /60	2.31	0.84
MUN	Russell Investments Tax Exmp Bd C	RTECX	C	(800) 832-6688	C- / 4.0	1.50	-2.94	-1.06 / 4	1.69 /54	1.33 /43	1.70	1.59
MUN	Russell Investments Tax Exmp Bd E	RTBEX	B+	(800) 832-6688	C+ / 5.9	1.68	-2.64	-0.32 /12	2.45 /72	2.08 /61	2.27	0.84
MUN	Russell Investments Tax Exmp Bd S	RLVSX	A	(800) 832-6688	C+ / 6.5	1.75	-2.52	-0.07 /17	2.71 /77	2.34 /67	2.71	0.59
MUH	Russell Investments Tx Ex HY Bd A	RTHAX	U	(800) 832-6688	U /	2.42	-3.61	2.62 /62	--	--	3.54	1.19
MUH	Russell Investments Tx Ex HY Bd C	RTHCX	U	(800) 832-6688	U /	2.28	-3.84	1.84 /55	--	--	2.90	1.94
MUH	Russell Investments Tx Ex HY Bd E	RTHEX	U	(800) 832-6688	U /	2.32	-3.60	2.52 /62	--	--	3.38	1.19
MUH	Russell Investments Tx Ex HY Bd S	RTHSX	U	(800) 832-6688	U /	2.48	-3.39	2.87 /64	--	--	3.92	0.94
COI	Ryan Labs Core Bond	RLCBX	U		U /	1.26	-1.87	3.03 /57	--	--	2.37	1.19
COI	Ryan Labs Long Credit	RLLCX	U		U /	3.52	-4.84	10.61 /80	--	--	3.74	1.12
EM	Rydex Emerging Markets Bond Strat	RYIEX	E	(800) 820-0888	D+ / 2.3	4.31	-2.35	8.19 /75	1.02 /28	--	4.92	1.76
EM	Rydex Emerging Markets Bond Strat	RYFTX	E	(800) 820-0888	D+ / 2.8	4.10	-2.55	7.04 /73	0.10 /13	--	5.36	2.50
EM	Rydex Emerging Markets Bond Strat	RYGTX	E	(800) 820-0888	C- / 4.1	4.30	-2.17	7.85 /74	0.86 /25	--	5.19	1.74
USL	Rydex Govt Lg Bd 1.2x Strgy A	RYABX	E+	(800) 820-0888	C / 5.0	2.24	-16.76	-7.67 / 0	6.91 /96	3.81 /70	1.00	1.20
USL	Rydex Govt Lg Bd 1.2x Strgy C	RYCGX	E+	(800) 820-0888	C+ / 5.7	2.05	-17.09	-8.35 / 0	6.09 /92	2.97 /57	0.25	1.95
GL	Rydex Govt Lg Bd 1.2x Strgy H	RYHBX	U	(800) 820-0888	U /	2.26	-16.79	-7.67 / 0	--	--	1.05	1.20
USL	Rydex Govt Lg Bd 1.2x Strgy Inv	RYGBX	D-	(800) 820-0888	B- / 7.1	2.30	-16.73	-7.50 / 0	7.10 /96	3.94 /72	1.31	0.94
COH	Rydex High Yld Stratgy A	RYHDX	C-	(800) 820-0888	B / 7.6	3.40	3.19	12.08 /83	4.31 /79	6.75 /96	1.81	1.54
COH	Rydex High Yld Stratgy C	RYHHX	C	(800) 820-0888	B / 8.0	3.20	2.78	11.23 /82	3.47 /68	5.91 /91	2.10	2.29
COH	Rydex High Yld Stratgy H	RYHGX	C+	(800) 820-0888	B+ / 8.7	3.40	3.15	12.04 /83	4.20 /78	6.76 /96	1.90	1.54
USS	Rydex Inv Govt Lg Bd Stgy A	RYAQX	E-	(800) 820-0888	E- / 0.0	-2.43	14.87	3.98 /62	-8.57 / 0	-5.24 / 0	0.00	3.76
USS	Rydex Inv Govt Lg Bd Stgy C	RYJCX	E-	(800) 820-0888	E- / 0.0	-2.62	14.43	3.22 /58	-9.25 / 0	-5.94 / 0	0.00	4.51
GL	Rydex Inv Govt Lg Bd Stgy H	RYHJX	U	(800) 820-0888	U /	-2.46	14.86	4.28 /64	--	--	0.00	3.62
USS	Rydex Inv Govt Lg Bd Stgy Inv	RYJUX	E-	(800) 820-0888	E- / 0.0	-2.38	15.03	4.26 /63	-8.33 / 0	-5.00 / 0	0.00	3.49
COH	Rydex Inv High Yld Strtgy A	RYILX	E-	(800) 820-0888	E- / 0.0	-3.19	-3.50	-11.79 / 0	-8.06 / 0	-10.20 / 0	0.00	1.52
COH	Rydex Inv High Yld Strtgy C	RYIYX	E-	(800) 820-0888	E- / 0.0	-3.38	-3.93	-12.50 / 0	-8.52 / 0	-10.76 / 0	0.00	2.27
COH	Rydex Inv High Yld Strtgy H	RYIHX	E-	(800) 820-0888	E- / 0.0	-2.94	-3.55	-10.81 / 0	-7.46 / 0	-9.82 / 0	0.00	1.52

● Denotes fund is closed to new investors
* Denotes fund is included in Section II

www.thestreetratings.com

RISK			NET ASSETS		ASSET							FUND MANAGER		MINIMUM		LOADS	
Risk Rating/Pts	3 Yr Avg Standard Deviation	Avg Dura-tion	NAV As of 2/28/17	Total $(Mil)	Cash %	Gov. Bond %	Muni. Bond %	Corp. Bond %	Other %	Portfolio Turnover Ratio	Avg Coupon Rate	Manager Quality Pct	Manager Tenure (Years)	Initial Purch. $	Additional Purch. $	Front End Load	Back End Load
D- /1.5	5.8	4.9	9.62	5	2	28	0	38	32	68	0.0	95	6	0	0	3.8	0.0
D- /1.5	5.7	4.9	9.57	8	2	28	0	38	32	68	0.0	94	6	0	0	0.0	0.0
D- /1.4	5.8	4.9	9.66	1	2	28	0	38	32	68	0.0	95	6	0	0	0.0	0.0
D- /1.4	5.8	4.9	9.65	1,405	2	28	0	38	32	68	0.0	96	6	0	0	0.0	0.0
D- /1.5	5.7	4.9	9.65	586	2	28	0	38	32	68	0.0	96	6	10,000,000	0	0.0	0.0
C /5.5	3.0	5.1	21.08	10	0	20	0	26	54	207	0.0	30	28	0	0	3.8	0.0
C /5.4	3.0	5.1	20.90	14	0	20	0	26	54	207	0.0	11	28	0	0	0.0	0.0
C /5.5	3.0	5.1	21.08	6	0	20	0	26	54	207	0.0	30	28	0	0	0.0	0.0
C /5.4	3.0	5.1	21.07	236	0	20	0	26	54	207	0.0	48	28	100,000	0	0.0	0.0
U /	N/A	5.1	21.13	1	0	20	0	26	54	207	0.0	N/A	28	0	0	0.0	0.0
C /5.5	3.0	5.1	21.05	509	0	20	0	26	54	207	0.0	42	28	0	0	0.0	0.0
C /5.5	3.0	5.1	21.09	155	0	20	0	26	54	207	0.0	54	28	10,000,000	0	0.0	0.0
A /9.3	0.9	1.7	19.13	21	2	28	0	23	47	113	0.0	59	10	0	0	3.8	0.0
A /9.4	0.9	1.7	18.98	45	2	28	0	23	47	113	0.0	25	10	0	0	0.0	0.0
A /9.4	0.9	1.7	19.19	2	2	28	0	23	47	113	0.0	59	10	0	0	0.0	0.0
U /	N/A	1.7	19.18	N/A	2	28	0	23	47	113	0.0	N/A	10	0	0	0.0	0.0
A /9.3	0.9	1.7	19.15	577	2	28	0	23	47	113	0.0	66	10	0	0	0.0	0.0
A /9.3	0.9	1.7	19.15	196	2	28	0	23	47	113	0.0	68	10	10,000,000	0	0.0	0.0
C /4.8	3.2	4.9	10.60	48	9	27	0	28	36	203	0.0	25	6	0	0	3.8	0.0
C /4.8	3.2	4.9	10.59	51	9	27	0	28	36	203	0.0	9	6	0	0	0.0	0.0
C /4.9	3.2	4.9	10.52	9	9	27	0	28	36	203	0.0	26	6	0	0	0.0	0.0
C /4.9	3.2	4.9	10.47	941	9	27	0	28	36	203	0.0	35	6	100,000	0	0.0	0.0
U /	N/A	4.9	10.51	1	9	27	0	28	36	203	0.0	N/A	6	0	0	0.0	0.0
C /4.8	3.2	4.9	10.63	3,301	9	27	0	28	36	203	0.0	33	6	0	0	0.0	0.0
C /4.8	3.2	4.9	10.49	814	9	27	0	28	36	203	0.0	42	6	10,000,000	0	0.0	0.0
B- /7.0	2.7	4.9	22.90	22	0	0	91	0	9	14	0.0	23	4	0	0	3.8	0.0
B- /7.0	2.7	4.9	22.77	29	0	0	91	0	9	14	0.0	9	4	0	0	0.0	0.0
C+ /6.9	2.7	4.9	22.89	4	0	0	91	0	9	14	0.0	24	4	0	0	0.0	0.0
C+ /6.9	2.7	4.9	22.81	1,463	0	0	91	0	9	14	0.0	32	4	0	0	0.0	0.0
U /	N/A	7.7	10.18	2	0	0	0	0	100	22	0.0	N/A	2	0	0	3.8	0.0
U /	N/A	7.7	10.17	1	0	0	0	0	100	22	0.0	N/A	2	0	0	0.0	0.0
U /	N/A	7.7	10.21	N/A	0	0	0	0	100	22	0.0	N/A	2	0	0	0.0	0.0
U /	N/A	7.7	10.19	342	0	0	0	0	100	22	0.0	N/A	2	0	0	0.0	0.0
U /	N/A	N/A	9.82	100	2	32	0	32	34	161	0.0	N/A	3	1,000,000	0	0.0	0.0
U /	N/A	N/A	10.20	67	0	0	0	0	100	0	0.0	N/A	N/A	1,000,000	0	0.0	0.0
E /0.3	8.4	N/A	71.32	N/A	88	10	0	0	2	21,555	0.0	90	4	2,500	0	4.8	0.0
E /0.3	8.3	N/A	68.68	N/A	88	10	0	0	2	21,555	0.0	84	4	2,500	0	0.0	0.0
E /0.3	8.3	N/A	70.91	1	88	10	0	0	2	21,555	0.0	89	4	2,500	0	0.0	0.0
E- /0.0	16.4	13.8	51.50	31	25	74	0	0	1	2,699	3.6	1	23	2,500	0	4.8	0.0
E- /0.0	16.4	13.8	51.15	2	25	74	0	0	1	2,699	3.6	0	23	2,500	0	0.0	0.0
U /	N/A	13.8	51.54	23	25	74	0	0	1	2,699	3.6	N/A	23	2,500	0	0.0	0.0
E- /0.0	16.4	13.8	51.11	28	25	74	0	0	1	2,699	3.6	2	23	2,500	0	0.0	0.0
D /1.9	4.8	0.1	24.65	17	33	66	0	0	1	521	0.0	80	10	2,500	0	4.8	0.0
D /1.8	4.9	0.1	22.26	5	33	66	0	0	1	521	0.0	65	10	2,500	0	0.0	0.0
D /1.8	4.8	0.1	24.63	393	33	66	0	0	1	521	0.0	79	10	2,500	0	0.0	0.0
E- /0.0	13.6	N/A	34.46	19	100	0	0	0	0	838	0.0	1	9	2,500	0	4.8	0.0
E- /0.0	13.6	N/A	30.45	23	100	0	0	0	0	838	0.0	1	9	2,500	0	0.0	0.0
U /	N/A	N/A	34.56	56	100	0	0	0	0	838	0.0	N/A	9	2,500	0	0.0	0.0
E- /0.0	13.6	N/A	35.75	76	100	0	0	0	0	838	0.0	2	9	2,500	0	0.0	0.0
D /1.7	5.0	N/A	66.16	1	99	0	0	0	1	1,722	0.0	0	10	2,500	0	4.8	0.0
D /1.8	4.9	N/A	62.02	1	99	0	0	0	1	1,722	0.0	0	10	2,500	0	0.0	0.0
D /1.7	5.0	N/A	67.75	2	99	0	0	0	1	1,722	0.0	0	10	2,500	0	0.0	0.0

Fund Type	Fund Name	Ticker Symbol	Overall Investment Rating	Phone	Performance Rating/Pts	3 Mo	6 Mo	1Yr / Pct	3Yr / Pct	5Yr / Pct	Dividend Yield	Expense Ratio
	99 Pct = Best							Total Return % through 2/28/17	Annualized		Incl. in Returns	
GEI	Rydex Strengthening Dlr 2x Strtgy A	RYSDX	C	(800) 820-0888	A+ / 9.9	-0.86	10.62	4.97 /66	13.86 /99	6.77 /96	0.00	1.71
GEI	Rydex Strengthening Dlr 2x Strtgy C	RYSJX	C	(800) 820-0888	A+ / 9.9	-1.05	10.19	4.18 /63	13.01 /99	5.98 /92	0.00	2.47
GEI	Rydex Strengthening Dlr 2x Strtgy H	RYSBX	C	(800) 820-0888	A+ / 9.9	-0.88	10.60	4.95 /66	13.85 /99	6.78 /96	0.00	1.72
GEI	Rydex Wekng Dlr 2x Stgry A	RYWDX	E-	(800) 820-0888	E- / 0.0	-0.03	-11.27	-8.07 / 0	-15.95 / 0	-10.79 / 0	0.00	1.72
GEI	Rydex Wekng Dlr 2x Stgry C	RYWJX	E-	(800) 820-0888	E- / 0.0	-0.21	-11.65	-8.73 / 0	-16.60 / 0	-11.46 / 0	0.00	2.47
GEI	Rydex Wekng Dlr 2x Stgry H	RYWBX	E-	(800) 820-0888	E- / 0.0	-0.03	-11.29	-8.09 / 0	-15.94 / 0	-10.79 / 0	0.00	1.72
* GES	SA Global Fixed Income	SAXIX	C	(800) 366-7266	D+ / 2.3	0.53	-0.73	0.61 /35	0.89 /26	0.95 /27	0.99	0.73
* GEI	SA US Fixed Income Fund	SAUFX	C	(800) 366-7266	D- / 1.5	0.25	0.06	0.43 /32	0.21 /17	0.11 /15	0.43	0.65
LP	Salient Select Opportunity Inst	FSOTX	C	(800) 999-6809	A+ / 9.9	8.36	11.29	38.13 /99	2.77 /57	--	3.14	2.12
GL	Salient Tactical Muni & Credit A	FLSLX	D-	(800) 999-6809	C / 4.6	3.44	-3.00	2.20 /51	3.99 /75	1.40 /33	2.22	1.96
GEL	Salient Tactical Muni & Credit Adv	FLSMX	C+	(800) 999-6809	B- / 7.4	3.58	-2.78	2.71 /55	4.47 /80	1.92 /41	2.86	1.51
MUS	Sanford C Bernstein CA Muni	SNCAX	B-	(212) 486-5800	C / 4.4	1.74	-1.94	-0.38 /11	1.67 /53	1.44 /45	2.09	0.63
MUN	Sanford C Bernstein Diversified Mun	SNDPX	B-	(800) 221-5672	C / 4.5	1.72	-1.89	-0.39 /11	1.71 /55	1.53 /47	1.99	0.55
* GES	Sanford C Bernstein II Int Dur Inst	SIIDX	C+	(800) 221-5672	C+ / 6.2	1.35	-1.64	3.53 /60	3.28 /66	2.91 /56	2.81	0.58
* GES	Sanford C Bernstein Interm Duration	SNIDX	C+	(212) 486-5800	C+ / 6.1	1.38	-1.57	3.57 /60	3.21 /64	2.80 /54	2.72	0.59
MUS	Sanford C Bernstein New York Muni	SNNYX	B+	(212) 486-5800	C / 5.1	1.83	-1.84	-0.12 /16	1.95 /61	1.53 /47	2.17	0.61
MUS	Sanford C Bernstein Sh Dur CA Mun	SDCMX	D	(212) 486-5800	E / 0.4	0.41	-0.48	-0.24 /14	-0.17 / 5	0.01 / 7	0.24	0.83
MUS	Sanford C Bernstein Sh Dur NY Mun	SDNYX	C	(212) 486-5800	D / 1.9	0.56	-0.07	0.24 /30	0.28 /20	0.32 /21	0.48	0.70
MUN	Sanford C Bernstein Sh-Dur Dvrs	SDDMX	C	(212) 486-5800	D / 1.8	0.75	0.02	0.21 /29	0.25 /20	0.35 /22	0.45	0.63
GES	Sanford C Bernstein Short Dur Plus	SNSDX	C	(212) 486-5800	D / 2.0	0.36	-0.04	0.78 /37	0.52 /21	0.48 /21	0.87	0.64
GEI	Saratoga Adv Tr Inv Qlty Bond C	SQBCX	D-	(800) 807-3863	E / 0.3	0.33	-0.79	0.20 /26	-0.01 / 5	-0.04 / 5	0.29	2.37
GEI	Saratoga Adv Tr Inv Qlty Bond I	SIBPX	D	(800) 807-3863	D- / 1.2	0.54	-0.56	0.89 /38	0.67 /23	0.73 /24	0.98	1.36
MUN	Saratoga Adv Tr-Municipal Bond C	SMBCX	E+	(800) 807-3863	E- / 0.2	1.48	-3.65	-2.01 / 1	-0.27 / 4	-0.43 / 3	0.11	3.96
MUN	Saratoga Adv Tr-Municipal Bond I	SMBPX	E+	(800) 807-3863	E- / 0.2	1.73	-3.29	-1.46 / 2	0.18 /18	0.15 /19	0.57	2.92
MUS	Saturna Idaho Tax-Exempt	NITEX	A+	(800) 728-8762	B+ / 8.3	2.32	-1.49	1.63 /53	3.60 /89	2.67 /74	5.03	0.67
GL	Saturna Sustainable Bond	SEBFX	U	(800) 728-8762	U /	2.08	-0.09	4.82 /66	--	--	2.49	1.02
GES	SC 529 CO FS Conservative AG	CNATX	B	(800) 345-6611	C / 4.3	1.64	0.71	5.07 /67	2.29 /48	2.64 /52	0.00	0.99
GES	SC 529 CO FS Conservative B		B-	(800) 345-6611	C- / 4.0	1.38	0.29	4.11 /63	1.40 /33	1.77 /39	0.00	1.74
GES	SC 529 CO FS Conservative C	CNBTX	B	(800) 345-6611	C / 4.5	1.51	0.43	4.42 /64	1.68 /38	2.02 /42	0.00	1.74
GES	SC 529 CO FS Conservative Dir		A+	(800) 345-6611	C+ / 5.9	1.69	0.74	4.37 /64	2.62 /54	2.90 /56	0.00	0.54
GES	SC 529 CO FS Conservative E	CNETX	B+	(800) 345-6611	C / 4.9	1.53	0.53	4.68 /65	1.93 /42	2.31 /46	0.00	1.24
GES	SC 529 CO FS Conservative Z		A	(800) 345-6611	C+ / 5.8	1.67	0.83	5.19 /67	2.46 /51	2.82 /55	0.00	0.74
COH	SC 529 CO FS Income Opps AG	CINAX	C-	(800) 345-6611	B / 8.0	3.87	3.08	12.63 /84	3.96 /75	5.58 /89	0.00	1.43
COH	SC 529 CO FS Income Opps B		C-	(800) 345-6611	B / 7.8	3.70	2.68	11.69 /83	3.08 /62	4.72 /81	0.00	2.18
COH	SC 529 CO FS Income Opps C	CICNX	C-	(800) 345-6611	B / 8.1	3.76	2.83	12.00 /83	3.36 /67	4.94 /83	0.00	2.18
COH	SC 529 CO FS Income Opps E	CINEX	C	(800) 345-6611	B+ / 8.3	3.82	2.93	12.25 /84	3.60 /70	5.23 /86	0.00	1.68
GEI	SC 529 CO FS Total Return Bond AG	CBADX	C+	(800) 345-6611	C / 4.8	1.55	-1.29	4.38 /64	2.91 /60	2.54 /50	0.00	1.09
GEI	SC 529 CO FS Total Return Bond B		C	(800) 345-6611	C / 4.4	1.32	-1.70	3.52 /60	2.02 /44	1.68 /37	0.00	1.84
GEI	SC 529 CO FS Total Return Bond C	CBCDX	C+	(800) 345-6611	C / 4.9	1.41	-1.55	3.77 /61	2.28 /48	1.91 /41	0.00	1.84
GEI	SC 529 CO FS Total Return Bond E	CEDBX	B-	(800) 345-6611	C / 5.3	1.48	-1.43	4.04 /62	2.53 /52	2.20 /45	0.00	1.34
USS	SC 529 CO FS US Govt Mortgage	CAGMX	B-	(800) 345-6611	C- / 3.7	0.66	-0.39	2.06 /49	2.47 /51	2.51 /50	0.00	1.25
USS	SC 529 CO FS US Govt Mortgage B		C+	(800) 345-6611	C- / 3.4	0.43	-0.84	1.22 /42	1.61 /37	1.67 /37	0.00	2.00
USS	SC 529 CO FS US Govt Mortgage C	CGCBX	B	(800) 345-6611	C- / 3.9	0.57	-0.64	1.52 /45	1.87 /41	1.90 /41	0.00	2.00
USS	SC 529 CO FS US Govt Mortgage E	CEGDX	C+	(800) 345-6611	C / 4.3	0.61	-0.53	1.77 /47	2.12 /45	2.18 /45	0.00	1.50
COI	Schroder Long Dur Inv-Gr Bd Inv	STWLX	D+	(800) 464-3108	B+ / 8.4	2.68	-7.12	6.46 /71	5.61 /89	5.41 /88	3.35	1.16
COI	Schroder Short Duration Bond Inv	SDBNX	U	(800) 464-3108	U /	0.53	-0.03	2.01 /49	--	--	1.38	2.66
COI	Schroder Short Duration Bond R6	SDBRX	U	(800) 464-3108	U /	0.53	-0.03	2.06 /49	--	--	1.43	2.51
GES	Schroder Total Return Fix Inc Inv	SBBIX	C-	(800) 464-3108	C / 5.1	1.85	-1.12	4.45 /64	2.27 /48	2.39 /48	2.85	0.64
MMT	Schwab Adv Cash Reserves Prem	SWZXX	C-	(800) 407-0256	D- / 1.0	0.10	0.17	0.20 /26	0.07 /11	0.05 /12	0.20	N/A
MMT	Schwab Adv Cash Reserves Sweep	SWQXX	C-	(800) 407-0256	E+ / 0.9	0.09	0.13	0.14 /24	0.05 /10	0.04 /10	0.14	N/A
MMF	Schwab AMT Tax-Free Money	SWFXX	D+	(800) 407-0256	E+ / 0.8	0.03	0.06	0.06 /22	0.03 /10	0.03 /12	0.06	N/A
MMF	Schwab AMT Tax-Free Money Val	SWWXX	C-	(800) 407-0256	D- / 1.2	0.07	0.15	0.17 /28	0.07 /14	0.05 /14	0.17	N/A

● Denotes fund is closed to new investors
* Denotes fund is included in Section II

Risk Rating/Pts	3 Yr Avg Standard Deviation	Avg Duration	NAV As of 2/28/17	Total $(Mil)	Cash %	Gov. Bond %	Muni. Bond %	Corp. Bond %	Other %	Portfolio Turnover Ratio	Avg Coupon Rate	Manager Quality Pct	Manager Tenure (Years)	Initial Purch. $	Additional Purch. $	Front End Load	Back End Load
E- /0.0	14.6	0.1	54.04	2	98	1	0	0	1	376	0.0	99	12	2,500	0	4.8	0.0
E- /0.0	14.6	0.1	49.08	1	98	1	0	0	1	376	0.0	99	12	2,500	0	0.0	0.0
E- /0.0	14.6	0.1	53.82	7	98	1	0	0	1	376	0.0	99	12	2,500	0	0.0	0.0
E- /0.0	14.5	N/A	64.26	N/A	100	0	0	0	0	699	0.0	0	12	2,500	0	4.8	0.0
E- /0.0	14.5	N/A	58.10	1	100	0	0	0	0	699	0.0	N/A	12	2,500	0	0.0	0.0
E- /0.0	14.5	N/A	64.19	3	100	0	0	0	0	699	0.0	0	12	2,500	0	0.0	0.0
A- /9.0	1.3	N/A	9.62	722	0	0	0	0	100	42	0.0	29	18	100,000	0	0.0	0.0
A+ /9.8	0.5	N/A	10.19	610	0	0	0	0	100	140	0.0	33	18	100,000	0	0.0	0.0
E- /0.0	13.3	N/A	24.44	4	18	0	0	3	79	104	0.0	66	6	100,000	0	0.0	0.0
C- /3.6	3.7	N/A	7.65	5	4	5	90	0	1	160	0.0	95	2	4,000	100	5.8	0.0
C- /3.6	3.7	N/A	7.63	28	4	5	90	0	1	160	0.0	85	2	0	0	0.0	0.0
B /7.7	2.4	4.2	14.22	1,109	0	5	94	0	1	12	5.0	14	15	25,000	0	0.0	0.0
B /7.7	2.4	4.0	14.31	5,237	0	4	94	0	2	11	5.0	15	28	25,000	0	0.0	0.0
C /5.3	3.1	5.4	14.95	613	0	26	0	27	47	146	3.6	67	12	3,000,000	0	0.0	0.0
C /5.3	3.0	5.3	13.12	3,333	0	23	0	26	51	146	3.6	65	12	25,000	0	0.0	0.0
B /7.6	2.5	4.2	13.97	1,546	2	4	92	0	2	17	5.0	19	18	25,000	0	0.0	0.0
A+ /9.8	0.6	1.6	12.38	14	5	0	89	4	2	34	4.9	18	23	25,000	0	0.0	0.0
A+ /9.7	0.6	1.6	12.46	45	9	0	90	0	1	35	4.4	28	23	25,000	0	0.0	0.0
A+ /9.7	0.6	1.4	12.58	157	1	0	96	1	2	42	4.6	27	15	25,000	0	0.0	0.0
A+ /9.6	0.7	2.1	11.69	293	4	34	0	23	39	76	1.6	36	12	25,000	0	0.0	0.0
B+ /8.7	1.6	N/A	9.58	N/A	0	0	0	0	100	37	0.0	7	2	250	0	0.0	2.0
B+ /8.7	1.6	N/A	9.57	7	0	0	0	0	100	37	0.0	19	2	250	0	0.0	2.0
B- /7.1	2.7	N/A	9.09	N/A	0	0	0	0	100	142	0.0	1	8	250	0	0.0	2.0
B- /7.0	2.7	N/A	9.08	1	0	0	0	0	100	142	0.0	1	8	250	0	0.0	2.0
B- /7.1	2.7	6.4	5.35	17	6	0	93	0	1	7	4.8	70	22	1,000	25	0.0	0.0
U /	N/A	5.0	9.77	10	5	11	0	81	3	4	0.0	N/A	2	10,000	25	0.0	0.0
B /8.1	2.1	N/A	15.54	109	0	0	0	0	100	0	0.0	81	N/A	250	50	2.8	0.0
B /8.2	2.1	N/A	13.93	2	0	0	0	0	100	0	0.0	67	N/A	250	50	0.0	0.0
B /8.2	2.1	N/A	14.16	50	0	0	0	0	100	0	0.0	73	N/A	250	50	0.0	0.0
B+ /8.4	1.9	N/A	16.23	81	0	0	0	0	100	0	0.0	82	N/A	250	50	0.0	0.0
B /8.1	2.1	N/A	15.22	5	0	0	0	0	100	0	0.0	78	N/A	250	50	0.0	0.0
B /8.2	2.1	N/A	15.81	4	0	0	0	0	100	0	0.0	83	N/A	250	50	0.0	0.0
D /1.7	5.0	N/A	28.44	6	0	0	0	0	100	7	0.0	57	N/A	250	50	2.8	0.0
D /1.7	5.1	N/A	24.93	N/A	0	0	0	0	100	7	0.0	20	N/A	250	50	0.0	0.0
D /1.7	5.0	N/A	25.10	2	0	0	0	0	100	7	0.0	28	N/A	250	50	0.0	0.0
D /1.7	5.0	N/A	26.39	N/A	0	0	0	0	100	7	0.0	37	N/A	250	50	0.0	0.0
C+ /6.7	2.8	N/A	18.33	5	0	0	0	0	100	320	0.0	65	N/A	250	50	2.8	0.0
C+ /6.5	2.8	N/A	16.17	N/A	0	0	0	0	100	320	0.0	26	N/A	250	50	0.0	0.0
C+ /6.7	2.8	N/A	16.53	2	0	0	0	0	100	320	0.0	36	N/A	250	50	0.0	0.0
C+ /6.5	2.8	N/A	16.50	N/A	0	0	0	0	100	320	0.0	52	N/A	250	50	0.0	0.0
B+ /8.5	1.8	N/A	15.33	1	0	0	0	0	100	121	0.0	82	N/A	250	50	2.8	0.0
B+ /8.5	1.8	N/A	14.12	N/A	0	0	0	0	100	121	0.0	71	N/A	250	50	0.0	0.0
B+ /8.5	1.8	N/A	14.06	1	0	0	0	0	100	121	0.0	76	N/A	250	50	0.0	0.0
B- /7.5	2.6	N/A	14.94	N/A	0	0	0	0	100	121	0.0	82	N/A	250	50	0.0	0.0
E /0.3	8.6	15.6	8.63	73	0	20	2	72	6	160	0.0	3	6	250,000	1,000	0.0	0.0
U /	N/A	1.8	10.01	N/A	0	0	0	0	100	59	0.0	N/A	2	250,000	1,000	0.0	0.0
U /	N/A	1.8	10.01	15	0	0	0	0	100	59	0.0	N/A	2	5,000,000	0	0.0	0.0
C /5.2	3.1	5.2	9.86	61	2	12	0	57	29	72	0.0	35	13	250,000	1,000	0.0	0.0
A+ /9.9	N/A	N/A	1.00	11,475	100	0	0	0	0	0	0.2	44	13	0	0	0.0	0.0
A+ /9.9	N/A	N/A	1.00	4,159	100	0	0	0	0	0	0.1	42	13	0	0	0.0	0.0
A+ /9.9	N/A	N/A	1.00	2,820	100	0	0	0	0	0	0.1	40	N/A	0	0	0.0	0.0
A+ /9.9	N/A	N/A	1.00	518	100	0	0	0	0	0	0.2	45	N/A	25,000	500	0.0	0.0

Fund Type	Fund Name	Ticker Symbol	Overall Investment Rating	Phone	Perfor-mance Rating/Pts	3 Mo	6 Mo	1Yr / Pct	3Yr / Pct	5Yr / Pct	Dividend Yield	Expense Ratio
MMF	Schwab CA Muni Money Sweep	SWCXX	D+	(800) 407-0256	E+ / 0.8	0.02	0.05	0.06 /22	0.03 /10	0.03 /12	0.06	N/A
MMF	Schwab CA Muni Money Val Adv	SWKXX	C-	(800) 407-0256	D- / 1.2	0.06	0.14	0.16 /28	0.07 /14	0.05 /14	0.16	N/A
MUS	Schwab California Tax-Free Bond Fd	SWCAX	C+	(800) 407-0256	C+ / 6.2	2.35	-3.00	-0.73 / 7	2.64 /76	2.65 /74	2.32	0.60
MMT	Schwab Cash Reserves	SWSXX	C-	(800) 407-0256	D- / 1.1	0.09	0.14	0.17 /25	0.10 /13	0.08 /14	0.17	N/A
USA	Schwab GNMA	SWGSX	C+	(800) 407-0256	C- / 3.6	0.21	-1.29	-0.20 /15	2.02 /44	1.51 /35	2.32	0.63
MMT	Schwab Government Money	SNVXX	U	(800) 407-0256	U /	0.04	0.06	0.08 /22	--	--	0.08	N/A
GL	Schwab Intermediate-Term Bond	SWIIX	C+	(800) 407-0256	C- / 3.5	0.63	-1.44	0.64 /36	1.78 /39	1.62 /36	1.87	0.64
MMT	Schwab Investor Money	SWRXX	C-	(800) 407-0256	D- / 1.0	0.11	0.18	0.20 /26	0.07 /11	0.05 /12	0.20	N/A
MMF	Schwab MA Muni Money Sweep	SWDXX	U	(800) 407-0256	U /	--	--	--	--	--	0.04	N/A
MMT	Schwab Money Market	SWMXX	D+	(800) 407-0256	E+ / 0.7	0.06	0.08	0.09 /22	0.04 / 9	0.03 / 9	0.09	N/A
MMF	Schwab Muni Money Premier	SWOXX	C	(800) 407-0256	D- / 1.5	0.12	0.25	0.35 /34	0.13 /16	0.09 /17	0.35	N/A
MMF	Schwab Muni Money Sel	SWLXX	C-	(800) 407-0256	D- / 1.4	0.09	0.20	0.25 /31	0.10 /15	0.07 /16	0.25	N/A
MMF	Schwab Muni Money Sweep	SWXXX	C-	(800) 407-0256	E+ / 0.9	0.03	0.08	0.08 /23	0.04 /11	0.03 /12	0.08	N/A
MMF	Schwab Muni Money Val Adv	SWTXX	C-	(800) 407-0256	D- / 1.2	0.07	0.15	0.17 /28	0.07 /14	0.05 /14	0.17	N/A
MMF	Schwab NJ Municipal Money Sweep	SWJXX	U	(800) 407-0256	U /	--	--	--	--	--	0.02	N/A
MMF	Schwab NY Muni Money Swep	SWNXX	D+	(800) 407-0256	E+ / 0.7	0.02	0.04	0.05 /22	0.03 /10	0.03 /12	0.05	N/A
MMF	Schwab NY Muni Money Val Adv	SWYXX	C-	(800) 407-0256	D- / 1.2	0.07	0.14	0.16 /28	0.07 /14	0.05 /14	0.16	N/A
MMF	Schwab PA Muni Money Fund Sweep	SWEXX	D+	(800) 407-0256	E+ / 0.8	0.03	0.05	0.05 /22	0.03 /10	0.02 / 9	0.05	N/A
MMT	Schwab Retirement Advantage	SWIXX	C-	(800) 407-0256	D- / 1.2	0.13	0.21	0.30 /29	0.11 /14	0.07 /13	0.30	N/A
USS ●	Schwab Short-Term Bond Market	SWBDX	C	(800) 407-0256	D+ / 2.5	0.54	-0.56	0.67 /36	0.96 /27	0.96 /27	1.21	0.62
*MUN	Schwab Tax-Free Bond Fund	SWNTX	B-	(800) 407-0256	C+ / 6.1	2.20	-2.64	-0.47 /10	2.53 /74	2.41 /69	2.24	0.57
*USL ●	Schwab Total Bond Market Fd	SWLBX	C-	(800) 407-0256	C / 4.3	1.00	-2.38	1.07 /40	2.39 /50	1.95 /41	2.26	0.54
GEI	Schwab Trs Inflation Prot Sec Index	SWRSX	E+	(800) 407-0256	C- / 4.0	1.20	-0.70	3.10 /57	1.68 /38	0.54 /22	1.78	0.05
MMT●	Schwab Trs Oblig Mny Val Adv	SNOXX	D+	(800) 407-0256	E+ / 0.7	0.05	0.08	0.10 /22	0.03 / 9	--	0.10	N/A
MMT	Schwab Value Adv Money Investor	SWVXX	C-	(800) 407-0256	D- / 1.3	0.13	0.23	0.32 /30	0.12 /14	0.08 /14	0.32	N/A
MMT	Schwab Value Adv Money Prem	SWAXX	C	(800) 407-0256	D- / 1.5	0.18	0.31	0.49 /33	0.20 /17	0.13 /16	0.49	N/A
MMT	Schwab Value Adv Money Select	SWBXX	C	(800) 407-0256	D- / 1.4	0.16	0.28	0.42 /32	0.16 /15	0.10 /15	0.42	N/A
MMT	Schwab Value Adv Money Ultra	SNAXX	C	(800) 407-0256	D- / 1.5	0.18	0.33	0.52 /34	0.22 /17	0.16 /17	0.52	N/A
GEI	Scout Core Bond Fund Institutional	SCCIX	C	(800) 996-2862	C- / 3.2	0.67	-2.28	0.76 /37	1.64 /37	1.98 /42	1.63	0.72
COI	Scout Core Bond Fund Y	SCCYX	D+	(800) 996-2862	D+ / 2.6	0.57	-2.47	0.41 /31	1.26 /31	1.63 /37	1.27	0.89
GEI	Scout Core Plus Bond Fund Inst	SCPZX	C+	(800) 996-2862	C- / 4.0	0.89	-1.88	2.86 /56	1.85 /40	2.62 /51	1.72	0.65
COI	Scout Core Plus Bond Fund Y	SCPYX	C-	(800) 996-2862	C- / 3.4	0.79	-2.07	2.47 /53	1.47 /35	2.25 /45	1.37	0.89
COI	Scout Low Duration Bond	SCLDX	B-	(800) 996-2862	C- / 3.0	0.39	0.20	1.95 /48	1.11 /29	--	1.33	1.03
GEL	Scout Unconstrained Bond Inst	SUBFX	D-	(800) 996-2862	C- / 3.5	0.69	0.31	6.72 /72	0.75 /24	3.74 /69	1.25	0.82
GEN	Scout Unconstrained Bond Y	SUBYX	E+	(800) 996-2862	C- / 3.1	0.60	0.24	6.48 /72	0.47 /21	--	0.43	1.11
MUH	SEI Asset Alloc-Def Strat All F	STDAX	C+	(800) 342-5734	A+ / 9.9	6.34	4.85	19.17 /99	8.26 /99	10.32 /99	3.90	1.34
COI	SEI Catholic Values Fixed Income F	CFVAX	U	(800) 342-5734	U /	1.33	-1.60	3.22 /58	--	--	2.35	1.10
COI	SEI Catholic Values Fixed Income Y	CFVYX	U	(800) 342-5734	U /	1.35	-1.65	3.32 /58	--	--	2.45	0.85
USA	SEI Daily Inc Tr-GNMA Bond F	SEGMX	B	(800) 342-5734	C / 4.4	0.36	-1.21	0.18 /25	2.51 /52	1.95 /41	2.03	0.69
USA	SEI Daily Inc Tr-GNMA Bond Y	SGMYX	U	(800) 342-5734	U /	0.40	-1.32	0.27 /28	--	--	2.24	0.45
MMT	SEI Daily Inc Tr-Government CAA	GFAXX	U	(800) 342-5734	U /	0.08	0.13	0.21 /26	--	--	0.21	N/A
MMT	SEI Daily Inc Tr-Government F	SEOXX	C-	(800) 342-5734	D- / 1.1	0.08	0.13	0.21 /26	0.09 /13	0.06 /13	0.21	N/A
*USS	SEI Daily Inc Tr-Sh Dur Gov Bd F	TCSGX	C	(800) 342-5734	D / 2.0	0.10	-0.42	0.37 /30	0.62 /22	0.58 /22	1.14	0.69
USS	SEI Daily Inc Tr-Sh Dur Gov Bd Y	SDGFX	U	(800) 342-5734	U /	-0.19	-0.95	-0.76 / 6	--	--	0.00	0.44
GES	SEI Daily Inc Tr-Ultra Sh Dur Bd F	SECPX	B-	(800) 342-5734	D+ / 2.6	0.42	0.59	1.56 /45	0.81 /25	1.04 /28	1.12	0.69
GEI	SEI Daily Inc Tr-Ultra Sh Dur Bd Y	SECYX	U	(800) 342-5734	U /	0.44	0.52	1.65 /46	--	--	1.20	0.44
*EM	SEI Inst Intl Emerging Mkts Debt F	SITEX	E+	(800) 342-5734	C / 4.9	6.25	-0.15	12.88 /85	0.67 /23	0.61 /23	1.51	1.61
EM	SEI Inst Intl Emerging Mkts Debt Y	SIEDX	U	(800) 342-5734	U /	6.40	0.02	13.27 /86	--	--	1.77	1.36
GL	SEI Inst Intl International Fx In F	SEFIX	C	(800) 342-5734	C+ / 5.9	0.48	-2.19	2.48 /53	3.62 /70	3.44 /64	1.69	1.07
GL	SEI Inst Intl International Fx In Y	SIFIX	U	(800) 342-5734	U /	0.65	-2.03	2.76 /55	--	--	1.97	0.82
*COI	SEI Inst Inv Core Fixed Income A	SCOAX	B+	(800) 342-5734	C+ / 6.0	1.29	-1.63	2.68 /54	3.22 /65	3.18 /60	2.63	0.37
*COH	SEI Inst Inv High Yield Bond A	SGYAX	B-	(800) 342-5734	A+ / 9.8	5.43	6.25	22.75 /98	5.02 /85	7.29 /97	6.34	0.56

● Denotes fund is closed to new investors
* Denotes fund is included in Section II

www.thestreetratings.com

RISK			NET ASSETS		ASSET							FUND MANAGER		MINIMUM		LOADS	
Risk Rating/Pts	3 Yr Avg Standard Deviation	Avg Dura-tion	NAV As of 2/28/17	Total $(Mil)	Cash %	Gov. Bond %	Muni. Bond %	Corp. Bond %	Other %	Portfolio Turnover Ratio	Avg Coupon Rate	Manager Quality Pct	Manager Tenure (Years)	Initial Purch. $	Additional Purch. $	Front End Load	Back End Load
A+ / 9.9	N/A	N/A	1.00	5,971	100	0	0	0	0	0	0.1	40	N/A	0	0	0.0	0.0
A+ / 9.9	N/A	N/A	1.00	812	100	0	0	0	0	0	0.2	44	N/A	25,000	500	0.0	0.0
C / 4.6	3.3	5.0	11.70	426	0	0	99	0	1	38	0.0	15	9	100	0	0.0	0.0
A+ / 9.9	N/A	N/A	1.00	39,750	100	0	0	0	0	0	0.2	N/A	N/A	0	0	0.0	0.0
B+ / 8.3	1.9	4.0	9.96	307	0	10	0	0	90	363	0.0	74	14	100	0	0.0	0.0
U /	N/A	N/A	1.00	989	100	0	0	0	0	0	0.1	N/A	N/A	25,000	500	0.0	0.0
B / 8.1	2.1	3.7	10.04	326	0	40	0	18	42	199	0.0	86	10	100	0	0.0	0.0
A+ / 9.9	N/A	N/A	1.00	614	100	0	0	0	0	0	0.2	44	N/A	1	1	0.0	0.0
U /	N/A	N/A	1.00	464	100	0	0	0	0	0	0.0	40	N/A	0	0	0.0	0.0
A+ / 9.9	N/A	N/A	1.00	8,870	100	0	0	0	0	0	0.1	40	9	0	0	0.0	0.0
A+ / 9.9	0.1	N/A	1.00	2,324	100	0	0	0	0	0	0.4	49	N/A	3,000,000	1	0.0	0.0
A+ / 9.9	N/A	N/A	1.00	545	100	0	0	0	0	0	0.3	47	N/A	1,000,000	1	0.0	0.0
A+ / 9.9	N/A	N/A	1.00	9,414	100	0	0	0	0	0	0.1	42	N/A	0	0	0.0	0.0
A+ / 9.9	N/A	N/A	1.00	542	100	0	0	0	0	0	0.2	45	N/A	25,000	500	0.0	0.0
U /	N/A	N/A	1.00	612	100	0	0	0	0	0	0.0	N/A	N/A	0	0	0.0	0.0
A+ / 9.9	N/A	N/A	1.00	1,511	100	0	0	0	0	0	0.1	41	N/A	0	0	0.0	0.0
A+ / 9.9	N/A	N/A	1.00	227	100	0	0	0	0	0	0.2	45	N/A	25,000	500	0.0	0.0
A+ / 9.9	N/A	N/A	1.00	394	100	0	0	0	0	0	0.1	41	N/A	0	0	0.0	0.0
A+ / 9.9	0.1	N/A	1.00	236	100	0	0	0	0	0	0.3	N/A	19	25,000	1	0.0	0.0
A- / 9.0	1.3	2.8	9.26	440	0	71	0	27	2	65	0.0	51	13	100	0	0.0	0.0
C+ / 5.6	3.0	4.8	11.57	651	1	0	98	0	1	54	0.0	19	9	100	0	0.0	0.0
C+ / 5.7	3.0	5.4	9.44	1,244	0	42	1	24	33	92	0.0	70	19	100	0	0.0	0.0
D+ / 2.8	4.0	7.8	11.11	333	0	100	0	0	0	24	0.0	8	11	0	0	0.0	0.0
A+ / 9.9	N/A	N/A	1.00	818	100	0	0	0	0	0	0.1	41	N/A	25,000	500	0.0	0.0
A+ / 9.9	0.1	N/A	1.00	8,038	100	0	0	0	0	0	0.3	47	25	25,000	500	0.0	0.0
A+ / 9.9	0.1	N/A	1.00	1,782	100	0	0	0	0	0	0.5	51	25	3,000,000	1	0.0	0.0
A+ / 9.9	0.1	N/A	1.00	2,097	100	0	0	0	0	0	0.4	50	25	1,000,000	1	0.0	0.0
A+ / 9.9	0.1	N/A	1.00	2,448	100	0	0	0	0	0	0.5	52	25	10,000,000	1	0.0	0.0
B / 7.7	2.4	3.4	11.28	193	5	49	0	21	25	453	3.7	29	16	100,000	100	0.0	0.0
B / 7.7	2.4	3.4	11.28	3	5	49	0	21	25	453	3.7	22	16	1,000	100	0.0	0.0
B- / 7.4	2.6	3.3	31.39	795	0	52	0	16	32	480	2.3	45	21	100,000	100	0.0	0.0
B- / 7.4	2.6	3.3	31.38	54	0	52	0	16	32	480	2.3	22	21	1,000	100	0.0	0.0
A+ / 9.6	0.8	1.5	10.04	49	4	7	0	37	52	94	3.1	64	5	1,000	100	0.0	0.0
C- / 3.9	3.6	-0.2	11.73	1,470	30	5	0	54	11	615	2.8	76	6	100,000	100	0.0	0.0
C- / 3.9	3.5	-0.2	11.79	130	30	5	0	54	11	615	2.8	71	6	1,000	100	0.0	0.0
E+ / 0.6	6.9	N/A	14.64	8	2	2	0	31	65	29	0.0	98	14	100,000	1,000	0.0	0.0
U /	N/A	6.9	9.94	111	0	0	0	0	100	216	0.0	N/A	2	500	100	0.0	0.0
U /	N/A	6.9	9.94	1	0	0	0	0	100	216	0.0	N/A	2	500	100	0.0	0.0
B / 8.2	2.0	1.6	10.50	113	8	0	0	0	92	718	0.0	80	16	0	0	0.0	0.0
U /	N/A	1.6	10.49	N/A	8	0	0	0	92	718	0.0	N/A	16	100,000	1,000	0.0	0.0
U /	N/A	N/A	1.00	26	100	0	0	0	0	0	0.2	N/A	3	0	0	0.0	0.0
A+ / 9.9	N/A	N/A	1.00	7,775	100	0	0	0	0	0	0.2	45	3	0	0	0.0	0.0
A / 9.4	0.9	1.6	10.43	777	16	35	0	0	49	245	0.0	N/A	14	0	0	0.0	0.0
U /	N/A	1.6	10.43	49	16	35	0	0	49	245	0.0	N/A	14	0	0	0.0	0.0
A+ / 9.9	0.3	0.7	9.32	264	1	6	5	53	35	115	0.0	66	18	0	0	0.0	0.0
U /	N/A	0.7	9.32	45	1	6	5	53	35	115	0.0	N/A	18	100,000	1,000	0.0	0.5
E- / 0.2	9.4	6.7	9.79	1,339	3	86	0	9	2	86	0.0	91	17	100,000	1,000	0.0	1.0
U /	N/A	6.7	9.82	97	3	86	0	9	2	86	0.0	N/A	17	100,000	1,000	0.0	1.0
C / 4.9	2.9	8.7	10.03	444	0	71	1	23	5	106	0.0	94	9	100,000	1,000	0.0	1.0
U /	N/A	8.7	10.01	26	0	71	1	23	5	106	0.0	N/A	9	100,000	1,000	0.0	0.0
C+ / 6.5	2.8	7.0	10.22	5,630	0	30	0	28	42	364	0.0	70	3	100,000	1,000	0.0	0.0
D- / 1.1	5.7	4.8	9.12	2,885	5	0	0	79	16	50	0.0	68	8	100,000	1,000	0.0	0.0

Fund Type	Fund Name	Ticker Symbol	Overall Investment Rating	Phone	Performance Rating/Pts	3 Mo	6 Mo	1Yr / Pct	3Yr / Pct	5Yr / Pct	Dividend Yield	Expense Ratio
COI	SEI Inst Inv Intermediate Dur Cr A	SIDCX	U	(800) 342-5734	U /	1.83	-1.90	4.85 /66	--	--	2.73	0.32
COI	SEI Inst Inv Limited Duration Bd A	SLDBX	U	(800) 342-5734	U /	0.41	0.16	1.37 /43	--	--	1.42	0.32
*GEI	SEI Inst Inv Long Dur Credit A	SLDAX	C-	(800) 342-5734	A- /9.1	3.10	-5.18	7.97 /74	6.15 /93	--	3.95	0.37
*COI	SEI Inst Inv Long Duration A	LDRAX	C-	(800) 342-5734	A- /9.0	3.30	-5.95	7.02 /73	6.26 /93	4.91 /83	4.03	0.37
GEI	SEI Inst Inv Tr Real Return Plus Fd	RRPAX	C-	(800) 342-5734	D+ /2.6	0.93	1.12	2.71 /55	0.52 /21	0.27 /19	1.22	0.29
*GEI	SEI Inst Inv Ultra Short Dur Bd A	SUSAX	B	(800) 342-5734	C- /3.2	0.49	0.76	1.99 /49	1.14 /30	1.33 /32	1.47	0.22
USA	SEI Inst Mgd Tr SIMT Consv Income	COIAX	U	(800) 342-5734	U /	0.18	0.29	--	--	--	0.00	N/A
MUN	SEI Inst Mgd Tr SIMT Tax Fr Consv F	TFCAX	U	(800) 342-5734	U /	0.11	0.23	--	--	--	0.00	N/A
MUN	SEI Inst Mgd Tr SIMT Tax Fr Consv Y	TFCYX	U	(800) 342-5734	U /	0.13	0.26	--	--	--	0.00	N/A
USA	SEI Inst Mgd Tr-SIMT Consv Income	COIYX	U	(800) 342-5734	U /	0.20	0.34	--	--	--	0.00	N/A
*EM	SEI Insti Inv Tr Emer Mrk Dbt Fd A	SEDAX	D-	(800) 342-5734	C+ /6.8	6.52	0.18	13.88 /87	1.68 /38	1.56 /35	3.44	0.95
GEI	SEI Institutional Mgd Real Return F	SRAAX	D+	(800) 342-5734	D /1.8	0.79	0.89	2.21 /51	0.13 /14	-0.11 / 4	0.00	0.80
GEI	SEI Institutional Mgd Real Return Y	SRYRX	U	(800) 342-5734	U /	0.79	0.99	2.31 /52	--	--	0.00	0.55
*COI	SEI Instl Managed Tr-Core Fix Inc F	TRLVX	C+	(800) 342-5734	C /5.4	1.42	-1.58	2.92 /56	2.97 /61	3.10 /59	2.34	0.86
COI	SEI Instl Managed Tr-Core Fix Inc I	SCXIX	C+	(800) 342-5734	C /5.0	1.37	-1.69	2.60 /54	2.74 /57	2.86 /56	2.12	1.11
COI	SEI Instl Managed Tr-Core Fix Inc Y	SCFYX	U	(800) 342-5734	U /	1.49	-1.46	3.17 /58	--	--	2.59	0.63
*GEI	SEI Instl Managed Tr-High Yld Bd F	SHYAX	C+	(800) 342-5734	A+ /9.7	5.26	6.31	22.81 /98	4.52 /81	6.60 /95	5.61	1.08
GEI	SEI Instl Managed Tr-High Yld Bd I	SEIYX	B-	(800) 342-5734	A /9.5	5.35	6.31	22.38 /98	3.87 /74	6.01 /92	5.35	1.32
COH	SEI Instl Managed Tr-High Yld Bd Y	SIYYX	U	(800) 342-5734	U /	5.33	6.44	23.12 /98	--	--	5.85	0.83
GEI	SEI Instl Mgd Tr-Enhanced Inc F	SEEAX	A-	(800) 342-5734	C /4.6	1.23	2.16	5.36 /68	1.69 /38	2.29 /46	2.24	1.05
GEI	SEI Instl Mgd Tr-Enhanced Inc I	SEIIX	B+	(800) 342-5734	C- /4.1	1.27	2.14	5.08 /67	1.42 /34	2.02 /42	1.96	1.26
GL	SEI Instl Mgd Tr-Enhanced Inc Y	SNHYX	U	(800) 342-5734	U /	1.41	2.37	5.52 /69	--	--	2.38	0.77
MUS	SEI Tax-Exempt Tr-CA Muni Bond F	SBDAX	D	(800) 342-5734	C /4.9	2.50	-2.88	-1.37 / 2	2.07 /64	1.98 /59	1.83	0.81
MUN	SEI Tax-Exempt Tr-CA Muni Bond Y	SCYYX	U	(800) 342-5734	U /	2.54	-2.90	-1.22 / 3	--	--	1.99	0.56
*MUN	SEI Tax-Exempt Tr-Intrm Term Muni	SEIMX	C	(800) 342-5734	C+ /5.7	2.24	-2.90	-0.41 /11	2.50 /73	2.27 /66	2.46	0.81
MUN	SEI Tax-Exempt Tr-Intrm Term Muni	SINYX	U	(800) 342-5734	U /	2.30	-2.70	-0.16 /15	--	--	2.72	0.56
MUS	SEI Tax-Exempt Tr-MA Muni Bond F	SMAAX	D-	(800) 342-5734	C /4.5	2.35	-3.20	-1.62 / 1	1.96 /61	1.65 /50	1.78	0.81
MUN	SEI Tax-Exempt Tr-MA Muni Bond Y	SMSYX	U	(800) 342-5734	U /	2.40	-3.13	-1.45 / 2	--	--	2.05	0.56
MUI	SEI Tax-Exempt Tr-NJ Muni Bond F	SENJX	C-	(800) 342-5734	C- /3.9	1.67	-2.59	-0.54 / 9	1.52 /49	1.45 /45	2.11	0.82
MUN	SEI Tax-Exempt Tr-NJ Muni Bond Y	SNJYX	U	(800) 342-5734	U /	1.71	-2.52	-0.30 /13	--	--	2.27	0.57
MUI	SEI Tax-Exempt Tr-NY Muni Bond F	SENYX	C-	(800) 342-5734	C /5.0	2.42	-2.45	-0.72 / 7	2.00 /62	1.65 /50	1.71	0.82
MUN	SEI Tax-Exempt Tr-NY Muni Bond Y	SNYYX	U	(800) 342-5734	U /	2.37	-2.38	-0.58 / 9	--	--	1.96	0.57
MUS	SEI Tax-Exempt Tr-PA Muni Bond F	SEPAX	D+	(800) 342-5734	C /4.4	2.20	-2.67	-1.01 / 4	1.78 /57	1.58 /48	1.91	0.80
MUN	SEI Tax-Exempt Tr-PA Muni Bond Y	SPAYX	U	(800) 342-5734	U /	2.24	-2.60	-0.95 / 5	--	--	2.06	0.55
*MUN	SEI Tax-Exempt Tr-Shrt Dur Muni F	SUMAX	C	(800) 342-5734	D /1.7	0.54	-0.16	0.05 /21	0.24 /20	0.39 /23	0.45	0.82
MUN	SEI Tax-Exempt Tr-Shrt Dur Muni Y	SHYMX	U	(800) 342-5734	U /	0.60	-0.03	0.30 /32	--	--	0.70	0.57
*MUN	SEI Tax-Exempt Tr-Tax Advtg Inc F	SEATX	A	(800) 342-5734	A+ /9.8	3.58	-2.31	3.93 /70	5.55 /98	5.30 /98	4.02	1.08
MUN	SEI Tax-Exempt Tr-Tax Advtg Inc Y	STAYX	U	(800) 342-5734	U /	3.64	-2.19	4.19 /71	--	--	4.28	0.83
*GEI	SEI US Fixed Income F	SUFAX	C	(800) 342-5734	C /4.3	1.05	-2.17	1.52 /45	2.47 /51	2.33 /47	1.83	0.86
GEI	SEI US Fixed Income Y	SUSWX	U	(800) 342-5734	U /	1.01	-2.05	1.67 /46	--	--	2.08	0.61
GEL	Semper MBS Total Return A	SEMOX	U	(888) 263-6443	U /	0.76	2.19	5.11 /67	--	--	4.80	1.01
GEN	Semper MBS Total Return Fund Inst	SEMMX	A+	(888) 263-6443	B /8.2	0.78	2.25	5.29 /68	4.81 /84	--	5.07	0.76
GEN	Semper MBS Total Return Fund Inv	SEMPX	A+	(888) 263-6443	B /7.9	0.76	2.17	5.08 /67	4.55 /81	--	4.87	1.01
GES	Semper Short Duration Inst	SEMIX	A	(888) 263-6443	C /4.5	0.79	1.59	3.05 /57	1.88 /41	1.91 /41	3.22	1.15
GES	Semper Short Duration Inv	SEMRX	B+	(888) 263-6443	C- /3.5	0.73	1.46	2.78 /55	1.19 /31	0.90 /26	2.96	1.36
USS	Sentinel Government Securities A	SEGSX	D	(800) 282-3863	D- /1.4	0.31	-1.89	-0.80 / 6	1.23 /31	0.50 /21	2.53	0.96
USS	Sentinel Government Securities C	SCGGX	D-	(800) 282-3863	E /0.5	0.10	-2.27	-1.70 / 1	0.42 /20	-0.30 / 4	1.76	1.74
USS	Sentinel Government Securities I	SIBWX	C-	(800) 282-3863	D+ /2.7	0.35	-1.79	-0.61 / 8	1.44 /34	0.73 /24	2.78	0.73
USS	Sentinel Low Duration Bond A	SSIGX	D+	(800) 282-3863	D /1.6	0.58	-0.63	2.61 /54	0.28 /18	0.19 /18	1.62	0.95
USS	Sentinel Low Duration Bond I	SSBDX	C	(800) 282-3863	D+ /2.5	0.68	-0.35	3.03 /57	0.63 /22	--	1.93	0.61
USS	Sentinel Low Duration Bond S	SSSGX	D+	(800) 282-3863	D /1.8	0.56	-0.57	2.59 /54	0.17 /16	0.03 / 9	1.49	1.07
GL	Sentinel Total Return Bond A	SATRX	D-	(800) 282-3863	D /2.1	1.40	-1.18	3.22 /58	0.97 /27	2.81 /55	2.16	0.97

● Denotes fund is closed to new investors
* Denotes fund is included in Section II

www.thestreetratings.com

RISK			NET ASSETS		ASSET					Portfolio Turnover Ratio	Avg Coupon Rate	FUND MANAGER		MINIMUM		LOADS	
Risk Rating/Pts	3 Yr Avg Standard Deviation	Avg Dura-tion	NAV As of 2/28/17	Total $(Mil)	Cash %	Gov. Bond %	Muni. Bond %	Corp. Bond %	Other %			Manager Quality Pct	Manager Tenure (Years)	Initial Purch. $	Additional Purch. $	Front End Load	Back End Load
U /	N/A	1.8	9.91	1,542	0	5	3	89	3	122	0.0	N/A	2	100,000	1,000	0.0	0.0
U /	N/A	7.4	9.96	1,296	0	33	4	35	28	134	0.0	N/A	3	100,000	1,000	0.0	0.0
E /0.4	7.6	14.5	10.11	3,225	0	2	8	88	2	74	0.0	39	5	100,000	1,000	0.0	0.0
E /0.3	8.2	14.5	8.30	2,297	4	22	5	65	4	72	0.0	13	13	100,000	1,000	0.0	0.0
B /8.2	2.0	3.1	9.69	158	0	99	0	0	1	80	0.0	22	8	100,000	1,000	0.0	0.0
A+ /9.9	0.3	1.2	10.00	526	48	0	1	28	23	103	0.0	74	6	100,000	1,000	0.0	0.0
U /	N/A	0.2	10.00	201	0	0	0	0	100	0	0.0	N/A	1	100,000	1,000	0.0	0.0
U /	N/A	0.6	10.00	150	0	0	0	0	100	0	0.0	N/A	1	100,000	1,000	0.0	0.0
U /	N/A	0.6	10.00	4	0	0	0	0	100	0	0.0	N/A	1	100,000	1,000	0.0	0.0
U /	N/A	0.2	10.00	19	0	0	0	0	100	0	0.0	N/A	1	100,000	1,000	0.0	0.0
E- /0.2	9.2	6.7	9.73	2,027	3	86	0	9	2	77	0.0	94	11	100,000	1,000	0.0	0.0
B+ /8.3	2.0	3.1	10.16	265	0	99	0	0	1	38	0.0	14	4	100,000	1,000	0.0	0.3
U /	N/A	3.1	10.19	19	0	99	0	0	1	38	0.0	N/A	4	100,000	1,000	0.0	0.3
C+ /6.1	2.9	5.2	11.18	1,879	3	31	0	26	40	336	0.0	61	12	100,000	1,000	0.0	0.6
C+ /6.3	2.9	5.2	11.17	9	3	31	0	26	40	336	0.0	55	12	100,000	1,000	0.0	0.6
U /	N/A	5.2	11.18	132	3	31	0	26	40	336	0.0	N/A	12	100,000	1,000	0.0	0.6
E+ /0.9	5.9	2.6	7.29	1,471	2	4	0	73	21	56	0.0	93	13	100,000	1,000	0.0	1.0
D- /1.4	5.8	2.6	7.03	13	2	4	0	73	21	56	0.0	91	13	100,000	1,000	0.0	1.0
U /	N/A	2.6	7.29	177	2	4	0	73	21	56	0.0	N/A	13	100,000	1,000	0.0	1.0
A- /9.0	1.2	1.0	7.54	75	2	2	0	39	57	90	0.0	81	11	100,000	1,000	0.0	0.8
A- /9.0	1.2	1.0	7.53	N/A	2	2	0	39	57	90	0.0	78	11	100,000	1,000	0.0	0.8
U /	N/A	1.0	7.54	7	2	2	0	39	57	90	0.0	N/A	11	100,000	1,000	0.0	0.8
C- /4.2	3.4	5.1	10.67	309	0	0	99	0	1	13	0.0	6	18	100,000	1,000	0.0	0.0
U /	N/A	5.1	10.66	19	0	0	99	0	1	13	0.0	N/A	18	100,000	1,000	0.0	0.0
C /4.9	3.2	5.6	11.52	1,759	0	0	99	0	1	15	0.0	14	18	100,000	1,000	0.0	0.5
U /	N/A	5.6	11.53	67	0	0	99	0	1	15	0.0	N/A	18	100,000	1,000	0.0	0.5
C- /3.8	3.6	5.5	10.48	71	0	0	99	0	1	9	0.0	4	18	100,000	1,000	0.0	0.0
U /	N/A	5.5	10.47	N/A	0	0	99	0	1	9	0.0	N/A	18	100,000	1,000	0.0	0.0
C+ /6.7	2.8	4.5	10.29	116	0	5	94	0	1	8	0.0	7	18	100,000	1,000	0.0	0.0
U /	N/A	4.5	10.29	N/A	0	5	94	0	1	8	0.0	N/A	18	100,000	1,000	0.0	0.0
C /5.0	3.1	5.1	10.68	192	3	0	96	0	1	15	0.0	8	18	100,000	1,000	0.0	0.0
U /	N/A	5.1	10.66	N/A	3	0	96	0	1	15	0.0	N/A	18	100,000	1,000	0.0	0.0
C /5.4	3.0	5.2	10.60	148	0	0	0	0	100	19	0.0	7	18	100,000	1,000	0.0	0.0
U /	N/A	5.2	10.60	N/A	0	0	0	0	100	19	0.0	N/A	18	100,000	1,000	0.0	0.0
A+ /9.8	0.5	5.2	10.01	1,351	0	0	99	0	1	49	0.0	32	6	100,000	1,000	0.0	0.0
U /	N/A	5.2	10.01	29	0	0	99	0	1	49	0.0	N/A	6	100,000	1,000	0.0	0.0
C- /3.5	3.8	6.6	10.24	1,061	0	6	71	8	15	24	0.0	83	10	100,000	1,000	0.0	0.0
U /	N/A	6.6	10.23	50	0	6	71	8	15	24	0.0	N/A	10	100,000	1,000	0.0	0.0
C+ /6.4	2.8	6.9	10.11	1,549	17	30	0	20	33	401	0.0	37	3	100,000	1,000	0.0	0.6
U /	N/A	6.9	10.10	154	17	30	0	20	33	401	0.0	N/A	3	100,000	1,000	0.0	0.6
U /	N/A	N/A	10.59	9	0	0	0	0	100	166	0.0	N/A	4	1,000	100	2.0	0.0
B+ /8.8	1.5	N/A	10.60	628	0	0	0	0	100	166	0.0	96	4	1,000,000	1,000	0.0	0.0
B+ /8.8	1.5	N/A	10.59	83	0	0	0	0	100	166	0.0	96	4	2,500	1,000	0.0	0.0
A+ /9.6	0.7	N/A	9.87	43	23	0	9	1	67	56	0.0	84	7	1,000,000	1,000	0.0	0.0
A+ /9.6	0.7	N/A	9.86	2	23	0	9	1	67	56	0.0	79	7	2,500	1,000	0.0	0.0
B /8.2	2.1	2.7	9.71	142	0	3	0	0	97	150	4.0	46	5	1,000	50	2.3	0.0
B /8.2	2.0	2.7	9.72	19	0	3	0	0	97	150	4.0	16	5	1,000	50	0.0	0.0
B /8.2	2.1	2.7	9.71	24	0	3	0	0	97	150	4.0	57	5	1,000,000	0	0.0	0.0
B+ /8.6	1.7	2.4	8.44	90	5	9	0	46	40	27	3.5	42	5	1,000	50	1.0	0.0
B+ /8.6	1.7	2.4	8.46	22	5	9	0	46	40	27	3.5	59	5	1,000,000	0	0.0	0.0
B+ /8.6	1.8	2.4	8.46	217	5	9	0	46	40	27	3.5	34	5	1,000	50	0.0	0.0
C+ /6.0	2.9	4.3	10.33	66	6	11	0	41	42	441	4.3	82	7	1,000	50	2.3	0.0

					PERFORMANCE						Incl. in Returns	
						Total Return % through 2/28/17						
									Annualized		Dividend	Expense
Fund Type	Fund Name	Ticker Symbol	Overall Investment Rating	Phone	Perfor-mance Rating/Pts	3 Mo	6 Mo	1Yr / Pct	3Yr / Pct	5Yr / Pct	Yield	Ratio
GL	Sentinel Total Return Bond C	SCTRX	E+	(800) 282-3863	D / 1.8	1.19	-1.63	2.25 /51	0.17 /16	2.14 /44	1.36	1.78
GL	Sentinel Total Return Bond I	SITRX	D	(800) 282-3863	C- / 3.3	1.44	-1.11	3.36 /59	1.12 /29	2.98 /58	2.35	0.77
GL	Sentinel Total Return Bond R3	SBRRX	U	(800) 282-3863	U /	1.50	-1.18	3.22 /58	--	--	2.21	3.40
GL	Sentinel Total Return Bond R6	STRRX	U	(800) 282-3863	U /	1.55	-1.08	3.41 /59	--	--	2.40	2.90
GEI	Sextant Bond Income Fund	SBIFX	D-	(800) 728-8762	C / 5.5	1.55	-3.11	2.91 /56	3.01 /61	2.52 /50	2.93	1.03
GEI	Sextant Short-Term Bond Fund	STBFX	C+	(800) 728-8762	D+ / 2.7	0.52	-0.04	1.49 /44	0.96 /27	0.86 /26	1.09	1.21
LP ●	Shenkman Floating Rate Hi Inc Inst	SFHIX	U	(855) 743-6562	U /	2.06	3.74	10.79 /81	--	--	4.10	0.83
COH	Shenkman Short Duration Hi Inc A	SCFAX	C	(855) 743-6562	C- / 3.9	1.53	1.79	5.55 /69	2.16 /46	--	2.57	1.74
COH	Shenkman Short Duration Hi Inc C	SCFCX	C+	(855) 743-6562	C- / 3.9	1.34	1.42	4.79 /66	1.44 /34	--	1.92	2.50
COH	Shenkman Short Duration Hi Inc F	SCFFX	B+	(855) 743-6562	C / 5.5	1.50	1.82	5.72 /69	2.40 /50	--	2.90	1.56
COH	Shenkman Short Duration Hi Inc Inst	SCFIX	A-	(855) 743-6562	C+ / 5.8	1.63	1.97	5.81 /70	2.53 /52	--	3.00	1.61
USS	Sht-Tm US Government Bond Direct	STUSX	D	(800) 955-9988	E / 0.5	0.10	-0.28	-0.07 /17	-0.02 / 5	-0.08 / 4	0.29	0.95
USS	Sht-Tm US Government Bond K	STUKX	D	(800) 955-9988	E / 0.3	0.00	-0.45	-0.55 / 9	-0.50 / 4	-0.57 / 3	0.00	1.45
GL	Sierra Strategic Income A	SSIZX	C+	(866) 738-4363	C / 5.1	2.33	0.55	6.98 /72	3.44 /68	3.81 /70	2.53	2.06
GL	Sierra Strategic Income C	SSICX	B+	(866) 738-4363	C+ / 6.5	2.19	0.27	6.39 /71	2.83 /58	3.19 /61	2.12	2.66
GL	Sierra Strategic Income I	SSIIX	A	(866) 738-4363	B- / 7.2	2.32	0.60	6.98 /72	3.44 /68	3.81 /70	2.68	2.06
GL	Sierra Strategic Income R	SSIRX	A	(866) 738-4363	B- / 7.5	2.43	0.74	7.31 /73	3.78 /73	4.14 /74	3.07	1.66
GL ●	Sierra Strategic Income Y	SSIYX	A	(866) 738-4363	B- / 7.5	2.39	0.74	7.23 /73	3.75 /72	4.14 /74	3.08	1.58
*MUS	Sit MN Tax Free Income	SMTFX	B+	(800) 332-5580	B / 7.7	2.00	-3.13	0.18 /28	3.55 /88	3.13 /82	3.13	0.82
MUN	Sit Tax Free Income Fund	SNTIX	A	(800) 332-5580	A / 9.4	2.43	-3.37	0.69 /40	5.01 /97	4.34 /96	3.59	0.89
*USS	Sit US Government Securities Fund	SNGVX	B-	(800) 332-5580	C- / 3.0	0.57	-0.54	0.16 /24	1.41 /33	0.88 /26	1.45	0.80
GEI	SMI Bond	SMIUX	U	(877) 764-3863	U /	0.84	-1.85	1.91 /48	--	--	2.01	4.48
GES	Spirit of America Income Fd A	SOAIX	C	(800) 452-4892	B- / 7.5	2.34	-2.12	4.93 /66	5.77 /90	4.85 /82	4.08	1.15
GEL	Spirit of America Income Fd C	SACTX	U	(800) 452-4892	U /	2.11	-2.25	--	--	--	0.00	N/A
MUH	Spirit of America Municipal TF Bd A	SOAMX	D	(800) 452-4892	C+ / 6.3	1.96	-3.28	0.55 /38	4.00 /93	2.53 /71	3.00	1.10
MUN	Spirit of America Municipal TF Bd C	SACFX	U	(800) 452-4892	U /	1.64	-3.61	--	--	--	0.00	N/A
GEI	SS Inst Income Inv	SSFIX	B-	(800) 843-2639	C+ / 5.6	1.38	-1.76	3.74 /61	2.82 /58	2.71 /53	2.38	0.23
GEI	SS Inst Income Svc	SSFSX	C+	(800) 843-2639	C / 5.2	1.30	-1.92	3.56 /60	2.59 /54	2.48 /49	2.13	0.48
COH	SSgA High Yield Bond A	SSHGX	U	(800) 843-2639	U /	3.90	4.41	14.83 /88	--	--	4.71	1.28
COH	SSgA High Yield Bond I	SSHJX	U	(800) 843-2639	U /	3.95	4.38	15.09 /89	--	--	5.24	1.03
COH	SSgA High Yield Bond K	SSHKX	U	(800) 843-2639	U /	4.00	4.62	15.31 /89	--	--	5.43	0.83
COH ●	SSgA High Yield Bond N	SSHYX	C	(800) 843-2639	B+ / 8.5	3.94	4.50	15.04 /89	3.27 /65	5.68 /90	5.20	1.08
GL	STAAR AltCat	SITAX	E	(800) 332-7738	D / 1.8	5.03	3.50	14.16 /87	-2.44 / 2	2.72 /53	0.00	2.56
GEI	STAAR Inv Trust General Bond Fund	SITGX	D-	(800) 332-7738	E / 0.5	-0.41	-1.03	0.70 /36	-0.06 / 5	0.30 /20	0.29	1.59
COI	STAAR Inv Trust Shrt Term Bond	SITBX	D	(800) 332-7738	E / 0.4	-0.11	-0.22	0.11 /23	-0.26 / 4	0.15 /17	0.00	1.47
GEN	Stadion Alternative Income A	TACFX	E+	(866) 383-7636	D+ / 2.6	-0.46	-1.45	0.96 /39	2.95 /60	--	1.70	1.74
GEL	Stadion Alternative Income C	TACCX	U	(866) 383-7636	U /	-0.71	-1.90	0.16 /24	--	--	1.40	2.19
GEL	Stadion Alternative Income I	TACSX	D-	(866) 383-7636	C / 5.5	-0.51	-1.33	1.19 /42	3.22 /65	--	2.03	1.30
COI	State Farm Bond A	BNSAX	D-	(800) 447-4930	C- / 3.4	0.91	-2.19	1.53 /45	2.55 /53	1.87 /40	2.23	0.65
COI	State Farm Bond B	BNSBX	D	(800) 447-4930	C- / 4.0	0.81	-2.39	1.12 /41	2.14 /45	1.47 /34	1.89	1.05
COI	State Farm Bond Inst	SFBIX	C-	(800) 447-4930	C / 5.1	0.97	-2.07	1.78 /47	2.80 /58	2.11 /44	2.55	0.40
COI	State Farm Bond LegB	SFBBX	D	(800) 447-4930	C- / 4.0	0.81	-2.38	1.13 /41	2.14 /45	1.47 /34	1.90	1.05
COI	State Farm Bond Premier	SFBAX	D-	(800) 447-4930	C- / 3.4	0.94	-2.14	1.51 /45	2.54 /53	1.87 /40	2.30	0.65
COI	State Farm Bond R1	SRBOX	D	(800) 447-4930	C- / 4.1	0.83	-2.26	1.20 /42	2.22 /47	1.55 /35	1.97	0.97
COI	State Farm Bond R2	SRBTX	D+	(800) 447-4930	C / 4.4	0.79	-2.25	1.32 /43	2.40 /50	1.73 /38	2.18	0.77
COI	State Farm Bond R3	SRBHX	C-	(800) 447-4930	C / 5.0	0.96	-2.10	1.71 /46	2.73 /57	2.04 /43	2.48	0.47
GEI	State Farm Interim	SFITX	C-	(800) 447-4930	D / 2.1	0.30	-0.81	-0.24 /14	0.83 /25	0.67 /23	1.17	0.17
MMT	State Farm Money Market Inst	SAIXX	U	(800) 447-4930	U /	0.01	0.01	0.01 /18	0.01 / 7	0.01 / 6	0.01	N/A
*MUN	State Farm Muni Bond	SFBDX	A+	(800) 447-4930	C+ / 6.8	1.95	-1.78	-0.01 /17	2.80 /79	2.53 /71	3.02	0.16
MUH	State Farm Tax Advant Bond A	TANAX	C-	(800) 447-4930	C+ / 5.7	1.90	-2.23	-0.21 /14	3.17 /84	2.46 /70	2.29	0.66
MUH	State Farm Tax Advant Bond B	TANBX	C	(800) 447-4930	C+ / 6.3	1.71	-2.51	-0.63 / 8	2.72 /77	2.05 /60	1.93	1.06
MUH	State Farm Tax Advant Bond LegB	SFTBX	C	(800) 447-4930	C+ / 6.5	1.71	-2.51	-0.63 / 8	2.77 /78	2.06 /60	1.92	1.06

● Denotes fund is closed to new investors
* Denotes fund is included in Section II

www.thestreetratings.com

RISK			NET ASSETS		ASSET					Portfolio Turnover Ratio	Avg Coupon Rate	FUND MANAGER		MINIMUM		LOADS	
Risk Rating/Pts	3 Yr Avg Standard Deviation	Avg Dura-tion	NAV As of 2/28/17	Total $(Mil)	Cash %	Gov. Bond %	Muni. Bond %	Corp. Bond %	Other %			Manager Quality Pct	Manager Tenure (Years)	Initial Purch. $	Additional Purch. $	Front End Load	Back End Load
C+ / 5.9	2.9	4.3	10.30	26	6	11	0	41	42	441	4.3	70	7	1,000	50	0.0	0.0
C+ / 5.9	2.9	4.3	10.34	216	6	11	0	41	42	441	4.3	83	7	1,000,000	0	0.0	0.0
U /	N/A	4.3	10.33	1	6	11	0	41	42	441	4.3	N/A	7	0	0	0.0	0.0
U /	N/A	4.3	10.34	1	6	11	0	41	42	441	4.3	N/A	7	1,000,000	0	0.0	0.0
D+ / 2.8	4.0	7.0	5.11	9	1	11	23	62	3	4	6.6	26	22	1,000	25	0.0	0.0
A / 9.3	0.9	2.6	5.03	11	6	11	0	81	2	13	5.4	57	22	1,000	25	0.0	0.0
U /	N/A	N/A	9.81	294	0	0	0	0	100	60	0.0	N/A	3	1,000,000	100,000	0.0	1.0
B- / 7.4	2.1	N/A	10.02	10	5	0	0	82	13	53	0.0	67	5	1,000	100	3.0	1.0
B- / 7.5	2.1	N/A	9.99	12	5	0	0	82	13	53	0.0	36	5	1,000	100	0.0	1.0
B- / 7.4	2.1	N/A	9.99	92	5	0	0	82	13	53	0.0	73	5	1,000	100	0.0	1.0
B- / 7.4	2.1	N/A	10.00	275	5	0	0	82	13	53	0.0	75	5	1,000,000	100,000	0.0	1.0
A+ / 9.8	0.5	1.2	10.13	5	0	96	0	0	4	47	1.3	26	14	1,000	100	0.0	0.0
A+ / 9.7	0.6	1.2	9.97	1	0	96	0	0	4	47	1.3	14	14	1,000	100	0.0	0.0
C+ / 6.2	2.9	N/A	21.17	63	45	1	28	2	24	115	0.0	94	6	10,000	1,000	5.8	0.0
C+ / 6.2	2.9	N/A	21.13	88	45	1	28	2	24	115	0.0	93	6	10,000	1,000	0.0	0.0
C+ / 6.3	2.9	N/A	21.20	98	45	1	28	2	24	115	0.0	94	6	10,000	1,000	0.0	0.0
C+ / 6.3	2.9	N/A	21.09	408	45	1	28	2	24	115	0.0	95	6	100,000	1,000	0.0	0.0
C+ / 6.2	2.9	N/A	21.03	N/A	45	1	28	2	24	115	0.0	95	6	20,000,000	0	0.0	0.0
C / 5.0	3.1	5.2	10.29	523	5	0	89	0	6	10	4.6	57	24	5,000	100	0.0	0.0
C- / 3.4	3.9	5.5	9.48	157	0	0	97	0	3	23	4.4	74	29	5,000	100	0.0	0.0
A / 9.3	0.9	1.4	10.94	654	1	0	0	0	99	29	6.4	74	30	5,000	100	0.0	0.0
U /	N/A	N/A	9.74	7	6	41	0	47	6	400	0.0	N/A	2	500	50	0.0	2.0
D+ / 2.9	4.1	N/A	11.90	221	5	0	72	8	15	9	0.0	88	8	500	50	4.8	0.0
U /	N/A	N/A	11.90	N/A	5	0	72	8	15	9	0.0	N/A	8	500	50	0.0	0.0
D+ / 2.3	3.7	10.3	9.39	105	0	0	100	0	0	11	5.5	52	8	500	50	4.8	0.0
U /	N/A	10.3	9.37	N/A	0	0	100	0	0	11	5.5	N/A	8	500	50	0.0	0.0
C+ / 6.2	2.9	5.4	9.41	278	0	19	0	36	45	219	6.3	61	N/A	5,000,000	0	0.0	0.0
C+ / 5.9	2.9	5.4	9.63	N/A	0	19	0	36	45	219	6.3	51	N/A	5,000,000	0	0.0	0.0
U /	N/A	3.7	7.64	N/A	6	0	0	93	1	77	0.0	N/A	5	2,000	0	3.8	0.0
U /	N/A	3.7	7.63	1	6	0	0	93	1	77	0.0	N/A	5	1,000,000	0	0.0	0.0
U /	N/A	3.7	7.63	26	6	0	0	93	1	77	0.0	N/A	5	10,000,000	0	0.0	0.0
D / 1.6	5.1	3.7	7.63	47	6	0	0	93	1	77	0.0	20	5	1,000	100	0.0	0.0
E- / 0.2	11.0	N/A	14.19	3	13	1	0	0	86	30	0.0	3	20	1,000	50	0.0	0.0
B+ / 8.5	1.8	N/A	9.67	1	5	10	4	78	3	17	3.9	15	20	1,000	50	0.0	0.0
A+ / 9.8	0.4	1.4	8.92	1	54	0	3	42	1	0	3.5	21	20	1,000	50	0.0	0.0
D+ / 2.6	4.3	N/A	10.04	8	2	0	0	0	98	18	0.0	69	5	1,000	250	5.8	0.0
U /	N/A	N/A	9.96	4	2	0	0	0	98	18	0.0	N/A	5	1,000	250	0.0	0.0
D+ / 2.7	4.2	N/A	10.02	105	2	0	0	0	98	18	0.0	76	5	500,000	0	0.0	0.0
C / 5.2	3.1	5.2	11.23	201	0	13	0	73	14	9	0.0	35	17	250	50	3.0	0.0
C / 5.2	3.1	5.2	11.22	10	0	13	0	73	14	9	0.0	22	17	250	50	0.0	0.0
C / 5.1	3.1	5.2	11.22	264	0	13	0	73	14	9	0.0	51	17	250	50	0.0	0.0
C / 5.1	3.1	5.2	11.24	2	0	13	0	73	14	9	0.0	21	17	250	50	0.0	0.0
C / 5.0	3.1	5.2	11.23	361	0	13	0	73	14	9	0.0	34	17	250	50	3.0	0.0
C / 5.2	3.1	5.2	11.23	4	0	13	0	73	14	9	0.0	25	17	0	0	0.0	0.0
C / 5.2	3.1	5.2	11.21	9	0	13	0	73	14	9	0.0	30	17	0	0	0.0	0.0
C / 5.2	3.1	5.2	11.23	2	0	13	0	73	14	9	0.0	48	17	0	0	0.0	0.0
B+ / 8.7	1.5	2.6	9.92	374	0	99	0	0	1	12	0.0	24	19	250	50	0.0	0.0
U /	N/A	N/A	1.00	82	100	0	0	0	0	0	0.0	N/A	N/A	250	50	0.0	0.0
B- / 7.5	2.6	4.4	8.63	700	0	0	98	0	2	10	0.0	50	19	250	50	0.0	0.0
C- / 4.2	2.9	4.4	11.76	101	1	3	93	0	3	4	0.0	50	17	250	50	3.0	0.0
C- / 4.2	2.9	4.4	11.75	2	1	3	93	0	3	4	0.0	26	17	250	50	0.0	0.0
C- / 4.2	2.9	4.4	11.75	N/A	1	3	93	0	3	4	0.0	29	17	250	50	0.0	0.0

Fund Type	Fund Name	Ticker Symbol	Overall Investment Rating	Phone	PERFORMANCE Performance Rating/Pts	Total Return % through 2/28/17			Annualized		Incl. in Returns	
						3 Mo	6 Mo	1Yr / Pct	3Yr / Pct	5Yr / Pct	Dividend Yield	Expense Ratio
MUH	State Farm Tax Advant Bond Premier	SFTAX	C-	(800) 447-4930	C+ / 5.7	1.84	-2.26	-0.15 / 15	3.19 / 84	2.47 / 70	2.35	0.56
COI	State Street Aggregate Bond Index	SSAFX	U	(800) 882-0052	U /	1.07	-2.21	1.22 / 42	--	--	2.22	0.19
COI	State Street Aggregate Bond Index A	SSFCX	U	(800) 882-0052	U /	0.91	-2.50	0.78 / 37	--	--	1.88	0.89
COI	State Street Aggregate Bond Index I	SSFDX	U	(800) 882-0052	U /	1.07	-2.28	1.13 / 41	--	--	2.20	0.64
COI	State Street Aggregate Bond Index K	SSFEX	U	(800) 882-0052	U /	0.97	-2.28	1.13 / 41	--	--	2.20	0.44
GEI	State Street Income VIS 1	SSIMX	C	(800) 843-2639	C / 4.5	1.19	-2.03	3.06 / 57	2.20 / 46	2.19 / 45	1.87	1.16
MMT	State Street Inst Liq Reserves Inv	SSVXX	C-	(800) 882-0052	E+ / 0.9	0.10	0.13	0.18 / 25	0.06 / 11	0.04 / 10	0.17	N/A
MMT	State Street Inst Liq Reserves Prem	SSIXX	C	(800) 882-0052	D / 1.7	0.18	0.30	0.53 / 34	0.26 / 18	0.21 / 19	0.52	N/A
MMT	State Street Treas MM Investment	TRVXX	U	(800) 882-0052	U /	--	--	--	--	--	0.01	N/A
MMT	State Street TreasPls MM Inv	TPVXX	U	(800) 882-0052	U /	--	--	--	--	--	0.01	N/A
MMT	State Street TreasPls MM Prem	TPIXX	C-	(800) 882-0052	D- / 1.1	0.10	0.15	0.24 / 27	0.09 / 13	0.06 / 13	0.24	N/A
MMT	State Street US Govt MM Inv	GVVXX	D+	(800) 882-0052	E+ / 0.6	0.02	0.02	0.02 / 19	0.01 / 7	--	0.02	N/A
MMT	State Street US Govt MM Premier	GVMXX	C-	(800) 882-0052	D- / 1.2	0.11	0.17	0.30 / 29	0.11 / 14	0.07 / 13	0.29	N/A
COI	Sterling Capital Corporate A	SCCMX	B+	(800) 228-1872	C / 5.3	1.70	-0.15	5.05 / 67	2.83 / 58	--	2.72	0.86
COI	Sterling Capital Corporate C	SCCNX	B	(800) 228-1872	C / 4.8	1.51	-0.62	4.17 / 63	2.07 / 44	--	2.03	1.61
GEL	Sterling Capital Corporate Inst	SCCPX	A+	(800) 228-1872	C+ / 6.5	1.76	-0.13	5.20 / 67	3.09 / 63	3.54 / 66	3.02	0.61
USS	Sterling Capital Interm US Govt A	BGVAX	D-	(800) 228-1872	D- / 1.0	0.45	-1.94	-0.77 / 6	1.02 / 28	0.73 / 24	1.90	0.96
USS ●	Sterling Capital Interm US Govt B	BUSGX	D-	(800) 228-1872	E / 0.5	0.26	-2.23	-1.43 / 2	0.29 / 18	-0.03 / 5	1.17	1.71
USS	Sterling Capital Interm US Govt C	BIUCX	D-	(800) 228-1872	E / 0.5	0.26	-2.31	-1.52 / 2	0.26 / 18	-0.05 / 5	1.18	1.71
USS	Sterling Capital Interm US Govt I	BBGVX	C-	(800) 228-1872	D+ / 2.5	0.51	-1.82	-0.52 / 9	1.27 / 32	0.96 / 27	2.20	0.71
MUS	Sterling Capital KY Interm TxFr A	BKTAX	D	(800) 228-1872	C- / 3.2	1.85	-2.61	-0.51 / 9	1.76 / 56	1.64 / 50	2.09	1.02
MUS	Sterling Capital KY Interm TxFr C	BKCAX	D	(800) 228-1872	D+ / 2.7	1.81	-2.83	-1.10 / 4	1.05 / 37	0.92 / 33	1.42	1.77
MUS	Sterling Capital KY Interm TxFr I	BKITX	C+	(800) 228-1872	C / 5.0	1.91	-2.50	-0.27 / 13	1.98 / 62	1.90 / 56	2.38	0.77
MUS	Sterling Capital MD Interm TxFr A	BMAAX	D	(800) 228-1872	C- / 3.1	1.84	-2.39	-0.84 / 6	1.76 / 56	1.47 / 46	1.76	0.95
MUS	Sterling Capital MD Interm TxFr C	BMDCX	D-	(800) 228-1872	D+ / 2.5	1.74	-2.67	-1.49 / 2	1.03 / 36	0.73 / 29	1.03	1.70
MUS	Sterling Capital MD Interm TxFr I	BMAIX	C+	(800) 228-1872	C / 5.0	1.90	-2.26	-0.59 / 8	2.02 / 63	1.74 / 52	2.05	0.70
MUS	Sterling Capital NC Interm TxFr A	BNCAX	D	(800) 228-1872	C- / 3.2	1.72	-2.82	-1.02 / 4	1.89 / 60	1.60 / 49	2.03	0.89
MUS	Sterling Capital NC Interm TxFr C	BBNCX	D-	(800) 228-1872	D+ / 2.5	1.53	-3.18	-1.76 / 1	1.13 / 39	0.82 / 31	1.31	1.64
MUS	Sterling Capital NC Interm TxFr I	BBNTX	C+	(800) 228-1872	C / 5.1	1.78	-2.69	-0.77 / 6	2.14 / 66	1.86 / 56	2.33	0.64
MUS	Sterling Capital SC Interm TxFr A	BASCX	D+	(800) 228-1872	C- / 3.6	1.94	-2.48	-0.85 / 5	1.99 / 62	1.76 / 53	1.74	0.91
MUS	Sterling Capital SC Interm TxFr C	BSCCX	D	(800) 228-1872	D+ / 2.9	1.75	-2.84	-1.59 / 1	1.23 / 41	0.99 / 35	1.01	1.66
MUS	Sterling Capital SC Interm TxFr I	BSCIX	B	(800) 228-1872	C / 5.5	2.01	-2.38	-0.53 / 9	2.25 / 68	2.01 / 59	2.03	0.66
COI	Sterling Capital Sec Opp Inst	SCSPX	A	(800) 228-1872	C / 5.3	0.56	-0.58	1.84 / 48	2.86 / 59	2.45 / 49	2.66	0.61
COI	Sterling Capital Securitized Opp A	SCSSX	B	(800) 228-1872	C- / 4.0	0.50	-0.80	1.58 / 45	2.60 / 54	--	2.36	0.86
COI	Sterling Capital Securitized Opp C	SCSTX	B-	(800) 228-1872	C- / 3.7	0.41	-1.07	0.93 / 39	1.89 / 41	--	1.65	1.61
USS	Sterling Capital Short Dur Bd A	BSGAX	C	(800) 228-1872	D / 1.9	0.59	0.14	1.84 / 48	0.87 / 26	1.25 / 31	2.37	0.80
USS	Sterling Capital Short Dur Bd C	BBSCX	C-	(800) 228-1872	D- / 1.4	0.40	-0.23	1.08 / 40	0.12 / 14	0.49 / 21	1.66	1.55
USS	Sterling Capital Short Dur Bd Inst	BBSGX	B	(800) 228-1872	C- / 3.1	0.65	0.27	2.09 / 50	1.12 / 29	1.50 / 34	2.67	0.55
GEI	Sterling Capital Tot Rtn Bd A	BICAX	D+	(800) 228-1872	D+ / 2.9	1.20	-1.67	3.24 / 58	2.72 / 56	2.65 / 52	2.77	0.81
GEI ●	Sterling Capital Tot Rtn Bd B	BICBX	C	(800) 228-1872	C- / 4.0	1.01	-2.04	2.36 / 52	1.95 / 42	1.86 / 40	2.17	1.56
GEI	Sterling Capital Tot Rtn Bd C	BICCX	C	(800) 228-1872	C- / 4.1	1.01	-2.03	2.47 / 53	1.96 / 42	1.88 / 40	2.18	1.56
GEI	Sterling Capital Tot Rtn Bd I	BIBTX	B+	(800) 228-1872	C+ / 5.9	1.26	-1.55	3.49 / 60	3.01 / 61	2.90 / 56	3.19	0.56
GEI	Sterling Capital Tot Rtn Bd R	BICRX	B-	(800) 228-1872	C / 5.0	1.14	-1.80	2.95 / 56	2.51 / 52	2.37 / 47	2.66	1.06
COI	Sterling Capital Ultra Short Bd A	BUSRX	C	(800) 228-1872	D / 1.8	0.21	0.33	1.03 / 40	0.47 / 21	--	1.43	0.78
COI	Sterling Capital Ultra Short Bd Ins	BUSIX	C+	(800) 228-1872	D+ / 2.4	0.27	0.46	1.38 / 44	0.72 / 23	--	1.69	0.53
MUS	Sterling Capital VA Interm TxFr A	BVAAX	D-	(800) 228-1872	D+ / 2.7	1.86	-2.86	-1.18 / 3	1.68 / 53	1.42 / 45	1.92	0.90
MUS	Sterling Capital VA Interm TxFr C	BVACX	E+	(800) 228-1872	D / 2.1	1.67	-3.22	-1.92 / 1	0.92 / 34	0.66 / 28	1.19	1.65
MUS	Sterling Capital VA Interm TxFr I	BVATX	C-	(800) 228-1872	C / 4.6	1.92	-2.74	-0.93 / 5	1.93 / 61	1.67 / 51	2.21	0.65
MUS	Sterling Capital WVA Interm TxFr A	BWVAX	C	(800) 228-1872	C- / 4.1	1.80	-2.25	-0.38 / 11	2.15 / 66	1.82 / 54	2.03	0.90
MUS	Sterling Capital WVA Interm TxFr C	BWVCX	C-	(800) 228-1872	C- / 3.4	1.61	-2.61	-1.03 / 4	1.38 / 45	1.08 / 37	1.31	1.65
MUS	Sterling Capital WVA Interm TxFr I	OWVAX	B+	(800) 228-1872	C+ / 6.0	1.86	-2.13	-0.13 / 16	2.37 / 71	2.08 / 61	2.33	0.65
GES	Steward Select Bond Fd Indv	SEAKX	C	(877) 420-4440	C- / 3.2	0.84	-1.55	1.23 / 42	1.50 / 35	1.27 / 31	1.81	0.95

RISK			NET ASSETS		ASSET					Portfolio Turnover Ratio	Avg Coupon Rate	FUND MANAGER		MINIMUM		LOADS	
Risk Rating/Pts	3 Yr Avg Standard Deviation	Avg Duration	NAV As of 2/28/17	Total $(Mil)	Cash %	Gov. Bond %	Muni. Bond %	Corp. Bond %	Other %			Manager Quality Pct	Manager Tenure (Years)	Initial Purch. $	Additional Purch. $	Front End Load	Back End Load
C /4.3	2.9	4.4	11.74	429	1	3	93	0	3	4	0.0	52	17	250	50	3.0	0.0
U /	N/A	5.5	9.96	414	2	41	0	23	34	62	0.0	N/A	3	0	0	0.0	0.0
U /	N/A	5.5	9.82	N/A	0	43	1	26	30	62	0.0	N/A	3	2,000	0	3.8	0.0
U /	N/A	5.5	9.83	12	0	43	1	26	30	62	0.0	N/A	3	1,000,000	0	0.0	0.0
U /	N/A	5.5	9.82	85	0	43	1	26	30	62	0.0	N/A	3	10,000,000	0	0.0	0.0
C+ /6.4	2.8	5.4	11.48	25	0	29	0	39	32	241	5.8	33	N/A	0	0	0.0	0.0
A+ /9.9	N/A	N/A	1.00	6	100	0	0	0	0	0	0.2	42	N/A	25,000,000	0	0.0	0.0
A+ /9.9	0.1	N/A	1.00	8,739	100	0	0	0	0	0	0.5	53	N/A	500,000,000	0	0.0	0.0
U /	N/A	N/A	1.00	577	100	0	0	0	0	0	0.0	N/A	N/A	25,000,000	0	0.0	0.0
U /	N/A	N/A	1.00	44	100	0	0	0	0	0	0.0	N/A	N/A	25,000,000	0	0.0	0.0
A+ /9.9	N/A	N/A	1.00	2,031	100	0	0	0	0	0	0.2	45	N/A	500,000,000	0	0.0	0.0
A+ /9.9	N/A	N/A	1.00	1,019	100	0	0	0	0	0	0.0	37	N/A	25,000,000	0	0.0	0.0
A+ /9.9	N/A	N/A	1.00	41,636	100	0	0	0	0	0	0.3	N/A	N/A	500,000,000	0	0.0	0.0
B /7.7	2.4	N/A	10.18	1	3	0	0	94	3	84	0.0	69	6	1,000	0	2.0	0.0
B /7.7	2.4	N/A	10.16	N/A	3	0	0	94	3	84	0.0	37	6	1,000	0	0.0	0.0
B /7.7	2.4	N/A	10.17	30	3	0	0	94	3	84	0.0	77	6	1,000,000	0	0.0	0.0
B /7.9	2.2	3.4	9.95	6	0	74	0	10	16	49	0.0	28	14	1,000	0	2.0	0.0
B /8.0	2.2	3.4	9.92	N/A	0	74	0	10	16	49	0.0	11	14	1,000	0	0.0	0.0
B /7.9	2.2	3.4	9.93	1	0	74	0	10	16	49	0.0	10	14	1,000	0	0.0	0.0
B /7.9	2.2	3.4	9.96	18	0	74	0	10	16	49	0.0	38	14	1,000,000	0	0.0	0.0
C+ /6.6	2.8	5.3	10.19	4	1	0	96	0	3	16	0.0	9	14	1,000	0	2.0	0.0
C+ /6.5	2.8	5.3	10.20	N/A	1	0	96	0	3	16	0.0	3	14	1,000	0	0.0	0.0
C+ /6.5	2.8	5.3	10.17	8	1	0	96	0	3	16	0.0	12	14	1,000,000	0	0.0	0.0
C+ /6.7	2.8	5.4	10.91	6	1	0	96	0	3	14	0.0	9	14	1,000	0	2.0	0.0
C+ /6.5	2.8	5.4	10.92	1	1	0	96	0	3	14	0.0	3	14	1,000	0	0.0	0.0
C+ /6.7	2.8	5.4	10.93	22	1	0	96	0	3	14	0.0	14	14	1,000,000	0	0.0	0.0
C+ /6.2	2.9	5.3	10.69	47	1	1	96	0	2	10	0.0	10	17	1,000	0	2.0	0.0
C+ /6.3	2.8	5.3	10.68	5	1	1	96	0	2	10	0.0	3	17	1,000	0	0.0	0.0
C+ /6.2	2.9	5.3	10.69	152	1	1	96	0	2	10	0.0	14	17	1,000,000	0	0.0	0.0
C+ /6.4	2.8	5.3	10.98	17	1	0	96	0	3	3	0.0	12	17	1,000	0	2.0	0.0
C+ /6.3	2.8	5.3	10.98	2	1	0	96	0	3	3	0.0	4	17	1,000	0	0.0	0.0
C+ /6.6	2.8	5.3	10.91	69	1	0	96	0	3	3	0.0	17	17	1,000,000	0	0.0	0.0
B+ /8.6	1.8	N/A	9.90	42	0	1	0	1	98	44	0.0	81	3	1,000,000	0	0.0	0.0
B+ /8.5	1.8	N/A	9.89	N/A	0	1	0	1	98	44	0.0	77	3	1,000	0	2.0	0.0
B+ /8.5	1.8	N/A	9.89	N/A	0	1	0	1	98	44	0.0	62	3	1,000	0	0.0	0.0
A /9.5	0.8	1.6	8.72	7	1	3	1	65	30	55	0.0	63	6	1,000	0	2.0	0.0
A /9.5	0.8	1.6	8.72	2	1	3	1	65	30	55	0.0	28	6	1,000	0	0.0	0.0
A /9.5	0.8	1.6	8.72	65	1	3	1	65	30	55	0.0	70	6	1,000,000	0	0.0	0.0
B- /7.0	2.7	4.5	10.51	68	0	11	6	34	49	65	0.0	60	9	1,000	0	5.8	0.0
B- /7.1	2.7	4.5	10.52	N/A	0	11	6	34	49	65	0.0	25	9	1,000	0	0.0	0.0
B- /7.2	2.7	4.5	10.53	8	0	11	6	34	49	65	0.0	27	9	1,000	0	0.0	0.0
B- /7.1	2.7	4.5	10.52	825	0	11	6	34	49	65	0.0	69	9	1,000,000	0	0.0	0.0
B- /7.2	2.7	4.5	10.47	N/A	0	11	6	34	49	65	0.0	54	9	1,000	0	0.0	0.0
A+ /9.9	0.3	N/A	9.79	7	2	0	2	53	43	43	0.0	55	5	1,000	0	0.5	0.0
A+ /9.9	0.3	N/A	9.79	42	2	0	2	53	43	43	0.0	64	5	1,000,000	0	0.0	0.0
C /5.5	3.0	5.2	11.65	31	3	1	93	0	3	16	0.0	6	17	1,000	0	2.0	0.0
C+ /5.6	3.0	5.2	11.65	1	3	1	93	0	3	16	0.0	2	17	1,000	0	0.0	0.0
C /5.5	3.0	5.2	11.65	77	3	1	93	0	3	16	0.0	9	17	1,000,000	0	0.0	0.0
B- /7.1	2.7	5.2	9.94	34	2	0	96	0	2	11	0.0	18	17	1,000	0	2.0	0.0
B- /7.2	2.7	5.2	9.95	1	2	0	96	0	2	11	0.0	6	17	1,000	0	0.0	0.0
B- /7.0	2.7	5.2	9.95	63	2	0	96	0	2	11	0.0	23	17	1,000,000	0	0.0	0.0
B /7.8	2.4	4.3	24.52	11	2	29	0	61	8	11	0.0	21	7	200	0	0.0	0.0

Fund Type	Fund Name	Ticker Symbol	Overall Investment Rating	Phone	Performance Rating/Pts	3 Mo	6 Mo	1Yr / Pct	3Yr / Pct	5Yr / Pct	Dividend Yield	Expense Ratio
GES	Steward Select Bond Fd Inst	SEACX	C+	(877) 420-4440	C- / 3.8	0.94	-1.40	1.58 /45	1.85 /41	1.64 /37	2.16	0.60
*EM	Stone Harbor Emerging Debt Inst	SHMDX	C+	(866) 699-8125	A+ /9.7	5.42	0.49	16.18 /90	5.83 /91	4.07 /73	6.23	0.68
EM	Stone Harbor Emg Mks Crp Dbt Fd	SHCDX	B	(866) 699-8125	A /9.3	4.00	1.38	12.90 /85	5.24 /87	4.73 /81	4.53	1.38
EM	Stone Harbor Emg Mkts Dbt All Inst	SHADX	U	(866) 699-8125	U /	6.23	0.31	14.38 /87	--	--	3.70	1.65
GEI	Stone Harbor High Yield Bond Inst	SHHYX	C-	(866) 699-8125	B /8.2	4.86	4.62	16.47 /91	2.61 /54	5.64 /90	5.28	0.65
COI	Stone Harbor Investment Grade Inst	SHIGX	C	(866) 699-8125	C /5.1	1.29	-1.76	3.06 /57	2.54 /53	--	2.24	1.43
GEN	Stone Harbor Strategic Income Inst	SHSIX	C	(866) 699-8125	B /7.7	3.37	1.17	10.18 /79	3.45 /68	--	3.88	1.58
USL ●	SunAmerica 2020 High Watermark A	HWKAX	E	(800) 858-8850	E- / 0.2	0.12	-1.63	-0.87 / 5	1.15 /30	0.59 /22	2.37	2.10
USL ●	SunAmerica 2020 High Watermark C		E+	(800) 858-8850	E+ / 0.8	-0.05	-2.02	-1.48 / 2	0.49 /21	-0.09 / 4	1.31	2.98
USL ●	SunAmerica 2020 High Watermark I		D-	(800) 858-8850	C- / 3.1	0.29	-1.35	-0.37 /12	1.65 /37	1.04 /28	3.03	2.07
GEI	SunAmerica VAL Co I Cap Conse Fd	VCCCX	C-	(800) 858-8850	C / 4.4	1.12	-2.35	1.33 /43	2.37 /49	2.21 /45	2.35	0.64
USS	SunAmerica VAL Co I Gov Sec Fd	VCGSX	D	(800) 858-8850	C- / 3.5	0.51	-2.68	-0.70 / 7	2.10 /45	1.44 /33	2.41	0.64
*GEI	SunAmerica VAL Co I Infln Prot Fd	VCTPX	D-	(800) 858-8850	C- / 3.6	1.61	-0.42	4.21 /63	1.12 /29	0.63 /23	0.25	0.59
GL	SunAmerica VAL Co I Intl Govt Bd Fd	VCIFX	E	(800) 858-8850	D /1.8	1.98	-4.87	2.16 /50	0.46 /20	0.73 /24	0.00	0.64
*GEI	SunAmerica VAL Co II Core Bond Fd	VCCBX	C+	(800) 858-8850	C /5.3	1.64	-1.42	3.43 /59	2.58 /53	2.62 /51	2.00	0.79
*GEI	SunAmerica VAL Co II High Yld Bd	VCHYX	B-	(800) 858-8850	A- /9.0	4.51	4.10	16.31 /91	3.84 /73	5.57 /89	4.35	0.99
*GEI	SunAmerica VAL Co II Strat Bond	VCSBX	C+	(800) 858-8850	B- /7.5	3.07	0.97	10.40 /80	3.22 /65	4.03 /73	3.94	0.88
*MUS	T Rowe Price CA Tax Free Bond	PRXCX	B+	(800) 638-5660	B+ /8.3	2.24	-3.82	-0.12 /16	4.09 /93	3.75 /91	3.27	0.50
MMT	T Rowe Price Cash Reserves	TSCXX	C-	(800) 638-5660	D- /1.0	0.09	0.15	0.18 /25	0.07 /11	0.04 /10	0.18	N/A
*COI	T Rowe Price Corporate Income	PRPIX	C-	(800) 638-5660	B- /7.0	2.19	-2.12	5.82 /70	3.63 /70	4.02 /73	3.15	0.62
COI	T Rowe Price Corporate Income I	TICCX	U	(800) 638-5660	U /	2.22	-2.06	5.94 /70	--	--	3.26	0.73
COH	T Rowe Price Credit Opptys	PRCPX	U	(800) 638-5660	U /	4.30	6.83	21.52 /98	--	--	4.75	1.67
COH	T Rowe Price Credit Opptys Adv	PAOPX	U	(800) 638-5660	U /	4.28	6.67	21.29 /97	--	--	4.67	2.45
EM	T Rowe Price Em Mkts Loc Cur	PRELX	E-	(800) 638-5660	E /0.5	7.17	0.73	14.52 /88	-2.34 / 2	-2.53 / 1	5.49	1.10
EM	T Rowe Price Emerg Mkts Corp Bd	PACEX	C+	(800) 638-5660	B+ /8.7	3.81	0.83	13.20 /85	4.72 /83	--	4.12	1.60
EM	T Rowe Price Emerg Mkts Corp Bd I	TECIX	U	(800) 638-5660	U /	4.01	1.13	13.65 /86	--	--	4.52	1.36
EM	T Rowe Price Emerg Mkts Corp Bd	TRECX	C+	(800) 638-5660	B+ /8.8	3.93	0.97	13.31 /86	4.83 /84	--	4.22	1.19
EM	T Rowe Price Emerging Markets Bd	PREMX	C+	(800) 638-5660	A+ /9.8	6.36	2.52	18.31 /94	6.74 /95	5.22 /86	6.37	0.93
EM	T Rowe Price Emerging Markets Bd A	PAIKX	U	(800) 638-5660	U /	6.27	2.37	17.97 /93	--	--	6.08	2.00
EM	T Rowe Price Emerging Markets Bd I	PRXIX	U	(800) 638-5660	U /	6.40	2.52	18.40 /94	--	--	6.52	0.86
EM	T Rowe Price Emg Mkts Loc Cur Adv	PAELX	E-	(800) 638-5660	E /0.4	7.14	0.67	14.23 /87	-2.45 / 2	-2.65 / 1	5.39	1.72
EM	T Rowe Price Emg Mkts Loc Cur I	TEIMX	U	(800) 638-5660	U /	7.42	1.03	14.86 /88	--	--	5.79	1.24
LP	T Rowe Price Floating Rate	PRFRX	A+	(800) 638-5660	B- /7.0	1.72	2.92	9.05 /77	3.39 /67	3.98 /72	4.11	0.79
LP	T Rowe Price Floating Rate Advisor	PAFRX	A+	(800) 638-5660	C+ /6.9	1.66	2.82	8.95 /76	3.32 /66	3.88 /71	3.91	1.08
MUS	T Rowe Price GA Tax-Free Bd	GTFBX	B	(800) 638-5660	B- /7.5	1.93	-3.42	-0.28 /13	3.51 /88	2.98 /80	2.99	0.54
GL	T Rowe Price Global High Inc Bd	RPIHX	U	(800) 638-5660	U /	4.49	4.16	18.96 /95	--	--	5.59	2.18
GL	T Rowe Price Global High Inc Bd Adv	PAIHX	U	(800) 638-5660	U /	4.43	4.04	18.72 /95	--	--	5.40	3.00
GL	T Rowe Price Global High Inc Bd I	RPOIX	U	(800) 638-5660	U /	4.53	4.13	19.04 /95	--	--	5.75	2.30
GES	T Rowe Price Global MS Bd	PRSNX	B-	(800) 638-5660	B /7.6	3.12	0.73	7.91 /74	3.69 /71	3.91 /71	3.44	0.83
GES	T Rowe Price Global MS Bd Adv	PRSAX	B-	(800) 638-5660	B- /7.4	3.14	0.59	7.63 /74	3.46 /68	3.70 /69	3.18	1.14
GL	T Rowe Price Global MS Bd I	PGMSX	U	(800) 638-5660	U /	3.25	0.79	--	--	--	0.00	0.70
*USA	T Rowe Price GNMA	PRGMX	B	(800) 638-5660	C- /4.0	0.36	-0.53	1.02 /40	2.03 /44	1.66 /37	2.86	0.59
MMT	T Rowe Price Government Money	PRRXX	D+	(800) 638-5660	E+ /0.6	0.03	0.03	0.03 /20	0.02 / 8	0.02 / 8	0.03	N/A
*COH ●	T Rowe Price High Yield	PRHYX	C+	(800) 638-5660	A- /9.2	4.68	5.40	18.93 /95	4.13 /77	6.60 /95	5.59	0.75
COH ●	T Rowe Price High Yield Adv	PAHIX	C+	(800) 638-5660	A- /9.0	4.66	5.35	18.86 /95	3.89 /74	6.35 /94	5.49	1.02
COH ●	T Rowe Price High Yield I	PRHIX	U	(800) 638-5660	U /	4.71	5.46	19.09 /95	--	--	5.71	0.60
US	T Rowe Price Infla-Protect Bond	PRIPX	E+	(800) 638-5660	C- /3.5	1.10	-1.06	2.49 /53	1.42 /34	0.37 /20	0.01	0.59
GEI	T Rowe Price Infla-Protect Bond I	TIIPX	U	(800) 638-5660	U /	1.02	-1.06	2.59 /54	--	--	0.02	0.97
EM	T Rowe Price Ins Emerging Mkts Bd	TREBX	B-	(800) 638-5660	A+ /9.9	6.44	3.36	18.64 /94	7.51 /97	6.13 /93	6.71	0.70
*GEI	T Rowe Price Inst Core Plus	TICPX	C+	(800) 638-5660	C+ /5.7	1.43	-1.78	3.38 /59	2.91 /60	2.94 /57	2.98	0.45
COH	T Rowe Price Inst Credit Opptys	TRXPX	U	(800) 638-5660	U /	4.78	7.50	22.64 /98	--	--	5.24	0.67
GL	T Rowe Price Inst Glbl Mlti-Sec Bd	RPGMX	B+	(800) 638-5660	B /8.2	3.48	1.12	8.84 /76	4.12 /77	--	3.72	0.56

● Denotes fund is closed to new investors
* Denotes fund is included in Section II

Risk Rating/Pts	3 Yr Avg Standard Deviation	Avg Dura-tion	NAV As of 2/28/17	Total $(Mil)	Cash %	Gov. Bond %	Muni. Bond %	Corp. Bond %	Other %	Portfolio Turnover Ratio	Avg Coupon Rate	Manager Quality Pct	Manager Tenure (Years)	Initial Purch. $	Additional Purch. $	Front End Load	Back End Load
B /7.7	2.4	4.3	24.41	146	2	29	0	61	8	11	0.0	32	7	25,000	1,000	0.0	0.0
E /0.5	7.6	6.3	10.44	1,500	0	0	0	0	100	90	5.7	99	10	1,000,000	250,000	0.0	0.0
D /2.0	5.1	4.5	9.06	15	1	3	0	94	2	127	5.6	98	10	1,000,000	250,000	0.0	0.0
U /	N/A	5.8	9.18	50	3	82	1	12	2	70	6.1	N/A	3	1,000,000	250,000	0.0	0.0
D- /1.5	5.8	4.5	8.34	215	0	0	0	0	100	48	6.2	81	10	1,000,000	250,000	0.0	0.0
C /5.4	3.0	N/A	10.25	17	11	20	0	36	33	52	0.0	33	4	1,000,000	250,000	0.0	0.0
D+ /2.6	4.4	N/A	9.80	39	8	23	0	53	16	26	0.0	82	4	1,000,000	250,000	0.0	0.0
C /5.4	3.0	N/A	8.75	18	2	97	0	0	1	0	0.0	25	13	500	100	5.8	0.0
C /5.4	3.0	N/A	8.83	2	2	97	0	0	1	0	0.0	10	13	500	100	0.0	0.0
C /5.2	3.1	N/A	8.76	7	2	97	0	0	1	0	0.0	48	13	0	0	0.0	0.0
C+ /6.1	2.9	6.2	9.71	209	0	22	0	33	45	71	3.4	32	15	0	0	0.0	0.0
C+ /5.6	3.0	5.8	10.49	143	4	35	0	6	55	17	2.8	59	6	0	0	0.0	0.0
C- /4.2	3.2	7.0	10.95	559	2	65	0	27	6	33	2.1	12	13	0	0	0.0	0.0
D- /1.5	5.5	7.7	11.34	198	2	89	0	7	2	95	3.8	87	8	0	0	0.0	0.0
C+ /5.9	2.9	6.2	11.14	1,029	2	15	0	42	41	139	3.8	47	15	0	0	0.0	0.0
D /1.9	5.2	5.2	7.88	627	7	0	0	90	3	36	6.3	90	8	0	0	0.0	0.0
C- /3.3	4.0	5.9	11.40	827	9	14	0	56	21	162	5.0	78	15	0	0	0.0	0.0
C- /3.6	3.7	5.2	11.35	615	1	0	98	0	1	13	5.0	54	14	2,500	100	0.0	0.0
A+ /9.9	N/A	N/A	1.00	5,297	100	0	0	0	0	0	0.2	44	8	25,000	1,000	0.0	0.0
D+ /2.6	4.2	7.8	9.54	836	0	0	0	0	100	49	3.9	35	14	2,500	100	0.0	0.0
U /	N/A	7.8	9.54	56	0	0	0	0	100	49	3.9	N/A	14	1,000,000	0	0.0	2.0
U /	N/A	N/A	8.68	42	7	0	0	86	7	101	0.0	N/A	2	2,500	100	0.0	2.0
U /	N/A	N/A	8.66	N/A	7	0	0	86	7	101	0.0	N/A	2	2,500	100	0.0	2.0
E- /0.1	12.0	N/A	6.57	248	4	92	0	3	1	90	0.0	59	6	2,500	100	0.0	2.0
D /1.8	5.4	5.5	10.38	1	8	2	0	83	7	115	6.7	97	2	2,500	100	0.0	2.0
U /	N/A	5.5	10.39	4	8	2	0	83	7	115	6.7	N/A	2	1,000,000	0	0.0	2.0
D /1.8	5.4	5.5	10.39	54	8	2	0	83	7	115	6.7	97	2	2,500	100	0.0	2.0
E+ /0.7	6.9	6.5	12.64	6,220	5	66	0	22	7	62	6.4	99	23	2,500	100	0.0	2.0
U /	N/A	6.5	12.64	1	5	66	0	22	7	62	6.4	N/A	23	2,500	100	0.0	2.0
U /	N/A	6.5	12.63	303	5	66	0	22	7	62	6.4	N/A	23	1,000,000	0	0.0	2.0
E- /0.1	12.0	N/A	6.56	N/A	4	92	0	3	1	90	0.0	56	6	2,500	100	0.0	2.0
U /	N/A	N/A	6.57	6	4	92	0	3	1	90	0.0	N/A	6	1,000,000	0	0.0	2.0
B /7.9	2.2	0.4	9.94	809	0	0	0	0	100	39	5.3	91	6	2,500	100	0.0	2.0
B /8.0	2.2	0.4	9.95	64	0	0	0	0	100	39	5.3	91	6	2,500	100	0.0	2.0
C /4.6	3.3	5.3	11.39	308	1	0	98	0	1	6	5.1	N/A	20	2,500	100	0.0	0.0
U /	N/A	N/A	10.26	46	0	0	0	0	100	79	0.0	N/A	2	2,500	100	0.0	2.0
U /	N/A	N/A	10.26	2	0	0	0	0	100	79	0.0	N/A	2	2,500	100	0.0	2.0
U /	N/A	N/A	10.25	15	0	0	0	0	100	79	0.0	N/A	2	1,000,000	0	0.0	2.0
C- /4.0	3.5	3.9	11.29	321	6	43	0	25	26	164	4.3	83	9	2,500	100	0.0	0.0
C- /4.0	3.5	3.9	11.30	18	6	43	0	25	26	164	4.3	80	9	2,500	100	0.0	0.0
U /	N/A	3.9	11.29	24	6	43	0	25	26	164	4.3	N/A	9	1,000,000	0	0.0	0.0
B+ /8.7	1.6	2.6	9.32	1,449	0	0	0	0	100	467	4.0	78	9	2,500	100	0.0	0.0
A+ /9.9	N/A	N/A	1.00	6,562	100	0	0	0	0	0	0.0	38	8	2,500	100	0.0	0.0
D- /1.4	5.3	3.2	6.76	7,941	3	0	0	83	14	68	6.9	44	21	2,500	100	0.0	2.0
D- /1.3	5.4	3.2	6.74	65	3	0	0	83	14	68	6.9	29	21	2,500	100	0.0	2.0
U /	N/A	3.2	6.76	2,044	3	0	0	83	14	68	6.9	N/A	21	1,000,000	0	0.0	2.0
C- /3.1	4.0	6.6	11.89	439	0	0	0	0	100	102	0.7	30	15	2,500	100	0.0	0.0
U /	N/A	6.6	11.90	45	0	0	0	0	100	102	0.7	N/A	15	1,000,000	0	0.0	0.0
D- /1.1	6.1	6.2	9.14	287	2	66	0	25	7	72	6.7	99	11	1,000,000	0	0.0	2.0
C+ /6.0	2.9	5.5	10.29	519	2	22	1	30	45	160	3.4	61	13	1,000,000	0	0.0	0.0
U /	N/A	N/A	8.55	25	4	0	0	88	8	106	0.0	N/A	2	1,000,000	0	0.0	2.0
C- /3.9	3.6	4.7	9.95	50	6	32	0	34	28	208	4.0	96	4	1,000,000	0	0.0	0.0

I. Index of Bond and Money Market Mutual Funds

Fund Type	Fund Name	Ticker Symbol	Overall Investment Rating	Phone	Performance Rating/Pts	3 Mo	6 Mo	1Yr / Pct	3Yr / Pct	5Yr / Pct	Dividend Yield	Expense Ratio
EM	T Rowe Price Inst Intl Bd	RPIIX	E-	(800) 638-5660	E- / 0.0	1.99	-7.42	1.26 /42	-2.29 / 2	-0.74 / 2	2.06	0.55
COI	T Rowe Price Inst Long Dur Cr	RPLCX	C-	(800) 638-5660	B+ / 8.8	3.32	-4.88	7.97 /74	5.71 /90	--	3.70	0.45
LP	T Rowe Price Instl Fltng Rate	RPIFX	A+	(800) 638-5660	B- / 7.4	1.79	3.02	9.47 /78	3.71 /72	4.51 /79	4.35	0.69
*LP	T Rowe Price Instl Fltng Rate F	PFFRX	A+	(800) 638-5660	B- / 7.2	1.75	2.94	9.33 /77	3.57 /70	4.39 /77	4.22	0.56
*COH ●	T Rowe Price Instl High Yield	TRHYX	C+	(800) 638-5660	A / 9.4	4.76	5.77	20.65 /97	4.37 /79	6.72 /96	5.93	0.50
MUH	T Rowe Price Int Tax-Fr Hi Yld	PRIHX	U	(800) 638-5660	U /	1.81	-2.66	0.78 /42	--	--	2.65	1.50
MUH	T Rowe Price Int Tax-Fr Hi Yld Adv	PRAHX	U	(800) 638-5660	U /	1.79	-2.71	0.68 /40	--	--	2.55	2.25
*GL	T Rowe Price Intl Bond	RPIBX	E-	(800) 638-5660	E- / 0.0	1.93	-7.38	1.05 /40	-2.59 / 1	-1.15 / 2	1.83	0.83
GL	T Rowe Price Intl Bond Adv	PAIBX	E-	(800) 638-5660	E- / 0.0	1.85	-7.60	0.78 /37	-2.89 / 1	-1.46 / 2	1.55	1.15
GL	T Rowe Price Intl Bond I	RPISX	U	(800) 638-5660	U /	1.96	-7.42	1.20 /42	--	--	1.99	0.82
*GEI	T Rowe Price Ltd Dur Inf Foc Bd	TRBFX	D+	(800) 638-5660	D / 2.0	0.70	0.70	2.32 /52	0.17 /16	0.08 /14	0.00	0.51
COI	T Rowe Price Ltd Dur Inf Foc Bd I	TRLDX	U	(800) 638-5660	U /	0.90	0.90	2.52 /53	--	--	0.00	0.35
MUS	T Rowe Price MD ShTm Tax-Free Bd	PRMDX	C	(800) 638-5660	D / 2.1	1.19	-0.55	--	0.43 /23	0.54 /25	0.77	0.55
*MUS	T Rowe Price MD Tax Free Bd	MDXBX	A+	(800) 638-5660	B / 8.0	1.80	-2.45	0.73 /41	3.64 /89	3.20 /83	3.39	0.46
MMF	T Rowe Price MD Tax-Free Money	TMDXX	U	(800) 638-5660	U /	--	--	--	--	--	0.01	N/A
*GEI	T Rowe Price New Income	PRCIX	C	(800) 638-5660	C / 4.8	1.18	-2.06	2.21 /51	2.48 /51	2.30 /46	2.54	0.55
GEI	T Rowe Price New Income Adv	PANIX	C-	(800) 638-5660	C / 4.4	1.12	-2.19	1.97 /49	2.25 /47	2.07 /43	2.31	0.78
COI	T Rowe Price New Income I	PRXEX	U	(800) 638-5660	U /	1.22	-2.09	2.37 /52	--	--	2.70	0.39
GEI	T Rowe Price New Income R	RRNIX	D+	(800) 638-5660	C- / 3.8	1.03	-2.45	1.63 /46	1.88 /41	1.74 /38	1.97	1.15
MUS	T Rowe Price NJ Tax-Free Bond	NJTFX	A-	(800) 638-5660	B / 7.9	1.66	-3.13	0.41 /35	3.73 /90	3.23 /84	3.24	0.52
MUS	T Rowe Price NY Tax Free Bd	PRNYX	A	(800) 638-5660	B+ / 8.3	1.98	-2.98	0.33 /33	3.95 /92	3.24 /84	3.32	0.51
*GES	T Rowe Price Short Term Bond	PRWBX	C+	(800) 638-5660	D+ / 2.8	0.42	0.18	1.82 /47	0.94 /27	1.09 /29	1.60	0.47
GES	T Rowe Price Short Term Bond Adv	PASHX	C	(800) 638-5660	D / 2.2	0.34	0.02	1.52 /45	0.57 /21	0.75 /24	1.30	0.75
COI	T Rowe Price Short Term Bond I	TBSIX	U	(800) 638-5660	U /	0.44	0.22	2.14 /50	--	--	1.70	0.36
*GES	T Rowe Price Spectrum Income	RPSIX	C+	(800) 638-5660	B- / 7.5	2.95	1.15	9.95 /79	3.32 /66	4.20 /75	3.41	0.69
MUN	T Rowe Price Summit Muni Inc Adv	PAIMX	B+	(800) 638-5660	B / 8.0	1.90	-3.62	0.01 /19	3.86 /92	--	3.03	0.75
*MUN	T Rowe Price Summit Muni Income	PRINX	A-	(800) 638-5660	B+ / 8.4	1.97	-3.50	0.27 /31	4.12 /94	3.65 /89	3.30	0.50
*MUN	T Rowe Price Summit Muni Intmdt	PRSMX	B	(800) 638-5660	C+ / 6.3	1.97	-2.66	-0.27 /13	2.66 /76	2.52 /71	2.63	0.50
MUN	T Rowe Price Summit Muni Intmdt	PAIFX	B-	(800) 638-5660	C+ / 5.8	1.99	-2.78	-0.52 / 9	2.40 /71	--	2.37	0.75
*MUH	T Rowe Price Tax-Free High Yield	PRFHX	B+	(800) 638-5660	A / 9.3	2.18	-3.36	1.64 /53	5.37 /98	4.99 /98	3.82	0.69
MUH	T Rowe Price Tax-Free High Yield Ad	PATFX	B+	(800) 638-5660	A- / 9.2	2.44	-3.19	1.84 /55	5.19 /97	--	3.48	0.63
*MUN	T Rowe Price Tax-Free Income	PRTAX	A	(800) 638-5660	B / 8.0	1.87	-2.94	0.25 /31	3.76 /90	3.28 /85	3.75	0.52
MUN	T Rowe Price Tax-Free Income Adv	PATAX	B+	(800) 638-5660	B- / 7.3	1.79	-3.10	-0.18 /15	3.36 /86	2.90 /78	3.40	0.86
*MUN	T Rowe Price Tax-Free Sh-Intmdt	PRFSX	C	(800) 638-5660	D+ / 2.8	1.45	-1.08	-0.26 /14	0.82 /32	1.05 /36	1.35	0.49
MUN	T Rowe Price Tax-Free Sh-Intmdt	PATIX	C-	(800) 638-5660	D / 2.1	1.55	-1.08	-0.44 /10	0.52 /24	--	0.99	0.87
COI	T Rowe Price Ultra Short Term Bond	TRBUX	B	(800) 638-5660	D+ / 2.9	0.36	0.68	2.08 /50	0.96 /32	--	1.26	0.40
*GEI	T Rowe Price US Bond Enhanced	PBDIX	C-	(800) 638-5660	C / 4.6	1.18	-2.19	1.76 /47	2.62 /54	2.24 /45	2.77	0.30
US	T Rowe Price US Treas Intmdt	PRTIX	E+	(800) 638-5660	D+ / 2.5	0.69	-3.00	-1.73 / 1	1.58 /36	1.00 /27	1.52	0.51
US	T Rowe Price US Treas Long-Term	PRULX	E+	(800) 638-5660	C+ / 6.1	1.76	-11.31	-4.70 / 0	5.33 /87	2.67 /52	2.50	0.52
MMT	T Rowe Price US Treasury Money	PRTXX	D+	(800) 638-5660	E+ / 0.7	0.03	0.03	0.04 /20	0.02 / 8	0.02 / 8	0.04	N/A
*MUS	T Rowe Price VA Tax-Free Bond	PRVAX	A+	(800) 638-5660	B / 8.0	1.76	-2.81	0.56 /38	3.71 /90	3.06 /81	3.21	0.47
USA	TCG Advantage Money Market Inst	GAIXX	U	(866) 707-8588	U /	0.14	0.24	0.45 /32	--	--	0.45	0.64
USA	TCG Cash Reserve Mny Mkt Inst	CRIXX	U	(866) 707-8588	U /	0.14	0.24	0.45 /32	--	--	0.45	0.64
USA	TCG Daily Liquidity Mny Mkt Inst	DLIXX	U	(866) 707-8588	U /	0.14	0.24	0.45 /32	--	--	0.45	0.64
USA	TCG Liquid Assets Money Market Inst	LSIXX	U	(866) 707-8588	U /	0.14	0.24	0.45 /32	--	--	0.45	0.64
USA	TCG Liquidity Plus Mny Mkt Inst	LPIXX	U	(866) 707-8588	U /	0.13	0.24	0.45 /32	--	--	0.45	0.64
USA	TCG Max Money Market Inst	GXIXX	U	(866) 707-8588	U /	0.14	0.24	0.44 /32	--	--	0.44	0.64
USA	TCG Premier Money Market Inst	GRIXX	U	(866) 707-8588	U /	0.14	0.24	0.44 /32	--	--	0.44	0.64
USA	TCG Primary Liquidity Mny Mkt Inst	GQIXX	U	(866) 707-8588	U /	0.14	0.24	0.45 /32	--	--	0.45	0.64
USA	TCG Select Money Market Inst	GLIXX	U	(866) 707-8588	U /	0.14	0.24	0.44 /32	--	--	0.44	0.64
USA	TCG Ultra Money Market Inst	GUIXX	U	(866) 707-8588	U /	0.14	0.24	0.45 /32	--	--	0.44	0.64
USS	TCW Core Fixed Income I	TGCFX	C+	(800) 386-3829	C / 4.3	0.85	-1.86	1.42 /44	2.28 /48	2.53 /50	1.77	0.50

● Denotes fund is closed to new investors
* Denotes fund is included in Section II

www.thestreetratings.com

RISK			NET ASSETS		ASSET					Portfolio Turnover Ratio	Avg Coupon Rate	FUND MANAGER		MINIMUM		LOADS	
Risk Rating/Pts	3 Yr Avg Standard Deviation	Avg Dura-tion	NAV As of 2/28/17	Total $(Mil)	Cash %	Gov. Bond %	Muni. Bond %	Corp. Bond %	Other %			Manager Quality Pct	Manager Tenure (Years)	Initial Purch. $	Additional Purch. $	Front End Load	Back End Load
E /0.4	7.6	9.0	8.33	325	4	74	1	17	4	63	3.5	55	3	1,000,000	0	0.0	2.0
E /0.5	7.5	N/A	10.34	36	3	7	0	88	2	56	0.0	12	4	1,000,000	0	0.0	0.0
B /7.9	2.3	0.4	10.09	4,378	7	0	0	70	23	50	5.2	92	8	1,000,000	0	0.0	2.0
B /7.9	2.3	0.4	10.08	529	7	0	0	70	23	50	5.2	92	8	2,500	100	0.0	2.0
D- /1.1	5.7	3.1	9.00	1,748	3	0	0	86	11	70	7.0	42	2	1,000,000	0	0.0	2.0
U /	N/A	N/A	10.15	52	0	0	99	0	1	16	0.0	N/A	3	2,500	100	0.0	2.0
U /	N/A	N/A	10.15	1	0	0	99	0	1	16	0.0	N/A	3	2,500	100	0.0	2.0
E /0.4	7.6	9.0	8.47	3,997	4	74	1	18	3	60	3.5	37	3	2,500	100	0.0	2.0
E /0.4	7.6	9.0	8.48	12	4	74	1	18	3	60	3.5	27	3	2,500	100	0.0	2.0
U /	N/A	9.0	8.47	573	4	74	1	18	3	60	3.5	N/A	3	1,000,000	0	0.0	2.0
B+ /8.4	1.9	2.5	5.03	7,348	0	72	0	18	10	105	0.6	15	N/A	2,500	100	0.0	0.0
U /	N/A	2.5	5.04	422	0	72	0	18	10	105	0.6	N/A	N/A	1,000,000	0	0.0	0.0
A- /9.1	1.1	2.2	5.20	206	0	0	99	0	1	24	4.7	19	21	2,500	100	0.0	0.0
C+ /6.7	2.8	4.2	10.68	2,178	1	0	98	0	1	7	5.0	69	17	2,500	100	0.0	0.0
U /	N/A	N/A	1.00	136	100	0	0	0	0	0	0.0	N/A	16	2,500	100	0.0	0.0
C+ /6.3	2.9	5.5	9.43	28,669	4	15	1	28	52	164	3.2	40	17	2,500	100	0.0	0.0
C+ /6.1	2.9	5.5	9.41	59	4	15	1	28	52	164	3.2	29	17	2,500	100	0.0	0.0
U /	N/A	5.5	9.42	2,456	4	15	1	28	52	164	3.2	N/A	17	1,000,000	0	0.0	0.0
C+ /6.2	2.9	5.5	9.42	9	4	15	1	28	52	164	3.2	19	17	2,500	100	0.0	0.0
C /4.7	3.2	4.7	11.87	368	1	0	98	0	1	8	5.1	59	17	2,500	100	0.0	0.0
C /4.8	3.2	4.6	11.53	472	1	0	98	0	1	12	5.1	65	17	2,500	100	0.0	0.0
A /9.4	0.8	1.8	4.72	4,265	0	6	0	51	43	44	2.3	59	2	2,500	100	0.0	0.0
A /9.3	0.9	1.8	4.71	78	0	6	0	51	43	44	2.3	35	2	2,500	100	0.0	0.0
U /	N/A	1.8	4.72	773	0	6	0	51	43	44	2.3	N/A	2	1,000,000	0	0.0	0.0
C- /3.4	3.8	5.2	12.58	6,349	3	23	0	34	40	18	4.7	82	19	2,500	100	0.0	0.0
C- /4.1	3.5	4.8	11.71	6	1	0	98	0	1	6	5.1	54	18	25,000	1,000	0.0	0.0
C- /4.1	3.5	4.8	11.71	1,231	1	0	98	0	1	6	5.1	63	18	25,000	1,000	0.0	0.0
C+ /6.0	2.9	4.5	11.75	4,246	1	0	98	0	1	12	5.1	24	24	25,000	1,000	0.0	0.0
C+ /6.0	2.9	4.5	11.75	6	1	0	98	0	1	12	5.1	17	24	25,000	1,000	0.0	0.0
D+ /2.7	3.8	5.2	11.77	4,034	0	0	0	0	100	13	5.3	81	15	2,500	100	0.0	2.0
D+ /2.8	3.7	5.2	11.83	452	0	0	0	0	100	13	5.3	79	15	2,500	100	0.0	2.0
C /5.0	3.1	4.5	10.07	1,957	0	0	99	0	1	8	5.2	62	10	2,500	100	0.0	0.0
C /5.0	3.1	4.5	10.07	592	0	0	99	0	1	8	5.2	45	10	2,500	100	0.0	0.0
B+ /8.6	1.7	2.9	5.58	1,920	0	0	99	0	1	15	5.0	14	23	2,500	100	0.0	0.0
B+ /8.6	1.7	2.9	5.58	15	0	0	99	0	1	15	5.0	9	23	2,500	100	0.0	0.0
A+ /9.8	0.5	N/A	5.01	330	0	11	0	61	28	99	0.0	68	4	2,500	100	0.0	0.0
C /5.4	3.0	5.6	10.95	655	0	25	3	33	39	96	3.3	37	17	2,500	100	0.0	0.5
C- /3.5	3.8	5.6	5.74	356	0	94	0	0	6	47	2.2	25	10	2,500	100	0.0	0.0
E- /0.2	11.0	18.0	12.36	361	1	94	0	0	5	36	3.4	31	14	2,500	100	0.0	0.0
A+ /9.9	N/A	N/A	1.00	2,068	100	0	0	0	0	0	0.0	39	8	2,500	100	0.0	0.0
C+ /5.9	2.9	4.7	11.90	1,159	1	0	98	0	1	11	5.0	66	20	2,500	100	0.0	0.0
U /	N/A	N/A	1.00	30	0	0	0	0	100	0	0.0	N/A	2	500	50	0.0	0.0
U /	N/A	N/A	1.00	30	0	0	0	0	100	0	0.0	N/A	1	500	50	0.0	0.0
U /	N/A	N/A	1.00	30	0	0	0	0	100	0	0.0	N/A	2	500	50	0.0	0.0
U /	N/A	N/A	1.00	30	0	0	0	0	100	0	0.0	N/A	2	500	50	0.0	0.0
U /	N/A	N/A	1.00	30	0	0	0	0	100	0	0.0	N/A	1	500	50	0.0	0.0
U /	N/A	N/A	1.00	30	0	0	0	0	100	0	0.0	N/A	1	500	50	0.0	0.0
U /	N/A	N/A	1.00	30	0	0	0	0	100	0	0.0	N/A	2	500	50	0.0	0.0
U /	N/A	N/A	1.00	30	0	0	0	0	100	0	0.0	N/A	1	500	50	0.0	0.0
U /	N/A	N/A	1.00	30	0	0	0	0	100	0	0.0	N/A	2	500	50	0.0	0.0
U /	N/A	N/A	1.00	30	0	0	0	0	100	0	0.0	N/A	1	500	50	0.0	0.0
B /7.6	2.5	4.9	10.94	1,303	0	33	0	22	45	283	2.7	73	7	2,000	250	0.0	0.0

						PERFORMANCE							
	99 Pct = Best 0 Pct = Worst						Total Return % through 2/28/17					Incl. in Returns	
			Ticker	Overall Investment		Perfor- mance				Annualized		Dividend	Expense
Fund Type	Fund Name		Symbol	Rating	Phone	Rating/Pts	3 Mo	6 Mo	1Yr / Pct	3Yr / Pct	5Yr / Pct	Yield	Ratio
USS	TCW Core Fixed Income N		TGFNX	C+	(800) 386-3829	C- / 3.8	0.79	-1.98	1.11 / 41	1.98 / 43	2.42 / 48	1.55	0.79
EM	TCW Emerging Markets Income I		TGEIX	C+	(800) 386-3829	A+ / 9.6	6.19	2.43	17.95 / 93	4.84 / 84	4.94 / 83	5.14	0.88
* EM	TCW Emerging Markets Income N		TGINX	C+	(800) 386-3829	A / 9.4	6.14	2.29	17.56 / 93	4.54 / 81	4.65 / 80	4.88	1.16
GL	TCW Emg Mkts Local Currency Inc I		TGWIX	E	(800) 386-3829	C- / 3.7	7.67	1.79	16.33 / 91	-1.37 / 2	-1.51 / 2	0.00	1.00
GL	TCW Emg Mkts Local Currency Inc N		TGWNX	E	(800) 386-3829	C- / 3.7	7.56	1.79	16.20 / 91	-1.37 / 2	-1.55 / 2	0.00	1.25
GL	TCW Global Bond I		TGGBX	E	(800) 386-3829	E- / 0.2	0.81	-4.05	0.21 / 26	-0.61 / 3	1.20 / 30	2.07	1.37
GL	TCW Global Bond N		TGGFX	E	(800) 386-3829	E- / 0.2	0.81	-4.05	0.21 / 26	-0.61 / 3	1.20 / 30	2.07	1.64
COH	TCW High Yield Bond I		TGHYX	B-	(800) 386-3829	B / 8.1	2.90	2.95	9.34 / 77	3.82 / 73	5.75 / 90	4.16	1.03
COH	TCW High Yield Bond N		TGHNX	C+	(800) 386-3829	B / 7.7	2.69	2.73	8.95 / 76	3.50 / 69	5.50 / 88	4.01	1.38
MTG	TCW Short Term Bond I		TGSMX	C+	(800) 386-3829	D / 2.1	0.21	0.54	0.99 / 39	0.53 / 21	0.85 / 25	0.99	1.57
MTG	TCW Total Return Bond I		TGLMX	C+	(800) 386-3829	C- / 4.2	0.73	-2.21	0.40 / 31	2.42 / 50	4.11 / 74	2.51	0.60
*MTG	TCW Total Return Bond N		TGMNX	C+	(800) 386-3829	C- / 3.7	0.56	-2.42	0.01 / 17	2.10 / 45	3.79 / 70	2.25	0.88
COI	TD 1 to 5 Year Corporate Bond Ptf		TDFPX	B		C- / 3.6	0.80	-0.21	2.19 / 51	1.51 / 35	--	1.86	0.83
COI	TD 5 to 10 Year Corporate Bd Ptf		TDFSX	D+		C+ / 6.0	1.46	-2.50	3.31 / 58	3.25 / 65	--	2.88	0.93
MMF	TD California Municipal Mny Mkt Inv		WCAXX	U		U /	--	--	--	--	--	0.01	N/A
GEI	TD Core Bond Adv		TDCBX	D+		C- / 3.8	0.78	-2.68	0.64 / 36	2.12 / 45	--	1.88	1.24
GEI	TD Core Bond Inst		TDBFX	D		C- / 3.9	0.79	-2.67	0.66 / 36	2.13 / 45	--	1.89	0.99
COH	TD High Yield Bond Adv		TDHYX	B-		B+ / 8.9	2.11	3.73	15.17 / 89	4.08 / 76	--	4.31	3.00
COH	TD High Yield Bond Inst		TDHBX	B-		A- / 9.0	2.14	3.87	15.32 / 89	4.13 / 77	--	4.34	2.68
MMT	TD Inst Treasury Obligs MM Com		TTCXX	U		U /	--	--	--	--	--	0.02	N/A
MMT	TD Inst Treasury Obligs MM IS		TDVXX	D+		E+ / 0.7	0.03	0.04	0.07 / 21	0.03 / 9	0.02 / 8	0.07	N/A
MMT	TD Money Market Inv		WTOXX	U		U /	--	--	--	--	--	0.02	N/A
MMT	TD Money Market Prem		NPLXX	D+		E+ / 0.7	0.03	0.04	0.04 / 20	0.02 / 8	0.02 / 8	0.04	N/A
MMT	TD Money Market Select		TDSXX	D+		E+ / 0.7	0.03	0.04	0.04 / 20	0.02 / 8	0.02 / 8	0.04	N/A
MMF	TD Municipal Investor		WTMXX	U		U /	--	--	--	--	--	0.01	N/A
MMF	TD NY Municipal Mny Mkt Inv		WNYXX	U		U /	--	--	--	--	--	0.01	N/A
COI	TD Short-Term Bond Adv		TDSHX	C+		D+ / 2.4	0.52	0.05	1.36 / 43	0.77 / 24	--	1.26	0.94
COI	TD Short-Term Bond Inst		TDSBX	C+		D+ / 2.4	0.52	0.05	1.36 / 43	0.77 / 24	0.83 / 25	1.25	0.68
MMT	TD US Government Commercial		TGCXX	U		U /	--	--	--	--	--	0.01	N/A
MMT	TD US Government Inv		WTUXX	U		U /	--	--	--	--	--	0.01	N/A
EM	Templeton Emerging Markets Bond A		FEMGX	C-	(800) 342-5236	B+ / 8.7	8.27	7.90	19.71 / 95	3.36 / 67	--	2.44	2.57
EM	Templeton Emerging Markets Bond		FEMZX	C	(800) 342-5236	A / 9.5	8.31	7.90	19.96 / 96	3.53 / 69	--	2.66	2.32
EM	Templeton Emerging Markets Bond C		FEMHX	C	(800) 342-5236	A- / 9.1	8.23	7.55	19.20 / 95	2.85 / 59	--	2.13	2.97
EM	Templeton Emerging Markets Bond R			C	(800) 342-5236	A / 9.3	8.31	7.97	19.68 / 95	3.13 / 63	--	2.07	2.82
EM	Templeton Emerging Markets Bond			C	(800) 342-5236	A / 9.5	8.45	8.02	20.09 / 96	3.61 / 70	--	2.76	4.95
* GL	Templeton Global Bond A		TPINX	D-	(800) 342-5236	C+ / 6.7	5.67	9.24	12.99 / 85	2.18 / 46	2.96 / 57	2.11	0.96
GL	Templeton Global Bond Adv		TGBAX	D+	(800) 321-8563	B / 8.1	5.77	9.32	13.23 / 86	2.42 / 50	3.21 / 61	2.45	0.71
GL	Templeton Global Bond C		TEGBX	D	(800) 342-5236	B- / 7.4	5.65	9.00	12.51 / 84	1.77 / 39	2.56 / 50	1.82	1.36
GL	Templeton Global Bond R		FGBRX	D	(800) 342-5236	B / 7.6	5.61	9.11	12.71 / 84	1.93 / 42	2.70 / 53	1.97	1.21
GL	Templeton Global Bond R6		FBNRX	C-	(800) 342-5236	B+ / 8.3	5.81	9.41	13.41 / 86	2.57 / 53	3.20 / 61	2.60	0.56
GL	Templeton Global Currency A		ICPHX	E-	(800) 342-5236	E- / 0.0	2.86	2.73	4.08 / 62	-4.63 / 0	-3.74 / 0	0.00	1.41
GL	Templeton Global Currency Advisor		ICHHX	E-	(800) 321-8563	E- / 0.1	2.95	2.95	4.42 / 64	-4.36 / 0	-3.47 / 0	0.00	1.16
* GL	Templeton Global Total Return A		TGTRX	D-	(800) 342-5236	B- / 7.2	5.76	9.44	15.93 / 90	2.24 / 47	3.72 / 69	2.59	1.08
GL	Templeton Global Total Return Adv		TTRZX	C-	(800) 321-8563	B+ / 8.6	5.81	9.56	16.18 / 90	2.49 / 52	3.99 / 72	2.93	0.83
GL	Templeton Global Total Return C		TTRCX	D	(800) 342-5236	B / 7.8	5.57	9.14	15.39 / 89	1.81 / 40	3.30 / 62	2.33	1.48
GL	Templeton Global Total Return R			D+	(800) 342-5236	B / 8.0	5.60	9.21	15.53 / 89	1.96 / 42	3.46 / 65	2.47	1.33
GL	Templeton Global Total Return R6		FTTRX	C-	(800) 342-5236	B+ / 8.7	5.85	9.63	16.35 / 91	2.59 / 54	4.07 / 73	3.06	0.70
GL	Templeton International Bond A		TBOAX	E+	(800) 342-5236	C- / 3.8	5.66	8.11	11.92 / 83	0.20 / 16	1.32 / 32	0.78	1.31
GL	Templeton International Bond Adv		FIBZX	D-	(800) 321-8563	C+ / 6.0	5.72	8.20	12.27 / 84	0.46 / 20	1.59 / 36	1.02	1.06
GL	Templeton International Bond C		FCNBX	E+	(800) 342-5236	C / 4.9	5.55	7.85	11.44 / 82	-0.18 / 4	0.93 / 27	0.42	1.71
GL	Templeton International Bond R			E+	(800) 342-5236	C / 5.1	5.51	7.88	11.54 / 82	-0.06 / 5	1.06 / 28	0.59	1.56
GEI	TETON Westwood Interm Bond A		WEAIX	E+	(800) 422-3554	E / 0.4	0.73	-2.27	0.53 / 34	0.93 / 26	0.59 / 22	1.10	1.47

● Denotes fund is closed to new investors
* Denotes fund is included in Section II

| RISK | | | NET ASSETS | | ASSET | | | | | Portfolio | Avg | FUND MANAGER | | MINIMUM | | LOADS | |
Risk Rating/Pts	3 Yr Avg Standard Deviation	Avg Dura-tion	NAV As of 2/28/17	Total $(Mil)	Cash %	Gov. Bond %	Muni. Bond %	Corp. Bond %	Other %	Portfolio Turnover Ratio	Avg Coupon Rate	Manager Quality Pct	Manager Tenure (Years)	Initial Purch. $	Additional Purch. $	Front End Load	Back End Load
B / 7.6	2.5	4.9	10.91	421	0	33	0	22	45	283	2.7	66	7	2,000	250	0.0	0.0
E+ / 0.7	6.6	6.4	8.37	2,769	3	64	0	31	2	215	6.2	98	7	2,000	250	0.0	0.0
E+ / 0.8	6.6	6.4	10.78	544	3	64	0	31	2	215	6.2	98	7	2,000	250	0.0	0.0
E- / 0.1	11.6	5.5	9.12	103	1	97	0	0	2	209	7.8	79	7	2,000	250	0.0	0.0
E- / 0.1	11.6	5.5	9.11	13	1	97	0	0	2	209	7.8	80	7	2,000	250	0.0	0.0
C- / 3.4	3.8	5.9	9.53	8	0	57	0	20	23	117	3.3	68	6	2,000	250	0.0	0.0
C- / 3.4	3.8	5.9	9.53	7	0	57	0	20	23	117	3.3	68	6	2,000	250	0.0	0.0
C- / 3.1	3.6	2.1	6.30	19	1	14	0	81	4	244	4.6	80	6	2,000	250	0.0	0.0
C- / 3.1	3.6	2.1	6.34	9	1	14	0	81	4	244	4.6	76	6	2,000	250	0.0	0.0
A+ / 9.9	0.4	0.6	8.68	9	1	49	0	24	26	46	1.5	56	7	2,000	250	0.0	0.0
B / 7.6	2.5	4.9	9.91	7,313	0	32	0	0	68	318	2.7	27	7	2,000	250	0.0	0.0
B / 7.7	2.4	4.9	10.22	2,342	0	32	0	0	68	318	2.7	20	7	2,000	250	0.0	0.0
B+ / 8.9	1.4	2.7	10.05	63	0	0	0	0	100	72	0.0	59	N/A	0	0	0.0	0.0
C- / 3.3	3.9	6.5	10.17	42	0	0	0	0	100	70	0.0	31	N/A	0	0	0.0	0.0
U /	N/A	N/A	1.00	151	100	0	0	0	0	0	0.0	N/A	N/A	0	0	0.0	0.0
C+ / 6.0	2.9	5.6	9.94	N/A	0	0	0	0	100	102	0.0	23	N/A	0	0	0.0	0.0
C+ / 5.8	3.0	5.6	9.94	41	0	0	0	0	100	102	0.0	22	N/A	0	0	0.0	0.0
D / 2.0	4.5	4.1	9.94	N/A	0	0	0	0	100	38	0.0	70	4	0	0	0.0	0.0
D / 2.0	4.5	4.1	9.95	9	0	0	0	0	100	38	0.0	71	4	0	0	0.0	0.0
U /	N/A	N/A	1.00	518	100	0	0	0	0	0	0.0	39	N/A	0	0	0.0	0.0
A+ / 9.9	N/A	N/A	1.00	312	100	0	0	0	0	0	0.1	41	N/A	0	0	0.0	0.0
U /	N/A	N/A	1.00	445	100	0	0	0	0	0	0.0	N/A	N/A	0	0	0.0	0.0
A+ / 9.9	N/A	N/A	1.00	61	100	0	0	0	0	0	0.0	39	N/A	100,000	5,000	0.0	0.0
A+ / 9.9	N/A	N/A	1.00	282	100	0	0	0	0	0	0.0	39	N/A	50,000	0	0.0	0.0
U /	N/A	N/A	1.00	402	100	0	0	0	0	0	0.0	N/A	22	0	0	0.0	0.0
U /	N/A	N/A	1.00	100	100	0	0	0	0	0	0.0	N/A	N/A	0	0	0.0	0.0
A / 9.5	0.8	1.8	10.16	N/A	3	11	3	61	22	116	0.0	48	8	0	0	0.0	0.0
A / 9.4	0.8	1.8	10.16	51	3	11	3	61	22	116	0.0	46	8	0	0	0.0	0.0
U /	N/A	N/A	1.00	92	100	0	0	0	0	0	0.0	N/A	N/A	0	0	0.0	0.0
U /	N/A	N/A	1.00	862	100	0	0	0	0	0	0.0	N/A	N/A	0	0	0.0	0.0
E+ / 0.6	7.5	N/A	9.27	14	22	67	0	9	2	40	0.0	95	4	1,000	0	4.3	0.0
E / 0.5	7.6	N/A	9.29	N/A	22	67	0	9	2	40	0.0	95	4	1,000	0	0.0	0.0
E / 0.5	7.7	N/A	9.26	1	22	67	0	9	2	40	0.0	94	4	1,000	0	0.0	0.0
E / 0.5	7.6	N/A	9.28	N/A	22	67	0	9	2	40	0.0	94	4	1,000	0	0.0	0.0
E / 0.5	7.7	N/A	9.29	N/A	22	67	0	9	2	40	0.0	95	4	1,000,000	0	0.0	0.0
E+ / 0.9	6.4	N/A	12.23	12,455	14	83	0	1	2	50	5.5	83	16	1,000	0	4.3	0.0
E+ / 0.9	6.4	N/A	12.18	20,559	14	83	0	1	2	50	5.5	85	16	1,000	0	0.0	0.0
E+ / 0.9	6.4	N/A	12.26	3,960	14	83	0	1	2	50	5.5	80	16	1,000	0	0.0	0.0
E+ / 0.9	6.4	N/A	12.23	295	14	83	0	1	2	50	5.5	81	16	1,000	0	0.0	0.0
E+ / 0.9	6.4	N/A	12.18	2,959	14	83	0	1	2	50	5.5	86	16	1,000,000	0	0.0	0.0
D- / 1.4	5.8	0.3	7.91	43	24	75	0	0	1	0	0.0	0	16	1,000	0	2.3	0.0
D- / 1.4	5.8	0.3	8.03	13	24	75	0	0	1	0	0.0	0	16	1,000,000	0	0.0	0.0
E+ / 0.8	6.7	0.4	12.30	1,171	16	81	0	0	3	44	5.9	84	9	1,000	0	4.3	0.0
E+ / 0.8	6.7	0.4	12.32	2,704	16	81	0	0	3	44	5.9	86	9	1,000	0	0.0	0.0
E+ / 0.8	6.7	0.4	12.28	472	16	81	0	0	3	44	5.9	81	9	1,000	0	0.0	0.0
E+ / 0.8	6.7	0.4	12.30	10	16	81	0	0	3	44	5.9	82	9	1,000	0	0.0	0.0
E+ / 0.7	6.8	0.4	12.31	890	16	81	0	0	3	44	5.9	87	9	1,000,000	0	0.0	0.0
D- / 1.2	6.0	0.8	10.83	84	36	63	0	0	1	106	4.9	56	10	1,000	0	4.3	0.0
D- / 1.2	6.1	0.8	10.84	245	36	63	0	0	1	106	4.9	65	10	1,000	0	0.0	0.0
D- / 1.2	6.0	0.8	10.84	11	36	63	0	0	1	106	4.9	34	10	1,000	0	0.0	0.0
D- / 1.2	6.1	0.8	10.82	N/A	36	63	0	0	1	106	4.9	41	10	1,000	0	0.0	0.0
B / 7.6	2.5	4.4	11.24	1	9	30	0	59	2	48	0.0	8	18	1,000	0	4.0	0.0

Fund Type	Fund Name	Ticker Symbol	Overall Investment Rating	Phone	Perfor-mance Rating/Pts	3 Mo	6 Mo	1Yr / Pct	3Yr / Pct	5Yr / Pct	Dividend Yield	Expense Ratio
GEI	TETON Westwood Interm Bond AAA	WEIBX	D	(800) 422-3554	D+ / 2.4	0.76	-2.22	0.63 / 35	1.03 / 28	0.69 / 23	1.24	1.37
GEI	TETON Westwood Interm Bond C	WECIX	D-	(800) 422-3554	E+ / 0.8	0.60	-2.55	-0.06 / 17	0.28 / 18	-0.07 / 5	0.49	2.12
GEI	TETON Westwood Interm Bond I	WEIIX	C-	(800) 422-3554	D+ / 2.8	0.73	-2.18	0.79 / 37	1.28 / 32	0.93 / 26	1.50	1.12
COH	Third Avenue Focused Credit Inst	TFCIX	E-	(800) 443-1021	E- / 0.0	11.59	15.93	24.82 / 99	-10.39 / 0	-0.73 / 2	47.98	0.88
*GEI	Thompson Bond	THOPX	B-	(800) 999-0887	B / 8.0	2.84	3.66	15.78 / 90	2.69 / 56	3.81 / 70	4.17	0.71
MUS	Thornburg CA Ltd Term Muni A	LTCAX	D+	(800) 847-0200	D / 2.2	1.52	-1.86	-1.04 / 4	1.22 / 41	1.54 / 47	1.27	0.94
MUS	Thornburg CA Ltd Term Muni C	LTCCX	C-	(800) 847-0200	D+ / 2.6	1.46	-2.05	-1.28 / 3	0.98 / 35	1.28 / 42	1.04	1.18
MUS	Thornburg CA Ltd Term Muni Inst	LTCIX	C+	(800) 847-0200	C- / 4.0	1.60	-1.78	-0.74 / 7	1.54 / 50	1.86 / 56	1.60	0.63
MUN	Thornburg Intermediate Muni A	THIMX	C-	(800) 847-0200	C- / 3.6	1.41	-2.97	-0.80 / 6	2.09 / 65	2.20 / 64	2.03	0.92
MUN	Thornburg Intermediate Muni C	THMCX	C	(800) 847-0200	C- / 4.0	1.26	-3.20	-1.19 / 3	1.76 / 56	1.86 / 56	1.74	1.28
MUN	Thornburg Intermediate Muni Inst	THMIX	B	(800) 847-0200	C+ / 5.7	1.49	-2.84	-0.50 / 9	2.40 / 71	2.52 / 71	2.38	0.62
*GES	Thornburg Limited Term Income A	THIFX	B	(800) 847-0200	C- / 3.9	0.83	-0.02	2.87 / 56	2.01 / 43	2.58 / 51	1.83	0.87
GES	Thornburg Limited Term Income C	THICX	B	(800) 847-0200	C- / 4.1	0.77	-0.13	2.65 / 54	1.78 / 39	2.35 / 47	1.65	1.10
GES	Thornburg Limited Term Income Inst	THIIX	A	(800) 847-0200	C / 5.1	0.84	0.09	3.24 / 58	2.37 / 50	2.94 / 57	2.22	0.52
GES	Thornburg Limited Term Income R3	THIRX	B+	(800) 847-0200	C / 4.3	0.79	-0.08	2.75 / 55	1.89 / 41	2.47 / 49	1.74	1.11
COI	Thornburg Limited Term Income R4	THRIX	B+	(800) 847-0200	C / 4.3	0.72	-0.16	2.74 / 55	1.92 / 42	—	1.73	1.66
COI	Thornburg Limited Term Income R5	THRRX	A-	(800) 847-0200	C / 4.9	0.88	0.08	3.08 / 57	2.25 / 47	—	2.06	0.67
*MUN	Thornburg Limited Term Muni A	LTMFX	D+	(800) 847-0200	D / 2.1	1.55	-1.73	-0.71 / 7	1.06 / 37	1.28 / 42	1.56	0.73
MUN	Thornburg Limited Term Muni C	LTMCX	C-	(800) 847-0200	D+ / 2.5	1.56	-1.84	-0.94 / 5	0.85 / 32	1.03 / 36	1.34	0.96
MUN	Thornburg Limited Term Muni Inst	LTMIX	C+	(800) 847-0200	C- / 3.8	1.63	-1.58	-0.40 / 11	1.38 / 45	1.59 / 49	1.90	0.41
USS	Thornburg Limited Term US Govt A	LTUSX	D+	(800) 847-0200	D / 1.6	0.19	-0.83	-0.17 / 15	0.91 / 26	0.71 / 24	1.50	0.92
USS	Thornburg Limited Term US Govt C	LTUCX	C-	(800) 847-0200	D / 1.8	0.12	-0.96	-0.44 / 10	0.64 / 22	0.43 / 21	1.24	1.21
USS	Thornburg Limited Term US Govt Inst	LTUIX	C+	(800) 847-0200	D+ / 2.7	0.27	-0.67	0.16 / 24	1.23 / 31	1.03 / 28	1.86	0.62
USS	Thornburg Limited Term US Govt R3	LTURX	C-	(800) 847-0200	D / 2.1	0.25	-0.86	-0.15 / 15	0.85 / 25	0.63 / 23	1.46	1.35
USS	Thornburg Limited Term US Govt R4	LTUGX	C-	(800) 847-0200	D / 2.1	0.17	-0.94	-0.24 / 14	0.91 / 26	—	1.45	1.13
USS	Thornburg Limited Term US Govt R5	LTGRX	C	(800) 847-0200	D+ / 2.6	0.25	-0.79	0.15 / 24	1.19 / 31	—	1.77	2.02
COI	Thornburg Low Duration Income A	TLDAX	C+	(800) 847-0200	D+ / 2.3	0.57	0.41	1.70 / 46	1.04 / 28	—	1.10	2.10
COI	Thornburg Low Duration Income I	TLDIX	B	(800) 847-0200	C- / 3.1	0.49	0.39	1.78 / 47	1.17 / 30	—	1.28	1.89
MUN	Thornburg Low Duration Municipal A	TLMAX	D	(800) 847-0200	E / 0.4	0.56	-0.02	0.04 / 21	0.22 / 19	—	0.36	2.85
MUN	Thornburg Low Duration Municipal I	TLMIX	C+	(800) 847-0200	D / 2.1	0.60	0.07	0.31 / 33	0.41 / 22	—	0.55	0.82
MUS	Thornburg NM Intermediate Muni A	THNMX	C	(800) 847-0200	C- / 3.3	1.14	-2.28	-0.79 / 6	1.90 / 60	1.69 / 51	2.25	0.98
MUS	Thornburg NM Intermediate Muni D	THNDX	C+	(800) 847-0200	C- / 3.9	1.02	-2.39	-1.10 / 4	1.66 / 53	1.43 / 45	2.06	1.20
MUS	Thornburg NM Intermediate Muni I	THNIX	A-	(800) 847-0200	C / 5.4	1.23	-2.13	-0.54 / 9	2.24 / 68	2.01 / 59	2.63	0.65
MUN	Thornburg NY Interm Muni I	TNYIX	B+	(800) 847-0200	C+ / 5.7	1.59	-2.42	-0.39 / 11	2.35 / 70	2.23 / 64	2.70	0.76
MUN	Thornburg NY Intermediate Muni A	THNYX	C	(800) 847-0200	C- / 3.6	1.51	-2.58	-0.71 / 7	2.03 / 63	1.91 / 57	2.33	1.05
GES	Thornburg Strategic Income Fd A	TSIAX	C-	(800) 847-0200	C / 5.5	2.47	2.08	10.55 / 80	2.67 / 55	4.74 / 81	2.74	1.23
GES	Thornburg Strategic Income Fd C	TSICX	C	(800) 847-0200	C+ / 6.4	2.33	1.81	9.96 / 79	2.09 / 45	4.15 / 74	2.32	1.97
GES	Thornburg Strategic Income Fd I	TSIIX	B	(800) 847-0200	B- / 7.5	2.57	2.27	10.96 / 81	2.99 / 61	5.08 / 85	3.21	0.89
GL	Thornburg Strategic Income Fd R3	TSIRX	B-	(800) 847-0200	B- / 7.1	2.47	2.00	10.47 / 80	2.60 / 54	—	2.87	2.70
GL	Thornburg Strategic Income Fd R4	TSRIX	B-	(800) 847-0200	B- / 7.2	2.47	2.09	10.56 / 80	2.73 / 57	—	2.87	2.64
GL	Thornburg Strategic Income Fd R5	TSRRX	B	(800) 847-0200	B- / 7.4	2.55	2.24	10.88 / 81	2.93 / 60	—	3.14	1.55
MUN	Thornburg Strategic Municipal Inc A	TSSAX	C	(800) 847-0200	C / 5.2	1.23	-3.34	-0.74 / 7	2.88 / 80	2.95 / 79	2.04	1.31
MUN	Thornburg Strategic Municipal Inc C	TSSCX	B-	(800) 847-0200	C+ / 5.7	1.14	-3.49	-1.05 / 4	2.59 / 75	2.66 / 74	1.76	1.70
MUN	Thornburg Strategic Municipal Inc I	TSSIX	A-	(800) 847-0200	B- / 7.1	1.30	-3.19	-0.43 / 11	3.23 / 85	3.28 / 85	2.40	0.93
*COH ●	Thrivent Diversified Inc Plus A	AAHYX	D+	(800) 847-4836	B- / 7.1	3.59	3.35	12.24 / 84	3.57 / 70	5.99 / 92	3.01	1.10
COH	Thrivent Diversified Inc Plus S	THYFX	C+	(800) 847-4836	B+ / 8.6	3.69	3.52	12.50 / 84	3.91 / 74	6.31 / 94	3.46	0.81
USS ●	Thrivent Government Bond A	TBFAX	E+	(800) 847-4836	D+ / 2.4	0.71	-2.48	-0.50 / 9	1.87 / 41	1.13 / 29	1.27	1.12
USS	Thrivent Government Bond S	TBFIX	D-	(800) 847-4836	C- / 3.5	0.73	-2.55	-0.46 / 10	2.08 / 45	1.39 / 33	1.33	0.57
COH ●	Thrivent High Yield A	LBHYX	D+	(800) 847-4836	B / 7.6	4.30	4.13	15.95 / 90	3.46 / 68	5.75 / 90	4.94	0.81
COH	Thrivent High Yield S	LBHIX	C+	(800) 847-4836	B+ / 8.9	4.36	4.26	16.25 / 91	3.69 / 71	6.07 / 93	5.43	0.50
GES ●	Thrivent Income A	LUBIX	D	(800) 847-4836	C / 5.3	2.16	-1.25	7.03 / 73	3.34 / 66	3.88 / 71	2.95	0.77
GES	Thrivent Income S	LBIIX	C+	(800) 847-4836	B- / 7.3	2.25	-1.10	7.38 / 73	3.70 / 71	4.25 / 75	3.41	0.41

● Denotes fund is closed to new investors
* Denotes fund is included in Section II

| RISK | | | NET ASSETS | | ASSET | | | | | | | FUND MANAGER | | MINIMUM | | LOADS | |
Risk Rating/Pts	3 Yr Avg Standard Deviation	Avg Dura-tion	NAV As of 2/28/17	Total $(Mil)	Cash %	Gov. Bond %	Muni. Bond %	Corp. Bond %	Other %	Portfolio Turnover Ratio	Avg Coupon Rate	Manager Quality Pct	Manager Tenure (Years)	Initial Purch. $	Additional Purch. $	Front End Load	Back End Load
B /7.6	2.5	4.4	11.25	4	9	30	0	59	2	48	0.0	10	18	1,000	0	0.0	0.0
B /7.6	2.5	4.4	10.68	1	9	30	0	59	2	48	0.0	3	18	1,000	0	0.0	0.0
B /7.6	2.5	4.4	11.25	13	9	30	0	59	2	48	0.0	14	18	500,000	0	0.0	0.0
E- /0.0	13.1	2.8	4.14	487	13	10	0	48	29	31	9.5	0	8	100,000	0	0.0	2.0
C- /3.2	4.0	1.3	11.41	2,363	2	4	2	82	10	29	6.6	86	25	250	50	0.0	0.0
B /7.9	2.2	3.4	13.66	165	0	0	99	0	1	16	3.8	10	6	5,000	100	1.5	0.0
B /7.9	2.2	3.4	13.67	61	0	0	99	0	1	16	3.8	7	6	5,000	100	0.0	0.0
B /7.9	2.2	3.4	13.67	447	0	0	99	0	1	16	3.8	16	6	2,500,000	100	0.0	0.0
B- /7.0	2.7	4.8	13.97	421	2	0	97	0	1	11	4.3	15	6	5,000	100	2.0	0.0
B- /7.1	2.7	4.8	13.98	156	2	0	97	0	1	11	4.3	10	6	5,000	100	0.0	0.0
C+ /6.8	2.8	4.8	13.95	894	2	0	97	0	1	11	4.3	22	6	2,500,000	100	0.0	0.0
B+ /8.8	1.5	2.4	13.39	1,079	4	10	2	52	32	21	2.7	71	10	5,000	100	1.5	0.0
B+ /8.8	1.5	2.4	13.37	629	4	10	2	52	32	21	2.7	65	10	5,000	100	0.0	0.0
B+ /8.8	1.5	2.4	13.39	2,891	4	10	2	52	32	21	2.7	78	10	2,500,000	100	0.0	0.0
B+ /8.8	1.5	2.4	13.40	96	4	10	2	52	32	21	2.7	68	10	0	0	0.0	0.0
B+ /8.8	1.5	2.4	13.38	7	4	10	2	52	32	21	2.7	69	10	0	0	0.0	0.0
B+ /8.8	1.5	2.4	13.39	78	4	10	2	52	32	21	2.7	75	10	0	0	0.0	0.0
B /8.2	2.0	3.5	14.32	1,473	0	0	100	0	0	15	4.1	10	6	5,000	100	1.5	0.0
B /8.1	2.1	3.5	14.35	661	0	0	100	0	0	15	4.1	7	6	5,000	100	0.0	0.0
B /8.2	2.1	3.5	14.32	5,075	0	0	100	0	0	15	4.1	16	6	2,500,000	100	0.0	0.0
A- /9.0	1.4	2.4	13.05	104	5	28	0	8	59	10	2.4	48	10	5,000	100	1.5	0.0
B+ /8.9	1.4	2.4	13.13	43	5	28	0	8	59	10	2.4	30	10	5,000	100	0.0	0.0
B+ /8.9	1.4	2.4	13.05	131	5	28	0	8	59	10	2.4	60	10	2,500,000	100	0.0	0.0
B+ /8.9	1.4	2.4	13.06	15	5	28	0	8	59	10	2.4	41	10	0	0	0.0	0.0
B+ /8.9	1.4	2.4	13.04	2	5	28	0	8	59	10	2.4	48	10	0	0	0.0	0.0
B+ /8.8	1.5	2.4	13.06	4	5	28	0	8	59	10	2.4	57	10	0	0	0.0	0.0
A+ /9.7	0.7	2.4	12.42	9	17	24	1	31	27	43	2.7	64	4	5,000	100	1.5	0.0
A+ /9.7	0.6	2.4	12.41	15	17	24	1	31	27	43	2.7	68	4	2,500,000	100	0.0	0.0
A+ /9.8	0.5	1.2	12.34	23	1	0	98	0	1	21	3.9	29	4	5,000	100	1.5	0.0
A+ /9.8	0.6	1.2	12.34	47	1	0	98	0	1	21	3.9	36	4	2,500,000	100	0.0	0.0
B /7.9	2.2	4.3	13.27	125	1	0	98	0	1	7	4.6	24	6	5,000	100	2.0	0.0
B /7.9	2.2	4.3	13.27	25	1	0	98	0	1	7	4.6	17	6	5,000	100	0.0	0.0
B /7.8	2.3	4.3	13.26	58	1	0	98	0	1	7	4.6	33	6	2,500,000	100	0.0	0.0
B- /7.2	2.6	4.6	12.96	22	0	0	99	0	1	7	4.8	24	6	2,500,000	100	0.0	0.0
B- /7.2	2.6	4.6	12.96	40	0	0	99	0	1	7	4.8	16	6	5,000	100	2.0	0.0
C /4.3	3.4	3.0	11.65	269	13	1	0	68	18	29	4.8	84	10	5,000	100	4.5	0.0
C /4.3	3.4	3.0	11.63	241	13	1	0	68	18	29	4.8	79	10	5,000	100	0.0	0.0
C /4.3	3.4	3.0	11.62	528	13	1	0	68	18	29	4.8	87	10	2,500,000	100	0.0	0.0
C /4.4	3.3	3.0	11.63	3	13	1	0	68	18	29	4.8	92	10	0	0	0.0	0.0
C /4.3	3.4	3.0	11.64	3	13	1	0	68	18	29	4.8	92	10	0	0	0.0	0.0
C /4.3	3.4	3.0	11.62	6	13	1	0	68	18	29	4.8	93	10	0	0	0.0	0.0
C+ /5.8	3.0	5.0	14.93	71	1	0	98	0	1	11	4.1	30	8	5,000	100	2.0	0.0
C+ /6.0	2.9	5.0	14.95	37	1	0	98	0	1	11	4.1	23	8	5,000	100	0.0	0.0
C+ /5.8	3.0	5.0	14.95	179	1	0	98	0	1	11	4.1	51	8	2,500,000	100	0.0	0.0
D /2.1	4.4	3.1	7.15	601	3	4	0	23	70	108	2.7	66	11	2,000	50	4.5	0.0
D /2.1	4.4	3.1	7.09	175	3	4	0	23	70	108	2.7	74	11	50,000	0	0.0	0.0
C /4.3	3.4	5.6	9.89	8	1	82	0	7	10	149	2.3	34	7	2,000	50	2.0	0.0
C- /4.2	3.4	5.6	9.89	54	1	82	0	7	10	149	2.3	48	7	50,000	0	0.0	0.0
D- /1.4	5.3	3.9	4.86	477	0	3	0	91	6	42	6.1	19	20	2,000	50	4.5	0.0
D- /1.5	5.2	3.9	4.86	239	0	3	0	91	6	42	6.1	27	20	50,000	0	0.0	0.0
C- /3.8	3.6	6.2	9.11	348	0	13	0	74	13	104	4.1	67	8	2,000	50	4.5	0.0
C- /3.8	3.6	6.2	9.10	464	0	13	0	74	13	104	4.1	75	8	50,000	0	0.0	0.0

Fund Type	Fund Name	Ticker Symbol	Overall Investment Rating	Phone	Performance Rating/Pts	3 Mo	6 Mo	1Yr / Pct	3Yr / Pct	5Yr / Pct	Dividend Yield	Expense Ratio
GEI ●	Thrivent Limited Maturity Bond A	LBLAX	B+	(800) 847-4836	C- / 3.9	0.80	0.66	3.14 /58	1.46 /34	1.49 /34	1.63	0.63
GEI	Thrivent Limited Maturity Bond S	THLIX	A-	(800) 847-4836	C- / 4.2	0.77	0.68	3.27 /58	1.67 /38	1.71 /38	1.84	0.38
MMT	Thrivent Money Market S	AALXX	U	(800) 847-4836	U /	0.01	0.01	0.01 /18	--	--	0.01	N/A
*MUN ●	Thrivent Municipal Bond A	AAMBX	D	(800) 847-4836	C / 4.9	1.93	-3.28	-0.26 /14	3.40 /87	2.81 /76	3.24	0.74
MUN	Thrivent Municipal Bond S	TMBIX	B+	(800) 847-4836	B / 7.8	1.99	-3.16	-0.02 /17	3.66 /90	3.07 /81	3.64	0.48
GEI ●	Thrivent Oppty Income Plus A	AAINX	B+	(800) 847-4836	C+ / 5.8	2.24	1.66	8.75 /76	3.14 /63	--	3.29	1.02
GEI	Thrivent Oppty Income Plus S	IIINX	A+	(800) 847-4836	B- / 7.5	2.30	1.76	8.97 /76	3.36 /67	--	3.65	0.71
COI	TIAA-CREF Bond Advisor	TIBHX	U	(800) 842-2252	U /	1.45	-1.40	3.57 /60	--	--	2.78	0.41
COI	TIAA-CREF Bond Index Adv	TBIAX	U	(800) 842-2252	U /	1.04	-2.33	1.13 /41	--	--	2.27	0.22
GEI	TIAA-CREF Bond Index Inst	TBIIX	D+	(800) 842-2252	C / 4.6	1.05	-2.31	1.16 /41	2.53 /52	2.09 /44	2.30	0.12
GEI	TIAA-CREF Bond Index Prem	TBIPX	D	(800) 842-2252	C / 4.3	1.11	-2.38	1.01 /40	2.37 /49	1.94 /41	2.15	0.27
GEI	TIAA-CREF Bond Index Retail	TBILX	D	(800) 842-2252	C- / 4.0	0.97	-2.47	0.83 /38	2.19 /46	1.73 /38	1.97	0.46
GEI	TIAA-CREF Bond Index Retire	TBIRX	D	(800) 842-2252	C- / 4.1	0.99	-2.43	0.91 /39	2.27 /48	1.82 /39	2.05	0.37
GEI	TIAA-CREF Bond Inst	TIBDX	B	(800) 842-2252	C+ / 6.2	1.55	-1.30	3.59 /60	3.25 /65	3.25 /62	2.80	0.31
COI	TIAA-CREF Bond Plus Advisor	TCBHX	U	(800) 842-2252	U /	1.71	-0.87	4.80 /66	--	--	3.05	0.41
GEI	TIAA-CREF Bond Plus Inst	TIBFX	B+	(800) 842-2252	C+ / 6.6	1.64	-0.93	4.74 /66	3.37 /67	3.57 /67	3.10	0.31
GEI	TIAA-CREF Bond Plus Prem	TBPPX	B+	(800) 842-2252	C+ / 6.4	1.71	-1.00	4.58 /65	3.21 /64	3.41 /64	2.95	0.46
GEI	TIAA-CREF Bond Plus Retail	TCBPX	B+	(800) 842-2252	C+ / 6.1	1.56	-1.08	4.41 /64	3.04 /62	3.23 /61	2.78	0.63
GEI	TIAA-CREF Bond Plus Retire	TCBRX	B+	(800) 842-2252	C+ / 6.2	1.58	-1.05	4.48 /64	3.11 /63	3.31 /62	2.85	0.56
GEI	TIAA-CREF Bond Prem	TIDPX	B	(800) 842-2252	C+ / 6.0	1.42	-1.46	3.43 /59	3.07 /62	3.08 /59	2.65	0.46
GEI	TIAA-CREF Bond Retail	TIORX	B-	(800) 842-2252	C+ / 5.7	1.46	-1.49	3.37 /59	2.93 /60	2.95 /57	2.50	0.62
GEI	TIAA-CREF Bond Retire	TIDRX	B	(800) 842-2252	C+ / 5.8	1.47	-1.46	3.42 /59	2.98 /61	2.98 /58	2.55	0.56
EM	TIAA-CREF Emerging Mkts Debt Adv	TEDHX	U	(800) 842-2252	U /	6.11	1.56	17.98 /94	--	--	5.01	0.76
EM	TIAA-CREF Emerging Mkts Debt Inst	TEDNX	U	(800) 842-2252	U /	6.12	1.57	17.96 /93	--	--	5.09	0.66
EM	TIAA-CREF Emerging Mkts Debt	TEDPX	U	(800) 842-2252	U /	6.09	1.40	17.68 /93	--	--	4.96	0.86
EM	TIAA-CREF Emerging Mkts Debt Ret	TEDTX	U	(800) 842-2252	U /	6.05	1.44	17.71 /93	--	--	4.87	0.94
EM	TIAA-CREF Emerging Mkts Debt Rtl	TEDLX	U	(800) 842-2252	U /	5.99	1.39	17.67 /93	--	--	4.74	0.97
COH	TIAA-CREF High Yield Fund Advisor	TIHHX	U	(800) 842-2252	U /	3.99	5.49	20.86 /97	--	--	5.57	0.46
COH	TIAA-CREF High Yield Fund Inst	TIHYX	C+	(800) 842-2252	A / 9.4	4.11	5.52	21.09 /97	4.53 /81	6.30 /94	5.65	0.36
COH	TIAA-CREF High Yield Fund Premier	TIHPX	C+	(800) 842-2252	A / 9.4	4.07	5.55	21.03 /97	4.37 /79	6.17 /93	5.51	0.51
COH	TIAA-CREF High Yield Fund Retail	TIYRX	C+	(800) 842-2252	A / 9.3	4.03	5.48	20.82 /97	4.25 /78	6.04 /92	5.39	0.63
COH	TIAA-CREF High Yield Fund Retire	TIHRX	C+	(800) 842-2252	A / 9.3	4.05	5.50	20.91 /97	4.30 /79	6.06 /92	5.41	0.61
GEI	TIAA-CREF Infltn Linkd Bd Advisor	TIIHX	U	(800) 842-2252	U /	1.16	0.03	2.50 /53	--	--	1.50	0.36
GEI	TIAA-CREF Infltn Linkd Bd Inst	TIILX	E+	(800) 842-2252	C- / 3.4	1.03	-0.01	2.36 /52	1.31 /32	0.31 /20	1.54	0.27
GEI	TIAA-CREF Infltn Linkd Bd Prmr	TIKPX	E+	(800) 842-2252	C- / 3.2	1.06	-0.08	2.21 /51	1.16 /30	0.15 /17	1.40	0.42
GEI	TIAA-CREF Infltn Linkd Bd Retail	TCILX	E+	(800) 842-2252	C- / 3.0	1.01	-0.15	2.10 /50	1.01 /28	0.01 / 5	1.26	0.58
GEI	TIAA-CREF Infltn Linkd Bd Retire	TIKRX	E+	(800) 842-2252	C- / 3.1	1.01	-0.11	2.16 /50	1.06 /29	0.07 /13	1.26	0.52
GL	TIAA-CREF Intl Bond Advisor	TIBNX	U	(800) 842-2252	U /	1.96	-1.91	--	--	--	0.00	N/A
GL	TIAA-CREF Intl Bond Inst	TIBWX	U	(800) 842-2252	U /	1.89	-1.97	--	--	--	0.00	N/A
GL	TIAA-CREF Intl Bond Premier	TIBLX	U	(800) 842-2252	U /	1.94	-1.93	--	--	--	0.00	N/A
GL	TIAA-CREF Intl Bond Retail	TIBEX	U	(800) 842-2252	U /	1.79	-2.08	--	--	--	0.00	N/A
GL	TIAA-CREF Intl Bond Retire	TIBVX	U	(800) 842-2252	U /	1.82	-2.05	--	--	--	0.00	N/A
MMT	TIAA-CREF Money Market Adv	TMHXX	U	(800) 842-2252	U /	0.10	0.16	0.26 /28	--	--	0.26	N/A
MMT	TIAA-CREF Money Market Inst	TCIXX	C-	(800) 842-2252	D- / 1.3	0.10	0.17	0.32 /30	0.13 /14	0.09 /15	0.32	N/A
MMT	TIAA-CREF Money Market Retail	TIRXX	U	(800) 842-2252	U /	--	--	--	--	--	0.01	N/A
COI	TIAA-CREF Sh Trm Bond Adv	TCTHX	U	(800) 842-2252	U /	0.61	0.36	2.12 /50	--	--	1.80	0.37
GEI	TIAA-CREF Sh Trm Bond Inst	TISIX	B	(800) 842-2252	C- / 3.4	0.71	0.48	2.14 /50	1.32 /32	1.51 /35	1.81	0.27
GEI	TIAA-CREF Sh Trm Bond Prmr	TSTPX	B	(800) 842-2252	C- / 3.2	0.67	0.40	1.98 /49	1.17 /30	1.36 /33	1.66	0.42
GEI	TIAA-CREF Sh Trm Bond Retail	TCTRX	B-	(800) 842-2252	D+ / 2.8	0.53	0.23	1.82 /47	0.98 /27	1.18 /30	1.50	0.58
GEI	TIAA-CREF Sh Trm Bond Retire	TISRX	B-	(800) 842-2252	C- / 3.0	0.65	0.36	1.88 /48	1.04 /28	1.26 /31	1.56	0.52
COI	TIAA-CREF Short-Term Bond Indx	TTBHX	U	(800) 842-2252	U /	0.37	-0.10	0.71 /36	--	--	1.01	0.44
COI	TIAA-CREF Short-Term Bond Indx	TNSHX	U	(800) 842-2252	U /	0.37	0.03	0.82 /38	--	--	1.02	0.45

● Denotes fund is closed to new investors
* Denotes fund is included in Section II

Risk Rating/Pts	3 Yr Avg Standard Deviation	Avg Dura-tion	NAV As of 2/28/17	Total $(Mil)	Cash %	Gov. Bond %	Muni. Bond %	Corp. Bond %	Other %	Portfolio Turnover Ratio	Avg Coupon Rate	Manager Quality Pct	Manager Tenure (Years)	Initial Purch. $	Additional Purch. $	Front End Load	Back End Load
A /9.3	0.9	1.8	12.46	351	0	29	0	36	35	81	2.4	72	18	2,500	100	0.0	0.0
A /9.3	0.9	1.8	12.45	488	0	29	0	36	35	81	2.4	76	18	50,000	0	0.0	0.0
U /	N/A	N/A	1.00	82	100	0	0	0	0	0	0.0	N/A	16	50,000	0	0.0	0.0
C /4.4	3.3	6.0	11.31	1,405	0	0	99	0	1	10	4.7	34	15	2,000	50	4.5	0.0
C /4.5	3.3	6.0	11.31	196	0	0	99	0	1	10	4.7	52	15	50,000	0	0.0	0.0
B- /7.2	2.7	2.9	10.23	259	2	16	0	25	57	147	4.4	85	15	2,000	50	4.5	0.0
B- /7.2	2.7	2.9	10.23	198	2	16	0	25	57	147	4.4	87	15	50,000	0	0.0	0.0
U /	N/A	5.4	10.32	N/A	0	20	5	34	41	309	3.6	N/A	14	0	0	0.0	0.0
U /	N/A	5.5	10.78	5	0	0	0	0	100	22	3.0	N/A	8	0	0	0.0	0.0
C /5.1	3.1	5.5	10.78	7,163	0	0	0	0	100	22	3.0	31	8	10,000,000	1,000	0.0	0.0
C /5.1	3.1	5.5	10.78	30	0	0	0	0	100	22	3.0	26	8	5,000,000	0	0.0	0.0
C /5.2	3.1	5.5	10.78	22	0	0	0	0	100	22	3.0	21	8	2,500	100	0.0	0.0
C /5.1	3.1	5.5	10.78	138	0	0	0	0	100	22	3.0	23	8	0	0	0.0	0.0
C+ /6.1	2.9	5.4	10.32	3,656	0	20	5	34	41	309	3.6	70	14	2,000,000	1,000	0.0	0.0
U /	N/A	5.4	10.39	2	0	25	3	32	40	293	3.8	N/A	11	0	0	0.0	0.0
C+ /6.3	2.9	5.4	10.38	2,778	0	25	3	32	40	293	3.8	75	11	2,000,000	1,000	0.0	0.0
C+ /6.1	2.9	5.4	10.38	41	0	25	3	32	40	293	3.8	71	11	1,000,000	0	0.0	0.0
C+ /6.3	2.9	5.4	10.40	264	0	25	3	32	40	293	3.8	68	11	2,500	100	0.0	0.0
C+ /6.3	2.9	5.4	10.39	307	0	25	3	32	40	293	3.8	70	11	0	0	0.0	0.0
C+ /6.5	2.8	5.4	10.32	28	0	20	5	34	41	309	3.6	66	14	1,000,000	0	0.0	0.0
C+ /6.2	2.9	5.4	10.50	90	0	20	5	34	41	309	3.6	61	14	2,500	100	0.0	0.0
C+ /6.2	2.9	5.4	10.51	225	0	20	5	34	41	309	3.6	63	14	0	0	0.0	0.0
U /	N/A	7.1	10.08	N/A	1	57	1	36	5	125	5.3	N/A	N/A	0	0	0.0	0.0
U /	N/A	7.1	10.07	302	1	57	1	36	5	125	5.3	N/A	N/A	2,000,000	1,000	0.0	0.0
U /	N/A	7.1	10.06	N/A	1	57	1	36	5	125	5.3	N/A	N/A	1,000,000	0	0.0	0.0
U /	N/A	7.1	10.06	7	1	57	1	36	5	125	5.3	N/A	N/A	0	0	0.0	0.0
U /	N/A	7.1	10.07	1	1	57	1	36	5	125	5.3	N/A	N/A	2,500	100	0.0	0.0
U /	N/A	4.0	9.88	4	1	6	0	76	17	50	6.6	N/A	11	0	0	0.0	0.0
E+ /0.9	6.0	4.0	9.89	2,430	1	6	0	76	17	50	6.6	34	11	2,000,000	1,000	0.0	2.0
E+ /0.9	6.0	4.0	9.90	138	1	6	0	76	17	50	6.6	30	11	0	0	0.0	2.0
E+ /0.9	5.9	4.0	9.94	608	1	6	0	76	17	50	6.6	27	11	2,500	100	0.0	2.0
E+ /0.9	5.9	4.0	9.90	352	1	6	0	76	17	50	6.6	29	11	0	0	0.0	2.0
U /	N/A	5.6	11.48	N/A	0	98	0	0	2	27	0.9	N/A	9	0	0	0.0	0.0
C- /3.5	3.8	5.6	11.47	2,221	0	98	0	0	2	27	0.9	6	9	2,000,000	1,000	0.0	0.0
C- /3.5	3.8	5.6	11.44	11	0	98	0	0	2	27	0.9	5	9	0	0	0.0	0.0
C- /3.5	3.8	5.6	11.19	122	0	98	0	0	2	27	0.9	4	9	2,500	100	0.0	0.0
C- /3.5	3.8	5.6	11.55	233	0	98	0	0	2	27	0.9	5	9	0	0	0.0	0.0
U /	N/A	8.3	9.63	1	0	0	0	0	100	0	3.4	N/A	1	0	0	0.0	0.0
U /	N/A	8.3	9.62	293	0	0	0	0	100	0	3.4	N/A	1	2,000,000	1,000	0.0	0.0
U /	N/A	8.3	9.63	1	0	0	0	0	100	0	3.4	N/A	1	0	0	0.0	0.0
U /	N/A	8.3	9.62	1	0	0	0	0	100	0	3.4	N/A	1	2,500	100	0.0	0.0
U /	N/A	8.3	9.62	2	0	0	0	0	100	0	3.4	N/A	1	0	0	0.0	0.0
U /	N/A	N/A	1.00	N/A	100	0	0	0	0	0	0.3	N/A	18	0	0	0.0	0.0
A+ /9.9	N/A	N/A	1.00	450	100	0	0	0	0	0	0.3	47	18	2,000,000	1,000	0.0	0.0
U /	N/A	N/A	1.00	321	100	0	0	0	0	0	0.0	N/A	18	2,500	100	0.0	0.0
U /	N/A	1.9	10.33	N/A	0	26	0	39	35	93	2.4	N/A	11	0	0	0.0	0.0
A+ /9.6	0.8	1.9	10.34	1,490	0	26	0	39	35	93	2.4	69	11	2,000,000	1,000	0.0	0.0
A+ /9.6	0.8	1.9	10.35	15	0	26	0	39	35	93	2.4	64	11	0	0	0.0	0.0
A /9.5	0.8	1.9	10.34	132	0	26	0	39	35	93	2.4	59	11	2,500	100	0.0	0.0
A /9.5	0.8	1.9	10.35	106	0	26	0	39	35	93	2.4	60	11	0	0	0.0	0.0
U /	N/A	1.9	9.97	N/A	0	0	0	0	100	53	1.3	N/A	2	0	0	0.0	0.0
U /	N/A	1.9	9.98	156	0	0	0	0	100	53	1.3	N/A	2	10,000,000	1,000	0.0	0.0

Fund Type	Fund Name	Ticker Symbol	Overall Investment Rating	Phone	Performance Rating/Pts	3 Mo	6 Mo	1Yr / Pct	3Yr / Pct	5Yr / Pct	Dividend Yield	Expense Ratio
	99 Pct = Best / 0 Pct = Worst							Total Return % through 2/28/17	Annualized		Incl. in Returns	
COI	TIAA-CREF Short-Term Bond Indx	TPSHX	U	(800) 842-2252	U /	0.34	-0.15	0.56 /34	--	--	0.86	0.84
COI	TIAA-CREF Short-Term Bond Indx	TESHX	U	(800) 842-2252	U /	0.21	-0.20	0.47 /33	--	--	0.77	0.80
COI	TIAA-CREF Short-Term Bond Indx	TRSHX	U	(800) 842-2252	U /	0.20	-0.21	0.45 /32	--	--	0.75	1.02
COI	TIAACREF Social Choice Bond Adv	TSBHX	U	(800) 842-2252	U /	1.25	-1.47	2.50 /53	--	--	2.32	0.50
COI	TIAACREF Social Choice Bond Inst	TSBIX	B	(800) 842-2252	C+ / 6.7	1.38	-1.40	2.65 /54	3.83 /73	--	2.48	0.41
COI	TIAACREF Social Choice Bond Prmr	TSBPX	B	(800) 842-2252	C+ / 6.5	1.34	-1.48	2.50 /53	3.68 /71	--	2.32	0.56
COI	TIAACREF Social Choice Bond Ret	TSBBX	B	(800) 842-2252	C+ / 6.3	1.22	-1.52	2.40 /52	3.58 /70	--	2.23	0.66
COI	TIAACREF Social Choice Bond Rtl	TSBRX	B	(800) 842-2252	C+ / 6.2	1.22	-1.54	2.27 /51	3.51 /69	--	2.20	0.69
MUN	TIAA-CREF T/E Bond Adv	TIXHX	U	(800) 842-2252	U /	1.99	-3.56	-0.67 / 7	--	--	2.16	0.42
MUN	TIAA-CREF T/E Bond Inst	TITIX	D+	(800) 842-2252	C / 5.5	2.10	-3.54	-0.66 / 7	2.38 /71	1.95 /58	2.17	0.36
MUN	TIAA-CREF T/E Bond Retail	TIXRX	D	(800) 842-2252	C / 4.8	1.93	-3.67	-0.93 / 5	2.09 /65	1.67 /51	1.89	0.63
GES	Timothy Plan Fixed Income A	TFIAX	D-	(800) 662-0201	E / 0.5	0.67	-2.02	1.27 /43	1.30 /32	0.91 /26	1.69	1.29
GES	Timothy Plan Fixed Income C	TFICX	D	(800) 662-0201	D / 1.6	0.41	-2.46	0.36 /30	0.52 /21	0.12 /16	0.88	2.04
COI	Timothy Plan Fixed Income I	TPFIX	C-	(800) 662-0201	C- / 3.3	0.74	-2.00	1.35 /43	1.57 /36	--	2.06	1.04
COH	Timothy Plan High Yield A	TPHAX	D-	(800) 662-0201	B- / 7.0	3.70	3.58	16.55 /91	2.78 /57	4.51 /79	3.63	1.31
COH	Timothy Plan High Yield C	TPHCX	D	(800) 662-0201	B- / 7.4	3.47	3.28	15.70 /90	1.99 /43	3.73 /69	2.88	2.06
COH	Timothy Plan High Yield I	TPHIX	C-	(800) 662-0201	B+ / 8.4	3.65	3.72	16.75 /91	3.02 /61	--	4.09	1.07
COH	Toews Tactical Income Fund	THHYX	B+	(877) 558-6397	A- / 9.0	4.07	3.77	13.44 /86	4.26 /78	5.67 /90	3.33	1.49
GL	Toews Unconstrained Income	TUIFX	A	(877) 558-6397	B- / 7.5	3.08	2.07	9.65 /78	3.15 /63	--	1.96	1.52
GEI	Touchstone Active Bond A	TOBAX	D+	(800) 543-0407	C- / 3.8	1.96	-0.76	5.42 /68	2.55 /53	2.60 /51	2.44	1.16
GEI	Touchstone Active Bond C	TODCX	C	(800) 543-0407	C / 4.5	1.73	-1.18	4.65 /65	1.79 /39	1.84 /40	2.03	2.03
COI	Touchstone Active Bond Instl	TOBIX	B	(800) 543-0407	C+ / 6.3	2.05	-0.60	5.78 /69	2.89 /59	2.94 /57	2.89	0.92
COI	Touchstone Active Bond Y	TOBYX	B	(800) 543-0407	C+ / 6.1	1.93	-0.73	5.59 /69	2.77 /57	2.86 /56	2.81	0.88
GES	Touchstone Flexible Income A	FFSAX	B	(800) 543-0407	C / 5.3	2.39	-0.61	4.89 /66	3.98 /75	3.99 /72	2.55	1.34
GES	Touchstone Flexible Income C	FRACX	A-	(800) 543-0407	C+ / 6.4	2.23	-0.98	4.20 /63	3.20 /64	3.24 /61	2.01	2.07
GEL	Touchstone Flexible Income Inst	TFSLX	A+	(800) 543-0407	B / 7.7	2.57	-0.43	5.25 /68	4.36 /79	--	3.05	0.96
GES	Touchstone Flexible Income Y	MXIIX	A+	(800) 543-0407	B- / 7.5	2.44	-0.48	5.14 /67	4.23 /78	4.26 /76	2.95	1.07
COH	Touchstone High Yield A	THYAX	D-	(800) 543-0407	C+ / 6.7	4.11	3.47	16.59 /91	2.46 /51	4.68 /81	4.47	1.15
COH	Touchstone High Yield C	THYCX	D-	(800) 543-0407	B- / 7.1	3.93	2.97	15.62 /89	1.69 /38	3.90 /71	3.98	1.87
COH	Touchstone High Yield Inst	THIYX	C-	(800) 543-0407	B+ / 8.3	4.23	3.60	17.01 /92	2.79 /58	5.07 /85	4.95	0.75
COH	Touchstone High Yield Y	THYYX	C-	(800) 543-0407	B / 8.2	4.21	3.56	16.76 /91	2.71 /56	4.94 /84	4.88	0.87
MUI	Touchstone Ohio Tax-Free Bond A	TOHAX	C-	(800) 543-0407	C- / 3.6	1.60	-2.76	-0.16 /15	2.79 /79	2.70 /74	2.89	1.13
MUI	Touchstone Ohio Tax-Free Bond C	TOHCX	C+	(800) 543-0407	C / 4.7	1.42	-3.12	-0.81 / 6	2.02 /63	1.95 /58	2.26	2.09
MUN	Touchstone Ohio Tax-Free Bond Inst	TOHIX	U	(800) 543-0407	U /	1.66	-2.65	--	--	--	0.00	N/A
MUN	Touchstone Ohio Tax-Free Bond Y	TOHYX	U	(800) 543-0407	U /	1.67	-2.63	--	--	--	0.00	N/A
GEI	Touchstone Tot Rtn Bond A	TCPAX	D-	(800) 543-0407	D+ / 2.4	0.88	-2.16	1.49 /44	2.34 /49	2.21 /45	2.58	1.27
GEI	Touchstone Tot Rtn Bond C	TCPCX	D	(800) 543-0407	C- / 3.1	0.69	-2.63	0.63 /35	1.58 /36	1.45 /34	1.95	2.28
GEI	Touchstone Tot Rtn Bond Inst	TCPNX	C+	(800) 543-0407	C / 5.0	0.97	-2.08	1.84 /48	2.73 /57	2.61 /51	3.07	0.62
GEI	Touchstone Tot Rtn Bond Y	TCPYX	C	(800) 543-0407	C / 4.8	0.94	-2.14	1.64 /46	2.61 /54	2.46 /49	2.96	0.71
GEI	Touchstone Ut Sh Dr Fxd Inc A	TSDAX	C	(800) 543-0407	D / 1.8	0.35	0.63	1.50 /45	0.83 /25	0.89 /26	1.25	0.99
GEI	Touchstone Ut Sh Dr Fxd Inc C	TSDCX	C	(800) 543-0407	D / 1.8	0.21	0.36	0.98 /39	0.32 /19	0.38 /20	0.76	1.48
GEI	Touchstone Ut Sh Dr Fxd Inc Inst	TSDIX	B	(800) 543-0407	C- / 3.0	0.33	0.69	1.71 /46	1.10 /29	1.17 /30	1.59	0.48
GEI	Touchstone Ut Sh Dr Fxd Inc Y	TSYYX	B	(800) 543-0407	C- / 3.0	0.43	0.77	1.77 /47	1.08 /29	1.15 /29	1.54	0.52
USS	Touchstone Ut Sh Dr Fxd Inc Z	TSDOX	B-	(800) 543-0407	D+ / 2.6	0.35	0.63	1.50 /45	0.83 /25	0.91 /26	1.28	0.76
COH	Transamerica Bond I2		C+	(888) 233-4339	B+ / 8.7	3.19	1.77	14.75 /88	3.97 /75	5.71 /90	2.32	0.70
COI	Transamerica Bond R6	TABSX	U	(888) 233-4339	U /	3.19	1.77	14.85 /88	--	--	2.40	0.70
GEI	Transamerica Core Bond I2		C+	(888) 233-4339	C / 4.8	0.97	-2.09	1.19 /42	2.70 /56	2.36 /47	2.83	0.52
EM	Transamerica Emerging Mkts Debt A	EMTAX	D	(888) 233-4339	B+ / 8.3	6.32	2.56	17.24 /92	4.02 /76	4.68 /81	2.78	1.11
EM	Transamerica Emerging Mkts Debt C	EMTCX	C-	(888) 233-4339	B+ / 8.7	6.12	2.16	16.34 /91	3.29 /66	3.96 /72	2.40	1.85
EM	Transamerica Emerging Mkts Debt I	EMTIX	C	(888) 233-4339	A / 9.4	6.36	2.67	17.43 /93	4.34 /79	5.04 /84	3.10	0.81
EM	Transamerica Emerging Mkts Debt I2		C	(888) 233-4339	A / 9.4	6.39	2.72	17.51 /93	4.46 /80	5.13 /85	3.17	0.71
EM	Transamerica Emerging Mkts Debt	TAEDX	U	(888) 233-4339	U /	6.39	2.84	17.82 /93	--	--	3.41	0.71

● Denotes fund is closed to new investors
* Denotes fund is included in Section II

www.thestreetratings.com

I. Index of Bond and Money Market Mutual Funds

RISK			NET ASSETS		ASSET							FUND MANAGER		MINIMUM		LOADS	
Risk Rating/Pts	3 Yr Avg Standard Deviation	Avg Dura-tion	NAV As of 2/28/17	Total $(Mil)	Cash %	Gov. Bond %	Muni. Bond %	Corp. Bond %	Other %	Portfolio Turnover Ratio	Avg Coupon Rate	Manager Quality Pct	Manager Tenure (Years)	Initial Purch. $	Additional Purch. $	Front End Load	Back End Load
U /	N/A	1.9	9.97	N/A	0	0	0	0	100	53	1.3	N/A	2	0	0	0.0	0.0
U /	N/A	1.9	9.97	10	0	0	0	0	100	53	1.3	N/A	2	0	0	0.0	0.0
U /	N/A	1.9	9.97	1	0	0	0	0	100	53	1.3	N/A	2	2,500	100	0.0	0.0
U /	N/A	5.6	10.20	102	0	26	11	32	31	107	3.3	N/A	5	0	0	0.0	0.0
C /5.4	3.0	5.6	10.20	577	0	26	11	32	31	107	3.3	79	5	2,000,000	1,000	0.0	0.0
C /5.4	3.0	5.6	10.20	17	0	26	11	32	31	107	3.3	77	5	0	0	0.0	0.0
C+ /5.6	3.0	5.6	10.20	262	0	26	11	32	31	107	3.3	76	5	0	0	0.0	0.0
C+ /5.9	2.9	5.6	10.19	111	0	26	11	32	31	107	3.3	76	5	2,500	100	0.0	0.0
U /	N/A	6.2	10.24	N/A	0	0	0	0	100	110	4.9	N/A	2	0	0	0.0	0.0
C- /4.1	3.5	6.2	10.24	3	0	0	0	0	100	110	4.9	8	2	2,000,000	1,000	0.0	0.0
C- /4.2	3.4	6.2	10.25	283	0	0	0	0	100	110	4.9	6	2	2,500	100	0.0	0.0
B- /7.5	2.5	4.2	10.21	85	2	32	0	31	35	40	0.0	13	13	1,000	0	4.5	0.0
B /7.6	2.5	4.2	9.82	10	2	32	0	31	35	40	0.0	5	13	1,000	0	0.0	0.0
B- /7.5	2.6	4.2	10.14	1	2	32	0	31	35	40	0.0	20	13	25,000	5,000	0.0	0.0
D- /1.0	5.9	N/A	9.31	43	7	0	0	92	1	27	0.0	4	10	1,000	0	4.5	0.0
D- /1.0	5.8	N/A	9.41	3	7	0	0	92	1	27	0.0	1	10	1,000	0	0.0	0.0
D- /1.0	5.8	N/A	9.32	5	7	0	0	92	1	27	0.0	6	10	25,000	5,000	0.0	0.0
C- /3.2	3.5	N/A	11.45	506	0	0	0	0	100	739	0.0	85	7	10,000	100	0.0	0.0
C+ /6.1	2.9	N/A	10.48	110	50	31	0	11	8	496	0.0	94	4	10,000	100	0.0	0.0
C+ /6.0	2.9	5.7	10.39	24	0	28	0	45	27	590	0.0	61	16	2,500	50	4.8	0.0
C+ /6.1	2.9	5.7	9.62	6	0	28	0	45	27	590	0.0	27	16	2,500	50	0.0	0.0
C+ /6.0	2.9	5.7	10.38	7	0	28	0	45	27	590	0.0	61	16	500,000	50	0.0	0.0
C+ /6.1	2.9	5.7	10.38	68	0	28	0	45	27	590	0.0	57	16	2,500	50	0.0	0.0
C+ /6.9	2.7	4.6	10.73	55	0	18	0	46	36	122	6.5	85	10	2,500	50	5.8	0.0
C+ /6.8	2.8	4.6	10.59	57	0	18	0	46	36	122	6.5	78	10	2,500	50	0.0	0.0
C+ /6.9	2.8	4.6	10.76	108	0	18	0	46	36	122	6.5	88	10	500,000	50	0.0	0.0
B- /7.0	2.7	4.6	10.76	465	0	18	0	46	36	122	6.5	87	10	2,500	50	0.0	0.0
E+ /0.9	6.0	4.0	8.31	21	1	1	0	96	2	56	0.0	2	18	2,500	50	4.8	0.0
E+ /0.9	6.0	4.0	8.29	15	1	1	0	96	2	56	0.0	1	18	2,500	50	0.0	0.0
E+ /0.9	6.0	4.0	8.54	123	1	1	0	96	2	56	0.0	4	18	500,000	50	0.0	0.0
E+ /0.9	6.0	4.0	8.54	94	1	1	0	96	2	56	0.0	3	18	2,500	50	0.0	0.0
C+ /6.9	2.7	4.4	11.47	46	0	0	100	0	0	27	0.0	35	31	2,500	50	4.8	0.0
B- /7.0	2.7	4.4	11.49	7	0	0	100	0	0	27	0.0	14	31	2,500	50	0.0	0.0
U /	N/A	4.4	11.47	N/A	0	0	100	0	0	27	0.0	N/A	31	500,000	50	0.0	0.0
U /	N/A	4.4	11.47	N/A	0	0	100	0	0	27	0.0	N/A	31	2,500	50	0.0	0.0
C+ /6.5	2.8	5.5	10.05	7	6	6	3	33	52	12	0.0	34	6	2,500	50	4.8	0.0
C+ /6.3	2.9	5.5	10.03	2	6	6	3	33	52	12	0.0	12	6	2,500	50	0.0	0.0
C+ /6.4	2.8	5.5	10.06	174	6	6	3	33	52	12	0.0	55	6	500,000	50	0.0	0.0
C+ /6.1	2.9	5.5	10.06	35	6	6	3	33	52	12	0.0	46	6	2,500	50	0.0	0.0
A+ /9.9	0.3	0.6	9.31	16	2	0	5	40	53	169	0.0	67	9	2,500	50	2.0	0.0
A+ /9.9	0.3	0.6	9.31	8	2	0	5	40	53	169	0.0	50	9	2,500	50	0.0	0.0
A+ /9.9	0.3	0.6	9.30	152	2	0	5	40	53	169	0.0	74	9	500,000	50	0.0	0.0
A+ /9.9	0.3	0.6	9.31	212	2	0	5	40	53	169	0.0	72	9	2,500	50	0.0	0.0
A+ /9.9	0.3	0.6	9.31	213	2	0	5	40	53	169	0.0	69	9	2,500	50	0.0	0.0
D /1.9	4.8	5.0	9.39	215	3	12	0	65	20	38	10.4	63	10	0	0	0.0	0.0
U /	N/A	5.0	9.39	1	3	12	0	65	20	38	10.4	N/A	10	0	0	0.0	0.0
C+ /6.8	2.8	5.6	9.92	1,110	6	27	0	24	43	22	12.4	56	2	0	0	0.0	0.0
E /0.4	7.8	4.9	10.61	33	3	65	2	28	2	257	9.6	97	6	1,000	50	4.8	0.0
E /0.4	7.8	4.9	10.54	14	3	65	2	28	2	257	9.6	96	6	1,000	50	0.0	0.0
E /0.4	7.8	4.9	10.64	431	3	65	2	28	2	257	9.6	98	6	1,000,000	0	0.0	0.0
E /0.4	7.8	4.9	10.64	207	3	65	2	28	2	257	9.6	98	6	0	0	0.0	0.0
U /	N/A	4.9	10.63	N/A	3	65	2	28	2	257	9.6	N/A	6	0	0	0.0	0.0

					PERFORMANCE						Incl. in Returns	
								Total Return % through 2/28/17				
			Overall		Perfor-				Annualized		Dividend	Expense
Fund		Ticker	Investment		mance						Yield	Ratio
Type	Fund Name	Symbol	Rating	Phone	Rating/Pts	3 Mo	6 Mo	1Yr / Pct	3Yr / Pct	5Yr / Pct		
COI	Transamerica Flexible Income A	IDITX	B+	(888) 233-4339	C / 5.4	2.64	1.61	8.28 /75	2.98 /61	4.42 /78	3.79	0.89
COI ●	Transamerica Flexible Income B	IFLBX	A-	(888) 233-4339	C+ / 5.8	2.31	1.08	7.35 /73	2.06 /44	3.52 /66	3.01	1.72
COI	Transamerica Flexible Income C	IFLLX	A	(888) 233-4339	C+ / 6.1	2.39	1.19	7.49 /73	2.25 /47	3.67 /68	3.22	1.60
COI	Transamerica Flexible Income I	TFXIX	A+	(888) 233-4339	B- / 7.4	2.72	1.77	8.58 /75	3.27 /65	4.71 /81	4.26	0.61
COI	Transamerica Flexible Income I2		A+	(888) 233-4339	B- / 7.5	2.88	1.84	8.84 /76	3.38 /67	4.82 /82	4.39	0.51
GEL	Transamerica Flexible Income R6	TAFLX	U	(888) 233-4339	U /	2.77	1.83	8.83 /76	--	--	4.38	0.52
LP	Transamerica Floating Rate A	TFLAX	A+	(888) 233-4339	C+ / 6.4	1.82	3.08	9.09 /77	3.61 /70	--	3.87	1.12
LP	Transamerica Floating Rate C	TFLCX	A+	(888) 233-4339	B- / 7.0	1.63	2.69	8.27 /75	2.87 /59	--	3.32	1.88
LP	Transamerica Floating Rate I	TFLIX	A+	(888) 233-4339	B / 8.0	1.98	3.20	9.14 /77	3.80 /73	--	4.30	0.89
LP	Transamerica Floating Rate I2		A+	(888) 233-4339	B / 8.1	1.90	3.23	9.42 /78	3.93 /74	--	4.36	0.81
GES	Transamerica High Yield Bond A	IHIYX	C	(888) 233-4339	B+ / 8.7	5.04	5.15	19.31 /95	4.12 /77	6.23 /94	4.98	1.01
GES ●	Transamerica High Yield Bond B	INCBX	C+	(888) 233-4339	A- / 9.0	4.93	4.83	18.45 /94	3.33 /66	5.40 /88	4.43	1.81
GES	Transamerica High Yield Bond C	INCLX	C+	(888) 233-4339	A- / 9.0	4.87	4.79	18.56 /94	3.38 /67	5.46 /88	4.56	1.74
COH	Transamerica High Yield Bond I	TDHIX	C+	(888) 233-4339	A / 9.5	5.09	5.28	19.66 /95	4.37 /79	6.49 /95	5.49	0.74
GES	Transamerica High Yield Bond I2		B	(888) 233-4339	A+ / 9.6	5.22	5.44	19.86 /96	4.52 /81	6.64 /95	5.58	0.64
COH	Transamerica High Yield Bond R6	TAHBX	U	(888) 233-4339	U /	4.73	4.37	18.66 /94	--	--	4.59	0.64
MUH	Transamerica High Yield Muni A	THAYX	C+	(888) 233-4339	A / 9.5	2.76	-5.63	-0.31 /13	6.59 /99	--	2.67	1.30
MUH	Transamerica High Yield Muni C	THCYX	B-	(888) 233-4339	A+ / 9.6	2.35	-6.05	-1.12 / 4	5.90 /98	--	1.84	2.05
MUH	Transamerica High Yield Muni I	THYIX	B	(888) 233-4339	A+ / 9.8	2.42	-5.81	-0.52 / 9	6.65 /99	--	2.47	1.08
GEI	Transamerica Inflation Opptys A	TIOAX	U	(888) 233-4339	U /	1.61	-0.27	5.20 /67	--	--	0.31	0.99
GEI	Transamerica Inflation Opptys C	TIOCX	U	(888) 233-4339	U /	1.36	-0.71	4.37 /64	--	--	0.20	1.78
GEI	Transamerica Inflation Opptys I	ITIOX	U	(888) 233-4339	U /	1.59	-0.26	5.41 /68	--	--	0.33	0.79
GEI	Transamerica Inflation Opptys I2		U	(888) 233-4339	U /	1.62	-0.12	5.55 /69	--	--	0.37	0.66
GEI	Transamerica Inflation Opptys R6	RTIOX	U	(888) 233-4339	U /	1.62	-0.12	--	--	--	0.00	N/A
COI	Transamerica Intermediate Bond I2		U	(888) 233-4339	U /	1.18	-1.92	1.95 /48	--	--	2.11	0.42
MUN	Transamerica Intermediate Muni A	TAMUX	C	(888) 233-4339	B- / 7.1	2.88	-3.70	-0.28 /13	4.55 /96	--	2.01	0.96
MUN	Transamerica Intermediate Muni C	TCMUX	C+	(888) 233-4339	B / 7.9	2.58	-4.14	-0.92 / 5	3.88 /92	--	1.45	1.71
MUN	Transamerica Intermediate Muni I	TIMUX	B+	(888) 233-4339	A- / 9.0	2.91	-3.71	-0.09 /16	4.64 /96	--	2.20	0.71
GEI	Transamerica Prt Core Bond	DVGCX	C+	(888) 233-4339	C / 4.6	1.17	-1.76	2.42 /52	2.31 /48	2.67 /52	2.04	0.96
COI	Transamerica Prt High Quality Bond	DVHQX	C	(888) 233-4339	D / 1.8	0.30	0.02	0.66 /36	0.39 /20	0.54 /22	1.48	0.99
COH	Transamerica Prt High Yield Bond	DVHYX	C+	(888) 233-4339	A / 9.5	5.29	5.47	20.16 /96	4.25 /78	6.31 /94	5.31	1.18
USS	Transamerica Prt Inflation-Prot Sec	DVIGX	E+	(888) 233-4339	D+ / 2.4	0.82	-1.02	2.50 /53	0.69 /23	0.03 / 9	0.84	1.04
GEI	Transamerica Prt Inst Core Bond	DICBX	B-	(888) 233-4339	C / 5.2	1.33	-1.52	2.83 /55	2.67 /55	2.99 /58	2.35	0.71
GEI	Transamerica Prt Inst High Qual Bd	DIHQX	C+	(888) 233-4339	D+ / 2.3	0.37	0.20	1.01 /40	0.72 /23	0.89 /26	1.80	0.76
COH	Transamerica Prt Inst High Yld Bd	DIHYX	C+	(888) 233-4339	A+ / 9.6	5.37	5.63	20.38 /96	4.48 /80	6.51 /95	5.47	0.91
USS	Transamerica Prt Inst Infl Prot Sec	DIIGX	E+	(888) 233-4339	C- / 3.1	0.91	-0.86	2.87 /56	1.06 /29	0.43 /21	1.28	0.80
*COI	Transamerica Short-Term Bond A	ITAAX	B-	(888) 233-4339	C- / 3.1	0.92	0.84	3.82 /61	1.51 /35	2.39 /48	2.12	0.84
COI	Transamerica Short-Term Bond C	ITACX	C+	(888) 233-4339	D+ / 2.8	0.72	0.45	3.03 /57	0.74 /24	1.62 /36	1.40	1.60
COI	Transamerica Short-Term Bond I	TSTIX	A-	(888) 233-4339	C / 4.4	0.87	0.93	3.96 /62	1.71 /38	2.59 /51	2.38	0.63
COI	Transamerica Short-Term Bond I2		A	(888) 233-4339	C / 4.6	0.90	0.88	4.05 /62	1.81 /40	2.69 /53	2.47	0.53
COI	Transamerica Short-Term Bond R6	TASTX	U	(888) 233-4339	U /	0.90	0.98	4.07 /62	--	--	2.48	0.53
GEI	Transamerica Total Return I2		C	(888) 233-4339	C / 5.5	2.11	-0.66	4.22 /63	2.53 /52	2.49 /49	0.45	0.78
USA	TransWestern Inst Sht Dur Govt Bond	TWSGX	C+	(855) 881-2380	D+ / 2.6	0.30	-0.31	0.59 /35	1.18 /30	1.05 /28	1.92	0.67
GES	Tributary Income Inst	FOINX	C+	(800) 662-4203	C / 5.0	1.33	-1.67	1.98 /49	2.62 /54	2.73 /53	2.70	1.19
COI	Tributary Income Inst Plus	FOIPX	B	(800) 662-4203	C / 5.2	1.37	-1.59	2.16 /50	2.77 /57	2.90 /56	2.88	0.85
MUN	Tributary Nebraska Tax Free InstIP	FONPX	D	(800) 662-4203	D / 1.9	1.74	-2.13	-0.42 /11	0.50 /24	-0.53 / 3	3.30	0.85
COI	Tributary Short/Int Bond Inst Plus	FOSPX	B	(800) 662-4203	C- / 3.6	0.79	0.49	2.24 /51	1.44 /34	1.94 /41	2.19	0.77
GEI	Tributary Short/Intmdt Bond Inst	FOSIX	B-	(800) 662-4203	C- / 3.2	0.74	0.28	1.92 /48	1.22 /31	1.68 /37	1.99	1.11
GEI	Trust for Credit UltSh Dur Gov Inv	TCUYX	C-	(800) 342-5828	D- / 1.2	0.12	0.13	0.27 /28	0.13 /14	--	0.58	0.44
MTG	Trust for Credit UltSh Dur Gov TCU	TCUUX	C-	(800) 342-5828	D- / 1.3	0.13	0.14	0.30 /29	0.16 /15	0.18 /18	0.61	0.41
USS	Trust for Credit Uns Sh Dur Ptf Inv	TCUEX	C-	(800) 342-5828	D- / 1.5	0.22	-0.31	0.18 /25	0.32 /19	--	0.80	0.43
GEI	Trust for Credit Uns Sh Dur TCU	TCUDX	C	(800) 342-5828	D / 1.6	0.23	-0.29	0.21 /26	0.35 /19	0.38 /20	0.83	0.40

● Denotes fund is closed to new investors
* Denotes fund is included in Section II

RISK			NET ASSETS		ASSET					Portfolio Turnover Ratio	Avg Coupon Rate	FUND MANAGER		MINIMUM		LOADS	
Risk Rating/Pts	3 Yr Avg Standard Deviation	Avg Dura-tion	NAV As of 2/28/17	Total $(Mil)	Cash %	Gov. Bond %	Muni. Bond %	Corp. Bond %	Other %			Manager Quality Pct	Manager Tenure (Years)	Initial Purch. $	Additional Purch. $	Front End Load	Back End Load
B /7.6	2.5	3.5	9.28	89	0	10	1	58	31	47	12.7	78	12	1,000	50	4.8	0.0
B /7.6	2.5	3.5	9.29	1	0	10	1	58	31	47	12.7	57	12	1,000	50	0.0	0.0
B /7.7	2.4	3.5	9.22	55	0	10	1	58	31	47	12.7	64	12	1,000	50	0.0	0.0
B /7.6	2.5	3.5	9.29	165	0	10	1	58	31	47	12.7	81	12	1,000,000	0	0.0	0.0
B /7.6	2.5	3.5	9.30	125	0	10	1	58	31	47	12.7	82	12	0	0	0.0	0.0
U /	N/A	3.5	9.29	5	0	10	1	58	31	47	12.7	N/A	12	0	0	0.0	0.0
B+ /8.3	2.0	0.5	10.00	24	5	0	0	79	16	50	4.7	92	4	1,000	50	4.8	0.0
B+ /8.3	2.0	0.5	10.00	12	5	0	0	79	16	50	4.7	88	4	1,000	50	0.0	0.0
B+ /8.3	1.9	0.5	9.97	40	5	0	0	79	16	50	4.7	93	4	1,000,000	0	0.0	0.0
B+ /8.3	2.0	0.5	10.00	442	5	0	0	79	16	50	4.7	93	4	0	0	0.0	0.0
D- /1.1	5.6	3.5	9.30	118	5	0	0	90	5	49	8.5	91	11	1,000	50	4.8	0.0
D /1.6	5.6	3.5	9.32	2	5	0	0	90	5	49	8.5	87	11	1,000	50	0.0	0.0
D- /1.5	5.7	3.5	9.26	50	5	0	0	90	5	49	8.5	87	11	1,000	50	0.0	0.0
D- /1.2	5.6	3.5	9.37	205	5	0	0	90	5	49	8.5	48	11	1,000,000	0	0.0	0.0
D /1.6	5.6	3.5	9.40	913	5	0	0	90	5	49	8.5	93	11	0	0	0.0	0.0
U /	N/A	3.5	9.40	15	5	0	0	90	5	49	8.5	N/A	11	0	0	0.0	0.0
D- /1.3	5.2	7.2	11.14	38	3	0	96	0	1	61	21.1	78	4	1,000	50	3.3	0.0
D- /1.3	5.2	7.2	11.16	13	3	0	96	0	1	61	21.1	64	4	1,000	50	0.0	0.0
D- /1.3	5.2	7.2	11.17	47	3	0	96	0	1	61	21.1	78	4	1,000,000	0	0.0	0.0
U /	N/A	6.6	9.93	1	1	82	0	10	7	39	9.5	N/A	3	1,000	50	4.8	0.0
U /	N/A	6.6	9.77	1	1	82	0	10	7	39	9.5	N/A	3	1,000	50	0.0	0.0
U /	N/A	6.6	9.98	N/A	1	82	0	10	7	39	9.5	N/A	3	1,000,000	0	0.0	0.0
U /	N/A	6.6	10.00	166	1	82	0	10	7	39	9.5	N/A	3	0	0	0.0	0.0
U /	N/A	6.6	10.00	N/A	1	82	0	10	7	39	9.5	N/A	3	0	0	0.0	0.0
U /	N/A	5.4	10.08	1,968	0	0	0	0	100	66	11.2	N/A	3	0	0	0.0	0.0
C- /3.0	4.1	6.0	11.14	351	8	0	91	0	1	34	8.0	54	5	1,000	50	4.8	0.0
C- /3.1	4.0	6.0	11.11	186	8	0	91	0	1	34	8.0	25	5	1,000	50	0.0	0.0
C- /3.0	4.1	6.0	11.19	666	8	0	91	0	1	34	8.0	57	5	1,000,000	0	0.0	0.0
C+ /6.9	2.7	5.4	12.94	367	0	32	0	34	34	46	11.8	35	3	5,000	0	0.0	0.0
A+ /9.7	0.7	1.6	11.11	102	1	15	0	26	58	70	9.6	34	27	5,000	0	0.0	0.0
D- /1.1	5.7	3.7	8.87	124	4	0	0	93	3	44	8.6	34	3	5,000	0	0.0	0.0
D+ /2.9	3.9	7.8	11.15	116	0	99	0	0	1	54	9.9	11	7	5,000	0	0.0	0.0
C+ /6.8	2.8	5.4	10.71	318	0	32	0	34	34	46	11.8	56	3	5,000	0	0.0	0.0
A+ /9.7	0.7	1.6	10.09	56	1	15	0	26	58	70	9.6	55	27	5,000	0	0.0	0.0
D- /1.1	5.7	3.7	8.86	356	4	0	0	93	3	44	8.6	50	3	5,000	0	0.0	0.0
C- /3.0	3.9	7.8	9.77	64	0	99	0	0	1	54	9.9	20	7	5,000	0	0.0	0.0
A /9.3	1.0	1.6	10.21	933	2	0	0	69	29	45	7.9	73	6	1,000	50	2.5	0.0
A /9.3	1.0	1.6	10.19	577	2	0	0	69	29	45	7.9	51	6	1,000	50	0.0	0.0
A /9.3	0.9	1.6	10.03	940	2	0	0	69	29	45	7.9	77	6	1,000,000	0	0.0	0.0
A /9.3	1.0	1.6	10.02	317	2	0	0	69	29	45	7.9	78	6	0	0	0.0	0.0
U /	N/A	1.6	10.02	1	2	0	0	69	29	45	7.9	N/A	6	0	0	0.0	0.0
C /4.8	3.2	5.6	10.07	563	0	31	1	25	43	31	13.2	46	3	0	0	0.0	0.0
A- /9.1	1.1	N/A	9.78	327	0	15	0	0	85	27	0.0	64	6	2,000,000	500,000	0.0	0.3
C+ /6.7	2.8	5.2	10.26	7	1	17	1	28	53	24	3.7	52	14	1,000	50	0.0	0.0
C+ /6.9	2.7	5.2	10.26	191	1	17	1	28	53	24	3.7	62	14	5,000,000	50	0.0	0.0
B /7.7	2.4	N/A	9.70	72	0	0	0	0	100	0	0.0	2	1	5,000,000	50	0.0	0.0
A /9.3	0.9	2.0	9.36	118	0	19	0	34	47	40	2.4	69	14	5,000,000	50	0.0	0.0
A /9.3	0.9	2.0	9.33	10	0	19	0	34	47	40	2.4	63	14	1,000	50	0.0	0.0
A+ /9.9	0.2	0.6	9.47	14	15	54	0	0	31	147	0.0	38	22	0	0	0.0	0.0
A+ /9.9	0.2	0.6	9.47	366	15	54	0	0	31	147	0.0	37	N/A	0	0	0.0	0.0
A+ /9.7	0.7	N/A	9.65	22	2	72	0	0	26	131	0.0	34	9	0	0	0.0	0.0
A+ /9.7	0.7	N/A	9.65	393	2	72	0	0	26	131	0.0	32	9	0	0	0.0	0.0

99 Pct = Best
0 Pct = Worst

Fund Type	Fund Name	Ticker Symbol	Overall Investment Rating	Phone	Performance Rating/Pts	PERFORMANCE — Total Return % through 2/28/17			Annualized		Incl. in Returns	
						3 Mo	6 Mo	1Yr / Pct	3Yr / Pct	5Yr / Pct	Dividend Yield	Expense Ratio
MUN	UBS Municipal Bond A	UMBAX	U	(888) 793-8637	U /	2.05	-3.10	-0.40 / 11	--	--	1.41	1.15
MUN	UBS Municipal Bond C	UMBCX	U	(888) 793-8637	U /	1.83	-3.34	-0.89 / 5	--	--	0.94	1.65
MUN	UBS Municipal Bond P	UMBPX	U	(888) 793-8637	U /	2.02	-2.98	-0.15 / 15	--	--	1.70	0.89
MMT	UBS Select Prime Inst	SELXX	C	(888) 793-8637	D- / 1.5	0.21	0.32	0.51 / 33	0.22 / 17	0.16 / 17	0.49	N/A
MMT	UBS Select Prime Investor	SPIXX	C-	(888) 793-8637	D- / 1.0	0.11	0.15	0.20 / 26	0.08 / 12	0.05 / 12	0.18	N/A
MMT	UBS Select Prime Pfd	SPPXX	C	(888) 793-8637	D / 1.7	0.22	0.34	0.55 / 34	0.26 / 18	0.20 / 18	0.52	N/A
MMT	UBS Select Treas Inst	SETXX	C-	(888) 793-8637	D- / 1.1	0.09	0.14	0.22 / 27	0.09 / 13	0.06 / 13	0.22	N/A
MMT	UBS Select Treas Pfd	STPXX	C-	(888) 793-8637	D- / 1.2	0.10	0.16	0.26 / 28	0.11 / 14	0.07 / 13	0.26	N/A
MMT	UBS Select Treasury Investor	STRXX	D+	(888) 793-8637	E+ / 0.6	0.03	0.03	0.03 / 20	0.02 / 8	0.02 / 8	0.03	N/A
MMF	UBS Tax-Free Investor	SFRXX	C-	(888) 793-8637	E+ / 0.9	0.05	0.09	0.09 / 24	0.04 / 11	0.03 / 12	0.09	N/A
GEI	Universal Inst Core Plus Fxd Inc I	UFIPX	A-	(800) 869-6397	B- / 7.5	1.79	0.19	7.08 / 73	3.92 / 74	4.09 / 74	1.90	0.76
GEI	Universal Inst Core Plus Fxd Inc II	UCFIX	B+	(800) 869-6397	B- / 7.3	1.70	0.09	6.83 / 72	3.65 / 71	3.82 / 70	1.65	1.01
EM	Universal Inst Emer Mrkt Debt I	UEMDX	C-	(800) 869-6397	B+ / 8.9	5.08	-0.25	13.32 / 86	4.40 / 80	3.47 / 65	5.53	1.09
EM	Universal Inst Emer Mrkt Debt II	UEDBX	C	(800) 869-6397	B+ / 8.9	5.26	-0.25	13.37 / 86	4.38 / 79	3.44 / 64	5.52	1.34
US	US Global Inv Govt Ultra-Short Bond	UGSDX	C-	(800) 873-8637	D / 1.6	0.15	-0.24	-0.03 / 17	0.39 / 20	0.25 / 19	0.44	1.13
GL	US Global Inv Near-Term Tax Free	NEARX	C	(800) 873-8637	D+ / 2.5	1.23	-1.12	-0.53 / 9	1.13 / 30	1.28 / 31	1.27	1.09
USS	US Govt Securities Direct	CAUSX	C-	(800) 955-9988	C- / 4.0	1.96	-1.02	1.15 / 41	1.93 / 42	0.99 / 27	4.50	0.82
USS	US Govt Securities K	CAUKX	D-	(800) 955-9988	D / 2.0	1.45	-1.73	-0.87 / 5	0.89 / 26	0.19 / 18	2.12	1.32
MUS	USAA California Bond Adviser	UXABX	B	(800) 382-8722	B / 7.7	2.21	-2.87	0.04 / 21	3.85 / 91	3.84 / 92	3.19	0.80
*MUS	USAA California Bond Fund	USCBX	A-	(800) 382-8722	B+ / 8.6	2.36	-2.67	0.38 / 35	4.14 / 94	4.11 / 94	3.44	0.56
GEN	USAA Flexible Income Adviser	UAFIX	E+	(800) 382-8722	C / 5.3	4.70	-0.79	10.68 / 80	1.46 / 34	--	1.82	1.36
GEN	USAA Flexible Income Fund	USFIX	D-	(800) 382-8722	C+ / 6.1	4.69	-0.76	10.87 / 81	1.68 / 38	--	1.99	1.00
GEN	USAA Flexible Income Institutional	UIFIX	D-	(800) 382-8722	C+ / 6.3	4.81	-0.64	11.08 / 81	1.87 / 41	--	2.08	0.89
USA	USAA Government Securities Adviser	UAGNX	C	(800) 382-8722	D+ / 2.7	0.15	-1.62	-0.26 / 14	1.41 / 33	1.02 / 28	1.79	0.95
USA	USAA Government Securities Fund	USGNX	C+	(800) 382-8722	C- / 3.2	0.21	-1.49	-0.09 / 16	1.68 / 38	1.37 / 33	2.07	0.51
USS	USAA Government Securities Inst	UIGSX	U	(800) 382-8722	U /	0.23	-1.45	-0.02 / 17	--	--	2.14	0.44
GL	USAA High Income Adviser	UHYOX	C+	(800) 382-8722	A / 9.3	4.93	5.63	22.83 / 98	3.52 / 69	6.39 / 95	5.37	1.21
*COH	USAA High Income Fund	USHYX	C+	(800) 382-8722	A / 9.4	5.00	5.77	23.09 / 98	3.79 / 73	6.66 / 96	5.67	0.84
COH	USAA High Income Institutional	UIHIX	C+	(800) 382-8722	A / 9.5	5.02	5.96	23.38 / 98	3.90 / 74	6.80 / 96	5.75	0.73
*USS	USAA Income Fund	USAIX	B-	(800) 382-8722	C+ / 6.7	2.11	-1.09	6.30 / 71	3.24 / 65	3.45 / 65	3.48	0.53
COI	USAA Income Fund Adv	UINCX	C+	(800) 382-8722	C+ / 6.4	2.06	-1.21	6.03 / 70	2.97 / 61	3.16 / 60	3.22	0.86
USS	USAA Income Fund Inst	UIINX	B-	(800) 382-8722	C+ / 6.8	2.13	-1.06	6.35 / 71	3.32 / 66	3.53 / 66	3.53	0.46
COI	USAA Intmdt-Trm Bd Fd Adv	UITBX	B	(800) 382-8722	C+ / 6.7	2.30	-0.11	7.65 / 74	2.87 / 59	3.97 / 72	3.51	0.86
GEI	USAA Intmdt-Trm Bd Fd Inst	UIITX	B+	(800) 382-8722	B- / 7.1	2.38	-0.04	7.99 / 74	3.23 / 65	4.33 / 77	3.82	0.54
*GEI	USAA Intmdt-Trm Bd Fund	USIBX	B+	(800) 382-8722	B- / 7.0	2.35	0.00	7.92 / 74	3.14 / 63	4.24 / 75	3.76	0.62
MMT	USAA Money Market Fund	USAXX	D+	(800) 382-8722	E+ / 0.8	0.06	0.10	0.10 / 22	0.04 / 9	0.03 / 9	0.10	N/A
MUS	USAA New York Bond Adv	UNYBX	B-	(800) 382-8722	C+ / 6.7	1.50	-2.89	0.04 / 21	3.20 / 84	2.65 / 74	3.28	0.85
GEI	USAA New York Bond Fund	USNYX	C	(800) 382-8722	C+ / 5.6	1.55	-2.76	0.26 / 28	3.43 / 68	2.93 / 56	3.51	0.66
GES	USAA Real Return Fund	USRRX	E+	(800) 382-8722	C / 4.4	3.27	1.71	12.22 / 84	0.16 / 15	1.55 / 35	0.12	1.19
GES	USAA Real Return Institutional	UIRRX	E+	(800) 382-8722	C / 4.6	3.37	1.71	12.21 / 84	0.29 / 18	1.71 / 38	0.13	0.99
COI	USAA Short Term Bond Adv	UASBX	B	(800) 382-8722	C- / 3.5	0.86	0.39	3.10 / 57	1.24 / 31	1.62 / 36	1.63	0.86
GEI	USAA Short Term Bond Inst	UISBX	B+	(800) 382-8722	C- / 4.0	0.83	0.45	3.48 / 60	1.55 / 36	1.97 / 42	1.99	0.51
*GEI	USAA Short Term Bond Retail Fund	USSBX	B+	(800) 382-8722	C- / 3.9	0.91	0.51	3.37 / 59	1.48 / 35	1.87 / 40	1.89	0.61
MUN	USAA T/E Short Term Adviser	UTESX	D	(800) 382-8722	E+ / 0.6	0.47	-0.76	-0.27 / 13	0.39 / 22	0.70 / 28	1.16	0.83
*MUN	USAA T/E Short Term Bond Fund	USSTX	C+	(800) 382-8722	D / 2.2	0.55	-0.71	--	0.58 / 26	0.94 / 34	1.43	0.55
MMF	USAA Tax Exempt-CA MM	UCAXX	U	(800) 382-8722	U /	--	--	--	--	--	0.28	N/A
MMF	USAA Tax Exempt-Money Market	USEXX	C-	(800) 382-8722	D- / 1.3	0.16	0.21	0.21 / 30	0.08 / 14	0.06 / 15	0.21	N/A
MMF	USAA Tax Exempt-NY MM	UNYXX	C-	(800) 382-8722	E+ / 0.9	0.03	0.07	0.08 / 23	0.05 / 12	0.03 / 12	0.08	N/A
MMF	USAA Tax VA Exempt MM	UVAXX	U	(800) 382-8722	U /	--	--	--	--	--	0.05	N/A
MUN	USAA Tax-Ex Intm-Trm Adviser	UTEIX	D	(800) 382-8722	C / 4.3	1.76	-3.91	-1.06 / 4	2.23 / 68	2.52 / 71	2.92	0.88
MUN	USAA Tax-Ex L Term Adviser	UTELX	B+	(800) 382-8722	B- / 7.2	1.85	-2.80	0.38 / 35	3.41 / 87	3.32 / 85	3.75	0.90
*MUN	USAA Tax-Exempt Interm-Term Fund	USATX	C	(800) 382-8722	C+ / 5.7	1.84	-3.78	-0.79 / 6	2.49 / 73	2.76 / 75	3.21	0.54

● Denotes fund is closed to new investors
* Denotes fund is included in Section II

RISK Rating/Pts	3 Yr Avg Standard Deviation	Avg Duration	NAV As of 2/28/17	Total $(Mil)	Cash %	Gov. Bond %	Muni. Bond %	Corp. Bond %	Other %	Portfolio Turnover Ratio	Avg Coupon Rate	Manager Quality Pct	Manager Tenure (Years)	Initial Purch. $	Additional Purch. $	Front End Load	Back End Load
U /	N/A	N/A	10.08	22	0	0	99	0	1	100	4.3	N/A	3	1,000	100	2.3	0.0
U /	N/A	N/A	10.07	7	0	0	99	0	1	100	4.3	N/A	3	1,000	100	0.0	0.0
U /	N/A	N/A	10.07	99	0	0	99	0	1	100	4.3	N/A	3	5,000,000	0	0.0	0.0
A+ /9.9	0.1	N/A	1.00	2,099	100	0	0	0	0	0	0.5	51	16	1,000,000	0	0.0	0.0
A+ /9.9	N/A	N/A	1.00	226	100	0	0	0	0	0	0.2	43	16	100,000	0	0.0	0.0
A+ /9.9	0.1	N/A	1.00	438	100	0	0	0	0	0	0.5	53	16	99,000,000	0	0.0	0.0
A+ /9.9	N/A	N/A	1.00	4,496	100	0	0	0	0	0	0.2	46	13	1,000,000	0	0.0	0.0
A+ /9.9	N/A	N/A	1.00	9,359	100	0	0	0	0	0	0.3	N/A	9	50,000,000	0	0.0	0.0
A+ /9.9	N/A	N/A	1.00	204	100	0	0	0	0	0	0.0	39	9	100,000	0	0.0	0.0
A+ /9.9	N/A	N/A	1.00	37	100	0	0	0	0	0	0.1	42	9	100,000	0	0.0	0.0
C /5.3	3.1	5.2	10.82	81	0	11	10	31	48	400	0.0	83	6	0	0	0.0	0.0
C /5.4	3.0	5.2	10.78	104	0	11	10	31	48	400	0.0	81	6	0	0	0.0	0.0
E+ /0.6	7.0	7.0	8.06	207	1	75	2	18	4	37	0.0	98	15	0	0	0.0	0.0
E+ /0.7	6.9	7.0	8.01	20	1	75	2	18	4	37	0.0	98	15	0	0	0.0	0.0
A- /9.1	1.2	N/A	2.00	55	3	96	0	0	1	60	0.0	36	28	5,000	100	0.0	0.0
B+ /8.8	1.5	2.9	2.22	93	5	0	94	0	1	15	6.0	80	27	5,000	100	0.0	0.0
C+ /6.5	2.8	4.9	10.24	18	0	92	0	0	8	18	3.1	59	14	1,000	100	0.0	0.0
C+ /6.7	2.8	4.9	10.27	5	0	92	0	0	8	18	3.1	16	14	1,000	100	0.0	0.0
C- /4.1	3.1	9.2	10.91	7	0	0	99	0	1	9	4.9	68	N/A	3,000	50	0.0	1.0
C- /4.0	3.1	9.2	10.93	669	0	0	99	0	1	9	4.9	73	N/A	3,000	50	0.0	0.0
E+ /0.8	6.6	N/A	9.29	5	7	19	5	28	41	36	0.0	3	N/A	3,000	50	0.0	1.0
E+ /0.8	6.6	N/A	9.29	50	7	19	5	28	41	36	0.0	5	N/A	3,000	50	0.0	0.0
E+ /0.9	6.5	N/A	9.31	23	7	19	5	28	41	36	0.0	6	N/A	1,000,000	0	0.0	0.0
B+ /8.6	1.8	2.1	9.80	5	1	14	4	0	81	14	5.4	60	N/A	3,000	50	0.0	0.0
B+ /8.5	1.8	2.1	9.80	397	1	14	4	0	81	14	5.4	67	N/A	3,000	50	0.0	0.0
U /	N/A	2.1	9.80	131	1	14	4	0	81	14	5.4	N/A	N/A	1,000,000	0	0.0	1.0
D- /1.2	6.0	2.9	8.28	10	0	0	0	0	100	36	7.6	95	1	3,000	50	0.0	1.0
E+ /0.8	6.0	2.9	8.26	1,193	0	0	0	0	100	36	7.6	16	1	3,000	50	0.0	1.0
E+ /0.9	6.0	2.9	8.26	963	0	0	0	0	100	36	7.6	18	1	1,000,000	0	0.0	1.0
C /4.8	3.2	3.7	13.02	3,419	0	11	8	64	17	11	5.8	84	1	3,000	50	0.0	0.0
C /4.8	3.2	3.7	12.99	139	0	11	8	64	17	11	5.8	52	1	3,000	50	0.0	0.0
C /4.8	3.2	3.7	13.01	3,457	0	11	8	64	17	11	5.8	85	1	1,000,000	0	0.0	0.0
C /5.4	3.0	3.2	10.54	89	1	6	4	74	15	18	8.9	59	1	3,000	50	0.0	0.0
C /5.4	3.0	3.2	10.55	1,961	1	6	4	74	15	18	8.9	76	1	1,000,000	0	0.0	0.0
C /5.5	3.0	3.2	10.55	1,850	1	6	4	74	15	18	8.9	75	1	3,000	50	0.0	0.0
A+ /9.9	N/A	N/A	1.00	4,799	100	0	0	0	0	0	0.1	42	N/A	1,000	50	0.0	0.0
C /5.0	2.8	8.7	11.85	6	2	0	97	0	1	10	4.7	54	N/A	3,000	50	0.0	1.0
C /5.1	2.8	8.7	11.88	209	2	0	97	0	1	10	4.7	79	N/A	3,000	50	0.0	0.0
D- /1.0	6.4	N/A	10.12	24	6	40	0	14	40	35	0.0	3	N/A	3,000	50	0.0	0.0
D- /1.0	6.3	N/A	10.13	46	6	40	0	14	40	35	0.0	4	N/A	3,000	50	0.0	0.0
A- /9.2	1.0	1.6	9.16	18	0	7	8	64	21	22	5.5	61	1	3,000	50	0.0	0.0
A- /9.2	1.0	1.6	9.15	1,856	0	7	8	64	21	22	5.5	72	1	1,000,000	0	0.0	0.0
A- /9.2	1.1	1.6	9.16	1,326	0	7	8	64	21	22	5.5	70	1	3,000	50	0.0	0.0
A /9.5	0.8	2.3	10.46	38	0	0	98	0	2	25	5.0	24	N/A	3,000	50	0.0	1.0
A /9.5	0.8	2.3	10.45	1,698	0	0	98	0	2	25	5.0	29	N/A	3,000	50	0.0	0.0
U /	N/A	N/A	1.00	248	100	0	0	0	0	0	0.3	53	N/A	3,000	50	0.0	0.0
A+ /9.9	0.1	N/A	1.00	2,066	100	0	0	0	0	0	0.2	N/A	N/A	3,000	50	0.0	0.0
A+ /9.9	N/A	N/A	1.00	68	100	0	0	0	0	0	0.1	42	N/A	3,000	50	0.0	0.0
U /	N/A	N/A	1.00	141	100	0	0	0	0	0	0.1	41	N/A	3,000	50	0.0	0.0
C /4.8	3.2	6.3	13.07	38	0	0	99	0	1	10	4.9	9	N/A	3,000	50	0.0	1.0
C /5.0	2.9	8.0	13.24	11	1	0	98	0	1	6	5.3	59	N/A	3,000	50	0.0	1.0
C /4.7	3.2	6.3	13.07	4,275	0	0	99	0	1	10	4.9	14	N/A	3,000	50	0.0	0.0

99 Pct = Best
0 Pct = Worst

Fund Type	Fund Name	Ticker Symbol	Overall Investment Rating	Phone	Performance Rating/Pts	Total Return % through 2/28/17			Annualized		Incl. in Returns	
						3 Mo	6 Mo	1Yr / Pct	3Yr / Pct	5Yr / Pct	Dividend Yield	Expense Ratio
*MUN	USAA Tax-Exempt Long Term Fund	USTEX	A	(800) 382-8722	B / 8.0	1.85	-2.71	0.64 /39	3.71 /90	3.64 /89	4.09	0.51
MMT	USAA Treasury Money Market	UATXX	D+	(800) 382-8722	E+ / 0.6	0.02	0.02	0.02 /19	0.01 / 7	--	0.02	N/A
MUN	USAA Ultra Short Term Bond Fund	UUSTX	B+	(800) 382-8722	C- / 3.8	0.47	0.51	2.28 /60	0.87 /33	1.31 /42	1.34	0.59
GEI	USAA Ultra Short Term Bond Inst	UUSIX	B-	(800) 382-8722	D+ / 2.8	0.37	0.50	2.13 /50	0.88 /26	--	1.29	0.57
MUS	USAA Virginia Bond Adv	UVABX	B+	(800) 382-8722	B- / 7.2	1.52	-2.51	0.51 /37	3.45 /87	3.02 /80	2.95	0.84
*GEI	USAA Virginia Bond Fund	USVAX	C+	(800) 382-8722	C+ / 6.1	1.58	-2.49	0.66 /36	3.67 /71	3.25 /62	3.20	0.60
MMT	VALIC Co II Govt MM II	VIIXX	U	(800) 858-8850	U /	0.01	0.01	0.02 /19	0.01 / 7	0.01 / 6	0.02	N/A
MMT	VALIC Company Government Mny	VCIXX	U	(800) 858-8850	U /	0.01	0.02	0.02 /19	0.01 / 7	0.01 / 6	0.02	N/A
COH	Value Line Core Bond Fund	VAGIX	D-	(800) 243-2729	C- / 3.5	1.04	-2.11	1.18 /42	1.72 /38	1.99 /42	1.81	1.17
MUH	Value Line Tax Exempt Fund	VLHYX	C-	(800) 243-2729	C+ / 6.0	1.98	-2.84	-0.46 /10	2.49 /73	2.03 /60	2.82	1.11
EM	VanEck Unconstrained EM Bd A	EMBAX	E-	(800) 826-1115	E / 0.3	6.08	3.64	10.20 /79	-1.15 / 2	--	3.99	1.44
EM	VanEck Unconstrained EM Bd C	EMBCX	E	(800) 826-1115	D / 1.7	5.83	3.31	9.40 /77	-1.87 / 2	--	4.40	2.68
EM	VanEck Unconstrained EM Bd I	EMBUX	E	(800) 826-1115	C- / 3.4	6.29	3.88	10.53 /80	-0.84 / 3	--	4.17	0.94
EM	VanEck Unconstrained EM Bd Y	EMBYX	E	(800) 826-1115	C- / 3.2	6.16	3.75	10.41 /80	-0.93 / 3	--	4.19	1.07
COH	Vanguard 529 High Yield Bond Port		B-	(800) 662-7447	A- / 9.2	3.83	3.79	14.41 /87	4.50 /81	5.89 /91	0.00	0.38
COI	Vanguard 529 Income		C+	(800) 662-7447	C- / 3.5	0.82	-0.81	1.53 /45	1.60 /36	1.13 /29	0.00	0.25
GEI	Vanguard 529 Inflation Pro Sec Port		E+	(800) 662-7447	C- / 4.1	1.36	-0.55	3.22 /58	1.71 /38	0.57 /22	0.00	0.32
GEI	Vanguard 529 Interest Acc Port		C+	(800) 662-7447	D / 2.0	0.33	0.50	1.00 /40	0.50 /21	0.35 /20	0.00	0.25
GEI	Vanguard 529 ND Income Fd		C	(800) 662-7447	C- / 3.0	0.53	-1.34	0.76 /37	1.42 /34	0.75 /24	0.00	0.85
GEI	Vanguard 529 PA Income Port		B+	(800) 662-7447	B- / 7.3	2.35	-0.06	5.77 /69	3.81 /73	4.14 /74	0.00	0.52
GEI	Vanguard 529 Ttl Bond Mkt Index Por		D	(800) 662-7447	C / 4.4	1.19	-2.40	1.25 /42	2.40 /50	1.97 /42	0.00	0.28
MUS	Vanguard CA Interm-Term T-E Adm	VCADX	B	(800) 662-7447	B- / 7.1	2.43	-2.76	-0.23 /14	3.09 /83	3.09 /81	2.72	0.12
*MUS	Vanguard CA Interm-Term T-E Inv	VCAIX	B	(800) 662-7447	B- / 7.0	2.41	-2.82	-0.33 /12	3.00 /82	3.00 /80	2.61	0.20
MUS	Vanguard CA Long-Term Tax-Exmpt	VCLAX	B	(800) 662-7447	B+ / 8.7	2.83	-4.02	0.08 /23	4.40 /95	4.03 /94	3.50	0.12
MUS	Vanguard CA Long-Term Tax-Exmpt	VCITX	B	(800) 662-7447	B+ / 8.6	2.81	-4.08	-0.02 /17	4.31 /95	3.95 /93	3.39	0.20
MMF	Vanguard CA T/F MM Inv	VCTXX	C	(800) 662-7447	D- / 1.5	0.13	0.26	0.37 /34	0.13 /17	0.09 /17	0.37	N/A
COI	Vanguard Core Bond Admiral	VCOBX	U	(800) 662-7447	U /	1.23	-2.06	--	--	--	0.00	N/A
EM	Vanguard Em Mkt Govt Bd Idx	VGAVX	B-	(800) 662-7447	A / 9.4	4.36	-0.12	11.56 /82	5.74 /90	--	4.64	0.33
EM	Vanguard Em Mkt Govt Bd Idx Inv	VGOVX	B-	(800) 662-7447	A / 9.3	4.37	-0.15	11.42 /82	5.61 /89	--	4.46	0.49
*US	Vanguard Extnd Durtn Trea Idx Inst	VEDTX	C-	(800) 662-7447	A- / 9.1	2.64	-16.42	-6.63 / 0	9.40 /99	4.53 /79	2.94	0.08
US	Vanguard Extnd Durtn Trea Idx	VEDIX	C-	(800) 662-7447	A- / 9.1	2.60	-16.42	-6.64 / 0	9.41 /99	4.55 /79	2.96	0.06
MMT	Vanguard Federal M/M Inv	VMFXX	C-	(800) 662-7447	D- / 1.3	0.11	0.19	0.34 /30	0.14 /15	0.09 /15	0.34	N/A
USA	Vanguard GNMA Adm	VFIJX	B+	(800) 662-7447	C / 4.8	0.43	-1.07	0.77 /37	2.67 /55	2.07 /43	2.33	0.11
*USA	Vanguard GNMA Inv	VFIIX	B+	(800) 662-7447	C / 4.6	0.41	-1.11	0.67 /36	2.57 /53	1.96 /41	2.23	0.21
COH	Vanguard High-Yield Corporate Adm	VWEAX	B	(800) 662-7447	A / 9.3	3.89	3.90	14.65 /88	4.72 /83	6.13 /93	5.43	0.13
*COH	Vanguard High-Yield Corporate Inv	VWEHX	B	(800) 662-7447	A / 9.3	3.87	3.85	14.53 /88	4.62 /82	6.02 /92	5.33	0.23
MUH	Vanguard High-Yield Tax-Exempt	VWALX	B	(800) 662-7447	A- / 9.1	2.36	-3.73	1.07 /46	4.58 /96	4.10 /94	3.85	0.12
*MUH	Vanguard High-Yield Tax-Exempt Inv	VWAHX	B	(800) 662-7447	B+ / 8.9	2.34	-3.78	0.96 /44	4.49 /96	4.01 /93	3.74	0.20
USS	Vanguard Infltn Pro Sec Adm	VAIPX	E+	(800) 662-7447	C / 4.4	1.29	-0.52	3.35 /59	1.88 /41	0.74 /24	3.44	0.10
USS	Vanguard Infltn Pro Sec Inst	VIPIX	E+	(800) 662-7447	C / 4.5	1.39	-0.46	3.43 /59	1.92 /42	0.78 /25	3.45	0.07
*USS	Vanguard Infltn Pro Sec Inv	VIPSX	E+	(800) 662-7447	C- / 4.2	1.22	-0.62	3.24 /58	1.77 /39	0.64 /23	3.33	0.20
GEI	Vanguard Interm-Term Bd Index Adm	VBILX	D-	(800) 662-7447	C / 5.4	1.33	-2.77	1.13 /41	3.12 /63	2.78 /54	2.61	0.09
*GEI	Vanguard Interm-Term Bd Index Inv	VBIIX	D-	(800) 662-7447	C / 5.2	1.30	-2.81	1.04 /40	3.03 /62	2.69 /53	2.52	0.16
GEI	Vanguard Interm-Term Invst-Grd Adm	VFIDX	C+	(800) 662-7447	C+ / 6.4	1.44	-1.59	3.46 /59	3.43 /68	3.50 /66	2.89	0.10
*GEI	Vanguard Interm-Term Invst-Grd Inv	VFICX	C+	(800) 662-7447	C+ / 6.2	1.42	-1.64	3.36 /59	3.32 /66	3.40 /64	2.79	0.20
MUN	Vanguard Interm-Term Tax-Exempt	VWIUX	B+	(800) 662-7447	C+ / 6.9	2.10	-2.55	-0.01 /17	2.90 /80	2.68 /74	2.88	0.12
*MUN	Vanguard Interm-Term Tax-Exempt	VWITX	B+	(800) 662-7447	C+ / 6.7	2.08	-2.61	-0.11 /16	2.80 /79	2.60 /73	2.77	0.20
US	Vanguard Interm-Term Treasury Adm	VFIUX	E+	(800) 662-7447	C- / 3.4	0.67	-2.42	-1.16 / 3	2.03 /44	1.50 /34	1.67	0.10
*US	Vanguard Interm-Term Treasury Inv	VFITX	E+	(800) 662-7447	C- / 3.2	0.65	-2.46	-1.26 / 3	1.93 /42	1.40 /33	1.56	0.20
GEI	Vanguard Interm-Tm Bd Idx Inst	VBIMX	D-	(800) 662-7447	C / 5.4	1.33	-2.76	1.15 /41	3.14 /63	2.81 /55	2.63	0.06
COI	Vanguard Interm-Tm Bd Idx Inst Plus	VBIUX	D-	(800) 662-7447	C / 5.4	1.33	-2.76	1.15 /41	3.16 /64	2.83 /55	2.64	0.04
*COI	Vanguard Intm-Term Corp Bd Idx	VICSX	C	(800) 662-7447	B- / 7.2	1.86	-1.80	5.25 /68	3.96 /75	4.11 /74	3.25	0.07

● Denotes fund is closed to new investors
* Denotes fund is included in Section II

www.thestreetratings.com

RISK			NET ASSETS		ASSET					Portfolio Turnover Ratio	Avg Coupon Rate	FUND MANAGER		MINIMUM		LOADS	
Risk Rating/Pts	3 Yr Avg Standard Deviation	Avg Dura-tion	NAV As of 2/28/17	Total $(Mil)	Cash %	Gov. Bond %	Muni. Bond %	Corp. Bond %	Other %			Manager Quality Pct	Manager Tenure (Years)	Initial Purch. $	Additional Purch. $	Front End Load	Back End Load
C / 5.0	2.9	8.0	13.25	2,346	1	0	98	0	1	6	5.3	67	N/A	3,000	50	0.0	0.0
A+ / 9.9	N/A	N/A	1.00	2,461	100	0	0	0	0	0	0.0	37	N/A	3,000	50	0.0	0.0
A+ / 9.7	0.7	N/A	9.99	371	1	0	9	67	23	20	0.0	67	N/A	3,000	50	0.0	0.0
A+ / 9.7	0.6	N/A	9.99	9	1	0	9	67	23	20	0.0	65	N/A	1,000,000	0	0.0	0.0
C / 5.4	2.8	7.6	11.21	25	0	0	99	0	1	3	5.3	64	N/A	3,000	50	0.0	1.0
C / 5.2	2.9	7.6	11.21	663	0	0	99	0	1	3	5.3	82	N/A	3,000	50	0.0	0.0
U /	N/A	N/A	1.00	135	100	0	0	0	0	0	0.0	N/A	N/A	0	0	0.0	0.0
U /	N/A	N/A	1.00	342	100	0	0	0	0	0	0.0	N/A	N/A	0	0	0.0	0.0
C / 4.6	2.8	5.4	14.85	66	1	16	2	48	33	34	0.0	76	7	1,000	250	0.0	0.0
C- / 4.1	3.0	5.1	9.80	62	1	0	98	0	1	6	0.0	18	7	1,000	250	0.0	0.0
E+ / 0.6	7.4	3.9	7.04	8	5	68	4	4	19	605	7.9	34	5	1,000	100	5.8	0.0
E+ / 0.6	7.3	3.9	6.78	3	5	68	4	4	19	605	7.9	13	5	1,000	100	0.0	0.0
E+ / 0.6	7.4	3.9	7.15	86	5	68	4	4	19	605	7.9	53	5	1,000,000	0	0.0	0.0
E+ / 0.6	7.4	3.9	7.12	23	5	68	4	4	19	605	7.9	49	5	1,000	100	0.0	0.0
D / 2.0	4.6	N/A	25.73	135	5	2	0	88	5	0	0.0	75	15	3,000	50	0.0	0.0
B / 7.9	2.2	N/A	15.90	761	25	48	0	12	15	0	0.0	29	15	3,000	50	0.0	0.0
D+ / 2.9	4.1	N/A	17.93	120	1	98	0	0	1	0	0.0	7	N/A	3,000	50	0.0	0.0
A+ / 9.9	0.2	N/A	12.07	444	0	0	0	0	100	0	0.0	62	N/A	3,000	50	0.0	0.0
B / 8.2	2.0	N/A	13.29	61	25	48	1	13	13	0	0.0	26	11	25	25	0.0	0.0
C / 5.0	3.1	N/A	16.12	145	0	38	1	20	41	0	0.0	83	11	25	25	0.0	0.0
C / 5.0	3.1	N/A	17.07	191	0	46	1	25	28	0	0.0	26	15	3,000	50	0.0	0.0
C / 4.8	3.2	4.9	11.62	9,928	0	0	99	0	1	17	4.4	28	4	50,000	100	0.0	0.0
C / 4.8	3.2	4.9	11.62	1,559	0	0	99	0	1	17	4.4	25	4	3,000	100	0.0	0.0
D+ / 2.8	4.1	5.8	11.89	3,174	0	0	99	0	1	14	4.4	44	6	50,000	100	0.0	0.0
D+ / 2.8	4.1	5.8	11.89	464	0	0	99	0	1	14	4.4	36	6	3,000	100	0.0	0.0
A+ / 9.9	0.1	N/A	1.00	3,678	100	0	0	0	0	0	0.4	48	N/A	3,000	100	0.0	0.0
U /	N/A	5.8	19.79	590	0	0	0	0	100	229	3.0	N/A	1	50,000	1	0.0	0.0
D / 1.7	5.5	6.4	19.91	205	0	0	0	0	100	20	5.6	99	4	10,000	100	0.0	0.0
D / 1.7	5.5	6.4	9.96	12	0	0	0	0	100	20	5.6	99	4	3,000	100	0.0	0.0
E- / 0.0	17.6	24.7	33.95	577	0	100	0	0	0	20	3.6	69	4	5,000,000	0	0.0	0.0
E- / 0.0	17.6	24.7	85.21	340	0	100	0	0	0	20	3.6	69	4	100,000,000	0	0.0	0.0
A+ / 9.9	N/A	N/A	1.00	71,348	100	0	0	0	0	0	0.3	48	10	3,000	100	0.0	0.0
B+ / 8.3	2.0	1.8	10.54	17,540	0	3	0	1	96	706	3.6	82	11	50,000	0	0.0	0.0
B+ / 8.3	2.0	1.8	10.54	7,999	0	3	0	1	96	706	3.6	81	11	3,000	1	0.0	0.0
D / 2.0	4.6	4.3	5.92	18,206	2	3	0	92	3	34	5.8	78	9	50,000	0	0.0	0.0
D / 2.0	4.6	4.3	5.92	4,161	2	3	0	92	3	34	5.8	77	9	3,000	1	0.0	0.0
D+ / 2.6	3.8	5.4	11.08	8,904	1	0	98	0	1	19	4.7	65	7	50,000	100	0.0	0.0
D+ / 2.6	3.8	5.4	11.08	1,783	1	0	98	0	1	19	4.7	62	7	3,000	100	0.0	0.0
D+ / 2.7	4.1	7.9	25.84	13,000	2	97	0	0	1	43	0.8	43	6	10,000	100	0.0	0.0
D+ / 2.7	4.1	7.9	10.53	8,876	2	97	0	0	1	43	0.8	43	6	5,000,000	100	0.0	0.0
D+ / 2.7	4.1	7.9	13.16	4,549	2	97	0	0	1	43	0.8	35	6	3,000	100	0.0	0.0
D+ / 2.9	4.1	6.5	11.33	12,275	0	56	0	42	2	51	2.8	22	9	10,000	100	0.0	0.0
D+ / 2.9	4.1	6.5	11.33	1,427	0	56	0	42	2	51	2.8	20	9	3,000	100	0.0	0.0
C / 4.7	3.2	5.5	9.72	25,527	0	9	0	75	16	70	3.3	68	9	50,000	0	0.0	0.0
C / 4.7	3.2	5.5	9.72	2,679	0	9	0	75	16	70	3.3	65	9	3,000	1	0.0	0.0
C+ / 5.9	2.9	4.6	13.98	47,084	1	0	97	0	2	9	4.5	30	4	50,000	0	0.0	0.0
C+ / 5.9	2.9	4.6	13.98	4,062	1	0	97	0	2	9	4.5	27	4	3,000	100	0.0	0.0
C- / 4.0	3.5	5.3	11.14	5,210	0	97	0	1	2	142	1.9	53	2	50,000	0	0.0	0.0
C- / 3.9	3.5	5.3	11.14	1,175	0	97	0	1	2	142	1.9	47	2	3,000	1	0.0	0.0
D+ / 2.9	4.1	6.5	11.33	2,699	0	56	0	42	2	51	2.8	23	9	5,000,000	100	0.0	0.0
D+ / 2.9	4.1	6.5	11.33	1,514	0	56	0	42	2	51	2.8	30	9	100,000,000	100	0.0	0.0
C- / 3.2	4.0	6.5	23.27	785	1	0	0	98	1	56	3.8	60	8	10,000	0	0.0	0.0

					PERFORMANCE							
	99 Pct = Best 0 Pct = Worst					Total Return % through 2/28/17					Incl. in Returns	
			Ticker Symbol	Overall Investment Rating	Perfor- mance				Annualized		Dividend	Expense
Fund Type	Fund Name				Rating/Pts	3 Mo	6 Mo	1Yr / Pct	3Yr / Pct	5Yr / Pct	Yield	Ratio
COI	Vanguard Intm-Term Corp Bd Idx Inst		VICBX	C	B- / 7.2	1.88	-1.78	5.29 /68	3.98 /75	4.15 /74	3.27	0.05
*USS	Vanguard Intm-Term Govt Bd Idx		VSIGX	E+	C- / 3.2	0.62	-2.47	-1.25 / 3	1.95 /42	1.46 /34	1.55	0.07
USS	Vanguard Intm-Term Govt Bd Idx Inst		VIIGX	E+	C- / 3.2	0.60	-2.50	-1.26 / 3	1.96 /42	1.49 /34	1.57	0.05
MUN	Vanguard Lmtd-Term Tax-Exempt		VMLUX	B-	C- / 3.5	1.43	-0.65	0.15 /27	1.07 /37	1.19 /39	1.62	0.12
*MUN	Vanguard Lmtd-Term Tax-Exempt Inv		VMLTX	C+	C- / 3.3	1.40	-0.70	0.05 /21	0.98 /35	1.10 /37	1.51	0.20
GEL	Vanguard Long Term Bd Idx Inst		VBLLX	D+	B+ / 8.5	3.18	-7.08	4.57 /65	5.95 /92	4.40 /77	3.92	0.06
COI	Vanguard Long Term Bd Idx Inst Plus		VBLIX	D+	B+ / 8.5	3.18	-7.08	4.58 /65	5.97 /92	4.42 /78	3.93	0.04
*GEL	Vanguard Long Term Bd Idx Investor		VBLTX	D	B+ / 8.4	3.16	-7.13	4.47 /64	5.84 /91	4.28 /76	3.82	0.16
COI	Vanguard Long-Term Corp Bd Idx		VLTCX	C	A / 9.4	4.09	-3.98	11.67 /82	5.99 /92	5.27 /87	4.26	0.07
COI	Vanguard Long-Term Corp Bd Idx		VLCIX	C	A / 9.4	4.07	-4.02	11.67 /83	5.99 /92	5.29 /87	4.29	0.05
USL	Vanguard Long-Term Govt Bd Idx		VLGSX	D-	B- / 7.1	1.86	-11.13	-4.33 / 0	6.15 /93	3.34 /63	2.65	0.07
USL	Vanguard Long-Term Govt Bd Idx		VLGIX	D-	B- / 7.1	1.84	-11.12	-4.32 / 0	6.19 /93	3.37 /63	2.68	0.05
GEI ●	Vanguard Long-Term Inv Gr Adm		VWETX	C-	A- / 9.2	3.34	-5.38	7.20 /73	6.44 /94	5.51 /89	4.26	0.12
*GEI ●	Vanguard Long-Term Inv Gr Inv		VWESX	C-	A- / 9.1	3.32	-5.43	7.10 /73	6.34 /94	5.40 /88	4.16	0.21
MUN	Vanguard Long-Term Tax-Exempt		VWLUX	B+	B+ / 8.7	2.41	-3.50	0.57 /38	4.28 /95	3.75 /91	3.69	0.12
*MUN	Vanguard Long-Term Tax-Exempt Inv		VWLTX	B+	B+ / 8.6	2.38	-3.56	0.46 /36	4.19 /94	3.66 /89	3.59	0.20
US	Vanguard Long-Term Treasury Adm		VUSUX	D-	B- / 7.1	1.89	-11.25	-4.33 / 0	6.19 /93	3.33 /63	2.81	0.10
*US	Vanguard Long-Term Treasury Inv		VUSTX	D-	B- / 7.0	1.87	-11.29	-4.43 / 0	6.08 /92	3.23 /61	2.71	0.20
*MUS	Vanguard MA Tax-Exempt Inv		VMATX	C+	B / 7.8	2.41	-3.83	-0.29 /13	3.73 /90	3.02 /80	2.99	0.16
*MTG	Vanguard Mort-Backed Secs Idx Adm		VMBSX	B	C / 4.3	0.60	-1.17	0.43 /32	2.39 /50	1.96 /41	1.79	0.07
MTG	Vanguard Mort-Backed Secs Idx Inst		VMBIX	B	C / 4.3	0.58	-1.17	0.46 /32	2.41 /50	--	1.80	0.05
MMF	Vanguard Municipal Money Mkt Inv		VMSXX	C	D / 1.7	0.14	0.28	0.42 /36	0.15 /17	0.10 /17	0.42	N/A
MUS	Vanguard NJ Long-Term Tax-Exempt		VNJUX	C+	B / 7.8	2.12	-4.09	0.61 /39	3.62 /89	3.23 /84	3.74	0.12
MUS	Vanguard NJ Long-Term Tax-Exempt		VNJTX	C+	B / 7.6	2.09	-4.14	0.50 /37	3.53 /88	3.14 /82	3.63	0.20
MMF	Vanguard NJ T/E Money Market		VNJXX	C	D- / 1.5	0.12	0.24	0.36 /34	0.13 /17	0.09 /17	0.36	N/A
MUS	Vanguard NY Long-Term Tax-Exempt		VNYUX	A-	B+ / 8.7	2.25	-3.38	0.40 /35	4.33 /95	3.62 /89	3.35	0.12
MUS	Vanguard NY Long-Term Tax-Exempt		VNYTX	A-	B+ / 8.6	2.23	-3.44	0.30 /32	4.24 /94	3.53 /88	3.24	0.20
MMF	Vanguard NY Tx-Ex MM Inv		VYFXX	C	D / 1.6	0.13	0.27	0.39 /35	0.14 /17	0.09 /17	0.39	N/A
COI	Vanguard OH College Adv Income			C+	C- / 3.6	0.72	-1.03	1.39 /44	1.71 /38	1.18 /30	0.00	0.27
*MUS	Vanguard OH Long-Term Tax-Exempt		VOHIX	A-	B+ / 8.9	2.42	-3.33	0.75 /41	4.40 /95	3.72 /90	3.24	0.16
MUS	Vanguard PA Long-Term Tax-Exempt		VPALX	A-	B+ / 8.7	2.38	-3.23	0.68 /40	4.26 /95	3.58 /89	3.66	0.12
MUS	Vanguard PA Long-Term Tax-Exempt		VPAIX	A-	B+ / 8.6	2.35	-3.29	0.57 /38	4.17 /94	3.49 /87	3.55	0.20
MMF	Vanguard PA T/F MM Inv		VPTXX	C	D / 1.6	0.12	0.26	0.37 /34	0.13 /17	0.09 /17	0.37	N/A
MMT	Vanguard Prime M/M Inv		VMMXX	C	D / 1.6	0.18	0.33	0.56 /34	0.22 /17	0.15 /17	0.55	N/A
MMT	Vanguard Prime MM Adm		VMRXX	C	D / 1.7	0.20	0.36	0.62 /35	0.28 /18	0.20 /18	0.61	N/A
GES	Vanguard Short-Term Bd Idx Admiral		VBIRX	C+	D+ / 2.8	0.48	-0.48	0.82 /38	1.15 /30	1.15 /29	1.50	0.09
COI	Vanguard Short-Term Bd Idx Ins Plus		VBIPX	C+	D+ / 2.8	0.49	-0.47	0.85 /38	1.19 /31	1.19 /30	1.52	0.04
COI	Vanguard Short-Term Bd Idx Inst		VBITX	C+	D+ / 2.8	0.50	-0.46	0.86 /38	1.18 /30	1.18 /30	1.52	0.06
*GES	Vanguard Short-Term Bd Idx Investor		VBISX	C	D+ / 2.6	0.48	-0.50	0.76 /37	1.07 /29	1.06 /28	1.42	0.16
*COI	Vanguard Short-Term Crp Bd Idx		VSCSX	B+	C / 4.3	1.00	0.04	2.98 /56	1.88 /41	2.31 /46	2.11	0.07
COI	Vanguard Short-Term Crp Bd Idx Inst		VSTBX	B+	C / 4.4	1.00	0.01	3.01 /57	1.90 /41	2.33 /47	2.14	0.05
USS	Vanguard Short-Term Federal Adm		VSGDX	C+	D+ / 2.6	0.35	-0.19	0.60 /35	1.04 /28	0.92 /26	1.19	0.10
*USS	Vanguard Short-Term Federal Inv		VSGBX	C	D+ / 2.4	0.33	-0.24	0.50 /33	0.94 /27	0.82 /25	1.09	0.20
USS	Vanguard Short-Term Gvt Bd Idx		VSBSX	C	D / 1.9	0.23	-0.16	0.25 /27	0.57 /21	0.53 /22	0.85	0.07
USS	Vanguard Short-Term Gvt Bd Idx Inst		VSBIX	C	D / 2.0	0.23	-0.11	0.32 /29	0.62 /22	0.56 /22	0.87	0.05
MUN	Vanguard Short-Term Tax-Exempt		VWSUX	B-	D+ / 2.7	0.71	0.08	0.56 /38	0.63 /27	0.70 /29	1.01	0.12
*MUN	Vanguard Short-Term Tax-Exempt		VWSTX	C+	D+ / 2.4	0.69	0.03	0.46 /36	0.54 /25	0.62 /27	0.90	0.20
US	Vanguard Short-Term Treasury Adm		VFIRX	C	D+ / 2.3	0.35	-0.10	0.45 /32	0.81 /25	0.70 /24	0.99	0.10
*US	Vanguard Short-Term Treasury Inv		VFISX	C	D / 2.1	0.33	-0.15	0.35 /30	0.71 /23	0.60 /23	0.89	0.20
GEI	Vanguard Sh-Term Invest-Grade		VFSUX	B+	C- / 4.2	0.77	0.00	2.80 /55	1.87 /41	2.14 /44	2.02	0.10
GEI	Vanguard Sh-Term Invest-Grade Inst		VFSIX	B+	C / 4.3	0.78	0.02	2.83 /56	1.90 /41	2.17 /44	2.05	0.07
*GEI	Vanguard Sh-Term Invest-Grade Inv		VFSTX	B+	C- / 4.1	0.75	-0.05	2.70 /55	1.77 /39	2.04 /43	1.92	0.20

● Denotes fund is closed to new investors
* Denotes fund is included in Section II

www.thestreetratings.com

Risk Rating/Pts	3 Yr Avg Standard Deviation	Avg Duration	NAV As of 2/28/17	Total $(Mil)	Cash %	Gov. Bond %	Muni. Bond %	Corp. Bond %	Other %	Portfolio Turnover Ratio	Avg Coupon Rate	Manager Quality Pct	Manager Tenure (Years)	Initial Purch. $	Additional Purch. $	Front End Load	Back End Load
C- /3.1	4.0	6.5	28.76	435	1	0	0	98	1	56	3.8	60	8	5,000,000	0	0.0	0.0
C- /4.1	3.5	5.2	21.70	691	0	99	0	0	1	37	2.0	34	4	10,000	0	0.0	0.0
C- /4.0	3.5	5.2	26.92	367	0	99	0	0	1	37	2.0	34	4	5,000,000	0	0.0	0.0
B+ /8.8	1.5	2.6	10.93	21,358	1	0	97	0	2	13	3.8	25	9	50,000	0	0.0	0.0
B+ /8.8	1.5	2.6	10.93	1,795	1	0	97	0	2	13	3.8	22	9	3,000	100	0.0	0.0
E- /0.2	8.8	14.9	13.75	2,390	1	42	5	51	1	42	4.7	6	4	5,000,000	100	0.0	0.0
E- /0.2	8.8	14.9	13.75	2,857	1	42	5	51	1	42	4.7	5	4	100,000,000	100	0.0	0.0
E- /0.2	8.8	14.9	13.75	2,709	1	42	5	51	1	42	4.7	5	4	3,000	100	0.0	0.0
E /0.3	8.2	13.7	24.24	112	0	0	0	99	1	59	5.3	8	8	10,000	0	0.0	0.0
E /0.3	8.2	13.7	30.08	470	0	0	0	99	1	59	5.3	8	8	5,000,000	0	0.0	0.0
E- /0.1	11.2	17.1	25.22	271	0	99	0	0	1	18	3.6	28	4	10,000	0	0.0	0.0
E- /0.1	11.2	17.1	32.01	169	0	99	0	0	1	18	3.6	29	4	5,000,000	0	0.0	0.0
E /0.3	7.9	13.8	10.21	10,585	4	5	13	76	2	35	4.4	36	4	50,000	0	0.0	0.0
E /0.3	7.9	13.8	10.21	4,157	4	5	13	76	2	35	4.4	32	4	3,000	1	0.0	0.0
C- /3.5	3.7	5.4	11.43	9,033	0	0	99	0	1	13	4.8	58	7	50,000	100	0.0	0.0
C- /3.5	3.7	5.4	11.43	926	0	0	99	0	1	13	4.8	55	7	3,000	100	0.0	0.0
E- /0.1	11.4	17.3	11.95	2,506	0	98	0	0	2	117	3.3	61	2	50,000	0	0.0	0.0
E- /0.1	11.4	17.3	11.95	998	0	98	0	0	2	117	3.3	58	2	3,000	1	0.0	0.0
C- /3.4	3.9	5.4	10.59	1,525	0	0	99	0	1	15	4.7	26	9	3,000	100	0.0	0.0
B+ /8.3	1.9	2.6	20.99	522	0	0	0	0	100	380	4.6	45	8	10,000	0	0.0	0.0
B+ /8.4	1.9	2.6	28.44	48	0	0	0	0	100	380	4.6	48	8	5,000,000	0	0.0	0.0
A+ /9.9	0.1	N/A	1.00	16,881	100	0	0	0	0	0	0.4	49	1	3,000	100	0.0	0.0
C- /3.0	4.1	5.4	11.73	1,750	0	0	99	0	1	25	4.5	19	1	50,000	100	0.0	0.0
C- /3.0	4.1	5.4	11.73	232	0	0	99	0	1	25	4.5	17	1	3,000	100	0.0	0.0
A+ /9.9	0.1	N/A	1.00	1,237	100	0	0	0	0	0	0.4	48	6	3,000	100	0.0	0.0
C- /3.9	3.5	5.2	11.59	3,566	0	0	99	0	1	17	4.9	66	4	50,000	100	0.0	0.0
C- /3.9	3.6	5.2	11.59	457	0	0	99	0	1	17	4.9	63	4	3,000	100	0.0	0.0
A+ /9.9	0.1	N/A	1.00	2,164	100	0	0	0	0	0	0.4	49	6	3,000	100	0.0	0.0
B /7.9	2.2	N/A	15.31	244	25	48	0	12	15	0	0.0	34	8	25	0	0.0	0.0
C- /3.7	3.7	5.3	12.37	1,124	0	0	99	0	1	21	4.6	64	9	3,000	100	0.0	0.0
C- /3.9	3.5	5.2	11.37	3,087	0	0	100	0	0	16	4.9	64	6	50,000	100	0.0	0.0
C- /3.9	3.5	5.2	11.37	318	0	0	100	0	0	16	4.9	61	6	3,000	100	0.0	0.0
A+ /9.9	0.1	N/A	1.00	1,953	100	0	0	0	0	0	0.4	48	2	3,000	100	0.0	0.0
A+ /9.9	0.1	N/A	1.00	87,240	100	0	0	0	0	0	0.6	52	14	3,000	100	0.0	0.0
A+ /9.9	0.1	N/A	1.00	12,143	100	0	0	0	0	0	0.6	54	14	5,000,000	100	0.0	0.0
B+ /8.9	1.4	2.8	10.45	15,437	0	72	0	26	2	52	1.9	40	4	10,000	100	0.0	0.0
B+ /8.9	1.4	2.8	10.45	4,302	0	72	0	26	2	52	1.9	51	4	100,000,000	100	0.0	0.0
B+ /8.9	1.4	2.8	10.45	4,912	0	72	0	26	2	52	1.9	51	4	5,000,000	100	0.0	0.0
B+ /8.9	1.4	2.8	10.45	1,820	0	72	0	26	2	52	1.9	35	4	3,000	100	0.0	0.0
B+ /8.8	1.5	2.8	21.67	2,394	0	0	0	99	1	57	3.4	67	8	10,000	0	0.0	0.0
B+ /8.8	1.5	2.8	26.52	1,192	0	0	0	99	1	57	3.4	67	8	5,000,000	0	0.0	0.0
A- /9.2	1.0	2.4	10.71	4,837	0	97	0	0	3	314	1.3	60	2	50,000	0	0.0	0.0
A- /9.2	1.1	2.4	10.71	830	0	97	0	0	3	314	1.3	57	2	3,000	1	0.0	0.0
A /9.5	0.8	1.9	20.26	435	1	98	0	0	1	64	1.5	47	4	10,000	0	0.0	0.0
A+ /9.6	0.8	1.9	25.46	193	1	98	0	0	1	64	1.5	50	4	5,000,000	0	0.0	0.0
A+ /9.8	0.5	1.4	15.78	13,294	0	0	97	0	3	29	3.0	52	1	50,000	0	0.0	0.0
A+ /9.8	0.5	1.4	15.78	1,239	0	0	97	0	3	29	3.0	46	1	3,000	100	0.0	0.0
A- /9.2	1.0	2.3	10.65	6,889	0	94	0	4	2	211	1.3	57	9	50,000	0	0.0	0.0
A- /9.2	1.0	2.3	10.65	907	0	94	0	4	2	211	1.3	53	9	3,000	1	0.0	0.0
A- /9.0	1.3	2.6	10.67	39,171	0	23	0	54	23	75	2.9	72	9	50,000	0	0.0	0.0
A- /9.0	1.3	2.6	10.67	10,172	0	23	0	54	23	75	2.9	73	9	5,000,000	1	0.0	0.0
A- /9.0	1.3	2.6	10.67	9,650	0	23	0	54	23	75	2.9	71	9	3,000	1	0.0	0.0

Fund Type	Fund Name	Ticker Symbol	Overall Investment Rating	Phone	Performance Rating/Pts	3 Mo	6 Mo	1Yr / Pct	3Yr / Pct	5Yr / Pct	Dividend Yield	Expense Ratio
	99 Pct = Best							Total Return % through 2/28/17	Annualized		Incl. in Returns	
GEI	Vanguard ST Inf Prot Sec Idx Adm	VTAPX	C-	(800) 662-7447	D+ / 2.4	0.84	1.05	2.46 /53	0.43 /20	--	0.76	0.08
GEI	Vanguard ST Inf Prot Sec Idx Inst	VTSPX	C-	(800) 662-7447	D+ / 2.4	0.85	1.05	2.50 /53	0.47 /21	--	0.80	0.05
*GEI	Vanguard ST Inf Prot Sec Idx Inv	VTIPX	C-	(800) 662-7447	D / 2.2	0.79	0.96	2.33 /52	0.33 /19	--	0.55	0.17
MUN	Vanguard Tax Exempt Bond Index	VTEAX	U	(800) 662-7447	U /	2.18	-2.90	0.24 /30	--	--	1.69	N/A
MUN	Vanguard Tax Exempt Bond Index	VTEBX	U	(800) 662-7447	U /	2.16	-2.90	0.19 /29	--	--	1.59	N/A
COI	Vanguard Total Bond Mkt II Idx Inst	VTBNX	D+	(800) 662-7447	C / 4.6	1.08	-2.38	1.35 /43	2.54 /53	2.12 /44	2.41	0.02
*COI	Vanguard Total Bond Mkt II Idx Inv	VTBIX	D+	(800) 662-7447	C / 4.5	1.06	-2.42	1.28 /43	2.48 /51	2.05 /43	2.34	0.09
GES	Vanguard Total Bond Mrkt Idx IPLUS	VBMPX	D+	(800) 662-7447	C / 4.7	1.23	-2.29	1.47 /44	2.59 /54	2.19 /45	2.48	0.04
GES	Vanguard Total Bond Mrkt Index Adm	VBTLX	D+	(800) 662-7447	C / 4.7	1.23	-2.30	1.45 /44	2.57 /53	2.17 /44	2.46	0.06
GES	Vanguard Total Bond Mrkt Index Inst	VBTIX	D+	(800) 662-7447	C / 4.7	1.23	-2.30	1.46 /44	2.58 /53	2.18 /45	2.47	0.05
*GES	Vanguard Total Bond Mrkt Index Inv	VBMFX	D+	(800) 662-7447	C / 4.5	1.20	-2.35	1.35 /43	2.47 /51	2.06 /43	2.36	0.16
GL	Vanguard Total Internatl Bd Idx Adm	VTABX	B	(800) 662-7447	C+ / 6.8	0.55	-2.00	2.00 /49	4.17 /77	--	1.86	0.14
GL	Vanguard Total Internatl Bd Idx Ins	VTIFX	B	(800) 662-7447	C+ / 6.9	0.53	-2.01	2.07 /50	4.23 /78	--	1.91	0.09
*GL	Vanguard Total Internatl Bd Idx Inv	VTIBX	B	(800) 662-7447	C+ / 6.8	0.54	-2.02	2.02 /49	4.15 /77	--	1.83	0.17
MMT	Vanguard Treas MM Inv	VUSXX	C-	(800) 662-7447	D- / 1.2	0.10	0.17	0.29 /29	0.12 /14	0.08 /14	0.29	N/A
GEI	Vanguard Ultra-Short-Term Bond	VUSFX	U	(800) 662-7447	U /	0.34	0.54	1.32 /43	--	--	1.11	0.12
GEI	Vanguard Ultra-Short-Term Bond Inv	VUBFX	U	(800) 662-7447	U /	0.37	0.50	1.24 /42	--	--	1.03	0.20
GEI	Vanguard WY College Inv Bon In Port		D	(800) 662-7447	C- / 4.1	1.18	-2.46	1.11 /41	2.23 /47	1.81 /39	0.00	0.52
GEI	Vanguard WY College Inv Income		C+	(800) 662-7447	C- / 3.5	0.70	-1.17	1.20 /42	1.66 /37	1.07 /28	0.00	0.52
US	Victory CEMP Market Neutral Inc A	CBHAX	D-	(888) 944-4367	C- / 3.9	3.67	2.83	4.51 /65	2.55 /53	--	2.51	1.27
US	Victory CEMP Market Neutral Inc C	CBHCX	D+	(888) 944-4367	C / 5.0	3.61	2.51	3.74 /61	1.78 /39	--	2.04	2.52
US	Victory CEMP Market Neutral Inc I	CBHIX	C+	(888) 944-4367	C+ / 6.6	3.85	2.95	4.75 /66	2.80 /58	--	2.90	1.03
LP	Victory Floating Rate A	RSFLX	C-	(800) 539-3863	B- / 7.1	1.87	3.48	14.85 /88	2.52 /52	3.96 /72	4.52	1.05
LP	Victory Floating Rate C	RSFCX	C-	(800) 539-3863	C+ / 6.7	1.64	3.05	13.92 /87	1.71 /38	3.16 /60	3.82	1.84
LP	Victory Floating Rate R	RSFKX	C-	(800) 539-3863	B- / 7.0	1.62	3.22	14.25 /87	1.98 /43	3.46 /65	4.09	1.41
LP	Victory Floating Rate Y	RSFYX	C+	(800) 539-3863	B / 7.8	1.78	3.45	14.96 /88	2.75 /57	4.19 /75	4.82	0.83
MUH	Victory High Income Municipal Bd A	RSHMX	B-	(800) 539-3863	B+ / 8.6	1.48	-4.23	-0.08 /16	5.03 /97	3.39 /86	4.20	0.93
MUH	Victory High Income Municipal Bd C	RSHCX	C+	(800) 539-3863	B / 8.2	1.31	-4.57	-0.82 / 6	4.24 /94	2.60 /73	3.51	1.71
MUH	Victory High Income Municipal Bd Y	RHMYX	B+	(800) 539-3863	A / 9.4	1.66	-4.01	0.28 /32	5.32 /98	3.65 /89	4.55	0.71
COH	Victory High Yield A	GUHYX	C	(800) 539-3863	A- / 9.2	6.11	7.02	22.27 /98	3.35 /67	5.58 /89	5.72	1.13
COH	Victory High Yield C	RHYCX	C	(800) 539-3863	A- / 9.0	6.05	6.78	21.58 /98	2.64 /55	4.86 /83	5.17	1.87
COH	Victory High Yield R	RHYKX	C	(800) 539-3863	A- / 9.2	5.99	6.81	21.78 /98	2.95 /60	5.19 /86	5.50	1.38
COH	Victory High Yield Y	RSYYX	C+	(800) 539-3863	A / 9.5	6.20	7.17	22.47 /98	3.61 /70	5.83 /91	6.10	0.92
USS	Victory INCORE Fund For Income A	IPFIX	C-	(800) 539-3863	D / 2.0	0.37	-1.04	-0.38 /11	1.42 /34	1.02 /28	5.16	0.94
USS	Victory INCORE Fund For Income C	VFFCX	D	(800) 539-3863	D- / 1.5	0.08	-1.42	-1.24 / 3	0.63 /22	0.23 /19	4.52	1.72
USA	Victory INCORE Fund For Income I	VFFIX	C+	(800) 539-3863	C- / 3.2	0.34	-0.90	-0.20 /15	1.67 /38	1.28 /31	5.56	0.65
USS	Victory INCORE Fund For Income R	GGIFX	C	(800) 539-3863	D+ / 2.8	0.38	-1.03	-0.37 /12	1.42 /34	1.01 /28	5.26	0.95
USA	Victory INCORE Fund For Income R6	VFFRX	U	(800) 539-3863	U /	0.44	-0.90	-0.11 /16	--	--	5.55	0.99
USA	Victory INCORE Fund For Income Y	VFFYX	C+	(800) 539-3863	C- / 3.2	0.32	-0.94	-0.18 /15	1.64 /37	--	5.47	0.90
COI	Victory INCORE Investment Quality A	GUIQX	C-	(800) 539-3863	C / 4.5	1.46	-1.25	4.05 /62	2.50 /52	2.50 /50	2.37	1.04
COI	Victory INCORE Investment Quality C	RIQCX	D+	(800) 539-3863	C- / 3.8	1.14	-1.77	3.13 /57	1.61 /37	1.64 /37	1.53	1.83
COI	Victory INCORE Investment Quality R	RIQKX	C+	(800) 539-3863	C / 4.7	1.37	-1.33	3.74 /61	2.12 /45	2.09 /44	2.02	1.47
COI	Victory INCORE Investment Quality Y	RSQYX	B	(800) 539-3863	C+ / 5.6	1.52	-1.13	4.27 /63	2.69 /56	2.67 /52	2.63	0.83
GEI	Victory INCORE Low Duration Bond	RLDAX	C	(800) 539-3863	D / 2.2	0.68	0.51	2.03 /49	1.02 /28	1.10 /29	0.99	0.83
GEI	Victory INCORE Low Duration Bond	RLDCX	C	(800) 539-3863	D / 1.8	0.43	0.15	1.29 /43	0.25 /18	0.33 /20	0.28	1.60
GEI	Victory INCORE Low Duration Bond	RLDKX	C+	(800) 539-3863	D+ / 2.3	0.52	0.37	1.59 /45	0.60 /22	0.68 /23	0.68	1.19
GEI	Victory INCORE Low Duration Bond	RSDYX	B	(800) 539-3863	C- / 3.4	0.64	0.62	2.28 /51	1.24 /31	1.32 /32	1.25	0.60
USS	Victory INCORE Total Return Bond A	MUCAX	D-	(800) 539-3863	C- / 3.3	1.50	-1.46	3.90 /62	1.69 /38	2.50 /50	3.39	1.14
USS	Victory INCORE Total Return Bond C	MUCCX	D-	(800) 539-3863	D+ / 2.9	1.33	-1.78	3.13 /57	0.94 /27	1.74 /38	2.70	2.06
COI	Victory INCORE Total Return Bond	MUCRX	U	(800) 539-3863	U /	1.50	-1.28	4.22 /63	--	--	3.77	1.65
USS	Victory INCORE Total Return Bond Y	MUCYX	D+	(800) 539-3863	C / 4.6	1.61	-1.27	4.21 /63	1.95 /42	2.76 /54	3.76	0.67
MUN	Victory National Muni A	VNMAX	C	(800) 539-3863	C- / 3.8	2.14	-2.22	0.07 /23	1.92 /60	1.61 /49	2.32	1.09

● Denotes fund is closed to new investors
* Denotes fund is included in Section II

www.thestreetratings.com

RISK			NET ASSETS		ASSET							FUND MANAGER		MINIMUM		LOADS	
Risk Rating/Pts	3 Yr Avg Standard Deviation	Avg Dura-tion	NAV As of 2/28/17	Total $(Mil)	Cash %	Gov. Bond %	Muni. Bond %	Corp. Bond %	Other %	Portfolio Turnover Ratio	Avg Coupon Rate	Manager Quality Pct	Manager Tenure (Years)	Initial Purch. $	Additional Purch. $	Front End Load	Back End Load
B+ / 8.6	1.7	2.7	24.77	4,252	0	99	0	0	1	28	0.8	24	5	10,000	100	0.0	0.0
B+ / 8.6	1.7	2.7	24.78	5,860	0	99	0	0	1	28	0.8	26	5	5,000,000	100	0.0	0.0
B+ / 8.6	1.7	2.7	24.75	5,329	0	99	0	0	1	28	0.8	21	5	3,000	100	0.0	0.0
U /	N/A	N/A	20.21	93	2	0	97	0	1	0	0.0	N/A	2	10,000	1	0.0	0.0
U /	N/A	N/A	10.11	2	2	0	97	0	1	0	0.0	N/A	2	3,000	1	0.0	0.0
C / 5.0	3.1	N/A	10.67	48,414	4	45	1	25	25	116	0.0	35	7	5,000,000	100	0.0	0.0
C / 5.0	3.1	N/A	10.67	72,531	4	45	1	25	25	116	0.0	33	7	3,000	100	0.0	0.0
C / 5.1	3.1	5.7	10.71	22,266	0	46	1	28	25	84	3.2	33	4	100,000,000	100	0.0	0.0
C / 5.1	3.1	5.7	10.71	74,510	0	46	1	28	25	84	3.2	32	4	10,000	100	0.0	0.0
C / 5.1	3.1	5.7	10.71	35,287	0	46	1	28	25	84	3.2	32	4	5,000,000	100	0.0	0.0
C / 5.1	3.1	5.7	10.71	5,940	0	46	1	28	25	84	3.2	28	4	3,000	100	0.0	0.0
C / 5.1	2.9	7.7	21.65	25,463	1	75	3	18	3	20	2.4	95	4	10,000	100	0.0	0.0
C / 5.1	2.9	7.7	32.49	18,525	1	75	3	18	3	20	2.4	95	4	5,000,000	100	0.0	0.0
C / 5.1	2.9	7.7	10.83	22,670	1	75	3	18	3	20	2.4	95	4	3,000	100	0.0	0.0
A+ / 9.9	N/A	N/A	1.00	14,646	100	0	0	0	0	0	0.3	47	20	50,000	100	0.0	0.0
U /	N/A	1.0	20.01	2,228	24	23	0	26	27	24	1.8	N/A	2	50,000	1	0.0	0.0
U /	N/A	1.0	10.01	142	24	23	0	26	27	24	1.8	N/A	2	3,000	1	0.0	0.0
C / 5.1	3.1	N/A	15.49	37	0	47	1	21	31	0	0.0	22	8	25	15	0.0	0.0
B / 8.0	2.1	N/A	14.34	247	25	48	0	10	17	0	0.0	31	8	25	15	0.0	0.0
C / 4.5	3.3	N/A	9.49	25	20	0	0	0	80	92	0.0	89	N/A	2,500	50	5.8	0.0
C / 4.4	3.4	N/A	9.42	1	20	0	0	0	80	92	0.0	83	N/A	2,500	50	0.0	0.0
C / 4.3	3.4	N/A	9.53	31	20	0	0	0	80	92	0.0	90	N/A	2,000,000	0	0.0	0.0
D+ / 2.8	4.2	0.6	9.72	205	2	0	0	72	26	29	5.1	82	8	2,500	100	2.0	0.0
D+ / 2.8	4.2	0.6	9.73	331	2	0	0	72	26	29	5.1	72	8	2,500	100	0.0	0.0
D+ / 2.8	4.2	0.6	9.72	1	2	0	0	72	26	29	5.1	77	8	1,000	0	0.0	0.0
D+ / 2.9	4.1	0.6	9.72	374	2	0	0	72	26	29	5.1	85	8	0	100	0.0	0.0
D+ / 2.8	3.7	5.8	10.47	31	3	0	96	0	1	53	5.4	80	3	2,500	100	2.0	0.0
D+ / 2.7	3.7	5.8	10.47	28	3	0	96	0	1	53	5.4	64	3	2,500	100	0.0	0.0
D+ / 2.8	3.7	5.8	10.48	34	3	0	96	0	1	53	5.4	82	3	0	100	0.0	0.0
E+ / 0.7	6.3	3.2	6.51	26	3	0	0	91	6	151	6.7	7	8	2,500	100	2.0	0.0
E+ / 0.7	6.3	3.2	6.53	23	3	0	0	91	6	151	6.7	2	8	2,500	100	0.0	0.0
E+ / 0.7	6.3	3.2	6.53	19	3	0	0	91	6	151	6.7	4	8	1,000	0	0.0	0.0
E+ / 0.8	6.2	3.2	6.48	6	3	0	0	91	6	151	6.7	11	8	0	100	0.0	0.0
B+ / 8.5	1.8	2.7	9.39	342	1	25	0	0	74	31	7.4	60	11	2,500	250	2.0	0.0
B+ / 8.4	1.8	2.7	9.31	65	1	25	0	0	74	31	7.4	24	11	2,500	250	0.0	0.0
B+ / 8.5	1.8	2.7	9.38	515	1	25	0	0	74	31	7.4	67	11	2,000,000	0	0.0	0.0
B+ / 8.5	1.8	2.7	9.40	71	1	25	0	0	74	31	7.4	60	11	0	0	0.0	0.0
U /	N/A	2.7	9.38	7	1	25	0	0	74	31	7.4	N/A	11	0	0	0.0	0.0
B+ / 8.5	1.8	2.7	9.39	7	1	25	0	0	74	31	7.4	66	11	0	0	0.0	0.0
C+ / 6.0	2.9	5.4	9.54	39	3	2	1	50	44	73	4.0	35	1	2,500	100	2.0	0.0
C+ / 6.0	2.9	5.4	9.53	8	3	2	1	50	44	73	4.0	12	1	2,500	100	0.0	0.0
C+ / 6.4	2.8	5.4	9.56	5	3	2	1	50	44	73	4.0	25	1	1,000	0	0.0	0.0
C+ / 6.4	2.8	5.4	9.53	6	3	2	1	50	44	73	4.0	53	1	0	100	0.0	0.0
A / 9.4	0.9	1.9	10.06	199	2	3	0	42	53	36	2.8	62	13	2,500	100	2.0	0.0
A / 9.5	0.8	1.9	10.05	109	2	3	0	42	53	36	2.8	28	13	2,500	100	0.0	0.0
A / 9.5	0.8	1.9	10.05	3	2	3	0	42	53	36	2.8	47	13	1,000	0	0.0	0.0
A / 9.5	0.8	1.9	10.06	335	2	3	0	42	53	36	2.8	70	13	0	100	0.0	0.0
C / 5.0	3.1	6.3	9.52	14	0	4	1	50	45	423	3.9	55	5	2,500	50	2.0	0.0
C / 5.0	3.1	6.3	9.59	3	0	4	1	50	45	423	3.9	22	5	2,500	50	0.0	0.0
U /	N/A	6.3	9.54	6	0	4	1	50	45	423	3.9	N/A	5	0	0	0.0	0.0
C / 5.2	3.1	6.3	9.54	81	0	4	1	50	45	423	3.9	64	5	1,000,000	0	0.0	0.0
B- / 7.1	2.7	4.2	10.65	50	3	0	96	0	1	61	4.6	14	23	2,500	250	2.0	0.0

Fund Type	Fund Name	Ticker Symbol	Overall Investment Rating	Phone	PERFORMANCE Performance Rating/Pts	Total Return % through 2/28/17 3 Mo	6 Mo	1Yr / Pct	Annualized 3Yr / Pct	5Yr / Pct	Incl. in Returns Dividend Yield	Expense Ratio
MUN	Victory National Muni Y	VNMYX	B+	(800) 539-3863	C+ / 5.7	2.11	-2.18	0.25 /31	2.19 /67	--	2.64	1.10
MUS	Victory OH Muni Bond A	SOHTX	C+	(800) 539-3863	C / 4.9	2.02	-2.28	0.31 /33	2.44 /72	2.02 /59	2.92	1.06
GEI	Victory Strategic Income A	RSIAX	B	(800) 539-3863	C / 5.2	2.09	1.48	7.49 /73	2.19 /46	2.94 /57	2.78	1.13
GEI	Victory Strategic Income C	RSICX	C+	(800) 539-3863	C / 4.7	1.88	0.99	6.63 /72	1.39 /33	2.11 /44	2.05	1.94
GEI	Victory Strategic Income R	RINKX	B	(800) 539-3863	C / 5.4	1.98	1.19	7.04 /73	1.79 /39	2.51 /50	2.44	1.42
GEI	Victory Strategic Income Y	RSRYX	A	(800) 539-3863	C+ / 6.3	2.15	1.51	7.66 /74	2.41 /50	3.15 /60	3.07	0.95
MUN	Victory Tax-Exempt A	GUTEX	D	(800) 539-3863	C / 5.1	2.37	-3.87	-0.84 / 6	2.81 /79	2.14 /62	3.42	0.91
MUN	Victory Tax-Exempt C	RETCX	D-	(800) 539-3863	C / 4.3	2.17	-4.25	-1.53 / 2	2.00 /62	1.33 /43	2.68	1.68
MUN	Victory Tax-Exempt Y	RSTYX	C	(800) 539-3863	C+ / 6.7	2.50	-3.81	-0.64 / 8	2.96 /81	2.28 /66	3.60	0.69
MUS	Viking Tax-Free Fund For MT A	VMTTX	C	(800) 601-5593	C / 4.3	1.52	-3.03	-0.68 / 7	2.55 /74	1.91 /57	2.58	1.15
MUN	Viking Tax-Free Fund For MT I	VMTIX	U	(800) 601-5593	U /	1.69	-2.82	--	--	--	0.00	N/A
MUS	Viking Tax-Free Fund For ND A	VNDFX	C+	(800) 601-5593	C / 5.0	1.65	-2.69	-0.35 /12	2.78 /78	2.07 /60	2.53	1.24
MUN	Viking Tax-Free Fund For ND I	VNDIX	U	(800) 601-5593	U /	1.71	-2.57	--	--	--	0.00	N/A
COH	Virtus Bond A	SAVAX	D-	(800) 243-1574	C / 4.3	2.34	-0.41	5.87 /70	2.52 /52	3.19 /61	2.88	1.18
COH ●	Virtus Bond B	SAVBX	D	(800) 243-1574	C / 4.6	2.13	-0.79	5.16 /67	1.74 /39	2.42 /48	2.33	1.93
COH	Virtus Bond C	SAVCX	D	(800) 243-1574	C / 4.6	2.12	-0.88	5.03 /67	1.73 /39	2.41 /48	2.31	1.93
COH	Virtus Bond I	SAVYX	C	(800) 243-1574	C+ / 6.3	2.46	-0.28	6.13 /71	2.80 /58	3.47 /65	3.19	0.93
MUS	Virtus California T/E Bond A	CTESX	C+	(800) 243-1574	B- / 7.2	2.57	-2.90	0.23 /30	3.90 /92	3.39 /86	2.94	1.21
MUS	Virtus California T/E Bond I	CTXEX	A-	(800) 243-1574	B+ / 8.7	2.64	-2.70	0.58 /38	4.14 /94	3.64 /89	3.29	0.96
EM	Virtus Emerging Markets Debt A	VEDAX	D	(800) 243-1574	B / 7.6	5.51	0.53	14.76 /88	3.68 /71	--	4.27	1.54
EM	Virtus Emerging Markets Debt C	VEDCX	D	(800) 243-1574	B / 7.8	5.32	0.16	13.79 /86	2.92 /60	--	3.71	2.29
EM	Virtus Emerging Markets Debt I	VIEDX	C-	(800) 243-1574	B+ / 8.9	5.69	0.77	15.05 /89	3.98 /75	--	4.69	1.29
COH	Virtus High Yield A	PHCHX	C	(800) 243-1574	B+ / 8.6	4.92	4.95	17.20 /92	4.01 /75	6.13 /93	4.65	1.43
COH ●	Virtus High Yield B	PHCCX	C	(800) 243-1574	B+ / 8.7	4.61	4.45	16.27 /91	3.19 /64	5.38 /87	4.25	2.18
COH	Virtus High Yield C	PGHCX	C	(800) 243-1574	B+ / 8.7	4.81	4.65	16.35 /91	3.23 /65	5.37 /87	4.20	2.18
COH	Virtus High Yield I	PHCIX	B-	(800) 243-1574	A / 9.4	4.73	4.82	17.18 /92	4.27 /78	--	5.07	1.18
GEI	Virtus Low Duration Income A	HIMZX	C+	(800) 243-1574	D+ / 2.8	0.78	0.05	2.54 /53	1.50 /35	2.17 /44	1.82	1.10
GEI	Virtus Low Duration Income C	PCMZX	C	(800) 243-1574	D+ / 2.4	0.59	-0.32	1.78 /47	0.75 /24	1.41 /33	1.12	1.85
GEI	Virtus Low Duration Income I	HIBIX	B+	(800) 243-1574	C- / 4.2	0.84	0.26	2.80 /55	1.79 /40	2.43 /48	2.12	0.85
*GES	Virtus Multi Sector Short Term B A	NARAX	B+	(800) 243-1574	C / 4.8	1.85	1.54	6.58 /72	2.13 /45	2.90 /56	2.87	1.00
GES ●	Virtus Multi Sector Short Term B B	PBARX	B+	(800) 243-1574	C / 4.5	1.31	0.88	5.65 /69	1.50 /35	2.32 /46	2.48	1.50
GES	Virtus Multi Sector Short Term B C	PSTCX	A-	(800) 243-1574	C / 5.3	1.76	1.40	6.23 /71	1.86 /41	2.65 /52	2.65	1.25
GES	Virtus Multi Sector Short Term B I	PIMSX	A+	(800) 243-1574	C+ / 6.2	2.12	1.67	6.83 /72	2.39 /50	3.20 /61	3.18	0.75
GES	Virtus Multi Sector Short Term B T	PMSTX	B	(800) 243-1574	C / 4.4	1.64	1.15	5.72 /69	1.36 /33	2.15 /44	2.16	1.75
GES	Virtus Multi-Sec Intermediate Bd A	NAMFX	C-	(800) 243-1574	B- / 7.4	4.13	2.72	14.12 /87	3.41 /67	4.55 /79	4.05	1.17
GES ●	Virtus Multi-Sec Intermediate Bd B	NBMFX	C-	(800) 243-1574	B- / 7.5	3.95	2.25	13.21 /85	2.61 /54	3.74 /69	3.50	1.92
GES	Virtus Multi-Sec Intermediate Bd C	NCMFX	C	(800) 243-1574	B / 7.6	4.00	2.31	13.24 /86	2.67 /55	3.77 /70	3.44	1.92
GES	Virtus Multi-Sec Intermediate Bd I	VMFIX	B-	(800) 243-1574	B+ / 8.7	4.29	2.84	14.39 /87	3.70 /71	4.83 /82	4.45	0.92
GL	Virtus Multi-Sec Intermediate Bd R6	VMFRX	U	(800) 243-1574	U /	4.31	2.88	14.48 /87	--	--	4.53	0.85
LP	Virtus Senior Floating Rate A	PSFRX	A	(800) 243-1574	C+ / 6.5	2.24	3.73	10.40 /80	2.81 /58	4.00 /73	3.69	1.08
LP	Virtus Senior Floating Rate C	PFSRX	A	(800) 243-1574	C+ / 6.4	2.05	3.34	9.57 /78	2.01 /43	3.22 /61	3.05	1.83
LP	Virtus Senior Floating Rate I	PSFIX	A+	(800) 243-1574	B / 7.6	2.31	3.86	10.69 /80	3.03 /62	4.26 /76	4.04	0.83
GEN	Virtus Strat Income A	VASBX	U	(800) 243-1574	U /	2.60	1.23	9.68 /78	--	--	3.09	2.42
GEN	Virtus Strat Income C	VSBCX	U	(800) 243-1574	U /	2.41	0.86	8.87 /76	--	--	2.47	3.17
GEL	Virtus Strat Income I	VISBX	U	(800) 243-1574	U /	2.66	1.36	9.96 /79	--	--	3.46	2.17
MUN	Virtus Tax Exempt Bond A	HXBZX	C	(800) 243-1574	C / 4.7	2.00	-2.50	-0.56 / 9	2.71 /77	2.30 /66	2.52	1.01
MUN	Virtus Tax Exempt Bond C	PXCZX	C-	(800) 243-1574	C / 4.6	1.90	-2.86	-1.30 / 2	1.97 /62	1.56 /48	1.83	1.76
MUN	Virtus Tax Exempt Bond I	HXBIX	B+	(800) 243-1574	C+ / 6.9	2.06	-2.39	-0.32 /12	2.96 /81	2.57 /72	2.84	0.76
EM	Voya Diversified Emerg Mkts Dbt A	IADEX	D	(800) 992-0180	B- / 7.0	4.48	-0.49	8.83 /76	3.59 /70	--	1.46	8.56
EM	Voya Diversified Emerg Mkts Dbt C	ICDEX	D	(800) 992-0180	C+ / 6.9	4.43	-0.83	8.22 /75	2.82 /58	--	1.19	9.31
EM	Voya Diversified Emerg Mkts Dbt I	IIDEX	C-	(800) 992-0180	B / 8.0	4.63	-0.34	9.36 /77	3.92 /74	--	1.64	8.17
EM	Voya Diversified Emerg Mkts Dbt W	IWDEX	C-	(800) 992-0180	B / 7.9	4.55	-0.43	9.15 /77	3.84 /73	--	1.67	8.31

● Denotes fund is closed to new investors
* Denotes fund is included in Section II

RISK			NET ASSETS		ASSET					Portfolio Turnover Ratio	Avg Coupon Rate	FUND MANAGER		MINIMUM		LOADS	
Risk Rating/Pts	3 Yr Avg Standard Deviation	Avg Dura- tion	NAV As of 2/28/17	Total $(Mil)	Cash %	Gov. Bond %	Muni. Bond %	Corp. Bond %	Other %			Manager Quality Pct	Manager Tenure (Years)	Initial Purch. $	Additional Purch. $	Front End Load	Back End Load
B- / 7.1	2.7	4.2	10.64	4	3	0	96	0	1	61	4.6	20	23	0	0	0.0	0.0
C+ / 6.5	2.8	4.6	10.89	35	5	0	94	0	1	39	4.5	21	23	2,500	250	2.0	0.0
B- / 7.3	2.6	1.8	10.06	36	3	12	0	70	15	41	4.1	76	8	2,500	100	2.0	0.0
B- / 7.2	2.7	1.8	10.10	12	3	12	0	70	15	41	4.1	54	8	2,500	100	0.0	0.0
B- / 7.2	2.7	1.8	10.11	3	3	12	0	70	15	41	4.1	68	8	1,000	0	0.0	0.0
B- / 7.1	2.7	1.8	10.00	12	3	12	0	70	15	41	4.1	78	8	0	100	0.0	0.0
C- / 3.9	3.5	5.6	9.76	48	0	0	99	0	1	39	5.0	13	24	2,500	100	2.0	0.0
C- / 3.9	3.6	5.6	9.76	32	0	0	99	0	1	39	5.0	4	24	2,500	100	0.0	0.0
C- / 3.8	3.6	5.6	9.76	31	0	0	99	0	1	39	5.0	15	24	0	100	0.0	0.0
C+ / 6.4	2.8	5.1	9.96	77	8	0	91	0	1	12	4.4	25	18	1,000	50	2.5	0.0
U /	N/A	5.1	9.97	1	8	0	91	0	1	12	4.4	N/A	18	1,000	50	0.0	0.0
C+ / 6.5	2.8	4.7	10.23	26	7	0	92	0	1	19	4.1	32	18	1,000	50	2.5	0.0
U /	N/A	4.7	10.23	N/A	7	0	92	0	1	19	4.1	N/A	18	1,000	50	0.0	0.0
C- / 4.1	3.0	5.2	11.17	43	1	11	1	50	37	64	4.6	70	5	2,500	100	3.8	0.0
C- / 4.0	3.0	5.2	10.87	N/A	1	11	1	50	37	64	4.6	37	5	2,500	100	0.0	0.0
C- / 4.0	3.0	5.2	10.91	8	1	11	1	50	37	64	4.6	37	5	2,500	100	0.0	0.0
C- / 4.0	3.0	5.2	11.35	23	1	11	1	50	37	64	4.6	75	5	100,000	0	0.0	0.0
C- / 4.0	3.5	5.8	11.66	18	14	0	85	0	1	21	5.0	54	21	2,500	100	2.8	0.0
C- / 4.1	3.5	5.8	11.64	10	14	0	85	0	1	21	5.0	63	21	100,000	0	0.0	0.0
E+ / 0.6	7.2	N/A	9.27	1	2	35	0	60	3	49	0.0	96	5	2,500	100	3.8	0.0
E+ / 0.7	7.2	N/A	9.26	N/A	2	35	0	60	3	49	0.0	95	5	2,500	100	0.0	0.0
E+ / 0.7	7.2	N/A	9.27	29	2	35	0	60	3	49	0.0	97	5	100,000	0	0.0	0.0
D- / 1.5	5.2	3.7	4.27	60	1	1	0	84	14	81	6.4	46	6	2,500	100	3.8	0.0
D / 1.6	5.1	3.7	4.15	N/A	1	1	0	84	14	81	6.4	17	6	2,500	100	0.0	0.0
D- / 1.5	5.2	3.7	4.20	4	1	1	0	84	14	81	6.4	17	6	2,500	100	0.0	0.0
D / 1.6	5.1	3.7	4.27	9	1	1	0	84	14	81	6.4	61	6	100,000	0	0.0	0.0
A- / 9.1	1.2	2.5	10.79	98	2	8	0	23	67	56	3.4	67	5	2,500	100	2.3	0.0
A- / 9.0	1.2	2.5	10.79	40	2	8	0	23	67	56	3.4	33	5	2,500	100	0.0	0.0
A- / 9.1	1.2	2.5	10.79	229	2	8	0	23	67	56	3.4	73	5	100,000	0	0.0	0.0
B+ / 8.3	2.0	2.5	4.76	1,242	1	7	0	38	54	53	4.5	80	24	2,500	100	2.3	0.0
B+ / 8.3	2.0	2.5	4.71	N/A	1	7	0	38	54	53	4.5	69	24	2,500	100	0.0	0.0
B / 8.1	2.1	2.5	4.82	1,273	1	7	0	38	54	53	4.5	73	24	2,500	100	0.0	0.0
B / 8.2	2.1	2.5	4.77	4,202	1	7	0	38	54	53	4.5	81	24	100,000	0	0.0	0.0
B / 8.1	2.1	2.5	4.81	443	1	7	0	38	54	53	4.5	62	24	2,500	100	0.0	0.0
D+ / 2.4	4.6	4.3	10.32	97	0	12	0	54	34	60	5.7	85	23	2,500	100	3.8	0.0
D+ / 2.4	4.6	4.3	10.28	1	0	12	0	54	34	60	5.7	77	23	2,500	100	0.0	0.0
D+ / 2.4	4.6	4.3	10.42	69	0	12	0	54	34	60	5.7	77	23	2,500	100	0.0	0.0
D+ / 2.4	4.6	4.3	10.33	149	0	12	0	54	34	60	5.7	87	23	100,000	0	0.0	0.0
U /	N/A	4.3	10.33	3	0	12	0	54	34	60	5.7	N/A	23	0	0	0.0	0.0
C+ / 6.9	2.7	0.4	9.54	234	0	0	0	21	79	48	4.6	87	5	2,500	100	2.8	0.0
B- / 7.0	2.7	0.4	9.55	111	0	0	0	21	79	48	4.6	80	5	2,500	100	0.0	0.0
C+ / 6.9	2.7	0.4	9.53	249	0	0	0	21	79	48	4.6	88	5	100,000	0	0.0	0.0
U /	N/A	4.1	9.98	1	0	0	0	0	100	98	0.0	N/A	3	2,500	100	3.8	0.0
U /	N/A	4.1	9.97	1	0	0	0	0	100	98	0.0	N/A	3	2,500	100	0.0	0.0
U /	N/A	4.1	9.97	29	0	0	0	0	100	98	0.0	N/A	3	100,000	0	0.0	0.0
C+ / 5.9	2.9	5.2	11.16	59	0	0	99	0	1	10	4.8	25	5	2,500	100	2.8	0.0
C+ / 5.9	2.9	5.2	11.17	22	0	0	99	0	1	10	4.8	10	5	2,500	100	0.0	0.0
C+ / 5.8	2.9	5.2	11.16	89	0	0	99	0	1	10	4.8	33	5	100,000	0	0.0	0.0
D- / 1.5	5.7	N/A	9.26	N/A	5	57	1	34	3	2	0.0	96	4	1,000	0	2.5	0.0
D- / 1.5	5.7	N/A	9.13	N/A	5	57	1	34	3	2	0.0	95	4	1,000	0	0.0	0.0
D- / 1.5	5.7	N/A	9.28	18	5	57	1	34	3	2	0.0	97	4	250,000	0	0.0	0.0
D / 1.6	5.6	N/A	9.26	N/A	5	57	1	34	3	2	0.0	96	4	1,000	0	0.0	0.0

Fund Type	Fund Name	Ticker Symbol	Overall Investment Rating	Phone	PERFORMANCE Perfor-mance Rating/Pts	Total Return % through 2/28/17 3 Mo	6 Mo	1Yr / Pct	Annualized 3Yr / Pct	5Yr / Pct	Incl. in Returns Dividend Yield	Expense Ratio
EM	Voya Emerg Markets Corporate Debt	IMCDX	B+	(800) 992-0180	A / 9.4	4.31	1.16	11.52 /82	5.53 /89	--	5.12	1.05
EM	Voya Emerg Mkts Hard Curr Debt P	IHCSX	B-	(800) 992-0180	A+ / 9.7	4.95	-0.47	12.23 /84	6.71 /95	--	5.95	0.82
EM	Voya Emg Mkts Local Currency Debt	ILCDX	E-	(800) 992-0180	E- / 0.2	5.74	-0.48	8.87 /76	-2.97 / 1	--	2.76	0.99
LP	Voya Floating Rate A	IFRAX	A-	(800) 992-0180	C+ / 6.3	1.37	2.79	9.07 /77	2.91 /60	4.06 /73	3.82	1.08
LP	Voya Floating Rate C	IFRCX	B+	(800) 992-0180	C+ / 6.1	1.19	2.41	8.14 /75	2.14 /46	3.28 /62	3.18	1.83
LP	Voya Floating Rate I	IFRIX	A+	(800) 992-0180	B- / 7.4	1.54	2.92	9.35 /77	3.20 /64	4.32 /76	4.18	0.79
LP	Voya Floating Rate P	IFRPX	A+	(800) 992-0180	B / 8.1	1.61	3.26	9.97 /79	3.86 /74	--	4.84	0.77
LP	Voya Floating Rate R	IFRRX	A	(800) 992-0180	C+ / 6.9	1.42	2.77	8.81 /76	2.69 /56	3.78 /70	3.68	1.33
LP	Voya Floating Rate W	IFRWX	A+	(800) 992-0180	B- / 7.4	1.44	2.92	9.33 /77	3.20 /64	4.31 /76	4.17	0.83
GL	Voya Global Bond A	INGBX	E	(800) 992-0180	E / 0.4	2.25	-1.96	4.32 /64	-0.20 / 4	0.49 /21	4.20	0.98
GL	● Voya Global Bond B	IGBBX	E	(800) 992-0180	E / 0.3	2.08	-2.35	3.58 /60	-0.94 / 3	-0.27 / 4	3.58	1.73
GL	Voya Global Bond C	IGBCX	E	(800) 992-0180	E / 0.3	2.07	-2.35	3.56 /60	-0.96 / 3	-0.27 / 4	3.56	1.73
GL	Voya Global Bond I	IGBIX	E	(800) 992-0180	D / 2.2	2.33	-1.83	4.63 /65	0.09 /12	0.76 /24	4.61	0.61
GL	Voya Global Bond O	IGBOX	E	(800) 992-0180	D / 1.8	2.30	-1.90	4.32 /64	-0.20 / 4	0.49 /21	4.41	0.98
GEI	Voya Global Bond Portfolio Adv	IOSAX	E	(800) 992-0180	D / 2.2	2.43	-1.92	5.02 /67	0.04 / 9	0.27 /19	1.70	1.18
GEI	Voya Global Bond Portfolio Inl	IOSIX	E+	(800) 992-0180	D+ / 2.9	2.52	-1.72	5.51 /69	0.50 /21	0.76 /24	2.12	0.68
GEI	Voya Global Bond Portfolio Svc	IOSSX	E	(800) 992-0180	D+ / 2.5	2.46	-1.84	5.18 /67	0.28 /18	0.52 /22	1.91	0.93
GL	Voya Global Bond R	IGBRX	E	(800) 992-0180	E+ / 0.9	2.19	-2.18	3.97 /62	-0.46 / 4	0.22 /19	4.07	1.23
GL	Voya Global Bond R6	IGBZX	E	(800) 992-0180	D / 2.2	2.44	-1.81	4.65 /65	0.11 /13	--	4.62	0.59
GL	Voya Global Bond W	IGBWX	E	(800) 992-0180	D / 2.1	2.37	-1.87	4.58 /65	0.05 / 9	0.75 /24	4.67	0.73
* USA	Voya GNMA Income A	LEXNX	C+	(800) 992-0180	C- / 3.1	0.35	-0.83	0.53 /34	2.23 /47	1.89 /40	2.72	0.93
USA	● Voya GNMA Income B	LEXBX	C	(800) 992-0180	D+ / 2.8	0.16	-1.21	-0.22 /14	1.42 /34	1.10 /29	1.93	1.68
USA	Voya GNMA Income C	LEGNX	C+	(800) 992-0180	D+ / 2.9	0.16	-1.09	-0.20 /15	1.47 /35	1.11 /29	1.94	1.68
USA	Voya GNMA Income I	LEINX	B+	(800) 992-0180	C / 4.6	0.42	-0.69	0.79 /37	2.51 /52	2.16 /44	3.06	0.64
USA	Voya GNMA Income W	IGMWX	B+	(800) 992-0180	C / 4.5	0.41	-0.71	0.75 /37	2.47 /51	2.14 /44	3.02	0.68
MMT	Voya Government Liquid Assets Inst	IPLXX	C-	(800) 992-0180	E+ / 0.9	0.07	0.10	0.15 /24	0.06 /11	0.06 /13	0.15	N/A
MMT	Voya Government Liquid Assets Svc	ISPXX	D+	(800) 992-0180	E+ / 0.6	0.01	0.01	0.01 /18	0.01 / 7	0.01 / 6	0.01	N/A
LP	Voya Govt Money Market Port I	IVMXX	D+	(800) 992-0180	E+ / 0.7	0.05	0.07	0.10 /22	0.04 / 9	0.04 /10	0.10	0.38
COH	Voya High Yield Bond A	IHYAX	C+	(800) 992-0180	B+ / 8.6	4.28	4.33	15.62 /89	4.00 /75	6.44 /95	4.90	1.07
COH	● Voya High Yield Bond B	INYBX	C	(800) 992-0180	B+ / 8.4	3.97	3.95	14.83 /88	3.22 /65	5.64 /90	4.34	1.82
COH	Voya High Yield Bond C	IMYCX	C	(800) 992-0180	B+ / 8.4	4.09	4.08	14.76 /88	3.22 /65	5.64 /90	4.29	1.82
COH	Voya High Yield Bond I	IHYIX	B-	(800) 992-0180	A / 9.3	4.38	4.51	16.07 /90	4.39 /80	6.83 /96	5.39	0.69
COH	Voya High Yield Bond P	IHYPX	B	(800) 992-0180	A+ / 9.6	4.40	4.83	16.79 /92	5.03 /85	--	5.99	0.67
COH	Voya High Yield Bond R	IRSTX	C+	(800) 992-0180	B+ / 8.9	4.09	4.20	15.38 /89	3.78 /73	--	4.82	1.32
COH	Voya High Yield Bond R6	VHYRX	U	(800) 992-0180	U /	4.37	4.63	--	--	--	0.00	N/A
COH	Voya High Yield Bond W	IHYWX	B-	(800) 992-0180	A / 9.3	4.21	4.46	15.90 /90	4.28 /78	6.78 /96	5.27	0.82
COH	Voya High Yield Institutional	IPIMX	B-	(800) 992-0180	A / 9.5	4.35	4.65	17.72 /93	4.59 /82	6.22 /94	6.76	0.49
COH	Voya High Yield Service	IPHYX	C+	(800) 992-0180	A / 9.4	4.29	4.42	17.44 /93	4.29 /79	5.94 /92	6.52	0.74
COH	Voya High Yield Service 2	IPYSX	C+	(800) 992-0180	A / 9.3	4.24	4.44	17.24 /92	4.18 /77	5.80 /91	6.37	0.89
COI	Voya Intermediate Bond A	IIBAX	C+	(800) 992-0180	C / 4.9	1.57	-1.22	3.43 /59	3.06 /62	3.43 /64	2.93	0.66
COI	● Voya Intermediate Bond B	IIBBX	C	(800) 992-0180	C / 4.6	1.29	-1.59	2.65 /54	2.24 /47	2.64 /52	2.24	1.41
COI	Voya Intermediate Bond C	IICCX	C	(800) 992-0180	C / 4.6	1.29	-1.59	2.66 /54	2.27 /48	2.66 /52	2.25	1.41
COI	Voya Intermediate Bond I	IICIX	B+	(800) 992-0180	C+ / 6.4	1.56	-1.15	3.67 /61	3.38 /67	3.75 /69	3.35	0.33
COI	Voya Intermediate Bond O	IDBOX	B	(800) 992-0180	C+ / 5.9	1.47	-1.31	3.33 /59	3.04 /62	3.41 /64	3.01	0.66
GEI	Voya Intermediate Bond Port Adv	IIBPX	B	(800) 992-0180	C+ / 5.8	1.54	-1.36	3.78 /61	2.91 /60	3.38 /64	2.49	1.04
GEI	Voya Intermediate Bond Port I	IPIIX	B+	(800) 992-0180	C+ / 6.5	1.66	-1.16	4.30 /64	3.32 /66	3.85 /70	2.92	0.54
* GEI	Voya Intermediate Bond Port S	IPISX	B	(800) 992-0180	C+ / 6.1	1.60	-1.23	4.08 /63	3.07 /62	3.58 /67	2.70	0.79
COI	Voya Intermediate Bond R	IIBOX	B-	(800) 992-0180	C / 5.5	1.51	-1.34	3.17 /58	2.81 /58	3.17 /60	2.76	0.91
COI	Voya Intermediate Bond R6	IIBZX	B+	(800) 992-0180	C+ / 6.5	1.66	-1.05	3.79 /61	3.43 /68	--	3.36	0.32
COI	Voya Intermediate Bond W	IIBWX	B+	(800) 992-0180	C+ / 6.3	1.54	-1.10	3.69 /61	3.29 /66	3.68 /68	3.26	0.41
COI	Voya Investment Grade Credit A	VACFX	U	(800) 992-0180	U /	2.55	-1.06	--	--	--	0.00	N/A
COI	Voya Investment Grade Credit I	VIGCX	U	(800) 992-0180	U /	2.62	-0.93	--	--	--	0.00	N/A

● Denotes fund is closed to new investors
* Denotes fund is included in Section II

294

www.thestreetratings.com

99 Pct = Best
0 Pct = Worst

RISK			NET ASSETS		ASSET							FUND MANAGER		MINIMUM		LOADS	
Risk Rating/Pts	3 Yr Avg Standard Deviation	Avg Dura-tion	NAV As of 2/28/17	Total $(Mil)	Cash %	Gov. Bond %	Muni. Bond %	Corp. Bond %	Other %	Portfolio Turnover Ratio	Avg Coupon Rate	Manager Quality Pct	Manager Tenure (Years)	Initial Purch. $	Additional Purch. $	Front End Load	Back End Load
D+ / 2.4	4.6	4.5	9.90	102	0	0	0	0	100	86	5.5	98	4	0	0	0.0	0.0
D- / 1.1	6.2	5.8	9.64	151	0	0	0	0	100	50	5.7	99	4	0	0	0.0	0.0
E- / 0.2	10.1	4.1	7.34	89	0	0	0	0	100	18	6.1	19	4	0	0	0.0	0.0
C+ / 6.9	2.3	53.3	9.95	71	6	0	0	5	89	46	4.9	87	7	1,000	0	2.5	0.0
C+ / 6.9	2.2	53.3	9.95	54	6	0	0	5	89	46	4.9	81	7	1,000	0	0.0	0.0
C+ / 6.9	2.3	53.3	9.95	1,123	6	0	0	5	89	46	4.9	89	7	250,000	0	0.0	0.0
C+ / 6.9	2.2	53.3	9.94	36	6	0	0	5	89	46	4.9	92	7	0	0	0.0	0.0
C+ / 6.8	2.3	53.3	9.94	118	6	0	0	5	89	46	4.9	86	7	0	0	0.0	0.0
C+ / 6.8	2.3	53.3	9.97	414	6	0	0	5	89	46	4.9	89	7	1,000	0	0.0	0.0
D+ / 2.4	4.6	6.5	9.76	39	0	32	0	25	43	256	3.5	78	6	1,000	0	2.5	0.0
D+ / 2.4	4.6	6.5	9.66	N/A	0	32	0	25	43	256	3.5	61	6	1,000	0	0.0	0.0
D+ / 2.4	4.6	6.5	9.70	19	0	32	0	25	43	256	3.5	60	6	1,000	0	0.0	0.0
D+ / 2.4	4.6	6.5	9.72	87	0	32	0	25	43	256	3.5	81	6	250,000	0	0.0	0.0
D+ / 2.4	4.6	6.5	9.55	2	0	32	0	25	43	256	3.5	78	6	1,000	0	0.0	0.0
D / 2.2	4.8	6.8	10.44	24	0	28	0	30	42	335	4.2	1	6	0	0	0.0	0.0
D / 2.2	4.8	6.8	10.62	164	0	28	0	30	42	335	4.2	3	6	0	0	0.0	0.0
D / 2.2	4.8	6.8	10.61	41	0	28	0	30	42	335	4.2	2	6	0	0	0.0	0.0
D+ / 2.4	4.6	6.5	9.73	6	0	32	0	25	43	256	3.5	73	6	0	0	0.0	0.0
D+ / 2.4	4.6	6.5	9.76	164	0	32	0	25	43	256	3.5	81	6	1,000,000	0	0.0	0.0
D+ / 2.4	4.5	6.5	9.54	57	0	32	0	25	43	256	3.5	80	6	1,000	0	0.0	0.0
B+ / 8.7	1.6	2.4	8.45	556	0	3	0	0	97	508	4.4	80	8	1,000	0	2.5	0.0
B+ / 8.7	1.6	2.4	8.40	N/A	0	3	0	0	97	508	4.4	65	8	1,000	0	0.0	0.0
B+ / 8.8	1.5	2.4	8.41	116	0	3	0	0	97	508	4.4	67	8	1,000	0	0.0	0.0
B+ / 8.7	1.6	2.4	8.46	475	0	3	0	0	97	508	4.4	82	8	250,000	0	0.0	0.0
B+ / 8.7	1.6	2.4	8.47	111	0	3	0	0	97	508	4.4	82	8	1,000	0	0.0	0.0
A+ / 9.9	N/A	N/A	1.00	64	100	0	0	0	0	0	0.2	43	13	0	0	0.0	0.0
A+ / 9.9	N/A	N/A	1.00	470	100	0	0	0	0	0	0.0	38	13	0	0	0.0	0.0
A+ / 9.9	N/A	N/A	1.00	482	0	0	0	0	100	0	0.0	37	13	0	0	0.0	0.0
D / 1.8	4.9	3.9	8.18	62	1	0	0	98	1	33	6.4	57	10	1,000	0	2.5	0.0
D / 1.8	4.9	3.9	8.17	N/A	1	0	0	98	1	33	6.4	22	10	1,000	0	0.0	0.0
D / 1.8	4.9	3.9	8.18	13	1	0	0	98	1	33	6.4	22	10	1,000	0	0.0	0.0
D / 1.8	4.9	3.9	8.17	231	1	0	0	98	1	33	6.4	67	10	250,000	0	0.0	0.0
D / 1.8	4.9	3.9	8.17	149	1	0	0	98	1	33	6.4	79	10	0	0	0.0	0.0
D / 1.8	4.9	3.9	8.18	N/A	1	0	0	98	1	33	6.4	46	10	0	0	0.0	0.0
U /	N/A	3.9	8.17	125	1	0	0	98	1	33	6.4	N/A	10	1,000,000	0	0.0	0.0
D / 1.8	4.9	3.9	8.19	89	1	0	0	98	1	33	6.4	65	10	1,000	0	0.0	0.0
D- / 1.5	5.2	3.8	10.14	57	4	0	0	95	1	33	6.4	65	3	0	0	0.0	0.0
D- / 1.5	5.2	3.8	10.13	482	4	0	0	95	1	33	6.4	56	3	0	0	0.0	0.0
D- / 1.5	5.2	3.8	10.15	6	4	0	0	95	1	33	6.4	53	3	0	0	0.0	0.0
C+ / 6.4	2.8	5.4	10.04	432	0	26	0	27	47	465	3.4	66	8	1,000	0	2.5	0.0
C+ / 6.3	2.9	5.4	10.01	N/A	0	26	0	27	47	465	3.4	30	8	1,000	0	0.0	0.0
C+ / 6.3	2.9	5.4	10.02	30	0	26	0	27	47	465	3.4	30	8	1,000	0	0.0	0.0
C+ / 6.3	2.9	5.4	10.03	1,520	0	26	0	27	47	465	3.4	72	8	250,000	0	0.0	0.0
C+ / 6.3	2.9	5.4	10.03	33	0	26	0	27	47	465	3.4	65	8	1,000	0	0.0	0.0
C+ / 6.3	2.9	5.5	12.62	311	0	17	0	39	44	346	3.7	63	8	0	0	0.0	0.0
C+ / 5.9	2.9	5.5	12.75	1,154	0	17	0	39	44	346	3.7	72	8	0	0	0.0	0.0
C+ / 6.2	2.9	5.5	12.67	2,851	0	17	0	39	44	346	3.7	67	8	0	0	0.0	0.0
C+ / 6.4	2.8	5.4	10.05	166	0	26	0	27	47	465	3.4	58	8	0	0	0.0	0.0
C+ / 6.3	2.9	5.4	10.03	770	0	26	0	27	47	465	3.4	74	8	1,000,000	0	0.0	0.0
C+ / 6.3	2.9	5.4	10.02	636	0	26	0	27	47	465	3.4	71	8	1,000	0	0.0	0.0
U /	N/A	7.3	10.90	N/A	0	0	0	0	100	490	4.0	N/A	5	1,000	0	0.0	0.0
U /	N/A	7.3	10.90	N/A	0	0	0	0	100	490	4.0	N/A	5	250,000	0	0.0	0.0

Fund Type	Fund Name	Ticker Symbol	Overall Investment Rating	Phone	PERFORMANCE Performance Rating/Pts	Total Return % through 2/28/17 3 Mo	6 Mo	1Yr / Pct	Annualized 3Yr / Pct	5Yr / Pct	Incl. in Returns Dividend Yield	Expense Ratio
COI	Voya Investment Grade Credit P	IIGPX	C+	(800) 992-0180	B+ / 8.6	2.67	-0.75	9.12 /77	4.83 /84	--	3.55	0.60
COI	Voya Investment Grade Credit R6	VIGTX	U	(800) 992-0180	U /	2.62	-0.93	--	--	--	0.00	N/A
GEI	Voya Investment Grade Credit SMA	ISCFX	C+	(800) 992-0180	B+ / 8.7	2.78	-0.62	9.22 /77	4.95 /85	4.94 /84	3.65	0.64
GEI	Voya Limited Maturity Bond Adv	IMBAX	C-	(800) 992-0180	D- / 1.5	0.38	-0.62	0.47 /33	0.28 /18	0.44 /21	1.30	0.88
GEI	Voya Limited Maturity Bond Inst	ILBPX	C	(800) 992-0180	D / 1.9	0.52	-1.08	0.30 /29	0.63 /22	0.88 /26	1.81	0.28
GEI	Voya Limited Maturity Bond Svc	ILMBX	C	(800) 992-0180	D / 1.8	0.46	-0.89	0.41 /31	0.48 /21	0.69 /24	1.61	0.53
MTG	Voya Securitized Credit I	VCFIX	U	(800) 992-0180	U /	2.01	1.67	6.03 /70	--	--	4.73	0.82
MTG	Voya Securitized Credit P	VSCFX	U	(800) 992-0180	U /	2.04	1.88	6.63 /72	--	--	5.11	0.74
LP	Voya Senior Income A	XSIAX	B+	(800) 992-0180	B+ / 8.3	2.45	4.75	14.59 /88	3.91 /74	6.29 /94	5.29	2.46
LP	● Voya Senior Income B	XSIBX	B+	(800) 992-0180	B+ / 8.3	2.34	4.52	14.00 /87	3.35 /67	5.75 /90	4.96	3.21
LP	Voya Senior Income C	XSICX	B+	(800) 992-0180	B+ / 8.4	2.25	4.42	13.96 /87	3.39 /67	5.76 /90	4.95	2.96
LP	Voya Senior Income I	XSIIX	A	(800) 992-0180	A- / 9.0	2.44	4.81	14.83 /88	4.16 /77	6.57 /95	5.69	2.21
LP	Voya Senior Income W	XSIWX	A	(800) 992-0180	A- / 9.0	2.51	4.87	14.87 /88	4.17 /77	6.58 /95	5.67	2.21
COI	Voya Short Term Bond A	IASBX	C	(800) 992-0180	D / 1.8	0.47	0.15	1.57 /45	0.93 /26	--	1.53	0.96
COI	Voya Short Term Bond C	ICSBX	C-	(800) 992-0180	D- / 1.5	0.39	-0.12	0.92 /39	0.17 /16	--	0.82	1.71
COI	Voya Short Term Bond I	IISBX	B	(800) 992-0180	C- / 3.1	0.42	0.18	1.75 /47	1.15 /30	--	1.75	0.63
COI	Voya Short Term Bond R	VSTRX	U	(800) 992-0180	U /	0.44	0.05	1.34 /43	--	--	1.23	1.21
COI	Voya Short Term Bond W	IWSBX	B	(800) 992-0180	C- / 3.0	0.51	0.25	1.80 /47	1.11 /29	--	1.69	0.71
GEI	Voya Strategic Income Opptys A	ISIAX	A+	(800) 992-0180	C+ / 6.8	2.03	2.80	7.48 /73	3.54 /69	--	4.38	1.25
GEI	Voya Strategic Income Opptys C	ISICX	A+	(800) 992-0180	C+ / 6.7	1.95	2.52	6.69 /72	2.79 /58	--	3.81	2.00
GEI	Voya Strategic Income Opptys I	IISIX	A+	(800) 992-0180	B / 8.0	2.13	3.12	7.90 /74	4.05 /76	--	4.89	0.87
GEI	Voya Strategic Income Opptys R	ISIRX	A+	(800) 992-0180	B- / 7.2	1.97	2.57	7.04 /73	3.31 /66	--	4.27	1.50
GL	Voya Strategic Income Opptys R6	VSIRX	U	(800) 992-0180	U /	2.04	2.94	7.72 /74	--	--	4.93	0.87
GEI	Voya Strategic Income Opptys W	ISIWX	A+	(800) 992-0180	B / 7.6	2.09	2.92	7.73 /74	3.65 /71	--	4.72	1.00
GEI	Voya US Bond Index Adv	ILUAX	D	(800) 992-0180	C- / 3.5	0.82	-2.56	0.75 /37	1.84 /40	1.37 /33	1.95	0.91
GEI	Voya US Bond Index I	ILBAX	D	(800) 992-0180	C- / 4.2	0.94	-2.40	1.20 /42	2.31 /48	1.89 /40	2.50	0.41
GEI	Voya US Bond Index S	ILABX	D	(800) 992-0180	C- / 3.9	0.88	-2.53	0.92 /39	2.09 /45	1.63 /37	2.22	0.66
GEI	VY BlackRock Infl Pro Bond Adv	IBRAX	E	(800) 992-0180	D / 2.1	0.89	-0.95	2.56 /54	0.45 /20	-0.39 / 3	0.12	1.16
GEI	VY BlackRock Infl Pro Bond Inst	IBRIX	E+	(800) 992-0180	C- / 3.2	1.13	-0.53	3.18 /58	1.06 /29	0.21 /18	0.70	0.56
GEI	VY BlackRock Infl Pro Bond Svc	IBRSX	E+	(800) 992-0180	D+ / 2.8	1.09	-0.69	2.94 /56	0.80 /24	-0.05 / 5	0.45	0.81
GEI	VY Pioneer High Yield I	IPHIX	C	(800) 992-0180	B+ / 8.9	4.57	4.99	19.97 /96	3.03 /62	6.35 /94	4.87	0.77
GEI	VY Pioneer High Yield S	IPHSX	C	(800) 992-0180	B+ / 8.7	4.59	4.86	19.81 /96	2.78 /57	6.09 /93	4.63	1.02
MTG	WA Adjustable Rate Income A	ARMZX	B-	(877) 534-4627	D+ / 2.7	0.85	1.30	3.49 /60	1.20 /31	1.78 /39	1.48	0.82
COI	WA Adjustable Rate Income C	LWAIX	C+	(877) 534-4627	D+ / 2.3	0.66	0.90	2.66 /54	0.37 /20	0.95 /27	0.70	1.64
MTG	● WA Adjustable Rate Income C1	ARMGX	B-	(877) 534-4627	D+ / 2.7	0.83	1.02	2.93 /56	0.63 /22	1.22 /30	0.95	1.38
MTG	WA Adjustable Rate Income I	SBAYX	A-	(877) 534-4627	C- / 4.0	0.91	1.40	3.70 /61	1.38 /33	1.97 /42	1.70	0.65
COI	WA Adjustable Rate Income IS	ARMLX	A	(877) 534-4627	C- / 4.2	1.03	1.55	3.89 /62	1.51 /35	--	1.78	0.56
MUS	WA CA Municipals A	SHRCX	C-	(877) 534-4627	C / 4.8	1.43	-3.24	-0.27 /13	3.32 /86	2.92 /79	3.81	0.72
MUS	WA CA Municipals C	SCACX	C+	(877) 534-4627	C+ / 6.1	1.28	-3.52	-0.78 / 6	2.74 /78	2.34 /67	3.39	1.28
MUS	WA CA Municipals I	LMCUX	B+	(877) 534-4627	B- / 7.4	1.46	-3.18	-0.15 /15	3.45 /87	3.04 /81	4.11	0.65
MMF	WA California Tax Free Mny Mkt A	LOAXX	D+	(888) 425-6432	E+ / 0.8	0.02	0.04	0.08 /23	0.03 /10	0.02 / 9	0.08	N/A
MMF	WA California Tax Free Mny Mkt N	CFAXX	U	(888) 425-6432	U /	--	--	--	--	--	0.04	N/A
COI	WA Core Bond A	WABAX	C-	(888) 425-6432	C / 4.6	1.60	-1.68	3.71 /61	3.36 /67	3.02 /58	1.96	0.91
COI	WA Core Bond C	WABCX	C	(888) 425-6432	C / 5.2	1.42	-1.95	2.99 /56	2.66 /55	2.29 /46	1.34	1.54
COI	● WA Core Bond C1	LWACX	C+	(888) 425-6432	C+ / 5.7	1.50	-1.87	3.29 /58	2.97 /61	2.63 /52	1.63	1.22
COI	WA Core Bond FI	WAPIX	B	(888) 425-6432	C+ / 6.4	1.59	-1.69	3.72 /61	3.42 /68	3.10 /59	2.05	0.81
COI	WA Core Bond I	WATFX	B+	(888) 425-6432	C+ / 6.9	1.69	-1.50	4.10 /63	3.77 /72	3.40 /64	2.42	0.54
COI	WA Core Bond IS	WACSX	B+	(888) 425-6432	C+ / 6.9	1.70	-1.48	4.12 /63	3.80 /73	3.46 /65	2.44	0.44
COI	WA Core Bond R	WABRX	C+	(888) 425-6432	C+ / 5.9	1.52	-1.82	3.32 /59	3.08 /62	2.74 /53	1.74	1.12
COI	WA Core Plus Bond C	WAPCX	C+	(888) 425-6432	C+ / 6.2	1.89	-1.39	4.52 /65	3.09 /63	2.91 /56	2.64	1.52
COI	● WA Core Plus Bond C1	LWCPX	B-	(888) 425-6432	C+ / 6.6	1.89	-1.32	4.76 /66	3.38 /67	3.22 /61	2.96	1.20
GEI	WA Core Plus Bond FI	WACIX	B	(888) 425-6432	B- / 7.1	1.99	-1.13	5.16 /67	3.81 /73	3.67 /68	3.34	0.84

● Denotes fund is closed to new investors
* Denotes fund is included in Section II

www.thestreetratings.com

RISK			NET ASSETS		ASSET							FUND MANAGER		MINIMUM		LOADS	
Risk Rating/Pts	3 Yr Avg Standard Deviation	Avg Dura-tion	NAV As of 2/28/17	Total $(Mil)	Cash %	Gov. Bond %	Muni. Bond %	Corp. Bond %	Other %	Portfolio Turnover Ratio	Avg Coupon Rate	Manager Quality Pct	Manager Tenure (Years)	Initial Purch. $	Additional Purch. $	Front End Load	Back End Load
D+ / 2.3	4.5	7.3	10.89	133	0	0	0	0	100	490	4.0	73	5	0	0	0.0	0.0
U /	N/A	7.3	10.90	N/A	0	0	0	0	100	490	4.0	N/A	5	1,000,000	0	0.0	0.0
D+ / 2.3	4.5	7.3	10.89	3	0	0	0	0	100	490	4.0	82	5	0	0	0.0	0.0
A / 9.5	0.8	1.9	9.77	23	2	29	0	45	24	325	1.9	27	8	0	0	0.0	0.0
A- / 9.2	1.0	1.9	9.97	165	2	29	0	45	24	325	1.9	45	8	0	0	0.0	0.0
A / 9.4	0.9	1.9	10.05	89	2	29	0	45	24	325	1.9	35	8	0	0	0.0	0.0
U /	N/A	2.8	10.05	121	0	0	0	0	100	35	3.7	N/A	N/A	250,000	0	0.0	0.0
U /	N/A	2.8	10.10	152	0	0	0	0	100	35	3.7	N/A	N/A	0	0	0.0	0.0
C- / 4.0	3.5	0.1	12.85	207	0	0	0	12	88	44	7.6	91	16	1,000	0	2.5	0.0
C- / 4.0	3.5	0.1	12.79	N/A	0	0	0	12	88	44	7.6	88	16	1,000	0	0.0	0.0
C- / 4.0	3.5	0.1	12.82	214	0	0	0	12	88	44	7.6	88	16	1,000	0	0.0	0.0
C- / 4.0	3.5	0.1	12.81	46	0	0	0	12	88	44	7.6	92	16	250,000	0	0.0	0.0
C- / 4.0	3.5	0.1	12.86	27	0	0	0	12	88	44	7.6	92	16	1,000	0	0.0	0.0
A+ / 9.6	0.8	1.9	9.84	7	0	18	0	52	30	109	2.5	58	5	1,000	0	2.5	0.0
A / 9.5	0.8	1.9	9.85	1	0	18	0	52	30	109	2.5	23	5	1,000	0	0.0	0.0
A+ / 9.6	0.8	1.9	9.84	13	0	18	0	52	30	109	2.5	64	5	250,000	0	0.0	0.0
U /	N/A	1.9	9.84	N/A	0	18	0	52	30	109	2.5	N/A	5	0	0	0.0	0.0
A+ / 9.6	0.8	1.9	9.85	N/A	0	18	0	52	30	109	2.5	64	5	1,000	0	0.0	0.0
B+ / 8.6	1.8	N/A	10.09	9	5	8	0	33	54	83	0.0	93	5	1,000	0	2.5	0.0
B+ / 8.6	1.7	N/A	9.94	2	5	8	0	33	54	83	0.0	89	5	1,000	0	0.0	0.0
B+ / 8.6	1.7	N/A	10.15	20	5	8	0	33	54	83	0.0	94	5	250,000	0	0.0	0.0
B+ / 8.6	1.8	N/A	10.01	4	5	8	0	33	54	83	0.0	92	5	0	0	0.0	0.0
U /	N/A	N/A	10.13	111	5	8	0	33	54	83	0.0	N/A	5	1,000,000	0	0.0	0.0
B+ / 8.6	1.8	N/A	10.06	3	5	8	0	33	54	83	0.0	93	5	1,000	0	0.0	0.0
C+ / 5.6	3.0	5.4	10.54	32	0	44	1	25	30	213	3.2	15	5	0	0	0.0	0.0
C / 5.3	3.1	5.4	10.58	3,034	0	44	1	25	30	213	3.2	25	5	0	0	0.0	0.0
C / 5.5	3.0	5.4	10.55	226	0	44	1	25	30	213	3.2	20	5	0	0	0.0	0.0
D+ / 2.8	3.9	7.8	9.26	53	2	72	0	24	2	470	12.9	1	7	0	0	0.0	0.0
D+ / 2.9	3.9	7.8	9.60	307	2	72	0	24	2	470	12.9	4	7	0	0	0.0	0.0
D+ / 2.8	4.0	7.8	9.52	187	2	72	0	24	2	470	12.9	2	7	0	0	0.0	0.0
D- / 1.0	6.3	3.7	11.92	102	2	0	0	71	27	28	5.5	89	11	0	0	0.0	0.0
D- / 1.0	6.4	3.7	11.91	4	2	0	0	71	27	28	5.5	87	11	0	0	0.0	0.0
A+ / 9.7	0.7	1.0	8.97	129	23	0	0	36	41	22	2.2	76	3	1,000	50	2.3	0.0
A+ / 9.7	0.7	1.0	8.94	2	23	0	0	36	41	22	2.2	N/A	3	1,000	50	0.0	0.0
A+ / 9.7	0.7	1.0	8.92	28	23	0	0	36	41	22	2.2	60	3	1,000	50	0.0	0.0
A+ / 9.7	0.7	1.0	8.95	21	23	0	0	36	41	22	2.2	79	3	1,000,000	0	0.0	0.0
A+ / 9.7	0.7	1.0	8.96	4	23	0	0	36	41	22	2.2	78	3	1,000,000	0	0.0	0.0
C / 5.0	3.1	5.4	15.92	395	0	0	99	0	1	9	4.9	46	10	1,000	50	4.3	0.0
C / 5.1	3.1	5.4	15.88	77	0	0	99	0	1	9	4.9	23	10	1,000	50	0.0	0.0
C / 5.1	3.1	5.4	15.92	94	0	0	99	0	1	9	4.9	54	10	1,000,000	0	0.0	0.0
A+ / 9.9	N/A	N/A	1.00	33	100	0	0	0	0	0	0.1	41	6	1,000	50	0.0	0.0
U /	N/A	N/A	1.00	2	100	0	0	0	0	0	0.0	39	25	0	0	0.0	0.0
C / 5.5	3.0	5.7	12.44	439	5	37	0	26	32	85	2.7	69	23	1,000	50	4.3	0.0
C / 5.4	3.0	5.7	12.45	57	5	37	0	26	32	85	2.7	40	23	1,000	50	0.0	0.0
C / 5.5	3.0	5.7	12.45	17	5	37	0	26	32	85	2.7	57	23	1,000	50	0.0	0.0
C / 5.5	3.0	5.7	12.45	182	5	37	0	26	32	85	2.7	70	23	0	0	0.0	0.0
C / 5.4	3.0	5.7	12.44	4,619	5	37	0	26	32	85	2.7	76	23	1,000,000	0	0.0	0.0
C / 5.5	3.0	5.7	12.46	2,501	5	37	0	26	32	85	2.7	77	23	0	0	0.0	0.0
C / 5.5	3.0	5.7	12.45	24	5	37	0	26	32	85	2.7	61	23	0	0	0.0	0.0
C / 4.8	3.2	6.1	11.55	185	0	35	0	33	32	93	3.6	57	12	1,000	50	0.0	0.0
C / 4.8	3.2	6.1	11.53	25	0	35	0	33	32	93	3.6	66	12	1,000	50	0.0	0.0
C / 4.8	3.2	6.1	11.54	403	0	35	0	33	32	93	3.6	78	12	0	0	0.0	0.0

Fund Type	Fund Name	Ticker Symbol	Overall Investment Rating	Phone	Performance Rating/Pts	3 Mo	6 Mo	1Yr / Pct	3Yr / Pct	5Yr / Pct	Dividend Yield	Expense Ratio
								Total Return % through 2/28/17	Annualized		Incl. in Returns	
GEI	WA Core Plus Bond I	WACPX	B+	(888) 425-6432	B- / 7.5	2.07	-0.95	5.65 /69	4.19 /77	3.99 /72	3.72	0.52
GEI	WA Core Plus Bond IS	WAPSX	B+	(888) 425-6432	B- / 7.5	2.08	-0.93	5.67 /69	4.22 /78	4.05 /73	3.75	0.42
COI	WA Core Plus Bond R	WAPRX	B-	(888) 425-6432	C+ / 6.8	1.90	-1.29	4.87 /66	3.51 /69	3.28 /62	3.06	1.12
COI	WA Core Plus BondA	WAPAX	C-	(888) 425-6432	C+ / 5.6	1.98	-1.13	5.27 /68	3.77 /72	3.62 /68	3.22	0.89
COI	WA Corporate Bond A	SIGAX	C	(877) 534-4627	B / 7.7	3.17	-0.04	11.48 /82	4.65 /82	5.14 /85	3.56	1.02
COI	WA Corporate Bond C	LWBOX	C	(877) 534-4627	B / 8.1	2.98	-0.40	10.73 /81	3.92 /74	4.43 /78	3.05	1.68
COI ●	WA Corporate Bond C1	SBILX	C+	(877) 534-4627	B+ / 8.3	2.98	-0.36	10.92 /81	4.14 /77	4.62 /80	3.26	1.48
COI	WA Corporate Bond I	SIGYX	B	(877) 534-4627	A- / 9.0	3.16	0.12	11.75 /83	4.97 /85	5.49 /88	4.05	0.69
COI	WA Corporate Bond P	LCBPX	C+	(877) 534-4627	B+ / 8.7	3.13	-0.12	11.31 /82	4.50 /81	4.99 /84	3.56	1.17
EM	WA Emerging Markets Debt A	LWEAX	D	(888) 425-6432	B- / 7.4	5.83	0.34	14.57 /88	3.51 /69	2.48 /49	3.99	1.37
EM	WA Emerging Markets Debt A2	WEMDX	D	(888) 425-6432	B- / 7.4	5.86	0.37	14.62 /88	3.57 /70	--	4.01	1.24
EM	WA Emerging Markets Debt C	WAEOX	D	(888) 425-6432	B / 7.8	5.89	0.04	14.00 /87	2.83 /58	1.84 /40	3.64	2.00
EM ●	WA Emerging Markets Debt C1	LWECX	D	(888) 425-6432	B / 8.0	5.65	0.08	14.00 /87	3.09 /63	2.06 /43	3.73	1.66
EM	WA Emerging Markets Debt FI	LMWDX	C	(888) 425-6432	A- / 9.1	6.16	0.34	14.91 /88	4.37 /79	3.00 /58	3.83	1.12
EM	WA Emerging Markets Debt Inst	SEMDX	C-	(888) 425-6432	B+ / 8.8	5.92	0.47	14.86 /88	3.89 /74	2.87 /56	4.40	0.98
EM	WA Emerging Markets Debt IS	LWISX	C-	(888) 425-6432	B+ / 8.9	5.95	0.52	14.98 /88	4.01 /75	--	4.49	0.94
COH	WA Global High Yield Bond A	SAHYX	D	(877) 534-4627	B / 7.7	5.17	5.14	21.99 /98	2.38 /50	5.22 /86	5.83	1.13
GL	WA Global High Yield Bond C	LWGOX	D+	(877) 534-4627	B / 8.0	4.99	4.77	21.12 /97	1.67 /38	4.48 /78	5.42	1.82
COH ●	WA Global High Yield Bond C1	SHYCX	D+	(877) 534-4627	B+ / 8.3	5.01	4.86	21.43 /97	1.89 /41	4.72 /81	5.63	1.61
COH	WA Global High Yield Bond I	SHYOX	C	(877) 534-4627	B+ / 8.9	5.24	5.28	22.31 /98	2.65 /55	5.52 /89	6.35	0.89
GL	WA Global High Yield Bond IS	LWGSX	C	(877) 534-4627	A- / 9.0	5.10	5.32	22.23 /98	2.70 /56	--	6.44	0.78
GL	WA Global Strategic Income A	SDSAX	C-	(877) 534-4627	B- / 7.0	4.11	2.33	13.08 /85	3.24 /65	4.38 /77	4.83	1.14
GL	WA Global Strategic Income C	LWSIX	C	(877) 534-4627	B- / 7.3	3.94	1.97	12.29 /84	2.48 /51	3.59 /67	4.34	1.85
GL ●	WA Global Strategic Income C1	SDSIX	C+	(877) 534-4627	B / 7.6	4.00	2.12	12.62 /84	2.83 /58	3.96 /72	4.65	1.54
GL	WA Global Strategic Income I	SDSYX	B	(877) 534-4627	B+ / 8.4	4.18	2.48	13.37 /86	3.55 /69	4.68 /81	5.33	0.86
GL	WA Global Strategic Income IS	WAGIX	U	(877) 534-4627	U /	4.20	2.53	13.44 /86	--	--	5.39	0.74
COH	WA High Yield A	WAYAX	D	(888) 425-6432	B / 7.7	4.51	5.26	23.19 /98	2.27 /48	5.56 /89	5.46	0.96
COH	WA High Yield A2	WHAYX	U	(888) 425-6432	U /	4.54	5.16	23.02 /98	--	--	5.49	0.98
COH	WA High Yield C	WAYCX	D	(888) 425-6432	B / 8.0	4.37	4.80	22.11 /98	1.54 /36	4.61 /80	5.01	1.73
COH	WA High Yield I	WAHYX	C	(888) 425-6432	A- / 9.0	4.63	5.32	23.33 /98	2.62 /54	5.70 /90	5.99	0.72
COH	WA High Yield IS	WAHSX	C	(888) 425-6432	A- / 9.0	4.59	5.30	23.45 /98	2.63 /55	5.77 /91	6.05	0.64
COH	WA High Yield R	WAYRX	C-	(888) 425-6432	B+ / 8.5	4.47	5.00	22.77 /98	2.01 /43	5.11 /85	5.42	1.52
GEI	WA Inflation Indexed Plus Bond A	WAFAX	E	(888) 425-6432	E / 0.3	1.36	-0.92	2.21 /51	0.42 /20	-0.19 / 4	0.98	0.65
GEI	WA Inflation Indexed Plus Bond C	WAFCX	E	(888) 425-6432	E / 0.5	1.24	-1.20	1.52 /45	-0.27 / 4	-0.93 / 2	0.87	1.30
GEI ●	WA Inflation Indexed Plus Bond C1	LWICX	E	(888) 425-6432	D- / 1.4	1.24	-1.08	1.74 /47	-0.02 / 5	-0.70 / 2	0.91	1.10
USS	WA Inflation Indexed Plus Bond FI	WATPX	E	(888) 425-6432	D / 2.1	1.36	-0.84	2.13 /50	0.40 /20	-0.27 / 4	1.02	0.64
USS	WA Inflation Indexed Plus Bond I	WAIIX	E+	(888) 425-6432	D+ / 2.6	1.38	-0.79	2.47 /53	0.71 /23	0.09 /14	1.10	0.38
USS	WA Inflation Indexed Plus Bond IS	WAFSX	E+	(888) 425-6432	D+ / 2.8	1.47	-0.68	2.58 /54	0.86 /25	0.21 /18	1.13	0.25
GEI	WA Inflation Indexed Plus Bond R	WAFRX	E	(888) 425-6432	D- / 1.5	1.23	-1.18	1.74 /47	0.05 / 9	-0.57 / 3	0.91	0.99
MMT	WA Inst Cash Reserves Inst	CARXX	C	(800) 331-1792	D / 1.7	0.20	0.35	0.57 /35	0.27 /18	0.21 /19	0.53	N/A
MMT	WA Inst Govt Reserves Inst	INGXX	C-	(888) 425-6432	D- / 1.3	0.11	0.19	0.33 /30	0.15 /15	0.11 /16	0.33	N/A
MMT	WA Inst Govt Reserves Inv	LGRXX	C-	(888) 425-6432	D- / 1.2	0.10	0.16	0.27 /28	0.10 /13	--	0.27	N/A
MMT	WA Inst Liquid Reserves Inst	CILXX	C	(800) 331-1792	D / 1.8	0.19	0.40	0.63 /35	0.30 /19	0.23 /19	0.57	N/A
MMT	WA Inst Liquid Reserves Inv	LLRXX	C	(800) 331-1792	D / 1.6	0.18	0.37	0.57 /35	0.24 /17	--	0.52	N/A
MMT	WA Inst US Treas Reserves Inst	CIIXX	C-	(800) 331-1792	D- / 1.1	0.08	0.14	0.23 /27	0.09 /13	0.06 /13	0.23	N/A
MUS	WA Int Maturity California Muni A	ITCAX	D	(877) 534-4627	C- / 3.6	1.18	-3.51	-1.71 / 1	2.39 /71	2.17 /63	2.67	0.78
MUS	WA Int Maturity California Muni C	SIMLX	D	(877) 534-4627	C- / 3.5	0.91	-3.91	-2.30 / 1	1.78 /57	1.56 /48	2.11	1.36
MUS	WA Int Maturity California Muni I	SICYX	C+	(877) 534-4627	C / 5.5	1.21	-3.42	-1.55 / 1	2.55 /74	2.33 /67	2.88	0.69
MUS	WA Int Maturity New York Muni A	IMNYX	D+	(877) 534-4627	C- / 3.1	1.01	-3.30	-1.45 / 2	2.08 /64	1.81 /54	2.96	0.75
MUS	WA Int Maturity New York Muni C	SINLX	D+	(877) 534-4627	C- / 3.0	0.86	-3.48	-2.04 / 1	1.50 /48	1.20 /40	2.41	1.35
MUS	WA Int Maturity New York Muni I	LMIIX	B-	(877) 534-4627	C / 5.0	1.05	-3.13	-1.31 / 2	2.26 /68	1.96 /58	3.18	0.67
COI	WA Intermediate Bond A	WATAX	C-	(888) 425-6432	C- / 3.0	1.33	-0.72	2.65 /54	2.29 /48	2.36 /47	1.79	0.82

● Denotes fund is closed to new investors
* Denotes fund is included in Section II

Risk Rating/Pts	3 Yr Avg Standard Deviation	Avg Duration	NAV As of 2/28/17	Total $(Mil)	Cash %	Gov. Bond %	Muni. Bond %	Corp. Bond %	Other %	Portfolio Turnover Ratio	Avg Coupon Rate	Manager Quality Pct	Manager Tenure (Years)	Initial Purch. $	Additional Purch. $	Front End Load	Back End Load
C / 4.7	3.2	6.1	11.54	11,312	0	35	0	33	32	93	3.6	82	12	1,000,000	0	0.0	0.0
C / 4.7	3.2	6.1	11.54	4,069	0	35	0	33	32	93	3.6	82	12	0	0	0.0	0.0
C / 4.7	3.2	6.1	11.52	144	0	35	0	33	32	93	3.6	68	12	0	0	0.0	0.0
C / 4.7	3.2	6.1	11.53	895	0	35	0	33	32	93	3.6	74	12	1,000	50	4.3	0.0
D+ / 2.3	4.5	7.0	12.35	263	1	11	3	80	5	95	4.9	76	7	1,000	50	4.3	0.0
D+ / 2.3	4.5	7.0	12.35	7	1	11	3	80	5	95	4.9	58	7	1,000	50	0.0	0.0
D+ / 2.3	4.5	7.0	12.27	11	1	11	3	80	5	95	4.9	65	7	1,000	50	0.0	0.0
D+ / 2.3	4.5	7.0	12.35	65	1	11	3	80	5	95	4.9	80	7	1,000,000	0	0.0	0.0
D+ / 2.3	4.5	7.0	12.34	61	1	11	3	80	5	95	4.9	73	7	0	50	0.0	0.0
E+ / 0.6	7.2	8.1	5.02	9	1	69	1	27	2	46	5.9	96	4	1,000	50	4.3	0.0
E+ / 0.6	7.2	8.1	5.01	3	1	69	1	27	2	46	5.9	96	4	1,000	50	4.3	0.0
E / 0.5	7.3	8.1	5.01	2	1	69	1	27	2	46	5.9	95	4	1,000	50	0.0	0.0
E / 0.5	7.2	8.1	5.05	N/A	1	69	1	27	2	46	5.9	95	4	1,000	50	0.0	0.0
E / 0.5	7.3	8.1	5.04	N/A	1	69	1	27	2	46	5.9	98	4	0	0	0.0	0.0
E+ / 0.6	7.1	8.1	5.01	69	1	69	1	27	2	46	5.9	97	4	1,000,000	0	0.0	0.0
E+ / 0.6	7.2	8.1	5.00	2	1	69	1	27	2	46	5.9	97	4	1,000,000	0	0.0	0.0
E+ / 0.7	6.7	4.9	6.47	165	0	15	2	75	8	71	6.4	1	11	1,000	50	4.3	0.0
E+ / 0.8	6.6	4.9	6.48	7	0	15	2	75	8	71	6.4	88	11	1,000	50	0.0	0.0
E+ / 0.7	6.7	4.9	6.54	41	0	15	2	75	8	71	6.4	1	11	1,000	50	0.0	0.0
E+ / 0.7	6.6	4.9	6.47	37	0	15	2	75	8	71	6.4	2	11	1,000,000	0	0.0	0.0
E+ / 0.8	6.6	4.9	6.46	105	0	15	2	75	8	71	6.4	93	11	0	0	0.0	0.0
D+ / 2.4	4.1	4.7	6.36	275	4	19	0	47	30	68	5.6	94	5	1,000	50	4.3	0.0
C- / 3.1	4.0	4.7	6.35	7	4	19	0	47	30	68	5.6	91	5	1,000	50	0.0	0.0
C- / 3.1	4.1	4.7	6.37	27	4	19	0	47	30	68	5.6	93	5	1,000	50	0.0	0.0
C- / 3.1	4.1	4.7	6.39	62	4	19	0	47	30	68	5.6	94	5	1,000,000	0	0.0	0.0
U /	N/A	4.7	6.39	1	4	19	0	47	30	68	5.6	N/A	5	1,000,000	0	0.0	0.0
E+ / 0.6	6.7	4.7	8.15	4	2	0	0	88	10	71	6.4	1	12	1,000	50	4.3	0.0
U /	N/A	4.7	8.16	23	2	0	0	88	10	71	6.4	N/A	12	1,000	50	4.3	0.0
E+ / 0.7	6.6	4.7	8.08	4	2	0	0	88	10	71	6.4	0	12	1,000	50	0.0	0.0
E+ / 0.7	6.7	4.7	8.09	85	2	0	0	88	10	71	6.4	2	12	1,000,000	0	0.0	0.0
E+ / 0.7	6.7	4.7	8.22	149	2	0	0	88	10	71	6.4	2	12	0	0	0.0	0.0
E+ / 0.6	6.7	4.7	8.10	N/A	2	0	0	88	10	71	6.4	1	12	0	0	0.0	0.0
C- / 3.1	3.7	8.3	11.10	23	12	87	0	0	1	69	1.0	2	3	1,000	50	4.3	0.0
C- / 3.0	3.8	8.3	10.82	2	12	87	0	0	1	69	1.0	1	3	1,000	50	0.0	0.0
C- / 3.1	3.7	8.3	10.93	1	12	87	0	0	1	69	1.0	1	3	1,000	50	0.0	0.0
C- / 3.1	3.7	8.3	11.02	2	12	87	0	0	1	69	1.0	7	3	0	0	0.0	0.0
D+ / 2.9	3.8	8.3	11.20	76	12	87	0	0	1	69	1.0	11	3	1,000,000	0	0.0	0.0
C- / 3.0	3.8	8.3	11.26	315	12	87	0	0	1	69	1.0	14	3	0	0	0.0	0.0
C- / 3.0	3.8	8.3	10.95	1	12	87	0	0	1	69	1.0	1	3	0	0	0.0	0.0
A+ / 9.9	0.1	N/A	1.00	3,158	100	0	0	0	0	0	0.5	54	N/A	1,000,000	50	0.0	0.0
A+ / 9.9	N/A	N/A	1.00	18,616	100	0	0	0	0	0	0.3	49	N/A	1,000,000	50	0.0	0.0
A+ / 9.9	N/A	N/A	1.00	313	100	0	0	0	0	0	0.3	N/A	N/A	1,000,000	50	0.0	0.0
A+ / 9.9	0.1	N/A	1.00	944	100	0	0	0	0	0	0.6	55	N/A	1,000,000	50	0.0	0.0
A+ / 9.9	0.1	N/A	1.00	28	100	0	0	0	0	0	0.5	52	N/A	1,000,000	50	0.0	0.0
A+ / 9.9	N/A	N/A	1.00	7,217	100	0	0	0	0	0	0.2	46	25	1,000,000	50	0.0	0.0
C+ / 5.9	2.9	4.8	8.73	74	0	0	99	0	1	4	4.8	19	19	1,000	50	2.3	0.0
C+ / 6.0	2.9	4.8	8.71	117	0	0	99	0	1	4	4.8	8	19	1,000	50	0.0	0.0
C+ / 5.8	3.0	4.8	8.76	30	0	0	99	0	1	4	4.8	22	19	1,000,000	0	0.0	0.0
B- / 7.1	2.7	4.7	8.66	131	0	0	99	0	1	5	4.9	17	19	1,000	50	2.3	0.0
B- / 7.0	2.7	4.7	8.67	67	0	0	99	0	1	5	4.9	8	19	1,000	50	0.0	0.0
B- / 7.0	2.7	4.7	8.65	45	0	0	99	0	1	5	4.9	22	19	1,000,000	0	0.0	0.0
B / 7.9	2.3	4.3	10.85	3	10	36	1	31	22	106	2.3	58	8	1,000	50	4.3	0.0

Fund Type	Fund Name	Ticker Symbol	Overall Investment Rating	Phone	Performance Rating/Pts	3 Mo	6 Mo	1Yr / Pct	3Yr / Pct	5Yr / Pct	Dividend Yield	Expense Ratio
								Total Return % through 2/28/17	Annualized		Incl. in Returns	
COI	WA Intermediate Bond C	WATCX	C+	(888) 425-6432	C- / 3.5	1.15	-1.08	1.88 /48	1.54 /36	1.63 /37	1.12	1.59
GEI	WA Intermediate Bond I	WATIX	A-	(888) 425-6432	C / 5.4	1.42	-0.55	2.99 /56	2.66 /55	2.75 /54	2.20	0.52
GEI	WA Intermediate Bond IS	WABSX	A-	(888) 425-6432	C / 5.5	1.44	-0.53	3.05 /57	2.74 /57	2.81 /55	2.26	0.46
COI	WA Intermediate Bond R	WATRX	B-	(888) 425-6432	C / 4.3	1.26	-0.87	2.34 /52	2.00 /43	2.08 /43	1.56	1.35
*MUN	WA Intermediate Term Muni A	SBLTX	C+	(877) 534-4627	C / 4.5	1.60	-2.84	-0.44 /10	2.53 /74	2.15 /62	3.12	0.74
MUN	WA Intermediate Term Muni C	SMLLX	C+	(877) 534-4627	C / 4.5	1.46	-3.11	-1.00 / 4	1.94 /61	1.57 /48	2.60	1.32
MUN	WA Intermediate Term Muni I	SBTYX	A	(877) 534-4627	C+ / 6.3	1.64	-2.77	-0.29 /13	2.68 /77	2.31 /66	3.34	0.65
MMT	WA Liquid Reserves A	LLAXX	C-	(888) 425-6432	D- / 1.3	0.11	0.33	0.37 /31	0.13 /14	0.08 /14	0.31	N/A
GL	WA Macro Opportunities A	LAAAX	C-	(800) 228-2121	B / 8.2	4.44	0.61	13.40 /86	4.75 /83	—	1.45	1.60
GL	WA Macro Opportunities C	LAACX	C	(800) 228-2121	B+ / 8.5	4.31	0.24	12.69 /84	4.01 /75	—	0.80	2.33
GL	WA Macro Opportunities FI	LAFIX	C+	(800) 228-2121	A- / 9.1	4.55	0.62	13.42 /86	4.74 /83	—	1.43	1.64
GL	WA Macro Opportunities I	LAOIX	C+	(800) 228-2121	A / 9.3	4.55	0.72	13.75 /86	4.98 /85	—	1.81	1.31
GL	WA Macro Opportunities IS	LAOSX	C+	(800) 228-2121	A / 9.3	4.54	0.81	13.82 /86	5.09 /86	—	1.89	1.22
MUN●	WA Managed Municipals 1	SMMOX	A-	(877) 534-4627	B / 8.1	1.90	-2.95	0.38 /35	3.80 /91	3.28 /85	3.90	0.57
*MUN	WA Managed Municipals A	SHMMX	C+	(877) 534-4627	C+ / 6.0	1.86	-3.05	0.29 /32	3.70 /90	3.19 /83	3.63	0.66
MUN	WA Managed Municipals C	SMMCX	B	(877) 534-4627	B- / 7.0	1.71	-3.32	-0.27 /13	3.10 /83	2.61 /73	3.21	1.23
MUN	WA Managed Municipals I	SMMYX	A-	(877) 534-4627	B / 8.1	1.87	-2.96	0.38 /35	3.80 /91	3.29 /85	3.88	0.58
MUS	WA Massachusetts Municipals A	SLMMX	D	(877) 534-4627	C / 4.5	0.95	-4.63	-1.30 / 2	3.48 /88	2.41 /69	2.97	0.87
MUS	WA Massachusetts Municipals C	SMALX	C-	(877) 534-4627	C+ / 5.8	0.81	-4.90	-1.85 / 1	2.91 /80	1.85 /55	2.53	1.42
MUS	WA Massachusetts Municipals I	LHMIX	B-	(877) 534-4627	B- / 7.3	1.06	-4.56	-1.15 / 3	3.66 /90	2.58 /72	3.25	0.78
USS ●	WA Mortgage Backed Securities 1	SGVSX	A	(877) 534-4627	C+ / 5.8	0.98	-0.36	1.52 /45	3.14 /63	3.83 /70	3.73	0.68
*USS	WA Mortgage Backed Securities A	SGVAX	C+	(877) 534-4627	C- / 3.5	0.91	-0.50	1.25 /42	2.87 /59	3.57 /67	3.31	0.94
MTG	WA Mortgage Backed Securities C	LWMSX	B-	(877) 534-4627	C- / 4.1	0.73	-0.76	0.63 /35	2.13 /45	2.82 /55	2.73	1.63
USS ●	WA Mortgage Backed Securities C1	SGSLX	B	(877) 534-4627	C / 4.5	0.81	-0.71	0.80 /37	2.39 /50	3.06 /59	3.00	1.40
USS	WA Mortgage Backed Securities I	SGSYX	A	(877) 534-4627	C+ / 5.8	0.98	-0.35	1.54 /45	3.18 /64	3.91 /71	3.73	0.65
MUH	WA Municipal High Income A	STXAX	C+	(877) 534-4627	B / 7.8	1.92	-3.42	1.40 /50	4.77 /97	3.73 /90	3.93	0.78
MUH	WA Municipal High Income C	SMHLX	B-	(877) 534-4627	B+ / 8.5	1.78	-3.72	0.81 /42	4.17 /94	3.14 /82	3.51	1.35
MUH	WA Municipal High Income I	LMHIX	A-	(877) 534-4627	A / 9.3	1.89	-3.38	1.53 /52	4.90 /97	3.88 /92	4.26	0.70
MUS	WA New Jersey Municipals A	SHNJX	D	(877) 534-4627	C- / 3.7	1.20	-3.90	-0.23 /14	2.85 /79	2.11 /62	3.60	0.76
MUS	WA New Jersey Municipals C	SNJLX	C-	(877) 534-4627	C / 4.9	1.06	-4.18	-0.79 / 6	2.24 /68	1.51 /47	3.17	1.33
MUS	WA New Jersey Municipals I	LNJIX	B	(877) 534-4627	C+ / 6.7	1.24	-3.82	-0.06 /17	3.02 /82	2.27 /66	3.93	0.70
MUS	WA New York Municipals A	SBNYX	C-	(877) 534-4627	C / 4.6	1.29	-3.53	-0.96 / 4	3.33 /86	2.20 /64	3.41	0.73
MUS	WA New York Municipals C	SBYLX	C+	(877) 534-4627	C+ / 5.8	1.14	-3.81	-1.53 / 2	2.74 /78	1.62 /49	2.96	1.30
MUS	WA New York Municipals I	SNPYX	A-	(877) 534-4627	B- / 7.3	1.32	-3.47	-0.83 / 6	3.47 /87	2.33 /67	3.69	0.62
MMF	WA NY Tax Free Money Market A	LNAXX	D+	(888) 425-6432	E+ / 0.8	0.02	0.04	0.06 /22	0.03 /10	0.02 / 9	0.06	N/A
MMF	WA NY Tax Free Money Market N	CIYXX	U	(888) 425-6432	U /	--	--	--	--	--	0.03	N/A
MUS	WA Oregon Municipals A	SHORX	C+	(877) 534-4627	C / 4.4	0.92	-3.44	-0.63 / 8	3.25 /85	2.22 /64	3.27	0.85
MUS	WA Oregon Municipals C	SORLX	B+	(877) 534-4627	C+ / 5.7	0.79	-3.72	-1.19 / 3	2.68 /77	1.66 /50	2.84	1.42
MUS	WA Oregon Municipals I	LMOOX	A+	(877) 534-4627	B- / 7.1	0.96	-3.45	-0.57 / 9	3.37 /86	2.36 /68	3.57	0.80
MUS	WA Pennsylvania Municipals A	SBPAX	A-	(877) 534-4627	C+ / 6.5	1.61	-2.35	0.97 /44	3.85 /91	2.54 /71	3.45	0.71
MUS	WA Pennsylvania Municipals C	SPALX	A+	(877) 534-4627	B- / 7.3	1.47	-2.64	0.31 /33	3.27 /85	1.96 /58	3.03	1.27
MUS	WA Pennsylvania Municipals I	LPPIX	A+	(877) 534-4627	B+ / 8.5	1.64	-2.30	1.00 /45	3.96 /93	2.65 /74	3.72	0.63
MMT	WA Premium Liquid Reserves	CIPXX	C-	(800) 331-1792	D- / 1.4	0.15	0.27	0.39 /31	0.14 /15	0.09 /15	0.32	N/A
MMT	WA Premium US Treasury Reserves	CIMXX	D+	(800) 331-1792	E+ / 0.7	0.02	0.03	0.08 /22	0.03 / 9	0.02 / 8	0.08	N/A
MMF	WA Select Tax Free Reserves Inv	LTFXX	C	(888) 425-6432	D- / 1.5	0.12	0.23	0.33 /33	0.12 /16	—	0.33	N/A
MUN	WA Short Duration Muni Income A	SHDAX	D	(877) 534-4627	E / 0.5	0.68	-0.43	0.09 /24	0.54 /25	0.75 /29	1.06	0.65
MUN	WA Short Duration Muni Income A2	SHDQX	U	(877) 534-4627	U /	0.59	-0.57	-0.16 /15	--	--	0.80	0.68
MUN	WA Short Duration Muni Income C	SHDLX	C-	(877) 534-4627	D- / 1.3	0.59	-0.60	-0.26 /14	0.19 /19	0.39 /23	0.73	1.01
MUN	WA Short Duration Muni Income I	SMDYX	C+	(877) 534-4627	D+ / 2.4	0.70	-0.40	0.17 /28	0.62 /27	0.84 /31	1.15	0.57
COI	WA Short Term Yield IS	LGSTX	U	(877) 534-4627	U /	0.20	0.48	1.00 /40	--	--	0.69	0.44
US	WA Short-Term Bond A	SBSTX	C	(877) 534-4627	D / 2.1	0.89	0.62	2.41 /52	0.98 /27	1.29 /31	1.57	0.77
COI	WA Short-Term Bond C	LWSOX	C	(877) 534-4627	D / 1.9	0.78	0.36	2.00 /49	0.22 /17	0.53 /22	0.94	1.55

99 Pct = Best
0 Pct = Worst

● Denotes fund is closed to new investors
* Denotes fund is included in Section II

www.thestreetratings.com

RISK			NET ASSETS		ASSET					Portfolio Turnover Ratio	Avg Coupon Rate	FUND MANAGER		MINIMUM		LOADS	
Risk Rating/Pts	3 Yr Avg Standard Deviation	Avg Dura-tion	NAV As of 2/28/17	Total $(Mil)	Cash %	Gov. Bond %	Muni. Bond %	Corp. Bond %	Other %			Manager Quality Pct	Manager Tenure (Years)	Initial Purch. $	Additional Purch. $	Front End Load	Back End Load
B /7.9	2.2	4.3	10.87	1	10	36	1	31	22	106	2.3	25	8	1,000	50	0.0	0.0
B /7.8	2.3	4.3	10.85	283	10	36	1	31	22	106	2.3	69	8	1,000,000	0	0.0	0.0
B /7.9	2.3	4.3	10.86	264	10	36	1	31	22	106	2.3	71	8	0	0	0.0	0.0
B /7.8	2.3	4.3	10.85	N/A	10	36	1	31	22	106	2.3	41	8	0	0	0.0	0.0
B- /7.2	2.6	4.5	6.38	1,233	0	0	99	0	1	8	4.9	29	10	1,000	50	2.3	0.0
B- /7.2	2.7	4.5	6.39	660	0	0	99	0	1	8	4.9	14	10	1,000	50	0.0	0.0
B- /7.2	2.6	4.5	6.38	733	0	0	99	0	1	8	4.9	34	10	1,000,000	0	0.0	0.0
A+ /9.9	0.1	N/A	1.00	21	100	0	0	0	0	0	0.3	47	N/A	1,000	50	0.0	0.0
D- /1.3	5.9	4.6	10.76	61	6	42	0	44	8	295	3.3	97	4	1,000	50	4.3	0.0
D- /1.3	5.9	4.6	10.67	29	6	42	0	44	8	295	3.3	96	4	1,000	50	0.0	0.0
D- /1.2	6.0	4.6	10.77	27	6	42	0	44	8	295	3.3	97	4	0	0	0.0	0.0
D- /1.3	6.0	4.6	10.75	660	6	42	0	44	8	295	3.3	97	4	1,000,000	0	0.0	0.0
D- /1.3	6.0	4.6	10.77	198	6	42	0	44	8	295	3.3	97	4	0	0	0.0	0.0
C /4.8	3.2	5.3	16.15	21	0	0	100	0	0	5	5.3	63	10	0	0	0.0	0.0
C /4.9	3.2	5.3	16.20	2,999	0	0	100	0	0	5	5.3	61	10	1,000	50	4.3	0.0
C /4.9	3.2	5.3	16.21	683	0	0	100	0	0	5	5.3	32	10	1,000	50	0.0	0.0
C /4.9	3.2	5.3	16.23	1,034	0	0	100	0	0	5	5.3	63	10	1,000,000	0	0.0	0.0
C- /4.2	3.4	6.3	12.54	56	0	0	99	0	1	15	5.1	38	11	1,000	50	4.3	0.0
C- /4.1	3.4	6.3	12.52	14	0	0	99	0	1	15	5.1	20	11	1,000	50	0.0	0.0
C- /4.1	3.4	6.3	12.54	29	0	0	99	0	1	15	5.1	51	11	1,000,000	0	0.0	0.0
B /8.0	2.1	3.6	10.54	32	0	4	0	14	82	137	3.8	86	4	0	0	0.0	0.0
B /8.0	2.1	3.6	10.53	535	0	4	0	14	82	137	3.8	84	4	1,000	50	4.3	0.0
B /8.0	2.2	3.6	10.53	31	0	4	0	14	82	137	3.8	35	4	1,000	50	0.0	0.0
B /8.0	2.1	3.6	10.54	14	0	4	0	14	82	137	3.8	80	4	1,000	50	0.0	0.0
B /8.0	2.1	3.6	10.58	224	0	4	0	14	82	137	3.8	86	4	1,000,000	0	0.0	0.0
D+ /2.9	3.6	5.8	14.09	300	0	0	99	0	1	9	5.6	78	10	1,000	50	4.3	0.0
D+ /2.8	3.6	5.8	14.01	105	0	0	99	0	1	9	5.6	65	10	1,000	50	0.0	0.0
C- /3.0	3.6	5.8	14.01	222	0	0	99	0	1	9	5.6	79	10	1,000,000	0	0.0	0.0
C /5.5	3.0	5.4	12.19	162	0	0	99	0	1	22	5.2	30	11	1,000	50	4.3	0.0
C /5.3	3.0	5.4	12.19	46	0	0	99	0	1	22	5.2	13	11	1,000	50	0.0	0.0
C /5.5	3.0	5.4	12.20	35	0	0	99	0	1	22	5.2	35	11	1,000,000	0	0.0	0.0
C+ /5.8	3.0	5.3	13.12	499	0	0	100	0	0	7	5.0	56	10	1,000	50	4.3	0.0
C+ /5.7	3.0	5.3	13.11	89	0	0	100	0	0	7	5.0	27	10	1,000	50	0.0	0.0
C+ /5.7	3.0	5.3	13.11	108	0	0	100	0	0	7	5.0	60	10	1,000,000	0	0.0	0.0
A+ /9.9	N/A	N/A	1.00	36	100	0	0	0	0	0	0.1	41	6	1,000	50	0.0	0.0
U /	N/A	N/A	1.00	38	100	0	0	0	0	0	0.0	39	32	0	0	0.0	0.0
C+ /6.9	2.8	5.2	10.23	48	0	0	99	0	1	8	4.9	63	11	1,000	50	4.3	0.0
C+ /6.8	2.8	5.2	10.18	16	0	0	99	0	1	8	4.9	35	11	1,000	50	0.0	0.0
C+ /6.9	2.8	5.2	10.23	22	0	0	99	0	1	8	4.9	66	11	1,000,000	0	0.0	0.0
C+ /6.8	2.8	4.7	12.77	117	0	0	99	0	1	17	5.0	75	10	1,000	50	4.3	0.0
C+ /6.9	2.8	4.7	12.71	68	0	0	99	0	1	17	5.0	61	10	1,000	50	0.0	0.0
C+ /6.9	2.7	4.7	12.76	30	0	0	99	0	1	17	5.0	77	10	1,000,000	0	0.0	0.0
A+ /9.9	0.1	N/A	1.00	24	100	0	0	0	0	0	0.3	47	N/A	100,000	50	0.0	0.0
A+ /9.9	N/A	N/A	1.00	109	100	0	0	0	0	0	0.1	41	26	100,000	50	0.0	0.0
A+ /9.9	0.1	N/A	1.00	33	100	0	0	0	0	0	0.3	47	N/A	1,000,000	50	0.0	0.0
A /9.4	0.8	1.7	5.08	306	0	0	100	0	0	30	3.4	28	14	1,000	50	2.3	0.0
U /	N/A	1.7	5.08	1	0	0	100	0	0	30	3.4	N/A	14	1,000	50	2.3	0.0
A /9.4	0.9	1.7	5.08	907	0	0	100	0	0	30	3.4	18	14	1,000	50	0.0	0.0
A /9.5	0.8	1.7	5.08	403	0	0	100	0	0	30	3.4	32	14	1,000,000	0	0.0	0.0
U /	N/A	0.2	10.01	N/A	0	0	0	0	100	36	0.0	N/A	3	1,000,000	0	0.0	0.0
A /9.4	0.9	2.4	3.87	41	10	1	0	55	34	34	2.3	68	3	1,000	50	2.3	0.0
A /9.4	0.9	2.4	3.87	8	10	1	0	55	34	34	2.3	24	3	1,000	50	0.0	0.0

					PERFORMANCE						Incl. in Returns	
99 Pct = Best / 0 Pct = Worst							Total Return % through 2/28/17					
					Perfor-mance				Annualized		Dividend	Expense
Fund Type	Fund Name	Ticker Symbol	Overall Investment Rating	Phone	Rating/Pts	3 Mo	6 Mo	1Yr / Pct	3Yr / Pct	5Yr / Pct	Yield	Ratio
US	● WA Short-Term Bond C1	SSTLX	C+	(877) 534-4627	D+ / 2.6	0.82	0.23	2.13 /50	0.71 /23	1.03 /28	1.33	1.04
US	WA Short-Term Bond I	SBSYX	B	(877) 534-4627	C- / 3.5	0.95	0.76	2.69 /55	1.26 /32	1.61 /36	1.88	0.50
COI	WA Short-Term Bond IS	LWSTX	B+	(877) 534-4627	C- / 3.6	0.97	0.79	2.75 /55	1.31 /32	1.58 /36	1.93	0.46
COI	WA Short-Term Bond R	LWARX	C+	(877) 534-4627	D+ / 2.7	1.08	0.47	2.35 /52	0.75 /24	--	1.29	1.15
MMF	WA Tax Free Reserves A	LWAXX	U	(888) 425-6432	U /	--	--	--	--	--	0.07	N/A
MMF	WA Tax Free Reserves C	LTCXX	U	(888) 425-6432	U /	--	--	--	--	--	0.04	N/A
MMF	WA Tax Free Reserves N	CIXXX	U	(888) 425-6432	U /	--	--	--	--	--	0.04	N/A
GL	WA Total Return Unconstrained A	WAUAX	B-	(888) 425-6432	C / 5.2	2.13	2.51	9.42 /78	2.49 /52	2.82 /55	2.62	1.40
GL	WA Total Return Unconstrained C	WAUCX	B+	(888) 425-6432	C+ / 5.9	2.07	2.29	8.79 /76	1.78 /39	2.06 /43	2.17	1.88
GL	WA Total Return Unconstrained FI	WARIX	A	(888) 425-6432	C+ / 6.9	2.15	2.55	9.58 /78	2.53 /52	2.87 /56	2.88	1.16
GL	WA Total Return Unconstrained I	WAARX	A	(888) 425-6432	B- / 7.2	2.21	2.68	9.85 /79	2.80 /58	3.13 /60	3.12	0.91
GL	WA Total Return Unconstrained IS	WAASX	A	(888) 425-6432	B- / 7.3	2.24	2.74	9.99 /79	2.87 /59	3.19 /61	3.24	0.80
GL	WA Total Return Unconstrained R	WAURX	B+	(888) 425-6432	C+ / 6.5	2.10	2.45	9.36 /77	2.26 /48	2.55 /50	2.68	1.42
MMT	WA US Treasury Reserves N	CISXX	U	(888) 425-6432	U /	--	--	--	--	--	0.03	N/A
COI	Waddell & Reed Adv Bond Fund A	UNBDX	D-	(888) 923-3355	D+ / 2.4	1.30	-2.08	3.30 /58	2.35 /49	2.02 /42	2.09	0.96
COI	● Waddell & Reed Adv Bond Fund B	WBABX	D-	(888) 923-3355	D+ / 2.6	1.13	-2.56	2.08 /50	1.03 /28	0.74 /24	0.86	2.26
COI	Waddell & Reed Adv Bond Fund C	WCABX	D-	(888) 923-3355	C- / 3.2	1.08	-2.49	2.41 /52	1.38 /33	1.07 /28	1.35	1.87
COI	Waddell & Reed Adv Bond Fund Y	WYABX	C	(888) 923-3355	C / 5.3	1.36	-1.94	3.59 /60	2.64 /55	2.31 /46	2.50	0.67
MMT	Waddell & Reed Adv Cash Mgmt A	UNCXX	D+	(888) 923-3355	E+ / 0.7	0.03	0.04	0.05 /21	0.03 / 9	0.03 /10	0.05	N/A
MMT	● Waddell & Reed Adv Cash Mgmt B	WCBXX	U	(888) 923-3355	U /	--	--	--	--	--	0.02	N/A
GL	Waddell & Reed Adv Global Bond A	UNHHX	E+	(888) 923-3355	D+ / 2.4	2.52	2.02	8.62 /76	1.02 /28	1.81 /39	1.46	1.19
GL	● Waddell & Reed Adv Global Bond B	WGBBX	E+	(888) 923-3355	D+ / 2.7	2.16	1.33	7.51 /73	-0.23 / 4	0.51 /22	0.26	2.54
GL	Waddell & Reed Adv Global Bond C	WGBCX	E+	(888) 923-3355	C- / 3.3	2.30	1.60	7.70 /74	0.18 /16	0.97 /27	0.72	2.02
GL	Waddell & Reed Adv Global Bond Y	WGBYX	D-	(888) 923-3355	C / 5.4	2.33	2.19	9.01 /76	1.38 /33	2.19 /45	1.90	0.83
USS	Waddell & Reed Adv Gov Secs A	UNGVX	E+	(888) 923-3355	E / 0.3	0.53	-2.75	-1.22 / 3	0.93 /27	0.27 /19	1.30	1.07
USS	● Waddell & Reed Adv Gov Secs B	WGVBX	E+	(888) 923-3355	E- / 0.2	0.25	-3.29	-2.33 / 1	-0.24 / 4	-0.88 / 2	0.20	2.24
USS	Waddell & Reed Adv Gov Secs C	WGVCX	E+	(888) 923-3355	E / 0.3	0.31	-3.18	-2.10 / 1	0.07 /11	-0.57 / 3	0.44	1.88
USS	Waddell & Reed Adv Gov Secs Y	WGVYX	D-	(888) 923-3355	D+ / 2.3	0.60	-2.61	-0.93 / 5	1.24 /31	0.58 /22	1.66	0.74
*COH	Waddell & Reed Adv High Income A	UNHIX	C-	(888) 923-3355	B+ / 8.3	4.61	6.47	22.04 /98	3.44 /68	7.09 /97	6.28	1.01
COH	● Waddell & Reed Adv High Income B	WBHIX	C-	(888) 923-3355	B+ / 8.5	4.30	5.83	20.55 /97	2.22 /47	5.86 /91	5.48	2.18
COH	Waddell & Reed Adv High Income C	WCHIX	C	(888) 923-3355	B+ / 8.8	4.41	6.04	21.05 /97	2.62 /54	6.25 /94	5.88	1.79
COH	Waddell & Reed Adv High Income Y	WYHIX	C+	(888) 923-3355	A / 9.5	4.66	6.58	22.33 /98	3.71 /72	7.38 /97	6.90	0.74
*MUN	Waddell & Reed Adv Muni Bond A	UNMBX	B+	(888) 923-3355	C / 5.1	1.51	-1.91	0.71 /41	3.15 /84	2.71 /75	2.75	0.90
MUN	● Waddell & Reed Adv Muni Bond B	WBMBX	B+	(888) 923-3355	C / 5.4	1.28	-2.39	-0.26 /14	2.18 /67	1.71 /52	1.90	1.82
MUN	Waddell & Reed Adv Muni Bond C	WCMBX	B+	(888) 923-3355	C / 5.5	1.29	-2.34	-0.16 /15	2.27 /69	1.83 /55	1.99	1.76
MUN	● Waddell & Reed Adv Muni Bond Y	WYMBX	U	(888) 923-3355	U /	1.55	-1.83	--	--	--	0.00	0.72
*MUH	Waddell & Reed Adv Muni High Inc A	UMUHX	B	(888) 923-3355	B / 8.1	1.94	-2.07	1.98 /57	4.76 /96	4.15 /94	4.37	0.90
MUH	● Waddell & Reed Adv Muni High Inc B	WBMHX	B+	(888) 923-3355	B / 8.2	1.72	-2.52	1.02 /45	3.76 /90	3.15 /82	3.59	1.87
MUH	Waddell & Reed Adv Muni High Inc C	WCMHX	B+	(888) 923-3355	B+ / 8.4	1.74	-2.47	1.14 /47	3.89 /92	3.29 /85	3.71	1.73
MUH	Waddell & Reed Adv Muni High Inc Y	WAMHX	U	(888) 923-3355	U /	1.99	-1.99	--	--	--	0.00	0.75
US	Wasatch Hoisington US Treasury	WHOSX	D-	(800) 551-1700	C+ / 6.8	1.69	-14.66	-5.86 / 0	7.03 /96	3.25 /62	2.17	0.67
GEI	Wasatch-1st Source Income Investor	FMEQX	C-	(800) 766-8938	D+ / 2.3	0.64	-0.70	1.02 /40	1.38 /33	1.23 /30	1.79	0.73
MUH	Wasmer Schroeder Hi Yld Muni Inst	WSHYX	U	(888) 263-6443	U /	1.76	-3.22	1.65 /53	--	--	3.82	0.96
GL	Wavelength Interest Rate Neutral	WAVLX	D-		C+ / 5.7	3.04	1.95	9.94 /79	1.45 /34	--	2.09	2.35
GEN	Weitz Core Plus Income Ins	WCPBX	U	(800) 232-4161	U /	1.10	-0.26	6.86 /72	--	--	2.57	1.38
GEN	Weitz Core Plus Income Inv	WCPNX	U	(800) 232-4161	U /	1.05	-0.37	6.65 /72	--	--	2.37	2.36
MUS	Weitz Nebraska Tax Free Income Fd	WNTFX	C	(800) 232-4161	D+ / 2.5	1.13	-1.14	-0.70 / 7	0.82 /32	0.91 /33	1.71	0.78
GEI	Weitz Short Dur Income Inst	WEFIX	B+	(800) 232-4161	C- / 4.0	0.73	0.21	3.28 /58	1.62 /37	1.88 /40	2.12	0.63
COI	Weitz Short Dur Income Inv	WSHNX	B	(800) 232-4161	C- / 3.6	0.67	0.02	3.03 /57	1.36 /33	1.66 /37	1.88	0.92
MMT	Wells Fargo 100% Trsry MM A	WFTXX	U	(800) 222-8222	U /	--	--	--	--	--	0.01	N/A
MMT	Wells Fargo 100% Trsry MM Adm	WTRXX	D+	(800) 222-8222	E+ / 0.8	0.06	0.07	0.09 /22	0.03 / 9	0.02 / 8	0.09	N/A
USA	Wells Fargo 100% Trsry MM Inst	WOTXX	U	(800) 222-8222	U /	0.08	0.12	0.19 /25	--	--	0.19	0.40

● Denotes fund is closed to new investors
* Denotes fund is included in Section II

www.thestreetratings.com

RISK Risk Rating/Pts	3 Yr Avg Standard Deviation	Avg Duration	NET ASSETS NAV As of 2/28/17	Total $(Mil)	ASSET Cash %	Gov. Bond %	Muni. Bond %	Corp. Bond %	Other %	Portfolio Turnover Ratio	Avg Coupon Rate	FUND MANAGER Manager Quality Pct	Manager Tenure (Years)	MINIMUM Initial Purch. $	Additional Purch. $	LOADS Front End Load	Back End Load
A /9.3	0.9	2.4	3.87	48	10	1	0	55	34	34	2.3	59	3	1,000	50	0.0	0.0
A /9.4	0.9	2.4	3.87	60	10	1	0	55	34	34	2.3	74	3	1,000,000	0	0.0	0.0
A /9.3	0.9	2.4	3.87	429	10	1	0	55	34	34	2.3	68	3	0	0	0.0	0.0
A /9.3	0.9	2.4	3.87	N/A	10	1	0	55	34	34	2.3	48	3	0	0	0.0	0.0
U /	N/A	N/A	1.00	73	100	0	0	0	0	0	0.1	42	N/A	1,000	50	0.0	0.0
U /	N/A	N/A	1.00	1	100	0	0	0	0	0	0.0	41	N/A	1,000	50	0.0	0.0
U /	N/A	N/A	1.00	14	100	0	0	0	0	0	0.0	41	N/A	0	0	0.0	0.0
C+/6.8	2.8	-0.5	10.45	206	8	24	0	42	26	59	3.4	90	11	1,000	50	4.3	0.0
C+/6.6	2.8	-0.5	10.45	17	8	24	0	42	26	59	3.4	85	11	1,000	50	0.0	0.0
C+/6.6	2.8	-0.5	10.44	178	8	24	0	42	26	59	3.4	90	11	0	0	0.0	0.0
C+/6.7	2.8	-0.5	10.45	744	8	24	0	42	26	59	3.4	91	11	1,000,000	0	0.0	0.0
C+/6.2	2.9	-0.5	10.43	73	8	24	0	42	26	59	3.4	92	11	0	0	0.0	0.0
C+/6.3	2.9	-0.5	10.45	N/A	8	24	0	42	26	59	3.4	88	11	0	0	0.0	0.0
U /	N/A	N/A	1.00	641	100	0	0	0	0	0	0.0	N/A	26	0	0	0.0	0.0
C /5.3	3.1	6.0	6.20	476	0	2	2	77	19	88	3.6	27	2	750	0	5.8	0.0
C /5.4	3.0	6.0	6.20	2	0	2	2	77	19	88	3.6	5	2	750	0	0.0	0.0
C /5.3	3.0	6.0	6.19	9	0	2	2	77	19	88	3.6	8	2	750	0	0.0	0.0
C /5.4	3.0	6.0	6.20	710	0	2	2	77	19	88	3.6	40	2	0	0	0.0	0.0
A+/9.9	N/A	N/A	1.00	1,433	100	0	0	0	0	0	0.1	41	19	750	0	0.0	0.0
U /	N/A	N/A	1.00	1	100	0	0	0	0	0	0.0	N/A	19	750	0	0.0	0.0
D+/2.8	4.2	2.5	3.71	265	2	32	1	58	7	16	4.6	81	15	750	0	5.8	0.0
D+/2.7	4.3	2.5	3.71	1	2	32	1	58	7	16	4.6	55	15	750	0	0.0	0.0
D+/2.8	4.2	2.5	3.71	5	2	32	1	58	7	16	4.6	68	15	750	0	0.0	0.0
D+/2.8	4.2	2.5	3.71	285	2	32	1	58	7	16	4.6	84	15	0	0	0.0	0.0
C+/6.6	2.8	5.0	5.41	101	0	54	0	4	42	43	2.7	17	2	750	0	4.3	0.0
C+/6.6	2.8	5.0	5.41	1	0	54	0	4	42	43	2.7	3	2	750	0	0.0	0.0
C+/6.6	2.8	5.0	5.41	3	0	54	0	4	42	43	2.7	5	2	750	0	0.0	0.0
C+/6.7	2.8	5.0	5.41	140	0	54	0	4	42	43	2.7	25	2	0	0	0.0	0.0
E+/0.8	6.1	3.1	6.81	1,219	1	0	0	82	17	38	7.4	9	3	750	0	5.8	0.0
E+/0.8	6.1	3.1	6.81	5	1	0	0	82	17	38	7.4	1	3	750	0	0.0	0.0
E+/0.8	6.1	3.1	6.81	35	1	0	0	82	17	38	7.4	3	3	750	0	0.0	0.0
E+/0.8	6.1	3.1	6.81	798	1	0	0	82	17	38	7.4	14	3	0	0	0.0	0.0
B /7.6	2.5	5.2	7.47	539	0	0	97	0	3	5	3.9	66	17	750	0	4.3	0.0
B /7.6	2.5	5.2	7.46	1	0	0	97	0	3	5	3.9	26	17	750	0	0.0	0.0
B-/7.5	2.5	5.2	7.46	14	0	0	97	0	3	5	3.9	27	17	750	0	0.0	0.0
U /	N/A	5.2	7.47	282	0	0	97	0	3	5	3.9	N/A	17	0	0	0.0	0.0
C-/3.9	3.1	6.1	4.77	660	1	0	97	1	1	4	5.7	83	9	750	0	4.3	0.0
C-/3.9	3.1	6.1	4.77	1	1	0	97	1	1	4	5.7	71	9	750	0	0.0	0.0
C-/3.9	3.1	6.1	4.77	22	1	0	97	1	1	4	5.7	73	9	750	0	0.0	0.0
U /	N/A	6.1	4.77	135	1	0	97	1	1	4	5.7	N/A	9	0	0	0.0	0.0
E-/0.0	13.5	22.9	15.87	288	1	98	0	0	1	59	1.8	58	21	2,000	100	0.0	2.0
B+/8.7	1.6	3.0	10.08	100	2	15	5	47	31	37	7.6	42	9	2,000	100	0.0	2.0
U /	N/A	4.7	10.44	102	4	0	95	0	1	27	5.0	N/A	3	100,000	500	0.0	1.0
D /1.8	5.4	N/A	9.89	21	6	31	0	54	9	103	0.0	86	4	100,000	100	0.0	0.0
U /	N/A	3.5	10.27	17	3	30	2	35	30	26	3.5	N/A	3	1,000,000	25	0.0	0.0
U /	N/A	3.5	10.27	6	3	30	2	35	30	26	3.5	N/A	3	2,500	25	0.0	0.0
A-/9.0	1.4	2.5	9.93	62	1	1	96	0	2	13	3.8	20	32	2,500	25	0.0	0.0
A-/9.1	1.2	2.2	12.35	1,107	0	24	0	41	35	23	3.1	71	21	1,000,000	25	0.0	0.0
A-/9.1	1.2	2.2	12.32	92	0	24	0	41	35	23	3.1	61	21	2,500	25	0.0	0.0
U /	N/A	N/A	1.00	339	100	0	0	0	0	0	0.0	N/A	N/A	1,000	100	0.0	0.0
A+/9.9	N/A	N/A	1.00	1,299	100	0	0	0	0	0	0.1	39	N/A	1,000,000	0	0.0	0.0
U /	N/A	N/A	1.00	4,090	0	0	0	0	100	0	0.0	N/A	N/A	10,000,000	0	0.0	0.0

								PERFORMANCE						
99 Pct = Best									Total Return % through 2/28/17				Incl. in Returns	
0 Pct = Worst					Perfor-						Annualized		Dividend	Expense
Fund		Ticker	Overall Investment		mance									
Type	Fund Name	Symbol	Rating	Phone	Rating/Pts	3 Mo	6 Mo	1Yr / Pct	3Yr / Pct	5Yr / Pct			Yield	Ratio
MMT	Wells Fargo 100% Trsry MM S	NWTXX	U	(800) 222-8222	U /	--	--	--	--	--			0.01	N/A
MMT	Wells Fargo 100% Trsry MM Swp		U	(800) 222-8222	U /	--	--	--	--	--			0.01	N/A
MTG	Wells Fargo Adj Rate Govt A	ESAAX	D	(800) 222-8222	E / 0.5	0.31	0.39	0.68 / 36	0.28 / 18	0.52 / 22			0.77	0.79
MTG	Wells Fargo Adj Rate Govt Adm	ESADX	C+	(800) 222-8222	D / 1.9	0.34	0.46	0.82 / 38	0.42 / 20	0.67 / 23			0.93	0.73
MTG	Wells Fargo Adj Rate Govt C	ESACX	D	(800) 222-8222	E / 0.3	0.24	0.13	0.04 / 20	-0.43 / 4	-0.20 / 4			0.04	1.54
MTG	Wells Fargo Adj Rate Govt I	EKIZX	C+	(800) 222-8222	D / 2.2	0.49	0.64	1.08 / 40	0.60 / 22	0.83 / 25			1.07	0.46
MUS	Wells Fargo CA Ltd Tax Fr A	SFCIX	C-	(800) 222-8222	D+ / 2.4	1.38	-1.62	-0.49 / 10	1.37 / 45	1.83 / 55			1.62	0.83
MUS	Wells Fargo CA Ltd Tax Fr Adm	SCTIX	B	(800) 222-8222	C / 4.3	1.54	-1.56	-0.23 / 14	1.60 / 51	2.04 / 60			1.85	0.77
MUS	Wells Fargo CA Ltd Tax Fr C	SFCCX	D+	(800) 222-8222	D / 1.9	1.29	-1.99	-1.23 / 3	0.61 / 27	1.07 / 37			0.89	1.58
MUN	Wells Fargo CA Ltd Tax Fr Inst	SFCNX	U	(800) 222-8222	U /	1.47	-1.52	-0.22 / 14	--	--			1.95	0.50
MUS	Wells Fargo CA Tax Fr A	SCTAX	D+	(800) 222-8222	C+ / 5.7	2.10	-4.28	-0.41 / 11	3.86 / 92	4.01 / 93			2.91	0.82
MUS	Wells Fargo CA Tax Fr Adm	SGCAX	B	(800) 222-8222	B / 8.2	2.06	-4.18	-0.21 / 14	4.07 / 93	4.20 / 95			3.25	0.76
MUS	Wells Fargo CA Tax Fr C	SCTCX	C-	(800) 222-8222	C+ / 6.6	1.88	-4.61	-1.17 / 3	3.10 / 83	3.22 / 84			2.27	1.57
MUN	Wells Fargo CA Tax Fr Inst	SGTIX	U	(800) 222-8222	U /	2.07	-4.14	-0.14 / 15	--	--			3.33	0.49
MMT	Wells Fargo Cash Inv MM Sel	WFQXX	C	(800) 222-8222	D / 1.7	0.20	0.36	0.57 / 35	0.28 / 18	0.21 / 19			0.52	N/A
MUS	Wells Fargo CO Tax Fr A	NWCOX	C-	(800) 222-8222	C+ / 5.8	2.11	-3.86	--	3.80 / 91	3.53 / 88			2.95	0.93
MUS	Wells Fargo CO Tax Fr Adm	NCOTX	B+	(800) 222-8222	B+ / 8.4	2.17	-3.74	0.25 / 31	4.09 / 93	3.79 / 91			3.35	0.87
MUS	Wells Fargo CO Tax Fr C	WCOTX	C	(800) 222-8222	C+ / 6.7	1.92	-4.21	-0.75 / 6	3.06 / 83	2.76 / 75			2.31	1.68
GEI	Wells Fargo Conv Income Inst	WCIIX	C+	(800) 222-8222	D / 2.2	0.28	0.53	1.15 / 41	0.61 / 22	--			0.95	0.36
GEI	Wells Fargo Core Bond A	MBFAX	D-	(800) 222-8222	D+ / 2.5	1.02	-2.11	1.33 / 43	2.36 / 49	2.33 / 47			1.32	0.83
GEI	Wells Fargo Core Bond Adm	MNTRX	C-	(800) 222-8222	C / 4.6	1.05	-2.06	1.49 / 44	2.44 / 51	2.42 / 48			1.46	0.77
GEI	Wells Fargo Core Bond C	MBFCX	D-	(800) 222-8222	C- / 3.1	0.84	-2.50	0.57 / 34	1.58 / 36	1.56 / 35			0.63	1.58
GEI	Wells Fargo Core Bond I	MBFIX	C	(800) 222-8222	C / 5.0	1.13	-1.93	1.69 / 46	2.73 / 57	2.71 / 53			1.75	0.50
COI	Wells Fargo Core Bond R	WTRRX	D	(800) 222-8222	C- / 3.9	0.89	-2.30	1.08 / 40	2.08 / 45	2.06 / 43			1.13	1.08
COI	Wells Fargo Core Bond R4	MBFRX	C-	(800) 222-8222	C / 4.8	1.10	-1.98	1.59 / 45	2.63 / 55	--			1.65	0.60
COI	Wells Fargo Core Bond R6	WTRIX	C	(800) 222-8222	C / 5.1	1.14	-1.98	1.74 / 47	2.78 / 57	--			1.80	0.45
USS	Wells Fargo Core Plus Bond A	STYAX	C-	(800) 222-8222	C+ / 5.8	2.31	-0.65	6.10 / 70	3.74 / 72	3.22 / 61			2.80	0.94
COI	Wells Fargo Core Plus Bond Adm	WIPDX	B	(800) 222-8222	B- / 7.3	2.26	-0.60	6.22 / 71	3.86 / 74	3.34 / 63			3.05	0.88
USS	Wells Fargo Core Plus Bond C	WFIPX	C+	(800) 222-8222	C+ / 6.2	2.11	-1.03	5.30 / 68	2.95 / 60	2.44 / 49			2.17	1.69
USS	Wells Fargo Core Plus Bond Inst	WIPIX	B	(800) 222-8222	B- / 7.5	2.31	-0.50	6.39 / 71	4.01 / 75	3.52 / 66			3.21	0.61
* MUN	Wells Fargo CoreBuilder A	WFCMX	B+	(800) 222-8222	B+ / 8.6	2.02	-3.53	-0.10 / 16	4.35 / 95	4.80 / 97			3.23	0.07
MMT	Wells Fargo Csh Inv MM Adm	WFAXX	C-	(800) 222-8222	D- / 1.3	0.16	0.26	0.37 / 31	0.14 / 15	0.09 / 15			0.32	N/A
MMT	Wells Fargo Csh Inv MM I	WFIXX	C	(800) 222-8222	D / 1.6	0.19	0.34	0.51 / 33	0.22 / 17	0.15 / 17			0.45	N/A
MMT	Wells Fargo Csh Inv MM S	NWIXX	C-	(800) 222-8222	D- / 1.1	0.12	0.19	0.21 / 26	0.08 / 12	0.05 / 12			0.15	N/A
GES	Wells Fargo Dvsfd Inc Bldr A	EKSAX	C+	(800) 222-8222	A+ / 9.6	4.89	5.34	18.09 / 94	6.38 / 94	7.81 / 98			3.22	1.07
GES	Wells Fargo Dvsfd Inc Bldr Adm	EKSDX	B	(800) 222-8222	A+ / 9.9	4.84	5.33	18.20 / 94	6.56 / 95	7.97 / 98			3.57	0.99
GES ●	Wells Fargo Dvsfd Inc Bldr B	EKSBX	B	(800) 222-8222	A+ / 9.7	4.68	4.94	17.35 / 93	5.54 / 89	6.94 / 96			2.70	1.82
GES	Wells Fargo Dvsfd Inc Bldr C	EKSCX	B	(800) 222-8222	A+ / 9.7	4.52	4.78	17.19 / 92	5.58 / 89	7.00 / 96			2.70	1.82
GES	Wells Fargo Dvsfd Inc Bldr Inst	EKSYX	B	(800) 222-8222	A+ / 9.9	5.07	5.61	18.64 / 94	6.83 / 95	8.23 / 98			3.75	0.74
USS	Wells Fargo Govt Secs A	SGVDX	E+	(800) 222-8222	E+ / 0.8	0.60	-2.44	-0.64 / 8	1.73 / 39	1.32 / 32			1.13	0.88
USS	Wells Fargo Govt Secs Adm	WGSDX	C-	(800) 222-8222	C- / 3.4	0.66	-2.33	-0.43 / 11	1.98 / 43	1.54 / 35			1.39	0.82
USS	Wells Fargo Govt Secs C	WGSCX	D-	(800) 222-8222	D / 1.9	0.42	-2.80	-1.38 / 2	1.00 / 28	0.57 / 22			0.42	1.63
USS	Wells Fargo Govt Secs I	SGVIX	C-	(800) 222-8222	C- / 3.7	0.69	-2.26	-0.27 / 13	2.11 / 45	1.70 / 38			1.55	0.55
MMT	Wells Fargo Gv MM A	WFGXX	U	(800) 222-8222	U /	--	--	--	--	--			0.01	N/A
MMT	Wells Fargo Gv MM Adm	WGAXX	D+	(800) 222-8222	E+ / 0.9	0.06	0.09	0.12 / 23	0.05 / 10	0.03 / 10			0.12	N/A
MMT	Wells Fargo Gv MM I	GVIXX	C-	(800) 222-8222	D- / 1.1	0.09	0.16	0.26 / 28	0.10 / 13	0.07 / 13			0.26	N/A
MMT	Wells Fargo Gv MM S	NWGXX	D+	(800) 222-8222	E+ / 0.6	0.02	0.02	0.03 / 20	0.02 / 8	0.01 / 6			0.03	N/A
MMT	Wells Fargo Gv MM Select	WFFXX	U	(800) 222-8222	U /	0.11	0.19	0.32 / 30	--	--			0.32	N/A
MMT	Wells Fargo Gv MM Sweep		U	(800) 222-8222	U /	--	--	--	--	--			0.01	N/A
MMT	Wells Fargo Heritage MM Adm	SHMXX	C-	(800) 222-8222	D- / 1.3	0.14	0.23	0.34 / 30	0.13 / 14	0.08 / 14			0.31	N/A
MMT	Wells Fargo Heritage MM Inst	SHIXX	C	(800) 222-8222	D- / 1.5	0.17	0.30	0.47 / 33	0.20 / 17	0.13 / 16			0.44	N/A
MMT	Wells Fargo Heritage MM Sel	WFJXX	C	(800) 222-8222	D / 1.7	0.19	0.34	0.55 / 34	0.27 / 18	0.20 / 18			0.51	N/A

● Denotes fund is closed to new investors
* Denotes fund is included in Section II

www.thestreetratings.com

RISK			NET ASSETS		ASSET							FUND MANAGER		MINIMUM		LOADS	
Risk Rating/Pts	3 Yr Avg Standard Deviation	Avg Dura-tion	NAV As of 2/28/17	Total $(Mil)	Cash %	Gov. Bond %	Muni. Bond %	Corp. Bond %	Other %	Portfolio Turnover Ratio	Avg Coupon Rate	Manager Quality Pct	Manager Tenure (Years)	Initial Purch. $	Additional Purch. $	Front End Load	Back End Load
U /	N/A	N/A	1.00	3,587	100	0	0	0	0	0	0.0	N/A	N/A	100,000	0	0.0	0.0
U /	N/A	N/A	1.00	667	100	0	0	0	0	0	0.0	N/A	N/A	0	0	0.0	0.0
A+ / 9.9	0.4	0.7	9.01	154	3	2	0	0	95	13	2.6	54	9	1,000	100	2.0	0.0
A+ / 9.9	0.4	0.7	9.01	34	3	2	0	0	95	13	2.6	60	9	1,000,000	0	0.0	0.0
A+ / 9.9	0.4	0.7	9.02	86	3	2	0	0	95	13	2.6	22	9	1,000	100	0.0	0.0
A+ / 9.8	0.4	0.7	9.02	528	3	2	0	0	95	13	2.6	65	9	1,000,000	0	0.0	0.0
B+ / 8.3	2.0	3.3	10.75	160	2	0	97	0	1	21	3.9	18	8	1,000	100	2.0	0.0
B+ / 8.3	2.0	3.3	10.59	139	2	0	97	0	1	21	3.9	23	8	1,000,000	0	0.0	0.0
B+ / 8.3	2.0	3.3	10.75	37	2	0	97	0	1	21	3.9	6	8	1,000	100	0.0	0.0
U /	N/A	3.3	10.58	346	2	0	97	0	1	21	3.9	N/A	8	1,000,000	0	0.0	0.0
C- / 3.6	3.7	6.3	11.69	476	1	0	98	0	1	17	3.9	37	8	1,000	100	4.5	0.0
C- / 3.6	3.7	6.3	11.71	217	1	0	98	0	1	17	3.9	52	8	1,000,000	0	0.0	0.0
C- / 3.5	3.8	6.3	11.92	60	1	0	98	0	1	17	3.9	14	8	1,000	100	0.0	0.0
U /	N/A	6.3	11.71	289	1	0	98	0	1	17	3.9	N/A	8	1,000,000	0	0.0	0.0
A+ / 9.9	0.1	N/A	1.00	871	100	0	0	0	0	0	0.5	54	N/A	50,000,000	0	0.0	0.0
C- / 3.8	3.6	6.0	10.83	39	3	0	96	0	1	13	4.9	43	12	1,000	100	4.5	0.0
C- / 3.8	3.6	6.0	10.83	52	3	0	96	0	1	13	4.9	58	12	1,000,000	0	0.0	0.0
C- / 3.8	3.6	6.0	10.84	9	3	0	96	0	1	13	4.9	17	12	1,000	100	0.0	0.0
A+ / 9.9	0.2	0.4	10.01	459	2	1	8	62	27	269	1.2	63	4	1,000,000	0	0.0	0.0
C+ / 5.6	3.0	5.7	13.10	415	0	35	1	21	43	667	2.8	29	14	1,000	100	4.5	0.0
C+ / 5.7	3.0	5.7	12.79	372	0	35	1	21	43	667	2.8	32	14	1,000,000	0	0.0	0.0
C / 5.5	3.0	5.7	12.97	62	0	35	1	21	43	667	2.8	10	14	1,000	100	0.0	0.0
C / 5.5	3.0	5.7	12.77	3,302	0	35	1	21	43	667	2.8	47	14	1,000,000	0	0.0	0.0
C+ / 5.6	3.0	5.7	12.78	15	0	35	1	21	43	667	2.8	24	14	0	0	0.0	0.0
C+ / 5.6	3.0	5.7	12.77	44	0	35	1	21	43	667	2.8	49	14	0	0	0.0	0.0
C+ / 5.6	3.0	5.7	12.77	682	0	35	1	21	43	667	2.8	55	14	0	0	0.0	0.0
C / 4.4	3.3	5.3	12.43	356	0	16	4	43	37	288	4.0	87	12	1,000	100	4.5	0.0
C / 4.5	3.3	5.3	12.41	57	0	16	4	43	37	288	4.0	73	12	1,000,000	0	0.0	0.0
C / 4.6	3.3	5.3	12.43	19	0	16	4	43	37	288	4.0	81	12	1,000	100	0.0	0.0
C / 4.5	3.3	5.3	12.44	98	0	16	4	43	37	288	4.0	89	12	1,000,000	0	0.0	0.0
C- / 3.7	3.7	3.6	11.57	559	0	0	99	0	1	21	3.8	68	9	0	0	0.0	0.0
A+ / 9.9	0.1	N/A	1.00	108	100	0	0	0	0	0	0.3	48	N/A	1,000,000	0	0.0	0.0
A+ / 9.9	0.1	N/A	1.00	752	100	0	0	0	0	0	0.5	51	N/A	10,000,000	0	0.0	0.0
A+ / 9.9	0.1	N/A	1.00	214	100	0	0	0	0	0	0.2	44	N/A	100,000	0	0.0	0.0
D- / 1.1	5.6	4.9	6.27	195	2	1	0	70	27	38	5.6	96	10	1,000	100	5.8	0.0
D / 1.6	5.6	4.9	6.14	47	2	1	0	70	27	38	5.6	97	10	1,000,000	0	0.0	0.0
D / 1.6	5.6	4.9	6.30	N/A	2	1	0	70	27	38	5.6	95	10	1,000	100	0.0	0.0
D / 1.7	5.5	4.9	6.28	145	2	1	0	70	27	38	5.6	95	10	1,000	100	0.0	0.0
D / 1.6	5.6	4.9	6.14	197	2	1	0	70	27	38	5.6	97	10	1,000,000	0	0.0	0.0
C+ / 6.9	2.7	4.5	10.88	431	0	32	1	1	66	397	3.4	51	7	1,000	100	4.5	0.0
C+ / 6.9	2.7	4.5	10.88	214	0	32	1	1	66	397	3.4	60	7	1,000,000	0	0.0	0.0
B- / 7.0	2.7	4.5	10.88	23	0	32	1	1	66	397	3.4	20	7	1,000	100	0.0	0.0
C+ / 6.9	2.7	4.5	10.87	436	0	32	1	1	66	397	3.4	64	7	1,000,000	0	0.0	0.0
U /	N/A	N/A	1.00	270	100	0	0	0	0	0	0.0	N/A	N/A	1,000	100	0.0	0.0
A+ / 9.9	N/A	N/A	1.00	490	100	0	0	0	0	0	0.1	42	N/A	1,000,000	0	0.0	0.0
A+ / 9.9	N/A	N/A	1.00	23,477	100	0	0	0	0	0	0.3	N/A	N/A	10,000,000	0	0.0	0.0
A+ / 9.9	N/A	N/A	1.00	2,993	100	0	0	0	0	0	0.0	38	N/A	100,000	0	0.0	0.0
U /	N/A	N/A	1.00	35,966	100	0	0	0	0	0	0.3	N/A	N/A	50,000,000	0	0.0	0.0
U /	N/A	N/A	1.00	N/A	100	0	0	0	0	0	0.0	N/A	N/A	0	0	0.0	0.0
A+ / 9.9	0.1	N/A	1.00	97	100	0	0	0	0	0	0.3	47	N/A	1,000,000	0	0.0	0.0
A+ / 9.9	0.1	N/A	1.00	1,035	100	0	0	0	0	0	0.4	50	N/A	10,000,000	0	0.0	0.0
A+ / 9.9	0.1	N/A	1.00	3,400	100	0	0	0	0	0	0.5	54	N/A	50,000,000	0	0.0	0.0

Fund Type	Fund Name	Ticker Symbol	Overall Investment Rating	Phone	Performance Rating/Pts	Total Return % through 2/28/17					Incl. in Returns	
						3 Mo	6 Mo	1Yr / Pct	Annualized 3Yr / Pct	5Yr / Pct	Dividend Yield	Expense Ratio
MMT	Wells Fargo Heritage MM Svc	WHTXX	C-	(800) 222-8222	D- / 1.1	0.12	0.18	0.24 / 27	0.09 / 13	0.06 / 13	0.21	N/A
MUH	Wells Fargo Hi Yld Muni Bd A	WHYMX	C	(800) 222-8222	B / 7.6	1.63	-4.54	-0.57 / 9	5.14 / 97	--	3.26	1.08
MUH	Wells Fargo Hi Yld Muni Bd Adm	WHYDX	B+	(800) 222-8222	A / 9.3	1.65	-4.50	-0.47 / 10	5.25 / 98	--	3.52	1.02
MUH	Wells Fargo Hi Yld Muni Bd C	WHYCX	C+	(800) 222-8222	B / 8.2	1.44	-4.90	-1.31 / 2	4.35 / 95	--	2.64	1.83
MUH	Wells Fargo Hi Yld Muni Bd Inst	WHYIX	B+	(800) 222-8222	A / 9.4	1.59	-4.43	-0.42 / 11	5.37 / 98	--	3.68	0.75
COH	Wells Fargo High Yld Bd Fd A	EKHAX	C	(800) 222-8222	B+ / 8.6	4.52	3.78	14.63 / 88	4.78 / 84	6.11 / 93	3.99	1.04
COH	Wells Fargo High Yld Bd Fd Adm	EKHYX	B-	(800) 222-8222	A / 9.4	4.56	3.85	14.45 / 87	5.00 / 85	6.34 / 94	4.35	0.98
COH ●	Wells Fargo High Yld Bd Fd B	EKHBX	C+	(800) 222-8222	B+ / 8.9	4.33	3.42	13.81 / 86	4.01 / 75	5.33 / 87	3.48	1.79
COH	Wells Fargo High Yld Bd Fd C	EKHCX	C+	(800) 222-8222	B+ / 8.8	4.33	3.40	13.78 / 86	4.00 / 75	5.33 / 87	3.46	1.79
COH	Wells Fargo High Yld Bd Inst	EKHIX	U	(800) 222-8222	U /	4.63	3.99	15.06 / 89	--	--	4.54	0.71
GL	Wells Fargo Intl Bd A	ESIYX	E-	(800) 222-8222	E- / 0.0	2.30	-8.44	0.10 / 22	-3.01 / 1	-1.51 / 2	0.00	1.06
GL	Wells Fargo Intl Bd Adm	ESIDX	E-	(800) 222-8222	E- / 0.0	2.29	-8.33	0.20 / 26	-2.85 / 1	-1.35 / 2	0.00	1.00
GL	Wells Fargo Intl Bd C	ESIVX	E-	(800) 222-8222	E- / 0.0	2.14	-8.73	-0.63 / 8	-3.74 / 1	-2.26 / 1	0.00	1.81
GL	Wells Fargo Intl Bd I	ESICX	E-	(800) 222-8222	E- / 0.1	2.38	-8.28	0.40 / 31	-2.69 / 1	-1.20 / 2	0.00	0.73
GL	Wells Fargo Intl Bd R6	ESIRX	E-	(800) 222-8222	E- / 0.1	2.38	-8.27	0.40 / 31	-2.67 / 1	--	0.00	0.68
MUN	Wells Fargo Intm Tax/AMT Fr A	WFTAX	D-	(800) 222-8222	D+ / 2.8	1.59	-3.35	-1.05 / 4	2.07 / 64	2.27 / 66	2.24	0.80
MUN	Wells Fargo Intm Tax/AMT Fr Adm	WFITX	C-	(800) 222-8222	C / 5.0	1.61	-3.30	-0.95 / 5	2.17 / 66	2.39 / 68	2.41	0.74
MUN	Wells Fargo Intm Tax/AMT Fr C	WFTFX	D-	(800) 222-8222	D+ / 2.8	1.40	-3.71	-1.79 / 1	1.31 / 44	1.51 / 47	1.54	1.55
MUN	Wells Fargo Intm Tax/AMT Fr I	WITIX	C	(800) 222-8222	C / 5.4	1.74	-3.14	-0.79 / 6	2.34 / 70	2.57 / 72	2.57	0.47
MMT	Wells Fargo MM A	STGXX	D+	(800) 222-8222	E+ / 0.7	0.06	0.07	0.07 / 21	0.03 / 9	0.02 / 8	0.07	N/A
MMT ●	Wells Fargo MM B		U	(800) 222-8222	U /	0.00	0.01	0.02 / 19	0.01 / 7	0.01 / 6	0.02	N/A
MMT	Wells Fargo MM Prm	WMPXX	U	(800) 222-8222	U /	0.17	0.28	--	--	--	0.00	N/A
MMT	Wells Fargo MM Svc	WMOXX	C-	(800) 222-8222	E+ / 0.9	0.10	0.13	0.15 / 24	0.06 / 11	0.04 / 10	0.15	N/A
MUS	Wells Fargo MN Tax Free A	NMTFX	C+	(800) 222-8222	C- / 3.9	1.49	-2.20	0.28 / 32	2.74 / 78	2.54 / 71	2.67	0.89
MUS	Wells Fargo MN Tax Free Adm	NWMIX	A+	(800) 222-8222	B- / 7.1	1.55	-2.08	0.44 / 36	2.97 / 81	2.78 / 76	3.05	0.83
MUS	Wells Fargo MN Tax Free C	WMTCX	B	(800) 222-8222	C / 4.8	1.40	-2.56	-0.47 / 10	1.98 / 62	1.78 / 54	2.03	1.64
MMF	Wells Fargo Mu Cash Mgmt MM Adm	WUCXX	C	(800) 222-8222	D / 1.6	0.12	0.30	0.38 / 35	0.14 / 17	0.10 / 17	0.33	N/A
MMF	Wells Fargo Mu Cash Mgmt MM I	EMMXX	C	(800) 222-8222	D / 1.8	0.15	0.36	0.49 / 37	0.18 / 18	0.13 / 18	0.43	N/A
MMF	Wells Fargo Mu Cash Mgmt MM S	EISXX	C-	(800) 222-8222	D- / 1.4	0.09	0.23	0.26 / 31	0.10 / 15	0.08 / 16	0.21	N/A
* MUN	Wells Fargo Muni Bd A	WMFAX	C	(800) 222-8222	C+ / 5.9	1.86	-3.06	0.57 / 38	3.68 / 90	3.79 / 91	2.93	0.79
MUN	Wells Fargo Muni Bd Adm	WMFDX	A-	(800) 222-8222	B / 8.2	1.80	-2.99	0.72 / 41	3.83 / 91	3.95 / 93	3.22	0.73
MUN	Wells Fargo Muni Bd C	WMFCX	B-	(800) 222-8222	C+ / 6.7	1.67	-3.33	-0.18 / 15	2.94 / 81	3.04 / 81	2.30	1.54
MUN	Wells Fargo Muni Bd Inst	WMBIX	A	(800) 222-8222	B+ / 8.4	1.93	-2.92	0.86 / 43	3.98 / 93	4.09 / 94	3.36	0.46
MMF	Wells Fargo Natl TF MM A	NWMXX	U	(800) 222-8222	U /	--	--	--	--	--	0.13	N/A
MMF	Wells Fargo Natl TF MM Adm	WNTXX	C	(800) 222-8222	D / 1.6	0.17	0.27	0.35 / 34	0.13 / 17	0.09 / 17	0.35	N/A
MMF	Wells Fargo Natl TF MM Prmr	WFNXX	C	(800) 222-8222	D / 1.7	0.20	0.32	0.45 / 36	0.16 / 18	0.11 / 18	0.45	N/A
MMF	Wells Fargo Natl TF MM S	MMIXX	C-	(800) 222-8222	D- / 1.4	0.14	0.20	0.22 / 30	0.09 / 15	0.06 / 15	0.22	N/A
MUS	Wells Fargo NC TF A	ENCMX	C-	(800) 222-8222	C- / 3.4	1.16	-2.86	-0.96 / 4	2.78 / 78	2.60 / 73	2.87	0.96
MUS	Wells Fargo NC TF C	ENCCX	C+	(800) 222-8222	C- / 4.2	0.97	-3.22	-1.70 / 1	1.98 / 62	1.83 / 55	2.23	1.71
MUS	Wells Fargo NC TF Inst	ENCYX	A	(800) 222-8222	C+ / 6.9	1.23	-2.71	-0.66 / 7	3.09 / 83	2.91 / 79	3.32	0.63
MUS	Wells Fargo PA Tax Fr A	EKVAX	C-	(800) 222-8222	C / 5.1	2.01	-3.27	-0.66 / 7	3.54 / 88	3.37 / 86	2.95	0.90
MUS	Wells Fargo PA Tax Fr C	EKVCX	C+	(800) 222-8222	C+ / 6.1	1.83	-3.64	-1.33 / 2	2.80 / 79	2.59 / 72	2.31	1.65
MUS	Wells Fargo PA Tax Fr Inst	EKVYX	A-	(800) 222-8222	B / 7.9	2.07	-3.15	-0.41 / 11	3.80 / 91	3.62 / 89	3.34	0.57
GEI	Wells Fargo Real Return A	IPBAX	E+	(800) 222-8222	C- / 3.7	1.95	-0.34	5.23 / 68	2.35 / 49	0.76 / 24	1.53	1.19
GEI	Wells Fargo Real Return Adm	IPBIX	D	(800) 222-8222	C+ / 6.0	1.93	-0.23	5.46 / 68	2.61 / 54	1.01 / 28	1.64	1.13
GEI	Wells Fargo Real Return C	IPBCX	E+	(800) 222-8222	C- / 4.2	1.77	-0.70	4.42 / 64	1.58 / 36	--	0.56	1.94
USS	Wells Fargo Sh Dur Gov A	MSDAX	D	(800) 222-8222	E / 0.5	0.27	-0.02	0.46 / 32	0.53 / 21	0.57 / 22	1.54	0.78
USS	Wells Fargo Sh Dur Gov Adm	MNSGX	C	(800) 222-8222	D / 2.1	0.22	-0.03	0.54 / 34	0.71 / 23	0.76 / 24	1.76	0.72
USS	Wells Fargo Sh Dur Gov C	MSDCX	D	(800) 222-8222	E / 0.4	-0.01	-0.49	-0.39 / 11	-0.22 / 4	-0.18 / 4	0.82	1.53
USS	Wells Fargo Sh Dur Gov I	WSGIX	C+	(800) 222-8222	D+ / 2.5	0.36	0.06	0.72 / 36	0.90 / 26	0.94 / 27	1.94	0.45
USS	Wells Fargo Sh Dur Gov R6	MSDRX	C+	(800) 222-8222	D+ / 2.6	0.38	0.19	0.87 / 38	0.95 / 27	--	1.99	0.40
GEI	Wells Fargo Sh-Tm Bd A	SSTVX	C+	(800) 222-8222	D / 2.2	0.58	0.34	1.96 / 49	1.11 / 29	1.31 / 32	1.34	0.82

● Denotes fund is closed to new investors
* Denotes fund is included in Section II

www.thestreetratings.com

Risk Rating/Pts	3 Yr Avg Standard Deviation	Avg Dura-tion	NAV As of 2/28/17	Total $(Mil)	Cash %	Gov. Bond %	Muni. Bond %	Corp. Bond %	Other %	Portfolio Turnover Ratio	Avg Coupon Rate	Manager Quality Pct	Manager Tenure (Years)	Initial Purch. $	Additional Purch. $	Front End Load	Back End Load
A+ / 9.9	N/A	N/A	1.00	60	100	0	0	0	0	0	0.2	45	N/A	100,000	0	0.0	0.0
D+ / 2.6	3.9	6.1	10.14	33	2	0	97	0	1	61	4.6	78	4	1,000	100	4.5	0.0
D+ / 2.5	4.0	6.1	10.14	19	2	0	97	0	1	61	4.6	78	4	1,000,000	0	0.0	0.0
D+ / 2.5	3.9	6.1	10.14	9	2	0	97	0	1	61	4.6	60	4	1,000	100	0.0	0.0
D+ / 2.6	3.9	6.1	10.13	67	2	0	97	0	1	61	4.6	80	4	1,000,000	0	0.0	0.0
D- / 1.5	5.2	5.0	3.36	337	1	0	0	89	10	75	5.8	76	4	1,000	100	4.5	0.0
D- / 1.5	5.2	5.0	3.36	41	1	0	0	89	10	75	5.8	79	4	1,000,000	0	0.0	0.0
D- / 1.4	5.3	5.0	3.36	1	1	0	0	89	10	75	5.8	57	4	1,000	100	0.0	0.0
D- / 1.5	5.2	5.0	3.36	68	1	0	0	89	10	75	5.8	59	4	1,000	100	0.0	0.0
U /	N/A	5.0	3.36	112	1	0	0	89	10	75	5.8	N/A	4	1,000,000	0	0.0	0.0
E / 0.3	8.7	6.7	9.62	49	0	78	2	18	2	96	3.8	33	24	1,000	100	4.5	0.0
E / 0.3	8.7	6.7	9.65	38	0	78	2	18	2	96	3.8	43	24	1,000,000	0	0.0	0.0
E / 0.3	8.7	6.7	9.37	4	0	78	2	18	2	96	3.8	12	24	1,000	100	0.0	0.0
E / 0.3	8.8	6.7	9.71	467	0	78	2	18	2	96	3.8	54	24	1,000,000	0	0.0	0.0
E / 0.3	8.7	6.7	9.73	7	0	78	2	18	2	96	3.8	54	24	0	0	0.0	0.0
C / 5.4	3.0	4.4	11.32	432	1	0	98	0	1	14	4.2	10	16	1,000	100	3.0	0.0
C / 5.5	3.0	4.4	11.33	360	1	0	98	0	1	14	4.2	11	16	1,000,000	0	0.0	0.0
C / 5.4	3.0	4.4	11.32	48	1	0	98	0	1	14	4.2	3	16	1,000	100	0.0	0.0
C / 5.4	3.0	4.4	11.34	1,687	1	0	98	0	1	14	4.2	14	16	1,000,000	0	0.0	0.0
A+ / 9.9	N/A	N/A	1.00	529	100	0	0	0	0	0	0.1	39	N/A	1,000	100	0.0	0.0
U /	N/A	N/A	1.00	N/A	100	0	0	0	0	0	0.0	N/A	N/A	1,000	100	0.0	0.0
U /	N/A	N/A	1.00	N/A	100	0	0	0	0	0	0.0	N/A	N/A	10,000,000	0	0.0	0.0
A+ / 9.9	N/A	N/A	1.00	21	100	0	0	0	0	0	0.2	42	N/A	100,000	0	0.0	0.0
B / 7.8	2.3	4.4	10.60	42	2	0	97	0	1	16	4.7	56	4	1,000	100	4.5	0.0
B / 7.7	2.4	4.4	10.59	114	2	0	97	0	1	16	4.7	62	4	1,000,000	0	0.0	0.0
B / 7.7	2.4	4.4	10.60	10	2	0	97	0	1	16	4.7	21	4	1,000	100	0.0	0.0
A+ / 9.9	0.1	N/A	1.00	3	100	0	0	0	0	0	0.3	49	N/A	1,000,000	0	0.0	0.0
A+ / 9.9	0.1	N/A	1.00	310	100	0	0	0	0	0	0.4	50	N/A	10,000,000	0	0.0	0.0
A+ / 9.9	0.1	N/A	1.00	24	100	0	0	0	0	0	0.2	N/A	N/A	100,000	0	0.0	0.0
C / 4.6	3.2	4.3	10.12	1,335	0	0	99	0	1	16	3.8	58	17	1,000	100	4.5	0.0
C / 4.8	3.2	4.3	10.12	131	0	0	99	0	1	16	3.8	64	17	1,000,000	0	0.0	0.0
C / 4.7	3.2	4.3	10.12	159	0	0	99	0	1	16	3.8	26	17	1,000	100	0.0	0.0
C / 4.6	3.2	4.3	10.12	980	0	0	99	0	1	16	3.8	67	17	1,000,000	0	0.0	0.0
U /	N/A	N/A	1.00	134	100	0	0	0	0	0	0.1	44	N/A	1,000	100	0.0	0.0
A+ / 9.9	0.1	N/A	1.00	157	100	0	0	0	0	0	0.4	49	N/A	1,000,000	0	0.0	0.0
A+ / 9.9	0.1	N/A	1.00	110	100	0	0	0	0	0	0.5	50	N/A	10,000,000	0	0.0	0.0
A+ / 9.9	0.1	N/A	1.00	74	100	0	0	0	0	0	0.2	N/A	N/A	100,000	0	0.0	0.0
B- / 7.2	2.7	4.3	10.09	32	1	0	98	0	1	7	5.0	41	8	1,000	100	4.5	0.0
B- / 7.2	2.7	4.3	10.09	5	1	0	98	0	1	7	5.0	15	8	1,000	100	0.0	0.0
B- / 7.1	2.7	4.3	10.09	40	1	0	98	0	1	7	5.0	58	8	1,000,000	0	0.0	0.0
C / 5.0	3.1	5.4	11.52	49	0	0	99	0	1	13	5.1	54	8	1,000	100	4.5	0.0
C / 4.9	3.2	5.4	11.50	18	0	0	99	0	1	13	5.1	21	8	1,000	100	0.0	0.0
C / 5.0	3.1	5.4	11.52	107	0	0	99	0	1	13	5.1	63	8	1,000,000	0	0.0	0.0
D+ / 2.4	4.5	4.9	9.99	29	2	69	0	12	17	29	1.6	18	12	1,000	100	4.5	0.0
D+ / 2.4	4.6	4.9	10.09	25	2	69	0	12	17	29	1.6	24	12	1,000,000	0	0.0	0.0
D+ / 2.4	4.6	4.9	9.85	5	2	69	0	12	17	29	1.6	6	12	1,000	100	0.0	0.0
A / 9.4	0.9	1.8	9.88	58	0	31	0	0	69	284	2.7	40	14	1,000	100	2.0	0.0
A / 9.4	0.8	1.8	9.89	111	0	31	0	0	69	284	2.7	54	14	1,000,000	0	0.0	0.0
A / 9.4	0.8	1.8	9.89	24	0	31	0	0	69	284	2.7	16	14	1,000	100	0.0	0.0
A / 9.5	0.8	1.8	9.89	623	0	31	0	0	69	284	2.7	60	14	1,000,000	0	0.0	0.0
A / 9.4	0.9	1.8	9.91	221	0	31	0	0	69	284	2.7	61	14	0	0	0.0	0.0
A+ / 9.6	0.8	1.9	8.75	244	4	3	5	52	36	59	3.2	65	13	1,000	100	2.0	0.0

Fund Type	Fund Name	Ticker Symbol	Overall Investment Rating	Phone	Performance Rating/Pts	3 Mo	6 Mo	1Yr / Pct	Annualized 3Yr / Pct	5Yr / Pct	Dividend Yield	Expense Ratio
GEI	Wells Fargo Sh-Tm Bd C	WFSHX	C	(800) 222-8222	D / 1.9	0.40	-0.03	1.20 /42	0.36 /19	0.55 /22	0.62	1.57
GEI	Wells Fargo Sh-Tm Bd I	SSHIX	B+	(800) 222-8222	C- / 3.6	0.64	0.46	2.20 /51	1.42 /34	1.62 /36	1.61	0.49
COH	Wells Fargo Sh-Tm Hi Yld A	SSTHX	B-	(800) 222-8222	C- / 4.2	1.10	1.36	4.66 /65	2.32 /49	3.05 /59	2.85	0.93
COH	Wells Fargo Sh-Tm Hi Yld Adm	WDHYX	A	(800) 222-8222	C+ / 5.8	1.14	1.44	4.83 /66	2.48 /51	3.22 /61	3.09	0.87
COH	Wells Fargo Sh-Tm Hi Yld C	WFHYX	B-	(800) 222-8222	C- / 4.2	0.92	0.99	3.88 /62	1.56 /36	2.28 /46	2.19	1.68
COH	Wells Fargo Sh-Tm Hi Yld Inst	STYIX	A	(800) 222-8222	C+ / 6.0	1.18	1.52	4.99 /67	2.63 /55	--	3.24	0.60
* MUN	Wells Fargo ST Muni Bd A	WSMAX	D	(800) 222-8222	E / 0.5	0.53	-0.79	-0.11 /16	0.53 /25	0.89 /33	1.19	0.75
MUN	Wells Fargo ST Muni Bd Adm	WSTMX	C	(800) 222-8222	D / 2.1	0.54	-0.68	0.02 /19	0.51 /24	0.89 /33	1.24	0.69
MUN	Wells Fargo ST Muni Bd C	WSSCX	D	(800) 222-8222	E / 0.3	0.35	-1.16	-0.85 / 5	-0.22 / 4	0.14 /19	0.46	1.50
MUN	Wells Fargo ST Muni Bd I	WSBIX	C+	(800) 222-8222	D+ / 2.7	0.59	-0.68	0.22 /30	0.77 /30	1.11 /38	1.45	0.42
* MUN	Wells Fargo Str Muni Bd A	VMPAX	C	(800) 222-8222	D / 2.2	0.93	-0.99	0.95 /44	1.65 /53	2.08 /61	1.40	0.82
MUN	Wells Fargo Str Muni Bd Adm	VMPYX	A	(800) 222-8222	C / 5.0	0.84	-0.93	0.96 /44	1.77 /56	2.22 /64	1.58	0.76
MUN ●	Wells Fargo Str Muni Bd B	VMPIX	C+	(800) 222-8222	D+ / 2.8	0.63	-1.37	0.08 /23	0.89 /33	1.30 /42	0.70	1.57
MUN	Wells Fargo Str Muni Bd C	DHICX	C+	(800) 222-8222	D+ / 2.8	0.74	-1.35	0.20 /29	0.89 /33	1.32 /43	0.70	1.57
MUN	Wells Fargo Str Muni Bd I	STRIX	A+	(800) 222-8222	C+ / 5.7	1.01	-0.72	1.28 /49	1.98 /62	--	1.79	0.49
GL	Wells Fargo Strategic Income A	WSIAX	D-	(800) 222-8222	C- / 4.0	2.80	2.67	9.95 /79	1.40 /33	--	2.25	1.54
GL	Wells Fargo Strategic Income Ad	WSIDX	C-	(800) 222-8222	C+ / 6.0	2.80	2.67	10.09 /79	1.55 /36	--	2.39	1.48
GL	Wells Fargo Strategic Income C	WSICX	D-	(800) 222-8222	C / 4.4	2.73	2.39	9.15 /77	0.64 /22	--	1.60	2.29
GL	Wells Fargo Strategic Income I	WSINX	C-	(800) 222-8222	C+ / 6.2	2.96	2.87	10.33 /80	1.70 /38	--	2.67	1.21
MMT	Wells Fargo Treas Pls MM Admin	WTPXX	D+	(800) 222-8222	E+ / 0.7	0.05	0.06	0.08 /22	0.03 / 9	0.02 / 8	0.08	N/A
MMT	Wells Fargo Treas Pls MM I	PISXX	C-	(800) 222-8222	D- / 1.1	0.09	0.14	0.22 /27	0.09 /13	0.06 /13	0.22	N/A
MMT	Wells Fargo Treas Pls MM S	PRVXX	D+	(800) 222-8222	E+ / 0.6	0.03	0.03	0.03 /20	0.02 / 8	0.02 / 8	0.03	N/A
MMT	Wells Fargo Treas Pls MM Sweep		U	(800) 222-8222	U /	--	--	--	--	--	0.01	N/A
GES	Wells Fargo Ult ST Inc A	SADAX	C	(800) 222-8222	D- / 1.5	0.27	0.42	1.65 /46	0.62 /22	0.74 /24	1.03	0.80
GES	Wells Fargo Ult ST Inc Adm	WUSDX	B-	(800) 222-8222	D+ / 2.6	0.43	0.49	1.93 /48	0.77 /24	0.90 /26	1.20	0.74
GES	Wells Fargo Ult ST Inc C	WUSTX	D+	(800) 222-8222	E / 0.5	0.09	0.05	0.90 /39	-0.15 / 5	-0.01 / 5	0.30	1.55
GES	Wells Fargo Ult ST Inc Instl	SADIX	B	(800) 222-8222	D+ / 2.9	0.48	0.59	2.01 /49	0.98 /27	1.10 /29	1.40	0.47
* MUN	Wells Fargo Ult-Sh Mun Inc A	SMAVX	D	(800) 222-8222	E / 0.3	0.16	-0.44	-0.11 /16	0.09 /15	0.21 /20	0.50	0.75
MUN	Wells Fargo Ult-Sh Mun Inc Adm	WUSMX	C-	(800) 222-8222	D- / 1.2	0.18	-0.40	-0.04 /17	0.16 /18	0.28 /21	0.58	0.69
MUN	Wells Fargo Ult-Sh Mun Inc C	WFUSX	D	(800) 222-8222	E- / 0.2	0.01	-0.84	-0.84 / 6	-0.65 / 3	-0.55 / 3	0.00	1.50
MUN	Wells Fargo Ult-Sh Mun Inc I	SMAIX	C+	(800) 222-8222	D / 1.9	0.23	-0.29	0.19 /29	0.39 /22	0.51 /25	0.81	0.42
MUS	Wells Fargo WI Tax Fr A	WWTFX	C-	(800) 222-8222	C- / 3.1	1.31	-2.32	-0.46 /10	2.50 /73	2.24 /65	2.23	0.93
MUS	Wells Fargo WI Tax Fr C	WWTCX	C+	(800) 222-8222	C- / 4.0	1.12	-2.68	-1.20 / 3	1.74 /56	1.48 /46	1.58	1.68
USL	WesMark Govt Bond Fund	WMBDX	C-	(800) 864-1013	D+ / 2.7	0.17	-1.78	-0.87 / 5	1.51 /35	0.97 /27	1.75	1.01
MUI	WesMark West Virginia Muni Bond	WMKMX	A-	(800) 864-1013	C+ / 5.9	1.55	-2.30	-0.50 /10	2.42 /72	1.99 /59	2.04	1.07
MUI	Westcore CO Tax Exempt	WTCOX	A	(800) 392-2673	C+ / 6.9	1.81	-2.60	-0.15 /15	2.95 /81	2.36 /68	2.71	0.77
COH	Westcore Flexible Income Inst	WILTX	B-	(800) 392-2673	A / 9.3	3.13	3.28	15.72 /90	5.36 /88	5.92 /92	4.67	1.03
COH	Westcore Flexible Income Rtl	WTLTX	B-	(800) 392-2673	A / 9.3	3.17	3.26	15.39 /89	5.18 /86	5.77 /91	4.41	0.98
GEI	Westcore Plus Bond Inst	WIIBX	B	(800) 392-2673	C+ / 5.9	1.51	-1.44	3.50 /60	3.02 /61	2.93 /56	3.48	0.55
* GEI	Westcore Plus Bond Rtl	WTIBX	B-	(800) 392-2673	C+ / 5.6	1.39	-1.57	3.32 /59	2.85 /59	2.75 /54	3.41	0.70
MMT	Western Asset Inst US Tr Ob MM Inst	LUIXX	C-	(888) 425-6432	D- / 1.2	0.09	0.17	0.31 /29	0.13 /14	--	0.31	N/A
COH	Western Asset Short Dur High Inc A	SHIAX	D-	(877) 534-4627	C+ / 6.5	3.98	5.82	21.17 /97	0.68 /23	4.60 /80	6.08	0.99
COH	Western Asset Short Dur High Inc C	LWHIX	D-	(877) 534-4627	C+ / 6.3	3.80	5.46	20.35 /96	-0.03 / 5	3.90 /71	5.56	1.69
COH ●	Western Asset Short Dur High Inc C1	SHICX	D-	(877) 534-4627	C+ / 6.7	3.86	5.59	20.84 /97	0.25 /18	4.17 /75	5.82	1.41
COH	Western Asset Short Dur High Inc I	SHIYX	D	(877) 534-4627	B- / 7.4	4.04	5.75	21.46 /97	0.92 /26	4.88 /83	6.50	0.72
COH	Western Asset Short Dur High Inc R	LWSRX	D-	(877) 534-4627	C+ / 6.8	3.91	5.66	21.00 /97	0.27 /18	--	5.87	1.32
COH	Westwood Opportunistic Hi Yld Inst	WWHYX	U	(866) 777-7818	U /	4.85	6.01	19.55 /95	--	--	5.84	5.97
COH	Westwood Opportunistic Hi Yld Ultra	WHYUX	U	(866) 777-7818	U /	4.89	5.97	19.69 /95	--	--	5.95	6.23
COH	Westwood Short Dur High Yield Inst	WHGHX	C-	(866) 777-7818	C+ / 6.3	2.49	3.08	10.03 /79	1.85 /41	3.33 /63	4.37	0.94
COH	Westwood Short Dur High Yld A	WSDAX	D	(866) 777-7818	C / 5.0	2.42	2.95	9.75 /78	1.63 /37	--	4.03	1.19
GL	Westwood Worldwide Inc Oppty Inst	WWIOX	U	(866) 777-7818	U /	4.80	2.77	11.01 /81	--	--	1.42	2.49
GEI	William Blair Bond I	WBFIX	A-	(800) 742-7272	C+ / 6.0	1.47	-1.11	4.48 /65	2.92 /60	3.13 /60	3.95	0.59

● Denotes fund is closed to new investors
* Denotes fund is included in Section II

www.thestreetratings.com

RISK			NET ASSETS		ASSET					Portfolio Turnover Ratio	Avg Coupon Rate	FUND MANAGER		MINIMUM		LOADS	
Risk Rating/Pts	3 Yr Avg Standard Deviation	Avg Duration	NAV As of 2/28/17	Total $(Mil)	Cash %	Gov. Bond %	Muni. Bond %	Corp. Bond %	Other %			Manager Quality Pct	Manager Tenure (Years)	Initial Purch. $	Additional Purch. $	Front End Load	Back End Load
A /9.5	0.8	1.9	8.74	13	4	3	5	52	36	59	3.2	30	13	1,000	100	0.0	0.0
A /9.5	0.8	1.9	8.76	251	4	3	5	52	36	59	3.2	71	13	1,000,000	0	0.0	0.0
B /7.9	1.7	1.1	8.09	279	1	2	0	85	12	32	5.1	77	19	1,000	100	3.0	0.0
B /8.0	1.6	1.1	8.09	175	1	2	0	85	12	32	5.1	80	19	1,000,000	0	0.0	0.0
B /7.9	1.7	1.1	8.09	119	1	2	0	85	12	32	5.1	60	19	1,000	100	0.0	0.0
B /8.0	1.7	1.1	8.08	897	1	2	0	85	12	32	5.1	81	19	1,000,000	0	0.0	0.0
A /9.4	0.9	1.1	9.83	1,969	0	0	97	0	3	16	2.6	27	17	1,000	100	2.0	0.0
A /9.5	0.8	1.1	9.84	73	0	0	97	0	3	16	2.6	28	17	1,000,000	0	0.0	0.0
A /9.4	0.9	1.1	9.83	68	0	0	97	0	3	16	2.6	10	17	1,000	100	0.0	0.0
A /9.4	0.8	1.1	9.85	3,141	0	0	97	0	3	16	2.6	35	17	1,000,000	0	0.0	0.0
B+ /8.9	1.4	1.4	8.88	686	0	0	98	0	2	53	2.5	56	7	1,000	100	4.0	0.0
B+ /8.9	1.4	1.4	8.87	195	0	0	98	0	2	53	2.5	61	7	1,000,000	0	0.0	0.0
B+ /8.9	1.4	1.4	8.85	N/A	0	0	98	0	2	53	2.5	23	7	1,000	100	0.0	0.0
B+ /8.9	1.4	1.4	8.91	150	0	0	98	0	2	53	2.5	22	7	1,000	100	0.0	0.0
B+ /8.9	1.4	1.4	8.88	878	0	0	98	0	2	53	2.5	67	7	1,000,000	0	0.0	0.0
C- /3.9	3.5	1.5	9.36	1	4	16	3	60	17	52	5.1	83	4	1,000	100	4.0	0.0
C- /3.9	3.6	1.5	9.40	1	4	16	3	60	17	52	5.1	85	4	1,000	0	0.0	0.0
C- /3.9	3.5	1.5	9.32	1	4	16	3	60	17	52	5.1	75	4	1,000	100	0.0	0.0
C- /3.9	3.5	1.5	9.36	24	4	16	3	60	17	52	5.1	86	4	1,000,000	0	0.0	0.0
A+ /9.9	N/A	N/A	1.00	123	100	0	0	0	0	0	0.1	39	N/A	1,000,000	0	0.0	0.0
A+ /9.9	N/A	N/A	1.00	10,671	100	0	0	0	0	0	0.2	45	N/A	10,000,000	0	0.0	0.0
A+ /9.9	N/A	N/A	1.00	1,827	100	0	0	0	0	0	0.0	38	N/A	100,000	0	0.0	0.0
U /	N/A	N/A	1.00	N/A	100	0	0	0	0	0	0.0	N/A	N/A	0	0	0.0	0.0
A+ /9.9	0.4	0.5	8.48	300	2	3	4	51	40	51	2.8	63	15	1,000	100	2.0	0.0
A+ /9.8	0.4	0.5	8.45	27	2	3	4	51	40	51	2.8	66	15	1,000,000	0	0.0	0.0
A+ /9.8	0.4	0.5	8.47	6	2	3	4	51	40	51	2.8	27	15	1,000	100	0.0	0.0
A+ /9.9	0.4	0.5	8.48	1,218	2	3	4	51	40	51	2.8	71	15	1,000,000	0	0.0	0.0
A+ /9.8	0.5	0.5	9.56	1,135	0	0	96	0	4	41	1.8	27	17	1,000	100	2.0	0.0
A+ /9.9	0.4	0.5	9.56	1,475	0	0	96	0	4	41	1.8	31	17	1,000,000	0	0.0	0.0
A+ /9.8	0.4	0.5	9.39	27	0	0	96	0	4	41	1.8	10	17	1,000	100	0.0	0.0
A+ /9.9	0.4	0.5	9.56	2,721	0	0	96	0	4	41	1.8	43	17	1,000,000	0	0.0	0.0
B /7.6	2.5	3.9	10.73	143	1	0	98	0	1	16	4.2	36	16	1,000	100	4.5	0.0
B /7.6	2.5	3.9	10.73	10	1	0	98	0	1	16	4.2	15	16	1,000	100	0.0	0.0
B /7.8	2.4	3.3	9.86	248	0	6	19	0	75	13	0.0	56	19	1,000	100	0.0	0.0
B- /7.4	2.6	4.4	10.40	117	0	0	97	0	3	15	0.0	28	11	1,000	100	0.0	0.0
C+ /6.4	2.8	5.0	11.40	203	2	5	91	0	2	30	0.0	36	12	2,500	25	0.0	0.0
D /1.8	4.9	4.4	8.87	19	1	0	0	90	9	37	0.0	83	8	500,000	0	0.0	2.0
D /1.9	4.8	4.4	8.99	59	1	0	0	90	9	37	0.0	82	8	2,500	25	0.0	2.0
C+ /6.3	2.9	4.8	10.55	128	0	11	8	40	41	51	0.0	65	N/A	500,000	0	0.0	0.0
C+ /6.1	2.9	4.8	10.66	1,058	0	11	8	40	41	51	0.0	59	N/A	2,500	25	0.0	0.0
A+ /9.9	N/A	N/A	1.00	186	100	0	0	0	0	0	0.3	48	N/A	1,000,000	50	0.0	0.0
E+ /0.7	6.5	2.6	5.42	316	0	0	0	81	19	64	6.4	0	11	1,000	50	2.3	0.0
E+ /0.7	6.5	2.6	5.42	74	0	0	0	81	19	64	6.4	0	11	1,000	50	0.0	0.0
E+ /0.7	6.5	2.6	5.45	74	0	0	0	81	19	64	6.4	0	11	1,000	50	0.0	0.0
E+ /0.7	6.5	2.6	5.44	154	0	0	0	81	19	64	6.4	0	11	1,000,000	0	0.0	0.0
E+ /0.7	6.5	2.6	5.42	N/A	0	0	0	81	19	64	6.4	0	11	0	0	0.0	0.0
U /	N/A	N/A	10.04	N/A	9	0	0	89	2	60	0.0	N/A	3	5,000	0	0.0	0.0
U /	N/A	N/A	10.03	4	9	0	0	89	2	60	0.0	N/A	3	250,000	0	0.0	0.0
C- /3.7	3.2	3.0	9.39	80	1	0	0	98	1	54	0.0	22	6	100,000	0	0.0	0.0
C- /3.7	3.2	3.0	9.39	1	1	0	0	98	1	54	0.0	17	6	5,000	0	2.3	0.0
U /	N/A	N/A	9.79	7	16	17	0	12	55	54	0.0	N/A	2	5,000	0	0.0	0.0
B- /7.3	2.6	5.6	10.35	329	0	7	0	42	51	32	5.1	73	10	500,000	0	0.0	0.0

Fund Type	Fund Name	Ticker Symbol	Overall Investment Rating	Phone	Performance Rating/Pts	3 Mo	6 Mo	1Yr / Pct	3Yr / Pct	5Yr / Pct	Dividend Yield	Expense Ratio
						Total Return % through 2/28/17			Annualized		Incl. in Returns	
COI	William Blair Bond Institutional	BBFIX	A	(800) 742-7272	C+ / 6.1	1.48	-1.08	4.54 /65	3.01 /61	3.25 /62	4.01	0.38
GEI	William Blair Bond N	WBBNX	B+	(800) 742-7272	C+ / 5.6	1.30	-1.30	4.22 /63	2.72 /56	2.93 /56	3.71	0.79
GEI	William Blair Income I	BIFIX	B+	(800) 742-7272	C / 4.3	0.76	-0.19	2.23 /51	2.01 /43	2.04 /43	3.14	0.55
GEI	William Blair Income N	WBRRX	B	(800) 742-7272	C- / 3.9	0.71	-0.29	2.01 /49	1.74 /39	1.81 /39	2.92	0.81
GEI	William Blair Low Duration I	WBLIX	B-	(800) 742-7272	D+ / 2.6	0.15	0.26	1.10 /41	0.94 /27	0.92 /26	2.43	0.59
GEI	William Blair Low Duration Inst	WBLJX	B-	(800) 742-7272	D+ / 2.7	0.16	0.28	1.13 /41	1.01 /28	1.02 /28	2.47	0.42
GEI	William Blair Low Duration N	WBLNX	C+	(800) 742-7272	D+ / 2.3	0.19	0.24	0.96 /39	0.78 /24	0.76 /24	2.18	0.77
GES	Wilmington Broad Market Bond A	AKIRX	E+	(800) 336-9970	D / 2.0	0.99	-2.38	1.47 /44	2.02 /44	2.01 /42	1.81	1.10
GES	Wilmington Broad Market Bond Inst	ARKIX	D+	(800) 336-9970	C / 4.4	0.97	-2.27	1.70 /46	2.37 /50	2.33 /47	2.24	0.85
GEI	Wilmington Intermediate Trm Bd A	GVITX	D-	(800) 336-9970	E / 0.4	0.59	-1.49	0.66 /36	1.18 /30	1.28 /31	1.28	1.18
GEI	Wilmington Intermediate Trm Bd Inst	ARIFX	C	(800) 336-9970	C- / 3.2	0.67	-1.42	0.89 /39	1.50 /35	1.59 /36	1.67	0.93
MUN	Wilmington Muni Bond A	WTABX	E+	(800) 336-9970	D+ / 2.3	2.34	-2.77	-0.84 / 6	2.16 /66	2.08 /61	1.55	1.09
MUN	Wilmington Muni Bond Inst	WTAIX	C	(800) 336-9970	C+ / 5.8	2.32	-2.65	-0.67 / 7	2.39 /71	2.33 /67	1.88	0.84
MUS	Wilmington NY Municipal Bond A	VNYFX	E+	(800) 336-9970	D / 1.9	2.02	-3.08	-1.09 / 4	2.01 /63	1.83 /55	1.47	1.23
MUS	Wilmington NY Municipal Bond Inst	VNYIX	C-	(800) 336-9970	C / 5.4	2.18	-2.96	-0.75 / 6	2.27 /69	2.10 /61	1.79	0.98
COI	Wilmington Short-Term Bd A	MVSAX	C-	(800) 336-9970	D- / 1.3	0.30	-0.19	0.99 /39	0.60 /22	0.84 /25	1.18	1.11
COI	Wilmington Short-Term Bd Inst	MVSTX	C+	(800) 336-9970	D+ / 2.5	0.46	0.04	1.35 /43	0.85 /25	1.11 /29	1.45	0.86
MMT	Wilmington U.S. Treasury MM Admn	ARMXX	U	(800) 336-9970	U /	--	--	--	--	--	0.03	N/A
MMT	Wilmington U.S. Treasury MM Select	VSTXX	D+	(800) 336-9970	E+ / 0.7	0.04	0.06	0.08 /22	0.03 / 9	0.02 / 8	0.08	N/A
MMT	Wilmington U.S. Treasury MM	VTSXX	U	(800) 336-9970	U /	--	--	--	--	--	0.02	N/A
MMT	Wilmington US Government MM	AIIXX	U	(800) 336-9970	U /	--	--	--	--	--	0.04	N/A
MMT	Wilmington US Government MM Inst	WGOXX	D+	(800) 336-9970	E+ / 0.9	0.06	0.09	0.12 /23	0.05 /10	--	0.12	N/A
MMT	Wilmington US Government MM	AKGXX	D+	(800) 336-9970	E+ / 0.8	0.04	0.06	0.09 /22	0.04 / 9	0.03 /10	0.09	N/A
MMT	Wilmington US Government MM	AGAXX	U	(800) 336-9970	U /	--	--	--	--	--	0.01	N/A
GL	Wilshire Income Opportunities Inv	WIORX	U	(888) 200-6796	U /	1.79	0.24	--	--	--	0.00	1.10
MTG	Wright Current Income	WCIFX	C	(800) 232-0013	C- / 3.2	0.12	-1.81	-0.84 / 6	1.84 /40	1.46 /34	3.57	1.18
GEN	Zeo Strategic Income I	ZEOIX	A+	(855) 936-3863	C+ / 5.6	0.81	1.29	4.83 /66	2.73 /57	3.29 /62	2.68	1.27
LP	Ziegler Floating Rate A	ZFLAX	U	(877) 568-7633	U /	1.58	3.09	--	--	--	0.00	N/A
LP	Ziegler Floating Rate C	ZFLCX	U	(877) 568-7633	U /	1.40	2.77	--	--	--	0.00	N/A
LP	Ziegler Floating Rate Instl	ZFLIX	U	(877) 568-7633	U /	1.64	3.23	--	--	--	0.00	N/A

99 Pct = Best
0 Pct = Worst

● Denotes fund is closed to new investors
* Denotes fund is included in Section II

www.thestreetratings.com

| RISK | | | NET ASSETS | | ASSET | | | | | | | FUND MANAGER | | MINIMUM | | LOADS | |
Risk Rating/Pts	3 Yr Avg Standard Deviation	Avg Dura-tion	NAV As of 2/28/17	Total $(Mil)	Cash %	Gov. Bond %	Muni. Bond %	Corp. Bond %	Other %	Portfolio Turnover Ratio	Avg Coupon Rate	Manager Quality Pct	Manager Tenure (Years)	Initial Purch. $	Additional Purch. $	Front End Load	Back End Load
B- /7.3	2.6	5.6	10.34	96	0	7	0	42	51	32	5.1	70	10	5,000,000	0	0.0	0.0
B- /7.3	2.6	5.6	10.45	123	0	7	0	42	51	32	5.1	70	10	2,500	1,000	0.0	0.0
B+ /8.9	1.4	3.3	8.81	57	2	6	0	35	57	21	4.1	72	15	500,000	0	0.0	0.0
B+ /8.9	1.4	3.3	8.87	52	2	6	0	35	57	21	4.1	66	15	2,500	1,000	0.0	0.0
A+ /9.8	0.5	1.0	9.05	196	7	0	0	21	72	106	2.7	66	8	500,000	0	0.0	0.0
A+ /9.8	0.5	1.0	9.05	52	7	0	0	21	72	106	2.7	68	8	5,000,000	0	0.0	0.0
A+ /9.8	0.5	1.0	9.06	7	7	0	0	21	72	106	2.7	61	8	2,500	1,000	0.0	0.0
C /5.3	3.0	5.5	9.77	5	0	29	0	44	27	44	5.7	18	21	1,000	25	4.5	0.0
C /5.5	3.0	5.5	9.60	502	0	29	0	44	27	44	5.7	29	21	1,000,000	25	0.0	0.0
B /8.0	2.2	4.0	9.85	3	0	47	0	50	3	32	0.0	17	21	1,000	25	4.5	0.0
B /8.0	2.2	4.0	9.85	133	0	47	0	50	3	32	0.0	26	21	1,000,000	25	0.0	0.0
C /4.7	3.2	5.4	13.06	33	3	1	93	0	3	32	0.0	8	6	1,000	25	4.5	0.0
C /4.8	3.2	5.4	13.06	254	3	1	93	0	3	32	0.0	12	6	1,000,000	25	0.0	0.0
C /4.7	3.2	5.3	10.49	18	0	0	99	0	1	24	0.0	7	5	1,000	25	4.5	0.0
C /4.8	3.2	5.3	10.50	69	0	0	99	0	1	24	0.0	10	5	1,000,000	25	0.0	0.0
A+ /9.6	0.8	1.9	9.99	7	0	19	0	69	12	104	0.0	37	21	1,000	25	1.8	0.0
A+ /9.6	0.8	1.9	10.00	66	0	19	0	69	12	104	0.0	54	21	1,000,000	25	0.0	0.0
U /	N/A	N/A	1.00	589	100	0	0	0	0	0	0.0	N/A	N/A	1,000	25	0.0	0.0
A+ /9.9	N/A	N/A	1.00	314	100	0	0	0	0	0	0.1	39	N/A	100,000	25	0.0	0.0
U /	N/A	N/A	1.00	N/A	100	0	0	0	0	0	0.0	N/A	N/A	0	0	0.0	0.0
U /	N/A	N/A	1.00	1,685	100	0	0	0	0	0	0.0	39	N/A	1,000	25	0.0	0.0
A+ /9.9	N/A	N/A	1.00	382	100	0	0	0	0	0	0.1	42	N/A	5,000,000	25	0.0	0.0
A+ /9.9	N/A	N/A	1.00	3,607	100	0	0	0	0	0	0.1	41	N/A	100,000	25	0.0	0.0
U /	N/A	N/A	1.00	1,389	100	0	0	0	0	0	0.0	N/A	N/A	0	0	0.0	0.0
U /	N/A	N/A	10.28	1	0	16	1	20	63	0	0.0	N/A	1	2,500	100	0.0	0.0
B /8.0	2.1	3.8	9.04	56	1	2	0	2	95	35	4.9	22	8	1,000	0	0.0	0.0
A- /9.0	1.3	N/A	9.96	240	0	0	0	0	100	135	0.0	88	6	5,000	1,000	0.0	1.0
U /	N/A	N/A	25.89	N/A	0	5	0	6	89	23	0.0	N/A	1	1,000	100	4.3	1.0
U /	N/A	N/A	25.87	N/A	0	5	0	6	89	23	0.0	N/A	1	1,000	100	0.0	0.0
U /	N/A	N/A	25.91	39	0	5	0	6	89	23	0.0	N/A	1	1,000,000	0	0.0	0.0

Section II

Analysis of Largest Bond and Money Market Mutual Funds

A summary analysis of the 381 largest retail

Fixed Income Mutual Funds

receiving a TheStreet Investment Rating.

Funds are listed in alphabetical order.

Section II Contents

1. Fund Name The name of the mutual fund as stated in its prospectus, which can sometimes differ slightly from the name that the company uses for advertising. If you cannot find the paritcular mutual fund you are interested in, or if you have any doubts regarding the precise name, verify the information with your broker or on your account statement. Also, use the fund's ticker symbol for confirmation.

2. Ticker Symbol The unique alphabetic symbol used for identifying and trading a specific mutual fund. No two funds can have the same ticker symbol, and the ticker symbol for mutual funds always ends with an "X".

A handful of funds currently show no associated ticker symbol. This means that the fund is either small or new since the NASD only assigns a ticker symbols to funds with at least $25 million in assets or 1,000 shareholders.

3. Investment Rating Our overall rating is measured on a scale from A to E based on each fund's risk-adjusted performance. Please see page 11 for specific descriptions of each letter grade. Also refer to page 7 for information on how our ratings are derived. Most important, when using this rating, please be sure to consider the warnings beginning on page 13 regarding the ratings' limitations and the underlying assumptions.

4. Major Rating Factors A synopsis of the key ratios and sub-factors that have most influenced the rating of a particular mutual fund, including an examination of the fund's performance, risk, and managerial performance. There may be additional factors which have influenced the rating but do not appear due to space limitations.

5. Services Offered Services and/or benefits offered by the fund.

6. Address The address of the company managing the fund.

7. Phone The telephone number of the company managing the fund. Call this number to receive a prospectus or other information about the fund.

8. Fund Family The umbrella group of mutual funds to which the fund belongs. In many cases, investors may move their assets from one fund to another within the same family at little or no cost.

9. Fund Type   The mutual fund's peer category based on its investment objective as stated in its prospectus.

COH	Corporate - High Yield	MMT	Money Market - Treas.
COI	Corporate - Inv. Grade	MTG	Mortgage
EM	Emerging Market	MUH	Municipal - High Yield
GEN	General	MUI	Municipal - Insured
GEI	General - Inv. Grade	MUN	Municipal - National
GEL	General - Long Term	MUS	Municipal - Single State
GES	General - Short & Interm.	USL	U.S. Gov.- Long Term
GL	Global	USS	U.S. Gov. - Short & Interm
LP	Loan Participation	USA	U.S. Gov. - Agency
MMF	Money Mkt - Tax Exempt	US	U.S. Gov. - Treasury

A blank fund type means that the mutual fund has not yet been categorized.

How to Read the Annualized Total Return Graph

The annualized total return graph provides a clearer picture of a fund's yearly financial performance. In addition to the solid line denoting the fund's calendar year returns for the last six years, the graph also shows the yearly return for a benchmark bond index for easy comparison using a dotted line. In the case of most bond funds, the index used is the Lehman Brothers Aggregate Bond Index; and for municipal bond funds, the index used is Lehman Brothers Municipals Index.

The top of the shaded area of the graph denotes the average returns for all funds within the same fund type. If the solid line falls into the shaded area, that means that the fund has performed below the average for its type.

How to Read the Historical Data Table

NAV:
The fund's share price as of the date indicated. A fund's NAV is computed by dividing the value of the fund's asset holdings, less accrued fees and expenses, by the number of its shares outstanding.

Risk Rating/Pts:
A letter grade rating based solely on the mutual fund's risk as determined by its monthly performance volatility over the trailing three years. Pts are rating points where 0=worst and 10=best.

Data Date:
The month-end or year-end as of date used for evaluating the mutual fund.

Data Date	Investment Rating	Net Assets ($Mil)	NAV	Performance Rating/Pts	Total Return Y-T-D	Risk Rating/Pts
2-17	C+	105	38.99	C+ / 6.3	20.69%	D+ / 2.9
2016	C	179	9.51	C+ / 6.4	-2.28%	D+ / 2.9
2015	C	470	10.45	C / 4.3	2.77%	C+ / 5.7
2014	B-	424	1.00	D- / 1.2	1.04%	B+ / 8.9
2013	B	159	42.37	C+ / 6.2	-1.66%	C / 5.3
2012	B-	155	41.31	C+ / 6.4	-1.41%	C+ / 5.2

Investment Rating:
Our overall opinion of the fund's risk-adjusted performance at the specified time period.

Net Assets $(Mil):
The total value of all of the fund's asset holdings (in millions) including stocks, bonds, cash, and other financial instruments, less accrued expenses and fees.

Performance Rating/Pts:
A letter grade rating based solely on the mutual fund's return to shareholders over the trailing three years, without any consideration for the amount of risk the fund poses. Pts are rating points where 0=worst and 10=best

Total Return Y-T-D:
The fund's total return to shareholders since the beginning of the calendar year specified.

AB Global Bond A (ANAGX)   B   Good

Fund Family: Alliance Bernstein Funds   **Phone:** (800) 221-5672
Address: P.O. Box 786003, San Antonio, TX 78278
Fund Type: GL - Global

Major Rating Factors: A moderate risk profile coupled with stable earnings characterizes AB Global Bond A which receives a TheStreet Investment Rating of B (Good). Volatility, as measured by standard deviation, is considered low for fixed income funds at 2.68. Another risk factor is the fund's fairly average duration of 5.7 years (i.e. average interest rate risk). The fund's risk rating is currently B- (Good).

The fund's performance rating is currently C (Fair). It has registered an average return of 3.68% over the last three years and is up 0.68% over the last three months. Factored into the performance evaluation is an expense ratio of 0.85% (average) and a 4.3% front-end load that is levied at the time of purchase.

Douglas J. Peebles has been running the fund for 25 years and currently receives a manager quality ranking of 94 (0=worst, 99=best). If you desire stability with a moderate level of risk then this fund is an excellent option.

Services Offered: Automated phone transactions, check writing, payroll deductions, bank draft capabilities, an IRA investment plan, a 401K investment plan and a systematic withdrawal plan.

Data Date	Investment Rating	Net Assets ($Mil)	NAV	Performance Rating/Pts	Total Return Y-T-D	Risk Rating/Pts
2-17	B	1,291	8.38	C / 5.2	0.68%	B- / 7.1
2016	B+	1,282	8.35	C+ / 6.1	5.37%	B- / 7.2
2015	C-	1,071	8.16	C / 4.6	0.48%	C+ / 5.7
2014	D	1,082	8.42	C- / 3.0	4.76%	C+ / 5.7
2013	D	1,238	8.24	D / 2.0	-2.15%	C+ / 6.7
2012	C+	1,579	8.62	C- / 3.6	7.02%	B- / 7.2

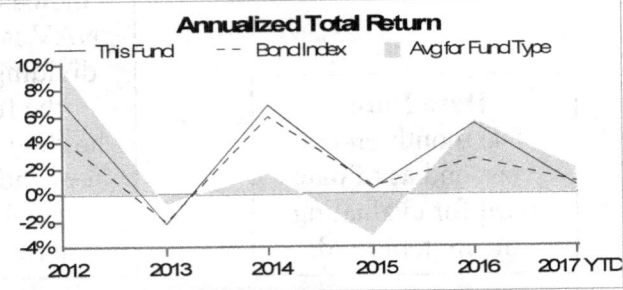

AB High Income A (AGDAX)   B-   Good

Fund Family: Alliance Bernstein Funds   **Phone:** (800) 221-5672
Address: P.O. Box 786003, San Antonio, TX 78278
Fund Type: GL - Global

Major Rating Factors: AB High Income A has adopted a very risky asset allocation strategy and currently receives an overall TheStreet Investment Rating of B- (Good). Volatility, as measured by standard deviation, is considered above average for fixed income funds at 5.39. Another risk factor is the fund's below average duration of 3.9 years (i.e. lower interest rate risk). The high level of risk (D, Weak) did however, reward investors with excellent performance.

The fund's performance rating is currently A (Excellent). It has registered an average return of 4.76% over the last three years and is up 3.18% over the last three months. Factored into the performance evaluation is an expense ratio of 0.85% (average) and a 4.3% front-end load that is levied at the time of purchase.

Douglas J. Peebles has been running the fund for 15 years and currently receives a manager quality ranking of 97 (0=worst, 99=best). If you are comfortable owning a very high risk investment, this fund may be an option.

Services Offered: Automated phone transactions, check writing, payroll deductions, bank draft capabilities, an IRA investment plan, a 401K investment plan and a systematic withdrawal plan.

Data Date	Investment Rating	Net Assets ($Mil)	NAV	Performance Rating/Pts	Total Return Y-T-D	Risk Rating/Pts
2-17	B-	2,039	8.86	A / 9.3	3.18%	D / 1.8
2016	C+	1,985	8.66	B+ / 8.8	15.17%	D / 1.9
2015	D	1,795	8.02	D / 2.2	-3.98%	D+ / 2.7
2014	C-	2,201	8.95	B- / 7.4	1.68%	D / 1.9
2013	C	2,589	9.38	A- / 9.2	6.62%	E+ / 0.9
2012	C+	2,563	9.50	A- / 9.1	18.54%	E / 0.5

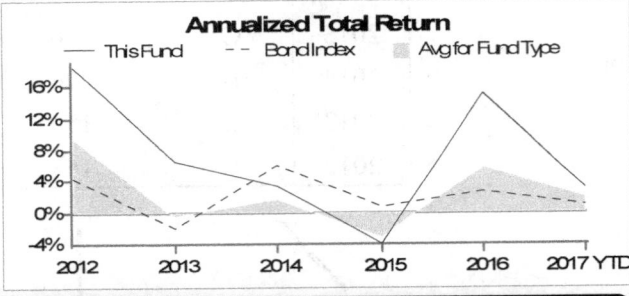

AB High Income Municipal A (ABTHX)   B   Good

Fund Family: Alliance Bernstein Funds   **Phone:** (800) 221-5672
Address: P.O. Box 786003, San Antonio, TX 78278
Fund Type: MUH - Municipal - High Yield

Major Rating Factors: AB High Income Municipal A has adopted a very risky asset allocation strategy and currently receives an overall TheStreet Investment Rating of B (Good). Volatility, as measured by standard deviation, is considered above average for fixed income funds at 4.77. Another risk factor is the fund's fairly average duration of 6.3 years (i.e. average interest rate risk). The high level of risk (D, Weak) did however, reward investors with excellent performance.

The fund's performance rating is currently A (Excellent). It has registered an average return of 6.01% over the last three years (9.95% taxable equivalent) and is up 2.17% over the last three months (3.59% taxable equivalent). Factored into the performance evaluation is an expense ratio of 0.88% (average) and a 3.0% front-end load that is levied at the time of purchase.

Robert B. Davidson, III has been running the fund for 7 years and currently receives a manager quality ranking of 77 (0=worst, 99=best). If you are comfortable owning a very high risk investment, this fund may be an option.

Services Offered: Automated phone transactions, payroll deductions, bank draft capabilities, an IRA investment plan, a 401K investment plan, wire transfers and a systematic withdrawal plan.

Data Date	Investment Rating	Net Assets ($Mil)	NAV	Performance Rating/Pts	Total Return Y-T-D	Risk Rating/Pts
2-17	B	781	11.07	A / 9.4	2.17%	D / 1.9
2016	B-	765	10.91	A+ / 9.6	-0.15%	D / 1.7
2015	C	738	11.37	A+ / 9.7	5.31%	E+ / 0.6
2014	C+	677	11.29	A+ / 9.9	17.19%	E+ / 0.6
2013	D+	522	10.11	B / 8.0	-7.95%	E+ / 0.6
2012	U	639	11.55	U / --	16.59%	U / --

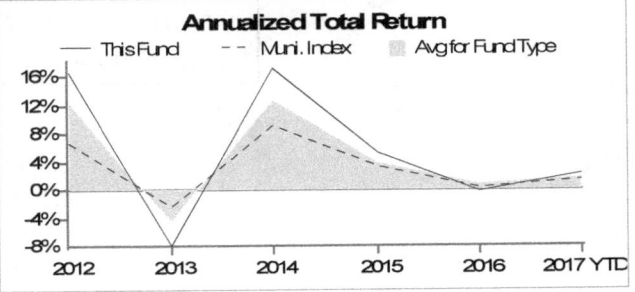

AB Municipal Income (MISHX)   B+   Good

Fund Family: Alliance Bernstein Funds   **Phone:** (800) 221-5672
Address: P.O. Box 786003, San Antonio, TX 78278
Fund Type: MUH - Municipal - High Yield
Major Rating Factors: AB Municipal Income has adopted a very risky asset allocation strategy and currently receives an overall TheStreet Investment Rating of B+ (Good). Volatility, as measured by standard deviation, is considered above average for fixed income funds at 4.74. The high level of risk (D, Weak) did however, reward investors with excellent performance.

The fund's performance rating is currently A+ (Excellent). It has registered an average return of 6.93% over the last three years (11.48% taxable equivalent) and is up 1.64% over the last three months (2.72% taxable equivalent). Factored into the performance evaluation is an expense ratio of 0.01% (very low).

Terrance T. Hults has been running the fund for 7 years and currently receives a manager quality ranking of 85 (0=worst, 99=best). If you are comfortable owning a very high risk investment, this fund may be an option.
Services Offered: Automated phone transactions, bank draft capabilities and wire transfers.

Data Date	Investment Rating	Net Assets ($Mil)	NAV	Performance Rating/Pts	Total Return Y-T-D	Risk Rating/Pts
2-17	B+	1,571	11.16	A+ / 9.9	1.64%	D / 1.9
2016	B	1,430	11.05	A+ / 9.9	1.81%	D / 1.7
2015	C	851	11.29	A+ / 9.9	5.82%	E+ / 0.6
2014	C+	528	11.16	A+ / 9.9	18.14%	E+ / 0.6
2013	C+	287	9.92	A+ / 9.6	-6.71%	E+ / 0.9

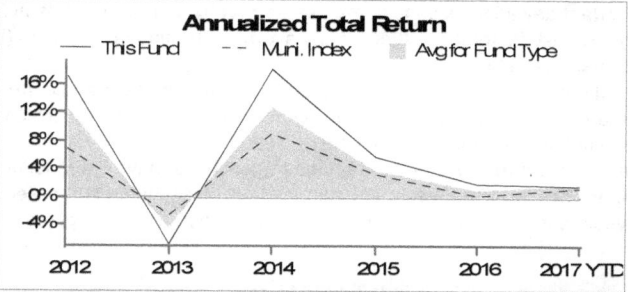

Annualized Total Return

AB Municipal Income Natl A (ALTHX)   C   Fair

Fund Family: Alliance Bernstein Funds   **Phone:** (800) 221-5672
Address: P.O. Box 786003, San Antonio, TX 78278
Fund Type: MUN - Municipal - National
Major Rating Factors: Middle of the road best describes AB Municipal Income Natl A whose TheStreet Investment Rating is currently a C (Fair). The fund has a performance rating of C+ (Fair) based on an average return of 3.61% over the last three years (5.98% taxable equivalent) and 1.12% over the last three months (1.85% taxable equivalent). Factored into the performance evaluation is an expense ratio of 0.80% (low) and a 3.0% front-end load that is levied at the time of purchase.

The fund's risk rating is currently C- (Fair). Volatility, as measured by standard deviation, is considered average for fixed income funds at 3.41. Another risk factor is the fund's below average duration of 4.7 years (i.e. lower interest rate risk).

Terrance T. Hults has been running the fund for 22 years and currently receives a manager quality ranking of 41 (0=worst, 99=best). If you desire an average level of risk, then this fund may be an option.
Services Offered: Automated phone transactions, check writing, payroll deductions, bank draft capabilities and a systematic withdrawal plan.

Data Date	Investment Rating	Net Assets ($Mil)	NAV	Performance Rating/Pts	Total Return Y-T-D	Risk Rating/Pts
2-17	C	614	10.12	C+ / 6.5	1.12%	C- / 4.2
2016	C+	618	10.06	C+ / 6.8	0.34%	C- / 4.1
2015	B-	613	10.33	B+ / 8.5	2.94%	C- / 4.1
2014	B+	588	10.38	B+ / 8.4	10.02%	C- / 3.8
2013	C	620	9.78	C+ / 6.2	-4.39%	C- / 4.2
2012	A+	775	10.60	B / 8.0	8.47%	C / 4.6

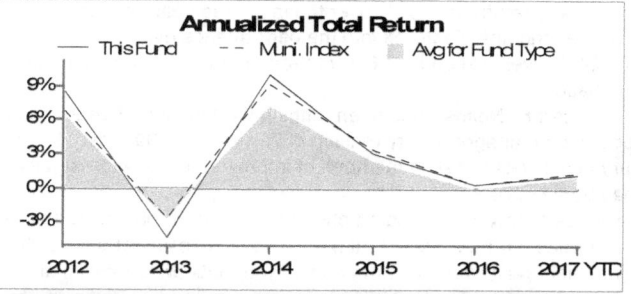

Annualized Total Return

American Century VP Infl Prot II (AIPTX)   D-   Weak

Fund Family: American Century Investment Funds   **Phone:** (800) 345-6488
Address: PO Box 419200, Kansas City, MO 64141
Fund Type: USL - US Government - Long Term
Major Rating Factors: American Century VP Infl Prot II receives a TheStreet Investment Rating of D- (Weak). The fund has a performance rating of C- (Fair) based on an average return of 1.39% over the last three years and 1.29% over the last three months. Factored into the performance evaluation is an expense ratio of 0.72% (low).

The fund's risk rating is currently C- (Fair). Volatility, as measured by standard deviation, is considered average for fixed income funds at 3.86. Another risk factor is the fund's fairly average duration of 6.9 years (i.e. average interest rate risk).

Brian Howell has been running the fund for 10 years and currently receives a manager quality ranking of 36 (0=worst, 99=best). If you desire an average level of risk, then this fund may be an option.
Services Offered: N/A

Data Date	Investment Rating	Net Assets ($Mil)	NAV	Performance Rating/Pts	Total Return Y-T-D	Risk Rating/Pts
2-17	D-	590	10.24	C- / 3.9	1.29%	C- / 3.4
2016	D-	581	10.11	C- / 3.9	4.39%	C- / 3.5
2015	D-	529	9.94	E+ / 0.9	-2.47%	D+ / 2.5
2014	E+	661	10.39	D / 1.6	3.30%	D / 2.2
2013	E+	689	10.45	D+ / 2.3	-8.48%	C- / 3.1
2012	C	1,314	12.03	C+ / 5.6	7.39%	C / 4.5

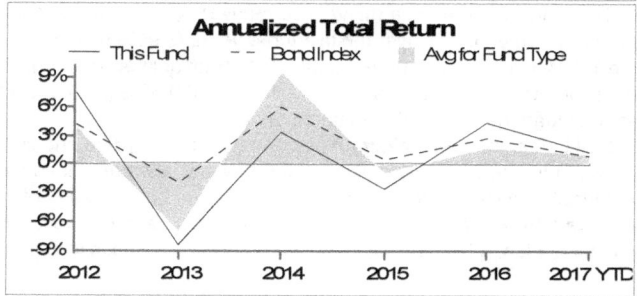

Annualized Total Return

American Funds Bd Fd of Amer A (ABNDX)   D   Weak

Fund Family: American Funds   **Phone:** (800) 421-0180
Address: 333 South Hope Street, Los Angeles, CA 90071
Fund Type: GEI - General - Investment Grade

Major Rating Factors: American Funds Bd Fd of Amer A receives a TheStreet Investment Rating of D (Weak). The fund has a performance rating of C- (Fair) based on an average return of 2.44% over the last three years and 1.07% over the last three months. Factored into the performance evaluation is an expense ratio of 0.61% (low) and a 3.8% front-end load that is levied at the time of purchase.

The fund's risk rating is currently C+ (Fair). Volatility, as measured by standard deviation, is considered average for fixed income funds at 2.97. Another risk factor is the fund's fairly average duration of 5.1 years (i.e. average interest rate risk).

John H. Smet has been running the fund for 28 years and currently receives a manager quality ranking of 33 (0=worst, 99=best). If you desire an average level of risk, then this fund may be an option.

Services Offered: Automated phone transactions, payroll deductions, bank draft capabilities, an IRA investment plan, a 401K investment plan, a Keogh investment plan, wire transfers and a systematic withdrawal plan.

Data Date	Investment Rating	Net Assets ($Mil)	NAV	Performance Rating/Pts	Total Return Y-T-D	Risk Rating/Pts
2-17	D	19,312	12.82	C- / 3.2	1.07%	C+ / 5.7
2016	D	19,407	12.72	C- / 3.4	2.74%	C+ / 5.7
2015	C-	18,548	12.59	C- / 3.6	0.23%	C+ / 5.9
2014	C-	18,663	12.81	C- / 3.5	5.53%	C+ / 6.7
2013	C-	19,325	12.40	D+ / 2.8	-1.99%	B- / 7.3
2012	C	24,142	12.95	C- / 3.1	5.89%	B / 7.6

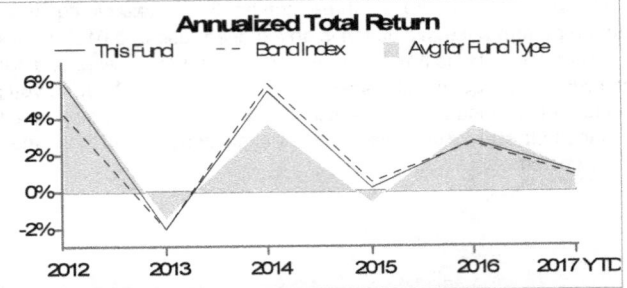

American Funds Cap World Bond A (CWBFX)   E-   Very Weak

Fund Family: American Funds   **Phone:** (800) 421-0180
Address: 333 South Hope Street, Los Angeles, CA 90071
Fund Type: GL - Global

Major Rating Factors: American Funds Cap World Bond A has adopted a very risky asset allocation strategy and currently receives an overall TheStreet Investment Rating of E- (Very Weak). Volatility, as measured by standard deviation, is considered above average for fixed income funds at 5.09. Unfortunately, the high level of risk (D, Weak) failed to pay off as investors endured poor performance.

The fund's performance rating is currently E- (Very Weak). It has registered an average return of -0.31% over the last three years and is up 1.90% over the last three months. Factored into the performance evaluation is an expense ratio of 0.94% (average) and a 3.8% front-end load that is levied at the time of purchase.

Robert H. Neithart has been running the fund for 18 years and currently receives a manager quality ranking of 79 (0=worst, 99=best). If you can tolerate very high levels of risk in the hope of improved future returns, holding this fund may be an option.

Services Offered: Automated phone transactions, payroll deductions, bank draft capabilities, an IRA investment plan, a 401K investment plan, a Keogh investment plan, wire transfers and a systematic withdrawal plan.

Data Date	Investment Rating	Net Assets ($Mil)	NAV	Performance Rating/Pts	Total Return Y-T-D	Risk Rating/Pts
2-17	E-	5,791	19.32	E- / 0.2	1.90%	D / 2.0
2016	E	5,830	18.96	E / 0.3	2.27%	D / 2.0
2015	D-	6,138	18.91	E+ / 0.7	-4.19%	C- / 3.3
2014	E+	7,028	19.85	D- / 1.4	1.59%	C- / 3.3
2013	E+	7,237	20.11	D / 1.9	-2.92%	C- / 3.0
2012	E-	8,376	21.20	D+ / 2.7	7.43%	D / 2.1

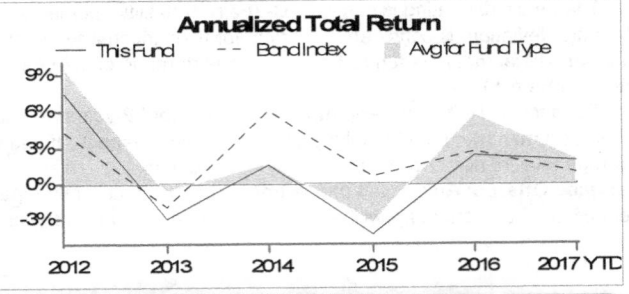

American Funds High Inc Muni Bnd A (AMHIX)   B   Good

Fund Family: American Funds   **Phone:** (800) 421-0180
Address: 333 South Hope Street, Los Angeles, CA 90071
Fund Type: MUH - Municipal - High Yield

Major Rating Factors: American Funds High Inc Muni Bnd A has adopted a risky asset allocation strategy and currently receives an overall TheStreet Investment Rating of B (Good). Volatility, as measured by standard deviation, is considered above average for fixed income funds at 3.72. Another risk factor is the fund's fairly average duration of 6.9 years (i.e. average interest rate risk). The high level of risk (D+, Weak) did however, reward investors with excellent performance.

The fund's performance rating is currently B+ (Good). It has registered an average return of 5.43% over the last three years (8.99% taxable equivalent) and is up 1.49% over the last three months (2.47% taxable equivalent). Factored into the performance evaluation is an expense ratio of 0.67% (low) and a 3.8% front-end load that is levied at the time of purchase.

Neil L. Langberg has been running the fund for 23 years and currently receives a manager quality ranking of 82 (0=worst, 99=best). If you are comfortable owning a high risk investment, this fund may be an option.

Services Offered: Automated phone transactions, payroll deductions, an IRA investment plan, a Keogh investment plan and a systematic withdrawal plan.

Data Date	Investment Rating	Net Assets ($Mil)	NAV	Performance Rating/Pts	Total Return Y-T-D	Risk Rating/Pts
2-17	B	3,407	15.41	B+ / 8.9	1.49%	D+ / 2.8
2016	B+	3,337	15.28	A / 9.4	1.54%	D+ / 2.6
2015	C+	2,931	15.62	A+ / 9.7	4.39%	D / 2.2
2014	B	2,563	15.58	A+ / 9.8	14.04%	D- / 1.4
2013	C+	2,121	14.26	B+ / 8.6	-3.41%	D+ / 2.3
2012	A+	2,441	15.42	A+ / 9.7	14.18%	C- / 3.0

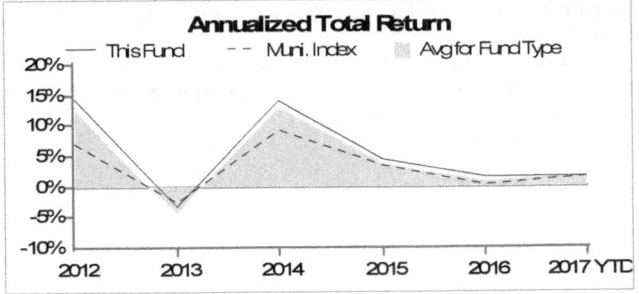

American Funds High Income Tr A (AHITX)   D+   Weak

Fund Family: American Funds   **Phone:** (800) 421-0180
Address: 333 South Hope Street, Los Angeles, CA 90071
Fund Type: COH - Corporate - High Yield
Major Rating Factors: American Funds High Income Tr A has adopted a very risky asset allocation strategy and currently receives an overall TheStreet Investment Rating of D+ (Weak). Volatility, as measured by standard deviation, is considered high for fixed income funds at 6.19. Another risk factor is the fund's below average duration of 3.4 years (i.e. lower interest rate risk). The high level of risk (E+, Very Weak) did however, reward investors with excellent performance.

The fund's performance rating is currently B (Good). It has registered an average return of 2.82% over the last three years and is up 2.79% over the last three months. Factored into the performance evaluation is an expense ratio of 0.71% (low) and a 3.8% front-end load that is levied at the time of purchase.

David C. Barclay has been running the fund for 28 years and currently receives a manager quality ranking of 3 (0=worst, 99=best). If you are comfortable owning a very high risk investment, this fund may be an option.
Services Offered: Automated phone transactions, payroll deductions, an IRA investment plan, a 401K investment plan, a Keogh investment plan, wire transfers and a systematic withdrawal plan.

Data Date	Investment Rating	Net Assets ($Mil)	NAV	Performance Rating/Pts	Total Return Y-T-D	Risk Rating/Pts
2-17	D+	11,925	10.46	B / 8.1	2.79%	E+ / 0.8
2016	D	11,736	10.26	B- / 7.5	16.31%	E+ / 0.8
2015	E	10,974	9.35	E+ / 0.7	-7.42%	D- / 1.2
2014	D	13,458	10.75	C+ / 6.0	0.53%	D / 2.2
2013	C	14,340	11.36	B+ / 8.8	6.44%	D- / 1.2
2012	C-	14,368	11.36	B / 7.8	14.52%	D- / 1.0

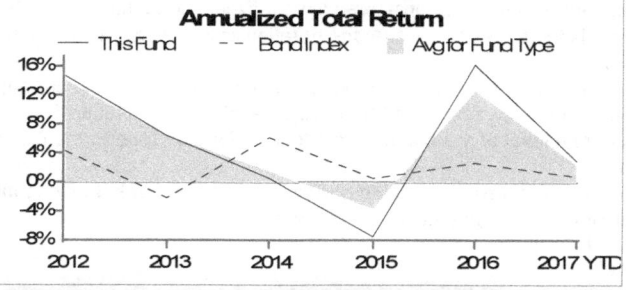

Annualized Total Return

American Funds Intm Bd Fd Amr A (AIBAX)   D+   Weak

Fund Family: American Funds   **Phone:** (800) 421-0180
Address: 333 South Hope Street, Los Angeles, CA 90071
Fund Type: GEI - General - Investment Grade
Major Rating Factors: Disappointing performance is the major factor driving the D+ (Weak) TheStreet Investment Rating for American Funds Intm Bd Fd Amr A. The fund currently has a performance rating of D (Weak) based on an average return of 1.14% over the last three years and 0.52% over the last three months. Factored into the performance evaluation is an expense ratio of 0.61% (low) and a 2.5% front-end load that is levied at the time of purchase.

The fund's risk rating is currently B+ (Good). Volatility, as measured by standard deviation, is considered low for fixed income funds at 1.81. Another risk factor is the fund's very low average duration of 2.9 years (i.e. low interest rate risk).

Mark A. Brett has been running the fund for 8 years and currently receives a manager quality ranking of 26 (0=worst, 99=best). This fund offers only a moderate level of risk but investors looking for strong performance are still waiting.
Services Offered: Automated phone transactions, payroll deductions, an IRA investment plan, a 401K investment plan, a Keogh investment plan, wire transfers and a systematic withdrawal plan.

Data Date	Investment Rating	Net Assets ($Mil)	NAV	Performance Rating/Pts	Total Return Y-T-D	Risk Rating/Pts
2-17	D+	7,075	13.39	D / 1.8	0.52%	B+ / 8.5
2016	C-	7,086	13.34	D / 2.0	1.13%	B+ / 8.6
2015	C	6,795	13.43	C- / 3.0	0.92%	B+ / 8.6
2014	D+	6,346	13.51	D- / 1.5	1.92%	B+ / 8.8
2013	D+	6,303	13.42	D- / 1.4	-1.17%	B+ / 8.9
2012	C-	7,162	13.76	D- / 1.3	2.70%	B+ / 8.8

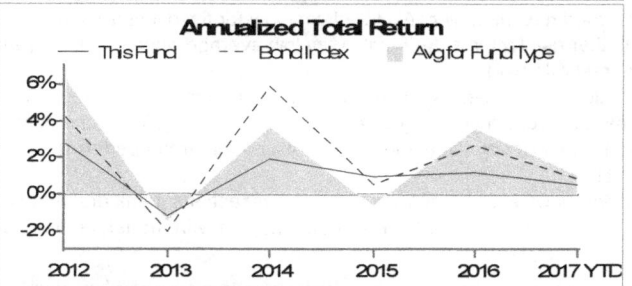

Annualized Total Return

American Funds Ltd Term T/E Bond A (LTEBX)   D+   Weak

Fund Family: American Funds   **Phone:** (800) 421-0180
Address: 333 South Hope Street, Los Angeles, CA 90071
Fund Type: MUN - Municipal - National
Major Rating Factors: Disappointing performance is the major factor driving the D+ (Weak) TheStreet Investment Rating for American Funds Ltd Term T/E Bond A. The fund currently has a performance rating of D (Weak) based on an average return of 1.24% over the last three years (2.05% taxable equivalent) and 0.98% over the last three months (1.62% taxable equivalent). Factored into the performance evaluation is an expense ratio of 0.59% (low) and a 2.5% front-end load that is levied at the time of purchase.

The fund's risk rating is currently B+ (Good). Volatility, as measured by standard deviation, is considered low for fixed income funds at 1.82. Another risk factor is the fund's below average duration of 3.1 years (i.e. lower interest rate risk).

Neil L. Langberg has been running the fund for 24 years and currently receives a manager quality ranking of 18 (0=worst, 99=best). This fund offers only a moderate level of risk but investors looking for strong performance are still waiting.
Services Offered: Automated phone transactions, payroll deductions, an IRA investment plan, a 401K investment plan, a Keogh investment plan and a systematic withdrawal plan.

Data Date	Investment Rating	Net Assets ($Mil)	NAV	Performance Rating/Pts	Total Return Y-T-D	Risk Rating/Pts
2-17	D+	2,989	15.65	D / 2.0	0.98%	B+ / 8.5
2016	C-	3,016	15.55	D / 2.0	-0.25%	B+ / 8.5
2015	A	2,762	15.91	C+ / 6.7	1.40%	B+ / 8.4
2014	C+	2,661	16.06	C- / 3.8	3.36%	B / 8.1
2013	A+	2,580	15.92	C+ / 6.2	-0.15%	B / 7.9
2012	C	2,703	16.34	C- / 3.9	3.81%	C+ / 6.6

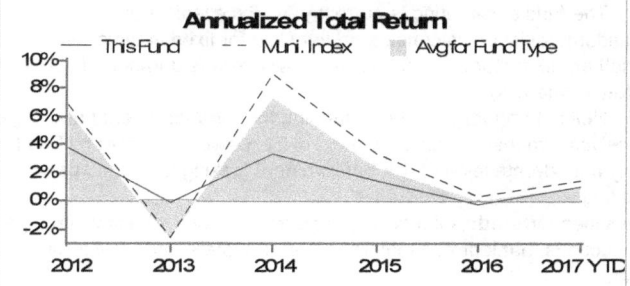

Annualized Total Return

American Funds Preservation A (PPVAX)

D+ **Weak**

Fund Family: American Funds
Phone: (800) 421-0180
Address: 333 South Hope Street, Los Angeles, CA 90071
Fund Type: GEI - General - Investment Grade

Major Rating Factors: Disappointing performance is the major factor driving the D+ (Weak) TheStreet Investment Rating for American Funds Preservation A. The fund currently has a performance rating of D (Weak) based on an average return of 1.09% over the last three years and 0.52% over the last three months. Factored into the performance evaluation is an expense ratio of 0.71% (low) and a 2.5% front-end load that is levied at the time of purchase.

The fund's risk rating is currently B+ (Good). Volatility, as measured by standard deviation, is considered low for fixed income funds at 1.63. Another risk factor is the fund's below average duration of 3.3 years (i.e. lower interest rate risk).

John H. Smet has been running the fund for 5 years and currently receives a manager quality ranking of 28 (0=worst, 99=best). This fund offers only a moderate level of risk but investors looking for strong performance are still waiting.

Services Offered: Automated phone transactions, bank draft capabilities, wire transfers and a systematic withdrawal plan.

Data Date	Investment Rating	Net Assets ($Mil)	NAV	Perfor- mance Rating/Pts	Total Return Y-T-D	Risk Rating/Pts
2-17	D+	785	9.91	D / 1.8	0.52%	B+ / 8.7
2016	C-	791	9.87	D / 2.0	1.28%	B+ / 8.7
2015	C	604	9.87	D+ / 2.8	0.56%	B+ / 8.8
2014	U	443	9.93	U / --	1.90%	U / --
2013	U	333	9.84	U / --	-1.10%	U / --
2012	U	256	10.06	U / --	0.00%	U / --

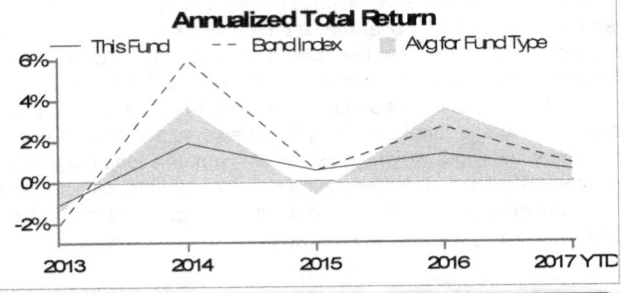

American Funds Sh-T Bd of Amr A (ASBAX)

D **Weak**

Fund Family: American Funds
Phone: (800) 421-0180
Address: 333 South Hope Street, Los Angeles, CA 90071
Fund Type: GES - General - Short & Inter. Term

Major Rating Factors: Very poor performance is the major factor driving the D (Weak) TheStreet Investment Rating for American Funds Sh-T Bd of Amr A. The fund currently has a performance rating of E+ (Very Weak) based on an average return of 0.63% over the last three years and 0.44% over the last three months. Factored into the performance evaluation is an expense ratio of 0.62% (low) and a 2.5% front-end load that is levied at the time of purchase.

The fund's risk rating is currently A (Excellent). Volatility, as measured by standard deviation, is considered very low for fixed income funds at 0.82. Another risk factor is the fund's very low average duration of 1.6 years (i.e. low interest rate risk).

John R. Queen has been running the fund for 6 years and currently receives a manager quality ranking of 42 (0=worst, 99=best). This fund offers only a moderate level of risk but investors looking for strong performance are still waiting.

Services Offered: Automated phone transactions, bank draft capabilities, an IRA investment plan, a 401K investment plan, wire transfers and a systematic withdrawal plan.

Data Date	Investment Rating	Net Assets ($Mil)	NAV	Perfor- mance Rating/Pts	Total Return Y-T-D	Risk Rating/Pts
2-17	D	3,157	9.96	E+ / 0.8	0.44%	A / 9.5
2016	D+	3,188	9.93	E+ / 0.7	1.02%	A / 9.5
2015	C	2,998	9.92	D+ / 2.3	0.36%	A / 9.5
2014	D+	2,972	9.98	E+ / 0.6	0.46%	A+ / 9.7
2013	D+	3,112	9.98	E / 0.4	-0.32%	A+ / 9.7
2012	D+	3,188	10.07	E / 0.5	0.81%	A+ / 9.7

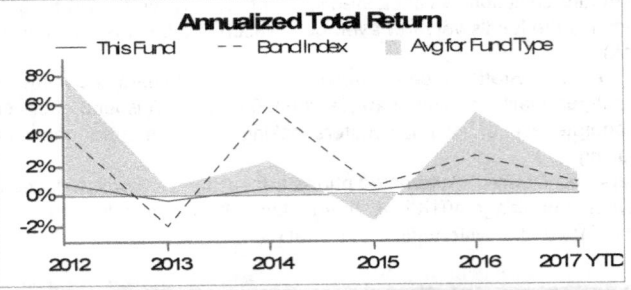

American Funds ST T/E Bnd Fd A (ASTEX)

D **Weak**

Fund Family: American Funds
Phone: (800) 421-0180
Address: 333 South Hope Street, Los Angeles, CA 90071
Fund Type: MUN - Municipal - National

Major Rating Factors: Very poor performance is the major factor driving the D (Weak) TheStreet Investment Rating for American Funds ST T/E Bnd Fd A. The fund currently has a performance rating of E (Very Weak) based on an average return of 0.52% over the last three years (0.86% taxable equivalent) and 0.89% over the last three months (1.47% taxable equivalent). Factored into the performance evaluation is an expense ratio of 0.59% (low) and a 2.5% front-end load that is levied at the time of purchase.

The fund's risk rating is currently A- (Excellent). Volatility, as measured by standard deviation, is considered very low for fixed income funds at 1.08. Another risk factor is the fund's very low average duration of 2.1 years (i.e. low interest rate risk).

Neil L. Langberg has been running the fund for 8 years and currently receives a manager quality ranking of 21 (0=worst, 99=best). This fund offers only a moderate level of risk but investors looking for strong performance are still waiting.

Services Offered: Automated phone transactions, check writing, payroll deductions, bank draft capabilities, wire transfers and a systematic withdrawal plan.

Data Date	Investment Rating	Net Assets ($Mil)	NAV	Perfor- mance Rating/Pts	Total Return Y-T-D	Risk Rating/Pts
2-17	D	737	10.11	E / 0.5	0.89%	A- / 9.1
2016	D	748	10.04	E / 0.5	-0.04%	A- / 9.2
2015	C	671	10.15	C- / 3.1	0.44%	A / 9.3
2014	C-	737	10.21	D- / 1.4	0.95%	A / 9.4
2013	C	735	10.22	D / 2.0	0.41%	A / 9.4
2012	C-	663	10.29	E+ / 0.9	1.63%	A / 9.4

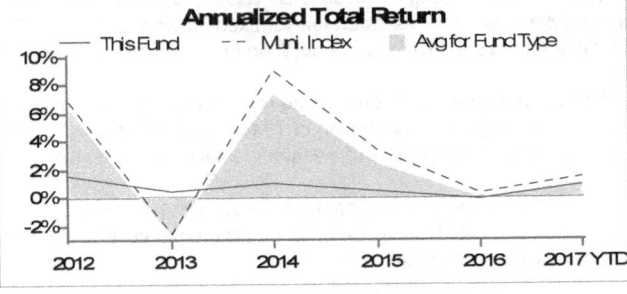

American Funds T/E Bd of America A (AFTEX)   C+   Fair

Fund Family: American Funds   **Phone:** (800) 421-0180
Address: 333 South Hope Street, Los Angeles, CA 90071
Fund Type: MUN - Municipal - National
Major Rating Factors: Middle of the road best describes American Funds T/E Bd of America A whose TheStreet Investment Rating is currently a C+ (Fair). The fund has a performance rating of C+ (Fair) based on an average return of 3.50% over the last three years (5.80% taxable equivalent) and 0.99% over the last three months (1.64% taxable equivalent). Factored into the performance evaluation is an expense ratio of 0.54% (very low) and a 3.8% front-end load that is levied at the time of purchase.

The fund's risk rating is currently C (Fair). Volatility, as measured by standard deviation, is considered average for fixed income funds at 3.07. Another risk factor is the fund's fairly average duration of 5.7 years (i.e. average interest rate risk).

Neil L. Langberg has been running the fund for 38 years and currently receives a manager quality ranking of 55 (0=worst, 99=best). If you desire an average level of risk, then this fund may be an option.

Services Offered: Automated phone transactions, payroll deductions, an IRA investment plan, a 401K investment plan, wire transfers and a systematic withdrawal plan.

Data Date	Investment Rating	Net Assets ($Mil)	NAV	Perfor- mance Rating/Pts	Total Return Y-T-D	Risk Rating/Pts
2-17	C+	9,326	12.80	C+ / 5.9	0.99%	C / 5.2
2016	C+	9,229	12.74	C+ / 6.4	0.35%	C / 4.9
2015	B	7,769	13.09	B+ / 8.7	3.12%	C / 4.7
2014	A-	7,071	13.11	B+ / 8.6	9.67%	C / 4.3
2013	B	6,590	12.37	B- / 7.4	-2.73%	C / 4.3
2012	B+	7,663	13.16	B- / 7.4	8.91%	C / 4.3

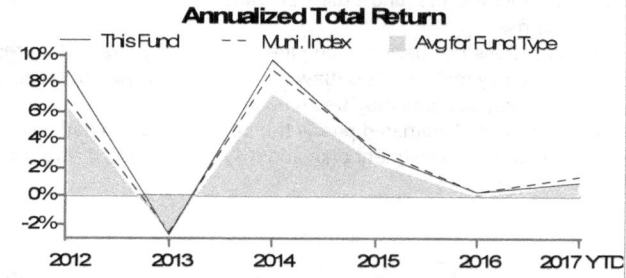

American Funds Tax-Exempt of CA A (TAFTX)   C   Fair

Fund Family: American Funds   **Phone:** (800) 421-0180
Address: 333 South Hope Street, Los Angeles, CA 90071
Fund Type: MUS - Municipal - Single State
Major Rating Factors: Middle of the road best describes American Funds Tax-Exempt of CA A whose TheStreet Investment Rating is currently a C (Fair). The fund has a performance rating of C+ (Fair) based on an average return of 3.62% over the last three years (5.99% taxable equivalent) and 1.02% over the last three months (1.69% taxable equivalent). Factored into the performance evaluation is an expense ratio of 0.60% (low) and a 3.8% front-end load that is levied at the time of purchase.

The fund's risk rating is currently C (Fair). Volatility, as measured by standard deviation, is considered average for fixed income funds at 3.36. Another risk factor is the fund's fairly average duration of 6.3 years (i.e. average interest rate risk).

Neil L. Langberg has been running the fund for 31 years and currently receives a manager quality ranking of 47 (0=worst, 99=best). If you desire an average level of risk, then this fund may be an option.

Services Offered: Automated phone transactions, payroll deductions, an IRA investment plan, a 401K investment plan and a systematic withdrawal plan.

Data Date	Investment Rating	Net Assets ($Mil)	NAV	Perfor- mance Rating/Pts	Total Return Y-T-D	Risk Rating/Pts
2-17	C	1,593	17.35	C+ / 6.0	1.02%	C / 4.3
2016	C	1,578	17.26	C+ / 6.7	-0.13%	C- / 4.1
2015	B+	1,458	17.81	A- / 9.1	3.38%	C / 4.3
2014	A	1,337	17.81	A- / 9.1	10.77%	C- / 4.1
2013	B+	1,208	16.65	B+ / 8.5	-2.31%	C- / 3.8
2012	A-	1,353	17.69	B+ / 8.7	9.96%	C- / 3.1

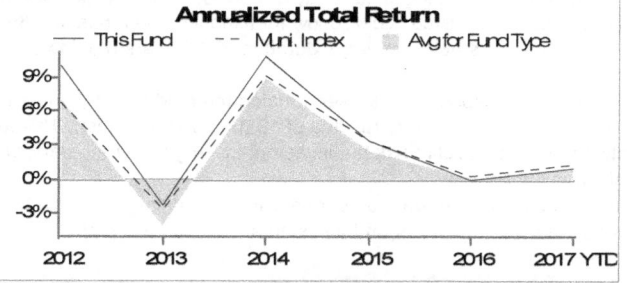

American Funds US Govt Sec A (AMUSX)   D-   Weak

Fund Family: American Funds   **Phone:** (800) 421-0180
Address: 333 South Hope Street, Los Angeles, CA 90071
Fund Type: USS - US Government - Short & Inter. Term
Major Rating Factors: Disappointing performance is the major factor driving the D- (Weak) TheStreet Investment Rating for American Funds US Govt Sec A. The fund currently has a performance rating of D (Weak) based on an average return of 1.90% over the last three years and 0.67% over the last three months. Factored into the performance evaluation is an expense ratio of 0.63% (low) and a 3.8% front-end load that is levied at the time of purchase.

The fund's risk rating is currently C+ (Fair). Volatility, as measured by standard deviation, is considered average for fixed income funds at 2.75. Another risk factor is the fund's below average duration of 3.8 years (i.e. lower interest rate risk).

Fergus N. MacDonald has been running the fund for 7 years and currently receives a manager quality ranking of 57 (0=worst, 99=best). This fund offers an average level of risk, but investors looking for strong performance will be frustrated.

Services Offered: Payroll deductions, an IRA investment plan, a 401K investment plan, a Keogh investment plan, wire transfers and a systematic withdrawal plan.

Data Date	Investment Rating	Net Assets ($Mil)	NAV	Perfor- mance Rating/Pts	Total Return Y-T-D	Risk Rating/Pts
2-17	D-	2,789	13.70	D / 1.9	0.67%	C+ / 6.8
2016	D	2,838	13.63	D+ / 2.4	0.75%	C+ / 6.6
2015	C-	2,629	13.85	C- / 3.8	1.52%	B- / 7.0
2014	D	2,626	14.03	D / 1.8	4.84%	B / 7.6
2013	D	2,914	13.52	D- / 1.0	-3.16%	B / 7.8
2012	D-	4,165	14.21	D / 1.8	2.10%	C+ / 6.9

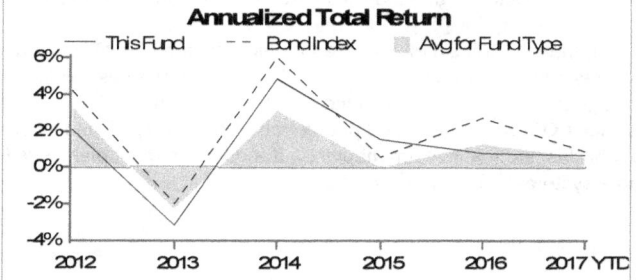

AMG Mgrs Loomis Sayles Bond N (MGFIX)

C   **Fair**

Fund Family: AMG Funds   **Phone:** (800) 548-4539
Address: 600 Steamboat Road, Greenwich, CT 06830
Fund Type: GEL - General - Long Term
Major Rating Factors: Middle of the road best describes AMG Mgrs Loomis Sayles Bond N whose TheStreet Investment Rating is currently a C (Fair). The fund has a performance rating of C+ (Fair) based on an average return of 2.66% over the last three years and 2.07% over the last three months. Factored into the performance evaluation is an expense ratio of 0.89% (average).

The fund's risk rating is currently C (Fair). Volatility, as measured by standard deviation, is considered average for fixed income funds at 3.35. Another risk factor is the fund's fairly average duration of 5.6 years (i.e. average interest rate risk).

Daniel J. Fuss has been running the fund for 23 years and currently receives a manager quality ranking of 66 (0=worst, 99=best). If you desire an average level of risk, then this fund may be an option.

Services Offered: Automated phone transactions, payroll deductions, bank draft capabilities, an IRA investment plan and a systematic withdrawal plan.

Data Date	Investment Rating	Net Assets ($Mil)	NAV	Performance Rating/Pts	Total Return Y-T-D	Risk Rating/Pts
2-17	C	1,223	26.63	C+ / 6.4	2.07%	C / 4.4
2016	C-	1,234	26.24	C+ / 5.8	5.15%	C / 4.5
2015	C-	1,576	26.20	C+ / 5.6	-2.15%	C / 5.1
2014	B+	1,946	27.88	B- / 7.5	5.81%	C / 4.9
2013	B+	1,545	27.33	B / 8.2	1.08%	C / 4.5
2012	B+	2,373	27.93	B / 7.6	12.04%	C / 4.4

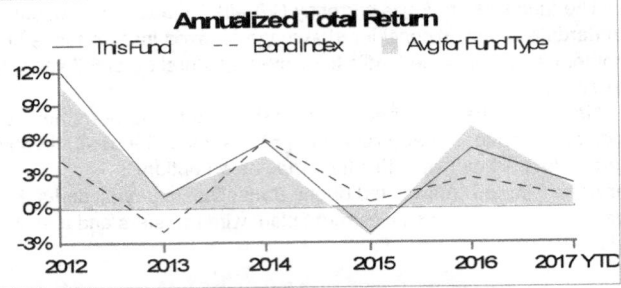

Annualized Total Return

Aquila Hawaiian Tax Free Trust A (HULAX)

D+   **Weak**

Fund Family: Aquila Funds   **Phone:** (800) 437-1020
Address: 380 Madison Aveneue, New York, NY 10017
Fund Type: MUN - Municipal - National
Major Rating Factors: Disappointing performance is the major factor driving the D+ (Weak) TheStreet Investment Rating for Aquila Hawaiian Tax Free Trust A. The fund currently has a performance rating of D+ (Weak) based on an average return of 2.15% over the last three years (3.56% taxable equivalent) and 1.31% over the last three months (2.17% taxable equivalent). Factored into the performance evaluation is an expense ratio of 0.83% (low) and a 4.0% front-end load that is levied at the time of purchase.

The fund's risk rating is currently B- (Good). Volatility, as measured by standard deviation, is considered low for fixed income funds at 2.66. Another risk factor is the fund's below average duration of 4.5 years (i.e. lower interest rate risk).

Stephen K. Rodgers has been running the fund for 32 years and currently receives a manager quality ranking of 18 (0=worst, 99=best). This fund offers only a moderate level of risk but investors looking for strong performance are still waiting.

Services Offered: Automated phone transactions, payroll deductions, bank draft capabilities, wire transfers and a systematic withdrawal plan.

Data Date	Investment Rating	Net Assets ($Mil)	NAV	Performance Rating/Pts	Total Return Y-T-D	Risk Rating/Pts
2-17	D+	664	11.34	D+ / 2.7	1.31%	B- / 7.2
2016	D	658	11.23	D+ / 2.3	-0.36%	B- / 7.2
2015	B	662	11.50	C+ / 6.4	2.07%	B- / 7.3
2014	D+	675	11.53	C- / 3.7	5.40%	C+/ 6.3
2013	D+	687	11.23	D+ / 2.9	-2.55%	C+/ 6.4
2012	D	773	11.83	D+ / 2.8	4.25%	C+/ 6.6

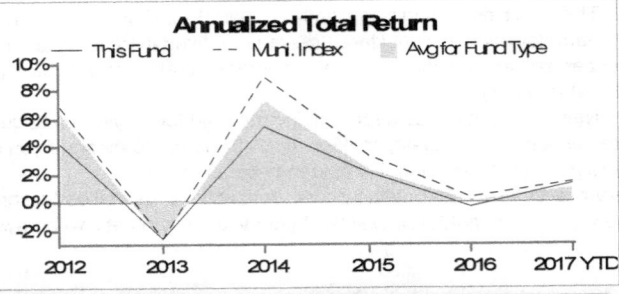

Annualized Total Return

Baird Aggregate Bond Inv (BAGSX)

C+   **Fair**

Fund Family: Baird Funds   **Phone:** (866) 442-2473
Address: 777 East Wisconsin Avenue, Milwaukee, WI 53202
Fund Type: COI - Corporate - Investment Grade
Major Rating Factors: Middle of the road best describes Baird Aggregate Bond Inv whose TheStreet Investment Rating is currently a C+ (Fair). The fund has a performance rating of C (Fair) based on an average return of 2.90% over the last three years and 0.96% over the last three months. Factored into the performance evaluation is an expense ratio of 0.55% (very low).

The fund's risk rating is currently C+ (Fair). Volatility, as measured by standard deviation, is considered average for fixed income funds at 2.93. Another risk factor is the fund's fairly average duration of 5.5 years (i.e. average interest rate risk).

Charles B. Groeschell has been running the fund for 17 years and currently receives a manager quality ranking of 59 (0=worst, 99=best). If you desire an average level of risk, then this fund may be an option.

Services Offered: Automated phone transactions, payroll deductions, bank draft capabilities, an IRA investment plan, a Keogh investment plan, wire transfers and a systematic withdrawal plan.

Data Date	Investment Rating	Net Assets ($Mil)	NAV	Performance Rating/Pts	Total Return Y-T-D	Risk Rating/Pts
2-17	C+	841	11.12	C / 5.4	0.96%	C+/ 5.9
2016	B-	809	11.05	C+ / 5.9	3.34%	C+/ 5.9
2015	C+	486	10.94	C+ / 6.6	0.21%	C+/ 5.9
2014	B+	242	11.15	C+ / 6.1	6.71%	C+/ 6.5
2013	B+	142	10.72	C+ / 5.8	-1.54%	B- / 7.1
2012	A	49	11.21	C / 5.5	7.72%	B- / 7.4

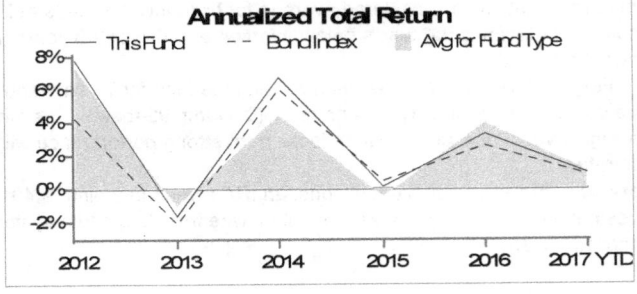

Annualized Total Return

Baird Core Plus Bond Inv (BCOSX)   B   Good

Fund Family: Baird Funds   **Phone:** (866) 442-2473
Address: 777 East Wisconsin Avenue, Milwaukee, WI 53202
Fund Type: GEI - General - Investment Grade
Major Rating Factors: Baird Core Plus Bond Inv receives a TheStreet
Investment Rating of B (Good). The fund has a performance rating of C+ (Fair)
based on an average return of 3.12% over the last three years and 1.15% over
the last three months. Factored into the performance evaluation is an expense
ratio of 0.55% (very low).

     The fund's risk rating is currently C+ (Fair). Volatility, as measured by
standard deviation, is considered average for fixed income funds at 2.95.
Another risk factor is the fund's fairly average duration of 5.4 years (i.e. average
interest rate risk).

     Gary A. Elfe has been running the fund for 17 years and currently receives a
manager quality ranking of 66 (0=worst, 99=best). If you desire an average level
of risk, then this fund may be an option.

Services Offered: Automated phone transactions, payroll deductions, bank draft
capabilities, an IRA investment plan, a Keogh investment plan, wire transfers
and a systematic withdrawal plan.

Data Date	Investment Rating	Net Assets ($Mil)	NAV	Performance Rating/Pts	Total Return Y-T-D	Risk Rating/Pts
2-17	B	2,935	11.55	C+ / 6.1	1.15%	C+ / 5.8
2016	B	2,882	11.46	C+ / 6.4	4.47%	C+ / 5.9
2015	C	2,173	11.26	C+ / 6.1	-0.11%	C / 5.5
2014	B	2,192	11.55	C+ / 5.8	6.27%	C+ / 6.1
2013	B+	1,046	11.16	C+ / 5.9	-1.61%	C+ / 6.7
2012	A	1,035	11.67	C+ / 5.9	7.80%	B- / 7.0

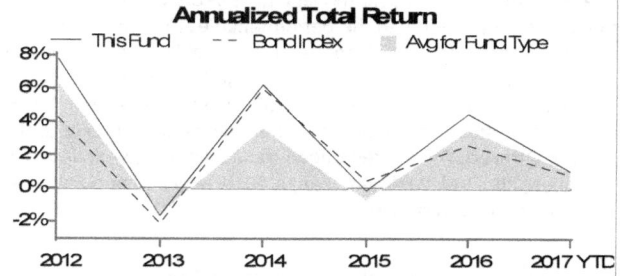

Berwyn Income Fund (BERIX)   C-   Fair

Fund Family: Berwyn Funds   **Phone:** (800) 992-6757
Address: C/O Ultimus Fund Solutions LLC, Cincinnati, OH 45246
Fund Type: GES - General - Short & Inter. Term
Major Rating Factors: Middle of the road best describes Berwyn Income Fund
whose TheStreet Investment Rating is currently a C- (Fair). The fund has a
performance rating of C+ (Fair) based on an average return of 2.69% over the
last three years and 1.10% over the last three months. Factored into the
performance evaluation is an expense ratio of 0.67% (low) and a 1.0% back-end
load levied at the time of sale.

     The fund's risk rating is currently C- (Fair). Volatility, as measured by
standard deviation, is considered average for fixed income funds at 3.80.
Another risk factor is the fund's very low average duration of 2.8 years (i.e. low
interest rate risk).

     Lee S. Grout has been running the fund for 15 years and currently receives
a manager quality ranking of 82 (0=worst, 99=best). If you desire an average
level of risk, then this fund may be an option.

Services Offered: Automated phone transactions, payroll deductions, bank draft
capabilities, an IRA investment plan and a systematic withdrawal plan.

Data Date	Investment Rating	Net Assets ($Mil)	NAV	Performance Rating/Pts	Total Return Y-T-D	Risk Rating/Pts
2-17	C-	1,741	13.74	C+ / 6.6	1.10%	C- / 3.4
2016	C	1,716	13.59	C+ / 6.8	8.73%	C- / 3.5
2015	C	1,747	12.85	B+ / 8.3	-3.30%	C- / 3.0
2014	C+	2,575	13.61	B+ / 8.6	3.32%	D / 2.1
2013	B+	2,107	14.01	A+ / 9.9	15.83%	D+ / 2.3
2012	E	1,448	13.15	C / 4.7	7.96%	D / 2.1

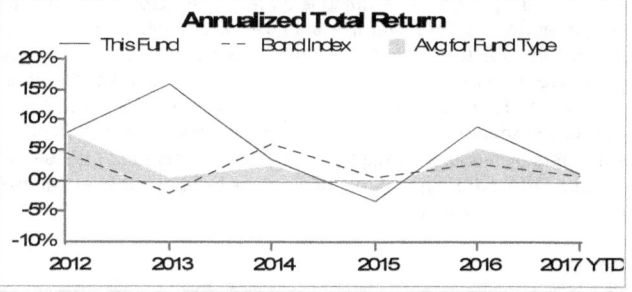

BlackRock Alloc Target Srs M (BRAMX)   B+   Good

Fund Family: BlackRock Funds   **Phone:** (800) 441-7762
Address: c/o PFPC, Inc., Providence, RI 02940
Fund Type: GEI - General - Investment Grade
Major Rating Factors: A moderate risk profile coupled with stable earnings
characterizes BlackRock Alloc Target Srs M which receives a TheStreet
Investment Rating of B+ (Good). Volatility, as measured by standard deviation, is
considered low for fixed income funds at 2.02. The fund's risk rating is currently
B (Good).

     The fund's performance rating is currently C (Fair). It has registered an
average return of 2.83% over the last three years and is up 0.52% over the last
three months. Factored into the performance evaluation is an expense ratio of
0.12% (very low).

     Michael Heilbronn has been running the fund for 6 years and currently
receives a manager quality ranking of 77 (0=worst, 99=best). If you desire
stability with a moderate level of risk then this fund is an excellent option.

Services Offered: Automated phone transactions, bank draft capabilities, wire
transfers and a systematic withdrawal plan.

Data Date	Investment Rating	Net Assets ($Mil)	NAV	Performance Rating/Pts	Total Return Y-T-D	Risk Rating/Pts
2-17	B+	596	9.72	C / 5.0	0.52%	B / 8.2
2016	A	588	9.72	C+ / 6.1	2.20%	B / 7.9
2015	B	533	9.80	B- / 7.4	1.52%	C+ / 5.9
2014	C+	464	9.98	C+ / 5.6	7.11%	C+ / 5.8

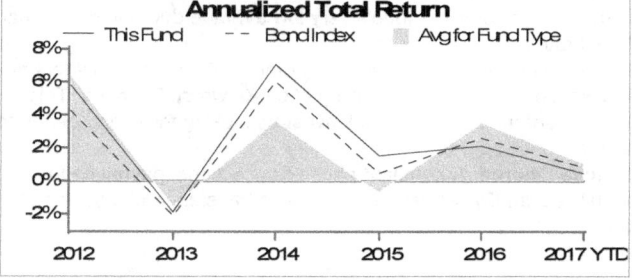

BlackRock Floating Rate Inc Inv A (BFRAX)

A+   Excellent

Fund Family: BlackRock Funds   **Phone:** (800) 441-7762
Address: c/o PFPC, Inc., Providence, RI 02940
Fund Type: LP - Loan Participation

Major Rating Factors: A moderate risk profile coupled with stable earnings characterizes BlackRock Floating Rate Inc Inv A which receives a TheStreet Investment Rating of A+ (Excellent). Volatility, as measured by standard deviation, is considered low for fixed income funds at 2.34. Another risk factor is the fund's very low average duration of 0.1 years (i.e. low interest rate risk). The fund's risk rating is currently B (Good).

The fund's performance rating is currently C+ (Fair). It has registered an average return of 3.24% over the last three years and is up 0.90% over the last three months. Factored into the performance evaluation is an expense ratio of 1.02% (average) and a 2.5% front-end load that is levied at the time of purchase.

C. Adrian Marshall has been running the fund for 8 years and currently receives a manager quality ranking of 90 (0=worst, 99=best). If you desire stability with a moderate level of risk then this fund is an excellent option.

Services Offered: Automated phone transactions, payroll deductions, bank draft capabilities, an IRA investment plan, a 401K investment plan, wire transfers and a systematic withdrawal plan.

Data Date	Investment Rating	Net Assets ($Mil)	NAV	Performance Rating/Pts	Total Return Y-T-D	Risk Rating/Pts
2-17	A+	643	10.26	C+/ 6.9	0.90%	B / 7.8
2016	A+	625	10.23	C+/ 6.7	7.62%	B / 7.9
2015	B+	540	9.89	C+/ 6.1	0.71%	B+/ 8.4
2014	B+	567	10.21	C / 4.6	1.20%	B / 8.2
2013	B+	750	10.51	B-/ 7.3	5.09%	C / 5.2
2012	E+	501	10.39	C-/ 3.2	8.29%	C-/ 4.1

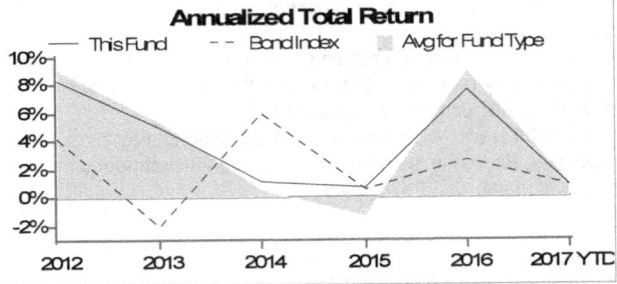

Annualized Total Return

BlackRock High Yield Bond Inv A (BHYAX)

C-   Fair

Fund Family: BlackRock Funds   **Phone:** (800) 441-7762
Address: c/o PFPC, Inc., Providence, RI 02940
Fund Type: COH - Corporate - High Yield

Major Rating Factors: BlackRock High Yield Bond Inv A has adopted a very risky asset allocation strategy and currently receives an overall TheStreet Investment Rating of C- (Fair). Volatility, as measured by standard deviation, is considered above average for fixed income funds at 5.49. Another risk factor is the fund's very low average duration of 1.2 years (i.e. low interest rate risk). The high level of risk (D-, Weak) did however, reward investors with excellent performance.

The fund's performance rating is currently B+ (Good). It has registered an average return of 3.75% over the last three years and is up 2.76% over the last three months. Factored into the performance evaluation is an expense ratio of 0.94% (average) and a 4.0% front-end load that is levied at the time of purchase.

James E. Keenan has been running the fund for 10 years and currently receives a manager quality ranking of 25 (0=worst, 99=best). If you are comfortable owning a very high risk investment, this fund may be an option.

Services Offered: Payroll deductions, bank draft capabilities, an IRA investment plan and a systematic withdrawal plan.

Data Date	Investment Rating	Net Assets ($Mil)	NAV	Performance Rating/Pts	Total Return Y-T-D	Risk Rating/Pts
2-17	C-	3,589	7.77	B+/ 8.4	2.76%	D-/ 1.2
2016	C-	3,573	7.63	B / 8.1	13.41%	D-/ 1.3
2015	D	2,622	7.13	D+/ 2.8	-4.33%	D-/ 1.2
2014	C	2,927	7.88	B+/ 8.3	3.04%	D / 1.8
2013	B-	4,283	8.21	A+/ 9.6	8.95%	D-/ 1.3
2012	C+	3,550	8.09	A-/ 9.1	16.77%	D-/ 1.0

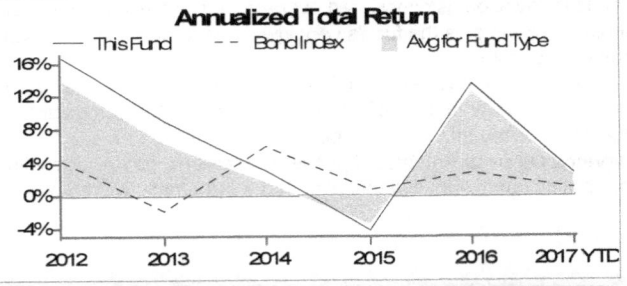

Annualized Total Return

BlackRock Low Duration Bond Inv A (BLDAX)

C   Fair

Fund Family: BlackRock Funds   **Phone:** (800) 441-7762
Address: c/o PFPC, Inc., Providence, RI 02940
Fund Type: GEI - General - Investment Grade

Major Rating Factors: Disappointing performance is the major factor driving the C (Fair) TheStreet Investment Rating for BlackRock Low Duration Bond Inv A. The fund currently has a performance rating of D (Weak) based on an average return of 1.07% over the last three years and 0.50% over the last three months. Factored into the performance evaluation is an expense ratio of 0.84% (low) and a 2.3% front-end load that is levied at the time of purchase.

The fund's risk rating is currently A (Excellent). Volatility, as measured by standard deviation, is considered very low for fixed income funds at 0.79. Another risk factor is the fund's very low average duration of 2.0 years (i.e. low interest rate risk).

Thomas F. Musmanno has been running the fund for 9 years and currently receives a manager quality ranking of 64 (0=worst, 99=best). This fund offers only a moderate level of risk but investors looking for strong performance are still waiting.

Services Offered: Automated phone transactions, payroll deductions, bank draft capabilities, an IRA investment plan, wire transfers and a systematic withdrawal plan.

Data Date	Investment Rating	Net Assets ($Mil)	NAV	Performance Rating/Pts	Total Return Y-T-D	Risk Rating/Pts
2-17	C	887	9.62	D / 2.1	0.50%	A / 9.5
2016	C+	887	9.60	D+/ 2.3	1.66%	A / 9.5
2015	C+	843	9.58	C-/ 4.0	0.48%	A-/ 9.2
2014	C	777	9.68	D+/ 2.4	1.18%	A-/ 9.1
2013	C+	1,605	9.75	C-/ 3.1	0.99%	A-/ 9.1
2012	C	578	9.83	D / 1.7	4.84%	A-/ 9.1

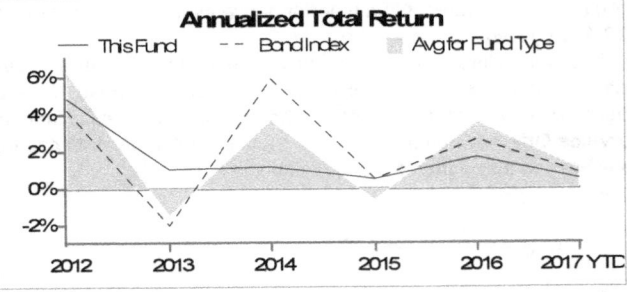

Annualized Total Return

BlackRock Natl Muni Inv A (MDNLX)   B+   Good

Fund Family: BlackRock Funds   **Phone:** (800) 441-7762
Address: c/o PFPC, Inc., Providence, RI 02940
Fund Type: MUN - Municipal - National

Major Rating Factors: A moderate risk profile coupled with stable earnings characterizes BlackRock Natl Muni Inv A which receives a TheStreet Investment Rating of B+ (Good). Volatility, as measured by standard deviation, is considered low for fixed income funds at 2.71. The fund's risk rating is currently B- (Good).

The fund's performance rating is currently C+ (Fair). It has registered an average return of 3.53% over the last three years (5.85% taxable equivalent) and is up 1.09% over the last three months (1.81% taxable equivalent). Factored into the performance evaluation is an expense ratio of 0.85% (average) and a 4.3% front-end load that is levied at the time of purchase.

Walter O'Connor has been running the fund for 21 years and currently receives a manager quality ranking of 68 (0=worst, 99=best). If you desire stability with a moderate level of risk then this fund is an excellent option.

Services Offered: Payroll deductions, bank draft capabilities and a systematic withdrawal plan.

Data Date	Investment Rating	Net Assets ($Mil)	NAV	Performance Rating/Pts	Total Return Y-T-D	Risk Rating/Pts
2-17	B+	2,327	10.78	C+ / 6.0	1.09%	B- / 7.0
2016	B+	2,313	10.72	C+ / 6.6	0.15%	C+ / 6.0
2015	B-	2,592	11.01	B+ / 8.6	3.35%	C- / 4.2
2014	B+	2,177	11.00	B+ / 8.6	10.06%	C- / 3.3
2013	C+	1,716	10.35	B / 7.6	-3.20%	C- / 3.5
2012	B+	2,055	11.09	B / 8.2	9.63%	C- / 3.4

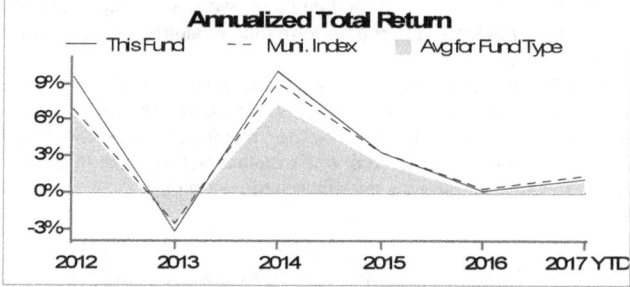

BlackRock Strat Muni Opps Inv A (MEMTX)   C   Fair

Fund Family: BlackRock Funds   **Phone:** (800) 441-7762
Address: c/o PFPC, Inc., Providence, RI 02940
Fund Type: MUN - Municipal - National

Major Rating Factors: Middle of the road best describes BlackRock Strat Muni Opps Inv A whose TheStreet Investment Rating is currently a C (Fair). The fund has a performance rating of C+ (Fair) based on an average return of 3.62% over the last three years (5.99% taxable equivalent) and 1.45% over the last three months (2.40% taxable equivalent). Factored into the performance evaluation is an expense ratio of 0.95% (average) and a 4.3% front-end load that is levied at the time of purchase.

The fund's risk rating is currently C- (Fair). Volatility, as measured by standard deviation, is considered average for fixed income funds at 3.51.

Theodore R. Jaeckel, Jr. has been running the fund for 11 years and currently receives a manager quality ranking of 52 (0=worst, 99=best). If you desire an average level of risk, then this fund may be an option.

Services Offered: Automated phone transactions, payroll deductions, wire transfers and a systematic withdrawal plan.

Data Date	Investment Rating	Net Assets ($Mil)	NAV	Performance Rating/Pts	Total Return Y-T-D	Risk Rating/Pts
2-17	C	1,091	11.30	C+ / 6.3	1.45%	C- / 4.0
2016	C-	1,082	11.19	C+ / 6.3	0.58%	C- / 3.9
2015	B-	934	11.53	B+ / 8.7	3.41%	C- / 4.0
2014	C+	618	11.45	B / 7.9	9.36%	C- / 3.2
2013	C	190	10.77	C+ / 6.9	-3.09%	C- / 3.7
2012	B+	216	11.51	B / 7.6	8.17%	C- / 3.9

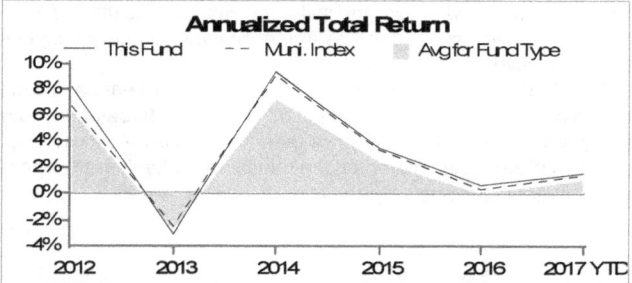

BlackRock Total Return Inv A (MDHQX)   D+   Weak

Fund Family: BlackRock Funds   **Phone:** (800) 441-7762
Address: c/o PFPC, Inc., Providence, RI 02940
Fund Type: GEI - General - Investment Grade

Major Rating Factors: BlackRock Total Return Inv A receives a TheStreet Investment Rating of D+ (Weak). The fund has a performance rating of C- (Fair) based on an average return of 3.08% over the last three years and 1.02% over the last three months. Factored into the performance evaluation is an expense ratio of 0.86% (average) and a 4.0% front-end load that is levied at the time of purchase.

The fund's risk rating is currently C+ (Fair). Volatility, as measured by standard deviation, is considered average for fixed income funds at 2.97. Another risk factor is the fund's below average duration of 4.9 years (i.e. lower interest rate risk).

Richard M. Rieder has been running the fund for 7 years and currently receives a manager quality ranking of 63 (0=worst, 99=best). If you desire an average level of risk, then this fund may be an option.

Services Offered: Automated phone transactions, bank draft capabilities, an IRA investment plan, wire transfers and a systematic withdrawal plan.

Data Date	Investment Rating	Net Assets ($Mil)	NAV	Performance Rating/Pts	Total Return Y-T-D	Risk Rating/Pts
2-17	D+	2,029	11.66	C- / 4.1	1.02%	C+ / 5.7
2016	C-	2,008	11.59	C / 4.6	3.19%	C+ / 5.7
2015	C-	2,291	11.51	C+ / 5.6	0.03%	C / 5.2
2014	B	1,236	11.86	C+ / 6.4	7.74%	C+ / 6.0
2013	C	965	11.40	C / 4.5	-0.50%	C+ / 6.5
2012	B-	1,102	11.83	C / 4.9	9.70%	C+ / 6.5

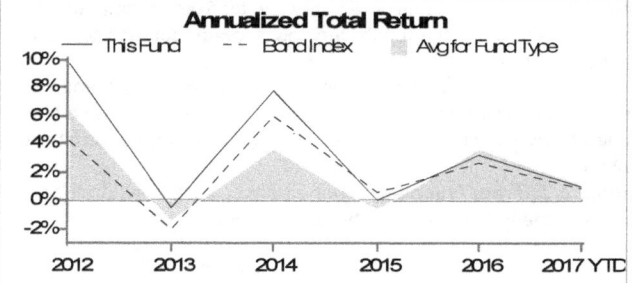

BNY Mellon Bond M (MPBFX)   C+   Fair

Fund Family: Mellon Funds   **Phone:** (800) 645-6561
Address: One Mellon Center, Pittsburgh, PA 15258
Fund Type: GEI - General - Investment Grade
Major Rating Factors: A moderate risk profile coupled with stable earnings characterizes BNY Mellon Bond M which receives a TheStreet Investment Rating of C+ (Fair). Volatility, as measured by standard deviation, is considered low for fixed income funds at 2.67. Another risk factor is the fund's fairly average duration of 5.1 years (i.e. average interest rate risk). The fund's risk rating is currently B- (Good).

The fund's performance rating is currently C (Fair). It has registered an average return of 2.25% over the last three years and is up 0.94% over the last three months. Factored into the performance evaluation is an expense ratio of 0.56% (very low).

John F. Flahive has been running the fund for 12 years and currently receives a manager quality ranking of 36 (0=worst, 99=best). If you desire stability with a moderate level of risk then this fund is an excellent option.
Services Offered: Automated phone transactions, bank draft capabilities, an IRA investment plan and a systematic withdrawal plan.

Data Date	Investment Rating	Net Assets ($Mil)	NAV	Perfor- mance Rating/Pts	Total Return Y-T-D	Risk Rating/Pts
2-17	C+	992	12.65	C / 4.4	0.94%	B- / 7.1
2016	C+	987	12.59	C / 4.6	2.52%	B- / 7.2
2015	C+	994	12.66	C+ / 5.7	0.70%	C+ / 6.7
2014	C	1,032	12.92	C- / 4.1	4.63%	C+ / 6.6
2013	C	1,100	12.72	C- / 3.8	-2.29%	B- / 7.5
2012	B-	1,300	13.58	C- / 3.4	6.04%	B+ / 8.4

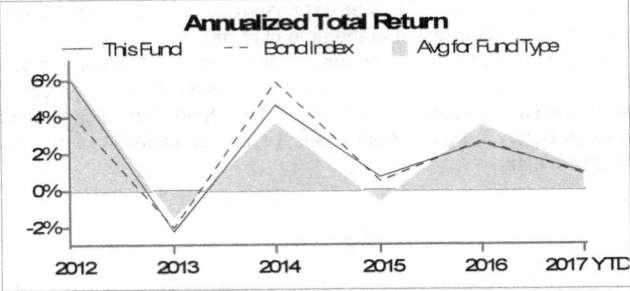

BNY Mellon Inter Bond M (MPIBX)   C+   Fair

Fund Family: Mellon Funds   **Phone:** (800) 645-6561
Address: One Mellon Center, Pittsburgh, PA 15258
Fund Type: GEI - General - Investment Grade
Major Rating Factors: A moderate risk profile coupled with stable earnings characterizes BNY Mellon Inter Bond M which receives a TheStreet Investment Rating of C+ (Fair). Volatility, as measured by standard deviation, is considered low for fixed income funds at 1.64. Another risk factor is the fund's below average duration of 3.2 years (i.e. lower interest rate risk). The fund's risk rating is currently B+ (Good).

The fund's performance rating is currently C- (Fair). It has registered an average return of 1.37% over the last three years and is up 0.65% over the last three months. Factored into the performance evaluation is an expense ratio of 0.56% (very low).

John F. Flahive has been running the fund for 11 years and currently receives a manager quality ranking of 37 (0=worst, 99=best). If you desire stability with a moderate level of risk then this fund is an excellent option.
Services Offered: Automated phone transactions, bank draft capabilities, an IRA investment plan and a systematic withdrawal plan.

Data Date	Investment Rating	Net Assets ($Mil)	NAV	Perfor- mance Rating/Pts	Total Return Y-T-D	Risk Rating/Pts
2-17	C+	851	12.52	C- / 3.3	0.65%	B+ / 8.7
2016	C+	877	12.48	C- / 3.4	2.02%	B+ / 8.7
2015	C+	857	12.49	C / 4.5	0.58%	B+ / 8.4
2014	C	904	12.66	D+ / 2.5	1.95%	B+ / 8.5
2013	C+	927	12.67	C- / 3.0	-1.30%	B+ / 8.6
2012	C	930	13.20	D / 2.2	4.15%	B+ / 8.8

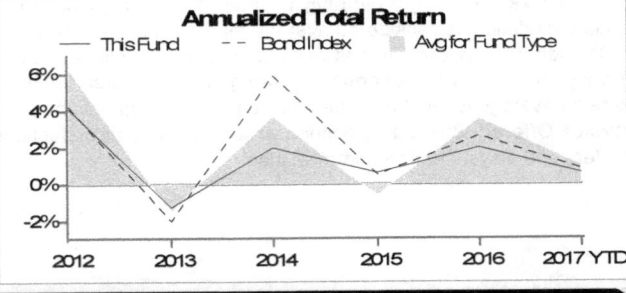

BNY Mellon National ST Muni Bd M (MPSTX)   C   Fair

Fund Family: Mellon Funds   **Phone:** (800) 645-6561
Address: One Mellon Center, Pittsburgh, PA 15258
Fund Type: MUI - Municipal - Insured
Major Rating Factors: Disappointing performance is the major factor driving the C (Fair) TheStreet Investment Rating for BNY Mellon National ST Muni Bd M. The fund currently has a performance rating of D (Weak) based on an average return of 0.44% over the last three years and 0.79% over the last three months. Factored into the performance evaluation is an expense ratio of 0.51% (very low).

The fund's risk rating is currently A (Excellent). Volatility, as measured by standard deviation, is considered very low for fixed income funds at 0.86. Another risk factor is the fund's very low average duration of 1.8 years (i.e. low interest rate risk).

John F. Flahive has been running the fund for 2 years and currently receives a manager quality ranking of 26 (0=worst, 99=best). This fund offers only a moderate level of risk but investors looking for strong performance are still waiting.
Services Offered: Automated phone transactions, bank draft capabilities, an IRA investment plan and a systematic withdrawal plan.

Data Date	Investment Rating	Net Assets ($Mil)	NAV	Perfor- mance Rating/Pts	Total Return Y-T-D	Risk Rating/Pts
2-17	C	911	12.76	D / 2.2	0.79%	A / 9.4
2016	C-	925	12.68	D / 1.7	-0.05%	A / 9.5
2015	B+	1,016	12.81	C / 5.3	0.37%	A / 9.5
2014	C	1,197	12.88	D / 2.0	0.71%	A / 9.5
2013	B-	1,272	12.90	D+ / 2.9	0.34%	A+ / 9.6
2012	C-	1,281	12.97	D- / 1.0	1.09%	A+ / 9.6

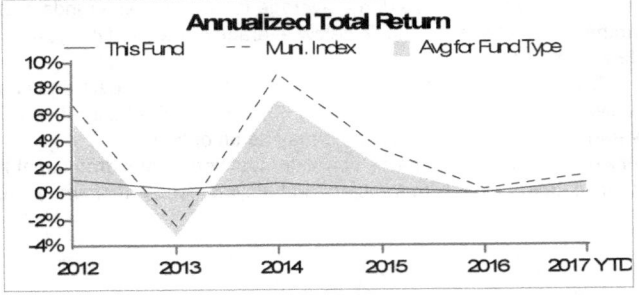

BNY Mellon Natl Int Muni M (MPNIX)   C+   Fair

Fund Family: Mellon Funds   **Phone:** (800) 645-6561
Address: One Mellon Center, Pittsburgh, PA 15258
Fund Type: MUN - Municipal - National
Major Rating Factors: Middle of the road best describes BNY Mellon Natl Int Muni M whose TheStreet Investment Rating is currently a C+ (Fair). The fund has a performance rating of C+ (Fair) based on an average return of 2.33% over the last three years (3.86% taxable equivalent) and 1.17% over the last three months (1.94% taxable equivalent). Factored into the performance evaluation is an expense ratio of 0.50% (very low).

The fund's risk rating is currently C+ (Fair). Volatility, as measured by standard deviation, is considered average for fixed income funds at 2.97. Another risk factor is the fund's below average duration of 4.5 years (i.e. lower interest rate risk).

John F. Flahive has been running the fund for 17 years and currently receives a manager quality ranking of 15 (0=worst, 99=best). If you desire an average level of risk, then this fund may be an option.

Services Offered: Automated phone transactions, bank draft capabilities, an IRA investment plan and a systematic withdrawal plan.

Data Date	Investment Rating	Net Assets ($Mil)	NAV	Performance Rating/Pts	Total Return Y-T-D	Risk Rating/Pts
2-17	C+	2,034	13.37	C+ / 5.8	1.17%	C+ / 5.6
2016	C+	2,030	13.27	C / 5.5	-0.29%	C+ / 5.8
2015	A+	2,063	13.74	B+ / 8.8	2.64%	B- / 7.0
2014	A-	1,918	13.75	B- / 7.1	5.99%	C+ / 5.9
2013	A+	1,665	13.34	B / 7.9	-1.46%	C+ / 6.1
2012	B	1,770	13.93	C+ / 6.0	5.25%	C / 5.5

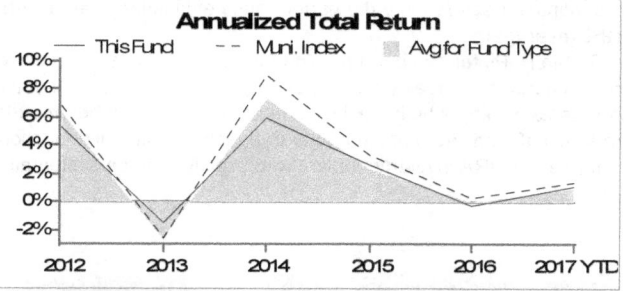

Annualized Total Return

Bridge Builder Core Bond (BBTBX)   C+   Fair

Fund Family: Bridge Builder Funds   **Phone:** (855) 823-3611
Address: c/o US Bancorp Fund Services L, Milwaukee, WI 53201
Fund Type: GEN - General
Major Rating Factors: Middle of the road best describes Bridge Builder Core Bond whose TheStreet Investment Rating is currently a C+ (Fair). The fund has a performance rating of C (Fair) based on an average return of 2.99% over the last three years and 1.02% over the last three months. Factored into the performance evaluation is an expense ratio of 0.37% (very low).

The fund's risk rating is currently C+ (Fair). Volatility, as measured by standard deviation, is considered average for fixed income funds at 2.94. Another risk factor is the fund's fairly average duration of 5.4 years (i.e. average interest rate risk).

Charles B. Groeschell has been running the fund for 4 years and currently receives a manager quality ranking of 60 (0=worst, 99=best). If you desire an average level of risk, then this fund may be an option.

Services Offered: Automated phone transactions, bank draft capabilities and wire transfers.

Data Date	Investment Rating	Net Assets ($Mil)	NAV	Performance Rating/Pts	Total Return Y-T-D	Risk Rating/Pts
2-17	C+	10,790	10.09	C / 5.5	1.02%	C+ / 5.9
2016	B-	10,573	10.03	C+ / 5.7	3.31%	C+ / 6.1
2015	U	9,954	10.03	U / --	0.82%	U / --
2014	U	7,677	10.21	U / --	5.91%	U / --

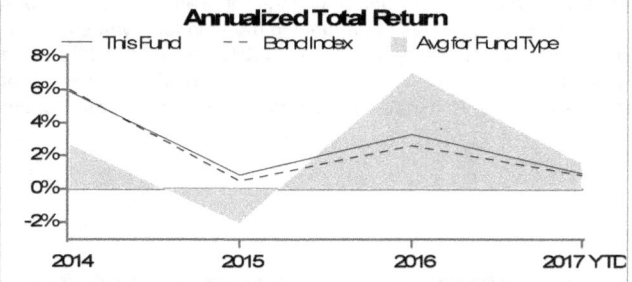

Annualized Total Return

CGCM Core Fixed Inc (TIIUX)   C+   Fair

Fund Family: Consulting Group Capital Markets   **Phone:** (800) 444-4273
Address: 2000 Westchester Avenue, Purchase, NY 10577
Fund Type: GEI - General - Investment Grade
Major Rating Factors: Middle of the road best describes CGCM Core Fixed Inc whose TheStreet Investment Rating is currently a C+ (Fair). The fund has a performance rating of C (Fair) based on an average return of 2.68% over the last three years and 1.07% over the last three months. Factored into the performance evaluation is an expense ratio of 0.54% (very low).

The fund's risk rating is currently C+ (Fair). Volatility, as measured by standard deviation, is considered average for fixed income funds at 2.87. Another risk factor is the fund's below average duration of 4.0 years (i.e. lower interest rate risk).

Michael C. Buchanan has been running the fund for 12 years and currently receives a manager quality ranking of 53 (0=worst, 99=best). If you desire an average level of risk, then this fund may be an option.

Services Offered: Payroll deductions and a systematic withdrawal plan.

Data Date	Investment Rating	Net Assets ($Mil)	NAV	Performance Rating/Pts	Total Return Y-T-D	Risk Rating/Pts
2-17	C+	712	8.07	C / 5.1	1.07%	C+ / 6.2
2016	C+	704	8.02	C / 5.3	2.89%	C+ / 6.3
2015	C+	798	8.09	C+ / 6.4	0.59%	C+ / 5.9
2014	B-	776	8.31	C / 5.5	5.70%	C+ / 6.3
2013	B	870	8.19	C / 5.1	-1.95%	B- / 7.2
2012	A-	933	8.57	C / 5.4	7.91%	B- / 7.4

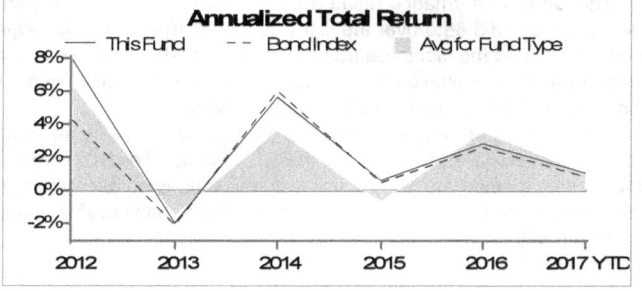

Annualized Total Return

CNR Fixed Income Opportunities N (RIMOX) | B+ | Good

Fund Family: CNR Funds | **Phone:** (888) 889-0799
Address: c/o SEI Inv Distribution Co., Oaks, PA 19456
Fund Type: GEI - General - Investment Grade

Major Rating Factors: CNR Fixed Income Opportunities N has adopted a risky asset allocation strategy and currently receives an overall TheStreet Investment Rating of B+ (Good). Volatility, as measured by standard deviation, is considered above average for fixed income funds at 4.20. The high level of risk (D+, Weak) did however, reward investors with excellent performance.

The fund's performance rating is currently A- (Excellent). It has registered an average return of 4.16% over the last three years and is up 1.64% over the last three months. Factored into the performance evaluation is an expense ratio of 1.12% (average).

Stefan P. Pinter has been running the fund for 6 years and currently receives a manager quality ranking of 95 (0=worst, 99=best). If you are comfortable owning a high risk investment, this fund may be an option.

Services Offered: Automated phone transactions, payroll deductions, bank draft capabilities, an IRA investment plan, wire transfers and a systematic withdrawal plan.

Data Date	Investment Rating	Net Assets ($Mil)	NAV	Performance Rating/Pts	Total Return Y-T-D	Risk Rating/Pts
2-17	B+	2,371	25.98	A- / 9.1	1.64%	D+ / 2.8
2016	B+	2,247	25.56	A- / 9.1	11.06%	C- / 3.1
2015	C	1,613	24.47	B / 7.6	1.81%	C- / 4.1
2014	C	1,338	25.73	C / 5.5	-0.04%	C / 5.4
2013	A+	1,125	27.26	B+ / 8.7	6.46%	C / 4.8
2012	D	653	27.20	C+ / 5.7	10.70%	C- / 3.2

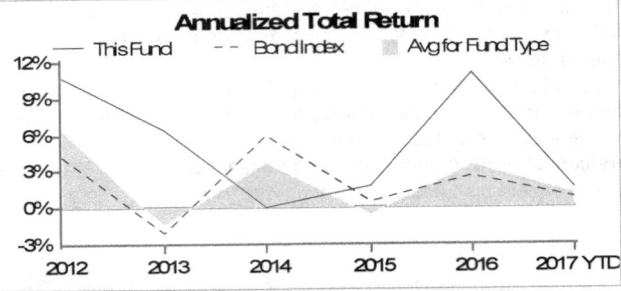

Annualized Total Return

Cohen and Steers Pref Sec&Inc A (CPXAX) | A- | Excellent

Fund Family: Cohen & Steers Funds | **Phone:** (800) 330-7348
Address: 280 Park Avenue, New York, NY 10017
Fund Type: GEI - General - Investment Grade

Major Rating Factors: Exceptional performance is the major factor driving the A- (Excellent) TheStreet Investment Rating for Cohen and Steers Pref Sec&Inc A. The fund currently has a performance rating of A (Excellent) based on an average return of 6.99% over the last three years and 3.57% over the last three months. Factored into the performance evaluation is an expense ratio of 1.19% (above average) and a 4.5% front-end load that is levied at the time of purchase.

The fund's risk rating is currently C- (Fair). Volatility, as measured by standard deviation, is considered average for fixed income funds at 4.10.

William F. Scapell has been running the fund for 7 years and currently receives a manager quality ranking of 96 (0=worst, 99=best). If you desire an average level of risk and strong performance, then this fund is a good option.

Services Offered: Automated phone transactions, bank draft capabilities and wire transfers.

Data Date	Investment Rating	Net Assets ($Mil)	NAV	Performance Rating/Pts	Total Return Y-T-D	Risk Rating/Pts
2-17	A-	932	13.77	A / 9.3	3.57%	C- / 3.0
2016	A-	967	13.41	A / 9.5	4.25%	C- / 3.2
2015	B+	738	13.57	A+ / 9.8	5.78%	C- / 3.9
2014	A	568	13.56	A+ / 9.7	11.61%	D+ / 2.9
2013	B	431	12.87	A / 9.4	2.55%	D / 2.2
2012	U	414	13.34	U / --	22.04%	U / --

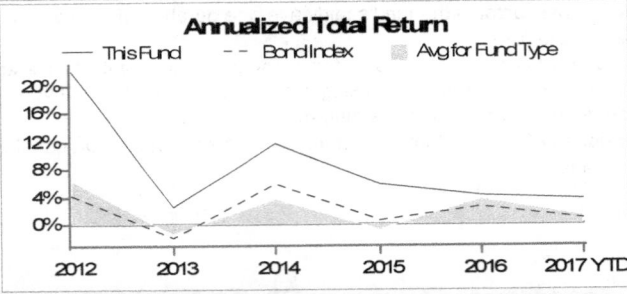

Annualized Total Return

Colorado Bond Shares Tax-Exempt (HICOX) | A+ | Excellent

Fund Family: Freedom Funds Management Company | **Phone:** (800) 572-0069
Address: 1200 17th Street, Denver, CO 80202
Fund Type: MUS - Municipal - Single State

Major Rating Factors: A moderate risk profile coupled with stable earnings characterizes Colorado Bond Shares Tax-Exempt which receives a TheStreet Investment Rating of A+ (Excellent). Volatility, as measured by standard deviation, is considered low for fixed income funds at 1.51. Another risk factor is the fund's fairly average duration of 5.7 years (i.e. average interest rate risk). The fund's risk rating is currently B+ (Good).

The fund's performance rating is currently C+ (Fair). It has registered an average return of 3.88% over the last three years (6.43% taxable equivalent) and is up 1.11% over the last three months (1.84% taxable equivalent). Factored into the performance evaluation is an expense ratio of 0.58% (low) and a 4.8% front-end load that is levied at the time of purchase.

Fred R. Kelly, Jr. has been running the fund for 27 years and currently receives a manager quality ranking of 89 (0=worst, 99=best). If you desire stability with a moderate level of risk then this fund is an excellent option.

Services Offered: Automated phone transactions, bank draft capabilities and a systematic withdrawal plan.

Data Date	Investment Rating	Net Assets ($Mil)	NAV	Performance Rating/Pts	Total Return Y-T-D	Risk Rating/Pts
2-17	A+	1,072	8.93	C+ / 6.6	1.11%	B+ / 8.8
2016	A+	1,045	8.89	C+ / 6.5	1.69%	B+ / 8.8
2015	A+	944	9.13	A- / 9.0	4.50%	A- / 9.1
2014	A+	905	9.10	C+ / 6.4	5.76%	A- / 9.1
2013	A+	860	8.99	C+ / 6.7	1.60%	A- / 9.1
2012	B+	894	9.23	C- / 3.6	5.14%	A / 9.3

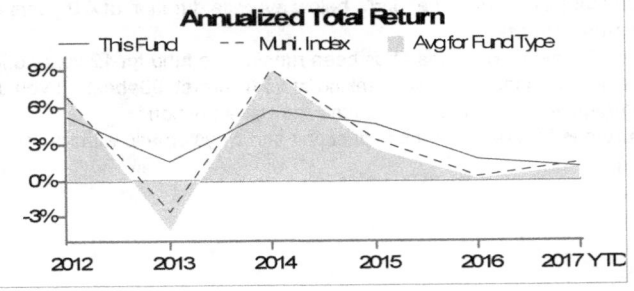

Annualized Total Return

Columbia CMG Ultra Short Term Bond (CMGUX)   C+   Fair

Fund Family: Columbia Threadneedle Investments   **Phone:** (800) 345-6611
Address: One Financial Center, Boston, MA 02111
Fund Type: GEI - General - Investment Grade
Major Rating Factors: Disappointing performance is the major factor driving the C+ (Fair) TheStreet Investment Rating for Columbia CMG Ultra Short Term Bond. The fund currently has a performance rating of D (Weak) based on an average return of 0.63% over the last three years and 0.28% over the last three months. Factored into the performance evaluation is an expense ratio of 0.26% (very low).

The fund's risk rating is currently A+ (Excellent). Volatility, as measured by standard deviation, is considered very low for fixed income funds at 0.27. Another risk factor is the fund's very low average duration of 0.5 years (i.e. low interest rate risk).

Leonard A. Aplet has been running the fund for 5 years and currently receives a manager quality ranking of 62 (0=worst, 99=best). This fund offers only a moderate level of risk but investors looking for strong performance are still waiting.
Services Offered: Automated phone transactions and bank draft capabilities.

Data Date	Investment Rating	Net Assets ($Mil)	NAV	Performance Rating/Pts	Total Return Y-T-D	Risk Rating/Pts
2-17	C+	1,795	9.01	D / 2.2	0.28%	A+ / 9.9
2016	C+	1,814	9.00	D+ / 2.4	1.10%	A+ / 9.9
2015	B	1,446	8.98	C / 4.3	0.30%	A+ / 9.9
2014	C	1,687	8.99	D / 1.6	0.36%	A+ / 9.9
2013	C	1,952	8.99	D- / 1.5	0.35%	A+ / 9.9
2012	C-	1,491	9.01	E+ / 0.6	1.38%	A+ / 9.9

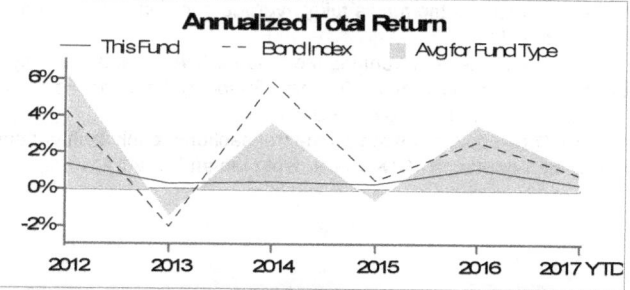

Annualized Total Return

Columbia High Yield Bond A (INEAX)   C-   Fair

Fund Family: Columbia Threadneedle Investments   **Phone:** (800) 345-6611
Address: One Financial Center, Boston, MA 02111
Fund Type: COH - Corporate - High Yield
Major Rating Factors: Columbia High Yield Bond A has adopted a very risky asset allocation strategy and currently receives an overall TheStreet Investment Rating of C- (Fair). Volatility, as measured by standard deviation, is considered above average for fixed income funds at 4.95. Another risk factor is the fund's below average duration of 4.2 years (i.e. lower interest rate risk). The high level of risk (D, Weak) did however, reward investors with excellent performance.

The fund's performance rating is currently B (Good). It has registered an average return of 4.28% over the last three years and is up 2.50% over the last three months. Factored into the performance evaluation is an expense ratio of 1.06% (average) and a 4.8% front-end load that is levied at the time of purchase.

Brian J. Lavin has been running the fund for 7 years and currently receives a manager quality ranking of 66 (0=worst, 99=best). If you are comfortable owning a very high risk investment, this fund may be an option.
Services Offered: Automated phone transactions, payroll deductions, bank draft capabilities, an IRA investment plan, a 401K investment plan and a systematic withdrawal plan.

Data Date	Investment Rating	Net Assets ($Mil)	NAV	Performance Rating/Pts	Total Return Y-T-D	Risk Rating/Pts
2-17	C-	1,134	2.97	B / 7.9	2.50%	D / 1.8
2016	C-	1,138	2.92	B / 7.8	11.14%	D / 1.8
2015	D	1,084	2.76	C / 4.7	-1.53%	D / 1.7
2014	C-	1,195	2.94	B / 7.6	3.68%	D / 1.9
2013	C	1,341	2.98	A- / 9.1	5.90%	E+ / 0.9
2012	C-	1,285	2.97	B+ / 8.3	15.61%	E+ / 0.8

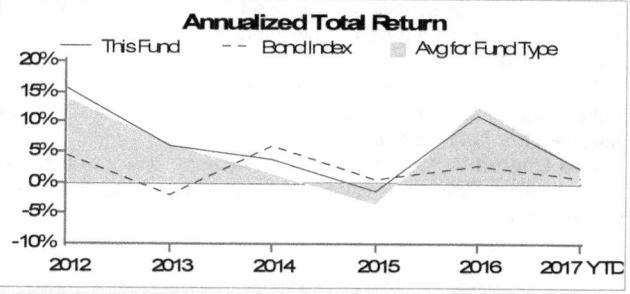

Annualized Total Return

Columbia Income Opportunities A (AIOAX)   D+   Weak

Fund Family: Columbia Threadneedle Investments   **Phone:** (800) 345-6611
Address: One Financial Center, Boston, MA 02111
Fund Type: COH - Corporate - High Yield
Major Rating Factors: Columbia Income Opportunities A has adopted a very risky asset allocation strategy and currently receives an overall TheStreet Investment Rating of D+ (Weak). Volatility, as measured by standard deviation, is considered above average for fixed income funds at 5.05. Another risk factor is the fund's below average duration of 4.3 years (i.e. lower interest rate risk). The high level of risk (D, Weak) did however, reward investors with excellent performance.

The fund's performance rating is currently B- (Good). It has registered an average return of 4.00% over the last three years and is up 2.39% over the last three months. Factored into the performance evaluation is an expense ratio of 1.13% (average) and a 4.8% front-end load that is levied at the time of purchase.

Brian J. Lavin has been running the fund for 14 years and currently receives a manager quality ranking of 58 (0=worst, 99=best). If you are comfortable owning a very high risk investment, this fund may be an option.
Services Offered: Automated phone transactions, payroll deductions, bank draft capabilities, an IRA investment plan, a 401K investment plan, wire transfers and a systematic withdrawal plan.

Data Date	Investment Rating	Net Assets ($Mil)	NAV	Performance Rating/Pts	Total Return Y-T-D	Risk Rating/Pts
2-17	D+	1,529	9.94	B- / 7.5	2.39%	D / 1.7
2016	D+	1,494	9.78	B- / 7.4	10.21%	D / 1.7
2015	D	1,376	9.29	C / 4.4	-1.15%	D- / 1.4
2014	D	1,636	9.90	C+ / 6.9	3.69%	D / 1.9
2013	C	1,508	10.02	B+ / 8.8	4.65%	D- / 1.4
2012	C	983	10.06	B / 8.0	14.11%	D- / 1.3

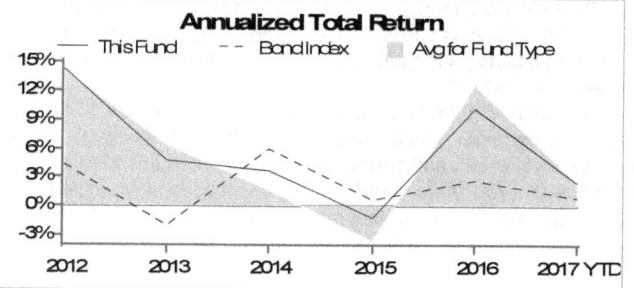

Annualized Total Return

Columbia MMrg Tot Rtn Bd Strat A (CMCPX)   B-   Good

Fund Family: Columbia Threadneedle Investments   **Phone:** (800) 345-6611
Address: One Financial Center, Boston, MA 02111
Fund Type: COI - Corporate - Investment Grade

Major Rating Factors: Columbia MMrg Tot Rtn Bd Strat A receives a TheStreet Investment Rating of B- (Good). The fund has a performance rating of C (Fair) based on an average return of 2.43% over the last three years and 1.15% over the last three months. Factored into the performance evaluation is an expense ratio of 0.81% (low).

The fund's risk rating is currently C+ (Fair). Volatility, as measured by standard deviation, is considered average for fixed income funds at 2.73. Another risk factor is the fund's fairly average duration of 5.2 years (i.e. average interest rate risk).

Brian Lavin has been running the fund for 5 years and currently receives a manager quality ranking of 43 (0=worst, 99=best). If you desire an average level of risk, then this fund may be an option.

Services Offered: Automated phone transactions, bank draft capabilities, an IRA investment plan, a 401K investment plan and wire transfers.

Data Date	Investment Rating	Net Assets ($Mil)	NAV	Perfor- mance Rating/Pts	Total Return Y-T-D	Risk Rating/Pts
2-17	B-	7,059	9.99	C / 4.9	1.15%	C+/ 6.9
2016	B-	6,108	9.91	C / 5.0	3.37%	B- / 7.0
2015	C	5,217	9.92	C / 5.2	-0.36%	B- / 7.0
2014	U	4,546	10.17	U / --	5.17%	U / --
2013	U	4,115	9.88	U / --	-1.72%	U / --
2012	U	4,966	10.27	U / --	0.00%	U / --

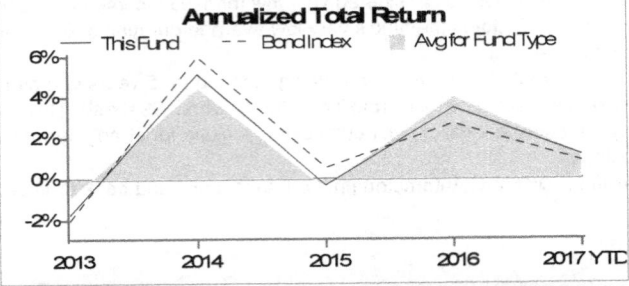

Columbia Strategic Income A (COSIX)   C   Fair

Fund Family: Columbia Threadneedle Investments   **Phone:** (800) 345-6611
Address: One Financial Center, Boston, MA 02111
Fund Type: GES - General - Short & Inter. Term

Major Rating Factors: Middle of the road best describes Columbia Strategic Income A whose TheStreet Investment Rating is currently a C (Fair). The fund has a performance rating of C+ (Fair) based on an average return of 3.68% over the last three years and 1.64% over the last three months. Factored into the performance evaluation is an expense ratio of 1.05% (average) and a 4.8% front-end load that is levied at the time of purchase.

The fund's risk rating is currently C- (Fair). Volatility, as measured by standard deviation, is considered average for fixed income funds at 3.77. Another risk factor is the fund's below average duration of 4.1 years (i.e. lower interest rate risk).

Brian J. Lavin has been running the fund for 7 years and currently receives a manager quality ranking of 91 (0=worst, 99=best). If you desire an average level of risk, then this fund may be an option.

Services Offered: Automated phone transactions, check writing, payroll deductions, bank draft capabilities, an IRA investment plan and a systematic withdrawal plan.

Data Date	Investment Rating	Net Assets ($Mil)	NAV	Perfor- mance Rating/Pts	Total Return Y-T-D	Risk Rating/Pts
2-17	C	1,713	5.98	C+/ 6.6	1.64%	C- / 3.5
2016	C-	1,763	5.91	C+/ 6.3	7.75%	C- / 3.6
2015	D	1,488	5.66	D+/ 2.7	0.24%	C- / 3.7
2014	D-	1,257	5.88	C / 4.4	3.67%	C- / 3.2
2013	C-	1,271	6.00	C+/ 6.3	0.07%	C- / 3.1
2012	D	1,508	6.42	C+/ 6.3	11.60%	D+/ 2.5

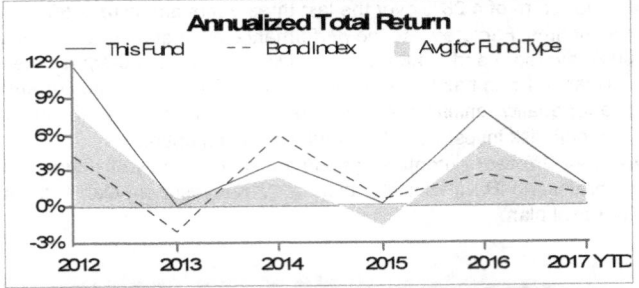

Columbia Strategic Municipal Inc A (INTAX)   B-   Good

Fund Family: Columbia Threadneedle Investments   **Phone:** (800) 345-6611
Address: One Financial Center, Boston, MA 02111
Fund Type: MUN - Municipal - National

Major Rating Factors: Strong performance is the major factor driving the B- (Good) TheStreet Investment Rating for Columbia Strategic Municipal Inc A. The fund currently has a performance rating of B (Good) based on an average return of 4.56% over the last three years (7.55% taxable equivalent) and 1.34% over the last three months (2.22% taxable equivalent). Factored into the performance evaluation is an expense ratio of 0.82% (low) and a 3.0% front-end load that is levied at the time of purchase.

The fund's risk rating is currently C- (Fair). Volatility, as measured by standard deviation, is considered average for fixed income funds at 3.55. Another risk factor is the fund's above average duration of 7.5 years (i.e. higher interest rate risk).

Catherine M. Stienstra has been running the fund for 10 years and currently receives a manager quality ranking of 72 (0=worst, 99=best). If you desire an average level of risk and strong performance, then this fund is a good option.

Services Offered: Automated phone transactions, payroll deductions, bank draft capabilities, an IRA investment plan, a 401K investment plan, a Keogh investment plan, wire transfers and a systematic withdrawal plan.

Data Date	Investment Rating	Net Assets ($Mil)	NAV	Perfor- mance Rating/Pts	Total Return Y-T-D	Risk Rating/Pts
2-17	B-	677	3.96	B / 7.9	1.34%	C- / 3.5
2016	B	663	3.93	B+/ 8.4	0.43%	C- / 3.5
2015	B	592	4.07	A / 9.4	3.95%	C- / 3.2
2014	B+	559	4.09	A / 9.3	12.26%	D+/ 2.9
2013	C+	520	3.80	B- / 7.5	-3.64%	C- / 3.1
2012	B	632	4.11	B+/ 8.3	10.73%	D+/ 2.9

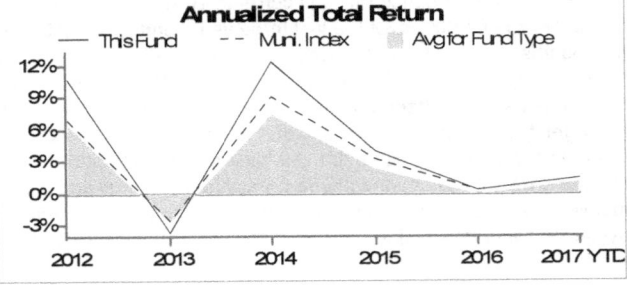

Columbia Tax-Exempt A (COLTX)　　　　　C　　　Fair

Fund Family: Columbia Threadneedle Investments　**Phone:** (800) 345-6611
Address: One Financial Center, Boston, MA 02111
Fund Type: MUN - Municipal - National
Major Rating Factors: Middle of the road best describes Columbia Tax-Exempt A whose TheStreet Investment Rating is currently a C (Fair). The fund has a performance rating of C+ (Fair) based on an average return of 3.81% over the last three years (6.31% taxable equivalent) and 1.27% over the last three months (2.10% taxable equivalent). Factored into the performance evaluation is an expense ratio of 0.72% (low) and a 3.0% front-end load that is levied at the time of purchase.

The fund's risk rating is currently C- (Fair). Volatility, as measured by standard deviation, is considered average for fixed income funds at 3.51. Another risk factor is the fund's above average duration of 7.3 years (i.e. higher interest rate risk).

Kimberly A. Campbell has been running the fund for 15 years and currently receives a manager quality ranking of 52 (0=worst, 99=best). If you desire an average level of risk, then this fund may be an option.

Services Offered: Automated phone transactions, check writing, payroll deductions, bank draft capabilities, an IRA investment plan and a systematic withdrawal plan.

Data Date	Investment Rating	Net Assets ($Mil)	NAV	Performance Rating/Pts	Total Return Y-T-D	Risk Rating/Pts
2-17	C	3,009	13.45	C+ / 6.7	1.27%	C- / 3.6
2016	C	3,037	13.37	C+ / 6.8	-0.56%	C- / 3.6
2015	B	3,263	13.99	A- / 9.1	3.56%	C- / 4.1
2014	A-	3,334	14.08	B+ / 8.7	11.00%	C- / 3.8
2013	C+	3,280	13.24	B- / 7.2	-3.41%	C- / 3.5
2012	C+	3,794	14.29	B / 7.6	8.99%	D+ / 2.8

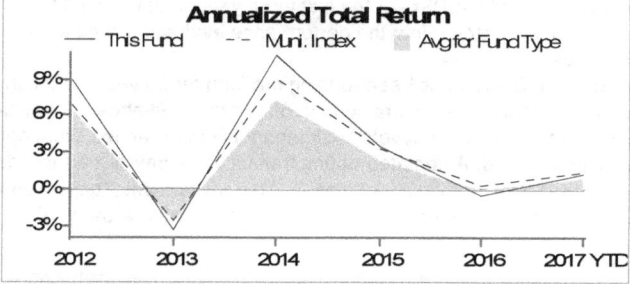

Columbia Total Return Bond A (LIBAX)　　　　　C　　　Fair

Fund Family: Columbia Threadneedle Investments　**Phone:** (800) 345-6611
Address: One Financial Center, Boston, MA 02111
Fund Type: COI - Corporate - Investment Grade
Major Rating Factors: Middle of the road best describes Columbia Total Return Bond A whose TheStreet Investment Rating is currently a C (Fair). The fund has a performance rating of C (Fair) based on an average return of 2.91% over the last three years and 1.08% over the last three months. Factored into the performance evaluation is an expense ratio of 0.90% (average) and a 3.0% front-end load that is levied at the time of purchase.

The fund's risk rating is currently C+ (Fair). Volatility, as measured by standard deviation, is considered average for fixed income funds at 2.86. Another risk factor is the fund's fairly average duration of 5.6 years (i.e. average interest rate risk).

Carl W. Pappo has been running the fund for 5 years and currently receives a manager quality ranking of 60 (0=worst, 99=best). If you desire an average level of risk, then this fund may be an option.

Services Offered: Automated phone transactions, payroll deductions, bank draft capabilities, an IRA investment plan, a 401K investment plan, wire transfers and a systematic withdrawal plan.

Data Date	Investment Rating	Net Assets ($Mil)	NAV	Performance Rating/Pts	Total Return Y-T-D	Risk Rating/Pts
2-17	C	893	9.01	C / 4.7	1.08%	C+ / 6.3
2016	C+	910	8.95	C / 4.9	4.51%	C+ / 6.4
2015	C-	1,105	8.92	C- / 3.0	0.11%	C+ / 6.6
2014	C-	1,274	9.19	C- / 3.6	5.20%	C+ / 6.8
2013	C-	1,604	8.95	C- / 3.0	-2.55%	B- / 7.0
2012	C+	428	9.47	C- / 3.8	7.09%	B- / 7.0

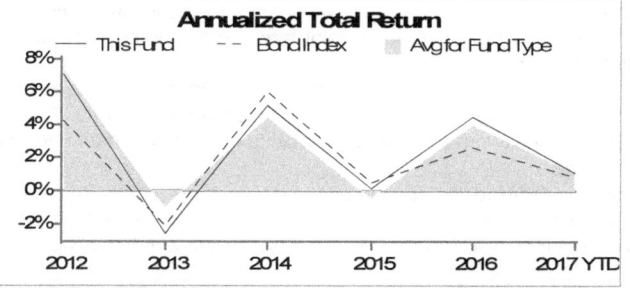

Columbia US Government Mortgage A (AUGAX)　　　　　B-　　　Good

Fund Family: Columbia Threadneedle Investments　**Phone:** (800) 345-6611
Address: One Financial Center, Boston, MA 02111
Fund Type: USS - US Government - Short & Inter. Term
Major Rating Factors: A moderate risk profile coupled with stable earnings characterizes Columbia US Government Mortgage A which receives a TheStreet Investment Rating of B- (Good). Volatility, as measured by standard deviation, is considered low for fixed income funds at 1.83. Another risk factor is the fund's below average duration of 3.3 years (i.e. lower interest rate risk). The fund's risk rating is currently B+ (Good).

The fund's performance rating is currently C- (Fair). It has registered an average return of 2.60% over the last three years and is up 0.71% over the last three months. Factored into the performance evaluation is an expense ratio of 0.97% (average) and a 3.0% front-end load that is levied at the time of purchase.

Jason J. Callan has been running the fund for 8 years and currently receives a manager quality ranking of 83 (0=worst, 99=best). If you desire stability with a moderate level of risk then this fund is an excellent option.

Services Offered: Automated phone transactions, payroll deductions, bank draft capabilities, an IRA investment plan, a 401K investment plan, a Keogh investment plan, wire transfers and a systematic withdrawal plan.

Data Date	Investment Rating	Net Assets ($Mil)	NAV	Performance Rating/Pts	Total Return Y-T-D	Risk Rating/Pts
2-17	B-	653	5.42	C- / 3.9	0.71%	B+ / 8.5
2016	B	670	5.40	C- / 4.1	2.18%	B+ / 8.5
2015	B	640	5.42	C / 5.2	1.07%	B+ / 8.6
2014	B-	568	5.52	C- / 3.8	5.51%	B+ / 8.4
2013	B	581	5.37	C- / 4.1	-1.54%	B+ / 8.4
2012	A	737	5.62	C / 4.7	6.95%	B+ / 8.6

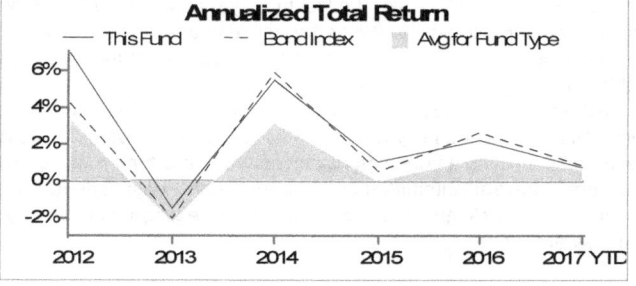

Commerce Bond (CFBNX)   A-   Excellent

Fund Family: Commerce Funds   **Phone:** (800) 995-6365
Address: PO Box 219525, Kansas, MO 64121
Fund Type: GEI - General - Investment Grade

Major Rating Factors: A moderate risk profile coupled with stable earnings characterizes Commerce Bond which receives a TheStreet Investment Rating of A- (Excellent). Volatility, as measured by standard deviation, is considered low for fixed income funds at 2.56. Another risk factor is the fund's fairly average duration of 5.2 years (i.e. average interest rate risk). The fund's risk rating is currently B- (Good).

The fund's performance rating is currently C+ (Fair). It has registered an average return of 2.89% over the last three years and is up 1.11% over the last three months. Factored into the performance evaluation is an expense ratio of 0.68% (low).

Scott M. Colbert has been running the fund for 23 years and currently receives a manager quality ranking of 69 (0=worst, 99=best). If you desire stability with a moderate level of risk then this fund is an excellent option.

Services Offered: Automated phone transactions, payroll deductions, bank draft capabilities, an IRA investment plan, a 401K investment plan, a Keogh investment plan, wire transfers and a systematic withdrawal plan.

Data Date	Investment Rating	Net Assets ($Mil)	NAV	Performance Rating/Pts	Total Return Y-T-D	Risk Rating/Pts
2-17	A-	1,078	19.88	C+ / 5.9	1.11%	B- / 7.4
2016	A-	1,064	19.77	C+ / 6.1	3.97%	B- / 7.4
2015	B+	981	19.67	C+ / 6.6	0.11%	B- / 7.3
2014	A-	879	20.35	C+ / 5.8	5.86%	B- / 7.5
2013	A	779	20.01	C+ / 6.0	-0.56%	B / 8.1
2012	A+	784	20.95	C / 5.4	7.26%	B / 8.2

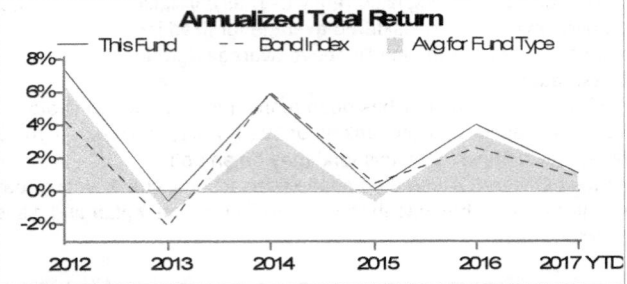

Delaware Diversified Income A (DPDFX)   D-   Weak

Fund Family: Delaware Investments   **Phone:** (800) 523-1918
Address: P.O. Box 219656, Kansas City, MO 64121
Fund Type: GES - General - Short & Inter. Term

Major Rating Factors: Disappointing performance is the major factor driving the D- (Weak) TheStreet Investment Rating for Delaware Diversified Income A. The fund currently has a performance rating of D+ (Weak) based on an average return of 2.15% over the last three years and 1.38% over the last three months. Factored into the performance evaluation is an expense ratio of 0.90% (average) and a 4.5% front-end load that is levied at the time of purchase.

The fund's risk rating is currently C (Fair). Volatility, as measured by standard deviation, is considered average for fixed income funds at 3.02. Another risk factor is the fund's fairly average duration of 5.8 years (i.e. average interest rate risk).

Paul C. Grillo, Jr. has been running the fund for 16 years and currently receives a manager quality ranking of 28 (0=worst, 99=best). This fund offers an average level of risk, but investors looking for strong performance will be frustrated.

Services Offered: Automated phone transactions, payroll deductions, bank draft capabilities, an IRA investment plan, a 401K investment plan, a Keogh investment plan, wire transfers and a systematic withdrawal plan.

Data Date	Investment Rating	Net Assets ($Mil)	NAV	Performance Rating/Pts	Total Return Y-T-D	Risk Rating/Pts
2-17	D-	994	8.67	D+ / 2.9	1.38%	C / 5.4
2016	D-	1,146	8.60	C- / 3.0	3.55%	C+ / 5.6
2015	D	1,568	8.57	D / 1.9	-1.15%	C / 4.7
2014	D	2,035	8.97	C- / 3.4	5.11%	C / 5.1
2013	D+	2,956	8.89	C- / 3.6	-1.37%	C+ / 5.6
2012	D+	4,750	9.35	C- / 3.4	6.86%	C+ / 6.0

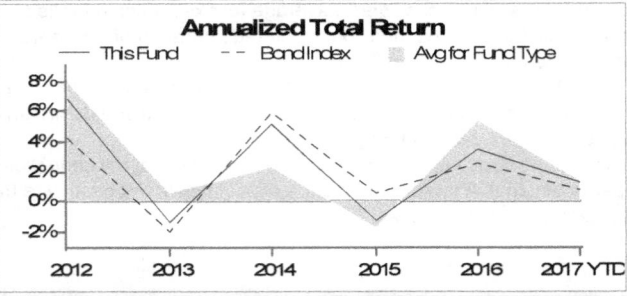

Deutsche High Income A (KHYAX)   D   Weak

Fund Family: Deutsche Funds   **Phone:** (800) 728-3337
Address: P.O. Box 219151, Kansas City, MO 64121
Fund Type: COH - Corporate - High Yield

Major Rating Factors: Deutsche High Income A has adopted a very risky asset allocation strategy and currently receives an overall TheStreet Investment Rating of D (Weak). Volatility, as measured by standard deviation, is considered above average for fixed income funds at 5.22. Another risk factor is the fund's below average duration of 4.4 years (i.e. lower interest rate risk). The high level of risk (D-, Weak) did however, reward investors with excellent performance.

The fund's performance rating is currently B- (Good). It has registered an average return of 3.52% over the last three years and is up 2.80% over the last three months. Factored into the performance evaluation is an expense ratio of 0.94% (average), a 4.5% front-end load that is levied at the time of purchase and a 2.0% back-end load levied at the time of sale.

Gary S. Russell has been running the fund for 11 years and currently receives a manager quality ranking of 23 (0=worst, 99=best). If you are comfortable owning a very high risk investment, this fund may be an option.

Services Offered: Automated phone transactions, payroll deductions, bank draft capabilities, an IRA investment plan, a 401K investment plan and a systematic withdrawal plan.

Data Date	Investment Rating	Net Assets ($Mil)	NAV	Performance Rating/Pts	Total Return Y-T-D	Risk Rating/Pts
2-17	D	797	4.77	B- / 7.3	2.80%	D- / 1.5
2016	D	794	4.68	C+ / 6.8	12.78%	D- / 1.5
2015	D-	820	4.37	D / 1.6	-3.47%	D / 1.6
2014	D	1,007	4.78	C+ / 6.2	1.90%	D / 2.0
2013	C	1,203	4.97	B+ / 8.9	7.04%	E+ / 0.9
2012	D	1,311	4.95	B / 7.7	14.73%	E+ / 0.7

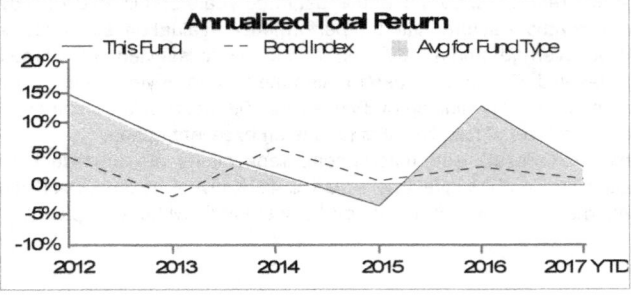

Deutsche Managed Municipal Bd A (SMLAX)
C+   Fair

Fund Family: Deutsche Funds   **Phone:** (800) 728-3337
Address: P.O. Box 219151, Kansas City, MO 64121
Fund Type: MUN - Municipal - National
Major Rating Factors: Middle of the road best describes Deutsche Managed Municipal Bd A whose TheStreet Investment Rating is currently a C+ (Fair). The fund has a performance rating of C+ (Fair) based on an average return of 3.67% over the last three years (6.08% taxable equivalent) and 1.12% over the last three months (1.85% taxable equivalent). Factored into the performance evaluation is an expense ratio of 0.80% (low) and a 2.8% front-end load that is levied at the time of purchase.

The fund's risk rating is currently C- (Fair). Volatility, as measured by standard deviation, is considered average for fixed income funds at 3.46. Another risk factor is the fund's below average duration of 4.9 years (i.e. lower interest rate risk).

Ashton P. Goodfield has been running the fund for 29 years and currently receives a manager quality ranking of 43 (0=worst, 99=best). If you desire an average level of risk, then this fund may be an option.
Services Offered: Automated phone transactions, check writing, payroll deductions, bank draft capabilities, an IRA investment plan, a 401K investment plan, wire transfers and a systematic withdrawal plan.

Data Date	Investment Rating	Net Assets ($Mil)	NAV	Performance Rating/Pts	Total Return Y-T-D	Risk Rating/Pts
2-17	C+	1,848	9.04	C+ / 6.7	1.12%	C- / 4.1
2016	C+	1,873	8.99	B- / 7.2	-0.08%	C- / 3.9
2015	C+	1,941	9.32	B+ / 8.9	2.94%	C- / 3.5
2014	B+	1,980	9.40	A- / 9.1	11.18%	D+ / 2.8
2013	C	1,901	8.80	C+ / 6.9	-3.94%	C- / 3.6
2012	B	2,363	9.53	B- / 7.5	9.52%	C- / 3.6

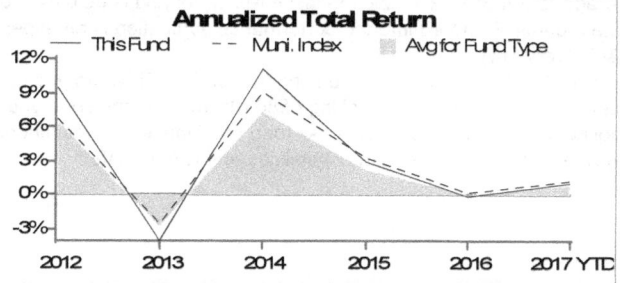

Deutsche Strategic Govt Sec A (KUSAX)
C-   Fair

Fund Family: Deutsche Funds   **Phone:** (800) 728-3337
Address: P.O. Box 219151, Kansas City, MO 64121
Fund Type: USS - US Government - Short & Inter. Term
Major Rating Factors: Disappointing performance is the major factor driving the C- (Fair) TheStreet Investment Rating for Deutsche Strategic Govt Sec A. The fund currently has a performance rating of D (Weak) based on an average return of 1.66% over the last three years and 0.51% over the last three months. Factored into the performance evaluation is an expense ratio of 0.81% (low) and a 2.8% front-end load that is levied at the time of purchase.

The fund's risk rating is currently B+ (Good). Volatility, as measured by standard deviation, is considered low for fixed income funds at 1.52. Another risk factor is the fund's below average duration of 3.4 years (i.e. lower interest rate risk).

Scott Agi has been running the fund for 3 years and currently receives a manager quality ranking of 75 (0=worst, 99=best). This fund offers only a moderate level of risk but investors looking for strong performance are still waiting.
Services Offered: Automated phone transactions, payroll deductions, bank draft capabilities, an IRA investment plan, a 401K investment plan and a systematic withdrawal plan.

Data Date	Investment Rating	Net Assets ($Mil)	NAV	Performance Rating/Pts	Total Return Y-T-D	Risk Rating/Pts
2-17	C-	838	7.91	D / 2.1	0.51%	B+ / 8.8
2016	C+	857	7.91	C- / 3.1	1.02%	B+ / 8.6
2015	D+	956	8.04	D+ / 2.5	-0.04%	C+ / 6.6
2014	D-	1,089	8.30	D / 2.2	6.02%	C+ / 6.2
2013	D-	1,197	8.09	E+ / 0.8	-4.37%	B- / 7.2
2012	C-	1,571	8.79	D / 2.0	2.36%	B+ / 8.5

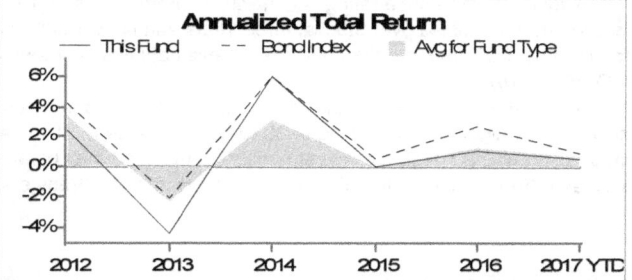

DFA CA Sht Trm Muni Bd Inst (DFCMX)
C+   Fair

Fund Family: Dimensional Fund Advisors   **Phone:** (800) 984-9472
Address: 6300 Bee Cave Road, Austin, TX 78746
Fund Type: MUS - Municipal - Single State
Major Rating Factors: Disappointing performance is the major factor driving the C+ (Fair) TheStreet Investment Rating for DFA CA Sht Trm Muni Bd Inst. The fund currently has a performance rating of D+ (Weak) based on an average return of 0.73% over the last three years (1.21% taxable equivalent) and 0.82% over the last three months (1.36% taxable equivalent). Factored into the performance evaluation is an expense ratio of 0.22% (very low).

The fund's risk rating is currently A- (Excellent). Volatility, as measured by standard deviation, is considered very low for fixed income funds at 1.15. Another risk factor is the fund's very low average duration of 2.6 years (i.e. low interest rate risk).

David A. Plecha has been running the fund for 10 years and currently receives a manager quality ranking of 27 (0=worst, 99=best). This fund offers only a moderate level of risk but investors looking for strong performance are still waiting.
Services Offered: Automated phone transactions, bank draft capabilities and wire transfers.

Data Date	Investment Rating	Net Assets ($Mil)	NAV	Performance Rating/Pts	Total Return Y-T-D	Risk Rating/Pts
2-17	C+	943	10.30	D+ / 2.7	0.82%	A- / 9.1
2016	C	899	10.23	D+ / 2.3	0.07%	A- / 9.1
2015	A+	833	10.31	C+ / 6.5	1.02%	A / 9.4
2014	C+	724	10.29	D / 2.1	0.80%	A+ / 9.7
2013	B	547	10.29	C- / 3.4	0.65%	A+ / 9.6
2012	C-	403	10.31	D- / 1.0	0.94%	A / 9.4

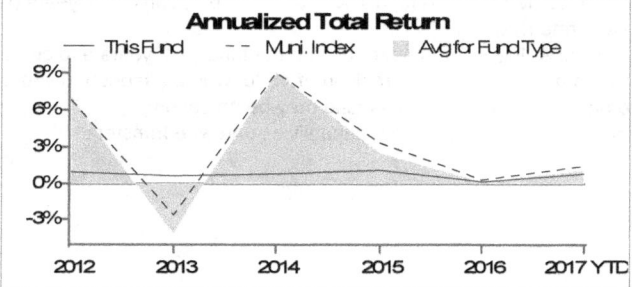

DFA Five Year Glbl Fixed Inc Inst (DFGBX)   C+   Fair

Fund Family: Dimensional Fund Advisors   **Phone:** (800) 984-9472
Address: 6300 Bee Cave Road, Austin, TX 78746
Fund Type: GL - Global

Major Rating Factors: A moderate risk profile coupled with stable earnings characterizes DFA Five Year Glbl Fixed Inc Inst which receives a TheStreet Investment Rating of C+ (Fair). Volatility, as measured by standard deviation, is considered low for fixed income funds at 2.10. Another risk factor is the fund's below average duration of 3.7 years (i.e. lower interest rate risk). The fund's risk rating is currently B (Good).

The fund's performance rating is currently C- (Fair). It has registered an average return of 1.82% over the last three years and is up 0.64% over the last three months. Factored into the performance evaluation is an expense ratio of 0.27% (very low).

David A. Plecha has been running the fund for 18 years and currently receives a manager quality ranking of 86 (0=worst, 99=best). If you desire stability with a moderate level of risk then this fund is an excellent option.
Services Offered: Bank draft capabilities and wire transfers.

Data Date	Investment Rating	Net Assets ($Mil)	NAV	Perfor-mance Rating/Pts	Total Return Y-T-D	Risk Rating/Pts
2-17	C+	12,772	10.94	C- / 3.7	0.64%	B / 8.1
2016	C+	12,413	10.87	C- / 3.9	1.79%	B / 8.2
2015	B+	11,298	10.90	C+ / 6.4	1.45%	B / 8.1
2014	C+	10,019	10.93	C- / 3.5	2.87%	B+ / 8.3
2013	B-	7,954	10.84	C- / 4.0	-0.41%	B / 8.1
2012	C-	6,477	11.15	D+ / 2.6	4.80%	B- / 7.4

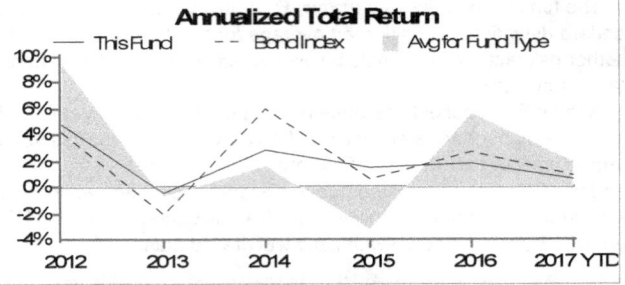
Annualized Total Return

DFA Infltn Protected Sec Port Inst (DIPSX)   E+   Very Weak

Fund Family: Dimensional Fund Advisors   **Phone:** (800) 984-9472
Address: 6300 Bee Cave Road, Austin, TX 78746
Fund Type: US - US Treasury

Major Rating Factors: DFA Infltn Protected Sec Port Inst has adopted a risky asset allocation strategy and currently receives an overall TheStreet Investment Rating of E+ (Very Weak). Volatility, as measured by standard deviation, is considered above average for fixed income funds at 4.52. Another risk factor is the fund's above average duration of 7.9 years (i.e. higher interest rate risk). Unfortunately, the high level of risk (D+, Weak) has only provided investors with average performance.

The fund's performance rating is currently C (Fair). It has registered an average return of 1.85% over the last three years and is up 1.54% over the last three months. Factored into the performance evaluation is an expense ratio of 0.12% (very low).

David A. Plecha has been running the fund for 11 years and currently receives a manager quality ranking of 38 (0=worst, 99=best). If you are comfortable owning a high risk investment, then this fund may be an option.
Services Offered: Automated phone transactions and wire transfers.

Data Date	Investment Rating	Net Assets ($Mil)	NAV	Perfor-mance Rating/Pts	Total Return Y-T-D	Risk Rating/Pts
2-17	E+	3,802	11.86	C / 4.3	1.54%	D+ / 2.3
2016	D-	3,627	11.68	C / 4.6	4.67%	D / 2.2
2015	E+	3,065	11.38	D- / 1.0	-1.22%	D- / 1.2
2014	E	2,737	11.60	D- / 1.4	3.36%	D- / 1.2
2013	E+	2,401	11.46	D+ / 2.8	-9.27%	D / 2.0
2012	C	2,591	12.80	C+ / 6.9	7.45%	D+ / 2.9

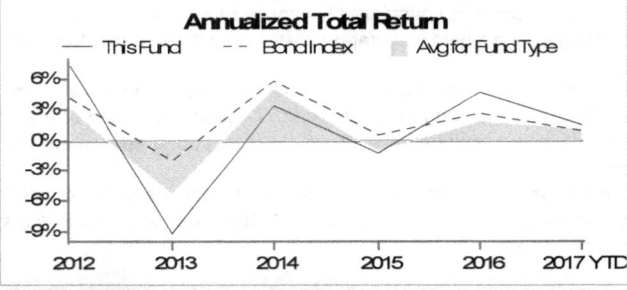
Annualized Total Return

DFA Intmdt Govt Fx Inc Inst (DFIGX)   E+   Very Weak

Fund Family: Dimensional Fund Advisors   **Phone:** (800) 984-9472
Address: 6300 Bee Cave Road, Austin, TX 78746
Fund Type: USS - US Government - Short & Inter. Term

Major Rating Factors: DFA Intmdt Govt Fx Inc Inst receives a TheStreet Investment Rating of E+ (Very Weak). The fund has a performance rating of C- (Fair) based on an average return of 2.32% over the last three years and 0.89% over the last three months. Factored into the performance evaluation is an expense ratio of 0.12% (very low).

The fund's risk rating is currently C- (Fair). Volatility, as measured by standard deviation, is considered average for fixed income funds at 3.78. Another risk factor is the fund's fairly average duration of 5.7 years (i.e. average interest rate risk).

David A. Plecha has been running the fund for 7 years and currently receives a manager quality ranking of 48 (0=worst, 99=best). If you desire an average level of risk, then this fund may be an option.
Services Offered: Bank draft capabilities and wire transfers.

Data Date	Investment Rating	Net Assets ($Mil)	NAV	Perfor-mance Rating/Pts	Total Return Y-T-D	Risk Rating/Pts
2-17	E+	4,040	12.44	C- / 3.6	0.89%	C- / 3.5
2016	D-	3,857	12.33	C- / 3.9	1.15%	C- / 3.6
2015	C	3,359	12.46	C+ / 6.1	1.77%	C / 4.7
2014	D	4,099	12.55	C- / 3.3	5.18%	C+ / 5.7
2013	D	3,294	12.26	C- / 3.3	-3.52%	C+ / 5.7
2012	D	3,158	13.02	C- / 3.7	3.71%	C+ / 5.6

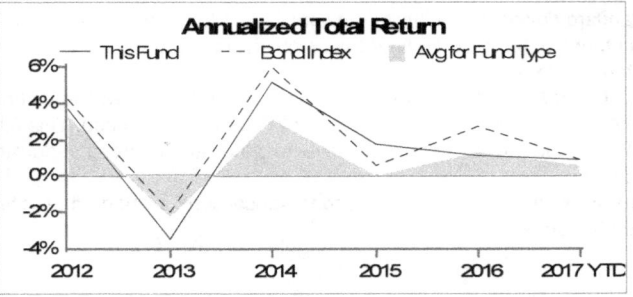
Annualized Total Return

DFA Intmdt Term Municipal Bd Inst (DFTIX)   B+   Good

Fund Family: Dimensional Fund Advisors   **Phone:** (800) 984-9472
Address: 6300 Bee Cave Road, Austin, TX 78746
Fund Type: MUN - Municipal - National

Major Rating Factors: A moderate risk profile coupled with stable earnings characterizes DFA Intmdt Term Municipal Bd Inst which receives a TheStreet Investment Rating of B+ (Good). Volatility, as measured by standard deviation, is considered low for fixed income funds at 2.67. Another risk factor is the fund's below average duration of 4.8 years (i.e. lower interest rate risk). The fund's risk rating is currently B- (Good).

The fund's performance rating is currently C (Fair). It has registered an average return of 2.14% over the last three years (3.54% taxable equivalent) and is up 1.31% over the last three months (2.17% taxable equivalent). Factored into the performance evaluation is an expense ratio of 0.23% (very low).

David A. Plecha has been running the fund for 5 years and currently receives a manager quality ranking of 23 (0=worst, 99=best). If you desire stability with a moderate level of risk then this fund is an excellent option.
Services Offered: Automated phone transactions, bank draft capabilities and wire transfers.

Data Date	Investment Rating	Net Assets ($Mil)	NAV	Performance Rating/Pts	Total Return Y-T-D	Risk Rating/Pts
2-17	B+	1,459	10.14	C / 5.5	1.31%	B- / 7.1
2016	B	1,406	10.03	C+ / 5.7	-0.15%	C+/ 6.9
2015	B+	963	10.18	B+ / 8.4	2.60%	C / 5.1
2014	U	561	10.07	U / --	5.49%	U / --
2013	U	310	9.70	U / --	-2.05%	U / --
2012	U	101	10.01	U / --	0.00%	U / --

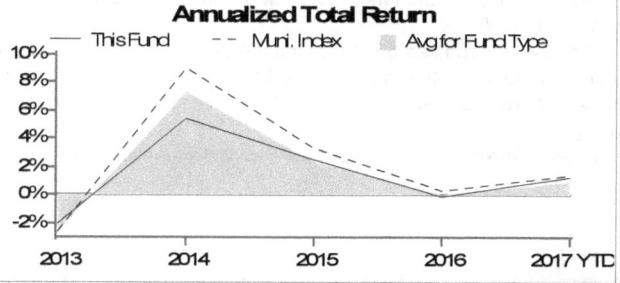

DFA Int-Term Extended Quality Inst (DFTEX)   D+   Weak

Fund Family: Dimensional Fund Advisors   **Phone:** (800) 984-9472
Address: 6300 Bee Cave Road, Austin, TX 78746
Fund Type: GL - Global

Major Rating Factors: DFA Int-Term Extended Quality Inst has adopted a risky asset allocation strategy and currently receives an overall TheStreet Investment Rating of D+ (Weak). Volatility, as measured by standard deviation, is considered above average for fixed income funds at 4.44. Another risk factor is the fund's fairly average duration of 6.9 years (i.e. average interest rate risk). Unfortunately, the high level of risk (D+, Weak) has only provided investors with average performance.

The fund's performance rating is currently C+ (Fair). It has registered an average return of 3.78% over the last three years and is up 1.46% over the last three months. Factored into the performance evaluation is an expense ratio of 0.22% (very low).

David A. Plecha has been running the fund for 7 years and currently receives a manager quality ranking of 95 (0=worst, 99=best). If you are comfortable owning a high risk investment, then this fund may be an option.
Services Offered: Automated phone transactions, bank draft capabilities and wire transfers.

Data Date	Investment Rating	Net Assets ($Mil)	NAV	Performance Rating/Pts	Total Return Y-T-D	Risk Rating/Pts
2-17	D+	1,483	10.66	C+ / 6.7	1.46%	D+/ 2.5
2016	C-	1,394	10.55	B- / 7.0	4.03%	D+/ 2.5
2015	C-	1,094	10.46	C+ / 6.9	1.28%	D+/ 2.6
2014	C-	2,313	10.73	C+ / 6.1	8.07%	C- / 3.5
2013	D+	1,523	10.28	C / 5.3	-3.81%	C- / 4.0
2012	U	919	10.99	U / --	8.27%	U / --

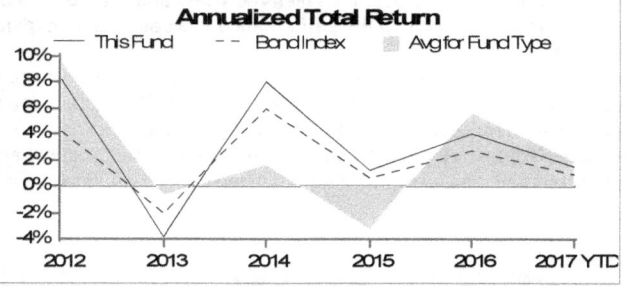

DFA Investment Grade Portfolio (DFAPX)   D   Weak

Fund Family: Dimensional Fund Advisors   **Phone:** (800) 984-9472
Address: 6300 Bee Cave Road, Austin, TX 78746
Fund Type: GL - Global

Major Rating Factors: DFA Investment Grade Portfolio receives a TheStreet Investment Rating of D (Weak). The fund has a performance rating of C (Fair) based on an average return of 2.92% over the last three years and 1.03% over the last three months. Factored into the performance evaluation is an expense ratio of 0.22% (very low).

The fund's risk rating is currently C- (Fair). Volatility, as measured by standard deviation, is considered average for fixed income funds at 3.47.

David A. Plecha has been running the fund for 6 years and currently receives a manager quality ranking of 93 (0=worst, 99=best). If you desire an average level of risk, then this fund may be an option.
Services Offered: Automated phone transactions, bank draft capabilities, an IRA investment plan, a 401K investment plan and wire transfers.

Data Date	Investment Rating	Net Assets ($Mil)	NAV	Performance Rating/Pts	Total Return Y-T-D	Risk Rating/Pts
2-17	D	6,766	10.80	C / 5.2	1.03%	C- / 4.1
2016	C-	6,297	10.69	C+ / 5.6	2.57%	C- / 4.1
2015	C	4,368	10.64	C+ / 6.8	1.61%	C / 4.3
2014	D+	2,612	10.73	C / 4.5	6.23%	C / 5.4
2013	U	1,717	10.35	U / --	-2.87%	U / --
2012	U	991	10.90	U / --	5.31%	U / --

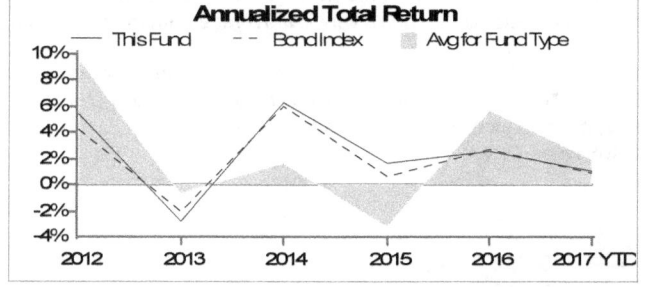

DFA One-Yr Fixed Inc Inst (DFIHX)   C+   Fair

Fund Family: Dimensional Fund Advisors   **Phone:** (800) 984-9472
Address: 6300 Bee Cave Road, Austin, TX 78746
Fund Type: GES - General - Short & Inter. Term

Major Rating Factors: Disappointing performance is the major factor driving the C+ (Fair) TheStreet Investment Rating for DFA One-Yr Fixed Inc Inst. The fund currently has a performance rating of D (Weak) based on an average return of 0.48% over the last three years and 0.23% over the last three months. Factored into the performance evaluation is an expense ratio of 0.17% (very low).

The fund's risk rating is currently A+ (Excellent). Volatility, as measured by standard deviation, is considered very low for fixed income funds at 0.36. Another risk factor is the fund's very low average duration of 1.0 years (i.e. low interest rate risk).

David A. Plecha has been running the fund for 34 years and currently receives a manager quality ranking of 54 (0=worst, 99=best). This fund offers only a moderate level of risk but investors looking for strong performance are still waiting.

Services Offered: Bank draft capabilities and wire transfers.

Data Date	Investment Rating	Net Assets ($Mil)	NAV	Perfor-mance Rating/Pts	Total Return Y-T-D	Risk Rating/Pts
2-17	C+	7,089	10.30	D / 2.0	0.23%	A+ / 9.9
2016	C+	6,947	10.29	D / 2.2	0.84%	A+ / 9.9
2015	B	7,610	10.28	C- / 4.2	0.31%	A+ / 9.9
2014	C	8,750	10.30	D- / 1.4	0.26%	A+ / 9.9
2013	C	8,540	10.31	D- / 1.2	0.34%	A+ / 9.9
2012	C-	7,636	10.32	E+ / 0.6	0.93%	A+ / 9.9

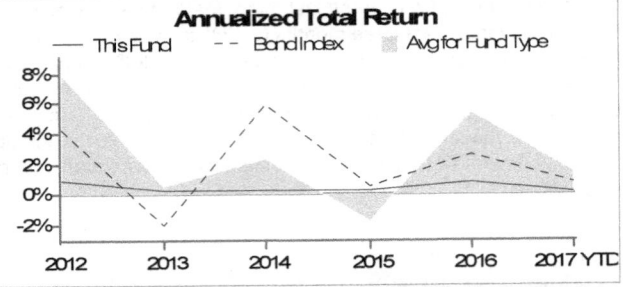

DFA S/T Extended Quality Port Inst (DFEQX)   B-   Good

Fund Family: Dimensional Fund Advisors   **Phone:** (800) 984-9472
Address: 6300 Bee Cave Road, Austin, TX 78746
Fund Type: GL - Global

Major Rating Factors: A moderate risk profile coupled with stable earnings characterizes DFA S/T Extended Quality Port Inst which receives a TheStreet Investment Rating of B- (Good). Volatility, as measured by standard deviation, is considered low for fixed income funds at 1.49. Another risk factor is the fund's very low average duration of 2.8 years (i.e. low interest rate risk). The fund's risk rating is currently B+ (Good).

The fund's performance rating is currently C- (Fair). It has registered an average return of 1.54% over the last three years and is up 0.62% over the last three months. Factored into the performance evaluation is an expense ratio of 0.22% (very low).

David J. Williams has been running the fund for 9 years and currently receives a manager quality ranking of 83 (0=worst, 99=best). If you desire stability with a moderate level of risk then this fund is an excellent option.

Services Offered: Automated phone transactions, bank draft capabilities, an IRA investment plan, wire transfers and a systematic withdrawal plan.

Data Date	Investment Rating	Net Assets ($Mil)	NAV	Perfor-mance Rating/Pts	Total Return Y-T-D	Risk Rating/Pts
2-17	B-	4,978	10.80	C- / 3.6	0.62%	B+ / 8.8
2016	B-	4,795	10.76	C- / 3.6	2.06%	B+ / 8.8
2015	A-	3,943	10.73	C+ / 5.9	1.15%	B+ / 8.9
2014	C+	3,961	10.79	D+ / 2.8	1.68%	B+ / 8.9
2013	B-	2,628	10.78	C- / 3.4	0.41%	A- / 9.0
2012	C	2,049	10.91	D / 1.9	3.63%	B+ / 8.9

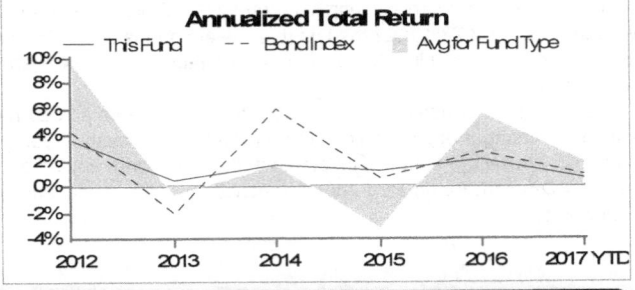

DFA Selectively Hedged Glb FI Ptf (DFSHX)   E+   Very Weak

Fund Family: Dimensional Fund Advisors   **Phone:** (800) 984-9472
Address: 6300 Bee Cave Road, Austin, TX 78746
Fund Type: GL - Global

Major Rating Factors: Disappointing performance is the major factor driving the E+ (Very Weak) TheStreet Investment Rating for DFA Selectively Hedged Glb FI Ptf. The fund currently has a performance rating of D (Weak) based on an average return of -0.37% over the last three years and 1.59% over the last three months. Factored into the performance evaluation is an expense ratio of 0.17% (very low).

The fund's risk rating is currently C- (Fair). Volatility, as measured by standard deviation, is considered average for fixed income funds at 3.48. Another risk factor is the fund's very low average duration of 2.8 years (i.e. low interest rate risk).

David A. Plecha currently receives a manager quality ranking of 63 (0=worst, 99=best). This fund offers an average level of risk, but investors looking for strong performance will be frustrated.

Services Offered: N/A

Data Date	Investment Rating	Net Assets ($Mil)	NAV	Perfor-mance Rating/Pts	Total Return Y-T-D	Risk Rating/Pts
2-17	E+	1,053	9.57	D / 1.7	1.59%	C- / 4.0
2016	E+	1,009	9.42	E+ / 0.6	3.27%	C / 4.3
2015	D	952	9.27	D- / 1.1	-3.17%	C- / 4.1
2014	E+	1,094	9.68	E+ / 0.7	-1.57%	C- / 3.6
2013	E+	956	9.99	D / 1.9	-1.11%	C- / 3.1
2012	E-	873	10.24	D / 1.7	4.22%	D+ / 2.4

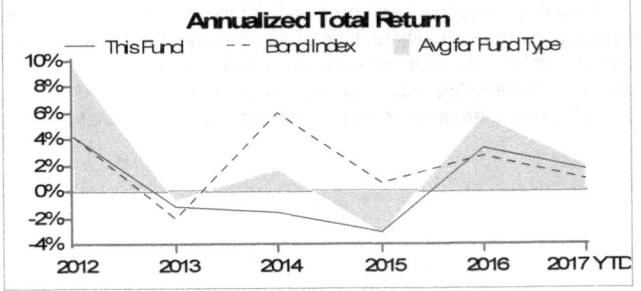

DFA Short Dur Real Ret Port Instl (DFAIX)   C+   Fair

Fund Family: Dimensional Fund Advisors   **Phone:** (800) 984-9472
Address: 6300 Bee Cave Road, Austin, TX 78746
Fund Type: GEI - General - Investment Grade
Major Rating Factors: A moderate risk profile coupled with stable earnings characterizes DFA Short Dur Real Ret Port Instl which receives a TheStreet Investment Rating of C+ (Fair). Volatility, as measured by standard deviation, is considered low for fixed income funds at 2.18. The fund's risk rating is currently B (Good).

The fund's performance rating is currently C- (Fair). It has registered an average return of 0.96% over the last three years and is up 0.91% over the last three months. Factored into the performance evaluation is an expense ratio of 0.24% (very low).

David A. Plecha has been running the fund for 4 years and currently receives a manager quality ranking of 44 (0=worst, 99=best). If you desire stability with a moderate level of risk then this fund is an excellent option.
Services Offered: Automated phone transactions, bank draft capabilities, an IRA investment plan, a 401K investment plan and wire transfers.

Data Date	Investment Rating	Net Assets ($Mil)	NAV	Performance Rating/Pts	Total Return Y-T-D	Risk Rating/Pts
2-17	C+	993	9.95	C- / 3.7	0.91%	B / 7.9
2016	C+	948	9.86	C- / 3.5	3.63%	B / 8.1
2015	U	738	9.65	U / --	0.46%	U / --
2014	U	674	9.73	U / --	-0.95%	U / --

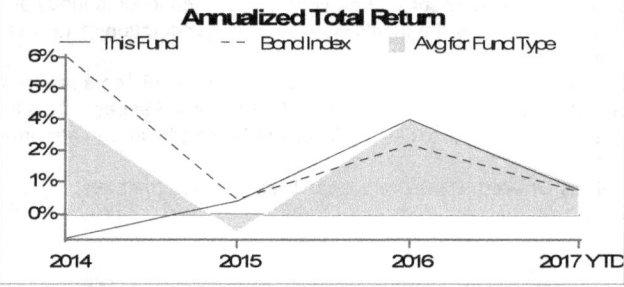

Annualized Total Return

DFA Short Term Municipal Bd Inst (DFSMX)   C+   Fair

Fund Family: Dimensional Fund Advisors   **Phone:** (800) 984-9472
Address: 6300 Bee Cave Road, Austin, TX 78746
Fund Type: MUN - Municipal - National
Major Rating Factors: Disappointing performance is the major factor driving the C+ (Fair) TheStreet Investment Rating for DFA Short Term Municipal Bd Inst. The fund currently has a performance rating of D+ (Weak) based on an average return of 0.73% over the last three years (1.21% taxable equivalent) and 0.94% over the last three months (1.56% taxable equivalent). Factored into the performance evaluation is an expense ratio of 0.22% (very low).

The fund's risk rating is currently A- (Excellent). Volatility, as measured by standard deviation, is considered very low for fixed income funds at 1.23. Another risk factor is the fund's very low average duration of 2.6 years (i.e. low interest rate risk).

David A. Plecha has been running the fund for 15 years and currently receives a manager quality ranking of 27 (0=worst, 99=best). This fund offers only a moderate level of risk but investors looking for strong performance are still waiting.
Services Offered: Automated phone transactions, bank draft capabilities and wire transfers.

Data Date	Investment Rating	Net Assets ($Mil)	NAV	Performance Rating/Pts	Total Return Y-T-D	Risk Rating/Pts
2-17	C+	2,237	10.19	D+ / 2.7	0.94%	A- / 9.0
2016	C	2,159	10.11	D / 2.2	0.05%	A- / 9.0
2015	A+	2,213	10.20	C+ / 6.4	1.15%	A / 9.4
2014	C	2,150	10.18	D / 1.8	0.57%	A+ / 9.7
2013	B-	1,842	10.21	D+ / 2.8	0.46%	A+ / 9.7
2012	C-	1,572	10.25	E+ / 0.9	0.73%	A / 9.5

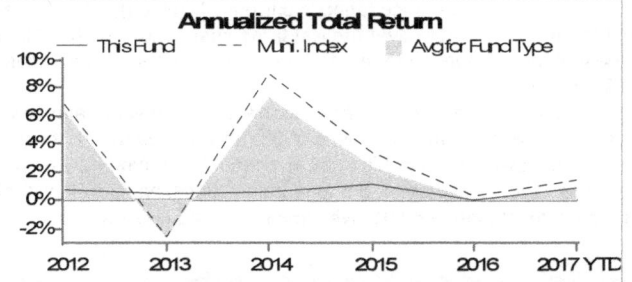

Annualized Total Return

DFA Short-Term Government Inst (DFFGX)   C   Fair

Fund Family: Dimensional Fund Advisors   **Phone:** (800) 984-9472
Address: 6300 Bee Cave Road, Austin, TX 78746
Fund Type: USS - US Government - Short & Inter. Term
Major Rating Factors: Disappointing performance is the major factor driving the C (Fair) TheStreet Investment Rating for DFA Short-Term Government Inst. The fund currently has a performance rating of D+ (Weak) based on an average return of 0.98% over the last three years and 0.28% over the last three months. Factored into the performance evaluation is an expense ratio of 0.19% (very low).

The fund's risk rating is currently B+ (Good). Volatility, as measured by standard deviation, is considered low for fixed income funds at 1.42. Another risk factor is the fund's very low average duration of 2.8 years (i.e. low interest rate risk).

David A. Plecha has been running the fund for 29 years and currently receives a manager quality ranking of 50 (0=worst, 99=best). This fund offers only a moderate level of risk but investors looking for strong performance are still waiting.
Services Offered: Bank draft capabilities and wire transfers.

Data Date	Investment Rating	Net Assets ($Mil)	NAV	Performance Rating/Pts	Total Return Y-T-D	Risk Rating/Pts
2-17	C	2,130	10.62	D+ / 2.3	0.28%	B+ / 8.9
2016	C	2,081	10.59	D+ / 2.6	0.99%	B+ / 8.9
2015	B	2,144	10.62	C / 4.9	0.99%	A- / 9.0
2014	C-	2,144	10.65	D / 1.8	1.25%	A- / 9.2
2013	C	1,807	10.62	D / 2.1	-0.45%	A- / 9.1
2012	C-	1,603	10.77	D- / 1.3	1.59%	A- / 9.1

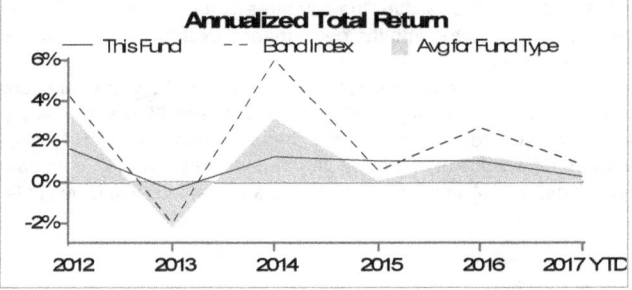

Annualized Total Return

DFA Two Year Glbl Fixed Inc Inst (DFGFX)

C+ **Fair**

Fund Family: Dimensional Fund Advisors **Phone:** (800) 984-9472
Address: 6300 Bee Cave Road, Austin, TX 78746
Fund Type: GL - Global

Major Rating Factors: Disappointing performance is the major factor driving the C+ (Fair) TheStreet Investment Rating for DFA Two Year Glbl Fixed Inc Inst. The fund currently has a performance rating of D (Weak) based on an average return of 0.62% over the last three years and 0.30% over the last three months. Factored into the performance evaluation is an expense ratio of 0.18% (very low).

The fund's risk rating is currently A+ (Excellent). Volatility, as measured by standard deviation, is considered very low for fixed income funds at 0.46. Another risk factor is the fund's very low average duration of 1.5 years (i.e. low interest rate risk).

David A. Plecha has been running the fund for 18 years and currently receives a manager quality ranking of 66 (0=worst, 99=best). This fund offers only a moderate level of risk but investors looking for strong performance are still waiting.

Services Offered: Bank draft capabilities and wire transfers.

Data Date	Investment Rating	Net Assets ($Mil)	NAV	Performance Rating/Pts	Total Return Y-T-D	Risk Rating/Pts
2-17	C+	4,911	9.97	D / 2.1	0.30%	A+ / 9.8
2016	C+	4,854	9.94	D+ / 2.3	0.95%	A+ / 9.8
2015	B	5,310	9.93	C / 4.4	0.33%	A+ / 9.9
2014	C	6,153	9.90	D- / 1.5	0.38%	A+ / 9.9
2013	C	5,659	10.01	D- / 1.4	0.46%	A+ / 9.9
2012	C-	4,653	10.04	E+ / 0.6	1.03%	A+ / 9.9

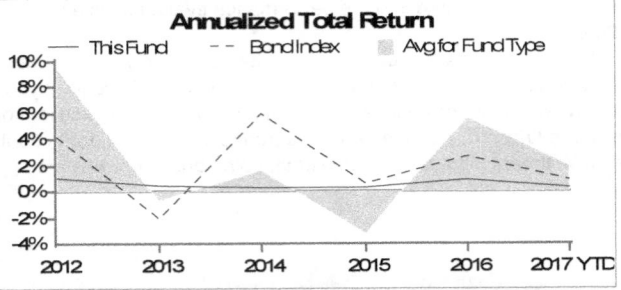

Annualized Total Return

DFA World ex US Govt Fxd Inc Inst (DWFIX)

C **Fair**

Fund Family: Dimensional Fund Advisors **Phone:** (800) 984-9472
Address: 6300 Bee Cave Road, Austin, TX 78746
Fund Type: GL - Global

Major Rating Factors: DFA World ex US Govt Fxd Inc Inst has adopted a very risky asset allocation strategy and currently receives an overall TheStreet Investment Rating of C (Fair). Volatility, as measured by standard deviation, is considered above average for fixed income funds at 4.49. Another risk factor is the fund's above average duration of 8.2 years (i.e. higher interest rate risk). The high level of risk (D, Weak) did however, reward investors with excellent performance.

The fund's performance rating is currently B (Good). It has registered an average return of 5.40% over the last three years and is up 0.50% over the last three months. Factored into the performance evaluation is an expense ratio of 0.22% (very low).

David A. Plecha has been running the fund for 6 years and currently receives a manager quality ranking of 98 (0=worst, 99=best). If you are comfortable owning a very high risk investment, this fund may be an option.

Services Offered: Automated phone transactions, bank draft capabilities, an IRA investment plan, a 401K investment plan and wire transfers.

Data Date	Investment Rating	Net Assets ($Mil)	NAV	Performance Rating/Pts	Total Return Y-T-D	Risk Rating/Pts
2-17	C	816	10.02	B / 7.9	0.50%	D / 2.2
2016	B-	785	9.97	A- / 9.0	5.55%	D+ / 2.4
2015	C	565	9.71	B / 8.2	0.85%	D+ / 2.8
2014	A-	385	10.34	B / 8.1	12.28%	C / 4.5
2013	U	262	10.03	U / --	-2.16%	U / --
2012	U	164	10.44	U / --	6.69%	U / --

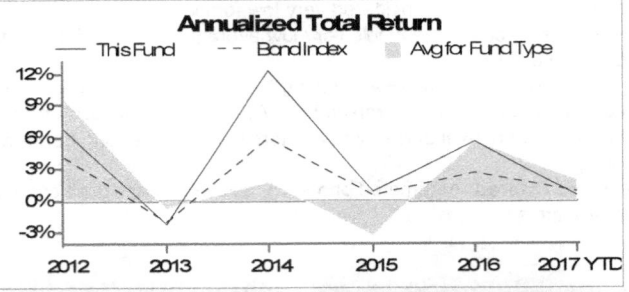

Annualized Total Return

Dodge & Cox Income Fund (DODIX)

A **Excellent**

Fund Family: Dodge & Cox **Phone:** (800) 621-3979
Address: 555 California Street, San Francisco, CA 94104
Fund Type: GEI - General - Investment Grade

Major Rating Factors: A moderate risk profile coupled with stable earnings characterizes Dodge & Cox Income Fund which receives a TheStreet Investment Rating of A (Excellent). Volatility, as measured by standard deviation, is considered low for fixed income funds at 2.69. Another risk factor is the fund's below average duration of 4.0 years (i.e. lower interest rate risk). The fund's risk rating is currently B- (Good).

The fund's performance rating is currently C+ (Fair). It has registered an average return of 3.06% over the last three years and is up 1.10% over the last three months. Factored into the performance evaluation is an expense ratio of 0.43% (very low).

Dana M. Emery has been running the fund for 28 years and currently receives a manager quality ranking of 78 (0=worst, 99=best). If you desire stability with a moderate level of risk then this fund is an excellent option.

Services Offered: Automated phone transactions, payroll deductions, bank draft capabilities, an IRA investment plan and a systematic withdrawal plan.

Data Date	Investment Rating	Net Assets ($Mil)	NAV	Performance Rating/Pts	Total Return Y-T-D	Risk Rating/Pts
2-17	A	47,060	13.74	C+ / 6.7	1.10%	B- / 7.1
2016	A	46,290	13.59	C+ / 6.9	5.61%	B- / 7.1
2015	B+	43,898	13.29	C+ / 6.6	-0.59%	B / 7.7
2014	A	39,128	13.78	C+ / 6.2	5.48%	B- / 7.5
2013	A	24,599	13.53	C+ / 6.4	0.64%	B- / 7.5
2012	B	26,539	13.86	C / 4.4	7.94%	B / 7.6

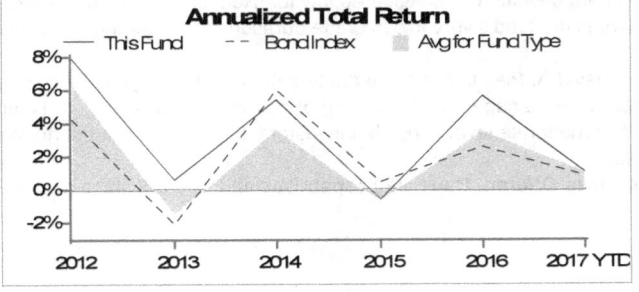

Annualized Total Return

DoubleLine Core Fixed Income N (DLFNX)   A-   Excellent

Fund Family: DoubleLine Funds   **Phone:** (877) 354-6311
Address: C/O US Bancorp Fund Services L, Milwaukee, WI 53201
Fund Type: GL - Global
Major Rating Factors: A moderate risk profile coupled with stable earnings characterizes DoubleLine Core Fixed Income N which receives a TheStreet Investment Rating of A- (Excellent). Volatility, as measured by standard deviation, is considered low for fixed income funds at 2.70. Another risk factor is the fund's below average duration of 4.4 years (i.e. lower interest rate risk). The fund's risk rating is currently B- (Good).

The fund's performance rating is currently C+ (Fair). It has registered an average return of 3.15% over the last three years and is up 1.23% over the last three months. Factored into the performance evaluation is an expense ratio of 0.48% (very low).

Jeffrey E. Gundlach has been running the fund for 7 years and currently receives a manager quality ranking of 94 (0=worst, 99=best). If you desire stability with a moderate level of risk then this fund is an excellent option.

Services Offered: Automated phone transactions, payroll deductions, bank draft capabilities, an IRA investment plan, a 401K investment plan, wire transfers and a systematic withdrawal plan.

Data Date	Investment Rating	Net Assets ($Mil)	NAV	Perfor-mance Rating/Pts	Total Return Y-T-D	Risk Rating/Pts
2-17	A-	1,065	10.87	C+ / 6.1	1.23%	B- / 7.0
2016	A-	1,049	10.78	C+ / 6.3	3.76%	B- / 7.0
2015	C+	845	10.67	C+ / 6.7	0.39%	C+ / 5.9
2014	B	511	10.98	C+ / 6.1	6.60%	C+ / 6.2
2013	A	388	10.70	B- / 7.2	-1.36%	C+ / 6.4
2012	U	795	11.33	U / --	7.89%	U / --

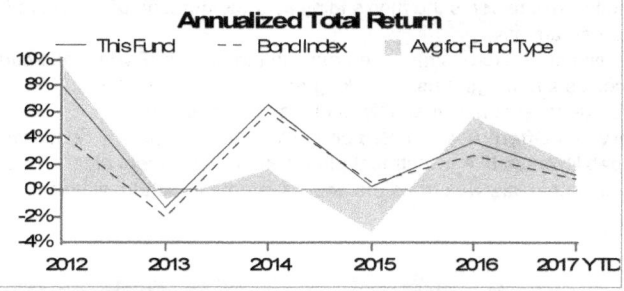

Annualized Total Return

DoubleLine Low Duration Bond N (DLSNX)   A-   Excellent

Fund Family: DoubleLine Funds   **Phone:** (877) 354-6311
Address: C/O US Bancorp Fund Services L, Milwaukee, WI 53201
Fund Type: COI - Corporate - Investment Grade
Major Rating Factors: A moderate risk profile coupled with stable earnings characterizes DoubleLine Low Duration Bond N which receives a TheStreet Investment Rating of A- (Excellent). Volatility, as measured by standard deviation, is considered very low for fixed income funds at 0.76. Another risk factor is the fund's very low average duration of 1.1 years (i.e. low interest rate risk). The fund's risk rating is currently A+ (Excellent).

The fund's performance rating is currently C- (Fair). It has registered an average return of 1.61% over the last three years and is up 0.62% over the last three months. Factored into the performance evaluation is an expense ratio of 0.69% (low).

Luz M. Padilla has been running the fund for 6 years and currently receives a manager quality ranking of 77 (0=worst, 99=best). If you desire stability with a moderate level of risk then this fund is an excellent option.

Services Offered: Automated phone transactions, payroll deductions, bank draft capabilities, an IRA investment plan, a 401K investment plan, wire transfers and a systematic withdrawal plan.

Data Date	Investment Rating	Net Assets ($Mil)	NAV	Perfor-mance Rating/Pts	Total Return Y-T-D	Risk Rating/Pts
2-17	A-	1,521	10.04	C- / 4.1	0.62%	A+ / 9.6
2016	B+	1,324	10.01	C- / 4.0	2.61%	A+ / 9.6
2015	A	1,140	9.98	C+ / 5.9	0.81%	A+ / 9.6
2014	B-	1,081	10.12	D+ / 2.8	1.35%	A+ / 9.6
2013	U	996	10.17	U / --	1.29%	U / --
2012	U	214	10.19	U / --	3.32%	U / --

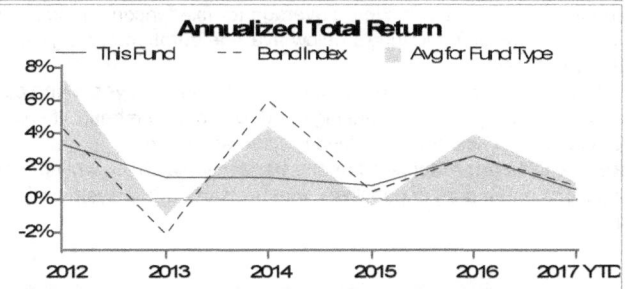

Annualized Total Return

DoubleLine Total Return Bond N (DLTNX)   A-   Excellent

Fund Family: DoubleLine Funds   **Phone:** (877) 354-6311
Address: C/O US Bancorp Fund Services L, Milwaukee, WI 53201
Fund Type: GES - General - Short & Inter. Term
Major Rating Factors: A moderate risk profile coupled with stable earnings characterizes DoubleLine Total Return Bond N which receives a TheStreet Investment Rating of A- (Excellent). Volatility, as measured by standard deviation, is considered low for fixed income funds at 2.02. Another risk factor is the fund's very low average duration of 2.6 years (i.e. low interest rate risk). The fund's risk rating is currently B (Good).

The fund's performance rating is currently C (Fair). It has registered an average return of 2.85% over the last three years and is up 0.67% over the last three months. Factored into the performance evaluation is an expense ratio of 0.72% (low).

Jeffrey E. Gundlach has been running the fund for 7 years and currently receives a manager quality ranking of 77 (0=worst, 99=best). If you desire stability with a moderate level of risk then this fund is an excellent option.

Services Offered: Automated phone transactions, payroll deductions, bank draft capabilities, an IRA investment plan, a 401K investment plan, wire transfers and a systematic withdrawal plan.

Data Date	Investment Rating	Net Assets ($Mil)	NAV	Perfor-mance Rating/Pts	Total Return Y-T-D	Risk Rating/Pts
2-17	A-	10,091	10.63	C / 5.1	0.67%	B / 8.2
2016	A	11,011	10.62	C+ / 6.0	1.92%	B / 7.9
2015	A	10,359	10.78	B / 7.8	2.07%	B- / 7.5
2014	A+	7,798	10.97	C+ / 6.7	6.47%	B- / 7.4
2013	A+	6,995	10.78	B- / 7.4	-0.23%	B / 7.9
2012	U	8,995	11.33	U / --	9.00%	U / --

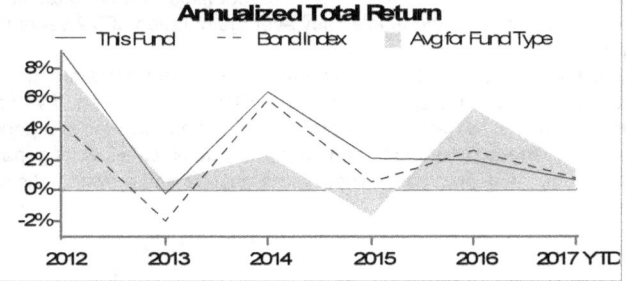

Annualized Total Return

Dreyfus Bond Market Index Inv (DBMIX)

D+   **Weak**

Fund Family: Dreyfus Funds   **Phone:** (800) 645-6561
Address: 144 Glenn Curtiss Boulevard, Uniondale, NY 11556
Fund Type: COI - Corporate - Investment Grade
Major Rating Factors: Dreyfus Bond Market Index Inv receives a TheStreet Investment Rating of D+ (Weak). The fund has a performance rating of C- (Fair) based on an average return of 2.13% over the last three years and 0.85% over the last three months. Factored into the performance evaluation is an expense ratio of 0.41% (very low).

The fund's risk rating is currently C+ (Fair). Volatility, as measured by standard deviation, is considered average for fixed income funds at 2.93. Another risk factor is the fund's fairly average duration of 5.5 years (i.e. average interest rate risk).

Nancy G. Rogers has been running the fund for 7 years and currently receives a manager quality ranking of 27 (0=worst, 99=best). If you desire an average level of risk, then this fund may be an option.

Services Offered: Automated phone transactions, payroll deductions, bank draft capabilities, an IRA investment plan, a 401K investment plan, a Keogh investment plan, wire transfers and a systematic withdrawal plan.

Data Date	Investment Rating	Net Assets ($Mil)	NAV	Performance Rating/Pts	Total Return Y-T-D	Risk Rating/Pts
2-17	D+	1,042	10.28	C- / 3.9	0.85%	C+ / 5.9
2016	C-	1,040	10.23	C / 4.3	2.08%	C+ / 6.0
2015	C	1,022	10.29	C / 5.3	0.05%	C+ / 6.4
2014	C	1,178	10.56	C- / 3.8	5.56%	B- / 7.0
2013	C-	878	10.32	C- / 3.2	-2.59%	B- / 7.4
2012	C	1,046	11.02	D+ / 2.9	3.69%	B- / 7.4

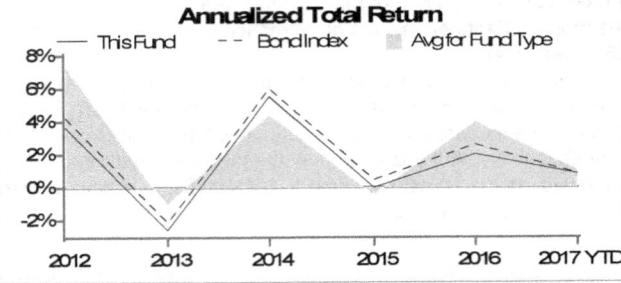

Annualized Total Return

Dreyfus Intermediate Muni Bd (DITEX)

C+   **Fair**

Fund Family: Dreyfus Funds   **Phone:** (800) 645-6561
Address: 144 Glenn Curtiss Boulevard, Uniondale, NY 11556
Fund Type: MUN - Municipal - National
Major Rating Factors: Middle of the road best describes Dreyfus Intermediate Muni Bd whose TheStreet Investment Rating is currently a C+ (Fair). The fund has a performance rating of C+ (Fair) based on an average return of 2.66% over the last three years (4.40% taxable equivalent) and 1.08% over the last three months (1.79% taxable equivalent). Factored into the performance evaluation is an expense ratio of 0.74% (low).

The fund's risk rating is currently C (Fair). Volatility, as measured by standard deviation, is considered average for fixed income funds at 3.23. Another risk factor is the fund's below average duration of 4.8 years (i.e. lower interest rate risk).

Thomas C. Casey has been running the fund for 6 years and currently receives a manager quality ranking of 16 (0=worst, 99=best). If you desire an average level of risk, then this fund may be an option.

Services Offered: Automated phone transactions, check writing, payroll deductions, bank draft capabilities, wire transfers and a systematic withdrawal plan.

Data Date	Investment Rating	Net Assets ($Mil)	NAV	Performance Rating/Pts	Total Return Y-T-D	Risk Rating/Pts
2-17	C+	726	13.53	C+ / 6.3	1.08%	C / 4.7
2016	C+	723	13.44	C+ / 6.4	-0.29%	C / 4.6
2015	A	766	13.97	A- / 9.1	3.00%	C / 5.5
2014	B+	789	14.02	B- / 7.5	7.21%	C / 5.2
2013	A-	790	13.44	B / 7.7	-1.86%	C / 5.4
2012	B	960	14.23	C+ / 6.4	4.88%	C / 5.3

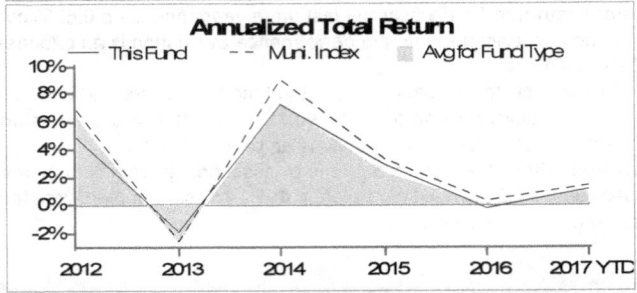

Annualized Total Return

Dreyfus Municipal Bond (DRTAX)

B-   **Good**

Fund Family: Dreyfus Funds   **Phone:** (800) 645-6561
Address: 144 Glenn Curtiss Boulevard, Uniondale, NY 11556
Fund Type: MUN - Municipal - National
Major Rating Factors: Strong performance is the major factor driving the B- (Good) TheStreet Investment Rating for Dreyfus Municipal Bond. The fund currently has a performance rating of B (Good) based on an average return of 3.68% over the last three years (6.09% taxable equivalent) and 1.29% over the last three months (2.14% taxable equivalent). Factored into the performance evaluation is an expense ratio of 0.73% (low).

The fund's risk rating is currently C- (Fair). Volatility, as measured by standard deviation, is considered average for fixed income funds at 3.71. Another risk factor is the fund's fairly average duration of 5.2 years (i.e. average interest rate risk).

Daniel A. Marques has been running the fund for 8 years and currently receives a manager quality ranking of 29 (0=worst, 99=best). If you desire an average level of risk and strong performance, then this fund is a good option.

Services Offered: Automated phone transactions, check writing, payroll deductions, bank draft capabilities, wire transfers and a systematic withdrawal plan.

Data Date	Investment Rating	Net Assets ($Mil)	NAV	Performance Rating/Pts	Total Return Y-T-D	Risk Rating/Pts
2-17	B-	1,357	11.58	B / 7.8	1.29%	C- / 3.6
2016	B	1,359	11.49	B / 8.2	-0.26%	C- / 3.5
2015	B+	1,436	11.88	A / 9.5	3.60%	C- / 4.0
2014	A	1,474	11.85	A- / 9.0	10.51%	C- / 3.9
2013	B	1,448	11.10	B / 7.6	-3.56%	C / 4.4
2012	B+	1,683	11.91	B- / 7.3	7.30%	C / 4.3

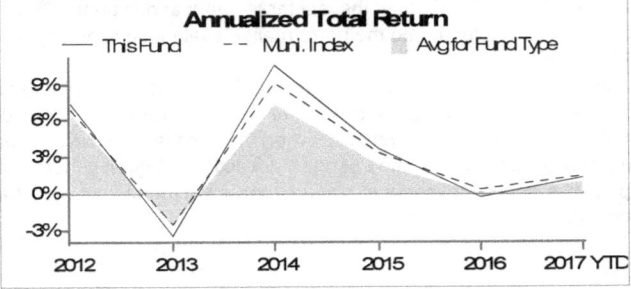

Annualized Total Return

Dreyfus NY Tax Exempt Bond (DRNYX)   B   Good

Fund Family: Dreyfus Funds   **Phone:** (800) 645-6561
Address: 144 Glenn Curtiss Boulevard, Uniondale, NY 11556
Fund Type: MUS - Municipal - Single State
Major Rating Factors: Strong performance is the major factor driving the B (Good) TheStreet Investment Rating for Dreyfus NY Tax Exempt Bond. The fund currently has a performance rating of B (Good) based on an average return of 3.51% over the last three years (5.81% taxable equivalent) and 1.26% over the last three months (2.09% taxable equivalent). Factored into the performance evaluation is an expense ratio of 0.73% (low).

The fund's risk rating is currently C- (Fair). Volatility, as measured by standard deviation, is considered average for fixed income funds at 3.39. Another risk factor is the fund's fairly average duration of 5.3 years (i.e. average interest rate risk).

Thomas C. Casey has been running the fund for 8 years and currently receives a manager quality ranking of 36 (0=worst, 99=best). If you desire an average level of risk and strong performance, then this fund is a good option.
Services Offered: Automated phone transactions, check writing, payroll deductions, bank draft capabilities, wire transfers and a systematic withdrawal plan.

Data Date	Investment Rating	Net Assets ($Mil)	NAV	Performance Rating/Pts	Total Return Y-T-D	Risk Rating/Pts
2-17	B	1,133	14.67	B / 7.7	1.26%	C- / 4.2
2016	B	1,127	14.56	B / 7.8	-0.05%	C / 4.3
2015	B+	1,172	15.02	A- / 9.1	3.61%	C / 4.3
2014	B	1,194	14.98	B / 7.9	8.96%	C- / 4.0
2013	C-	1,171	14.24	C+ / 5.7	-4.68%	C / 4.4
2012	B	1,408	15.50	C+ / 6.9	6.36%	C / 4.3

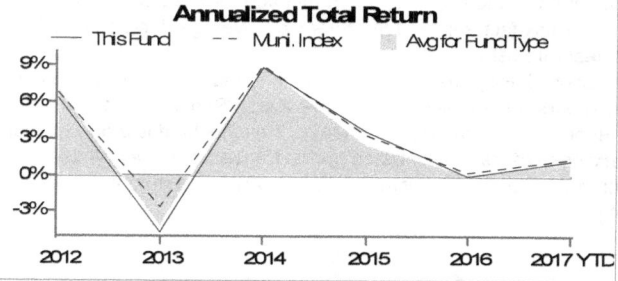

Dupree KY Tax Free Income (KYTFX)   A   Excellent

Fund Family: Dupree Funds   **Phone:** (800) 866-0614
Address: P.O. Box 1149, Lexington, KY 40507
Fund Type: MUS - Municipal - Single State
Major Rating Factors: Dupree KY Tax Free Income receives a TheStreet Investment Rating of A (Excellent). The fund has a performance rating of C+ (Fair) based on an average return of 2.73% over the last three years (4.52% taxable equivalent) and 0.76% over the last three months (1.26% taxable equivalent). Factored into the performance evaluation is an expense ratio of 0.55% (very low).

The fund's risk rating is currently C+ (Fair). Volatility, as measured by standard deviation, is considered average for fixed income funds at 2.75. Another risk factor is the fund's fairly average duration of 5.1 years (i.e. average interest rate risk).

Vincent Harrison has been running the fund for 18 years and currently receives a manager quality ranking of 33 (0=worst, 99=best). If you desire an average level of risk, then this fund may be an option.
Services Offered: Automated phone transactions, payroll deductions, bank draft capabilities, an IRA investment plan, wire transfers and a systematic withdrawal plan.

Data Date	Investment Rating	Net Assets ($Mil)	NAV	Performance Rating/Pts	Total Return Y-T-D	Risk Rating/Pts
2-17	A	982	7.70	C+ / 6.6	0.76%	C+ / 6.8
2016	A	977	7.68	B- / 7.1	0.25%	C+ / 6.6
2015	A	989	7.90	A- / 9.0	2.51%	C+ / 5.9
2014	A	988	7.96	B / 8.2	7.66%	C / 5.1
2013	A	930	7.65	B / 8.1	-2.02%	C / 5.3
2012	B+	996	8.09	C+ / 6.8	6.09%	C / 5.1

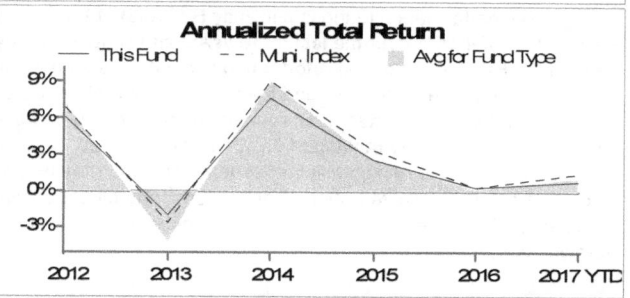

Eaton Vance Float Rate Advtage A (EAFAX)   B+   Good

Fund Family: Eaton Vance Funds   **Phone:** (800) 262-1122
Address: The Eaton Vance Building, Boston, MA 02109
Fund Type: LP - Loan Participation
Major Rating Factors: Strong performance is the major factor driving the B+ (Good) TheStreet Investment Rating for Eaton Vance Float Rate Advtage A. The fund currently has a performance rating of B+ (Good) based on an average return of 3.87% over the last three years and 1.22% over the last three months. Factored into the performance evaluation is an expense ratio of 1.36% (above average) and a 2.3% front-end load that is levied at the time of purchase.

The fund's risk rating is currently C- (Fair). Volatility, as measured by standard deviation, is considered average for fixed income funds at 3.72. Another risk factor is the fund's very low average duration of 0.3 years (i.e. low interest rate risk).

Scott H. Page has been running the fund for 21 years and currently receives a manager quality ranking of 91 (0=worst, 99=best). If you desire an average level of risk and strong performance, then this fund is a good option.
Services Offered: Automated phone transactions, payroll deductions, bank draft capabilities, an IRA investment plan, a 401K investment plan, wire transfers and a systematic withdrawal plan.

Data Date	Investment Rating	Net Assets ($Mil)	NAV	Performance Rating/Pts	Total Return Y-T-D	Risk Rating/Pts
2-17	B+	1,826	10.89	B+ / 8.5	1.22%	C- / 3.6
2016	B+	1,708	10.83	B+ / 8.4	12.67%	C- / 3.9
2015	D+	1,549	10.10	D+ / 2.9	-1.84%	C+ / 6.1
2014	A-	1,984	10.79	C / 5.4	0.69%	B / 7.9
2013	A-	2,280	11.20	B+ / 8.3	5.62%	C / 4.5
2012	D-	1,048	11.10	C+ / 6.2	10.53%	D / 2.1

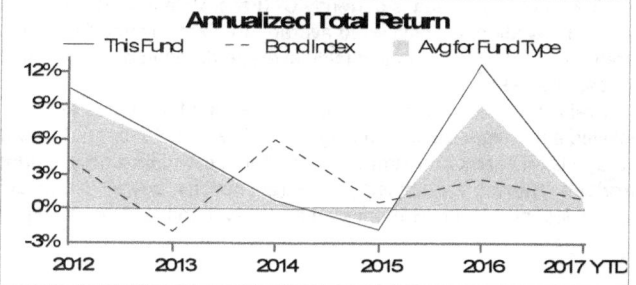

Eaton Vance Floating Rate A (EVBLX)   B+   Good

Fund Family: Eaton Vance Funds   **Phone:** (800) 262-1122
Address: The Eaton Vance Building, Boston, MA 02109
Fund Type: LP - Loan Participation
Major Rating Factors: Strong performance is the major factor driving the B+ (Good) TheStreet Investment Rating for Eaton Vance Floating Rate A. The fund currently has a performance rating of B (Good) based on an average return of 3.21% over the last three years and 1.10% over the last three months. Factored into the performance evaluation is an expense ratio of 1.03% (average) and a 2.3% front-end load that is levied at the time of purchase.

The fund's risk rating is currently C (Fair). Volatility, as measured by standard deviation, is considered average for fixed income funds at 3.19. Another risk factor is the fund's very low average duration of 0.3 years (i.e. low interest rate risk).

Scott H. Page has been running the fund for 16 years and currently receives a manager quality ranking of 88 (0=worst, 99=best). If you desire an average level of risk and strong performance, then this fund is a good option.

Services Offered: Automated phone transactions, payroll deductions, bank draft capabilities, an IRA investment plan, a 401K investment plan and a systematic withdrawal plan.

Data Date	Investment Rating	Net Assets ($Mil)	NAV	Performance Rating/Pts	Total Return Y-T-D	Risk Rating/Pts
2-17	B+	1,177	9.31	B / 7.6	1.10%	C / 4.8
2016	B+	1,134	9.26	B- / 7.4	10.93%	C / 5.2
2015	C-	1,204	8.69	D+ / 2.3	-1.91%	B- / 7.5
2014	B	1,688	9.21	C- / 4.0	0.37%	B+ / 8.6
2013	B+	2,739	9.50	C+ / 6.9	4.54%	C+ / 6.1
2012	E+	1,695	9.43	C- / 3.8	8.12%	C- / 3.5

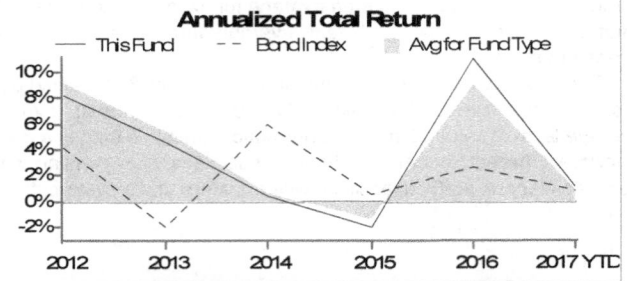

Eaton Vance Income Fd of Boston A (EVIBX)   C   Fair

Fund Family: Eaton Vance Funds   **Phone:** (800) 262-1122
Address: The Eaton Vance Building, Boston, MA 02109
Fund Type: COH - Corporate - High Yield
Major Rating Factors: Eaton Vance Income Fd of Boston A has adopted a very risky asset allocation strategy and currently receives an overall TheStreet Investment Rating of C (Fair). Volatility, as measured by standard deviation, is considered above average for fixed income funds at 4.68. Another risk factor is the fund's below average duration of 3.3 years (i.e. lower interest rate risk). The high level of risk (D, Weak) did however, reward investors with excellent performance.

The fund's performance rating is currently B (Good). It has registered an average return of 4.15% over the last three years and is up 2.13% over the last three months. Factored into the performance evaluation is an expense ratio of 1.00% (average) and a 4.8% front-end load that is levied at the time of purchase.

Michael W. Weilheimer has been running the fund for 16 years and currently receives a manager quality ranking of 65 (0=worst, 99=best). If you are comfortable owning a very high risk investment, this fund may be an option.

Services Offered: Automated phone transactions, payroll deductions, bank draft capabilities, an IRA investment plan, a 401K investment plan and a systematic withdrawal plan.

Data Date	Investment Rating	Net Assets ($Mil)	NAV	Performance Rating/Pts	Total Return Y-T-D	Risk Rating/Pts
2-17	C	1,600	5.80	B / 8.0	2.13%	D / 1.9
2016	C	1,631	5.73	B / 8.0	12.66%	D / 2.0
2015	D	1,258	5.40	C- / 3.9	-2.05%	D / 2.2
2014	C	1,490	5.86	C+ / 6.8	2.54%	C- / 3.3
2013	C+	1,906	6.06	A- / 9.1	7.29%	D / 1.8
2012	C	1,966	6.00	B / 7.8	13.40%	D / 1.6

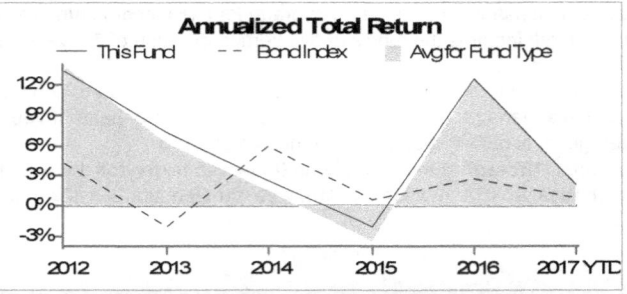

Eaton Vance National Muni Inc A (EANAX)   B+   Good

Fund Family: Eaton Vance Funds   **Phone:** (800) 262-1122
Address: The Eaton Vance Building, Boston, MA 02109
Fund Type: MUN - Municipal - National
Major Rating Factors: Strong performance is the major factor driving the B+ (Good) TheStreet Investment Rating for Eaton Vance National Muni Inc A. The fund currently has a performance rating of B+ (Good) based on an average return of 5.15% over the last three years (8.53% taxable equivalent) and 0.74% over the last three months (1.23% taxable equivalent). Factored into the performance evaluation is an expense ratio of 0.76% (low) and a 4.8% front-end load that is levied at the time of purchase.

The fund's risk rating is currently C- (Fair). Volatility, as measured by standard deviation, is considered average for fixed income funds at 3.67. Another risk factor is the fund's fairly average duration of 5.2 years (i.e. average interest rate risk).

Craig R. Brandon has been running the fund for 4 years and currently receives a manager quality ranking of 81 (0=worst, 99=best). If you desire an average level of risk and strong performance, then this fund is a good option.

Services Offered: Automated phone transactions, payroll deductions, bank draft capabilities, an IRA investment plan and a systematic withdrawal plan.

Data Date	Investment Rating	Net Assets ($Mil)	NAV	Performance Rating/Pts	Total Return Y-T-D	Risk Rating/Pts
2-17	B+	1,670	9.77	B+ / 8.3	0.74%	C- / 3.7
2016	A-	1,706	9.76	A / 9.5	1.72%	C- / 3.3
2015	C-	1,890	9.96	A- / 9.0	4.30%	E+ / 0.7
2014	C+	2,061	9.93	A+ / 9.6	14.83%	E / 0.5
2013	D-	1,957	9.04	C+ / 6.1	-7.46%	E / 0.5
2012	B-	2,854	10.26	A- / 9.0	14.21%	D- / 1.4

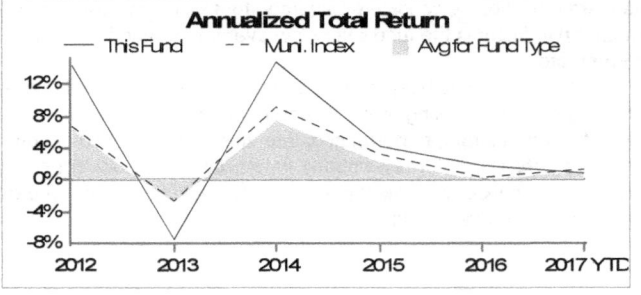

Eaton Vance Short Dur Strat Inc A (ETSIX)   C+   Fair

Fund Family: Eaton Vance Funds   **Phone:** (800) 262-1122
Address: The Eaton Vance Building, Boston, MA 02109
Fund Type: GL - Global
Major Rating Factors: Middle of the road best describes Eaton Vance Short
Dur Strat Inc A whose TheStreet Investment Rating is currently a C+ (Fair). The
fund has a performance rating of C+ (Fair) based on an average return of 2.98%
over the last three years and 0.76% over the last three months. Factored into the
performance evaluation is an expense ratio of 1.06% (average) and a 2.3%
front-end load that is levied at the time of purchase.

The fund's risk rating is currently C (Fair). Volatility, as measured by
standard deviation, is considered average for fixed income funds at 3.27.
Another risk factor is the fund's very low average duration of 1.2 years (i.e. low
interest rate risk).

Mark S. Venezia has been running the fund for 27 years and currently
receives a manager quality ranking of 90 (0=worst, 99=best). If you desire an
average level of risk, then this fund may be an option.

Services Offered: Automated phone transactions, payroll deductions, bank draft
capabilities, an IRA investment plan, a Keogh investment plan and a systematic
withdrawal plan.

Data Date	Investment Rating	Net Assets ($Mil)	NAV	Performance Rating/Pts	Total Return Y-T-D	Risk Rating/Pts
2-17	C+	867	7.38	C+ / 6.7	0.76%	C / 4.6
2016	C+	874	7.37	C+ / 6.5	5.54%	C / 4.9
2015	D+	1,176	7.27	C- / 3.1	-0.81%	C+ / 5.7
2014	C-	857	7.64	C / 4.5	4.34%	C / 5.5
2013	D	1,039	7.83	C- / 3.9	0.36%	C / 5.0
2012	E+	1,476	8.18	D+ / 2.8	8.51%	C / 5.2

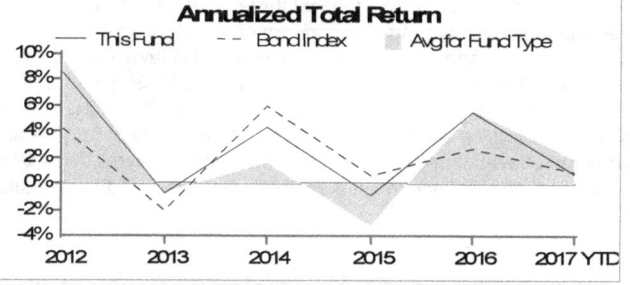

Elfun Tax Exempt Income (ELFTX)   A-   Excellent

Fund Family: State Street Global Advisors Funds   **Phone:** (800) 843-2639
Address: 1290 Broadway, Denver, CO 80203
Fund Type: MUN - Municipal - National
Major Rating Factors: Strong performance is the major factor driving the A-
(Excellent) TheStreet Investment Rating for Elfun Tax Exempt Income. The fund
currently has a performance rating of B (Good) based on an average return of
3.75% over the last three years (6.21% taxable equivalent) and 1.18% over the
last three months (1.95% taxable equivalent). Factored into the performance
evaluation is an expense ratio of 0.20% (very low).

The fund's risk rating is currently C (Fair). Volatility, as measured by
standard deviation, is considered average for fixed income funds at 3.26.
Another risk factor is the fund's fairly average duration of 6.7 years (i.e. average
interest rate risk).

Michael J. Caufield currently receives a manager quality ranking of 58
(0=worst, 99=best). If you desire an average level of risk and strong
performance, then this fund is a good option.

Services Offered: Automated phone transactions, payroll deductions, bank draft
capabilities, an IRA investment plan, wire transfers and a systematic withdrawal
plan.

Data Date	Investment Rating	Net Assets ($Mil)	NAV	Performance Rating/Pts	Total Return Y-T-D	Risk Rating/Pts
2-17	A-	1,494	11.54	B / 8.1	1.18%	C / 4.6
2016	A-	1,492	11.48	B+ / 8.5	0.42%	C / 4.4
2015	B	1,585	11.88	A- / 9.2	3.22%	C- / 3.8
2014	B+	1,621	11.97	B+ / 8.8	9.85%	C- / 3.5
2013	B-	1,569	11.34	B- / 7.4	-4.05%	C- / 3.9
2012	B+	1,785	12.32	B / 7.8	7.45%	C- / 3.8

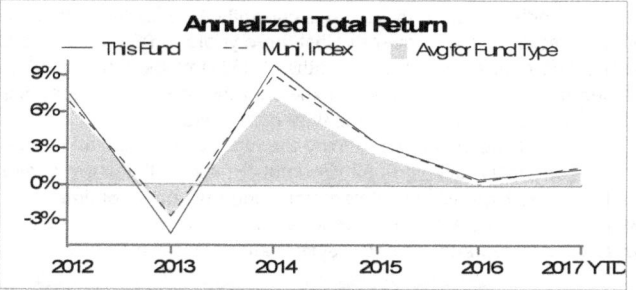

Federated Bond Fund A (FDBAX)   C-   Fair

Fund Family: Federated Investors Funds   **Phone:** (800) 341-7400
Address: 4000 Ericcson Drive, Warrendale, PA 15086
Fund Type: COI - Corporate - Investment Grade
Major Rating Factors: Middle of the road best describes Federated Bond Fund
A whose TheStreet Investment Rating is currently a C- (Fair). The fund has a
performance rating of C+ (Fair) based on an average return of 3.71% over the
last three years and 2.17% over the last three months. Factored into the
performance evaluation is an expense ratio of 1.01% (average) and a 4.5%
front-end load that is levied at the time of purchase.

The fund's risk rating is currently C- (Fair). Volatility, as measured by
standard deviation, is considered average for fixed income funds at 3.97.
Another risk factor is the fund's fairly average duration of 6.3 years (i.e. average
interest rate risk).

Brian S. Ruffner has been running the fund for 4 years and currently
receives a manager quality ranking of 61 (0=worst, 99=best). If you desire an
average level of risk, then this fund may be an option.

Services Offered: Automated phone transactions, payroll deductions, bank draft
capabilities, an IRA investment plan, a 401K investment plan, wire transfers and
a systematic withdrawal plan.

Data Date	Investment Rating	Net Assets ($Mil)	NAV	Performance Rating/Pts	Total Return Y-T-D	Risk Rating/Pts
2-17	C-	642	9.20	C+ / 6.6	2.17%	C- / 3.2
2016	C-	664	9.06	C+ / 6.2	8.22%	C- / 3.4
2015	D	681	8.73	D+ / 2.5	-1.95%	C- / 4.0
2014	C	892	9.40	C+ / 5.7	5.85%	C / 4.8
2013	C+	889	9.27	C+ / 6.3	0.83%	C / 4.6
2012	C+	943	9.62	C+ / 5.8	10.22%	C / 4.7

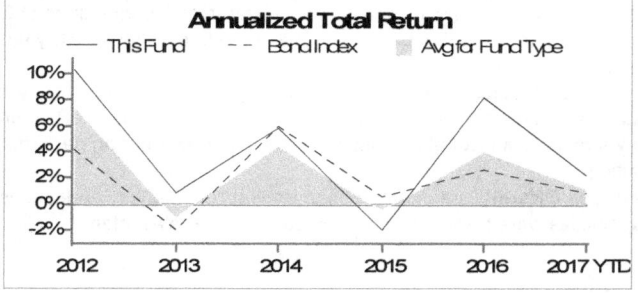

Federated High Income Bond A (FHIIX)

C   **Fair**

Fund Family: Federated Investors Funds   **Phone:** (800) 341-7400
Address: 4000 Ericcson Drive, Warrendale, PA 15086
Fund Type: COH - Corporate - High Yield

Major Rating Factors: Federated High Income Bond A has adopted a very risky asset allocation strategy and currently receives an overall TheStreet Investment Rating of C (Fair). Volatility, as measured by standard deviation, is considered above average for fixed income funds at 5.39. Another risk factor is the fund's below average duration of 3.6 years (i.e. lower interest rate risk). The high level of risk (D-, Weak) did however, reward investors with excellent performance.

The fund's performance rating is currently B+ (Good). It has registered an average return of 4.27% over the last three years and is up 2.79% over the last three months. Factored into the performance evaluation is an expense ratio of 1.01% (average) and a 4.5% front-end load that is levied at the time of purchase.

Mark E. Durbiano has been running the fund for 30 years and currently receives a manager quality ranking of 51 (0=worst, 99=best). If you are comfortable owning a very high risk investment, this fund may be an option.

Services Offered: Automated phone transactions, payroll deductions, bank draft capabilities, an IRA investment plan, wire transfers and a systematic withdrawal plan.

Data Date	Investment Rating	Net Assets ($Mil)	NAV	Performance Rating/Pts	Total Return Y-T-D	Risk Rating/Pts
2-17	C	650	7.65	B+ / 8.6	2.79%	D- / 1.3
2016	C-	636	7.50	B / 8.2	14.31%	D- / 1.4
2015	D-	634	6.92	D / 1.6	-3.28%	D / 1.8
2014	D	776	7.56	C+/ 6.2	2.14%	D+ / 2.7
2013	C+	887	7.84	B+ / 8.8	6.69%	D / 1.7
2012	C-	940	7.82	B- / 7.4	14.28%	D- / 1.5

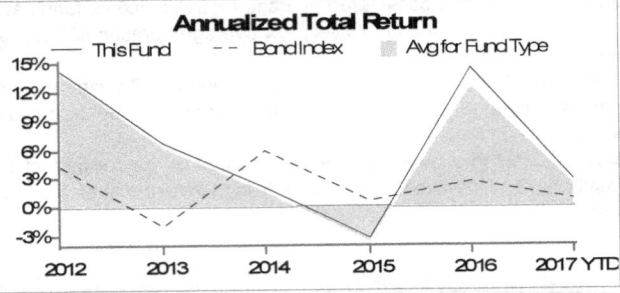

Annualized Total Return

Federated Muni & Stock Advantage A (FMUAX)

B-   **Good**

Fund Family: Federated Investors Funds   **Phone:** (800) 341-7400
Address: 4000 Ericcson Drive, Warrendale, PA 15086
Fund Type: MUH - Municipal - High Yield

Major Rating Factors: Federated Muni & Stock Advantage A has adopted a very risky asset allocation strategy and currently receives an overall TheStreet Investment Rating of B- (Good). Volatility, as measured by standard deviation, is considered above average for fixed income funds at 4.46. Another risk factor is the fund's fairly average duration of 6.2 years (i.e. average interest rate risk). The high level of risk (D, Weak) did however, reward investors with excellent performance.

The fund's performance rating is currently A- (Excellent). It has registered an average return of 4.20% over the last three years (6.96% taxable equivalent) and is up 2.81% over the last three months (4.65% taxable equivalent). Factored into the performance evaluation is an expense ratio of 1.07% (average) and a 5.5% front-end load that is levied at the time of purchase.

John L. Nichol has been running the fund for 14 years and currently receives a manager quality ranking of 92 (0=worst, 99=best). If you are comfortable owning a very high risk investment, this fund may be an option.

Services Offered: Automated phone transactions, payroll deductions, bank draft capabilities, wire transfers and a systematic withdrawal plan.

Data Date	Investment Rating	Net Assets ($Mil)	NAV	Performance Rating/Pts	Total Return Y-T-D	Risk Rating/Pts
2-17	B-	654	12.87	A- / 9.1	2.81%	D / 2.1
2016	C	653	12.56	B / 7.9	6.23%	D / 2.1
2015	C-	590	12.11	A- / 9.0	-0.97%	D- / 1.1
2014	C+	556	12.57	A / 9.4	7.00%	D- / 1.3
2013	A-	390	12.20	A+/ 9.9	8.79%	D+/ 2.6
2012	C+	307	11.59	B / 8.1	9.07%	D / 1.9

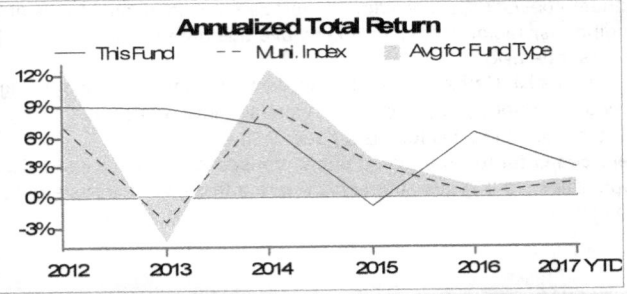

Annualized Total Return

Federated Muni Ultrashrt A (FMUUX)

D   **Weak**

Fund Family: Federated Investors Funds   **Phone:** (800) 341-7400
Address: 4000 Ericcson Drive, Warrendale, PA 15086
Fund Type: MUI - Municipal - Insured

Major Rating Factors: Very poor performance is the major factor driving the D (Weak) TheStreet Investment Rating for Federated Muni Ultrashrt A. The fund currently has a performance rating of E (Very Weak) based on an average return of 0.06% over the last three years and 0.18% over the last three months. Factored into the performance evaluation is an expense ratio of 0.98% (average) and a 2.0% front-end load that is levied at the time of purchase.

The fund's risk rating is currently A+ (Excellent). Volatility, as measured by standard deviation, is considered very low for fixed income funds at 0.28. Another risk factor is the fund's very low average duration of 0.3 years (i.e. low interest rate risk).

Jeffrey A. Kozemchak has been running the fund for 17 years and currently receives a manager quality ranking of 33 (0=worst, 99=best). This fund offers only a moderate level of risk but investors looking for strong performance are still waiting.

Services Offered: Automated phone transactions, payroll deductions, bank draft capabilities, wire transfers and a systematic withdrawal plan.

Data Date	Investment Rating	Net Assets ($Mil)	NAV	Performance Rating/Pts	Total Return Y-T-D	Risk Rating/Pts
2-17	D	803	9.99	E / 0.3	0.18%	A+/ 9.9
2016	D+	792	9.98	E+ / 0.6	0.28%	A+/ 9.9
2015	C	911	9.99	D+/ 2.3	-0.35%	A+/ 9.9
2014	D+	1,289	10.04	E+ / 0.7	0.33%	A+/ 9.9
2013	C-	1,597	10.03	E+ / 0.7	0.09%	A+/ 9.9
2012	C-	2,069	10.05	E / 0.4	0.59%	A+/ 9.9

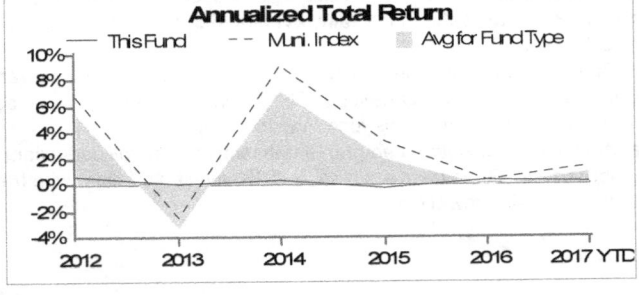

Annualized Total Return

Fidelity Adv Float-Rate Hi-Inc A (FFRAX)   C+   Fair

Fund Family: Fidelity Advisor   **Phone:** (800) 522-7297
Address: 245 Summer Street, Boston, MA 02210
Fund Type: LP - Loan Participation
Major Rating Factors: Middle of the road best describes Fidelity Adv Float-Rate Hi-Inc A whose TheStreet Investment Rating is currently a C+ (Fair). The fund has a performance rating of C+ (Fair) based on an average return of 2.71% over the last three years and 0.87% over the last three months. Factored into the performance evaluation is an expense ratio of 0.99% (average), a 2.8% front-end load that is levied at the time of purchase and a 1.0% back-end load levied at the time of sale.

The fund's risk rating is currently C (Fair). Volatility, as measured by standard deviation, is considered average for fixed income funds at 3.11. Another risk factor is the fund's very low average duration of 0.3 years (i.e. low interest rate risk).

Eric Mollenhauer has been running the fund for 4 years and currently receives a manager quality ranking of 85 (0=worst, 99=best). If you desire an average level of risk, then this fund may be an option.

Services Offered: Automated phone transactions, payroll deductions, bank draft capabilities, an IRA investment plan, a 401K investment plan, a Keogh investment plan, wire transfers and a systematic withdrawal plan.

Data Date	Investment Rating	Net Assets ($Mil)	NAV	Perfor-mance Rating/Pts	Total Return Y-T-D	Risk Rating/Pts
2-17	C+	796	9.69	C+ / 6.3	0.87%	C / 5.1
2016	B-	755	9.66	C+ / 6.2	9.72%	C+ / 5.6
2015	C-	772	9.14	D / 1.7	-1.44%	B / 8.0
2014	C	1,038	9.63	D+ / 2.6	0.02%	B+ / 8.4
2013	C	1,693	9.98	C / 4.9	3.62%	C / 5.4
2012	E	1,333	9.94	D+ / 2.4	6.61%	C- / 3.9

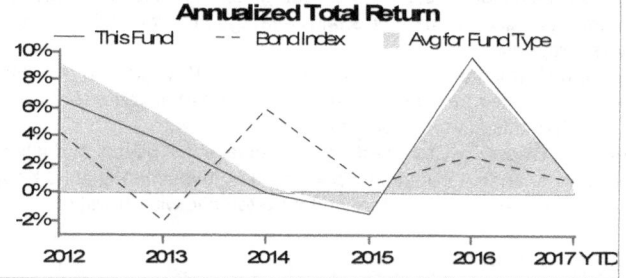

Fidelity Adv Hi Income Advantage A (FAHDX)   C+   Fair

Fund Family: Fidelity Advisor   **Phone:** (800) 522-7297
Address: 245 Summer Street, Boston, MA 02210
Fund Type: COH - Corporate - High Yield
Major Rating Factors: Fidelity Adv Hi Income Advantage A has adopted a very risky asset allocation strategy and currently receives an overall TheStreet Investment Rating of C+ (Fair). Volatility, as measured by standard deviation, is considered high for fixed income funds at 6.71. Another risk factor is the fund's below average duration of 3.8 years (i.e. lower interest rate risk). The high level of risk (E+, Very Weak) did however, reward investors with excellent performance.

The fund's performance rating is currently A (Excellent). It has registered an average return of 5.20% over the last three years and is up 4.31% over the last three months. Factored into the performance evaluation is an expense ratio of 1.04% (average), a 4.0% front-end load that is levied at the time of purchase and a 1.0% back-end load levied at the time of sale.

Harley J. Lank has been running the fund for 8 years and currently receives a manager quality ranking of 55 (0=worst, 99=best). If you are comfortable owning a very high risk investment, this fund may be an option.

Services Offered: Automated phone transactions, payroll deductions, bank draft capabilities, an IRA investment plan, a 401K investment plan, a Keogh investment plan, wire transfers and a systematic withdrawal plan.

Data Date	Investment Rating	Net Assets ($Mil)	NAV	Perfor-mance Rating/Pts	Total Return Y-T-D	Risk Rating/Pts
2-17	C+	612	11.09	A / 9.5	4.31%	E+ / 0.6
2016	C-	588	10.70	B+ / 8.5	13.36%	E+ / 0.7
2015	D	591	9.89	C / 5.1	-3.01%	E+ / 0.8
2014	C	666	10.69	B+ / 8.8	3.86%	D- / 1.2
2013	C	701	10.73	A / 9.5	9.99%	E / 0.3
2012	C-	714	10.32	B+ / 8.6	18.03%	E- / 0.2

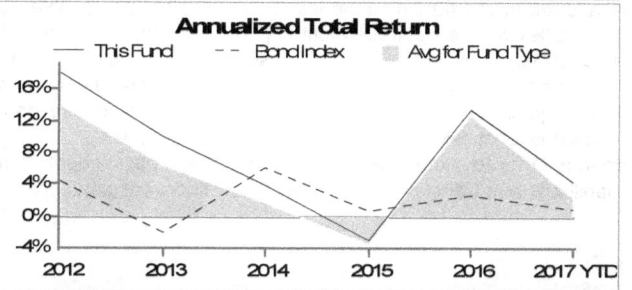

Fidelity Adv Strategic Income A (FSTAX)   C-   Fair

Fund Family: Fidelity Advisor   **Phone:** (800) 522-7297
Address: 245 Summer Street, Boston, MA 02210
Fund Type: GES - General - Short & Inter. Term
Major Rating Factors: Middle of the road best describes Fidelity Adv Strategic Income A whose TheStreet Investment Rating is currently a C- (Fair). The fund has a performance rating of C+ (Fair) based on an average return of 3.38% over the last three years and 2.62% over the last three months. Factored into the performance evaluation is an expense ratio of 1.00% (average) and a 4.0% front-end load that is levied at the time of purchase.

The fund's risk rating is currently C- (Fair). Volatility, as measured by standard deviation, is considered average for fixed income funds at 4.10. Another risk factor is the fund's below average duration of 4.9 years (i.e. lower interest rate risk).

Mark J. Notkin has been running the fund for 18 years and currently receives a manager quality ranking of 83 (0=worst, 99=best). If you desire an average level of risk, then this fund may be an option.

Services Offered: Automated phone transactions, payroll deductions, bank draft capabilities, an IRA investment plan, a 401K investment plan, a Keogh investment plan, wire transfers and a systematic withdrawal plan.

Data Date	Investment Rating	Net Assets ($Mil)	NAV	Perfor-mance Rating/Pts	Total Return Y-T-D	Risk Rating/Pts
2-17	C-	3,120	12.13	C+ / 6.8	2.62%	C- / 3.0
2016	D+	3,093	11.89	C+ / 5.9	8.51%	C- / 3.3
2015	D	3,268	11.32	D / 1.7	-1.84%	C- / 3.7
2014	D	3,792	11.92	C- / 4.1	3.52%	C / 4.3
2013	C-	4,206	12.10	C+ / 5.6	0.08%	C- / 4.1
2012	D-	5,573	12.69	C / 5.4	10.57%	C- / 3.0

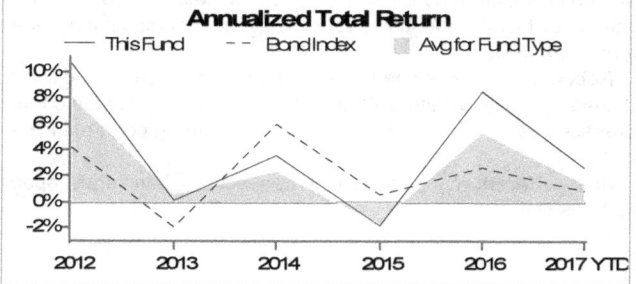

Fidelity Advisor Total Bond A (FEPAX)   C-   Fair

Fund Family: Fidelity Advisor   **Phone:** (800) 522-7297
Address: 245 Summer Street, Boston, MA 02210
Fund Type: GEI - General - Investment Grade
Major Rating Factors: Middle of the road best describes Fidelity Advisor Total Bond A whose TheStreet Investment Rating is currently a C- (Fair). The fund has a performance rating of C (Fair) based on an average return of 2.99% over the last three years and 1.34% over the last three months. Factored into the performance evaluation is an expense ratio of 0.75% (low) and a 4.0% front-end load that is levied at the time of purchase.

The fund's risk rating is currently C (Fair). Volatility, as measured by standard deviation, is considered average for fixed income funds at 3.08. Another risk factor is the fund's fairly average duration of 5.3 years (i.e. average interest rate risk).

Ford O'Neil has been running the fund for 13 years and currently receives a manager quality ranking of 66 (0=worst, 99=best). If you desire an average level of risk, then this fund may be an option.
Services Offered: Automated phone transactions, payroll deductions, bank draft capabilities, an IRA investment plan, a 401K investment plan, a Keogh investment plan, wire transfers and a systematic withdrawal plan.

Data Date	Investment Rating	Net Assets ($Mil)	NAV	Performance Rating/Pts	Total Return Y-T-D	Risk Rating/Pts
2-17	C-	1,210	10.62	C / 4.8	1.34%	C / 5.2
2016	C-	1,155	10.52	C / 4.8	5.53%	C / 5.4
2015	D+	1,141	10.26	D+ / 2.4	-0.73%	C+ / 5.7
2014	D+	738	10.68	C- / 3.6	5.22%	C+ / 6.3
2013	C-	515	10.44	C- / 3.6	-1.33%	B- / 7.0
2012	C+	663	10.96	C- / 3.5	6.27%	B / 7.8

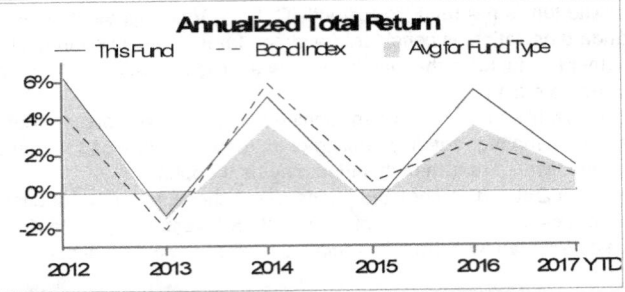

Annualized Total Return

Fidelity CA Ltd Term Tax-Free Bd (FCSTX)   B   Good

Fund Family: Fidelity Investments   **Phone:** (800) 544-8544
Address: 245 Summer Street, Boston, MA 02210
Fund Type: MUS - Municipal - Single State
Major Rating Factors: A moderate risk profile coupled with stable earnings characterizes Fidelity CA Ltd Term Tax-Free Bd which receives a TheStreet Investment Rating of B (Good). Volatility, as measured by standard deviation, is considered low for fixed income funds at 1.78. Another risk factor is the fund's below average duration of 3.1 years (i.e. lower interest rate risk). The fund's risk rating is currently B+ (Good).

The fund's performance rating is currently C- (Fair). It has registered an average return of 1.40% over the last three years (2.32% taxable equivalent) and is up 1.22% over the last three months (2.02% taxable equivalent). Factored into the performance evaluation is an expense ratio of 0.48% (very low).

Cormac Cullen has been running the fund for 1 year and currently receives a manager quality ranking of 25 (0=worst, 99=best). If you desire stability with a moderate level of risk then this fund is an excellent option.
Services Offered: Automated phone transactions, payroll deductions, bank draft capabilities, wire transfers and a systematic withdrawal plan.

Data Date	Investment Rating	Net Assets ($Mil)	NAV	Performance Rating/Pts	Total Return Y-T-D	Risk Rating/Pts
2-17	B	765	10.59	C- / 4.0	1.22%	B+ / 8.5
2016	C+	754	10.49	C- / 3.3	-0.47%	B+ / 8.6
2015	A+	788	10.72	B / 7.8	1.70%	B+ / 8.9
2014	B+	782	10.73	C- / 4.2	3.25%	B+ / 8.8
2013	A	689	10.59	C / 5.2	0.30%	B+ / 8.8
2012	C+	790	10.80	D+ / 2.3	2.44%	B+ / 8.9

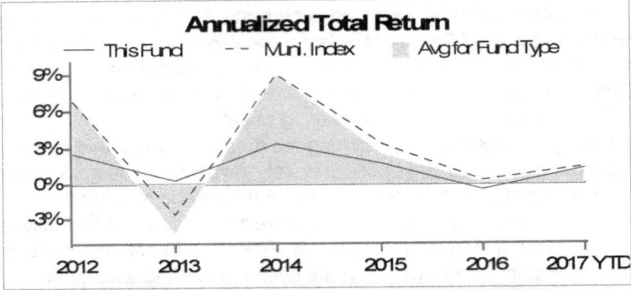

Annualized Total Return

Fidelity Conservative Inc Bond (FCONX)   C+   Fair

Fund Family: Fidelity Investments   **Phone:** (800) 544-8544
Address: 245 Summer Street, Boston, MA 02210
Fund Type: GEN - General
Major Rating Factors: Disappointing performance is the major factor driving the C+ (Fair) TheStreet Investment Rating for Fidelity Conservative Inc Bond. The fund currently has a performance rating of D (Weak) based on an average return of 0.57% over the last three years and 0.26% over the last three months. Factored into the performance evaluation is an expense ratio of 0.40% (very low).

The fund's risk rating is currently A+ (Excellent). Volatility, as measured by standard deviation, is considered very low for fixed income funds at 0.20. Another risk factor is the fund's very low average duration of 0.3 years (i.e. low interest rate risk).

Robert Galuszka has been running the fund for 2 years and currently receives a manager quality ranking of 63 (0=worst, 99=best). This fund offers only a moderate level of risk but investors looking for strong performance are still waiting.
Services Offered: Automated phone transactions, bank draft capabilities and wire transfers.

Data Date	Investment Rating	Net Assets ($Mil)	NAV	Performance Rating/Pts	Total Return Y-T-D	Risk Rating/Pts
2-17	C+	1,739	10.04	D / 2.2	0.26%	A+ / 9.9
2016	C+	1,600	10.03	D+ / 2.3	0.95%	A+ / 9.9
2015	B	1,089	10.02	C / 4.5	0.35%	A+ / 9.9
2014	C	1,433	10.03	D / 1.6	0.21%	A+ / 9.9
2013	U	1,563	10.04	U / --	0.62%	U / --
2012	U	1,033	10.03	U / --	1.38%	U / --

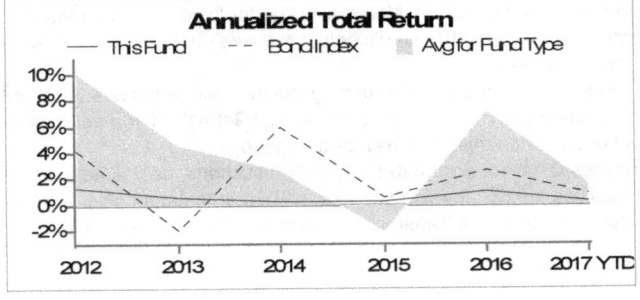

Annualized Total Return

Fidelity Focused High Income (FHIFX)   C   Fair

Fund Family: Fidelity Investments   **Phone:** (800) 544-8544
Address: 245 Summer Street, Boston, MA 02210
Fund Type: COH - Corporate - High Yield
Major Rating Factors: Fidelity Focused High Income has adopted a very risky asset allocation strategy and currently receives an overall TheStreet Investment Rating of C (Fair). Volatility, as measured by standard deviation, is considered above average for fixed income funds at 5.25. Another risk factor is the fund's below average duration of 3.9 years (i.e. lower interest rate risk). The high level of risk (D-, Weak) did however, reward investors with excellent performance.

The fund's performance rating is currently B+ (Good). It has registered an average return of 3.70% over the last three years and is up 2.24% over the last three months. Factored into the performance evaluation is an expense ratio of 0.85% (average) and a 1.0% back-end load levied at the time of sale.

Matthew J. Conti has been running the fund for 13 years and currently receives a manager quality ranking of 31 (0=worst, 99=best). If you are comfortable owning a very high risk investment, this fund may be an option.
Services Offered: Automated phone transactions, payroll deductions, bank draft capabilities, an IRA investment plan, a Keogh investment plan, wire transfers and a systematic withdrawal plan.

Data Date	Investment Rating	Net Assets ($Mil)	NAV	Performance Rating/Pts	Total Return Y-T-D	Risk Rating/Pts
2-17	C	594	8.62	B+ / 8.5	2.24%	D- / 1.4
2016	C	612	8.49	B+ / 8.3	10.94%	D- / 1.5
2015	D	727	8.01	C / 4.7	-1.93%	D / 1.7
2014	C-	592	8.55	C+ / 6.5	2.45%	C- / 3.1
2013	B-	744	9.00	B+ / 8.9	4.44%	D+ / 2.4
2012	C	929	9.39	B- / 7.5	11.69%	D / 1.8

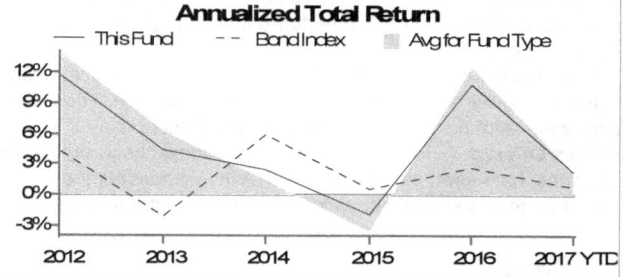

Fidelity GNMA Fund (FGMNX)   B   Good

Fund Family: Fidelity Investments   **Phone:** (800) 544-8544
Address: 245 Summer Street, Boston, MA 02210
Fund Type: USA - US Government/Agency
Major Rating Factors: A moderate risk profile coupled with stable earnings characterizes Fidelity GNMA Fund which receives a TheStreet Investment Rating of B (Good). Volatility, as measured by standard deviation, is considered low for fixed income funds at 1.79. Another risk factor is the fund's very low average duration of 2.7 years (i.e. low interest rate risk). The fund's risk rating is currently B+ (Good).

The fund's performance rating is currently C (Fair). It has registered an average return of 2.33% over the last three years and is up 0.42% over the last three months. Factored into the performance evaluation is an expense ratio of 0.45% (very low).

William W. Irving has been running the fund for 13 years and currently receives a manager quality ranking of 80 (0=worst, 99=best). If you desire stability with a moderate level of risk then this fund is an excellent option.
Services Offered: Automated phone transactions, check writing, payroll deductions, bank draft capabilities, an IRA investment plan, a 401K investment plan, a Keogh investment plan, wire transfers and a systematic withdrawal plan.

Data Date	Investment Rating	Net Assets ($Mil)	NAV	Performance Rating/Pts	Total Return Y-T-D	Risk Rating/Pts
2-17	B	5,586	11.44	C / 4.3	0.42%	B+ / 8.5
2016	A-	6,035	11.43	C / 5.3	1.63%	B+ / 8.3
2015	B+	5,911	11.52	C+ / 6.9	1.20%	B- / 7.0
2014	C	6,442	11.66	C- / 4.0	6.26%	C+ / 6.9
2013	C	6,901	11.21	C- / 3.4	-2.17%	B / 7.7
2012	C+	10,916	11.74	C- / 3.0	2.98%	B+ / 8.4

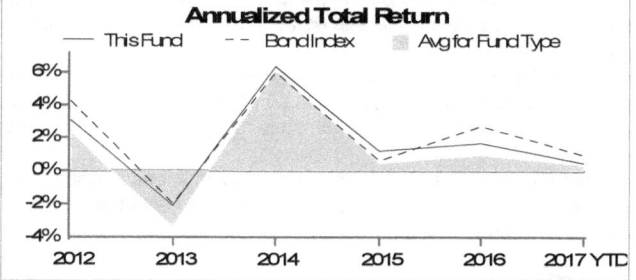

Fidelity High Income (SPHIX)   C+   Fair

Fund Family: Fidelity Investments   **Phone:** (800) 544-8544
Address: 245 Summer Street, Boston, MA 02210
Fund Type: COI - Corporate - Investment Grade
Major Rating Factors: Fidelity High Income has adopted a very risky asset allocation strategy and currently receives an overall TheStreet Investment Rating of C+ (Fair). Volatility, as measured by standard deviation, is considered above average for fixed income funds at 6.23. Another risk factor is the fund's below average duration of 3.5 years (i.e. lower interest rate risk). The high level of risk (D-, Weak) did however, reward investors with excellent performance.

The fund's performance rating is currently A (Excellent). It has registered an average return of 3.96% over the last three years and is up 3.15% over the last three months. Factored into the performance evaluation is an expense ratio of 0.73% (low) and a 1.0% back-end load levied at the time of sale.

Frederick D. Hoff, Jr. has been running the fund for 17 years and currently receives a manager quality ranking of 81 (0=worst, 99=best). If you are comfortable owning a very high risk investment, this fund may be an option.
Services Offered: Automated phone transactions, payroll deductions, bank draft capabilities, an IRA investment plan, a Keogh investment plan, wire transfers and a systematic withdrawal plan.

Data Date	Investment Rating	Net Assets ($Mil)	NAV	Performance Rating/Pts	Total Return Y-T-D	Risk Rating/Pts
2-17	C+	4,659	8.91	A / 9.4	3.15%	D- / 1.1
2016	C	4,665	8.71	A- / 9.1	15.97%	D- / 1.1
2015	D-	4,163	7.95	D / 1.7	-5.40%	D / 1.9
2014	C	5,365	8.90	B- / 7.5	1.53%	D+ / 2.9
2013	C+	6,001	9.37	A / 9.4	6.68%	E+ / 0.9
2012	C-	6,494	9.34	B+ / 8.4	14.89%	E+ / 0.6

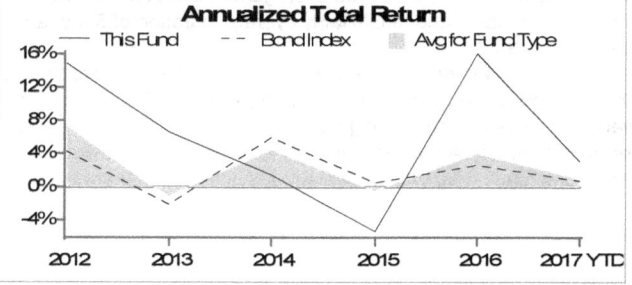

Fidelity Intermediate Bond (FTHRX)

B-   **Good**

Fund Family: Fidelity Investments   **Phone:** (800) 544-8544
Address: 245 Summer Street, Boston, MA 02210
Fund Type: GEI - General - Investment Grade

Major Rating Factors: A moderate risk profile coupled with stable earnings characterizes Fidelity Intermediate Bond which receives a TheStreet Investment Rating of B- (Good). Volatility, as measured by standard deviation, is considered low for fixed income funds at 2.19. Another risk factor is the fund's below average duration of 4.0 years (i.e. lower interest rate risk). The fund's risk rating is currently B (Good).

The fund's performance rating is currently C- (Fair). It has registered an average return of 2.01% over the last three years and is up 0.82% over the last three months. Factored into the performance evaluation is an expense ratio of 0.45% (very low).

Robert Galuszza has been running the fund for 4 years and currently receives a manager quality ranking of 50 (0=worst, 99=best). If you desire stability with a moderate level of risk then this fund is an excellent option.

Services Offered: Automated phone transactions, check writing, payroll deductions, bank draft capabilities, an IRA investment plan, a 401K investment plan, a Keogh investment plan and a systematic withdrawal plan.

Data Date	Investment Rating	Net Assets ($Mil)	NAV	Performance Rating/Pts	Total Return Y-T-D	Risk Rating/Pts
2-17	B-	3,141	10.84	C- / 4.2	0.82%	B / 7.9
2016	B-	3,201	10.79	C / 4.4	2.76%	B / 8.0
2015	B	3,080	10.73	C+ / 5.7	0.68%	B / 8.0
2014	C+	3,342	10.93	C- / 3.6	3.31%	B / 8.2
2013	B+	3,325	10.83	C / 4.7	-0.64%	B / 8.2
2012	B-	4,067	11.14	C- / 3.6	4.93%	B / 8.0

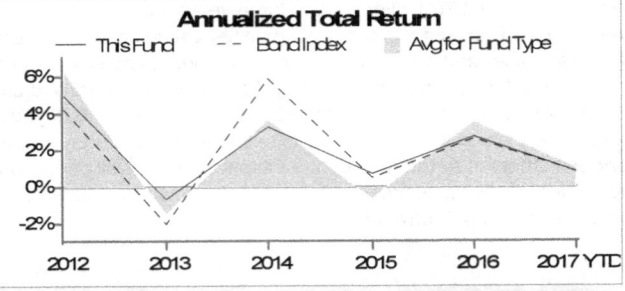

Annualized Total Return

Fidelity Intermediate Government (FSTGX)

D+   **Weak**

Fund Family: Fidelity Investments   **Phone:** (800) 544-8544
Address: 245 Summer Street, Boston, MA 02210
Fund Type: USS - US Government - Short & Inter. Term

Major Rating Factors: Disappointing performance is the major factor driving the D+ (Weak) TheStreet Investment Rating for Fidelity Intermediate Government. The fund currently has a performance rating of D+ (Weak) based on an average return of 1.18% over the last three years and 0.41% over the last three months. Factored into the performance evaluation is an expense ratio of 0.45% (very low).

The fund's risk rating is currently B (Good). Volatility, as measured by standard deviation, is considered low for fixed income funds at 2.18. Another risk factor is the fund's below average duration of 3.8 years (i.e. lower interest rate risk).

William W. Irving has been running the fund for 9 years and currently receives a manager quality ranking of 33 (0=worst, 99=best). This fund offers only a moderate level of risk but investors looking for strong performance are still waiting.

Services Offered: Automated phone transactions, check writing, payroll deductions, bank draft capabilities, an IRA investment plan, a Keogh investment plan and a systematic withdrawal plan.

Data Date	Investment Rating	Net Assets ($Mil)	NAV	Performance Rating/Pts	Total Return Y-T-D	Risk Rating/Pts
2-17	D+	611	10.47	D+ / 2.3	0.41%	B / 7.9
2016	C-	665	10.45	D+ / 2.8	0.88%	B / 8.0
2015	C+	714	10.57	C / 5.0	0.81%	B+ / 8.3
2014	C-	770	10.68	D+ / 2.3	2.60%	B+ / 8.6
2013	C	869	10.54	D+ / 2.6	-1.26%	B+ / 8.5
2012	D+	1,097	10.85	D / 1.8	1.97%	B / 8.0

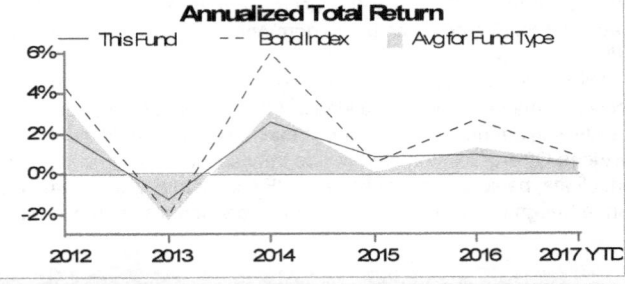

Annualized Total Return

Fidelity MA Muni Inc Fd (FDMMX)

C+   **Fair**

Fund Family: Fidelity Investments   **Phone:** (800) 544-8544
Address: 245 Summer Street, Boston, MA 02210
Fund Type: MUS - Municipal - Single State

Major Rating Factors: Strong performance is the major factor driving the C+ (Fair) TheStreet Investment Rating for Fidelity MA Muni Inc Fd. The fund currently has a performance rating of B- (Good) based on an average return of 3.56% over the last three years (5.90% taxable equivalent) and 0.80% over the last three months (1.32% taxable equivalent). Factored into the performance evaluation is an expense ratio of 0.46% (very low).

The fund's risk rating is currently C- (Fair). Volatility, as measured by standard deviation, is considered average for fixed income funds at 3.61. Another risk factor is the fund's fairly average duration of 6.8 years (i.e. average interest rate risk).

Kevin J. Ramundo has been running the fund for 7 years and currently receives a manager quality ranking of 29 (0=worst, 99=best). If you desire an average level of risk and strong performance, then this fund is a good option.

Services Offered: Automated phone transactions, check writing, payroll deductions, bank draft capabilities and a systematic withdrawal plan.

Data Date	Investment Rating	Net Assets ($Mil)	NAV	Performance Rating/Pts	Total Return Y-T-D	Risk Rating/Pts
2-17	C+	2,119	12.02	B- / 7.4	0.80%	C- / 3.8
2016	B	2,110	11.98	B / 8.0	-0.11%	C- / 3.8
2015	B	2,232	12.50	A / 9.3	3.36%	C- / 3.8
2014	B+	2,170	12.52	B+ / 8.8	9.96%	C- / 3.6
2013	B-	1,981	11.79	B- / 7.5	-3.46%	C- / 3.9
2012	B+	2,547	12.69	B / 7.6	7.18%	C / 4.3

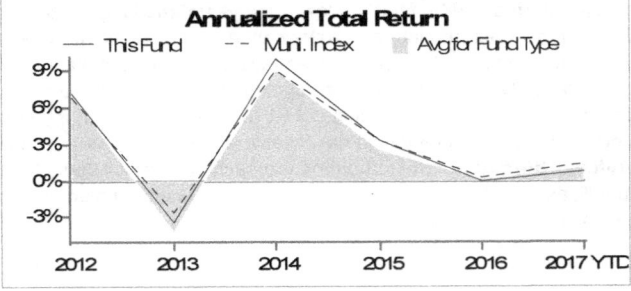

Annualized Total Return

Fidelity MI Muni Inc (FMHTX)   B   Good

Fund Family: Fidelity Investments   **Phone:** (800) 544-8544
Address: 245 Summer Street, Boston, MA 02210
Fund Type: MUS - Municipal - Single State
Major Rating Factors: Strong performance is the major factor driving the B
(Good) TheStreet Investment Rating for Fidelity MI Muni Inc. The fund currently
has a performance rating of B- (Good) based on an average return of 3.54%
over the last three years (5.86% taxable equivalent) and 0.89% over the last
three months (1.47% taxable equivalent). Factored into the performance
evaluation is an expense ratio of 0.49% (very low).

The fund's risk rating is currently C (Fair). Volatility, as measured by
standard deviation, is considered average for fixed income funds at 3.28.
Another risk factor is the fund's fairly average duration of 5.9 years (i.e. average
interest rate risk).

Cormac Cullen has been running the fund for 1 year and currently receives a
manager quality ranking of 47 (0=worst, 99=best). If you desire an average level
of risk and strong performance, then this fund is a good option.
Services Offered: Automated phone transactions, check writing, payroll
deductions, bank draft capabilities and a systematic withdrawal plan.

Data Date	Investment Rating	Net Assets ($Mil)	NAV	Performance Rating/Pts	Total Return Y-T-D	Risk Rating/Pts
2-17	B	654	11.99	B- / 7.5	0.89%	C / 4.5
2016	B+	651	11.94	B / 7.9	-0.16%	C / 4.5
2015	A	633	12.38	A / 9.4	3.61%	C / 5.4
2014	A+	569	12.33	B+ / 8.5	9.23%	C / 5.2
2013	B+	529	11.70	B- / 7.0	-2.75%	C+ / 5.7
2012	A	693	12.54	C+ / 6.7	6.19%	C+ / 6.0

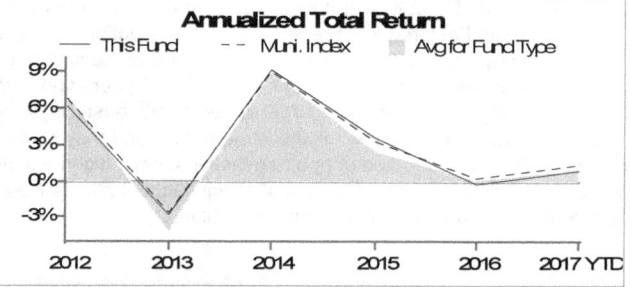

Fidelity MN Muni Inc (FIMIX)   B+   Good

Fund Family: Fidelity Investments   **Phone:** (800) 544-8544
Address: 245 Summer Street, Boston, MA 02210
Fund Type: MUS - Municipal - Single State
Major Rating Factors: Fidelity MN Muni Inc receives a TheStreet Investment
Rating of B+ (Good). The fund has a performance rating of C+ (Fair) based on
an average return of 2.83% over the last three years (4.69% taxable equivalent)
and 1.00% over the last three months (1.66% taxable equivalent). Factored into
the performance evaluation is an expense ratio of 0.50% (very low).

The fund's risk rating is currently C+ (Fair). Volatility, as measured by
standard deviation, is considered average for fixed income funds at 2.95.
Another risk factor is the fund's fairly average duration of 5.6 years (i.e. average
interest rate risk).

Kevin J. Ramundo has been running the fund for 7 years and currently
receives a manager quality ranking of 28 (0=worst, 99=best). If you desire an
average level of risk, then this fund may be an option.
Services Offered: Automated phone transactions, check writing, payroll
deductions, bank draft capabilities and a systematic withdrawal plan.

Data Date	Investment Rating	Net Assets ($Mil)	NAV	Performance Rating/Pts	Total Return Y-T-D	Risk Rating/Pts
2-17	B+	527	11.48	C+ / 6.7	1.00%	C+ / 5.8
2016	B+	522	11.42	C+ / 6.6	0.08%	C+ / 5.9
2015	A+	505	11.75	B+ / 8.9	3.00%	C+ / 6.8
2014	A	506	11.77	B- / 7.2	6.85%	C+ / 6.0
2013	A-	480	11.39	B- / 7.0	-1.91%	C+ / 6.2
2012	B	558	11.99	C+ / 5.7	4.91%	C+ / 6.0

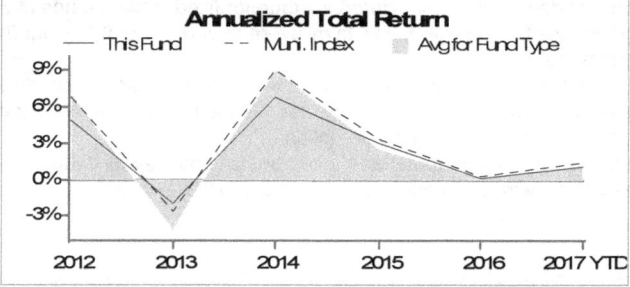

Fidelity Municipal Inc (FHIGX)   C+   Fair

Fund Family: Fidelity Investments   **Phone:** (800) 544-8544
Address: 245 Summer Street, Boston, MA 02210
Fund Type: MUH - Municipal - High Yield
Major Rating Factors: Fidelity Municipal Inc has adopted a risky asset
allocation strategy and currently receives an overall TheStreet Investment Rating
of C+ (Fair). Volatility, as measured by standard deviation, is considered above
average for fixed income funds at 3.69. Another risk factor is the fund's fairly
average duration of 6.6 years (i.e. average interest rate risk). The high level of
risk (D+, Weak) did however, reward investors with excellent performance.

The fund's performance rating is currently B (Good). It has registered an
average return of 3.77% over the last three years (6.24% taxable equivalent) and
is up 1.11% over the last three months (1.84% taxable equivalent). Factored into
the performance evaluation is an expense ratio of 0.48% (very low).

Kevin J. Ramundo has been running the fund for 7 years and currently
receives a manager quality ranking of 33 (0=worst, 99=best). If you are
comfortable owning a high risk investment, this fund may be an option.
Services Offered: Automated phone transactions, check writing, payroll
deductions, bank draft capabilities and a systematic withdrawal plan.

Data Date	Investment Rating	Net Assets ($Mil)	NAV	Performance Rating/Pts	Total Return Y-T-D	Risk Rating/Pts
2-17	C+	5,417	12.91	B / 7.8	1.11%	D+ / 2.8
2016	C+	5,473	12.86	B+ / 8.3	-0.01%	D+ / 2.8
2015	B-	5,756	13.44	A / 9.5	3.31%	C- / 3.0
2014	B+	5,733	13.53	A- / 9.2	10.59%	C- / 3.0
2013	B	5,331	12.68	B / 8.2	-2.94%	C- / 3.4
2012	B+	6,783	13.57	B / 8.2	7.92%	C- / 3.5

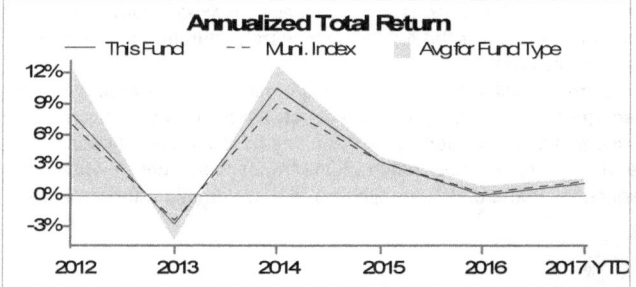

Fidelity New Markets Income (FNMIX)   C+   Fair

Fund Family: Fidelity Investments   **Phone:** (800) 544-8544
Address: 245 Summer Street, Boston, MA 02210
Fund Type: EM - Emerging Market
Major Rating Factors: Fidelity New Markets Income has adopted a very risky asset allocation strategy and currently receives an overall TheStreet Investment Rating of C+ (Fair). Volatility, as measured by standard deviation, is considered high for fixed income funds at 7.51. Another risk factor is the fund's fairly average duration of 5.9 years (i.e. average interest rate risk). The high level of risk (E, Very Weak) did however, reward investors with excellent performance.

The fund's performance rating is currently A+ (Excellent). It has registered an average return of 7.02% over the last three years and is up 4.07% over the last three months. Factored into the performance evaluation is an expense ratio of 0.86% (average) and a 1.0% back-end load levied at the time of sale.

John H. Carlson has been running the fund for 22 years and currently receives a manager quality ranking of 99 (0=worst, 99=best). If you are comfortable owning a very high risk investment, this fund may be an option.
Services Offered: Automated phone transactions, payroll deductions, bank draft capabilities, an IRA investment plan, a 401K investment plan, a Keogh investment plan and a systematic withdrawal plan.

Data Date	Investment Rating	Net Assets ($Mil)	NAV	Perfor- mance Rating/Pts	Total Return Y-T-D	Risk Rating/Pts
2-17	C+	5,231	16.09	A+ / 9.9	4.07%	E / 0.4
2016	C	4,818	15.60	A+ / 9.7	14.70%	E / 0.4
2015	E+	3,978	14.52	D / 1.9	0.24%	E / 0.3
2014	D-	4,513	15.26	C / 5.5	4.32%	E / 0.3
2013	D	4,514	15.59	B- / 7.2	-6.41%	E+ / 0.6
2012	B	7,243	17.80	A+ / 9.7	20.02%	D- / 1.3

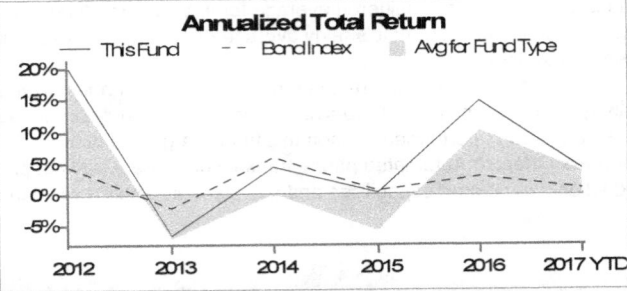

Fidelity NJ Muni Income Fd (FNJHX)   C-   Fair

Fund Family: Fidelity Investments   **Phone:** (800) 544-8544
Address: 245 Summer Street, Boston, MA 02210
Fund Type: MUS - Municipal - Single State
Major Rating Factors: Middle of the road best describes Fidelity NJ Muni Income Fd whose TheStreet Investment Rating is currently a C- (Fair). The fund has a performance rating of C+ (Fair) based on an average return of 2.91% over the last three years (4.82% taxable equivalent) and 0.76% over the last three months (1.26% taxable equivalent). Factored into the performance evaluation is an expense ratio of 0.48% (very low).

The fund's risk rating is currently C- (Fair). Volatility, as measured by standard deviation, is considered average for fixed income funds at 3.84. Another risk factor is the fund's fairly average duration of 6.2 years (i.e. average interest rate risk).

Cormac Cullen has been running the fund for 1 year and currently receives a manager quality ranking of 11 (0=worst, 99=best). If you desire an average level of risk, then this fund may be an option.
Services Offered: Automated phone transactions, payroll deductions, bank draft capabilities, wire transfers and a systematic withdrawal plan.

Data Date	Investment Rating	Net Assets ($Mil)	NAV	Perfor- mance Rating/Pts	Total Return Y-T-D	Risk Rating/Pts
2-17	C-	523	11.53	C+ / 6.6	0.76%	C- / 3.4
2016	C	529	11.50	B- / 7.2	0.51%	C- / 3.4
2015	B-	548	11.88	B+ / 8.9	1.98%	C- / 3.8
2014	B+	601	12.06	B+ / 8.4	8.94%	C- / 4.2
2013	B	580	11.44	B- / 7.2	-2.91%	C / 4.5
2012	B+	683	12.25	C+ / 6.8	6.38%	C / 4.9

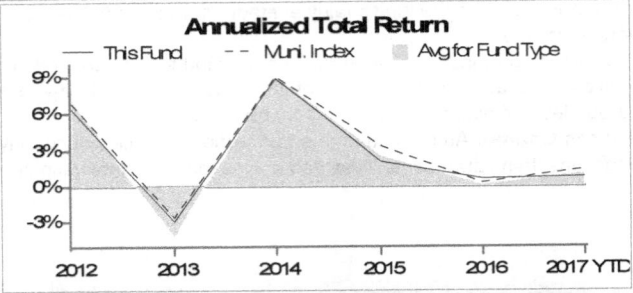

Fidelity OH Muni Inc (FOHFX)   B   Good

Fund Family: Fidelity Investments   **Phone:** (800) 544-8544
Address: 245 Summer Street, Boston, MA 02210
Fund Type: MUS - Municipal - Single State
Major Rating Factors: Strong performance is the major factor driving the B (Good) TheStreet Investment Rating for Fidelity OH Muni Inc. The fund currently has a performance rating of B (Good) based on an average return of 4.08% over the last three years (6.76% taxable equivalent) and 1.01% over the last three months (1.67% taxable equivalent). Factored into the performance evaluation is an expense ratio of 0.48% (very low).

The fund's risk rating is currently C- (Fair). Volatility, as measured by standard deviation, is considered average for fixed income funds at 3.77. Another risk factor is the fund's fairly average duration of 6.9 years (i.e. average interest rate risk).

Cormac Cullen has been running the fund for 1 year and currently receives a manager quality ranking of 48 (0=worst, 99=best). If you desire an average level of risk and strong performance, then this fund is a good option.
Services Offered: Automated phone transactions, check writing, payroll deductions, bank draft capabilities and a systematic withdrawal plan.

Data Date	Investment Rating	Net Assets ($Mil)	NAV	Perfor- mance Rating/Pts	Total Return Y-T-D	Risk Rating/Pts
2-17	B	652	11.95	B / 8.2	1.01%	C- / 3.5
2016	B+	656	11.91	B+ / 8.7	0.19%	C- / 3.5
2015	B	634	12.29	A+ / 9.6	4.24%	C- / 3.6
2014	A	597	12.26	A- / 9.0	10.26%	C- / 3.9
2013	B	535	11.48	B- / 7.4	-3.16%	C / 4.4
2012	A-	646	12.39	B- / 7.3	7.14%	C / 5.1

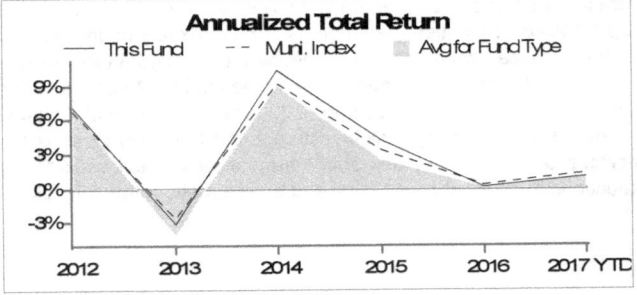

Fidelity Series Emerg Mrkts Dbt (FEDCX) C+ Fair

Fund Family: Fidelity Advisor   **Phone:** (800) 522-7297
Address: 245 Summer Street, Boston, MA 02210
Fund Type: EM - Emerging Market
Major Rating Factors: Fidelity Series Emerg Mrkts Dbt has adopted a very risky asset allocation strategy and currently receives an overall TheStreet Investment Rating of C+ (Fair). Volatility, as measured by standard deviation, is considered high for fixed income funds at 7.14. Another risk factor is the fund's fairly average duration of 5.6 years (i.e. average interest rate risk). The high level of risk (E+, Very Weak) did however, reward investors with excellent performance.

The fund's performance rating is currently A+ (Excellent). It has registered an average return of 6.93% over the last three years and is up 3.73% over the last three months. Factored into the performance evaluation is an expense ratio of 0.82% (low).

Jonathan M. Kelly has been running the fund for 6 years and currently receives a manager quality ranking of 99 (0=worst, 99=best). If you are comfortable owning a very high risk investment, this fund may be an option.
Services Offered: Automated phone transactions, bank draft capabilities, an IRA investment plan and wire transfers.

Data Date	Investment Rating	Net Assets ($Mil)	NAV	Performance Rating/Pts	Total Return Y-T-D	Risk Rating/Pts
2-17	C+	603	10.24	A+ / 9.9	3.73%	E+ / 0.7
2016	C+	525	9.96	A+ / 9.7	15.70%	E+ / 0.6
2015	D-	480	9.16	C- / 3.0	1.51%	E / 0.5
2014	D-	531	9.61	C / 4.9	1.87%	E / 0.5
2013	U	581	10.05	U / --	-4.22%	U / --
2012	U	675	11.15	U / --	19.09%	U / --

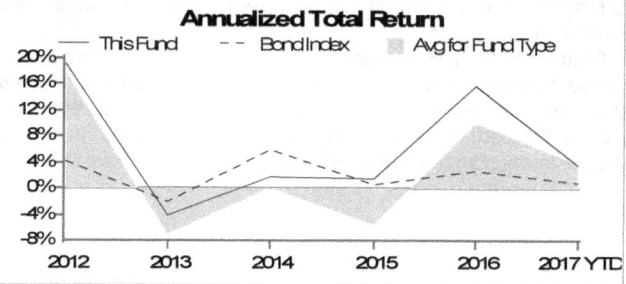
Annualized Total Return

Fidelity Series Inf-Pro Bd Idx F (FFIPX) D- Weak

Fund Family: Fidelity Investments   **Phone:** (800) 544-8544
Address: 245 Summer Street, Boston, MA 02210
Fund Type: GEI - General - Investment Grade
Major Rating Factors: Fidelity Series Inf-Pro Bd Idx F receives a TheStreet Investment Rating of D- (Weak). The fund has a performance rating of C- (Fair) based on an average return of 1.22% over the last three years and 0.93% over the last three months. Factored into the performance evaluation is an expense ratio of 0.05% (very low).

The fund's risk rating is currently C (Fair). Volatility, as measured by standard deviation, is considered average for fixed income funds at 3.28. Another risk factor is the fund's below average duration of 3.7 years (i.e. lower interest rate risk).

Brandon Bettencourt has been running the fund for 3 years and currently receives a manager quality ranking of 11 (0=worst, 99=best). If you desire an average level of risk, then this fund may be an option.
Services Offered: Automated phone transactions, payroll deductions, bank draft capabilities, an IRA investment plan, a 401K investment plan, wire transfers and a systematic withdrawal plan.

Data Date	Investment Rating	Net Assets ($Mil)	NAV	Performance Rating/Pts	Total Return Y-T-D	Risk Rating/Pts
2-17	D-	1,249	9.88	C- / 3.6	0.93%	C / 4.5
2016	D-	1,251	9.79	C- / 3.6	4.12%	C / 4.6
2015	D	903	9.54	D- / 1.3	-0.77%	C- / 3.8
2014	E+	591	9.65	E+ / 0.7	0.95%	C / 4.5
2013	D-	717	10.05	D / 2.1	-5.65%	C / 5.1
2012	C-	3,692	11.36	C- / 3.6	4.92%	C+/ 6.4

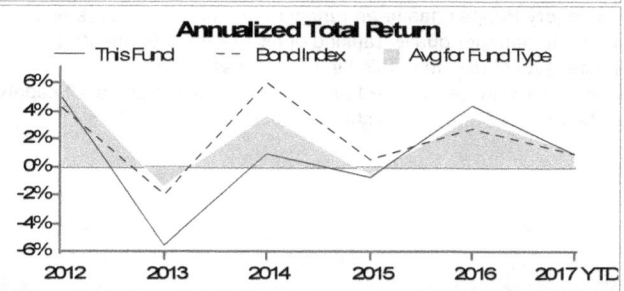
Annualized Total Return

Fidelity Srs Inv Grade Bond (FSIGX) C+ Fair

Fund Family: Fidelity Investments   **Phone:** (800) 544-8544
Address: 245 Summer Street, Boston, MA 02210
Fund Type: GEI - General - Investment Grade
Major Rating Factors: Middle of the road best describes Fidelity Srs Inv Grade Bond whose TheStreet Investment Rating is currently a C+ (Fair). The fund has a performance rating of C+ (Fair) based on an average return of 2.94% over the last three years and 1.22% over the last three months. Factored into the performance evaluation is an expense ratio of 0.45% (very low).

The fund's risk rating is currently C (Fair). Volatility, as measured by standard deviation, is considered average for fixed income funds at 3.11. Another risk factor is the fund's fairly average duration of 5.6 years (i.e. average interest rate risk).

Ford O'Neil has been running the fund for 9 years and currently receives a manager quality ranking of 58 (0=worst, 99=best). If you desire an average level of risk, then this fund may be an option.
Services Offered: Automated phone transactions, bank draft capabilities, wire transfers and a systematic withdrawal plan.

Data Date	Investment Rating	Net Assets ($Mil)	NAV	Performance Rating/Pts	Total Return Y-T-D	Risk Rating/Pts
2-17	C+	11,859	11.18	C+/ 6.0	1.22%	C / 5.1
2016	C+	11,757	11.09	C+/ 6.1	4.35%	C / 5.2
2015	C	12,304	11.03	C+/ 5.6	-0.24%	C / 5.5
2014	C	12,889	11.45	C / 4.8	5.88%	C+/ 6.2
2013	C+	11,959	11.11	C / 4.7	-1.96%	C+/ 6.8
2012	B-	13,653	11.59	C- / 4.2	5.50%	B- / 7.5

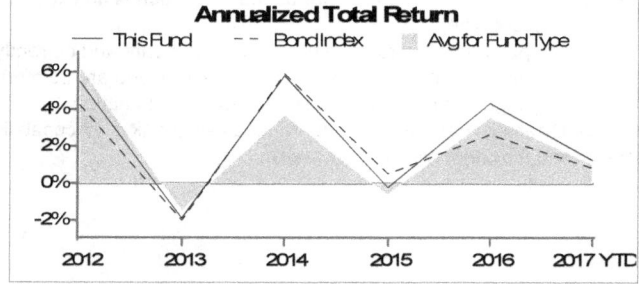
Annualized Total Return

Fidelity Strat Adv Short Duration (FAUDX)

B **Good**

Fund Family: Fidelity Investments
Phone: (800) 544-8544
Address: 245 Summer Street, Boston, MA 02210
Fund Type: COI - Corporate - Investment Grade

Major Rating Factors: A moderate risk profile coupled with stable earnings characterizes Fidelity Strat Adv Short Duration which receives a TheStreet Investment Rating of B (Good). Volatility, as measured by standard deviation, is considered very low for fixed income funds at 0.51. The fund's risk rating is currently A+ (Excellent).

The fund's performance rating is currently C- (Fair). It has registered an average return of 1.03% over the last three years and is up 0.40% over the last three months. Factored into the performance evaluation is an expense ratio of 0.76% (low).

Gregory H. Pappas has been running the fund for 6 years and currently receives a manager quality ranking of 69 (0=worst, 99=best). If you desire stability with a moderate level of risk then this fund is an excellent option.

Services Offered: Automated phone transactions, bank draft capabilities, an IRA investment plan, a 401K investment plan and wire transfers.

Data Date	Investment Rating	Net Assets ($Mil)	NAV	Performance Rating/Pts	Total Return Y-T-D	Risk Rating/Pts
2-17	B	9,093	10.04	C- / 3.1	0.40%	A+ / 9.8
2016	B	8,603	10.02	C- / 3.1	1.86%	A+ / 9.8
2015	B+	7,192	9.97	C / 4.8	0.48%	A+ / 9.8
2014	C	7,100	10.03	D / 1.9	0.69%	A+ / 9.8
2013	U	6,511	10.06	U / --	0.54%	U / --
2012	U	4,985	10.09	U / --	1.81%	U / --

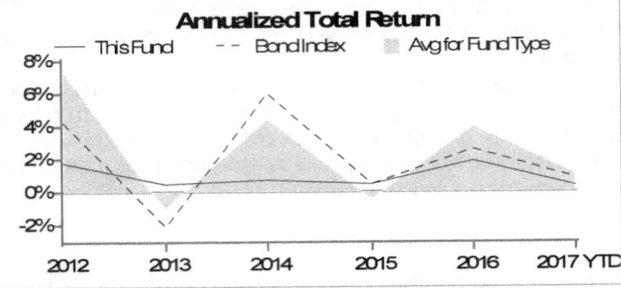

Annualized Total Return

Fidelity Strategic Advisers Cor Inc (FPCIX)

B+ **Good**

Fund Family: Fidelity Investments
Phone: (800) 544-8544
Address: 245 Summer Street, Boston, MA 02210
Fund Type: GEI - General - Investment Grade

Major Rating Factors: Fidelity Strategic Advisers Cor Inc receives a TheStreet Investment Rating of B+ (Good). The fund has a performance rating of C+ (Fair) based on an average return of 2.93% over the last three years and 1.26% over the last three months. Factored into the performance evaluation is an expense ratio of 0.73% (low).

The fund's risk rating is currently C+ (Fair). Volatility, as measured by standard deviation, is considered average for fixed income funds at 2.82.

Gregory Pappas has been running the fund for 10 years and currently receives a manager quality ranking of 66 (0=worst, 99=best). If you desire an average level of risk, then this fund may be an option.

Services Offered: Automated phone transactions, bank draft capabilities, wire transfers and a systematic withdrawal plan.

Data Date	Investment Rating	Net Assets ($Mil)	NAV	Performance Rating/Pts	Total Return Y-T-D	Risk Rating/Pts
2-17	B+	30,089	10.50	C+ / 6.1	1.26%	C+ / 6.5
2016	B+	28,850	10.41	C+ / 6.1	4.39%	C+ / 6.6
2015	C	28,195	10.34	C+ / 5.8	-0.02%	C+ / 6.2
2014	C+	19,161	10.66	C / 5.4	5.37%	C+ / 6.3
2013	B	16,225	10.43	C / 5.2	-1.57%	B- / 7.0
2012	A-	11,891	10.90	C / 5.2	7.82%	B / 7.6

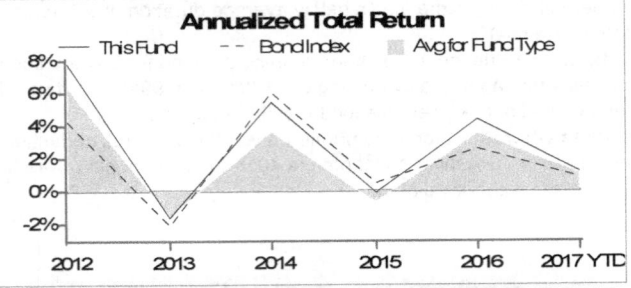

Annualized Total Return

Fidelity Strategic Advisers Inc Opp (FPIOX)

C+ **Fair**

Fund Family: Fidelity Investments
Phone: (800) 544-8544
Address: 245 Summer Street, Boston, MA 02210
Fund Type: COH - Corporate - High Yield

Major Rating Factors: Fidelity Strategic Advisers Inc Opp has adopted a very risky asset allocation strategy and currently receives an overall TheStreet Investment Rating of C+ (Fair). Volatility, as measured by standard deviation, is considered above average for fixed income funds at 5.58. The high level of risk (D-, Weak) did however, reward investors with excellent performance.

The fund's performance rating is currently A- (Excellent). It has registered an average return of 3.65% over the last three years and is up 2.95% over the last three months. Factored into the performance evaluation is an expense ratio of 1.14% (above average).

Greg Pappas has been running the fund for 10 years and currently receives a manager quality ranking of 19 (0=worst, 99=best). If you are comfortable owning a very high risk investment, this fund may be an option.

Services Offered: Automated phone transactions, bank draft capabilities, wire transfers and a systematic withdrawal plan.

Data Date	Investment Rating	Net Assets ($Mil)	NAV	Performance Rating/Pts	Total Return Y-T-D	Risk Rating/Pts
2-17	C+	3,302	9.56	A- / 9.2	2.95%	D- / 1.2
2016	C	3,474	9.36	A- / 9.0	13.52%	D- / 1.2
2015	D	3,973	8.71	C / 4.4	-3.86%	D- / 1.5
2014	C	4,144	9.75	B / 8.0	1.80%	D / 1.9
2013	C+	4,307	10.26	A+ / 9.6	8.06%	E+ / 0.8
2012	C	3,952	10.11	B+ / 8.7	15.25%	E / 0.5

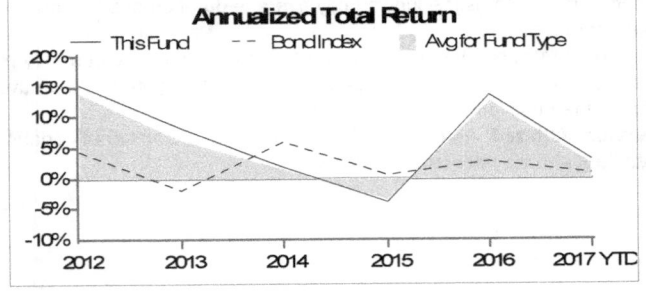

Annualized Total Return

Fidelity Strategic Income Fund (FSICX)   C+   Fair

Fund Family: Fidelity Investments   **Phone:** (800) 544-8544
Address: 245 Summer Street, Boston, MA 02210
Fund Type: GL - Global

Major Rating Factors: Fidelity Strategic Income Fund has adopted a risky asset allocation strategy and currently receives an overall TheStreet Investment Rating of C+ (Fair). Volatility, as measured by standard deviation, is considered above average for fixed income funds at 4.16. Another risk factor is the fund's below average duration of 4.8 years (i.e. lower interest rate risk). The high level of risk (D+, Weak) did however, reward investors with excellent performance.

The fund's performance rating is currently B (Good). It has registered an average return of 3.60% over the last three years and is up 2.54% over the last three months. Factored into the performance evaluation is an expense ratio of 0.71% (low).

Mark J. Notkin has been running the fund for 18 years and currently receives a manager quality ranking of 95 (0=worst, 99=best). If you are comfortable owning a high risk investment, this fund may be an option.

Services Offered: Automated phone transactions, payroll deductions, bank draft capabilities, an IRA investment plan, a 401K investment plan, a Keogh investment plan, wire transfers and a systematic withdrawal plan.

Data Date	Investment Rating	Net Assets ($Mil)	NAV	Performance Rating/Pts	Total Return Y-T-D	Risk Rating/Pts
2-17	C+	7,669	10.87	B / 8.1	2.54%	D+/ 2.8
2016	C+	7,449	10.66	B / 7.6	8.76%	C- / 3.1
2015	D+	7,334	10.15	C- / 4.0	-1.62%	C- / 3.6
2014	C-	8,370	10.69	C+/ 5.8	3.78%	C- / 4.2
2013	C+	8,407	10.85	B- / 7.2	0.38%	C- / 4.0
2012	C	10,493	11.37	C+/ 6.8	10.90%	D+/ 2.9

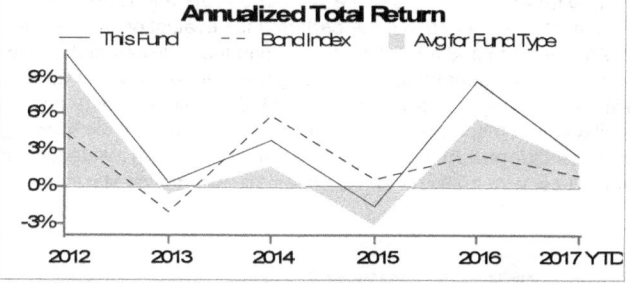

Fidelity Tax Free Bond Fd (FTABX)   B   Good

Fund Family: Fidelity Investments   **Phone:** (800) 544-8544
Address: 245 Summer Street, Boston, MA 02210
Fund Type: MUN - Municipal - National

Major Rating Factors: Strong performance is the major factor driving the B (Good) TheStreet Investment Rating for Fidelity Tax Free Bond Fd. The fund currently has a performance rating of B (Good) based on an average return of 3.89% over the last three years (6.44% taxable equivalent) and 1.06% over the last three months (1.76% taxable equivalent). Factored into the performance evaluation is an expense ratio of 0.46% (very low).

The fund's risk rating is currently C- (Fair). Volatility, as measured by standard deviation, is considered average for fixed income funds at 3.62. Another risk factor is the fund's fairly average duration of 6.6 years (i.e. average interest rate risk).

Mark Sommer has been running the fund for 7 years and currently receives a manager quality ranking of 46 (0=worst, 99=best). If you desire an average level of risk and strong performance, then this fund is a good option.

Services Offered: Automated phone transactions, payroll deductions, bank draft capabilities, wire transfers and a systematic withdrawal plan.

Data Date	Investment Rating	Net Assets ($Mil)	NAV	Performance Rating/Pts	Total Return Y-T-D	Risk Rating/Pts
2-17	B	3,153	11.33	B / 8.1	1.06%	C- / 3.8
2016	B+	3,092	11.27	B+/ 8.6	0.37%	C- / 3.7
2015	B	2,983	11.66	A / 9.5	3.21%	C- / 3.7
2014	A+	2,819	11.71	A / 9.3	10.73%	C- / 4.2
2013	B+	2,208	10.97	B+/ 8.4	-2.83%	C- / 4.0
2012	A+	2,481	11.72	B / 8.2	8.18%	C / 4.4

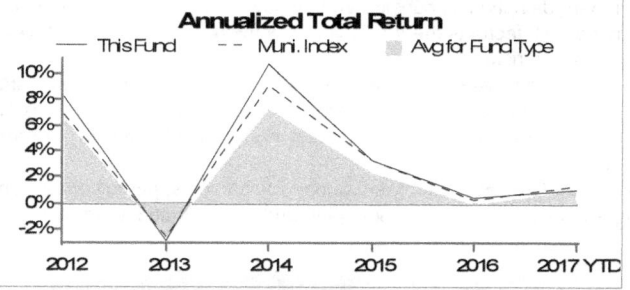

First Inv Fund for Income A (FIFIX)   D-   Weak

Fund Family: First Investors Funds   **Phone:** (800) 423-4026
Address: 110 Wall Street, New York, NY 10005
Fund Type: COH - Corporate - High Yield

Major Rating Factors: First Inv Fund for Income A has adopted a very risky asset allocation strategy and currently receives an overall TheStreet Investment Rating of D- (Weak). Volatility, as measured by standard deviation, is considered above average for fixed income funds at 4.82. Another risk factor is the fund's below average duration of 4.0 years (i.e. lower interest rate risk). Unfortunately, the high level of risk (D, Weak) has only provided investors with average performance.

The fund's performance rating is currently C+ (Fair). It has registered an average return of 2.78% over the last three years and is up 2.03% over the last three months. Factored into the performance evaluation is an expense ratio of 1.23% (above average) and a 5.8% front-end load that is levied at the time of purchase.

Clinton J. Comeaux has been running the fund for 8 years and currently receives a manager quality ranking of 15 (0=worst, 99=best). If you are comfortable owning a very high risk investment, then this fund may be an option.

Services Offered: Automated phone transactions, payroll deductions, bank draft capabilities, an IRA investment plan, a 401K investment plan and a systematic withdrawal plan.

Data Date	Investment Rating	Net Assets ($Mil)	NAV	Performance Rating/Pts	Total Return Y-T-D	Risk Rating/Pts
2-17	D-	569	2.50	C+/ 5.9	2.03%	D / 1.9
2016	D-	562	2.47	C+/ 5.8	10.90%	D / 1.9
2015	D-	552	2.34	D / 1.8	-2.28%	D / 1.9
2014	D-	603	2.52	C / 4.9	0.56%	D+/ 2.7
2013	C+	658	2.64	B+/ 8.8	6.22%	D- / 1.5
2012	D+	614	2.63	B- / 7.3	13.11%	D- / 1.4

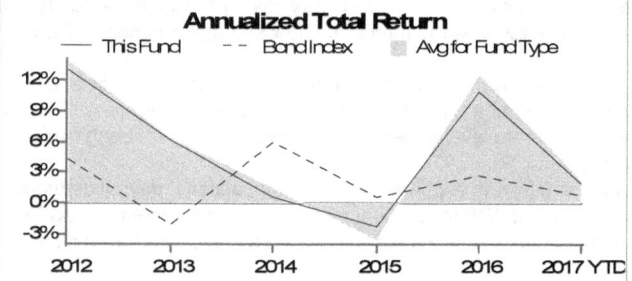

First Inv Tax Exempt Income A (FITAX)

C **Fair**

Fund Family: First Investors Funds **Phone:** (800) 423-4026
Address: 110 Wall Street, New York, NY 10005
Fund Type: MUI - Municipal - Insured
Major Rating Factors: A moderate risk profile coupled with stable earnings characterizes First Inv Tax Exempt Income A which receives a TheStreet Investment Rating of C (Fair). Volatility, as measured by standard deviation, is considered low for fixed income funds at 2.27. Another risk factor is the fund's below average duration of 3.5 years (i.e. lower interest rate risk). The fund's risk rating is currently B (Good).

The fund's performance rating is currently C- (Fair). It has registered an average return of 2.94% over the last three years and is up 0.79% over the last three months. Factored into the performance evaluation is an expense ratio of 1.00% (average) and a 5.8% front-end load that is levied at the time of purchase.

Clark D. Wagner has been running the fund for 26 years and currently receives a manager quality ranking of 66 (0=worst, 99=best). If you desire stability with a moderate level of risk then this fund is an excellent option.
Services Offered: Automated phone transactions, payroll deductions, bank draft capabilities, wire transfers and a systematic withdrawal plan.

Data Date	Investment Rating	Net Assets ($Mil)	NAV	Performance Rating/Pts	Total Return Y-T-D	Risk Rating/Pts
2-17	C	612	9.51	C- / 3.4	0.79%	B / 7.9
2016	B-	606	9.50	C / 4.6	0.12%	B / 7.6
2015	C+	626	9.87	B- / 7.3	2.54%	C / 4.5
2014	C	644	10.01	C+ / 6.7	8.88%	C- / 3.7
2013	D+	639	9.56	C / 5.0	-3.18%	C- / 4.1
2012	D	722	10.27	C / 4.9	7.23%	C- / 4.0

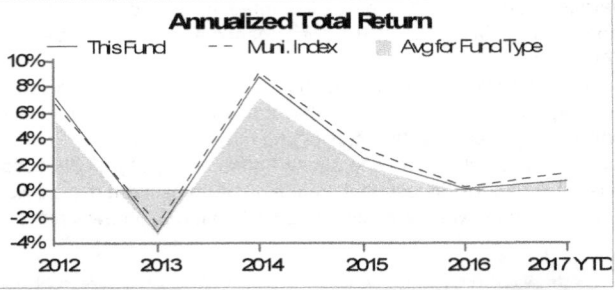

FPA New Income Inc (FPNIX)

B- **Good**

Fund Family: FPA Funds **Phone:** (800) 982-4372
Address: 11400 West Olympic Blvd, Los Angeles, CA 90064
Fund Type: GEI - General - Investment Grade
Major Rating Factors: Disappointing performance is the major factor driving the B- (Good) TheStreet Investment Rating for FPA New Income Inc. The fund currently has a performance rating of D+ (Weak) based on an average return of 1.30% over the last three years and 0.50% over the last three months. Factored into the performance evaluation is an expense ratio of 0.58% (low) and a 2.0% back-end load levied at the time of sale.

The fund's risk rating is currently A+ (Excellent). Volatility, as measured by standard deviation, is considered very low for fixed income funds at 0.74. Another risk factor is the fund's very low average duration of 1.3 years (i.e. low interest rate risk).

Thomas H. Atteberry has been running the fund for 13 years and currently receives a manager quality ranking of 73 (0=worst, 99=best). This fund offers only a moderate level of risk but investors looking for strong performance are still waiting.
Services Offered: Automated phone transactions, payroll deductions, bank draft capabilities, an IRA investment plan and a systematic withdrawal plan.

Data Date	Investment Rating	Net Assets ($Mil)	NAV	Performance Rating/Pts	Total Return Y-T-D	Risk Rating/Pts
2-17	B-	4,927	10.02	D+ / 2.8	0.50%	A+ / 9.6
2016	B-	4,952	9.97	C- / 3.0	2.53%	A+ / 9.6
2015	C	5,357	9.95	C- / 3.2	0.15%	A / 9.5
2014	C+	5,622	10.12	D / 2.2	2.07%	A+ / 9.6
2013	C	5,176	10.27	D / 1.8	0.67%	A+ / 9.7
2012	C-	5,043	10.64	E+ / 0.6	2.18%	A+ / 9.9

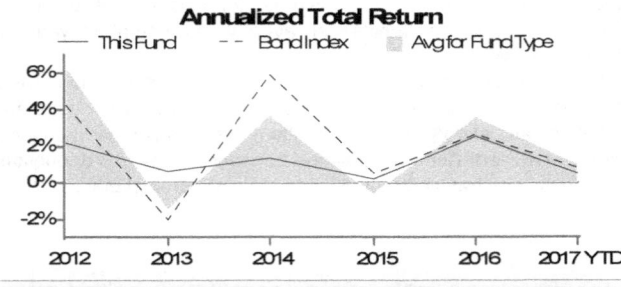

Franklin Adjustable US Govt Sec A (FISAX)

D **Weak**

Fund Family: Franklin Templeton Investments **Phone:** (800) 342-5236
Address: One Franklin Parkway, San Mateo, CA 94403
Fund Type: USS - US Government - Short & Inter. Term
Major Rating Factors: Very poor performance is the major factor driving the D (Weak) TheStreet Investment Rating for Franklin Adjustable US Govt Sec A. The fund currently has a performance rating of E (Very Weak) based on an average return of -0.04% over the last three years and 0.16% over the last three months. Factored into the performance evaluation is an expense ratio of 0.91% (average) and a 2.3% front-end load that is levied at the time of purchase.

The fund's risk rating is currently A+ (Excellent). Volatility, as measured by standard deviation, is considered very low for fixed income funds at 0.40. Another risk factor is the fund's very low average duration of 0.8 years (i.e. low interest rate risk).

Roger A. Bayston has been running the fund for 26 years and currently receives a manager quality ranking of 33 (0=worst, 99=best). This fund offers only a moderate level of risk but investors looking for strong performance are still waiting.
Services Offered: Automated phone transactions, payroll deductions, bank draft capabilities, an IRA investment plan, a 401K investment plan, a Keogh investment plan, wire transfers and a systematic withdrawal plan.

Data Date	Investment Rating	Net Assets ($Mil)	NAV	Performance Rating/Pts	Total Return Y-T-D	Risk Rating/Pts
2-17	D	632	8.37	E / 0.3	0.16%	A+ / 9.8
2016	D+	652	8.38	E / 0.5	0.09%	A+ / 9.8
2015	C	842	8.50	D / 2.0	-0.68%	A+ / 9.8
2014	C-	1,030	8.66	D- / 1.1	0.65%	A+ / 9.8
2013	C-	1,086	8.70	E+ / 0.9	-0.16%	A+ / 9.8
2012	C-	1,278	8.84	E / 0.5	1.42%	A+ / 9.8

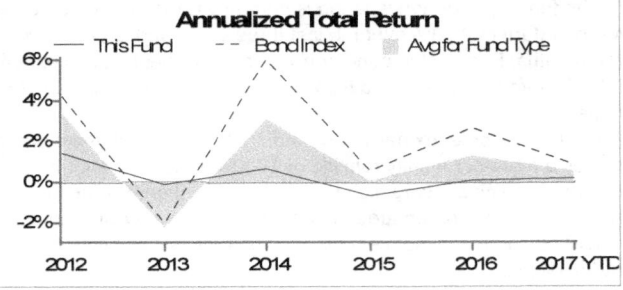

Franklin Arizona Tax-Free Inc A (FTAZX)   C+   Fair

Fund Family: Franklin Templeton Investments   **Phone:** (800) 342-5236
Address: One Franklin Parkway, San Mateo, CA 94403
Fund Type: MUS - Municipal - Single State
Major Rating Factors: Middle of the road best describes Franklin Arizona Tax-Free Inc A whose TheStreet Investment Rating is currently a C+ (Fair). The fund has a performance rating of C+ (Fair) based on an average return of 3.66% over the last three years (6.06% taxable equivalent) and 0.96% over the last three months (1.59% taxable equivalent). Factored into the performance evaluation is an expense ratio of 0.62% (low) and a 4.3% front-end load that is levied at the time of purchase.

The fund's risk rating is currently C (Fair). Volatility, as measured by standard deviation, is considered average for fixed income funds at 3.08. Another risk factor is the fund's below average duration of 4.6 years (i.e. lower interest rate risk).

Carrie Higgins has been running the fund for 25 years and currently receives a manager quality ranking of 65 (0=worst, 99=best). If you desire an average level of risk, then this fund may be an option.

Services Offered: Automated phone transactions, payroll deductions, bank draft capabilities, wire transfers and a systematic withdrawal plan.

Data Date	Investment Rating	Net Assets ($Mil)	NAV	Performance Rating/Pts	Total Return Y-T-D	Risk Rating/Pts
2-17	C+	776	10.78	C+ / 6.0	0.96%	C / 5.2
2016	B-	794	10.74	C+ / 6.9	1.01%	C / 4.8
2015	C	786	11.00	B / 7.6	1.86%	C- / 3.4
2014	B	810	11.21	B+ / 8.4	11.08%	C- / 3.1
2013	D	807	10.50	C / 5.1	-4.98%	C- / 3.5
2012	C+	975	11.50	C+ / 6.9	8.81%	C- / 3.3

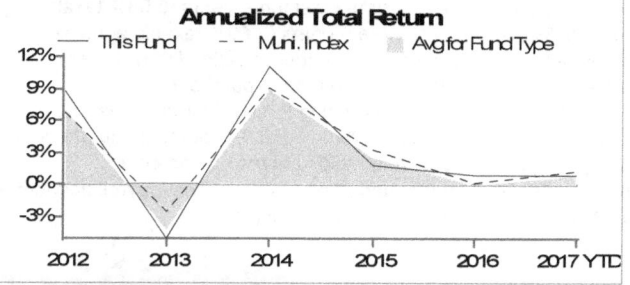

Franklin CA Interm Tax-Free A (FKCIX)   C-   Fair

Fund Family: Franklin Templeton Investments   **Phone:** (800) 342-5236
Address: One Franklin Parkway, San Mateo, CA 94403
Fund Type: MUS - Municipal - Single State
Major Rating Factors: Middle of the road best describes Franklin CA Interm Tax-Free A whose TheStreet Investment Rating is currently a C- (Fair). The fund has a performance rating of C+ (Fair) based on an average return of 3.07% over the last three years (5.08% taxable equivalent) and 1.20% over the last three months (1.99% taxable equivalent). Factored into the performance evaluation is an expense ratio of 0.63% (low) and a 2.3% front-end load that is levied at the time of purchase.

The fund's risk rating is currently C (Fair). Volatility, as measured by standard deviation, is considered average for fixed income funds at 3.36. Another risk factor is the fund's fairly average duration of 5.2 years (i.e. average interest rate risk).

John W. Wiley has been running the fund for 25 years and currently receives a manager quality ranking of 23 (0=worst, 99=best). If you desire an average level of risk, then this fund may be an option.

Services Offered: Automated phone transactions, payroll deductions, bank draft capabilities, wire transfers and a systematic withdrawal plan.

Data Date	Investment Rating	Net Assets ($Mil)	NAV	Performance Rating/Pts	Total Return Y-T-D	Risk Rating/Pts
2-17	C-	940	11.93	C+ / 5.7	1.20%	C / 4.3
2016	C-	954	11.84	C+ / 5.7	-0.11%	C / 4.4
2015	B+	924	12.17	B+ / 8.8	2.68%	C / 5.1
2014	A-	875	12.19	B / 8.1	8.34%	C / 4.8
2013	B+	781	11.60	B / 7.8	-1.69%	C / 4.8
2012	B	791	12.18	C+ / 6.9	6.38%	C / 4.4

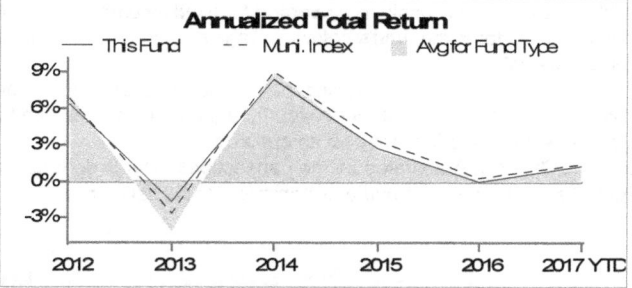

Franklin California H/Y Muni A (FCAMX)   C+   Fair

Fund Family: Franklin Templeton Investments   **Phone:** (800) 342-5236
Address: One Franklin Parkway, San Mateo, CA 94403
Fund Type: MUH - Municipal - High Yield
Major Rating Factors: Franklin California H/Y Muni A has adopted a very risky asset allocation strategy and currently receives an overall TheStreet Investment Rating of C+ (Fair). Volatility, as measured by standard deviation, is considered above average for fixed income funds at 4.65. Another risk factor is the fund's fairly average duration of 7.0 years (i.e. average interest rate risk). The high level of risk (D, Weak) did however, reward investors with excellent performance.

The fund's performance rating is currently B+ (Good). It has registered an average return of 5.83% over the last three years (9.65% taxable equivalent) and is up 1.47% over the last three months (2.43% taxable equivalent). Factored into the performance evaluation is an expense ratio of 0.65% (low) and a 4.3% front-end load that is levied at the time of purchase.

John W. Wiley has been running the fund for 23 years and currently receives a manager quality ranking of 75 (0=worst, 99=best). If you are comfortable owning a very high risk investment, this fund may be an option.

Services Offered: Automated phone transactions, payroll deductions, bank draft capabilities and a systematic withdrawal plan.

Data Date	Investment Rating	Net Assets ($Mil)	NAV	Performance Rating/Pts	Total Return Y-T-D	Risk Rating/Pts
2-17	C+	1,367	10.64	B+ / 8.9	1.47%	D / 1.8
2016	B-	1,368	10.55	A / 9.3	1.08%	D / 1.8
2015	C+	1,332	10.82	A+ / 9.8	5.24%	D / 1.7
2014	B-	1,262	10.70	A+ / 9.8	14.68%	D- / 1.1
2013	C+	1,094	9.77	A- / 9.1	-3.71%	D- / 1.5
2012	A-	1,303	10.61	A+ / 9.8	13.39%	D / 1.9

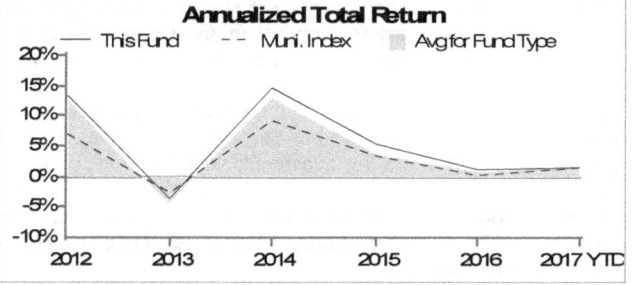

Franklin California Tx-Fr Inc A (FKTFX)　　　C+　　Fair

Fund Family: Franklin Templeton Investments　　**Phone:** (800) 342-5236
Address: One Franklin Parkway, San Mateo, CA 94403
Fund Type: MUS - Municipal - Single State
Major Rating Factors: Franklin California Tx-Fr Inc A has adopted a risky asset allocation strategy and currently receives an overall TheStreet Investment Rating of C+ (Fair). Volatility, as measured by standard deviation, is considered above average for fixed income funds at 4.31. Another risk factor is the fund's fairly average duration of 6.8 years (i.e. average interest rate risk). The high level of risk (D+, Weak) did however, reward investors with excellent performance.

The fund's performance rating is currently B (Good). It has registered an average return of 4.88% over the last three years (8.08% taxable equivalent) and is up 1.57% over the last three months (2.60% taxable equivalent). Factored into the performance evaluation is an expense ratio of 0.57% (very low) and a 4.3% front-end load that is levied at the time of purchase.

John W. Wiley has been running the fund for 26 years and currently receives a manager quality ranking of 60 (0=worst, 99=best). If you are comfortable owning a high risk investment, this fund may be an option.
Services Offered: Automated phone transactions, payroll deductions, bank draft capabilities and a systematic withdrawal plan.

Data Date	Investment Rating	Net Assets ($Mil)	NAV	Performance Rating/Pts	Total Return Y-T-D	Risk Rating/Pts
2-17	C+	12,536	7.39	B / 7.9	1.57%	D+ / 2.7
2016	C+	12,622	7.32	B+ / 8.3	0.81%	D+ / 2.6
2015	C+	11,552	7.52	A / 9.3	3.61%	D+ / 2.9
2014	B+	11,560	7.55	A / 9.5	13.54%	D+ / 2.8
2013	C	10,843	6.94	B- / 7.3	-3.85%	D+ / 2.5
2012	B-	12,695	7.54	B / 8.2	10.16%	D+ / 2.6

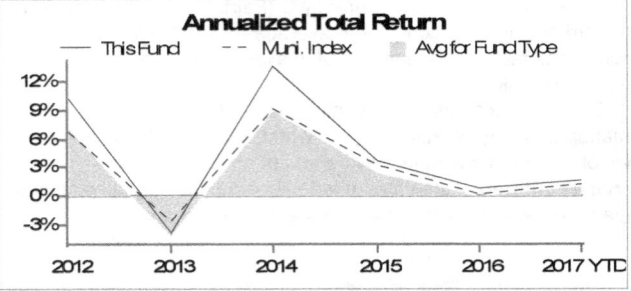

Franklin Colorado Tax-Free Inc A (FRCOX)　　　B+　　Good

Fund Family: Franklin Templeton Investments　　**Phone:** (800) 342-5236
Address: One Franklin Parkway, San Mateo, CA 94403
Fund Type: MUS - Municipal - Single State
Major Rating Factors: Franklin Colorado Tax-Free Inc A receives a TheStreet Investment Rating of B+ (Good). The fund has a performance rating of C+ (Fair) based on an average return of 3.88% over the last three years (6.43% taxable equivalent) and 1.12% over the last three months (1.85% taxable equivalent). Factored into the performance evaluation is an expense ratio of 0.65% (low) and a 4.3% front-end load that is levied at the time of purchase.

The fund's risk rating is currently C+ (Fair). Volatility, as measured by standard deviation, is considered average for fixed income funds at 2.90. Another risk factor is the fund's below average duration of 4.1 years (i.e. lower interest rate risk).

Carrie Higgins has been running the fund for 25 years and currently receives a manager quality ranking of 74 (0=worst, 99=best). If you desire an average level of risk, then this fund may be an option.
Services Offered: Automated phone transactions, payroll deductions, bank draft capabilities, wire transfers and a systematic withdrawal plan.

Data Date	Investment Rating	Net Assets ($Mil)	NAV	Performance Rating/Pts	Total Return Y-T-D	Risk Rating/Pts
2-17	B+	560	11.66	C+ / 6.7	1.12%	C+ / 6.1
2016	B+	567	11.60	B- / 7.4	1.40%	C / 5.5
2015	C	539	11.87	B- / 7.4	2.00%	C- / 3.2
2014	C+	539	12.09	B / 8.1	10.97%	D+ / 2.8
2013	D	530	11.34	C / 5.2	-5.32%	C- / 3.2
2012	C	653	12.44	C+ / 6.7	8.42%	C- / 3.0

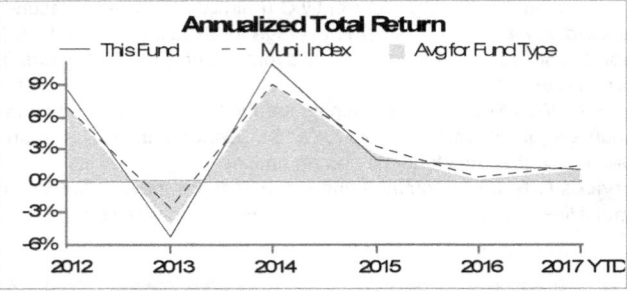

Franklin Fdrl Lmtd Trm T/F Inc A (FFTFX)　　　D　　Weak

Fund Family: Franklin Templeton Investments　　**Phone:** (800) 342-5236
Address: One Franklin Parkway, San Mateo, CA 94403
Fund Type: MUN - Municipal - National
Major Rating Factors: Very poor performance is the major factor driving the D (Weak) TheStreet Investment Rating for Franklin Fdrl Lmtd Trm T/F Inc A. The fund currently has a performance rating of E (Very Weak) based on an average return of 0.45% over the last three years (0.75% taxable equivalent) and 0.52% over the last three months (0.86% taxable equivalent). Factored into the performance evaluation is an expense ratio of 0.69% (low) and a 2.3% front-end load that is levied at the time of purchase.

The fund's risk rating is currently A+ (Excellent). Volatility, as measured by standard deviation, is considered very low for fixed income funds at 0.70. Another risk factor is the fund's very low average duration of 1.3 years (i.e. low interest rate risk).

James P. Conn has been running the fund for 14 years and currently receives a manager quality ranking of 32 (0=worst, 99=best). This fund offers only a moderate level of risk but investors looking for strong performance are still waiting.
Services Offered: Automated phone transactions, payroll deductions, bank draft capabilities, an IRA investment plan, a 401K investment plan, wire transfers and a systematic withdrawal plan.

Data Date	Investment Rating	Net Assets ($Mil)	NAV	Performance Rating/Pts	Total Return Y-T-D	Risk Rating/Pts
2-17	D	835	10.37	E / 0.4	0.52%	A+ / 9.7
2016	D+	810	10.33	E+ / 0.6	0.05%	A+ / 9.6
2015	C+	868	10.41	C- / 3.4	0.42%	A / 9.5
2014	C	906	10.46	D / 1.8	1.09%	A / 9.5
2013	B-	968	10.45	C- / 3.3	0.37%	A / 9.3
2012	C-	762	10.55	D- / 1.5	1.96%	A- / 9.0

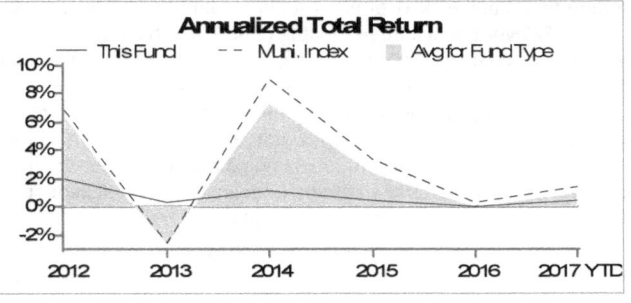

Franklin Fed Interm-Trm T/F Inc A (FKITX)   C-   Fair

Fund Family: Franklin Templeton Investments   **Phone:** (800) 342-5236
Address: One Franklin Parkway, San Mateo, CA 94403
Fund Type: MUN - Municipal - National
Major Rating Factors: Middle of the road best describes Franklin Fed Interm-Trm T/F Inc A whose TheStreet Investment Rating is currently a C- (Fair). The fund has a performance rating of C- (Fair) based on an average return of 2.28% over the last three years (3.78% taxable equivalent) and 1.08% over the last three months (1.79% taxable equivalent). Factored into the performance evaluation is an expense ratio of 0.66% (low) and a 2.3% front-end load that is levied at the time of purchase.

The fund's risk rating is currently C+ (Fair). Volatility, as measured by standard deviation, is considered average for fixed income funds at 2.90. Another risk factor is the fund's below average duration of 4.5 years (i.e. lower interest rate risk).

John B. Pomeroy has been running the fund for 25 years and currently receives a manager quality ranking of 16 (0=worst, 99=best). If you desire an average level of risk, then this fund may be an option.
Services Offered: Automated phone transactions, payroll deductions, bank draft capabilities and a systematic withdrawal plan.

Data Date	Investment Rating	Net Assets ($Mil)	NAV	Performance Rating/Pts	Total Return Y-T-D	Risk Rating/Pts
2-17	C-	1,966	12.11	C- / 4.0	1.08%	C+ / 6.0
2016	C-	2,011	12.03	C / 4.3	-0.57%	C+ / 5.8
2015	B	1,895	12.40	B / 8.0	2.45%	C / 5.1
2014	C+	1,806	12.41	C+ / 6.4	6.86%	C / 4.9
2013	B	1,880	11.93	B- / 7.1	-2.49%	C / 4.7
2012	B-	2,175	12.57	C+ / 6.7	5.55%	C / 4.3

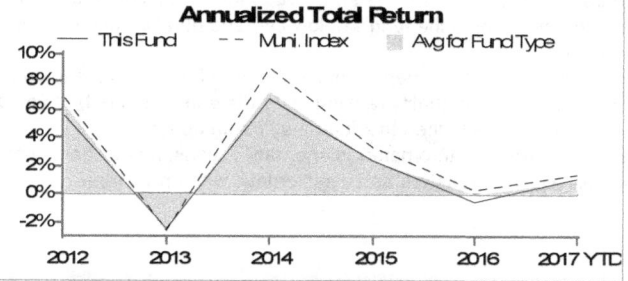

Franklin Federal Tax-Free Inc A (FKTIX)   B   Good

Fund Family: Franklin Templeton Investments   **Phone:** (800) 342-5236
Address: One Franklin Parkway, San Mateo, CA 94403
Fund Type: MUN - Municipal - National
Major Rating Factors: Franklin Federal Tax-Free Inc A receives a TheStreet Investment Rating of B (Good). The fund has a performance rating of C+ (Fair) based on an average return of 3.76% over the last three years (6.23% taxable equivalent) and 1.00% over the last three months (1.66% taxable equivalent). Factored into the performance evaluation is an expense ratio of 0.61% (low) and a 4.3% front-end load that is levied at the time of purchase.

The fund's risk rating is currently C+ (Fair). Volatility, as measured by standard deviation, is considered average for fixed income funds at 2.93. Another risk factor is the fund's below average duration of 4.3 years (i.e. lower interest rate risk).

Sheila A. Amoroso has been running the fund for 30 years and currently receives a manager quality ranking of 69 (0=worst, 99=best). If you desire an average level of risk, then this fund may be an option.
Services Offered: Automated phone transactions, payroll deductions, bank draft capabilities and a systematic withdrawal plan.

Data Date	Investment Rating	Net Assets ($Mil)	NAV	Performance Rating/Pts	Total Return Y-T-D	Risk Rating/Pts
2-17	B	9,552	12.05	C+ / 6.2	1.00%	C+ / 5.9
2016	B	8,127	12.01	B- / 7.1	0.70%	C / 5.3
2015	C+	8,244	12.38	B / 8.1	2.44%	C- / 3.6
2014	B+	8,622	12.55	B+ / 8.6	11.21%	C- / 3.3
2013	C	8,059	11.74	C+ / 6.7	-4.46%	C- / 3.6
2012	B	9,320	12.78	B- / 7.5	9.03%	C- / 3.6

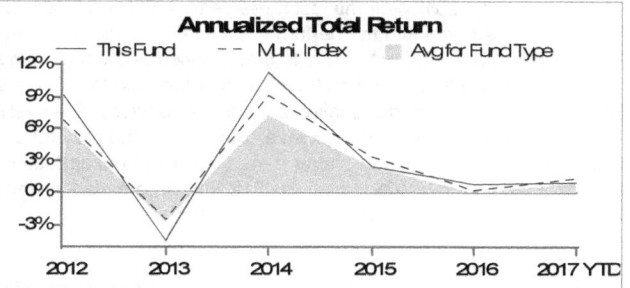

Franklin Floating Rate Dly-Acc A (FAFRX)   B   Good

Fund Family: Franklin Templeton Investments   **Phone:** (800) 342-5236
Address: One Franklin Parkway, San Mateo, CA 94403
Fund Type: LP - Loan Participation
Major Rating Factors: Strong performance is the major factor driving the B (Good) TheStreet Investment Rating for Franklin Floating Rate Dly-Acc A. The fund currently has a performance rating of B- (Good) based on an average return of 3.19% over the last three years and 0.52% over the last three months. Factored into the performance evaluation is an expense ratio of 0.86% (average) and a 2.3% front-end load that is levied at the time of purchase.

The fund's risk rating is currently C (Fair). Volatility, as measured by standard deviation, is considered average for fixed income funds at 3.29. Another risk factor is the fund's very low average duration of 0.2 years (i.e. low interest rate risk).

Justin Ma has been running the fund for 4 years and currently receives a manager quality ranking of 87 (0=worst, 99=best). If you desire an average level of risk and strong performance, then this fund is a good option.
Services Offered: Automated phone transactions, payroll deductions, bank draft capabilities, an IRA investment plan, a 401K investment plan, a Keogh investment plan, wire transfers and a systematic withdrawal plan.

Data Date	Investment Rating	Net Assets ($Mil)	NAV	Performance Rating/Pts	Total Return Y-T-D	Risk Rating/Pts
2-17	B	1,465	8.89	B- / 7.5	0.52%	C / 4.5
2016	B+	1,387	8.89	B / 7.7	11.62%	C / 4.8
2015	C-	1,493	8.33	D / 2.2	-2.12%	B- / 7.2
2014	B	1,743	8.91	C- / 4.0	0.49%	B+ / 8.5
2013	B	2,022	9.21	C+ / 6.4	4.53%	C+ / 5.7
2012	E+	1,327	9.13	C- / 3.2	8.06%	C / 4.8

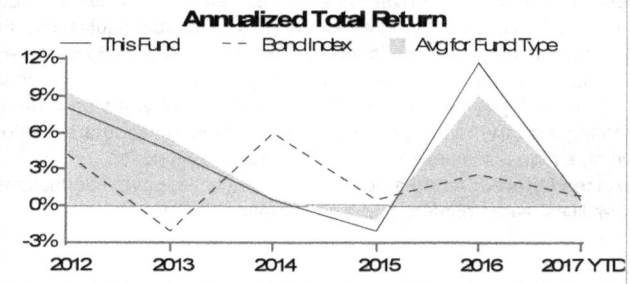

Franklin Florida Tax-Free Inc A (FRFLX)   B   Good

Fund Family: Franklin Templeton Investments   **Phone:** (800) 342-5236
Address: One Franklin Parkway, San Mateo, CA 94403
Fund Type: MUS - Municipal - Single State
Major Rating Factors: Franklin Florida Tax-Free Inc A receives a TheStreet
Investment Rating of B (Good). The fund has a performance rating of C+ (Fair)
based on an average return of 3.60% over the last three years (5.96% taxable
equivalent) and 1.09% over the last three months (1.81% taxable equivalent).
Factored into the performance evaluation is an expense ratio of 0.64% (low) and
a 4.3% front-end load that is levied at the time of purchase.

The fund's risk rating is currently C+ (Fair). Volatility, as measured by
standard deviation, is considered average for fixed income funds at 2.87.
Another risk factor is the fund's below average duration of 4.0 years (i.e. lower
interest rate risk).

Stella S. Wong has been running the fund for 30 years and currently
receives a manager quality ranking of 71 (0=worst, 99=best). If you desire an
average level of risk, then this fund may be an option.

Services Offered: Automated phone transactions, payroll deductions, bank draft
capabilities, wire transfers and a systematic withdrawal plan.

Data Date	Investment Rating	Net Assets ($Mil)	NAV	Performance Rating/Pts	Total Return Y-T-D	Risk Rating/Pts
2-17	B	643	10.88	C+/ 6.2	1.09%	C+/ 6.2
2016	B+	661	10.83	B-/ 7.2	1.30%	C / 5.5
2015	C-	688	11.11	C+/ 6.8	2.53%	C- / 3.0
2014	D+	717	11.28	C+/ 6.3	9.86%	C- / 3.0
2013	E+	771	10.73	D / 1.6	-6.22%	C- / 3.7
2012	C+	1,024	11.91	C / 5.5	6.57%	C / 5.4

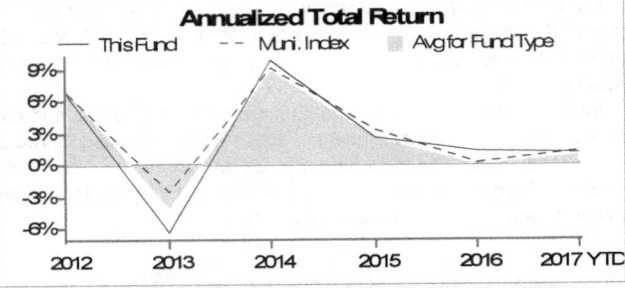

Annualized Total Return

Franklin High Income A (FHAIX)   D+   Weak

Fund Family: Franklin Templeton Investments   **Phone:** (800) 342-5236
Address: One Franklin Parkway, San Mateo, CA 94403
Fund Type: COH - Corporate - High Yield
Major Rating Factors: Franklin High Income A has adopted a very risky asset
allocation strategy and currently receives an overall TheStreet Investment Rating
of D+ (Weak). Volatility, as measured by standard deviation, is considered high
for fixed income funds at 8.03. Another risk factor is the fund's below average
duration of 4.0 years (i.e. lower interest rate risk). The high level of risk (E, Very
Weak) did however, reward investors with excellent performance.

The fund's performance rating is currently B+ (Good). It has registered an
average return of 2.20% over the last three years and is up 3.60% over the last
three months. Factored into the performance evaluation is an expense ratio of
0.79% (low) and a 4.3% front-end load that is levied at the time of purchase.

Christopher J. Molumphy has been running the fund for 26 years and
currently receives a manager quality ranking of 0 (0=worst, 99=best). If you are
comfortable owning a very high risk investment, this fund may be an option.

Services Offered: Automated phone transactions, payroll deductions, bank draft
capabilities, an IRA investment plan, a 401K investment plan, a Keogh
investment plan and a systematic withdrawal plan.

Data Date	Investment Rating	Net Assets ($Mil)	NAV	Performance Rating/Pts	Total Return Y-T-D	Risk Rating/Pts
2-17	D+	2,848	1.91	B+/ 8.4	3.60%	E / 0.3
2016	D-	2,777	1.86	B- / 7.4	19.32%	E / 0.3
2015	E-	2,961	1.66	E / 0.3	-10.74%	E / 0.5
2014	D-	3,624	1.98	C+/ 5.7	-0.39%	D- / 1.3
2013	C+	3,804	2.11	A / 9.5	7.64%	E+/ 0.8
2012	C-	3,704	2.09	B+/ 8.3	15.71%	E+/ 0.6

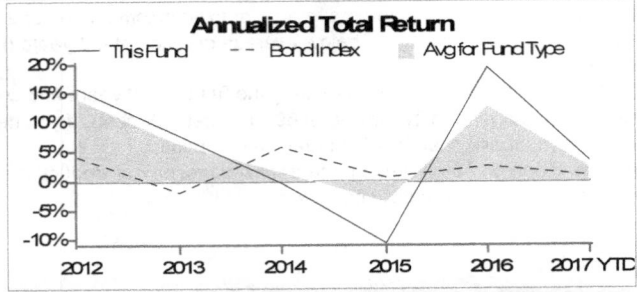

Annualized Total Return

Franklin High Yld Tax-Free Inc A (FRHIX)   C   Fair

Fund Family: Franklin Templeton Investments   **Phone:** (800) 342-5236
Address: One Franklin Parkway, San Mateo, CA 94403
Fund Type: MUH - Municipal - High Yield
Major Rating Factors: Franklin High Yld Tax-Free Inc A has adopted a risky
asset allocation strategy and currently receives an overall TheStreet Investment
Rating of C (Fair). Volatility, as measured by standard deviation, is considered
above average for fixed income funds at 3.90. Another risk factor is the fund's
fairly average duration of 5.7 years (i.e. average interest rate risk). The high level
of risk (D+, Weak) did however, reward investors with excellent performance.

The fund's performance rating is currently B (Good). It has registered an
average return of 4.76% over the last three years (7.88% taxable equivalent) and
is up 1.33% over the last three months (2.20% taxable equivalent). Factored into
the performance evaluation is an expense ratio of 0.67% (low) and a 4.3%
front-end load that is levied at the time of purchase.

John W. Wiley has been running the fund for 24 years and currently receives
a manager quality ranking of 71 (0=worst, 99=best). If you are comfortable
owning a high risk investment, this fund may be an option.

Services Offered: Automated phone transactions, payroll deductions, bank draft
capabilities, wire transfers and a systematic withdrawal plan.

Data Date	Investment Rating	Net Assets ($Mil)	NAV	Performance Rating/Pts	Total Return Y-T-D	Risk Rating/Pts
2-17	C	5,039	10.25	B / 7.7	1.33%	D+/ 2.6
2016	C+	5,104	10.19	B+/ 8.7	1.15%	D+/ 2.5
2015	C-	5,003	10.51	B+/ 8.5	3.18%	D / 1.6
2014	C+	5,175	10.63	A- / 9.2	13.87%	D- / 1.0
2013	D-	5,076	9.77	C+/ 5.6	-6.73%	D / 1.7
2012	B+	6,489	10.94	A- / 9.0	11.06%	D+/ 2.3

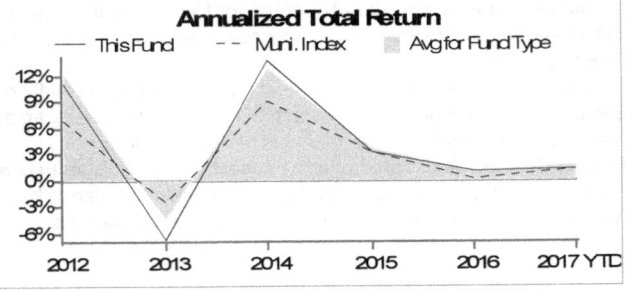

Annualized Total Return

Franklin Low Dur Totl Return A (FLDAX)   C+   Fair

Fund Family: Franklin Templeton Investments   **Phone:** (800) 342-5236
Address: One Franklin Parkway, San Mateo, CA 94403
Fund Type: GEI - General - Investment Grade
Major Rating Factors: Disappointing performance is the major factor driving the C+ (Fair) TheStreet Investment Rating for Franklin Low Dur Totl Return A. The fund currently has a performance rating of D+ (Weak) based on an average return of 1.13% over the last three years and 0.62% over the last three months. Factored into the performance evaluation is an expense ratio of 0.97% (average) and a 2.3% front-end load that is levied at the time of purchase.

The fund's risk rating is currently A- (Excellent). Volatility, as measured by standard deviation, is considered very low for fixed income funds at 1.02. Another risk factor is the fund's very low average duration of 1.4 years (i.e. low interest rate risk).

Christopher J. Molumphy has been running the fund for 13 years and currently receives a manager quality ranking of 71 (0=worst, 99=best). This fund offers only a moderate level of risk but investors looking for strong performance are still waiting.

Services Offered: Automated phone transactions, payroll deductions, bank draft capabilities, an IRA investment plan, a 401K investment plan, a Keogh investment plan and a systematic withdrawal plan.

Data Date	Investment Rating	Net Assets ($Mil)	NAV	Performance Rating/Pts	Total Return Y-T-D	Risk Rating/Pts
2-17	C+	1,471	9.86	D+ / 2.7	0.62%	A- / 9.2
2016	C+	1,490	9.83	D+ / 2.5	2.68%	A- / 9.2
2015	C	1,637	9.74	D+ / 2.7	-0.59%	A / 9.3
2014	C-	1,585	10.00	D / 1.8	0.19%	B+ / 8.9
2013	C	1,315	10.13	D+ / 2.3	1.22%	B+ / 8.7
2012	D	967	10.24	D- / 1.2	4.08%	B+ / 8.3

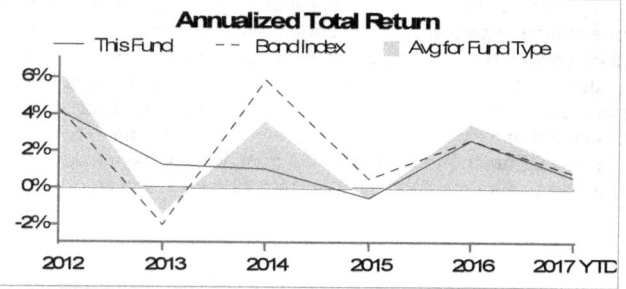

Franklin MI Tax-Free Inc A (FTTMX)   C   Fair

Fund Family: Franklin Templeton Investments   **Phone:** (800) 342-5236
Address: One Franklin Parkway, San Mateo, CA 94403
Fund Type: MUI - Municipal - Insured
Major Rating Factors: Middle of the road best describes Franklin MI Tax-Free Inc A whose TheStreet Investment Rating is currently a C (Fair). The fund has a performance rating of C (Fair) based on an average return of 3.19% over the last three years and 0.90% over the last three months. Factored into the performance evaluation is an expense ratio of 0.64% (low) and a 4.3% front-end load that is levied at the time of purchase.

The fund's risk rating is currently C+ (Fair). Volatility, as measured by standard deviation, is considered average for fixed income funds at 2.98. Another risk factor is the fund's below average duration of 4.5 years (i.e. lower interest rate risk).

John B. Pomeroy has been running the fund for 28 years and currently receives a manager quality ranking of 59 (0=worst, 99=best). If you desire an average level of risk, then this fund may be an option.
Services Offered: Automated phone transactions, payroll deductions, bank draft capabilities, wire transfers and a systematic withdrawal plan.

Data Date	Investment Rating	Net Assets ($Mil)	NAV	Performance Rating/Pts	Total Return Y-T-D	Risk Rating/Pts
2-17	C	867	11.52	C / 5.2	0.90%	C+ / 5.6
2016	C+	875	11.48	C+ / 6.6	1.26%	C / 4.9
2015	C-	894	11.74	C+ / 6.6	0.80%	C- / 3.9
2014	B	954	12.06	B- / 7.4	10.95%	C / 4.3
2013	D-	967	11.30	D+ / 2.4	-5.15%	C / 5.1
2012	C-	1,256	12.36	C / 4.3	6.09%	C / 5.3

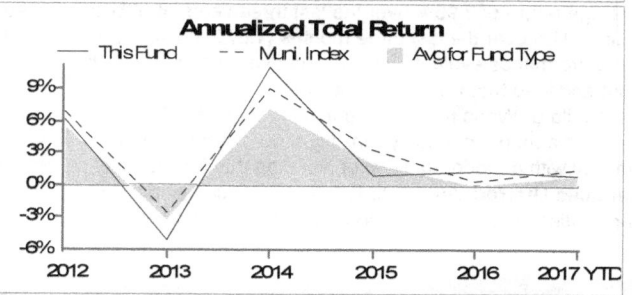

Franklin Missouri Tax-Free Inc A (FRMOX)   B-   Good

Fund Family: Franklin Templeton Investments   **Phone:** (800) 342-5236
Address: One Franklin Parkway, San Mateo, CA 94403
Fund Type: MUS - Municipal - Single State
Major Rating Factors: Franklin Missouri Tax-Free Inc A receives a TheStreet Investment Rating of B- (Good). The fund has a performance rating of C (Fair) based on an average return of 3.30% over the last three years (5.46% taxable equivalent) and 0.76% over the last three months (1.26% taxable equivalent). Factored into the performance evaluation is an expense ratio of 0.64% (low) and a 4.3% front-end load that is levied at the time of purchase.

The fund's risk rating is currently C+ (Fair). Volatility, as measured by standard deviation, is considered average for fixed income funds at 2.83. Another risk factor is the fund's below average duration of 4.2 years (i.e. lower interest rate risk).

Carrie Higgins has been running the fund for 25 years and currently receives a manager quality ranking of 66 (0=worst, 99=best). If you desire an average level of risk, then this fund may be an option.
Services Offered: Automated phone transactions, payroll deductions, bank draft capabilities, wire transfers and a systematic withdrawal plan.

Data Date	Investment Rating	Net Assets ($Mil)	NAV	Performance Rating/Pts	Total Return Y-T-D	Risk Rating/Pts
2-17	B-	871	11.74	C / 5.5	0.76%	C+ / 6.5
2016	B+	883	11.72	C+ / 6.8	1.35%	C+ / 5.9
2015	C-	865	11.98	C+ / 6.5	2.37%	C- / 3.7
2014	C-	877	12.13	C+ / 6.1	9.08%	C- / 3.5
2013	D-	915	11.56	C- / 3.1	-5.83%	C- / 3.9
2012	C	1,135	12.73	C+ / 6.0	6.82%	C- / 3.9

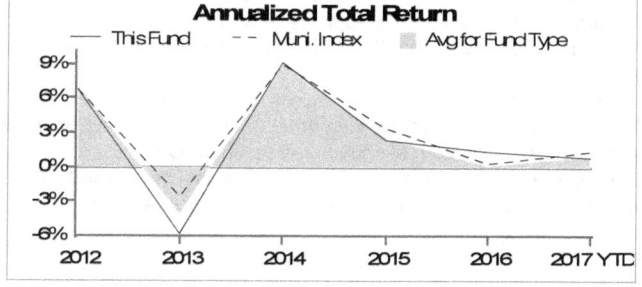

Franklin MN Tax-Free Inc A (FMINX)　　　C+　　Fair

Fund Family: Franklin Templeton Investments　**Phone:** (800) 342-5236
Address: One Franklin Parkway, San Mateo, CA 94403
Fund Type: MUI - Municipal - Insured

Major Rating Factors: A moderate risk profile coupled with stable earnings characterizes Franklin MN Tax-Free Inc A which receives a TheStreet Investment Rating of C+ (Fair). Volatility, as measured by standard deviation, is considered low for fixed income funds at 2.63. Another risk factor is the fund's below average duration of 3.9 years (i.e. lower interest rate risk). The fund's risk rating is currently B- (Good).

The fund's performance rating is currently C (Fair). It has registered an average return of 2.84% over the last three years and is up 0.90% over the last three months. Factored into the performance evaluation is an expense ratio of 0.64% (low) and a 4.3% front-end load that is levied at the time of purchase.

John B. Pomeroy has been running the fund for 28 years and currently receives a manager quality ranking of 46 (0=worst, 99=best). If you desire stability with a moderate level of risk then this fund is an excellent option.
Services Offered: Automated phone transactions, payroll deductions, bank draft capabilities, wire transfers and a systematic withdrawal plan.

Data Date	Investment Rating	Net Assets ($Mil)	NAV	Performance Rating/Pts	Total Return Y-T-D	Risk Rating/Pts
2-17	C+	709	12.27	C / 4.3	0.90%	B- / 7.2
2016	C+	708	12.22	C / 4.8	0.27%	B- / 7.0
2015	C	720	12.56	B- / 7.0	2.15%	C / 4.8
2014	C+	712	12.69	C+ / 6.4	8.17%	C / 4.4
2013	C-	739	12.12	C / 5.3	-3.77%	C / 4.5
2012	C	891	13.00	C+ / 5.6	6.60%	C / 4.7

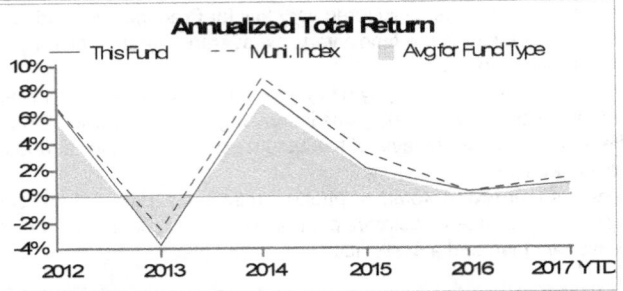

Franklin NC Tax-Free Inc A (FXNCX)　　　B-　　Good

Fund Family: Franklin Templeton Investments　**Phone:** (800) 342-5236
Address: One Franklin Parkway, San Mateo, CA 94403
Fund Type: MUS - Municipal - Single State

Major Rating Factors: A moderate risk profile coupled with stable earnings characterizes Franklin NC Tax-Free Inc A which receives a TheStreet Investment Rating of B- (Good). Volatility, as measured by standard deviation, is considered low for fixed income funds at 2.61. Another risk factor is the fund's below average duration of 3.9 years (i.e. lower interest rate risk). The fund's risk rating is currently B- (Good).

The fund's performance rating is currently C (Fair). It has registered an average return of 2.95% over the last three years (4.89% taxable equivalent) and is up 1.01% over the last three months (1.67% taxable equivalent). Factored into the performance evaluation is an expense ratio of 0.64% (low) and a 4.3% front-end load that is levied at the time of purchase.

Stella S. Wong has been running the fund for 30 years and currently receives a manager quality ranking of 60 (0=worst, 99=best). If you desire stability with a moderate level of risk then this fund is an excellent option.
Services Offered: Automated phone transactions, payroll deductions, bank draft capabilities, wire transfers and a systematic withdrawal plan.

Data Date	Investment Rating	Net Assets ($Mil)	NAV	Performance Rating/Pts	Total Return Y-T-D	Risk Rating/Pts
2-17	B-	759	11.70	C / 4.8	1.01%	B- / 7.3
2016	B	778	11.65	C+ / 5.8	1.15%	C+ / 6.9
2015	D+	799	11.92	C- / 4.0	1.55%	C- / 3.8
2014	D	834	12.16	C / 5.3	8.67%	C- / 3.4
2013	E+	889	11.64	D / 1.9	-6.75%	C- / 3.8
2012	C	1,146	12.93	C+ / 5.8	6.96%	C- / 4.2

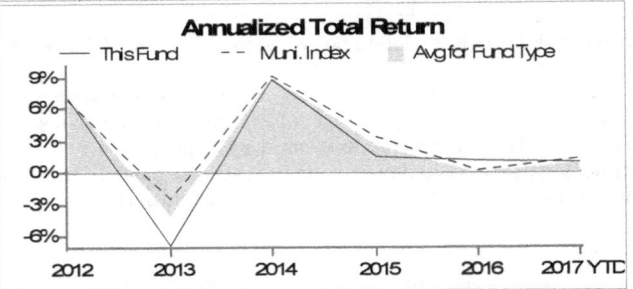

Franklin New Jersey TaxFree Inc A (FRNJX)　　　C+　　Fair

Fund Family: Franklin Templeton Investments　**Phone:** (800) 342-5236
Address: One Franklin Parkway, San Mateo, CA 94403
Fund Type: MUN - Municipal - National

Major Rating Factors: Middle of the road best describes Franklin New Jersey TaxFree Inc A whose TheStreet Investment Rating is currently a C+ (Fair). The fund has a performance rating of C (Fair) based on an average return of 3.04% over the last three years (5.03% taxable equivalent) and 0.80% over the last three months (1.32% taxable equivalent). Factored into the performance evaluation is an expense ratio of 0.64% (low) and a 4.3% front-end load that is levied at the time of purchase.

The fund's risk rating is currently C+ (Fair). Volatility, as measured by standard deviation, is considered average for fixed income funds at 2.79. Another risk factor is the fund's below average duration of 3.7 years (i.e. lower interest rate risk).

Stella S. Wong has been running the fund for 29 years and currently receives a manager quality ranking of 59 (0=worst, 99=best). If you desire an average level of risk, then this fund may be an option.
Services Offered: Automated phone transactions, payroll deductions, bank draft capabilities, wire transfers and a systematic withdrawal plan.

Data Date	Investment Rating	Net Assets ($Mil)	NAV	Performance Rating/Pts	Total Return Y-T-D	Risk Rating/Pts
2-17	C+	752	11.45	C / 5.0	0.80%	C+ / 6.7
2016	B	760	11.43	C+ / 6.2	1.60%	C+ / 6.1
2015	C-	815	11.69	C+ / 5.6	1.33%	C- / 3.7
2014	D+	903	11.99	C+ / 5.8	8.92%	C- / 3.6
2013	D-	1,011	11.46	D+ / 2.5	-5.50%	C- / 3.7
2012	D+	1,271	12.58	C / 5.2	6.13%	C- / 4.0

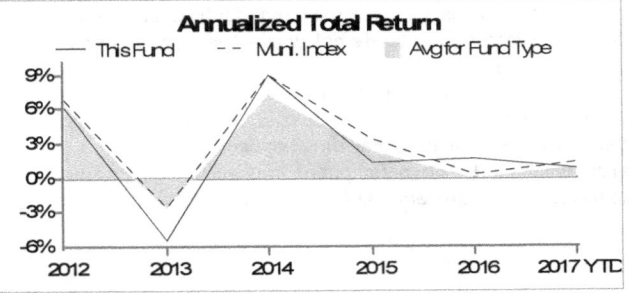

Franklin New York Tax-Free Inc A (FNYTX)   B   Good

Fund Family: Franklin Templeton Investments   **Phone:** (800) 342-5236
Address: One Franklin Parkway, San Mateo, CA 94403
Fund Type: MUS - Municipal - Single State
Major Rating Factors: A moderate risk profile coupled with stable earnings characterizes Franklin New York Tax-Free Inc A which receives a TheStreet Investment Rating of B (Good). Volatility, as measured by standard deviation, is considered low for fixed income funds at 2.52. Another risk factor is the fund's below average duration of 3.7 years (i.e. lower interest rate risk). The fund's risk rating is currently B- (Good).

The fund's performance rating is currently C (Fair). It has registered an average return of 3.02% over the last three years (5.00% taxable equivalent) and is up 0.86% over the last three months (1.42% taxable equivalent). Factored into the performance evaluation is an expense ratio of 0.61% (low) and a 4.3% front-end load that is levied at the time of purchase.

John B. Pomeroy has been running the fund for 28 years and currently receives a manager quality ranking of 64 (0=worst, 99=best). If you desire stability with a moderate level of risk then this fund is an excellent option.
Services Offered: Automated phone transactions, payroll deductions, bank draft capabilities, an IRA investment plan and a systematic withdrawal plan.

Data Date	Investment Rating	Net Assets ($Mil)	NAV	Perfor-mance Rating/Pts	Total Return Y-T-D	Risk Rating/Pts
2-17	B	3,970	11.21	C / 4.7	0.86%	B- / 7.5
2016	B+	4,002	11.18	C+ / 5.8	0.88%	B- / 7.2
2015	C	4,178	11.48	C+ / 6.5	1.51%	C / 4.3
2014	C	4,451	11.72	C+ / 6.5	9.28%	C- / 4.0
2013	D-	4,637	11.15	C- / 3.4	-4.65%	C- / 4.2
2012	D+	5,692	12.13	C / 4.8	6.40%	C / 4.3

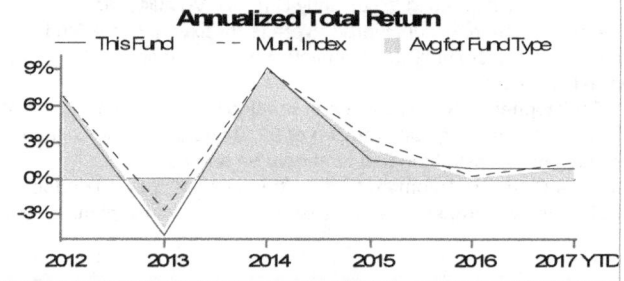

Franklin NY Interm Tax-Free Inc A (FKNIX)   D+   Weak

Fund Family: Franklin Templeton Investments   **Phone:** (800) 342-5236
Address: One Franklin Parkway, San Mateo, CA 94403
Fund Type: MUS - Municipal - Single State
Major Rating Factors: Franklin NY Interm Tax-Free Inc A receives a TheStreet Investment Rating of D+ (Weak). The fund has a performance rating of C (Fair) based on an average return of 2.62% over the last three years (4.34% taxable equivalent) and 1.04% over the last three months (1.72% taxable equivalent). Factored into the performance evaluation is an expense ratio of 0.65% (low) and a 2.3% front-end load that is levied at the time of purchase.

The fund's risk rating is currently C (Fair). Volatility, as measured by standard deviation, is considered average for fixed income funds at 3.16. Another risk factor is the fund's below average duration of 5.0 years (i.e. lower interest rate risk).

John B. Pomeroy has been running the fund for 25 years and currently receives a manager quality ranking of 17 (0=worst, 99=best). If you desire an average level of risk, then this fund may be an option.
Services Offered: Automated phone transactions, payroll deductions, bank draft capabilities and a systematic withdrawal plan.

Data Date	Investment Rating	Net Assets ($Mil)	NAV	Perfor-mance Rating/Pts	Total Return Y-T-D	Risk Rating/Pts
2-17	D+	533	11.53	C / 4.7	1.04%	C / 4.9
2016	D+	544	11.46	C / 4.9	-0.25%	C / 4.8
2015	B	534	11.78	B / 8.1	2.79%	C / 5.0
2014	C+	531	11.77	C+ / 6.2	7.03%	C / 4.7
2013	C+	599	11.31	C+ / 6.5	-2.63%	C / 4.5
2012	C	642	11.94	C+ / 6.0	4.90%	C- / 4.1

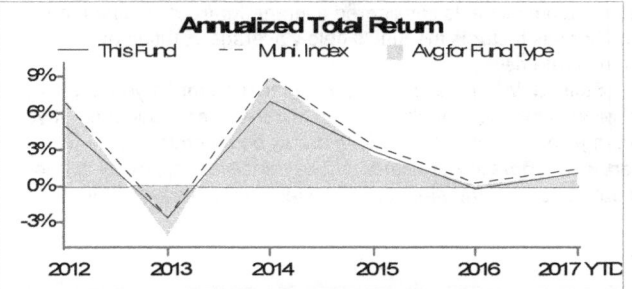

Franklin Ohio Tax-Free Inc A (FTOIX)   B   Good

Fund Family: Franklin Templeton Investments   **Phone:** (800) 342-5236
Address: One Franklin Parkway, San Mateo, CA 94403
Fund Type: MUI - Municipal - Insured
Major Rating Factors: Franklin Ohio Tax-Free Inc A receives a TheStreet Investment Rating of B (Good). The fund has a performance rating of C+ (Fair) based on an average return of 3.86% over the last three years and 0.74% over the last three months. Factored into the performance evaluation is an expense ratio of 0.63% (low) and a 4.3% front-end load that is levied at the time of purchase.

The fund's risk rating is currently C+ (Fair). Volatility, as measured by standard deviation, is considered average for fixed income funds at 2.98. Another risk factor is the fund's below average duration of 4.2 years (i.e. lower interest rate risk).

James P. Conn has been running the fund for 18 years and currently receives a manager quality ranking of 70 (0=worst, 99=best). If you desire an average level of risk, then this fund may be an option.
Services Offered: Automated phone transactions, payroll deductions, bank draft capabilities, wire transfers and a systematic withdrawal plan.

Data Date	Investment Rating	Net Assets ($Mil)	NAV	Perfor-mance Rating/Pts	Total Return Y-T-D	Risk Rating/Pts
2-17	B	1,142	12.56	C+ / 6.4	0.74%	C+ / 5.6
2016	B+	1,162	12.53	B- / 7.4	0.94%	C / 5.2
2015	C+	1,155	12.82	B / 8.2	3.31%	C- / 3.4
2014	C+	1,149	12.85	B / 7.8	10.24%	C- / 3.1
2013	D	1,170	12.11	C / 5.0	-4.42%	C- / 3.4
2012	D+	1,423	13.13	C / 5.4	7.43%	C- / 3.6

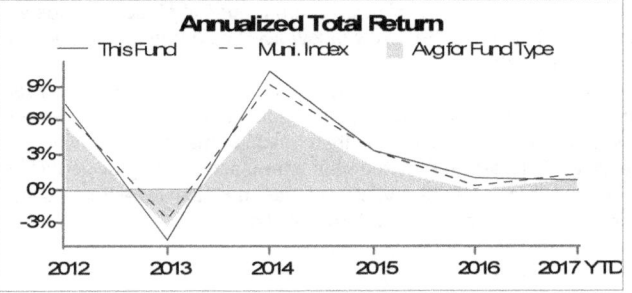

Franklin Oregon Tax-Free Inc A (FRORX) C Fair

Fund Family: Franklin Templeton Investments   **Phone:** (800) 342-5236
Address: One Franklin Parkway, San Mateo, CA 94403
Fund Type: MUS - Municipal - Single State
Major Rating Factors: Middle of the road best describes Franklin Oregon Tax-Free Inc A whose TheStreet Investment Rating is currently a C (Fair). The fund has a performance rating of C+ (Fair) based on an average return of 3.41% over the last three years (5.65% taxable equivalent) and 0.99% over the last three months (1.64% taxable equivalent). Factored into the performance evaluation is an expense ratio of 0.63% (low) and a 4.3% front-end load that is levied at the time of purchase.

The fund's risk rating is currently C (Fair). Volatility, as measured by standard deviation, is considered average for fixed income funds at 3.07. Another risk factor is the fund's below average duration of 4.7 years (i.e. lower interest rate risk).

Christopher S. Sperry has been running the fund for 17 years and currently receives a manager quality ranking of 55 (0=worst, 99=best). If you desire an average level of risk, then this fund may be an option.
Services Offered: Automated phone transactions, payroll deductions, bank draft capabilities, wire transfers and a systematic withdrawal plan.

Data Date	Investment Rating	Net Assets ($Mil)	NAV	Performance Rating/Pts	Total Return Y-T-D	Risk Rating/Pts
2-17	C	967	11.60	C+ / 5.6	0.99%	C / 5.2
2016	C+	975	11.55	C+ / 6.5	0.99%	C / 4.8
2015	C-	937	11.83	C+ / 6.7	2.32%	C- / 3.3
2014	D+	944	11.99	C+ / 6.4	9.78%	C- / 3.0
2013	E+	933	11.36	D+ / 2.4	-6.27%	C- / 3.5
2012	C	1,178	12.57	C+ / 5.7	6.86%	C- / 4.2

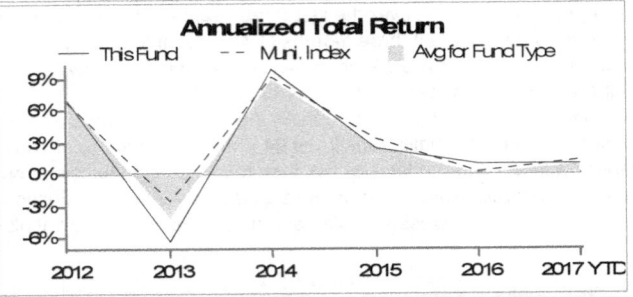

Franklin PA Tax-Free Inc A (FRPAX) A- Excellent

Fund Family: Franklin Templeton Investments   **Phone:** (800) 342-5236
Address: One Franklin Parkway, San Mateo, CA 94403
Fund Type: MUS - Municipal - Single State
Major Rating Factors: Franklin PA Tax-Free Inc A receives a TheStreet Investment Rating of A- (Excellent). The fund has a performance rating of C+ (Fair) based on an average return of 3.79% over the last three years (6.28% taxable equivalent) and 1.12% over the last three months (1.85% taxable equivalent). Factored into the performance evaluation is an expense ratio of 0.64% (low) and a 4.3% front-end load that is levied at the time of purchase.

The fund's risk rating is currently C+ (Fair). Volatility, as measured by standard deviation, is considered average for fixed income funds at 2.84. Another risk factor is the fund's below average duration of 4.0 years (i.e. lower interest rate risk).

Stella S. Wong has been running the fund for 31 years and currently receives a manager quality ranking of 76 (0=worst, 99=best). If you desire an average level of risk, then this fund may be an option.
Services Offered: Automated phone transactions, payroll deductions, bank draft capabilities, wire transfers and a systematic withdrawal plan.

Data Date	Investment Rating	Net Assets ($Mil)	NAV	Performance Rating/Pts	Total Return Y-T-D	Risk Rating/Pts
2-17	A-	951	10.12	C+ / 6.6	1.12%	C+ / 6.4
2016	A-	963	10.07	B / 7.6	1.80%	C+ / 5.6
2015	C-	958	10.26	C+ / 6.7	1.89%	C- / 3.2
2014	C	991	10.47	B- / 7.2	10.62%	D+ / 2.9
2013	D-	1,036	9.87	C- / 3.2	-6.15%	C- / 3.2
2012	C	1,285	10.93	C+ / 6.4	7.41%	C- / 3.3

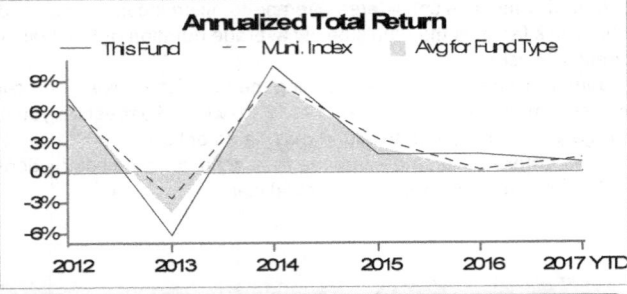

Franklin Strategic Income A (FRSTX) D- Weak

Fund Family: Franklin Templeton Investments   **Phone:** (800) 342-5236
Address: One Franklin Parkway, San Mateo, CA 94403
Fund Type: GEN - General
Major Rating Factors: Franklin Strategic Income A receives a TheStreet Investment Rating of D- (Weak). The fund has a performance rating of C (Fair) based on an average return of 1.77% over the last three years and 1.79% over the last three months. Factored into the performance evaluation is an expense ratio of 0.92% (average) and a 4.3% front-end load that is levied at the time of purchase.

The fund's risk rating is currently C- (Fair). Volatility, as measured by standard deviation, is considered average for fixed income funds at 3.96. Another risk factor is the fund's below average duration of 3.5 years (i.e. lower interest rate risk).

Christopher J. Molumphy has been running the fund for 23 years and currently receives a manager quality ranking of 69 (0=worst, 99=best). If you desire an average level of risk, then this fund may be an option.
Services Offered: Automated phone transactions, payroll deductions, an IRA investment plan, a 401K investment plan, a Keogh investment plan, wire transfers and a systematic withdrawal plan.

Data Date	Investment Rating	Net Assets ($Mil)	NAV	Performance Rating/Pts	Total Return Y-T-D	Risk Rating/Pts
2-17	D-	4,007	9.78	C / 4.7	1.79%	C- / 3.3
2016	D-	4,101	9.63	C- / 3.8	7.98%	C- / 3.4
2015	D	4,774	9.15	D- / 1.2	-4.26%	C- / 3.9
2014	D	5,230	10.00	C / 4.7	1.67%	C- / 4.0
2013	C	4,939	10.46	B- / 7.3	3.20%	D+ / 2.7
2012	D-	4,490	10.68	C+ / 6.0	12.35%	D / 2.1

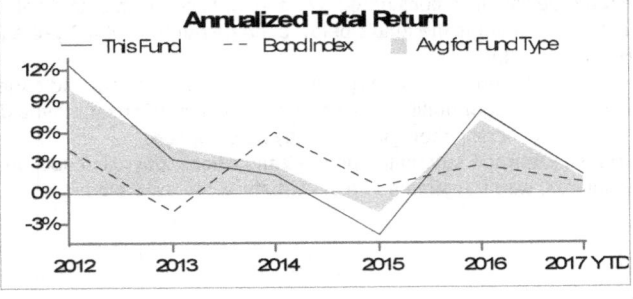

Franklin Total Return A (FKBAX)　　　　　　　　　　　D　　Weak

Fund Family: Franklin Templeton Investments　　**Phone:** (800) 342-5236
Address: One Franklin Parkway, San Mateo, CA 94403
Fund Type: GEI - General - Investment Grade
Major Rating Factors: Disappointing performance is the major factor driving the D (Weak) TheStreet Investment Rating for Franklin Total Return A. The fund currently has a performance rating of D+ (Weak) based on an average return of 2.02% over the last three years and 1.03% over the last three months. Factored into the performance evaluation is an expense ratio of 0.94% (average) and a 4.3% front-end load that is levied at the time of purchase.

The fund's risk rating is currently C+ (Fair). Volatility, as measured by standard deviation, is considered average for fixed income funds at 2.79. Another risk factor is the fund's fairly average duration of 5.6 years (i.e. average interest rate risk).

Christopher J. Molumphy has been running the fund for 19 years and currently receives a manager quality ranking of 36 (0=worst, 99=best). This fund offers an average level of risk, but investors looking for strong performance will be frustrated.

Services Offered: Automated phone transactions, payroll deductions, bank draft capabilities, an IRA investment plan, a 401K investment plan, a Keogh investment plan, wire transfers and a systematic withdrawal plan.

Data Date	Investment Rating	Net Assets ($Mil)	NAV	Perfor- mance Rating/Pts	Total Return Y-T-D	Risk Rating/Pts
2-17	D	3,304	9.72	D+ / 2.8	1.03%	C+ / 6.7
2016	D	3,452	9.66	D+ / 2.8	2.83%	C+ / 6.8
2015	D+	3,536	9.56	D+ / 2.4	-1.59%	C+ / 5.6
2014	D	3,282	10.04	C- / 3.7	4.47%	C / 5.3
2013	C-	2,969	9.85	C- / 4.1	-0.98%	C+ / 5.7
2012	C+	3,225	10.33	C / 4.5	8.33%	C+ / 6.0

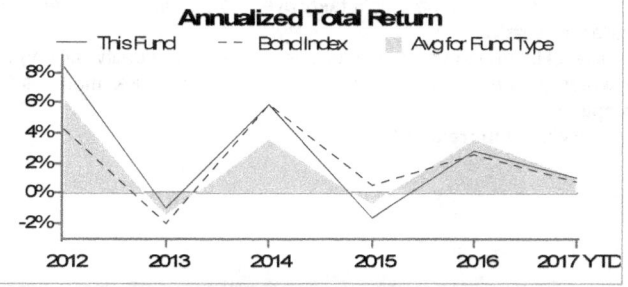

Franklin US Government Sec A (FKUSX)　　　　　　　D　　Weak

Fund Family: Franklin Templeton Investments　　**Phone:** (800) 342-5236
Address: One Franklin Parkway, San Mateo, CA 94403
Fund Type: USS - US Government - Short & Inter. Term
Major Rating Factors: Very poor performance is the major factor driving the D (Weak) TheStreet Investment Rating for Franklin US Government Sec A. The fund currently has a performance rating of E+ (Very Weak) based on an average return of 1.46% over the last three years and 0.36% over the last three months. Factored into the performance evaluation is an expense ratio of 0.76% (low) and a 4.3% front-end load that is levied at the time of purchase.

The fund's risk rating is currently B+ (Good). Volatility, as measured by standard deviation, is considered low for fixed income funds at 1.39. Another risk factor is the fund's very low average duration of 2.6 years (i.e. low interest rate risk).

Roger A. Bayston has been running the fund for 24 years and currently receives a manager quality ranking of 71 (0=worst, 99=best). This fund offers only a moderate level of risk but investors looking for strong performance are still waiting.

Services Offered: Automated phone transactions, payroll deductions, bank draft capabilities, an IRA investment plan, a 401K investment plan, a Keogh investment plan and a systematic withdrawal plan.

Data Date	Investment Rating	Net Assets ($Mil)	NAV	Perfor- mance Rating/Pts	Total Return Y-T-D	Risk Rating/Pts
2-17	D	3,913	6.19	E+ / 0.8	0.36%	B+ / 8.9
2016	C-	4,098	6.20	D / 2.1	0.67%	B+ / 8.7
2015	C	4,137	6.35	C- / 3.6	0.94%	B+ / 8.3
2014	D	4,279	6.50	D / 1.7	4.31%	B / 8.2
2013	D+	4,782	6.45	D- / 1.2	-1.68%	B+ / 8.5
2012	D+	6,614	6.80	D- / 1.4	1.53%	B+ / 8.6

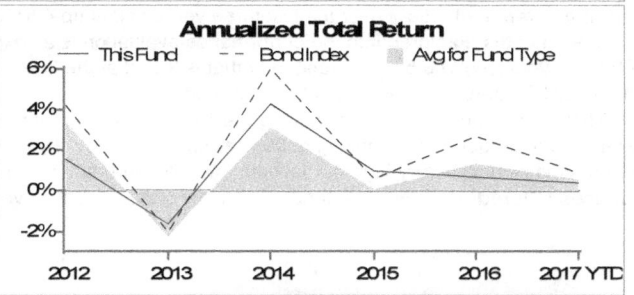

Franklin Virginia Tax-Free Inc A (FRVAX)　　　　　　B+　　Good

Fund Family: Franklin Templeton Investments　　**Phone:** (800) 342-5236
Address: One Franklin Parkway, San Mateo, CA 94403
Fund Type: MUS - Municipal - Single State
Major Rating Factors: A moderate risk profile coupled with stable earnings characterizes Franklin Virginia Tax-Free Inc A which receives a TheStreet Investment Rating of B+ (Good). Volatility, as measured by standard deviation, is considered low for fixed income funds at 2.70. Another risk factor is the fund's below average duration of 3.8 years (i.e. lower interest rate risk). The fund's risk rating is currently B- (Good).

The fund's performance rating is currently C+ (Fair). It has registered an average return of 3.37% over the last three years (5.58% taxable equivalent) and is up 0.92% over the last three months (1.52% taxable equivalent). Factored into the performance evaluation is an expense ratio of 0.65% (low) and a 4.3% front-end load that is levied at the time of purchase.

Stella S. Wong has been running the fund for 30 years and currently receives a manager quality ranking of 69 (0=worst, 99=best). If you desire stability with a moderate level of risk then this fund is an excellent option.

Services Offered: Automated phone transactions, payroll deductions, bank draft capabilities, wire transfers and a systematic withdrawal plan.

Data Date	Investment Rating	Net Assets ($Mil)	NAV	Perfor- mance Rating/Pts	Total Return Y-T-D	Risk Rating/Pts
2-17	B+	523	11.31	C+ / 5.9	0.92%	B- / 7.0
2016	A-	533	11.27	C+ / 6.8	1.79%	C+ / 6.6
2015	C-	536	11.47	C+ / 6.0	1.77%	C- / 3.8
2014	C-	554	11.69	C+ / 6.1	9.13%	C- / 3.5
2013	D-	592	11.13	D+ / 2.7	-5.80%	C- / 3.8
2012	C-	772	12.24	C / 5.4	6.80%	C- / 4.2

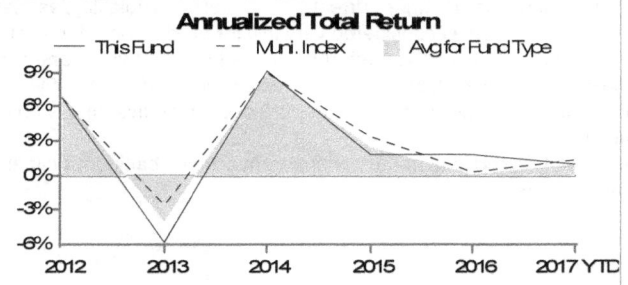

GE RSP Income (GESLX)
B-   **Good**

Fund Family: GE Investment Funds   **Phone:** (800) 242-0134
Address: PO Box 9838, Providence, RI 02940
Fund Type: GES - General - Short & Inter. Term

Major Rating Factors: GE RSP Income receives a TheStreet Investment Rating of B- (Good). The fund has a performance rating of C+ (Fair) based on an average return of 2.86% over the last three years and 1.10% over the last three months. Factored into the performance evaluation is an expense ratio of 0.17% (very low).

The fund's risk rating is currently C+ (Fair). Volatility, as measured by standard deviation, is considered average for fixed income funds at 2.87. Another risk factor is the fund's fairly average duration of 6.0 years (i.e. average interest rate risk).

Mark H. Johnson currently receives a manager quality ranking of 61 (0=worst, 99=best). If you desire an average level of risk, then this fund may be an option.

Services Offered: N/A

Data Date	Investment Rating	Net Assets ($Mil)	NAV	Performance Rating/Pts	Total Return Y-T-D	Risk Rating/Pts
2-17	B-	2,417	11.46	C+ / 5.6	1.10%	C+ / 6.2
2016	B-	2,424	11.38	C+ / 5.7	3.51%	C+ / 6.3
2015	B	2,465	11.36	C+ / 6.8	0.35%	C+ / 6.8
2014	B	2,608	11.67	C / 5.3	5.83%	B- / 7.2
2013	B+	2,601	11.33	C+ / 5.9	-0.84%	B- / 7.3
2012	B+	2,932	11.75	C / 4.6	5.87%	B / 7.8

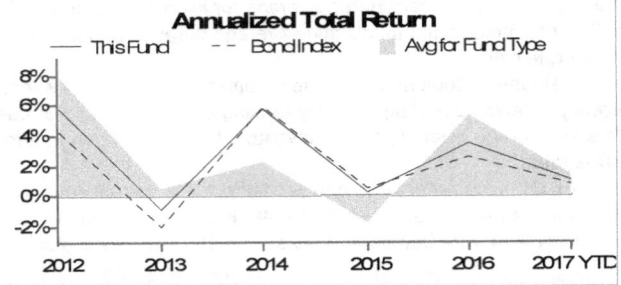

GMO Emerging Country Debt III (GMCDX)
C+   **Fair**

Fund Family: GMO Funds   **Phone:** N/A
Address: 40 Rowes Wharf, Boston, MA 02110
Fund Type: EM - Emerging Market

Major Rating Factors: GMO Emerging Country Debt III has adopted a very risky asset allocation strategy and currently receives an overall TheStreet Investment Rating of C+ (Fair). Volatility, as measured by standard deviation, is considered high for fixed income funds at 7.90. Another risk factor is the fund's below average duration of 4.7 years (i.e. lower interest rate risk). The high level of risk (E, Very Weak) did however, reward investors with excellent performance.

The fund's performance rating is currently A+ (Excellent). It has registered an average return of 7.56% over the last three years and is up 4.81% over the last three months. Factored into the performance evaluation is an expense ratio of 0.54% (very low), a 0.5% front-end load that is levied at the time of purchase and a 0.5% back-end load levied at the time of sale.

Thomas F. Cooper has been running the fund for 23 years and currently receives a manager quality ranking of 99 (0=worst, 99=best). If you are comfortable owning a very high risk investment, this fund may be an option.
Services Offered: However, the fund is currently closed to new investors.

Data Date	Investment Rating	Net Assets ($Mil)	NAV	Performance Rating/Pts	Total Return Y-T-D	Risk Rating/Pts
2-17	C+	1,067	28.99	A+ / 9.9	4.81%	E / 0.4
2016	C	929	27.66	A+ / 9.6	13.86%	E / 0.4
2015	D+	828	8.68	C+ / 6.1	0.02%	E / 0.4
2014	C-	855	9.33	B+ / 8.8	5.98%	E- / 0.2
2013	C	492	9.61	A+ / 9.6	-1.18%	E- / 0.2
2012	B-	573	10.32	A+ / 9.9	26.73%	E- / 0.2

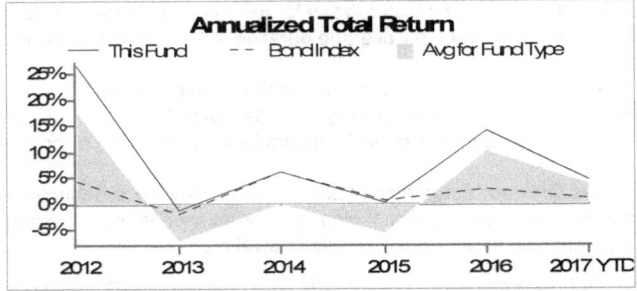

GMO Opportunistic Income VI (GMODX)
A+   **Excellent**

Fund Family: GMO Funds   **Phone:** N/A
Address: 40 Rowes Wharf, Boston, MA 02110
Fund Type: GEI - General - Investment Grade

Major Rating Factors: Strong performance is the major factor driving the A+ (Excellent) TheStreet Investment Rating for GMO Opportunistic Income VI. The fund currently has a performance rating of B (Good) based on an average return of 4.08% over the last three years and 1.90% over the last three months. Factored into the performance evaluation is an expense ratio of 0.50% (very low), a 0.4% front-end load that is levied at the time of purchase and a 0.4% back-end load levied at the time of sale.

The fund's risk rating is currently A- (Excellent). Volatility, as measured by standard deviation, is considered very low for fixed income funds at 1.18.

Benjamin L. Inker has been running the fund for 3 years and currently receives a manager quality ranking of 95 (0=worst, 99=best). If you desire only a moderate level of risk and strong performance, then this fund is an excellent option.

Services Offered: Automated phone transactions, bank draft capabilities and wire transfers.

Data Date	Investment Rating	Net Assets ($Mil)	NAV	Performance Rating/Pts	Total Return Y-T-D	Risk Rating/Pts
2-17	A+	1,511	25.78	B / 7.8	1.90%	A- / 9.1
2016	A+	1,472	25.30	B- / 7.2	5.14%	A- / 9.2
2015	U	1,672	24.68	U / --	1.67%	U / --
2014	U	1,806	24.69	U / --	0.00%	U / --

GMO US Treasury (GUSTX)   C   Fair

Fund Family: GMO Funds   **Phone:** N/A
Address: 40 Rowes Wharf, Boston, MA 02110
Fund Type: US - US Treasury
Major Rating Factors: Disappointing performance is the major factor driving the C (Fair) TheStreet Investment Rating for GMO US Treasury. The fund currently has a performance rating of D (Weak) based on an average return of 0.25% over the last three years and 0.09% over the last three months. Factored into the performance evaluation is an expense ratio of 0.10% (very low).

The fund's risk rating is currently A+ (Excellent). Volatility, as measured by standard deviation, is considered very low for fixed income funds at 0.08.

Benjamin L. Inker has been running the fund for 3 years and currently receives a manager quality ranking of 52 (0=worst, 99=best). This fund offers only a moderate level of risk but investors looking for strong performance are still waiting.
Services Offered: Automated phone transactions, bank draft capabilities, wire transfers and a systematic withdrawal plan.

Data Date	Investment Rating	Net Assets ($Mil)	NAV	Performance Rating/Pts	Total Return Y-T-D	Risk Rating/Pts
2-17	C	2,666	25.00	D / 1.6	0.09%	A+ / 9.9
2016	C	2,949	25.00	D / 1.9	0.49%	A+ / 9.9
2015	B-	3,972	24.99	C- / 3.8	0.11%	A+ / 9.9
2014	C-	2,187	25.00	D- / 1.1	0.08%	A+ / 9.9
2013	C-	1,802	25.00	E+ / 0.8	0.14%	A+ / 9.9
2012	D+	2,959	25.00	E / 0.3	0.10%	A+ / 9.9

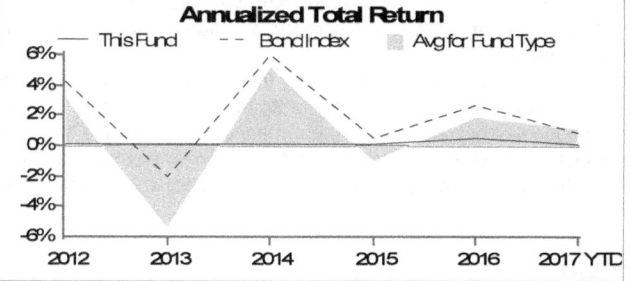

Goldman Sachs Strategic Income A (GSZAX)   E+   Very Weak

Fund Family: Goldman Sachs Funds   **Phone:** (800) 526-7384
Address: P.O. Box 06050, Chicago, IL 60050
Fund Type: GL - Global
Major Rating Factors: Very poor performance is the major factor driving the E+ (Very Weak) TheStreet Investment Rating for Goldman Sachs Strategic Income A. The fund currently has a performance rating of E+ (Very Weak) based on an average return of -0.05% over the last three years and 0.76% over the last three months. Factored into the performance evaluation is an expense ratio of 0.91% (average) and a 3.8% front-end load that is levied at the time of purchase.

The fund's risk rating is currently C (Fair). Volatility, as measured by standard deviation, is considered average for fixed income funds at 3.13. Another risk factor is the fund's very low average duration of -0.4 years (i.e. low interest rate risk).

Jonathan A. Beinner has been running the fund for 7 years and currently receives a manager quality ranking of 26 (0=worst, 99=best). This fund offers an average level of risk, but investors looking for strong performance will be frustrated.
Services Offered: Automated phone transactions, payroll deductions, bank draft capabilities, an IRA investment plan, a 401K investment plan, wire transfers and a systematic withdrawal plan.

Data Date	Investment Rating	Net Assets ($Mil)	NAV	Performance Rating/Pts	Total Return Y-T-D	Risk Rating/Pts
2-17	E+	864	9.69	E+ / 0.9	0.76%	C / 5.0
2016	E+	884	9.64	E / 0.5	2.19%	C / 5.4
2015	D+	1,703	9.62	D / 2.1	-2.40%	C+ / 5.9
2014	C	2,987	10.28	C / 5.0	-0.84%	C+ / 5.7
2013	B+	2,945	10.66	B- / 7.3	6.07%	C / 5.1
2012	U	522	10.34	U / --	13.34%	U / --

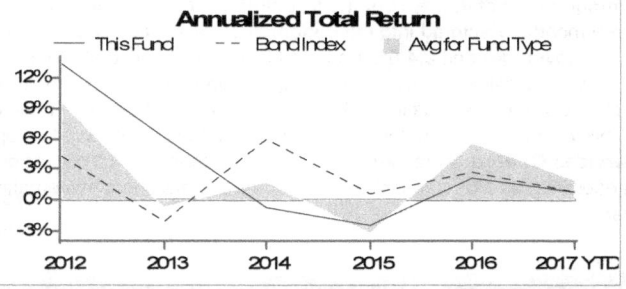

Guggenheim Floating Rate Strat A (GIFAX)   A+   Excellent

Fund Family: Guggenheim Investments Funds   **Phone:** (800) 820-0888
Address: 9601 Blackwell Road, Rockville, MD 20850
Fund Type: LP - Loan Participation
Major Rating Factors: A moderate risk profile coupled with stable earnings characterizes Guggenheim Floating Rate Strat A which receives a TheStreet Investment Rating of A+ (Excellent). Volatility, as measured by standard deviation, is considered low for fixed income funds at 2.15. Another risk factor is the fund's very low average duration of 0.3 years (i.e. low interest rate risk). The fund's risk rating is currently B (Good).

The fund's performance rating is currently C+ (Fair). It has registered an average return of 3.50% over the last three years and is up 0.70% over the last three months. Factored into the performance evaluation is an expense ratio of 1.19% (above average) and a 3.0% front-end load that is levied at the time of purchase.

Byron S. Minerd has been running the fund for 6 years and currently receives a manager quality ranking of 91 (0=worst, 99=best). If you desire stability with a moderate level of risk then this fund is an excellent option.
Services Offered: Automated phone transactions, payroll deductions, bank draft capabilities, an IRA investment plan, wire transfers and a systematic withdrawal plan.

Data Date	Investment Rating	Net Assets ($Mil)	NAV	Performance Rating/Pts	Total Return Y-T-D	Risk Rating/Pts
2-17	A+	536	26.11	C+ / 6.8	0.70%	B / 8.0
2016	A+	491	26.06	B- / 7.0	7.44%	B / 8.2
2015	A+	391	25.23	B- / 7.3	1.08%	B+ / 8.6
2014	A+	286	26.03	C+ / 6.3	2.45%	B+ / 8.3
2013	U	447	26.77	U / --	6.97%	U / --
2012	U	64	26.37	U / --	11.50%	U / --

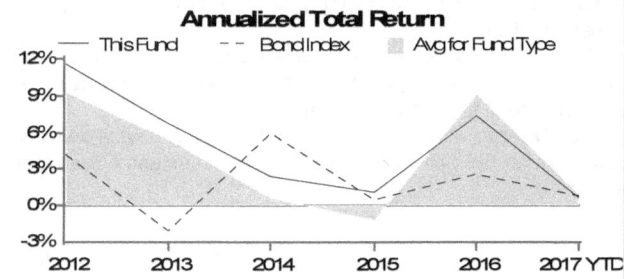

Guggenheim Macro Opportunities A (GIOAX)

A+   Excellent

Fund Family: Guggenheim Investments Funds   **Phone:** (800) 820-0888
Address: 9601 Blackwell Road, Rockville, MD 20850
Fund Type: GEL - General - Long Term

Major Rating Factors: Strong performance is the major factor driving the A+ (Excellent) TheStreet Investment Rating for Guggenheim Macro Opportunities A. The fund currently has a performance rating of B (Good) based on an average return of 4.09% over the last three years and 1.61% over the last three months. Factored into the performance evaluation is an expense ratio of 1.57% (above average) and a 4.0% front-end load that is levied at the time of purchase.

The fund's risk rating is currently C+ (Fair). Volatility, as measured by standard deviation, is considered average for fixed income funds at 2.84. Another risk factor is the fund's very low average duration of -0.1 years (i.e. low interest rate risk).

Byron S. Minerd has been running the fund for 6 years and currently receives a manager quality ranking of 94 (0=worst, 99=best). If you desire an average level of risk and strong performance, then this fund is a good option.

Services Offered: Automated phone transactions, payroll deductions, bank draft capabilities, an IRA investment plan, wire transfers and a systematic withdrawal plan.

Data Date	Investment Rating	Net Assets ($Mil)	NAV	Performance Rating/Pts	Total Return Y-T-D	Risk Rating/Pts
2-17	A+	828	26.58	B / 8.0	1.61%	C+/ 6.4
2016	A+	762	26.33	B+ / 8.5	10.59%	C+/ 6.3
2015	C-	779	25.16	C / 4.6	-1.51%	C+/ 5.7
2014	A-	644	26.83	B- / 7.5	5.14%	C / 5.3
2013	U	325	26.70	U / --	3.82%	U / --
2012	U	128	27.05	U / --	14.38%	U / --

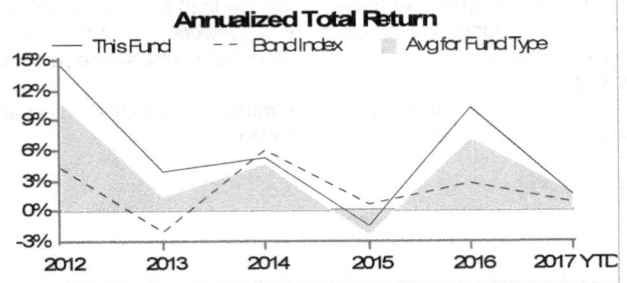
Annualized Total Return

Guggenheim Total Return Bond A (GIBAX)

A+   Excellent

Fund Family: Guggenheim Investments Funds   **Phone:** (800) 820-0888
Address: 9601 Blackwell Road, Rockville, MD 20850
Fund Type: GEI - General - Investment Grade

Major Rating Factors: A moderate risk profile coupled with stable earnings characterizes Guggenheim Total Return Bond A which receives a TheStreet Investment Rating of A+ (Excellent). Volatility, as measured by standard deviation, is considered low for fixed income funds at 2.27. Another risk factor is the fund's below average duration of 4.4 years (i.e. lower interest rate risk). The fund's risk rating is currently B (Good).

The fund's performance rating is currently C+ (Fair). It has registered an average return of 4.32% over the last three years and is up 1.48% over the last three months. Factored into the performance evaluation is an expense ratio of 1.10% (average) and a 4.0% front-end load that is levied at the time of purchase.

Byron S. Minerd has been running the fund for 6 years and currently receives a manager quality ranking of 89 (0=worst, 99=best). If you desire stability with a moderate level of risk then this fund is an excellent option.

Services Offered: Automated phone transactions, payroll deductions, bank draft capabilities, an IRA investment plan, wire transfers and a systematic withdrawal plan.

Data Date	Investment Rating	Net Assets ($Mil)	NAV	Performance Rating/Pts	Total Return Y-T-D	Risk Rating/Pts
2-17	A+	639	26.64	C+ / 6.8	1.48%	B / 7.9
2016	A+	608	26.41	B- / 7.1	5.79%	B / 7.8
2015	B	463	26.06	B- / 7.3	0.87%	C+/ 6.3
2014	A+	212	26.95	B / 7.6	7.84%	C+/ 6.0
2013	U	67	26.16	U / --	1.48%	U / --
2012	U	83	26.99	U / --	12.90%	U / --

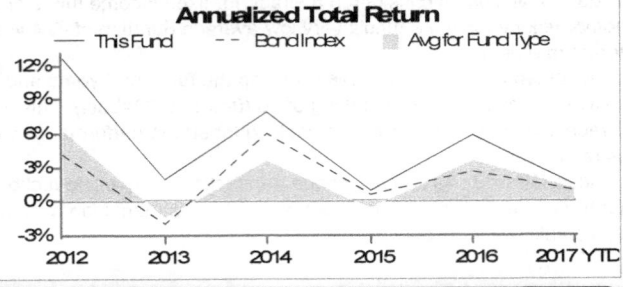
Annualized Total Return

Harbor Bond Inst (HABDX)

C   Fair

Fund Family: Harbor Funds   **Phone:** (800) 422-1050
Address: 111 South Wacker Drive, Chicago, IL 60606
Fund Type: GEI - General - Investment Grade

Major Rating Factors: Middle of the road best describes Harbor Bond Inst whose TheStreet Investment Rating is currently a C (Fair). The fund has a performance rating of C+ (Fair) based on an average return of 2.62% over the last three years and 1.59% over the last three months. Factored into the performance evaluation is an expense ratio of 0.60% (low).

The fund's risk rating is currently C (Fair). Volatility, as measured by standard deviation, is considered average for fixed income funds at 3.25. Another risk factor is the fund's fairly average duration of 5.6 years (i.e. average interest rate risk).

Mark R. Kiesel has been running the fund for 3 years and currently receives a manager quality ranking of 48 (0=worst, 99=best). If you desire an average level of risk, then this fund may be an option.

Services Offered: Automated phone transactions, payroll deductions, bank draft capabilities, an IRA investment plan, wire transfers and a systematic withdrawal plan.

Data Date	Investment Rating	Net Assets ($Mil)	NAV	Performance Rating/Pts	Total Return Y-T-D	Risk Rating/Pts
2-17	C	2,260	11.52	C+/ 5.8	1.59%	C / 4.6
2016	C-	2,284	11.34	C / 5.2	3.24%	C / 4.9
2015	C-	2,776	11.47	C+/ 5.8	0.23%	C / 4.8
2014	C	3,886	12.06	C+/ 5.7	4.78%	C / 5.2
2013	C	6,345	11.95	C / 4.9	-1.46%	C / 5.5
2012	C+	7,688	12.48	C / 4.9	9.32%	C+/ 6.1

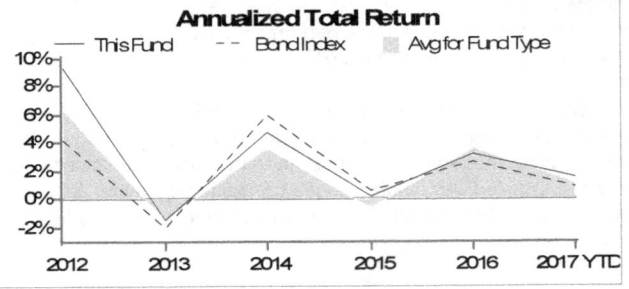
Annualized Total Return

Hartford Floating Rate A (HFLAX)   C+   Fair

Fund Family: Hartford Mutual Funds   **Phone:** (888) 843-7824
Address: P.O. Box 64387, St. Paul, MN 55164
Fund Type: LP - Loan Participation

Major Rating Factors: Strong performance is the major factor driving the C+ (Fair) TheStreet Investment Rating for Hartford Floating Rate A. The fund currently has a performance rating of B- (Good) based on an average return of 2.99% over the last three years and 1.27% over the last three months. Factored into the performance evaluation is an expense ratio of 0.99% (average) and a 3.0% front-end load that is levied at the time of purchase.

The fund's risk rating is currently C- (Fair). Volatility, as measured by standard deviation, is considered average for fixed income funds at 3.79. Another risk factor is the fund's very low average duration of 0.3 years (i.e. low interest rate risk).

Brion S. Johnson currently receives a manager quality ranking of 85 (0=worst, 99=best). If you desire an average level of risk and strong performance, then this fund is a good option.

Services Offered: Automated phone transactions, payroll deductions, bank draft capabilities, an IRA investment plan, a 401K investment plan, a Keogh investment plan, wire transfers and a systematic withdrawal plan.

Data Date	Investment Rating	Net Assets ($Mil)	NAV	Perfor-mance Rating/Pts	Total Return Y-T-D	Risk Rating/Pts
2-17	C+	853	8.73	B- / 7.4	1.27%	C- / 3.5
2016	C+	873	8.67	B- / 7.1	11.17%	C- / 3.8
2015	D	997	8.13	D / 1.8	-2.14%	C / 5.2
2014	C	1,443	8.66	C- / 3.8	-0.25%	B- / 7.3
2013	B	2,064	9.03	B- / 7.1	5.08%	C / 4.7
2012	E	1,777	8.94	C- / 4.2	9.18%	D+ / 2.3

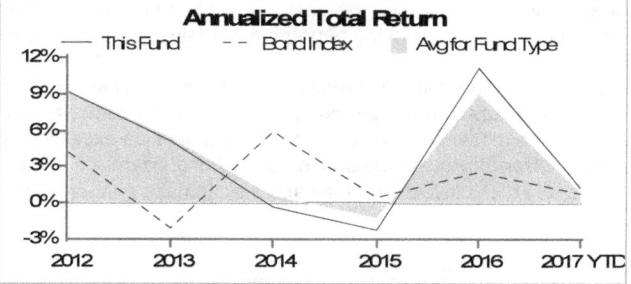

Hartford Short Duration A (HSDAX)   C+   Fair

Fund Family: Hartford Mutual Funds   **Phone:** (888) 843-7824
Address: P.O. Box 64387, St. Paul, MN 55164
Fund Type: COI - Corporate - Investment Grade

Major Rating Factors: A moderate risk profile coupled with stable earnings characterizes Hartford Short Duration A which receives a TheStreet Investment Rating of C+ (Fair). Volatility, as measured by standard deviation, is considered very low for fixed income funds at 1.13. Another risk factor is the fund's very low average duration of 1.8 years (i.e. low interest rate risk). The fund's risk rating is currently A- (Excellent).

The fund's performance rating is currently C- (Fair). It has registered an average return of 1.40% over the last three years and is up 0.53% over the last three months. Factored into the performance evaluation is an expense ratio of 0.90% (average) and a 2.0% front-end load that is levied at the time of purchase.

Timothy E. Smith has been running the fund for 5 years and currently receives a manager quality ranking of 66 (0=worst, 99=best). If you desire stability with a moderate level of risk then this fund is an excellent option.

Services Offered: Automated phone transactions, payroll deductions, bank draft capabilities, an IRA investment plan, a 401K investment plan, a Keogh investment plan, wire transfers and a systematic withdrawal plan.

Data Date	Investment Rating	Net Assets ($Mil)	NAV	Perfor-mance Rating/Pts	Total Return Y-T-D	Risk Rating/Pts
2-17	C+	517	9.86	C- / 3.0	0.53%	A- / 9.1
2016	C+	532	9.84	C- / 3.1	3.01%	A- / 9.1
2015	C+	481	9.72	C- / 3.9	0.53%	A- / 9.1
2014	C	474	9.83	D+ / 2.3	0.81%	A- / 9.0
2013	C+	446	9.93	C- / 3.2	1.08%	B+ / 8.9
2012	C-	295	10.03	D / 1.6	4.62%	A- / 9.0

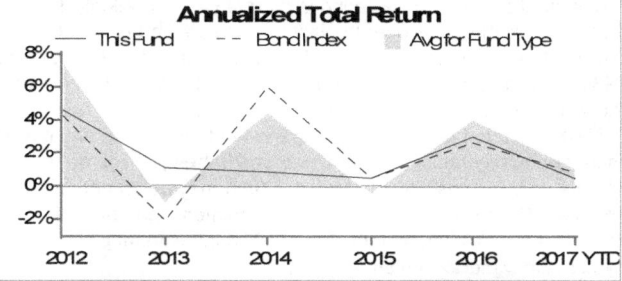

Hartford Total Return Bond A (ITBAX)   D-   Weak

Fund Family: Hartford Mutual Funds   **Phone:** (888) 843-7824
Address: P.O. Box 64387, St. Paul, MN 55164
Fund Type: GEI - General - Investment Grade

Major Rating Factors: Hartford Total Return Bond A receives a TheStreet Investment Rating of D- (Weak). The fund has a performance rating of C- (Fair) based on an average return of 2.35% over the last three years and 1.20% over the last three months. Factored into the performance evaluation is an expense ratio of 0.88% (average) and a 4.5% front-end load that is levied at the time of purchase.

The fund's risk rating is currently C (Fair). Volatility, as measured by standard deviation, is considered average for fixed income funds at 3.00. Another risk factor is the fund's fairly average duration of 5.3 years (i.e. average interest rate risk).

Campe E. Goodman has been running the fund for 5 years and currently receives a manager quality ranking of 35 (0=worst, 99=best). If you desire an average level of risk, then this fund may be an option.

Services Offered: Automated phone transactions, payroll deductions, bank draft capabilities, an IRA investment plan, a 401K investment plan, wire transfers and a systematic withdrawal plan.

Data Date	Investment Rating	Net Assets ($Mil)	NAV	Perfor-mance Rating/Pts	Total Return Y-T-D	Risk Rating/Pts
2-17	D-	736	10.31	C- / 3.3	1.20%	C / 5.5
2016	D	740	10.23	C- / 3.2	3.68%	C+ / 5.7
2015	D+	677	10.13	D / 2.1	-0.93%	C / 5.3
2014	D	613	10.48	C- / 3.5	5.24%	C+ / 5.8
2013	C-	570	10.40	C- / 3.2	-1.78%	C+ / 6.7
2012	C+	710	10.84	C- / 3.3	7.10%	B / 8.1

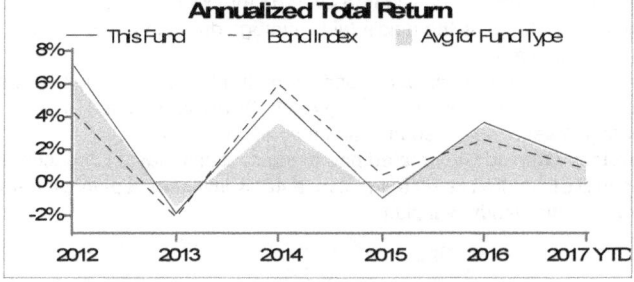

Homestead Short Term Bond (HOSBX)

A+   Excellent

Fund Family: Homestead Funds   **Phone:** (800) 258-3030
Address: c/o BFDS, Kansas, MO 64121
Fund Type: GES - General - Short & Inter. Term

Major Rating Factors: A moderate risk profile coupled with stable earnings characterizes Homestead Short Term Bond which receives a TheStreet Investment Rating of A+ (Excellent). Volatility, as measured by standard deviation, is considered low for fixed income funds at 1.93. Another risk factor is the fund's very low average duration of 2.6 years (i.e. low interest rate risk). The fund's risk rating is currently B+ (Good).

The fund's performance rating is currently C+ (Fair). It has registered an average return of 2.34% over the last three years and is up 0.64% over the last three months. Factored into the performance evaluation is an expense ratio of 0.74% (low).

Douglas G. Kern has been running the fund for 26 years and currently receives a manager quality ranking of 83 (0=worst, 99=best). If you desire stability with a moderate level of risk then this fund is an excellent option.

Services Offered: Automated phone transactions, payroll deductions, bank draft capabilities, an IRA investment plan and a systematic withdrawal plan.

Data Date	Investment Rating	Net Assets ($Mil)	NAV	Performance Rating/Pts	Total Return Y-T-D	Risk Rating/Pts
2-17	A+	536	5.21	C+ / 6.3	0.64%	B+ / 8.3
2016	B-	540	5.19	C- / 3.3	1.75%	A / 9.5
2015	A	542	5.18	C+ / 6.0	0.43%	A / 9.4
2014	B	571	5.23	C- / 3.4	1.56%	A / 9.4
2013	A-	535	5.22	C- / 4.2	1.64%	A / 9.5
2012	C+	426	5.22	D / 2.1	4.58%	A / 9.4

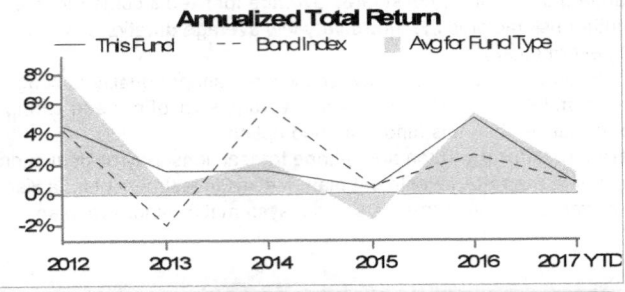

Hotchkis and Wiley High Yield A (HWHAX)

C   Fair

Fund Family: Hotchkis & Wiley Funds   **Phone:** (866) 493-8637
Address: 725 S. Figueroa Street, Los Angeles, CA 90017
Fund Type: COH - Corporate - High Yield

Major Rating Factors: Hotchkis and Wiley High Yield A has adopted a very risky asset allocation strategy and currently receives an overall TheStreet Investment Rating of C (Fair). Volatility, as measured by standard deviation, is considered high for fixed income funds at 6.00. Another risk factor is the fund's below average duration of 3.7 years (i.e. lower interest rate risk). The high level of risk (E+, Very Weak) did however, reward investors with excellent performance.

The fund's performance rating is currently A- (Excellent). It has registered an average return of 4.13% over the last three years and is up 3.67% over the last three months. Factored into the performance evaluation is an expense ratio of 0.99% (average), a 3.8% front-end load that is levied at the time of purchase and a 2.0% back-end load levied at the time of sale.

Mark T. Hudoff has been running the fund for 8 years and currently receives a manager quality ranking of 24 (0=worst, 99=best). If you are comfortable owning a very high risk investment, this fund may be an option.

Services Offered: Automated phone transactions, payroll deductions, bank draft capabilities, an IRA investment plan, a 401K investment plan, wire transfers and a systematic withdrawal plan.

Data Date	Investment Rating	Net Assets ($Mil)	NAV	Performance Rating/Pts	Total Return Y-T-D	Risk Rating/Pts
2-17	C	523	12.25	A- / 9.0	3.67%	E+ / 0.9
2016	D+	533	11.93	B / 7.9	15.69%	D- / 1.0
2015	D-	565	10.98	D- / 1.4	-4.56%	D / 1.8
2014	C-	604	12.32	B- / 7.1	0.90%	D+ / 2.7
2013	C+	490	12.99	A+ / 9.6	8.85%	E+ / 0.8
2012	C+	177	12.80	A- / 9.2	17.61%	E / 0.4

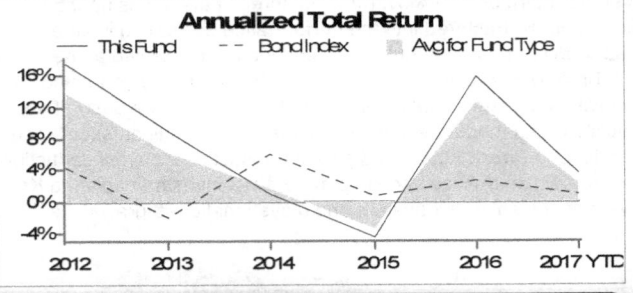

Invesco Core Plus Bond A (ACPSX)

C   Fair

Fund Family: Invesco Investments Funds   **Phone:** (800) 959-4246
Address: P.O. Box 4739, Houston, TX 77210
Fund Type: GEI - General - Investment Grade

Major Rating Factors: Middle of the road best describes Invesco Core Plus Bond A whose TheStreet Investment Rating is currently a C (Fair). The fund has a performance rating of C+ (Fair) based on an average return of 3.68% over the last three years and 1.32% over the last three months. Factored into the performance evaluation is an expense ratio of 0.95% (average) and a 4.3% front-end load that is levied at the time of purchase.

The fund's risk rating is currently C (Fair). Volatility, as measured by standard deviation, is considered average for fixed income funds at 3.05. Another risk factor is the fund's fairly average duration of 5.6 years (i.e. average interest rate risk).

Chuck E. Burge has been running the fund for 8 years and currently receives a manager quality ranking of 78 (0=worst, 99=best). If you desire an average level of risk, then this fund may be an option.

Services Offered: Automated phone transactions, payroll deductions, bank draft capabilities, an IRA investment plan, a 401K investment plan, wire transfers and a systematic withdrawal plan.

Data Date	Investment Rating	Net Assets ($Mil)	NAV	Performance Rating/Pts	Total Return Y-T-D	Risk Rating/Pts
2-17	C	716	10.79	C+ / 5.6	1.32%	C / 5.3
2016	C+	689	10.70	C+ / 5.6	5.02%	C / 5.5
2015	C-	534	10.52	C / 5.4	0.28%	C / 5.1
2014	C+	383	10.86	C / 5.3	7.01%	C+ / 5.9
2013	C	313	10.57	C / 4.4	-0.44%	C+ / 6.4
2012	C	330	10.99	C- / 3.4	7.95%	B- / 7.1

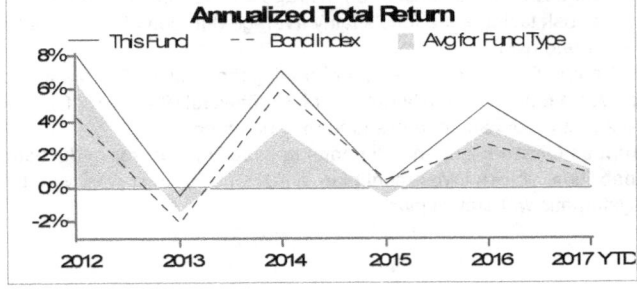

Invesco Corporate Bond A (ACCBX)   C-   Fair

Fund Family: Invesco Investments Funds   **Phone:** (800) 959-4246
Address: P.O. Box 4739, Houston, TX 77210
Fund Type: GEI - General - Investment Grade
Major Rating Factors: Invesco Corporate Bond A has adopted a risky asset allocation strategy and currently receives an overall TheStreet Investment Rating of C- (Fair). Volatility, as measured by standard deviation, is considered above average for fixed income funds at 4.36. Another risk factor is the fund's fairly average duration of 7.0 years (i.e. average interest rate risk). The high level of risk (D+, Weak) did however, reward investors with excellent performance.

The fund's performance rating is currently B- (Good). It has registered an average return of 4.28% over the last three years and is up 2.28% over the last three months. Factored into the performance evaluation is an expense ratio of 0.90% (average) and a 4.3% front-end load that is levied at the time of purchase.

Chuck E. Burge has been running the fund for 7 years and currently receives a manager quality ranking of 77 (0=worst, 99=best). If you are comfortable owning a high risk investment, this fund may be an option.

Services Offered: Automated phone transactions, payroll deductions, bank draft capabilities, an IRA investment plan, a 401K investment plan, a Keogh investment plan, wire transfers and a systematic withdrawal plan.

Data Date	Investment Rating	Net Assets ($Mil)	NAV	Performance Rating/Pts	Total Return Y-T-D	Risk Rating/Pts
2-17	C-	947	7.31	B- / 7.2	2.28%	D+ / 2.4
2016	C-	935	7.19	B- / 7.1	8.06%	D+ / 2.5
2015	D+	854	6.90	C- / 4.2	-1.62%	D+ / 2.8
2014	C+	838	7.28	C+ / 6.9	8.00%	C- / 3.8
2013	C	766	7.01	C+ / 6.4	-0.05%	C- / 3.8
2012	C	889	7.29	C+ / 5.8	11.44%	C- / 3.9

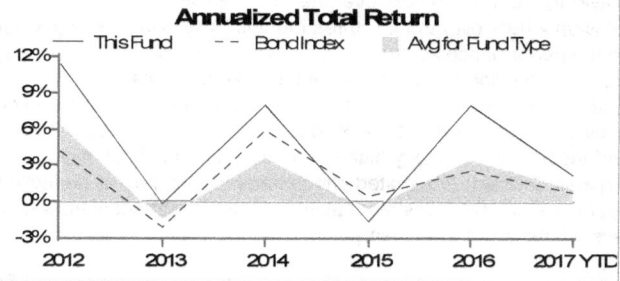

Invesco Floating Rate A (AFRAX)   B-   Good

Fund Family: Invesco Investments Funds   **Phone:** (800) 959-4246
Address: P.O. Box 4739, Houston, TX 77210
Fund Type: LP - Loan Participation
Major Rating Factors: Strong performance is the major factor driving the B- (Good) TheStreet Investment Rating for Invesco Floating Rate A. The fund currently has a performance rating of B (Good) based on an average return of 3.10% over the last three years and 1.24% over the last three months. Factored into the performance evaluation is an expense ratio of 1.12% (average) and a 2.5% front-end load that is levied at the time of purchase.

The fund's risk rating is currently C- (Fair). Volatility, as measured by standard deviation, is considered average for fixed income funds at 3.70.

Thomas Ewald has been running the fund for 11 years and currently receives a manager quality ranking of 87 (0=worst, 99=best). If you desire an average level of risk and strong performance, then this fund is a good option.
Services Offered: Automated phone transactions, payroll deductions, an IRA investment plan and a systematic withdrawal plan.

Data Date	Investment Rating	Net Assets ($Mil)	NAV	Performance Rating/Pts	Total Return Y-T-D	Risk Rating/Pts
2-17	B-	729	7.62	B / 7.6	1.24%	C- / 3.6
2016	C+	700	7.58	B- / 7.3	11.12%	C- / 4.0
2015	C-	690	7.14	D+ / 2.3	-2.87%	B- / 7.4
2014	B+	868	7.72	C / 5.3	0.86%	B / 7.9
2013	A-	1,093	7.99	B / 7.9	5.88%	C / 5.1
2012	D-	513	7.87	C / 5.0	10.12%	C- / 3.0

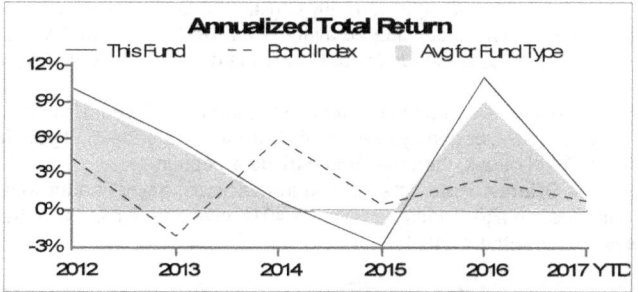

Invesco High Yield A (AMHYX)   D   Weak

Fund Family: Invesco Investments Funds   **Phone:** (800) 959-4246
Address: P.O. Box 4739, Houston, TX 77210
Fund Type: COH - Corporate - High Yield
Major Rating Factors: Invesco High Yield A has adopted a very risky asset allocation strategy and currently receives an overall TheStreet Investment Rating of D (Weak). Volatility, as measured by standard deviation, is considered above average for fixed income funds at 5.63. Another risk factor is the fund's below average duration of 4.1 years (i.e. lower interest rate risk). The high level of risk (D-, Weak) did however, reward investors with excellent performance.

The fund's performance rating is currently B- (Good). It has registered an average return of 3.00% over the last three years and is up 2.53% over the last three months. Factored into the performance evaluation is an expense ratio of 1.03% (average) and a 4.3% front-end load that is levied at the time of purchase.

Scott C. Roberts has been running the fund for 7 years and currently receives a manager quality ranking of 8 (0=worst, 99=best). If you are comfortable owning a very high risk investment, this fund may be an option.
Services Offered: Automated phone transactions, payroll deductions, bank draft capabilities, an IRA investment plan, a 401K investment plan, a Keogh investment plan, wire transfers and a systematic withdrawal plan.

Data Date	Investment Rating	Net Assets ($Mil)	NAV	Performance Rating/Pts	Total Return Y-T-D	Risk Rating/Pts
2-17	D	826	4.21	B- / 7.2	2.53%	D- / 1.1
2016	D-	791	4.14	C+ / 6.5	11.28%	D- / 1.2
2015	D-	752	3.93	D / 2.2	-3.09%	E+ / 0.9
2014	D	863	4.29	B- / 7.1	1.12%	D- / 1.4
2013	C	1,068	4.49	A- / 9.2	7.04%	E+ / 0.8
2012	C-	1,097	4.44	B+ / 8.4	17.51%	E+ / 0.6

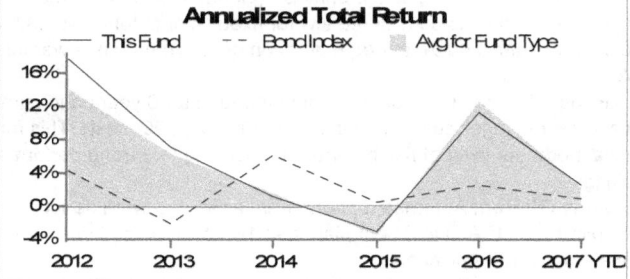

Invesco High Yield Municipal A (ACTHX)
B+   Good

Fund Family: Invesco Investments Funds   **Phone:** (800) 959-4246
Address: P.O. Box 4739, Houston, TX 77210
Fund Type: MUH - Municipal - High Yield
Major Rating Factors: Invesco High Yield Municipal A has adopted a very risky asset allocation strategy and currently receives an overall TheStreet Investment Rating of B+ (Good). Volatility, as measured by standard deviation, is considered above average for fixed income funds at 4.32. Another risk factor is the fund's above average duration of 8.3 years (i.e. higher interest rate risk). The high level of risk (D, Weak) did however, reward investors with excellent performance.

The fund's performance rating is currently A+ (Excellent). It has registered an average return of 6.92% over the last three years (11.46% taxable equivalent) and is up 2.09% over the last three months (3.46% taxable equivalent). Factored into the performance evaluation is an expense ratio of 0.93% (average) and a 4.3% front-end load that is levied at the time of purchase.

James D. Phillips has been running the fund for 15 years and currently receives a manager quality ranking of 88 (0=worst, 99=best). If you are comfortable owning a very high risk investment, this fund may be an option.
Services Offered: Automated phone transactions, payroll deductions, bank draft capabilities, an IRA investment plan, a 401K investment plan, wire transfers and a systematic withdrawal plan.

Data Date	Investment Rating	Net Assets ($Mil)	NAV	Performance Rating/Pts	Total Return Y-T-D	Risk Rating/Pts
2-17	B+	4,907	9.87	A+ / 9.7	2.09%	D / 2.0
2016	B	4,644	9.75	A+ / 9.8	1.36%	D / 1.9
2015	C	4,797	10.10	A+ / 9.8	6.25%	D- / 1.0
2014	C+	4,779	9.99	A+ / 9.8	16.55%	E+ / 0.9
2013	C-	4,019	9.04	B- / 7.5	-5.56%	D- / 1.5
2012	A	4,872	10.12	A+ / 9.7	13.92%	D+ / 2.4

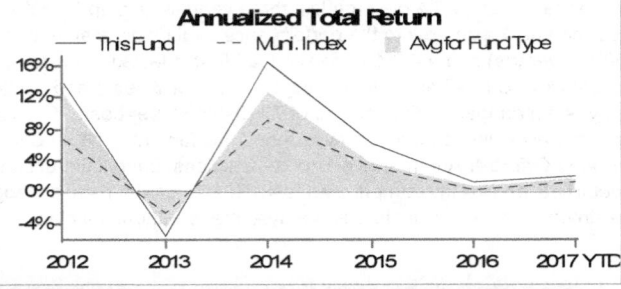

Annualized Total Return

Invesco Intm Term Municipal Inc A (VKLMX)
C   Fair

Fund Family: Invesco Investments Funds   **Phone:** (800) 959-4246
Address: P.O. Box 4739, Houston, TX 77210
Fund Type: MUN - Municipal - National
Major Rating Factors: Middle of the road best describes Invesco Intm Term Municipal Inc A whose TheStreet Investment Rating is currently a C (Fair). The fund has a performance rating of C (Fair) based on an average return of 2.94% over the last three years (4.87% taxable equivalent) and 1.02% over the last three months (1.69% taxable equivalent). Factored into the performance evaluation is an expense ratio of 0.90% (average) and a 2.5% front-end load that is levied at the time of purchase.

The fund's risk rating is currently C (Fair). Volatility, as measured by standard deviation, is considered average for fixed income funds at 3.02. Another risk factor is the fund's fairly average duration of 5.6 years (i.e. average interest rate risk).

Robert J. Stryker has been running the fund for 12 years and currently receives a manager quality ranking of 29 (0=worst, 99=best). If you desire an average level of risk, then this fund may be an option.
Services Offered: Automated phone transactions, payroll deductions, bank draft capabilities, an IRA investment plan, a 401K investment plan, wire transfers and a systematic withdrawal plan.

Data Date	Investment Rating	Net Assets ($Mil)	NAV	Performance Rating/Pts	Total Return Y-T-D	Risk Rating/Pts
2-17	C	701	10.97	C / 5.2	1.02%	C / 5.4
2016	C	705	10.91	C / 5.1	-0.19%	C / 5.5
2015	A	605	11.21	B+ / 8.7	2.87%	C+ / 6.2
2014	A-	475	11.20	B- / 7.5	7.77%	C+ / 5.6
2013	B+	397	10.73	C+ / 6.6	-1.80%	C+ / 5.9
2012	B+	390	11.28	C+ / 6.1	5.95%	C+ / 5.8

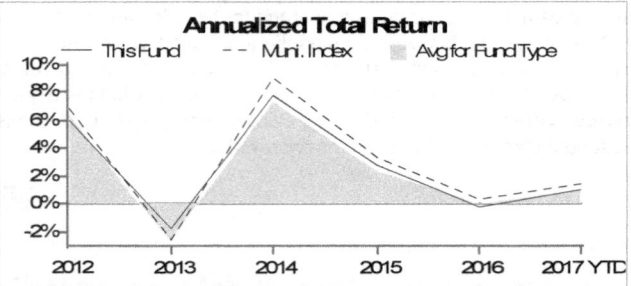

Annualized Total Return

Invesco Limited Term Muni Inc A (ATFAX)
C-   Fair

Fund Family: Invesco Investments Funds   **Phone:** (800) 959-4246
Address: P.O. Box 4739, Houston, TX 77210
Fund Type: MUN - Municipal - National
Major Rating Factors: Disappointing performance is the major factor driving the C- (Fair) TheStreet Investment Rating for Invesco Limited Term Muni Inc A. The fund currently has a performance rating of D (Weak) based on an average return of 1.43% over the last three years (2.37% taxable equivalent) and 0.99% over the last three months (1.64% taxable equivalent). Factored into the performance evaluation is an expense ratio of 0.61% (low) and a 2.5% front-end load that is levied at the time of purchase.

The fund's risk rating is currently B+ (Good). Volatility, as measured by standard deviation, is considered low for fixed income funds at 1.87. Another risk factor is the fund's below average duration of 3.5 years (i.e. lower interest rate risk).

Robert J. Stryker has been running the fund for 6 years and currently receives a manager quality ranking of 21 (0=worst, 99=best). This fund offers only a moderate level of risk but investors looking for strong performance are still waiting.
Services Offered: Automated phone transactions, payroll deductions, bank draft capabilities, an IRA investment plan, a 401K investment plan, wire transfers and a systematic withdrawal plan.

Data Date	Investment Rating	Net Assets ($Mil)	NAV	Performance Rating/Pts	Total Return Y-T-D	Risk Rating/Pts
2-17	C-	1,275	11.31	D / 2.2	0.99%	B+ / 8.4
2016	C-	1,294	11.23	D / 2.2	-0.56%	B+ / 8.4
2015	A	1,135	11.50	C+ / 6.9	1.40%	B / 8.1
2014	B-	930	11.60	C / 4.9	4.39%	B- / 7.2
2013	A	975	11.43	C+ / 6.9	-0.78%	C+ / 6.5
2012	C+	1,158	11.86	C / 5.0	4.91%	C+ / 5.9

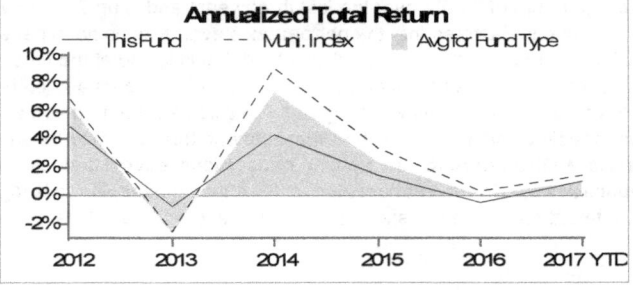

Annualized Total Return

Invesco Municipal Income A (VKMMX)   C   Fair

Fund Family: Invesco Investments Funds   **Phone:** (800) 959-4246
Address: P.O. Box 4739, Houston, TX 77210
Fund Type: MUN - Municipal - National
Major Rating Factors: Middle of the road best describes Invesco Municipal Income A whose TheStreet Investment Rating is currently a C (Fair). The fund has a performance rating of C+ (Fair) based on an average return of 4.09% over the last three years (6.77% taxable equivalent) and 1.37% over the last three months (2.27% taxable equivalent). Factored into the performance evaluation is an expense ratio of 0.93% (average) and a 4.3% front-end load that is levied at the time of purchase.

The fund's risk rating is currently C- (Fair). Volatility, as measured by standard deviation, is considered average for fixed income funds at 3.48. Another risk factor is the fund's above average duration of 7.5 years (i.e. higher interest rate risk).

Robert J. Stryker has been running the fund for 12 years and currently receives a manager quality ranking of 61 (0=worst, 99=best). If you desire an average level of risk, then this fund may be an option.

Services Offered: Automated phone transactions, payroll deductions, bank draft capabilities, a 401K investment plan, wire transfers and a systematic withdrawal plan.

Data Date	Investment Rating	Net Assets ($Mil)	NAV	Performance Rating/Pts	Total Return Y-T-D	Risk Rating/Pts
2-17	C	1,924	13.22	C+ / 6.6	1.37%	C- / 3.7
2016	C	1,911	13.12	C+ / 6.8	0.07%	C- / 3.6
2015	C+	1,703	13.64	B+ / 8.9	3.70%	C- / 3.2
2014	B+	1,635	13.72	B+ / 8.8	11.00%	C- / 3.4
2013	C+	1,540	12.89	C+ / 6.9	-3.47%	C- / 3.8
2012	B-	1,535	13.93	B- / 7.5	8.93%	C- / 3.4

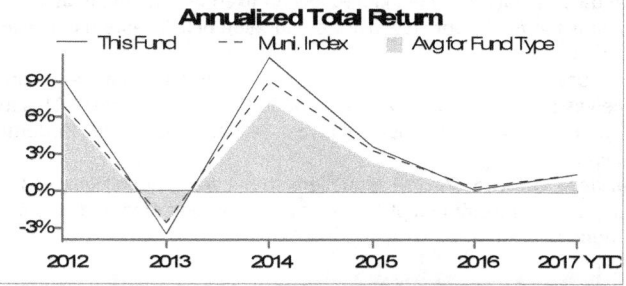

Annualized Total Return

Invesco US Government A (AGOVX)   E+   Very Weak

Fund Family: Invesco Investments Funds   **Phone:** (800) 959-4246
Address: P.O. Box 4739, Houston, TX 77210
Fund Type: USS - US Government - Short & Inter. Term
Major Rating Factors: Very poor performance is the major factor driving the E+ (Very Weak) TheStreet Investment Rating for Invesco US Government A. The fund currently has a performance rating of E (Very Weak) based on an average return of 1.51% over the last three years and 0.45% over the last three months. Factored into the performance evaluation is an expense ratio of 0.95% (average) and a 4.3% front-end load that is levied at the time of purchase.

The fund's risk rating is currently C+ (Fair). Volatility, as measured by standard deviation, is considered average for fixed income funds at 2.74. Another risk factor is the fund's below average duration of 5.0 years (i.e. lower interest rate risk).

Brian Schneider has been running the fund for 8 years and currently receives a manager quality ranking of 35 (0=worst, 99=best). This fund offers an average level of risk, but investors looking for strong performance will be frustrated.

Services Offered: Automated phone transactions, payroll deductions, bank draft capabilities, an IRA investment plan, a 401K investment plan, a Keogh investment plan, wire transfers and a systematic withdrawal plan.

Data Date	Investment Rating	Net Assets ($Mil)	NAV	Performance Rating/Pts	Total Return Y-T-D	Risk Rating/Pts
2-17	E+	559	8.84	E / 0.5	0.45%	C+ / 6.9
2016	D-	572	8.83	D- / 1.3	1.38%	B- / 7.0
2015	D+	602	8.87	D / 1.9	0.18%	B- / 7.4
2014	D	627	8.99	D- / 1.4	3.85%	B / 7.8
2013	D	678	8.83	E+ / 0.9	-2.88%	B- / 7.5
2012	E+	849	9.30	D- / 1.5	2.21%	C+ / 6.3

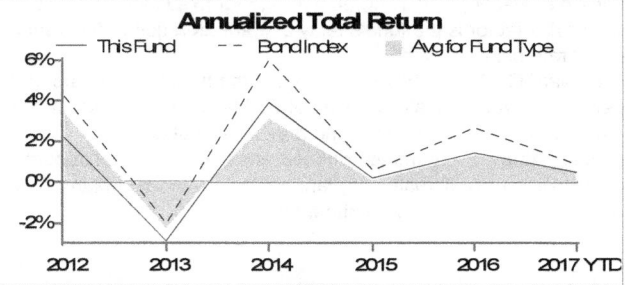

Annualized Total Return

Ivy High Income A (WHIAX)   C-   Fair

Fund Family: Ivy Funds   **Phone:** (800) 777-6472
Address: PO Box 29217, Shawnee Mission, KS 66201
Fund Type: COH - Corporate - High Yield
Major Rating Factors: Ivy High Income A has adopted a very risky asset allocation strategy and currently receives an overall TheStreet Investment Rating of C- (Fair). Volatility, as measured by standard deviation, is considered high for fixed income funds at 6.34. Another risk factor is the fund's below average duration of 3.1 years (i.e. lower interest rate risk). The high level of risk (E+, Very Weak) did however, reward investors with excellent performance.

The fund's performance rating is currently B+ (Good). It has registered an average return of 3.39% over the last three years and is up 3.08% over the last three months. Factored into the performance evaluation is an expense ratio of 0.96% (average) and a 5.8% front-end load that is levied at the time of purchase.

Chad Gunther has been running the fund for 3 years and currently receives a manager quality ranking of 8 (0=worst, 99=best). If you are comfortable owning a very high risk investment, this fund may be an option.

Services Offered: Payroll deductions, bank draft capabilities, an IRA investment plan, a 401K investment plan, a Keogh investment plan and a systematic withdrawal plan.

Data Date	Investment Rating	Net Assets ($Mil)	NAV	Performance Rating/Pts	Total Return Y-T-D	Risk Rating/Pts
2-17	C-	1,397	7.64	B+ / 8.6	3.08%	E+ / 0.7
2016	D	1,360	7.49	B / 7.7	16.75%	E+ / 0.8
2015	E+	2,358	6.94	E+ / 0.9	-7.41%	D- / 1.5
2014	B-	3,285	8.07	B / 7.6	1.48%	C- / 3.7
2013	A-	3,743	8.64	A+ / 9.8	10.20%	D+ / 2.6
2012	B	2,777	8.54	A- / 9.0	16.89%	D / 2.0

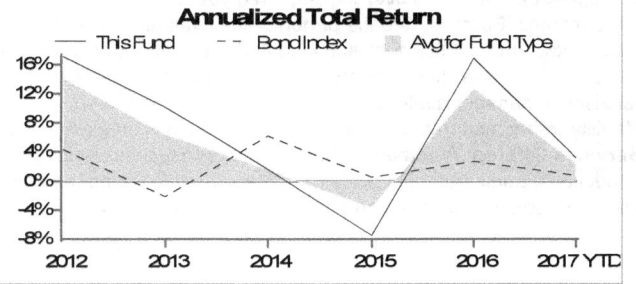

Annualized Total Return

Ivy Limited-Term Bond A (WLTAX)   C-   Fair

Fund Family: Ivy Funds   **Phone:** (800) 777-6472
Address: PO Box 29217, Shawnee Mission, KS 66201
Fund Type: GES - General - Short & Inter. Term
Major Rating Factors: Disappointing performance is the major factor driving the C- (Fair) TheStreet Investment Rating for Ivy Limited-Term Bond A. The fund currently has a performance rating of D (Weak) based on an average return of 1.05% over the last three years and 0.54% over the last three months. Factored into the performance evaluation is an expense ratio of 0.88% (average) and a 2.5% front-end load that is levied at the time of purchase.

The fund's risk rating is currently B+ (Good). Volatility, as measured by standard deviation, is considered low for fixed income funds at 1.54. Another risk factor is the fund's very low average duration of 2.9 years (i.e. low interest rate risk).

Susan K. Regan has been running the fund for 3 years and currently receives a manager quality ranking of 30 (0=worst, 99=best). This fund offers only a moderate level of risk but investors looking for strong performance are still waiting.

Services Offered: Payroll deductions, bank draft capabilities, an IRA investment plan, a 401K investment plan, a Keogh investment plan and a systematic withdrawal plan.

Data Date	Investment Rating	Net Assets ($Mil)	NAV	Performance Rating/Pts	Total Return Y-T-D	Risk Rating/Pts
2-17	C-	575	10.81	D / 1.8	0.54%	B+ / 8.7
2016	C-	654	10.78	D / 2.0	2.01%	B+ / 8.8
2015	C-	1,515	10.74	D+ / 2.4	0.45%	B+ / 8.7
2014	D	1,520	10.84	D- / 1.2	0.85%	B+ / 8.7
2013	C-	1,368	10.90	D- / 1.5	-0.73%	B+ / 8.8
2012	D+	1,179	11.20	D- / 1.1	2.67%	B+ / 8.9

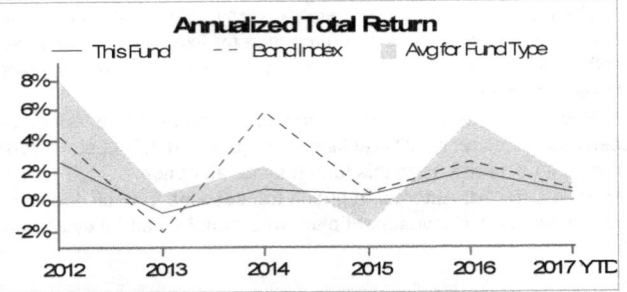

J Hancock Bond A (JHNBX)   C+   Fair

Fund Family: John Hancock Funds   **Phone:** (800) 257-3336
Address: 601 Congress Street, Boston, MA 02210
Fund Type: GEI - General - Investment Grade
Major Rating Factors: Middle of the road best describes J Hancock Bond A whose TheStreet Investment Rating is currently a C+ (Fair). The fund has a performance rating of C (Fair) based on an average return of 3.16% over the last three years and 1.49% over the last three months. Factored into the performance evaluation is an expense ratio of 0.93% (average) and a 4.0% front-end load that is levied at the time of purchase.

The fund's risk rating is currently C+ (Fair). Volatility, as measured by standard deviation, is considered average for fixed income funds at 2.85. Another risk factor is the fund's fairly average duration of 5.0 years (i.e. average interest rate risk).

Howard C. Greene has been running the fund for 15 years and currently receives a manager quality ranking of 73 (0=worst, 99=best). If you desire an average level of risk, then this fund may be an option.

Services Offered: Automated phone transactions, payroll deductions, bank draft capabilities, an IRA investment plan, a 401K investment plan, a Keogh investment plan and a systematic withdrawal plan.

Data Date	Investment Rating	Net Assets ($Mil)	NAV	Performance Rating/Pts	Total Return Y-T-D	Risk Rating/Pts
2-17	C+	1,690	15.80	C / 4.9	1.49%	C+ / 6.3
2016	C+	1,878	15.65	C / 4.9	4.46%	C+ / 6.4
2015	C-	1,768	15.46	C / 5.1	-0.18%	C / 5.2
2014	B	1,522	16.02	C+ / 6.5	6.63%	C / 5.4
2013	C+	1,316	15.75	C+ / 6.0	0.46%	C / 5.4
2012	A-	1,295	16.42	C+ / 6.7	11.49%	C+ / 5.9

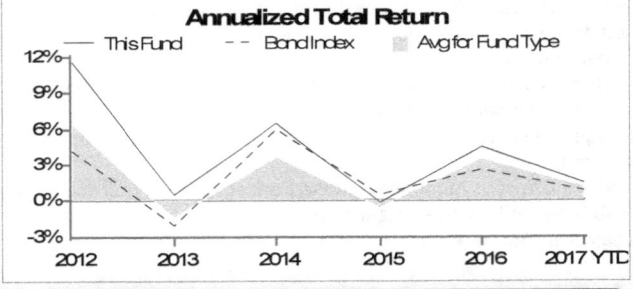

J Hancock Income A (JHFIX)   C   Fair

Fund Family: John Hancock Funds   **Phone:** (800) 257-3336
Address: 601 Congress Street, Boston, MA 02210
Fund Type: GL - Global
Major Rating Factors: A moderate risk profile coupled with stable earnings characterizes J Hancock Income A which receives a TheStreet Investment Rating of C (Fair). Volatility, as measured by standard deviation, is considered low for fixed income funds at 2.11. Another risk factor is the fund's below average duration of 3.6 years (i.e. lower interest rate risk). The fund's risk rating is currently B (Good).

The fund's performance rating is currently C- (Fair). It has registered an average return of 2.12% over the last three years and is up 1.12% over the last three months. Factored into the performance evaluation is an expense ratio of 0.82% (low) and a 4.0% front-end load that is levied at the time of purchase.

Daniel S. Janis, III has been running the fund for 18 years and currently receives a manager quality ranking of 89 (0=worst, 99=best). If you desire stability with a moderate level of risk then this fund is an excellent option.

Services Offered: Automated phone transactions, check writing, payroll deductions, bank draft capabilities, an IRA investment plan, a 401K investment plan, a Keogh investment plan and a systematic withdrawal plan.

Data Date	Investment Rating	Net Assets ($Mil)	NAV	Performance Rating/Pts	Total Return Y-T-D	Risk Rating/Pts
2-17	C	691	6.43	C- / 3.0	1.12%	B / 8.1
2016	C	812	6.39	C- / 3.3	3.21%	B / 8.0
2015	C	908	6.37	C / 5.2	0.44%	C+ / 6.1
2014	C	1,050	6.56	C+ / 5.6	3.70%	C / 4.8
2013	D	1,336	6.58	C+ / 5.8	2.00%	D+ / 2.4
2012	D-	1,754	6.75	C+ / 6.4	11.57%	D / 1.8

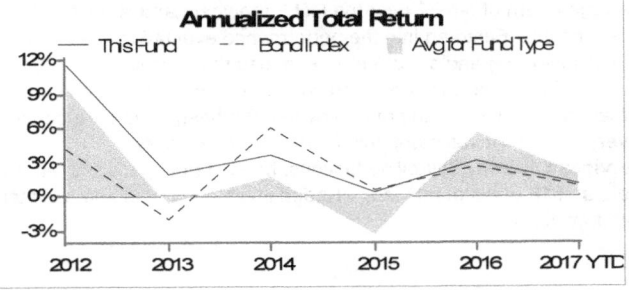

J Hancock Strat Income Opp A (JIPAX)   B+   Good

Fund Family: John Hancock Funds   **Phone:** (800) 257-3336
Address: 601 Congress Street, Boston, MA 02210
Fund Type: GL - Global
Major Rating Factors: A moderate risk profile coupled with stable earnings characterizes J Hancock Strat Income Opp A which receives a TheStreet Investment Rating of B+ (Good). Volatility, as measured by standard deviation, is considered low for fixed income funds at 2.24. Another risk factor is the fund's very low average duration of 2.8 years (i.e. low interest rate risk). The fund's risk rating is currently B (Good).

The fund's performance rating is currently C (Fair). It has registered an average return of 2.86% over the last three years and is up 1.23% over the last three months. Factored into the performance evaluation is an expense ratio of 1.11% (average) and a 4.0% front-end load that is levied at the time of purchase.

Daniel S. Janis, III has been running the fund for 11 years and currently receives a manager quality ranking of 92 (0=worst, 99=best). If you desire stability with a moderate level of risk then this fund is an excellent option.

Services Offered: Automated phone transactions, payroll deductions, bank draft capabilities, wire transfers and a systematic withdrawal plan.

Data Date	Investment Rating	Net Assets ($Mil)	NAV	Performance Rating/Pts	Total Return Y-T-D	Risk Rating/Pts
2-17	B+	585	10.70	C / 4.9	1.23%	B / 7.9
2016	B+	1,081	10.61	C / 5.1	4.73%	B / 7.8
2015	C+	1,141	10.36	C+/ 6.1	0.79%	C+/ 6.1
2014	C+	1,089	10.86	C+/ 6.3	4.45%	C / 4.7
2013	D	1,186	10.79	C+/ 6.1	2.41%	D / 2.1
2012	D-	1,022	11.13	C+/ 6.6	11.84%	D / 1.6

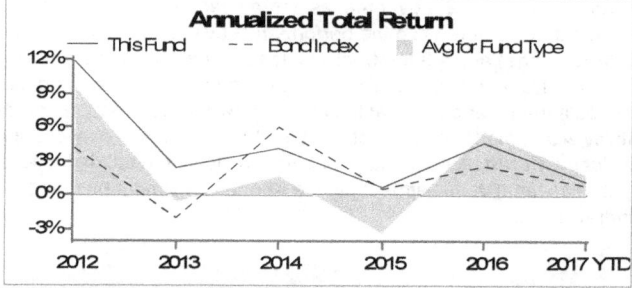

Janus Flexible Bond A (JDFAX)   D-   Weak

Fund Family: Janus Funds   **Phone:** (800) 295-2687
Address: 151 Detroit Street, Denver, CO 80206
Fund Type: GEI - General - Investment Grade
Major Rating Factors: Disappointing performance is the major factor driving the D- (Weak) TheStreet Investment Rating for Janus Flexible Bond A. The fund currently has a performance rating of D (Weak) based on an average return of 1.93% over the last three years and 0.91% over the last three months. Factored into the performance evaluation is an expense ratio of 0.81% (low) and a 4.8% front-end load that is levied at the time of purchase.

The fund's risk rating is currently B- (Good). Volatility, as measured by standard deviation, is considered low for fixed income funds at 2.67. Another risk factor is the fund's fairly average duration of 5.5 years (i.e. average interest rate risk).

Darrell W. Watters has been running the fund for 10 years and currently receives a manager quality ranking of 25 (0=worst, 99=best). This fund offers only a moderate level of risk but investors looking for strong performance are still waiting.

Services Offered: Automated phone transactions, payroll deductions, bank draft capabilities, an IRA investment plan, a 401K investment plan, wire transfers and a systematic withdrawal plan.

Data Date	Investment Rating	Net Assets ($Mil)	NAV	Performance Rating/Pts	Total Return Y-T-D	Risk Rating/Pts
2-17	D-	616	10.34	D / 2.0	0.91%	B- / 7.1
2016	D	682	10.29	D+/ 2.3	2.38%	B- / 7.1
2015	C-	698	10.30	D+/ 2.9	-0.14%	B- / 7.3
2014	C	661	10.56	C- / 3.9	4.72%	B- / 7.3
2013	B-	637	10.37	C / 4.5	-0.28%	B / 7.7
2012	C+	829	10.82	C- / 3.7	7.83%	B- / 7.2

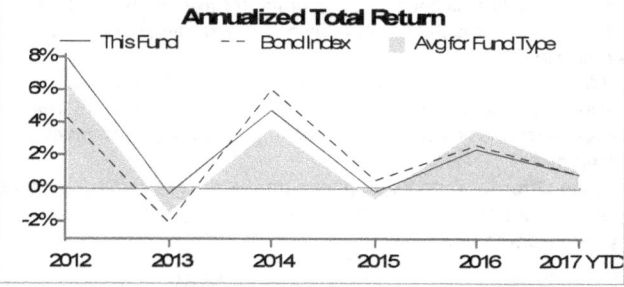

JPMorgan Core Bond A (PGBOX)   D   Weak

Fund Family: JPMorgan Funds   **Phone:** (800) 480-4111
Address: 522 Fifth Avenue, New York, NY 10036
Fund Type: GEI - General - Investment Grade
Major Rating Factors: Disappointing performance is the major factor driving the D (Weak) TheStreet Investment Rating for JPMorgan Core Bond A. The fund currently has a performance rating of D+ (Weak) based on an average return of 2.20% over the last three years and 0.87% over the last three months. Factored into the performance evaluation is an expense ratio of 0.99% (average) and a 3.8% front-end load that is levied at the time of purchase.

The fund's risk rating is currently C+ (Fair). Volatility, as measured by standard deviation, is considered average for fixed income funds at 2.78. Another risk factor is the fund's fairly average duration of 5.5 years (i.e. average interest rate risk).

Barbara E. Miller has been running the fund for 2 years and currently receives a manager quality ranking of 29 (0=worst, 99=best). This fund offers an average level of risk, but investors looking for strong performance will be frustrated.

Services Offered: Automated phone transactions, payroll deductions, bank draft capabilities, an IRA investment plan, a Keogh investment plan and a systematic withdrawal plan.

Data Date	Investment Rating	Net Assets ($Mil)	NAV	Performance Rating/Pts	Total Return Y-T-D	Risk Rating/Pts
2-17	D	2,571	11.55	D+/ 2.5	0.87%	C+/ 6.7
2016	D	2,685	11.49	D+/ 2.8	2.10%	C+/ 6.8
2015	C-	2,956	11.55	C- / 3.4	0.51%	B- / 7.5
2014	C-	4,754	11.76	C- / 3.1	5.04%	B / 7.7
2013	C-	5,210	11.48	D+/ 2.6	-1.92%	B / 8.1
2012	C+	6,565	12.07	D+/ 2.8	4.82%	B+/ 8.3

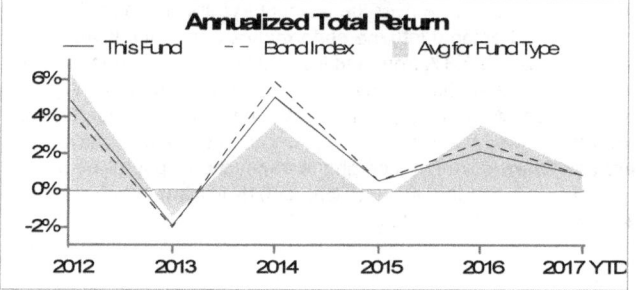

JPMorgan Core Plus Bond A (ONIAX)　　　　C　　Fair

Fund Family: JPMorgan Funds　　　**Phone:** (800) 480-4111
Address: 522 Fifth Avenue, New York, NY 10036
Fund Type: GL - Global
Major Rating Factors: A moderate risk profile coupled with stable earnings characterizes JPMorgan Core Plus Bond A which receives a TheStreet Investment Rating of C (Fair). Volatility, as measured by standard deviation, is considered low for fixed income funds at 2.70. Another risk factor is the fund's fairly average duration of 5.7 years (i.e. average interest rate risk). The fund's risk rating is currently B- (Good).

The fund's performance rating is currently C- (Fair). It has registered an average return of 2.82% over the last three years and is up 1.12% over the last three months. Factored into the performance evaluation is an expense ratio of 1.03% (average) and a 3.8% front-end load that is levied at the time of purchase.

Richard D. Figuly has been running the fund for 11 years and currently receives a manager quality ranking of 93 (0=worst, 99=best). If you desire stability with a moderate level of risk then this fund is an excellent option.
Services Offered: Automated phone transactions, payroll deductions, bank draft capabilities, an IRA investment plan, a Keogh investment plan and a systematic withdrawal plan.

Data Date	Investment Rating	Net Assets ($Mil)	NAV	Perfor-mance Rating/Pts	Total Return Y-T-D	Risk Rating/Pts
2-17	C	1,074	8.22	C- / 4.0	1.12%	B- / 7.0
2016	C+	1,078	8.16	C / 4.3	3.78%	B- / 7.0
2015	C	795	8.06	C / 5.1	0.02%	B- / 7.0
2014	B	517	8.31	C / 4.9	6.04%	B- / 7.4
2013	B	335	8.16	C / 4.9	0.07%	B / 7.7
2012	B	569	8.51	C / 4.3	6.97%	B / 7.7

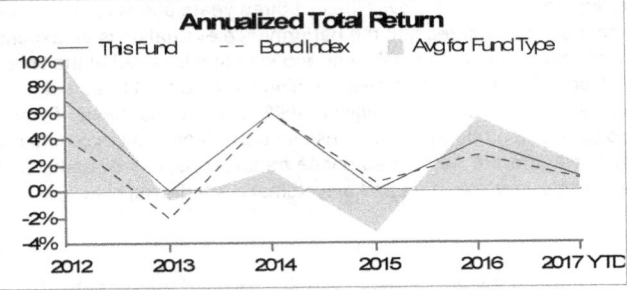

Annualized Total Return

JPMorgan Government Bond A (OGGAX)　　　　E+　　Very Weak

Fund Family: JPMorgan Funds　　　**Phone:** (800) 480-4111
Address: 522 Fifth Avenue, New York, NY 10036
Fund Type: USS - US Government - Short & Inter. Term
Major Rating Factors: Disappointing performance is the major factor driving the E+ (Very Weak) TheStreet Investment Rating for JPMorgan Government Bond A. The fund currently has a performance rating of D (Weak) based on an average return of 1.92% over the last three years and 0.68% over the last three months. Factored into the performance evaluation is an expense ratio of 1.14% (above average) and a 3.8% front-end load that is levied at the time of purchase.

The fund's risk rating is currently C+ (Fair). Volatility, as measured by standard deviation, is considered average for fixed income funds at 2.99. Another risk factor is the fund's fairly average duration of 5.2 years (i.e. average interest rate risk).

Michael J. Sais has been running the fund for 21 years and currently receives a manager quality ranking of 52 (0=worst, 99=best). This fund offers an average level of risk, but investors looking for strong performance will be frustrated.
Services Offered: Automated phone transactions, payroll deductions, bank draft capabilities, an IRA investment plan, a 401K investment plan, wire transfers and a systematic withdrawal plan.

Data Date	Investment Rating	Net Assets ($Mil)	NAV	Perfor-mance Rating/Pts	Total Return Y-T-D	Risk Rating/Pts
2-17	E+	529	10.54	D / 1.8	0.68%	C+ / 5.6
2016	D-	535	10.50	D+ / 2.4	1.29%	C / 5.5
2015	D+	605	10.62	D+ / 2.5	0.71%	C+ / 5.6
2014	D-	655	10.93	D / 2.1	5.25%	C+ / 6.0
2013	D-	708	10.85	D / 1.8	-3.85%	C / 5.5
2012	E+	799	11.63	D+ / 2.8	3.28%	C / 5.2

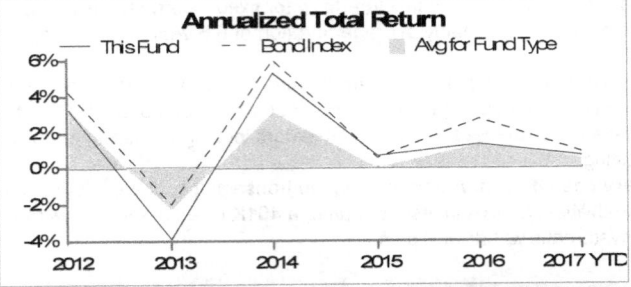

Annualized Total Return

JPMorgan High Yield A (OHYAX)　　　　C-　　Fair

Fund Family: JPMorgan Funds　　　**Phone:** (800) 480-4111
Address: 522 Fifth Avenue, New York, NY 10036
Fund Type: COH - Corporate - High Yield
Major Rating Factors: JPMorgan High Yield A has adopted a very risky asset allocation strategy and currently receives an overall TheStreet Investment Rating of C- (Fair). Volatility, as measured by standard deviation, is considered above average for fixed income funds at 5.57. Another risk factor is the fund's below average duration of 4.2 years (i.e. lower interest rate risk). The high level of risk (D-, Weak) did however, reward investors with excellent performance.

The fund's performance rating is currently B (Good). It has registered an average return of 3.48% over the last three years and is up 2.59% over the last three months. Factored into the performance evaluation is an expense ratio of 0.72% (low) and a 3.8% front-end load that is levied at the time of purchase.

James P. Shanahan, Jr. has been running the fund for 19 years and currently receives a manager quality ranking of 15 (0=worst, 99=best). If you are comfortable owning a very high risk investment, this fund may be an option.
Services Offered: Automated phone transactions, payroll deductions, bank draft capabilities, an IRA investment plan, a 401K investment plan, wire transfers and a systematic withdrawal plan.

Data Date	Investment Rating	Net Assets ($Mil)	NAV	Perfor-mance Rating/Pts	Total Return Y-T-D	Risk Rating/Pts
2-17	C-	981	7.44	B / 8.1	2.59%	D- / 1.2
2016	D+	973	7.31	B / 7.7	13.56%	D- / 1.2
2015	D-	811	6.80	D / 1.7	-4.75%	D / 1.6
2014	C-	809	7.55	B- / 7.1	2.37%	D+ / 2.6
2013	C+	1,020	7.95	B+ / 8.9	6.85%	D- / 1.3
2012	C-	1,021	8.10	B / 7.7	14.48%	D- / 1.0

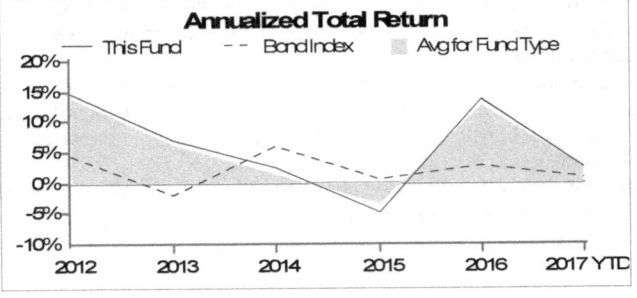

Annualized Total Return

JPMorgan Short Duration Bond A (OGLVX)   D   Weak

Fund Family: JPMorgan Funds   **Phone:** (800) 480-4111
Address: 522 Fifth Avenue, New York, NY 10036
Fund Type: GEI - General - Investment Grade
Major Rating Factors: Very poor performance is the major factor driving the D (Weak) TheStreet Investment Rating for JPMorgan Short Duration Bond A. The fund currently has a performance rating of E (Very Weak) based on an average return of 0.43% over the last three years and 0.21% over the last three months. Factored into the performance evaluation is an expense ratio of 0.92% (average) and a 2.3% front-end load that is levied at the time of purchase.

The fund's risk rating is currently A (Excellent). Volatility, as measured by standard deviation, is considered very low for fixed income funds at 0.78. Another risk factor is the fund's very low average duration of 1.8 years (i.e. low interest rate risk).

Gregg F. Hrivnak has been running the fund for 11 years and currently receives a manager quality ranking of 30 (0=worst, 99=best). This fund offers only a moderate level of risk but investors looking for strong performance are still waiting.

Services Offered: Automated phone transactions, payroll deductions, bank draft capabilities, an IRA investment plan, a 401K investment plan, wire transfers and a systematic withdrawal plan.

Data Date	Investment Rating	Net Assets ($Mil)	NAV	Perfor-mance Rating/Pts	Total Return Y-T-D	Risk Rating/Pts
2-17	D	536	10.81	E / 0.4	0.21%	A / 9.5
2016	D+	557	10.80	E+ / 0.7	0.79%	A / 9.5
2015	C	533	10.79	D+ / 2.4	0.17%	A+ / 9.6
2014	D+	230	10.85	E+ / 0.8	0.47%	A+ / 9.7
2013	C-	242	10.87	E+ / 0.9	-0.22%	A+ / 9.6
2012	D+	292	10.98	E+ / 0.6	1.41%	A+ / 9.6

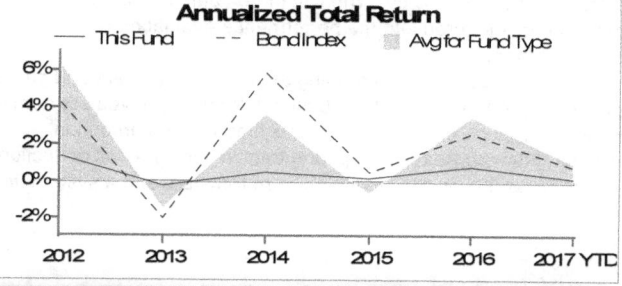

Annualized Total Return

JPMorgan Strategic Income Opp A (JSOAX)   B+   Good

Fund Family: JPMorgan Funds   **Phone:** (800) 480-4111
Address: 522 Fifth Avenue, New York, NY 10036
Fund Type: GL - Global
Major Rating Factors: A moderate risk profile coupled with stable earnings characterizes JPMorgan Strategic Income Opp A which receives a TheStreet Investment Rating of B+ (Good). Volatility, as measured by standard deviation, is considered low for fixed income funds at 2.67. Another risk factor is the fund's very low average duration of 1.7 years (i.e. low interest rate risk). The fund's risk rating is currently B- (Good).

The fund's performance rating is currently C+ (Fair). It has registered an average return of 2.34% over the last three years and is up 1.57% over the last three months. Factored into the performance evaluation is an expense ratio of 1.28% (above average) and a 3.8% front-end load that is levied at the time of purchase.

William H. Eigen, III has been running the fund for 9 years and currently receives a manager quality ranking of 89 (0=worst, 99=best). If you desire stability with a moderate level of risk then this fund is an excellent option.

Services Offered: Automated phone transactions, payroll deductions, bank draft capabilities, a 401K investment plan, a Keogh investment plan, wire transfers and a systematic withdrawal plan.

Data Date	Investment Rating	Net Assets ($Mil)	NAV	Perfor-mance Rating/Pts	Total Return Y-T-D	Risk Rating/Pts
2-17	B+	1,531	11.69	C+ / 5.8	1.57%	B- / 7.1
2016	B	1,502	11.57	C / 5.0	8.92%	B- / 7.5
2015	D+	1,967	11.07	D- / 1.4	-2.37%	B / 7.9
2014	C	3,774	11.69	D+/ 2.7	-0.14%	B+/ 8.8
2013	C-	4,694	11.86	C- / 3.9	2.78%	C+/ 6.6
2012	E	2,293	11.80	D / 2.0	7.82%	C / 4.9

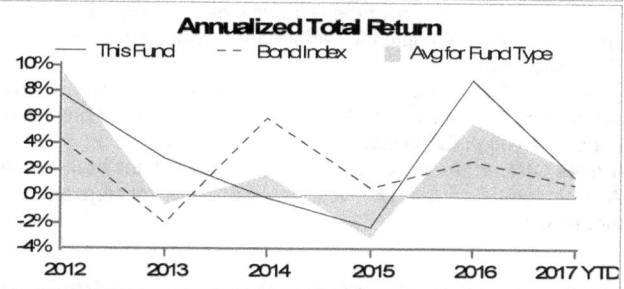

Annualized Total Return

KP Fixed Income Instl (KPFIX)   A-   Excellent

Fund Family: KP Funds   **Phone:** (855) 457-3637
Address: c/o SEI Investments, Oaks, PA 19456
Fund Type: GEI - General - Investment Grade
Major Rating Factors: A moderate risk profile coupled with stable earnings characterizes KP Fixed Income Instl which receives a TheStreet Investment Rating of A- (Excellent). Volatility, as measured by standard deviation, is considered low for fixed income funds at 2.54. The fund's risk rating is currently B- (Good).

The fund's performance rating is currently C+ (Fair). It has registered an average return of 2.84% over the last three years and is up 1.01% over the last three months. Factored into the performance evaluation is an expense ratio of 0.35% (very low).

Gregory C. Allen has been running the fund for 3 years and currently receives a manager quality ranking of 68 (0=worst, 99=best). If you desire stability with a moderate level of risk then this fund is an excellent option.

Services Offered: Automated phone transactions, bank draft capabilities, a 401K investment plan and wire transfers.

Data Date	Investment Rating	Net Assets ($Mil)	NAV	Perfor-mance Rating/Pts	Total Return Y-T-D	Risk Rating/Pts
2-17	A-	1,296	9.96	C+/ 5.7	1.01%	B- / 7.5
2016	U	1,070	9.86	U / --	4.08%	U / --
2015	U	920	9.78	U / --	0.47%	U / --
2014	U	826	10.00	U / --	0.00%	U / --

Asset Composition
For: KP Fixed Income Instl

Cash & Cash Equivalent:	10%
Government Bonds:	42%
Municipal Bonds:	0%
Corporate Bonds:	22%
Other:	26%

Loomis Sayles Bond Ret (LSBRX)

D   **Weak**

Fund Family: Loomis Sayles Funds   **Phone:** (800) 633-3330
Address: PO Box 219594, Kansas, MO 61421
Fund Type: GES - General - Short & Inter. Term

Major Rating Factors: Loomis Sayles Bond Ret has adopted a very risky asset allocation strategy and currently receives an overall TheStreet Investment Rating of D (Weak). Volatility, as measured by standard deviation, is considered above average for fixed income funds at 5.78. Another risk factor is the fund's below average duration of 3.6 years (i.e. lower interest rate risk). The high level of risk (D-, Weak) did however, reward investors with excellent performance.

The fund's performance rating is currently B- (Good). It has registered an average return of 2.02% over the last three years and is up 3.35% over the last three months. Factored into the performance evaluation is an expense ratio of 0.89% (average).

Daniel J. Fuss has been running the fund for 26 years and currently receives a manager quality ranking of 69 (0=worst, 99=best). If you are comfortable owning a very high risk investment, this fund may be an option.

Services Offered: Automated phone transactions, payroll deductions, bank draft capabilities, an IRA investment plan, wire transfers and a systematic withdrawal plan.

Data Date	Investment Rating	Net Assets ($Mil)	NAV	Performance Rating/Pts	Total Return Y-T-D	Risk Rating/Pts
2-17	D	3,891	13.89	B- / 7.3	3.35%	D- / 1.4
2016	D-	3,908	13.50	C / 5.3	8.40%	D- / 1.5
2015	D	5,355	12.82	D / 2.1	-7.06%	D / 2.0
2014	C	8,498	14.76	B+ / 8.4	4.49%	D / 1.7
2013	C+	8,370	15.09	A- / 9.2	5.52%	D- / 1.5
2012	C+	8,771	15.06	B+ / 8.5	14.77%	D- / 1.4

Annualized Total Return

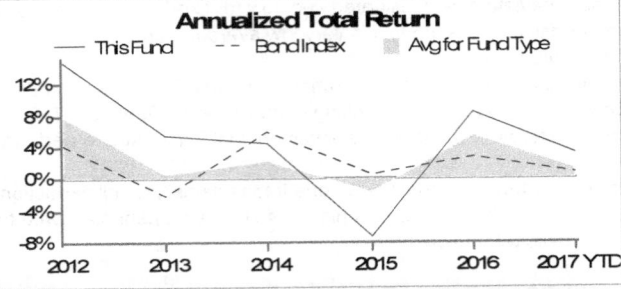

Loomis Sayles Fixed Inc Fd (LSFIX)

C   **Fair**

Fund Family: Loomis Sayles Funds   **Phone:** (800) 633-3330
Address: PO Box 219594, Kansas, MO 61421
Fund Type: GEI - General - Investment Grade

Major Rating Factors: Loomis Sayles Fixed Inc Fd has adopted a very risky asset allocation strategy and currently receives an overall TheStreet Investment Rating of C (Fair). Volatility, as measured by standard deviation, is considered above average for fixed income funds at 5.29. Another risk factor is the fund's below average duration of 4.0 years (i.e. lower interest rate risk). The high level of risk (D, Weak) did however, reward investors with excellent performance.

The fund's performance rating is currently B (Good). It has registered an average return of 2.80% over the last three years and is up 3.16% over the last three months. Factored into the performance evaluation is an expense ratio of 0.57% (very low).

Daniel J. Fuss has been running the fund for 22 years and currently receives a manager quality ranking of 81 (0=worst, 99=best). If you are comfortable owning a very high risk investment, this fund may be an option.

Services Offered: Automated phone transactions, bank draft capabilities, an IRA investment plan, a 401K investment plan, wire transfers and a systematic withdrawal plan.

Data Date	Investment Rating	Net Assets ($Mil)	NAV	Performance Rating/Pts	Total Return Y-T-D	Risk Rating/Pts
2-17	C	1,088	13.39	B / 8.0	3.16%	D / 1.9
2016	D+	1,093	12.98	B- / 7.0	9.94%	D / 1.9
2015	D	1,190	12.23	C- / 4.1	-6.03%	D / 2.0
2014	C+	1,442	13.90	B+ / 8.7	4.62%	D / 1.7
2013	B-	1,213	14.45	A+ / 9.6	6.88%	D- / 1.5
2012	C+	1,172	14.43	B+ / 8.8	15.65%	D- / 1.5

Annualized Total Return

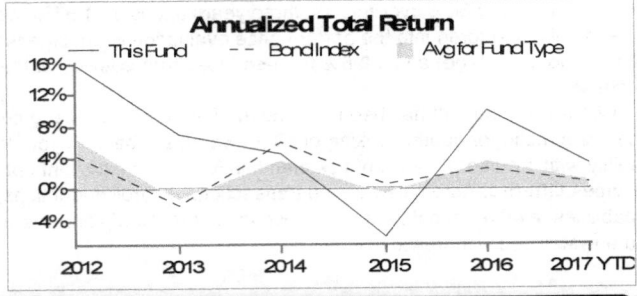

Loomis Sayles Inst High Income Inst (LSHIX)

C+   **Fair**

Fund Family: Loomis Sayles Funds   **Phone:** (800) 633-3330
Address: PO Box 219594, Kansas, MO 61421
Fund Type: COH - Corporate - High Yield

Major Rating Factors: Loomis Sayles Inst High Income Inst has adopted a very risky asset allocation strategy and currently receives an overall TheStreet Investment Rating of C+ (Fair). Volatility, as measured by standard deviation, is considered high for fixed income funds at 7.65. Another risk factor is the fund's below average duration of 4.0 years (i.e. lower interest rate risk). The high level of risk (E, Very Weak) did however, reward investors with excellent performance.

The fund's performance rating is currently A+ (Excellent). It has registered an average return of 3.85% over the last three years and is up 3.81% over the last three months. Factored into the performance evaluation is an expense ratio of 0.68% (low).

Daniel J. Fuss has been running the fund for 21 years and currently receives a manager quality ranking of 4 (0=worst, 99=best). If you are comfortable owning a very high risk investment, this fund may be an option.

Services Offered: Automated phone transactions, bank draft capabilities, an IRA investment plan, a 401K investment plan, wire transfers and a systematic withdrawal plan.

Data Date	Investment Rating	Net Assets ($Mil)	NAV	Performance Rating/Pts	Total Return Y-T-D	Risk Rating/Pts
2-17	C+	761	6.81	A+ / 9.7	3.81%	E / 0.4
2016	C	735	6.56	A+ / 9.6	18.95%	E / 0.4
2015	D-	593	5.85	C- / 3.2	-10.27%	E / 0.5
2014	C+	657	7.24	A+ / 9.6	5.17%	E+ / 0.9
2013	C+	667	7.65	A+ / 9.9	15.07%	E / 0.4
2012	C	626	7.47	B+ / 8.8	17.98%	E / 0.3

Annualized Total Return

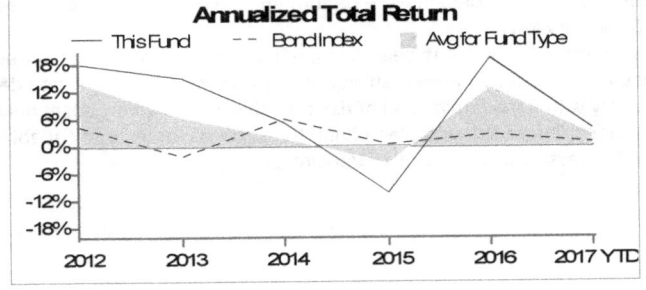

Lord Abbett Bond Debenture A (LBNDX)   B-   Good

Fund Family: Lord Abbett Funds   **Phone:** (888) 522-2388
Address: 90 Hudson Street, Jersey City, NJ 07302
Fund Type: COH - Corporate - High Yield

Major Rating Factors: Lord Abbett Bond Debenture A has adopted a very risky asset allocation strategy and currently receives an overall TheStreet Investment Rating of B- (Good). Volatility, as measured by standard deviation, is considered above average for fixed income funds at 5.08. Another risk factor is the fund's below average duration of 4.5 years (i.e. lower interest rate risk). The high level of risk (D, Weak) did however, reward investors with excellent performance.

The fund's performance rating is currently A (Excellent). It has registered an average return of 4.84% over the last three years and is up 2.78% over the last three months. Factored into the performance evaluation is an expense ratio of 0.82% (low) and a 2.3% front-end load that is levied at the time of purchase.

Robert A. Lee has been running the fund for 4 years and currently receives a manager quality ranking of 76 (0=worst, 99=best). If you are comfortable owning a very high risk investment, this fund may be an option.

Services Offered: Automated phone transactions, payroll deductions, an IRA investment plan, a 401K investment plan and a systematic withdrawal plan.

Data Date	Investment Rating	Net Assets ($Mil)	NAV	Performance Rating/Pts	Total Return Y-T-D	Risk Rating/Pts
2-17	B-	4,173	8.09	A / 9.3	2.78%	D / 1.6
2016	C+	4,266	7.93	A- / 9.1	12.35%	D / 1.6
2015	C-	4,175	7.40	C+ / 6.9	-1.74%	D / 2.0
2014	C+	4,513	7.93	B+ / 8.3	4.52%	D+ / 2.4
2013	C+	4,771	8.15	A- / 9.1	7.79%	D- / 1.4
2012	D	4,840	8.14	B- / 7.1	13.22%	D- / 1.3

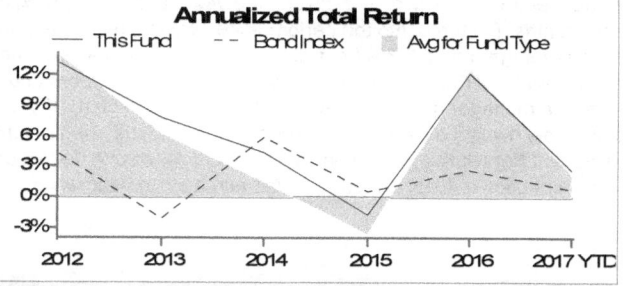

Lord Abbett Floating Rate A (LFRAX)   A+   Excellent

Fund Family: Lord Abbett Funds   **Phone:** (888) 522-2388
Address: 90 Hudson Street, Jersey City, NJ 07302
Fund Type: LP - Loan Participation

Major Rating Factors: Strong performance is the major factor driving the A+ (Excellent) TheStreet Investment Rating for Lord Abbett Floating Rate A. The fund currently has a performance rating of B (Good) based on an average return of 3.73% over the last three years and 0.97% over the last three months. Factored into the performance evaluation is an expense ratio of 0.80% (low) and a 2.3% front-end load that is levied at the time of purchase.

The fund's risk rating is currently B- (Good). Volatility, as measured by standard deviation, is considered low for fixed income funds at 2.61. Another risk factor is the fund's very low average duration of 0.5 years (i.e. low interest rate risk).

Jeffrey D. Lapin has been running the fund for 5 years and currently receives a manager quality ranking of 92 (0=worst, 99=best). If you desire only a moderate level of risk and strong performance, then this fund is an excellent option.

Services Offered: Automated phone transactions, payroll deductions, bank draft capabilities, a 401K investment plan, wire transfers and a systematic withdrawal plan.

Data Date	Investment Rating	Net Assets ($Mil)	NAV	Performance Rating/Pts	Total Return Y-T-D	Risk Rating/Pts
2-17	A+	3,523	9.26	B / 7.7	0.97%	B- / 7.3
2016	A+	3,341	9.24	B / 7.8	9.89%	B- / 7.5
2015	B	2,270	8.80	C+ / 6.2	0.35%	B- / 7.5
2014	A-	2,600	9.16	C / 5.4	0.93%	B / 8.0
2013	A-	3,595	9.50	B / 7.9	5.89%	C / 4.9
2012	E+	1,449	9.41	C- / 4.2	10.12%	D+ / 2.9

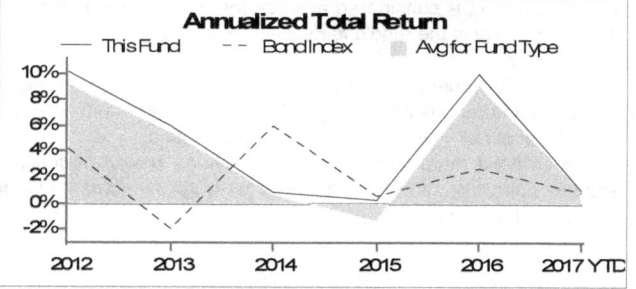

Lord Abbett High Yield A (LHYAX)   B-   Good

Fund Family: Lord Abbett Funds   **Phone:** (888) 522-2388
Address: 90 Hudson Street, Jersey City, NJ 07302
Fund Type: COH - Corporate - High Yield

Major Rating Factors: Lord Abbett High Yield A has adopted a very risky asset allocation strategy and currently receives an overall TheStreet Investment Rating of B- (Good). Volatility, as measured by standard deviation, is considered above average for fixed income funds at 5.64. Another risk factor is the fund's below average duration of 4.4 years (i.e. lower interest rate risk). The high level of risk (D-, Weak) did however, reward investors with excellent performance.

The fund's performance rating is currently A+ (Excellent). It has registered an average return of 5.57% over the last three years and is up 3.12% over the last three months. Factored into the performance evaluation is an expense ratio of 0.94% (average) and a 2.3% front-end load that is levied at the time of purchase.

Steven F. Rocco has been running the fund for 7 years and currently receives a manager quality ranking of 78 (0=worst, 99=best). If you are comfortable owning a very high risk investment, this fund may be an option.

Services Offered: Automated phone transactions, payroll deductions, an IRA investment plan, a 401K investment plan and a systematic withdrawal plan.

Data Date	Investment Rating	Net Assets ($Mil)	NAV	Performance Rating/Pts	Total Return Y-T-D	Risk Rating/Pts
2-17	B-	1,673	7.67	A+ / 9.7	3.12%	D- / 1.1
2016	C+	1,783	7.51	A+ / 9.6	15.84%	D- / 1.2
2015	D+	965	6.89	C+ / 6.7	-2.26%	D / 1.6
2014	C+	842	7.46	B+ / 8.7	3.47%	D / 2.0
2013	B-	870	7.81	A+ / 9.8	9.70%	D- / 1.1
2012	C+	752	7.85	B+ / 8.8	16.51%	E+ / 0.8

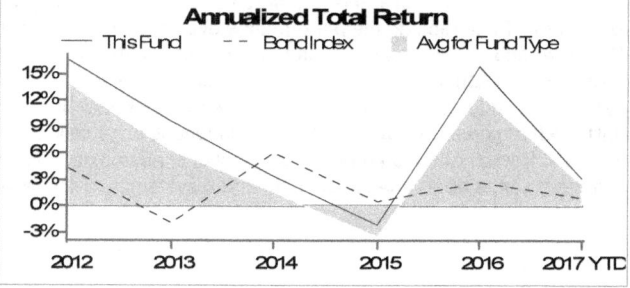

Lord Abbett Income A (LAGVX)

C   **Fair**

Fund Family: Lord Abbett Funds   **Phone:** (888) 522-2388
Address: 90 Hudson Street, Jersey City, NJ 07302
Fund Type: COI - Corporate - Investment Grade

Major Rating Factors: Lord Abbett Income A has adopted a risky asset allocation strategy and currently receives an overall TheStreet Investment Rating of C (Fair). Volatility, as measured by standard deviation, is considered above average for fixed income funds at 4.41. Another risk factor is the fund's fairly average duration of 5.7 years (i.e. average interest rate risk). The high level of risk (D+, Weak) did however, reward investors with excellent performance.

The fund's performance rating is currently B (Good). It has registered an average return of 3.84% over the last three years and is up 2.04% over the last three months. Factored into the performance evaluation is an expense ratio of 0.90% (average) and a 2.3% front-end load that is levied at the time of purchase.

Andrew H. O'Brien has been running the fund for 19 years and currently receives a manager quality ranking of 63 (0=worst, 99=best). If you are comfortable owning a high risk investment, this fund may be an option.

Services Offered: Automated phone transactions, payroll deductions, an IRA investment plan, a 401K investment plan and a systematic withdrawal plan.

Data Date	Investment Rating	Net Assets ($Mil)	NAV	Performance Rating/Pts	Total Return Y-T-D	Risk Rating/Pts
2-17	C	890	2.82	B / 7.7	2.04%	D+ / 2.6
2016	C	898	2.78	B- / 7.4	8.73%	D+ / 2.7
2015	D	978	2.66	C- / 3.0	-3.09%	C- / 3.6
2014	B-	1,129	2.87	B- / 7.3	7.23%	C- / 4.1
2013	B	1,024	2.82	B / 7.7	0.28%	C- / 4.2
2012	A-	1,191	3.00	B- / 7.5	12.51%	C / 4.6

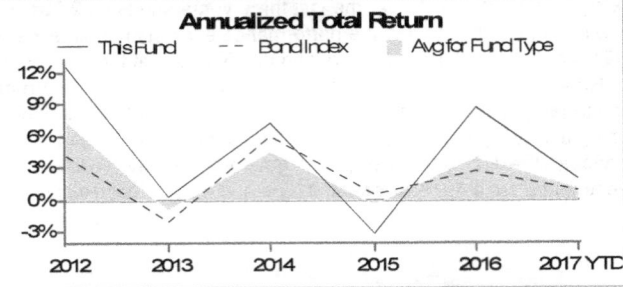

Annualized Total Return

Lord Abbett Interm Tax Free A (LISAX)

D+   **Weak**

Fund Family: Lord Abbett Funds   **Phone:** (888) 522-2388
Address: 90 Hudson Street, Jersey City, NJ 07302
Fund Type: MUN - Municipal - National

Major Rating Factors: Lord Abbett Interm Tax Free A receives a TheStreet Investment Rating of D+ (Weak). The fund has a performance rating of C (Fair) based on an average return of 2.87% over the last three years (4.75% taxable equivalent) and 1.49% over the last three months (2.47% taxable equivalent). Factored into the performance evaluation is an expense ratio of 0.71% (low) and a 2.3% front-end load that is levied at the time of purchase.

The fund's risk rating is currently C (Fair). Volatility, as measured by standard deviation, is considered average for fixed income funds at 3.27. Another risk factor is the fund's fairly average duration of 5.1 years (i.e. average interest rate risk).

Daniel S. Solender has been running the fund for 11 years and currently receives a manager quality ranking of 21 (0=worst, 99=best). If you desire an average level of risk, then this fund may be an option.

Services Offered: Automated phone transactions, payroll deductions, an IRA investment plan, a 401K investment plan, a Keogh investment plan and a systematic withdrawal plan.

Data Date	Investment Rating	Net Assets ($Mil)	NAV	Performance Rating/Pts	Total Return Y-T-D	Risk Rating/Pts
2-17	D+	1,682	10.65	C / 5.2	1.49%	C / 4.6
2016	D+	1,711	10.54	C / 5.0	-0.65%	C / 4.4
2015	B+	1,709	10.88	B+ / 8.6	2.86%	C / 4.9
2014	B+	1,541	10.88	B / 7.6	8.35%	C / 4.9
2013	B-	1,596	10.34	C+ / 6.5	-2.82%	C / 5.2
2012	A-	2,181	11.01	C+ / 6.9	6.40%	C / 5.5

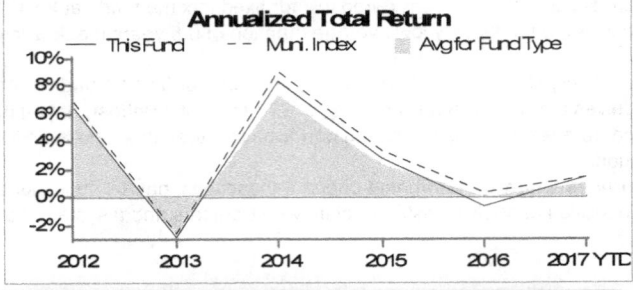

Annualized Total Return

Lord Abbett Shrt Duration Inc A (LALDX)

B+   **Good**

Fund Family: Lord Abbett Funds   **Phone:** (888) 522-2388
Address: 90 Hudson Street, Jersey City, NJ 07302
Fund Type: GEI - General - Investment Grade

Major Rating Factors: A moderate risk profile coupled with stable earnings characterizes Lord Abbett Shrt Duration Inc A which receives a TheStreet Investment Rating of B+ (Good). Volatility, as measured by standard deviation, is considered very low for fixed income funds at 1.29. Another risk factor is the fund's very low average duration of 2.0 years (i.e. low interest rate risk). The fund's risk rating is currently A- (Excellent).

The fund's performance rating is currently C- (Fair). It has registered an average return of 1.98% over the last three years and is up 0.64% over the last three months. Factored into the performance evaluation is an expense ratio of 0.60% (low) and a 2.3% front-end load that is levied at the time of purchase.

Andrew H. O'Brien has been running the fund for 19 years and currently receives a manager quality ranking of 80 (0=worst, 99=best). If you desire stability with a moderate level of risk then this fund is an excellent option.

Services Offered: Automated phone transactions, payroll deductions, an IRA investment plan, a 401K investment plan and a systematic withdrawal plan.

Data Date	Investment Rating	Net Assets ($Mil)	NAV	Performance Rating/Pts	Total Return Y-T-D	Risk Rating/Pts
2-17	B+	10,725	4.31	C- / 4.0	0.64%	A- / 9.0
2016	B	11,002	4.31	C- / 4.1	4.01%	A- / 9.0
2015	B-	11,056	4.31	C / 4.5	0.43%	A- / 9.0
2014	B-	12,594	4.46	C- / 3.3	1.73%	B+ / 8.9
2013	A-	13,132	4.55	C / 4.8	1.62%	B+ / 8.8
2012	C+	11,684	4.65	D+ / 2.7	6.64%	B+ / 8.8

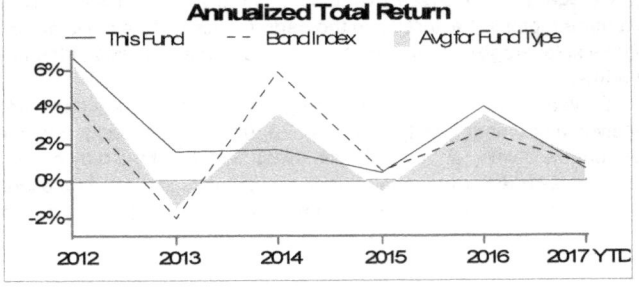

Annualized Total Return

Lord Abbett Shrt Duration Tax-Fr A (LSDAX)   D-   Weak

Fund Family: Lord Abbett Funds   **Phone:** (888) 522-2388
Address: 90 Hudson Street, Jersey City, NJ 07302
Fund Type: MUN - Municipal - National

Major Rating Factors: Very poor performance is the major factor driving the D-(Weak) TheStreet Investment Rating for Lord Abbett Shrt Duration Tax-Fr A. The fund currently has a performance rating of E (Very Weak) based on an average return of 0.54% over the last three years (0.89% taxable equivalent) and 0.90% over the last three months (1.49% taxable equivalent). Factored into the performance evaluation is an expense ratio of 0.70% (low) and a 2.3% front-end load that is levied at the time of purchase.

The fund's risk rating is currently A- (Excellent). Volatility, as measured by standard deviation, is considered very low for fixed income funds at 1.33. Another risk factor is the fund's very low average duration of 2.2 years (i.e. low interest rate risk).

Daniel S. Solender has been running the fund for 9 years and currently receives a manager quality ranking of 15 (0=worst, 99=best). This fund offers only a moderate level of risk but investors looking for strong performance are still waiting.

Services Offered: Automated phone transactions, payroll deductions, bank draft capabilities, an IRA investment plan, a 401K investment plan, wire transfers and a systematic withdrawal plan.

Data Date	Investment Rating	Net Assets ($Mil)	NAV	Performance Rating/Pts	Total Return Y-T-D	Risk Rating/Pts
2-17	D-	875	15.56	E / 0.4	0.90%	A- / 9.0
2016	D	938	15.45	E / 0.5	-0.66%	A- / 9.0
2015	B-	1,078	15.72	C / 4.4	0.71%	A- / 9.2
2014	C	1,255	15.77	D / 2.0	1.58%	A- / 9.2
2013	C+	1,363	15.70	D+ / 2.7	0.02%	A / 9.3
2012	C	1,564	15.91	D- / 1.4	2.16%	A / 9.4

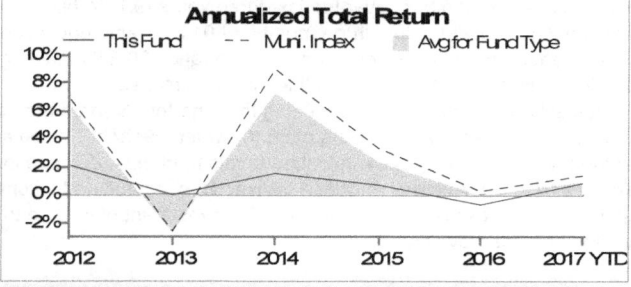

Annualized Total Return

Lord Abbett Tax Free Natl A (LANSX)   B-   Good

Fund Family: Lord Abbett Funds   **Phone:** (888) 522-2388
Address: 90 Hudson Street, Jersey City, NJ 07302
Fund Type: MUN - Municipal - National

Major Rating Factors: Strong performance is the major factor driving the B-(Good) TheStreet Investment Rating for Lord Abbett Tax Free Natl A. The fund currently has a performance rating of B (Good) based on an average return of 4.41% over the last three years (7.30% taxable equivalent) and 1.58% over the last three months (2.62% taxable equivalent). Factored into the performance evaluation is an expense ratio of 0.77% (low) and a 2.3% front-end load that is levied at the time of purchase.

The fund's risk rating is currently C- (Fair). Volatility, as measured by standard deviation, is considered average for fixed income funds at 3.92. Another risk factor is the fund's fairly average duration of 6.4 years (i.e. average interest rate risk).

Daniel S. Solender has been running the fund for 11 years and currently receives a manager quality ranking of 58 (0=worst, 99=best). If you desire an average level of risk and strong performance, then this fund is a good option.

Services Offered: Automated phone transactions, payroll deductions, an IRA investment plan, a 401K investment plan and a systematic withdrawal plan.

Data Date	Investment Rating	Net Assets ($Mil)	NAV	Performance Rating/Pts	Total Return Y-T-D	Risk Rating/Pts
2-17	B-	1,461	11.12	B / 7.9	1.58%	C- / 3.3
2016	B-	1,473	11.01	B+ / 8.4	0.36%	C- / 3.2
2015	C	1,445	11.35	B+ / 8.9	3.28%	D / 2.2
2014	C+	1,440	11.39	A+ / 9.6	12.83%	D- / 1.1
2013	C	1,379	10.49	B / 7.8	-6.11%	D / 2.0
2012	A	1,769	11.62	A+ / 9.7	13.75%	D+ / 2.5

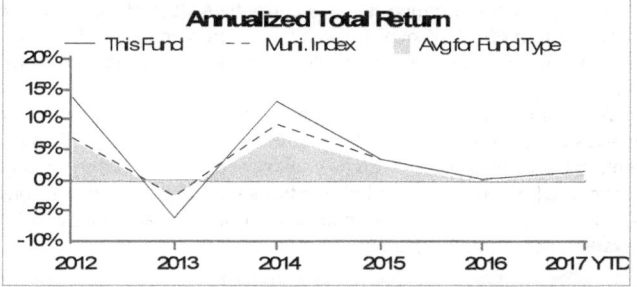

Annualized Total Return

Lord Abbett Total Return A (LTRAX)   C+   Fair

Fund Family: Lord Abbett Funds   **Phone:** (888) 522-2388
Address: 90 Hudson Street, Jersey City, NJ 07302
Fund Type: GEI - General - Investment Grade

Major Rating Factors: Middle of the road best describes Lord Abbett Total Return A whose TheStreet Investment Rating is currently a C+ (Fair). The fund has a performance rating of C (Fair) based on an average return of 2.78% over the last three years and 1.21% over the last three months. Factored into the performance evaluation is an expense ratio of 0.83% (low) and a 2.3% front-end load that is levied at the time of purchase.

The fund's risk rating is currently C+ (Fair). Volatility, as measured by standard deviation, is considered average for fixed income funds at 2.82. Another risk factor is the fund's fairly average duration of 5.4 years (i.e. average interest rate risk).

Andrew H. O'Brien has been running the fund for 19 years and currently receives a manager quality ranking of 62 (0=worst, 99=best). If you desire an average level of risk, then this fund may be an option.

Services Offered: Automated phone transactions, payroll deductions, an IRA investment plan, a 401K investment plan and a systematic withdrawal plan.

Data Date	Investment Rating	Net Assets ($Mil)	NAV	Performance Rating/Pts	Total Return Y-T-D	Risk Rating/Pts
2-17	C+	1,292	10.34	C / 4.7	1.21%	C+/ 6.5
2016	C+	1,319	10.26	C / 4.9	4.05%	C+/ 6.6
2015	C-	1,223	10.17	C / 4.3	-0.64%	C+/ 6.5
2014	C+	959	10.55	C / 5.0	6.12%	C+/ 6.6
2013	B-	829	10.30	C / 5.0	-1.40%	B- / 7.2
2012	B+	959	10.77	C / 4.6	7.73%	B / 8.0

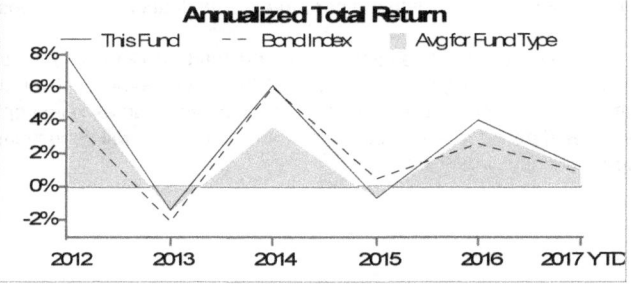

Annualized Total Return

Lord Abbett Tx Fr High Yld Muni A (HYMAX)

B+   **Good**

Fund Family: Lord Abbett Funds   **Phone:** (888) 522-2388
Address: 90 Hudson Street, Jersey City, NJ 07302
Fund Type: MUH - Municipal - High Yield
Major Rating Factors: Lord Abbett Tx Fr High Yld Muni A has adopted a risky asset allocation strategy and currently receives an overall TheStreet Investment Rating of B+ (Good). Volatility, as measured by standard deviation, is considered above average for fixed income funds at 3.98. Another risk factor is the fund's above average duration of 7.4 years (i.e. higher interest rate risk). The high level of risk (D+, Weak) did however, reward investors with excellent performance.

The fund's performance rating is currently A+ (Excellent). It has registered an average return of 5.90% over the last three years (9.77% taxable equivalent) and is up 2.42% over the last three months (4.01% taxable equivalent). Factored into the performance evaluation is an expense ratio of 0.87% (average) and a 2.3% front-end load that is levied at the time of purchase.

Daniel S. Solender has been running the fund for 13 years and currently receives a manager quality ranking of 85 (0=worst, 99=best). If you are comfortable owning a high risk investment, this fund may be an option.
Services Offered: Automated phone transactions, payroll deductions, bank draft capabilities, an IRA investment plan, a 401K investment plan, wire transfers and a systematic withdrawal plan.

Data Date	Investment Rating	Net Assets ($Mil)	NAV	Perfor- mance Rating/Pts	Total Return Y-T-D	Risk Rating/Pts
2-17	B+	1,128	11.63	A+ / 9.7	2.42%	D+ / 2.3
2016	B+	1,100	11.44	A+ / 9.8	2.64%	D / 2.2
2015	C-	1,139	11.64	A- / 9.2	3.66%	E+ / 0.6
2014	C+	1,165	11.76	A+ / 9.8	14.50%	E+ / 0.6
2013	D-	982	10.77	C / 5.5	-6.99%	D- / 1.0
2012	A-	1,250	12.16	A+ / 9.7	17.99%	D / 2.1

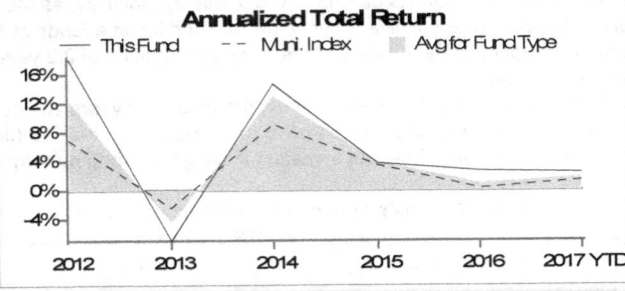

MainStay High Yield Corp Bond C (MYHCX)

C+   **Fair**

Fund Family: MainStay Funds   **Phone:** (800) 624-6782
Address: 51 Madison Avenue, New York, NY 10010
Fund Type: COH - Corporate - High Yield
Major Rating Factors: MainStay High Yield Corp Bond C has adopted a very risky asset allocation strategy and currently receives an overall TheStreet Investment Rating of C+ (Fair). Volatility, as measured by standard deviation, is considered above average for fixed income funds at 5.14. Another risk factor is the fund's below average duration of 3.5 years (i.e. lower interest rate risk). The high level of risk (D, Weak) did however, reward investors with excellent performance.

The fund's performance rating is currently A- (Excellent). It has registered an average return of 3.92% over the last three years and is up 2.31% over the last three months. Factored into the performance evaluation is an expense ratio of 1.77% (high).

Andrew M. Susser has been running the fund for 4 years and currently receives a manager quality ranking of 38 (0=worst, 99=best). If you are comfortable owning a very high risk investment, this fund may be an option.
Services Offered: Automated phone transactions, payroll deductions, bank draft capabilities, an IRA investment plan, a 401K investment plan, wire transfers and a systematic withdrawal plan.

Data Date	Investment Rating	Net Assets ($Mil)	NAV	Perfor- mance Rating/Pts	Total Return Y-T-D	Risk Rating/Pts
2-17	C+	744	5.79	A- / 9.2	2.31%	D / 1.6
2016	C+	670	5.71	A- / 9.2	14.66%	D / 1.6
2015	D	610	5.27	C- / 3.1	-2.52%	D+ / 2.6
2014	C-	746	5.71	C+ / 6.0	0.49%	C- / 3.9
2013	B+	808	6.02	A- / 9.0	5.31%	C- / 3.1
2012	C	832	6.08	B- / 7.5	12.19%	D+ / 2.3

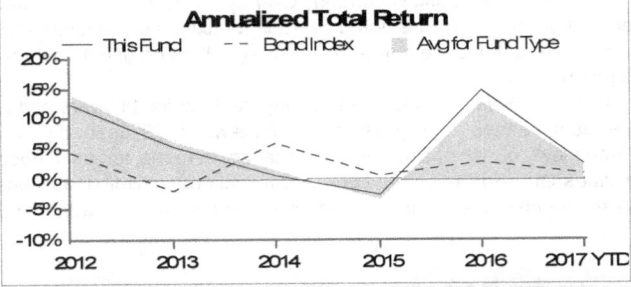

Manning & Napier Unconstrained Bd S (EXCPX)

B+   **Good**

Fund Family: Manning & Napier Funds   **Phone:** (800) 466-3863
Address: 290 Woodcliff Drive, Fairport, NY 14450
Fund Type: COI - Corporate - Investment Grade
Major Rating Factors: A moderate risk profile coupled with stable earnings characterizes Manning & Napier Unconstrained Bd S which receives a TheStreet Investment Rating of B+ (Good). Volatility, as measured by standard deviation, is considered low for fixed income funds at 2.02. The fund's risk rating is currently B (Good).

The fund's performance rating is currently C (Fair). It has registered an average return of 1.77% over the last three years and is up 0.97% over the last three months. Factored into the performance evaluation is an expense ratio of 0.77% (low).

R. Keith Harwood has been running the fund for 12 years and currently receives a manager quality ranking of 57 (0=worst, 99=best). If you desire stability with a moderate level of risk then this fund is an excellent option.
Services Offered: Automated phone transactions, payroll deductions, bank draft capabilities and wire transfers.

Data Date	Investment Rating	Net Assets ($Mil)	NAV	Perfor- mance Rating/Pts	Total Return Y-T-D	Risk Rating/Pts
2-17	B+	835	10.43	C / 4.8	0.97%	B / 8.2
2016	B+	845	10.33	C / 5.0	4.08%	B / 8.2
2015	C-	835	10.12	C / 4.4	-0.88%	C+ / 6.3
2014	C	680	10.53	C / 5.5	3.18%	C / 5.2
2013	B-	654	10.65	B- / 7.0	-0.02%	C / 4.6
2012	B	631	11.27	C+ / 6.8	10.94%	C / 4.7

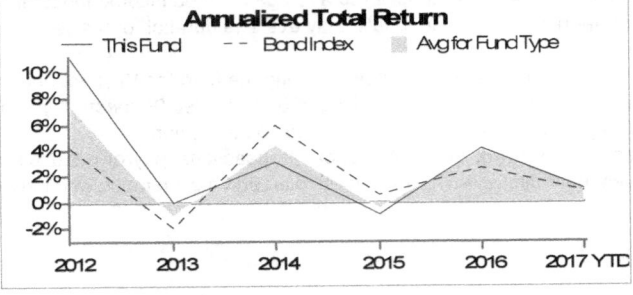

Metropolitan West Low Dur Bd M (MWLDX)   B-   Good

Fund Family: Metropolitan West Fund   **Phone:** (800) 496-8298
Address: 11766 Wilshire Boulevard, Los Angeles, CA 90025
Fund Type: GEI - General - Investment Grade

Major Rating Factors: Disappointing performance is the major factor driving the B- (Good) TheStreet Investment Rating for Metropolitan West Low Dur Bd M. The fund currently has a performance rating of D+ (Weak) based on an average return of 0.86% over the last three years and 0.30% over the last three months. Factored into the performance evaluation is an expense ratio of 0.62% (low).

The fund's risk rating is currently A+ (Excellent). Volatility, as measured by standard deviation, is considered very low for fixed income funds at 0.50. Another risk factor is the fund's very low average duration of 1.4 years (i.e. low interest rate risk).

Stephen M. Kane has been running the fund for 20 years and currently receives a manager quality ranking of 63 (0=worst, 99=best). This fund offers only a moderate level of risk but investors looking for strong performance are still waiting.

Services Offered: Automated phone transactions, check writing, payroll deductions, bank draft capabilities and a systematic withdrawal plan.

Data Date	Investment Rating	Net Assets ($Mil)	NAV	Performance Rating/Pts	Total Return Y-T-D	Risk Rating/Pts
2-17	B-	1,302	8.72	D+ / 2.6	0.30%	A+ / 9.8
2016	B-	1,323	8.71	D+ / 2.8	1.23%	A+ / 9.8
2015	A	1,515	8.72	C+ / 5.8	0.21%	A / 9.5
2014	B+	1,991	8.80	C / 4.3	1.39%	B+ / 8.9
2013	A	1,858	8.79	C / 5.4	1.92%	B+ / 8.8
2012	B	1,128	8.79	C- / 4.1	7.54%	B / 7.9

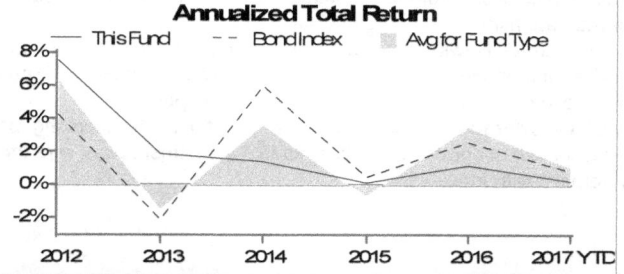

Annualized Total Return

Metropolitan West Tot Ret Bond M (MWTRX)   B-   Good

Fund Family: Metropolitan West Fund   **Phone:** (800) 496-8298
Address: 11766 Wilshire Boulevard, Los Angeles, CA 90025
Fund Type: GEI - General - Investment Grade

Major Rating Factors: A moderate risk profile coupled with stable earnings characterizes Metropolitan West Tot Ret Bond M which receives a TheStreet Investment Rating of B- (Good). Volatility, as measured by standard deviation, is considered low for fixed income funds at 2.53. Another risk factor is the fund's below average duration of 4.9 years (i.e. lower interest rate risk). The fund's risk rating is currently B- (Good).

The fund's performance rating is currently C (Fair). It has registered an average return of 2.34% over the last three years and is up 0.86% over the last three months. Factored into the performance evaluation is an expense ratio of 0.67% (low).

Stephen M. Kane has been running the fund for 20 years and currently receives a manager quality ranking of 49 (0=worst, 99=best). If you desire stability with a moderate level of risk then this fund is an excellent option.

Services Offered: Automated phone transactions, check writing, payroll deductions, bank draft capabilities and a systematic withdrawal plan.

Data Date	Investment Rating	Net Assets ($Mil)	NAV	Performance Rating/Pts	Total Return Y-T-D	Risk Rating/Pts
2-17	B-	15,316	10.60	C / 4.4	0.86%	B- / 7.5
2016	B-	15,535	10.54	C / 4.7	2.32%	B- / 7.5
2015	B	16,048	10.62	C+ / 6.9	-0.04%	C+ / 6.9
2014	A+	14,117	10.91	B- / 7.3	5.83%	C+ / 6.5
2013	A+	10,074	10.55	B- / 7.3	0.20%	B- / 7.1
2012	A+	10,124	10.90	B- / 7.4	11.41%	C+ / 6.7

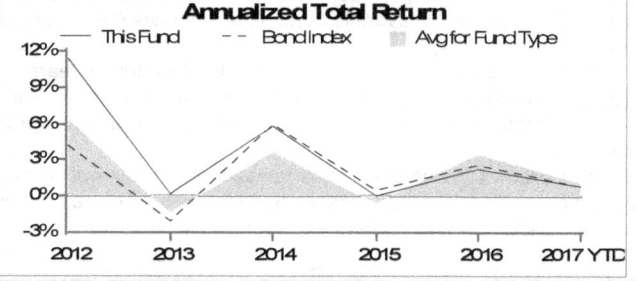

Annualized Total Return

Metropolitan West Uncons Bond M (MWCRX)   A+   Excellent

Fund Family: Metropolitan West Fund   **Phone:** (800) 496-8298
Address: 11766 Wilshire Boulevard, Los Angeles, CA 90025
Fund Type: GEL - General - Long Term

Major Rating Factors: A moderate risk profile coupled with stable earnings characterizes Metropolitan West Uncons Bond M which receives a TheStreet Investment Rating of A+ (Excellent). Volatility, as measured by standard deviation, is considered very low for fixed income funds at 0.96. Another risk factor is the fund's very low average duration of 1.4 years (i.e. low interest rate risk). The fund's risk rating is currently A (Excellent).

The fund's performance rating is currently C (Fair). It has registered an average return of 2.20% over the last three years and is up 0.92% over the last three months. Factored into the performance evaluation is an expense ratio of 1.05% (average).

Stephen M. Kane has been running the fund for 6 years and currently receives a manager quality ranking of 84 (0=worst, 99=best). If you desire stability with a moderate level of risk then this fund is an excellent option.

Services Offered: Automated phone transactions, payroll deductions, bank draft capabilities, an IRA investment plan, a 401K investment plan, wire transfers and a systematic withdrawal plan.

Data Date	Investment Rating	Net Assets ($Mil)	NAV	Performance Rating/Pts	Total Return Y-T-D	Risk Rating/Pts
2-17	A+	1,432	11.89	C / 5.3	0.92%	A / 9.3
2016	A	823	11.82	C / 5.2	3.50%	A / 9.3
2015	A+	866	11.71	C+ / 6.9	-0.04%	B+ / 8.7
2014	A+	463	11.93	B / 7.9	3.36%	C+ / 6.8
2013	U	266	11.76	U / --	2.87%	U / --
2012	U	64	11.74	U / --	15.78%	U / --

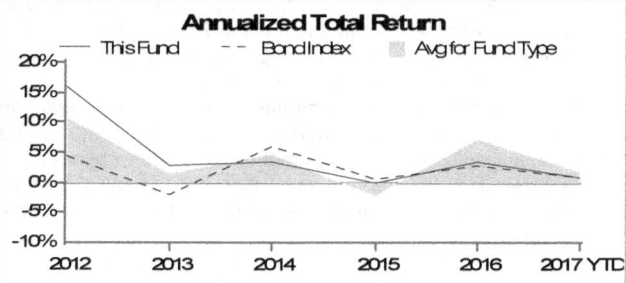

Annualized Total Return

MFS Corporate Bond A (MFBFX)

D   Weak

Fund Family: MFS Funds
Phone: (800) 225-2606
Address: P.O. Box 55824, Boston, MA 02205
Fund Type: GEI - General - Investment Grade

Major Rating Factors: MFS Corporate Bond A receives a TheStreet Investment Rating of D (Weak). The fund has a performance rating of C (Fair) based on an average return of 3.31% over the last three years and 1.52% over the last three months. Factored into the performance evaluation is an expense ratio of 0.82% (low) and a 4.3% front-end load that is levied at the time of purchase.

The fund's risk rating is currently C- (Fair). Volatility, as measured by standard deviation, is considered average for fixed income funds at 3.71. Another risk factor is the fund's fairly average duration of 6.8 years (i.e. average interest rate risk).

Richard O. Hawkins has been running the fund for 12 years and currently receives a manager quality ranking of 61 (0=worst, 99=best). If you desire an average level of risk, then this fund may be an option.

Services Offered: Automated phone transactions, check writing, payroll deductions, bank draft capabilities, an IRA investment plan, wire transfers and a systematic withdrawal plan.

Data Date	Investment Rating	Net Assets ($Mil)	NAV	Performance Rating/Pts	Total Return Y-T-D	Risk Rating/Pts
2-17	D	1,551	13.88	C / 5.0	1.52%	C- / 3.6
2016	D	1,709	13.75	C / 5.1	5.81%	C- / 3.8
2015	D+	1,548	13.42	C- / 3.9	-0.36%	C / 4.3
2014	C+	1,500	13.98	C+ / 6.6	5.69%	C / 4.8
2013	C	1,463	13.71	C+ / 5.7	-0.51%	C / 4.6
2012	C+	1,746	14.29	C+ / 6.1	10.44%	C / 4.5

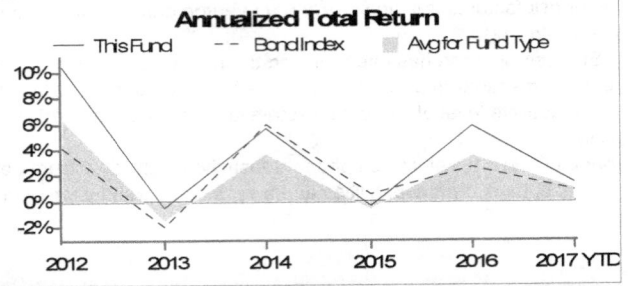

Annualized Total Return

MFS Government Securities Fund A (MFGSX)

E+   Very Weak

Fund Family: MFS Funds
Phone: (800) 225-2606
Address: P.O. Box 55824, Boston, MA 02205
Fund Type: USS - US Government - Short & Inter. Term

Major Rating Factors: Very poor performance is the major factor driving the E+ (Very Weak) TheStreet Investment Rating for MFS Government Securities Fund A. The fund currently has a performance rating of E (Very Weak) based on an average return of 1.42% over the last three years and 0.64% over the last three months. Factored into the performance evaluation is an expense ratio of 0.88% (average) and a 4.3% front-end load that is levied at the time of purchase.

The fund's risk rating is currently B- (Good). Volatility, as measured by standard deviation, is considered low for fixed income funds at 2.56. Another risk factor is the fund's below average duration of 4.5 years (i.e. lower interest rate risk).

Geoffrey L. Schechter has been running the fund for 11 years and currently receives a manager quality ranking of 35 (0=worst, 99=best). This fund offers only a moderate level of risk but investors looking for strong performance are still waiting.

Services Offered: Automated phone transactions, check writing, payroll deductions, bank draft capabilities, an IRA investment plan, a 401K investment plan, wire transfers and a systematic withdrawal plan.

Data Date	Investment Rating	Net Assets ($Mil)	NAV	Performance Rating/Pts	Total Return Y-T-D	Risk Rating/Pts
2-17	E+	684	9.84	E / 0.4	0.64%	B- / 7.4
2016	D-	701	9.82	E+ / 0.7	0.52%	B- / 7.4
2015	C-	690	9.99	D / 2.2	0.27%	B / 7.6
2014	C-	692	10.16	D+ / 2.7	4.63%	B / 7.7
2013	D-	696	9.92	E / 0.5	-2.96%	B / 7.9
2012	D-	888	10.48	D- / 1.3	2.08%	B / 7.6

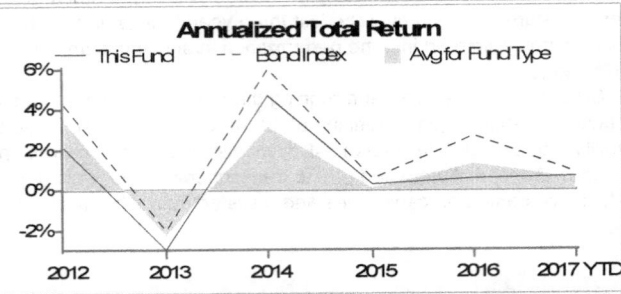

Annualized Total Return

MFS Municipal High Income A (MMHYX)

B+   Good

Fund Family: MFS Funds
Phone: (800) 225-2606
Address: P.O. Box 55824, Boston, MA 02205
Fund Type: MUH - Municipal - High Yield

Major Rating Factors: MFS Municipal High Income A has adopted a risky asset allocation strategy and currently receives an overall TheStreet Investment Rating of B+ (Good). Volatility, as measured by standard deviation, is considered above average for fixed income funds at 3.86. Another risk factor is the fund's fairly average duration of 6.9 years (i.e. average interest rate risk). The high level of risk (D+, Weak) did however, reward investors with excellent performance.

The fund's performance rating is currently A (Excellent). It has registered an average return of 6.12% over the last three years (10.13% taxable equivalent) and is up 1.64% over the last three months (2.72% taxable equivalent). Factored into the performance evaluation is an expense ratio of 0.71% (low) and a 4.3% front-end load that is levied at the time of purchase.

Geoffrey L. Schechter has been running the fund for 15 years and currently receives a manager quality ranking of 86 (0=worst, 99=best). If you are comfortable owning a high risk investment, this fund may be an option.

Services Offered: Automated phone transactions, payroll deductions, bank draft capabilities, an IRA investment plan, a 401K investment plan and a systematic withdrawal plan.

Data Date	Investment Rating	Net Assets ($Mil)	NAV	Performance Rating/Pts	Total Return Y-T-D	Risk Rating/Pts
2-17	B+	1,646	8.07	A / 9.4	1.64%	D+ / 2.6
2016	B+	1,771	8.00	A+ / 9.9	1.81%	D+ / 2.5
2015	C	1,911	8.19	A / 9.5	5.03%	D- / 1.4
2014	B-	1,527	8.14	A+ / 9.8	14.74%	E+ / 0.9
2013	D+	1,407	7.43	B- / 7.0	-6.02%	D / 1.7
2012	A	2,107	8.31	A+ / 9.7	13.94%	D+ / 2.3

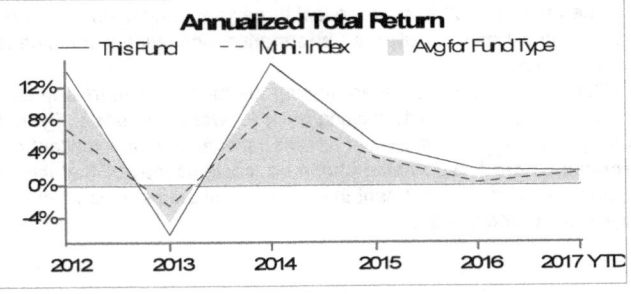

Annualized Total Return

MFS Municipal Income A (MFIAX)   B   Good

Fund Family: MFS Funds
Address: P.O. Box 55824, Boston, MA 02205
Fund Type: MUN - Municipal - National
Phone: (800) 225-2606

Major Rating Factors: Strong performance is the major factor driving the B (Good) TheStreet Investment Rating for MFS Municipal Income A. The fund currently has a performance rating of B- (Good) based on an average return of 4.25% over the last three years (7.04% taxable equivalent) and 1.15% over the last three months (1.90% taxable equivalent). Factored into the performance evaluation is an expense ratio of 0.78% (low) and a 4.3% front-end load that is levied at the time of purchase.

The fund's risk rating is currently C (Fair). Volatility, as measured by standard deviation, is considered average for fixed income funds at 3.12. Another risk factor is the fund's fairly average duration of 5.9 years (i.e. average interest rate risk).

Geoffrey L. Schechter has been running the fund for 19 years and currently receives a manager quality ranking of 74 (0=worst, 99=best). If you desire an average level of risk and strong performance, then this fund is a good option.

Services Offered: Automated phone transactions, check writing, payroll deductions, bank draft capabilities, an IRA investment plan, a 401K investment plan and a systematic withdrawal plan.

Data Date	Investment Rating	Net Assets ($Mil)	NAV	Performance Rating/Pts	Total Return Y-T-D	Risk Rating/Pts
2-17	B	1,225	8.64	B- / 7.1	1.15%	C / 5.0
2016	B	1,293	8.59	B / 7.6	0.99%	C / 4.8
2015	C+	808	8.81	B+ / 8.3	3.33%	C- / 3.6
2014	B+	764	8.83	A / 9.3	10.85%	D+ / 2.6
2013	D+	726	8.25	C+ / 5.9	-4.99%	D+ / 2.9
2012	B	1,009	9.01	B / 7.9	10.46%	C- / 3.0

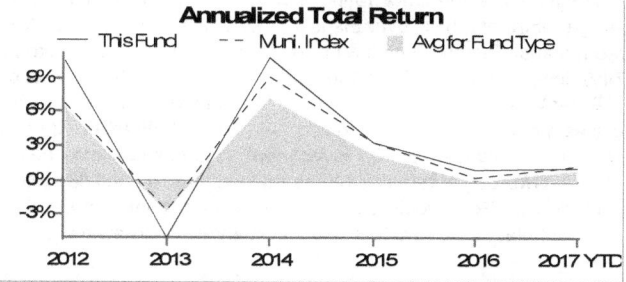

MFS Municipal Lmtd Maturity A (MTLFX)   C-   Fair

Fund Family: MFS Funds
Address: P.O. Box 55824, Boston, MA 02205
Fund Type: MUN - Municipal - National
Phone: (800) 225-2606

Major Rating Factors: Disappointing performance is the major factor driving the C- (Fair) TheStreet Investment Rating for MFS Municipal Lmtd Maturity A. The fund currently has a performance rating of D+ (Weak) based on an average return of 1.45% over the last three years (2.40% taxable equivalent) and 0.95% over the last three months (1.57% taxable equivalent). Factored into the performance evaluation is an expense ratio of 0.80% (low) and a 2.5% front-end load that is levied at the time of purchase.

The fund's risk rating is currently B+ (Good). Volatility, as measured by standard deviation, is considered low for fixed income funds at 1.91. Another risk factor is the fund's below average duration of 3.3 years (i.e. lower interest rate risk).

Geoffrey L. Schechter has been running the fund for 17 years and currently receives a manager quality ranking of 21 (0=worst, 99=best). This fund offers only a moderate level of risk but investors looking for strong performance are still waiting.

Services Offered: Automated phone transactions, check writing, payroll deductions, bank draft capabilities, an IRA investment plan, a 401K investment plan and a systematic withdrawal plan.

Data Date	Investment Rating	Net Assets ($Mil)	NAV	Performance Rating/Pts	Total Return Y-T-D	Risk Rating/Pts
2-17	C-	632	8.07	D+ / 2.4	0.95%	B+ / 8.4
2016	C-	698	8.02	D+ / 2.3	0.05%	B+ / 8.5
2015	A	680	8.17	C+ / 6.5	1.75%	B+ / 8.6
2014	C	677	8.16	C- / 3.0	3.12%	B+ / 8.5
2013	B	706	8.04	C- / 4.0	-0.84%	B+ / 8.6
2012	C+	653	8.25	D+ / 2.5	3.05%	B+ / 8.6

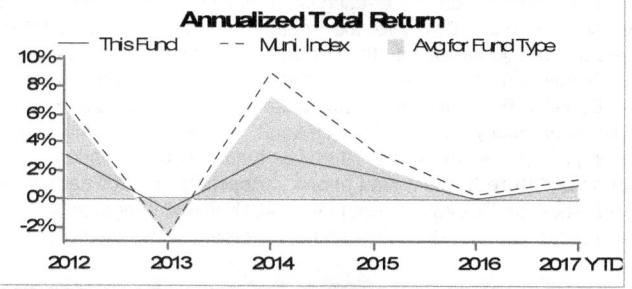

MFS Total Return Bond A (MRBFX)   D+   Weak

Fund Family: MFS Funds
Address: P.O. Box 55824, Boston, MA 02205
Fund Type: GEI - General - Investment Grade
Phone: (800) 225-2606

Major Rating Factors: MFS Total Return Bond A receives a TheStreet Investment Rating of D+ (Weak). The fund has a performance rating of C- (Fair) based on an average return of 2.52% over the last three years and 1.13% over the last three months. Factored into the performance evaluation is an expense ratio of 0.89% (average) and a 4.3% front-end load that is levied at the time of purchase.

The fund's risk rating is currently C+ (Fair). Volatility, as measured by standard deviation, is considered average for fixed income funds at 2.77. Another risk factor is the fund's fairly average duration of 5.4 years (i.e. average interest rate risk).

Robert D. Persons has been running the fund for 11 years and currently receives a manager quality ranking of 52 (0=worst, 99=best). If you desire an average level of risk, then this fund may be an option.

Services Offered: Automated phone transactions, check writing, payroll deductions, bank draft capabilities, an IRA investment plan, a 401K investment plan, wire transfers and a systematic withdrawal plan.

Data Date	Investment Rating	Net Assets ($Mil)	NAV	Performance Rating/Pts	Total Return Y-T-D	Risk Rating/Pts
2-17	D+	1,680	10.64	C- / 3.3	1.13%	C+ / 6.7
2016	C-	1,801	10.57	C- / 3.5	3.54%	C+ / 6.9
2015	C+	1,617	10.50	C+ / 5.7	-0.53%	C+ / 6.6
2014	B	1,380	10.90	C+ / 5.6	5.68%	C+ / 6.8
2013	C	1,076	10.67	C- / 3.8	-1.04%	B- / 7.0
2012	C+	1,090	11.11	C- / 3.8	7.40%	B- / 7.5

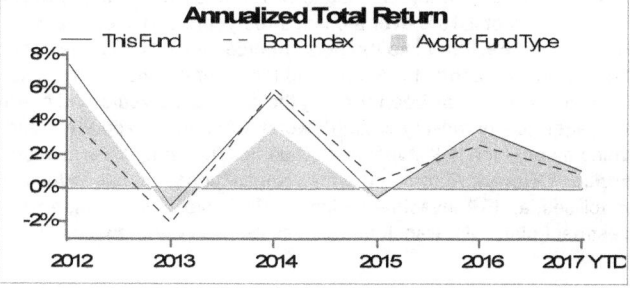

Natixis Loomis Sayles Cor Pl Bd A (NEFRX)

D-   Weak

Fund Family: Natixis Funds   **Phone:** (800) 225-5478

Address: P.O. Box 219579, Kansas City, MO 64121

Fund Type: GEI - General - Investment Grade

Major Rating Factors: Natixis Loomis Sayles Cor Pl Bd A has adopted a risky asset allocation strategy and currently receives an overall TheStreet Investment Rating of D- (Weak). Volatility, as measured by standard deviation, is considered above average for fixed income funds at 4.11. Another risk factor is the fund's fairly average duration of 6.3 years (i.e. average interest rate risk). Unfortunately, the high level of risk (D+, Weak) has only provided investors with average performance.

The fund's performance rating is currently C (Fair). It has registered an average return of 2.51% over the last three years and is up 1.67% over the last three months. Factored into the performance evaluation is an expense ratio of 0.74% (low) and a 4.3% front-end load that is levied at the time of purchase.

Peter W. Palfrey has been running the fund for 21 years and currently receives a manager quality ranking of 38 (0=worst, 99=best). If you are comfortable owning a high risk investment, then this fund may be an option.

Services Offered: Automated phone transactions, payroll deductions, bank draft capabilities, an IRA investment plan, a 401K investment plan, a Keogh investment plan, wire transfers and a systematic withdrawal plan.

Data Date	Investment Rating	Net Assets ($Mil)	NAV	Performance Rating/Pts	Total Return Y-T-D	Risk Rating/Pts
2-17	D-	740	12.82	C / 4.4	1.67%	D+ / 2.9
2016	D-	743	12.66	C / 4.6	7.19%	C- / 3.0
2015	D	809	12.19	D- / 1.3	-4.20%	C- / 3.1
2014	D+	851	13.04	C / 5.5	6.18%	C- / 3.9
2013	C+	418	12.76	C+ / 6.4	-0.82%	C / 4.4
2012	A-	559	13.39	C+ / 6.7	11.31%	C+ / 5.7

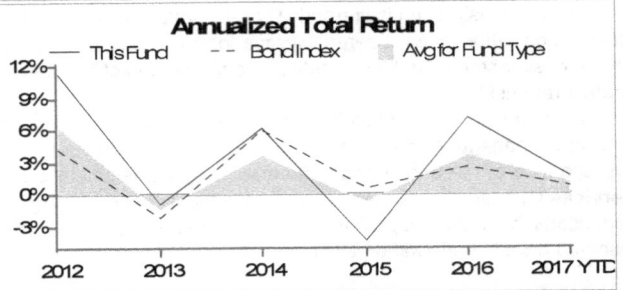

Natixis Loomis Sayles Invst Gr Bd A (LIGRX)

E+   Very Weak

Fund Family: Natixis Funds   **Phone:** (800) 225-5478

Address: P.O. Box 219579, Kansas City, MO 64121

Fund Type: GEI - General - Investment Grade

Major Rating Factors: Natixis Loomis Sayles Invst Gr Bd A has adopted a risky asset allocation strategy and currently receives an overall TheStreet Investment Rating of E+ (Very Weak). Volatility, as measured by standard deviation, is considered above average for fixed income funds at 4.44. Another risk factor is the fund's below average duration of 4.0 years (i.e. lower interest rate risk). Unfortunately, the high level of risk (D+, Weak) has only provided investors with average performance.

The fund's performance rating is currently C- (Fair). It has registered an average return of 1.63% over the last three years and is up 2.21% over the last three months. Factored into the performance evaluation is an expense ratio of 0.83% (low) and a 4.3% front-end load that is levied at the time of purchase.

Daniel J. Fuss has been running the fund for 21 years and currently receives a manager quality ranking of 31 (0=worst, 99=best). If you are comfortable owning a high risk investment, then this fund may be an option.

Services Offered: Automated phone transactions, payroll deductions, bank draft capabilities, an IRA investment plan, a 401K investment plan, a Keogh investment plan, wire transfers and a systematic withdrawal plan.

Data Date	Investment Rating	Net Assets ($Mil)	NAV	Performance Rating/Pts	Total Return Y-T-D	Risk Rating/Pts
2-17	E+	955	10.99	C- / 3.6	2.21%	D+ / 2.5
2016	E+	958	10.79	D+ / 2.8	5.99%	D+ / 2.6
2015	D-	1,432	10.84	D- / 1.2	-5.33%	D+ / 2.8
2014	D	1,983	11.86	C+ / 5.6	4.88%	D+ / 2.8
2013	C-	2,358	11.89	C+ / 6.7	1.02%	D+ / 2.7
2012	C-	3,024	12.62	C+ / 6.5	11.98%	D+ / 2.7

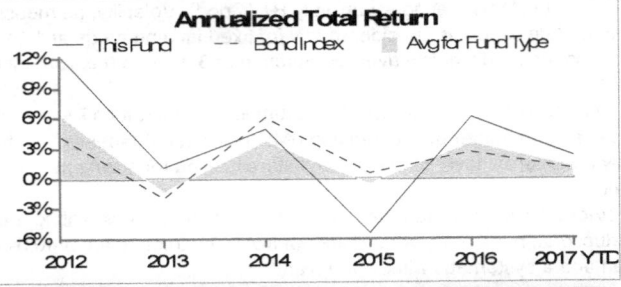

Natixis Loomis Sayles Strat Inc A (NEFZX)

D-   Weak

Fund Family: Natixis Funds   **Phone:** (800) 225-5478

Address: P.O. Box 219579, Kansas City, MO 64121

Fund Type: GEL - General - Long Term

Major Rating Factors: Natixis Loomis Sayles Strat Inc A has adopted a very risky asset allocation strategy and currently receives an overall TheStreet Investment Rating of D- (Weak). Volatility, as measured by standard deviation, is considered above average for fixed income funds at 6.38. Another risk factor is the fund's below average duration of 3.3 years (i.e. lower interest rate risk). Unfortunately, the high level of risk (D-, Weak) has only provided investors with average performance.

The fund's performance rating is currently C+ (Fair). It has registered an average return of 2.19% over the last three years and is up 3.26% over the last three months. Factored into the performance evaluation is an expense ratio of 0.94% (average) and a 4.3% front-end load that is levied at the time of purchase.

Daniel J. Fuss has been running the fund for 22 years and currently receives a manager quality ranking of 73 (0=worst, 99=best). If you are comfortable owning a very high risk investment, then this fund may be an option.

Services Offered: Automated phone transactions, payroll deductions, bank draft capabilities, an IRA investment plan, a 401K investment plan, a Keogh investment plan, wire transfers and a systematic withdrawal plan.

Data Date	Investment Rating	Net Assets ($Mil)	NAV	Performance Rating/Pts	Total Return Y-T-D	Risk Rating/Pts
2-17	D-	2,229	14.50	C+ / 6.4	3.26%	D- / 1.0
2016	E+	2,259	14.12	C- / 3.9	8.27%	E+ / 0.9
2015	D-	2,875	13.67	D+ / 2.7	-7.64%	E+ / 0.7
2014	C	4,433	16.29	B+ / 8.7	5.65%	D- / 1.0
2013	C+	5,601	16.36	A+ / 9.6	10.87%	E+ / 0.6
2012	D	5,068	15.47	B- / 7.3	13.56%	E+ / 0.8

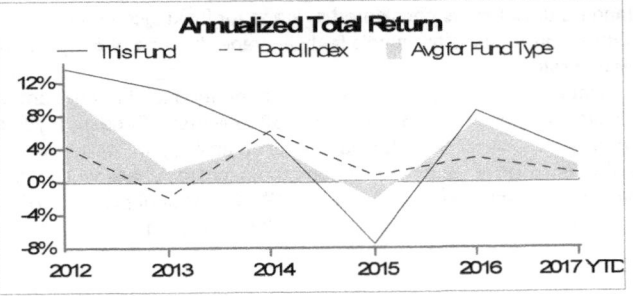

Northern Bond Index (NOBOX)   C-   Fair

Fund Family: Northern Funds   **Phone:** (800) 595-9111
Address: PO Box 75986, Chicago, IL 60675
Fund Type: MTG - Mortgage
Major Rating Factors: Middle of the road best describes Northern Bond Index whose TheStreet Investment Rating is currently a C- (Fair). The fund has a performance rating of C (Fair) based on an average return of 2.50% over the last three years and 0.92% over the last three months. Factored into the performance evaluation is an expense ratio of 0.18% (very low).

The fund's risk rating is currently C+ (Fair). Volatility, as measured by standard deviation, is considered average for fixed income funds at 2.94. Another risk factor is the fund's fairly average duration of 5.4 years (i.e. average interest rate risk).

Louis R. D'Arienzo has been running the fund for 10 years and currently receives a manager quality ranking of 17 (0=worst, 99=best). If you desire an average level of risk, then this fund may be an option.

Services Offered: Automated phone transactions, payroll deductions, bank draft capabilities, an IRA investment plan, a 401K investment plan, wire transfers and a systematic withdrawal plan.

Data Date	Investment Rating	Net Assets ($Mil)	NAV	Performance Rating/Pts	Total Return Y-T-D	Risk Rating/Pts
2-17	C-	2,569	10.51	C / 4.5	0.92%	C+ / 5.8
2016	C	2,618	10.46	C / 4.9	2.33%	C+ / 5.9
2015	C+	2,497	10.50	C+ / 6.2	0.50%	C+ / 6.5
2014	C	2,579	10.74	C- / 4.2	5.93%	B- / 7.0
2013	C	2,232	10.42	C- / 3.8	-2.29%	B- / 7.4
2012	C	2,614	10.96	C- / 3.2	4.05%	B- / 7.2

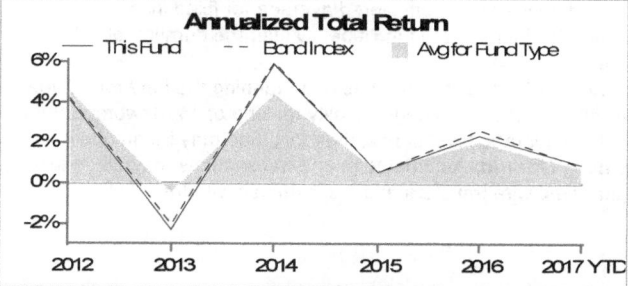

Northern Fixed Income (NOFIX)   C   Fair

Fund Family: Northern Funds   **Phone:** (800) 595-9111
Address: PO Box 75986, Chicago, IL 60675
Fund Type: GL - Global
Major Rating Factors: Middle of the road best describes Northern Fixed Income whose TheStreet Investment Rating is currently a C (Fair). The fund has a performance rating of C (Fair) based on an average return of 2.66% over the last three years and 1.15% over the last three months. Factored into the performance evaluation is an expense ratio of 0.49% (very low).

The fund's risk rating is currently C (Fair). Volatility, as measured by standard deviation, is considered average for fixed income funds at 3.03. Another risk factor is the fund's fairly average duration of 5.4 years (i.e. average interest rate risk).

Bradley Camden has been running the fund for 6 years and currently receives a manager quality ranking of 92 (0=worst, 99=best). If you desire an average level of risk, then this fund may be an option.

Services Offered: Automated phone transactions, payroll deductions, bank draft capabilities, an IRA investment plan, a 401K investment plan, wire transfers and a systematic withdrawal plan.

Data Date	Investment Rating	Net Assets ($Mil)	NAV	Performance Rating/Pts	Total Return Y-T-D	Risk Rating/Pts
2-17	C	1,191	10.17	C / 5.3	1.15%	C / 5.4
2016	C	1,261	10.10	C / 5.5	3.23%	C / 5.5
2015	C	1,380	10.04	C+ / 6.2	-0.16%	C / 5.0
2014	C+	1,945	10.40	C+ / 5.6	6.19%	C+ / 5.6
2013	B	1,534	10.09	C+ / 5.7	-1.49%	C+ / 6.4
2012	B	1,763	10.63	C / 4.5	7.15%	B- / 7.5

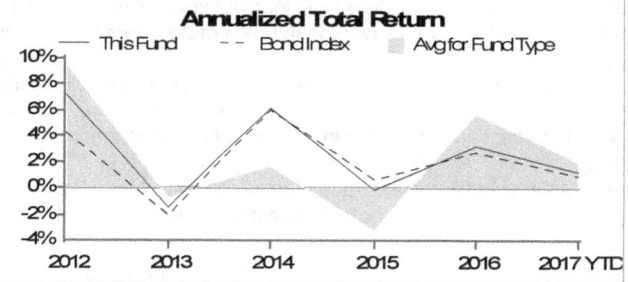

Northern HY Fixed Income (NHFIX)   C   Fair

Fund Family: Northern Funds   **Phone:** (800) 595-9111
Address: PO Box 75986, Chicago, IL 60675
Fund Type: COH - Corporate - High Yield
Major Rating Factors: Northern HY Fixed Income has adopted a very risky asset allocation strategy and currently receives an overall TheStreet Investment Rating of C (Fair). Volatility, as measured by standard deviation, is considered above average for fixed income funds at 5.37. Another risk factor is the fund's below average duration of 4.0 years (i.e. lower interest rate risk). The high level of risk (D-, Weak) did however, reward investors with excellent performance.

The fund's performance rating is currently B+ (Good). It has registered an average return of 3.23% over the last three years and is up 2.46% over the last three months. Factored into the performance evaluation is an expense ratio of 0.82% (low) and a 2.0% back-end load levied at the time of sale.

Richard J. Inzunza has been running the fund for 10 years and currently receives a manager quality ranking of 15 (0=worst, 99=best). If you are comfortable owning a very high risk investment, this fund may be an option.

Services Offered: Bank draft capabilities and a systematic withdrawal plan.

Data Date	Investment Rating	Net Assets ($Mil)	NAV	Performance Rating/Pts	Total Return Y-T-D	Risk Rating/Pts
2-17	C	4,706	6.89	B+ / 8.4	2.46%	D- / 1.3
2016	C-	4,664	6.79	B / 8.0	11.26%	D- / 1.4
2015	D	4,982	6.48	C / 4.5	-3.04%	D / 1.7
2014	C-	4,814	7.08	B / 7.6	2.11%	D / 2.2
2013	C+	5,575	7.49	A / 9.5	7.69%	D- / 1.1
2012	C-	5,926	7.55	B+ / 8.4	15.05%	E+ / 0.6

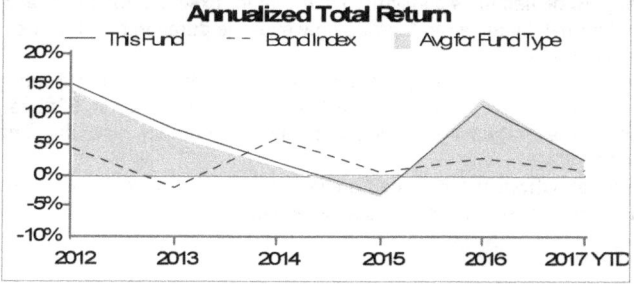

Northern Intermed Tax Exempt (NOITX)

C+ **Fair**

Fund Family: Northern Funds **Phone:** (800) 595-9111
Address: PO Box 75986, Chicago, IL 60675
Fund Type: MUN - Municipal - National

Major Rating Factors: Middle of the road best describes Northern Intermed Tax Exempt whose TheStreet Investment Rating is currently a C+ (Fair). The fund has a performance rating of C+ (Fair) based on an average return of 2.46% over the last three years (4.07% taxable equivalent) and 0.74% over the last three months (1.23% taxable equivalent). Factored into the performance evaluation is an expense ratio of 0.51% (very low).

The fund's risk rating is currently C (Fair). Volatility, as measured by standard deviation, is considered average for fixed income funds at 3.16. Another risk factor is the fund's below average duration of 4.6 years (i.e. lower interest rate risk).

Timothy T. A. McGregor has been running the fund for 19 years and currently receives a manager quality ranking of 14 (0=worst, 99=best). If you desire an average level of risk, then this fund may be an option.

Services Offered: Automated phone transactions, payroll deductions, bank draft capabilities, wire transfers and a systematic withdrawal plan.

Data Date	Investment Rating	Net Assets ($Mil)	NAV	Performance Rating/Pts	Total Return Y-T-D	Risk Rating/Pts
2-17	C+	2,790	10.39	C+ / 6.0	0.74%	C / 4.9
2016	C+	2,843	10.35	C+ / 6.4	-0.08%	C / 4.7
2015	B+	3,079	10.72	B+ / 8.9	2.78%	C / 5.1
2014	B	2,969	10.69	B- / 7.3	6.84%	C / 4.7
2013	B+	2,279	10.24	B / 7.6	-2.23%	C / 4.8
2012	C+	2,449	10.75	C+ / 5.8	5.02%	C / 4.7

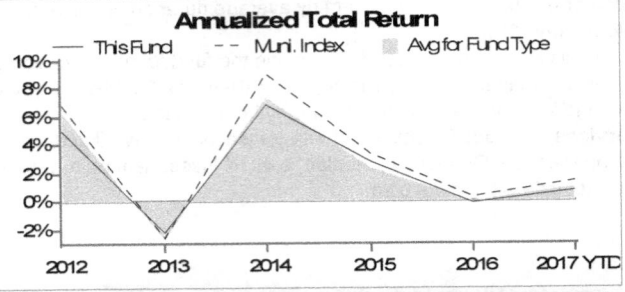

Northern Short-Interm Tax-Ex (NSITX)

C- **Fair**

Fund Family: Northern Funds **Phone:** (800) 595-9111
Address: PO Box 75986, Chicago, IL 60675
Fund Type: MUH - Municipal - High Yield

Major Rating Factors: Disappointing performance is the major factor driving the C- (Fair) TheStreet Investment Rating for Northern Short-Interm Tax-Ex. The fund currently has a performance rating of D+ (Weak) based on an average return of 0.73% over the last three years (1.21% taxable equivalent) and 0.98% over the last three months (1.62% taxable equivalent). Factored into the performance evaluation is an expense ratio of 0.49% (very low).

The fund's risk rating is currently B (Good). Volatility, as measured by standard deviation, is considered low for fixed income funds at 1.54. Another risk factor is the fund's very low average duration of 2.5 years (i.e. low interest rate risk).

Timothy P. Blair has been running the fund for 10 years and currently receives a manager quality ranking of 15 (0=worst, 99=best). This fund offers only a moderate level of risk but investors looking for strong performance are still waiting.

Services Offered: Automated phone transactions, payroll deductions, bank draft capabilities, wire transfers and a systematic withdrawal plan.

Data Date	Investment Rating	Net Assets ($Mil)	NAV	Performance Rating/Pts	Total Return Y-T-D	Risk Rating/Pts
2-17	C-	1,063	10.35	D+ / 2.6	0.98%	B / 8.2
2016	C-	1,057	10.27	D / 2.2	-0.30%	B+ / 8.3
2015	A	1,188	10.44	C+ / 6.7	1.15%	B+ / 8.7
2014	C	1,402	10.45	D+ / 2.4	1.38%	B+ / 8.7
2013	B-	1,216	10.45	C- / 3.5	0.08%	B+ / 8.8
2012	D	1,062	10.60	D- / 1.2	1.25%	B+ / 8.6

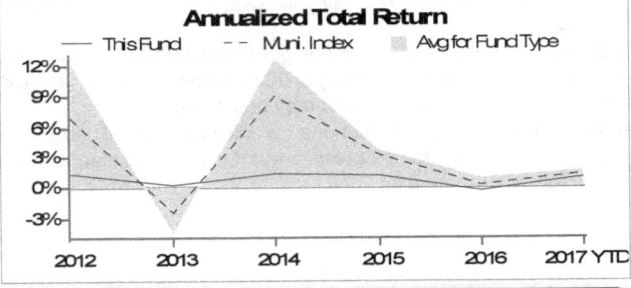

Northern Tax Exempt (NOTEX)

B+ **Good**

Fund Family: Northern Funds **Phone:** (800) 595-9111
Address: PO Box 75986, Chicago, IL 60675
Fund Type: MUN - Municipal - National

Major Rating Factors: Strong performance is the major factor driving the B+ (Good) TheStreet Investment Rating for Northern Tax Exempt. The fund currently has a performance rating of B (Good) based on an average return of 3.80% over the last three years (6.29% taxable equivalent) and 0.80% over the last three months (1.32% taxable equivalent). Factored into the performance evaluation is an expense ratio of 0.49% (very low).

The fund's risk rating is currently C (Fair). Volatility, as measured by standard deviation, is considered average for fixed income funds at 3.36. Another risk factor is the fund's below average duration of 4.7 years (i.e. lower interest rate risk).

Timothy T. A. McGregor has been running the fund for 19 years and currently receives a manager quality ranking of 56 (0=worst, 99=best). If you desire an average level of risk and strong performance, then this fund is a good option.

Services Offered: Automated phone transactions, payroll deductions, bank draft capabilities, wire transfers and a systematic withdrawal plan.

Data Date	Investment Rating	Net Assets ($Mil)	NAV	Performance Rating/Pts	Total Return Y-T-D	Risk Rating/Pts
2-17	B+	1,114	10.56	B / 8.1	0.80%	C / 4.3
2016	A-	1,160	10.53	B+ / 8.9	0.32%	C- / 4.1
2015	B	994	10.81	A / 9.5	3.69%	C- / 3.5
2014	B+	823	10.79	A- / 9.1	10.46%	C- / 3.3
2013	B	808	10.13	B+ / 8.4	-3.65%	C- / 3.5
2012	B	1,211	11.02	B / 7.9	7.93%	C- / 3.2

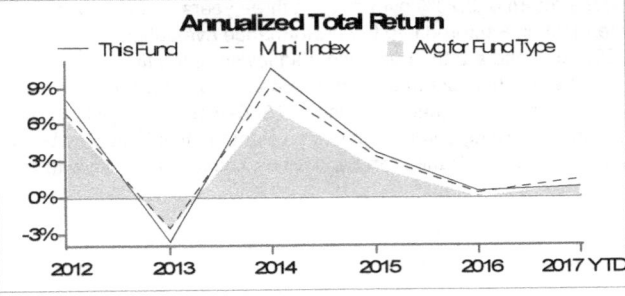

Northern Tax-Advtged Ult-Sh Fxd Inc (NTAUX)   C+   Fair

Fund Family: Northern Funds   **Phone:** (800) 595-9111
Address: PO Box 75986, Chicago, IL 60675
Fund Type: MTG - Mortgage
Major Rating Factors: Disappointing performance is the major factor driving the C+ (Fair) TheStreet Investment Rating for Northern Tax-Advtged Ult-Sh Fxd Inc. The fund currently has a performance rating of D (Weak) based on an average return of 0.61% over the last three years and 0.43% over the last three months. Factored into the performance evaluation is an expense ratio of 0.26% (very low).

    The fund's risk rating is currently A+ (Excellent). Volatility, as measured by standard deviation, is considered very low for fixed income funds at 0.33. Another risk factor is the fund's very low average duration of 0.9 years (i.e. low interest rate risk).

    Patrick Quinn has been running the fund for 8 years and currently receives a manager quality ranking of 58 (0=worst, 99=best). This fund offers only a moderate level of risk but investors looking for strong performance are still waiting.

Services Offered: Automated phone transactions, payroll deductions, bank draft capabilities, wire transfers and a systematic withdrawal plan.

Data Date	Investment Rating	Net Assets ($Mil)	NAV	Performance Rating/Pts	Total Return Y-T-D	Risk Rating/Pts
2-17	C+	3,507	10.14	D / 2.2	0.43%	A+ / 9.9
2016	C+	3,254	10.11	D+ / 2.3	0.83%	A+ / 9.9
2015	B+	3,311	10.11	C / 4.8	0.35%	A+ / 9.9
2014	C	2,904	10.14	D / 1.8	0.52%	A+ / 9.9
2013	C	2,632	10.15	D / 1.8	0.75%	A+ / 9.9
2012	C-	1,827	10.14	E+ / 0.6	1.35%	A+ / 9.9

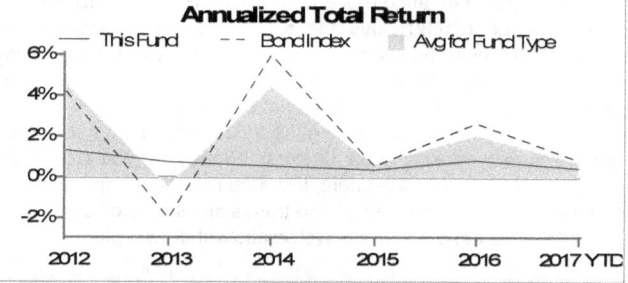

Northern Ultra-Short Fixed Income (NUSFX)   B-   Good

Fund Family: Northern Funds   **Phone:** (800) 595-9111
Address: PO Box 75986, Chicago, IL 60675
Fund Type: GEI - General - Investment Grade
Major Rating Factors: Disappointing performance is the major factor driving the B- (Good) TheStreet Investment Rating for Northern Ultra-Short Fixed Income. The fund currently has a performance rating of D+ (Weak) based on an average return of 0.92% over the last three years and 0.49% over the last three months. Factored into the performance evaluation is an expense ratio of 0.26% (very low).

    The fund's risk rating is currently A+ (Excellent). Volatility, as measured by standard deviation, is considered very low for fixed income funds at 0.51. Another risk factor is the fund's very low average duration of 1.0 years (i.e. low interest rate risk).

    Christina Fletcher has been running the fund for 5 years and currently receives a manager quality ranking of 65 (0=worst, 99=best). This fund offers only a moderate level of risk but investors looking for strong performance are still waiting.

Services Offered: Automated phone transactions, payroll deductions, bank draft capabilities, wire transfers and a systematic withdrawal plan.

Data Date	Investment Rating	Net Assets ($Mil)	NAV	Performance Rating/Pts	Total Return Y-T-D	Risk Rating/Pts
2-17	B-	2,115	10.21	D+ / 2.8	0.49%	A+ / 9.8
2016	B-	2,163	10.18	D+ / 2.8	1.52%	A+ / 9.8
2015	B+	1,570	10.14	C / 4.9	0.51%	A+ / 9.8
2014	C	1,636	10.18	D / 2.0	0.55%	A+ / 9.7
2013	C+	1,450	10.21	D / 2.2	0.77%	A+ / 9.6
2012	C-	944	10.21	E+ / 0.7	2.43%	A+ / 9.8

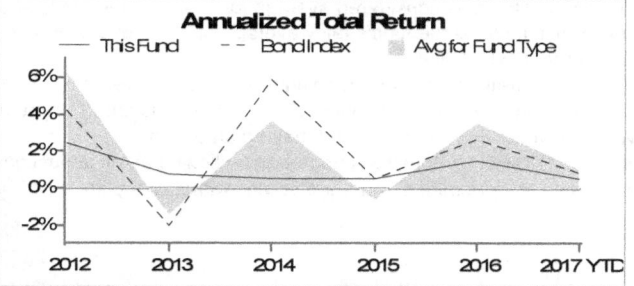

Nuveen All Amer Muni A (FLAAX)   C   Fair

Fund Family: Nuveen Investor Services   **Phone:** (800) 257-8787
Address: P.O. Box 8530, Boston, MA 02266
Fund Type: MUN - Municipal - National
Major Rating Factors: Nuveen All Amer Muni A has adopted a risky asset allocation strategy and currently receives an overall TheStreet Investment Rating of C (Fair). Volatility, as measured by standard deviation, is considered above average for fixed income funds at 3.98. Another risk factor is the fund's above average duration of 7.6 years (i.e. higher interest rate risk). The high level of risk (D+, Weak) did however, reward investors with excellent performance.

    The fund's performance rating is currently B (Good). It has registered an average return of 4.72% over the last three years (7.82% taxable equivalent) and is up 1.51% over the last three months (2.50% taxable equivalent). Factored into the performance evaluation is an expense ratio of 0.70% (low) and a 4.2% front-end load that is levied at the time of purchase.

    John V. Miller has been running the fund for 7 years and currently receives a manager quality ranking of 64 (0=worst, 99=best). If you are comfortable owning a high risk investment, this fund may be an option.

Services Offered: Automated phone transactions, payroll deductions, bank draft capabilities, wire transfers and a systematic withdrawal plan.

Data Date	Investment Rating	Net Assets ($Mil)	NAV	Performance Rating/Pts	Total Return Y-T-D	Risk Rating/Pts
2-17	C	1,273	11.33	B / 7.6	1.51%	D+ / 2.8
2016	C+	1,267	11.23	B / 8.0	0.30%	D+ / 2.7
2015	C+	1,066	11.61	A- / 9.1	3.77%	D+ / 2.9
2014	B-	937	11.63	A / 9.5	13.38%	D / 1.6
2013	C	898	10.70	B / 7.9	-4.75%	D / 2.1
2012	A-	1,195	11.70	A / 9.3	11.30%	D+ / 2.6

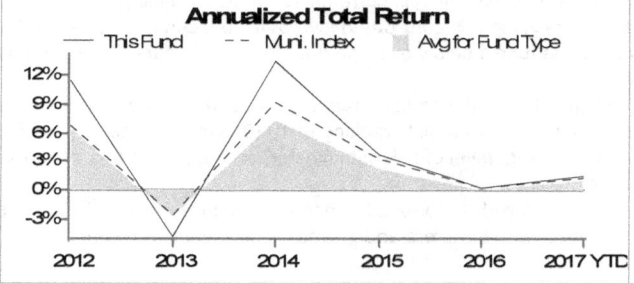

Nuveen High Yield Muni Bond A (NHMAX)

B-   **Good**

Fund Family: Nuveen Investor Services
Phone: (800) 257-8787
Address: P.O. Box 8530, Boston, MA 02266
Fund Type: MUH - Municipal - High Yield
Major Rating Factors: Nuveen High Yield Muni Bond A has adopted a very risky asset allocation strategy and currently receives an overall TheStreet Investment Rating of B- (Good). Volatility, as measured by standard deviation, is considered above average for fixed income funds at 4.93. Another risk factor is the fund's above average duration of 9.4 years (i.e. higher interest rate risk). The high level of risk (D-, Weak) did however, reward investors with excellent performance.

The fund's performance rating is currently A+ (Excellent). It has registered an average return of 6.80% over the last three years (11.26% taxable equivalent) and is up 2.28% over the last three months (3.78% taxable equivalent). Factored into the performance evaluation is an expense ratio of 0.83% (low) and a 4.2% front-end load that is levied at the time of purchase.

John V. Miller has been running the fund for 17 years and currently receives a manager quality ranking of 83 (0=worst, 99=best). If you are comfortable owning a very high risk investment, this fund may be an option.
Services Offered: Automated phone transactions, payroll deductions, bank draft capabilities, wire transfers and a systematic withdrawal plan.

Data Date	Investment Rating	Net Assets ($Mil)	NAV	Performance Rating/Pts	Total Return Y-T-D	Risk Rating/Pts
2-17	B-	4,389	16.68	A+ / 9.7	2.28%	D- / 1.4
2016	B-	4,181	16.46	A+ / 9.8	1.30%	D- / 1.1
2015	C	3,798	17.14	A+ / 9.9	4.83%	E / 0.5
2014	C+	3,440	17.27	A+ / 9.9	19.13%	E / 0.5
2013	C+	2,416	15.36	A+ / 9.6	-4.69%	E / 0.5
2012	B+	2,896	17.14	A+ / 9.9	20.92%	D- / 1.2

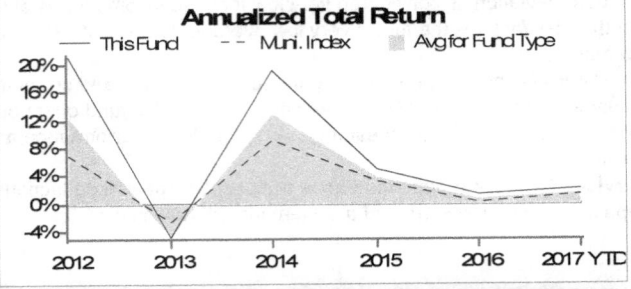

Nuveen Intmdt Duration Muni Bond A (NMBAX)

D-   **Weak**

Fund Family: Nuveen Investor Services
Phone: (800) 257-8787
Address: P.O. Box 8530, Boston, MA 02266
Fund Type: MUN - Municipal - National
Major Rating Factors: Nuveen Intmdt Duration Muni Bond A receives a TheStreet Investment Rating of D- (Weak). The fund has a performance rating of C- (Fair) based on an average return of 2.63% over the last three years (4.36% taxable equivalent) and 1.37% over the last three months (2.27% taxable equivalent). Factored into the performance evaluation is an expense ratio of 0.68% (low) and a 3.0% front-end load that is levied at the time of purchase.

The fund's risk rating is currently C- (Fair). Volatility, as measured by standard deviation, is considered average for fixed income funds at 3.39. Another risk factor is the fund's fairly average duration of 5.6 years (i.e. average interest rate risk).

Paul L. Brennan has been running the fund for 10 years and currently receives a manager quality ranking of 12 (0=worst, 99=best). If you desire an average level of risk, then this fund may be an option.
Services Offered: Automated phone transactions, payroll deductions, bank draft capabilities, wire transfers and a systematic withdrawal plan.

Data Date	Investment Rating	Net Assets ($Mil)	NAV	Performance Rating/Pts	Total Return Y-T-D	Risk Rating/Pts
2-17	D-	1,049	9.02	C- / 4.2	1.37%	C- / 4.2
2016	D-	1,111	8.94	C- / 3.8	-0.68%	C / 4.3
2015	B+	589	9.26	B+ / 8.4	2.84%	C+ / 5.6
2014	B+	1,111	9.26	C+ / 6.9	7.31%	C / 5.4
2013	B-	643	8.89	C+ / 5.8	-1.78%	C+ / 6.1
2012	B-	485	9.34	C / 4.9	5.79%	C+ / 6.4

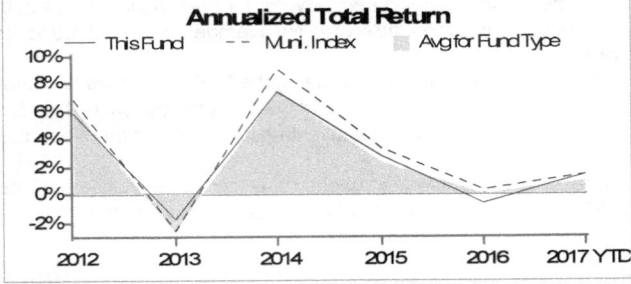

Nuveen Ltd Term Muni A (FLTDX)

D-   **Weak**

Fund Family: Nuveen Investor Services
Phone: (800) 257-8787
Address: P.O. Box 8530, Boston, MA 02266
Fund Type: MUN - Municipal - National
Major Rating Factors: Disappointing performance is the major factor driving the D- (Weak) TheStreet Investment Rating for Nuveen Ltd Term Muni A. The fund currently has a performance rating of D- (Weak) based on an average return of 1.07% over the last three years (1.77% taxable equivalent) and 1.13% over the last three months (1.87% taxable equivalent). Factored into the performance evaluation is an expense ratio of 0.63% (low) and a 2.5% front-end load that is levied at the time of purchase.

The fund's risk rating is currently B (Good). Volatility, as measured by standard deviation, is considered low for fixed income funds at 2.09. Another risk factor is the fund's below average duration of 3.2 years (i.e. lower interest rate risk).

Paul L. Brennan has been running the fund for 11 years and currently receives a manager quality ranking of 10 (0=worst, 99=best). This fund offers only a moderate level of risk but investors looking for strong performance are still waiting.
Services Offered: Automated phone transactions, payroll deductions, bank draft capabilities, wire transfers and a systematic withdrawal plan.

Data Date	Investment Rating	Net Assets ($Mil)	NAV	Performance Rating/Pts	Total Return Y-T-D	Risk Rating/Pts
2-17	D-	1,212	10.88	D- / 1.1	1.13%	B / 8.1
2016	D-	1,229	10.79	E+ / 0.6	-1.02%	B / 8.2
2015	A	1,168	11.10	C+ / 6.9	1.68%	B+ / 8.7
2014	C+	1,136	11.12	C- / 3.2	3.05%	B+ / 8.6
2013	B+	1,307	11.00	C / 4.9	-0.08%	B+ / 8.6
2012	C	1,362	11.22	D+ / 2.5	2.89%	B+ / 8.3

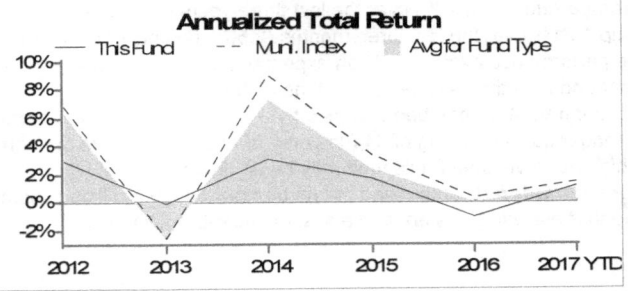

Nuveen Short Dur Hi Yld Muni A (NVHAX)   C   Fair

Fund Family: Nuveen Investor Services   **Phone:** (800) 257-8787
Address: P.O. Box 8530, Boston, MA 02266
Fund Type: MUH - Municipal - High Yield
Major Rating Factors: Middle of the road best describes Nuveen Short Dur Hi
Yld Muni A whose TheStreet Investment Rating is currently a C (Fair). The fund
has a performance rating of C+ (Fair) based on an average return of 3.64% over
the last three years (6.03% taxable equivalent) and 1.09% over the last three
months (1.81% taxable equivalent). Factored into the performance evaluation is
an expense ratio of 0.83% (low) and a 2.5% front-end load that is levied at the
time of purchase.

The fund's risk rating is currently C- (Fair). Volatility, as measured by
standard deviation, is considered average for fixed income funds at 3.23.

John V. Miller has been running the fund for 4 years and currently receives a
manager quality ranking of 59 (0=worst, 99=best). If you desire an average level
of risk, then this fund may be an option.

Services Offered: Automated phone transactions, payroll deductions, bank draft
capabilities, wire transfers and a systematic withdrawal plan.

Data Date	Investment Rating	Net Assets ($Mil)	NAV	Perfor-mance Rating/Pts	Total Return Y-T-D	Risk Rating/Pts
2-17	C	762	9.84	C+ / 6.6	1.09%	C- / 3.6
2016	C	622	9.79	C+ / 6.6	0.18%	C- / 3.7
2015	U	780	10.10	U / --	2.81%	U / --
2014	U	575	10.16	U / --	9.76%	U / --
2013	U	269	9.59	U / --	0.00%	U / --

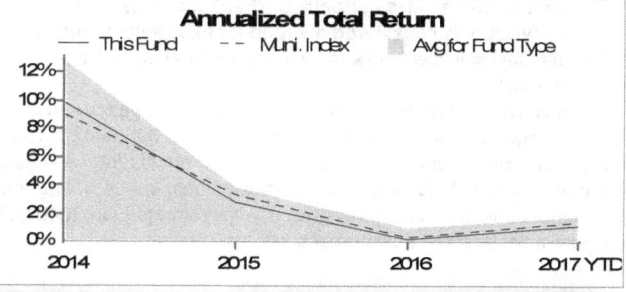

Old Westbury Fixed Income (OWFIX)   D   Weak

Fund Family: Old Westbury Funds   **Phone:** (800) 607-2200
Address: 630 5th Ave., New York, NY 10111
Fund Type: GEI - General - Investment Grade
Major Rating Factors: Disappointing performance is the major factor driving the
D (Weak) TheStreet Investment Rating for Old Westbury Fixed Income. The fund
currently has a performance rating of D (Weak) based on an average return of
0.83% over the last three years and 0.54% over the last three months. Factored
into the performance evaluation is an expense ratio of 0.74% (low).

The fund's risk rating is currently B (Good). Volatility, as measured by
standard deviation, is considered low for fixed income funds at 1.94. Another risk
factor is the fund's above average duration of 8.5 years (i.e. higher interest rate
risk).

David W. Rossmiller has been running the fund for 5 years and currently
receives a manager quality ranking of 14 (0=worst, 99=best). This fund offers
only a moderate level of risk but investors looking for strong performance are still
waiting.

Services Offered: Automated phone transactions, payroll deductions, bank draft
capabilities, an IRA investment plan, a 401K investment plan and a Keogh
investment plan.

Data Date	Investment Rating	Net Assets ($Mil)	NAV	Perfor-mance Rating/Pts	Total Return Y-T-D	Risk Rating/Pts
2-17	D	780	11.11	D / 2.0	0.54%	B / 7.9
2016	D+	754	11.05	D / 2.2	0.77%	B / 8.0
2015	C+	583	11.11	C / 4.4	0.58%	B+ / 8.4
2014	C-	564	11.19	D / 2.2	1.49%	B+ / 8.6
2013	C	535	11.20	D+ / 2.9	-0.92%	B+ / 8.5
2012	D	484	11.56	D / 2.0	3.19%	B / 7.6

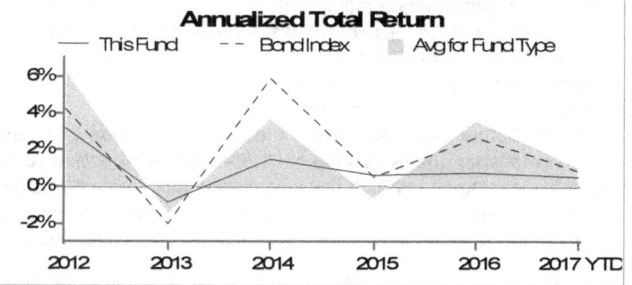

Old Westbury Muni Bond (OWMBX)   C-   Fair

Fund Family: Old Westbury Funds   **Phone:** (800) 607-2200
Address: 630 5th Ave., New York, NY 10111
Fund Type: MUN - Municipal - National
Major Rating Factors: A moderate risk profile coupled with stable earnings
characterizes Old Westbury Muni Bond which receives a TheStreet Investment
Rating of C- (Fair). Volatility, as measured by standard deviation, is considered
low for fixed income funds at 2.37. Another risk factor is the fund's fairly average
duration of 6.3 years (i.e. average interest rate risk). The fund's risk rating is
currently B (Good).

The fund's performance rating is currently C- (Fair). It has registered an
average return of 1.11% over the last three years (1.84% taxable equivalent) and
is up 0.77% over the last three months (1.28% taxable equivalent). Factored into
the performance evaluation is an expense ratio of 0.70% (low).

Bruce A. Whiteford has been running the fund for 19 years and currently
receives a manager quality ranking of 7 (0=worst, 99=best). If you desire stability
with a moderate level of risk then this fund is an excellent option.

Services Offered: Automated phone transactions, payroll deductions, bank draft
capabilities, a 401K investment plan and a Keogh investment plan.

Data Date	Investment Rating	Net Assets ($Mil)	NAV	Perfor-mance Rating/Pts	Total Return Y-T-D	Risk Rating/Pts
2-17	C-	2,055	11.85	C- / 3.0	0.77%	B / 7.7
2016	C-	1,927	11.76	D+ / 2.9	-0.35%	B / 7.8
2015	A	1,378	11.99	B- / 7.3	1.84%	B / 8.2
2014	C	1,340	11.94	C- / 3.2	2.61%	B / 8.0
2013	B+	1,199	11.82	C / 5.0	-1.35%	B / 7.8
2012	D-	1,097	12.18	C- / 3.2	2.57%	C+ / 5.7

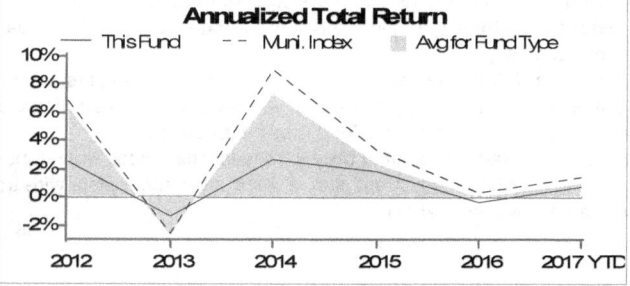

Oppeneheimer Rochester CA Muni A (OPCAX)

A- **Excellent**

Fund Family: OppenheimerFunds
Phone: (888) 470-0862
Address: P.O. Box 219534, Denver, CO 80217
Fund Type: MUS - Municipal - Single State

Major Rating Factors: Exceptional performance is the major factor driving the A- (Excellent) TheStreet Investment Rating for Oppeneheimer Rochester CA Muni A. The fund currently has a performance rating of A (Excellent) based on an average return of 5.61% over the last three years (9.29% taxable equivalent) and 1.65% over the last three months (2.73% taxable equivalent). Factored into the performance evaluation is an expense ratio of 1.22% (above average) and a 4.8% front-end load that is levied at the time of purchase.

The fund's risk rating is currently C- (Fair). Volatility, as measured by standard deviation, is considered average for fixed income funds at 3.96. Another risk factor is the fund's fairly average duration of 5.6 years (i.e. average interest rate risk).

Scott S. Cottier has been running the fund for 15 years and currently receives a manager quality ranking of 86 (0=worst, 99=best). If you desire an average level of risk and strong performance, then this fund is a good option.

Services Offered: Automated phone transactions, check writing, payroll deductions, bank draft capabilities, an IRA investment plan, a 401K investment plan, wire transfers and a systematic withdrawal plan.

Data Date	Investment Rating	Net Assets ($Mil)	NAV	Performance Rating/Pts	Total Return Y-T-D	Risk Rating/Pts
2-17	A-	869	8.27	A / 9.3	1.65%	C- / 3.3
2016	B+	847	8.21	A+ / 9.8	3.46%	D+ / 2.7
2015	C	876	8.36	A- / 9.1	3.75%	D- / 1.2
2014	C+	937	8.51	A+ / 9.8	14.78%	E+ / 0.8
2013	C	879	7.85	A- / 9.1	-5.53%	D- / 1.0
2012	B+	1,144	8.84	A+ / 9.9	18.37%	D- / 1.3

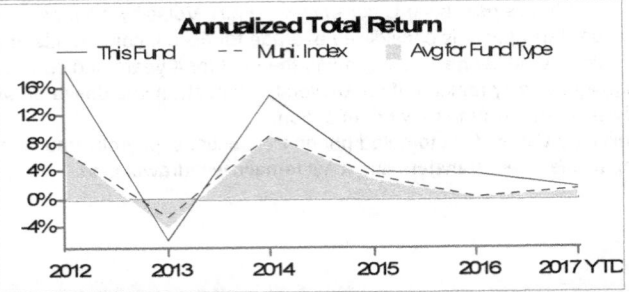
Annualized Total Return

Oppeneheimer Rochester Hi Yld Mun A (ORNAX)

B+ **Good**

Fund Family: OppenheimerFunds
Phone: (888) 470-0862
Address: P.O. Box 219534, Denver, CO 80217
Fund Type: MUH - Municipal - High Yield

Major Rating Factors: Oppeneheimer Rochester Hi Yld Mun A has adopted a very risky asset allocation strategy and currently receives an overall TheStreet Investment Rating of B+ (Good). Volatility, as measured by standard deviation, is considered above average for fixed income funds at 5.04. Another risk factor is the fund's fairly average duration of 6.8 years (i.e. average interest rate risk). The high level of risk (D, Weak) did however, reward investors with excellent performance.

The fund's performance rating is currently A+ (Excellent). It has registered an average return of 7.47% over the last three years (12.37% taxable equivalent) and is up 3.58% over the last three months (5.93% taxable equivalent). Factored into the performance evaluation is an expense ratio of 0.99% (average) and a 4.8% front-end load that is levied at the time of purchase.

Scott S. Cottier has been running the fund for 15 years and currently receives a manager quality ranking of 91 (0=worst, 99=best). If you are comfortable owning a very high risk investment, this fund may be an option.

Services Offered: Automated phone transactions, check writing, payroll deductions, bank draft capabilities, wire transfers and a systematic withdrawal plan.

Data Date	Investment Rating	Net Assets ($Mil)	NAV	Performance Rating/Pts	Total Return Y-T-D	Risk Rating/Pts
2-17	B+	3,110	7.09	A+ / 9.9	3.58%	D / 1.7
2016	B	2,965	6.92	A+ / 9.9	5.00%	D- / 1.4
2015	C-	3,003	7.02	A / 9.4	4.79%	E / 0.4
2014	C+	3,296	7.16	A+ / 9.8	16.13%	E / 0.4
2013	C-	3,296	6.61	B+ / 8.4	-6.63%	E / 0.4
2012	B	4,393	7.63	A+ / 9.9	18.85%	E+ / 0.9

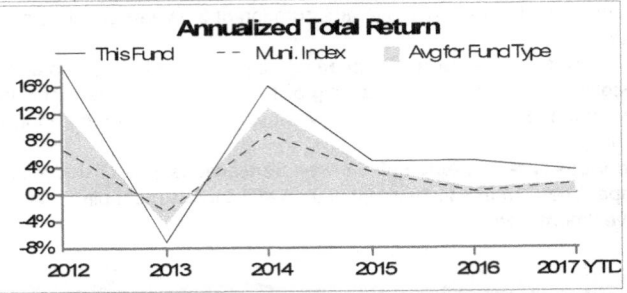
Annualized Total Return

Oppenheimer Core Bond A (OPIGX)

D **Weak**

Fund Family: OppenheimerFunds
Phone: (888) 470-0862
Address: P.O. Box 219534, Denver, CO 80217
Fund Type: GEI - General - Investment Grade

Major Rating Factors: Oppenheimer Core Bond A receives a TheStreet Investment Rating of D (Weak). The fund has a performance rating of C- (Fair) based on an average return of 2.79% over the last three years and 1.14% over the last three months. Factored into the performance evaluation is an expense ratio of 0.96% (average) and a 4.8% front-end load that is levied at the time of purchase.

The fund's risk rating is currently C+ (Fair). Volatility, as measured by standard deviation, is considered average for fixed income funds at 2.89. Another risk factor is the fund's very low average duration of 2.1 years (i.e. low interest rate risk).

Krishna K. Memani has been running the fund for 8 years and currently receives a manager quality ranking of 58 (0=worst, 99=best). If you desire an average level of risk, then this fund may be an option.

Services Offered: Automated phone transactions, check writing, payroll deductions, an IRA investment plan, a 401K investment plan, wire transfers and a systematic withdrawal plan.

Data Date	Investment Rating	Net Assets ($Mil)	NAV	Performance Rating/Pts	Total Return Y-T-D	Risk Rating/Pts
2-17	D	601	6.81	C- / 3.3	1.14%	C+ / 6.1
2016	D+	611	6.76	C- / 3.7	2.75%	C+ / 6.0
2015	C	508	6.74	C / 5.3	0.51%	C+ / 5.7
2014	B-	479	6.92	C+ / 5.7	6.76%	C+ / 6.0
2013	B+	363	6.73	C+ / 6.1	0.10%	C+ / 6.5
2012	A-	453	7.00	C+ / 6.0	9.72%	C+ / 6.6

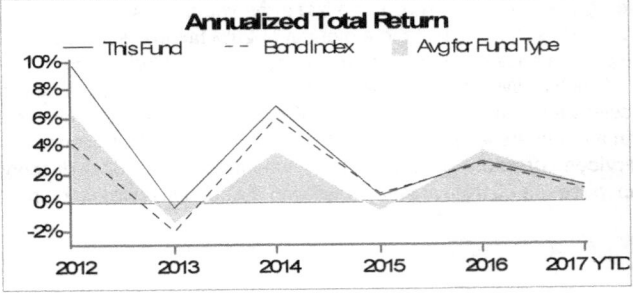
Annualized Total Return

Oppenheimer Global Strategic Inc A (OPSIX)   D   Weak

Fund Family: OppenheimerFunds   **Phone:** (888) 470-0862
Address: P.O. Box 219534, Denver, CO 80217
Fund Type: GES - General - Short & Inter. Term
Major Rating Factors: Oppenheimer Global Strategic Inc A receives a TheStreet Investment Rating of D (Weak). The fund has a performance rating of C (Fair) based on an average return of 2.39% over the last three years and 2.18% over the last three months. Factored into the performance evaluation is an expense ratio of 1.04% (average) and a 4.8% front-end load that is levied at the time of purchase.

The fund's risk rating is currently C- (Fair). Volatility, as measured by standard deviation, is considered average for fixed income funds at 3.69. Another risk factor is the fund's below average duration of 4.3 years (i.e. lower interest rate risk).

Krishna K. Memani has been running the fund for 8 years and currently receives a manager quality ranking of 70 (0=worst, 99=best). If you desire an average level of risk, then this fund may be an option.

Services Offered: Automated phone transactions, payroll deductions, bank draft capabilities, an IRA investment plan, a 401K investment plan, a Keogh investment plan, wire transfers and a systematic withdrawal plan.

Data Date	Investment Rating	Net Assets ($Mil)	NAV	Performance Rating/Pts	Total Return Y-T-D	Risk Rating/Pts
2-17	D	3,388	3.94	C / 4.9	2.18%	C- / 3.7
2016	D-	3,416	3.88	C- / 3.6	6.35%	C- / 4.0
2015	D-	3,805	3.79	D- / 1.2	-2.35%	D+ / 2.8
2014	D-	4,528	4.05	C / 4.3	2.63%	C- / 3.3
2013	D-	5,326	4.13	C / 4.5	-0.28%	D+ / 2.3
2012	C-	6,398	4.36	B- / 7.1	13.48%	D / 1.8

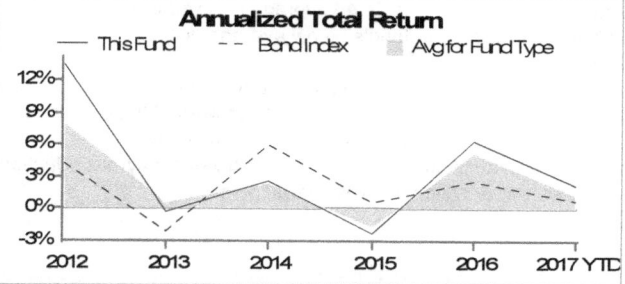

Oppenheimer Intl Bond A (OIBAX)   E+   Very Weak

Fund Family: OppenheimerFunds   **Phone:** (888) 470-0862
Address: P.O. Box 219534, Denver, CO 80217
Fund Type: GL - Global
Major Rating Factors: Oppenheimer Intl Bond A has adopted a very risky asset allocation strategy and currently receives an overall TheStreet Investment Rating of E+ (Very Weak). Volatility, as measured by standard deviation, is considered above average for fixed income funds at 5.00. Another risk factor is the fund's below average duration of 4.6 years (i.e. lower interest rate risk). Unfortunately, the high level of risk (D, Weak) has only provided investors with average performance.

The fund's performance rating is currently C- (Fair). It has registered an average return of 1.57% over the last three years and is up 2.76% over the last three months. Factored into the performance evaluation is an expense ratio of 1.02% (average) and a 4.8% front-end load that is levied at the time of purchase.

Hemant Baijal has been running the fund for 4 years and currently receives a manager quality ranking of 90 (0=worst, 99=best). If you are comfortable owning a very high risk investment, then this fund may be an option.

Services Offered: Automated phone transactions, payroll deductions, bank draft capabilities, an IRA investment plan, a 401K investment plan, a Keogh investment plan, wire transfers and a systematic withdrawal plan.

Data Date	Investment Rating	Net Assets ($Mil)	NAV	Performance Rating/Pts	Total Return Y-T-D	Risk Rating/Pts
2-17	E+	1,413	5.72	C- / 3.4	2.76%	D / 2.0
2016	E	1,429	5.61	E+ / 0.6	6.13%	D / 2.1
2015	D-	1,797	5.52	E / 0.4	-3.72%	D+ / 2.7
2014	E	2,838	5.92	D- / 1.3	0.32%	D- / 1.5
2013	E-	4,379	6.08	E+ / 0.9	-3.90%	E+ / 0.9
2012	E-	5,869	6.58	C- / 3.5	10.77%	E / 0.4

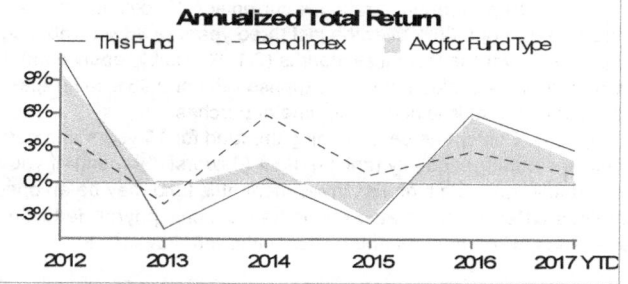

Oppenheimer Limited-Term Bond A (OUSGX)   C+   Fair

Fund Family: OppenheimerFunds   **Phone:** (888) 470-0862
Address: P.O. Box 219534, Denver, CO 80217
Fund Type: USS - US Government - Short & Inter. Term
Major Rating Factors: Disappointing performance is the major factor driving the C+ (Fair) TheStreet Investment Rating for Oppenheimer Limited-Term Bond A. The fund currently has a performance rating of D+ (Weak) based on an average return of 1.33% over the last three years and 0.55% over the last three months. Factored into the performance evaluation is an expense ratio of 0.90% (average) and a 2.3% front-end load that is levied at the time of purchase.

The fund's risk rating is currently A- (Excellent). Volatility, as measured by standard deviation, is considered very low for fixed income funds at 1.04. Another risk factor is the fund's very low average duration of 2.1 years (i.e. low interest rate risk).

Peter A. Strzalkowski has been running the fund for 8 years and currently receives a manager quality ranking of 74 (0=worst, 99=best). This fund offers only a moderate level of risk but investors looking for strong performance are still waiting.

Services Offered: Automated phone transactions, payroll deductions, bank draft capabilities, an IRA investment plan, a 401K investment plan, a Keogh investment plan and a systematic withdrawal plan.

Data Date	Investment Rating	Net Assets ($Mil)	NAV	Performance Rating/Pts	Total Return Y-T-D	Risk Rating/Pts
2-17	C+	696	4.54	D+ / 2.6	0.55%	A- / 9.2
2016	C+	713	4.53	D+ / 2.7	2.11%	A- / 9.2
2015	C+	713	4.53	C- / 3.7	0.45%	A- / 9.0
2014	C-	705	9.24	D / 2.2	1.74%	B+ / 8.7
2013	A-	613	9.37	C / 5.0	0.65%	B+ / 8.5
2012	D	761	9.56	D+ / 2.5	3.89%	B- / 7.0

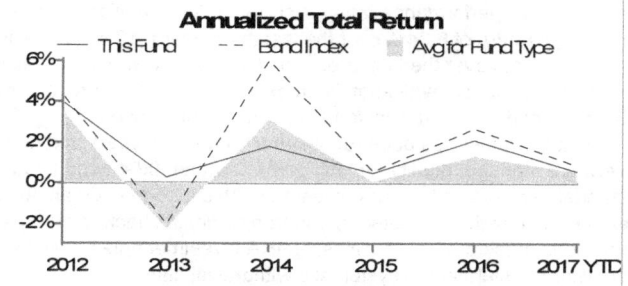

Oppenheimer Ltd Term NY Muni A (LTNYX)
D- **Weak**

Fund Family: OppenheimerFunds
Phone: (888) 470-0862
Address: P.O. Box 219534, Denver, CO 80217
Fund Type: MUS - Municipal - Single State
Major Rating Factors: Oppenheimer Ltd Term NY Muni A receives a TheStreet Investment Rating of D- (Weak). The fund has a performance rating of C (Fair) based on an average return of 1.88% over the last three years (3.11% taxable equivalent) and 1.62% over the last three months (2.68% taxable equivalent). Factored into the performance evaluation is an expense ratio of 0.85% (average) and a 2.3% front-end load that is levied at the time of purchase.

The fund's risk rating is currently C- (Fair). Volatility, as measured by standard deviation, is considered average for fixed income funds at 3.61. Another risk factor is the fund's below average duration of 3.7 years (i.e. lower interest rate risk).

Scott S. Cottier has been running the fund for 15 years and currently receives a manager quality ranking of 29 (0=worst, 99=best). If you desire an average level of risk, then this fund may be an option.
Services Offered: Automated phone transactions, payroll deductions, bank draft capabilities and a systematic withdrawal plan.

Data Date	Investment Rating	Net Assets ($Mil)	NAV	Performance Rating/Pts	Total Return Y-T-D	Risk Rating/Pts
2-17	D-	1,602	2.98	C / 4.7	1.62%	C- / 3.8
2016	D	1,615	2.95	C / 5.0	1.63%	C- / 3.7
2015	D	1,855	3.01	D / 1.9	-1.01%	C- / 3.1
2014	D	2,344	3.16	C / 4.8	7.16%	C- / 3.8
2013	D-	2,792	3.06	E+ / 0.9	-6.29%	C / 5.3
2012	A-	3,803	3.39	C+ / 5.7	6.13%	C+ / 6.8

Annualized Total Return

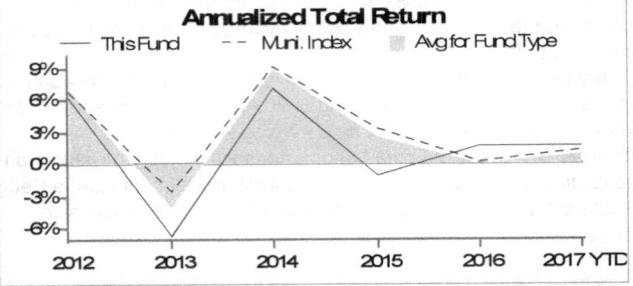

Oppenheimer Rochester AMT-Fr NY M A (OPNYX)
B+ **Good**

Fund Family: OppenheimerFunds
Phone: (888) 470-0862
Address: P.O. Box 219534, Denver, CO 80217
Fund Type: MUS - Municipal - Single State
Major Rating Factors: Oppenheimer Rochester AMT-Fr NY M A has adopted a risky asset allocation strategy and currently receives an overall TheStreet Investment Rating of B+ (Good). Volatility, as measured by standard deviation, is considered above average for fixed income funds at 4.44. Another risk factor is the fund's fairly average duration of 6.3 years (i.e. average interest rate risk). The high level of risk (D+, Weak) did however, reward investors with excellent performance.

The fund's performance rating is currently A (Excellent). It has registered an average return of 5.65% over the last three years (9.36% taxable equivalent) and is up 1.27% over the last three months (2.10% taxable equivalent). Factored into the performance evaluation is an expense ratio of 0.96% (average) and a 4.8% front-end load that is levied at the time of purchase.

Scott S. Cottier has been running the fund for 15 years and currently receives a manager quality ranking of 84 (0=worst, 99=best). If you are comfortable owning a high risk investment, this fund may be an option.
Services Offered: Automated phone transactions, payroll deductions, bank draft capabilities, wire transfers and a systematic withdrawal plan.

Data Date	Investment Rating	Net Assets ($Mil)	NAV	Performance Rating/Pts	Total Return Y-T-D	Risk Rating/Pts
2-17	B+	914	11.08	A / 9.3	1.27%	D+ / 2.5
2016	B+	906	11.02	A+ / 9.8	4.09%	D / 2.2
2015	C-	936	11.10	B / 7.6	4.18%	E+ / 0.6
2014	C-	983	11.24	B+ / 8.8	14.21%	E / 0.5
2013	E	963	10.42	D / 1.8	-10.67%	E+ / 0.6
2012	B	1,199	12.33	A+ / 9.6	13.66%	D- / 1.3

Annualized Total Return

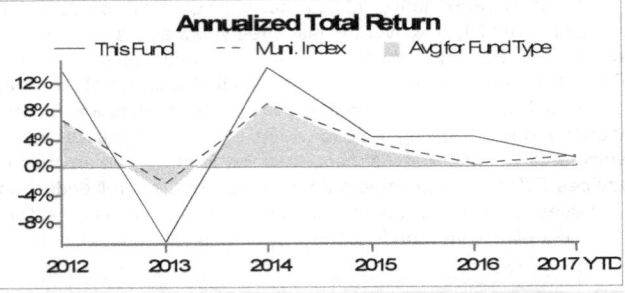

Oppenheimer Rochester AMT-Free Muni (OPTAX)
A- **Excellent**

Fund Family: OppenheimerFunds
Phone: (888) 470-0862
Address: P.O. Box 219534, Denver, CO 80217
Fund Type: MUN - Municipal - National
Major Rating Factors: Oppenheimer Rochester AMT-Free Muni has adopted a risky asset allocation strategy and currently receives an overall TheStreet Investment Rating of A- (Excellent). Volatility, as measured by standard deviation, is considered above average for fixed income funds at 4.16. Another risk factor is the fund's fairly average duration of 6.1 years (i.e. average interest rate risk). The high level of risk (D+, Weak) did however, reward investors with excellent performance.

The fund's performance rating is currently A+ (Excellent). It has registered an average return of 6.34% over the last three years (10.50% taxable equivalent) and is up 2.44% over the last three months (4.04% taxable equivalent). Factored into the performance evaluation is an expense ratio of 0.98% (average) and a 4.8% front-end load that is levied at the time of purchase.

Scott S. Cottier has been running the fund for 15 years and currently receives a manager quality ranking of 89 (0=worst, 99=best). If you are comfortable owning a high risk investment, this fund may be an option.
Services Offered: Automated phone transactions, check writing, payroll deductions, bank draft capabilities, an IRA investment plan, a 401K investment plan, wire transfers and a systematic withdrawal plan.

Data Date	Investment Rating	Net Assets ($Mil)	NAV	Performance Rating/Pts	Total Return Y-T-D	Risk Rating/Pts
2-17	A-	1,218	6.83	A+ / 9.7	2.44%	D+ / 2.8
2016	B+	1,194	6.73	A+ / 9.8	2.50%	D+ / 2.6
2015	C	1,273	6.94	A / 9.5	5.19%	E+ / 0.8
2014	C+	1,319	7.01	A+ / 9.8	15.64%	E+ / 0.6
2013	C	1,332	6.43	A / 9.3	-6.68%	E+ / 0.6
2012	B	1,924	7.29	A+ / 9.9	18.96%	E+ / 0.9

Annualized Total Return

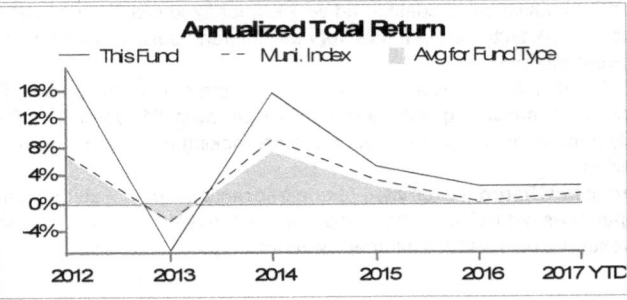

Oppenheimer Rochester Ltd Term M A (OPITX)   C   Fair

Fund Family: OppenheimerFunds **Phone:** (888) 470-0862
Address: P.O. Box 219534, Denver, CO 80217
Fund Type: MUN - Municipal - National
Major Rating Factors: Middle of the road best describes Oppenheimer
Rochester Ltd Term M A whose TheStreet Investment Rating is currently a C
(Fair). The fund has a performance rating of C (Fair) based on an average return
of 2.10% over the last three years (3.48% taxable equivalent) and 1.36% over
the last three months (2.25% taxable equivalent). Factored into the performance
evaluation is an expense ratio of 0.92% (average) and a 2.3% front-end load that
is levied at the time of purchase.

The fund's risk rating is currently C (Fair). Volatility, as measured by
standard deviation, is considered average for fixed income funds at 3.04.
Another risk factor is the fund's very low average duration of 2.2 years (i.e. low
interest rate risk).

Scott S. Cottier has been running the fund for 15 years and currently
receives a manager quality ranking of 68 (0=worst, 99=best). If you desire an
average level of risk, then this fund may be an option.
Services Offered: Automated phone transactions, payroll deductions, bank draft
capabilities, wire transfers and a systematic withdrawal plan.

Data Date	Investment Rating	Net Assets ($Mil)	NAV	Performance Rating/Pts	Total Return Y-T-D	Risk Rating/Pts
2-17	C	963	4.50	C / 5.4	1.36%	C / 5.3
2016	C+	976	4.47	C+ / 6.2	3.02%	C / 5.0
2015	D	1,212	4.51	D+ / 2.4	-1.71%	C- / 4.0
2014	B-	1,794	14.34	C+ / 6.6	7.20%	C / 4.9
2013	C	2,430	13.92	C / 4.7	-4.08%	C+ / 5.8
2012	A+	3,477	15.11	B- / 7.0	7.47%	C+ / 6.8

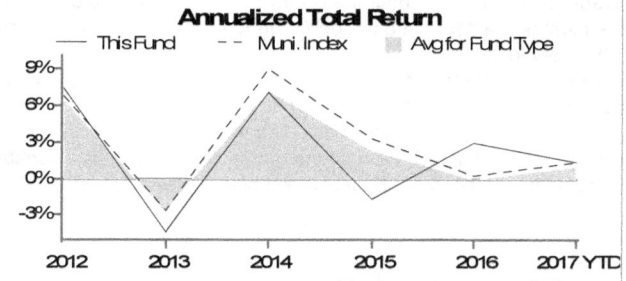

Oppenheimer Rochester Muni A (RMUNX)   B+   Good

Fund Family: OppenheimerFunds **Phone:** (888) 470-0862
Address: P.O. Box 219534, Denver, CO 80217
Fund Type: MUS - Municipal - Single State
Major Rating Factors: Oppenheimer Rochester Muni A has adopted a very
risky asset allocation strategy and currently receives an overall TheStreet
Investment Rating of B+ (Good). Volatility, as measured by standard deviation, is
considered above average for fixed income funds at 4.97. Another risk factor is
the fund's fairly average duration of 7.0 years (i.e. average interest rate risk).
The high level of risk (D, Weak) did however, reward investors with excellent
performance.

The fund's performance rating is currently A+ (Excellent). It has registered
an average return of 5.99% over the last three years (9.92% taxable equivalent)
and is up 2.35% over the last three months (3.89% taxable equivalent). Factored
into the performance evaluation is an expense ratio of 0.86% (average) and a
4.8% front-end load that is levied at the time of purchase.

Scott S. Cottier has been running the fund for 15 years and currently
receives a manager quality ranking of 87 (0=worst, 99=best). If you are
comfortable owning a very high risk investment, this fund may be an option.
Services Offered: Automated phone transactions, payroll deductions, bank draft
capabilities and a systematic withdrawal plan.

Data Date	Investment Rating	Net Assets ($Mil)	NAV	Performance Rating/Pts	Total Return Y-T-D	Risk Rating/Pts
2-17	B+	4,510	14.88	A+ / 9.7	2.35%	D / 2.1
2016	B	4,419	14.68	A+ / 9.9	6.05%	D / 1.9
2015	D	4,461	14.68	C / 5.2	1.95%	E / 0.4
2014	C-	4,988	15.35	B+ / 8.8	14.44%	E / 0.5
2013	E-	4,957	14.29	E / 0.4	-10.87%	E+ / 0.6
2012	B	6,731	17.02	A / 9.5	12.94%	D / 1.6

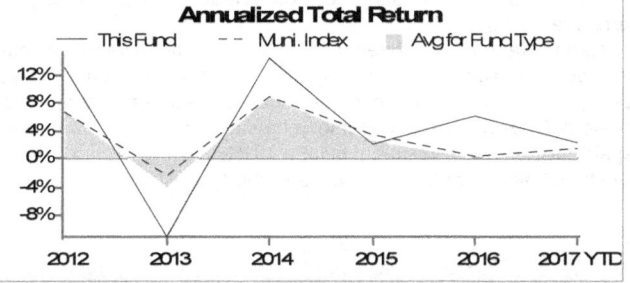

Oppenheimer Sen-Floating Rate A (OOSAX)   B+   Good

Fund Family: OppenheimerFunds **Phone:** (888) 470-0862
Address: P.O. Box 219534, Denver, CO 80217
Fund Type: LP - Loan Participation
Major Rating Factors: Strong performance is the major factor driving the B+
(Good) TheStreet Investment Rating for Oppenheimer Sen-Floating Rate A. The
fund currently has a performance rating of B+ (Good) based on an average
return of 3.76% over the last three years and 1.26% over the last three months.
Factored into the performance evaluation is an expense ratio of 1.11% (average)
and a 3.5% front-end load that is levied at the time of purchase.

The fund's risk rating is currently C- (Fair). Volatility, as measured by
standard deviation, is considered average for fixed income funds at 3.48.
Another risk factor is the fund's very low average duration of 0.1 years (i.e. low
interest rate risk).

Joseph J. Welsh has been running the fund for 18 years and currently
receives a manager quality ranking of 90 (0=worst, 99=best). If you desire an
average level of risk and strong performance, then this fund is a good option.
Services Offered: Automated phone transactions, payroll deductions, bank draft
capabilities, an IRA investment plan, a Keogh investment plan, wire transfers
and a systematic withdrawal plan.

Data Date	Investment Rating	Net Assets ($Mil)	NAV	Performance Rating/Pts	Total Return Y-T-D	Risk Rating/Pts
2-17	B+	4,556	8.20	B+ / 8.3	1.26%	C- / 4.0
2016	B-	4,407	8.15	B / 8.0	12.70%	C- / 3.5
2015	C-	4,237	7.60	D+ / 2.6	-2.06%	B- / 7.0
2014	B	5,602	8.11	C / 4.4	0.55%	B+ / 8.4
2013	A	7,097	8.43	B / 7.6	6.41%	C+ / 5.7
2012	D-	3,055	8.30	C / 4.8	8.44%	C- / 3.2

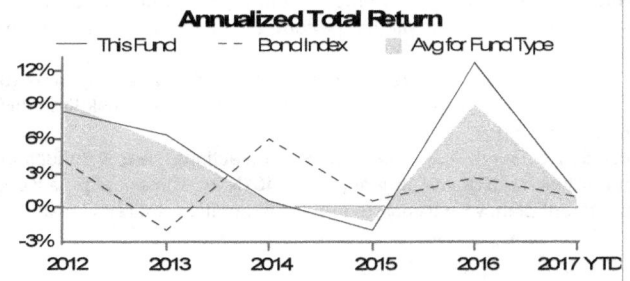

Opportunistic Income A (ENIAX)

A+   Excellent

Fund Family: SEI Financial Management Corp   **Phone:** (800) 342-5734
Address: One Freedom Valley Drive, Oaks, PA 19456
Fund Type: GL - Global
Major Rating Factors: A moderate risk profile coupled with stable earnings characterizes Opportunistic Income A which receives a TheStreet Investment Rating of A+ (Excellent). Volatility, as measured by standard deviation, is considered very low for fixed income funds at 0.99. Another risk factor is the fund's very low average duration of 2.6 years (i.e. low interest rate risk). The fund's risk rating is currently A- (Excellent).

The fund's performance rating is currently C+ (Fair). It has registered an average return of 2.38% over the last three years and is up 0.74% over the last three months. Factored into the performance evaluation is an expense ratio of 0.53% (very low).

Timothy E. Smith has been running the fund for 10 years and currently receives a manager quality ranking of 88 (0=worst, 99=best). If you desire stability with a moderate level of risk then this fund is an excellent option.

Services Offered: Automated phone transactions, bank draft capabilities, an IRA investment plan, a 401K investment plan and wire transfers.

Data Date	Investment Rating	Net Assets ($Mil)	NAV	Perfor- mance Rating/Pts	Total Return Y-T-D	Risk Rating/Pts
2-17	A+	2,207	8.22	C+ / 5.9	0.74%	A- / 9.2
2016	A+	2,196	8.16	C+ / 5.8	4.20%	A- / 9.2
2015	A+	2,169	8.05	C+ / 6.9	0.91%	A- / 9.2
2014	A-	1,967	8.18	C / 4.7	2.07%	A- / 9.0

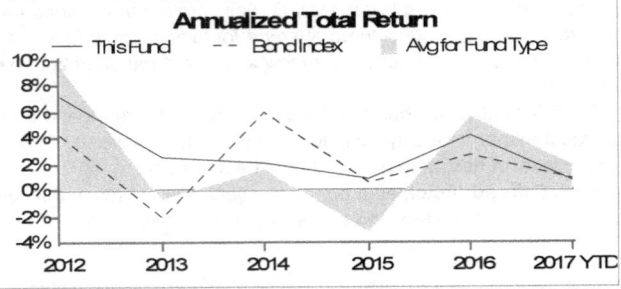

Osterweis Strategic Income (OSTIX)

B+   Good

Fund Family: Osterweis Funds   **Phone:** (800) 700-3316
Address: One Maritime Plaza, San Francisco, CA 94111
Fund Type: GES - General - Short & Inter. Term
Major Rating Factors: Strong performance is the major factor driving the B+ (Good) TheStreet Investment Rating for Osterweis Strategic Income. The fund currently has a performance rating of B+ (Good) based on an average return of 3.51% over the last three years and 1.25% over the last three months. Factored into the performance evaluation is an expense ratio of 0.83% (low).

The fund's risk rating is currently C- (Fair). Volatility, as measured by standard deviation, is considered average for fixed income funds at 3.67. Another risk factor is the fund's very low average duration of 1.2 years (i.e. low interest rate risk).

Carl P. Kaufman has been running the fund for 15 years and currently receives a manager quality ranking of 93 (0=worst, 99=best). If you desire an average level of risk and strong performance, then this fund is a good option.

Services Offered: Automated phone transactions, payroll deductions, bank draft capabilities, an IRA investment plan, a 401K investment plan, a Keogh investment plan, wire transfers and a systematic withdrawal plan.

Data Date	Investment Rating	Net Assets ($Mil)	NAV	Perfor- mance Rating/Pts	Total Return Y-T-D	Risk Rating/Pts
2-17	B+	5,381	11.35	B+ / 8.6	1.25%	C- / 3.7
2016	B	5,063	11.21	B+ / 8.7	10.95%	C- / 3.1
2015	C	5,252	10.66	C+ / 6.4	-0.93%	C / 5.0
2014	A	6,269	11.39	C+ / 5.9	1.26%	B / 7.7
2013	A+	5,664	11.84	B+ / 8.4	6.58%	B / 7.6
2012	C	2,749	11.65	C / 5.0	8.55%	C / 5.3

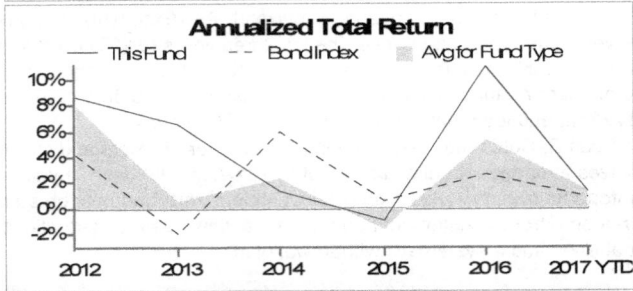

Payden Low Duration Investor (PYSBX)

B   Good

Fund Family: Payden & Rygel Funds   **Phone:** (888) 409-8007
Address: P.O. Box 1611, Milwaukee, WI 53201
Fund Type: GEI - General - Investment Grade
Major Rating Factors: A moderate risk profile coupled with stable earnings characterizes Payden Low Duration Investor which receives a TheStreet Investment Rating of B (Good). Volatility, as measured by standard deviation, is considered very low for fixed income funds at 0.64. Another risk factor is the fund's very low average duration of 1.6 years (i.e. low interest rate risk). The fund's risk rating is currently A+ (Excellent).

The fund's performance rating is currently C- (Fair). It has registered an average return of 1.04% over the last three years and is up 0.51% over the last three months. Factored into the performance evaluation is an expense ratio of 0.57% (very low).

Eric Hovey currently receives a manager quality ranking of 67 (0=worst, 99=best). If you desire stability with a moderate level of risk then this fund is an excellent option.

Services Offered: Automated phone transactions, payroll deductions, bank draft capabilities, an IRA investment plan, a 401K investment plan, a Keogh investment plan, wire transfers and a systematic withdrawal plan.

Data Date	Investment Rating	Net Assets ($Mil)	NAV	Perfor- mance Rating/Pts	Total Return Y-T-D	Risk Rating/Pts
2-17	B	847	10.09	C- / 3.1	0.51%	A+ / 9.7
2016	B-	846	10.06	C- / 3.0	1.85%	A+ / 9.7
2015	B	910	10.00	C / 4.7	0.43%	A / 9.5
2014	C+	939	10.07	D+ / 2.5	0.71%	A / 9.3
2013	C+	960	10.15	C- / 3.0	0.56%	A- / 9.1
2012	C	585	10.24	D- / 1.5	4.27%	A- / 9.2

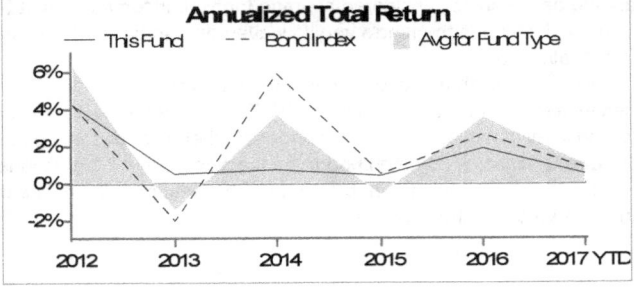

Performance Trust Strategic Bond (PTIAX)   A+   Excellent

Fund Family: Performance Funds   **Phone:** (800) 737-3676
Address: PO Box 182484, Columbus, OH 43218
Fund Type: GEI - General - Investment Grade
Major Rating Factors: Strong performance is the major factor driving the A+ (Excellent) TheStreet Investment Rating for Performance Trust Strategic Bond. The fund currently has a performance rating of B (Good) based on an average return of 5.01% over the last three years and 1.51% over the last three months. Factored into the performance evaluation is an expense ratio of 0.89% (average) and a 2.0% back-end load levied at the time of sale.

The fund's risk rating is currently B (Good). Volatility, as measured by standard deviation, is considered low for fixed income funds at 2.05.

Anthony J. Harris has been running the fund for 7 years and currently receives a manager quality ranking of 93 (0=worst, 99=best). If you desire only a moderate level of risk and strong performance, then this fund is an excellent option.

Services Offered: Automated phone transactions, payroll deductions, bank draft capabilities, wire transfers and a systematic withdrawal plan.

Data Date	Investment Rating	Net Assets ($Mil)	NAV	Perfor-mance Rating/Pts	Total Return Y-T-D	Risk Rating/Pts
2-17	A+	834	22.48	B / 7.8	1.51%	B / 8.2
2016	A+	778	22.35	B+ / 8.3	4.61%	B / 7.9
2015	B	227	22.55	B+ / 8.5	3.48%	C / 4.8
2014	A+	157	22.87	B+ / 8.5	8.91%	C / 5.1
2013	A+	152	21.98	B+ / 8.3	0.01%	C+/ 5.8
2012	U	119	22.90	U / --	14.51%	U / --

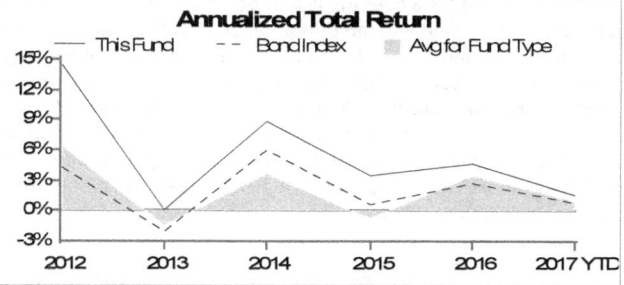

Annualized Total Return

PIMCO Fixed Income SHares C (FXICX)   D+   Weak

Fund Family: Allianz Global Investors   **Phone:** (800) 988-8380
Address: 1345 Avenue of the Americas, New York, NY 10105
Fund Type: GEI - General - Investment Grade
Major Rating Factors: PIMCO Fixed Income SHares C receives a TheStreet Investment Rating of D+ (Weak). The fund has a performance rating of C+ (Fair) based on an average return of 1.98% over the last three years and 1.73% over the last three months. Factored into the performance evaluation is an expense ratio of 0.03% (very low).

The fund's risk rating is currently C- (Fair). Volatility, as measured by standard deviation, is considered average for fixed income funds at 3.65.

David L. Braun has been running the fund for 1 year and currently receives a manager quality ranking of 78 (0=worst, 99=best). If you desire an average level of risk, then this fund may be an option.

Services Offered: Automated phone transactions, bank draft capabilities and wire transfers.

Data Date	Investment Rating	Net Assets ($Mil)	NAV	Perfor-mance Rating/Pts	Total Return Y-T-D	Risk Rating/Pts
2-17	D+	1,349	10.15	C+/ 5.7	1.73%	C- / 3.7
2016	D-	1,302	10.05	C- / 4.0	0.82%	C- / 4.0
2015	C-	1,554	10.42	B- / 7.2	1.73%	C- / 3.2
2014	C	1,971	11.43	B- / 7.4	2.78%	D+/ 2.8
2013	C+	3,134	12.19	B+ / 8.8	1.67%	D / 1.6

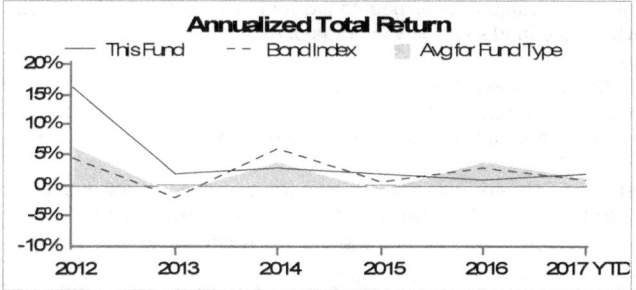

Annualized Total Return

PIMCO Fixed Income SHares M (FXIMX)   C   Fair

Fund Family: Allianz Global Investors   **Phone:** (800) 988-8380
Address: 1345 Avenue of the Americas, New York, NY 10105
Fund Type: GEI - General - Investment Grade
Major Rating Factors: PIMCO Fixed Income SHares M has adopted a very risky asset allocation strategy and currently receives an overall TheStreet Investment Rating of C (Fair). Volatility, as measured by standard deviation, is considered above average for fixed income funds at 5.46. The high level of risk (D, Weak) did however, reward investors with excellent performance.

The fund's performance rating is currently B (Good). It has registered an average return of 4.29% over the last three years and is up 2.47% over the last three months. Factored into the performance evaluation is an expense ratio of 0.06% (very low).

David L. Braun has been running the fund for 1 year and currently receives a manager quality ranking of 48 (0=worst, 99=best). If you are comfortable owning a very high risk investment, this fund may be an option.

Services Offered: Automated phone transactions, bank draft capabilities and wire transfers.

Data Date	Investment Rating	Net Assets ($Mil)	NAV	Perfor-mance Rating/Pts	Total Return Y-T-D	Risk Rating/Pts
2-17	C	1,362	10.13	B / 8.0	2.47%	D / 1.8
2016	C-	1,327	9.95	B / 7.6	8.53%	D / 1.8
2015	C-	1,578	9.87	C+/ 6.0	-0.45%	D+/ 2.6
2014	C+	1,998	10.37	C+/ 6.8	4.87%	C- / 3.9
2013	B+	2,981	10.58	B / 7.9	-0.56%	C / 4.5

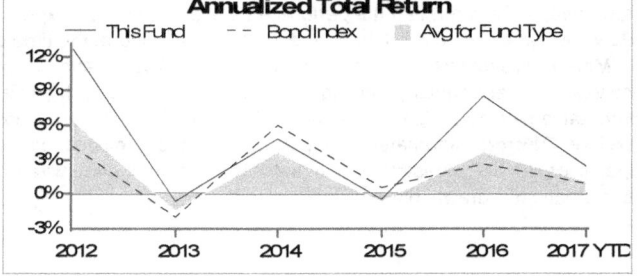

Annualized Total Return

PIMCO High Yield A (PHDAX)

C   **Fair**

Fund Family: PIMCO Funds   **Phone:** (800) 426-0107
Address: 840 Newport Center Drive, Newport Beach, CA 92660
Fund Type: COH - Corporate - High Yield

Major Rating Factors: PIMCO High Yield A has adopted a very risky asset allocation strategy and currently receives an overall TheStreet Investment Rating of C (Fair). Volatility, as measured by standard deviation, is considered above average for fixed income funds at 5.21. Another risk factor is the fund's below average duration of 3.5 years (i.e. lower interest rate risk). The high level of risk (D-, Weak) did however, reward investors with excellent performance.

The fund's performance rating is currently B+ (Good). It has registered an average return of 4.19% over the last three years and is up 2.54% over the last three months. Factored into the performance evaluation is an expense ratio of 0.91% (average) and a 3.8% front-end load that is levied at the time of purchase.

Andrew R. Jessop has been running the fund for 7 years and currently receives a manager quality ranking of 56 (0=worst, 99=best). If you are comfortable owning a very high risk investment, this fund may be an option.

Services Offered: Automated phone transactions, payroll deductions, bank draft capabilities, an IRA investment plan, a 401K investment plan, wire transfers and a systematic withdrawal plan.

Data Date	Investment Rating	Net Assets ($Mil)	NAV	Perfor-mance Rating/Pts	Total Return Y-T-D	Risk Rating/Pts
2-17	C	583	8.96	B+ / 8.4	2.54%	D- / 1.5
2016	C-	560	8.81	B / 8.2	12.30%	D / 1.6
2015	D	637	8.26	C- / 3.6	-2.22%	D / 1.8
2014	C-	758	9.14	B- / 7.0	2.95%	D+ / 2.6
2013	C	1,064	9.61	B+ / 8.7	5.40%	D- / 1.2
2012	C-	1,256	9.64	B / 7.8	14.17%	D- / 1.0

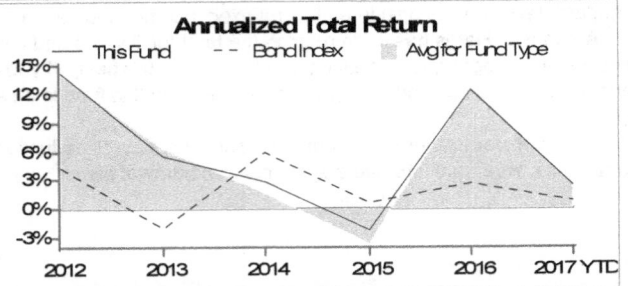

Annualized Total Return

PIMCO Income Fund A (PONAX)

A+   **Excellent**

Fund Family: PIMCO Funds   **Phone:** (800) 426-0107
Address: 840 Newport Center Drive, Newport Beach, CA 92660
Fund Type: GEI - General - Investment Grade

Major Rating Factors: Strong performance is the major factor driving the A+ (Excellent) TheStreet Investment Rating for PIMCO Income Fund A. The fund currently has a performance rating of B+ (Good) based on an average return of 5.53% over the last three years and 2.05% over the last three months. Factored into the performance evaluation is an expense ratio of 0.85% (average) and a 3.8% front-end load that is levied at the time of purchase.

The fund's risk rating is currently B- (Good). Volatility, as measured by standard deviation, is considered low for fixed income funds at 2.56. Another risk factor is the fund's very low average duration of 2.6 years (i.e. low interest rate risk).

Daniel J. Ivascyn has been running the fund for 10 years and currently receives a manager quality ranking of 96 (0=worst, 99=best). If you desire only a moderate level of risk and strong performance, then this fund is an excellent option.

Services Offered: Automated phone transactions, payroll deductions, bank draft capabilities, an IRA investment plan, a 401K investment plan, a Keogh investment plan, wire transfers and a systematic withdrawal plan.

Data Date	Investment Rating	Net Assets ($Mil)	NAV	Perfor-mance Rating/Pts	Total Return Y-T-D	Risk Rating/Pts
2-17	A+	8,615	12.20	B+ / 8.8	2.05%	B- / 7.5
2016	A+	8,155	12.06	B+ / 8.9	8.29%	B- / 7.5
2015	B-	6,548	11.73	B / 8.1	2.19%	C / 4.5
2014	A+	5,179	12.33	A- / 9.2	6.79%	C- / 4.1
2013	A+	4,856	12.26	A+ / 9.6	4.43%	C / 4.4
2012	A+	3,065	12.36	A+ / 9.8	21.72%	C- / 4.1

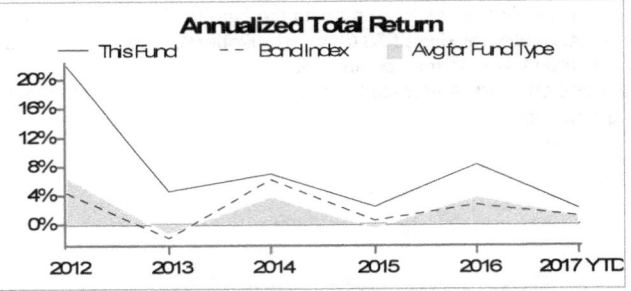

Annualized Total Return

PIMCO Investment Grade Corp A (PBDAX)

C-   **Fair**

Fund Family: PIMCO Funds   **Phone:** (800) 426-0107
Address: 840 Newport Center Drive, Newport Beach, CA 92660
Fund Type: COI - Corporate - Investment Grade

Major Rating Factors: PIMCO Investment Grade Corp A has adopted a risky asset allocation strategy and currently receives an overall TheStreet Investment Rating of C- (Fair). Volatility, as measured by standard deviation, is considered above average for fixed income funds at 4.30. Another risk factor is the fund's fairly average duration of 6.7 years (i.e. average interest rate risk). The high level of risk (D+, Weak) did however, reward investors with excellent performance.

The fund's performance rating is currently B- (Good). It has registered an average return of 4.52% over the last three years and is up 1.92% over the last three months. Factored into the performance evaluation is an expense ratio of 0.93% (average) and a 3.8% front-end load that is levied at the time of purchase.

Mark R. Kiesel has been running the fund for 15 years and currently receives a manager quality ranking of 72 (0=worst, 99=best). If you are comfortable owning a high risk investment, this fund may be an option.

Services Offered: Automated phone transactions, payroll deductions, bank draft capabilities, an IRA investment plan, a 401K investment plan, wire transfers and a systematic withdrawal plan.

Data Date	Investment Rating	Net Assets ($Mil)	NAV	Perfor-mance Rating/Pts	Total Return Y-T-D	Risk Rating/Pts
2-17	C-	1,001	10.35	B- / 7.2	1.92%	D+ / 2.7
2016	C-	1,002	10.21	B- / 7.0	6.56%	D+ / 2.8
2015	D+	916	9.92	C / 4.9	-0.14%	D+ / 2.7
2014	C+	956	10.55	B- / 7.5	8.33%	C- / 3.1
2013	C-	1,202	10.24	C+ / 6.4	-2.08%	C- / 3.4
2012	B	1,728	11.12	B / 7.9	14.55%	C- / 3.5

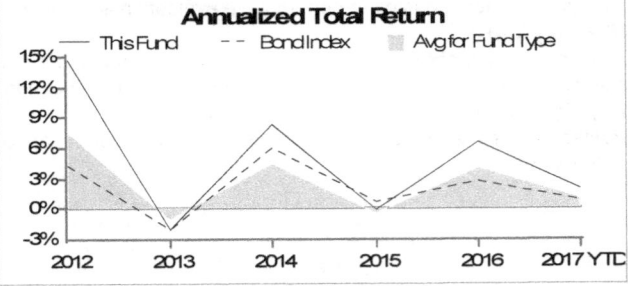

Annualized Total Return

PIMCO Low Duration A (PTLAX)   C-   Fair

Fund Family: PIMCO Funds   **Phone:** (800) 426-0107
Address: 840 Newport Center Drive, Newport Beach, CA 92660
Fund Type: GEI - General - Investment Grade
Major Rating Factors: Disappointing performance is the major factor driving the C- (Fair) TheStreet Investment Rating for PIMCO Low Duration A. The fund currently has a performance rating of D (Weak) based on an average return of 0.63% over the last three years and 0.36% over the last three months. Factored into the performance evaluation is an expense ratio of 0.85% (average) and a 2.3% front-end load that is levied at the time of purchase.

The fund's risk rating is currently A- (Excellent). Volatility, as measured by standard deviation, is considered very low for fixed income funds at 1.23. Another risk factor is the fund's very low average duration of 1.9 years (i.e. low interest rate risk).

Jerome M. Schneider has been running the fund for 3 years and currently receives a manager quality ranking of 50 (0=worst, 99=best). This fund offers only a moderate level of risk but investors looking for strong performance are still waiting.

Services Offered: Automated phone transactions, payroll deductions, bank draft capabilities, an IRA investment plan, a 401K investment plan, wire transfers and a systematic withdrawal plan.

Data Date	Investment Rating	Net Assets ($Mil)	NAV	Performance Rating/Pts	Total Return Y-T-D	Risk Rating/Pts
2-17	C-	864	9.86	D / 1.7	0.36%	A- / 9.0
2016	C-	914	9.85	D / 1.9	1.56%	A- / 9.0
2015	C-	1,212	9.86	D+ / 2.5	0.32%	B+ / 8.7
2014	D+	1,731	10.04	D / 2.0	0.43%	B+ / 8.5
2013	C-	3,306	10.33	D+ / 2.4	-0.23%	B+ / 8.4
2012	C-	3,650	10.51	D / 1.8	5.81%	B+ / 8.4

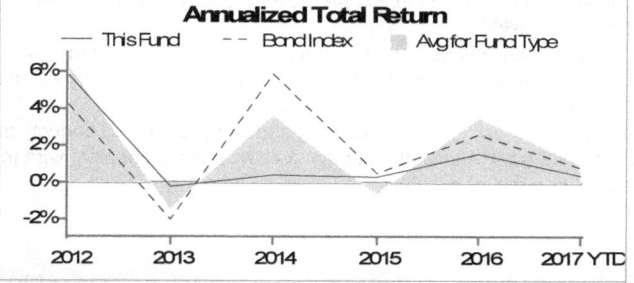

Annualized Total Return

PIMCO Real Return A (PRTNX)   E   Very Weak

Fund Family: PIMCO Funds   **Phone:** (800) 426-0107
Address: 840 Newport Center Drive, Newport Beach, CA 92660
Fund Type: GEI - General - Investment Grade
Major Rating Factors: PIMCO Real Return A has adopted a very risky asset allocation strategy and currently receives an overall TheStreet Investment Rating of E (Very Weak). Volatility, as measured by standard deviation, is considered above average for fixed income funds at 4.66. Unfortunately, the high level of risk (D, Weak) failed to pay off as investors endured very poor performance.

The fund's performance rating is currently D (Weak). It has registered an average return of 1.07% over the last three years and is up 1.64% over the last three months. Factored into the performance evaluation is an expense ratio of 0.98% (average) and a 3.8% front-end load that is levied at the time of purchase.

Mihir P. Worah has been running the fund for 10 years and currently receives a manager quality ranking of 2 (0=worst, 99=best). If you can tolerate very high levels of risk in the hope of improved future returns, holding this fund may be an option.

Services Offered: Automated phone transactions, payroll deductions, bank draft capabilities, an IRA investment plan, a 401K investment plan, wire transfers and a systematic withdrawal plan.

Data Date	Investment Rating	Net Assets ($Mil)	NAV	Performance Rating/Pts	Total Return Y-T-D	Risk Rating/Pts
2-17	E	1,747	11.09	D / 2.1	1.64%	D / 2.1
2016	E+	1,766	10.92	D / 2.2	4.62%	D / 2.2
2015	E	1,949	10.51	E / 0.4	-3.14%	D- / 1.0
2014	E	2,319	10.92	E+ / 0.6	3.01%	D- / 1.1
2013	E	2,988	10.97	E+ / 0.9	-9.41%	D / 2.2
2012	D+	5,124	12.27	C+ / 5.7	8.82%	C- / 3.3

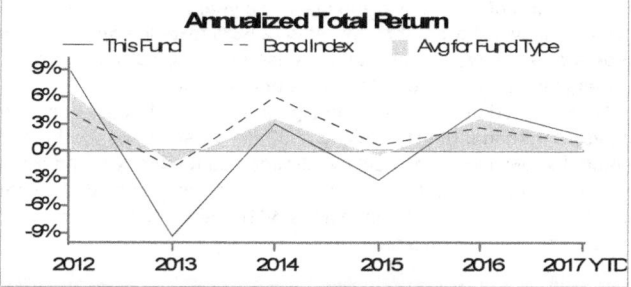

Annualized Total Return

PIMCO Short Term A (PSHAX)   C+   Fair

Fund Family: PIMCO Funds   **Phone:** (800) 426-0107
Address: 840 Newport Center Drive, Newport Beach, CA 92660
Fund Type: GEI - General - Investment Grade
Major Rating Factors: A moderate risk profile coupled with stable earnings characterizes PIMCO Short Term A which receives a TheStreet Investment Rating of C+ (Fair). Volatility, as measured by standard deviation, is considered very low for fixed income funds at 1.03. The fund's risk rating is currently A- (Excellent).

The fund's performance rating is currently C- (Fair). It has registered an average return of 1.40% over the last three years and is up 0.40% over the last three months. Factored into the performance evaluation is an expense ratio of 0.72% (low) and a 2.3% front-end load that is levied at the time of purchase.

Jerome M. Schneider has been running the fund for 6 years and currently receives a manager quality ranking of 83 (0=worst, 99=best). If you desire stability with a moderate level of risk then this fund is an excellent option.

Services Offered: Automated phone transactions, payroll deductions, bank draft capabilities, an IRA investment plan, a 401K investment plan, wire transfers and a systematic withdrawal plan.

Data Date	Investment Rating	Net Assets ($Mil)	NAV	Performance Rating/Pts	Total Return Y-T-D	Risk Rating/Pts
2-17	C+	876	9.82	C- / 3.0	0.40%	A- / 9.2
2016	C+	803	9.80	C- / 3.0	2.30%	A- / 9.2
2015	B-	603	9.73	C / 4.3	1.11%	A / 9.3
2014	C	685	9.75	D / 1.7	0.71%	A / 9.5
2013	C-	1,100	9.85	D- / 1.3	0.59%	A / 9.4
2012	D+	1,364	9.88	E+ / 0.7	3.18%	A / 9.5

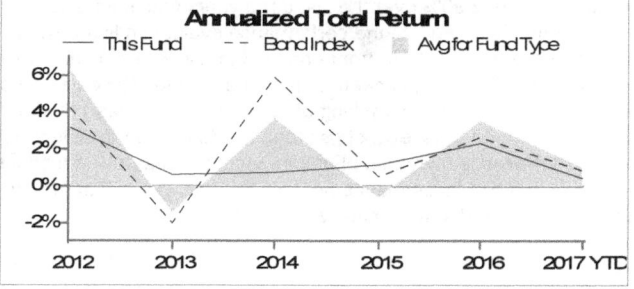

Annualized Total Return

PIMCO Total Return A (PTTAX)

D-   **Weak**

Fund Family: PIMCO Funds   **Phone:** (800) 426-0107
Address: 840 Newport Center Drive, Newport Beach, CA 92660
Fund Type: GEI - General - Investment Grade
Major Rating Factors: PIMCO Total Return A receives a TheStreet Investment Rating of D- (Weak). The fund has a performance rating of C- (Fair) based on an average return of 2.18% over the last three years and 1.59% over the last three months. Factored into the performance evaluation is an expense ratio of 0.86% (average) and a 3.8% front-end load that is levied at the time of purchase.

The fund's risk rating is currently C (Fair). Volatility, as measured by standard deviation, is considered average for fixed income funds at 3.31. Another risk factor is the fund's fairly average duration of 5.6 years (i.e. average interest rate risk).

Mark R. Kiesel has been running the fund for 3 years and currently receives a manager quality ranking of 25 (0=worst, 99=best). If you desire an average level of risk, then this fund may be an option.

Services Offered: Automated phone transactions, payroll deductions, bank draft capabilities, an IRA investment plan, a 401K investment plan, wire transfers and a systematic withdrawal plan.

Data Date	Investment Rating	Net Assets ($Mil)	NAV	Performance Rating/Pts	Total Return Y-T-D	Risk Rating/Pts
2-17	D-	5,628	10.15	C- / 3.4	1.59%	C / 4.4
2016	D-	5,945	10.03	D+ / 2.7	2.20%	C / 4.7
2015	D+	8,439	10.07	D+ / 2.7	0.33%	C / 4.4
2014	D	14,122	10.66	C- / 4.0	4.28%	C / 4.9
2013	D	21,616	10.69	C- / 3.1	-2.30%	C / 5.1
2012	C	27,665	11.24	C / 4.4	9.95%	C+/ 5.8

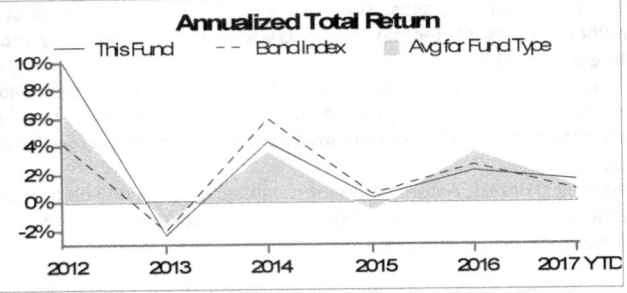

Annualized Total Return

Pioneer AMT-Free Muni A (PBMFX)

C-   **Fair**

Fund Family: Pioneer Investments   **Phone:** (800) 225-6292
Address: P.O. Box 55014, Boston, MA 02205
Fund Type: MUN - Municipal - National
Major Rating Factors: Pioneer AMT-Free Muni A has adopted a risky asset allocation strategy and currently receives an overall TheStreet Investment Rating of C- (Fair). Volatility, as measured by standard deviation, is considered above average for fixed income funds at 4.39. Another risk factor is the fund's fairly average duration of 6.6 years (i.e. average interest rate risk). The high level of risk (D+, Weak) did however, reward investors with excellent performance.

The fund's performance rating is currently B- (Good). It has registered an average return of 4.49% over the last three years (7.44% taxable equivalent) and is up 1.53% over the last three months (2.53% taxable equivalent). Factored into the performance evaluation is an expense ratio of 0.83% (low) and a 4.5% front-end load that is levied at the time of purchase.

David J. Eurkus has been running the fund for 11 years and currently receives a manager quality ranking of 33 (0=worst, 99=best). If you are comfortable owning a high risk investment, this fund may be an option.

Services Offered: Automated phone transactions, payroll deductions, bank draft capabilities, an IRA investment plan, a 401K investment plan, wire transfers and a systematic withdrawal plan.

Data Date	Investment Rating	Net Assets ($Mil)	NAV	Performance Rating/Pts	Total Return Y-T-D	Risk Rating/Pts
2-17	C-	684	14.27	B- / 7.1	1.53%	D+/ 2.6
2016	C	692	14.12	B / 7.7	-0.49%	D+/ 2.4
2015	C	708	14.60	A / 9.3	4.50%	D / 2.0
2014	B-	698	14.49	A / 9.5	13.62%	D- / 1.2
2013	C-	648	13.25	B- / 7.5	-5.33%	D / 1.8
2012	B+	823	14.56	A / 9.3	12.86%	D / 2.0

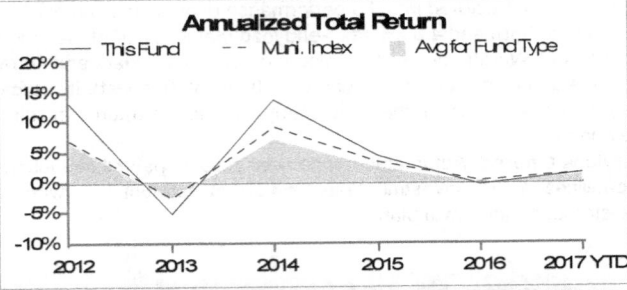

Annualized Total Return

Pioneer Bond Fund A (PIOBX)

B-   **Good**

Fund Family: Pioneer Investments   **Phone:** (800) 225-6292
Address: P.O. Box 55014, Boston, MA 02205
Fund Type: GEI - General - Investment Grade
Major Rating Factors: A moderate risk profile coupled with stable earnings characterizes Pioneer Bond Fund A which receives a TheStreet Investment Rating of B- (Good). Volatility, as measured by standard deviation, is considered low for fixed income funds at 2.12. Another risk factor is the fund's below average duration of 4.3 years (i.e. lower interest rate risk). The fund's risk rating is currently B (Good).

The fund's performance rating is currently C- (Fair). It has registered an average return of 2.90% over the last three years and is up 0.98% over the last three months. Factored into the performance evaluation is an expense ratio of 0.98% (average) and a 4.5% front-end load that is levied at the time of purchase.

Kenneth J. Taubes has been running the fund for 19 years and currently receives a manager quality ranking of 79 (0=worst, 99=best). If you desire stability with a moderate level of risk then this fund is an excellent option.

Services Offered: Automated phone transactions, payroll deductions, bank draft capabilities, an IRA investment plan, a 401K investment plan, a Keogh investment plan and a systematic withdrawal plan.

Data Date	Investment Rating	Net Assets ($Mil)	NAV	Performance Rating/Pts	Total Return Y-T-D	Risk Rating/Pts
2-17	B-	1,181	9.67	C- / 4.2	0.98%	B / 8.0
2016	B	1,180	9.62	C / 4.6	4.19%	B / 8.0
2015	C+	1,034	9.51	C / 4.9	-0.01%	B / 7.9
2014	B+	949	9.80	C / 5.2	5.94%	B / 7.6
2013	B+	531	9.60	C / 4.9	0.49%	B / 8.0
2012	B+	544	9.93	C / 4.3	8.64%	B / 8.2

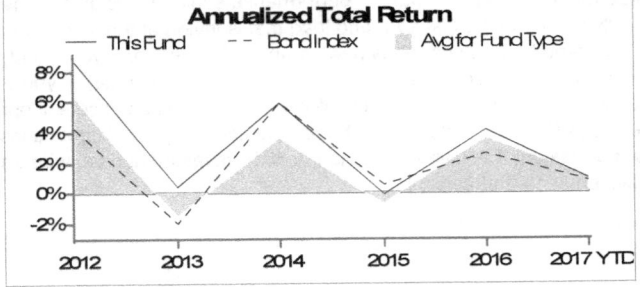

Annualized Total Return

Pioneer High Yield A (TAHYX)   D   Weak

Fund Family: Pioneer Investments   **Phone:** (800) 225-6292
Address: P.O. Box 55014, Boston, MA 02205
Fund Type: COH - Corporate - High Yield
Major Rating Factors: Pioneer High Yield A has adopted a very risky asset
allocation strategy and currently receives an overall TheStreet Investment Rating
of D (Weak). Volatility, as measured by standard deviation, is considered high for
fixed income funds at 6.22. Another risk factor is the fund's below average
duration of 3.4 years (i.e. lower interest rate risk). The high level of risk (E+, Very
Weak) did however, reward investors with excellent performance.

    The fund's performance rating is currently B (Good). It has registered an
average return of 2.87% over the last three years and is up 3.06% over the last
three months. Factored into the performance evaluation is an expense ratio of
1.17% (above average) and a 4.5% front-end load that is levied at the time of
purchase.

    Andrew D. Feltus has been running the fund for 10 years and currently
receives a manager quality ranking of 4 (0=worst, 99=best). If you are
comfortable owning a very high risk investment, this fund may be an option.
Services Offered: Automated phone transactions, payroll deductions, bank draft
capabilities, an IRA investment plan, a 401K investment plan, a Keogh
investment plan, wire transfers and a systematic withdrawal plan.

Data Date	Investment Rating	Net Assets ($Mil)	NAV	Perfor-mance Rating/Pts	Total Return Y-T-D	Risk Rating/Pts
2-17	D	547	9.72	B / 7.8	3.06%	E+ / 0.8
2016	D-	544	9.50	B- / 7.0	14.15%	E+ / 0.8
2015	E+	579	8.76	D / 2.0	-4.89%	E+ / 0.6
2014	D	826	9.74	B- / 7.1	-0.15%	E+ / 0.9
2013	C	1,182	10.67	A / 9.4	12.31%	E- / 0.2
2012	D-	1,254	10.33	B- / 7.4	14.98%	E- / 0.1

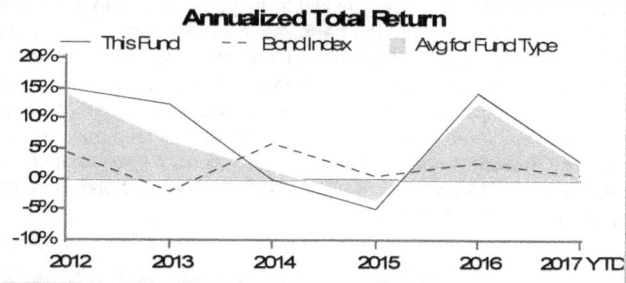

Pioneer Multi-Asset Ultrasht Inc A (MAFRX)   C+   Fair

Fund Family: Pioneer Investments   **Phone:** (800) 225-6292
Address: P.O. Box 55014, Boston, MA 02205
Fund Type: GL - Global
Major Rating Factors: Disappointing performance is the major factor driving the
C+ (Fair) TheStreet Investment Rating for Pioneer Multi-Asset Ultrasht Inc A.
The fund currently has a performance rating of D (Weak) based on an average
return of 1.08% over the last three years and 0.24% over the last three months.
Factored into the performance evaluation is an expense ratio of 0.63% (low) and
a 2.5% front-end load that is levied at the time of purchase.

    The fund's risk rating is currently A+ (Excellent). Volatility, as measured by
standard deviation, is considered very low for fixed income funds at 0.39.
Another risk factor is the fund's very low average duration of 0.3 years (i.e. low
interest rate risk).

    Craig D. Sterling currently receives a manager quality ranking of 76
(0=worst, 99=best). This fund offers only a moderate level of risk but investors
looking for strong performance are still waiting.
Services Offered: Automated phone transactions, payroll deductions, bank draft
capabilities, an IRA investment plan, wire transfers and a systematic withdrawal
plan.

Data Date	Investment Rating	Net Assets ($Mil)	NAV	Perfor-mance Rating/Pts	Total Return Y-T-D	Risk Rating/Pts
2-17	C+	762	9.98	D / 2.2	0.24%	A+ / 9.9
2016	C+	702	9.98	D+ / 2.4	2.06%	A+ / 9.9
2015	C+	696	9.94	C- / 3.3	0.52%	A+ / 9.9
2014	C	708	10.01	D / 1.7	0.70%	A+ / 9.8
2013	U	533	10.06	U / --	0.88%	U / --
2012	U	283	10.08	U / --	2.90%	U / --

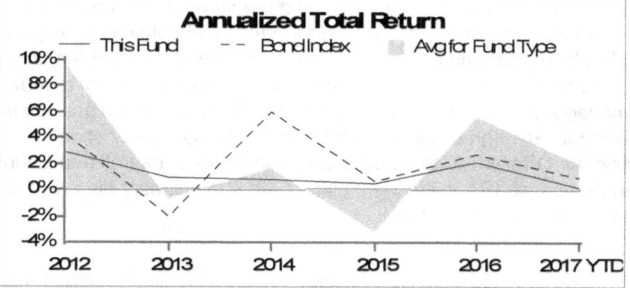

Pioneer Strategic Income A (PSRAX)   B   Good

Fund Family: Pioneer Investments   **Phone:** (800) 225-6292
Address: P.O. Box 55014, Boston, MA 02205
Fund Type: GES - General - Short & Inter. Term
Major Rating Factors: Pioneer Strategic Income A receives a TheStreet
Investment Rating of B (Good). The fund has a performance rating of C+ (Fair)
based on an average return of 3.34% over the last three years and 1.59% over
the last three months. Factored into the performance evaluation is an expense
ratio of 1.05% (average) and a 4.5% front-end load that is levied at the time of
purchase.

    The fund's risk rating is currently C+ (Fair). Volatility, as measured by
standard deviation, is considered average for fixed income funds at 2.88.
Another risk factor is the fund's below average duration of 4.1 years (i.e. lower
interest rate risk).

    Kenneth J. Taubes has been running the fund for 18 years and currently
receives a manager quality ranking of 86 (0=worst, 99=best). If you desire an
average level of risk, then this fund may be an option.
Services Offered: Automated phone transactions, payroll deductions, bank draft
capabilities, a 401K investment plan and a systematic withdrawal plan.

Data Date	Investment Rating	Net Assets ($Mil)	NAV	Perfor-mance Rating/Pts	Total Return Y-T-D	Risk Rating/Pts
2-17	B	1,201	10.73	C+ / 6.2	1.59%	C+ / 6.2
2016	B	1,232	10.62	C+ / 6.0	7.64%	C+ / 6.5
2015	D+	1,271	10.21	D+ / 2.7	-1.46%	C+ / 6.1
2014	C+	1,523	10.73	C / 5.5	4.62%	C / 5.5
2013	C	1,872	10.81	C+ / 5.9	1.51%	C / 4.9
2012	C	2,142	11.28	C+ / 5.7	11.22%	C / 4.6

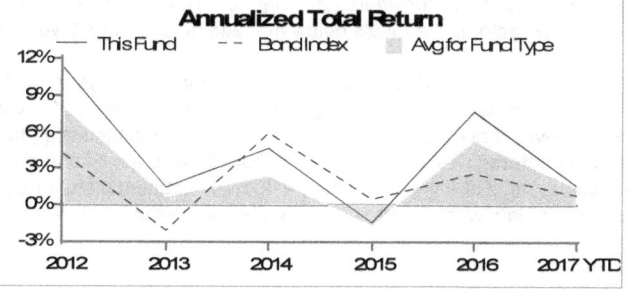

Principal Glb Divers Income A (PGBAX) C+ Fair

Fund Family: Principal Financial Group   **Phone:** (800) 222-5852
Address: P.O. Box 8024, Boston, MA 02266
Fund Type: GL - Global
Major Rating Factors: Principal Glb Divers Income A has adopted a very risky asset allocation strategy and currently receives an overall TheStreet Investment Rating of C+ (Fair). Volatility, as measured by standard deviation, is considered above average for fixed income funds at 4.96. Another risk factor is the fund's below average duration of 3.8 years (i.e. lower interest rate risk). The high level of risk (D, Weak) did however, reward investors with excellent performance.

The fund's performance rating is currently B+ (Good). It has registered an average return of 4.27% over the last three years and is up 3.23% over the last three months. Factored into the performance evaluation is an expense ratio of 1.09% (average) and a 3.8% front-end load that is levied at the time of purchase.

Kelly A. Grossman has been running the fund for 7 years and currently receives a manager quality ranking of 96 (0=worst, 99=best). If you are comfortable owning a very high risk investment, this fund may be an option.
Services Offered: Automated phone transactions, payroll deductions, bank draft capabilities, an IRA investment plan, a 401K investment plan, wire transfers and a systematic withdrawal plan.

Data Date	Investment Rating	Net Assets ($Mil)	NAV	Perfor- mance Rating/Pts	Total Return Y-T-D	Risk Rating/Pts
2-17	C+	1,945	13.84	B+ / 8.3	3.23%	D / 2.1
2016	C-	2,013	13.51	B- / 7.4	9.30%	D / 2.1
2015	D+	2,124	13.05	C+ / 5.9	-2.52%	D / 1.6
2014	C+	2,437	14.03	B+ / 8.4	6.20%	D+ / 2.3
2013	C	2,597	14.12	B+ / 8.7	5.79%	D- / 1.2
2012	C-	2,202	13.96	B+ / 8.4	15.65%	E / 0.4

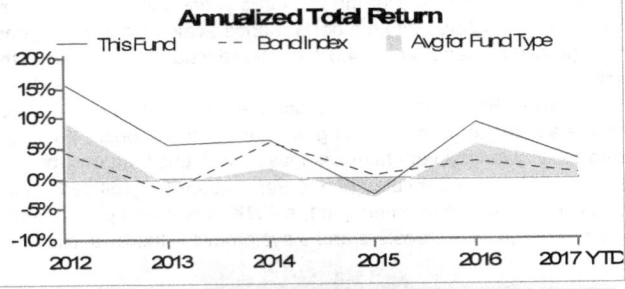

Principal High Yield A (CPHYX) C+ Fair

Fund Family: Principal Financial Group   **Phone:** (800) 222-5852
Address: P.O. Box 8024, Boston, MA 02266
Fund Type: COH - Corporate - High Yield
Major Rating Factors: Principal High Yield A has adopted a very risky asset allocation strategy and currently receives an overall TheStreet Investment Rating of C+ (Fair). Volatility, as measured by standard deviation, is considered above average for fixed income funds at 5.35. Another risk factor is the fund's below average duration of 3.4 years (i.e. lower interest rate risk). The high level of risk (D-, Weak) did however, reward investors with excellent performance.

The fund's performance rating is currently A- (Excellent). It has registered an average return of 4.48% over the last three years and is up 2.93% over the last three months. Factored into the performance evaluation is an expense ratio of 0.88% (average) and a 3.8% front-end load that is levied at the time of purchase.

Darrin E. Smith has been running the fund for 5 years and currently receives a manager quality ranking of 59 (0=worst, 99=best). If you are comfortable owning a very high risk investment, this fund may be an option.
Services Offered: Automated phone transactions, payroll deductions, bank draft capabilities, an IRA investment plan, a 401K investment plan, wire transfers and a systematic withdrawal plan.

Data Date	Investment Rating	Net Assets ($Mil)	NAV	Perfor- mance Rating/Pts	Total Return Y-T-D	Risk Rating/Pts
2-17	C+	987	7.47	A- / 9.2	2.93%	D- / 1.4
2016	C	943	7.32	B+ / 8.9	14.65%	D- / 1.4
2015	D	847	6.77	D+ / 2.7	-2.95%	D / 1.8
2014	C-	1,100	7.39	B- / 7.1	2.11%	D+ / 2.6
2013	C+	1,947	7.76	A- / 9.1	7.01%	D- / 1.3
2012	C	1,864	7.87	B / 8.0	15.25%	D- / 1.1

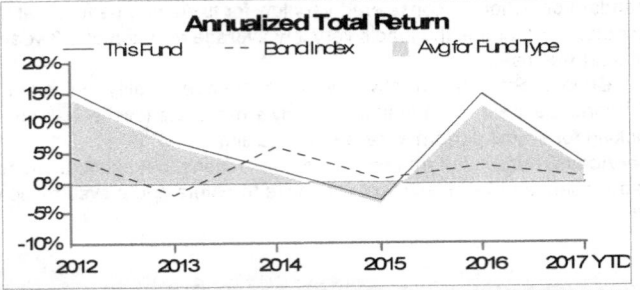

Principal Preferred Sec A (PPSAX) A+ Excellent

Fund Family: Principal Financial Group   **Phone:** (800) 222-5852
Address: P.O. Box 8024, Boston, MA 02266
Fund Type: USS - US Government - Short & Inter. Term
Major Rating Factors: Exceptional performance is the major factor driving the A+ (Excellent) TheStreet Investment Rating for Principal Preferred Sec A. The fund currently has a performance rating of A- (Excellent) based on an average return of 6.30% over the last three years and 3.58% over the last three months. Factored into the performance evaluation is an expense ratio of 1.07% (average) and a 3.8% front-end load that is levied at the time of purchase.

The fund's risk rating is currently C (Fair). Volatility, as measured by standard deviation, is considered average for fixed income funds at 3.29. Another risk factor is the fund's below average duration of 4.6 years (i.e. lower interest rate risk).

Lewis P. Jacoby, IV has been running the fund for 15 years and currently receives a manager quality ranking of 97 (0=worst, 99=best). If you desire an average level of risk and strong performance, then this fund is a good option.
Services Offered: Automated phone transactions, payroll deductions, bank draft capabilities, an IRA investment plan, a 401K investment plan, a Keogh investment plan, wire transfers and a systematic withdrawal plan.

Data Date	Investment Rating	Net Assets ($Mil)	NAV	Perfor- mance Rating/Pts	Total Return Y-T-D	Risk Rating/Pts
2-17	A+	715	10.23	A- / 9.0	3.58%	C / 4.5
2016	A-	796	9.95	B+ / 8.4	3.39%	C / 4.7
2015	B+	770	10.16	A- / 9.2	4.69%	C / 4.7
2014	A	829	10.27	A / 9.3	11.24%	C- / 3.7
2013	C	962	9.87	B / 7.7	1.47%	D / 2.2
2012	B-	1,217	10.53	A- / 9.0	18.87%	D / 1.6

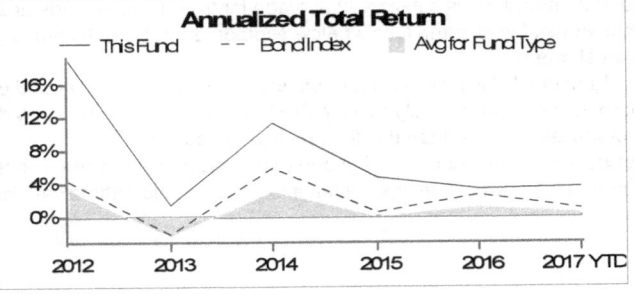

Prudential High Yield A (PBHAX)

C+   **Fair**

Fund Family: Prudential Investments   **Phone:** (800) 225-1852
Address: Gateway Center Three, Newark, NJ 07102
Fund Type: COH - Corporate - High Yield
Major Rating Factors: Prudential High Yield A has adopted a very risky asset allocation strategy and currently receives an overall TheStreet Investment Rating of C+ (Fair). Volatility, as measured by standard deviation, is considered above average for fixed income funds at 5.57. Another risk factor is the fund's below average duration of 3.9 years (i.e. lower interest rate risk). The high level of risk (D-, Weak) did however, reward investors with excellent performance.

The fund's performance rating is currently A- (Excellent). It has registered an average return of 4.84% over the last three years and is up 3.21% over the last three months. Factored into the performance evaluation is an expense ratio of 0.82% (low) and a 4.5% front-end load that is levied at the time of purchase.

Michael J. Collins has been running the fund for 16 years and currently receives a manager quality ranking of 64 (0=worst, 99=best). If you are comfortable owning a very high risk investment, this fund may be an option.
Services Offered: Payroll deductions, an IRA investment plan, a 401K investment plan and a systematic withdrawal plan.

Data Date	Investment Rating	Net Assets ($Mil)	NAV	Perfor-mance Rating/Pts	Total Return Y-T-D	Risk Rating/Pts
2-17	C+	1,334	5.57	A- / 9.2	3.21%	D- / 1.2
2016	C	1,347	5.45	B+ / 8.8	14.98%	D- / 1.2
2015	D	1,112	5.05	D+ / 2.7	-2.87%	D / 1.9
2014	C-	1,264	5.53	C+ / 6.9	2.53%	D+ / 2.6
2013	C+	1,342	5.73	A- / 9.1	6.95%	D / 1.6
2012	C	1,401	5.71	B / 8.0	14.07%	D- / 1.4

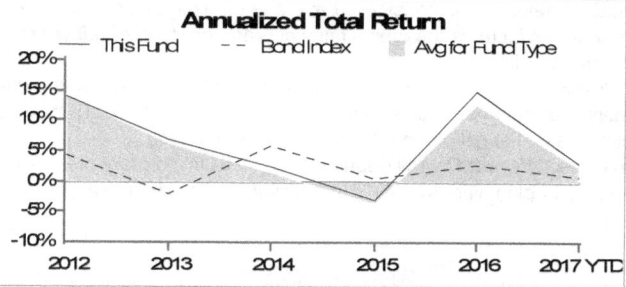

Annualized Total Return

Prudential National Muni A (PRNMX)

C-   **Fair**

Fund Family: Prudential Investments   **Phone:** (800) 225-1852
Address: Gateway Center Three, Newark, NJ 07102
Fund Type: MUN - Municipal - National
Major Rating Factors: Middle of the road best describes Prudential National Muni A whose TheStreet Investment Rating is currently a C- (Fair). The fund has a performance rating of C+ (Fair) based on an average return of 3.41% over the last three years (5.65% taxable equivalent) and 1.05% over the last three months (1.74% taxable equivalent). Factored into the performance evaluation is an expense ratio of 0.84% (low) and a 4.0% front-end load that is levied at the time of purchase.

The fund's risk rating is currently C (Fair). Volatility, as measured by standard deviation, is considered average for fixed income funds at 3.27. Another risk factor is the fund's fairly average duration of 6.5 years (i.e. average interest rate risk).

Robert S. Tipp has been running the fund for 13 years and currently receives a manager quality ranking of 38 (0=worst, 99=best). If you desire an average level of risk, then this fund may be an option.
Services Offered: Payroll deductions, a 401K investment plan and a systematic withdrawal plan.

Data Date	Investment Rating	Net Assets ($Mil)	NAV	Perfor-mance Rating/Pts	Total Return Y-T-D	Risk Rating/Pts
2-17	C-	570	14.78	C+ / 5.6	1.05%	C / 4.6
2016	C	573	14.71	C+ / 6.2	0.30%	C / 4.3
2015	C	597	15.18	B / 8.1	3.00%	C- / 3.4
2014	C+	630	15.28	B / 8.0	9.85%	D+ / 2.6
2013	C-	622	14.43	C+ / 5.7	-4.38%	C- / 3.6
2012	C+	742	15.67	C+ / 6.7	8.69%	C- / 3.8

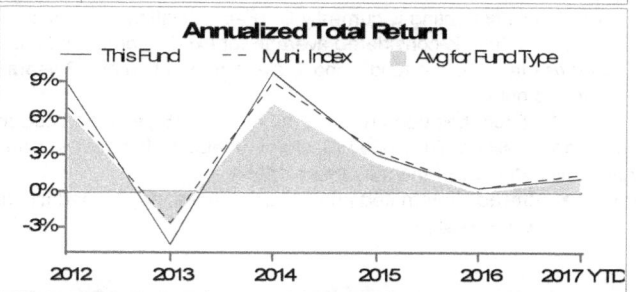

Annualized Total Return

Prudential Short-Term Corp Bond A (PBSMX)

C   **Fair**

Fund Family: Prudential Investments   **Phone:** (800) 225-1852
Address: Gateway Center Three, Newark, NJ 07102
Fund Type: COI - Corporate - Investment Grade
Major Rating Factors: Disappointing performance is the major factor driving the C (Fair) TheStreet Investment Rating for Prudential Short-Term Corp Bond A. The fund currently has a performance rating of D+ (Weak) based on an average return of 1.49% over the last three years and 0.75% over the last three months. Factored into the performance evaluation is an expense ratio of 0.77% (low) and a 3.3% front-end load that is levied at the time of purchase.

The fund's risk rating is currently B+ (Good). Volatility, as measured by standard deviation, is considered low for fixed income funds at 1.38. Another risk factor is the fund's very low average duration of 2.7 years (i.e. low interest rate risk).

Malcolm J. Dalrymple has been running the fund for 18 years and currently receives a manager quality ranking of 58 (0=worst, 99=best). This fund offers only a moderate level of risk but investors looking for strong performance are still waiting.
Services Offered: Payroll deductions, an IRA investment plan, a 401K investment plan and a systematic withdrawal plan.

Data Date	Investment Rating	Net Assets ($Mil)	NAV	Perfor-mance Rating/Pts	Total Return Y-T-D	Risk Rating/Pts
2-17	C	1,348	11.05	D+ / 2.4	0.75%	B+ / 8.9
2016	C	1,861	11.01	D+ / 2.4	2.50%	B+ / 8.9
2015	C+	1,803	11.00	C- / 3.8	0.81%	B+ / 8.9
2014	C	2,189	11.19	D+ / 2.4	1.41%	B+ / 8.8
2013	C+	2,785	11.33	C- / 3.2	0.89%	B+ / 8.7
2012	C-	2,597	11.56	D / 1.7	5.23%	B+ / 8.5

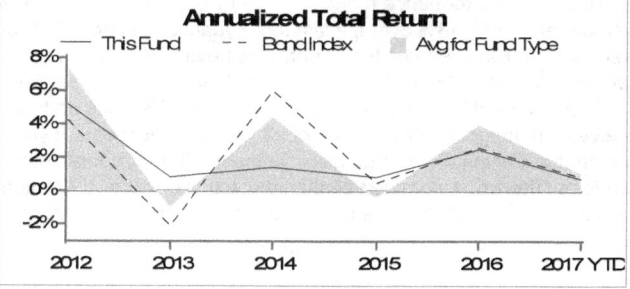

Annualized Total Return

Prudential Total Return Bond A (PDBAX)   D   Weak

Fund Family: Prudential Investments   **Phone:** (800) 225-1852
Address: Gateway Center Three, Newark, NJ 07102
Fund Type: GES - General - Short & Inter. Term
Major Rating Factors: Prudential Total Return Bond A receives a TheStreet Investment Rating of D (Weak). The fund has a performance rating of C (Fair) based on an average return of 3.42% over the last three years and 1.64% over the last three months. Factored into the performance evaluation is an expense ratio of 0.80% (low) and a 4.5% front-end load that is levied at the time of purchase.

The fund's risk rating is currently C- (Fair). Volatility, as measured by standard deviation, is considered average for fixed income funds at 3.53. Another risk factor is the fund's fairly average duration of 5.8 years (i.e. average interest rate risk).

Robert S. Tipp has been running the fund for 15 years and currently receives a manager quality ranking of 61 (0=worst, 99=best). If you desire an average level of risk, then this fund may be an option.

Services Offered: Payroll deductions, an IRA investment plan, a 401K investment plan, wire transfers and a systematic withdrawal plan.

Data Date	Investment Rating	Net Assets ($Mil)	NAV	Performance Rating/Pts	Total Return Y-T-D	Risk Rating/Pts
2-17	D	3,061	14.30	C / 4.9	1.64%	C- / 3.9
2016	D	3,648	14.13	C / 4.6	4.54%	C- / 4.2
2015	D+	3,051	14.01	C- / 3.9	-0.37%	C- / 4.2
2014	C-	1,862	14.46	C / 5.5	6.78%	C / 4.8
2013	C	1,145	14.02	C / 5.4	-1.17%	C / 5.2
2012	B	1,207	14.68	C+/ 5.7	9.59%	C+/ 6.1

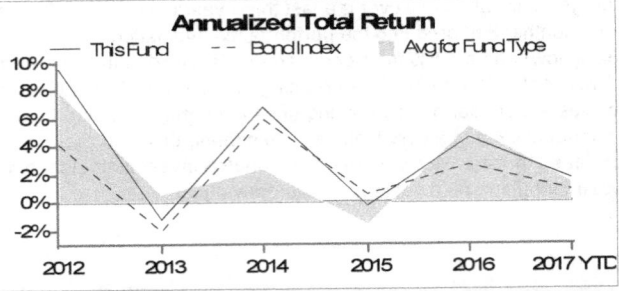

Annualized Total Return

Putnam CA Tax Exempt Income A (PCTEX)   C-   Fair

Fund Family: Putnam Funds   **Phone:** (800) 225-1581
Address: One Post Office Square, Boston, MA 02109
Fund Type: MUS - Municipal - Single State
Major Rating Factors: Middle of the road best describes Putnam CA Tax Exempt Income A whose TheStreet Investment Rating is currently a C- (Fair). The fund has a performance rating of C+ (Fair) based on an average return of 3.87% over the last three years (6.41% taxable equivalent) and 1.31% over the last three months (2.17% taxable equivalent). Factored into the performance evaluation is an expense ratio of 0.74% (low) and a 4.0% front-end load that is levied at the time of purchase.

The fund's risk rating is currently C- (Fair). Volatility, as measured by standard deviation, is considered average for fixed income funds at 3.49. Another risk factor is the fund's above average duration of 7.3 years (i.e. higher interest rate risk).

Paul M. Drury has been running the fund for 15 years and currently receives a manager quality ranking of 53 (0=worst, 99=best). If you desire an average level of risk, then this fund may be an option.

Services Offered: Automated phone transactions, payroll deductions and a systematic withdrawal plan.

Data Date	Investment Rating	Net Assets ($Mil)	NAV	Performance Rating/Pts	Total Return Y-T-D	Risk Rating/Pts
2-17	C-	1,150	8.02	C+/ 6.4	1.31%	C- / 3.6
2016	C-	1,150	7.96	C+/ 6.5	0.08%	C- / 3.7
2015	C+	1,221	8.23	B+/ 8.8	3.01%	C- / 3.4
2014	B+	1,266	8.29	A- / 9.0	10.92%	C- / 3.1
2013	C+	1,269	7.77	B / 7.8	-3.20%	C- / 3.1
2012	B	1,563	8.36	B+/ 8.5	9.58%	D+/ 2.5

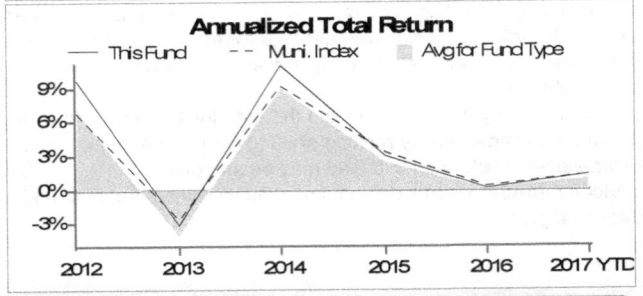

Annualized Total Return

Putnam Diversified Income A (PDINX)   E+   Very Weak

Fund Family: Putnam Funds   **Phone:** (800) 225-1581
Address: One Post Office Square, Boston, MA 02109
Fund Type: GES - General - Short & Inter. Term
Major Rating Factors: Putnam Diversified Income A has adopted a very risky asset allocation strategy and currently receives an overall TheStreet Investment Rating of E+ (Very Weak). Volatility, as measured by standard deviation, is considered above average for fixed income funds at 5.80. Another risk factor is the fund's very low average duration of 0.3 years (i.e. low interest rate risk). Unfortunately, the high level of risk (D-, Weak) has only provided investors with average performance.

The fund's performance rating is currently C (Fair). It has registered an average return of 1.18% over the last three years and is up 1.51% over the last three months. Factored into the performance evaluation is an expense ratio of 0.98% (average) and a 4.0% front-end load that is levied at the time of purchase.

D. William Kohli has been running the fund for 23 years and currently receives a manager quality ranking of 93 (0=worst, 99=best). If you are comfortable owning a very high risk investment, then this fund may be an option.

Services Offered: Automated phone transactions, payroll deductions, an IRA investment plan, a 401K investment plan and a systematic withdrawal plan.

Data Date	Investment Rating	Net Assets ($Mil)	NAV	Performance Rating/Pts	Total Return Y-T-D	Risk Rating/Pts
2-17	E+	1,285	7.05	C / 5.3	1.51%	D- / 1.4
2016	E+	1,258	7.01	C- / 3.5	5.10%	D- / 1.5
2015	D	1,785	7.05	C- / 3.6	-2.92%	C- / 3.2
2014	C	2,276	7.61	C+/ 6.1	0.96%	C / 4.4
2013	C-	2,551	7.92	B / 7.7	7.85%	D / 1.9
2012	E+	1,752	7.77	C / 5.1	12.72%	D / 1.8

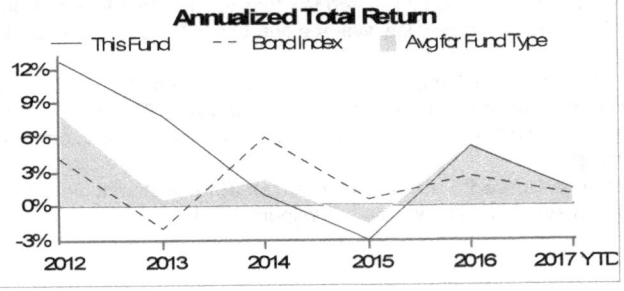

Annualized Total Return

Putnam High Yield Trust A (PHIGX)   C-   Fair

Fund Family: Putnam Funds   **Phone:** (800) 225-1581
Address: One Post Office Square, Boston, MA 02109
Fund Type: COH - Corporate - High Yield
Major Rating Factors: Putnam High Yield Trust A has adopted a very risky
asset allocation strategy and currently receives an overall TheStreet Investment
Rating of C- (Fair). Volatility, as measured by standard deviation, is considered
above average for fixed income funds at 5.87. Another risk factor is the fund's
below average duration of 3.4 years (i.e. lower interest rate risk). The high level
of risk (D-, Weak) did however, reward investors with excellent performance.

The fund's performance rating is currently B+ (Good). It has registered an
average return of 3.62% over the last three years and is up 2.39% over the last
three months. Factored into the performance evaluation is an expense ratio of
1.02% (average) and a 4.0% front-end load that is levied at the time of purchase.

Paul D. Scanlon has been running the fund for 15 years and currently
receives a manager quality ranking of 13 (0=worst, 99=best). If you are
comfortable owning a very high risk investment, this fund may be an option.
Services Offered: Automated phone transactions, payroll deductions, an IRA
investment plan and a systematic withdrawal plan.

Data Date	Investment Rating	Net Assets ($Mil)	NAV	Perfor-mance Rating/Pts	Total Return Y-T-D	Risk Rating/Pts
2-17	C-	795	7.77	B+ / 8.4	2.39%	D- / 1.0
2016	D+	798	7.65	B / 8.1	15.08%	D- / 1.0
2015	D-	832	7.01	D- / 1.5	-5.04%	D- / 1.3
2014	C-	920	7.80	B- / 7.2	1.79%	D+ / 2.3
2013	C	1,113	8.07	A- / 9.0	7.69%	E+ / 0.7
2012	D	1,187	7.95	B / 7.7	15.66%	E / 0.5

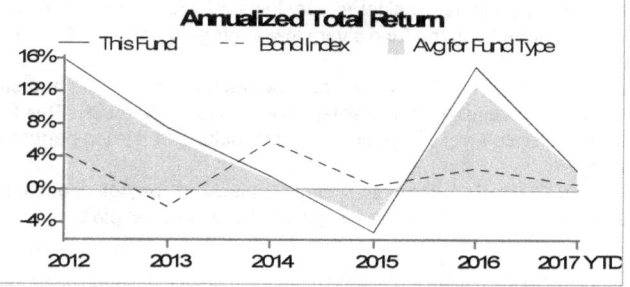

Putnam Income Fund A (PINCX)   D+   Weak

Fund Family: Putnam Funds   **Phone:** (800) 225-1581
Address: One Post Office Square, Boston, MA 02109
Fund Type: GES - General - Short & Inter. Term
Major Rating Factors: A moderate risk profile coupled with stable earnings
characterizes Putnam Income Fund A which receives a TheStreet Investment
Rating of D+ (Weak). Volatility, as measured by standard deviation, is
considered low for fixed income funds at 2.72. Another risk factor is the fund's
fairly average duration of 5.9 years (i.e. average interest rate risk). The fund's
risk rating is currently B- (Good).

The fund's performance rating is currently C- (Fair). It has registered an
average return of 1.46% over the last three years and is up 1.77% over the last
three months. Factored into the performance evaluation is an expense ratio of
0.86% (average) and a 4.0% front-end load that is levied at the time of purchase.

Michael V. Salm has been running the fund for 10 years and currently
receives a manager quality ranking of 59 (0=worst, 99=best). If you desire
stability with a moderate level of risk then this fund is an excellent option.
Services Offered: Automated phone transactions, payroll deductions, an IRA
investment plan, a 401K investment plan, a Keogh investment plan and a
systematic withdrawal plan.

Data Date	Investment Rating	Net Assets ($Mil)	NAV	Perfor-mance Rating/Pts	Total Return Y-T-D	Risk Rating/Pts
2-17	D+	749	6.87	C- / 3.0	1.77%	B- / 7.0
2016	D	767	6.79	D+ / 2.3	2.04%	B- / 7.0
2015	C-	1,073	6.87	C- / 3.2	-1.75%	B- / 7.5
2014	B+	1,066	7.20	C+ / 6.0	5.13%	C+ / 6.9
2013	A	779	7.14	B- / 7.0	2.06%	C+ / 6.6
2012	B	876	7.27	C / 5.3	10.59%	C+ / 6.3

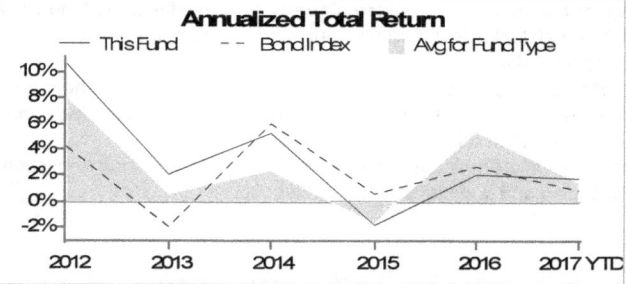

Putnam NY Tax Exempt Income A (PTEIX)   C+   Fair

Fund Family: Putnam Funds   **Phone:** (800) 225-1581
Address: One Post Office Square, Boston, MA 02109
Fund Type: MUS - Municipal - Single State
Major Rating Factors: Middle of the road best describes Putnam NY Tax
Exempt Income A whose TheStreet Investment Rating is currently a C+ (Fair).
The fund has a performance rating of C+ (Fair) based on an average return of
3.53% over the last three years (5.85% taxable equivalent) and 1.01% over the
last three months (1.67% taxable equivalent). Factored into the performance
evaluation is an expense ratio of 0.75% (low) and a 4.0% front-end load that is
levied at the time of purchase.

The fund's risk rating is currently C (Fair). Volatility, as measured by
standard deviation, is considered average for fixed income funds at 3.07.
Another risk factor is the fund's fairly average duration of 6.6 years (i.e. average
interest rate risk).

Paul M. Drury has been running the fund for 15 years and currently receives
a manager quality ranking of 56 (0=worst, 99=best). If you desire an average
level of risk, then this fund may be an option.
Services Offered: Automated phone transactions, payroll deductions, bank draft
capabilities and a systematic withdrawal plan.

Data Date	Investment Rating	Net Assets ($Mil)	NAV	Perfor-mance Rating/Pts	Total Return Y-T-D	Risk Rating/Pts
2-17	C+	888	8.43	C+ / 5.8	1.01%	C / 5.2
2016	C+	892	8.39	C+ / 6.1	0.46%	C / 5.1
2015	C+	919	8.63	B / 7.8	2.81%	C / 4.5
2014	B-	950	8.69	B- / 7.4	9.51%	C- / 4.1
2013	D	953	8.23	C- / 4.0	-4.54%	C- / 4.0
2012	C+	1,183	8.95	C+ / 6.2	7.26%	C / 4.3

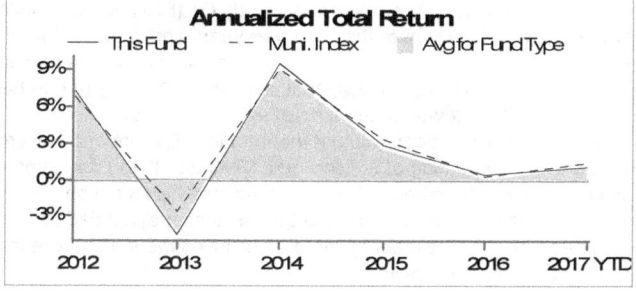

Putnam Short Duration Income A (PSDTX)

C+ **Fair**

Fund Family: Putnam Funds   **Phone:** (800) 225-1581
Address: One Post Office Square, Boston, MA 02109
Fund Type: COI - Corporate - Investment Grade

Major Rating Factors: Disappointing performance is the major factor driving the C+ (Fair) TheStreet Investment Rating for Putnam Short Duration Income A. The fund currently has a performance rating of D (Weak) based on an average return of 0.61% over the last three years and 0.25% over the last three months. Factored into the performance evaluation is an expense ratio of 0.54% (very low).

The fund's risk rating is currently A+ (Excellent). Volatility, as measured by standard deviation, is considered very low for fixed income funds at 0.20. Another risk factor is the fund's very low average duration of 0.1 years (i.e. low interest rate risk).

Joanne M. Driscoll has been running the fund for 6 years and currently receives a manager quality ranking of 64 (0=worst, 99=best). This fund offers only a moderate level of risk but investors looking for strong performance are still waiting.

Services Offered: Automated phone transactions, payroll deductions, bank draft capabilities, wire transfers and a systematic withdrawal plan.

Data Date	Investment Rating	Net Assets ($Mil)	NAV	Performance Rating/Pts	Total Return Y-T-D	Risk Rating/Pts
2-17	C+	3,532	10.05	D / 2.2	0.25%	A+ / 9.9
2016	C+	3,007	10.04	D+ / 2.4	0.97%	A+ / 9.9
2015	B+	1,339	10.02	C / 4.6	0.27%	A+ / 9.9
2014	C	1,479	10.04	D / 1.6	0.51%	A+ / 9.9
2013	U	1,176	10.04	U / --	0.59%	U / --
2012	U	419	10.04	U / --	0.94%	U / --

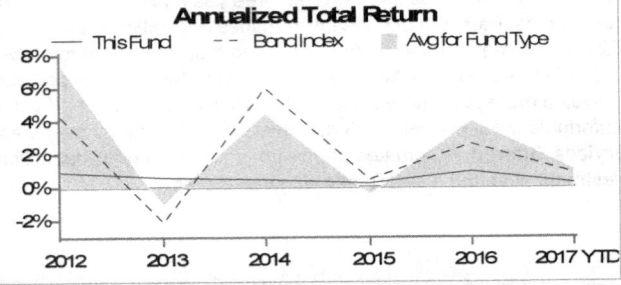

Annualized Total Return

Putnam Tax Exempt Income A (PTAEX)

B- **Good**

Fund Family: Putnam Funds   **Phone:** (800) 225-1581
Address: One Post Office Square, Boston, MA 02109
Fund Type: MUN - Municipal - National

Major Rating Factors: Putnam Tax Exempt Income A receives a TheStreet Investment Rating of B- (Good). The fund has a performance rating of C+ (Fair) based on an average return of 3.55% over the last three years (5.88% taxable equivalent) and 1.06% over the last three months (1.76% taxable equivalent). Factored into the performance evaluation is an expense ratio of 0.75% (low) and a 4.0% front-end load that is levied at the time of purchase.

The fund's risk rating is currently C+ (Fair). Volatility, as measured by standard deviation, is considered average for fixed income funds at 2.93. Another risk factor is the fund's fairly average duration of 6.4 years (i.e. average interest rate risk).

Paul M. Drury has been running the fund for 15 years and currently receives a manager quality ranking of 62 (0=worst, 99=best). If you desire an average level of risk, then this fund may be an option.

Services Offered: Automated phone transactions, payroll deductions, bank draft capabilities and a systematic withdrawal plan.

Data Date	Investment Rating	Net Assets ($Mil)	NAV	Performance Rating/Pts	Total Return Y-T-D	Risk Rating/Pts
2-17	B-	826	8.50	C+ / 5.9	1.06%	C+ / 5.9
2016	B-	836	8.46	C+ / 6.2	0.37%	C / 5.5
2015	C+	874	8.74	B / 8.0	2.64%	C / 4.5
2014	B+	904	8.84	B / 8.2	9.92%	C- / 4.2
2013	C	910	8.37	C+ / 6.2	-4.10%	C- / 4.0
2012	B+	1,153	9.08	B- / 7.5	8.79%	C- / 4.1

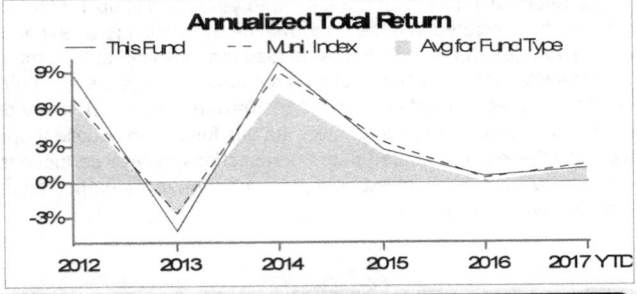

Annualized Total Return

Putnam Tax-Free Hi-Yield A (PTHAX)

D **Weak**

Fund Family: Putnam Funds   **Phone:** (800) 225-1581
Address: One Post Office Square, Boston, MA 02109
Fund Type: COH - Corporate - High Yield

Major Rating Factors: Putnam Tax-Free Hi-Yield A has adopted a risky asset allocation strategy and currently receives an overall TheStreet Investment Rating of D (Weak). Volatility, as measured by standard deviation, is considered above average for fixed income funds at 3.81. Another risk factor is the fund's above average duration of 7.2 years (i.e. higher interest rate risk). Unfortunately, the high level of risk (D+, Weak) has only provided investors with average performance.

The fund's performance rating is currently C+ (Fair). It has registered an average return of 5.34% over the last three years and is up 1.90% over the last three months. Factored into the performance evaluation is an expense ratio of 0.83% (low), a 4.0% front-end load that is levied at the time of purchase and a 1.0% back-end load levied at the time of sale.

Paul M. Drury has been running the fund for 15 years and currently receives a manager quality ranking of 96 (0=worst, 99=best). If you are comfortable owning a high risk investment, then this fund may be an option.

Services Offered: Automated phone transactions, payroll deductions, bank draft capabilities, an IRA investment plan, a 401K investment plan, wire transfers and a systematic withdrawal plan.

Data Date	Investment Rating	Net Assets ($Mil)	NAV	Performance Rating/Pts	Total Return Y-T-D	Risk Rating/Pts
2-17	D	739	12.29	C+ / 6.3	1.90%	D+ / 2.4
2016	D	734	12.14	C+ / 6.4	0.90%	D+ / 2.4
2015	C-	771	12.53	B / 8.1	4.35%	D / 1.9
2014	D+	815	12.53	B / 7.9	13.70%	D- / 1.1
2013	D-	770	11.53	C / 4.3	-5.41%	D / 2.0
2012	D+	951	12.76	C+ / 6.5	13.01%	D+ / 2.4

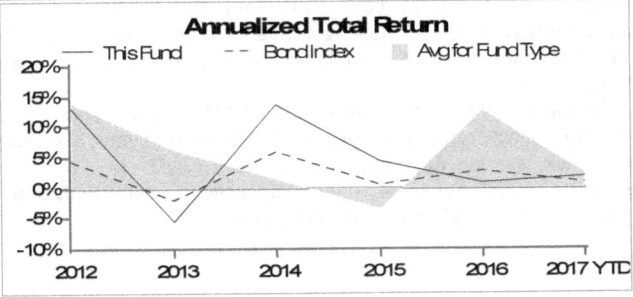

Annualized Total Return

Putnam US Govt Income Tr A (PGSIX)   D   Weak

Fund Family: Putnam Funds   **Phone:** (800) 225-1581
Address: One Post Office Square, Boston, MA 02109
Fund Type: USS - US Government - Short & Inter. Term
Major Rating Factors: Disappointing performance is the major factor driving the D (Weak) TheStreet Investment Rating for Putnam US Govt Income Tr A. The fund currently has a performance rating of D- (Weak) based on an average return of 1.11% over the last three years and 0.28% over the last three months. Factored into the performance evaluation is an expense ratio of 0.85% (average) and a 4.0% front-end load that is levied at the time of purchase.

The fund's risk rating is currently B+ (Good). Volatility, as measured by standard deviation, is considered low for fixed income funds at 1.68. Another risk factor is the fund's below average duration of 3.2 years (i.e. lower interest rate risk).

Michael V. Salm has been running the fund for 10 years and currently receives a manager quality ranking of 78 (0=worst, 99=best). This fund offers only a moderate level of risk but investors looking for strong performance are still waiting.

Services Offered: Automated phone transactions, payroll deductions, an IRA investment plan, a 401K investment plan and a systematic withdrawal plan.

Data Date	Investment Rating	Net Assets ($Mil)	NAV	Performance Rating/Pts	Total Return Y-T-D	Risk Rating/Pts
2-17	D	697	13.03	D- / 1.4	0.28%	B+ / 8.6
2016	C-	719	13.06	D+ / 2.5	0.63%	B+ / 8.4
2015	C	811	13.36	C- / 4.2	-0.26%	B- / 7.3
2014	C-	881	13.73	C- / 3.0	5.49%	B- / 7.3
2013	D+	930	13.26	D / 1.9	-0.48%	B / 8.0
2012	D+	1,203	13.53	D- / 1.4	3.31%	B+ / 8.6

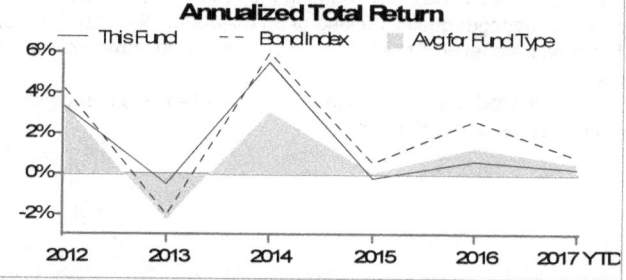

Annualized Total Return

RidgeWorth Seix US Gvt Sec US Bd I (SIGVX)   C+   Fair

Fund Family: RidgeWorth Funds   **Phone:** (888) 784-3863
Address: 50 Hurt Plaza, Atlanta, GA 30303
Fund Type: USS - US Government - Short & Inter. Term
Major Rating Factors: Disappointing performance is the major factor driving the C+ (Fair) TheStreet Investment Rating for RidgeWorth Seix US Gvt Sec US Bd I. The fund currently has a performance rating of D (Weak) based on an average return of 0.50% over the last three years and 0.18% over the last three months. Factored into the performance evaluation is an expense ratio of 0.41% (very low).

The fund's risk rating is currently A+ (Excellent). Volatility, as measured by standard deviation, is considered very low for fixed income funds at 0.24. Another risk factor is the fund's very low average duration of 0.3 years (i.e. low interest rate risk).

James F. Keegan has been running the fund for 3 years and currently receives a manager quality ranking of 61 (0=worst, 99=best). This fund offers only a moderate level of risk but investors looking for strong performance are still waiting.

Services Offered: Automated phone transactions and a systematic withdrawal plan.

Data Date	Investment Rating	Net Assets ($Mil)	NAV	Performance Rating/Pts	Total Return Y-T-D	Risk Rating/Pts
2-17	C+	1,344	10.02	D / 2.0	0.18%	A+ / 9.9
2016	C+	1,391	10.02	D+ / 2.3	0.64%	A+ / 9.9
2015	B	1,520	10.05	C- / 4.1	-0.03%	A+ / 9.9
2014	C	1,728	10.13	D / 1.8	0.91%	A+ / 9.9
2013	C	2,099	10.11	D / 1.6	0.05%	A+ / 9.9
2012	C-	2,388	10.17	E+ / 0.7	1.55%	A+ / 9.9

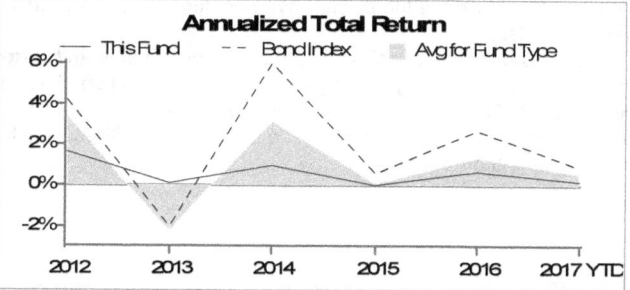

Annualized Total Return

SA Global Fixed Income (SAXIX)   C   Fair

Fund Family: SA Funds   **Phone:** (800) 366-7266
Address: 3055 Olin Avenue, San Jose, CA 95128
Fund Type: GES - General - Short & Inter. Term
Major Rating Factors: Disappointing performance is the major factor driving the C (Fair) TheStreet Investment Rating for SA Global Fixed Income. The fund currently has a performance rating of D+ (Weak) based on an average return of 0.89% over the last three years and 0.52% over the last three months. Factored into the performance evaluation is an expense ratio of 0.73% (low).

The fund's risk rating is currently A- (Excellent). Volatility, as measured by standard deviation, is considered very low for fixed income funds at 1.31.

David A. Plecha has been running the fund for 18 years and currently receives a manager quality ranking of 29 (0=worst, 99=best). This fund offers only a moderate level of risk but investors looking for strong performance are still waiting.

Services Offered: Automated phone transactions, bank draft capabilities, an IRA investment plan and wire transfers.

Data Date	Investment Rating	Net Assets ($Mil)	NAV	Performance Rating/Pts	Total Return Y-T-D	Risk Rating/Pts
2-17	C	722	9.62	D+ / 2.3	0.52%	A- / 9.0
2016	C	714	9.57	D+ / 2.4	0.93%	A- / 9.0
2015	B-	741	9.60	C / 4.4	0.27%	A- / 9.0
2014	C	751	9.65	D+ / 2.3	1.47%	A- / 9.2
2013	C-	631	9.62	D / 1.9	-0.49%	A- / 9.0
2012	D+	564	9.86	D- / 1.1	2.80%	A- / 9.0

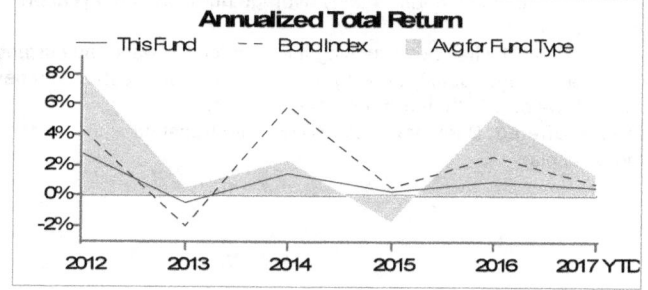

Annualized Total Return

SA US Fixed Income Fund (SAUFX)   C   Fair

Fund Family: SA Funds   **Phone:** (800) 366-7266
Address: 3055 Olin Avenue, San Jose, CA 95128
Fund Type: GEI - General - Investment Grade

Major Rating Factors: Disappointing performance is the major factor driving the C (Fair) TheStreet Investment Rating for SA US Fixed Income Fund. The fund currently has a performance rating of D- (Weak) based on an average return of 0.21% over the last three years and 0.20% over the last three months. Factored into the performance evaluation is an expense ratio of 0.65% (low).

The fund's risk rating is currently A+ (Excellent). Volatility, as measured by standard deviation, is considered very low for fixed income funds at 0.51.

David A. Plecha has been running the fund for 18 years and currently receives a manager quality ranking of 33 (0=worst, 99=best). This fund offers only a moderate level of risk but investors looking for strong performance are still waiting.

Services Offered: Bank draft capabilities, an IRA investment plan, a 401K investment plan and wire transfers.

Data Date	Investment Rating	Net Assets ($Mil)	NAV	Performance Rating/Pts	Total Return Y-T-D	Risk Rating/Pts
2-17	C	610	10.19	D- / 1.5	0.20%	A+ / 9.8
2016	C	607	10.17	D / 1.6	0.63%	A+ / 9.8
2015	C	610	10.15	D+ / 2.9	0.06%	A+ / 9.8
2014	D+	594	10.17	E+ / 0.8	-0.17%	A+ / 9.9
2013	C-	459	10.19	E+ / 0.7	-0.27%	A+ / 9.9
2012	C-	392	10.22	E / 0.5	0.31%	A+ / 9.9

Annualized Total Return

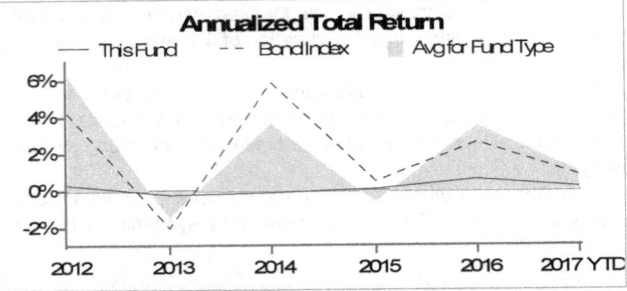

Sanford C Bernstein II Int Dur Inst (SIIDX)   C+   Fair

Fund Family: Alliance Bernstein Funds   **Phone:** (800) 221-5672
Address: P.O. Box 786003, San Antonio, TX 78278
Fund Type: GES - General - Short & Inter. Term

Major Rating Factors: Middle of the road best describes Sanford C Bernstein II Int Dur Inst whose TheStreet Investment Rating is currently a C+ (Fair). The fund has a performance rating of C+ (Fair) based on an average return of 3.28% over the last three years and 0.92% over the last three months. Factored into the performance evaluation is an expense ratio of 0.58% (low).

The fund's risk rating is currently C (Fair). Volatility, as measured by standard deviation, is considered average for fixed income funds at 3.05. Another risk factor is the fund's fairly average duration of 5.4 years (i.e. average interest rate risk).

Greg Wilensky has been running the fund for 12 years and currently receives a manager quality ranking of 67 (0=worst, 99=best). If you desire an average level of risk, then this fund may be an option.

Services Offered: Payroll deductions, bank draft capabilities, wire transfers and a systematic withdrawal plan.

Data Date	Investment Rating	Net Assets ($Mil)	NAV	Performance Rating/Pts	Total Return Y-T-D	Risk Rating/Pts
2-17	C+	613	14.95	C+ / 6.2	0.92%	C / 5.3
2016	B	598	14.88	C+ / 6.6	4.30%	C / 5.4
2015	C+	613	14.86	C+ / 6.5	0.42%	C / 5.5
2014	C+	647	15.42	C / 5.1	6.59%	C+ / 6.3
2013	C+	701	15.35	C / 4.3	-2.03%	C+ / 6.9
2012	B	1,039	16.23	C / 4.5	5.53%	B- / 7.3

Annualized Total Return

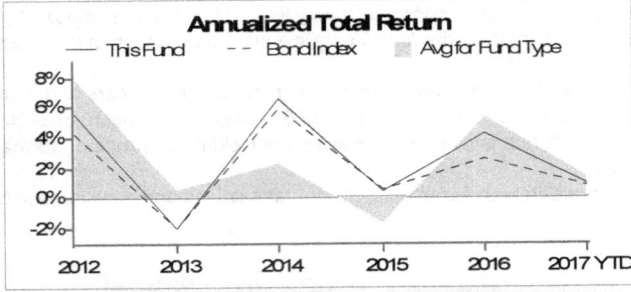

Sanford C Bernstein Interm Duration (SNIDX)   C+   Fair

Fund Family: Bernstein Funds   **Phone:** (212) 486-5800
Address: 1345 Avenue of the Americas, New York, NY 10105
Fund Type: GES - General - Short & Inter. Term

Major Rating Factors: Middle of the road best describes Sanford C Bernstein Interm Duration whose TheStreet Investment Rating is currently a C+ (Fair). The fund has a performance rating of C+ (Fair) based on an average return of 3.21% over the last three years and 1.05% over the last three months. Factored into the performance evaluation is an expense ratio of 0.59% (low).

The fund's risk rating is currently C (Fair). Volatility, as measured by standard deviation, is considered average for fixed income funds at 3.04. Another risk factor is the fund's fairly average duration of 5.3 years (i.e. average interest rate risk).

Greg Wilensky has been running the fund for 12 years and currently receives a manager quality ranking of 65 (0=worst, 99=best). If you desire an average level of risk, then this fund may be an option.

Services Offered: Bank draft capabilities, wire transfers and a systematic withdrawal plan.

Data Date	Investment Rating	Net Assets ($Mil)	NAV	Performance Rating/Pts	Total Return Y-T-D	Risk Rating/Pts
2-17	C+	3,333	13.12	C+ / 6.1	1.05%	C / 5.3
2016	B-	3,301	13.04	C+ / 6.4	4.14%	C / 5.4
2015	C	3,338	13.01	C+ / 6.3	0.31%	C / 5.5
2014	C+	3,597	13.53	C / 5.0	6.59%	C+ / 6.3
2013	C	3,840	13.35	C- / 4.0	-2.36%	C+ / 6.9
2012	C+	4,616	14.09	C / 4.3	5.26%	B- / 7.0

Annualized Total Return

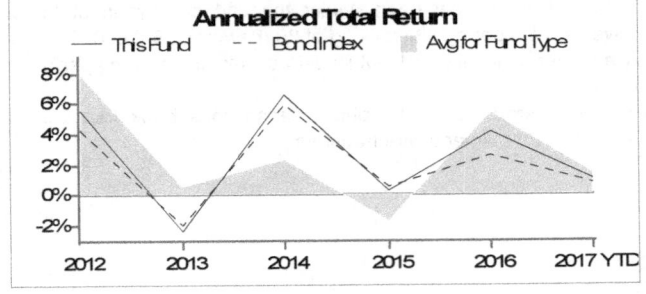

Schwab Tax-Free Bond Fund (SWNTX)   B-   Good

Fund Family: Schwab Funds   **Phone:** (800) 407-0256
Address: P.O. Box 8283, Boston, MA 02266
Fund Type: MUN - Municipal - National

Major Rating Factors: Schwab Tax-Free Bond Fund receives a TheStreet Investment Rating of B- (Good). The fund has a performance rating of C+ (Fair) based on an average return of 2.53% over the last three years (4.19% taxable equivalent) and 1.18% over the last three months (1.95% taxable equivalent). Factored into the performance evaluation is an expense ratio of 0.57% (very low).

The fund's risk rating is currently C+ (Fair). Volatility, as measured by standard deviation, is considered average for fixed income funds at 2.98. Another risk factor is the fund's below average duration of 4.8 years (i.e. lower interest rate risk).

Kenneth M. Salinger has been running the fund for 9 years and currently receives a manager quality ranking of 19 (0=worst, 99=best). If you desire an average level of risk, then this fund may be an option.

Services Offered: Automated phone transactions, payroll deductions, bank draft capabilities and wire transfers.

Data Date	Investment Rating	Net Assets ($Mil)	NAV	Performance Rating/Pts	Total Return Y-T-D	Risk Rating/Pts
2-17	B-	651	11.57	C+ / 6.1	1.18%	C+ / 5.6
2016	C+	666	11.48	C+ / 5.9	-0.36%	C+ / 5.7
2015	A+	650	11.88	B+ / 8.9	2.65%	C+ / 6.9
2014	A	642	11.89	B / 7.6	6.54%	C+ / 5.8
2013	A+	591	11.53	B / 8.2	-1.32%	C+ / 6.2
2012	A	713	11.96	C+ / 6.9	5.55%	C+ / 5.9

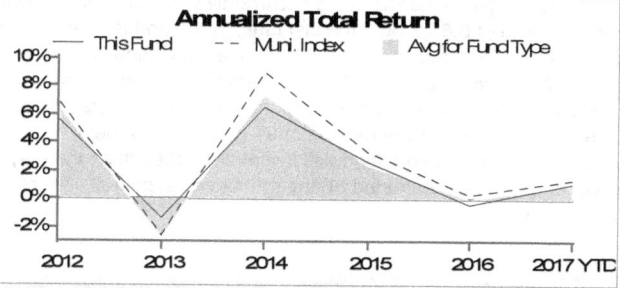

Schwab Total Bond Market Fd (SWLBX)   C-   Fair

Fund Family: Schwab Funds   **Phone:** (800) 407-0256
Address: P.O. Box 8283, Boston, MA 02266
Fund Type: USL - US Government - Long Term

Major Rating Factors: Middle of the road best describes Schwab Total Bond Market Fd whose TheStreet Investment Rating is currently a C- (Fair). The fund has a performance rating of C (Fair) based on an average return of 2.39% over the last three years and 0.92% over the last three months. Factored into the performance evaluation is an expense ratio of 0.54% (very low).

The fund's risk rating is currently C+ (Fair). Volatility, as measured by standard deviation, is considered average for fixed income funds at 2.97. Another risk factor is the fund's fairly average duration of 5.4 years (i.e. average interest rate risk).

Steven Hung has been running the fund for 19 years and currently receives a manager quality ranking of 70 (0=worst, 99=best). If you desire an average level of risk, then this fund may be an option.

Services Offered: Automated phone transactions, payroll deductions, bank draft capabilities, an IRA investment plan, a 401K investment plan, a Keogh investment plan and wire transfers. However, the fund is currently closed to new investors.

Data Date	Investment Rating	Net Assets ($Mil)	NAV	Performance Rating/Pts	Total Return Y-T-D	Risk Rating/Pts
2-17	C-	1,244	9.44	C / 4.3	0.92%	C+ / 5.7
2016	C-	1,365	9.39	C / 4.7	2.23%	C+ / 5.9
2015	C+	1,355	9.39	C+ / 5.9	0.29%	C+ / 6.4
2014	C	1,266	9.57	C- / 4.0	5.83%	B- / 7.1
2013	C	890	9.25	C- / 3.4	-2.38%	B / 7.6
2012	C	927	9.70	C- / 3.0	3.80%	B / 7.6

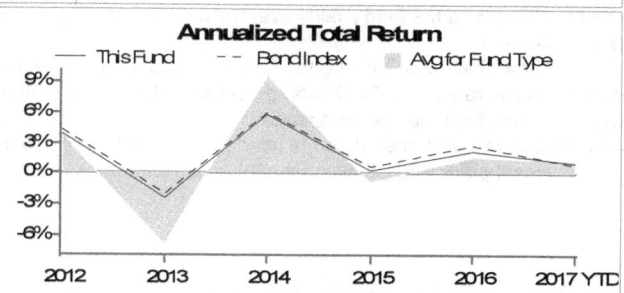

SEI Daily Inc Tr-Sh Dur Gov Bd F (TCSGX)   C   Fair

Fund Family: SEI Financial Management Corp   **Phone:** (800) 342-5734
Address: One Freedom Valley Drive, Oaks, PA 19456
Fund Type: USS - US Government - Short & Inter. Term

Major Rating Factors: Disappointing performance is the major factor driving the C (Fair) TheStreet Investment Rating for SEI Daily Inc Tr-Sh Dur Gov Bd F. The fund currently has a performance rating of D (Weak) based on an average return of 0.62% over the last three years and 0.08% over the last three months. Factored into the performance evaluation is an expense ratio of 0.69% (low).

The fund's risk rating is currently A (Excellent). Volatility, as measured by standard deviation, is considered very low for fixed income funds at 0.88. Another risk factor is the fund's very low average duration of 1.6 years (i.e. low interest rate risk).

This fund offers only a moderate level of risk but investors looking for strong performance are still waiting.

Services Offered: Automated phone transactions and bank draft capabilities.

Data Date	Investment Rating	Net Assets ($Mil)	NAV	Performance Rating/Pts	Total Return Y-T-D	Risk Rating/Pts
2-17	C	777	10.43	D / 2.0	0.08%	A / 9.4
2016	C	808	10.44	D+ / 2.3	1.21%	A / 9.4
2015	C	782	10.43	D+ / 2.9	-0.57%	A / 9.3
2014	C-	715	10.50	D- / 1.5	0.73%	A / 9.5
2013	C	716	10.52	D / 1.7	-0.37%	A / 9.4
2012	C-	708	10.65	D- / 1.0	1.48%	A / 9.5

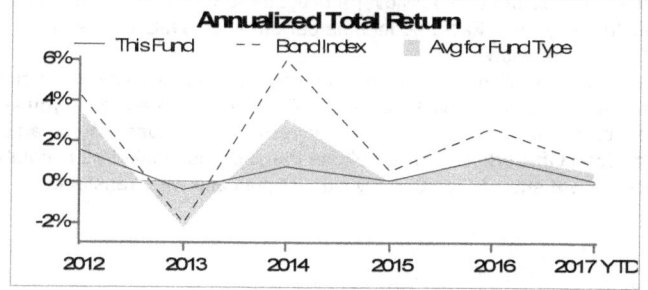

SEI Inst Intl Emerging Mkts Debt F (SITEX)

E+   Very Weak

Fund Family: SEI Financial Management Corp   **Phone:** (800) 342-5734
Address: One Freedom Valley Drive, Oaks, PA 19456
Fund Type: EM - Emerging Market

Major Rating Factors: SEI Inst Intl Emerging Mkts Debt F has adopted a very risky asset allocation strategy and currently receives an overall TheStreet Investment Rating of E+ (Very Weak). Volatility, as measured by standard deviation, is considered high for fixed income funds at 9.36. Another risk factor is the fund's fairly average duration of 6.7 years (i.e. average interest rate risk). Unfortunately, the high level of risk (E-, Very Weak) has only provided investors with average performance.

The fund's performance rating is currently C (Fair). It has registered an average return of 0.67% over the last three years and is up 4.37% over the last three months. Factored into the performance evaluation is an expense ratio of 1.61% (above average) and a 1.0% back-end load levied at the time of sale.

David S. Aniloff has been running the fund for 17 years and currently receives a manager quality ranking of 91 (0=worst, 99=best). If you are comfortable owning a very high risk investment, then this fund may be an option.
Services Offered: Automated phone transactions, payroll deductions and bank draft capabilities.

Data Date	Investment Rating	Net Assets ($Mil)	NAV	Performance Rating/Pts	Total Return Y-T-D	Risk Rating/Pts
2-17	E+	1,339	9.79	C / 4.9	4.37%	E- / 0.2
2016	E-	1,268	9.38	E+ / 0.6	9.40%	E- / 0.2
2015	E-	1,258	8.71	E- / 0.1	-9.12%	E / 0.3
2014	E-	1,322	9.63	E+ / 0.8	-1.20%	E / 0.3
2013	E	1,164	10.02	D+ / 2.3	-9.59%	E / 0.4
2012	B-	1,221	11.57	A / 9.4	17.54%	D- / 1.1

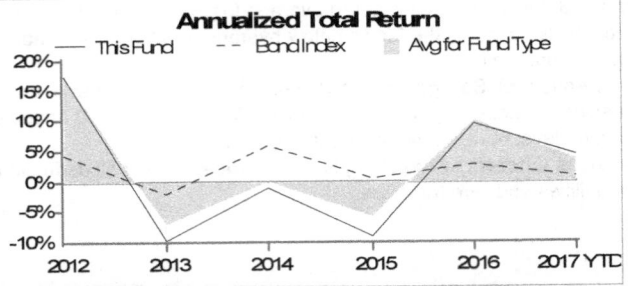

Annualized Total Return

SEI Inst Inv Core Fixed Income A (SCOAX)

B+   Good

Fund Family: SEI Financial Management Corp   **Phone:** (800) 342-5734
Address: One Freedom Valley Drive, Oaks, PA 19456
Fund Type: COI - Corporate - Investment Grade

Major Rating Factors: SEI Inst Inv Core Fixed Income A receives a TheStreet Investment Rating of B+ (Good). The fund has a performance rating of C+ (Fair) based on an average return of 3.22% over the last three years and 1.03% over the last three months. Factored into the performance evaluation is an expense ratio of 0.37% (very low).

The fund's risk rating is currently C+ (Fair). Volatility, as measured by standard deviation, is considered average for fixed income funds at 2.82. Another risk factor is the fund's fairly average duration of 7.0 years (i.e. average interest rate risk).

Erin Garrett has been running the fund for 3 years and currently receives a manager quality ranking of 70 (0=worst, 99=best). If you desire an average level of risk, then this fund may be an option.
Services Offered: Automated phone transactions, bank draft capabilities, an IRA investment plan, a 401K investment plan and wire transfers.

Data Date	Investment Rating	Net Assets ($Mil)	NAV	Performance Rating/Pts	Total Return Y-T-D	Risk Rating/Pts
2-17	B+	5,630	10.22	C+ / 6.0	1.03%	C+ / 6.5
2016	B+	5,461	10.16	C+ / 6.3	3.36%	C+ / 6.6
2015	B-	5,180	10.20	B- / 7.2	0.85%	C+ / 5.9
2014	A-	6,295	10.59	C+ / 6.1	6.76%	B- / 7.1

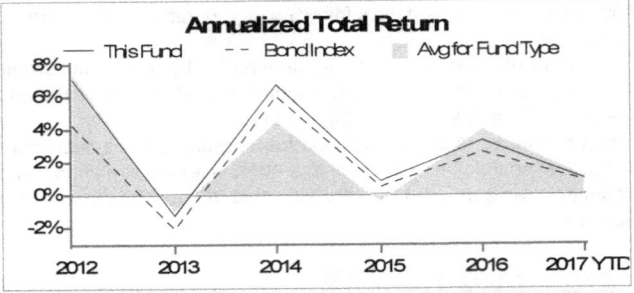

Annualized Total Return

SEI Inst Inv High Yield Bond A (SGYAX)

B-   Good

Fund Family: SEI Financial Management Corp   **Phone:** (800) 342-5734
Address: One Freedom Valley Drive, Oaks, PA 19456
Fund Type: COH - Corporate - High Yield

Major Rating Factors: SEI Inst Inv High Yield Bond A has adopted a very risky asset allocation strategy and currently receives an overall TheStreet Investment Rating of B- (Good). Volatility, as measured by standard deviation, is considered above average for fixed income funds at 5.69. Another risk factor is the fund's below average duration of 4.8 years (i.e. lower interest rate risk). The high level of risk (D-, Weak) did however, reward investors with excellent performance.

The fund's performance rating is currently A+ (Excellent). It has registered an average return of 5.02% over the last three years and is up 3.06% over the last three months. Factored into the performance evaluation is an expense ratio of 0.56% (very low).

Michael E. Schroer has been running the fund for 8 years and currently receives a manager quality ranking of 68 (0=worst, 99=best). If you are comfortable owning a very high risk investment, this fund may be an option.
Services Offered: Automated phone transactions, bank draft capabilities, an IRA investment plan, a 401K investment plan and wire transfers.

Data Date	Investment Rating	Net Assets ($Mil)	NAV	Performance Rating/Pts	Total Return Y-T-D	Risk Rating/Pts
2-17	B-	2,885	9.12	A+ / 9.8	3.06%	D- / 1.1
2016	C+	2,870	8.94	A+ / 9.7	17.19%	D- / 1.1
2015	D	2,296	8.22	C / 4.4	-4.16%	D / 2.1
2014	B+	2,205	9.22	B+ / 8.6	2.54%	C- / 3.6

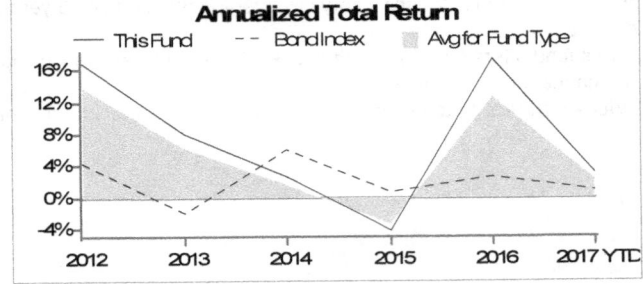

Annualized Total Return

SEI Inst Inv Long Dur Credit A (SLDAX)   C-   Fair

Fund Family: SEI Financial Management Corp   **Phone:** (800) 342-5734
Address: One Freedom Valley Drive, Oaks, PA 19456
Fund Type: GEI - General - Investment Grade

Major Rating Factors: SEI Inst Inv Long Dur Credit A has adopted a very risky asset allocation strategy and currently receives an overall TheStreet Investment Rating of C- (Fair). Volatility, as measured by standard deviation, is considered high for fixed income funds at 7.62. Another risk factor is the fund's very high average duration of 14.5 years (i.e. very high interest rate risk). The high level of risk (E, Very Weak) did however, reward investors with excellent performance.

The fund's performance rating is currently A- (Excellent). It has registered an average return of 6.15% over the last three years and is up 2.05% over the last three months. Factored into the performance evaluation is an expense ratio of 0.37% (very low).

Jack Sommers has been running the fund for 5 years and currently receives a manager quality ranking of 39 (0=worst, 99=best). If you are comfortable owning a very high risk investment, this fund may be an option.

Services Offered: Automated phone transactions, bank draft capabilities, an IRA investment plan, a 401K investment plan and wire transfers.

Data Date	Investment Rating	Net Assets ($Mil)	NAV	Performance Rating/Pts	Total Return Y-T-D	Risk Rating/Pts
2-17	C-	3,225	10.11	A- / 9.1	2.05%	E / 0.4
2016	C	3,120	9.97	A / 9.5	8.50%	E / 0.4
2015	D+	3,024	9.57	B- / 7.2	-2.71%	E / 0.3
2014	U	3,151	10.47	U / --	17.04%	U / --

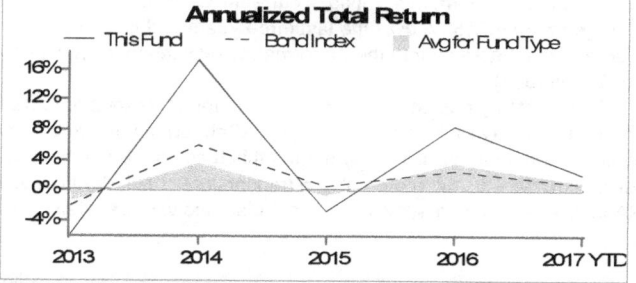

Annualized Total Return

SEI Inst Inv Long Duration A (LDRAX)   C-   Fair

Fund Family: SEI Financial Management Corp   **Phone:** (800) 342-5734
Address: One Freedom Valley Drive, Oaks, PA 19456
Fund Type: COI - Corporate - Investment Grade

Major Rating Factors: SEI Inst Inv Long Duration A has adopted a very risky asset allocation strategy and currently receives an overall TheStreet Investment Rating of C- (Fair). Volatility, as measured by standard deviation, is considered high for fixed income funds at 8.19. Another risk factor is the fund's very high average duration of 14.5 years (i.e. very high interest rate risk). The high level of risk (E, Very Weak) did however, reward investors with excellent performance.

The fund's performance rating is currently A- (Excellent). It has registered an average return of 6.26% over the last three years and is up 2.39% over the last three months. Factored into the performance evaluation is an expense ratio of 0.37% (very low).

Tad Rivelle has been running the fund for 13 years and currently receives a manager quality ranking of 13 (0=worst, 99=best). If you are comfortable owning a very high risk investment, this fund may be an option.

Services Offered: Automated phone transactions.

Data Date	Investment Rating	Net Assets ($Mil)	NAV	Performance Rating/Pts	Total Return Y-T-D	Risk Rating/Pts
2-17	C-	2,297	8.30	A- / 9.0	2.39%	E / 0.3
2016	C	2,430	8.16	A / 9.5	8.20%	E / 0.3
2015	D	2,781	8.07	C+ / 5.8	-3.69%	E / 0.3
2014	C-	3,967	9.13	A- / 9.1	19.00%	E / 0.3

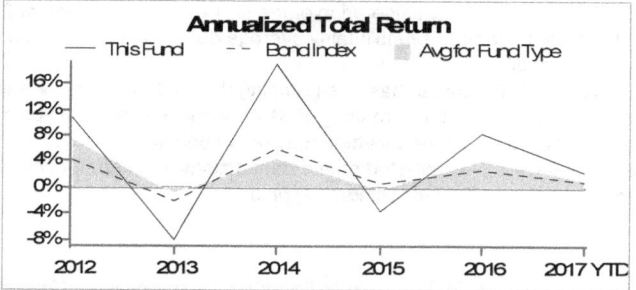

Annualized Total Return

SEI Inst Inv Ultra Short Dur Bd A (SUSAX)   B   Good

Fund Family: SEI Financial Management Corp   **Phone:** (800) 342-5734
Address: One Freedom Valley Drive, Oaks, PA 19456
Fund Type: GEI - General - Investment Grade

Major Rating Factors: A moderate risk profile coupled with stable earnings characterizes SEI Inst Inv Ultra Short Dur Bd A which receives a TheStreet Investment Rating of B (Good). Volatility, as measured by standard deviation, is considered very low for fixed income funds at 0.32. Another risk factor is the fund's very low average duration of 1.2 years (i.e. low interest rate risk). The fund's risk rating is currently A+ (Excellent).

The fund's performance rating is currently C- (Fair). It has registered an average return of 1.14% over the last three years and is up 0.36% over the last three months. Factored into the performance evaluation is an expense ratio of 0.22% (very low).

Timothy E. Smith has been running the fund for 6 years and currently receives a manager quality ranking of 74 (0=worst, 99=best). If you desire stability with a moderate level of risk then this fund is an excellent option.

Services Offered: Automated phone transactions, bank draft capabilities, a 401K investment plan and wire transfers.

Data Date	Investment Rating	Net Assets ($Mil)	NAV	Performance Rating/Pts	Total Return Y-T-D	Risk Rating/Pts
2-17	B	526	10.00	C- / 3.2	0.36%	A+ / 9.9
2016	B	523	9.99	C- / 3.3	1.85%	A+ / 9.9
2015	A-	614	9.95	C / 5.4	0.73%	A+ / 9.9
2014	C+	742	10.00	D+ / 2.3	0.74%	A+ / 9.8
2013	U	612	10.03	U / --	0.92%	U / --
2012	U	406	10.04	U / --	2.80%	U / --

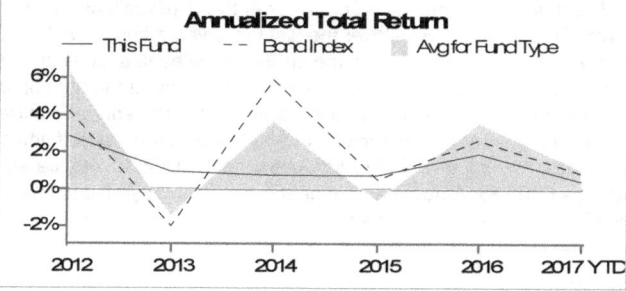

Annualized Total Return

SEI Insti Inv Tr Emer Mrk Dbt Fd A (SEDAX)   D-   Weak

Fund Family: SEI Financial Management Corp   **Phone:** (800) 342-5734
Address: One Freedom Valley Drive, Oaks, PA 19456
Fund Type: EM - Emerging Market
Major Rating Factors: SEI Insti Inv Tr Emer Mrk Dbt Fd A has adopted a very risky asset allocation strategy and currently receives an overall TheStreet Investment Rating of D- (Weak). Volatility, as measured by standard deviation, is considered high for fixed income funds at 9.23. Another risk factor is the fund's fairly average duration of 6.7 years (i.e. average interest rate risk). Unfortunately, the high level of risk (E-, Very Weak) has only provided investors with average performance.

The fund's performance rating is currently C+ (Fair). It has registered an average return of 1.68% over the last three years and is up 4.51% over the last three months. Factored into the performance evaluation is an expense ratio of 0.95% (average).

Peter J. Wilby has been running the fund for 11 years and currently receives a manager quality ranking of 94 (0=worst, 99=best). If you are comfortable owning a very high risk investment, then this fund may be an option.
Services Offered: Automated phone transactions, bank draft capabilities, an IRA investment plan, a 401K investment plan and wire transfers.

Data Date	Investment Rating	Net Assets ($Mil)	NAV	Performance Rating/Pts	Total Return Y-T-D	Risk Rating/Pts
2-17	D-	2,027	9.73	C+ / 6.8	4.51%	E- / 0.2
2016	E	1,963	9.31	C- / 3.0	10.46%	E- / 0.2
2015	E-	1,771	8.73	E- / 0.2	-8.10%	E / 0.3
2014	E	1,658	9.59	D / 2.2	-0.25%	E / 0.3

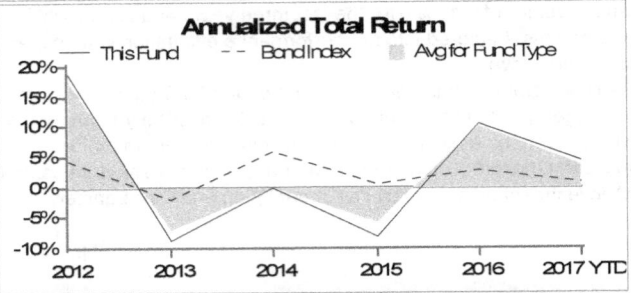
Annualized Total Return

SEI Instl Managed Tr-Core Fix Inc F (TRLVX)   C+   Fair

Fund Family: SEI Financial Management Corp   **Phone:** (800) 342-5734
Address: One Freedom Valley Drive, Oaks, PA 19456
Fund Type: COI - Corporate - Investment Grade
Major Rating Factors: Middle of the road best describes SEI Instl Managed Tr-Core Fix Inc F whose TheStreet Investment Rating is currently a C+ (Fair). The fund has a performance rating of C (Fair) based on an average return of 2.97% over the last three years and 1.12% over the last three months. Factored into the performance evaluation is an expense ratio of 0.86% (average) and a 0.6% back-end load levied at the time of sale.

The fund's risk rating is currently C+ (Fair). Volatility, as measured by standard deviation, is considered average for fixed income funds at 2.89. Another risk factor is the fund's fairly average duration of 5.2 years (i.e. average interest rate risk).

Michael C. Buchanan has been running the fund for 12 years and currently receives a manager quality ranking of 61 (0=worst, 99=best). If you desire an average level of risk, then this fund may be an option.
Services Offered: Automated phone transactions, bank draft capabilities, wire transfers and a systematic withdrawal plan.

Data Date	Investment Rating	Net Assets ($Mil)	NAV	Performance Rating/Pts	Total Return Y-T-D	Risk Rating/Pts
2-17	C+	1,879	11.18	C / 5.4	1.12%	C+ / 6.1
2016	B-	1,887	11.10	C+ / 5.7	3.35%	C+ / 6.2
2015	C+	2,025	11.22	C+ / 6.4	0.27%	C+ / 6.3
2014	B+	2,065	11.58	C+ / 6.0	6.56%	C+ / 6.9
2013	B+	1,920	11.14	C+ / 5.6	-1.56%	B / 7.6
2012	A+	2,190	11.64	C+ / 6.2	8.08%	C+ / 6.9

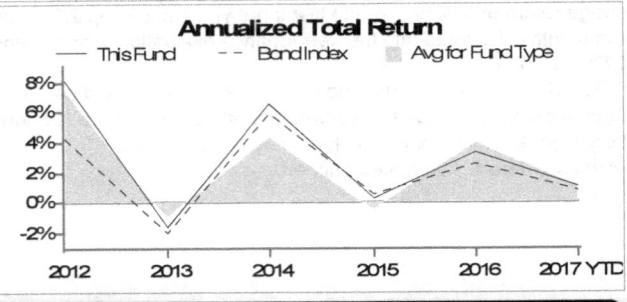
Annualized Total Return

SEI Instl Managed Tr-High Yld Bd F (SHYAX)   C+   Fair

Fund Family: SEI Financial Management Corp   **Phone:** (800) 342-5734
Address: One Freedom Valley Drive, Oaks, PA 19456
Fund Type: GEI - General - Investment Grade
Major Rating Factors: SEI Instl Managed Tr-High Yld Bd F has adopted a very risky asset allocation strategy and currently receives an overall TheStreet Investment Rating of C+ (Fair). Volatility, as measured by standard deviation, is considered high for fixed income funds at 5.89. Another risk factor is the fund's very low average duration of 2.6 years (i.e. low interest rate risk). The high level of risk (E+, Very Weak) did however, reward investors with excellent performance.

The fund's performance rating is currently A+ (Excellent). It has registered an average return of 4.52% over the last three years and is up 3.00% over the last three months. Factored into the performance evaluation is an expense ratio of 1.08% (average) and a 1.0% back-end load levied at the time of sale.

Robert L. Cook has been running the fund for 13 years and currently receives a manager quality ranking of 93 (0=worst, 99=best). If you are comfortable owning a very high risk investment, this fund may be an option.
Services Offered: Automated phone transactions, payroll deductions, bank draft capabilities, wire transfers and a systematic withdrawal plan.

Data Date	Investment Rating	Net Assets ($Mil)	NAV	Performance Rating/Pts	Total Return Y-T-D	Risk Rating/Pts
2-17	C+	1,471	7.29	A+ / 9.7	3.00%	E+ / 0.9
2016	B-	1,442	7.14	A / 9.5	17.22%	D- / 1.4
2015	D-	1,492	6.58	D / 1.9	-5.06%	D / 1.9
2014	B+	1,703	7.44	B / 7.8	1.91%	C / 4.3
2013	B+	2,055	7.75	A+ / 9.6	6.95%	D+ / 2.4
2012	B	1,848	7.72	A / 9.3	15.78%	D- / 1.5

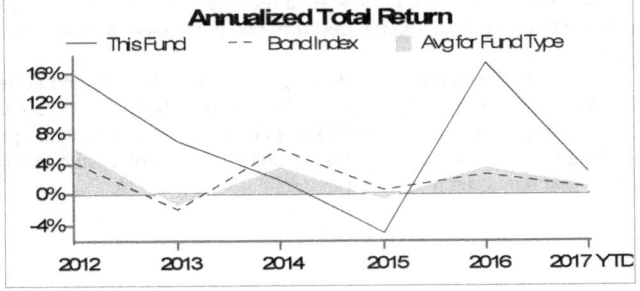
Annualized Total Return

SEI Tax-Exempt Tr-Intrm Term Muni F (SEIMX)　　　C　　Fair

Fund Family: SEI Financial Management Corp　　**Phone:** (800) 342-5734
Address: One Freedom Valley Drive, Oaks, PA 19456
Fund Type: MUN - Municipal - National

Major Rating Factors: Middle of the road best describes SEI Tax-Exempt Tr-Intrm Term Muni F whose TheStreet Investment Rating is currently a C (Fair). The fund has a performance rating of C+ (Fair) based on an average return of 2.50% over the last three years (4.14% taxable equivalent) and 1.12% over the last three months (1.85% taxable equivalent). Factored into the performance evaluation is an expense ratio of 0.81% (low) and a 0.5% back-end load levied at the time of sale.

The fund's risk rating is currently C (Fair). Volatility, as measured by standard deviation, is considered average for fixed income funds at 3.16. Another risk factor is the fund's fairly average duration of 5.6 years (i.e. average interest rate risk).

Joseph R. Baxter has been running the fund for 18 years and currently receives a manager quality ranking of 14 (0=worst, 99=best). If you desire an average level of risk, then this fund may be an option.
Services Offered: Automated phone transactions and bank draft capabilities.

Data Date	Investment Rating	Net Assets ($Mil)	NAV	Performance Rating/Pts	Total Return Y-T-D	Risk Rating/Pts
2-17	C	1,759	11.52	C+/ 5.7	1.12%	C / 4.9
2016	C	1,702	11.44	C+/ 5.6	-0.27%	C / 4.9
2015	A	1,567	11.75	B+/ 8.8	2.74%	C+/ 6.1
2014	B+	1,389	11.73	B- / 7.1	6.60%	C / 5.5
2013	A-	1,127	11.29	B- / 7.3	-1.93%	C+/ 5.7
2012	B+	1,013	11.83	C+/ 6.5	5.30%	C+/ 5.7

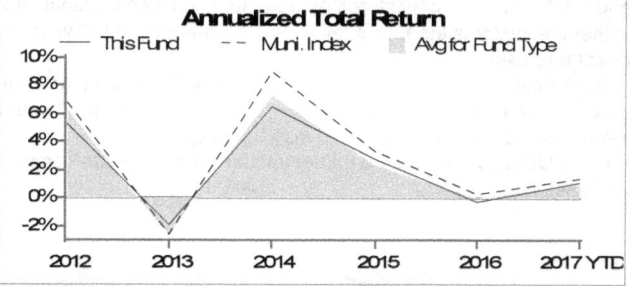

Annualized Total Return

SEI Tax-Exempt Tr-Shrt Dur Muni F (SUMAX)　　　C　　Fair

Fund Family: SEI Financial Management Corp　　**Phone:** (800) 342-5734
Address: One Freedom Valley Drive, Oaks, PA 19456
Fund Type: MUN - Municipal - National

Major Rating Factors: Disappointing performance is the major factor driving the C (Fair) TheStreet Investment Rating for SEI Tax-Exempt Tr-Shrt Dur Muni F. The fund currently has a performance rating of D (Weak) based on an average return of 0.24% over the last three years (0.40% taxable equivalent) and 0.49% over the last three months (0.81% taxable equivalent). Factored into the performance evaluation is an expense ratio of 0.82% (low).

The fund's risk rating is currently A+ (Excellent). Volatility, as measured by standard deviation, is considered very low for fixed income funds at 0.45. Another risk factor is the fund's fairly average duration of 5.2 years (i.e. average interest rate risk).

Kristian J. Lind has been running the fund for 6 years and currently receives a manager quality ranking of 32 (0=worst, 99=best). This fund offers only a moderate level of risk but investors looking for strong performance are still waiting.
Services Offered: Automated phone transactions, bank draft capabilities and wire transfers.

Data Date	Investment Rating	Net Assets ($Mil)	NAV	Performance Rating/Pts	Total Return Y-T-D	Risk Rating/Pts
2-17	C	1,351	10.01	D / 1.7	0.49%	A+/ 9.8
2016	D+	1,363	9.97	E+/ 0.8	-0.28%	A+/ 9.8
2015	B+	1,451	10.04	C / 4.9	0.18%	A+/ 9.9
2014	C	1,211	10.05	D / 1.7	0.54%	A+/ 9.9
2013	C+	1,030	10.04	D / 2.0	0.39%	A+/ 9.9
2012	C-	841	10.06	E+/ 0.7	0.89%	A+/ 9.9

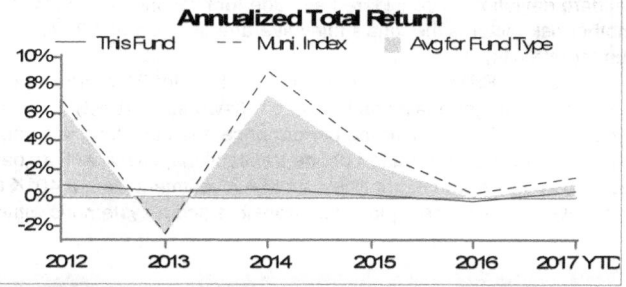

Annualized Total Return

SEI Tax-Exempt Tr-Tax Advtg Inc F (SEATX)　　　A　　Excellent

Fund Family: SEI Financial Management Corp　　**Phone:** (800) 342-5734
Address: One Freedom Valley Drive, Oaks, PA 19456
Fund Type: MUN - Municipal - National

Major Rating Factors: Exceptional performance is the major factor driving the A (Excellent) TheStreet Investment Rating for SEI Tax-Exempt Tr-Tax Advtg Inc F. The fund currently has a performance rating of A+ (Excellent) based on an average return of 5.55% over the last three years (9.19% taxable equivalent) and 2.66% over the last three months (4.40% taxable equivalent). Factored into the performance evaluation is an expense ratio of 1.08% (average).

The fund's risk rating is currently C- (Fair). Volatility, as measured by standard deviation, is considered average for fixed income funds at 3.79. Another risk factor is the fund's fairly average duration of 6.6 years (i.e. average interest rate risk).

Lewis P. Jacoby, IV has been running the fund for 10 years and currently receives a manager quality ranking of 83 (0=worst, 99=best). If you desire an average level of risk and strong performance, then this fund is a good option.
Services Offered: Automated phone transactions.

Data Date	Investment Rating	Net Assets ($Mil)	NAV	Performance Rating/Pts	Total Return Y-T-D	Risk Rating/Pts
2-17	A	1,061	10.24	A+/ 9.8	2.66%	C- / 3.5
2016	A	1,032	10.04	A+/ 9.7	1.74%	C- / 3.5
2015	B	1,082	10.26	A+/ 9.8	5.50%	D+/ 2.8
2014	B+	852	10.11	A+/ 9.8	11.24%	D / 2.1
2013	B	593	9.43	B+/ 8.7	-3.46%	C- / 3.2
2012	A+	484	10.20	A+/ 9.8	15.97%	C- / 3.5

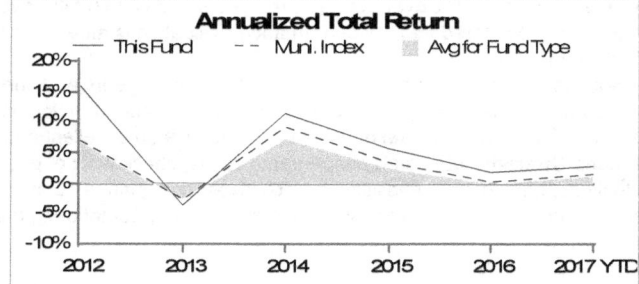

Annualized Total Return

SEI US Fixed Income F (SUFAX)   C   Fair

Fund Family: SEI Financial Management Corp   **Phone:** (800) 342-5734
Address: One Freedom Valley Drive, Oaks, PA 19456
Fund Type: GEI - General - Investment Grade
Major Rating Factors: Middle of the road best describes SEI US Fixed Income F whose TheStreet Investment Rating is currently a C (Fair). The fund has a performance rating of C (Fair) based on an average return of 2.47% over the last three years and 0.91% over the last three months. Factored into the performance evaluation is an expense ratio of 0.86% (average) and a 0.6% back-end load levied at the time of sale.

The fund's risk rating is currently C+ (Fair). Volatility, as measured by standard deviation, is considered average for fixed income funds at 2.83. Another risk factor is the fund's fairly average duration of 6.9 years (i.e. average interest rate risk).

S. Kenneth Leech has been running the fund for 3 years and currently receives a manager quality ranking of 37 (0=worst, 99=best). If you desire an average level of risk, then this fund may be an option.
Services Offered: Automated phone transactions, bank draft capabilities and wire transfers.

Data Date	Investment Rating	Net Assets ($Mil)	NAV	Performance Rating/Pts	Total Return Y-T-D	Risk Rating/Pts
2-17	C	1,549	10.11	C / 4.3	0.91%	C+/ 6.4
2016	C	1,479	10.05	C / 4.7	2.41%	C+/ 6.6
2015	C	1,121	10.16	C+/ 5.7	0.33%	C+/ 6.0
2014	B-	1,134	10.44	C / 4.7	5.91%	B- / 7.2
2013	B-	1,009	10.08	C / 4.4	-2.24%	B / 7.8
2012	B+	941	10.52	C- / 4.2	6.00%	B / 8.2

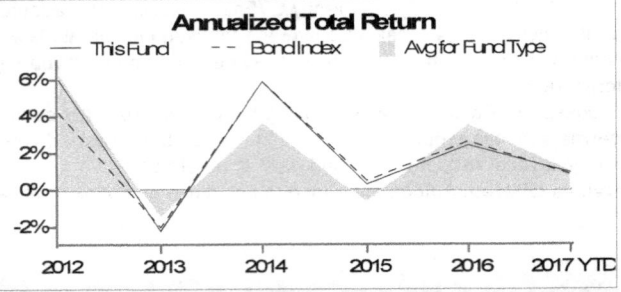

Annualized Total Return

Sit MN Tax Free Income (SMTFX)   B+   Good

Fund Family: Sit Mutual Funds   **Phone:** (800) 332-5580
Address: P.O. Box 9763, Providence, RI 02940
Fund Type: MUS - Municipal - Single State
Major Rating Factors: Strong performance is the major factor driving the B+ (Good) TheStreet Investment Rating for Sit MN Tax Free Income. The fund currently has a performance rating of B (Good) based on an average return of 3.55% over the last three years (5.88% taxable equivalent) and 0.92% over the last three months (1.52% taxable equivalent). Factored into the performance evaluation is an expense ratio of 0.82% (low).

The fund's risk rating is currently C (Fair). Volatility, as measured by standard deviation, is considered average for fixed income funds at 3.14. Another risk factor is the fund's fairly average duration of 5.2 years (i.e. average interest rate risk).

Michael C. Brilley has been running the fund for 24 years and currently receives a manager quality ranking of 57 (0=worst, 99=best). If you desire an average level of risk and strong performance, then this fund is a good option.
Services Offered: Automated phone transactions, check writing, payroll deductions, bank draft capabilities, an IRA investment plan, a 401K investment plan, a Keogh investment plan, wire transfers and a systematic withdrawal plan.

Data Date	Investment Rating	Net Assets ($Mil)	NAV	Performance Rating/Pts	Total Return Y-T-D	Risk Rating/Pts
2-17	B+	523	10.29	B / 7.7	0.92%	C / 5.0
2016	A-	509	10.25	B+/ 8.4	0.16%	C / 4.5
2015	A-	481	10.55	A / 9.4	3.56%	C / 4.8
2014	A+	425	10.53	B+/ 8.9	9.89%	C / 4.8
2013	A	341	9.93	B / 8.1	-3.10%	C / 5.2
2012	A+	395	10.64	B / 8.1	7.24%	C+/ 6.0

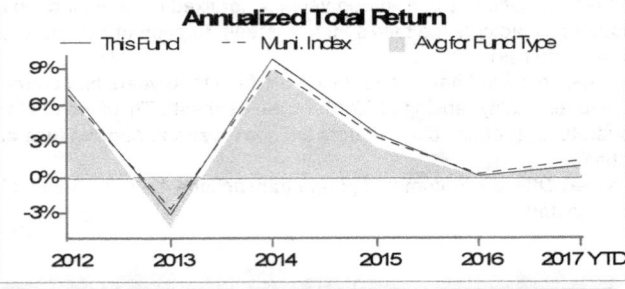

Annualized Total Return

Sit US Government Securities Fund (SNGVX)   B-   Good

Fund Family: Sit Mutual Funds   **Phone:** (800) 332-5580
Address: P.O. Box 9763, Providence, RI 02940
Fund Type: USS - US Government - Short & Inter. Term
Major Rating Factors: A moderate risk profile coupled with stable earnings characterizes Sit US Government Securities Fund which receives a TheStreet Investment Rating of B- (Good). Volatility, as measured by standard deviation, is considered very low for fixed income funds at 0.91. Another risk factor is the fund's very low average duration of 1.4 years (i.e. low interest rate risk). The fund's risk rating is currently A (Excellent).

The fund's performance rating is currently C- (Fair). It has registered an average return of 1.41% over the last three years and is up 0.54% over the last three months. Factored into the performance evaluation is an expense ratio of 0.80% (low).

Michael C. Brilley has been running the fund for 30 years and currently receives a manager quality ranking of 74 (0=worst, 99=best). If you desire stability with a moderate level of risk then this fund is an excellent option.
Services Offered: Automated phone transactions, check writing, payroll deductions, bank draft capabilities, an IRA investment plan, a 401K investment plan, a Keogh investment plan, wire transfers and a systematic withdrawal plan.

Data Date	Investment Rating	Net Assets ($Mil)	NAV	Performance Rating/Pts	Total Return Y-T-D	Risk Rating/Pts
2-17	B-	654	10.94	C- / 3.0	0.54%	A / 9.3
2016	B-	663	10.91	C- / 3.0	0.55%	A / 9.4
2015	B+	601	11.01	C / 5.1	1.48%	A- / 9.2
2014	C	586	11.06	D / 2.1	2.21%	A- / 9.2
2013	C-	790	11.02	D- / 1.2	-2.24%	A- / 9.2
2012	C	1,739	11.36	D- / 1.3	1.75%	A / 9.4

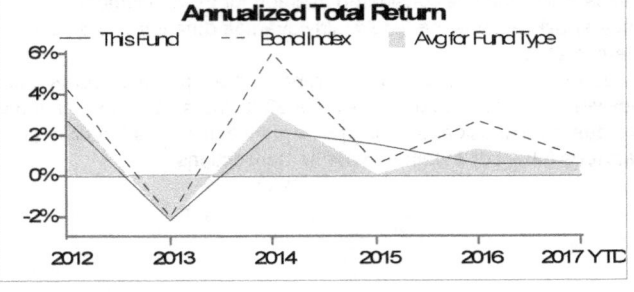

Annualized Total Return

State Farm Muni Bond (SFBDX)   A+   Excellent

Fund Family: State Farm Funds   **Phone:** (800) 447-4930
Address: P.O. Box 219548, Kansas City, MO 64121
Fund Type: MUN - Municipal - National
Major Rating Factors: A moderate risk profile coupled with stable earnings characterizes State Farm Muni Bond which receives a TheStreet Investment Rating of A+ (Excellent). Volatility, as measured by standard deviation, is considered low for fixed income funds at 2.55. Another risk factor is the fund's below average duration of 4.4 years (i.e. lower interest rate risk). The fund's risk rating is currently B- (Good).

The fund's performance rating is currently C+ (Fair). It has registered an average return of 2.80% over the last three years (4.64% taxable equivalent) and is up 0.99% over the last three months (1.64% taxable equivalent). Factored into the performance evaluation is an expense ratio of 0.16% (very low).

Robert M. Reardon, Jr. has been running the fund for 19 years and currently receives a manager quality ranking of 50 (0=worst, 99=best). If you desire stability with a moderate level of risk then this fund is an excellent option.
Services Offered: Automated phone transactions, payroll deductions, bank draft capabilities, wire transfers and a systematic withdrawal plan.

Data Date	Investment Rating	Net Assets ($Mil)	NAV	Performance Rating/Pts	Total Return Y-T-D	Risk Rating/Pts
2-17	A+	700	8.63	C+ / 6.8	0.99%	B- / 7.5
2016	A+	702	8.59	B- / 7.1	0.27%	B- / 7.4
2015	A+	681	8.82	A- / 9.0	2.96%	C+ / 6.6
2014	A-	658	8.84	B- / 7.4	6.76%	C+ / 5.7
2013	A	631	8.57	B / 7.8	-1.54%	C+ / 5.8
2012	B	680	9.02	C+ / 6.1	4.86%	C+ / 5.7

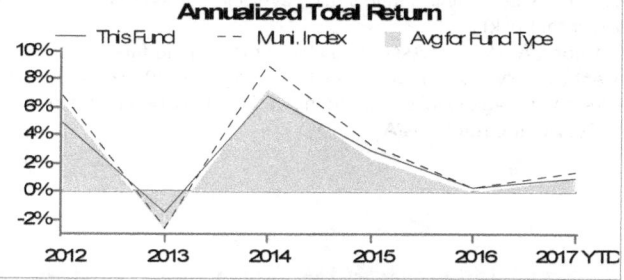

Stone Harbor Emerging Debt Inst (SHMDX)   C+   Fair

Fund Family: Stone Harbor Investment Funds   **Phone:** (866) 699-8125
Address: 31 West 52nd Street, New York, NY 10019
Fund Type: EM - Emerging Market
Major Rating Factors: Stone Harbor Emerging Debt Inst has adopted a very risky asset allocation strategy and currently receives an overall TheStreet Investment Rating of C+ (Fair). Volatility, as measured by standard deviation, is considered high for fixed income funds at 7.58. Another risk factor is the fund's fairly average duration of 6.3 years (i.e. average interest rate risk). The high level of risk (E, Very Weak) did however, reward investors with excellent performance.

The fund's performance rating is currently A+ (Excellent). It has registered an average return of 5.83% over the last three years and is up 3.86% over the last three months. Factored into the performance evaluation is an expense ratio of 0.68% (low).

Pablo Cisilino has been running the fund for 10 years and currently receives a manager quality ranking of 99 (0=worst, 99=best). If you are comfortable owning a very high risk investment, this fund may be an option.
Services Offered: Automated phone transactions, bank draft capabilities, wire transfers and a systematic withdrawal plan.

Data Date	Investment Rating	Net Assets ($Mil)	NAV	Performance Rating/Pts	Total Return Y-T-D	Risk Rating/Pts
2-17	C+	1,500	10.44	A+ / 9.7	3.86%	E / 0.5
2016	C	1,596	10.12	A / 9.3	14.13%	E / 0.5
2015	E	1,646	9.48	D- / 1.1	-0.90%	E / 0.4
2014	E+	2,094	10.19	C- / 3.3	2.87%	E / 0.4
2013	E+	1,887	10.40	C- / 3.8	-8.77%	E / 0.4
2012	B-	1,720	11.97	A / 9.5	17.00%	E+ / 0.7

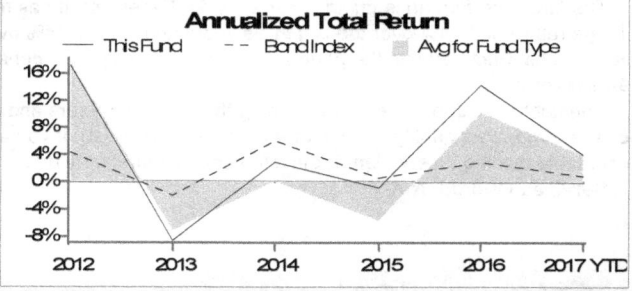

SunAmerica VAL Co I Infln Prot Fd (VCTPX)   D-   Weak

Fund Family: AIG Funds   **Phone:** (800) 858-8850
Address: C/O BFDS, Kansas City, MO 64121
Fund Type: GEI - General - Investment Grade
Major Rating Factors: SunAmerica VAL Co I Infln Prot Fd receives a TheStreet Investment Rating of D- (Weak). The fund has a performance rating of C- (Fair) based on an average return of 1.12% over the last three years and 1.70% over the last three months. Factored into the performance evaluation is an expense ratio of 0.59% (low).

The fund's risk rating is currently C- (Fair). Volatility, as measured by standard deviation, is considered average for fixed income funds at 3.19. Another risk factor is the fund's above average duration of 7.0 years (i.e. higher interest rate risk).

Robert A. Vanden Assem has been running the fund for 13 years and currently receives a manager quality ranking of 12 (0=worst, 99=best). If you desire an average level of risk, then this fund may be an option.
Services Offered: N/A

Data Date	Investment Rating	Net Assets ($Mil)	NAV	Performance Rating/Pts	Total Return Y-T-D	Risk Rating/Pts
2-17	D-	559	10.95	C- / 3.6	1.70%	C- / 4.2
2016	D-	501	10.81	C- / 3.2	3.80%	C / 4.5
2015	D-	458	10.56	E+ / 0.9	-3.01%	C- / 3.2
2014	D-	497	11.12	D / 2.0	2.97%	C- / 3.3
2013	D-	435	11.07	C- / 3.0	-6.97%	C- / 3.2
2012	C	452	11.90	C+ / 6.7	8.03%	C- / 3.4

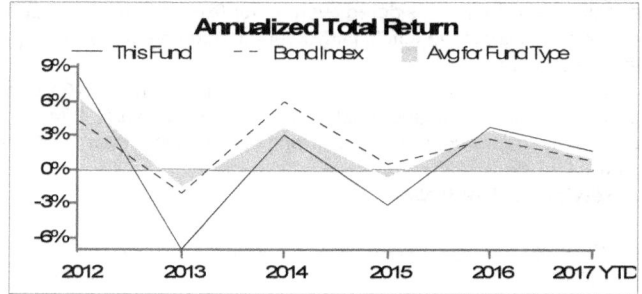

SunAmerica VAL Co II Core Bond Fd (VCCBX)

C+   Fair

Fund Family: AIG Funds
Phone: (800) 858-8850
Address: C/O BFDS, Kansas City, MO 64121
Fund Type: GEI - General - Investment Grade

Major Rating Factors: Middle of the road best describes SunAmerica VAL Co II Core Bond Fd whose TheStreet Investment Rating is currently a C+ (Fair). The fund has a performance rating of C (Fair) based on an average return of 2.58% over the last three years and 1.27% over the last three months. Factored into the performance evaluation is an expense ratio of 0.79% (low).

The fund's risk rating is currently C+ (Fair). Volatility, as measured by standard deviation, is considered average for fixed income funds at 2.94. Another risk factor is the fund's fairly average duration of 6.2 years (i.e. average interest rate risk).

Robert A. Vanden Assem has been running the fund for 15 years and currently receives a manager quality ranking of 47 (0=worst, 99=best). If you desire an average level of risk, then this fund may be an option.

Services Offered: N/A

Data Date	Investment Rating	Net Assets ($Mil)	NAV	Performance Rating/Pts	Total Return Y-T-D	Risk Rating/Pts
2-17	C+	1,029	11.14	C / 5.3	1.27%	C+ / 5.9
2016	C+	1,024	11.00	C / 5.3	3.44%	C+ / 6.1
2015	C	1,179	10.88	C / 5.5	-0.20%	C / 5.5
2014	C+	956	11.13	C / 5.2	5.44%	C+ / 5.9
2013	C+	866	10.83	C / 5.0	-1.81%	C+ / 6.4
2012	B+	603	11.03	C / 5.3	7.38%	C+ / 6.8

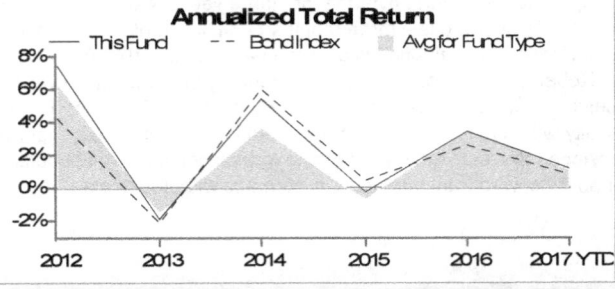

SunAmerica VAL Co II High Yld Bd Fd (VCHYX)

B-   Good

Fund Family: AIG Funds
Phone: (800) 858-8850
Address: C/O BFDS, Kansas City, MO 64121
Fund Type: GEI - General - Investment Grade

Major Rating Factors: SunAmerica VAL Co II High Yld Bd Fd has adopted a very risky asset allocation strategy and currently receives an overall TheStreet Investment Rating of B- (Good). Volatility, as measured by standard deviation, is considered above average for fixed income funds at 5.17. Another risk factor is the fund's fairly average duration of 5.2 years (i.e. average interest rate risk). The high level of risk (D, Weak) did however, reward investors with excellent performance.

The fund's performance rating is currently A- (Excellent). It has registered an average return of 3.84% over the last three years and is up 2.74% over the last three months. Factored into the performance evaluation is an expense ratio of 0.99% (average).

Christopher A. Jones has been running the fund for 8 years and currently receives a manager quality ranking of 90 (0=worst, 99=best). If you are comfortable owning a very high risk investment, this fund may be an option.

Services Offered: N/A

Data Date	Investment Rating	Net Assets ($Mil)	NAV	Performance Rating/Pts	Total Return Y-T-D	Risk Rating/Pts
2-17	B-	627	7.88	A- / 9.0	2.74%	D / 1.9
2016	C+	635	7.67	B+ / 8.9	12.90%	D / 2.0
2015	D	487	7.12	C- / 3.9	-3.66%	D / 2.0
2014	B-	411	7.76	B / 7.6	2.85%	C- / 3.9
2013	B	392	7.92	A- / 9.2	5.18%	D / 2.1
2012	C+	343	7.53	B+ / 8.4	13.75%	D- / 1.3

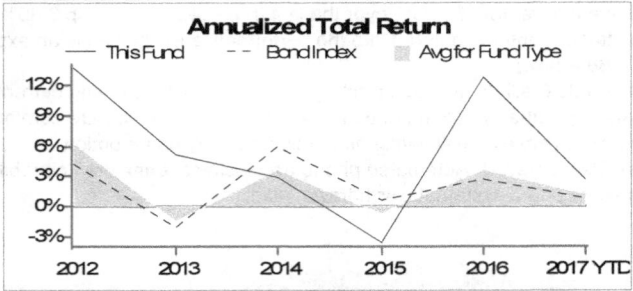

SunAmerica VAL Co II Strat Bond (VCSBX)

C+   Fair

Fund Family: AIG Funds
Phone: (800) 858-8850
Address: C/O BFDS, Kansas City, MO 64121
Fund Type: GEI - General - Investment Grade

Major Rating Factors: Strong performance is the major factor driving the C+ (Fair) TheStreet Investment Rating for SunAmerica VAL Co II Strat Bond. The fund currently has a performance rating of B- (Good) based on an average return of 3.22% over the last three years and 2.06% over the last three months. Factored into the performance evaluation is an expense ratio of 0.88% (average).

The fund's risk rating is currently C- (Fair). Volatility, as measured by standard deviation, is considered average for fixed income funds at 3.96. Another risk factor is the fund's fairly average duration of 5.9 years (i.e. average interest rate risk).

Robert A. Vanden Assem has been running the fund for 15 years and currently receives a manager quality ranking of 78 (0=worst, 99=best). If you desire an average level of risk and strong performance, then this fund is a good option.

Services Offered: N/A

Data Date	Investment Rating	Net Assets ($Mil)	NAV	Performance Rating/Pts	Total Return Y-T-D	Risk Rating/Pts
2-17	C+	827	11.40	B- / 7.5	2.06%	C- / 3.3
2016	C+	825	11.17	B- / 7.3	8.17%	C- / 3.4
2015	D	768	10.79	C- / 3.6	-1.93%	C- / 3.2
2014	C-	778	11.50	C+ / 6.3	3.95%	C- / 3.7
2013	C+	713	11.60	B / 7.6	0.26%	C- / 3.3
2012	C+	676	11.57	B- / 7.4	12.41%	D+ / 2.7

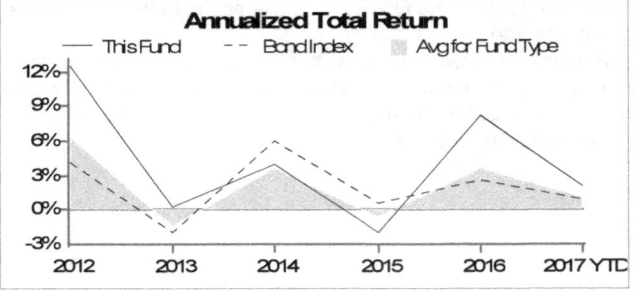

T Rowe Price CA Tax Free Bond (PRXCX)   B+   Good

Fund Family: T. Rowe Price Funds   **Phone:** (800) 638-5660
Address: 100 East Pratt Street, Baltimore, MD 21202
Fund Type: MUS - Municipal - Single State

Major Rating Factors: Strong performance is the major factor driving the B+ (Good) TheStreet Investment Rating for T Rowe Price CA Tax Free Bond. The fund currently has a performance rating of B+ (Good) based on an average return of 4.09% over the last three years (6.77% taxable equivalent) and 1.06% over the last three months (1.76% taxable equivalent). Factored into the performance evaluation is an expense ratio of 0.50% (very low).

The fund's risk rating is currently C- (Fair). Volatility, as measured by standard deviation, is considered average for fixed income funds at 3.69. Another risk factor is the fund's fairly average duration of 5.2 years (i.e. average interest rate risk).

Konstantine B. Mallas has been running the fund for 14 years and currently receives a manager quality ranking of 54 (0=worst, 99=best). If you desire an average level of risk and strong performance, then this fund is a good option.

Services Offered: Automated phone transactions, check writing, payroll deductions, bank draft capabilities, wire transfers and a systematic withdrawal plan.

Data Date	Investment Rating	Net Assets ($Mil)	NAV	Perfor- mance Rating/Pts	Total Return Y-T-D	Risk Rating/Pts
2-17	B+	615	11.35	B+ / 8.3	1.06%	C- / 3.6
2016	B+	581	11.29	B+ / 8.9	0.07%	C- / 3.5
2015	B+	513	11.65	A+ / 9.7	3.84%	C- / 3.7
2014	A	500	11.61	A+ / 9.6	11.41%	C- / 3.5
2013	B+	399	10.81	B+ / 8.7	-2.76%	C- / 3.8
2012	A+	414	11.55	B+ / 8.7	9.28%	C- / 4.0

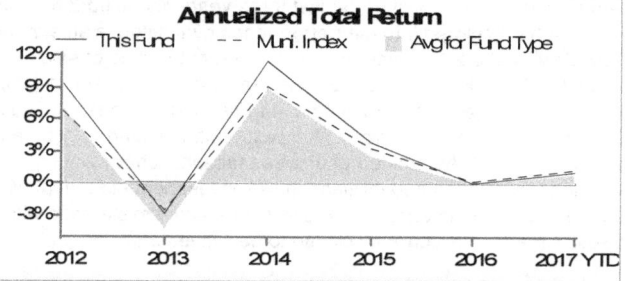

T Rowe Price Corporate Income (PRPIX)   C-   Fair

Fund Family: T. Rowe Price Funds   **Phone:** (800) 638-5660
Address: 100 East Pratt Street, Baltimore, MD 21202
Fund Type: COI - Corporate - Investment Grade

Major Rating Factors: T Rowe Price Corporate Income has adopted a risky asset allocation strategy and currently receives an overall TheStreet Investment Rating of C- (Fair). Volatility, as measured by standard deviation, is considered above average for fixed income funds at 4.18. Another risk factor is the fund's above average duration of 7.8 years (i.e. higher interest rate risk). The high level of risk (D+, Weak) did however, reward investors with excellent performance.

The fund's performance rating is currently B- (Good). It has registered an average return of 3.63% over the last three years and is up 1.70% over the last three months. Factored into the performance evaluation is an expense ratio of 0.62% (low).

David A. Tiberii has been running the fund for 14 years and currently receives a manager quality ranking of 35 (0=worst, 99=best). If you are comfortable owning a high risk investment, this fund may be an option.

Services Offered: Automated phone transactions, check writing, payroll deductions, bank draft capabilities, an IRA investment plan, a 401K investment plan, a Keogh investment plan, wire transfers and a systematic withdrawal plan.

Data Date	Investment Rating	Net Assets ($Mil)	NAV	Perfor- mance Rating/Pts	Total Return Y-T-D	Risk Rating/Pts
2-17	C-	836	9.54	B- / 7.0	1.70%	D+ / 2.6
2016	C-	836	9.43	B- / 7.0	5.09%	D+ / 2.6
2015	C-	708	9.26	C+ / 6.8	-0.67%	D+ / 2.8
2014	C+	623	9.71	B / 7.6	8.26%	C- / 3.4
2013	C+	554	9.45	B- / 7.3	-1.42%	C- / 3.7
2012	B-	683	10.16	B- / 7.4	11.16%	C- / 3.4

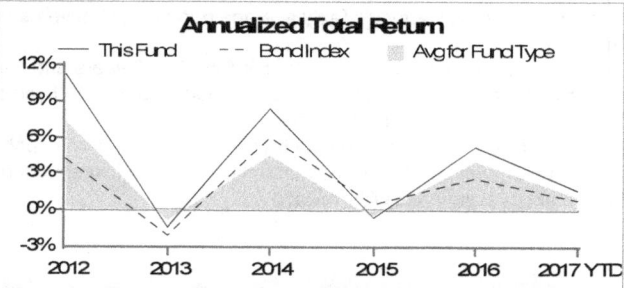

T Rowe Price GNMA (PRGMX)   B   Good

Fund Family: T. Rowe Price Funds   **Phone:** (800) 638-5660
Address: 100 East Pratt Street, Baltimore, MD 21202
Fund Type: USA - US Government/Agency

Major Rating Factors: A moderate risk profile coupled with stable earnings characterizes T Rowe Price GNMA which receives a TheStreet Investment Rating of B (Good). Volatility, as measured by standard deviation, is considered low for fixed income funds at 1.63. Another risk factor is the fund's very low average duration of 2.6 years (i.e. low interest rate risk). The fund's risk rating is currently B+ (Good).

The fund's performance rating is currently C- (Fair). It has registered an average return of 2.03% over the last three years and is up 0.45% over the last three months. Factored into the performance evaluation is an expense ratio of 0.59% (low).

Andrew C. McCormick has been running the fund for 9 years and currently receives a manager quality ranking of 78 (0=worst, 99=best). If you desire stability with a moderate level of risk then this fund is an excellent option.

Services Offered: Automated phone transactions, check writing, payroll deductions, bank draft capabilities, an IRA investment plan, a 401K investment plan, a Keogh investment plan, wire transfers and a systematic withdrawal plan.

Data Date	Investment Rating	Net Assets ($Mil)	NAV	Perfor- mance Rating/Pts	Total Return Y-T-D	Risk Rating/Pts
2-17	B	1,449	9.32	C- / 4.0	0.45%	B+ / 8.7
2016	B+	1,480	9.32	C / 4.9	1.68%	B+ / 8.5
2015	B	1,559	9.43	C+ / 6.3	0.86%	B- / 7.5
2014	C	1,644	9.64	C- / 3.5	5.43%	B- / 7.3
2013	C-	1,534	9.43	D+ / 2.6	-2.41%	B / 8.1
2012	C+	1,810	10.01	D+ / 2.5	2.84%	B+ / 8.8

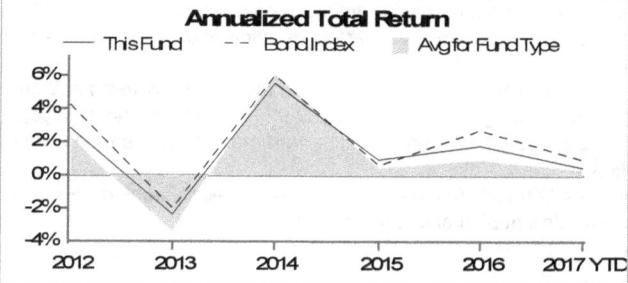

T Rowe Price High Yield (PRHYX)   C+   Fair

Fund Family: T. Rowe Price Funds   **Phone:** (800) 638-5660
Address: 100 East Pratt Street, Baltimore, MD 21202
Fund Type: COH - Corporate - High Yield
Major Rating Factors: T Rowe Price High Yield has adopted a very risky asset allocation strategy and currently receives an overall TheStreet Investment Rating of C+ (Fair). Volatility, as measured by standard deviation, is considered above average for fixed income funds at 5.34. Another risk factor is the fund's below average duration of 3.2 years (i.e. lower interest rate risk). The high level of risk (D-, Weak) did however, reward investors with excellent performance.

The fund's performance rating is currently A- (Excellent). It has registered an average return of 4.13% over the last three years and is up 2.61% over the last three months. Factored into the performance evaluation is an expense ratio of 0.75% (low) and a 2.0% back-end load levied at the time of sale.

Mark J. Vaselkiv has been running the fund for 21 years and currently receives a manager quality ranking of 44 (0=worst, 99=best). If you are comfortable owning a very high risk investment, this fund may be an option.
Services Offered: Automated phone transactions, check writing, payroll deductions, bank draft capabilities, an IRA investment plan, a 401K investment plan, a Keogh investment plan, wire transfers and a systematic withdrawal plan. However, the fund is currently closed to new investors.

Data Date	Investment Rating	Net Assets ($Mil)	NAV	Performance Rating/Pts	Total Return Y-T-D	Risk Rating/Pts
2-17	C+	7,941	6.76	A- / 9.2	2.61%	D- / 1.4
2016	C+	7,710	6.65	A- / 9.1	14.51%	D- / 1.4
2015	D	8,036	6.18	C / 4.8	-3.26%	D- / 1.4
2014	C-	8,379	6.78	B / 7.9	2.00%	D / 1.8
2013	C+	8,739	7.15	A+ / 9.7	9.07%	E+ / 0.7
2012	C-	7,902	6.98	B+ / 8.5	15.24%	E / 0.5

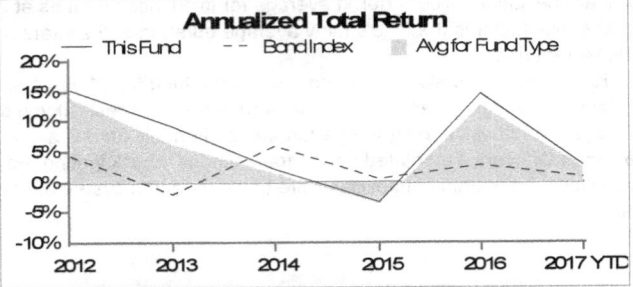

Annualized Total Return

T Rowe Price Inst Core Plus (TICPX)   C+   Fair

Fund Family: T. Rowe Price Funds   **Phone:** (800) 638-5660
Address: 100 East Pratt Street, Baltimore, MD 21202
Fund Type: GEI - General - Investment Grade
Major Rating Factors: Middle of the road best describes T Rowe Price Inst Core Plus whose TheStreet Investment Rating is currently a C+ (Fair). The fund has a performance rating of C+ (Fair) based on an average return of 2.91% over the last three years and 1.18% over the last three months. Factored into the performance evaluation is an expense ratio of 0.45% (very low).

The fund's risk rating is currently C+ (Fair). Volatility, as measured by standard deviation, is considered average for fixed income funds at 2.92. Another risk factor is the fund's fairly average duration of 5.5 years (i.e. average interest rate risk).

Brian J. Brennan has been running the fund for 13 years and currently receives a manager quality ranking of 61 (0=worst, 99=best). If you desire an average level of risk, then this fund may be an option.
Services Offered: Automated phone transactions, bank draft capabilities, an IRA investment plan, a 401K investment plan, a Keogh investment plan, wire transfers and a systematic withdrawal plan.

Data Date	Investment Rating	Net Assets ($Mil)	NAV	Performance Rating/Pts	Total Return Y-T-D	Risk Rating/Pts
2-17	C+	519	10.29	C+ / 5.7	1.18%	C+ / 6.0
2016	B-	500	10.22	C+ / 5.8	3.78%	C+ / 6.1
2015	C	601	10.14	C+ / 6.3	0.13%	C+ / 5.7
2014	C+	562	10.45	C / 5.5	5.98%	C+ / 6.2
2013	B-	323	10.20	C / 5.2	-1.45%	C+ / 6.7
2012	A-	215	10.73	C / 4.9	7.17%	B / 7.8

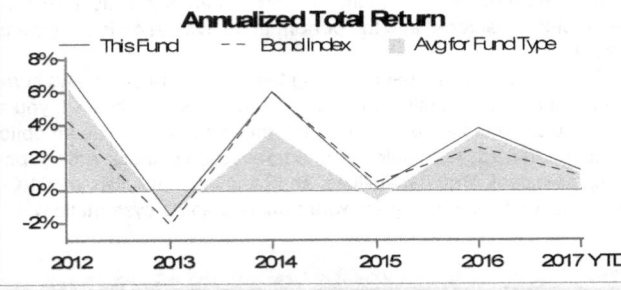

Annualized Total Return

T Rowe Price Instl Fltng Rate F (PFFRX)   A+   Excellent

Fund Family: T. Rowe Price Funds   **Phone:** (800) 638-5660
Address: 100 East Pratt Street, Baltimore, MD 21202
Fund Type: LP - Loan Participation
Major Rating Factors: Strong performance is the major factor driving the A+ (Excellent) TheStreet Investment Rating for T Rowe Price Instl Fltng Rate F. The fund currently has a performance rating of B- (Good) based on an average return of 3.57% over the last three years and 0.69% over the last three months. Factored into the performance evaluation is an expense ratio of 0.56% (very low) and a 2.0% back-end load levied at the time of sale.

The fund's risk rating is currently B (Good). Volatility, as measured by standard deviation, is considered low for fixed income funds at 2.27. Another risk factor is the fund's very low average duration of 0.4 years (i.e. low interest rate risk).

Paul M. Massaro has been running the fund for 8 years and currently receives a manager quality ranking of 92 (0=worst, 99=best). If you desire only a moderate level of risk and strong performance, then this fund is an excellent option.
Services Offered: Automated phone transactions, bank draft capabilities, an IRA investment plan and wire transfers.

Data Date	Investment Rating	Net Assets ($Mil)	NAV	Performance Rating/Pts	Total Return Y-T-D	Risk Rating/Pts
2-17	A+	529	10.08	B- / 7.2	0.69%	B / 7.9
2016	A+	535	10.08	B- / 7.4	7.98%	B / 8.0
2015	A-	871	9.74	C+ / 6.9	1.35%	B / 7.8
2014	A-	638	10.02	C / 5.0	1.58%	B+ / 8.5
2013	B+	856	10.28	B- / 7.2	5.12%	C / 5.2
2012	U	658	10.20	U / --	8.17%	U / --

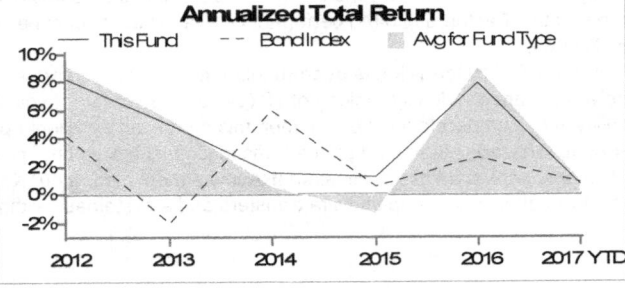

Annualized Total Return

T Rowe Price Instl High Yield (TRHYX)   C+   Fair

Fund Family: T. Rowe Price Funds   **Phone:** (800) 638-5660
Address: 100 East Pratt Street, Baltimore, MD 21202
Fund Type: COH - Corporate - High Yield
Major Rating Factors: T Rowe Price Instl High Yield has adopted a very risky asset allocation strategy and currently receives an overall TheStreet Investment Rating of C+ (Fair). Volatility, as measured by standard deviation, is considered above average for fixed income funds at 5.69. Another risk factor is the fund's below average duration of 3.1 years (i.e. lower interest rate risk). The high level of risk (D-, Weak) did however, reward investors with excellent performance.

The fund's performance rating is currently A (Excellent). It has registered an average return of 4.37% over the last three years and is up 2.71% over the last three months. Factored into the performance evaluation is an expense ratio of 0.50% (very low) and a 2.0% back-end load levied at the time of sale.

Mark J. Vaselkiv has been running the fund for 2 years and currently receives a manager quality ranking of 42 (0=worst, 99=best). If you are comfortable owning a very high risk investment, this fund may be an option.
Services Offered: Automated phone transactions, bank draft capabilities, an IRA investment plan, a 401K investment plan, a Keogh investment plan, wire transfers and a systematic withdrawal plan. However, the fund is currently closed to new investors.

Data Date	Investment Rating	Net Assets ($Mil)	NAV	Performance Rating/Pts	Total Return Y-T-D	Risk Rating/Pts
2-17	C+	1,748	9.00	A / 9.4	2.71%	D- / 1.1
2016	C+	1,704	8.85	A / 9.4	15.92%	D- / 1.1
2015	D	1,925	8.15	C- / 3.8	-3.90%	D- / 1.2
2014	C-	2,249	9.07	B / 7.8	2.28%	D / 1.8
2013	C+	2,872	9.71	A+ / 9.6	8.53%	E+ / 0.9
2012	C	2,611	9.76	B+ / 8.5	14.79%	E+ / 0.6

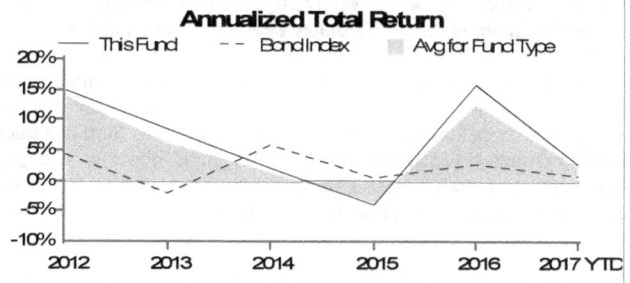

T Rowe Price Intl Bond (RPIBX)   E-   Very Weak

Fund Family: T. Rowe Price Funds   **Phone:** (800) 638-5660
Address: 100 East Pratt Street, Baltimore, MD 21202
Fund Type: GL - Global
Major Rating Factors: T Rowe Price Intl Bond has adopted a very risky asset allocation strategy and currently receives an overall TheStreet Investment Rating of E- (Very Weak). Volatility, as measured by standard deviation, is considered high for fixed income funds at 7.63. Unfortunately, the high level of risk (E, Very Weak) failed to pay off as investors endured poor performance.

The fund's performance rating is currently E- (Very Weak). It has registered an average return of -2.59% over the last three years and is up 2.23% over the last three months. Factored into the performance evaluation is an expense ratio of 0.83% (low) and a 2.0% back-end load levied at the time of sale.

Arif Hussain has been running the fund for 3 years and currently receives a manager quality ranking of 37 (0=worst, 99=best). If you can tolerate very high levels of risk in the hope of improved future returns, holding this fund may be an option.
Services Offered: Automated phone transactions, check writing, payroll deductions, bank draft capabilities, an IRA investment plan, a 401K investment plan, a Keogh investment plan, wire transfers and a systematic withdrawal plan.

Data Date	Investment Rating	Net Assets ($Mil)	NAV	Performance Rating/Pts	Total Return Y-T-D	Risk Rating/Pts
2-17	E-	3,997	8.47	E- / 0.0	2.23%	E / 0.4
2016	E-	3,944	8.31	E- / 0.1	2.21%	E / 0.4
2015	E	5,231	8.27	E / 0.3	-5.71%	D- / 1.5
2014	E-	4,523	8.94	E- / 0.2	-3.77%	D- / 1.2
2013	E	4,906	9.50	D- / 1.2	-3.81%	D- / 1.4
2012	E-	4,972	10.10	D+ / 2.3	6.11%	E / 0.5

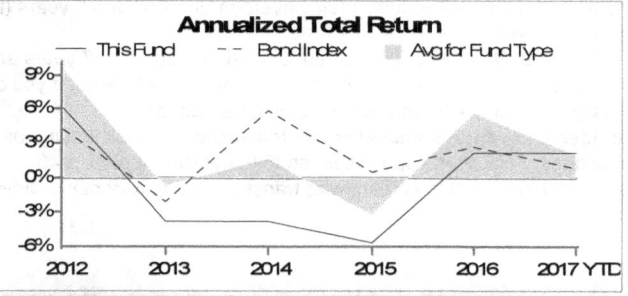

T Rowe Price Ltd Dur Inf Foc Bd (TRBFX)   D+   Weak

Fund Family: T. Rowe Price Funds   **Phone:** (800) 638-5660
Address: 100 East Pratt Street, Baltimore, MD 21202
Fund Type: GEI - General - Investment Grade
Major Rating Factors: Disappointing performance is the major factor driving the D+ (Weak) TheStreet Investment Rating for T Rowe Price Ltd Dur Inf Foc Bd. The fund currently has a performance rating of D (Weak) based on an average return of 0.17% over the last three years and 0.60% over the last three months. Factored into the performance evaluation is an expense ratio of 0.51% (very low).

The fund's risk rating is currently B+ (Good). Volatility, as measured by standard deviation, is considered low for fixed income funds at 1.90. Another risk factor is the fund's very low average duration of 2.5 years (i.e. low interest rate risk).

Stephen Bartolini currently receives a manager quality ranking of 15 (0=worst, 99=best). This fund offers only a moderate level of risk but investors looking for strong performance are still waiting.
Services Offered: Automated phone transactions, payroll deductions, bank draft capabilities, wire transfers and a systematic withdrawal plan.

Data Date	Investment Rating	Net Assets ($Mil)	NAV	Performance Rating/Pts	Total Return Y-T-D	Risk Rating/Pts
2-17	D+	7,348	5.03	D / 2.0	0.60%	B+ / 8.4
2016	D+	7,070	5.00	D / 1.9	2.12%	B+ / 8.5

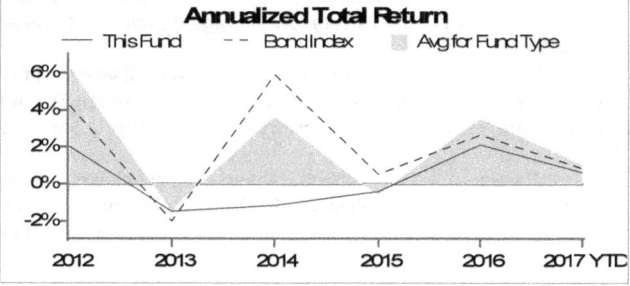

T Rowe Price MD Tax Free Bd (MDXBX)

A+ Excellent

Fund Family: T. Rowe Price Funds **Phone:** (800) 638-5660
Address: 100 East Pratt Street, Baltimore, MD 21202
Fund Type: MUS - Municipal - Single State

Major Rating Factors: Strong performance is the major factor driving the A+ (Excellent) TheStreet Investment Rating for T Rowe Price MD Tax Free Bd. The fund currently has a performance rating of B (Good) based on an average return of 3.64% over the last three years (6.03% taxable equivalent) and 0.95% over the last three months (1.57% taxable equivalent). Factored into the performance evaluation is an expense ratio of 0.46% (very low).

The fund's risk rating is currently C+ (Fair). Volatility, as measured by standard deviation, is considered average for fixed income funds at 2.78. Another risk factor is the fund's below average duration of 4.2 years (i.e. lower interest rate risk).

Hugh D. McGuirk has been running the fund for 17 years and currently receives a manager quality ranking of 69 (0=worst, 99=best). If you desire an average level of risk and strong performance, then this fund is a good option.

Services Offered: Automated phone transactions, check writing, payroll deductions, bank draft capabilities, an IRA investment plan, a 401K investment plan, a Keogh investment plan, wire transfers and a systematic withdrawal plan.

Data Date	Investment Rating	Net Assets ($Mil)	NAV	Perfor-mance Rating/Pts	Total Return Y-T-D	Risk Rating/Pts
2-17	A+	2,178	10.68	B / 8.0	0.95%	C+ / 6.7
2016	A+	2,191	10.64	B+ / 8.7	0.91%	C+ / 6.1
2015	A-	2,073	10.90	A / 9.3	3.18%	C / 4.7
2014	A+	2,020	10.95	B+ / 8.9	9.35%	C / 4.4
2013	A-	1,875	10.39	B / 8.2	-2.75%	C / 4.6
2012	A	2,100	11.09	B / 7.7	7.57%	C / 4.9

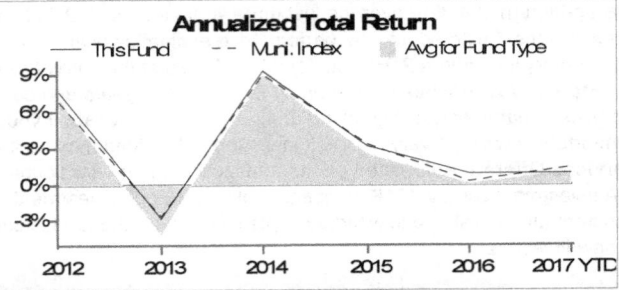

Annualized Total Return

T Rowe Price New Income (PRCIX)

C Fair

Fund Family: T. Rowe Price Funds **Phone:** (800) 638-5660
Address: 100 East Pratt Street, Baltimore, MD 21202
Fund Type: GEI - General - Investment Grade

Major Rating Factors: Middle of the road best describes T Rowe Price New Income whose TheStreet Investment Rating is currently a C (Fair). The fund has a performance rating of C (Fair) based on an average return of 2.48% over the last three years and 1.07% over the last three months. Factored into the performance evaluation is an expense ratio of 0.55% (very low).

The fund's risk rating is currently C+ (Fair). Volatility, as measured by standard deviation, is considered average for fixed income funds at 2.86. Another risk factor is the fund's fairly average duration of 5.5 years (i.e. average interest rate risk).

Daniel O. Shackelford has been running the fund for 17 years and currently receives a manager quality ranking of 40 (0=worst, 99=best). If you desire an average level of risk, then this fund may be an option.

Services Offered: Automated phone transactions, check writing, payroll deductions, bank draft capabilities, an IRA investment plan, a 401K investment plan, a Keogh investment plan, wire transfers and a systematic withdrawal plan.

Data Date	Investment Rating	Net Assets ($Mil)	NAV	Perfor-mance Rating/Pts	Total Return Y-T-D	Risk Rating/Pts
2-17	C	28,669	9.43	C / 4.8	1.07%	C+ / 6.3
2016	C+	28,067	9.37	C / 4.9	2.65%	C+ / 6.4
2015	C	27,969	9.36	C+ / 5.8	0.16%	C+ / 5.9
2014	C	28,136	9.58	C / 4.7	5.75%	C+ / 6.4
2013	C	21,532	9.30	C- / 4.1	-2.26%	C+ / 6.9
2012	B	20,368	9.85	C- / 3.9	5.87%	B / 7.9

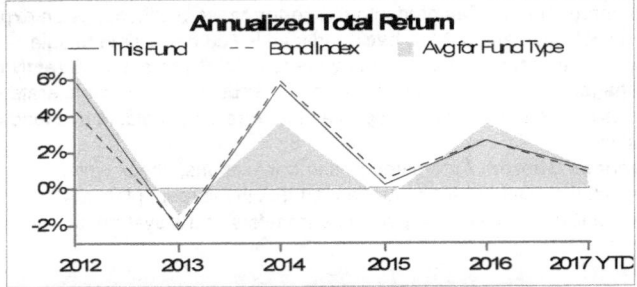

Annualized Total Return

T Rowe Price Short Term Bond (PRWBX)

C+ Fair

Fund Family: T. Rowe Price Funds **Phone:** (800) 638-5660
Address: 100 East Pratt Street, Baltimore, MD 21202
Fund Type: GES - General - Short & Inter. Term

Major Rating Factors: Disappointing performance is the major factor driving the C+ (Fair) TheStreet Investment Rating for T Rowe Price Short Term Bond. The fund currently has a performance rating of D+ (Weak) based on an average return of 0.94% over the last three years and 0.49% over the last three months. Factored into the performance evaluation is an expense ratio of 0.47% (very low).

The fund's risk rating is currently A (Excellent). Volatility, as measured by standard deviation, is considered very low for fixed income funds at 0.84. Another risk factor is the fund's very low average duration of 1.8 years (i.e. low interest rate risk).

Michael F. Reinartz has been running the fund for 2 years and currently receives a manager quality ranking of 59 (0=worst, 99=best). This fund offers only a moderate level of risk but investors looking for strong performance are still waiting.

Services Offered: Automated phone transactions, check writing, payroll deductions, bank draft capabilities, an IRA investment plan, a 401K investment plan, a Keogh investment plan, wire transfers and a systematic withdrawal plan.

Data Date	Investment Rating	Net Assets ($Mil)	NAV	Perfor-mance Rating/Pts	Total Return Y-T-D	Risk Rating/Pts
2-17	C+	4,265	4.72	D+ / 2.8	0.49%	A / 9.4
2016	C+	4,310	4.71	D+ / 2.8	1.58%	A / 9.4
2015	B	5,617	4.71	C / 4.6	0.59%	A / 9.4
2014	C	6,314	4.75	D / 2.0	0.60%	A / 9.4
2013	C+	6,202	4.79	D+ / 2.4	0.30%	A / 9.4
2012	C-	5,848	4.85	D- / 1.1	2.87%	A / 9.4

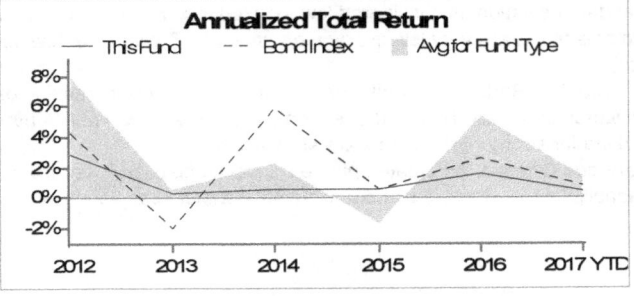

Annualized Total Return

T Rowe Price Spectrum Income (RPSIX)   C+   Fair

Fund Family: T. Rowe Price Funds   **Phone:** (800) 638-5660
Address: 100 East Pratt Street, Baltimore, MD 21202
Fund Type: GES - General - Short & Inter. Term

Major Rating Factors: Strong performance is the major factor driving the C+ (Fair) TheStreet Investment Rating for T Rowe Price Spectrum Income. The fund currently has a performance rating of B- (Good) based on an average return of 3.32% over the last three years and 2.07% over the last three months. Factored into the performance evaluation is an expense ratio of 0.69% (low).

The fund's risk rating is currently C- (Fair). Volatility, as measured by standard deviation, is considered average for fixed income funds at 3.80. Another risk factor is the fund's fairly average duration of 5.2 years (i.e. average interest rate risk).

Edmund M. Notzon III, Ph.D has been running the fund for 19 years and currently receives a manager quality ranking of 82 (0=worst, 99=best). If you desire an average level of risk and strong performance, then this fund is a good option.

Services Offered: Automated phone transactions, check writing, payroll deductions, bank draft capabilities, an IRA investment plan, a 401K investment plan, a Keogh investment plan, wire transfers and a systematic withdrawal plan.

Data Date	Investment Rating	Net Assets ($Mil)	NAV	Performance Rating/Pts	Total Return Y-T-D	Risk Rating/Pts
2-17	C+	6,349	12.58	B- / 7.5	2.07%	C- / 3.4
2016	C+	6,259	12.39	B- / 7.2	8.19%	C- / 3.7
2015	C-	6,054	11.89	C+/ 5.6	-2.11%	C- / 4.1
2014	C+	6,722	12.70	C+/ 6.6	3.88%	C / 4.6
2013	B	6,472	12.76	B / 8.1	3.02%	C- / 3.8
2012	D+	6,600	13.00	C+/ 6.1	10.17%	D+/ 2.7

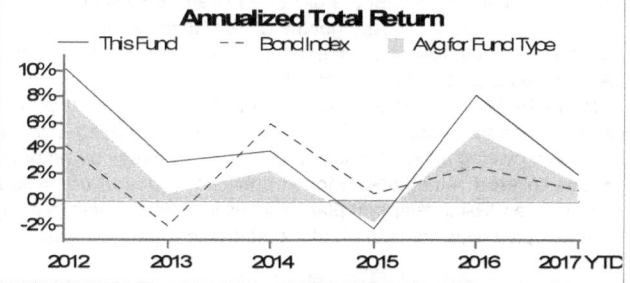

Annualized Total Return

T Rowe Price Summit Muni Income (PRINX)   A-   Excellent

Fund Family: T. Rowe Price Funds   **Phone:** (800) 638-5660
Address: 100 East Pratt Street, Baltimore, MD 21202
Fund Type: MUN - Municipal - National

Major Rating Factors: Strong performance is the major factor driving the A- (Excellent) TheStreet Investment Rating for T Rowe Price Summit Muni Income. The fund currently has a performance rating of B+ (Good) based on an average return of 4.12% over the last three years (6.82% taxable equivalent) and 0.99% over the last three months (1.64% taxable equivalent). Factored into the performance evaluation is an expense ratio of 0.50% (very low).

The fund's risk rating is currently C- (Fair). Volatility, as measured by standard deviation, is considered average for fixed income funds at 3.46. Another risk factor is the fund's below average duration of 4.8 years (i.e. lower interest rate risk).

Konstantine B. Mallas has been running the fund for 18 years and currently receives a manager quality ranking of 63 (0=worst, 99=best). If you desire an average level of risk and strong performance, then this fund is a good option.

Services Offered: Automated phone transactions, check writing, payroll deductions, bank draft capabilities, an IRA investment plan, a 401K investment plan, a Keogh investment plan, wire transfers and a systematic withdrawal plan.

Data Date	Investment Rating	Net Assets ($Mil)	NAV	Performance Rating/Pts	Total Return Y-T-D	Risk Rating/Pts
2-17	A-	1,231	11.71	B+/ 8.4	0.99%	C- / 4.1
2016	A	1,234	11.66	A- / 9.1	0.42%	C- / 4.0
2015	B	1,006	11.99	A+/ 9.6	3.47%	C- / 3.4
2014	A-	965	11.99	A / 9.5	11.56%	D+/ 2.9
2013	B+	733	11.14	B+/ 8.5	-3.74%	C- / 3.5
2012	A+	824	12.01	A- / 9.0	9.87%	C- / 3.8

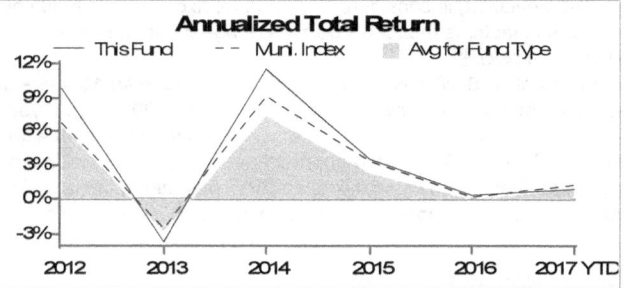

Annualized Total Return

T Rowe Price Summit Muni Intmdt (PRSMX)   B   Good

Fund Family: T. Rowe Price Funds   **Phone:** (800) 638-5660
Address: 100 East Pratt Street, Baltimore, MD 21202
Fund Type: MUN - Municipal - National

Major Rating Factors: T Rowe Price Summit Muni Intmdt receives a TheStreet Investment Rating of B (Good). The fund has a performance rating of C+ (Fair) based on an average return of 2.66% over the last three years (4.40% taxable equivalent) and 0.96% over the last three months (1.59% taxable equivalent). Factored into the performance evaluation is an expense ratio of 0.50% (very low).

The fund's risk rating is currently C+ (Fair). Volatility, as measured by standard deviation, is considered average for fixed income funds at 2.91. Another risk factor is the fund's below average duration of 4.5 years (i.e. lower interest rate risk).

Charles B. Hill has been running the fund for 24 years and currently receives a manager quality ranking of 24 (0=worst, 99=best). If you desire an average level of risk, then this fund may be an option.

Services Offered: Automated phone transactions, check writing, payroll deductions, bank draft capabilities, an IRA investment plan, a 401K investment plan, a Keogh investment plan, wire transfers and a systematic withdrawal plan.

Data Date	Investment Rating	Net Assets ($Mil)	NAV	Performance Rating/Pts	Total Return Y-T-D	Risk Rating/Pts
2-17	B	4,246	11.75	C+/ 6.3	0.96%	C+/ 6.0
2016	B	4,049	11.69	C+/ 6.6	-0.05%	C+/ 5.9
2015	A+	3,904	12.00	A- / 9.1	2.82%	C+/ 6.4
2014	A	3,932	11.98	B / 7.8	7.05%	C+/ 5.6
2013	A+	2,976	11.49	B / 8.0	-1.16%	C+/ 6.0
2012	B	2,296	11.96	C+/ 6.0	5.29%	C+/ 5.7

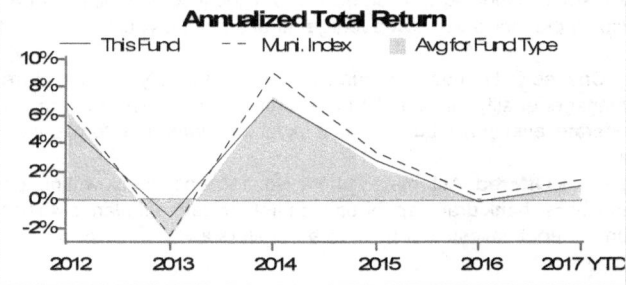

Annualized Total Return

T Rowe Price Tax-Free High Yield (PRFHX)   B+   Good

Fund Family: T. Rowe Price Funds   **Phone:** (800) 638-5660
Address: 100 East Pratt Street, Baltimore, MD 21202
Fund Type: MUH - Municipal - High Yield

Major Rating Factors: T Rowe Price Tax-Free High Yield has adopted a risky asset allocation strategy and currently receives an overall TheStreet Investment Rating of B+ (Good). Volatility, as measured by standard deviation, is considered above average for fixed income funds at 3.76. Another risk factor is the fund's fairly average duration of 5.2 years (i.e. average interest rate risk). The high level of risk (D+, Weak) did however, reward investors with excellent performance.

The fund's performance rating is currently A (Excellent). It has registered an average return of 5.37% over the last three years (8.89% taxable equivalent) and is up 1.32% over the last three months (2.19% taxable equivalent). Factored into the performance evaluation is an expense ratio of 0.69% (low) and a 2.0% back-end load levied at the time of sale.

James M. Murphy has been running the fund for 15 years and currently receives a manager quality ranking of 81 (0=worst, 99=best). If you are comfortable owning a high risk investment, this fund may be an option.

Services Offered: Automated phone transactions, payroll deductions, bank draft capabilities, an IRA investment plan, a 401K investment plan, a Keogh investment plan, wire transfers and a systematic withdrawal plan.

Data Date	Investment Rating	Net Assets ($Mil)	NAV	Performance Rating/Pts	Total Return Y-T-D	Risk Rating/Pts
2-17	B+	4,034	11.77	A / 9.3	1.32%	D+ / 2.7
2016	B+	3,989	11.69	A+ / 9.7	1.39%	D+ / 2.5
2015	C+	3,362	11.97	A+ / 9.7	3.82%	D / 1.9
2014	B-	3,240	12.00	A+ / 9.8	14.99%	D- / 1.2
2013	C+	2,267	10.89	B+ / 8.6	-4.51%	D / 2.0
2012	A+	2,554	11.92	A+ / 9.7	13.66%	D+ / 2.8

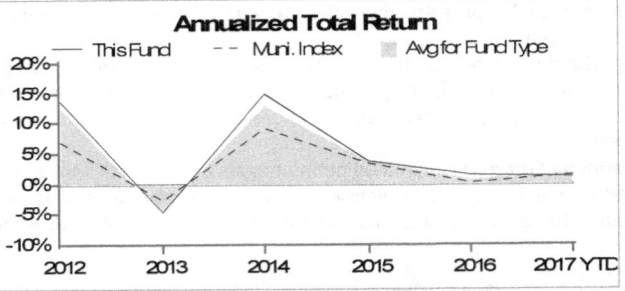

Annualized Total Return

T Rowe Price Tax-Free Income (PRTAX)   A   Excellent

Fund Family: T. Rowe Price Funds   **Phone:** (800) 638-5660
Address: 100 East Pratt Street, Baltimore, MD 21202
Fund Type: MUN - Municipal - National

Major Rating Factors: Strong performance is the major factor driving the A (Excellent) TheStreet Investment Rating for T Rowe Price Tax-Free Income. The fund currently has a performance rating of B (Good) based on an average return of 3.76% over the last three years (6.23% taxable equivalent) and 1.03% over the last three months (1.71% taxable equivalent). Factored into the performance evaluation is an expense ratio of 0.52% (very low).

The fund's risk rating is currently C (Fair). Volatility, as measured by standard deviation, is considered average for fixed income funds at 3.13. Another risk factor is the fund's below average duration of 4.5 years (i.e. lower interest rate risk).

Konstantine B. Mallas has been running the fund for 10 years and currently receives a manager quality ranking of 62 (0=worst, 99=best). If you desire an average level of risk and strong performance, then this fund is a good option.

Services Offered: Automated phone transactions, check writing, payroll deductions, bank draft capabilities, an IRA investment plan, a 401K investment plan, a Keogh investment plan, wire transfers and a systematic withdrawal plan.

Data Date	Investment Rating	Net Assets ($Mil)	NAV	Performance Rating/Pts	Total Return Y-T-D	Risk Rating/Pts
2-17	A	1,957	10.07	B / 8.0	1.03%	C / 5.0
2016	A	1,946	10.03	B+ / 8.7	0.33%	C / 4.6
2015	B+	1,854	10.37	A / 9.4	3.13%	C- / 4.0
2014	A	1,822	10.44	A / 9.3	10.53%	C- / 3.6
2013	B+	1,681	9.82	B / 8.2	-3.41%	C- / 4.0
2012	A	1,888	10.57	B / 8.2	8.58%	C- / 4.2

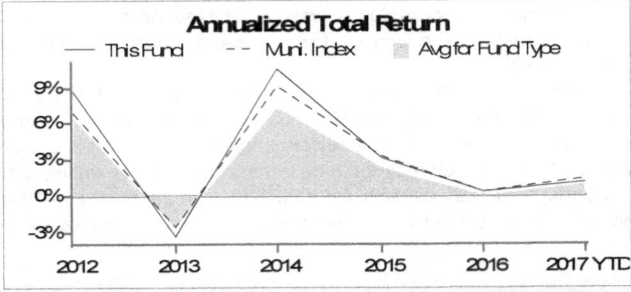

Annualized Total Return

T Rowe Price Tax-Free Sh-Intmdt (PRFSX)   C   Fair

Fund Family: T. Rowe Price Funds   **Phone:** (800) 638-5660
Address: 100 East Pratt Street, Baltimore, MD 21202
Fund Type: MUN - Municipal - National

Major Rating Factors: Disappointing performance is the major factor driving the C (Fair) TheStreet Investment Rating for T Rowe Price Tax-Free Sh-Intmdt. The fund currently has a performance rating of D+ (Weak) based on an average return of 0.82% over the last three years (1.36% taxable equivalent) and 0.97% over the last three months (1.61% taxable equivalent). Factored into the performance evaluation is an expense ratio of 0.49% (very low).

The fund's risk rating is currently B+ (Good). Volatility, as measured by standard deviation, is considered low for fixed income funds at 1.68. Another risk factor is the fund's very low average duration of 2.9 years (i.e. low interest rate risk).

Charles B. Hill has been running the fund for 23 years and currently receives a manager quality ranking of 14 (0=worst, 99=best). This fund offers only a moderate level of risk but investors looking for strong performance are still waiting.

Services Offered: Automated phone transactions, check writing, payroll deductions, bank draft capabilities, an IRA investment plan, a 401K investment plan, a Keogh investment plan, wire transfers and a systematic withdrawal plan.

Data Date	Investment Rating	Net Assets ($Mil)	NAV	Performance Rating/Pts	Total Return Y-T-D	Risk Rating/Pts
2-17	C	1,920	5.58	D+ / 2.8	0.97%	B+ / 8.6
2016	C-	2,049	5.54	D+ / 2.4	-0.29%	B+ / 8.7
2015	A+	2,081	5.63	B- / 7.1	1.05%	B+ / 8.9
2014	B-	2,112	5.65	C- / 3.4	1.90%	B+ / 8.9
2013	A+	1,916	5.63	C / 5.5	0.53%	B+ / 8.9
2012	C+	1,922	5.69	D / 2.2	2.15%	A- / 9.0

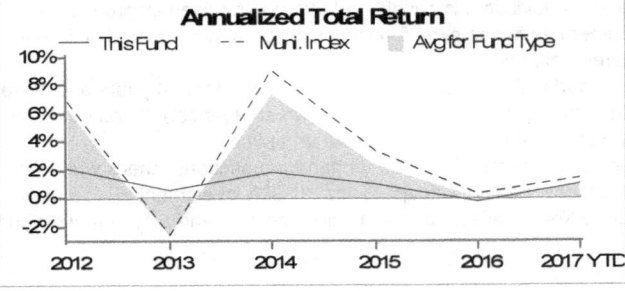

Annualized Total Return

T Rowe Price US Bond Enhanced Index (PBDIX)   C-   Fair

Fund Family: T. Rowe Price Funds   **Phone:** (800) 638-5660
Address: 100 East Pratt Street, Baltimore, MD 21202
Fund Type: GEI - General - Investment Grade
Major Rating Factors: Middle of the road best describes T Rowe Price US Bond Enhanced Index whose TheStreet Investment Rating is currently a C- (Fair). The fund has a performance rating of C (Fair) based on an average return of 2.62% over the last three years and 1.02% over the last three months. Factored into the performance evaluation is an expense ratio of 0.30% (very low) and a 0.5% back-end load levied at the time of sale.

The fund's risk rating is currently C (Fair). Volatility, as measured by standard deviation, is considered average for fixed income funds at 3.02. Another risk factor is the fund's fairly average duration of 5.6 years (i.e. average interest rate risk).

Robert M. Larkins has been running the fund for 17 years and currently receives a manager quality ranking of 37 (0=worst, 99=best). If you desire an average level of risk, then this fund may be an option.

Services Offered: Automated phone transactions, payroll deductions, bank draft capabilities, an IRA investment plan, a 401K investment plan, a Keogh investment plan, wire transfers and a systematic withdrawal plan.

Data Date	Investment Rating	Net Assets ($Mil)	NAV	Performance Rating/Pts	Total Return Y-T-D	Risk Rating/Pts
2-17	C-	655	10.95	C / 4.6	1.02%	C / 5.4
2016	C-	657	10.89	C / 4.9	2.70%	C / 5.5
2015	C+	595	10.90	C+/ 5.9	0.28%	C+/ 6.3
2014	C+	616	11.19	C / 4.3	6.12%	B- / 7.0
2013	C	556	10.87	C- / 3.7	-2.18%	B- / 7.5
2012	C	833	11.52	C- / 3.2	4.42%	B- / 7.5

Annualized Total Return

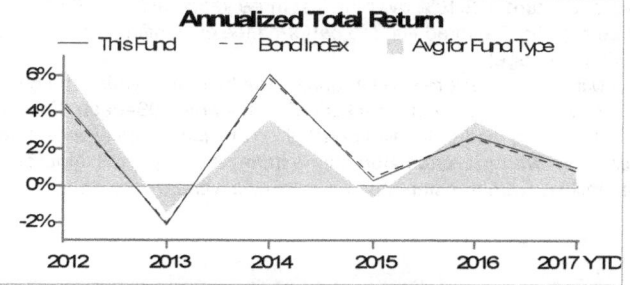

T Rowe Price VA Tax-Free Bond (PRVAX)   A+   Excellent

Fund Family: T. Rowe Price Funds   **Phone:** (800) 638-5660
Address: 100 East Pratt Street, Baltimore, MD 21202
Fund Type: MUS - Municipal - Single State
Major Rating Factors: Strong performance is the major factor driving the A+ (Excellent) TheStreet Investment Rating for T Rowe Price VA Tax-Free Bond. The fund currently has a performance rating of B (Good) based on an average return of 3.71% over the last three years (6.14% taxable equivalent) and 0.88% over the last three months (1.46% taxable equivalent). Factored into the performance evaluation is an expense ratio of 0.47% (very low).

The fund's risk rating is currently C+ (Fair). Volatility, as measured by standard deviation, is considered average for fixed income funds at 2.94. Another risk factor is the fund's below average duration of 4.7 years (i.e. lower interest rate risk).

Hugh D. McGuirk has been running the fund for 20 years and currently receives a manager quality ranking of 66 (0=worst, 99=best). If you desire an average level of risk and strong performance, then this fund is a good option.

Services Offered: Automated phone transactions, check writing, payroll deductions, bank draft capabilities, an IRA investment plan, a 401K investment plan, wire transfers and a systematic withdrawal plan.

Data Date	Investment Rating	Net Assets ($Mil)	NAV	Performance Rating/Pts	Total Return Y-T-D	Risk Rating/Pts
2-17	A+	1,159	11.90	B / 8.0	0.88%	C+/ 5.9
2016	A+	1,165	11.86	B+/ 8.8	0.71%	C / 5.2
2015	B	1,069	12.15	A / 9.3	3.36%	C- / 3.9
2014	B+	985	12.16	B+/ 8.8	9.84%	C- / 3.6
2013	B	878	11.46	B / 7.9	-3.50%	C- / 4.0
2012	B+	1,004	12.31	B- / 7.4	7.31%	C / 4.3

Annualized Total Return

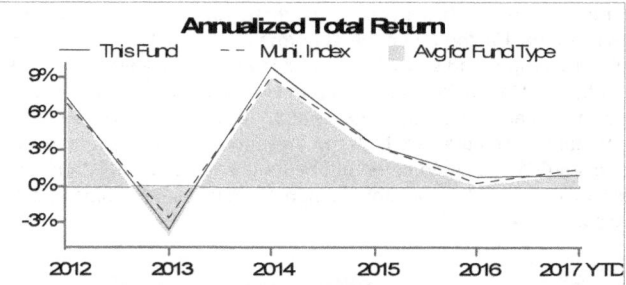

TCW Emerging Markets Income N (TGINX)   C+   Fair

Fund Family: TCW Funds   **Phone:** (800) 386-3829
Address: 865 S Figueroa St, Los Angeles, CA 90017
Fund Type: EM - Emerging Market
Major Rating Factors: TCW Emerging Markets Income N has adopted a very risky asset allocation strategy and currently receives an overall TheStreet Investment Rating of C+ (Fair). Volatility, as measured by standard deviation, is considered high for fixed income funds at 6.59. Another risk factor is the fund's fairly average duration of 6.3 years (i.e. average interest rate risk). The high level of risk (E+, Very Weak) did however, reward investors with excellent performance.

The fund's performance rating is currently A (Excellent). It has registered an average return of 4.54% over the last three years and is up 4.13% over the last three months. Factored into the performance evaluation is an expense ratio of 1.16% (above average).

David I. Robbins has been running the fund for 7 years and currently receives a manager quality ranking of 98 (0=worst, 99=best). If you are comfortable owning a very high risk investment, this fund may be an option.

Services Offered: Automated phone transactions, payroll deductions, bank draft capabilities, a 401K investment plan, wire transfers and a systematic withdrawal plan.

Data Date	Investment Rating	Net Assets ($Mil)	NAV	Performance Rating/Pts	Total Return Y-T-D	Risk Rating/Pts
2-17	C+	544	10.78	A / 9.4	4.13%	E+/ 0.8
2016	C-	527	10.44	B+/ 8.4	13.99%	E+/ 0.8
2015	E	513	9.62	E+/ 0.9	-2.84%	E+/ 0.7
2014	D-	681	10.40	C / 4.9	0.59%	E / 0.5
2013	D-	1,298	10.83	C+/ 6.7	-5.03%	E- / 0.2
2012	C+	1,448	12.02	A+/ 9.9	22.26%	E- / 0.2

Annualized Total Return

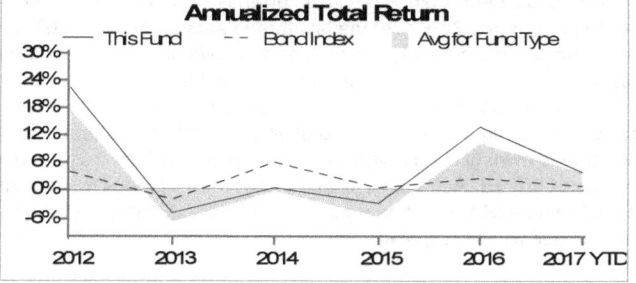

TCW Total Return Bond N (TGMNX)   C+   Fair

Fund Family: TCW Funds   **Phone:** (800) 386-3829
Address: 865 S Figueroa St, Los Angeles, CA 90017
Fund Type: MTG - Mortgage

Major Rating Factors: A moderate risk profile coupled with stable earnings characterizes TCW Total Return Bond N which receives a TheStreet Investment Rating of C+ (Fair). Volatility, as measured by standard deviation, is considered low for fixed income funds at 2.41. Another risk factor is the fund's below average duration of 4.9 years (i.e. lower interest rate risk). The fund's risk rating is currently B (Good).

The fund's performance rating is currently C- (Fair). It has registered an average return of 2.10% over the last three years and is up 0.68% over the last three months. Factored into the performance evaluation is an expense ratio of 0.88% (average).

Mitchell A. Flack has been running the fund for 7 years and currently receives a manager quality ranking of 20 (0=worst, 99=best). If you desire stability with a moderate level of risk then this fund is an excellent option.
Services Offered: Automated phone transactions, payroll deductions, bank draft capabilities, wire transfers and a systematic withdrawal plan.

Data Date	Investment Rating	Net Assets ($Mil)	NAV	Perfor- mance Rating/Pts	Total Return Y-T-D	Risk Rating/Pts
2-17	C+	2,342	10.22	C- / 3.7	0.68%	B / 7.7
2016	C+	2,481	10.19	C- / 4.1	1.20%	B / 7.7
2015	A	2,409	10.45	B- / 7.5	0.72%	B / 7.6
2014	A+	2,212	10.64	B / 7.8	5.48%	C+/ 6.5
2013	A+	2,417	10.34	B / 8.0	1.42%	B- / 7.1
2012	A+	2,475	10.63	B- / 7.4	13.05%	B- / 7.1

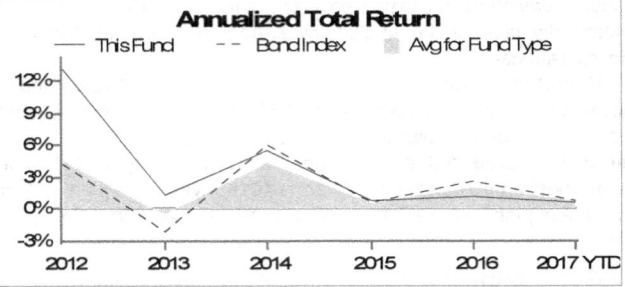

Templeton Global Bond A (TPINX)   D-   Weak

Fund Family: Franklin Templeton Investments   **Phone:** (800) 342-5236
Address: One Franklin Parkway, San Mateo, CA 94403
Fund Type: GL - Global

Major Rating Factors: Templeton Global Bond A has adopted a very risky asset allocation strategy and currently receives an overall TheStreet Investment Rating of D- (Weak). Volatility, as measured by standard deviation, is considered high for fixed income funds at 6.39. Another risk factor is the fund's very low average duration of 0.0 years (i.e. low interest rate risk). Unfortunately, the high level of risk (E+, Very Weak) has only provided investors with average performance.

The fund's performance rating is currently C+ (Fair). It has registered an average return of 2.18% over the last three years and is up 2.33% over the last three months. Factored into the performance evaluation is an expense ratio of 0.96% (average) and a 4.3% front-end load that is levied at the time of purchase.

Michael Hasenstab has been running the fund for 16 years and currently receives a manager quality ranking of 83 (0=worst, 99=best). If you are comfortable owning a very high risk investment, then this fund may be an option.
Services Offered: Automated phone transactions, payroll deductions, bank draft capabilities, an IRA investment plan, a 401K investment plan and a systematic withdrawal plan.

Data Date	Investment Rating	Net Assets ($Mil)	NAV	Perfor- mance Rating/Pts	Total Return Y-T-D	Risk Rating/Pts
2-17	D-	12,455	12.23	C+ / 6.7	2.33%	E+ / 0.9
2016	E+	12,768	12.00	C- / 4.2	6.22%	E+ / 0.9
2015	E+	18,502	11.58	D- / 1.2	-4.26%	D- / 1.5
2014	D-	22,017	12.46	C / 5.5	1.58%	E+ / 0.7
2013	D-	26,428	13.14	C+/ 6.1	2.22%	E / 0.3
2012	E+	25,903	13.38	C+/ 6.6	15.80%	E- / 0.2

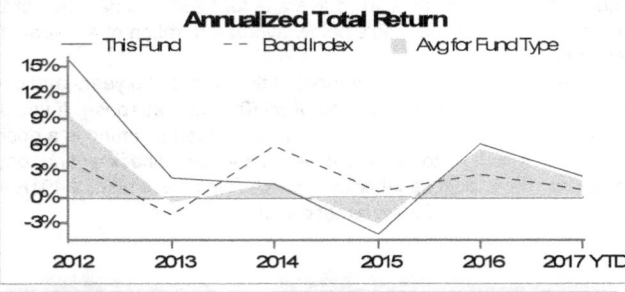

Templeton Global Total Return A (TGTRX)   D-   Weak

Fund Family: Franklin Templeton Investments   **Phone:** (800) 342-5236
Address: One Franklin Parkway, San Mateo, CA 94403
Fund Type: GL - Global

Major Rating Factors: Templeton Global Total Return A has adopted a very risky asset allocation strategy and currently receives an overall TheStreet Investment Rating of D- (Weak). Volatility, as measured by standard deviation, is considered high for fixed income funds at 6.73. Another risk factor is the fund's very low average duration of 0.4 years (i.e. low interest rate risk). The high level of risk (E+, Very Weak) did however, reward investors with excellent performance.

The fund's performance rating is currently B- (Good). It has registered an average return of 2.24% over the last three years and is up 2.20% over the last three months. Factored into the performance evaluation is an expense ratio of 1.08% (average) and a 4.3% front-end load that is levied at the time of purchase.

Michael Hasenstab has been running the fund for 9 years and currently receives a manager quality ranking of 84 (0=worst, 99=best). If you are comfortable owning a very high risk investment, this fund may be an option.
Services Offered: Automated phone transactions, payroll deductions, bank draft capabilities, an IRA investment plan, a 401K investment plan, wire transfers and a systematic withdrawal plan.

Data Date	Investment Rating	Net Assets ($Mil)	NAV	Perfor- mance Rating/Pts	Total Return Y-T-D	Risk Rating/Pts
2-17	D-	1,171	12.30	B- / 7.2	2.20%	E+/ 0.8
2016	E+	1,175	12.09	C / 4.9	8.41%	E+ / 0.7
2015	E+	1,696	11.48	D- / 1.1	-4.88%	D- / 1.1
2014	D-	1,986	12.54	C+/ 6.3	0.37%	E / 0.5
2013	D+	2,166	13.48	B / 8.2	3.55%	E- / 0.2
2012	C-	1,402	13.62	B+/ 8.6	19.03%	E- / 0.2

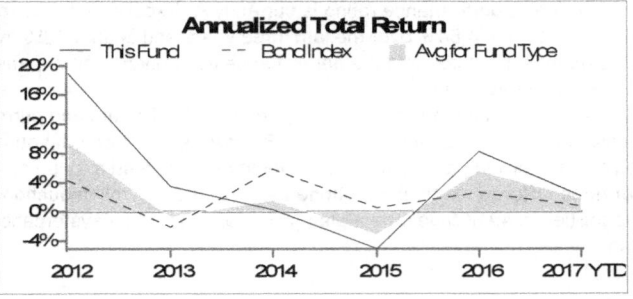

Thompson Bond (THOPX)　　　　　　　B-　　　Good

Fund Family: Thompson IM Funds　　　　**Phone:** (800) 999-0887
Address: 918 Deming Way, Madison, WI 53717
Fund Type: GEI - General - Investment Grade

Major Rating Factors: Strong performance is the major factor driving the B- (Good) TheStreet Investment Rating for Thompson Bond. The fund currently has a performance rating of B (Good) based on an average return of 2.69% over the last three years and 1.78% over the last three months. Factored into the performance evaluation is an expense ratio of 0.71% (low).

　　The fund's risk rating is currently C- (Fair). Volatility, as measured by standard deviation, is considered average for fixed income funds at 3.98. Another risk factor is the fund's very low average duration of 1.3 years (i.e. low interest rate risk).

　　John W. Thompson has been running the fund for 25 years and currently receives a manager quality ranking of 86 (0=worst, 99=best). If you desire an average level of risk and strong performance, then this fund is a good option.

Services Offered: Automated phone transactions, payroll deductions, bank draft capabilities, an IRA investment plan, a 401K investment plan, wire transfers and a systematic withdrawal plan.

Data Date	Investment Rating	Net Assets ($Mil)	NAV	Perfor-mance Rating/Pts	Total Return Y-T-D	Risk Rating/Pts
2-17	B-	2,363	11.41	B / 8.0	1.78%	C- / 3.2
2016	C+	2,107	11.21	B- / 7.5	10.42%	C- / 3.5
2015	C-	2,503	10.60	D / 2.2	-2.86%	B- / 7.3
2014	B	3,525	11.40	C / 4.6	0.96%	B / 7.6
2013	A+	2,353	11.74	B- / 7.4	2.82%	B / 7.9
2012	B	1,354	11.86	C / 4.7	9.34%	B- / 7.2

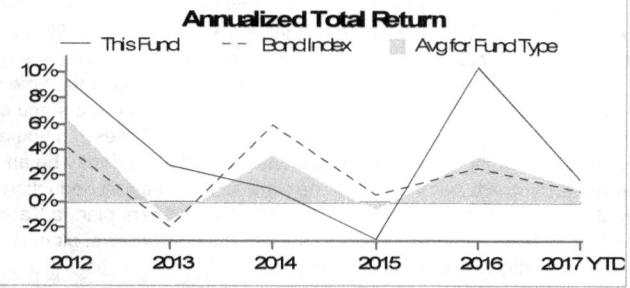

Thornburg Limited Term Income A (THIFX)　　　B　　　Good

Fund Family: Thornburg Funds　　　　**Phone:** (800) 847-0200
Address: 119 East Marcy Street, Santa Fe, NM 87501
Fund Type: GES - General - Short & Inter. Term

Major Rating Factors: A moderate risk profile coupled with stable earnings characterizes Thornburg Limited Term Income A which receives a TheStreet Investment Rating of B (Good). Volatility, as measured by standard deviation, is considered low for fixed income funds at 1.49. Another risk factor is the fund's very low average duration of 2.4 years (i.e. low interest rate risk). The fund's risk rating is currently B+ (Good).

　　The fund's performance rating is currently C- (Fair). It has registered an average return of 2.01% over the last three years and is up 0.67% over the last three months. Factored into the performance evaluation is an expense ratio of 0.87% (average) and a 1.5% front-end load that is levied at the time of purchase.

　　Jason H. Brady has been running the fund for 10 years and currently receives a manager quality ranking of 71 (0=worst, 99=best). If you desire stability with a moderate level of risk then this fund is an excellent option.

Services Offered: Automated phone transactions, payroll deductions, bank draft capabilities, an IRA investment plan, wire transfers and a systematic withdrawal plan.

Data Date	Investment Rating	Net Assets ($Mil)	NAV	Perfor-mance Rating/Pts	Total Return Y-T-D	Risk Rating/Pts
2-17	B	1,079	13.39	C- / 3.9	0.67%	B+ / 8.8
2016	B	1,091	13.34	C / 4.3	3.12%	B+ / 8.7
2015	B-	984	13.18	C / 5.0	0.47%	B+ / 8.4
2014	B-	933	13.38	C- / 4.1	3.47%	B / 8.2
2013	A-	936	13.28	C / 5.1	-0.17%	B+ / 8.4
2012	B	1,137	13.73	C- / 3.7	7.50%	B+ / 8.5

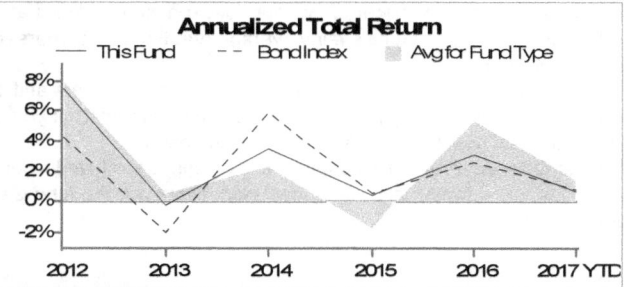

Thornburg Limited Term Muni A (LTMFX)　　　D+　　　Weak

Fund Family: Thornburg Funds　　　　**Phone:** (800) 847-0200
Address: 119 East Marcy Street, Santa Fe, NM 87501
Fund Type: MUN - Municipal - National

Major Rating Factors: Disappointing performance is the major factor driving the D+ (Weak) TheStreet Investment Rating for Thornburg Limited Term Muni A. The fund currently has a performance rating of D (Weak) based on an average return of 1.06% over the last three years (1.76% taxable equivalent) and 0.99% over the last three months (1.64% taxable equivalent). Factored into the performance evaluation is an expense ratio of 0.73% (low) and a 1.5% front-end load that is levied at the time of purchase.

　　The fund's risk rating is currently B (Good). Volatility, as measured by standard deviation, is considered low for fixed income funds at 2.03. Another risk factor is the fund's below average duration of 3.5 years (i.e. lower interest rate risk).

　　Christopher M. Ryon has been running the fund for 6 years and currently receives a manager quality ranking of 10 (0=worst, 99=best). This fund offers only a moderate level of risk but investors looking for strong performance are still waiting.

Services Offered: Automated phone transactions, payroll deductions, bank draft capabilities, an IRA investment plan, wire transfers and a systematic withdrawal plan.

Data Date	Investment Rating	Net Assets ($Mil)	NAV	Perfor-mance Rating/Pts	Total Return Y-T-D	Risk Rating/Pts
2-17	D+	1,473	14.32	D / 2.1	0.99%	B / 8.2
2016	D+	1,620	14.22	D / 1.8	-0.69%	B+ / 8.3
2015	A+	1,692	14.54	B- / 7.1	1.50%	B+ / 8.7
2014	B-	1,858	14.55	C- / 3.6	2.99%	B+ / 8.5
2013	A+	2,190	14.37	C+ / 5.8	-0.19%	B+ / 8.4
2012	C+	2,232	14.66	C- / 3.2	3.07%	B / 8.1

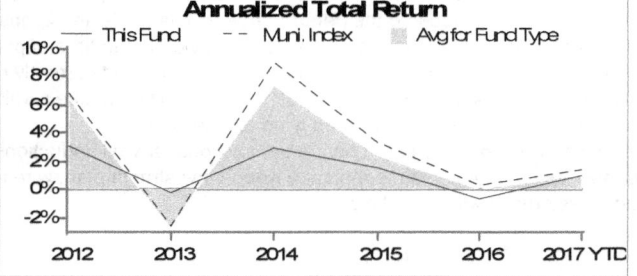

Thrivent Diversified Inc Plus A (AAHYX)   D+   Weak

Fund Family: Thrivent Mutual Funds   **Phone:** (800) 847-4836
Address: P.O. Box 219348, Kansas City, MO 64121
Fund Type: COH - Corporate - High Yield

Major Rating Factors: Thrivent Diversified Inc Plus A has adopted a very risky asset allocation strategy and currently receives an overall TheStreet Investment Rating of D+ (Weak). Volatility, as measured by standard deviation, is considered above average for fixed income funds at 4.36. Another risk factor is the fund's below average duration of 3.1 years (i.e. lower interest rate risk). The high level of risk (D, Weak) did however, reward investors with excellent performance.

The fund's performance rating is currently B- (Good). It has registered an average return of 3.57% over the last three years and is up 2.58% over the last three months. Factored into the performance evaluation is an expense ratio of 1.10% (average) and a 4.5% front-end load that is levied at the time of purchase.

Mark L. Simenstad has been running the fund for 11 years and currently receives a manager quality ranking of 66 (0=worst, 99=best). If you are comfortable owning a very high risk investment, this fund may be an option.

Services Offered: Automated phone transactions, payroll deductions, bank draft capabilities, an IRA investment plan, a 401K investment plan, a Keogh investment plan, wire transfers and a systematic withdrawal plan. However, the fund is currently closed to new investors.

Data Date	Investment Rating	Net Assets ($Mil)	NAV	Performance Rating/Pts	Total Return Y-T-D	Risk Rating/Pts
2-17	D+	601	7.15	B- / 7.1	2.58%	D / 2.1
2016	D-	591	7.00	C / 5.5	6.70%	D / 2.2
2015	C-	586	6.79	B / 7.6	-0.62%	D+/ 2.4
2014	C+	567	7.10	B+/ 8.3	3.54%	D / 2.1
2013	C+	459	7.25	A / 9.4	10.40%	D- / 1.3
2012	D-	290	6.82	B- / 7.2	14.08%	E+/ 0.8

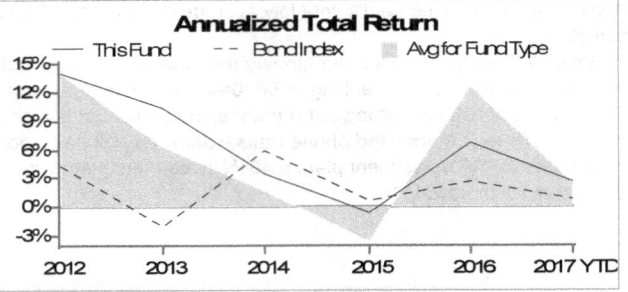

Thrivent Municipal Bond A (AAMBX)   D   Weak

Fund Family: Thrivent Mutual Funds   **Phone:** (800) 847-4836
Address: P.O. Box 219348, Kansas City, MO 64121
Fund Type: MUN - Municipal - National

Major Rating Factors: Thrivent Municipal Bond A receives a TheStreet Investment Rating of D (Weak). The fund has a performance rating of C (Fair) based on an average return of 3.40% over the last three years (5.63% taxable equivalent) and 0.91% over the last three months (1.51% taxable equivalent). Factored into the performance evaluation is an expense ratio of 0.74% (low) and a 4.5% front-end load that is levied at the time of purchase.

The fund's risk rating is currently C (Fair). Volatility, as measured by standard deviation, is considered average for fixed income funds at 3.31. Another risk factor is the fund's fairly average duration of 6.0 years (i.e. average interest rate risk).

Janet I. Grangaard has been running the fund for 15 years and currently receives a manager quality ranking of 34 (0=worst, 99=best). If you desire an average level of risk, then this fund may be an option.

Services Offered: Automated phone transactions, payroll deductions, bank draft capabilities and a systematic withdrawal plan. However, the fund is currently closed to new investors.

Data Date	Investment Rating	Net Assets ($Mil)	NAV	Performance Rating/Pts	Total Return Y-T-D	Risk Rating/Pts
2-17	D	1,405	11.31	C / 4.9	0.91%	C / 4.4
2016	D+	1,410	11.27	C / 5.3	-0.20%	C / 4.4
2015	C+	1,463	11.67	B / 8.2	3.10%	C- / 4.2
2014	B-	1,454	11.71	B / 7.7	9.61%	C- / 3.7
2013	C-	1,361	11.07	C+/ 5.9	-3.55%	C- / 4.0
2012	B-	1,537	11.91	C+/ 6.2	7.58%	C / 4.8

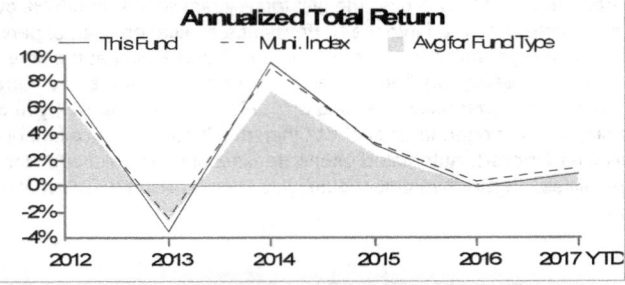

Transamerica Short-Term Bond A (ITAAX)   B-   Good

Fund Family: Transamerica Funds   **Phone:** (888) 233-4339
Address: P.O. Box 219945, Kansas City, MO 64121
Fund Type: COI - Corporate - Investment Grade

Major Rating Factors: A moderate risk profile coupled with stable earnings characterizes Transamerica Short-Term Bond A which receives a TheStreet Investment Rating of B- (Good). Volatility, as measured by standard deviation, is considered very low for fixed income funds at 0.96. Another risk factor is the fund's very low average duration of 1.6 years (i.e. low interest rate risk). The fund's risk rating is currently A (Excellent).

The fund's performance rating is currently C- (Fair). It has registered an average return of 1.51% over the last three years and is up 0.75% over the last three months. Factored into the performance evaluation is an expense ratio of 0.84% (low) and a 2.5% front-end load that is levied at the time of purchase.

Doug Weih has been running the fund for 6 years and currently receives a manager quality ranking of 73 (0=worst, 99=best). If you desire stability with a moderate level of risk then this fund is an excellent option.

Services Offered: Automated phone transactions, payroll deductions, bank draft capabilities, an IRA investment plan, a Keogh investment plan, wire transfers and a systematic withdrawal plan.

Data Date	Investment Rating	Net Assets ($Mil)	NAV	Performance Rating/Pts	Total Return Y-T-D	Risk Rating/Pts
2-17	B-	933	10.21	C- / 3.1	0.75%	A / 9.3
2016	C+	923	10.17	C- / 3.0	2.90%	A / 9.3
2015	B-	944	10.10	C / 4.5	0.30%	A- / 9.2
2014	B-	1,017	10.28	C- / 3.3	1.37%	A- / 9.0
2013	B+	984	10.38	C / 4.5	2.20%	A- / 9.0
2012	C+	800	10.47	D+/ 2.3	6.55%	B+/ 8.9

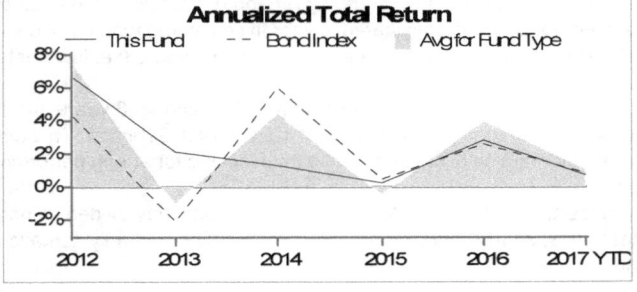

USAA California Bond Fund (USCBX)   A-   Excellent

Fund Family: USAA Group   **Phone:** (800) 382-8722
Address: 9800 Fredricksburg Road, San Antonio, TX 78288
Fund Type: MUS - Municipal - Single State

Major Rating Factors: Strong performance is the major factor driving the A-
(Excellent) TheStreet Investment Rating for USAA California Bond Fund. The
fund currently has a performance rating of B+ (Good) based on an average
return of 4.14% over the last three years (6.86% taxable equivalent) and 1.13%
over the last three months (1.87% taxable equivalent). Factored into the
performance evaluation is an expense ratio of 0.56% (very low).

The fund's risk rating is currently C- (Fair). Volatility, as measured by
standard deviation, is considered average for fixed income funds at 3.09.
Another risk factor is the fund's above average duration of 9.2 years (i.e. higher
interest rate risk).

John Spear currently receives a manager quality ranking of 73 (0=worst,
99=best). If you desire an average level of risk and strong performance, then this
fund is a good option.

Services Offered: Automated phone transactions, payroll deductions, bank draft
capabilities, an IRA investment plan and a systematic withdrawal plan.

Data Date	Investment Rating	Net Assets ($Mil)	NAV	Performance Rating/Pts	Total Return Y-T-D	Risk Rating/Pts
2-17	A-	669	10.93	B+ / 8.6	1.13%	C- / 4.0
2016	A-	668	10.87	A / 9.4	0.12%	C- / 3.5
2015	B-	683	11.23	A+ / 9.8	3.66%	D+ / 2.7
2014	B	666	11.25	A+ / 9.7	12.61%	D / 1.6
2013	B	600	10.39	A+ / 9.7	-2.95%	D / 2.0
2012	B+	679	11.15	A+ / 9.7	11.16%	D / 1.8

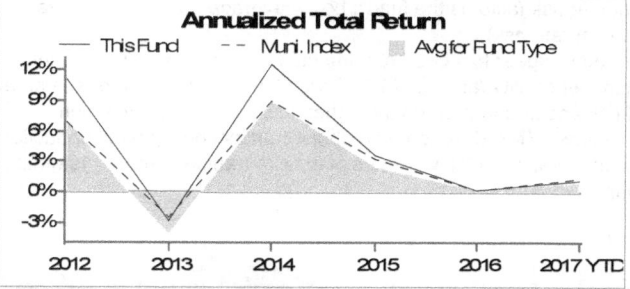

USAA High Income Fund (USHYX)   C+   Fair

Fund Family: USAA Group   **Phone:** (800) 382-8722
Address: 9800 Fredricksburg Road, San Antonio, TX 78288
Fund Type: COH - Corporate - High Yield

Major Rating Factors: USAA High Income Fund has adopted a very risky asset
allocation strategy and currently receives an overall TheStreet Investment Rating
of C+ (Fair). Volatility, as measured by standard deviation, is considered high for
fixed income funds at 6.03. Another risk factor is the fund's very low average
duration of 2.9 years (i.e. low interest rate risk). The high level of risk (E+, Very
Weak) did however, reward investors with excellent performance.

The fund's performance rating is currently A (Excellent). It has registered an
average return of 3.79% over the last three years and is up 3.04% over the last
three months. Factored into the performance evaluation is an expense ratio of
0.84% (low) and a 1.0% back-end load levied at the time of sale.

John Spear has been running the fund for 1 year and currently receives a
manager quality ranking of 16 (0=worst, 99=best). If you are comfortable owning
a very high risk investment, this fund may be an option.

Services Offered: Automated phone transactions, payroll deductions, bank draft
capabilities, an IRA investment plan, wire transfers and a systematic withdrawal
plan.

Data Date	Investment Rating	Net Assets ($Mil)	NAV	Performance Rating/Pts	Total Return Y-T-D	Risk Rating/Pts
2-17	C+	1,193	8.26	A / 9.4	3.04%	E+ / 0.8
2016	C	1,144	8.08	A / 9.3	17.91%	E+ / 0.9
2015	D-	1,105	7.29	D- / 1.3	-8.56%	D / 1.6
2014	B	1,389	8.45	B+ / 8.6	3.53%	D+ / 2.9
2013	B	1,338	8.69	A+ / 9.7	8.47%	D- / 1.5
2012	B-	1,154	8.66	A / 9.3	16.53%	D- / 1.1

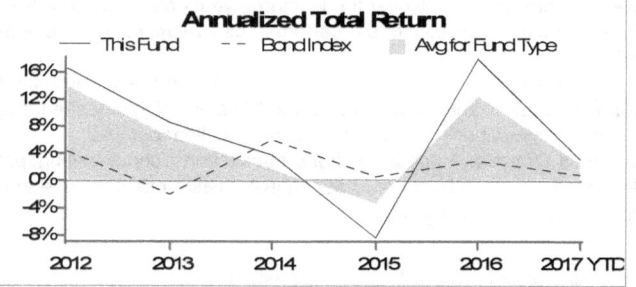

USAA Income Fund (USAIX)   B-   Good

Fund Family: USAA Group   **Phone:** (800) 382-8722
Address: 9800 Fredricksburg Road, San Antonio, TX 78288
Fund Type: USS - US Government - Short & Inter. Term

Major Rating Factors: USAA Income Fund receives a TheStreet Investment
Rating of B- (Good). The fund has a performance rating of C+ (Fair) based on an
average return of 3.24% over the last three years and 1.56% over the last three
months. Factored into the performance evaluation is an expense ratio of 0.53%
(very low).

The fund's risk rating is currently C (Fair). Volatility, as measured by
standard deviation, is considered average for fixed income funds at 3.20.
Another risk factor is the fund's below average duration of 3.7 years (i.e. lower
interest rate risk).

John Spear has been running the fund for 1 year and currently receives a
manager quality ranking of 84 (0=worst, 99=best). If you desire an average level
of risk, then this fund may be an option.

Services Offered: Automated phone transactions, payroll deductions, bank draft
capabilities, an IRA investment plan, wire transfers and a systematic withdrawal
plan.

Data Date	Investment Rating	Net Assets ($Mil)	NAV	Performance Rating/Pts	Total Return Y-T-D	Risk Rating/Pts
2-17	B-	3,419	13.02	C+ / 6.7	1.56%	C / 4.8
2016	C+	3,332	12.88	C+ / 6.6	5.84%	C / 5.0
2015	C	3,458	12.60	C+ / 5.8	-1.11%	C+ / 6.2
2014	B+	3,228	13.20	C+ / 5.8	5.89%	B- / 7.1
2013	A	2,628	12.94	C+ / 6.2	-0.18%	B / 7.8
2012	A+	2,790	13.47	C / 5.0	7.00%	B+ / 8.3

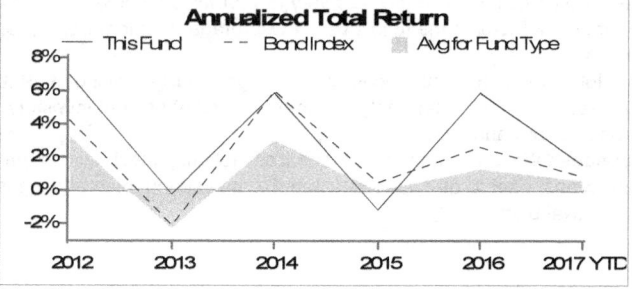

USAA Intmdt-Trm Bd Fund (USIBX)

B+   **Good**

Fund Family: USAA Group   **Phone:** (800) 382-8722
Address: 9800 Fredricksburg Road, San Antonio, TX 78288
Fund Type: GEI - General - Investment Grade
Major Rating Factors: Strong performance is the major factor driving the B+ (Good) TheStreet Investment Rating for USAA Intmdt-Trm Bd Fund. The fund currently has a performance rating of B- (Good) based on an average return of 3.14% over the last three years and 1.85% over the last three months. Factored into the performance evaluation is an expense ratio of 0.62% (low).

The fund's risk rating is currently C (Fair). Volatility, as measured by standard deviation, is considered average for fixed income funds at 3.01. Another risk factor is the fund's below average duration of 3.2 years (i.e. lower interest rate risk).

John Spear has been running the fund for 1 year and currently receives a manager quality ranking of 75 (0=worst, 99=best). If you desire an average level of risk and strong performance, then this fund is a good option.

Services Offered: Automated phone transactions, payroll deductions, bank draft capabilities, an IRA investment plan, wire transfers and a systematic withdrawal plan.

Data Date	Investment Rating	Net Assets ($Mil)	NAV	Perfor-mance Rating/Pts	Total Return Y-T-D	Risk Rating/Pts
2-17	B+	1,850	10.55	B- / 7.0	1.85%	C / 5.5
2016	B+	1,802	10.42	C+ / 6.7	6.69%	C+ / 5.8
2015	C	1,967	10.15	C / 5.2	-2.32%	C+ / 6.4
2014	A+	2,020	10.83	B- / 7.3	5.75%	C+ / 6.3
2013	A+	1,747	10.68	B / 8.1	1.30%	C+ / 6.2
2012	A+	1,795	11.01	B / 8.1	11.23%	C+ / 5.8

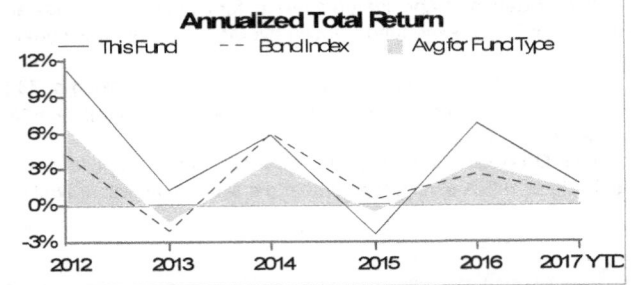

Annualized Total Return

USAA Short Term Bond Retail Fund (USSBX)

B+   **Good**

Fund Family: USAA Group   **Phone:** (800) 382-8722
Address: 9800 Fredricksburg Road, San Antonio, TX 78288
Fund Type: GEI - General - Investment Grade
Major Rating Factors: A moderate risk profile coupled with stable earnings characterizes USAA Short Term Bond Retail Fund which receives a TheStreet Investment Rating of B+ (Good). Volatility, as measured by standard deviation, is considered very low for fixed income funds at 1.05. Another risk factor is the fund's very low average duration of 1.6 years (i.e. low interest rate risk). The fund's risk rating is currently A- (Excellent).

The fund's performance rating is currently C- (Fair). It has registered an average return of 1.48% over the last three years and is up 0.64% over the last three months. Factored into the performance evaluation is an expense ratio of 0.61% (low).

John Spear has been running the fund for 1 year and currently receives a manager quality ranking of 70 (0=worst, 99=best). If you desire stability with a moderate level of risk then this fund is an excellent option.

Services Offered: Automated phone transactions, check writing, payroll deductions, bank draft capabilities, an IRA investment plan, wire transfers and a systematic withdrawal plan.

Data Date	Investment Rating	Net Assets ($Mil)	NAV	Perfor-mance Rating/Pts	Total Return Y-T-D	Risk Rating/Pts
2-17	B+	1,326	9.16	C- / 3.9	0.64%	A- / 9.2
2016	B	1,339	9.13	C- / 3.9	3.01%	A- / 9.2
2015	B+	1,786	9.03	C / 5.1	0.00%	A- / 9.2
2014	B-	1,690	9.18	C- / 3.1	1.66%	A- / 9.2
2013	B+	1,625	9.19	C- / 3.9	1.01%	A / 9.3
2012	C+	1,648	9.28	D / 1.9	4.09%	A / 9.5

Asset Composition
For: USAA Short Term Bond Retail Fund

Cash & Cash Equivalent:	0%
Government Bonds:	7%
Municipal Bonds:	8%
Corporate Bonds:	64%
Other:	21%

USAA T/E Short Term Bond Fund (USSTX)

C+   **Fair**

Fund Family: USAA Group   **Phone:** (800) 382-8722
Address: 9800 Fredricksburg Road, San Antonio, TX 78288
Fund Type: MUN - Municipal - National
Major Rating Factors: Disappointing performance is the major factor driving the C+ (Fair) TheStreet Investment Rating for USAA T/E Short Term Bond Fund. The fund currently has a performance rating of D (Weak) based on an average return of 0.58% over the last three years (0.96% taxable equivalent) and 0.43% over the last three months (0.71% taxable equivalent). Factored into the performance evaluation is an expense ratio of 0.55% (very low).

The fund's risk rating is currently A (Excellent). Volatility, as measured by standard deviation, is considered very low for fixed income funds at 0.80. Another risk factor is the fund's very low average duration of 2.3 years (i.e. low interest rate risk).

John Spear currently receives a manager quality ranking of 29 (0=worst, 99=best). This fund offers only a moderate level of risk but investors looking for strong performance are still waiting.

Services Offered: Automated phone transactions, check writing, payroll deductions, bank draft capabilities, an IRA investment plan and a systematic withdrawal plan.

Data Date	Investment Rating	Net Assets ($Mil)	NAV	Perfor-mance Rating/Pts	Total Return Y-T-D	Risk Rating/Pts
2-17	C+	1,698	10.45	D / 2.2	0.43%	A / 9.5
2016	C	1,689	10.43	D+ / 2.3	-0.12%	A / 9.5
2015	A+	1,806	10.59	C+ / 6.6	0.57%	A+ / 9.7
2014	B	1,994	10.69	C- / 3.4	1.54%	A+ / 9.6
2013	A+	2,087	10.70	C+ / 5.6	0.65%	A / 9.5
2012	B-	2,168	10.83	D+ / 2.6	2.52%	A / 9.4

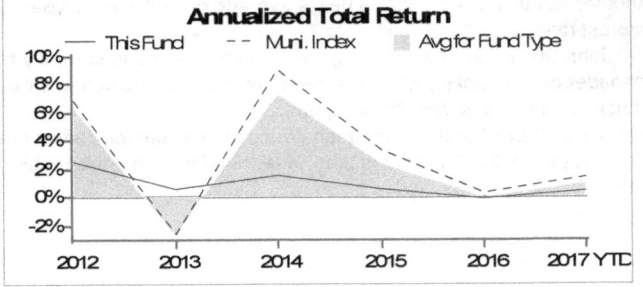

Annualized Total Return

USAA Tax-Exempt Interm-Term Fund (USATX)   C   Fair

Fund Family: USAA Group   **Phone:** (800) 382-8722
Address: 9800 Fredricksburg Road, San Antonio, TX 78288
Fund Type: MUN - Municipal - National

Major Rating Factors: Middle of the road best describes USAA Tax-Exempt Interm-Term Fund whose TheStreet Investment Rating is currently a C (Fair). The fund has a performance rating of C+ (Fair) based on an average return of 2.49% over the last three years (4.12% taxable equivalent) and 0.79% over the last three months (1.31% taxable equivalent). Factored into the performance evaluation is an expense ratio of 0.54% (very low).

The fund's risk rating is currently C (Fair). Volatility, as measured by standard deviation, is considered average for fixed income funds at 3.20. Another risk factor is the fund's fairly average duration of 6.3 years (i.e. average interest rate risk).

John Spear currently receives a manager quality ranking of 14 (0=worst, 99=best). If you desire an average level of risk, then this fund may be an option.
Services Offered: Automated phone transactions, payroll deductions, bank draft capabilities, an IRA investment plan and a systematic withdrawal plan.

Data Date	Investment Rating	Net Assets ($Mil)	NAV	Performance Rating/Pts	Total Return Y-T-D	Risk Rating/Pts
2-17	C	4,275	13.07	C+ / 5.7	0.79%	C / 4.7
2016	C	4,283	13.04	C+ / 5.9	-0.50%	C / 4.7
2015	A+	4,034	13.52	A- / 9.2	2.62%	B- / 7.0
2014	A+	3,757	13.61	B+ / 8.6	7.37%	C+/ 5.7
2013	A+	2,996	13.12	B+ / 8.8	-1.04%	C+/ 5.8
2012	A+	3,321	13.75	B / 7.9	7.21%	C+/ 5.6

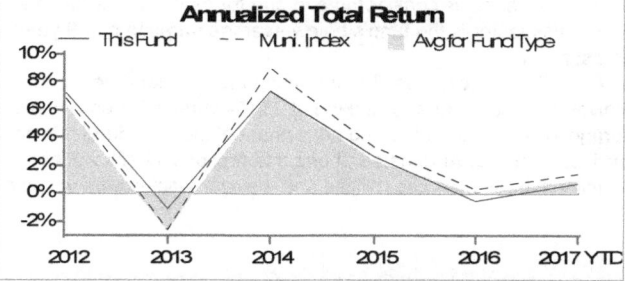

USAA Tax-Exempt Long Term Fund (USTEX)   A   Excellent

Fund Family: USAA Group   **Phone:** (800) 382-8722
Address: 9800 Fredricksburg Road, San Antonio, TX 78288
Fund Type: MUN - Municipal - National

Major Rating Factors: Strong performance is the major factor driving the A (Excellent) TheStreet Investment Rating for USAA Tax-Exempt Long Term Fund. The fund currently has a performance rating of B (Good) based on an average return of 3.71% over the last three years (6.14% taxable equivalent) and 0.97% over the last three months (1.61% taxable equivalent). Factored into the performance evaluation is an expense ratio of 0.51% (very low).

The fund's risk rating is currently C (Fair). Volatility, as measured by standard deviation, is considered average for fixed income funds at 2.92. Another risk factor is the fund's above average duration of 7.9 years (i.e. higher interest rate risk).

John Spear currently receives a manager quality ranking of 67 (0=worst, 99=best). If you desire an average level of risk and strong performance, then this fund is a good option.
Services Offered: Automated phone transactions, payroll deductions, bank draft capabilities, an IRA investment plan and a systematic withdrawal plan.

Data Date	Investment Rating	Net Assets ($Mil)	NAV	Performance Rating/Pts	Total Return Y-T-D	Risk Rating/Pts
2-17	A	2,346	13.25	B / 8.0	0.97%	C / 5.0
2016	A	2,337	13.21	A- / 9.0	0.65%	C / 4.3
2015	B	2,357	13.66	A / 9.5	3.32%	C- / 3.4
2014	A-	2,345	13.79	A / 9.5	10.54%	C- / 3.1
2013	A-	2,457	13.01	A- / 9.2	-2.79%	C- / 3.4
2012	A-	2,826	13.94	A- / 9.2	9.81%	D+/ 2.8

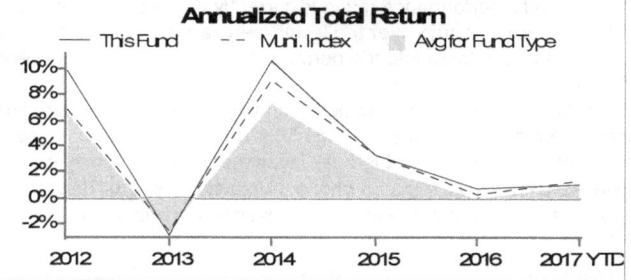

USAA Virginia Bond Fund (USVAX)   C+   Fair

Fund Family: USAA Group   **Phone:** (800) 382-8722
Address: 9800 Fredricksburg Road, San Antonio, TX 78288
Fund Type: GEI - General - Investment Grade

Major Rating Factors: Middle of the road best describes USAA Virginia Bond Fund whose TheStreet Investment Rating is currently a C+ (Fair). The fund has a performance rating of C+ (Fair) based on an average return of 3.67% over the last three years and 0.68% over the last three months. Factored into the performance evaluation is an expense ratio of 0.60% (low).

The fund's risk rating is currently C (Fair). Volatility, as measured by standard deviation, is considered average for fixed income funds at 2.88. Another risk factor is the fund's above average duration of 7.6 years (i.e. higher interest rate risk).

John Spear currently receives a manager quality ranking of 82 (0=worst, 99=best). If you desire an average level of risk, then this fund may be an option.
Services Offered: Automated phone transactions, bank draft capabilities, an IRA investment plan and a systematic withdrawal plan.

Data Date	Investment Rating	Net Assets ($Mil)	NAV	Performance Rating/Pts	Total Return Y-T-D	Risk Rating/Pts
2-17	C+	663	11.21	C+ / 6.1	0.68%	C / 5.2
2016	B-	654	11.19	C+ / 6.9	0.82%	C / 4.6
2015	C+	632	11.46	B+ / 8.4	2.78%	C- / 3.7
2014	C+	631	11.56	B- / 7.4	10.78%	C- / 3.7
2013	C	578	10.84	C+ / 6.1	-3.15%	C- / 4.1
2012	D-	660	11.64	C- / 4.2	7.77%	C / 4.5

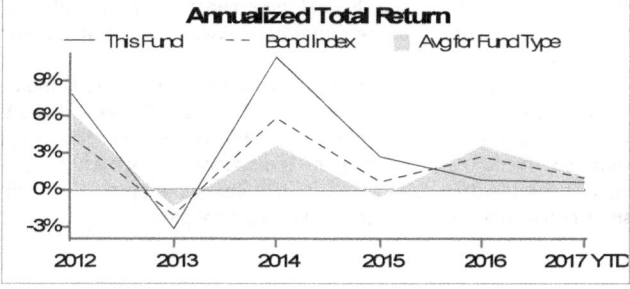

Vanguard CA Interm-Term T-E Inv (VCAIX)

B   **Good**

Fund Family: Vanguard Funds   **Phone:** (800) 662-7447
Address: Vanguard Financial Center, Valley Forge, PA 19482
Fund Type: MUS - Municipal - Single State

Major Rating Factors: Strong performance is the major factor driving the B (Good) TheStreet Investment Rating for Vanguard CA Interm-Term T-E Inv. The fund currently has a performance rating of B- (Good) based on an average return of 3.00% over the last three years (4.97% taxable equivalent) and 1.21% over the last three months (2.00% taxable equivalent). Factored into the performance evaluation is an expense ratio of 0.20% (very low).

The fund's risk rating is currently C (Fair). Volatility, as measured by standard deviation, is considered average for fixed income funds at 3.19. Another risk factor is the fund's below average duration of 4.9 years (i.e. lower interest rate risk).

Adam M. Ferguson has been running the fund for 4 years and currently receives a manager quality ranking of 25 (0=worst, 99=best). If you desire an average level of risk and strong performance, then this fund is a good option.

Services Offered: Automated phone transactions, check writing, payroll deductions, bank draft capabilities and a systematic withdrawal plan.

Data Date	Investment Rating	Net Assets ($Mil)	NAV	Performance Rating/Pts	Total Return Y-T-D	Risk Rating/Pts
2-17	B	1,559	11.62	B- / 7.0	1.21%	C / 4.8
2016	B-	1,539	11.53	B- / 7.1	-0.18%	C / 4.6
2015	A	1,509	11.85	A / 9.5	3.18%	C / 5.4
2014	A+	1,471	11.81	B+ / 8.7	8.00%	C / 5.0
2013	A+	1,200	11.27	B+ / 8.8	-0.83%	C / 5.2
2012	A	1,344	11.74	B- / 7.5	6.63%	C / 5.0

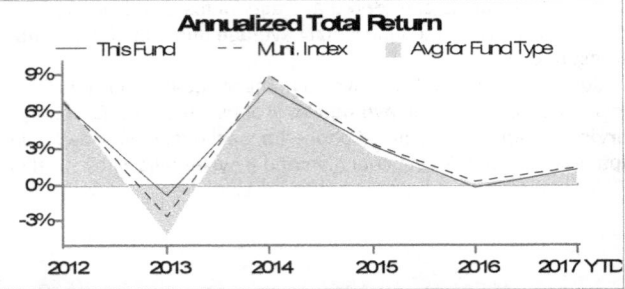

Annualized Total Return

Vanguard Extnd Durtn Trea Idx Inst (VEDTX)

C-   **Fair**

Fund Family: Vanguard Funds   **Phone:** (800) 662-7447
Address: Vanguard Financial Center, Valley Forge, PA 19482
Fund Type: US - US Treasury

Major Rating Factors: Vanguard Extnd Durtn Trea Idx Inst has adopted a very risky asset allocation strategy and currently receives an overall TheStreet Investment Rating of C- (Fair). Volatility, as measured by standard deviation, is considered high for fixed income funds at 17.56. Another risk factor is the fund's very high average duration of 24.7 years (i.e. very high interest rate risk). The high level of risk (E-, Very Weak) did however, reward investors with excellent performance.

The fund's performance rating is currently A- (Excellent). It has registered an average return of 9.40% over the last three years and is up 3.03% over the last three months. Factored into the performance evaluation is an expense ratio of 0.08% (very low).

Joshua C. Barrickman has been running the fund for 4 years and currently receives a manager quality ranking of 69 (0=worst, 99=best). If you are comfortable owning a very high risk investment, this fund may be an option.

Services Offered: Automated phone transactions, payroll deductions, bank draft capabilities, wire transfers and a systematic withdrawal plan.

Data Date	Investment Rating	Net Assets ($Mil)	NAV	Performance Rating/Pts	Total Return Y-T-D	Risk Rating/Pts
2-17	C-	577	33.95	A- / 9.1	3.03%	E- / 0.0
2016	C-	530	32.95	A / 9.5	-0.72%	E- / 0.0
2015	D+	486	34.12	B / 7.8	-4.43%	E- / 0.0
2014	C	522	37.21	A+ / 9.9	45.66%	E- / 0.0
2013	E+	398	26.48	C / 5.2	-20.86%	E- / 0.0
2012	C+	438	35.08	A+ / 9.9	3.25%	E- / 0.0

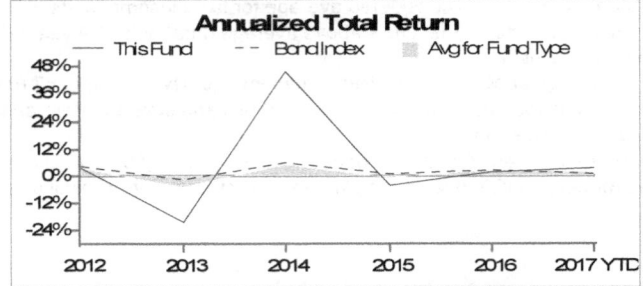

Annualized Total Return

Vanguard GNMA Inv (VFIIX)

B+   **Good**

Fund Family: Vanguard Funds   **Phone:** (800) 662-7447
Address: Vanguard Financial Center, Valley Forge, PA 19482
Fund Type: USA - US Government/Agency

Major Rating Factors: A moderate risk profile coupled with stable earnings characterizes Vanguard GNMA Inv which receives a TheStreet Investment Rating of B+ (Good). Volatility, as measured by standard deviation, is considered low for fixed income funds at 1.96. Another risk factor is the fund's very low average duration of 1.8 years (i.e. low interest rate risk). The fund's risk rating is currently B+ (Good).

The fund's performance rating is currently C (Fair). It has registered an average return of 2.57% over the last three years and is up 0.38% over the last three months. Factored into the performance evaluation is an expense ratio of 0.21% (very low).

Michael F. Garrett has been running the fund for 11 years and currently receives a manager quality ranking of 81 (0=worst, 99=best). If you desire stability with a moderate level of risk then this fund is an excellent option.

Services Offered: Automated phone transactions, check writing, payroll deductions, bank draft capabilities, an IRA investment plan, a Keogh investment plan, wire transfers and a systematic withdrawal plan.

Data Date	Investment Rating	Net Assets ($Mil)	NAV	Performance Rating/Pts	Total Return Y-T-D	Risk Rating/Pts
2-17	B+	7,999	10.54	C / 4.6	0.38%	B+ / 8.3
2016	A-	8,088	10.54	C+ / 5.7	1.85%	B / 8.1
2015	B+	8,577	10.66	B- / 7.1	1.33%	C+ / 6.8
2014	C	9,140	10.82	C- / 4.0	6.65%	C+ / 6.8
2013	C-	9,541	10.42	C- / 3.0	-2.22%	B / 7.7
2012	C+	14,100	10.91	D+ / 2.7	2.35%	B+ / 8.6

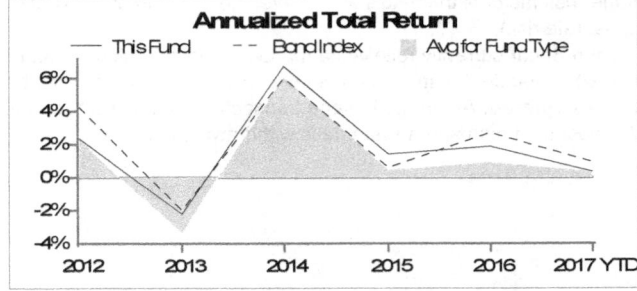

Annualized Total Return

Vanguard High-Yield Corporate Inv (VWEHX)   B   Good

Fund Family: Vanguard Funds   **Phone:** (800) 662-7447
Address: Vanguard Financial Center, Valley Forge, PA 19482
Fund Type: COH - Corporate - High Yield
Major Rating Factors: Vanguard High-Yield Corporate Inv has adopted a very risky asset allocation strategy and currently receives an overall TheStreet Investment Rating of B (Good). Volatility, as measured by standard deviation, is considered above average for fixed income funds at 4.62. Another risk factor is the fund's below average duration of 4.3 years (i.e. lower interest rate risk). The high level of risk (D, Weak) did however, reward investors with excellent performance.

The fund's performance rating is currently A (Excellent). It has registered an average return of 4.62% over the last three years and is up 2.45% over the last three months. Factored into the performance evaluation is an expense ratio of 0.23% (very low).

Michael L Hong has been running the fund for 9 years and currently receives a manager quality ranking of 77 (0=worst, 99=best). If you are comfortable owning a very high risk investment, this fund may be an option.
Services Offered: Automated phone transactions, check writing, payroll deductions, bank draft capabilities, an IRA investment plan, a Keogh investment plan, wire transfers and a systematic withdrawal plan.

Data Date	Investment Rating	Net Assets ($Mil)	NAV	Perfor- mance Rating/Pts	Total Return Y-T-D	Risk Rating/Pts
2-17	B	4,161	5.92	A / 9.3	2.45%	D / 2.0
2016	B-	3,972	5.83	A- / 9.2	11.19%	D / 2.0
2015	C-	3,804	5.54	C+/ 6.9	-1.39%	D / 2.2
2014	C+	4,151	5.97	B+/ 8.3	4.58%	D+/ 2.7
2013	B	4,371	6.03	A / 9.5	4.54%	D / 1.8
2012	B-	5,638	6.11	B+/ 8.9	14.36%	D- / 1.5

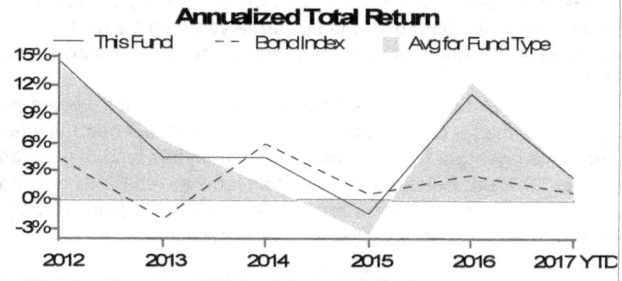

Vanguard High-Yield Tax-Exempt Inv (VWAHX)   B   Good

Fund Family: Vanguard Funds   **Phone:** (800) 662-7447
Address: Vanguard Financial Center, Valley Forge, PA 19482
Fund Type: MUH - Municipal - High Yield
Major Rating Factors: Vanguard High-Yield Tax-Exempt Inv has adopted a risky asset allocation strategy and currently receives an overall TheStreet Investment Rating of B (Good). Volatility, as measured by standard deviation, is considered above average for fixed income funds at 3.83. Another risk factor is the fund's fairly average duration of 5.4 years (i.e. average interest rate risk). The high level of risk (D+, Weak) did however, reward investors with excellent performance.

The fund's performance rating is currently B+ (Good). It has registered an average return of 4.49% over the last three years (7.44% taxable equivalent) and is up 1.26% over the last three months (2.09% taxable equivalent). Factored into the performance evaluation is an expense ratio of 0.20% (very low).

Mathew M. Kiselak has been running the fund for 7 years and currently receives a manager quality ranking of 62 (0=worst, 99=best). If you are comfortable owning a high risk investment, this fund may be an option.
Services Offered: Automated phone transactions, check writing, payroll deductions, bank draft capabilities, an IRA investment plan, wire transfers and a systematic withdrawal plan.

Data Date	Investment Rating	Net Assets ($Mil)	NAV	Perfor- mance Rating/Pts	Total Return Y-T-D	Risk Rating/Pts
2-17	B	1,783	11.08	B+/ 8.9	1.26%	D+/ 2.6
2016	B+	1,736	11.01	A / 9.4	0.83%	D+/ 2.6
2015	B	1,628	11.32	A+/ 9.8	4.13%	D+/ 2.9
2014	B+	1,516	11.28	A+/ 9.6	11.62%	D+/ 2.7
2013	B+	1,264	10.50	B+/ 8.6	-3.22%	C- / 3.4
2012	A	1,606	11.29	A- / 9.0	9.36%	C- / 3.1

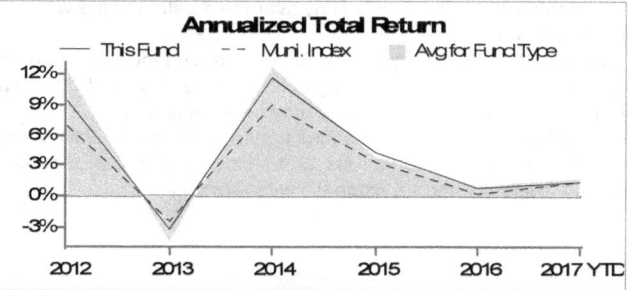

Vanguard Infltn Pro Sec Inv (VIPSX)   E+   Very Weak

Fund Family: Vanguard Funds   **Phone:** (800) 662-7447
Address: Vanguard Financial Center, Valley Forge, PA 19482
Fund Type: USS - US Government - Short & Inter. Term
Major Rating Factors: Vanguard Infltn Pro Sec Inv has adopted a risky asset allocation strategy and currently receives an overall TheStreet Investment Rating of E+ (Very Weak). Volatility, as measured by standard deviation, is considered above average for fixed income funds at 4.06. Another risk factor is the fund's above average duration of 7.9 years (i.e. higher interest rate risk). Unfortunately, the high level of risk (D+, Weak) has only provided investors with average performance.

The fund's performance rating is currently C- (Fair). It has registered an average return of 1.77% over the last three years and is up 1.39% over the last three months. Factored into the performance evaluation is an expense ratio of 0.20% (very low).

Gemma Wright-Casparius has been running the fund for 6 years and currently receives a manager quality ranking of 35 (0=worst, 99=best). If you are comfortable owning a high risk investment, then this fund may be an option.
Services Offered: Automated phone transactions, check writing, payroll deductions, bank draft capabilities and wire transfers.

Data Date	Investment Rating	Net Assets ($Mil)	NAV	Perfor- mance Rating/Pts	Total Return Y-T-D	Risk Rating/Pts
2-17	E+	4,549	13.16	C- / 4.2	1.39%	D+/ 2.7
2016	D-	4,496	12.98	C / 4.5	4.52%	D+/ 2.8
2015	D-	4,847	12.84	D- / 1.0	-1.83%	D / 2.0
2014	E+	5,604	13.18	D / 1.6	3.83%	D- / 1.5
2013	E+	6,578	12.98	D+/ 2.3	-8.92%	D+/ 2.4
2012	C-	16,075	14.53	C+/ 6.0	6.77%	C- / 3.1

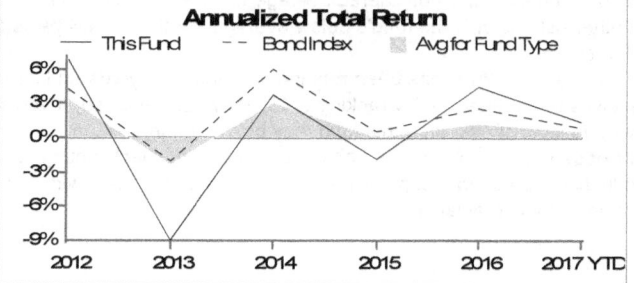

Vanguard Interm-Term Bd Index Inv (VBIIX)   D-   Weak

Fund Family: Vanguard Funds   **Phone:** (800) 662-7447
Address: Vanguard Financial Center, Valley Forge, PA 19482
Fund Type: GEI - General - Investment Grade
Major Rating Factors: Vanguard Interm-Term Bd Index Inv has adopted a risky asset allocation strategy and currently receives an overall TheStreet Investment Rating of D- (Weak). Volatility, as measured by standard deviation, is considered above average for fixed income funds at 4.13. Another risk factor is the fund's fairly average duration of 6.5 years (i.e. average interest rate risk). Unfortunately, the high level of risk (D+, Weak) has only provided investors with average performance.

The fund's performance rating is currently C (Fair). It has registered an average return of 3.03% over the last three years and is up 1.22% over the last three months. Factored into the performance evaluation is an expense ratio of 0.16% (very low).

Joshua C. Barrickman has been running the fund for 9 years and currently receives a manager quality ranking of 20 (0=worst, 99=best). If you are comfortable owning a high risk investment, then this fund may be an option.

Services Offered: Automated phone transactions, check writing, payroll deductions, bank draft capabilities, an IRA investment plan, a Keogh investment plan, wire transfers and a systematic withdrawal plan.

Data Date	Investment Rating	Net Assets ($Mil)	NAV	Performance Rating/Pts	Total Return Y-T-D	Risk Rating/Pts
2-17	D-	1,427	11.33	C / 5.2	1.22%	D+ / 2.9
2016	D	1,472	11.24	C+ / 5.6	2.75%	D+ / 2.9
2015	C-	1,402	11.26	C+ / 6.5	1.21%	C- / 3.1
2014	D+	1,551	11.46	C / 5.2	6.85%	C- / 4.1
2013	C-	1,558	11.09	C / 5.3	-3.54%	C / 4.5
2012	C+	2,120	11.96	C+ / 6.3	6.91%	C / 4.5

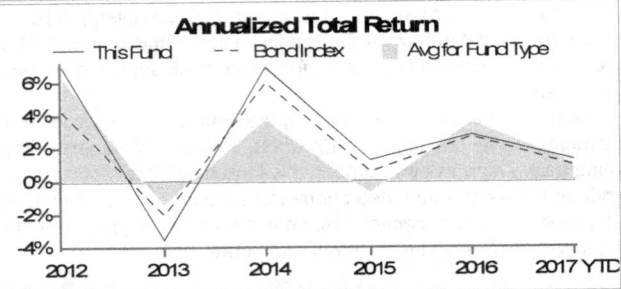

Vanguard Interm-Term Invst-Grd Inv (VFICX)   C+   Fair

Fund Family: Vanguard Funds   **Phone:** (800) 662-7447
Address: Vanguard Financial Center, Valley Forge, PA 19482
Fund Type: GEI - General - Investment Grade
Major Rating Factors: Middle of the road best describes Vanguard Interm-Term Invst-Grd Inv whose TheStreet Investment Rating is currently a C+ (Fair). The fund has a performance rating of C+ (Fair) based on an average return of 3.32% over the last three years and 1.27% over the last three months. Factored into the performance evaluation is an expense ratio of 0.20% (very low).

The fund's risk rating is currently C (Fair). Volatility, as measured by standard deviation, is considered average for fixed income funds at 3.23. Another risk factor is the fund's fairly average duration of 5.5 years (i.e. average interest rate risk).

Gregory S. Nassour has been running the fund for 9 years and currently receives a manager quality ranking of 65 (0=worst, 99=best). If you desire an average level of risk, then this fund may be an option.

Services Offered: Automated phone transactions, check writing, payroll deductions, bank draft capabilities, an IRA investment plan, a Keogh investment plan, wire transfers and a systematic withdrawal plan.

Data Date	Investment Rating	Net Assets ($Mil)	NAV	Performance Rating/Pts	Total Return Y-T-D	Risk Rating/Pts
2-17	C+	2,679	9.72	C+ / 6.2	1.27%	C / 4.7
2016	C+	2,686	9.64	C+ / 6.4	3.83%	C / 4.7
2015	C+	2,669	9.64	B- / 7.2	1.53%	C / 4.7
2014	C+	2,874	9.83	C+ / 6.1	5.81%	C / 5.1
2013	B-	3,143	9.67	C+ / 6.6	-1.37%	C / 5.1
2012	B+	4,957	10.32	C+ / 6.8	9.14%	C / 5.1

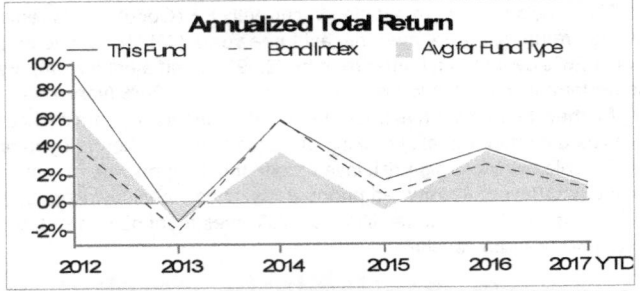

Vanguard Interm-Term Tax-Exempt Inv (VWITX)   B+   Good

Fund Family: Vanguard Funds   **Phone:** (800) 662-7447
Address: Vanguard Financial Center, Valley Forge, PA 19482
Fund Type: MUN - Municipal - National
Major Rating Factors: Vanguard Interm-Term Tax-Exempt Inv receives a TheStreet Investment Rating of B+ (Good). The fund has a performance rating of C+ (Fair) based on an average return of 2.80% over the last three years (4.64% taxable equivalent) and 1.10% over the last three months (1.82% taxable equivalent). Factored into the performance evaluation is an expense ratio of 0.20% (very low).

The fund's risk rating is currently C+ (Fair). Volatility, as measured by standard deviation, is considered average for fixed income funds at 2.93. Another risk factor is the fund's below average duration of 4.6 years (i.e. lower interest rate risk).

James M. D'Arcy has been running the fund for 4 years and currently receives a manager quality ranking of 27 (0=worst, 99=best). If you desire an average level of risk, then this fund may be an option.

Services Offered: Automated phone transactions, check writing, payroll deductions, bank draft capabilities, an IRA investment plan, wire transfers and a systematic withdrawal plan.

Data Date	Investment Rating	Net Assets ($Mil)	NAV	Performance Rating/Pts	Total Return Y-T-D	Risk Rating/Pts
2-17	B+	4,062	13.98	C+ / 6.7	1.10%	C+ / 5.9
2016	B+	4,052	13.89	C+ / 6.8	0.08%	C+ / 5.7
2015	A+	4,422	14.26	A- / 9.1	2.86%	C+ / 6.1
2014	A	4,702	14.27	B / 8.0	7.25%	C / 5.2
2013	A	4,624	13.72	B / 8.1	-1.55%	C / 5.5
2012	B+	6,892	14.38	C+ / 6.6	5.70%	C / 5.3

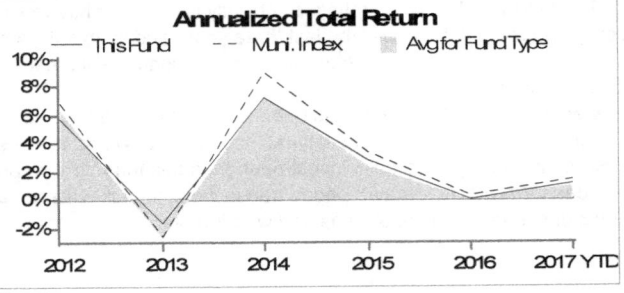

Vanguard Interm-Term Treasury Inv (VFITX)   E+   Very Weak

Fund Family: Vanguard Funds   **Phone:** (800) 662-7447
Address: Vanguard Financial Center, Valley Forge, PA 19482
Fund Type: US - US Treasury
Major Rating Factors: Vanguard Interm-Term Treasury Inv receives a
TheStreet Investment Rating of E+ (Very Weak). The fund has a performance
rating of C- (Fair) based on an average return of 1.93% over the last three years
and 0.70% over the last three months. Factored into the performance evaluation
is an expense ratio of 0.20% (very low).

The fund's risk rating is currently C- (Fair). Volatility, as measured by
standard deviation, is considered average for fixed income funds at 3.52.
Another risk factor is the fund's fairly average duration of 5.3 years (i.e. average
interest rate risk).

Gemma Wright-Casparius has been running the fund for 2 years and
currently receives a manager quality ranking of 47 (0=worst, 99=best). If you
desire an average level of risk, then this fund may be an option.
Services Offered: Automated phone transactions, check writing, payroll
deductions, bank draft capabilities, an IRA investment plan, a Keogh investment
plan, wire transfers and a systematic withdrawal plan.

Data Date	Investment Rating	Net Assets ($Mil)	NAV	Perfor-mance Rating/Pts	Total Return Y-T-D	Risk Rating/Pts
2-17	E+	1,175	11.14	C- / 3.2	0.70%	C- / 3.9
2016	D-	1,208	11.09	C- / 3.7	1.19%	C- / 4.1
2015	C-	1,307	11.26	C+ / 5.6	1.50%	C / 4.8
2014	D	1,358	11.37	D+ / 2.8	4.32%	C+ / 5.8
2013	D	1,469	11.12	C- / 3.2	-3.09%	C+ / 5.6
2012	D-	2,081	11.70	C- / 3.5	2.67%	C / 5.0

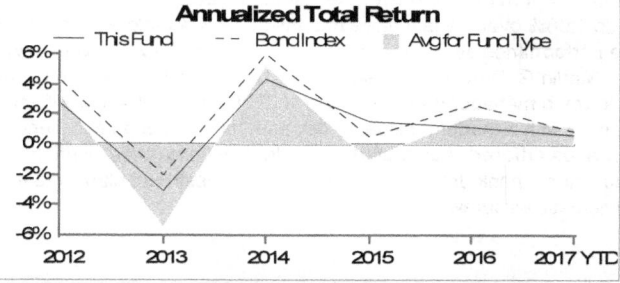

Vanguard Intm-Term Corp Bd Idx Adm (VICSX)   C   Fair

Fund Family: Vanguard Funds   **Phone:** (800) 662-7447
Address: Vanguard Financial Center, Valley Forge, PA 19482
Fund Type: COI - Corporate - Investment Grade
Major Rating Factors: Strong performance is the major factor driving the C
(Fair) TheStreet Investment Rating for Vanguard Intm-Term Corp Bd Idx Adm.
The fund currently has a performance rating of B- (Good) based on an average
return of 3.96% over the last three years and 1.51% over the last three months.
Factored into the performance evaluation is an expense ratio of 0.07% (very
low).

The fund's risk rating is currently C- (Fair). Volatility, as measured by
standard deviation, is considered average for fixed income funds at 4.01.
Another risk factor is the fund's fairly average duration of 6.4 years (i.e. average
interest rate risk).

Joshua C. Barrickman has been running the fund for 8 years and currently
receives a manager quality ranking of 60 (0=worst, 99=best). If you desire an
average level of risk and strong performance, then this fund is a good option.
Services Offered: Automated phone transactions, bank draft capabilities, wire
transfers and a systematic withdrawal plan.

Data Date	Investment Rating	Net Assets ($Mil)	NAV	Perfor-mance Rating/Pts	Total Return Y-T-D	Risk Rating/Pts
2-17	C	785	23.27	B- / 7.2	1.51%	C- / 3.2
2016	C+	702	23.04	B- / 7.4	5.30%	C- / 3.2
2015	C-	467	22.60	B- / 7.2	0.93%	C- / 3.1
2014	C+	301	23.14	B- / 7.3	7.45%	C- / 3.7
2013	C+	73	22.27	B- / 7.3	-1.79%	C- / 3.5
2012	U	54	23.57	U / --	11.39%	U / --

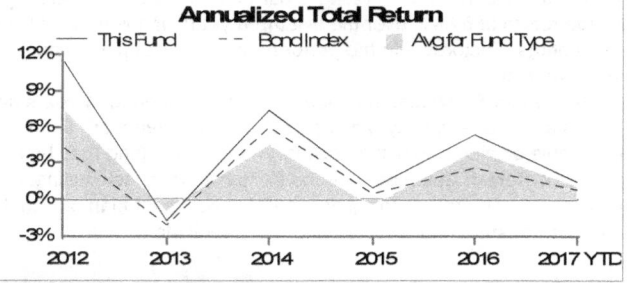

Vanguard Intm-Term Govt Bd Idx Adm (VSIGX)   E+   Very Weak

Fund Family: Vanguard Funds   **Phone:** (800) 662-7447
Address: Vanguard Financial Center, Valley Forge, PA 19482
Fund Type: USS - US Government - Short & Inter. Term
Major Rating Factors: Vanguard Intm-Term Govt Bd Idx Adm receives a
TheStreet Investment Rating of E+ (Very Weak). The fund has a performance
rating of C- (Fair) based on an average return of 1.95% over the last three years
and 0.71% over the last three months. Factored into the performance evaluation
is an expense ratio of 0.07% (very low).

The fund's risk rating is currently C- (Fair). Volatility, as measured by
standard deviation, is considered average for fixed income funds at 3.45.
Another risk factor is the fund's fairly average duration of 5.2 years (i.e. average
interest rate risk).

Joshua C. Barrickman has been running the fund for 4 years and currently
receives a manager quality ranking of 34 (0=worst, 99=best). If you desire an
average level of risk, then this fund may be an option.
Services Offered: Automated phone transactions, bank draft capabilities, wire
transfers and a systematic withdrawal plan.

Data Date	Investment Rating	Net Assets ($Mil)	NAV	Perfor-mance Rating/Pts	Total Return Y-T-D	Risk Rating/Pts
2-17	E+	691	21.70	C- / 3.2	0.71%	C- / 4.1
2016	D-	707	21.60	C- / 3.7	1.10%	C- / 4.2
2015	C	434	21.72	C+ / 5.9	1.65%	C / 5.2
2014	D	262	21.73	D+ / 2.8	4.22%	C+ / 6.1
2013	D+	158	21.18	C- / 3.5	-2.74%	C+ / 5.8
2012	U	52	22.13	U / --	2.63%	U / --

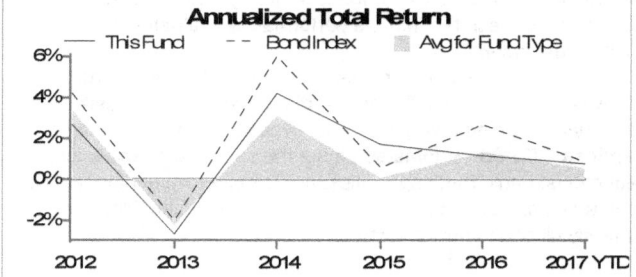

Vanguard Lmtd-Term Tax-Exempt Inv (VMLTX)   C+   Fair

Fund Family: Vanguard Funds   **Phone:** (800) 662-7447
Address: Vanguard Financial Center, Valley Forge, PA 19482
Fund Type: MUN - Municipal - National

Major Rating Factors: A moderate risk profile coupled with stable earnings characterizes Vanguard Lmtd-Term Tax-Exempt Inv which receives a TheStreet Investment Rating of C+ (Fair). Volatility, as measured by standard deviation, is considered low for fixed income funds at 1.50. Another risk factor is the fund's very low average duration of 2.6 years (i.e. low interest rate risk). The fund's risk rating is currently B+ (Good).

The fund's performance rating is currently C- (Fair). It has registered an average return of 0.98% over the last three years (1.62% taxable equivalent) and is up 1.08% over the last three months (1.79% taxable equivalent). Factored into the performance evaluation is an expense ratio of 0.20% (very low).

Marlin G. Brown has been running the fund for 9 years and currently receives a manager quality ranking of 22 (0=worst, 99=best). If you desire stability with a moderate level of risk then this fund is an excellent option.

Services Offered: Automated phone transactions, check writing, payroll deductions, bank draft capabilities, an IRA investment plan, wire transfers and a systematic withdrawal plan.

Data Date	Investment Rating	Net Assets ($Mil)	NAV	Performance Rating/Pts	Total Return Y-T-D	Risk Rating/Pts
2-17	C+	1,795	10.93	C- / 3.3	1.08%	B+ / 8.8
2016	C	1,830	10.84	D+ / 2.7	-0.16%	B+ / 8.8
2015	A+	2,037	11.02	B- / 7.3	1.32%	A- / 9.1
2014	C+	2,270	11.04	C- / 3.1	1.79%	A- / 9.1
2013	A-	2,341	11.02	C / 4.6	0.49%	A- / 9.1
2012	C	2,693	11.15	D / 1.7	1.77%	A- / 9.2

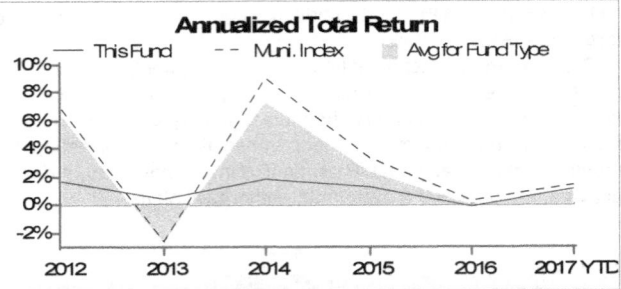

Vanguard Long Term Bd Idx Investor (VBLTX)   D   Weak

Fund Family: Vanguard Funds   **Phone:** (800) 662-7447
Address: Vanguard Financial Center, Valley Forge, PA 19482
Fund Type: GEL - General - Long Term

Major Rating Factors: Vanguard Long Term Bd Idx Investor has adopted a very risky asset allocation strategy and currently receives an overall TheStreet Investment Rating of D (Weak). Volatility, as measured by standard deviation, is considered high for fixed income funds at 8.82. Another risk factor is the fund's very high average duration of 14.9 years (i.e. very high interest rate risk). The high level of risk (E-, Very Weak) did however, reward investors with excellent performance.

The fund's performance rating is currently B+ (Good). It has registered an average return of 5.84% over the last three years and is up 2.41% over the last three months. Factored into the performance evaluation is an expense ratio of 0.16% (very low).

Christopher E. Wrazen has been running the fund for 4 years and currently receives a manager quality ranking of 5 (0=worst, 99=best). If you are comfortable owning a very high risk investment, this fund may be an option.

Services Offered: Automated phone transactions, check writing, payroll deductions, bank draft capabilities, an IRA investment plan, a Keogh investment plan, wire transfers and a systematic withdrawal plan.

Data Date	Investment Rating	Net Assets ($Mil)	NAV	Performance Rating/Pts	Total Return Y-T-D	Risk Rating/Pts
2-17	D	2,709	13.75	B+ / 8.4	2.41%	E- / 0.2
2016	C-	2,595	13.51	A- / 9.1	6.41%	E- / 0.2
2015	D	2,449	13.20	C+ / 5.8	-3.47%	E- / 0.2
2014	C-	2,594	14.26	B+ / 8.9	19.72%	E / 0.3
2013	D-	2,019	12.41	C+ / 6.4	-9.13%	E- / 0.2
2012	C+	2,904	14.27	A- / 9.2	8.49%	E / 0.3

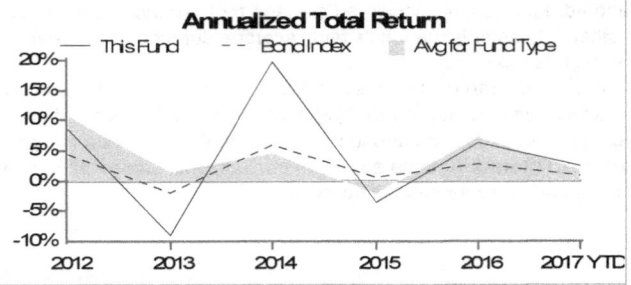

Vanguard Long-Term Inv Gr Inv (VWESX)   C-   Fair

Fund Family: Vanguard Funds   **Phone:** (800) 662-7447
Address: Vanguard Financial Center, Valley Forge, PA 19482
Fund Type: GEI - General - Investment Grade

Major Rating Factors: Vanguard Long-Term Inv Gr Inv has adopted a very risky asset allocation strategy and currently receives an overall TheStreet Investment Rating of C- (Fair). Volatility, as measured by standard deviation, is considered high for fixed income funds at 7.94. Another risk factor is the fund's very high average duration of 13.8 years (i.e. very high interest rate risk). The high level of risk (E, Very Weak) did however, reward investors with excellent performance.

The fund's performance rating is currently A- (Excellent). It has registered an average return of 6.34% over the last three years and is up 2.18% over the last three months. Factored into the performance evaluation is an expense ratio of 0.21% (very low).

Gregory S. Nassour has been running the fund for 4 years and currently receives a manager quality ranking of 32 (0=worst, 99=best). If you are comfortable owning a very high risk investment, this fund may be an option.

Services Offered: Automated phone transactions, check writing, payroll deductions, bank draft capabilities, an IRA investment plan, a Keogh investment plan, wire transfers and a systematic withdrawal plan. However, the fund is currently closed to new investors.

Data Date	Investment Rating	Net Assets ($Mil)	NAV	Performance Rating/Pts	Total Return Y-T-D	Risk Rating/Pts
2-17	C-	4,157	10.21	A- / 9.1	2.18%	E / 0.3
2016	C	4,103	10.06	A+ / 9.6	7.82%	E / 0.3
2015	D+	4,042	9.90	B / 7.7	-2.21%	E / 0.3
2014	C	4,482	10.75	A / 9.4	18.17%	E / 0.4
2013	D+	3,962	9.65	B / 8.0	-5.87%	E / 0.4
2012	C+	4,472	10.85	A / 9.3	11.66%	E / 0.5

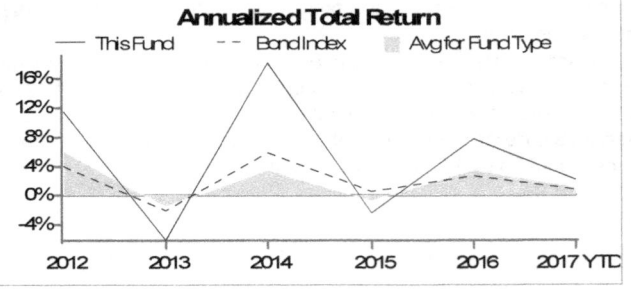

Vanguard Long-Term Tax-Exempt Inv (VWLTX)   B+   Good

Fund Family: Vanguard Funds   **Phone:** (800) 662-7447
Address: Vanguard Financial Center, Valley Forge, PA 19482
Fund Type: MUN - Municipal - National

Major Rating Factors: Strong performance is the major factor driving the B+ (Good) TheStreet Investment Rating for Vanguard Long-Term Tax-Exempt Inv. The fund currently has a performance rating of B+ (Good) based on an average return of 4.19% over the last three years (6.94% taxable equivalent) and 1.01% over the last three months (1.67% taxable equivalent). Factored into the performance evaluation is an expense ratio of 0.20% (very low).

The fund's risk rating is currently C- (Fair). Volatility, as measured by standard deviation, is considered average for fixed income funds at 3.74. Another risk factor is the fund's fairly average duration of 5.4 years (i.e. average interest rate risk).

Mathew M. Kiselak has been running the fund for 7 years and currently receives a manager quality ranking of 55 (0=worst, 99=best). If you desire an average level of risk and strong performance, then this fund is a good option.

Services Offered: Automated phone transactions, check writing, payroll deductions, bank draft capabilities, an IRA investment plan, wire transfers and a systematic withdrawal plan.

Data Date	Investment Rating	Net Assets ($Mil)	NAV	Perfor-mance Rating/Pts	Total Return Y-T-D	Risk Rating/Pts
2-17	B+	926	11.43	B+ / 8.6	1.01%	C- / 3.5
2016	A-	923	11.38	A- / 9.2	0.63%	C- / 3.5
2015	B+	931	11.75	A+ / 9.7	3.97%	C- / 3.8
2014	A	955	11.74	A / 9.4	11.07%	C- / 3.7
2013	A-	943	11.01	B+ / 8.4	-2.95%	C- / 4.2
2012	A	1,094	11.80	B / 8.1	8.08%	C / 4.4

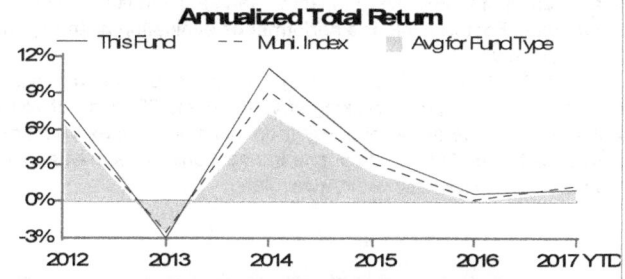

Vanguard Long-Term Treasury Inv (VUSTX)   D-   Weak

Fund Family: Vanguard Funds   **Phone:** (800) 662-7447
Address: Vanguard Financial Center, Valley Forge, PA 19482
Fund Type: US - US Treasury

Major Rating Factors: Vanguard Long-Term Treasury Inv has adopted a very risky asset allocation strategy and currently receives an overall TheStreet Investment Rating of D- (Weak). Volatility, as measured by standard deviation, is considered high for fixed income funds at 11.38. Another risk factor is the fund's very high average duration of 17.3 years (i.e. very high interest rate risk). The high level of risk (E-, Very Weak) did however, reward investors with excellent performance.

The fund's performance rating is currently B- (Good). It has registered an average return of 6.08% over the last three years and is up 2.23% over the last three months. Factored into the performance evaluation is an expense ratio of 0.20% (very low).

Gemma Wright-Casparius has been running the fund for 2 years and currently receives a manager quality ranking of 58 (0=worst, 99=best). If you are comfortable owning a very high risk investment, this fund may be an option.

Services Offered: Automated phone transactions, check writing, payroll deductions, bank draft capabilities, an IRA investment plan, a Keogh investment plan, wire transfers and a systematic withdrawal plan.

Data Date	Investment Rating	Net Assets ($Mil)	NAV	Perfor-mance Rating/Pts	Total Return Y-T-D	Risk Rating/Pts
2-17	D-	998	11.95	B- / 7.0	2.23%	E- / 0.1
2016	D	1,006	11.74	B / 8.1	1.20%	E- / 0.1
2015	D+	1,074	12.19	B- / 7.3	-1.54%	E- / 0.1
2014	C-	1,190	13.05	B+ / 8.9	25.28%	E- / 0.2
2013	E	963	10.90	C- / 3.2	-13.03%	E- / 0.1
2012	C-	1,491	13.07	B+ / 8.5	3.47%	E- / 0.1

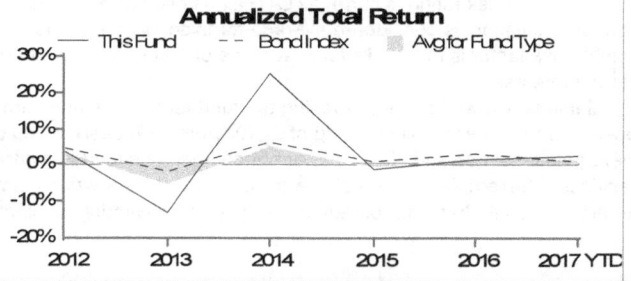

Vanguard MA Tax-Exempt Inv (VMATX)   C+   Fair

Fund Family: Vanguard Funds   **Phone:** (800) 662-7447
Address: Vanguard Financial Center, Valley Forge, PA 19482
Fund Type: MUS - Municipal - Single State

Major Rating Factors: Strong performance is the major factor driving the C+ (Fair) TheStreet Investment Rating for Vanguard MA Tax-Exempt Inv. The fund currently has a performance rating of B (Good) based on an average return of 3.73% over the last three years (6.18% taxable equivalent) and 0.96% over the last three months (1.59% taxable equivalent). Factored into the performance evaluation is an expense ratio of 0.16% (very low).

The fund's risk rating is currently C- (Fair). Volatility, as measured by standard deviation, is considered average for fixed income funds at 3.87. Another risk factor is the fund's fairly average duration of 5.4 years (i.e. average interest rate risk).

Marlin G. Brown has been running the fund for 9 years and currently receives a manager quality ranking of 26 (0=worst, 99=best). If you desire an average level of risk and strong performance, then this fund is a good option.

Services Offered: Automated phone transactions, check writing, payroll deductions, bank draft capabilities, wire transfers and a systematic withdrawal plan.

Data Date	Investment Rating	Net Assets ($Mil)	NAV	Perfor-mance Rating/Pts	Total Return Y-T-D	Risk Rating/Pts
2-17	C+	1,525	10.59	B / 7.8	0.96%	C- / 3.4
2016	B	1,487	10.54	B+ / 8.4	-0.12%	C- / 3.4
2015	B+	1,286	10.92	A+ / 9.6	3.95%	C- / 3.6
2014	B+	1,170	10.85	B+ / 8.9	10.29%	C- / 3.6
2013	B	981	10.22	B / 7.6	-3.32%	C- / 4.1
2012	B	1,111	10.92	C+ / 6.9	6.46%	C / 4.5

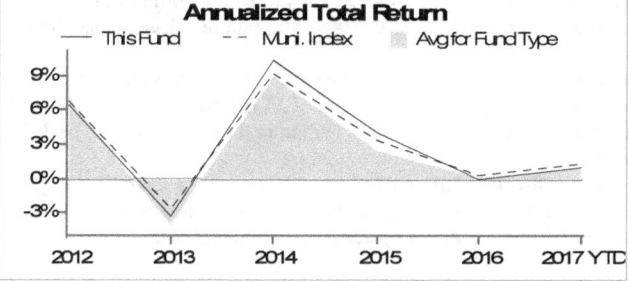

Vanguard Mort-Backed Secs Idx Adm (VMBSX)   B   Good

Fund Family: Vanguard Funds   **Phone:** (800) 662-7447
Address: Vanguard Financial Center, Valley Forge, PA 19482
Fund Type: MTG - Mortgage
Major Rating Factors: A moderate risk profile coupled with stable earnings
characterizes Vanguard Mort-Backed Secs Idx Adm which receives a TheStreet
Investment Rating of B (Good). Volatility, as measured by standard deviation, is
considered low for fixed income funds at 1.94. Another risk factor is the fund's
very low average duration of 2.5 years (i.e. low interest rate risk). The fund's risk
rating is currently B+ (Good).

The fund's performance rating is currently C (Fair). It has registered an
average return of 2.39% over the last three years and is up 0.55% over the last
three months. Factored into the performance evaluation is an expense ratio of
0.07% (very low).

William D. Baird has been running the fund for 8 years and currently
receives a manager quality ranking of 45 (0=worst, 99=best). If you desire
stability with a moderate level of risk then this fund is an excellent option.
Services Offered: Automated phone transactions, bank draft capabilities, wire
transfers and a systematic withdrawal plan.

Data Date	Investment Rating	Net Assets ($Mil)	NAV	Performance Rating/Pts	Total Return Y-T-D	Risk Rating/Pts
2-17	B	522	20.99	C / 4.3	0.55%	B+ / 8.3
2016	B+	544	20.94	C / 5.0	1.42%	B+ / 8.3
2015	A	442	21.08	B- / 7.2	1.44%	B / 8.0
2014	B-	394	21.20	C- / 3.9	5.77%	B / 8.1
2013	C+	272	20.43	C- / 3.0	-1.29%	B+ / 8.6
2012	C	306	20.90	D / 2.1	2.54%	B+ / 8.9

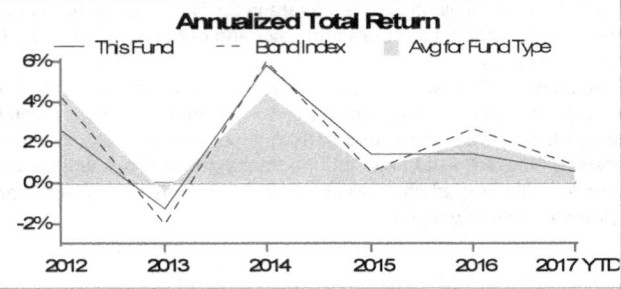
Annualized Total Return

Vanguard OH Long-Term Tax-Exmpt Inv (VOHIX)   A-   Excellent

Fund Family: Vanguard Funds   **Phone:** (800) 662-7447
Address: Vanguard Financial Center, Valley Forge, PA 19482
Fund Type: MUS - Municipal - Single State
Major Rating Factors: Strong performance is the major factor driving the A-
(Excellent) TheStreet Investment Rating for Vanguard OH Long-Term
Tax-Exmpt Inv. The fund currently has a performance rating of B+ (Good) based
on an average return of 4.40% over the last three years (7.29% taxable
equivalent) and 0.94% over the last three months (1.56% taxable equivalent).
Factored into the performance evaluation is an expense ratio of 0.16% (very
low).

The fund's risk rating is currently C- (Fair). Volatility, as measured by
standard deviation, is considered average for fixed income funds at 3.68.
Another risk factor is the fund's fairly average duration of 5.3 years (i.e. average
interest rate risk).

Marlin G. Brown has been running the fund for 9 years and currently
receives a manager quality ranking of 64 (0=worst, 99=best). If you desire an
average level of risk and strong performance, then this fund is a good option.
Services Offered: Automated phone transactions, check writing, payroll
deductions, bank draft capabilities and a systematic withdrawal plan.

Data Date	Investment Rating	Net Assets ($Mil)	NAV	Performance Rating/Pts	Total Return Y-T-D	Risk Rating/Pts
2-17	A-	1,124	12.37	B+ / 8.9	0.94%	C- / 3.7
2016	A-	1,112	12.32	A / 9.4	0.98%	C- / 3.5
2015	B	1,019	12.65	A+ / 9.7	4.25%	C- / 3.4
2014	A	978	12.61	A / 9.3	11.20%	C- / 3.5
2013	B	872	11.81	B / 8.0	-3.16%	C- / 3.9
2012	B+	1,023	12.71	B- / 7.5	7.47%	C / 4.5

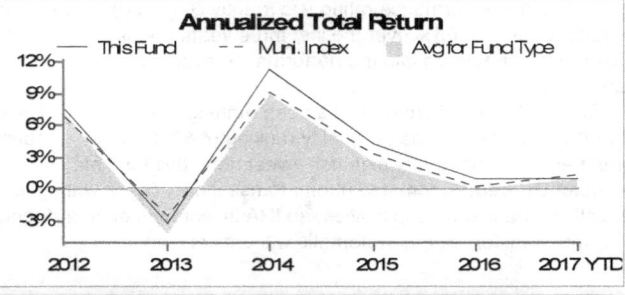
Annualized Total Return

Vanguard Short-Term Bd Idx Investor (VBISX)   C   Fair

Fund Family: Vanguard Funds   **Phone:** (800) 662-7447
Address: Vanguard Financial Center, Valley Forge, PA 19482
Fund Type: GES - General - Short & Inter. Term
Major Rating Factors: Disappointing performance is the major factor driving the
C (Fair) TheStreet Investment Rating for Vanguard Short-Term Bd Idx Investor.
The fund currently has a performance rating of D+ (Weak) based on an average
return of 1.07% over the last three years and 0.43% over the last three months.
Factored into the performance evaluation is an expense ratio of 0.16% (very
low).

The fund's risk rating is currently B+ (Good). Volatility, as measured by
standard deviation, is considered low for fixed income funds at 1.38. Another risk
factor is the fund's very low average duration of 2.8 years (i.e. low interest rate
risk).

Joshua C. Barrickman has been running the fund for 4 years and currently
receives a manager quality ranking of 35 (0=worst, 99=best). This fund offers
only a moderate level of risk but investors looking for strong performance are still
waiting.
Services Offered: Automated phone transactions, check writing, payroll
deductions, bank draft capabilities, an IRA investment plan, a Keogh investment
plan, wire transfers and a systematic withdrawal plan.

Data Date	Investment Rating	Net Assets ($Mil)	NAV	Performance Rating/Pts	Total Return Y-T-D	Risk Rating/Pts
2-17	C	1,820	10.45	D+ / 2.6	0.43%	B+ / 8.9
2016	C+	2,217	10.43	D+ / 2.8	1.41%	B+ / 8.9
2015	B	2,325	10.43	C / 5.0	0.85%	A- / 9.0
2014	C	2,667	10.48	D / 2.0	1.16%	A / 9.3
2013	C	3,003	10.49	D+ / 2.4	0.07%	A- / 9.2
2012	C-	3,185	10.63	D- / 1.3	1.95%	A- / 9.1

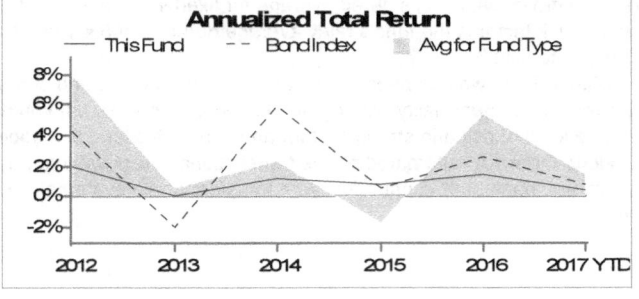
Annualized Total Return

Vanguard Short-Term Crp Bd Idx Adm (VSCSX)   B+   Good

Fund Family: Vanguard Funds   **Phone:** (800) 662-7447
Address: Vanguard Financial Center, Valley Forge, PA 19482
Fund Type: COI - Corporate - Investment Grade
Major Rating Factors: A moderate risk profile coupled with stable earnings characterizes Vanguard Short-Term Crp Bd Idx Adm which receives a TheStreet Investment Rating of B+ (Good). Volatility, as measured by standard deviation, is considered low for fixed income funds at 1.48. Another risk factor is the fund's very low average duration of 2.8 years (i.e. low interest rate risk). The fund's risk rating is currently B+ (Good).

The fund's performance rating is currently C (Fair). It has registered an average return of 1.88% over the last three years and is up 0.84% over the last three months. Factored into the performance evaluation is an expense ratio of 0.07% (very low).

Joshua C. Barrickman has been running the fund for 8 years and currently receives a manager quality ranking of 67 (0=worst, 99=best). If you desire stability with a moderate level of risk then this fund is an excellent option.
Services Offered: Automated phone transactions, bank draft capabilities, wire transfers and a systematic withdrawal plan.

Data Date	Investment Rating	Net Assets ($Mil)	NAV	Perfor- mance Rating/Pts	Total Return Y-T-D	Risk Rating/Pts
2-17	B+	2,394	21.67	C / 4.3	0.84%	B+ / 8.8
2016	B+	2,061	21.56	C / 4.3	2.63%	B+ / 8.8
2015	A	1,341	21.45	C+/ 6.6	1.23%	B+ / 8.8
2014	B	937	21.63	C- / 3.8	1.98%	B+ / 8.7
2013	A-	198	21.64	C / 5.1	1.37%	B+ / 8.5
2012	U	33	21.79	U / --	5.74%	U / --

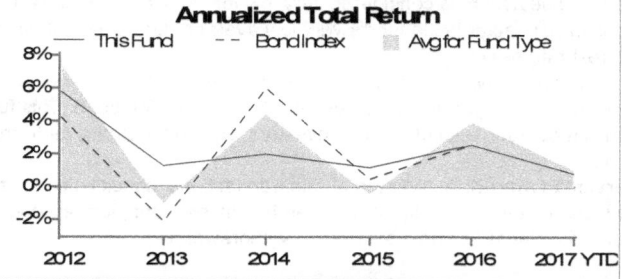

Vanguard Short-Term Federal Inv (VSGBX)   C   Fair

Fund Family: Vanguard Funds   **Phone:** (800) 662-7447
Address: Vanguard Financial Center, Valley Forge, PA 19482
Fund Type: USS - US Government - Short & Inter. Term
Major Rating Factors: Disappointing performance is the major factor driving the C (Fair) TheStreet Investment Rating for Vanguard Short-Term Federal Inv. The fund currently has a performance rating of D+ (Weak) based on an average return of 0.94% over the last three years and 0.36% over the last three months. Factored into the performance evaluation is an expense ratio of 0.20% (very low).

The fund's risk rating is currently A- (Excellent). Volatility, as measured by standard deviation, is considered very low for fixed income funds at 1.05. Another risk factor is the fund's very low average duration of 2.3 years (i.e. low interest rate risk).

Brian W. Quigley has been running the fund for 2 years and currently receives a manager quality ranking of 57 (0=worst, 99=best). This fund offers only a moderate level of risk but investors looking for strong performance are still waiting.
Services Offered: Automated phone transactions, check writing, payroll deductions, bank draft capabilities, an IRA investment plan, a Keogh investment plan, wire transfers and a systematic withdrawal plan.

Data Date	Investment Rating	Net Assets ($Mil)	NAV	Perfor- mance Rating/Pts	Total Return Y-T-D	Risk Rating/Pts
2-17	C	830	10.71	D+/ 2.4	0.36%	A- / 9.2
2016	C+	832	10.69	D+/ 2.7	1.14%	A- / 9.1
2015	B	826	10.71	C / 4.7	0.73%	A- / 9.2
2014	C	928	10.76	D / 1.8	1.17%	A / 9.4
2013	C	1,520	10.70	D / 1.8	-0.35%	A / 9.4
2012	C-	1,999	10.80	D- / 1.0	1.44%	A / 9.3

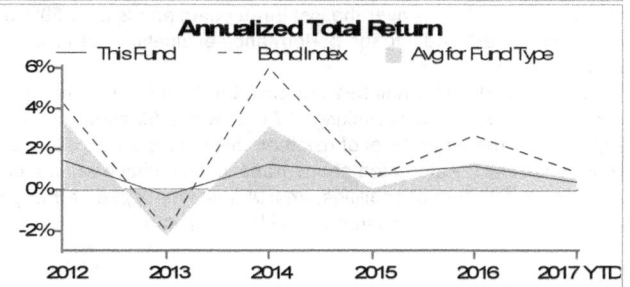

Vanguard Short-Term Tax-Exempt Inv (VWSTX)   C+   Fair

Fund Family: Vanguard Funds   **Phone:** (800) 662-7447
Address: Vanguard Financial Center, Valley Forge, PA 19482
Fund Type: MUN - Municipal - National
Major Rating Factors: Disappointing performance is the major factor driving the C+ (Fair) TheStreet Investment Rating for Vanguard Short-Term Tax-Exempt Inv. The fund currently has a performance rating of D+ (Weak) based on an average return of 0.54% over the last three years (0.89% taxable equivalent) and 0.54% over the last three months (0.89% taxable equivalent). Factored into the performance evaluation is an expense ratio of 0.20% (very low).

The fund's risk rating is currently A+ (Excellent). Volatility, as measured by standard deviation, is considered very low for fixed income funds at 0.52. Another risk factor is the fund's very low average duration of 1.4 years (i.e. low interest rate risk).

Justin A. Schwartz has been running the fund for 1 year and currently receives a manager quality ranking of 46 (0=worst, 99=best). This fund offers only a moderate level of risk but investors looking for strong performance are still waiting.
Services Offered: Automated phone transactions, check writing, payroll deductions, bank draft capabilities, an IRA investment plan, wire transfers and a systematic withdrawal plan.

Data Date	Investment Rating	Net Assets ($Mil)	NAV	Perfor- mance Rating/Pts	Total Return Y-T-D	Risk Rating/Pts
2-17	C+	1,239	15.78	D+/ 2.4	0.54%	A+/ 9.8
2016	C+	1,208	15.72	D+/ 2.3	0.36%	A+/ 9.8
2015	A	1,361	15.80	C / 5.5	0.45%	A+/ 9.8
2014	C+	1,670	15.84	D / 2.0	0.65%	A+/ 9.9
2013	B-	1,817	15.85	D+/ 2.5	0.47%	A+/ 9.9
2012	C-	2,071	15.91	E+/ 0.8	0.99%	A+/ 9.9

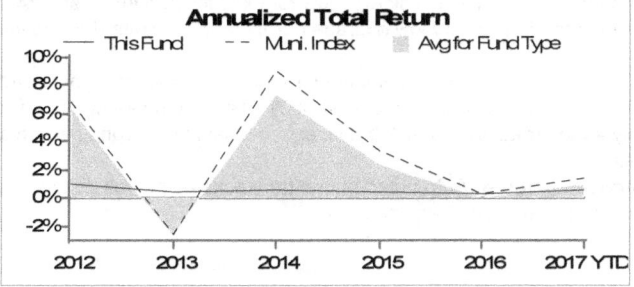

Vanguard Short-Term Treasury Inv (VFISX)　　　C　Fair

Fund Family: Vanguard Funds　　　**Phone:** (800) 662-7447
Address: Vanguard Financial Center, Valley Forge, PA 19482
Fund Type: US - US Treasury
Major Rating Factors: Disappointing performance is the major factor driving the
C (Fair) TheStreet Investment Rating for Vanguard Short-Term Treasury Inv.
The fund currently has a performance rating of D (Weak) based on an average
return of 0.71% over the last three years and 0.24% over the last three months.
Factored into the performance evaluation is an expense ratio of 0.20% (very
low).

　　The fund's risk rating is currently A- (Excellent). Volatility, as measured by
standard deviation, is considered very low for fixed income funds at 1.03.
Another risk factor is the fund's very low average duration of 2.3 years (i.e. low
interest rate risk).

　　Gregory S. Nassour has been running the fund for 9 years and currently
receives a manager quality ranking of 53 (0=worst, 99=best). This fund offers
only a moderate level of risk but investors looking for strong performance are still
waiting.

Services Offered: Automated phone transactions, check writing, payroll
deductions, bank draft capabilities, an IRA investment plan, a Keogh investment
plan, wire transfers and a systematic withdrawal plan.

Data Date	Investment Rating	Net Assets ($Mil)	NAV	Performance Rating/Pts	Total Return Y-T-D	Risk Rating/Pts
2-17	C	907	10.65	D / 2.1	0.24%	A- / 9.2
2016	C	910	10.64	D+ / 2.4	1.08%	A- / 9.2
2015	B-	986	10.65	C / 4.3	0.45%	A / 9.4
2014	C-	1,049	10.69	D- / 1.5	0.71%	A+ / 9.6
2013	C-	1,167	10.68	D- / 1.5	-0.10%	A / 9.5
2012	D+	1,484	10.74	E+ / 0.8	0.69%	A / 9.4

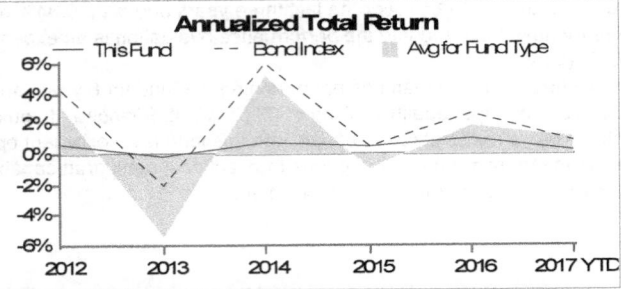

Vanguard Sh-Term Invest-Grade Inv (VFSTX)　　　B+　Good

Fund Family: Vanguard Funds　　　**Phone:** (800) 662-7447
Address: Vanguard Financial Center, Valley Forge, PA 19482
Fund Type: GEI - General - Investment Grade
Major Rating Factors: A moderate risk profile coupled with stable earnings
characterizes Vanguard Sh-Term Invest-Grade Inv which receives a TheStreet
Investment Rating of B+ (Good). Volatility, as measured by standard deviation, is
considered very low for fixed income funds at 1.27. Another risk factor is the
fund's very low average duration of 2.6 years (i.e. low interest rate risk). The
fund's risk rating is currently A- (Excellent).

　　The fund's performance rating is currently C- (Fair). It has registered an
average return of 1.77% over the last three years and is up 0.69% over the last
three months. Factored into the performance evaluation is an expense ratio of
0.20% (very low).

　　Gregory S. Nassour has been running the fund for 9 years and currently
receives a manager quality ranking of 71 (0=worst, 99=best). If you desire
stability with a moderate level of risk then this fund is an excellent option.

Services Offered: Automated phone transactions, check writing, payroll
deductions, bank draft capabilities, an IRA investment plan, a Keogh investment
plan, wire transfers and a systematic withdrawal plan.

Data Date	Investment Rating	Net Assets ($Mil)	NAV	Performance Rating/Pts	Total Return Y-T-D	Risk Rating/Pts
2-17	B+	9,650	10.67	C- / 4.1	0.69%	A- / 9.0
2016	B+	9,527	10.63	C- / 4.2	2.72%	A- / 9.0
2015	A	9,987	10.56	C+ / 6.2	1.03%	A- / 9.0
2014	B-	10,954	10.66	C- / 3.2	1.76%	A- / 9.0
2013	B	11,732	10.70	C- / 3.9	0.97%	A- / 9.0
2012	C	12,229	10.83	D / 2.0	4.52%	A- / 9.0

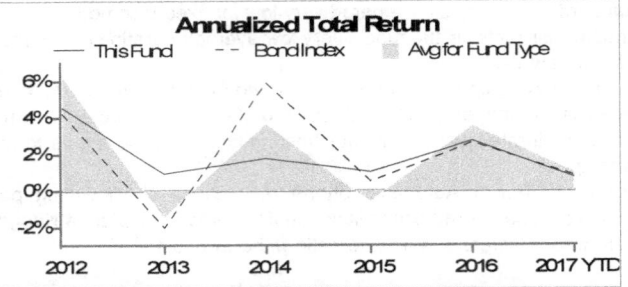

Vanguard ST Inf Prot Sec Idx Inv (VTIPX)　　　C-　Fair

Fund Family: Vanguard Funds　　　**Phone:** (800) 662-7447
Address: Vanguard Financial Center, Valley Forge, PA 19482
Fund Type: GEI - General - Investment Grade
Major Rating Factors: Disappointing performance is the major factor driving the
C- (Fair) TheStreet Investment Rating for Vanguard ST Inf Prot Sec Idx Inv. The
fund currently has a performance rating of D (Weak) based on an average return
of 0.33% over the last three years and 0.49% over the last three months.
Factored into the performance evaluation is an expense ratio of 0.17% (very
low).

　　The fund's risk rating is currently B+ (Good). Volatility, as measured by
standard deviation, is considered low for fixed income funds at 1.74. Another risk
factor is the fund's very low average duration of 2.7 years (i.e. low interest rate
risk).

　　Joshua C. Barrickman has been running the fund for 5 years and currently
receives a manager quality ranking of 21 (0=worst, 99=best). This fund offers
only a moderate level of risk but investors looking for strong performance are still
waiting.

Services Offered: Automated phone transactions, payroll deductions, bank draft
capabilities and wire transfers.

Data Date	Investment Rating	Net Assets ($Mil)	NAV	Performance Rating/Pts	Total Return Y-T-D	Risk Rating/Pts
2-17	C-	5,329	24.75	D / 2.2	0.49%	B+ / 8.6
2016	C-	5,179	24.63	D+ / 2.3	2.59%	B+ / 8.6
2015	C-	4,617	24.14	D / 1.8	-0.21%	B+ / 8.7
2014	U	4,596	24.19	U / --	-1.28%	U / --
2013	U	3,917	24.68	U / --	-1.62%	U / --

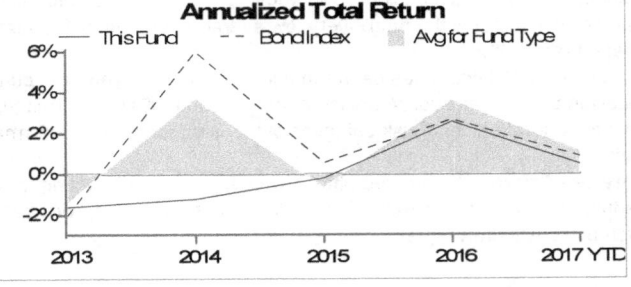

Vanguard Total Bond Mkt II Idx Inv (VTBIX)   D+   Weak

Fund Family: Vanguard Funds   **Phone:** (800) 662-7447
Address: Vanguard Financial Center, Valley Forge, PA 19482
Fund Type: COI - Corporate - Investment Grade
Major Rating Factors: Vanguard Total Bond Mkt II Idx Inv receives a TheStreet Investment Rating of D+ (Weak). The fund has a performance rating of C (Fair) based on an average return of 2.48% over the last three years and 0.95% over the last three months. Factored into the performance evaluation is an expense ratio of 0.09% (very low).

The fund's risk rating is currently C (Fair). Volatility, as measured by standard deviation, is considered average for fixed income funds at 3.12.

Joshua C. Barrickman has been running the fund for 7 years and currently receives a manager quality ranking of 33 (0=worst, 99=best). If you desire an average level of risk, then this fund may be an option.
Services Offered: Automated phone transactions, payroll deductions, bank draft capabilities, an IRA investment plan, a 401K investment plan, wire transfers and a systematic withdrawal plan.

Data Date	Investment Rating	Net Assets ($Mil)	NAV	Performance Rating/Pts	Total Return Y-T-D	Risk Rating/Pts
2-17	D+	72,531	10.67	C / 4.5	0.95%	C / 5.0
2016	C-	68,381	10.61	C / 4.8	2.44%	C / 5.1
2015	C	55,324	10.60	C+/ 6.0	0.28%	C+/ 6.1
2014	C	54,268	10.84	C- / 4.2	5.93%	B- / 7.0
2013	C	47,497	10.49	C- / 3.7	-2.26%	B- / 7.2
2012	C	45,758	10.97	C- / 3.2	3.91%	B- / 7.2

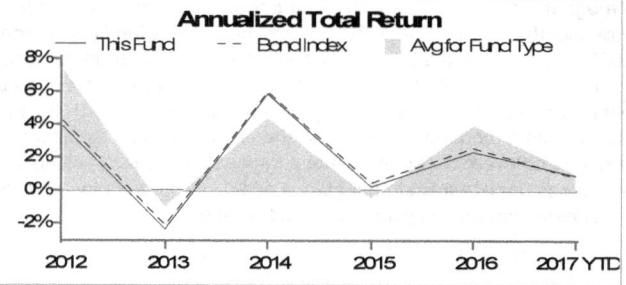

Vanguard Total Bond Mrkt Index Inv (VBMFX)   D+   Weak

Fund Family: Vanguard Funds   **Phone:** (800) 662-7447
Address: Vanguard Financial Center, Valley Forge, PA 19482
Fund Type: GES - General - Short & Inter. Term
Major Rating Factors: Vanguard Total Bond Mrkt Index Inv receives a TheStreet Investment Rating of D+ (Weak). The fund has a performance rating of C (Fair) based on an average return of 2.47% over the last three years and 0.96% over the last three months. Factored into the performance evaluation is an expense ratio of 0.16% (very low).

The fund's risk rating is currently C (Fair). Volatility, as measured by standard deviation, is considered average for fixed income funds at 3.11. Another risk factor is the fund's fairly average duration of 5.7 years (i.e. average interest rate risk).

Joshua C. Barrickman has been running the fund for 4 years and currently receives a manager quality ranking of 28 (0=worst, 99=best). If you desire an average level of risk, then this fund may be an option.
Services Offered: Automated phone transactions, check writing, payroll deductions, bank draft capabilities, an IRA investment plan, a Keogh investment plan, wire transfers and a systematic withdrawal plan.

Data Date	Investment Rating	Net Assets ($Mil)	NAV	Performance Rating/Pts	Total Return Y-T-D	Risk Rating/Pts
2-17	D+	5,940	10.71	C / 4.5	0.96%	C / 5.1
2016	C-	5,969	10.65	C / 4.8	2.50%	C / 5.1
2015	C	6,565	10.64	C+/ 6.0	0.30%	C+/ 6.1
2014	C	7,076	10.87	C- / 4.1	5.76%	B- / 7.0
2013	C	7,939	10.56	C- / 3.7	-2.26%	B- / 7.2
2012	C	11,794	11.09	C- / 3.2	4.05%	B- / 7.1

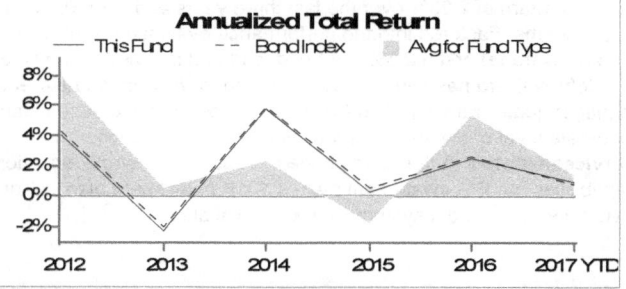

Vanguard Total Internatl Bd Idx Inv (VTIBX)   B   Good

Fund Family: Vanguard Funds   **Phone:** (800) 662-7447
Address: Vanguard Financial Center, Valley Forge, PA 19482
Fund Type: GL - Global
Major Rating Factors: Vanguard Total Internatl Bd Idx Inv receives a TheStreet Investment Rating of B (Good). The fund has a performance rating of C+ (Fair) based on an average return of 4.15% over the last three years and 0.07% over the last three months. Factored into the performance evaluation is an expense ratio of 0.17% (very low).

The fund's risk rating is currently C (Fair). Volatility, as measured by standard deviation, is considered average for fixed income funds at 2.91. Another risk factor is the fund's above average duration of 7.7 years (i.e. higher interest rate risk).

Joshua C. Barrickman has been running the fund for 4 years and currently receives a manager quality ranking of 95 (0=worst, 99=best). If you desire an average level of risk, then this fund may be an option.
Services Offered: Automated phone transactions, payroll deductions, bank draft capabilities and wire transfers.

Data Date	Investment Rating	Net Assets ($Mil)	NAV	Performance Rating/Pts	Total Return Y-T-D	Risk Rating/Pts
2-17	B	22,670	10.83	C+/ 6.8	0.07%	C / 5.1
2016	A	21,711	10.84	B / 7.8	4.67%	C+/ 5.8
2015	U	20,429	10.55	U / --	1.04%	U / --
2014	U	14,883	10.61	U / --	8.83%	U / --
2013	U	12,583	9.91	U / --	0.00%	U / --

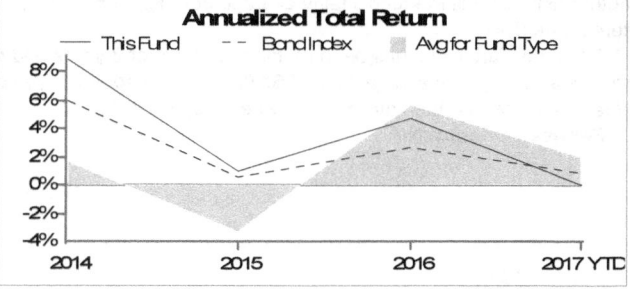

Virtus Multi Sector Short Term B A (NARAX)
B+   **Good**

Fund Family: Virtus Mutual Funds   **Phone:** (800) 243-1574
Address: C/O State Street Bank & Trust, Boston, MA 02266
Fund Type: GES - General - Short & Inter. Term

Major Rating Factors: A moderate risk profile coupled with stable earnings characterizes Virtus Multi Sector Short Term B A which receives a TheStreet Investment Rating of B+ (Good). Volatility, as measured by standard deviation, is considered low for fixed income funds at 1.96. Another risk factor is the fund's very low average duration of 2.5 years (i.e. low interest rate risk). The fund's risk rating is currently B+ (Good).

The fund's performance rating is currently C (Fair). It has registered an average return of 2.13% over the last three years and is up 1.36% over the last three months. Factored into the performance evaluation is an expense ratio of 1.00% (average) and a 2.3% front-end load that is levied at the time of purchase.

David L. Albrycht has been running the fund for 24 years and currently receives a manager quality ranking of 80 (0=worst, 99=best). If you desire stability with a moderate level of risk then this fund is an excellent option.

Services Offered: Automated phone transactions, check writing, payroll deductions, an IRA investment plan, a 401K investment plan, a Keogh investment plan and a systematic withdrawal plan.

Data Date	Investment Rating	Net Assets ($Mil)	NAV	Perfor- mance Rating/Pts	Total Return Y-T-D	Risk Rating/Pts
2-17	B+	1,242	4.76	C / 4.8	1.36%	B+ / 8.3
2016	B	1,244	4.72	C- / 4.2	4.97%	B+ / 8.5
2015	C	1,496	4.63	C- / 3.3	0.07%	B / 8.1
2014	C-	1,811	4.76	C- / 3.6	1.03%	B- / 7.0
2013	B-	3,560	4.86	C+ / 6.0	1.52%	C+ / 5.7
2012	C	3,259	4.96	C / 5.0	9.40%	C / 4.8

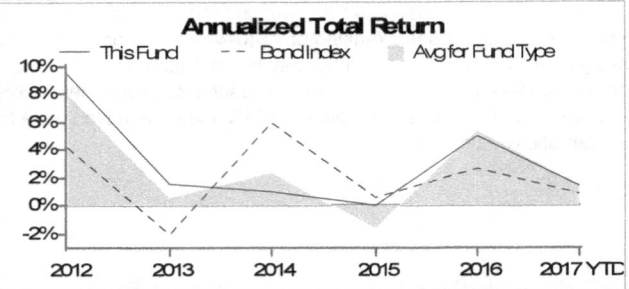

Voya GNMA Income A (LEXNX)
C+   **Fair**

Fund Family: Voya Investments LLC   **Phone:** (800) 992-0180
Address: 7337 East Doubletree Ranch Roa, Scottsdale, AZ 85258
Fund Type: USA - US Government/Agency

Major Rating Factors: A moderate risk profile coupled with stable earnings characterizes Voya GNMA Income A which receives a TheStreet Investment Rating of C+ (Fair). Volatility, as measured by standard deviation, is considered low for fixed income funds at 1.57. Another risk factor is the fund's very low average duration of 2.4 years (i.e. low interest rate risk). The fund's risk rating is currently B+ (Good).

The fund's performance rating is currently C- (Fair). It has registered an average return of 2.23% over the last three years and is up 0.39% over the last three months. Factored into the performance evaluation is an expense ratio of 0.93% (average) and a 2.5% front-end load that is levied at the time of purchase.

Jeffrey Dutra has been running the fund for 8 years and currently receives a manager quality ranking of 80 (0=worst, 99=best). If you desire stability with a moderate level of risk then this fund is an excellent option.

Services Offered: Automated phone transactions, payroll deductions, bank draft capabilities, an IRA investment plan, a 401K investment plan, a Keogh investment plan and a systematic withdrawal plan.

Data Date	Investment Rating	Net Assets ($Mil)	NAV	Perfor- mance Rating/Pts	Total Return Y-T-D	Risk Rating/Pts
2-17	C+	556	8.45	C- / 3.1	0.39%	B+ / 8.7
2016	B	580	8.45	C- / 3.9	1.68%	B+ / 8.7
2015	B	541	8.55	C+ / 5.6	1.60%	B / 8.1
2014	C-	525	8.68	D+ / 2.7	4.93%	B / 8.2
2013	C-	601	8.56	D+ / 2.4	-1.84%	B+ / 8.4
2012	C+	744	9.02	D+ / 2.3	2.87%	B+ / 8.8

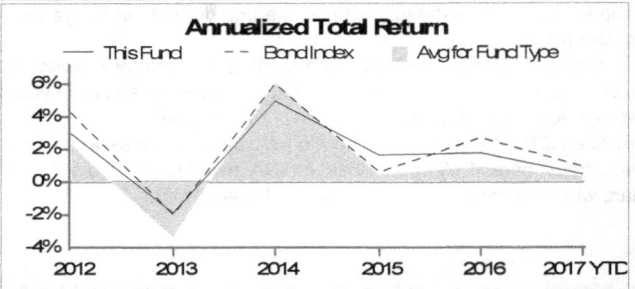

Voya Intermediate Bond Port S (IPISX)
B   **Good**

Fund Family: Voya Investments LLC   **Phone:** (800) 992-0180
Address: 7337 East Doubletree Ranch Roa, Scottsdale, AZ 85258
Fund Type: GEI - General - Investment Grade

Major Rating Factors: Voya Intermediate Bond Port S receives a TheStreet Investment Rating of B (Good). The fund has a performance rating of C+ (Fair) based on an average return of 3.07% over the last three years and 1.26% over the last three months. Factored into the performance evaluation is an expense ratio of 0.79% (low).

The fund's risk rating is currently C+ (Fair). Volatility, as measured by standard deviation, is considered average for fixed income funds at 2.88. Another risk factor is the fund's fairly average duration of 5.5 years (i.e. average interest rate risk).

Christine Hurtsellers has been running the fund for 8 years and currently receives a manager quality ranking of 67 (0=worst, 99=best). If you desire an average level of risk, then this fund may be an option.

Services Offered: N/A

Data Date	Investment Rating	Net Assets ($Mil)	NAV	Perfor- mance Rating/Pts	Total Return Y-T-D	Risk Rating/Pts
2-17	B	2,851	12.67	C+ / 6.1	1.26%	C+ / 6.2
2016	B	2,880	12.58	C+ / 6.4	4.19%	C+ / 6.2
2015	C+	3,171	12.44	C+ / 6.9	-0.02%	C+ / 5.7
2014	B+	3,478	12.83	C+ / 6.7	6.48%	C+ / 5.9
2013	A	1,120	12.43	B- / 7.0	-0.38%	C+ / 6.4
2012	A+	1,229	12.89	C+ / 6.6	9.08%	C+ / 6.7

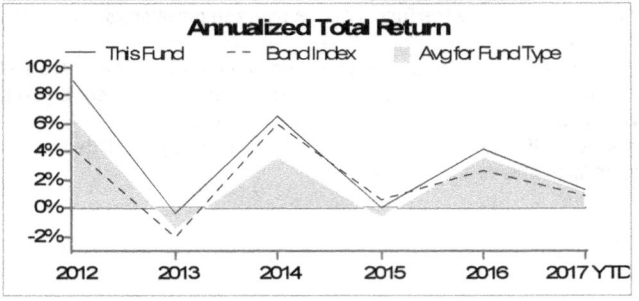

WA Intermediate Term Muni A (SBLTX)   C+   Fair

Fund Family: Legg Mason Partners Funds   **Phone:** (877) 534-4627
Address: 100 Light Street, Baltimore, MD 21202
Fund Type: MUN - Municipal - National

Major Rating Factors: A moderate risk profile coupled with stable earnings characterizes WA Intermediate Term Muni A which receives a TheStreet Investment Rating of C+ (Fair). Volatility, as measured by standard deviation, is considered low for fixed income funds at 2.64. Another risk factor is the fund's below average duration of 4.5 years (i.e. lower interest rate risk). The fund's risk rating is currently B- (Good).

The fund's performance rating is currently C (Fair). It has registered an average return of 2.53% over the last three years (4.19% taxable equivalent) and is up 0.85% over the last three months (1.41% taxable equivalent). Factored into the performance evaluation is an expense ratio of 0.74% (low) and a 2.3% front-end load that is levied at the time of purchase.

Robert E. Amodeo has been running the fund for 10 years and currently receives a manager quality ranking of 29 (0=worst, 99=best). If you desire stability with a moderate level of risk then this fund is an excellent option.

Services Offered: Automated phone transactions, payroll deductions, bank draft capabilities, an IRA investment plan and a systematic withdrawal plan.

Data Date	Investment Rating	Net Assets ($Mil)	NAV	Perfor-mance Rating/Pts	Total Return Y-T-D	Risk Rating/Pts
2-17	C+	1,233	6.38	C / 4.5	0.85%	B- / 7.2
2016	C+	1,276	6.36	C / 4.9	-0.15%	B- / 7.0
2015	B	1,348	6.57	B / 7.8	2.21%	C+ / 5.8
2014	B	1,296	6.63	B- / 7.2	7.45%	C / 4.6
2013	B-	1,215	6.37	C+ / 6.9	-3.37%	C / 4.7
2012	B-	1,459	6.81	C+ / 6.6	7.22%	C / 4.6

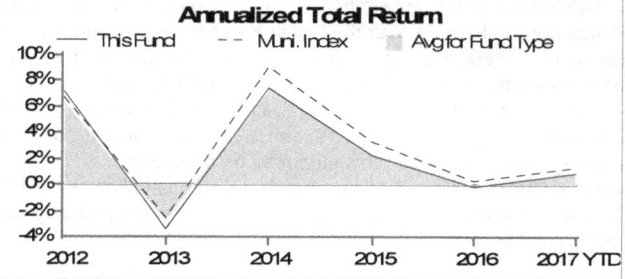

WA Managed Municipals A (SHMMX)   C+   Fair

Fund Family: Legg Mason Partners Funds   **Phone:** (877) 534-4627
Address: 100 Light Street, Baltimore, MD 21202
Fund Type: MUN - Municipal - National

Major Rating Factors: Middle of the road best describes WA Managed Municipals A whose TheStreet Investment Rating is currently a C+ (Fair). The fund has a performance rating of C+ (Fair) based on an average return of 3.70% over the last three years (6.13% taxable equivalent) and 1.14% over the last three months (1.89% taxable equivalent). Factored into the performance evaluation is an expense ratio of 0.66% (low) and a 4.3% front-end load that is levied at the time of purchase.

The fund's risk rating is currently C (Fair). Volatility, as measured by standard deviation, is considered average for fixed income funds at 3.16. Another risk factor is the fund's fairly average duration of 5.3 years (i.e. average interest rate risk).

Robert E. Amodeo has been running the fund for 10 years and currently receives a manager quality ranking of 61 (0=worst, 99=best). If you desire an average level of risk, then this fund may be an option.

Services Offered: Automated phone transactions, payroll deductions, bank draft capabilities and a systematic withdrawal plan.

Data Date	Investment Rating	Net Assets ($Mil)	NAV	Perfor-mance Rating/Pts	Total Return Y-T-D	Risk Rating/Pts
2-17	C+	2,999	16.20	C+ / 6.0	1.14%	C / 4.9
2016	C+	2,951	16.12	C+ / 6.4	0.11%	C / 4.6
2015	C	2,983	16.70	B / 8.2	2.75%	C- / 3.4
2014	B	2,755	16.88	B+ / 8.7	10.92%	D+ / 2.8
2013	C	2,761	15.83	B / 7.7	-4.35%	D+ / 2.4
2012	B-	3,670	17.23	B / 8.0	10.13%	D+ / 2.6

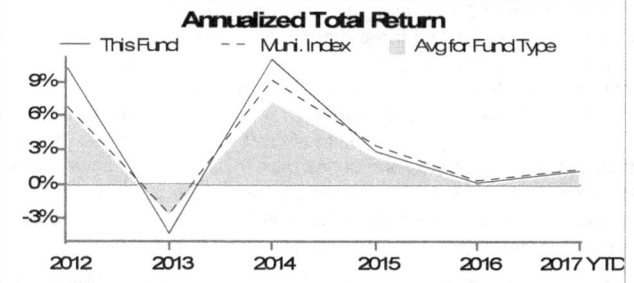

WA Mortgage Backed Securities A (SGVAX)   C+   Fair

Fund Family: Legg Mason Partners Funds   **Phone:** (877) 534-4627
Address: 100 Light Street, Baltimore, MD 21202
Fund Type: USS - US Government - Short & Inter. Term

Major Rating Factors: A moderate risk profile coupled with stable earnings characterizes WA Mortgage Backed Securities A which receives a TheStreet Investment Rating of C+ (Fair). Volatility, as measured by standard deviation, is considered low for fixed income funds at 2.11. Another risk factor is the fund's below average duration of 3.6 years (i.e. lower interest rate risk). The fund's risk rating is currently B (Good).

The fund's performance rating is currently C- (Fair). It has registered an average return of 2.87% over the last three years and is up 0.81% over the last three months. Factored into the performance evaluation is an expense ratio of 0.94% (average) and a 4.3% front-end load that is levied at the time of purchase.

Anup Agarwal has been running the fund for 4 years and currently receives a manager quality ranking of 84 (0=worst, 99=best). If you desire stability with a moderate level of risk then this fund is an excellent option.

Services Offered: Automated phone transactions, payroll deductions, bank draft capabilities, an IRA investment plan, a 401K investment plan, wire transfers and a systematic withdrawal plan.

Data Date	Investment Rating	Net Assets ($Mil)	NAV	Perfor-mance Rating/Pts	Total Return Y-T-D	Risk Rating/Pts
2-17	C+	535	10.53	C- / 3.5	0.81%	B / 8.0
2016	C+	548	10.49	C- / 3.7	1.23%	B / 8.1
2015	A	550	10.73	B- / 7.2	1.98%	B / 8.2
2014	A	464	10.90	C+ / 5.8	6.46%	B / 8.1
2013	A	491	10.66	C / 5.4	1.71%	B+ / 8.4
2012	B+	507	10.88	C / 4.4	7.77%	B / 8.1

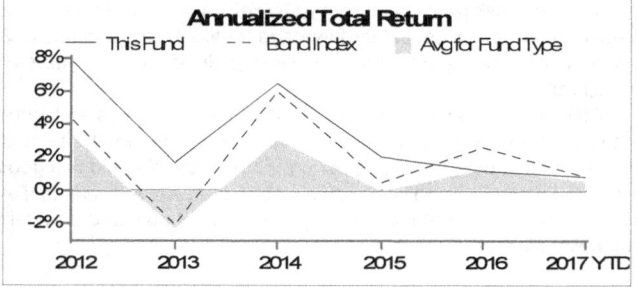

Waddell & Reed Adv High Income A (UNHIX)

C-   **Fair**

Fund Family: Waddell & Reed Funds   **Phone:** (888) 923-3355
Address: 6300 Lamar Avenue, Shawnee Mission, KS 66201
Fund Type: COH - Corporate - High Yield

Major Rating Factors: Waddell & Reed Adv High Income A has adopted a very risky asset allocation strategy and currently receives an overall TheStreet Investment Rating of C- (Fair). Volatility, as measured by standard deviation, is considered high for fixed income funds at 6.12. Another risk factor is the fund's below average duration of 3.1 years (i.e. lower interest rate risk). The high level of risk (E+, Very Weak) did however, reward investors with excellent performance.

The fund's performance rating is currently B+ (Good). It has registered an average return of 3.44% over the last three years and is up 2.81% over the last three months. Factored into the performance evaluation is an expense ratio of 1.01% (average) and a 5.8% front-end load that is levied at the time of purchase.

Chad Gunther has been running the fund for 3 years and currently receives a manager quality ranking of 9 (0=worst, 99=best). If you are comfortable owning a very high risk investment, this fund may be an option.

Services Offered: Payroll deductions, bank draft capabilities, an IRA investment plan, a 401K investment plan, a Keogh investment plan and a systematic withdrawal plan.

Data Date	Investment Rating	Net Assets ($Mil)	NAV	Performance Rating/Pts	Total Return Y-T-D	Risk Rating/Pts
2-17	C-	1,219	6.81	B+ / 8.3	2.81%	E+ / 0.8
2016	D+	1,184	6.69	B / 7.8	16.33%	E+ / 0.8
2015	E+	1,742	6.18	D- / 1.2	-6.87%	D- / 1.4
2014	B-	1,967	7.12	B+ / 8.3	1.92%	C- / 3.0
2013	B	1,841	7.60	A+ / 9.9	10.81%	D / 1.7
2012	B-	1,641	7.55	A- / 9.1	19.07%	D- / 1.5

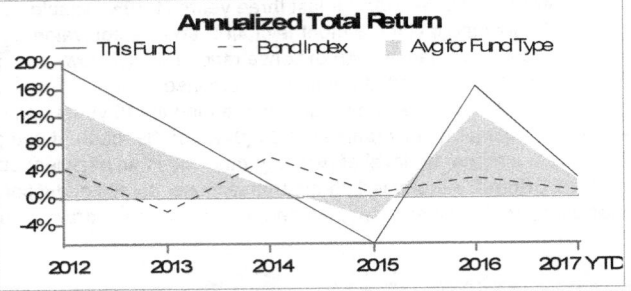

Annualized Total Return

Waddell & Reed Adv Muni Bond A (UNMBX)

B+   **Good**

Fund Family: Waddell & Reed Funds   **Phone:** (888) 923-3355
Address: 6300 Lamar Avenue, Shawnee Mission, KS 66201
Fund Type: MUN - Municipal - National

Major Rating Factors: A moderate risk profile coupled with stable earnings characterizes Waddell & Reed Adv Muni Bond A which receives a TheStreet Investment Rating of B+ (Good). Volatility, as measured by standard deviation, is considered low for fixed income funds at 2.47. Another risk factor is the fund's fairly average duration of 5.2 years (i.e. average interest rate risk). The fund's risk rating is currently B (Good).

The fund's performance rating is currently C (Fair). It has registered an average return of 3.15% over the last three years (5.22% taxable equivalent) and is up 0.74% over the last three months (1.23% taxable equivalent). Factored into the performance evaluation is an expense ratio of 0.90% (average) and a 4.3% front-end load that is levied at the time of purchase.

Bryan J. Bailey has been running the fund for 17 years and currently receives a manager quality ranking of 66 (0=worst, 99=best). If you desire stability with a moderate level of risk then this fund is an excellent option.

Services Offered: Automated phone transactions, payroll deductions, bank draft capabilities, an IRA investment plan, a 401K investment plan, a Keogh investment plan and a systematic withdrawal plan.

Data Date	Investment Rating	Net Assets ($Mil)	NAV	Performance Rating/Pts	Total Return Y-T-D	Risk Rating/Pts
2-17	B+	539	7.47	C / 5.1	0.74%	B / 7.6
2016	A-	548	7.44	C+ / 6.1	0.69%	B- / 7.4
2015	B	861	7.60	B / 7.9	2.68%	C+ / 5.7
2014	B+	862	7.61	B- / 7.4	8.59%	C / 5.0
2013	C	836	7.23	C+ / 5.6	-3.29%	C / 5.0
2012	B+	971	7.72	C+ / 6.6	7.65%	C / 5.3

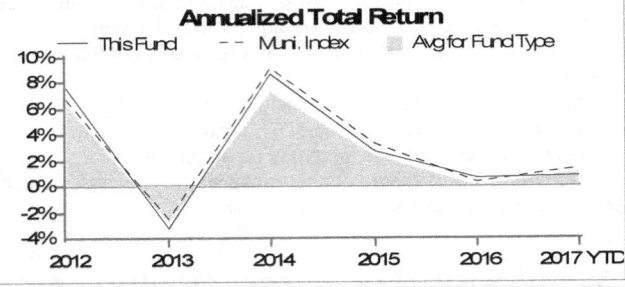

Annualized Total Return

Waddell & Reed Adv Muni High Inc A (UMUHX)

B   **Good**

Fund Family: Waddell & Reed Funds   **Phone:** (888) 923-3355
Address: 6300 Lamar Avenue, Shawnee Mission, KS 66201
Fund Type: MUH - Municipal - High Yield

Major Rating Factors: Strong performance is the major factor driving the B (Good) TheStreet Investment Rating for Waddell & Reed Adv Muni High Inc A. The fund currently has a performance rating of B (Good) based on an average return of 4.76% over the last three years (7.88% taxable equivalent) and 1.37% over the last three months (2.27% taxable equivalent). Factored into the performance evaluation is an expense ratio of 0.90% (average) and a 4.3% front-end load that is levied at the time of purchase.

The fund's risk rating is currently C- (Fair). Volatility, as measured by standard deviation, is considered average for fixed income funds at 3.07. Another risk factor is the fund's fairly average duration of 6.1 years (i.e. average interest rate risk).

Michael J. Walls has been running the fund for 9 years and currently receives a manager quality ranking of 83 (0=worst, 99=best). If you desire an average level of risk and strong performance, then this fund is a good option.

Services Offered: Payroll deductions, bank draft capabilities, an IRA investment plan, a 401K investment plan, a Keogh investment plan and a systematic withdrawal plan.

Data Date	Investment Rating	Net Assets ($Mil)	NAV	Performance Rating/Pts	Total Return Y-T-D	Risk Rating/Pts
2-17	B	660	4.77	B / 8.1	1.37%	C- / 3.9
2016	B+	675	4.74	B+ / 8.4	0.51%	C- / 3.8
2015	C+	835	4.93	A- / 9.2	3.78%	D+ / 2.8
2014	B+	802	4.96	A / 9.4	12.72%	D+ / 2.3
2013	C-	724	4.62	C+ / 6.6	-4.02%	C- / 3.0
2012	A	817	5.05	A- / 9.0	11.19%	C- / 3.1

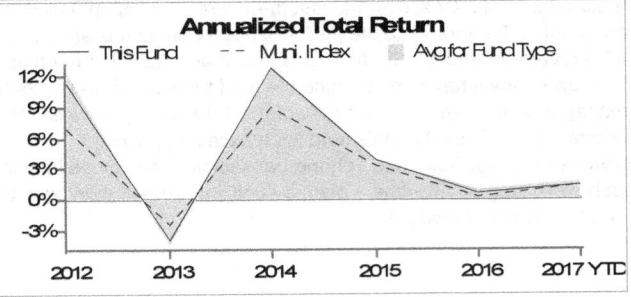

Annualized Total Return

Wells Fargo CoreBuilder A (WFCMX)   B+   Good

Fund Family: Wells Fargo Advantage Funds   **Phone:** (800) 222-8222
Address: PO Box 8266, Boston, MA 02266
Fund Type: MUN - Municipal - National

Major Rating Factors: Strong performance is the major factor driving the B+ (Good) TheStreet Investment Rating for Wells Fargo CoreBuilder A. The fund currently has a performance rating of B+ (Good) based on an average return of 4.35% over the last three years (7.20% taxable equivalent) and 1.11% over the last three months (1.84% taxable equivalent). Factored into the performance evaluation is an expense ratio of 0.07% (very low).

The fund's risk rating is currently C- (Fair). Volatility, as measured by standard deviation, is considered average for fixed income funds at 3.66. Another risk factor is the fund's below average duration of 3.6 years (i.e. lower interest rate risk).

Robert J. Miller has been running the fund for 9 years and currently receives a manager quality ranking of 68 (0=worst, 99=best). If you desire an average level of risk and strong performance, then this fund is a good option.

Services Offered: N/A

Data Date	Investment Rating	Net Assets ($Mil)	NAV	Performance Rating/Pts	Total Return Y-T-D	Risk Rating/Pts
2-17	B+	559	11.57	B+ / 8.6	1.11%	C- / 3.7
2016	A-	541	11.51	A / 9.3	-0.76%	C- / 3.5
2015	A-	361	11.96	A+ / 9.9	4.38%	C- / 4.1
2014	A+	222	11.86	A+ / 9.9	13.27%	C- / 3.7
2013	A+	105	10.99	A+ / 9.8	-1.37%	C / 4.5
2012	A+	50	11.61	A+ / 9.9	12.81%	C / 5.4

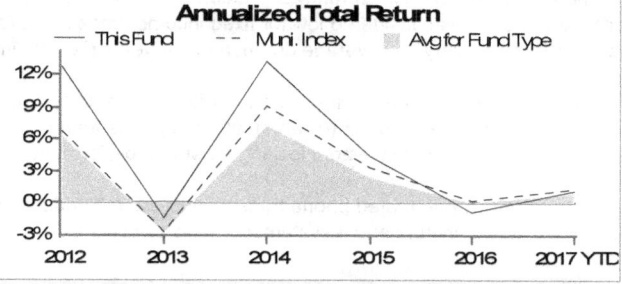

Wells Fargo Muni Bd A (WMFAX)   C   Fair

Fund Family: Wells Fargo Advantage Funds   **Phone:** (800) 222-8222
Address: PO Box 8266, Boston, MA 02266
Fund Type: MUN - Municipal - National

Major Rating Factors: Middle of the road best describes Wells Fargo Muni Bd A whose TheStreet Investment Rating is currently a C (Fair). The fund has a performance rating of C+ (Fair) based on an average return of 3.68% over the last three years (6.09% taxable equivalent) and 0.98% over the last three months (1.62% taxable equivalent). Factored into the performance evaluation is an expense ratio of 0.79% (low) and a 4.5% front-end load that is levied at the time of purchase.

The fund's risk rating is currently C (Fair). Volatility, as measured by standard deviation, is considered average for fixed income funds at 3.24. Another risk factor is the fund's below average duration of 4.3 years (i.e. lower interest rate risk).

Lyle J. Fitterer has been running the fund for 17 years and currently receives a manager quality ranking of 58 (0=worst, 99=best). If you desire an average level of risk, then this fund may be an option.

Services Offered: Automated phone transactions, payroll deductions, bank draft capabilities, an IRA investment plan, a 401K investment plan, a Keogh investment plan, wire transfers and a systematic withdrawal plan.

Data Date	Investment Rating	Net Assets ($Mil)	NAV	Performance Rating/Pts	Total Return Y-T-D	Risk Rating/Pts
2-17	C	1,335	10.12	C+ / 5.9	0.98%	C / 4.6
2016	C+	1,357	10.08	C+ / 6.8	0.17%	C- / 4.2
2015	B+	2,017	10.43	A- / 9.1	3.26%	C / 4.4
2014	A+	1,625	10.45	A- / 9.2	11.08%	C- / 4.2
2013	B+	1,620	9.76	B / 8.2	-1.94%	C / 4.5
2012	A+	1,819	10.34	B+ / 8.4	10.28%	C / 5.5

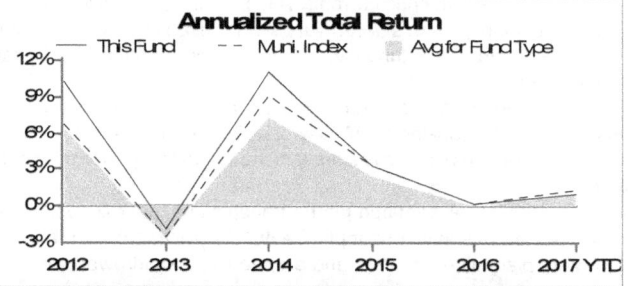

Wells Fargo ST Muni Bd A (WSMAX)   D   Weak

Fund Family: Wells Fargo Advantage Funds   **Phone:** (800) 222-8222
Address: PO Box 8266, Boston, MA 02266
Fund Type: MUN - Municipal - National

Major Rating Factors: Very poor performance is the major factor driving the D (Weak) TheStreet Investment Rating for Wells Fargo ST Muni Bd A. The fund currently has a performance rating of E (Very Weak) based on an average return of 0.53% over the last three years (0.88% taxable equivalent) and 0.53% over the last three months (0.88% taxable equivalent). Factored into the performance evaluation is an expense ratio of 0.75% (low) and a 2.0% front-end load that is levied at the time of purchase.

The fund's risk rating is currently A (Excellent). Volatility, as measured by standard deviation, is considered very low for fixed income funds at 0.85. Another risk factor is the fund's very low average duration of 1.1 years (i.e. low interest rate risk).

Lyle J. Fitterer has been running the fund for 17 years and currently receives a manager quality ranking of 27 (0=worst, 99=best). This fund offers only a moderate level of risk but investors looking for strong performance are still waiting.

Services Offered: Automated phone transactions, payroll deductions, bank draft capabilities, an IRA investment plan, a Keogh investment plan, wire transfers and a systematic withdrawal plan.

Data Date	Investment Rating	Net Assets ($Mil)	NAV	Performance Rating/Pts	Total Return Y-T-D	Risk Rating/Pts
2-17	D	1,969	9.83	E / 0.5	0.53%	A / 9.4
2016	D	2,052	9.80	E+ / 0.6	-0.26%	A / 9.4
2015	B+	3,540	9.94	C / 5.1	0.54%	A+ / 9.8
2014	C+	2,101	9.99	D+ / 2.5	1.56%	A+ / 9.8
2013	B+	1,687	9.94	C- / 3.5	0.71%	A+ / 9.7
2012	C+	1,553	9.99	D- / 1.5	2.32%	A+ / 9.7

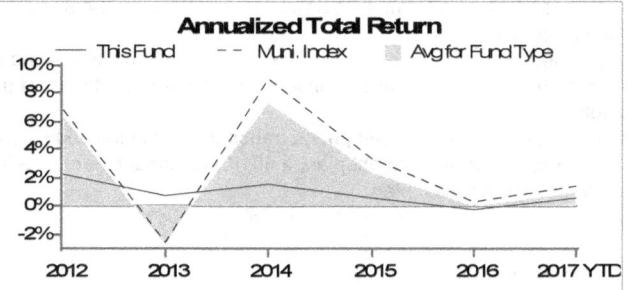

Wells Fargo Str Muni Bd A (VMPAX)

C **Fair**

Fund Family: Wells Fargo Advantage Funds **Phone:** (800) 222-8222
Address: PO Box 8266, Boston, MA 02266
Fund Type: MUN - Municipal - National

Major Rating Factors: Disappointing performance is the major factor driving the C (Fair) TheStreet Investment Rating for Wells Fargo Str Muni Bd A. The fund currently has a performance rating of D (Weak) based on an average return of 1.65% over the last three years (2.73% taxable equivalent) and 0.74% over the last three months (1.23% taxable equivalent). Factored into the performance evaluation is an expense ratio of 0.82% (low) and a 4.0% front-end load that is levied at the time of purchase.

The fund's risk rating is currently B+ (Good). Volatility, as measured by standard deviation, is considered low for fixed income funds at 1.37. Another risk factor is the fund's very low average duration of 1.4 years (i.e. low interest rate risk).

Lyle J. Fitterer has been running the fund for 7 years and currently receives a manager quality ranking of 56 (0=worst, 99=best). This fund offers only a moderate level of risk but investors looking for strong performance are still waiting.

Services Offered: Automated phone transactions, payroll deductions, bank draft capabilities, wire transfers and a systematic withdrawal plan.

Data Date	Investment Rating	Net Assets ($Mil)	NAV	Performance Rating/Pts	Total Return Y-T-D	Risk Rating/Pts
2-17	C	686	8.88	D / 2.2	0.74%	B+ / 8.9
2016	C	681	8.84	D+ / 2.7	0.36%	B+ / 8.8
2015	A+	638	8.98	B- / 7.3	1.53%	B+ / 8.8
2014	B+	603	8.99	C / 4.5	4.55%	B+ / 8.9
2013	A-	569	8.80	C / 4.6	0.60%	A- / 9.0
2012	C+	578	8.95	D+ / 2.3	4.33%	A / 9.5

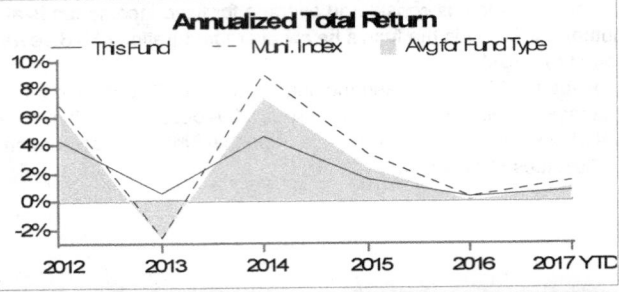

Wells Fargo Ult-Sh Mun Inc A (SMAVX)

D **Weak**

Fund Family: Wells Fargo Advantage Funds **Phone:** (800) 222-8222
Address: PO Box 8266, Boston, MA 02266
Fund Type: MUN - Municipal - National

Major Rating Factors: Very poor performance is the major factor driving the D (Weak) TheStreet Investment Rating for Wells Fargo Ult-Sh Mun Inc A. The fund currently has a performance rating of E (Very Weak) based on an average return of 0.09% over the last three years (0.15% taxable equivalent) and 0.21% over the last three months (0.35% taxable equivalent). Factored into the performance evaluation is an expense ratio of 0.75% (low) and a 2.0% front-end load that is levied at the time of purchase.

The fund's risk rating is currently A+ (Excellent). Volatility, as measured by standard deviation, is considered very low for fixed income funds at 0.46. Another risk factor is the fund's very low average duration of 0.5 years (i.e. low interest rate risk).

Lyle J. Fitterer has been running the fund for 17 years and currently receives a manager quality ranking of 27 (0=worst, 99=best). This fund offers only a moderate level of risk but investors looking for strong performance are still waiting.

Services Offered: Automated phone transactions, payroll deductions, bank draft capabilities, an IRA investment plan, a 401K investment plan, a Keogh investment plan, wire transfers and a systematic withdrawal plan.

Data Date	Investment Rating	Net Assets ($Mil)	NAV	Performance Rating/Pts	Total Return Y-T-D	Risk Rating/Pts
2-17	D	1,135	9.56	E / 0.3	0.21%	A+ / 9.8
2016	D+	1,160	9.55	E / 0.5	-0.26%	A+ / 9.8
2015	C	1,287	9.62	D+ / 2.8	0.11%	A+ / 9.9
2014	D+	1,114	4.82	E+ / 0.8	0.29%	A+ / 9.9
2013	C-	1,734	4.82	D- / 1.0	0.31%	A+ / 9.9
2012	C-	2,307	4.82	E / 0.5	0.73%	A+ / 9.9

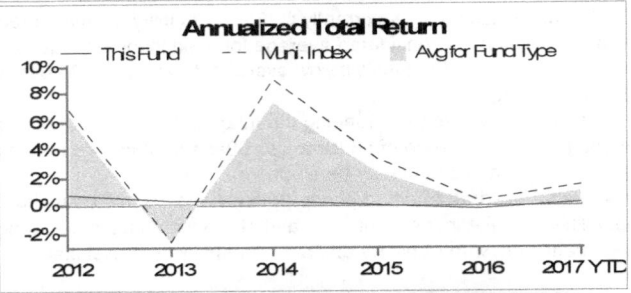

Westcore Plus Bond Rtl (WTIBX)

B- **Good**

Fund Family: Westcore Funds **Phone:** (800) 392-2673
Address: 370 17th Street, Denver, CO 80202
Fund Type: GEI - General - Investment Grade

Major Rating Factors: Westcore Plus Bond Rtl receives a TheStreet Investment Rating of B- (Good). The fund has a performance rating of C+ (Fair) based on an average return of 2.85% over the last three years and 1.26% over the last three months. Factored into the performance evaluation is an expense ratio of 0.70% (low).

The fund's risk rating is currently C+ (Fair). Volatility, as measured by standard deviation, is considered average for fixed income funds at 2.89. Another risk factor is the fund's below average duration of 4.8 years (i.e. lower interest rate risk).

Kenneth A. Harris currently receives a manager quality ranking of 59 (0=worst, 99=best). If you desire an average level of risk, then this fund may be an option.

Services Offered: Automated phone transactions, payroll deductions, bank draft capabilities, an IRA investment plan, a 401K investment plan, wire transfers and a systematic withdrawal plan.

Data Date	Investment Rating	Net Assets ($Mil)	NAV	Performance Rating/Pts	Total Return Y-T-D	Risk Rating/Pts
2-17	B-	1,058	10.66	C+ / 5.6	1.26%	C+ / 6.1
2016	B-	1,069	10.59	C+ / 5.8	3.82%	C+ / 6.1
2015	C+	1,311	10.55	C+ / 6.3	0.01%	C+ / 6.2
2014	C+	1,357	10.92	C / 5.1	5.90%	C+ / 6.7
2013	B+	1,215	10.71	C / 5.3	-1.23%	B- / 7.5
2012	C+	1,457	11.24	C- / 3.6	5.67%	B / 7.8

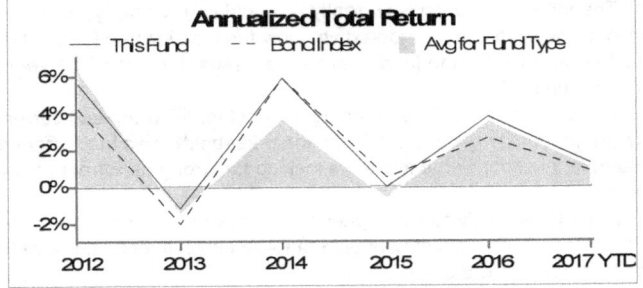

Section III

Top 200 Bond Mutual Funds

A compilation of those

Fixed Income Mutual Funds

receiving the highest TheStreet Investment Ratings.

Funds are listed in order by Overall Investment Rating.

Section III Contents

This section contains a summary analysis of each of the top 200 bond mutual funds as determined by their overall TheStreet Investment Rating. You can use this section to identify those mutual funds that have achieved the best possible combination of total return on investment and reduced risk over the past three years. Consult each fund's individual Performance Rating and Risk Rating to find the fund that best matches your investing style.

In order to optimize the utility of our top and bottom fund lists, rather than listing all funds in a multi-class series, a single fund from each series is selected for display as the primary share class. Whenever possible, the selected fund is one that a retail investor would be most likely to choose. This share class may not be appropriate for every investor, so please consult with your financial advisor, the fund company, and the fund's prospectus before placing your trade.

1. **Fund Type**

The mutual fund's peer category based on its investment objective as stated in its prospectus.

COH	Corporate - High Yield	MMT	Money Market - Treas.
COI	Corporate - Inv. Grade	MTG	Mortgage
EM	Emerging Market	MUH	Municipal - High Yield
GEN	General	MUI	Municipal - Insured
GEI	General - Inv. Grade	MUN	Municipal - National
GEL	General - Long Term	MUS	Municipal - Single State
GES	General - Short & Interm.	USL	U.S. Gov.- Long Term
GL	Global	USS	U.S. Gov. - Short & Interm
LP	Loan Participation	USA	U.S. Gov. - Agency
MMF	Money Mkt - Tax Exempt	US	U.S. Gov. - Treasury

A blank fund type means that the mutual fund has not yet been categorized.

2. **Fund Name**

The name of the mutual fund as stated in its prospectus, which can sometimes differ slightly from the name that the company uses for advertising. If you cannot find the particular mutual fund you are interested in, or if you have any doubts regarding the precise name, verify the information with your broker or on your account statement. Also, use the fund's ticker symbol for confirmation. (See column 3.)

3. **Ticker Symbol**

The unique alphabetic symbol used for identifying and trading a specific mutual fund. No two funds can have the same ticker symbol, and the ticker symbol for mutual funds always ends with an "X".

A handful of funds currently show no associated ticker symbol. This means that the fund is either small or new since the NASD only assigns a ticker symbol to funds with at least $25 million in assets or 1,000 shareholders.

4.	**Overall Investment Rating**	Our overall rating is measured on a scale from A to E based on each fund's risk-adjusted performance. Please see page 11 for specific descriptions of each letter grade. Also, refer to page 7 for information on how our ratings are derived. Most important, when using this rating, please be sure to consider the warnings beginning on page 13 regarding the ratings' limitations and the underlying assumptions.
5.	**Phone**	The telephone number of the company managing the fund. Call this number to receive a prospectus or other information about the fund.
6.	**Net Asset Value (NAV)**	The fund's share price as of the date indicated. A fund's NAV is computed by dividing the value of the fund's asset holdings, less accrued fees and expenses, by the number of its shares outstanding.
7.	**Performance Rating/Points**	A letter grade rating based solely on the mutual fund's financial performance over the trailing three years, without any consideration for the amount of risk the fund poses. Like the overall Investment Rating, the Performance Rating is measured on a scale from A to E for ease of interpretation. The points score indicates where the Performance Rating falls on a scale of 0 to 10.
		In the case of funds investing in municipal or other tax-free securities, this rating is based on the taxable equivalent return of the fund assuming the maximum marginal U.S. tax rate (35%).
8.	**1-Year Total Return**	The total return the fund has provided investors over the preceding twelve months. This total return figure is computed based on the fund's dividend distributions and share price appreciation/depreciation during the period, net of the expenses and fees it imposes on its shareholders. Although the total return figure does not reflect an adjustment for any loads the fund may carry, such adjustments have been made in deriving TheStreet Investment Ratings.
9.	**1-Year Total Return Percentile**	The fund's percentile rank based on its one-year performance compared to that of all other fixed income funds in existence for at least one year. A score of 99 is the best possible, indicating that the fund outperformed 99% of the other mutual funds. Zero is the worst possible percentile score.
		In the case of funds investing in municipal or other tax-free securities, this percentile rank is based on the taxable equivalent return of the fund assuming the maximum marginal U.S. tax rate (35%).
10.	**3-Year Total Return**	The total annual return the fund has provided investors over the preceding three years.

11. 3-Year Total Return Percentile

The fund's percentile rank based on its three-year performance compared to that of all other fixed income funds in existence for at least three years. A score of 99 is the best possible, indicating that the fund outperformed 99% of the other mutual funds. Zero is the worst possible percentile score.

In the case of funds investing in municipal or other tax-free securities, this percentile rank is based on the taxable equivalent return of the fund assuming the maximum marginal U.S. tax rate (35%).

12. 5-Year Total Return

The total annual return the fund has provided investors over the preceding five years.

13. 5-Year Total Return Percentile

The fund's percentile rank based on its five-year performance compared to that of all other fixed income funds in existence for at least five years. A score of 99 is the best possible, indicating that the fund outperformed 99% of the other mutual funds. Zero is the worst possible percentile score.

In the case of funds investing in municipal or other tax-free securities, this percentile rank is based on the taxable equivalent return of the fund assuming the maximum marginal U.S. tax rate (35%).

14. Risk Rating/Points

A letter grade rating based solely on the mutual fund's risk as determined by its monthly performance volatility over the trailing three years and the underlying credit risk and interest rate risk of its investment portfolio. The risk rating does not take into consideration the overall financial performance the fund has achieved or the total return it has provided to its shareholders. Like the overall Investment Rating, the Risk Rating is measured on a scale from A to E for ease of interpretation. The points score indicates where the Risk Rating falls on a scale of 0 to 10.

15. Manager Quality Percentile

The manager quality percentile is based on a ranking of the fund's alpha, a statistical measure representing the difference between a fund's actual returns and its expected performance given its level of risk. Fund managers who have been able to exceed the fund's statistically expected performance receive a high percentile rank with 99 representing the best possible score. At the other end of the spectrum, fund managers who have actually detracted from the fund's expected performance receive a low percentile rank with 0 representing the worst possible score.

16. Manager Tenure

The number of years the current manager has been managing the fund. Since fund managers who deliver substandard returns are usually replaced, a long tenure is usually a good sign that shareholders are satisfied that the fund is achieving its stated objectives.

Fund Type	Fund Name	Ticker Symbol	Overall Investment Rating	Phone	Net Asset Value As of 2/28/17	Performance Rating/Pts	1Yr / Pct	3Yr / Pct	5Yr / Pct	Risk Rating/Pts	Mgr. Quality Pct	Mgr. Tenure (Years)
USS	Principal Preferred Sec A	PPSAX	A+	(800) 222-5852	10.23	A- /9.0	9.14 /77	6.30 /93	7.09 /96	C /4.5	97	15
GEI	PIMCO Income Fund A	PONAX	A+	(800) 426-0107	12.20	B+ /8.8	10.72 /81	5.53 /89	8.03 /98	B- /7.5	96	10
MUS	Saturna Idaho Tax-Exempt	NITEX	A+	(800) 728-8762	5.35	B+ /8.3	1.63 /53	3.60 /89	2.67 /74	B- /7.1	70	22
MUS	T Rowe Price MD Tax Free Bd	MDXBX	A+	(800) 638-5660	10.68	B /8.0	0.73 /41	3.64 /89	3.20 /83	C+ /6.7	69	17
MUS	T Rowe Price VA Tax-Free Bond	PRVAX	A+	(800) 638-5660	11.90	B /8.0	0.56 /38	3.71 /90	3.06 /81	C+ /5.9	66	20
GL	Federated Floating Rt Str Inc Inst	FFRSX	A+	(800) 341-7400	10.02	B /7.8	9.63 /78	3.52 /69	4.01 /73	B /8.2	93	2
LP	Lord Abbett Floating Rate A	LFRAX	A+	(888) 522-2388	9.26	B /7.7	11.78 /83	3.73 /72	4.86 /83	B- /7.3	92	5
MUS	Dupree AL Tax Free Income	DUALX	A+	(800) 866-0614	12.20	B- /7.5	0.50 /37	3.36 /86	3.01 /80	C+ /6.9	64	16
LP	T Rowe Price Instl Fltng Rate F	PFFRX	A+	(800) 638-5660	10.08	B- /7.2	9.33 /77	3.57 /70	4.39 /77	B /7.9	92	8
GES	J Hancock VIT Strat Inc Opps I	JESNX	A+	(800) 257-3336	13.59	B- /7.2	6.29 /71	3.47 /68	4.76 /81	B /7.8	88	13
MUS	Lee Fnl Hawaii-Muni Bond Inv	SURFX	A+		11.03	B- /7.1	-0.09 /16	3.13 /84	2.81 /76	B /7.6	65	2
MUN	BMO Intermediate Tax Free Y	MITFX	A+	(800) 236-3863	11.15	C+ /6.9	0.10 /24	2.93 /81	2.72 /75	B- /7.2	51	2
LP	BlackRock Floating Rate Inc Inv A	BFRAX	A+	(800) 441-7762	10.26	C+ /6.9	9.56 /78	3.24 /65	4.15 /74	B /7.8	90	8
USS	Morgan Stanley Mortgage Sec Tr A	MTGAX	A+	(800) 869-6397	8.49	C+ /6.8	7.28 /73	4.23 /78	4.92 /83	B /8.0	93	3
MUN	State Farm Muni Bond	SFBDX	A+	(800) 447-4930	8.63	C+ /6.8	-0.01 /17	2.80 /79	2.53 /71	B- /7.5	50	19
GL	Payden Global Fixed Inc Investor	PYGFX	A+	(888) 409-8007	8.98	C+ /6.7	3.50 /60	3.73 /72	3.75 /69	B /7.6	94	9
MUS	Colorado Bond Shares	HICOX	A+	(800) 572-0069	8.93	C+ /6.6	2.01 /57	3.88 /92	3.71 /90	B+ /8.8	89	27
GEI	Frost Total Return Bond Inv	FATRX	A+	(866) 777-7818	10.44	C+ /6.6	7.02 /73	2.80 /58	4.22 /75	B /8.0	81	15
USS	Guggenheim Investment Grade Bd	SIUSX	A+	(800) 820-0888	18.27	C+ /6.5	6.20 /71	4.14 /77	4.59 /80	B /8.0	93	5
GEI	CM Advisors Fixed Income	CMFIX	A+	(800) 664-4888	11.57	C+ /6.3	7.95 /74	2.36 /49	1.92 /41	B /8.2	79	6
GES	Homestead Short Term Bond	HOSBX	A+	(800) 258-3030	5.21	C+ /6.3	5.27 /68	2.34 /49	2.47 /49	B+ /8.3	83	26
GEI	Ave Maria Bond	AVEFX	A+	(866) 283-6274	11.29	C+ /6.2	4.92 /66	2.85 /59	3.47 /65	B+ /8.3	85	14
MUS	Oppeneheimer Rochester PA Muni	OPATX	A	(888) 470-0862	10.40	A+ /9.7	5.37 /75	6.05 /99	3.84 /91	C- /3.2	91	15
MUN	Dupree Taxable Muni Bd Srs	DUTMX	A	(800) 866-0614	10.50	A+ /9.6	2.08 /58	5.31 /98	4.96 /97	C- /3.2	88	7
MUN	Sit Tax Free Income Fund	SNTIX	A	(800) 332-5580	9.48	A /9.4	0.69 /40	5.01 /97	4.34 /96	C- /3.4	74	29
USS	Nuveen Preferred Securities A	NPSAX	A	(800) 257-8787	17.22	A- /9.0	11.35 /82	6.19 /93	8.02 /98	C- /4.0	98	11
MUS	T Rowe Price NY Tax Free Bd	PRNYX	A	(800) 638-5660	11.53	B+ /8.3	0.33 /33	3.95 /92	3.24 /84	C /4.8	65	17
GEI	● RiverNorth/DoubleLine Strat Inc R	RNDLX	A	(888) 848-7549	10.61	B /8.1	10.38 /80	4.41 /80	5.13 /85	C+ /5.6	91	7
MUN	USAA Tax-Exempt Long Term	USTEX	A	(800) 382-8722	13.25	B /8.0	0.64 /39	3.71 /90	3.64 /89	C /5.0	67	N/A
MUN	T Rowe Price Tax-Free Income	PRTAX	A	(800) 638-5660	10.07	B /8.0	0.25 /31	3.76 /90	3.28 /85	C /5.0	62	10
GES	BlackRock Crdt Strategies Inc Inv	BMSAX	A	(800) 441-7762	10.19	B- /7.2	9.75 /78	3.53 /69	4.82 /82	C+ /6.1	91	5
LP	Columbia Floating Rate A	RFRAX	A	(800) 345-6611	9.08	B- /7.1	11.84 /83	3.29 /66	4.52 /79	C+ /6.6	89	11
GL	WA Total Return Unconstrained FI	WARIX	A	(888) 425-6432	10.44	C+ /6.9	9.58 /78	2.53 /52	2.87 /56	C+ /6.6	90	11
MUI	Westcore CO Tax Exempt	WTCOX	A	(800) 392-2673	11.40	C+ /6.9	-0.15 /15	2.95 /81	2.36 /68	C+ /6.4	36	12
MUS	Dupree TN Tax-Free Income	TNTIX	A	(800) 866-0614	11.34	C+ /6.7	-0.12 /16	2.91 /80	2.64 /73	C+ /6.7	44	13
GEI	Dodge & Cox Income Fund	DODIX	A	(800) 621-3979	13.74	C+ /6.7	6.70 /72	3.06 /62	3.38 /63	B- /7.1	78	28
MUS	Dupree KY Tax Free Income	KYTFX	A	(800) 866-0614	7.70	C+ /6.6	0.11 /25	2.73 /77	2.56 /72	C+ /6.8	33	18
LP	Virtus Senior Floating Rate A	PSFRX	A	(800) 243-1574	9.54	C+ /6.5	10.40 /80	2.81 /58	4.00 /73	C+ /6.9	87	5
LP	● MainStay Floating Rate B	MXFBX	A	(800) 624-6782	9.38	C+ /6.3	9.36 /77	2.07 /44	2.81 /55	B- /7.1	81	13
GEI	Nationwide Core Plus Bond R6	NWCIX	A	(800) 848-0920	10.21	C+ /6.2	4.31 /64	3.08 /62	3.47 /65	B- /7.5	73	15
GEI	Metropolitan West Strategic Inc M	MWSTX	A	(800) 496-8298	8.06	C /4.6	4.08 /62	1.82 /40	4.07 /73	A- /9.2	81	14
MUN	Oppenheimer Rochester AMT-Free	OPTAX	A-	(888) 470-0862	6.83	A+ /9.7	3.73 /69	6.34 /99	6.00 /99	D+ /2.8	89	15
GEI	Cohen and Steers Pref Sec&Inc A	CPXAX	A-	(800) 330-7348	13.77	A /9.3	10.71 /80	6.99 /96	8.28 /99	C- /3.0	96	7
MUS	Oppeneheimer Rochester CA Muni	OPCAX	A-	(888) 470-0862	8.27	A /9.3	4.11 /71	5.61 /98	5.51 /99	C- /3.3	86	15
MUS	Vanguard OH Long-Term	VOHIX	A-	(800) 662-7447	12.37	B+ /8.9	0.75 /41	4.40 /95	3.72 /90	C- /3.7	64	9
GES	Changing Parameters	CPMPX	A-	(866) 618-3456	10.26	B+ /8.7	12.45 /84	4.05 /76	4.61 /80	C- /3.9	91	10
MUS	Vanguard NY Long-Term	VNYTX	A-	(800) 662-7447	11.59	B+ /8.6	0.30 /32	4.24 /94	3.53 /88	C- /3.9	63	4
MUS	USAA California Bond Fund	USCBX	A-	(800) 382-8722	10.93	B+ /8.6	0.38 /35	4.14 /94	4.11 /94	C- /4.0	73	N/A
MUS	Vanguard PA Long-Term	VPAIX	A-	(800) 662-7447	11.37	B+ /8.6	0.57 /38	4.17 /94	3.49 /87	C- /3.9	61	6
MUN	T Rowe Price Summit Muni Income	PRINX	A-	(800) 638-5660	11.71	B+ /8.4	0.27 /31	4.12 /94	3.65 /89	C- /4.1	63	18
GEI	BlackRock Managed Income Inv A	BLADX	A-	(800) 441-7762	10.02	B /8.1	8.89 /76	4.17 /77	3.53 /66	C /4.6	84	8
MUN	Elfun Tax Exempt Income	ELFTX	A-	(800) 843-2639	11.54	B /8.1	0.44 /36	3.75 /90	2.93 /79	C /4.6	58	N/A

● Denotes fund is closed to new investors

Fund Type	Fund Name	Ticker Symbol	Overall Investment Rating	Phone	Net Asset Value As of 2/28/17	Performance Rating/Pts	Annualized Total Return Through 2/28/17 1Yr / Pct	3Yr / Pct	5Yr / Pct	Risk Rating/Pts	Mgr. Quality Pct	Mgr. Tenure (Years)
MUS	Dupree MS Tax Free Income	DUMSX	A-	(800) 866-0614	12.00	B /8.0	0.36 /34	3.73 /90	3.13 /82	C /4.9	63	17
MUS	T Rowe Price NJ Tax-Free Bond	NJTFX	A-	(800) 638-5660	11.87	B /7.9	0.41 /35	3.73 /90	3.23 /84	C /4.7	59	17
MUS	Fidelity PA Muni Inc	FPXTX	A-	(800) 544-8544	11.01	B /7.8	0.27 /31	3.64 /89	3.15 /82	C /5.1	59	15
GEI	Cavalier Adaptive Income Inst	CADTX	A-	(877) 773-3863	10.41	B /7.7	9.82 /79	3.02 /61	2.99 /58	C /5.0	82	1
MUS	AB Municipal Income II VA A	AVAAX	A-	(800) 221-5672	11.04	C+ /6.9	0.48 /37	3.77 /90	2.73 /75	C+ /6.0	68	22
MUS	Franklin PA Tax-Free Inc A	FRPAX	A-	(800) 342-5236	10.12	C+ /6.6	1.61 /53	3.79 /91	2.61 /73	C+ /6.4	76	31
MUS	WA Pennsylvania Municipals A	SBPAX	A-	(877) 534-4627	12.77	C+ /6.5	0.97 /44	3.85 /91	2.54 /71	C+ /6.8	75	10
MUS	Franklin Alabama Tax-Free Inc A	FRALX	A-	(800) 342-5236	11.16	C+ /6.3	1.67 /54	3.63 /89	2.76 /75	C+ /6.8	74	28
LP	Voya Floating Rate A	IFRAX	A-	(800) 992-0180	9.95	C+ /6.3	9.07 /77	2.91 /60	4.06 /73	C+ /6.9	87	7
MUS	Madison Tax Free Virginia Y	GTVAX	A-	(800) 877-6089	11.41	C+ /6.2	-0.49 /10	2.61 /76	1.97 /58	B- /7.0	29	20
GL	DoubleLine Core Fixed Income N	DLFNX	A-	(877) 354-6311	10.87	C+ /6.1	3.81 /61	3.15 /63	3.23 /61	B- /7.0	94	7
COI	Payden Core Bond Adviser	PYCWX	A-	(888) 409-8007	10.56	C+ /6.0	3.90 /62	2.97 /60	3.08 /59	B- /7.1	67	20
GES	ICON Bond C	IOBCX	A-	(800) 764-0442	9.48	C+ /6.0	6.34 /71	2.42 /50	2.53 /50	B- /7.4	71	6
GEI	Commerce Bond	CFBNX	A-	(800) 995-6365	19.88	C+ /5.9	3.98 /62	2.89 /59	3.14 /60	B- /7.4	69	23
MUI	WesMark West Virginia Muni Bond	WMKMX	A-	(800) 864-1013	10.40	C+ /5.9	-0.50 /10	2.42 /72	1.99 /59	B- /7.4	28	11
GES	AdvisorOne CLS Flexible Income N	CLFLX	A-	(866) 811-0225	10.25	C+ /5.8	5.52 /69	2.42 /50	2.34 /47	B- /7.5	71	3
COI	Federated Interm Corp Bd Instl	FIIFX	A-	(800) 341-7400	9.25	C /5.5	4.75 /66	2.47 /51	3.34 /63	B /7.6	58	4
GEI	WA Intermediate Bond IS	WABSX	A-	(888) 425-6432	10.86	C /5.5	3.05 /57	2.74 /57	2.81 /55	B /7.9	71	8
GES	DoubleLine Total Return Bond N	DLTNX	A-	(877) 354-6311	10.63	C /5.1	1.11 /41	2.85 /59	3.43 /64	B /8.2	77	7
MTG	Federated Mortgage Fund Inst	FGFIX	A-	(800) 341-7400	9.57	C /4.9	2.00 /49	2.62 /54	2.10 /44	B+ /8.5	65	14
GEI	SEI Instl Mgd Tr-Enhanced Inc F	SEEAX	A-	(800) 342-5734	7.54	C /4.6	5.36 /68	1.69 /38	2.29 /46	A- /9.0	81	11
MUH	Oppenheimer Rochester Hi Yld	ORNAX	B+	(888) 470-0862	7.09	A+ /9.9	7.13 /81	7.47 /99	6.59 /99	D /1.7	91	15
MUH	MainStay High Yield Muni Bond C	MMHDX	B+	(800) 624-6782	12.14	A+ /9.9	2.48 /61	6.40 /99	5.49 /99	D /2.0	84	7
MUH	Invesco High Yield Municipal A	ACTHX	B+	(800) 959-4246	9.87	A+ /9.7	2.53 /62	6.92 /99	5.74 /99	D /2.0	88	15
MUS	Oppenheimer Rochester Muni A	RMUNX	B+	(888) 470-0862	14.88	A+ /9.7	6.99 /81	5.99 /98	3.99 /93	D /2.1	87	15
MUH	Lord Abbett Tx Fr High Yld Muni A	HYMAX	B+	(888) 522-2388	11.63	A+ /9.7	3.59 /69	5.90 /98	5.30 /98	D+ /2.3	85	13
MUH	PIMCO High Yield Muni Bond A	PYMAX	B+	(800) 426-0107	8.77	A+ /9.6	2.36 /60	5.95 /98	5.05 /98	D /2.1	80	2
MUH	MFS Municipal High Income A	MMHYX	B+	(800) 225-2606	8.07	A /9.4	1.91 /56	6.12 /99	5.03 /98	D+ /2.6	86	15
MUS	Oppenheimer Rochester AMT-Fr	OPNYX	B+	(888) 470-0862	11.08	A /9.3	4.42 /72	5.65 /98	3.89 /92	D+ /2.5	84	15
MUH	T Rowe Price Tax-Free High Yield	PRFHX	B+	(800) 638-5660	11.77	A /9.3	1.64 /53	5.37 /98	4.99 /98	D+ /2.7	81	15
COH	Hundredfold Select Alternative Svc	SFHYX	B+	(855) 582-8006	22.72	A- /9.2	14.09 /87	4.14 /77	5.07 /85	D+ /2.6	82	13
GEI	CNR Fixed Income Opportunities N	RIMOX	B+	(888) 889-0799	25.98	A- /9.1	15.63 /90	4.16 /77	5.58 /89	D+ /2.8	95	6
MUN	Eaton Vance High Yield Muni Inc A	ETHYX	B+	(800) 262-1122	8.68	A- /9.1	1.03 /45	6.27 /99	5.42 /99	D+ /2.7	84	13
COI	Diamond Hill Corporate Credit A	DSIAX	B+	(614) 255-3333	11.27	A- /9.0	15.58 /89	5.22 /86	5.60 /89	C- /3.3	93	11
MUS ●	Oppenheimer Rochester Ohio Muni	OROHX	B+	(888) 470-0862	10.06	A- /9.0	4.02 /71	5.23 /97	4.29 /95	C- /3.1	81	11
COI	Payden Corporate Bond Investor	PYACX	B+	(888) 409-8007	11.03	B+ /8.8	8.28 /75	5.17 /86	5.29 /87	C- /3.2	84	N/A
MUS ●	Oppenheimer Rochester NC Muni	OPNCX	B+	(888) 470-0862	10.89	B+ /8.8	4.13 /71	4.95 /97	2.87 /78	C- /3.1	86	11
GES	Osterweis Strategic Income	OSTIX	B+	(800) 700-3316	11.35	B+ /8.6	15.03 /88	3.51 /69	4.90 /83	C- /3.7	93	15
MUN	Vanguard Long-Term Tax-Exempt	VWLTX	B+	(800) 662-7447	11.43	B+ /8.6	0.46 /36	4.19 /94	3.66 /89	C- /3.5	55	7
MUS	Northern CA T/E Bond	NCATX	B+	(800) 595-9111	11.49	B+ /8.5	-0.45 /10	4.32 /95	3.97 /93	C- /3.4	57	20
LP	Eaton Vance Float Rate Advtage A	EAFAX	B+	(800) 262-1122	10.89	B+ /8.5	15.82 /90	3.87 /74	4.93 /83	C- /3.6	91	21
MUN	Eaton Vance National Muni Inc A	EANAX	B+	(800) 262-1122	9.77	B+ /8.3	2.02 /57	5.15 /97	3.98 /93	C- /3.7	81	4
MUS	T Rowe Price CA Tax Free Bond	PRXCX	B+	(800) 638-5660	11.35	B+ /8.3	-0.12 /16	4.09 /93	3.75 /91	C- /3.6	54	14
LP	Oppenheimer Sen-Floating Rate A	OOSAX	B+	(888) 470-0862	8.20	B+ /8.3	16.53 /91	3.76 /72	4.75 /81	C- /4.0	90	18
LP	Voya Senior Income A	XSIAX	B+	(800) 992-0180	12.85	B+ /8.3	14.59 /88	3.91 /74	6.29 /94	C- /4.0	91	16
MUS	Fidelity AZ Muni Income Fd	FSAZX	B+	(800) 544-8544	11.91	B /8.1	-0.17 /15	3.91 /92	3.29 /85	C- /4.0	53	7
MUN	Northern Tax Exempt	NOTEX	B+	(800) 595-9111	10.56	B /8.1	0.19 /28	3.80 /91	3.25 /84	C /4.3	56	19
LP	Eaton Vance Flt-Rate and Hi Inc A	EVFHX	B+	(800) 262-1122	9.44	B /7.9	13.86 /87	3.46 /68	4.43 /78	C /4.5	90	17
MUS	Sit MN Tax Free Income	SMTFX	B+	(800) 332-5580	10.29	B /7.7	0.18 /28	3.55 /88	3.13 /82	C /5.0	57	24
LP	Eaton Vance Floating Rate A	EVBLX	B+	(800) 262-1122	9.31	B /7.6	13.62 /86	3.21 /64	3.98 /72	C /4.8	88	16
GEI	Universal Inst Core Plus Fxd Inc II	UCFIX	B+	(800) 869-6397	10.78	B- /7.3	6.83 /72	3.65 /71	3.82 /70	C /5.4	81	6
GEI	USAA Intmdt-Trm Bd Fund	USIBX	B+	(800) 382-8722	10.55	B- /7.0	7.92 /74	3.14 /63	4.24 /75	C /5.5	75	1

● Denotes fund is closed to new investors

Data as of February 28, 2017

Fund Type	Fund Name	Ticker Symbol	Overall Investment Rating	Phone	Net Asset Value As of 2/28/17	Performance Rating/Pts	Annualized Total Return Through 2/28/17 1Yr / Pct	3Yr / Pct	5Yr / Pct	Risk Rating/Pts	Mgr. Quality Pct	Mgr. Tenure (Years)
	99 Pct = Best *0 Pct = Worst*					**PERFORMANCE**				**RISK**	**FUND MGR**	
MUI	Pacific Capital Tax-Free Secs Y	PTXFX	B+	(888) 739-1390	10.10	C+ /6.7	-0.38 /11	2.86 /80	2.44 /69	C+ /5.6	28	13
MUS	Franklin Colorado Tax-Free Inc A	FRCOX	B+	(800) 342-5236	11.66	C+ /6.7	1.30 /49	3.88 /92	2.87 /77	C+ /6.1	74	25
MUS	Fidelity MN Muni Inc	FIMIX	B+	(800) 544-8544	11.48	C+ /6.7	-0.06 /17	2.83 /79	2.34 /67	C+ /5.8	28	7
MUN	Vanguard Interm-Term Tax-Exempt	VWITX	B+	(800) 662-7447	13.98	C+ /6.7	-0.11 /16	2.80 /79	2.60 /73	C+ /5.9	27	4
GEI	J Hancock Active Bond 1	JIADX	B+	(800) 257-3336	10.06	C+ /6.2	4.31 /64	3.08 /62	3.61 /67	C+ /6.6	70	12
GEI	TiAA-CREF Bond Plus Retail	TCBPX	B+	(800) 842-2252	10.40	C+ /6.1	4.41 /64	3.04 /62	3.23 /61	C+ /6.3	68	11
MUN	BlackRock Natl Muni Inv A	MDNLX	B+	(800) 441-7762	10.78	C+ /6.0	0.66 /40	3.53 /88	3.31 /85	B- /7.0	68	21
MUS	Franklin Virginia Tax-Free Inc A	FRVAX	B+	(800) 342-5236	11.31	C+ /5.9	1.49 /51	3.37 /86	2.30 /66	B- /7.0	69	30
MUS	Oppeneheimer Rochester LT CA	OLCAX	B+	(888) 470-0862	3.20	C+ /5.8	2.29 /60	2.56 /75	2.55 /71	B- /7.2	59	13
GL	JPMorgan Strategic Income Opp A	JSOAX	B+	(800) 480-4111	11.69	C+ /5.8	11.60 /82	2.34 /49	3.15 /60	B- /7.1	89	9
GEI ●	Thrivent Oppty Income Plus A	AAINX	B+	(800) 847-4836	10.23	C+ /5.8	8.75 /76	3.14 /63	--	B- /7.2	85	15
MUS	MFS MD Municipal Bond A	MFSMX	B+	(800) 225-2606	10.77	C+ /5.7	0.61 /39	3.48 /88	2.35 /67	B- /7.0	66	18
MUI	Commerce Kansas T/F Intm Bond	KTXIX	B+	(800) 995-6365	19.14	C+ /5.7	-0.43 /10	2.37 /71	1.97 /58	B- /7.2	24	17
GEI	William Blair Bond N	WBBNX	B+	(800) 742-7272	10.45	C+ /5.6	4.22 /63	2.72 /56	2.93 /56	B- /7.3	70	10
MUS	Franklin Kentucky Tax-Free Inc A	FRKYX	B+	(800) 342-5236	11.01	C+ /5.6	0.85 /43	3.38 /86	2.62 /73	B- /7.5	72	21
COI	MSIF Short Duration Income A	MLDAX	B+	(800) 354-8185	8.16	C /5.5	8.64 /76	2.73 /56	2.38 /47	B- /7.4	86	6
COI	Transamerica Flexible Income A	IDITX	B+	(888) 233-4339	9.28	C /5.4	8.28 /75	2.98 /61	4.42 /78	B /7.6	78	12
MUN	Eaton Vance VA Municipal Income	ETVAX	B+	(800) 262-1122	7.95	C /5.3	1.35 /50	3.27 /85	2.61 /73	B /7.7	72	10
COH	Pioneer Floating Rate Fund Class	FLARX	B+	(800) 225-6292	6.81	C /5.2	8.44 /75	2.80 /58	3.71 /69	B- /7.4	80	10
MUI	First Inv MI Tax Exempt A	FTMIX	B+	(800) 423-4026	11.98	C /5.2	0.06 /22	3.77 /91	2.45 /69	B- /7.5	79	26
MUN	Waddell & Reed Adv Muni Bond A	UNMBX	B+	(888) 923-3355	7.47	C /5.1	0.71 /41	3.15 /84	2.71 /75	B /7.6	66	17
MUI	First Inv PA Tax Exempt A	FTPAX	B+	(800) 423-4026	13.02	C /4.9	0.78 /42	3.45 /87	2.83 /77	B /7.9	78	26
GL	J Hancock Strat Income Opp A	JIPAX	B+	(800) 257-3336	10.70	C /4.9	5.87 /70	2.86 /59	4.00 /73	B /7.9	92	11
GES	Virtus Multi Sector Short Term B A	NARAX	B+	(800) 243-1574	4.76	C /4.8	6.58 /72	2.13 /45	2.90 /56	B+ /8.3	80	24
USA	Vanguard GNMA Inv	VFIIX	B+	(800) 662-7447	10.54	C /4.6	0.67 /36	2.57 /53	1.96 /41	B+ /8.3	81	11
MUS	1919 Maryland Tax-Free Income A	LMMDX	B+	(844) 828-1919	15.92	C /4.6	1.39 /50	2.72 /77	2.10 /61	B+ /8.3	73	10
COI	Vanguard Short-Term Crp Bd Idx	VSCSX	B+	(800) 662-7447	21.67	C /4.3	2.98 /56	1.88 /41	2.31 /46	B+ /8.8	67	8
MUN	Oppenheimer Rochester Sht Term	ORSTX	B+	(888) 470-0862	3.73	C- /4.1	0.82 /42	1.93 /60	1.91 /57	A- /9.2	74	7
GEI	Vanguard Sh-Term Invest-Grade	VFSTX	B+	(800) 662-7447	10.67	C- /4.1	2.70 /55	1.77 /39	2.04 /43	A- /9.0	71	9
GEI	Weitz Short Dur Income Inst	WEFIX	B+	(800) 232-4161	12.35	C- /4.0	3.28 /58	1.62 /37	1.88 /40	A- /9.1	71	21
GEI	Lord Abbett Shrt Duration Inc A	LALDX	B+	(888) 522-2388	4.31	C- /4.0	4.69 /65	1.98 /43	2.57 /51	A- /9.0	80	19
GEI	USAA Short Term Bond Retail	USSBX	B+	(800) 382-8722	9.16	C- /3.9	3.37 /59	1.48 /35	1.87 /40	A- /9.2	70	1
GEI ●	Thrivent Limited Maturity Bond A	LBLAX	B+	(800) 847-4836	12.46	C- /3.9	3.14 /58	1.46 /34	1.49 /34	A /9.3	72	18
MUN	USAA Ultra Short Term Bond Fund	UUSTX	B+	(800) 382-8722	9.99	C- /3.8	2.28 /60	0.87 /33	1.31 /42	A+ /9.7	67	N/A
GL	BBH Limited Duration Class N	BBBMX	B+	(800) 625-5759	10.17	C- /3.7	3.44 /59	1.20 /31	1.47 /34	A+ /9.7	77	6
GES	Semper Short Duration Inv	SEMRX	B+	(888) 263-6443	9.86	C- /3.5	2.78 /55	1.19 /31	0.90 /26	A+ /9.6	79	7
EM	BlackRock Emg Mkts Flex Dyn Bd	BAEDX	B	(800) 441-7762	9.68	A+ /9.8	17.51 /93	6.80 /95	4.26 /76	D- /1.4	99	6
COI	Angel Oak High Yield Opps Inst	ANHIX	B	(877) 625-3042	11.94	A+ /9.7	20.93 /97	4.75 /83	6.31 /94	D /1.6	88	8
COH	PIA High Yield Institutional	PHYSX	B	(800) 251-1970	10.32	A+ /9.6	18.33 /94	4.80 /84	6.74 /96	D /1.9	77	7
MUH	BlackRock High Yld Muni Inv A	MDYHX	B	(800) 441-7762	9.34	A /9.5	1.68 /54	6.46 /99	5.06 /98	D /1.7	82	11
MUH	Pioneer High Income Municipal A	PIMAX	B	(800) 225-6292	7.21	A /9.5	3.01 /65	6.07 /99	5.50 /99	D /2.0	81	11
MUH	Goldman Sachs High Yield Muni A	GHYAX	B	(800) 526-7384	9.31	A /9.4	4.89 /73	6.19 /99	5.65 /99	D /2.1	88	17
MUH	AB High Income Municipal A	ABTHX	B	(800) 221-5672	11.07	A /9.4	0.97 /44	6.01 /98	5.19 /98	D /1.9	77	7
MUH	Delaware Natl HY Muni Bd A	CXHYX	B	(800) 523-1918	10.77	A /9.3	1.84 /55	6.07 /99	5.22 /98	D /2.2	82	14
COH	Vanguard High-Yield Corporate Inv	VWEHX	B	(800) 662-7447	5.92	A /9.3	14.53 /88	4.62 /82	6.02 /92	D /2.0	77	9
MUH	Northern High Yield Muni	NHYMX	B	(800) 595-9111	8.68	A- /9.0	0.17 /28	4.77 /97	4.20 /95	D+ /2.6	71	19
MUH	Vanguard High-Yield Tax-Exempt	VWAHX	B	(800) 662-7447	11.08	B+ /8.9	0.96 /44	4.49 /96	4.01 /93	D+ /2.6	62	7
MUH	Columbia High Yield Municipal A	LHIAX	B	(800) 345-6611	10.49	B+ /8.9	1.48 /51	5.23 /97	4.84 /97	D+ /2.5	80	8
MUH	American Funds High Inc Muni Bnd	AMHIX	B	(800) 421-0180	15.41	B+ /8.9	1.75 /54	5.43 /98	5.38 /98	D+ /2.8	82	23
MUS ●	Oppenheimer Rochester AZ Muni	ORAZX	B	(888) 470-0862	10.50	B+ /8.7	6.14 /78	4.48 /96	2.83 /77	D+ /2.8	87	11
COH	Brandes Separately Mgd Acct Res	SMARX	B	(800) 237-7119	8.89	B+ /8.6	13.04 /85	4.22 /78	5.71 /90	D+ /2.8	85	12
MUS	Vanguard CA Long-Term	VCITX	B	(800) 662-7447	11.89	B+ /8.6	-0.02 /17	4.31 /95	3.95 /93	D+ /2.8	36	6

● Denotes fund is closed to new investors

Fund Type	Fund Name	Ticker Symbol	Overall Investment Rating	Phone	Net Asset Value As of 2/28/17	Performance Rating/Pts	Annualized Total Return Through 2/28/17			Risk Rating/Pts	Mgr. Quality Pct	Mgr. Tenure (Years)
	99 Pct = Best 0 Pct = Worst						1Yr / Pct	3Yr / Pct	5Yr / Pct			
MUH	Ivy Municipal High Income A	IYIAX	B	(800) 777-6472	5.14	B+ /8.6	1.94 /56	5.18 /97	4.01 /93	C- /3.3	84	8
MUS	BlackRock NY Muni Oppty Inv A	MENKX	B	(800) 441-7762	11.03	B+ /8.4	2.08 /58	5.04 /97	3.75 /91	C- /3.1	74	11
MUS ●	Oppenheimer Rochester MA Muni	ORMAX	B	(888) 470-0862	10.28	B+ /8.3	3.50 /68	4.66 /96	3.05 /81	C- /3.6	83	11
MUN ●	MainStay Tax Free Bond Fund B	MKTBX	B	(800) 624-6782	9.82	B+ /8.3	0.10 /24	4.15 /94	3.56 /88	C- /3.4	62	8
MUS	Fidelity OH Muni Inc	FOHFX	B	(800) 544-8544	11.95	B /8.2	-0.22 /14	4.08 /93	3.40 /86	C- /3.5	48	1
MUH	Waddell & Reed Adv Muni High Inc	UMUHX	B	(888) 923-3355	4.77	B /8.1	1.98 /57	4.76 /96	4.15 /94	C- /3.9	83	9
MUN	Fidelity Tax Free Bond Fd	FTABX	B	(800) 544-8544	11.33	B /8.1	0.10 /24	3.89 /92	3.51 /88	C- /3.8	46	7
MUS	Dreyfus NY Tax Exempt Bond	DRNYX	B	(800) 645-6561	14.67	B /7.7	0.16 /27	3.51 /88	2.41 /69	C- /4.2	36	8
MUN	PIMCO Unconstrained Tax Mnged	ATMAX	B	(800) 426-0107	10.43	B /7.6	9.78 /89	2.19 /67	2.25 /65	C- /4.2	84	2
MUS	Fidelity MD Muni Income Fd	SMDMX	B	(800) 544-8544	11.18	B /7.6	-0.12 /16	3.51 /88	2.60 /72	C- /4.1	33	15
MUS	Fidelity MI Muni Inc	FMHTX	B	(800) 544-8544	11.99	B- /7.5	-0.48 /10	3.54 /88	2.89 /78	C /4.5	47	1
GL	CGCM Intl Fixed Inc	TIFUX	B	(800) 444-4273	7.61	B- /7.5	5.26 /68	4.40 /80	3.81 /70	C /4.3	96	3
LP	RidgeWorth Seix Fltng Rt Hg Inc A	SFRAX	B	(888) 784-3863	8.79	B- /7.5	13.62 /86	3.30 /66	4.28 /76	C- /4.2	89	11
MUS	T Rowe Price GA Tax-Free Bd	GTFBX	B	(800) 638-5660	11.39	B- /7.5	-0.28 /13	3.51 /88	2.98 /80	C /4.6	N/A	20
LP	Franklin Floating Rate Dly-Acc A	FAFRX	B	(800) 342-5236	8.89	B- /7.5	14.02 /87	3.19 /64	3.93 /71	C /4.5	87	4
MUS	Northern AZ Tax Exempt	NOAZX	B	(800) 595-9111	10.53	B- /7.4	0.01 /18	3.28 /85	2.95 /79	C /4.3	28	18
MUS	BlackRock CA Muni Opptys A	MECMX	B	(800) 441-7762	12.34	B- /7.3	1.12 /46	4.27 /95	3.54 /88	C /4.6	75	24
GEI	WA Core Plus Bond FI	WACIX	B	(888) 425-6432	11.54	B- /7.1	5.16 /67	3.81 /73	3.67 /68	C /4.8	78	12
MUN	MFS Municipal Income A	MFIAX	B	(800) 225-2606	8.64	B- /7.1	0.87 /43	4.25 /94	3.40 /86	C /5.0	74	19
MUS	MFS PA Municipal Bond A	MFPAX	B	(800) 225-2606	10.19	B- /7.1	0.87 /43	4.24 /94	3.11 /82	C /4.9	73	18
MUS ●	Oppenheimer Rochester MN Muni	OPAMX	B	(888) 470-0862	12.73	B- /7.0	0.71 /40	4.39 /95	3.92 /92	C /5.1	78	11
MUS	Vanguard CA Interm-Term T-E Inv	VCAIX	B	(800) 662-7447	11.62	B- /7.0	-0.33 /12	3.00 /82	3.00 /80	C /4.8	25	4
GEI	Henderson Strategic Income A	HFAAX	B	(866) 443-6337	9.39	C+ /6.9	8.37 /75	4.33 /79	5.59 /89	C /5.0	90	9
LP	AIG Sr Floating Rate A	SASFX	B	(800) 858-8850	8.12	C+ /6.9	13.03 /85	3.01 /61	4.16 /74	C /5.0	88	8
MUS	Dupree NC Tax Free Income	NTFIX	B	(800) 866-0614	11.40	C+ /6.9	-0.14 /15	3.02 /82	2.74 /75	C /5.0	30	13
MUI	GuideMark Tax-Exempt Fixed Inc	GMTEX	B	(888) 278-5809	11.29	C+ /6.8	-0.44 /10	2.99 /82	2.27 /65	C /5.4	30	11
MUN	Federated Interm Muni Trust Y	FIMYX	B	(800) 341-7400	9.95	C+ /6.8	0.33 /33	2.87 /80	2.54 /71	C /5.1	25	22
MUS	Franklin MA Tax-Free Inc A	FMISX	B	(800) 342-5236	11.63	C+ /6.7	0.61 /39	4.08 /93	2.81 /76	C /5.5	75	28
MUS	Delaware Tax-Free Pennsylvania A	DELIX	B	(800) 523-1918	8.01	C+ /6.6	0.75 /41	4.06 /93	3.07 /81	C /5.3	72	14
MUI	Franklin Ohio Tax-Free Inc A	FTOIX	B	(800) 342-5236	12.56	C+ /6.4	0.51 /37	3.86 /91	2.94 /79	C+ /5.6	70	18
COI	WA Core Bond FI	WAPIX	B	(888) 425-6432	12.45	C+ /6.4	3.72 /61	3.42 /68	3.10 /59	C /5.5	70	23
MUN	T Rowe Price Summit Muni Intmdt	PRSMX	B	(800) 638-5660	11.75	C+ /6.3	-0.27 /13	2.66 /76	2.52 /71	C+ /6.0	24	24
MUS	Nuveen MD Muni Bond A	NMDAX	B	(800) 257-8787	10.57	C+ /6.3	0.62 /39	3.75 /90	2.69 /74	C+ /6.0	69	1
MUS	Franklin Florida Tax-Free Inc A	FRFLX	B	(800) 342-5236	10.88	C+ /6.2	1.02 /45	3.60 /89	2.41 /69	C+ /6.2	71	30
GES	Pioneer Strategic Income A	PSRAX	B	(800) 225-6292	10.73	C+ /6.2	9.79 /78	3.34 /66	4.12 /74	C+ /6.2	86	18
MUN	Franklin Federal Tax-Free Inc A	FKTIX	B	(800) 342-5236	12.05	C+ /6.2	0.56 /38	3.76 /90	3.21 /83	C+ /5.9	69	30
GEI	Baird Core Plus Bond Inv	BCOSX	B	(866) 442-2473	11.55	C+ /6.1	4.18 /63	3.12 /63	3.15 /60	C+ /5.8	66	17
MUS	MFS AL Municipal Bond Fund A	MFALX	B	(800) 225-2606	10.12	C+ /6.1	0.21 /29	3.75 /90	2.78 /76	C+ /6.3	70	18
MUS	Commerce Missouri T/F Intm Bd	CFMOX	B	(800) 995-6365	19.26	C+ /5.9	-0.10 /16	2.31 /69	2.00 /59	C+ /6.5	19	18
GEI	Voya Intermediate Bond Port Adv	IIBPX	B	(800) 992-0180	12.62	C+ /5.8	3.78 /61	2.91 /60	3.38 /64	C+ /6.3	63	8
GEI	TIAA-CREF Bond Retire	TIDRX	B	(800) 842-2252	10.51	C+ /5.8	3.42 /59	2.98 /61	2.98 /58	C+ /6.2	63	14
MUS	Franklin Georgia Tax-Free Inc A	FTGAX	B	(800) 342-5236	11.99	C+ /5.8	0.68 /40	3.56 /88	2.83 /77	C+ /6.2	67	21
MUS	CA Tax-Free Income Direct	CFNTX	B	(800) 955-9988	11.44	C /5.5	-0.48 /10	2.27 /68	2.36 /68	B- /7.0	20	14
GES	Touchstone Flexible Income A	FFSAX	B	(800) 543-0407	10.73	C /5.3	4.89 /66	3.98 /75	3.99 /72	C+ /6.9	85	10

● Denotes fund is closed to new investors

Section IV

Bottom 200 Bond Mutual Funds

A compilation of those

Fixed Income Mutual Funds

receiving the lowest TheStreet Investment Ratings.

Funds are listed in order by Overall Investment Rating.

Section IV Contents

This section contains a summary analysis of each of the bottom 200 bond mutual funds as determined by their overall TheStreet Investment Rating. Typically, these funds have invested in securities with excessive credit and/or interest rate risk. As such, these are the funds that you should generally avoid since they have historically underperformed most other mutual funds given the level of risk in their underlying investments.

In order to optimize the utility of our top and bottom fund lists, rather than listing all funds in a multi-class series, a single fund from each series is selected for display as the primary share class. Whenever possible, the selected fund is one that a retail investor would be most likely to choose. This share class may not be appropriate for every investor, so please consult with your financial advisor, the fund company, and the fund's prospectus before placing your trade.

1. Fund Type   The mutual fund's peer category based on its investment objective as stated in its prospectus.

COH	Corporate - High Yield	MMT	Money Market - Treas.
COI	Corporate - Inv. Grade	MTG	Mortgage
EM	Emerging Market	MUH	Municipal - High Yield
GEN	General	MUI	Municipal - Insured
GEI	General - Inv. Grade	MUN	Municipal - National
GEL	General - Long Term	MUS	Municipal - Single State
GES	General - Short & Interm.	USL	U.S. Gov.- Long Term
GL	Global	USS	U.S. Gov. - Short & Interm
LP	Loan Participation	USA	U.S. Gov. - Agency
MMF	Money Mkt - Tax Exempt	US	U.S. Gov. - Treasury

A blank fund type means that the mutual fund has not yet been categorized.

2. Fund Name   The name of the mutual fund as stated in its prospectus, which can sometimes differ slightly from the name that the company uses for advertising. If you cannot find the particular mutual fund you are interested in, or if you have any doubts regarding the precise name, verify the information with your broker or on your account statement. Also, use the fund's ticker symbol for confirmation. (See column 3.)

3. Ticker Symbol   The unique alphabetic symbol used for identifying and trading a specific mutual fund. No two funds can have the same ticker symbol, and the ticker symbol for mutual funds always ends with an "X".

A handful of funds currently show no associated ticker symbol. This means that the fund is either small or new since the NASD only assigns a ticker symbol to funds with at least $25 million in assets or 1,000 shareholders.

4. Overall Investment Rating

Our overall rating is measured on a scale from A to E based on each fund's risk-adjusted performance. Please see page 11 for specific descriptions of each letter grade. Also, refer to page 7 for information on how our ratings are derived. Most important, when using this rating, please be sure to consider the warnings beginning on page 13 regarding the ratings' limitations and the underlying assumptions.

5. Phone

The telephone number of the company managing the fund. Call this number to receive a prospectus or other information about the fund.

6. Net Asset Value (NAV)

The fund's share price as of the date indicated. A fund's NAV is computed by dividing the value of the fund's asset holdings, less accrued fees and expenses, by the number of its shares outstanding.

7. Performance Rating/Points

A letter grade rating based solely on the mutual fund's financial performance over the trailing three years, without any consideration for the amount of risk the fund poses. Like the overall Investment Rating, the Performance Rating is measured on a scale from A to E for ease of interpretation. The points score indicates where the Performance Rating falls on a scale of 0 to 10.

In the case of funds investing in municipal or other tax-free securities, this rating is based on the taxable equivalent return of the fund assuming the maximum marginal U.S. tax rate (35%).

8. 1-Year Total Return

The total return the fund has provided investors over the preceding twelve months. This total return figure is computed based on the fund's dividend distributions and share price appreciation/depreciation during the period, net of the expenses and fees it imposes on its shareholders. Although the total return figure does not reflect an adjustment for any loads the fund may carry, such adjustments have been made in deriving TheStreet Investment Ratings.

9. 1-Year Total Return Percentile

The fund's percentile rank based on its one-year performance compared to that of all other fixed income funds in existence for at least one year. A score of 99 is the highest possible, indicating that the fund outperformed 99% of the other mutual funds. Zero is the lowest possible percentile score.

In the case of funds investing in municipal or other tax-free securities, this percentile rank is based on the taxable equivalent return of the fund assuming the maximum marginal U.S. tax rate (35%).

10. 3-Year Total Return

The total annual return the fund has provided investors over the preceding three years.

11.	**3-Year Total Return Percentile**	The fund's percentile rank based on its three-year performance compared to that of all other fixed income funds in existence for at least three years. A score of 99 is the highest possible, indicating that the fund outperformed 99% of the other mutual funds. Zero is the lowest possible percentile score.
		In the case of funds investing in municipal or other tax-free securities, this percentile rank is based on the taxable equivalent return of the fund assuming the maximum marginal U.S. tax rate (35%).
12.	**5-Year Total Return**	The total annual return the fund has provided investors over the preceding five years.
13.	**5-Year Total Return Percentile**	The fund's percentile rank based on its five-year performance compared to that of all other fixed income funds in existence for at least five years. A score of 99 is the highest possible, indicating that the fund outperformed 99% of the other mutual funds. Zero is the lowest possible percentile score.
		In the case of funds investing in municipal or other tax-free securities, this percentile rank is based on the taxable equivalent return of the fund assuming the maximum marginal U.S. tax rate (35%).
14.	**Risk Rating/Points**	A letter grade rating based solely on the mutual fund's risk as determined by its monthly performance volatility over the trailing three years and the underlying credit risk and interest rate risk of its investment portfolio. The risk rating does not take into consideration the overall financial performance the fund has achieved or the total return it has provided to its shareholders. Like the overall Investment Rating, the Risk Rating is measured on a scale from A to E for ease of interpretation. The points score indicates where the Risk Rating falls on a scale of 0 to 10.
15.	**Manager Quality Percentile**	The manager quality percentile is based on a ranking of the fund's alpha, a statistical measure representing the difference between a fund's actual returns and its expected performance given its level of risk. Fund managers who have been able to exceed the fund's statistically expected performance receive a high percentile rank with 99 representing the highest possible score. At the other end of the spectrum, fund managers who have actually detracted from the fund's expected performance receive a low percentile rank with 0 representing the lowest possible score.
16.	**Manager Tenure**	The number of years the current manager has been managing the fund. Since fund managers who deliver substandard returns are usually replaced, a long tenure is usually a good sign that shareholders are satisfied that the fund is achieving its stated objectives.

Fund Type	Fund Name	Ticker Symbol	Overall Investment Rating	Phone	Net Asset Value As of 2/28/17	Performance Rating/Pts	1Yr / Pct	3Yr / Pct	5Yr / Pct	Risk Rating/Pts	Mgr. Quality Pct	Mgr. Tenure (Years)
GEI	Rydex Wekng Dlr 2x Stgry A	RYWDX	E-	(800) 820-0888	64.26	E- /0.0	-8.07 /0	-15.95 /0	-10.79 /0	E- /0.0	0	12
USS	PIMCO StocksPLUS Short A	PSSAX	E-	(800) 426-0107	9.25	E- /0.0	-14.51 /0	-9.78 /0	-11.51 /0	E /0.3	0	3
MTG	ProFunds-Falling US Dollar Svc	FDPSX	E-	(888) 776-3637	15.64	E- /0.0	-6.29 /0	-10.51 /0	-7.63 /0	E+ /0.7	0	8
COH	Rydex Inv High Yld Strtgy A	RYILX	E-	(800) 820-0888	66.16	E- /0.0	-11.79 /0	-8.06 /0	-10.20 /0	D /1.7	0	10
COH	Access Flex Bear High Yield Inv	AFBIX	E-	(888) 776-3637	39.06	E- /0.0	-14.53 /0	-8.63 /0	-11.20 /0	D /1.6	0	12
GEI	Credit Suisse Cmdty Rtn Strat A	CRSAX	E-	(877) 927-2874	5.01	E- /0.0	16.51 /91	-12.70 /0	-10.08 /0	E- /0.0	0	11
GEI	Credit Suisse Commdty Ret Str	CCRSX	E-	(877) 927-2874	4.42	E- /0.0	16.32 /91	-12.69 /0	-10.11 /0	E- /0.0	0	11
USS	Rydex Inv Govt Lg Bd Stgy A	RYAQX	E-	(800) 820-0888	34.46	E- /0.0	3.98 /62	-8.57 /0	-5.24 /0	E- /0.0	1	9
GL	Federated Prudent DollarBear A	PSAFX	E-	(800) 341-7400	9.42	E- /0.0	-3.29 /0	-5.52 /0	-4.82 /0	D- /1.2	0	3
US	Direxion Mo 7-10 Year Tr Br 2X Inv	DXKSX	E-	(800) 851-0511	30.38	E- /0.0	3.05 /57	-8.69 /0	-7.30 /0	E- /0.2	0	13
GL	American Century Intl Bond A	AIBDX	E-	(800) 345-6488	12.12	E- /0.0	-1.38 /2	-3.66 /1	-2.36 /1	E /0.5	8	8
EM	EuroPac International Bond A	EPIBX	E-	(888) 558-5851	8.13	E- /0.0	5.72 /69	-4.84 /0	-3.25 /1	E /0.4	1	7
GL	Federated Global Total Return Bd	FTIIX	E-	(800) 341-7400	9.50	E- /0.0	-3.72 /0	-2.95 /1	-2.25 /1	E /0.5	21	15
GL	Wells Fargo Intl Bd A	ESIYX	E-	(800) 222-8222	9.62	E- /0.0	0.10 /22	-3.01 /1	-1.51 /2	E /0.3	33	24
EM	Dreyfus Eme Mkts Dbt LC A	DDBAX	E-	(800) 782-6620	11.50	E- /0.0	11.43 /82	-4.81 /0	-3.53 /0	E- /0.1	2	9
EM	Invesco Emerg Mkts Flexible Bond	IAEMX	E-	(800) 959-4246	6.56	E- /0.0	7.67 /74	-4.59 /0	-4.03 /0	E /0.5	0	2
GL	Laudus Mondrian Intl Govt Fxd Inc	LIFNX	E-	(800) 407-0256	9.22	E- /0.0	-2.67 /0	-3.16 /1	-2.78 /1	E /0.4	20	N/A
GL	Templeton Global Currency A	ICPHX	E-	(800) 342-5236	7.91	E- /0.0	4.08 /62	-4.63 /0	-3.74 /0	D- /1.4	0	16
GL	Columbia Global Bond A	IGBFX	E-	(800) 345-6611	5.62	E- /0.0	0.72 /36	-2.45 /2	-2.00 /1	D /1.8	9	4
GES	AB All Mkt Real Return A	AMTAX	E-	(800) 221-5672	8.51	E- /0.0	23.44 /98	-6.72 /0	-4.09 /0	E- /0.0	0	2
GL	T Rowe Price Intl Bond	RPIBX	E-	(800) 638-5660	8.47	E- /0.0	1.05 /40	-2.59 /1	-1.15 /2	E /0.4	37	3
EM	T Rowe Price Inst Intl Bd	RPIIX	E-	(800) 638-5660	8.33	E- /0.0	1.26 /42	-2.29 /2	-0.74 /2	E /0.4	55	3
EM	Goldman Sachs Local Emg Mkt	GAMDX	E-	(800) 526-7384	6.22	E- /0.1	12.70 /84	-3.74 /1	-3.37 /0	E- /0.0	12	9
GL	PACE Global Fx Inc Inve A	PWFAX	E-	(888) 793-8637	9.67	E- /0.1	-0.77 /6	-0.28 /4	-0.61 /3	E+ /0.8	84	22
GL	Invesco World Bond A	AUBAX	E-	(800) 959-4246	10.02	E- /0.1	4.88 /66	-1.37 /2	0.11 /15	E+ /0.6	75	7
GL	PIMCO Foreign Bd Fd (Unhgd) A	PFUAX	E-	(800) 426-0107	9.47	E- /0.1	4.04 /62	-1.08 /3	-0.22 /4	E /0.5	79	3
LP	Driehaus Select Credit Fund	DRSLX	E-	(800) 560-6111	8.03	E- /0.1	9.42 /78	-3.53 /1	-0.36 /3	D /1.8	0	7
GL	Dreyfus Intl Bond A	DIBAX	E-	(800) 645-6561	15.03	E- /0.1	2.43 /53	-0.56 /3	0.53 /22	D- /1.0	79	11
EM	PIMCO Emerging Local Bond A	PELAX	E-	(800) 426-0107	7.21	E- /0.1	14.35 /87	-3.27 /1	-3.50 /0	E- /0.1	20	11
GL	American Funds Cap World Bond	CWBFX	E-	(800) 421-0180	19.32	E- /0.2	2.00 /49	-0.31 /4	0.46 /21	D /2.0	79	18
GL	MFS Global Bond Fund A	MGBAX	E-	(800) 225-2606	8.60	E- /0.2	1.37 /43	-1.09 /3	-1.32 /2	D- /1.5	70	7
GL	Lord Abbett Emerg Mkts Currency	LDMAX	E-	(888) 522-2388	5.26	E- /0.2	10.04 /79	-2.23 /2	-1.70 /1	E /0.5	18	10
US	American Century MA Real Rtn A	ASIDX	E-	(800) 345-6488	9.68	E- /0.2	9.50 /78	-1.49 /2	-1.47 /2	D /2.0	2	7
GL	PIMCO Emerging Markets	PLMAX	E-	(800) 426-0107	8.91	E- /0.2	11.00 /81	-1.92 /2	-1.57 /2	E /0.5	26	12
GL	Prudential Global Total Return A	GTRAX	E-	(800) 225-1852	6.39	E /0.4	2.83 /55	0.93 /26	2.12 /44	E+ /0.9	91	15
GL	Janus Global Bond A	JGBAX	E	(800) 295-2687	9.34	E- /0.1	--	-0.25 /4	1.01 /27	D+ /2.5	76	3
GEI	Dreyfus Opportunistic Fixed Inc A	DSTAX	E	(800) 782-6620	11.28	E- /0.2	5.60 /69	-1.06 /3	1.23 /30	C- /3.1	8	7
USL	● SunAmerica 2020 High Watermark	HWKAX	E	(800) 858-8850	8.75	E- /0.2	-0.87 /5	1.15 /30	0.59 /22	C /5.4	25	13
USS	Nationwide Govt Bond A	NUSAX	E	(800) 848-0920	9.92	E /0.3	-2.15 /1	0.76 /24	0.62 /23	C /4.4	9	20
GEI	Franklin Real Return A	FRRAX	E	(800) 342-5236	10.24	E /0.3	7.34 /73	-0.65 /3	-0.07 /4	C- /3.0	3	13
GL	Loomis Sayles Glbl Bd Ret	LSGLX	E	(800) 633-3330	15.39	E /0.3	4.07 /62	-0.76 /3	0.24 /19	D /1.9	74	17
GL	Voya Global Bond A	INGBX	E	(800) 992-0180	9.76	E /0.4	4.32 /64	-0.20 /4	0.49 /21	D+ /2.4	78	6
GEI	Principal Infl Prot A	PITAX	E	(800) 222-5852	8.45	E /0.5	2.47 /53	0.71 /23	-0.07 /5	D+ /2.9	2	7
MUS	New Hampshire Municipal	NHMUX	E	(800) 601-5593	10.42	E /0.5	-2.52 /0	1.44 /47	1.30 /42	C- /4.1	2	14
GL	PIMCO Glb Advantage Strategy Bd	PGSAX	E	(800) 426-0107	10.44	E+ /0.7	8.66 /76	-0.47 /4	0.27 /19	D /2.1	67	6
USS	MFS Inflation Adjusted Bond A	MIAAX	E	(800) 225-2606	10.39	E+ /0.9	2.44 /53	1.06 /28	-0.06 /5	C- /3.1	16	14
GES	BlackRock Inflation Prot Bond Inv	BPRAX	E	(800) 441-7762	10.52	D- /1.0	3.25 /58	0.84 /25	0.10 /15	C- /3.0	4	7
USS	American Ind US Infl Protected A	FNIHX	E	(866) 410-2006	10.67	D- /1.1	2.63 /54	1.07 /29	0.02 /7	D+ /2.6	17	11
GL	J Hancock Global Bond NAV		E	(800) 257-3336	12.01	D- /1.1	1.89 /48	0.26 /18	0.95 /27	D /1.6	86	2
GES	Fidelity Adv Inflation-Protect Bd A	FIPAX	E	(800) 522-7297	11.93	D- /1.4	2.54 /53	1.10 /29	0.02 /7	C- /3.0	3	13
GL	Nuveen Inflation Protected Sec A	FAIPX	E	(800) 257-8787	11.07	D- /1.5	2.69 /55	1.14 /30	0.31 /20	C- /3.2	85	13
GL	BlackRock Strategic Global Bd Inv	MDWIX	E	(800) 441-7762	5.88	D- /1.5	5.32 /68	0.77 /24	2.09 /43	D+ /2.6	86	6

● Denotes fund is closed to new investors

						PERFORMANCE				RISK	FUND MGR	
	99 Pct = Best 0 Pct = Worst				Net Asset Value As of 2/28/17	Perform-ance Rating/Pts	Annualized Total Return Through 2/28/17			Risk Rating/Pts	Mgr. Quality Pct	Mgr. Tenure (Years)
Fund Type	Fund Name	Ticker Symbol	Overall Investment Rating	Phone			1Yr / Pct	3Yr / Pct	5Yr / Pct			
GL	Putnam Global Income A	PGGIX	E	(800) 225-1581	11.83	D /1.7	6.24 /71	0.62 /22	1.77 /39	D+ /2.9	82	23
GL	STAAR AltCat	SITAX	E	(800) 332-7738	14.19	D /1.8	14.16 /87	-2.44 / 2	2.72 /53	E- / 0.2	3	20
GL	SunAmerica VAL Co I Intl Govt Bd	VCIFX	E	(800) 858-8850	11.34	D /1.8	2.16 /50	0.46 /20	0.73 /24	D- /1.5	87	8
GEI	Cutler Fixed Income Fund	CALFX	E	(888) 288-5374	8.68	D /1.9	-0.31 /13	1.03 /28	0.71 /24	D+ /2.5	8	30
GEI	MassMutual Premier Infl-PI A	MPSAX	E	(800) 542-6767	10.24	D /1.9	3.48 /60	1.51 /35	0.35 /20	C- /3.0	6	14
GL	LM BW Global Opportunities Bond	GOBAX	E	(877) 534-4627	10.46	D /2.0	6.14 /71	0.92 /26	1.65 /37	E / 0.4	91	11
GL	PIMCO Global Bond (Unhedged) D	PGBDX	E	(800) 426-0107	9.13	D /2.1	3.96 /62	0.31 /19	0.85 /25	D /1.9	86	3
GL	Aberdeen Global Unconstrained FI	CUGAX	E	(866) 667-9231	10.15	D /2.1	9.55 /78	0.43 /20	0.69 /23	D+ /2.4	82	8
GEI	Goldman Sachs Infl Prot Secs A	GSAPX	E	(800) 526-7384	10.48	D /2.1	3.30 /58	1.37 /33	0.39 /20	C- /3.1	7	10
USS	WA Inflation Indexed Plus Bond FI	WATPX	E	(888) 425-6432	11.02	D /2.1	2.13 /50	0.40 /20	-0.27 / 4	C- /3.1	7	3
GEI	PIMCO Real Return A	PRTNX	E	(800) 426-0107	11.09	D /2.1	4.85 /66	1.07 /29	0.42 /21	D /2.1	2	10
GEI	J Hancock Absolute Ret Curr A	JCUAX	E	(800) 257-3336	9.41	D /2.1	3.18 /58	1.09 /29	2.47 /49	E+ / 0.7	87	6
GEI	VY BlackRock Infl Pro Bond Adv	IBRAX	E	(800) 992-0180	9.26	D /2.1	2.56 /54	0.45 /20	-0.39 / 3	D+ /2.8	1	7
GEI	Voya Global Bond Portfolio Adv	IOSAX	E	(800) 992-0180	10.44	D /2.2	5.02 /67	0.04 / 9	0.27 /19	D /2.2	1	6
GL	AMG Mgrs Global Income Opp N	MGGBX	E	(800) 548-4539	19.59	D /2.2	6.82 /72	0.20 /16	1.52 /35	D- /1.0	86	15
GL	LM BW International Opptys Bd IS	LMOTX	E	(877) 534-4627	11.14	D /2.2	5.59 /69	-0.08 / 5	1.60 /36	E / 0.4	87	8
USL	Deutsche Global Inflation A	TIPAX	E	(800) 728-3337	10.10	D+ /2.3	2.88 /56	1.44 /34	-0.07 / 4	D+ /2.3	22	7
US	Direxion Mo 7-10 Year Tr Bl 2X Inv	DXKLX	E	(800) 851-0511	34.14	D+ /2.4	-8.47 / 0	3.22 /65	1.44 /33	E- /0.2	1	11
EM	Deutsche Enh Emg Mrkts Fxd Inc	SZEAX	E	(800) 728-3337	9.41	D+ /2.7	10.98 /81	0.52 /21	1.63 /37	E+ / 0.9	82	6
COH	Catalyst/SMH High Income A	HIIFX	E	(866) 447-4228	3.91	C- /3.3	46.00 /99	-5.28 / 0	-1.69 / 1	E- / 0.0	0	9
EM	Eaton Vance Emer Market Local	EEIAX	E	(800) 262-1122	6.17	C- /3.4	17.57 /93	-0.11 / 5	-2.49 / 1	E- / 0.1	89	9
EM	Oppenheimer Em Mkts Local Debt	OEMAX	E	(888) 470-0862	7.17	C- /3.5	15.90 /90	0.05 / 9	-0.79 / 2	E- / 0.2	89	2
GL	TCW Emg Mkts Local Currency Inc	TGWNX	E	(800) 386-3829	9.11	C- /3.7	16.20 /91	-1.37 / 2	-1.55 / 2	E- / 0.1	80	7
USS	First Inv Government A	FIGVX	E+	(800) 423-4026	10.46	E- /0.1	-1.52 / 2	0.59 /22	0.41 /21	B / 7.8	16	5
USS	AIG US Gov Sec A	SGTAX	E+	(800) 858-8850	9.17	E- /0.1	-2.83 / 0	0.69 /23	0.02 / 7	C+ /6.6	16	3
MUN	Saratoga Adv Tr-Municipal Bond C	SMBCX	E+	(800) 807-3863	9.09	E- /0.2	-2.01 / 1	-0.27 / 4	-0.43 / 3	B- /7.1	1	8
USS	Waddell & Reed Adv Gov Secs A	UNGVX	E+	(888) 923-3355	5.41	E /0.3	-1.22 / 3	0.93 /27	0.27 /19	C+ /6.6	17	2
GEI	TETON Westwood Interm Bond A	WEAIX	E+	(800) 422-3554	11.24	E /0.4	0.53 /34	0.93 /26	0.59 /22	B / 7.6	8	18
USS	American Century Govt Bond A	ABTAX	E+	(800) 345-6488	10.97	E /0.4	-1.02 / 4	1.40 /33	0.86 /25	B- /7.2	32	15
USS	MFS Government Securities Fund	MFGSX	E+	(800) 225-2606	9.84	E /0.4	-0.96 / 4	1.42 /34	1.00 /27	B- /7.4	35	11
USS	Fidelity Adv Govt Inc A	FVIAX	E+	(800) 522-7297	10.22	E /0.5	-1.14 / 3	1.58 /36	1.18 /30	C+ /6.1	34	10
USS	Invesco US Government A	AGOVX	E+	(800) 959-4246	8.84	E /0.5	-0.14 /15	1.51 /35	0.98 /27	C+ /6.9	35	8
GL	Eaton Vance Dvsfd Currency	EAIIX	E+	(800) 262-1122	8.81	E+ /0.6	5.38 /68	0.16 /15	-0.46 / 3	C+ /5.7	65	9
USS	Wells Fargo Govt Secs A	SGVDX	E+	(800) 222-8222	10.88	E+ /0.8	-0.64 / 8	1.73 /39	1.32 /32	C+ /6.9	51	7
GL	Goldman Sachs Strategic Income	GSZAX	E+	(800) 526-7384	9.69	E+ /0.9	6.40 /71	-0.05 / 5	3.03 /58	C / 5.0	26	7
USS	Prudential Government Income A	PGVAX	E+	(800) 225-1852	9.55	D- /1.0	-0.24 /14	1.74 /39	1.51 /35	C+ /6.5	49	14
US	Hartford Inflation Plus A	HIPAX	E+	(888) 843-7824	10.90	D- /1.2	3.56 /60	0.86 /25	-0.19 / 4	C / 5.0	30	2
MUN	Nationwide HighMark Natl Int TFB	NWJOX	E+	(800) 848-0920	10.52	D- /1.4	-1.50 / 2	1.15 /39	1.40 /44	C / 5.3	3	21
GEI	Dreyfus Interm Term Inc A	DRITX	E+	(800) 645-6561	13.35	D /1.6	2.19 /51	1.48 /35	2.02 /42	C+ /5.9	12	9
GL	DFA Selectively Hedged Glb FI Ptf	DFSHX	E+	(800) 984-9472	9.57	D /1.7	4.47 /64	-0.37 / 4	0.07 /13	C- / 4.0	63	N/A
MUN	American Century Int Tax-Fr Bd A	TWWOX	E+	(800) 345-6488	11.19	D /1.7	-0.76 / 6	1.86 /59	1.67 /51	C+ /6.1	8	11
GEI	Federated Real Return Bond A	RRFAX	E+	(800) 341-7400	10.44	D /1.7	5.81 /70	0.68 /23	0.24 /19	C / 4.7	28	11
GL	Deutsche Enhanced Global Bond A	SZGAX	E+	(800) 728-3337	9.15	D /1.8	3.89 /62	1.04 /28	1.41 /33	C- / 3.5	84	6
USS	JPMorgan Government Bond A	OGGAX	E+	(800) 480-4111	10.54	D /1.8	-0.57 / 9	1.92 /42	1.35 /32	C+ /5.6	52	21
MUS	Wilmington NY Municipal Bond A	VNYFX	E+	(800) 336-9970	10.49	D /1.9	-1.09 / 4	2.01 /63	1.83 /55	C / 4.7	7	5
GES	Wilmington Broad Market Bond A	AKIRX	E+	(800) 336-9970	9.77	D /2.0	1.47 /44	2.02 /44	2.01 /42	C / 5.3	18	21
MUS	PNC Ohio Intermediate Tax-Ex	POXAX	E+	(800) 551-2145	10.41	D+ /2.3	-1.19 / 3	1.80 /57	1.49 /46	C / 5.3	6	8
MUN	Wilmington Muni Bond A	WTABX	E+	(800) 336-9970	13.06	D+ /2.3	-0.84 / 6	2.16 /66	2.08 /61	C / 4.7	8	6
GL	Waddell & Reed Adv Global Bond	UNHHX	E+	(888) 923-3355	3.71	D+ /2.4	8.62 /76	1.02 /28	1.81 /39	D+ /2.8	81	15
USS	● Thrivent Government Bond A	TBFAX	E+	(800) 847-4836	9.89	D+ /2.4	-0.50 / 9	1.87 /41	1.13 /29	C / 4.3	34	7
USS	Transamerica Prt Inflation-Prot Sec	DVIGX	E+	(888) 233-4339	11.15	D+ /2.4	2.50 /53	0.69 /23	0.03 / 9	D+ /2.9	11	7
US	Columbia US Treasury Index A	LUTAX	E+	(800) 345-6611	11.02	D+ /2.5	-1.49 / 2	1.56 /36	0.99 /27	C- /4.2	28	7

● Denotes fund is closed to new investors

Fund Type	Fund Name	Ticker Symbol	Overall Investment Rating	Phone	Net Asset Value As of 2/28/17	PERFORMANCE Performance Rating/Pts	Annualized Total Return Through 2/28/17 1Yr / Pct	3Yr / Pct	5Yr / Pct	RISK Risk Rating/Pts	FUND MGR Mgr. Quality Pct	Mgr. Tenure (Years)
US	T Rowe Price US Treas Intmdt	PRTIX	E+	(800) 638-5660	5.74	D+ /2.5	-1.73 / 1	1.58 / 36	1.00 / 27	C- / 3.5	25	10
MUH	JPMorgan CA Tax Free Bond A	JCBAX	E+	(800) 480-4111	10.78	D+ /2.5	-0.95 / 5	2.09 / 65	2.11 / 61	C- / 4.2	11	13
GEI	Dreyfus Infl Adjusted Sec Inv	DIAVX	E+	(800) 645-6561	12.64	D+ /2.6	2.04 / 49	0.75 / 24	-0.18 / 4	C- / 3.5	6	12
MUN	PACE Muni Fxd Inc Inve A	PMUAX	E+	(888) 793-8637	12.86	D+ /2.6	-0.82 / 6	2.32 / 69	2.02 / 59	C / 4.5	9	17
US	Northern US Treasury Index	BTIAX	E+	(800) 637-1380	21.39	D+ /2.9	-1.43 / 2	1.81 / 40	1.22 / 30	C- / 4.2	37	8
GL	GuideStone Infl Protected Bd Inv	GIPZX	E+	(888) 984-8433	10.38	C- /3.0	2.61 / 54	1.00 / 28	0.06 / 12	C- / 3.4	83	3
GEI	TIAA-CREF Infltn Linkd Bd Retail	TCILX	E+	(800) 842-2252	11.19	C- /3.0	2.10 / 50	1.01 / 28	0.01 / 5	C- / 3.5	4	9
MUS	Dreyfus MA Muni A	PSMAX	E+	(800) 782-6620	11.41	C- /3.0	-1.43 / 2	2.69 / 77	1.90 / 56	C- / 4.0	11	6
COI	AB Bond Inflation Strat A	ABNAX	E+	(800) 221-5672	10.86	C- /3.0	5.76 / 69	1.64 / 37	0.92 / 26	C- / 3.8	11	7
US	Vanguard Interm-Term Treasury	VFITX	E+	(800) 662-7447	11.14	C- /3.2	-1.26 / 3	1.93 / 42	1.40 / 33	C- / 3.9	47	2
USS	Vanguard Intm-Term Govt Bd Idx	VSIGX	E+	(800) 662-7447	21.70	C- /3.2	-1.25 / 3	1.95 / 42	1.46 / 34	C- / 4.1	34	4
GEI	American Century Infl Adj Bd A	AIAVX	E+	(800) 345-6488	11.67	C- /3.3	3.44 / 59	1.12 / 29	0.02 / 7	D+ / 2.9	4	11
GL	Oppenheimer Intl Bond A	OIBAX	E+	(888) 470-0862	5.72	C- /3.4	9.42 / 78	1.57 / 36	1.55 / 35	D / 2.0	90	4
US	Fidelity Intrm Treasury Inv	FIBIX	E+	(800) 544-8544	10.70	C- /3.4	-2.09 / 1	2.33 / 49	1.56 / 35	D+ / 2.4	35	3
USL	Loomis Sayles Infl Prot Sec Inst	LSGSX	E+	(800) 633-3330	10.49	C- /3.4	3.03 / 57	1.26 / 31	0.40 / 20	D+ / 2.7	26	5
US	T Rowe Price Infla-Protect Bond	PRIPX	E+	(800) 638-5660	11.89	C- /3.5	2.49 / 53	1.42 / 34	0.37 / 20	C- / 3.1	30	15
GEN	Iron Strategic Income Fd Inv	IRNIX	E+	(800) 408-4682	10.79	C- /3.5	8.01 / 74	0.41 / 20	2.48 / 49	C- / 3.8	54	11
GEI	Natixis Loomis Sayles Invst Gr Bd	LIGRX	E+	(800) 225-5478	10.99	C- /3.6	8.54 / 75	1.63 / 37	3.01 / 58	D+ / 2.5	31	21
GL	Leader Total Return Inv	LCTRX	E+	(800) 711-9164	9.62	C- /3.6	12.69 / 84	-0.49 / 4	3.49 / 65	D / 2.0	31	7
USS	DFA Intmdt Govt Fx Inc Inst	DFIGX	E+	(800) 984-9472	12.44	C- /3.6	-1.27 / 3	2.32 / 48	1.75 / 38	C- / 3.5	48	7
GEI	Columbia Inflation Protected Sec A	APSAX	E+	(800) 345-6611	9.38	C- /3.7	10.09 / 79	1.02 / 28	0.33 / 20	D / 1.7	5	5
GEI	Wells Fargo Real Return A	IPBAX	E+	(800) 222-8222	9.99	C- /3.7	5.23 / 68	2.35 / 49	0.76 / 24	D+ / 2.4	18	12
GL	Ivy Global Bond A	IVSAX	E+	(800) 777-6472	9.67	C- /3.7	10.48 / 80	1.57 / 36	2.18 / 44	D+ / 2.6	86	9
GL	Templeton International Bond A	TBOAX	E+	(800) 342-5236	10.83	C- /3.8	11.92 / 83	0.20 / 16	1.32 / 32	D- / 1.2	56	10
GEI	J Hancock Real Return Bond NAV		E+	(800) 257-3336	11.14	C- /3.9	4.61 / 65	1.24 / 31	0.47 / 21	D+ / 2.5	4	9
GL	Aberdeen Asia Bond Inst Service	ABISX	E+	(866) 667-9231	10.01	C- /3.9	5.26 / 68	1.40 / 33	0.51 / 21	D- / 1.3	90	10
GEI	Schwab Trs Inflation Prot Sec	SWRSX	E+	(800) 407-0256	11.11	C- /4.0	3.10 / 57	1.68 / 38	0.54 / 22	D+ / 2.8	8	11
US	Harbor Real Return Inst	HARRX	E+	(800) 422-1050	9.42	C- /4.1	5.04 / 67	1.30 / 32	0.53 / 22	D / 2.2	31	12
USS	Vanguard Infltn Pro Sec Inv	VIPSX	E+	(800) 662-7447	13.16	C- /4.2	3.24 / 58	1.77 / 39	0.64 / 23	D+ / 2.7	35	6
US	DFA Infltn Protected Sec Port Inst	DIPSX	E+	(800) 984-9472	11.86	C /4.3	3.02 / 57	1.85 / 40	0.74 / 24	D+ / 2.3	38	11
GES	USAA Real Return Fund	USRRX	E+	(800) 382-8722	10.12	C /4.4	12.22 / 84	0.16 / 15	1.55 / 35	D- / 1.0	3	N/A
COI	Oppenheimer Corporate Bond A	OFIAX	E+	(888) 470-0862	10.73	C /4.4	6.36 / 71	2.93 / 60	4.20 / 75	D+ / 2.7	19	7
GES	Northeast Investors Trust	NTHEX	E+	(800) 225-6704	4.74	C /4.8	35.60 / 99	-3.55 / 1	2.53 / 50	E- / 0.0	2	N/A
USS	Hussman Strategic Total Return	HSTRX	E+	(800) 487-7626	12.04	C /4.8	3.60 / 60	2.77 / 57	0.57 / 22	D- / 1.0	71	15
USL	PIMCO Long Term US Govt A	PFGAX	E+	(800) 426-0107	6.02	C /4.9	-3.95 / 0	5.46 / 88	2.99 / 58	E- / 0.1	14	10
EM	SEI Inst Intl Emerging Mkts Debt F	SITEX	E+	(800) 342-5734	9.79	C /4.9	12.88 / 85	0.67 / 23	0.61 / 23	E- / 0.2	91	17
USA	ProFunds-US Government Plus	GVPSX	E+	(888) 776-3637	49.04	C /5.0	-8.64 / 0	5.62 / 89	1.47 / 34	E- / 0.0	1	8
USL	Rydex Govt Lg Bd 1.2x Strgy A	RYABX	E+	(800) 820-0888	51.50	C /5.0	-7.67 / 0	6.91 / 96	3.81 / 70	E- / 0.0	1	23
COI	Federated Emerging Mkt Debt A	IHIAX	E+	(800) 341-7400	8.47	C /5.2	11.94 / 83	1.84 / 40	2.21 / 45	E / 0.3	7	4
GES	Putnam Diversified Income A	PDINX	E+	(800) 225-1581	7.05	C /5.3	15.03 / 89	1.18 / 30	3.84 / 70	D- / 1.4	93	23
GEI	American Century Zero Cpn 2025	BTTRX	E+	(800) 345-6488	96.09	C+ /5.6	-2.97 / 0	4.27 / 78	2.78 / 54	E+ / 0.7	6	11
GEI	Calvert Long Term Income A	CLDAX	E+	(800) 368-2745	16.56	C+ /5.9	5.47 / 68	4.70 / 83	4.56 / 79	E / 0.5	10	4
US	Dreyfus US Treasury Long Term	DRGBX	E+	(800) 645-6561	18.40	C+ /6.1	-4.72 / 0	5.29 / 87	2.53 / 50	E- / 0.2	37	9
US	T Rowe Price US Treas Long-Term	PRULX	E+	(800) 638-5660	12.36	C+ /6.1	-4.70 / 0	5.33 / 87	2.67 / 52	E- / 0.2	31	14
USS	Nuveen Intermediate Government	FIGAX	D-	(800) 257-8787	8.65	E- /0.2	-1.63 / 1	0.54 / 21	0.59 / 22	B / 8.1	17	15
USS	Manor Bond Fund	MNRBX	D-	(800) 787-3334	10.30	E- /0.2	-1.81 / 1	-0.38 / 4	-0.40 / 3	B+ / 8.8	7	19
GEI	Saratoga Adv Tr Inv Qlty Bond C	SQBCX	D-	(800) 807-3863	9.58	E /0.3	0.20 / 26	-0.01 / 5	-0.04 / 5	B+ / 8.7	7	2
US	JPMorgan Treasury and Agency A	OTABX	D-	(800) 480-4111	9.34	E /0.3	-0.27 / 13	0.20 / 16	0.12 / 16	A- / 9.2	26	N/A
USS	Putnam American Government A	PAGVX	D-	(800) 225-1581	8.61	E /0.3	0.33 / 30	0.70 / 23	1.16 / 30	B+ / 8.5	33	10
USS	Federated USG Sec:2-5yrs R	FIGKX	D-	(800) 341-7400	10.88	E /0.3	-1.06 / 4	-0.14 / 5	-0.48 / 3	B+ / 8.4	7	4
MUN	Fidelity Adv Ltd Term Muni Inc A	FASHX	D-	(800) 522-7297	10.53	E /0.3	-0.57 / 9	0.57 / 26	0.76 / 30	B+ / 8.7	10	14
MUN	PNC Tax Exempt Limited Mat Bond	PDLAX	D-	(800) 551-2145	10.33	E /0.4	-0.66 / 7	0.70 / 29	0.69 / 28	B+ / 8.6	11	10

● Denotes fund is closed to new investors

	99 Pct = Best 0 Pct = Worst				Net Asset	PERFORMANCE				RISK	FUND MGR	
			Overall		Value	Perform- ance	Annualized Total Return Through 2/28/17				Mgr. Quality	Mgr. Tenure
Fund Type	Fund Name	Ticker Symbol	Investment Rating	Phone	As of 2/28/17	Rating/Pts	1Yr / Pct	3Yr / Pct	5Yr / Pct	Risk Rating/Pts	Pct	(Years)
MUN	JPMorgan Short Term Muni Bond	OSTAX	D-	(800) 480-4111	10.48	E /0.4	-0.69 / 7	0.51 / 24	0.49 / 24	B+ / 8.4	6	11
MUI	Dreyfus Sh-Intmd Muni Bd A	DMBAX	D-	(800) 645-6561	12.94	E /0.4	-0.30 / 13	0.43 / 22	0.63 / 27	B+ / 8.9	12	8
MUN	Lord Abbett Shrt Duration Tax-Fr A	LSDAX	D-	(888) 522-2388	15.56	E /0.4	-0.51 / 9	0.54 / 25	0.75 / 29	A- / 9.0	15	9
GEI	Leader Short-Term Bond Inv	LCCMX	D-	(800) 711-9164	9.02	E /0.4	3.17 / 58	-0.94 / 3	1.52 / 35	B / 7.9	7	12
GES	PNC Intermediate Bond A	PBFAX	D-	(800) 551-2145	10.87	E /0.4	0.99 / 39	1.06 / 29	1.15 / 29	B / 8.1	17	15
GEI	Wilmington Intermediate Trm Bd A	GVITX	D-	(800) 336-9970	9.85	E /0.4	0.66 / 36	1.18 / 30	1.28 / 31	B / 8.0	17	21
USS ●	MainStay Government Fund B	MCSGX	D-	(800) 624-6782	8.33	E /0.5	-1.66 / 1	0.35 / 19	0.11 / 15	B / 8.2	16	6
GEI	STAAR Inv Trust General Bond	SITGX	D-	(800) 332-7738	9.67	E /0.5	0.70 / 36	-0.06 / 5	0.30 / 20	B+ / 8.5	15	20
USA	American Century Ginnie Mae A	BGNAX	D-	(800) 345-6488	10.55	E /0.5	-0.22 / 14	1.43 / 34	1.11 / 29	B+ / 8.6	65	11
USA	Dreyfus GNMA Fund A	GPGAX	D-	(800) 782-6620	15.00	E /0.5	-0.03 / 17	1.43 / 34	1.16 / 29	B+ / 8.6	65	2
USS	J Hancock Government Inc A	JHGIX	D-	(800) 257-3336	9.38	E /0.5	-0.47 / 10	1.44 / 34	1.56 / 35	B / 7.7	48	19
USS	PNC Government Mortgage A	POMAX	D-	(800) 551-2145	8.99	E /0.5	-0.55 / 9	1.53 / 35	1.04 / 28	B+ / 8.3	62	15
GES	Timothy Plan Fixed Income A	TFIAX	D-	(800) 662-0201	10.21	E /0.5	1.27 / 43	1.30 / 32	0.91 / 26	B- / 7.5	13	13
GEI	American Century SD Inf Prot Bd A	APOAX	D-	(800) 345-6488	10.19	E+ /0.7	2.90 / 56	0.11 / 13	-0.12 / 4	B+ / 8.3	13	11
USS	Goldman Sachs Govt Income A	GSGOX	D-	(800) 526-7384	14.67	E+ /0.8	-0.70 / 7	1.49 / 35	1.15 / 29	B / 7.6	43	4
USS	Federated Govt Inc Securities A	FGOAX	D-	(800) 341-7400	8.79	E+ /0.8	-0.26 / 13	1.66 / 37	1.33 / 32	B / 7.8	58	14
MUN	Centre Active US Tax Exempt Inv	DHBRX	D-	(800) 955-7175	10.05	D- /1.0	-2.06 / 1	1.47 / 47	1.04 / 36	B- / 7.2	9	2
USS	Sterling Capital Interm US Govt A	BGVAX	D-	(800) 228-1872	9.95	D- /1.0	-0.77 / 6	1.02 / 28	0.73 / 24	B / 7.9	28	14
MUN	Nuveen Ltd Term Muni A	FLTDX	D-	(800) 257-8787	10.88	D- /1.1	-0.92 / 5	1.07 / 37	1.29 / 42	B / 8.1	10	11
MUI	JPMorgan Tax Aware Real Return	TXRAX	D-	(800) 480-4111	9.52	D- /1.3	2.78 / 63	0.66 / 28	0.46 / 24	B- / 7.3	11	12
GEI	JPMorgan Intermediate T/F Bd A	JITAX	D-	(800) 480-4111	10.94	D /1.8	-0.78 / 6	1.81 / 40	1.61 / 36	C+ / 6.4	28	12
COI	Dunham Corporate/Government	DACGX	D-	(888) 338-6426	13.67	D /1.8	3.44 / 59	1.45 / 34	1.91 / 41	C+ / 6.5	16	4
GES	PNC Bond A	PAAAX	D-	(800) 551-2145	10.23	D /1.9	1.28 / 43	1.90 / 41	1.68 / 37	C+ / 6.4	20	15
USS	American Funds US Govt Sec A	AMUSX	D-	(800) 421-0180	13.70	D /1.9	-0.34 / 12	1.90 / 41	1.29 / 31	C+ / 6.8	57	7
GEI	Janus Flexible Bond A	JDFAX	D-	(800) 295-2687	10.34	D /2.0	1.90 / 48	1.93 / 42	2.56 / 50	B- / 7.1	25	10
GES	Nuveen Core Bond A	FAIIX	D-	(800) 257-8787	9.69	D /2.0	1.47 / 44	1.58 / 36	1.82 / 39	C+ / 5.8	12	17
GEI	MassMutual Premier Core Bond A	MMCBX	D-	(800) 542-6767	10.55	D /2.1	2.83 / 55	1.84 / 40	2.00 / 42	C+ / 5.7	18	22
GEI	MainStay Indexed Bond Inv	MIXNX	D-	(800) 624-6782	10.67	D /2.1	0.72 / 36	1.73 / 39	1.36 / 32	C+ / 5.8	13	13
MUS	Columbia AMT-Fr NC Intm Muni Bd	NNCIX	D-	(800) 345-6611	10.29	D /2.1	-1.05 / 4	1.69 / 54	1.55 / 47	C+ / 6.4	7	6
MUS	American Century CA IT TxFr Bd A	BCIAX	D-	(800) 345-6488	11.74	D /2.1	-0.74 / 6	2.08 / 64	2.07 / 60	C+ / 5.8	10	15
GL	Sentinel Total Return Bond A	SATRX	D-	(800) 282-3863	10.33	D /2.1	3.22 / 58	0.97 / 27	2.81 / 55	C+ / 6.0	82	7
GEI	PNC Total Return Advantage A	PTVAX	D-	(800) 551-2145	10.70	D /2.1	3.05 / 57	1.73 / 39	1.98 / 42	C+ / 6.6	20	15
COI	Eaton Vance Core Bond A	EAGIX	D-	(800) 262-1122	9.75	D /2.1	1.79 / 47	2.06 / 44	2.15 / 44	C+ / 6.4	25	7
MUN	Dreyfus Tax Sensitive Tot Ret Bd A	DSDAX	D-	(800) 645-6561	22.61	D+ /2.3	-0.43 / 11	2.11 / 65	1.92 / 57	C / 5.4	10	16
MUS	Columbia AMT-Fr CT Intm Muni Bd	LCTAX	D-	(800) 345-6611	10.55	D+ /2.3	-0.95 / 5	1.76 / 56	1.59 / 49	C+ / 6.7	9	15
USS	Federated Tot Ret Gov Bond Svc	FTGSX	D-	(800) 341-7400	10.77	D+ /2.3	-0.98 / 4	1.32 / 32	0.92 / 26	C+ / 5.7	24	14
GEI	American Century Diversified Bd A	ADFAX	D-	(800) 345-6488	10.71	D+ /2.3	1.49 / 44	2.22 / 47	1.87 / 40	C+ / 6.0	27	16
MUN	Neuberger Berman Muni Int Bd A	NMNAX	D-	(800) 877-9700	11.62	D+ /2.3	-0.79 / 6	2.07 / 64	1.88 / 56	C+ / 6.5	13	7
USS	Delaware Strategic Income Fund A	DEGGX	D-	(800) 523-1918	8.29	D+ /2.4	1.98 / 49	2.07 / 44	2.32 / 46	C+ / 6.2	65	20
COI	Waddell & Reed Adv Bond Fund A	UNBDX	D-	(888) 923-3355	6.20	D+ /2.4	3.30 / 58	2.35 / 49	2.02 / 42	C / 5.3	27	2
MUS	Maine Municipal	MEMUX	D-	(800) 601-5593	10.74	D+ /2.4	-1.38 / 2	1.88 / 59	1.69 / 51	C+ / 5.9	8	14
LP	Deutsche Floating Rate A	DFRAX	D-	(800) 728-3337	8.42	D+ /2.5	7.83 / 74	0.35 / 19	2.43 / 48	C / 5.5	27	10
GEI	Wells Fargo Core Bond A	MBFAX	D-	(800) 222-8222	13.10	D+ /2.5	1.33 / 43	2.36 / 49	2.33 / 47	C+ / 5.6	29	14
MUS	Nationwide HighMark CA Int TF Bd	NWJKX	D-	(800) 848-0920	9.99	D+ /2.5	-1.44 / 2	1.66 / 53	1.80 / 54	C+ / 5.9	6	4

Section V

Performance:
100 Best and Worst
Bond Mutual Funds

A compilation of those

Fixed Income Mutual Funds

receiving the highest and lowest Performance Ratings.

Funds are listed in order by Performance Rating.

Section V Contents

This section contains a summary analysis of each of the top 100 and bottom 100 bond mutual funds as determined by their TheStreet Performance Rating. Since the Performance Rating does not take into consideration the amount of risk a fund poses, the selection of funds presented here is based solely on each fund's financial performance over the past three years.

In order to optimize the utility of our top and bottom fund lists, rather than listing all funds in a multi-class series, a single fund from each series is selected for display as the primary share class. Whenever possible, the selected fund is one that a retail investor would be most likely to choose. This share class may not be appropriate for every investor, so please consult with your financial advisor, the fund company, and the fund's prospectus before placing your trade.

You can use this section to identify those funds that have historically given shareholders the highest returns on their investments. A word of caution though: past performance is not necessarily indicative of future results. While these funds have provided the highest returns, some of them may be currently overvalued and due for a correction.

1. **Fund Type**

The mutual fund's peer category based on its investment objective as stated in its prospectus.

COH	Corporate - High Yield	MMT	Money Market - Treas.
COI	Corporate - Inv. Grade	MTG	Mortgage
EM	Emerging Market	MUH	Municipal - High Yield
GEN	General	MUI	Municipal - Insured
GEI	General - Inv. Grade	MUN	Municipal - National
GEL	General - Long Term	MUS	Municipal - Single State
GES	General - Short & Interm.	USL	U.S. Gov.- Long Term
GL	Global	USS	U.S. Gov. - Short & Interm
LP	Loan Participation	USA	U.S. Gov. - Agency
MMF	Money Mkt - Tax Exempt	US	U.S. Gov. - Treasury

A blank fund type means that the mutual fund has not yet been categorized.

2. **Fund Name**

The name of the mutual fund as stated in its prospectus, which can sometimes differ slightly from the name that the company uses for advertising. If you cannot find the particular mutual fund you are interested in, or if you have any doubts regarding the precise name, verify the information with your broker or on your account statement. Also, use the fund's ticker symbol for confirmation. (See column 3.)

3. **Ticker Symbol**

The unique alphabetic symbol used for identifying and trading a specific mutual fund. No two funds can have the same ticker symbol, and the ticker symbol for mutual funds always ends with an "X".

A handful of funds currently show no associated ticker symbol. This means that the fund is either small or new since the NASD only assigns a ticker symbol to funds with at least $25 million in assets or 1,000 shareholders.

4.	**Overall Investment Rating**	Our overall rating is measured on a scale from A to E based on each fund's risk-adjusted performance. Please see page 11 for specific descriptions of each letter grade. Also, refer to page 7 for information on how our ratings are derived. Most important, when using this rating, please be sure to consider the warnings beginning on page 13 regarding the ratings' limitations and the underlying assumptions.
5.	**Phone**	The telephone number of the company managing the fund. Call this number to receive a prospectus or other information about the fund.
6.	**Net Asset Value (NAV)**	The fund's share price as of the date indicated. A fund's NAV is computed by dividing the value of the fund's asset holdings, less accrued fees and expenses, by the number of its shares outstanding.
7.	**Performance Rating/Points**	A letter grade rating based solely on the mutual fund's financial performance over the trailing three years, without any consideration for the amount of risk the fund poses. Like the overall Investment Rating, the Performance Rating is measured on a scale from A to E for ease of interpretation. The points score indicates where the Performance Rating falls on a scale of 0 to 10.
		In the case of funds investing in municipal or other tax-free securities, this rating is based on the taxable equivalent return of the fund assuming the maximum marginal U.S. tax rate (35%).
8.	**1-Year Total Return**	The total return the fund has provided investors over the preceding twelve months. This total return figure is computed based on the fund's dividend distributions and share price appreciation/depreciation during the period, net of the expenses and fees it imposes on its shareholders. Although the total return figure does not reflect an adjustment for any loads the fund may carry, such adjustments have been made in deriving TheStreet Investment Ratings.
9.	**1-Year Total Return Percentile**	The fund's percentile rank based on its one-year performance compared to that of all other fixed income funds in existence for at least one year. A score of 99 is the best possible, indicating that the fund outperformed 99% of the other mutual funds. Zero is the worst possible percentile score.
		In the case of funds investing in municipal or other tax-free securities, this percentile rank is based on the taxable equivalent return of the fund assuming the maximum marginal U.S. tax rate (35%).
10.	**3-Year Total Return**	The total annual return the fund has provided investors over the preceding three years.

11. **3-Year Total Return Percentile**	The fund's percentile rank based on its three-year performance compared to that of all other fixed income funds in existence for at least three years. A score of 99 is the best possible, indicating that the fund outperformed 99% of the other mutual funds. Zero is the worst possible percentile score.
	In the case of funds investing in municipal or other tax-free securities, this percentile rank is based on the taxable equivalent return of the fund assuming the maximum marginal U.S. tax rate (35%).
12. **5-Year Total Return**	The total annual return the fund has provided investors over the preceding five years.
13. **5-Year Total Return Percentile**	The fund's percentile rank based on its five-year performance compared to that of all other fixed income funds in existence for at least five years. A score of 99 is the best possible, indicating that the fund outperformed 99% of the other mutual funds. Zero is the worst possible percentile score.
	In the case of funds investing in municipal or other tax-free securities, this percentile rank is based on the taxable equivalent return of the fund assuming the maximum marginal U.S. tax rate (35%).
14. **Risk Rating/Points**	A letter grade rating based solely on the mutual fund's risk as determined by its monthly performance volatility over the trailing three years and the underlying credit risk and interest rate risk of its investment portfolio. The risk rating does not take into consideration the overall financial performance the fund has achieved or the total return it has provided to its shareholders. Like the overall Investment Rating, the Risk Rating is measured on a scale from A to E for ease of interpretation. The points score indicates where the Risk Rating falls on a scale of 0 to 10.
15. **Manager Quality Percentile**	The manager quality percentile is based on a ranking of the fund's alpha, a statistical measure representing the difference between a fund's actual returns and its expected performance given its level of risk. Fund managers who have been able to exceed the fund's statistically expected performance receive a high percentile rank with 99 representing the highest possible score. At the other end of the spectrum, fund managers who have actually detracted from the fund's expected performance receive a low percentile rank with 0 representing the lowest possible score.
16. **Manager Tenure**	The number of years the current manager has been managing the fund. Since fund managers who deliver substandard returns are usually replaced, a long tenure is usually a good sign that shareholders are satisfied that the fund is achieving its stated objectives.

Fund Type	Fund Name	Ticker Symbol	Overall Investment Rating	Phone	Net Asset Value As of 2/28/17	PERFORMANCE Perform-ance Rating/Pts	Annualized Total Return Through 2/28/17 1Yr / Pct	3Yr / Pct	5Yr / Pct	RISK Risk Rating/Pts	FUND MGR Mgr. Quality Pct	Mgr. Tenure (Years)
	99 Pct = Best *0 Pct = Worst*											
MUH	MainStay High Yield Muni Bond C	MMHDX	B+	(800) 624-6782	12.14	A+ /9.9	2.48 /61	6.40 /99	5.49 /99	D / 2.0	84	7
MUH	Oppenheimer Rochester Hi Yld	ORNAX	B+	(888) 470-0862	7.09	A+ /9.9	7.13 /81	7.47 /99	6.59 /99	D / 1.7	91	15
EM	T Rowe Price Ins Emerging Mkts	TREBX	B-	(800) 638-5660	9.14	A+ /9.9	18.64 /94	7.51 /97	6.13 /93	D- / 1.1	99	11
MUH	SEI Asset Alloc-Def Strat All F	STDAX	C+	(800) 342-5734	14.64	A+ /9.9	19.17 /99	8.26 /99	10.32 /99	E+ / 0.6	98	14
EM	Fidelity New Markets Income	FNMIX	C+	(800) 544-8544	16.09	A+ /9.9	18.72 /95	7.02 /96	5.74 /90	E / 0.4	99	22
EM ●	GMO Emerging Country Debt III	GMCDX	C+		28.99	A+ /9.9	19.47 /95	7.56 /97	7.87 /98	E / 0.4	99	23
GES	Metropolitan West Alpha Trak 500	MWATX	C+	(800) 496-8298	8.96	A+ /9.9	35.34 /99	13.01 /99	16.54 /99	E- / 0.2	99	19
GEI	Columbia Abs Rtn Currency & Inc	RACWX	C+	(800) 345-6611	10.90	A+ /9.9	9.30 /77	12.21 /99	5.18 /86	E- / 0.1	99	11
MTG	PIMCO StkPlus Intl (DH) A	PIPAX	C	(800) 426-0107	7.60	A+ /9.9	26.71 /99	6.07 /92	10.96 /99	E- / 0.0	98	2
GEI	Rydex Strengthening Dlr 2x Strtgy	RYSDX	C	(800) 820-0888	54.04	A+ /9.9	4.97 /66	13.86 /99	6.77 /96	E- / 0.0	99	12
GEN	J Hancock VIT Value I	JEVLX	C	(800) 257-3336	22.17	A+ /9.9	32.97 /99	6.07 /92	11.88 /99	E- / 0.0	99	20
GEI	Fairholme Focused Income	FOCIX	C+	(866) 202-2263	12.55	A+ /9.9	42.47 /99	6.55 /94	10.45 /99	E- / 0.0	99	8
EM	BlackRock Emg Mkts Flex Dyn Bd	BAEDX	B	(800) 441-7762	9.68	A+ /9.8	17.51 /93	6.80 /95	4.26 /76	D- / 1.4	99	6
EM	T Rowe Price Emerging Markets	PREMX	C+	(800) 638-5660	12.64	A+ /9.8	18.31 /94	6.74 /95	5.22 /86	E+ / 0.7	99	23
GEI	PIMCO Long Term Credit Inst	PTCIX	C+	(800) 426-0107	11.71	A+ /9.8	13.18 /85	7.28 /96	7.24 /97	E / 0.3	69	8
MUS	Oppenheimer Rochester PA Muni	OPATX	A	(888) 470-0862	10.40	A+ /9.7	5.37 /75	6.05 /99	3.84 /91	C- / 3.2	91	15
MUN	Oppenheimer Rochester AMT-Free	OPTAX	A-	(888) 470-0862	6.83	A+ /9.7	3.73 /69	6.34 /99	6.00 /99	D+ / 2.8	89	15
MUH	Lord Abbett Tx Fr High Yld Muni A	HYMAX	B+	(888) 522-2388	11.63	A+ /9.7	3.59 /69	5.90 /98	5.30 /98	D+ / 2.3	85	13
MUS	Oppenheimer Rochester Muni A	RMUNX	B+	(888) 470-0862	14.88	A+ /9.7	6.99 /81	5.99 /98	3.99 /93	D / 2.1	87	15
MUH	Invesco High Yield Municipal A	ACTHX	B+	(800) 959-4246	9.87	A+ /9.7	2.53 /62	6.92 /99	5.74 /99	D / 2.0	88	15
COI	Angel Oak High Yield Opps Inst	ANHIX	B	(877) 625-3042	11.94	A+ /9.7	20.93 /97	4.75 /83	6.31 /94	D / 1.6	88	8
MUH	Nuveen High Yield Muni Bond A	NHMAX	B-	(800) 257-8787	16.68	A+ /9.7	2.45 /61	6.80 /99	6.98 /99	D- / 1.4	83	17
COH	J Hancock US High Yield Bd NAV		B-	(800) 257-3336	11.38	A+ /9.7	20.94 /97	4.71 /83	6.00 /92	D- / 1.2	62	12
COH	Lord Abbett High Yield A	LHYAX	B-	(888) 522-2388	7.67	A+ /9.7	21.58 /98	5.57 /89	7.79 /98	D- / 1.1	78	7
GEI	SEI Instl Managed Tr-High Yld Bd	SHYAX	C+	(800) 342-5734	7.29	A+ /9.7	22.81 /98	4.52 /81	6.60 /95	E+ / 0.9	93	13
MUS ●	Oppenheimer Rochester VA Muni	ORVAX	C+	(888) 470-0862	8.23	A+ /9.7	9.27 /87	5.37 /98	2.85 /77	E+ / 0.6	77	11
EM	Stone Harbor Emerging Debt Inst	SHMDX	C+	(866) 699-8125	10.44	A+ /9.7	16.18 /90	5.83 /91	4.07 /73	E / 0.5	99	10
COH	Loomis Sayles Inst High Income	LSHIX	C+	(800) 633-3330	6.81	A+ /9.7	27.63 /99	3.85 /73	8.00 /98	E / 0.4	4	21
EM	Fidelity Adv Emerging Mkts Inc A	FMKAX	C+	(800) 522-7297	14.20	A+ /9.7	18.36 /94	6.62 /95	5.33 /87	E / 0.4	99	22
MUN	Dupree Taxable Muni Bd Srs	DUTMX	A	(800) 866-0614	10.50	A+ /9.6	2.08 /58	5.31 /98	4.96 /97	C- / 3.2	88	7
MUH	PIMCO High Yield Muni Bond A	PYMAX	B+	(800) 426-0107	8.77	A+ /9.6	2.36 /60	5.95 /98	5.05 /98	D / 2.1	80	2
COH	PIA High Yield Institutional	PHYSX	B	(800) 251-1970	10.32	A+ /9.6	18.33 /94	4.80 /84	6.74 /96	D / 1.9	77	7
GES	Wells Fargo Dvsfd Inc Bldr A	EKSAX	C+	(800) 222-8222	6.27	A+ /9.6	18.09 /94	6.38 /94	7.81 /98	D- / 1.1	96	10
EM	DoubleLine Em Mkts Fxd Inc N	DLENX	C+	(877) 354-6311	10.50	A+ /9.6	18.33 /94	5.08 /85	4.67 /80	D- / 1.0	98	7
COH	Federated High Yield Trust Svc	FHYTX	C+	(800) 341-7400	6.89	A+ /9.6	20.02 /96	5.02 /85	8.09 /98	E+ / 0.7	54	33
MUH	Pioneer High Income Municipal A	PIMAX	B	(800) 225-6292	7.21	A /9.5	3.01 /65	6.07 /99	5.50 /99	D / 2.0	81	11
MUH	BlackRock High Yld Muni Inv A	MDYHX	B	(800) 441-7762	9.34	A /9.5	1.68 /54	6.46 /99	5.06 /98	D / 1.7	82	11
COH	Federated Instl High Yld Bond	FIHBX	B-	(800) 341-7400	10.06	A /9.5	18.69 /94	5.14 /86	6.97 /96	D- / 1.3	74	15
COH	Transamerica Prt High Yield Bond	DVHYX	C+	(888) 233-4339	8.87	A /9.5	20.16 /96	4.25 /78	6.31 /94	D- / 1.1	34	3
EM	Payden Emerging Market Bond	PYEWX	C+	(888) 409-8007	13.80	A /9.5	13.61 /86	5.58 /89	4.55 /79	D- / 1.0	99	17
MUH	Nuveen CA High Yield Muni Bd A	NCHAX	C+	(800) 257-8787	9.35	A /9.5	0.25 /31	6.67 /99	6.69 /99	E+ / 0.9	73	11
EM	Franklin Emg Mkt Debt	FEMDX	C+	(800) 342-5236	11.31	A /9.5	18.26 /94	4.50 /81	4.72 /81	E+ / 0.7	97	11
COH	Fidelity Adv Hi Income Advantage	FAHDX	C+	(800) 522-7297	11.09	A /9.5	22.41 /98	5.20 /86	7.61 /97	E+ / 0.6	55	8
MUN	Sit Tax Free Income Fund	SNTIX	A	(800) 332-5580	9.48	A /9.4	0.69 /40	5.01 /97	4.34 /96	C- / 3.4	74	29
MUH	MFS Municipal High Income A	MMHYX	B+	(800) 225-2606	8.07	A /9.4	1.91 /56	6.12 /99	5.03 /98	D+ / 2.6	86	15
MUH	Goldman Sachs High Yield Muni A	GHYAX	B	(800) 526-7384	9.31	A /9.4	4.89 /73	6.19 /99	5.65 /99	D / 2.1	88	17
MUH	AB High Income Municipal A	ABTHX	B	(800) 221-5672	11.07	A /9.4	0.97 /44	6.01 /98	5.19 /98	D / 1.9	77	7
COH	Voya High Yield Service	IPHYX	C+	(800) 992-0180	10.13	A /9.4	17.44 /93	4.29 /79	5.94 /92	D- / 1.5	56	3
GEI	Northern Multi-Mgr HY Oppty	NMHYX	C+	(800) 595-9111	10.05	A /9.4	21.69 /98	4.03 /76	6.19 /93	D- / 1.4	92	5
COI	Fidelity High Income	SPHIX	C+	(800) 544-8544	8.91	A /9.4	21.79 /98	3.96 /75	5.91 /91	D- / 1.1	81	17
COH	CNR High Yield Bond N	CHBAX	C+	(888) 889-0799	8.01	A /9.4	21.23 /97	3.88 /74	6.00 /92	D- / 1.1	25	6
COH ●	T Rowe Price Instl High Yield	TRHYX	C+	(800) 638-5660	9.00	A /9.4	20.65 /97	4.37 /79	6.72 /96	D- / 1.1	42	2

● Denotes fund is closed to new investors

Fund Type	Fund Name	Ticker Symbol	Overall Investment Rating	Phone	Net Asset Value As of 2/28/17	PERFORMANCE Perform-ance Rating/Pts	Annualized Total Return Through 2/28/17 1Yr / Pct	3Yr / Pct	5Yr / Pct	RISK Risk Rating/Pts	FUND MGR Mgr. Quality Pct	Mgr. Tenure (Years)
	99 Pct = Best *0 Pct = Worst*											
MUH	AMG GW&K Muni Enhanced Yield	GWMNX	C+	(800) 548-4539	9.50	A /9.4	0.17 /28	5.35 /98	4.18 /95	D- / 1.0	33	12
EM	TCW Emerging Markets Income N	TGINX	C+	(800) 386-3829	10.78	A /9.4	17.56 /93	4.54 /81	4.65 /80	E+ / 0.8	98	7
COH	USAA High Income Fund	USHYX	C+	(800) 382-8722	8.26	A /9.4	23.09 /98	3.79 /73	6.66 /96	E+ / 0.8	16	1
COI	Vanguard Long-Term Corp Bd Idx	VLTCX	C	(800) 662-7447	24.24	A /9.4	11.67 /82	5.99 /92	5.27 /87	E / 0.3	8	8
MUS	Oppeneheimer Rochester CA Muni	OPCAX	A-	(888) 470-0862	8.27	A /9.3	4.11 /71	5.61 /98	5.51 /99	C- / 3.3	86	15
GEI	Cohen and Steers Pref Sec&Inc A	CPXAX	A-	(800) 330-7348	13.77	A /9.3	10.71 /80	6.99 /96	8.28 /99	C- / 3.0	96	7
MUH	T Rowe Price Tax-Free High Yield	PRFHX	B+	(800) 638-5660	11.77	A /9.3	1.64 /53	5.37 /98	4.99 /98	D+ / 2.7	81	15
MUS	Oppenheimer Rochester AMT-Fr	OPNYX	B+	(888) 470-0862	11.08	A /9.3	4.42 /72	5.65 /98	3.89 /92	D+ / 2.5	84	15
MUH	Delaware Natl HY Muni Bd A	CXHYX	B	(800) 523-1918	10.77	A /9.3	1.84 /55	6.07 /99	5.22 /98	D / 2.2	82	14
COH	Vanguard High-Yield Corporate Inv	VWEHX	B	(800) 662-7447	5.92	A /9.3	14.53 /88	4.62 /82	6.02 /92	D / 2.0	77	9
COH	Westcore Flexible Income Rtl	WTLTX	B-	(800) 392-2673	8.99	A /9.3	15.39 /89	5.18 /86	5.77 /91	D / 1.9	82	8
GL	AB High Income A	AGDAX	B-	(800) 221-5672	8.86	A /9.3	20.70 /97	4.76 /83	6.95 /96	D / 1.8	97	15
COH	Lord Abbett Bond Debenture A	LBNDX	B-	(888) 522-2388	8.09	A /9.3	18.04 /94	4.84 /84	6.50 /95	D / 1.6	76	4
COH	TIAA-CREF High Yield Fund Retire	TIHRX	C+	(800) 842-2252	9.90	A /9.3	20.91 /97	4.30 /79	6.06 /92	E+ / 0.9	29	11
COH	Hundredfold Select Alternative Svc	SFHYX	B+	(855) 582-8006	22.72	A- /9.2	14.09 /87	4.14 /77	5.07 /85	D+ / 2.6	82	13
COH	Guggenheim High Yield A	SIHAX	C+	(800) 820-0888	11.46	A- /9.2	21.15 /97	4.98 /85	7.64 /97	D / 1.7	78	5
COH ●	MainStay High Yield Corp Bond B	MKHCX	C+	(800) 624-6782	5.78	A- /9.2	18.56 /94	3.87 /74	5.42 /88	D / 1.6	37	4
COH ●	T Rowe Price High Yield	PRHYX	C+	(800) 638-5660	6.76	A- /9.2	18.93 /95	4.13 /77	6.60 /95	D- / 1.4	44	21
COH	Principal High Yield A	CPHYX	C+	(800) 222-5852	7.47	A- /9.2	19.56 /95	4.48 /80	6.51 /95	D- / 1.4	59	5
COH	Prudential High Yield A	PBHAX	C+	(800) 225-1852	5.57	A- /9.2	20.00 /96	4.84 /84	6.53 /95	D- / 1.2	64	16
COH	Victory High Yield A	GUHYX	C	(800) 539-3863	6.51	A- /9.2	22.27 /98	3.35 /67	5.58 /89	E+ / 0.7	7	8
COH	J Hancock High Yield NAV		C	(800) 257-3336	8.27	A- /9.2	24.95 /99	2.63 /55	5.93 /92	E / 0.5	1	11
GL	Nuveen High Income Bond A	FJSIX	C	(800) 257-8787	7.95	A- /9.2	32.82 /99	2.50 /52	5.75 /90	E / 0.3	91	12
GEI	CNR Fixed Income Opportunities N	RIMOX	B+	(888) 889-0799	25.98	A- /9.1	15.63 /90	4.16 /77	5.58 /89	D+ / 2.8	95	6
MUN	Eaton Vance High Yield Muni Inc A	ETHYX	B+	(800) 262-1122	8.68	A- /9.1	1.03 /45	6.27 /99	5.42 /99	D+ / 2.7	84	13
MUH	Federated Muni & Stock	FMUAX	B-	(800) 341-7400	12.87	A- /9.1	9.80 /89	4.20 /94	5.98 /99	D / 2.1	92	14
COH	MassMutual Premier High Yield A	MPHAX	C+	(800) 542-6767	9.13	A- /9.1	19.70 /95	4.82 /84	7.72 /98	D / 1.6	75	7
GL	PIMCO High Yield Spectrum A	PHSAX	C+	(800) 426-0107	10.00	A- /9.1	19.90 /96	4.42 /80	6.86 /96	D- / 1.5	96	7
COH	MFS Global High Yield A	MHOAX	C+	(800) 225-2606	6.24	A- /9.1	17.65 /93	3.73 /72	5.63 /89	D- / 1.2	21	12
GEI	Nuveen Symphony Credit Oppty A	NCOAX	C	(800) 257-8787	20.76	A- /9.1	25.98 /99	3.49 /69	6.33 /94	E+ / 0.8	91	7
COH	Permanent Portfolio Versatile Bd I	PRVBX	C	(800) 531-5142	59.65	A- /9.1	19.94 /96	3.59 /70	4.11 /74	E+ / 0.8	37	14
GEI ●	Vanguard Long-Term Inv Gr Inv	VWESX	C-	(800) 662-7447	10.21	A- /9.1	7.10 /73	6.34 /94	5.40 /88	E / 0.3	32	4
US	Vanguard Extnd Durtn Trea Idx Inst	VEDTX	C-	(800) 662-7447	33.95	A- /9.1	-6.63 / 0	9.40 /99	4.53 /79	E- / 0.0	69	4
GEI	PIMCO Extended Duration P	PEDPX	C-	(800) 426-0107	7.55	A- /9.1	-5.95 / 0	9.45 /99	4.30 /76	E- / 0.0	0	10
USS	Principal Preferred Sec A	PPSAX	A+	(800) 222-5852	10.23	A- /9.0	9.14 /77	6.30 /93	7.09 /96	C / 4.5	97	15
USS	Nuveen Preferred Securities A	NPSAX	A	(800) 257-8787	17.22	A- /9.0	11.35 /82	6.19 /93	8.02 /98	C- / 4.0	98	11
COI	Diamond Hill Corporate Credit A	DSIAX	B+	(614) 255-3333	11.27	A- /9.0	15.58 /89	5.22 /86	5.60 /89	C- / 3.3	93	11
MUS ●	Oppenheimer Rochester Ohio Muni	OROHX	B+	(888) 470-0862	10.06	A- /9.0	4.02 /71	5.23 /97	4.29 /95	C- / 3.1	81	11
MUH	Northern High Yield Muni	NHYMX	B	(800) 595-9111	8.68	A- /9.0	0.17 /28	4.77 /97	4.20 /95	D+ / 2.6	71	19
LP	Invesco Senior Loan A	VSLAX	B-	(800) 959-4246	6.68	A- /9.0	20.95 /97	3.89 /74	6.11 /93	D / 2.2	89	10
COI	BMO TCH Corporate Income Y	MCIYX	B-	(800) 236-3863	12.96	A- /9.0	15.31 /89	4.47 /80	4.90 /83	D / 2.1	74	9
GEI	SunAmerica VAL Co II High Yld Bd	VCHYX	B-	(800) 858-8850	7.88	A- /9.0	16.31 /91	3.84 /73	5.57 /89	D / 1.9	90	8
COH	Principal High Yield Fund I Inst	PYHIX	C	(800) 222-5852	10.00	A- /9.0	17.61 /93	3.58 /70	5.89 /91	D- / 1.1	17	10
COH	AMG Mgrs High Yield N	MHHAX	C	(800) 548-4539	7.84	A- /9.0	19.76 /96	3.85 /73	5.96 /92	D- / 1.0	19	16
COH	Hotchkis and Wiley High Yield A	HWHAX	C	(866) 493-8637	12.25	A- /9.0	23.14 /98	4.13 /77	6.85 /96	E+ / 0.9	24	8
COH	WA High Yield IS	WAHSX	C	(888) 425-6432	8.22	A- /9.0	23.45 /98	2.63 /55	5.77 /91	E+ / 0.7	2	12
GEI	PIMCO Long Dur Total Return P	PLRPX	C-	(800) 426-0107	10.70	A- /9.0	6.80 /72	6.18 /93	4.69 /81	E / 0.3	11	10
MUS	Vanguard OH Long-Term	VOHIX	A-	(800) 662-7447	12.37	B+ /8.9	0.75 /41	4.40 /95	3.72 /90	C- / 3.7	64	9

● Denotes fund is closed to new investors

 Data as of February 28, 2017

Fund Type	Fund Name	Ticker Symbol	Overall Investment Rating	Phone	Net Asset Value As of 2/28/17	Performance Rating/Pts	1Yr / Pct	3Yr / Pct	5Yr / Pct	Risk Rating/Pts	Mgr. Quality Pct	Mgr. Tenure (Years)
	99 Pct = Best *0 Pct = Worst*											
USS	Rydex Inv Govt Lg Bd Stgy A	RYAQX	E-	(800) 820-0888	34.46	E- /0.0	3.98 /62	-8.57 / 0	-5.24 / 0	E- / 0.0	1	9
GEI	Credit Suisse Cmdty Rtn Strat A	CRSAX	E-	(877) 927-2874	5.01	E- /0.0	16.51 /91	-12.70 / 0	-10.08 / 0	E- / 0.0	0	11
GEI	Rydex Wekng Dlr 2x Stgry A	RYWDX	E-	(800) 820-0888	64.26	E- /0.0	-8.07 / 0	-15.95 / 0	-10.79 / 0	E- / 0.0	0	12
GEI	Credit Suisse Commdty Ret Str	CCRSX	E-	(877) 927-2874	4.42	E- /0.0	16.32 /91	-12.69 / 0	-10.11 / 0	E- / 0.0	0	11
GES	AB All Mkt Real Return A	AMTAX	E-	(800) 221-5672	8.51	E- /0.0	23.44 /98	-6.72 / 0	-4.09 / 0	E- / 0.0	0	2
EM	Dreyfus Eme Mkts Dbt LC A	DDBAX	E-	(800) 782-6620	11.50	E- /0.0	11.43 /82	-4.81 / 0	-3.53 / 0	E- / 0.1	2	9
US	Direxion Mo 7-10 Year Tr Br 2X Inv	DXKSX	E-	(800) 851-0511	30.38	E- /0.0	3.05 /57	-8.69 / 0	-7.30 / 0	E- / 0.2	0	13
GL	Wells Fargo Intl Bd A	ESIYX	E-	(800) 222-8222	9.62	E- /0.0	0.10 /22	-3.01 / 1	-1.51 / 2	E / 0.3	33	24
USS	PIMCO StocksPLUS Short A	PSSAX	E-	(800) 426-0107	9.25	E- /0.0	-14.51 / 0	-9.78 / 0	-11.51 / 0	E / 0.3	0	3
EM	T Rowe Price Inst Intl Bd	RPIIX	E-	(800) 638-5660	8.33	E- /0.0	1.26 /42	-2.29 / 2	-0.74 / 2	E / 0.4	55	3
GL	Laudus Mondrian Intl Govt Fxd Inc	LIFNX	E-	(800) 407-0256	9.22	E- /0.0	-2.67 / 0	-3.16 / 1	-2.78 / 1	E / 0.4	20	N/A
EM	EuroPac International Bond A	EPIBX	E-	(888) 558-5851	8.13	E- /0.0	5.72 /69	-4.84 / 0	-3.25 / 1	E / 0.4	1	7
GL	T Rowe Price Intl Bond	RPIBX	E-	(800) 638-5660	8.47	E- /0.0	1.05 /40	-2.59 / 1	-1.15 / 2	E / 0.4	37	3
GL	American Century Intl Bond A	AIBDX	E-	(800) 345-6488	12.12	E- /0.0	-1.38 / 2	-3.66 / 1	-2.36 / 1	E / 0.5	8	8
EM	Invesco Emerg Mkts Flexible Bond	IAEMX	E-	(800) 959-4246	6.56	E- /0.0	7.67 /74	-4.59 / 0	-4.03 / 0	E / 0.5	0	2
GL	Federated Global Total Return Bd	FTIIX	E-	(800) 341-7400	9.50	E- /0.0	-3.72 / 0	-2.95 / 1	-2.25 / 1	E / 0.5	21	15
MTG	ProFunds-Falling US Dollar Svc	FDPSX	E-	(888) 776-3637	15.64	E- /0.0	-6.29 / 0	-10.51 / 0	-7.63 / 0	E+ / 0.7	0	8
GL	Federated Prudent DollarBear A	PSAFX	E-	(800) 341-7400	9.42	E- /0.0	-3.29 / 0	-5.52 / 0	-4.82 / 0	D- / 1.2	0	3
GL	Templeton Global Currency A	ICPHX	E-	(800) 342-5236	7.91	E- /0.0	4.08 /62	-4.63 / 0	-3.74 / 0	D- / 1.4	0	16
COH	Access Flex Bear High Yield Inv	AFBIX	E-	(888) 776-3637	39.06	E- /0.0	-14.53 / 0	-8.63 / 0	-11.20 / 0	D / 1.6	0	12
COH	Rydex Inv High Yld Strtgy A	RYILX	E-	(800) 820-0888	66.16	E- /0.0	-11.79 / 0	-8.06 / 0	-10.20 / 0	D / 1.7	0	10
GL	Columbia Global Bond A	IGBFX	E-	(800) 345-6611	5.62	E- /0.0	0.72 /36	-2.45 / 2	-2.00 / 1	D / 1.8	9	4
EM	Goldman Sachs Local Emg Mkt	GAMDX	E-	(800) 526-7384	6.22	E- /0.1	12.70 /84	-3.74 / 1	-3.37 / 0	E- / 0.0	12	9
EM	PIMCO Emerging Local Bond A	PELAX	E-	(800) 426-0107	7.21	E- /0.1	14.35 /87	-3.27 / 1	-3.50 / 0	E- / 0.1	20	11
GL	PIMCO Foreign Bd Fd (Unhgd) A	PFUAX	E-	(800) 426-0107	9.47	E- /0.1	4.04 /62	-1.08 / 3	-0.22 / 4	E / 0.5	79	3
GL	Invesco World Bond A	AUBAX	E-	(800) 959-4246	10.02	E- /0.1	4.88 /66	-1.37 / 2	0.11 /15	E+ / 0.6	75	7
GL	PACE Global Fx Inc Inve A	PWFAX	E-	(888) 793-8637	9.67	E- /0.1	-0.77 / 6	-0.28 / 4	-0.61 / 3	E+ / 0.8	84	22
GL	Dreyfus Intl Bond A	DIBAX	E-	(800) 645-6561	15.03	E- /0.1	2.43 /53	-0.56 / 3	0.53 /22	D- / 1.0	79	11
LP	Driehaus Select Credit Fund	DRSLX	E-	(800) 560-6111	8.03	E- /0.1	9.42 /78	-3.53 / 1	-0.36 / 3	D / 1.8	0	7
GL	Janus Global Bond A	JGBAX	E	(800) 295-2687	9.34	E- /0.1	--	-0.25 / 4	1.01 /27	D+ / 2.5	76	6
USS	AIG US Gov Sec A	SGTAX	E+	(800) 858-8850	9.17	E- /0.1	-2.83 / 0	0.69 /23	0.02 / 7	C+ / 6.6	16	3
USS	First Inv Government A	FIGVX	E+	(800) 423-4026	10.46	E- /0.1	-1.52 / 2	0.59 /22	0.41 /21	B / 7.8	16	5
GL	PIMCO Emerging Markets	PLMAX	E-	(800) 426-0107	8.91	E- /0.2	11.00 /81	-1.92 / 2	-1.57 / 2	E / 0.5	26	12
GL	Lord Abbett Emerg Mkts Currency	LDMAX	E-	(888) 522-2388	5.26	E- /0.2	10.04 /79	-2.23 / 2	-1.70 / 1	E / 0.5	18	10
GL	MFS Global Bond Fund A	MGBAX	E-	(800) 225-2606	8.60	E- /0.2	1.37 /43	-1.09 / 3	-1.32 / 2	D- / 1.5	70	7
GL	American Funds Cap World Bond	CWBFX	E-	(800) 421-0180	19.32	E- /0.2	2.00 /49	-0.31 / 4	0.46 /21	D / 2.0	79	18
US	American Century MA Real Rtn A	ASIDX	E-	(800) 345-6488	9.68	E- /0.2	9.50 /78	-1.49 / 2	-1.47 / 2	D / 2.0	2	7
GEI	Dreyfus Opportunistic Fixed Inc A	DSTAX	E	(800) 782-6620	11.28	E- /0.2	5.60 /69	-1.06 / 3	1.23 /30	C- / 3.1	8	7
USL ●	SunAmerica 2020 High Watermark	HWKAX	E	(800) 858-8850	8.75	E- /0.2	-0.87 / 5	1.15 /30	0.59 /22	C / 5.4	25	13
MUN	Saratoga Adv Tr-Municipal Bond C	SMBCX	E+	(800) 807-3863	9.09	E- /0.2	-2.01 / 1	-0.27 / 4	-0.43 / 3	B- / 7.1	1	8
USS	Nuveen Intermediate Government	FIGAX	D-	(800) 257-8787	8.65	E- /0.2	-1.63 / 1	0.54 /21	0.59 /22	B / 8.1	17	15
USS	Manor Bond Fund	MNRBX	D-	(800) 787-3334	10.30	E- /0.2	-1.81 / 1	-0.38 / 4	-0.40 / 3	B+ / 8.8	7	19
USS	Davis Government Bond A	RFBAX	D	(800) 279-0279	5.36	E- /0.2	-0.45 /10	0.32 /19	0.13 /16	A / 9.4	31	18
MUN	BlackRock Short Term Muni Inv A	MELMX	D	(800) 441-7762	10.14	E- /0.2	-0.18 /15	0.06 /12	0.17 /19	A / 9.5	18	10
GEI	AB Short Duration A	ADPAX	D	(800) 221-5672	11.70	E- /0.2	0.42 /31	0.24 /17	0.16 /17	A+ / 9.6	27	12
GL	Loomis Sayles Glbl Bd Ret	LSGLX	E	(800) 633-3330	15.39	E /0.3	4.07 /62	-0.76 / 3	0.24 /19	D / 1.9	74	17
GEI	Franklin Real Return A	FRRAX	E	(800) 342-5236	10.24	E /0.3	7.34 /73	-0.65 / 3	-0.07 / 4	C- / 3.0	3	13
USS	Nationwide Govt Bond A	NUSAX	E	(800) 848-0920	9.92	E /0.3	-2.15 / 1	0.76 /24	0.62 /23	C / 4.4	9	20
USS	Waddell & Reed Adv Gov Secs A	UNGVX	E+	(888) 923-3355	5.41	E /0.3	-1.22 / 3	0.93 /27	0.27 /19	C+ / 6.6	17	2
USS	Federated USG Sec:2-5yrs R	FIGKX	D-	(800) 341-7400	10.88	E /0.3	-1.06 / 4	-0.14 / 5	-0.48 / 3	B+ / 8.4	7	4
USS	Putnam American Government A	PAGVX	D-	(800) 225-1581	8.61	E /0.3	0.33 /30	0.70 /23	1.16 /30	B+ / 8.5	33	10
MUN	Fidelity Adv Ltd Term Muni Inc A	FASHX	D-	(800) 522-7297	10.53	E /0.3	-0.57 / 9	0.57 /26	0.76 /30	B+ / 8.7	10	14

● Denotes fund is closed to new investors

Fund Type	Fund Name	Ticker Symbol	Overall Investment Rating	Phone	Net Asset Value As of 2/28/17	Perform-ance Rating/Pts	Annualized Total Return Through 2/28/17			Risk Rating/Pts	Mgr. Quality Pct	Mgr. Tenure (Years)
							1Yr / Pct	3Yr / Pct	5Yr / Pct			
GEI	Saratoga Adv Tr Inv Qlty Bond C	SQBCX	D-	(800) 807-3863	9.58	E /0.3	0.20 /26	-0.01 / 5	-0.04 / 5	B+ / 8.7	7	2
US	JPMorgan Treasury and Agency A	OTABX	D-	(800) 480-4111	9.34	E /0.3	-0.27 /13	0.20 /16	0.12 /16	A- / 9.2	26	N/A
MUS	PIMCO CA Sh Duration Muni Inc A	PCDAX	D	(800) 426-0107	9.88	E /0.3	-0.28 /13	0.23 /19	0.24 /20	A / 9.3	17	6
USS	Eaton Vance Govt Obligation A	EVGOX	D	(800) 262-1122	6.38	E /0.3	0.49 /33	0.90 /26	0.78 /25	A / 9.5	63	3
USS	American Century Sh-Term Govt A	TWAVX	D	(800) 345-6488	9.59	E /0.3	-0.24 /14	0.04 / 9	-0.07 / 4	A / 9.5	22	15
GEI	Neuberger Berman Short Dur Bd A	NSHAX	D	(800) 877-9700	7.44	E /0.3	0.35 /30	0.28 /18	0.78 /25	A+ / 9.7	30	11
MUN	Wells Fargo Ult-Sh Mun Inc A	SMAVX	D	(800) 222-8222	9.56	E /0.3	-0.11 /16	0.09 /15	0.21 /20	A+ / 9.8	27	17
USS	Franklin Adjustable US Govt Sec A	FISAX	D	(800) 342-5236	8.37	E /0.3	0.50 /33	-0.04 / 5	0.20 /18	A+ / 9.8	33	26
USS	Federated Gov Ultrashort Dur A	FGUAX	D	(800) 341-7400	9.82	E /0.3	0.18 /25	-0.14 / 5	-0.14 / 4	A+ / 9.9	31	20
US	Permanent Portfolio Short-Tm Trs I	PRTBX	D	(800) 531-5142	64.70	E /0.3	-0.14 /15	-0.45 / 4	-0.51 / 3	A+ / 9.9	20	14
MUI	Federated Muni Ultrashrt A	FMUUX	D	(800) 341-7400	9.99	E /0.3	0.52 /37	0.06 /12	0.16 /19	A+ / 9.9	33	17
GL	Prudential Global Total Return A	GTRAX	E-	(800) 225-1852	6.39	E /0.4	2.83 /55	0.93 /26	2.12 /44	E+ / 0.9	91	15
GL	Voya Global Bond A	INGBX	E	(800) 992-0180	9.76	E /0.4	4.32 /64	-0.20 / 4	0.49 /21	D+ / 2.4	78	6
USS	American Century Govt Bond A	ABTAX	E+	(800) 345-6488	10.97	E /0.4	-1.02 / 4	1.40 /33	0.86 /25	B- / 7.2	32	15
USS	MFS Government Securities Fund	MFGSX	E+	(800) 225-2606	9.84	E /0.4	-0.96 / 4	1.42 /34	1.00 /27	B- / 7.4	35	11
GEI	TETON Westwood Interm Bond A	WEAIX	E+	(800) 422-3554	11.24	E /0.4	0.53 /34	0.93 /26	0.59 /22	B / 7.6	8	18
GEI	Leader Short-Term Bond Inv	LCCMX	D-	(800) 711-9164	9.02	E /0.4	3.17 /58	-0.94 / 3	1.52 /35	B / 7.9	7	12
GEI	Wilmington Intermediate Trm Bd A	GVITX	D-	(800) 336-9970	9.85	E /0.4	0.66 /36	1.18 /30	1.28 /31	B / 8.0	17	21
GES	PNC Intermediate Bond A	PBFAX	D-	(800) 551-2145	10.87	E /0.4	0.99 /39	1.06 /29	1.15 /29	B / 8.1	17	15
MUN	JPMorgan Short Term Muni Bond	OSTAX	D-	(800) 480-4111	10.48	E /0.4	-0.69 / 7	0.51 /24	0.49 /24	B+ / 8.4	6	11
MUN	PNC Tax Exempt Limited Mat Bond	PDLAX	D-	(800) 551-2145	10.33	E /0.4	-0.66 / 7	0.70 /29	0.69 /28	B+ / 8.6	11	10
MUI	Dreyfus Sh-Intmd Muni Bd A	DMBAX	D-	(800) 645-6561	12.94	E /0.4	-0.30 /13	0.43 /22	0.63 /27	B+ / 8.9	12	8
MUN	Lord Abbett Shrt Duration Tax-Fr A	LSDAX	D-	(888) 522-2388	15.56	E /0.4	-0.51 / 9	0.54 /25	0.75 /29	A- / 9.0	15	9
MUS	RidgeWorth Seix Short-Trm Muni	SMMAX	D	(888) 784-3863	9.94	E /0.4	0.12 /25	0.43 /23	0.70 /28	A- / 9.2	22	6
MUN	PIMCO Short Duration Muni Inc A	PSDAX	D	(800) 426-0107	8.40	E /0.4	-0.10 /16	0.39 /22	0.48 /24	A- / 9.2	19	3
GEI	JPMorgan Short Duration Bond A	OGLVX	D	(800) 480-4111	10.81	E /0.4	0.55 /34	0.43 /20	0.47 /21	A / 9.5	30	11
GEI	RidgeWorth Seix Sh-Term Bond A	STSBX	D	(888) 784-3863	9.96	E /0.4	0.39 /31	0.37 /19	0.68 /23	A / 9.5	28	3
MUN	Franklin Fdrl Lmtd Trm T/F Inc A	FFTFX	D	(800) 342-5236	10.37	E /0.4	0.05 /21	0.45 /23	0.69 /28	A+ / 9.7	32	14
MUS	Sanford C Bernstein Sh Dur CA	SDCMX	D	(212) 486-5800	12.38	E /0.4	-0.24 /14	-0.17 / 5	0.01 / 7	A+ / 9.8	18	23
MUN	Eaton Vance Floating-Rte Muni Inc	EXFLX	D	(800) 262-1122	9.80	E /0.4	0.72 /41	0.26 /20	0.14 /19	A+ / 9.8	37	13
COI	STAAR Inv Trust Shrt Term Bond	SITBX	D	(800) 332-7738	8.92	E /0.4	0.11 /23	-0.26 / 4	0.15 /17	A+ / 9.8	21	20
GEI	Principal Infl Prot A	PITAX	E	(800) 222-5852	8.45	E /0.5	2.47 /53	0.71 /23	-0.07 / 5	D+ / 2.9	2	7
MUS	New Hampshire Municipal	NHMUX	E	(800) 601-5593	10.42	E /0.5	-2.52 / 0	1.44 /47	1.30 /42	C- / 4.1	2	14
USS	Fidelity Adv Govt Inc A	FVIAX	E+	(800) 522-7297	10.22	E /0.5	-1.14 / 3	1.58 /36	1.18 /30	C+ / 6.1	34	10
USS	Invesco US Government A	AGOVX	E+	(800) 959-4246	8.84	E /0.5	-0.14 /15	1.51 /35	0.98 /27	C+ / 6.9	35	8
GES	Timothy Plan Fixed Income A	TFIAX	D-	(800) 662-0201	10.21	E /0.5	1.27 /43	1.30 /32	0.91 /26	B- / 7.5	13	13
USS	J Hancock Government Inc A	JHGIX	D-	(800) 257-3336	9.38	E /0.5	-0.47 /10	1.44 /34	1.56 /35	B / 7.7	48	19
USS ●	MainStay Government Fund B	MCSGX	D-	(800) 624-6782	8.33	E /0.5	-1.66 / 1	0.35 /19	0.11 /15	B / 8.2	16	6
USS	PNC Government Mortgage A	POMAX	D-	(800) 551-2145	8.99	E /0.5	-0.55 / 9	1.53 /35	1.04 /28	B+ / 8.3	62	15
GEI	STAAR Inv Trust General Bond	SITGX	D-	(800) 332-7738	9.67	E /0.5	0.70 /36	-0.06 / 5	0.30 /20	B+ / 8.5	15	20
USA	American Century Ginnie Mae A	BGNAX	D-	(800) 345-6488	10.55	E /0.5	-0.22 /14	1.43 /34	1.11 /29	B+ / 8.6	65	11
USA	Dreyfus GNMA Fund A	GPGAX	D-	(800) 782-6620	15.00	E /0.5	-0.03 /17	1.43 /34	1.16 /29	B+ / 8.6	65	2
MUN	American Funds ST T/E Bnd Fd A	ASTEX	D	(800) 421-0180	10.11	E /0.5	0.20 /29	0.52 /24	0.70 /28	A- / 9.1	21	8
MUN	Deutsche Short Term Muni Bond A	SRMAX	D	(800) 728-3337	10.11	E /0.5	-0.01 /17	0.55 /25	0.60 /26	A- / 9.2	24	14
USS	Natixis Loomis Say Ltd Trm	NEFLX	D	(800) 225-5478	11.36	E /0.5	0.10 /22	0.65 /22	0.84 /25	A- / 9.2	41	16
MUN	Nuveen Short Term Municipal	FSHAX	D	(800) 257-8787	10.05	E /0.5	0.06 /22	0.56 /25	0.91 /33	A / 9.3	29	15
USS	Oppenheimer Limited Term Govt A	OPGVX	D	(888) 470-0862	4.42	E /0.5	0.24 /27	0.62 /22	0.78 /25	A / 9.3	45	8
MUN	WA Short Duration Muni Income A	SHDAX	D	(877) 534-4627	5.08	E /0.5	0.09 /24	0.54 /25	0.75 /29	A / 9.4	28	14

Section VI

Risk:
100 Best and Worst
Bond Mutual Funds

A compilation of those

Fixed Income Mutual Funds

receiving the highest and lowest Risk Ratings.

Funds are listed in order by Risk Rating.

Section VI Contents

This section contains a summary analysis of each of the top 100 and bottom 100 bond mutual funds as determined by their TheStreet Risk Rating. Since the Risk Rating does not take into consideration a fund's overall financial performance, the selection of funds presented here is based solely on each fund's level of credit risk and interest rate risk.

In order to optimize the utility of our top and bottom fund lists, rather than listing all funds in a multi-class series, a single fund from each series is selected for display as the primary share class. Whenever possible, the selected fund is one that a retail investor would be most likely to choose. This share class may not be appropriate for every investor, so please consult with your financial advisor, the fund company, and the fund's prospectus before placing your trade.

You can use this section to identify those funds that have historically given shareholders the most consistent returns on their investments. A word of caution though: consistency in the past is not necessarily indicative of future results. While these funds have provided the most stable returns, it is possible for a fund manager – especially a newly appointed fund manager – to suddenly shift the fund's investment focus which could lead to greater volatility.

1. **Fund Type**   The mutual fund's peer category based on its investment objective as stated in its prospectus.

COH	Corporate - High Yield	MMT	Money Market - Treas.
COI	Corporate - Inv. Grade	MTG	Mortgage
EM	Emerging Market	MUH	Municipal - High Yield
GEN	General	MUI	Municipal - Insured
GEI	General - Inv. Grade	MUN	Municipal - National
GEL	General - Long Term	MUS	Municipal - Single State
GES	General - Short & Interm.	USL	U.S. Gov.- Long Term
GL	Global	USS	U.S. Gov. - Short & Interm
LP	Loan Participation	USA	U.S. Gov. - Agency
MMF	Money Mkt - Tax Exempt	US	U.S. Gov. - Treasury

A blank fund type means that the mutual fund has not yet been categorized.

2. **Fund Name**   The name of the mutual fund as stated in its prospectus, which can sometimes differ slightly from the name that the company uses for advertising. If you cannot find the particular mutual fund you are interested in, or if you have any doubts regarding the precise name, verify the information with your broker or on your account statement. Also, use the fund's ticker symbol for confirmation. (See column 3.)

3. **Ticker Symbol**   The unique alphabetic symbol used for identifying and trading a specific mutual fund. No two funds can have the same ticker symbol, and the ticker symbol for mutual funds always ends with an "X".

A handful of funds currently show no associated ticker symbol. This means that the fund is either small or new since the NASD only assigns a ticker symbol to funds with at least $25 million in assets or 1,000 shareholders.

4. Overall Investment Rating

Our overall rating is measured on a scale from A to E based on each fund's risk-adjusted performance. Please see page 11 for specific descriptions of each letter grade. Also, refer to page 7 for information on how our ratings are derived. Most important, when using this rating, please be sure to consider the warnings beginning on page 13 regarding the ratings' limitations and the underlying assumptions.

5. Phone

The telephone number of the company managing the fund. Call this number to receive a prospectus or other information about the fund.

6. Net Asset Value (NAV)

The fund's share price as of the date indicated. A fund's NAV is computed by dividing the value of the fund's asset holdings, less accrued fees and expenses, by the number of its shares outstanding.

7. Performance Rating/Points

A letter grade rating based solely on the mutual fund's financial performance over the trailing three years, without any consideration for the amount of risk the fund poses. Like the overall Investment Rating, the Performance Rating is measured on a scale from A to E for ease of interpretation. The points score indicates where the Performance Rating falls on a scale of 0 to 10.

In the case of funds investing in municipal or other tax-free securities, this rating is based on the taxable equivalent return of the fund assuming the maximum marginal U.S. tax rate (35%).

8. 1-Year Total Return

The total return the fund has provided investors over the preceeding twelve months. This total return figure is computed based on the fund's dividend distributions and share price appreciation/depreciation during the period, net of the expenses and fees it imposes on its shareholders. Although the total return figure does not reflect an adjustment for any loads the fund may carry, such adjustments have been made in deriving TheStreet Investment Ratings.

9. 1-Year Total Return Percentile

The fund's percentile rank based on its one-year performance compared to that of all other fixed income funds in existence for at least one year. A score of 99 is the best possible, indicating that the fund outperformed 99% of the other mutual funds. Zero is the worst possible percentile score.

In the case of funds investing in municipal or other tax-free securities, this percentile rank is based on the taxable equivalent return of the fund assuming the maximum marginal U.S. tax rate (35%).

10. 3-Year Total Return

The total annual return the fund has provided investors over the preceeding three years.

11. 3-Year Total Return Percentile

The fund's percentile rank based on its three-year performance compared to that of all other fixed income funds in existence for at least three years. A score of 99 is the best possible, indicating that the fund outperformed 99% of the other mutual funds. Zero is the worst possible percentile score.

In the case of funds investing in municipal or other tax-free securities, this percentile rank is based on the taxable equivalent return of the fund assuming the maximum marginal U.S. tax rate (35%).

12. 5-Year Total Return

The total annual return the fund has provided investors over the preceeding five years.

13. 5-Year Total Return Percentile

The fund's percentile rank based on its five-year performance compared to that of all other fixed income funds in existence for at least five years. A score of 99 is the best possible, indicating that the fund outperformed 99% of the other mutual funds. Zero is the worst possible percentile score.

In the case of funds investing in municipal or other tax-free securities, this percentile rank is based on the taxable equivalent return of the fund assuming the maximum marginal U.S. tax rate (35%).

14. Risk Rating/Points

A letter grade rating based solely on the mutual fund's risk as determined by its monthly performance volatility over the trailing three years and the underlying credit risk and interest rate risk of its investment portfolio. The risk rating does not take into consideration the overall financial performance the fund has achieved or the total return it has provided to its shareholders. Like the overall Investment Rating, the Risk Rating is measured on a scale from A to E for ease of interpretation. The points score indicates where the Risk Rating falls on a scale of 0 to 10.

15. Manager Quality Percentile

The manager quality percentile is based on a ranking of the fund's alpha, a statistical measure representing the difference between a fund's actual returns and its expected performance given its level of risk. Fund managers who have been able to exceed the fund's statistically expected performance receive a high percentile rank with 99 representing the highest possible score. At the other end of the spectrum, fund managers who have actually detracted from the fund's expected performance receive a low percentile rank with 0 representing the lowest possible score.

16. Manager Tenure

The number of years the current manager has been managing the fund. Since fund managers who deliver substandard returns are usually replaced, a long tenure is usually a good sign that shareholders are satisfied that the fund is achieving its stated objectives.

99 Pct = Best
0 Pct = Worst

Fund Type	Fund Name	Ticker Symbol	Overall Investment Rating	Phone	Net Asset Value As of 2/28/17	Perform-ance Rating/Pts	1Yr / Pct	3Yr / Pct	5Yr / Pct	Risk Rating/Pts	Mgr. Quality Pct	Mgr. Tenure (Years)
GEI	Payden Limited Maturity Investor	PYLMX	B-	(888) 409-8007	9.47	D+ /2.6	1.70 /46	0.79 /24	0.87 /26	A+ / 9.9	66	N/A
GES	SEI Daily Inc Tr-Ultra Sh Dur Bd F	SECPX	B-	(800) 342-5734	9.32	D+ /2.6	1.56 /45	0.81 /25	1.04 /28	A+ / 9.9	66	18
USS	Touchstone Ut Sh Dr Fxd Inc Z	TSDOX	B-	(800) 543-0407	9.31	D+ /2.6	1.50 /45	0.83 /25	0.91 /26	A+ / 9.9	69	9
GEI	RidgeWorth Seix Ultra Short Bond I	SISSX	B-	(888) 784-3863	9.96	D+ /2.6	1.70 /46	0.78 /24	0.93 /26	A+ / 9.9	66	3
MUN	Alpine Ultra Short Muni Inc Inst	ATOIX	C+	(888) 785-5578	10.04	D+ /2.5	0.73 /41	0.61 /27	0.57 /26	A+ / 9.9	63	N/A
MUN	BMO Ultra Sht Tax-Free Y	MUYSX	C+	(800) 236-3863	10.07	D+ /2.3	0.57 /38	0.48 /24	0.62 /27	A+ / 9.9	56	2
GEI	Columbia CMG Ultra Short Term	CMGUX	C+	(800) 345-6611	9.01	D /2.2	1.15 /41	0.63 /22	0.63 /23	A+ / 9.9	62	5
MTG	Northern Tax-Advtged Ult-Sh Fxd	NTAUX	C+	(800) 595-9111	10.14	D /2.2	1.03 /40	0.61 /22	0.74 /24	A+ / 9.9	58	8
GEI	Metropolitan West Ultra Short Bnd	MWUSX	C+	(800) 496-8298	4.27	D /2.1	1.11 /41	0.57 /21	1.45 /34	A+ / 9.9	61	14
MTG	TCW Short Term Bond I	TGSMX	C+	(800) 386-3829	8.68	D /2.1	0.99 /39	0.53 /21	0.85 /25	A+ / 9.9	56	7
GES	DFA One-Yr Fixed Inc Inst	DFIHX	C+	(800) 984-9472	10.30	D /2.0	0.79 /37	0.48 /21	0.52 /22	A+ / 9.9	54	34
USS	RidgeWorth Seix US Gvt Sec US	SIGVX	C+	(888) 784-3863	10.02	D /2.0	0.87 /38	0.50 /21	0.57 /22	A+ / 9.9	61	3
MTG	Federated Adj Rate Sec Inst	FEUGX	C	(800) 341-7400	9.69	D /1.7	0.70 /36	0.28 /18	0.33 /20	A+ / 9.9	48	22
US	GMO US Treasury	GUSTX	C		25.00	D /1.6	0.49 /33	0.25 /18	0.20 /18	A+ / 9.9	52	3
GES	Wells Fargo Ult ST Inc A	SADAX	C	(800) 222-8222	8.48	D- /1.5	1.65 /46	0.62 /22	0.74 /24	A+ / 9.9	63	15
MTG	Trust for Credit UltSh Dur Gov TCU	TCUUX	C-	(800) 342-5828	9.47	D- /1.3	0.30 /29	0.16 /15	0.18 /18	A+ / 9.9	37	N/A
GEI	PNC Ultra Short Bond A	PSBAX	D+	(800) 551-2145	9.95	E /0.5	0.60 /35	0.14 /14	0.10 /15	A+ / 9.9	37	15
MTG	Wells Fargo Adj Rate Govt A	ESAAX	D	(800) 222-8222	9.01	E /0.5	0.68 /36	0.28 /18	0.52 /22	A+ / 9.9	54	9
USS	Federated Gov Ultrashort Dur A	FGUAX	D	(800) 341-7400	9.82	E /0.3	0.18 /25	-0.14 / 5	-0.14 / 4	A+ / 9.9	31	20
US	Permanent Portfolio Short-Tm Trs I	PRTBX	D	(800) 531-5142	64.70	E /0.3	-0.14 /15	-0.45 / 4	-0.51 / 3	A+ / 9.9	20	14
MUI	Federated Muni Ultrashrt A	FMUUX	D	(800) 341-7400	9.99	E /0.3	0.52 /37	0.06 /12	0.16 /19	A+ / 9.9	33	17
GEI	Northern Ultra-Short Fixed Income	NUSFX	B-	(800) 595-9111	10.21	D+ /2.8	1.83 /47	0.92 /26	1.05 /28	A+ / 9.8	65	5
GEI	Metropolitan West Low Dur Bd M	MWLDX	B-	(800) 496-8298	8.72	D+ /2.6	1.45 /44	0.86 /25	2.09 /43	A+ / 9.8	63	20
US	RidgeWorth Seix Ltd Dur I	SAMLX	C+	(888) 784-3863	9.93	D+ /2.5	1.74 /47	0.68 /23	0.65 /23	A+ / 9.8	67	15
MTG	PIA Short-Term Securities Adv	PIASX	C+	(800) 251-1970	10.03	D+ /2.4	1.68 /46	0.72 /23	0.57 /22	A+ / 9.8	62	N/A
GEI	Calvert Ultra-Short Inc A	CULAX	C+	(800) 368-2745	15.62	D+ /2.4	2.43 /53	0.92 /26	1.11 /29	A+ / 9.8	72	5
MUN	Vanguard Short-Term Tax-Exempt	VWSTX	C+	(800) 662-7447	15.78	D+ /2.4	0.46 /36	0.54 /25	0.62 /27	A+ / 9.8	46	1
GEI	Pioneer Short Term Income A	STABX	C+	(800) 225-6292	9.53	D+ /2.3	2.33 /52	1.20 /31	1.69 /37	A+ / 9.8	74	11
GEI	William Blair Low Duration N	WBLNX	C+	(800) 742-7272	9.06	D+ /2.3	0.96 /39	0.78 /24	0.76 /24	A+ / 9.8	61	8
GL	DFA Two Year Glbl Fixed Inc Inst	DFGFX	C+	(800) 984-9472	9.97	D /2.1	0.85 /38	0.62 /22	0.63 /23	A+ / 9.8	66	18
GEI	LWAS DFA Two Year Fixed	DFCFX	C+	(800) 984-9472	9.99	D /2.0	0.79 /37	0.57 /21	0.52 /22	A+ / 9.8	53	N/A
USS	AMG Mgrs Amundi Short DurGov	MGSDX	C+	(800) 548-4539	9.63	D /2.0	1.25 /42	0.46 /20	0.62 /23	A+ / 9.8	61	25
MUN	SEI Tax-Exempt Tr-Shrt Dur Muni	SUMAX	C	(800) 342-5734	10.01	D /1.7	0.05 /21	0.24 /20	0.39 /23	A+ / 9.8	32	6
GEI	JPMorgan Limited Duration Bd A	ONUAX	C	(800) 480-4111	9.99	D /1.6	1.13 /41	0.86 /25	1.98 /42	A+ / 9.8	63	22
GEI	SA US Fixed Income Fund	SAUFX	C	(800) 366-7266	10.19	D- /1.5	0.43 /32	0.21 /17	0.11 /15	A+ / 9.8	33	18
GEI	Goldman Sachs Enhanced Inc A	GEIAX	C-	(800) 526-7384	9.45	D- /1.3	1.67 /46	0.33 /19	0.40 /20	A+ / 9.8	55	9
MTG	Goldman Sachs Hi Qual Fltg R A	GSAMX	C-	(800) 526-7384	8.72	D- /1.1	1.87 /48	0.18 /16	0.24 /19	A+ / 9.8	56	9
USS	Dreyfus Ultra Short Income Z	DSIGX	D+	(800) 645-6561	10.08	E+ /0.9	0.66 /36	-0.03 / 5	0.04 /10	A+ / 9.8	35	1
GES	Federated Ultra Short Bd A	FULAX	D+	(800) 341-7400	9.11	E+ /0.8	1.44 /44	0.41 /20	0.64 /23	A+ / 9.8	52	19
USS	Sht-Tm US Government Bond	STUSX	D	(800) 955-9988	10.13	E /0.5	-0.07 /17	-0.02 / 5	-0.08 / 4	A+ / 9.8	26	14
MUS	Sanford C Bernstein Sh Dur CA	SDCMX	D	(212) 486-5800	12.38	E /0.4	-0.24 /14	-0.17 / 5	0.01 / 7	A+ / 9.8	18	23
MUN	Eaton Vance Floating-Rte Muni Inc	EXFLX	D	(800) 262-1122	9.80	E /0.4	0.72 /41	0.26 /20	0.14 /19	A+ / 9.8	37	13
COI	STAAR Inv Trust Shrt Term Bond	SITBX	D	(800) 332-7738	8.92	E /0.4	0.11 /23	-0.26 / 4	0.15 /17	A+ / 9.8	21	20
MUN	Wells Fargo Ult-Sh Mun Inc A	SMAVX	D	(800) 222-8222	9.56	E /0.3	-0.11 /16	0.09 /15	0.21 /20	A+ / 9.8	29	17
USS	Franklin Adjustable US Govt Sec A	FISAX	D	(800) 342-5236	8.37	E /0.3	0.50 /33	-0.04 / 5	0.20 /18	A+ / 9.8	33	26
MUN	USAA Ultra Short Term Bond Fund	UUSTX	B+	(800) 382-8722	9.99	C- /3.8	2.28 /60	0.87 /33	1.31 /42	A+ / 9.7	67	N/A
GL	BBH Limited Duration Class N	BBBMX	B+	(800) 625-5759	10.17	C- /3.7	3.44 /59	1.20 /31	1.47 /34	A+ / 9.7	77	6
GEI	Payden Low Duration Investor	PYSBX	B	(888) 409-8007	10.09	C- /3.1	2.17 /50	1.04 /28	1.41 /33	A+ / 9.7	67	N/A
GL	Payden Global Low Duration	PYGSX	B-	(888) 409-8007	10.04	C- /3.0	2.11 /50	0.98 /27	1.69 /37	A+ / 9.7	75	N/A
MTG	WA Adjustable Rate Income A	ARMZX	B-	(877) 534-4627	8.97	D+ /2.7	3.49 /60	1.20 /31	1.78 /39	A+ / 9.7	76	3
MUS	Sanford C Bernstein Sh Dur NY	SDNYX	C	(212) 486-5800	12.46	D /1.9	0.24 /30	0.28 /20	0.32 /21	A+ / 9.7	28	23
MUN	Sanford C Bernstein Sh-Dur Dvrs	SDDMX	C	(212) 486-5800	12.58	D /1.8	0.21 /29	0.25 /20	0.35 /22	A+ / 9.7	27	15

● Denotes fund is closed to new investors

Fund Type	Fund Name	Ticker Symbol	Overall Investment Rating	Phone	Net Asset Value As of 2/28/17	Performance Rating/Pts	1Yr / Pct	3Yr / Pct	5Yr / Pct	Risk Rating/Pts	Mgr. Quality Pct	Mgr. Tenure (Years)
USS	LWAS DFA Two Year Government	DFYGX	C	(800) 984-9472	9.85	D /1.8	0.38 /31	0.41 /20	0.34 /20	A+ /9.7	42	16
COI	Transamerica Prt High Quality	DVHQX	C	(888) 233-4339	11.11	D /1.8	0.66 /36	0.39 /20	0.54 /22	A+ /9.7	34	27
GEI	Trust for Credit Uns Sh Dur TCU	TCUDX	C	(800) 342-5828	9.65	D /1.6	0.21 /26	0.35 /19	0.38 /20	A+ /9.7	32	9
MTG	AMF Ultra Short Mortgage Fund	ASARX	C	(800) 527-3713	7.11	D /1.6	-0.04 /17	0.34 /19	0.80 /25	A+ /9.7	33	8
GES	Federated Short Term Inc A	FTIAX	C-	(800) 341-7400	8.50	D- /1.4	1.14 /41	0.37 /19	0.60 /22	A+ /9.7	34	22
GEI	MFS Limited Maturity A	MQLFX	C-	(800) 225-2606	5.98	D- /1.3	1.63 /46	0.70 /23	1.05 /28	A+ /9.7	52	N/A
USS	Goldman Sachs Short Dur Gov A	GSSDX	D	(800) 526-7384	9.98	E /0.5	0.53 /34	0.32 /19	0.30 /20	A+ /9.7	36	9
MUN	Franklin Fdrl Lmtd Trm T/F Inc A	FFTFX	D	(800) 342-5236	10.37	E /0.4	0.05 /21	0.45 /23	0.69 /28	A+ /9.7	32	14
GEI	Neuberger Berman Short Dur Bd A	NSHAX	D	(800) 877-9700	7.44	E /0.3	0.35 /30	0.28 /18	0.78 /25	A+ /9.7	30	11
GES	Semper Short Duration Inv	SEMRX	B+	(888) 263-6443	9.86	C- /3.5	2.78 /55	1.19 /31	0.90 /26	A+ /9.6	79	7
GEI	FPA New Income Inc	FPNIX	B-	(800) 982-4372	10.02	D+ /2.8	2.94 /56	1.30 /32	1.41 /33	A+ /9.6	73	13
GEI	BMO Short-Term Income Y	MSINX	B-	(800) 236-3863	9.36	D+ /2.8	1.67 /46	0.99 /27	1.25 /31	A+ /9.6	60	5
GEI	● Fidelity Short-Term Bond	FSHBX	C+	(800) 544-8544	8.60	D+ /2.6	1.25 /42	0.95 /27	1.12 /29	A+ /9.6	58	10
GEI	Cavanal Hill Limited Dur NL Inv	APSTX	C+	(800) 762-7085	9.52	D /2.2	0.56 /34	0.80 /24	1.50 /34	A+ /9.6	52	23
GEI	Wells Fargo Sh-Tm Bd A	SSTVX	C+	(800) 222-8222	8.75	D /2.2	1.96 /49	1.11 /29	1.31 /32	A+ /9.6	65	13
GEI	American Century Sh Duration A	ACSQX	C	(800) 345-6488	10.26	D /1.9	1.88 /48	0.89 /26	0.82 /25	A+ /9.6	59	N/A
GEI	Columbia Short Term Bond A	NSTRX	C	(800) 345-6611	9.99	D /1.9	1.46 /44	0.65 /22	0.86 /26	A+ /9.6	N/A	13
USS	Federated USG Sec:1-3yrs Y	FSGTX	C-	(800) 341-7400	10.34	D- /1.4	0.49 /33	0.21 /17	0.07 /13	A+ /9.6	31	4
COI	Wilmington Short-Term Bd A	MVSAX	C-	(800) 336-9970	9.99	D- /1.3	0.99 /39	0.60 /22	0.84 /25	A+ /9.6	37	21
GEI	PNC Ltd Maturity Bond A	PLFAX	D	(800) 551-2145	10.16	E /0.5	0.43 /32	0.40 /20	0.42 /21	A+ /9.6	31	15
GES	MainStay Tax Adv Sht-Tm Bd	MYTBX	D	(800) 624-6782	9.58	E /0.5	-0.09 /16	0.20 /16	0.13 /16	A+ /9.6	24	2
GEI	AB Short Duration A	ADPAX	D	(800) 221-5672	11.70	E- /0.2	0.42 /31	0.24 /17	0.16 /17	A+ /9.6	27	12
COI	Frost Low Duration Bond Inv	FADLX	B-	(866) 777-7818	10.24	C- /3.0	1.76 /47	1.07 /29	1.24 /31	A /9.5	62	15
GEI	TIAA-CREF Sh Trm Bond Retail	TCTRX	B-	(800) 842-2252	10.34	D+ /2.8	1.82 /47	0.98 /27	1.18 /30	A /9.5	59	11
MUN	USAA T/E Short Term Bond Fund	USSTX	C+	(800) 382-8722	10.45	D /2.2	--	0.58 /26	0.94 /34	A /9.5	29	N/A
GEI	BlackRock Low Duration Bond Inv	BLDAX	C	(800) 441-7762	9.62	D /2.1	1.93 /48	1.07 /29	1.65 /37	A /9.5	64	9
GEI	Nuveen Short Term Bond A	FALTX	C	(800) 257-8787	9.85	D /2.0	2.42 /52	0.92 /26	1.55 /35	A /9.5	64	13
USS	Vanguard Short-Term Gvt Bd Idx	VSBSX	C	(800) 662-7447	20.26	D /1.9	0.25 /27	0.57 /21	0.53 /22	A /9.5	47	4
USS	Sterling Capital Short Dur Bd A	BSGAX	C	(800) 228-1872	8.72	D /1.9	1.84 /48	0.87 /26	1.25 /31	A /9.5	63	6
GEI	Voya Limited Maturity Bond Adv	IMBAX	C-	(800) 992-0180	9.77	D- /1.5	0.47 /33	0.28 /18	0.44 /21	A /9.5	27	8
USS	BNY Mellon ST US Gov Sec M	MPSUX	C-	(800) 645-6561	11.71	D- /1.3	-0.09 /16	0.27 /18	0.18 /18	A /9.5	30	17
GES	American Funds Sh-T Bd of Amr A	ASBAX	D	(800) 421-0180	9.96	E+ /0.8	1.04 /40	0.63 /22	0.50 /21	A /9.5	42	6
GEI	JPMorgan Short Duration Bond A	OGLVX	D	(800) 480-4111	10.81	E /0.4	0.55 /34	0.43 /20	0.47 /21	A /9.5	30	11
GEI	RidgeWorth Seix Sh-Term Bond A	STSBX	D	(888) 784-3863	9.96	E /0.4	0.39 /31	0.37 /19	0.68 /23	A /9.5	28	3
USS	Eaton Vance Govt Obligation A	EVGOX	D	(800) 262-1122	6.38	E /0.3	0.49 /33	0.90 /26	0.78 /25	A /9.5	63	3
USS	American Century Sh-Term Govt A	TWAVX	D	(800) 345-6488	9.59	E /0.3	-0.24 /14	0.04 / 9	-0.07 / 4	A /9.5	22	15
MUN	BlackRock Short Term Muni Inv A	MELMX	D	(800) 441-7762	10.14	E- /0.2	-0.18 /15	0.06 /12	0.17 /19	A /9.5	18	10
GES	Baird Short-Term Bond Inst	BSBIX	B	(866) 442-2473	9.68	C- /3.6	2.25 /51	1.47 /34	1.84 /39	A /9.4	71	13
GES	T Rowe Price Short Term Bond	PRWBX	C+	(800) 638-5660	4.72	D+ /2.8	1.82 /47	0.94 /27	1.09 /29	A /9.4	59	2
GEI	Northern Short Bond	BSBAX	C+	(800) 637-1380	18.88	D+ /2.8	2.06 /49	0.86 /25	1.14 /29	A /9.4	56	7
COI	TD Short-Term Bond Inst	TDSBX	C+		10.16	D+ /2.4	1.36 /43	0.77 /24	0.83 /25	A /9.4	46	8
GEI	Victory INCORE Low Duration	RLDAX	C	(800) 539-3863	10.06	D /2.2	2.03 /49	1.02 /28	1.10 /29	A /9.4	62	13
MUI	BNY Mellon National ST Muni Bd	MPSTX	C	(800) 645-6561	12.76	D /2.2	0.38 /35	0.44 /23	0.54 /25	A /9.4	26	2
US	WA Short-Term Bond A	SBSTX	C	(877) 534-4627	3.87	D /2.1	2.41 /52	0.98 /27	1.29 /31	A /9.4	68	3
USS	SEI Daily Inc Tr-Sh Dur Gov Bd F	TCSGX	C	(800) 342-5734	10.43	D /2.0	0.37 /30	0.62 /22	0.58 /22	A /9.4	N/A	14
GEI	Nationwide HighMark Sht Term Bd	NWJSX	C-	(800) 848-0920	9.94	D- /1.4	1.52 /45	0.71 /23	0.84 /25	A /9.4	44	13
MUN	Columbia Sh-Term Muni Bd A	NSMMX	D	(800) 345-6611	10.35	E+ /0.6	--	0.27 /20	0.47 /24	A /9.4	20	5
MUN	WA Short Duration Muni Income A	SHDAX	D	(877) 534-4627	5.08	E /0.5	0.09 /24	0.54 /25	0.75 /29	A /9.4	28	14

● Denotes fund is closed to new investors

						PERFORMANCE				RISK	FUND MGR	
99 Pct = Best *0 Pct = Worst*			Overall		Net Asset Value As of	Perform-ance	Annualized Total Return Through 2/28/17			Risk	Mgr. Quality	Mgr. Tenure
Fund Type	Fund Name	Ticker Symbol	Investment Rating	Phone	2/28/17	Rating/Pts	1Yr / Pct	3Yr / Pct	5Yr / Pct	Rating/Pts	Pct	(Years)
USS	Rydex Inv Govt Lg Bd Stgy A	RYAQX	E-	(800) 820-0888	34.46	E- /0.0	3.98 /62	-8.57 / 0	-5.24 / 0	E- /0.0	1	9
GEI	Credit Suisse Cmdty Rtn Strat A	CRSAX	E-	(877) 927-2874	5.01	E- /0.0	16.51 /91	-12.70 / 0	-10.08 / 0	E- /0.0	0	11
GEI	Rydex Wekng Dlr 2x Stgry A	RYWDX	E-	(800) 820-0888	64.26	E- /0.0	-8.07 / 0	-15.95 / 0	-10.79 / 0	E- /0.0	0	12
GEI	Credit Suisse Commdty Ret Str	CCRSX	E-	(877) 927-2874	4.42	E- /0.0	16.32 /91	-12.69 / 0	-10.11 / 0	E- /0.0	0	11
GES	AB All Mkt Real Return A	AMTAX	E-	(800) 221-5672	8.51	E- /0.0	23.44 /98	-6.72 / 0	-4.09 / 0	E- /0.0	0	2
EM	Goldman Sachs Local Emg Mkt	GAMDX	E-	(800) 526-7384	6.22	E- /0.1	12.70 /84	-3.74 / 1	-3.37 / 0	E- /0.0	12	9
COH	Catalyst/SMH High Income A	HIIFX	E	(866) 447-4228	3.91	C- /3.3	46.00 /99	-5.28 / 0	-1.69 / 1	E- /0.0	0	9
GES	Northeast Investors Trust	NTHEX	E+	(800) 225-6704	4.74	C /4.8	35.60 /99	-3.55 / 1	2.53 /50	E- /0.0	2	N/A
USL	Rydex Govt Lg Bd 1.2x Strgy A	RYABX	E+	(800) 820-0888	51.50	C /5.0	-7.67 / 0	6.91 /96	3.81 /70	E- /0.0	1	23
USA	ProFunds-US Government Plus	GVPSX	E+	(888) 776-3637	49.04	C /5.0	-8.64 / 0	5.62 /89	1.47 /34	E- /0.0	1	8
US	Wasatch Hoisington US Treasury	WHOSX	D-	(800) 551-1700	15.87	C+ /6.8	-5.86 / 0	7.03 /96	3.25 /62	E- /0.0	58	21
EM	Janus Emerging Markets A	JMFAX	D+	(800) 295-2687	8.68	B+ /8.8	29.19 /99	2.84 /59	-0.15 / 4	E- /0.0	96	5
US	Vanguard Extnd Durtn Trea Idx Inst	VEDTX	C-	(800) 662-7447	33.95	A- /9.1	-6.63 / 0	9.40 /99	4.53 /79	E- /0.0	69	4
GEI	PIMCO Extended Duration P	PEDPX	C-	(800) 426-0107	7.55	A- /9.1	-5.95 / 0	9.45 /99	4.30 /76	E- /0.0	0	10
MTG	PIMCO StkPlus Intl (DH) A	PIPAX	C	(800) 426-0107	7.60	A+ /9.9	26.71 /99	6.07 /92	10.96 /99	E- /0.0	98	2
GEI	Rydex Strengthening Dlr 2x Strtgy	RYSDX	C	(800) 820-0888	54.04	A+ /9.9	4.97 /66	13.86 /99	6.77 /96	E- /0.0	99	12
GEN	J Hancock VIT Value I	JEVLX	C	(800) 257-3336	22.17	A+ /9.9	32.97 /99	6.07 /92	11.88 /99	E- /0.0	99	20
GEI	Fairholme Focused Income	FOCIX	C+	(866) 202-2263	12.55	A+ /9.9	42.47 /99	6.55 /94	10.45 /99	E- /0.0	99	8
EM	Dreyfus Eme Mkts Dbt LC A	DDBAX	E-	(800) 782-6620	11.50	E- /0.0	11.43 /82	-4.81 / 0	-3.53 / 0	E- /0.1	2	9
EM	PIMCO Emerging Local Bond A	PELAX	E-	(800) 426-0107	7.21	E- /0.1	14.35 /87	-3.27 / 1	-3.50 / 0	E- /0.1	20	11
EM	Eaton Vance Emer Market Local	EEIAX	E	(800) 262-1122	6.17	C- /3.4	17.57 /93	-0.11 / 5	-2.49 / 1	E- /0.1	89	9
GL	TCW Emg Mkts Local Currency Inc	TGWNX	E	(800) 386-3829	9.11	C- /3.7	16.20 /91	-1.37 / 2	-1.55 / 2	E- /0.1	80	7
USL	PIMCO Long Term US Govt A	PFGAX	E+	(800) 426-0107	6.02	C /4.9	-3.95 / 0	5.46 /88	2.99 /58	E- /0.1	14	10
US	Fidelity Lg-T Tre Bd In Inv	FLBIX	D-	(800) 544-8544	12.80	C+ /6.8	-4.66 / 0	6.00 /92	3.19 /60	E- /0.1	53	3
US	Vanguard Long-Term Treasury Inv	VUSTX	D-	(800) 662-7447	11.95	B- /7.0	-4.43 / 0	6.08 /92	3.23 /61	E- /0.1	58	2
USL	Vanguard Long-Term Govt Bd Idx	VLGSX	D-	(800) 662-7447	25.22	B- /7.1	-4.33 / 0	6.15 /93	3.34 /63	E- /0.1	28	4
GEI	Columbia Abs Rtn Currency & Inc	RACWX	C+	(800) 345-6611	10.90	A+ /9.9	9.30 /77	12.21 /99	5.18 /86	E- /0.1	99	11
US	Direxion Mo 7-10 Year Tr Br 2X Inv	DXKSX	E-	(800) 851-0511	30.38	E- /0.0	3.05 /57	-8.69 / 0	-7.30 / 0	E- /0.2	0	13
GL	STAAR AltCat	SITAX	E	(800) 332-7738	14.19	D /1.8	14.16 /87	-2.44 / 2	2.72 /53	E- /0.2	3	20
US	Direxion Mo 7-10 Year Tr Bl 2X Inv	DXKLX	E	(800) 851-0511	34.14	D+ /2.4	-8.47 / 0	3.22 /65	1.44 /33	E- /0.2	1	11
EM	Oppenheimer Em Mkts Local Debt	OEMAX	E	(888) 470-0862	7.17	C- /3.5	15.90 /90	0.05 / 9	-0.79 / 2	E- /0.2	89	2
EM	SEI Inst Intl Emerging Mkts Debt F	SITEX	E+	(800) 342-5734	9.79	C /4.9	12.88 /85	0.67 /23	0.61 /23	E- /0.2	91	17
US	T Rowe Price US Treas Long-Term	PRULX	E+	(800) 638-5660	12.36	C+ /6.1	-4.70 / 0	5.33 /87	2.67 /52	E- /0.2	31	14
US	Dreyfus US Treasury Long Term	DRGBX	E+	(800) 645-6561	18.40	C+ /6.1	-4.72 / 0	5.29 /87	2.53 /50	E- /0.2	37	9
GEL	Vanguard Long Term Bd Idx	VBLTX	D	(800) 662-7447	13.75	B+ /8.4	4.47 /64	5.84 /91	4.28 /76	E- /0.2	5	4
GES	Metropolitan West Alpha Trak 500	MWATX	C+	(800) 496-8298	8.96	A+ /9.9	35.34 /99	13.01 /99	16.54 /99	E- /0.2	99	19
GL	Wells Fargo Intl Bd A	ESIYX	E-	(800) 222-8222	9.62	E- /0.0	0.10 /22	-3.01 / 1	-1.51 / 2	E /0.3	33	24
USS	PIMCO StocksPLUS Short A	PSSAX	E-	(800) 426-0107	9.25	E- /0.0	-14.51 / 0	-9.78 / 0	-11.51 / 0	E /0.3	0	3
COI	Federated Emerging Mkt Debt A	IHIAX	E+	(800) 341-7400	8.47	C /5.2	11.94 /83	1.84 /40	2.21 /45	E /0.3	7	4
GEI	PIMCO Real Return Asset P	PRTPX	D-	(800) 426-0107	8.39	C+ /6.5	7.81 /74	2.90 /59	1.11 /29	E /0.3	1	10
GEI	API Multi Asset Income A	APIUX	D	(800) 544-6060	10.41	B /7.7	23.71 /99	2.42 /50	5.54 /89	E /0.3	85	20
COH	Franklin High Income A	FHAIX	D+	(800) 342-5236	1.91	B+ /8.4	27.58 /99	2.20 /46	5.26 /86	E /0.3	0	26
GL	● MainStay Global High Income B	MGHBX	D+	(800) 624-6782	10.28	B+ /8.6	17.00 /92	3.36 /67	3.21 /61	E /0.3	96	6
EM	PIMCO Emerging Markets Bond A	PAEMX	C-	(800) 426-0107	10.40	B+ /8.8	17.97 /93	4.41 /80	3.73 /69	E /0.3	98	5
GEI	PIMCO Long Dur Total Return P	PLRPX	C-	(800) 426-0107	10.70	A- /9.0	6.80 /72	6.18 /93	4.69 /81	E /0.3	11	10
GEI	● Vanguard Long-Term Inv Gr Inv	VWESX	C-	(800) 662-7447	10.21	A- /9.1	7.10 /73	6.34 /94	5.40 /88	E /0.3	32	4
GL	Nuveen High Income Bond A	FJSIX	C	(800) 257-8787	7.95	A- /9.2	32.82 /99	2.50 /52	5.75 /90	E /0.3	91	12
COI	Vanguard Long-Term Corp Bd Idx	VLTCX	C	(800) 662-7447	24.24	A /9.4	11.67 /82	5.99 /92	5.27 /87	E /0.3	8	8
GEI	PIMCO Long Term Credit Inst	PTCIX	C+	(800) 426-0107	11.71	A+ /9.8	13.18 /85	7.28 /96	7.24 /97	E /0.3	69	8
EM	T Rowe Price Inst Intl Bd	RPIIX	E-	(800) 638-5660	8.33	E- /0.0	1.26 /42	-2.29 / 2	-0.74 / 2	E /0.4	55	3
GL	Laudus Mondrian Intl Govt Fxd Inc	LIFNX	E-	(800) 407-0256	9.22	E- /0.0	-2.67 / 0	-3.16 / 1	-2.78 / 1	E /0.4	20	N/A
EM	EuroPac International Bond A	EPIBX	E-	(888) 558-5851	8.13	E- /0.0	5.72 /69	-4.84 / 0	-3.25 / 1	E /0.4	1	7

● Denotes fund is closed to new investors

						PERFORMANCE	Annualized Total Return Through 2/28/17			RISK	FUND MGR	
Fund Type	Fund Name	Ticker Symbol	Overall Investment Rating	Phone	Net Asset Value As of 2/28/17	Perform-ance Rating/Pts	1Yr / Pct	3Yr / Pct	5Yr / Pct	Risk Rating/Pts	Mgr. Quality Pct	Mgr. Tenure (Years)
GL	T Rowe Price Intl Bond	RPIBX	E-	(800) 638-5660	8.47	E- /0.0	1.05 /40	-2.59 / 1	-1.15 / 2	E /0.4	37	3
GL	LM BW Global Opportunities Bond	GOBAX	E	(877) 534-4627	10.46	D /2.0	6.14 /71	0.92 /26	1.65 /37	E /0.4	91	11
GL	LM BW International Opptys Bd IS	LMOTX	E	(877) 534-4627	11.14	D /2.2	5.59 /69	-0.08 / 5	1.60 /36	E /0.4	87	8
COI	Delaware Extended Duration Bd A	DEEAX	D-	(800) 523-1918	6.39	C+ /6.9	7.49 /73	4.72 /83	5.49 /88	E /0.4	5	10
EM	J Hancock Emerg Markets Debt A	JMKAX	C-	(800) 257-3336	9.44	B+ /8.8	17.97 /93	4.66 /82	3.99 /72	E /0.4	98	4
COH	Loomis Sayles Inst High Income	LSHIX	C+	(800) 633-3330	6.81	A+ /9.7	27.63 /99	3.85 /73	8.00 /98	E /0.4	4	21
EM	Fidelity Adv Emerging Mkts Inc A	FMKAX	C+	(800) 522-7297	14.20	A+ /9.7	18.36 /94	6.62 /95	5.33 /87	E /0.4	99	22
EM	Fidelity New Markets Income	FNMIX	C+	(800) 544-8544	16.09	A+ /9.9	18.72 /95	7.02 /96	5.74 /90	E /0.4	99	22
EM	● GMO Emerging Country Debt III	GMCDX	C+		28.99	A+ /9.9	19.47 /95	7.56 /97	7.87 /98	E /0.4	99	23
GL	American Century Intl Bond A	AIBDX	E-	(800) 345-6488	12.12	E- /0.0	-1.38 / 2	-3.66 / 1	-2.36 / 1	E /0.5	8	8
EM	Invesco Emerg Mkts Flexible Bond	IAEMX	E-	(800) 959-4246	6.56	E- /0.0	7.67 /74	-4.59 / 0	-4.03 / 0	E /0.5	0	2
GL	Federated Global Total Return Bd	FTIIX	E-	(800) 341-7400	9.50	E- /0.0	-3.72 / 0	-2.95 / 1	-2.25 / 1	E /0.5	21	15
GL	PIMCO Foreign Bd Fd (Unhgd) A	PFUAX	E-	(800) 426-0107	9.47	E- /0.1	4.04 /62	-1.08 / 3	-0.22 / 4	E /0.5	79	3
GL	PIMCO Emerging Markets	PLMAX	E-	(800) 426-0107	8.91	E- /0.2	11.00 /81	-1.92 / 2	-1.57 / 2	E /0.5	26	12
GL	Lord Abbett Emerg Mkts Currency	LDMAX	E-	(888) 522-2388	5.26	E- /0.2	10.04 /79	-2.23 / 2	-1.70 / 1	E /0.5	18	10
GEI	Calvert Long Term Income A	CLDAX	E+	(800) 368-2745	16.56	C+ /5.9	5.47 /68	4.70 /83	4.56 /79	E /0.5	10	4
COH	First Eagle High Yield I	FEHIX	C-	(800) 334-2143	9.08	B+ /8.9	24.20 /99	2.56 /53	5.17 /86	E /0.5	1	N/A
COH	J Hancock High Yield NAV		C	(800) 257-3336	8.27	A- /9.2	24.95 /99	2.63 /55	5.93 /92	E /0.5	1	11
EM	Stone Harbor Emerging Debt Inst	SHMDX	C+	(866) 699-8125	10.44	A+ /9.7	16.18 /90	5.83 /91	4.07 /73	E /0.5	99	10
GL	Invesco World Bond A	AUBAX	E-	(800) 959-4246	10.02	E- /0.1	4.88 /66	-1.37 / 2	0.11 /15	E /0.5	75	7
EM	WA Emerging Markets Debt A	LWEAX	D	(888) 425-6432	5.02	B- /7.4	14.57 /88	3.51 /69	2.48 /49	E+ /0.6	96	4
EM	PIMCO EM Corporate Bond Inst	PEMIX	D+	(800) 426-0107	10.61	B /8.2	17.28 /92	2.39 /50	3.55 /66	E+ /0.6	92	1
COH	RidgeWorth Seix High Income A	SAHIX	D+	(888) 784-3863	6.53	B+ /8.3	22.00 /98	3.35 /67	5.87 /91	E+ /0.6	4	6
EM	Columbia Emerging Markets Bond	REBAX	C-	(800) 345-6611	11.55	B+ /8.5	16.23 /91	4.77 /83	3.97 /72	E+ /0.6	98	6
COH	Loomis Sayles High Income A	NEFHX	C-	(800) 225-5478	4.31	B+ /8.8	21.71 /98	3.82 /73	6.26 /94	E+ /0.6	7	15
COH	Fidelity Adv Hi Income Advantage	FAHDX	C+	(800) 522-7297	11.09	A /9.5	22.41 /98	5.20 /86	7.61 /97	E+ /0.6	55	8
MUS	● Oppenheimer Rochester VA Muni	ORVAX	C+	(888) 470-0862	8.23	A+ /9.7	9.27 /87	5.37 /98	2.85 /77	E+ /0.6	77	11
MUH	SEI Asset Alloc-Def Strat All F	STDAX	C+	(800) 342-5734	14.64	A+ /9.9	19.17 /99	8.26 /99	10.32 /99	E+ /0.6	98	14
MTG	ProFunds-Falling US Dollar Svc	FDPSX	E-	(888) 776-3637	15.64	E- /0.0	-6.29 / 0	-10.51 / 0	-7.63 / 0	E+ /0.7	0	8I
GEI	J Hancock Absolute Ret Curr A	JCUAX	E	(800) 257-3336	9.41	D /2.1	3.18 /58	1.09 /29	2.47 /49	E+ /0.7	87	6
GEI	American Century Zero Cpn 2025	BTTRX	E+	(800) 345-6488	96.09	C+ /5.6	-2.97 / 0	4.27 /78	2.78 /54	E+ /0.7	6	11
COH	Western Asset Short Dur High Inc	SHIAX	D-	(877) 534-4627	5.42	C+ /6.5	21.17 /97	0.68 /23	4.60 /80	E+ /0.7	0	6
COH	WA Global High Yield Bond A	SAHYX	D	(877) 534-4627	6.47	B /7.7	21.99 /98	2.38 /50	5.22 /86	E+ /0.7	1	11
COH	Ivy High Income A	WHIAX	C-	(800) 777-6472	7.64	B+ /8.6	23.90 /99	3.39 /67	6.68 /96	E+ /0.7	8	3
EM	Universal Inst Emer Mrkt Debt II	UEDBX	C	(800) 869-6397	8.01	B+ /8.9	13.37 /86	4.38 /79	3.44 /64	E+ /0.7	98	15
COH	WA High Yield IS	WAHSX	C	(888) 425-6432	8.22	A- /9.0	23.45 /98	2.63 /55	5.77 /91	E+ /0.7	2	12
COH	Victory High Yield A	GUHYX	C	(800) 539-3863	6.51	A- /9.2	22.27 /98	3.35 /67	5.58 /89	E+ /0.7	7	8
EM	Franklin Emg Mkt Debt	FEMDX	C+	(800) 342-5236	11.31	A /9.5	18.26 /94	4.50 /81	4.72 /81	E+ /0.7	97	11
COH	Federated High Yield Trust Svc	FHYTX	C+	(800) 341-7400	6.89	A+ /9.6	20.02 /96	5.02 /85	8.09 /98	E+ /0.7	54	33
EM	T Rowe Price Emerging Markets	PREMX	C+	(800) 638-5660	12.64	A+ /9.8	18.31 /94	6.74 /95	5.22 /86	E+ /0.7	99	23
GL	PACE Global Fx Inc Inve A	PWFAX	E-	(888) 793-8637	9.67	E- /0.1	-0.77 / 6	-0.28 / 4	-0.61 / 3	E+ /0.8	84	22
GL	Templeton Global Total Return A	TGTRX	D-	(800) 342-5236	12.30	B- /7.2	15.93 /90	2.24 /47	3.72 /69	E+ /0.8	84	9
COH	AllianzGI High Yield Bond A	AYBAX	D	(800) 988-8380	9.31	B- /7.5	19.30 /95	2.60 /54	5.15 /85	E+ /0.8	3	21
COH	Pioneer High Yield A	TAHYX	D	(800) 225-6292	9.72	B /7.8	19.80 /96	2.87 /59	6.02 /92	E+ /0.8	4	10
COH	American Funds High Income Tr A	AHITX	D+	(800) 421-0180	10.46	B /8.1	21.40 /97	2.82 /58	5.14 /85	E+ /0.8	3	28
COH	Waddell & Reed Adv High Income	UNHIX	C-	(888) 923-3355	6.81	B+ /8.3	22.04 /98	3.44 /68	7.09 /97	E+ /0.8	9	3
GEI	Nuveen Symphony Credit Oppty A	NCOAX	C	(800) 257-8787	20.76	A- /9.1	25.98 /99	3.49 /69	6.33 /94	E+ /0.8	91	7
COH	Permanent Portfolio Versatile Bd I	PRVBX	C	(800) 531-5142	59.65	A- /9.1	19.94 /96	3.59 /70	4.11 /74	E+ /0.8	37	14

99 Pct = Best
0 Pct = Worst

● Denotes fund is closed to new investors

Data as of February 28, 2017

Section VII

Top-Rated Bond
Mutual Funds
by Risk Category

A compilation of those

Fixed Income Mutual Funds

receiving the highest TheStreet Investment Ratings

within each risk grade.

Funds are listed in order by Overall Investment Rating.

Section VII Contents

This section contains a summary analysis of the top 100 rated bond and money market mutual funds within each risk grade. Based on your personal risk tolerance, each page shows those funds that have achieved the best financial performance over the past three years.

In order to optimize the utility of our top and bottom fund lists, rather than listing all funds in a multi-class series, a single fund from each series is selected for display as the primary share class. Whenever possible, the selected fund is one that a retail investor would be most likely to choose. This share class may not be appropriate for every investor, so please consult with your financial advisor, the fund company, and the fund's prospectus before placing your trade.

Take the Investor Profile Quiz in the Appendix for assistance in determining your own risk tolerance level. Then you can use this section to identify those funds that are most appropriate for your investing style.

Note that increased risk does not always mean increased performance. Most of the riskiest mutual funds in the E (Very Weak) Risk Rating category have also provided very poor returns to their shareholders. Funds in the D and E Risk Rating categories generally represent speculative ventures that should not be entered into lightly.

1. Fund Type   The mutual fund's peer category based on its investment objective as stated in its prospectus.

COH	Corporate - High Yield	MMT	Money Market - Treas.
COI	Corporate - Inv. Grade	MTG	Mortgage
EM	Emerging Market	MUH	Municipal - High Yield
GEN	General	MUI	Municipal - Insured
GEI	General - Inv. Grade	MUN	Municipal - National
GEL	General - Long Term	MUS	Municipal - Single State
GES	General - Short & Interm.	USL	U.S. Gov.- Long Term
GL	Global	USS	U.S. Gov. - Short & Interm
LP	Loan Participation	USA	U.S. Gov. - Agency
MMF	Money Mkt - Tax Exempt	US	U.S. Gov. - Treasury

A blank fund type means that the mutual fund has not yet been categorized.

2. Fund Name   The name of the mutual fund as stated in its prospectus, which can sometimes differ slightly from the name that the company uses for advertising. If you cannot find the particular mutual fund you are interested in, or if you have any doubts regarding the precise name, verify the information with your broker or on your account statement. Also, use the fund's ticker symbol for confirmation. (See column 3.)

3. Ticker Symbol

The unique alphabetic symbol used for identifying and trading a specific mutual fund. No two funds can have the same ticker symbol, and the ticker symbol for mutual funds always ends with an "X".

A handful of funds currently show no associated ticker symbol. This means that the fund is either small or new since the NASD only assigns a ticker symbol to funds with at least $25 million in assets or 1,000 shareholders.

4. Overall Investment Rating

Our overall rating is measured on a scale from A to E based on each fund's risk-adjusted performance. Please see page 11 for specific descriptions of each letter grade. Also, refer to page 7 for information on how our ratings are derived. Most important, when using this rating, please be sure to consider the warnings beginning on page 13 regarding the ratings' limitations and the underlying assumptions.

5. Phone

The telephone number of the company managing the fund. Call this number to receive a prospectus or other information about the fund.

6. Net Asset Value (NAV)

The fund's share price as of the date indicated. A fund's NAV is computed by dividing the value of the fund's asset holdings, less accrued fees and expenses, by the number of its shares outstanding.

7. Performance Rating/Points

A letter grade rating based solely on the mutual fund's financial performance over the trailing three years, without any consideration for the amount of risk the fund poses. Like the overall Investment Rating, the Performance Rating is measured on a scale from A to E for ease of interpretation. The points score indicates where the Performance Rating falls on a scale of 0 to 10.

In the case of funds investing in municipal or other tax-free securities, this rating is based on the taxable equivalent return of the fund assuming the maximum marginal U.S. tax rate (35%).

8. 1-Year Total Return

The total return the fund has provided investors over the preceeding twelve months. This total return figure is computed based on the fund's dividend distributions and share price appreciation/depreciation during the period, net of the expenses and fees it imposes on its shareholders. Although the total return figure does not reflect an adjustment for any loads the fund may carry, such adjustments have been made in deriving TheStreet Investment Ratings.

9. 1-Year Total Return Percentile

The fund's percentile rank based on its one-year performance compared to that of all other fixed income funds in existence for at least one year. A score of 99 is the best possible, indicating that the fund outperformed 99% of the other mutual funds. Zero is the worst possible percentile score.

In the case of funds investing in municipal or other tax-free securities, this percentile rank is based on the taxable equivalent return of the fund assuming the maximum marginal U.S. tax rate (35%).

10. 3-Year Total Return

The total annual return the fund has provided investors over the preceeding three years.

11. 3-Year Total Return Percentile

The fund's percentile rank based on its three-year performance compared to that of all other fixed income funds in existence for at least three years. A score of 99 is the best possible, indicating that the fund outperformed 99% of the other mutual funds. Zero is the worst possible percentile score.

In the case of funds investing in municipal or other tax-free securities, this percentile rank is based on the taxable equivalent return of the fund assuming the maximum marginal U.S. tax rate (35%).

12. 5-Year Total Return

The total annual return the fund has provided investors over the preceeding five years.

13. 5-Year Total Return Percentile

The fund's percentile rank based on its five-year performance compared to that of all other fixed income funds in existence for at least five years. A score of 99 is the best possible, indicating that the fund outperformed 99% of the other mutual funds. Zero is the worst possible percentile score.

In the case of funds investing in municipal or other tax-free securities, this percentile rank is based on the taxable equivalent return of the fund assuming the maximum marginal U.S. tax rate (35%).

14. Risk Rating/Points

A letter grade rating based solely on the mutual fund's risk as determined by its monthly performance volatility over the trailing three years and the underlying credit risk and interest rate risk of its investment portfolio. The risk rating does not take into consideration the overall financial performance the fund has achieved or the total return it has provided to its shareholders. Like the overall Investment Rating, the Risk Rating is measured on a scale from A to E for ease of interpretation. The points score indicates where the Risk Rating falls on a scale of 0 to 10.

15. Manager Quality Percentile

The manager quality percentile is based on a ranking of the fund's alpha, a statistical measure representing the difference between a fund's actual returns and its expected performance given its level of risk. Fund managers who have been able to exceed the fund's statistically expected performance receive a high percentile rank with 99 representing the highest possible score. At the other end of the spectrum, fund managers who have actually detracted from the fund's expected performance receive a low percentile rank with 0 representing the lowest possible score.

16. Manager Tenure

The number of years the current manager has been managing the fund. Since fund managers who deliver substandard returns are usually replaced, a long tenure is usually a good sign that shareholders are satisfied that the fund is achieving its stated objectives.

VII. Top-Rated Bond Mutual Funds In The A Risk Category

99 Pct = Best
0 Pct = Worst

Fund Type	Fund Name	Ticker Symbol	Overall Investment Rating	Phone	Net Asset Value As of 2/28/17	Performance Rating/Pts	1Yr / Pct	3Yr / Pct	5Yr / Pct	Risk Rating/Pts	Mgr. Quality Pct	Mgr. Tenure (Years)
GEI	Metropolitan West Strategic Inc M	MWSTX	A	(800) 496-8298	8.06	C /4.6	4.08 /62	1.82 /40	4.07 /73	A- /9.2	81	14
GEI	SEI Instl Mgd Tr-Enhanced Inc F	SEEAX	A-	(800) 342-5734	7.54	C /4.6	5.36 /68	1.69 /38	2.29 /46	A- /9.0	81	11
MUN	Oppenheimer Rochester Sht Term	ORSTX	B+	(888) 470-0862	3.73	C- /4.1	0.82 /42	1.93 /60	1.91 /57	A- /9.2	74	7
GEI	Vanguard Sh-Term Invest-Grade	VFSTX	B+	(800) 662-7447	10.67	C- /4.1	2.70 /55	1.77 /39	2.04 /43	A- /9.0	71	9
GEI	Weitz Short Dur Income Inst	WEFIX	B+	(800) 232-4161	12.35	C- /4.0	3.28 /58	1.62 /37	1.88 /40	A- /9.1	71	21
GEI	Lord Abbett Shrt Duration Inc A	LALDX	B+	(888) 522-2388	4.31	C- /4.0	4.69 /65	1.98 /43	2.57 /51	A- /9.0	80	19
GEI	● Thrivent Limited Maturity Bond A	LBLAX	B+	(800) 847-4836	12.46	C- /3.9	3.14 /58	1.46 /34	1.49 /34	A /9.3	72	18
GEI	USAA Short Term Bond Retail	USSBX	B+	(800) 382-8722	9.16	C- /3.9	3.37 /59	1.48 /35	1.87 /40	A- /9.2	70	1
MUN	USAA Ultra Short Term Bond Fund	UUSTX	B+	(800) 382-8722	9.99	C- /3.8	2.28 /60	0.87 /33	1.31 /42	A+ /9.7	67	N/A
GL	BBH Limited Duration Class N	BBBMX	B+	(800) 625-5759	10.17	C- /3.7	3.44 /59	1.20 /31	1.47 /34	A+ /9.7	77	6
GES	Semper Short Duration Inv	SEMRX	B+	(888) 263-6443	9.86	C- /3.5	2.78 /55	1.19 /31	0.90 /26	A+ /9.6	79	7
GES	Baird Short-Term Bond Inst	BSBIX	B	(866) 442-2473	9.68	C- /3.6	2.25 /51	1.47 /34	1.84 /39	A /9.4	71	13
GEI	Payden Low Duration Investor	PYSBX	B	(888) 409-8007	10.09	C- /3.1	2.17 /50	1.04 /28	1.41 /33	A+ /9.7	67	N/A
GEI	Tributary Short/Intmdt Bond Inst	FOSIX	B-	(800) 662-4203	9.33	C- /3.2	1.92 /48	1.22 /31	1.68 /37	A /9.3	63	14
COI	Transamerica Short-Term Bond A	ITAAX	B-	(888) 233-4339	10.21	C- /3.1	3.82 /61	1.51 /35	2.39 /48	A /9.3	73	6
GL	Payden Global Low Duration	PYGSX	B-	(888) 409-8007	10.04	C- /3.0	2.11 /50	0.98 /27	1.69 /37	A+ /9.7	75	N/A
COI	Frost Low Duration Bond Inv	FADLX	B-	(866) 777-7818	10.24	C- /3.0	1.76 /47	1.07 /29	1.24 /31	A /9.5	62	15
USS	Sit US Government Securities	SNGVX	B-	(800) 332-5580	10.94	C- /3.0	0.16 /24	1.41 /33	0.88 /26	A /9.3	74	30
GEI	Northern Ultra-Short Fixed Income	NUSFX	B-	(800) 595-9111	10.21	D+ /2.8	1.83 /47	0.92 /26	1.05 /28	A+ /9.8	65	5
GEI	FPA New Income Inc	FPNIX	B-	(800) 982-4372	10.02	D+ /2.8	2.94 /56	1.30 /32	1.41 /33	A+ /9.6	73	13
GEI	BMO Short-Term Income Y	MSINX	B-	(800) 236-3863	9.36	D+ /2.8	1.67 /46	0.99 /27	1.25 /31	A+ /9.6	60	5
GEI	TIAA-CREF Sh Trm Bond Retail	TCTRX	B-	(800) 842-2252	10.34	D+ /2.8	1.82 /47	0.98 /27	1.18 /30	A /9.5	59	11
MTG	WA Adjustable Rate Income A	ARMZX	B-	(877) 534-4627	8.97	D+ /2.7	3.49 /60	1.20 /31	1.78 /39	A+ /9.7	76	3
GEI	Payden Limited Maturity Investor	PYLMX	B-	(888) 409-8007	9.47	D+ /2.6	1.70 /46	0.79 /24	0.87 /26	A+ /9.9	66	N/A
USS	Touchstone Ut Sh Dr Fxd Inc Z	TSDOX	B-	(800) 543-0407	9.31	D+ /2.6	1.50 /45	0.83 /25	0.91 /26	A+ /9.9	69	9
GES	SEI Daily Inc Tr-Ultra Sh Dur Bd F	SECPX	B-	(800) 342-5734	9.32	D+ /2.6	1.56 /45	0.81 /25	1.04 /28	A+ /9.9	66	18
GEI	RidgeWorth Seix Ultra Short Bond I	SISSX	B-	(888) 784-3863	9.96	D+ /2.6	1.70 /46	0.78 /24	0.93 /26	A+ /9.9	66	3
GEI	Metropolitan West Low Dur Bd M	MWLDX	B-	(800) 496-8298	8.72	D+ /2.6	1.45 /44	0.86 /25	2.09 /43	A+ /9.8	63	20
GEI	PIMCO Short Term A	PSHAX	C+	(800) 426-0107	9.82	C- /3.0	3.42 /59	1.40 /33	1.41 /33	A- /9.2	83	6
COI	Hartford Short Duration A	HSDAX	C+	(888) 843-7824	9.86	C- /3.0	3.50 /60	1.40 /33	1.81 /39	A- /9.1	66	5
GEI	Invesco Short Term Bond A	STBAX	C+	(800) 959-4246	8.61	D+ /2.9	3.39 /59	1.49 /35	1.74 /38	A- /9.2	72	8
GEI	Northern Short Bond	BSBAX	C+	(800) 637-1380	18.88	D+ /2.8	2.06 /49	0.86 /25	1.14 /29	A /9.4	56	7
GES	T Rowe Price Short Term Bond	PRWBX	C+	(800) 638-5660	4.72	D+ /2.8	1.82 /47	0.94 /27	1.09 /29	A /9.4	59	2
USS	Eaton Vance Sh Duration Gov Inc	EALDX	C+	(800) 262-1122	8.28	D+ /2.8	2.26 /51	1.47 /34	1.32 /32	A /9.3	83	3
GEI	Virtus Low Duration Income A	HIMZX	C+	(800) 243-1574	10.79	D+ /2.8	2.54 /53	1.50 /35	2.17 /44	A- /9.1	67	5
GEI	Sextant Short-Term Bond Fund	STBFX	C+	(800) 728-8762	5.03	D+ /2.7	1.49 /44	0.96 /27	0.86 /26	A /9.3	57	22
GEI	Franklin Low Dur Totl Return A	FLDAX	C+	(800) 342-5236	9.86	D+ /2.7	3.85 /61	1.13 /30	1.40 /33	A- /9.2	71	13
GEI	PIMCO Low Duration ESG Admin	PDRAX	C+	(800) 426-0107	9.49	D+ /2.7	2.32 /52	0.72 /23	1.39 /33	A- /9.1	55	3
MUS	DFA CA Sht Trm Muni Bd Inst	DFCMX	C+	(800) 984-9472	10.30	D+ /2.7	-0.04 /17	0.73 /29	0.76 /30	A- /9.1	27	10
MUN	DFA Short Term Municipal Bd Inst	DFSMX	C+	(800) 984-9472	10.19	D+ /2.7	0.03 /20	0.73 /29	0.68 /28	A- /9.0	27	15
GEI	● Fidelity Short-Term Bond	FSHBX	C+	(800) 544-8544	8.60	D+ /2.6	1.25 /42	0.95 /27	1.12 /29	A+ /9.6	58	10
GEI	Principal Short-Term Income Fd A	SRHQX	C+	(800) 222-5852	12.19	D+ /2.6	2.36 /52	1.37 /33	1.75 /38	A /9.3	67	7
USS	Oppenheimer Limited-Term Bond A	OUSGX	C+	(888) 470-0862	4.54	D+ /2.6	2.79 /55	1.33 /32	1.62 /36	A- /9.2	74	8
MUN	Alpine Ultra Short Muni Inc Inst	ATOIX	C+	(888) 785-5578	10.04	D+ /2.5	0.73 /41	0.61 /27	0.57 /26	A+ /9.9	63	N/A
US	RidgeWorth Seix Ltd Dur I	SAMLX	C+	(888) 784-3863	9.93	D+ /2.5	1.74 /47	0.68 /23	0.65 /23	A+ /9.8	67	15
GEI	PIMCO Low Duration II Admin	PDFAX	C+	(800) 426-0107	9.75	D+ /2.5	2.52 /53	0.61 /22	1.07 /28	A- /9.1	49	3
MUN	Vanguard Short-Term Tax-Exempt	VWSTX	C+	(800) 662-7447	15.78	D+ /2.4	0.46 /36	0.54 /25	0.62 /27	A+ /9.9	46	1
GEI	Calvert Ultra-Short Inc A	CULAX	C+	(800) 368-2745	15.62	D+ /2.4	2.43 /53	0.92 /26	1.11 /29	A+ /9.8	72	5
MTG	PIA Short-Term Securities Adv	PIASX	C+	(800) 251-1970	10.03	D+ /2.4	1.68 /46	0.72 /23	0.57 /22	A+ /9.8	62	N/A
COI	TD Short-Term Bond Inst	TDSBX	C+		10.16	D+ /2.4	1.36 /43	0.77 /24	0.83 /25	A /9.4	46	8
MUN	BMO Ultra Sht Tax-Free Y	MUYSX	C+	(800) 236-3863	10.07	D+ /2.3	0.57 /38	0.48 /24	0.62 /27	A+ /9.9	56	2
GEI	Pioneer Short Term Income A	STABX	C+	(800) 225-6292	9.53	D+ /2.3	2.33 /52	1.20 /31	1.69 /37	A+ /9.8	74	11

● Denotes fund is closed to new investors

VII. Top-Rated Bond Mutual Funds In The A Risk Category

Fund Type	Fund Name	Ticker Symbol	Overall Investment Rating	Phone	Net Asset Value As of 2/28/17	Performance Rating/Pts	1Yr / Pct	3Yr / Pct	5Yr / Pct	Risk Rating/Pts	Mgr. Quality Pct	Mgr. Tenure (Years)
GEI	William Blair Low Duration N	WBLNX	C+	(800) 742-7272	9.06	D+ /2.3	0.96 /39	0.78 /24	0.76 /24	A+ / 9.8	61	8
GEI	Columbia CMG Ultra Short Term	CMGUX	C+	(800) 345-6611	9.01	D /2.2	1.15 /41	0.63 /22	0.63 /23	A+ / 9.9	62	5
MTG	Northern Tax-Advtged Ult-Sh Fxd	NTAUX	C+	(800) 595-9111	10.14	D /2.2	1.03 /40	0.61 /22	0.74 /24	A+ / 9.9	58	8
GEI	Wells Fargo Sh-Tm Bd A	SSTVX	C+	(800) 222-8222	8.75	D /2.2	1.96 /49	1.11 /29	1.31 /32	A+ / 9.6	65	13
GEI	Cavanal Hill Limited Dur NL Inv	APSTX	C+	(800) 762-7085	9.52	D /2.2	0.56 /34	0.80 /24	1.50 /34	A+ / 9.6	52	23
MUN	USAA T/E Short Term Bond Fund	USSTX	C+	(800) 382-8722	10.45	D /2.2	--	0.58 /26	0.94 /34	A / 9.5	29	N/A
GEI	Metropolitan West Ultra Short Bnd	MWUSX	C+	(800) 496-8298	4.27	D /2.1	1.11 /41	0.57 /21	1.45 /34	A+ / 9.9	61	14
MTG	TCW Short Term Bond I	TGSMX	C+	(800) 386-3829	8.68	D /2.1	0.99 /39	0.53 /21	0.85 /25	A+ / 9.9	56	7
GL	DFA Two Year Glbl Fixed Inc Inst	DFGFX	C+	(800) 984-9472	9.97	D /2.1	0.85 /38	0.62 /22	0.63 /23	A+ / 9.8	66	18
USS	RidgeWorth Seix US Gvt Sec US	SIGVX	C+	(888) 784-3863	10.02	D /2.0	0.87 /38	0.50 /21	0.57 /22	A+ / 9.9	61	3
GES	DFA One-Yr Fixed Inc Inst	DFIHX	C+	(800) 984-9472	10.30	D /2.0	0.79 /37	0.48 /21	0.52 /22	A+ / 9.9	54	34
GEI	LWAS DFA Two Year Fixed	DFCFX	C+	(800) 984-9472	9.99	D /2.0	0.79 /37	0.57 /21	0.52 /22	A+ / 9.8	53	N/A
USS	AMG Mgrs Amundi Short DurGov	MGSDX	C+	(800) 548-4539	9.63	D /2.0	1.25 /42	0.46 /20	0.62 /23	A+ / 9.8	61	25
USS ●	Schwab Short-Term Bond Market	SWBDX	C	(800) 407-0256	9.26	D+ /2.5	0.67 /36	0.96 /27	0.96 /27	A- / 9.0	51	13
MUS	Weitz Nebraska Tax Free Income	WNTFX	C	(800) 232-4161	9.93	D+ /2.5	-0.70 / 7	0.82 /32	0.91 /33	A- / 9.0	20	32
USS	Vanguard Short-Term Federal Inv	VSGBX	C	(800) 662-7447	10.71	D+ /2.4	0.50 /33	0.94 /27	0.82 /25	A- / 9.2	57	2
GES	SA Global Fixed Income	SAXIX	C	(800) 366-7266	9.62	D+ /2.3	0.61 /35	0.89 /26	0.95 /27	A- / 9.0	29	18
MUI	BNY Mellon National ST Muni Bd	MPSTX	C	(800) 645-6561	12.76	D /2.2	0.38 /35	0.44 /23	0.54 /25	A / 9.4	26	2
GEI	Victory INCORE Low Duration	RLDAX	C	(800) 539-3863	10.06	D /2.2	2.03 /49	1.02 /28	1.10 /29	A / 9.4	62	13
GEI	BlackRock Low Duration Bond Inv	BLDAX	C	(800) 441-7762	9.62	D /2.1	1.93 /48	1.07 /29	1.65 /37	A / 9.5	64	9
US	WA Short-Term Bond A	SBSTX	C	(877) 534-4627	3.87	D /2.1	2.41 /52	0.98 /27	1.29 /31	A / 9.4	68	3
US	Vanguard Short-Term Treasury Inv	VFISX	C	(800) 662-7447	10.65	D /2.1	0.35 /30	0.71 /23	0.60 /23	A- / 9.2	53	9
MUS	T Rowe Price MD ShTm Tax-Free	PRMDX	C	(800) 638-5660	5.20	D /2.1	--	0.43 /23	0.54 /25	A- / 9.1	19	21
GEI	Nuveen Short Term Bond A	FALTX	C	(800) 257-8787	9.85	D /2.0	2.42 /52	0.92 /26	1.55 /35	A / 9.5	64	13
USS	SEI Daily Inc Tr-Sh Dur Gov Bd F	TCSGX	C	(800) 342-5734	10.43	D /2.0	0.37 /30	0.62 /22	0.58 /22	A / 9.4	N/A	14
GEI	MassMutual Premier Short Dur Bd	MSHAX	C	(800) 542-6767	10.09	D /2.0	2.41 /52	1.28 /32	1.35 /32	A- / 9.1	63	19
MUS	Sanford C Bernstein Sh Dur NY	SDNYX	C	(212) 486-5800	12.46	D /1.9	0.24 /30	0.28 /20	0.32 /21	A+ / 9.7	28	23
GEI	American Century Sh Duration A	ACSQX	C	(800) 345-6488	10.26	D /1.9	1.88 /48	0.89 /26	0.82 /25	A+ / 9.6	59	N/A
GEI	Columbia Short Term Bond A	NSTRX	C	(800) 345-6611	9.99	D /1.9	1.46 /44	0.65 /23	0.86 /26	A+ / 9.6	N/A	13
USS	Vanguard Short-Term Gvt Bd Idx	VSBSX	C	(800) 662-7447	20.26	D /1.9	0.25 /27	0.57 /21	0.53 /22	A / 9.5	47	4
USS	Sterling Capital Short Dur Bd A	BSGAX	C	(800) 228-1872	8.72	D /1.9	1.84 /48	0.87 /26	1.25 /31	A / 9.5	63	6
USS	LWAS DFA Two Year Government	DFYGX	C	(800) 984-9472	9.85	D /1.8	0.38 /31	0.41 /20	0.34 /20	A+ / 9.7	42	16
COI	Transamerica Prt High Quality	DVHQX	C	(888) 233-4339	11.11	D /1.8	0.66 /36	0.39 /20	0.54 /22	A+ / 9.7	34	27
MUN	Sanford C Bernstein Sh-Dur Dvrs	SDDMX	C	(212) 486-5800	12.58	D /1.8	0.21 /29	0.25 /20	0.35 /22	A+ / 9.7	27	15
MTG	Federated Adj Rate Sec Inst	FEUGX	C	(800) 341-7400	9.69	D /1.7	0.70 /36	0.28 /18	0.33 /20	A+ / 9.9	48	22
MUN	SEI Tax-Exempt Tr-Shrt Dur Muni	SUMAX	C	(800) 342-5734	10.01	D /1.7	0.05 /21	0.24 /20	0.39 /23	A+ / 9.8	32	6
US	GMO US Treasury	GUSTX	C		25.00	D /1.6	0.49 /33	0.25 /18	0.20 /18	A+ / 9.9	52	3
GEI	JPMorgan Limited Duration Bd A	ONUAX	C	(800) 480-4111	9.99	D /1.6	1.13 /41	0.86 /25	1.98 /42	A+ / 9.8	63	22
GEI	Trust for Credit Uns Sh Dur TCU	TCUDX	C	(800) 342-5828	9.65	D /1.6	0.21 /26	0.35 /19	0.38 /20	A+ / 9.7	32	9
MTG	AMF Ultra Short Mortgage Fund	ASARX	C	(800) 527-3713	7.11	D /1.6	-0.04 /17	0.34 /19	0.80 /25	A+ / 9.7	33	8
GES	Wells Fargo Ult ST Inc A	SADAX	C	(800) 222-8222	8.48	D- /1.5	1.65 /46	0.62 /22	0.74 /24	A+ / 9.9	63	15
GEI	SA US Fixed Income Fund	SAUFX	C	(800) 366-7266	10.19	D- /1.5	0.43 /32	0.21 /17	0.11 /15	A+ / 9.8	33	18
USS	Delaware Limited-Term Diver Inc A	DTRIX	C-	(800) 523-1918	8.48	D /2.1	1.81 /47	1.30 /32	0.76 /24	A- / 9.0	66	18
GEI	Dreyfus Short Term Inc D	DSTIX	C-	(800) 782-6620	10.35	D /2.0	1.36 /43	0.43 /20	1.02 /28	A- / 9.1	23	9
USS	Commerce Short Term Govt	CFSTX	C-	(800) 995-6365	17.17	D /2.0	0.40 /31	0.62 /22	0.80 /25	A- / 9.1	36	23
USS	Homestead Short Term Govt Sec	HOSGX	C-	(800) 258-3030	5.17	D /1.9	-0.07 /16	0.64 /22	0.60 /23	A- / 9.1	37	22
GEI	Croft Income	CLINX	C-	(800) 551-0990	9.66	D /1.9	3.32 /58	0.66 /22	0.98 /27	A- / 9.0	40	22
USS	Payden US Government Adv	PYUWX	C-	(888) 409-8007	10.48	D /1.9	-0.10 /16	0.65 /22	0.58 /22	A- / 9.0	34	N/A

VII. Top-Rated Bond Mutual Funds In The B Risk Category

99 Pct = Best
0 Pct = Worst

Fund Type	Fund Name	Ticker Symbol	Overall Investment Rating	Phone	Net Asset Value As of 2/28/17	PERFORMANCE Perform-ance Rating/Pts	Annualized Total Return Through 2/28/17 1Yr / Pct	3Yr / Pct	5Yr / Pct	RISK Risk Rating/Pts	FUND MGR Mgr. Quality Pct	Mgr. Tenure (Years)
GEI	PIMCO Income Fund A	PONAX	A+	(800) 426-0107	12.20	B+ /8.8	10.72 /81	5.53 /89	8.03 /98	B- /7.5	96	10
MUS	Saturna Idaho Tax-Exempt	NITEX	A+	(800) 728-8762	5.35	B+ /8.3	1.63 /53	3.60 /89	2.67 /74	B- /7.1	70	22
GL	Federated Floating Rt Str Inc Inst	FFRSX	A+	(800) 341-7400	10.02	B /7.8	9.63 /78	3.52 /69	4.01 /73	B /8.2	93	2
LP	Lord Abbett Floating Rate A	LFRAX	A+	(888) 522-2388	9.26	B /7.7	11.78 /83	3.73 /72	4.86 /83	B- /7.3	92	5
LP	T Rowe Price Instl Fltng Rate F	PFFRX	A+	(800) 638-5660	10.08	B- /7.2	9.33 /77	3.57 /70	4.39 /77	B /7.9	92	8
GES	J Hancock VIT Strat Inc Opps I	JESNX	A+	(800) 257-3336	13.59	B- /7.2	6.29 /71	3.47 /68	4.76 /81	B /7.8	88	13
MUS	Lee Fnl Hawaii-Muni Bond Inv	SURFX	A+		11.03	B- /7.1	-0.09 /16	3.13 /84	2.81 /76	B /7.6	65	2
LP	BlackRock Floating Rate Inc Inv A	BFRAX	A+	(800) 441-7762	10.26	C+ /6.9	9.56 /78	3.24 /65	4.15 /74	B /7.8	90	8
MUN	BMO Intermediate Tax Free Y	MITFX	A+	(800) 236-3863	11.15	C+ /6.9	0.10 /24	2.93 /81	2.72 /75	B- /7.2	51	2
USS	Morgan Stanley Mortgage Sec Tr A	MTGAX	A+	(800) 869-6397	8.49	C+ /6.8	7.28 /73	4.23 /78	4.92 /83	B /8.0	93	3
MUN	State Farm Muni Bond	SFBDX	A+	(800) 447-4930	8.63	C+ /6.8	-0.01 /17	2.80 /79	2.53 /71	B- /7.5	50	19
GL	Payden Global Fixed Inc Investor	PYGFX	A+	(888) 409-8007	8.98	C+ /6.7	3.50 /60	3.73 /72	3.75 /69	B /7.6	94	9
MUS	Colorado Bond Shares	HICOX	A+	(800) 572-0069	8.93	C+ /6.6	2.01 /57	3.88 /92	3.71 /90	B+ /8.8	89	27
GEI	Frost Total Return Bond Inv	FATRX	A+	(866) 777-7818	10.44	C+ /6.6	7.02 /73	2.80 /58	4.22 /75	B /8.0	81	15
USS	Guggenheim Investment Grade Bd	SIUSX	A+	(800) 820-0888	18.27	C+ /6.5	6.20 /71	4.14 /77	4.59 /80	B /8.0	93	5
GES	Homestead Short Term Bond	HOSBX	A+	(800) 258-3030	5.21	C+ /6.3	5.27 /68	2.34 /49	2.47 /49	B+ /8.3	83	26
GEI	CM Advisors Fixed Income	CMFIX	A+	(800) 664-4888	11.57	C+ /6.3	7.95 /74	2.36 /49	1.92 /41	B /8.2	79	6
GEI	Ave Maria Bond	AVEFX	A+	(866) 283-6274	11.29	C+ /6.2	4.92 /66	2.85 /59	3.47 /65	B+ /8.3	85	14
GEI	Dodge & Cox Income Fund	DODIX	A	(800) 621-3979	13.74	C+ /6.7	6.70 /72	3.06 /62	3.38 /63	B- /7.1	78	28
LP	● MainStay Floating Rate B	MXFBX	A	(800) 624-6782	9.38	C+ /6.3	9.36 /77	2.07 /44	2.81 /55	B- /7.1	81	13
GEI	Nationwide Core Plus Bond R6	NWCIX	A	(800) 848-0920	10.21	C+ /6.2	4.31 /64	3.08 /62	3.47 /65	B- /7.5	73	15
MUS	Madison Tax Free Virginia Y	GTVAX	A-	(800) 877-6089	11.41	C+ /6.2	-0.49 /10	2.61 /76	1.97 /58	B- /7.0	29	20
GL	DoubleLine Core Fixed Income N	DLFNX	A-	(877) 354-6311	10.87	C+ /6.1	3.81 /61	3.15 /63	3.23 /61	B- /7.0	94	7
GES	ICON Bond C	IOBCX	A-	(800) 764-0442	9.48	C+ /6.0	6.34 /71	2.42 /50	2.53 /50	B- /7.4	71	6
COI	Payden Core Bond Adviser	PYCWX	A-	(888) 409-8007	10.56	C+ /6.0	3.90 /62	2.97 /60	3.08 /59	B- /7.1	67	20
GEI	Commerce Bond	CFBNX	A-	(800) 995-6365	19.88	C+ /5.9	3.98 /62	2.89 /59	3.14 /60	B- /7.4	69	23
MUI	WesMark West Virginia Muni Bond	WMKMX	A-	(800) 864-1013	10.40	C+ /5.9	-0.50 /10	2.42 /72	1.99 /59	B- /7.4	28	11
GES	AdvisorOne CLS Flexible Income N	CLFLX	A-	(866) 811-0225	10.25	C+ /5.8	5.52 /69	2.42 /50	2.34 /47	B- /7.5	71	3
GEI	WA Intermediate Bond IS	WABSX	A-	(888) 425-6432	10.86	C /5.5	3.05 /57	2.74 /57	2.81 /55	B /7.9	71	8
COI	Federated Interm Corp Bd Instl	FIIFX	A-	(800) 341-7400	9.25	C /5.5	4.75 /66	2.47 /51	3.34 /63	B /7.6	58	4
GES	DoubleLine Total Return Bond N	DLTNX	A-	(877) 354-6311	10.63	C /5.1	1.11 /41	2.85 /59	3.43 /64	B /8.2	77	7
MTG	Federated Mortgage Fund Inst	FGFIX	A-	(800) 341-7400	9.57	C /4.9	2.00 /49	2.62 /54	2.10 /44	B+ /8.5	65	14
MUN	BlackRock Natl Muni Inv A	MDNLX	B+	(800) 441-7762	10.78	C+ /6.0	0.66 /40	3.53 /88	3.31 /85	B- /7.0	68	21
MUS	Franklin Virginia Tax-Free Inc A	FRVAX	B+	(800) 342-5236	11.31	C+ /5.9	1.49 /51	3.37 /86	2.30 /66	B- /7.0	69	30
MUS	Oppenheimer Rochester LT CA	OLCAX	B+	(888) 470-0862	3.20	C+ /5.8	2.29 /60	2.56 /75	2.55 /71	B- /7.2	59	13
GEI	● Thrivent Oppty Income Plus A	AAINX	B+	(800) 847-4836	10.23	C+ /5.8	8.75 /76	3.14 /63	--	B- /7.2	85	15
GL	JPMorgan Strategic Income Opp A	JSOAX	B+	(800) 480-4111	11.69	C+ /5.8	11.60 /82	2.34 /49	3.15 /60	B- /7.1	89	9
MUI	Commerce Kansas T/F Intm Bond	KTXIX	B+	(800) 995-6365	19.14	C+ /5.7	-0.43 /10	2.37 /71	1.97 /58	B- /7.2	24	17
MUS	MFS MD Municipal Bond A	MFSMX	B+	(800) 225-2606	10.77	C+ /5.7	0.61 /39	3.48 /88	2.35 /67	B- /7.0	66	18
MUS	Franklin Kentucky Tax-Free Inc A	FRKYX	B+	(800) 342-5236	11.01	C+ /5.6	0.85 /43	3.38 /86	2.62 /73	B- /7.5	72	21
GEI	William Blair Bond N	WBBNX	B+	(800) 742-7272	10.45	C+ /5.6	4.22 /63	2.72 /56	2.93 /56	B- /7.3	70	10
COI	MSIF Short Duration Income A	MLDAX	B+	(800) 354-8185	8.16	C /5.5	8.64 /76	2.73 /56	2.38 /47	B- /7.4	86	6
COI	Transamerica Flexible Income A	IDITX	B+	(888) 233-4339	9.28	C /5.4	8.28 /75	2.98 /61	4.42 /78	B /7.6	78	12
MUN	Eaton Vance VA Municipal Income	ETVAX	B+	(800) 262-1122	7.95	C /5.3	1.35 /50	3.27 /85	2.61 /73	B /7.7	72	10
MUI	First Inv MI Tax Exempt A	FTMIX	B+	(800) 423-4026	11.98	C /5.2	0.06 /22	3.77 /91	2.45 /69	B- /7.5	79	26
COH	Pioneer Floating Rate Fund Class	FLARX	B+	(800) 225-6292	6.81	C /5.2	8.44 /75	2.80 /58	3.71 /69	B- /7.4	80	10
MUN	Waddell & Reed Adv Muni Bond A	UNMBX	B+	(888) 923-3355	7.47	C /5.1	0.71 /41	3.15 /84	2.71 /75	B /7.6	66	17
GL	J Hancock Strat Income Opp A	JIPAX	B+	(800) 257-3336	10.70	C /4.9	5.87 /70	2.86 /59	4.00 /73	B /7.9	92	11
MUI	First Inv PA Tax Exempt A	FTPAX	B+	(800) 423-4026	13.02	C /4.9	0.78 /42	3.45 /87	2.83 /77	B /7.9	78	26
GES	Virtus Multi Sector Short Term B A	NARAX	B+	(800) 243-1574	4.76	C /4.8	6.58 /72	2.13 /45	2.90 /56	B+ /8.3	80	24
MUS	1919 Maryland Tax-Free Income A	LMMDX	B+	(844) 828-1919	15.92	C /4.6	1.39 /50	2.72 /77	2.10 /61	B+ /8.3	73	10
USA	Vanguard GNMA Inv	VFIIX	B+	(800) 662-7447	10.54	C /4.6	0.67 /36	2.57 /53	1.96 /41	B+ /8.3	81	11

● Denotes fund is closed to new investors

Fund Type	Fund Name	Ticker Symbol	Overall Investment Rating	Phone	Net Asset Value As of 2/28/17	Performance Rating/Pts	1Yr / Pct	3Yr / Pct	5Yr / Pct	Risk Rating/Pts	Mgr. Quality Pct	Mgr. Tenure (Years)
COI	Vanguard Short-Term Crp Bd Idx	VSCSX	B+	(800) 662-7447	21.67	C /4.3	2.98 /56	1.88 /41	2.31 /46	B+ / 8.8	67	8
MUS	CA Tax-Free Income Direct	CFNTX	B	(800) 955-9988	11.44	C /5.5	-0.48 /10	2.27 /68	2.36 /68	B- / 7.0	20	14
GEI	Victory Strategic Income A	RSIAX	B	(800) 539-3863	10.06	C /5.2	7.49 /73	2.19 /46	2.94 /57	B- / 7.3	76	8
GL	AB Global Bond A	ANAGX	B	(800) 221-5672	8.38	C /5.2	4.46 /64	3.68 /71	3.21 /61	B- / 7.1	94	25
GES	Natixis Loomis Sayles Strat Alpha	LABAX	B	(800) 225-5478	9.94	C /5.1	9.64 /78	2.46 /51	3.17 /60	B- / 7.3	87	7
GL	Eaton Vance Glb Mac Abslut Ret A	EAGMX	B	(800) 262-1122	9.04	C /4.7	5.03 /67	3.24 /65	1.93 /41	B / 7.9	92	20
GEI	Highland Fixed Income A	HFBAX	B	(877) 665-1287	12.92	C /4.7	6.17 /71	2.83 /58	2.36 /47	B / 7.6	75	3
MUS	Franklin New York Tax-Free Inc A	FNYTX	B	(800) 342-5236	11.21	C /4.7	0.61 /39	3.02 /82	2.25 /65	B- / 7.5	64	28
GEI	Loomis Sayles Intm Dur Bd Y	LSDIX	B	(800) 225-5478	10.24	C /4.5	2.38 /52	2.19 /46	2.37 /47	B / 8.1	60	12
USA	SEI Daily Inc Tr-GNMA Bond F	SEGMX	B	(800) 342-5734	10.50	C /4.4	0.18 /25	2.51 /52	1.95 /41	B / 8.2	80	16
USA	Fidelity GNMA Fund	FGMNX	B	(800) 544-8544	11.44	C /4.3	0.69 /36	2.33 /49	1.95 /41	B+ / 8.5	80	13
MTG	Vanguard Mort-Backed Secs Idx	VMBSX	B	(800) 662-7447	20.99	C /4.3	0.43 /32	2.39 /50	1.96 /41	B+ / 8.3	45	8
COI	Federated Sht-Interm Tot Ret B	FGCIX	B	(800) 341-7400	10.33	C- /4.2	3.88 /62	1.69 /38	1.80 /39	B+ / 8.6	61	4
USS	AMG Mgrs Amundi Intmd Gov N	MGIDX	B	(800) 548-4539	10.67	C- /4.2	0.47 /33	2.37 /49	2.13 /44	B+ / 8.4	80	25
MUN	Cavanal Hill Intmdt TxFr Bd NL Inv	APTFX	B	(800) 762-7085	10.96	C- /4.2	-0.29 /13	1.52 /49	1.32 /42	B+ / 8.3	21	24
MTG	Advisors Series Trust PIA MBS	PMTGX	B	(800) 251-1970	9.53	C- /4.2	0.44 /32	2.38 /50	2.00 /42	B+ / 8.3	38	11
MUI	First Inv NC Tax Exempt B	FMTQX	B	(800) 423-4026	13.18	C- /4.2	-1.30 / 2	1.82 /58	1.22 /40	B / 8.2	28	25
USS	BMO Mortgage Income Y	MRGIX	B	(800) 236-3863	9.16	C- /4.2	0.70 /34	2.38 /50	1.88 /40	B / 8.1	78	N/A
GEI	CNR Intermediate Fixed Income N	RIMCX	B	(888) 889-0799	26.20	C- /4.1	2.54 /53	1.84 /40	2.31 /46	B+ / 8.4	55	4
GEI	New Covenant Income	NCICX	B	(877) 835-4531	23.13	C- /4.1	1.75 /47	2.02 /44	1.70 /38	B+ / 8.3	57	3
USA	T Rowe Price GNMA	PRGMX	B	(800) 638-5660	9.32	C- /4.0	1.02 /40	2.03 /44	1.66 /37	B+ / 8.7	78	9
MUS	Fidelity CA Ltd Term Tax-Free Bd	FCSTX	B	(800) 544-8544	10.59	C- /4.0	-0.27 /13	1.40 /46	1.46 /45	B+ / 8.5	25	1
GEI	William Blair Income N	WBRRX	B	(800) 742-7272	8.87	C- /3.9	2.01 /49	1.74 /39	1.81 /39	B+ / 8.9	66	15
GES	Thornburg Limited Term Income A	THIFX	B	(800) 847-0200	13.39	C- /3.9	2.87 /56	2.01 /43	2.58 /51	B+ / 8.8	71	10
GL	Putnam Absolute Return 100 A	PARTX	B	(800) 225-1581	9.99	C- /3.8	5.32 /68	1.15 /30	1.41 /33	B+ / 8.9	76	9
MUS	Franklin NC Tax-Free Inc A	FXNCX	B-	(800) 342-5236	11.70	C /4.8	1.18 /47	2.95 /81	1.83 /55	B- / 7.3	60	30
MUS	Kansas Municipal	KSMUX	B-	(800) 601-5593	10.69	C /4.7	0.10 /24	2.57 /75	2.25 /65	B- / 7.4	34	21
GEI	PIMCO Moderate Duration Fund P	PMOPX	B-	(800) 426-0107	10.15	C /4.6	3.36 /59	1.89 /41	2.56 /50	B / 7.7	50	3
MUN	Frost Municipal Bond Inv	FAUMX	B-	(866) 777-7818	10.34	C /4.6	-0.70 / 7	1.81 /57	1.63 /50	B / 7.6	15	15
MUS	Putnam MN Tax Exempt Inc II A	PXMNX	B-	(800) 225-1581	9.20	C /4.5	0.04 /21	2.94 /81	2.52 /71	B- / 7.4	55	15
MUS	Brown Advisory Maryland Bond Inv	BIAMX	B-	(800) 540-6807	10.52	C /4.4	-0.19 /15	1.70 /54	1.37 /44	B / 7.6	12	3
GEI	Metropolitan West Tot Ret Bond M	MWTRX	B-	(800) 496-8298	10.60	C /4.4	1.52 /45	2.34 /49	3.54 /66	B- / 7.5	49	20
MUN	Glenmede Intermediate Muni Port	GTCMX	B-	(800) 442-8299	10.89	C /4.3	-0.13 /15	1.58 /51	1.47 /46	B / 7.8	15	6
GEI	Pioneer Bond Fund A	PIOBX	B-	(800) 225-6292	9.67	C- /4.2	4.94 /66	2.90 /59	3.51 /66	B / 8.0	79	19
GEI	Fidelity Intermediate Bond	FTHRX	B-	(800) 544-8544	10.84	C- /4.2	2.23 /51	2.01 /43	2.13 /44	B / 7.9	50	4
COH	Wells Fargo Sh-Tm Hi Yld A	SSTHX	B-	(800) 222-8222	8.09	C- /4.2	4.66 /65	2.32 /49	3.05 /59	B / 7.9	77	19
GL	JPMorgan Unconstrained Debt A	JSIAX	B-	(800) 480-4111	9.89	C- /4.1	6.76 /72	2.06 /44	2.71 /53	B / 8.1	88	7
USS	Columbia US Government	AUGAX	B-	(800) 345-6611	5.42	C- /3.9	2.34 /52	2.60 /54	2.65 /52	B+ / 8.5	83	8
USA	Payden GNMA Adv	PYGWX	B-	(888) 409-8007	9.57	C- /3.8	0.33 /30	2.07 /44	1.49 /34	B+ / 8.4	77	N/A
MTG	HC Capital US Mtg/Asst Bckd Fl	HCASX	B-	(800) 242-9596	9.60	C- /3.8	0.08 /21	2.06 /44	1.74 /38	B+ / 8.3	29	4
GEI	Brown Advisory Interm Income Inv	BIAIX	B-	(800) 540-6807	10.56	C- /3.8	1.49 /44	1.88 /41	1.51 /35	B+ / 8.3	50	25
GL	DFA S/T Extended Quality Port Inst	DFEQX	B-	(800) 984-9472	10.80	C- /3.6	1.92 /48	1.54 /35	1.65 /37	B+ / 8.8	83	9
USS	Payden Kravitz Cash Bal Plan Ret	PKCRX	B-	(888) 409-8007	9.87	C- /3.5	4.47 /64	0.94 /27	1.29 /31	B+ / 8.8	72	N/A
MUN	WA Intermediate Term Muni A	SBLTX	C+	(877) 534-4627	6.38	C /4.5	-0.44 /10	2.53 /74	2.15 /62	B- / 7.2	29	10
GEI	Parnassus Income Fd-Fixed Inc	PRFIX	C+	(800) 999-3505	16.54	C /4.4	2.04 /49	2.19 /46	1.56 /35	B- / 7.5	37	4
MUS	Delaware Tax Free MN Intmdt A	DXCCX	C+	(800) 523-1918	10.98	C /4.4	-0.16 /15	2.54 /74	2.16 /63	B- / 7.4	31	14
GEI	BNY Mellon Bond M	MPBFX	C+	(800) 645-6561	12.65	C /4.4	1.90 /48	2.25 /47	2.09 /43	B- / 7.1	36	12
MUI	Franklin MN Tax-Free Inc A	FMINX	C+	(800) 342-5236	12.27	C /4.3	0.10 /24	2.84 /79	2.35 /67	B- / 7.2	46	28

VII. Top-Rated Bond Mutual Funds In The C Risk Category   **Spring 2017**

99 Pct = Best
0 Pct = Worst

Fund Type	Fund Name	Ticker Symbol	Overall Investment Rating	Phone	Net Asset Value As of 2/28/17	Performance Rating/Pts	1Yr / Pct	3Yr / Pct	5Yr / Pct	Risk Rating/Pts	Mgr. Quality Pct	Mgr. Tenure (Years)
USS	Principal Preferred Sec A	PPSAX	A+	(800) 222-5852	10.23	A- /9.0	9.14 /77	6.30 /93	7.09 /96	C /4.5	97	15
MUS	T Rowe Price MD Tax Free Bd	MDXBX	A+	(800) 638-5660	10.68	B /8.0	0.73 /41	3.64 /89	3.20 /83	C+ /6.7	69	17
MUS	T Rowe Price VA Tax-Free Bond	PRVAX	A+	(800) 638-5660	11.90	B /8.0	0.56 /38	3.71 /90	3.06 /81	C+ /5.9	66	20
MUS	Dupree AL Tax Free Income	DUALX	A+	(800) 866-0614	12.20	B- /7.5	0.50 /37	3.36 /86	3.01 /80	C+ /6.9	64	16
MUS	Oppenheimer Rochester PA Muni	OPATX	A	(888) 470-0862	10.40	A+ /9.7	5.37 /75	6.05 /99	3.84 /91	C- /3.2	91	15
MUN	Dupree Taxable Muni Bd Srs	DUTMX	A	(800) 866-0614	10.50	A+ /9.6	2.08 /58	5.31 /98	4.96 /97	C- /3.2	88	7
MUN	Sit Tax Free Income Fund	SNTIX	A	(800) 332-5580	9.48	A /9.4	0.69 /40	5.01 /97	4.34 /96	C- /3.4	74	29
USS	Nuveen Preferred Securities A	NPSAX	A	(800) 257-8787	17.22	A- /9.0	11.35 /82	6.19 /93	8.02 /98	C- /4.0	98	11
MUS	T Rowe Price NY Tax Free Bd	PRNYX	A	(800) 638-5660	11.53	B+ /8.3	0.33 /33	3.95 /92	3.24 /84	C /4.8	65	17
GEI ●	RiverNorth/DoubleLine Strat Inc R	RNDLX	A	(888) 848-7549	10.61	B /8.1	10.38 /80	4.41 /80	5.13 /85	C+ /5.6	91	7
MUN	T Rowe Price Tax-Free Income	PRTAX	A	(800) 638-5660	10.07	B /8.0	0.25 /31	3.76 /90	3.28 /85	C /5.0	62	10
MUN	USAA Tax-Exempt Long Term	USTEX	A	(800) 382-8722	13.25	B /8.0	0.64 /39	3.71 /90	3.64 /89	C /5.0	67	N/A
GES	BlackRock Crdt Strategies Inc Inv	BMSAX	A	(800) 441-7762	10.19	B- /7.2	9.75 /78	3.53 /69	4.82 /82	C+ /6.1	91	5
LP	Columbia Floating Rate A	RFRAX	A	(800) 345-6611	9.08	B- /7.1	11.84 /83	3.29 /66	4.52 /79	C+ /6.6	89	11
GL	WA Total Return Unconstrained Fl	WARIX	A	(888) 425-6432	10.44	C+ /6.9	9.58 /78	2.53 /52	2.87 /56	C+ /6.6	90	11
MUI	Westcore CO Tax Exempt	WTCOX	A	(800) 392-2673	11.40	C+ /6.9	-0.15 /15	2.95 /81	2.36 /68	C+ /6.4	36	12
MUS	Dupree TN Tax-Free Income	TNTIX	A	(800) 866-0614	11.34	C+ /6.7	-0.12 /16	2.91 /80	2.64 /73	C+ /6.7	44	13
MUS	Dupree KY Tax Free Income	KYTFX	A	(800) 866-0614	7.70	C+ /6.6	0.11 /25	2.73 /77	2.56 /72	C+ /6.8	33	18
LP	Virtus Senior Floating Rate A	PSFRX	A	(800) 243-1574	9.54	C+ /6.5	10.40 /80	2.81 /58	4.00 /73	C+ /6.9	87	5
MUS	Oppeneheimer Rochester CA Muni	OPCAX	A-	(888) 470-0862	8.27	A /9.3	4.11 /71	5.61 /98	5.51 /99	C- /3.3	86	15
GEI	Cohen and Steers Pref Sec&Inc A	CPXAX	A-	(800) 330-7348	13.77	A /9.3	10.71 /80	6.99 /96	8.28 /99	C- /3.0	96	7
MUS	Vanguard OH Long-Term	VOHIX	A-	(800) 662-7447	12.37	B+ /8.9	0.75 /41	4.40 /95	3.72 /90	C- /3.7	64	9
GES	Changing Parameters	CPMPX	A-	(866) 618-3456	10.26	B+ /8.7	12.45 /84	4.05 /76	4.61 /80	C- /3.9	91	10
MUS	USAA California Bond Fund	USCBX	A-	(800) 382-8722	10.93	B+ /8.6	0.38 /35	4.14 /94	4.11 /94	C- /4.0	73	N/A
MUS	Vanguard PA Long-Term	VPAIX	A-	(800) 662-7447	11.37	B+ /8.6	0.57 /38	4.17 /94	3.49 /87	C- /3.9	61	6
MUS	Vanguard NY Long-Term	VNYTX	A-	(800) 662-7447	11.59	B+ /8.6	0.30 /32	4.24 /94	3.53 /88	C- /3.9	63	4
MUN	T Rowe Price Summit Muni Income	PRINX	A-	(800) 638-5660	11.71	B+ /8.4	0.27 /31	4.12 /94	3.65 /89	C- /4.1	63	18
MUN	Elfun Tax Exempt Income	ELFTX	A-	(800) 843-2639	11.54	B /8.1	0.44 /36	3.75 /90	2.93 /79	C /4.6	58	N/A
GEI	BlackRock Managed Income Inv A	BLADX	A-	(800) 441-7762	10.02	B /8.1	8.89 /76	4.17 /77	3.53 /66	C /4.6	84	8
MUS	Dupree MS Tax Free Income	DUMSX	A-	(800) 866-0614	12.00	B /8.0	0.36 /34	3.73 /90	3.13 /82	C /4.9	63	17
MUS	T Rowe Price NJ Tax-Free Bond	NJTFX	A-	(800) 638-5660	11.87	B /7.9	0.41 /35	3.73 /90	3.23 /84	C /4.7	59	17
MUS	Fidelity PA Muni Inc	FPXTX	A-	(800) 544-8544	11.01	B /7.8	0.27 /31	3.64 /89	3.15 /82	C /5.1	59	15
GEI	Cavalier Adaptive Income Inst	CADTX	A-	(877) 773-3863	10.41	B /7.7	9.82 /79	3.02 /61	2.99 /58	C /5.0	82	1
MUS	AB Municipal Income II VA A	AVAAX	A-	(800) 221-5672	11.04	C+ /6.9	0.48 /37	3.77 /90	2.73 /75	C+ /6.0	68	22
MUS	Franklin PA Tax-Free Inc A	FRPAX	A-	(800) 342-5236	10.12	C+ /6.6	1.61 /53	3.79 /91	2.61 /73	C+ /6.4	76	31
MUS	WA Pennsylvania Municipals A	SBPAX	A-	(877) 534-4627	12.77	C+ /6.5	0.97 /44	3.85 /91	2.54 /71	C+ /6.8	75	10
LP	Voya Floating Rate A	IFRAX	A-	(800) 992-0180	9.95	C+ /6.3	9.07 /77	2.91 /60	4.06 /73	C+ /6.9	87	7
MUS	Franklin Alabama Tax-Free Inc A	FRALX	A-	(800) 342-5236	11.16	C+ /6.3	1.67 /54	3.63 /89	2.76 /75	C+ /6.8	74	28
COI	Diamond Hill Corporate Credit A	DSIAX	B+	(614) 255-3333	11.27	A- /9.0	15.58 /89	5.22 /86	5.60 /89	C- /3.3	93	11
MUS ●	Oppenheimer Rochester Ohio Muni	OROHX	B+	(888) 470-0862	10.06	A- /9.0	4.02 /71	5.23 /97	4.29 /95	C- /3.1	81	11
COI	Payden Corporate Bond Investor	PYACX	B+	(888) 409-8007	11.03	B+ /8.8	8.28 /75	5.17 /86	5.29 /87	C- /3.2	84	N/A
MUS ●	Oppenheimer Rochester NC Muni	OPNCX	B+	(888) 470-0862	10.89	B+ /8.8	4.13 /71	4.95 /97	2.87 /78	C- /3.1	86	11
GES	Osterweis Strategic Income	OSTIX	B+	(800) 700-3316	11.35	B+ /8.6	15.03 /88	3.51 /69	4.90 /83	C- /3.7	93	15
MUN	Vanguard Long-Term Tax-Exempt	VWLTX	B+	(800) 662-7447	11.43	B+ /8.6	0.46 /36	4.19 /94	3.66 /89	C- /3.5	55	7
LP	Eaton Vance Float Rate Advtage A	EAFAX	B+	(800) 262-1122	10.89	B+ /8.5	15.82 /90	3.87 /74	4.93 /83	C- /3.6	91	21
MUS	Northern CA T/E Bond	NCATX	B+	(800) 595-9111	11.49	B+ /8.5	-0.45 /10	4.32 /95	3.97 /93	C- /3.4	57	20
LP	Voya Senior Income A	XSIAX	B+	(800) 992-0180	12.85	B+ /8.3	14.59 /88	3.91 /74	6.29 /94	C- /4.0	91	16
LP	Oppenheimer Sen-Floating Rate A	OOSAX	B+	(888) 470-0862	8.20	B+ /8.3	16.53 /91	3.76 /72	4.75 /81	C- /4.0	90	18
MUN	Eaton Vance National Muni Inc A	EANAX	B+	(800) 262-1122	9.77	B+ /8.3	2.02 /57	5.15 /97	3.98 /93	C- /3.7	81	4
MUS	T Rowe Price CA Tax Free Bond	PRXCX	B+	(800) 638-5660	11.35	B+ /8.3	-0.12 /16	4.09 /93	3.75 /91	C- /3.6	54	14
MUN	Northern Tax Exempt	NOTEX	B+	(800) 595-9111	10.56	B /8.1	0.19 /28	3.80 /91	3.25 /84	C /4.3	56	19
MUS	Fidelity AZ Muni Income Fd	FSAZX	B+	(800) 544-8544	11.91	B /8.1	-0.17 /15	3.91 /92	3.29 /85	C- /4.0	53	7

● Denotes fund is closed to new investors

Fund Type	Fund Name	Ticker Symbol	Overall Investment Rating	Phone	Net Asset Value As of 2/28/17	Performance Rating/Pts	1Yr / Pct	3Yr / Pct	5Yr / Pct	Risk Rating/Pts	Mgr. Quality Pct	Mgr. Tenure (Years)
LP	Eaton Vance Flt-Rate and Hi Inc A	EVFHX	B+	(800) 262-1122	9.44	B / 7.9	13.86 / 87	3.46 / 68	4.43 / 78	C / 4.5	90	17
MUS	Sit MN Tax Free Income	SMTFX	B+	(800) 332-5580	10.29	B / 7.7	0.18 / 28	3.55 / 88	3.13 / 82	C / 5.0	57	24
LP	Eaton Vance Floating Rate A	EVBLX	B+	(800) 262-1122	9.31	B / 7.6	13.62 / 86	3.21 / 64	3.98 / 72	C / 4.8	88	16
GEI	Universal Inst Core Plus Fxd Inc II	UCFIX	B+	(800) 869-6397	10.78	B- / 7.3	6.83 / 72	3.65 / 71	3.82 / 70	C / 5.4	81	6
GEI	USAA Intmdt-Trm Bd Fund	USIBX	B+	(800) 382-8722	10.55	B- / 7.0	7.92 / 74	3.14 / 63	4.24 / 75	C / 5.5	75	1
MUS	Franklin Colorado Tax-Free Inc A	FRCOX	B+	(800) 342-5236	11.66	C+ / 6.7	1.30 / 49	3.88 / 92	2.87 / 77	C+ / 6.1	74	25
MUN	Vanguard Interm-Term Tax-Exempt	VWITX	B+	(800) 662-7447	13.98	C+ / 6.7	-0.11 / 16	2.80 / 79	2.60 / 73	C+ / 5.9	27	4
MUS	Fidelity MN Muni Inc	FIMIX	B+	(800) 544-8544	11.48	C+ / 6.7	-0.06 / 17	2.83 / 79	2.34 / 67	C+ / 5.8	28	7
MUI	Pacific Capital Tax-Free Secs Y	PTXFX	B+	(888) 739-1390	10.10	C+ / 6.7	-0.38 / 11	2.86 / 80	2.44 / 69	C+ / 5.6	28	13
GEI	J Hancock Active Bond 1	JIADX	B+	(800) 257-3336	10.06	C+ / 6.2	4.31 / 64	3.08 / 62	3.61 / 67	C+ / 6.6	70	12
GEI	TiAA-CREF Bond Plus Retail	TCBPX	B+	(800) 842-2252	10.40	C+ / 6.1	4.41 / 64	3.04 / 62	3.23 / 61	C+ / 6.3	68	11
MUH	Ivy Municipal High Income A	IYIAX	B	(800) 777-6472	5.14	B+ / 8.6	1.94 / 56	5.18 / 97	4.01 / 93	C- / 3.3	84	8
MUS	BlackRock NY Muni Oppty Inv A	MENKX	B	(800) 441-7762	11.03	B+ / 8.4	2.08 / 58	5.04 / 97	3.75 / 91	C- / 3.1	74	11
MUS ●	Oppenheimer Rochester MA Muni	ORMAX	B	(888) 470-0862	10.28	B+ / 8.3	3.50 / 68	4.66 / 96	3.05 / 81	C- / 3.6	83	11
MUN ●	MainStay Tax Free Bond Fund B	MKTBX	B	(800) 624-6782	9.82	B+ / 8.3	0.10 / 24	4.15 / 94	3.56 / 88	C- / 3.4	62	8
MUS	Fidelity OH Muni Inc	FOHFX	B	(800) 544-8544	11.95	B / 8.2	-0.22 / 14	4.08 / 93	3.40 / 86	C- / 3.5	48	1
MUH	Waddell & Reed Adv Muni High Inc	UMUHX	B	(888) 923-3355	4.77	B / 8.1	1.98 / 57	4.76 / 96	4.15 / 94	C- / 3.9	83	9
MUN	Fidelity Tax Free Bond Fd	FTABX	B	(800) 544-8544	11.33	B / 8.1	0.10 / 24	3.89 / 92	3.51 / 88	C- / 3.8	46	7
MUS	Dreyfus NY Tax Exempt Bond	DRNYX	B	(800) 645-6561	14.67	B / 7.7	0.16 / 27	3.51 / 88	2.41 / 69	C- / 4.2	36	8
MUN	PIMCO Unconstrained Tax Mnged	ATMAX	B	(800) 426-0107	10.43	B / 7.6	9.78 / 89	2.19 / 67	2.25 / 65	C- / 4.2	84	2
MUS	Fidelity MD Muni Income Fd	SMDMX	B	(800) 544-8544	11.18	B / 7.6	-0.12 / 16	3.51 / 88	2.60 / 72	C- / 4.1	33	15
MUS	T Rowe Price GA Tax-Free Bd	GTFBX	B	(800) 638-5660	11.39	B- / 7.5	-0.28 / 13	3.51 / 88	2.98 / 80	C / 4.6	N/A	20
MUS	Fidelity MI Muni Inc	FMHTX	B	(800) 544-8544	11.99	B- / 7.5	-0.48 / 10	3.54 / 88	2.89 / 78	C / 4.5	47	1
LP	Franklin Floating Rate Dly-Acc A	FAFRX	B	(800) 342-5236	8.89	B- / 7.5	14.02 / 87	3.19 / 64	3.93 / 71	C / 4.5	87	4
GL	CGCM Intl Fixed Inc	TIFUX	B	(800) 444-4273	7.61	B- / 7.5	5.26 / 68	4.40 / 80	3.81 / 70	C / 4.3	96	3
LP	RidgeWorth Seix Fltng Rt Hg Inc A	SFRAX	B	(888) 784-3863	8.79	B- / 7.5	13.62 / 86	3.30 / 66	4.28 / 76	C- / 4.2	89	11
MUS	Northern AZ Tax Exempt	NOAZX	B	(800) 595-9111	10.53	B- / 7.4	0.01 / 18	3.28 / 85	2.95 / 79	C / 4.3	28	18
MUS	BlackRock CA Muni Opptys A	MECMX	B	(800) 441-7762	12.34	B- / 7.3	1.12 / 46	4.27 / 95	3.54 / 88	C / 4.6	75	24
MUN	MFS Municipal Income A	MFIAX	B	(800) 225-2606	8.64	B- / 7.1	0.87 / 43	4.25 / 94	3.40 / 86	C / 5.0	74	19
MUS	MFS PA Municipal Bond A	MFPAX	B	(800) 225-2606	10.19	B- / 7.1	0.87 / 43	4.24 / 94	3.11 / 82	C / 4.9	73	18
GEI	WA Core Plus Bond FI	WACIX	B	(888) 425-6432	11.54	B- / 7.1	5.16 / 67	3.81 / 73	3.67 / 68	C / 4.8	78	12
MUS ●	Oppenheimer Rochester MN Muni	OPAMX	B	(888) 470-0862	12.73	B- / 7.0	0.71 / 40	4.39 / 95	3.92 / 92	C / 5.1	78	11
MUS	Vanguard CA Interm-Term T-E Inv	VCAIX	B	(800) 662-7447	11.62	B- / 7.0	-0.33 / 12	3.00 / 82	3.00 / 80	C / 4.8	25	4
LP	AIG Sr Floating Rate A	SASFX	B	(800) 858-8850	8.12	C+ / 6.9	13.03 / 85	3.01 / 61	4.16 / 74	C / 5.0	88	8
GEI	Henderson Strategic Income A	HFAAX	B	(866) 443-6337	9.39	C+ / 6.9	8.37 / 75	4.33 / 79	5.59 / 89	C / 5.0	90	9
MUS	Dupree NC Tax Free Income	NTFIX	B	(800) 866-0614	11.40	C+ / 6.9	-0.14 / 15	3.02 / 82	2.74 / 75	C / 5.0	30	13
MUI	GuideMark Tax-Exempt Fixed Inc	GMTEX	B	(888) 278-5809	11.29	C+ / 6.8	-0.44 / 10	2.99 / 82	2.27 / 65	C / 5.4	30	11
MUN	Federated Interm Muni Trust Y	FIMYX	B	(800) 341-7400	9.95	C+ / 6.8	0.33 / 33	2.87 / 80	2.54 / 71	C / 5.1	25	22
MUS	Franklin MA Tax-Free Inc A	FMISX	B	(800) 342-5236	11.63	C+ / 6.7	0.61 / 39	4.08 / 93	2.81 / 76	C / 5.5	75	28
MUS	Delaware Tax-Free Pennsylvania A	DELIX	B	(800) 523-1918	8.01	C+ / 6.6	0.75 / 41	4.06 / 93	3.07 / 81	C / 5.3	72	14
MUI	Franklin Ohio Tax-Free Inc A	FTOIX	B	(800) 342-5236	12.56	C+ / 6.4	0.51 / 37	3.86 / 91	2.94 / 79	C+ / 5.6	70	18
COI	WA Core Bond FI	WAPIX	B	(888) 425-6432	12.45	C+ / 6.4	3.72 / 61	3.42 / 68	3.10 / 59	C / 5.5	70	23
MUN	T Rowe Price Summit Muni Intmdt	PRSMX	B	(800) 638-5660	11.75	C+ / 6.3	-0.27 / 13	2.66 / 76	2.52 / 71	C+ / 6.0	24	24
MUS	Nuveen MD Muni Bond A	NMDAX	B	(800) 257-8787	10.57	C+ / 6.3	0.62 / 39	3.75 / 90	2.69 / 74	C+ / 6.0	69	1
GES	Pioneer Strategic Income A	PSRAX	B	(800) 225-6292	10.73	C+ / 6.2	9.79 / 78	3.34 / 66	4.12 / 74	C+ / 6.2	86	18
MUS	Franklin Florida Tax-Free Inc A	FRFLX	B	(800) 342-5236	10.88	C+ / 6.2	1.02 / 45	3.60 / 89	2.41 / 69	C+ / 6.2	71	30
MUN	Franklin Federal Tax-Free Inc A	FKTIX	B	(800) 342-5236	12.05	C+ / 6.2	0.56 / 38	3.76 / 90	3.21 / 83	C+ / 5.9	69	30
MUS	MFS AL Municipal Bond Fund A	MFALX	B	(800) 225-2606	10.12	C+ / 6.1	0.21 / 29	3.75 / 90	2.78 / 76	C+ / 6.3	70	18

Fund Type	Fund Name	Ticker Symbol	Overall Investment Rating	Phone	Net Asset Value As of 2/28/17	Performance Rating/Pts	1Yr / Pct	3Yr / Pct	5Yr / Pct	Risk Rating/Pts	Mgr. Quality Pct	Mgr. Tenure (Years)
MUN	Oppenheimer Rochester AMT-Free	OPTAX	A-	(888) 470-0862	6.83	A+ /9.7	3.73 /69	6.34 /99	6.00 /99	D+ / 2.8	89	15
MUH	MainStay High Yield Muni Bond C	MMHDX	B+	(800) 624-6782	12.14	A+ /9.9	2.48 /61	6.40 /99	5.49 /99	D / 2.0	84	7
MUH	Oppeneheimer Rochester Hi Yld	ORNAX	B+	(888) 470-0862	7.09	A+ /9.9	7.13 /81	7.47 /99	6.59 /99	D / 1.7	91	15
MUH	Lord Abbett Tx Fr High Yld Muni A	HYMAX	B+	(888) 522-2388	11.63	A+ /9.7	3.59 /69	5.90 /98	5.30 /98	D+ / 2.3	85	13
MUS	Oppenheimer Rochester Muni A	RMUNX	B+	(888) 470-0862	14.88	A+ /9.7	6.99 /81	5.99 /98	3.99 /93	D / 2.1	87	15
MUH	Invesco High Yield Municipal A	ACTHX	B+	(800) 959-4246	9.87	A+ /9.7	2.53 /62	6.92 /99	5.74 /99	D / 2.0	88	15
MUH	PIMCO High Yield Muni Bond A	PYMAX	B+	(800) 426-0107	8.77	A+ /9.6	2.36 /60	5.95 /98	5.05 /98	D / 2.1	80	2
MUH	MFS Municipal High Income A	MMHYX	B+	(800) 225-2606	8.07	A /9.4	1.91 /56	6.12 /99	5.03 /98	D+ / 2.6	86	15
MUH	T Rowe Price Tax-Free High Yield	PRFHX	B+	(800) 638-5660	11.77	A /9.3	1.64 /53	5.37 /98	4.99 /98	D+ / 2.7	81	15
MUS	Oppenheimer Rochester AMT-Fr	OPNYX	B+	(888) 470-0862	11.08	A /9.3	4.42 /72	5.65 /98	3.89 /92	D+ / 2.5	84	15
COH	Hundredfold Select Alternative Svc	SFHYX	B+	(855) 582-8006	22.72	A- /9.2	14.09 /87	4.14 /77	5.07 /85	D+ / 2.6	82	13
GEI	CNR Fixed Income Opportunities N	RIMOX	B+	(888) 889-0799	25.98	A- /9.1	15.63 /90	4.16 /77	5.58 /89	D+ / 2.8	95	6
MUN	Eaton Vance High Yield Muni Inc A	ETHYX	B+	(800) 262-1122	8.68	A- /9.1	1.03 /45	6.27 /99	5.42 /99	D+ / 2.7	84	13
EM	BlackRock Emg Mkts Flex Dyn Bd	BAEDX	B	(800) 441-7762	9.68	A+ /9.8	17.51 /93	6.80 /95	4.26 /76	D- / 1.4	99	6
COI	Angel Oak High Yield Opps Inst	ANHIX	B	(877) 625-3042	11.94	A+ /9.7	20.93 /97	4.75 /83	6.31 /94	D / 1.6	88	8
COH	PIA High Yield Institutional	PHYSX	B	(800) 251-1970	10.32	A+ /9.6	18.33 /94	4.80 /84	6.74 /96	D / 1.9	77	7
MUH	Pioneer High Income Municipal A	PIMAX	B	(800) 225-6292	7.21	A /9.5	3.01 /65	6.07 /99	5.50 /99	D / 2.0	81	11
MUH	BlackRock High Yld Muni Inv A	MDYHX	B	(800) 441-7762	9.34	A /9.5	1.68 /54	6.46 /99	5.06 /98	D / 1.7	82	11
MUH	Goldman Sachs High Yield Muni A	GHYAX	B	(800) 526-7384	9.31	A /9.4	4.89 /73	6.19 /99	5.65 /99	D / 2.1	88	17
MUH	AB High Income Municipal A	ABTHX	B	(800) 221-5672	11.07	A /9.4	0.97 /44	6.01 /98	5.19 /98	D / 1.9	77	7
MUH	Delaware Natl HY Muni Bd A	CXHYX	B	(800) 523-1918	10.77	A /9.3	1.84 /55	6.07 /99	5.22 /98	D / 2.2	82	14
COH	Vanguard High-Yield Corporate Inv	VWEHX	B	(800) 662-7447	5.92	A /9.3	14.53 /88	4.62 /82	6.02 /92	D / 2.0	77	9
MUH	Northern High Yield Muni	NHYMX	B	(800) 595-9111	8.68	A- /9.0	0.17 /28	4.77 /97	4.20 /95	D+ / 2.6	71	19
MUH	American Funds High Inc Muni Bnd	AMHIX	B	(800) 421-0180	15.41	B+ /8.9	1.75 /54	5.43 /98	5.38 /98	D+ / 2.8	82	23
MUH	Vanguard High-Yield Tax-Exempt	VWAHX	B	(800) 662-7447	11.08	B+ /8.9	0.96 /44	4.49 /96	4.01 /93	D+ / 2.6	62	7
MUH	Columbia High Yield Municipal A	LHIAX	B	(800) 345-6611	10.49	B+ /8.9	1.48 /51	5.23 /97	4.84 /97	D+ / 2.5	80	8
MUS ●	Oppenheimer Rochester AZ Muni	ORAZX	B	(888) 470-0862	10.50	B+ /8.7	6.14 /78	4.48 /96	2.83 /77	D+ / 2.8	87	11
MUS	Vanguard CA Long-Term	VCITX	B	(800) 662-7447	11.89	B+ /8.6	-0.02 /17	4.31 /95	3.95 /93	D+ / 2.8	36	6
COH	Brandes Separately Mgd Acct Res	SMARX	B	(800) 237-7119	8.89	B+ /8.6	13.04 /85	4.22 /78	5.71 /90	D+ / 2.8	85	12
EM	T Rowe Price Ins Emerging Mkts	TREBX	B-	(800) 638-5660	9.14	A+ /9.9	18.64 /94	7.51 /97	6.13 /93	D- / 1.1	99	11
MUH	Nuveen High Yield Muni Bond A	NHMAX	B-	(800) 257-8787	16.68	A+ /9.7	2.45 /61	6.80 /99	6.98 /99	D- / 1.4	83	17
COH	J Hancock US High Yield Bd NAV		B-	(800) 257-3336	11.38	A+ /9.7	20.94 /97	4.71 /83	6.00 /92	D- / 1.2	62	12
COH	Lord Abbett High Yield A	LHYAX	B-	(888) 522-2388	7.67	A+ /9.7	21.58 /98	5.57 /89	7.79 /98	D- / 1.1	78	7
COH	Federated Instl High Yld Bond	FIHBX	B-	(800) 341-7400	10.06	A /9.5	18.69 /94	5.14 /86	6.97 /96	D- / 1.3	74	15
COH	Westcore Flexible Income Rtl	WTLTX	B-	(800) 392-2673	8.99	A /9.3	15.39 /89	5.18 /86	5.77 /91	D / 1.9	82	8
GL	AB High Income A	AGDAX	B-	(800) 221-5672	8.86	A /9.3	20.70 /97	4.76 /83	6.95 /96	D / 1.8	97	15
COH	Lord Abbett Bond Debenture A	LBNDX	B-	(888) 522-2388	8.09	A /9.3	18.04 /94	4.84 /84	6.50 /95	D / 1.6	76	4
MUH	Federated Muni & Stock	FMUAX	B-	(800) 341-7400	12.87	A- /9.1	9.80 /89	4.20 /94	5.98 /99	D / 2.1	92	14
LP	Invesco Senior Loan A	VSLAX	B-	(800) 959-4246	6.68	A- /9.0	20.95 /97	3.89 /74	6.11 /93	D / 2.2	89	10
COI	BMO TCH Corporate Income Y	MCIYX	B-	(800) 236-3863	12.96	A- /9.0	15.31 /89	4.47 /80	4.90 /83	D / 2.1	74	9
GEI	SunAmerica VAL Co II High Yld Bd	VCHYX	B-	(800) 858-8850	7.88	A- /9.0	16.31 /91	3.84 /73	5.57 /89	D / 1.9	90	8
MUH	Prudential Muni High Income A	PRHAX	B-	(800) 225-1852	10.07	B+ /8.8	1.40 /50	5.43 /98	4.72 /97	D / 2.2	78	13
MUH	Federated Muni High Yield Advn A	FMOAX	B-	(800) 341-7400	8.78	B+ /8.7	1.34 /49	5.50 /98	4.91 /97	D+ / 2.4	81	8
MUH	Victory High Income Municipal Bd	RSHMX	B-	(800) 539-3863	10.47	B+ /8.6	-0.08 /16	5.03 /97	3.39 /86	D+ / 2.8	80	3
USS	MSIF Trust Core Plus Fix Inc A	MFXAX	B-	(800) 354-8185	10.92	B+ /8.6	12.57 /84	5.58 /89	5.13 /85	D+ / 2.4	95	6
GES	Wells Fargo Dvsfd Inc Bldr A	EKSAX	C+	(800) 222-8222	6.27	A+ /9.6	18.09 /94	6.38 /94	7.81 /98	D- / 1.1	96	10
EM	DoubleLine Em Mkts Fxd Inc N	DLENX	C+	(877) 354-6311	10.50	A+ /9.6	18.33 /94	5.08 /85	4.67 /80	D- / 1.0	98	7
COH	Transamerica Prt High Yield Bond	DVHYX	C+	(888) 233-4339	8.87	A /9.5	20.16 /96	4.25 /78	6.31 /94	D- / 1.1	34	3
EM	Payden Emerging Market Bond	PYEWX	C+	(888) 409-8007	13.80	A /9.5	13.61 /86	5.58 /89	4.55 /79	D- / 1.0	99	17
COH	Voya High Yield Service	IPHYX	C+	(800) 992-0180	10.13	A /9.4	17.44 /93	4.29 /79	5.94 /92	D- / 1.5	56	3
GEI	Northern Multi-Mgr HY Oppty	NMHYX	C+	(800) 595-9111	10.05	A /9.4	21.69 /98	4.03 /76	6.19 /93	D- / 1.4	92	5
COI	Fidelity High Income	SPHIX	C+	(800) 544-8544	8.91	A /9.4	21.79 /98	3.96 /75	5.91 /91	D- / 1.1	81	17

● Denotes fund is closed to new investors

Fund Type	Fund Name	Ticker Symbol	Overall Investment Rating	Phone	Net Asset Value As of 2/28/17	Performance Rating/Pts	1Yr / Pct	3Yr / Pct	5Yr / Pct	Risk Rating/Pts	Mgr. Quality Pct	Mgr. Tenure (Years)
COH	CNR High Yield Bond N	CHBAX	C+	(888) 889-0799	8.01	A /9.4	21.23 /97	3.88 /74	6.00 /92	D- / 1.1	25	6
COH ●	T Rowe Price Instl High Yield	TRHYX	C+	(800) 638-5660	9.00	A /9.4	20.65 /97	4.37 /79	6.72 /96	D- / 1.1	42	2
MUH	AMG GW&K Muni Enhanced Yield	GWMNX	C+	(800) 548-4539	9.50	A /9.4	0.17 /28	5.35 /98	4.18 /95	D- / 1.0	33	12
COH	Guggenheim High Yield A	SIHAX	C+	(800) 820-0888	11.46	A- /9.2	21.15 /97	4.98 /85	7.64 /97	D / 1.7	78	5
COH ●	MainStay High Yield Corp Bond B	MKHCX	C+	(800) 624-6782	5.78	A- /9.2	18.56 /94	3.87 /74	5.42 /88	D / 1.6	37	4
COH	Principal High Yield A	CPHYX	C+	(800) 222-5852	7.47	A- /9.2	19.56 /95	4.48 /80	6.51 /95	D- / 1.4	59	5
COH ●	T Rowe Price High Yield	PRHYX	C+	(800) 638-5660	6.76	A- /9.2	18.93 /95	4.13 /77	6.60 /95	D- / 1.4	44	21
COH	Prudential High Yield A	PBHAX	C+	(800) 225-1852	5.57	A- /9.2	20.00 /96	4.84 /84	6.53 /95	D- / 1.2	64	16
COH	MassMutual Premier High Yield A	MPHAX	C+	(800) 542-6767	9.13	A- /9.1	19.70 /95	4.82 /84	7.72 /98	D / 1.6	75	7
GL	PIMCO High Yield Spectrum A	PHSAX	C+	(800) 426-0107	10.00	A- /9.1	19.90 /96	4.42 /80	6.86 /96	D- / 1.5	96	7
COH	MFS Global High Yield A	MHOAX	C+	(800) 225-2606	6.24	A- /9.1	17.65 /93	3.73 /72	5.63 /89	D- / 1.2	21	12
MUH	Franklin California H/Y Muni A	FCAMX	C+	(800) 342-5236	10.64	B+ /8.9	1.16 /47	5.83 /98	5.23 /98	D / 1.8	75	23
GEI	Voya Investment Grade Credit	ISCFX	C+	(800) 992-0180	10.89	B+ /8.7	9.22 /77	4.95 /85	4.94 /84	D+ / 2.3	82	5
COH	Voya High Yield Bond A	IHYAX	C+	(800) 992-0180	8.18	B+ /8.6	15.62 /89	4.00 /75	6.44 /95	D / 1.8	57	10
MUS	Oppenheimer Rochester NJ Muni	ONJAX	C+	(888) 470-0862	9.38	B+ /8.5	3.98 /71	4.86 /97	3.11 /82	D+ / 2.5	84	15
GEI	Invesco Income Allocation A	ALAAX	C+	(800) 959-4246	11.44	B+ /8.5	12.91 /85	5.42 /88	6.66 /95	D+ / 2.3	93	3
COH	Eaton Vance High Inc Opp Fund A	ETHIX	C+	(800) 262-1122	4.55	B+ /8.5	14.99 /88	4.72 /83	7.02 /96	D / 1.9	77	21
GL	GMO Currency Hedged Intl Bond	GMHBX	C+		26.50	B+ /8.4	2.79 /55	5.93 /91	6.04 /92	D / 2.0	98	3
GL	Principal Glb Divers Income A	PGBAX	C+	(800) 222-5852	13.84	B+ /8.3	14.19 /87	4.27 /78	6.21 /94	D / 2.1	96	7
MUS	Nuveen CA Muni Bond A	NCAAX	C+	(800) 257-8787	11.00	B /8.2	0.36 /34	5.18 /97	4.84 /97	D+ / 2.7	73	14
GL	Fidelity Strategic Income Fund	FSICX	C+	(800) 544-8544	10.87	B /8.1	11.62 /82	3.60 /70	4.10 /74	D+ / 2.8	95	18
MUS	Franklin California Tx-Fr Inc A	FKTFX	C+	(800) 342-5236	7.39	B /7.9	1.22 /48	4.88 /97	4.25 /95	D+ / 2.7	60	26
MUH	WA Municipal High Income A	STXAX	C+	(877) 534-4627	14.09	B /7.8	1.40 /50	4.77 /97	3.73 /90	D+ / 2.9	78	10
MUH	Fidelity Municipal Inc	FHIGX	C+	(800) 544-8544	12.91	B /7.8	-0.13 /15	3.77 /91	3.37 /86	D+ / 2.8	33	7
COH	Principal High Yield Fund I Inst	PYHIX	C	(800) 222-5852	10.00	A- /9.0	17.61 /93	3.58 /70	5.89 /91	D- / 1.1	17	10
COH	AMG Mgrs High Yield N	MHHAX	C	(800) 548-4539	7.84	A- /9.0	19.76 /96	3.85 /73	5.96 /92	D- / 1.0	19	16
MUH	Dreyfus High Yld Muni Bd A	DHYAX	C	(800) 645-6561	11.80	B+ /8.9	2.69 /63	5.88 /98	4.77 /97	D- / 1.2	62	6
COH	PACE High Yield Invst A	PHIAX	C	(888) 793-8637	10.04	B+ /8.8	20.85 /97	3.94 /75	6.22 /94	D- / 1.1	25	2
GL	Russell Investments Glbl Opp Crd	RGCYX	C	(800) 832-6688	9.65	B+ /8.7	15.00 /88	3.64 /71	4.61 /80	D- / 1.5	96	6
GES	Transamerica High Yield Bond A	IHIYX	C	(888) 233-4339	9.30	B+ /8.7	19.31 /95	4.12 /77	6.23 /94	D- / 1.1	91	11
USS	Eaton Vance Core Plus Bond A	EBABX	C	(800) 262-1122	11.69	B+ /8.6	16.06 /90	4.91 /84	3.78 /70	D / 1.6	94	8
COH	Virtus High Yield A	PHCHX	C	(800) 243-1574	4.27	B+ /8.6	17.20 /92	4.01 /75	6.13 /93	D- / 1.5	46	6
COH	Wells Fargo High Yld Bd Fd A	EKHAX	C	(800) 222-8222	3.36	B+ /8.6	14.63 /88	4.78 /84	6.11 /93	D- / 1.5	76	4
COH	Federated High Income Bond A	FHIIX	C	(800) 341-7400	7.65	B+ /8.6	17.79 /93	4.27 /78	6.14 /93	D- / 1.3	51	30
COH ●	SSgA High Yield Bond N	SSHYX	C	(800) 843-2639	7.63	B+ /8.5	15.04 /89	3.27 /65	5.68 /90	D / 1.6	20	5
COH	Fidelity Focused High Income	FHIFX	C	(800) 544-8544	8.62	B+ /8.5	14.52 /88	3.70 /71	4.94 /83	D- / 1.4	31	13
COH	PIMCO High Yield A	PHDAX	C	(800) 426-0107	8.96	B+ /8.4	15.65 /90	4.19 /77	5.83 /91	D- / 1.5	56	7
COH	Northern HY Fixed Income	NHFIX	C	(800) 595-9111	6.89	B+ /8.4	17.51 /93	3.23 /65	5.79 /91	D- / 1.3	15	10
MUS ●	Oppenheimer Rochester MD Muni	ORMDX	C	(888) 470-0862	9.59	B+ /8.3	5.85 /76	4.29 /95	2.27 /66	D / 1.7	82	11
GES	PIMCO Diversified Income A	PDVAX	C	(800) 426-0107	10.75	B /8.2	13.45 /86	4.51 /81	4.86 /83	D / 2.1	88	1
COH	Payden High Income Adviser	PYHWX	C	(888) 409-8007	6.56	B /8.2	12.01 /83	3.50 /69	5.15 /86	D / 2.0	51	5
GEI	Loomis Sayles Fixed Inc Fd	LSFIX	C	(800) 633-3330	13.39	B /8.0	15.01 /88	2.80 /58	5.26 /86	D / 1.9	81	22
COH	Eaton Vance Income Fd of Boston	EVIBX	C	(800) 262-1122	5.80	B /8.0	14.93 /88	4.15 /77	6.10 /93	D / 1.9	65	16
COH	Access Flex High Yield Inv	FYAIX	C	(888) 776-3637	33.27	B /7.9	9.88 /79	3.60 /70	5.64 /90	D / 2.1	76	13
GL	Janus High-Yield A	JHYAX	C	(800) 295-2687	8.58	B /7.8	15.91 /90	3.61 /70	5.84 /91	D / 2.2	94	9
COI	Lord Abbett Income A	LAGVX	C	(888) 522-2388	2.82	B /7.7	12.18 /84	3.84 /73	4.64 /80	D+ / 2.6	63	19
MUH	Franklin High Yld Tax-Free Inc A	FRHIX	C	(800) 342-5236	10.25	B /7.7	1.19 /47	4.76 /96	3.74 /90	D+ / 2.6	71	24
COH	Lazard US Corporate Income Open	LZHOX	C	(800) 821-6474	4.93	B /7.7	10.59 /80	3.58 /70	5.16 /86	D+ / 2.3	63	14

VII. Top-Rated Bond Mutual Funds In The E Risk Category

Fund Type	Fund Name	Ticker Symbol	Overall Investment Rating	Phone	Net Asset Value As of 2/28/17	Performance Rating/Pts	1Yr / Pct	3Yr / Pct	5Yr / Pct	Risk Rating/Pts	Mgr. Quality Pct	Mgr. Tenure (Years)
MUH	SEI Asset Alloc-Def Strat All F	STDAX	C+	(800) 342-5734	14.64	A+ /9.9	19.17 /99	8.26 /99	10.32 /99	E+ / 0.6	98	14
EM ●	GMO Emerging Country Debt III	GMCDX	C+		28.99	A+ /9.9	19.47 /95	7.56 /97	7.87 /98	E / 0.4	99	23
EM	Fidelity New Markets Income	FNMIX	C+	(800) 544-8544	16.09	A+ /9.9	18.72 /95	7.02 /96	5.74 /90	E / 0.4	99	22
GES	Metropolitan West Alpha Trak 500	MWATX	C+	(800) 496-8298	8.96	A+ /9.9	35.34 /99	13.01 /99	16.54 /99	E- / 0.2	99	19
GEI	Columbia Abs Rtn Currency & Inc	RACWX	C+	(800) 345-6611	10.90	A+ /9.9	9.30 /77	12.21 /99	5.18 /86	E- / 0.1	99	11
GEI	Fairholme Focused Income	FOCIX	C+	(866) 202-2263	12.55	A+ /9.9	42.47 /99	6.55 /94	10.45 /99	E- / 0.0	99	8
EM	T Rowe Price Emerging Markets	PREMX	C+	(800) 638-5660	12.64	A+ /9.8	18.31 /94	6.74 /95	5.22 /86	E+ / 0.7	99	23
GEI	PIMCO Long Term Credit Inst	PTCIX	C+	(800) 426-0107	11.71	A+ /9.8	13.18 /85	7.28 /96	7.24 /97	E / 0.3	69	8
GEI	SEI Instl Managed Tr-High Yld Bd	SHYAX	C+	(800) 342-5734	7.29	A+ /9.7	22.81 /98	4.52 /81	6.60 /95	E+ / 0.9	93	13
MUS ●	Oppenheimer Rochester VA Muni	ORVAX	C+	(888) 470-0862	8.23	A+ /9.7	9.27 /87	5.37 /98	2.85 /77	E+ / 0.6	77	11
EM	Stone Harbor Emerging Debt Inst	SHMDX	C+	(866) 699-8125	10.44	A+ /9.7	16.18 /90	5.83 /91	4.07 /73	E / 0.5	99	10
COH	Loomis Sayles Inst High Income	LSHIX	C+	(800) 633-3330	6.81	A+ /9.7	27.63 /99	3.85 /73	8.00 /98	E / 0.4	4	21
EM	Fidelity Adv Emerging Mkts Inc A	FMKAX	C+	(800) 522-7297	14.20	A+ /9.7	18.36 /94	6.62 /95	5.33 /87	E / 0.4	99	22
COH	Federated High Yield Trust Svc	FHYTX	C+	(800) 341-7400	6.89	A+ /9.6	20.02 /96	5.02 /85	8.09 /98	E+ / 0.7	54	33
MUH	Nuveen CA High Yield Muni Bd A	NCHAX	C+	(800) 257-8787	9.35	A /9.5	0.25 /31	6.67 /99	6.69 /99	E+ / 0.9	73	11
EM	Franklin Emg Mkt Debt	FEMDX	C+	(800) 342-5236	11.31	A /9.5	18.26 /94	4.50 /81	4.72 /81	E+ / 0.7	97	11
COH	Fidelity Adv Hi Income Advantage	FAHDX	C+	(800) 522-7297	11.09	A /9.5	22.41 /98	5.20 /86	7.61 /97	E+ / 0.6	55	8
EM	TCW Emerging Markets Income N	TGINX	C+	(800) 386-3829	10.78	A /9.4	17.56 /93	4.54 /81	4.65 /80	E+ / 0.8	98	7
COH	USAA High Income Fund	USHYX	C+	(800) 382-8722	8.26	A /9.4	23.09 /98	3.79 /73	6.66 /96	E+ / 0.8	16	1
COH	TIAA-CREF High Yield Fund Retire	TIHRX	C+	(800) 842-2252	9.90	A /9.3	20.91 /97	4.30 /79	6.06 /92	E+ / 0.9	29	11
GEN	J Hancock VIT Value I	JEVLX	C	(800) 257-3336	22.17	A+ /9.9	32.97 /99	6.07 /92	11.88 /99	E- / 0.0	99	20
MTG	PIMCO StkPlus Intl (DH) A	PIPAX	C	(800) 426-0107	7.60	A+ /9.9	26.71 /99	6.07 /92	10.96 /99	E- / 0.0	98	2
GEI	Rydex Strengthening Dlr 2x Strtgy	RYSDX	C	(800) 820-0888	54.04	A+ /9.9	4.97 /66	13.86 /99	6.77 /96	E- / 0.0	99	12
COI	Vanguard Long-Term Corp Bd Idx	VLTCX	C	(800) 662-7447	24.24	A /9.4	11.67 /82	5.99 /92	5.27 /87	E / 0.3	8	8
COH	Victory High Yield A	GUHYX	C	(800) 539-3863	6.51	A- /9.2	22.27 /98	3.35 /67	5.58 /89	E+ / 0.7	7	8
COH	J Hancock High Yield NAV		C	(800) 257-3336	8.27	A- /9.2	24.95 /99	2.63 /55	5.93 /92	E / 0.5	1	11
GL	Nuveen High Income Bond A	FJSIX	C	(800) 257-8787	7.95	A- /9.2	32.82 /99	2.50 /52	5.75 /90	E / 0.3	91	12
COH	Permanent Portfolio Versatile Bd I	PRVBX	C	(800) 531-5142	59.65	A- /9.1	19.94 /96	3.59 /70	4.11 /74	E+ / 0.8	37	14
GEI	Nuveen Symphony Credit Oppty A	NCOAX	C	(800) 257-8787	20.76	A- /9.1	25.98 /99	3.49 /69	6.33 /94	E+ / 0.8	91	7
COH	Hotchkis and Wiley High Yield A	HWHAX	C	(866) 493-8637	12.25	A- /9.0	23.14 /98	4.13 /73	6.85 /96	E+ / 0.9	24	8
COH	WA High Yield IS	WAHSX	C	(888) 425-6432	8.22	A- /9.0	23.45 /98	2.63 /55	5.77 /91	E+ / 0.7	2	12
EM	Universal Inst Emer Mrkt Debt II	UEDBX	C	(800) 869-6397	8.01	B+ /8.9	13.37 /86	4.38 /79	3.44 /64	E+ / 0.7	98	15
GEI ●	Vanguard Long-Term Inv Gr Inv	VWESX	C-	(800) 662-7447	10.21	A- /9.1	7.10 /73	6.34 /94	5.40 /88	E / 0.3	32	4
US	Vanguard Extnd Durtn Trea Idx Inst	VEDTX	C-	(800) 662-7447	33.95	A- /9.1	-6.63 / 0	9.40 /99	4.53 /79	E- / 0.0	69	4
GEI	PIMCO Extended Duration P	PEDPX	C-	(800) 426-0107	7.55	A- /9.1	-5.95 / 0	9.45 /99	4.30 /76	E- / 0.0	0	10
GEI	PIMCO Long Dur Total Return P	PLRPX	C-	(800) 426-0107	10.70	A- /9.0	6.80 /72	6.18 /93	4.69 /81	E / 0.3	11	10
COH	First Eagle High Yield I	FEHIX	C-	(800) 334-2143	9.08	B+ /8.9	24.20 /99	2.56 /53	5.17 /86	E / 0.5	1	N/A
COH	Loomis Sayles High Income A	NEFHX	C-	(800) 225-5478	4.31	B+ /8.8	21.71 /98	3.82 /73	6.26 /94	E+ / 0.6	7	15
EM	J Hancock Emerg Markets Debt A	JMKAX	C-	(800) 257-3336	9.44	B+ /8.8	17.97 /93	4.66 /82	3.99 /72	E / 0.4	98	4
EM	PIMCO Emerging Markets Bond A	PAEMX	C-	(800) 426-0107	10.40	B+ /8.8	17.97 /93	4.41 /80	3.73 /69	E / 0.3	98	5
COH	Pax High Yield Inv	PAXHX	C-	(800) 767-1729	6.86	B+ /8.7	21.20 /97	2.25 /47	4.82 /82	E+ / 0.9	2	2
COH	Ivy High Income A	WHIAX	C-	(800) 777-6472	7.64	B+ /8.6	23.90 /99	3.39 /67	6.68 /96	E+ / 0.7	8	3
EM	Columbia Emerging Markets Bond	REBAX	C-	(800) 345-6611	11.55	B+ /8.5	16.23 /91	4.77 /83	3.97 /72	E+ / 0.6	98	6
COH	Waddell & Reed Adv High Income	UNHIX	C-	(888) 923-3355	6.81	B+ /8.3	22.04 /98	3.44 /68	7.09 /97	E+ / 0.8	9	3
EM	Janus Emerging Markets A	JMFAX	D+	(800) 295-2687	8.68	B+ /8.8	29.19 /99	2.84 /59	-0.15 / 4	E- / 0.0	96	5
GL ●	MainStay Global High Income B	MGHBX	D+	(800) 624-6782	10.28	B+ /8.6	17.00 /92	3.36 /67	3.21 /61	E / 0.3	96	6
COH	Franklin High Income A	FHAIX	D+	(800) 342-5236	1.91	B+ /8.4	27.58 /99	2.20 /46	5.26 /86	E / 0.3	0	26
COH	RidgeWorth Seix High Income A	SAHIX	D+	(888) 784-3863	6.53	B+ /8.3	22.00 /98	3.35 /67	5.87 /91	E+ / 0.6	4	6
EM	PIMCO EM Corporate Bond Inst	PEMIX	D+	(800) 426-0107	10.61	B /8.2	17.28 /92	2.39 /50	3.55 /66	E+ / 0.6	92	1
COH	J Hancock High Yield A	JHHBX	D+	(800) 257-3336	3.54	B /8.1	20.68 /97	2.96 /60	7.03 /96	E+ / 0.9	6	8
COH	CGCM High Yield	THYUX	D+	(800) 444-4273	3.87	B /8.1	19.81 /96	1.91 /41	5.01 /84	E+ / 0.9	1	12
COH	American Funds High Income Tr A	AHITX	D+	(800) 421-0180	10.46	B /8.1	21.40 /97	2.82 /58	5.14 /85	E+ / 0.8	3	28

● Denotes fund is closed to new investors

www.thestreetratings.com

					Net Asset Value As of 2/28/17	PERFORMANCE					RISK	FUND MGR	
	99 Pct = Best 0 Pct = Worst			Overall Investment Rating		Perform-ance Rating/Pts	Annualized Total Return Through 2/28/17			Risk Rating/Pts	Mgr. Quality Pct	Mgr. Tenure (Years)
Fund Type	Fund Name	Ticker Symbol					1Yr / Pct	3Yr / Pct	5Yr / Pct			
COH	Putnam High Yield Advantage A	PHYIX	D+	(800) 225-1581	5.92	B /8.0	19.31 /95	3.55 /69	5.79 /91	E+ / 0.9	11	15
GEL	Vanguard Long Term Bd Idx	VBLTX	D	(800) 662-7447	13.75	B+ /8.4	4.47 /64	5.84 /91	4.28 /76	E- / 0.2	5	4
GEI	J Hancock Global Income A	JYGAX	D	(800) 257-3336	9.48	B /7.8	16.13 /90	3.61 /70	4.06 /73	E+ / 0.9	82	8
COH	Pioneer High Yield A	TAHYX	D	(800) 225-6292	9.72	B /7.8	19.80 /96	2.87 /59	6.02 /92	E+ / 0.8	4	10
COH	WA Global High Yield Bond A	SAHYX	D	(877) 534-4627	6.47	B /7.7	21.99 /98	2.38 /50	5.22 /86	E+ / 0.7	1	11
GEI	API Multi Asset Income A	APIUX	D	(800) 544-6060	10.41	B /7.7	23.71 /99	2.42 /50	5.54 /89	E / 0.3	85	20
COH	AllianzGI High Yield Bond A	AYBAX	D	(800) 988-8380	9.31	B- /7.5	19.30 /95	2.60 /54	5.15 /85	E+ / 0.8	3	21
EM	WA Emerging Markets Debt A	LWEAX	D	(888) 425-6432	5.02	B- /7.4	14.57 /88	3.51 /69	2.48 /49	E+ / 0.6	96	4
GL	Templeton Global Total Return A	TGTRX	D-	(800) 342-5236	12.30	B- /7.2	15.93 /90	2.24 /47	3.72 /69	E+ / 0.8	84	9
USL	Vanguard Long-Term Govt Bd Idx	VLGSX	D-	(800) 662-7447	25.22	B- /7.1	-4.33 / 0	6.15 /93	3.34 /63	E- / 0.1	28	4
US	Vanguard Long-Term Treasury Inv	VUSTX	D-	(800) 662-7447	11.95	B- /7.0	-4.43 / 0	6.08 /92	3.23 /61	E- / 0.1	58	2
COI	Delaware Extended Duration Bd A	DEEAX	D-	(800) 523-1918	6.39	C+ /6.9	7.49 /73	4.72 /83	5.49 /88	E / 0.4	5	10
US	Fidelity Lg-T Tre Bd In Inv	FLBIX	D-	(800) 544-8544	12.80	C+ /6.8	-4.66 / 0	6.00 /92	3.19 /60	E- / 0.1	53	3
US	Wasatch Hoisington US Treasury	WHOSX	D-	(800) 551-1700	15.87	C+ /6.8	-5.86 / 0	7.03 /96	3.25 /62	E- / 0.0	58	21
GL	Templeton Global Bond A	TPINX	D-	(800) 342-5236	12.23	C+ /6.7	12.99 /85	2.18 /46	2.96 /57	E+ / 0.9	83	16
COH	Touchstone High Yield A	THYAX	D-	(800) 543-0407	8.31	C+ /6.7	16.59 /91	2.46 /51	4.68 /81	E+ / 0.9	2	18
COH	Western Asset Short Dur High Inc	SHIAX	D-	(877) 534-4627	5.42	C+ /6.5	21.17 /97	0.68 /23	4.60 /80	E+ / 0.7	0	11
GEI	PIMCO Real Return Asset P	PRTPX	D-	(800) 426-0107	8.39	C+ /6.5	7.81 /74	2.90 /59	1.11 /29	E / 0.3	1	10
COH	Delaware High-Yield Opps A	DHOAX	D-	(800) 523-1918	3.85	C+ /6.0	16.96 /92	1.63 /37	5.14 /85	E+ / 0.9	1	5
US	Dreyfus US Treasury Long Term	DRGBX	E+	(800) 645-6561	18.40	C+ /6.1	-4.72 / 0	5.29 /87	2.53 /50	E- / 0.2	37	9
US	T Rowe Price US Treas Long-Term	PRULX	E+	(800) 638-5660	12.36	C+ /6.1	-4.70 / 0	5.33 /87	2.67 /52	E- / 0.2	31	14
GEI	Calvert Long Term Income A	CLDAX	E+	(800) 368-2745	16.56	C+ /5.9	5.47 /68	4.70 /83	4.56 /79	E / 0.5	10	4
GEI	American Century Zero Cpn 2025	BTTRX	E+	(800) 345-6488	96.09	C+ /5.6	-2.97 / 0	4.27 /78	2.78 /54	E+ / 0.7	6	11
COI	Federated Emerging Mkt Debt A	IHIAX	E+	(800) 341-7400	8.47	C /5.2	11.94 /83	1.84 /40	2.21 /45	E / 0.3	7	4
USA	ProFunds-US Government Plus	GVPSX	E+	(888) 776-3637	49.04	C /5.0	-8.64 / 0	5.62 /89	1.47 /34	E- / 0.0	1	8
USL	Rydex Govt Lg Bd 1.2x Strgy A	RYABX	E+	(800) 820-0888	51.50	C /5.0	-7.67 / 0	6.91 /96	3.81 /70	E- / 0.0	1	23
EM	SEI Inst Intl Emerging Mkts Debt F	SITEX	E+	(800) 342-5734	9.79	C /4.9	12.88 /85	0.67 /23	0.61 /23	E- / 0.2	91	17
USL	PIMCO Long Term US Govt A	PFGAX	E+	(800) 426-0107	6.02	C /4.9	-3.95 / 0	5.46 /88	2.99 /58	E- / 0.1	14	10
GES	Northeast Investors Trust	NTHEX	E+	(800) 225-6704	4.74	C /4.8	35.60 /99	-3.55 / 1	2.53 /50	E- / 0.0	2	N/A
GL	TCW Emg Mkts Local Currency Inc	TGWNX	E	(800) 386-3829	9.11	C- /3.7	16.20 /91	-1.37 / 2	-1.55 / 2	E- / 0.1	80	7
EM	Oppenheimer Em Mkts Local Debt	OEMAX	E	(888) 470-0862	7.17	C- /3.5	15.90 /90	0.05 / 9	-0.79 / 2	E- / 0.2	89	2
EM	Eaton Vance Emer Market Local	EEIAX	E	(800) 262-1122	6.17	C- /3.4	17.57 /93	-0.11 / 5	-2.49 / 1	E- / 0.1	89	9
COH	Catalyst/SMH High Income A	HIIFX	E	(866) 447-4228	3.91	C- /3.3	46.00 /99	-5.28 / 0	-1.69 / 1	E- / 0.0	0	9
EM	Deutsche Enh Emg Mrkts Fxd Inc	SZEAX	E	(800) 728-3337	9.41	D+ /2.7	10.98 /81	0.52 /21	1.63 /37	E+ / 0.9	82	6
US	Direxion Mo 7-10 Year Tr Bl 2X Inv	DXKLX	E	(800) 851-0511	34.14	D+ /2.4	-8.47 / 0	3.22 /65	1.44 /33	E- / 0.2	1	11
GL	LM BW International Opptys Bd IS	LMOTX	E	(877) 534-4627	11.14	D /2.2	5.59 /69	-0.08 / 5	1.60 /36	E / 0.4	87	8
GEI	J Hancock Absolute Ret Curr A	JCUAX	E	(800) 257-3336	9.41	D /2.1	3.18 /58	1.09 /29	2.47 /49	E+ / 0.7	87	6
GL	LM BW Global Opportunities Bond	GOBAX	E	(877) 534-4627	10.46	D /2.0	6.14 /71	0.92 /26	1.65 /37	E / 0.4	91	11
GL	STAAR AltCat	SITAX	E	(800) 332-7738	14.19	D /1.8	14.16 /87	-2.44 / 2	2.72 /53	E- / 0.2	3	20
GL	Prudential Global Total Return A	GTRAX	E-	(800) 225-1852	6.39	E /0.4	2.83 /55	0.93 /26	2.12 /44	E+ / 0.9	91	15
GL	Lord Abbett Emerg Mkts Currency	LDMAX	E-	(888) 522-2388	5.26	E- /0.2	10.04 /79	-2.23 / 2	-1.70 / 1	E / 0.5	18	10
GL	PIMCO Emerging Markets	PLMAX	E-	(800) 426-0107	8.91	E- /0.2	11.00 /81	-1.92 / 2	-1.57 / 2	E / 0.5	26	12
GL	PACE Global Fx Inc Inve A	PWFAX	E-	(888) 793-8637	9.67	E- /0.1	-0.77 / 6	-0.28 / 4	-0.61 / 3	E+ / 0.8	84	22
GL	Invesco World Bond A	AUBAX	E-	(800) 959-4246	10.02	E- /0.1	4.88 /66	-1.37 / 2	0.11 /15	E+ / 0.6	75	7
GL	PIMCO Foreign Bd Fd (Unhgd) A	PFUAX	E-	(800) 426-0107	9.47	E- /0.1	4.04 /62	-1.08 / 3	-0.22 / 4	E / 0.5	79	3
EM	PIMCO Emerging Local Bond A	PELAX	E-	(800) 426-0107	7.21	E- /0.1	14.35 /87	-3.27 / 1	-3.50 / 0	E- / 0.1	20	11
EM	Goldman Sachs Local Emg Mkt	GAMDX	E-	(800) 526-7384	6.22	E- /0.1	12.70 /84	-3.74 / 1	-3.37 / 0	E- / 0.0	12	9
MTG	ProFunds-Falling US Dollar Svc	FDPSX	E-	(888) 776-3637	15.64	E- /0.0	-6.29 / 0	-10.51 / 0	-7.63 / 0	E+ / 0.7	0	8

Section VIII

Top-Rated Bond
Mutual Funds
by Fund Type

A compilation of those

Fixed Income Mutual Funds

receiving the highest TheStreet Investment Rating

within each type of fund.

Funds are listed in order by Overall Investment Rating.

Section VIII Contents

This section contains a summary analysis of the top rated 100 bond and money market mutual funds within each fund type. If you are looking for a particular type of mutual fund, these pages show those funds that have achieved the best combination of risk and financial performance over the past three years.

In order to optimize the utility of our top and bottom fund lists, rather than listing all funds in a multi-class series, a single fund from each series is selected for display as the primary share class. Whenever possible, the selected fund is one that a retail investor would be most likely to choose. This share class may not be appropriate for every investor, so please consult with your financial advisor, the fund company, and the fund's prospectus before placing your trade.

1. Fund Type
The mutual fund's peer category based on its investment objective as stated in its prospectus.

COH	Corporate - High Yield	MMT	Money Market - Treas.
COI	Corporate - Inv. Grade	MTG	Mortgage
EM	Emerging Market	MUH	Municipal - High Yield
GEN	General	MUI	Municipal - Insured
GEI	General - Inv. Grade	MUN	Municipal - National
GEL	General - Long Term	MUS	Municipal - Single State
GES	General - Short & Interm.	USL	U.S. Gov.- Long Term
GL	Global	USS	U.S. Gov. - Short & Interm
LP	Loan Participation	USA	U.S. Gov. - Agency
MMF	Money Mkt - Tax Exempt	US	U.S. Gov. - Treasury

A blank fund type means that the mutual fund has not yet been categorized.

2. Fund Name
The name of the mutual fund as stated in its prospectus, which can sometimes differ slightly from the name that the company uses for advertising. If you cannot find the particular mutual fund you are interested in, or if you have any doubts regarding the precise name, verify the information with your broker or on your account statement. Also, use the fund's ticker symbol for confirmation. (See column 3.)

3. Ticker Symbol
The unique alphabetic symbol used for identifying and trading a specific mutual fund. No two funds can have the same ticker symbol, and the ticker symbol for mutual funds always ends with an "X".

A handful of funds currently show no associated ticker symbol. This means that the fund is either small or new since the NASD only assigns a ticker symbol to funds with at least $25 million in assets or 1,000 shareholders.

4. Overall Investment Rating

Our overall rating is measured on a scale from A to E based on each fund's risk-adjusted performance. Please see page 11 for specific descriptions of each letter grade. Also, refer to page 7 for information on how our ratings are derived. Most important, when using this rating, please be sure to consider the warnings beginning on page 13 regarding the ratings' limitations and the underlying assumptions.

5. Phone

The telephone number of the company managing the fund. Call this number to receive a prospectus or other information about the fund.

6. Net Asset Value (NAV)

The fund's share price as of the date indicated. A fund's NAV is computed by dividing the value of the fund's asset holdings, less accrued fees and expenses, by the number of its shares outstanding.

7. Performance Rating/Points

A letter grade rating based solely on the mutual fund's financial performance over the trailing three years, without any consideration for the amount of risk the fund poses. Like the overall Investment Rating, the Performance Rating is measured on a scale from A to E for ease of interpretation. The points score indicates where the Performance Rating falls on a scale of 0 to 10.

In the case of funds investing in municipal or other tax-free securities, this rating is based on the taxable equivalent return of the fund assuming the maximum marginal U.S. tax rate (35%).

8. 1-Year Total Return

The total return the fund has provided investors over the preceding twelve months. This total return figure is computed based on the fund's dividend distributions and share price appreciation/depreciation during the period, net of the expenses and fees it imposes on its shareholders. Although the total return figure does not reflect an adjustment for any loads the fund may carry, such adjustments have been made in deriving TheStreet Investment Ratings.

9. 1-Year Total Return Percentile

The fund's percentile rank based on its one-year performance compared to that of all other fixed income funds in existence for at least one year. A score of 99 is the best possible, indicating that the fund outperformed 99% of the other mutual funds. Zero is the worst possible percentile score.

In the case of funds investing in municipal or other tax-free securities, this percentile rank is based on the taxable equivalent return of the fund assuming the maximum marginal U.S. tax rate (35%).

10. 3-Year Total Return

The total annual return the fund has provided investors over the preceding three years.

11. 3-Year Total Return Percentile

The fund's percentile rank based on its three-year performance compared to that of all other fixed income funds in existence for at least three years. A score of 99 is the best possible, indicating that the fund outperformed 99% of the other mutual funds. Zero is the worst possible percentile score.

In the case of funds investing in municipal or other tax-free securities, this percentile rank is based on the taxable equivalent return of the fund assuming the maximum marginal U.S. tax rate (35%).

12. 5-Year Total Return

The total annual return the fund has provided investors over the preceding five years.

13. 5-Year Total Return Percentile

The fund's percentile rank based on its five-year performance compared to that of all other fixed income funds in existence for at least five years. A score of 99 is the best possible, indicating that the fund outperformed 99% of the other mutual funds. Zero is the worst possible percentile score.

In the case of funds investing in municipal or other tax-free securities, this percentile rank is based on the taxable equivalent return of the fund assuming the maximum marginal U.S. tax rate (35%).

14. Risk Rating/Points

A letter grade rating based solely on the mutual fund's risk as determined by its monthly performance volatility over the trailing three years and the underlying credit risk and interest rate risk of its investment portfolio. The risk rating does not take into consideration the overall financial performance the fund has achieved or the total return it has provided to its shareholders. Like the overall Investment Rating, the Risk Rating is measured on a scale from A to E for ease of interpretation. The points score indicates where the Risk Rating falls on a scale of 0 to 10.

15. Manager Quality Percentile

The manager quality percentile is based on a ranking of the fund's alpha, a statistical measure representing the difference between a fund's actual returns and its expected performance given its level of risk. Fund managers who have been able to exceed the fund's statistically expected performance receive a high percentile rank with 99 representing the highest possible score. At the other end of the spectrum, fund managers who have actually detracted from the fund's expected performance receive a low percentile rank with 0 representing the lowest possible score.

16. Manager Tenure

The number of years the current manager has been managing the fund. Since fund managers who deliver substandard returns are usually replaced, a long tenure is usually a good sign that shareholders are satisfied that the fund is achieving its stated objectives.

99 Pct = Best
0 Pct = Worst

Fund Type	Fund Name	Ticker Symbol	Overall Investment Rating	Phone	Net Asset Value As of 2/28/17	Perform-ance Rating/Pts	1Yr / Pct	3Yr / Pct	5Yr / Pct	Risk Rating/Pts	Mgr. Quality Pct	Mgr. Tenure (Years)
COH	Hundredfold Select Alternative Svc	SFHYX	B+	(855) 582-8006	22.72	A- / 9.2	14.09 / 87	4.14 / 77	5.07 / 85	D+ / 2.6	82	13
COH	Pioneer Floating Rate Fund Class	FLARX	B+	(800) 225-6292	6.81	C / 5.2	8.44 / 75	2.80 / 58	3.71 / 69	B- / 7.4	80	10
COH	PIA High Yield Institutional	PHYSX	B	(800) 251-1970	10.32	A+ / 9.6	18.33 / 94	4.80 / 84	6.74 / 96	D / 1.9	77	7
COH	Vanguard High-Yield Corporate Inv	VWEHX	B	(800) 662-7447	5.92	A / 9.3	14.53 / 88	4.62 / 82	6.02 / 92	D / 2.0	77	9
COH	Brandes Separately Mgd Acct Res	SMARX	B	(800) 237-7119	8.89	B+ / 8.6	13.04 / 85	4.22 / 78	5.71 / 90	D+ / 2.8	85	12
COH	J Hancock US High Yield Bd NAV		B-	(800) 257-3336	11.38	A+ / 9.7	20.94 / 97	4.71 / 83	6.00 / 92	D- / 1.2	62	12
COH	Lord Abbett High Yield A	LHYAX	B-	(888) 522-2388	7.67	A+ / 9.7	21.58 / 98	5.57 / 89	7.79 / 98	D- / 1.1	78	7
COH	Federated Instl High Yld Bond	FIHBX	B-	(800) 341-7400	10.06	A / 9.5	18.69 / 94	5.14 / 86	6.97 / 96	D- / 1.3	74	15
COH	Westcore Flexible Income Rtl	WTLTX	B-	(800) 392-2673	8.99	A / 9.3	15.39 / 89	5.18 / 86	5.77 / 91	D / 1.9	82	8
COH	Lord Abbett Bond Debenture A	LBNDX	B-	(888) 522-2388	8.09	A / 9.3	18.04 / 94	4.84 / 84	6.50 / 95	D / 1.6	76	4
COH	Credit Suisse Floating Rate HI A	CHIAX	B-	(877) 927-2874	6.90	B- / 7.3	12.68 / 84	3.84 / 73	4.63 / 80	C / 4.3	85	12
COH	Wells Fargo Sh-Tm Hi Yld A	SSTHX	B-	(800) 222-8222	8.09	C- / 4.2	4.66 / 65	2.32 / 49	3.05 / 59	B / 7.9	77	19
COH	Loomis Sayles Inst High Income	LSHIX	C+	(800) 633-3330	6.81	A+ / 9.7	27.63 / 99	3.85 / 73	8.00 / 98	E / 0.4	4	21
COH	Federated High Yield Trust Svc	FHYTX	C+	(800) 341-7400	6.89	A+ / 9.6	20.02 / 96	5.02 / 85	8.09 / 98	E+ / 0.7	54	33
COH	Transamerica Prt High Yield Bond	DVHYX	C+	(888) 233-4339	8.87	A / 9.5	20.16 / 96	4.25 / 78	6.31 / 94	D- / 1.1	34	3
COH	Fidelity Adv Hi Income Advantage	FAHDX	C+	(800) 522-7297	11.09	A / 9.5	22.41 / 98	5.20 / 86	7.61 / 97	E+ / 0.6	55	8
COH	Voya High Yield Service	IPHYX	C+	(800) 992-0180	10.13	A / 9.4	17.44 / 93	4.29 / 79	5.94 / 92	D- / 1.5	56	3
COH	CNR High Yield Bond N	CHBAX	C+	(888) 889-0799	8.01	A / 9.4	21.23 / 97	3.88 / 74	6.00 / 92	D- / 1.1	25	6
COH ●	T Rowe Price Instl High Yield	TRHYX	C+	(800) 638-5660	9.00	A / 9.4	20.65 / 97	4.37 / 79	6.72 / 96	D- / 1.1	42	2
COH	USAA High Income Fund	USHYX	C+	(800) 382-8722	8.26	A / 9.4	23.09 / 98	3.79 / 73	6.66 / 96	E+ / 0.8	16	1
COH	TIAA-CREF High Yield Fund Retire	TIHRX	C+	(800) 842-2252	9.90	A / 9.3	20.91 / 97	4.30 / 79	6.06 / 92	E+ / 0.9	29	11
COH	Guggenheim High Yield A	SIHAX	C+	(800) 820-0888	11.46	A- / 9.2	21.15 / 97	4.98 / 85	7.64 / 97	D / 1.7	78	5
COH ●	MainStay High Yield Corp Bond B	MKHCX	C+	(800) 624-6782	5.78	A- / 9.2	18.56 / 94	3.87 / 74	5.42 / 88	D / 1.6	37	4
COH	Principal High Yield A	CPHYX	C+	(800) 222-5852	7.47	A- / 9.2	19.56 / 95	4.48 / 80	6.51 / 95	D- / 1.4	59	5
COH ●	T Rowe Price High Yield	PRHYX	C+	(800) 638-5660	6.76	A- / 9.2	18.93 / 95	4.13 / 77	6.60 / 95	D- / 1.4	44	21
COH	Prudential High Yield A	PBHAX	C+	(800) 225-1852	5.57	A- / 9.2	20.00 / 96	4.84 / 84	6.53 / 95	D- / 1.2	64	16
COH	MassMutual Premier High Yield A	MPHAX	C+	(800) 542-6767	9.13	A- / 9.1	19.70 / 95	4.82 / 84	7.72 / 98	D / 1.6	75	7
COH	MFS Global High Yield A	MHOAX	C+	(800) 225-2606	6.24	A- / 9.1	17.65 / 93	3.73 / 72	5.63 / 89	D- / 1.2	21	12
COH	Voya High Yield Bond A	IHYAX	C+	(800) 992-0180	8.18	B+ / 8.6	15.62 / 89	4.00 / 75	6.44 / 95	D / 1.8	57	10
COH	Eaton Vance High Inc Opp Fund A	ETHIX	C+	(800) 262-1122	4.55	B+ / 8.5	14.99 / 88	4.72 / 83	7.02 / 96	D / 1.9	77	21
COH	Buffalo High Yield Fund	BUFHX	C+	(800) 492-8332	11.24	B / 7.7	10.54 / 80	3.75 / 72	5.51 / 89	C- / 3.3	79	14
COH	TCW High Yield Bond N	TGHNX	C+	(800) 386-3829	6.34	B / 7.7	8.95 / 76	3.50 / 69	5.50 / 88	C- / 3.1	76	6
COH	Putnam Floating Rate Income A	PFLRX	C+	(800) 225-1581	8.63	C+ / 6.6	10.39 / 80	2.50 / 52	3.92 / 71	C- / 4.2	64	12
COH	Aquila Three Peaks High Inc A	ATPAX	C+	(800) 437-1020	8.57	C+ / 5.6	5.86 / 70	3.49 / 68	4.47 / 78	C / 5.5	85	11
COH	Victory High Yield A	GUHYX	C	(800) 539-3863	6.51	A- / 9.2	22.27 / 98	3.35 / 67	5.58 / 89	E+ / 0.7	7	8
COH	J Hancock High Yield NAV		C	(800) 257-3336	8.27	A- / 9.2	24.95 / 99	2.63 / 55	5.93 / 92	E / 0.5	1	11
COH	Permanent Portfolio Versatile Bd I	PRVBX	C	(800) 531-5142	59.65	A- / 9.1	19.94 / 96	3.59 / 70	4.11 / 74	E+ / 0.8	37	14
COH	Principal High Yield Fund I Inst	PYHIX	C	(800) 222-5852	10.00	A- / 9.0	17.61 / 93	3.58 / 70	5.89 / 91	D- / 1.1	17	10
COH	AMG Mgrs High Yield N	MHHAX	C	(800) 548-4539	7.84	A- / 9.0	19.76 / 96	3.85 / 73	5.96 / 92	D- / 1.0	19	16
COH	Hotchkis and Wiley High Yield A	HWHAX	C	(866) 493-8637	12.25	A- / 9.0	23.14 / 98	4.13 / 77	6.85 / 96	E+ / 0.9	24	8
COH	WA High Yield IS	WAHSX	C	(888) 425-6432	8.22	A- / 9.0	23.45 / 98	2.63 / 55	5.77 / 91	E+ / 0.7	2	12
COH	PACE High Yield Invst A	PHIAX	C	(888) 793-8637	10.04	B+ / 8.8	20.85 / 97	3.94 / 75	6.22 / 94	D- / 1.1	25	2
COH	Virtus High Yield A	PHCHX	C	(800) 243-1574	4.27	B+ / 8.6	17.20 / 92	4.01 / 75	6.13 / 93	D- / 1.5	46	6
COH	Wells Fargo High Yld Bd Fd A	EKHAX	C	(800) 222-8222	3.36	B+ / 8.6	14.63 / 88	4.78 / 84	6.11 / 93	D- / 1.5	76	4
COH	Federated High Income Bond A	FHIIX	C	(800) 341-7400	7.65	B+ / 8.6	17.79 / 93	4.27 / 78	6.14 / 93	D- / 1.3	51	30
COH ●	SSgA High Yield Bond N	SSHYX	C	(800) 843-2639	7.63	B+ / 8.5	15.04 / 89	3.27 / 65	5.68 / 90	D / 1.6	20	5
COH	Fidelity Focused High Income	FHIFX	C	(800) 544-8544	8.62	B+ / 8.5	14.52 / 88	3.70 / 71	4.94 / 83	D- / 1.4	31	13
COH	PIMCO High Yield A	PHDAX	C	(800) 426-0107	8.96	B+ / 8.4	15.65 / 90	4.19 / 77	5.83 / 91	D- / 1.5	56	7
COH	Northern HY Fixed Income	NHFIX	C	(800) 595-9111	6.89	B+ / 8.4	17.51 / 93	3.23 / 65	5.79 / 91	D- / 1.3	15	10
COH	Payden High Income Adviser	PYHWX	C	(888) 409-8007	6.56	B / 8.2	12.01 / 83	3.50 / 69	5.15 / 86	D / 2.0	51	5
COH	Eaton Vance Income Fd of Boston	EVIBX	C	(800) 262-1122	5.80	B / 8.0	14.93 / 88	4.15 / 77	6.10 / 93	D / 1.9	65	16
COH	Access Flex High Yield Inv	FYAIX	C	(888) 776-3637	33.27	B / 7.9	9.88 / 79	3.60 / 70	5.64 / 90	D / 2.1	76	13

● Denotes fund is closed to new investors

Fund Type	Fund Name	Ticker Symbol	Overall Investment Rating	Phone	Net Asset Value As of 2/28/17	PERFORMANCE Perform-ance Rating/Pts	Annualized Total Return Through 2/28/17 1Yr / Pct	3Yr / Pct	5Yr / Pct	RISK Risk Rating/Pts	FUND MGR Mgr. Quality Pct	Mgr. Tenure (Years)
COI	Payden Core Bond Adviser	PYCWX	A-	(888) 409-8007	10.56	C+ /6.0	3.90 /62	2.97 /60	3.08 /59	B- /7.1	67	20
COI	Federated Interm Corp Bd Instl	FIIFX	A-	(800) 341-7400	9.25	C /5.5	4.75 /66	2.47 /51	3.34 /63	B /7.6	58	4
COI	Diamond Hill Corporate Credit A	DSIAX	B+	(614) 255-3333	11.27	A- /9.0	15.58 /89	5.22 /86	5.60 /89	C- /3.3	93	11
COI	Payden Corporate Bond Investor	PYACX	B+	(888) 409-8007	11.03	B+ /8.8	8.28 /75	5.17 /86	5.29 /87	C- /3.2	84	N/A
COI	MSIF Short Duration Income A	MLDAX	B+	(800) 354-8185	8.16	C /5.5	8.64 /76	2.73 /56	2.38 /47	B- /7.4	86	6
COI	Transamerica Flexible Income A	IDITX	B+	(888) 233-4339	9.28	C /5.4	8.28 /75	2.98 /61	4.42 /78	B /7.6	78	12
COI	Vanguard Short-Term Crp Bd Idx	VSCSX	B+	(800) 662-7447	21.67	C /4.3	2.98 /56	1.88 /41	2.31 /46	B+ /8.8	67	8
COI	Angel Oak High Yield Opps Inst	ANHIX	B	(877) 625-3042	11.94	A+ /9.7	20.93 /97	4.75 /83	6.31 /94	D /1.6	88	8
COI	WA Core Bond FI	WAPIX	B	(888) 425-6432	12.45	C+ /6.4	3.72 /61	3.42 /68	3.10 /59	C /5.5	70	23
COI	Federated Sht-Interm Tot Ret B	FGCIX	B	(800) 341-7400	10.33	C- /4.2	3.88 /62	1.69 /38	1.80 /39	B+ /8.6	61	4
COI	BMO TCH Corporate Income Y	MCIYX	B-	(800) 236-3863	12.96	A- /9.0	15.31 /89	4.47 /80	4.90 /83	D /2.1	74	9
COI	Transamerica Short-Term Bond A	ITAAX	B-	(888) 233-4339	10.21	C- /3.1	3.82 /61	1.51 /35	2.39 /48	A /9.3	73	6
COI	Frost Low Duration Bond Inv	FADLX	B-	(866) 777-7818	10.24	C- /3.0	1.76 /47	1.07 /29	1.24 /31	A /9.5	62	15
COI	Fidelity High Income	SPHIX	C+	(800) 544-8544	8.91	A /9.4	21.79 /98	3.96 /75	5.91 /91	D- /1.1	81	17
COI	SEI Instl Managed Tr-Core Fix Inc	TRLVX	C+	(800) 342-5734	11.18	C /5.4	2.92 /56	2.97 /61	3.10 /59	C+ /6.1	61	12
COI	Baird Aggregate Bond Inv	BAGSX	C+	(866) 442-2473	11.12	C /5.4	2.50 /53	2.90 /59	3.06 /59	C+ /5.9	59	17
COI	Mutual of America Inst Bond	MABOX	C+	(800) 914-8716	9.89	C /5.4	3.75 /61	2.63 /55	2.50 /49	C+ /5.8	55	21
COI	Voya Intermediate Bond A	IIBAX	C+	(800) 992-0180	10.04	C /4.9	3.43 /59	3.06 /62	3.43 /64	C+ /6.4	66	8
COI	Hartford Short Duration A	HSDAX	C+	(888) 843-7824	9.86	C- /3.0	3.50 /60	1.40 /33	1.81 /39	A- /9.1	66	5
COI	CNR Corporate Bond N	CCBAX	C+	(888) 889-0799	10.41	D+ /2.7	2.56 /54	0.83 /25	1.34 /32	B+ /8.9	27	16
COI	TD Short-Term Bond Inst	TDSBX	C+		10.16	D+ /2.4	1.36 /43	0.77 /24	0.83 /25	A /9.4	46	8
COI	Vanguard Long-Term Corp Bd Idx	VLTCX	C	(800) 662-7447	24.24	A /9.4	11.67 /82	5.99 /92	5.27 /87	E /0.3	8	8
COI	Lord Abbett Income A	LAGVX	C	(888) 522-2388	2.82	B /7.7	12.18 /84	3.84 /73	4.64 /80	D+ /2.6	63	19
COI	WA Corporate Bond A	SIGAX	C	(877) 534-4627	12.35	B /7.7	11.48 /82	4.65 /82	5.14 /85	D+ /2.3	76	7
COI	Vanguard Intm-Term Corp Bd Idx	VICSX	C	(800) 662-7447	23.27	B- /7.2	5.25 /68	3.96 /75	4.11 /74	C- /3.2	60	8
COI	HC Capital US Corp FI Sec HC	HCXSX	C	(800) 242-9596	9.91	C+ /6.7	6.19 /71	3.36 /67	2.69 /53	C- /3.3	34	N/A
COI	Principal Income Fd A	CMPIX	C	(800) 222-5852	9.52	C /4.8	5.58 /69	2.51 /52	3.20 /61	C+ /5.8	37	12
COI	Columbia Total Return Bond A	LIBAX	C	(800) 345-6611	9.01	C /4.7	4.45 /64	2.91 /59	2.60 /51	C+ /6.3	60	5
COI	Eaton Vance Short Dur Real	EARRX	C	(800) 262-1122	9.91	C- /3.2	6.43 /71	0.92 /26	1.04 /28	B /7.8	41	N/A
COI	Prudential Short-Term Corp Bond	PBSMX	C	(800) 225-1852	11.05	D+ /2.4	2.76 /55	1.49 /35	1.91 /41	B+ /8.9	58	18
COI	Transamerica Prt High Quality	DVHQX	C	(888) 233-4339	11.11	D /1.8	0.66 /36	0.39 /20	0.54 /22	A+ /9.7	34	27
COI	PIA BBB Bond MACS	PBBBX	C-	(800) 251-1970	9.22	B- /7.4	8.50 /75	3.65 /71	3.77 /69	D /2.1	24	14
COI	PIMCO Investment Grade Corp A	PBDAX	C-	(800) 426-0107	10.35	B- /7.2	7.71 /74	4.52 /81	4.91 /83	D+ /2.7	72	15
COI	T Rowe Price Corporate Income	PRPIX	C-	(800) 638-5660	9.54	B- /7.0	5.82 /70	3.63 /70	4.02 /73	D+ /2.6	35	14
COI	Federated Bond Fund A	FDBAX	C-	(800) 341-7400	9.20	C+ /6.6	10.31 /80	3.71 /72	4.27 /76	C- /3.2	61	4
COI	Victory INCORE Investment Quality	GUIQX	C-	(800) 539-3863	9.54	C /4.5	4.05 /62	2.50 /52	2.50 /50	C+ /6.0	35	1
COI	Scout Core Plus Bond Fund Y	SCPYX	C-	(800) 996-2862	31.38	C- /3.4	2.47 /53	1.47 /35	2.25 /45	B- /7.4	22	21
COI	Calvert Short Duration Income A	CSDAX	C-	(800) 368-2745	16.04	D /1.8	3.66 /61	1.29 /32	1.98 /42	A- /9.0	56	4
COI	Wilmington Short-Term Bd A	MVSAX	C-	(800) 336-9970	9.99	D- /1.3	0.99 /39	0.60 /22	0.84 /25	A+ /9.6	37	21
COI	Dreyfus Bond Market Index Inv	DBMIX	D+	(800) 645-6561	10.28	C- /3.9	0.91 /39	2.13 /45	1.73 /38	C+ /5.9	27	7
COI	Federated Tot Ret Bd A	TLRAX	D+	(800) 341-7400	10.86	C- /3.7	4.82 /66	2.56 /53	2.41 /48	C+ /6.4	44	4
COI	Madison Core Bond A	MBOAX	D+	(800) 877-6089	9.98	D+ /2.7	2.65 /54	2.28 /48	1.51 /35	B- /7.4	42	8
COI	Eagle Investment Grade Bond A	EGBAX	D+	(800) 421-4184	14.78	D /2.0	1.47 /44	1.59 /36	1.32 /32	B+ /8.3	44	7
COI	Nuveen Strategic Income A	FCDDX	D	(800) 257-8787	10.66	C+ /6.3	13.35 /86	2.81 /58	4.39 /77	D /2.2	33	17
COI	Nationwide Bond A	NBDAX	D	(800) 848-0920	9.63	C- /3.4	2.79 /55	2.09 /45	2.64 /52	C /5.5	27	13
COI	Domini Impact Bond Inv	DSBFX	D	(800) 498-1351	11.15	C- /3.2	2.48 /53	1.98 /43	1.45 /34	C+ /5.8	21	2
COI	Columbia Bond A	CNDAX	D	(800) 345-6611	8.44	C- /3.0	2.70 /55	2.57 /53	2.08 /43	C+ /6.0	45	7
COI	FDP BlacRock Franklin Temp TR	MDFFX	D	(800) 441-7762	10.17	D+ /2.7	4.16 /63	1.86 /41	2.28 /46	C+ /6.9	25	12
COI	JPMorgan Inflation Managed Bond	JIMAX	D	(800) 480-4111	10.34	D /1.7	3.63 /60	0.85 /25	0.69 /23	B /7.8	18	7
COI	STAAR Inv Trust Shrt Term Bond	SITBX	D	(800) 332-7738	8.92	E /0.4	0.11 /23	-0.26 / 4	0.15 /17	A+ /9.8	21	20
COI	Delaware Extended Duration Bd A	DEEAX	D-	(800) 523-1918	6.39	C+ /6.9	7.49 /73	4.72 /83	5.49 /88	E /0.4	5	10
COI	Fidelity Advisor Corporate Bond A	FCBAX	D-	(800) 522-7297	11.40	C+ /5.7	7.72 /74	3.37 /67	3.61 /67	D+ /2.6	28	7

Denotes fund is closed to new investors

Data as of February 28, 2017

Fund Type	Fund Name	Ticker Symbol	Overall Investment Rating	Phone	Net Asset Value As of 2/28/17	Performance Rating/Pts	Annualized Total Return Through 2/28/17			Risk Rating/Pts	Mgr. Quality Pct	Mgr. Tenure (Years)
							1Yr / Pct	3Yr / Pct	5Yr / Pct			
EM	BlackRock Emg Mkts Flex Dyn Bd	BAEDX	B	(800) 441-7762	9.68	A+ /9.8	17.51 /93	6.80 /95	4.26 /76	D- / 1.4	99	6
EM	T Rowe Price Ins Emerging Mkts	TREBX	B-	(800) 638-5660	9.14	A+ /9.9	18.64 /94	7.51 /97	6.13 /93	D- / 1.1	99	11
EM	● GMO Emerging Country Debt III	GMCDX	C+		28.99	A+ /9.9	19.47 /95	7.56 /97	7.87 /98	E / 0.4	99	23
EM	Fidelity New Markets Income	FNMIX	C+	(800) 544-8544	16.09	A+ /9.9	18.72 /95	7.02 /96	5.74 /90	E / 0.4	99	22
EM	T Rowe Price Emerging Markets	PREMX	C+	(800) 638-5660	12.64	A+ /9.8	18.31 /94	6.74 /95	5.22 /86	E+ / 0.7	99	23
EM	Stone Harbor Emerging Debt Inst	SHMDX	C+	(866) 699-8125	10.44	A+ /9.7	16.18 /90	5.83 /91	4.07 /73	E / 0.5	99	10
EM	Fidelity Adv Emerging Mkts Inc A	FMKAX	C+	(800) 522-7297	14.20	A+ /9.7	18.36 /94	6.62 /95	5.33 /87	E / 0.4	99	22
EM	DoubleLine Em Mkts Fxd Inc N	DLENX	C+	(877) 354-6311	10.50	A+ /9.6	18.33 /94	5.08 /85	4.67 /80	D- / 1.0	98	7
EM	Payden Emerging Market Bond	PYEWX	C+	(888) 409-8007	13.80	A /9.5	13.61 /86	5.58 /89	4.55 /79	D- / 1.0	99	17
EM	Franklin Emg Mkt Debt	FEMDX	C+	(800) 342-5236	11.31	A /9.5	18.26 /94	4.50 /81	4.72 /81	E+ / 0.7	97	11
EM	TCW Emerging Markets Income N	TGINX	C+	(800) 386-3829	10.78	A /9.4	17.56 /93	4.54 /81	4.65 /80	E+ / 0.8	98	7
EM	Universal Inst Emer Mrkt Debt II	UEDBX	C	(800) 869-6397	8.01	B+ /8.9	13.37 /86	4.38 /79	3.44 /64	E+ / 0.7	98	15
EM	J Hancock Emerg Markets Debt A	JMKAX	C-	(800) 257-3336	9.44	B+ /8.8	17.97 /93	4.66 /82	3.99 /72	E / 0.4	98	4
EM	PIMCO Emerging Markets Bond A	PAEMX	C-	(800) 426-0107	10.40	B+ /8.8	17.97 /93	4.41 /80	3.73 /69	E / 0.3	98	5
EM	Goldman Sachs Emg Mkts Debt A	GSDAX	C-	(800) 526-7384	12.73	B+ /8.5	12.35 /84	6.06 /92	5.17 /86	D- / 1.0	99	14
EM	Columbia Emerging Markets Bond	REBAX	C-	(800) 345-6611	11.55	B+ /8.5	16.23 /91	4.77 /83	3.97 /72	E+ / 0.6	98	6
EM	MFS Emerging Markets Debt A	MEDAX	C-	(800) 225-2606	14.76	B /7.7	11.63 /82	4.62 /82	4.13 /74	D- / 1.5	98	19
EM	Janus Emerging Markets A	JMFAX	D+	(800) 295-2687	8.68	B+ /8.8	29.19 /99	2.84 /59	-0.15 / 4	E- / 0.0	96	5
EM	PIMCO EM Corporate Bond Inst	PEMIX	D+	(800) 426-0107	10.61	B /8.2	17.28 /92	2.39 /50	3.55 /66	E+ / 0.6	92	1
EM	JPMorgan Emerg Mkt Debt A	JEDAX	D	(800) 480-4111	8.15	B- /7.5	11.14 /81	4.16 /77	3.95 /72	D- / 1.3	97	1
EM	WA Emerging Markets Debt A	LWEAX	D	(888) 425-6432	5.02	B- /7.4	14.57 /88	3.51 /69	2.48 /49	E+ / 0.6	96	4
EM	SEI Inst Intl Emerging Mkts Debt F	SITEX	E+	(800) 342-5734	9.79	C /4.9	12.88 /85	0.67 /23	0.61 /23	E- / 0.2	91	17
EM	Oppenheimer Em Mkts Local Debt	OEMAX	E	(888) 470-0862	7.17	C- /3.5	15.90 /90	0.05 / 9	-0.79 / 2	E- / 0.2	89	2
EM	Eaton Vance Emer Market Local	EEIAX	E	(800) 262-1122	6.17	C- /3.4	17.57 /93	-0.11 / 5	-2.49 / 1	E- / 0.1	89	9
EM	Deutsche Enh Emg Mrkts Fxd Inc	SZEAX	E	(800) 728-3337	9.41	D+ /2.7	10.98 /81	0.52 /21	1.63 /37	E+ / 0.9	82	6
EM	PIMCO Emerging Local Bond A	PELAX	E-	(800) 426-0107	7.21	E- /0.1	14.35 /87	-3.27 / 1	-3.50 / 0	E- / 0.1	20	11
EM	Goldman Sachs Local Emg Mkt	GAMDX	E-	(800) 526-7384	6.22	E- /0.1	12.70 /84	-3.74 / 1	-3.37 / 0	E- / 0.0	12	9
EM	Invesco Emerg Mkts Flexible Bond	IAEMX	E-	(800) 959-4246	6.56	E- /0.0	7.67 /74	-4.59 / 0	-4.03 / 0	E / 0.5	0	2
EM	T Rowe Price Inst Intl Bd	RPIIX	E-	(800) 638-5660	8.33	E- /0.0	1.26 /42	-2.29 / 2	-0.74 / 2	E / 0.4	55	3
EM	EuroPac International Bond A	EPIBX	E-	(888) 558-5851	8.13	E- /0.0	5.72 /69	-4.84 / 0	-3.25 / 1	E / 0.4	1	7
EM	Dreyfus Eme Mkts Dbt LC A	DDBAX	E-	(800) 782-6620	11.50	E- /0.0	11.43 /82	-4.81 / 0	-3.53 / 0	E- / 0.1	2	9

● Denotes fund is closed to new investors

Fund Type	Fund Name	Ticker Symbol	Overall Investment Rating	Phone	Net Asset Value As of 2/28/17	Perform-ance Rating/Pts	1Yr / Pct	3Yr / Pct	5Yr / Pct	Risk Rating/Pts	Mgr. Quality Pct	Mgr. Tenure (Years)
GEI	PIMCO Income Fund A	PONAX	A+	(800) 426-0107	12.20	B+ /8.8	10.72 /81	5.53 /89	8.03 /98	B- /7.5	96	10
GEI	Frost Total Return Bond Inv	FATRX	A+	(866) 777-7818	10.44	C+ /6.6	7.02 /73	2.80 /58	4.22 /75	B /8.0	81	15
GEI	CM Advisors Fixed Income	CMFIX	A+	(800) 664-4888	11.57	C+ /6.3	7.95 /74	2.36 /49	1.92 /41	B /8.2	79	6
GEI	Ave Maria Bond	AVEFX	A+	(866) 283-6274	11.29	C+ /6.2	4.92 /66	2.85 /59	3.47 /65	B+ /8.3	85	14
GEI ●	RiverNorth/DoubleLine Strat Inc R	RNDLX	A	(888) 848-7549	10.61	B /8.1	10.38 /80	4.41 /80	5.13 /85	C+ /5.6	91	7
GEI	Dodge & Cox Income Fund	DODIX	A	(800) 621-3979	13.74	C+ /6.7	6.70 /72	3.06 /62	3.38 /63	B- /7.1	78	28
GEI	Nationwide Core Plus Bond R6	NWCIX	A	(800) 848-0920	10.21	C+ /6.2	4.31 /64	3.08 /62	3.47 /65	B- /7.5	73	15
GEI	Metropolitan West Strategic Inc M	MWSTX	A	(800) 496-8298	8.06	C /4.6	4.08 /62	1.82 /40	4.07 /73	A- /9.2	81	14
GEI	Cohen and Steers Pref Sec&Inc A	CPXAX	A-	(800) 330-7348	13.77	A /9.3	10.71 /80	6.99 /96	8.28 /99	C- /3.0	96	7
GEI	BlackRock Managed Income Inv A	BLADX	A-	(800) 441-7762	10.02	B /8.1	8.89 /76	4.17 /77	3.53 /66	C /4.6	84	8
GEI	Cavalier Adaptive Income Inst	CADTX	A-	(877) 773-3863	10.41	B /7.7	9.82 /79	3.02 /61	2.99 /58	C /5.0	82	1
GEI	Commerce Bond	CFBNX	A-	(800) 995-6365	19.88	C+ /5.9	3.98 /62	2.89 /59	3.14 /60	B- /7.4	69	23
GEI	WA Intermediate Bond IS	WABSX	A-	(888) 425-6432	10.86	C /5.5	3.05 /57	2.74 /57	2.81 /55	B /7.9	71	8
GEI	SEI Instl Mgd Tr-Enhanced Inc F	SEEAX	A-	(800) 342-5734	7.54	C /4.6	5.36 /68	1.69 /38	2.29 /46	A- /9.0	81	11
GEI	CNR Fixed Income Opportunities N	RIMOX	B+	(888) 889-0799	25.98	A- /9.1	15.63 /90	4.16 /77	5.58 /89	D+ /2.8	95	6
GEI	Universal Inst Core Plus Fxd Inc II	UCFIX	B+	(800) 869-6397	10.78	B- /7.3	6.83 /72	3.65 /71	3.82 /70	C /5.4	81	6
GEI	USAA Intmdt-Trm Bd Fund	USIBX	B+	(800) 382-8722	10.55	B- /7.0	7.92 /74	3.14 /63	4.24 /75	C /5.5	75	1
GEI	J Hancock Active Bond 1	JIADX	B+	(800) 257-3336	10.06	C+ /6.2	4.31 /64	3.08 /62	3.61 /67	C+ /6.6	70	12
GEI	TiAA-CREF Bond Plus Retail	TCBPX	B+	(800) 842-2252	10.40	C+ /6.1	4.41 /64	3.04 /62	3.23 /61	C+ /6.3	68	11
GEI ●	Thrivent Oppty Income Plus A	AAINX	B+	(800) 847-4836	10.23	C+ /5.8	8.75 /76	3.14 /63	--	B- /7.2	85	15
GEI	William Blair Bond N	WBBNX	B+	(800) 742-7272	10.45	C+ /5.6	4.22 /63	2.72 /56	2.93 /56	B- /7.3	70	10
GEI	Vanguard Sh-Term Invest-Grade	VFSTX	B+	(800) 662-7447	10.67	C- /4.1	2.70 /55	1.77 /39	2.04 /43	A- /9.0	71	9
GEI	Weitz Short Dur Income Inst	WEFIX	B+	(800) 232-4161	12.35	C- /4.0	3.28 /58	1.62 /37	1.88 /40	A- /9.1	71	21
GEI	Lord Abbett Shrt Duration Inc A	LALDX	B+	(888) 522-2388	4.31	C- /4.0	4.69 /65	1.98 /43	2.57 /51	A- /9.0	80	19
GEI ●	Thrivent Limited Maturity Bond A	LBLAX	B+	(800) 847-4836	12.46	C- /3.9	3.14 /58	1.46 /34	1.49 /34	A /9.3	72	18
GEI	USAA Short Term Bond Retail	USSBX	B+	(800) 382-8722	9.16	C- /3.9	3.37 /59	1.48 /35	1.87 /40	A- /9.2	70	1
GEI	WA Core Plus Bond FI	WACIX	B	(888) 425-6432	11.54	B- /7.1	5.16 /67	3.81 /73	3.67 /68	C /4.8	78	12
GEI	Henderson Strategic Income A	HFAAX	B	(866) 443-6337	9.39	C+ /6.9	8.37 /75	4.33 /79	5.59 /89	C /5.0	90	9
GEI	Baird Core Plus Bond Inv	BCOSX	B	(866) 442-2473	11.55	C+ /6.1	4.18 /63	3.12 /63	3.15 /60	C+ /5.8	66	17
GEI	Voya Intermediate Bond Port Adv	IIBPX	B	(800) 992-0180	12.62	C+ /5.8	3.78 /61	2.91 /60	3.38 /64	C+ /6.3	63	8
GEI	TIAA-CREF Bond Retire	TIDRX	B	(800) 842-2252	10.51	C+ /5.8	3.42 /59	2.98 /61	2.98 /58	C+ /6.2	63	14
GEI	Victory Strategic Income A	RSIAX	B	(800) 539-3863	10.06	C /5.2	7.49 /73	2.19 /46	2.94 /57	B- /7.3	76	8
GEI	Highland Fixed Income A	HFBAX	B	(877) 665-1287	12.92	C /4.7	6.17 /71	2.83 /58	2.36 /47	B /7.6	75	3
GEI	Loomis Sayles Intm Dur Bd Y	LSDIX	B	(800) 225-5478	10.24	C /4.5	2.38 /52	2.19 /46	2.37 /47	B /8.1	60	12
GEI	CNR Intermediate Fixed Income N	RIMCX	B	(888) 889-0799	26.20	C- /4.1	2.54 /53	1.84 /40	2.31 /46	B+ /8.4	55	4
GEI	New Covenant Income	NCICX	B	(877) 835-4531	23.13	C- /4.1	1.75 /47	2.02 /44	1.70 /38	B+ /8.3	57	3
GEI	William Blair Income N	WBRRX	B	(800) 742-7272	8.87	C- /3.9	2.01 /49	1.74 /39	1.81 /39	B+ /8.9	66	15
GEI	Payden Low Duration Investor	PYSBX	B	(888) 409-8007	10.09	C- /3.1	2.17 /50	1.04 /28	1.41 /33	A+ /9.7	67	N/A
GEI	SunAmerica VAL Co II High Yld Bd	VCHYX	B-	(800) 858-8850	7.88	A- /9.0	16.31 /91	3.84 /73	5.57 /89	D /1.9	90	8
GEI	Thompson Bond	THOPX	B-	(800) 999-0887	11.41	B /8.0	15.78 /90	2.69 /56	3.81 /70	C- /3.2	86	25
GEI	Elfun Income	EINFX	B-	(800) 843-2639	11.36	C+ /5.6	3.69 /61	2.80 /58	2.72 /53	C+ /6.2	61	N/A
GEI	SS Inst Income Inv	SSFIX	B-	(800) 843-2639	9.41	C+ /5.6	3.74 /61	2.82 /58	2.71 /53	C+ /6.2	61	N/A
GEI	Westcore Plus Bond Rtl	WTIBX	B-	(800) 392-2673	10.66	C+ /5.6	3.32 /59	2.85 /58	2.75 /54	C+ /6.1	59	N/A
GEI	PIMCO Moderate Duration Fund P	PMOPX	B-	(800) 426-0107	10.15	C /4.6	3.36 /59	1.89 /41	2.56 /50	B /7.7	50	3
GEI	Metropolitan West Tot Ret Bond M	MWTRX	B-	(800) 496-8298	10.60	C /4.4	1.52 /45	2.34 /49	3.54 /66	B- /7.5	49	20
GEI	Pioneer Bond Fund A	PIOBX	B-	(800) 225-6292	9.67	C- /4.2	4.94 /66	2.90 /59	3.51 /66	B /8.0	79	19
GEI	Fidelity Intermediate Bond	FTHRX	B-	(800) 544-8544	10.84	C- /4.2	2.23 /51	2.01 /43	2.13 /44	B /7.9	50	4
GEI	Brown Advisory Interm Income Inv	BIAIX	B-	(800) 540-6807	10.56	C- /3.8	1.49 /44	1.88 /41	1.51 /35	B+ /8.3	50	25
GEI	Tributary Short/Intmdt Bond Inst	FOSIX	B-	(800) 662-4203	9.33	C- /3.2	1.92 /48	1.22 /31	1.68 /37	A /9.3	63	14
GEI	Northern Ultra-Short Fixed Income	NUSFX	B-	(800) 595-9111	10.21	D+ /2.8	1.83 /47	0.92 /26	1.05 /28	A+ /9.8	65	5
GEI	BMO Short-Term Income Y	MSINX	B-	(800) 236-3863	9.36	D+ /2.8	1.67 /46	0.99 /27	1.25 /31	A+ /9.6	60	5
GEI	FPA New Income Inc	FPNIX	B-	(800) 982-4372	10.02	D+ /2.8	2.94 /56	1.30 /32	1.41 /33	A+ /9.6	73	13

Fund Type	Fund Name	Ticker Symbol	Overall Investment Rating	Phone	Net Asset Value As of 2/28/17	PERFORMANCE					RISK	FUND MGR	
	99 Pct = Best 0 Pct = Worst					Perform-ance Rating/Pts	Annualized Total Return Through 2/28/17			Risk Rating/Pts	Mgr. Quality Pct	Mgr. Tenure (Years)
							1Yr / Pct	3Yr / Pct	5Yr / Pct			
GEL	AMG Mgrs Loomis Sayles Bond N	MGFIX	C	(800) 548-4539	26.63	C+ /6.4	7.44 /73	2.66 /55	3.86 /70	C /4.4	66	23
GEL	Vanguard Long Term Bd Idx	VBLTX	D	(800) 662-7447	13.75	B+ /8.4	4.47 /64	5.84 /91	4.28 /76	E- /0.2	5	4
GEL	J Hancock Short Duration Opp A	JMBAX	D	(800) 257-3336	9.67	C /4.4	8.77 /76	1.58 /36	2.42 /48	C /4.6	74	8
GEL	Natixis Loomis Sayles Strat Inc A	NEFZX	D-	(800) 225-5478	14.50	C+ /6.4	15.67 /90	2.19 /46	5.24 /86	D- /1.0	73	22

● Denotes fund is closed to new investors

Fund Type	Fund Name	Ticker Symbol	Overall Investment Rating	Phone	Net Asset Value As of 2/28/17	Perform-ance Rating/Pts	Annualized Total Return Through 2/28/17			Risk Rating/Pts	Mgr. Quality Pct	Mgr. Tenure (Years)
	99 Pct = Best / 0 Pct = Worst						1Yr / Pct	3Yr / Pct	5Yr / Pct			
GES	J Hancock VIT Strat Inc Opps I	JESNX	A+	(800) 257-3336	13.59	B- /7.2	6.29 /71	3.47 /68	4.76 /81	B /7.8	88	13
GES	Homestead Short Term Bond	HOSBX	A+	(800) 258-3030	5.21	C+ /6.3	5.27 /68	2.34 /49	2.47 /49	B+ /8.3	83	26
GES	BlackRock Crdt Strategies Inc Inv	BMSAX	A	(800) 441-7762	10.19	B- /7.2	9.75 /78	3.53 /69	4.82 /82	C+ /6.1	91	5
GES	Changing Parameters	CPMPX	A-	(866) 618-3456	10.26	B+ /8.7	12.45 /84	4.05 /76	4.61 /80	C- /3.9	91	10
GES	ICON Bond C	IOBCX	A-	(800) 764-0442	9.48	C+ /6.0	6.34 /71	2.42 /50	2.53 /50	B- /7.4	71	6
GES	AdvisorOne CLS Flexible Income N	CLFLX	A-	(866) 811-0225	10.25	C+ /5.8	5.52 /69	2.42 /50	2.34 /47	B- /7.5	71	3
GES	DoubleLine Total Return Bond N	DLTNX	A-	(877) 354-6311	10.63	C /5.1	1.11 /41	2.85 /59	3.43 /64	B /8.2	77	7
GES	Osterweis Strategic Income	OSTIX	B+	(800) 700-3316	11.35	B+ /8.6	15.03 /88	3.51 /69	4.90 /83	C- /3.7	93	15
GES	Virtus Multi Sector Short Term B A	NARAX	B+	(800) 243-1574	4.76	C /4.8	6.58 /72	2.13 /45	2.90 /56	B+ /8.3	80	24
GES	Semper Short Duration Inv	SEMRX	B+	(888) 263-6443	9.86	C- /3.5	2.78 /55	1.19 /31	0.90 /26	A+ /9.6	79	7
GES	Pioneer Strategic Income A	PSRAX	B	(800) 225-6292	10.73	C+ /6.2	9.79 /78	3.34 /66	4.12 /74	C+ /6.2	86	18
GES	Touchstone Flexible Income A	FFSAX	B	(800) 543-0407	10.73	C /5.3	4.89 /66	3.98 /75	3.99 /72	C+ /6.9	85	10
GES	Natixis Loomis Sayles Strat Alpha	LABAX	B	(800) 225-5478	9.94	C /5.1	9.64 /78	2.46 /51	3.17 /60	B- /7.3	87	7
GES	Thornburg Limited Term Income A	THIFX	B	(800) 847-0200	13.39	C- /3.9	2.87 /56	2.01 /43	2.58 /51	B+ /8.8	71	10
GES	Baird Short-Term Bond Inst	BSBIX	B	(866) 442-2473	9.68	C- /3.6	2.25 /51	1.47 /34	1.84 /39	A /9.4	71	13
GES	T Rowe Price Global MS Bd Adv	PRSAX	B-	(800) 638-5660	11.30	B- /7.4	7.63 /74	3.46 /68	3.70 /69	C- /4.0	80	9
GES	GE RSP Income	GESLX	B-	(800) 242-0134	11.46	C+ /5.6	3.49 /60	2.86 /59	2.76 /54	C+ /6.2	61	N/A
GES	SEI Daily Inc Tr-Ultra Sh Dur Bd F	SECPX	B-	(800) 342-5734	9.32	D+ /2.6	1.56 /45	0.81 /25	1.04 /28	A+ /9.9	66	18
GES	Metropolitan West Alpha Trak 500	MWATX	C+	(800) 496-8298	8.96	A+ /9.9	35.34 /99	13.01 /99	16.54 /99	E- /0.2	99	19
GES	Wells Fargo Dvsfd Inc Bldr A	EKSAX	C+	(800) 222-8222	6.27	A+ /9.6	18.09 /94	6.38 /94	7.81 /98	D- /1.1	96	10
GES	T Rowe Price Spectrum Income	RPSIX	C+	(800) 638-5660	12.58	B- /7.5	9.95 /79	3.32 /66	4.20 /75	C- /3.4	82	19
GES	MFS Strategic Income A	MFIOX	C+	(800) 225-2606	6.56	C+ /6.8	9.18 /77	2.71 /56	3.64 /68	C- /4.2	73	6
GES	Sanford C Bernstein II Int Dur Inst	SIIDX	C+	(800) 221-5672	14.95	C+ /6.2	3.53 /60	3.28 /66	2.91 /56	C /5.3	67	12
GES	Sanford C Bernstein Interm	SNIDX	C+	(212) 486-5800	13.12	C+ /6.1	3.57 /60	3.21 /64	2.80 /54	C /5.3	65	12
GES	Tributary Income Inst	FOINX	C+	(800) 662-4203	10.26	C /5.0	1.98 /49	2.62 /54	2.73 /53	C+ /6.7	52	14
GES	Steward Select Bond Fd Inst	SEACX	C+	(877) 420-4440	24.41	C- /3.8	1.58 /45	1.85 /41	1.64 /37	B /7.7	32	7
GES	T Rowe Price Short Term Bond	PRWBX	C+	(800) 638-5660	4.72	D+ /2.8	1.82 /47	0.94 /27	1.09 /29	A /9.4	59	2
GES	DFA One-Yr Fixed Inc Inst	DFIHX	C+	(800) 984-9472	10.30	D /2.0	0.79 /37	0.48 /21	0.52 /22	A+ /9.9	54	34
GES	Transamerica High Yield Bond A	IHIYX	C	(888) 233-4339	9.30	B+ /8.7	19.31 /95	4.12 /77	6.23 /94	D- /1.1	91	11
GES	PIMCO Diversified Income A	PDVAX	C	(800) 426-0107	10.75	B /8.2	13.45 /86	4.51 /81	4.86 /83	D /2.1	88	1
GES	Spirit of America Income Fd A	SOAIX	C	(800) 452-4892	11.90	B- /7.5	4.93 /66	5.77 /90	4.85 /82	D+ /2.9	88	8
GES	Columbia Strategic Income A	COSIX	C	(800) 345-6611	5.98	C+ /6.6	10.61 /80	3.68 /71	4.08 /73	C- /3.5	91	8
GES	Vanguard Short-Term Bd Idx	VBISX	C	(800) 662-7447	10.45	D+ /2.6	0.76 /37	1.07 /29	1.06 /28	B+ /8.9	35	4
GES	SA Global Fixed Income	SAXIX	C	(800) 366-7266	9.62	D+ /2.3	0.61 /35	0.89 /26	0.95 /27	A- /9.0	29	18
GES	Wells Fargo Ult ST Inc A	SADAX	C	(800) 222-8222	8.48	D- /1.5	1.65 /46	0.62 /22	0.74 /24	A+ /9.9	63	15
GES	PIMCO Low Duration Income A	PFIAX	C-	(800) 426-0107	8.43	B /7.7	17.21 /92	2.67 /55	3.84 /70	D /1.6	92	1
GES	Virtus Multi-Sec Intermediate Bd A	NAMFX	C-	(800) 243-1574	10.32	B- /7.4	14.12 /87	3.41 /67	4.55 /79	D+ /2.4	85	23
GES	Fidelity Adv Strategic Income A	FSTAX	C-	(800) 522-7297	12.13	C+ /6.8	11.45 /82	3.38 /67	3.84 /70	C- /3.0	83	18
GES	Berwyn Income Fund	BERIX	C-	(800) 992-6757	13.74	C+ /6.6	9.76 /78	2.69 /56	5.65 /90	C- /3.4	82	15
GES	Thornburg Strategic Income Fd A	TSIAX	C-	(800) 847-0200	11.65	C /5.5	10.55 /80	2.67 /55	4.74 /81	C /4.3	84	10
GES	Deutsche Core Fixed Income A	SFXAX	C-	(800) 728-3337	9.95	C- /3.1	2.83 /55	2.44 /51	2.56 /50	B- /7.3	54	3
GES	Eaton Vance Mult-Str Absolute Rtn	EADDX	C-	(800) 262-1122	8.70	D /2.0	2.89 /56	1.62 /37	0.92 /26	B+ /8.9	71	13
GES	Ivy Limited-Term Bond A	WLTAX	C-	(800) 777-6472	10.81	D /1.8	1.75 /47	1.05 /28	0.96 /27	B+ /8.7	30	3
GES	Federated Short Term Inc A	FTIAX	C-	(800) 341-7400	8.50	D- /1.4	1.14 /41	0.37 /19	0.60 /22	A+ /9.7	34	22
GES	Federated Strategic Income Fund	STIAX	D+	(800) 341-7400	9.06	B- /7.2	14.08 /87	3.45 /68	3.77 /69	D /2.1	87	4
GES	Vanguard Total Bond Mrkt Index	VBMFX	D+	(800) 662-7447	10.71	C /4.5	1.35 /43	2.47 /51	2.06 /43	C /5.1	28	4
GES	Hartford Unconstrained Bond A	HTIAX	D+	(888) 843-7824	9.60	C- /3.3	7.61 /74	1.51 /35	1.69 /37	C+ /6.7	72	5
GES	Putnam Income Fund A	PINCX	D+	(800) 225-1581	6.87	C- /3.0	6.01 /70	1.46 /34	3.50 /66	B- /7.0	59	10
GES	Deutsche Fixed Income Opps A	SDUAX	D+	(800) 728-3337	8.59	D+ /2.6	6.49 /72	0.63 /22	1.62 /36	B /7.7	74	7
GES	Federated Ultra Short Bd A	FULAX	D+	(800) 341-7400	9.11	E+ /0.8	1.44 /44	0.41 /20	0.64 /23	A+ /9.8	52	19
GES	Loomis Sayles Bond Ret	LSBRX	D	(800) 633-3330	13.89	B- /7.3	14.68 /88	2.02 /44	4.33 /76	D- /1.4	69	26
GES ●	Thrivent Income A	LUBIX	D	(800) 847-4836	9.11	C /5.3	7.03 /73	3.34 /66	3.88 /71	C- /3.8	67	8

● Denotes fund is closed to new investors

Data as of February 28, 2017

Fund Type	Fund Name	Ticker Symbol	Overall Investment Rating	Phone	Net Asset Value As of 2/28/17	PERFORMANCE Perform-ance Rating/Pts	Annualized Total Return Through 2/28/17 1Yr / Pct	3Yr / Pct	5Yr / Pct	RISK Risk Rating/Pts	FUND MGR Mgr. Quality Pct	Mgr. Tenure (Years)
	99 Pct = Best 0 Pct = Worst											
GL	Federated Floating Rt Str Inc Inst	FFRSX	A+	(800) 341-7400	10.02	B /7.8	9.63 /78	3.52 /69	4.01 /73	B /8.2	93	2
GL	Payden Global Fixed Inc Investor	PYGFX	A+	(888) 409-8007	8.98	C+ /6.7	3.50 /60	3.73 /72	3.75 /69	B /7.6	94	9
GL	WA Total Return Unconstrained FI	WARIX	A	(888) 425-6432	10.44	C+ /6.9	9.58 /78	2.53 /52	2.87 /56	C+ /6.6	90	11
GL	DoubleLine Core Fixed Income N	DLFNX	A-	(877) 354-6311	10.87	C+ /6.1	3.81 /61	3.15 /63	3.23 /61	B- /7.0	94	7
GL	JPMorgan Strategic Income Opp A	JSOAX	B+	(800) 480-4111	11.69	C+ /5.8	11.60 /82	2.34 /49	3.15 /60	B- /7.1	89	9
GL	J Hancock Strat Income Opp A	JIPAX	B+	(800) 257-3336	10.70	C /4.9	5.87 /70	2.86 /59	4.00 /73	B /7.9	92	11
GL	BBH Limited Duration Class N	BBBMX	B+	(800) 625-5759	10.17	C- /3.7	3.44 /59	1.20 /31	1.47 /34	A+ /9.7	77	6
GL	CGCM Intl Fixed Inc	TIFUX	B	(800) 444-4273	7.61	B- /7.5	5.26 /68	4.40 /80	3.81 /70	C /4.3	96	3
GL	AB Global Bond A	ANAGX	B	(800) 221-5672	8.38	C /5.2	4.46 /64	3.68 /71	3.21 /61	B- /7.1	94	25
GL	Eaton Vance Glb Mac Abslut Ret A	EAGMX	B	(800) 262-1122	9.04	C /4.7	5.03 /67	3.24 /65	1.93 /41	B /7.9	92	20
GL	Putnam Absolute Return 100 A	PARTX	B	(800) 225-1581	9.99	C- /3.8	5.32 /68	1.15 /30	1.41 /33	B+ /8.9	76	9
GL	AB High Income A	AGDAX	B-	(800) 221-5672	8.86	A /9.3	20.70 /97	4.76 /83	6.95 /96	D /1.8	97	15
GL	PIMCO Foreign Bond (US Hedged)	PFOAX	B-	(800) 426-0107	10.51	B- /7.5	5.65 /69	5.27 /87	5.42 /88	C- /4.1	97	3
GL	PIMCO Global Bond (US Hedged)	PAIIX	B-	(800) 426-0107	10.21	C+ /6.7	5.47 /68	4.48 /80	4.34 /77	C /4.8	96	3
GL	JPMorgan Unconstrained Debt A	JSIAX	B-	(800) 480-4111	9.89	C- /4.1	6.76 /72	2.06 /44	2.71 /53	B /8.1	88	7
GL	DFA S/T Extended Quality Port Inst	DFEQX	B-	(800) 984-9472	10.80	C- /3.6	1.92 /48	1.54 /35	1.65 /37	B+ /8.8	83	9
GL	Payden Global Low Duration	PYGSX	B-	(888) 409-8007	10.04	C- /3.0	2.11 /50	0.98 /27	1.69 /37	A+ /9.7	75	N/A
GL	PIMCO High Yield Spectrum A	PHSAX	C+	(800) 426-0107	10.00	A- /9.1	19.90 /96	4.42 /80	6.86 /96	D- /1.5	96	7
GL	GMO Currency Hedged Intl Bond	GMHBX	C+		26.50	B+ /8.4	2.79 /55	5.93 /91	6.04 /92	D /2.0	98	3
GL	Principal Glb Divers Income A	PGBAX	C+	(800) 222-5852	13.84	B+ /8.3	14.19 /87	4.27 /78	6.21 /94	D /2.1	96	7
GL	Fidelity Strategic Income Fund	FSICX	C+	(800) 544-8544	10.87	B /8.1	11.62 /82	3.60 /70	4.10 /74	D+ /2.8	95	18
GL	Eaton Vance Short Dur Strat Inc A	ETSIX	C+	(800) 262-1122	7.38	C+ /6.7	9.53 /78	2.98 /61	2.75 /54	C /4.6	90	27
GL	Aberdeen Total Return Bond A	BJBGX	C+	(866) 667-9231	13.13	C /5.0	3.30 /58	2.53 /52	2.08 /43	C+ /6.0	92	15
GL	DFA Five Year Glbl Fixed Inc Inst	DFGBX	C+	(800) 984-9472	10.94	C- /3.7	0.97 /39	1.82 /40	1.98 /42	B /8.1	86	18
GL	Goldman Sachs Glbl Income A	GSGIX	C+	(800) 526-7384	12.22	C- /3.7	2.13 /50	2.80 /58	3.31 /62	B /7.8	92	22
GL	Schwab Intermediate-Term Bond	SWIIX	C+	(800) 407-0256	10.04	C- /3.5	0.64 /36	1.78 /39	1.62 /36	B /8.1	86	10
GL	DFA Two Year Glbl Fixed Inc Inst	DFGFX	C+	(800) 984-9472	9.97	D /2.1	0.85 /38	0.62 /22	0.63 /23	A+ /9.8	66	18
GL	Nuveen High Income Bond A	FJSIX	C	(800) 257-8787	7.95	A- /9.2	32.82 /99	2.50 /52	5.75 /90	E /0.3	91	12
GL	Russell Investments Glbl Opp Crd	RGCYX	C	(800) 832-6688	9.65	B+ /8.7	15.00 /88	3.64 /71	4.61 /80	D- /1.5	96	6
GL	Janus High-Yield A	JHYAX	C	(800) 295-2687	8.58	B /7.8	15.91 /90	3.61 /70	5.84 /91	D /2.2	94	9
GL	SEI Inst Intl International Fx In F	SEFIX	C	(800) 342-5734	10.03	C+ /5.9	2.48 /53	3.62 /70	3.44 /64	C /4.9	94	9
GL	Northern Fixed Income	NOFIX	C	(800) 595-9111	10.17	C /5.3	3.31 /58	2.66 /55	2.82 /55	C /5.4	92	6
GL	AB Unconstrained Bond A	AGSAX	C	(800) 221-5672	8.62	C /4.7	7.97 /74	2.06 /44	2.44 /48	C+ /6.2	86	21
GL	JPMorgan Core Plus Bond A	ONIAX	C	(800) 480-4111	8.22	C- /4.0	3.34 /59	2.82 /58	3.13 /60	B- /7.0	93	11
GL	MassMutual Select Total Ret Bd	MSPGX	C	(800) 542-6767	9.81	C- /3.7	1.73 /46	1.79 /39	2.33 /47	B /7.6	87	N/A
GL	J Hancock Income A	JHFIX	C	(800) 257-3336	6.43	C- /3.0	3.23 /58	2.12 /45	3.45 /64	B /8.1	89	18
GL	US Global Inv Near-Term Tax Free	NEARX	C	(800) 873-8637	2.22	D+ /2.5	-0.53 / 9	1.13 /30	1.28 /31	B+ /8.8	80	27
GL	WA Global Strategic Income A	SDSAX	C-	(877) 534-4627	6.36	B- /7.0	13.08 /85	3.24 /65	4.38 /77	D+ /2.4	94	5
GL	● MainStay Global High Income B	MGHBX	D+	(800) 624-6782	10.28	B+ /8.6	17.00 /92	3.36 /67	3.21 /61	E /0.3	96	6
GL	GuideStone Global Bond Inv	GGBFX	D+	(888) 984-8433	9.92	B- /7.5	14.34 /87	2.54 /52	3.46 /65	D /1.6	93	11
GL	Hartford Strategic Income A	HSNAX	D+	(888) 843-7824	8.76	C+ /6.9	12.69 /84	3.28 /66	3.71 /69	D /2.2	95	5
GL	Putnam Absolute Return 300 A	PTRNX	D+	(800) 225-1581	9.77	C /4.6	9.10 /77	0.93 /26	2.11 /44	C /4.9	70	9
GL	Dreyfus/Standish Global Fixed Inc	DHGAX	D+	(800) 645-6561	21.18	C- /3.1	1.68 /46	2.61 /54	3.28 /62	C+ /6.9	91	11
GL	Janus Short-Term Bond A	JSHAX	D	(800) 295-2687	3.02	E+ /0.7	1.45 /44	0.57 /21	1.13 /29	A /9.3	67	10
GL	Templeton Global Total Return A	TGTRX	D-	(800) 342-5236	12.30	B- /7.2	15.93 /90	2.24 /47	3.72 /69	E+ /0.8	84	9
GL	Templeton Global Bond A	TPINX	D-	(800) 342-5236	12.23	C+ /6.7	12.99 /85	2.18 /46	2.96 /57	E+ /0.9	83	16
GL	Pioneer Global High Yield A	PGHYX	D-	(800) 225-6292	8.85	C+ /6.3	18.35 /94	1.73 /39	4.02 /73	D- /1.0	88	16
GL	Aberdeen Global High Income A	BJBHX	D-	(866) 667-9231	8.92	C+ /5.6	16.14 /90	0.06 /10	4.18 /75	D /1.6	61	15
GL	Putnam Absolute Return 700 A	PDMAX	D-	(800) 225-1581	11.71	C /5.2	8.43 /75	2.82 /58	3.83 /70	D+ /2.3	90	9
GL	● MainStay Unconstrained Bond B	MASBX	D-	(800) 624-6782	8.77	C /5.0	11.13 /81	0.87 /26	2.81 /55	D+ /2.7	78	8
GL	Goldman Sachs Inv Gr Cdt A	GSGAX	D-	(800) 526-7384	9.10	C /4.5	5.67 /69	2.81 /58	3.52 /66	D+ /2.8	93	14
GL	Pioneer Global Multisector Income	PGABX	D-	(800) 225-6292	10.42	C- /3.1	5.43 /68	2.03 /44	2.06 /43	C /4.7	90	10

● Denotes fund is closed to new investors

Fund Type	Fund Name	Ticker Symbol	Overall Investment Rating	Phone	Net Asset Value As of 2/28/17	PERFORMANCE Perform-ance Rating/Pts	Annualized Total Return Through 2/28/17			RISK Risk Rating/Pts	FUND MGR Mgr. Quality Pct	Mgr. Tenure (Years)
							1Yr / Pct	3Yr / Pct	5Yr / Pct			
	99 Pct = Best											
	0 Pct = Worst											
LP	Lord Abbett Floating Rate A	LFRAX	A+	(888) 522-2388	9.26	B /7.7	11.78 /83	3.73 /72	4.86 /83	B- /7.3	92	5
LP	T Rowe Price Instl Fltng Rate F	PFFRX	A+	(800) 638-5660	10.08	B- /7.2	9.33 /77	3.57 /70	4.39 /77	B /7.9	92	8
LP	BlackRock Floating Rate Inc Inv A	BFRAX	A+	(800) 441-7762	10.26	C+ /6.9	9.56 /78	3.24 /65	4.15 /74	B /7.8	90	8
LP	Columbia Floating Rate A	RFRAX	A	(800) 345-6611	9.08	B- /7.1	11.84 /83	3.29 /66	4.52 /79	C+ /6.6	89	11
LP	Virtus Senior Floating Rate A	PSFRX	A	(800) 243-1574	9.54	C+ /6.5	10.40 /80	2.81 /58	4.00 /73	C+ /6.9	87	5
LP	● MainStay Floating Rate B	MXFBX	A	(800) 624-6782	9.38	C+ /6.3	9.36 /77	2.07 /44	2.81 /55	B- /7.1	81	13
LP	Voya Floating Rate A	IFRAX	A-	(800) 992-0180	9.95	C+ /6.3	9.07 /77	2.91 /60	4.06 /73	C+ /6.9	87	7
LP	Eaton Vance Float Rate Advtage A	EAFAX	B+	(800) 262-1122	10.89	B+ /8.5	15.82 /90	3.87 /74	4.93 /83	C- /3.6	91	21
LP	Oppenheimer Sen-Floating Rate A	OOSAX	B+	(888) 470-0862	8.20	B+ /8.3	16.53 /91	3.76 /72	4.75 /81	C- /4.0	90	18
LP	Voya Senior Income A	XSIAX	B+	(800) 992-0180	12.85	B+ /8.3	14.59 /88	3.91 /74	6.29 /94	C- /4.0	91	16
LP	Eaton Vance Flt-Rate and Hi Inc A	EVFHX	B+	(800) 262-1122	9.44	B /7.9	13.86 /87	3.46 /68	4.43 /78	C /4.5	90	17
LP	Eaton Vance Floating Rate A	EVBLX	B+	(800) 262-1122	9.31	B /7.6	13.62 /86	3.21 /64	3.98 /72	C /4.8	88	16
LP	Franklin Floating Rate Dly-Acc A	FAFRX	B	(800) 342-5236	8.89	B- /7.5	14.02 /87	3.19 /64	3.93 /71	C /4.5	87	4
LP	RidgeWorth Seix Fltng Rt Hg Inc A	SFRAX	B	(888) 784-3863	8.79	B- /7.5	13.62 /86	3.30 /66	4.28 /76	C- /4.2	89	11
LP	AIG Sr Floating Rate A	SASFX	B	(800) 858-8850	8.12	C+ /6.9	13.03 /85	3.01 /61	4.16 /74	C /5.0	88	8
LP	Invesco Senior Loan A	VSLAX	B-	(800) 959-4246	6.68	A- /9.0	20.95 /97	3.89 /74	6.11 /93	D /2.2	89	10
LP	Invesco Floating Rate A	AFRAX	B-	(800) 959-4246	7.62	B /7.6	14.94 /88	3.10 /63	4.53 /79	C- /3.6	87	11
LP	Neuberger Berman Floating Rt Inc	NFIAX	B-	(800) 877-9700	9.96	C /5.1	9.54 /78	2.49 /52	3.47 /65	C+ /6.7	84	8
LP	Hartford Floating Rate A	HFLAX	C+	(888) 843-7824	8.73	B- /7.4	14.73 /88	2.99 /61	4.07 /73	C- /3.5	85	N/A
LP	Fidelity Adv Float-Rate Hi-Inc A	FFRAX	C+	(800) 522-7297	9.69	C+ /6.3	12.18 /84	2.71 /56	3.37 /63	C /5.1	85	4
LP	Delaware Floating Rate Fd A	DDFAX	C+	(800) 523-1918	8.38	D+ /2.8	5.42 /68	1.03 /28	1.79 /39	B+ /8.9	68	7
LP	Victory Floating Rate A	RSFLX	C-	(800) 539-3863	9.72	B- /7.1	14.85 /88	2.52 /52	3.96 /72	D+ /2.8	82	8
LP	Highland Floating Rate Opps A	HFRAX	D	(877) 665-1287	7.40	B- /7.5	21.26 /97	1.84 /40	6.92 /96	D- /1.3	68	5
LP	Deutsche Floating Rate A	DFRAX	D-	(800) 728-3337	8.42	D+ /2.5	7.83 /74	0.35 /19	2.43 /48	C /5.5	27	10
LP	Driehaus Select Credit Fund	DRSLX	E-	(800) 560-6111	8.03	E- /0.1	9.42 /78	-3.53 / 1	-0.36 / 3	D /1.8	0	7

● Denotes fund is closed to new investors

www.thestreetratings.com

Data as of February 28, 2017

Fund Type	Fund Name	Ticker Symbol	Overall Investment Rating	Phone	Net Asset Value As of 2/28/17	PERFORMANCE Performance Rating/Pts	Annualized Total Return Through 2/28/17 1Yr / Pct	3Yr / Pct	5Yr / Pct	RISK Risk Rating/Pts	FUND MGR Mgr. Quality Pct	Mgr. Tenure (Years)
	99 Pct = Best 0 Pct = Worst											
MMF	Federated T/F Oblig Fund Wealth	TBIXX	C	(800) 341-7400	1.00	D /1.8	0.57 /38	0.21 /19	0.13 /18	A+ / 9.9	52	N/A
MMF	Federated Municipal Obl Cap	MFCXX	C	(800) 341-7400	1.00	D /1.7	0.41 /35	0.16 /18	0.11 /17	A+ / 9.9	50	N/A
MMF	Fidelity MM Tax Exempt Select	FSXXX	C	(800) 544-8544	1.00	D /1.7	0.40 /35	0.17 /18	0.11 /18	A+ / 9.9	50	N/A
MMF	Dreyfus Muni Cash Mgmt Plus Inv	DVMXX	C	(800) 645-6561	1.00	D /1.7	0.53 /38	0.18 /18	0.11 /17	A+ / 9.9	49	21
MMF	Vanguard Municipal Money Mkt Inv	VMSXX	C	(800) 662-7447	1.00	D /1.7	0.42 /36	0.15 /17	0.10 /17	A+ / 9.9	49	1
MMF	Goldman Sachs Inv Tx Ex MM Inst	FTXXX	C	(800) 526-7384	1.00	D /1.6	0.38 /35	0.13 /16	0.09 /17	A+ / 9.9	49	N/A
MMF	Vanguard PA T/F MM Inv	VPTXX	C	(800) 662-7447	1.00	D /1.6	0.37 /34	0.13 /17	0.09 /17	A+ / 9.9	48	2
MMF	Vanguard NY Tx-Ex MM Inv	VYFXX	C	(800) 662-7447	1.00	D /1.6	0.39 /35	0.14 /17	0.09 /17	A+ / 9.9	49	6
MMF	Federated Inst Tx Fr Cash Tr Prmr	FTFXX	C	(800) 341-7400	1.00	D /1.6	0.39 /35	0.14 /17	0.08 /16	A+ / 9.9	49	N/A
MMF	Invesco Tax-Free Cash Rsv Inst	TFPXX	C	(800) 959-4246	1.00	D- /1.5	0.34 /34	0.12 /16	0.10 /17	A+ / 9.9	47	N/A
MMF	Vanguard NJ T/E Money Market	VNJXX	C	(800) 662-7447	1.00	D- /1.5	0.36 /34	0.13 /17	0.09 /17	A+ / 9.9	48	6
MMF	Invesco Premier Tax-Ex Port Inst	PEIXX	C	(800) 959-4246	1.00	D- /1.5	0.34 /34	0.12 /16	0.08 /16	A+ / 9.9	48	N/A
MMF	MSILF T/E Portfolio Cshmgt	MTMXX	C	(800) 354-8185	1.00	D- /1.5	0.40 /35	0.14 /17	0.09 /17	A+ / 9.9	49	N/A
MMF	Fidelity MA AMT T/F MM Fd	FMSXX	C	(800) 544-8544	1.00	D- /1.5	0.25 /31	0.13 /16	0.09 /17	A+ / 9.9	48	2
MMF	Vanguard CA T/F MM Inv	VCTXX	C	(800) 662-7447	1.00	D- /1.5	0.37 /34	0.13 /17	0.09 /17	A+ / 9.9	48	N/A
MMF	Invesco Tax-Exempt Cash A	ACSXX	C	(800) 959-4246	1.00	D- /1.4	0.18 /28	0.13 /16	0.11 /18	A+ / 9.9	49	N/A
MMF	Fidelity CA AMT T/F MM Fd	FSPXX	C	(800) 544-8544	1.00	D- /1.4	0.28 /32	0.10 /15	0.07 /15	A+ / 9.9	46	2
MMF	BlackRock Liqdty MuniCash Port D	MCDXX	C-		1.00	D- /1.4	0.27 /31	0.10 /15	0.06 /14	A+ / 9.9	N/A	N/A
MMF	Wells Fargo Mu Cash Mgmt MM S	EISXX	C-	(800) 222-8222	1.00	D- /1.4	0.26 /31	0.10 /15	0.08 /16	A+ / 9.9	N/A	N/A
MMF	Fidelity Municipal MM Fund	FTEXX	C-	(800) 544-8544	1.00	D- /1.3	0.20 /29	0.08 /14	0.05 /14	A+ / 9.9	44	14
MMF	Fidelity AZ Muni Money Market	FSAXX	C-	(800) 544-8544	1.00	D- /1.3	0.21 /29	0.08 /14	0.05 /14	A+ / 9.9	47	11
MMF	USAA Tax Exempt-Money Market	USEXX	C-	(800) 382-8722	1.00	D- /1.3	0.21 /30	0.08 /14	0.06 /15	A+ / 9.9	N/A	N/A
MMF	Fidelity NY AMT T/F MM Svc	FNOXX	C-	(800) 544-8544	1.00	D- /1.2	0.14 /27	0.08 /14	0.06 /15	A+ / 9.9	46	6
MMF	Federated GA Muni Cash Tr	GAMXX	C-	(800) 341-7400	1.00	D- /1.1	0.14 /27	0.07 /13	0.05 /14	A+ / 9.9	44	N/A
MMF	Federated MI Muni Cash Svc	MIMXX	C-	(800) 341-7400	1.00	D- /1.1	0.13 /26	0.06 /12	0.04 /12	A+ / 9.9	43	22
MMF	Fidelity NJ AMT T/F MM Svc	FNNXX	C-	(800) 544-8544	1.00	D- /1.1	0.14 /27	0.07 /13	0.05 /14	A+ / 9.9	44	7
MMF	Fidelity CA Muni Money Market	FCFXX	C-	(800) 544-8544	1.00	D- /1.1	0.15 /27	0.06 /12	0.04 /12	A+ / 9.9	42	2
MMF	Fidelity CT Muni Money Market	FCMXX	C-	(800) 544-8544	1.00	D- /1.0	0.12 /25	0.05 /11	0.03 /11	A+ / 9.9	43	2
MMF	Fidelity NJ Municipal Money Market	FNJXX	C-	(800) 544-8544	1.00	D- /1.0	0.12 /25	0.05 /12	0.03 /11	A+ / 9.9	41	7
MMF	Fidelity PA Muni MM Fd	FPTXX	C-	(800) 544-8544	1.00	D- /1.0	0.12 /25	0.05 /12	0.03 /11	A+ / 9.9	43	6
MMF	Schwab Muni Money Sweep	SWXXX	C-	(800) 407-0256	1.00	E+ /0.9	0.08 /23	0.04 /11	0.03 /12	A+ / 9.9	42	N/A
MMF	USAA Tax Exempt-NY MM	UNYXX	C-	(800) 382-8722	1.00	E+ /0.9	0.08 /23	0.05 /12	0.03 /12	A+ / 9.9	42	N/A
MMF	JPMorgan CA Mun MM Morgan	VCAXX	C-	(800) 480-4111	1.00	E+ /0.9	0.08 /23	0.04 /11	0.03 /11	A+ / 9.9	41	N/A
MMF	Dreyfus AMT-Free T/E Cash Mgmt	DEVXX	D+	(800) 645-6561	1.00	E+ /0.9	0.10 /24	0.04 /10	0.02 / 9	A+ / 9.9	41	N/A
MMF	Schwab CA Muni Money Sweep	SWCXX	D+	(800) 407-0256	1.00	E+ /0.8	0.06 /22	0.03 /10	0.03 /12	A+ / 9.9	40	N/A
MMF	Schwab AMT Tax-Free Money	SWFXX	D+	(800) 407-0256	1.00	E+ /0.8	0.06 /22	0.03 /10	0.03 /12	A+ / 9.9	40	N/A
MMF	Schwab PA Muni Money Fund	SWEXX	D+	(800) 407-0256	1.00	E+ /0.8	0.05 /22	0.03 /10	0.02 / 9	A+ / 9.9	41	N/A
MMF	JPMorgan Tax Free MM Morgan	VTMXX	D+	(800) 480-4111	1.00	E+ /0.8	0.05 /22	0.03 /10	0.02 / 9	A+ / 9.9	40	N/A
MMF	JPMorgan NY Mun MM Morgan	VNYXX	D+	(800) 480-4111	1.00	E+ /0.8	0.06 /22	0.03 /10	0.02 / 9	A+ / 9.9	40	N/A
MMF	Dreyfus AMT-F NY Muni Csh Mgmt	DVYXX	D+	(800) 645-6561	1.00	E+ /0.7	0.06 /22	0.02 / 8	0.01 / 7	A+ / 9.9	39	N/A
MMF	Schwab NY Muni Money Swep	SWNXX	D+	(800) 407-0256	1.00	E+ /0.7	0.05 /22	0.03 /10	0.03 /12	A+ / 9.9	41	N/A
MMF	BNY Mellon National Muni MM Inv	MNTXX	D+	(800) 645-6561	1.00	E+ /0.7	0.07 /23	0.02 / 8	0.01 / 7	A+ / 9.9	39	N/A

● Denotes fund is closed to new investors

Fund Type	Fund Name	Ticker Symbol	Overall Investment Rating	Phone	Net Asset Value As of 2/28/17	Performance Rating/Pts	Annualized Total Return Through 2/28/17			Risk Rating/Pts	Mgr. Quality Pct	Mgr. Tenure (Years)
	99 Pct = Best *0 Pct = Worst*						1Yr / Pct	3Yr / Pct	5Yr / Pct			
MMT	WA Inst Liquid Reserves Inst	CILXX	C	(800) 331-1792	1.00	D /1.8	0.63 /35	0.30 /19	0.23 /19	A+ / 9.9	55	N/A
MMT	Invesco Liquid Assets Inst	LAPXX	C	(800) 959-4246	1.00	D /1.7	0.58 /35	0.27 /18	0.21 /19	A+ / 9.9	54	N/A
MMT	Vanguard Prime M/M Inv	VMMXX	C	(800) 662-7447	1.00	D /1.6	0.56 /34	0.22 /17	0.15 /17	A+ / 9.9	52	14
MMT	Goldman Sachs Fin Sq MM Inst	FSMXX	C	(800) 526-7384	1.00	D /1.6	0.53 /34	0.26 /18	0.20 /18	A+ / 9.9	53	N/A
MMT	Goldman Sachs Fin Sq Pr Oblg	FPOXX	C	(800) 526-7384	1.00	D /1.6	0.53 /34	0.23 /17	0.16 /17	A+ / 9.9	52	N/A
MMT	Invesco STIC Prime Inst	SRIXX	C	(800) 959-4246	1.00	D- /1.5	0.41 /31	0.21 /17	0.16 /17	A+ / 9.9	52	N/A
MMT	Invesco Premier Portfolio Inst	IPPXX	C	(800) 959-4246	1.00	D- /1.5	0.51 /33	0.22 /17	0.16 /17	A+ / 9.9	52	N/A
MMT	Federated Prime Cash Obl Wealth	PCOXX	C	(800) 341-7400	1.00	D- /1.5	0.49 /33	0.22 /17	0.17 /17	A+ / 9.9	51	21
MMT	Federated Inst Money Mkt Mgt Inst	MMPXX	C	(800) 341-7400	1.00	D- /1.5	0.43 /32	0.24 /17	0.19 /18	A+ / 9.9	53	N/A
MMT	MSILF Prime Portfolio IS	MPEXX	C	(800) 354-8185	1.00	D- /1.5	0.48 /33	0.20 /16	0.15 /17	A+ / 9.9	51	N/A
MMT	BlackRock-Lq TempCash Instl	TMCXX	C	(800) 441-7762	1.00	D- /1.4	0.39 /31	0.19 /16	0.16 /17	A+ / 9.9	51	N/A
MMT	Harbor Money Market Inst	HARXX	C	(800) 422-1050	1.00	D- /1.4	0.38 /31	0.19 /16	0.15 /17	A+ / 9.9	51	14
MMT	Fidelity Spartan Money Market	SPRXX	C	(800) 544-8544	1.00	D- /1.4	0.43 /32	0.16 /15	0.10 /15	A+ / 9.9	49	N/A
MMT	Federated Inst Prime Value Obl	PVCXX	C	(800) 341-7400	1.00	D- /1.4	0.44 /32	0.18 /16	0.13 /16	A+ / 9.9	49	N/A
MMT	Dreyfus Prime Money Market	CZAXX	C	(800) 645-6561	1.00	D- /1.4	0.45 /32	0.16 /15	0.10 /15	A+ / 9.9	49	N/A
MMT	MSILF Money Mkt Cshmgt	MSHXX	C	(800) 354-8185	1.00	D- /1.4	0.43 /32	0.17 /16	0.11 /16	A+ / 9.9	49	N/A
MMT	Fidelity Cash-MM III	FCOXX	C-	(800) 544-8544	1.00	D- /1.3	0.33 /30	0.12 /14	0.08 /14	A+ / 9.9	46	6
MMT	Schwab Value Adv Money Investor	SWVXX	C-	(800) 407-0256	1.00	D- /1.3	0.32 /30	0.12 /14	0.08 /14	A+ / 9.9	47	25
MMT	Vanguard Federal M/M Inv	VMFXX	C-	(800) 662-7447	1.00	D- /1.3	0.34 /30	0.14 /15	0.09 /15	A+ / 9.9	48	10
MMT	Invesco Gov and Agency Inst	AGPXX	C-	(800) 959-4246	1.00	D- /1.3	0.32 /30	0.14 /15	0.09 /15	A+ / 9.9	48	N/A
MMT	BlackRock Liqdty TempFd Dollar	TDOXX	C-	(800) 441-7762	1.00	D- /1.3	0.35 /30	0.14 /15	0.09 /14	A+ / 9.9	46	N/A
MMT	Fidelity Prime MM III	FCDXX	C-	(800) 522-7297	1.00	D- /1.3	0.32 /29	0.12 /14	0.07 /13	A+ / 9.9	N/A	2
MMT	Goldman Sachs Fin Sq Govt Inst	FGTXX	C-	(800) 526-7384	1.00	D- /1.3	0.33 /30	0.13 /14	0.09 /15	A+ / 9.9	47	N/A
MMT	Gabelli US Treasury Money Mkt	GABXX	C-	(800) 422-3554	1.00	D- /1.2	0.28 /28	0.10 /13	0.07 /13	A+ / 9.9	N/A	25
MMT	Invesco Treasury Inst	TRPXX	C-	(800) 959-4246	1.00	D- /1.2	0.27 /28	0.11 /13	0.08 /14	A+ / 9.9	N/A	N/A
MMT	AB Government Exchange	AEAXX	C-	(800) 221-5672	1.00	D- /1.2	0.22 /26	0.14 /15	0.13 /16	A+ / 9.9	48	N/A
MMT	Dreyfus Inst Pref Govt Mny Mkt	DSHXX	C-	(800) 426-9363	1.00	D- /1.2	0.29 /29	0.11 /13	0.08 /14	A+ / 9.9	N/A	N/A
MMT	Vanguard Treas MM Inv	VUSXX	C-	(800) 662-7447	1.00	D- /1.2	0.29 /29	0.12 /14	0.08 /14	A+ / 9.9	47	20
MMT	Schwab Retirement Advantage	SWIXX	C-	(800) 407-0256	1.00	D- /1.2	0.30 /29	0.11 /14	0.07 /13	A+ / 9.9	N/A	19
MMT	Invesco Premier US Gv Mny Port	IUGXX	C-	(800) 959-4246	1.00	D- /1.2	0.29 /29	0.12 /14	0.08 /14	A+ / 9.9	46	N/A
MMT	Federated Inst Prime 60 Day Prem	FMTXX	C-	(800) 341-7400	1.00	D- /1.1	0.28 /28	0.09 /12	0.06 /12	A+ / 9.9	44	26
MMT	Dreyfus Basic Money Market	DBAXX	C-	(800) 645-6561	1.00	D- /1.1	0.25 /27	0.09 /12	0.05 /11	A+ / 9.9	44	N/A
MMT	Goldman Sachs Fin Sq Treas Sol	FEDXX	C-	(800) 526-7384	1.00	D- /1.1	0.24 /27	0.10 /13	0.06 /12	A+ / 9.9	46	N/A
MMT	Schwab Cash Reserves	SWSXX	C-	(800) 407-0256	1.00	D- /1.1	0.17 /25	0.10 /13	0.08 /14	A+ / 9.9	N/A	N/A
MMT	MSILF Govt Portfolio Inv	MVVXX	C-	(800) 354-8185	1.00	D- /1.1	0.21 /26	0.10 /13	0.08 /14	A+ / 9.9	N/A	N/A
MMT	SEI Daily Inc Tr-Government F	SEOXX	C-	(800) 342-5734	1.00	D- /1.1	0.21 /26	0.09 /13	0.06 /13	A+ / 9.9	45	3
MMT	Invesco Trs Obligations Inst	TSPXX	C-	(800) 959-4246	1.00	D- /1.1	0.19 /26	0.11 /14	0.08 /14	A+ / 9.9	47	N/A
MMT	BlackRock-Money Market Prtf Inv A	PINXX	C-	(800) 441-7762	1.00	D- /1.1	0.25 /27	0.10 /13	0.06 /12	A+ / 9.9	45	9
MMT	BlackRock-Lq T-Fund Instl	TSTXX	C-	(800) 441-7762	1.00	D- /1.1	0.25 /27	0.10 /13	0.07 /13	A+ / 9.9	N/A	N/A
MMT	Goldman Sachs Fin Sq Tre Instr	FTIXX	C-	(800) 526-7384	1.00	D- /1.1	0.24 /27	0.09 /12	0.05 /11	A+ / 9.9	44	N/A
MMT	Wells Fargo Csh Inv MM S	NWIXX	C-	(800) 222-8222	1.00	D- /1.1	0.21 /26	0.08 /12	0.05 /12	A+ / 9.9	44	N/A
MMT	PNC Government Money Market A	PGAXX	C-	(800) 551-2145	1.00	D- /1.1	0.20 /26	0.09 /13	0.06 /13	A+ / 9.9	46	N/A
MMT	BlackRock-Lq Federal Tr Instl	TFFXX	C-	(800) 441-7762	1.00	D- /1.1	0.25 /27	0.10 /13	0.06 /12	A+ / 9.9	45	N/A
MMT	Federated Trust For US Trs Obl	TTOXX	C-	(800) 341-7400	1.00	D- /1.1	0.24 /27	0.09 /13	0.05 /11	A+ / 9.9	44	N/A
MMT	Dreyfus Inst Tr Agcy Cash Adv	DHLXX	C-	(800) 426-9363	1.00	D- /1.0	0.23 /27	0.08 /11	0.05 /11	A+ / 9.9	44	N/A
MMT	Fidelity US Treasury Income Port I	FSIXX	C-	(800) 544-8544	1.00	D- /1.0	0.21 /26	0.08 /12	0.05 /11	A+ / 9.9	44	N/A
MMT	Schwab Investor Money	SWRXX	C-	(800) 407-0256	1.00	D- /1.0	0.20 /26	0.07 /11	0.05 /12	A+ / 9.9	44	N/A
MMT	BlackRock Liqdty Treas Tr Fd Inst	TTTXX	C-	(800) 221-8120	1.00	D- /1.0	0.22 /27	0.08 /11	0.05 /11	A+ / 9.9	44	N/A
MMT	Federated US Trs Csh Res Instl	UTIXX	C-	(800) 341-7400	1.00	D- /1.0	0.21 /26	0.08 /11	0.05 /11	A+ / 9.9	44	23
MMT	PIMCO Government Money Market	AMAXX	C-	(800) 426-0107	1.00	D- /1.0	0.18 /25	0.08 /12	0.06 /13	A+ / 9.9	45	6
MMT	T Rowe Price Cash Reserves	TSCXX	C-	(800) 638-5660	1.00	D- /1.0	0.18 /25	0.07 /11	0.04 /10	A+ / 9.9	44	8
MMT	American Century Prime MM Inv	BPRXX	C-	(800) 345-6488	1.00	E+ /0.9	0.16 /24	0.06 /10	0.04 /10	A+ / 9.9	42	N/A

Denotes fund is closed to new investors

Fund Type	Fund Name	Ticker Symbol	Overall Investment Rating	Phone	Net Asset Value As of 2/28/17	PERFORMANCE Perform- ance Rating/Pts	Annualized Total Return Through 2/28/17			RISK Risk Rating/Pts	FUND MGR Mgr. Quality Pct	Mgr. Tenure (Years)
	99 Pct = Best *0 Pct = Worst*						1Yr / Pct	3Yr / Pct	5Yr / Pct			
MTG	Federated Mortgage Fund Inst	FGFIX	A-	(800) 341-7400	9.57	C /4.9	2.00 /49	2.62 /54	2.10 /44	B+ / 8.5	65	14
MTG	Vanguard Mort-Backed Secs Idx	VMBSX	B	(800) 662-7447	20.99	C /4.3	0.43 /32	2.39 /50	1.96 /41	B+ / 8.3	45	8
MTG	Advisors Series Trust PIA MBS	PMTGX	B	(800) 251-1970	9.53	C- /4.2	0.44 /32	2.38 /50	2.00 /42	B+ / 8.3	38	11
MTG	Prudential Corporate Bond Z	TGMBX	B-	(800) 225-1852	11.11	B- /7.5	7.52 /73	3.92 /74	2.85 /55	C- / 3.8	74	2
MTG	HC Capital US Mtg/Asst Bckd Fl	HCASX	B-	(800) 242-9596	9.60	C- /3.8	0.08 /21	2.06 /44	1.74 /38	B+ / 8.3	29	4
MTG	WA Adjustable Rate Income A	ARMZX	B-	(877) 534-4627	8.97	D+ /2.7	3.49 /60	1.20 /31	1.78 /39	A+ / 9.7	76	3
MTG	PIMCO Mortgage-Backd Sec A	PMRAX	C+	(800) 426-0107	10.45	C- /3.7	1.80 /47	2.71 /56	2.43 /48	B+ / 8.4	63	5
MTG	TCW Total Return Bond N	TGMNX	C+	(800) 386-3829	10.22	C- /3.7	0.01 /17	2.10 /45	3.79 /70	B / 7.7	20	7
MTG	Mgd Acct Srs BlackRock US Mtg	BMPAX	C+	(800) 441-7762	10.27	C- /3.6	1.69 /46	2.89 /59	3.21 /61	B+ / 8.3	67	8
MTG	American Funds Mortgage Fund A	MFAAX	C+	(800) 421-0180	10.10	C- /3.2	1.16 /41	2.50 /52	1.89 /40	B / 8.2	58	7
MTG ●	Franklin Strategic Mortgage Port	FSMIX	C+	(800) 342-5236	9.36	C- /3.1	1.15 /41	2.64 /55	3.07 /59	B+ / 8.4	62	24
MTG	PIA Short-Term Securities Adv	PIASX	C+	(800) 251-1970	10.03	D+ /2.4	1.68 /46	0.72 /23	0.57 /22	A+ / 9.8	62	N/A
MTG	Northern Tax-Advtged Ult-Sh Fxd	NTAUX	C+	(800) 595-9111	10.14	D /2.2	1.03 /40	0.61 /22	0.74 /24	A+ / 9.9	58	8
MTG	TCW Short Term Bond I	TGSMX	C+	(800) 386-3829	8.68	D /2.1	0.99 /39	0.53 /21	0.85 /25	A+ / 9.9	56	7
MTG	PIMCO StkPlus Intl (DH) A	PIPAX	C	(800) 426-0107	7.60	A+ /9.9	26.71 /99	6.07 /92	10.96 /99	E- / 0.0	98	2
MTG	Wright Current Income	WCIFX	C	(800) 232-0013	9.04	C- /3.2	-0.84 / 6	1.84 /40	1.46 /34	B / 8.0	22	8
MTG	RidgeWorth Seix US Mtg A	SLTMX	C	(888) 784-3863	11.10	C- /3.1	0.10 /22	2.33 /49	1.75 /38	B / 8.1	32	10
MTG	JPMorgan Mortgage Backed Sec A	OMBAX	C	(800) 480-4111	11.45	D+ /2.9	0.78 /37	2.39 /50	2.24 /45	B+ / 8.4	59	12
MTG	Federated Adj Rate Sec Inst	FEUGX	C	(800) 341-7400	9.69	D /1.7	0.70 /36	0.28 /18	0.33 /20	A+ / 9.9	48	22
MTG	AMF Ultra Short Mortgage Fund	ASARX	C	(800) 527-3713	7.11	D /1.6	-0.04 /17	0.34 /19	0.80 /25	A+ / 9.7	33	8
MTG	Northern Bond Index	NOBOX	C-	(800) 595-9111	10.51	C /4.5	1.17 /41	2.50 /52	2.08 /43	C+ / 5.8	17	10
MTG	Goldman Sachs US Mtge A	GSUAX	C-	(800) 526-7384	10.47	D+ /2.5	0.50 /33	2.27 /48	2.39 /48	B+ / 8.4	43	14
MTG	Principal Govt & High Qual Bd A	CMPGX	C-	(800) 222-5852	10.54	D+ /2.5	0.01 /17	1.84 /40	1.72 /38	B / 8.1	20	7
MTG	Fidelity Adv Mortgage Secs A	FMGAX	C-	(800) 522-7297	11.18	D+ /2.4	0.31 /29	2.28 /48	1.94 /41	B / 8.2	33	9
MTG	BlackRock GNMA Port Inv A	BGPAX	C-	(800) 441-7762	9.69	D /1.9	0.29 /28	1.90 /41	1.65 /37	B+ / 8.6	34	8
MTG	Trust for Credit UltSh Dur Gov TCU	TCUUX	C-	(800) 342-5828	9.47	D- /1.3	0.30 /29	0.16 /15	0.18 /18	A+ / 9.9	37	N/A
MTG	Goldman Sachs Hi Qual Fltg R A	GSAMX	C-	(800) 526-7384	8.72	D- /1.1	1.87 /48	0.18 /16	0.24 /19	A+ / 9.8	56	9
MTG	Pacific Financial Tactical Inv	PFTLX	D	(888) 451-8734	9.35	E+ /0.6	2.30 /52	-0.50 / 4	1.07 /28	A- / 9.0	11	10
MTG	Wells Fargo Adj Rate Govt A	ESAAX	D	(800) 222-8222	9.01	E /0.5	0.68 /36	0.28 /18	0.52 /22	A+ / 9.9	54	9
MTG	ProFunds-Falling US Dollar Svc	FDPSX	E-	(888) 776-3637	15.64	E- /0.0	-6.29 / 0	-10.51 / 0	-7.63 / 0	E+ / 0.7	0	8

● Denotes fund is closed to new investors

www.thestreetratings.com

Fund Type	Fund Name	Ticker Symbol	Overall Investment Rating	Phone	Net Asset Value As of 2/28/17	Perform-ance Rating/Pts	Annualized Total Return Through 2/28/17			Risk Rating/Pts	Mgr. Quality Pct	Mgr. Tenure (Years)
							1Yr / Pct	3Yr / Pct	5Yr / Pct			
MUH	MainStay High Yield Muni Bond C	MMHDX	B+	(800) 624-6782	12.14	A+ /9.9	2.48 /61	6.40 /99	5.49 /99	D / 2.0	84	7
MUH	Oppeneheimer Rochester Hi Yld	ORNAX	B+	(888) 470-0862	7.09	A+ /9.9	7.13 /81	7.47 /99	6.59 /99	D / 1.7	91	15
MUH	Lord Abbett Tx Fr High Yld Muni A	HYMAX	B+	(888) 522-2388	11.63	A+ /9.7	3.59 /69	5.90 /98	5.30 /98	D+ / 2.3	85	13
MUH	Invesco High Yield Municipal A	ACTHX	B+	(800) 959-4246	9.87	A+ /9.7	2.53 /62	6.92 /99	5.74 /99	D / 2.0	88	15
MUH	PIMCO High Yield Muni Bond A	PYMAX	B+	(800) 426-0107	8.77	A+ /9.6	2.36 /60	5.95 /98	5.05 /98	D / 2.1	80	2
MUH	MFS Municipal High Income A	MMHYX	B+	(800) 225-2606	8.07	A /9.4	1.91 /56	6.12 /99	5.03 /98	D+ / 2.6	86	15
MUH	T Rowe Price Tax-Free High Yield	PRFHX	B+	(800) 638-5660	11.77	A /9.3	1.64 /53	5.37 /98	4.99 /98	D+ / 2.7	81	15
MUH	Pioneer High Income Municipal A	PIMAX	B	(800) 225-6292	7.21	A /9.5	3.01 /65	6.07 /99	5.50 /99	D / 2.0	81	11
MUH	BlackRock High Yld Muni Inv A	MDYHX	B	(800) 441-7762	9.34	A /9.5	1.68 /54	6.46 /99	5.06 /98	D / 1.7	82	11
MUH	Goldman Sachs High Yield Muni A	GHYAX	B	(800) 526-7384	9.31	A /9.4	4.89 /73	6.19 /99	5.65 /99	D / 2.1	88	17
MUH	AB High Income Municipal A	ABTHX	B	(800) 221-5672	11.07	A /9.4	0.97 /44	6.01 /98	5.19 /98	D / 1.9	77	7
MUH	Delaware Natl HY Muni Bd A	CXHYX	B	(800) 523-1918	10.77	A /9.3	1.84 /55	6.07 /99	5.22 /98	D / 2.2	82	14
MUH	Northern High Yield Muni	NHYMX	B	(800) 595-9111	8.68	A- /9.0	0.17 /28	4.77 /97	4.20 /95	D+ / 2.6	71	19
MUH	American Funds High Inc Muni Bnd	AMHIX	B	(800) 421-0180	15.41	B+ /8.9	1.75 /54	5.43 /98	5.38 /98	D+ / 2.8	82	23
MUH	Vanguard High-Yield Tax-Exempt	VWAHX	B	(800) 662-7447	11.08	B+ /8.9	0.96 /44	4.49 /96	4.01 /93	D+ / 2.6	62	7
MUH	Columbia High Yield Municipal A	LHIAX	B	(800) 345-6611	10.49	B+ /8.9	1.48 /51	5.23 /97	4.84 /97	D+ / 2.5	80	8
MUH	Ivy Municipal High Income A	IYIAX	B	(800) 777-6472	5.14	B+ /8.6	1.94 /56	5.18 /97	4.01 /93	C- / 3.3	84	8
MUH	Waddell & Reed Adv Muni High Inc	UMUHX	B	(888) 923-3355	4.77	B /8.1	1.98 /57	4.76 /96	4.15 /94	C- / 3.9	83	9
MUH	Nuveen High Yield Muni Bond A	NHMAX	B-	(800) 257-8787	16.68	A+ /9.7	2.45 /61	6.80 /99	6.98 /99	D- / 1.4	83	17
MUH	Federated Muni & Stock	FMUAX	B-	(800) 341-7400	12.87	A- /9.1	9.80 /89	4.20 /94	5.98 /99	D / 2.1	92	14
MUH	Prudential Muni High Income A	PRHAX	B-	(800) 225-1852	10.07	B+ /8.8	1.40 /50	5.43 /98	4.72 /97	D / 2.2	78	13
MUH	Federated Muni High Yield Advn A	FMOAX	B-	(800) 341-7400	8.78	B+ /8.7	1.34 /49	5.50 /98	4.91 /97	D+ / 2.4	81	8
MUH	Victory High Income Municipal Bd	RSHMX	B-	(800) 539-3863	10.47	B+ /8.6	-0.08 /16	5.03 /97	3.39 /86	D+ / 2.8	80	3
MUH	SEI Asset Alloc-Def Strat All F	STDAX	C+	(800) 342-5734	14.64	A+ /9.9	19.17 /99	8.26 /99	10.32 /99	E+ / 0.6	98	14
MUH	Nuveen CA High Yield Muni Bd A	NCHAX	C+	(800) 257-8787	9.35	A /9.5	0.25 /31	6.67 /99	6.69 /99	E+ / 0.9	73	11
MUH	AMG GW&K Muni Enhanced Yield	GWMNX	C+	(800) 548-4539	9.50	A /9.4	0.17 /28	5.35 /98	4.18 /95	D- / 1.0	33	12
MUH	Franklin California H/Y Muni A	FCAMX	C+	(800) 342-5236	10.64	B+ /8.9	1.16 /47	5.83 /98	5.23 /98	D / 1.8	75	23
MUH	WA Municipal High Income A	STXAX	C+	(877) 534-4627	14.09	B /7.8	1.40 /50	4.77 /97	3.73 /90	D+ / 2.9	78	10
MUH	Fidelity Municipal Inc	FHIGX	C+	(800) 544-8544	12.91	B /7.8	-0.13 /15	3.77 /91	3.37 /86	D+ / 2.8	33	7
MUH	Deutsche Strat High Yield T/F A	NOTAX	C+	(800) 728-3337	12.09	B /7.7	1.31 /49	4.25 /94	3.55 /88	C- / 3.1	67	19
MUH	Dreyfus High Yld Muni Bd A	DHYAX	C	(800) 645-6561	11.80	B+ /8.9	2.69 /63	5.88 /98	4.77 /97	D- / 1.2	62	6
MUH	Franklin High Yld Tax-Free Inc A	FRHIX	C	(800) 342-5236	10.25	B /7.7	1.19 /47	4.76 /96	3.74 /90	D+ / 2.6	71	24
MUH	J Hancock High Yield Muni Bond A	JHTFX	C	(800) 257-3336	7.93	B /7.6	1.46 /51	4.55 /96	3.55 /88	D+ / 2.4	70	2
MUH	American Century CA Hi-Yld Muni	CAYAX	C-	(800) 345-6488	10.31	B /7.6	0.31 /33	4.94 /97	4.53 /96	D / 2.2	61	30
MUH	American Century High Yld Muni A	AYMAX	C-	(800) 345-6488	9.32	B- /7.4	0.67 /40	4.67 /96	4.18 /95	D+ / 2.3	60	19
MUH	Value Line Tax Exempt Fund	VLHYX	C-	(800) 243-2729	9.80	C+ /6.0	-0.46 /10	2.49 /73	2.03 /60	C- / 4.1	18	7
MUH	State Farm Tax Advant Bond A	TANAX	C-	(800) 447-4930	11.76	C+ /5.7	-0.21 /14	3.17 /84	2.46 /70	C- / 4.2	50	17
MUH	Northern Short-Interm Tax-Ex	NSITX	C-	(800) 595-9111	10.35	D+ /2.6	-0.29 /13	0.73 /29	0.76 /30	B / 8.2	15	10
MUH	Delaware MN HY Muni Bond A	DVMHX	D+	(800) 523-1918	10.64	C+ /5.6	0.45 /36	3.59 /89	3.09 /81	C- / 4.0	62	14
MUH	Spirit of America Municipal TF Bd A	SOAMX	D	(800) 452-4892	9.39	C+ /6.3	0.55 /38	4.00 /93	2.53 /71	D+ / 2.3	52	8
MUH	Fidelity Adv Muni Income A	FAMUX	D-	(800) 522-7297	12.93	C /5.0	-0.64 / 8	3.40 /87	3.07 /81	D+ / 2.8	22	11
MUH	Hartford Municipal Opportunities A	HHMAX	D-	(888) 843-7824	8.45	C /4.7	-0.03 /17	3.22 /85	3.20 /83	C- / 3.4	27	5
MUH	Federated Ohio Municipal Inc Fund	OMIAX	D-	(800) 341-7400	11.05	C /4.3	0.40 /35	2.98 /82	2.68 /74	C- / 3.8	28	22
MUH	Columbia AMT-Fr Intm Muni Bond	LITAX	D-	(800) 345-6611	10.44	C- /3.9	-0.53 / 9	2.45 /72	2.26 /65	C / 4.3	19	8
MUH	JPMorgan CA Tax Free Bond A	JCBAX	E+	(800) 480-4111	10.78	D+ /2.5	-0.95 / 5	2.09 /65	2.11 /61	C- / 4.2	11	13

Fund Type	Fund Name	Ticker Symbol	Overall Investment Rating	Phone	Net Asset Value As of 2/28/17	PERFORMANCE Perform-ance Rating/Pts	Annualized Total Return Through 2/28/17 1Yr / Pct	3Yr / Pct	5Yr / Pct	RISK Risk Rating/Pts	FUND MGR Mgr. Quality Pct	Mgr. Tenure (Years)
MUI	Westcore CO Tax Exempt	WTCOX	A	(800) 392-2673	11.40	C+ /6.9	-0.15 /15	2.95 /81	2.36 /68	C+ / 6.4	36	12
MUI	WesMark West Virginia Muni Bond	WMKMX	A-	(800) 864-1013	10.40	C+ /5.9	-0.50 /10	2.42 /72	1.99 /59	B- / 7.4	28	11
MUI	Pacific Capital Tax-Free Secs Y	PTXFX	B+	(888) 739-1390	10.10	C+ /6.7	-0.38 /11	2.86 /80	2.44 /69	C+ / 5.6	28	13
MUI	Commerce Kansas T/F Intm Bond	KTXIX	B+	(800) 995-6365	19.14	C+ /5.7	-0.43 /10	2.37 /71	1.97 /58	B- / 7.2	24	17
MUI	First Inv MI Tax Exempt A	FTMIX	B+	(800) 423-4026	11.98	C /5.2	0.06 /22	3.77 /91	2.45 /69	B- / 7.5	79	26
MUI	First Inv PA Tax Exempt A	FTPAX	B+	(800) 423-4026	13.02	C /4.9	0.78 /42	3.45 /87	2.83 /77	B / 7.9	78	26
MUI	GuideMark Tax-Exempt Fixed Inc	GMTEX	B	(888) 278-5809	11.29	C+ /6.8	-0.44 /10	2.99 /82	2.27 /65	C / 5.4	30	11
MUI	Franklin Ohio Tax-Free Inc A	FTOIX	B	(800) 342-5236	12.56	C+ /6.4	0.51 /37	3.86 /91	2.94 /79	C+ / 5.6	70	18
MUI	First Inv NC Tax Exempt B	FMTQX	B	(800) 423-4026	13.18	C- /4.2	-1.30 / 2	1.82 /58	1.22 /40	B / 8.2	28	25
MUI	BNY Mellon PA Inter Muni Bond M	MPPIX	C+	(800) 645-6561	12.00	C /5.4	-0.10 /16	2.13 /65	1.70 /51	C+ / 6.0	12	17
MUI	Franklin MN Tax-Free Inc A	FMINX	C+	(800) 342-5236	12.27	C /4.3	0.10 /24	2.84 /79	2.35 /67	B- / 7.2	46	28
MUI	First Inv OH Tax Exempt A	FIOHX	C+	(800) 423-4026	12.38	C- /4.0	-0.16 /15	3.28 /85	2.49 /70	B / 7.7	70	26
MUI	First Inv NY Tax Exempt A	FNYFX	C+	(800) 423-4026	14.26	C- /3.9	-0.01 /17	3.20 /84	2.41 /69	B- / 7.5	64	26
MUI	Putnam AMT Free Ins Mun A	PPNAX	C	(800) 225-1581	14.94	C /5.5	-0.19 /15	3.50 /88	2.94 /79	C / 5.0	53	15
MUI	Franklin MI Tax-Free Inc A	FTTMX	C	(800) 342-5236	11.52	C /5.2	1.23 /48	3.19 /84	2.43 /69	C+ / 5.6	59	28
MUI	First Inv Tax Exempt Opps A	EIITX	C	(800) 423-4026	16.58	C /4.9	-0.02 /17	3.72 /90	3.00 /80	C+ / 5.8	67	26
MUI	First Inv Tax Exempt Income A	FITAX	C	(800) 423-4026	9.51	C- /3.4	-0.03 /17	2.94 /81	2.59 /72	B / 7.9	66	26
MUI	CNR CA Tax-Exempt Bond N	CCTEX	C	(888) 889-0799	10.55	C- /3.1	-0.63 / 8	1.08 /37	1.28 /41	B / 8.1	10	8
MUI	First Inv CT Tax Exempt A	FICTX	C	(800) 423-4026	13.22	C- /3.1	-0.08 /16	2.84 /79	2.22 /64	B / 7.8	60	26
MUI	BNY Mellon National ST Muni Bd	MPSTX	C	(800) 645-6561	12.76	D /2.2	0.38 /35	0.44 /23	0.54 /25	A / 9.4	26	2
MUI	Aquila Narragansett TxFr Income A	NITFX	C-	(800) 437-1020	10.60	C /5.1	-0.31 /13	3.31 /86	2.60 /72	C / 5.3	47	17
MUI	SEI Tax-Exempt Tr-NY Muni Bond	SENYX	C-	(800) 342-5734	10.68	C /5.0	-0.72 / 7	2.00 /62	1.65 /50	C / 5.0	8	18
MUI	SEI Tax-Exempt Tr-NJ Muni Bond	SENJX	C-	(800) 342-5734	10.29	C- /3.9	-0.54 / 9	1.52 /49	1.45 /45	C+ / 6.7	7	18
MUI	Touchstone Ohio Tax-Free Bond A	TOHAX	C-	(800) 543-0407	11.47	C- /3.6	-0.16 /15	2.79 /79	2.70 /74	C+ / 6.9	35	31
MUI	First Inv MA Tax Exempt A	FIMAX	C-	(800) 423-4026	11.74	C- /3.4	-0.10 /16	3.02 /82	2.27 /65	C+ / 6.7	51	26
MUI	First Inv CA Tax Exempt A	FICAX	D+	(800) 423-4026	12.63	C /4.8	-0.18 /15	3.65 /89	3.23 /84	C / 5.1	60	26
MUI	First Inv NJ Tax Exempt A	FINJX	D+	(800) 423-4026	12.75	C- /3.7	0.45 /36	3.03 /82	2.24 /64	C+ / 6.0	37	26
MUI	First Inv MN Tax Exempt A	FIMNX	D+	(800) 423-4026	11.95	D /2.1	-0.20 /14	2.30 /69	2.11 /61	B / 8.1	51	26
MUI	First Inv VA Tax Exempt A	FIVAX	D	(800) 423-4026	12.89	D+ /2.9	-0.36 /12	2.83 /79	2.07 /60	C+ / 6.4	32	26
MUI	JPMorgan OH Municipal A	ONOHX	D	(800) 480-4111	10.59	D /2.2	-0.59 / 8	1.85 /59	1.66 /50	B- / 7.5	15	23
MUI	Federated Muni Ultrashrt A	FMUUX	D	(800) 341-7400	9.99	E /0.3	0.52 /37	0.06 /12	0.16 /19	A+ / 9.9	33	17
MUI	First Inv OR Tax Exempt A	FTORX	D-	(800) 423-4026	13.36	C- /3.1	-0.24 /14	2.91 /80	1.98 /59	C+ / 5.6	30	25
MUI	JPMorgan Tax Aware Real Return	TXRAX	D-	(800) 480-4111	9.52	D- /1.3	2.78 /63	0.66 /28	0.46 /24	B- / 7.3	11	12
MUI	Dreyfus Sh-Intmd Muni Bd A	DMBAX	D-	(800) 645-6561	12.94	E /0.4	-0.30 /13	0.43 /22	0.63 /27	B+ / 8.9	12	8

• Denotes fund is closed to new investors

Fund Type	Fund Name	Ticker Symbol	Overall Investment Rating	Phone	Net Asset Value As of 2/28/17	Performance Rating/Pts	1Yr / Pct	3Yr / Pct	5Yr / Pct	Risk Rating/Pts	Mgr Quality Pct	Mgr Tenure (Years)
MUN	BMO Intermediate Tax Free Y	MITFX	A+	(800) 236-3863	11.15	C+ /6.9	0.10 /24	2.93 /81	2.72 /75	B- /7.2	51	2
MUN	State Farm Muni Bond	SFBDX	A+	(800) 447-4930	8.63	C+ /6.8	-0.01 /17	2.80 /79	2.53 /71	B- /7.5	50	19
MUN	Dupree Taxable Muni Bd Srs	DUTMX	A	(800) 866-0614	10.50	A+ /9.6	2.08 /58	5.31 /98	4.96 /97	C- /3.2	88	7
MUN	Sit Tax Free Income Fund	SNTIX	A	(800) 332-5580	9.48	A /9.4	0.69 /40	5.01 /97	4.34 /96	C- /3.4	74	29
MUN	T Rowe Price Tax-Free Income	PRTAX	A	(800) 638-5660	10.07	B /8.0	0.25 /31	3.76 /90	3.28 /85	C /5.0	62	10
MUN	USAA Tax-Exempt Long Term	USTEX	A	(800) 382-8722	13.25	B /8.0	0.64 /39	3.71 /90	3.64 /89	C /5.0	67	N/A
MUN	Oppenheimer Rochester AMT-Free	OPTAX	A-	(888) 470-0862	6.83	A+ /9.7	3.73 /69	6.34 /99	6.00 /99	D+ /2.8	89	15
MUN	T Rowe Price Summit Muni Income	PRINX	A-	(800) 638-5660	11.71	B+ /8.4	0.27 /31	4.12 /94	3.65 /89	C- /4.1	63	18
MUN	Elfun Tax Exempt Income	ELFTX	A-	(800) 843-2639	11.54	B /8.1	0.44 /36	3.75 /90	2.93 /79	C /4.6	58	N/A
MUN	Eaton Vance High Yield Muni Inc A	ETHYX	B+	(800) 262-1122	8.68	A- /9.1	1.03 /45	6.27 /99	5.42 /99	D+ /2.7	84	13
MUN	Vanguard Long-Term Tax-Exempt	VWLTX	B+	(800) 662-7447	11.43	B+ /8.6	0.46 /36	4.19 /94	3.66 /89	C- /3.5	55	7
MUN	Eaton Vance National Muni Inc A	EANAX	B+	(800) 262-1122	9.77	B+ /8.3	2.02 /57	5.15 /97	3.98 /93	C- /3.7	81	4
MUN	Northern Tax Exempt	NOTEX	B+	(800) 595-9111	10.56	B /8.1	0.19 /28	3.80 /91	3.25 /84	C /4.3	56	19
MUN	Vanguard Interm-Term Tax-Exempt	VWITX	B+	(800) 662-7447	13.98	C+ /6.7	-0.11 /16	2.80 /79	2.60 /73	C+ /5.9	27	4
MUN	BlackRock Natl Muni Inv A	MDNLX	B+	(800) 441-7762	10.78	C+ /6.0	0.66 /40	3.53 /88	3.31 /85	B- /7.0	68	21
MUN	Eaton Vance VA Municipal Income	ETVAX	B+	(800) 262-1122	7.95	C /5.3	1.35 /50	3.27 /85	2.61 /73	B /7.7	72	10
MUN	Waddell & Reed Adv Muni Bond A	UNMBX	B+	(888) 923-3355	7.47	C /5.1	0.71 /41	3.15 /84	2.71 /75	B /7.6	66	17
MUN	Oppenheimer Rochester Sht Term	ORSTX	B+	(888) 470-0862	3.73	C- /4.1	0.82 /42	1.93 /60	1.91 /57	A- /9.2	74	7
MUN	USAA Ultra Short Term Bond Fund	UUSTX	B+	(800) 382-8722	9.99	C- /3.8	2.28 /60	0.87 /33	1.31 /42	A+ /9.7	67	N/A
MUN ●	MainStay Tax Free Bond Fund B	MKTBX	B	(800) 624-6782	9.82	B+ /8.3	0.10 /24	4.15 /94	3.56 /88	C- /3.4	62	8
MUN	Fidelity Tax Free Bond Fd	FTABX	B	(800) 544-8544	11.33	B /8.1	0.10 /24	3.89 /92	3.51 /88	C- /3.8	46	7
MUN	PIMCO Unconstrained Tax Mnged	ATMAX	B	(800) 426-0107	10.43	B /7.6	9.78 /89	2.19 /67	2.25 /65	C- /4.2	84	2
MUN	MFS Municipal Income A	MFIAX	B	(800) 225-2606	8.64	B- /7.1	0.87 /43	4.25 /94	3.40 /86	C /5.0	74	19
MUN	Federated Interm Muni Trust Y	FIMYX	B	(800) 341-7400	9.95	C+ /6.8	0.33 /33	2.87 /80	2.54 /71	C /5.1	25	22
MUN	T Rowe Price Summit Muni Intmdt	PRSMX	B	(800) 638-5660	11.75	C+ /6.3	-0.27 /13	2.66 /76	2.52 /71	C+ /6.0	24	24
MUN	Franklin Federal Tax-Free Inc A	FKTIX	B	(800) 342-5236	12.05	C+ /6.2	0.56 /38	3.76 /90	3.21 /83	C+ /5.9	69	30
MUN	Cavanal Hill Intmdt TxFr Bd NL Inv	APTFX	B	(800) 762-7085	10.96	C- /4.2	-0.29 /13	1.52 /49	1.32 /42	B+ /8.3	21	24
MUN	Columbia Strategic Municipal Inc A	INTAX	B-	(800) 345-6611	3.96	B /7.9	0.89 /43	4.56 /96	4.11 /94	C- /3.5	72	10
MUN	Lord Abbett Tax Free Natl A	LANSX	B-	(888) 522-2388	11.12	B /7.9	0.36 /34	4.41 /95	3.85 /92	C- /3.3	58	11
MUN	Dreyfus Municipal Bond	DRTAX	B-	(800) 645-6561	11.58	B /7.8	-0.09 /16	3.68 /90	3.08 /81	C- /3.6	29	8
MUN	Madison Tax Free National Y	GTFHX	B-	(800) 877-6089	10.77	C+ /6.9	-0.47 /10	3.04 /83	2.31 /66	C /4.6	26	20
MUN	Schwab Tax-Free Bond Fund	SWNTX	B-	(800) 407-0256	11.57	C+ /6.1	-0.47 /10	2.53 /74	2.41 /69	C+ /5.6	19	9
MUN	Putnam Tax Exempt Income A	PTAEX	B-	(800) 225-1581	8.50	C+ /5.9	0.37 /34	3.55 /88	2.98 /80	C+ /5.9	62	15
MUN	Frost Municipal Bond Inv	FAUMX	B-	(866) 777-7818	10.34	C /4.6	-0.70 / 7	1.81 /57	1.63 /50	B /7.6	15	15
MUN	Glenmede Intermediate Muni Port	GTCMX	B-	(800) 442-8299	10.89	C /4.3	-0.13 /15	1.58 /51	1.47 /46	B /7.8	15	6
MUN	Lord Abbett AMT Free Municipal	LATAX	C+	(888) 522-2388	15.72	B /7.6	0.40 /35	4.21 /94	3.37 /86	C- /3.3	48	7
MUN	PIMCO Municipal Bond A	PMLAX	C+	(800) 426-0107	9.63	B- /7.4	0.71 /40	3.94 /92	3.47 /87	C- /3.6	48	2
MUN	Eaton Vance AMT-Free Muni	ETMBX	C+	(800) 262-1122	9.03	C+ /6.9	0.41 /35	4.38 /95	3.65 /89	C- /4.1	72	12
MUN	Deutsche Managed Municipal Bd A	SMLAX	C+	(800) 728-3337	9.04	C+ /6.7	0.11 /25	3.67 /90	3.22 /84	C- /4.1	43	29
MUN	Dreyfus Intermediate Muni Bd	DITEX	C+	(800) 645-6561	13.53	C+ /6.3	-0.48 /10	2.66 /76	2.39 /68	C /4.7	16	6
MUN	Northern Intermed Tax Exempt	NOITX	C+	(800) 595-9111	10.39	C+ /6.0	-0.32 /12	2.46 /73	2.20 /63	C /4.9	14	19
MUN	WA Managed Municipals A	SHMMX	C+	(877) 534-4627	16.20	C+ /6.0	0.29 /32	3.70 /90	3.19 /83	C /4.9	61	10
MUN	American Funds T/E Bd of America	AFTEX	C+	(800) 421-0180	12.80	C+ /5.9	0.28 /32	3.50 /88	3.32 /85	C /5.2	55	38
MUN	Commerce National T/F Intm Bd	CFNLX	C+	(800) 995-6365	19.29	C+ /5.8	-0.16 /15	2.34 /70	2.21 /64	C /5.0	14	18
MUN	BNY Mellon NY Int TxEx Inv	MNYIX	C+	(800) 645-6561	10.99	C /5.5	-0.35 /12	2.28 /69	1.83 /55	C+ /5.8	15	10
MUN	Eaton Vance CT Municipal Income	ETCTX	C+	(800) 262-1122	10.13	C /5.4	0.48 /37	3.55 /88	2.52 /71	C+ /6.0	65	3
MUN	Franklin New Jersey TaxFree Inc A	FRNJX	C+	(800) 342-5236	11.45	C /5.0	1.43 /51	3.04 /83	2.01 /59	C+ /6.7	59	29
MUN	WA Intermediate Term Muni A	SBLTX	C+	(877) 534-4627	6.38	C /4.5	-0.44 /10	2.53 /74	2.15 /62	B- /7.2	29	10
MUN	Eaton Vance MD Municipal Income	ETMDX	C+	(800) 262-1122	8.82	C- /4.2	0.52 /37	2.90 /80	2.48 /70	B /7.7	58	13
MUN	Eaton Vance Nat Ltd Mat Muni Inc	EXNAX	C+	(800) 262-1122	9.85	C- /4.2	-0.48 /10	2.32 /69	2.08 /61	B- /7.2	23	3
MUN	Hartford Municipal Real Return A	HTNAX	C+	(888) 843-7824	9.19	C- /4.1	2.56 /62	2.25 /68	1.92 /57	B- /7.2	49	N/A
MUN	Vanguard Lmtd-Term Tax-Exempt	VMLTX	C+	(800) 662-7447	10.93	C- /3.3	0.05 /21	0.98 /35	1.10 /37	B+ /8.8	22	9

99 Pct = Best
0 Pct = Worst

Fund Type	Fund Name	Ticker Symbol	Overall Investment Rating	Phone	Net Asset Value As of 2/28/17	PERFORMANCE Perform-ance Rating/Pts	Annualized Total Return Through 2/28/17 1Yr / Pct	3Yr / Pct	5Yr / Pct	RISK Risk Rating/Pts	FUND MGR Mgr. Quality Pct	Mgr. Tenure (Years)
MUS	Saturna Idaho Tax-Exempt	NITEX	A+	(800) 728-8762	5.35	B+ /8.3	1.63 /53	3.60 /89	2.67 /74	B- / 7.1	70	22
MUS	T Rowe Price MD Tax Free Bd	MDXBX	A+	(800) 638-5660	10.68	B /8.0	0.73 /41	3.64 /89	3.20 /83	C+ / 6.7	69	17
MUS	T Rowe Price VA Tax-Free Bond	PRVAX	A+	(800) 638-5660	11.90	B /8.0	0.56 /38	3.71 /90	3.06 /81	C+ / 5.9	66	20
MUS	Dupree AL Tax Free Income	DUALX	A+	(800) 866-0614	12.20	B- /7.5	0.50 /37	3.36 /86	3.01 /80	C+ / 6.9	64	16
MUS	Lee Fnl Hawaii-Muni Bond Inv	SURFX	A+		11.03	B- /7.1	-0.09 /16	3.13 /84	2.81 /76	B / 7.6	65	2
MUS	Colorado Bond Shares	HICOX	A+	(800) 572-0069	8.93	C+ /6.6	2.01 /57	3.88 /92	3.71 /90	B+ / 8.8	89	27
MUS	Oppeneheimer Rochester PA Muni	OPATX	A	(888) 470-0862	10.40	A+ /9.7	5.37 /75	6.05 /99	3.84 /91	C- / 3.2	91	15
MUS	T Rowe Price NY Tax Free Bd	PRNYX	A	(800) 638-5660	11.53	B+ /8.3	0.33 /33	3.95 /92	3.24 /84	C / 4.8	65	17
MUS	Dupree TN Tax-Free Income	TNTIX	A	(800) 866-0614	11.34	C+ /6.7	-0.12 /16	2.91 /80	2.64 /73	C+ / 6.7	44	13
MUS	Dupree KY Tax Free Income	KYTFX	A	(800) 866-0614	7.70	C+ /6.6	0.11 /25	2.73 /77	2.56 /72	C+ / 6.8	33	18
MUS	Oppenheimer Rochester CA Muni	OPCAX	A-	(888) 470-0862	8.27	A /9.3	4.11 /71	5.61 /98	5.51 /99	C- / 3.3	86	15
MUS	Vanguard OH Long-Term	VOHIX	A-	(800) 662-7447	12.37	B+ /8.9	0.75 /41	4.40 /95	3.72 /90	C- / 3.7	64	9
MUS	USAA California Bond Fund	USCBX	A-	(800) 382-8722	10.93	B+ /8.6	0.38 /35	4.14 /94	4.11 /94	C- / 4.0	73	N/A
MUS	Vanguard PA Long-Term	VPAIX	A-	(800) 662-7447	11.37	B+ /8.6	0.57 /38	4.17 /94	3.49 /87	C- / 3.9	61	6
MUS	Vanguard NY Long-Term	VNYTX	A-	(800) 662-7447	11.59	B+ /8.6	0.30 /32	4.24 /94	3.53 /88	C- / 3.9	63	4
MUS	Dupree MS Tax Free Income	DUMSX	A-	(800) 866-0614	12.00	B /8.0	0.36 /34	3.73 /90	3.13 /82	C / 4.9	63	17
MUS	T Rowe Price NJ Tax-Free Bond	NJTFX	A-	(800) 638-5660	11.87	B /7.9	0.41 /35	3.73 /90	3.23 /84	C / 4.7	59	17
MUS	Fidelity PA Muni Inc	FPXTX	A-	(800) 544-8544	11.01	B /7.8	0.27 /31	3.64 /89	3.15 /82	C / 5.1	59	15
MUS	AB Municipal Income II VA A	AVAAX	A-	(800) 221-5672	11.04	C+ /6.9	0.48 /37	3.77 /90	2.73 /75	C+ / 6.0	68	22
MUS	Franklin PA Tax-Free Inc A	FRPAX	A-	(800) 342-5236	10.12	C+ /6.6	1.61 /53	3.79 /91	2.61 /73	C+ / 6.4	76	31
MUS	WA Pennsylvania Municipals A	SBPAX	A-	(877) 534-4627	12.77	C+ /6.5	0.97 /44	3.85 /91	2.54 /71	C+ / 6.8	75	10
MUS	Franklin Alabama Tax-Free Inc A	FRALX	A-	(800) 342-5236	11.16	C+ /6.3	1.67 /54	3.63 /89	2.76 /75	C+ / 6.8	74	28
MUS	Madison Tax Free Virginia Y	GTVAX	A-	(800) 877-6089	11.41	C+ /6.2	-0.49 /10	2.61 /76	1.97 /58	B- / 7.0	29	20
MUS	Oppenheimer Rochester Muni A	RMUNX	B+	(888) 470-0862	14.88	A+ /9.7	6.99 /81	5.99 /98	3.99 /93	D / 2.1	87	15
MUS	Oppenheimer Rochester AMT-Fr	OPNYX	B+	(888) 470-0862	11.08	A /9.3	4.42 /72	5.65 /98	3.89 /92	D+ / 2.5	84	15
MUS ●	Oppenheimer Rochester Ohio Muni	OROHX	B+	(888) 470-0862	10.06	A- /9.0	4.02 /71	5.23 /97	4.29 /95	C- / 3.1	81	11
MUS ●	Oppenheimer Rochester NC Muni	OPNCX	B+	(888) 470-0862	10.89	B+ /8.8	4.13 /71	4.95 /97	2.87 /78	C- / 3.1	86	11
MUS	Northern CA T/E Bond	NCATX	B+	(800) 595-9111	11.49	B+ /8.5	-0.45 /10	4.32 /95	3.97 /93	C- / 3.4	57	20
MUS	T Rowe Price CA Tax Free Bond	PRXCX	B+	(800) 638-5660	11.35	B+ /8.3	-0.12 /16	4.09 /93	3.75 /91	C- / 3.6	54	14
MUS	Fidelity AZ Muni Income Fd	FSAZX	B+	(800) 544-8544	11.91	B /8.1	-0.17 /15	3.91 /92	3.29 /85	C- / 4.0	53	7
MUS	Sit MN Tax Free Income	SMTFX	B+	(800) 332-5580	10.29	B /7.7	0.18 /28	3.55 /88	3.13 /82	C / 5.0	57	24
MUS	Franklin Colorado Tax-Free Inc A	FRCOX	B+	(800) 342-5236	11.66	C+ /6.7	1.30 /49	3.88 /92	2.87 /77	C+ / 6.1	74	25
MUS	Fidelity MN Muni Inc	FIMIX	B+	(800) 544-8544	11.48	C+ /6.7	-0.06 /17	2.83 /79	2.34 /67	C+ / 5.8	28	7
MUS	Franklin Virginia Tax-Free Inc A	FRVAX	B+	(800) 342-5236	11.31	C+ /5.9	1.49 /51	3.37 /86	2.30 /66	B- / 7.0	69	30
MUS	Oppenheimer Rochester LT CA	OLCAX	B+	(888) 470-0862	3.20	C+ /5.8	2.29 /60	2.56 /75	2.55 /71	B- / 7.2	59	13
MUS	MFS MD Municipal Bond A	MFSMX	B+	(800) 225-2606	10.77	C+ /5.7	0.61 /39	3.48 /88	2.35 /67	B- / 7.0	66	18
MUS	Franklin Kentucky Tax-Free Inc A	FRKYX	B+	(800) 342-5236	11.01	C+ /5.6	0.85 /43	3.38 /86	2.62 /73	B- / 7.5	72	21
MUS	1919 Maryland Tax-Free Income A	LMMDX	B+	(844) 828-1919	15.92	C /4.6	1.39 /50	2.72 /77	2.10 /61	B+ / 8.3	73	10
MUS ●	Oppenheimer Rochester AZ Muni	ORAZX	B	(888) 470-0862	10.50	B+ /8.7	6.14 /78	4.48 /96	2.83 /77	D+ / 2.8	87	11
MUS	Vanguard CA Long-Term	VCITX	B	(800) 662-7447	11.89	B+ /8.6	-0.02 /17	4.31 /95	3.95 /93	D+ / 2.8	36	6
MUS	BlackRock NY Muni Oppty Inv A	MENKX	B	(800) 441-7762	11.03	B+ /8.4	2.08 /58	5.04 /97	3.75 /91	C- / 3.1	74	11
MUS ●	Oppenheimer Rochester MA Muni	ORMAX	B	(888) 470-0862	10.28	B+ /8.3	3.50 /68	4.66 /96	3.05 /81	C- / 3.6	83	11
MUS	Fidelity OH Muni Inc	FOHFX	B	(800) 544-8544	11.95	B /8.2	-0.22 /14	4.08 /93	3.40 /86	C- / 3.5	48	1
MUS	Dreyfus NY Tax Exempt Bond	DRNYX	B	(800) 645-6561	14.67	B /7.7	0.16 /27	3.51 /88	2.41 /69	C- / 4.2	36	8
MUS	Fidelity MD Muni Income Fd	SMDMX	B	(800) 544-8544	11.18	B /7.6	-0.12 /16	3.51 /88	2.60 /72	C- / 4.1	33	15
MUS	T Rowe Price GA Tax-Free Bd	GTFBX	B	(800) 638-5660	11.39	B- /7.5	-0.28 /13	3.51 /88	2.98 /80	C / 4.6	N/A	20
MUS	Fidelity MI Muni Inc	FMHTX	B	(800) 544-8544	11.99	B- /7.5	-0.48 /10	3.54 /88	2.89 /78	C / 4.5	47	1
MUS	Northern AZ Tax Exempt	NOAZX	B	(800) 595-9111	10.53	B- /7.4	0.01 /18	3.28 /85	2.95 /79	C / 4.3	28	18
MUS	BlackRock CA Muni Opptys A	MECMX	B	(800) 441-7762	12.34	B- /7.3	1.12 /46	4.27 /95	3.54 /88	C / 4.6	75	24
MUS	MFS PA Municipal Bond A	MFPAX	B	(800) 225-2606	10.19	B- /7.1	0.87 /43	4.24 /94	3.11 /82	C / 4.9	73	18
MUS ●	Oppenheimer Rochester MN Muni	OPAMX	B	(888) 470-0862	12.73	B- /7.0	0.71 /40	4.39 /95	3.92 /92	C / 5.1	78	11
MUS	Vanguard CA Interm-Term T-E Inv	VCAIX	B	(800) 662-7447	11.62	B- /7.0	-0.33 /12	3.00 /82	3.00 /80	C / 4.8	25	4

● Denotes fund is closed to new investors

Fund Type	Fund Name	Ticker Symbol	Overall Investment Rating	Phone	Net Asset Value As of 2/28/17	PERFORMANCE Performance Rating/Pts	Annualized Total Return Through 2/28/17			RISK Risk Rating/Pts	FUND MGR Mgr. Quality Pct	Mgr. Tenure (Years)
	99 Pct = Best *0 Pct = Worst*						1Yr / Pct	3Yr / Pct	5Yr / Pct			
USL ●	Schwab Total Bond Market Fd	SWLBX	C-	(800) 407-0256	9.44	C /4.3	1.07 /40	2.39 /50	1.95 /41	C+ / 5.7	70	19
USL	WesMark Govt Bond Fund	WMBDX	C-	(800) 864-1013	9.86	D+ /2.7	-0.87 / 5	1.51 /35	0.97 /27	B / 7.8	56	19
USL	Vanguard Long-Term Govt Bd Idx	VLGSX	D-	(800) 662-7447	25.22	B- /7.1	-4.33 / 0	6.15 /93	3.34 /63	E- / 0.1	28	4
USL	Dupree Interm Government Bond	DPIGX	D-	(800) 866-0614	10.25	C /4.8	-0.90 / 5	3.10 /63	2.08 /43	C- / 3.6	76	18
USL	American Century VP Infl Prot II	AIPTX	D-	(800) 345-6488	10.24	C- /3.9	4.26 /63	1.39 /33	0.48 /21	C- / 3.4	36	10
USL	HC Capital US Govt FI Sec HC	HCUSX	D-	(800) 242-9596	9.79	D+ /2.8	-1.18 / 3	1.67 /38	0.63 /23	C / 5.4	37	N/A
USL	Rydex Govt Lg Bd 1.2x Strgy A	RYABX	E+	(800) 820-0888	51.50	C /5.0	-7.67 / 0	6.91 /96	3.81 /70	E- / 0.0	1	23
USL	PIMCO Long Term US Govt A	PFGAX	E+	(800) 426-0107	6.02	C /4.9	-3.95 / 0	5.46 /88	2.99 /58	E- / 0.1	14	10
USL	Loomis Sayles Infl Prot Sec Inst	LSGSX	E+	(800) 633-3330	10.49	C- /3.4	3.03 /57	1.26 /31	0.40 /20	D+ / 2.7	26	5
USL	Deutsche Global Inflation A	TIPAX	E	(800) 728-3337	10.10	D+ /2.3	2.88 /56	1.44 /34	-0.07 / 4	D+ / 2.3	22	7
USL ●	SunAmerica 2020 High Watermark	HWKAX	E	(800) 858-8850	8.75	E- /0.2	-0.87 / 5	1.15 /30	0.59 /22	C / 5.4	25	13

Fund Type	Fund Name	Ticker Symbol	Overall Investment Rating	Phone	Net Asset Value As of 2/28/17	Perform- ance Rating/Pts	Annualized Total Return Through 2/28/17			Risk Rating/Pts	Mgr. Quality Pct	Mgr. Tenure (Years)
							1Yr / Pct	3Yr / Pct	5Yr / Pct			
USS	Principal Preferred Sec A	PPSAX	A+	(800) 222-5852	10.23	A- /9.0	9.14 /77	6.30 /93	7.09 /96	C /4.5	97	15
USS	Morgan Stanley Mortgage Sec Tr A	MTGAX	A+	(800) 869-6397	8.49	C+ /6.8	7.28 /73	4.23 /78	4.92 /83	B /8.0	93	3
USS	Guggenheim Investment Grade Bd	SIUSX	A+	(800) 820-0888	18.27	C+ /6.5	6.20 /71	4.14 /77	4.59 /80	B /8.0	93	5
USS	Nuveen Preferred Securities A	NPSAX	A	(800) 257-8787	17.22	A- /9.0	11.35 /82	6.19 /93	8.02 /98	C- /4.0	98	11
USS	AMG Mgrs Amundi Intmd Gov N	MGIDX	B	(800) 548-4539	10.67	C- /4.2	0.47 /33	2.37 /49	2.13 /44	B+ /8.4	80	25
USS	BMO Mortgage Income Y	MRGIX	B	(800) 236-3863	9.16	C- /4.2	0.70 /36	2.38 /50	1.88 /40	B /8.1	78	N/A
USS	MSIF Trust Core Plus Fix Inc A	MFXAX	B-	(800) 354-8185	10.92	B+ /8.6	12.57 /84	5.58 /89	5.13 /85	D+ /2.4	95	6
USS	USAA Income Fund	USAIX	B-	(800) 382-8722	13.02	C+ /6.7	6.30 /71	3.24 /65	3.45 /65	C /4.8	84	1
USS	Columbia US Government	AUGAX	B-	(800) 345-6611	5.42	C- /3.9	2.34 /52	2.60 /54	2.65 /52	B+ /8.5	83	8
USS	Payden Kravitz Cash Bal Plan Ret	PKCRX	B-	(888) 409-8007	9.87	C- /3.5	4.47 /64	0.94 /27	1.29 /31	B+ /8.8	72	N/A
USS	Sit US Government Securities	SNGVX	B-	(800) 332-5580	10.94	C- /3.0	0.16 /24	1.41 /33	0.88 /26	A /9.3	74	30
USS	Touchstone Ut Sh Dr Fxd Inc Z	TSDOX	B-	(800) 543-0407	9.31	D+ /2.6	1.50 /45	0.83 /25	0.91 /26	A+ /9.9	69	9
USS	TCW Core Fixed Income N	TGFNX	C+	(800) 386-3829	10.91	C- /3.8	1.11 /41	1.98 /43	2.42 /48	B /7.6	66	7
USS	Federated Govt Income Trust Inst	FICMX	C+	(800) 341-7400	10.16	C- /3.7	0.13 /23	1.96 /42	1.55 /35	B+ /8.4	74	17
USS	WA Mortgage Backed Securities A	SGVAX	C+	(877) 534-4627	10.53	C- /3.5	1.25 /42	2.87 /59	3.57 /67	B /8.0	84	4
USS	Invesco Quality Income A	VKMGX	C+	(800) 959-4246	12.08	C- /3.3	1.19 /42	2.83 /58	2.48 /49	B /8.1	83	7
USS	Eaton Vance Sh Duration Gov Inc	EALDX	C+	(800) 262-1122	8.28	D+ /2.8	2.26 /51	1.47 /34	1.32 /32	A /9.3	83	3
USS	Oppenheimer Limited-Term Bond A	OUSGX	C+	(888) 470-0862	4.54	D+ /2.6	2.79 /55	1.33 /32	1.62 /36	A- /9.2	74	8
USS	RidgeWorth Seix US Gvt Sec US	SIGVX	C+	(888) 784-3863	10.02	D /2.0	0.87 /38	0.50 /21	0.57 /22	A+ /9.9	61	3
USS	AMG Mgrs Amundi Short DurGov	MGSDX	C+	(800) 548-4539	9.63	D /2.0	1.25 /42	0.46 /20	0.62 /23	A+ /9.8	61	25
USS	Eaton Vance Core Plus Bond A	EBABX	C	(800) 262-1122	11.69	B+ /8.6	16.06 /90	4.91 /84	3.78 /70	D /1.6	94	8
USS	Glenmede Core Fixed Income Port	GTCGX	C	(800) 442-8299	10.98	C- /3.7	0.51 /33	1.99 /43	1.62 /36	B /7.6	65	18
USS	Hartford US Govt Sec HLS Fd IA	HAUSX	C	(888) 843-7824	10.35	C- /3.4	0.19 /25	1.78 /39	1.53 /35	B /7.8	61	5
USS ●	Schwab Short-Term Bond Market	SWBDX	C	(800) 407-0256	9.26	D+ /2.5	0.67 /36	0.96 /27	0.96 /27	A- /9.0	51	13
USS	Vanguard Short-Term Federal Inv	VSGBX	C	(800) 662-7447	10.71	D+ /2.4	0.50 /33	0.94 /27	0.82 /25	A- /9.2	57	2
USS	DFA Short-Term Government Inst	DFFGX	C	(800) 984-9472	10.62	D+ /2.3	-0.14 /15	0.98 /27	0.87 /26	B+ /8.9	50	29
USS	SEI Daily Inc Tr-Sh Dur Gov Bd F	TCSGX	C	(800) 342-5734	10.43	D /2.0	0.37 /30	0.62 /22	0.58 /22	A /9.4	N/A	14
USS	Vanguard Short-Term Gvt Bd Idx	VSBSX	C	(800) 662-7447	20.26	D /1.9	0.25 /27	0.57 /21	0.53 /22	A /9.5	47	4
USS	Sterling Capital Short Dur Bd A	BSGAX	C	(800) 228-1872	8.72	D /1.9	1.84 /48	0.87 /26	1.25 /31	A /9.5	63	6
USS	LWAS DFA Two Year Government	DFYGX	C	(800) 984-9472	9.85	D /1.8	0.38 /31	0.41 /20	0.34 /20	A+ /9.7	42	16
USS	Wells Fargo Core Plus Bond A	STYAX	C-	(800) 222-8222	12.43	C+ /5.8	6.10 /70	3.74 /72	3.22 /61	C /4.4	87	12
USS	PACE Mtg Backed Sec Fixed Inc	PFXAX	C-	(888) 793-8637	12.82	D+ /2.4	1.29 /43	2.26 /48	1.74 /38	B /8.2	77	4
USS	Delaware Limited-Term Diver Inc A	DTRIX	C-	(800) 523-1918	8.48	D /2.1	1.81 /47	1.30 /32	0.76 /24	A- /9.0	66	18
USS	Deutsche Strategic Govt Sec A	KUSAX	C-	(800) 728-3337	7.91	D /2.1	0.35 /30	1.66 /37	1.05 /28	B+ /8.8	75	3
USS	Commerce Short Term Govt	CFSTX	C-	(800) 995-6365	17.17	D /2.0	0.40 /31	0.62 /22	0.80 /25	A- /9.1	36	23
USS	Access Cap Community Invs A	ACASX	C-	(800) 422-2766	9.03	D /2.0	-0.06 /17	1.95 /42	1.62 /36	B+ /8.6	75	11
USS	Victory INCORE Fund For Income	IPFIX	C-	(800) 539-3863	9.39	D /2.0	-0.38 /11	1.42 /34	1.02 /28	B+ /8.5	60	11
USS	Homestead Short Term Govt Sec	HOSGX	C-	(800) 258-3030	5.17	D /1.9	-0.07 /16	0.64 /22	0.60 /23	A- /9.1	37	22
USS	Payden US Government Adv	PYUWX	C-	(888) 409-8007	10.48	D /1.9	-0.10 /16	0.65 /22	0.58 /22	A- /9.0	34	N/A
USS	Fidelity Limited Term Government	FFXSX	C-	(800) 544-8544	9.94	D /1.9	-0.38 /11	0.70 /23	0.66 /23	B+ /8.9	32	9
USS	Northern Short-Int US Govt	NSIUX	C-	(800) 595-9111	9.82	D /1.8	-0.52 / 9	0.66 /23	0.43 /21	B+ /8.7	28	4
USS	J Hancock Sh Tm Govt Inc NAV		C-	(800) 257-3336	9.47	D /1.7	-0.33 /12	0.50 /21	0.42 /21	A- /9.1	32	N/A
USS	Federated USG Sec:1-3yrs Y	FSGTX	C-	(800) 341-7400	10.34	D- /1.4	0.49 /33	0.21 /17	0.07 /13	A+ /9.6	31	4
USS	BNY Mellon ST US Gov Sec M	MPSUX	C-	(800) 645-6561	11.71	D- /1.3	-0.09 /16	0.27 /18	0.18 /18	A /9.5	30	17
USS	Morgan Stanley US Govt Sec Tr A	USGAX	D+	(800) 869-6397	8.70	D+ /2.5	1.11 /41	2.36 /49	1.93 /41	B /7.8	76	5
USS	Fidelity Intermediate Government	FSTGX	D+	(800) 544-8544	10.47	D+ /2.3	-0.69 / 7	1.18 /30	1.05 /28	B /7.9	33	9
USS	Federated Fund for US Govt Sec A	FUSGX	D+	(800) 341-7400	7.39	D /1.7	0.27 /28	1.88 /41	1.50 /34	B+ /8.4	72	14
USS	Thornburg Limited Term US Govt A	LTUSX	D+	(800) 847-0200	13.05	D /1.6	-0.17 /15	0.91 /26	0.71 /24	A- /9.0	48	10
USS	Sentinel Low Duration Bond A	SSIGX	D+	(800) 282-3863	8.44	D /1.6	2.61 /54	0.28 /18	0.19 /18	B+ /8.6	42	5
USS	Dreyfus Ultra Short Income Z	DSIGX	D+	(800) 645-6561	10.08	E+ /0.9	0.66 /36	-0.03 / 5	0.04 /10	A+ /9.8	35	1
USS	SunAmerica VAL Co I Gov Sec Fd	VCGSX	D	(800) 858-8850	10.49	C- /3.5	-0.70 / 7	2.10 /45	1.44 /33	C+ /5.6	59	6
USS	Northern US Government	NOUGX	D	(800) 595-9111	9.65	D /2.1	-1.13 / 3	1.15 /30	0.70 /24	B /7.7	28	4

● Denotes fund is closed to new investors

Fund Type	Fund Name	Ticker Symbol	Overall Investment Rating	Phone	Net Asset Value As of 2/28/17	Perform-ance Rating/Pts	Annualized Total Return Through 2/28/17			Risk Rating/Pts	Mgr. Quality Pct	Mgr. Tenure (Years)
	99 Pct = Best *0 Pct = Worst*						1Yr / Pct	3Yr / Pct	5Yr / Pct			
USA	Vanguard GNMA Inv	VFIIX	B+	(800) 662-7447	10.54	C /4.6	0.67 /36	2.57 /53	1.96 /41	B+ / 8.3	81	11
USA	SEI Daily Inc Tr-GNMA Bond F	SEGMX	B	(800) 342-5734	10.50	C /4.4	0.18 /25	2.51 /52	1.95 /41	B / 8.2	80	16
USA	Fidelity GNMA Fund	FGMNX	B	(800) 544-8544	11.44	C /4.3	0.69 /36	2.33 /49	1.95 /41	B+ / 8.5	80	13
USA	T Rowe Price GNMA	PRGMX	B	(800) 638-5660	9.32	C- /4.0	1.02 /40	2.03 /44	1.66 /37	B+ / 8.7	78	9
USA	Payden GNMA Adv	PYGWX	B-	(888) 409-8007	9.57	C- /3.8	0.33 /30	2.07 /44	1.49 /34	B+ / 8.4	77	N/A
USA	Schwab GNMA	SWGSX	C+	(800) 407-0256	9.96	C- /3.6	-0.20 /15	2.02 /44	1.51 /35	B+ / 8.3	74	14
USA	USAA Government Securities Fund	USGNX	C+	(800) 382-8722	9.80	C- /3.2	-0.09 /16	1.68 /38	1.37 /33	B+ / 8.5	67	N/A
USA	Voya GNMA Income A	LEXNX	C+	(800) 992-0180	8.45	C- /3.1	0.53 /34	2.23 /47	1.89 /40	B+ / 8.7	80	8
USA	PIMCO GNMA A	PAGNX	C-	(800) 426-0107	11.14	D /2.2	0.65 /36	1.97 /43	1.57 /36	B+ / 8.6	76	5
USA	Deutsche GNMA A	GGGGX	C-	(800) 728-3337	13.82	D /2.0	0.44 /32	1.58 /36	1.01 /27	B+ / 8.8	74	2
USA	American Century Ginnie Mae A	BGNAX	D-	(800) 345-6488	10.55	E /0.5	-0.22 /14	1.43 /34	1.11 /29	B+ / 8.6	65	11
USA	Dreyfus GNMA Fund A	GPGAX	D-	(800) 782-6620	15.00	E /0.5	-0.03 /17	1.43 /34	1.16 /29	B+ / 8.6	65	2
USA	ProFunds-US Government Plus	GVPSX	E+	(888) 776-3637	49.04	C /5.0	-8.64 / 0	5.62 /89	1.47 /34	E- / 0.0	1	8

Fund Type	Fund Name	Ticker Symbol	Overall Investment Rating	Phone	Net Asset Value As of 2/28/17	Performance Rating/Pts	1Yr / Pct	3Yr / Pct	5Yr / Pct	Risk Rating/Pts	Mgr. Quality Pct	Mgr. Tenure (Years)
US	RidgeWorth Seix Ltd Dur I	SAMLX	C+	(888) 784-3863	9.93	D+ /2.5	1.74 /47	0.68 /23	0.65 /23	A+ / 9.8	67	15
US	WA Short-Term Bond A	SBSTX	C	(877) 534-4627	3.87	D /2.1	2.41 /52	0.98 /27	1.29 /31	A / 9.4	68	3
US	Vanguard Short-Term Treasury Inv	VFISX	C	(800) 662-7447	10.65	D /2.1	0.35 /30	0.71 /23	0.60 /23	A- / 9.2	53	9
US	GMO US Treasury	GUSTX	C		25.00	D /1.6	0.49 /33	0.25 /18	0.20 /18	A+ / 9.9	52	3
US	Vanguard Extnd Durtn Trea Idx Inst	VEDTX	C-	(800) 662-7447	33.95	A- /9.1	-6.63 / 0	9.40 /99	4.53 /79	E- / 0.0	69	4
US	Invesco Sh Dur Infl Pro A	LMTAX	C-	(800) 959-4246	10.58	D /1.9	2.04 /49	0.89 /26	0.53 /22	B+ / 8.9	61	8
US	Fidelity S/T TyBd In Inv	FSBIX	C-	(800) 544-8544	10.39	D /1.9	-0.25 /14	0.72 /23	0.62 /23	B+ / 8.8	36	3
US	US Global Inv Govt Ultra-Short	UGSDX	C-	(800) 873-8637	2.00	D /1.6	-0.03 /17	0.39 /20	0.25 /19	A- / 9.1	36	28
US	Dreyfus US Treasury Intermediate	DRGIX	D	(800) 645-6561	13.21	D /1.6	-1.04 / 4	0.67 /23	0.41 /20	B / 8.0	23	9
US	Permanent Portfolio Short-Tm Trs I	PRTBX	D	(800) 531-5142	64.70	E /0.3	-0.14 /15	-0.45 / 4	-0.51 / 3	A+ / 9.9	20	14
US	Vanguard Long-Term Treasury Inv	VUSTX	D-	(800) 662-7447	11.95	B- /7.0	-4.43 / 0	6.08 /92	3.23 /61	E- / 0.1	58	2
US	Fidelity Lg-T Tre Bd In Inv	FLBIX	D-	(800) 544-8544	12.80	C+ /6.8	-4.66 / 0	6.00 /92	3.19 /60	E- / 0.1	53	3
US	Wasatch Hoisington US Treasury	WHOSX	D-	(800) 551-1700	15.87	C+ /6.8	-5.86 / 0	7.03 /96	3.25 /62	E- / 0.0	58	21
US	American Century Zero Cpn 2020	BTTTX	D-	(800) 345-6488	103.15	C- /3.9	-0.44 /10	2.29 /48	1.75 /38	C- / 4.2	65	11
US	JPMorgan Treasury and Agency A	OTABX	D-	(800) 480-4111	9.34	E /0.3	-0.27 /13	0.20 /16	0.12 /16	A- / 9.2	26	N/A
US	Dreyfus US Treasury Long Term	DRGBX	E+	(800) 645-6561	18.40	C+ /6.1	-4.72 / 0	5.29 /87	2.53 /50	E- / 0.2	37	9
US	T Rowe Price US Treas Long-Term	PRULX	E+	(800) 638-5660	12.36	C+ /6.1	-4.70 / 0	5.33 /87	2.67 /52	E- / 0.2	31	14
US	DFA Infltn Protected Sec Port Inst	DIPSX	E+	(800) 984-9472	11.86	C /4.3	3.02 /57	1.85 /40	0.74 /24	D+ / 2.3	38	11
US	Harbor Real Return Inst	HARRX	E+	(800) 422-1050	9.42	C- /4.1	5.04 /67	1.30 /32	0.53 /22	D / 2.2	31	12
US	T Rowe Price Infla-Protect Bond	PRIPX	E+	(800) 638-5660	11.89	C- /3.5	2.49 /53	1.42 /34	0.37 /20	C- / 3.1	30	15
US	Fidelity Intrm Treasury Inv	FIBIX	E+	(800) 544-8544	10.70	C- /3.4	-2.09 / 1	2.33 /49	1.56 /35	D+ / 2.4	35	3
US	Vanguard Interm-Term Treasury	VFITX	E+	(800) 662-7447	11.14	C- /3.2	-1.26 / 3	1.93 /42	1.40 /33	C- / 3.9	47	2
US	Northern US Treasury Index	BTIAX	E+	(800) 637-1380	21.39	D+ /2.9	-1.43 / 2	1.81 /40	1.22 /30	C- / 4.2	37	8
US	Columbia US Treasury Index A	LUTAX	E+	(800) 345-6611	11.02	D+ /2.5	-1.49 / 2	1.56 /36	0.99 /27	C- / 4.2	28	7
US	T Rowe Price US Treas Intmdt	PRTIX	E+	(800) 638-5660	5.74	D+ /2.5	-1.73 / 1	1.58 /36	1.00 /27	C- / 3.5	25	10
US	Hartford Inflation Plus A	HIPAX	E+	(888) 843-7824	10.90	D- /1.2	3.56 /60	0.86 /25	-0.19 / 4	C / 5.0	30	2
US	Direxion Mo 7-10 Year Tr Bl 2X Inv	DXKLX	E	(800) 851-0511	34.14	D+ /2.4	-8.47 / 0	3.22 /65	1.44 /33	E- / 0.2	1	11
US	American Century MA Real Rtn A	ASIDX	E-	(800) 345-6488	9.68	E- /0.2	9.50 /78	-1.49 / 2	-1.47 / 2	D / 2.0	2	7
US	Direxion Mo 7-10 Year Tr Br 2X Inv	DXKSX	E-	(800) 851-0511	30.38	E- /0.0	3.05 /57	-8.69 / 0	-7.30 / 0	E- / 0.2	0	13

● Denotes fund is closed to new investors

Appendix

What is a Mutual Fund?

Picking individual stocks is difficult and buying individual bonds can be expensive. Mutual funds were introduced to allow the small investor to participate in the stock and bond market for just a small initial investment. Mutual funds are pools of stocks or bonds that are managed by investment professionals. First, an investment company organizes the fund and collects the money from investors. The company then takes that money and pays a portfolio manager to invest it in stocks, bonds, money market instruments and other types of securities.

Most funds fit within one of two main categories, open-ended funds or closed-end funds. Open-ended funds issue new shares when investors put in money and redeem shares when investors withdraw money. The price of a share is determined by dividing the total net assets of the fund by the number of shares outstanding.

On the other hand, closed-end funds issue a fixed number of shares in an initial public offering, trading thereafter in the open market like a stock. Open-end funds are the most common type of mutual fund. Investing in either class of funds means you own a share of the portfolio, so you participate in the fund's gains and losses.

There are more than 20,000 different mutual funds, each with a stated investment objective. Here are descriptions for five of the most popular types of funds:

Stock funds: A mutual fund which invests mainly in stocks. These funds are more actively traded than other more conservative funds. The stocks chosen may vary widely according to the fund's investment strategy.

Bond funds: A mutual fund which invests in bonds, in an effort to provide stable income while preserving principal as much as possible. These funds invest in medium- to long-term bonds issued by corporations and governments.

Index funds: A mutual fund that aims to match the performance of a specific index, such as the S&P 500. Index funds tend to have fewer expenses than other funds because portfolio decisions are automatic and transactions are infrequent.

Balanced funds: A mutual fund that buys a combination of stocks and bonds, in order to supply both income and capital growth while ensuring a minimal amount of risk for investors.

Money market funds: An open-end mutual fund which invests only in stable, short-term securities. The fund's value remains at a constant $1 per share, but only those administered by banks are government insured.

Investing in a mutual fund has several advantages over owning a single stock or bond. For example, funds offer instant portfolio diversification by giving you ownership of many stocks or bonds simultaneously. This diversification protects you in case a part of your investment takes a sudden downturn. You also get the benefit of having a professional handling your investment, though a management fee is charged for these services, typically 1% or 2% a year. You should be aware that the fund may also levy other fees and that you will likely have to pay a sales commission (known as a load) if you purchase the fund from a financial adviser.

The fund manager's strategy is laid out in the fund's prospectus, which is the official name for the legal document that contains financial information about the fund, including its history, its officers and its performance. Mutual fund investments are fully liquid so you can easily get in or out by just placing an order through a broker.

Investor Profile Quiz

We recognize that each person approaches his or her investment decisions from a unique perspective. A mutual fund that is perfect for someone else may be totally inappropriate for you due to factors such as:

- How much risk you are comfortable taking
- Your age and the number of years you have before retirement
- Your income level and tax rate
- Your other existing investments and personal net worth
- Preconceived expectations about investment performance

The following quiz will help you quantify your tolerance for risk based on your own personal life situation. As you read through each question, circle the letter next to the single answer that you feel most accurately describes your current position. Keep in mind that there are no "correct" answers to this quiz, only answers that are helpful in assessing your investment style. So don't worry about how your answer might be perceived by others; just try to be as honest and accurate as possible.

Then at the end of the quiz, use the point totals listed on the right side of the page to compute your test score. Once you've added up your total points, refer to the corresponding investor profile for an evaluation of your personal risk tolerance. Each profile also lists the page number where you will find the top performing mutual funds matching your risk profile.

		Points	Your Score
1.	I am currently investing to pay for:		
	a. Retirement	0 pts	
	b. College	0 pts	
	c. A house	0 pts	
2.	I expect I will need to liquidate some or all of this investment in:		
	a. 2 years or less	0 pts	
	b. 2 to 5 years	5 pts	
	c. 5 to 10 years	8 pts	
	d. 10 years or more	10 pts	
3.	My age group is		
	a. Under 30	10 pts	
	b. 30 to 44	9 pts	
	c. 45 to 60	7 pts	
	d. 60 to 74	5 pts	
	e. 75 and older	1 pts	
4.	I am currently looking to invest money through:		
	a. An IRA or other tax-deferred account	0 pts	
	b. A fully taxable account	0 pts	

5.	I have a cash reserve equal to 3 to 6 months expenses.		
	a. Yes	10 pts	
	b. No	1 pts	
6.	My primary source of income is:		
	a. Salary and other earnings from my primary occupation	7 pts	
	b. Earnings from my investment portfolio	5 pts	
	c. Retirement pension and/or Social Security	3 pts	
7.	I will need regular income from this investment now or in the near future.		
	a. Yes	6 pts	
	b. No	10 pts	
8.	Over the long run, I expect this investment to average returns of:		
	a. 8% annually or less	0 pts	
	b. 8% to 12% annually	6 pts	
	c. 12% to 15% annually	8 pts	
	d. 15% to 20% annually	10 pts	
	e. Over 20% annually	18 pts	
9.	The worst loss I would be comfortable accepting on my investment is:		
	a. Less than 5%. Stability of principal is very important to me.	1 pts	
	b. 5% to 10%. Modest periodic declines are acceptable.	3 pts	
	c. 10% to 15%. I understand that there may be losses in the short run but over the long term, higher risk investments will offer highest returns.	8 pts	
	d. Over 15%. You don't get high returns without taking risk. I'm looking for maximum capital gains and understand that my funds can substantially decline.	15 pts	
10.	If the bond market were to suddenly decline by 15%, which of the following would most likely be your reaction?		
	a. I should have left the market long ago, at the first sign of trouble.	3 pts	
	b. I should have substantially exited the bond market by now to limit my exposure.	5 pts	
	c. I'm still in the bond market but I've got my finger on the trigger.	7 pts	
	d. I'm staying fully invested so I'll be ready for the next bull market.	10 pts	
11.	The best defense against a bear market in bonds is:		
	a. A defensive market timing system that avoids large losses.	4 pts	
	b. A potent offense that will make big gains in the next bond bull market.	10 pts	
12.	The best strategy to employ during bear markets is:		
	a. Move to cash. It's the only safe hiding place.	5 pts	
	b. Short the market and try to make a profit as it declines.	10 pts	
	c. Wait it out because the market will eventually recover.	8 pts	

13.	I would classify myself as:		
	a. A buy-and-hold investor who rides out all the peaks and valleys.	10 pts	
	b. A market timer who wants to capture the major bull markets.	7 pts	
	c. A market timer who wants to avoid the major bear markets.	5 pts	
14.	My attitude regarding trading activity is:		
	a. Active trading is costly and unproductive.	0 pts	
	b. I don't mind frequent trades as long as I'm making money	2 pts	
	c. Occasional trading is okay but too much activity is not good.	1 pts	
15.	If the 30-year U.S. Treasury Bond advanced strongly over the last 12 months, my investment should have:		
	a. Grown even more than the market.	10 pts	
	b. Approximated the performance of the broad market.	5 pts	
	c. Focused on reducing the risk of loss in a bond bear market, even if it meant giving up some upside potential in the bull market.	2 pts	

		Extensive	Some	None	
16.	I have experience (extensive, some, or none) with the following types of investments.				
	a. U.S. stocks or stock mutual funds	2 pts	1 pts	0 pts	
	b. International stock funds	2 pts	1 pts	0 pts	
	c. Bonds or bond funds	1 pts	0 pts	0 pts	
	d. Futures and/or options	5 pts	3 pts	0 pts	
	e. Managed futures or funds	3 pts	1 pts	0 pts	
	f. Real estate	2 pts	1 pts	0 pts	
	g. Private hedge funds	3 pts	1 pts	0 pts	
	h. Privately managed accounts	2 pts	1 pts	0 pts	

17.	Excluding my primary residence, this investment represents ___% of my investment holdings.		
	a. Less than 5%	10 pts	
	b. 5% to 10%	7 pts	
	c. 10% to 20%	5 pts	
	d. 20% to 30%	3 pts	
	e. 30% or more	1 pts	
		TOTAL	

Under 58 pts   **Very Conservative.** You appear to be very risk averse with capital preservation as your primary goal. As such, most bond mutual funds may be a little too risky for your taste, especially in a turbulent market environment. We would recommend you stick to the safest bond and money market mutual funds where your income stream is predictable and more secure. To find them, turn to pages 490 - 491 listing the top performing fixed income mutual funds receiving a risk rating in the A (Excellent) range, our best risk rating.

58 to 77 pts   **Conservative.** Based on your responses, it appears that you are more concerned about minimizing the risk to your principal than you are about maximizing your returns. Don't worry, there are plenty of good mutual funds that offer strong returns with very little volatility. As a starting point, we recommend you turn to pages 492 – 493 where you will find a list of the top performing funds receiving a risk rating in the B (Good) range.

78 to 108 pts   **Moderate.** You are prepared to take on a little added risk in order to enhance your investment returns. This is probably the most common approach to mutual fund investing. To select a mutual fund matching your style, we recommend you turn to pages 494 - 495. There you can easily pick from the top performing mutual funds receiving a risk rating in the C (Fair) range.

109 to 129 pts   **Aggressive.** You appear to be ready to ride out almost any financial storm on your way toward maximizing your investment returns. You understand that the only way to make large returns on your investments is by taking on added risk, and your personal situation seems to allow for that approach. We recommend you use pages 494 - 497 as a starting point for selecting a high performing mutual fund with a risk rating in the C (Fair) or D (Weak) range.

Over 129 pts   **Very Aggressive.** Based on your responses, you appear to be leaning heavily toward speculation. Your primary concern is maximizing your investment growth, and you are prepared to take on as much risk as necessary in order to do so. To this end, turn to page 498 - 499 where you'll find the highest performing mutual funds with a risk rating in the E (Very Weak) range. These investments have historically been extremely volatile, oftentimes investing in bonds that are currently out of favor. As such, they are highly speculative investments that could provide superior results if you can stomach the volatility and uncertainty. For a list of the top performing bond mutual funds regardless of risk category, turn to page 470. Also see Section VII in *TheStreet Ratings Guide to Stock Mutual Funds* and Section VI in *TheStreet Ratings Guide to Common Stocks*.

Performance Benchmarks

The following benchmarks represent the average performance for all mutual funds within each bond or money market fund type category. Comparing an individual mutual fund's returns to these benchmarks is yet another way to assess its performance. For the top performing funds within each of the following categories, turn to Section VIII, Top-Rated Bond Mutual Funds by Fund Type, beginning on page 506. You can also use this information to compare the average performance of one category of funds to another (updated through Feb. 28, 2017).

		3 Month Total Return %	1 Year Total Return %	Refer to page:
COH	Corporate - High Yield	4.04%	16.75%	506
COI	Corporate - Investment Grade	1.47%	4.41%	507
EM	Emerging Market Income	5.45%	14.14%	508
GEI	General Bd - Investment Grade	1.39%	3.99%	509
GEL	General Bd - Long	2.79%	10.12%	510
GES	General Bd - Short & Interm	2.12%	7.40%	511
MTG	General Mortgage	0.91%	2.30%	516
GL	Global Income	2.79%	7.93%	512
LP	Loan Participation	2.22%	11.90%	513
GEN	Multi-Sector Bond	2.36%	10.32%	
MUH	Municipal - High Yield	2.56%	1.68%	517
MUI	Municipal - Insured	1.56%	-0.11%	518
MUN	Municipal - National	1.78%	0.09%	519
MUS	Municipal - Single State	1.84%	0.07%	520
MMF	Ret Munic/Tax-Exempt (Stab)	0.08%	0.20%	514
MMT	Ret/Prime/US Gov/Treas (Stab)	0.08%	0.18%	515
USL	US Government - Long	1.01%	-0.51%	521
USS	US Government - Short & Interm	0.57%	0.87%	522
USA	US Government/Agency	0.29%	0.05%	523
US	US Treasury	1.19%	0.55%	524

Fund Type Descriptions

<u>COH - Corporate - High Yield</u> - Seeks high current income by investing a minimum of 65% of its assets in generally low-quality corporate debt issues.

<u>COI - Corporate - Investment Grade</u> - Seeks current income by investing a minimum of 65% in investment grade corporate debt issues. Investment grade securities must be BBB or higher, as rated by Standard & Poor's.

<u>EM - Emerging Market</u> - Seeks income by investing in income producing securities from emerging market countries.

<u>GEN - General</u> - Seeks income by investing without geographic boundary in corporate debt, government debt or preferred securities. Investments are not tied to any specific maturity or duration.

<u>GEI - General - Investment Grade</u> - Seeks income by investing in investment grade domestic or foreign corporate debt, government debt and preferred securities.

<u>GEL - General - Long Term</u> - Seeks income by investing in corporate debt, government debt and preferred securities with maturities over 10 years or an average duration over 6 years.

<u>GES - General - Short & Intermediate Term</u> - Seeks income by investing in corporate debt, government debt and preferred securities with an average maturity under 10 years or an average duration under 6 years.

<u>GL - Global</u> - Invests a minimum of 65% in fixed income securities issued by domestic and/or foreign governments.

<u>LP - Loan Participation</u> - Invests a minimum of 65% of its assets in loan interests.

<u>MMF - Ret Munic/Tax-Exempt (Stab)</u> - Seeks tax-free income and stability by investing in high-quality, short-term obligations which are exempt from federal and the taxation of a specified state.

<u>MMT - Ret/Prime/US Gov/Treas (Stab)</u> - Seeks income and stability by investing in high-quality, short-term obligations issued by the U.S. Government, corporations, financial institutions, and other entities.

<u>MTG - Mortgage</u> - Invests a minimum of 65% of its assets in a broad range of mortgage or mortgage-related securities, including those issued by the U.S. government and by government related and private organizations.

<u>MUH - Municipal - High Yield</u> - Seeks tax-free income by investing a minimum of 65% of its assets in generally low-quality issues from any state municipality.

<u>MUI - Municipal - Insured</u> - Seeks federally tax-free income by investing a minimum of 65% of its assets in municipal debt obligations that are insured as to timely payment of principal and interest.

<u>MUN - Municipal - National</u> - Seeks federally tax-free income by investing at least 65% in issues from any state municipality.

MUS - Municipal - Single State - Seeks tax-free income by investing in issues which are exempt from federal and the taxation of a specified state.

USL - U.S. Government - Long Term - Invests a minimum of 65% in securities issued or guaranteed by the Government, its agencies or instrumentalities with maturities over 10 years or an average duration over 6 years.

USS - U.S. Government - Short and Intermediate Term - Invests a minimum of 65% in securities issued or guaranteed by the Government, its agencies or instrumentalities with maturities under 10 years or an average duration under 6 years.

USA - U.S. Government - Agency - Invests a minimum of 65% in securities issued or guaranteed by the Government, its agencies or instrumentalities. Investments are not tied to any specific maturity or duration.

US - U.S. Government - Treasury - Invests a minimum of 65% of its assets in securities issued and backed by the full faith and credit of the U.S. government.

Share Class Descriptions

Many mutual funds have several classes of shares, each with different fees and associated sales charges. While there is no official standardization of mutual fund classes we have compiled a list of those most frequently seen. Ultimately you must consult a fund's prospectus for particular share class designations and what they mean. Federal regulation requires that the load, or sales charge, not exceed 8.5% of the investment purchase.

Class	Description
A	**Front End Load**. Sales charge is paid at the time of purchase and is deducted from the investment amount.
B	**Back End Load**. Also known as contingent deferred sales charge (CDSC); the sales charge is imposed if the fund is sold. Class B shares usually convert to Class A shares after six to eight years from the date of purchase.
C	**Level Load**. A set sales charge paid annually for as long as the fund is held. This class is especially beneficial to the short–term investor.
D	**Flexible.** Class D shares can be anything a fund company wants. Check the fund prospectus for the details regarding a specific fund's fee structure.
I	**Institutional**. No sales charge is collected due to the size of the order. This class usually requires a minimum investment of $100,000.
M	**Mid Load**. Similar to Class A, but with a lower front end load and higher expense ratio (see page 19 for more information on expense ratios).
N	**No Load.** No sales fee is imposed.
R	**No Load**. No sales fee is imposed and fund must be held in a qualified retirement account.
T	**Mid Load**. Similar to Class A, but with a lower front end load and higher expense ratio (see page 19 for more information on expense ratios).
Y	**Institutional**. No sales charge is collected due to the size of the order. This class usually requires a minimum investment of $100,000.
Z	**No Load**. Fund is only available for purchase to employees of the mutual fund company, as an employee benefit. No sales fee is imposed.